Stephen Walther
Kevin Hoffman
Nate Dudek

ASP.NET 4

UNLEASHED

SAMS | 800 East 96th Street, Indianapolis, Indiana 46240 USA

ASP.NET 4 Unleashed

ISBN-13: 978-0-672-33112-1

ISBN-10: 0-672-33112-8

Library of Congress Cataloging-in-Publication Data:

Walther, Stephen.

ASP.NET 4.0 unleashed / Stephen Walther, Kevin Hoffman, Nate Dudek.

    p. cm.

Includes index.

ISBN 978-0-672-33112-1

1. Active server pages. 2. Web sites—Design. 3. Web site development. 4. Microsoft .NET. I. Hoffman, Kevin. II. Dudek, Nate. III. Title.

TK5105.8885.A26W3517 2011

006.7'882—dc22

                                2010034058

Printed in the United States of America

First Printing September 2010

Trademarks

All terms mentioned in this book that are known to be trademarks or service marks have been appropriately capitalized. Sams Publishing cannot attest to the accuracy of this information. Use of a term in this book should not be regarded as affecting the validity of any trademark or service mark.

Warning and Disclaimer

Every effort has been made to make this book as complete and as accurate as possible, but no warranty or fitness is implied. The information provided is on an "as is" basis. The authors and the publisher shall have neither liability nor responsibility to any person or entity with respect to any loss or damages arising from the information contained in this book.

Bulk Sales

Sams Publishing offers excellent discounts on this book when ordered in quantity for bulk purchases or special sales. For more information, please contact

   U.S. Corporate and Government Sales
   1-800-382-3419
   corpsales@pearsontechgroup.com

For sales outside of the U.S., please contact

   International Sales
   international@pearson.com

Editor-in-Chief
Karen Gettman

Executive Editor
Neil Rowe

Development Editor
Mark Renfrow

Managing Editor
Kristy Hart

Project Editors
Jovana San Nicolas-Shirley and
Alexandra Maurer

Copy Editor
Apostrophe Editing Services

Indexer
WordWise Publishing Services LLC

Proofreader
Debbie Williams

Technical Editor
J. Boyd Nolan

Publishing Coordinator
Cindy Teeters

Cover Designer
Gary Adair

Composition
Gloria Schurick

Contents at a Glance

Table of Contents

About the Authors

Stephen Walther is a Senior Program Manager on the Microsoft ASP.NET team. He works on ASP.NET Web Forms and ASP.NET Ajax. Before joining Microsoft, his company provided training and consulting for organizations such as NASA, Boeing, Lockheed Martin, the National Science Foundation, and Verizon. Walther got his start with the World Wide Web by dropping out of MIT and developing two large commercial websites. He created the Collegescape website, used by more than 200 colleges (including Harvard, Stanford, and MIT) to accept online college applications. He also developed the CityAuction website, the auction website used by both Snap! and CitySearch. He is the author of several editions of ASP.NET Unleashed.

Kevin Hoffman has been programming since he was 10 years old, when he got his hands on a Commodore VIC-20 and learned BASIC. He has eaten, slept, and breathed code ever since. He has written applications for scientific instruments, military applications, small businesses, and Fortune 500 enterprises on virtually every platform and language ranging from Symbol Barcode readers running PalmOS to the iPhone, ASP.NET, Rails, and everything in between. Kevin is the chief systems architect for Exclaim Computing, where he builds custom architectures and application solutions for a wide range of clients and industries. He regularly contributes to articles for magazines such as *MSDN Magazine* and is the author of the Kotan Code blog (http://www.kotancode.com).

Nate Dudek is the development lead for Exclaim Computing, a company focused on providing technology solutions for a variety of platforms, including mobile, web, enterprise, and cloud computing. He has presented at conferences, written several articles, and is constantly mentoring and teaching developers on software development best practices, software architecture, and new technologies.

For the past ten years, Nate has architected and developed software for a variety of industries, including real-time systems for power utilities, enterprise resource planning systems for service-based companies, and eCommerce systems for web businesses. He holds a B.S. degree in computer science from Clarkson University with a minor in software engineering and mathematics. Nate writes about all areas of technology on his blog, Caffeine Dependency Injection, at http://www.caffeinedi.com.

Dedications

Kevin Hoffman: I would like to dedicate this book to my daughter, through whose eyes the world is a vast, amazing place filled with wondrous things from crab cakes to pyramids, from Jeopardy! answers to hot rods.

Nate Dudek: To my parents, Fred and Linda Dudek—the smartest people I know.

Acknowledgments

The authors would like to thank the publishing team for working with us on this book. Special thanks to Neil, Mark, J. Boyd, and others. Thank you for your valuable feedback, answers, and hard work on this book. Without you all, this book would not be possible.

First and foremost I would like to acknowledge the tireless work of Stephen Walther, the original author of the core material of this book for ASP.NET 3.5. Second, I would like to acknowledge Microsoft. ASP.NET 1.0 was a great start to a promising future for web developers and ASP.NET 4.0 is as robust and full-featured a web development platform as you can find today. Additionally I would like to thank all the staff at SAMS Publishing—putting together a book of this size is a Herculean effort, and they should be congratulated.

—Kevin Hoffman

First, I want to thank my wife Leanne for all her support and encouragement and for putting up with my long hours working on this book.

I want to thank Kevin Hoffman for his endless knowledge, his "wordsmithing" capabilities, and his teamwork in completing the book. I also want to thank Neil Rowe for his support and for providing us with everything we needed to make this book a reality.

For their guidance and support, I'd like to thank Mario Harik, Michael Luca, and Len Bertelli.

Last, but certainly not least, I want to thank Stephen Walther for writing the first three versions of the ASP.NET Unleashed series—an exhaustingly thorough core that makes up the foundation of this book.

—Nate Dudek

We Want to Hear from You!

As the reader of this book, *you* are our most important critic and commentator. We value your opinion and want to know what we're doing right, what we could do better, what areas you'd like to see us publish in, and any other words of wisdom you're willing to pass our way.

You can email or write me directly to let me know what you did or didn't like about this book—as well as what we can do to make our books stronger.

Please note that I cannot help you with technical problems related to the topic of this book, and that due to the high volume of mail I receive, I might not be able to reply to every message.

When you write, please be sure to include this book's title and authors as well as your name and phone or email address. I will carefully review your comments and share them with the authors and editors who worked on the book.

E-mail: feedback@samspublishing.com

Mail: Neil Rowe
            Executive Editor
            Sams Publishing
            800 East 96th Street
            Indianapolis, IN 46240 USA

Reader Services

Visit our website and register this book at www.informit.com/title/9780672331121 for convenient access to any updates, downloads, or errata that might be available for this book.

Introduction

Web development has been rapidly evolving over the years. The features and functionality that today's web developers are asked to produce are exponentially more involved and complex than they were just a few years ago. As the demands of today's business and commercial software grow, so too must the power of the tools and development frameworks developers use every day.

Even in the years since ASP.NET was first introduced, it has undergone dramatic growth in terms of ease of use, power, flexibility, scalability, and time to market. Some of the largest websites hosted on the Internet have ASP.NET and the .NET Framework to thank for their speed, power, and scalability including Dell, MySpace, and Microsoft.

Whether you plan on building the next greatest social network, a simple blogging site, or a year-long project to build a suite of Line of Business applications for the enterprise—ASP.NET might be the right tool for the job.

Who Should Read This Book?

ASP.NET 4 Unleashed is for professional programmers who need to create rich, interactive websites. This book is a comprehensive reference for building websites with all the tools and technology that are part of the ever-growing ASP.NET umbrella. There are hundreds of code samples on the accomanying website that you can use to immediately begin building your website.

If you are new to building websites with ASP.NET, you can use this book to learn everything you need to know to build a website with the ASP.NET Framework. If you are an experienced ASP.NET developer, you can use this book to refresh your memory on some lesser-used features and learn about the new features in ASP.NET 4.

What Do You Need to Know Before You Read This Book?

To get the most out of this book, you should have a decent familiarity with the core concepts of the .NET Framework. This book can be used as a reference for ASP.NET veterans as well as serve as a full, cover-to-cover learning experience for developers new to building ASP.NET web applications. The samples are designed to be clear and easy to read, regardless of whether your background is in VB.NET or C#.

To get the most from the database chapters, you should have some experience working with a database, such as Microsoft SQL Server, Oracle, or Microsoft Access. Purely to make the samples easier to install and test, the data-driven samples either work from data files or from SQL Server databases.

If you want to run every sample from this book, you should be running at least Windows Vista, Windows Server 2008, or Windows 7 for best results. You should also have the latest version of Internet Information Server (IIS) installed and some version of Visual Studio 2010 installed.

Changes to This Book

This edition of the book reflects many important transitions in the ASP.NET Framework. There are several new chapters in this book that cover features introduced in ASP.NET 4, such as a new charting control, a new URL routing engine, use of the ADO.NET Entity Framework and WCF Data Services and much more.

Another area that has seen large amounts of change and improvement in ASP.NET 4 is the use of client-side scripting such as Ajax. The entire Ajax section of this book has been completely redone since the previous version.

How This Book Is Organized

Although we encourage you to read this book from start to finish, reading chapter by chapter, some experienced ASP.NET developers might want to pick and choose chapters and skip the ones that are review. If necessary, you can use this book solely as a reference and jump to a chapter only when the need arises. It might be helpful, therefore, to have an idea of the overall organization of this book.

▶ **Part I: Building ASP.NET Pages**—Provides you with an overview of the basic controls included in the ASP.NET Framework. You learn how to build interactive Web Forms with the form controls. You also learn how to validate form data with the validation controls. Finally, you learn how to upload files and display interactive calendars and wizards with the rich controls.

▶ **Part II: Designing ASP.NET Websites**—Discusses how you can create a common layout and style for the pages on your website. You learn how to use Master Pages to share content across multiple pages. You also learn how to use Themes to create a consistent page style.

▶ **Part III: Performing Data Access**—Focuses on data access. You learn how to use the ListView and GridView controls to display, page, sort, and edit a set of database records. You learn how to use the DetailsView and FormView controls to display and edit a single database record at a time. WCF Data Services are introduced in this section.

▶ **Part IV: Building Components**—Focuses on building custom components. You learn how to design and create multitiered applications. You also learn how to build data access components by taking advantage of both LINQ to SQL and ADO.NET.

▶ **Part V: Site Navigation**—Discusses the various navigation controls included in the ASP.NET Framework, such as the `TreeView` and `Menu` controls. You learn how to use these controls with a Site Map to allow users to easily navigate a website. You also learn how to use the `VirtualPathProvider` class to abstract a website from the file system.

▶ **Part VI: Security**—Focuses on the Login controls and Membership API. You learn how to create a user registration and authentication system. You learn how to store Membership information in either a SQL Server database or Active Directory.

▶ **Part VII: Building ASP.NET Applications**—Discusses a variety of topics related to building ASP.NET applications. For example, you learn how to improve the performance of your ASP.NET applications by taking advantage of caching. You also learn how to localize your ASP.NET applications so that they can be easily translated and presented in multiple human languages.

▶ **Part VIII: Custom Control Building**—Concentrates on extending the ASP.NET Framework with custom controls. For example, you learn how to create custom data access controls that work like the `ListView` and `GridView` controls.

▶ **Part IX: ASP.NET AJAX**—Concentrates on extending the ASP.NET Framework with custom controls. For example, you learn how to create custom data access controls that work like the `ListView` and `GridView` controls.

NOTE

The book's website contains all of the code samples found in this book in C# and VB.NET. The code samples are posted online at www.informit.com/title/9780672331121 in the Books Section of the website.

Overview of the ASP.NET Framework

Let's start by building a simple ASP.NET page.

> **NOTE**
>
> For information on installing ASP.NET, see the last section of this chapter.

If you use Visual Web Developer or Visual Studio, you first need to create a new website. Start Visual Web Developer and select File, New Web Site. The New Web Site dialog box appears (see Figure 1.1). Enter the folder in which you want your new website to be created (such as "Chapter1") in the Location field and click the OK button.

> **NOTE**
>
> When you create a new website, you might receive an error message warning you that you need to enable script debugging in Internet Explorer. You need to enable script debugging to build Ajax applications. We discuss Ajax later in the book.

After you create a new website, you can add an ASP.NET page to it. Select Web Site, Add New Item. Select Web Form and enter the value `FirstPage.aspx` in the Name field. Make sure that both the Place Code in Separate File and Select Master Page check boxes are unchecked, and click the Add button to create the new ASP.NET page (see Figure 1.2).

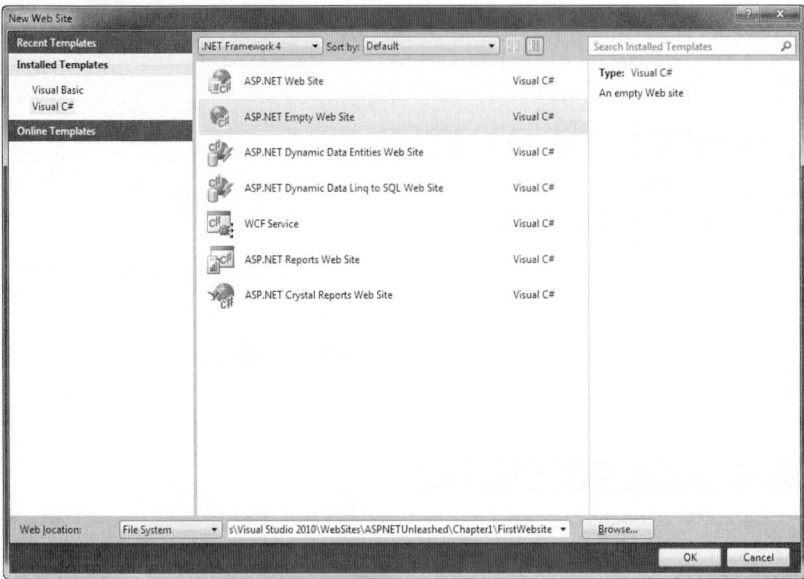

FIGURE 1.1   Creating a new website.

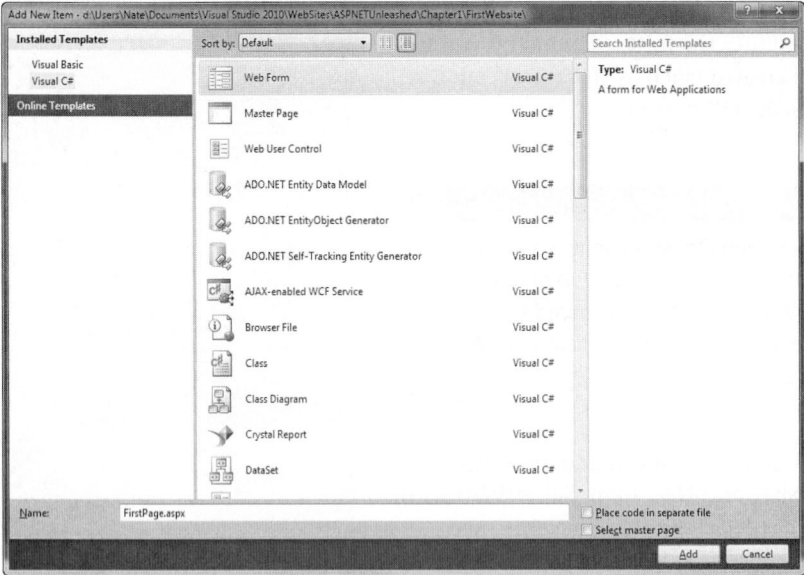

FIGURE 1.2   Adding a new ASP.NET page.

Make sure that your code for `FirstPage.aspx` looks like the code contained in Listing 1.1.

LISTING 1.1   FirstPage.aspx

```
<%@ Page Language="C#" %>
<!DOCTYPE html PUBLIC "-//W3C//DTD XHTML 1.0 Transitional//EN"
"http://www.w3.org/TR/xhtml1/DTD/xhtml1-transitional.dtd">
<script runat="server">

    void Page_Load()
    {
        lblServerTime.Text = DateTime.Now.ToString();
    }

</script>
<html xmlns="http://www.w3.org/1999/xhtml" >
<head>
    <title>First Page</title>
</head>
<body>
    <form id="form1" runat="server">
    <div>

    Welcome to ASP.NET 4.0! The current date and time is:

    <asp:Label
        id="lblServerTime"
        Runat="server" />

    </div>
    </form>
</body>
</html>
```

NOTE

The book's website contains all the code samples found in this book in both C# and VB.NET.

The ASP.NET page in Listing 1.1 displays a brief message and the server's current date and time. You can view the page in Listing 1.1 in a browser by right-clicking the page and selecting View in Browser (see Figure 1.3).

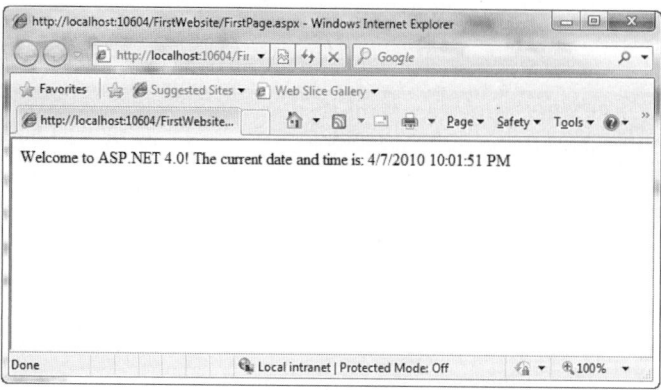

FIGURE 1.3   Viewing `FirstPage.aspx` in a browser.

The page in Listing 1.1 is an extremely simple page. However, it does illustrate the most common elements of an ASP.NET page. The page contains a directive, a code declaration block, and a page render block.

The first line, in Listing 1.1, contains a directive that looks like this:

```
<%@ Page Language="C#" %>
```

A directive always begins with the special characters `<%@` and ends with the characters `%>`. Directives are used primarily to provide the compiler with the information it needs to compile the page.

For example, the directive in Listing 1.1 indicates that the code contained in the page is C# code. The page is compiled by the C# compiler and not another compiler, such as the Visual Basic .NET (VB.NET) compiler.

The next part of the page begins with the opening `<script runat="server">` tag and ends with the closing `</script>` tag. The `<script>` tag contains the *code declaration block*.

The code declaration block contains all the methods used in the page. It contains all the page's functions and subroutines. The code declaration block in Listing 1.1 includes a single method named `Page_Load()`, which looks like this:

```
void Page_Load()
{
    lblServerTime.Text = DateTime.Now.ToString();
}
```

This method assigns the current date and time to the `Text` property of a `Label` control contained in the body of the page named `lblServerTime`.

The `Page_Load()` method is an example of an event handler. This method handles the `Page Load` event. Every time the page loads, the method automatically executes and assigns the current date and time to the `Label` control.

The final part of the page is called the *page render block*, which contains everything rendered to the browser. In Listing 1.1, the render block includes everything between the opening and closing <html> tags.

The majority of the page render block consists of everyday HTML. For example, the page contains the standard HTML <head> and <body> tags. In Listing 1.1, two special things are contained in the page render block.

First, notice that the page contains a <form> tag that looks like this:

```
<form id="form1" runat="server">
```

This is an example of an ASP.NET control. Because the tag includes a runat="server" attribute, the tag represents an ASP.NET control that executes on the server.

ASP.NET pages are often called *web form* pages because they almost always contain a server-side form element.

The page render block also contains a Label control. The Label control is declared with the <asp:Label> tag. In Listing 1.1, the Label control is used to display the current date and time.

Controls are the heart of ASP.NET Framework. Most of the ink contained in this book is devoted to describing the properties and features of ASP.NET controls. Controls are discussed in more detail shortly; however, first you need to understand .NET Framework.

> **NOTE**
>
> By default, ASP.NET pages are compatible with the XHTML 1.0 Transitional standard. The page in Listing 1.1 includes an XHTML 1.0 Transitional DOCTYPE. For details on how ASP.NET Framework complies with both XHTML and accessibility standards, see the article at the Microsoft MSDN website (msdn.Microsoft.com), "Building ASP.NET 2.0 Web Sites Using Web Standards."

ASP.NET and the .NET Framework

ASP.NET is part of the Microsoft .NET Framework. To build ASP.NET pages, you need to take advantage of the features of .NET Framework, which consists of two parts: the Framework Class Library and the Common Language Runtime.

Understanding the Framework Class Library

The .NET Framework contains thousands of classes that you can use when building an application. Framework Class Library was designed to make it easier to perform the most common programming tasks. Following are just a few examples of the classes in the framework:

- ▶ **File class**—Enables you to represent a file on your hard drive. You can use the File class to check whether a file exists, create a new file, delete a file, and perform many other file-related tasks.

- ▶ **Graphics class**—Enables you to work with different types of images such as GIF, PNG, BMP, and JPEG. You can use the Graphics class to draw rectangles, arcs, ellipses, and other elements on an image

- ▶ **Random class**—Enables you to generate a random number.

- ▶ **SmtpClient class**—Enables you to send email. You can use the SmtpClient class to send emails that contain attachments and HTML content.

Framework has only four examples of classes. The .NET Framework contains more than 13,000 classes you can use when building applications.

You can view all the classes contained in the framework by opening the Microsoft .NET Framework SDK documentation on Microsoft's .NET Framework Developer Center website and expanding the Class Library node (see Figure 1.4). The SDK documentation website is located at http://msdn.microsoft.com/en-us/netframework/default.aspx.

Each class in the Framework can include properties, methods, and events. The properties, methods, and events exposed by a class are the members of a class. For example, following is a partial list of the members of the SmtpClient class:

- ▶ Properties

    - ▶ **Host**—The name or IP address of your email server

    - ▶ **Port**—The number of the port to use when sending an email message

- ▶ Methods

    - ▶ **Send**—Enables you to send an email message synchronously

    - ▶ **SendAsync**—Enables you to send an email message asynchronously

- ▶ Events

    - ▶ **SendCompleted**—Raised when an asynchronous send operation completes

If you know the members of a class, you know everything that you can do with a class. For example, the SmtpClient class includes two properties named Host and Port, which enable you to specify the email server and port to use when sending an email message.

The SmtpClient class also includes two methods you can use to send an email: Send() and SendAsync(). The Send method blocks further program execution until the send operation is completed. The SendAsync() method, on the other hand, sends the email asynchronously. Unlike the Send() method, the SendAsync() method does not wait to check whether the send operation was successful.

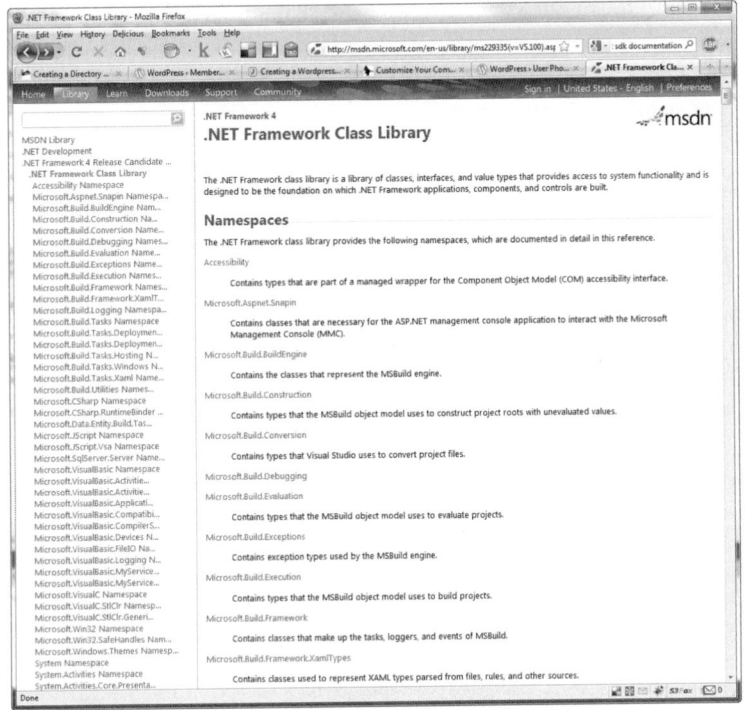

FIGURE 1.4   The online Microsoft .NET Framework SDK documentation.

Finally, the `SmtpClient` class includes an event named `SendCompleted`, which is raised when an asynchronous send operation completes. You can create an event handler for the `SendCompleted` event that displays a message when the email has been successfully sent.

The page in Listing 1.2 sends an email by using the `SmtpClient` class and calling its `Send()` method.

LISTING 1.2   SendMail.aspx

```
<%@ Page Language="C#" %>
<%@ Import Namespace="System.Net.Mail" %>
<!DOCTYPE html PUBLIC "-//W3C//DTD XHTML 1.0 Transitional//EN"
"http://www.w3.org/TR/xhtml1/DTD/xhtml1-transitional.dtd">
<script runat="server">

    void Page_Load()
    {
        SmtpClient client = new SmtpClient();
        client.Host = "localhost";
        client.Port = 25;
        client.Send("nate@somewhere", "nate@exclaimcomputing.com",
            "Beware!", "Watch out for zombies!");
```

```
    }

</script>
<html xmlns="http://www.w3.org/1999/xhtml" >
<head id="Head1" runat="server">
    <title>Send Mail</title>
</head>
<body>
    <form id="form1" runat="server">
    <div>
    Email sent!

    </div>
    </form>
</body>
</html>
```

The page in Listing 1.2 calls the `SmtpClient Send()` method to send the email. The first parameter is the from: address; the second parameter is the to: address; the third parameter is the subject; and the final parameter is the body of the email.

WARNING

The page in Listing 1.2 sends the email by using the local SMTP Server. If your SMTP Server is not enabled, you receive the error An Existing Connection Was Forcibly Closed by the Remote Host. You can enable your local SMTP Server by opening Internet Information Services, right-clicking Default SMTP Virtual Server, and selecting Start.

Understanding Namespaces

There are more than 13,000 classes in .NET Framework. This is an overwhelming number. If Microsoft simply jumbled all the classes together, you would never find anything. Fortunately, Microsoft divided the classes in the framework into separate namespaces.

A *namespace* is simply a category. For example, all the classes related to working with the file system are located in the `System.IO` namespace. All the classes for working a Microsoft SQL Server database are located in the `System.Data.SqlClient` namespace.

Before you can use a class in a page, you must indicate the namespace associated with the class. There are multiple ways of doing this.

First, you can fully qualify a class name with its namespace. For example, because the `File` class is contained in the `System.IO` namespace, you can use the following statement to check whether a file exists:

```
System.IO.File.Exists("SomeFile.txt")
```

Specifying a namespace every time you use a class can quickly become tedious. (It involves a lot of typing.) A second option is to import a namespace.

You can add an <$I<%@ Import % directive><%@ Import %> directive to a page to import a particular namespace. In Listing 1.2, we imported the System.Net.Mail namespace because the SmtpClient is part of this namespace. The page in Listing 1.2 includes the following directive near the top of the page:

```
<%@ Import Namespace="System.Net.Mail" %>
```

After you import a particular namespace, you can use all the classes in that namespace without qualifying the class names.

Finally, if you discover that you use a namespace in multiple pages in your application, you can configure all the pages in your application to recognize the namespace.

NOTE

A web configuration file is a special type of file that you can add to your application to configure your application. Be aware that the file is an XML file and, therefore, all the tags contained in the file are case-sensitive. You can add a web configuration file to your application by selecting Web Site, Add New Item Web Configuration File. Chapter 34, "Configuring Applications," discusses web configuration files in detail.

If you add the web configuration file in Listing 1.3 to your application, you do not need to import the System.Net.Mail namespace in a page to use the classes from this namespace. For example, if you include the Web.config file in your project, you can remove the <%@ Import %> directive from the page in Listing 1.2.

LISTING 1.3   Web.Config

```xml
<?xml version="1.0"?>
<configuration>
    <system.web>
      <pages>
        <namespaces>
          <add namespace="System.Net.Mail"/>
        </namespaces>
      </pages>
    </system.web>
</configuration>
```

You don't have to import every namespace. ASP.NET gives you the most commonly used namespaces for free:

- ▶ `System`
- ▶ `System.Collections`
- ▶ `System.Collections.Generic`
- ▶ `System.Collections.Specialized`
- ▶ `System.ComponentModel.DataAnnotations`
- ▶ `System.Configuration`
- ▶ `System.Data.Entity.Linq`
- ▶ `System.Data.Linq`
- ▶ `System.Text`
- ▶ `System.Text.RegularExpressions`
- ▶ `System.Web`
- ▶ `System.Web.Caching`
- ▶ `System.Web.DynamicData`
- ▶ `System.Web.SessionState`
- ▶ `System.Web.Security`
- ▶ `System.Web.Profile`
- ▶ `System.Web.UI`
- ▶ `System.Web.UI.WebControls`
- ▶ `System.Web.UI.WebControls.WebParts`
- ▶ `System.Web.UI.HtmlControls`
- ▶ `System.Xml.Linq`

The default namespaces are listed inside the pages element in the root web configuration file located at the following path:

`\Windows\Microsoft.NET\Framework\v4.0.30128\Config\Web.Config`

Understanding Assemblies

An assembly is the actual `.dll` file on your hard drive in which the classes in .NET Framework are stored. For example, all the classes contained in the ASP.NET Framework are located in an assembly named `System.Web.dll`.

More accurately, an assembly is the primary unit of deployment, security, and version control in .NET Framework. Because an assembly can span multiple files, an assembly is often referred to as a "logical" dll.

The two types of assemblies are private and shared. A private assembly can be used by only a single application. A shared assembly, on the other hand, can be used by all applications located on the same server.

Shared assemblies are located in the Global Assembly Cache (GAC). For example, the System.Web.dll assembly and all the other assemblies included with.NET Framework are located in the Global Assembly Cache.

NOTE

The Global Assembly Cache is located physically in your computer's \WINDOWS\Assembly folder.

Before you can use a class contained in an assembly in your application, you must add a reference to the assembly. By default, an ASP.NET 4 application references the most common assemblies contained in the Global Assembly Cache:

- ▶ mscorlib.dll

- ▶ Microsoft.CSharp

- ▶ System.dll

- ▶ System.Configuration.dll

- ▶ System.Web.dll

- ▶ System.Data.dll

- ▶ System.Web.Services.dll

- ▶ System.Xml.dll

- ▶ System.Drawing.dll

- ▶ System.EnterpriseServices.dll

- ▶ System.IdentityModel.dll

- ▶ System.Runtime.Serialization.dll

- ▶ System.ServiceModel.dll

- ▶ System.ServiceModel.Activation.dll

- ▶ System.ServiceModel.Web.dll

- ▶ System.Activities.dll

- ▶ System.ServiceModel.Activities.dll

- ▶ System.WorkflowServices.dll

- ▶ System.Core.dll

- ▶ System.Web.Extensions.dll

- ▶ System.Data.DataSetExtensions.dll

- ▶ System.Xml.Linq.dll

- ▶ System.ComponentModel.DataAnnotations.dll

- ▶ System.Web.DynamicData.dll

- ▶ System.Data.Entity.dll

- ▶ System.Web.Entity.dll

- ▶ System.Data.Linq.dll

- ▶ System.Data.Entity.Design.dll

- ▶ System.Web.ApplicationServices.dll

All these assemblies are part of .NET 4 Framework. Websites created on previous versions of .NET referenced a different set of assemblies.

> **NOTE**
>
> You can target a website to work with .NET Framework 2.0, .NET Framework 3.0, .NET Framework 3.5, or .NET Framework 4. Within Visual Web Developer, select Website, Start Options and the Build tab. You can select the framework to target from a drop-down list.

To use any particular class in .NET Framework, you must do two things. First, your application must reference the assembly that contains the class. Second, your application must import the namespace associated with the class.

In most cases, you won't worry about referencing the necessary assembly because the most common assemblies are referenced automatically. However, if you need to use a specialized assembly, you need to add a reference explicitly to the assembly. For example, if you need to interact with Active Directory by using the classes in the System.DirectoryServices namespace, you need to add a reference to the System.DirectoryServices.dll assembly to your application.

Each class entry in .NET Framework SDK documentation lists the assembly and namespace associated with the class. For example, if you look up the MessageQueue class in the documentation, you discover that this class is located in the System.Messaging namespace located in the System.Messaging.dll assembly.

If you use Visual Web Developer, you can add a reference to an assembly explicitly by selecting Web Site, Add Reference, and the name of the assembly that you need to reference. For example, adding a reference to the System.Messaging.dll assembly results in the web configuration file in Listing 1.4 being added to your application.

LISTING 1.4 Web.Config

```xml
<?xml version="1.0"?>
<configuration>
<system.web>
  <compilation>
  <assemblies>
  <add
    assembly="System.Messaging, Version=4.0.0.0,
    Culture=neutral, PublicKeyToken=B03F5F7F11D50A3A" />
  </assemblies>
  </compilation>
</system.web>
</configuration>
```

If you prefer not to use Visual Web Developer, you can add the reference to the System.Messaging.dll assembly by creating the file in Listing 1.4 manually.

Understanding the Common Language Runtime

The second part of .NET Framework is the Common Language Runtime (CLR). The CLR is responsible for executing your application code.

When you write an application for .NET Framework with a language such as C# or Visual Basic .NET, your source code is never compiled directly into machine code. Instead, the C# or Visual Basic compiler converts your code into a special language named Microsoft Intermediate Language (MSIL).

MSIL looks like an object-oriented assembly language; however, unlike a typical assembly language, it is not CPU-specific. MSIL is a low-level and platform-independent language.

When your application actually executes, the MSIL code is just-in-time compiled into machine code by the JITTER (the Just-In-Time compiler). Normally, your entire application is not compiled from MSIL into machine code. Instead, only the methods actually called during execution are compiled.

In reality, .NET Framework understands only one language: MSIL. However, you can write applications using languages such as Visual Basic .NET and C# for .NET Framework because .NET Framework includes compilers for these languages that enable you to compile your code into MSIL.

You can write code for .NET Framework using any one of dozens of different languages, including

- ▶ Ada
- ▶ Apl
- ▶ Caml
- ▶ COBOL
- ▶ Eiffel
- ▶ Forth
- ▶ Fortran
- ▶ JavaScript
- ▶ Oberon
- ▶ PERL
- ▶ Pascal
- ▶ PHP
- ▶ Python
- ▶ RPG
- ▶ Ruby
- ▶ Scheme
- ▶ Small Talk

The vast majority of developers building ASP.NET applications write the applications in either C# or Visual Basic .NET. Many of the other .NET languages in the preceding list are academic experiments. Once upon a time, if you wanted to become a developer, you concentrated on becoming proficient at a particular language. For example, you became a C++ programmer, a COBOL programmer, or a Visual Basic Programmer.

For .NET Framework, however, knowing a particular language is not particularly important. The choice of which language to use when building a .NET application is largely a preference choice. If you like case-sensitivity and curly braces, you should use the C# programming language. If you want to be lazy about casing and you don't like semicolons, write your code with Visual Basic .NET.

All the real action in .NET Framework happens in the Framework Class Library. If you want to become a good programmer using Microsoft technologies, you need to learn how to use the methods, properties, and events of the 13,000 classes included in the Framework. From the point of view of .NET Framework, it doesn't matter whether you use these classes from a Visual Basic .NET or C# application.

> **NOTE**
>
> All the code samples in this book were written in both C# and Visual Basic. All of the code samples can be found on the book's website.

Understanding ASP.NET Controls

ASP.NET controls are the heart of ASP.NET Framework. An ASP.NET control is a .NET class that executes on the server and renders certain content to the browser. For example, in the first ASP.NET page created at the beginning of this chapter, a Label control was used to display the current date and time. The ASP.NET framework includes more than 90 controls, which enable you to do everything from displaying a list of database records to displaying a randomly rotating banner advertisement.

This section provides an overview of the controls included in ASP.NET Framework. You also learn how to handle events raised by controls and how to take advantage of View State.

Overview of ASP.NET Controls

The ASP.NET Framework contains more than 90 controls. These controls can be divided into seven groups:

- **Standard Controls**—Enable you to render standard form elements such as buttons, input fields, and labels. We examine these controls in detail in Chapter 2, "Using the Standard Controls."

- **Validation Controls**—Enable you to validate form data before you submit the data to the server. For example, you can use a RequiredFieldValidator control to check whether a user entered a value for a required input field. These controls are discussed in Chapter 3, "Using the Validation Controls."

- **Rich Controls**—Enable you to render things such as calendars, file upload buttons, rotating banner advertisements, and multistep wizards. Chapter 4, "Using the Rich Controls," discusses these controls.

- **Data Controls**—Enable you to work with data such as database data. For example, you can use these controls to submit new records to a database table or display a list of database records. Part III, "Performing Data Access," discusses these controls.

- **Navigation Controls**—Enable you to display standard navigation elements such as menus, tree views, and bread crumb trails. Chapter 22, "Using the Navigation Controls," discusses these controls.

▶ **Login Controls**—Enables you to display login, change password, and registration forms. Chapter 26, "Using the Login Controls," discusses these controls.

▶ **HTML Controls**—Enable you to convert any HTML tag into a server-side control. This group of controls are discussed in the next section.

With the exception of the HTML controls, you declare and use all ASP.NET controls in a page in exactly the same way. For example, if you want to display a text input field in a page, you can declare a `TextBox` control like this:

```
<asp:TextBox id="TextBox1" runat="Server" />
```

This control declaration looks like the declaration for an HTML tag. Remember, however, unlike an HTML tag, a control is a .NET class that executes on the server and not in the web browser.

When the TextBox control is rendered to the browser, it renders the following content:

```
<input name="TextBox1" type="text" id="TextBox1" />
```

The first part of the control declaration, the `asp:` prefix, indicates the namespace for the control. All the standard ASP.NET controls are contained in the `System.Web.UI.WebControls` namespace. The prefix `asp:` represents this namespace.

Next, the declaration contains the name of the control being declared. In this case, a `TextBox` control is declared.

This declaration also includes an ID attribute. You use the ID to refer to the control in the page within your code. Every control must have a unique ID.

NOTE

You should always assign an ID attribute to every control even when you don't need to program against it. If you don't provide an ID attribute, certain features of ASP.NET Framework (such as two-way databinding) won't work.

The declaration also includes a `runat="Server"` attribute. This attribute marks the tag as representing a server-side control. If you neglect to include this attribute, the `TextBox` tag would be passed, without being executed, to the browser. The browser would simply ignore the tag.

Finally, notice that the tag ends with a forward slash. The forward slash is shorthand for creating a closing `</asp:TextBox>` tag. You can, if you prefer, declare the `TextBox` control like this:

```
<asp:TextBox id="TextBox1" runat="server"></asp:TextBox>
```

In this case, the opening tag does not contain a forward slash and an explicit closing tag is included.

Understanding HTML Controls

You declare HTML controls in a different way than you declare standard ASP.NET controls. The ASP.NET Framework enables you to take any HTML tag (real or imaginary) and add a runat="server" attribute to the tag. The runat="server" attribute converts the HTML tag into a server-side ASP.NET control.

For example, the page in Listing 1.5 contains a <span> tag, which has been converted into an ASP.NET control.

LISTING 1.5   HtmlControls.aspx

```
<%@ Page Language="C#" %>
<!DOCTYPE html PUBLIC "-//W3C//DTD XHTML 1.0 Transitional//EN"
"http://www.w3.org/TR/xhtml1/DTD/xhtml1-transitional.dtd">
<script runat="server">

    void Page_Load()
    {
        spanNow.InnerText = DateTime.Now.ToString("T");
    }

</script>
<html xmlns="http://www.w3.org/1999/xhtml" >
<head id="Head1" runat="server">
    <title>HTML Controls</title>
</head>
<body>
    <form id="form1" runat="server">
    <div>

    At the tone, the time will be:
    <span id="spanNow" runat="server" />

    </div>
    </form>
</body>
</html>
```

The <span> tag in Listing 1.5 looks just like a normal HTML <span> tag except for the addition of the runat="server" attribute.

Because the <span> tag in Listing 1.5 is a server-side HTML control, you can program against it. In Listing 1.5, the current date and time are assigned to the <span> tag in the Page_Load() method.

The HTML controls are included in ASP.NET Framework to make it easier to convert existing HTML pages to use ASP.NET Framework. I rarely use the HTML controls in this book because, in general, the standard ASP.NET controls provide all the same functionality and more.

Understanding and Handling Control Events

The majority of ASP.NET controls support one or more events. For example, the ASP.NET Button control supports the Click event. The Click event is raised on the server after you click the button rendered by the Button control in the browser.

The page in Listing 1.6 illustrates how you can write code that executes when a user clicks the button rendered by the Button control (in other words, it illustrates how you can create a Click event handler):

LISTING 1.6   ShowButtonClick.aspx

```
<%@ Page Language="C#" %>
<!DOCTYPE html PUBLIC "-//W3C//DTD XHTML 1.0 Transitional//EN"
"http://www.w3.org/TR/xhtml1/DTD/xhtml1-transitional.dtd">
<script runat="server">

    protected void btnSubmit_Click(object sender, EventArgs e)
    {
        Label1.Text = "Thanks!";
    }
</script>
<html xmlns="http://www.w3.org/1999/xhtml" >
<head id="Head1" runat="server">
    <title>Show Button Click</title>
</head>
<body>
    <form id="form1" runat="server">
    <div>

    <asp:Button
        id="btnSubmit"
        Text="Click Here"
        OnClick="btnSubmit_Click"
        Runat="server" />

    <br /><br />
```

```
    <asp:Label
        id="Label1"
        Runat="server" />

    </div>
    </form>
</body>
</html>
```

Notice that the Button control in Listing 1.6 includes an OnClick attribute. This attribute points to a subroutine named btnSubmit_Click(). The btnSubmit_Click() subroutine is the handler for the Button Click event. This subroutine executes whenever you click the button (see Figure 1.5).

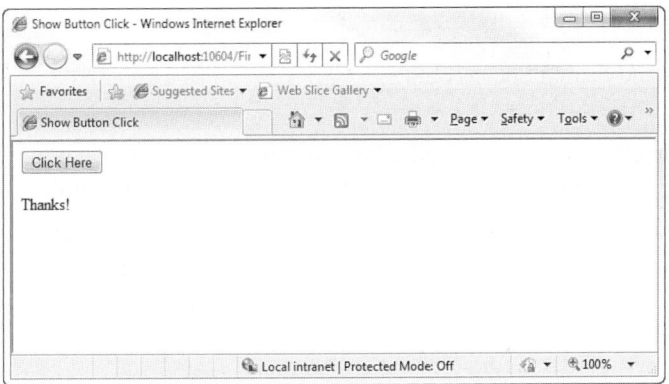

FIGURE 1.5   Raising a Click event.

You can add an event handler automatically to a control in multiple ways when using Visual Web Developer. In Source view, add a handler by selecting a control from the top-left drop-down list and selecting an event from the top-right drop-down list. The event handler code is added to the page automatically (see Figure 1.6).

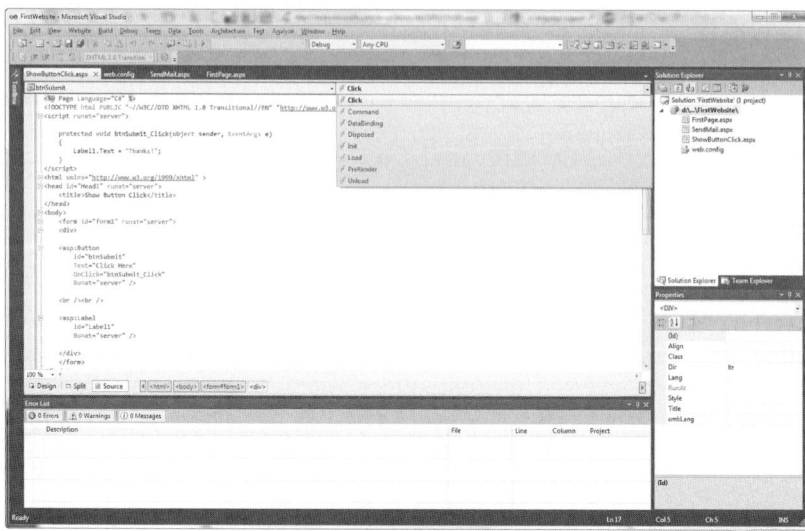

FIGURE 1.6   Adding an event handler from Source view.

In Design view, you can double-click a control to add a handler for the control's default event. Double-clicking a control switches you to Source view and adds the event handler.

Finally, from Design view, after selecting a control on the designer surface, you can add an event handler from the Properties window by clicking the Events button (the lightning bolt) and double-clicking next to the name of any of the events (see Figure 1.7).

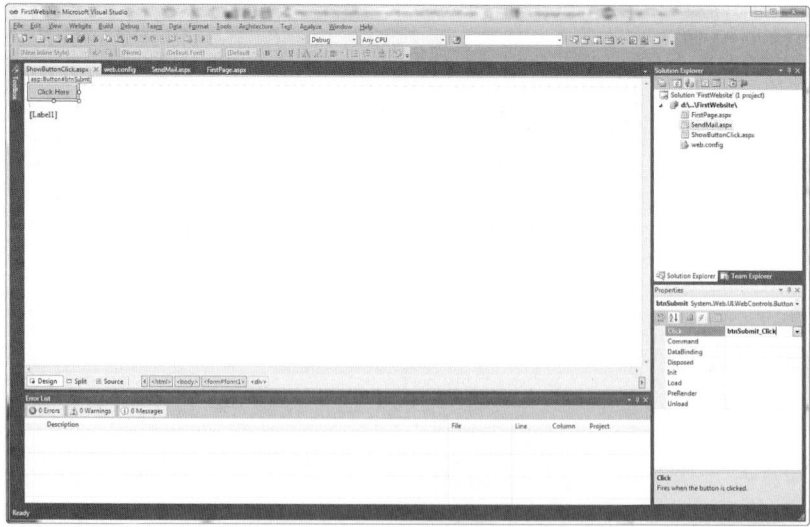

FIGURE 1.7   Adding an event handler from the Properties window.

You need to understand that all ASP.NET control events happen on the server. For example, the Click event is not raised when you actually click a button. The Click event is not raised until the page containing the Button control is posted back to the server.

The ASP.NET Framework is a server-side web application framework. The .NET Framework code that you write executes on the server and not within the web browser. From the perspective of ASP.NET, nothing happens until the page is posted back to the server and can execute within the context of .NET Framework.

Notice that two parameters are passed to the btnSubmit_Click() handler in Listing 1.6. All event handlers for ASP.NET controls have the same general signature.

The first parameter, the object parameter named sender, represents the control that raised the event. In other words, it represents the Button control that you clicked.

You can wire multiple controls in a page to the same event handler and use this first parameter to determine the particular control that raised the event. For example, the page in Listing 1.7 includes two Button controls. When you click either Button control, the text displayed by the Button control is updated (see Figure 1.8).

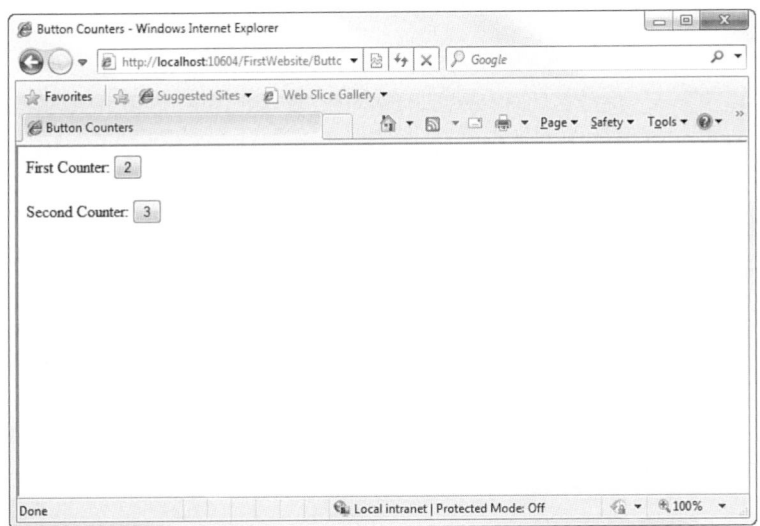

FIGURE 1.8   Handling two Button controls with one event handler.

LISTING 1.7   ButtonCounters.aspx

```
<%@ Page Language="C#" %>
<!DOCTYPE html PUBLIC "-//W3C//DTD XHTML 1.0 Transitional//EN"
"http://www.w3.org/TR/xhtml1/DTD/xhtml1-transitional.dtd">
<script runat="server">

    protected void Button_Click(object sender, EventArgs e)
```

```
    {
        Button btn = (Button)sender;
        btn.Text = (Int32.Parse(btn.Text) + 1).ToString();
    }
</script>
<html xmlns="http://www.w3.org/1999/xhtml" >
<head id="Head1" runat="server">
    <title>Button Counters</title>
</head>
<body>
    <form id="form1" runat="server">
    <div>

    First Counter:
    <asp:Button
        id="Button1"
        Text="0"
        OnClick="Button_Click"
        Runat="server" />

    <br /><br />

    Second Counter:
    <asp:Button
        id="Button2"
        Text="0"
        OnClick="Button_Click"
        Runat="server" />

    </div>
    </form>
</body>
</html>
```

The second parameter passed to the Click event handler, the EventArgs parameter named e, represents any additional event information associated with the event. No additional event information is associated with clicking a button, so this second parameter does not represent anything useful in either Listing 1.6 or Listing 1.7.

When you click an ImageButton control instead of a Button control, on the other hand, additional event information is passed to the event handler. When you click an ImageButton control, the X and Y coordinates of where you clicked are passed to the handler.

The page in Listing 1.8 contains an `ImageButton` control that displays a picture. When you click the picture, the X and Y coordinates of the spot you clicked display in a Label control (see Figure 1.9).

LISTING 1.8   `ShowEventArgs.aspx`

```
<%@ Page Language="C#" %>
<!DOCTYPE html PUBLIC "-//W3C//DTD XHTML 1.0 Transitional//EN"
"http://www.w3.org/TR/xhtml1/DTD/xhtml1-transitional.dtd">
<script runat="server">

    protected void btnElephant_Click(object sender, ImageClickEventArgs e)
    {
        lblX.Text = e.X.ToString();
        lblY.Text = e.Y.ToString();
    }
</script>
<html xmlns="http://www.w3.org/1999/xhtml" >
<head id="Head1" runat="server">
    <title>Show EventArgs</title>
</head>
<body>
    <form id="form1" runat="server">
    <div>

    <asp:ImageButton
        id="btnElephant"
        ImageUrl="Elephant.jpg"
        Runat="server" OnClick="btnElephant_Click" />

    <br />
    X Coordinate:
    <asp:Label
        id="lblX"
        Runat="server" />
    <br />
    Y Coordinate:
    <asp:Label
        id="lblY"
        Runat="server" />

    </div>
    </form>
</body>
</html>
```

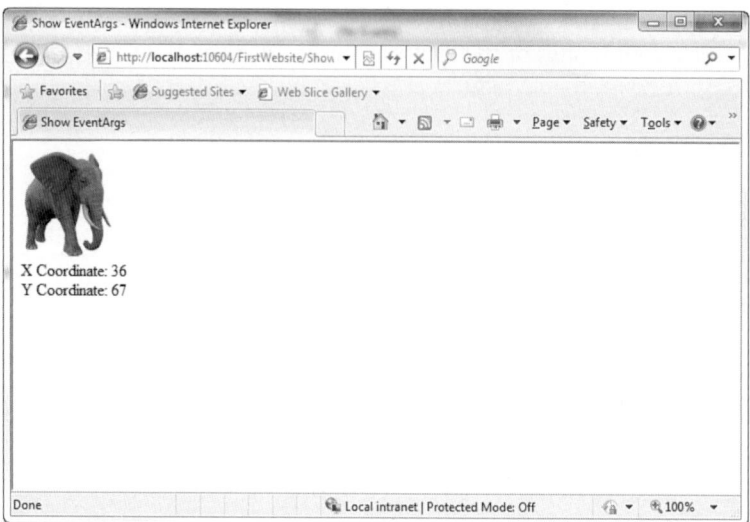

FIGURE 1.9   Clicking an `ImageButton`.

The second parameter passed to the `btnElephant_Click()` method is an `ImageClickEventArgs` parameter. Whenever the second parameter is not the default `EventArgs` parameter, you know that additional event information is passed to the handler.

Understanding View State

The HTTP protocol, the fundamental protocol of the World Wide Web, is a stateless protocol. Each time you request a web page from a website, from the website's perspective, you are a completely new person.

The ASP.NET Framework, however, manages to transcend this limitation of the HTTP protocol. For example, if you assign a value to a Label control's `Text` property, the Label control retains this value across multiple page requests.

Consider the page in Listing 1.9. This page contains a Button control and a Label control. Each time you click the Button control, the value displayed by the Label control is incremented by 1 (see Figure 1.10). How does the Label control preserve its value across postbacks to the web server?

LISTING 1.9 ShowViewState.aspx

```
<%@ Page Language="C#" %>
<!DOCTYPE html PUBLIC "-//W3C//DTD XHTML 1.0 Transitional//EN"
"http://www.w3.org/TR/xhtml1/DTD/xhtml1-transitional.dtd">
<script runat="server">

    protected void btnAdd_Click(object sender, EventArgs e)
    {
        lblCounter.Text = (Int32.Parse(lblCounter.Text) + 1).ToString();
    }
</script>
<html xmlns="http://www.w3.org/1999/xhtml" >
<head id="Head1" runat="server">
    <title>Show  View State</title>
</head>
<body>
    <form id="form1" runat="server">
    <div>

    <asp:Button
        id="btnAdd"
        Text="Add"
        OnClick="btnAdd_Click"
        Runat="server" />

    <asp:Label
        id="lblCounter"
        Text="0"
        Runat="server" />

    </div>
    </form>
</body>
</html>
```

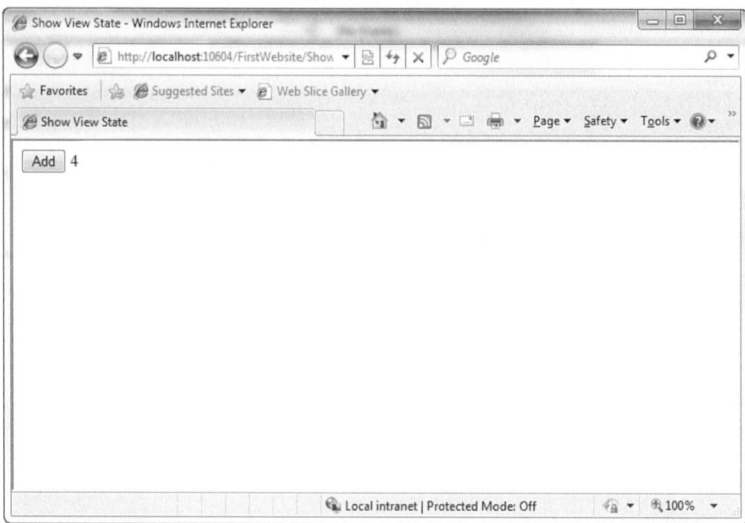

FIGURE 1.10   Preserving state between postbacks.

The ASP.NET Framework uses a trick called View State. If you open the page in Listing 1.9 in your browser and select View Source, you notice that the page includes a hidden form field named __VIEWSTATE that looks like this:

```
<input type="hidden" name="__VIEWSTATE" id="__
  VIEWSTATE" value="/wEPDwUKLTc2ODE1OTYxNw9kFgICBA9kFgIC
  Aw8PFgIeBFRleHQFATFkZGT3tMnThg9KZpGak55p367vfInj1w==" />
```

This hidden form field contains the value of the Label control's Text property (and the values of any other control properties stored in View State). When the page is posted back to the server, ASP.NET Framework rips apart this string and re-creates the values of all the properties stored in View State. In this way, ASP.NET Framework preserves the state of control properties across postbacks to the web server.

By default, View State is enabled for every control in ASP.NET Framework. If you change the background color of a Calendar control, the new background color is remembered across postbacks. If you change the selected item in a DropDownList, the selected item is remembered across postbacks. The values of these properties are automatically stored in View State.

View State is a good thing, but sometimes it can be too much of a good thing. The __VIEWSTATE hidden form field can become large. Stuffing too much data into View State can slow down the rendering of a page because the contents of the hidden field must be pushed back and forth between the web server and web browser.

You can determine how much View State each control contained in a page is consuming by enabling tracing for a page (see Figure 1.11). The page in Listing 1.10 includes a Trace="true" attribute in its <%@ Page %> directive, which enables tracing.

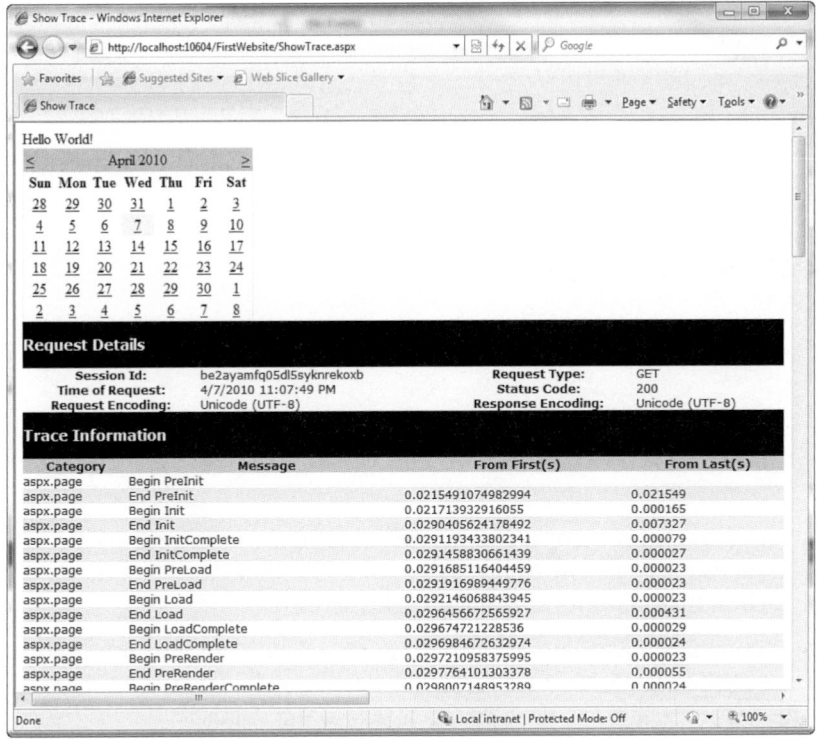

FIGURE 1.11   Viewing View State size for each control.

LISTING 1.10   ShowTrace.aspx

```
<%@ Page Language="C#" Trace="true" %>
<!DOCTYPE html PUBLIC "-//W3C//DTD XHTML 1.0 Transitional//EN"
"http://www.w3.org/TR/xhtml1/DTD/xhtml1-transitional.dtd">
<script runat="server">

    void Page_Load()
    {
        Label1.Text = "Hello World!";
        Calendar1.TodaysDate = DateTime.Now;
    }

</script>
<html xmlns="http://www.w3.org/1999/xhtml" >
<head id="Head1" runat="server">
    <title>Show Trace</title>
</head>
<body>
```

```
    <form id="form1" runat="server">
    <div>

    <asp:Label
        id="Label1"
        Runat="server" />
    <asp:Calendar
        id="Calendar1"
        TodayDayStyle-BackColor="Yellow"
        Runat="server" />

    </div>
    </form>
</body>
</html>
```

When you open the page in Listing 1.10, additional information about the page is appended to the bottom of the page. The Control Tree section displays the amount of View State used by each ASP.NET control contained in the page.

Every ASP.NET control includes a property named EnableViewState. If you set this property to the value False, View State is disabled for the control. In that case, the values of the control properties are not remembered across postbacks to the server.

For example, the page in Listing 1.11 contains two Label controls and a Button control. The first Label has View State disabled, and the second Label has View State enabled. When you click the button, only the value of the second Label control is incremented past 1.

LISTING 1.11   DisableViewState.aspx

```
<%@ Page Language="C#" %>
<!DOCTYPE html PUBLIC "-//W3C//DTD XHTML 1.0 Transitional//EN"
"http://www.w3.org/TR/xhtml1/DTD/xhtml1-transitional.dtd">
<script runat="server">

    protected void btnAdd_Click(object sender, EventArgs e)
    {
        Label1.Text = (Int32.Parse(Label1.Text) + 1).ToString();
        Label2.Text = (Int32.Parse(Label2.Text) + 1).ToString();
    }
</script>
<html xmlns="http://www.w3.org/1999/xhtml" >
<head id="Head1" runat="server">
    <title>Disable  View State</title>
</head>
```

```
<body>
    <form id="form1" runat="server">
    <div>

    Label 1:
    <asp:Label
        id="Label1"
        EnableViewState="false"
        Text="0"
        Runat="server" />

    <br />

    Label 2:
    <asp:Label
        id="Label2"
        Text="0"
        Runat="server" />

    <br /><br />

    <asp:Button
        id="btnAdd"
        Text="Add"
        OnClick="btnAdd_Click"
        Runat="server" />

    </div>
    </form>
</body>
</html>
```

Sometimes, you might want to disable View State even when you aren't concerned with the size of the __VIEWSTATE hidden form field. For example, if you use a Label control to display a form validation error message, you might want to start from scratch each time the page is submitted. In that case, simply disable View State for the Label control.

> **NOTE**
>
> The ASP.NET Framework version 2.0 introduced a new feature called Control State, which is similar to View State except that it is used to preserve only critical state information. For example, the GridView control uses Control State to store the selected row. Even if you disable View State, the GridView control remembers which row is selected.

Understanding ASP.NET Pages

This section examines ASP.NET pages in more detail. You learn about dynamic compilation and code-behind files. We also discuss the events supported by the Page class.

Understanding Dynamic Compilation

Strangely enough, when you create an ASP.NET page, you are actually creating the source code for a .NET class. You are creating a new instance of the `System.Web.UI.Page` class. The entire contents of an ASP.NET page, including all script and HTML content, are compiled into a .NET class.

When you request an ASP.NET page, ASP.NET Framework checks for a .NET class that corresponds to the page. If a corresponding class does not exist, the Framework automatically compiles the page into a new class and stores the compiled class (the assembly) in the Temporary ASP.NET Files folder located at the following path:

```
\WINDOWS\Microsoft.NET\Framework\v4.0.30128\Temporary ASP.NET Files
```

The next time anyone requests the same page in the future, the page is not compiled again. The previously compiled class is executed, and the results are returned to the browser.

Even if you unplug your web server, move to Borneo for 3 years, and start up your web server again, the next time someone requests the same page, the page does not need to be recompiled. The compiled class is preserved in the Temporary ASP.NET Files folder until the source code for your application is modified.

When the class is added to the Temporary ASP.NET Files folder, a file dependency is created between the class and the original ASP.NET page. If the ASP.NET page is modified in any way, the corresponding .NET class is automatically deleted. The next time someone requests the page, the Framework automatically compiles the modified page source into a new .NET class.

This process is called *dynamic compilation*, which enables ASP.NET applications to support thousands of simultaneous users. Unlike an ASP Classic page, for example, an ASP.NET page does not need to be parsed and compiled every time it is requested. An ASP.NET page is compiled only when an application is modified.

> **NOTE**
>
> You can precompile an entire ASP.NET application by using the `aspnet_compiler.exe` command-line tool. If you precompile an application, users don't experience the compilation delay resulting from the first page request.

NOTE

You can disable dynamic compilation for a single page, the pages in a folder, or an entire website with the `CompilationMode` attribute. When the `CompilationMode` attribute is used with the `<%@ Page %>` directive, it enables you to disable dynamic compilation for a single page. When the `compilationMode` attribute is used with the pages element in a web configuration file, it enables you to disable dynamic compilation for an entire folder or application.

Disabling compilation is useful when you have thousands of pages in a website and you don't want to load too many assemblies into memory. When the `CompilationMode` attribute is set to the value `Never`, the page is never compiled, and an assembly is never generated for the page. The page is interpreted at runtime.

You cannot disable compilation for pages that include server-side code. In particular, a no compile page cannot include a server-side `<script>...</script>` block. On the other hand, a no compile page can contain ASP.NET controls and databinding expressions.

If you are curious, I've included the source code for the class that corresponds to the `FirstPage.aspx` page in Listing 1.12. (I cleaned up the code and made it shorter to save space.) I copied this file from the Temporary ASP.NET Files folder after enabling debugging for the application.

LISTING 1.12   `FirstPage.aspx` Source

```
namespace ASP
{
    using System.Web.Security;
    using System.Web;
    using System.Web.SessionState;
    using System.Text;
    using System.Collections.Specialized;
    using System.Web.Profile;
    using System.Net.Mail;
    using System.Collections;
    using System.Web.UI.WebControls.WebParts;
    using System.Configuration;
    using System;
    using System.Web.Caching;
    using System.Web.UI;
    using System.Text.RegularExpressions;
    using System.Web.UI.WebControls;
    using System.Web.UI.HtmlControls;
```

```
[System.Runtime.CompilerServices.CompilerGlobalScopeAttribute()]
public class firstpage_aspx : global::System.Web.UI.Page,
System.Web.SessionState.IRequiresSessionState, System.Web.IHttpHandler
{
    protected global::System.Web.UI.WebControls.Label lblServerTime;
    protected global::System.Web.UI.HtmlControls.HtmlForm form1;
    private static bool @__initialized;
    private static object @__fileDependencies;

    void Page_Load()
    {
        lblServerTime.Text = DateTime.Now.ToString();
    }

    public firstpage_aspx()
    {
        string[] dependencies;
        ((global::System.Web.UI.Page)(this)).AppRelativeVirtualPath =
➥"~/FirstPage.aspx";
        if ((global::ASP.firstpage_aspx.@__initialized == false))
        {
            dependencies = new string[1];
            dependencies[0] = "~/FirstPage.aspx";
            global::ASP.firstpage_aspx.@__fileDependencies =
this.GetWrappedFileDependencies(dependencies);
            global::ASP.firstpage_aspx.@__initialized = true;
        }
        this.Server.ScriptTimeout = 30000000;
    }

    protected System.Web.Profile.DefaultProfile Profile
    {
        get
        {
            return ((System.Web.Profile.DefaultProfile)(this.Context.Profile));
        }
    }

    protected System.Web.HttpApplication ApplicationInstance
    {
        get
        {
            return ((System.Web.HttpApplication)(this.Context.Application
➥Instance));
        }
```

```
        }

        private global::System.Web.UI.WebControls.Label @__BuildControllbl
➥ServerTime()
        {
        ...code...
        }

        private global::System.Web.UI.HtmlControls.HtmlForm @__BuildControlform1()
        {
        ...code...
        }

        private void @__BuildControlTree(firstpage_aspx @__ctrl)
        {
        ...code...
        }

        protected override void FrameworkInitialize()
        {
            base.FrameworkInitialize();
            this.@__BuildControlTree(this);
            this.AddWrappedFileDependencies(global::ASP.firstpage_aspx.@__file
➥Dependencies);
            this.Request.ValidateInput();
        }

        public override int GetTypeHashCode()
        {
            return 243955639;
        }

        public override void ProcessRequest(System.Web.HttpContext context)
        {
            base.ProcessRequest(context);
        }
    }
}
```

The class in Listing 1.12 inherits from the System.Web.UI.Page class. The ProcessRequest() method is called by ASP.NET Framework when the page is displayed. This method builds the page's control tree, which is the subject of the next section.

Understanding Control Trees

In the previous section, you learned that an ASP.NET page is actually the source code for a .NET class. Alternatively, you can think of an ASP.NET page as a bag of controls. More accurately, because some controls might contain child controls, you can think of an ASP.NET page as a control tree.

For example, the page in Listing 1.13 contains a DropDownList control and a Button control. Furthermore, because the `<%@ Page %>` directive has the `Trace="true"` attribute, tracing is enabled for the page.

LISTING 1.13   ShowControlTree.aspx

```
<%@ Page Language="C#" Trace="true" %>
<!DOCTYPE html PUBLIC "-//W3C//DTD XHTML 1.0 Transitional//EN"
"http://www.w3.org/TR/xhtml1/DTD/xhtml1-transitional.dtd">
<html xmlns="http://www.w3.org/1999/xhtml" >
<head id="Head1" runat="server">
    <title>Show Control Tree</title>
</head>
<body>
    <form id="form1" runat="server">
    <div>

    <asp:DropDownList
        id="DropDownList1"
        Runat="server">
        <asp:ListItem Text="Oranges" />
        <asp:ListItem Text="Apples" />
    </asp:DropDownList>

    <asp:Button
        id="Button1"
        Text="Submit"
        Runat="server" />

    </div>
    </form>
</body>
</html>
```

When you open the page in Listing 1.13 in your browser, you can see the control tree for the page appended to the bottom of the page. It looks like this:

```
__Page ASP.showcontroltree_aspx
    ctl02 System.Web.UI.LiteralControl
```

```
ctl00 System.Web.UI.HtmlControls.HtmlHead
    ctl01 System.Web.UI.HtmlControls.HtmlTitle
ctl03 System.Web.UI.LiteralControl
form1 System.Web.UI.HtmlControls.HtmlForm
    ctl04 System.Web.UI.LiteralControl
    DropDownList1 System.Web.UI.WebControls.DropDownList
    ctl05 System.Web.UI.LiteralControl
    Button1 System.Web.UI.WebControls.Button
    ctl06 System.Web.UI.LiteralControl
ctl07
```

The root node in the control tree is the page itself. The page has an ID of __Page. The page class contains all the other controls in its child controls collection. The control tree also contains an instance of the HtmlForm class named form1. This control is the server-side form tag contained in the page. It contains all the other form controls—the DropDownList and Button controls—as child controls.

Several LiteralControl controls are interspersed between the other controls in the control tree. What are these controls?

Remember that everything in an ASP.NET page is converted into a .NET class, including any HTML or plain text content in a page. The LiteralControl class represents the HTML content in the page (including any carriage returns between tags).

NOTE

Normally, you refer to a control in a page by its ID. However, there are situations in which this is not possible. In those cases, you can use the FindControl() method of the Control class to retrieve a control with a particular ID. The FindControl() method is similar to the JavaScript getElementById() method.

Using Code-Behind Pages

The ASP.NET Framework (and Visual Web Developer) enables you to create two different types of ASP.NET pages. You can create both single-file and two-file ASP.NET pages.

All the code samples in this book are written as single-file ASP.NET pages. In a single-file ASP.NET page, a single file contains both the page code and page controls. The page code is contained in a <script runat="server"> tag.

As an alternative to a single-file ASP.NET page, you can create a two-file ASP.NET page. A two-file ASP.NET page is normally referred to as a *code-behind* page. In a code-behind page, the page code is contained in a separate file.

NOTE

Code-behind pages work in a different way after ASP.NET 2.0 Framework than they did in ASP.NET 1.x Framework. In ASP.NET 1.x, the two halves of a code-behind page were related by inheritance. After ASP.NET 2.0 Framework, the two halves of a code-behind page are related by a combination of partial classes and inheritance.

For example, Listing 1.14 and Listing 1.15 contain the two halves of a code-behind page.

VISUAL WEB DEVELOPER NOTE

When using Visual Web Developer, you create a code-behind page by selecting Web Site, Add New Item and selecting the Web Form Item and checking the Place Code in Separate File check box before adding the page.

LISTING 1.14   FirstPageCodeBehind.aspx

```
<%@ Page Language="C#" AutoEventWireup="true" CodeFile="FirstPageCodeBehind.aspx.cs
"Inherits="FirstPageCodeBehind" %>
<!DOCTYPE html PUBLIC "-//W3C//DTD XHTML 1.0 Transitional//EN"
"http://www.w3.org/TR/xhtml1/DTD/xhtml1-transitional.dtd">
<html xmlns="http://www.w3.org/1999/xhtml" >
<head id="Head1" runat="server">
    <title>First Page Code-Behind</title>
</head>
<body>
    <form id="form1" runat="server">
    <div>

    <asp:Button
        id="Button1"
        Text="Click Here"
        OnClick="Button1_Click"
        Runat="server" />

    <br /><br />

    <asp:Label
        id="Label1"
        Runat="server" />
```

```
        </div>
    </form>
</body>
</html>
```

LISTING 1.15 FirstPageCodeBehind.aspx.cs

```csharp
using System;
using System.Collections.Generic;
using System.Web;
using System.Web.UI;
using System.Web.UI.WebControls;

public partial class FirstPageCodeBehind : System.Web.UI.Page
{
    protected void Page_Load(object sender, EventArgs e)
    {
        Label1.Text = "Click the Button";
    }

    protected void Button1_Click(object sender, EventArgs e)
    {
        Label1.Text = "Thanks!";
    }
}
```

The page in Listing 1.14 is called the *presentation page*. It contains a Button control and a Label control. However, the page does not contain any code. All the code is contained in the code-behind file.

VISUAL WEB DEVELOPER NOTE

You can flip to the code-behind file for a page by right-clicking a page and selecting View Code.

The code-behind the file in Listing 1.15 contains the Page_Load() and Button1_Click() handlers. The code-behind file in Listing 1.15 does not contain any controls.

Notice that the page in Listing 1.14 includes both a CodeFile and Inherits attribute in its <%@ Page %> directive. These attributes link the page to its code-behind file.

How Code-Behind Works: The Ugly Details

In the early versions of ASP.NET Framework (ASP.NET 1.x), two classes were generated by a code-behind page. One class corresponded to the presentation page, and one class corresponded to the code-behind file. These classes were related to one another through class inheritance. The presentation page class inherited from the code-behind file class.

The problem with this method of associating presentation pages with their code-behind files was that it was brittle. Inheritance is a one-way relationship. Anything that is true of the mother is true of the daughter, but not the other way around. Any control that you declared in the presentation page was required to be declared in the code-behind file. Furthermore, the control had to be declared with exactly the same ID. Otherwise, the inheritance relationship would be broken and events raised by a control could not be handled in the code-behind file.

In the beta version of ASP.NET 2.0, a completely different method of associating presentation pages with their code-behind files was used. This new method was far less brittle. The two halves of a code-behind page were no longer related through inheritance, but through a new technology supported by .NET 2.0 Framework called *partial classes*.

> **NOTE**
>
> Chapter 17, "Building Components," discusses partial classes.

Partial classes enable you to declare a class in more than one physical file. When the class is compiled, one class is generated from all the partial classes. Any members of one partial class—including any private fields, methods, and properties—are accessible to any other partial classes of the same class. This makes sense because partial classes are combined eventually to create one final class.

The advantage of using partial classes is that you don't need to worry about declaring a control in both the presentation page and code-behind file. Anything that you declare in the presentation page is available automatically in the code-behind file, and anything you declare in the code-behind file is available automatically in the presentation page.

The beta version of ASP.NET 2.0 Framework used partial classes to relate a presentation page with its code-behind file. However, certain advanced features of ASP.NET 1.x Framework were not compatible with using partial classes. To support these advanced features, a more complex method of associating presentation pages with code-behind files is used in the final release of ASP.NET 2.0 Framework. This method is still the standard in ASP.NET 4.

Since version 2.0 of ASP.NET, the framework uses a combination of inheritance and partial classes to relate presentation pages and code-behind files. Three classes are generated whenever you create a code-behind page.

The first two classes correspond to the presentation page. For example, when you create the FirstPageCodeBehind.aspx page, the following two classes are generated automatically in the Temporary ASP.NET Files folder:

```
public partial class FirstPageCodeBehind
{
    protected System.Web.UI.WebControls.Button Button1;
    protected System.Web.UI.WebControls.Label Label1;

    ... additional code ...
}

public class firstpagecodebehind_aspx : FirstPageCodeBehind
{
    ... additional code ...
}
```

A third class is generated that corresponds to the code-behind file. Corresponding to the
FirstPageCodeBehind.aspx.cs file, the following class is generated:

```
public partial class FirstPageCodeBehind : System.Web.UI.Page
{
    protected void Page_Load(object sender, EventArgs e)
    {
        Label1.Text = "Click the Button";
    }

    protected void Button1_Click(object sender, EventArgs e)
    {
        Label1.Text = "Thanks!";
    }
}
```

The firstpagecodebehind_aspx class is executed when the FirstPageCodeBehind.aspx
page is requested from a browser. This class inherits from the FirstPageCodeBehind class.
The FirstPageCodeBehind class is a partial class. It gets generated twice: once by the
presentation page and once by the code-behind file.

The ASP.NET Framework uses a combination of partial classes and inheritance to relate
presentation pages and code-behind files. Because the page and code-behind classes are
partial classes, unlike the previous version of ASP.NET, you no longer need to declare
controls in both the presentation and code-behind page. Any control declared in the
presentation page is accessible in the code-behind file automatically. Because the page
class inherits from the code-behind class, ASP.NET Framework continues to support
advanced features of ASP.NET 1.x Framework, such as custom base Page classes.

Deciding Between Single-File and Code-Behind Pages

So, when should you use single-file ASP.NET pages and when should you use code-behind
pages? This decision is a preference choice. There are intense arguments over this topic
contained in blogs spread across the Internet.

I've heard it argued that code-behind pages are superior to single-file pages because code-behind pages enable you to more cleanly separate your user interface from your application logic. The problem with this argument is that the normal justification for separating your user interface from your application logic is code reuse. Building code-behind pages doesn't promote code reuse. A better way to reuse application logic across multiple pages is to build separate component libraries. (Part IV of this book explores this topic.)

Ultimately, it is a personal preference. The majority of enterprise projects that we have worked on utilize code-behind pages, but single-file pages are perfectly acceptable under the right circumstances.

Handling Page Events

Whenever you request an ASP.NET page, a particular set of events is raised in a particular sequence. This sequence of events is called the *page execution lifecycle*.

For example, we have already used the Page Load event in previous code samples. You normally use the Page Load event to initialize the properties of controls contained in a page. However, the Page Load event is only one event supported by the Page class.

Following is the sequence of events raised whenever you request a page:

1. PreInit
2. Init
3. InitComplete
4. PreLoad
5. Load
6. LoadComplete
7. PreRender
8. PreRenderComplete
9. SaveStateComplete
10. Unload

Why so many events? Different things happen and different information is available at different stages in the page execution lifecycle.

For example, View State is not loaded until after the InitComplete event. Data posted to the server from a form control, such as a TextBox control, is also not available until after this event.

Ninety-nine percent of the time, you won't handle any of these events except for the Load and the PreRender events. The difference between these two events is that the Load event happens before any control events, and the PreRender event happens after any control events.

The page in Listing 1.16 illustrates the difference between the Load and PreRender events. The page contains three event handlers: one for the Load event, one for the Button Click event, and one for the `PreRender` event. Each handler adds a message to a Label control (Figure 1.12).

LISTING 1.16 ShowPageEvents.aspx

```
<%@ Page Language="C#" %>
<!DOCTYPE html PUBLIC "-//W3C//DTD XHTML 1.0 Transitional//EN"
"http://www.w3.org/TR/xhtml1/DTD/xhtml1-transitional.dtd">
<script runat="server">

    void Page_Load(object sender, EventArgs e)
    {
        Label1.Text = "Page Load";
    }

    void Button1_Click(object sender, EventArgs e)
    {
        Label1.Text += "<br />Button Click";
    }

    void Page_PreRender()
    {
        Label1.Text += "<br />Page PreRender";
    }
</script>
<html xmlns="http://www.w3.org/1999/xhtml" >
<head id="Head1" runat="server">
    <title>Show Page Events</title>
</head>
<body>
    <form id="form1" runat="server">
    <div>

    <asp:Button
        id="Button1"
        Text="Click Here"
        OnClick="Button1_Click"
        Runat="server" />

    <br /><br />

    <asp:Label
        id="Label1"
        Runat="server" />

    </div>
```

```
    </form>
</body>
</html>
```

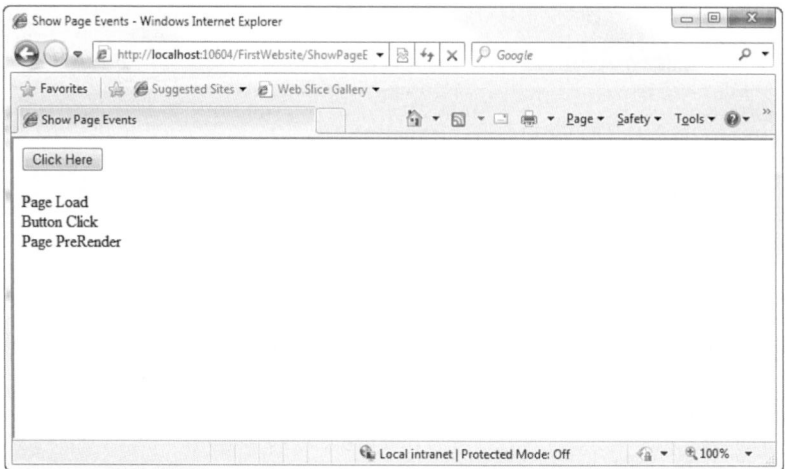

FIGURE 1.12   Viewing the sequence of page events.

When you click the Button control, the Click event does not happen on the server until after the Load event and before the PreRender event.

The other thing you should notice about the page in Listing 1.16 is the way the event handlers are wired to the Page events. ASP.NET pages support a feature named AutoEventWireUp, which is enabled by default. If you name a subroutine Page_Load(), the subroutine automatically handles the Page Load event; if you name a subroutine Page_PreRender(), the subroutine automatically handles the Page PreRender event, and so on.

> **WARNING**
>
> AutoEventWireUp does not work for every page event. For example, it does not work for the Page_InitComplete() event.

Using the Page.IsPostBack Property

The Page class includes a property called the IsPostBack property, which you can use to detect whether the page has already been posted back to the server.

Because of View State, when you initialize a control property, you do not want to initialize the property every time a page loads. Because View State saves the state of control properties across page posts, you typically initialize a control property only once, when the page first loads.

Many controls don't work correctly if you reinitialize the properties of the control with each page load. In these cases, you must use the IsPostBack property to detect whether the page has been posted.

The page in Listing 1.17 illustrates how you can use the Page.IsPostBack property when adding items to a DropDownList control.

LISTING 1.17   ShowIsPostBack.aspx

```
<%@ Page Language="C#" %>
<!DOCTYPE html PUBLIC "-//W3C//DTD XHTML 1.0 Transitional//EN"
"http://www.w3.org/TR/xhtml1/DTD/xhtml1-transitional.dtd">
<script runat="server">

    void Page_Load()
    {
        if (!Page.IsPostBack)
        {
            // Create collection of items
            ArrayList items = new ArrayList();
            items.Add("Apples");
            items.Add("Oranges");

            // Bind to DropDownList
            DropDownList1.DataSource = items;
            DropDownList1.DataBind();
        }
    }

    protected void Button1_Click(object sender, EventArgs e)
    {
        Label1.Text = DropDownList1.SelectedItem.Text;
    }
</script>
<html xmlns="http://www.w3.org/1999/xhtml" >
<head id="Head1" runat="server">
    <title>Show IsPostBack</title>
</head>
<body>
    <form id="form1" runat="server">
    <div>

    <asp:DropDownList
        id="DropDownList1"
        Runat="server" />

    <asp:Button
```

```
        id="Button1"
        Text="Select"
        OnClick="Button1_Click"
        Runat="server" />

    <br /><br />

    You selected:
    <asp:Label
        id="Label1"
        Runat="server" />

    </div>
    </form>
</body>
</html>
```

In Listing 1.17, the code in the Page_Load() event handler executes only once when the page first loads. When you post the page again, the IsPostBack property returns True and the code contained in the Page_Load() handler is skipped.

If you remove the IsPostBack check from the Page_Load() method, you get a strange result. The DropDownList always displays its first item as the selected item. Binding the DropDownList to a collection of items reinitializes the DropDownList control. Therefore, you want to bind the DropDownList control only once, when the page first loads.

Debugging and Tracing ASP.NET Pages

The sad fact of life is that you spend the majority of your development time when building applications debugging the application. In this section, you learn how to get detailed error messages when developing ASP.NET pages. You also learn how you can display custom trace messages that you can use when debugging a page.

Debugging ASP.NET Pages

If you need to view detailed error messages when you execute a page, you need to enable debugging for either the page or your entire application. You can enable debugging for a page by adding a Debug="true" attribute to the <%@ Page %> directive. For example, the page in Listing 1.18 has debugging enabled.

LISTING 1.18   ShowError.aspx

```
<%@ Page Language="C#" Debug="true" %>
<!DOCTYPE html PUBLIC "-//W3C//DTD XHTML 1.0 Transitional//EN"
"http://www.w3.org/TR/xhtml1/DTD/xhtml1-transitional.dtd">
<script runat="server">

    void Page_Load()
```

```
    {
        int zero = 0;
        Label1.Text = (1 / zero).ToString();
    }

</script>
<html xmlns="http://www.w3.org/1999/xhtml" >
<head id="Head1" runat="server">
    <title>Show Error</title>
</head>
<body>
    <form id="form1" runat="server">
    <div>

    <asp:Label
        id="Label1"
        Runat="server" />

    </div>
    </form>
</body>
</html>
```

When you open the page in Listing 1.18 in your web browser, a detailed error message
displays (see Figure 1.13).

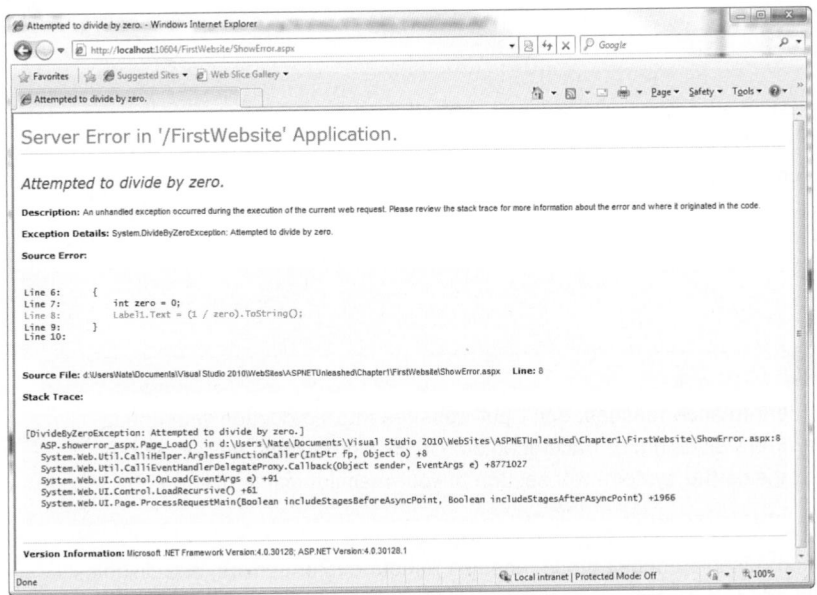

FIGURE 1.13 Viewing a detailed error message.

WARNING

Make sure that you disable debugging before placing your application into production. When an application is compiled in debug mode, the compiler can't make certain performance optimizations.

Rather than enable debugging for a single page, you can enable debugging for an entire application by adding the web configuration file in Listing 1.19 to your application.

LISTING 1.19   Web.Config

```xml
<?xml version="1.0"?>
<configuration>
<system.web>
  <compilation debug="true" />
</system.web>
</configuration>
```

When debugging an ASP.NET application located on a remote web server, you need to disable custom errors. For security reasons, by default, ASP.NET Framework doesn't display error messages when you request a page from a remote machine. When custom errors are enabled, you don't see errors on a remote machine. The modified web configuration file in Listing 1.20 disables custom errors.

LISTING 1.20   Web.Config

```xml
<?xml version="1.0"?>
<configuration>
<system.web>
  <compilation debug="true" />
  <customErrors mode="Off" />
</system.web>
</configuration>
```

WARNING

For security and performance reasons, don't put websites into production with debug enabled, custom errors disabled, or trace enabled. On your production server, add the following element inside the system.web section of your machine.config file:

```
<deployment retail="true"/>
```

Adding this element disables debug mode, enables remote custom errors, and disables trace. You should add this element to the machine.config file located on all your production servers.

Debugging Pages with Visual Web Developer

If you use Visual Web Developer, you can display compilation error messages by performing a build on a page or an entire website. Select Build, Build Page or Build, Build Web Site. A list of compilation error messages and warnings appears in the Error List window (see Figure 1.14). You can double-click any of the errors to navigate directly to the code that caused the error.

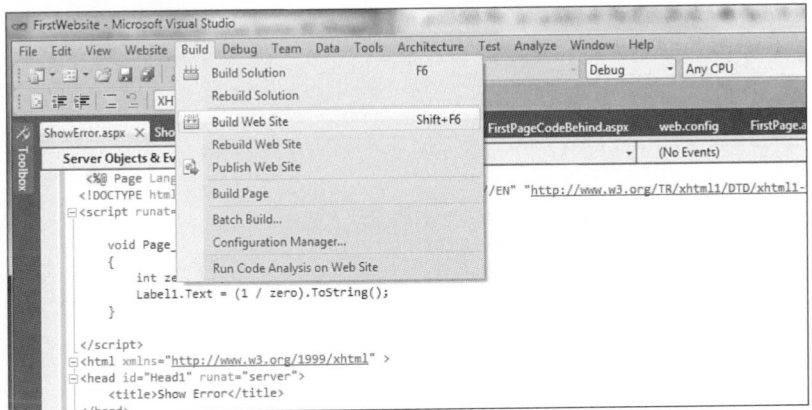

FIGURE 1.14   Performing a build in Visual Web Developer.

If you need to perform more advanced debugging, you can use the Visual Web Developer's debugger. The debugger enables you to set breakpoints and step line by line through your code. You set a breakpoint by double-clicking the left-most column in Source view. When you add a breakpoint, a red circle appears (see Figure 1.15).

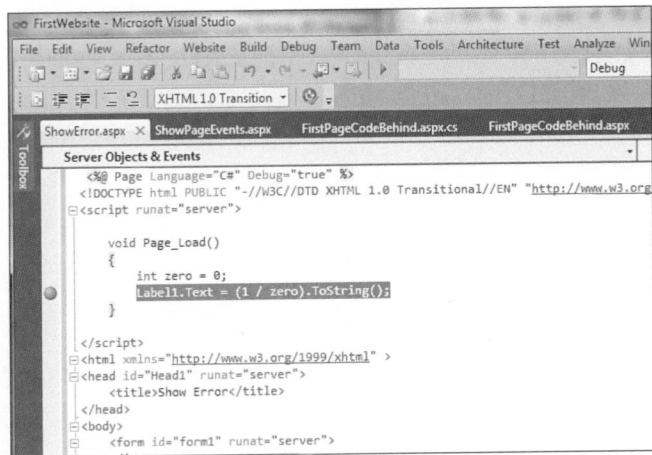

FIGURE 1.15   Setting a breakpoint.

After you set a breakpoint, run your application by selecting Debug, Start Debugging. Execution stops when the breakpoint is hit. At that point, you can hover your mouse over any variable or control property to view the current value of the variable or control property.

> **NOTE**
>
> You can designate one of the pages in your application as the Start Page. That way, whenever you run your application, the Start Page is executed regardless of the page that you have open. Set the Start Page by right-clicking a page in the Solution Explorer window and selecting Set As Start Page.

After you hit a breakpoint, you can continue execution by selecting Step Into, Step Over, or Step Out from the Debug menu or the toolbar. Here's an explanation of each of these options:

▶ **Step Into**—Executes the next line of code

▶ **Step Over**—Executes the next line of code without leaving the current method

▶ **Step Out**—Executes the next line of code and returns to the method that called the current method

When you finish debugging a page, you can continue, stop, or restart your application by selecting a particular option from the Debug menu or the toolbar.

Tracing Page Execution

If you want to output trace messages while a page executes, you can enable tracing for a particular page or an entire application. The ASP.NET Framework supports both page-level tracing and application-level tracing.

The page in Listing 1.21 illustrates how you can take advantage of page-level tracing.

LISTING 1.21   PageTrace.aspx

```
<%@ Page Language="C#" Trace="true" %>
<!DOCTYPE html PUBLIC "-//W3C//DTD XHTML 1.0 Transitional//EN"
"http://www.w3.org/TR/xhtml1/DTD/xhtml1-transitional.dtd">
<script runat="server">

    void Page_Load()
    {
        for (int counter = 0; counter < 10; counter++)
        {
            ListBox1.Items.Add("item " + counter.ToString());
            Trace.Warn("counter=" + counter.ToString());
```

```
            }
        }

    </script>
    <html xmlns="http://www.w3.org/1999/xhtml" >
    <head id="Head1" runat="server">
        <title>Page Trace</title>
    </head>
    <body>
        <form id="form1" runat="server">
        <div>

        <asp:ListBox
            id="ListBox1"
            Runat="server" />

        </div>
        </form>
    </body>
    </html>
```

The `<%@ Page %>` directive in Listing 1.21 includes a `trace="true"` attribute. This attribute enables tracing and causes a Trace Information section to be appended to the bottom of the page (see Figure 1.16).

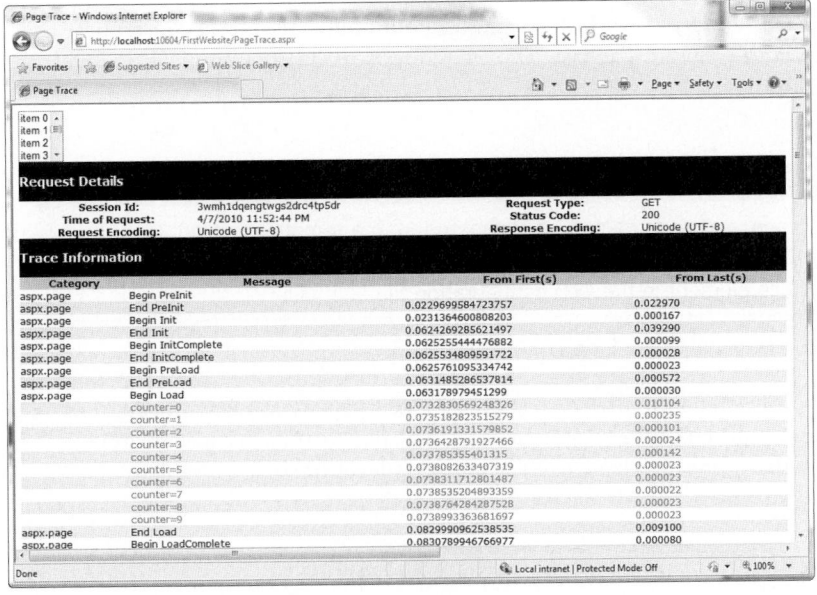

FIGURE 1.16   Viewing page trace information.

Notice, furthermore, that the Page_Load() handler uses the Trace.Warn() method to write messages to the Trace Information section. You can output any string to the Trace Information section that you want. In Listing 1.21, the current value of a variable named counter displays.

You need to take advantage of page tracing when you want to determine exactly what is happening when a page executes. You can call the Trace.Warn() method wherever you need in your code. Because the Trace Information section appears even when an error exists on your page, you can use tracing to diagnose the causes of any page errors.

One disadvantage of page tracing is that everyone in the world gets to see your trace information. You can get around this problem by taking advantage of application-level tracing. When application-level tracing is enabled, trace information appears only when you request a special page named Trace.axd.

To enable application-level tracing, you need to add the web configuration file in Listing 1.22 to your application.

LISTING 1.22 Web.Config

```
<?xml version="1.0"?>
<configuration>
<system.web>
    <trace enabled="true" />
</system.web>
</configuration>
```

After you add the Web.Config file in Listing 1.22 to your application, you can request the Trace.axd page in your browser. The last 10 page requests made after application-level tracing is enabled display.

> **WARNING**
>
> By default, the Trace.axd page cannot be requested from a remote machine. If you need to access the Trace.axd page remotely, you need to add a localOnly="false" attribute to the trace element in the web configuration file.

If you click the View Details link next to any of the listed page requests, you can view all the trace messages outputted by the page. Messages written with the Trace.Warn() method display by the Trace.axd page even when page-level tracing is disabled.

NOTE

You can use the new `writeToDiagnosticsTrace` attribute of the `trace` element to write all trace messages to the Output window of Visual Web Developer when you run an application. You can use the new `mostRecent` attribute to display the last 10 page requests rather than the 10 page requests after tracing was enabled.

WARNING

If you don't enable the `mostRecent` attribute when application level tracing is enabled, tracing stops after 10 pages.

Installing ASP.NET

The easiest way to install ASP.NET Framework is to install Visual Web Developer Express. You can download the latest version of Visual Web Developer from www.ASP.net, which is the official Microsoft ASP.NET website.

Installing Visual Web Developer Express also installs the following components:

▶ Microsoft .NET Framework version 4

▶ SQL Server Express

Visual Web Developer Express is compatible with the following operating systems:

▶ Windows XP (x86) Service Pack 3

▶ Windows XP (x64) Service Pack 2

▶ Windows Server 2003 Service Pack 2

▶ Windows Server 2003 R2

▶ Windows Server 2008 Service Pack 2

▶ Windows Server 2008 R2

▶ Windows Vista

▶ Windows 7

You can install Visual Web Developer Express on a computer that already has other versions of Visual Studio or Visual Web Developer installed. Different versions of the development environments can coexist peacefully.

Furthermore, the same web server can serve ASP.NET 1.1 pages, ASP.NET 2.0 pages, ASP.NET 3.0 pages, ASP.NET 3.5 pages, and ASP.NET 4 pages. Each version of .NET Framework is installed in the following folder:

```
C:\WINDOWS\Microsoft.NET\Framework
```

For example, on my computer, I have the following six versions of .NET Framework installed (version 1.0, version 1.1, version 2.0, version 3.0, version 3.5, and version 4):

```
C:\WINDOWS\Microsoft.NET\Framework\v1.0.3705
C:\WINDOWS\Microsoft.NET\Framework\v1.1.4322
C:\WINDOWS\Microsoft.NET\Framework\v2.0.50727
C:\WINDOWS\Microsoft.NET\Framework\v3.0
C:\WINDOWS\Microsoft.NET\Framework\v3.5
C:\WINDOWS\Microsoft.NET\Framework\v4.0.30128
```

> **NOTE**
>
> The Framework directory contains the 32-bit (x86) version of .NET. If you are running on a 64-bit (x64) operating system, you also have another directory named Framework64.

All the folders except for v3.0 and v3.5 include a command-line tool named aspnet_regiis.exe. You can use this tool to associate a particular virtual directory on your machine with a particular version of .NET Framework.

For example, executing the following command from a command prompt located in the v1.0.3705, v1.1.4322, v2.0.50727, or v4.0.30128 folders enables the 1.0, 1.1, 2.0, or 4 version of ASP.NET for a virtual directory named MyApplication:

```
aspnet_regiis -s W3SVC/1/ROOT/MyApplication
```

By executing the aspnet_regiis.exe tool located in the different .NET Framework version folders, you can map a particular virtual directory to any version of ASP.NET Framework.

The .NET Frameworks 3.0 and 3.5 work differently than earlier versions. The 3.0 and 3.5 versions build on top of the existing .NET Framework 2.0. To use these versions of .NET Framework, you need to add the correct assembly references to your website and use the correct versions of the C# or VB.NET compilers. You reference these assemblies and configure the compiler within your application's web.config file. When you create a new website in Visual Web Developer, the necessary configuration settings are included in your web.config file automatically. The .NET Framework 4 is the first version since 2.0 that does not build off of a previous version.

You also have the option of targeting a particular version of .NET Framework. To do this, select Website, Start Options and select the Build tab. You can choose to target .NET Framework 2.0, .NET Framework 3.0, .NET Framework 3.5, or .NET Framework 4 (see Figure 1.17).

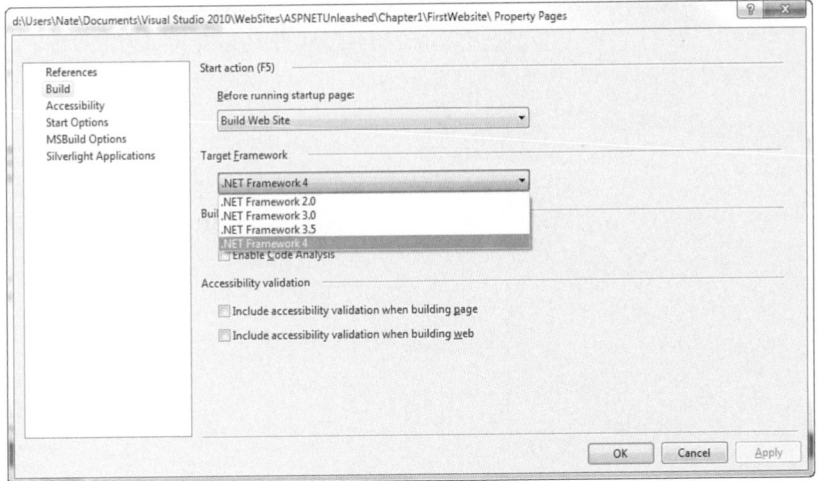

FIGURE 1.17   Targeting a particular version of .NET Framework.

NOTE

If you load an existing ASP.NET 2.0, 3.0, or 3.5 website into Visual Web Developer 2010, Visual Web Developer prompts you to upgrade the website to ASP.NET 4. When Visual Web Developer upgrades your website, it modifies your web.config file.

Summary

In this chapter, you were introduced to ASP.NET 4 Framework. First, we built a simple ASP.NET page. You learned about the three main elements of an ASP.NET page: directives, code declaration blocks, and page render blocks.

Next, we discussed .NET Framework. You learned about the 13,000 classes contained in the Framework Class Library and about the features of the Common Language Runtime.

You also were provided with an overview of ASP.NET controls. You learned about the different groups of controls included in .NET Framework. You also learned how to handle control events and take advantage of View State.

We also discussed ASP.NET pages. You learned how ASP.NET pages are dynamically compiled when they are first requested. We also examined how you can divide a single-file ASP.NET page into a code-behind page. You learned how to debug and trace the execution of an ASP.NET page.

At the end of the chapter we covered installation issues in getting ASP.NET Framework up and running. You learned how to map different Virtual Directories to different versions of ASP.NET Framework. You also learned how to target different versions of .NET Framework in your web configuration file.

CHAPTER 2

Using the Standard Controls

In this chapter, you learn how to use the core controls contained in ASP.NET 4 Framework. These are controls that you use in just about any ASP.NET application that you build.

You learn how to display information to users by using the Label and Literal controls. You learn how to accept user input with the TextBox, CheckBox, and RadioButton controls. You also learn how to submit forms with the button controls.

At the end of this chapter, you learn how to group form fields with the Panel control. Finally, you learn how to link from one page to another with the HyperLink control.

Displaying Information

The ASP.NET Framework includes two controls you can use to display text in a page: the Label control and the Literal control. Whereas the Literal control simply displays text, the Label control supports several additional formatting properties.

Using the Label Control

Whenever you need to modify the text displayed in a page dynamically, you can use the Label control. For example, the page in Listing 2.1 dynamically modifies the value of a Label control's Text property to display the current time (see Figure 2.1).

LISTING 2.1   ShowLabel.aspx

```
<%@ Page Language="C#" %>
<!DOCTYPE html PUBLIC "-//W3C//DTD XHTML 1.0 Transitional//EN"
"http://www.w3.org/TR/xhtml1/DTD/xhtml1-transitional.dtd">
<script runat="server">

    void Page_Load()
    {
        lblTime.Text = DateTime.Now.ToString("T");
    }
</script>
<html xmlns="http://www.w3.org/1999/xhtml" >
<head id="Head1" runat="server">
    <title>Show Label</title>
</head>
<body>
    <form id="form1" runat="server">
    <div>

    <asp:Label
        id="lblTime"
        Runat="server" />

    </div>
    </form>
</body>
</html>
```

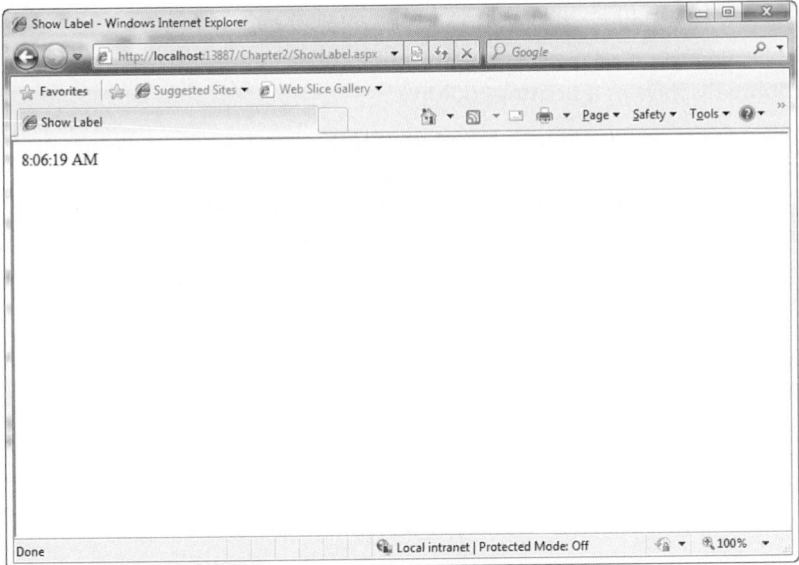

FIGURE 2.1   Displaying the time with a Label control.

Any string that you assign to the Label control's Text property is displayed by the Label when the control is rendered. You can assign simple text to the Text property, or you can assign HTML content.

As an alternative to assigning text to the Text property, you can place the text between the Label control's opening and closing tags. Any text that you place before the opening and closing tags is assigned to the Text property.

By default, a Label control renders its contents in an HTML <span> tag. Whatever value you assign to the Text property is rendered to the browser enclosed in a <span> tag.

The Label control supports several properties you can use to format the text displayed by the Label (this is not a complete list):

▶ **BackColor**—Enables you to change the background color of the label.

▶ **BorderColor**—Enables you to set the color of a border rendered around the label.

▶ **BorderStyle**—Enables you to display a border around the label. Possible values are NotSet, None, Dotted, Dashed, Solid, Double, Groove, Ridge, Inset, and Outset.

▶ **BorderWidth**—Enables you to set the size of a border rendered around the label.

▶ **CssClass**—Enables you to associate a Cascading Style Sheet class with the label.

▶ **Font**—Enables you to set the label's font properties.

▶ **ForeColor**—Enables you to set the color of the content rendered by the label.

▶ **Style**—Enables you to assign style attributes to the label.

▶ **ToolTip**—Enables you to set a label's title attribute. (In Microsoft Internet Explorer, the title attribute displays as a floating tooltip.)

In general, I recommend that you avoid using the formatting properties and take advantage of Cascading Style Sheets to format the rendered output of the Label control. The page in Listing 2.2 contains two Label controls: The first is formatted with properties and the second is formatted with a Cascading Style Sheet (see Figure 2.2).

LISTING 2.2   FormatLabel.aspx

```
<%@ Page Language="C#" %>
<!DOCTYPE html PUBLIC "-//W3C//DTD XHTML 1.0 Transitional//EN"
  "http://www.w3.org/TR/xhtml1/DTD/xhtml1-transitional.dtd">
<html xmlns="http://www.w3.org/1999/xhtml" >
<head id="Head1" runat="server">
    <style type="text/css">
        div
        {
            padding:10px;
        }
        .labelStyle
        {
            color:red;
            background-color:yellow;
            border:Solid 2px Red;
        }
    </style>
    <title>Format Label</title>
</head>
<body>
    <form id="form1" runat="server">
    <div>

    <asp:Label
        id="lblFirst"
        Text="First Label"
        ForeColor="Red"
        BackColor="Yellow"
        BorderStyle="Solid"
        BorderWidth="2"
        BorderColor="red"
        Runat="server" />

    <br /><br />
```

```
<asp:Label
    id="lblSecond"
    Text="Second Label"
    CssClass="labelStyle"
    Runat="server" />

    </div>
    </form>
</body>
</html>
```

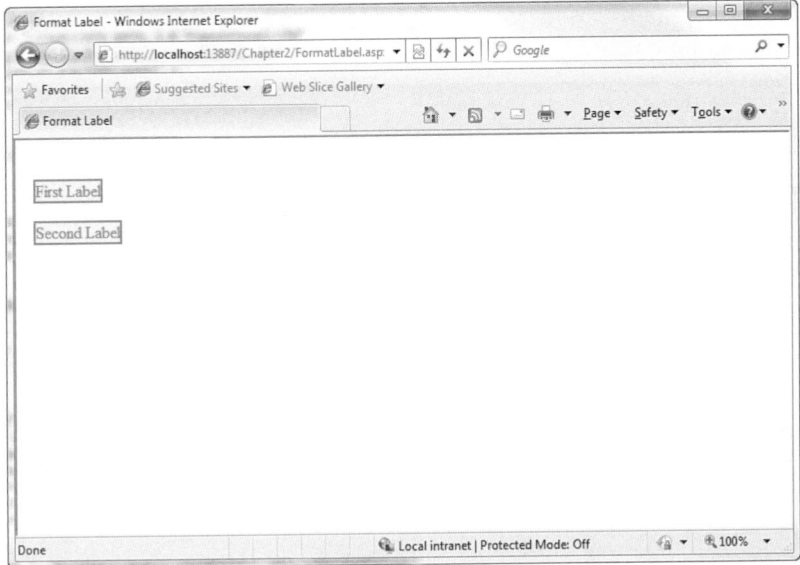

FIGURE 2.2   Formatting a label.

You should use a Label control when labeling the fields in an HTML form. The Label control includes a property named the AssociatedControlID property. You can set this property to point at an ASP.NET control that represents a form field.

For example, the page in Listing 2.3 contains a simple form that contains fields for entering a first and last name. Label controls label the two TextBox controls.

LISTING 2.3   LabelForm.aspx

```
<%@ Page Language="C#" %>
<!DOCTYPE html PUBLIC "-//W3C//DTD XHTML 1.0 Transitional//EN"
"http://www.w3.org/TR/xhtml1/DTD/xhtml1-transitional.dtd">
<html xmlns="http://www.w3.org/1999/xhtml" >
<head id="Head1" runat="server">
```

```
        <title>Label Form</title>
    </head>
    <body>
        <form id="form1" runat="server">
        <div>

        <asp:Label
            id="lblFirstName"
            Text="First Name:"
            AssociatedControlID="txtFirstName"
            Runat="server" />
        <br />
        <asp:TextBox
            id="txtFirstName"
            Runat="server" />

        <br /><br />

        <asp:Label
            id="lblLastName"
            Text="Last Name:"
            AssociatedControlID="txtLastName"
            Runat="server" />
        <br />
        <asp:TextBox
            id="txtLastName"
            Runat="server" />

        </div>
        </form>
    </body>
</html>
```

When you provide a `Label` control with an `AssociatedControlID` property, the `Label` control is rendered as an HTML `<label>` tag instead of an HTML `<span>` tag. For example, if you select View Source on your web browser, you see that the first `Label` in Listing 2.3 renders the following content to the browser:

```
<label for="txtFirstName" id="lblFirstName">First Name:</label>
```

Always use a `Label` control with an `AssociatedControlID` property when labeling form fields. This is important when you need to make your website accessible to persons with disabilities. If someone uses an assistive device, such as a screen reader, to interact with your website, the `AssociatedControlID` property enables the assistive device to associate the correct label with the correct form field.

A side benefit of using the AssociatedControlID property is that clicking a label when this property is set automatically changes the form focus to the associated form input field.

> **WEB STANDARDS NOTE**
>
> Both the WCAG 1.0 and Section 508 accessibility guidelines require you to use the `<label for>` tag when labeling form fields. For more information, see http://www.w3.org/wai and http://www.Section508.gov.

Using the `Literal` Control

The Literal control is similar to the Label control. You can use the Literal control to display text or HTML content in a browser. However, unlike the Label control, the Literal control does not render its content inside of a <span> tag.

For example, the page in Listing 2.4 uses a Literal control in the page's <head> tag to dynamically modify the title displayed in the browser title bar. The current date displays in the Literal control (see Figure 2.3).

LISTING 2.4   ShowLiteral.aspx

```
<%@ Page Language="C#" %>
<!DOCTYPE html PUBLIC "-//W3C//DTD XHTML 1.0 Transitional//EN"
"http://www.w3.org/TR/xhtml1/DTD/xhtml1-transitional.dtd">
<script runat="server">
    void Page_Load()
    {
        ltlTitle.Text = DateTime.Now.ToString("D");
    }
</script>
<html xmlns="http://www.w3.org/1999/xhtml" >
<head>
    <title><asp:Literal id="ltlTitle" Runat="Server" /></title>
</head>
<body>
    <form id="form1" runat="server">
    <div>

    <h1>Look in the title bar</h1>

    </div>
    </form>
```

```
</body>
</html>
```

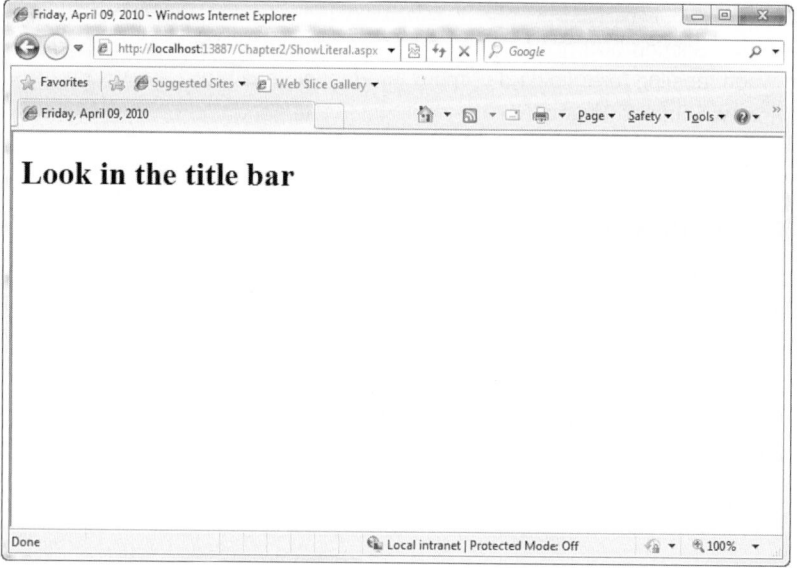

FIGURE 2.3   Modifying the browser title with a Literal control.

If you used a Label control in Listing 2.4 instead of a Literal control, the uninterpreted <span> tags would appear in the browser title bar.

NOTE

The page in Listing 2.4 uses a format specifier to format the date before assigning the date to the Label control. The D format specifier causes the date to be formatted in a long format. You can use several standard format specifiers with the ToString() method to format dates, times, currency amounts, and numbers. For a list of these format specifiers, look up the Format Specifiers topic in the index of the Microsoft .NET Framework SDK Documentation.

Because the contents of a Literal control are not contained in a <span> tag, the Literal control does not support any of the formatting properties supported by the <span> tag. For example, the Literal control does not support either the CssClass or BackColor properties.

The `Literal` control does support one property not supported by the `Label` control: the `Mode` property. The `Mode` property enables you to encode HTML content and accepts any of the following three values:

▶ **PassThrough**—Displays the contents of the control without encoding.

▶ **Encode**—Displays the contents of the control after HTML encoding the content.

▶ **Transform**—Displays the contents of the control after stripping markup not supported by the requesting device.

For example, the page in Listing 2.5 contains three `Literal` controls set to the three possible values of the `Mode` property (see Figure 2.4).

LISTING 2.5   ShowLiteralMode.aspx

```
<%@ Page Language="C#" %>
<!DOCTYPE html PUBLIC "-//W3C//DTD XHTML 1.0 Transitional//EN"
"http://www.w3.org/TR/xhtml1/DTD/xhtml1-transitional.dtd">
<html xmlns="http://www.w3.org/1999/xhtml" >
<head id="Head1" runat="server">
    <title>Show Literal Mode</title>
</head>
<body>
    <form id="form1" runat="server">
    <div>

    <asp:Literal
        id="ltlFirst"
        Mode="PassThrough"
        Text="<hr />"
        Runat="server" />

    <br /><br />

    <asp:Literal
        id="ltlSecond"
        Mode="Encode"
        Text="<hr />"
        Runat="server" />

    <br /><br />

    <asp:Literal
        id="ltlThird"
        Mode="Transform"
        Text="<hr />"
```

```
        Runat="server" />

    </div>
    </form>
</body>
</html>
```

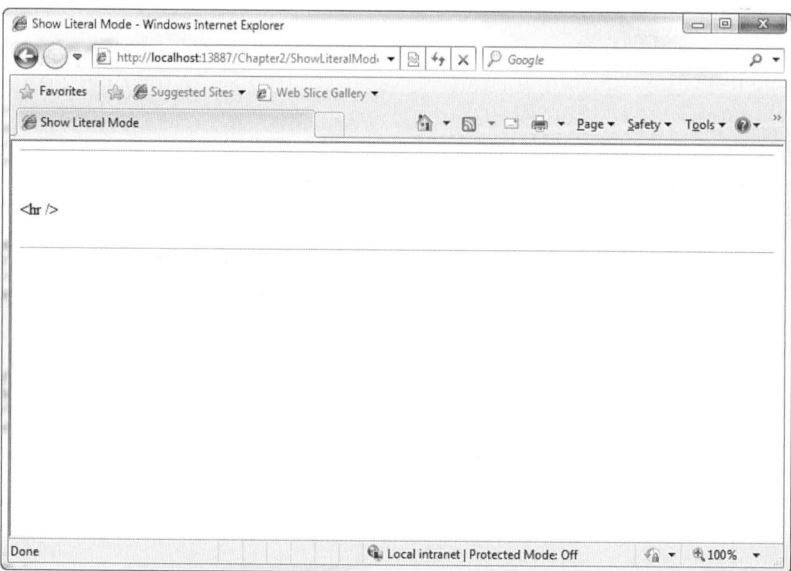

FIGURE 2.4   Three values of the Literal control's Mode property.

When you request the page in Listing 2.5 with a web browser, the first Literal control displays a horizontal rule; the second Literal control displays the uninterpreted <hr /> tag; and the final Literal control displays another horizontal rule. If you request the page from a device (such as a WML cell phone) that does not support the <hr> tag, the third <hr /> tag is stripped.

Accepting User Input

The ASP.NET Framework includes several controls that you can use to gather user input. In this section, you learn how to use the TextBox, CheckBox, and RadioButton controls. These controls correspond to the standard types of HTML input tags.

Using the TextBox Control

You can use the TextBox control to display three different types of input fields depending on the value of its TextMode property. The TextMode property accepts the following three values:

▶ **SingleLine**—Displays a single-line input field.

▶ **MultiLine**—Displays a multiline input field.

▶ **Password**—Displays a single-line input field in which the text is hidden.

The page in Listing 2.6 contains three TextBox controls that illustrate all three of the TextMode values (see Figure 2.5).

LISTING 2.6   ShowTextBox.aspx

```
<%@ Page Language="C#" %>
<!DOCTYPE html PUBLIC "-//W3C//DTD XHTML 1.0 Transitional//EN"
"http://www.w3.org/TR/xhtml1/DTD/xhtml1-transitional.dtd">
<html xmlns="http://www.w3.org/1999/xhtml" >
<head id="Head1" runat="server">
    <title>Show TextBox</title>
</head>
<body>
    <form id="form1" runat="server">
    <div>

    <asp:TextBox
        id="txtUserName"
        TextMode="SingleLine"
        Runat="server" />

    <br /><br />

    <asp:TextBox
        id="txtPassword"
        TextMode="Password"
        Runat="server" />

    <br /><br />

    <asp:TextBox
        id="txtComments"
        TextMode="MultiLine"
        Runat="server" />

    </div>
    </form>
</body>
</html>
```

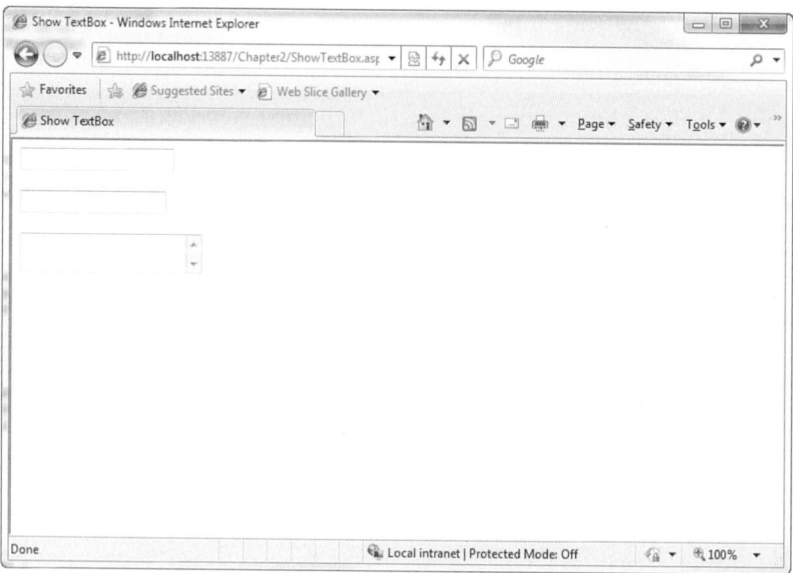

FIGURE 2.5   Displaying TextBox controls with different values for TextMode.

You can use the following properties to control the rendering characteristics of the TextBox control (this is not a complete list):

▶ **AccessKey**—Enables you to specify a key that navigates to the TextBox control.

▶ **AutoCompleteType**—Enables you to associate an AutoComplete class with the TextBox control.

▶ **AutoPostBack**—Enables you to post the form containing the TextBox back to the server automatically when the contents of the TextBox is changed.

▶ **Columns**—Enables you to specify the number of columns to display.

▶ **Enabled**—Enables you to disable the text box.

▶ **MaxLength**—Enables you to specify the maximum length of data that a user can enter in a text box. (This does not work when TextMode is set to Multiline.)

▶ **ReadOnly**—Enables you to prevent users from changing the text in a text box.

▶ **Rows**—Enables you to specify the number of rows to display.

▶ **TabIndex**—Enables you to specify the tab order of the text box.

▶ **Wrap**—Enables you to specify whether text word-wraps when the TextMode is set to Multiline.

The TextBox control also supports the following method:

▶ **Focus**—Enables you to set the initial form focus to the text box.

And, the TextBox control supports the following event:

▶ **TextChanged**—Raised on the server when the contents of the text box are changed.

When the AutoPostBack property has the value True, the form containing the TextBox is automatically posted back to the server when the contents of the TextBox changes. For example, the page in Listing 2.7 contains a simple search form. If you modify the contents of the text box and tab out of the TextBox control, the form is automatically posted back to the server, and the contents of the TextBox display (see Figure 2.6).

LISTING 2.7   TextBoxAutoPostBack.aspx

```
<%@ Page Language="C#" %>
<!DOCTYPE html PUBLIC "-//W3C//DTD XHTML 1.0 Transitional//EN"
"http://www.w3.org/TR/xhtml1/DTD/xhtml1-transitional.dtd">
<script runat="server">

    protected void txtSearch_TextChanged(object sender, EventArgs e)
    {
        lblSearchResults.Text = "Search for: " + txtSearch.Text;
    }
</script>
<html xmlns="http://www.w3.org/1999/xhtml" >
<head id="Head1" runat="server">
    <title>TextBox AutoPostBack</title>
</head>
<body>
    <form id="form1" runat="server">
    <div>

    <asp:Label
        id="lblSearch"
        Text="Search:"
        Runat="server" />
    <asp:TextBox
        id="txtSearch"
        AutoPostBack="true"
        OnTextChanged="txtSearch_TextChanged"
        Runat="server" />

    <hr />

    <asp:Label
        id="lblSearchResults"
        Runat="server" />
```

```
    </div>
    </form>
</body>
</html>
```

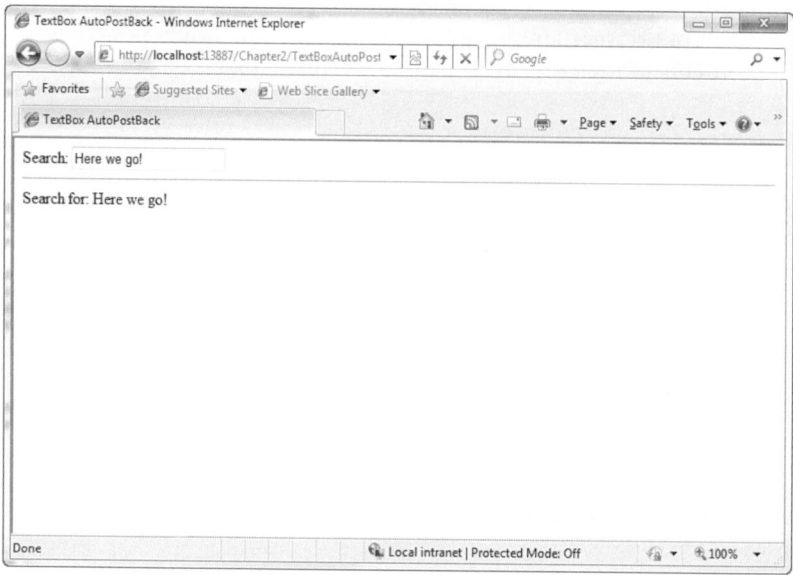

FIGURE 2.6   Reloading a form automatically when the contents of a form field change.

In Listing 2.7, the TextBox control's TextChanged event is handled. This event is raised on the server when the contents of the TextBox have been changed. You can handle this event even when you don't use the AutoPostBack property.

WEB STANDARDS NOTE

You should avoid using the AutoPostBack property for accessibility reasons. Creating a page that automatically reposts the server can be confusing to someone using an assistive device such as a screen reader. A better way to send data back to the server and dynamically update the page without a PostBack is to utilize features of Microsoft AJAX, JavaScript, or jQuery. This approach often results in a cleaner, faster page.

Notice that the TextBox control also includes a property that enables you to associate the TextBox with a particular AutoComplete class. When AutoComplete is enabled, the user does not need to reenter common information—such as a first name, last name, or phone number—in a form field. If the user has not disabled AutoComplete on his browser, his browser prompts him to enter the same value that he entered previously for the form field (even if the user entered the value for a form field at a different website).

You can disable auto-complete by adding an `AutoComplete="Off"` attribute to the `TextBox`. This is useful when you want to use ASP.NET AJAX Control Toolkit `AutoComplete` control, and you don't want the browser auto-complete to interfere with the Ajax auto-complete.

For example, the page in Listing 2.8 asks for your first name, last name, and phone number. Each `TextBox` control is associated with a particular `AutoComplete` class. The `AutoComplete` class specifies the type of information associated with the form field. After you complete the form once, if you return to the same form in the future, you are prompted to enter the same responses (see Figure 2.7).

LISTING 2.8   ShowAutoComplete.aspx

```
<%@ Page Language="C#" %>
<!DOCTYPE html PUBLIC "-//W3C//DTD XHTML 1.0 Transitional//EN"
"http://www.w3.org/TR/xhtml1/DTD/xhtml1-transitional.dtd">
<html xmlns="http://www.w3.org/1999/xhtml" >
<head id="Head1" runat="server">
    <title>Show AutoComplete</title>
</head>
<body>
    <form id="form1" runat="server">
    <div>

    <asp:Label
        id="lblFirstName"
        Text="First Name:"
        AssociatedControlID="txtFirstName"
        Runat="server" />
    <br />
    <asp:TextBox
        id="txtFirstName"
        AutoCompleteType="FirstName"
        Runat="server" />
    <br /><br />
    <asp:Label
        id="lblLastname"
        Text="Last Name:"
        AssociatedControlID="txtLastName"
        Runat="server" />
    <br />
    <asp:TextBox
        id="txtLastName"
```

```
        AutoCompleteType="LastName"
        Runat="server" />
    <br /><br />
    <asp:Button
        id="btnSubmit"
        Text="Submit"
        Runat="server" />

    </div>
    </form>
</body>
</html>
```

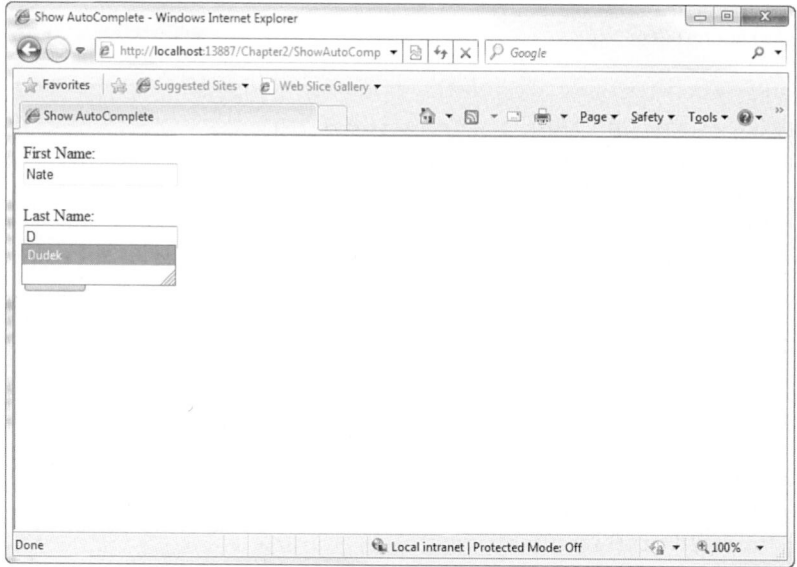

FIGURE 2.7   Using AutoComplete with the TextBox control.

> **NOTE**
>
> When using Internet Explorer, you can configure AutoComplete by selecting Tools,
> Internet Options, Content, and clicking the AutoComplete button. The ASP.NET Framework
> does not support AutoComplete for other browsers such as FireFox or Opera.

Finally, the TextBox control supports the Focus() method. You can use the Focus()
method to shift the initial form focus to a particular TextBox control. By default, no form
field has focus when a page first opens. If you want to make it easier for users to complete
a form, you can set the focus automatically to a particular TextBox control contained in a
form.

For example, the page in Listing 2.9 sets the focus to the first of two form fields.

LISTING 2.9   TextBoxFocus.aspx

```
<%@ Page Language="C#" %>
<!DOCTYPE html PUBLIC "-//W3C//DTD XHTML 1.0 Transitional//EN"
"http://www.w3.org/TR/xhtml1/DTD/xhtml1-transitional.dtd">
<script runat="server">

    void Page_Load()
    {
        txtFirstName.Focus();
    }

</script>
<html xmlns="http://www.w3.org/1999/xhtml" >
<head id="Head1" runat="server">
    <title>TextBox Focus</title>
</head>
<body>
    <form id="form1" runat="server">
    <div>

    <asp:Label
        id="lblFirstName"
        Text="First Name:"
        AssociatedControlID="txtFirstName"
        Runat="server" />
    <br />
    <asp:TextBox
        id="txtFirstName"
        AutoCompleteType="FirstName"
        Runat="server" />
    <br /><br />
    <asp:Label
        id="lblLastname"
        Text="Last Name:"
        AssociatedControlID="txtLastName"
        Runat="server" />
    <br />
    <asp:TextBox
        id="txtLastName"
        AutoCompleteType="LastName"
        Runat="server" />
    <br /><br />
    <asp:Button
```

```
            id="btnSubmit"
            Text="Submit"
            Runat="server" />

    </div>
    </form>
</body>
</html>
```

In Listing 2.9, the `Page_Load()` event handler sets the form focus to the `txtFirstName` TextBox control.

> **NOTE**
>
> You can also set the form focus by setting either the `Page.SetFocus()` method or the server-side `HtmlForm` control's `DefaultFocus` property.

Using the CheckBox Control

The `CheckBox` control enables you to display, well, a check box. The page in Listing 2.10 illustrates how you can use the `CheckBox` control in a newsletter signup form (see Figure 2.8).

LISTING 2.10   ShowCheckBox.aspx

```
<%@ Page Language="C#" %>
<!DOCTYPE html PUBLIC "-//W3C//DTD XHTML 1.0 Transitional//EN"
"http://www.w3.org/TR/xhtml1/DTD/xhtml1-transitional.dtd">
<script runat="server">

    protected void btnSubmit_Click(object sender, EventArgs e)
    {
        lblResult.Text = chkNewsletter.Checked.ToString();
    }
</script>
<html xmlns="http://www.w3.org/1999/xhtml" >
<head id="Head1" runat="server">
    <title>Show CheckBox</title>
</head>
<body>
    <form id="form1" runat="server">
    <div>

    <asp:CheckBox
        id="chkNewsletter"
```

```
            Text="Receive Newsletter?"
            Runat="server" />
        <br />
        <asp:Button
            id="btnSubmit"
            Text="Submit"
            OnClick="btnSubmit_Click"
            Runat="server" />
        <hr />

        <asp:Label
            id="lblResult"
            Runat="server" />

    </div>
    </form>
</body>
</html>
```

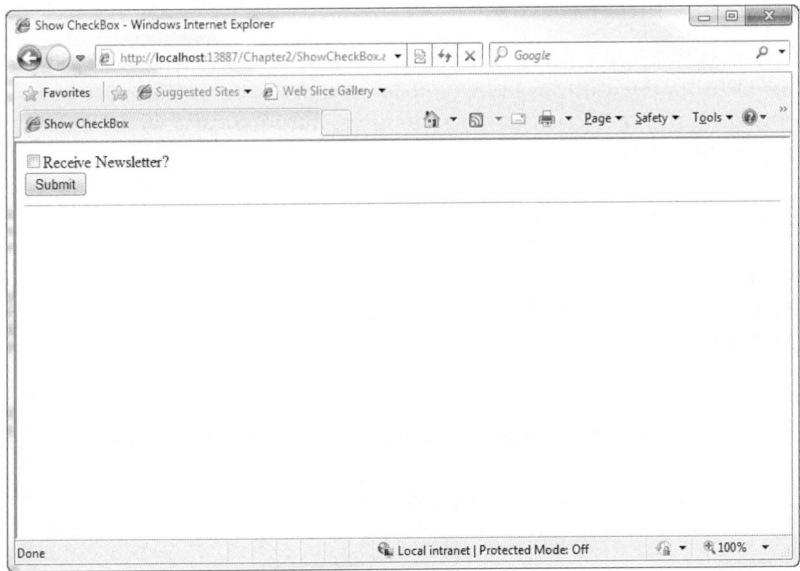

FIGURE 2.8   Displaying a CheckBox control.

In Listing 2.10, the Checked property determines whether the user has checked the check box. Notice that the CheckBox includes a Text property that labels the CheckBox. If you use this property, the proper (accessibility standards-compliant) HTML <label> tag is generated for the TextBox.

The CheckBox control supports the following properties (this is not a complete list):

- ▶ **AccessKey**—Enables you to specify a key that navigates to the TextBox control.
- ▶ **AutoPostBack**—Enables you to post the form containing the CheckBox back to the server automatically when the CheckBox is checked or unchecked.
- ▶ **Checked**—Enables you to get or set whether the CheckBox is checked.
- ▶ **Enabled**—Enables you to disable the TextBox.
- ▶ **TabIndex**—Enables you to specify the tab order of the check box.
- ▶ **Text**—Enables you to provide a label for the check box.
- ▶ **TextAlign**—Enables you to align the label for the check box. Possible values are Left and Right.

The CheckBox control also supports the following method:

- ▶ **Focus**—Enables you to set the initial form focus to the check box.

And the CheckBox control supports the following event:

- ▶ **CheckedChanged**—Raised on the server when the check box is checked or unchecked.

Notice that the CheckBox control, like the TextBox control, supports the AutoPostBack property. The page in Listing 2.11 illustrates how you can use the AutoPostBack property to post the form containing the check box back to the server automatically when the check box is checked or unchecked.

LISTING 2.11   CheckBoxAutoPostBack.aspx

```
<%@ Page Language="C#" %>
<!DOCTYPE html PUBLIC "-//W3C//DTD XHTML 1.0 Transitional//EN"
"http://www.w3.org/TR/xhtml1/DTD/xhtml1-transitional.dtd">
<script runat="server">

    protected void chkNewsletter_CheckedChanged(object sender, EventArgs e)
    {
        lblResult.Text = chkNewsletter.Checked.ToString();
    }
</script>

<html xmlns="http://www.w3.org/1999/xhtml" >
<head id="Head1" runat="server">
    <title>CheckBox AutoPostBack</title>
</head>
<body>
    <form id="form1" runat="server">
    <div>
```

```
<asp:CheckBox
    id="chkNewsletter"
    Text="Receive Newsletter?"
    AutoPostBack="true"
    OnCheckedChanged="chkNewsletter_CheckedChanged"
    Runat="server" />
<hr />

<asp:Label
    id="lblResult"
    Runat="server" />

</div>
</form>
</body>
</html>
```

NOTE

The ASP.NET Framework also includes the `CheckBoxList` control that enables you to display a list of check boxes automatically. This control is discussed in detail in Chapter 10, "Using List Controls."

Using the `RadioButton` Control

You always use the `RadioButton` control in a group. Only one radio button in a group of `RadioButton` controls can be checked at a time.

For example, the page in Listing 2.12 contains three RadioButton controls (see Figure 2.9).

LISTING 2.12   ShowRadioButton.aspx

```
<%@ Page Language="C#" %>
<!DOCTYPE html PUBLIC "-//W3C//DTD XHTML 1.0 Transitional//EN"
"http://www.w3.org/TR/xhtml1/DTD/xhtml1-transitional.dtd">
<script runat="server">

    protected void btnSubmit_Click(object sender, EventArgs e)
    {
        if (rdlMagazine.Checked)
            lblResult.Text = rdlMagazine.Text;
        if (rdlTelevision.Checked)
            lblResult.Text = rdlTelevision.Text;
        if (rdlOther.Checked)
            lblResult.Text = rdlOther.Text;
```

```
        }
</script>
<html xmlns="http://www.w3.org/1999/xhtml" >
<head id="Head1" runat="server">
    <title>Show RadioButton</title>
</head>
<body>
    <form id="form1" runat="server">
    <div>

    How did you hear about our Website?

    <ul>
        <li>
        <asp:RadioButton
            id="rdlMagazine"
            Text="Magazine Article"
            GroupName="Source"
            Runat="server" />
        </li>
        <li>
        <asp:RadioButton
            id="rdlTelevision"
            Text="Television Program"
            GroupName="Source"
            Runat="server" />
        </li>
        <li>
        <asp:RadioButton
            id="rdlOther"
            Text="Other Source"
            GroupName="Source"
            Runat="server" />
        </li>
    </ul>

    <asp:Button
        id="btnSubmit"
        Text="Submit"
        Runat="server" OnClick="btnSubmit_Click" />
    <hr />

    <asp:Label
        id="lblResult"
        Runat="server" />
```

```
      </div>
    </form>
  </body>
</html>
```

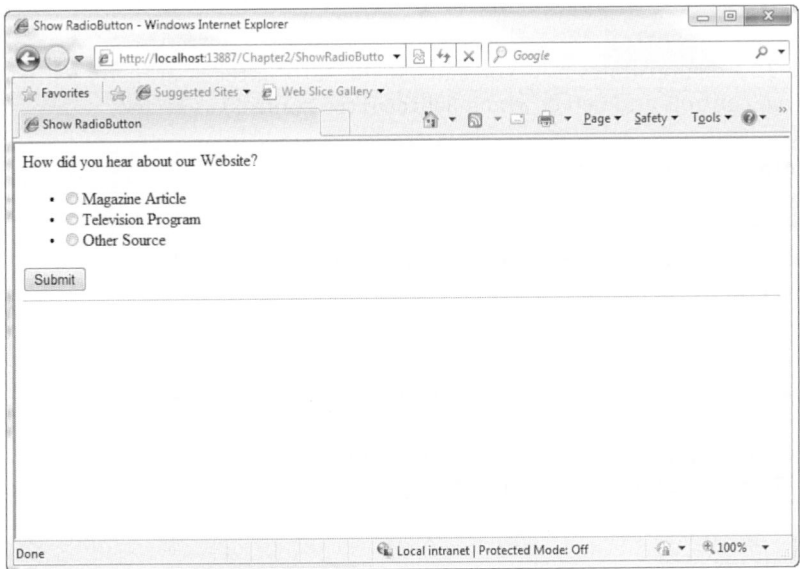

FIGURE 2.9   Displaying RadioButton.

The RadioButton controls in Listing 2.12 are grouped together with the RadioButton control's GroupName property. Only one of the three RadioButton controls can be checked at a time.

The RadioButton control supports the following properties (this is not a complete list):

▶ **AccessKey**—Enables you to specify a key that navigates to the RadioButton control.

▶ **AutoPostBack**—Enables you to post the form containing the RadioButton back to the server automatically when the radio button is checked or unchecked.

▶ **Checked**—Enables you to get or set whether the RadioButton control is checked.

▶ **Enabled**—Enables you to disable the RadioButton.

▶ **GroupName**—Enables you to group RadioButton controls.

▶ **TabIndex**—Enables you to specify the tab order of the RadioButton control.

▶ **Text**—Enables you to label the RadioButton control.

▶ **TextAlign**—Enables you to align the RadioButton label. Possible values are Left and Right.

The RadioButton control supports the following method:

▶ Focus—Enables you to set the initial form focus to the RadioButton control.

Finally, the RadioButton control supports the following event:

▶ CheckedChanged—Raised on the server when the RadioButton is checked or unchecked.

The page in Listing 2.13 demonstrates how you can use the AutoPostBack property with a group of RadioButton controls and detect which RadioButton control is selected.

LISTING 2.13   RadioButtonAutoPostBack.aspx

```
<%@ Page Language="C#" %>
<!DOCTYPE html PUBLIC "-//W3C//DTD XHTML 1.0 Transitional//EN"
"http://www.w3.org/TR/xhtml1/DTD/xhtml1-transitional.dtd">
<script runat="server">

    protected void RadioButton_CheckedChanged(object sender, EventArgs e)
    {
        RadioButton selectedRadioButton = (RadioButton)sender;
        lblResult.Text = selectedRadioButton.Text;
    }
</script>
<html xmlns="http://www.w3.org/1999/xhtml" >
<head id="Head1" runat="server">
    <title>RadioButton AutoPostBack</title>
</head>
<body>
    <form id="form1" runat="server">
    <div>
    How did you hear about our Website?

    <ul>
        <li>
        <asp:RadioButton
            id="rdlMagazine"
            Text="Magazine Article"
            GroupName="Source"
            AutoPostBack="true"
            OnCheckedChanged="RadioButton_CheckedChanged"
            Runat="server" />
        </li>
        <li>
        <asp:RadioButton
```

```
            id="rdlTelevision"
            Text="Television Program"
            GroupName="Source"
            AutoPostBack="true"
            OnCheckedChanged="RadioButton_CheckedChanged"
            Runat="server" />
    </li>
    <li>
    <asp:RadioButton
            id="rdlOther"
            Text="Other Source"
            GroupName="Source"
            AutoPostBack="true"
            OnCheckedChanged="RadioButton_CheckedChanged"
            Runat="server" />
    </li>
    </ul>

    <hr />

    <asp:Label
        id="lblResult"
        Runat="server" />

    </div>
    </form>
</body>
</html>
```

In Listing 2.13, when you select a RadioButton control, the page is automatically posted back to the server, and the value of the Text property of the selected RadioButton control displays. Notice that all three of the RadioButton controls are associated with the same CheckedChanged event handler. The first parameter passed to the handler represents the particular RadioButton that was changed.

NOTE

The ASP.NET Framework also includes the RadioButtonList control, which enables you to display a list of radio buttons automatically. This control is discussed in detail in Chapter 10.

2

Submitting Form Data

The ASP.NET Framework includes three controls you can use to submit a form to the server: Button, LinkButton, and ImageButton. These controls have the same function, but each control has a distinct appearance.

In this section, you learn how to use each of these three types of buttons in a page. Next, you learn how to associate client-side scripts with server-side Button controls. You also learn how to use a button control to post a form to a page other than the current page. Finally, you learn how to handle a button control's Command event.

Using the Button Control

The Button control renders a push button that you can use to submit a form to the server. For example, the page in Listing 2.14 contains a Button control. When you click the Button control, the time displayed by a Label control is updated (see Figure 2.10).

LISTING 2.14   ShowButton.aspx

```
<%@ Page Language="C#" %>
<!DOCTYPE html PUBLIC "-//W3C//DTD XHTML 1.0 Transitional//EN"
"http://www.w3.org/TR/xhtml1/DTD/xhtml1-transitional.dtd">
<script runat="server">

    protected void btnSubmit_Click(object sender, EventArgs e)
    {
        lblTime.Text = DateTime.Now.ToString("T");
    }
</script>
<html xmlns="http://www.w3.org/1999/xhtml" >
<head id="Head1" runat="server">
    <title>Show Button</title>
</head>
<body>
    <form id="form1" runat="server">
    <div>

    <asp:Button
        id="btnSubmit"
        Text="Submit"
        OnClick="btnSubmit_Click"
        Runat="server" />

    <br /><br />
```

```
    <asp:Label
        id="lblTime"
        Runat="server" />

    </div>
    </form>
</body>
</html>
```

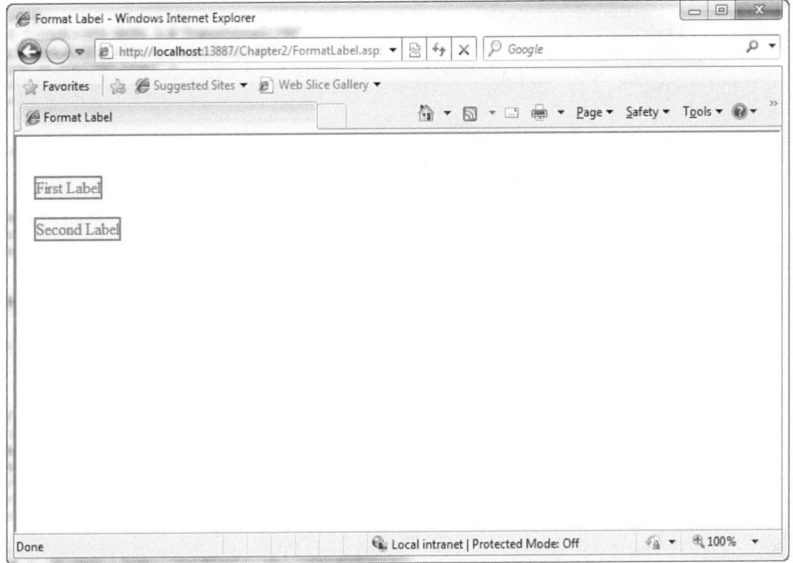

FIGURE 2.10   Displaying a `Button` control.

The `Button` control supports the following properties (this is not a complete list):

▶ **AccessKey**—Enables you to specify a key that navigates to the `Button` control.

▶ **CommandArgument**—Enables you to specify a command argument passed to the `Command` event.

▶ **CommandName**—Enables you to specify a command name passed to the `Command` event.

▶ **Enabled**—Enables you to disable the `Button` control.

▶ **OnClientClick**—Enables you to specify a client-side script that executes when the button is clicked.

▶ **PostBackUrl**—Enables you to post a form to a particular page.

▶ **TabIndex**—Enables you to specify the tab order of the `Button` control.

▶ **Text**—Enables you to label the `Button` control.

▶ **UseSubmitBehavior**—Enables you to use JavaScript to post a form.

The `Button` control also supports the following method:

▶ **Focus**—Enables you to set the initial form focus to the `Button` control.

The `Button` control also supports the following two events:

▶ **Click**—Raised when the `Button` control is clicked.

▶ **Command**—Raised when the Button control is clicked. The `CommandName` and `CommandArgument` are passed to this event.

Using the **LinkButton** Control

The `LinkButton` control, like the `Button` control, enables you to post a form to the server. Unlike a `Button` control, however, the `LinkButton` control renders a link instead of a push button.

The page in Listing 2.15 contains a simple form. The form includes a `LinkButton` control that enables you to submit the form to the server and display the contents of the form fields (see Figure 2.11).

LISTING 2.15   ShowLinkButton.aspx

```
<%@ Page Language="C#" %>
<!DOCTYPE html PUBLIC "-//W3C//DTD XHTML 1.0 Transitional//EN"
"http://www.w3.org/TR/xhtml1/DTD/xhtml1-transitional.dtd">
<script runat="server">

    protected void lnkSubmit_Click(object sender, EventArgs e)
    {
        lblResults.Text = "First Name: " + txtFirstName.Text;
        lblResults.Text += "<br />Last Name: " + txtLastName.Text;
    }
</script>
<html xmlns="http://www.w3.org/1999/xhtml" >
<head id="Head1" runat="server">
    <title>Show LinkButton</title>
</head>
<body>
    <form id="form1" runat="server">
    <div>
```

```
    <asp:Label
        id="lblFirstName"
        Text="First Name:"
        AssociatedControlID="txtFirstName"
        Runat="server" />
    <br />
    <asp:TextBox
        id="txtFirstName"
        Runat="server" />
    <br /><br />
    <asp:Label
        id="lblLastName"
        Text="Last Name:"
        AssociatedControlID="txtLastName"
        Runat="server" />
    <br />
    <asp:TextBox
        id="txtLastName"
        Runat="server" />
    <br /><br />
    <asp:LinkButton
        id="lnkSubmit"
        Text="Submit"
        OnClick="lnkSubmit_Click"
        Runat="server" />

    <br /><br />
    <asp:Label
        id="lblResults"
        Runat="server" />

    </div>
    </form>
</body>
</html>
```

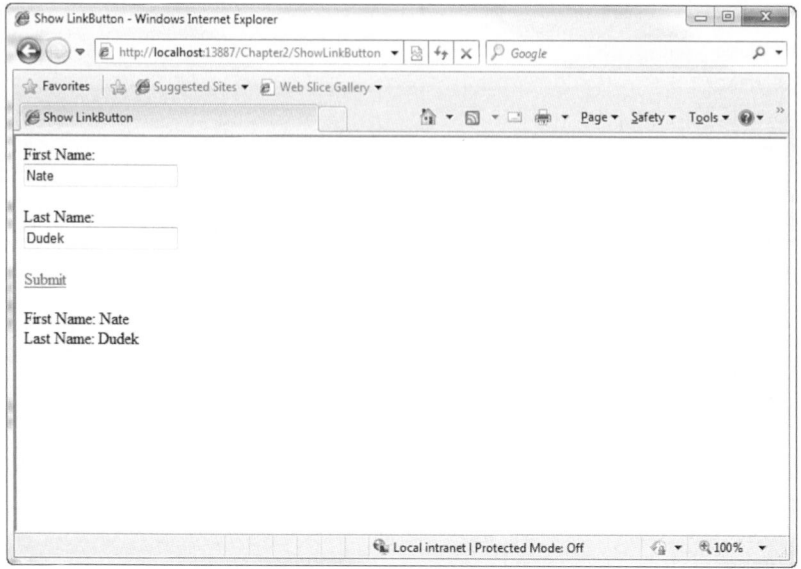

FIGURE 2.11   Displaying a `LinkButton` control.

Behind the scenes, the `LinkButton` control uses JavaScript to post the form back to the server. The hyperlink rendered by the `LinkButton` control looks like this:

```
<a id="lnkSubmit" href="javascript:__doPostBack('lnkSubmit','')">Submit</a>
```

Clicking the `LinkButton` invokes the `JavaScript __doPostBack()` method, which posts the form to the server. When the form is posted, the values of all the other form fields in the page are also posted to the server.

The `LinkButton` control supports the following properties (this is not a complete list):

- **AccessKey**—Enables you to specify a key that navigates to the `Button` control.
- **CommandArgument**—Enables you to specify a command argument passed to the Command event.
- **CommandName**—Enables you to specify a command name passed to the `Command` event.
- **Enabled**—Enables you to disable the `LinkButton` control.
- **OnClientClick**—Enables you to specify a client-side script that executes when the `LinkButton` is clicked.
- **PostBackUrl**—Enables you to post a form to a particular page.

▶ **TabIndex**—Enables you to specify the tab order of the `LinkButton` control.

▶ **Text**—Enables you to label the `LinkButton` control.

The `LinkButton` control also supports the following method:

▶ **Focus**—Enables you to set the initial form focus to the `LinkButton` control

The `LinkButton` control also supports the following two events:

▶ **Click**—Raised when the `LinkButton` control is clicked.

▶ **Command**—Raised when the `LinkButton` control is clicked. The `CommandName` and `CommandArgument` are passed to this event.

Using the `ImageButton` Control

The `ImageButton` control, like the `Button` and `LinkButton` controls, enables you to post a form to the server. However, the `ImageButton` control always displays an image.

The page in Listing 2.16 contains an `ImageButton` control that posts a simple form back to the server (see Figure 2.12).

LISTING 2.16   ShowImageButton.aspx

```
<%@ Page Language="C#" %>
<!DOCTYPE html PUBLIC "-//W3C//DTD XHTML 1.0 Transitional//EN"
"http://www.w3.org/TR/xhtml1/DTD/xhtml1-transitional.dtd">
<script runat="server">

    protected void btnSubmit_Click(object sender, ImageClickEventArgs e)
    {
        lblResults.Text = "First Name: " + txtFirstName.Text;
        lblResults.Text += "<br />Last Name: " + txtLastName.Text;
    }
</script>
<html xmlns="http://www.w3.org/1999/xhtml" >
<head id="Head1" runat="server">
    <title>Show ImageButton</title>
</head>
<body>
    <form id="form1" runat="server">
    <div>

    <asp:Label
        id="lblFirstName"
        Text="First Name:"
        AssociatedControlID="txtFirstName"
```

```
            Runat="server" />
    <br />
    <asp:TextBox
        id="txtFirstName"
        Runat="server" />
    <br /><br />
    <asp:Label
        id="lblLastName"
        Text="Last Name:"
        AssociatedControlID="txtLastName"
        Runat="server" />
    <br />
    <asp:TextBox
        id="txtLastName"
        Runat="server" />
    <br /><br />
    <asp:ImageButton
        id="btnSubmit"
        ImageUrl="Submit.gif"
        AlternateText="Submit Form"
        Runat="server" OnClick="btnSubmit_Click" />

    <br /><br />
    <asp:Label
        id="lblResults"
        Runat="server" />

    </div>
    </form>
</body>
</html>
```

The ImageButton in Listing 2.16 includes both an ImageUrl and AlternateText property. The ImageUrl contains the path to the image that the ImageButton displays. The AlternateText property provides alternate text for the image used by screen readers and text-only browsers.

WEB STANDARDS NOTE

Always include alternate text for any image. The accessibility guidelines require it. Furthermore, remember that some people turn off images in their browsers for a faster surfing experience.

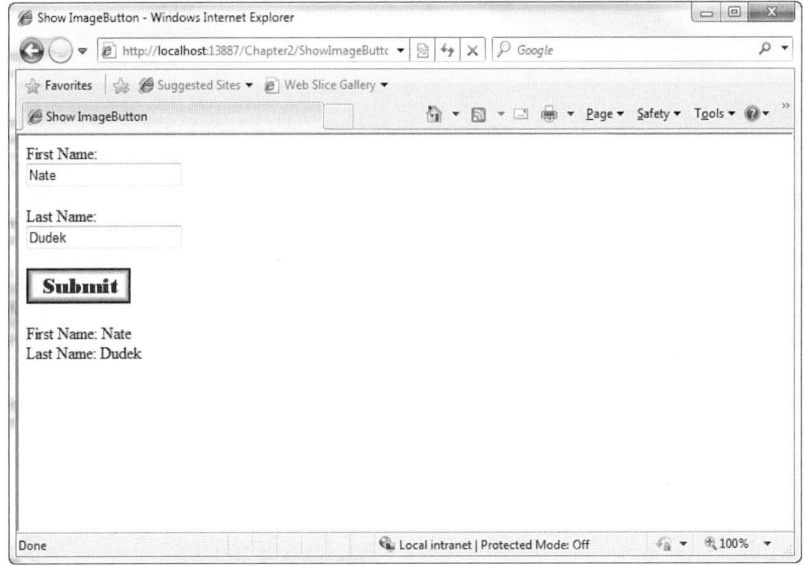

FIGURE 2.12   Displaying an `ImageButton` control.

The event handler for an `Image` control's `Click` event is different than that for the other button controls. The second parameter passed to the event handler is an instance of the `ImageClickEventArgs` class. This class has the following properties:

▶ X—The x coordinate relative to the image the user clicked.

▶ Y—The y coordinate relative to the image the user clicked.

You can use the `ImageButton` control to create a simple image map. For example, the page in Listing 2.17 contains an `ImageButton` that displays an image of a target. If you click the center of the target, a success message is displayed (see Figure 2.13).

LISTING 2.17   `ImageButtonTarget.aspx`

```
<%@ Page Language="C#" %>
<!DOCTYPE html PUBLIC "-//W3C//DTD XHTML 1.0 Transitional//EN"
"http://www.w3.org/TR/xhtml1/DTD/xhtml1-transitional.dtd">
<script runat="server">

    protected void btnTarget_Click(object sender, ImageClickEventArgs e)
    {
        if ((e.X > 90 && e.X < 110) && (e.Y > 90 && e.Y < 110))
            lblResult.Text = "You hit the target!";
        else
            lblResult.Text = "You missed!";
    }
```

```
</script>
<html xmlns="http://www.w3.org/1999/xhtml" >
<head id="Head1" runat="server">
    <title>ImageButton Target</title>
</head>
<body>
    <form id="form1" runat="server">
    <div>

    <asp:ImageButton
        id="btnTarget"
        ImageUrl="Target.gif"
        Runat="server" OnClick="btnTarget_Click" />

    <br /><br />

    <asp:Label
        id="lblResult"
        Runat="server" />

    </div>
    </form>
</body>
</html>
```

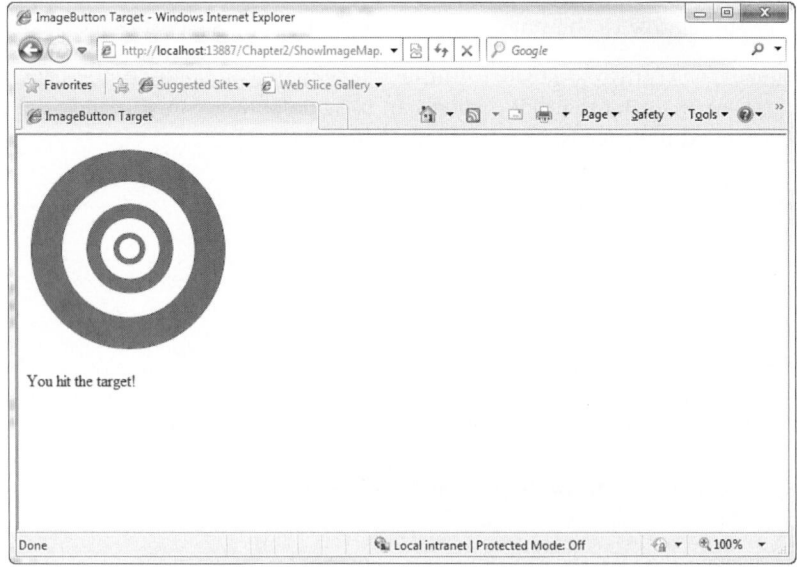

FIGURE 2.13   Retrieving X and Y coordinates from an ImageButton.

WEB STANDARDS NOTE

The ImageButton can create a server-side image map. Server-side image maps are not accessible to persons with disabilities. A better method for creating an ImageMap is to use the ImageMap control, which enables you to create a client-side image map. The ImageMap control is discussed in the next section of this chapter.

The ImageButton control supports the following properties (this is not a complete list):

▶ **AccessKey**—Enables you to specify a key that navigates to the ImageButton control.

▶ **AlternateText**—Enables you to provide alternate text for the image (required for accessibility).

▶ **DescriptionUrl**—Enables you to provide a link to a page that contains a detailed description of the image (required to make a complex image accessible).

▶ **CommandArgument**—Enables you to specify a command argument that is passed to the Command event.

▶ **CommandName**—Enables you to specify a command name passed to the Command event.

▶ **Enabled**—Enables you to disable the ImageButton control.

▶ **GenerateEmptyAlternateText**—Enables you to set the AlternateText property to an empty string.

▶ **ImageAlign**—Enables you to align the image relative to other HTML elements in the page. Possible values are AbsBottom, AbsMiddle, Baseline, Bottom, Left, Middle, NotSet, Right, TextTop, and Top.

▶ **ImageUrl**—Enables you to specify the URL to the image.

▶ **OnClientClick**—Enables you to specify a client-side script that executes when the ImageButton is clicked.

▶ **PostBackUrl**—Enables you to post a form to a particular page.

▶ **TabIndex**—Enables you to specify the tab order of the ImageButton control.

The ImageButton control also supports the following method:

▶ **Focus**—Enables you to set the initial form focus to the ImageButton control.

The ImageButton control also supports the following two events:

▶ **Click**—Raised when the ImageButton control is clicked.

▶ **Command**—Raised when the ImageButton control is clicked. The CommandName and CommandArgument are passed to this event.

Using Client Scripts with Button Controls

All three Button controls support an OnClientClick property. You can use this property to execute any client-side code that you need when a button is clicked. The page in Listing 2.18 illustrates how you can use the OnClientClick property to display a confirmation dialog box (see Figure 2.14).

LISTING 2.18   ButtonOnClientClick.aspx

```
<%@ Page Language="C#" %>
<!DOCTYPE html PUBLIC "-//W3C//DTD XHTML 1.0 Transitional//EN"
"http://www.w3.org/TR/xhtml1/DTD/xhtml1-transitional.dtd">
<script runat="server">

    protected void btnDelete_Click(object sender, EventArgs e)
    {
        lblResult.Text = "All pages deleted!";
    }
</script>
<html xmlns="http://www.w3.org/1999/xhtml" >
<head id="Head1" runat="server">
    <title>Button OnClientClick</title>
</head>
<body>
    <form id="form1" runat="server">
    <div>

    <asp:Button
        id="btnDelete"
        Text="Delete Website"
        OnClick="btnDelete_Click"
        OnClientClick="return confirm('Are you sure?');"
        Runat="server" />

    <br /><br />

    <asp:Label
        id="lblResult"
        Runat="server" />

    </div>
    </form>
</body>
</html>
```

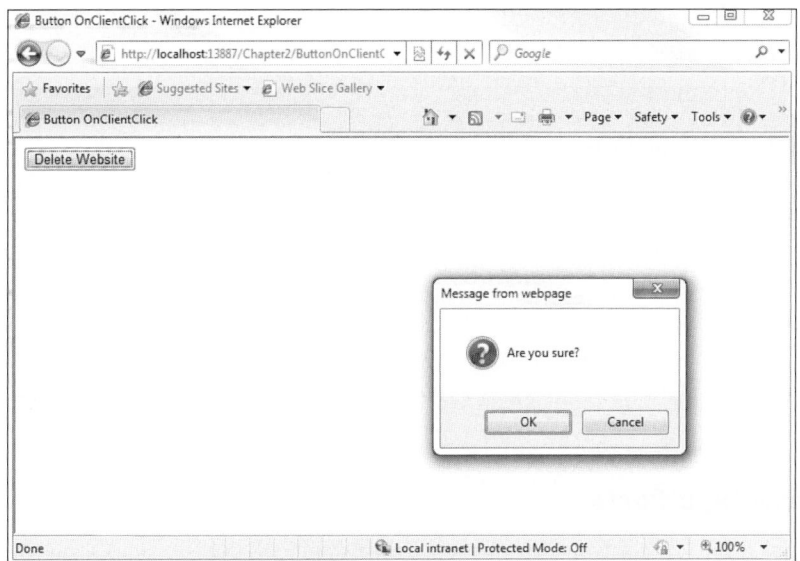

FIGURE 2.14   Displaying a client-side confirmation dialog box.

In Listing 2.18, the Button control includes an OnClientClick property, which executes a JavaScript script when you click the button on the client. The script displays a confirmation dialog box. If the confirmation box returns False, the button click is canceled, and the form containing the button is not posted to the server.

Because the button controls, like most ASP.NET controls, support expando attributes, you can handle other client-side events simply by adding an arbitrary attribute to the control. If ASP.NET Framework does not recognize an attribute declared on a button control, the framework simply passes the attribute to the browser.

For example, the page in Listing 2.19 contains a button control that includes onmouseover and onmouseout attributes. When you hover your mouse over the button, the text displayed in the button is changed.

LISTING 2.19   ButtonExpando.aspx

```
<%@ Page Language="C#" %>
<!DOCTYPE html PUBLIC "-//W3C//DTD XHTML 1.0 Transitional//EN"
"http://www.w3.org/TR/xhtml1/DTD/xhtml1-transitional.dtd">
<html xmlns="http://www.w3.org/1999/xhtml" >
<head id="Head1" runat="server">
    <title>Button Expando</title>
</head>
<body>
    <form id="form1" runat="server">
    <div>
```

```
<asp:Button
    id="btnSubmit"
    Text="Submit"
    onmouseover="this.value='Click Here!'"
    onmouseout="this.value='Submit'"
    Runat="server" />


    </div>
    </form>
</body>
</html>
```

Performing Cross-Page Posts

By default, if you click a button control, the page containing the control is posted back to itself, and the same page is reloaded. However, you can use the PostBackUrl property to post form data to another page.

For example, the page in Listing 2.20 includes a search form. The Button control in the page posts the form to another page named ButtonSearchResults.aspx. The ButtonSearchResults.aspx page is contained in Listing 2.21.

LISTING 2.20   ButtonSearch.aspx

```
<%@ Page Language="C#" %>
<!DOCTYPE html PUBLIC "-//W3C//DTD XHTML 1.0 Transitional//EN"
"http://www.w3.org/TR/xhtml1/DTD/xhtml1-transitional.dtd">
<html xmlns="http://www.w3.org/1999/xhtml" >
<head id="Head1" runat="server">
    <title>Button Search</title>
</head>
<body>
    <form id="form1" runat="server">
    <div>

    <asp:Label
        id="lblSearch"
        Text="Search:"
        Runat="server" />
    <asp:TextBox
        id="txtSearch"
        Runat="server" />
```

```
<asp:Button
    id="btnSearch"
    Text="Go!"
    PostBackUrl="ButtonSearchResults.aspx"
    Runat="server" />
</div>
</form>
</body>
</html>
```

LISTING 2.21   ButtonSearchResults.aspx

```
<%@ Page Language="C#" %>
<!DOCTYPE html PUBLIC "-//W3C//DTD XHTML 1.0 Transitional//EN"
"http://www.w3.org/TR/xhtml1/DTD/xhtml1-transitional.dtd">
<script runat="server">

    void Page_Load()
    {
        if (PreviousPage != null)
        {
            TextBox txtSearch = (TextBox)PreviousPage.FindControl("txtSearch");
            lblSearch.Text = String.Format("Search For: {0}", txtSearch.Text);
        }
    }

</script>
<html xmlns="http://www.w3.org/1999/xhtml" >
<head id="Head1" runat="server">
    <title>Button Search Results</title>
</head>
<body>
    <form id="form1" runat="server">
    <div>

    <asp:Label
        id="lblSearch"
        Runat="server" />

    </div>
    </form>
</body>
</html>
```

In the `Page_Load` event handler in Listing 2.21, the `PreviousPage` property gets a reference to the previous page (the `ButtonSearch.aspx` page in Listing 2.20). Next, the `FindControl()` method retrieves the `txtSearch TextBox` control from the previous page. Finally, the value entered into the `TextBox` displays in a label on the page.

As an alternative to using the `FindControl()` method to retrieve a particular control from the previous page, you can expose the control through a page property. The page in Listing 2.22 exposes the `txtSearch TextBox` through a property named `SearchString`. The page posts the form data to a page named `ButtonSearchResultsTyped.aspx`, contained in Listing 2.23.

LISTING 2.22 `ButtonSearchTyped.aspx`

```
<%@ Page Language="C#" %>
<!DOCTYPE html PUBLIC "-//W3C//DTD XHTML 1.0 Transitional//EN"
"http://www.w3.org/TR/xhtml1/DTD/xhtml1-transitional.dtd">
<script runat="server">

    public string SearchString
    {
        get { return txtSearch.Text; }
    }

</script>
<html xmlns="http://www.w3.org/1999/xhtml" >
<head id="Head1" runat="server">
    <title>Button Search Typed</title>
</head>
<body>
    <form id="form1" runat="server">
    <div>

    <asp:Label
        id="lblSearch"
        Text="Search:"
        Runat="server" />
    <asp:TextBox
        id="txtSearch"
        Runat="server" />
    <asp:Button
        id="btnSearch"
        Text="Go!"
        PostBackUrl="ButtonSearchResultsTyped.aspx"
        Runat="server" />
    </div>
    </form>
```

```
</body>
</html>
```

LISTING 2.23   ButtonSearchResultsTyped.aspx

```
<%@ Page Language="C#" %>
<%@ PreviousPageType VirtualPath="~/ButtonSearchTyped.aspx" %>
<!DOCTYPE html PUBLIC "-//W3C//DTD XHTML 1.0 Transitional//EN"
"http://www.w3.org/TR/xhtml1/DTD/xhtml1-transitional.dtd">
<script runat="server">

    void Page_Load()
    {
        if (Page.PreviousPage != null)
        {
            lblSearch.Text = String.Format("Search For: {0}", PreviousPage.
➥SearchString);
        }
    }

</script>
<html xmlns="http://www.w3.org/1999/xhtml" >
<head id="Head1" runat="server">
    <title>Button Search Results Typed</title>
</head>
<body>
    <form id="form1" runat="server">
    <div>

    <asp:Label
        id="lblSearch"
        Runat="server" />

    </div>
    </form>
</body>
</html>
```

Notice that the page in Listing 2.23 includes a <%@ PreviousPageType %> directive. This directive casts the value returned by the PreviousPage property as an instance of the ButtonSearchTyped class. Without this directive, the PreviousPage property would return the previous page as an instance of the generic Page class.

You can use either method when performing cross-page posts. The first method provides you with an untyped method of retrieving values from the previous page, and the second method provides you with a typed method.

Specifying a Default Button

You can specify a default button for a form by using the `DefaultButton` property of the server-side `Form` control. If you specify a default button, pressing the keyboard Enter key invokes the button.

For example, the page in Listing 2.24 contains a simple search form. The `<form>` tag sets the `btnSearch` `Button` control as the default button on the page.

LISTING 2.24   `ButtonDefaultButton.aspx`

```
<%@ Page Language="C#" %>
<!DOCTYPE html PUBLIC "-//W3C//DTD XHTML 1.0 Transitional//EN"
"http://www.w3.org/TR/xhtml1/DTD/xhtml1-transitional.dtd">
<script runat="server">

    protected void btnSearch_Click(object sender, EventArgs e)
    {
        lblResult.Text = "Search for: " + txtSearch.Text;
    }
</script>
<html xmlns="http://www.w3.org/1999/xhtml" >
<head id="Head1" runat="server">
    <title>Button Default Button</title>
</head>
<body>
    <form id="form1" defaultbutton="btnSearch" runat="server">
    <div>

    <asp:Label
        id="lblSearch"
        Text="Search:"
        AssociatedControlID="txtSearch"
        Runat="server" />
    <asp:TextBox
        id="txtSearch"
        Runat="server" />
    <asp:Button
        id="btnSearch"
        Text="Search"
        OnClick="btnSearch_Click"
        Runat="server" />
```

```
<asp:Button
    id="btnCancel"
    Text="Cancel"
    Runat="server" />

<hr />

<asp:Label
    id="lblResult"
    Runat="server" />

</div>
</form>
</body>
</html>
```

If you open the page in Listing 2.24, type a search phrase, and press the keyboard Enter key, the form is submitted to the server. Pressing the Enter key causes the btnSearch_Click event handler to execute because the btnSearch button is the default button on the page.

Handling the Command Event

All three Button controls support both the Click event and the Command event. The difference between these events is that you can pass a command name and command argument to a Command event handler but not to a Click event handler.

For example, the page in Listing 2.25 contains two Button controls and a BulletedList control. When you click the first button, the items displayed by the BulletedList control are sorted in ascending order, and when you click the second button, the items displayed by the BulletedList control are sorted in descending order (see Figure 2.15).

LISTING 2.25 ButtonCommand.aspx

```
<%@ Page Language="C#" %>
<%@ Import Namespace="System.Collections.Generic" %>
<!DOCTYPE html PUBLIC "-//W3C//DTD XHTML 1.0 Transitional//EN"
"http://www.w3.org/TR/xhtml1/DTD/xhtml1-transitional.dtd">
<script runat="server">
```

```
    private List<String> groceries = new List<String>();

    void Page_Load()
    {
        groceries.Add("Milk");
        groceries.Add("Steak");
        groceries.Add("Fish");
    }

    protected void Sort_Command(object sender, CommandEventArgs e)
    {
        if (e.CommandName == "Sort")
        {
            switch (e.CommandArgument.ToString())
            {
                case "ASC":
                    groceries.Sort(SortASC);
                    break;
                case "DESC":
                    groceries.Sort(SortDESC);
                    break;
            }
        }
    }

    void Page_PreRender()
    {
        bltGroceries.DataSource = groceries;
        bltGroceries.DataBind();
    }

    int SortASC(string x, string y)
    {
        return String.Compare(x, y);
    }

    int SortDESC(string x, string y)
    {
        return String.Compare(x, y) * -1;
    }

</script>
<html xmlns="http://www.w3.org/1999/xhtml" >
```

```
<head id="Head1" runat="server">
    <title>Button Command</title>
</head>
<body>
    <form id="form1" runat="server">
    <div>

    <asp:Button
        id="btnSortAsc"
        Text="Sort ASC"
        CommandName="Sort"
        CommandArgument="ASC"
        OnCommand="Sort_Command"
        Runat="server" />

    <asp:Button
        id="btnSortDESC"
        Text="Sort DESC"
        CommandName="Sort"
        CommandArgument="DESC"
        OnCommand="Sort_Command"
        Runat="server" />

    <br /><br />

    <asp:BulletedList
        id="bltGroceries"
        Runat="server" />

    </div>
    </form>
</body>
</html>
```

Both Button controls include CommandName and CommandArgument properties. Furthermore, both Button controls are wired to the same Sort_Command() event handler. This event handler checks the CommandName and CommandArgument properties when determining how the elements in the BulletedList should be sorted.

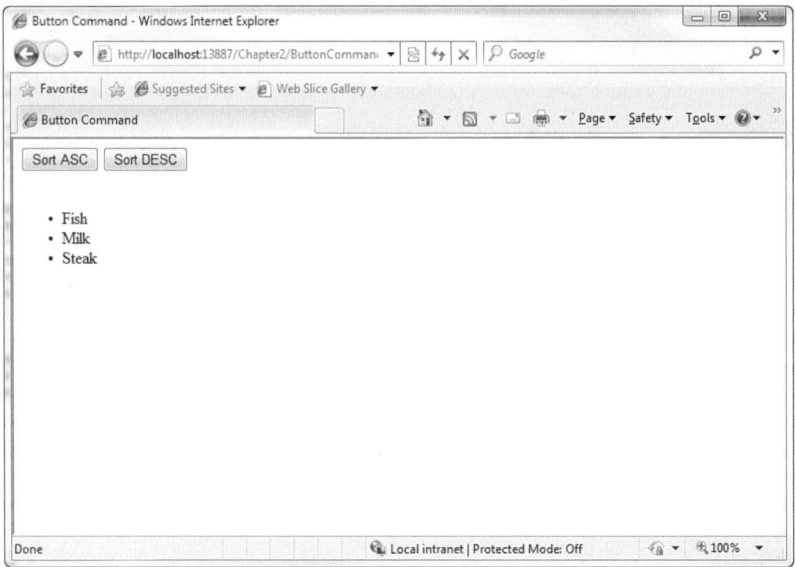

FIGURE 2.15   Handling the Command event.

Displaying Images

The ASP.NET Framework includes two controls for displaying images: Image and ImageMap. The Image control simply displays an image. The ImageMap control enables you to create a client-side, clickable, image map.

Using the Image Control

The page in Listing 2.26 randomly displays one of three images. The image is displayed by setting the ImageUrl property of the Image control contained in the body of the page.

LISTING 2.26   ShowImage.aspx

```
<%@ Page Language="C#" %>
<!DOCTYPE html PUBLIC "-//W3C//DTD XHTML 1.0 Transitional//EN"
"http://www.w3.org/TR/xhtml1/DTD/xhtml1-transitional.dtd">
<script runat="server">

    void Page_Load()
    {
        Random rnd = new Random();
        switch (rnd.Next(3))
        {
```

```
            case 0:
                imgRandom.ImageUrl = "Picture1.gif";
                imgRandom.AlternateText = "Picture 1";
                break;
            case 1:
                imgRandom.ImageUrl = "Picture2.gif";
                imgRandom.AlternateText = "Picture 2";
                break;
            case 2:
                imgRandom.ImageUrl = "Picture3.gif";
                imgRandom.AlternateText = "Picture 3";
                break;
        }
    }

</script>
<html xmlns="http://www.w3.org/1999/xhtml" >
<head id="Head1" runat="server">
    <title>Show Image</title>
</head>
<body>
    <form id="form1" runat="server">
    <div>

    <asp:Image
        id="imgRandom"
        Runat="server" />

    </div>
    </form>
</body>
</html>
```

The Image control supports the following properties (this is not a complete list):

▶ **AlternateText**—Enables you to provide alternate text for the image (required for accessibility).

▶ **DescriptionUrl**—Enables you to provide a link to a page that contains a detailed description of the image (required to make a complex image accessible).

▶ **GenerateEmptyAlternateText**—Enables you to set the AlternateText property to an empty string.

- ▶ **ImageAlign**—Enables you to align the image relative to other HTML elements in the page. Possible values are AbsBottom, AbsMiddle, Baseline, Bottom, Left, Middle, NotSet, Right, TextTop, and Top.

- ▶ **ImageUrl**—Enables you to specify the URL to the image.

The Image control supports three methods for supplying alternate text. If an image represents page content, you should supply a value for the AlternateText property. For example, if you have an image for your company's logo, you should assign the text "My Company Logo" to the AlternateText property.

If an Image control represents something complex—such as a bar chart, pie graph, or company organizational chart— you should supply a value for the DescriptionUrl property. The DescriptionUrl property links to a page that contains a long textual description of the image.

Finally, if the image is used purely for decoration (it expresses no content), you should set the GenerateEmptyAlternateText property to the value True. When this property has the value True, an alt="" attribute is included in the rendered <img> tag. Screen readers know to ignore images with empty alt attributes.

Using the **ImageMap** Control

The ImageMap control enables you to create a client-side image map. An image map displays an image. When you click different areas of the image, things happen.

For example, you can use an image map as a fancy navigation bar. In that case, clicking different areas of the image map navigates to different pages in your website.

You also can use an image map as an input mechanism. For example, you can click different product images to add a particular product to a shopping cart.

An ImageMap control is composed out of instances of the HotSpot class. A HotSpot defines the clickable regions in an image map. The ASP.NET Framework ships with three HotSpot classes:

- ▶ **CircleHotSpot**—Enables you to define a circular region in an image map.

- ▶ **PolygonHotSpot**—Enables you to define an irregularly shaped region in an image map.

- ▶ **RectangleHotSpot**—Enables you to define a rectangular region in an image map.

The page in Listing 2.27 contains a navigation bar created with an ImageMap control, which contains three RectangleHotSpots that delimit the three buttons displayed by the navigation bar (see Figure 2.16).

LISTING 2.27   ImageMapNavigate.aspx

```
<%@ Page Language="C#" %>
<!DOCTYPE html PUBLIC "-//W3C//DTD XHTML 1.0 Transitional//EN"
"http://www.w3.org/TR/xhtml1/DTD/xhtml1-transitional.dtd">
<html xmlns="http://www.w3.org/1999/xhtml" >
<head id="Head1" runat="server">
    <title>ImageMap Navigate</title>
</head>
<body>
    <form id="form1" runat="server">
    <div>

    <asp:ImageMap
        id="mapNavigate"
        ImageUrl="ImageBar.jpg"
        Runat="server">
        <asp:RectangleHotSpot
            NavigateUrl="Home.aspx"
            Left="0"
            Top="0"
            Right="100"
            Bottom="50"
            AlternateText="Navigate to Home" />
        <asp:RectangleHotSpot
            NavigateUrl="Products.aspx"
            Left="100"
            Top="0"
            Right="200"
            Bottom="50"
            AlternateText="Navigate to Products" />
        <asp:RectangleHotSpot
            NavigateUrl="Services.aspx"
            Left="200"
            Top="0"
            Right="300"
            Bottom="50"
            AlternateText="Navigate to Services" />
    </asp:ImageMap>

    </div>
    </form>
</body>
</html>
```

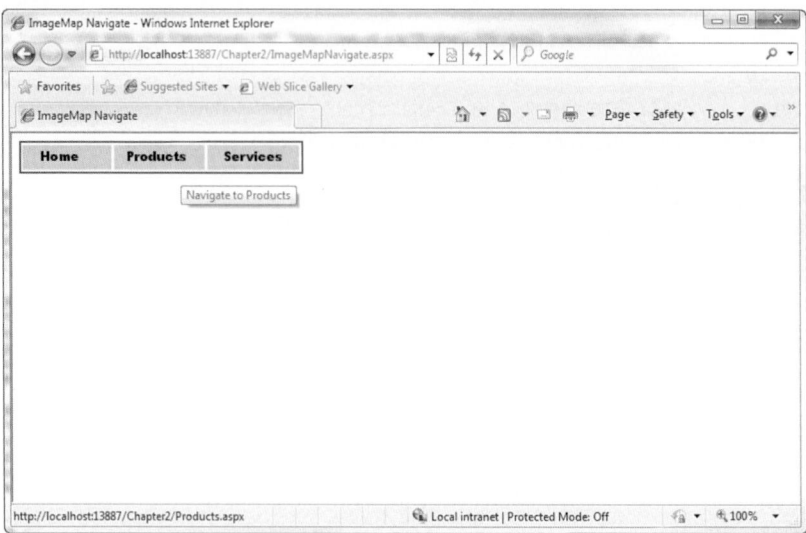

FIGURE 2.16   Navigating with an `ImageMap` control.

Each `RectangleHotSpot` includes `Left`, `Top`, `Right`, and `Bottom` properties that describe the area of the rectangle. Each `RectangleHotSpot` also includes a `NavigateUrl` property that contains the URL to which the region of the image map links.

Rather than use an image map to link to different pages, you can use it to post back to the same page. For example, the page in Listing 2.28 uses an `ImageMap` control to display a menu. When you click different menu items represented by different regions of the image map, the text contained in the `TextBox` control is changed (see Figure 2.17).

LISTING 2.28   `ImageMapPostBack.aspx`

```
<%@ Page Language="C#" %>
<!DOCTYPE html PUBLIC "-//W3C//DTD XHTML 1.0 Transitional//EN"
"http://www.w3.org/TR/xhtml1/DTD/xhtml1-transitional.dtd">
<script runat="server">

    protected void mapMenu_Click(object sender, ImageMapEventArgs e)
    {
        switch (e.PostBackValue)
        {
            case "ToUpper":
                txtText.Text = txtText.Text.ToUpper();
                break;
            case "ToLower":
                txtText.Text = txtText.Text.ToLower();
                break;
```

```
                case "Erase":
                    txtText.Text = String.Empty;
                    break;
            }
        }
</script>
<html xmlns="http://www.w3.org/1999/xhtml" >
<head id="Head1" runat="server">
    <title>ImageMap PostBack</title>
</head>
<body>
    <form id="form1" runat="server">
    <div>

    <asp:ImageMap
        id="mapMenu"
        ImageUrl="MenuBar.gif"
        HotSpotMode="PostBack"
        Runat="server" OnClick="mapMenu_Click">
        <asp:RectangleHotSpot
            PostBackValue="ToUpper"
            Left="0"
            Top="0"
            Right="100"
            Bottom="30"
            AlternateText="To Uppercase" />
        <asp:RectangleHotSpot
            PostBackValue="ToLower"
            Left="100"
            Top="0"
            Right="200"
            Bottom="30"
            AlternateText="To Lowercase" />
        <asp:RectangleHotSpot
            PostBackValue="Erase"
            Left="200"
            Top="0"
            Right="300"
            Bottom="30"
            AlternateText="Erase Text" />
    </asp:ImageMap>

    <br />

    <asp:TextBox
        id="txtText"
```

2

```
            TextMode="MultiLine"
            Columns="40"
            Rows="5"
            Runat="server" />

    </div>
    </form>
</body>
</html>
```

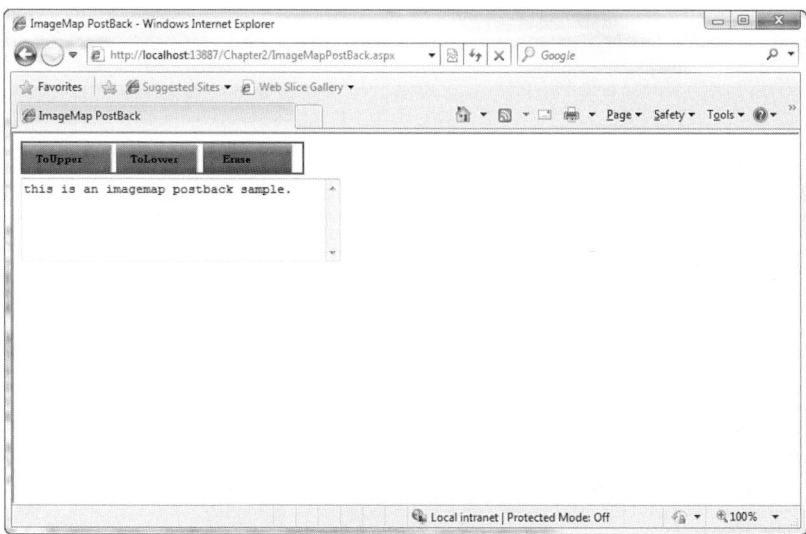

FIGURE 2.17   Posting back to the server with an ImageMap control.

Notice that the ImageMap control has its HotSpotMode property set to the value PostBack. Also, the ImageMap is wired to a Click event handler named mapMenu_Click.

Each HotSpot contained in the ImageMap control has a PostBackValue property. The mapMenu_Click handler reads the PostBackValue from the region clicked and modifies the text displayed by the TextBox control.

The ImageMap control supports the following properties (this is not a complete list):

▶ **AccessKey**—Enables you to specify a key that navigates to the ImageMap control.

▶ **AlternateText**—Enables you to provide alternate text for the image (required for accessibility).

▶ **DescriptionUrl**—Enables you to provide a link to a page that contains a detailed description of the image (required to make a complex image accessible).

▶ **GenerateEmptyAlternateText**—Enables you to set the `AlternateText` property to an empty string.

▶ **HotSpotMode**—Enables you to specify the behavior of the image map when you click a region. Possible values are `Inactive`, `Navigate`, `NotSet`, and `PostBack`.

▶ **HotSpots**—Enables you to retrieve the collection of `HotSpots` contained in the `ImageMap` control.

▶ **ImageAlign**—Enables you to align the image map with other HTML elements in the page. Possible values are `AbsBottom`, `AbsMiddle`, `Baseline`, `Bottom`, `Left`, `Middle`, `NotSet`, `Right`, `TextTop`, and `Top`.

▶ **ImageUrl**—Enables you to specify the URL to the image.

▶ **TabIndex**—Enables you to specify the tab order of the `ImageMap` control.

▶ **Target**—Enables you to open a page in a new window.

The `ImageMap` control also supports the following method:

▶ **Focus**—Enables you to set the initial form focus to the `ImageMap` control.

Finally, the `ImageMap` control supports the following event:

▶ **Click**—Raised when you click a region of the `ImageMap` and the `HotSpotMode` property is set to the value `PostBack`.

Using the Panel Control

The `Panel` control enables you to work with a group of ASP.NET controls.

For example, you can use a `Panel` control to hide or show a group of ASP.NET controls. The page in Listing 2.29 contains a list of `RadioButton` controls which can be used to select your favorite programming language. The last `RadioButton` is labeled `Other`. If you select the `Other` radio button, the contents of a `Panel` control are revealed (see Figure 2.18).

LISTING 2.29   ShowPanel.aspx

```
<%@ Page Language="C#" %>
<!DOCTYPE html PUBLIC "-//W3C//DTD XHTML 1.0 Transitional//EN"
"http://www.w3.org/TR/xhtml1/DTD/xhtml1-transitional.dtd">
<script runat="server">

    protected void btnSubmit_Click(object sender, EventArgs e)
    {
        if (rdlOther.Checked)
            pnlOther.Visible = true;
        else
            pnlOther.Visible = false;
```

```
        }
</script>
<html xmlns="http://www.w3.org/1999/xhtml" >
<head id="Head1" runat="server">
    <title>Show Panel</title>
</head>
<body>
    <form id="form1" runat="server">
    <div>

    Select your favorite programming language:
    <br /><br />
    <asp:RadioButton
        id="rdlVisualBasic"
        GroupName="language"
        Text="Visual Basic"
        Runat="server" />
    <br /><br />
    <asp:RadioButton
        id="rdlCSharp"
        GroupName="language"
        Text="C#"
        Runat="server" />
    <br /><br />
    <asp:RadioButton
        id="rdlOther"
        GroupName="language"
        Text="Other Language"
        Runat="server" />
    <br />
    <asp:Panel
        id="pnlOther"
        Visible="false"
        Runat="server">

        <asp:Label
            id="lblOther"
            Text="Other Language:"
            AssociatedControlID="txtOther"
            Runat="server" />
        <asp:TextBox
            id="txtOther"
            Runat="server" />

    </asp:Panel>
```

```
    <br /><br />

    <asp:Button
        id="btnSubmit"
        Text="Submit"
        Runat="server" OnClick="btnSubmit_Click" />

    </div>
    </form>
</body>
</html>
```

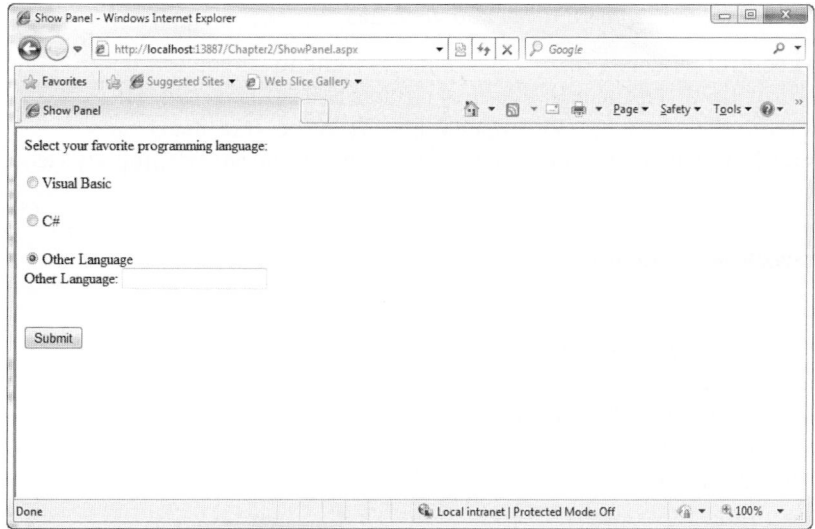

FIGURE 2.18   Hiding and displaying controls with the Panel control.

Notice that the Panel control is declared with a Visible property that has the value False. Because the Visible property is set to the value False, the Panel control and any controls contained in the Panel control are not rendered when the page is requested.

If you select the RadioButton control labeled Other, the Visible property is set to the value True and the contents of the Panel control display.

> **NOTE**
>
> Every control in ASP.NET supports the Visible property. When Visible is set to the value False, the control does not render its contents.

The Panel control supports the following properties (this is not a complete list):

▶ **DefaultButton**—Enables you to specify the default button in a Panel. The default button is invoked when you press the Enter button.

▶ **Direction**—Enables you to get or set the direction in which controls that display text are rendered. Possible values are NotSet, LeftToRight, and RightToLeft.

▶ **GroupingText**—Enables you to render the Panel control as a fieldset with a particular legend.

▶ **HorizontalAlign**—Enables you to specify the horizontal alignment of the contents of the Panel. Possible values are Center, Justify, Left, NotSet, and Right.

▶ **ScrollBars**—Enables you to display scrollbars around the panel's contents. Possible values are Auto, Both, Horizontal, None, and Vertical.

By default, a Panel control renders a <div> tag around its contents. If you set the GroupingText property, however, the Panel control renders a <fieldset> tag. The value that you assign to the GroupingText property appears in the <fieldset> tag's <legend> tag. Listing 2.30 demonstrates how you can use the GroupingText property (see Figure 2.19).

LISTING 2.30 PanelGroupingText.aspx

```
<%@ Page Language="C#" %>
<!DOCTYPE html PUBLIC "-//W3C//DTD XHTML 1.0 Transitional//EN"
"http://www.w3.org/TR/xhtml1/DTD/xhtml1-transitional.dtd">
<html xmlns="http://www.w3.org/1999/xhtml" >
<head id="Head1" runat="server">
    <title>Panel Grouping Text</title>
</head>
<body>
    <form id="form1" runat="server">
    <div>

    <asp:Panel
        id="pnlContact"
        GroupingText="Contact Information"
        Runat="server">

    <asp:Label
        id="lblFirstName"
        Text="First Name:"
        AssociatedControlID="txtFirstName"
        Runat="server" />
    <br />
    <asp:TextBox
        id="txtFirstName"
```

```
            AutoCompleteType="FirstName"
            Runat="server" />
        <br /><br />
        <asp:Label
            id="lblLastname"
            Text="Last Name:"
            AssociatedControlID="txtLastName"
            Runat="server" />
        <br />
        <asp:TextBox
            id="txtLastName"
            AutoCompleteType="LastName"
            Runat="server" />
        <br /><br />
        <asp:Button
            id="btnSubmit"
            Text="Submit"
            Runat="server" />

    </asp:Panel>

    </div>
    </form>
</body>
</html>
```

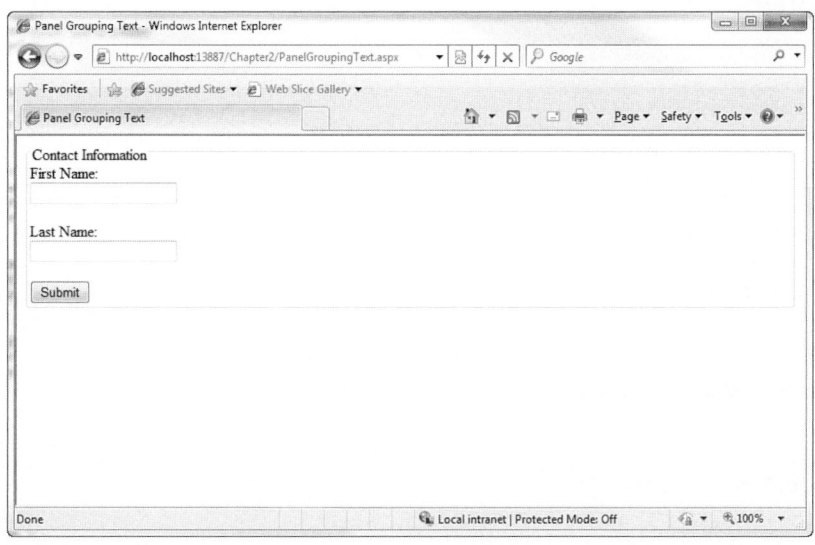

FIGURE 2.19   Setting the GroupingText property.

WEB STANDARDS NOTE

According to the accessibility guidelines, you should use <fieldset> tags when group-ing related form fields in long forms.

The ScrollBars property enables you to display scrollbars around a panel's contents. For example, the page in Listing 2.31 contains a Panel control that contains a BulletedList control that displays 100 items. The panel is configured to scroll when its contents over-flow its width or height (see Figure 2.20).

LISTING 2.31   PanelScrollBars.aspx

```
<%@ Page Language="C#" %>
<!DOCTYPE html PUBLIC "-//W3C//DTD XHTML 1.0 Transitional//EN"
"http://www.w3.org/TR/xhtml1/DTD/xhtml1-transitional.dtd">
<script runat="server">

    void Page_Load()
    {
        for (int i = 0; i < 100; i++)
            bltList.Items.Add("Item " + i.ToString());
    }

</script>
<html xmlns="http://www.w3.org/1999/xhtml" >
<head id="Head1" runat="server">
    <style type="text/css">
        html
        {
            background-color:silver;
        }
        .contents
        {
            background-color:white;
            width:200px;
            height:200px;
        }
    </style>
    <title>Panel ScrollBars</title>
</head>
<body>
    <form id="form1" runat="server">
    <div>
```

```
<asp:Panel
    id="pnlContent"
    ScrollBars="Auto"
    CssClass="contents"
    Runat="server">
    <asp:BulletedList
        id="bltList"
        Runat="server" />
</asp:Panel>

</div>
</form>
</body>
</html>
```

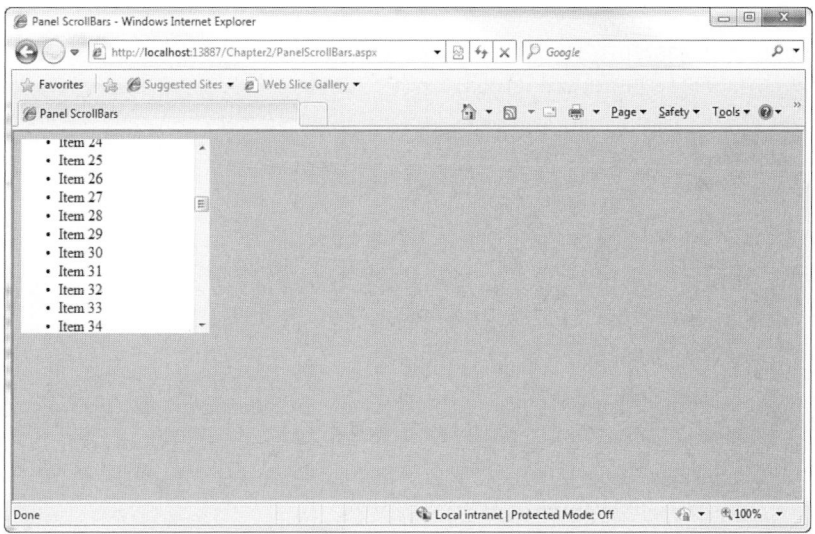

FIGURE 2.20   Displaying scrollbars with a Panel control.

WEB STANDARDS NOTE

Don't use the values Horizontal or Vertical with the ScrollBars property when you
want the scrollbars to appear in browsers other than Microsoft Internet Explorer. If you
want the scrollbars to appear in FireFox and Opera, use either the value Auto or Both.

When enabling scrollbars with the `Panel` control, you must specify a particular width and height to display the scrollbars. In Listing 2.31, the width and height are specified in a Cascading Style Sheet class. Alternatively, you can specify the width and height with the `Panel` control's `Width` and `Height` properties.

Using the HyperLink Control

The `HyperLink` control enables you to create a link to a page. Unlike the `LinkButton` control, the `HyperLink` control does not submit a form to a server.

For example, the page in Listing 2.32 displays a hyperlink that randomly links to a page in your application.

LISTING 2.32   ShowHyperLink.aspx

```
<%@ Page Language="C#" %>
<%@ Import Namespace="System.IO" %>
<!DOCTYPE html PUBLIC "-//W3C//DTD XHTML 1.0 Transitional//EN"
"http://www.w3.org/TR/xhtml1/DTD/xhtml1-transitional.dtd">
<script runat="server">

    void Page_Load()
    {
        lnkRandom.NavigateUrl = GetRandomFile();
    }


    string GetRandomFile()
    {
        string[] files = Directory.GetFiles(MapPath(Request.ApplicationPath),
➥"*.aspx");
        Random rnd = new Random();
        string rndFile = files[rnd.Next(files.Length)];
        return Path.GetFileName(rndFile);
    }

</script>
<html xmlns="http://www.w3.org/1999/xhtml" >
<head id="Head1" runat="server">
    <title>Show HyperLink</title>
</head>
<body>
    <form id="form1" runat="server">
    <div>

    <asp:HyperLink
```

```
        id="lnkRandom"
        Text="Random Link"
        Runat="server" />

    </div>
    </form>
</body>
</html>
```

In the Page_Load event handler in Listing 2.32, a random filename from the current application is assigned to the NavigateUrl property of the HyperLink control.

The HyperLink control supports the following properties (this is not a complete list):

- ▶ **Enabled**—Enables you to disable the hyperlink.

- ▶ **ImageUrl**—Enables you to specify an image for the hyperlink.

- ▶ **NavigateUrl**—Enables you to specify the URL represented by the hyperlink.

- ▶ **Target**—Enables you to open a new window.

- ▶ **Text**—Enables you to label the hyperlink.

Notice that you can specify an image for the HyperLink control by setting the ImageUrl property. If you set both the Text and ImageUrl properties, the ImageUrl property takes precedence.

Summary

In this chapter, you were introduced to the core controls of ASP.NET 4 Framework. You learned how to display information using the Label and Literal controls. You also learned how to accept user input using the TextBox, CheckBox, and RadioButton controls.

In the second part of this chapter, you learned how to use the different button controls—Button, LinkButton, and ImageButton—to submit a form. You learned how to post forms between pages. You also learned how to set a default button.

Finally, we discussed the Panel and HyperLink controls. You learned how to hide and display a group of controls with the Panel control. You also learned how to create dynamic links with the HyperLink control.

Using the Validation Controls

In this chapter, you learn how to validate form fields when a form is submitted to the web server. You can use the validation controls to prevent users from submitting the wrong type of data into a database table. For example, you can use validation controls to prevent a user from submitting the value "Apple" for a birth date field.

In the first part of this chapter, you are provided with an overview of the standard validation controls included in the ASP.NET 4 Framework. You learn how to control how validation errors display, how to highlight validation error messages, and how to use validation groups. You are provided with sample code for using each of the standard validation controls.

Next, we extend the basic validation controls with our own custom validation controls. For example, you learn how to create an AjaxValidator control that enables you to call a server-side validation function from the client.

Overview of the Validation Controls

ASP.NET 4 includes six validation controls:

▶ **RequiredFieldValidator**—Enables you to require a user to enter a value in a form field.

▶ **RangeValidator**—Enables you to check whether a value falls between a certain minimum and maximum value.

▶ **CompareValidator**—Enables you to compare a value against another value or perform a data type check.

- ▶ **RegularExpressionValidator**—Enables you to compare a value against a regular expression.

- ▶ **CustomValidator**—Enables you to perform custom validation.

- ▶ **ValidationSummary**—Enables you to display a summary of all validation errors in a page.

You can associate the validation controls with any form controls included in ASP.NET Framework. For example, if you want to require a user to enter a value into a TextBox control, you can associate a RequiredFieldValidator control with the TextBox control.

> **NOTE**
>
> Technically, you can use the validation controls with any control decorated with the ValidationProperty attribute.

Listing 3.1 contains a simple order entry form. It contains three TextBox controls that enable you to enter a product name, product price, and product quantity. The validation controls validate each of the form fields.

LISTING 3.1   OrderForm.aspx

```
<%@ Page Language="C#" %>
<!DOCTYPE html PUBLIC "-//W3C//DTD XHTML 1.0 Transitional//EN"
"http://www.w3.org/TR/xhtml1/DTD/xhtml1-transitional.dtd">
<script runat="server">

    void btnSubmit_Click(Object sender, EventArgs e)
    {
        if (Page.IsValid)
        {
            lblResult.Text = @"<br />Product: " + txtProductName.Text
                + "<br />Price: " + txtProductPrice.Text
                + "<br />Quantity: " + txtProductQuantity.Text;
        }
    }
</script>
<html xmlns="http://www.w3.org/1999/xhtml" >
<head id="Head1" runat="server">
    <title>Order Form</title>
</head>
<body>
    <form id="form1" runat="server">
    <div>
```

```
<fieldset>
<legend>Product Order Form</legend>

<asp:Label
    id="lblProductName"
    Text="Product Name:"
    AssociatedControlID="txtProductName"
    Runat="server" />
<br />
<asp:TextBox
    id="txtProductName"
    Runat="server" />
<asp:RequiredFieldValidator
    id="reqProductName"
    ControlToValidate="txtProductName"
    Text="(Required)"
    Runat="server" />

<br /><br />

<asp:Label
    id="lblProductPrice"
    Text="Product Price:"
    AssociatedControlID="txtProductPrice"
    Runat="server" />
<br />
<asp:TextBox
    id="txtProductPrice"
    Columns="5"
    Runat="server" />
<asp:RequiredFieldValidator
    id="reqProductPrice"
    ControlToValidate="txtProductPrice"
    Text="(Required)"
    Display="Dynamic"
    Runat="server" />
<asp:CompareValidator
    id="cmpProductPrice"
    ControlToValidate="txtProductPrice"
    Text="(Invalid Price)"
    Operator="DataTypeCheck"
    Type="Currency"
    Runat="server" />

<br /><br />
```

```
<asp:Label
    id="lblProductQuantity"
    Text="Product Quantity:"
    AssociatedControlID="txtProductQuantity"
    Runat="server" />
<br />
<asp:TextBox
    id="txtProductQuantity"
    Columns="5"
    Runat="server" />
<asp:RequiredFieldValidator
    id="reqProductQuantity"
    ControlToValidate="txtProductQuantity"
    Text="(Required)"
    Display="Dynamic"
    Runat="server" />
<asp:CompareValidator
    id="CompareValidator1"
    ControlToValidate="txtProductQuantity"
    Text="(Invalid Quantity)"
    Operator="DataTypeCheck"
    Type="Integer"
    Runat="server" />

<br /><br />

<asp:Button
    id="btnSubmit"
    Text="Submit Product Order"
    OnClick="btnSubmit_Click"
    Runat="server" />

</fieldset>

<asp:Label
    id="lblResult"
    Runat="server" />


</div>
</form>
</body>
</html>
```

A separate `RequiredFieldValidator` control is associated with each of the three form fields. If you attempt to submit the form in Listing 3.1 without entering a value for a field, a validation error message display (see Figure 3.1).

Each `RequiredFieldValidator` associates with a particular control through its `ControlToValidate` property. This property accepts the name of the control to validate on the page.

`CompareValidator` controls associate with the `txtProductPrice` and `txtProductQuantity` `TextBox` controls. The first `CompareValidator` checks whether the `txtProductPrice` text field contains a currency value, and the second `CompareValidator` checks whether the `txtProductQuantity` text field contains an integer value.

There is nothing wrong with associating more than one validation control with a form field. If you need to make a form field required and check the data type entered into the form field, you need to associate both a `RequiredFieldValidator` and `CompareValidator` control with the form field.

Finally, the `Page.IsValid` property is checked in the `Page_Load()` handler before the form data displays. When using the validation controls, you should always check the `Page.IsValid` property before doing anything with the data submitted to a page. This property returns the value `true` when, and only when, no validation errors are on the page.

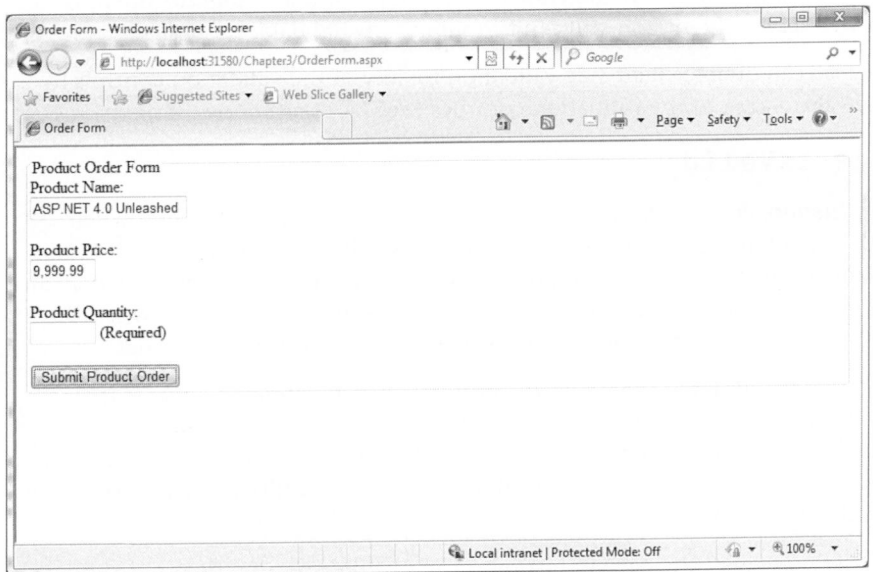

FIGURE 3.1   Displaying a validation error message.

Validation Controls and JavaScript

By default, the validation controls perform validation on both the client (the browser) and the server. The validation controls use client-side JavaScript. This is great from a user experience perspective because you get immediate feedback whenever you enter an invalid value into a form field.

> **NOTE**
>
> The RequiredFieldValidator does not perform client-side validation until after you attempt to submit a form at least once or you enter and remove data in a form field.

Almost all desktop browsers support client-side JavaScript. Supported browsers include Internet Explorer, Firefox, Chrome, Safari, and Opera. It is becoming more common to browse the web on mobile devices such as cell phones. Many of these mobile browsers do not yet support JavaScript.

You can use the validation controls with browsers that do not support JavaScript (or do not have JavaScript enabled). If a browser does not support JavaScript, the form must be posted back to the server before a validation error message displays.

Even when validation happens on the client, validation is still performed on the server. This is done for security reasons. If someone creates a fake form and submits the form data to your web server, the person still can't to submit invalid data.

If you prefer, you can disable client-side validation for any of the validation controls by assigning the value False to the validation control's EnableClientScript property.

Using Page.IsValid

As previously mentioned, you should always check the Page.IsValid property when working with data submitted with a form that contains validation controls. Each of the validation controls includes an IsValid property that returns the value True when a validation error doesn't exist. The Page.IsValid property returns the value True when the IsValid property for of the validation controls in a page returns the value True.

It is easy to forget to check the Page.IsValid property. When you use a browser that supports JavaScript with the validation controls, you are prevented from submitting a form back to the server when validation errors exist. However, if someone requests a page using a browser that does not support JavaScript, the page is submitted back to the server even when validation errors exist.

For example, if you request the page in Listing 3.1 with a browser that does not support JavaScript and submit the form without entering form data, the btnSubmit_Click() handler executes on the server. The Page.IsValid property is used in Listing 3.1 to prevent down-level browsers from displaying invalid form data.

WARNING

Unfortunately, many developers have made the mistake of forgetting to include a check of the `Page.IsValid` property several times when building applications. Because you do not normally develop a web application with JavsaScript disabled in your browser, you won't notice the problem described in this section until you start getting invalid data in your database tables.

Setting the Display Property

All the validation controls include a `Display` property that determines how the validation error message is rendered. This property accepts any of the following three possible values:

- Static
- Dynamic
- None

By default, the `Display` property has the value `Static`. When the `Display` property has this value, the validation error message rendered by the validation control looks like this:

```
<span id="reqProductName" style="visibility:hidden;">(Required)</span>
```

The error message is rendered in a `<span>` tag that includes a Cascading Style Sheet (CSS) style attribute that sets the visibility of the `<span>` tag to `hidden`.

If, on the other hand, you set the `Display` property to the value `Dynamic`, the error message is rendered like this:

```
<span id="reqProductName" style="display:none;">(Required)</span>
```

In this case, a CSS `display` attribute hides the contents of the `<span>` tag.

NOTE

In previous versions of ASP.NET, all `<span>` tags rendered by validators would also have "color:Red" in the style attribute. To become more standards-compliant, this inline styling is not present in ASP.NET 4. Instead, you should define a CSS class for your validation messages and set the CssClass property on each validator to style your messages.

You can use both the visibility and display attributes to hide text in a browser. However, text hidden with the `visibility` attribute still occupies screen real estate. Text hidden with the `display` attribute, on the other hand, does not occupy screen real estate.

In general, you should set a validation control's `Display` property to the value `Dynamic`. That way, if other content displays next to the validation control, the content is not pushed to the right. All modern browsers (Internet Explorer, Firefox, Chrome, Safari, and Opera) support the CSS `display` attribute.

The third possible value of the `Display` property is `None`. If you prefer, you can prevent the individual validation controls from displaying an error message and display the error messages with a `ValidationSummary` control. You learn how to use the `ValidationSummary` control later in this chapter.

Highlighting Validation Errors

When a validation control displays a validation error, the control displays the value of its `Text` property. Normally, you assign a simple text string, such as `"(Required)"` to the `Text` property; however, the `Text` property accepts any HTML string.

For example, the page in Listing 3.2 displays an image when you submit the form without entering a value for the First Name text field (see Figure 3.2).

LISTING 3.2   `ValidationImage.aspx`

```
<%@ Page Language="C#" %>
<!DOCTYPE html PUBLIC "-//W3C//DTD XHTML 1.0 Transitional//EN"
"http://www.w3.org/TR/xhtml1/DTD/xhtml1-transitional.dtd">
<html xmlns="http://www.w3.org/1999/xhtml" >
<head id="Head1" runat="server">
    <title>Validation Image</title>
</head>
<body>
    <form id="form1" runat="server">
    <div>

    <asp:Label
        id="lblFirstName"
        Text="First Name"
        AssociatedControlID="txtFirstName"
        Runat="server" />
    <br />
    <asp:TextBox
        id="txtFirstName"
        Runat="server" />
    <asp:RequiredFieldValidator
        id="reqFirstName"
        ControlToValidate="txtFirstName"
        Text="<img src='Error.gif' alt='First name is required.' />"
        Runat="server" />
```

```
    <br /><br />

    <asp:Button
        id="btnSubmit"
        Text="Submit"
        Runat="server" />

    </div>
    </form>
</body>
</html>
```

In Listing 3.2, the Text property contains an HTML <img> tag. When a validation error occurs, the image represented by the <img> tag displays.

Another way that you can emphasize errors is to take advantage of the SetFocusOnError property supported by all the validation controls. When this property has the value True, the form focus automatically shifts to the control associated with the validation control when a validation error occurs.

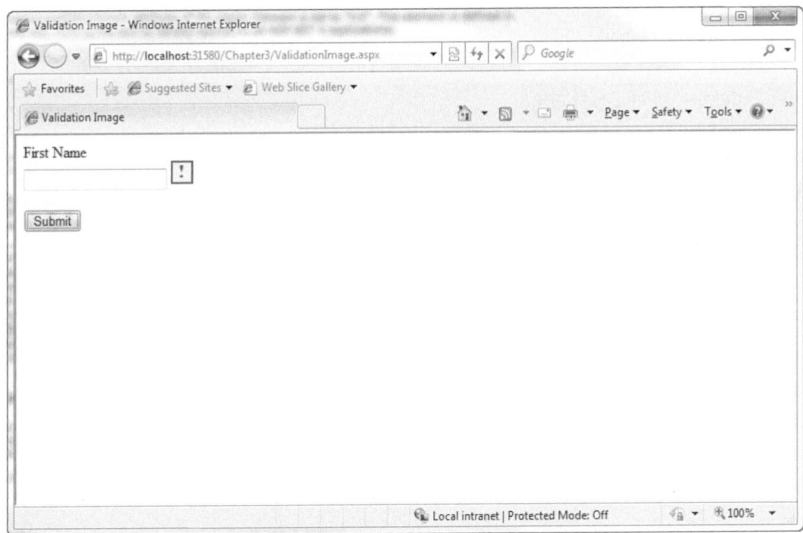

FIGURE 3.2   Displaying an image for a validation error.

For example, the page in Listing 3.3 contains two TextBox controls that are both validated with RequiredFieldValidator controls. Both RequiredFieldValidator controls have their SetFocusOnError properties enabled. If you provide a value for the first text field and not the second text field and submit the form, the form focus automatically shifts to the second form field.

LISTING 3.3   ShowSetFocusOnError.aspx

```
<%@ Page Language="C#" %>
<!DOCTYPE html PUBLIC "-//W3C//DTD XHTML 1.0 Transitional//EN"
"http://www.w3.org/TR/xhtml1/DTD/xhtml1-transitional.dtd">
<html xmlns="http://www.w3.org/1999/xhtml" >
<head id="Head1" runat="server">
    <title>Show SetFocusOnError</title>
</head>
<body>
    <form id="form1" runat="server">
    <div>

    <asp:Label
        id="lblFirstName"
        Text="First Name"
        AssociatedControlID="txtFirstName"
        Runat="server" />
    <br />
    <asp:TextBox
        id="txtFirstName"
        Runat="server" />
    <asp:RequiredFieldValidator
        id="reqFirstName"
        ControlToValidate="txtFirstName"
        Text="(Required)"
        SetFocusOnError="true"
        Runat="server" />

    <br /><br />

    <asp:Label
        id="lblLastName"
        Text="Last Name"
        AssociatedControlID="txtLastName"
        Runat="server" />
    <br />
    <asp:TextBox
        id="txtLastname"
        Runat="server" />
    <asp:RequiredFieldValidator
        id="reqLastName"
        ControlToValidate="txtLastName"
        Text="(Required)"
        SetFocusOnError="true"
        Runat="server" />
```

```
    <br /><br />

    <asp:Button
        id="btnSubmit"
        Text="Submit"
        Runat="server" />

    </div>
    </form>
</body>
</html>
```

Finally, if you want to really emphasize the controls associated with a validation error, you can take advantage of the `Page.Validators` property. This property exposes the collection of all the validation controls in a page. In Listing 3.4, the `Page.Validators` property highlights each control that has a validation error (see Figure 3.3).

LISTING 3.4   `ShowValidators.aspx`

```
<%@ Page Language="C#" %>
<!DOCTYPE html PUBLIC "-//W3C//DTD XHTML 1.0 Transitional//EN"
"http://www.w3.org/TR/xhtml1/DTD/xhtml1-transitional.dtd">
<script runat="server">

    void Page_PreRender()
    {
        foreach (BaseValidator valControl in Page.Validators)
        {
            WebControl assControl =
(WebControl)Page.FindControl(valControl.ControlToValidate);
            if (!valControl.IsValid)
                assControl.BackColor = System.Drawing.Color.Yellow;
            else
                assControl.BackColor = System.Drawing.Color.White;
        }
    }
</script>
<html xmlns="http://www.w3.org/1999/xhtml" >
<head id="Head1" runat="server">
    <title>Show Validators</title>
</head>
<body>
    <form id="form1" runat="server">
    <div>
```

```
<asp:Label
    id="lblFirstName"
    Text="First Name"
    AssociatedControlID="txtFirstName"
    Runat="server" />
<br />
<asp:TextBox
    id="txtFirstName"
    Runat="server" />
<asp:RequiredFieldValidator
    id="reqFirstName"
    ControlToValidate="txtFirstName"
    Text="(Required)"
    EnableClientScript="false"
    Runat="server" />

<br /><br />

<asp:Label
    id="lblLastName"
    Text="Last Name"
    AssociatedControlID="txtLastName"
    Runat="server" />
<br />
<asp:TextBox
    id="txtLastname"
    Runat="server" />
<asp:RequiredFieldValidator
    id="reqLastName"
    ControlToValidate="txtLastName"
    Text="(Required)"
    EnableClientScript="false"
    Runat="server" />

 <br /><br />

 <asp:Button
    id="btnSubmit"
    Text="Submit"
    Runat="server" />

</div>
</form>
</body>
</html>
```

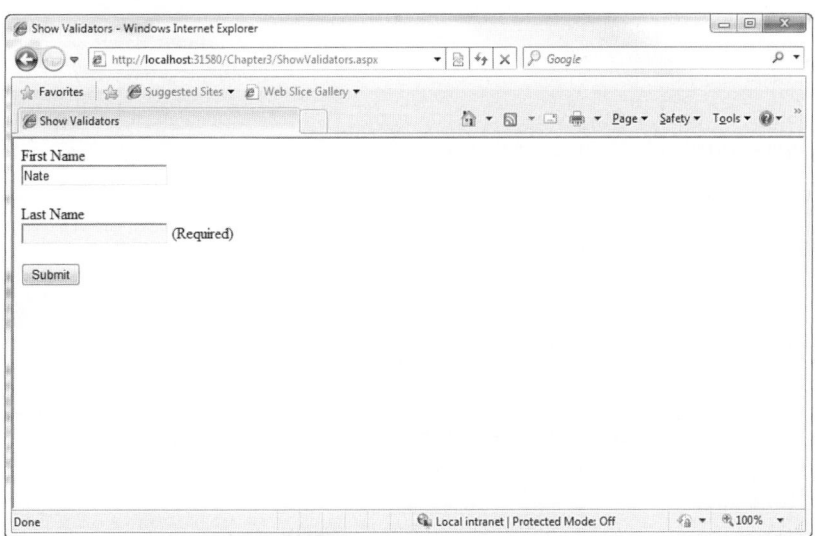

FIGURE 3.3   Changing the background color of form fields.

The `Page.Validators` property is used in the `Page_PreRender()` handler. The `IsValid` property is checked for each control in the `Page.Validators` collection. If `IsValid` returns `False`, the control validated by the validation control is highlighted with a yellow background color.

Using Validation Groups

In the first version of the ASP.NET Framework, there was no easy way to add two forms to the same page. If you added more than one form to a page, and both forms contained validation controls, the validation controls in both forms were evaluated regardless of which form you submitted.

For example, imagine that you wanted to create a page that contained both a login and registration form. The login form appeared in the left column and the registration form appeared in the right column. If both forms included validation controls, submitting the login form caused any validation controls contained in the registration form to be evaluated.

Since the release of ASP.NET 2.0, you no longer face this limitation. The ASP.NET 2.0 Framework introduced the idea of validation groups. A validation group enables you to group related form fields together.

For example, the page in Listing 3.5 contains both a login and registration form, and both forms contain independent sets of validation controls.

LISTING 3.5   ShowValidationGroups.aspx

```
<%@ Page Language="C#" %>
<!DOCTYPE html PUBLIC "-//W3C//DTD XHTML 1.0 Transitional//EN"
"http://www.w3.org/TR/xhtml1/DTD/xhtml1-transitional.dtd">
<script runat="server">

    void btnLogin_Click(Object sender, EventArgs e)
    {
        if (Page.IsValid)
            lblLoginResult.Text = "Log in successful!";
    }

    void btnRegister_Click(Object sender, EventArgs e)
    {
        if (Page.IsValid)
            lblRegisterResult.Text = "Registration successful!";
    }
</script>
<html xmlns="http://www.w3.org/1999/xhtml" >
<head id="Head1" runat="server">
    <style type="text/css">
        html
        {
            background-color:silver;
        }
        .column
        {
            float:left;
            width:300px;
            margin-left:10px;
            background-color:white;
            border:solid 1px black;
            padding:10px;
        }

    </style>
    <title>Show Validation Groups</title>
</head>
<body>
    <form id="form1" runat="server">

    <div class="column">
```

```
<fieldset>
<legend>Login</legend>
<p>
Please log in to our Website.
</p>
<asp:Label
    id="lblUserName"
    Text="User Name:"
    AssociatedControlID="txtUserName"
    Runat="server" />
<br />
<asp:TextBox
    id="txtUserName"
    Runat="server" />
<asp:RequiredFieldValidator
    id="reqUserName"
    ControlToValidate="txtUserName"
    Text="(Required)"
    ValidationGroup="LoginGroup"
    Runat="server" />
<br /><br />
<asp:Label
    id="lblPassword"
    Text="Password:"
    AssociatedControlID="txtPassword"
    Runat="server" />
<br />
<asp:TextBox
    id="txtPassword"
    TextMode="Password"
    Runat="server" />
<asp:RequiredFieldValidator
    id="reqPassword"
    ControlToValidate="txtPassword"
    Text="(Required)"
    ValidationGroup="LoginGroup"
    Runat="server" />
<br /><br />
<asp:Button
    id="btnLogin"
    Text="Login"
    ValidationGroup="LoginGroup"
    Runat="server" OnClick="btnLogin_Click" />
```

```
</fieldset>

<asp:Label
    id="lblLoginResult"
    Runat="server" />

</div>

<div class="column">
<fieldset>
<legend>Register</legend>
<p>
If you do not have a User Name, please
register at our Website.
</p>
<asp:Label
    id="lblFirstName"
    Text="First Name:"
    AssociatedControlID="txtFirstName"
    Runat="server" />
<br />
<asp:TextBox
    id="txtFirstName"
    Runat="server" />
<asp:RequiredFieldValidator
    id="reqFirstName"
    ControlToValidate="txtFirstName"
    Text="(Required)"
    ValidationGroup="RegisterGroup"
    Runat="server" />
<br /><br />
<asp:Label
    id="lblLastName"
    Text="Last Name:"
    AssociatedControlID="txtLastName"
    Runat="server" />
<br />
<asp:TextBox
    id="txtLastName"
    Runat="server" />
<asp:RequiredFieldValidator
    id="reqLastName"
    ControlToValidate="txtLastName"
    Text="(Required)"
    ValidationGroup="RegisterGroup"
    Runat="server" />
```

```
    <br /><br />
    <asp:Button
        id="btnRegister"
        Text="Register"
        ValidationGroup="RegisterGroup"
        Runat="server" OnClick="btnRegister_Click" />
    </fieldset>

    <asp:Label
        id="lblRegisterResult"
        Runat="server" />

    </div>

    </form>
</body>
</html>
```

The validation controls and the button controls all include ValidationGroup properties. The controls associated with the login form all have the value "LoginGroup" assigned to their ValidationGroup properties. The controls associated with the register form all have the value "RegisterGroup" assigned to their ValidationGroup properties.

Because the form fields are grouped into different validation groups, you can submit the two forms independently. Submitting the Login form does not trigger the validation controls in the Register form (see Figure 3.4).

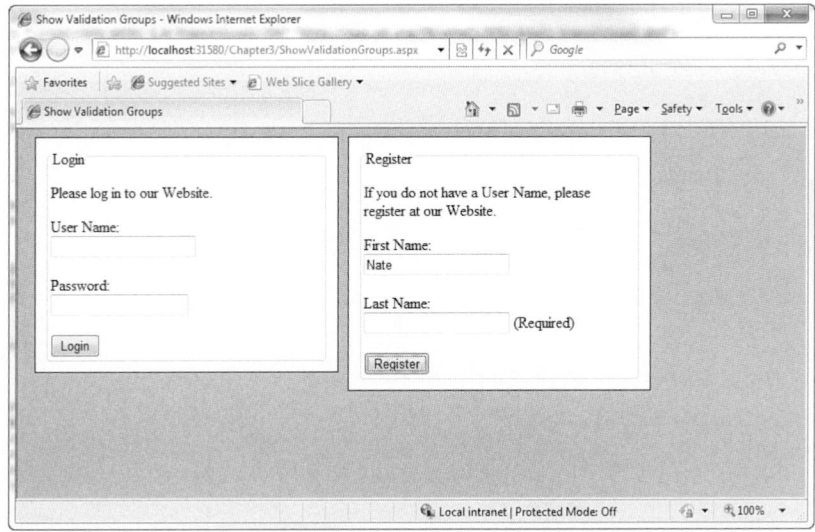

FIGURE 3.4   Using validation groups.

You can assign any string to the `ValidationGroup` property. The only purpose of the string is to associate different controls in a form together into different groups.

> **NOTE**
>
> Using validation groups is particularly important when working with Web Parts because multiple Web Parts with different forms might be added to the same page.

Disabling Validation

All the button controls—`Button`, `LinkButton`, and `ImageButton`—include a `CausesValidation` property. If you assign the value `False` to this property, clicking the button bypasses any validation in the page.

Bypassing validation is useful when creating a Cancel button. For example, the page in Listing 3.6 includes a Cancel button that redirects the user back to the `Default.aspx` page.

LISTING 3.6   ShowDisableValidation.aspx

```
<%@ Page Language="C#" %>
<!DOCTYPE html PUBLIC "-//W3C//DTD XHTML 1.0 Transitional//EN"
"http://www.w3.org/TR/xhtml1/DTD/xhtml1-transitional.dtd">
<script runat="server">

    void btnCancel_Click(Object sender, EventArgs e)
    {
        Response.Redirect("~/Default.aspx");
    }
</script>
<html xmlns="http://www.w3.org/1999/xhtml" >
<head id="Head1" runat="server">
    <title>Show Disable Validation</title>
</head>
<body>
    <form id="form1" runat="server">
    <div>

    <asp:Label
        id="lblFirstName"
        Text="First Name:"
        AssociatedControlID="txtFirstName"
        Runat="server" />
    <asp:TextBox
        id="txtFirstName"
        Runat="server" />
```

```
<asp:RequiredFieldValidator
    id="reqFirstName"
    ControlToValidate="txtFirstName"
    Text="(Required)"
    Runat="server" />
<br /><br />
<asp:Button
    id="btnSubmit"
    Text="Submit"
    Runat="server" />
<asp:Button
    id="btnCancel"
    Text="Cancel"
    OnClick="btnCancel_Click"
    CausesValidation="false"
    Runat="server" />

</div>
</form>
</body>
</html>
```

The Cancel button in Listing 3.6 includes the CausesValidation property with the value False. If the button did not include this property, the RequiredFieldValidator control would prevent you from submitting the form when you click the Cancel button.

Using the RequiredFieldValidator Control

The RequiredFieldValidator control enables you to require a user to enter a value into a form field before submitting the form. You must set two important properties when using the RequiredFieldValidator control:

▶ **ControlToValidate**—The ID of the form field validated.

▶ **Text**—The error message displayed when validation fails.

The page in Listing 3.7 illustrates how you can use the RequiredFieldValidator control to require a user to enter both a first and last name (see Figure 3.5).

LISTING 3.7   ShowRequiredFieldValidator.aspx

```
<%@ Page Language="C#" %>
<!DOCTYPE html PUBLIC "-//W3C//DTD XHTML 1.0 Transitional//EN"
"http://www.w3.org/TR/xhtml1/DTD/xhtml1-transitional.dtd">
<html xmlns="http://www.w3.org/1999/xhtml" >
<head id="Head1" runat="server">
    <title>Show RequiredFieldValidator</title>
</head>
<body>
    <form id="form1" runat="server">
    <div>

    <asp:Label
        id="lblFirstName"
        Text="First Name:"
        AssociatedControlID="txtFirstName"
        Runat="server" />
    <br />
    <asp:TextBox
        id="txtFirstName"
        Runat="server" />
    <asp:RequiredFieldValidator
        id="reqFirstName"
        ControlToValidate="txtFirstName"
        Text="(Required)"
        Runat="server" />

    <br /><br />

    <asp:Label
        id="lblLastName"
        Text="Last Name:"
        AssociatedControlID="txtLastName"
        Runat="server" />
    <br />
    <asp:TextBox
        id="txtLastName"
        Runat="server" />
    <asp:RequiredFieldValidator
        id="reqLastName"
        ControlToValidate="txtLastName"
        Text="(Required)"
        Runat="server" />
```

```
        <br /><br />

        <asp:Button
            id="btnSubmit"
            Text="Submit"
            Runat="server" />

        </div>
        </form>
</body>
</html>
```

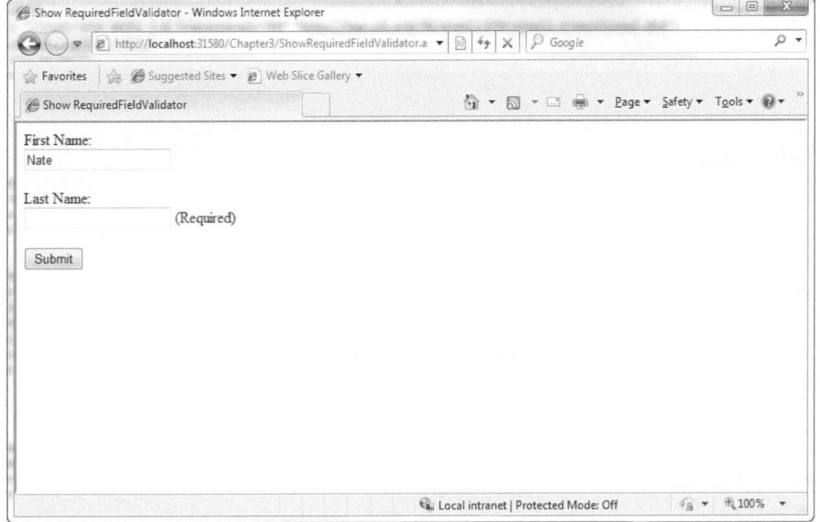

FIGURE 3.5   Requiring a user to enter form field values.

By default, the RequiredFieldValidator checks for a nonempty string (spaces don't count). If you enter anything into the form field associated with the RequiredFieldValidator, the RequiredFieldValidator does not display its validation error message.

You can use the RequiredFieldValidator control's InitialValue property to specify a default value other than an empty string. For example, the page in Listing 3.8 uses a RequiredFieldValidator to validate a DropDownList control (see Figure 3.6).

LISTING 3.8   ShowInitialValue.aspx

```
<%@ Page Language="C#" %>
<!DOCTYPE html PUBLIC "-//W3C//DTD XHTML 1.0 Transitional//EN"
"http://www.w3.org/TR/xhtml1/DTD/xhtml1-transitional.dtd">
<script runat="server">

    void btnSubmit_Click(Object sender, EventArgs e)
    {
        if (Page.IsValid)
            lblResult.Text = dropFavoriteColor.SelectedValue;
    }
</script>
<html xmlns="http://www.w3.org/1999/xhtml" >
<head id="Head1" runat="server">
    <title>Show Initial Value</title>
</head>
<body>
    <form id="form1" runat="server">
    <div>

    <asp:Label
        id="lblFavoriteColor"
        Text="Favorite Color:"
        AssociatedControlID="dropFavoriteColor"
        Runat="server" />
    <br />
    <asp:DropDownList
        id="dropFavoriteColor"
        Runat="server">
        <asp:ListItem Text="Select Color" Value="none" />
        <asp:ListItem Text="Red" Value="Red" />
        <asp:ListItem Text="Blue" Value="Blue" />
        <asp:ListItem Text="Green" Value="Green" />
    </asp:DropDownList>
    <asp:RequiredFieldValidator
        id="reqFavoriteColor"
        Text="(Required)"
        InitialValue="none"
        ControlToValidate="dropFavoriteColor"
        Runat="server" />

    <br /><br />

    <asp:Button
        id="btnSubmit"
```

```
        Text="Submit"
        Runat="server" OnClick="btnSubmit_Click" />

    <hr />

    <asp:Label
        id="lblResult"
        Runat="server" />

    </div>
    </form>
</body>
</html>
```

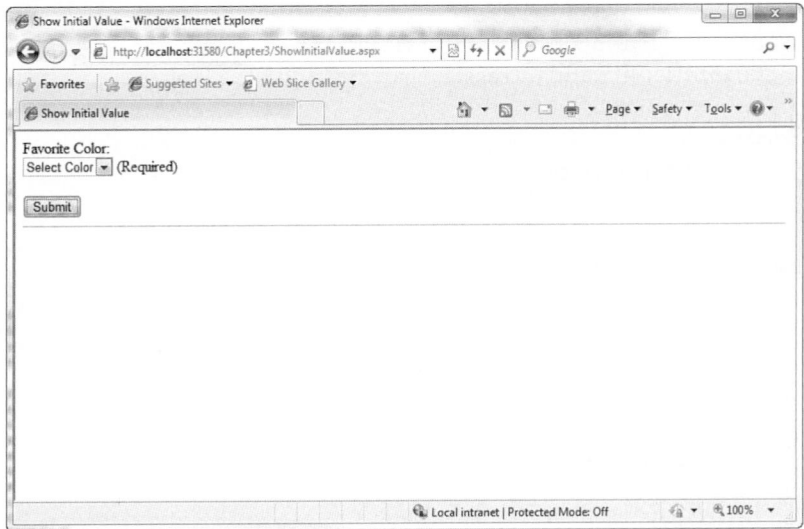

FIGURE 3.6   Using a `RequiredFieldValidator` with a `DropDownList` control.

The first list item displayed by the `DropDownList` control displays the text `"Select Color"`. If you submit the form without selecting a color from the `DropDownList` control, a validation error message displays.

The `RequiredFieldValidator` control includes an `InitialValue` property. The value of the first list from the `DropDownList` control is assigned to this property.

Using the RangeValidator Control

The `RangeValidator` control enables you to check whether the value of a form field falls between a certain minimum and maximum value. You must set five properties when using this control:

▶ **ControlToValidate**—The ID of the form field validated.

▶ **Text**—The error message displayed when validation fails.

▶ **MinimumValue**—The minimum value of the validation range.

▶ **MaximumValue**—The maximum value of the validation range.

▶ **Type**—The type of comparison to perform. Possible values are String, Integer, Double, Date, and Currency.

For example, the page in Listing 3.9 includes a RangeValidator that validates an age form field. If you do not enter an age between 5 and 100, a validation error displays (see Figure 3.7).

LISTING 3.9   ShowRangeValidator.aspx

```
<%@ Page Language="C#" %>
<!DOCTYPE html PUBLIC "-//W3C//DTD XHTML 1.0 Transitional//EN"
"http://www.w3.org/TR/xhtml1/DTD/xhtml1-transitional.dtd">
<html xmlns="http://www.w3.org/1999/xhtml" >
<head id="Head1" runat="server">
    <title>Show RangeValidator</title>
</head>
<body>
    <form id="form1" runat="server">
    <div>

    <asp:Label
        id="lblAge"
        Text="Age:"
        AssociatedControlID="txtAge"
        Runat="server" />
    <asp:TextBox
        id="txtAge"
        Runat="server" />
    <asp:RangeValidator
        id="reqAge"
        ControlToValidate="txtAge"
        Text="(Invalid Age)"
        MinimumValue="5"
        MaximumValue="100"
        Type="Integer"
        Runat="server" />

    <br /><br />

    <asp:Button
```

```
        id="btnSubmit"
        Text="Submit"
        Runat="server" />

    </div>
    </form>
</body>
</html>
```

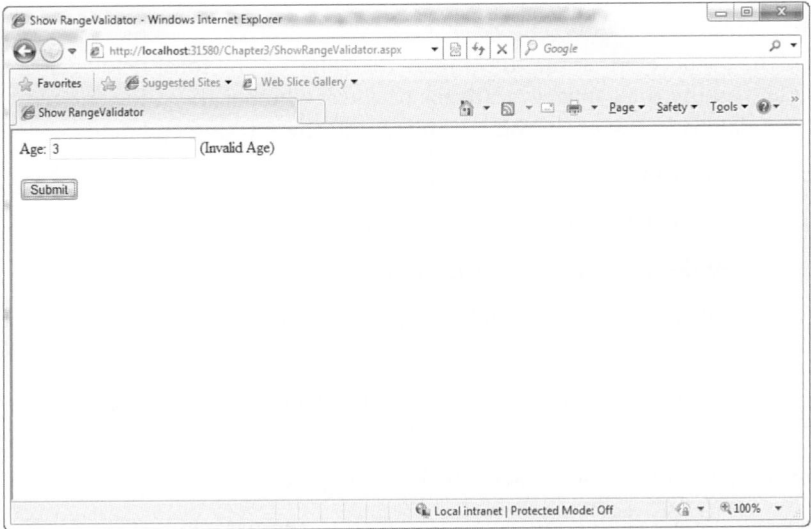

FIGURE 3.7   Validating a form field against a range of values.

If you submit the form in Listing 3.9 with an age less than 5 or greater than 100, the validation error message displays. The validation message also displays if you enter a value that is not a number. If the value entered into the form field cannot be converted into the data type represented by the RangeValidator control's Type property, the error message displays.

If you don't enter any value into the age field and submit the form, no error message displays. If you want to require a user to enter a value, you must associate a RequiredFieldValidator with the form field.

Don't forget to set the Type property when using the RangeValidator control. By default, the Type property has the value String, and the RangeValidator performs a string comparison to determine whether a value falls between the minimum and maximum value.

Using the `CompareValidator` Control

The `CompareValidator` control enables you to perform three different types of validation tasks. You can use the `CompareValidator` to perform a data type check. In other words, you can use the control to determine whether a user has entered the proper type of value into a form field, such as a date in a birth date field.

You also can use the `CompareValidator` to compare the value entered into a form field against a fixed value. For example, if you build an auction website, you can use the `CompareValidator` to check whether a new minimum bid is greater than the previous minimum bid.

Finally, you can use the `CompareValidator` to compare the value of one form field against another. For example, you use the `CompareValidator` to check whether the value entered into the meeting start date is less than the value entered into the meeting end date.

The `CompareValidator` has six important properties:

- **`ControlToValidate`**—The ID of the form field validated.

- **`Text`**—The error message displayed when validation fails.

- **`Type`**—The type of value compared. Possible values are `String`, `Integer`, `Double`, `Date`, and `Currency`.

- **`Operator`**—The type of comparison to perform. Possible values are `DataTypeCheck`, `Equal`, `GreaterThan`, `GreaterThanEqual`, `LessThan`, `LessThanEqual`, and `NotEqual`.

- **`ValueToCompare`**—The fixed value against which to compare.

- **`ControlToCompare`**—The ID of a control against which to compare.

The page in Listing 3.10 illustrates how you can use the `CompareValidator` to perform a data type check. The page contains a birth date field. If you enter a value that is not a date, the validation error message displays (see Figure 3.8).

LISTING 3.10   ShowDataTypeCheck.aspx

```
<%@ Page Language="C#" %>
<!DOCTYPE html PUBLIC "-//W3C//DTD XHTML 1.0 Transitional//EN"
"http://www.w3.org/TR/xhtml1/DTD/xhtml1-transitional.dtd">
<html xmlns="http://www.w3.org/1999/xhtml" >
<head id="Head1" runat="server">
    <title>Show Data Type Check</title>
</head>
<body>
    <form id="form1" runat="server">
    <div>

    <asp:Label
        id="lblBirthDate"
```

```
        Text="Birth Date:"
        AssociatedControlID="txtBirthDate"
        Runat="server" />
    <asp:TextBox
        id="txtBirthDate"
        Runat="server" />
    <asp:CompareValidator
        id="cmpBirthDate"
        Text="(Invalid Date)"
        ControlToValidate="txtBirthDate"
        Type="Date"
        Operator="DataTypeCheck"
        Runat="server" />

    <br /><br />

    <asp:Button
        id="btnSubmit"
        Text="Submit"
        Runat="server" />

    </div>
    </form>
</body>
</html>
```

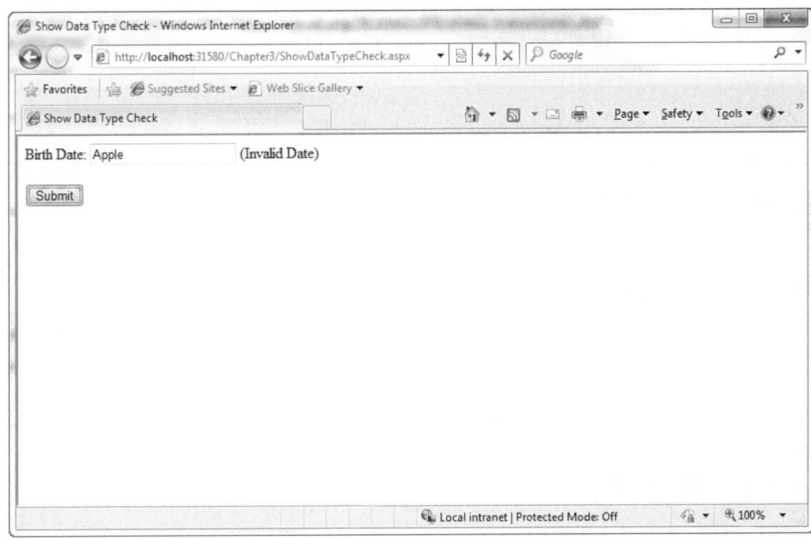

FIGURE 3.8   Performing a data type check.

The page in Listing 3.10 contains a CompareValidator control. Its Type property has the value Date, and its Operator property has the value DataTypeCheck. If you enter a value other than a date into the birth date field, the validation error message displays.

WARNING

An important limitation of the CompareValidator concerns how it performs a data type check. You cannot enter a long date into the form in Listing 3.10 (for example, December 25, 1966). You must enter a short date (for example, 12/25/1966). When validating currency amounts, you cannot enter the currency symbol. If these limitations concern you, you can use either the RegularExpression or CustomValidator controls to perform a more flexible data type check.

You can also use the CompareValidator to perform a comparison against a fixed value. For example, the page in Listing 3.11 uses a CompareValidator to check whether a date entered into a form field is greater than the current date (see Figure 3.9).

LISTING 3.11 ShowFixedValue.aspx

```
<%@ Page Language="C#" %>
<!DOCTYPE html PUBLIC "-//W3C//DTD XHTML 1.0 Transitional//EN"
"http://www.w3.org/TR/xhtml1/DTD/xhtml1-transitional.dtd">
<script runat="server">

    void Page_Load()
    {
        cmpDate.ValueToCompare = DateTime.Now.ToString("d");
    }
</script>
<html xmlns="http://www.w3.org/1999/xhtml" >
<head id="Head1" runat="server">
    <title>Show Fixed Value</title>
</head>
<body>
    <form id="form1" runat="server">
    <div>

    <asp:Label
        id="lblDate"
        Text="Date:"
        AssociatedControlID="txtDate"
        Runat="server" />
```

```
<asp:TextBox
    id="txtDate"
    Runat="server" />
<asp:CompareValidator
    id="cmpDate"
    Text="(Date must be greater than now)"
    ControlToValidate="txtDate"
    Type="Date"
    Operator="GreaterThan"
    Runat="server" />

<br /><br />

<asp:Button
    id="btnSubmit"
    Text="Submit"
    Runat="server" />

</div>
</form>
</body>
</html>
```

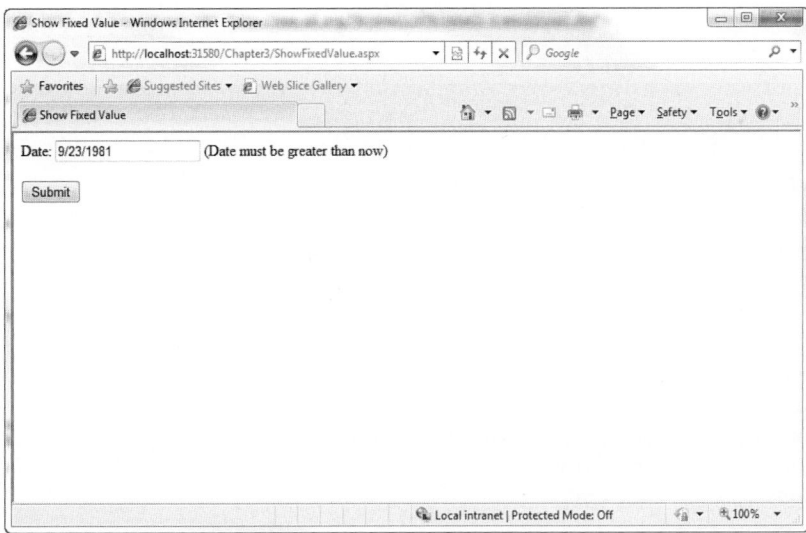

FIGURE 3.9   Comparing a form field against a fixed value.

Finally, you can use a `CompareValidator` to compare the value of one form field against another form field. The page in Listing 3.12 contains a meeting start date and meeting end date field. If you enter a value into the first field that is greater than the second field, a validation error displays (see Figure 3.10).

LISTING 3.12 ShowCompareValues.aspx

```
<%@ Page Language="C#" %>
<!DOCTYPE html PUBLIC "-//W3C//DTD XHTML 1.0 Transitional//EN"
"http://www.w3.org/TR/xhtml1/DTD/xhtml1-transitional.dtd">
<html xmlns="http://www.w3.org/1999/xhtml" >
<head id="Head1" runat="server">
    <title>Show Compare Values</title>
</head>
<body>
    <form id="form1" runat="server">
    <div>

    <asp:Label
        id="lblStartDate"
        Text="Start Date:"
        Runat="server" />
    <asp:TextBox
        id="txtStartDate"
        Runat="server" />

    <br /><br />

    <asp:Label
        id="lblEndDate"
        Text="End Date:"
        Runat="server" />
    <asp:TextBox
        id="txtEndDate"
        Runat="server" />
    <asp:CompareValidator
        id="cmpDate"
        Text="(End date must be greater than start date)"
        ControlToValidate="txtEndDate"
        ControlToCompare="txtStartDate"
        Type="Date"
        Operator="GreaterThan"
        Runat="server" />

    <br /><br />
```

```
<asp:Button
    id="btnSubmit"
    Text="Submit"
    Runat="server" />

</div>
</form>
</body>
</html>
```

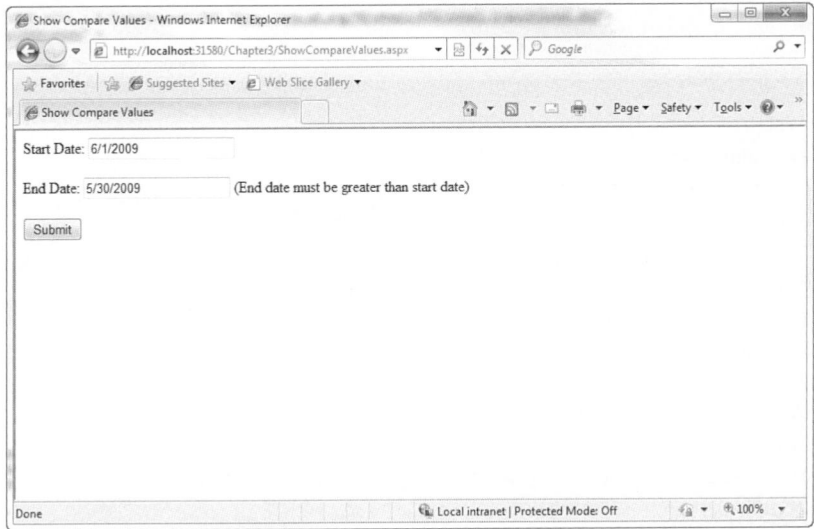

FIGURE 3.10   Comparing two form fields.

Just like the RangeValidator, the CompareValidator does not display an error if you don't enter a value into the form field being validated. If you want to require that a user enter a value, you must associate a RequiredFieldValidator control with the field.

Using the **RegularExpressionValidator** Control

The RegularExpressionValidator control enables you to compare the value of a form field against a regular expression. You can use a regular expression to represent string patterns such as email addresses, Social Security numbers, phone numbers, dates, currency amounts, and product codes.

For example, the page in Listing 3.13 enables you to validate an email address (see Figure 3.11).

LISTING 3.13   ShowRegularExpressionValidator.aspx

```
<%@ Page Language="C#" %>
<!DOCTYPE html PUBLIC "-//W3C//DTD XHTML 1.0 Transitional//EN"
"http://www.w3.org/TR/xhtml1/DTD/xhtml1-transitional.dtd">
<html xmlns="http://www.w3.org/1999/xhtml" >
<head id="Head1" runat="server">
    <title>Show RegularExpressionValidator</title>
</head>
<body>
    <form id="form1" runat="server">
    <div>

    <asp:Label
        id="lblEmail"
        Text="Email Address:"
        AssociatedControlID="txtEmail"
        Runat="server" />
    <asp:TextBox
        id="txtEmail"
        Runat="server" />
    <asp:RegularExpressionValidator
        id="regEmail"
        ControlToValidate="txtEmail"
        Text="(Invalid email)"
        ValidationExpression="\w+([-+.']\w+)*@\w+([-.]\w+)*\.\w+([-.]\w+)*"
        Runat="server" />

    <br /><br />

    <asp:Button
        id="btnSubmit"
        Text="Submit"
        Runat="server" />

    </div>
    </form>
</body>
</html>
```

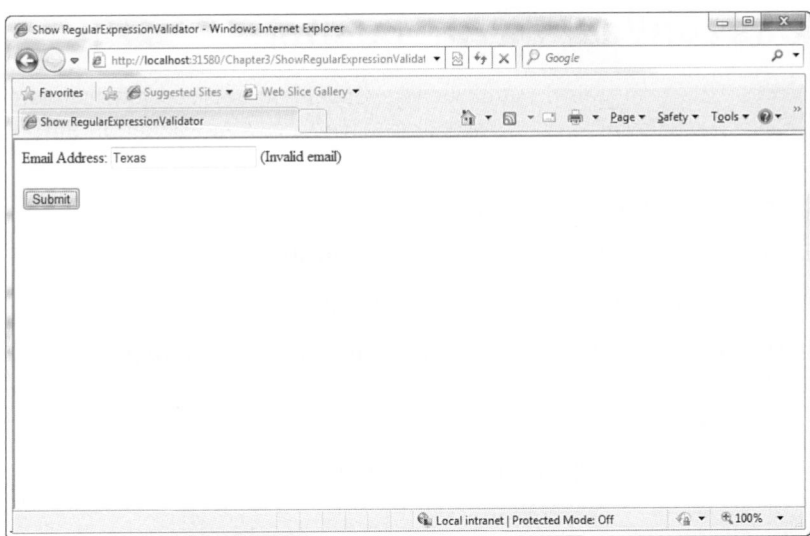

FIGURE 3.11   Validating an email address.

The regular expression is assigned to the `RegularExpressionValidator` control's `ValidationExpression` property. It looks like this:

```
\w+([-+.']\w+)*@\w+([-.]\w+)*\.\w+([-.]\w+)*
```

Regular expressions are not fun to read. This pattern matches a simple email address. The \w expression represents any nonwhitespace character. Therefore, roughly, this regular expression matches an email address that contains nonwhitespace characters, followed by an @ sign, followed by nonwhitespace characters, followed by a period, followed by more nonwhitespace characters.

> **NOTE**
>
> There are huge collections of regular expression patterns living on the Internet. A popular website for finding regular expressions is http://regexlib.com/.

Just like the other validation controls, the `RegularExpressionValidator` doesn't validate a form field unless the form field contains a value. To make a form field required, you must associate a `RequiredFieldValidator` control with the form field.

> **VISUAL WEB DEVELOPER NOTE**
>
> If you open the property sheet for a `RegularExpressionValidator` control in Design view and select the `ValidationExpression` property, you can view a number of canned regular expressions. Visual Web Developer includes regular expressions for patterns such as email addresses, phone numbers, and Social Security numbers.

Using the `CustomValidator` Control

If none of the other validation controls perform the type of validation that you need, you can always use the `CustomValidator` control. You can associate a custom validation function with the `CustomValidator` control.

The `CustomValidator` control has three important properties:

- ▶ **`ControlToValidate`**—The ID of the form field being validated.

- ▶ **`Text`**—The error message displayed when validation fails.

- ▶ **`ClientValidationFunction`**—The name of a client-side function used to perform client-side validation.

The `CustomValidator` also supports one event:

- ▶ **`ServerValidate`**—This event is raised when the `CustomValidator` performs validation.

You associate your custom validation function with the `CustomValidator` control by handling the `ServerValidate` event.

For example, imagine that you want to validate the length of a string entered into a form field. You want to ensure that a user does not enter more than 10 characters into a multiline `TextBox` control. The page in Listing 3.14 contains an event handler for a `CustomValidator` control's `ServerValidate` event, which checks the string's length.

LISTING 3.14   ShowCustomValidator.aspx

```
<%@ Page Language="C#" %>
<!DOCTYPE html PUBLIC "-//W3C//DTD XHTML 1.0 Transitional//EN"
"http://www.w3.org/TR/xhtml1/DTD/xhtml1-transitional.dtd">
<script runat="server">

    void valComments_ServerValidate(Object source, ServerValidateEventArgs args)
    {
        if (args.Value.Length > 10)
            args.IsValid = false;
        else
            args.IsValid = true;
    }
</script>
<html xmlns="http://www.w3.org/1999/xhtml" >
<head id="Head1" runat="server">
    <title>Show CustomValidator</title>
</head>
<body>
    <form id="form1" runat="server">
```

```
    <div>

    <asp:Label
        id="lblComments"
        Text="Comments:"
        AssociatedControlID="txtComments"
        Runat="server" />
    <br />
    <asp:TextBox
        id="txtComments"
        TextMode="MultiLine"
        Columns="30"
        Rows="5"
        Runat="server" />
    <asp:CustomValidator
        id="valComments"
        ControlToValidate="txtComments"
        Text="(Comments must be less than 10 characters)"
        OnServerValidate="valComments_ServerValidate"
        Runat="server" />

    <br /><br />

    <asp:Button
        id="btnSubmit"
        Text="Submit"
        Runat="server" />

    </div>
    </form>
</body>
</html>
```

The second parameter passed to the `ServerValidate` event handler is an instance of the `ServerValidateEventArgs` class. This class has three properties:

▶ **Value**—Represents the value of the form field being validated.

▶ **IsValid**—Represents whether validation fails or succeeds.

▶ **ValidateEmptyText**—Represents whether validation is performed when the form field being validated does not contain a value.

In Listing 3.14, if the string represented by the `Value` property is longer than 10 characters, the value `False` is assigned to the `IsValid` property and validation fails. Otherwise, the value `True` is assigned to the `IsValid` property and the input field passes the validation check (see Figure 3.12).

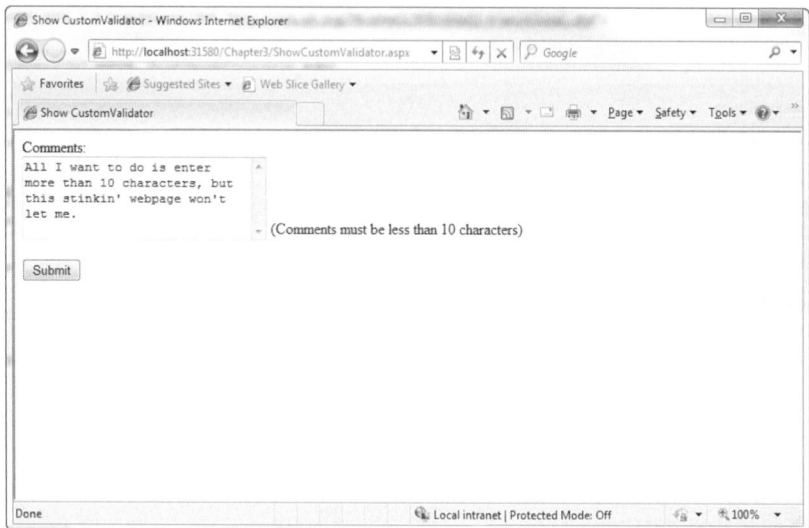

FIGURE 3.12   Validating field length with the `CustomValidator` control.

The `ServerValidate` event handler in Listing 3.14 is a server-side function. Therefore, validation does not occur until the page is posted back to the web server. If you want to perform validation on both the client (browser) and server, you need to supply a client-side validation function.

WARNING

If you don't associate a client validation function with a `CustomValidator` control, the `CustomValidator` doesn't render an error message until you post the page back to the server. Because the other validation controls prevent a page from posting if the page contains any validation errors, you won't see the error message rendered by the `CustomValidator` control until you pass every other validation check in a page.

The page in Listing 3.15 illustrates how you can associate a client-side validation function with the `CustomValidator` control. This page also checks the length of the string entered into a `TextBox` control. However, it checks the length on both the browser and server.

LISTING 3.15   ShowCustomValidatorJS.aspx

```
<%@ Page Language="C#" %>
<!DOCTYPE html PUBLIC "-//W3C//DTD XHTML 1.0 Transitional//EN"
"http://www.w3.org/TR/xhtml1/DTD/xhtml1-transitional.dtd">
<script runat="server">

    void valComments_ServerValidate(Object source, ServerValidateEventArgs args)
```

```
    {
        if (args.Value.Length > 10)
            args.IsValid = false;
        else
            args.IsValid = true;
    }
</script>
<html xmlns="http://www.w3.org/1999/xhtml" >
<head id="Head1" runat="server">
    <script type="text/javascript">

    function valComments_ClientValidate(source, args)
    {
        if (args.Value.length > 10)
            args.IsValid = false;
        else
            args.IsValid = true;
    }

    </script>
    <title>Show CustomValidator with JavaScript</title>
</head>
<body>
    <form id="form1" runat="server">
    <div>

    <asp:Label
        id="lblComments"
        Text="Comments:"
        AssociatedControlID="txtComments"
        Runat="server" />
    <br />
    <asp:TextBox
        id="txtComments"
        TextMode="MultiLine"
        Columns="30"
        Rows="5"
        Runat="server" />
    <asp:CustomValidator
        id="valComments"
        ControlToValidate="txtComments"
        Text="(Comments must be less than 10 characters)"
        OnServerValidate="valComments_ServerValidate"
        ClientValidationFunction="valComments_ClientValidate"
        Runat="server" />
```

```
        <br /><br />

        <asp:Button
            id="btnSubmit"
            Text="Submit"
            Runat="server" />

        </div>
        </form>
</body>
</html>
```

The `CustomValidator` control in Listing 3.15 includes a `ClientValidationFunction` property. This property contains the name of a JavaScript function defined in the page's <head> tag.

The JavaScript validation function accepts the same two parameters as the server-side validation function. The first parameter represents the `CustomValidator` control, and the second parameter represents an object that includes both a `Value` and an `IsValid` property. The client-side function is nearly identical to the server-side function (with the important difference that it is written in JavaScript).

Unlike the `RangeValidator`, `CompareValidator`, and `RegularExpressionValidator` controls, you can validate a form field with the `CustomValidator` control even when the form field is left blank. The `CustomValidator` control includes a property named the `ValidateEmptyText` property. You can use this property to cause the `CustomValidator` control to validate a form field even when the user hasn't entered a value into the form field. For example, the page in Listing 3.16 contains a `TextBox` that requires a product code that contains exactly four characters.

LISTING 3.16   ShowValidateEmptyText.aspx

```
<%@ Page Language="C#" %>
<!DOCTYPE html PUBLIC "-//W3C//DTD XHTML 1.0 Transitional//EN"
"http://www.w3.org/TR/xhtml1/DTD/xhtml1-transitional.dtd">
<script runat="server">

    void valProductCode_ServerValidate(Object source, ServerValidateEventArgs args)
    {
        if (args.Value.Length == 4)
            args.IsValid = true;
        else
            args.IsValid = false;
    }
</script>
<html xmlns="http://www.w3.org/1999/xhtml" >
```

```
<head id="Head1" runat="server">
    <title>Show Validate Empty Text</title>
</head>
<body>
    <form id="form1" runat="server">
    <div>

    <asp:Label
        id="lblProductCode"
        Text="Product Code:"
        AssociatedControlID="txtProductCode"
        Runat="server" />
    <br />
    <asp:TextBox
        id="txtProductCode"
        Runat="server" />
    <asp:CustomValidator
        id="valProductCode"
        ControlToValidate="txtProductCode"
        Text="(Invalid product code)"
        ValidateEmptyText="true"
        OnServerValidate="valProductCode_ServerValidate"
        Runat="server" />

    <br /><br />

    <asp:Button
        id="btnSubmit"
        Text="Submit"
        Runat="server" />

    </div>
    </form>
</body>
</html>
```

The CustomValidator control in Listing 3.16 includes a ValidateEmptyText property that has the value True. If the ValidateEmptyText property was not included, and you submitted the form without entering any data, no validation error would display.

Finally, unlike the other validation controls, you are not required to associate the CustomValidator control with any form field. In other words, you don't need to include a ControlToValidate property.

For example, the page in Listing 3.17 contains a timed test. If you don't answer the question within 5 seconds, the CustomValidator control displays a validation error message (see Figure 3.13).

LISTING 3.17   TimedTest.aspx

```
<%@ Page Language="C#" %>
<!DOCTYPE html PUBLIC "-//W3C//DTD XHTML 1.0 Transitional//EN"
"http://www.w3.org/TR/xhtml1/DTD/xhtml1-transitional.dtd">
<script runat="server">

    void Page_Load()
    {
        if (!Page.IsPostBack)
            ResetStartTime();
    }


    void btnAgain_Click(Object sender, EventArgs e)
    {
        ResetStartTime();
    }


    void ResetStartTime()
    {
        Session["StartTime"] = DateTime.Now;
    }



    void valAnswer_ServerValidate(Object source, ServerValidateEventArgs args)
    {
        DateTime startTime = (DateTime)Session["StartTime"];
        if (startTime.AddSeconds(5) > DateTime.Now)
            args.IsValid = true;
        else
            args.IsValid = false;
    }
</script>
<html xmlns="http://www.w3.org/1999/xhtml" >
<head id="Head1" runat="server">
    <title>Timed Test</title>
</head>
<body>
```

```
<form id="form1" runat="server">
<div>

<p>
You have 5 seconds to answer the following question:
</p>

<asp:Label
    id="lblQuestion"
    Text="What was Aristotle's first name?"
    AssociatedControlID="txtAnswer"
    Runat="server" />
<br />
<asp:TextBox
    id="txtAnswer"
    Runat="server" />
<asp:CustomValidator
    id="valAnswer"
    Text="(You answered too slowly!)"
    OnServerValidate="valAnswer_ServerValidate"
    Runat="server"  />

<br /><br />

<asp:Button
    id="btnSubmit"
    Text="Submit"
    Runat="server" />

<asp:Button
    id="btnAgain"
    Text="Try Again!"
    CausesValidation="false"
    OnClick="btnAgain_Click"
    Runat="server" />

</div>
</form>
</body>
</html>
```

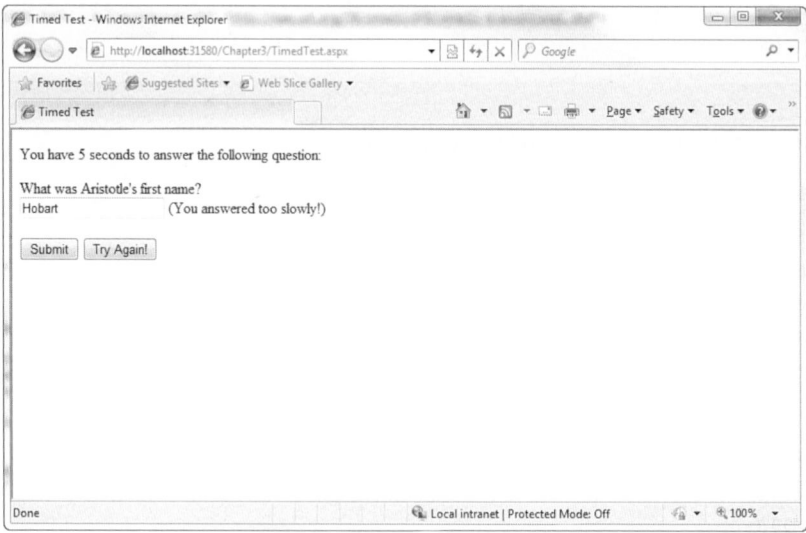

FIGURE 3.13   Performing validation against no particular field.

Using the ValidationSummary Control

The ValidationSummary control enables you to display a list of all the validation errors in a page in one location. This control is particularly useful when working with large forms. If a user enters the wrong value for a form field located toward the end of the page, the user might never see the error message. If you use the ValidationSummary control, however, you can always display a list of errors at the top of the form.

Each of the validation controls includes an ErrorMessage property. We have not been using the ErrorMessage property to represent the validation error message. Instead, we have used the Text property.

The distinction between the ErrorMessage and Text property is that any message that you assign to the ErrorMessage property appears in the ValidationSummary control, and any message that you assign to the Text property appears in the body of the page. Normally, you want to keep the error message for the Text property short (for example, "Required!"). The message assigned to the ErrorMessage property, on the other hand, should identify the form field that has the error (for example, "First name is required!").

> **NOTE**
>
> If you don't assign a value to the Text property, the value of the ErrorMessage property displays in both the ValidationSummary control and the body of the page.

The page in Listing 3.18 illustrates how you can use the ValidationSummary control to display a summary of error messages (see Figure 3.14).

LISTING 3.18 ShowValidationSummary.aspx

```
<%@ Page Language="C#" %>
<!DOCTYPE html PUBLIC "-//W3C//DTD XHTML 1.0 Transitional//EN"
"http://www.w3.org/TR/xhtml1/DTD/xhtml1-transitional.dtd">
<html xmlns="http://www.w3.org/1999/xhtml" >
<head id="Head1" runat="server">
    <title>Show ValidationSummary</title>
</head>
<body>
    <form id="form1" runat="server">
    <div>

    <asp:ValidationSummary
        id="ValidationSummary1"
        Runat="server" />

    <asp:Label
        id="lblFirstName"
        Text="First Name:"
        AssociatedControlID="txtFirstName"
        Runat="server" />
    <br />
    <asp:TextBox
        id="txtFirstName"
        Runat="server" />
    <asp:RequiredFieldValidator
        id="reqFirstName"
        Text="(Required)"
        ErrorMessage="First Name is required"
        ControlToValidate="txtFirstName"
        Runat="server" />

    <br /><br />

    <asp:Label
        id="lblLastName"
        Text="Last Name:"
        AssociatedControlID="txtLastName"
        Runat="server" />
    <br />
    <asp:TextBox
```

```
        id="txtLastName"
        Runat="server" />
    <asp:RequiredFieldValidator
        id="reqLastName"
        Text="(Required)"
        ErrorMessage="Last Name is required"
        ControlToValidate="txtLastName"
        Runat="server" />

    <br /><br />

    <asp:Button
        id="btnSubmit"
        Text="Submit"
        Runat="server" />

    </div>
    </form>
</body>
</html>
```

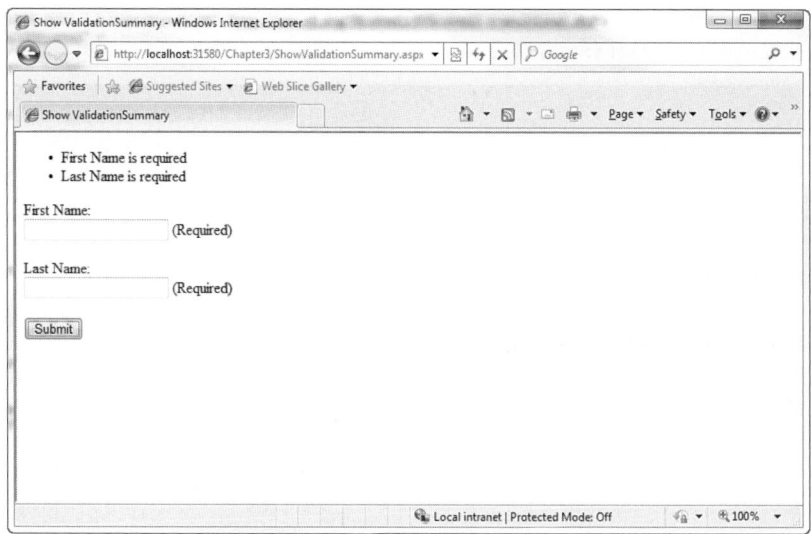

FIGURE 3.14   Displaying a validation summary.

If you submit the form in Listing 3.18 without entering a value for the first and last name, validation error messages appear in both the body of the page and in the ValidationSummary control.

The ValidationSummary control supports the following properties:

- ▶ **DisplayMode**—Enables you to specify how the error messages are formatted. Possible values are BulletList, List, and SingleParagraph.

- ▶ **HeaderText**—Enables you to display header text above the validation summary.

- ▶ **ShowMessageBox**—Enables you to display a pop-up alert box.

- ▶ **ShowSummary**—Enables you to hide the validation summary in the page.

If you set the ShowMessageBox property to the value True and the ShowSummary property to the value False, you can display the validation summary only within a pop-up alert box. For example, the page in Listing 3.19 displays a validation summary in an alert box (see Figure 3.15).

LISTING 3.19   ShowSummaryPopup.aspx

```
<%@ Page Language="C#" %>
<!DOCTYPE html PUBLIC "-//W3C//DTD XHTML 1.0 Transitional//EN"
"http://www.w3.org/TR/xhtml1/DTD/xhtml1-transitional.dtd">
<html xmlns="http://www.w3.org/1999/xhtml" >
<head id="Head1" runat="server">
    <title>Show Summary Popup</title>
</head>
<body>
    <form id="form1" runat="server">
    <div>

    <asp:ValidationSummary
        id="ValidationSummary1"
        ShowMessageBox="true"
        ShowSummary="false"
        Runat="server" />

    <asp:Label
        id="lblFirstName"
        Text="First Name:"
        AssociatedControlID="txtFirstName"
        Runat="server" />
    <br />
    <asp:TextBox
        id="txtFirstName"
        Runat="server" />
```

```
<asp:RequiredFieldValidator
    id="reqFirstName"
    ErrorMessage="First Name is required"
    ControlToValidate="txtFirstName"
    Display="None"
    Runat="server" />

<br /><br />

<asp:Label
    id="lblLastName"
    Text="Last Name:"
    AssociatedControlID="txtLastName"
    Runat="server" />
<br />
<asp:TextBox
    id="txtLastName"
    Runat="server" />
<asp:RequiredFieldValidator
    id="reqLastName"
    ErrorMessage="Last Name is required"
    ControlToValidate="txtLastName"
    Display="None"
    Runat="server" />

<br /><br />

<asp:Button
    id="btnSubmit"
    Text="Submit"
    Runat="server" />

</div>
</form>
</body>
</html>
```

Both of the RequiredFieldValidator controls have their Display properties set to the value None. The validation error messages appear only in the alert box.

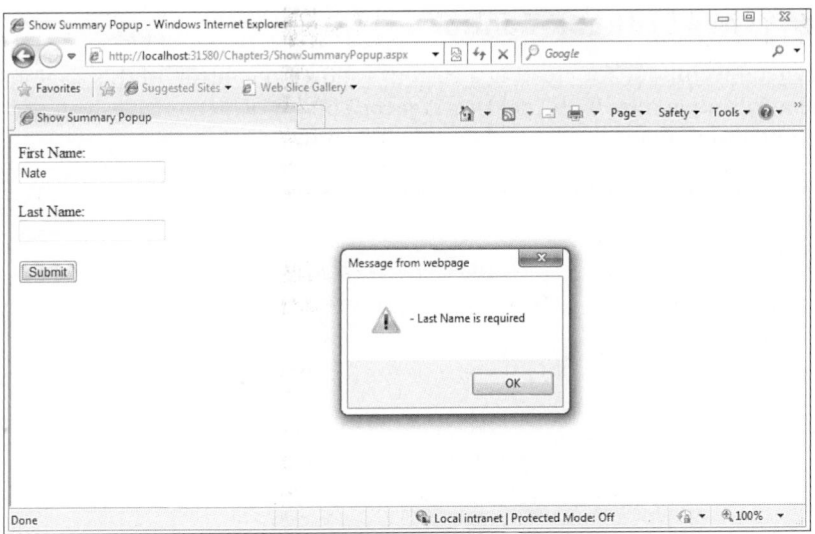

FIGURE 3.15   Displaying a validation summary in an alert box.

Creating Custom Validation Controls

In this final section, you learn how to create custom validation controls. We create two custom controls. First, we create a LengthValidator control that enables you to validate the length of an entry in a form field. Next, we create an AjaxValidator control. The AjaxValidator control performs validation on the client by passing information back to a custom function defined on the server.

You create a new validation control by deriving a new control from the BaseValidator class. As its name implies, the BaseValidator class is the base class for all the validation controls, including the RequiredFieldValidator and RegularExpressionValidator controls.

The BaseValidator class is a MustInherit (abstract) class, which requires you to implement a single method:

▶ **EvaluateIsValid**—Returns true when the form field being validated is valid.

The BaseValidator class also includes several other methods that you can override or otherwise use. The most useful of these methods follows:

▶ **GetControlValidationValue**—Enables you to retrieve the value of the control being validated.

When you create a custom validation control, you override the EvaluateIsValid() method and, within the EvaluateIsValid() method, you call GetControlValidationValue to get the value of the form field being validated.

Creating a `LengthValidator` Control

To illustrate the general technique for creating a custom validation control, in this section we create an extremely simple one. It's a `LengthValidator` control, which enables you to validate the length of a form field.

The code for the `LengthValidator` control is contained in Listing 3.20.

LISTING 3.20   LengthValidator.cs

```csharp
using System;
using System.Web.UI;
using System.Web.UI.WebControls;

namespace myControls
{
    /// <summary>
    /// Validates the length of an input field
    /// </summary>
    public class LengthValidator : BaseValidator
    {
        int _maximumLength = 0;

        public int MaximumLength
        {
            get { return _maximumLength; }
            set { _maximumLength = value; }
        }

        protected override bool EvaluateIsValid()
        {
            String value = this.GetControlValidationValue(this.ControlToValidate);
            if (value.Length > _maximumLength)
                return false;
            else
                return true;
        }
    }
}
```

Listing 3.20 contains a class that inherits from the `BaseValidator` class. The new class overrides the `EvaluateIsValid` method. The value from the control being validated is retrieved with the help of the `GetControlValidationValue()` method, and the length of the value is compared against the `MaximumLength` property.

> **NOTE**
>
> To use the class in Listing 3.20, you need to add the class to your application's `App_Code` folder by right-clicking the App_Code folder and choosing to add a new item. Any class added to this special folder is automatically compiled by the ASP.NET Framework.

The page in Listing 3.21 uses the `LengthValidator` control to validate the length of a comment input field (see Figure 3.16).

LISTING 3.21 `ShowLengthValidator.aspx`

```aspx
<%@ Page Language="C#" %>
<%@ Register TagPrefix="custom" Namespace="myControls" %>
<!DOCTYPE html PUBLIC "-//W3C//DTD XHTML 1.0 Transitional//EN"
"http://www.w3.org/TR/xhtml1/DTD/xhtml1-transitional.dtd">
<html xmlns="http://www.w3.org/1999/xhtml" >
<head id="Head1" runat="server">
    <title>Show Length Validator</title>
</head>
<body>
    <form id="form1" runat="server">
    <div>

    <asp:Label
        id="lblComments"
        Text="Comments:"
        AssociatedControlID="txtComments"
        Runat="server" />
    <br />
    <asp:TextBox
        id="txtComments"
        TextMode="MultiLine"
        Columns="30"
        Rows="2"
        Runat="server" />
    <custom:LengthValidator
        id="valComments"
        ControlToValidate="txtComments"
        Text="(Must be less than 10 characters)"
        MaximumLength="10"
        Runat="server" />

    <br /><br />
```

```
<asp:Button
    id="btnSubmit"
    Text="Submit"
    Runat="server" />

</div>
</form>
</body>
</html>
```

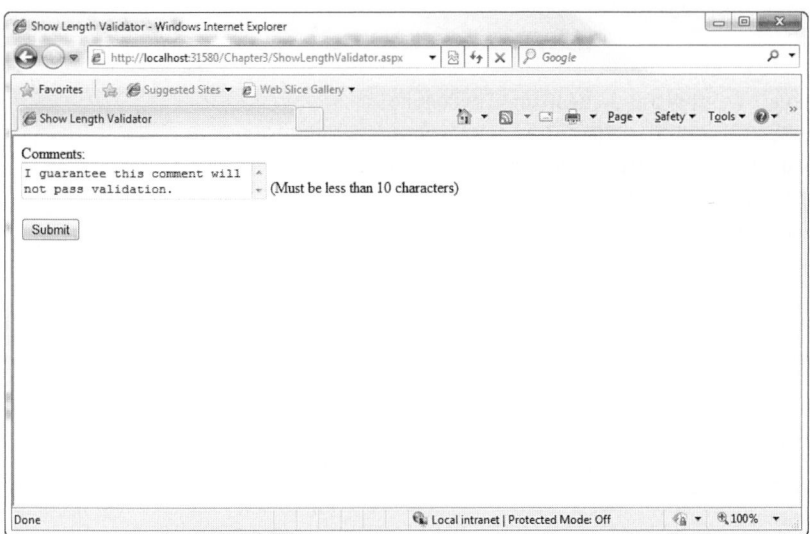

FIGURE 3.16   Validating the length of a field with the `LengthValidator` control.

The `LengthValidator` is registered at the top of the page with the `<%@ Register %>` directive. If you need to use the control in multiple pages in your application, you can alternatively register the control in the `<pages>` section of your application's web configuration file.

Creating an `AjaxValidator` Control

In this section, we create an extremely useful control named the `AjaxValidator` control. Like the `CustomValidator` control, the `AjaxValidator` control enables you to create a custom server-side validation function. Unlike the `CustomValidator` control, however, the `AjaxValidator` control enables you to call the custom validation function from the browser.

The `AjaxValidator` control uses AJAX (Asynchronous JavaScript and XML) to call the server-side validation function from the client. The advantage of using AJAX is that no postback to the server is apparent to the user.

For example, imagine that you create a website registration form and you need to validate a User Name field. You want to make sure that the User Name entered does not already exist in the database. The `AjaxValidator` enables you to call a server-side validation function from the client to check whether the User Name is unique in the database.

The code for the `AjaxValidator` control is contained in Listing 3.22.

LISTING 3.22 AjaxValidator.cs

3

```
using System;
using System.Web;
using System.Web.UI;
using System.Web.UI.WebControls;

namespace myControls
{
    /// <summary>
    /// Enables you to perform custom validation on both the client and server
    /// </summary>
    public class AjaxValidator : BaseValidator, ICallbackEventHandler
    {
        public event ServerValidateEventHandler ServerValidate;

        string _controlToValidateValue;

        protected override void OnPreRender(EventArgs e)
        {
            String eventRef = Page.ClientScript.GetCallbackEventReference
              (
                this,
                "",
                "",
                ""
              );

            // Register include file
            String includeScript =
                  Page.ResolveClientUrl("~/ClientScripts/AjaxValidator.js");
            Page.ClientScript.RegisterClientScriptInclude("AjaxValidator",
                  includeScript);

            // Register startup script
            String startupScript =
```

```csharp
String.Format("document.getElementById('{0}').evaluationfunction =
'AjaxValidatorEvaluateIsValid';", this.ClientID);
        Page.ClientScript.RegisterStartupScript(this.GetType(),
"AjaxValidator", startupScript, true);

        base.OnPreRender(e);
    }

    /// <summary>
    /// Only do the AJAX on browsers that support it
    /// </summary>
    protected override bool DetermineRenderUplevel()
    {
        return Context.Request.Browser.SupportsCallback;
    }

    /// <summary>
    /// Server method called by client AJAX call
    /// </summary>
    public string GetCallbackResult()
    {
        return ExecuteValidationFunction(_controlToValidateValue).ToString();
    }

    /// <summary>
    /// Return callback result to client
    /// </summary>
    public void RaiseCallbackEvent(string eventArgument)
    {
        _controlToValidateValue = eventArgument;
    }

    /// <summary>
    /// Server-side method for validation
    /// </summary>
    protected override bool EvaluateIsValid()
    {
        string controlToValidateValue =
this.GetControlValidationValue(this.ControlToValidate);
        return ExecuteValidationFunction(controlToValidateValue);
    }

    /// <summary>
    /// Performs the validation for both server and client
    /// </summary>
    private bool ExecuteValidationFunction(String controlToValidateValue)
```

```
        {
            ServerValidateEventArgs args = new ServerValidateEventArgs
➥(controlToValidateValue, this.IsValid);
            if (ServerValidate != null)
                ServerValidate(this, args);
            return args.IsValid;
        }


    }

}
```

The control in Listing 3.22 inherits from the `BaseValidator` class. It also implements the `ICallbackEventHandler` interface. The `ICallbackEventHandler` interface defines two methods called on the server when an AJAX request is made from the client.

In the `OnPreRender()` method, a JavaScript include file and startup script are registered. The JavaScript include file contains the client-side functions called when the `AjaxValidator` validates a form field on the client. The startup script associates the client-side `AjaxValidatorEvaluateIsValid()` function with the `AjaxValidator` control. The client-side validation framework automatically calls this JavaScript function when performing validation.

The JavaScript functions used by the `AjaxValidator` control are contained in Listing 3.23.

LISTING 3.23 AjaxValidator.js

```
// Performs AJAX call back to server
function AjaxValidatorEvaluateIsValid(val)
{
    var value = ValidatorGetValue(val.controltovalidate);
    WebForm_DoCallback(val.id, value, AjaxValidatorResult, val,
AjaxValidatorError, true);
    return true;
}


// Called when result is returned from server
function AjaxValidatorResult(returnValue, context)
{
    if (returnValue == 'True')
        context.isvalid = true;
    else
        context.isvalid = false;
    ValidatorUpdateDisplay(context);
}
```

```
// If there is an error, show it
function AjaxValidatorError(message)
{
    alert('Error: ' + message);
}
```

The `AjaxValidatorEvaluateIsValid()` JavaScript method initiates an AJAX call by calling the `WebForm_DoCallback()` method. This method calls the server-side validation function associated with the `AjaxValidator` control. When the AJAX call completes, the `AjaxValidatorResult()` method is called. This method updates the display of the validation control on the client.

The page in Listing 3.24 illustrates how you can use the `AjaxValidator` control. This page handles the `AjaxValidator` control's `ServerValidate` event to associate a custom validation function with the control.

The page in Listing 3.24 contains a form that includes fields for entering a username and favorite color. When you submit the form, the values of these fields are inserted into a database table named Users.

In Listing 3.24, the validation function checks whether a username already exists in the database. If you enter a username that already exists, a validation error message displays. The message displays in the browser before you submit the form back to the server (see Figure 3.17).

It is important to realize that you can associate any server-side validation function with the `AjaxValidator`. You can perform a database lookup, call a web service, or perform a complex mathematical function. Whatever function you define on the server is automatically called on the client.

LISTING 3.24   ShowAjaxValidator.aspx

```
<%@ Page Language="C#" %>
<%@ Register TagPrefix="custom" Namespace="myControls" %>
<%@ Import Namespace="System.Data.SqlClient" %>
<%@ Import Namespace="System.Web.Configuration" %>
<!DOCTYPE html PUBLIC "-//W3C//DTD XHTML 1.0 Transitional//EN"
"http://www.w3.org/TR/xhtml1/DTD/xhtml1-transitional.dtd">
<script runat="server">

    /// <summary>
    /// Validation function that is called on both the client and server
    /// </summary>
    protected void AjaxValidator1_ServerValidate(object source,
➥ServerValidateEventArgs args)
    {
        if (UserNameExists(args.Value))
```

```
            args.IsValid = false;
        else
            args.IsValid = true;
    }


    /// <summary>
    /// Returns true when user name already exists
    /// in Users database table
    /// </summary>
    private bool UserNameExists(string userName)
    {
        string conString =
WebConfigurationManager.ConnectionStrings["UsersDB"].ConnectionString;
        SqlConnection con = new SqlConnection(conString);
        SqlCommand cmd = new SqlCommand("SELECT COUNT(*)
➥FROM Users WHERE UserName=@UserName", con);
        cmd.Parameters.AddWithValue("@UserName", userName);
        bool result = false;
        using (con)
        {
            con.Open();
            int count = (int)cmd.ExecuteScalar();
            if (count > 0)
                result = true;
        }
        return result;
    }


    /// <summary>
    /// Insert new user name to Users database table
    /// </summary>
    protected void btnSubmit_Click(object sender, EventArgs e)
    {
        string conString =
WebConfigurationManager.ConnectionStrings["UsersDB"].ConnectionString;
        SqlConnection con = new SqlConnection(conString);
        SqlCommand cmd = new SqlCommand("INSERT Users (UserName,FavoriteColor)
➥VALUES (@UserName,@FavoriteColor)", con);
        cmd.Parameters.AddWithValue("@UserName", txtUserName.Text);
        cmd.Parameters.AddWithValue("@FavoriteColor", txtFavoriteColor.Text);
        using (con)
        {
            con.Open();
            cmd.ExecuteNonQuery();
        }
```

```
            txtUserName.Text = String.Empty;
            txtFavoriteColor.Text = String.Empty;
        }
    </script>
    <html xmlns="http://www.w3.org/1999/xhtml" >
    <head runat="server">
        <title>Show AjaxValidator</title>
    </head>
    <body>
        <form id="form1" runat="server">
        <div>

        <asp:Label
            id="lblUserName"
            Text="User Name:"
            AssociatedControlID="txtUserName"
            Runat="server" />
        <asp:TextBox
            id="txtUserName"
            Runat="server" />
        <custom:AjaxValidator
            id="AjaxValidator1"
            ControlToValidate="txtUserName"
            Text="User name already taken!"
            OnServerValidate="AjaxValidator1_ServerValidate"
            Runat="server" />

        <br /><br />
        <asp:Label
            id="lblFavoriteColor"
            Text="Favorite Color:"
            AssociatedControlID="txtFavoriteColor"
            Runat="server" />
        <asp:TextBox
            id="txtFavoriteColor"
            Runat="server" />

        <br /><br />
        <asp:Button
            id="btnSubmit"
            Text="Submit"
            Runat="server" OnClick="btnSubmit_Click" />
```

```
    </div>
    </form>
</body>
</html>
```

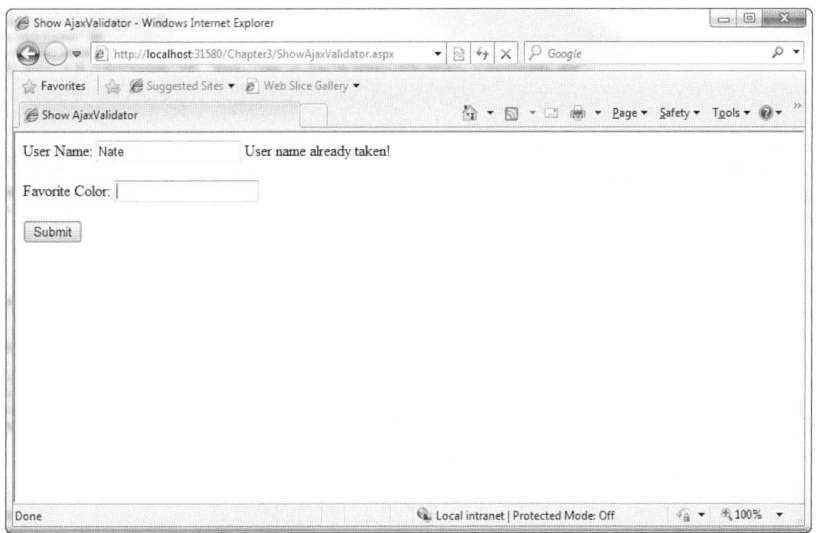

FIGURE 3.17   Using the `AjaxValidator` to check whether a username is unique.

Summary

In this chapter, you learned how to perform form validation with the ASP.NET 4 Framework. First, you were provided with an overview of all the standard validation controls. You learned how to highlight validation error messages and how to take advantage of validation groups to simulate multiple forms in a single page.

In the final section of this chapter, you learned how to create custom validation controls by deriving new controls from the `BaseValidator` control. You saw the creation of a custom `LengthValidator` and `AjaxValidator` control.

CHAPTER 4

Using the Rich Controls

In previous chapters we examined the ASP.NET controls that you use in just about any application. In this chapter we examine a more specialized set of controls known collectively as the *rich controls*.

In the first section, you learn how to accept file uploads at your website. For example, you learn how to allow users to upload images, Microsoft Word documents, or Microsoft Excel spreadsheets.

Next, you learn how to work with the Calendar control. You can use the Calendar control as a date picker. You can also use the Calendar control to display upcoming events (such as a meeting schedule).

We also discuss the AdRotator control. This control enables you to display banner advertisements randomly on your website. The control enables you to store a list of advertisements in an XML file or a database table.

Next, you learn about the MultiView control. This control enables you to hide and display areas of content on a page. You learn how to use this control to divide a page into different tabs.

In the following section, you learn about the Wizard control, which enables you to display multistep forms. This control is useful when you need to divide a long form into multiple subforms.

Finally, you learn how to display Silverlight content on your page. Silverlight controls enable you to add rich, interactive media to your website. You learn how to add Silverlight content to your page and display alternative content when a user doesn't have Silverlight installed on their computer.

Accepting File Uploads

The FileUpload control enables users to upload files to your web application. After the file is uploaded, you can store the file anywhere you please. Normally, you store the file either on the file system or in a database. This section explores both options.

The FileUpload control supports the following properties (this is not a complete list):

▶ **Enabled**—Enables you to disable the FileUpload control.

▶ **FileBytes**—Enables you to get the uploaded file contents as a byte array.

▶ **FileContent**—Enables you to get the uploaded file contents as a stream.

▶ **FileName**—Enables you to get the name of the file uploaded.

▶ **HasFile**—Returns True when a file has been uploaded.

▶ **PostedFile**—Enables you to get the uploaded file wrapped in the HttpPostedFile object.

The FileUpload control also supports the following methods:

▶ **Focus**—Enables you to shift the form focus to the FileUpload control.

▶ **SaveAs**—Enables you to save the uploaded file to the file system.

The FileUpload control's PostedFile property enables you to retrieve the uploaded file wrapped in an HttpPostedFile object. This object exposes additional information about the uploaded file.

The HttpPostedFile class has the following properties (this is not a complete list):

▶ **ContentLength**—Enables you to get the size of the uploaded file in bytes.

▶ **ContentType**—Enables you to get the MIME type of the uploaded file.

▶ **FileName**—Enables you to get the name of the uploaded file.

▶ **InputStream**—Enables you to retrieve the uploaded file as a stream.

The HttpPostedFile class also supports the following method:

▶ **SaveAs**—Enables you to save the uploaded file to the file system.

Some redundancy exists here. For example, you can get the name of the uploaded file by using either the FileUpload.FileName property or the HttpPostedFile.FileName property. You can save a file by using either the FileUpload.SaveAs() method or the HttpPostedFile.SaveAs() method.

> **NOTE**
>
> Adding a `FileUpload` control to a page automatically adds a
> `enctype="multipart/form-data"` attribute to the server-side `<form>` tag.

Saving Files to the File System

The page in Listing 4.1 illustrates how you can upload images to an application by using
the `FileUpload` control.

LISTING 4.1   `FileUploadFile.aspx`

```
<%@ Page Language="C#" %>
<%@ Import Namespace="System.IO" %>
<!DOCTYPE html PUBLIC "-//W3C//DTD XHTML 1.0 Transitional//EN"
"http://www.w3.org/TR/xhtml1/DTD/xhtml1-transitional.dtd">
<script runat="server">

    protected void btnAdd_Click(object sender, EventArgs e)
    {
        if (upImage.HasFile)
        {
            if (CheckFileType(upImage.FileName))
            {
                String filePath = "~/UploadImages/" + upImage.FileName;
                upImage.SaveAs(MapPath(filePath));
            }
        }
    }

    bool CheckFileType(string fileName)
    {
        string ext = Path.GetExtension(fileName);
        switch (ext.ToLower())
        {
            case ".gif":
                return true;
            case ".png":
                return true;
            case ".jpg":
                return true;
```

4

```
            case ".jpeg":
                return true;
            default:
                return false;
        }
    }

    void Page_PreRender()
    {
        string upFolder = MapPath("~/UploadImages/");
        DirectoryInfo dir = new DirectoryInfo(upFolder);
        dlstImages.DataSource = dir.GetFiles();
        dlstImages.DataBind();
    }
</script>
<html xmlns="http://www.w3.org/1999/xhtml" >
<head id="Head1" runat="server">
    <title>FileUpload File</title>
</head>
<body>
    <form id="form1" runat="server">
    <div>

    <asp:Label
        id="lblImageFile"
        Text="Image File:"
        AssociatedControlID="upImage"
        Runat="server" />

    <asp:FileUpload
        id="upImage"
        Runat="server" />

    <br /><br />

    <asp:Button
        id="btnAdd"
        Text="Add Image"
        OnClick="btnAdd_Click"
        Runat="server" />

    <hr />

    <asp:DataList
```

```
        id="dlstImages"
        RepeatColumns="3"
        runat="server">
        <ItemTemplate>
        <asp:Image ID="Image1"
            ImageUrl='<%# Eval("Name", "~/UploadImages/{0}") %>'
            style="width:200px"
            Runat="server" />
        <br />
        <%# Eval("Name") %>
        </ItemTemplate>
    </asp:DataList>

    </div>
    </form>
</body>
</html>
```

Listing 4.1 includes both a `FileUpload` control and a `DataList` control. When you upload a file, the file is saved to a folder named `UploadImages`. The `DataList` control automatically displays the contents of the `UploadImages` folder. The result is an image gallery (see Figure 4.1).

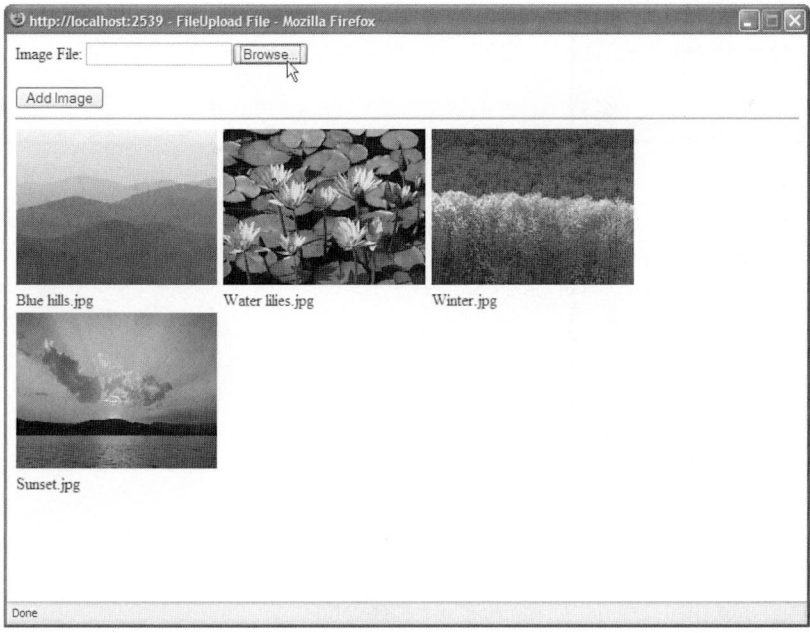

FIGURE 4.1 Displaying a photo gallery.

The page includes a method named CheckFileType(), which prevents users from uploading a file that does not have the .gif, .jpeg, .jpg, or .png extension. The method restricts the type of file that can be uploaded based on the file extension.

NOTE

The HTML 4.01 specifications define an accept attribute that you can use to filter the files that can be uploaded. Unfortunately, no browser supports the accept attribute, so you must perform filtering on the server (or use some JavaScript to check the filename extension on the client).

To save a file to the file system, the Windows account associated with the ASP.NET page must have sufficient permissions to save the file. For Windows 2003 and Windows 2008 servers, an ASP.NET page executes in the security context of the NETWORK SERVICE account. In the case of every other operating system, an ASP.NET page executes in the security context of the ASPNET account.

To enable ASP.NET Framework to save an uploaded file to a particular folder, you need to right-click the folder within Windows Explorer, select the Security tab, and provide either the NETWORK SERVICE or ASPNET account Write permissions for the folder (see Figure 4.2).

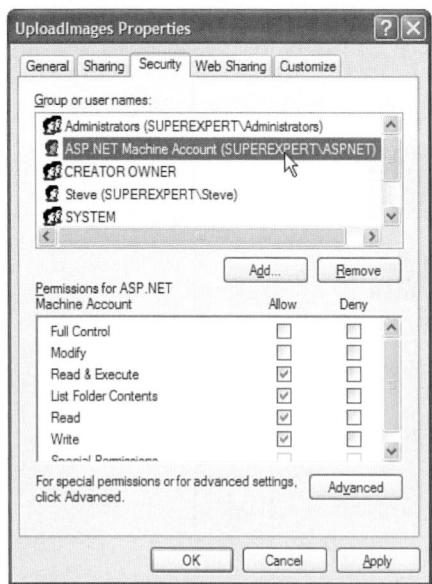

FIGURE 4.2   Adding Write permissions for the ASPNET account.

Saving Files to a Database

You also can use the `FileUpload` control to save files to a database table. Saving and retrieving files from a database can place more stress on your server. However, it does have certain advantages. First, you can avoid file system permissions issues. Second, saving files to a database enables you to more easily back up your information.

The page in Listing 4.2 enables you to save Microsoft Word documents to a database table (see Figure 4.3).

LISTING 4.2   `FileUploadDatabase.aspx`

```
<%@ Page Language="C#" %>
<%@ Import Namespace="System.IO" %>
<!DOCTYPE html PUBLIC "-//W3C//DTD XHTML 1.0 Transitional//EN"
"http://www.w3.org/TR/xhtml1/DTD/xhtml1-transitional.dtd">
<script runat="server">

    protected void btnAdd_Click(object sender, EventArgs e)
    {
        if (upFile.HasFile)
        {
            if (CheckFileType(upFile.FileName))
                srcFiles.Insert();
        }
    }

    bool CheckFileType(string fileName)
    {
        return (Path.GetExtension(fileName).ToLower() == ".doc"
            || Path.GetExtension(fileName).ToLower() == ".docx");
    }

</script>
<html xmlns="http://www.w3.org/1999/xhtml" >
<head id="Head1" runat="server">
    <style type="text/css">
        .fileList li
        {
            margin-bottom:5px;
        }
    </style>
    <title>FileUpload Database</title>
</head>
<body>
    <form id="form1" runat="server">
    <div>
```

```
<asp:Label
    id="lblFile"
    Text="Word Document:"
    AssociatedControlID="upFile"
    Runat="server" />

<asp:FileUpload
    id="upFile"
    Runat="server" />

<asp:Button
    id="btnAdd"
    Text="Add Document"
    OnClick="btnAdd_Click"
    Runat="server" />

<hr />

<asp:Repeater
    id="rptFiles"
    DataSourceID="srcFiles"
    Runat="server">
    <HeaderTemplate>
    <ul class="fileList">
    </HeaderTemplate>
    <ItemTemplate>
    <li>
    <asp:HyperLink
        id="lnkFile"
        Text='<%#Eval("FileName")%>'
        NavigateUrl='<%#Eval("Id", "~/FileHandler.ashx?id={0}")%>'
        Runat="server" />
    </li>
    </ItemTemplate>
    <FooterTemplate>
    </ul>
    </FooterTemplate>
</asp:Repeater>

<asp:SqlDataSource
    id="srcFiles"
    ConnectionString="Server=.\SQLExpress;Integrated Security=True;
        AttachDbFileName=¦DataDirectory¦FilesDB.mdf;User Instance=True"
    SelectCommand="SELECT Id,FileName FROM Files"
    InsertCommand="INSERT Files (FileName,FileBytes) VALUES
➥(@FileName,@FileBytes)"
```

```
        Runat="server">
        <InsertParameters>
            <asp:ControlParameter Name="FileName" ControlID="upFile"
PropertyName="FileName" />
            <asp:ControlParameter Name="FileBytes" ControlID="upFile"
PropertyName="FileBytes" />
        </InsertParameters>
    </asp:SqlDataSource>

    </div>
    </form>
</body>
</html>
```

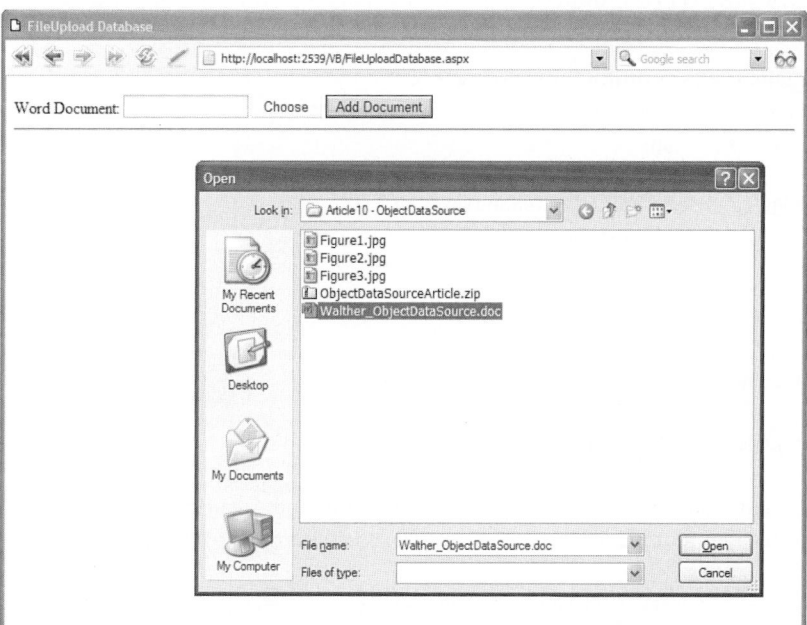

FIGURE 4.3   Uploading Microsoft Word documents.

When you submit the form in Listing 4.2, the btnAdd_Click() method executes. This method checks the file extension to verify that the file is a Microsoft Word document. Next, the SqlDataSource control's Insert() method is called to insert the values of the FileUpload control's FileName and FileBytes properties into a local SQL Express database table. The SQL Express database table, named Files, looks like this:

Column Name	Data Type
Id	`Int (IDENTITY)`
FileName	`NVarchar(50)`
FileBytes	`Varbinary(max)`

The page also displays a list of the current Microsoft Word documents in the database. You can click any file and view the contents of the file. Exactly what happens when you click a file is browser (and browser settings) dependent. With Microsoft Internet Explorer, for example, the document opens directly in the browser.

Clicking the name of a document links you to a page named `FileHandler.ashx`. The `FileHandler.ashx` file is a generic HTTP Handler file. Chapter 25, "Using the ASP.NET URL Routing Engine," discusses HTTP Handlers in detail. An HTTP Handler enables you to execute code when someone makes a request for a file with a certain path.

The `FileHandler.ashx` file is contained in Listing 4.3.

LISTING 4.3   `FileHandler.ashx`

```
<%@ WebHandler Language="C#" Class="FileHandler" %>


using System;
using System.Web;
using System.Data;
using System.Data.SqlClient;

public class FileHandler : IHttpHandler {

    const string conString = @"Server=.\SQLExpress;Integrated Security=True;
        AttachDbFileName=¦DataDirectory¦FilesDB.mdf;User Instance=True";

    public void ProcessRequest (HttpContext context) {
        context.Response.ContentType = "application/msword";

        SqlConnection con = new SqlConnection(conString);
        SqlCommand cmd = new SqlCommand("SELECT FileBytes FROM Files WHERE
➥Id=@Id", con);
        cmd.Parameters.AddWithValue("@Id", context.Request["Id"]);
        using (con)
        {
            con.Open();
            byte[] file = (byte[])cmd.ExecuteScalar();
            context.Response.BinaryWrite(file);
        }
```

```
    }

    public bool IsReusable {
        get {
            return false;
        }
    }

}
```

When the `FileHandler.aspx` page is requested, the `ProcessRequest()` method executes. This method grabs a query string item named `Id` and retrieves the matching record from the Files database table. The record contains the contents of a Microsoft Word document as a byte array. The byte array is sent to the browser with the `Response.BinaryWrite()` method.

Uploading Large Files

You must do extra work when uploading large files. You don't want to consume your entire server's memory by placing the entire file in memory. When working with a large file, you need to work with the file in more manageable chunks.

First, you need to configure your application to handle large files. Two configuration settings have an effect on posting large files to the server: the `httpRuntime maxRequestLength` and `httpRuntime requestLengthDiskThreshold` settings.

The `maxRequestLength` setting places a limit on the largest form post that the server can accept. By default, you cannot post a form that contains more than 4MB of data—if you try, you get an exception. If you need to upload a file that contains more than four megabytes of data, you need to change this setting.

The `requestLengthDiskThreshold` setting determines how a form post is buffered to the file system. In an older version of ASP.NET (ASP.NET 1.1), uploading a large file could do horrible things to your server. The entire file was uploaded into the server memory. While a 10-megabyte video file was uploaded, for example, 10 megabytes of server memory was consumed.

The ASP.NET 4 Framework enables you to buffer large files onto the file system. When the size of the file passes the `requestLengthDiskThreshold` setting, the remainder of the file is buffered to the file system (in the Temporary ASP.NET Files folder).

By default, the ASP.NET framework is configured to buffer any post larger than 80KB to a file buffer. If you are not happy with this setting, you can modify the `requestLengthDiskThreshold` to configure a new threshold (The `requestLengthDiskThreshold` setting must be less than the `maxRequestLength` setting.)

The web configuration file in Listing 4.4 enables files up to 10MB to be posted. It also changes the buffering threshold to 100KB. Changing the buffering threshold controls the amount of information stored in memory before it is flushed to disk.

LISTING 4.4   Web.Config

```
<?xml version="1.0"?>
<configuration>
<system.web>
  <httpRuntime
      maxRequestLength="10240"
      requestLengthDiskThreshold="100" />
</system.web>
</configuration>
```

When working with large files, you must be careful about the way that you handle the file when storing or retrieving the file from a data store. For example, when saving or retrieving a file from a database table, you should never load the entire file into memory.

The page in Listing 4.5 demonstrates how you can save a large file to a database table efficiently.

LISTING 4.5   FileUploadLarge.aspx

```
<%@ Page Language="C#" %>
<%@ Import Namespace="System.IO" %>
<%@ Import Namespace="System.Data" %>
<%@ Import Namespace="System.Data.SqlClient" %>
<!DOCTYPE html PUBLIC "-//W3C//DTD XHTML 1.0 Transitional//EN"
"http://www.w3.org/TR/xhtml1/DTD/xhtml1-transitional.dtd">
<script runat="server">

    const string conString = @"Server=.\SQLExpress;Integrated Security=True;
        AttachDbFileName=¦DataDirectory¦FilesDB.mdf;User Instance=True";


    void btnAdd_Click(Object s, EventArgs e)
    {
        if (upFile.HasFile)
        {
            if (CheckFileType(upFile.FileName))
            {
                AddFile(upFile.FileName, upFile.FileContent);
                rptFiles.DataBind();
            }
        }
    }


    bool CheckFileType(string fileName)
    {
```

```
        return Path.GetExtension(fileName).ToLower() == ".doc";
    }
    void AddFile(string fileName, Stream upload)
    {
        SqlConnection con = new SqlConnection(conString);

        SqlCommand cmd = new SqlCommand("INSERT Files (FileName) Values
➥(@FileName);" +
            "SELECT @Identity = SCOPE_IDENTITY()", con);

        cmd.Parameters.AddWithValue("@FileName", fileName);
        SqlParameter idParm = cmd.Parameters.Add("@Identity", SqlDbType.Int);
        idParm.Direction = ParameterDirection.Output;

        using (con)
        {
            con.Open();
            cmd.ExecuteNonQuery();
            int newFileId = (int)idParm.Value;
            StoreFile(newFileId, upload, con);
        }
    }

    void StoreFile(int fileId, Stream upload, SqlConnection connection)
    {
        int bufferLen = 8040;
        BinaryReader br = new BinaryReader(upload);
        byte[] chunk = br.ReadBytes(bufferLen);

        SqlCommand cmd = new SqlCommand("UPDATE Files SET FileBytes=@Buffer WHERE
Id=@FileId", connection);
        cmd.Parameters.AddWithValue("@FileId", fileId);
        cmd.Parameters.Add("@Buffer", SqlDbType.VarBinary, bufferLen).Value = chunk;
        cmd.ExecuteNonQuery();


        SqlCommand cmdAppend = new SqlCommand("UPDATE Files SET FileBytes
➥.WRITE(@Buffer,NULL, 0) WHERE Id=@FileId", connection);
        cmdAppend.Parameters.AddWithValue("@FileId", fileId);
        cmdAppend.Parameters.Add("@Buffer", SqlDbType.VarBinary, bufferLen);
        chunk = br.ReadBytes(bufferLen);

        while (chunk.Length > 0)
        {
            cmdAppend.Parameters["@Buffer"].Value = chunk;
            cmdAppend.ExecuteNonQuery();
```

```
            chunk = br.ReadBytes(bufferLen);
        }

        br.Close();
    }
}

</script>
<html xmlns="http://www.w3.org/1999/xhtml" >
<head id="Head1" runat="server">
    <title>FileUpload Large</title>
</head>
<body>
    <form id="form1" runat="server">
    <div>

    <asp:Label
        id="lblFile"
        Text="Word Document:"
        AssociatedControlID="upFile"
        Runat="server" />

    <asp:FileUpload
        id="upFile"
        Runat="server" />

    <asp:Button
        id="btnAdd"
        Text="Add Document"
        OnClick="btnAdd_Click"
        Runat="server" />

    <hr />

    <asp:Repeater
        id="rptFiles"
        DataSourceID="srcFiles"
        Runat="server">
        <HeaderTemplate>
        <ul class="fileList">
        </HeaderTemplate>
        <ItemTemplate>
        <li>
        <asp:HyperLink
            id="lnkFile"
```

```
            Text='<%#Eval("FileName")%>'
            NavigateUrl='<%#Eval("Id", "~/FileHandlerLarge.ashx?id={0}")%>'
            Runat="server" />
        </li>
        </ItemTemplate>
        <FooterTemplate>
        </ul>
        </FooterTemplate>
    </asp:Repeater>

    <asp:SqlDataSource
        id="srcFiles"
        ConnectionString="Server=.\SQLExpress;Integrated Security=True;
            AttachDbFileName=¦DataDirectory¦FilesDB.mdf;User Instance=True"
        SelectCommand="SELECT Id,FileName FROM Files"
        Runat="server" />

    </div>
    </form>
</body>
</html>
```

In Listing 4.5, the AddFile() method is called. This method adds a new row to the Files database table that contains the filename. Next, the StoreFile() method is called. This method adds the actual bytes of the uploaded file to the database. The file contents are divided into 8040-byte chunks. The SQL UPDATE statement includes a .WRITE clause used when the FileBytes database column is updated.

NOTE

Microsoft recommends that you set the buffer size to multiples of 8,040 when using the .WRITE clause to update database data.

The page in Listing 4.5 never represents the entire uploaded file in memory. The file is yanked into memory from the file system in 8,040-byte chunks and fed to SQL Server in chunks.

When you click a filename, the FileHandlerLarge.ashx HTTP Handler executes. This handler retrieves the selected file from the database and sends it to the browser. The handler is contained in Listing 4.6.

LISTING 4.6   `FileHandlerLarge.ashx`

```
<%@ WebHandler Language="C#" Class="FileHandlerLarge" %>

using System;
using System.Web;
using System.Data;
using System.Data.SqlClient;

public class FileHandlerLarge : IHttpHandler {

    const string conString = @"Server=.\SQLExpress;Integrated Security=True;
        AttachDbFileName=¦DataDirectory¦FilesDB.mdf;User Instance=True";

    public void ProcessRequest (HttpContext context) {
        context.Response.Buffer = false;
        context.Response.ContentType = "application/msword";

        SqlConnection con = new SqlConnection(conString);
        SqlCommand cmd = new SqlCommand("SELECT FileBytes FROM Files WHERE
➥Id=@Id", con);
        cmd.Parameters.AddWithValue("@Id", context.Request["Id"]);
        using (con)
        {
            con.Open();
            SqlDataReader reader = cmd.ExecuteReader
➥(CommandBehavior.SequentialAccess);
            if (reader.Read())
            {
                int bufferSize = 8040;
                byte[] chunk = new byte[bufferSize];
                long retCount;
                long startIndex = 0;

                retCount = reader.GetBytes(0, startIndex, chunk, 0, bufferSize);


                while (retCount == bufferSize)
                {
                    context.Response.BinaryWrite(chunk);

                    startIndex += bufferSize;
                    retCount = reader.GetBytes(0, startIndex, chunk, 0, bufferSize);
```

```
            }

            byte[] actualChunk = new Byte[retCount - 1];
            Buffer.BlockCopy(chunk, 0, actualChunk, 0, (int)retCount - 1);
            context.Response.BinaryWrite(actualChunk);
        }
    }
}

public bool IsReusable {
    get {
        return false;
    }
}
}
```

The HTTP Handler in Listing 4.6 uses a `SqlDataReader` to retrieve a file from the database. The `SqlDataReader` is retrieved with a `CommandBehavior.SequentialAccess` parameter that enables the `SqlDataReader` to load data as a stream. The contents of the database column are pulled into memory in 8,040-byte chunks. The chunks are written to the browser with the `Response.BinaryWrite()` method.

Response buffering is disabled for the handler. The `Response.Buffer` property is set to the value `False`. Because buffering is disabled, the output of the handler is not buffered in server memory before being transmitted to the browser.

> **WARNING**
>
> The method of working with large files described in this section only works with SQL Server 2005 and SQL Server 2008. When using earlier versions of SQL Server, you need to use the `TEXTPTR()` function instead of the `.WRITE` clause.

Displaying a Calendar

The `Calendar` control enables you to display a calendar. You can use the calendar as a date picker or to display a list of upcoming events.

The page in Listing 4.7 displays a simple calendar with the `Calendar` control (see Figure 4.4).

LISTING 4.7   ShowCalendar.aspx

```
<%@ Page Language="C#" %>
<!DOCTYPE html PUBLIC "-//W3C//DTD XHTML 1.0 Transitional//EN"
"http://www.w3.org/TR/xhtml1/DTD/xhtml1-transitional.dtd">
<html xmlns="http://www.w3.org/1999/xhtml" >
<head id="Head1" runat="server">
    <title>Show Calendar</title>
</head>
<body>
    <form id="form1" runat="server">
    <div>

    <asp:Calendar
        id="Calendar1"
        Runat="server" />

    </div>
    </form>
</body>
</html>
```

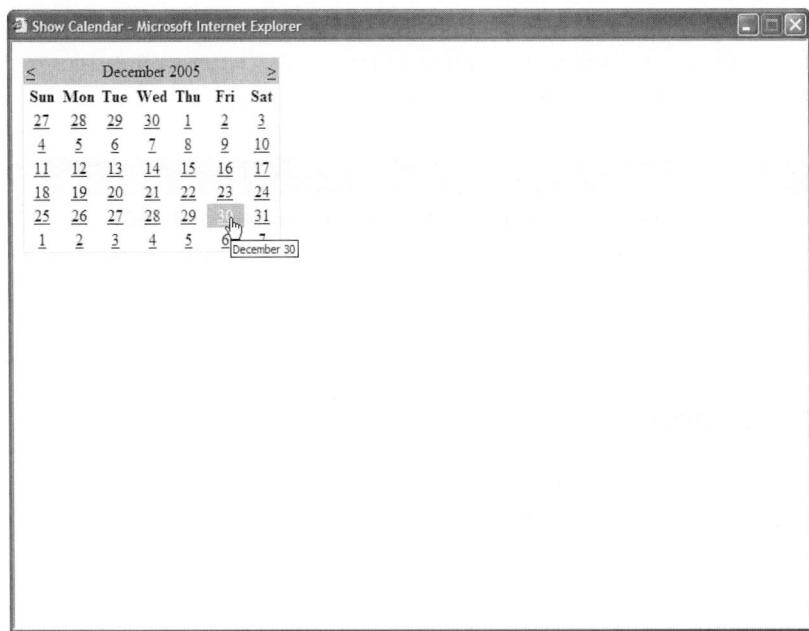

FIGURE 4.4   Displaying a calendar with the Calendar control.

The `Calendar` control supports the following properties (this is not a complete list):

▶ **DayNameFormat**—Enables you to specify the appearance of the days of the week. Possible values are `FirstLetter`, `FirstTwoLetters`, `Full`, `Short`, and `Shortest`.

▶ **NextMonthText**—Enables you to specify the text that appears for the next month link.

▶ **NextPrevFormat**—Enables you to specify the format of the next month and previous month link. Possible values are `CustomText`, `FullMonth`, and `ShortMonth`.

▶ **PrevMonthText**—Enables you to specify the text that appears for the previous month link.

▶ **SelectedDate**—Enables you to get or set the selected date.

▶ **SelectedDates**—Enables you to get or set a collection of selected dates.

▶ **SelectionMode**—Enables you to specify how dates are selected. Possible values are `Day`, `DayWeek`, `DayWeekMonth`, and `None`.

▶ **SelectMonthText**—Enables you to specify the text that appears for selecting a month.

▶ **SelectWeekText**—Enables you to specify the text that appears for selecting a week.

▶ **ShowDayHeader**—Enables you to hide or display the day names at the top of the `Calendar` control.

▶ **ShowNextPrevMonth**—Enables you to hide or display the links for the next and previous months.

▶ **ShowTitle**—Enables you to hide or display the title bar displayed at the top of the calendar.

▶ **TitleFormat**—Enables you to format the title bar. Possible values are `Month` and `MonthYear`.

▶ **TodaysDate**—Enables you to specify the current date. This property defaults to the current date on the server.

▶ **VisibleDate**—Enables you to specify the month displayed by the `Calendar` control. This property defaults to displaying the month that contains the date specified by `TodaysDate`.

The `Calendar` control also supports the following events:

▶ **DayRender**—Raised as each day is rendered.

▶ **SelectionChanged**—Raised when a new day, week, or month is selected.

▶ **VisibleMonthChanged**—Raised when the next or previous month link is clicked.

The SelectionMode property enables you to change the behavior of the calendar so that you can not only select days, but also select weeks or months. The page in Listing 4.8 illustrates how you can use the SelectionMode property with the SelectedDates property to select multiple dates (see Figure 4.5).

LISTING 4.8   CalendarSelectionMode.aspx

```
<%@ Page Language="C#" %>
<!DOCTYPE html PUBLIC "-//W3C//DTD XHTML 1.0 Transitional//EN"
"http://www.w3.org/TR/xhtml1/DTD/xhtml1-transitional.dtd">
<script runat="server">

    protected void btnSubmit_Click(object sender, EventArgs e)
    {
        bltResults.DataSource = Calendar1.SelectedDates;
        bltResults.DataBind();
    }
</script>
<html xmlns="http://www.w3.org/1999/xhtml" >
<head id="Head1" runat="server">
    <title>Calendar SelectionMode</title>
</head>
<body>
    <form id="form1" runat="server">
    <div>

    <asp:Calendar
        id="Calendar1"
        SelectionMode="DayWeekMonth"
        runat="server" />
    <br /><br />

    <asp:Button
        id="btnSubmit"
        Text="Submit"
        OnClick="btnSubmit_Click"
        Runat="server" />

    <hr />

    <asp:BulletedList
        id="bltResults"
        DataTextFormatString="{0:d}"
        Runat="server" />
```

```
        </div>
        </form>
    </body>
    </html>
```

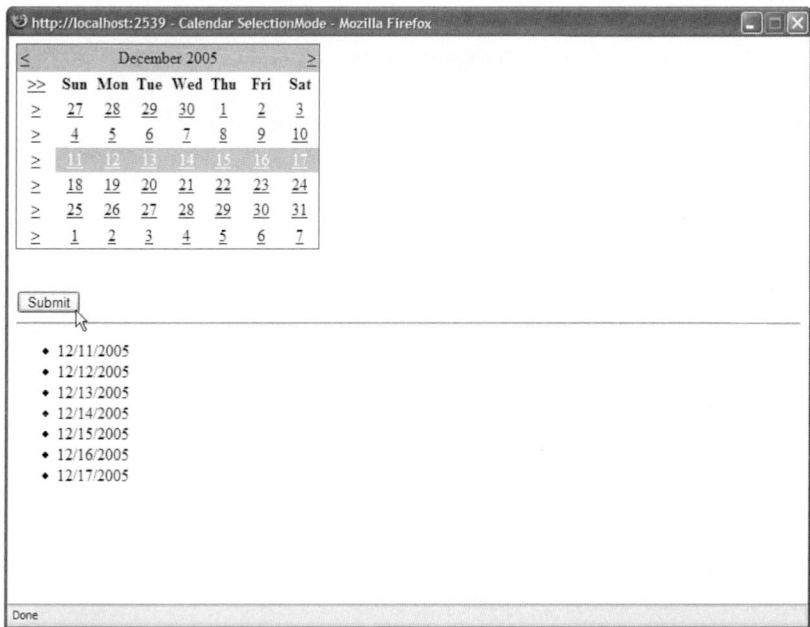

FIGURE 4.5   Selecting weeks and months with a `Calendar` control.

When you select a date, or group of dates, from the `Calendar` control in Listing 4.8, the set of selected dates display in a `BulletedList` control.

Creating a Pop-Up Date Picker

You can use a `Calendar` control to create a fancy pop-up date picker if you are willing to add a little JavaScript and some Cascading Style Sheet (CSS) rules to a page. The page in Listing 4.9 contains a `TextBox` and `Calendar` control (see Figure 4.6).

The `Calendar` control is hidden until you click the calendar image. The `#datePicker` style sheet rules sets the display property to `none`. When you click the image of the calendar, the JavaScript `displayCalendar()` function executes and sets the CSS display property to the value `block`.

When you select a date from the calendar, the page is posted back to the server and the `SelectionChanged` server-side event is raised. The `SelectionChanged` event handler updates the `TextBox` control with the selected date.

LISTING 4.9   CalendarJS.aspx

```
<%@ Page Language="C#" %>
<!DOCTYPE html PUBLIC "-//W3C//DTD XHTML 1.0 Transitional//EN"
"http://www.w3.org/TR/xhtml1/DTD/xhtml1-transitional.dtd">
<script runat="server">

    protected void calEventDate_SelectionChanged(object sender, EventArgs e)
    {
        txtEventDate.Text = calEventDate.SelectedDate.ToString("d");
    }

    protected void btnSubmit_Click(object sender, EventArgs e)
    {
        lblResult.Text = "You picked: " + txtEventDate.Text;
    }
</script>
<html xmlns="http://www.w3.org/1999/xhtml" >
<head id="Head1" runat="server">
    <script type="text/javascript">

        function displayCalendar()
        {
            var datePicker = document.getElementById('datePicker');
            datePicker.style.display = 'block';
        }

    </script>
    <style type="text/css">
        #datePicker
        {
            display:none;
            position:absolute;
            border:solid 2px black;
            background-color:white;
        }
        .content
        {
            width:400px;
            background-color:white;
            margin:auto;
            padding:10px;
        }
        html
        {
```

```
            background-color:silver;
        }
    </style>
    <title>Calendar with JavaScript</title>
</head>
<body>
    <form id="form1" runat="server">
    <div class="content">

    <asp:Label
        id="lblEventDate"
        Text="Event Date:"
        AssociatedControlID="txtEventDate"
        Runat="server" />
    <asp:TextBox
        id="txtEventDate"
        Runat="server" />
    <img src="Calendar.gif" onclick="displayCalendar()" />

    <div id="datePicker">
    <asp:Calendar
        id="calEventDate"
        OnSelectionChanged="calEventDate_SelectionChanged"
        Runat="server" />
    </div>

    <br />
    <asp:Button
        id="btnSubmit"
        Text="Submit"
        Runat="server" OnClick="btnSubmit_Click" />

    <hr />

    <asp:Label
        id="lblResult"
        Runat="server" />

    </div>
    </form>
</body>
</html>
```

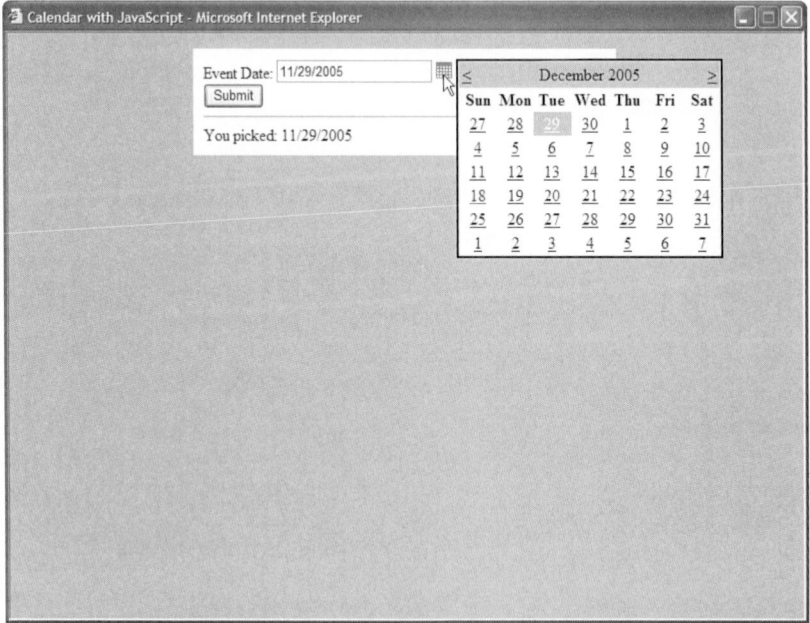

FIGURE 4.6 Displaying a pop-up calendar.

Rendering a Calendar from a Database Table

You also can use the Calendar control to display events in a calendar. In this section, we build a simple schedule application that enables you to insert, update, and delete calendar entries. Each schedule entry is highlighted in a Calendar control (see Figure 4.7).

The code for the schedule application is contained in Listing 4.10.

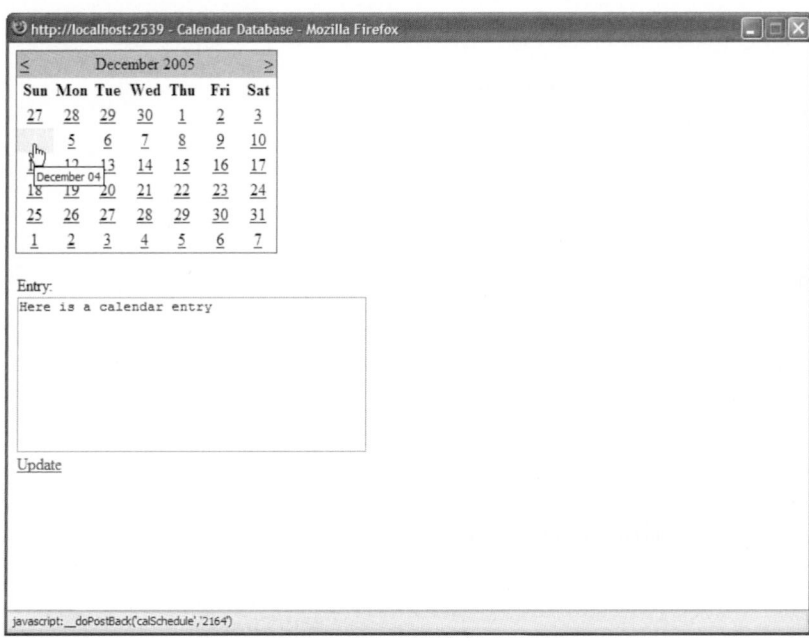

FIGURE 4.7   Displaying a calendar from a database.

LISTING 4.10   `CalendarDatabase.aspx`

```csharp
<%@ Page Language="C#" ValidateRequest="false" %>
<%@ Import Namespace="System.Data" %>
<!DOCTYPE html PUBLIC "-//W3C//DTD XHTML 1.0 Transitional//EN"
"http://www.w3.org/TR/xhtml1/DTD/xhtml1-transitional.dtd">
<script runat="server">

    DataView schedule = new DataView();

    void Page_Load()
    {
        if (calSchedule.SelectedDate == DateTime.MinValue)
            calSchedule.SelectedDate = calSchedule.TodaysDate;
    }

    void Page_PreRender()
    {
        schedule = (DataView)srcCalendar.Select(DataSourceSelectArguments.Empty);
        schedule.Sort = "EntryDate";
    }
```

```
    protected void calSchedule_DayRender(object sender, DayRenderEventArgs e)
    {
        if (schedule.FindRows(e.Day.Date).Length > 0)
            e.Cell.BackColor = System.Drawing.Color.Yellow;
    }
</script>
<html xmlns="http://www.w3.org/1999/xhtml" >
<head id="Head1" runat="server">
    <title>Calendar Database</title>
</head>
<body>
    <form id="form1" runat="server">
    <div>

    <asp:Calendar
        id="calSchedule"
        OnDayRender="calSchedule_DayRender"
        Runat="server" />


    <br />

    <asp:FormView
        id="frmSchedule"
        AllowPaging="True"
        DataKeyNames="EntryDate"
        DataSourceID="srcSchedule"
        Runat="server">
        <EmptyDataTemplate>
        <asp:LinkButton
            id="btnNew"
            Text="Add Entry"
            CommandName="New"
            Runat="server" />
        </EmptyDataTemplate>
        <ItemTemplate>
        <h1><%# Eval("EntryDate", "{0:D}") %></h1>
        <%# Eval("Entry") %>
        <br /><br />
        <asp:LinkButton
            Id="btnEdit"
            Text="Edit Entry"
            CommandName="Edit"
            Runat="server" />
        <asp:LinkButton
            Id="lnkDelete"
```

```
        Text="Delete Entry"
        CommandName="Delete"
        OnClientClick="return confirm('Delete entry?');"
        Runat="server" />
</ItemTemplate>
<EditItemTemplate>
<asp:Label
    id="lblEntry"
    Text="Entry:"
    AssociatedControlID="txtEntry"
    Runat="server" />
<br />
<asp:TextBox
    id="txtEntry"
    Text='<%#Bind("Entry") %>'
    TextMode="MultiLine"
    Columns="40"
    Rows="8"
    Runat="server" />
<br />
<asp:LinkButton
    id="btnUpdate"
    Text="Update"
    CommandName="Update"
    Runat="server" />
</EditItemTemplate>
<InsertItemTemplate>
<asp:Label
    id="lblEntry"
    Text="Entry:"
    AssociatedControlID="txtEntry"
    Runat="server" />
<br />
<asp:TextBox
    id="txtEntry"
    Text='<%#Bind("Entry") %>'
    TextMode="MultiLine"
    Columns="40"
    Rows="8"
    Runat="server" />
<br />
<asp:Button
    id="btnInsert"
    Text="Insert"
    CommandName="Insert"
    Runat="server" />
```

4

```
            </InsertItemTemplate>
        </asp:FormView>

        <asp:SqlDataSource
            id="srcSchedule"
            ConnectionString="Server=.\SQLExpress;Integrated Security=True;
                AttachDbFileName=¦DataDirectory¦ScheduleDB.mdf;User Instance=True"
            SelectCommand="SELECT EntryDate,Entry FROM Schedule WHERE
➥EntryDate=@EntryDate"
            InsertCommand="INSERT Schedule (EntryDate,Entry) VALUES
➥(@EntryDate,@Entry)"
            UpdateCommand="UPDATE Schedule SET Entry=@Entry WHERE EntryDate=@EntryDate"
            DELETECommand="DELETE Schedule WHERE EntryDate=@EntryDate"
            Runat="server">
            <SelectParameters>
            <asp:ControlParameter
                Name="EntryDate"
                ControlID="calSchedule"
                PropertyName="SelectedDate" />
            </SelectParameters>
            <InsertParameters>
            <asp:ControlParameter
                Name="EntryDate"
                ControlID="calSchedule"
                PropertyName="SelectedDate" />
            </InsertParameters>
        </asp:SqlDataSource>

        <asp:SqlDataSource
            id="srcCalendar"
            ConnectionString="Server=.\SQLExpress;Integrated Security=True;
                AttachDbFileName=¦DataDirectory¦ScheduleDB.mdf;User Instance=True"
            SelectCommand="SELECT EntryDate FROM Schedule"
            Runat="server">
        </asp:SqlDataSource>

        </div>
        </form>
</body>
</html>
```

The page in Listing 4.10 saves and loads entries from a SQL Express database named ScheduleDB. The contents of the schedule are contained in a table named Schedule that has the following schema:

Column Name	Data Type
EntryDate	DateTime
Entry	Nvarchar(max)

The tricky part in Listing 4.10 is the code for highlighting the current entries in the calendar. In the `Page_PreRender` event handler, a list of all the current entries is retrieved from the database. The list is represented by a `DataView` object.

The `DayRender` event is raised when the `Calendar` renders each day (table cell). In the `DayRender` event handler in Listing 4.10, if an entry is in the database that corresponds to the day being rendered, the day is highlighted with a yellow background color.

Displaying Advertisements

The `AdRotator` control enables you to randomly display different advertisements in a page. You can store the list of advertisements in either an XML file or in a database table.

The `AdRotator` control supports the following properties (this is not a complete list):

- ▶ **AdvertisementFile**—Enables you to specify the path to an XML file that contains a list of banner advertisements.

- ▶ **AlternateTextField**—Enables you to specify the name of the field for displaying alternate text for the banner advertisement image. The default value is `AlternateText`.

- ▶ **DataMember**—Enables you to bind to a particular data member in the data source.

- ▶ **DataSource**—Enables you to specify a data source programmatically for the list of banner advertisements.

- ▶ **DataSourceID**—Enables you to bind to a data source declaratively.

- ▶ **ImageUrlField**—Enables you to specify the name of the field for the image URL for the banner advertisement. The default value for this field is `ImageUrl`.

- ▶ **KeywordFilter**—Enables you to filter advertisements by a single keyword.

- ▶ **NavigateUrlField**—Enables you to specify the name of the field for the advertisement link. The default value for this field is `NavigateUrl`.

- ▶ **Target**—Enables you to open a new window when a user clicks the banner advertisement.

The `AdRotator` control also supports the following event:

- ▶ **AdCreated**—Raised after the `AdRotator` control selects an advertisement but before the `AdRotator` control renders the advertisement.

The `AdRotator` control includes a `KeywordFilter` property. You can provide each banner advertisement with a keyword and then filter the advertisements displayed by the `AdRotator` control by using the value of the `KeywordFilter` property.

This property can be used in multiple ways. For example, if you display more than one advertisement in the same page, you can filter the advertisements by page regions. You can use the `KeywordFilter` to show the big banner advertisement on the top of the page and box ads on the side of the page.

You can also use the `KeywordFilter` property to filter advertisements by website section. For example, you might want to show different advertisements on your website's home page than on your website's search page.

> **NOTE**
>
> If you cache a page that contains an `AdRotator` control, the `AdRotator` control is excluded from the cache. In other words, even if you cache a page, randomly selected banner advertisements still display. The `AdRotator` control takes advantage of a feature of the ASP.NET Framework called post-cache substitution. You learn more about this feature in Chapter 29, "Caching Application Pages and Data."

Storing Advertisements in an XML File

You can store the list of advertisements that the AdRotator displays in an XML file by setting the `AdRotator` control's `AdvertisementFile` property. For example, the page in Listing 4.11 contains three `AdRotator` controls that retrieve banner advertisements from an XML file named `AdList.xml` (see Figure 4.8).

LISTING 4.11 `AdRotatorXML.aspx`

```
<%@ Page Language="C#" %>
<!DOCTYPE html PUBLIC "-//W3C//DTD XHTML 1.0 Transitional//EN"
"http://www.w3.org/TR/xhtml1/DTD/xhtml1-transitional.dtd">
<html xmlns="http://www.w3.org/1999/xhtml" >
<head id="Head1" runat="server">
    <style type="text/css">
        html
        {
            background-color:silver;
        }
        .content
        {
            background-color:white;
            padding:10px;
            border:solid 1px black;
            margin:auto;
            width:400px;
```

```
                text-align:center;
            }
            .box
            {
                float:right;
                padding:10px;
                border-left:solid 1px black;
            }
            .clear
            {
                clear:both;
            }
    </style>
    <title>AdRotator XML</title>
</head>
<body>
    <form id="form1" runat="server">
    <div class="content">

    <asp:AdRotator
        id="AdRotator1"
        AdvertisementFile="~/App_Data/AdList.xml"
        KeywordFilter="banner"
        CssClass="banner"
        Runat="server" />

    <br />

    <div class="box">
        <asp:AdRotator
            id="AdRotator2"
            AdvertisementFile="~/App_Data/AdList.xml"
            KeywordFilter="box"
            Runat="server" />
        <br /><br />
        <asp:AdRotator
            id="AdRotator3"
            AdvertisementFile="~/App_Data/AdList.xml"
            KeywordFilter="box"
            Runat="server" />
    </div>


    <br />Here is the body text in the page.
    <br />Here is the body text in the page.
    <br />Here is the body text in the page.
```

4

```
        <br />Here is the body text in the page.

        <br class="clear" />
        </div>
        </form>
</body>
</html>
```

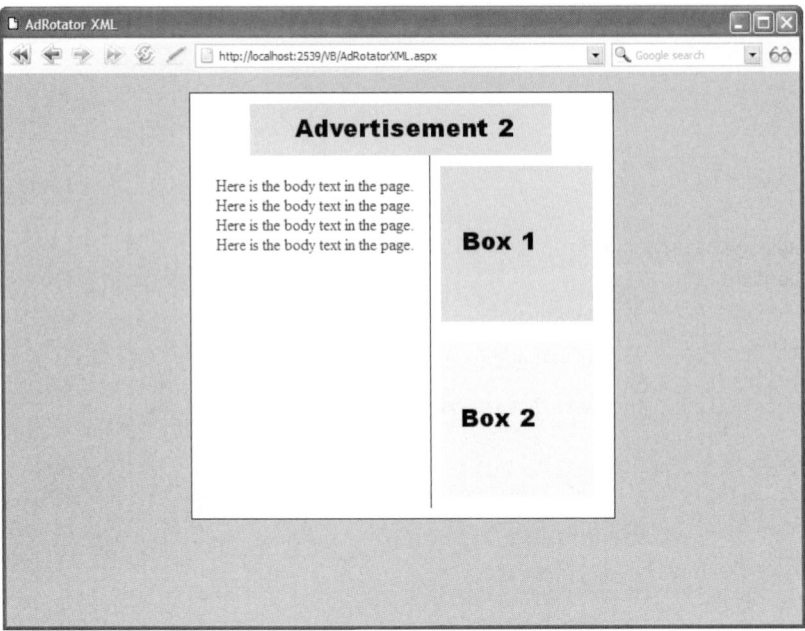

FIGURE 4.8   Displaying advertisements from an XML file.

The page in Listing 4.11 contains an AdRotator control that displays a banner advertisement at the top of the page. The page also contains two AdRotator controls that display box advertisements on the right of the page.

The first AdRotator has a KeyworldFilter property that has the value banner, and the remaining two AdRotator controls have KeywordFilter properties with the value box. The first AdRotator displays only banner advertisements, and the remaining two AdRotator controls display only box advertisements.

All three AdRotator controls get their list of banner advertisements from a file named AdList.xml. This file is located in the App_Data folder for security reasons. The files in the App_Data folder cannot be opened in a web browser.

> **NOTE**
>
> There is nothing wrong with assigning different XML files to different `AdRotator` controls. For example, you could create distinct `BannerAd.xml` and `BoxAd.xml` files, and then you would not have to worry about the `KeywordFilter` property.

The file in Listing 4.12 contains the contents of the `AdList.xml` file.

LISTING 4.12 `AdList.xml`

```xml
<?xml version="1.0" encoding="utf-8" ?>
<Advertisements>
  <!-- Banner Advertisements -->
  <Ad>
    <ImageUrl>~/Ads/BannerAd1.gif</ImageUrl>
    <Width>300</Width>
    <Height>50</Height>
    <NavigateUrl>http://www.AspWorkshops.com</NavigateUrl>
    <AlternateText>Banner Advertisement 1</AlternateText>
    <Impressions>50</Impressions>
    <Keyword>banner</Keyword>
  </Ad>
  <Ad>
    <ImageUrl>~/Ads/BannerAd2.gif</ImageUrl>
    <Width>300</Width>
    <Height>50</Height>
    <NavigateUrl>http://www.AspWorkshops.com</NavigateUrl>
    <AlternateText>Banner Advertisement 2</AlternateText>
    <Impressions>25</Impressions>
    <Keyword>banner</Keyword>
  </Ad>
  <Ad>
    <ImageUrl>~/Ads/BannerAd3.gif</ImageUrl>
    <Width>300</Width>
    <Height>50</Height>
    <NavigateUrl>http://www.AspWorkshops.com</NavigateUrl>
    <AlternateText>Banner Advertisement 3</AlternateText>
    <Impressions>25</Impressions>
    <Keyword>banner</Keyword>
  </Ad>
  <!-- Box Advertisements -->
  <Ad>
    <ImageUrl>~/Ads/BoxAd1.gif</ImageUrl>
    <Width>150</Width>
```

```
      <Height>150</Height>
      <NavigateUrl>http://www.AspWorkshops.com</NavigateUrl>
      <AlternateText>Box Advertisement 1</AlternateText>
      <Impressions>50</Impressions>
      <Keyword>box</Keyword>
   </Ad>
   <Ad>
      <ImageUrl>~/Ads/BoxAd2.gif</ImageUrl>
      <Width>150</Width>
      <Height>150</Height>
      <NavigateUrl>http://www.AspWorkshops.com</NavigateUrl>
      <AlternateText>Box Advertisement 2</AlternateText>
      <Impressions>50</Impressions>
      <Keyword>box</Keyword>
   </Ad>
</Advertisements>
```

The Impressions attribute in the file in Listing 4.12 determines how often each banner advertisement displays. For example, the first banner advertisement displays 50% of the time, and the remaining two banner advertisements display 25% of the time.

Storing Advertisements in a Database Table

Rather than store the list of advertisements in an XML file, you can store the list in a database table. For example, the AdRotator control contained in Listing 4.13 is bound to a SqlDataSource control. The SqlDataSource control represents the contents of a database table named AdList, which is located in a SQL Express database named AdListDB.

LISTING 4.13   AdRotatorDatabase.aspx

```
<%@ Page Language="C#" %>
<!DOCTYPE html PUBLIC "-//W3C//DTD XHTML 1.0 Transitional//EN"
"http://www.w3.org/TR/xhtml1/DTD/xhtml1-transitional.dtd">
<html xmlns="http://www.w3.org/1999/xhtml" >
<head id="Head1" runat="server">
    <title>AdRotator Database</title>
</head>
<body>
    <form id="form1" runat="server">
    <div>

    <asp:AdRotator
        id="AdRotator1"
        DataSourceID="srcAds"
```

```
        Runat="server" />

    <asp:SqlDataSource
        id="srcAds"
        ConnectionString="Server=.\SQLExpress;Integrated Security=True;
            AttachDbFileName=¦DataDirectory¦AdListDB.mdf;User Instance=True"
        SelectCommand="SELECT ImageUrl, Width, Height, NavigateUrl, AlternateText,
Keyword, Impressions
            FROM AdList"
        Runat="server" />

    </div>
    </form>
</body>
</html>
```

To use the page in Listing 4.13, you need to create the AdList database table. This table has the following schema:

Column Name	Data Type
Id	Int (IDENTITY)
ImageUrl	Varchar(250)
Width	Int
Height	Int
NavigateUrl	Varchar(250)
AlternateText	NVarchar(100)
Keyword	NVarchar(50)
Impressions	Int

The columns in the AdList database table correspond to the attributes in the AdList.xml file discussed in the previous section.

Tracking Impressions and Transfers

Normally, when you display advertisements, you do it to make money. Your advertisers want statistics on how often their advertisements display (the number of impressions) and how often their advertisements are clicked (the number of transfers).

To track the number of times that an advertisement displays, you need to handle the AdRotator control's AdCreated event. To track the number of times that an advertisement is clicked, you need to create a redirect handler.

WARNING

If you create an event handler for the AdCreated event and you cache the page, the content rendered by the AdRotator control is also cached. When handling the AdCreated event, use partial page caching to cache only part of a page and not the AdRotator control itself.

The page in Listing 4.14 displays a banner advertisement with the AdRotator control. The page includes an event handler for the AdRotator control's AdCreated event.

LISTING 4.14   AdRotatorTrack.aspx

```
<%@ Page Language="C#" %>
<!DOCTYPE html PUBLIC "-//W3C//DTD XHTML 1.0 Transitional//EN"
"http://www.w3.org/TR/xhtml1/DTD/xhtml1-transitional.dtd">
<script runat="server">

    protected void AdRotator1_AdCreated(object sender, AdCreatedEventArgs e)
    {
        // Update Impressions
        srcAds.InsertParameters["AdId"].DefaultValue =
➥e.AdProperties["Id"].ToString();
        srcAds.Insert();

        // Change NavigateUrl to redirect page
        e.NavigateUrl = "~/AdHandler.ashx?id=" + e.AdProperties["Id"].ToString();
    }
</script>
<html xmlns="http://www.w3.org/1999/xhtml" >
<head id="Head1" runat="server">
    <title>AdRotator Track</title>
</head>
<body>
    <form id="form1" runat="server">
    <div>

    <asp:AdRotator
        id="AdRotator1"
        DataSourceID="srcAds"
        OnAdCreated="AdRotator1_AdCreated"
        Runat="server" />
    <asp:SqlDataSource
        id="srcAds"
        ConnectionString="Server=.\SQLExpress;Integrated Security=True;
```

```
            AttachDbFileName=¦DataDirectory¦AdListDB.mdf;User Instance=True"
        SelectCommand="SELECT Id, ImageUrl, Width, Height, NavigateUrl,
➥AlternateText,Keyword, Impressions
            FROM AdList"
        InsertCommand="INSERT AdStats (AdId, EntryDate, Type) VALUES (@AdId,
➥GetDate(), 0)"
        Runat="server">
        <InsertParameters>
        <asp:Parameter Name="AdId" Type="int32" />
        </InsertParameters>
    </asp:SqlDataSource>

    </div>
    </form>
</body>
</html>
```

The AdCreated event handler does two things. First, it inserts a new record into a database table named AdStats, which records an advertisement impression. Second, the handler modifies the NavigateUrl so that the user is redirected to a handler named AdHandler.ashx.

The AdStats database table looks like this:

Column Name	Data Type
Id	Int (IDENTITY)
AdId	Int
EntryDate	DateTime
Type	Int

The Type column records the type of entry. The value 0 represents an advertisement impression, and the value 1 represents an advertisement transfer.

When you click an advertisement, you link to a file named AdHandler.ashx. This file is contained in Listing 4.15.

LISTING 4.15   `AdHandler.ashx`

```csharp
<%@ WebHandler Language="C#" Class="AdHandler" %>

using System;
using System.Web;
using System.Data;
using System.Data.SqlClient;

public class AdHandler : IHttpHandler {

    const string conString = @"Server=.\SQLExpress;Integrated Security=True;
            AttachDbFileName=¦DataDirectory¦AdListDB.mdf;User Instance=True";

    public void ProcessRequest (HttpContext context)
    {
        int AdId = Int32.Parse(context.Request["Id"]);

        SqlConnection con = new SqlConnection(conString);
        string navigateUrl = String.Empty;
        using (con)
        {
            con.Open();
            UpdateTransferStats(AdId, con);
            navigateUrl = GetNavigateUrl(AdId, con);
        }

        if (!String.IsNullOrEmpty(navigateUrl))
            context.Response.Redirect(navigateUrl);
    }

    void UpdateTransferStats(int advertisementId, SqlConnection con)
    {
        string cmdText = "INSERT AdStats (AdId, EntryDate, Type) VALUES " +
            "(@AdId, GetDate(), 1)";
        SqlCommand cmd = new SqlCommand(cmdText, con);
        cmd.Parameters.AddWithValue("@AdId", advertisementId);
        cmd.ExecuteNonQuery();
    }

    string GetNavigateUrl(int advertisementId, SqlConnection con)
    {
        string cmdText = "SELECT NavigateUrl FROM AdList WHERE Id=@AdId";
        SqlCommand cmd = new SqlCommand(cmdText, con);
        cmd.Parameters.AddWithValue("@AdId", advertisementId);
```

```
        return cmd.ExecuteScalar().ToString();
    }

    public bool IsReusable
    {
        get
        {
            return false;
        }
    }

}
```

The handler in Listing 4.15 performs two tasks. First, it inserts a new record into the AdStats database table, recording that a transfer is taking place. Next, it grabs the NavigateUrl from the AdList database table and sends the user to the advertiser's website.

The final page displays advertiser statistics from the AdStats database table (see Figure 4.9). This page is contained in Listing 4.16.

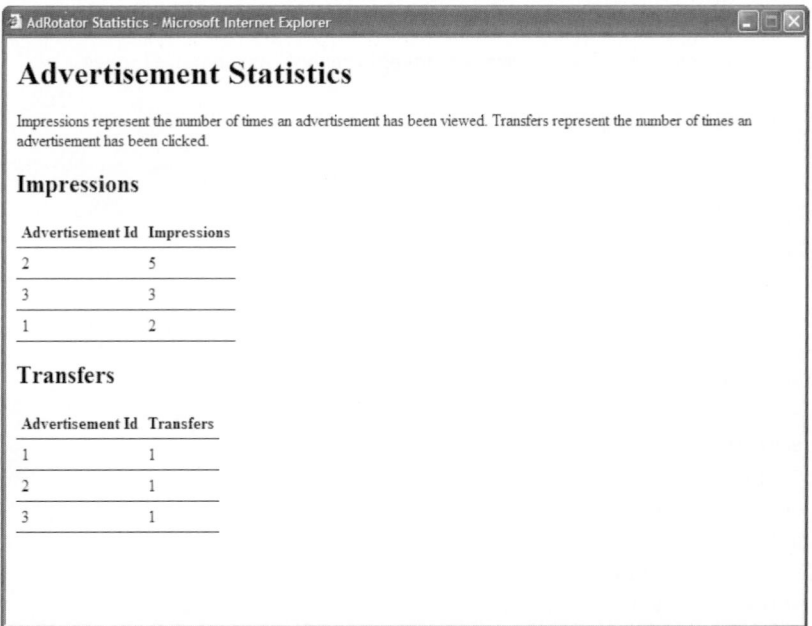

FIGURE 4.9   Displaying advertiser statistics.

LISTING 4.16 AdRotatorStats.aspx

```
<%@ Page Language="C#" %>
<!DOCTYPE html PUBLIC "-//W3C//DTD XHTML 1.0 Transitional//EN"
"http://www.w3.org/TR/xhtml1/DTD/xhtml1-transitional.dtd">
<html xmlns="http://www.w3.org/1999/xhtml" >
<head id="Head1" runat="server">
    <style type="text/css">
        .grid td,.grid th
        {
            border-bottom:solid 1px black;
            padding:5px;
        }
    </style>
    <title>AdRotator Statistics</title>
</head>
<body>
    <form id="form1" runat="server">
    <div>

    <h1>Advertisement Statistics</h1>
    Impressions represent the number of times an advertisement has been viewed.
    Transfers represent the number of times an advertisement has been clicked.

    <h2>Impressions</h2>

    <asp:GridView
        id="grdImpressions"
        DataSourceID="srcImpressions"
        AutoGenerateColumns="false"
        GridLines="None"
        CssClass="grid"
        Runat="server">
        <Columns>
        <asp:BoundField
            DataField="AdId"
            HeaderText="Advertisement Id" />
        <asp:BoundField
            DataField="Impressions"
            HeaderText="Impressions" />
        </Columns>
    </asp:GridView>

    <asp:SqlDataSource
        id="srcImpressions"
        ConnectionString="Server=.\SQLExpress;Integrated Security=True;
```

```
            AttachDbFileName=¦DataDirectory¦AdListDB.mdf;User Instance=True"
        SelectCommand="SELECT AdId,Count(*) As Impressions
            FROM AdStats
            WHERE Type=0
            GROUP BY AdId
            ORDER BY Impressions DESC"
        Runat="server" />


    <h2>Transfers</h2>

    <asp:GridView
        id="grdTransfers"
        DataSourceID="srcTransfers"
        AutoGenerateColumns="false"
        GridLines="None"
        CssClass="grid"
        Runat="server">
        <Columns>
        <asp:BoundField
            DataField="AdId"
            HeaderText="Advertisement Id" />
        <asp:BoundField
            DataField="Transfers"
            HeaderText="Transfers" />
        </Columns>
    </asp:GridView>

    <asp:SqlDataSource
        id="srcTransfers"
        ConnectionString="Server=.\SQLExpress;Integrated Security=True;
            AttachDbFileName=¦DataDirectory¦AdListDB.mdf;User Instance=True"
        SelectCommand="SELECT AdId,Count(*) As Transfers
            FROM AdStats
            WHERE Type=1
            GROUP BY AdId
            ORDER BY Transfers DESC"
        Runat="server" />

    </div>
    </form>
</body>
</html>
```

The page in Listing 4.16 contains two GridView controls bound to two SqlDataSource controls. The first GridView displays statistics on impressions, and the second GridView displays statistics on transfers.

Displaying Different Page Views

The `MultiView` control enables you to hide and display different areas of a page. This control is useful when you need to create a tabbed page. It is also useful when you need to divide a long form into multiple forms.

The `MultiView` control contains one or more `View` controls. You use the `MultiView` control to select a particular `View` control to render. (The selected `View` control is the `Active View`.) The contents of the remaining `View` controls are hidden. You can render only one `View` control at a time.

The `MultiView` control supports the following properties (this is not a complete list):

- ▶ **ActiveViewIndex**—Enables you to select the `View` control to render by index.

- ▶ **Views**—Enables you to retrieve the collection of `View` controls contained in the `MultiView` control.

The `MultiView` control also supports the following methods:

- ▶ **GetActiveView**—Enables you to retrieve the selected `View` control.

- ▶ **SetActiveView**—Enables you to select the active view.

Finally, the `MultiView` control supports the following event:

- ▶ **ActiveViewChanged**—Raised when a new `View` control is selected.

The `View` control does not support any special properties or methods. Its primary purpose is to act as a container for other controls. However, the `View` control does support the following two events:

- ▶ **Activate**—Raised when the view becomes the selected view in the `MultiView` control.

- ▶ **Deactivate**—Raised when another view becomes the selected view in the `MultiView` control.

Displaying a Tabbed Page View

When you use the `MultiView` control with the `Menu` control, you can create a tabbed page view. (To make it look pretty, you need to use some CSS.)

For example, the page in Listing 4.17 contains a `MultiView` control with three `View` controls. The `Menu` control switches between the `View` controls (see Figure 4.10).

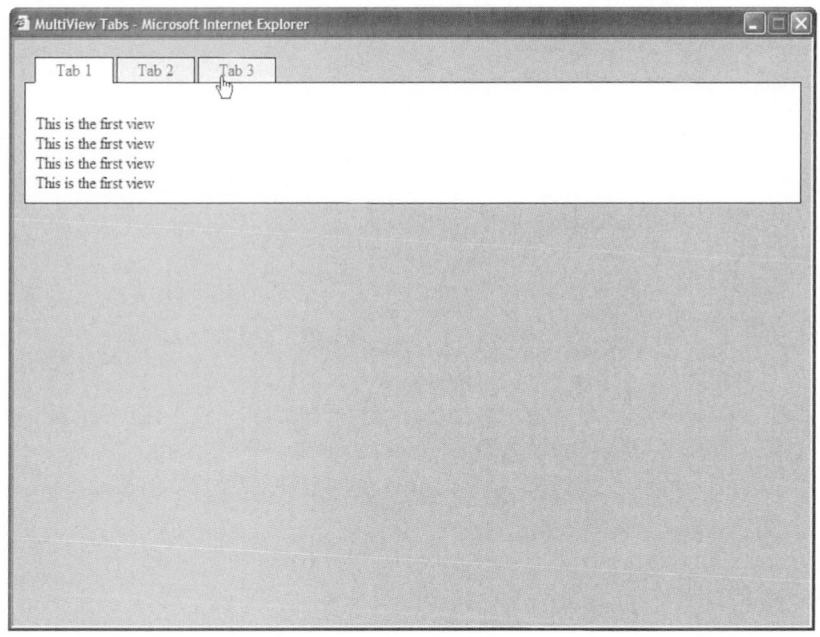

FIGURE 4.10   Displaying a tabbed page with the MultiView control.

LISTING 4.17   MultiViewTabs.aspx

```
<%@ Page Language="C#" %>
<!DOCTYPE html PUBLIC "-//W3C//DTD XHTML 1.0 Transitional//EN"
"http://www.w3.org/TR/xhtml1/DTD/xhtml1-transitional.dtd">
<script runat="server">

    protected void Menu1_MenuItemClick(object sender, MenuEventArgs e)
    {
        int index = Int32.Parse(e.Item.Value);
        MultiView1.ActiveViewIndex = index;
    }
</script>
<html xmlns="http://www.w3.org/1999/xhtml" >
<head id="Head1" runat="server">
    <style type="text/css">
        html
        {
            background-color:silver;
        }
        .tabs
        {
```

4

```
            position:relative;
            top:1px;
            left:10px;
        }
        .tab
        {
            border:solid 1px black;
            background-color:#eeeeee;
            padding:2px 10px;
        }
        .selectedTab
        {
            background-color:white;
            border-bottom:solid 1px white;
        }
        .tabContents
        {
            border:solid 1px black;
            padding:10px;
            background-color:white;
        }
    </style>
    <title>MultiView Tabs</title>
</head>
<body>
    <form id="form1" runat="server">
    <div>
    <asp:Menu
        id="Menu1"
        Orientation="Horizontal"
        StaticMenuItemStyle-CssClass="tab"
        StaticSelectedStyle-CssClass="selectedTab"
        CssClass="tabs"
        OnMenuItemClick="Menu1_MenuItemClick"
        Runat="server">
        <Items>
        <asp:MenuItem Text="Tab 1" Value="0" Selected="true" />
        <asp:MenuItem Text="Tab 2" Value="1" />
        <asp:MenuItem Text="Tab 3" Value="2" />
        </Items>
    </asp:Menu>

    <div class="tabContents">
    <asp:MultiView
        id="MultiView1"
        ActiveViewIndex="0"
```

```
        Runat="server">
        <asp:View ID="View1" runat="server">
            <br />This is the first view
            <br />This is the first view
            <br />This is the first view
            <br />This is the first view
        </asp:View>
        <asp:View ID="View2" runat="server">
            <br />This is the second view
            <br />This is the second view
            <br />This is the second view
            <br />This is the second view
        </asp:View>
        <asp:View ID="View3" runat="server">
            <br />This is the third view
            <br />This is the third view
            <br />This is the third view
            <br />This is the third view
        </asp:View>
    </asp:MultiView>
    </div>

    </div>
    </form>
</body>
</html>
```

In Listing 4.17, the Menu control is associated with a CSS class named tabs. This class relatively positions the Menu control down one pixel to merge the bottom border of the Menu control with the top border of the <div> tag that contains the MultiView. Because the selected tab has a white bottom border, the border between the selected tab and the tab contents disappears.

Displaying a Multipart Form

You can use the MultiView control to divide a large form into several subforms. You can associate particular commands with button controls contained in a MultiView. When the button is clicked, the MultiView changes the active view.

The MultiView control recognizes the following commands:

▶ **NextView**—Causes the MultiView to activate the next View control.

▶ **PrevView**—Causes the MultiView to activate the previous View control.

▶ **SwitchViewByID**—Causes the MultiView to activate the view specified by the button control's CommandArgument.

▶ **SwitchViewByIndex**—Causes the `MultiView` to activate the view specified by the button control's `CommandArgument`.

You can use these commands with any of the button controls—`Button`, `LinkButton`, and `ImageButton`—by setting the button control's `CommandName` property and, in the case of the `SwitchViewByID` and `SwitchViewByIndex`, by setting the `CommandArgument` property.

The page in Listing 4.18 illustrates how you can use the `NextView` command to create a multipart form.

LISTING 4.18   MultiViewForm.aspx

```
<%@ Page Language="C#" %>
<!DOCTYPE html PUBLIC "-//W3C//DTD XHTML 1.0 Transitional//EN"
"http://www.w3.org/TR/xhtml1/DTD/xhtml1-transitional.dtd">
<script runat="server">

    protected void View3_Activate(object sender, EventArgs e)
    {
        lblFirstNameResult.Text = txtFirstName.Text;
        lblColorResult.Text = txtColor.Text;
    }
</script>
<html xmlns="http://www.w3.org/1999/xhtml" >
<head id="Head1" runat="server">
    <title>MultiView Form</title>
</head>
<body>
    <form id="form1" runat="server">
    <div>

    <asp:MultiView
        id="MultiView1"
        ActiveViewIndex="0"
        Runat="server">
        <asp:View ID="View1" runat="server">
        <h1>Step 1</h1>
        <asp:Label
            id="lblFirstName"
            Text="Enter Your First Name:"
            AssociatedControlID="txtFirstName"
            Runat="server" />
        <br />
        <asp:TextBox
            id="txtFirstName"
            Runat="server" />
```

```
    <br /><br />

    <asp:Button
        id="btnNext"
        Text="Next"
        CommandName="NextView"
        Runat="server" />

</asp:View>
<asp:View ID="View2" runat="server">
<h1>Step 2</h1>
<asp:Label
    id="Label1"
    Text="Enter Your Favorite Color:"
    AssociatedControlID="txtColor"
    Runat="server" />
<br />
<asp:TextBox
    id="txtColor"
    Runat="server" />

    <br /><br />

    <asp:Button
        id="Button1"
        Text="Next"
        CommandName="NextView"
        Runat="server" />

</asp:View>
<asp:View ID="View3" runat="server" OnActivate="View3_Activate">
<h1>Summary</h1>
Your First Name:
<asp:Label
    id="lblFirstNameResult"
    Runat="server" />
<br /><br />
Your Favorite Color:
<asp:Label
    id="lblColorResult"
    Runat="server" />
</asp:View>
</asp:MultiView>
```

4

```
    </div>
    </form>
</body>
</html>
```

The first two `View` controls in Listing 4.18 contain a `Button` control. These `Button` controls both have a `CommandName` property set to the value `NextView`.

Displaying a Wizard

You can use the `Wizard` control, like the `MultiView` control, to divide a large form into multiple subforms. The `Wizard` control, however, supports many advanced features not supported by the `MultiView` control.

The `Wizard` control contains one or more `WizardStep` child controls. Only one `WizardStep` displays at a time.

The `Wizard` control supports the following properties (this is not a complete list):

- ▶ **ActiveStep**—Enables you to retrieve the active `WizardStep` control.

- ▶ **ActiveStepIndex**—Enables you to set or get the index of the active `WizardStep` control.

- ▶ **CancelDestinationPageUrl**—Enables you to specify the URL where the user is sent when the Cancel button is clicked.

- ▶ **DisplayCancelButton**—Enables you to hide or display the Cancel button.

- ▶ **DisplaySideBar**—Enables you to hide or display the `Wizard` control's side bar. The side bar displays a list of all the wizard steps.

- ▶ **FinishDestinationPageUrl**—Enables you to specify the URL where the user is sent when the Finish button is clicked.

- ▶ **HeaderText**—Enables you to specify the header text that appears at the top of the `Wizard` control.

- ▶ **WizardSteps**—Enables you to retrieve the `WizardStep` controls contained in the `Wizard` control.

The Wizard control also supports the following templates:

- ▶ **FinishNavigationTemplate**—Enables you to control the appearance of the navigation area of the finish step.

- ▶ **HeaderTemplate**—Enables you control the appearance of the header area of the `Wizard` control.

- ▶ **SideBarTemplate**—Enables you to control the appearance of the side bar area of the `Wizard` control.

► **StartNavigationTemplate**—Enables you to control the appearance of the navigation area of the start step.

► **StepNavigationTemplate**—Enables you to control the appearance of the navigation area of steps that are not start, finish, or complete steps.

The Wizard control also supports the following methods:

► **GetHistory()**—Enables you to retrieve the collection of WizardStep controls that have been accessed.

► **GetStepType()**—Enables you to return the type of WizardStep at a particular index. Possible values are Auto, Complete, Finish, Start, and Step.

► **MoveTo()**—Enables you to move to a particular WizardStep.

The Wizard control also supports the following events:

► **ActiveStepChanged**—Raised when a new WizardStep becomes the active step.

► **CancelButtonClick**—Raised when the Cancel button is clicked.

► **FinishButtonClick**—Raised when the Finish button is clicked.

► **NextButtonClick**—Raised when the Next button is clicked.

► **PreviousButtonClick**—Raised when the Previous button is clicked.

► **SideBarButtonClick**—Raised when a side bar button is clicked.

A Wizard control contains one or more WizardStep controls that represent steps in the wizard. The WizardStep control supports the following properties:

► **AllowReturn**—Enables you to prevent or allow a user to return to this step from a future step.

► **Name**—Enables you to return the name of the WizardStep control.

► **StepType**—Enables you to get or set the type of wizard step. Possible values are Auto, Complete, Finish, Start and Step.

► **Title**—Enables you to get or set the title of the WizardStep. The title displays in the wizard side bar.

► **Wizard**—Enables you to retrieve the Wizard control containing the WizardStep.

The WizardStep also supports the following two events:

► **Activate**—Raised when a WizardStep becomes active.

► **Deactivate**—Raised when another WizardStep becomes active.

The StepType property is the most important property. This property determines how a WizardStep is rendered. The default value of StepType is Auto. When StepType is set to the value Auto, the position of the WizardStep in the WizardSteps collection determines how the WizardStep renders.

You can explicitly set the StepType property to a particular value. If you set StepType to the value Start, a Previous button is not rendered. If you set the StepType to Step, both Previous and Next buttons are rendered. If you set StepType to the value Finish, Previous and Finish buttons are rendered. Finally, when StepType is set to the value Complete, no buttons are rendered.

The page in Listing 4.19 illustrates how you can use a Wizard control to display a multiple part form (see Figure 4.11).

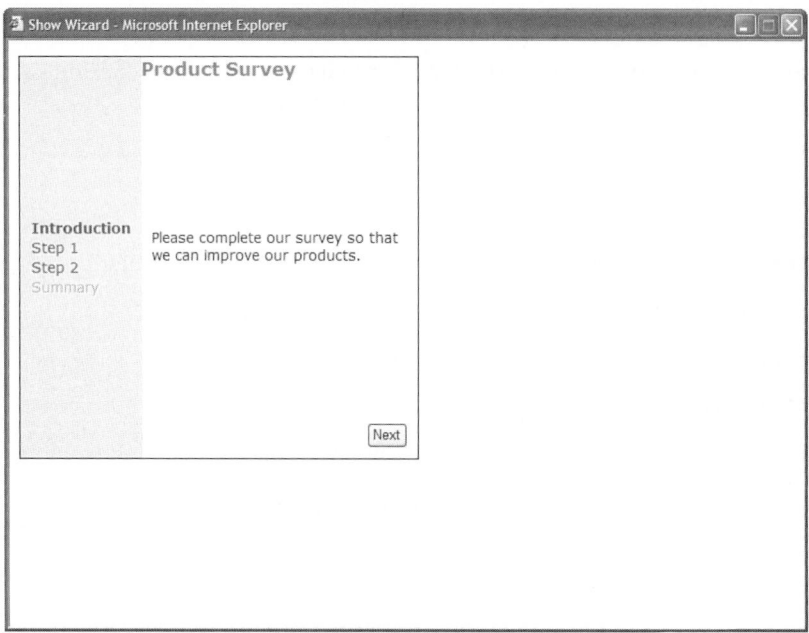

FIGURE 4.11   Displaying a wizard with the Wizard control.

LISTING 4.19   ShowWizard.aspx

```
<%@ Page Language="C#" %>
<!DOCTYPE html PUBLIC "-//W3C//DTD XHTML 1.0 Transitional//EN"
"http://www.w3.org/TR/xhtml1/DTD/xhtml1-transitional.dtd">
<script runat="server">

    protected void Wizard1_FinishButtonClick(object sender,
➥WizardNavigationEventArgs e)
    {
        lblSSNResult.Text = txtSSN.Text;
        lblPhoneResult.Text = txtPhone.Text;
    }
</script>
<html xmlns="http://www.w3.org/1999/xhtml" >
```

```
<head id="Head1" runat="server">
    <style type="text/css">
        .wizard
        {
            border:solid 1px black;
            font:14px Verdana,Sans-Serif;
            width:400px;
            height:300px;
        }
        .header
        {
            color:gray;
            font:bold 18px Verdana,Sans-Serif;
        }
        .sideBar
        {
            background-color:#eeeeee;
            padding:10px;
            width:100px;
        }
        .sideBar a
        {
            text-decoration:none;
        }
        .step
        {
            padding:10px;
        }
    </style>
    <title>Show Wizard</title>
</head>
<body>
    <form id="form1" runat="server">
    <div>

    <asp:Wizard
        id="Wizard1"
        HeaderText="Product Survey"
        OnFinishButtonClick="Wizard1_FinishButtonClick"
        CssClass="wizard"
        HeaderStyle-CssClass="header"
        SideBarStyle-CssClass="sideBar"
        StepStyle-CssClass="step"
        Runat="server">
        <WizardSteps>
        <asp:WizardStep ID="WizardStep1" Title="Introduction">
```

```
        Please complete our survey so that we can improve our
        products.
        </asp:WizardStep>
        <asp:WizardStep ID="WizardStep2" Title="Step 1">
        <asp:Label
            id="lblSSN"
            Text="Social Security Number:"
            AssociatedControlID="txtSSN"
            Runat="server" />
        <br />
        <asp:TextBox
            id="txtSSN"
            Runat="server" />
        </asp:WizardStep>
        <asp:WizardStep ID="WizardStep3" Title="Step 2" StepType="Finish">
        <asp:Label
            id="lblPhone"
            Text="Phone Number:"
            AssociatedControlID="txtPhone"
            Runat="server" />
        <br />
        <asp:TextBox
            id="txtPhone"
            Runat="server" />
        </asp:WizardStep>
        <asp:WizardStep ID="WizardStep4" Title="Summary" StepType="Complete">
        <h1>Summary</h1>
        Social Security Number:
        <asp:Label
            id="lblSSNResult"
            Runat="server" />
        <br /><br />
        Phone Number:
        <asp:Label
            id="lblPhoneResult"
            Runat="server" />
        </asp:WizardStep>
        </WizardSteps>
    </asp:Wizard>

    </div>
    </form>
</body>
</html>
```

The `Wizard` control in Listing 4.19 contains four `WizardStep` controls. The `StepType` property is explicitly set for the last two `WizardStep` controls. When the `Finish WizardStep` is rendered, a Finish button is rendered. When the `Complete WizardStep` is rendered, no buttons are rendered.

The `Wizard` control's `FinishButtonClick` event is handled with a method named `Wizard1_FinishButtonClick()`. This method updates the final `WizardStep` with a summary of the answers entered in the previous `WizardStep` controls.

Displaying Silverlight Content

Silverlight is a framework that enables you to incorporate rich, animated, interactive content to your website. To display this content, your website visitors must have the Silverlight runtime installed on their computer.

> **NOTE**
>
> You can download and install the Microsoft Silverlight runtime (for both Windows and Macintosh) from http://www.silverlight.net.

Unlike the other controls we discussed in this chapter, Silverlight content is not added to an ASP.NET application using a server control. Instead, a standard HTML `object` element is used to add the content. You should set the following attributes on the `object`:

- ▶ **Width**—The width of your Silverlight control, in pixels.

- ▶ **Height**—The height of your Silverlight control, in pixels.

- ▶ **Data**—Indicates the type of object you use, which should be set to "data:application/x-silverlight-2,".

- ▶ **Type**—Indicates the type of object you use, which should be set to "application/x-silverlight-2".

Silverlight applications are stored in a file with an extension of .xap; XAP files are similar to EXEs and DLLs in that they are the compiled binary versions of source code. The Silverlight content that you want to use on your page must be on your web server in XAP format. Then, the `source` parameter on the HTML `object` must be set to the path of the XAP file.

```
<object id="SilverlightContent" width="400" height="300"
    data="data:application/x-silverlight-2,"
    type="application/x-silverlight-2">
    <param name="source" value="SilverlightApplication1.xap" />
</object>
```

NOTE

Silverlight applications are built using the Silverlight SDK and Visual Studio using specific markup called XAML. Building the actual Silverlight content is beyond the scope of this book. For more information on building applications in Silverlight, check out *Silverlight 4 Unleashed* from SAMS Press.

You can specify several other parameters on your Silverlight HTML `object` to customize the content (this is not a complete list):

▶ **Background**—The color to set the background to.

▶ **MinRuntimeVersion**—The minimum version of Silverlight required.

▶ **AutoUpgrade**—Indicates whether to automatically upgrade to the required version of Silverlight if it is not installed.

▶ **OnError**—The name of a JavaScript function that should get called if an error occurs.

If Silverlight is not installed on the user's computer, you can display alternative content by providing standard HTML before the closing `</object>` tag. A common practice is to display the default installation image that links to the Silverlight download page.

The listing in 4.20 illustrates how to display a Silverlight control on your page and demonstrates the usage of the preceding parameters. Alternative content also displays if the user doesn't have Silverlight installed (see Figure 4.12).

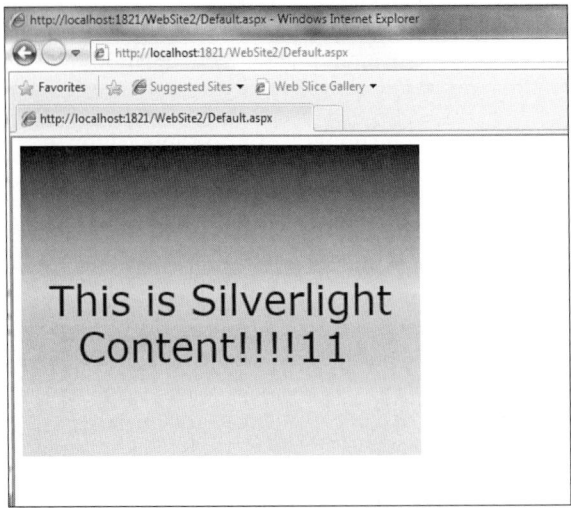

FIGURE 4.12   Displaying Silverlight content with an `object` tag.

LISTING 4.20   ShowSilverlight.aspx

```
<%@ Page Language="C#" %>


<!DOCTYPE html PUBLIC "-//W3C//DTD XHTML 1.0 Transitional//EN"
"http://www.w3.org/TR/xhtml1/DTD/xhtml1-transitional.dtd">
<html xmlns="http://www.w3.org/1999/xhtml">
<head id="head" runat="server">
    <script type="text/javascript">
        function onSilverlightError(sender, args) {
            var appSource = "";
            if (sender != null && sender != 0) {
                appSource = sender.getHost().Source;
            }

            var errorType = args.ErrorType;
            var iErrorCode = args.ErrorCode;

            if (errorType == "ImageError" ||
                errorType == "MediaError") {
                return;
            }

            var errMsg = "Unhandled Error in Silverlight Application "
                + appSource + "\n";

            errMsg += "Code: " + iErrorCode + "    \n";
            errMsg += "Category: " + errorType + "        \n";
            errMsg += "Message: " + args.ErrorMessage + "      \n";

            if (errorType == "ParserError") {
                errMsg += "File: " + args.xamlFile + "      \n";
                errMsg += "Line: " + args.lineNumber + "      \n";
                errMsg += "Position: " + args.charPosition + "      \n";
            }
            else if (errorType == "RuntimeError") {
                if (args.lineNumber != 0) {
                    errMsg += "Line: " + args.lineNumber + "      \n";
                    errMsg += "Position: " + args.charPosition +
                        "      \n";
                }
                errMsg += "MethodName: " + args.methodName + "      \n";
            }
```

```
                throw new Error(errMsg);
            }
    </script>
</head>
<body>
    <object id="SilverlightContent" width="400" height="300"
        data="data:application/x-silverlight-2,"
        type="application/x-silverlight-2">
        <param name="source" value="SilverlightApplication1.xap" />
        <param name="onerror" value="onSilverlightError" />
        <param name="background" value="black" />
        <param name="minRuntimeVersion" value="3.0.40624.0" />
        <param name="autoUpgrade" value="true" />
        <a href="http://go.microsoft.com/fwlink/?LinkID=149156"
                style="text-decoration: none;">
            <img src="http://go.microsoft.com/fwlink/?LinkId=108181"
                alt="Get Microsoft Silverlight"
                style="border-style: none" />
        </a>
    </object>
</body>
</html>
```

Listing 4.20 displays a simple web page with a Silverlight control. The SilverlightApplication1.xap file is located in the same folder as our web page, as the source tag indicates. The background of the control is set to black, and we require a minimum version of Silverlight 3. If a user visits this page and has only Silverlight 1 or 2 installed, they are automatically prompted to upgrade to the newer version. The a and img HTML tags toward the bottom of the object display only if the user does not have the Silverlight runtime installed and shows the default Get Microsoft Silverlight installation button.

Summary

This chapter tackled the rich controls. You learned how to perform file uploads with the FileUpload control. You also saw how to accept and display large file uploads by dividing the file into smaller chunks.

You also learned how to use the Calendar control to display a date picker and render a schedule of events. Using a tiny bit of JavaScript, you learned how to create a fancy pop-up date picker.

This chapter also discussed the AdRotator control. You learned how to store a list of advertisements in both an XML file and a database table. You also learned how to track advertisement impressions and transfers and build a statistics page.

You also learned how to use the `MultiView` control to display different views of a page. You learned how to create a tabbed page by using the `MultiView` control with the `Menu` control. You also learned how to use the `MultiView` to divide a large form into multiple subforms.

We also discussed the `Wizard` control. You learned how to use the `Wizard` control to render navigation elements automatically for completing a multistep task.

Finally, you learned how to add rich content to your site with Silverlight. You learned how to add Silverlight and how to display alternative content when a user doesn't have Silverlight installed.

4

Designing Websites with Master Pages

A Master Page enables you to share the same content among multiple content pages in a website. You can use a Master Page to create a common page layout. For example, if you want all the pages in your website to share a three-column layout, you can create the layout once in a Master Page and apply the layout to multiple content pages.

You also can use Master Pages to display common content in multiple pages. For example, if you want to display a standard header and footer in each page in your website, you can create the standard header and footer in a Master Page.

By taking advantage of Master Pages, you can make your website easier to maintain, extend, and modify. If you need to add a new page to your website that looks just like the other pages in your website, you simply need to apply the same Master Page to the new content page. If you decide to completely modify the design of your website, you do not need to change every content page. You can modify just a single Master Page to dramatically change the appearance of all the pages in your application.

In this chapter, you learn how to create Master Pages and apply them to content pages. It describes how you can apply a Master Page to an entire application by registering the Master Page in the web configuration file.

It also explores different methods of modifying content in a Master Page from individual content pages. For example, you learn how to change the title displayed by a Master Page for each content page.

Finally, you learn how to load Master Pages dynamically. Loading Master Pages dynamically is useful when you need to co-brand one website with another website, or when you want to enable individual website users to customize the appearance of your website.

Creating Master Pages

You create a Master Page by creating a file that ends with the .master extension. You can locate a Master Page file any place within an application. Furthermore, you can add multiple Master Pages to the same application.

For example, Listing 5.1 contains a simple Master Page.

LISTING 5.1 SimpleMaster.master

```
<%@ Master Language="C#" %>
<!DOCTYPE html PUBLIC "-//W3C//DTD XHTML 1.1//EN"
"http://www.w3.org/TR/xhtml11/DTD/xhtml11.dtd">
<html xmlns="http://www.w3.org/1999/xhtml" >
<head id="Head1" runat="server">
    <style type="text/css">
        html
        {
            background-color:silver;
            font:14px Arial,Sans-Serif;
        }
        .content
        {
            margin:auto;
            width:700px;
            background-color:white;
            border:Solid 1px black;
        }
        .leftColumn
        {
            float:left;
            padding:5px;
            width:200px;
            border-right:Solid 1px black;
            height:700px;

        }
        .rightColumn
        {
            float:left;
            padding:5px;
        }
        .clear
        {
            clear:both;
        }
```

```
        </style>
        <title>Simple Master</title>
    </head>
<body>
        <form id="form1" runat="server">
        <div class="content">
            <div class="leftColumn">

                <asp:contentplaceholder
                    id="ContentPlaceHolder1"
                    runat="server"/>

            </div>
            <div class="rightColumn">

                <asp:contentplaceholder
                    id="ContentPlaceHolder2"
                    runat="server"/>

            </div>
            <br class="clear" />
        </div>
        </form>
</body>
</html>
```

The Master Page in Listing 5.1 looks similar to a normal ASP.NET page. You can place almost all the same elements in a Master Page that you can place in an ASP.NET page, including HTML, server-side scripts, and ASP.NET controls.

VISUAL WEB DEVELOPER NOTE

You create a Master Page in Visual Web Developer by selecting the Website menu option, Add New Item, and the Master Page item.

You can see two special things about the Master Page in Listing 5.1. First, the file contains a <%@ Master %> directive instead of the normal <%@ Page %> directive. Second, the Master Page includes two ContentPlaceHolder controls.

When the Master Page merges with a particular content page, the content from the content page appears in the areas marked by ContentPlaceHolder controls. You can add as many ContentPlaceHolders to a Master Page as you need.

> **WARNING**
>
> You can't do some things in a Master Page that you can do in a content page. For example, you cannot cache a Master Page with the OutputCache directive. You also cannot apply a theme to a Master Page.

The Master Page in Listing 5.1 creates a two-column page layout. Each ContentPlaceHolder control is contained in a separate <div> tag. Cascading Style Sheet rules position the two <div> tags into a two-column page layout (see Figure 5.1).

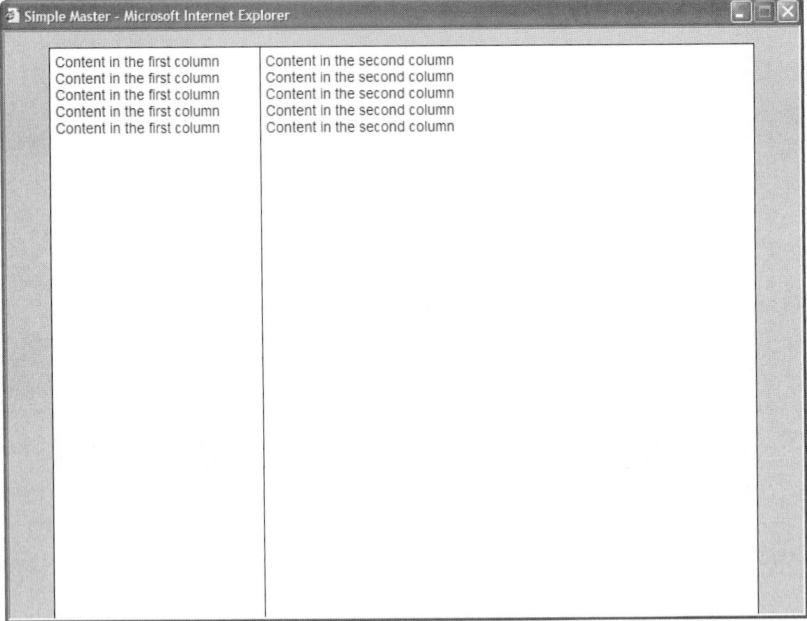

FIGURE 5.1   Creating a two-column Master Page.

> **WEB STANDARDS NOTE**
>
> The Master Page uses Cascading Style Sheets (CSS) to create the page layout. You should strive to avoid using HTML tables for layout. Use HTML tables to display only tabular information.

The content page in Listing 5.2 uses the Master Page that was just created.

LISTING 5.2   SimpleContent.aspx

```
<%@ Page Language="C#" MasterPageFile="~/SimpleMaster.master" %>


<asp:Content
    ID="Content1"
    ContentPlaceHolderID="ContentPlaceHolder1"
    Runat="Server">
    Content in the first column
    <br />Content in the first column
    <br />Content in the first column
    <br />Content in the first column
    <br />Content in the first column
</asp:Content>

<asp:Content
    ID="Content2"
    ContentPlaceHolderID="ContentPlaceHolder2"
    Runat="Server">
    Content in the second column
    <br />Content in the second column
    <br />Content in the second column
    <br />Content in the second column
    <br />Content in the second column
</asp:Content>
```

When you open the page in Listing 5.2 in a web browser, the contents of the page merge with the Master Page.

VISUAL WEB DEVELOPER NOTE

In Visual Web Developer, you create an ASP.NET page associated with a particular Master Page by selecting Website, Add New Item, and Web Form. Next, check the check box labeled Select Master Page. When you click Add, a dialog box appears that enables you to select a Master Page.

The Master Page is associated with the content page through the MasterPageFile attribute included in the <%@ Page %> directive. This attribute contains the virtual path to a Master Page.

The content page does not contain any of the standard opening and closing XHTML tags. All these tags are contained in the Master Page. All the content contained in the content page must be added with Content controls.

You must place all the content contained in a content page within the Content controls. If you attempt to place any content outside these controls, you get an exception.

The Content control includes a ContentPlaceHolderID property. This property points to the ID of a ContentPlaceHolder control contained in the Master Page.

Within a Content control, you can place anything that you would normally add to an ASP.NET page, including XHTML tags and ASP.NET controls.

Creating Default Content

You don't need to associate a Content control with every ContentPlaceHolder control contained in a Master Page. You can provide default content in a ContentPlaceHolder control, and the default content appears unless it is overridden in a particular content page.

For example, the Master Page in Listing 5.3 includes an additional column, which displays a banner advertisement (see Figure 5.2). The banner advertisement is contained in a ContentPlaceHolder control named contentAd.

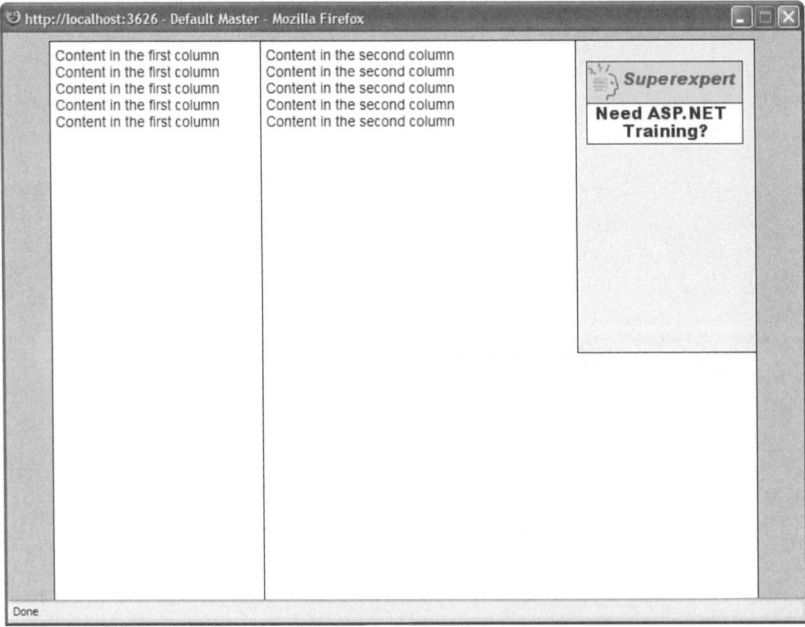

FIGURE 5.2   Displaying default content in a Master Page.

LISTING 5.3 DefaultMaster.master

```
<%@ Master Language="C#" %>
<!DOCTYPE html PUBLIC "-//W3C//DTD XHTML 1.1//EN"
"http://www.w3.org/TR/xhtml11/DTD/xhtml11.dtd">
<html xmlns="http://www.w3.org/1999/xhtml" >
<head id="Head1" runat="server">
    <style type="text/css">
        html
        {
            background-color:silver;
            font:14px Arial,Sans-Serif;
        }
        .content
        {
            margin:auto;
            width:700px;
            background-color:white;
            border:Solid 1px black;
        }
        .leftColumn
        {
            float:left;
            padding:5px;
            width:200px;
            border-right:Solid 1px black;
            height:700px;

        }
        .middleColumn
        {
            float:left;
            padding:5px;
        }
        .rightColumn
        {
            float:right;
            width:175px;
            height:300px;
            border-left:solid 1px black;
            border-bottom:solid 1px black;
            background-color:#eeeeee;
            text-align:center;
        }
```

```
            .ad
            {
                margin-top:20px;
            }
            .clear
            {
                clear:both;
            }
        </style>
        <title>Default Master</title>
    </head>
    <body>
        <form id="form1" runat="server">
        <div class="content">
            <div class="leftColumn">

                <asp:contentplaceholder
                    id="ContentPlaceHolder1"
                    runat="server"/>
            </div>
            <div class="middleColumn">
                <asp:ContentPlaceholder
                    id="ContentPlaceHolder2"
                    runat="server" />

            </div>
            <div class="rightColumn">

                <asp:ContentPlaceHolder
                    id="contentAd"
                    Runat="server">
                    <asp:Image
                        id="imgAd"
                        ImageUrl="~/BannerAd.gif"
                        CssClass="ad"
                        AlternateText="Advertisement for Superexpert ASP Workshops"
                        Runat="server" />
                </asp:ContentPlaceHolder>

            </div>
            <br class="clear" />
        </div>
        </form>
    </body>
    </html>
```

The content page in Listing 5.4 uses the Master Page in Listing 5.3. It does not include a Content control that corresponds to the contentAd control in the Master Page. When you open the page in a browser, the default banner advertisement displays.

LISTING 5.4 DefaultContent.aspx

```
<%@ Page Language="C#" MasterPageFile="~/DefaultMaster.master" %>


<asp:Content
    ID="Content1"
    ContentPlaceHolderID="ContentPlaceHolder1"
    Runat="Server">
    Content in the first column
    <br />Content in the first column
    <br />Content in the first column
    <br />Content in the first column
    <br />Content in the first column
</asp:Content>

<asp:Content
    ID="Content2"
    ContentPlaceHolderID="ContentPlaceHolder2"
    Runat="Server">
    Content in the second column
    <br />Content in the second column
    <br />Content in the second column
    <br />Content in the second column
    <br />Content in the second column
</asp:Content>
```

Of course, you do have the option of adding a Content control that overrides the default content contained in the contentAd control in the Master Page. For example, you might want to display different banner advertisements in different sections of your website.

> **NOTE**
>
> You can nest ContentPlaceHolder controls in a Master Page. If you do this, you have the option of overriding greater or smaller areas of content in the Master Page.

Nesting Master Pages

When building a large website, you might need to create multiple levels of Master Pages. For example, you might want to create a single sitewide Master Page that applies to all the content pages in your website. In addition, you might need to create multiple sectionwide Master Pages that apply to only the pages contained in a particular section.

You can nest Master Pages as many levels as you need. For example, Listing 5.5 contains a Master Page named Site.master, which displays a logo image and contains a single content area. It also contains sitewide navigation links.

LISTING 5.5 Site.master

```
<%@ Master Language="C#" %>
<!DOCTYPE html PUBLIC "-//W3C//DTD XHTML 1.1//EN"
"http://www.w3.org/TR/xhtml11/DTD/xhtml11.dtd">
<html xmlns="http://www.w3.org/1999/xhtml" >
<head id="Head1" runat="server">
    <style type="text/css">
        html
        {
            background-color:DarkGreen;
            font:14px Georgia,Serif;
        }
        .content
        {
            width:700px;
            margin:auto;
            border-style:solid;
            background-color:white;
            padding:10px;
        }
        .tabstrip
        {
            padding:3px;
            border-top:solid 1px black;
            border-bottom:solid 1px black;
        }
        .tabstrip a
        {
            font:14px Arial;
            color:DarkGreen;
            text-decoration:none;
        }
        .column
        {
            float:left;
            padding:10px;
            border-right:solid 1px black;
        }
        .rightColumn
        {
            float:left;
```

```
                padding:10px;
            }
            .clear
            {
                clear:both;
            }
        </style>
        <title>Site Master</title>
    </head>
    <body>
        <form id="form1" runat="server">

        <div class="content">
            <asp:Image
                id="imgLogo"
                ImageUrl="~/Images/SiteLogo.gif"
                AlternateText="Website Logo"
                Runat="server" />

            <div class="tabstrip">
            <asp:HyperLink
                id="lnkProducts"
                Text="Products"
                NavigateUrl="~/Products.aspx"
                Runat="server" />
             
            <asp:HyperLink
                id="lnkServices"
                Text="Services"
                NavigateUrl="~/Services.aspx"
                Runat="server" />
            </div>
            <asp:contentplaceholder id="ContentPlaceHolder1" runat="server">
            </asp:contentplaceholder>
            <br class="clear" />
            copyright &copy; 2007 by the Company
        </div>
        </form>
    </body>
</html>
```

The Master Pages in Listing 5.6 and Listing 5.7 are nested Master Pages. Both Master Pages include a MasterPageFile attribute that points to the Site.master Master Page.

LISTING 5.6   SectionProducts.master

```
<%@ Master Language="C#" MasterPageFile="~/Site.master" %>


<asp:Content
    id="Content1"
    ContentPlaceHolderID="ContentPlaceHolder1"
    Runat="server">
    <div class="column">
        <asp:ContentPlaceHolder
            id="ContentPlaceHolder1"
            Runat="server" />
    </div>
    <div class="column">
        <asp:ContentPlaceHolder
            id="ContentPlaceHolder2"
            Runat="server" />
    </div>
    <div class="rightColumn">
        <asp:ContentPlaceHolder
            id="ContentPlaceHolder3"
            Runat="server" />
    </div>
</asp:Content>
```

LISTING 5.7   SectionServices.master

```
<%@ Master Language="C#" MasterPageFile="~/Site.master" %>


<asp:Content
    id="Content1"
    ContentPlaceHolderID="ContentPlaceHolder1"
    Runat="server">
    <div class="column">
        <asp:ContentPlaceHolder
            id="ContentPlaceHolder1"
            Runat="server" />
    </div>
    <div class="rightColumn">
        <asp:ContentPlaceHolder
            id="ContentPlaceHolder2"
            Runat="server" />
    </div>
</asp:Content>
```

The Master Page in Listing 5.6 creates a three-column page layout, and the Master Page in Listing 5.7 creates a two-column page layout.

The Products.aspx page in Listing 5.8 uses the SectionProducts.master Master Page. When you request the Products.aspx page, the contents of Site.master, SectionProducts.master, and Products.aspx are combined to generate the rendered output (see Figure 5.3).

FIGURE 5.3   Nesting Master Pages to display the Products.aspx page.

LISTING 5.8   Products.aspx

```
<%@ Page Language="C#" MasterPageFile="~/SectionProducts.master" %>


<asp:Content
    ID="Content1"
    ContentPlaceHolderID="ContentPlaceHolder1"
    Runat="Server">
    Products, Products, Products
    <br />Products, Products, Products
    <br />Products, Products, Products
    <br />Products, Products, Products
    <br />Products, Products, Products
</asp:Content>
```

```
<asp:Content
    ID="Content2"
    ContentPlaceHolderID="ContentPlaceHolder2"
    Runat="Server">
    Products, Products, Products
    <br />Products, Products, Products
    <br />Products, Products, Products
    <br />Products, Products, Products
    <br />Products, Products, Products
</asp:Content>

<asp:Content
    ID="Content3"
    ContentPlaceHolderID="ContentPlaceHolder3"
    Runat="Server">
    Products, Products, Products
    <br />Products, Products, Products
    <br />Products, Products, Products
    <br />Products, Products, Products
    <br />Products, Products, Products
</asp:Content>
```

The Services.aspx page in Listing 5.9 uses the SectionService.master Master Page.
When this page is opened in a browser, the contents of Site.master,
SectionServices.master, and Services.aspx combine to generate the rendered output
(see Figure 5.4).

LISTING 5.9   Services.aspx

```
<%@ Page Language="C#" MasterPageFile="~/SectionServices.master" Title="Services" %>

<asp:Content
    ID="Content1"
    ContentPlaceHolderID="ContentPlaceHolder1"
    Runat="Server">
    Services, Services, Services
    <br />Services, Services, Services
    <br />Services, Services, Services
    <br />Services, Services, Services
    <br />Services, Services, Services
</asp:Content>
<asp:Content
    ID="Content2"
    ContentPlaceHolderID="ContentPlaceHolder2"
    Runat="Server">
```

```
         Services, Services, Services, Services, Services
         <br />Services, Services, Services, Services, Services
         <br />Services, Services, Services, Services, Services
         <br />Services, Services, Services, Services, Services
         <br />Services, Services, Services, Services, Services
</asp:Content>
```

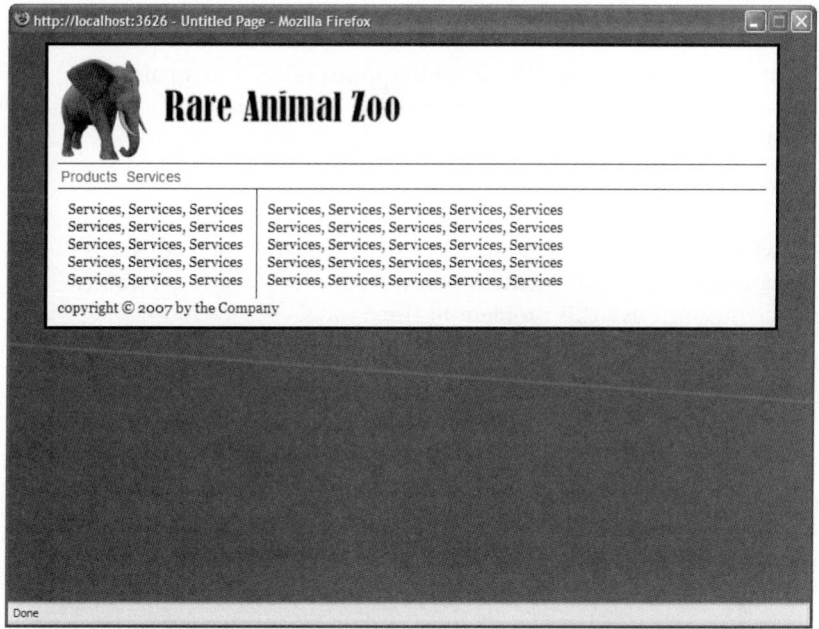

FIGURE 5.4   Nesting Master Pages to display the `Services.aspx` pages.

Using Images and Hyperlinks in Master Pages

You must be careful when using relative URLs in a Master Page. For example, you must be careful when adding images and links to a Master Page. Relative URLs are interpreted in different ways, depending on whether they are used with HTML tags or ASP.NET controls.

If you use a relative URL with an ASP.NET control, the URL is interpreted relative to the Master Page. For example, suppose that you add the following ASP.NET Image control to a Master Page:

```
<asp:Image ImageUrl="Picture.gif" Runat="Server" />
```

The `ImageUrl` property contains a relative URL. If the Master Page is in a folder named `MasterPages`, the URL is interpreted like this:

```
/MasterPages/Picture.gif
```

Even if a content page is in a completely different folder, the `ImageUrl` is interpreted relative to the folder that contains the Master Page and not relative to the content page.

The situation is completely different in the case of HTML elements. If an HTML element such as an <img> or <a> tag includes a relative URL, the relative URL is interpreted relative to the content page. For example, suppose you add the following <img> tag to a Master Page:

```
<img src="Picture.gif" />
```

The `src` attribute contains a relative URL, which is interpreted relative to a particular content page. For example, if you request a content page in a folder named `ContentPages`, the relative URL is interpreted like this:

```
/ContentPages/Picture.gif
```

Using relative URLs with HTML elements is especially tricky because the URL keeps changing with each content page. If you request content pages from different folders, the relative URL changes. You can solve this problem in three ways.

First, you can replace all the HTML elements that use relative URLs with ASP.NET controls. An ASP.NET control automatically reinterprets a relative URL as relative to the Master Page.

NOTE

Relative URLs used by ASP.NET controls in a Master Page are automatically reinterpreted relative to the Master Page. This process of reinterpretation is called *rebasing*. Only ASP.NET control properties decorated with the `UrlProperty` attribute are rebased.

Second, you can avoid relative URLs and use absolute URLs. For example, if your application is named MyApp, you can use the following <img> tag to display an image file located in the `MasterPages` folder:

```
<img src="/MyApp/MasterPages/Picture.gif" />
```

The disadvantage of using absolute URLs is that they make it difficult to change the location of a web application. If the name of your application changes, the absolute URLs no longer work and you end up with a bunch of broken images and links.

The final option is to use the `Page.ResolveUrl()` method to translate an application-relative URL into an absolute URL. This approach is illustrated with the page in Listing 5.10. The `Page.ResolveUrl()` method is used with the <img> tag in the body of the Master Page, which displays the website logo.

LISTING 5.10   MasterPages\ImageMaster.master

```
<%@ Master Language="C#" %>
<!DOCTYPE html PUBLIC "-//W3C//DTD XHTML 1.1//EN"
"http://www.w3.org/TR/xhtml11/DTD/xhtml11.dtd">
<html xmlns="http://www.w3.org/1999/xhtml" >
<head id="Head1" runat="server">
    <title>Image Master</title>
</head>
<body>
    <form id="form1" runat="server">
    <div>

    <img src='<%=Page.ResolveUrl("~/MasterPages/Logo.gif") %>' alt="Website Logo" />

    <asp:contentplaceholder id="ContentPlaceHolder1" runat="server" />

    </div>
    </form>
</body>
</html>
```

The Master Page in Listing 5.10 is in a folder named MasterPages. This folder also includes an image named Logo.gif. This image displays with the following HTML tag:

```
<img src='<%=Page.ResolveUrl("~/MasterPages/Logo.gif") %>' alt="Website Logo" />
```

The Page.ResolveUrl() method converts the tilde into the correct path for the current application directory.

The content page in Listing 5.11 uses the Master Page and correctly displays the website logo (see Figure 5.5):

LISTING 5.11   ImageContent.aspx

```
<%@ Page Language="C#" MasterPageFile="~/MasterPages/ImageMaster.master" %>


<asp:Content
    ID="Content1"
    ContentPlaceHolderID="ContentPlaceHolder1"
    Runat="Server">

    <h1>Content</h1>

</asp:Content>
```

FIGURE 5.5   Displaying a Master Page relative image.

Registering Master Pages in Web Configuration

You can apply a Master Page to every content page in a particular folder or every content page in an entire application. Rather than add a `MasterPageFile` attribute to individual content pages, you can add a configuration option to the web configuration file.

For example, the web configuration file in Listing 5.12 applies the `SimpleMaster.master` Master Page to every page contained in the same folder (or subfolder) as the web configuration file.

LISTING 5.12   FolderA\Web.Config

```
<?xml version="1.0"?>
<configuration>
<system.web>
  <pages masterPageFile="~/SimpleMaster.master" />
</system.web>
</configuration>
```

The Master Page is applied only to content pages. If a page does not contain any `Content` controls—it is a normal ASP.NET page— the Master Page is ignored.

You can override the Master Page configured in the web configuration file in the case of a particular content page. In other words, a `MasterPageFile` attribute in a content page takes precedence over a Master Page specified in the web configuration file.

Modifying Master Page Content

Master Pages enable you to display the same content in multiple content pages. You quickly discover that you need to override the content displayed by a Master Page in the case of particular content pages.

For example, normally the Master Page contains the opening and closing HTML tags, including the `<title>` tag. This means that every content page displays the same title. Normally, you want each page to display a unique title.

In this section, you learn multiple techniques of modifying Master Page content from a content page.

Using the `Title` Attribute

If you need to modify only the title displayed in each content page, you can take advantage of the `<%@ Page %>` directive's `Title` attribute. This attribute accepts any string value.

For example, the page in Listing 5.13 includes a `Title` attribute, which sets the title of the current content page to the value `Content Page Title`.

LISTING 5.13   TitleContent.aspx

```
<%@ Page Language="C#" MasterPageFile="~/SimpleMaster.master"
  Title="Content Page Title" %>

<asp:Content
    ID="Content1"
    ContentPlaceHolderID="ContentPlaceHolder1"
    Runat="Server">
    Content in the first column
    <br />Content in the first column
    <br />Content in the first column
    <br />Content in the first column
    <br />Content in the first column
</asp:Content>

<asp:Content
    ID="Content2"
    ContentPlaceHolderID="ContentPlaceHolder2"
    Runat="Server">
```

```
    Content in the second column
    <br />Content in the second column
    <br />Content in the second column
    <br />Content in the second column
    <br />Content in the second column
</asp:Content>
```

There is one requirement for the Title attribute to work. The HTML <head> tag in the Master Page must be a server-side Head tag. In other words, the <head> tag must include the runat="server" attribute. When you create a new Web Form or Master Page in Visual Web Developer, a server-side <head> tag is automatically created.

Using the Page Header Property

If you need to programmatically change the Title or CSS rules included in a Master Page, you can use the Page.Header property. This property returns an object that implements the IPageHeader interface. This interface has the following two properties:

▶ StyleSheet

▶ Title

For example, the content page in Listing 5.14 uses the SimpleMaster.master Master Page. It changes the Title and background color of the Master Page.

LISTING 5.14   HeaderContent.aspx

```
<%@ Page Language="C#" MasterPageFile="~/SimpleMaster.master" %>
<script runat="server">

    void Page_Load()
    {
        // Change the title
        Page.Header.Title = String.Format("Header Content ({0})", DateTime.Now);

        // Change the background color
        Style myStyle = new Style();
        myStyle.BackColor = System.Drawing.Color.Red;
        Page.Header.StyleSheet.CreateStyleRule(myStyle, null, "html");
    }

</script>
<asp:Content
    ID="Content1"
    ContentPlaceHolderID="ContentPlaceHolder1"
    Runat="Server">
    Content in the first column
    <br />Content in the first column
```

```
    <br />Content in the first column
    <br />Content in the first column
    <br />Content in the first column
</asp:Content>

<asp:Content
    ID="Content2"
    ContentPlaceHolderID="ContentPlaceHolder2"
    Runat="Server">
    Content in the second column
    <br />Content in the second column
    <br />Content in the second column
    <br />Content in the second column
    <br />Content in the second column
</asp:Content>
```

The Page.Header property returns the server-side <head> tag contained in the Master Page. You can cast the object returned by this property to an HTMLHead control.

You can modify other header tags by using page properties. For example, the page in Listing 5.15 modifies the Master Page <meta> tags (the tags used by search engines when indexing a page).

LISTING 5.15   MetaContent.aspx

```
<%@ Page Language="C#" MasterPageFile="~/SimpleMaster.master" %>

<script runat="server">

    void Page_Load()
    {
        // Create Meta Description
        Page.MetaDescription = "A sample of using the ASP.NET 4.0 Meta Properties";

        // Create Meta Keywords
        Page.MetaKeywords = "MetaDescription,MetaKeywords,ASP.NET";
    }

</script>

<asp:Content
    ID="Content1"
    ContentPlaceHolderID="ContentPlaceHolder1"
    Runat="Server">
    Content in the first column
```

```
    <br />Content in the first column
    <br />Content in the first column
    <br />Content in the first column
    <br />Content in the first column
</asp:Content>

<asp:Content
    ID="Content2"
    ContentPlaceHolderID="ContentPlaceHolder2"
    Runat="Server">
    Content in the second column
    <br />Content in the second column
    <br />Content in the second column
    <br />Content in the second column
    <br />Content in the second column
</asp:Content>
```

The Page_Load() method in Listing 5.15 uses two page-level properties. The first represents a Meta Description tag, and the second represents a Meta Keywords tag. When the page is rendered, the following tags are added to the <head> tag:

```
<meta name="description" content="A sample of using HtmlMeta controls" />
<meta name="keywords" content="HtmlMeta,Page.Header,ASP.NET" />
```

Exposing Master Page Properties

You can expose properties and methods from a Master Page and modify the properties and methods from a particular content page. For example, the Master Page in Listing 5.16 includes a public property named BodyTitle.

LISTING 5.16   PropertyMaster.master

```
<%@ Master Language="C#" %>
<!DOCTYPE html PUBLIC "-//W3C//DTD XHTML 1.1//EN"
"http://www.w3.org/TR/xhtml11/DTD/xhtml11.dtd">
<script runat="server">

    public string BodyTitle
    {
        get { return ltlBodyTitle.Text; }
        set { ltlBodyTitle.Text = value; }
    }
```

```
</script>
<html xmlns="http://www.w3.org/1999/xhtml" >
<head id="Head1" runat="server">
    <style type="text/css">
        html
        {
            background-color:silver;
        }
        .content
        {
            margin:auto;
            width:700px;
            background-color:white;
            padding:10px;
        }
        h1
        {
            border-bottom:solid 1px blue;
        }
    </style>
    <title>Property Master</title>
</head>
<body>
    <form id="form1" runat="server">
    <div class="content">
    <h1><asp:Literal ID="ltlBodyTitle" runat="server" /></h1>
    <asp:contentplaceholder
        id="ContentPlaceHolder1"
        runat="server" />
    </div>
    </form>
</body>
</html>
```

The BodyTitle property enables you to assign a title rendered in a header tag in the body of the page (see Figure 5.6).

Because the BodyTitle property is exposed as a public property, you can modify it from a particular content page. The page in Listing 5.17 assigns the value "The Body Title" to the BodyTitle property.

LISTING 5.17 PropertyContent.aspx

```
<%@ Page Language="C#" MasterPageFile="~/PropertyMaster.master" %>
<%@ MasterType VirtualPath="~/PropertyMaster.master" %>
<script runat="server">

    void Page_Load()
    {
        if (!Page.IsPostBack)
        {
            Master.BodyTitle = "The Body Title";
        }
    }
</script>
<asp:Content
    ID="Content1"
    ContentPlaceHolderID="ContentPlaceHolder1"
    Runat="Server">
    Content, Content, Content, Content
    <br />Content, Content, Content, Content
    <br />Content, Content, Content, Content
    <br />Content, Content, Content, Content
    <br />Content, Content, Content, Content
</asp:Content>
```

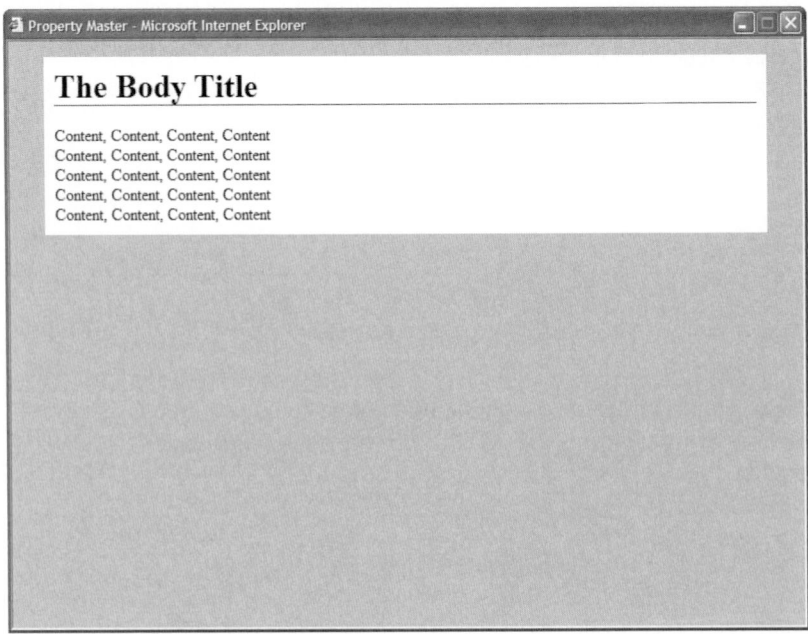

FIGURE 5.6 Displaying a body title.

You should notice several things about the page in Listing 5.17. First, you can refer to the Master Page by using the `Master` property. In the `Page_Load()` method in Listing 5.17, the `BodyTitle` property of the Master Page is assigned a value with the following line of code:

```
Master.BodyTitle = "The Body Title";
```

The page in Listing 5.17 includes a `<%@ MasterType %>` directive. This directive automatically casts the value of the Master property to the type of the Master Page. In other words, it casts the Master Page to the `PropertyMaster` type instead of the generic `MasterPage` type.

If you want to refer to a custom property in a Master Page, such as the `BodyTitle` property, the value of the `Master` property must be cast to the right type. The `BodyTitle` property is not a property of the generic `MasterPage` class, but it is a property of the `PropertyMaster` class.

Using `FindControl` with Master Pages

In the previous section, you learned how to modify a property of a control located in a Master Page from a content page by exposing a property from the Master Page. You have an alternative here. If you need to modify a control in a Master Page, you can use the `FindControl()` method in a content page.

For example, the Master Page in Listing 5.18 includes a Literal control named `BodyTitle`. This Master Page does not include any custom properties.

LISTING 5.18 FindMaster.master

```
<%@ Master Language="C#" %>
<!DOCTYPE html PUBLIC "-//W3C//DTD XHTML 1.1//EN"
"http://www.w3.org/TR/xhtml11/DTD/xhtml11.dtd">
<html xmlns="http://www.w3.org/1999/xhtml" >
<head id="Head1" runat="server">
    <style type="text/css">
        html
        {
            background-color:silver;
        }
        .content
        {
            margin:auto;
            width:700px;
            background-color:white;
            padding:10px;
        }
        h1
        {
```

```
                border-bottom:solid 1px blue;
            }

        </style>
        <title>Find Master</title>
</head>
<body>
        <form id="form1" runat="server">
        <div class="content">
        <h1><asp:Literal ID="ltlBodyTitle" runat="server" /></h1>
        <asp:contentplaceholder
            id="ContentPlaceHolder1"
            runat="server" />
        </div>
        </form>
</body>
</html>
```

The content page in Listing 5.19 modifies the Text property of the Literal control located in the Master Page. The content page uses the FindControl() method to retrieve the Literal control from the Master Page.

LISTING 5.19 FindContent.aspx

```
<%@ Page Language="C#" MasterPageFile="~/FindMaster.master" %>
<script runat="server">

    void Page_Load()
    {
        if (!Page.IsPostBack)
        {
            Literal ltlBodyTitle = (Literal)Master.FindControl("ltlBodyTitle");
            ltlBodyTitle.Text = "The Body Title";
        }
    }
</script>
<asp:Content
    ID="Content1"
    ContentPlaceHolderID="ContentPlaceHolder1"
    Runat="Server">
    Content, Content, Content, Content
    <br />Content, Content, Content, Content
    <br />Content, Content, Content, Content
```

```
    <br />Content, Content, Content, Content
    <br />Content, Content, Content, Content
</asp:Content>
```

The FindControl() method enables you to search a naming container for a control with a particular ID. The method returns a reference to the control.

Loading Master Pages Dynamically

You can associate different Master Pages dynamically with a content page. This is useful in two situations.

First, you can enable the users of your website to customize the appearance of the website by loading different Master Pages. You can display a menu of Master Pages and allow your users to pick their favorite layout.

Another situation in which loading Master Pages dynamically is useful concerns co-branding. Imagine that your company needs to make its website look like a partner website. When users link to your website from the partner website, you don't want users to know that they are traveling to a new website. You can maintain this illusion by dynamically loading different Master Pages based on a query string passed from a partner website.

A Master Page is merged with a content page early in the page execution life cycle. This means that you cannot dynamically load a Master Page during the Page Load event. The only event during which you can load a Master Page is during the Page PreInit event. This is the first event raised during the page execution life cycle.

For example, the content page in Listing 5.20 dynamically loads one of two Master Pages named Dynamic1.master and Dynamic2.master.

LISTING 5.20   DynamicContent.aspx

```
<%@ Page Language="C#" MasterPageFile="~/Dynamic1.master" %>
<script runat="server">

    protected void Page_PreInit(object sender, EventArgs e)
    {
        if (Request["master"] != null)
        {
            switch (Request["master"])
            {
                case "Dynamic1":
                    Profile.MasterPageFile = "Dynamic1.master";
                    break;
```

```
                case "Dynamic2":
                    Profile.MasterPageFile = "Dynamic2.master";
                    break;
            }
        }

        MasterPageFile = Profile.MasterPageFile;
    }
</script>

<asp:Content
    ID="Content1"
    ContentPlaceHolderID="ContentPlaceHolder1"
    Runat="Server">

    Select a Master Page:
    <ul class="selectMaster">
        <li>
        <a href="DynamicContent.aspx?master=Dynamic1">Dynamic Master 1</a>
        </li>
        <li>
        <a href="DynamicContent.aspx?master=Dynamic2">Dynamic Master 2</a>
        </li>
    </ul>

</asp:Content>
```

The page in Listing 5.20 contains two links. Both links include a query string parameter named master, which represents the name of a Master Page. When you click the first link, the Dynamic1.master Master Page loads (see Figure 5.7) and when you click the second link, the Dynamic2.master Master Page loads (see Figure 5.8).

The page in Listing 5.20 includes a Page_PreInit() event handler. This handler grabs the value of the master query string parameter and assigns the value of this parameter to a Profile property. Next, the value of the Profile property is assigned to the page's MasterPageFile property. Assigning a value to the MasterPageFile property causes a Master Page to be dynamically loaded.

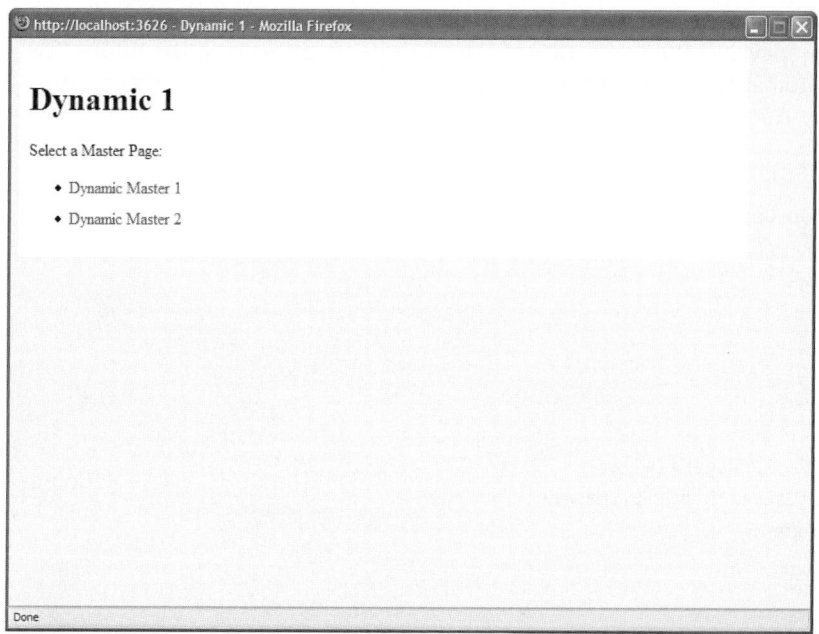

FIGURE 5.7   Displaying the Dynamic1 Master Page.

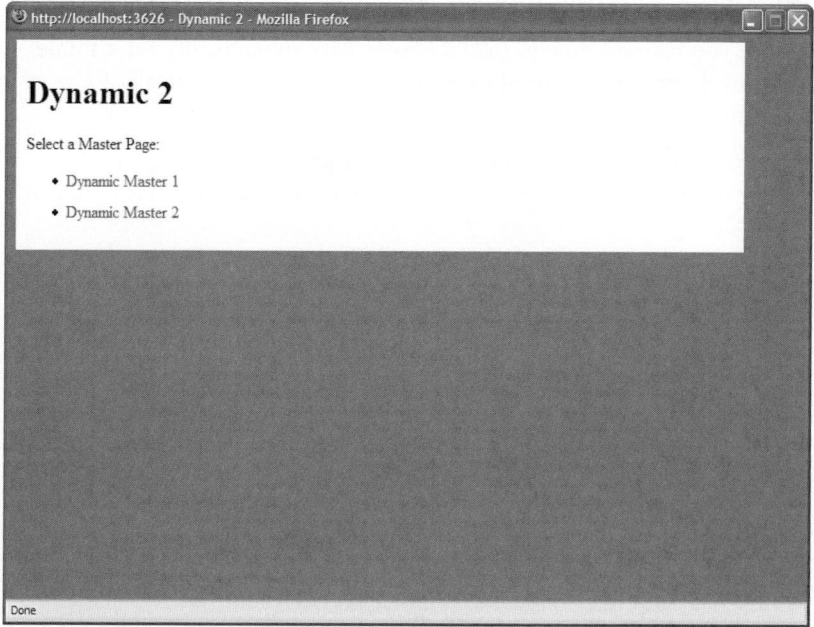

FIGURE 5.8   Displaying the Dynamic2 Master Page.

Because the name of the Master Page is assigned to a `Profile` property, the selected Master Page loads for a user even if the user returns to the website many years in the future. The `Profile` object automatically persists the values of its properties for a user across multiple visits to a website. The `Profile` is defined in the web configuration file contained in Listing 5.21.

LISTING 5.21   Web.Config

```
<?xml version="1.0"?>
<configuration>
  <system.web>
    <profile>
      <properties>
        <add
          name="MasterPageFile"
          defaultValue="Dynamic1.master" />
      </properties>
    </profile>
  </system.web>
</configuration>
```

Loading Master Pages Dynamically for Multiple Content Pages

In the previous section, you learned how to load a Master Page dynamically for a single page in a website. However, what if you need to load a Master Page dynamically for every content page in a website?

The easiest way to apply the same logic to multiple content pages is to create a new base `Page` class. The file in Listing 5.22 contains a new base `Page` class named `DynamicMasterPage`.

> **NOTE**
>
> Add the file in Listing 5.22 to your application's App_Code folder.

LISTING 5.22   DynamicMasterPage.cs

```
using System;
using System.Web.UI;
using System.Web.Profile;
```

```
public class DynamicMasterPage : Page
{

    protected override void OnPreInit(EventArgs e)
    {
        this.MasterPageFile = (string)Context.Profile["MasterPageFile"];
        base.OnPreInit(e);
    }


}
```

The class in Listing 5.22 inherits from the Page class. However, it overrides the base Page class's OnPreInit() method and adds the logic for loading a Master Page dynamically.

After you create a new base Page class, you need to register it in the web configuration file. The web configuration file in Listing 5.23 contains the necessary settings.

LISTING 5.23 Web.config

```
<?xml version="1.0"?>
<configuration>
  <system.web>

    <pages pageBaseType="DynamicMasterPage" />

    <profile>
      <properties>
        <add
          name="MasterPageFile"
          defaultValue="Dynamic1.master" />
      </properties>
    </profile>
  </system.web>
</configuration>
```

After you register the DynamicMasterPage class as the base Page class, every page in your application automatically inherits from the new base class. Every page inherits the new OnPreInit() method, and every page loads a Master Page dynamically.

Summary

In this chapter, you learned how to share the same content among multiple pages in an application by taking advantage of Master Pages. In the first section, you learned how to create a Master Page and apply it to multiple content pages. You also learned how to nest Master Pages and how to register a Master Page in the web configuration file.

The next section explored various techniques of modifying a Master Page from a particular content page. You learned how to use the `Title` attribute, use the `Page.Header` property, expose properties in a Master Page, and use the `FindControl()` method.

Finally, you learned how you can dynamically load different Master Pages and associate a particular Master Page with a particular content page at runtime. You learned how you can save a user's Master Page preference by using the `Profile` object.

Designing Websites with Themes

An ASP.NET Theme enables you to apply a consistent style to the pages in your website. You can use a Theme to control the appearance of both the HTML elements and ASP.NET controls that appear in a page.

Themes are different than Master Pages. A Master Page enables you to share content across multiple pages in a website. A Theme, on the other hand, enables you to control the appearance of the content.

In this chapter, you learn how to create and apply ASP.NET Themes. First, you learn how to create Skins, which enable you to modify the properties of an ASP.NET control that have an effect on its appearance. You learn how to create both Default and Named Skins.

Next, you learn how to format both HTML elements and ASP.NET controls by adding Cascading Style Sheets (CSS) to a Theme, which enable you to control the appearance and layout of pages in a website in a standards-compliant manner.

You also learn how you can create Global Themes, which can be used by multiple applications located on the same server. You learn how to use Global Themes with both file systems and HTTP-based websites.

Finally, you learn how to load Themes and Skins dynamically at runtime. You build a page that each user of a website can customize by skinning.

Creating Themes

You create a Theme by adding a new folder to a special folder in your application named App_Themes. Each folder that you add to the App_Themes folder represents a different Theme.

If the App_Themes folder doesn't exist in your application, you can create it. It must be located in the root of your application.

VISUAL WEB DEVELOPER NOTE

When using Visual Web Developer, you can create a new Theme folder by right-clicking the name of your project in the Solution Explorer window and selecting Add Folder, Theme Folder.

A Theme folder can contain a variety of different types of files, including images and text files. You also can organize the contents of a Theme folder by adding multiple subfolders to a Theme folder.

Following are the most important types of files in a Theme folder:

▶ Skin Files

▶ Cascading Style Sheet Files

In the following sections, you learn how to add both Skin files and CSS files to a Theme.

WARNING

Be careful about how you name your Theme (the folder name). The contents of a Theme folder are automatically compiled in the background into a new class. Don't name a Theme with a class name that conflicts with an existing class name in your project.

Adding Skins to Themes

A Theme can contain one or more Skin files. A Skin enables you to modify any of the properties of an ASP.NET control that have an effect on its appearance.

For example, imagine that you decide that you want every TextBox control in your web application to appear with a yellow background color and a dotted border. If you add the file in Listing 6.1 to the Simple Theme (the App_Themes\Simple folder), you can modify the appearance of all TextBox controls in all pages that use the Simple Theme.

LISTING 6.1 Simple\TextBox.skin

```
<asp:TextBox
    BackColor="Yellow"
    BorderStyle="Dotted"
    Runat="Server" />
```

The Skin file in Listing 6.1 is named `TextBox.skin`. You can name a Skin file anything you want. I recommend following a naming convention in which you name the Skin file after the name of the control that the Skin modifies.

A Theme folder can contain a single Skin file that contains Skins for hundreds of controls. Alternatively, a Theme can contain hundreds of Skin files, each of which contains a single Skin. It doesn't matter how you organize your Skins into files because everything in a Theme folder eventually gets compiled into one Theme class.

The Skin file in Listing 6.1 contains a declaration of a `TextBox` control. The `TextBox` control includes a `BackColor` property set to the value Yellow and a `BorderStyle` property set to the value Dotted.

The `TextBox` control includes a `Runat="Server"` attribute, but it does not include an `ID` attribute. You must always include a `Runat` attribute, but you can never include the `ID` attribute when declaring a control in a Skin.

> **NOTE**
>
> You can't create a Skin that applies to the properties of a User Control. However, you can skin the controls contained inside a User Control.

The Skin is applied to every page to which the Simple Theme is applied. For example, the page in Listing 6.2 uses the Simple Theme.

LISTING 6.2 ShowSkin.aspx

```
<%@ Page Language="C#" Theme="Simple" %>
<!DOCTYPE html PUBLIC "-//W3C//DTD XHTML 1.1//EN"
"http://www.w3.org/TR/xhtml11/DTD/xhtml11.dtd">
<html xmlns="http://www.w3.org/1999/xhtml" >
<head runat="server">
    <title>Show Skin</title>
</head>
<body>
    <form id="form1" runat="server">
    <div>

    <asp:TextBox
```

```
        Runat="server" />

    </div>
    </form>
</body>
</html>
```

The page in Listing 6.2 includes a Theme attribute in its `<%@ Page %>` directive. This attribute causes the Simple Theme to be applied to the page.

When you open the page in Listing 6.2, the Label control appears with a yellow background color and dotted border. This is the background color and border specified by the Theme (see Figure 6.1).

Only certain control properties are "themeable." In other words, you can create a Skin file that modifies only certain properties of a control. In general, you can use a Skin to modify properties that have an effect on a control's appearance but not its behavior. For example, you can modify the `BackColor` property of a `TextBox` control but not its `AutoPostBack` property.

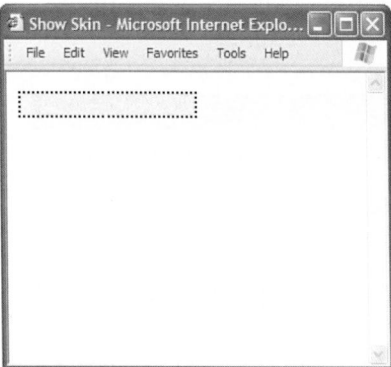

FIGURE 6.1   Using a TextBox Skin.

NOTE

By default, all control properties are themeable (can be modified in a Skin file). However, certain control properties are decorated with the `Themeable(False)` attribute, which disables theming.

Creating Named Skins

In the previous section, we created something called a Default Skin. A Default Skin is applied to every instance of a control of a certain type. For example, a Default Skin is applied to every instance of a TextBox control.

You also have the option of creating a Named Skin. When you create a Named Skin, you can decide when you want to apply the Skin. For example, you might want required fields in a form to appear with a red border. In that case, you can create a Named Skin and apply the Skin to only particular TextBox controls.

The Skin in Listing 6.3 contains both a Default Skin and a Named Skin for a TextBox control.

LISTING 6.3   Simple2\TextBox.skin

```
<asp:TextBox
    SkinID="DashedTextBox"
    BorderStyle="Dashed"
    BorderWidth="5px"
    Runat="Server" />

<asp:TextBox
    BorderStyle="Double"
    BorderWidth="5px"
    Runat="Server" />
```

The first TextBox in Listing 6.3 is an example of a Named Skin and includes a SkinID property. The SkinID property represents the name of the Named Skin. You use the value of this property when applying the Skin in a page.

The file in Listing 6.3 also includes a Default Skin for a TextBox control. The Default Skin does not include a SkinID property. If a TextBox control in a page is not associated with a Named Skin, the Default Skin is applied to the TextBox.

A Theme can contain only one Default Skin for each type of control. However, a Theme can contain as many Named Skins as you want. Each Named Skin must have a unique name.

The page in Listing 6.4 contains two TextBox controls. The first TextBox control includes a SkinID attribute. This attribute causes the Named Skin to be applied to the control. The second TextBox, on the other hand, does not include a SkinID property. The Default Skin is applied to the second TextBox control.

LISTING 6.4   ShowNamedSkin.aspx

```
<%@ Page Language="C#" Theme="Simple2" %>
<!DOCTYPE html PUBLIC "-//W3C//DTD XHTML 1.1//EN"
"http://www.w3.org/TR/xhtml11/DTD/xhtml11.dtd">
<html xmlns="http://www.w3.org/1999/xhtml" >
<head runat="server">
    <title>Show Named Skin</title>
</head>
<body>
    <form id="form1" runat="server">
    <div>

    <asp:TextBox
        id="txtFirstName"
        SkinID="DashedTextBox"
        Runat="server" />

    <br /><br />

    <asp:TextBox
        id="txtLastName"
        Runat="server" />

    </div>
    </form>
</body>
</html>
```

When you open the page in Listing 6.4, the first TextBox appears with a dashed border, and the second TextBox appears with a double border (see Figure 6.2).

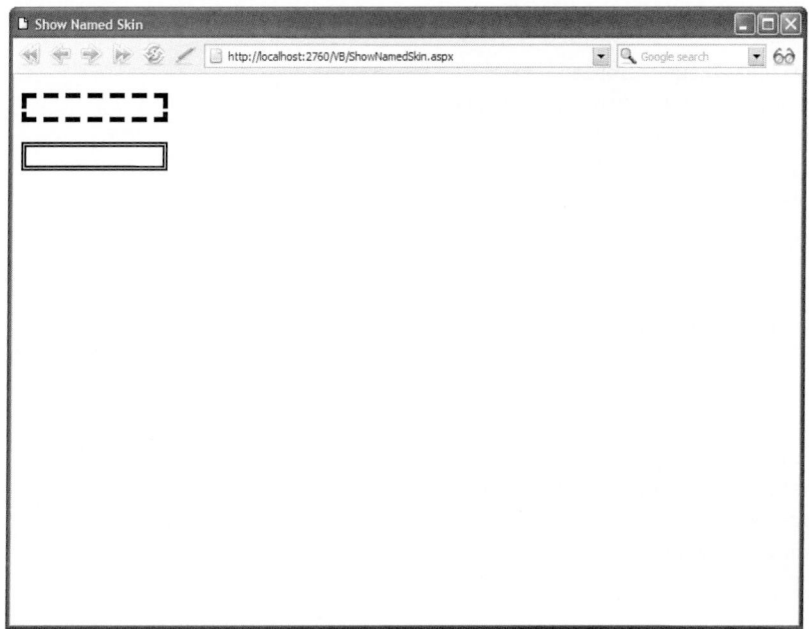

FIGURE 6.2   Using Named Skins.

Themes Versus `StyleSheetThemes`

When you apply a Theme to a page, the Skins in the Theme override any existing properties of the controls in the page. In other words, properties in a Skin override properties in a page.

For example, imagine that you create the Skin in Listing 6.5.

LISTING 6.5   Simple3\Label.skin

```
<asp:Label
    BackColor="Orange"
    Runat="Server" />
```

The Skin in Listing 6.5 sets the background color of all Label controls to the color Orange.

Now, image that you apply the Skin in Listing 6.5 to the ASP.NET page in Listing 6.6.

LISTING 6.6   ShowSkinTheme.aspx

```
<%@ Page Language="C#" Theme="Simple3" %>
<!DOCTYPE html PUBLIC "-//W3C//DTD XHTML 1.1//EN"
"http://www.w3.org/TR/xhtml11/DTD/xhtml11.dtd">
<html xmlns="http://www.w3.org/1999/xhtml" >
<head runat="server">
    <title>Show Skin Theme</title>
</head>
<body>
    <form id="form1" runat="server">
    <div>

    <asp:Label
        id="Label1"
        Text="What color background do I have?"
        BackColor="red"
        Runat="server" />

    </div>
    </form>
</body>
</html>
```

The page in Listing 6.6 includes a Label that has a BackColor property that is set to the value Red. However, when you open the page, the BackColor declared in the Skin overrides the BackColor declared in the page, and the Label displays with an orange background.

The default behavior of Themes makes it easy to modify the design of an existing website. You can override any existing control properties that have an effect on the appearance of the control.

However, there are situations in which you might want to override Skin properties. For example, you might want to display every Label in your website with an orange background color except for one Label. In that case, it would be nice if there were a way to override the Skin property.

You can override Skin properties by applying a Theme to a page with the StyleSheetTheme attribute instead of the Theme attribute. For example, the page in Listing 6.7 uses the StyleSheetTheme attribute to apply the Simple3 Theme to the page.

LISTING 6.7   ShowSkinStyleSheetTheme.aspx

```
<%@ Page Language="C#" StyleSheetTheme="Simple3" %>
<!DOCTYPE html PUBLIC "-//W3C//DTD XHTML 1.1//EN"
"http://www.w3.org/TR/xhtml11/DTD/xhtml11.dtd">
<html xmlns="http://www.w3.org/1999/xhtml" >
<head id="Head1" runat="server">
    <title>Show Skin Style Sheet Theme</title>
</head>
<body>
    <form id="form1" runat="server">
    <div>

    <asp:Label
        id="Label1"
        Text="What color background do I have?"
        BackColor="red"
        Runat="server" />

    </div>
    </form>
</body>
</html>
```

The <%@Page %> directive in Listing 6.7 includes a StyleSheetTheme attribute. When you open the page in Listing 6.7 in a web browser, the Label displays with a red background color instead of the orange background color specified by the Theme.

Disabling Themes

Every ASP.NET control includes an EnableTheming property. You can use the EnableTheming property to prevent a Skin from being applied to a particular control in a page.

For example, the page in Listing 6.8 contains two Calendar controls. The second Calendar control has its EnableTheming property set to the value False (see Figure 6.3).

LISTING 6.8   ShowEnableTheming.aspx

```
<%@ Page Language="C#" Theme="Simple4" %>
<html xmlns="http://www.w3.org/1999/xhtml" >
<head runat="server">
    <title>Show EnableTheming</title>
</head>
```

```
<body>
    <form id="form1" runat="server">
    <div>

    <asp:Calendar
        id="Calendar1"
        Runat="server" />

    <br /><br />

    <asp:Calendar
        id="Calendar2"
        EnableTheming="false"
        Runat="server" />

    </div>
    </form>
</body>
</html>
```

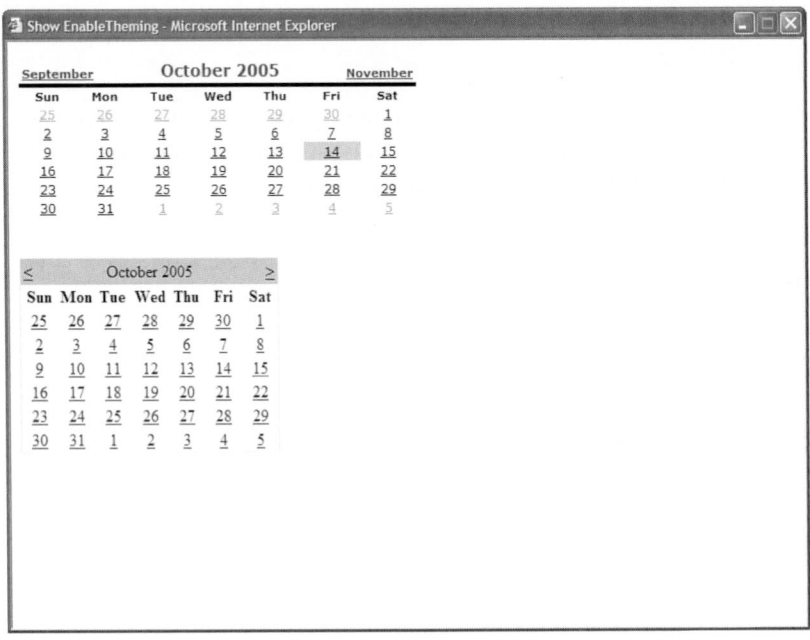

FIGURE 6.3   Disabling a Theme.

The page in Listing 6.8 includes a Theme attribute that applies the Simple Theme to the page. The Simple Theme includes the Skin in Listing 6.9.

LISTING 6.9   Simple4\Calendar.skin

```
<asp:Calendar
    BackColor="White"
    BorderColor="White"
    BorderWidth="1px"
    Font-Names="Verdana"
    Font-Size="9pt"
    ForeColor="Black"
    NextPrevFormat="FullMonth"
    Width="400px"
    Runat="Server">
    <SelectedDayStyle
        BackColor="#333399"
        ForeColor="White" />
    <OtherMonthDayStyle
        ForeColor="#999999" />
    <TodayDayStyle
        BackColor="#CCCCCC" />
    <NextPrevStyle
        Font-Bold="True"
        Font-Size="8pt"
        ForeColor="#333333"
        VerticalAlign="Bottom" />
    <DayHeaderStyle
        Font-Bold="True"
        Font-Size="8pt" />
    <TitleStyle
        BackColor="White"
        BorderColor="Black"
        BorderWidth="4px"
        Font-Bold="True"
        Font-Size="12pt"
        ForeColor="#333399" />
</asp:Calendar>
```

When you open the page in Listing 6.9 in a web browser, the Skin is applied to the first Calendar control but not the second Calendar control.

Registering Themes in the Web Configuration File

Rather than add the `Theme` or `StyleSheetTheme` attribute to each and every page to which you want to apply a Theme, you can register a Theme for all pages in your application in the web configuration file.

The Web.Config file in Listing 6.10 applies the Site Theme to every page in an application.

LISTING 6.10   Web.Config

```
<?xml version="1.0"?>
<configuration>
<system.web>

  <pages theme="Site" />

</system.web>
</configuration>
```

Rather than use the `theme` attribute, you can use the `styleSheetTheme` attribute to apply a Theme to the pages in an application. If you use the `styleSheetTheme` attribute, you can override particular Skin properties in a page.

The web configuration file in Listing 6.11 includes the `styleSheetTheme` attribute.

LISTING 6.11   Web.Config

```
<?xml version="1.0"?>
<configuration>
<system.web>

  <pages styleSheetTheme="Site" />

</system.web>
</configuration>
```

After you enable a Theme for an application, you can disable the Theme for a particular page by using the `EnableTheming` attribute with the `<%@ Page %>` directive. For example, the page in Listing 6.12 disables any Themes configured in the web configuration file.

LISTING 6.12   DisablePageTheme.aspx

```
<%@ Page Language="C#" EnableTheming="false" %>
<!DOCTYPE html PUBLIC "-//W3C//DTD XHTML 1.1//EN"
"http://www.w3.org/TR/xhtml11/DTD/xhtml11.dtd">
<html xmlns="http://www.w3.org/1999/xhtml" >
```

```
<head runat="server">
    <title>Disable Page Theme</title>
</head>
<body>
    <form id="form1" runat="server">
    <div>

    <asp:Label
        id="Label1"
        Text="Don't Theme Me!"
        Runat="server" />

    </div>
    </form>
</body>
</html>
```

Adding Cascading Style Sheets to Themes

As an alternative to Skins, you can use a CSS file to control the appearance of both the HTML elements and ASP.NET controls contained in a page. If you add a CSS file to a Theme folder, the CSS is automatically applied to every page to which the Theme is applied.

For example, the CSS in Listing 6.13 contains style rules applied to several different HTML elements in a page.

LISTING 6.13   App_Themes\StyleTheme\SimpleStyle.css

```
html
{
    background-color:gray;
    font:14px Georgia,Serif;
}

.content
{
    margin:auto;
    width:600px;
    border:solid 1px black;
    background-color:White;
    padding:10px;
}
```

```
h1
{
    color:Gray;
    font-size:18px;
    border-bottom:solid 1px orange;
}

label
{
    font-weight:bold;
}

input
{
    background-color:Yellow;
    border:double 3px orange;
}

.button
{
    background-color:#eeeeee;
}
```

If you add the SimpleStyle.css file to a Theme named StyleTheme (a folder named
StyleTheme in the App_Themes folder), the Cascading Style Sheet is applied automatically
to the page in Listing 6.14.

LISTING 6.14 ShowSimpleCSS.aspx

```
<%@ Page Language="C#" Theme="StyleTheme" %>
<!DOCTYPE html PUBLIC "-//W3C//DTD XHTML 1.1//EN"
"http://www.w3.org/TR/xhtml11/DTD/xhtml11.dtd">
<html xmlns="http://www.w3.org/1999/xhtml" >
<head id="Head1" runat="server">
    <title>Show Simple CSS</title>
</head>
<body>
    <form id="form1" runat="server">
    <div class="content">

    <h1>Registration Form</h1>

    <asp:Label
        id="lblFirstName"
        Text="First Name:"
```

```
            AssociatedControlID="txtFirstName"
            Runat="server" />
        <br />
        <asp:TextBox
            id="txtFirstName"
            Runat="server" />

        <br /><br />

        <asp:Label
            id="lblLastName"
            Text="Last Name:"
            AssociatedControlID="txtLastName"
            Runat="server" />
        <br />
        <asp:TextBox
            id="txtLastName"
            Runat="server" />

        <br /><br />

        <asp:Button
            id="btnSubmit"
            Text="Submit Form"
            CssClass="button"
            Runat="server" />

    </div>
    </form>
</body>
</html>
```

The CSS is used to style several HTML elements in Listing 6.14 (see Figure 6.4). For example, the Style Sheet sets the background color of the page to the value Gray. It also centers the <div> tag containing the page content.

Because an ASP.NET control renders HTML, the Style Sheet also styles the HTML rendered by the ASP.NET Label, TextBox, and Button controls. An ASP.NET Label control renders an HTML <label> tag and the Style Sheet formats all <label> tags in bold. Both a TextBox control and a Button control render HTML <input> tags. The Style Sheet modifies the border and background color of the <input> tag.

The Button control includes a CssClass attribute. By providing a control with a CssClass attribute, you can target a particular control (or set of controls) in a CSS. In this case, the background color of the <input> tag rendered by the Button control is set to the value #eeeeee (light gray).

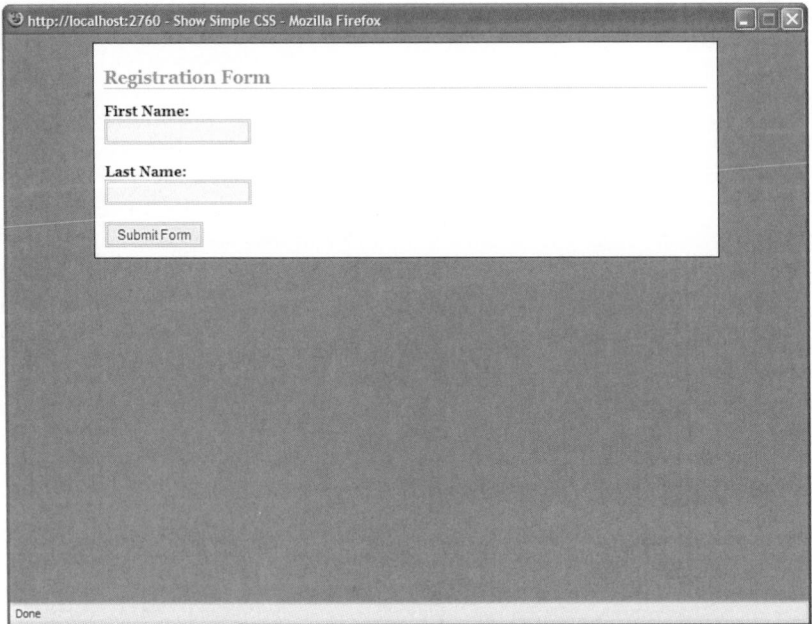

FIGURE 6.4   Styling with Cascading Style Sheets.

I recommend that you do all your web page design by using the method discussed in this section. You should place all your page design in an external CSS located in a Theme folder. In particular, you should not modify the appearance of a control by modifying its properties. Furthermore, you should avoid using Skin files.

The advantage of using Cascading Style Sheets is that they result in leaner and faster loading pages. The more content that you can place in an external Style Sheet, the less content must be loaded each time you make a page request. The contents of an external Style Sheet can be loaded and cached by a browser and applied to all pages in a web application.

If, on the other hand, you modify the appearance of a control by modifying its properties, additional content must be rendered to the browser each time you make a page request. For example, if you modify a Label control's BackColor property, an additional Style attribute is rendered when the Label control is rendered.

Using Skins is no different than setting control properties. Skins also result in bloated pages. For example, if you create a Skin for a Label control, the properties of the Label Skin must be merged with each Label control on each page before the Label is rendered.

> **NOTE**
>
> In this book, I try to avoid formatting controls by using control properties. Instead, I perform all the formatting in a Style Sheet embedded in the page (using the `<style>` tag). I would prefer to place all the control formatting in an external Style Sheet, but that would require creating a separate file for each code sample, which would make this book much longer than it already threatens to be.

Adding Multiple Cascading Style Sheets to a Theme

You can add as many CSS files to a Theme folder as you need. When you add multiple Cascading Style Sheets to a Theme, all the Cascading Style Sheets are applied to a page when the Theme is applied to a page.

The order in which an external Style Sheet is linked to a page can be important. For example, style sheet rules in one Style Sheet can override style sheet rules in another Style Sheet.

When you add multiple Style Sheets to a Theme, the style sheets are linked to a page in alphabetical order (in the order of the Style Sheet filename). For example, if the Theme contains three Style Sheet files named `ThemeA.css`, `ThemeB.css`, and `ThemeC.css`, the following three links are added to a page:

```
<link href="App_Themes/Simple/ThemeA.css" type="text/css" rel="stylesheet" />
<link href="App_Themes/Simple/ThemeB.css" type="text/css" rel="stylesheet" />
<link href="App_Themes/Simple/ThemeC.css" type="text/css" rel="stylesheet" />
```

If you want to control the order in which Style Sheets are applied to a page, you need to follow a naming convention.

Changing Page Layouts with Cascading Style Sheets

Because you can use a Cascading Style Sheet to change the layout of a page, you can use a Theme to control page layout.

For example, the page in Listing 6.15 contains three `<div>` tags. By default, if you open the page, the contents of the `<div>` tags are stacked one on top of another (see Figure 6.5).

FIGURE 6.5   Page without Cascading Style Sheet.

LISTING 6.15   ShowLayout.aspx

```
<%@ Page Language="C#" %>
<!DOCTYPE html PUBLIC "-//W3C//DTD XHTML 1.1//EN"
"http://www.w3.org/TR/xhtml11/DTD/xhtml11.dtd">
<html xmlns="http://www.w3.org/1999/xhtml" >
<head runat="server">
    <title>Show Layout</title>
</head>
<body>
    <form id="form1" runat="server">

    <div id="div1">
        First div content
        <br />First div content
        <br />First div content
        <br />First div content
        <br />First div content
    </div>

    <div id="div2">
        Second div content
```

```
            <br />Second div content
            <br />Second div content
            <br />Second div content
            <br />Second div content
        </div>

        <div id="div3">
            Third div content
            <br />Third div content
            <br />Third div content
            <br />Third div content
            <br />Third div content
        </div>

        </form>
</body>
</html>
```

If you add the Cascading Style Sheet in Listing 6.16, you can modify the layout of the
<div> tags (see Figure 6.6). The Style Sheet in Listing 6.16 displays the <div> tags in three
columns. (The Stylesheet floats each of the <div> tags.) You can appy this stylesheet to
your page using the following line of code in the <head> tag:

```
<link href="float.css" type="text/css" rel="stylesheet" />
```

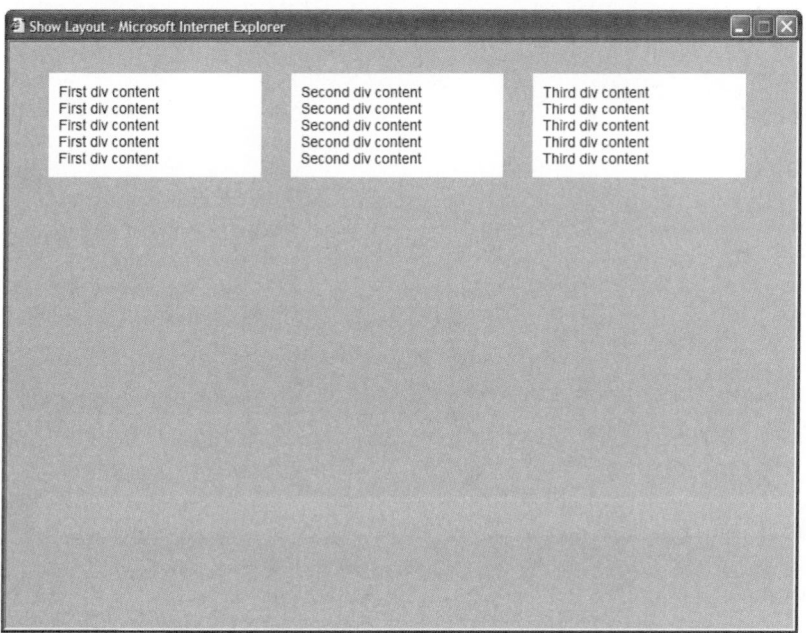

FIGURE 6.6   Using a floating layout.

LISTING 6.16 Float.css

```
html
{
    background-color:Silver;
    font:14px Arial,Sans-Serif;
}

#div1
{
    float:left;
    width:25%;
    margin:15px;
    padding:10px;
    background-color:White;
}

#div2
{
    float:left;
    width:25%;
    margin:15px;
    padding:10px;
    background-color:White;
}

#div3
{
    float:left;
    width:25%;
    margin:15px;
    padding:10px;
    background-color:White;
}
```

Alternatively, you can position the <div> tags absolutely by using the left and top style properties. The Style Sheet in Listing 6.17 reverses the order in which the three <div> tags are displayed (see Figure 6.7).

NOTE

The Cascading Style Sheets in this section work equally well with Internet Explorer, Firefox, and Opera.

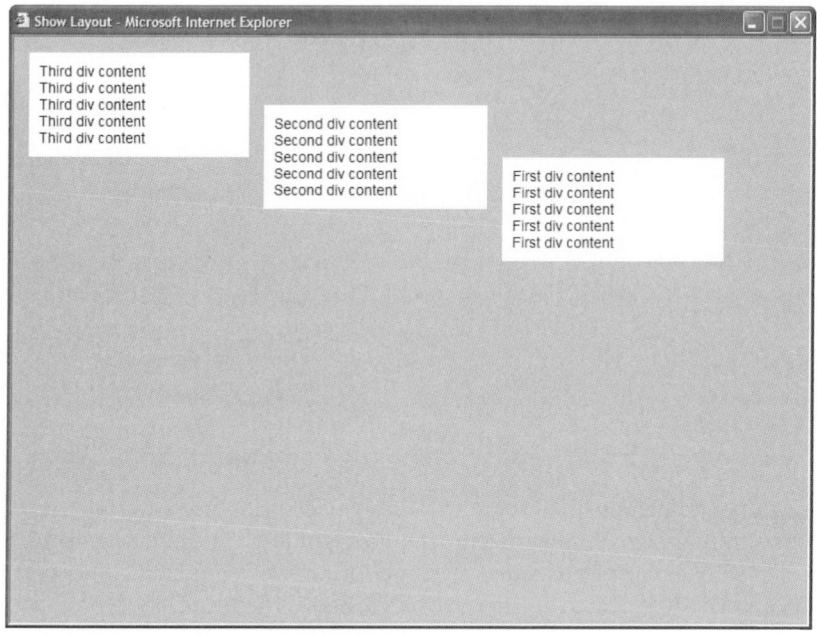

FIGURE 6.7   Using an absolute layout.

LISTING 6.17   Absolute.css

```
html
{
    background-color:Silver;
    font:14px Arial,Sans-Serif;
}

#div3
{
    position:absolute;
    left:15px;
    top:15px;
    width:200px;
    padding:10px;
    background-color:White;
}

#div2
{
    position:absolute;
    left:250px;
    top:65px;
```

```
    width:200px;
    padding:10px;
    background-color:White;
}

#div1
{
    position:absolute;
    left:485px;
    top:115px;
    width:200px;
    padding:10px;
    background-color:White;
}
```

The point of this section is to demonstrate that Cascading Style Sheets are powerful. You can create elaborate website designs simply by creating the right Style Sheet. If you want to see some samples of some amazing website designs performed with Cascading Style Sheets, visit the CSS Zen Garden located at http://www.CSSZenGarden.com.

Creating Global Themes

You can share the same Theme among multiple web applications running on the same web server. A Global Theme can contain both Skin files and CSS files. Creating a Global Theme is useful when you want to create one companywide website design and apply it to all your company's applications.

You create a Global Theme by adding the Theme to the Themes folder located at the following path:

```
WINDOWS\Microsoft.NET\Framework\[version]\ASP.NETClientFiles\Themes
```

After you add a Theme folder to this path, you can immediately start using the Theme in any file system-based website.

If you want to use the Theme in an HTTP-based website, you need to perform an additional step. You must add the Theme folder to the following path:

```
Inetpub\wwwroot\aspnet_client\system_web\[version]\Themes
```

You can copy the Theme to this folder manually or you can use the aspnet_regiis tool to copy the Theme folder. Execute the aspnet_regiis tool from the command line like this:

```
aspnet_regiis -c
```

The `aspnet_regiis` tool is located in the Windows\Microsoft.NET\Framework\[version] folder. You can open a command prompt and navigate to this folder to execute the tool. Alternatively, if you have installed the Microsoft .NET Framework SDK, you can execute the tool by opening the SDK Command Prompt from the Microsoft .NET Framework SDK program group.

Applying Themes Dynamically

You might want to enable each user of your website to customize the appearance of your website by selecting different Themes. Some website users might prefer a green Theme, and other website users might prefer a pink Theme.

You can dynamically apply a Theme to a page by handling the Page `PreInit` event. This event is the first event raised when you request a page. You cannot apply a Theme dynamically in a later event such as the Page `Load` or `PreRender` events.

For example, the page in Listing 6.18 applies either the Green Theme or the Pink Theme to the page depending on which link you click in the page body (see Figure 6.8).

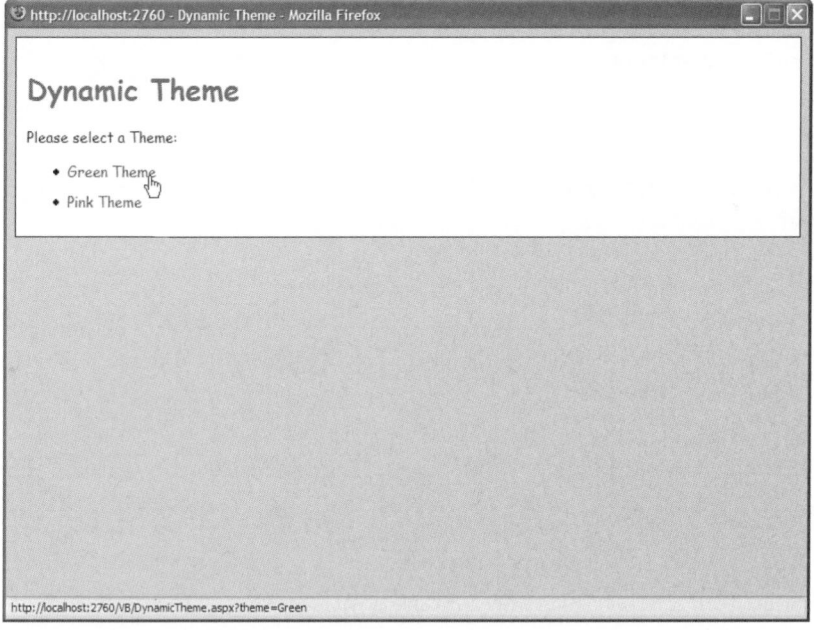

FIGURE 6.8   Selecting a Theme programmatically.

LISTING 6.18   DynamicTheme.aspx

```
<%@ Page Language="C#" %>
<!DOCTYPE html PUBLIC "-//W3C//DTD XHTML 1.1//EN"
"http://www.w3.org/TR/xhtml11/DTD/xhtml11.dtd">
<script runat="server">

    protected void Page_PreInit(object sender, EventArgs e)
    {
        if (Request["theme"] != null)
        {
            switch (Request["theme"])
            {
                case "Green":
                    Profile.userTheme = "GreenTheme";
                    break;
                case "Pink":
                    Profile.userTheme = "PinkTheme";
                    break;
            }
        }
        Theme = Profile.userTheme;
    }
</script>

<html xmlns="http://www.w3.org/1999/xhtml" >
<head runat="server">
    <title>Dynamic Theme</title>
</head>
<body>
    <form id="form1" runat="server">
    <div class="content">

    <h1>Dynamic Theme</h1>

    Please select a Theme:
    <ul>
    <li>
        <a href="DynamicTheme.aspx?theme=Green">Green Theme</a>
    </li>
    <li>
        <a href="DynamicTheme.aspx?theme=Pink">Pink Theme</a>
    </li>
    </ul>
```

```
    </div>
    </form>
</body>
</html>
```

A particular Theme is applied to the page with the help of the Theme property. You can assign the name of any Theme (Theme folder) to this property in the Page PreInit event, and the Theme will be applied to the page.

The selected Theme is stored in the Profile object. When you store information in the Profile object, the information is preserved across multiple visits to the website. So, if a user selects a favorite Theme once, the Theme is applied every time the user returns to the website in the future.

The Profile is defined in the web configuration file in Listing 6.19.

LISTING 6.19   Web.Config

```
<?xml version="1.0"?>
<configuration>
  <system.web>
    <profile>
      <properties>
        <add name="UserTheme" />
      </properties>
    </profile>
  </system.web>
</configuration>
```

Because the control tree has not been created when the PreInit event is raised, you can't refer to any controls in a page. Hyperlinks are used in Listing 6.18 to select a Theme. You could not use a DropDownList control because the DropDownList control would not have been created.

> **NOTE**
>
> If you need to load a Theme dynamically for multiple pages in an application, you can override the OnPreInit() method of the base Page class. This technique is discussed in the "Loading Master Pages Dynamically for Multiple Content Pages" section of Chapter 5, "Designing Websites with Master Pages."

Applying Skins Dynamically

You can apply skins dynamically to particular controls in a page. In the Page PreInit event, you can modify a control's SkinID property programmatically.

For example, the page in Listing 6.20 enables a user to select a favorite skin for a `GridView` control. The `GridView` control displays a list of movies (see Figure 6.9).

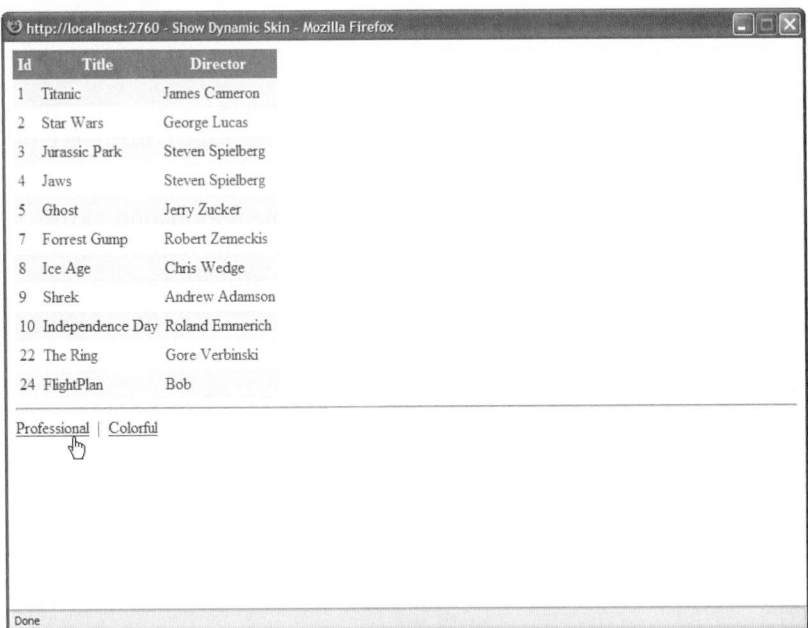

FIGURE 6.9   Applying a Skin programmatically.

LISTING 6.20   ShowDynamicSkin.aspx

```
<%@ Page Language="C#" Theme="DynamicSkin" %>
<!DOCTYPE html PUBLIC "-//W3C//DTD XHTML 1.1//EN"
"http://www.w3.org/TR/xhtml11/DTD/xhtml11.dtd">
<script runat="server">

    protected void Page_PreInit(object sender, EventArgs e)
    {
        if (Request["skin"] != null)
        {
            switch (Request["skin"])
            {
                case "professional":
                    grdMovies.SkinID = "Professional";
                    break;
                case "colorful":
                    grdMovies.SkinID = "Colorful";
```

```
                    break;
            }
        }
    }
</script>
<html xmlns="http://www.w3.org/1999/xhtml" >
<head runat="server">
    <title>Show Dynamic Skin</title>
</head>
<body>
    <form id="form1" runat="server">
    <div>

    <asp:GridView
        id="grdMovies"
        DataSourceID="srcMovies"
        Runat="server" />

     <asp:SqlDataSource
        id="srcMovies"
        ConnectionString="<%$ ConnectionStrings:Movies %>"
        SelectCommand="SELECT Id,Title,Director FROM Movies"
        Runat="server" />

    <hr />

    <a href="showdynamicskin.aspx?skin=professional">Professional</a>
     | 
    <a href="showdynamicskin.aspx?skin=colorful">Colorful</a>

    </div>
    </form>
</body>
</html>
```

A hyperlink is used to select a particular Skin. The Skin is applied to the GridView in the PreInit event when a particular value is assigned to the GridView control's SkinID property.

Of course, I don't recommend doing this. It makes more sense to use a CSS and modify a control's CssClass property. This alternative approach is demonstrated by the page in Listing 6.21.

LISTING 6.21 ShowDynamicCSS.aspx

```
<%@ Page Language="C#" Theme="DynamicSkin" %>
<!DOCTYPE html PUBLIC "-//W3C//DTD XHTML 1.1//EN"
"http://www.w3.org/TR/xhtml11/DTD/xhtml11.dtd">
<script runat="server">

    protected void btnSubmit_Click(object sender, EventArgs e)
    {
        grdMovies.CssClass = ddlCssClass.SelectedItem.Text;
    }
</script>
<html xmlns="http://www.w3.org/1999/xhtml" >
<head id="Head1" runat="server">
    <title>Show Dynamic CSS</title>
</head>
<body>
    <form id="form1" runat="server">
    <div>

    <asp:GridView
        id="grdMovies"
        DataSourceID="srcMovies"
        HeaderStyle-CssClass="Header"
        AlternatingRowStyle-CssClass="Alternating"
        GridLines="none"
        Runat="server" />

     <asp:SqlDataSource
        id="srcMovies"
        ConnectionString="<%$ ConnectionStrings:Movies %>"
        SelectCommand="SELECT Id,Title,Director FROM Movies"
        Runat="server" />

    <hr />

    <asp:Label
        id="lblCssClass"
        Text="Select Style:"
        AssociatedControlID="ddlCssClass"
        Runat="server" />
    <asp:DropDownList
        id="ddlCssClass"
        Runat="server">
```

```
        <asp:ListItem Text="Professional" />
        <asp:ListItem Text="Colorful" />
    </asp:DropDownList>
    <asp:Button
        id="btnSubmit"
        Text="Select"
        Runat="server" OnClick="btnSubmit_Click" />

    </div>
    </form>
</body>
</html>
```

Note that in this code sample, unlike the previous one, you can use a `DropDownList` and `Button` control to change the appearance of the `GridView` control when modifying the `CssClass` property. Because you can modify the `CssClass` property during any event before the page is rendered, you can handle the `Button Click` event to modify the value of the `CssClass` property (see Figure 6.10).

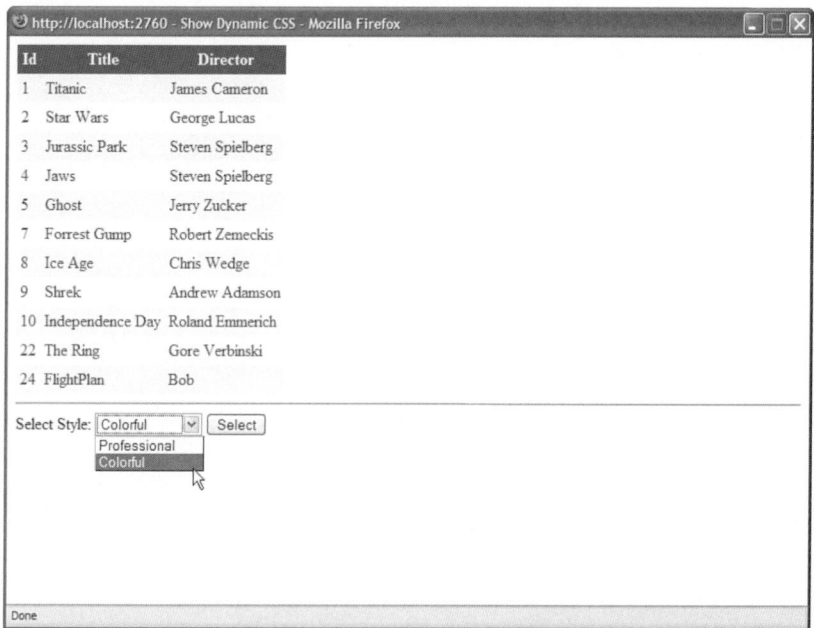

FIGURE 6.10   Modifying a `CssClass` programmatically.

Summary

In this chapter, you learned how to create a consistent look for your website by taking advantage of ASP.NET Themes. In the first section, you learned how to modify the appearance of controls in a page with Skins. You learned how to create both Default and Named Skins. You also learned how to apply a Theme by using the `Theme` attribute and `StyleSheetTheme` attribute.

Next, you learned how to add Cascading Style Sheets to Themes. I recommended that you take advantage of Cascading Style Sheets and avoid Skins whenever possible.

We also discussed how you can create Global Themes. You learned how to create a Theme that you can apply to every application executing on a web server.

Finally, you learned how to dynamically apply Themes. You learned how to use the `PreInit` event to dynamically apply either an entire Theme or a particular Skin at runtime.

CHAPTER 7

Creating Custom Controls with User Controls

A web User control enables you to build a new control from existing controls. By taking advantage of User controls, you can easily extend ASP.NET Framework with your own custom controls.

Imagine, for example, that you need to display the same address form in multiple pages in a web application. The address form consists of several TextBox and Validation controls for entering address information. If you want to avoid declaring all the TextBox and Validation controls in multiple pages, you can wrap these controls inside a web User control.

Anytime you discover that you need to display the same user interface elements in multiple pages, you should consider wrapping the elements inside a User control. By taking advantage of User controls, you make your website easier to maintain and extend.

In this chapter, you learn how to build custom controls with User controls by starting with the basics. You learn how to create a simple User control and expose properties and events from the User control.

You then examine how you can use AJAX with a User control. You learn how to modify the content displayed by a User control without posting the page that contains the User control back to the web server.

Finally, you learn how you can load User controls dynamically. You learn how to load a User control at runtime and inject the User control into a page. In the final section of this chapter, dynamically loaded User controls are used to build a multipage wizard.

Creating User Controls

Let's start by building a simple User control that randomly displays one image from a folder of images (see Figure 7.1). The code for the User control is contained in Listing 7.1.

FIGURE 7.1   Displaying an image with the `RandomImage` User control.

LISTING 7.1   RandomImage.ascx

```
<%@ Control Language="C#" ClassName="RandomImage" %>
<%@ Import Namespace="System.IO" %>

<script runat="server">

    void Page_Load()
    {
        string imageToDisplay = GetRandomImage();
        imgRandom.ImageUrl = Path.Combine("~/Images", imageToDisplay);
        lblRandom.Text = imageToDisplay;
    }

    private string GetRandomImage()
    {
        Random rnd = new Random();
```

```
        string[] images = Directory.GetFiles(MapPath("~/Images"), "*.jpg");
        string imageToDisplay = images[rnd.Next(images.Length)];
        return Path.GetFileName(imageToDisplay);
    }

</script>

<asp:Image
    id="imgRandom"
    Width="300px"
    Runat="server" />
<br />
<asp:Label
    id="lblRandom"
     Runat="server" />
```

VISUAL WEB DEVELOPER NOTE

You create a new User control in Visual Web Developer by selecting website, Add New Item, and the Web User control item.

The file in Listing 7.1 closely resembles a standard ASP.NET page. Like a standard ASP.NET page, the User control contains a `Page_Load()` event handler. Also, the User control contains standard controls such as ASP.NET Image and Label controls.

User controls are closely related to ASP.NET pages. Both the `UserControl` class and the `Page` class derive from the base `TemplateControl` class. Because they derive from the same base class, they share many of the same methods, properties, and events.

The important difference between an ASP.NET page and a User control is that a User control is something you can declare in an ASP.NET page. When you build a User control, you build a custom control.

The file in Listing 7.1 ends with the `.ascx` extension. You cannot request this file directly from a web browser. To use the `RandomImage` User control, you must declare the control in an ASP.NET page.

The page in Listing 7.2 contains the `RandomImage` User control. When you open the page, a random image displays.

LISTING 7.2   ShowRandomImage.aspx

```
<%@ Page Language="C#" %>
<%@ Register TagPrefix="user" TagName="RandomImage" Src="~/RandomImage.ascx" %>
<!DOCTYPE html PUBLIC "-//W3C//DTD XHTML 1.1//EN"
```

```
"http://www.w3.org/TR/xhtml11/DTD/xhtml11.dtd">
<html xmlns="http://www.w3.org/1999/xhtml" >
<head id="Head1" runat="server">
    <title>Show RandomImage</title>
</head>
<body>
    <form id="form1" runat="server">
    <div>

    <user:RandomImage
        ID="RandomImage1"
        Runat="server" />

    </div>
    </form>
</body>
</html>
```

Before you can use a web User control in a page, you must register it. The page in Listing 7.2 includes a `<%@ Register %>` directive that contains the following three attributes:

▶ **TagPrefix**—Indicates the namespace that you want to associate with the User control for the current page. You can use any string that you want.

▶ **TagName**—Indicates the name that you want to associate with the User control for the current page. You can use any string that you want.

▶ **Src**—Indicates the virtual path to the User control (the path to the `.ascx` file).

The `RandomImage` User control is declared in the body of the page. It looks like this:

```
<user:RandomImage ID="RandomImage1" Runat="Server" />
```

The declaration of the User control uses the `TagPrefix` and `TagName` specified in the `<%@ Register %>` directive. Furthermore, you provide a User control with both an `ID` and a `Runat` attribute, just as you would for any standard ASP.NET control.

VISUAL WEB DEVELOPER NOTE

You can add a User control to a page in Visual Web Developer simply by dragging the User control from the Solution Explorer window onto the Design surface. The `<%@ Register %>` directive is automatically added to the source of the page.

Registering User Controls in the Web Configuration File

As an alternative to registering a User control in each page in which you need to use it by using the `<%@ Register %>` directive, you can register a User control once for an entire application. You can register a User control in an application's web configuration file.

For example, the web configuration file in Listing 7.3 registers the `RandomImage` control for the application.

LISTING 7.3   Web.Config

```xml
<?xml version="1.0"?>
<configuration>
<system.web>
  <pages>
    <controls>
      <add
        tagPrefix="user"
        tagName="RandomImage"
        src="~/UserControls/RandomImage.ascx"/>
    </controls>
  </pages>
</system.web>
</configuration>
```

After you register a User control in the web configuration file, you can simply declare the User control in any page. For example, the page in Listing 7.4 contains an instance of the `RandomImage` User control, but it does not include the `<%@ Register %>` directive.

LISTING 7.4   ShowAppRegister.aspx

```aspx
<%@ Page Language="C#" %>
<!DOCTYPE html PUBLIC "-//W3C//DTD XHTML 1.1//EN"
"http://www.w3.org/TR/xhtml11/DTD/xhtml11.dtd">
<html xmlns="http://www.w3.org/1999/xhtml" >
<head id="Head1" runat="server">
    <title>Show Application Register</title>
</head>
<body>
    <form id="form1" runat="server">
    <div>

    <user:RandomImage
        ID="RandomImage1"
        Runat="Server" />
```

```
        </div>
    </form>
</body>
</html>
```

You need to be aware of one important limitation when registering a User control in the web configuration file. A User control cannot be located in the same folder as a page that uses it. For that reason, you should create all your User controls in a subfolder.

Exposing Properties from a User Control

The RandomImage User control always displays an image from the Images folder. It would be nice if you could specify the name of the folder that contains the images so that you could use different folder paths in different applications. You can do this by exposing a property from the RandomImage User control.

The modified RandomImage control in Listing 7.5, named PropertyRandomImage, exposes a property named ImageFolderPath.

LISTING 7.5   PropertyRandomImage.ascx

```
<%@ Control Language="C#" ClassName="PropertyRandomImage" %>
<%@ Import Namespace="System.IO" %>
<script runat="server">

    private string _imageFolderPath = "~/Images";

    public string ImageFolderPath
    {
        get { return _imageFolderPath; }
        set { _imageFolderPath = value; }
    }

    void Page_Load()
    {
        string imageToDisplay = GetRandomImage();
        imgRandom.ImageUrl = Path.Combine(_imageFolderPath, imageToDisplay);
        lblRandom.Text = imageToDisplay;
    }

    private string GetRandomImage()
    {
        Random rnd = new Random();
        string[] images = Directory.GetFiles(MapPath(imageFolderPath), "*.jpg");
        string imageToDisplay = images[rnd.Next(images.Length)];
        return Path.GetFileName(imageToDisplay);
```

```
    }
</script>

<asp:Image
    id="imgRandom"
    Width="300px"
    Runat="server" />
<br />
<asp:Label
    id="lblRandom"
    Runat="server" />
```

After you expose a property in a User control, you can set the property either declaratively or programmatically. The page in Listing 7.6 sets the `ImageFolderPath` property declaratively.

LISTING 7.6   ShowDeclarative.aspx

```
<%@ Page Language="C#" %>
<%@ Register TagPrefix="user" TagName="PropertyRandomImage"
Src="~/PropertyRandomImage.ascx" %>
<!DOCTYPE html PUBLIC "-//W3C//DTD XHTML 1.1//EN"
"http://www.w3.org/TR/xhtml11/DTD/xhtml11.dtd">
<html xmlns="http://www.w3.org/1999/xhtml" >
<head id="Head1" runat="server">
    <title>Show Declarative</title>
</head>
<body>
    <form id="form1" runat="server">
    <div>

    <user:PropertyRandomImage
        ID="PropertyRandomImage1"
        ImageFolderPath="~/Images2"
        Runat="server" />

    </div>
    </form>
</body>
</html>
```

The `PropertyRandomImage` User control in Listing 7.6 includes an `ImageFolderPath` property. When you request the page, the random images are retrieved from the Images2 folder.

VISUAL WEB DEVELOPER NOTE

Any properties that you add to a User control appear in both Intellisense and the Property window.

The page in Listing 7.7 demonstrates how you can set the `ImageFolderPath` programmatically.

LISTING 7.7   ShowProgrammatic.aspx

```
<%@ Page Language="C#" %>
<%@ Register TagPrefix="user" TagName="PropertyRandomImage"
Src="~/PropertyRandomImage.ascx" %>
<!DOCTYPE html PUBLIC "-//W3C//DTD XHTML 1.1//EN"
"http://www.w3.org/TR/xhtml11/DTD/xhtml11.dtd">
<script runat="server">

    protected void Page_Load(object sender, EventArgs e)
    {
        PropertyRandomImage1.ImageFolderPath = "~/Images2";
    }
</script>
<html xmlns="http://www.w3.org/1999/xhtml" >
<head id="Head1" runat="server">
    <title>Show Programmatic</title>
</head>
<body>
    <form id="form1" runat="server">
    <div>

    <user:PropertyRandomImage
        ID="PropertyRandomImage1"
        Runat="server" />

    </div>
    </form>
</body>
</html>
```

The page in Listing 7.7 includes a `Page_Load()` event handler. This handler programmatically sets the `ImageFolderPath` to the value `Images2`.

Exposing Events from a User Control

You can expose custom events from a User control. After you expose the event, you can handle the event in the page that contains the User control.

Exposing events is useful when you need to pass information up to the containing page. Imagine, for example, that you want to create a custom tab strip with a User control. When a user clicks a tab, you want to change the content displayed in the page (see Figure 7.2).

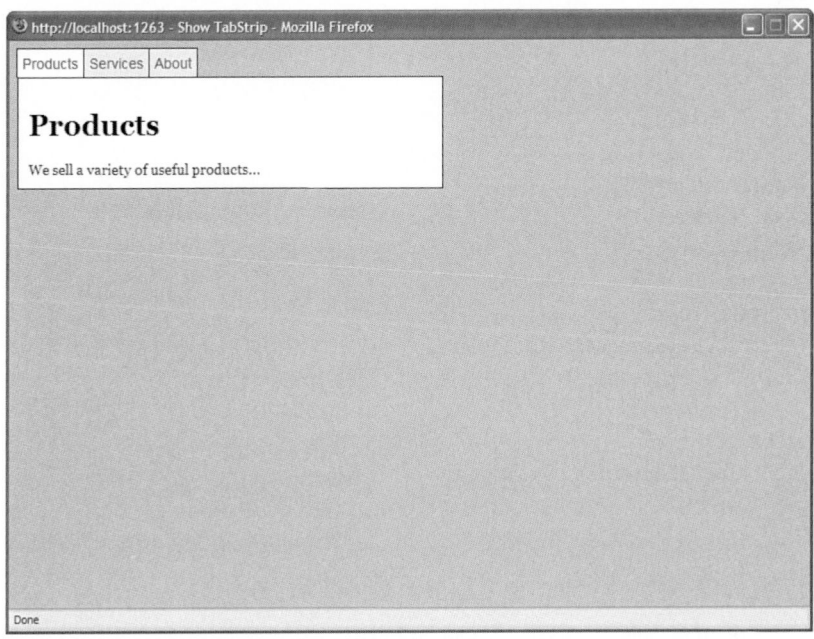

FIGURE 7.2   Displaying a tab strip with a User control.

The User control in Listing 7.8 contains the code for a simple tab strip.

LISTING 7.8   TabStrip.ascx

```
<%@ Control Language="C#" ClassName="TabStrip" %>
<%@ Import Namespace="System.Collections.Generic" %>
<script runat="server">

    public event EventHandler TabClick;

    /// <summary>
    /// The index of the selected tab
    /// </summary>
```

```
    public int SelectedIndex
    {
        get { return dlstTabStrip.SelectedIndex; }
    }

    /// <summary>
    /// Create the tabs
    /// </summary>
    void Page_Load()
    {
        if (!Page.IsPostBack)
        {
            // Create the tabs
            List<string> tabs = new List<string>();
            tabs.Add("Products");
            tabs.Add("Services");
            tabs.Add("About");

            // Bind tabs to the DataList
            dlstTabStrip.DataSource = tabs;
            dlstTabStrip.DataBind();

            // Select first tab
            dlstTabStrip.SelectedIndex = 0;
        }
    }

    /// <summary>
    /// This method executes when a user clicks a tab
    /// </summary>
    protected void dlstTabStrip_SelectedIndexChanged(object sender, EventArgs e)
    {
        if (TabClick != null)
            TabClick(this, EventArgs.Empty);
    }
</script>

<asp:DataList
    id="dlstTabStrip"
    RepeatDirection="Horizontal"
    OnSelectedIndexChanged="dlstTabStrip_SelectedIndexChanged"
    CssClass="tabs"
    ItemStyle-CssClass="tab"
    SelectedItemStyle-CssClass="selectedTab"
    Runat="server">
    <ItemTemplate>
```

```
    <asp:LinkButton
        id="lnkTab"
        Text='<%# Container.DataItem %>'
        CommandName="Select"
        Runat="server" />
    </ItemTemplate>
</asp:DataList>
```

The tab strip is created with the help of a `DataList` control. The `DataList` control displays links for each of the items created in the `Page_Load()` event handler.

The `TabStrip` control exposes an event named `TabClick`. This event is raised in the `dlstTabStrip_SelectedIndexChanged()` event handler when a user clicks a tab.

The page in Listing 7.9 uses the `TabStrip` control to display different content depending on the tab selected.

LISTING 7.9   ShowTabStrip.aspx

```
<%@ Page Language="C#" %>
<%@ Register TagPrefix="user" TagName="TabStrip" Src="~/TabStrip.ascx" %>
<!DOCTYPE html PUBLIC "-//W3C//DTD XHTML 1.1//EN"
"http://www.w3.org/TR/xhtml11/DTD/xhtml11.dtd">
<script runat="server">

    protected void TabStrip1_TabClick(object sender, EventArgs e)
    {
        MultiView1.ActiveViewIndex = TabStrip1.SelectedIndex;
    }
</script>
<html xmlns="http://www.w3.org/1999/xhtml" >
<head id="Head1" runat="server">
    <style type="text/css">
        html
        {
            background-color:silver;
            font:14px Georgia,Serif;
        }
        .tabs a
        {
            color:blue;
            text-decoration:none;
            font:14px Arial,Sans-Serif;
        }
        .tab
        {
```

```
            background-color:#eeeeee;
            padding:5px;
            border:Solid 1px black;
            border-bottom:none;
        }
        .selectedTab
        {
            background-color:white;
            padding:5px;
            border:Solid 1px black;
            border-bottom:none;
        }
        .views
        {
            background-color:white;
            width:400px;
            border:Solid 1px black;
            padding:10px;
        }
    </style>
    <title>Show TabStrip</title>
</head>
<body>
    <form id="form1" runat="server">
    <div>

    <user:TabStrip
        ID="TabStrip1"
        OnTabClick="TabStrip1_TabClick"
        Runat="Server" />

    <div class="views">
    <asp:MultiView
        id="MultiView1"
        ActiveViewIndex="0"
        Runat="server">
        <asp:View ID="Products" runat="server">
            <h1>Products</h1>
            We sell a variety of useful products...
        </asp:View>
        <asp:View ID="Services" runat="server">
            <h1>Services</h1>
            We offer a number of services...
```

```
        </asp:View>
        <asp:View ID="About" runat="server">
            <h1>About</h1>
            We were the first company to offer products and services...
        </asp:View>
    </asp:MultiView>
    </div>

    </div>
    </form>
</body>
</html>
```

The page in Listing 7.9 includes an event handler for the `TabStrip` control's `TabClick` event. When you click a tab, the index of the selected tab is retrieved from the tab strip, and the `View` control with the matching index displays.

VISUAL WEB DEVELOPER NOTE

You can add a `TabClick` event handler to the `TabStrip` control by selecting the `TabStrip` control from the top-left drop-down list and selecting the `TabClick` event from the top-right drop-down list.

NOTE

The ASP.NET Framework includes a Menu control that you can use to create both tab-strips and pop-up menus. This control is discussed in Chapter 4, "Using the Rich Controls," and Chapter 22, "Using the Navigation Controls."

Creating an AddressForm Control

Let's end this section by creating a generally useful Web User control. We build an AddressForm User control that you can reuse in multiple pages or reuse multiple times in a single page (see Figure 7.3).

The AddressForm User control is contained in Listing 7.10.

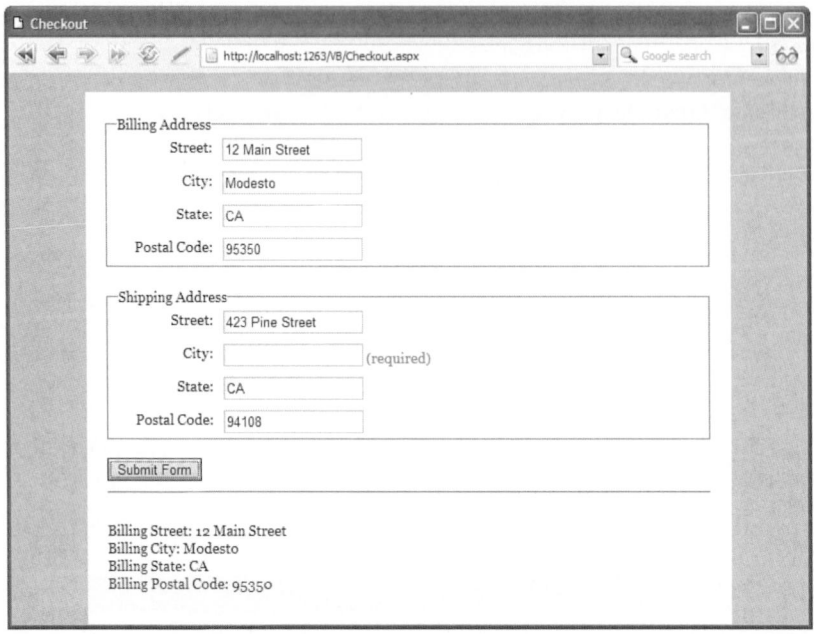

FIGURE 7.3   Displaying multiple address forms with the `AddressForm` User control.

LISTING 7.10   `AddressForm.ascx`

```
<%@ Control Language="C#" ClassName="AddressForm" %>
<script runat="server">

    public string Title
    {
        get { return ltlTitle.Text; }
        set { ltlTitle.Text = value; }
    }

    public string Street
    {
        get { return txtStreet.Text; }
        set { txtStreet.Text = value; }
    }

    public string City
    {
        get { return txtCity.Text; }
        set { txtCity.Text = value; }
    }
```

```
    public string State
    {
        get { return txtState.Text; }
        set { txtState.Text = value; }
    }

    public string PostalCode
    {
        get { return txtPostalCode.Text; }
        set { txtPostalCode.Text = value; }
    }

</script>

<fieldset>
<legend>
    <asp:Literal
        ID="ltlTitle"
        Text="Address Form"
        runat="server" />
</legend>

<div class="addressLabel">
<asp:Label
    ID="lblStreet"
    Text="Street:"
    AssociatedControlID="txtStreet"
    Runat="server" />
</div>
<div class="addressField">
<asp:TextBox
    ID="txtStreet"
    Runat="server" />
<asp:RequiredFieldValidator
    ID="reqStreet"
    Text="(required)"
    ControlToValidate="txtStreet"
    Runat="server" />
</div>

<br class="clear" />

<div class="addressLabel">
<asp:Label
    ID="lblCity"
    Text="City:"
```

```
        AssociatedControlID="txtCity"
        Runat="server" />
</div>
<div class="addressField">
<asp:TextBox
    ID="txtCity"
    Runat="server" />
<asp:RequiredFieldValidator
    ID="reqCity"
    Text="(required)"
    ControlToValidate="txtCity"
    Runat="server" />
</div>

<br class="clear" />

<div class="addressLabel">
<asp:Label
    ID="lblState"
    Text="State:"
    AssociatedControlID="txtState"
    Runat="server" />
</div>
<div class="addressField">
<asp:TextBox
    ID="txtState"
    Runat="server" />
<asp:RequiredFieldValidator
    ID="reqState"
    Text="(required)"
    ControlToValidate="txtState"
    Runat="server" />
</div>

<br class="clear" />

<div class="addressLabel">
<asp:Label
    ID="lblPostalCode"
    Text="Postal Code:"
    AssociatedControlID="txtPostalCode"
    Runat="server" />
</div>
<div class="addressField">
<asp:TextBox
    ID="txtPostalCode"
```

```
    Runat="server" />
<asp:RequiredFieldValidator
    ID="RequiredFieldValidator1"
    Text="(required)"
    ControlToValidate="txtPostalCode"
    Runat="server" />
</div>

<br class="clear" />

</fieldset>
```

The AddressForm control contains form controls for entering your street, city, state, and postal code. Each of these fields is validated by a RequiredFieldValidator control. Finally, the AddressForm includes a Label that can provide a title for the control.

The AddressForm exposes all its form fields with properties. The control includes public Street, City, State, and PostalCode property, which you can read from the containing page.

The page in Listing 7.11 illustrates how you can use the AddressForm control in a page.

LISTING 7.11   Checkout.aspx

```
<%@ Page Language="C#" %>
<%@ Register TagPrefix="user" TagName="AddressForm" Src="~/AddressForm.ascx" %>
<!DOCTYPE html PUBLIC "-//W3C//DTD XHTML 1.1//EN"
"http://www.w3.org/TR/xhtml11/DTD/xhtml11.dtd">
<script runat="server">

    protected void btnSubmit_Click(object sender, EventArgs e)
    {
        // Show Billing Address Form Results
        ltlResults.Text = "<br />Billing Street: " + AddressForm1.Street;
        ltlResults.Text += "<br />Billing  City: " + AddressForm1.City;
        ltlResults.Text += "<br />Billing  State: " + AddressForm1.State;
        ltlResults.Text += "<br />Billing Postal Code: " + AddressForm1.PostalCode;


        ltlResults.Text += "<br /><br />";


        // Show Shipping Address Form Results
        ltlResults.Text += "<br />Shipping Street: " + AddressForm2.Street;
        ltlResults.Text += "<br />Shipping  City: " + AddressForm2.City;
        ltlResults.Text += "<br />Shipping  State: " + AddressForm2.State;
        ltlResults.Text += "<br />Shipping Postal Code: " + AddressForm2.PostalCode;
    }
</script>
```

```
<html xmlns="http://www.w3.org/1999/xhtml" >
<head id="Head1" runat="server">
    <style type="text/css">
        html
        {
            background-color:silver;
            font:14px Georgia,Serif;
        }
        .content
        {
            background-color:white;
            width:600px;
            margin:auto;
            padding:20px;
        }
        .addressLabel
        {
            float:left;
            width:100px;
            padding:5px;
            text-align:right;
        }
        .addressField
        {
            float:left;
            padding:5px;
        }
        .clear
        {
            clear:both;
        }

    </style>
    <title>Checkout</title>
</head>
<body>
    <form id="form1" runat="server">
    <div class="content">

    <user:AddressForm
        id="AddressForm1"
        Title="Billing Address"
        Runat="server" />

    <br />
```

```
<user:AddressForm
    id="AddressForm2"
    Title="Shipping Address"
    Runat="server" />

<br />

<asp:Button
    ID="btnSubmit"
    Text="Submit Form"
    OnClick="btnSubmit_Click"
    Runat="server" />

<hr />

<asp:Literal
    id="ltlResults"
    Runat="server" />

</div>
</form>
</body>
</html>
```

The page in Listing 7.11 contains two instances of the AddressForm control: a Billing Address and Shipping Address. When you click the Button control, the address information is retrieved from the AddressForm controls and displayed in a Literal control. (In a real application, you would grab the data and store it in a database.)

WEB STANDARDS NOTE

The AddressForm User control does not use an HTML table to lay out its controls. You should strive to avoid using tables except when displaying tabular information. Instead, Cascading Style Sheet (CSS) rules are used to position the form elements.

AJAX and User Controls

Ajax (Asynchronous JavaScript and XML) enables you to update content in a page without posting the page back to the server. Behind the scenes, AJAX uses the XMLHttp ActiveX component (in the case of Microsoft Internet Explorer 6.0) or the XMLHttpRequest intrinsic browser object (in the case of other browsers such as FireFox and Internet Explorer 8.0).

We explore the topic of Ajax in depth in Part IX, "ASP.NET AJAX." In this section, I want to provide you with a quick sample of using Ajax with a User control. The User control in

Listing 7.12 randomly displays one of three quotations. The quotation is updated automatically every 5 seconds (see Figure 7.4).

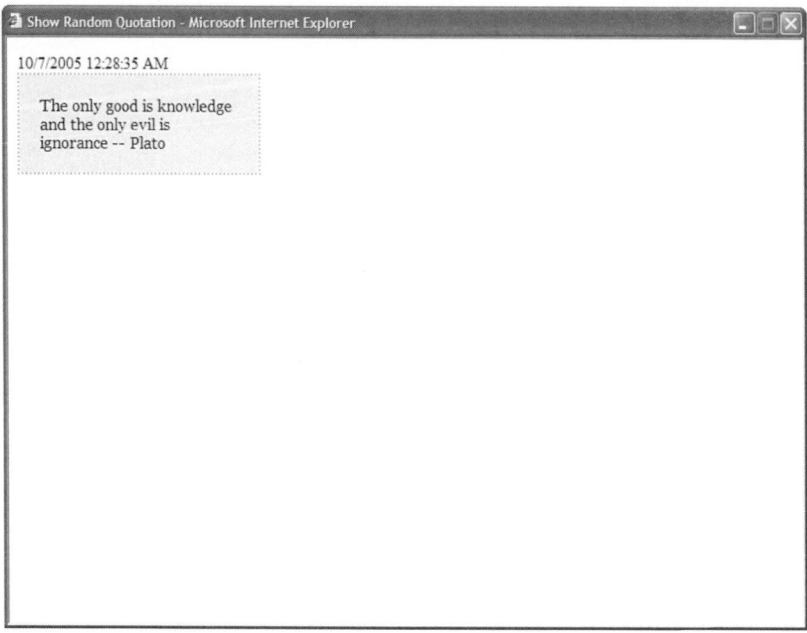

FIGURE 7.4   Using AJAX to display a random quotation.

LISTING 7.12   RandomQuotation.ascx

```
<%@ Control Language="C#" ClassName="RandomQuotation" %>
<%@ Import Namespace="System.Collections.Generic" %>
<script runat="server">

    void Page_Load()
    {
        List<string> quotes = new List<string>();
        quotes.Add("All paid jobs absorb and degrade the mind -- Aristotle");
        quotes.Add("No evil can happen to a good man, either in life or after death
-- Plato");
        quotes.Add("The only good is knowledge and the only evil is ignorance --
Plato");
        Random rnd = new Random();
        lblQuote.Text = quotes[rnd.Next(quotes.Count)];
    }
</script>
```

```
<asp:ScriptManager ID="sm1" runat="server" />
<asp:Timer ID="Timer1" Interval="5000" runat="server" />

<asp:UpdatePanel ID="up1" runat="server">
<Triggers>
    <asp:AsyncPostBackTrigger ControlID="Timer1" />
</Triggers>
<ContentTemplate>
    <div class="quote">
    <asp:Label
        id="lblQuote"
        Runat="server" />
    </div>
</ContentTemplate>
</asp:UpdatePanel>
```

A random quotation is assigned to the Label control in the Page_Load() method in Listing 7.12. The Label control is contained in an UpdatePanel control. The UpdatePanel marks an area of the page that is refreshed without a postback (an Ajax zone). The UpdatePanel control is associated with a Timer control. The Timer control causes the UpdatePanel to refresh its content every 5 seconds (an interval of 5,000 milliseconds).

The page in Listing 7.13 illustrates how you can use the RandomQuotation User control. It contains the User control and also displays the current time.

LISTING 7.13   ShowRandomQuotation.aspx

```
<%@ Page Language="C#" %>
<%@ Register TagPrefix="user" TagName="RandomQuotation"
  Src="~/RandomQuotation.ascx" %>
<!DOCTYPE html PUBLIC "-//W3C//DTD XHTML 1.1//EN"
"http://www.w3.org/TR/xhtml11/DTD/xhtml11.dtd">
<html xmlns="http://www.w3.org/1999/xhtml" >
<head id="Head1" runat="server">
    <style type="text/css">
        .quote
        {
            width:200px;
            padding:20px;
            border:Dotted 2px orange;
            background-color:#eeeeee;
            font:16px Georgia,Serif;
        }
    </style>
    <title>Show Random Quotation</title>
```

```
</head>
<body>
    <form id="form1" runat="server">
    <div>

    <%= DateTime.Now %>
    <br />

    <user:RandomQuotation
        id="RandomQuotation1"
        Runat="server" />

    </div>
    </form>
</body>
</html>
```

The random quotation is updated, but the time on the page does not change. Only the area of the page that contains the random quotation is updated.

Dynamically Loading User Controls

You can dynamically load a User control at runtime and display it in a page. Imagine, for example, that you want to display different featured products randomly on the home page of your website. However, you want to display each featured product with a completely different layout. In that case, you can create a separate User control for each product and load one of the User controls randomly at runtime.

You load a User control with the `Page.LoadControl()` method, which returns an instance of the `Control` class that you can add to a page. Typically, you add the User control to a `PlaceHolder` control that you have declared on the page.

> **NOTE**
>
> The `PlaceHolder` control was designed to do absolutely nothing. It simply acts as a placeholder on the page where you can add other controls.

For example, the page in Listing 7.14 randomly loads one of the controls from the FeaturedProducts folder and adds the control to the page.

LISTING 7.14 ShowFeaturedProduct.aspx

```
<%@ Page Language="C#" %>
<%@ Import Namespace="System.IO" %>
<!DOCTYPE html PUBLIC "-//W3C//DTD XHTML 1.1//EN"
"http://www.w3.org/TR/xhtml11/DTD/xhtml11.dtd">
<script runat="server">

    const string randomFolder = "~/FeaturedProducts";

    protected void Page_Load(object sender, EventArgs e)
    {
        string featuredProductPath = GetRandomProductPath();
        Control featuredProduct = Page.LoadControl(featuredProductPath);
        PlaceHolder1.Controls.Add(featuredProduct);
    }

    private string GetRandomProductPath()
    {
        Random rnd = new Random();
        string[] files = Directory.GetFiles(MapPath(randomFolder), "*.ascx");
        string featuredProductPath =
➥Path.GetFileName(files[rnd.Next(files.Length)]);
        return Path.Combine(randomFolder, featuredProductPath);
    }

</script>
<html xmlns="http://www.w3.org/1999/xhtml" >
<head id="Head1" runat="server">
    <title>Show Featured Products</title>
</head>
<body>
    <form id="form1" runat="server">
    <div>

    <asp:PlaceHolder
        id="PlaceHolder1"
        Runat="server" />

    </div>
    </form>
</body>
</html>
```

Using the Reference Directive

When you load a User control with the `Page.LoadControl()` method, the User control is returned as an instance of the `System.Web.UI.Control` class. This means that if the User control includes any custom properties, the properties aren't available when you dynamically load the User control.

If you dynamically load a User control, you need to cast the control to the correct type before you can access any of the control's custom properties. To get a reference to a User control's type, you must use the `<%@ Reference %>` directive.

For example, imagine that you need to create a form that displays different questions depending on the answers that a user provides for previous questions. In that case, you can dynamically load different User controls that contain the different sets of questions.

For example, the page in Listing 7.15 contains a survey form. The first question asks you whether you currently use ASP Classic or ASP.NET. Depending on your answer, the remainder of the form displays different questions (see Figure 7.5).

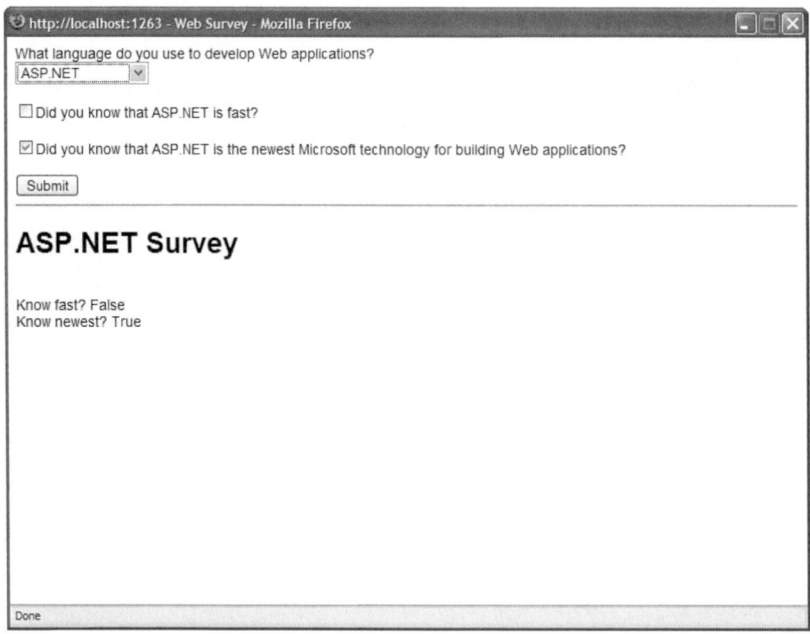

FIGURE 7.5   Displaying a survey form with dynamically loaded questions.

LISTING 7.15   WebSurvey.aspx

```
<%@ Page Language="C#" %>
<%@ Reference Control="~/ASPSurvey.ascx" %>
<%@ Reference Control="~/ASPNetSurvey.ascx" %>
<!DOCTYPE html PUBLIC "-//W3C//DTD XHTML 1.1//EN"
"http://www.w3.org/TR/xhtml11/DTD/xhtml11.dtd">
<script runat="server">

    private Control _survey = null;

    void Page_Load()
    {
        switch (ddlLanguage.SelectedIndex)
        {
            case 1:
                _survey = Page.LoadControl("ASPSurvey.ascx");
                break;
            case 2:
                _survey = Page.LoadControl("ASPNetSurvey.ascx");
                break;
        }

        if (_survey != null)
            PlaceHolder1.Controls.Add(_survey);
    }

    protected void btnSubmit_Click(object sender, EventArgs e)
    {
        switch (ddlLanguage.SelectedIndex)
        {
            case 1:
                ASPSurvey aspResults = (ASPSurvey)_survey;
                ltlResults.Text = "<h1>ASP Survey</h1>";
                ltlResults.Text += "<br />Know slow? " +
                ➥aspResults.KnowSlow.ToString();
                ltlResults.Text += "<br />Know outdated? " +
                ➥aspResults.KnowOutdated.ToString();
                break;
            case 2:
                ASPNetSurvey aspNetResults = (ASPNetSurvey)_survey;
                ltlResults.Text = "<h1>ASP.NET Survey</h1>";
                ltlResults.Text += "<br />Know fast? " +
                ➥aspNetResults.KnowFast.ToString();
                ltlResults.Text += "<br />Know newest? " +
                ➥aspNetResults.KnowNewest.ToString();
```

7

```
                    break;
            }
        }
</script>
<html xmlns="http://www.w3.org/1999/xhtml" >
<head id="Head1" runat="server">
    <style type="text/css">
        html
        {
            font:14px Arial,Sans-Serif;
        }
    </style>
    <title>Web Survey</title>
</head>
<body>
    <form id="form1" runat="server">
    <div>

    <asp:Label
        id="lblLanguage"
        Text="What language do you use to develop Web applications?"
        Runat="server" />
    <br />
    <asp:DropDownList
        id="ddlLanguage"
        ToolTip="Web application language (reloads form)"
        AutoPostBack="true"
        Runat="server">
        <asp:ListItem Text="Select Language" />
        <asp:ListItem Text="ASP Classic"  />
        <asp:ListItem Text="ASP.NET" />
    </asp:DropDownList>

    <br /><br />

    <asp:PlaceHolder
        id="PlaceHolder1"
        Runat="server" />

    <asp:Button
        id="btnSubmit"
        Text="Submit"
        OnClick="btnSubmit_Click"
        Runat="server" />
```

```
    <hr />

    <asp:Literal
        id="ltlResults"
        Runat="server" />

    </div>
    </form>
</body>
</html>
```

WEB STANDARDS NOTE

The DropDownList control in Listing 7.15 reloads the page automatically when you select a new option. You should never reload a page without warning the user because this can be confusing for someone who uses an assistive device such as a screen reader. In Listing 7.15, a warning is added to the ToolTip property of the DropDownList control.

Depending on the user's selection from the DropDownList control, one of two User controls is loaded in the Page_Load() event handler: ASPSurvey.ascx or ASPNetSurvey.ascx. These controls are contained in Listing 7.16 and Listing 7.17.

When you submit the survey form, the btnSubmit_Click() method executes. This method casts the User control loaded in the form to the correct type. It casts the User control to either the ASPSurvey or the ASPNetSurvey type.

The page in Listing 7.16 includes two <%@ Reference %> directives. These reference directives enable you to cast the User control to the correct type so that you can access custom properties of the control such as the KnowSlow and KnowOutdated properties.

LISTING 7.16   ASPSurvey.ascx

```
<%@ Control Language="C#" ClassName="ASPSurvey" %>
<script runat="server">

    public bool KnowSlow
    {
        get { return chkSlow.Checked; }
    }

    public bool KnowOutdated
    {
```

```
        get { return chkOutdated.Checked; }
    }

</script>

<asp:CheckBox
    id="chkSlow"
    Text="Did you know that ASP Classic is slow?"
    Runat="server" />

<br /><br />

<asp:CheckBox
    id="chkOutdated"
    Text="Did you know that ASP Classic is outdated?"
    Runat="server" />
<br /><br />
```

LISTING 7.17   ASPNetSurvey.ascx

```
<%@ Control Language="C#" ClassName="ASPNetSurvey" %>
<script runat="server">

    public bool KnowFast
    {
        get { return chkFast.Checked; }
    }

    public bool KnowNewest
    {
        get { return chkNewest.Checked; }
    }

</script>
<asp:CheckBox
    id="chkFast"
    Text="Did you know that ASP.NET is fast?"
    Runat="server" />

<br /><br />

<asp:CheckBox
    id="chkNewest"
```

```
    Text="Did you know that ASP.NET is the newest Microsoft
        technology for building Web applications?"
    Runat="server" />
<br /><br />
```

Creating a Multipage Wizard

This final section discusses how you can create a multipage wizard by dynamically loading different User controls into the same page. This is going to be a complicated sample, but it is a realistic sample of situations when you would want to load User controls dynamically (see Figure 7.6).

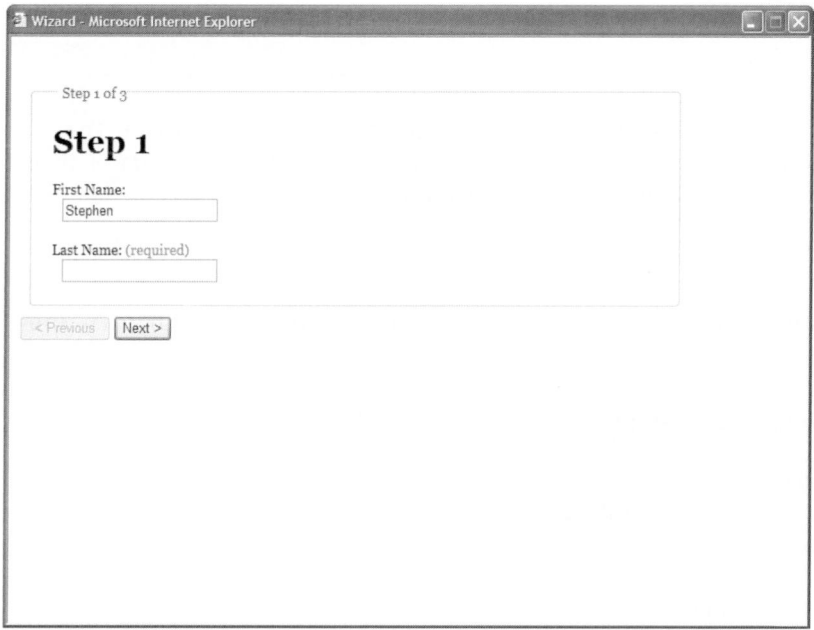

FIGURE 7.6   Displaying a wizard with a series of User controls.

Imagine that you must create a form with 200 questions in it. Displaying all 200 questions to a user in a single form would be overwhelming. Instead, it makes more sense to break the form into multiple pages. Each page of questions can be represented with a User control.

First, you need to define an interface, named the IWizardStep interface, which all the User controls will implement. An interface enables you to know, in advance, that a User control supports a particular set of properties or methods.

NOTE

You need to add the interface in Listing 7.18 to your application's App_Code folder. In Visual Web Developer, create the interface by selecting Website, Add New Item, select Class. Visual Web Developer prompts you to create the App_Code folder.

The IWizardStep interface is contained in Listing 7.18.

LISTING 7.18   IWizardStep.cs

```csharp
public interface IWizardStep
{
    void LoadStep();
    bool NextStep();
}
```

The interface in Listing 7.18 contains two methods: LoadStep() and NextStep(). The LoadStep() method is called when a User control is first loaded. The NextStep() method is called when the Next button is clicked in the wizard.

The NextStep() method returns a Boolean value. If the NextStep() method returns the value False, the user doesn't advance to the next wizard step.

This wizard consists of the three wizard steps contained in Listing 7.19, Listing 7.20, and Listing 7.21.

LISTING 7.19   WizardSteps\Step1.ascx

```
<%@ Control Language="C#" ClassName="Step1" %>
<%@ Implements Interface="IWizardStep" %>
<script runat="server">

    public void LoadStep()
    {
        if (Session["FirstName"] != null)
            txtFirstName.Text = (string)Session["FirstName"];
        if (Session["LastName"] != null)
            txtLastName.Text = (string)Session["LastName"];
    }

    public bool NextStep()
    {
        if (Page.IsValid)
        {

            Session["FirstName"] = txtFirstName.Text;
```

```
            Session["LastName"] = txtLastName.Text;
            return true;
        }
        return false;
    }
</script>
<h1>Step 1</h1>

<asp:Label
    id="lblFirstName"
    Text="First Name:"
    AssociatedControlID="txtFirstName"
    Runat="server" />
<asp:RequiredFieldValidator
    id="reqFirstName"
    Text="(required)"
    ControlToValidate="txtFirstName"
    Runat="server" />
<br />
<asp:TextBox
    id="txtFirstName"
    Runat="server" />

<br /><br />

<asp:Label
    id="lblLastName"
    Text="Last Name:"
    AssociatedControlID="txtLastName"
    Runat="server" />
<asp:RequiredFieldValidator
    id="reqLastName"
    Text="(required)"
    ControlToValidate="txtLastName"
    Runat="server" />
<br />
<asp:TextBox
    id="txtLastName"
    Runat="server" />
```

The wizard step in Listing 7.19 contains a simple form that contains Textbox controls
for the user's first and last name. Both TextBox controls are validated with
RequiredFieldValidator controls.

The User control in Listing 7.19 implements the IWizardStep interface. It contains an
<%@ Implements %> directive at the top of the control.

The `LoadStep()` method assigns values to the `txtFirstName` and `txtLastName` TextBox controls from Session state. The `NextStep()` method grabs the values from the `txtFirstName` and `txtLastName` TextBox controls and assigns the values to Session state.

The second step of the Wizard is contained in Listing 7.20.

LISTING 7.20   WizardSteps\Step2.ascx

```
<%@ Control Language="C#" ClassName="Step2" %>
<%@ Implements Interface="IWizardStep" %>
<script runat="server">

    public void LoadStep()
    {
        if (Session["FavoriteColor"] != null)
            txtFavoriteColor.Text = (string)Session["FavoriteColor"];
    }

    public bool NextStep()
    {
        if (Page.IsValid)
        {
            Session["FavoriteColor"] = txtFavoriteColor.Text;
            return true;
        }
        return false;
    }
</script>

<h1>Step 2</h1>

<asp:Label
    id="lblFavoriteColor"
    Text="Favorite Color:"
    AssociatedControlID="txtFavoriteColor"
    Runat="server" />
<asp:RequiredFieldValidator
    id="reqFavoriteColor"
    Text="(required)"
    ControlToValidate="txtFavoriteColor"
    Runat="server" />
<br />
<asp:TextBox
    id="txtFavoriteColor"
    Runat="server" />
```

The User control in Listing 7.20 also implements the IWizardStep interface. In this step, the user enters a favorite color.

The final wizard step is contained in Listing 7.21.

LISTING 7.21 WizardSteps\Step3.ascx

```
<%@ Control Language="C#" ClassName="Step3" %>
<%@ Implements Interface="IWizardStep" %>
<script runat="server">

    public void LoadStep()
    {
        lblFirstName.Text = (string)Session["FirstName"];
        lblLastName.Text = (string)Session["LastName"];
        lblFavoriteColor.Text = (string)Session["FavoriteColor"];
    }

    public bool NextStep()
    {
        return false;
    }
</script>

<h1>Step 3</h1>

First Name:
<asp:Label
    id="lblFirstName"
    Runat="server" />
<br />
Last Name:
<asp:Label
    id="lblLastName"
    Runat="server" />
<br />
Favorite Color:
<asp:Label
    id="lblFavoriteColor"
    Runat="server" />
```

The wizard step in Listing 7.21 displays a summary of answers that the user has provided in the first two wizard steps (see Figure 7.7). It also implements the IWizardStep interface. Because this is the final wizard step, the NextStep() method always returns the value False.

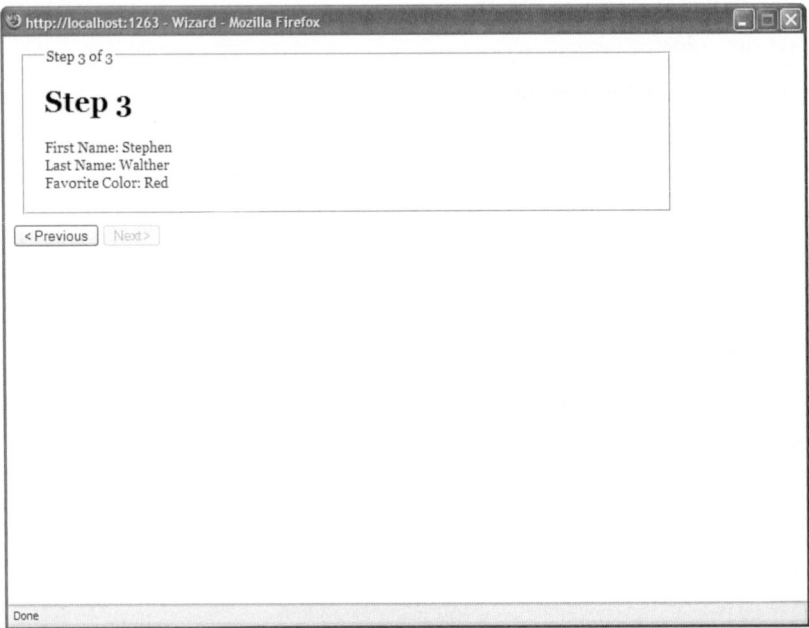

FIGURE 7.7   Displaying the wizard summary step.

The page in Listing 7.22 contains the actual wizard. This page loads each of the wizard steps.

LISTING 7.22   Wizard.aspx

```
<%@ Page Language="C#" %>
<%@ Import Namespace="System.Collections.Generic" %>
<!DOCTYPE html PUBLIC "-//W3C//DTD XHTML 1.1//EN"
"http://www.w3.org/TR/xhtml11/DTD/xhtml11.dtd">
<script runat="server">

    private List<String> _wizardSteps = new List<String>();
    private Control _currentStep;

    /// <summary>
    /// The current step in the Wizard
    /// </summary>
    public int StepIndex
    {
        get
        {
            if (ViewState["StepIndex"] == null)
                return 0;
```

```
            else
                return (int)ViewState["StepIndex"];
        }
        set
        {
            ViewState["StepIndex"] = value;
        }
    }


    /// <summary>
    /// Load the list of wizard steps and load
    /// current step
    /// </summary>
    void Page_Load()
    {
        _wizardSteps.Add("~/WizardSteps/Step1.ascx");
        _wizardSteps.Add("~/WizardSteps/Step2.ascx");
        _wizardSteps.Add("~/WizardSteps/Step3.ascx");

        LoadWizardStep();
    }


    /// <summary>
    /// Load the current wizard step
    /// </summary>
    private void LoadWizardStep()
    {
        _currentStep = Page.LoadControl(_wizardSteps[StepIndex]);
        _currentStep.ID = "ctlWizardStep";
        plhWizardStep.Controls.Clear();
        plhWizardStep.Controls.Add(_currentStep);
        ((IWizardStep)_currentStep).LoadStep();
        ltlStep.Text = String.Format("Step {0} of {1}", StepIndex + 1,
_wizardSteps.Count);
    }


    /// <summary>
    /// Disable the Previous and Next
    /// buttons when appropriate
    /// </summary>
    void Page_PreRender()
    {
        btnPrevious.Enabled = StepIndex > 0;
        btnNext.Enabled = StepIndex < _wizardSteps.Count - 1;
    }
```

```csharp
/// <summary>
/// Execute the step's NextStep() method
/// and move to the next step
/// </summary>
protected void btnNext_Click(object sender, EventArgs e)
{
    bool success = ((IWizardStep)_currentStep).NextStep();
    if (success)
    {
        if (StepIndex < _wizardSteps.Count - 1)
        {
            StepIndex++;
            LoadWizardStep();
        }
    }
}


/// <summary>
/// Move to the previous step
/// </summary>
protected void btnPrevious_Click(object sender, EventArgs e)
{
    if (StepIndex > 0)
    {
        StepIndex--;
        LoadWizardStep();
    }
}
</script>
<html xmlns="http://www.w3.org/1999/xhtml" >
<head id="Head1" runat="server">
    <style type="text/css">
        html
        {
            font:14px Georgia,Serif;
        }
        fieldset
        {
            display:block;
            width:600px;
            padding:20px;
            margin:10px;
        }
    </style>
    <title>Wizard</title>
```

```
</head>
<body>
    <form id="form1" runat="server">
    <div>

    <asp:Label
        id="lblStepNumber"
        Runat="server" />

    <fieldset>
    <legend><asp:Literal ID="ltlStep" runat="server" /></legend>
        <asp:PlaceHolder
            id="plhWizardStep"
            Runat="server" />
    </fieldset>

    <asp:Button
        id="btnPrevious"
        Text="&lt; Previous"
        CausesValidation="false"
        OnClick="btnPrevious_Click"
        Runat="server" />

    <asp:Button
        id="btnNext"
        Text="Next &gt;"
        OnClick="btnNext_Click"
        Runat="server" />

    </div>
    </form>
</body>
</html>
```

The list of wizard steps is created in the Page_Load() method. The path to each wizard step User control is added to a collection of wizard steps.

The StepIndex property represents the index of the wizard step to display. The value of this property is stored in ViewState so that the value is available across multiple page requests.

The current wizard step is loaded by the LoadWizardStep() method. This method uses the StepIndex to grab the path to the current wizard step. Next, it uses the Page.LoadControl() method to actually load the wizard step User control.

After the LoadWizardStep() method loads the current wizard step, it calls the control's LoadStep() method and initializes the control.

The page also contains a Previous and Next button. When you click the Previous button, the btnPrevious_Click() method is called and the StepIndex is reduced by one. When you click the Next button, the btnNext_Click() method is called.

The btnNext_Click() method first calls the current wizard step's NextStep() method. If this method returns the value True, one is added to the StepIndex property, and the next wizard step is loaded. Otherwise, if the NextStep() method returns false, the next wizard step is not loaded.

Summary

In this chapter, you learned how to build custom controls by creating User controls. The first section covered the basics of User controls. You learned how to create a User control and register it both in a page and in a Web configuration file. You learned how to add custom properties and events to a User control.

The next topic was caching and User controls. You learned how to cache the rendered content of a User control in server memory. You also learned how to share the same cached content across multiple pages.

You also explored the topic of AJAX and User controls. You learned how to update content in a User control without posting the page that contains the User control back to the web server.

Finally, you learned how to add User controls dynamically to a page. You learned how to use the <%@ Reference %> directive to cast a User control to a particular type. You also saw a series of User controls loaded dynamically to create a multipage wizard.

CHAPTER 8

Overview of Data Access

Any web application worth writing involves data access. In this chapter, you learn how to take advantage of the rich set of controls included in ASP.NET 4 Framework for working with data.

You learn how to take advantage of the DataBound controls to display data in your ASP.NET pages. You also learn how to take advantage of the DataSource controls to represent different sources of data such as databases, XML files, and business objects.

Next, you are provided with an overview of Microsoft SQL Server 2008 Express, which is the royalty-free database included with Visual Web Developer. You learn how to connect to this database and use it for all your data access needs.

Finally, at the end of this chapter, we build a database-driven application, which illustrates how you can use many of the Data controls discussed in this chapter. We build an Employee Directory application.

Using DataBound Controls

You use DataBound controls to generate your application's user interface for working with data. The DataBound controls display and edit database data, XML data, or just about any other type of data you can imagine.

There are three main types of DataBound controls: list controls, tabular DataBound controls, and hierarchical DataBound.

Working with List Controls

List controls display simple option lists. The ASP.NET 4 Framework includes the following five list controls:

- ▶ **BulletedList**— Displays a bulleted list of items. Each item can be displayed as text, a link button, or a hyperlink.

- ▶ **CheckBoxList**—Displays a list of check boxes. Multiple check boxes in the list can be selected.

- ▶ **DropDownList**—Displays a drop-down list. Only one item in the drop-down list can be selected.

- ▶ **ListBox**—Displays a list box. You can configure this control so that only one item in the list can be selected or multiple items can be selected.

- ▶ **RadioButtonList**—Displays a list of radio buttons. Only one radio button can be selected.

All five controls inherit from the same base `ListControl` class. This means that all these controls share a core set of properties and methods. In Chapter 10, "Using List Controls," you can find detailed instructions on how to use each of the list controls.

The examples in this chapter rely on local databases. You can simply copy the database files (the `.mdf` files) from code examples found on the book's website. We'll discuss the SQL Server 2008 Express database engine that allows you to utilize these files later in the chapter.

The page in Listing 8.1 illustrates how to use all five list controls to display the same set of database records (see Figure 8.1).

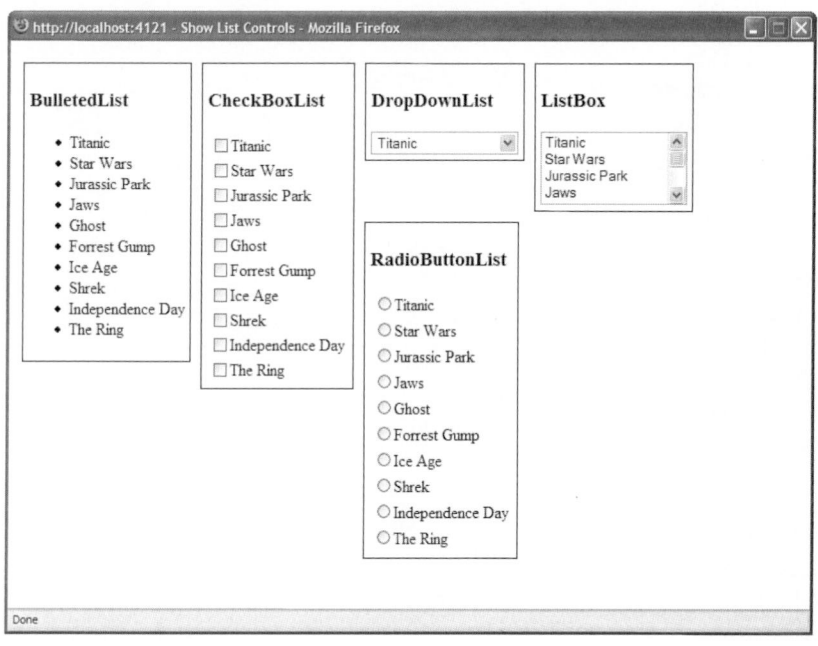

FIGURE 8.1   Using list controls.

LISTING 8.1   ShowListControls.aspx

```
<%@ Page Language="C#" %>
<!DOCTYPE html PUBLIC "-//W3C//DTD XHTML 1.1//EN"
"http://www.w3.org/TR/xhtml11/DTD/xhtml11.dtd">
<html xmlns="http://www.w3.org/1999/xhtml" >
<head id="Head1" runat="server">
    <style type="text/css">
        .floater
        {
            float:left;
            border:solid 1px black;
            padding:5px;
            margin:5px;
        }
    </style>
    <title>Show List Controls</title>
</head>
<body>
    <form id="form1" runat="server">

    <div class="floater">
    <h3>BulletedList</h3>
```

```
<asp:BulletedList
    id="BulletedList1"
    DataSourceId="srcMovies"
    DataTextField="Title"
    Runat="server" />
</div>

<div class="floater">
<h3>CheckBoxList</h3>
<asp:CheckBoxList
    id="CheckBoxList1"
    DataSourceId="srcMovies"
    DataTextField="Title"
    Runat="server" />
</div>

<div class="floater">
<h3>DropDownList</h3>
<asp:DropDownList
    id="DropDownList1"
    DataSourceId="srcMovies"
    DataTextField="Title"
    Runat="server" />
</div>

<div class="floater">
<h3>ListBox</h3>
<asp:ListBox
    id="ListBox1"
    DataSourceId="srcMovies"
    DataTextField="Title"
    Runat="server" />
</div>

<div class="floater">
<h3>RadioButtonList</h3>
<asp:RadioButtonList
    id="RadioButtonList1"
    DataSourceId="srcMovies"
    DataTextField="Title"
    Runat="server" />
</div>

<asp:SqlDataSource
    id="srcMovies"
    ConnectionString="Data Source=.\SQLExpress;
```

```
            AttachDbFilename=¦DataDirectory¦MyDatabase.mdf;
            Integrated Security=True;User Instance=True"
        SelectCommand="SELECT Title FROM Movies"
        Runat="server" />

    </form>
</body>
</html>
```

In Listing 8.1, each list control is bound to a SqlDataSource control which represents the contents of the Movies database table. For example, the BulletedList control is bound to the DataSource control like this:

```
<asp:BulletedList
    id="BulletedList1"
    DataSourceID="srcMovies"
    DataTextField="Title"
    Runat="server" />

<asp:SqlDataSource
    id="srcMovies"
    ConnectionString="Data Source=.\SQLExpress;
        AttachDbFilename=¦DataDirectory¦MyDatabase.mdf;
        Integrated Security=True;User Instance=True"
    SelectCommand="SELECT Title FROM Movies"
    Runat="server" />
```

The BulletedList control includes a DataSourceID attribute, which points to the ID of the SqlDataSource control. The DataSourceID attribute associates a DataBound control with a DataSource control.

Working with Tabular DataBound Controls

The tabular DataBound controls are the main set of controls that you use when working with database data. These controls enable you to display and, in some cases, modify data retrieved from a database or other type of data source.

Six tabular DataBound controls can be divided into two types: those that display multiple data items at a time and those that display a single data item at a time.

First, you can use any of the following controls to display a set of data items:

▶ **GridView**—Displays a set of data items in an HTML table. For example, you can use the GridView control to display all the records contained in the Movies database table. This control enables you to display, sort, page, select, and edit data.

▶ **DataList**—Displays a set of data items in an HTML table. Unlike the GridView control, more than one data item can display in a single row.

▶ **Repeater**—Displays a set of data items using a template. Unlike the GridView and DataList controls, a Repeater control does not automatically render an HTML table.

▶ **ListView**—Displays a set of data items using a template. Unlike the Repeater control, the ListView control supports sorting, paging, and editing database data.

You can use either of the following two controls to display a single data item at a time:

▶ **DetailsView**—Displays a single data item in an HTML table. For example, you can use the DetailsView control to display a single record from the Movies database table. This control enables you to display, page, edit, and add data.

▶ **FormView**—Uses a template to display a single data item. Unlike the DetailsView, a FormView enables you to use to layout a form by using templates.

NOTE

What happened to the DataGrid? The DataGrid was included in ASP.NET 1.x Framework, but it no longer appears in the Toolbox in Visual Web Developer. The DataGrid is officially deprecated. You should use the GridView control instead because the GridView is more powerful. For backward-compatibility reasons, the DataGrid is included in ASP.NET 4 Framework so that you can still use it in your pages.

The page in Listing 8.2 illustrates how you can use each of the tabular DataBound controls (see Figure 8.2).

FIGURE 8.2   Using tabular DataBound controls.

LISTING 8.2   ShowTabularDataBound.aspx

```
<%@ Page Language="C#" %>
<!DOCTYPE html PUBLIC "-//W3C//DTD XHTML 1.1//EN"
"http://www.w3.org/TR/xhtml11/DTD/xhtml11.dtd">
<html xmlns="http://www.w3.org/1999/xhtml" >
<head id="Head1" runat="server">
    <style type="text/css">
        .floater
        {
            float:left;
            border:solid 1px black;
            padding:5px;
            margin:5px;
        }
    </style>
    <title>Show Tabular Databound Controls</title>
</head>
<body>
    <form id="form1" runat="server">

    <div class="floater">
    <h3>GridView</h3>
    <asp:GridView
        id="GridView1"
        DataSourceId="srcMovies"
        Runat="server" />
    </div>



    <div class="floater">
    <h3>DataList</h3>
    <asp:DataList
        id="DataList1"
        DataSourceId="srcMovies"
        RepeatColumns="2"
        Runat="server">
        <ItemTemplate>
        <%#Eval("Title")%>
        <i>directed by</i>
        <%#Eval("Director")%>
        </ItemTemplate>
    </asp:DataList>
    </div>
```

8

```
    <div class="floater">
    <h3>DetailsView</h3>
    <asp:DetailsView
        id="DetailsView1"
        DataSourceId="srcMovies"
        AllowPaging="true"
        Runat="server" />
    </div>

    <div class="floater">
    <h3>FormView</h3>
    <asp:FormView
        id="FormView1"
        DataSourceId="srcMovies"
        AllowPaging="true"
        Runat="server">
        <ItemTemplate>
        <%#Eval("Title")%>
        <i>directed by</i>
        <%#Eval("Director")%>
        </ItemTemplate>
    </asp:FormView>
    </div>
<br style="clear:both" />


    <div class="floater">
    <h3>Repeater</h3>
    <asp:Repeater
        id="Repeater1"
        DataSourceId="srcMovies"
        Runat="server">
        <ItemTemplate>
        <%#Eval("Title")%>
        <i>directed by</i>
        <%#Eval("Director")%>
        </ItemTemplate>
    </asp:Repeater>
    </div>

    <div class="floater">
    <h3>ListView</h3>
    <asp:ListView
        id="ListView1"
        DataSourceId="srcMovies"
        Runat="server">
```

```
        <LayoutTemplate>
        <div id="itemContainer" runat="server">
        </div>
        <asp:DataPager ID="pager1" PageSize="3" runat="server">
        <Fields>
            <asp:NumericPagerField />
        </Fields>
        </asp:DataPager>
        </LayoutTemplate>
        <ItemTemplate>
        <%#Eval("Title")%>
        <i>directed by</i>
        <%#Eval("Director")%>
        </ItemTemplate>
    </asp:ListView>
    </div>

    <asp:SqlDataSource
        id="srcMovies"
        ConnectionString="Data Source=.\SQLExpress;
            AttachDbFilename=|DataDirectory|MyDatabase.mdf;
            Integrated Security=True;User Instance=True"
        SelectCommand="SELECT TOP 5 Title,Director FROM Movies"
        Runat="server" />

    </form>
</body>
</html>
```

For the moment, don't worry too much about formatting the controls. Each of the tabular DataBound controls supports an abundance of properties that modify the control's behavior and appearance. The GridView control gets a detailed examination in Chapter 11, "Using the GridView Control." The DetailsView and FormView controls are covered in Chapter 12, "Using the DetailsView and FormView Controls." The focus of Chapter 13, "Using the Repeater and DataList Controls," is the Repeater and DataList controls. Finally, the new ListView control is discussed in Chapter 14, "Using the ListView and DataPager Controls."

Working with Hierarchical DataBound Controls

A hierarchical DataBound control can display nested data items. For example, you can use hierarchical DataBound controls to display the folder and page structure of your website, the contents of an XML file, or a set of master/detail database records.

The ASP.NET 4 Framework includes two hierarchical DataBound controls:

- ▶ **Menu**—Displays data items in a static or dynamic menu.

- ▶ **TreeView**—Displays data items in a tree.

The page in Listing 8.3 illustrates how you can use both the Menu and TreeView controls. Both controls are bound to an XmlDataSource control, which represents the XML file in Listing 8.4 (see Figure 8.3).

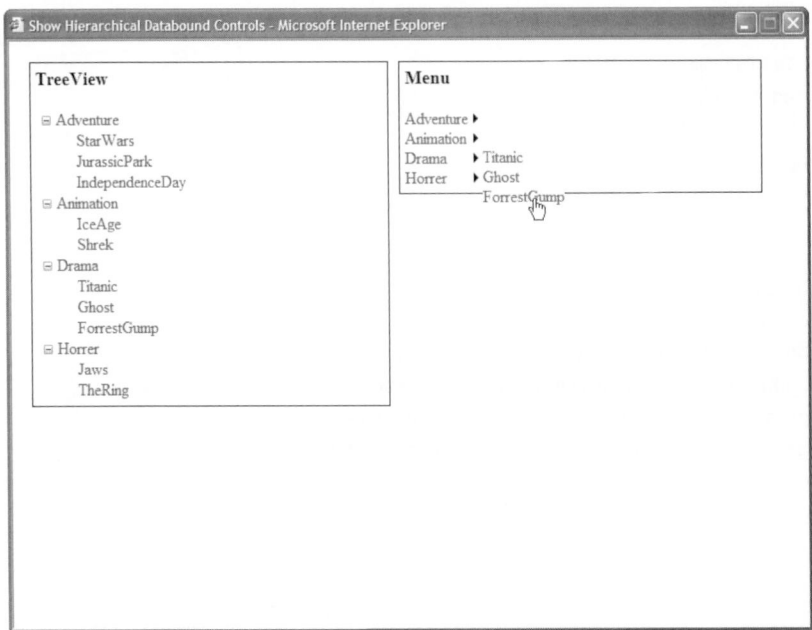

FIGURE 8.3   Using hierarchical DataBound controls.

LISTING 8.3   ShowHierarchicalDataBound.aspx

```
<%@ Page Language="C#" %>
<!DOCTYPE html PUBLIC "-//W3C//DTD XHTML 1.1//EN"
"http://www.w3.org/TR/xhtml11/DTD/xhtml11.dtd">
<html xmlns="http://www.w3.org/1999/xhtml" >
<head id="Head1" runat="server">
    <style type="text/css">
        .floater
        {
            float:left;
            width:45%;
```

```
            border:solid 1px black;
            padding:5px;
            margin:5px;
        }
    </style>
    <title>Show Hierarchical Databound Controls</title>
</head>
<body>
    <form id="form1" runat="server">

    <div class="floater">
    <h3>TreeView</h3>
    <asp:TreeView
        id="CheckBoxList1"
        DataSourceId="srcMovies"
        Runat="server" />
    </div>

    <div class="floater">
    <h3>Menu</h3>
    <asp:Menu
        id="BulletedList1"
        DataSourceId="srcMovies"
        Runat="server" />
    </div>

    <asp:XmlDataSource
        id="srcMovies"
        DataFile="~/Movies.xml"
        XPath="/movies/*"
        Runat="server" />

    </form>
</body>
</html>
```

LISTING 8.4 Movies.xml

```
<?xml version="1.0" encoding="utf-8" ?>
<movies>
  <Adventure>
    <StarWars />
    <JurassicPark />
    <IndependenceDay />
```

```
  </Adventure>
  <Animation>
    <IceAge />
    <Shrek />
  </Animation>
  <Drama>
    <Titanic />
    <Ghost />
    <ForrestGump />
  </Drama>
  <Horror>
    <Jaws />
    <TheRing />
  </Horror>
</movies>
```

Again, don't worry about the appearance of the Menu and TreeView controls in the page rendered by Listing 8.3. Both controls support a rich set of options for modifying the control's appearance. We examine the properties of both of these hierarchical controls in detail in Chapter 22, "Using the Navigation Controls."

Working with Other Controls

You can bind any control in ASP.NET Framework to the data items represented by a data source. Imagine, for example, that you want to display a photo gallery. In that case, you might want to bind a set of Image controls to a data source.

You can bind any ASP.NET control to a data item by adding the control to a template. For example, the page in Listing 8.5 automatically displays all the pictures in a folder named Photos (see Figure 8.4).

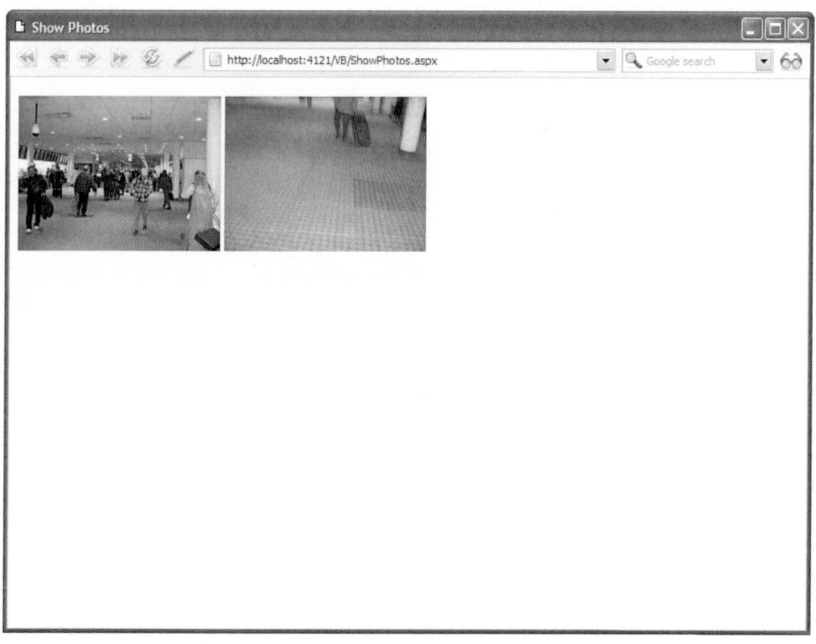

FIGURE 8.4   Binding images to a data source.

LISTING 8.5   ShowPhotos.aspx

```csharp
<%@ Page Language="C#" %>
<%@ Import Namespace="System.IO" %>
<%@ Import Namespace="System.Collections.Generic" %>
<!DOCTYPE html PUBLIC "-//W3C//DTD XHTML 1.1//EN"
"http://www.w3.org/TR/xhtml11/DTD/xhtml11.dtd">
<script runat="server">

    /// <summary>
    /// Bind photos to Repeater
    /// </summary>
    void Page_Load()
    {
        if (!Page.IsPostBack)
        {
            Repeater1.DataSource = GetPhotos();
            Repeater1.DataBind();
        }
    }

    /// <summary>
```

8

```
    /// Get list of photos from Photo folder
    /// </summary>
    public List<String> GetPhotos()
    {
        List<string> photos = new List<string>();
        string photoPath = MapPath("~/Photos");
        string[] files = Directory.GetFiles(photoPath);
        foreach (string photo in files)
            photos.Add("~/Photos/" + Path.GetFileName(photo));
        return photos;
    }

</script>
<html xmlns="http://www.w3.org/1999/xhtml" >
<head id="Head1" runat="server">
    <title>Show Photos</title>
</head>
<body>
    <form id="form1" runat="server">
    <div>

    <asp:Repeater
        id="Repeater1"
        runat="server">
        <ItemTemplate>
            <asp:Image
                id="Image1"
                Width="200px"
                ImageUrl='<%# Container.DataItem %>'
                Runat="server" />
        </ItemTemplate>
    </asp:Repeater>

    </div>
    </form>
</body>
</html>
```

The Repeater control contains an `ItemTemplate`, and the `ItemTemplate` contains an ASP.NET Image control. The `Image` control displays each of the photographs from the Photos folder.

Using DataSource Controls

You bind a `DataBound` control to a `DataSource` control. A `DataSource` control represents a particular type of data.

The ASP.NET 4 Framework includes the following six `DataSource` controls:

▶ **SqlDataSource**—Represents data retrieved from a SQL relational database, including Microsoft SQL Server, Oracle, or DB2.

▶ **LinqDataSource**—Represents a LINQ to SQL query.

▶ **AccessDataSource**—Represents data retrieved from a Microsoft Access database.

▶ **ObjectDataSource**—Represents data retrieved from a business object.

▶ **XmlDataSource**—Represents data retrieved from an XML document.

▶ **SiteMapDataSource**—Represents data retrieved from a Site Map Provider. A Site Map Provider represents the page and folder structure of a website.

The ASP.NET Framework contains two basic types of `DataSource` controls. The `SqlDataSource`, `AccessDataSource`, `LinqDataSource`, and `ObjectDataSource` controls all derive from the base `DataSourceControl` class. These controls can be used to represent tabular data. The `XmlDataSource` and `SiteMapDataSource` controls, on the other hand, derive from the base `HierarchicalDataSourceControl` control. These two controls can be used to represent both tabular and hierarchical data.

A `DataBound` control is associated with a particular data source control through its `DataSourceID` property. For example, the page in Listing 8.6 contains a `GridView` control bound to a `SqlDataSource` control (see Figure 8.5).

8

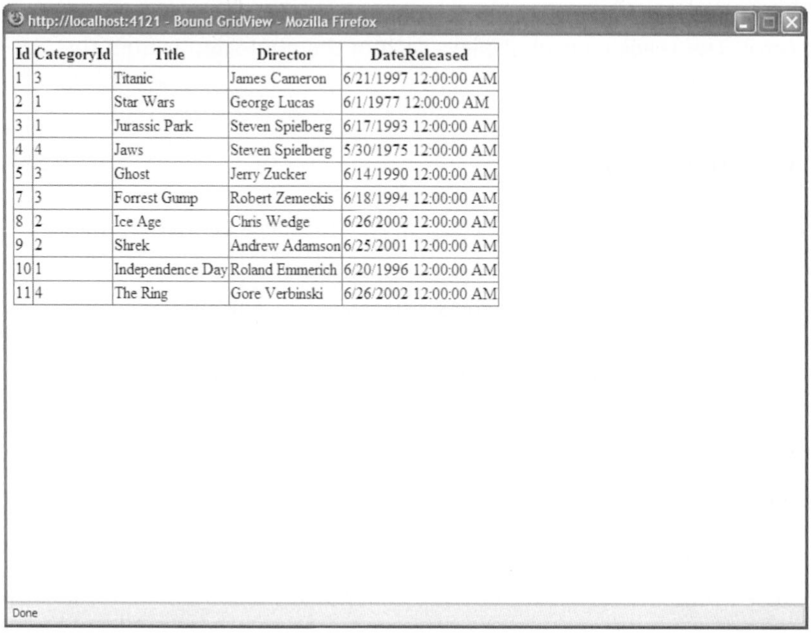

Id	CategoryId	Title	Director	DateReleased
1	3	Titanic	James Cameron	6/21/1997 12:00:00 AM
2	1	Star Wars	George Lucas	6/1/1977 12:00:00 AM
3	1	Jurassic Park	Steven Spielberg	6/17/1993 12:00:00 AM
4	4	Jaws	Steven Spielberg	5/30/1975 12:00:00 AM
5	3	Ghost	Jerry Zucker	6/14/1990 12:00:00 AM
7	3	Forrest Gump	Robert Zemeckis	6/18/1994 12:00:00 AM
8	2	Ice Age	Chris Wedge	6/26/2002 12:00:00 AM
9	2	Shrek	Andrew Adamson	6/25/2001 12:00:00 AM
10	1	Independence Day	Roland Emmerich	6/20/1996 12:00:00 AM
11	4	The Ring	Gore Verbinski	6/26/2002 12:00:00 AM

FIGURE 8.5 Using the `SqlDataSource` control.

LISTING 8.6 `BoundGridView.aspx`

```
<%@ Page Language="C#" %>
<!DOCTYPE html PUBLIC "-//W3C//DTD XHTML 1.1//EN"
"http://www.w3.org/TR/xhtml11/DTD/xhtml11.dtd">
<html xmlns="http://www.w3.org/1999/xhtml" >
<head id="Head1" runat="server">
    <title>Bound GridView</title>
</head>
<body>
    <form id="form1" runat="server">
    <div>

    <asp:GridView
        id="GridView1"
        DataSourceId="srcMovies"
        Runat="server" />

    <asp:SqlDataSource
        id="srcMovies"
```

```
        ConnectionString="Data Source=.\SQLExpress;
            AttachDbFilename=|DataDirectory|MyDatabase.mdf;
            Integrated Security=True;User Instance=True"
        SelectCommand="SELECT * FROM Movies"
        Runat="server" />

    </div>
    </form>
</body>
</html>
```

Using ASP.NET Parameters with DataSource Controls

Many of the DataSource controls support ASP.NET parameters. You use ASP.NET parameters to modify the commands that a DataSource control executes.

Different types of DataSource controls use ASP.NET parameters to represent different types of things. When you use ASP.NET parameters with a SqlDataSource control, the ASP.NET parameters represent ADO.NET parameters. In other words, they represent parameters used with SQL statements.

When you use parameters with the ObjectDataSource control, the ASP.NET parameters represent method parameters. They represent parameters passed to a particular method of a business object.

The SqlDataSource, AccessDataSource, LinqDataSource, and ObjectDataSource controls all support the following types of Parameter objects:

- ▶ **Parameter**—Represents an arbitrary static value.

- ▶ **ControlParameter**—Represents the value of a control or page property.

- ▶ **CookieParameter**—Represents the value of a browser cookie.

- ▶ **FormParameter**—Represents the value of an HTML form field.

- ▶ **ProfileParameter**—Represents the value of a Profile property.

- ▶ **QueryStringParameter**—Represents the value of a query string field.

- ▶ **SessionParameter**—Represents the value of an item stored in Session state.

For example, the page in Listing 8.7 contains a DropDownList, GridView, and SqlDataSource control. The DropDownList displays a list of movie categories. When you select a new category, the GridView displays matching movies (see Figure 8.6).

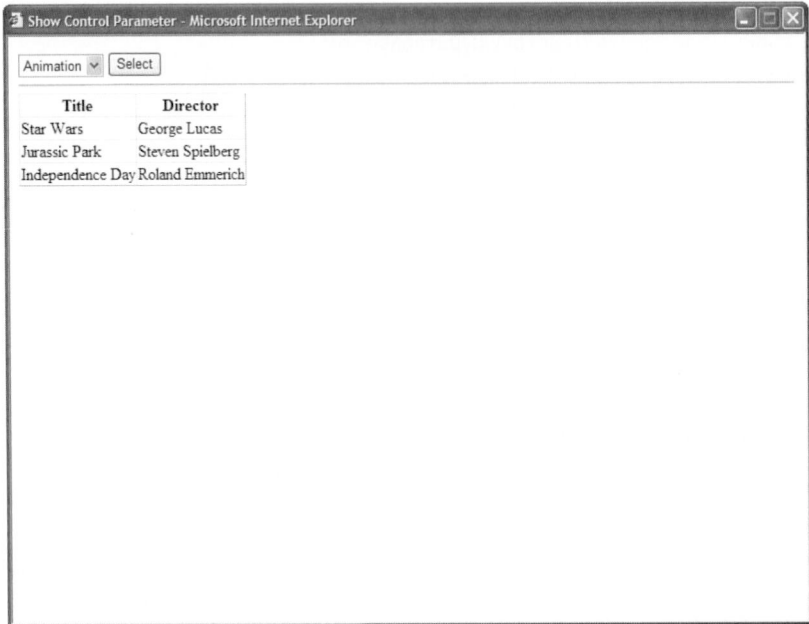

FIGURE 8.6   Using the `ControlParameter` object.

LISTING 8.7   ShowControlParameter.aspx

```
<%@ Page Language="C#" %>
<!DOCTYPE html PUBLIC "-//W3C//DTD XHTML 1.1//EN"
"http://www.w3.org/TR/xhtml11/DTD/xhtml11.dtd">
<html xmlns="http://www.w3.org/1999/xhtml" >
<head id="Head1" runat="server">
    <title>Show Control Parameter</title>
</head>
<body>
    <form id="form1" runat="server">
    <div>

    <asp:DropDownList
        id="ddlMovieCategory"
        DataSourceID="srcMovieCategories"
        DataTextField="Name"
        DataValueField="Id"
        Runat="server" />

    <asp:Button
        id="btnSelect"
```

```
            Text="Select"
            ToolTip="Select Movie"
            Runat="server" />

    <hr />

    <asp:GridView
        id="grdMovies"
        DataSourceID="srcMovies"
        Runat="server" />

    <asp:SqlDataSource
        id="srcMovieCategories"
        ConnectionString="Server=.\SQLExpress;
        Trusted_Connection=True;AttachDbFileName=|DataDirectory|MyDatabase.mdf;
        User Instance=True"
        SelectCommand="SELECT Id,Name FROM MovieCategories"
        Runat="server" />


    <asp:SqlDataSource
        id="srcMovies"
        ConnectionString="Data Source=.\SQLExpress;
            AttachDbFilename=|DataDirectory|MyDatabase.mdf;
            Integrated Security=True;User Instance=True"
        SelectCommand="SELECT Title,Director FROM Movies
            WHERE CategoryId=@Id"
        Runat="server">
        <SelectParameters>
            <asp:ControlParameter
                Name="Id"
                Type="int32"
                ControlID="ddlMovieCategory" />
        </SelectParameters>
    </asp:SqlDataSource>

    </div>
    </form>
</body>
</html>
```

The SqlDataSource control includes a ControlParameter object. The ControlParameter represents the selected item in the DropDownList control. The value of the ControlParameter is used in the SqlDataSource control's SelectCommand to select movies that match the category selected in the DropDownList control.

Using Programmatic DataBinding

When you bind a DataBound control to a DataSource control, you can take advantage of *declarative databinding*. When you use declarative databinding, ASP.NET Framework handles all the messy details of deciding when to retrieve the data items represented by a DataSource control.

In certain situations, you want to handle these messy details yourself. For example, you might want to force a GridView control to refresh the data it displays after you add a new record to a database table. Or you might want to bind a DataBound control to a data source that can't be easily represented by one of the existing DataSource controls. In these situations, you want to use *programmatic databinding*.

> **NOTE**
>
> The ASP.NET 1.x Framework supported only programmatic databinding. The first version of the Framework did not include any of the DataSource controls.

Every DataBound control has a DataSource property and a DataBind() method. By using this property and method, you can programmatically associate a DataBound control with a data source.

For example, the page in Listing 8.8 displays a list of all the fonts installed on your computer (see Figure 8.7).

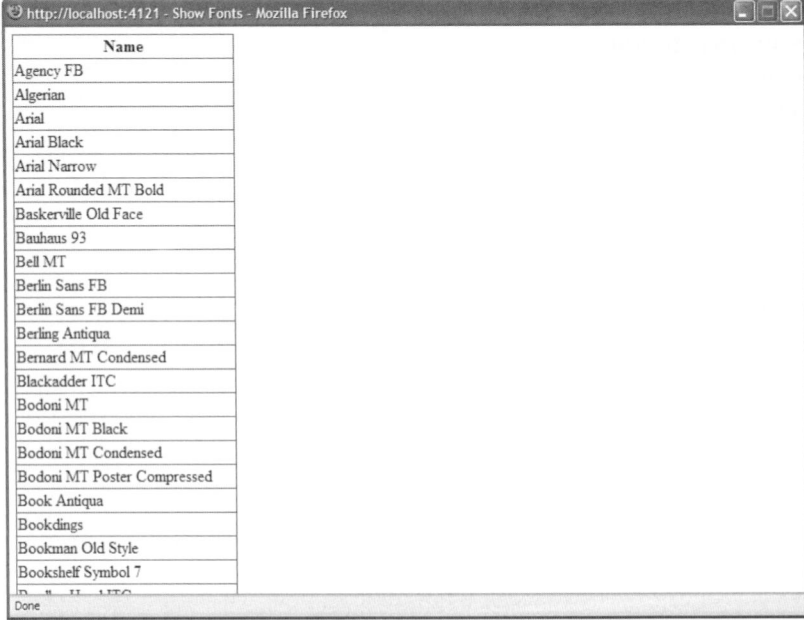

FIGURE 8.7   Programmatic databinding.

LISTING 8.8 ShowFonts.aspx

```csharp
<%@ Page Language="C#" %>
<%@ Import Namespace="System.Drawing.Text" %>
<!DOCTYPE html PUBLIC "-//W3C//DTD XHTML 1.1//EN"
"http://www.w3.org/TR/xhtml11/DTD/xhtml11.dtd">
<script runat="server">

    void Page_Load()
    {
        if (!Page.IsPostBack)
        {
            InstalledFontCollection fonts = new InstalledFontCollection();
            GridView1.DataSource = fonts.Families;
            GridView1.DataBind();
        }
    }
</script>
<html xmlns="http://www.w3.org/1999/xhtml" >
<head id="Head1" runat="server">
    <title>Show Fonts</title>
</head>
<body>
    <form id="form1" runat="server">
    <div>

    <asp:GridView
        id="GridView1"
        Runat="server" />

    </div>
    </form>
</body>
</html>
```

8

NOTE

The programmatic databinding in Listing 8.8 could have been avoided by taking advantage of the ObjectDataSource control. This DataSource control is discussed in detail in Chapter 18, "Using the ObjectDataSource Control."

The list of fonts is displayed by a GridView control. The actual list of fonts is retrieved from the InstalledFontCollection class (which inhabits the System.Drawing.Text namespace). The list of fonts is assigned to the GridView control's DataSource property, and the DataBind() method is called.

In Listing 8.8, a collection of fonts has been assigned to the DataSource property. In general, you can assign any object that implements the IEnumerable interface to the DataSource property. For example, you can assign collections, arrays, DataSets, DataReaders, DataViews, and enumerations to the DataSource property.

> **NOTE**
>
> Particular DataBound controls support different data sources. For example, you can assign any object that implements the IEnumerable or ITypedList interface to the DataSource property of a GridView control.

When you call the DataBind() method, the GridView control actually retrieves its data from the data source. The control iterates through all the items represented by the data source and displays each item. If you neglect to call the DataBind() method, the control never displays anything.

The GridView is bound to its data source only when the page is requested for the first time. The Page.IsPostBack property determines whether the page has been posted back to the server. You don't need to rebind the GridView to its data source every time the page is requested because the GridView uses View State to remember the data items that it displays.

You can't mix declarative and programmatic databinding. If you attempt to use both the DataSource and DataSourceID properties, you get an exception.

On the other hand, you can call the DataBind() method even when you have declaratively bound a control to a DataSource control. When you explicitly call DataBind(), the DataBound control grabs the data items from its DataSource control again. Explicitly calling DataBind() is useful when you want to refresh the data displayed by a DataBound control.

Understanding Templates and DataBinding Expressions

Almost all the DataBound controls support templates. You can use a template to format the layout and appearance of each of the data items that a DataBound control displays. Within a template, you can use a DataBinding expression to display the value of a data item.

In this section, you learn about the different kinds of templates and DataBinding expressions that you can use with the DataBound controls.

Using Templates

Every DataBound control included in ASP.NET 4 Framework supports templates with the sole exception of the TreeView control. The Repeater, DataList, ListView, and FormView controls all require you to use templates. If you don't supply a template, these controls display nothing. The GridView, DetailsView, and Menu controls also support templates, but they do not require a template.

For example, when you use the Repeater control, you must supply an ItemTemplate. The Repeater control uses the ItemTemplate to format each of the records that it displays. Listing 8.9 contains a Repeater control that formats each of the records from the Movies database table (see Figure 8.8).

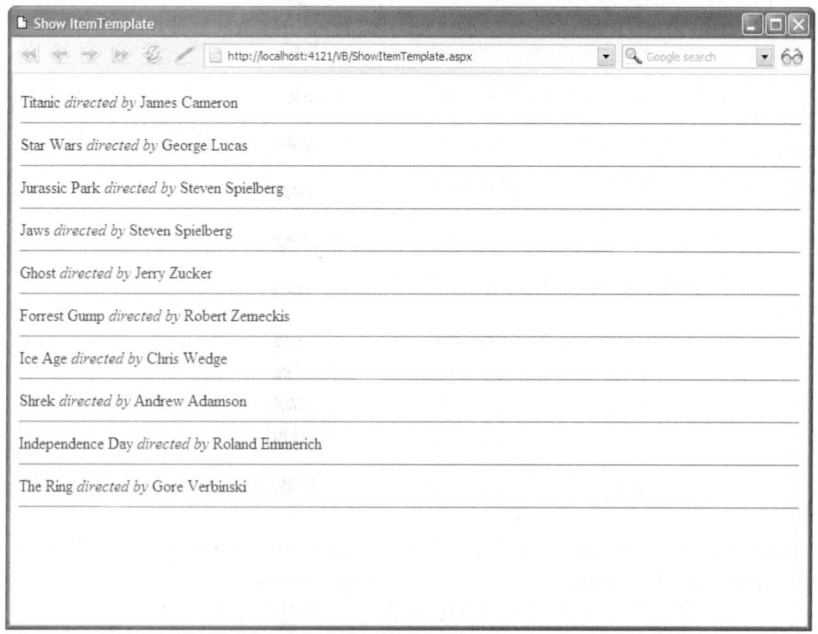

FIGURE 8.8   Using an ItemTemplate.

LISTING 8.9   ShowItemTemplate.aspx

```
<%@ Page Language="C#" %>
<!DOCTYPE html PUBLIC "-//W3C//DTD XHTML 1.1//EN"
"http://www.w3.org/TR/xhtml11/DTD/xhtml11.dtd">
<html xmlns="http://www.w3.org/1999/xhtml" >
<head id="Head1" runat="server">
    <title>Show ItemTemplate</title>
</head>
<body>
    <form id="form1" runat="server">
```

```
    <div>

    <asp:Repeater
        id="Repeater1"
        DataSourceId="srcMovies"
        Runat="server">
        <ItemTemplate>
        <%#Eval("Title")%>
        <i>directed by</i>
        <%#Eval("Director")%>
        <hr />
        </ItemTemplate>
    </asp:Repeater>


    <asp:SqlDataSource
        id="srcMovies"
        ConnectionString="Data Source=.\SQLExpress;
            AttachDbFilename=¦DataDirectory¦MyDatabase.mdf;
            Integrated Security=True;User Instance=True"
        SelectCommand="SELECT Title,Director FROM Movies"
        Runat="server" />

    </div>
    </form>
</body>
</html>
```

A template can contain HTML, DataBinding expressions, and other controls. In Listing 8.9, the template includes the following two DataBinding expressions:

```
<%# Eval("Title") %>
<%# Eval("Director") %>
```

The first DataBinding expression displays the value of the Title column and the second DataBinding expression displays the value of the Director column.

A template can contain other controls—even other DataBound controls. For example, the page in Listing 8.10 displays a list of hyperlinks (see Figure 8.9).

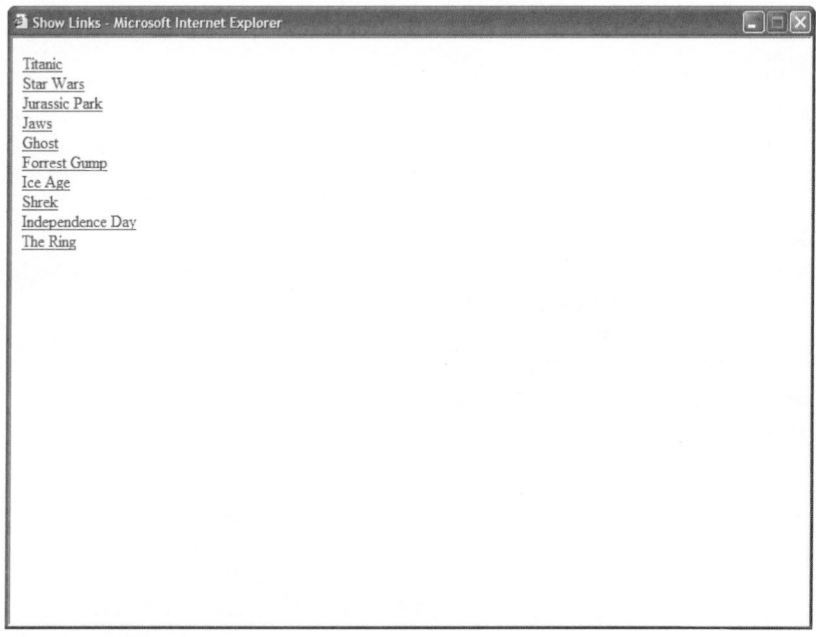

FIGURE 8.9   Displaying a list of hyperlinks.

LISTING 8.10   ShowLinks.aspx

```
<%@ Page Language="C#" %>
<!DOCTYPE html PUBLIC "-//W3C//DTD XHTML 1.1//EN"
"http://www.w3.org/TR/xhtml11/DTD/xhtml11.dtd">
<html xmlns="http://www.w3.org/1999/xhtml" >
<head id="Head1" runat="server">
    <title>Show Links</title>
</head>
<body>
    <form id="form1" runat="server">
    <div>

    <asp:Repeater
        id="Repeater1"
        DataSourceId="srcMovies"
        Runat="server">
        <ItemTemplate>

        <asp:HyperLink
            id="HyperLink1"
            Text='<%# Eval("Title") %>'
            NavigateUrl='<%# Eval("Id", "Details.aspx?id={0}") %>'
```

8

```
            runat="server" />
        <br />

        </ItemTemplate>
    </asp:Repeater>


    <asp:SqlDataSource
        id="srcMovies"
        ConnectionString="Data Source=.\SQLExpress;
            AttachDbFilename=|DataDirectory|MyDatabase.mdf;
            Integrated Security=True;User Instance=True"
        SelectCommand="SELECT Id, Title FROM Movies"
        Runat="server" />

    </div>
    </form>
</body>
</html>
```

In Listing 8.10, a HyperLink control displays for each item from the data source. The HyperLink control displays the movie title and links to a details page for the movie.

Using DataBinding Expressions

A DataBinding expression is a special type of expression not evaluated until runtime. You mark a databinding expression in a page by wrapping the expression in opening <%# and closing %> brackets.

A DataBinding expression isn't evaluated until a control's DataBinding event is raised. When you bind a DataBound control to a DataSource control declaratively, this event is raised automatically. When you bind a DataSource control to a data source programmatically, the DataBinding event is raised when you call the DataBind() method.

For example, the page in Listing 8.11 contains a DataList control that contains a template that includes two DataBinding expressions.

LISTING 8.11   ShowDataList.aspx

```
<%@ Page Language="C#" %>
<!DOCTYPE html PUBLIC "-//W3C//DTD XHTML 1.1//EN"
"http://www.w3.org/TR/xhtml11/DTD/xhtml11.dtd">
<html xmlns="http://www.w3.org/1999/xhtml" >
```

```
<head id="Head1" runat="server">
    <title>Show DataList</title>
</head>
<body>
    <form id="form1" runat="server">
    <div>

    <asp:DataList
        id="DataList1"
        DataSourceId="srcMovies"
        Runat="server">
        <ItemTemplate>
        <b>Movie Title:</b>
        <%#Eval("Title")%>
        <br />
        <b>Date Released:</b>
        <%#Eval("DateReleased", "{0:D}") %>
        <hr />
        </ItemTemplate>
    </asp:DataList>

    <asp:SqlDataSource
        id="srcMovies"
        ConnectionString="Data Source=.\SQLExpress;
            AttachDbFilename=|DataDirectory|MyDatabase.mdf;
            Integrated Security=True;User Instance=True"
        SelectCommand="SELECT Title,Director,DateReleased FROM Movies"
        Runat="server" />

    </div>
    </form>
</body>
</html>
```

The first DataBinding expression displays the title of the movie and the second
DataBinding expression displays the date the movie was released (see Figure 8.10).

Both DataBinding expressions call the Eval() method. The Eval() method is a protected
method of the Page class. Behind the scenes, the Page.Eval() method calls the static
(shared) DataBinder.Eval() method. If you want to be verbose, instead of using the
Eval() method, you could use the following two expressions:

```
<%# DataBinder.Eval(Container.DataItem, "Title") %>
<%# DataBinder.Eval(Container.DataItem, "DateReleased", "{0:D}" ) %>
```

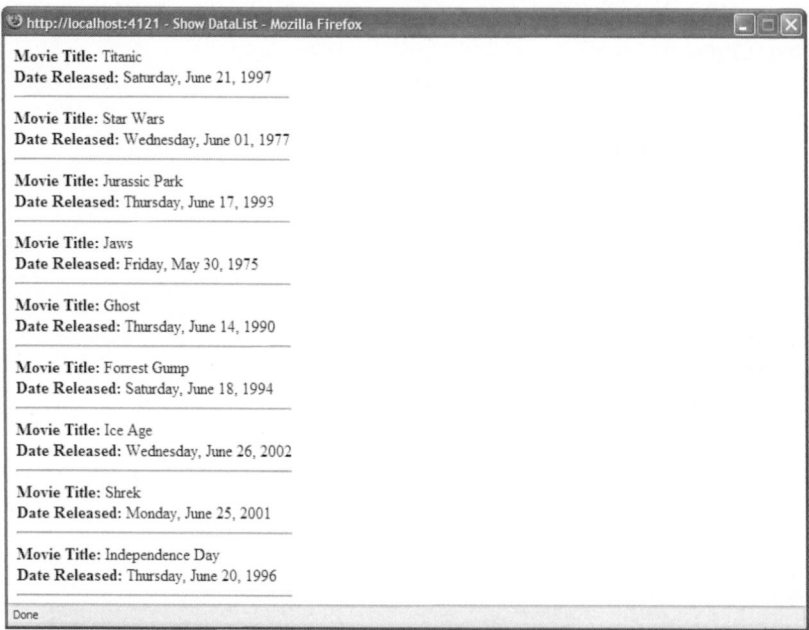

FIGURE 8.10   Using databinding expressions.

In ASP.NET version 1.x, you had to use `DataBinder.Eval()` when displaying data items in a template. However, Microsoft took pity on programmers after ASP.NET 2.0 and provided us with the shorter syntax.

> **NOTE**
>
> Technically, the `Eval()` method uses reflection when evaluating the data item to find a property with a certain name. You do pay a performance penalty when you use reflection.
>
> As an alternative, you can improve the performance of your DataBinding expressions by casting the data items to a particular type like this:
>
> ```
> <%# ((System.Data.DataRowView)Container.DataItem)["Title"] %>
> ```

The second DataBinding expression in Listing 8.11 includes a second parameter. The `Eval()` method, optionally, accepts a format string. You can use the format string to format values such as dates and currency amounts. In Listing 8.11, the format string formats the DateReleased column as a long date.

You can call other methods than the Eval() method in a DataBinding expression. For example, the DataBinding expression in Listing 8.12 calls a method named FormatTitle() to format the movie titles.

LISTING 8.12   FormatMovieTitles.aspx

```
<%@ Page Language="C#" %>
<!DOCTYPE html PUBLIC "-//W3C//DTD XHTML 1.1//EN"
"http://www.w3.org/TR/xhtml11/DTD/xhtml11.dtd">
<script runat="server">

    public string FormatTitle(Object title)
    {
        return "<b>" + title.ToString().ToUpper() + "</b>";
    }

</script>
<html xmlns="http://www.w3.org/1999/xhtml" >
<head id="Head1" runat="server">
    <title>Format Movie Titles</title>
</head>
<body>
    <form id="form1" runat="server">
    <div>

    <asp:Repeater
        id="Repeater1"
        DataSourceId="srcMovies"
        Runat="server">
        <ItemTemplate>
        <%# FormatTitle(Eval("Title")) %>
        <hr />
        </ItemTemplate>
    </asp:Repeater>


    <asp:SqlDataSource
        id="srcMovies"
        ConnectionString="Data Source=.\SQLExpress;
```

```
                AttachDbFilename=|DataDirectory|MyDatabase.mdf;
                Integrated Security=True;User Instance=True"
            SelectCommand="SELECT Title FROM Movies"
            Runat="server" />

    </div>
    </form>
</body>
</html>
```

The `FormatTitle()` method is defined in the page in Listing 8.12. This method formats each of the titles displayed by the `Repeater` control by making each title bold and upper-case (see Figure 8.11).

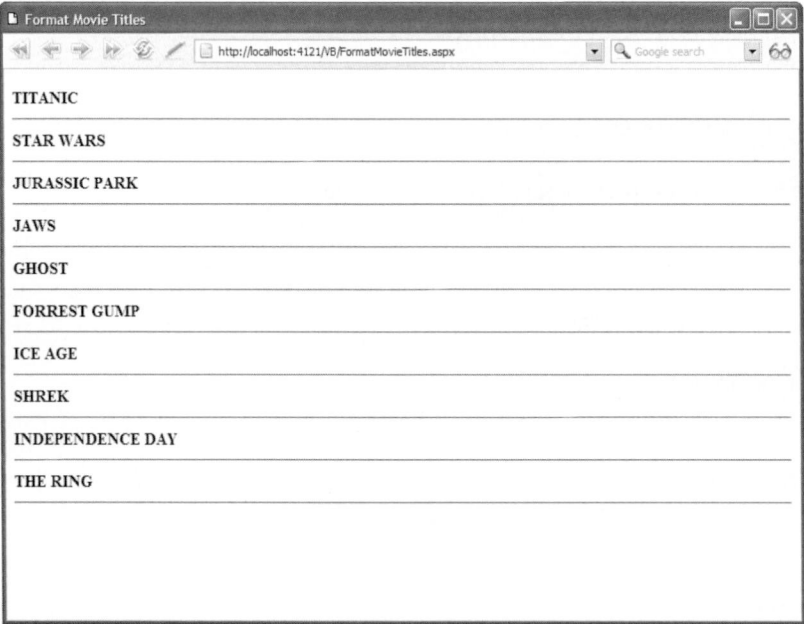

FIGURE 8.11   Formatting movie titles.

Using Two-Way DataBinding Expressions

The ASP.NET Framework actually supports two types of templates and two types of DataBinding expressions. The ASP.NET Framework supports both one-way DataBinding expressions and two-way DataBinding expressions.

Up to this point, we have used one-way DataBinding expressions exclusively. In a one-way DataBinding expression, you use the DataBinding expression to display the value of a data item. You use the `Eval()` method to display the value of a one-way DataBinding expression.

In a two-way DataBinding expression, you not only can display the value of a data item, you also can modify the value of a data item. You use the `Bind()` method when working with a two-way DataBinding expression.

For example, the page in Listing 8.13 contains a `FormView` control that includes a template for editing a movie record in the Movies database table (see Figure 8.12).

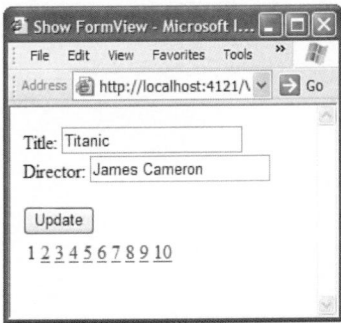

FIGURE 8.12   Editing a movie.

LISTING 8.13   ShowFormView.aspx

```
<%@ Page Language="C#" %>
<!DOCTYPE html PUBLIC "-//W3C//DTD XHTML 1.1//EN"
"http://www.w3.org/TR/xhtml11/DTD/xhtml11.dtd">
<html xmlns="http://www.w3.org/1999/xhtml" >
<head id="Head1" runat="server">
    <title>Show FormView</title>
</head>
<body>
    <form id="form1" runat="server">
    <div>

    <asp:FormView
        id="FormView1"
        DataKeyNames="Id"
        DataSourceId="srcMovies"
        DefaultMode="Edit"
        AllowPaging="true"
        Runat="server">
        <EditItemTemplate>
        <asp:Label
            id="lblTitle"
            Text="Title:"
            AssociatedControlID="txtTitle"
            Runat="server" />
```

```
        <asp:TextBox
            id="txtTitle"
            Text='<%#Bind("Title")%>'
            Runat="server" />
        <br />
        <asp:Label
            id="lblDirector"
            Text="Director:"
            AssociatedControlID="txtDirector"
            Runat="server" />
        <asp:TextBox
            id="txtDirector"
            Text='<%#Bind("Director")%>'
            Runat="server" />
        <br />
        <asp:Button
            id="btnUpdate"
            Text="Update"
            CommandName="Update"
            Runat="server" />
        </EditItemTemplate>
    </asp:FormView>

    <asp:SqlDataSource
        id="srcMovies"
        ConnectionString="Data Source=.\SQLExpress;
            AttachDbFilename=|DataDirectory|MyDatabase.mdf;
            Integrated Security=True;User Instance=True"
        SelectCommand="SELECT Id, Title,Director,DateReleased FROM Movies"
        UpdateCommand="UPDATE Movies SET Title=@Title,
            Director=@Director WHERE Id=@Id"
        Runat="server" />


    </div>
    </form>
</body>
</html>
```

The FormView contains an EditItemTemplate. The EditItemTemplate contains three TextBox controls. Each TextBox control has a two-way DataBinding expression assigned to its Text property.

The DataBinding expressions associate the TextBox control properties with the properties of the data item being edited. When you click the Update button, any changes you make to the Text properties are updated in the Movies database table.

NOTE

Templates that support one-way databinding implement the ITemplate interface, and templates that support two-way databinding implement the IBindableTemplate interface.

Overview of SQL Server 2008 Express

Microsoft SQL Server 2008 Express is the version of SQL Server bundled with Visual Web Developer. You can also download this database engine from the Microsoft website (http://www.microsoft.com/express/Database/). SQL Server Express is used for almost all the database examples in this book.

In this section, you are provided with a brief overview of the features of this database. You also learn how to connect to SQL Server Express.

Features of SQL Server Express

One of the most important features of SQL Server 2008 Express is that it is a royalty-free database engine. You can download it and use it for free in your applications. You also can distribute the database in commercial applications that you produce for others without paying royalties to Microsoft. (Registration at the Microsoft site is required to do this.)

Microsoft SQL Server 2008 Express uses the same database engine as the full retail version of SQL Server 2008. However, because it is a free product, Microsoft has limited some of its features to encourage you to upgrade to the full version of SQL Server 2008.

First, unlike the full version of SQL Server 2008, a SQL Server Express database can be no larger than 4 gigabytes. Furthermore, SQL Server Express is limited to using 1 gigabyte of RAM. Also, SQL Server Express uses only a single processor even when used on a multi-processor server.

SQL Server Express also does not support several of the advanced features of the full version of SQL Server 2008. For example, it doesn't support Analysis Services, Notification Services, English Query, Data Transformation Services, or OLAP.

NOTE

The version of SQL Server Express bundled with Visual Web Developer does not include support for Full-Text Search or Reporting Services. If you need these services, you can download a version of SQL Server Express that supports Full-Text Search and Reporting Services from the Microsoft website.

However, SQL Server Express does not have a Workload Governor. The performance of a SQL Server Express database is never throttled. This means that you can use SQL Server Express for small websites without worrying about performance limitations.

Finally, like the full version of SQL Server 2008, SQL Server Express supports the Common Language Runtime. In other words, you can use C# or Visual Basic .NET to create stored procedures, triggers, user-defined functions, and user-defined types.

SQL Server 2008 Express Management Tools

You can use three tools to create new database objects when using SQL Server 2008 Express. You can use Database Explorer in Visual Web Developer, Microsoft SQL Server Management Studio Express, and SQLCMD utility.

The Database Explorer included in Visual Web Developer provides you with a user-friendly interface for working with database objects (see Figure 8.13). I assume that you use the Database Explorer for the database samples in this book.

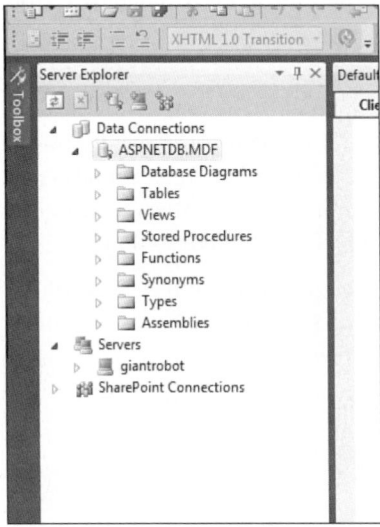

FIGURE 8.13   The Database Explorer window in Visual Web Developer.

Alternatively, you can use Microsoft SQL Server Management Studio Express. You can download Management Studio from the Microsoft site at http://www.microsoft.com/sqlserver/2008/en/us/express.aspx. This tool enables you to browse database objects and execute SQL queries (see Figure 8.14).

Finally, SQL Server 2008 Express includes a command-line tool named SQLCMD. You can use the SQLCMD tool to fire off SQL queries from the Command Prompt (see Figure 8.15). This alternative is the most painful, but it works.

You use SQLCMD by opening a command prompt and connecting to your database with the following command:

```
SQLCMD -S .\SQLExpress
```

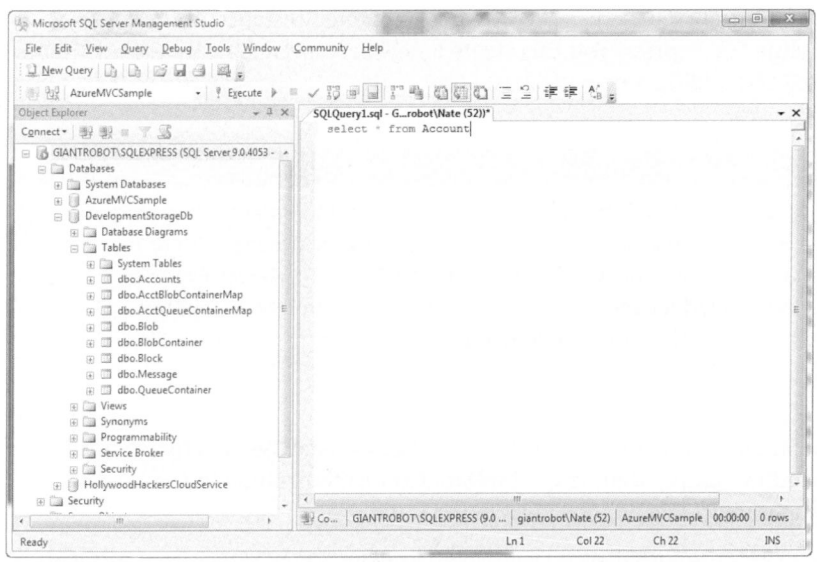

FIGURE 8.14   Using the Microsoft SQL Server Management Studio Express.

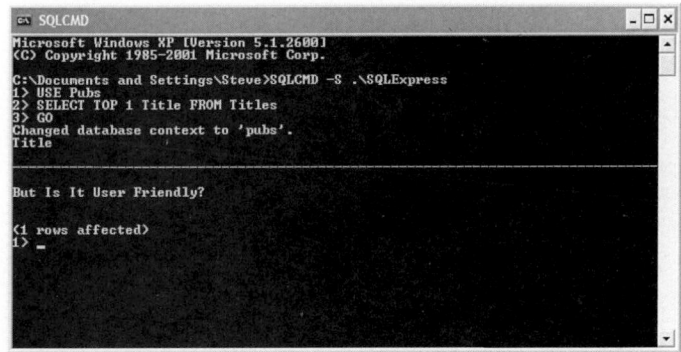

FIGURE 8.15   Executing a SQL query with SQLCMD.

Next, you can enter SQL statements at the command prompt. The statements are not executed until you type **GO.** You can get help using SQLCMD by typing :HELP after starting the tool. When you finish using the tool, type EXIT to quit.

Server Databases Versus Local Databases

You can create two different types of databases with SQL Server Express: Server and Local.

By default, when you install SQL Server 2008 Express, a named instance of the server is created with the name SQLExpress. You can create a new Server database by connecting to the named instance and adding a new database.

If you own Visual Studio 2010, you can create a new Server database directly from the Server Explorer window. Simply right-click the Data Connections node in the Server Explorer window, and select Create New SQL Server Database.

Unfortunately, you can't use Visual Web Developer to create a new Server database. This option is grayed out. If you need to create a new Server database, and you don't have the full version of Visual Studio, you need to use Microsoft SQL Server Management Studio Express as discussed in the previous section (see Figure 8.16).

FIGURE 8.16   Creating a new Server database.

When you create a Server database, the database is attached and available to any application running on the server. You can connect to the database easily from any ASP.NET application.

For example, the following connection string enables you to connect to a Server database named MyData:

```
Data Source=.\SQLExpress;Initial Catalog=MyData;Integrated Security=True
```

> **NOTE**
>
> There are many different ways to write a connection string that does the same thing. For example, instead of the Data Source parameter, you can use the Server parameter, and instead of the Initial Catalog parameter, you can use the Database parameter. For a list of all the keywords supported when connecting to a Microsoft SQL Server database, see the `SqlConnection.ConnectionString` entry in the Microsoft .NET Framework SDK documentation.

The other option is to create a Local database instead of a Server database. When you create a Local database, you create the database in your project. The database file is added to the App_Data folder in your website.

Here are the steps for creating a Local database in Visual Web Developer:

1. Open the Add New Item dialog box by selecting the website, Add New Item (see Figure 8.17).

2. Select Sql Database and provide the database with a name (for example, `MyLocalData.mdf`).

3. Click Add.

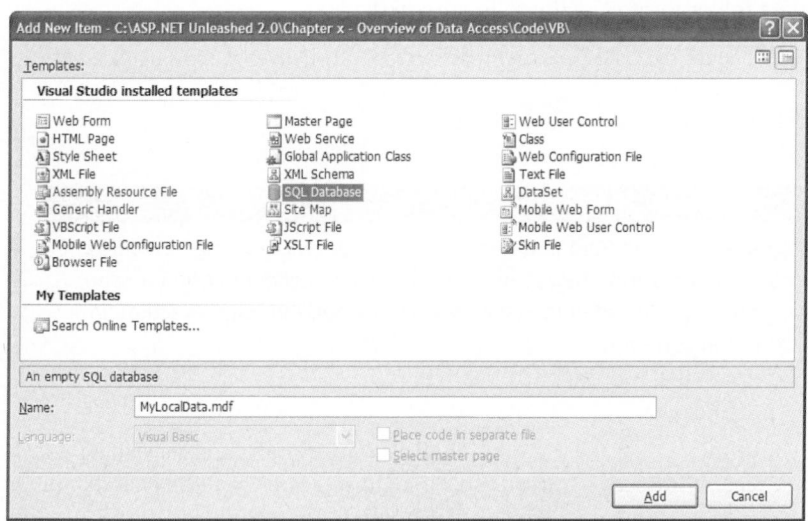

FIGURE 8.17   Creating a new Local database.

When you click Add, Visual Web Developer warns you that it needs to create the App_Data folder (if the folder doesn't already exist). The MyLocalData.mdf file will be added to this folder. Click OK to create the new folder.

You can connect to a Local database named MyLocalData.mdf by using the following connection string:

```
Data Source=.\SQLEXPRESS;AttachDbFilename=|DataDirectory|MyLocalData.mdf;
Integrated Security=True;User Instance=True
```

When you connect to the MyLocalData.mdf file, the database is attached automatically to Microsoft SQL Server Express.

The connection string includes an AttachDbFilename parameter. This parameter represents the physical path to a database file (.mdf file). The keyword ¦DataDirectory¦ is used in the path. The |DataDirectory| keyword represents a website's App_Data folder.

Instead of using the |DataDirectory| keyword, you could supply the entire physical path to a database file. The advantage of using the |DataDirectory| keyword is that you can move your web application easily to a new location without needing to change the connection string.

The connection string also includes a User Instance parameter. Creating a User Instance connection enables you to connect to a Local database without using an Administrator account. Because the ASPNET account is not an Administrator account, you need to add this parameter to use Local databases from ASP.NET pages.

Including the User Instance parameter in a connection string causes a separate user instance of SQL Server to execute with the security context of the user. The first time a user creates a User Instance connection, copies of the system databases are copied to a user's application data folder located at the following path:

```
C:\Users\[Username]\AppData\Local\Microsoft\Microsoft SQL Server Data\SQLEXPRESS
```

A separate set of system databases is created for each user.

> **NOTE**
>
> By default, when a page is served from Internet Information Server, the page executes in the security context of either the ASPNET or Network Service account. When a page is served from the web server included in Visual Web Developer, the page executes in the security context of the current user.

One of the primary advantages of using a Local database rather than a Server database is that a Local database can be moved easily to a new location. If you email a Local database file (the .mdf file stored in the App_Data folder) to a friend, your friend can start using the database immediately. The only requirement is that your friend has SQL Server Express installed on a computer.

Sample Database-Driven Web Application

The following chapters get into all the gritty details of the Data controls. Before you get lost in the details, however, I want to provide you with a sample of a data-driven web application. I want to provide you with a real-world application that illustrates what can be built with the Data controls.

In this section, a complete Employee Directory application is built, which supports displaying, adding, editing, and deleting employee information. The sample application includes all the necessary form field validation.

One of the amazing things about ASP.NET 4 Framework is how much the Framework simplifies data access. The sample application consists of a single page that contains little code. Writing the same application with ASP.NET 1.x Framework would require pages of code. (I won't even mention how much code it would require to write the same application in ASP Classic.)

Because the Employee Directory application includes all the required validation code, the page is a little too long to include in the pages of this book. However, it is included on the book's website. Open the page named `EmployeeDirectory.aspx`.

After you open the `EmployeeDirectory.aspx` page in your browser, you see a list of employees. This list is rendered by a `GridView` control (see Figure 8.18).

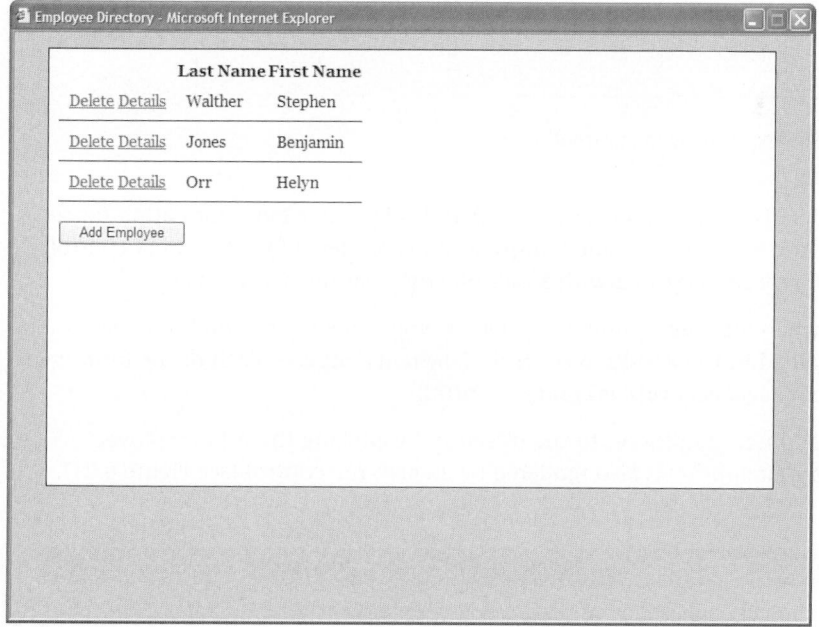

FIGURE 8.18   Displaying a list of employees with the `GridView` control.

Next to each employee, there is a Delete link and a Details link. If you click Delete, the selected employee is deleted from the database. A client-side confirmation dialog box appears when you click the Delete link (see Figure 8.19). This dialog box is added to each of the Delete links in the grdEmployees_RowCreated() method. This method is called automatically by the GridView control as the GridView creates each row.

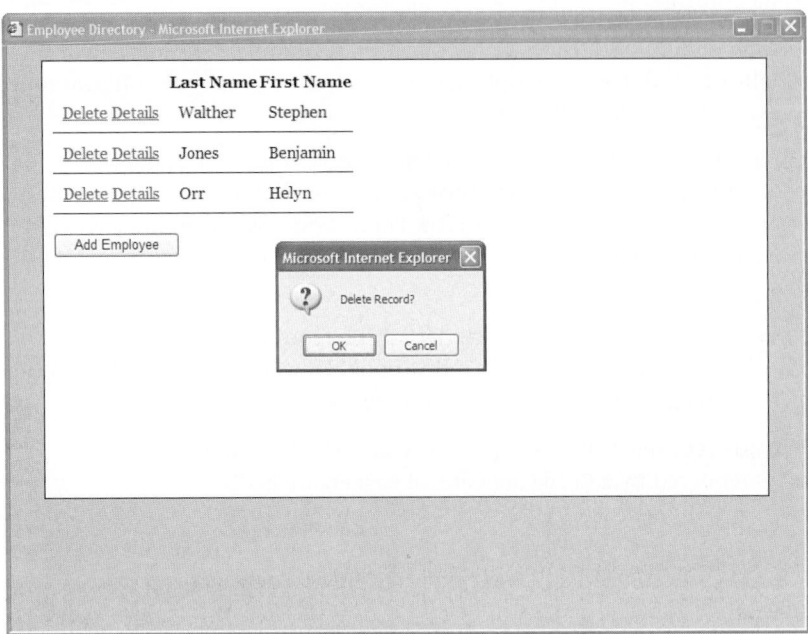

FIGURE 8.19   Deleting employee information.

If you click the Details link, a window appears that displays detailed information for the Employee (see Figure 8.20). The detailed information is rendered by a FormView control. The window that appears is created with an absolutely positioned <div> tag.

If you click Edit when viewing a employee's details, you can edit the employee record. The edit form is contained in the FormView control's EditItemTemplate. Each of the form fields is associated with a RequiredFieldValidator control.

Finally, you can add new employees to the directory by clicking the Add Employee button. The form that appears is also rendered by a FormView control (see Figure 8.21).

WEB STANDARDS NOTE

The Employee Directory application works great in Internet Explorer 6+, Firefox 1.0+, and Opera 8.0+. The only feature of the application that breaks Web standards is the use of the Drop Shadow filter around the pop-up window. The Drop Shadow effect works only in Internet Explorer.

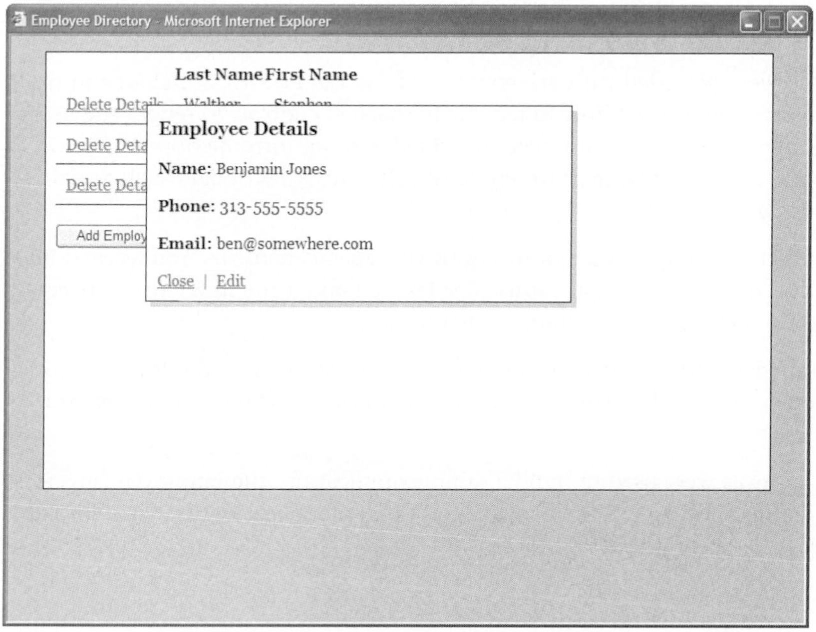

FIGURE 8.20   Displaying employee details.

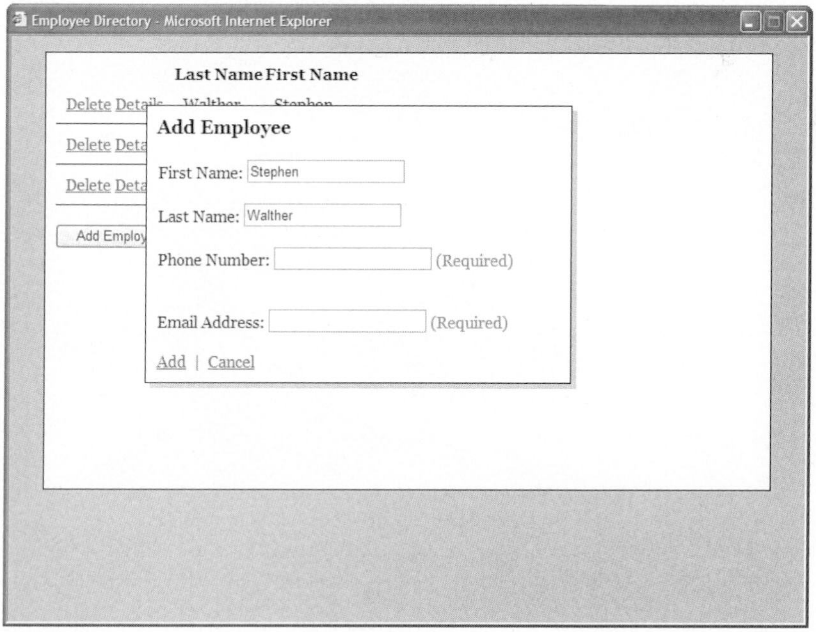

FIGURE 8.21   Adding a new employee.

Summary

In this chapter, you were provided with an overview of the Data controls included in the ASP.NET 4 Framework. You learned how to use the DataBound controls to render the user interface for working with data. You also were provided with an introduction to the DataSource controls, which can be used to represent different types of data such as database data and XML data.

You also learned about two important features of the DataBound controls. You learned how to use Templates and databinding expressions. You learned about the difference between one-way databinding and two-way databinding expressions.

Next, you were provided with an overview of SQL Server 2008 Express. You learned how to create a SQL Server Express database. You also learned how to create both Server and Local databases.

Finally, the Data controls were used to build a sample application: the Employee Directory application. You learned how to use the controls to build an application that enables you to list, edit, insert, and delete database records.

Using the SqlDataSource Control

The SqlDataSource control enables you to quickly and easily represent a SQL database in a web page. In many cases, you can take advantage of the SqlDataSource control to write a database-driven web page without writing a single line of code.

You use the SqlDataSource control to represent a connection and set of commands that can be executed against a SQL database. You can use the SqlDataSource control when working with Microsoft SQL Server, Microsoft SQL Server Express, Microsoft Access, Oracle, DB2, MySQL, or just about any other SQL relational database ever created by man.

> **NOTE**
>
> Although you can use the SqlDataSource control when working with Microsoft Access, the ASP.NET Framework does include the AccessDataSource control, which was designed specifically for Microsoft Access. Because using Microsoft Access for a website is not recommended, this book doesn't discuss the AccessDataSource control.

The SqlDataSource control is built on top of ADO.NET. Under the covers, the SqlDataSource uses ADO.NET objects such as the DataSet, DataReader, and Command objects. Because the SqlDataSource control is a control, it enables you to use these ADO.NET objects declaratively rather than programmatically.

The SqlDataSource control is a nonvisual control—it doesn't render anything. You use the SqlDataSource control with other controls, such as the GridView or FormView controls, to display and edit database data. The SqlDataSource control can also be used to issue SQL commands against a database programmatically.

> **NOTE**
>
> The SqlDataSource control is not an appropriate control to use when building more complicated multitier applications. The SqlDataSource control forces you to mix your data access layer with your user interface layer. If you want to build a more cleanly architected multi-tier application, you should use the ObjectDataSource control to represent your database data.
>
> The ObjectDataSource is discussed in detail in Chapter 18, "Using the ObjectDataSource Control."

In this chapter, you learn how to represent connections and commands with the SqlDataSource control. You also learn how to use different types of parameters when executing commands. Finally, you learn how to improve the performance of your database-driven applications by taking advantage of the SqlDataSource control's support for caching database data.

Creating Database Connections

You can use the SqlDataSource control to connect to just about any SQL relational database server. In this section, you learn how to connect to Microsoft SQL Server and other databases such as Oracle. You also learn how you can store the database connection string used by SqlDataSource securely in your web configuration files.

Connecting to Microsoft SQL Server

By default, the SqlDataSource control is configured to connect to Microsoft SQL Server version 7.0 or higher. The default provider used by the SqlDataSource control is the ADO.NET provider for Microsoft SQL Server.

You represent a database connection string with the SqlDataSource control's ConnectionString property. For example, the page in Listing 9.1 includes a SqlDataSource control that connects to a local SQL Server 2008 database (see Figure 9.1).

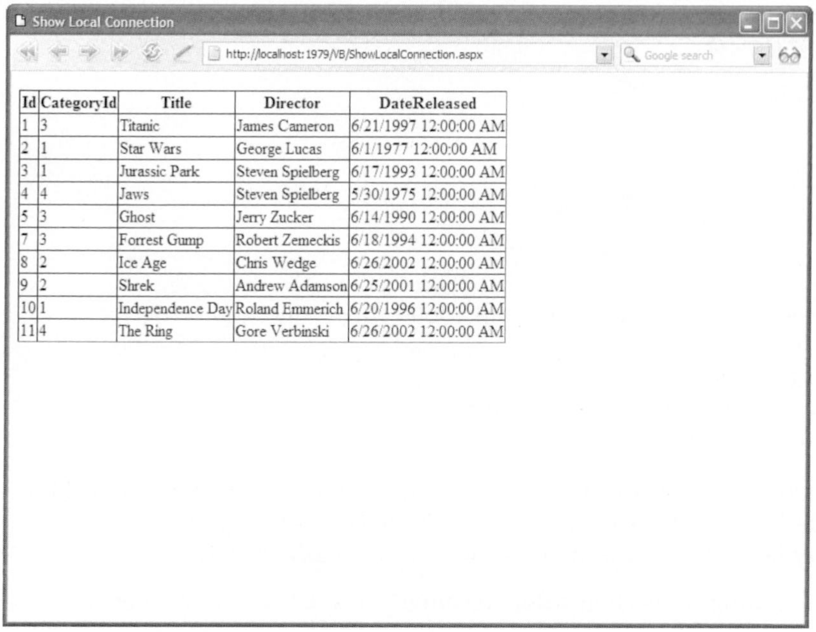

Id	CategoryId	Title	Director	DateReleased
1	3	Titanic	James Cameron	6/21/1997 12:00:00 AM
2	1	Star Wars	George Lucas	6/1/1977 12:00:00 AM
3	1	Jurassic Park	Steven Spielberg	6/17/1993 12:00:00 AM
4	4	Jaws	Steven Spielberg	5/30/1975 12:00:00 AM
5	3	Ghost	Jerry Zucker	6/14/1990 12:00:00 AM
7	3	Forrest Gump	Robert Zemeckis	6/18/1994 12:00:00 AM
8	2	Ice Age	Chris Wedge	6/26/2002 12:00:00 AM
9	2	Shrek	Andrew Adamson	6/25/2001 12:00:00 AM
10	1	Independence Day	Roland Emmerich	6/20/1996 12:00:00 AM
11	4	The Ring	Gore Verbinski	6/26/2002 12:00:00 AM

FIGURE 9.1 Displaying the Movies database table.

LISTING 9.1 ShowLocalConnection.aspx

```
<%@ Page Language="C#" %>
<!DOCTYPE html PUBLIC "-//W3C//DTD XHTML 1.1//EN"
"http://www.w3.org/TR/xhtml11/DTD/xhtml11.dtd">
<html xmlns="http://www.w3.org/1999/xhtml" >
<head id="Head1" runat="server">
    <title>Show Local Connection</title>
</head>
<body>
    <form id="form1" runat="server">
    <div>

    <asp:GridView
        id="grdMovies"
        DataSourceID="srcMovies"
        Runat="server" />

    <asp:SqlDataSource
        id="srcMovies"
        SelectCommand="SELECT * FROM Movies"
        ConnectionString="Data Source=.\SQLEXPRESS;
            AttachDbFilename=|DataDirectory|MyDatabase.mdf;
```

```
                Integrated Security=True;User Instance=True"
            Runat="server" />


    </div>
    </form>
</body>
</html>
```

In Listing 9.1, the SqlDataSource control uses the following connection string:

```
Data Source=.\SQLEXPRESS;
AttachDbFilename=|DataDirectory|MyDatabase.mdf;
Integrated Security=True;User Instance=True
```

This connection string connects to an instance of SQL Server Express located on the local machine and a database file named MyDatabase.mdf. The connection string uses Integrated Security (a Trusted Connection) to connect to the local database.

You can use the following connection string to connect to a database located on a remote server.

```
Data Source=DataServer;Initial Catalog=Northwind;
User ID=webuser;Password=secret
```

This database connection string connects to a SQL Server database located on a remote machine named DataServer. The connection string connects to a database named Northwind.

This second connection string uses SQL Standard Security instead of Integrated Security. It contains a user ID and password associated with a SQL Server login.

WARNING

For security reasons, you should never include a connection string that contains security credentials in an ASP.NET page. Theoretically, no one should see the source of an ASP.NET page. However, Microsoft does not have a perfect track record. Later in this section, you learn how to store connection strings in the web configuration file (and encrypt them).

The .NET Framework includes a utility class, named the SqlConnectionBuilder class, that you can use when working with SQL connection strings. This class automatically converts any connection string into a canonical representation. It also exposes properties for extracting and modifying individual connection string parameters, such as the Password parameters.

For example, the page in Listing 9.2 automatically converts any connection string into its canonical representation (see Figure 9.2).

FIGURE 9.2   Converting a connection string.

LISTING 9.2   `SqlConnectionStringBuilder.aspx`

```
<%@ Page Language="C#" %>
<%@ Import Namespace="System.Data.SqlClient" %>
<!DOCTYPE html PUBLIC "-//W3C//DTD XHTML 1.1//EN"
"http://www.w3.org/TR/xhtml11/DTD/xhtml11.dtd">
<script runat="server">

    protected void btnConvert_Click(object sender, EventArgs e)
    {
        SqlConnectionStringBuilder builder = new
SqlConnectionStringBuilder(txtConnectionString.Text);
        lblResult.Text = builder.ConnectionString;
    }
</script>
<html xmlns="http://www.w3.org/1999/xhtml" >
<head id="Head1" runat="server">
    <title>SQL Connection String Builder</title>
</head>
```

```
<body>
    <form id="form1" runat="server">
    <div>

    <asp:TextBox
        id="txtConnectionString"
        Columns="60"
        Runat="Server" />
    <asp:Button
        id="btnConvert"
        Text="Convert"
        OnClick="btnConvert_Click"
        Runat="Server" />

    <hr />

    <asp:Label
        id="lblResult"
        Runat="server" />

    </div>
    </form>
</body>
</html>
```

After opening the page in Listing 9.2, if you enter a connection string that looks like this:

```
Server=localhost;UID=webuser;pwd=secret;database=Northwind
```

the page converts the connection string to look like this:

```
Data Source=localhost;Initial Catalog=Northwind;User ID=webuser;Password=secret
```

Connecting to Other Databases

If you need to connect to any database server other than Microsoft SQL Server, you need to modify the SqlDataSource control's ProviderName property.

The .NET Framework includes the following providers:

- ▶ **System.Data.OracleClient**—Use the ADO.NET provider for Oracle when connecting to an Oracle database.

- ▶ **System.Data.OleDb**—Use the OLE DB provider when connecting to a data source that supports an OLE DB provider.

- ▶ **System.Data.Odbc**—Use the ODBC provider when connecting to a data source with an ODBC driver.

> **NOTE**
>
> You can configure additional providers that you can use with the `SqlDataSource` control by adding new entries to the `<DbProviderFactories>` section of the `Machine.config` file.

For performance reasons, you should always use the native ADO.NET provider for a database. However, if your database does not have an ADO.NET provider, you need to use either OLE DB or ODBC to connect to the database. Almost every database under the sun has either an OLE DB provider or an ODBC driver.

For example, the page in Listing 9.3 uses the ADO.NET Oracle provider to connect to an Oracle database.

LISTING 9.3   ConnectOracle.aspx

```
<%@ Page Language="C#" %>
<!DOCTYPE html PUBLIC "-//W3C//DTD XHTML 1.1//EN"
 "http://www.w3.org/TR/xhtml11/DTD/xhtml11.dtd">
<html xmlns="http://www.w3.org/1999/xhtml" >
<head id="Head1" runat="server">
    <title>Connect Oracle</title>
</head>
<body>
    <form id="form1" runat="server">
    <div>

    <asp:GridView
        id="grdOrders"
        DataSourceID="srcOrders"
        Runat="server" />

    <asp:SqlDataSource
        id="srcOrders"
        ProviderName="System.Data.OracleClient"
        SelectCommand="SELECT * FROM Orders"
        ConnectionString="Data Source=OracleDB;Integrated Security=yes"
        Runat="server" />

    </div>
    </form>
</body>
</html>
```

In Listing 9.3, the `ProviderName` property is set to the value `System.Data.OracleClient`. The connection uses the native ADO.NET Oracle provider instead of the default provider for Microsoft SQL Server.

> **NOTE**
>
> To connect to an Oracle database, you need to install the Oracle client software on your web server.

> **NOTE**
>
> Oracle has produced its own native ADO.NET provider. You can download the Oracle provider at `http://www.oracle.com/technology/tech/windows/odpnet/index.html`

Storing Connection Strings in the Web Configuration File

Storing connection strings in your pages is a bad idea for three reasons. First, it is not a good practice from the perspective of security. In theory, no one should ever view the source code of your ASP.NET pages. In practice, however, hackers have discovered security flaws in ASP.NET Framework. To sleep better at night, you should store your connection strings in a separate file.

Also, adding a connection string to every page makes it difficult to manage a website. If you ever need to change your password, you need to change every page that contains it. If, on the other hand, you store the connection string in one file, you can update the password by modifying the single file.

Finally, storing a connection string in a page can, potentially, hurt the performance of your application. The ADO.NET provider for SQL Server automatically uses connection pooling to improve your application's data access performance. Instead of being destroyed when they are closed, the connections are kept alive so that they can be put back into service quickly when the need arises. However, only connections created with the same connection strings are pooled together. (An exact character-by-character match is made.) Adding the same connection string to multiple pages is a recipe for defeating the benefits of connection pooling.

For these reasons, you should always place your connection strings in the web configuration file. The `Web.Config` file in Listing 9.4 includes a `connectionStrings` section.

LISTING 9.4   Web.Config

```
<?xml version="1.0"?>
<configuration>
  <connectionStrings>
    <add name="Movies" connectionString="Data Source=.\SQLEXPRESS;
      AttachDbFilename=¦DataDirectory¦MyDatabase.mdf;Integrated Security=True;
User Instance=True" />
```

```
    </connectionStrings>
</configuration>
```

You can add as many connection strings to the `connectionStrings` section as you want. The page in Listing 9.5 includes a `SqlDataSource` that uses the Movies connection string.

LISTING 9.5 `ShowMovies.aspx`

```
<%@ Page Language="C#" %>
<!DOCTYPE html PUBLIC "-//W3C//DTD XHTML 1.1//EN"
 "http://www.w3.org/TR/xhtml11/DTD/xhtml11.dtd">
<html xmlns="http://www.w3.org/1999/xhtml" >
<head id="Head1" runat="server">
    <title>Show Movies</title>
</head>
<body>
    <form id="form1" runat="server">
    <div>

    <asp:GridView
        id="grdMovies"
        DataSourceID="srcMovies"
        Runat="server" />

    <asp:SqlDataSource
        id="srcMovies"
        SelectCommand="SELECT * FROM Movies"
        ConnectionString="<%$ ConnectionStrings:Movies %>"
        Runat="server" />

    </div>
    </form>
</body>
</html>
```

The expression `<%$ ConnectionStrings:Movies %>` is used to represent the connection string. This expression is not case-sensitive.

Rather than add a connection string to your project's web configuration file, you can add the connection string to a web configuration file higher in the folder hierarchy. For example, you can add the connection string to the root `Web.Config` file and make it available to all applications running on your server. The root `Web.Config` file is located at the following path:

```
C:\WINDOWS\Microsoft.NET\Framework\[v4.0.30319]\CONFIG
```

Encrypting Connection Strings

You can encrypt the <connectionStrings> section of a web configuration file. For example, Listing 9.6 contains an encrypted version of the Web.Config file that was created in Listing 9.4.

LISTING 9.6   Web.Config

```
<?xml version="1.0"?>
<configuration>
  <protectedData>
    <protectedDataSections>
      <add name="connectionStrings" provider="RsaProtectedConfigurationProvider"
        inheritedByChildren="false" />
    </protectedDataSections>
  </protectedData>
  <connectionStrings>
    <EncryptedData Type="http://www.w3.org/2001/04/xmlenc#Element"
      xmlns="http://www.w3.org/2001/04/xmlenc#">
      <EncryptionMethod Algorithm="http://www.w3.org/2001/04/xmlenc
#tripledes-cbc" />
      <KeyInfo xmlns="http://www.w3.org/2000/09/xmldsig#">
        <EncryptedKey Recipient="" xmlns="http://www.w3.org/2001/04/xmlenc#">
          <EncryptionMethod Algorithm="http://www.w3.org/2001/04/xmlenc#rsa-1_5" />
          <KeyInfo xmlns="http://www.w3.org/2000/09/xmldsig#">
            <KeyName>Rsa Key</KeyName>
          </KeyInfo>
          <CipherData>
            <CipherValue>MPLyXy7PoZ8E5VPk6K/azkGumO5tpeuWRzxx4PfgKeFwFccKx/
8Zc7app++0
4c/dX7jA3uvNniFHTW6eKvrkLOsW2m6MxaeeLEfR9ME51Gy5jLa1KIXfTXKuJbXeZdiwrjCRdIqQpEj4fGZvr
3KkwI5HbGAqgK4Uu7IfBajdTJM=</CipherValue>
          </CipherData>
        </EncryptedKey>
      </KeyInfo>
      <CipherData>
        <CipherValue>CgnD74xMkcr7N4fgaHZNMps+e+if7dnEZ8xFw07kOBexaX+KyJvqtPuZiD2hW
Dpqt5EOw6YM0Fs2uI5ocetbb74+d4kfHorC0bEjLEV+zcsJVGi2dZ80ll6sW+Y99osupaxOfrL3ld3mphM
Yrpcf+xafAs05s2x7H77TY01Y1goRaQ77tnkEIrQNQsHk/5eeptcE+A8scZSlaolFRNSSCdyO1TiKjPHF+
MtI/8qzr2T6yjYM5Z+ZQ5TeiVvpg/6VD7K7dArIDmkFMTuQgdQBSJUQ23dZ5V9Ja9HxqMGCea9NomBdhGC
0sabDLxyPdOzGEAqOyxWKxqQM6Y0JyZKtPDg==</CipherValue>
      </CipherData>
    </EncryptedData>
  </connectionStrings>
</configuration>
```

The contents of the <connectionStrings> section are no longer visible. However, an ASP.NET page can continue to read the value of the Movie database connection string by using the <%$ ConnectionStrings:Movie %> expression.

The easiest way to encrypt the <connectionStrings> section is to use the aspnet_regiis command-line tool. This tool is located in the following folder:

```
C:\WINDOWS\Microsoft.NET\Framework\v2.0.50727 \
```

Executing the following command encrypts the <connectionStrings> section of a Web.Config file located in a folder with the path c:\Websites\MyWebsite:

```
aspnet_regiis -pef connectionStrings "c:\Websites\MyWebsite"
```

The -pef option (Protect Encrypt Filepath) encrypts a particular configuration section located at a particular path.

You can decrypt a section with the -pdf option like this:

```
aspnet_regiis -pdf connectionStrings "c:\Websites\MyWebsite"
```

NOTE

Web configuration encryption options are discussed in more detail in Chapter 34, "Configuring Applications."

Executing Database Commands

In this section, you learn how to represent and execute SQL commands with the SqlDataSource control. In particular, you learn how to execute both inline SQL statements and external stored procedures. You also learn how to capture and gracefully handle errors that result from executing SQL commands.

Executing Inline SQL Statements

You can use the SqlDataSource control to represent four different types of SQL commands. The control supports the following four properties:

▶ SelectCommand

▶ InsertCommand

▶ UpdateCommand

▶ DeleteCommand

You can assign any SQL statement to any of these properties. For example, the page in Listing 9.7 uses all four properties to enable selecting, inserting, updating, and deleting records from the Movies database table (see Figure 9.3).

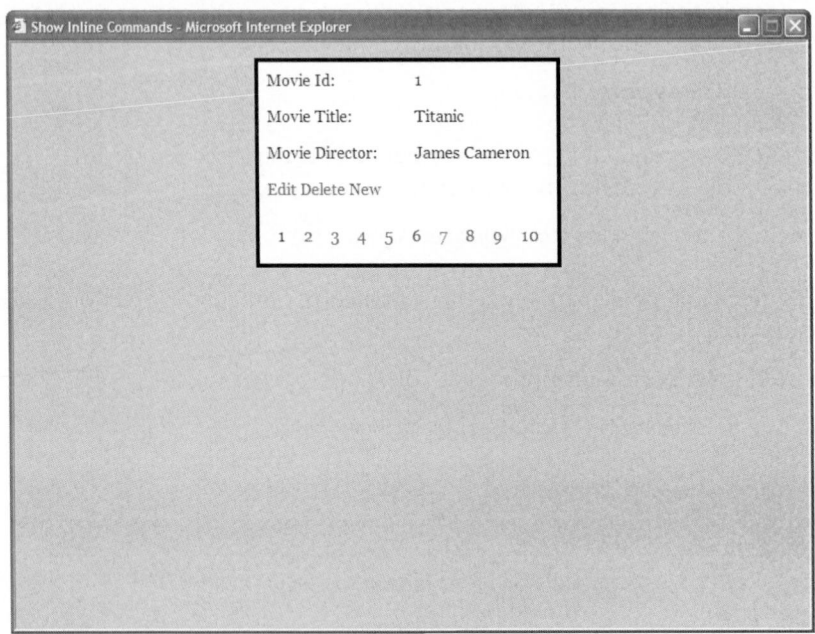

FIGURE 9.3   Executing inline SQL commands.

LISTING 9.7   ShowInlineCommands.aspx

```
<%@ Page Language="C#" %>
<!DOCTYPE html PUBLIC "-//W3C//DTD XHTML 1.1//EN"
  "http://www.w3.org/TR/xhtml11/DTD/xhtml11.dtd">
<html xmlns="http://www.w3.org/1999/xhtml" >
<head id="Head1" runat="server">
    <style type="text/css">
        .detailsView
        {
            margin:0px auto;
            border:solid 4px black;
            background-color:white;
        }
        .detailsView td
        {
            padding:8px;
```

```
        }
        html
        {
            background-color:silver;
            font-family:Georgia, Serif;
        }
        a
        {
            color:blue;
            text-decoration:none;
        }
    </style>
    <title>Show Inline Commands</title>
</head>
<body>
    <form id="form1" runat="server">
    <div>

    <asp:DetailsView
        id="dtlMovies"
        DataSourceID="srcMovies"
        DataKeyNames="Id"
        AllowPaging="true"
        AutoGenerateEditButton="true"
        AutoGenerateInsertButton="true"
        AutoGenerateDeleteButton="true"
        AutoGenerateRows="false"
        CssClass="detailsView"
        PagerSettings-Mode="NumericFirstLast"
        Runat="server">
        <Fields>
        <asp:BoundField DataField="Id"
            HeaderText="Movie Id:" ReadOnly="true" InsertVisible="false" />
        <asp:BoundField DataField="Title" HeaderText="Movie Title:" />
        <asp:BoundField DataField="Director" HeaderText="Movie Director:" />
        </Fields>
    </asp:DetailsView>

    <asp:SqlDataSource
        id="srcMovies"
        SelectCommand="SELECT Id,Title,Director FROM Movies"
        InsertCommand="INSERT Movies (Title,Director,CategoryId,DateReleased)
            VALUES (@Title, @Director,0,'12/15/1966')"
        UpdateCommand="UPDATE Movies SET Title=@Title,
            Director=@Director WHERE Id=@Id"
```

6

```
        DeleteCommand="DELETE Movies WHERE Id=@Id"
        ConnectionString="<%$ ConnectionStrings:Movies %>"
        Runat="server" />

    </div>
    </form>
</body>
</html>
```

The page in Listing 9.7 contains a DetailsView control bound to a SqlDataSource control. You can click the Edit link to update an existing record, the New link to insert a new record, or the Delete link to delete an existing record. The DataBound control takes advantage of all four SQL commands supported by the SqlDataSource control.

Executing Stored Procedures

The SqlDataSource control can represent SQL stored procedures just as easily as it can represent inline SQL commands. You can indicate that a command represents a stored procedure by assigning the value StoredProcedure to any of the following properties:

- ▶ SelectCommandType

- ▶ InsertCommandType

- ▶ UpdateCommandType

- ▶ DeleteCommandType

You can create a new stored procedure in Visual Web Developer by opening the Database Explorer window, expanding a Data Connection, right-clicking Stored Procedures, and clicking Add New Stored Procedure (see Figure 9.4).

The stored procedure in Listing 9.8 returns a count of the number of movies in each movie category.

LISTING 9.8   CountMoviesInCategory

```
CREATE PROCEDURE CountMoviesInCategory
AS
SELECT Name As Category, Count(*) As Count
FROM Movies
INNER JOIN MovieCategories
ON CategoryId = MovieCategories.Id
GROUP BY Name
```

The page in Listing 9.9 uses the CountMoviesInCategory stored procedure to display a report with a GridView control (see Figure 9.5).

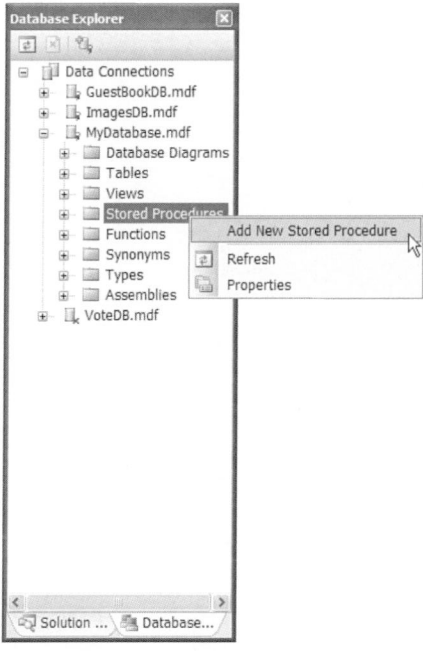

FIGURE 9.4   Creating a new stored procedure in Visual Web Developer.

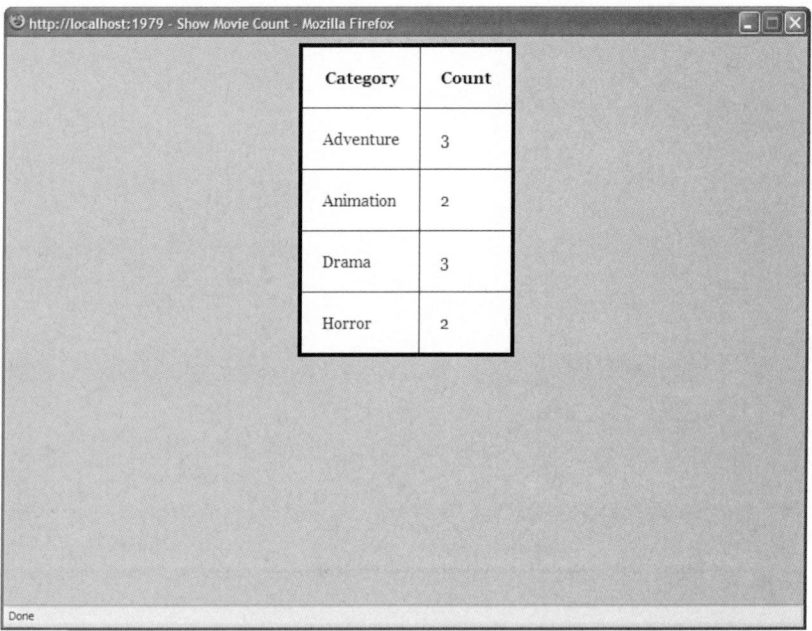

FIGURE 9.5   Showing count of movies in category.

LISTING 9.9 ShowMovieCount.aspx

```
<%@ Page Language="C#" %>
<!DOCTYPE html PUBLIC "-//W3C//DTD XHTML 1.1//EN"
 "http://www.w3.org/TR/xhtml11/DTD/xhtml11.dtd">
<html xmlns="http://www.w3.org/1999/xhtml" >
<head id="Head1" runat="server">
    <style type="text/css">
        .gridView
        {
            margin:0px auto;
            border:solid 4px black;
            background-color:white;
        }
        .gridView td, .gridView th
        {
            padding:20px;
        }
        html
        {
            background-color:silver;
            font-family:Georgia, Serif;
        }
    </style>
    <title>Show Movie Count</title>
</head>
<body>
    <form id="form1" runat="server">
    <div>

    <asp:GridView
        id="grdMovies"
        DataSourceID="srcMovies"
        CssClass="gridView"
        Runat="server" />

    <asp:SqlDataSource
        id="srcMovies"
        SelectCommand="CountMoviesInCategory"
        SelectCommandType="StoredProcedure"
        ConnectionString="<%$ ConnectionStrings:Movies %>"
        Runat="server" />
```

```
      </div>
      </form>
  </body>
  </html>
```

Filtering Database Rows

The `SqlDataSource` control includes a `FilterExpression` property that enables you to filter the rows returned by the control. You can define complex Boolean filters that include parameters with this property.

For example, the page in Listing 9.10 retrieves all movies that have titles that match the string entered into the `TextBox` control (see Figure 9.6).

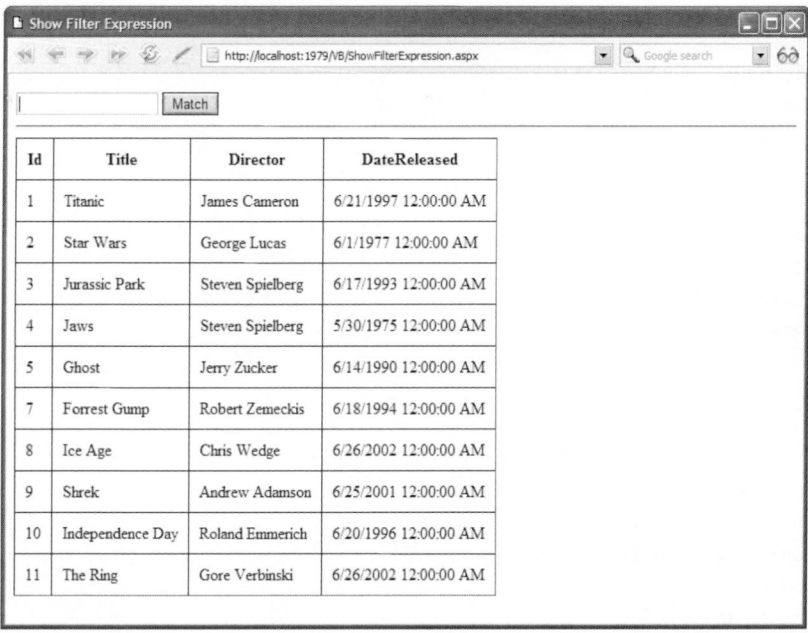

FIGURE 9.6   Show matching movies.

LISTING 9.10   ShowFilterExpression.aspx

```
<%@ Page Language="C#" %>
<!DOCTYPE html PUBLIC "-//W3C//DTD XHTML 1.1//EN"
 "http://www.w3.org/TR/xhtml11/DTD/xhtml11.dtd">
<html xmlns="http://www.w3.org/1999/xhtml" >
<head id="Head1" runat="server">
    <style type="text/css">
```

```
        td, th
        {
            padding:10px;
        }

    </style>
    <title>Show Filter Expression</title>
</head>
<body>
    <form id="form1" runat="server">
    <div>

    <asp:TextBox
        id="txtTitle"
        Runat="server" />
    <asp:Button
        id="btnMatch"
        Text="Match"
        Runat="server" />
    <hr />

    <asp:GridView
        id="grdMovies"
        DataSourceId="srcMovies"
        Runat="server" />

    <asp:SqlDataSource
        id="srcMovies"
        SelectCommand="SELECT Id,Title,Director,DateReleased
            FROM Movies"
        FilterExpression="Title LIKE '{0}%'"
        ConnectionString="<%$ ConnectionStrings:Movies %>"
        Runat="server">
        <FilterParameters>
            <asp:ControlParameter Name="Title" ControlID="txtTitle" />
        </FilterParameters>
    </asp:SqlDataSource>

    </div>
    </form>
</body>
</html>
```

In Listing 9.10, the FilterExpression includes the LIKE operator and the % wildcard character. The LIKE operator performs partial matches on the movie titles.

The filter expression includes a {0} placeholder. The value of the txtTitle TextBox is plugged into this placeholder. You can use multiple parameters and multiple placeholders with the FilterExpression property.

NOTE

Behind the scenes, the SqlDataSource control uses the DataView.RowFilter property to filter database rows. You can find detailed documentation on proper filter syntax by looking up the DataColumn.Expression property in the .NET Framework SDK Documentation.

Using the FilterExpression property is especially useful when caching the data represented by a SqlDataSource. For example, you can cache the entire contents of the movies database table in memory and use the FilterExpression property to filter the movies displayed on a page. You can display different sets of movies depending on a user's selection from a drop-down list of movie categories.

Changing the Data Source Mode

The SqlDataSource control can represent the data that it retrieves in two different ways. It can represent the data using either an ADO.NET DataSet or an ADO.NET DataReader.

By default, the SqlDataSource represents records using the ADO.NET DataSet object. The DataSet object provides a static, memory-resident representation of data.

NOTE

Technically, the SqlDataSource control returns a DataView and not a DataSet. Because, by default, the SqlDataSourceMode enumeration is set to the value DataSet, I continue to refer to DataSets instead of DataViews.

Some features of the DataBound controls work only when the controls are bound to a DataSet. For example, the GridView control supports client-side sorting and filtering only when the control is bound to a DataSet.

The other option is to represent the data that a SqlDataSource control returns with a DataReader object. The advantage of using DataReader is that it offers significantly better performance than the DataSet object. The DataReader represents a fast, forward-only representation of data. If you want to grab some database records and display the records in the fastest possible way, use the DataReader object.

For example, the page in Listing 9.11 retrieves the records from the Movies database by using DataReader.

LISTING 9.11   `ShowDataSourceMode.aspx`

```
<%@ Page Language="C#" %>
<!DOCTYPE html PUBLIC "-//W3C//DTD XHTML 1.1//EN"
 "http://www.w3.org/TR/xhtml11/DTD/xhtml11.dtd">
<html xmlns="http://www.w3.org/1999/xhtml" >
<head id="Head1" runat="server">
    <title>Show Data Source Mode</title>
</head>
<body>
    <form id="form1" runat="server">
    <div>

    <asp:GridView
        id="grdMovies"
        DataSourceID="srcMovies"
        Runat="server" />

    <asp:SqlDataSource
        id="srcMovies"
        DataSourceMode="DataReader"
        SelectCommand="SELECT * FROM Movies"
        ConnectionString="<%$ ConnectionStrings:Movies %>"
        Runat="server" />

    </div>
    </form>
</body>
</html>
```

The `SqlDataSource` control's `DataSourceMode` property is set to the value `DataReader`.

Handling SQL Command Execution Errors

Whenever you build a software application, you need to plan for failure. Databases go down, users enter unexpected values in form fields, and networks get clogged. It is miraculous that the Internet works at all.

You can handle errors thrown by the `SqlDataSource` control by handling any or all of the following four events:

▶ **Deleted**—Happens immediately after the `SqlDataSource` executes its delete command.

▶ **Inserted**—Happens immediately after the `SqlDataSource` executes its insert command.

▶ **Selected**—Happens immediately after the `SqlDataSource` executes its `select` command.

▶ **Updated**—Happens immediately after the `SqlDataSource` executes its `delete` command.

Each of these events is passed an EventArgs parameter that includes any exceptions raised when the command was executed. For example, in the SELECT command in Listing 9.12, movies are retrieved from the DontExist database table instead of the Movies database table.

LISTING 9.12   HandleError.aspx

```
<%@ Page Language="C#" %>
<!DOCTYPE html PUBLIC "-//W3C//DTD XHTML 1.1//EN"
"http://www.w3.org/TR/xhtml11/DTD/xhtml11.dtd">


<script runat="server">
    protected void srcMovies_Selected(object sender, SqlDataSourceStatusEventArgs e)
    {
        if (e.Exception != null)
        {
            lblError.Text = e.Exception.Message;
            e.ExceptionHandled = true;
        }
    }
</script>


<html xmlns="http://www.w3.org/1999/xhtml" >
<head id="Head1" runat="server">
    <style type="text/css">
        .error
        {
            display:block;
            color:red;
            font:bold 16px Arial;
            margin:10px;
        }
    </style>
    <title>Handle Error</title>
</head>
<body>
    <form id="form1" runat="server">
    <div>

    <asp:Label
```

```
        id="lblError"
        EnableViewState="false"
        CssClass="error"
        Runat="server" />

    <asp:GridView
        id="grdMovies"
        DataSourceID="srcMovies"
        Runat="server" />

    <asp:SqlDataSource
        id="srcMovies"
        SelectCommand="SELECT * FROM DontExist"
        ConnectionString="<%$ ConnectionStrings:Movies %>"
        OnSelected="srcMovies_Selected"
        Runat="server" />

    </div>
    </form>
</body>
</html>
```

If the page in Listing 9.12 is opened in a web browser, an exception is raised when the SqlDataSource control attempts to retrieve the rows from the DontExist database table. (Because it doesn't exist.) In the srcMovies_Selected() method, the exception is detected and displayed in a Label control.

The ExceptionHandled property suppresses the exception. If you do not set ExceptionHandled to true, the page explodes (see Figure 9.7).

As an alternative to handling exceptions at the level of the SqlDataSource control, you can handle the exception at the level of a DataBound control. The GridView, DetailsView, and FormView controls all include events that expose the Exception and ExceptionHandled properties.

For example, the page in Listing 9.13 includes a GridView that handles the exception raised when you attempt to edit the contents of the DontExist database table.

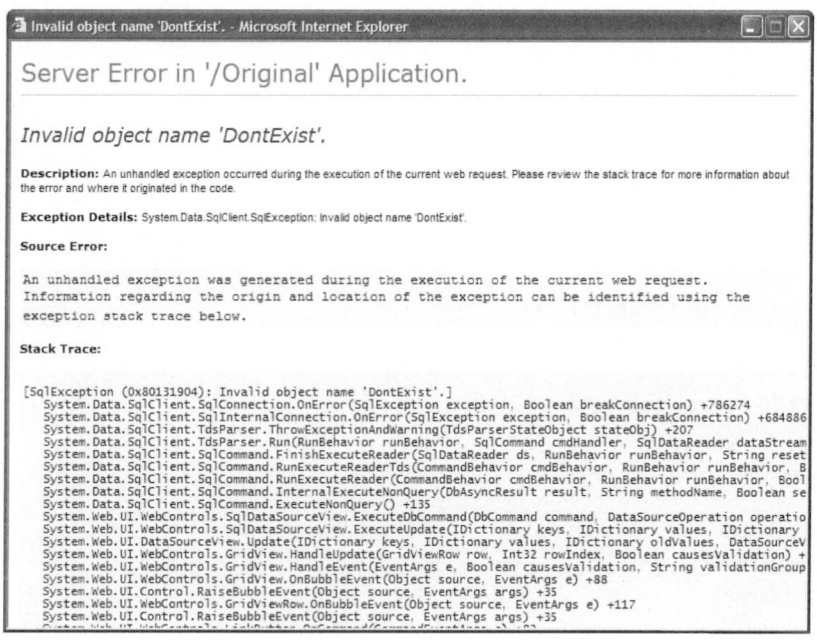

FIGURE 9.7   An unhandled exception.

LISTING 9.13   `GridViewHandleError.aspx`

```
<%@ Page Language="C#" %>
<!DOCTYPE html PUBLIC "-//W3C//DTD XHTML 1.1//EN"
"http://www.w3.org/TR/xhtml11/DTD/xhtml11.dtd">
<script runat="server">

    protected void grdMovies_RowUpdated(object sender, GridViewUpdatedEventArgs e)
    {
        if (e.Exception != null)
        {
            lblError.Text = e.Exception.Message;
            e.ExceptionHandled = true;
        }
    }
</script>

<html xmlns="http://www.w3.org/1999/xhtml" >
<head id="Head1" runat="server">
```

```
    <style type="text/css">
        .error
        {
            display:block;
            color:red;
            font:bold 16px Arial;
            margin:10px;
        }
    </style>
    <title>GridView Handle Error</title>
</head>
<body>
    <form id="form1" runat="server">
    <div>

    <asp:Label
        id="lblError"
        EnableViewState="false"
        CssClass="error"
        Runat="server" />

    <asp:GridView
        id="grdMovies"
        DataKeyNames="Id"
        AutoGenerateEditButton="true"
        DataSourceID="srcMovies"
        OnRowUpdated="grdMovies_RowUpdated"
        Runat="server"  />

    <asp:SqlDataSource
        id="srcMovies"
        SelectCommand="SELECT Id,Title FROM Movies"
        UpdateCommand="UPDATE DontExist SET Title=@Title
            WHERE Id=@ID"
        ConnectionString="<%$ ConnectionStrings:Movies %>"
        Runat="server" />

    </div>
    </form>
</body>
</html>
```

After you open the page in Listing 9.13, you can click the Edit link next to any record to edit the record. If you click the Update link, an exception is raised because the update command attempts to update the DontExist database table. The exception is handled by the GridView control's RowUpdated event handler.

You can handle an exception at both the level of the SqlDataSource control and the level of a DataBound control. The SqlDataSource control's events are raised before the corresponding events are raised for the DataBound control. If you handle an exception by using the ExceptionHandled property in the SqlDataSource control's event handler, the exception is not promoted to the DataSource control's event handler.

Canceling Command Execution

You can cancel SqlDataSource commands when some criterion is not met. For example, you might want to validate the parameters that you use with the command before executing the command.

You can cancel a command by handling any of the following events exposed by the SqlDataSource control:

- ▶ **Deleting**—Happens immediately before the SqlDataSource executes its delete command.

- ▶ **Filtering**—Happens immediately before the SqlDataSource filters its data.

- ▶ **Inserting**—Happens immediately before the SqlDataSource executes its insert command.

- ▶ **Selecting**—Happens immediately before the SqlDataSource executes its select command.

- ▶ **Updating**—Happens immediately before the SqlDataSource executes its delete command.

For example, the page in Listing 9.14 contains a DetailsView control bound to a SqlDataSource control that represents the contents of the Movies database table. The DetailsView control enables you to update a particular movie record; however, if you leave one of the fields blank, the update command is canceled (see Figure 9.8).

6

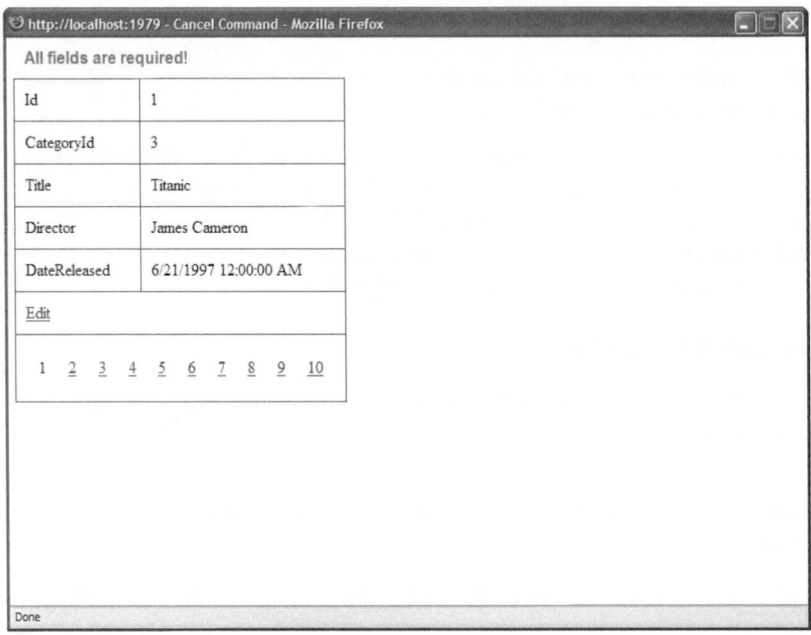

FIGURE 9.8   Canceling a command when a field is blank.

LISTING 9.14   CancelCommand.aspx

```
<%@ Page Language="C#" %>
<%@ Import Namespace="System.Data.SqlClient" %>
<!DOCTYPE html PUBLIC "-//W3C//DTD XHTML 1.1//EN"
"http://www.w3.org/TR/xhtml11/DTD/xhtml11.dtd">
<script runat="server">

    /// <summary>
    /// Iterate through all parameters and check for null
    /// </summary>
    protected void srcMovies_Updating(object sender, SqlDataSourceCommandEventArgs e)
    {
        foreach (SqlParameter param in e.Command.Parameters)
        if (param.Value == null)
        {
            e.Cancel = true;
            lblError.Text = "All fields are required!";
        }
    }
</script>

<html xmlns="http://www.w3.org/1999/xhtml" >
<head id="Head1" runat="server">
```

```
    <style type="text/css">
        .error
        {
            display:block;
            color:red;
            font:bold 16px Arial;
            margin:10px;
        }
        td,th
        {
            padding:10px;
        }
    </style>
    <title>Cancel Command</title>
</head>
<body>
    <form id="form1" runat="server">
    <div>

    <asp:Label
        id="lblError"
        EnableViewState="false"
        CssClass="error"
        Runat="server" />

    <asp:DetailsView
        id="dtlMovie"
        DataSourceID="srcMovies"
        DataKeyNames="Id"
        AllowPaging="true"
        AutoGenerateEditButton="true"
        Runat="server" />

    <asp:SqlDataSource
        id="srcMovies"
        SelectCommand="SELECT * FROM Movies"
        UpdateCommand="UPDATE Movies SET Title=@Title,
            Director=@Director,DateReleased=@DateReleased
            WHERE Id=@id"
        ConnectionString="<%$ ConnectionStrings:Movies %>"
        Runat="server" OnUpdating="srcMovies_Updating" />

    </div>
    </form>
</body>
</html>
```

The page in Listing 9.14 includes a srcMovies_Updating() method. In this method, each parameter associated with the update command is compared against the value Nothing (null). If one of the parameters is null, an error message displays in a Label control.

Using ASP.NET Parameters with the SqlDataSource Control

You can use any of the following ASP.NET Parameter objects with the SqlDataSource control:

- ▶ **Parameter**—Represents an arbitrary static value.
- ▶ **ControlParameter**—Represents the value of a control or page property.
- ▶ **CookieParameter**—Represents the value of a browser cookie.
- ▶ **FormParameter**—Represents the value of an HTML form field.
- ▶ **ProfileParameter**—Represents the value of a Profile property.
- ▶ **QueryStringParameter**—Represents the value of a query string field.
- ▶ **SessionParameter**—Represents the value of an item stored in Session state.

The SqlDataSource control includes five collections of ASP.NET parameters: SelectParameters, InsertParameters, DeleteParameters, UpdateParameters, and FilterParameters. You can use these parameter collections to associate a particular ASP.NET parameter with a particular SqlDataSource command or filter.

In the following sections, you learn how to use each of these different types of parameter objects.

Using the ASP.NET Parameter Object

The ASP.NET parameter object has the following properties:

- ▶ **ConvertEmptyStringToNull**—When true, if a parameter represents an empty string, the empty string converts to the value Nothing (null) before the associated command executes.
- ▶ **DefaultValue**—When a parameter has the value Nothing (null), the DefaultValue is used for the value of the parameter.
- ▶ **Direction**—Indicates the direction of the parameter. Possible values are Input, InputOutput, Output, and ReturnValue.
- ▶ **Name**—Indicates the name of the parameter. Do not use the @ character when indicating the name of an ASP.NET parameter.
- ▶ **Size**—Indicates the data size of the parameter.

▶ **Type**—Indicates the .NET Framework type of the parameter. You can assign any value from the `TypeCode` enumeration to this property.

You can use the ASP.NET parameter object to indicate several parameter properties explicitly, such as a parameter's type, size, and default value.

For example, the page in Listing 9.15 contains a `DetailsView` control bound to a `SqlDataSource` control. You can use the page to update records in the Movies database table (see Figure 9.9).

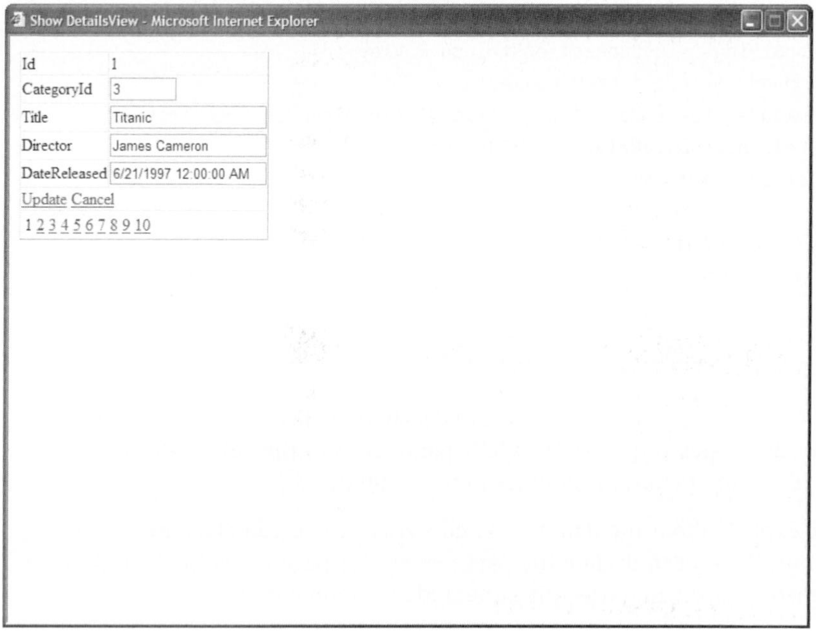

FIGURE 9.9   Updating movie records.

LISTING 9.15   `ShowDetailsView.aspx`

```
<%@ Page Language="C#" %>
<!DOCTYPE html PUBLIC "-//W3C//DTD XHTML 1.1//EN"
    "http://www.w3.org/TR/xhtml11/DTD/xhtml11.dtd">
<html xmlns="http://www.w3.org/1999/xhtml" >
<head id="Head1" runat="server">
    <title>Show DetailsView</title>
</head>
<body>
    <form id="form1" runat="server">
    <div>

    <asp:DetailsView
```

```
            id="dtlMovie"
            DataKeyNames="Id"
            DataSourceID="srcMovies"
            AutoGenerateEditButton="true"
            DefaultMode="Edit"
            AllowPaging="true"
            runat="server" />

        <asp:SqlDataSource
            id="srcMovies"
            ConnectionString="<%$ ConnectionStrings:Movies %>"
            SelectCommand="Select * FROM Movies"
            UpdateCommand="UPDATE Movies SET Title=@Title,Director=@Director,
                DateReleased=@DateReleased WHERE Id=@id"
            Runat="server" />

    </div>
    </form>
</body>
</html>
```

In Listing 9.15, no ASP.NET parameter objects are declared explicitly. The DetailsView control automatically creates and adds ADO.NET parameters to the SqlDataSource control's update command before the command is executed.

If you want to be explicit about the data types and sizes of the parameters used by a SqlDataSource control, you can declare the parameters. The page in Listing 9.16 declares each of the parameters used when executing the update command.

LISTING 9.16   ShowDetailsViewExplicit.aspx

```
<%@ Page Language="C#" %>
<!DOCTYPE html PUBLIC "-//W3C//DTD XHTML 1.1//EN"
  "http://www.w3.org/TR/xhtml11/DTD/xhtml11.dtd">
<html xmlns="http://www.w3.org/1999/xhtml" >
<head id="Head1" runat="server">
    <title>Show DetailsView Explicit</title>
</head>
<body>
    <form id="form1" runat="server">
    <div>
```

```
<asp:DetailsView
    id="dtlMovie"
    DataKeyNames="Id"
    DataSourceID="srcMovies"
    AutoGenerateEditButton="true"
    DefaultMode="Edit"
    AllowPaging="true"
    runat="server" />

<asp:SqlDataSource
    id="srcMovies"
    ConnectionString="<%$ ConnectionStrings:Movies %>"
    SelectCommand="Select * FROM Movies"
    UpdateCommand="UPDATE Movies SET Title=@Title,Director=@Director,
        DateReleased=@DateReleased WHERE Id=@id"
    Runat="server">
    <UpdateParameters>
      <asp:Parameter Name="Title"
        Type="String" Size="100" DefaultValue="Untitled" />
      <asp:Parameter Name="Director"
        Type="String" Size="100" DefaultValue="Alan Smithee" />
      <asp:Parameter Name="DateReleased" Type="DateTime" />
      <asp:Parameter Name="id" Type="int32" />
    </UpdateParameters>
</asp:SqlDataSource>
</div>
</form>
</body>
</html>
```

In Listing 9.16, each of the parameters used by the update command is provided with an explicit data type. For example, the DateReleased parameter is declared to be a DateTime parameter. (If you didn't assign an explicit type to this parameter, it would default to a string.)

Furthermore, the Title and Director parameters are provided with default values. If you edit a movie record and do not supply a title or director, the default values are used.

NOTE

Another situation in which explicitly declaring Parameter objects is useful is when you need to explicitly order the parameters. For example, the order of parameters is important when you use the OLE DB provider with Microsoft Access.

Using the ASP.NET `ControlParameter` Object

You use the `ControlParameter` object to represent the value of a control property. You can use it to represent the value of any control contained in the same page as the `SqlDataSource` control.

The `ControlParameter` object includes all the properties of the `Parameter` object and these additional properties:

- **`ControlID`**—The ID of the control that the parameter represents.

- **`PropertyName`**—The name of the property that the parameter represents.

For example, the page in Listing 9.17 includes a `DropDownList` control and a `DetailsView` control. When you select a movie from the `DropDownList`, details for the movie display in the `DetailsView` control (see Figure 9.10).

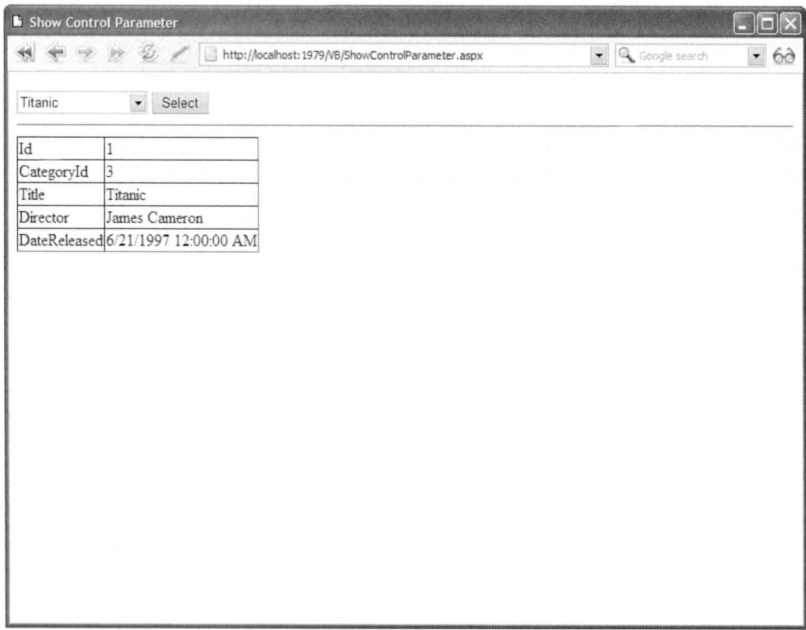

FIGURE 9.10   Show matching movies for each movie category.

LISTING 9.17   ShowControlParameter.aspx

```
<%@ Page Language="C#" %>
<!DOCTYPE html PUBLIC "-//W3C//DTD XHTML 1.1//EN"
   "http://www.w3.org/TR/xhtml11/DTD/xhtml11.dtd">
<html xmlns="http://www.w3.org/1999/xhtml" >
<head id="Head1" runat="server">
    <title>Show Control Parameter</title>
```

```
</head>
<body>
    <form id="form1" runat="server">
    <div>

    <asp:DropDownList
        id="ddlMovies"
        DataSourceID="srcMovies"
        DataTextField="Title"
        DataValueField="Id"
        Runat="server" />
    <asp:Button
        id="btnSelect"
        Text="Select"
        Runat="server" />

    <hr />

    <asp:DetailsView
        id="dtlMovie"
        DataSourceID="srcMovieDetails"
        Runat="server" />

    <asp:SqlDataSource
        id="srcMovies"
        SelectCommand="SELECT Id,Title FROM Movies"
        ConnectionString="<%$ ConnectionStrings:Movies %>"
        Runat="server" />

    <asp:SqlDataSource
        id="srcMovieDetails"
        SelectCommand="SELECT * FROM Movies
            WHERE Id=@Id"
        ConnectionString="<%$ ConnectionStrings:Movies %>"
        Runat="server">
        <SelectParameters>
            <asp:ControlParameter Name="Id" ControlID="ddlMovies"
                PropertyName="SelectedValue" />
        </SelectParameters>
    </asp:SqlDataSource>

    </div>
    </form>
</body>
</html>
```

6

The second SqlDataSource control in Listing 9.17 includes a ControlParameter object. The ControlParameter represents the ID of the selected movie in the DropDownList control.

When using a ControlParameter, you must always set the value of the ControlID property to point to a control on the page. On the other hand, you are not always required to set the PropertyName property. If you do not set PropertyName, the ControlParameter object automatically looks for a property decorated with the ControlValueProperty attribute. Because the SelectedValue property of the DropDownList control is decorated with this attribute, you do not need to set this property in Listing 9.17.

Because the Page class derives from the control class, you can use the ControlParameter object to represent the value of a Page property.

For example, the page in Listing 9.18 contains a simple guestbook that connects to a database called "GuestBook". When a user adds a new entry to the guestbook, the user's remote IP address is saved automatically with the guestbook entry (see Figure 9.11).

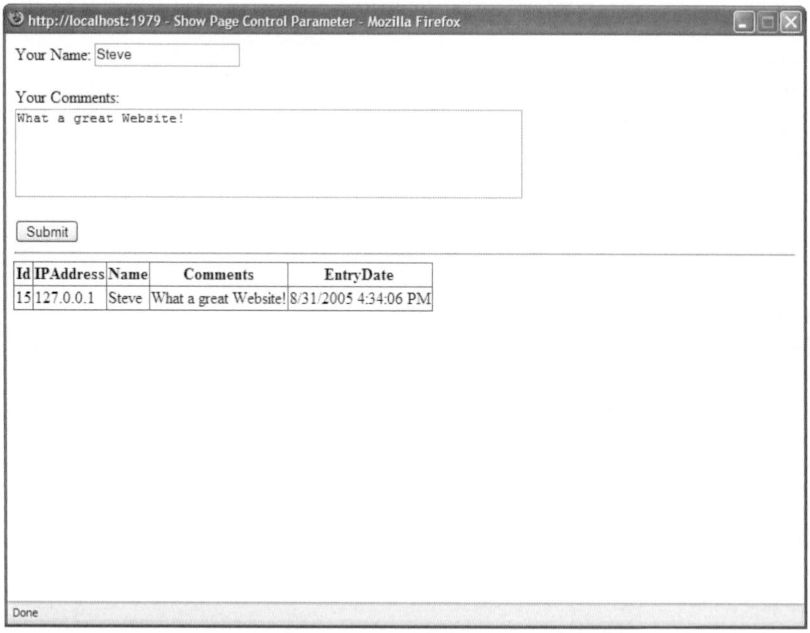

FIGURE 9.11   Saving an IP address in guest book entries.

LISTING 9.18   ShowPageControlParameter.aspx

```
<%@ Page Language="C#" %>
<!DOCTYPE html PUBLIC "-//W3C//DTD XHTML 1.1//EN"
"http://www.w3.org/TR/xhtml11/DTD/xhtml11.dtd">
<script runat="server">

    public string IPAddress
    {
        get { return Request.UserHostAddress; }
    }

</script>
<html xmlns="http://www.w3.org/1999/xhtml" >
<head id="Head1" runat="server">
    <title>Show Page Control Parameter</title>
</head>
<body>
    <form id="form1" runat="server">
    <div>

    <asp:FormView
        id="frmGuestBook"
        DataSourceID="srcGuestBook"
        DefaultMode="Insert"
        runat="server">
        <InsertItemTemplate>
        <asp:Label
            id="lblName"
            Text="Your Name:"
            AssociatedControlID="txtName"
            Runat="server" />
        <asp:TextBox
            id="txtName"
            Text='<%# Bind("Name") %>'
            Runat="server" />
        <br /><br />
        <asp:Label
            id="Label1"
            Text="Your Comments:"
            AssociatedControlID="txtComments"
            Runat="server" />
        <br />
        <asp:TextBox
            id="txtComments"
```

9

```
            Text='<%# Bind("Comments") %>'
            TextMode="MultiLine"
            Columns="60"
            Rows="4"
            Runat="server" />
        <br /><br />
        <asp:Button
            id="btnSubmit"
            Text="Submit"
            CommandName="Insert"
            Runat="server" />
        </InsertItemTemplate>
    </asp:FormView>

    <hr />

    <asp:GridView
        id="grdGuestBook"
        DataSourceID="srcGuestBook"
        Runat="server" />

    <asp:SqlDataSource
        id="srcGuestBook"
        SelectCommand="SELECT * FROM GuestBook ORDER BY Id DESC"
        InsertCommand="INSERT GuestBook (IPAddress,Name,Comments)
            VALUES (@IPAddress,@Name,
        ConnectionString="<%$ ConnectionStrings:GuestBook %>"
        Runat="server">
        <InsertParameters>
            <asp:ControlParameter Name="IPAddress" ControlID="__page"
                PropertyName="IPAddress" />
        </InsertParameters>
    </asp:SqlDataSource>

    </div>
    </form>
</body>
</html>
```

The ControlID property is set to the value __page. This value is the automatically generated ID for the Page class. The PropertyName property has the value IPAddress. This property is defined in the page.

Using the ASP.NET CookieParameter Object

The CookieParameter object represents a browser-side cookie. The CookieParameter includes all the properties of the base Parameter class and the following additional property:

▶ **CookieName**—The name of the browser cookie.

The page in Listing 9.19 illustrates how you can use the CookieParameter object. The page contains a voting form that you can use to vote for your favorite color. A cookie is added to the user's browser to identify the user and prevent someone from cheating by voting more than once (see Figure 9.12).

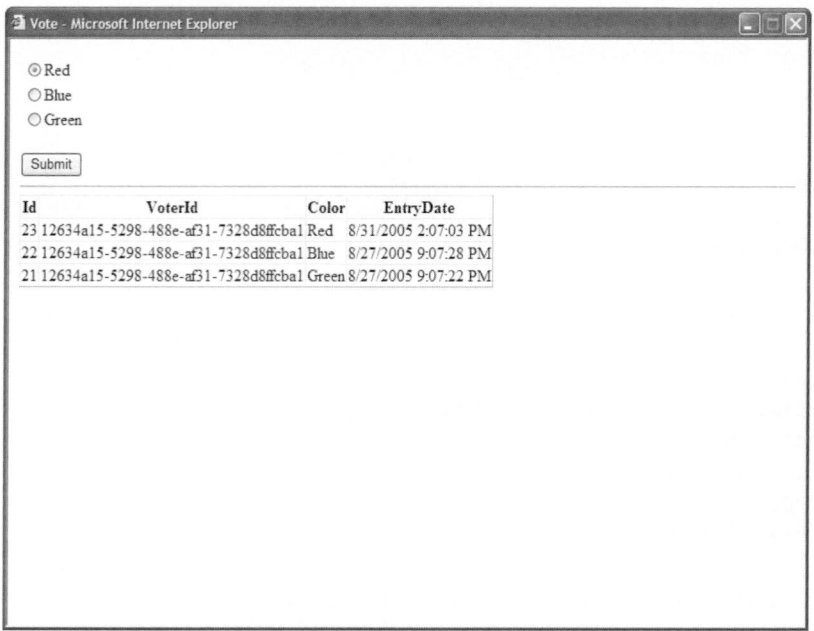

FIGURE 9.12   Vote on your favorite color.

LISTING 9.19   Vote.aspx

```
<%@ Page Language="C#" %>
<!DOCTYPE html PUBLIC "-//W3C//DTD XHTML 1.1//EN"
"http://www.w3.org/TR/xhtml11/DTD/xhtml11.dtd">
<script runat="server">

    void Page_Load()
    {
        if (Request.Cookies["VoterId"] == null)
        {
            string identifier = Guid.NewGuid().ToString();
```

```
            HttpCookie voteCookie = new HttpCookie("VoterId", identifier);
            voteCookie.Expires = DateTime.MaxValue;
            Response.AppendCookie(voteCookie);
        }
    }

</script>
<html xmlns="http://www.w3.org/1999/xhtml" >
<head id="Head1" runat="server">
    <title>Vote</title>
</head>
<body>
    <form id="form1" runat="server">
    <div>

    <asp:FormView
        id="frmVote"
        DataSourceID="srcVote"
        DefaultMode="Insert"
        Runat="server">
        <InsertItemTemplate>
        <asp:Label
            id="lblFavoriteColor"
            AssociatedControlID="rdlFavoriteColor"
            Runat="server" />
        <asp:RadioButtonList
            id="rdlFavoriteColor"
            SelectedValue='<%#Bind("Color")%>'
            Runat="server">
            <asp:ListItem Value="Red" Text="Red" Selected="True" />
            <asp:ListItem Value="Blue" Text="Blue" />
            <asp:ListItem Value="Green" Text="Green" />
        </asp:RadioButtonList>
        <br />
        <asp:Button
            id="btnSubmit"
            Text="Submit"
            CommandName="Insert"
            Runat="server" />
        </InsertItemTemplate>
    </asp:FormView>
```

```
<hr />

<asp:GridView
    id="grdVote"
    DataSourceID="srcVote"
    Runat="server" />

<asp:SqlDataSource
    id="srcVote"
    SelectCommand="SELECT * FROM Vote
        ORDER BY Id DESC"
    InsertCommand="INSERT Vote (VoterId,Color)
        VALUES (@VoterId,@Color)"
    ConnectionString="<%$ ConnectionStrings:Vote %>"
    Runat="server">
    <InsertParameters>
        <asp:CookieParameter Name="VoterId"
            CookieName="VoterId" />
    </InsertParameters>
</asp:SqlDataSource>

    </div>
    </form>
</body>
</html>
```

The cookie is added in the Page_Load() method. A unique identifier (GUID) is generated to identify the user uniquely.

Using the ASP.NET `FormParameter` Object

The FormParameter object represents a form field submitted to the server. Typically, you never work directly with browser form fields because their functionality is encapsulated in the ASP.NET form controls.

The page in Listing 9.20 contains a client-side HTML form that enables you to enter a movie title and director. When the form is submitted to the server, the values of the form fields are saved to the Movies database table (see Figure 9.13).

6

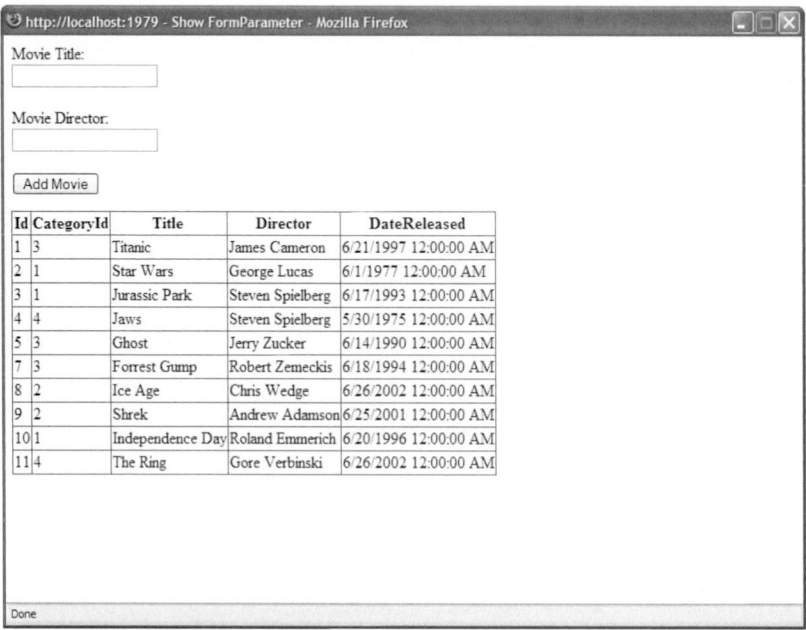

FIGURE 9.13   Using a client-side HTML form.

LISTING 9.20   ShowFormParameter.aspx

```
<%@ Page Language="C#" %>
<!DOCTYPE html PUBLIC "-//W3C//DTD XHTML 1.1//EN"
"http://www.w3.org/TR/xhtml11/DTD/xhtml11.dtd">
<script runat="server">

    void Page_Load()
    {
        if (Request.Form["AddMovie"] != null)
            srcMovies.Insert();
    }

</script>
<html xmlns="http://www.w3.org/1999/xhtml" >
<head id="Head1" runat="server">
    <title>Show FormParameter</title>
</head>
<body>
    <form action="ShowFormParameter.aspx" method="post">

    <label for="txtTitle">Movie Title:</label>
    <br />
```

```
    <input name="txtTitle" />

    <br /><br />

    <label for="txtDirector">Movie Director:</label>
    <br />
    <input name="txtDirector" />

    <br /><br />
    <input name="AddMovie" type="submit" value="Add Movie" />

    </form>

    <form id="form1" runat="server">
    <div>

    <asp:GridView
        id="grdMovies"
        DataSourceID="srcMovies"
        Runat="server" />

    <asp:SqlDataSource
        id="srcMovies"
        SelectCommand="SELECT * FROM Movies"
        InsertCommand="INSERT Movies (Title,Director,CategoryId,DateReleased)
            VALUES (@Title,@Director,0,'12/25/1966')"
        ConnectionString="<%$ ConnectionStrings:Movies %>"
        Runat="server">
        <InsertParameters>
            <asp:FormParameter Name="Title"
                FormField="txtTitle" DefaultValue="Untitled" />
            <asp:FormParameter Name="Director"
                FormField="txtDirector" DefaultValue="Allen Smithee" />
        </InsertParameters>
    </asp:SqlDataSource>

    </div>
    </form>
</body>
</html>
```

You check whether a form field named AddMovie exists in the Page_Load() method. This is the name of the submit button. If this field exists, you know that the client-side form was submitted and the SqlDataSource control's Insert() method can be called to add the form fields to the database.

Using the ASP.NET ProfileParameter Object

The `ProfileParameter` object enables you to represent any of the properties of the `Profile` object. The `ProfileParameter` includes all the properties of the `Parameter` class and the following property:

▶ **PropertyName**—Indicates the namex of the `Profile` property associated with this `ProfileParameter`.

For example, imagine that you build a Guest Book application and you want to allow users to enter their display names when adding entries to a guest book. You can add a `DisplayName` property to the `Profile` object with the web configuration file in Listing 9.21.

LISTING 9.21 Web.config

```
<?xml version="1.0"?>
<configuration>
  <connectionStrings>
    <add name="GuestBook" connectionString="Data Source=.\SQLEXPRESS;
      AttachDbFilename=¦DataDirectory¦GuestBookDB.mdf;
Integrated Security=True;User Instance=True" />
  </connectionStrings>

  <system.web>
    <profile enabled="true">
      <properties>
        <add name="DisplayName" defaultValue="Anonymous" />
      </properties>
    </profile>
  </system.web>

</configuration>
```

> **NOTE**
>
> The `Profile` object automatically stores user-specific information across visits to a website. The Profile object is discussed in detail in Chapter 28, "Maintaining Application State."

The web configuration file in Listing 9.21 includes the definition of a `Profile` property named `DisplayName`. The default value of this property is `Anonymous`.

The page in Listing 9.22 uses the `ProfileParameter` object to read the value of the `DisplayName` property automatically when new entries are added to a Guest Book.

LISTING 9.22   `ShowProfileParameter.aspx`

```
<%@ Page Language="C#" %>
<!DOCTYPE html PUBLIC "-//W3C//DTD XHTML 1.1//EN"
  "http://www.w3.org/TR/xhtml11/DTD/xhtml11.dtd">
<html xmlns="http://www.w3.org/1999/xhtml" >
<head id="Head1" runat="server">
    <title>Show ProfileParameter</title>
</head>
<body>
    <form id="form1" runat="server">
    <div>

    <asp:FormView
        id="frmGuestBook"
        DataSourceID="srcGuestBook"
        DefaultMode="Insert"
        Runat="server">
        <InsertItemTemplate>
        <asp:Label
            id="lblComments"
            Text="Enter Your Comments:"
            Runat="server" />
        <br />
        <asp:TextBox
            id="txtComments"
            Text='<%# Bind("Comments") %>'
            TextMode="MultiLine"
            Columns="50"
            Rows="4"
            Runat="server" />
        <br />
        <asp:Button
            id="btnInsert"
            Text="Add Comments"
            CommandName="Insert"
            Runat="server" />
        </InsertItemTemplate>
    </asp:FormView>

    <hr />

    <asp:GridView
        id="grdGuestBook"
        DataSourceID="srcGuestBook"
        Runat="server" />
```

6

```
    <asp:SqlDataSource
        id="srcGuestBook"
        SelectCommand="SELECT Name,Comments,EntryDate
            FROM GuestBook ORDER BY Id DESC"
        InsertCommand="INSERT GuestBook (Name,Comments)
            VALUES (@Name,@Comments)"
        ConnectionString="<%$ ConnectionStrings:GuestBook %>"
        Runat="server">
        <InsertParameters>
            <asp:ProfileParameter Name="Name" PropertyName="DisplayName" />
        </InsertParameters>
    </asp:SqlDataSource>

    </div>
    </form>
</body>
</html>
```

The SqlDataSource control in Listing 9.22 includes a ProfileParameter object. This object represents the DisplayName profile property.

Using the QueryStringParameter Object

The QueryStringParameter object can represent any query string passed to a page. The QueryStringParameter class includes all the properties of the base Parameter class with the addition of the following property:

▶ **QueryStringField**—The name of the query string that the QueryStringParameter represents.

This type of parameter is particularly useful when you build Master/Detail pages. For example, the page in Listing 9.23 displays a list of movie titles. Each movie title links to a page that contains detailed information for the movie.

LISTING 9.23   ShowQueryStringParameterMaster.aspx

```
<%@ Page Language="C#" %>
<!DOCTYPE html PUBLIC "-//W3C//DTD XHTML 1.1//EN"
 "http://www.w3.org/TR/xhtml11/DTD/xhtml11.dtd">
<html xmlns="http://www.w3.org/1999/xhtml" >
<head id="Head1" runat="server">
    <title>Show QueryStringParameter Master</title>
</head>
<body>
    <form id="form1" runat="server">
    <div>
```

```
    <asp:GridView
        id="grdMovies"
        DataSourceId="srcMovies"
        AutoGenerateColumns="false"
        ShowHeader="false"
        Runat="server">
        <Columns>
        <asp:HyperLinkField
            DataTextField="Title"
            DataNavigateUrlFields="Id"
            DataNavigateUrlFormatString=
➥"ShowQueryStringParameterDetails.aspx?id={0}" />
        </Columns>
    </asp:GridView>

    <asp:SqlDataSource
        id="srcMovies"
        SelectCommand="SELECT * FROM Movies"
        ConnectionString="<%$ ConnectionStrings:Movies %>"
        Runat="server" />

    </div>
    </form>
</body>
</html>
```

The ID of the movie is passed to the ShowQueryStringParameterDetails.aspx page. The
movie ID is passed in a query string field named id.

The page in Listing 9.24 displays detailed information for a particular movie.

LISTING 9.24   ShowQueryStringParameterDetails.aspx

```
<%@ Page Language="C#" %>
<!DOCTYPE html PUBLIC "-//W3C//DTD XHTML 1.1//EN"
    "http://www.w3.org/TR/xhtml11/DTD/xhtml11.dtd">
<html xmlns="http://www.w3.org/1999/xhtml" >
<head id="Head1" runat="server">
    <title>Show QueryStringParameter Details</title>
</head>
<body>
    <form id="form1" runat="server">
    <div>
```

9

```
<asp:DetailsView
    id="dtlMovie"
    DataSourceID="srcMovie"
    Runat="server" />

<asp:HyperLink
    Runat="server"
    Text="Back..."
    NavigateUrl="~/ShowQueryStringParameterMaster.aspx" />

<asp:SqlDataSource
    id="srcMovie"
    SelectCommand="SELECT * FROM Movies
        WHERE Id=@Id"
    ConnectionString="<%$ ConnectionStrings:Movies %>"
    Runat="server">
    <SelectParameters>
        <asp:QueryStringParameter
            Name="Id"
            QueryStringField="Id" />
    </SelectParameters>
</asp:SqlDataSource>

</div>
</form>
</body>
</html>
```

The SqlDataSource control in Listing 9.24 includes a QueryStringParameter. The QueryStringParameter supplies the movie ID in the SqlDataSource control's SelectCommand.

Using the SessionParameter Object

The SessionParameter object enables you to represent any item stored in Session state. The SessionParameter object includes all the properties of the base Parameter class and the following property:

▶ **SessionField**—The name of the item stored in Session state that the SessionParameter represents.

NOTE

Session state is discussed in detail in Chapter 28.

The page in Listing 9.25 contains a `GridView` that displays a list of movies matching a movie category. The movie category is stored in Session state.

LISTING 9.25   ShowSessionParameter.aspx

```
<%@ Page Language="C#" %>
<!DOCTYPE html PUBLIC "-//W3C//DTD XHTML 1.1//EN"
"http://www.w3.org/TR/xhtml11/DTD/xhtml11.dtd">
<script runat="server">

    void Page_Load()
    {
        Session["MovieCategoryName"] = "Animation";
    }

</script>
<html xmlns="http://www.w3.org/1999/xhtml" >
<head id="Head1" runat="server">
    <title>Show SessionParameter</title>
</head>
<body>
    <form id="form1" runat="server">
    <div>

    <asp:GridView
        id="grdMovies"
        DataSourceID="srcMovies"
        Runat="server" />

    <asp:SqlDataSource
        id="srcMovies"
        SelectCommand="SELECT Name As Category,Title,Director
            FROM Movies
            INNER JOIN MovieCategories
            ON CategoryId = MovieCategories.id
            WHERE Name=@Name"
        ConnectionString="<%$ ConnectionStrings:Movies %>"
        Runat="server">
        <SelectParameters>
        <asp:SessionParameter
            Name="Name"
            SessionField="MovieCategoryName" />
        </SelectParameters>
    </asp:SqlDataSource>
```

6

```
      </div>
      </form>
</body>
</html>
```

The current movie category is added to the Session object in the Page_Load() method. The SqlDataSource reads the MovieCategoryName item from Session state when it retrieves the list of movies that the GridView displays.

Programmatically Executing SqlDataSource Commands

You aren't required to use the SqlDataSource control only when working with DataBound controls. You can create parameters and execute the commands represented by a SqlDataSource control by working directly with the properties and methods of the SqlDataSource control in your code.

In this section, you learn how to add parameters programmatically to a SqlDataSource control. You also learn how to execute select, insert, update, and delete commands when using the SqlDataSource control.

Adding ADO.NET Parameters

Under the covers, the SqlDataSource control uses ADO.NET objects such as the ADO.NET DataSet, DataReader, Parameter, and Command objects to interact with a database. In particular, any ASP.NET Parameter objects that you declare when working with the SqlDataSource control get converted into ADO.NET Parameter objects.

In some cases, you want to work directly with these ADO.NET Parameter objects when using the SqlDataSource control. For example, you might want to add additional ADO.NET parameters programmatically before executing a command.

The page in Listing 9.26 automatically adds an ADO.NET Parameter that represents the current user's username to the command that the SqlDataSource executes.

LISTING 9.26   AddParameter.aspx

```
<%@ Page Language="C#" %>
<%@ Import Namespace="System.Data.SqlClient" %>
<!DOCTYPE html PUBLIC "-//W3C//DTD XHTML 1.1//EN"
"http://www.w3.org/TR/xhtml11/DTD/xhtml11.dtd">
<script runat="server">

    protected void srcGuestBook_Inserting(object sender,
➥SqlDataSourceCommandEventArgs e)
```

```
        {
            e.Command.Parameters.Add(new SqlParameter("@Name", User.Identity.Name));
        }
</script>

<html xmlns="http://www.w3.org/1999/xhtml" >
<head id="Head1" runat="server">
    <title>Show ProfileParameter</title>
</head>
<body>
    <form id="form1" runat="server">
    <div>

    <asp:FormView
        id="frmGuestBook"
        DataSourceID="srcGuestBook"
        DefaultMode="Insert"
        Runat="server">
        <InsertItemTemplate>
        <asp:Label
            id="lblComments"
            Text="Enter Your Comments:"
            Runat="server" />
        <br />
        <asp:TextBox
            id="txtComments"
            Text='<%# Bind("Comments") %>'
            TextMode="MultiLine"
            Columns="50"
            Rows="4"
            Runat="server" />
        <br />
        <asp:Button
            id="btnInsert"
            Text="Add Comments"
            CommandName="Insert"
            Runat="server" />
        </InsertItemTemplate>
    </asp:FormView>

    <hr />

    <asp:GridView
```

6

```
        id="grdGuestBook"
        DataSourceID="srcGuestBook"
        Runat="server" />

    <asp:SqlDataSource
        id="srcGuestBook"
        SelectCommand="SELECT Name,Comments,EntryDate
            FROM GuestBook ORDER BY Id DESC"
        InsertCommand="INSERT GuestBook (Name,Comments)
            VALUES (@Name,@Comments)"
        ConnectionString="<%$ ConnectionStrings:GuestBook %>"
        Runat="server" OnInserting="srcGuestBook_Inserting" />

    </div>
    </form>
</body>
</html>
```

The page in Listing 9.26 includes a `srcGuestBook_Inserting()` event handler, which executes immediately before the `SqlDataSource` control executes its insert command. In the event handler, a new ADO.NET `Parameter` is added to the insert command, which represents the current user's username.

> **NOTE**
>
> The names of ADO.NET parameters, unlike ASP.NET parameters, always start with the character @.

Executing `Insert`, `Update`, and `Delete` Commands

The `SqlDataSource` control has methods that correspond to each of the different types of commands that it represents:

▸ **Delete**—Enables you to execute a SQL delete command.

▸ **Insert**—Enables you to execute a SQL insert command.

▸ **Select**—Enables you to execute a SQL select command.

▸ **Update**—Enables you to execute a SQL update command.

For example, the page in Listing 9.27 contains a form for adding new entries to the GuestBook database table. This form is not contained in a `DataBound` control such as the `FormView` or `DetailsView` controls. The form is contained in the body of the page. When you click the Add Entry button, the `SqlDataSource` control's `Insert()` method is executed.

LISTING 9.27 `ExecuteInsert.aspx`

```
<%@ Page Language="C#" %>
<!DOCTYPE html PUBLIC "-//W3C//DTD XHTML 1.1//EN"
"http://www.w3.org/TR/xhtml11/DTD/xhtml11.dtd">
<script runat="server">

    /// <summary>
    /// When button clicked, execute Insert command
    /// </summary>
    protected void btnAddEntry_Click(object sender, EventArgs e)
    {
        srcGuestBook.InsertParameters["Name"].DefaultValue = txtName.Text;
        srcGuestBook.InsertParameters["Comments"].DefaultValue = txtComments.Text;
        srcGuestBook.Insert();
    }
</script>

<html xmlns="http://www.w3.org/1999/xhtml" >
<head id="Head1" runat="server">
    <title>Execute Insert</title>
</head>
<body>
    <form id="form1" runat="server">
    <div>

    <asp:Label
        id="lblName"
        Text="Name:"
        AssociatedControlId="txtName"
        Runat="server" />
    <br />
    <asp:TextBox
        id="txtName"
        Runat="server" />

    <br /><br />

    <asp:Label
        id="lblComments"
        Text="Comments:"
        AssociatedControlId="txtComments"
        Runat="server" />
    <br />
    <asp:TextBox
```

6

```
        id="txtComments"
        TextMode="MultiLine"
        Columns="50"
        Rows="2"
        Runat="server" />

    <br /><br />

    <asp:Button
        id="btnAddEntry"
        Text="Add Entry"
        Runat="server" OnClick="btnAddEntry_Click" />

    <hr />

    <asp:GridView
        id="grdGuestBook"
        DataSourceId="srcGuestBook"
        Runat="server" />

    <asp:SqlDataSource
        id="srcGuestBook"
        ConnectionString="<%$ ConnectionStrings:GuestBook %>"
        SelectCommand="SELECT Name,Comments FROM GuestBook
            ORDER BY Id DESC"
        InsertCommand="INSERT GuestBook (Name,Comments)
            VALUES (@Name,@Comments)"
        Runat="server">
        <InsertParameters>
            <asp:Parameter Name="Name" />
            <asp:Parameter Name="Comments" />
        </InsertParameters>
    </asp:SqlDataSource>

    </div>
    </form>
</body>
</html>
```

Executing Select Commands

The procedure for executing a select command is different from executing insert, update, and delete commands because a select command returns data. This section discusses how you can execute the SqlDataSource control's Select() method programmatically and represent the data that the method returns.

Remember that a `SqlDataSource` control can return either a `DataView` or `DataReader` depending on the value of its `DataSourceMode` property. The `SqlDataSource` control's `Select()` method returns an object of type `IEnumerable`. Both `DataViews` and `DataReaders` implement the `IEnumerable` interface.

To understand how you can call the `Select()` method programmatically, look at the following simple photo gallery application. This application enables you to upload images to a database table and display them in a page (see Figure 9.14).

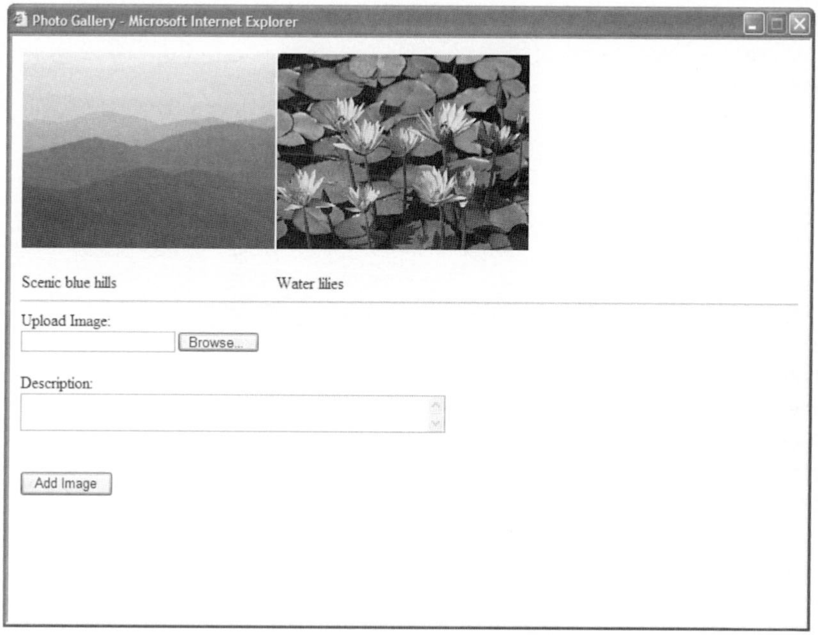

FIGURE 9.14   A photo gallery application.

First, you need to create the page that displays the images and contains the form for adding new images. The `PhotoGallery.aspx` page is contained in Listing 9.28.

LISTING 9.28   `PhotoGallery.aspx`

```
<%@ Page Language="C#" %>
<!DOCTYPE html PUBLIC "-//W3C//DTD XHTML 1.1//EN"
  "http://www.w3.org/TR/xhtml11/DTD/xhtml11.dtd">
<html xmlns="http://www.w3.org/1999/xhtml" >
<head id="Head1" runat="server">
    <title>Photo Gallery</title>
</head>
<body>
    <form id="form1" runat="server">
```

```
<div>

<asp:DataList
    id="dlstImages"
    DataSourceID="srcImages"
    RepeatColumns="3"
    Runat="server">
    <ItemTemplate>
    <asp:Image ID="Image1"
        ImageUrl='<%# String.Format("DynamicImage.ashx?id={0}", Eval("Id")) %>'
        Width="250"
        Runat="server" />
    <br />
    <%# Eval("Description") %>
</ItemTemplate>
</asp:DataList>

<hr />

<asp:FormView
    id="frmImage"
    DataSourceID="srcImages"
    DefaultMode="Insert"
    Runat="server">
    <InsertItemTemplate>
    <asp:Label
        id="lblImage"
        Text="Upload Image:"
        AssociatedControlId="upImage"
        Runat="server" />
    <br />
    <asp:FileUpload
        id="upImage"
        FileBytes='<%# Bind("Image") %>'
        Runat="server" />

    <br /><br />

    <asp:Label
        id="lblDescription"
        Text="Description:"
        AssociatedControlID="txtDescription"
        Runat="server" />
    <br />
    <asp:TextBox
```

```
            id="txtDescription"
            Text='<%# Bind("Description") %>'
            TextMode="MultiLine"
            Columns="50"
            Rows="2"
            Runat="server" />

    <br /><br />

    <asp:Button
        id="btnInsert"
        Text="Add Image"
        CommandName="Insert"
        Runat="server" />
    </InsertItemTemplate>
</asp:FormView>

<asp:SqlDataSource
    id="srcImages"
    SelectCommand="SELECT ID,Description FROM Images"
    InsertCommand="INSERT Images (Image,Description)
        VALUES (@Image,@Description)"
    ConnectionString="<%$ ConnectionStrings:Images %>"
    Runat="server" />

</div>
</form>
</body>
</html>
```

The page in Listing 9.28 has a FormView control that contains a FileUpload control. You can use the FileUpload control to upload images from your local hard drive to the application's database table.

Also, the page contains a DataList control that displays the image. The Image control contained in the DataList control's ItemTemplate points to a file named DynamicImage.ashx, which represents an HTTP Handler that renders a particular image. The DynamicImage.ashx handler is contained in Listing 9.29.

NOTE

HTTP handlers are discussed in detail in Chapter 31, "Working with the HTTP Runtime."

LISTING 9.29   DynamicImage.ashx

```csharp
<%@ WebHandler Language="C#" Class="DynamicImage" %>


using System.Data;
using System.Web;
using System.Web.Configuration;
using System.Web.UI;
using System.Web.UI.WebControls;


/// <summary>
/// Displays an image corresponding to the Id passed
/// in a query string field
/// </summary>
public class DynamicImage : IHttpHandler
{

    public void ProcessRequest (HttpContext context)
    {
        // Get the Id of the image to display
        string imageId = context.Request.QueryString["Id"];

        // Use SqlDataSource to grab image bytes
        SqlDataSource src = new SqlDataSource();
        src.ConnectionString =
WebConfigurationManager.ConnectionStrings["Images"].ConnectionString;
        src.SelectCommand = "SELECT Image FROM Images WHERE Id=" + imageId;

        // Return a DataView

        DataView view = (DataView)src.Select(DataSourceSelectArguments.Empty);
        context.Response.BinaryWrite( (byte[])view[0]["Image"]);

        // Return a DataReader
        //src.DataSourceMode = SqlDataSourceMode.DataReader;
        //IDataReader reader =
 (IDataReader)src.Select(DataSourceSelectArguments.Empty);
        //reader.Read();
        //context.Response.BinaryWrite((byte[])reader["Image"]);
        //reader.Close();

    }

    public bool IsReusable
    {
```

```
        get
        {
            return false;
        }
    }

}
```

In the `ProcessRequest()` method, an instance of the `SqlDataSource` control is created. The `SqlDataSource` control's `ConnectionString` and `SelectCommand` properties are initialized. Finally, the `SqlDataSource` control's `Select()` command is executed, and the results are rendered with the `Response.BinaryWrite()` method.

The return value from the `Select()` method is cast explicitly to a `DataView` object. You need to cast the return value to either a `DataView` or `IDataReader` for it to work with the results of the `Select()` method.

In Listing 9.29, the image bytes are returned in a `DataView`. To illustrate how you can use the `Select()` method to return a DataReader, I also included the code for returning the image with a `DataReader`, but I added comments to the code so that it won't execute.

Caching Database Data with the `SqlDataSource` Control

The easiest way to dramatically improve the performance of a database-driven website is through caching. Retrieving data from a database is one of the slowest operations that you can perform in a web page. Retrieving data from memory, on the other hand, is lightning fast. The `SqlDataSource` control makes it easy to cache data in your server's memory.

Caching is discussed in detail in Chapter 29, "Caching Application Pages and Data." In that chapter, you learn about all the different caching options supported by the `SqlDataSource` control. However, because it is so easy to cache data with the `SqlDataSource` control and caching has such a dramatic impact on performance, I want to provide you with a quick sample of how you can use the `SqlDataSource` control to cache data.

The page in Listing 9.30 displays a list of movies cached in memory.

LISTING 9.30 `CacheSqlDataSource.aspx`

```
<%@ Page Language="C#" %>
<!DOCTYPE html PUBLIC "-//W3C//DTD XHTML 1.1//EN"
"http://www.w3.org/TR/xhtml11/DTD/xhtml11.dtd">
<script runat="server">
```

9

```
     protected void srcMovies_Selecting(object sender,
➥SqlDataSourceSelectingEventArgs e)
     {
         lblMessage.Text = "Retrieving data from database";
     }
</script>
<html xmlns="http://www.w3.org/1999/xhtml" >
<head id="Head1" runat="server">
    <title>Cache SqlDataSource</title>
</head>
<body>
    <form id="form1" runat="server">
    <div>

    <asp:Label
        id="lblMessage"
        EnableViewState="false"
        Runat="server" />
    <br /><br />

    <asp:GridView
        id="grdMovies"
        DataSourceID="srcMovies"
        Runat="server" />

    <asp:SqlDataSource
        id="srcMovies"
        EnableCaching="True"
        CacheDuration="3600"
        SelectCommand="SELECT * FROM Movies"
        ConnectionString="<%$ ConnectionStrings:Movies %>"
        Runat="server" OnSelecting="srcMovies_Selecting" />

    </div>
    </form>
</body>
</html>
```

In Listing 9.30, two properties of the SqlDataSource control related to caching are set. First, the EnableCaching property is set to the value True. Next, the CacheDuration property is set to a value that represents 3,600 seconds (1 hour). The movies are cached in memory for a maximum of 1 hour. If you don't supply a value for the CacheDuration property, the default value is Infinite.

The page in Listing 9.30 includes a `srcMovies_Selecting()` event handler. This handler is called only when the movies are retrieved from the database rather than from memory. In other words, you can use this event handler to detect when the movies are dropped from the cache (see Figure 9.15).

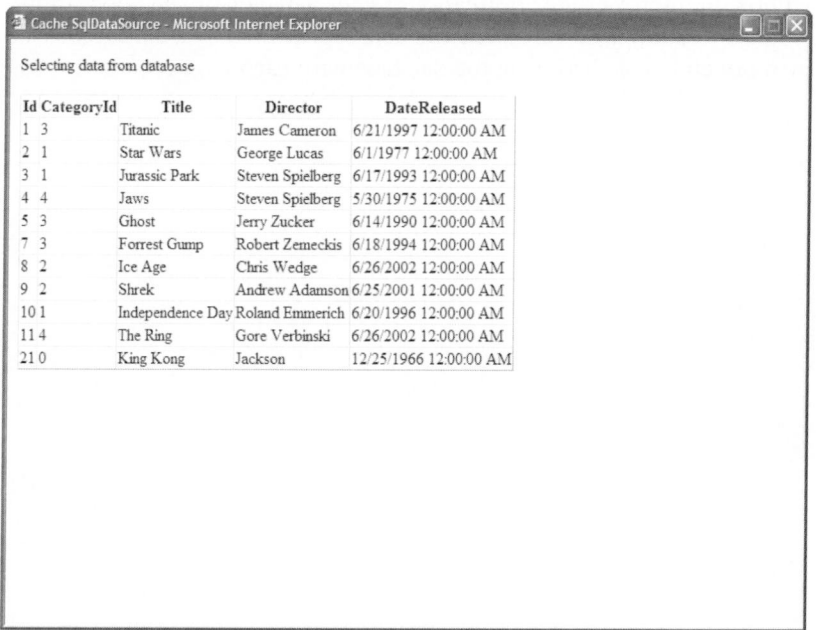

FIGURE 9.15   Caching the data represented by a `SqlDataSource` control.

The page in Listing 9.30 illustrates only one type of caching that you can use with the `SqlDataSource` control. In Chapter 29, you learn about all the advanced caching options supported by the `SqlDataSource` control. For example, by taking advantage of SQL cache dependencies, you can reload the cached data represented by a `SqlDataSource` control automatically when data in a database is changed. For more information, see the final section of Chapter 25, "Using the ASP.Net URL Routing Engine."

Summary

In this chapter, you learned how to use the `SqlDataSource` control to connect and execute commands against a SQL relational database. In the first section, you learned how to represent database connection strings with the `SqlDataSource` control. You learned how to store connection strings in the web configuration file and encrypt the connection strings.

Next, you learned how to execute both inline SQL commands and stored procedures. You also learned how to cancel commands and handle errors gracefully.

This chapter also discussed the different types of ASP.NET parameters that you can use with the `SqlDataSource` control. You learned how to use the `Parameter`, `ControlParameter`, `CookieParameter`, `FormParameter`, `ProfileParameter`, `SessionParameter`, and `QueryStringParameter` objects.

Finally, you learned how to improve the performance of your database-driven applications through caching. You learned how you can cache the data represented by a `SqlDataSource` control in server memory and avoid accessing the database with each page request.

Using List Controls

The List controls enable you to display simple lists of options. For example, you can use the RadioButtonList control to display a group of radio buttons or the BulletedList control to display a list of links.

In this chapter, you learn how to use each of the List controls included in the ASP.NET Framework. In particular, we discusses the DropDownList, RadioButtonList, ListBox, CheckBoxList, and BulletedList controls. You learn how to bind the different types of List controls to a data source such as a database table. You also learn how to work directly with the list items contained by a List control.

Finally, at the end of this chapter, you learn how to build a custom List control. We create a client-side multiselect List control that enables you to select multiple list items at a time.

Overview of the List Controls

The five List controls inherit from the base ListControl class. This means that all the List controls share a common set of properties and methods. This section provides you with an overview of the common features of the List controls.

Declaring List Items

The List controls render a list of options. Each option is represented by an instance of the ListItem class. For example, you can use the page in Listing 10.1 to render a set of options for selecting your favorite movie (see Figure 10.1).

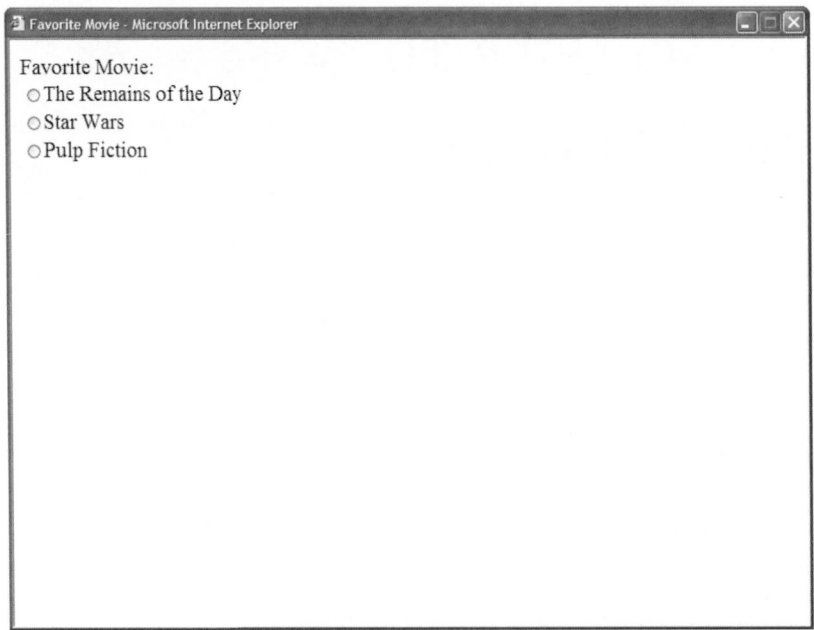

FIGURE 10.1   Displaying a list of movies.

LISTING 10.1   FavoriteMovie.aspx

```
<%@ Page Language="C#" %>
<!DOCTYPE html PUBLIC "-//W3C//DTD XHTML 1.1//EN"
"http://www.w3.org/TR/xhtml11/DTD/xhtml11.dtd">
<html xmlns="http://www.w3.org/1999/xhtml" >
<head id="Head1" runat="server">
    <title>Favorite Movie</title>
</head>
<body>
    <form id="form1" runat="server">
    <div>

    <asp:Label
        id="lblMovies"
        Text="Favorite Movie:"
        AssociatedControlID="rblMovies"
        Runat="server" />
```

```
    <asp:RadioButtonList
        id="rblMovies"
        Runat="server">
        <asp:ListItem
            Text="The Remains of the Day"
            Value="movie1" />
        <asp:ListItem
            Text="Star Wars"
            Value="movie2" />
        <asp:ListItem
            Text="Pulp Fiction"
            Value="movie3" />
    </asp:RadioButtonList>

    </div>
    </form>
</body>
</html>
```

The page in Listing 10.1 contains a `RadioButtonList` control that contains three `ListItem` controls that correspond to the three radio buttons. All the List controls use the `ListItem` control to represent individual list items.

The `ListItem` control supports the following five properties:

- ▶ **Attributes** — Enables you to add HTML attributes to a list item.
- ▶ **Enabled** — Enables you to disable a list item.
- ▶ **Selected**—Enables you to mark a list item as selected.
- ▶ **Text** — Enables you to specify the text displayed by the List Item.
- ▶ **Value** – Enables you to specify a hidden value associated with the List Item.

You use the `Text` property to indicate the text that you want the option to display, and the `Value` property to indicate a hidden value associated with the option. For example, the hidden value might represent the value of a primary key column in a database table.

The `Selected` property enables you to show a list item as selected. Selected radio buttons and check boxes appear checked. The selected option in a `DropDownList` is the default option displayed. Selected options in a `ListBox` appear highlighted. And in the case of a `BulletedList` control, the `selected` property has no effect whatsoever.

The `Enabled` property has different effects when used with different List controls. When you set a `ListItem` control's `Enabled` property to the value `False` when using the `DropDownList` or `ListBox` controls, the list item is not rendered to the browser. When you use this property with a `CheckBoxList`, `RadioButtonList`, or `BulletedList` control, the list item is ghosted and nonfunctional.

Binding to a Data Source

You can bind any of the List controls to a data source. The List controls support both declarative databinding and programmatic databinding.

For example, the page in Listing 10.2 contains a DropDownList control bound to the Movies database table with declarative databinding (see Figure 10.2).

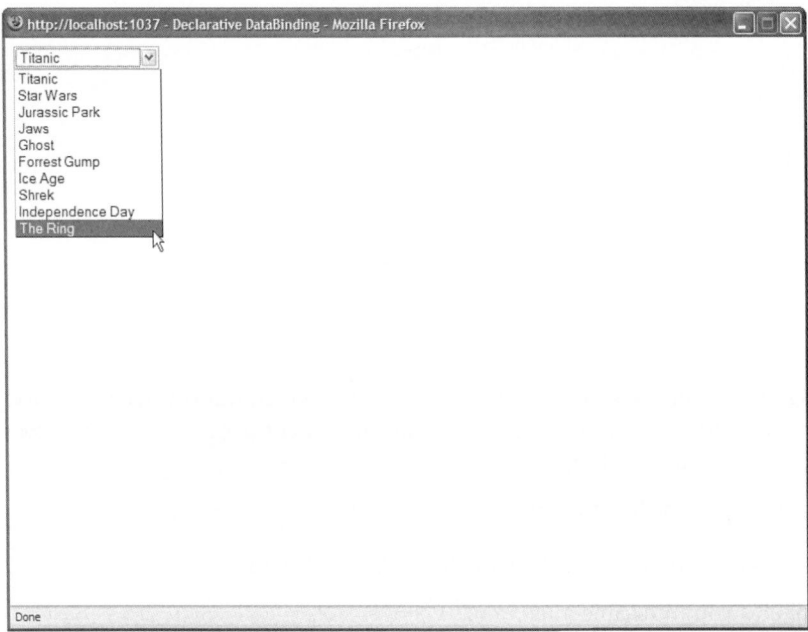

FIGURE 10.2   Displaying list items with declarative databinding.

LISTING 10.2   DeclarativeDataBinding.aspx

```
<%@ Page Language="C#" %>
<!DOCTYPE html PUBLIC "-//W3C//DTD XHTML 1.1//EN"
"http://www.w3.org/TR/xhtml11/DTD/xhtml11.dtd">
<html xmlns="http://www.w3.org/1999/xhtml" >
<head id="Head1" runat="server">
    <title>Declarative DataBinding</title>
</head>
<body>
```

```
<form id="form1" runat="server">
<div>

<asp:DropDownList
    id="ddlMovies"
    DataSourceID="srcMovies"
    DataTextField="Title"
    DataValueField="Id"
    Runat="server" />

<asp:SqlDataSource
    id="srcMovies"
    SelectCommand="SELECT Id, Title FROM Movies"
    ConnectionString="<%$ ConnectionStrings:Movies %>"
    Runat="server" />

</div>
</form>
</body>
</html>
```

The DropDownList control's DataSourceID property points to the ID of the SqlDataSource control. When you open the page in Listing 10.2, the SqlDataSource control retrieves the records from the Movies database table. The DropDownList control grabs these records from the SqlDataSource control and creates a ListItem control for each data item.

The DropDownList control has both its DataTextField and DataValueField properties set. When the DropDownList control creates each of its list items, it uses the values of the DataTextField and DataValueField properties to set the Text and Value properties of each list item.

As an alternative to declarative databinding, you can programmatically bind any of the List controls to a data source. For example, the page in Listing 10.3 binds a ListBox control to a collection that represents a shopping cart (see Figure 10.3).

10

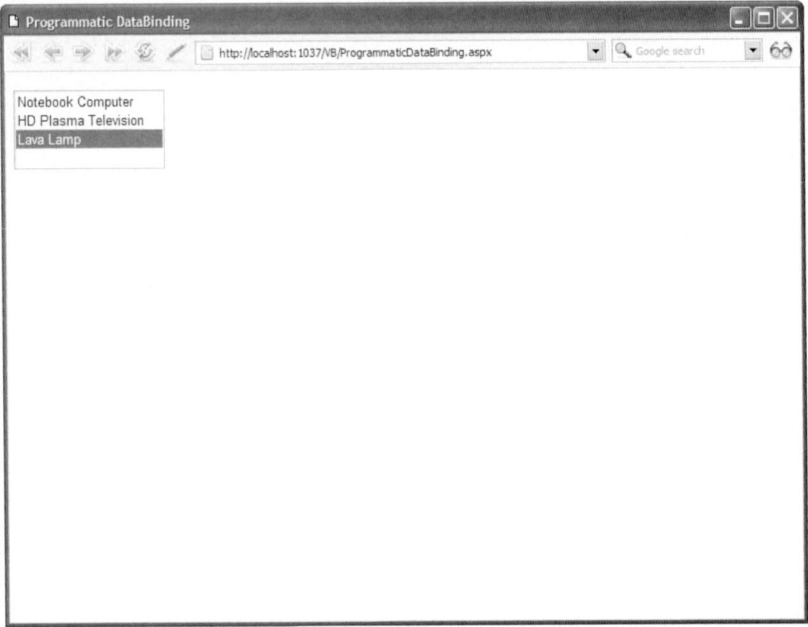

FIGURE 10.3   Show list items with programmatic binding.

LISTING 10.3   ProgrammaticDataBinding.aspx

```csharp
<%@ Page Language="C#" %>
<%@ Import Namespace="System.Collections.Generic" %>
<!DOCTYPE html PUBLIC "-//W3C//DTD XHTML 1.1//EN"
"http://www.w3.org/TR/xhtml11/DTD/xhtml11.dtd">
<script runat="server">

    /// <summary>
    /// Represents an item in the
    /// shopping cart
    /// </summary>
    public class CartItem
    {
        private int _id;
        public string _description;

        public int Id
        {
            get { return _id; }
        }

        public string Description
```

```
            {
                get { return _description; }
            }

            public CartItem(int id, string description)
            {
                _id = id;
                _description = description;
            }
        }

        void Page_Load()
        {
            if (!IsPostBack)
            {
                // Create shopping cart
                List<CartItem> shoppingCart = new List<CartItem>();
                shoppingCart.Add(new CartItem(1, "Notebook Computer"));
                shoppingCart.Add(new CartItem(2, "HD Plasma Television"));
                shoppingCart.Add(new CartItem(3, "Lava Lamp"));

                // Bind ListBox to shopping cart
                lstShoppingCart.DataSource = shoppingCart;
                lstShoppingCart.DataBind();
            }
        }
</script>

<html xmlns="http://www.w3.org/1999/xhtml" >
<head id="Head1" runat="server">
    <title>Programmatic DataBinding</title>
</head>
<body>
    <form id="form1" runat="server">
    <div>

    <asp:ListBox
        id="lstShoppingCart"
        DataTextField="Description"
        DataValueField="Id"
        Runat="server" />

    </div>
    </form>
</body>
</html>
```

In Listing 10.3, the `ListBox` is bound to the collection in the `Page_Load()` method. The `DataTextField` and `DataValueField` properties of the `ListBox` control represent properties of the `CartItem` class.

> **NOTE**
>
> A List control's `DataTextField` and `DataValueField` properties can refer to any public property of a class, but you cannot bind a List control to a public field.

Determining the Selected List Item

Displaying options with the List controls is all very nice, but at some point you need to determine which option a user has selected. The List controls support three properties that you can use to determine the selected list item:

▶ `SelectedIndex` — Gets or sets the index of the selected list item.

▶ `SelectedItem` — Gets the first selected list item.

▶ `SelectedValue` — Gets or sets the value of the first selected list item.

For example, the page in Listing 10.4 enables you to select an item from the `DropDownList` control and display the value of the selected item's `Text` property (see Figure 10.4).

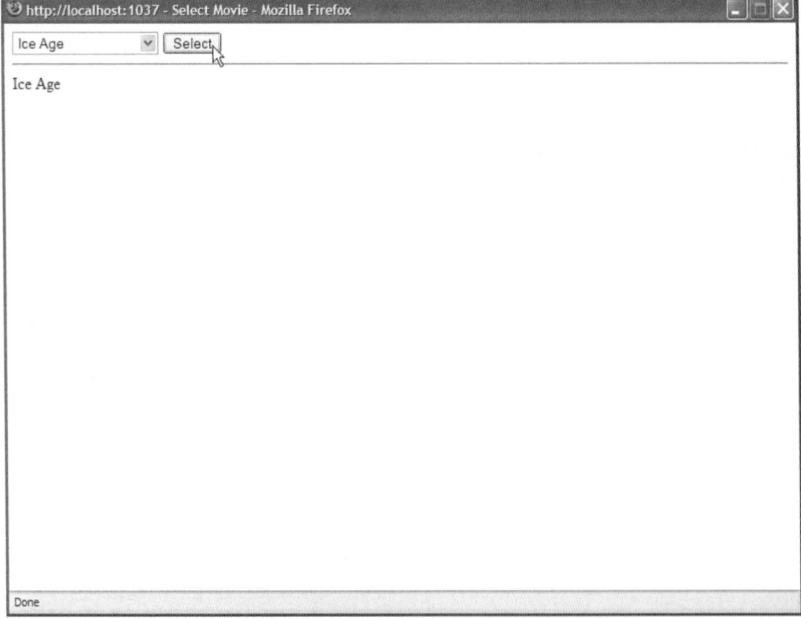

FIGURE 10.4   Selecting an item from a `DropDownList` control.

LISTING 10.4 SelectMovie.aspx

```
<%@ Page Language="C#" %>
<!DOCTYPE html PUBLIC "-//W3C//DTD XHTML 1.1//EN"
"http://www.w3.org/TR/xhtml11/DTD/xhtml11.dtd">
<script runat="server">

    protected void btnSelect_Click(object sender, EventArgs e)
    {
        lblSelectedMovie.Text = ddlMovies.SelectedItem.Text;
    }
</script>
<html xmlns="http://www.w3.org/1999/xhtml" >
<head id="Head1" runat="server">
    <title>Select Movie</title>
</head>
<body>
    <form id="form1" runat="server">
    <div>

    <asp:DropDownList
        id="ddlMovies"
        DataSourceID="srcMovies"
        DataTextField="Title"
        DataValueField="Id"
        Runat="server" />

    <asp:Button
        id="btnSelect"
        Text="Select"
        OnClick="btnSelect_Click"
        Runat="server" />

    <hr />

    <asp:Label
        id="lblSelectedMovie"
        Runat="server" />

    <asp:SqlDataSource
        id="srcMovies"
        SelectCommand="SELECT Id, Title FROM Movies"
        ConnectionString="<%$ ConnectionStrings:Movies %>"
        Runat="server" />

    </div>
```

```
    </form>
</body>
</html>
```

The `SelectedItem` property retrieves the selected `ListItem` control from the `DropDownList` control. The value of the selected item's `Text` property displays in the `Label` control.

You can use these properties when you want to associate a List control with another `DataBound` control. For example, the page in Listing 10.5 contains a `DropDownList` control that displays a list of movie categories and a `GridView` control that displays a list of movies that match the selected category (see Figure 10.5).

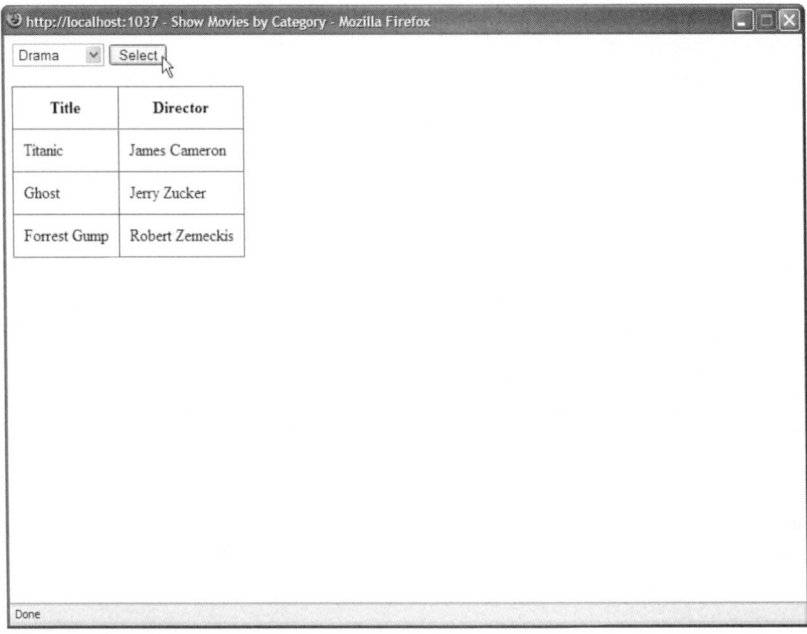

FIGURE 10.5   Master/Details form with a list control.

LISTING 10.5   ShowMoviesByCategory.aspx

```
<%@ Page Language="C#" %>
<!DOCTYPE html PUBLIC "-//W3C//DTD XHTML 1.1//EN"
"http://www.w3.org/TR/xhtml11/DTD/xhtml11.dtd">
<html xmlns="http://www.w3.org/1999/xhtml" >
<head id="Head1" runat="server">
    <style type="text/css">
        .gridView
        {
```

```
            margin-top:20px;
        }
        .gridView td, .gridView th
        {
            padding:10px;
        }
    </style>
    <title>Show Movies by Category</title>
</head>
<body>
    <form id="form1" runat="server">
    <div>

    <asp:DropDownList
        id="ddlMovieCategory"
        DataSourceID="srcMovieCategories"
        DataTextField="Name"
        DataValueField="Id"
        Runat="server" />

    <asp:Button
        id="btnSelect"
        Text="Select"
        Runat="server" />

    <asp:GridView
        id="grdMovies"
        DataSourceID="srcMovies"
        CssClass="gridView"
        Runat="server" />

    <asp:SqlDataSource
        id="srcMovieCategories"
        SelectCommand="SELECT Id, Name FROM MovieCategories"
        ConnectionString="<%$ ConnectionStrings:Movies %>"
        Runat="server" />

    <asp:SqlDataSource
        id="srcMovies"
        SelectCommand="SELECT Title,Director FROM Movies
            WHERE CategoryId=@Id"
        ConnectionString="<%$ ConnectionStrings:Movies %>"
        Runat="server">
        <SelectParameters>
```

10

```
        <asp:ControlParameter
            Name="Id"
            ControlID="ddlMovieCategory"
            PropertyName="SelectedValue" />
        </SelectParameters>
    </asp:SqlDataSource>

    </div>
    </form>
</body>
</html>
```

The DropDownList control is bound to the srcMovieCategories SqlDataSource control, and the GridView control is bound to the srcMovies SqlDataSource control. The srcMovies SqlDataSource control includes a ControlParameter, which represents the SelectedValue property of the DropDownList control. When you select a movie category from the DropDownList control, the selected value changes, and the GridView control displays a list of matching movies.

Appending Data Items

You can mix the list items that you declare in a List control and the list items that are added to the control when it is bound to a data source. This is useful when you want to display a default selection.

For example, imagine that you create a form in which you want to require a user to pick an item from a List control. In this situation, you should add a default item to the List control so that you can detect whether a user has actually picked an item.

You can mix declarative list items with databound list items by assigning the value True to the AppendDataBoundItems property. The page in Listing 10.6 illustrates how you can add a default list item to a List control (see Figure 10.6).

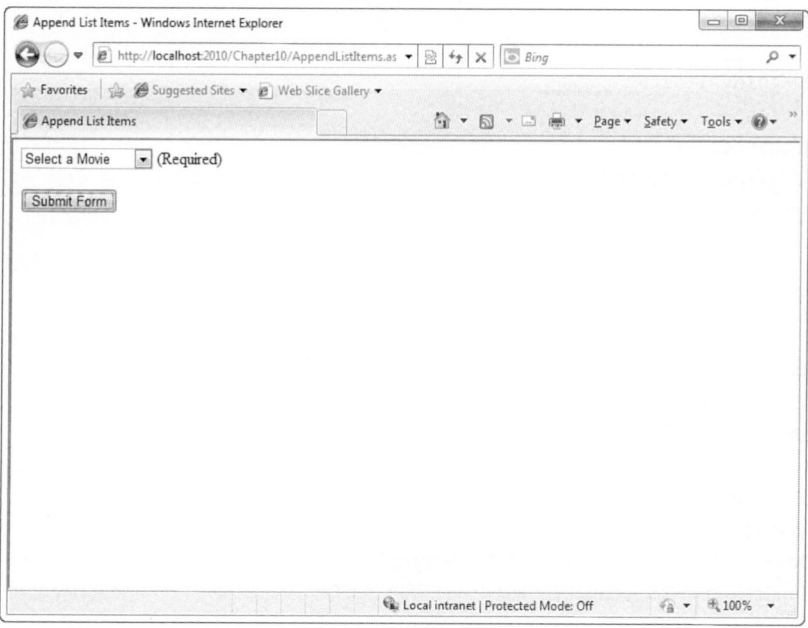

FIGURE 10.6   Displaying a default list item.

LISTING 10.6   `AppendListItems.aspx`

```
<%@ Page Language="C#" %>
<!DOCTYPE html PUBLIC "-//W3C//DTD XHTML 1.1//EN"
"http://www.w3.org/TR/xhtml11/DTD/xhtml11.dtd">
<html xmlns="http://www.w3.org/1999/xhtml" >
<head id="Head1" runat="server">
    <title>Append List Items</title>
</head>
<body>
    <form id="form1" runat="server">
    <div>

    <asp:DropDownList
        id="ddlMovies"
        DataSourceID="srcMovies"
        DataTextField="Title"
        DataValueField="Id"
        AppendDataBoundItems="True"
        Runat="server">
        <asp:ListItem
            Text="Select a Movie"
            Value="" />
```

10

```
</asp:DropDownList>

<asp:RequiredFieldValidator
    id="valMovies"
    Text="(Required)"
    ControlToValidate="ddlMovies"
    Runat="server" />

<br /><br />

<asp:Button
    id="btnSubmit"
    Text="Submit Form"
    Runat="server" />

<asp:SqlDataSource
    id="srcMovies"
    SelectCommand="SELECT Id, Title FROM Movies"
    ConnectionString="<%$ ConnectionStrings:Movies %>"
    Runat="server" />

    </div>
    </form>
</body>
</html>
```

The page in Listing 10.6 includes both a DropDownList control and a RequiredFieldValidator control. The DropDownList control includes a list item that displays the text Select a Movie. The Value property of this list item is set to the empty string. If you attempt to submit the form without selecting a list item other than the default list item, the RequiredFieldValidator displays an error message.

The DropDownList control includes an AppendDataBoundItems property that is set to the value True. If you neglect to set this property, the databound list items overwrite any declarative list items.

Enabling Automatic PostBacks

All the List controls, except for the BulletedList control, support a property named the AutoPostBack property. When this property is assigned the value True, the form containing the List control is automatically posted back to the server whenever a new selection is made.

For example, the page in Listing 10.7 contains a DropDownList control that has its AutoPostBack property enabled. When you select a new item from the DropDownList control, the page is automatically posted back to the server and the Label control displays the selected item.

LISTING 10.7   AutoPostBackListControl.aspx

```
<%@ Page Language="C#" %>
<!DOCTYPE html PUBLIC "-//W3C//DTD XHTML 1.1//EN"
"http://www.w3.org/TR/xhtml11/DTD/xhtml11.dtd">
<script runat="server">

    protected void ddlMovies_SelectedIndexChanged(object sender, EventArgs e)
    {
        lblSelectedMovie.Text = ddlMovies.SelectedItem.Text;
    }
</script>
<html xmlns="http://www.w3.org/1999/xhtml" >
<head id="Head1" runat="server">
    <title>AutoPostBack List Control</title>
</head>
<body>
    <form id="form1" runat="server">
    <div>

    <asp:DropDownList
        id="ddlMovies"
        DataSourceID="srcMovies"
        DataTextField="Title"
        DataValueField="Id"
        AutoPostBack="true"
        OnSelectedIndexChanged="ddlMovies_SelectedIndexChanged"
        Runat="server" />

    <br /><br />

    <asp:Label
        id="lblSelectedMovie"
        Runat="server" />

    <asp:SqlDataSource
        id="srcMovies"
```

```
        SelectCommand="SELECT Id, Title FROM Movies"
        ConnectionString="<%$ ConnectionStrings:Movies %>"
        Runat="server" />

    </div>
    </form>
</body>
</html>
```

When you enable the `AutoPostBack` property, a JavaScript `onchange()` event handler is added to the List control. The `onchange` event is supported by all recent browsers including Firefox 1.0 and Opera 8.0.

The `DropDownList` control has a `SelectedIndexChanged` event handler named `ddlMovies_SelectedIndexChanged()`. The `SelectedIndexChanged` event is raised whenever you make a new selection in the List control (independent of the `AutoPostBack` property). The `ddlMovies_SelectedIndexChanged()` method displays the selected list item in a Label control.

WEB STANDARDS NOTE

You should avoid using the `AutoPostBack` property because it creates accessibility problems for persons with disabilities. If you can't use a mouse, and you are interacting with a website through the keyboard, having a page post back to the server whenever you make a selection change is a frustrating experience.

Using the Items Collection

All the list items rendered by a List control are contained in the List control's list item collection. This collection is exposed by the `Items` property.

You can work directly with the list items in this collection. For example, you can add or remove particular list items, or you can change the order of the list items.

The page in Listing 10.8 contains two `ListBox` controls and two button controls. When you click the Add button, a list item is moved from the first `ListBox` to the second `ListBox` control. When you click Remove, the list item is moved back to the original List control (see Figure 10.7).

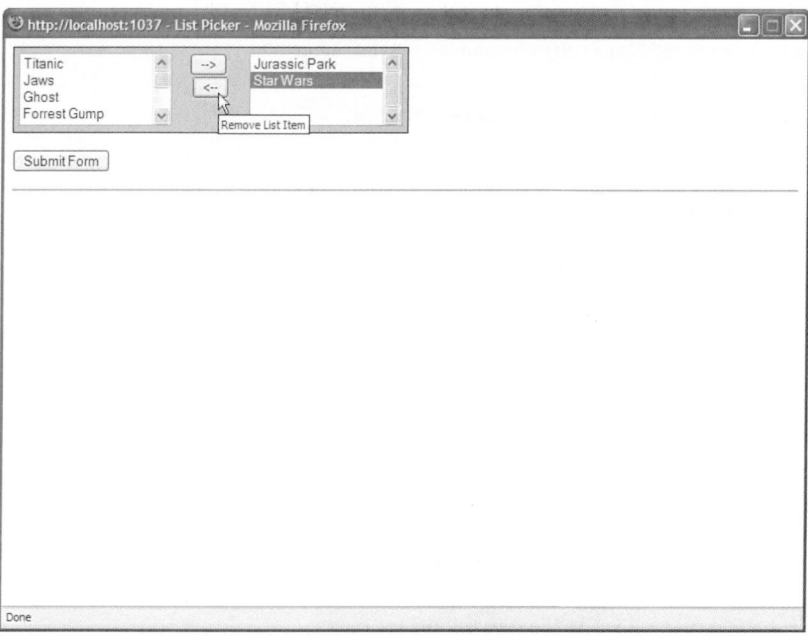

FIGURE 10.7   Using the ListPicker to select list items.

LISTING 10.8   ListPicker.aspx

```
<%@ Page Language="C#" %>
<!DOCTYPE html PUBLIC "-//W3C//DTD XHTML 1.1//EN"
"http://www.w3.org/TR/xhtml11/DTD/xhtml11.dtd">
<script runat="server">

    /// <summary>
    /// Move item from All Movies to Favorite Movies
    /// </summary>
    protected void btnAdd_Click(object sender, EventArgs e)
    {
        ListItem item = lstAllMovies.SelectedItem;
        if (item != null)
        {
            lstAllMovies.Items.Remove(item);
            lstFavoriteMovies.ClearSelection();
            lstFavoriteMovies.Items.Add(item);
        }
    }


    /// <summary>
    /// Move item from Favorite Movies to All Movies
```

10

```
    /// </summary>
    protected void btnRemove_Click(object sender, EventArgs e)
    {
        ListItem item = lstFavoriteMovies.SelectedItem;
        if (item != null)
        {
            lstFavoriteMovies.Items.Remove(item);
            lstAllMovies.ClearSelection();
            lstAllMovies.Items.Add(item);
        }
    }


    /// <summary>
    /// When the form is submitted,
    /// show the contents of the
    /// Favorite Movies ListBox
    /// </summary>
    protected void btnSubmit_Click(object sender, EventArgs e)
    {
        foreach (ListItem item in lstFavoriteMovies.Items)
            lblResults.Text += "<li>" + item.Text;
    }
</script>
<html xmlns="http://www.w3.org/1999/xhtml" >
<head id="Head1" runat="server">
    <style type="text/css">
        .listPicker
        {
            border:solid 1px black;
            padding:5px;
            width:380px;
            background-color:silver;
        }
        .listPicker select
        {
            width:100%;
        }
    </style>
    <title>List Picker</title>
</head>
<body>
    <form id="form1" runat="server">
```

```
<div class="listPicker">
<div style="float:left;width:40%">
<asp:ListBox
    id="lstAllMovies"
    DataSourceID="srcMovies"
    DataTextField="Title"
    DataValueField="Id"
    Runat="server" />
</div>
<div style="float:left;width:20%;text-align:center">
<asp:Button
    id="btnAdd"
    Text="--&gt;"
    ToolTip="Add List Item"
    Runat="server" OnClick="btnAdd_Click" />
<br />
<asp:Button
    id="btnRemove"
    Text="&lt;--"
    ToolTip="Remove List Item"
    Runat="server" OnClick="btnRemove_Click" />
</div>
<div style="float:left;width:40%">
<asp:ListBox
    id="lstFavoriteMovies"
    Runat="server" />
</div>
<br style="clear:both" />
</div>

<p>
<asp:Button
    id="btnSubmit"
    Text="Submit Form"
    Runat="server" OnClick="btnSubmit_Click" />
</p>

<hr />

<asp:Label
    id="lblResults"
    EnableViewState="false"
    Runat="server" />
```

```
<asp:SqlDataSource
    id="srcMovies"
    SelectCommand="SELECT Id, Title FROM Movies"
    ConnectionString="<%$ ConnectionStrings:Movies %>"
    Runat="server" />

    </form>
</body>
</html>
```

The first ListBox in Listing 10.8 is bound to the Movies database table. You can use the ListBox controls to pick your favorite movies by moving movie titles from the first ListBox to the second ListBox.

When you click the Add button, the btnAdd_Click() method executes. This method grabs the selected item from the All Movies ListBox and adds it to the Favorite Movies ListBox. The Remove button does exactly the opposite.

Both the btnAdd_Click() and btnRemove_Click() methods call the ClearSelection() method of the ListBox class. This method iterates through all the list items and sets the Selected property for each list item to the value False. If multiple list items are selected, an exception is thrown.

NOTE

One problem with the page discussed in this section is that the page must be posted back to the server each time you move an item from the first ListBox to the second ListBox. At the end of this chapter, you learn how to create a MultiSelectList control, which uses a client-side script to get around this limitation.

Working with the DropDownList Control

The DropDownList control enables you to display a list of options while requiring a minimum of screen real estate. A user can select only one option at a time when using this control.

The page in Listing 10.9 illustrates how you can use the DropDownList control to display all the movie titles from the Movies database table (see Figure 10.8).

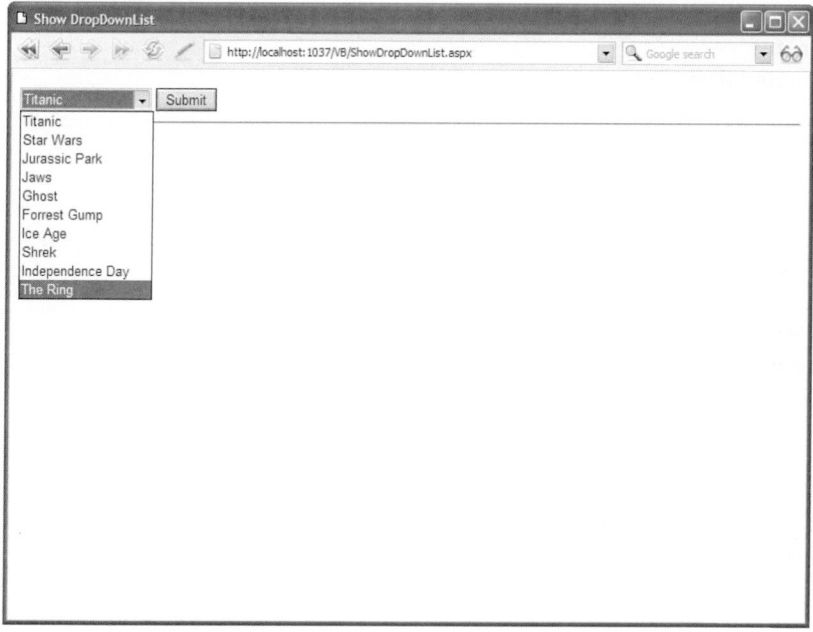

FIGURE 10.8   Displaying list items with the DropDownList control.

LISTING 10.9   ShowDropDownList.aspx

```
<%@ Page Language="C#" %>
<!DOCTYPE html PUBLIC "-//W3C//DTD XHTML 1.1//EN"
"http://www.w3.org/TR/xhtml11/DTD/xhtml11.dtd">
<script runat="server">

    protected void btnSubmit_Click(object sender, EventArgs e)
    {
        lblMovie.Text = ddlMovies.SelectedItem.Text;
    }
</script>
<html xmlns="http://www.w3.org/1999/xhtml" >
<head id="Head1" runat="server">
    <title>Show DropDownList</title>
</head>
<body>
    <form id="form1" runat="server">
    <div>
```

```
<asp:DropDownList
    id="ddlMovies"
    DataSourceID="srcMovies"
    DataTextField="Title"
    DataValueField="Id"
    Runat="server" />

<asp:Button
    id="btnSubmit"
    Text="Submit"
    OnClick="btnSubmit_Click"
    Runat="server" />

<hr />

<asp:Label
    id="lblMovie"
    Runat="server" />

<asp:SqlDataSource
    id="srcMovies"
    SelectCommand="SELECT Id, Title FROM Movies"
    ConnectionString="<%$ ConnectionStrings:Movies %>"
    Runat="server" />

</div>
</form>
</body>
</html>
```

The DropDownList control renders an HTML <select> tag. One problem with the HTML <select> tag is that it has an infinite z index. In other words, you can't place other objects, such as an absolutely positioned <div> tag, in front of a DropDownList control in a page.

One way to get around this problem is to use a third-party control such as the EasyListBox control (available at http://www.EasyListBox.com). This control works fine when other objects are layered over it. It also supports several advanced features such as multiple columns and images in list items.

Working with the **RadioButtonList** Control

The RadioButtonList control, like the DropDownList control, enables a user to select only one list item at a time. The RadioButttonList control displays a list of radio buttons that can be arranged either horizontally or vertically.

The page in Listing 10.10 illustrates how you can use the RadioButtonList control to display a list of movie titles (see Figure 10.9).

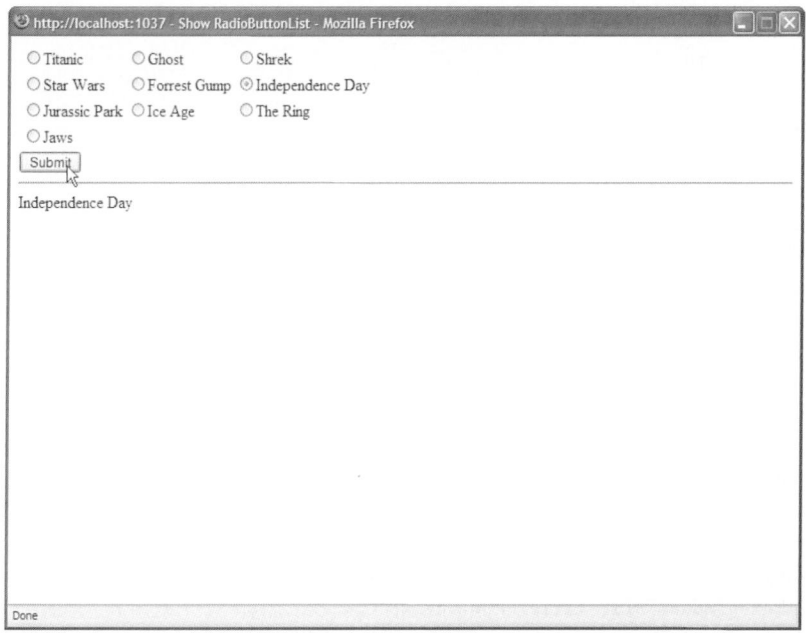

FIGURE 10.9   Displaying list items with the RadioButtonList control.

LISTING 10.10   ShowRadioButtonList.aspx

```
<%@ Page Language="C#" %>
<!DOCTYPE html PUBLIC "-//W3C//DTD XHTML 1.1//EN"
"http://www.w3.org/TR/xhtml11/DTD/xhtml11.dtd">
<script runat="server">

    protected void btnSubmit_Click(object sender, EventArgs e)
    {
        lblMovie.Text = rblMovies.SelectedItem.Text;
    }
</script>
<html xmlns="http://www.w3.org/1999/xhtml" >
<head id="Head1" runat="server">
```

10

```
        <title>Show RadioButtonList</title>
</head>
<body>
    <form id="form1" runat="server">
    <div>

    <asp:RadioButtonList
        id="rblMovies"
        DataSourceID="srcMovies"
        DataTextField="Title"
        DataValueField="Id"
        RepeatColumns="3"
        Runat="server" />

    <asp:Button
        id="btnSubmit"
        Text="Submit"
        Runat="server" OnClick="btnSubmit_Click" />

    <hr />

    <asp:Label
        id="lblMovie"
        Runat="server" />

    <asp:SqlDataSource
        id="srcMovies"
        SelectCommand="SELECT Id, Title FROM Movies"
        ConnectionString="<%$ ConnectionStrings:Movies %>"
        Runat="server" />

    </div>
    </form>
</body>
</html>
```

In Listing 10.10, the radio buttons are rendered in a three-column layout. The
RadioButtonList control includes three properties that have an effect on its layout:

▶ **RepeatColumns**—The number of columns of radio buttons to display.

▶ **RepeatDirection**—The direction that the radio buttons repeat. Possible values are
Horizontal and Vertical.

▶ **RepeatLayout**—Determines whether the radio buttons display in an HTML table.
Possible values are Table and Flow.

By default, the radio buttons rendered by the RadioButtonList control are rendered in an HTML table. If you set the RepeatLayout property to the value Flow, the radio buttons are not rendered in a table. Even when the RadioButtonList renders its items in Flow layout mode, you can specify multiple columns.

Working with the ListBox Control

The ListBox control is similar to the DropDownList control with two important differences. First, the ListBox control requires more screen real estate because it always displays a certain number of list items. Furthermore, unlike the DropDownList control, the ListBox control enables a user to select multiple items.

The page in Listing 10.11 illustrates how you can enable a user to select a single item from a ListBox control (see Figure 10.10).

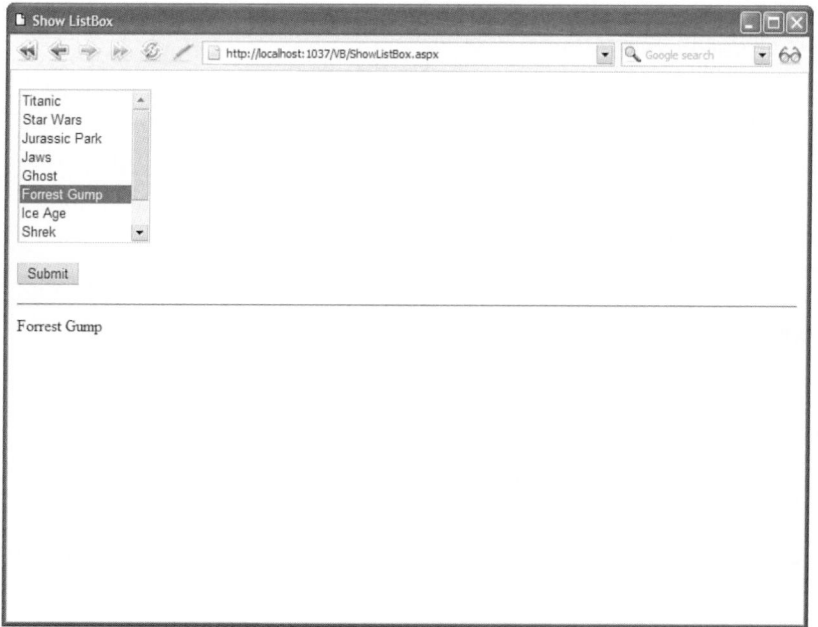

FIGURE 10.10   Displaying list items with the ListBox control.

LISTING 10.11   ShowListBox.aspx

```
<%@ Page Language="C#" %>
<!DOCTYPE html PUBLIC "-//W3C//DTD XHTML 1.1//EN"
"http://www.w3.org/TR/xhtml11/DTD/xhtml11.dtd">
<script runat="server">

    protected void btnSubmit_Click(object sender, EventArgs e)
    {
        lblMovie.Text = lstMovies.SelectedItem.Text;
    }
</script>
<html xmlns="http://www.w3.org/1999/xhtml" >
<head id="Head1" runat="server">
    <title>Show ListBox</title>
</head>
<body>
    <form id="form1" runat="server">
    <div>

    <asp:ListBox
        id="lstMovies"
        DataSourceID="srcMovies"
        DataTextField="Title"
        DataValueField="Id"
        Rows="8"
        Runat="server" />

    <p>
    <asp:Button
        id="btnSubmit"
        Text="Submit"
        OnClick="btnSubmit_Click"
        Runat="server" />
    </p>

    <hr />

    <asp:Label
        id="lblMovie"
        Runat="server" />

    <asp:SqlDataSource
        id="srcMovies"
```

```
        SelectCommand="SELECT Id, Title FROM Movies"
        ConnectionString="<%$ ConnectionStrings:Movies %>"
        Runat="server" />

    </div>
    </form>
</body>
</html>
```

The ListBox control in Listing 10.11 includes a Rows property. The Rows property determines the number of list items that the ListBox displays.

You can also configure the ListBox control to enable a user to select multiple items. This is illustrated in the page in Listing 10.12 (see Figure 10.11).

FIGURE 10.11   Selecting multiple list items.

LISTING 10.12   ShowMultipleListBox.aspx

```
<%@ Page Language="C#" %>
<!DOCTYPE html PUBLIC "-//W3C//DTD XHTML 1.1//EN"
"http://www.w3.org/TR/xhtml11/DTD/xhtml11.dtd">
<script runat="server">
```

```
    protected void btnSubmit_Click(object sender, EventArgs e)
    {
        foreach (ListItem item in lstMovies.Items)
            if (item.Selected)
                lblMovie.Text += "<li>" + item.Text;
    }
</script>
<html xmlns="http://www.w3.org/1999/xhtml" >
<head id="Head1" runat="server">
    <title>Show Multiple ListBox</title>
</head>
<body>
    <form id="form1" runat="server">
    <div>

    <asp:ListBox
        id="lstMovies"
        DataSourceID="srcMovies"
        DataTextField="Title"
        DataValueField="Id"
        SelectionMode="Multiple"
        Runat="server" />

    <p>
    <asp:Button
        id="btnSubmit"
        Text="Submit"
        OnClick="btnSubmit_Click"
        Runat="server" />
    </p>

    <hr />

    <asp:Label
        id="lblMovie"
        EnableViewState="false"
        Runat="server" />

     <asp:SqlDataSource
         id="srcMovies"
         SelectCommand="SELECT Id, Title FROM Movies"
```

```
        ConnectionString="<%$ ConnectionStrings:Movies %>"
        Runat="server" />

    </div>
    </form>
</body>
</html>
```

The `ListBox` in Listing 10.12 includes a `SelectionMode` property that is set to the value `Multiple`. A user can select multiple items from the `ListBox` by using the Ctrl or Shift key when clicking more than one list item.

> **WARNING**
>
> Most users don't understand how to select multiple items from a `ListBox` control. If you want to allow users to pick multiple items, a better approach is to use either the `CheckBoxList` control (discussed in the next section) or the `MultiSelectList` control (discussed in the final section).

When you click the Submit button in Listing 10.12, all the selected list items display in a Label control. The `SelectedItem`, `SelectedIndex`, and `SelectedValue` properties return only the first list item selected. When multiple items are selected, you need to iterate through the Items collection of the `ListBox` control to detect the selected items.

Working with the `CheckBoxList` Control

The `CheckBoxList` control renders a list of check boxes, which can be rendered horizontally or vertically. Unlike the other List controls, a user always can select multiple items when using a `CheckBoxList` control.

For example, the page in Listing 10.13 contains a `CheckBoxList` control that renders its list items in two columns (see Figure 10.12).

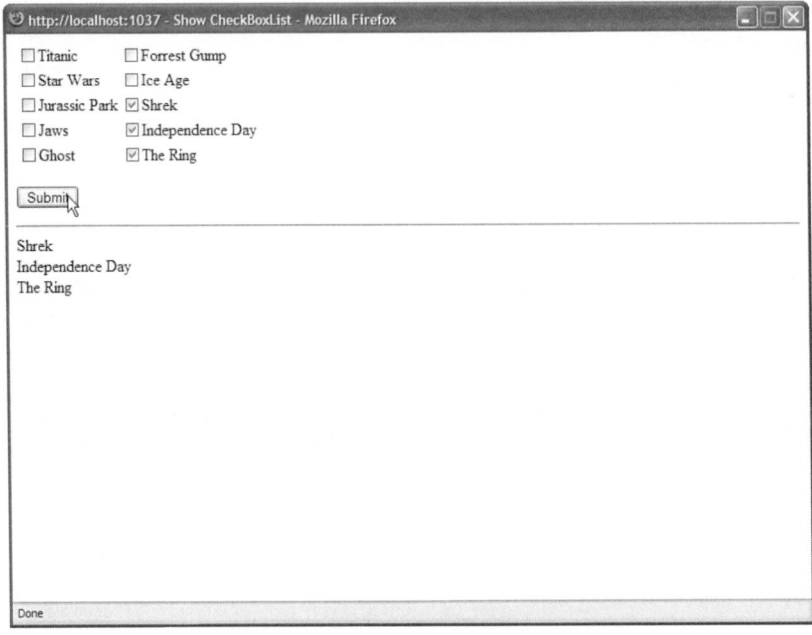

FIGURE 10.12   Displaying list items with the CheckBoxList control.

LISTING 10.13   ShowCheckBoxList.aspx

```
<%@ Page Language="C#" %>
<!DOCTYPE html PUBLIC "-//W3C//DTD XHTML 1.1//EN"
"http://www.w3.org/TR/xhtml11/DTD/xhtml11.dtd">
<script runat="server">

    protected void btnSubmit_Click(object sender, EventArgs e)
    {
        foreach (ListItem item in cblMovies.Items)
            if (item.Selected)
                lblMovie.Text += "<li>" + item.Text;
    }
</script>
<html xmlns="http://www.w3.org/1999/xhtml" >
<head id="Head1" runat="server">
    <title>Show CheckBoxList</title>
</head>
<body>
    <form id="form1" runat="server">
    <div>
```

```
<asp:CheckBoxList
    id="cblMovies"
    DataSourceID="srcMovies"
    DataTextField="Title"
    DataValueField="Id"
    RepeatColumns="2"
    Runat="server" />

<p>
<asp:Button
    id="btnSubmit"
    Text="Submit"
    OnClick="btnSubmit_Click"
    Runat="server" />
</p>

<hr />

<asp:Label
    id="lblMovie"
    EnableViewState="false"
    Runat="server" />

<asp:SqlDataSource
    id="srcMovies"
    SelectCommand="SELECT Id, Title FROM Movies"
    ConnectionString="<%$ ConnectionStrings:Movies %>"
    Runat="server" />

</div>
</form>
</body>
</html>
```

When you click the Submit button, the values of the Text property of any selected check boxes display in a Label control. The selected check boxes are retrieved from the CheckBoxList control's Items property.

The CheckBoxList control includes three properties that affect its layout:

▶ **RepeatColumns**—The number of columns of check boxes to display.

▶ **RepeatDirection**—The direction in which the check boxes are rendered. Possible values are Horizontal and Vertical.

▶ **RepeatLayout**—Determines whether the check boxes display in an HTML table. Possible values are Table and Flow.

10

Normally, a CheckBoxList control renders its list items in an HTML table. When the RepeatLayout property is set to the value Flow, the items are not rendered in a table.

Working with the BulletedList Control

The BulletedList control renders either an unordered (bulleted) or ordered (numbered) list. Each list item can be rendered as plain text, a LinkButton control, or a link to another web page.

For example, the page in Listing 10.14 uses the BulletedList control to render an unordered list of movies (see Figure 10.13).

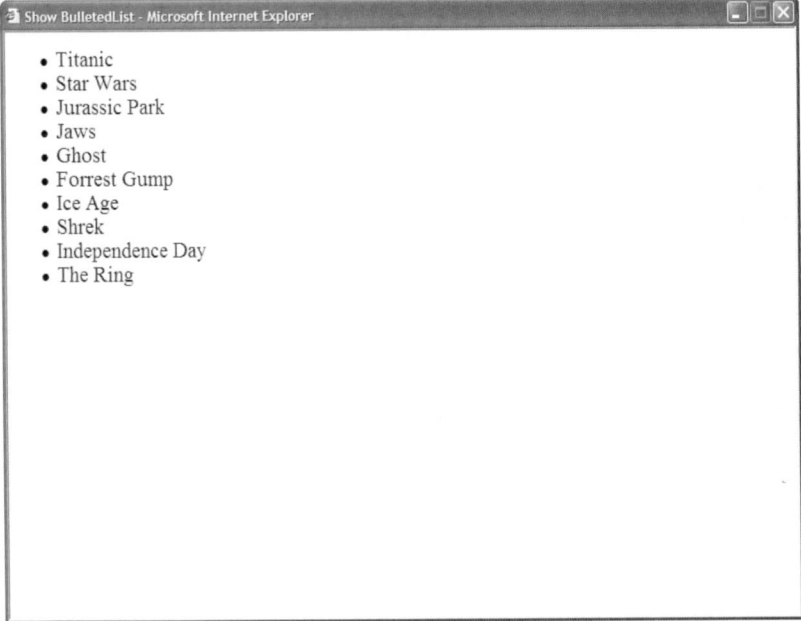

FIGURE 10.13   Displaying a list items with the BulletedList control.

LISTING 10.14   ShowBulletedList.aspx

```
<%@ Page Language="C#" %>
<!DOCTYPE html PUBLIC "-//W3C//DTD XHTML 1.1//EN"
"http://www.w3.org/TR/xhtml11/DTD/xhtml11.dtd">
<html xmlns="http://www.w3.org/1999/xhtml" >
<head id="Head1" runat="server">
    <title>Show BulletedList</title>
</head>
```

```
<body>
    <form id="form1" runat="server">
    <div>

    <asp:BulletedList
        id="blMovies"
        DataSourceID="srcMovies"
        DataTextField="Title"
        Runat="server" />

    <asp:SqlDataSource
        id="srcMovies"
        SelectCommand="SELECT Title FROM Movies"
        ConnectionString="<%$ ConnectionStrings:Movies %>"
        Runat="server" />

    </div>
    </form>
</body>
</html>
```

You can control the appearance of the bullets that appear for each list item with the
BulletStyle property. This property accepts the following values:

► Circle

► CustomImage

► Disc

► LowerAlpha

► LowerRoman

► NotSet

► Numbered

► Square

► UpperAlpha

► UpperRoman

You can set BulletStyle to Numbered to display a numbered list. If you set this property
to the value CustomImage and assign an image path to the BulletImageUrl property, you
can associate an image with each list item. For example, the page in Listing 10.15
displays an image named Bullet.gif with each list item (see Figure 10.14).

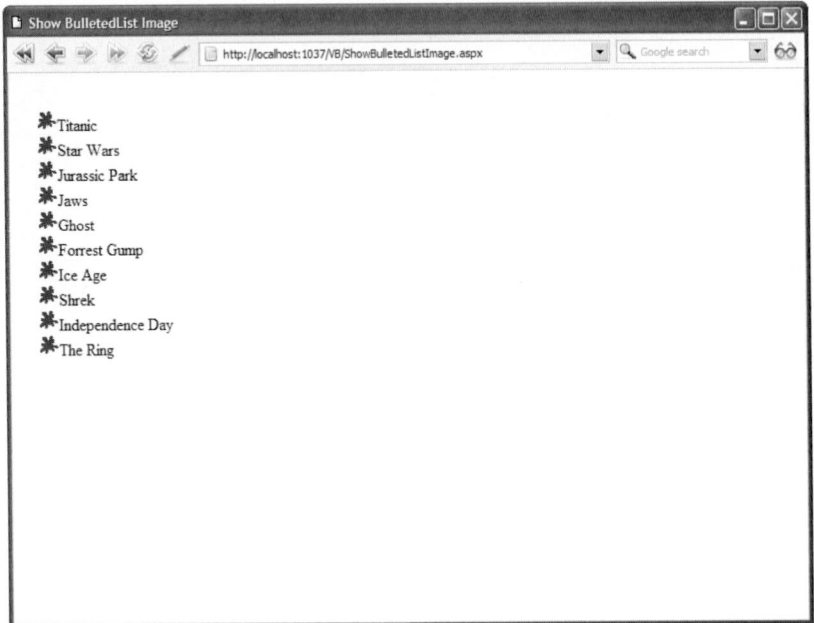

FIGURE 10.14   Displaying image bullets.

LISTING 10.15   ShowBulletedListImage.aspx

```
<%@ Page Language="C#" %>
<!DOCTYPE html PUBLIC "-//W3C//DTD XHTML 1.1//EN"
"http://www.w3.org/TR/xhtml11/DTD/xhtml11.dtd">
<html xmlns="http://www.w3.org/1999/xhtml" >
<head id="Head1" runat="server">
    <title>Show BulletedList Image</title>
</head>
<body>
    <form id="form1" runat="server">
    <div>

    <asp:BulletedList
        id="blMovies"
        DataSourceID="srcMovies"
        DataTextField="Title"
        BulletStyle="CustomImage"
        BulletImageUrl="~/Images/Bullet.gif"
        Runat="server" />
```

```
    <asp:SqlDataSource
        id="srcMovies"
        SelectCommand="SELECT Title FROM Movies"
        ConnectionString="<%$ ConnectionStrings:Movies %>"
        Runat="server" />

    </div>
    </form>
</body>
</html>
```

You can modify the appearance of each list item by modifying the value of the DisplayMode property. This property accepts one of the following values from the BulletedListDisplayMode enumeration:

▶ **HyperLink**—Each list item renders as a link to another page.

▶ **LinkButton**—Each list item renders by a LinkButton control.

▶ **Text**—Each list item renders as plain text.

For example, the page in Listing 10.16 displays a list of links to other websites (see Figure 10.15).

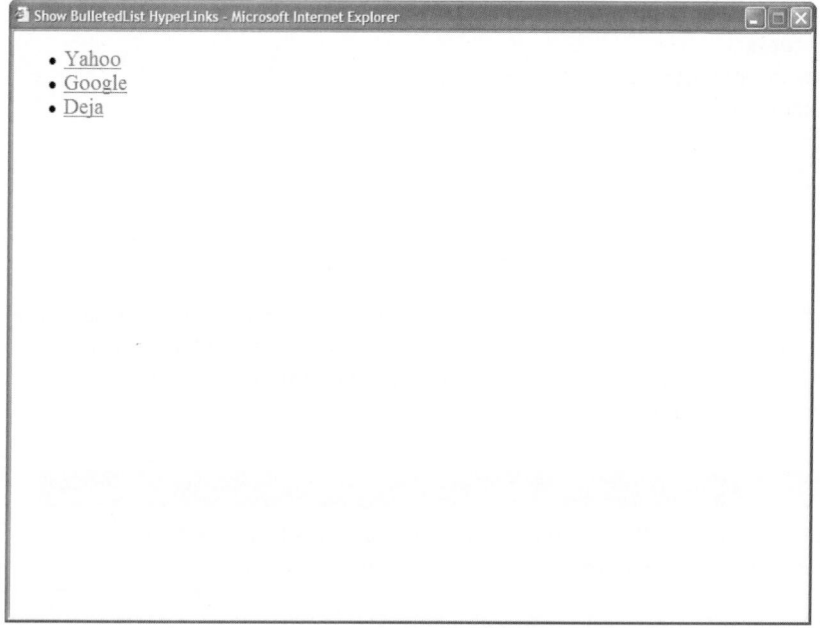

FIGURE 10.15   Displaying list items as hyperlinks.

10

LISTING 10.16   ShowBulletedListHyperLinks.aspx

```
<%@ Page Language="C#" %>
<!DOCTYPE html PUBLIC "-//W3C//DTD XHTML 1.1//EN"
"http://www.w3.org/TR/xhtml11/DTD/xhtml11.dtd">
<html xmlns="http://www.w3.org/1999/xhtml" >
<head id="Head1" runat="server">
    <title>Show BulletedList HyperLinks</title>
</head>
<body>
    <form id="form1" runat="server">

    <asp:BulletedList
        id="blWebsites"
        DisplayMode="HyperLink"
        Target="_blank"
        Runat="server">
        <asp:ListItem
            Text="Yahoo"
            Value="http://www.Yahoo.com" />
        <asp:ListItem
            Text="Google"
            Value="http://www.Google.com" />
        <asp:ListItem
            Text="Deja"
            Value="http://www.Deja.com" />
    </asp:BulletedList>

    </form>
</body>
</html>
```

Each list item has both its Text and Value properties set. The Text property contains the text that displays for the list item, and the Value property contains the URL for the other website. The Target property is set to the value blank. When you click one of the hyperlinks, the page opens in a new window.

WARNING

The BulletedList control is different from the other List controls because it does not support the SelectedIndex, SelectedItem, and SelectedValue properties.

Creating a Custom List Control

All the List controls inherit from the base `ListControl` class. If you are not happy with the existing List controls, you can build your own.

In this section, we create a custom List control named the `MultiSelectList` control that renders two list boxes and an Add and Remove button. You can click the buttons to move items between the two list boxes (see Figure 10.16).

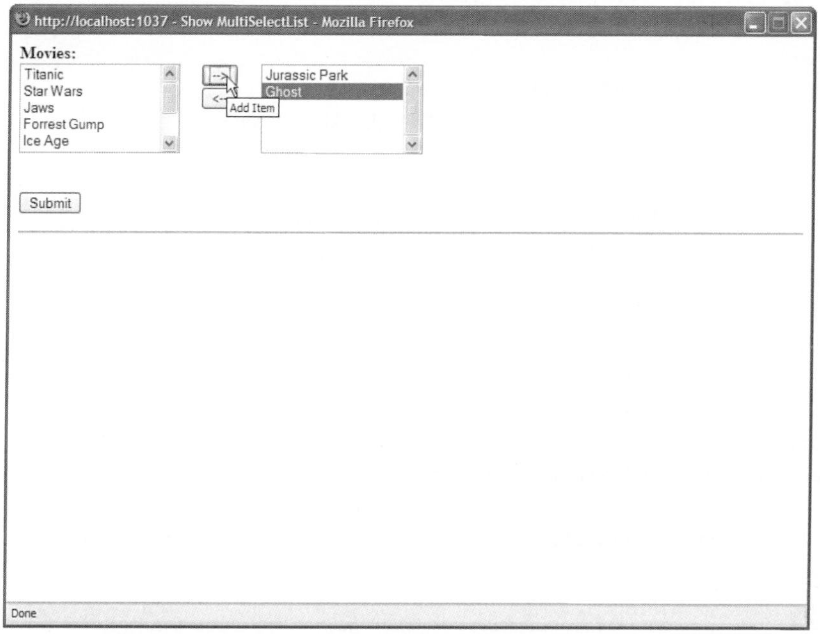

FIGURE 10.16   Using the `MultiSelectList` control.

The custom control uses client-side JavaScript to move the items between the two list boxes. Using JavaScript enables you to avoid posting the page back to the server each time a list item is moved. The client-side JavaScript is standards-compliant so it works with all web browsers, such as Internet Explorer, Firefox, Safari, and Opera.

The code for the custom `MultiSelectList` is contained in Listing 10.17.

LISTING 10.17   MultiSelectList.cs

```
using System;
using System.Data;
using System.Configuration;
using System.Web;
using System.Web.Security;
```

```
using System.Web.UI;
using System.Web.UI.WebControls;
using System.Web.UI.WebControls.WebParts;
using System.Web.UI.HtmlControls;

namespace MyControls
{
    /// <summary>
    /// Enables you to select mulitple list items
    /// from two list boxes
    /// </summary>
    [ValidationProperty("SelectedItem")]
    public class MultiSelectList : ListControl, IPostBackDataHandler
    {
        private int _rows = 5;
        private Unit _UnSelectedWidth = Unit.Parse("300px");
        private Unit _SelectedWidth = Unit.Parse("300px");


        /// <summary>
        /// This control is contained in a div
        /// tag
        /// </summary>
        protected override HtmlTextWriterTag TagKey
        {
            get { return HtmlTextWriterTag.Div; }
        }

        protected override void AddAttributesToRender(HtmlTextWriter writer)
        {
            writer.AddStyleAttribute("position", "relative");
            base.AddAttributesToRender(writer);
        }

        /// <summary>
        /// The number of rows of list items to display
        /// </summary>
        public int Rows
        {
            get { return _rows; }
            set { _rows = value; }
        }


        /// <summary>
        /// Name passed to client-side script
```

```
        /// </summary>
        private string BaseName
        {
            get { return ClientID + ClientIDSeparator; }
        }

        /// <summary>
        /// Name of unselected items list box
        /// </summary>
        private string UnselectedListName
        {
            get { return BaseName + "unselected"; }
        }

        /// <summary>
        /// Name of selected items list box
        /// </summary>
        private string SelectedListName
        {
            get { return BaseName + "selected"; }
        }

        /// <summary>
        /// Name of hidden input field
        /// </summary>
        private string HiddenName
        {
            get { return BaseName + "hidden"; }
        }

        /// <summary>
        /// Register client scripts
        /// </summary>
        protected override void OnPreRender(EventArgs e)
        {
            Page.RegisterRequiresPostBack(this);

            // Register hidden field
            Page.ClientScript.RegisterHiddenField
➥(HiddenName, String.Empty);

            // Register Include File
            if (!Page.ClientScript.IsClientScriptIncludeRegistered
➥("MultiSelectList"))
                Page.ClientScript.RegisterClientScriptInclude("MultiSelectList",
Page.ResolveUrl("~/ClientScripts/MultiSelectList.js"));
```

```
            // Register submit script
            string submitScript = String.Format("multiSelectList_submit('{0}')",
BaseName);
            Page.ClientScript.RegisterOnSubmitStatement(this.GetType(),
➥this.ClientID, submitScript);

            base.OnPreRender(e);
        }

        /// <summary>
        /// Render list boxes and buttons
        /// </summary>
        protected override void RenderContents(HtmlTextWriter writer)
        {

            // Render Unselected
            RenderUnselected(writer);

            // Render Buttons
            RenderButtons(writer);

            // Render Selected
            RenderSelected(writer);

            // Render clear break
            writer.AddStyleAttribute("clear", "both");
            writer.RenderBeginTag(HtmlTextWriterTag.Br);
            writer.RenderEndTag();
        }

        /// <summary>
        /// Render the buttons
        /// </summary>
        private void RenderButtons(HtmlTextWriter writer)
        {
            writer.AddStyleAttribute("float", "left");
            writer.AddStyleAttribute(HtmlTextWriterStyle.Padding, "10px");
            writer.AddStyleAttribute(HtmlTextWriterStyle.TextAlign, "center");
            writer.RenderBeginTag(HtmlTextWriterTag.Div);

            string addScript = String.Format("return multiSelectList_add('{0}');",
BaseName);
            writer.AddAttribute(HtmlTextWriterAttribute.Onclick, addScript);
            writer.AddAttribute(HtmlTextWriterAttribute.Title, "Add Item");
            writer.RenderBeginTag(HtmlTextWriterTag.Button);
            writer.Write("--&gt;");
```

```
                writer.RenderEndTag();
                writer.WriteBreak();
                string removeScript = String.Format("return
multiSelectList_remove('{0}');", BaseName);
                writer.AddAttribute(HtmlTextWriterAttribute.Onclick, removeScript);
                writer.AddAttribute(HtmlTextWriterAttribute.Title, "Remove Item");
                writer.RenderBeginTag(HtmlTextWriterTag.Button);
                writer.Write("&lt;--");
                writer.RenderEndTag();

                writer.RenderEndTag();
            }

            /// <summary>
            /// Render unselected list box
            /// </summary>
            private void RenderUnselected(HtmlTextWriter writer)
            {
                writer.AddStyleAttribute("float", "left");
                writer.AddAttribute(HtmlTextWriterAttribute.Size, _rows.ToString());
                writer.AddStyleAttribute(HtmlTextWriterStyle.Width,
_UnSelectedWidth.ToString());
                writer.AddAttribute(HtmlTextWriterAttribute.Id, UnselectedListName);
                writer.AddAttribute(HtmlTextWriterAttribute.Name, UnselectedListName);
                writer.AddAttribute(HtmlTextWriterAttribute.Multiple, "true");
                writer.RenderBeginTag(HtmlTextWriterTag.Select);
                foreach (ListItem item in Items)
                    if (!item.Selected)
                        RenderListItem(writer, item);
                writer.RenderEndTag();
            }

            /// <summary>
            /// Render selected list items
            /// </summary>
            private void RenderSelected(HtmlTextWriter writer)
            {
                writer.AddStyleAttribute("float", "left");
                writer.AddAttribute(HtmlTextWriterAttribute.Size, _rows.ToString());
                writer.AddStyleAttribute(HtmlTextWriterStyle.Width,
_SelectedWidth.ToString());
                writer.AddAttribute(HtmlTextWriterAttribute.Id, SelectedListName);
                writer.AddAttribute(HtmlTextWriterAttribute.Name, SelectedListName);
                writer.AddAttribute(HtmlTextWriterAttribute.Multiple, "true");
                writer.RenderBeginTag(HtmlTextWriterTag.Select);
                foreach (ListItem item in Items)
```

```
            if (item.Selected)
                RenderListItem(writer, item);
        writer.RenderEndTag();
    }


    /// <summary>
    /// Render a list item
    /// </summary>
    private void RenderListItem(HtmlTextWriter writer, ListItem item)
    {
        writer.AddAttribute(HtmlTextWriterAttribute.Value, item.Value);
        writer.RenderBeginTag(HtmlTextWriterTag.Option);
        writer.Write(item.Text);
        writer.RenderEndTag();
    }


    /// <summary>
    /// Process postback data
    /// </summary>
    public bool LoadPostData(string postDataKey,
System.Collections.Specialized.NameValueCollection postCollection)
    {
        EnsureDataBound();
        ClearSelection();

        string values = postCollection[HiddenName];
        if (values != String.Empty)
        {
            string[] splitValues = values.Split(',');
            foreach (string value in splitValues)
            {
                Items.FindByValue(value).Selected = true;
            }
        }
        return false;
    }


    /// <summary>
    /// Required by the IPostBackDataHandler interface
    /// </summary>
    public void RaisePostDataChangedEvent()
    {
    }
  }
}
```

The TagKey property of the base ListControl class is overridden. The elements of the control are contained in an HTML <div> tag.

The MultiSelectList renders its user interface in the RenderContents() method. This method renders the two list boxes and button controls. Each unselected list item renders in the first list box and each selected item renders in the second list box.

Furthermore, the MultiSelectList control implements the IPostBackDataHandler interface. When a user posts a page that contains the MultiSelectList control to the server, each item that the user selected is retrieved, and the Items collection of the List control is updated.

The control takes advantage of a client-side JavaScript library contained in a MultiSelectList.js file. This JavaScript library is registered in the control's OnPreRender() method. The MultiSelectList.js library is contained in Listing 10.18.

LISTING 10.18 MultiSelectList.js

```javascript
function multiSelectList_add(baseName)
{
    var unselectedList = document.getElementById(baseName + 'unselected');
    var selectedList = document.getElementById(baseName + 'selected');

    // Copy selected items
    var selectedItems = Array.clone(unselectedList.options);

    for (var i=0;i < selectedItems.length;i++)
    {
        if (selectedItems[i].selected)
        {
            var item = unselectedList.removeChild(selectedItems[i]);
            selectedList.appendChild(item);
        }
    }
    // Prevent post
    return false;
}

function multiSelectList_remove(baseName)
{
    var unselectedList = document.getElementById(baseName + 'unselected');
    var selectedList = document.getElementById(baseName + 'selected');

    // Copy unselected items
    var selectedItems = Array.clone(selectedList.options);

    for (var i=0;i < selectedItems.length;i++)
```

```
    {
        if (selectedItems[i].selected)
        {
            var item = selectedList.removeChild(selectedItems[i]);
            unselectedList.appendChild(item);
        }
    }
    // Prevent post
    return false;
}


// This function executes when the page
// is submitted. It stuffs all of the
// selected items into a hidden field
function multiSelectList_submit(baseName)
{

    var hidden = document.getElementById(baseName + 'hidden');
    var selectedList = document.getElementById(baseName + 'selected');
    var values = new Array();
    for (var i=0;i<selectedList.options.length;i++)
        values.push(selectedList.options[i].value);
    hidden.value = values.join(',');
}

Array.clone = function(arrItems)
{
  var results = [];
  for (var i=0;i < arrItems.length; i++)
    results.push(arrItems[i]);
  return results;
};
```

Listing 10.18 contains three JavaScript functions. The first two functions simply move list items from one list box to the other list box. The multiSelectList_submit() function is called immediately before a page containing the MultiSelectList control posts to the server. This control records each of the selected list items (the items in the second list box) to a hidden form field.

The page in Listing 10.19 illustrates how you can use the MultiSelectList control.

LISTING 10.19   ShowMultiSelectList.aspx

```
<%@ Page Language="C#" %>
<%@ Register TagPrefix="custom" Namespace="MyControls" %>
<!DOCTYPE html PUBLIC "-//W3C//DTD XHTML 1.1//EN"
```

```
"http://www.w3.org/TR/xhtml11/DTD/xhtml11.dtd">
<script runat="server">

    protected void btnSubmit_Click(object sender, EventArgs e)
    {
        foreach (ListItem item in MultiSelectList1.Items)
            if (item.Selected)
                lblSelected.Text += String.Format("<li>{0}
➥({1})",item.Text,item.Value);
    }
</script>
<html xmlns="http://www.w3.org/1999/xhtml" >
<head id="Head1" runat="server">
    <title>Show MultiSelectList</title>
</head>
<body>
    <form id="form1" runat="server">
    <div>

    <b>Movies:</b>
    <asp:RequiredFieldValidator
        id="val"
        ControlToValidate="MultiSelectList1"
        Text="Required"
        Runat="server" />

    <custom:MultiSelectList
        id="MultiSelectList1"
        DataSourceID="srcMovies"
        DataTextField="Title"
        DataValueField="Id"
        Runat="server" />

    <asp:SqlDataSource
        id="srcMovies"
        SelectCommand="SELECT Id, Title FROM Movies"
        ConnectionString="<%$ ConnectionStrings:Movies %>"
        Runat="server" />

    <p>
    <asp:Button
        id="btnSubmit"
        Text="Submit"
        Runat="server" OnClick="btnSubmit_Click" />
    </p>
```

10

```
    <hr />

    <asp:Label
        id="lblSelected"
        EnableViewState="false"
        Runat="server" />

    </div>
    </form>
</body>
</html>
```

In the page in Listing 10.19, the `MultiSelectList` control is bound to a `SqlDataSource` control, which represents the contents of the Movies database table. You can select movie titles in the `MultiSelectList` control by moving movie titles from one list box to the second list box. When you click the Submit button, the selected movies display in a Label control.

Summary

In this chapter, you learned how to use List controls to display simple option lists. You saw the `DropDownList`, `RadioButtonList`, `ListBox`, `CheckBoxList`, and `BulletedList` controls.

You also saw the common features of the List controls. You learned how to append data items to a List control and automatically post a form containing a List control back to the server.

Finally, you worked through the creation of a custom List control, which involved deriving a new control from the base `ListControl` class. The custom List control takes advantage of client-side JavaScript to enable users to select multiple list items without requiring a page to post back to the server when each item is selected.

Using the GridView Control

The GridView control is the workhorse of ASP.NET Framework. It is one of the most feature-rich and complicated of all the ASP.NET controls. The GridView control enables you to display, select, sort, page, and edit data items such as database records.

> **NOTE**
>
> The GridView control supersedes the DataGrid control included in the ASP.NET 1.x Framework. The DataGrid control is still included in ASP.NET 4 for backward compatibility, but you should use the GridView instead because it is a more powerful control.

In this chapter, you learn everything you ever wanted to know about the GridView control. You learn how to use all the basic features of the GridView control. For example, you learn how to use this control to display, select, sort, page, and edit database records. You also learn how to use AJAX with the GridView control when sorting and paging records.

You also get the chance to tackle several advanced topics. For example, you learn how to highlight certain rows in a GridView depending on the data the row represents. You also learn how to display column summaries.

Finally, you learn how to extend the GridView control by building custom GridView fields. At the end of this chapter, we build a LongTextField, a DeleteButtonField, and a ValidatedField.

GridView Control Fundamentals

In this section, you learn how to take advantage of all the basic features of the GridView control. In particular, you learn how to display, select, sort, page, and edit database data with a GridView control. We also discuss GridView formatting options.

Displaying Data

GridView renders its data items in an HTML table. Each data item renders in a distinct HTML table row. For example, the page in Listing 11.1 demonstrates how you can use GridView to display the contents of the Movies database table (see Figure 11.1).

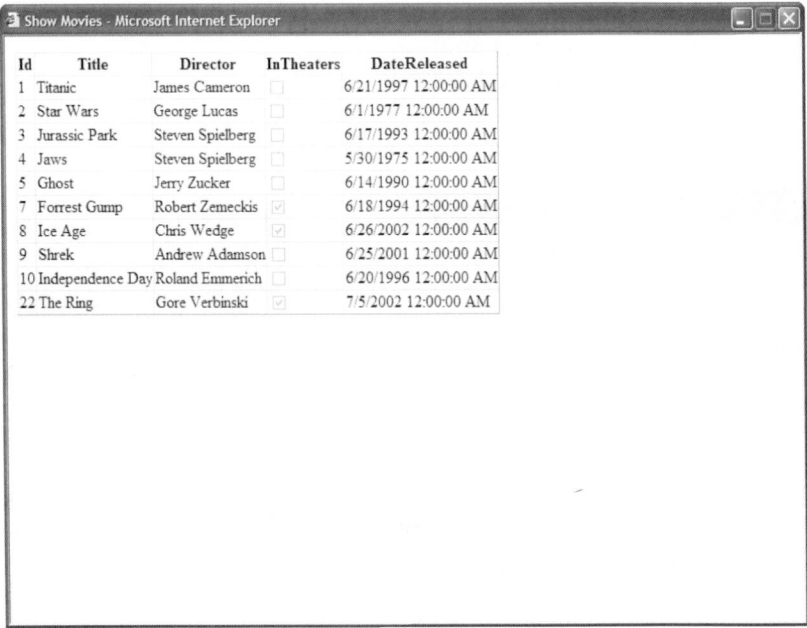

FIGURE 11.1   Displaying data with the GridView control.

LISTING 11.1   ShowMovies.aspx

```
<%@ Page Language="C#" %>
<!DOCTYPE html PUBLIC "-//W3C//DTD XHTML 1.1//EN"
   "http://www.w3.org/TR/xhtml11/DTD/xhtml11.dtd">
<html xmlns="http://www.w3.org/1999/xhtml" >
<head id="Head1" runat="server">
    <title>Show Movies</title>
</head>
<body>
```

```
<form id="form1" runat="server">
<div>

<asp:GridView
    id="grdMovies"
    DataSourceID="srcMovies"
    Runat="server" />

<asp:SqlDataSource
    id="srcMovies"
    ConnectionString="<%$ ConnectionStrings:Movies %>"
    SelectCommand="SELECT Id,Title,Director,InTheaters,DateReleased
        FROM Movies"
    Runat="server" />

</div>
</form>
</body>
</html>
```

In Listing 11.1, the GridView control is bound to a SqlDataSource control, which represents the Movies database table. The GridView associates with its data source through its DataSourceID property.

The GridView control automatically renders a check box for any Boolean fields. In the case of Listing 11.1, GridView renders a check box for the InTheaters database column. For all other types of fields, GridView simply renders the contents of the field.

WEB STANDARDS NOTE

The GridView control was designed to meet XHTML and accessibility guidelines. For example, the control uses the <th> tag to render its headers. Furthermore, each header tag includes a scope="col" attribute.

VISUAL WEB DEVELOPER NOTE

You can add a GridView and SqlDataSource control to a page quickly by dragging a database table from the Database Explorer window onto a page in Design view. When you drag a database table onto the page, a SqlDataSource is automatically created, which retrieves all the rows and all the columns from a database table.

The GridView control also supports programmatic databinding. In Listing 11.2, the GridView control displays a list of shopping list items represented by a Generic List collection.

LISTING 11.2   ShowShoppingList.aspx

```
<%@ Page Language="C#" %>
<%@ Import Namespace="System.Collections.Generic" %>
<!DOCTYPE html PUBLIC "-//W3C//DTD XHTML 1.1//EN"
"http://www.w3.org/TR/xhtml11/DTD/xhtml11.dtd">
<script runat="server">

    void Page_Load()
    {
        // Build shopping list
        List<string> shoppingList = new List<string>();
        shoppingList.Add("Bread");
        shoppingList.Add("Milk");
        shoppingList.Add("Beer");
        shoppingList.Add("Waffles");

        // Bind to GridView
        grdShoppingList.DataSource = shoppingList;
        grdShoppingList.DataBind();
    }

</script>
<html xmlns="http://www.w3.org/1999/xhtml" >
<head id="Head1" runat="server">
    <title>Show Shopping List</title>
</head>
<body>
    <form id="form1" runat="server">
    <div>

    <asp:GridView
        id="grdShoppingList"
        Runat="server" />

    </div>
    </form>
</body>
</html>
```

GridView is bound to the shopping list in the Page_Load() method. Its DataSource property points to the List collection, and its DataBind() method is called to load the items from the List collection and display them.

Selecting Data

You can allow a user to select a particular row in a GridView control. This is useful when you want to build single-page Master/Details forms. For example, the page in Listing 11.3 contains two GridView controls. The first GridView displays a list of movie categories. When you select a category, the second GridView displays a list of matching movies (see Figure 11.2).

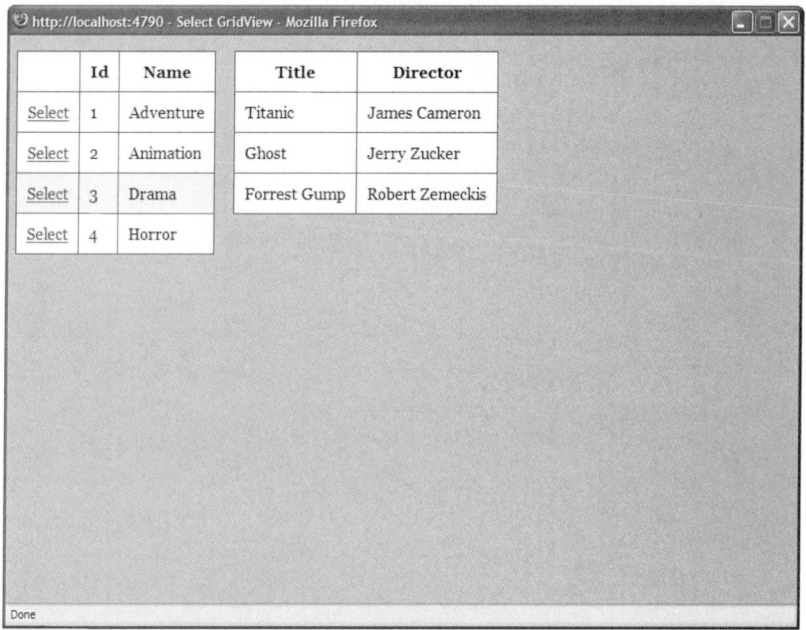

FIGURE 11.2   Selecting a GridView row.

LISTING 11.3   SelectGridView.aspx

```
<%@ Page Language="C#" %>
<!DOCTYPE html PUBLIC "-//W3C//DTD XHTML 1.1//EN"
    "http://www.w3.org/TR/xhtml11/DTD/xhtml11.dtd">
<html xmlns="http://www.w3.org/1999/xhtml" >
<head id="Head1" runat="server">
    <style type="text/css">
        html
        {
            background-color:silver;
```

```
            font-family:Georgia, Serif;
        }
        .gridView
        {
            float:left;
            margin-right:20px;
            background-color:white;
        }
        .gridView td, .gridView th
        {
            padding:10px;
        }
        .selectedRow
        {
            background-color:yellow;
        }
    </style>
    <title>Select GridView</title>
</head>
<body>
    <form id="form1" runat="server">
    <div>

    <asp:GridView
        id="grdMovieCategories"
        DataKeyNames="Id"
        DataSourceID="srcMovieCategories"
        AutoGenerateSelectButton="true"
        SelectedRowStyle-CssClass="selectedRow"
        CssClass="gridView"
        Runat="server" />

    <asp:GridView
        id="grdMovies"
        DataSourceID="srcMovies"
        CssClass="gridView"
        Runat="server" />

    <asp:SqlDataSource
        id="srcMovieCategories"
        ConnectionString="<%$ ConnectionStrings:Movies %>"
        SelectCommand="SELECT Id, Name FROM MovieCategories"
        Runat="server" />
```

```
<asp:SqlDataSource
    id="srcMovies"
    ConnectionString="<%$ ConnectionStrings:Movies %>"
    SelectCommand="SELECT Title,Director FROM Movies
        WHERE CategoryId=@CategoryId"
    Runat="server">
    <SelectParameters>
    <asp:ControlParameter
        Name="CategoryId"
        ControlID="grdMovieCategories"
        PropertyName="SelectedValue" />
    </SelectParameters>
</asp:SqlDataSource>

    </div>
    </form>
</body>
</html>
```

The first `GridView` has its `AutoGenerateSelectButton` property enabled. When this property has the value `True`, a `Select` link displays next to each row.

You can determine which row is selected in a `GridView` control by using any of the following methods:

▶ **SelectedDataKey()**—Returns the `DataKey` object associated with the selected row. (This is useful when there are multiple data keys.)

▶ **SelectedIndex()**—Returns the (zero-based) index of the selected row.

▶ **SelectedValue()**—Returns the data key associated with the selected row.

▶ **SelectedRow()**—Returns the actual row (`GridViewRow` object) associated with the selected row.

In most cases, you use the `SelectedValue()` method to determine the value associated with a particular row. The `SelectedValue()` method returns the data key associated with a row. The following section discusses data keys.

NOTE

When a user changes the page in `GridView`, you might not want the selected row to remain in the selected state when new data populates. You can set the `PersistedSelection` property to True to avoid this. When the user changes a `GridView` page, the selection goes away, and if they go back to the original page, the selection reappears.

Using Data Keys

You associate a value with each row in a GridView by providing a value for the GridView control's DataKeyNames property. You can assign the name of a single database column to this property, or you can assign a comma-separated list of column names to this property.

For example, the Employees database table uses two columns—the employee first and last name—as a primary key. The page in Listing 11.4 displays employee details when you select a particular employee (see Figure 11.3).

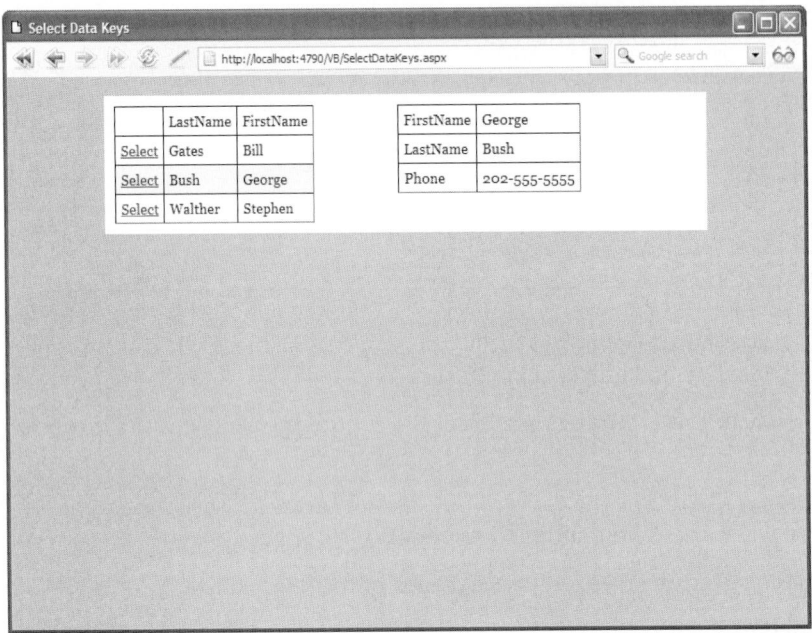

FIGURE 11.3   Displaying employee details.

LISTING 11.4   SelectDataKeys.aspx

```
<%@ Page Language="C#" %>
<!DOCTYPE html PUBLIC "-//W3C//DTD XHTML 1.1//EN"
    "http://www.w3.org/TR/xhtml11/DTD/xhtml11.dtd">
<html xmlns="http://www.w3.org/1999/xhtml" >
<head id="Head1" runat="server">
    <style type="text/css">
        html
        {
            background-color:silver;
        }
        .content
        {
```

```
                width:600px;
                margin:auto;
                background-color:white;
            }
            .column
            {
                float:left;
                padding:10px;
                width:265px;
            }
            .column td,.column th
            {
                padding:5px;
                font:14px Georgia, Serif
            }
            .selectedRow
            {
                background-color:yellow;
            }
        </style>
        <title>Select Data Keys</title>
</head>
<body>
    <form id="form1" runat="server">
    <div class="content">
    <div class="column">

    <asp:GridView
        id="grdEmployees"
        DataSourceID="srcEmployees"
        DataKeyNames="LastName,FirstName"
        AutoGenerateSelectButton="true"
        SelectedRowStyle-CssClass="selectedRow"
        Runat="server" />

    </div>
    <div class="column">

    <asp:DetailsView
        id="dtlEmployees"
        DataSourceID="srcEmployeeDetails"
        Runat="server" />

    </div>
```

```
        <br style="clear:both" />
        </div>

        <asp:SqlDataSource
            id="srcEmployees"
            ConnectionString="<%$ ConnectionStrings:Employees %>"
            SelectCommand="SELECT LastName,FirstName
                FROM Employees"
            Runat="server" />

        <asp:SqlDataSource
            id="srcEmployeeDetails"
            ConnectionString="<%$ ConnectionStrings:Employees %>"
            SelectCommand="SELECT * FROM Employees
                WHERE FirstName=@FirstName AND LastName=@LastName"
            Runat="server">
            <SelectParameters>
            <asp:ControlParameter
                Name="FirstName"
                ControlID="grdEmployees"
                PropertyName='SelectedDataKey("FirstName")' />
            <asp:ControlParameter
                Name="LastName"
                ControlID="grdEmployees"
                PropertyName='SelectedDataKey("LastName")' />
            </SelectParameters>
        </asp:SqlDataSource>

    </form>
</body>
</html>
```

In Listing 11.4, the `SelectedDataKey()` method retrieves the primary key of the selected
employee. The `SelectedDataKey()` method is used in both of the `ControlParameters`
contained in the second `SqlDataSource` control. If you use `SelectedValue()` instead of
`SelectedDataKey()`, you can return only the value of the first data key and not both
values.

A `GridView` stores data keys in a collection called the `DataKeys` collection. This collection
is exposed by the `GridView` control's `DataKeys` property. You can retrieve the data key associated with any row by using a statement that looks like this:

```
Object key = GridView1.DataKeys[6].Value;
```

This statement returns the value of the data key associated with the seventh row in the GridView. (Remember that the rows collection is zero-based.) If you have assigned multiple data keys to each row, you can use a statement that looks like this:

```
Object key = GridView1.DataKeys[6].Values["LastName"];
```

This statement retrieves the value of the LastName key for the seventh row in the GridView.

Sorting Data

You can sort the rows rendered by a GridView control by enabling the AllowSorting property. For example, the page in Listing 11.5 illustrates how you can sort the contents of the Movies database table.

LISTING 11.5   SortGrid.aspx

```
<%@ Page Language="C#" %>
<!DOCTYPE html PUBLIC "-//W3C//DTD XHTML 1.1//EN"
    "http://www.w3.org/TR/xhtml11/DTD/xhtml11.dtd">
<html xmlns="http://www.w3.org/1999/xhtml" >
<head id="Head1" runat="server">
    <title>Sort Grid</title>
</head>
<body>
    <form id="form1" runat="server">
    <div>

    <asp:GridView
        id="grdMovies"
        DataSourceID="srcMovies"
        AllowSorting="true"
        Runat="server" />

    <asp:SqlDataSource
        id="srcMovies"
        ConnectionString="<%$ ConnectionStrings:Movies %>"
        SelectCommand="SELECT Id,Title,DateReleased FROM Movies"
        Runat="server" />

    </div>
    </form>
</body>
</html>
```

When `AllowSorting` has the value `True`, column headers render as links. When you click a column header, you can sort the rows contained in the `GridView` in the order of the selected column.

> **NOTE**
>
> When using explicitly specified fields with a `GridView`, such as `BoundFields`, you need to specify values for the fields' `SortExpression` properties. Otherwise, nothing happens when you click a header.

The `GridView` supports ascending and descending sorts. In other words, if you click a column header more than once, the rows toggle between being sorted in ascending and descending order.

Sorting with AJAX

By default, whenever you click a column header to sort the rows contained in a `GridView`, the page containing the `GridView` is posted back to the server. When sorting records with the `GridView` control, you can avoid posting the entire page back to the server by taking advantage of Ajax (Asynchronous JavaScript and XML).

We get into the details of Ajax in Part IX, "ASP.NET AJAX." In this section, I provide you with a quick code sample that demonstrates how to use Ajax with the `GridView` control. The page in Listing 11.6 illustrates how you can take advantage of AJAX when sorting records.

LISTING 11.6   `AjaxSorting.aspx`

```
<%@ Page Language="C#" %>
<!DOCTYPE html PUBLIC "-//W3C//DTD XHTML 1.1//EN"
"http://www.w3.org/TR/xhtml11/DTD/xhtml11.dtd">
<html xmlns="http://www.w3.org/1999/xhtml" >
<head id="Head1" runat="server">
    <title>AJAX Sorting</title>
</head>
<body>
    <form id="form1" runat="server">
    <div>

    <asp:ScriptManager ID="sm1" runat="server" />

    <%= DateTime.Now.ToString("T") %>

    <asp:UpdatePanel ID="up1" runat="server">
    <ContentTemplate>
    <asp:GridView
```

```
        id="grdMovies"
        DataSourceID="srcMovies"
        AllowSorting="true"
        EnableSortingAndPagingCallbacks="true"
        Runat="server" />
    </ContentTemplate>
    </asp:UpdatePanel>

    <asp:SqlDataSource
        id="srcMovies"
        ConnectionString="<%$ ConnectionStrings:Movies %>"
        SelectCommand="SELECT Id,Title,DateReleased FROM Movies"
        Runat="server" />

    </div>
    </form>
</body>
</html>
```

GridView in Listing 11.6 is contained in an UpdatePanel control. When you sort GridView, only the region of the page contained in the UpdatePanel is updated.

The current time displays at the top of the page. The time is not updated when you sort the records in GridView. The entire page is not posted back to the server; only the content of the UpdatePanel control is updated.

> **NOTE**
>
> An alternative method for Ajax sorting with the GridView control is to enable the GridView control's EnableSortingAndPagingCallbacks property. I don't suggest that you use this method because it limits the types of fields that you can add to GridView. For example, if you enable EnableSortingAndPagingCallbacks, you can't use TemplateFields with GridView. The UpdatePanel control is not subject to these same limitations.

Customizing the Sorting Interface

You can customize the appearance of the sort links by handling the GridView control's RowDataBound event. This event is raised for each row rendered by GridView after GridView is bound to its data source.

For example, the page in Listing 11.7 displays an image that represents whether a column is sorted in ascending or descending order (see Figure 11.4).

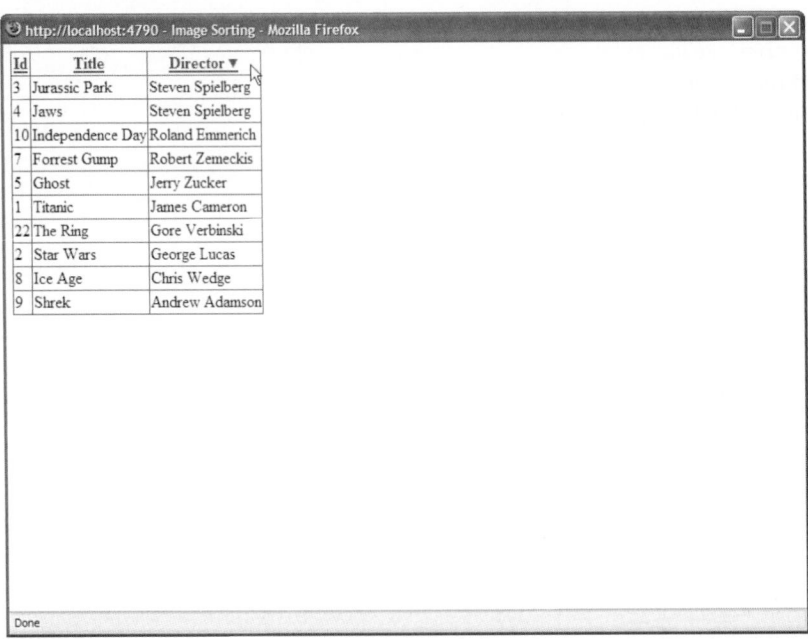

FIGURE 11.4   Displaying an image when sorting.

LISTING 11.7   ImageSorting.aspx

```
<%@ Page Language="C#" %>
<!DOCTYPE html PUBLIC "-//W3C//DTD XHTML 1.1//EN"
"http://www.w3.org/TR/xhtml11/DTD/xhtml11.dtd">
<script runat="server">

    protected void grdMovies_RowDataBound(object sender, GridViewRowEventArgs e)
    {
        if (e.Row.RowType == DataControlRowType.Header)
        {
            foreach (TableCell cell in e.Row.Cells)
            {
                LinkButton sortLink = (LinkButton)cell.Controls[0];
                if (sortLink.Text == grdMovies.SortExpression)
                {
                    if (grdMovies.SortDirection == SortDirection.Ascending)
                        sortLink.Text += " <img src='asc.gif' title='Sort
➥ascending' />";
                    else
                        sortLink.Text += " <img src='desc.gif' title='Sort
➥descending' />";
```

```
                }
            }
        }
    }
</script>
<html xmlns="http://www.w3.org/1999/xhtml" >
<head id="Head1" runat="server">
    <style type="text/css">
        img
        {
            border:0px;
        }
    </style>
    <title>Image Sorting</title>
</head>
<body>
    <form id="form1" runat="server">
    <div>

    <asp:GridView
        id="grdMovies"
        DataSourceID="srcMovies"
        AllowSorting="true"
        Runat="server" OnRowDataBound="grdMovies_RowDataBound" />

    <asp:SqlDataSource
        id="srcMovies"
        ConnectionString="<%$ ConnectionStrings:Movies %>"
        SelectCommand="SELECT Id,Title,Director FROM Movies"
        Runat="server" />

    </div>
    </form>
</body>
</html>
```

In Listing 11.7, the image is added to the header row in the grdMovies_RowDataBound()
method. The current row's RowType property is checked to verify that the row is a header
row. Next, an HTML <img> tag is added to the LinkButton that matches the column
currently selected for sorting.

If you need to completely customize the appearance of the sorting user interface, you can
call the GridView control's Sort() method programmatically. Listing 11.8 illustrates this
approach (see Figure 11.5).

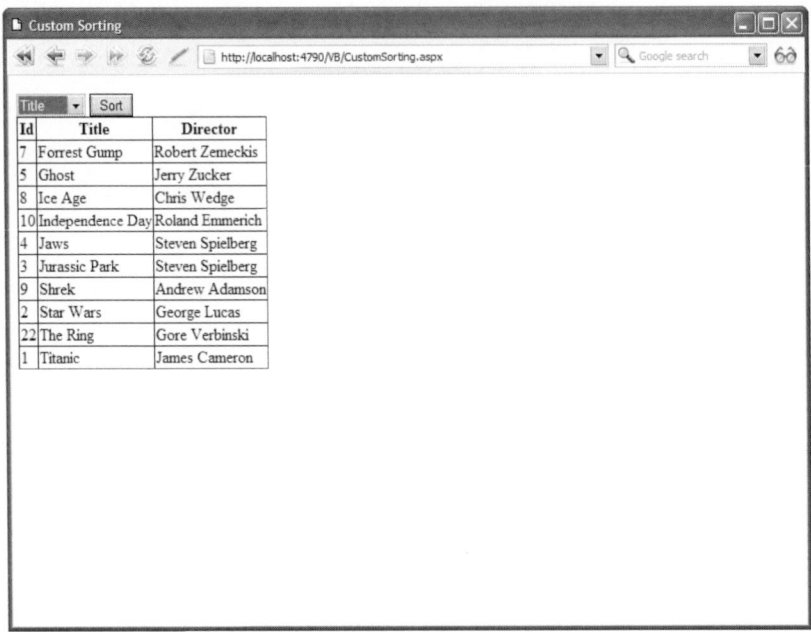

FIGURE 11.5   Displaying a custom sorting interface.

LISTING 11.8   CustomSorting.aspx

```
<%@ Page Language="C#" %>
<!DOCTYPE html PUBLIC "-//W3C//DTD XHTML 1.1//EN"
"http://www.w3.org/TR/xhtml11/DTD/xhtml11.dtd">
<script runat="server">

    protected void btnSort_Click(object sender, EventArgs e)
    {
        grdMovies.Sort(ddlSort.Text, SortDirection.Ascending);
    }
</script>
<html xmlns="http://www.w3.org/1999/xhtml" >
<head id="Head1" runat="server">
    <title>Custom Sorting</title>
</head>
<body>
    <form id="form1" runat="server">
    <div>
```

```
    <asp:DropDownList
        id="ddlSort"
        Runat="server">
        <asp:ListItem Text="Id" />
        <asp:ListItem Text="Title" />
        <asp:ListItem Text="Director" />
    </asp:DropDownList>
    <asp:Button
        id="btnSort"
        Text="Sort"
        Runat="server" OnClick="btnSort_Click" />

    <asp:GridView
        id="grdMovies"
        DataSourceID="srcMovies"
        Runat="server" />

    <asp:SqlDataSource
        id="srcMovies"
        ConnectionString="<%$ ConnectionStrings:Movies %>"
        SelectCommand="SELECT Id,Title,Director FROM Movies"
        Runat="server" />

    </div>
    </form>
</body>
</html>
```

The page in Listing 11.8 includes a DropDownList control, which you can use to sort the contents of the GridView. When a list item is selected from the DropDownList control and the Sort button is clicked, the btnSort_Click() method executes. This method calls the Sort() method of the GridView control to sort the contents of GridView.

Paging Through Data

When working with a large number of database rows, it is useful to display the rows in different pages. You can enable paging with the GridView control by enabling its AllowPaging property.

For example, the page in Listing 11.9 enables you to page through the records in the Movies database table (see Figure 11.6).

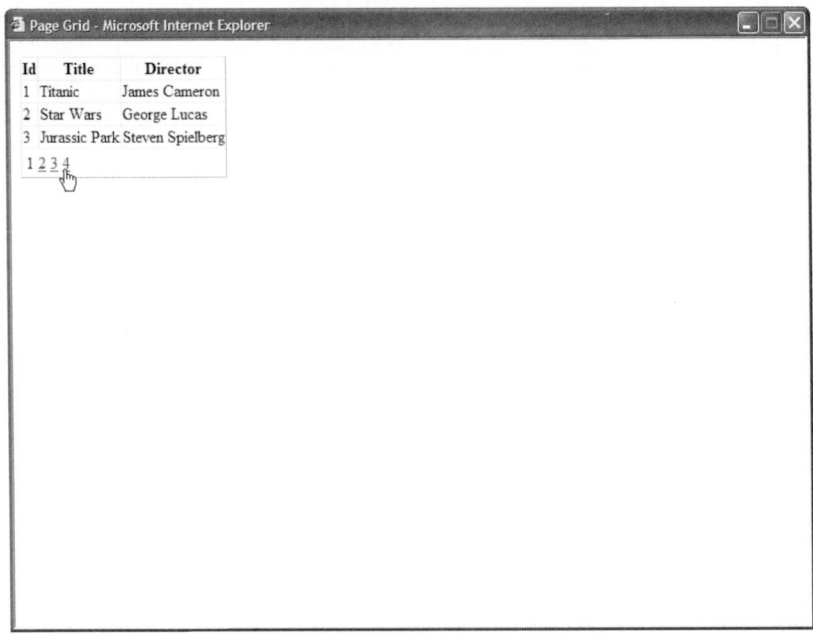

FIGURE 11.6   Paging through records in a `GridView` control.

LISTING 11.9   `PageGrid.aspx`

```
<%@ Page Language="C#" %>
<!DOCTYPE html PUBLIC "-//W3C//DTD XHTML 1.1//EN"
    "http://www.w3.org/TR/xhtml11/DTD/xhtml11.dtd">
<html xmlns="http://www.w3.org/1999/xhtml" >
<head id="Head1" runat="server">
    <title>Page Grid</title>
</head>
<body>
    <form id="form1" runat="server">
    <div>

    <asp:GridView
        id="grdMovies"
        DataSourceID="srcMovies"
        AllowPaging="true"
        PageSize="3"
        Runat="server" />

    <asp:SqlDataSource
        id="srcMovies"
```

```
        ConnectionString="<%$ ConnectionStrings:Movies %>"
        SelectCommand="SELECT Id,Title,Director FROM Movies"
        Runat="server" />

    </div>
    </form>
</body>
</html>
```

The GridView in Listing 11.9 displays three database records per page. You can modify the number of records displayed per page by modifying the GridView control's PageSize property. (If you don't specify a value for PageSize, the GridView defaults to displaying 10 records per page.)

WARNING

This section describes how you can enable *user interface paging* with the GridView control. When you use user interface paging, all the database records load into memory and divide into separate pages. For example, when paging through a database table that contains three billion database records, all three billion records load into memory even when you display only three records in a single page. You should not use user interface paging when working with large sets of data. Instead, use the ObjectDataSource control's support for *data source paging*. This option is discussed in Chapter 18, "Using the ObjectDataSource Control."

Paging with AJAX

The default behavior of the GridView control is to post back to the server every time you navigate to a new page of records; however, there is an alternative. You can take advantage of AJAX when paging through records with the GridView control.

The page in Listing 11.10 illustrates how you can use AJAX with the GridView control.

LISTING 11.10   AjaxPaging.aspx

```
<%@ Page Language="C#" %>
<!DOCTYPE html PUBLIC "-//W3C//DTD XHTML 1.1//EN"
"http://www.w3.org/TR/xhtml11/DTD/xhtml11.dtd">
<html xmlns="http://www.w3.org/1999/xhtml" >
<head id="Head1" runat="server">
    <title>AJAX Page</title>
</head>
<body>
    <form id="form1" runat="server">
    <div>
```

```
<asp:ScriptManager ID="sm1" runat="server" />

<%= DateTime.Now.ToString("T") %>

<asp:UpdatePanel ID="up1" runat="server">
<ContentTemplate>

<asp:GridView
    id="grdMovies"
    DataSourceID="srcMovies"
    AllowPaging="true"
    EnableSortingAndPagingCallbacks="true"
    PageSize="3"
    Runat="server" />

</ContentTemplate>
</asp:UpdatePanel>

<asp:SqlDataSource
    id="srcMovies"
    ConnectionString="<%$ ConnectionStrings:Movies %>"
    SelectCommand="SELECT Id,Title,Director FROM Movies"
    Runat="server" />

</div>
</form>
</body>
</html>
```

The page in Listing 11.10 includes an UpdatePanel control. Because the GridView is contained in the UpdatePanel, the page containing GridView is not posted back to the server when you page through GridView.

The page in Listing 11.10 displays the current time at the top of the page. When you page through the records rendered by the GridView control, the time does not change. Only the contents of the GridView control are modified.

Customizing the Paging Interface

By default, when paging is enabled, GridView renders a list of page numbers at the bottom of the grid. You can modify the user interface for paging through records by modifying the GridView control's PagerSettings property. For example, the page in Listing 11.11 contains a GridView that renders First, Previous, Next, and Last links at both the top and bottom of GridView (see Figure 11.7).

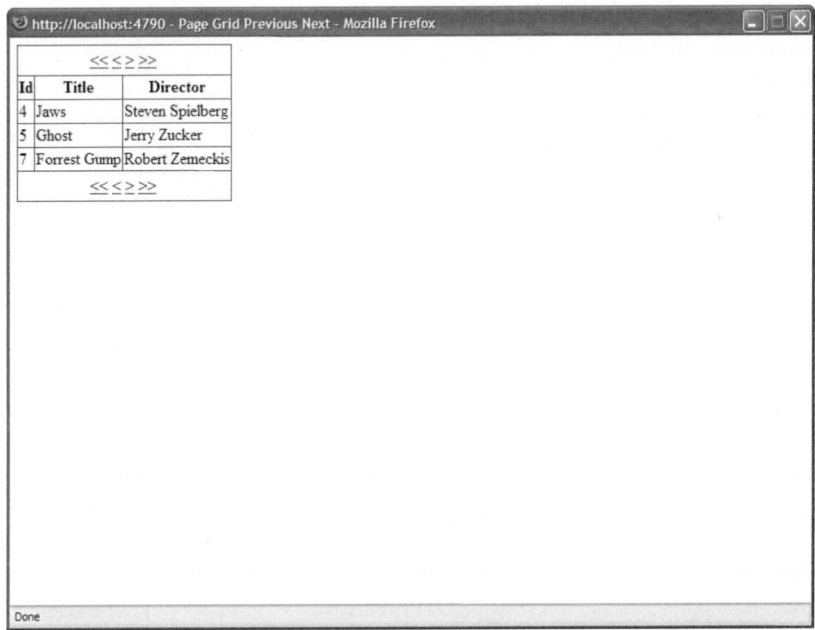

FIGURE 11.7   Modifying pager settings.

LISTING 11.11   PageGridPreviousNext.aspx

```
<%@ Page Language="C#" %>
<!DOCTYPE html PUBLIC "-//W3C//DTD XHTML 1.1//EN"
    "http://www.w3.org/TR/xhtml11/DTD/xhtml11.dtd">
<html xmlns="http://www.w3.org/1999/xhtml" >
<head id="Head1" runat="server">
    <title>Page Grid Previous Next</title>
</head>
<body>
    <form id="form1" runat="server">
    <div>

    <asp:GridView
        id="grdMovies"
        DataSourceID="srcMovies"
        AllowPaging="true"
        PageSize="3"
        PagerSettings-Mode="NextPreviousFirstLast"
        PagerSettings-Position="TopAndBottom"
        PagerStyle-HorizontalAlign="Center"
        Runat="server" />
```

```
<asp:SqlDataSource
    id="srcMovies"
    ConnectionString="<%$ ConnectionStrings:Movies %>"
    SelectCommand="SELECT Id,Title,Director FROM Movies"
    Runat="server" />

</div>
</form>
</body>
</html>
```

The PagerSettings class supports the following properties:

▶ **FirstPageImageUrl**—Enables you to display an image for the first page link.

▶ **FirstPageText**—Enables you to specify the text for the first page link.

▶ **LastPageImageUrl**—Enables you to display an image for the last page link.

▶ **LastPageText**—Enables you to specify the text for the last page link.

▶ **Mode**—Enables you to select a display mode for the pager user interface. Possible values are NextPrevious, NextPreviousFirstLast, Numeric, and NumericFirstLast.

▶ **NextPageImageUrl**—Enables you to display an image for the next page link.

▶ **NextPageText**—Enables you to specify the text for the next page link.

▶ **PageButtonCount**—Enables you to specify the number of page number links to display.

▶ **Position**—Enables you to specify the position of the paging user interface. Possible values are Bottom, Top, TopAndBottom.

▶ **PreviousPageImageUrl**—Enables you to display an image for the previous page link.

▶ **PreviousPageText**—Enables you to specify the text for the previous page link.

▶ **Visible**—Enables you to hide the paging user interface.

The PageButtonCount requires more explanation. Imagine that you display the contents of a database table that contains 3 billion records and you display two records per page. In that case, you need to render an overwhelming number of page numbers. The PageButtonCount property enables you to limit the number of page numbers displayed at once. When PageButtonCount has a value less than the number of page numbers, GridView renders ellipses, which enables a user to move between ranges of page numbers.

The GridView control includes a PagerTemplate, which enables you to completely customize the appearance of the paging user interface. For example, the page in Listing 11.12 uses a Menu control in a PagerTemplate to display a list of page numbers. The

PagerTemplate also includes two LinkButton controls, which represent a Previous and Next link (see Figure 11.8).

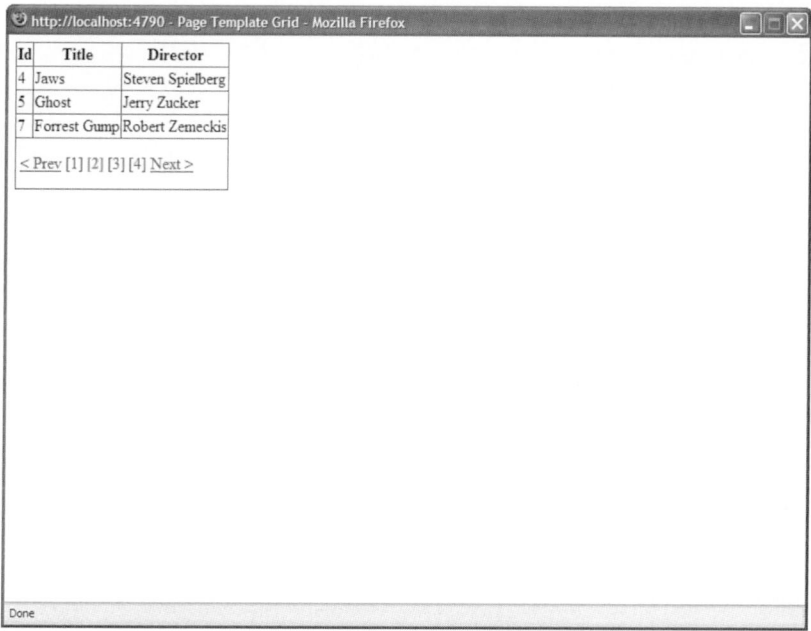

FIGURE 11.8   Using a template for the paging interface.

LISTING 11.12   PageTemplateGrid.aspx

```
<%@ Page Language="C#" %>
<!DOCTYPE html PUBLIC "-//W3C//DTD XHTML 1.1//EN"
"http://www.w3.org/TR/xhtml11/DTD/xhtml11.dtd">

<script runat="server">

    protected void grdMovies_DataBound(object sender, EventArgs e)
    {
        Menu menuPager = (Menu)grdMovies.BottomPagerRow.FindControl("menuPager");
        for (int i = 0; i < grdMovies.PageCount; i++)
        {
            MenuItem item = new MenuItem();
            item.Text = String.Format("",i + 1);
            item.Value = i.ToString();
            if (grdMovies.PageIndex == i)
                item.Selected = true;
            menuPager.Items.Add(item);
        }
```

```
        }

        protected void menuPager_MenuItemClick(object sender, MenuEventArgs e)
        {
            grdMovies.PageIndex = Int32.Parse(e.Item.Value);
        }
</script>

<html xmlns="http://www.w3.org/1999/xhtml" >
<head id="Head1" runat="server">
    <style type="text/css">
        .menu td
        {
            padding:5px 0px;
        }
        .selectedPage a
        {
            font-weight:bold;
            color:red;
        }
    </style>
    <title>Page Template Grid</title>
</head>
<body>
    <form id="form1" runat="server">
    <div>

    <asp:GridView
        id="grdMovies"
        DataSourceID="srcMovies"
        AllowPaging="true"
        PageSize="3"
        Runat="server" OnDataBound="grdMovies_DataBound">
        <PagerTemplate>
        <table>
        <tr><td>
        <asp:LinkButton
            id="lnkPrevious"
            Text="&lt; Prev"
            CommandName="Page"
            CommandArgument="Prev"
            ToolTip="Previous Page"
            Runat="server" />
        </td><td>
        <asp:Menu
            id="menuPager"
```

```
            Orientation="Horizontal"
            OnMenuItemClick="menuPager_MenuItemClick"
            StaticSelectedStyle-CssClass="selectedPage"
            CssClass="menu"
            Runat="server" />
    </td><td>
    <asp:LinkButton
        id="lnkNext"
        Text="Next &gt;"
        CommandName="Page"
        CommandArgument="Next"
        ToolTip="Next Page"
        Runat="server" />
    </td></tr>
    </table>
    </PagerTemplate>
</asp:GridView>

<asp:SqlDataSource
    id="srcMovies"
    ConnectionString="<%$ ConnectionStrings:Movies %>"
    SelectCommand="SELECT Id,Title,Director FROM Movies"
    Runat="server" />

</div>
</form>
</body>
</html>
```

The `GridView` in Listing 11.12 includes a `PagerTemplate` that contains a `Menu` control. When `GridView` is bound to its data source, the `grdMovies_DataBound()` method executes and creates menu items that correspond to each page in `GridView`. When you click a menu item, the page index of `GridView` is updated.

To customize the `PagerTemplate`, you can add button controls to the template such as the `Button`, `ImageButton`, or `LinkButton` controls. Set the `CommandName` property of the Button control to the value `Page` and the `CommandArgument` property to one of the following values:

▶ **Next**—Causes the `GridView` to display the next page of data items.

▶ **Prev**—Causes the `GridView` to display the previous page of data items.

▶ **First**—Causes the `GridView` to display the first page of data items.

▶ **Last**—Causes the `GridView` to display the last page of data items.

▶ **Integer Value**—Causes the `GridView` to display a particular page of data items.

Editing Data

The GridView control also enables you to edit database data. The amazing thing is that you can use the GridView to edit the contents of a database table row without writing a single line of code.

The page in Listing 11.13 illustrates how you can update and delete records in the Movies database table by using the GridView control (see Figure 11.9).

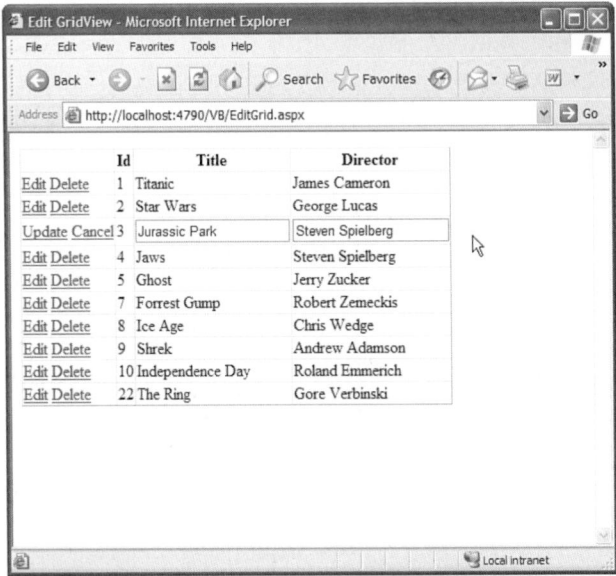

FIGURE 11.9   Editing records with the GridView.

LISTING 11.13   EditGrid.aspx

```
<%@ Page Language="C#" MaintainScrollPositionOnPostback="true" %>
<!DOCTYPE html PUBLIC "-//W3C//DTD XHTML 1.1//EN"
   "http://www.w3.org/TR/xhtml11/DTD/xhtml11.dtd">
<html xmlns="http://www.w3.org/1999/xhtml" >
<head id="Head1" runat="server">
    <title>Edit GridView</title>
</head>
<body>
    <form id="form1" runat="server">
    <div>

    <asp:GridView
        id="grdMovies"
        DataSourceID="srcMovies"
```

```
            DataKeyNames="Id"
            AutoGenerateEditButton="true"
            AutoGenerateDeleteButton="true"
            Runat="server" />

    <asp:SqlDataSource
        id="srcMovies"
        ConnectionString="<%$ ConnectionStrings:Movies %>"
        SelectCommand="SELECT Id,Title,Director FROM Movies"
        UpdateCommand="UPDATE Movies SET Title=@Title, Director=@Director
            WHERE Id=@Id"
        DeleteCommand="DELETE Movies WHERE Id=@Id"
        Runat="server" />

    </div>
    </form>
</body>
</html>
```

In Listing 11.13, the `GridView` control has both its `AutoGenerateEditButton` and `AutoGenerateDeleteButton` properties enabled. When these properties are enabled, Edit and Delete links are automatically rendered next to each row in the `GridView`.

NOTE

You can take advantage of the `<%@ Page %>` directive's `MaintainScrollPositionOnPostback` attribute to scroll a page back automatically to the same position whenever the page is posted back to the server. For example, if you add this attribute and click an Edit link rendered by a `GridView`, the page automatically scrolls to the record being edited. This attribute works with Internet Explorer 6+, Firefox 1+, and Opera 8+.

When you click an Edit link, you can edit a particular database row. The `GridView` automatically renders a check box for any Boolean columns and a text field for any other type of column.

NOTE

The `GridView` control does not support inserting new records into a database table. If you need to insert new records, use the `ListView`, `DetailsView`, or `FormView` control.

Furthermore, the GridView control includes a DataKeyNames property. When editing and deleting rows with the GridView, you need to assign the name of the primary key field from the database table being modified to this property. In Listing 11.13, the Movies ID column is assigned to the DataKeyNames property.

Finally, the SqlDataSource control associated with the GridView control includes a SelectCommand, UpdateCommand, and DeleteCommand property. These properties contain the SQL statements executed when you display, insert, and delete records with the GridView control.

The SQL statements contained in both the UpdateCommand and DeleteCommand include parameters. For example, the UpdateCommand looks like this:

```
UPDATE Movies SET Title=@Title, Director=@Director
WHERE Id=@Id
```

The @Title and @Director parameters represent the new values for these columns that a user enters when updating a record with the GridView control. The @Id parameter represents the primary key column from the database table.

Handling Concurrency Issues

The GridView control can track both the original and modified value of each database column. The GridView control tracks the original and updated values of a column so that you can handle concurrency conflicts. Imagine that you are building a massive order entry system. Your company has hundreds of employees modifying orders with a page that contains a GridView control. If two employees open the same customer record at the same time, one employee might overwrite changes made by the other employee. You can prevent this type of concurrency conflict by using the page in Listing 11.14.

LISTING 11.14   Concurrency.aspx

```
<%@ Page Language="C#" %>
<!DOCTYPE html PUBLIC "-//W3C//DTD XHTML 1.1//EN"
"http://www.w3.org/TR/xhtml11/DTD/xhtml11.dtd">

<script runat="server">

    protected void srcMovies_Updated(object sender, SqlDataSourceStatusEventArgs e)
    {
        if (e.AffectedRows == 0)
            lblMessage.Text = "Could not update record";
    }
</script>

<html xmlns="http://www.w3.org/1999/xhtml" >
<head id="Head1" runat="server">
    <title>Concurrency</title>
</head>
```

```
<body>
    <form id="form1" runat="server">
    <div>

    <asp:Label ID="lblMessage" EnableViewState="false" runat="server" />

    <asp:GridView
        id="grdMovies"
        DataSourceID="srcMovies"
        DataKeyNames="Id"
        AutoGenerateEditButton="true"
        Runat="server" />

    <asp:SqlDataSource
        id="srcMovies"
        ConflictDetection="CompareAllValues"
        OldValuesParameterFormatString="original_{0}"
        ConnectionString="<%$ ConnectionStrings:Movies %>"
        SelectCommand="SELECT Id,Title,Director FROM Movies"
        UpdateCommand="UPDATE Movies SET Title=@Title, Director=@Director
            WHERE Id=@original_Id AND Title=@original_Title AND
Director=@original_Director"
        Runat="server" OnUpdated="srcMovies_Updated" />

    </div>
    </form>
</body>
</html>
```

In Listing 11.14, the SqlDataSource control includes both a ConflictDetection and
OldValuesParameterFormatString property. These two properties cause the SqlDataSource
control to track both the original and modified versions of each column.

The ConflictDetection property can have one of the following two values:

▶ CompareAllValues

▶ OverwriteChanges

By default, the ConflictDetection property has the value OverwriteChanges, which
causes the SqlDataSource control to overwrite the previous value of a column with its
new value. When ConflictDetection is set to the value CompareAllValues, the
SqlDataSource tracks both the original and modified version of each column.

The OldValuesParameterFormatString property provides a distinguishing name for the
original value of a column. For example, the value of the SqlDataSource control's
UpdateCommand looks like this:

```
UPDATE Movies SET Title=@Title, Director=@Director
WHERE Id=@original_Id AND Title=@original_Title
AND Director=@original_Director
```

The @original_Id, @original_Title, and @original_Director parameters represent the original values of these columns. If the value of the Title or Director columns has changed in the underlying database, the record is not updated. In other words, if someone else beats you to the record change, your modifications are ignored.

The page in Listing 11.14 includes an Updated event handler for the SqlDataSource control. If there is a concurrency conflict, no records will be affected by the update. The event handler displays an error message when the e.AffectedRows property has the value 0.

Displaying Empty Data

GridView includes two properties that enable you to display content when no results are returned from the GridView control's data source. You can use either the EmptyDataText property or the EmptyDataTemplate property to handle empty data.

For example, the page in Listing 11.15 contains a movie search form. If you enter a search string that does not match the start of any movie title, the contents of the EmptyDataText property display (see Figure 11.10).

FIGURE 11.10   Displaying a message when no records match.

LISTING 11.15   ShowEmptyDataText.aspx

```
<%@ Page Language="C#" %>
<!DOCTYPE html PUBLIC "-//W3C//DTD XHTML 1.1//EN"
"http://www.w3.org/TR/xhtml11/DTD/xhtml11.dtd">
<script runat="server">

    protected void btnSubmit_Click(object sender, EventArgs e)
    {
        grdMovies.Visible = true;
    }
</script>

<html xmlns="http://www.w3.org/1999/xhtml" >
<head id="Head1" runat="server">
    <title>Show Empty Data Text</title>
</head>
<body>
    <form id="form1" runat="server">
    <div>

    <asp:TextBox
        id="txtTitle"
        Runat="server" />
    <asp:Button
        id="btnSubmit"
        Text="Search"
        OnClick="btnSubmit_Click"
        Runat="server" />
    <hr />

    <asp:GridView
        id="grdMovies"
        DataSourceID="srcMovies"
        EmptyDataText="<img src='sad.gif'/> No Matching Movies!"
        Visible="false"
        Runat="server" />

    <asp:SqlDataSource
        id="srcMovies"
        ConnectionString="<%$ ConnectionStrings:Movies %>"
        SelectCommand="SELECT Title,Director FROM Movies
            WHERE Title LIKE @Title+'%'"
        Runat="server">
        <SelectParameters>
        <asp:ControlParameter
```

```
            Name="Title"
            ControlID="txtTitle"
            PropertyName="Text" />
        </SelectParameters>
    </asp:SqlDataSource>

    </div>
    </form>
</body>
</html>
```

If you use the search form in Listing 11.15 to search for a movie that doesn't exist, an icon of a frowning face and the text No Matching Movies! is displayed.

The initial value of the GridView control's Visible property is set to False. The GridView displays only after you click the button. If you did not add this additional logic, the EmptyDataText message would display when the page first opens.

As an alternative to using the EmptyDataText property, you can use an EmptyDataTemplate to display content when a data source does not return any results. For example, the page in Listing 11.16 prompts you to enter a new movie when no matching movies are found (see Figure 11.11).

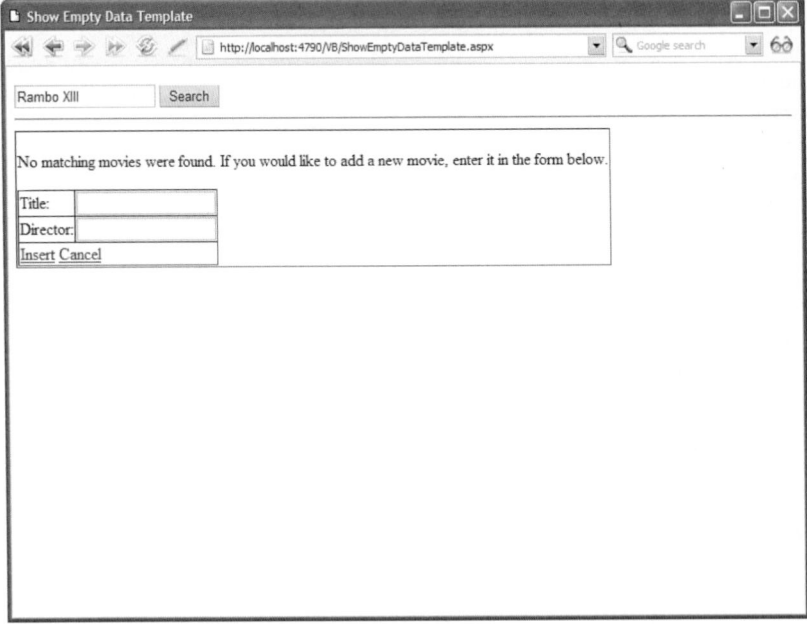

FIGURE 11.11   Displaying a template when no records match.

LISTING 11.16   ShowEmptyDataTemplate.aspx

```
<%@ Page Language="C#" %>
<!DOCTYPE html PUBLIC "-//W3C//DTD XHTML 1.1//EN"
"http://www.w3.org/TR/xhtml11/DTD/xhtml11.dtd">
<script runat="server">

    protected void btnSubmit_Click(object sender, EventArgs e)
    {
        grdMovies.Visible = true;
    }

    protected void dtlMovie_ItemInserted(object sender,
➥DetailsViewInsertedEventArgs e)
    {
        txtTitle.Text = (string)e.Values["Title"];
        grdMovies.DataBind();
    }
</script>

<html xmlns="http://www.w3.org/1999/xhtml" >
<head id="Head1" runat="server">
    <title>Show Empty Data Template</title>
</head>
<body>
    <form id="form1" runat="server">
    <div>

    <asp:TextBox
        id="txtTitle"
        Runat="server" />
    <asp:Button
        id="btnSubmit"
        Text="Search"
        OnClick="btnSubmit_Click"
        Runat="server" />
    <hr />

    <asp:GridView
        id="grdMovies"
        DataSourceID="srcMovies"
        Visible="false"
        Runat="server">
        <EmptyDataTemplate>
        <p>
        No matching movies were found. If you would like
```

```
        to add a new movie, enter it in the form below.
    </p>
    <asp:DetailsView
        id="dtlMovie"
        DataSourceID="srcMovies"
        DefaultMode="Insert"
        AutoGenerateInsertButton="true"
        AutoGenerateRows="false"
        Runat="server" OnItemInserted="dtlMovie_ItemInserted">
        <Fields>
        <asp:BoundField
            HeaderText="Title:"
            DataField="Title" />
        <asp:BoundField
            HeaderText="Director:"
            DataField="Director" />
        </Fields>
    </asp:DetailsView>

    </EmptyDataTemplate>
</asp:GridView>

<asp:SqlDataSource
    id="srcMovies"
    ConnectionString="<%$ ConnectionStrings:Movies %>"
    SelectCommand="SELECT Title,Director FROM Movies
        WHERE Title LIKE @Title+'%'"
    InsertCommand="INSERT Movies (Title, Director)
        VALUES (@Title, @Director)"
    Runat="server">
    <SelectParameters>
    <asp:ControlParameter
        Name="Title"
        ControlID="txtTitle"
        PropertyName="Text" />
    </SelectParameters>
</asp:SqlDataSource>

    </div>
    </form>
</body>
</html>
```

The EmptyDataTemplate in Listing 11.16 contains some text and a DetailsView control that you can use to insert a new movie into the Movies database table. You can add any HTML content or ASP.NET controls to EmptyDataTemplate that you need.

Formatting the `GridView` Control

The `GridView` control includes a rich set of formatting properties that you can use to modify its appearance. I recommend that you don't use most of these properties because using these properties results in bloated pages. Instead, I recommend that you use Cascading Style Sheets (CSS) to format the `GridView` control.

The `GridView` control includes a `CssClass` property. The control also exposes several `Style` objects that include the `CssClass` property:

- ▶ **`AlternatingRowStyle`**—Enables you to format every other row.
- ▶ **`FooterStyle`**—Enables you to format the footer row.
- ▶ **`HeaderStyle`**—Enables you to format the header row.
- ▶ **`PagerStyle`**—Enables you to format the pager row.
- ▶ **`RowStyle`**—Enables you to format each row.
- ▶ **`SelectedRowStyle`**—Enables you to format the selected row.

For example, the page in Listing 11.17 contains a `GridView` control formatted with CSS rules (see Figure 11.12).

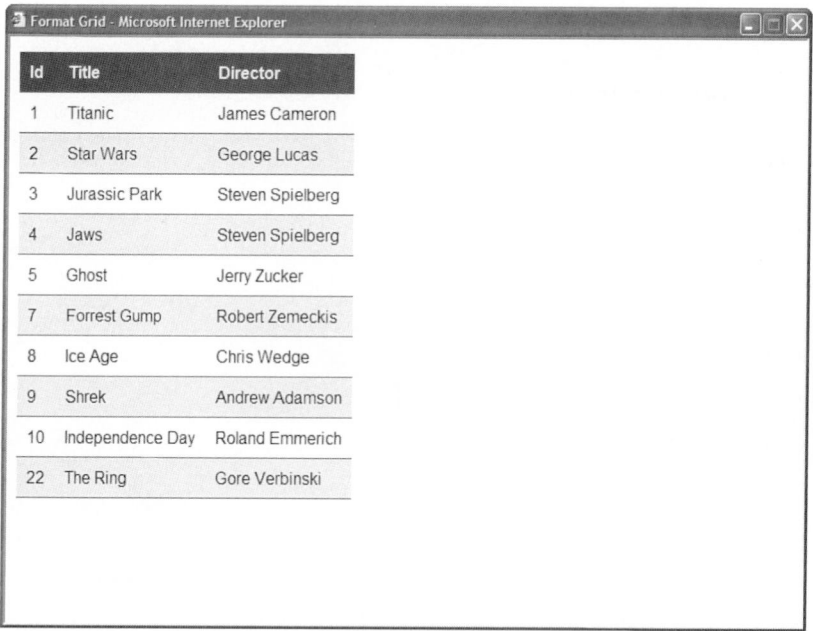

FIGURE 11.12 A `GridView` control formatted with CSS.

LISTING 11.17   FormatGrid.aspx

```
<%@ Page Language="C#" %>
<!DOCTYPE html PUBLIC "-//W3C//DTD XHTML 1.1//EN"
    "http://www.w3.org/TR/xhtml11/DTD/xhtml11.dtd">
<html xmlns="http://www.w3.org/1999/xhtml" >
<head id="Head1" runat="server">
    <style type="text/css">
        .grid
        {
            font:16px Arial, Sans-Serif;
        }
        .grid td, .grid th
        {
            padding:10px;
        }
        .header
        {
            text-align:left;
            color:white;
            background-color:blue;
        }
        .row td
        {
            border-bottom:solid 1px blue;
        }
        .alternating
        {
            background-color:#eeeeee;
        }
        .alternating td
        {
            border-bottom:solid 1px blue;
        }
    </style>
    <title>Format Grid</title>
</head>
<body>
    <form id="form1" runat="server">
    <div>

    <asp:GridView
        id="grdMovies"
        DataSourceID="srcMovies"
        GridLines="None"
        CssClass="grid"
```

```
        HeaderStyle-CssClass="header"
        RowStyle-CssClass="row"
        AlternatingRowStyle-CssClass="alternating"
        Runat="server" />

    <asp:SqlDataSource
        id="srcMovies"
        ConnectionString="<%$ ConnectionStrings:Movies %>"
        SelectCommand="SELECT Id,Title,Director FROM Movies"
        Runat="server" />

    </div>
    </form>
</body>
</html>
```

In Listing 11.17, the column header text is left-aligned. Also, banding is added to the table rendered by GridView. Alternating rows render with a gray background.

The GridView control has a few formatting properties that you might need to use even when formatting GridView with Cascading Style Sheets. For example, in Listing 11.17, the GridLines property was assigned the value None to suppress the default rendering of borders around each table cell. Following is a list of these properties:

- ▶ **GridLines**—Renders borders around table cells. Possible values are Both, Vertical, Horizontal, and None.

- ▶ **ShowFooter**—When True, renders a footer row at the bottom of the GridView.

- ▶ **ShowHeader**—When True, renders a header row at the top of the GridView.

Using `ViewState` with the `GridView` Control

By default, the GridView control stores the values of all the columns contained in all the rows that it renders in ViewState. In other words, all the rows that the GridView retrieves from its data source are stuffed in a hidden form field.

The advantage of using ViewState is that the GridView does not need to query the database for the same set of records every time a page containing GridView displays. The records are retrieved from the database only when the page first loads.

The disadvantage of using ViewState is that it means that a lot of information might need to be pushed over the wire to a user's browser. All ViewState information is stored in a hidden form field. When a large number of rows display, this hidden form field can become enormous. When ViewState becomes too large, it can significantly impact a page's performance.

You can disable ViewState by assigning the value False to the GridView control's EnableViewState property. Even if you disable ViewState, you can still display, sort, page, and edit database records with the GridView control. (GridView uses ControlState to track vital state information.) When displaying a large number of records, you should turn ViewState off.

You can view the amount of ViewState that GridView uses by enabling tracing for the page that contains GridView. Add the Trace="True" attribute to the Page directive like this:

```
<%@ Page Trace="true" %>
```

When tracing is enabled, a Control Tree section is appended to the end of a page when the page renders in a browser. The Control Tree section displays the ViewState size used by each control contained in the page.

Using Fields with the GridView Control

In all the sample code in the previous section, the GridView control was used to render automatically an HTML table that contains a list of data items. However, there is a problem with allowing GridView to render its columns automatically. The result does not look professional.

For example, the column headers are simply the names of the underlying database columns. Displaying the column name EntryDate as a column header seems, well, a little cheesy. We really need to specify custom column headers.

Another problem with enabling GridView to render its columns automatically is that you give up any control over column formatting. For example, the BoxOfficeTotals column displays as a decimal amount without any currency formatting. The EntryDate column always displays in short-date and long-time format.

Furthermore, it would be nice to display the values of certain columns as images, drop-down lists, or hyperlinks. If you use the automatically generated columns, you are stuck with the user interface you are given. The solution to all these problems is to specify explicitly the fields that GridView displays. The GridView control supports the following types of fields:

- ▶ **BoundField**—Enables you to display the value of a data item as text.
- ▶ **CheckBoxField**—Enables you to display the value of a data item as a check box.
- ▶ **CommandField**—Enables you to display links for editing, deleting, and selecting rows.
- ▶ **ButtonField**—Enables you to display the value of a data item as a button (image button, link button, or push button).
- ▶ **HyperLinkField**—Enables you to display the value of a data item as a link.

▶ **ImageField**—Enables you to display the value of a data item as an image.

▶ **TemplateField**—Enables you to customize the appearance of a data item.

The following sections examine how you can take advantage of each of these different types of fields.

NOTE

You can create custom fields that work with the `GridView` control. This option is explored in the final section of this chapter.

Using **BoundFields**

A `BoundField` always displays the value of a data item as text when a row is in normal display mode. When a row is selected for editing, a `BoundField` displays the value of a data item in a single-line text field.

The most important three properties of the `BoundField` class are the `DataField`, `DataFormatString`, and `HeaderText` properties. The page in Listing 11.18 illustrates how to use these properties when displaying a list of movies (see Figure 11.13).

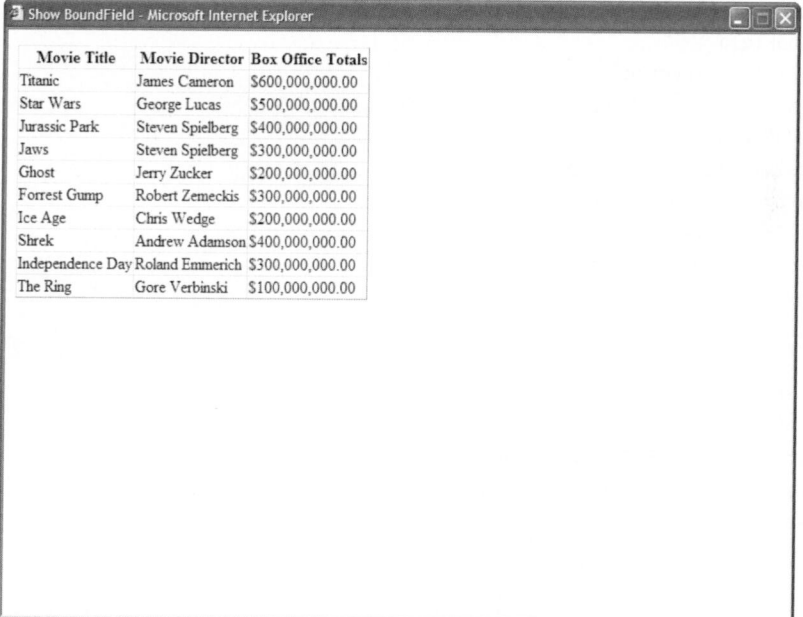

Movie Title	Movie Director	Box Office Totals
Titanic	James Cameron	$600,000,000.00
Star Wars	George Lucas	$500,000,000.00
Jurassic Park	Steven Spielberg	$400,000,000.00
Jaws	Steven Spielberg	$300,000,000.00
Ghost	Jerry Zucker	$200,000,000.00
Forrest Gump	Robert Zemeckis	$300,000,000.00
Ice Age	Chris Wedge	$200,000,000.00
Shrek	Andrew Adamson	$400,000,000.00
Independence Day	Roland Emmerich	$300,000,000.00
The Ring	Gore Verbinski	$100,000,000.00

FIGURE 11.13   Using `BoundFields` with the `GridView` control.

LISTING 11.18   ShowBoundField.aspx

```
<%@ Page Language="C#" %>
<!DOCTYPE html PUBLIC "-//W3C//DTD XHTML 1.1//EN"
    "http://www.w3.org/TR/xhtml11/DTD/xhtml11.dtd">
<html xmlns="http://www.w3.org/1999/xhtml" >
<head id="Head1" runat="server">
    <title>Show BoundField</title>
</head>
<body>
    <form id="form1" runat="server">
    <div>

    <asp:GridView
        id="grdMovies"
        DataSourceID="srcMovies"
        AutoGenerateColumns="false"
        Runat="server">
        <Columns>
        <asp:BoundField
            DataField="Title"
            HeaderText="Movie Title" />
        <asp:BoundField
            DataField="Director"
            HeaderText="Movie Director" />
        <asp:BoundField
            DataField="BoxOfficeTotals"
            DataFormatString="{0:c}"
            HtmlEncode="false"
            HeaderText="Box Office Totals" />
        </Columns>
    </asp:GridView>

    <asp:SqlDataSource
        id="srcMovies"
        ConnectionString="<%$ ConnectionStrings:Movies %>"
        SelectCommand="SELECT * FROM Movies"
        Runat="server" />

    </div>
    </form>
</body>
</html>
```

The GridView control includes an AutoGenerateColumns property assigned the value False. If you don't disable automatically generated columns, both columns represented by the BoundFields and all the columns from the data source display redundantly.

In Listing 11.18, BoundFields display the Title, Director, and BoxOfficeTotals columns. The DataField property represents the column that a BoundField displays. The HeaderText property determines the column header.

The BoundField used to display the BoxOfficeTotals column includes a DataFormatString property. This format string formats the values of the BoxOfficeTotals column as a currency amount.

> **NOTE**
>
> For more information about string formatting, see the Formatting Types topic in the Microsoft .NET Framework Documentation.

A BoundField supports several other useful properties:

- **AccessibleHeaderText**—Enables you to add an HTML abbr attribute to the column header.

- **ApplyFormatInEditMode**—Enables you to apply the DataFormatString to the field when the row is in edit display mode.

- **ConvertEmptyStringToNull**—Enables you to convert an empty string "" into the value Nothing (null) when editing a column.

- **DataField**—Enables you to specify the name of the field that the BoundField displays.

- **DataFormatString**—Enables you to use a format string to format a data item.

- **FooterStyle**—Enables you to format the column footer.

- **FooterText**—Enables you to display text in the column footer.

- **HeaderImageUrl**—Enables you to display an image in the column header.

- **HeaderStyle**—Enables you to format the column header.

- **HeaderText**—Enables you to display text in the column header.

- **HtmlEncode**—Enables you to HTML-encode the value of a data item, which enables you to avoid script injection attacks.

- **InsertVisible**—Enables you to not display a column when inserting a new record (does not apply to the GridView control).

- **ItemStyle**—Enables you to format a data item.

- **NullDisplayText**—Enables you to specify text displayed when a data item has the value Nothing (null).

▶ **ReadOnly**—Enables you to prevent the data item from being edited in edit mode.

▶ **ShowHeader**—Enables you to display the column header.

▶ **SortExpression**—Enables you to associate a sort expression with the column.

▶ **Visible**—Enables you to hide a column.

Using `CheckBoxFields`

A CheckBoxField, as you can probably guess, displays a check box. When a row is not in edit mode, the check box displays but is disabled.

The page in Listing 11.19 illustrates how you can use a CheckBoxField (see Figure 11.14).

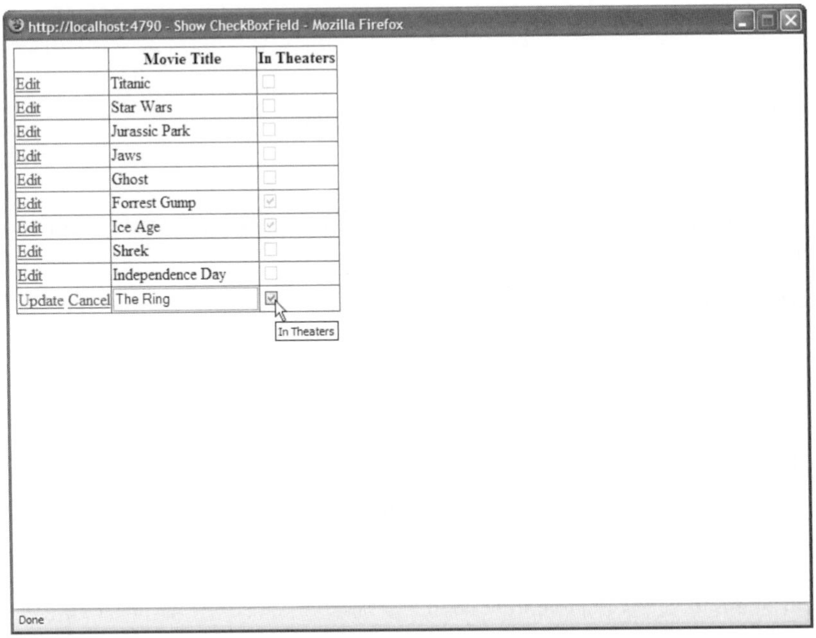

FIGURE 11.14   Using the CheckBoxField with the GridView control.

LISTING 11.19   ShowCheckBoxField.aspx

```
<%@ Page Language="C#" %>
<!DOCTYPE html PUBLIC "-//W3C//DTD XHTML 1.1//EN"
    "http://www.w3.org/TR/xhtml11/DTD/xhtml11.dtd">
<html xmlns="http://www.w3.org/1999/xhtml" >
<head id="Head1" runat="server">
    <title>Show CheckBoxField</title>
</head>
```

```
<body>
    <form id="form1" runat="server">
    <div>

    <asp:GridView
        id="grdMovies"
        DataSourceID="srcMovies"
        DataKeyNames="Id"
        AutoGenerateColumns="false"
        AutoGenerateEditButton="true"
        Runat="server">
        <Columns>
        <asp:BoundField
            DataField="Title"
            HeaderText="Movie Title" />
        <asp:CheckBoxField
            DataField="InTheaters"
            HeaderText="In Theaters" />
        </Columns>
    </asp:GridView>

    <asp:SqlDataSource
        id="srcMovies"
        ConnectionString="<%$ ConnectionStrings:Movies %>"
        SelectCommand="SELECT Id,Title,InTheaters FROM Movies"
        UpdateCommand="UPDATE Movies SET
            Title=@Title, InTheaters=@InTheaters
            WHERE Id=@Id"
        Runat="server" />

    </div>
    </form>
</body>
</html>
```

The CheckBoxField inherits from the BoundField class, so it includes all the properties of the BoundField class. It also supports the following property:

▸ **Text**—Displays text next to each check box.

Using CommandFields

You can use a CommandField to customize the appearance of the Edit, Delete, Update, Cancel, and Select buttons displayed by the GridView control. For example, the page in Listing 11.20 uses icons for the standard edit buttons (see Figure 11.15).

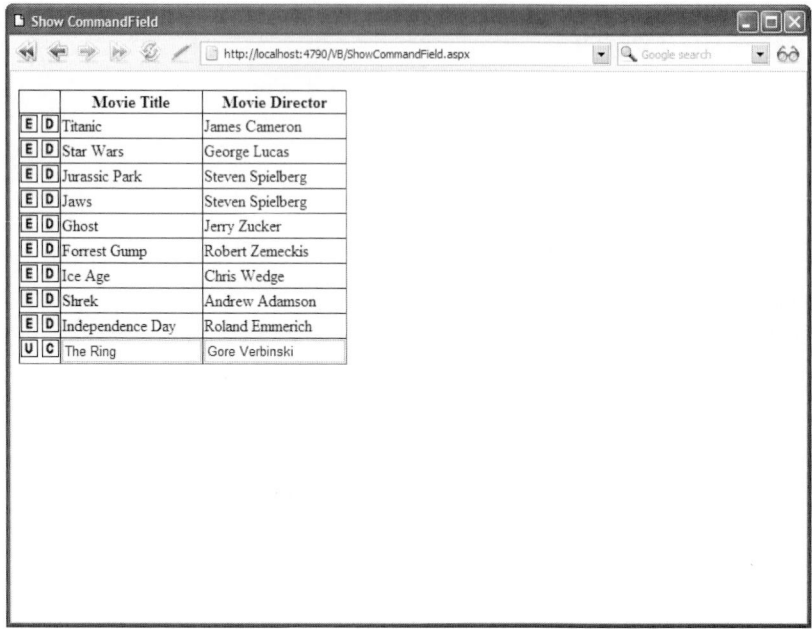

FIGURE 11.15   Using a `CommandField` with the `GridView` control.

LISTING 11.20   ShowCommandField.aspx

```csharp
<%@ Page Language="C#" %>
<!DOCTYPE html PUBLIC "-//W3C//DTD XHTML 1.1//EN"
  "http://www.w3.org/TR/xhtml11/DTD/xhtml11.dtd">
<html xmlns="http://www.w3.org/1999/xhtml" >
<head id="Head1" runat="server">
    <title>Show CommandField</title>
</head>
<body>
    <form id="form1" runat="server">
    <div>

    <asp:GridView
        id="grdMovies"
        DataSourceID="srcMovies"
        DataKeyNames="Id"
        AutoGenerateColumns="false"
        Runat="server">
        <Columns>
        <asp:CommandField
            ButtonType="Image"
```

```
                ShowEditButton="true"
                EditText="Edit Movie"
                EditImageUrl="Edit.gif"
                UpdateText="Update Movie"
                UpdateImageUrl="Update.gif"
                ShowCancelButton="true"
                CancelText="Cancel Edit"
                CancelImageUrl="Cancel.gif"
                ShowDeleteButton="true"
                DeleteText="Delete Movie"
                DeleteImageUrl="Delete.gif" />
        <asp:BoundField
            DataField="Title"
            HeaderText="Movie Title" />
        <asp:BoundField
            DataField="Director"
            HeaderText="Movie Director" />
        </Columns>
    </asp:GridView>

    <asp:SqlDataSource
        id="srcMovies"
        ConnectionString="<%$ ConnectionStrings:Movies %>"
        SelectCommand="SELECT Id,Title,Director FROM Movies"
        UpdateCommand="UPDATE Movies SET
            Title=@Title, Director=@Director
            WHERE Id=@Id"
        DeleteCommand="DELETE Movies
            WHERE Id=@Id"
        Runat="server" />

    </div>
    </form>
</body>
</html>
```

You do not enable the AutoGenerateEditButton or AutoGenerateDeleteButton properties when using a CommandField. Instead, you use the CommandField to set up the standard editing buttons explicitly.

The CommandField supports the following properties:

▶ **ButtonType**—Enables you to specify the type of button displayed by the CommandField. Possible values are Button, Image, and Link.

▶ **CancelImageUrl**—Enables you to specify an image to display for the Cancel button.

- ▶ **CancelText**—Enables you to specify the text to display for the Cancel button.
- ▶ **CausesValidation**—Enables you to disable validation when an Edit button is clicked.
- ▶ **DeleteImageUrl**—Enables you to specify an image to display for the Delete button.
- ▶ **DeleteText**—Enables you to specify the text to display for the Delete button.
- ▶ **EditImageUrl**—Enables you to specify an image to display for the Edit button.
- ▶ **EditText**—Enables you to specify the text to display for the Edit button.
- ▶ **InsertImageUrl**—Enables you to specify an image to display for the Insert button.
- ▶ **InsertText**—Enables you to specify the text to display for the Insert button.
- ▶ **NewImageUrl**—Enables you to specify an image to display for the New button (does not apply to GridView).
- ▶ **NewText**—Enables you to specify the text to display for the New button.
- ▶ **SelectImageUrl**—Enables you to specify the image to display for the Select button.
- ▶ **SelectText**—Enables you to specify the text to display for the Select button.
- ▶ **ShowCancelButton**—Enables you to display the Cancel button.
- ▶ **ShowDeleteButton**—Enables you to display the Delete button.
- ▶ **ShowEditButton**—Enables you to display the Edit button.
- ▶ **ShowInsertButton**—Enables you to display the Insert button (does not apply to GridView).
- ▶ **ShowSelectButton**—Enables you to display the Select button.
- ▶ **UpdateImageUrl**—Enables you to specify the image to display for the Update button.
- ▶ **UpdateText**—Enables you to specify the text to display for the Update button.
- ▶ **ValidationGroup**—Enables you to associate the edit buttons with a validation group.

Using Button Fields

You use a ButtonField to display a button in a GridView. You can use ButtonField to represent a custom command or one of the standard edit commands.

For example, GridView in Listing 11.21 contains two ButtonFields that a user can click to change the display order of the movie category records (see Figure 11.16).

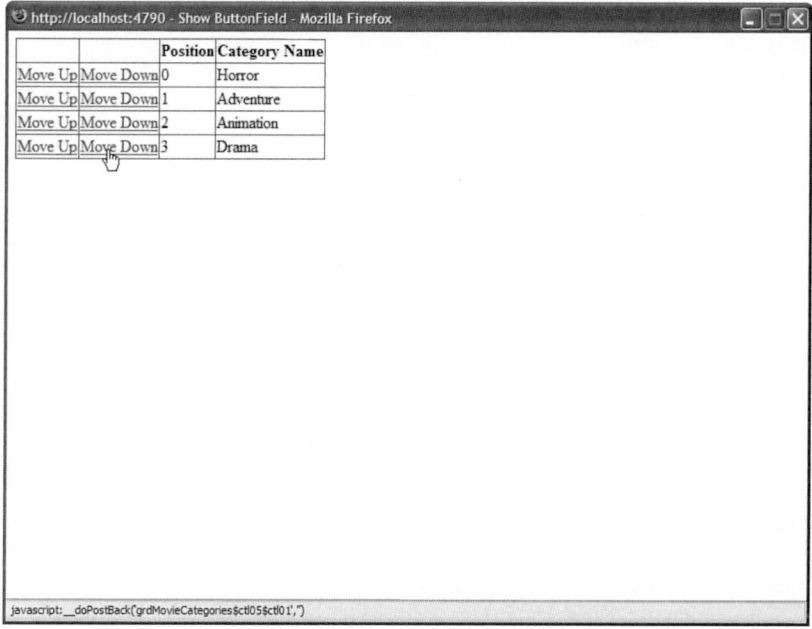

FIGURE 11.16   Using ButtonFields with the GridView control.

LISTING 11.21   ShowButtonField.aspx

```
<%@ Page Language="C#" %>
<!DOCTYPE html PUBLIC "-//W3C//DTD XHTML 1.1//EN"
"http://www.w3.org/TR/xhtml11/DTD/xhtml11.dtd">
<script runat="server">

    protected void grdMovieCategories_RowCommand(object sender,
➥GridViewCommandEventArgs e)
    {
        int index = Int32.Parse((string)e.CommandArgument);
        int id = (int)grdMovieCategories.DataKeys[index].Values["Id"];
        int position = (int)grdMovieCategories.DataKeys[index].Values["Position"];
        switch (e.CommandName)
        {
            case "Up":
                position--;
                break;
            case "Down":
                position++;
                break;
        }
        srcMovieCategories.UpdateParameters["Id"].DefaultValue = id.ToString();
```

```
        srcMovieCategories.UpdateParameters["Position"].DefaultValue =
position.ToString();
        srcMovieCategories.Update();
    }
</script>
<html xmlns="http://www.w3.org/1999/xhtml" >
<head id="Head1" runat="server">
    <title>Show ButtonField</title>
</head>
<body>
    <form id="form1" runat="server">
    <div>

    <asp:GridView
        id="grdMovieCategories"
        DataSourceID="srcMovieCategories"
        DataKeyNames="Id,Position"
        AutoGenerateColumns="false"
        OnRowCommand="grdMovieCategories_RowCommand"
        Runat="server">
        <Columns>
        <asp:ButtonField
            Text="Move Up"
            CommandName="Up" />
        <asp:ButtonField
            Text="Move Down"
            CommandName="Down" />
        <asp:BoundField
            DataField="Position"
            HeaderText="Position" />
        <asp:BoundField
            DataField="Name"
            HeaderText="Category Name" />
        </Columns>
    </asp:GridView>

    <asp:SqlDataSource
        id="srcMovieCategories"
        ConnectionString="<%$ ConnectionStrings:Movies %>"
        SelectCommand="SELECT Id, Name, Position FROM MovieCategories
            ORDER BY Position"
        UpdateCommand="UPDATE MovieCategories SET
            Position=@Position WHERE Id=@Id"
        Runat="server">
        <UpdateParameters>
```

```
        <asp:Parameter
            Name="Id" />
        <asp:Parameter
            Name="Position" />
        </UpdateParameters>
    </asp:SqlDataSource>

    </div>
    </form>
</body>
</html>
```

When you click either the Move Up or Move Down buttons in the page in Listing 11.21, the `GridView` control's `RowCommand` event is raised. This event is handled by the `grdMovieCategories_RowCommand()` method.

The `grdMovieCategories_RowCommand()` method retrieves the index of the row containing the button that was clicked. The row index is grabbed from the `GridViewCommandEventArgs`'s `CommandArgument` property passed as the second parameter to the event handler.

The `grdMovieCategories_RowCommand()` method updates the position of a record by setting the `SqlDataSource` control's `Update` parameters and calling the `SqlDataSource` control's `Update()` method.

A `ButtonField` supports the following properties:

- ▶ **ButtonType**—Enables you to specify the type of button displayed by the `CommandField`. Possible values are Button, Image, and Link.

- ▶ **CausesValidation**—Enables you to disable validation when the button is clicked.

- ▶ **CommandName**—Enables you to associate a standard edit command with the `ButtonField`. Possible values include Delete, Edit, Update, and Cancel.

- ▶ **DataTextField**—Enables you to use a data column to specify the button text.

- ▶ **DataTextFormatString**—Enables you to format the button text.

- ▶ **Text**—Enables you to specify the button text.

- ▶ **ValidationGroup**—Enables you to associate the button with a validation group.

You can use `CommandName` to associate a `ButtonField` with one of the standard edit commands. For example, you can create a Delete button by assigning the value `Delete` to the `CommandName` property.

Using HyperLink Fields

You use HyperLinkField to create a link to another page; HyperLinkField is particularly useful when you need to build two page Master/Detail forms.

For example, the page in Listing 11.22 displays a list of movie categories, and the page in Listing 11.23 displays a list of movies that match the selected category.

LISTING 11.22   Master.aspx

```
<%@ Page Language="C#" %>
<html xmlns="http://www.w3.org/1999/xhtml" >
<head id="Head1" runat="server">
    <title>Master</title>
</head>
<body>
    <form id="form1" runat="server">
    <div>

    <asp:GridView
        id="grdMovieCategories"
        DataSourceID="srcMovieCategories"
        AutoGenerateColumns="false"
        Runat="server">
        <Columns>
        <asp:HyperLinkField
            HeaderText="Movie Categories"
            DataTextField="Name"
            DataNavigateUrlFields="Id"
            DataNavigateUrlFormatString="Details.aspx?id={0}" />
        </Columns>
    </asp:GridView>

    <asp:SqlDataSource
        id="srcMovieCategories"
        ConnectionString="<%$ ConnectionStrings:Movies %>"
        SelectCommand="SELECT Id, Name FROM MovieCategories"
        Runat="server" />

    </div>
    </form>
</body>
</html>
```

LISTING 11.23 `Details.aspx`

```
<%@ Page Language="C#" %>
<!DOCTYPE html PUBLIC "-//W3C//DTD XHTML 1.1//EN"
  "http://www.w3.org/TR/xhtml11/DTD/xhtml11.dtd">
<html xmlns="http://www.w3.org/1999/xhtml" >
<head id="Head1" runat="server">
    <title>Details</title>
</head>
<body>
    <form id="form1" runat="server">
    <div>

    <asp:GridView
        id="grdMovies"
        DataSourceID="srcMovies"
        Runat="server" />

    <asp:SqlDataSource
        id="srcMovies"
        ConnectionString="<%$ ConnectionStrings:Movies %>"
        SelectCommand="SELECT Title,Director FROM Movies
            WHERE CategoryId=@CategoryId"
        Runat="server">
        <SelectParameters>
        <asp:QueryStringParameter
            Name="CategoryId"
            QueryStringField="id" />
        </SelectParameters>
    </asp:SqlDataSource>

    </div>
    </form>
</body>
</html>
```

The page in Listing 11.22 includes a `GridView` control that contains `HyperLinkField`, which creates a link to the `Details.aspx` page and passes the movie category ID as a query string parameter.

The `HyperLinkField` looks like this:

```
<asp:HyperLinkField
    HeaderText="Movie Categories"
    DataTextField="Name"
```

```
DataNavigateUrlFields="Id"
DataNavigateUrlFormatString="Details.aspx?id={0}" />
```

The `DataNavigateUrlFields` property represents the fields used with the `DataNavigateFormatString`, which plugs the value of the ID column from the `DataNavigateUrlFields` into the `{0}` placeholder.

> **NOTE**
>
> The `DataNavigateUrlFields` property accepts a comma-separated list of column names. You can use multiple placeholders in `DataNavigateUrlFormatString`.

When you link to the page in Listing 11.23, the list of matching movies displays. The `SqlDataSource` control includes a `QueryStringParameter` that represents the movie category ID query string parameter.

You also can use `HyperLinkFields` when working with frames. For example, the page in Listing 11.24 employs `GridView` to display a list of movies. The page also includes `iframe` (inline frame), which displays details for a particular movie; `iframe` displays the page contained in Listing 11.25 (see Figure 11.17).

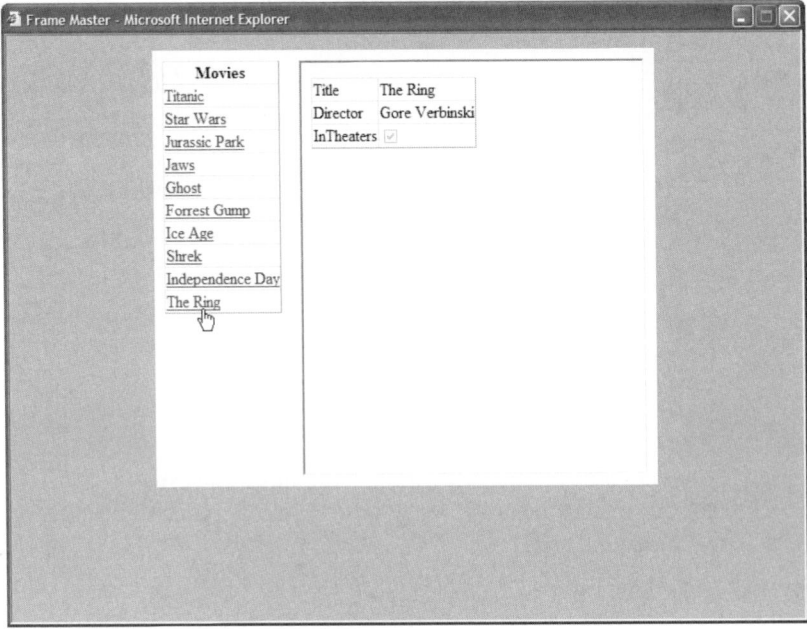

FIGURE 11.17   Displaying a single-page Master/Detail form.

LISTING 11.24   FrameMaster.aspx

```aspx
<%@ Page Language="C#" %>
<!DOCTYPE html PUBLIC "-//W3C//DTD XHTML 1.0 Transitional//EN"
    "http://www.w3.org/TR/xhtml1/DTD/xhtml1-transitional.dtd">
<html xmlns="http://www.w3.org/1999/xhtml" >
<head id="Head1" runat="server">
    <style type="text/css">
        html
        {
            background-color:silver;
        }
        .content
        {
            width:500px;
            margin:auto;
            background-color:white;
        }
        .column
        {
            padding:10px;
            float:left;
        }
        #FrameDetails
        {
            width:100%;
            height:400px;
        }
    </style>
    <title>Frame Master</title>
</head>
<body>
    <form id="form1" runat="server">
    <div class="content">

    <div class="column">

    <asp:GridView
        id="grdMovies"
        DataSourceID="srcMovies"
        AutoGenerateColumns="false"
        Runat="server">
        <Columns>
        <asp:HyperLinkField
            HeaderText="Movies"
            DataTextField="Title"
```

```
            DataNavigateUrlFields="Id"
            DataNavigateUrlFormatString="FrameDetails.aspx?id={0}"
            Target="FrameDetails" />
        </Columns>
    </asp:GridView>

    <asp:SqlDataSource
        id="srcMovies"
        ConnectionString="<%$ ConnectionStrings:Movies %>"
        SelectCommand="SELECT * FROM Movies"
        Runat="server" />

    </div>
    <div class="column">

    <iframe name="FrameDetails" id="FrameDetails"></iframe>

    </div>

    <br style="clear:both" />
    </div>
    </form>
</body>
</html>
```

LISTING 11.25   FrameDetails.aspx

```
<%@ Page Language="C#" %>
<!DOCTYPE html PUBLIC "-//W3C//DTD XHTML 1.0 Transitional//EN"
    "http://www.w3.org/TR/xhtml1/DTD/xhtml1-transitional.dtd">
<html xmlns="http://www.w3.org/1999/xhtml" >
<head id="Head1" runat="server">
    <title>Frame Details</title>
</head>
<body>
    <form id="form1" runat="server">
    <div>

    <asp:DetailsView
        id="dtlMovie"
        DataSourceID="srcMovieDetails"
        Runat="server" />

    <asp:SqlDataSource
```

```
        id="srcMovieDetails"
        ConnectionString="<%$ ConnectionStrings:Movies %>"
        SelectCommand="SELECT Title, Director, InTheaters
            FROM Movies WHERE Id=@MovieId"
        Runat="server">
        <SelectParameters>
        <asp:QueryStringParameter
            Name="MovieId"
            QueryStringField="id" />
        </SelectParameters>
    </asp:SqlDataSource>

    </div>
    </form>
</body>
</html>
```

The HyperLinkField contained in Listing 11.24 includes a Target property, which contains the name of the iframe. When you click a movie link, the FrameDetails.aspx page opens in the named iframe.

HyperLinkField supports the following properties:

▶ **DataNavigateUrlFields**—Represents the field or fields from the data source to use with DataNavigateUrlFormatString.

▶ **DataNavigateUrlFormatString**—Represents a format string that can be used to create the hyperlink.

▶ **DataTextField**—Represents a field from the data source to use for the hyperlink label.

▶ **DataTextFormatString**—Represents a format string that can be used to format the hyperlink label.

▶ **NavigateUrl**—Represents a fixed link to another page.

▶ **Target**—Represents the target of a link. Possible values include blank, parent, self, and top. You can also supply the name of a frame or iframe.

▶ **Text**—Represents fixed text to display as the label for the hyperlink.

Using ImageFields

You use ImageField to display an image stored on the server's hard drive. You can't use ImageField to display images stored in a database table.

The page in Listing 11.26 illustrates how you can use ImageField when creating a simple photo gallery (see Figure 11.18).

FIGURE 11.18 Using ImageField with the GridView control.

LISTING 11.26 ShowImageField.aspx

```
<%@ Page Language="C#" %>
<!DOCTYPE html PUBLIC "-//W3C//DTD XHTML 1.1//EN"
"http://www.w3.org/TR/xhtml11/DTD/xhtml11.dtd">
<script runat="server">

    protected void frmPhoto_ItemInserting(object sender, FormViewInsertEventArgs e)
    {
        // Get the FileUpload control
        FileUpload upPhoto = (FileUpload)frmPhoto.FindControl("upPhoto");
        srcImages.InsertParameters["FileName"].DefaultValue = upPhoto.FileName;

        string savePath = MapPath("~/Photos/" + upPhoto.FileName);
        // Save contents to file system
        upPhoto.SaveAs(savePath);
    }
</script>
```

```
<html xmlns="http://www.w3.org/1999/xhtml" >
<head id="Head1" runat="server">
    <title>Show ImageField</title>
</head>
<body>
    <form id="form1" runat="server">
    <div>

    <asp:GridView
        id="grdImages"
        DataSourceID="srcImages"
        AutoGenerateColumns="false"
        ShowHeader="false"
        Runat="server">
        <Columns>
        <asp:ImageField
            DataImageUrlField="FileName"
            DataImageUrlFormatString="~/Photos/{0}"
            DataAlternateTextField="AltText"
            ControlStyle-Width="200px" />
        </Columns>
    </asp:GridView>

    <asp:SqlDataSource
        id="srcImages"
        ConnectionString="<%$ ConnectionStrings:Photos %>"
        SelectCommand="SELECT FileName, AltText FROM Photos"
        InsertCommand="INSERT Photos (FileName, AltText)
            VALUES (@FileName, @AltText)"
        Runat="server">
        <InsertParameters>
            <asp:Parameter Name="FileName" />
        </InsertParameters>
    </asp:SqlDataSource>

    <hr />
    <asp:FormView
        id="frmPhoto"
        DefaultMode="Insert"
        DataSourceID="srcImages"
        OnItemInserting="frmPhoto_ItemInserting"
        Runat="server">
        <InsertItemTemplate>
        <h1>Add Photo</h1>
        <asp:Label
```

```
                id="lblPhoto"
                Text="Photo:"
                AssociatedControlID="upPhoto"
                Runat="server" />
        <br />
        <asp:FileUpload
                id="upPhoto"
                Runat="server" />
        <br />
        <asp:Label
                id="lblAltText"
                Text="Alternate Text:"
                AssociatedControlID="txtAltText"
                Runat="server" />
        <br />
        <asp:TextBox
                id="txtAltText"
                Text='<%# Bind("AltText") %>'
                Columns="50"
                Runat="server" />
        <br />
        <asp:Button
                id="btnInsert"
                Text="Add New Photo"
                CommandName="Insert"
                Runat="server" />
        </InsertItemTemplate>
    </asp:FormView>

    </div>
    </form>
</body>
</html>
```

The GridView in Listing 11.26 contains ImageField that looks like this:

```
<asp:ImageField
    DataImageUrlField="FileName"
    DataImageUrlFormatString="~/Photos/{0}"
    DataAlternateTextField="AltText"
    ControlStyle-Width="200px" />
```

The DataImageUrlField property contains the name of a field from the data source that represents the path to an image on the server hard drive. The DataImageUrlFormatString enables you to format this path. Finally, the DataAlternateTextField enables you to specify the value of the alt attribute used by the <img> tag.

WEB STANDARDS NOTE

Always supply an alt attribute for your <img> tags so that blind users of your web application can interpret an image's meaning. In the case of purely decorative images, create an empty alt attribute (alt="").

An ImageField supports the following properties:

- ▶ **AlternateText**—Enables you to specify fixed alternate text.
- ▶ **DataAlternateTextField**—Enables you to specify a field that represents the alternate text.
- ▶ **DataAlternateTextFormatString**—Enables you to format the alternate text.
- ▶ **DataImageUrlField**—Enables you to specify a field that represents the image path.
- ▶ **DataImageUrlFormatString**—Enables you to format the image path.
- ▶ **NullImageUrl**—Enables you to specify an alternate image when the DataImageUrlField is Nothing (null).

Using `TemplateFields`

A TemplateField enables you to add any content to a GridView column that you need, which can contain HTML, DataBinding expressions, or ASP.NET controls.

TemplateFields are particularly useful when you use GridView to edit database records. You can use TemplateField to customize the user interface and add validation to the fields being edited.

For example, the page in Listing 11.27 contains a GridView that enables you to edit the records contained in the Movies database table. TemplateFields render the user interface for editing the movie title and category columns (see Figure 11.19).

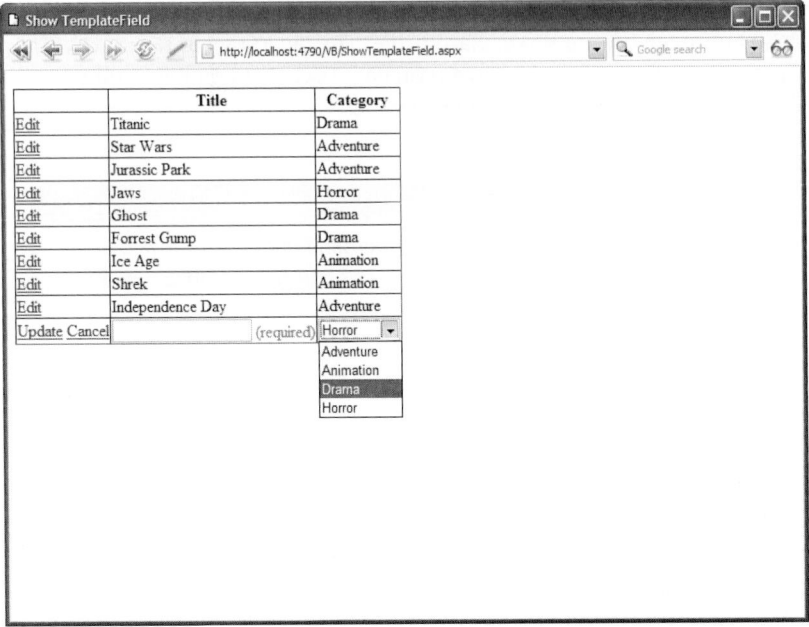

FIGURE 11.19   Using TemplateFields with the GridView control.

LISTING 11.27   ShowTemplateField.aspx

```
<%@ Page Language="C#" %>
<!DOCTYPE html PUBLIC "-//W3C//DTD XHTML 1.1//EN"
  "http://www.w3.org/TR/xhtml11/DTD/xhtml11.dtd">
<html xmlns="http://www.w3.org/1999/xhtml" >
<head id="Head1" runat="server">
    <title>Show TemplateField</title>
</head>
<body>
    <form id="form1" runat="server">
    <div>

    <asp:GridView
        id="grdMovies"
        DataSourceID="srcMovies"
        DataKeyNames="Id"
        AutoGenerateColumns="false"
        AutoGenerateEditButton="true"
        Runat="server">
        <Columns>
        <asp:TemplateField HeaderText="Title">
```

```
        <ItemTemplate>
        <%# Eval("Title") %>
        </ItemTemplate>
        <EditItemTemplate>
        <asp:TextBox
            id="txtTitle"
            Text='<%# Bind("Title") %>'
            Runat="server" />
        <asp:RequiredFieldValidator
            id="valTitle"
            ControlToValidate="txtTitle"
            Text="(required)"
            Runat="server" />
        </EditItemTemplate>
    </asp:TemplateField>
    <asp:TemplateField HeaderText="Category">
        <ItemTemplate>
        <%# Eval("Name") %>
        </ItemTemplate>
        <EditItemTemplate>
        <asp:DropDownList
            id="ddlCategory"
            DataSourceID="srcMovieCategories"
            DataTextField="Name"
            DataValueField="Id"
            SelectedValue='<%# Bind("CategoryId") %>'
            Runat="server" />
        </EditItemTemplate>
    </asp:TemplateField>
    </Columns>
</asp:GridView>

<asp:SqlDataSource
    id="srcMovies"
    ConnectionString='<%$ ConnectionStrings:Movies %>'
    SelectCommand="SELECT Movies.Id, Title, CategoryId, Name
        FROM Movies JOIN MovieCategories
        ON MovieCategories.Id = Movies.CategoryId"
    UpdateCommand="UPDATE Movies SET Title=@Title, CategoryId=@CategoryId
        WHERE Id=@Id"
    Runat="server" />

<asp:SqlDataSource
    id="srcMovieCategories"
    ConnectionString='<%$ ConnectionStrings:Movies %>'
```

```
        SelectCommand="SELECT Id, Name FROM MovieCategories"
        Runat="server" />

    </div>
    </form>
</body>
</html>
```

GridView in Listing 11.27 contains two `TemplateFields`. The first `TemplateField` enables you to display and edit the value of the Title column. The contents of `ItemTemplate` display when a row *is not* selected for editing. The contents of `EditItemTemplate` display when the row *is* selected for editing.

`EditItemTemplate` for the Title column includes a `RequiredFieldValidator` control. This `RequiredFieldValidator` control prevents a user from updating a record without entering a value for the Title column.

The second `TemplateField` displays the value of the movie category column. `EditItemTemplate` contains a `DropDownList` control, which enables you to change the movie category associated with the record being edited.

`TemplateField` supports the following six types of templates:

▶ **AlternatingItemTemplate**—The contents of this template display for every other row rendered by `GridView`.

▶ **EditItemTemplate**—The contents of this template display when a row is selected for editing.

▶ **FooterTemplate**—The contents of this template display in the column footer.

▶ **HeaderTemplate**—The contents of this template display in the column header.

▶ **InsertItemTemplate**—The contents of this template display when a new data item is inserted (does not apply to the `GridView` control).

▶ **ItemTemplate**—The contents of this template display for every row rendered by the `GridView`.

Working with `GridView` Control Events

The `GridView` control includes a rich set of events that you can handle to customize the control's behavior and appearance. These events can be divided into three groups.

First, the `GridView` control supports the following set of events raised when the control displays its rows:

▶ **DataBinding**—Raised immediately before GridView is bound to its data source.

▶ **DataBound**—Raised immediately after GridView is bound to its data source.

▶ **RowCreated**—Raised when each row in GridView is created.

▶ **RowDataBound**—Raised when each row in GridView is bound to data.

Second, the GridView control includes the following set of events raised when you edit records:

▶ **RowCommand**—Raised when an event is raised by a control contained in GridView.

▶ **RowUpdating**—Raised immediately before GridView updates a record.

▶ **RowUpdated**—Raised immediately after GridView updates a record.

▶ **RowDeleting**—Raised immediately before GridView deletes a record.

▶ **RowDeleted**—Raised immediately after GridView deletes a record.

▶ **RowCancelingEdit**—Raised when you cancel updating a record.

Finally, the GridView control supports the following events related to sorting, selecting, and paging:

▶ **PageIndexChanging**—Raised immediately before the current page changes.

▶ **PageIndexChanged**—Raised immediately after the current page changes.

▶ **Sorting**—Raised immediately before sorting.

▶ **Sorted**—Raised immediately after sorting.

▶ **SelectedIndexChanging**—Raised immediately before a row is selected.

▶ **SelectedIndexChanged**—Raised immediately after a row is selected.

In this section, you learn how to handle the RowDataBound event (my favorite event included with the GridView control) to create GridView special effects. You learn how to handle the RowDataBound event to highlight particular rows and show column summaries, and create nested Master/Detail forms.

Highlighting GridView Rows

Imagine that you want to highlight particular rows in GridView. For example, when displaying a table of sales totals, you might want to highlight the rows in which the sales are greater than a certain amount.

You can modify the appearance of individual rows in a GridView control by handling the RowDataBound event. For example, the page in Listing 11.28 displays every movie that has a box office total greater than $300,000.00 with a yellow background color (see Figure 11.20).

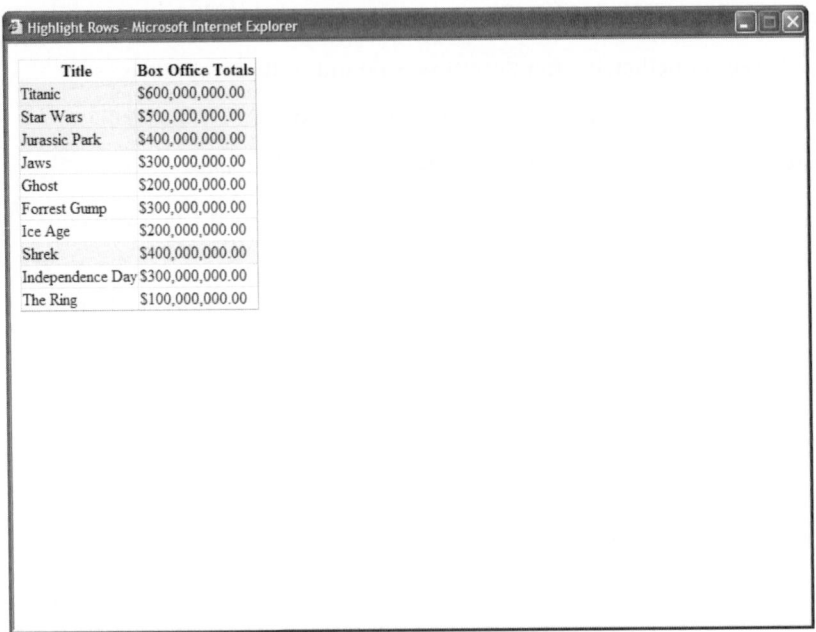

FIGURE 11.20 Highlighting rows in the GridView control.

LISTING 11.28 HighlightRows.aspx

```
<%@ Page Language="C#" %>
<!DOCTYPE html PUBLIC "-//W3C//DTD XHTML 1.1//EN"
"http://www.w3.org/TR/xhtml11/DTD/xhtml11.dtd">
<script runat="server">

    protected void grdMovies_RowDataBound(object sender, GridViewRowEventArgs e)
    {
        if (e.Row.RowType == DataControlRowType.DataRow)
        {
            decimal boxOfficeTotals = (decimal)DataBinder.Eval(e.Row.DataItem,
"BoxOfficeTotals");
            if (boxOfficeTotals > 300000000)
                e.Row.BackColor = System.Drawing.Color.Yellow;
        }
    }
</script>
<html xmlns="http://www.w3.org/1999/xhtml" >
<head id="Head1" runat="server">
    <title>Highlight Rows</title>
</head>
```

```
<body>
    <form id="form1" runat="server">
    <div>

    <asp:GridView
        id="grdMovies"
        DataSourceID="srcMovies"
        OnRowDataBound="grdMovies_RowDataBound"
        AutoGenerateColumns="false"
        Runat="server">
        <Columns>
        <asp:BoundField
            DataField="Title"
            HeaderText="Title" />
        <asp:BoundField
            DataField="BoxOfficeTotals"
            DataFormatString="{0:c}"
            HtmlEncode="false"
            HeaderText="Box Office Totals" />
        </Columns>
    </asp:GridView>

    <asp:SqlDataSource
        id="srcMovies"
        ConnectionString="<%$ ConnectionStrings:Movies %>"
        SelectCommand="SELECT * FROM Movies"
        Runat="server" />

    </div>
    </form>
</body>
</html>
```

In Listing 11.28, the `grdMovies_RowDataBound()` method is executed when `GridView` renders each of its rows (including its header and footer). The second parameter passed to this event handler is an instance of the `GridViewRowEventArgs` class. This class exposes a `GridViewRow` object that represents the row being bound.

The `GridViewRow` object supports several useful properties (this is not a complete list):

▶ **Cells**—Represents the collection of table row cells associated with the row being bound.

▶ **DataItem**—Represents the data item associated with the row being bound.

▶ **DataItemIndex**—Represents the index of the data item in its DataSet associated with the row being bound.

- **RowIndex**—Represents the index of the row being bound.
- **RowState**—Represents the state of the row being bound. Possible values are `Alternate`, `Normal`, `Selected`, and `Edit`. Because these values can be combined (for example, `RowState` can be `Alternate  Edit`), use a bitwise comparison `RowState`.
- **RowType**—Represents the type of row being bound. Possible values are `DataRow`, `Footer`, `Header`, `NullRow`, `Pager`, and `Separator`.

In Listing 11.28, the `RowType` property verifies that the row is `DataRow` (not a header row or some other type of row). The `DataItem` property retrieves the database record associated with the row. The `DataBinder.Eval()` method retrieves the value of the `BoxOfficeColumn`.

Displaying Column Summaries

Imagine that you want to display a column total at the bottom of a column. In that case, you can handle the `GridView RowDataBound` event to sum the values in a column and display the summary in the column footer.

For example, the page in Listing 11.29 contains a `GridView` control that displays a summary column representing the total box office sales of all movies (see Figure 11.21).

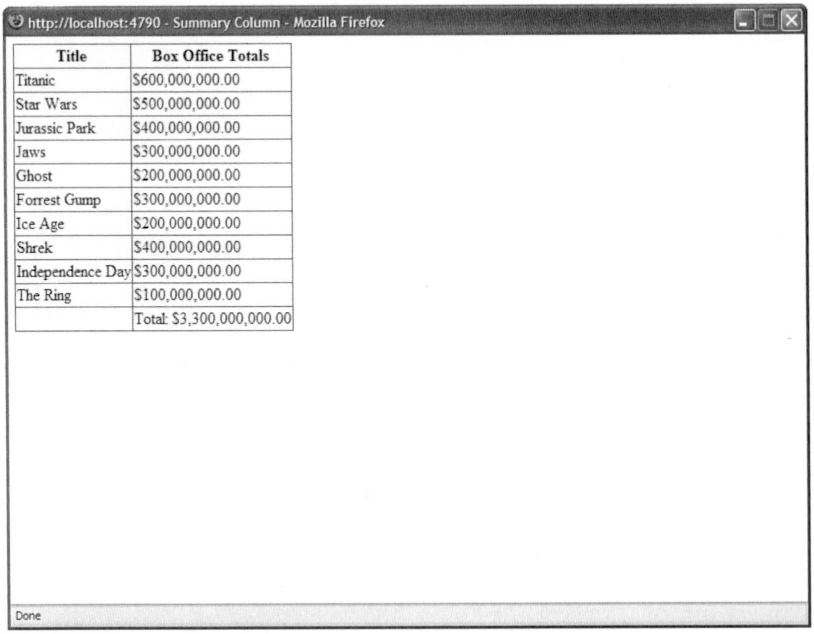

Title	Box Office Totals
Titanic	$600,000,000.00
Star Wars	$500,000,000.00
Jurassic Park	$400,000,000.00
Jaws	$300,000,000.00
Ghost	$200,000,000.00
Forrest Gump	$300,000,000.00
Ice Age	$200,000,000.00
Shrek	$400,000,000.00
Independence Day	$300,000,000.00
The Ring	$100,000,000.00
	Total: $3,300,000,000.00

FIGURE 11.21 Displaying a column summary.

LISTING 11.29   SummaryColumn.aspx

```
<%@ Page Language="C#" %>
<!DOCTYPE html PUBLIC "-//W3C//DTD XHTML 1.1//EN"
"http://www.w3.org/TR/xhtml11/DTD/xhtml11.dtd">
<script runat="server">

    private decimal _boxOfficeTotalsTotal = 0;

    protected void grdMovies_RowDataBound(object sender, GridViewRowEventArgs e)
    {
        if (e.Row.RowType == DataControlRowType.DataRow)
        {
            decimal boxOfficeTotals = (decimal)DataBinder.Eval(e.Row.DataItem,
"BoxOfficeTotals");
            _boxOfficeTotalsTotal += boxOfficeTotals;
        }
        if (e.Row.RowType == DataControlRowType.Footer)
        {
            Label lblSummary = (Label)e.Row.FindControl("lblSummary");
            lblSummary.Text = String.Format("Total: {0:c}", _boxOfficeTotalsTotal);
        }
    }
</script>
<html xmlns="http://www.w3.org/1999/xhtml" >
<head id="Head1" runat="server">
    <title>Summary Column</title>
</head>
<body>
    <form id="form1" runat="server">
    <div>

    <asp:GridView
        id="grdMovies"
        DataSourceID="srcMovies"
        OnRowDataBound="grdMovies_RowDataBound"
        AutoGenerateColumns="false"
        ShowFooter="true"
        Runat="server">
        <Columns>
        <asp:BoundField
            DataField="Title"
            HeaderText="Title" />
        <asp:TemplateField HeaderText="Box Office Totals">
        <ItemTemplate>
            <%# Eval("BoxOfficeTotals", "{0:c}") %>
```

```
            </ItemTemplate>
            <FooterTemplate>
                <asp:Label
                    id="lblSummary"
                    Runat="server" />
            </FooterTemplate>
            </asp:TemplateField>
            </Columns>
        </asp:GridView>

        <asp:SqlDataSource
            id="srcMovies"
            ConnectionString="<%$ ConnectionStrings:Movies %>"
            SelectCommand="SELECT * FROM Movies"
            Runat="server" />

        </div>
        </form>
</body>
</html>
```

The GridView control uses a TemplateField to represent the BoxOfficeTotals column. The TemplateField includes a <FooterTemplate> that contains a Label control. The grdMovies_RowDataBound() method displays the total of the box office totals in this Label control.

Displaying Nested Master/Details Forms

You also can handle the RowDataBound event to create nested Master/Details forms. The page in Listing 11.30 displays a list of movie categories and displays a list of matching movies under each category (see Figure 11.22).

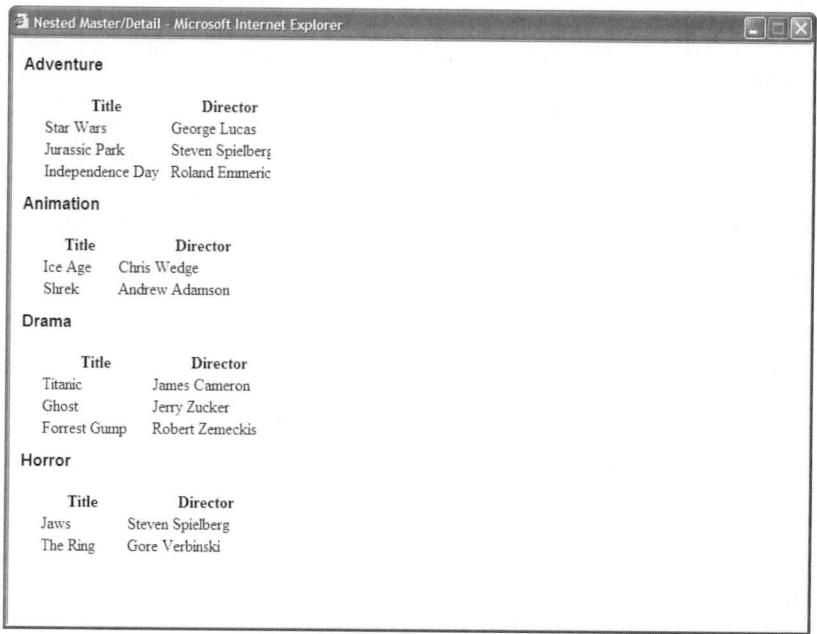

FIGURE 11.22   Displaying a nested Master/Detail form.

LISTING 11.30   NestedMasterDetail.aspx

```
<%@ Page Language="C#" %>
<!DOCTYPE html PUBLIC "-//W3C//DTD XHTML 1.1//EN"
"http://www.w3.org/TR/xhtml11/DTD/xhtml11.dtd">
<script runat="server">

    protected void grdMovieCategories_RowDataBound(object sender,
➥GridViewRowEventArgs e)
    {
        if (e.Row.RowType == DataControlRowType.DataRow)
        {
            int categoryId = (int)DataBinder.Eval(e.Row.DataItem,"Id");
            SqlDataSource srcMovies = (SqlDataSource)e.Row.FindControl("srcMovies");
            srcMovies.SelectParameters["CategoryId"].DefaultValue =
categoryId.ToString();
        }
    }

</script>
<html xmlns="http://www.w3.org/1999/xhtml" >
<head id="Head1" runat="server">
    <style type="text/css">
```

```
        .categories h1
        {
            font:bold 16px Arial, Sans-Serif;
        }
        .movies
        {
            margin-left:20px;
            margin-bottom:10px;
            width:100%;
        }
    </style>
    <title>Nested Master/Detail</title>
</head>
<body>
    <form id="form1" runat="server">
    <div>

    <asp:GridView
        id="grdMovies"
        DataSourceID="srcMovieCategories"
        OnRowDataBound="grdMovieCategories_RowDataBound"
        AutoGenerateColumns="false"
        CssClass="categories"
        ShowHeader="false"
        GridLines="none"
        Runat="server">
        <Columns>
        <asp:TemplateField>
        <ItemTemplate>
            <h1><%# Eval("Name") %></h1>
            <asp:GridView
                id="grdMovies"
                DataSourceId="srcMovies"
                CssClass="movies"
                GridLines="none"
                Runat="server" />

            <asp:SqlDataSource
                id="srcMovies"
                ConnectionString="<%$ ConnectionStrings:Movies %>"
                SelectCommand="SELECT Title,Director FROM Movies
                    WHERE CategoryId=@CategoryId"
                Runat="server">
                <SelectParameters>
                    <asp:Parameter Name="CategoryId" />
                </SelectParameters>
```

```
            </asp:SqlDataSource>
        </ItemTemplate>
        </asp:TemplateField>
        </Columns>
    </asp:GridView>

    <asp:SqlDataSource
        id="srcMovieCategories"
        ConnectionString="<%$ ConnectionStrings:Movies %>"
        SelectCommand="SELECT Id,Name FROM MovieCategories"
        Runat="server" />



    </div>
    </form>
</body>
</html>
```

The grdMovieCategories_RowDataBound() method handles the RowDataBound event. This event handler grabs the movie category ID from the current row's DataItem property. Next, it retrieves the SqlDataSource control contained in the grdMovieCategories TemplateField. Finally, it assigns the movie category ID to a parameter contained in the SqlDataSource control's SelectParameters collection.

NOTE

You must use the FindControl() method to get the SqlDataSource control from the TemplateField. The templates in a TemplateField each create their own naming containers to prevent naming collisions. The FindControl() method enables you to search a naming container for a control with a matching ID.

Extending the `GridView` Control

Like any other control in the ASP.NET Framework, if you don't like any aspect of the GridView control, you always have the option of extending the control. In this section, you learn how to extend the GridView control with custom fields.

To create a custom field, you can inherit a new class from any of the existing fields or any of the following base classes:

▶ **DataControlField**—The base class for all fields.

▶ **ButtonFieldBase**—The base class for all button fields, such as the ButtonField and CommandField.

In this section, you learn how to create a long text field, a delete button field, and a validated field.

Creating a LongTextField

None of the existing GridView fields do a good job of handling large amounts of text. You can fix this problem by creating a custom field, named the LongTextField, which you can use to display the value of text columns regardless of the length of the text.

In normal display mode, LongTextField displays the text in a scrolling <div> tag. In edit display mode, the text appears in a multiline TextBox control (see Figure 11.23).

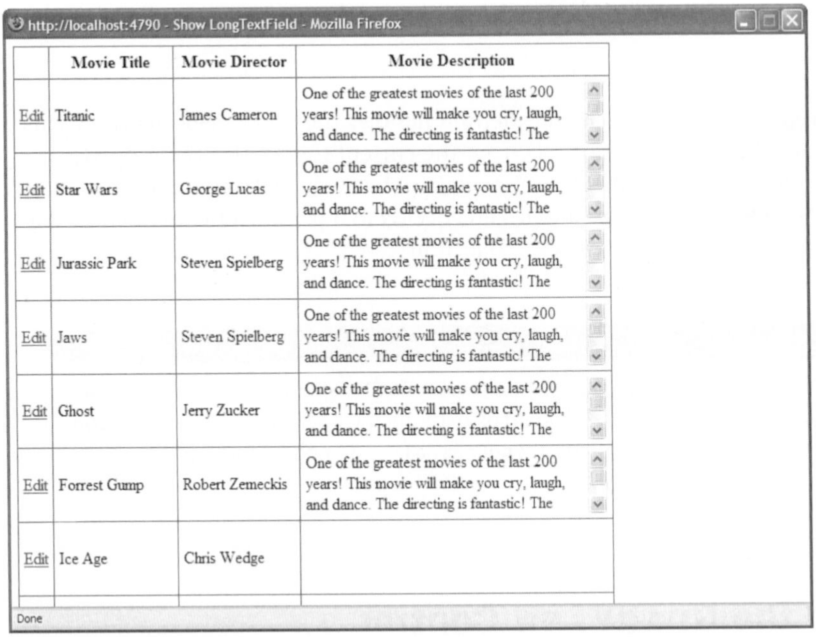

FIGURE 11.23   Displaying a long text field.

To create a custom field, a new class must be inherited from the base BoundField control. The custom LongTextField is contained in Listing 11.31.

LISTING 11.31 LongTextField.cs

```csharp
using System;
using System.Web.UI;
using System.Web.UI.WebControls;
using System.Web.UI.HtmlControls;

namespace myControls
{
    /// <summary>
    /// Enables you to display a long text field
    /// </summary>
    public class LongTextField : BoundField
    {
        private Unit _width = new Unit("250px");
        private Unit _height = new Unit("60px");

        /// <summary>
        /// The Width of the field
        /// </summary>
        public Unit Width
        {
            get { return _width; }
            set { _width = value; }
        }

        /// <summary>
        /// The Height of the field
        /// </summary>
        public Unit Height
        {
            get { return _height; }
            set { _height = value; }
        }

        /// <summary>
        /// Builds the contents of the field
        /// </summary>
        protected override void InitializeDataCell(DataControlFieldCell cell,
DataControlRowState rowState)
        {
            // If not editing, show in scrolling div
            if ((rowState & DataControlRowState.Edit) == 0)
            {
                HtmlGenericControl div = new HtmlGenericControl("div");
                div.Attributes["class"] = "longTextField";
```

```
        div.Style[HtmlTextWriterStyle.Width] = _width.ToString();
        div.Style[HtmlTextWriterStyle.Height] = _height.ToString();
        div.Style[HtmlTextWriterStyle.Overflow] = "auto";

        div.DataBinding += new EventHandler(div_DataBinding);

        cell.Controls.Add(div);
    }
    else
    {
        TextBox txtEdit = new TextBox();
        txtEdit.TextMode = TextBoxMode.MultiLine;
        txtEdit.Width = _width;
        txtEdit.Height = _height;

        txtEdit.DataBinding += new EventHandler(txtEdit_DataBinding);

        cell.Controls.Add(txtEdit);
    }
}

/// <summary>
/// Called when databound in display mode
/// </summary>
void div_DataBinding(object s, EventArgs e)
{
    HtmlGenericControl div = (HtmlGenericControl)s;

    // Get the field value
    Object value = this.GetValue(div.NamingContainer);

    // Assign the formatted value
    div.InnerText = this.FormatDataValue(value, this.HtmlEncode);
}

/// <summary>
/// Called when databound in edit mode
/// </summary>
void txtEdit_DataBinding(object s, EventArgs e)
{
    TextBox txtEdit = (TextBox)s;

    // Get the field value
    Object value = this.GetValue(txtEdit.NamingContainer);

    // Assign the formatted value
```

```
            txtEdit.Text = this.FormatDataValue(value, this.HtmlEncode);
        }

    }
}
```

In Listing 11.31, the `InitializeDataCell()` method is overridden. This method is responsible for creating all the controls that the custom field contains.

First, a check is made to determine whether the field is rendered when the row is selected for editing. A bitwise comparison must be performed with the `rowState` parameter because the `rowState` parameter can contain combinations of the values `Alternate`, `Normal`, `Selected`, and `Edit` (for example, `RowState` can be both `Alternate` and `Edit`).

When the row is not in edit mode, a `<div>` tag is created to contain the text. `HtmlGenericControl` represents the `<div>` tag. When `GridView` is bound to its data source, the `<div>` tags get the value of its `innerText` property from the `div_DataBinding()` method.

When the row is selected for editing, a multiline `TextBox` control is created. When `GridView` is bound to its data source, the `TextBox` control's `Text` property gets its value from the `txtEdit_DataBinding()` method.

You can experiment with `LongTextField` with the page in Listing 11.32. This page uses `LongTextField` to display the value of the Movie Description column.

LISTING 11.32   ShowLongTextField.aspx

```
<%@ Page Language="C#" %>
<%@ Register TagPrefix="custom" Namespace="myControls" %>
<!DOCTYPE html PUBLIC "-//W3C//DTD XHTML 1.1//EN"
    "http://www.w3.org/TR/xhtml11/DTD/xhtml11.dtd">
<html xmlns="http://www.w3.org/1999/xhtml" >
<head id="Head1" runat="server">
    <style type="text/css">
        .grid td, .grid th
        {
            padding:5px;
        }
    </style>
    <title>Show LongTextField</title>
</head>
<body>
    <form id="form1" runat="server">
    <div>

    <asp:GridView
```

```
        id="grdMovies"
        CssClass="grid"
        DataSourceID="srcMovies"
        DataKeyNames="Id"
        AutoGenerateColumns="false"
        AutoGenerateEditButton="true"
        Runat="server">
        <Columns>
        <asp:BoundField
            DataField="Title"
            HeaderText="Movie Title" />
        <asp:BoundField
            DataField="Director"
            HeaderText="Movie Director" />
        <custom:LongTextField
            DataField="Description"
            Width="300px"
            Height="60px"
            HeaderText="Movie Description" />
        </Columns>
    </asp:GridView>

    <asp:SqlDataSource
        id="srcMovies"
        ConnectionString="<%$ ConnectionStrings:Movies %>"
        SelectCommand="SELECT Id, Title, Director, Description
            FROM Movies"
        UpdateCommand="UPDATE Movies SET
            Title=@Title,Director=@Director,Description=
            WHERE Id=@Id"
        Runat="server" />

    </div>
    </form>
</body>
</html>
```

Creating a `DeleteButtonField`

I don't like the Delete button rendered by the `GridView` control's `CommandField`. The problem is that it does not provide you with any warning before you delete a record. In this section, we fix this problem by creating a Delete button that displays a client-side confirmation dialog box (see Figure 11.24).

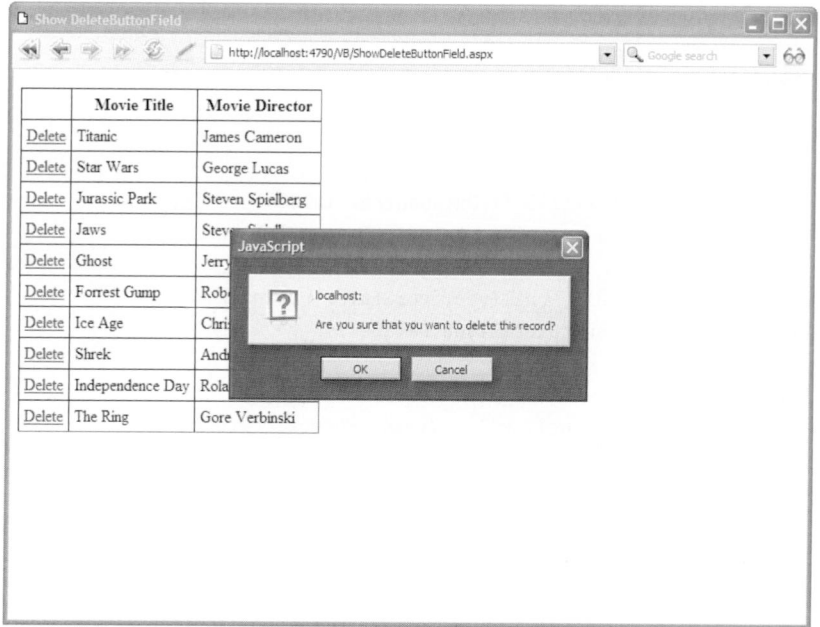

FIGURE 11.24   Displaying a confirmation dialog box.

DeleteButtonField inherits from the ButtonField class. The code for the custom field is contained in Listing 11.33.

LISTING 11.33   DeleteButtonField.cs

```
using System;
using System.Web.UI.WebControls;

namespace myControls
{
    /// <summary>
    /// Displays a confirmation before deleting a record
    /// </summary>
    public class DeleteButtonField : ButtonField
    {
        private string _confirmText = "Delete this record?";

        public string ConfirmText
        {
            get { return _confirmText; }
            set { _confirmText = value; }
        }
```

```
        public DeleteButtonField()
        {
            this.CommandName = "Delete";
            this.Text = "Delete";
        }

        public override void InitializeCell(DataControlFieldCell cell,
DataControlCellType cellType, DataControlRowState rowState, int rowIndex)
        {
            base.InitializeCell(cell, cellType, rowState, rowIndex);
            if (cellType == DataControlCellType.DataCell)
            {
                WebControl button = (WebControl)cell.Controls[0];
                button.Attributes["onclick"] = String.Format("return
➥confirm('{0}');", _confirmText);
            }
        }

    }
}
```

Most of the work in Listing 11.33 is handled by the base ButtonField class. The
InitializeCell() method is overridden so that the button can be grabbed. The button is
added to the cell by the base ButtonField's InitializeCell() method.

To create the confirmation dialog box, an onclick attribute is added to the button. If the
JavaScript confirm statement returns false, the button click is canceled.

You can test the DeleteButtonField with the page in Listing 11.34. This page enables you
to delete records from the Movies database table.

LISTING 11.34   ShowDeleteButtonField.aspx

```
<%@ Page Language="C#" %>
<%@ Register TagPrefix="custom" Namespace="myControls" %>
<!DOCTYPE html PUBLIC "-//W3C//DTD XHTML 1.1//EN"
  "http://www.w3.org/TR/xhtml11/DTD/xhtml11.dtd">
<html xmlns="http://www.w3.org/1999/xhtml" >
<head id="Head1" runat="server">
    <style type="text/css">
        .grid td, .grid th
        {
            padding:5px;
        }
    </style>
```

```
        <title>Show DeleteButtonField</title>
    </head>
<body>
    <form id="form1" runat="server">
    <div>

    <asp:GridView
        id="grdMovies"
        CssClass="grid"
        DataSourceID="srcMovies"
        DataKeyNames="Id"
        AutoGenerateColumns="false"
        Runat="server">
        <Columns>
        <custom:DeleteButtonField
            ConfirmText="Are you sure that you want to delete this record?" />
        <asp:BoundField
            DataField="Title"
            HeaderText="Movie Title" />
        <asp:BoundField
            DataField="Director"
            HeaderText="Movie Director" />
        </Columns>
    </asp:GridView>

    <asp:SqlDataSource
        id="srcMovies"
        ConnectionString="<%$ ConnectionStrings:Movies %>"
        SelectCommand="SELECT Id, Title, Director FROM Movies"
        DeleteCommand="DELETE Movies WHERE Id=@Id"
        Runat="server" />

    </div>
    </form>
</body>
</html>
```

Creating a ValidatedField

In this final section, we create a ValidatedField custom field, which automatically validates the data that a user enters into GridView when editing a record. ValidatedField uses RequiredFieldValidator to check whether a user has entered a value, and CompareValidator to check whether the value is the correct data type (see Figure 11.25).

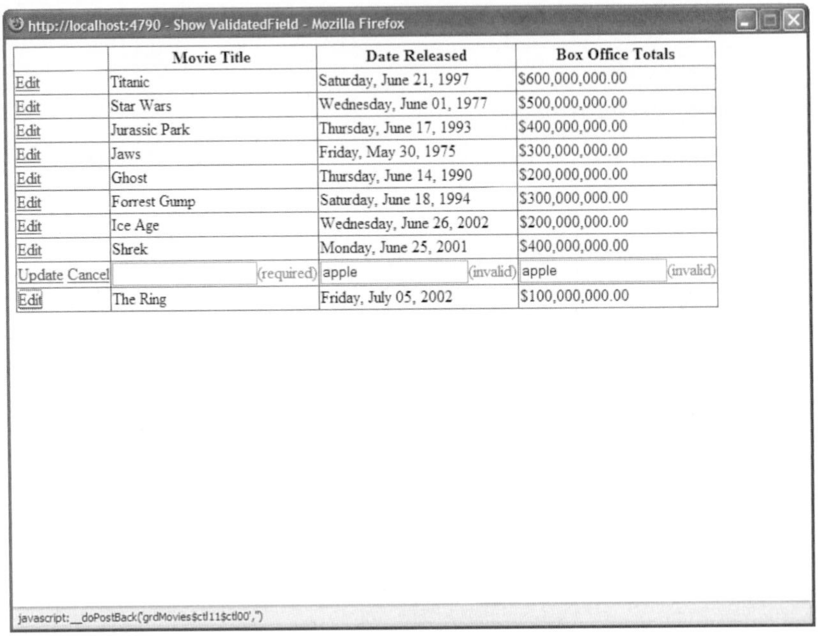
http://localhost:4790 - Show ValidatedField - Mozilla Firefox
Movie Title
Date Released
Box Office Totals
Edit Titanic Saturday, June 21, 1997 $600,000,000.00
Edit Star Wars Wednesday, June 01, 1977 $500,000,000.00
Edit Jurassic Park Thursday, June 17, 1993 $400,000,000.00
Edit Jaws Friday, May 30, 1975 $300,000,000.00
Edit Ghost Thursday, June 14, 1990 $200,000,000.00
Edit Forrest Gump Saturday, June 18, 1994 $300,000,000.00
Edit Ice Age Wednesday, June 26, 2002 $200,000,000.00
Edit Shrek Monday, June 25, 2001 $400,000,000.00
Update Cancel (required) apple (invalid) apple (invalid)
Edit The Ring Friday, July 05, 2002 $100,000,000.00
javascript:__doPostBack('grdMovies$ctl11$ctl00','')

FIGURE 11.25 Using `ValidatedField` to edit a record.

`ValidatedField` is a composite field. The field contains three child controls—a `TextBox`, `RequiredFieldValidator`, and `CompareValidator`—wrapped up in a container control.

The code for the `ValidatedField` is too long to include in this chapter. The entire source code (in both C# and VB.NET) can be downloaded from the book's website.

The source code for the `ValidatedField` contains two classes. It contains the `ValidatedField` class and the `EditContainer` class.

The `ValidatedField` class derives from the `BoundField` class and overrides the `InitializeDataCell()` method. When a row is not selected for editing, the field simply displays the value of the data item associated with it. When a row is selected for editing, the field creates a new `EditContainer` control.

The `EditContainer` control contains a `TextBox`, `RequiredFieldValidator`, and `CompareValidator`; `EditContainer` implements the `INamingContainer` interface. Implementing this interface prevents naming collisions when more than one instance of `ValidatedField` is used in a `GridView` row.

`ValidatedField` is used in the page in Listing 11.35. This page contains a `GridView` control that you can use to edit the Movies database table. The `GridView` control includes three `ValidatedFields`: for the Title, DateReleased, and BoxOfficeTotals columns.

If you edit a column and attempt to submit the column without entering a value, a validation error displays. Furthermore, if you attempt to enter a value that is not a date for the DateReleased column or a value that is not a currency amount for the BoxOfficeTotals column, a validation error displays.

LISTING 11.35 ShowValidatedField.aspx

```
<%@ Page Language="C#" %>
<%@ Register TagPrefix="custom" Namespace="myControls" %>
<!DOCTYPE html PUBLIC "-//W3C//DTD XHTML 1.1//EN"
    "http://www.w3.org/TR/xhtml11/DTD/xhtml11.dtd">
<html xmlns="http://www.w3.org/1999/xhtml" >
<head id="Head1" runat="server">
    <title>Show ValidatedField</title>
</head>
<body>
    <form id="form1" runat="server">
    <div>

    <asp:GridView
        id="grdMovies"
        DataKeyNames="Id"
        DataSourceID="srcMovies"
        AutoGenerateEditButton="true"
        AutoGenerateColumns="false"
        Runat="server">
        <Columns>
        <custom:ValidatedField
            DataField="Title"
            HeaderText="Movie Title" />
        <custom:ValidatedField
            DataField="DateReleased"
            DataFormatString="{0:D}"
            HtmlEncode="false"
            ValidationDataType="Date"
            HeaderText="Date Released" />
        <custom:ValidatedField
            DataField="BoxOfficeTotals"
            DataFormatString="{0:c}"
            HtmlEncode="false"
            ValidationDataType="Currency"
            HeaderText="Box Office Totals" />
        </Columns>
    </asp:GridView>
```

```
<asp:SqlDataSource
    id="srcMovies"
    ConnectionString="<%$ ConnectionStrings:Movies %>"
    SelectCommand="SELECT * FROM Movies"
    UpdateCommand="UPDATE Movies SET Title=@Title,
        DateReleased=@DateReleased, BoxOfficeTotals=@BoxOfficeTotals
        WHERE Id=@Id"
    Runat="server" />

</div>
</form>
</body>
</html>
```

Summary

In this chapter, you learned how to use the GridView control to display, select, sort, page, and edit database records. You also learn how to customize the appearance of the columns rendered by a column by using different types of fields. In particular, you learned how to use BoundFields, CheckboxFields, CommandFields, ImageFields, TemplateFields, ButtonFields, and HyperLinkFields.

Next, you learned how to handle the RowDataBound event to create GridView special effects. For example, you learned how to add column summaries to a GridView.

Finally, you learned how to extend the GridView control with custom fields. We created custom fields, which enable you to display large text fields, display a confirmation dialog box before a record is deleted, and display validation error messages when editing a record.

Using the DetailsView and FormView Controls

The DetailsView and FormView controls, the subject of this chapter, enable you to work with a single data item at a time. Both controls enable you to display, edit, insert, and delete data items such as database records. Furthermore, both controls enable you to page forward and backward through a set of data items.

The difference between the two controls concerns the user interface that the controls render. The DetailsView control always renders each field in a separate HTML table row. The FormView control, on the other hand, uses a template that enables you to completely customize the user interface rendered by the control.

Using the DetailsView Control

In this section, you learn how to use the DetailsView control when working with database records. In particular, you learn how to display, page, edit, insert, and delete database records with the DetailsView. You also learn how to format the appearance of the DetailsView control.

Displaying Data with the DetailsView Control

A DetailsView control renders an HTML table that displays the contents of a single database record. The DetailsView supports both declarative and programmatic databinding.

For example, the page in Listing 12.1 displays a record from the Movies database table, using declarative databinding (see Figure 12.1).

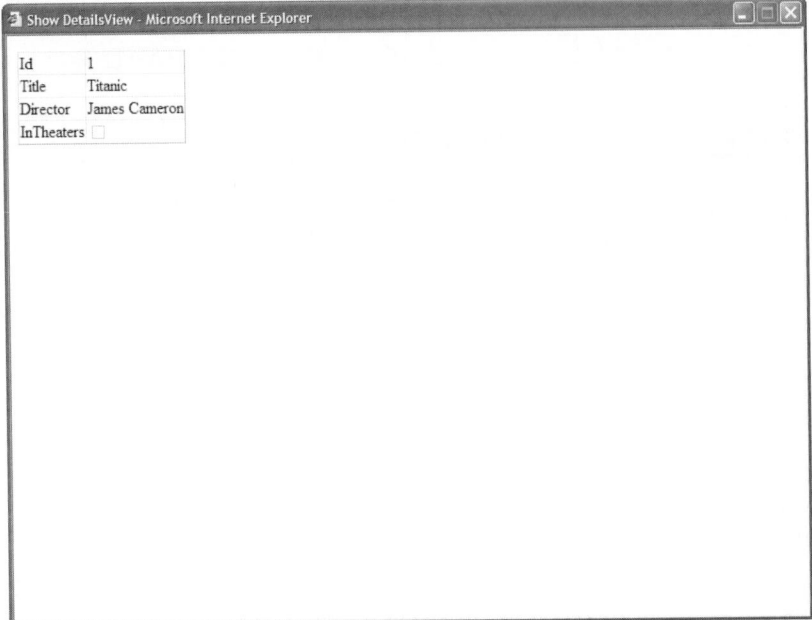

FIGURE 12.1   Displaying a movie record.

LISTING 12.1   ShowDetailsView.aspx

```
<%@ Page Language="C#" %>
<!DOCTYPE html PUBLIC "-//W3C//DTD XHTML 1.1//EN"
    "http://www.w3.org/TR/xhtml11/DTD/xhtml11.dtd">
<html xmlns="http://www.w3.org/1999/xhtml" >
<head id="Head1" runat="server">
    <title>Show DetailsView</title>
</head>
<body>
    <form id="form1" runat="server">
    <div>

    <asp:DetailsView
        id="dtlMovies"
        DataSourceID="srcMovies"
        Runat="server" />

    <asp:SqlDataSource
        id="srcMovies"
        ConnectionString="<%$ ConnectionStrings:Movies %>"
        SelectCommand="SELECT Id,Title,Director,InTheaters FROM Movies
```

```
        WHERE Id=1"
      Runat="server" />

  </div>
  </form>
</body>
</html>
```

In Listing 12.1, the SQL Select statement associated with the SqlDataSource control retrieves the first movie from the Movies database table. The DetailsView control is bound to the SqlDataSource control through its DataSourceID property.

You also can bind a DetailsView control programmatically to a data source. The page in Listing 12.2 contains a DetailsView bound to a collection of employees.

LISTING 12.2   ShowEmployee.aspx

```
<%@ Page Language="C#" %>
<%@ Import Namespace="System.Collections.Generic" %>
<!DOCTYPE html PUBLIC "-//W3C//DTD XHTML 1.1//EN"
"http://www.w3.org/TR/xhtml11/DTD/xhtml11.dtd">
<script runat="server">

    /// <summary>
    /// Represents an employee
    /// </summary>
    public class Employee
    {
        public string _firstName;
        public string _lastName;
        public bool _retired;

        public string FirstName
        {
            get { return _firstName; }
        }

        public string LastName
        {
            get { return _lastName; }
        }

        public bool Retired
        {
            get { return _retired; }
```

```
        }

        public Employee(string firstName, string lastName, bool retired)
        {
            _firstName = firstName;
            _lastName = lastName;
            _retired = retired;
        }
    }

    /// <summary>
    /// Load employees into DetailsView
    /// </summary>
    void Page_Load()
    {
        // Create employees collection with one employee
        Employee newEmployee = new Employee("Steve", "Walther", false);
        List<Employee> employees = new List<Employee>();
        employees.Add(newEmployee);

        // Bind employees to DetailsView
        dtlMovies.DataSource = employees;
        dtlMovies.DataBind();
    }

</script>
<html xmlns="http://www.w3.org/1999/xhtml" >
<head id="Head1" runat="server">
    <title>Show Employee</title>
</head>
<body>
    <form id="form1" runat="server">
    <div>

    <asp:DetailsView
        id="dtlMovies"
        Runat="server" />

    </div>
    </form>
</body>
</html>
```

In Listing 12.2, an `Employee` class is defined, which contains properties for the employee first name, last name, and retirement status. In the `Page_Load()` method, a new employee is created and added to a generic collection. This collection is bound to the `DetailsView` control.

Using Fields with the `DetailsView` Control

If you need more control over the appearance of the `DetailsView`, including the particular order in which columns display, you can use fields with the `DetailsView` control, which supports exactly the same fields as the `GridView` control:

- ▶ **BoundField**—Enables you to display the value of a data item as text.

- ▶ **CheckBoxField**—Enables you to display the value of a data item as a check box.

- ▶ **CommandField**—Enables you to display links for editing, deleting, and selecting rows.

- ▶ **ButtonField**—Enables you to display the value of a data item as a button (image button, link button, or push button).

- ▶ **HyperLinkField**—Enables you to display the value of a data item as a link.

- ▶ **ImageField**—Enables you to display the value of a data item as an image.

- ▶ **TemplateField**—Enables you to customize the appearance of a data item.

> **NOTE**
>
> Another option is to create custom fields for the `DetailsView` control. You can create custom fields that work with the `DetailsView` control in exactly the same way as you create custom fields that work with the `GridView` control. Custom fields for the `GridView` control are discussed in the final section of Chapter 11, "Using the GridView Control."

The page in Listing 12.3 contains a `DetailsView` control that contains three `BoundFields`. The `BoundFields` display the values of the Title, Director, and BoxOfficeTotals database columns (see Figure 12.2).

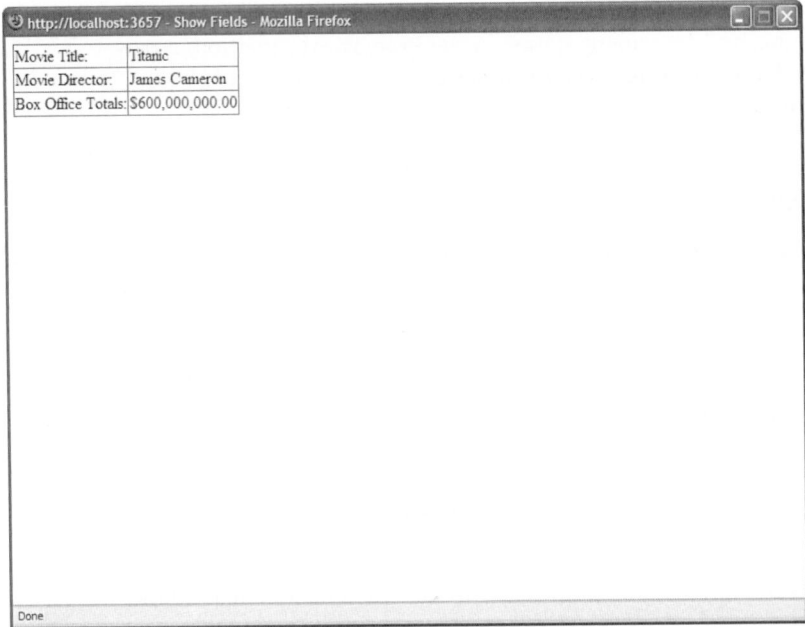

FIGURE 12.2 Using BoundFields with the DetailsView control.

LISTING 12.3 ShowFields.aspx

```
<%@ Page Language="C#" %>
<!DOCTYPE html PUBLIC "-//W3C//DTD XHTML 1.1//EN"
  "http://www.w3.org/TR/xhtml11/DTD/xhtml11.dtd">
<html xmlns="http://www.w3.org/1999/xhtml" >
<head id="Head1" runat="server">
    <title>Show Fields</title>
</head>
<body>
    <form id="form1" runat="server">
    <div>

    <asp:DetailsView
        id="dtlMovies"
        DataSourceID="srcMovies"
        AutoGenerateRows="false"
        Runat="server">
        <Fields>
        <asp:BoundField
            DataField="Title"
```

```
                    HeaderText="Movie Title:" />
            <asp:BoundField
                DataField="Director"
                HeaderText="Movie Director:" />
            <asp:BoundField
                DataField="BoxOfficeTotals"
                DataFormatString="{0:c}"
                HeaderText="Box Office Totals:" />
        </Fields>
    </asp:DetailsView>

    <asp:SqlDataSource
        id="srcMovies"
        ConnectionString="<%$ ConnectionStrings:Movies %>"
        SelectCommand="SELECT Id,Title,Director,BoxOfficeTotals FROM Movies
            WHERE Id=1"
        Runat="server" />

    </div>
    </form>
</body>
</html>
```

The DetailsView control has an AutoGenerateRows property that has the value False.
When you specify fields for a DetailsView control, you want to include this property so
that the fields do not appear more than once.

Each of the BoundFields in Listing 12.3 includes a HeaderText attribute that is used to
specify the label for the field. In addition, the BoundField associated with the
BoxOfficeTotals column includes a DataFormatString property that formats the value of
the column as a currency amount.

Displaying Empty Data with the DetailsView Control

The DetailsView control includes two properties that you can use to display a message
when no results are returned from its data source. You can use the EmptyDataText property
to display an HTML string, or the EmptyDataTemplate property to display more complicated content.

For example, SqlDataSource in Listing 12.4 does not return a record because no record in
the Movies database table has an ID of -1.

LISTING 12.4   ShowEmptyDataText.aspx

```
<%@ Page Language="C#" %>
<!DOCTYPE html PUBLIC "-//W3C//DTD XHTML 1.1//EN"
  "http://www.w3.org/TR/xhtml11/DTD/xhtml11.dtd">
<html xmlns="http://www.w3.org/1999/xhtml" >
<head id="Head1" runat="server">
    <title>Show Empty Data Text</title>
</head>
<body>
    <form id="form1" runat="server">
    <div>

    <asp:DetailsView
        id="dtlMovies"
        DataSourceID="srcMovies"
        EmptyDataText="<b>No Matching Record!</b>"
        Runat="server" />

    <asp:SqlDataSource
        id="srcMovies"
        ConnectionString="<%$ ConnectionStrings:Movies %>"
        SelectCommand="SELECT Id,Title,Director,InTheaters FROM Movies
            WHERE Id=-1"
        Runat="server" />

    </div>
    </form>
</body>
</html>
```

When you open the page in Listing 12.4, the contents of the EmptyDataText property display.

If you need to display more complicated content when no results are returned, such as ASP.NET controls, you can specify an EmptyDataTemplate. The page in Listing 12.5 illustrates how you can use the EmptyDataTemplate to display complicated HTML content (see Figure 12.3).

No Matching Results!

Please select a different record.

FIGURE 12.3   Displaying content when no results are returned.

LISTING 12.5   ShowEmptyDataTemplate.aspx

```
<%@ Page Language="C#" %>
<!DOCTYPE html PUBLIC "-//W3C//DTD XHTML 1.1//EN"
"http://www.w3.org/TR/xhtml11/DTD/xhtml11.dtd">
<html xmlns="http://www.w3.org/1999/xhtml" >
<head id="Head1" runat="server">
    <style type="text/css">
        .noMatch
        {
            background-color:#ffff66;
            padding:10px;
            font-family:Arial,Sans-Serif;
        }
        .noMatch h1
        {
            color:red;
            font-size:16px;
            font-weight:bold;
        }
    </style>
    <title>Show Empty Data Template</title>
```

```
</head>
<body>
    <form id="form1" runat="server">
    <div>

    <asp:DetailsView
        id="dtlMovies"
        DataSourceID="srcMovies"
        Runat="server">
        <EmptyDataTemplate>
        <div class="noMatch">
            <h1>No Matching Results!</h1>
            Please select a different record.
        </div>
        </EmptyDataTemplate>
    </asp:DetailsView>

    <asp:SqlDataSource
        id="srcMovies"
        ConnectionString="<%$ ConnectionStrings:Movies %>"
        SelectCommand="SELECT Id,Title,Director,InTheaters FROM Movies
            WHERE Id=-1"
        Runat="server" />

    </div>
    </form>
</body>
</html>
```

Paging through Data with the `DetailsView` Control

You can use the `DetailsView` to page through a set of database records by enabling the `DetailsView` control's `AllowPaging` property. The page in Listing 12.6 illustrates how you can page through the records in the Movies database table (see Figure 12.4).

FIGURE 12.4   Paging through records with the `DetailsView` control.

LISTING 12.6   ShowPaging.aspx

```
<%@ Page Language="C#" %>
<!DOCTYPE html PUBLIC "-//W3C//DTD XHTML 1.1//EN"
    "http://www.w3.org/TR/xhtml11/DTD/xhtml11.dtd">
<html xmlns="http://www.w3.org/1999/xhtml" >
<head id="Head1" runat="server">
    <title>Show Paging</title>
</head>
<body>
    <form id="form1" runat="server">
    <div>

    <asp:DetailsView
        id="dtlMovies"
        DataSourceID="srcMovies"
        AllowPaging="true"
        Runat="server" />

    <asp:SqlDataSource
        id="srcMovies"
        ConnectionString="<%$ ConnectionStrings:Movies %>"
```

```
        SelectCommand="SELECT Id,Title,Director,InTheaters FROM Movies"
        Runat="server" />

    </div>
    </form>
</body>
</html>
```

> **WARNING**
>
> In this section, you learn how to take advantage of user interface paging when paging
> through records with the DetailsView control. Although user interface paging is con-
> venient, it is not efficient. When working with large sets of records, you should use
> data source paging. This option is described in Chapter 18, "Using the
> ObjectDataSource Control."

Paging with AJAX

By default, when you page through records with the DetailsView control, the page is
posted back to the server each and every time you click a page number. As an alternative,
you can take advantage of AJAX to page through records. When you take advantage of
AJAX, only the DetailsView control and not the entire page is updated when you navigate to a new page of records.

> **NOTE**
>
> Ajax (Asynchronous JavaScript and XML) enables you to retrieve content from a web
> server without reloading the page. Ajax works with all modern browsers including
> Microsoft Internet Explorer, Firefox, Safari, Chrome, and Opera.

The page in Listing 12.7 illustrates how you can use AJAX with the DetailsView control.

LISTING 12.7   ShowAJAX.aspx

```
<%@ Page Language="C#" %>
<!DOCTYPE html PUBLIC "-//W3C//DTD XHTML 1.1//EN"
"http://www.w3.org/TR/xhtml11/DTD/xhtml11.dtd">
<html xmlns="http://www.w3.org/1999/xhtml" >
<head id="Head1" runat="server">
    <title>Show Paging</title>
</head>
<body>
    <form id="form1" runat="server">
    <div>
```

```
    <asp:ScriptManager id="sm1" runat="server" />

    <%= DateTime.Now %>

    <asp:UpdatePanel id="up1" runat="Server">
    <ContentTemplate>

    <asp:DetailsView
        id="dtlMovies"
        DataSourceID="srcMovies"
        AllowPaging="true"
        EnablePagingCallbacks="true"
        Runat="server" />

    </ContentTemplate>
    </asp:UpdatePanel>

    <asp:SqlDataSource
        id="srcMovies"
        ConnectionString="<%$ ConnectionStrings:Movies %>"
        SelectCommand="SELECT Id,Title,Director,InTheaters FROM Movies"
        Runat="server" />

    </div>
    </form>
</body>
</html>
```

The DetailsView control in Listing 12.7 is contained inside of an UpdatePanel control. When you page through the records displayed by the DetailsView control, only the content inside the UpdatePanel is updated.

Furthermore, the page in Listing 12.7 displays the current time. The time is not updated when you navigate to a new page of records. The time is not updated because the entire page is not updated. When you navigate to a new page, only the contents of the DetailsView are updated.

NOTE

The DetailsView control has an EnablePagingCallbacks property that also enables Ajax. This is a holdover property from the ASP.NET 2.0 Framework. UpdatePanel is a more flexible method of doing Ajax.

Customizing the Paging Interface

You can customize the appearance of the paging interface by modifying the PagerSettings property. For example, the DetailsView control in Listing 12.8 displays first, previous, next, and last links instead of page numbers (see Figure 12.5).

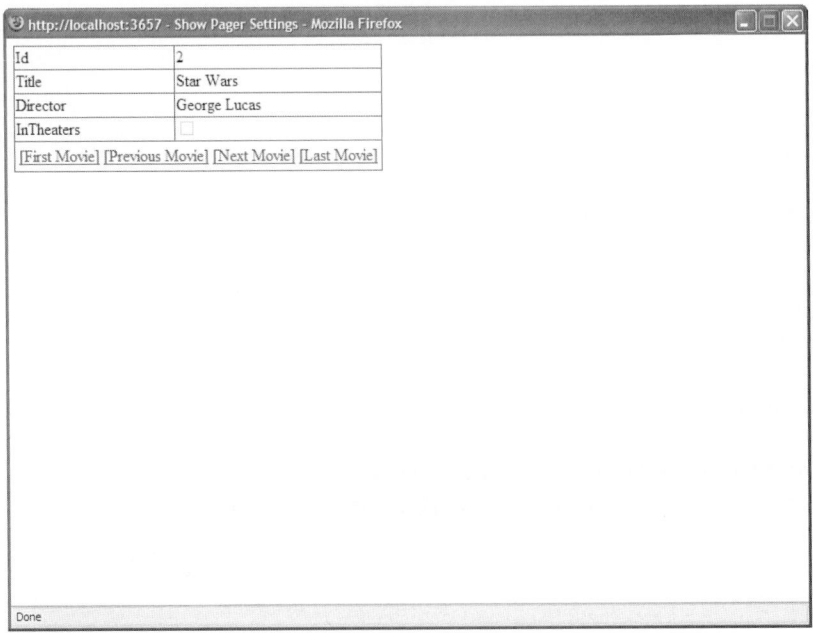

FIGURE 12.5   Using PagerSettings to customize the paging interface.

LISTING 12.8   ShowPagerSettings.aspx

```
<%@ Page Language="C#" %>
<!DOCTYPE html PUBLIC "-//W3C//DTD XHTML 1.1//EN"
   "http://www.w3.org/TR/xhtml11/DTD/xhtml11.dtd">
<html xmlns="http://www.w3.org/1999/xhtml" >
<head id="Head1" runat="server">
    <title>Show Pager Settings</title>
</head>
<body>
    <form id="form1" runat="server">
    <div>

    <asp:DetailsView
        id="dtlMovies"
        DataSourceID="srcMovies"
        AllowPaging="true"
        Runat="server">
```

```
        <PagerSettings
            Mode="NextPreviousFirstLast"
            FirstPageText="[First Movie]"
            LastPageText="[Last Movie]"
            NextPageText="[Next Movie]"
            PreviousPageText="[Previous Movie]" />
    </asp:DetailsView>

    <asp:SqlDataSource
        id="srcMovies"
        ConnectionString="<%$ ConnectionStrings:Movies %>"
        SelectCommand="SELECT Id,Title,Director,InTheaters FROM Movies"
        Runat="server" />

    </div>
    </form>
</body>
</html>
```

The `PagerSettings` class supports the following properties:

▶ **FirstPageImageUrl**—Enables you to display an image for the first page link.

▶ **FirstPageText**—Enables you to specify the text for the first page link.

▶ **LastPageImageUrl**—Enables you to display an image for the last page link.

▶ **LastPageText**—Enables you to specify the text for the last page link.

▶ **Mode**—Enables you to select a display mode for the pager user interface. Possible values are NextPrevious, NextPreviousFirstLast, Numeric, and NumericFirstLast.

▶ **NextPageImageUrl**—Enables you to specify the text for the next page link.

▶ **NextPageText**—Enables you to specify the text for the next page link.

▶ **PageButtonCount**—Enables you to specify the number of page number links to display.

▶ **Position**—Enables you to specify the position of the paging user interface. Possible values are Bottom, Top, TopAndBottom.

▶ **PreviousPageImageUrl**—Enables you to display an image for the previous page link.

▶ **PreviousPageText**—Enables you to specify the text for the previous page link.

▶ **Visible**—Enables you to hide the paging user interface.

If you need to customize the paging interface completely, you can use a template. For example, the page in Listing 12.9 displays a list of page numbers in a drop-down list control (see Figure 12.6).

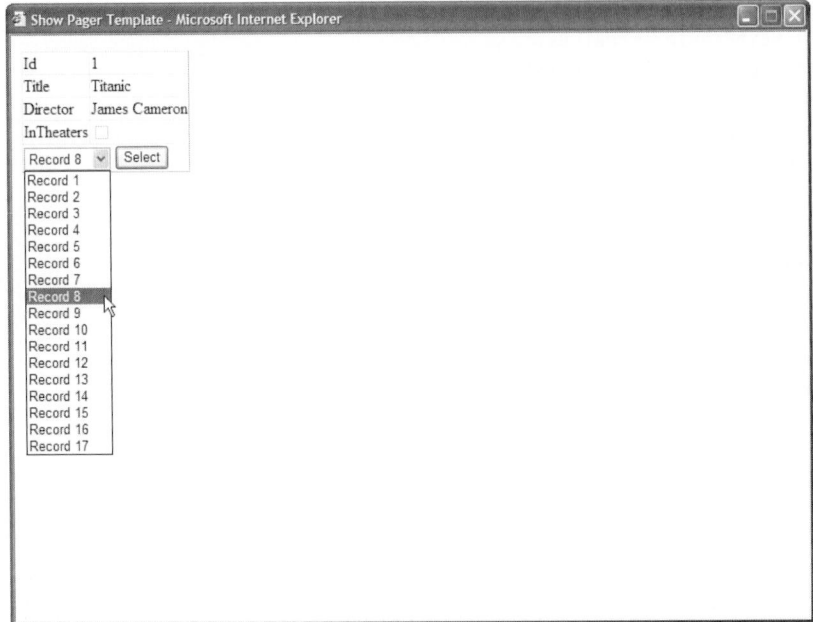

FIGURE 12.6   Using a `PagerTemplate` to customize the paging interface.

LISTING 12.9   ShowPagerTemplate.aspx

```
<%@ Page Language="C#" %>
<!DOCTYPE html PUBLIC "-//W3C//DTD XHTML 1.1//EN"
"http://www.w3.org/TR/xhtml11/DTD/xhtml11.dtd">
<script runat="server">

    protected void dtlMovies_DataBound(object sender, EventArgs e)
    {
        DropDownList ddlPager =
(DropDownList)dtlMovies.BottomPagerRow.Cells[0].FindControl("ddlPager");
        for (int i = 0; i < dtlMovies.PageCount; i++)
        {
            ListItem item = new ListItem( String.Format("Record {0}",i+1),
➥i.ToString());
            if (dtlMovies.PageIndex == i)
                item.Selected = true;
            ddlPager.Items.Add(item);
        }
    }
```

```
        protected void btnPage_Click(object sender, EventArgs e)
        {
            DropDownList ddlPager =
(DropDownList)dtlMovies.BottomPagerRow.Cells[0].FindControl("ddlPager");
            dtlMovies.PageIndex = Int32.Parse(ddlPager.SelectedValue);
        }
</script>
<html xmlns="http://www.w3.org/1999/xhtml" >
<head id="Head1" runat="server">
    <title>Show Pager Template</title>
</head>
<body>
    <form id="form1" runat="server">
    <div>

    <asp:DetailsView
        id="dtlMovies"
        DataSourceID="srcMovies"
        AllowPaging="true"
        OnDataBound="dtlMovies_DataBound"
        Runat="server">
        <PagerTemplate>
            <asp:DropDownList
                id="ddlPager"
                Runat="server" />
            <asp:Button
                id="btnPage"
                Text="Select"
                Runat="server" OnClick="btnPage_Click" />
        </PagerTemplate>
    </asp:DetailsView>

    <asp:SqlDataSource
        id="srcMovies"
        ConnectionString="<%$ ConnectionStrings:Movies %>"
        SelectCommand="SELECT Id,Title,Director,InTheaters FROM Movies"
        Runat="server" />

    </div>
    </form>
</body>
</html>
```

After you open the page in Listing 12.9, you can select a record from the DropDownList control and navigate to the record by clicking the Button control.

Updating Data with the `DetailsView` Control

You can use the `DetailsView` control to update existing database records. To update an existing record, assign the value True to the `DetailsView` control's `AutoGenerateEditButton` property, as illustrated in Listing 12.10 (see Figure 12.7).

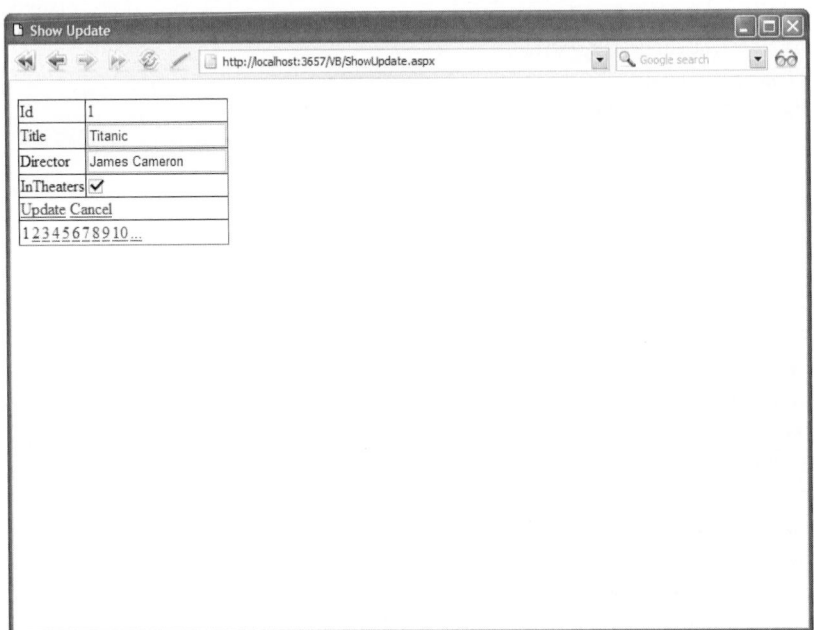

FIGURE 12.7   Editing a record with the `DetailsView` control.

LISTING 12.10   ShowUpdate.aspx

```
<%@ Page Language="C#" %>
<!DOCTYPE html PUBLIC "-//W3C//DTD XHTML 1.1//EN"
    "http://www.w3.org/TR/xhtml11/DTD/xhtml11.dtd">
<html xmlns="http://www.w3.org/1999/xhtml" >
<head id="Head1" runat="server">
    <title>Show Update</title>
</head>
<body>
    <form id="form1" runat="server">
    <div>
```

```
<asp:DetailsView
    id="dtlMovies"
    DataKeyNames="Id"
    AutoGenerateEditButton="true"
    AllowPaging="true"
    DataSourceID="srcMovies"
    Runat="server" />

<asp:SqlDataSource
    id="srcMovies"
    ConnectionString="<%$ ConnectionStrings:Movies %>"
    SelectCommand="SELECT Id,Title,Director,InTheaters FROM Movies"
    UpdateCommand="UPDATE Movies SET Title=@Title,Director=@Director,
        InTheaters=@InTheaters WHERE Id=@Id"
    Runat="server" />

</div>
</form>
</body>
</html>
```

When you open the page in Listing 12.10, the record appears in Read Only mode. You can click the Edit button to switch the DetailsView into Edit mode and update the record.

The DetailsView control includes a DataKeyNames property and an AutoGenerateEditButton property. The DataKeyNames property contains the name of the primary key column. The AutoGenerateEditButton property automatically generates the user interface for editing the record.

The SqlDataSource control includes an UpdateCommand. The UpdateCommand updates the Title, Director, and InTheaters database columns.

If you want the DetailsView control to initially appear in Edit mode, you can set the DetailsView control's DefaultMode property to the value Edit. For example, the page in Listing 12.11 contains a Master/Detail form. If you select any of the records in GridView, you can edit the record with the DetailsView control (see Figure 12.8).

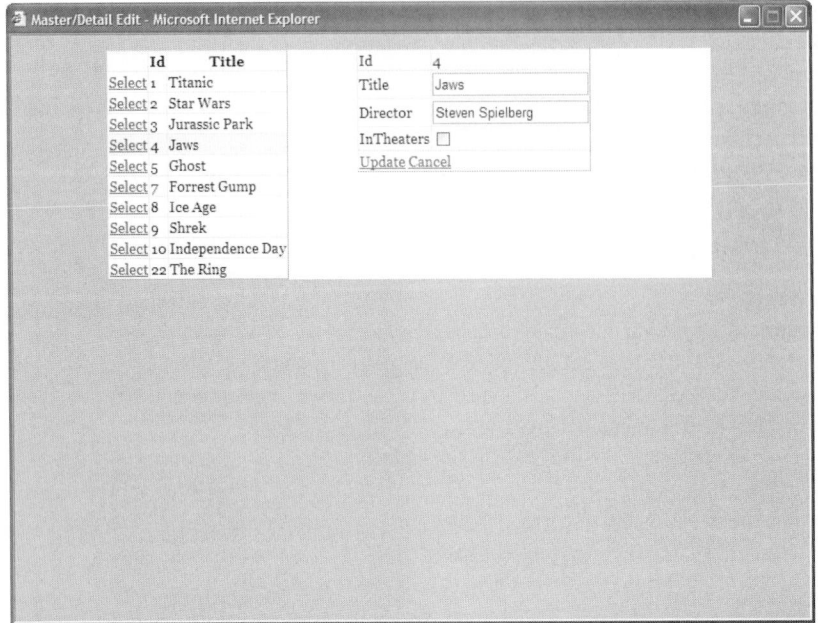

FIGURE 12.8   Displaying a Master/Detail form with the `DetailsView` control.

LISTING 12.11   MasterDetailEdit.aspx

```
<%@ Page Language="C#" %>
<!DOCTYPE html PUBLIC "-//W3C//DTD XHTML 1.1//EN"
"http://www.w3.org/TR/xhtml11/DTD/xhtml11.dtd">
<script runat="server">

    void Page_Load()
    {
        if (!Page.IsPostBack)
            grdMovies.SelectedIndex = 0;
    }


    protected void dtlMovies_ItemUpdated(object sender, DetailsViewUpdatedEventArgs
➡e)
    {
        grdMovies.DataBind();
    }
</script>
<html xmlns="http://www.w3.org/1999/xhtml" >
<head id="Head1" runat="server">
    <style type="text/css">
        html
```

```
            {
                background-color:silver;
                font:14px Georgia,Serif;
            }
            .content
            {
                margin:auto;
                width:600px;
                background-color:white;
            }
            .column
            {
                float:left;
                width:250px;
            }
            .selectedRow
            {
                background-color:yellow;
            }
        </style>
        <title>Master/Detail Edit</title>
</head>
<body>
        <form id="form1" runat="server">
        <div class="content">

        <div class="column">
        <asp:GridView
            id="grdMovies"
            DataSourceID="srcMovies"
            DataKeyNames="Id"
            AutoGenerateSelectButton="true"
            SelectedRowStyle-CssClass="selectedRow"
            Runat="server" />
        </div>

        <div class="column">
        <asp:DetailsView
            id="dtlMovies"
            DefaultMode="Edit"
            AutoGenerateEditButton="true"
            AllowPaging="true"
            DataSourceID="srcMovieDetails"
            DataKeyNames="Id"
            Runat="server" OnItemUpdated="dtlMovies_ItemUpdated" />
```

12

```
<asp:SqlDataSource
    id="srcMovies"
    ConnectionString="<%$ ConnectionStrings:Movies %>"
    SelectCommand="SELECT Id,Title FROM Movies"
    Runat="server" />
</div>

<asp:SqlDataSource
    id="srcMovieDetails"
    ConnectionString="<%$ ConnectionStrings:Movies %>"
    SelectCommand="SELECT Id,Title,Director,InTheaters FROM
        Movies WHERE Id=@MovieId"
    UpdateCommand="UPDATE Movies SET Title=@Title,Director=@Director,
        InTheaters=@InTheaters WHERE Id=@Id"
    Runat="server">
    <SelectParameters>
        <asp:ControlParameter Name="MovieId" ControlID="grdMovies" />
    </SelectParameters>
</asp:SqlDataSource>

</div>
</form>
</body>
</html>
```

The `DetailsView` control includes a `DefaultMode` property set to the value `Edit`. When you select a record, the record displays by `DetailsView` in Edit mode by default.

Using Templates When Editing

By default, you don't get any validation when editing records with the `DetailsView` control. In other words, there is nothing to prevent you from attempting to submit a null value to a database column that does not accept null values. If you need to perform validation, you need to use templates with the `DetailsView` control.

The page in Listing 12.12 uses `TemplateFields` for the Title and BoxOfficeTotals columns. Both `TemplateFields` contain a `RequiredFieldValidator`. The BoxOfficeTotals column also includes a CompareValidator to check whether the value entered is a currency value (see Figure 12.9).

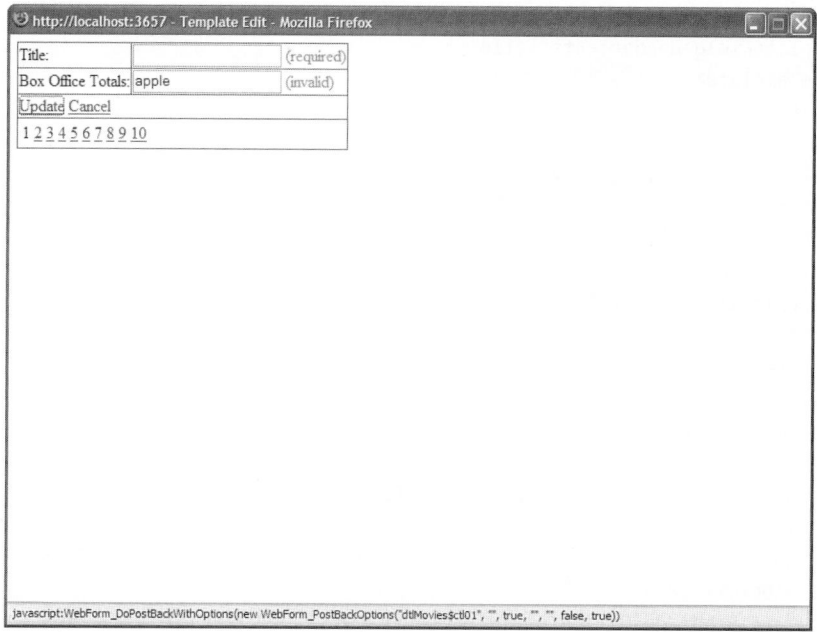

FIGURE 12.9   Using a template when editing with the DetailsView control.

LISTING 12.12   TemplateEdit.aspx

```
<%@ Page Language="C#" %>
<!DOCTYPE html PUBLIC "-//W3C//DTD XHTML 1.1//EN"
  "http://www.w3.org/TR/xhtml11/DTD/xhtml11.dtd">
<html xmlns="http://www.w3.org/1999/xhtml" >
<head id="Head1" runat="server">
    <title>Template Edit</title>
</head>
<body>
    <form id="form1" runat="server">
    <div>

    <asp:DetailsView
        id="dtlMovies"
        AutoGenerateRows="false"
        AutoGenerateEditButton="true"
        AllowPaging="true"
        DefaultMode="Edit"
        DataSourceID="srcMovies"
        DataKeyNames="Id"
        Runat="server">
```

```
        <Fields>
        <asp:TemplateField HeaderText="Title:">
        <EditItemTemplate>
        <asp:TextBox
            id="txtTitle"
            Text='<%# Bind("Title") %>'
            runat="server" />
        <asp:RequiredFieldValidator
            id="reqTitle"
            ControlToValidate="txtTitle"
            Text="(required)"
            Display="Dynamic"
            Runat="server" />
        </EditItemTemplate>
        </asp:TemplateField>
        <asp:TemplateField HeaderText="Box Office Totals:">
        <EditItemTemplate>
        <asp:TextBox
            id="txtBoxOfficeTotals"
            Text='<%# Bind("BoxOfficeTotals", "{0:f}") %>'
            runat="server" />
        <asp:RequiredFieldValidator
            id="reqBoxOfficeTotals"
            ControlToValidate="txtBoxOfficeTotals"
            Text="(required)"
            Display="Dynamic"
            Runat="server" />
        <asp:CompareValidator
            id="cmpBoxOfficeTotals"
            ControlToValidate="txtBoxOfficeTotals"
            Text="(invalid)"
            Display="Dynamic"
            Operator="DataTypeCheck"
            Type="currency"
            Runat="server" />
        </EditItemTemplate>
        </asp:TemplateField>
        </Fields>
    </asp:DetailsView>

    <asp:SqlDataSource
        id="srcMovies"
        ConnectionString="<%$ ConnectionStrings:Movies %>"
        SelectCommand="SELECT Id,Title,BoxOfficeTotals FROM Movies"
        UpdateCommand="UPDATE Movies SET Title=@Title,
            BoxOfficeTotals=@BoxOfficeTotals WHERE Id=@Id"
```

```
        Runat="server" />

    </div>
    </form>
</body>
</html>
```

If you attempt to edit a record, and you do not provide a value for the Title or BoxOfficeTotals columns, a validation error displays. Also, if you enter anything other than a currency amount for the BoxOfficeTotals column, a validation error message displays.

Handling Concurrency Issues

What happens when two users edit the same record at the same time? By default, the last user to update the database record wins. In other words, one user can overwrite changes made by another user.

Imagine that Sally opens a page to edit a database record. After opening the page, Sally leaves for her 2-week vacation in Las Vegas. While Sally is vacationing, Jim edits the same record and submits his changes. When Sally returns from vacation, she submits her changes. Any modifications that Jim makes are overwritten by Sally's changes.

If you need to prevent this scenario, you can take advantage of optimistic concurrency. The SqlDataSource control's ConflictDetection property supports the following two values:

- ▶ CompareAllValues
- ▶ OverwriteChanges

By default, the ConflictDetection property has the value OverwriteChanges. If you set this property to the value CompareAllValues, the SqlDataSource tracks both the original and modified versions of each column.

For example, the page in Listing 12.13 doesn't enable a user to update a record when the original record has been modified after the user has opened the page.

LISTING 12.13   Concurrency.aspx

```
<%@ Page Language="C#" %>
<!DOCTYPE html PUBLIC "-//W3C//DTD XHTML 1.1//EN"
"http://www.w3.org/TR/xhtml11/DTD/xhtml11.dtd">

<script runat="server">

    protected void srcMovies_Updated(object sender, SqlDataSourceStatusEventArgs e)
    {
        if (e.AffectedRows == 0)
            lblMessage.Text = "Could not update record";
```

```
        }
</script>

<html xmlns="http://www.w3.org/1999/xhtml" >
<head id="Head1" runat="server">
    <title>Concurrency</title>
</head>
<body>
    <form id="form1" runat="server">
    <div>

    <asp:Label ID="lblMessage" EnableViewState="false" runat="server" />

    <asp:DetailsView
        id="dtlMovies"
        DataKeyNames="Id"
        AutoGenerateEditButton="true"
        AllowPaging="true"
        DataSourceID="srcMovies"
        Runat="server" />

    <asp:SqlDataSource
        id="srcMovies"
        ConnectionString="<%$ ConnectionStrings:Movies %>"
        SelectCommand="SELECT Id,Title,Director,InTheaters FROM Movies"
        UpdateCommand="UPDATE Movies
            SET Title=@Title,Director=@Director,InTheaters=
            WHERE Title=@original_Title
            AND Director=@original_Director
            AND InTheaters=@InTheaters
            AND Id=@original_Id"
        ConflictDetection="CompareAllValues"
        OldValuesParameterFormatString="original_{0}"
        Runat="server" OnUpdated="srcMovies_Updated" />

    </div>
    </form>
</body>
</html>
```

Notice the contents of UpdateCommand in Listing 12.13. The current values are compared against the original values for each database column when updating a record. If the current and original values don't match, the record is not updated.

The SqlDataSource has both its ConflictDetection and OldValuesParameterFormat
String properties set. The OldValuesParameterFormatString specifies the prefix added to
the parameters that represent the original field values.

If there is a concurrency conflict, the e.AffectedRows property passed to the Updated
event handler will have the value 0. In Listing 12.13, a message is displayed in a Label
control when a record cannot be updated.

Inserting Data with the DetailsView Control

You can use the DetailsView control to insert new records into a database table. For
example, the page in Listing 12.14 enables you to insert a new record into the Movies
database table.

LISTING 12.14   ShowInsert.aspx

```
<%@ Page Language="C#" %>
<!DOCTYPE html PUBLIC "-//W3C//DTD XHTML 1.1//EN"
  "http://www.w3.org/TR/xhtml11/DTD/xhtml11.dtd">
<html xmlns="http://www.w3.org/1999/xhtml" >
<head id="Head1" runat="server">
    <title>Show Insert</title>
</head>
<body>
    <form id="form1" runat="server">
    <div>

    <asp:DetailsView
        id="dtlMovies"
        AllowPaging="true"
        DataSourceID="srcMovies"
        AutoGenerateInsertButton="true"
        Runat="server" />

    <asp:SqlDataSource
        id="srcMovies"
        ConnectionString="<%$ ConnectionStrings:Movies %>"
        SelectCommand="SELECT Title,Director,InTheaters FROM Movies"
        InsertCommand="INSERT Movies (Title,Director,InTheaters)
            VALUES (@Title,@Director,
        Runat="server" />

    </div>
    </form>
</body>
</html>
```

The DetailsView control in Listing 12.14 includes an AutoGenerateInsertButton property that has the value True. This property automatically generates the user interface for inserting a new record.

After you open the page in Listing 12.14, you can click the New button to display a form for inserting a new record. When you click the Insert button, the SQL command represented by the SqlDataSource control's InsertCommand property is executed.

If you want the DetailsView control to display an insert form by default, you can assign the value Insert to the DetailsView control's DefaultMode property. This approach is illustrated by the page in Listing 12.15 (see Figure 12.10).

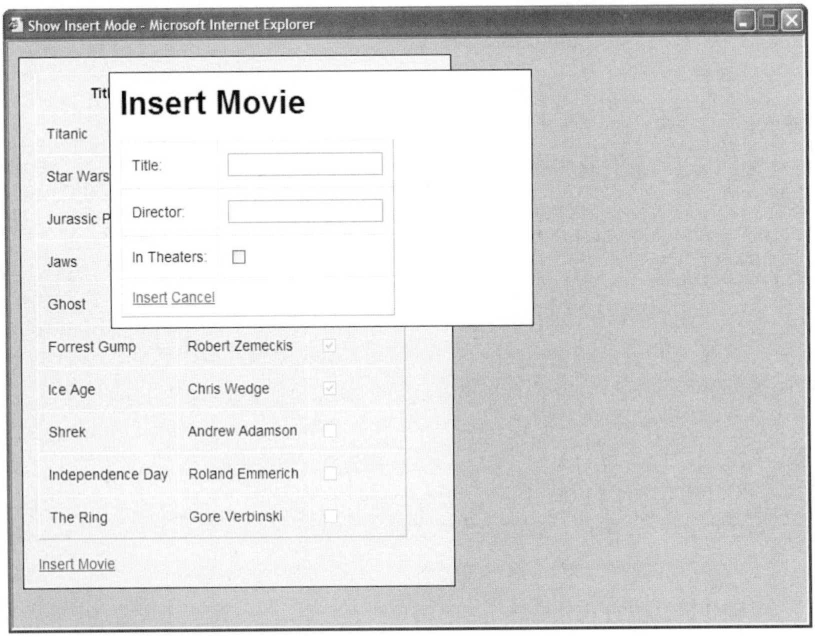

FIGURE 12.10 Inserting a record with the DetailsView control.

LISTING 12.15 ShowInsertMode.aspx

```
<%@ Page Language="C#" %>
<!DOCTYPE html PUBLIC "-//W3C//DTD XHTML 1.1//EN"
   "http://www.w3.org/TR/xhtml11/DTD/xhtml11.dtd">
<html xmlns="http://www.w3.org/1999/xhtml" >
<head id="Head1" runat="server">
    <style type="text/css">
        html
        {
            background-color:silver;
```

```
                font:14px Arial,Sans-Serif;
            }
            td,th
            {
                padding:10px;
            }
            #divDisplay
            {
                border:solid 1px black;
                width:400px;
                padding:15px;
                background-color:#eeeeee;
            }
            #divInsert
            {
                display:none;
                border:solid 1px black;
                width:400px;
                position:absolute;
                top:30px;
                left:100px;
                padding:10px;
                background-color:white;
            }

    </style>
    <script type="text/javascript">
        function showInsert()
        {
            var divInsert = document.getElementById('divInsert');
            divInsert.style.display = 'block';
        }
    </script>
    <title>Show Insert Mode</title>
</head>
<body>
    <form id="form1" runat="server">
    <div id="divDisplay">
    <asp:GridView
        id="grdMovies"
        DataSourceID="srcMovies"
        Runat="server" />
    <br />
    <a href="JavaScript:showInsert();">Insert Movie</a>
    </div>
```

12

```
<div id="divInsert">
<h1>Insert Movie</h1>
<asp:DetailsView
    id="dtlMovies"
    DataSourceID="srcMovies"
    AutoGenerateInsertButton="true"
    AutoGenerateRows="false"
    DefaultMode="Insert"
    Runat="server">
    <Fields>
    <asp:BoundField
        DataField="Title"
        HeaderText="Title:" />
    <asp:BoundField
        DataField="Director"
        HeaderText="Director:" />
    <asp:CheckBoxField
        DataField="InTheaters"
        HeaderText="In Theaters:" />
    </Fields>
</asp:DetailsView>
</div>

<asp:SqlDataSource
    id="srcMovies"
    ConnectionString="<%$ ConnectionStrings:Movies %>"
    SelectCommand="SELECT Title,Director,InTheaters FROM Movies"
    InsertCommand="INSERT Movies (Title,Director,InTheaters)
        VALUES (@Title,@Director,
    Runat="server" />

</form>
</body>
</html>
```

The page in Listing 12.15 contains both a GridView and DetailsView control. The
DetailsView control is hidden until you click the Insert Movie link. This link executes a
JavaScript function named ShowInsert(), which displays the DetailsView control.

NOTE

You can hide a column when a DetailsView control is in Insert mode with the
BoundField control's InsertVisible property. This property is useful, for example,
when you want to prevent users from inserting a value for an identity column.

Deleting Data with the `DetailsView` Control

You can delete records with the `DetailsView` control by enabling its `AutoGenerateDelete Button` property. The page in Listing 12.16 enables you to both insert and delete records in the Movies database table.

LISTING 12.16   `ShowDelete.aspx`

```
<%@ Page Language="C#" %>
<!DOCTYPE html PUBLIC "-//W3C//DTD XHTML 1.1//EN"
    "http://www.w3.org/TR/xhtml11/DTD/xhtml11.dtd">
<html xmlns="http://www.w3.org/1999/xhtml" >
<head id="Head1" runat="server">
    <title>Show Delete</title>
</head>
<body>
    <form id="form1" runat="server">
    <div>

    <asp:DetailsView
        id="dtlMovies"
        AllowPaging="true"
        DataSourceID="srcMovies"
        DataKeyNames="Id"
        AutoGenerateInsertButton="true"
        AutoGenerateDeleteButton="true"
        AutoGenerateRows="false"
        Runat="server">
        <Fields>
        <asp:BoundField
            DataField="Id"
            HeaderText="ID:"
            InsertVisible="false" />
        <asp:BoundField
            DataField="Title"
            HeaderText="Title:" />
        <asp:BoundField
            DataField="Director"
            HeaderText="Director:" />
        <asp:CheckBoxField
            DataField="InTheaters"
            HeaderText="In Theaters:" />
        </Fields>
    </asp:DetailsView>

    <asp:SqlDataSource
```

```
    id="srcMovies"
    ConnectionString="<%$ ConnectionStrings:Movies %>"
    SelectCommand="SELECT Id,Title,Director,InTheaters FROM Movies"
    InsertCommand="INSERT Movies (Title,Director,InTheaters)
        VALUES (@Title,@Director,
    DeleteCommand="DELETE Movies WHERE id=@Id"
    Runat="server" />

    </div>
    </form>
</body>
</html>
```

When deleting records, you need to supply a value for the DetailsView control's DataKeyNames property. A parameter named @Id represents the value of the ID column in the DeleteCommand property.

Working with DetailsView Control Events

The DetailsView control supports the following events:

▶ **DataBinding**—Raised immediately before the DetailsView control is bound to its data source.

▶ **DataBound**—Raised immediately after the DetailsView control is bound to its data source.

▶ **ItemCommand**—Raised when any control contained in the DetailsView raises an event (for example, when you click a button rendered by a ButtonField).

▶ **ItemCreated**—Raised when a DetailsView renders a data item.

▶ **ItemDeleting**—Raised immediately before a data item is deleted.

▶ **ItemDeleted**—Raised immediately after a data item is deleted.

▶ **ItemInserting**—Raised immediately before a data item is inserted.

▶ **ItemInserted**—Raised immediately after a data item is inserted.

▶ **ItemUpdating**—Raised immediately before a data item is updated.

▶ **ItemUpdated**—Raised immediately after a data item is updated.

▶ **ModeChanging**—Raised immediately before the DetailsView control's mode is changed.

▶ **ModeChanged**—Raised immediately after the DetailsView control's mode is changed.

▶ **PageIndexChanging**—Raised immediately before the current page is changed.

▶ **PageIndexChanged**—Raised immediately after the current page is changed.

Several of these events reflect similar events exposed by the DataSource controls. For example, the SqlDataSource control includes Inserting and Inserted events, which mirror the DetailsView control's ItemInserting and ItemInserted events.

The page in Listing 12.17 demonstrates how to use the ItemInserted event to handle any errors that might be raised when inserting a new record into a database table (see Figure 12.11).

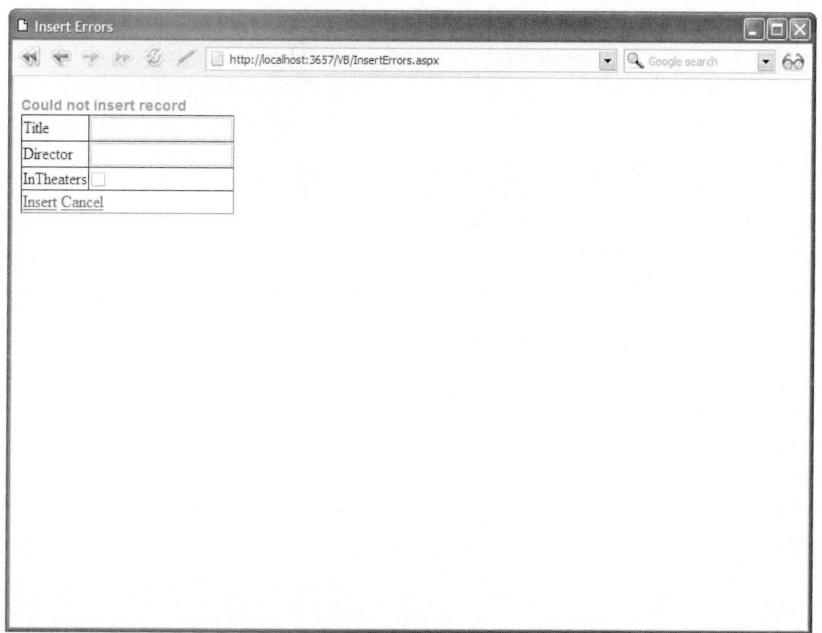

FIGURE 12.11   Handling database insert errors.

LISTING 12.17   InsertErrors.aspx

```
<%@ Page Language="C#" %>
<!DOCTYPE html PUBLIC "-//W3C//DTD XHTML 1.1//EN"
"http://www.w3.org/TR/xhtml11/DTD/xhtml11.dtd">
<script runat="server">

    protected void dtlMovies_ItemInserted(object sender,
➥DetailsViewInsertedEventArgs e)
    {
        if (e.Exception != null)
        {
            e.ExceptionHandled = true;
            e.KeepInInsertMode = true;
            lblError.Visible = true;
```

```
            }
        }
</script>
<html xmlns="http://www.w3.org/1999/xhtml" >
<head id="Head1" runat="server">
    <style type="text/css">
        .error
        {
            color:red;
            font:bold 14px Arial,Sans-Serif;
        }
    </style>
    <title>Insert Errors</title>
</head>
<body>
    <form id="form1" runat="server">
    <div>

    <asp:Label
        id="lblError"
        Text="Could not insert record"
        Visible="false"
        EnableViewState="false"
        CssClass="error"
        Runat="server" />

    <asp:DetailsView
        id="dtlMovies"
        AllowPaging="true"
        DataSourceID="srcMovies"
        AutoGenerateInsertButton="true"
        OnItemInserted="dtlMovies_ItemInserted"
        Runat="server" />

    <asp:SqlDataSource
        id="srcMovies"
        ConnectionString="<%$ ConnectionStrings:Movies %>"
        SelectCommand="SELECT Title,Director,InTheaters FROM Movies"
        InsertCommand="INSERT Movies (Title,Director,InTheaters)
            VALUES (@Title,@Director,
        Runat="server" />

    </div>
    </form>
</body>
</html>
```

If you attempt to insert a record without providing values for the Title or Director column, the error message contained in the Label control displays.

When you insert a record, the `DetailsView` control raises the `ItemInserted` event. The second parameter passed to the event handler for this method contains a property that exposes any exceptions raised when inserting the record. In Listing 12.17, if there is an exception, the exception is suppressed with the `ExceptionHandled` property. Furthermore, the `KeepInInsertMode` property prevents the `DetailsView` from automatically switching out of Insert mode.

Formatting the `DetailsView` Control

The `DetailsView` control includes an abundance of properties for formatting the control. I recommend that you format the `DetailsView` control by taking advantage of Cascading Style Sheets (CSS). All the following properties expose a Style object that includes a `CssClass` property:

▶ **CssClass**—Enables you to associate a style sheet class with the `DetailsView` control.

▶ **AlternatingRowStyle**—Represents every other row rendered by the `DetailsView` control.

▶ **CommandRowStyle**—Represents the row that contains the edit buttons.

▶ **EditRowStyle**—Represents rows when the `DetailsView` control is in Edit mode.

▶ **EmptyDataRowStyle**—Represents the row displayed when the data source does not return any data items.

▶ **FieldHeaderStyle**—Represents the cell displayed for the field labels.

▶ **FooterStyle**—Represents the footer row.

▶ **HeaderStyle**—Represents the header row.

▶ **InsertRowStyle**—Represents rows when the `DetailsView` control is in Insert mode.

▶ **PagerStyle**—Represents the row or rows that display the paging user interface.

▶ **RowStyle**—Represents the rows displayed by the `DetailsView` control.

Furthermore, you can take advantage of the following properties when formatting a DetailsView control:

▶ **GridLines**—Enables you to specify the appearance of the rules that appear around the cells of the table rendered by a `DetailsView` control. Possible values are None, Horizontal, Vertical, and Both.

▶ **HeaderText**—Enables you to specify text that appears in the header of the DetailsView control.

▶ **FooterText**—Enables you to specify text that appears in the footer of the
DetailsView control.

The page in Listing 12.18 uses several of these properties to format a DetailsView control
(see Figure 12.12).

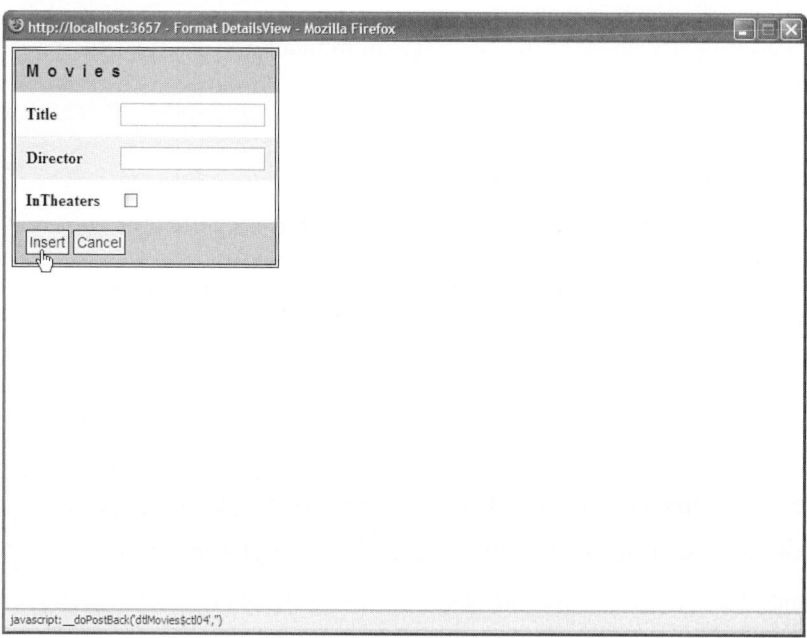

FIGURE 12.12   Formatting a DetailsView control with CSS.

LISTING 12.18   FormatDetailsView.aspx

```
<%@ Page Language="C#" %>
<!DOCTYPE html PUBLIC "-//W3C//DTD XHTML 1.1//EN"
  "http://www.w3.org/TR/xhtml11/DTD/xhtml11.dtd">
<html xmlns="http://www.w3.org/1999/xhtml" >
<head id="Head1" runat="server">
    <style type="text/css">
        .movies td,.movies th
        {
            padding:10px;
        }
        .movies
        {
            border:double 4px black;
        }
        .header
```

```
        {
            letter-spacing:8px;
            font:bold 16px Arial,Sans-Serif;
            background-color:silver;
        }
        .fieldHeader
        {
            font-weight:bold;
        }
        .alternating
        {
            background-color:#eeeeee;
        }
        .command
        {
            background-color:silver;
        }
        .command a
        {
            color:black;
            background-color:#eeeeee;
            font:14px Arials,Sans-Serif;
            text-decoration:none;
            padding:3px;
            border:solid 1px black;
        }
        .command a:hover
        {
            background-color:yellow;
        }
        .pager td
        {
            padding:2px;
        }
    </style>
    <title>Format DetailsView</title>
</head>
<body>
    <form id="form1" runat="server">
    <div>

    <asp:DetailsView
        id="dtlMovies"
        DataSourceID="srcMovies"
        AutoGenerateInsertButton="true"
        AllowPaging="true"
```

```
        GridLines="None"
        HeaderText="Movies"
        CssClass="movies"
        HeaderStyle-CssClass="header"
        FieldHeaderStyle-CssClass="fieldHeader"
        AlternatingRowStyle-CssClass="alternating"
        CommandRowStyle-CssClass="command"
        PagerStyle-CssClass="pager"
        Runat="server" />

    <asp:SqlDataSource
        id="srcMovies"
        ConnectionString="<%$ ConnectionStrings:Movies %>"
        SelectCommand="SELECT Title,Director,InTheaters FROM Movies"
        InsertCommand="INSERT Movies (Title,Director,InTheaters)
            VALUES (@Title,@Director,
        Runat="server" />

    </div>
    </form>
</body>
</html>
```

Using the `FormView` Control

You can use the `FormView` control to do anything that you can do with the `DetailsView` control. Just as you can with the `DetailsView` control, you can use the `FormView` control to display, page, edit, insert, and delete database records. However, unlike the `DetailsView` control, the `FormView` control is entirely template-driven.

I use the `FormView` control much more than the `DetailsView` control. The `FormView` control provides you with more control over the layout of a form. Furthermore, adding validation controls to `FormView` is easier than adding validation controls to a `DetailsView` control.

WEB STANDARDS NOTE

By default, the `FormView` control renders an HTML table. It creates an HTML table that contains a single cell. In ASP.NET 4, you can disable this by setting the `RenderOuterTable` property to `False`. This enables you to style the output using CSS styles.

Displaying Data with the `FormView` Control

You can display a database record with the `FormView` control by using an `ItemTemplate`. For example, the page in Listing 12.19 displays a record from the Movies database table (see Figure 12.13).

FIGURE 12.13   Displaying a database record with the `FormView` control.

LISTING 12.19   ShowFormView.aspx

```
<%@ Page Language="C#" %>
<!DOCTYPE html PUBLIC "-//W3C//DTD XHTML 1.1//EN"
  "http://www.w3.org/TR/xhtml11/DTD/xhtml11.dtd">
<html xmlns="http://www.w3.org/1999/xhtml" >
<head id="Head1" runat="server">
    <style type="text/css">
    html
    {
        background-color:silver;
    }
    #content
    {
        margins:auto;
        width:600px;
        padding:10px;
```

```
            background-color:white;
            font:14px Georgia,Serif;
        }
        </style>
        <title>Show FormView</title>
</head>
<body>
    <form id="form1" runat="server">
    <div id="content">

    <asp:FormView
        id="frmMovies"
        DataSourceID="srcMovies"
        Runat="server">
        <ItemTemplate>
        <h1><%# Eval("Title") %></h1>
        <b>Directed By:</b>
        <%# Eval("Director") %>
        <br />
        <b>Box Office Totals:</b>
        <%#Eval("BoxOfficeTotals", "{0:c}") %>
        </ItemTemplate>
    </asp:FormView>

    <asp:SqlDataSource
        id="srcMovies"
        ConnectionString="<%$ ConnectionStrings:Movies %>"
        SelectCommand="SELECT Id,Title,Director,BoxOfficeTotals FROM Movies
            WHERE Id=1"
        Runat="server" />

    </div>
    </form>
</body>
</html>
```

The `FormView` control's `DataSourceID` property points to the `SqlDataSource` control. The `SqlDataSource` control retrieves the first record from the Movies database table.

The `ItemTemplate` contains databinding expressions that display the values of the Title, Director, and BoxOfficeTotals columns. The `Eval()` method retrieves the values of these columns. The databinding expression for the BoxOfficeTotals column formats the value of the column as a currency amount.

Paging Through Data with the `FormView` Control

You can allow users to navigate through a set of data items by allowing paging. You can allow the `FormView` control to automatically render the paging interface, or you can use a `PagerTemplate` to customize the paging interface.

The page in Listing 12.20 automatically renders an additional row that contains buttons for navigating between data items.

LISTING 12.20 ShowFormViewPaging.aspx

```aspx
<%@ Page Language="C#" %>
<!DOCTYPE html PUBLIC "-//W3C//DTD XHTML 1.1//EN"
  "http://www.w3.org/TR/xhtml11/DTD/xhtml11.dtd">
<html xmlns="http://www.w3.org/1999/xhtml" >
<head id="Head1" runat="server">
    <style type="text/css">
    html
    {
        background-color:silver;
    }
    #content
    {
        margins:auto;
        width:600px;
        padding:10px;
        background-color:white;
        font:14px Georgia,Serif;
    }
    a
    {
        color:blue;
    }
    </style>
    <title>Show FormView Paging</title>
</head>
<body>
    <form id="form1" runat="server">
    <div id="content">

    <asp:FormView
        id="frmMovies"
        DataSourceID="srcMovies"
        AllowPaging="true"
        Runat="server">
        <ItemTemplate>
        <h1><%# Eval("Title") %></h1>
```

```
        <b>Directed By:</b>
        <%# Eval("Director") %>
        <br />
        <b>Box Office Totals:</b>
        <%#Eval("BoxOfficeTotals", "{0:c}") %>
        </ItemTemplate>
    </asp:FormView>

    <asp:SqlDataSource
        id="srcMovies"
        ConnectionString="<%$ ConnectionStrings:Movies %>"
        SelectCommand="SELECT Id,Title,Director,BoxOfficeTotals FROM Movies"
        Runat="server" />

    </div>
    </form>
</body>
</html>
```

The FormView in Listing 12.20 includes an AllowPaging property assigned the value True. Adding this property generates the paging interface automatically.

NOTE

You can enable Ajax paging for a FormView control in exactly the same way you enable Ajax paging for a GridView or DetailsView control. If you wrap the FormView control in an UpdatePanel, you can page through the records in FormView without performing a noticeable postback to the server.

WARNING

This section describes user interface paging, which is not an efficient method to use when paging through large record sets because all the data must be loaded into memory. In Chapter 18, you learn how to implement data source paging.

You can customize the appearance of the automatically rendered paging interface with the PagerSettings property, which exposes the PagerSettings class. The PagerSettings class supports the following properties:

▶ **FirstPageImageUrl**—Enables you to display an image for the first page link.

▶ **FirstPageText**—Enables you to specify the text for the first page link.

▶ **LastPageImageUrl**—Enables you to display an image for the last page link.

▶ **LastPageText**—Enables you to specify the text for the last page link.

▶ **Mode**—Enables you to select a display mode for the pager user interface. Possible values are NextPrevious, NextPreviousFirstLast, Numeric, and NumericFirstLast.

▶ **NextPageImageUrl**—Enables you to specify the text for the next page link.

▶ **NextPageText**—Enables you to specify the text for the next page link.

▶ **PageButtonCount**—Enables you to specify the number of page number links to display.

▶ **Position**—Enables you to specify the position of the paging user interface. Possible values are Bottom, Top, and TopAndBottom.

▶ **PreviousPageImageUrl**—Enables you to display an image for the previous page link.

▶ **PreviousPageText**—Enables you to specify the text for the previous page link.

▶ **Visible**—Enables you to hide the paging user interface.

If you need to customize the appearance of the paging interface completely, you can create a PagerTemplate. The page in Listing 12.21 uses the PagerTemplate to create a custom paging interface. The PagerTemplate displays the current page number. It also contains buttons for navigating to the previous and next page (see Figure 12.14).

FIGURE 12.14 Using a PagerTemplate with the FormView control.

LISTING 12.21   ShowFormViewPagerTemplate.aspx

```
<%@ Page Language="C#" %>
<!DOCTYPE html PUBLIC "-//W3C//DTD XHTML 1.1//EN"
    "http://www.w3.org/TR/xhtml11/DTD/xhtml11.dtd">
<html xmlns="http://www.w3.org/1999/xhtml" >
<head id="Head1" runat="server">
    <style type="text/css">
    html
    {
        background-color:silver;
    }
    #content
    {
        margins:auto;
        width:600px;
        padding:10px;
        background-color:white;
        font:14px Georgia,Serif;
    }
    .frmMovies
    {
        width:100%;
    }
    </style>
    <title>Show FormView Pager Template</title>
</head>
<body>
    <form id="form1" runat="server">
    <div id="content">

    <asp:FormView
        id="frmMovies"
        DataSourceID="srcMovies"
        AllowPaging="true"
        CssClass="frmMovies"
        Runat="server">
        <ItemTemplate>
        <h1><%# Eval("Title") %></h1>
        <b>Directed By:</b>
        <%# Eval("Director") %>
        <br />
        <b>Box Office Totals:</b>
        <%#Eval("BoxOfficeTotals", "{0:c}") %>
```

```
        </ItemTemplate>
        <PagerTemplate>
        <hr />
        <div style="float:left">
        Page: <%# frmMovies.PageIndex + 1 %>
        </div>

        <div style="float:right;white-space:nowrap">
        <asp:LinkButton
            id="lnkPrevious"
            Text="Previous Page"
            CommandName="Page"
            CommandArgument="Prev"
            Runat="server" />
        |
        <asp:LinkButton
            id="lnkNext"
            Text="Next Page"
            CommandName="Page"
            CommandArgument="Next"
            Runat="server" />
        </div>
        </PagerTemplate>
    </asp:FormView>

    <asp:SqlDataSource
        id="srcMovies"
        ConnectionString="<%$ ConnectionStrings:Movies %>"
        SelectCommand="SELECT Id,Title,Director,BoxOfficeTotals FROM Movies"
        Runat="server" />

    </div>
    </form>
</body>
</html>
```

Each button contained in the PagerTemplate has both a CommandName and CommandArgument property. The CommandName is set to the value Page. CommandArgument specifies a particular type of paging operation.

You can use the following values for the CommandArgument property:

▶ **First**—Navigates to the first page.

▶ **Last**—Navigates to the last page.

▶ **Prev**—Navigates to the previous page.

▶ **Next**—Navigates to the next page.

▶ **number**—Navigates to a particular page number.

Editing Data with the `FormView` Control

You can edit a database record with the FormView control. For example, you can use the page in Listing 12.22 to edit any of the records in the Movies database table (see Figure 12.15).

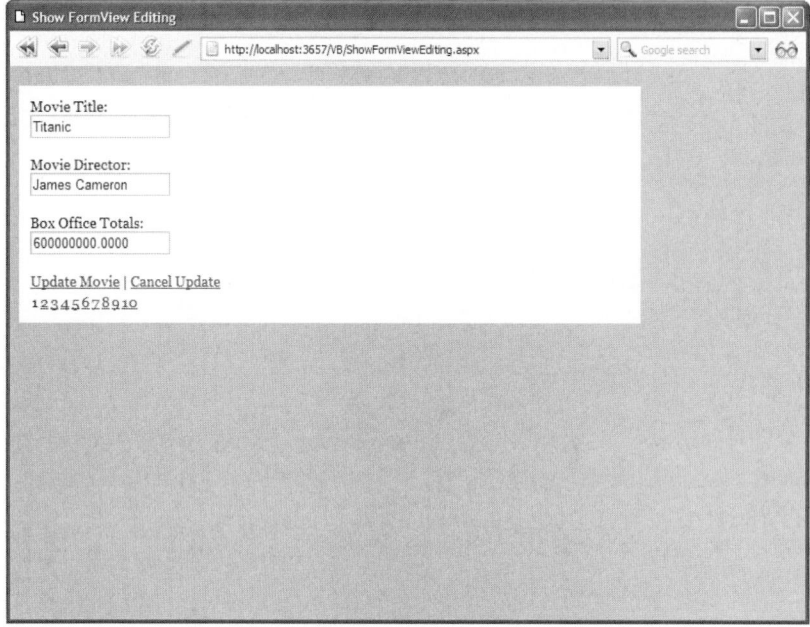

FIGURE 12.15   Editing a record with the FormView control.

LISTING 12.22   ShowFormViewEditing.aspx

```
<%@ Page Language="C#" %>
<!DOCTYPE html PUBLIC "-//W3C//DTD XHTML 1.1//EN"
   "http://www.w3.org/TR/xhtml11/DTD/xhtml11.dtd">
<html xmlns="http://www.w3.org/1999/xhtml" >
<head id="Head1" runat="server">
    <style type="text/css">
    html
    {
        background-color:silver;
    }
    #content
```

```
    {
        margins:auto;
        width:600px;
        padding:10px;
        background-color:white;
        font:14px Georgia,Serif;
    }
    a
    {
        color:blue;
    }
    </style>
    <title>Show FormView Editing</title>
</head>
<body>
    <form id="form1" runat="server">
    <div id="content">

    <asp:FormView
        id="frmMovies"
        DataSourceID="srcMovies"
        DataKeyNames="Id"
        AllowPaging="true"
        Runat="server">
        <ItemTemplate>
        <h1><%# Eval("Title") %></h1>
        <b>Directed By:</b>
        <%# Eval("Director") %>
        <br />
        <b>Box Office Totals:</b>
        <%#Eval("BoxOfficeTotals", "{0:c}") %>
        <hr />
        <asp:LinkButton
            id="lnkEdit"
            Text="Edit Movie"
            CommandName="Edit"
            Runat="server" />
        </ItemTemplate>
        <EditItemTemplate>
        <asp:Label
            id="lblTitle"
            Text="Movie Title:"
            AssociatedControlID="txtTitle"
            Runat="server" />
        <br />
        <asp:TextBox
```

```
            id="txtTitle"
            Text='<%# Bind("Title") %>'
            Runat="server" />
        <br /><br />
        <asp:Label
            id="lblDirector"
            Text="Movie Director:"
            AssociatedControlID="txtDirector"
            Runat="server" />
        <br />
        <asp:TextBox
            id="txtDirector"
            Text='<%# Bind("Director") %>'
            Runat="server" />
        <br /><br />
        <asp:Label
            id="lblBoxOfficeTotals"
            Text="Box Office Totals:"
            AssociatedControlID="txtBoxOfficeTotals"
            Runat="server" />
        <br />
        <asp:TextBox
            id="txtBoxOfficeTotals"
            Text='<%# Bind("BoxOfficeTotals") %>'
            Runat="server" />
        <br /><br />
        <asp:LinkButton
            id="lnkUpdate"
            Text="Update Movie"
            CommandName="Update"
            Runat="server" />
        |
        <asp:LinkButton
            id="lnkCancel"
            Text="Cancel Update"
            CommandName="Cancel"
            Runat="server" />
    </EditItemTemplate>
</asp:FormView>

<asp:SqlDataSource
    id="srcMovies"
    ConnectionString="<%$ ConnectionStrings:Movies %>"
    SelectCommand="SELECT Id,Title,Director,BoxOfficeTotals
        FROM Movies"
```

```
        UpdateCommand="UPDATE Movies SET Title=@Title,
            Director=@Director,BoxOfficeTotals=@BoxOfficeTotals
            WHERE Id=@Id"
        Runat="server" />

    </div>
    </form>
</body>
</html>
```

You should notice several things about the FormView control in Listing 12.22. First, the FormView control includes a DataKeyNames property that contains the name of the primary key from the data source. You need to specify a primary key when editing records.

Next, the FormView control's ItemTemplate includes a LinkButton that looks like this:

```
<asp:LinkButton
  id="lnkEdit"
  Text="Edit Movie"
  CommandName="Edit"
  Runat="server" />
```

This LinkButton includes a CommandName property with the value Edit. Clicking the link switches the FormView control into Edit mode. You could use any other control here that supports the CommandName property such as a Button or ImageButton control.

Next, the FormView control includes an EditItemTemplate. This template contains the form for editing the record. Each form field uses a two-way databinding expression. For example, the form field for editing the movie title looks like this:

```
<asp:TextBox
  id="txtTitle"
  Text='<%# Bind("Title") %>'
  Runat="server" />
```

The Bind("Title") method binds the Title column to the Text property of the TextBox control.

Finally, the EditItemTemplate includes both a LinkButton for updating the database record and a LinkButton for canceling the update. The LinkButton for updating the record looks like this:

```
<asp:LinkButton
    id="lnkUpdate"
    Text="Update Movie"
    CommandName="Update"
    Runat="server" />
```

This `LinkButton` includes a `CommandName` property, which has the value `Update`. When you click this `LinkButton`, the SQL statement represented by the `SqlDataSource` control's `UpdateCommand` is executed.

> **NOTE**
>
> If you want the `FormView` control to be in Edit mode by default, you can assign the value `Edit` to the `FormView` control's `DefaultMode` property.

Inserting Data with the `FormView` Control

You can use the `FormView` control to insert new records into a database table. For example, the page in Listing 12.23 enables you to insert a new movie record into the Movies database table.

LISTING 12.23   `ShowFormViewInserting.aspx`

```
<%@ Page Language="C#" %>
<!DOCTYPE html PUBLIC "-//W3C//DTD XHTML 1.1//EN"
    "http://www.w3.org/TR/xhtml11/DTD/xhtml11.dtd">
<html xmlns="http://www.w3.org/1999/xhtml" >
<head id="Head1" runat="server">
    <style type="text/css">
    html
    {
        background-color:silver;
    }
    #content
    {
        margins:auto;
        width:600px;
        padding:10px;
        background-color:white;
        font:14px Georgia,Serif;
    }
    a
    {
        color:blue;
    }
    </style>
    <title>Show FormView Inserting</title>
</head>
<body>
    <form id="form1" runat="server">
    <div id="content">
```

```
<asp:FormView
    id="frmMovies"
    DataSourceID="srcMovies"
    AllowPaging="true"
    Runat="server">
    <ItemTemplate>
    <h1><%# Eval("Title") %></h1>
    <b>Directed By:</b>
    <%# Eval("Director") %>
    <br />
    <b>In Theaters:</b>
    <%#Eval("InTheaters") %>
    <hr />
    <asp:LinkButton
        id="lnkNew"
        Text="New Movie"
        CommandName="New"
        Runat="server" />
    </ItemTemplate>
    <InsertItemTemplate>
    <asp:Label
        id="lblTitle"
        Text="Movie Title:"
        AssociatedControlID="txtTitle"
        Runat="server" />
    <br />
    <asp:TextBox
        id="txtTitle"
        Text='<%# Bind("Title") %>'
        Runat="server" />
    <br /><br />
    <asp:Label
        id="lblDirector"
        Text="Movie Director:"
        AssociatedControlID="txtDirector"
        Runat="server" />
    <br />
    <asp:TextBox
        id="txtDirector"
        Text='<%# Bind("Director") %>'
        Runat="server" />
    <br /><br />
    <asp:CheckBox
        id="chkInTheaters"
        Text="In Theaters"
        Checked='<%# Bind("InTheaters") %>'
```

```
                    Runat="server" />
            <br /><br />
            <asp:LinkButton
                id="lnkInsert"
                Text="Insert Movie"
                CommandName="Insert"
                Runat="server" />
            |
            <asp:LinkButton
                id="lnkCancel"
                Text="Cancel Insert"
                CommandName="Cancel"
                Runat="server" />
        </InsertItemTemplate>
    </asp:FormView>

    <asp:SqlDataSource
        id="srcMovies"
        ConnectionString="<%$ ConnectionStrings:Movies %>"
        SelectCommand="SELECT Id,Title,Director,InTheaters
            FROM Movies"
        InsertCommand="INSERT Movies (Title,Director,InTheaters)
            VALUES (@Title,@Director,
        Runat="server" />

    </div>
    </form>
</body>
</html>
```

You should notice several things about the page in Listing 12.23. First, ItemTemplate
includes a LinkButton control that looks like this:

```
<asp:LinkButton
  id="lnkNew"
  Text="New Movie"
  CommandName="New"
  Runat="server" />
```

When you click this `LinkButton` control, the `FormView` switches into Insert mode and displays the contents of the `InsertTemplate`. The `CommandName` property has the value `New`.

The `FormView` control includes `InsertItemTemplate` that contains the form for inserting a new movie record. Each form field uses a two-way databinding expression. For example, the `InTheaters` `CheckBox` looks like this:

```
<asp:CheckBox
  id="chkInTheaters"
  Text="In Theaters"
  Checked='<%# Bind("InTheaters") %>'
  Runat="server" />
```

The `Bind("InTheaters")` method binds the value of the `CheckBox` control's `Checked` property to the `InTheaters` database column.

The `InsertItemTemplate` contains a `LinkButton` for inserting the record and a `LinkButton` for canceling the insert operation. The `LinkButton` for inserting a record looks like this:

```
<asp:LinkButton
  id="lnkInsert"
  Text="Insert Movie"
  CommandName="Insert"
  Runat="server" />
```

This `LinkButton` control includes a `CommandName` property that has the value `Insert`. When you click the `LinkButton`, the SQL command represented by the `SqlDataSource` control's `InsertCommand` is executed.

> **NOTE**
>
> You can place the `FormView` control into Insert mode by default by assigning the value `Insert` to the control's `DefaultMode` property.

Deleting Data with the `FormView` Control

You can use the `FormView` control to delete database records. For example, the page in Listing 12.24 enables you to delete records from the Movies database table (see Figure 12.16).

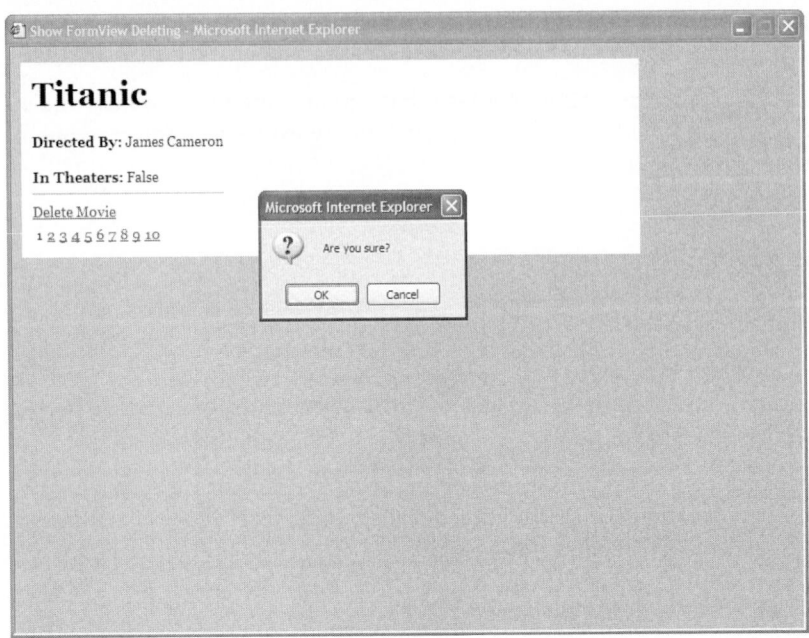

FIGURE 12.16   Deleting a record with the `FormView` control.

LISTING 12.24   `ShowFormViewDeleting.aspx`

```
<%@ Page Language="C#" %>
<!DOCTYPE html PUBLIC "-//W3C//DTD XHTML 1.1//EN"
    "http://www.w3.org/TR/xhtml11/DTD/xhtml11.dtd">
<html xmlns="http://www.w3.org/1999/xhtml" >
<head id="Head1" runat="server">
    <style type="text/css">
    html
    {
        background-color:silver;
    }
    #content
    {
        margins:auto;
        width:600px;
        padding:10px;
        background-color:white;
        font:14px Georgia,Serif;
    }
    a
    {
```

```
        color:blue;
    }
    </style>
    <title>Show FormView Deleting</title>
</head>
<body>
    <form id="form1" runat="server">
    <div id="content">

    <asp:FormView
        id="frmMovies"
        DataSourceID="srcMovies"
        DataKeyNames="Id"
        AllowPaging="true"
        Runat="server">
        <ItemTemplate>
        <h1><%# Eval("Title") %></h1>
        <b>Directed By:</b>
        <%# Eval("Director") %>
        <br />
        <b>In Theaters:</b>
        <%#Eval("InTheaters") %>
        <hr />
        <asp:LinkButton
            id="lnkDelete"
            Text="Delete Movie"
            CommandName="Delete"
            OnClientClick="return confirm('Are you sure?');"
            Runat="server" />
        </ItemTemplate>
    </asp:FormView>

    <asp:SqlDataSource
        id="srcMovies"
        ConnectionString="<%$ ConnectionStrings:Movies %>"
        SelectCommand="SELECT Id,Title,Director,InTheaters
            FROM Movies"
        DeleteCommand="DELETE Movies WHERE Id=@Id"
        Runat="server" />

    </div>
    </form>
</body>
</html>
```

The FormView control includes a DataKeyNames property, which contains the name of the primary key column from the data source. When deleting records with the FormView control, you need to indicate the primary key column.

Furthermore, the ItemTemplate includes a LinkButton for deleting a record. The LinkButton looks like this:

```
<asp:LinkButton
  id="lnkDelete"
  Text="Delete Movie"
  CommandName="Delete"
  OnClientClick="return confirm('Are you sure?');"
  Runat="server" />
```

This LinkButton includes a CommandName property that has the value Delete. When you click the LinkButton, the SQL command represented by the SqlDataSource control's DeleteCommand property is executed.

Also, the LinkButton includes an OnClientClick property that calls the JavaScript confirm() method to display a confirmation dialog box. This extra script prevents users from accidentally deleting database records.

Summary

In this chapter, you learned how to work with individual database records by using the DetailsView and FormView controls. You learned how to use both controls to display, page, edit, insert, and delete database records. You also learned how to format the appearance of both controls.

CHAPTER 13

Using the Repeater and DataList Controls

Both the Repeater and DataList controls—the subjects of this chapter—enable you to display a set of data items at a time. For example, you can use these controls to display all the rows contained in a database table.

The Repeater control is entirely template-driven. You can format the rendered output of the control in any way that you want. For example, you can use the Repeater control to display records in a bulleted list, a set of HTML tables, or even in a comma-delimited list.

The DataList control is also template-driven. However, unlike the Repeater control, the default behavior of the DataList control is to render its contents into an HTML table. The DataList control renders each record from its data source into a separate HTML table cell.

In this chapter, you learn how to use both of these controls to display database data. You also learn how to use each of the different types of templates that each of the controls supports. Finally, you can see how to handle the different types of events that the controls expose.

Using the Repeater Control

The Repeater control provides you with the maximum amount of flexibility in rendering a set of database records. You can format the output of the Repeater control in any way that you want. In this section, you learn how to display data with the Repeater control and handle Repeater control events.

Displaying Data with the **Repeater** Control

To display data with the `Repeater` control, you must create an `ItemTemplate`. For example, the page in Listing 13.1 displays the contents of the Movies database table (see Figure 13.1).

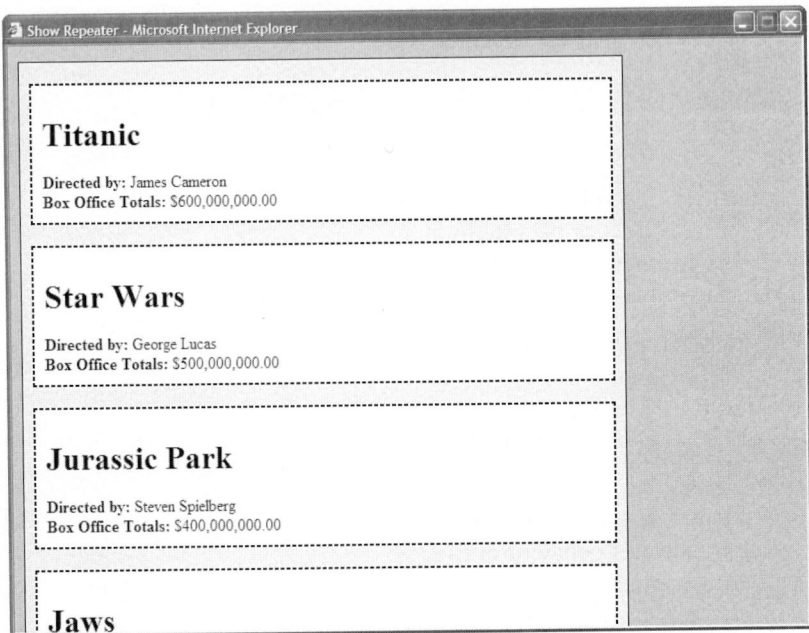

FIGURE 13.1   Displaying data with a `Repeater` control.

LISTING 13.1   ShowRepeater.aspx

```
<%@ Page Language="C#" %>
<!DOCTYPE html PUBLIC "-//W3C//DTD XHTML 1.1//EN"
  "http://www.w3.org/TR/xhtml11/DTD/xhtml11.dtd">
<html xmlns="http://www.w3.org/1999/xhtml" >
<head id="Head1" runat="server">
    <style type="text/css">
    html
    {
        background-color:silver;
    }
    .content
    {
        width:600px;
        border:solid 1px black;
        background-color:#eeeeee;
    }
```

```
        .movies
        {
            margin:20px 10px;
            padding:10px;
            border:dashed 2px black;
            background-color:white;
        }
        </style>
        <title>Show Repeater</title>
    </head>
<body>
        <form id="form1" runat="server">
        <div class="content">

        <asp:Repeater
            id="rptMovies"
            DataSourceID="srcMovies"
            Runat="server">
            <ItemTemplate>
            <div class="movies">
            <h1><%#Eval("Title") %></h1>
            <b>Directed by:</b> <%# Eval("Director") %>
            <br />
            <b>Box Office Totals:</b> <%# Eval("BoxOfficeTotals","{0:c}") %>
            </div>
            </ItemTemplate>
        </asp:Repeater>

        <asp:SqlDataSource
            id="srcMovies"
            ConnectionString="<%$ ConnectionStrings:Movies %>"
            SelectCommand="SELECT Title,Director,BoxOfficeTotals
                FROM Movies"
            Runat="server" />

        </div>
        </form>
</body>
</html>
```

The Repeater control in Listing 13.1 displays each record in a separate HTML <div> tag. A databinding expression is used to display the value of each column.

In Listing 13.1, declarative databinding is used to bind the Repeater to the SqlDataSource. You also can databind a Repeater control programmatically.

For example, the page in Listing 13.2 contains a Repeater control that renders a JavaScript array. The Repeater control is programmatically databound to the list of files in the Photos directory.

LISTING 13.2   ShowRepeaterPhotos.aspx

```
<%@ Page Language="C#" %>
<%@ Import Namespace="System.IO" %>
<!DOCTYPE html PUBLIC "-//W3C//DTD XHTML 1.1//EN"
"http://www.w3.org/TR/xhtml11/DTD/xhtml11.dtd">
<script runat="server">

    void Page_Load()
    {
        if (!Page.IsPostBack)
        {
            DirectoryInfo dir = new DirectoryInfo(MapPath("~/Photos"));
            rptPhotos.DataSource = dir.GetFiles("*.jpg");
            rptPhotos.DataBind();
        }
    }
</script>
<html xmlns="http://www.w3.org/1999/xhtml" >
<head id="Head1" runat="server">
    <style type="text/css">
        .photo
        {
            width:400px;
            background-color:white;
            filter:progid:DXImageTransform.Microsoft.Fade(duration=2);
        }
    </style>
    <script type="text/javascript">
    var photos = new Array();
    window.setInterval(showImage, 5000);

    function showImage()
    {
        if (photos.length > 0)
        {
            var index = Math.floor(Math.random() * photos.length);
            var image = document.getElementById('imgPhoto');
            image.src = photos[index];
            if (image.filters)
            {
                image.filters[0].Apply();
```

```
                    image.filters[0].Play();
                }
            }
        }
        </script>
        <title>Show Repeater Photos</title>
</head>
<body>
    <form id="form1" runat="server">
    <div>


    <img id="imgPhoto" alt="" class="photo" />
    <script type="text/javascript">
    <asp:Repeater
        id="rptPhotos"
        Runat="server">
        <ItemTemplate>
        <%# Eval("Name", "photos.push('Photos/{0}')") %>
        </ItemTemplate>
    </asp:Repeater>
    showImage();
    </script>

    </div>
    </form>
</body>
</html>
```

The page in Listing 13.2 randomly displays a different photo every 5 seconds. A random image is selected from the JavaScript array and displayed by the JavaScript showImage() function. An Internet Explorer transition filter is used to create a fade-in effect.

WEB STANDARDS NOTE

The transition filter is an Internet Explorer-only extension to Cascading Style Sheets (CSS). The page still works with Opera and Firefox, but you don't get the fade-in effect.

Using Templates with the Repeater Control

The Repeater control supports five different types of templates:

▶ **ItemTemplate**—Formats each item from the data source.

▶ **AlternatingItemTemplate**—Formats every other item from the data source.

- **SeparatorTemplate**—Formats between each item from the data source.
- **HeaderTemplate**—Formats before all items from the data source.
- **FooterTemplate**—Formats after all items from the data source.

You are required to use only an `ItemTemplate`; the other types of templates can be used at your own discretion. The order in which you declare the templates in the `Repeater` control does not matter.

You can use the `SeparatorTemplate` to create a banding effect (as in old-time computer paper). In other words, you can use the `SeparatorTemplate` to display alternating rows with a different background color. This approach is illustrated by the page in Listing 13.3 (see Figure 13.2).

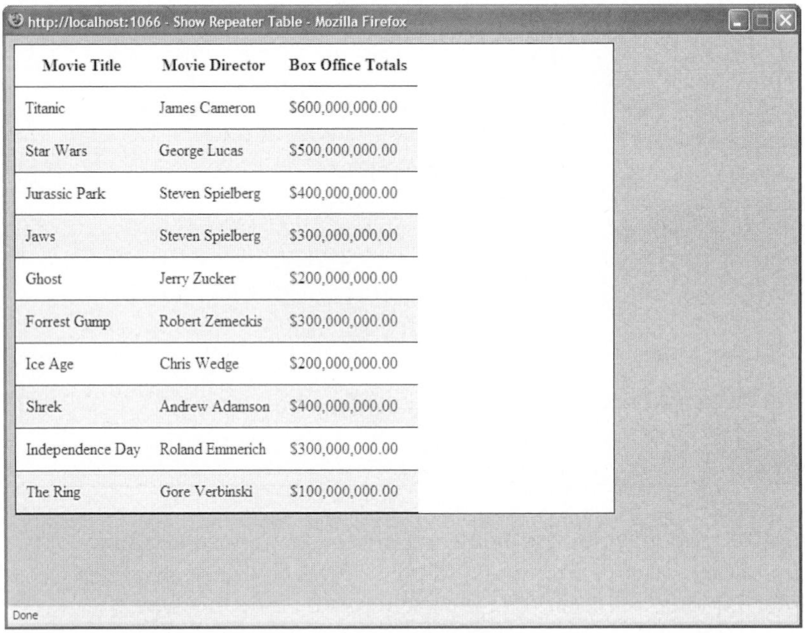

Movie Title	Movie Director	Box Office Totals
Titanic	James Cameron	$600,000,000.00
Star Wars	George Lucas	$500,000,000.00
Jurassic Park	Steven Spielberg	$400,000,000.00
Jaws	Steven Spielberg	$300,000,000.00
Ghost	Jerry Zucker	$200,000,000.00
Forrest Gump	Robert Zemeckis	$300,000,000.00
Ice Age	Chris Wedge	$200,000,000.00
Shrek	Andrew Adamson	$400,000,000.00
Independence Day	Roland Emmerich	$300,000,000.00
The Ring	Gore Verbinski	$100,000,000.00

FIGURE 13.2 Displaying an HTML table with the `Repeater` control.

LISTING 13.3 `ShowRepeaterTable.aspx`

```
<%@ Page Language="C#" %>
<!DOCTYPE html PUBLIC "-//W3C//DTD XHTML 1.1//EN"
  "http://www.w3.org/TR/xhtml11/DTD/xhtml11.dtd">
<html xmlns="http://www.w3.org/1999/xhtml" >
<head id="Head1" runat="server">
    <style type="text/css">
    html
    {
```

```
        background-color:silver;
    }
    .content
    {
        width:600px;
        border:solid 1px black;
        background-color:white;
    }
    .movies
    {
        border-collapse:collapse;
    }
    .movies th,.movies td
    {
        padding:10px;
        border-bottom:1px solid black;
    }
    .alternating
    {
        background-color:#eeeeee;
    }
    </style>
    <title>Show Repeater Table</title>
</head>
<body>
    <form id="form1" runat="server">
    <div class="content">

    <asp:Repeater
        id="rptMovies"
        DataSourceID="srcMovies"
        Runat="server">
        <HeaderTemplate>
        <table class="movies">
        <tr>
            <th>Movie Title</th>
            <th>Movie Director</th>
            <th>Box Office Totals</th>
        </tr>
        </HeaderTemplate>
        <ItemTemplate>
        <tr>
            <td><%#Eval("Title") %></td>
            <td><%#Eval("Director") %></td>
            <td><%#Eval("BoxOfficeTotals","{0:c}") %></td>
```

```
            </tr>
        </ItemTemplate>
        <AlternatingItemTemplate>
        <tr class="alternating">
            <td><%#Eval("Title") %></td>
            <td><%#Eval("Director") %></td>
            <td><%#Eval("BoxOfficeTotals","{0:c}") %></td>
        </tr>
        </AlternatingItemTemplate>
        <FooterTemplate>
        </table>
        </FooterTemplate>
    </asp:Repeater>

    <asp:SqlDataSource
        id="srcMovies"
        ConnectionString="<%$ ConnectionStrings:Movies %>"
        SelectCommand="SELECT Title,Director,BoxOfficeTotals
            FROM Movies"
        Runat="server" />

    </div>
    </form>
</body>
</html>
```

The Repeater control in Listing 13.3 renders an HTML table in which every other row appears with a gray background color. This Repeater control uses four out of five of the templates supported by Repeater: the ItemTemplate, AlternatingItemTemplate, HeaderTemplate, and FooterTemplate.

The AlternatingItemTemplate contains almost exactly the same content as the ItemTemplate. The only difference is that the <tr> tag includes a class attribute that changes its background color.

The SeparatorTemplate is used to add content between each data item from the data source. For example, the page in Listing 13.4 uses a SeparatorItemTemplate to create a tab strip with the Repeater control (see Figure 13.3).

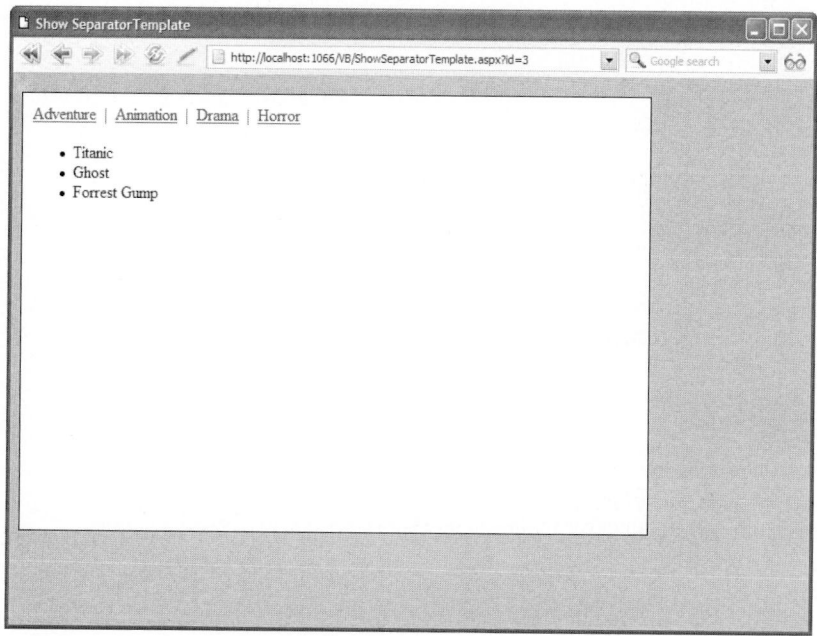

FIGURE 13.3   Displaying a tab strip with the `Repeater` control.

LISTING 13.4   ShowSeparatorTemplate.aspx

```
<%@ Page Language="C#" %>
<!DOCTYPE html PUBLIC "-//W3C//DTD XHTML 1.1//EN"
    "http://www.w3.org/TR/xhtml11/DTD/xhtml11.dtd">
<html xmlns="http://www.w3.org/1999/xhtml" >
<head id="Head1" runat="server">
    <style type="text/css">
    html
    {
        background-color:silver;
    }
    .content
    {
        width:600px;
        height:400px;
        padding:10px;
        border:solid 1px black;
        background-color:white;
    }
    a
    {
        color:blue;
```

```
        }
        </style>
        <title>Show SeparatorTemplate</title>
</head>
<body>
    <form id="form1" runat="server">
    <div class="content">

    <asp:Repeater
        id="rptMovieCategories"
        DataSourceID="srcMovieCategories"
        Runat="server">
        <ItemTemplate>
        <asp:HyperLink
            id="lnkMenu"
            Text='<%#Eval("Name")%>'
            NavigateUrl='<%#Eval("Id","ShowSeparatorTemplate.aspx?id={0}")%>'
            Runat="server" />
        </ItemTemplate>
        <SeparatorTemplate>
         | 
        </SeparatorTemplate>
    </asp:Repeater>

    <asp:Repeater
        id="rptMovies"
        DataSourceID="srcMovies"
        Runat="server">
        <HeaderTemplate>
        <ul>
        </HeaderTemplate>
        <ItemTemplate>
        <li><%#Eval("Title")%></li>
        </ItemTemplate>
        <FooterTemplate>
        </ul>
        </FooterTemplate>
    </asp:Repeater>

    <asp:SqlDataSource
        id="srcMovieCategories"
        ConnectionString="<%$ ConnectionStrings:Movies %>"
        SelectCommand="SELECT Id, Name
            FROM MovieCategories"
        Runat="server" />
```

```
<asp:SqlDataSource
    id="srcMovies"
    ConnectionString="<%$ ConnectionStrings:Movies %>"
    SelectCommand="SELECT Title FROM Movies
        WHERE CategoryId=@CategoryId"
    Runat="server">
    <SelectParameters>
    <asp:QueryStringParameter
        Name="CategoryId"
        QueryStringField="Id" />
    </SelectParameters>
</asp:SqlDataSource>

</div>
</form>
</body>
</html>
```

The page in Listing 13.4 contains two Repeater controls. The first Repeater control displays a tab strip of movie categories. The second Repeater control displays a bulleted list of matching movies.

Handling Repeater Control Events

The Repeater control supports the following events:

▶ **DataBinding**—Raised when the Repeater control is bound to its data source.

▶ **ItemCommand**—Raised when a control contained in the Repeater control raises an event.

▶ **ItemCreated**—Raised when each Repeater item is created.

▶ **ItemDataBound**—Raised when each Repeater item is bound.

The page in Listing 13.5 illustrates how you can use the DataBinding, ItemCommand, and ItemDataBound events. This page uses a Repeater control to update, delete, and insert database records (see Figure 13.4).

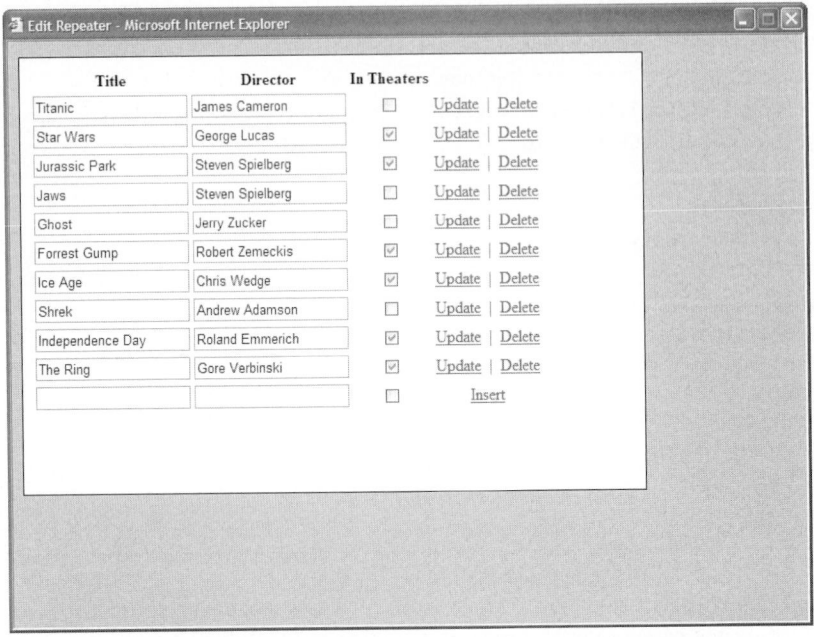

FIGURE 13.4   Editing database records with the Repeater control.

LISTING 13.5   EditRepeater.aspx

```csharp
<%@ Page Language="C#" %>
<!DOCTYPE html PUBLIC "-//W3C//DTD XHTML 1.1//EN"
"http://www.w3.org/TR/xhtml11/DTD/xhtml11.dtd">

<script runat="server">

    // The name of the primary key column
    string DataKeyName = "Id";

    /// <summary>
    /// Stores the primary keys in ViewState
    /// </summary>
    Hashtable Keys
    {
        get
        {
            if (ViewState["Keys"] == null)
                ViewState["Keys"] = new Hashtable();
            return (Hashtable)ViewState["Keys"];
        }
    }
```

```csharp
/// <summary>
/// Build the primary key collection
/// </summary>
protected void rptMovies_ItemDataBound(object sender, RepeaterItemEventArgs e)
{
    if (e.Item.ItemType == ListItemType.Item || e.Item.ItemType ==
ListItemType.AlternatingItem)
    {
        Keys.Add(e.Item.ItemIndex, DataBinder.Eval(e.Item.DataItem, "Id"));
    }
}


/// <summary>
/// Clear the primary keys when Repeater is rebound
/// to its data source
/// </summary>
protected void rptMovies_DataBinding(object sender, EventArgs e)
{
    Keys.Clear();
}


/// <summary>
/// When you click the Update,Insert, or Delete
/// button, this method executes
/// </summary>
protected void rptMovies_ItemCommand(object source, RepeaterCommandEventArgs e)
{
    switch (e.CommandName)
    {
        case "Update":
            UpdateMovie(e);
            break;
        case "Insert":
            InsertMovie(e);
            break;
        case "Delete":
            DeleteMovie(e);
            break;
    }
}


/// <summary>
/// Update a movie record
/// </summary>
void UpdateMovie(RepeaterCommandEventArgs e)
```

13

```
    {
        // Get the form fields
        TextBox txtTitle = (TextBox)e.Item.FindControl("txtTitle");
        TextBox txtDirector = (TextBox)e.Item.FindControl("txtDirector");
        CheckBox chkInTheaters = (CheckBox)e.Item.FindControl("chkInTheaters");

        // Set the DataSource parameters
        srcMovies.UpdateParameters["Id"].DefaultValue =
Keys[e.Item.ItemIndex].ToString();
        srcMovies.UpdateParameters["Title"].DefaultValue = txtTitle.Text;
        srcMovies.UpdateParameters["Director"].DefaultValue = txtDirector.Text;
        srcMovies.UpdateParameters["InTheaters"].DefaultValue =
chkInTheaters.Checked.ToString();

        // Fire the UpdateCommand
        srcMovies.Update();
    }


    /// <summary>
    /// Insert a movie record
    /// </summary>
    void InsertMovie(RepeaterCommandEventArgs e)
    {
        // Get the form fields
        TextBox txtTitle = (TextBox)e.Item.FindControl("txtTitle");
        TextBox txtDirector = (TextBox)e.Item.FindControl("txtDirector");
        CheckBox chkInTheaters = (CheckBox)e.Item.FindControl("chkInTheaters");

        // Set the DataSource parameters
        srcMovies.InsertParameters["Title"].DefaultValue = txtTitle.Text;
        srcMovies.InsertParameters["Director"].DefaultValue = txtDirector.Text;
        srcMovies.InsertParameters["InTheaters"].DefaultValue =
chkInTheaters.Checked.ToString();

        // Fire the InsertCommand
        srcMovies.Insert();
    }


    /// <summary>
    /// Delete a movie record
    /// </summary>
    void DeleteMovie(RepeaterCommandEventArgs e)
    {
        // Set the DataSource parameters
        srcMovies.DeleteParameters["Id"].DefaultValue =
Keys[e.Item.ItemIndex].ToString();
```

```
            // Fire the DeleteCommand
            srcMovies.Delete();


        }

</script>
<html xmlns="http://www.w3.org/1999/xhtml" >
<head id="Head1" runat="server">
    <style type="text/css">
    html
    {
        background-color:silver;
    }
    .content
    {
        width:600px;
        height:400px;
        padding:10px;
        border:solid 1px black;
        background-color:white;
    }
    .movies td
    {
        text-align:center;
    }
    a
    {
        color:blue;
    }
    </style>
    <title>Edit Repeater</title>
</head>
<body>
    <form id="form1" runat="server">
    <div class="content">

    <asp:Repeater
        id="rptMovies"
        DataSourceID="srcMovies"
        Runat="server" OnItemCommand="rptMovies_ItemCommand"
OnItemDataBound="rptMovies_ItemDataBound" OnDataBinding="rptMovies_DataBinding">
        <HeaderTemplate>
        <table class="movies">
        <tr>
            <th>Title</th>
            <th>Director</th>
```

13

```
        <th>In Theaters</th>
    </tr>
</HeaderTemplate>
<ItemTemplate>
<tr>
    <td>
    <asp:TextBox
        id="txtTitle"
        Text='<%#Eval("Title")%>'
        Runat="server" />
    </td>
    <td>
    <asp:TextBox
        id="txtDirector"
        Text='<%#Eval("Director")%>'
        Runat="server" />
    </td>
    <td>
    <asp:CheckBox
        id="chkInTheaters"
        Checked='<%#Eval("InTheaters")%>'
        Runat="server" />
    </td>
    <td>
    <asp:LinkButton
        id="lnkUpdate"
        CommandName="Update"
        Text="Update"
        Runat="server" />
     | 
    <asp:LinkButton
        id="lnkDelete"
        CommandName="Delete"
        Text="Delete"
        OnClientClick="return confirm('Are you sure?');"
        Runat="server" />
    </td>
</tr>
</ItemTemplate>
<FooterTemplate>
<tr>
    <td>
    <asp:TextBox
        id="txtTitle"
        Runat="server" />
    </td>
```

```
                <td>
                <asp:TextBox
                    id="txtDirector"
                    Runat="server" />
                </td>
                <td>
                <asp:CheckBox
                    id="chkInTheaters"
                    Runat="server" />
                </td>
                <td>
                <asp:LinkButton
                    id="lnkInsert"
                    CommandName="Insert"
                    Text="Insert"
                    Runat="server" />
                </td>
        </tr>
        </table>
        </FooterTemplate>
</asp:Repeater>

<asp:SqlDataSource
    id="srcMovies"
    ConnectionString="<%$ ConnectionStrings:Movies %>"
    SelectCommand="SELECT Id,Title,Director,InTheaters
        FROM Movies"
    UpdateCommand="UPDATE Movies SET Title=@Title,
        Director=@Director,InTheaters=@InTheaters
        WHERE Id=@Id"
    InsertCommand="INSERT Movies (Title,Director,InTheaters)
        VALUES (@Title,@Director,
    DeleteCommand="DELETE Movies WHERE Id=@Id"
    Runat="server">
    <UpdateParameters>
        <asp:Parameter Name="Id" />
        <asp:Parameter Name="Title" />
        <asp:Parameter Name="Director" />
        <asp:Parameter Name="InTheaters" />
    </UpdateParameters>
    <InsertParameters>
        <asp:Parameter Name="Title" />
        <asp:Parameter Name="Director" />
        <asp:Parameter Name="InTheaters" />
    </InsertParameters>
    <DeleteParameters>
```

13

```
            <asp:Parameter Name="Id" />
        </DeleteParameters>
    </asp:SqlDataSource>

    </div>
    </form>
</body>
</html>
```

In Listing 13.5, the ItemDataBound event handler builds a collection of primary keys from the data source. The collection of primary keys is stored in ViewState so that they will be available after a postback to the server.

The DataBinding event handler clears the primary key collection when the Repeater is rebound to its data source (after a record is updated or deleted). If you don't clear the collection, you get duplicates of the primary keys and an exception is raised.

The ItemCommand event handler takes care of processing the button click events. When you click an Insert, Update, or Delete button, the event bubbles up and raises the ItemCommmand event. The ItemCommand event handler grabs the values from the form fields and calls the Insert(), Update(), or Delete() methods of the SqlDataSource control.

Using the DataList Control

The DataList control, like the Repeater control, is template driven. Unlike the Repeater control, by default, the DataList renders an HTML table. Because the DataList uses a particular layout to render its content, you are provided with more formatting options when using the DataList control.

In this section, you learn how to use the DataList control to display data. You also learn how to render database records in both single-column and multicolumn HTML tables. We also explore how you can edit data with the DataList control.

Displaying Data with the DataList Control

To display data with the DataList control, you must supply the control with an ItemTemplate. The contents of the ItemTemplate are rendered for each data item from the data source.

For example, the page in Listing 13.6 uses a DataList to display the contents of the Movies database table. The ItemTemplate displays the values of the Title, Director, and BoxOfficeTotals columns (see Figure 13.5).

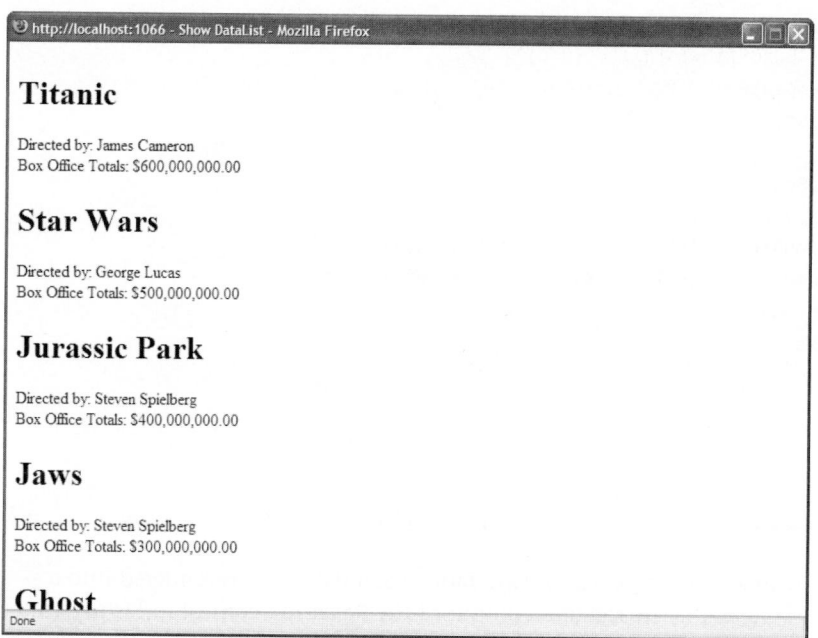

FIGURE 13.5   Displaying database records with the `DataList` control.

LISTING 13.6   ShowDataList.aspx

```
<%@ Page Language="C#" %>
<!DOCTYPE html PUBLIC "-//W3C//DTD XHTML 1.1//EN"
    "http://www.w3.org/TR/xhtml11/DTD/xhtml11.dtd">
<html xmlns="http://www.w3.org/1999/xhtml" >
<head id="Head1" runat="server">
    <title>Show DataList</title>
</head>
<body>
    <form id="form1" runat="server">
    <div>

    <asp:DataList
        id="dlstMovies"
        DataSourceID="srcMovies"
        Runat="server">
        <ItemTemplate>
        <h1><%#Eval("Title")%></h1>
        Directed by:
        <%#Eval("Director") %>
        <br />
```

```
        Box Office Totals:
        <%#Eval("BoxOfficeTotals","{0:c}") %>
        </ItemTemplate>
    </asp:DataList>

    <asp:SqlDataSource
        id="srcMovies"
        ConnectionString="<%$ ConnectionStrings:Movies %>"
        SelectCommand="SELECT Title,Director,BoxOfficeTotals
            FROM Movies"
        Runat="server" />

    </div>
    </form>
</body>
</html>
```

The DataList in Listing 13.6 renders an HTML table. Each data item is rendered into a separate table cell (<td> tag). The rendered output of the DataList control in Listing 13.6 looks like this:

```
<table id="dlstMovies" cellspacing="0" border="0"
  style="border-collapse:collapse;">
<tr>
  <td>
  <h1>Titanic</h1>
  Directed by:
  James Cameron
  <br />
  Box Office Totals:
  $600,000,000.00
  </td>
</tr>
<tr>
  <td>
  <h1>Star Wars</h1>
  Directed by:
  George Lucas
  <br />
  Box Office Totals:
  $500,000,000.00
  </td>
</tr>
...
</table>
```

The default behavior of the DataList control is to render an HTML table. However, you can override this default behavior and display the contents of each data item in a separate HTML <span> tag. This approach is illustrated in Listing 13.7.

LISTING 13.7 ShowFlowDataList.aspx

```
<%@ Page Language="C#" %>
<html xmlns="http://www.w3.org/1999/xhtml" >
<head id="Head1" runat="server">
    <title>Show Flow DataList</title>
</head>
<body>
    <form id="form1" runat="server">
    <div>

    <asp:DataList
        id="dlstMovies"
        DataSourceID="srcMovies"
        RepeatLayout="Flow"
        Runat="server">
        <ItemTemplate>
        <%#Eval("Title")%>
        </ItemTemplate>
    </asp:DataList>

    <asp:SqlDataSource
        id="srcMovies"
        ConnectionString="<%$ ConnectionStrings:Movies %>"
        SelectCommand="SELECT Title FROM Movies"
        Runat="server" />

    </div>
    </form>
</body>
</html>
```

The DataList control in Listing 13.7 includes a RepeatLayout property that has the value Flow. Each movie title is rendered in a <span> tag followed by a line-break tag (<br>).

The RepeatLayout property accepts one of the following two values:

▶ **Table**—Data Items are rendered in HTML table cells.

▶ **Flow**—Data Items are rendered in HTML <span> tags.

Displaying Data in Multiple Columns

You can render the contents of a DataList control into a multicolumn table in which each data item occupies a separate table cell. Two properties modify the layout of the HTML table rendered by the DataList control:

▶ **RepeatColumns**—The number of columns to display.

▶ **RepeatDirection**—The direction to render the cells. Possible values are Horizontal and Vertical.

For example, the page in Listing 13.8 displays the contents of the Movies database table in a three-column layout (see Figure 13.6).

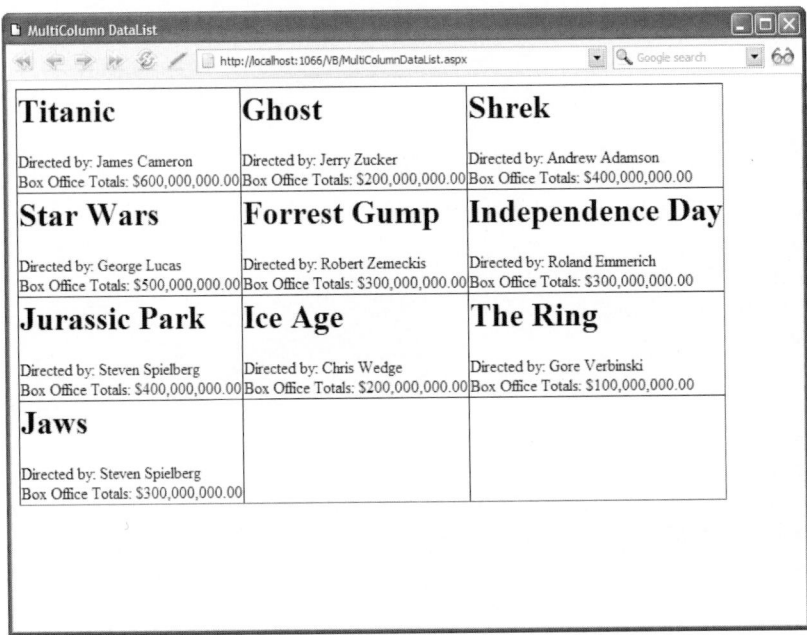

FIGURE 13.6   Displaying a multicolumn DataList.

LISTING 13.8   MultiColumnDataList.aspx

```
<%@ Page Language="C#" %>
<html xmlns="http://www.w3.org/1999/xhtml" >
<head id="Head1" runat="server">
    <title>MultiColumn DataList</title>
</head>
<body>
    <form id="form1" runat="server">
    <div>
```

```
<asp:DataList
    id="dlstMovies"
    DataSourceID="srcMovies"
    RepeatColumns="3"
    GridLines="Both"
    Runat="server">
    <ItemTemplate>
    <h1><%#Eval("Title")%></h1>
    Directed by:
    <%#Eval("Director") %>
    <br />
    Box Office Totals:
    <%#Eval("BoxOfficeTotals","{0:c}") %>
    </ItemTemplate>
</asp:DataList>

<asp:SqlDataSource
    id="srcMovies"
    ConnectionString="<%$ ConnectionStrings:Movies %>"
    SelectCommand="SELECT Title,Director,BoxOfficeTotals
        FROM Movies"
    Runat="server" />

</div>
</form>
</body>
</html>
```

The DataList control in Listing 13.8 includes a RepeatColumns property that has the value 3.

If you set the RepeatDirection property to the value Horizontal and do not assign a value to the RepeatColumns property, the DataList renders its data items horizontally without end.

NOTE

You can display data items in multiple columns when the DataList is in Flow layout mode. In that case, <br> tags create the row breaks.

Using Templates with the DataList Control

The DataList control supports all the same templates as the Repeater control:

▶ **ItemTemplate**—Formats each item from the data source.

▶ **AlternatingItemTemplate**—Formats every other item from the data source.

▶ **SeparatorTemplate**—Formats between each item from the data source.

▶ **HeaderTemplate**—Formats before all items from the data source.

▶ **FooterTemplate**—Formats after all items from the data source.

In addition, the DataList supports the following templates:

▶ **EditItemTemplate**—Displays when a row is selected for editing.

▶ **SelectedItemTemplate**—Displays when a row is selected.

The DataList control in Listing 13.9 includes both a HeaderTemplate and a FooterTemplate. The HeaderTemplate contains the caption for the table. The FooterTemplate contains a Label control that displays the total for all the preceding rows (see Figure 13.7).

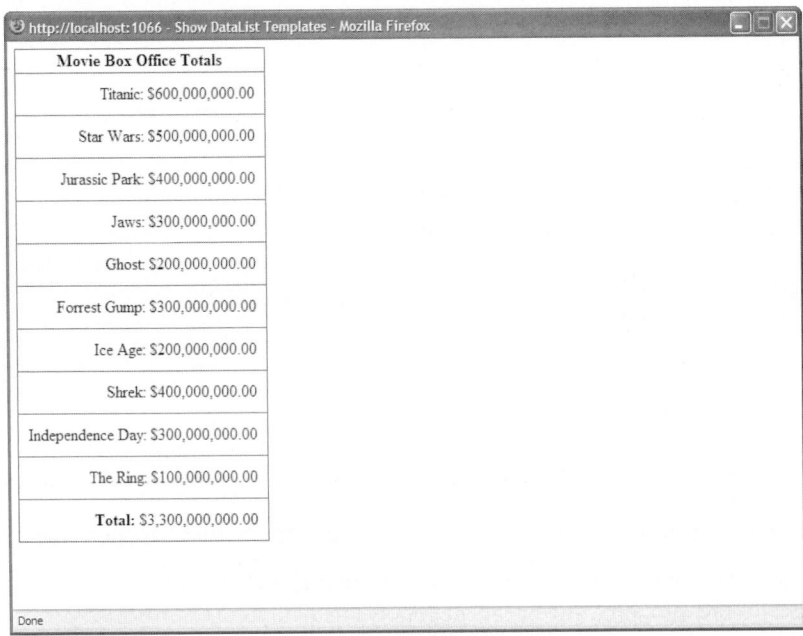

FIGURE 13.7   Displaying a HeaderTemplate and FooterTemplate.

LISTING 13.9   ShowDataListTemplates.aspx

```
<%@ Page Language="C#" %>
<!DOCTYPE html PUBLIC "-//W3C//DTD XHTML 1.1//EN"
"http://www.w3.org/TR/xhtml11/DTD/xhtml11.dtd">
<script runat="server">

    decimal totals;

    protected void dlstMovies_ItemDataBound(object sender, DataListItemEventArgs e)
    {
```

```
            if (e.Item.DataItem != null)
                totals += (decimal)DataBinder.Eval(e.Item.DataItem, "BoxOfficeTotals");
            if (e.Item.ItemType == ListItemType.Footer)
            {
                Label lblTotal = (Label)e.Item.FindControl("lblTotal");
                lblTotal.Text = totals.ToString("c");
            }
        }
    }
</script>
<html xmlns="http://www.w3.org/1999/xhtml" >
<head id="Head1" runat="server">
    <style type="text/css">
    .movies td
    {
        padding:10px;
        text-align:right;
    }
    </style>
    <title>Show DataList Templates</title>
</head>
<body>
    <form id="form1" runat="server">
    <div>

    <asp:DataList
        id="dlstMovies"
        DataSourceID="srcMovies"
        GridLines="Horizontal"
        UseAccessibleHeader="true"
        OnItemDataBound="dlstMovies_ItemDataBound"
        CssClass="movies"
        Runat="server" >
        <HeaderTemplate>
        Movie Box Office Totals
        </HeaderTemplate>
        <ItemTemplate>
        <%#Eval("Title")%>:
        <%#Eval("BoxOfficeTotals","{0:c}") %>
        </ItemTemplate>
        <FooterTemplate>
        <b>Total:</b>
        <asp:Label
            id="lblTotal"
            Runat="server" />
        </FooterTemplate>
    </asp:DataList>
```

```
    <asp:SqlDataSource
        id="srcMovies"
        ConnectionString="<%$ ConnectionStrings:Movies %>"
        SelectCommand="SELECT Title,BoxOfficeTotals
            FROM Movies"
        Runat="server" />

    </div>
    </form>
</body>
</html>
```

The total displayed in the FooterTemplate is calculated by the ItemDataBound event handler. The Label control is extracted by the FindControl() method and the total is assigned to the control's Text property.

Selecting Data with the DataList Control

You can use a DataList control as a menu by taking advantage of the control's SelectedValue property. For example, the page in Listing 13.10 enables you to pick a movie category and display a list of matching movies (see Figure 13.8).

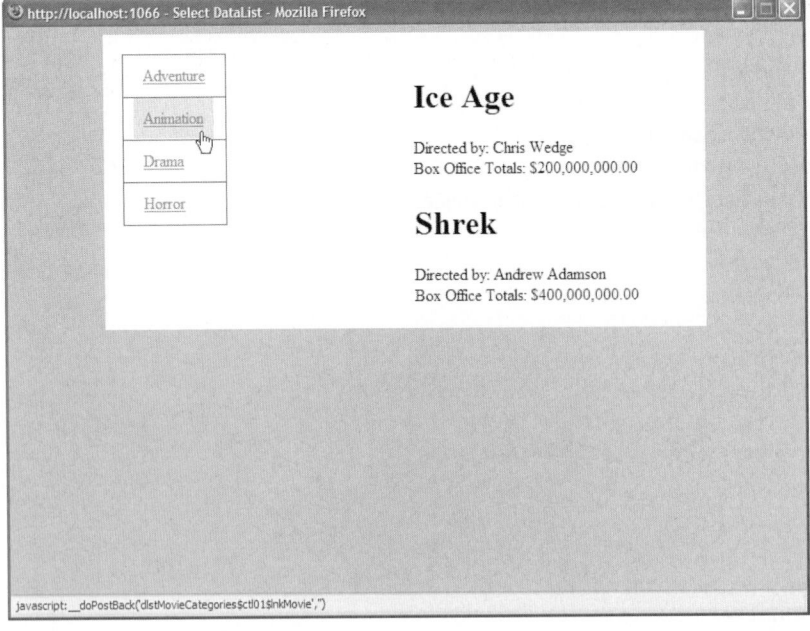

FIGURE 13.8   Selecting a row in the DataList.

LISTING 13.10   SelectDataList.aspx

```
<%@ Page Language="C#" %>
<!DOCTYPE html PUBLIC "-//W3C//DTD XHTML 1.1//EN"
    "http://www.w3.org/TR/xhtml11/DTD/xhtml11.dtd">
<html xmlns="http://www.w3.org/1999/xhtml" >
<head id="Head1" runat="server">
    <style type="text/css">
    html
    {
        background-color:orange;
    }
    .content
    {
        margin:auto;
        width:600px;
        background-color:white;
    }
    .column
    {
        float:left;
        width:250px;
        padding:20px;
    }
    .movies td
    {
        padding:10px;
    }
    a
    {
        padding:10px;
        color:red;
    }
    a:hover
    {
        background-color:Gold;
    }
    </style>
    <title>Select DataList</title>
</head>
<body>
    <form id="form1" runat="server">
    <div class="content">

    <div class="column">
    <asp:DataList
```

```
        id="dlstMovieCategories"
        DataSourceID="srcMovieCategories"
        DataKeyField="Id"
        GridLines="Both"
        CssClass="movies"
        Runat="server">
        <ItemTemplate>
        <asp:LinkButton
            id="lnkMovie"
            Text='<%#Eval("Name") %>'
            CommandName="Select"
            Runat="server" />
        </ItemTemplate>
    </asp:DataList>
    </div>

    <div class="column">
    <asp:DataList
        id="dlstMovieDetails"
        DataSourceID="srcMovieDetails"
        Runat="server">
        <ItemTemplate>
        <h1><%#Eval("Title")%></h1>
        Directed by:
        <%#Eval("Director") %>
        <br />
        Box Office Totals:
        <%#Eval("BoxOfficeTotals","{0:c}") %>
        </ItemTemplate>
    </asp:DataList>
    </div>
    <br style="clear:both" />
    </div>

    <asp:SqlDataSource
        id="srcMovieCategories"
        ConnectionString="<%$ ConnectionStrings:Movies %>"
        SelectCommand="SELECT Id, Name FROM MovieCategories"
        Runat="server" />

    <asp:SqlDataSource
        id="srcMovieDetails"
        ConnectionString="<%$ ConnectionStrings:Movies %>"
        SelectCommand="SELECT Title,Director,BoxOfficeTotals
            FROM Movies WHERE CategoryId=@CategoryId"
```

```
      Runat="server">
      <SelectParameters>
      <asp:ControlParameter
          Name="CategoryId"
          ControlID="dlstMovieCategories"
          PropertyName="SelectedValue" />
      </SelectParameters>
    </asp:SqlDataSource>
    </form>
</body>
</html>
```

The page in Listing 13.10 contains two DataList controls. The first control displays a menu of movie categories and the second DataList control displays a list of matching movies.

The first DataList in Listing 13.10 includes a DataKeyField property. The DataKeyField property accepts the name of a primary key column from the data source. When this property is set, the DataList control's DataKeys collection is populated with the primary keys from the data source when the control is bound to its data source.

The first DataList contains a LinkButton inside its ItemTemplate, which looks like this:

```
<asp:LinkButton
  id="lnkMovie"
  Text='<%#Eval("Name") %>'
  CommandName="Select"
  Runat="server" />
```

Because the LinkButton control's CommandName property has the value Select, clicking the button changes the value of the DataList control's SelectedValue property. The DataList control's SelectedValue property is used by the second SqlDataSource control to return movies that match the selected category.

> **NOTE**
>
> Unlike the GridView, DetailsView, ListView, and FormView controls, you cannot assign the names of multiple primary key columns to the DataKeyField property.

Editing Data with the DataList Control

You can use the DataList control to edit database records. However, editing with the DataList control requires more coding than editing with other DataBound controls, such as the GridView, FormView, or DetailsView controls.

The page in Listing 13.11 illustrates how you can edit and delete database records with the DataList control (see Figure 13.9).

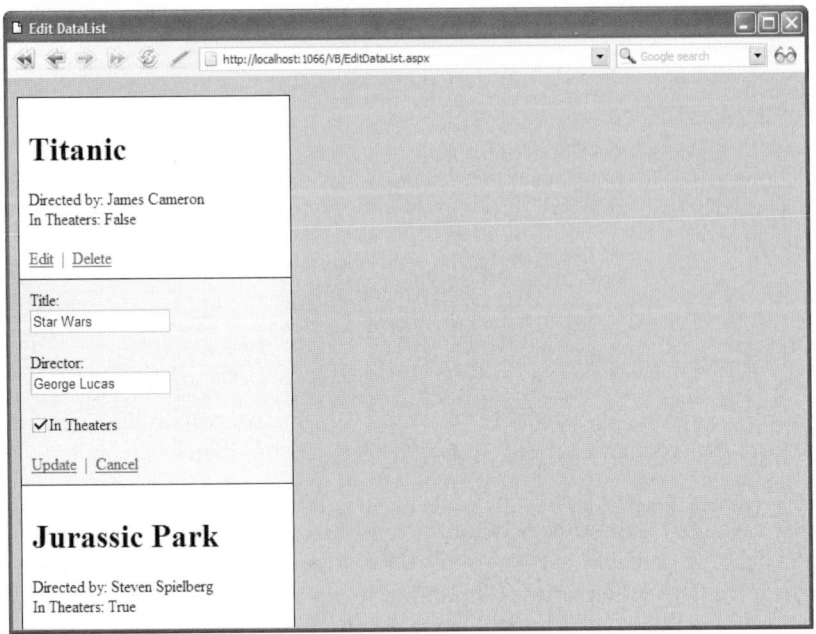

FIGURE 13.9   Editing database records with the DataList control.

LISTING 13.11   EditDataList.aspx

```
<%@ Page Language="C#" MaintainScrollPositionOnPostback="true" %>
<!DOCTYPE html PUBLIC "-//W3C//DTD XHTML 1.1//EN"
"http://www.w3.org/TR/xhtml11/DTD/xhtml11.dtd">
<script runat="server">

    protected void dlstMovies_EditCommand(object source, DataListCommandEventArgs e)
    {
        dlstMovies.EditItemIndex = e.Item.ItemIndex;
        dlstMovies.DataBind();
    }

    protected void dlstMovies_UpdateCommand(object source,
➥DataListCommandEventArgs e)
    {
        // Get form fields
        TextBox txtTitle = (TextBox)e.Item.FindControl("txtTitle");
        TextBox txtDirector = (TextBox)e.Item.FindControl("txtDirector");
        CheckBox chkInTheaters = (CheckBox)e.Item.FindControl("chkInTheaters");

        // Assign parameters
        srcMovies.UpdateParameters["Id"].DefaultValue =
dlstMovies.DataKeys[e.Item.ItemIndex].ToString();
```

```
        srcMovies.UpdateParameters["Title"].DefaultValue = txtTitle.Text;
        srcMovies.UpdateParameters["Director"].DefaultValue = txtDirector.Text;
        srcMovies.UpdateParameters["InTheaters"].DefaultValue =
chkInTheaters.Checked.ToString();

        // Call SqlDataSource Update
        srcMovies.Update();

        // Take out of Edit mode
        dlstMovies.EditItemIndex = -1;
    }

    protected void dlstMovies_DeleteCommand(object source,
➥DataListCommandEventArgs e)
    {
        // Assign parameters
        srcMovies.DeleteParameters["Id"].DefaultValue =
dlstMovies.DataKeys[e.Item.ItemIndex].ToString();

        // Call SqlDataSource Delete
        srcMovies.Delete();
    }

    protected void dlstMovies_CancelCommand(object source,
➥DataListCommandEventArgs e)
    {
        dlstMovies.EditItemIndex = -1;
        dlstMovies.DataBind();
    }
</script>
<html xmlns="http://www.w3.org/1999/xhtml">
<head id="Head1" runat="server">
    <style type="text/css">
    html
    {
        background-color:silver;
    }
    .movies
    {
        background-color:white;
    }
    .movies td,.movies th
    {
        padding:10px;
        border:solid 1px black;
    }
```

```
    .edit
    {
        background-color:yellow;
    }
    a
    {
        color:blue;
    }
    </style>
    <title>Edit DataList</title>
</head>
<body>
    <form id="form1" runat="server">
    <div>

    <asp:DataList
        id="dlstMovies"
        DataSourceID="srcMovies"
        DataKeyField="Id"
        GridLines="None"
        OnEditCommand="dlstMovies_EditCommand"
        OnCancelCommand="dlstMovies_CancelCommand"
        OnUpdateCommand="dlstMovies_UpdateCommand"
        OnDeleteCommand="dlstMovies_DeleteCommand"
        CssClass="movies"
        EditItemStyle-CssClass="edit"
        Runat="server">
        <ItemTemplate>
        <h1><%#Eval("Title")%></h1>
        Directed by:
        <%#Eval("Director") %>
        <br />
        In Theaters:
        <%#Eval("InTheaters") %>
        <br /><br />
        <asp:LinkButton
            id="lnkEdit"
            CommandName="Edit"
            Text="Edit"
            Runat="server" />
         | 
        <asp:LinkButton
            id="lnkDelete"
            CommandName="Delete"
            Text="Delete"
            OnClientClick="return confirm('Are you sure?');"
```

```
        Runat="server" />
    </ItemTemplate>
    <EditItemTemplate>
    <asp:Label
        id="lblTitle"
        Text="Title:"
        AssociatedControlID="txtTitle"
        Runat="server" />
    <br />
    <asp:TextBox
        id="txtTitle"
        Text='<%#Eval("Title")%>'
        Runat="server" />
    <br /><br />
    <asp:Label
        id="lblDirector"
        Text="Director:"
        AssociatedControlID="txtDirector"
        Runat="server" />
    <br />
    <asp:TextBox
        id="txtDirector"
        Text='<%#Eval("Director")%>'
        Runat="server" />
    <br /><br />
    <asp:CheckBox
        id="chkInTheaters"
        Text="In Theaters"
        Checked='<%#Eval("InTheaters")%>'
        Runat="server" />
    <br /><br />
    <asp:LinkButton
        id="lnkUpdate"
        CommandName="Update"
        Text="Update"
        Runat="server" />
      | 
    <asp:LinkButton
        id="lnkCancel"
        CommandName="Cancel"
        Text="Cancel"
        Runat="server" />
    </EditItemTemplate>
</asp:DataList>

<asp:SqlDataSource
```

```
        id="srcMovies"
        ConnectionString="<%$ ConnectionStrings:Movies %>"
        SelectCommand="SELECT Id,Title,Director,InTheaters
            FROM Movies"
        UpdateCommand="UPDATE Movies SET Title=@Title,
            Director=@Director,InTheaters=@InTheaters
            WHERE Id=@Id"
        DeleteCommand="DELETE Movies WHERE Id=@Id"
        Runat="server">
        <UpdateParameters>
            <asp:Parameter Name="Id" />
            <asp:Parameter Name="Title" />
            <asp:Parameter Name="Director" />
            <asp:Parameter Name="InTheaters" />
        </UpdateParameters>
        <DeleteParameters>
            <asp:Parameter Name="Id" />
        </DeleteParameters>
    </asp:SqlDataSource>

    </div>
    </form>
</body>
</html>
```

The ItemTemplate contained in the DataList in Listing 13.11 includes an Edit LinkButton and a Delete LinkButton. When you click the Edit LinkButton, the DataList raises its EditCommand event and the dlstMovies_Edit() method is executed. Clicking the Delete LinkButton raises the DeleteCommand event and the dlstMovies_Delete() method is executed.

The dlstMovies_Edit() method sets the EditItemIndex property of the DataList control. The EditItemTemplate is displayed for the item in the DataList that matches the EditItemIndex.

The EditItemTemplate includes form fields for editing a movie record and an Update and Cancel LinkButton. These LinkButtons raise the UpdateCommand and CancelCommand events, and execute the corresponding event handlers.

> **NOTE**
>
> The <%@ Page %> directive includes a MaintainScrollPositionOnPostback attribute. This attribute causes a page to scroll to the same position whenever you post the page back to the server. For example, when you click the Edit link next to a row in the DataList, the page scrolls to the Edit link that you clicked.

Formatting the DataList Control

The DataList control includes a rich set of properties that you can use to format the HTML rendered by the control. If you want to associate Cascading Style Sheet (CSS) rules with different elements of the DataList, you can take advantage of any of the following properties:

- **CssClass**—Enables you to associate a CSS class with the DataList.

- **AlternatingItemStyle**—Enables you to format every other row of DataList.

- **EditItemStyle**—Enables you to format the DataList row selected for editing.

- **FooterStyle**—Enables you to format the footer row of DataList.

- **HeaderStyle**—Enables you to format the header row of DataList.

- **ItemStyle**—Enables you to format each row displayed by DataList.

- **SelectedItemStyle**—Enables you to format the selected row in DataList.

- **SeparatorStyle**—Enables you to format the row separator displayed by DataList.

When formatting the DataList, you also need to work with the following properties:

- **GridLines**—Enables you to add rules around the cells in the DataList. Possible values are None, Horizontal, Vertical, and Both.

- **ShowFooter**—Enables you to show or hide the footer row.

- **ShowHeader**—Enables you to show or hide the header row.

- **UseAccessibleHeader**—Enables you to render HTML <th> tags instead of <td> tags for the cells in the header row.

WEB STANDARDS NOTE

To make a page that contains a DataList more accessible to persons with disabilities, you should always include a HeaderTemplate and enable the UserAccessibleHeader property.

The page in Listing 13.12 illustrates how you can take advantage of several of these formatting properties (see Figure 13.10).

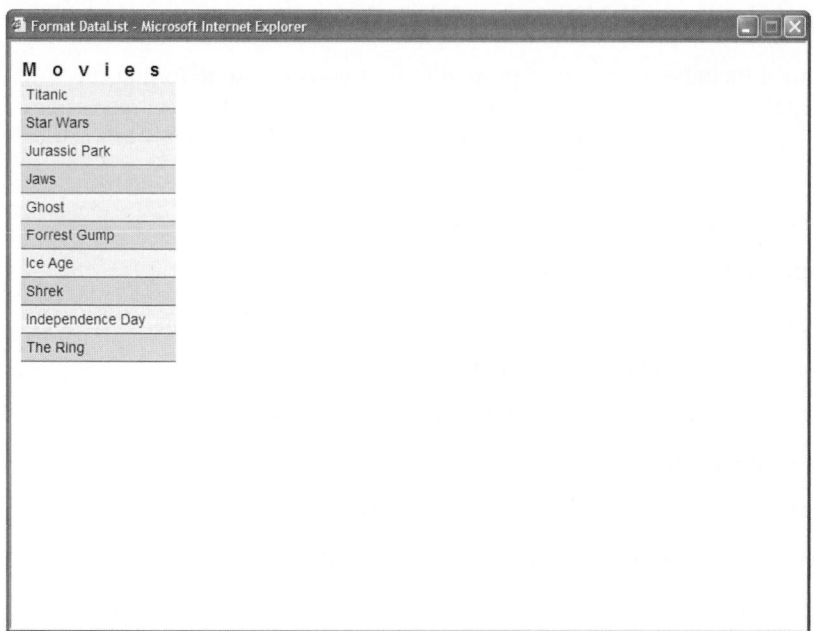

FIGURE 13.10   Formatting a DataList.

LISTING 13.12   FormatDataList.aspx

```
<%@ Page Language="C#" %>
<!DOCTYPE html PUBLIC "-//W3C//DTD XHTML 1.1//EN"
    "http://www.w3.org/TR/xhtml11/DTD/xhtml11.dtd">
<html xmlns="http://www.w3.org/1999/xhtml" >
<head id="Head1" runat="server">
    <style type="text/css">
    html
    {
        background-color:#Silver;
    }
    .movies
    {
        font:14px Arial,Sans-Serif;
    }
    .header
    {
        font-size:18px;
        letter-spacing:15px;
    }
    .item
    {
```

```
         padding:5px;
         background-color:#eeeeee;
         border-bottom:Solid 1px blue;
     }
     .alternating
     {
         padding:5px;
         background-color:LightBlue;
         border-bottom:Solid 1px blue;
     }
     </style>
     <title>Format DataList</title>
</head>
<body>
     <form id="form1" runat="server">
     <div>

     <asp:DataList
         id="dlstMovies"
         DataSourceID="srcMovies"
         UseAccessibleHeader="true"
         CssClass="movies"
         HeaderStyle-CssClass="header"
         ItemStyle-CssClass="item"
         AlternatingItemStyle-CssClass="alternating"
         Runat="server">
         <HeaderTemplate>
         Movies
         </HeaderTemplate>
         <ItemTemplate>
         <%#Eval("Title")%>
         </ItemTemplate>
     </asp:DataList>

     <asp:SqlDataSource
         id="srcMovies"
         ConnectionString="<%$ ConnectionStrings:Movies %>"
         SelectCommand="SELECT Title FROM Movies"
         Runat="server" />

     </div>
     </form>
</body>
</html>
```

Summary

In this chapter, you learned how to use the Repeater control and the DataList control to display a set of database records. First, you learned how to use the Repeater control to display and edit database records. For example, you learned how to use the Repeater control to enable users to edit, delete, and insert database records.

In the second half of this chapter, you learned how to work with the DataList control. You learned how to render both single and multicolumn tables with the DataList control. You also learned how to select rows with the DataList control. Finally, you learned how to edit records using the DataList control.

CHAPTER 14

Using the ListView and DataPager Controls

In this chapter, we examine the two databound controls that were introduced in version 3.5 of .NET Framework: the ListView and the DataPager controls. The ListView control is extremely flexible. You can use it in many of the same situations in which you would have used the GridView, DataList, FormView, or Repeater control in the past.

The DataPager control works with the ListView control. It enables you to add support for paging to a ListView control.

Using the ListView Control

You can think of the ListView control as a super-flexible GridView control. Like a GridView control, the ListView control can be used to display, edit, delete, select, page through, and sort database data. However, unlike the GridView, the ListView control is entirely template-driven. Furthermore, unlike the GridView control, you can use the ListView control to insert new data into a database.

You also can think of the ListView control as a replacement for the DataList control. Like a DataList control, the ListView control can be used to display database records in multiple columns. For example, you can use the ListView control to render a photo gallery.

Finally, you can think of the ListView control as a super-fancy Repeater control. Like a Repeater control, the ListView control is entirely template driven. However, unlike a Repeater control, the ListView control can be used to edit, page through, and sort database data.

The ListView control supports the following templates:

▶ **LayoutTemplate**—Specifies the containing element for the contents of the ListView.

▶ **ItemTemplate**—Formats each item rendered by the ListView.

▶ **ItemSeparatorTemplate**—Displays content between each item rendered by the ListView.

▶ **GroupTemplate**—Specifies the containing element for a group of items rendered by the ListView.

▶ **GroupSeparatorTemplate**—Displays content between each group of items rendered by the ListView.

▶ **EmptyItemTemplate**—Renders content for the remaining items in a GroupTemplate.

▶ **EmptyDataTemplate**—Specifies content that displays when no items are returned from the ListView control's data source.

▶ **SelectedItemTemplate**—Specifies the content displayed for the selected item in the ListView.

▶ **AlternatingItemTemplate**—Renders different content for alternating items in a ListView.

▶ **EditItemTemplate**—Renders content for editing an item in a ListView.

▶ **InsertItemTemplate**—Renders content for inserting a new item in a ListView.

You learn how to use these various types of templates in the following sections.

Using the LayoutTemplate and ItemTemplate

Let's start with a ListView control simple scenario in which you might want to use the ListView control. Suppose that you have a set of database records that you want to display in a set of HTML <div> tags. The page in Listing 14.1 illustrates how you can use the LayoutTemplate and ItemTemplate templates to display the records from the Movie database table.

LISTING 14.1 SimpleListView.aspx

```
<%@ Page Language="C#" %>
<!DOCTYPE html PUBLIC "-//W3C//DTD XHTML 1.0 Transitional//EN"
 "http://www.w3.org/TR/xhtml1/DTD/xhtml1-transitional.dtd">
<html xmlns="http://www.w3.org/1999/xhtml">
<head id="Head1" runat="server">
    <title>Simple ListView</title>
</head>
<body>
    <form id="form1" runat="server">
    <div>
```

```
<asp:ListView
    ID="lstMovies"
    DataSourceId="srcMovies"
    runat="server">
    <LayoutTemplate>
        <div
                            style="border:dashed 1px black">
            <asp:Placeholder
             id="itemPlaceholder"
             runat="server" />
        </div>
    </LayoutTemplate>
    <ItemTemplate>
        <div style="border:solid 1px black">
        <%# Eval("Title") %>
        </div>
    </ItemTemplate>
    <AlternatingItemTemplate>
        <div style="border:solid 1px black;background-color:Silver">
        <%# Eval("Title") %>
        </div>
    </AlternatingItemTemplate>
    <EmptyDataTemplate>
        No records found
    </EmptyDataTemplate>
</asp:ListView>

<asp:SqlDataSource
    id="srcMovies"
    SelectCommand="SELECT Id, Title, Director FROM Movies"
    ConnectionString='<%$ ConnectionStrings:Movies %>'
    Runat="server" />

    </div>
    </form>
</body>
</html>
```

The ListView control in Listing 14.1 contains five templates. First, the LayoutTemplate creates a single containing <div> tag for all the items rendered by the ListView. The content contained in the LayoutTemplate is rendered once and only once. In the page in Listing 14.1, the LayoutTemplate displays a <div> tag with a dashed border (see Figure 14.1).

> **NOTE**
>
> In ASP.NET 3.5, the LayoutTemplate was required and it needed to contain a server-side control with an ID of itemContainer. In ASP.NET 4, LayoutTemplate is no longer required.

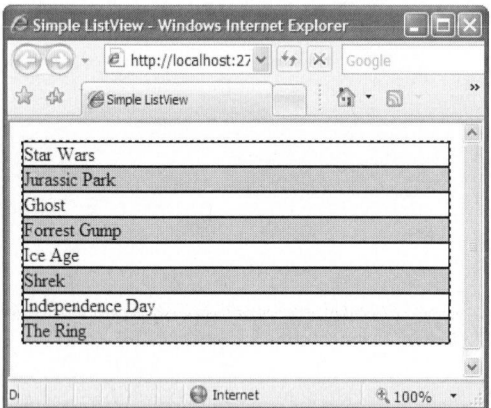

FIGURE 14.1   Displaying database records with a ListView control.

The ItemTemplate renders each of the items from the data source (or every other item when an AlternatingItemTemplate is present). In Listing 14.1, the ItemTemplate renders a <div> tag with a solid border. A data-binding expression is used with the <div> tag to display the value of the database Title column.

The AlternatingItemTemplate is optional. If it is present, every other item displayed by the ListView control is rendered with the AlternatingItemTemplate. In Listing 14.1, the AlternatingItemTemplate is used to give alternating items a silver background color.

Finally, the EmptyDataTemplate displays content when no results are retrieved from the data source. In Listing 14.1, the EmptyDataTemplate is used to display the text No Records Found when no items are returned from the data source.

You can use the ListView control to render any HTML elements you can imagine. You can use the ListView control to render bulleted lists, an HTML table, a blog tag cloud, or even the elements of a JavaScript array. For example, the page in Listing 14.2 uses a ListView control to render an HTML table.

LISTING 14.2   TableListView.aspx

```
<%@ Page Language="C#" %>
<!DOCTYPE html PUBLIC "-//W3C//DTD XHTML 1.0 Transitional//EN"
 "http://www.w3.org/TR/xhtml1/DTD/xhtml1-transitional.dtd">
<html xmlns="http://www.w3.org/1999/xhtml">
<head id="Head1" runat="server">
```

```
            <title>Table ListView</title>
    </head>
    <body>
        <form id="form1" runat="server">
        <div>

            <asp:ListView
                ID="lstMovies"
                DataSourceId="srcMovies"
                runat="server">
                <LayoutTemplate>
                    <table>
                    <thead>
                        <tr>
                            <th>Title</th>
                            <th>Director</th>
                        </tr>
                    </thead>
                    <tbody>
                            <asp:Placeholder
                            id="itemPlaceholder"
                            runat="server" />
                    </tbody>
                    </table>
                </LayoutTemplate>
                <ItemTemplate>
                    <tr>
                        <td><%# Eval("Title") %></td>
                        <td><%# Eval("Director") %></td>
                    </tr>
                </ItemTemplate>
                <EmptyDataTemplate>
                    No records found
                </EmptyDataTemplate>
            </asp:ListView>

            <asp:SqlDataSource
                id="srcMovies"
                SelectCommand="SELECT Id, Title, Director FROM Movie"
                ConnectionString='<%$ ConnectionStrings:con %>'
                Runat="server" />
        </div>
        </form>
    </body>
</html>
```

Notice that the itemContainer in Listing 14.2 is the <tbody> element. The <tbody> element contains each row of the table. Each row is rendered by the ItemTemplate (see Figure 14.2).

FIGURE 14.2   Displaying a table with a ListView control.

Using the GroupTemplate

You can use the ListView control's GroupTemplate to group multiple items together. Grouping items is useful when you want to display items in multiple columns. For example, you might want to display a photo gallery in which three pictures are displayed per row.

The page in Listing 14.3 displays a set of photographs within a series of HTML <div> tags. A maximum of three photographs display in each <div> tag (see Figure 14.3).

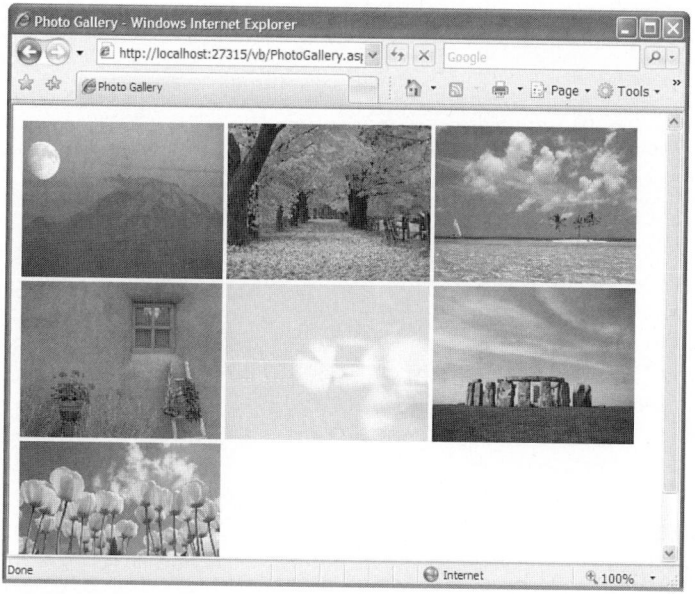

FIGURE 14.3   Displaying a photo gallery with a ListView control.

LISTING 14.3   PhotoGallery.aspx

```
<%@ Page Language="C#" %>
<%@ Import Namespace="System.Collections.Generic" %>
<!DOCTYPE html PUBLIC "-//W3C//DTD XHTML 1.0 Transitional//EN"
 "http://www.w3.org/TR/xhtml1/DTD/xhtml1-transitional.dtd">
<script runat="server">

    void Page_Load()
    {
        List<string> photos = new List<string>();
        photos.Add( "~/Images/Ascent.jpg" );
        photos.Add( "~/Images/Autumn.jpg" );
        photos.Add( "~/Images/Azul.jpg" );
        photos.Add( "~/Images/Home.jpg" );
        photos.Add( "~/Images/Peace.jpg" );
        photos.Add( "~/Images/Stonehenge.jpg" );
        photos.Add( "~/Images/Tulips.jpg" );

        lstPhotos.DataSource = photos;
        lstPhotos.DataBind();
    }
</script>
<html xmlns="http://www.w3.org/1999/xhtml">
```

```
<head runat="server">
    <title>Photo Gallery</title>
</head>
<body>
    <form id="form1" runat="server">
    <div>

    <asp:ListView
        ID="lstPhotos"
        GroupItemCount="3"
        runat="server">
        <LayoutTemplate><asp:Placeholder
                id="groupPlaceholder"
                runat="server" />          </LayoutTemplate>
        <GroupTemplate>
            <div>
                <asp:Placeholder
                id="itemPlaceholder"
                runat="server" />
            </div>
        </GroupTemplate>
        <ItemTemplate>
            <asp:Image
                id="imgPhoto"
                ImageUrl='<%# Container.DataItem %>'
                Width="200px"
                Runat="server" />
        </ItemTemplate>
    </asp:ListView>

    </div>
    </form>
</body>
</html>
```

In Listing 14.3, the photographs are represented with a List collection. The List is bound
to the ListView programmatically in the Page_Load() method.

Notice that the ListView includes a LayoutTemplate, GroupTemplate, and ItemTemplate.
In previous listings, the LayoutTemplate included an element with an ID of
itemContainer. In this listing, the LayoutTemplate includes an element with an ID of
groupContainer. The contents of the GroupTemplate are added to the element in the
LayoutTemplate with an ID of groupContainer.

The GroupTemplate includes the itemContainer element. The contents of the
ItemTemplate are rendered within the itemContainer element in the GroupTemplate.

Notice that the `ListView` control includes a `GroupItemCount` attribute. This property determines the number of items displayed in a `GroupTemplate` before a new `GroupTemplate` is created.

> **NOTE**
>
> The `ListView` control also supports an `EmptyItemTemplate` that can be used to render content for the leftover items in a `GroupTemplate`. For example, if you set the `GroupItemCount` property to 3 and there are four items, the contents of the `EmptyItemTemplate` display for the final two items.

Selecting a Row

You can set up the `ListView` control so you can use it to select items. This is useful when you want to create a master/detail form.

For example, the page in Listing 14.4 contains two `ListView` controls. The first `ListView` works like a tab strip. It enables you to select a movie category. The second `ListView` displays a numbered list of matching movies.

LISTING 14.4   `MasterDetail.aspx`

```
<%@ Page Language="C#" %>
<!DOCTYPE html PUBLIC "-//W3C//DTD XHTML 1.0 Transitional//EN"
 "http://www.w3.org/TR/xhtml1/DTD/xhtml1-transitional.dtd">
<html xmlns="http://www.w3.org/1999/xhtml">
<head runat="server">
    <title>Master/Detail</title>
    <style type="text/css">

        .categoryContainer div
        {
            width: 100px;
            font-size:small;
            border: 1px solid black;
            float:left;
            padding:3px;
            margin:3px;
        }

        .categoryContainer a
        {
            text-decoration:none;
        }

        .categoryContainer div:hover
        {
```

```
            background-color:#eeeeee;
        }

        #selected
        {
            background-color:silver;
        }

    </style>
</head>
<body>
    <form id="form1" runat="server">
    <div>

        <asp:ListView
            ID="lstMovieCategories"
            DataSourceId="srcMovieCategory"
            DataKeyNames="Id"
            runat="server">
            <LayoutTemplate>
                <div
                    id="itemContainer"
                    class="categoryContainer"
                    runat="server">
                </div>
            </LayoutTemplate>
            <ItemTemplate>
                <div>
                <asp:LinkButton
                    id="lnkSelect"
                    Text='<%# Eval("Name") %>'
                    CommandName="Select"
                    Runat="server" />
                </div>
            </ItemTemplate>
            <SelectedItemTemplate>
                <div id="selected">
                <%# Eval("Name") %>
                </div>
            </SelectedItemTemplate>
        </asp:ListView>

        <br style="clear:both" /><br />

        <asp:ListView
            ID="lstMovies"
```

```
            DataSourceId="srcMovies"
            runat="server">
            <LayoutTemplate>
                <ol
                    id="itemContainer"
                    runat="server">
                </ol>
            </LayoutTemplate>
            <ItemTemplate>
                <li><%# Eval("Title") %></li>
            </ItemTemplate>
        </asp:ListView>

        <asp:SqlDataSource
            id="srcMovieCategory"
            SelectCommand="SELECT Id, Name FROM MovieCategory"
            ConnectionString='<%$ ConnectionStrings:con %>'
            Runat="server" />

        <asp:SqlDataSource
            id="srcMovies"
            SelectCommand="SELECT Title FROM Movie
                WHERE CategoryId=@CategoryId"
            ConnectionString='<%$ ConnectionStrings:con %>'
            Runat="server">
            <SelectParameters>
                <asp:ControlParameter
                    Name="CategoryId"
                    ControlID="lstMovieCategories" />
            </SelectParameters>
        </asp:SqlDataSource>
    </div>
    </form>
</body>
</html>
```

The first ListView control in Listing 14.4 renders something resembling a tab strip (see Figure 14.4). Notice that this ListView control has its DataKeyNames property set. Setting the DataKeyNames property causes the ListView control to build a hidden collection of primary key values when the ListView is bound to its data source. Each item in the ListView is associated with an ID value.

FIGURE 14.4   Displaying a master/detail form with a ListView control.

Furthermore, notice that the ListView control includes a SelectedItemTemplate. The contents of this template are rendered for the selected item in the ListView. You select an item by clicking one of the links rendered by the ListView control's ItemTemplate. The links are rendered with a LinkButton control. Notice that the CommandName property of the LinkButton has the value Select. This magic command name causes the ListView to change the selected item.

The second ListView control uses the first ListView control as the source value for a select parameter. When you select a new item in the first ListView control, the second ListView control displays matching movies.

Sorting Database Data

You can sort the items in a ListView control by adding one or more button controls to ListView that have a CommandName property set to the value Sort and a CommandArgument property set to the name of a property to sort by. For example, the page in Listing 14.5 contains a ListView control that renders an HTML table. You can click the column headers to sort the table by a particular column (see Figure 14.5).

FIGURE 14.5   Sorting data with the ListView control.

LISTING 14.5   SortListView.aspx

```
<%@ Page Language="C#" %>
<!DOCTYPE html PUBLIC "-//W3C//DTD XHTML 1.0 Transitional//EN"
 "http://www.w3.org/TR/xhtml1/DTD/xhtml1-transitional.dtd">
<html xmlns="http://www.w3.org/1999/xhtml">
<head id="Head1" runat="server">
    <title>Sort ListView</title>
</head>
<body>
    <form id="form1" runat="server">
    <div>

        <asp:ListView
            ID="lstMovies"
            DataSourceId="srcMovies"
            runat="server">
            <LayoutTemplate>
                <table>
                <thead>
                    <tr>
                        <th>
                        <asp:LinkButton
                            id="lnkTitle"
```

```
                                Text="Title"
                                CommandName="Sort"
                                CommandArgument="Title"
                                Runat="server" />
                        </th>
                        <th>
                        <asp:LinkButton
                                id="LinkButton1"
                                Text="Director"
                                CommandName="Sort"
                                CommandArgument="Director"
                                Runat="server" />
                        </th>
                    </tr>
                </thead>
                <tbody id="itemContainer" runat="server">
                </tbody>
                </table>
            </LayoutTemplate>
            <ItemTemplate>
                <tr>
                    <td><%# Eval("Title") %></td>
                    <td><%# Eval("Director") %></td>
                </tr>
            </ItemTemplate>
            <EmptyDataTemplate>
                No records found
            </EmptyDataTemplate>
        </asp:ListView>

        <asp:SqlDataSource
            id="srcMovies"
            SelectCommand="SELECT Id, Title, Director FROM Movie"
            ConnectionString='<%$ ConnectionStrings:con %>'
            Runat="server" />
    </div>
    </form>
</body>
</html>
```

The two LinkButtons used for sorting the items in the ListView are contained in the
LayoutTemplate. Both LinkButtons have a CommandName property set to the value Sort.
The first LinkButton sorts by the Title property and the second LinkButton sorts by the
Director property.

Editing Database Data

You can use the ListView control to update, delete, and insert items. The page in Listing 14.6 illustrates how you can use the ListView to modify or delete the records in the Movie database table (see Figure 14.6).

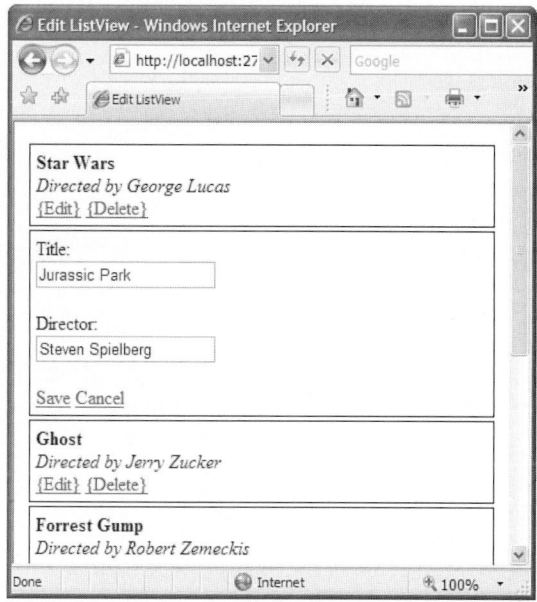

FIGURE 14.6   Editing database data with the ListView control.

LISTING 14.6   EditListView.aspx

```
<%@ Page Language="C#" %>


<!DOCTYPE html PUBLIC "-//W3C//DTD XHTML 1.0 Transitional//EN"
  "http://www.w3.org/TR/xhtml1/DTD/xhtml1-transitional.dtd">

<style type="text/css">

    .movie
    {
       border: solid 1px black;
       padding:5px;
       margin:3px;
    }

    .edit
    {
        background-color:lightyellow;
```

```
        }

</style>

<html xmlns="http://www.w3.org/1999/xhtml">
<head runat="server">
    <title>Edit ListView</title>
</head>
<body>
    <form id="form1" runat="server">
    <div>

        <asp:ListView
            ID="lstMovies"
            DataSourceId="srcMovies"
            DataKeyNames="Id"
            runat="server">
            <LayoutTemplate>
                <div
                    id="itemContainer"
                    runat="server">
                </div>
            </LayoutTemplate>
            <ItemTemplate>
                <div class="movie">
                <strong><%# Eval("Title") %></strong>
                <br />
                <em>Directed by <%# Eval("Director") %></em>
                <br />
                <asp:LinkButton
                    id="lnkEdit"
                    Text="{Edit}"
                    CommandName="Edit"
                    Runat="server" />
                <asp:LinkButton
                    id="lnkDelete"
                    Text="{Delete}"
                    CommandName="Delete"
                    OnClientClick="return confirm('Delete this movie?')"
                    Runat="server" />
                </div>
            </ItemTemplate>
            <EditItemTemplate>
                <div class="movie edit">
```

```
            <asp:Label
                id="lblTitle"
                Text="Title:"
                AssociatedControlID="txtTitle"
                Runat="server" />
            <br />
            <asp:TextBox
                id="txtTitle"
                Text='<%# Bind("Title") %>'
                Runat="server" />

            <br /><br />

            <asp:Label
                id="lblDirector"
                Text="Director:"
                AssociatedControlID="txtDirector"
                Runat="server" />
            <br />
            <asp:TextBox
                id="txtDirector"
                Text='<%# Bind("Director") %>'
                Runat="server" />

            <br /><br />
            <asp:LinkButton
                id="lnkUpdate"
                Text="Save"
                CommandName="Update"
                Runat="server" />
          <asp:LinkButton
                id="lnkCancel"
                Text="Cancel"
                CommandName="Cancel"
                Runat="server" />
            </div>
        </EditItemTemplate>
</asp:ListView>

<asp:SqlDataSource
    id="srcMovies"
    SelectCommand="SELECT Id, Title, Director FROM Movie"
    UpdateCommand="Update Movie SET Title=@Title, Director=@Director
        WHERE Id=@Id"
```

```
            DeleteCommand="Delete Movie WHERE Id=@Id"
            ConnectionString='<%$ ConnectionStrings:con %>'
            Runat="server" />

    </div>
    </form>
</body>
</html>
```

The ListView control in Listing 14. 6 has an ItemTemplate that contains two LinkButtons. The first LinkButton has a CommandName property set to the value Edit and the second LinkButton has a CommandName property set to the value Delete. When you click the first LinkButton, the ListView control's EditItemTemplate displays. When you click the second LinkButton, the current database record is deleted (after you confirm that you really want to delete the movie record).

The EditItemTemplate contains a form for editing a movie record. The form contains two TextBox controls that have two-way data-binding expressions assigned to their Text properties. The form also contains two LinkButton controls. The first LinkButton control has a CommandName of Update. When you click this button, the database is updated with the form changes and the EditItemTemplate switches back to the normal ItemTemplate. If you click the Cancel button, the EditItemTemplate switches to an ItemTemplate without updating the database.

When editing with a ListView, you need to assign the primary key column names to the ListView control's DataKeyNames property. The ListView control uses this to determine which database record to update.

Notice that all the ListView editing is driven by the following magic command names: Edit, Delete, Update, and Cancel. By setting button control CommandName properties to these magic command names, you can control how the ListView edits items.

You also can use the ListView control to insert new records into a database table. The ListView control supports an InsertItemTemplate. The page in Listing 14.7 illustrates how you can use the InsertItemTemplate to create a simple customer feedback form (see Figure 14.7).

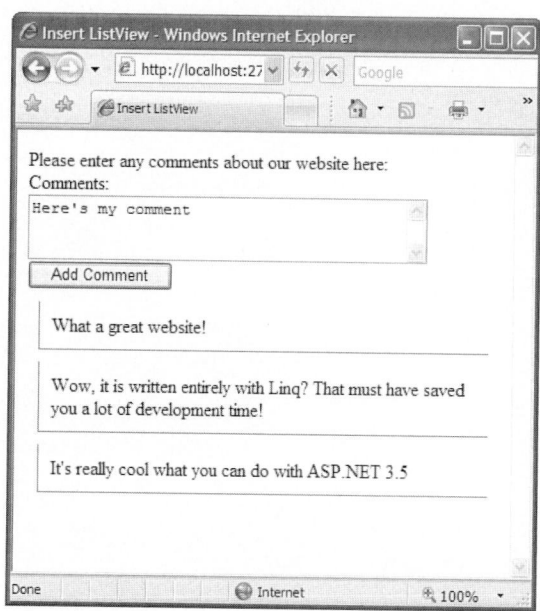

FIGURE 14.7   Inserting new records with the ListView control.

LISTING 14.7   InsertListView.aspx

```
<%@ Page Language="C#" %>
<!DOCTYPE html PUBLIC "-//W3C//DTD XHTML 1.0 Transitional//EN"
 "http://www.w3.org/TR/xhtml1/DTD/xhtml1-transitional.dtd">
<html xmlns="http://www.w3.org/1999/xhtml">
<head id="Head1" runat="server">
    <title>Insert ListView</title>
    <style type="text/css">

    .comment
    {
        margin:10px;
        padding: 10px;
        border-left:solid 1px gray;
        border-bottom:solid 1px gray;
    }

    </style>
</head>
<body>
    <form id="form1" runat="server">
    <div>
```

```
<asp:ListView
    ID="lstFeedback"
    DataSourceId="srcFeedback"
    InsertItemPosition="FirstItem"
    runat="server">
    <LayoutTemplate>
        <div
            id="itemContainer"
            runat="server">
        </div>
    </LayoutTemplate>
    <ItemTemplate>
        <div class="comment">
        <%# Eval("Comment") %>
        </div>
    </ItemTemplate>
    <InsertItemTemplate>
        <div>
        Please enter any comments
        about our website here:
        <br />
        <asp:Label
            id="lblComments"
            Text="Comments:"
            AssociatedControlID="txtComment"
            Runat="server" />
        <br />
        <asp:TextBox
            id="txtComment"
            Text='<%# Bind("Comment") %>'
            TextMode="MultiLine"
            Columns="40"
            Rows="3"
            Runat="server" />
        <br />
        <asp:Button
            id="lnkInsert"
            Text="Add Comment"
            CommandName="Insert"
            Runat="server" />
        </div>
    </InsertItemTemplate>
</asp:ListView>

<asp:SqlDataSource
    id="srcFeedback"
```

```
          SelectCommand="SELECT Id, Comment FROM Feedback"
          InsertCommand="INSERT Feedback (Comment) VALUES (@Comment)"
          ConnectionString='<%$ ConnectionStrings:con %>'
          Runat="server" />

     </div>
     </form>
</body>
</html>
```

The `InsertItemTemplate` appears only when you set the `ListView` control's `InsertItemPosition` property. You can set this property to the value `FirstItem`, `LastItem`, or `None`. In Listing 14.7, it's set to the value `FirstItem` so that the insert form appears above all the current items.

The `InsertItemTemplate` contains a single `TextBox` control that has its `Text` property set to a data-binding expression. The template also contains a `Button` control that has a `CommandName` property set to the value `Insert`. When you click the button, the new item is inserted into the database.

Using the DataPager Control

The `DataPager` control displays a user interface for navigating through multiple pages of items. The `DataPager` control works with any control that supports the `IPageableItemContainer` interface. Unfortunately, there is currently only a single control that supports this interface: the `ListView` control. So this means that you can only use the `DataPager` with the `ListView` control.

The `DataPager` control includes the following properties:

- ▶ **PageSize**—Gets or sets the number of items to display at a time.

- ▶ **PagedControlId**—Gets or sets the control to page. (The control must implement `IPageableItemContainer`.)

- ▶ **Fields**—Gets the fields contained by the `DataPager`.

- ▶ **StartRowIndex**—Gets the index of the first item to show.

- ▶ **MaximumRows**—Gets the maximum number of rows to retrieve from the data source.

- ▶ **TotalRowCount**—Gets the total number of items available from the data source.

You set the `PageSize` to control the number of items to display per page. The `PagerControlId` property is optional. If you place the `DataPager` within the `ListView` control's `LayoutTemplate`, you don't need to set the `PagerControlId` property. If, on the other hand, you place the `DataPager` outside of the `ListView` control, you need to set the `PagerControlId` property to the ID of the `ListView`.

If you add a DataPager to a page and do nothing else, the DataPager won't render anything. To display a user interface for the DataPager, you need to add one or more fields to the DataPager. The DataPager control supports the following fields:

▶ **NextPreviousPagerField**—Used to display Next, Previous, First, and Last links.

▶ **NumericPagerField**—Used to display Next, Previous, and page numbers links.

▶ **TemplatePagerField**—Used to create a custom user interface for paging.

The page in Listing 14.8 demonstrates how you can use the DataPager control to page through movies displayed by a ListView control (see Figure 14.8).

FIGURE 14.8   Using a DataPager control with the ListView control.

LISTING 14.8   DataPagerListView.aspx

```
<%@ Page Language="C#" %>
<!DOCTYPE html PUBLIC "-//W3C//DTD XHTML 1.0 Transitional//EN"
 "http://www.w3.org/TR/xhtml1/DTD/xhtml1-transitional.dtd">
<html xmlns="http://www.w3.org/1999/xhtml">
<head id="Head1" runat="server">
    <title>DataPager ListView</title>
</head>
<body>
    <form id="form1" runat="server">
    <div>

        <asp:ListView
            ID="lstMovies"
            DataSourceId="srcMovies"
            runat="server">
            <LayoutTemplate>
                <ol
```

```
                        id="itemContainer"
                        runat="server">
                    </ol>
                    <asp:DataPager
                        id="pg"
                        PageSize="2"
                        Runat="server">
                        <Fields>
                            <asp:NextPreviousPagerField
                                ShowFirstPageButton="true"
                                ShowPreviousPageButton="true"
                                ShowNextPageButton="false"
                                ShowLastPageButton="false" />
                            <asp:NumericPagerField />
                            <asp:NextPreviousPagerField
                                ShowFirstPageButton="false"
                                ShowPreviousPageButton="false"
                                ShowNextPageButton="true"
                                ShowLastPageButton="true" />
                        </Fields>
                    </asp:DataPager>

                </LayoutTemplate>
                <ItemTemplate>
                    <li>
                    <%# Eval("Title") %>
                    </li>
                </ItemTemplate>
            </asp:ListView>

            <asp:SqlDataSource
                id="srcMovies"
                SelectCommand="SELECT Id, Title, Director FROM Movie"
                ConnectionString='<%$ ConnectionStrings:con %>'
                Runat="server" />
        </div>
        </form>
    </body>
    </html>
```

The DataPager contains three fields: NextPreviousPagerField, NumericPagerField, and NextPreviousPagerField. Notice that the DataPager contains two NextPreviousPagerFields. The first one displays the First and Previous links, and the second one displays the Next and Last links.

Creating a Custom User Interface for Paging

If you need total and complete control over the paging user interface, you can use the TemplatePagerField to customize the appearance of the DataPager. The page in Listing 14.9 illustrates how you can use the TemplatePagerField.

LISTING 14.9   DataPagerTemplate.aspx

```
<%@ Page Language="C#" %>
<!DOCTYPE html PUBLIC "-//W3C//DTD XHTML 1.0 Transitional//EN"
 "http://www.w3.org/TR/xhtml1/DTD/xhtml1-transitional.dtd">
<script runat="server">

    protected void pg_PagerCommand(object sender, DataPagerCommandEventArgs e)
    {
        e.NewMaximumRows = e.Item.Pager.MaximumRows;
        switch (e.CommandName)
        {
            case "Previous":
                if (e.Item.Pager.StartRowIndex > 0)
                    e.NewStartRowIndex = e.Item.Pager.StartRowIndex - 2;
                break;

            case "Next":
                e.NewStartRowIndex = e.Item.Pager.StartRowIndex + 2;
                break;
        }
    }

</script>
<html xmlns="http://www.w3.org/1999/xhtml">
<head id="Head1" runat="server">
    <title>DataPager Template</title>
</head>
<body>
    <form id="form1" runat="server">
    <div>

        <asp:ListView
            ID="lstMovies"
            DataSourceId="srcMovies"
            runat="server">
            <LayoutTemplate>
                <ul
                    id="itemContainer"
```

```
                    runat="server">
            </ul>
            <asp:DataPager
                id="pg"
                PageSize="2"
                Runat="server">
                <Fields>
                    <asp:TemplatePagerField
                        OnPagerCommand="pg_PagerCommand">
                        <PagerTemplate>
                        <asp:LinkButton
                            id="lnkPrevious"
                            Text="Previous"
                            CommandName="Previous"
                            Runat="server" />
                        <asp:LinkButton
                            id="lnkNext"
                            Text="Next"
                            CommandName="Next"
                            Runat="server" />
                        </PagerTemplate>
                    </asp:TemplatePagerField>
                </Fields>
            </asp:DataPager>

        </LayoutTemplate>
        <ItemTemplate>
            <li>
            <%# Eval("Title") %>
            </li>
        </ItemTemplate>
    </asp:ListView>

    <asp:SqlDataSource
        id="srcMovies"
        SelectCommand="SELECT Id, Title, Director FROM Movie"
        ConnectionString='<%$ ConnectionStrings:con %>'
        Runat="server" />

    </div>
    </form>
</body>
</html>
```

The TemplatePagerField in Listing 14.9 contains two LinkButton controls (see Figure 14.9). The first LinkButton has a CommandName set to the value Previous, and the second LinkButton control has a CommandName set to the value Next.

FIGURE 14.9   Creating a custom paging user interface.

The page also contains an event handler for the TemplatePagerField's PagerCommand event. The actual work of paging is done within this event handler. The second argument passed to the event handler is an instance of the DataPagerCommandEventArgs class. You change the current page by assigning new values to this object's NewStartRowIndex and NewMaximumRows properties.

Data Source Paging with the DataPager Control

You can take advantage of the DataPager control when performing data source paging. The page in Listing 14.10 contains a ListView control bound to a LinqDataSource control. Because the LinqDataSource control has its AutoPage property set to the value true, it performs paging on the database server.

> **NOTE**
>
> The LinqDataSource control and LINQ to SQL are discussed in Chapter 20, "Data Access with LINQ to SQL."

LISTING 14.10   DataPagerDataSource.aspx

```
<%@ Page Language="C#" Trace="true" %>
<!DOCTYPE html PUBLIC "-//W3C//DTD XHTML 1.0 Transitional//EN"
 "http://www.w3.org/TR/xhtml1/DTD/xhtml1-transitional.dtd">
<html xmlns="http://www.w3.org/1999/xhtml">
<head runat="server">
    <title>DataPager DataSource Paging</title>
```

```
        </head>
        <body>
            <form id="form1" runat="server">
            <div>


            <asp:ListView
                ID="lstMovies"
                DataSourceId="srcMovies"
                runat="server">
                <LayoutTemplate>
                    <ol
                        id="itemContainer"
                        runat="server">
                    </ol>
                    <asp:DataPager
                        id="pg"
                        PageSize="2"
                        Runat="server">
                        <Fields>
                            <asp:NumericPagerField />
                        </Fields>
                    </asp:DataPager>

                </LayoutTemplate>
                <ItemTemplate>
                    <li>
                    <%# Eval("Title") %>
                    </li>
                </ItemTemplate>
            </asp:ListView>


            <asp:LinqDataSource
                id="srcMovies"
                ContextTypeName="MyDatabaseDataContext"
                TableName="Movies"
                AutoPage="true"
                Runat="server" />

            </div>
            </form>
        </body>
        </html>
```

14

So that you can verify that the paging is happening through the database, I've set the DataContext to log to ASP.NET trace. If you look at the Trace Information section at the bottom of the page, you can see the actual SQL commands executed by the LinqDataSource control (see Figure 14.10).

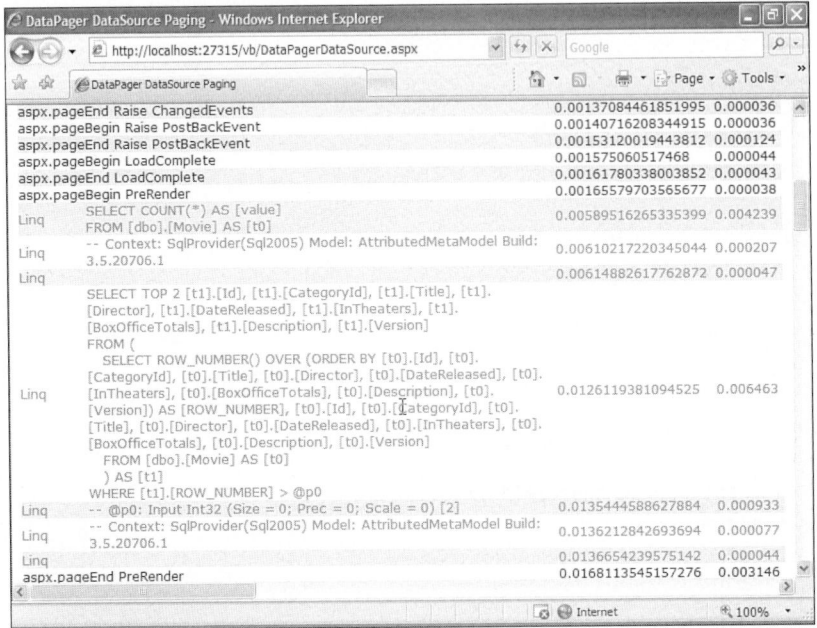

FIGURE 14.10   Performing data source paging with the DataPager control.

Summary

I'm a huge fan of the new ListView and DataPager controls. I'm constantly running into layout limitations when using the GridView control. Because ListView is entirely template-driven, it is not subject to these same limitations.

In this chapter, you learned how to use the ListView control to display, sort, edit, and insert data. You also learned how to take advantage of the DataPager control to add paging to the ListView control. You learned how to create a custom pager template and how to perform data source paging.

Using the Chart Control

Not too long ago, the only way to add robust charting and graphing capabilities to your application was to buy a third-party control suite. This was mainly due to the complexity involved; the task of writing your own chart control was too time-consuming and error-prone. This has recently changed.

In 2008, Microsoft released a free charting control that enabled developers to add rich, browser-based charts to ASP.NET 3.5 web applications. These components are now part of ASP.NET 4 and are included by default with the .NET Framework.

This chapter shows you how to use ASP.NET Chart Control to add dynamic, data bound graphics such as bar graphs or pie charts to your web application. We provide an overview of Chart Control and the different types of charts and graphs that it can produce. We cover the different ways you can customize a chart's appearance by modifying the plotting area and adding borders, backgrounds, and legends. Finally, we show you how to extend your charts with Ajax by adding tooltips, drill-down functionality, and other interactive features.

To get the most out of this chapter, we recommend that you run the samples in your environment and play around with changes to configurations and options to see how it alters the behavior of the charts.

Chart Control Fundamentals

In this section, you learn how to use the Chart control to provide graphical representations of data. You also learn how to group, sort, and filter data to customize the way your chart displays.

Displaying Data with the Chart Control

The Chart control has three main components:

▶ **Series**—Developers familiar with charting and graphing terminology recognize this term immediately. A series is a collection of data points. Different types of charts render a series in different ways, but the underlying format for specifying a series of data points remains the same.

▶ **Chart area**—Define the plot areas for which a series is plotted. For instance, a line graph would be defined as a single plot area. If you want to display a line graph and a bar graph on a single chart, you would define two chart areas.

▶ **Data points**—A single point of data within a series. As you read through this chapter you see more about what data points look like and how they are used.

Series, chart areas, and data points can all be specified either declaratively or programmatically. The page in Listing 15.1 displays a simple chart showing the number of movies in different categories using declarative data binding (see Figure 15.1).

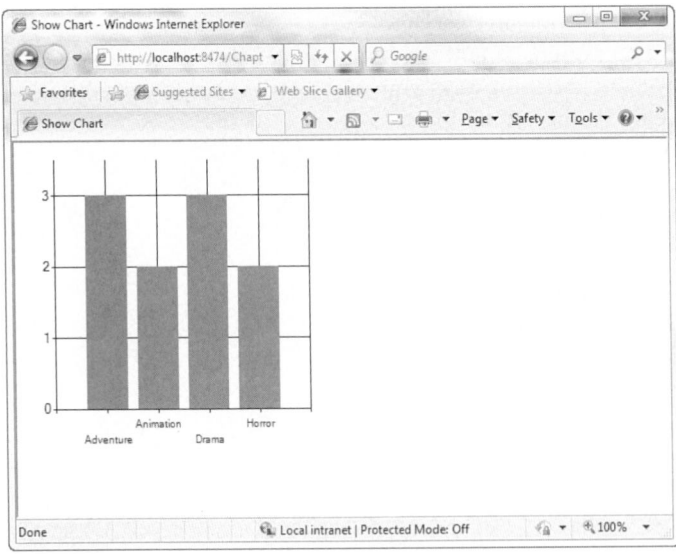

FIGURE 15.1   Displaying a chart of movie categories.

LISTING 15.1 ShowChart.aspx

```
<%@ Page Language="C#" %>
<%@ Register Assembly="System.Web.DataVisualization,
    Version=4.0.0.0, Culture=neutral, PublicKeyToken=31bf3856ad364e35"
    Namespace="System.Web.UI.DataVisualization.Charting" TagPrefix="asp" %>
<!DOCTYPE html PUBLIC "-//W3C//DTD XHTML 1.1//EN"
    "http://www.w3.org/TR/xhtml11/DTD/xhtml11.dtd">
<html xmlns="http://www.w3.org/1999/xhtml" >
<head id="Head1" runat="server">
    <title>Show Chart</title>
</head>
<body>
    <form id="form1" runat="server">
    <div>

    <asp:Chart ID="chtMovies" runat="server" DataSourceID="srcMovies">
            <Series>
                <asp:Series Name="MovieCategorySeries"
                                XValueMember="Category" YValueMembers="Count" >
                </asp:Series>
            </Series>
            <ChartAreas>
                <asp:ChartArea Name="MovieChartArea">
                </asp:ChartArea>
            </ChartAreas>
        </asp:Chart>

    <asp:SqlDataSource
        id="srcMovies"
        ConnectionString="<%$ ConnectionStrings:Movies %>"
        SelectCommand="CountMoviesInCategory"
        SelectCommandType="StoredProcedure"
        Runat="server" />
    </div>
    </form>
</body>
</html>
```

In Listing 15.1, we reuse the `CountMoviesInCategory` stored procedure from Chapter 9, "Using the SqlDataSource Control." The `Chart` is bound to the `SqlDataSource` control through the `DataSourceID` property, and the chart's x-and y-axes are associated to the dataset's returned columns through the `XValueMember` and `YValueMembers` properties on the `Series`.

Unlike the previous chapter's code samples, we have an additional `Register` declaration at the top of the page. Although the `Chart` control is shipped as part of the .NET 4 Framework, it is still located in a separate assembly and requires an explicit declaration to include it in the page.

> **NOTE**
>
> In addition to the Register declaration, you need to modify your web.config file to get the Chart functionality to work. The Chart control uses a separate HTTP Handler to render the image, and by default, your application isn't aware of it. Add the following section to the system.web section of the web.config file, and your charts render the following:
>
> ```
> <httpHandlers>
>         <add path="ChartImg.axd" verb="GET,HEAD"
> type="System.Web.UI.DataVisualization.Charting.ChartHttpHandler,
> System.Web.DataVisualization, Version=4.0.0.0, Culture=neutral,
> PublicKeyToken=31bf3856ad364e35" validate="false" />
>     </httpHandlers>
> ```
>
> You can read more about how the Chart renders to the browser later in this chapter.

The default chart type is `Column`, which displays each data point as a vertical bar. You can change the way the data points display by setting the `ChartType` property on the `Series`. Listing 15.2 shows the same data as a line graph (see Figure 15.2):

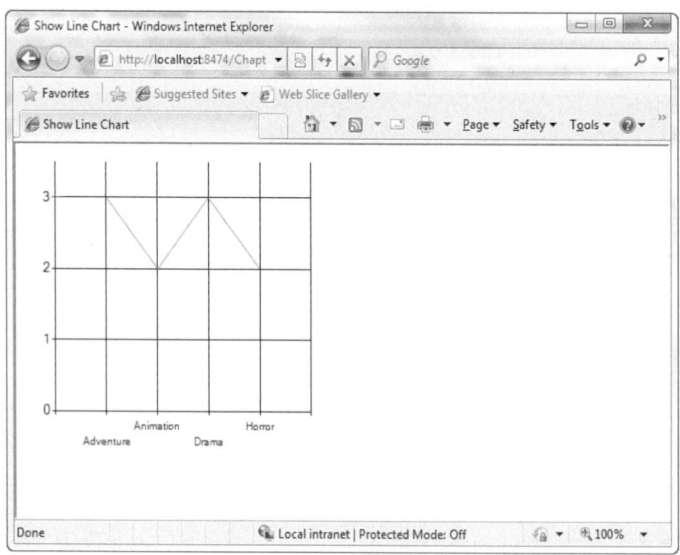

FIGURE 15.2   Displaying a line chart.

LISTING 15.2   ShowLineChart.aspx

```
<%@ Page Language="C#" %>
<%@ Register Assembly="System.Web.DataVisualization,
    Version=4.0.0.0, Culture=neutral, PublicKeyToken=31bf3856ad364e35"
    Namespace="System.Web.UI.DataVisualization.Charting" TagPrefix="asp" %>
<!DOCTYPE html PUBLIC "-//W3C//DTD XHTML 1.1//EN"
    "http://www.w3.org/TR/xhtml11/DTD/xhtml11.dtd">
<html xmlns="http://www.w3.org/1999/xhtml" >
<head id="Head1" runat="server">
    <title>Show Line Chart</title>
</head>
<body>
    <form id="form1" runat="server">
    <div>

    <asp:Chart ID="chtMovies" runat="server" DataSourceID="srcMovies">
        <Series>
            <asp:Series Name="MovieCategorySeries" ChartType="Line"
                            XValueMember="Category" YValueMembers="Count" >
            </asp:Series>
        </Series>
        <ChartAreas>
            <asp:ChartArea Name="MovieChartArea">
            </asp:ChartArea>
        </ChartAreas>
    </asp:Chart>

    <asp:SqlDataSource
        id="srcMovies"
        ConnectionString="<%$ ConnectionStrings:Movies %>"
        SelectCommand="CountMoviesInCategory"
        SelectCommandType="StoredProcedure"
        Runat="server" />
    </div>
    </form>
</body>
</html>
```

Charting is a massive topic and has consumed entire books in the past. You can use more than 30 different chart types to provide visualizations of your data. In the interest of keeping this chapter small and easy to read, the following provides an overview of just a few of the available chart types:

- ▶ **Area**—Shows the rate of change over time by shading the area under the line

- ▶ **Bar**—Similar to a Column chart but displays the values horizontally instead of vertically

- ▶ **Line**—Displays changes in data by rendering data points as a single continuous line

- ▶ **Point**—Displays each value as a point on the chart

- ▶ **Pie**—Shows how much each data point contributes to the entire data set by rendering it as a percentage

- ▶ **Box Plot**—Shows how data is distributed across a data set by displaying one or more boxes

- ▶ **Candlestick**—Commonly used to display stock information, such as the high and low values, along with the opening and closing prices

NOTE

You can find the complete set of possible chart types on the MSDN website at http://msdn.microsoft.com/en-us/library/dd489233(VS.100).aspx.

Sorting and Filtering Data

An instance of a chart control contains a `DataManipulator` property that can be used to sort and filter the chart data. You can sort any series in the chart by any axis (X, Y, Y2, and so on), and you can choose to sort in either an ascending or descending order. The `DataManipulator` property provides a `Sort` method to do this.

To use the sorting functionality, your chart must already be populated with data. To ensure this, we wait until the `OnDataBound` event to invoke our sorting code. Listing 15.3 sorts the movie categories from highest count to lowest count by executing the `chtMovies_DataBound` method after it binds to the `SqlDataSource` (see Figure 15.3).

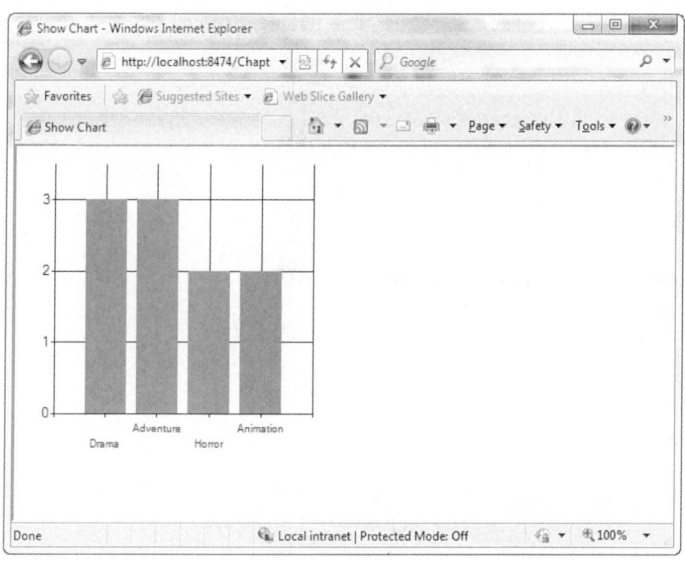

FIGURE 15.3   Sorting a chart.

LISTING 15.3   SortChart.aspx

```
<%@ Page Language="C#" %>


<%@ Register Assembly="System.Web.DataVisualization,
    Version=4.0.0.0, Culture=neutral, PublicKeyToken=31bf3856ad364e35"
Namespace="System.Web.UI.DataVisualization.Charting"
    TagPrefix="asp" %>
<!DOCTYPE html PUBLIC "-//W3C//DTD XHTML 1.1//EN"
    "http://www.w3.org/TR/xhtml11/DTD/xhtml11.dtd">


<script runat="server">
    void chtMovies_DataBound(object sender, EventArgs e)
    {
        chtMovies.DataManipulator.Sort(PointSortOrder.Descending, "Y",
➥"MovieCategorySeries");
    }
</script>


<html xmlns="http://www.w3.org/1999/xhtml">
<head id="Head1" runat="server">
    <title>Show Chart</title>
</head>
<body>
    <form id="form1" runat="server">
    <div>
```

```
        <asp:Chart ID="chtMovies" runat="server" DataSourceID="srcMovies"
OnDataBound="chtMovies_DataBound">
            <Series>
                <asp:Series Name="MovieCategorySeries" XValueMember="Category"
YValueMembers="Count">
                </asp:Series>
            </Series>
            <ChartAreas>
                <asp:ChartArea Name="MovieChartArea">
                </asp:ChartArea>
            </ChartAreas>
        </asp:Chart>
        <asp:SqlDataSource ID="srcMovies" ConnectionString="<%$
➥ConnectionStrings:Movies %>"
            SelectCommand="CountMoviesInCategory"
SelectCommandType="StoredProcedure" runat="server" />
    </div>
    </form>
</body>
</html>
```

Filtering chart data is similar to sorting it. The DataManipulator provides a FilterTopN method that enables you to only display the top "n" number of data points. For example, Listing 15.4 shows only the three movie categories with the highest counts (see Figure 15.4).

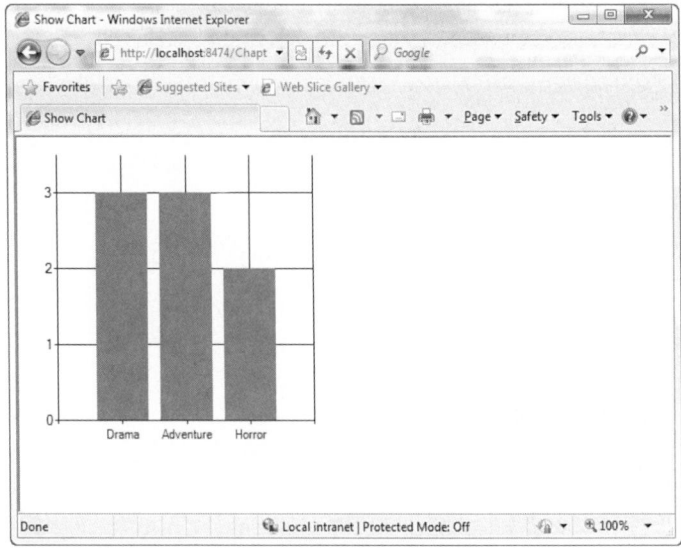

FIGURE 15.4   Filtering chart data.

LISTING 15.4 FilterChart.aspx

```
<%@ Page Language="C#" %>


<%@ Register Assembly="System.Web.DataVisualization,
    Version=4.0.0.0, Culture=neutral, PublicKeyToken=31bf3856ad364e35"
Namespace="System.Web.UI.DataVisualization.Charting"
    TagPrefix="asp" %>
<!DOCTYPE html PUBLIC "-//W3C//DTD XHTML 1.1//EN"
    "http://www.w3.org/TR/xhtml11/DTD/xhtml11.dtd">


<script runat="server">
    void chtMovies_DataBound(object sender, EventArgs e)
    {
        chtMovies.DataManipulator.FilterTopN(3, "MovieCategorySeries",
"MovieCategorySeries", "Y", true);
    }
</script>


<html xmlns="http://www.w3.org/1999/xhtml">
<head id="Head1" runat="server">
    <title>Show Chart</title>
</head>
<body>
    <form id="form1" runat="server">
    <div>
        <asp:Chart ID="chtMovies" runat="server" DataSourceID="srcMovies"
OnDataBound="chtMovies_DataBound">
            <Series>
                <asp:Series Name="MovieCategorySeries" XValueMember="Category"
YValueMembers="Count">
                </asp:Series>
            </Series>
            <ChartAreas>
                <asp:ChartArea Name="MovieChartArea">
                </asp:ChartArea>
            </ChartAreas>
        </asp:Chart>
        <asp:SqlDataSource ID="srcMovies" ConnectionString="<%$
➥ConnectionStrings:Movies %>"
            SelectCommand="CountMoviesInCategory" SelectCommandType="StoredProcedure"
runat="server" />
    </div>
    </form>
</body>
</html>
```

15

> **NOTE**
>
> It is also possible to define custom sorts and filters for your chart. The `DataManipulator` provides a `Sort` method that takes an object of type `IComparer` as a parameter, along with a `Filter` method that takes an object of type `IDataPointFilter` as a parameter. You can write classes that implement these inter-faces and build the logic that sorts or filters your data however you like.

Using Statistical Formulas

Statistical analysis goes hand in hand with charting and data visualization, and the ASP.NET charting control provides a wealth of functionality in this area. The `DataManipulator` property makes it easy to add statistical analyses to your charts. You can use the `Statistics` property on the `DataManipulator` to perform statistical analyses on data series without having to hand-write custom algorithms. (Though you can do that too, if necessary.)

The code in Listing 15.5 illustrates adding a label to the top of a page that contains a chart showing the mean value of a series of data points (see Figure 15.5).

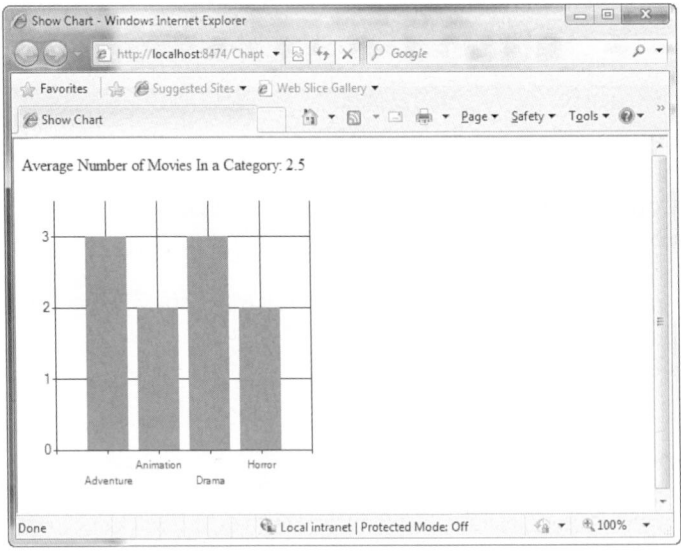

FIGURE 15.5   Displaying the mean.

LISTING 15.5   `ShowMean.aspx`

```
<%@ Page Language="C#" %>
<%@ Register Assembly="System.Web.DataVisualization,
    Version=4.0.0.0, Culture=neutral, PublicKeyToken=31bf3856ad364e35"
    Namespace="System.Web.UI.DataVisualization.Charting" TagPrefix="asp" %>
```

```
<!DOCTYPE html PUBLIC "-//W3C//DTD XHTML 1.1//EN"
    "http://www.w3.org/TR/xhtml11/DTD/xhtml11.dtd">

<script runat="server">
    void chtMovies_DataBound(object sender, EventArgs e)
    {
        lblAverage.Text =
chtMovies.DataManipulator.Statistics.Mean("MovieCategorySeries").ToString();
    }
</script>

<html xmlns="http://www.w3.org/1999/xhtml" >
<head id="Head1" runat="server">
    <title>Show Chart</title>
</head>
<body>
    <form id="form1" runat="server">
    <div>

    <p>Average Number of Movies In a Category: <asp:Label ID="lblAverage"
➥runat="server" /></p>

    <asp:Chart ID="chtMovies" runat="server" DataSourceID="srcMovies"
OnDataBound="chtMovies_DataBound">
            <Series>
                <asp:Series Name="MovieCategorySeries"
                                XValueMember="Category" YValueMembers="Count" >
                </asp:Series>
            </Series>
            <ChartAreas>
                <asp:ChartArea Name="MovieChartArea">
                </asp:ChartArea>
            </ChartAreas>
        </asp:Chart>

    <asp:SqlDataSource
        id="srcMovies"
        ConnectionString="<%$ ConnectionStrings:Movies %>"
        SelectCommand="CountMoviesInCategory"
        SelectCommandType="StoredProcedure"
        Runat="server" />
    </div>
    </form>
</body>
</html>
```

15

You can also use these calculated statistics to display *strip lines*—a band across any axis to bring attention to a value or range of values. Strip lines can be defined declaratively on any axis within ChartArea. Listing 15.6 adds a strip line to display the average count (mean) within the chart by declaring a StripLine on the AxisY axis (see Figure 15.6).

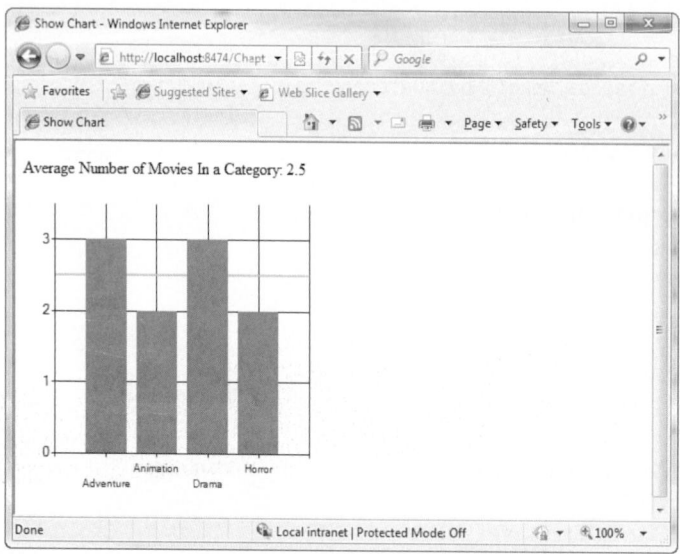

FIGURE 15.6   Displaying a strip line.

LISTING 15.6   ShowMeanStripLine.aspx

```
<%@ Page Language="C#" %>
<%@ Register Assembly="System.Web.DataVisualization,
    Version=4.0.0.0, Culture=neutral, PublicKeyToken=31bf3856ad364e35"
    Namespace="System.Web.UI.DataVisualization.Charting" TagPrefix="asp" %>
<!DOCTYPE html PUBLIC "-//W3C//DTD XHTML 1.1//EN"
    "http://www.w3.org/TR/xhtml11/DTD/xhtml11.dtd">

<script runat="server">
    void chtMovies_DataBound(object sender, EventArgs e)
    {
        double average =
➥chtMovies.DataManipulator.Statistics.Mean("MovieCategorySeries");

        lblAverage.Text = average.ToString();
        chtMovies.ChartAreas["MovieChartArea"].AxisY.StripLines[0].IntervalOffset =
average;
    }
</script>
```

```
<html xmlns="http://www.w3.org/1999/xhtml" >
<head id="Head1" runat="server">
    <title>Show Chart</title>
</head>
<body>
    <form id="form1" runat="server">
    <div>

    <p>Average Number of Movies In a Category: <asp:Label ID="lblAverage"
➥runat="server" /></p>

    <asp:Chart ID="chtMovies" runat="server" DataSourceID="srcMovies"
OnDataBound="chtMovies_DataBound">
            <Series>
                <asp:Series Name="MovieCategorySeries"
                            XValueMember="Category" YValueMembers="Count" >
                </asp:Series>
            </Series>
            <ChartAreas>
                <asp:ChartArea Name="MovieChartArea">
                    <AxisY>
                        <StripLines>
                            <asp:StripLine BorderColor="Orange" BorderWidth="2" />
                        </StripLines>
                    </AxisY>
                </asp:ChartArea>
            </ChartAreas>
        </asp:Chart>

    <asp:SqlDataSource
        id="srcMovies"
        ConnectionString="<%$ ConnectionStrings:Movies %>"
        SelectCommand="CountMoviesInCategory"
        SelectCommandType="StoredProcedure"
        Runat="server" />
    </div>
    </form>
</body>
</html>
```

The Statistics property provides common formulas such as mean, median, normal distribution, correlation, and covariance. Advanced calculations specific to financial analyses can be performed by using the FinancialFormula method on the DataManipulator object. Some common financial formulas that can be calculated with the FinancialFormula method follow:

▶ **MovingAverage**—An average of data calculated over a period of time.

▶ **ExponentialMovingAverage**—Similar to a MovingAverage, except recent days have more weight in the calculation.

▶ **Forecasting**—Predicts the future values by analyzing the historical data.

▶ **MassIndex**—Predicts the reversal of a trend by comparing the difference and range between the high and low values in a dataset.

▶ **StandardDeviation**—Calculates the difference between values in a dataset.

Listing 15.7 demonstrates how to perform financial analysis on a sample set of data and display it as a series (see Figure 15.7).

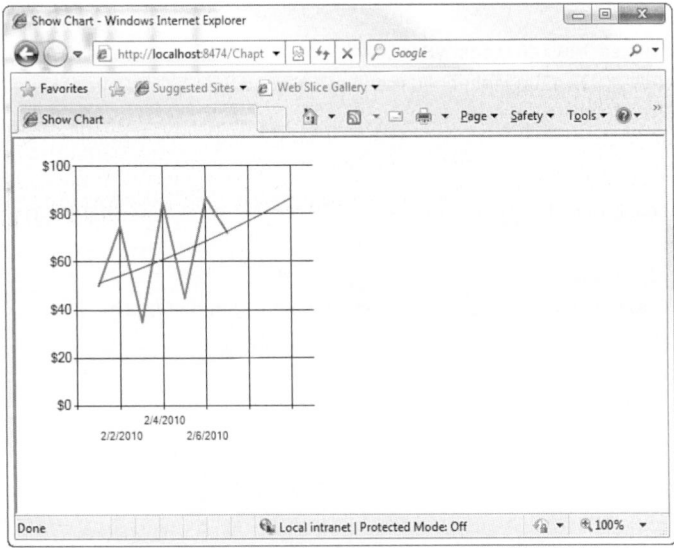

FIGURE 15.7   Displaying a financial analysis series.

LISTING 15.7   ShowFinancialAnalysis.aspx

```
<%@ Page Language="C#" %>
<%@ Register Assembly="System.Web.DataVisualization,
    Version=4.0.0.0, Culture=neutral, PublicKeyToken=31bf3856ad364e35"
    Namespace="System.Web.UI.DataVisualization.Charting" TagPrefix="asp" %>
<!DOCTYPE html PUBLIC "-//W3C//DTD XHTML 1.1//EN"
    "http://www.w3.org/TR/xhtml11/DTD/xhtml11.dtd">

<script runat="server">
    void PopulateData()
    {
```

```
        chtPrices.Series["PriceSeries"].Points.AddXY("2/1/2010", 50);
        chtPrices.Series["PriceSeries"].Points.AddXY("2/2/2010", 75);
        chtPrices.Series["PriceSeries"].Points.AddXY("2/3/2010", 35);
        chtPrices.Series["PriceSeries"].Points.AddXY("2/4/2010", 85);
        chtPrices.Series["PriceSeries"].Points.AddXY("2/5/2010", 45);
        chtPrices.Series["PriceSeries"].Points.AddXY("2/6/2010", 87);
        chtPrices.Series["PriceSeries"].Points.AddXY("2/7/2010", 72);
    }

    void Page_Load()
    {
        PopulateData();

        chtPrices.DataManipulator.FinancialFormula(FinancialFormula.Forecasting,
    "Exponential,3,false,false", "PriceSeries", "ForecastSeries");
    }
</script>

<html xmlns="http://www.w3.org/1999/xhtml" >
<head id="Head1" runat="server">
    <title>Show Chart</title>
</head>
<body>
    <form id="form1" runat="server">
    <div>

    <asp:Chart ID="chtPrices" runat="server" >
            <Series>
                <asp:Series Name="PriceSeries" ChartType="Line" Color="Red"
BorderWidth="2"></asp:Series>
                <asp:Series Name="ForecastSeries" ChartType="Line"
➥Color="Blue"></asp:Series>
            </Series>
            <ChartAreas>
                <asp:ChartArea Name="PriceChartArea">
                    <AxisY>
                        <LabelStyle Format="C0" />
                    </AxisY>
                </asp:ChartArea>
            </ChartAreas>
        </asp:Chart>
    </div>
    </form>
</body>
</html>
```

15

> **NOTE**
>
> The second parameter in the `FinancialFormula` method is a string representing a set of parameters for the analysis. This parameter set is different for every formula. The Forecasting formula used in Listing 15.7 uses a parameter set of `RegressionType`, `Period`, `ApproxError`, `ForecastError` that enables you to optionally customize how the analysis is performed.
>
> You can find the complete set of parameters for every formula on the MSDN website.

The statistical and financial formulas built into the `Chart` control make it easy to add powerful analyses to your web applications with little custom code. In the past, adding things such as striplines and performing additional calculations on a data series was either something you had to code yourself or something that cost a great deal of extra money when buying charting controls from vendors. With ASP.NET 4, all that functionality is not only available, but also it is available in an easily accessible, easy to use API.

Customizing a Chart's Appearance

The `Chart` control enables you to customize almost every aspect of its appearance. In addition to customizing the plot area, specifying border details, adding axis titles, and inserting legends, the `Chart` control also enables you to easily render your data in 3D.

Customizing the Background and Plotting Area

The `Chart` control provides many properties to customize almost every aspect of the background and plotting area, including the background color, border colors and widths, gradients, and data point colors. Some of the properties you can use to customize a chart's appearance follow:

- ▶ **BackColor**—The color of the chart's background.

- ▶ **BackGradientStyle**—Specifies how a gradient should be applied to the background.

- ▶ **BackSecondaryColor**—The secondary color used for background gradients.

- ▶ **Palette**—Specifies the color palette to use for chart's data points.

- ▶ **BorderSkin-SkinStyle**—Provides a number of built-in styles to render a shaded, three-dimensional border around the entire chart.

Most of these properties apply to the `ChartArea` as well, so you can customize the actual plotting area differently from the overall chart's appearance. Furthermore, many of them also apply to the `Series`, so you can control the appearance of your data points.

Listing 15.8 demonstrates some of the styles you can apply to a chart, including a left-to-right background gradient, a colored chart area background, and an embossed border around the chart (see Figure 15.8).

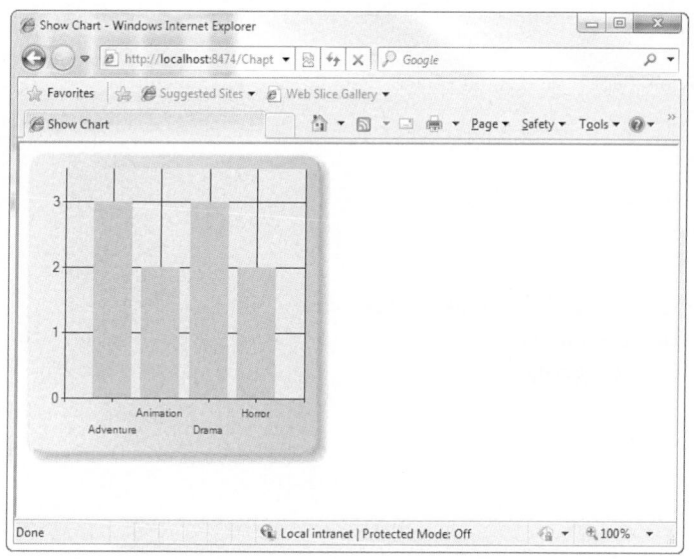

FIGURE 15.8   Customizing a chart's appearance.

LISTING 15.8   ChartAppearance.aspx

```
<%@ Page Language="C#" %>
<%@ Register Assembly="System.Web.DataVisualization,
    Version=4.0.0.0, Culture=neutral, PublicKeyToken=31bf3856ad364e35"
    Namespace="System.Web.UI.DataVisualization.Charting" TagPrefix="asp" %>
<!DOCTYPE html PUBLIC "-//W3C//DTD XHTML 1.1//EN"
    "http://www.w3.org/TR/xhtml11/DTD/xhtml11.dtd">
<html xmlns="http://www.w3.org/1999/xhtml" >
<head id="Head1" runat="server">
    <title>Show Chart</title>
</head>
<body>
    <form id="form1" runat="server">
    <div>

    <asp:Chart ID="chtMovies" runat="server" DataSourceID="srcMovies"
➥BackColor="AliceBlue"
BackGradientStyle="LeftRight" BackSecondaryColor="SkyBlue" Palette="Pastel"
BorderSkin-SkinStyle="Emboss" >
            <Series>
                <asp:Series Name="MovieCategorySeries"
                                XValueMember="Category" YValueMembers="Count" >
                </asp:Series>
```

```
            </Series>
            <ChartAreas>
                <asp:ChartArea Name="MovieChartArea" BackColor="AntiqueWhite">
                </asp:ChartArea>
            </ChartAreas>
        </asp:Chart>

    <asp:SqlDataSource
        id="srcMovies"
        ConnectionString="<%$ ConnectionStrings:Movies %>"
        SelectCommand="CountMoviesInCategory"
        SelectCommandType="StoredProcedure"
        Runat="server" />
    </div>
    </form>
</body>
</html>
```

The Chart control also provides many options for displaying titles and legends. You can provide a chart title declaratively in the Titles section under the Chart. Similarly, axis titles and their styles can be defined declaratively in the ChartArea.

There is also a Legends section under the Chart property that enables you to define a chart legend and position it wherever you want. Listing 15.9 demonstrates how to add a legend and titles to a chart (see Figure 15.9).

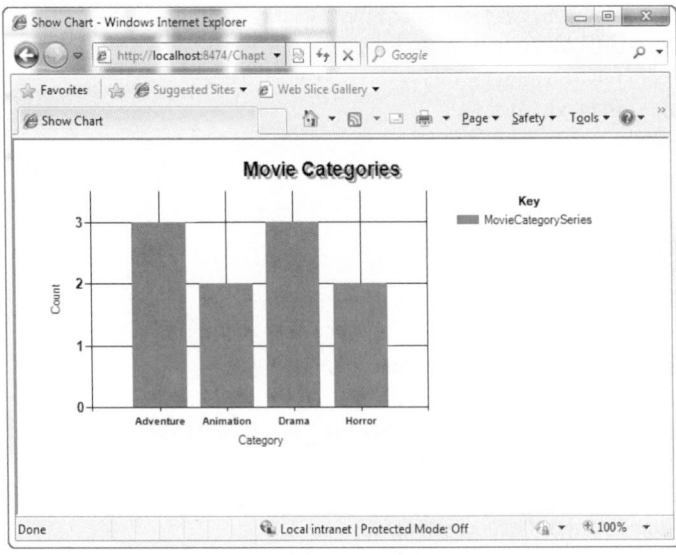

FIGURE 15.9   Adding titles and a legend.

LISTING 15.9   ShowChartTitles.aspx

```
<%@ Page Language="C#" %>
<%@ Register Assembly="System.Web.DataVisualization,
    Version=4.0.0.0, Culture=neutral, PublicKeyToken=31bf3856ad364e35"
    Namespace="System.Web.UI.DataVisualization.Charting" TagPrefix="asp" %>
<!DOCTYPE html PUBLIC "-//W3C//DTD XHTML 1.1//EN"
    "http://www.w3.org/TR/xhtml11/DTD/xhtml11.dtd">
<html xmlns="http://www.w3.org/1999/xhtml" >
<head id="Head1" runat="server">
    <title>Show Chart</title>
</head>
<body>
    <form id="form1" runat="server">
    <div>

    <asp:Chart ID="chtMovies" runat="server" DataSourceID="srcMovies" Width="600">
    <Titles>
        <asp:Title Font="Arial, 14pt, style=Bold" ShadowOffset="3" Text="Movie
Categories"Alignment="TopCenter" />
    </Titles>
    <Legends>
        <asp:Legend LegendStyle="Row" Title="Key" BackColor="Transparent" />
    </Legends>
            <Series>
                <asp:Series Name="MovieCategorySeries"
                                XValueMember="Category" YValueMembers="Count" >
                </asp:Series>
            </Series>
            <ChartAreas>
                <asp:ChartArea Name="MovieChartArea">
                    <AxisX Title="Category">
                        <LabelStyle Font="Arial, 12pt, style=Bold" />
                    </AxisX>
                    <AxisY Title="Count">
                        <LabelStyle Font="Arial, 12pt, style=Bold" />
                    </AxisY>
                </asp:ChartArea>
            </ChartAreas>
        </asp:Chart>

    <asp:SqlDataSource
        id="srcMovies"
        ConnectionString="<%$ ConnectionStrings:Movies %>"
        SelectCommand="CountMoviesInCategory"
        SelectCommandType="StoredProcedure"
```

```
            Runat="server" />
    </div>
    </form>
</body>
</html>
```

By default, the legend is placed on the right of the chart. In Listing 15.9, we set the `Width` property on the `Chart` to give it more space; otherwise, the default width would have been used, and the actual chart area would have rendered significantly smaller.

Three-Dimensional Charts

With all the powerful and flexible functionality that we have seen so far that comes with the ASP.NET charting control, it would be easy to assume that to get 3D charts we have to do a bunch of difficult low-level customization and coding. Thankfully, this is not the case, and 3-D charting is every bit as easy to use as 2D charting.

To turn on 3D charts, you simply modify the `Area3DStyle` set of properties. If you look at the property editor in the designer for a `ChartArea`, you see a collapsible section called `Area3DStyle`. The first and most important property here is the `Enabled` property. When enabled, you can change a host of 3D-related properties including the rotation angles, lighting, perspective, depth, and more.

Figure 15.10 shows a 3D number chart depicting the number of zombie sightings of various types.

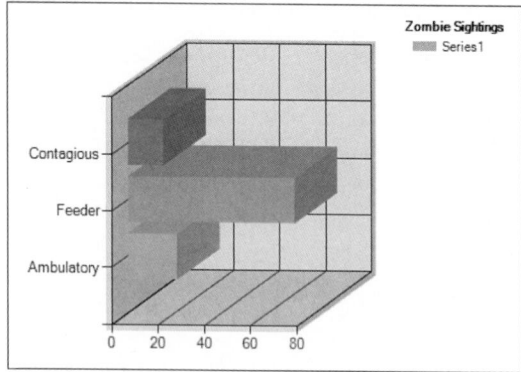

FIGURE 15.10   Using 3D charts.

Go back through some of the samples already created in this chapter, turn on 3D for the charting areas, and play with the various properties to see how they affect the look and feel of the final chart.

Drill-Down Reports

Those of us who have created reports for business stakeholders and customers alike know that rendering the chart is merely the tip of the iceberg. People want to know where the data came from and want their charts to be interactive.

Again, this is where we typically end up spending large amounts of money for complicated third-party vendor control suites that enable for the injection of code to enable for drill-downs and clickable charts. As we've seen throughout this chapter, ASP.NET Chart Control actually builds images rendered in-place on the page. If this is the case, then how can we create clickable data points?

One of the most powerful features within ASP.NET Chart Control is that we can assign a value to the Url property of any given data point. This means we can click any dot in a scatter plot diagram, or we can click any bar in a bar graph, and we will be redirected to that URL.

To see how this works, let's take a look at the ASPx markup that produced the preceding chart illustrating the various types of zombie sightings within a given data series:

```
<asp:Chart ID="zombieChart" runat="server" Width="500" Height="350"
    Palette="EarthTones">
    <Series>
        <asp:Series ChartArea="MainChartArea" ChartType="Bar" Name="Series1"
            Palette="EarthTones" Legend="Legend1">
        </asp:Series>
    </Series>

    <ChartAreas>
        <asp:ChartArea Name="MainChartArea">
            <Area3DStyle Enable3D="True"></Area3DStyle>
        </asp:ChartArea>
    </ChartAreas>
    <Legends>
        <asp:Legend Name="Legend1" Title="Zombie Sightings">
        </asp:Legend>
    </Legends>
</asp:Chart>
```

Given this chart, we want to make it so that when you click a particular bar for that type of sighting, you are redirected to a drill-down page displaying a chronologically sorted list of all zombie sightings of that type. To do this, we assign a URL to each of the data points in the graph, as shown here in the Page_Load() event handler for this page:

```
private DataPoint LastAddedPoint
{
    get
    {
```

15

```
        return zombieChart.Series[0].Points[zombieChart.Series[0].Points.Count - 1];
    }
}

protected void Page_Load(object sender, EventArgs e)
{
    zombieChart.Series[0].Points.AddXY("Ambulatory", 21);
    LastAddedPoint.Url = string.Format("~/ZombieSightings.aspx?type=Ambulatory");

    zombieChart.Series[0].Points.AddXY("Feeder", 72);
    LastAddedPoint.Url = string.Format("~/ZombieSightings.aspx?type=Feeder");

    zombieChart.Series[0].Points.AddXY("Contagious", 15);
    LastAddedPoint.Url = string.Format("~/ZombieSightings.aspx?type=Contagious");
}
```

Now when you run this application and you hover the mouse over each of the bar graph data points, you see the appropriate URL show up in the status bar at the bottom of your browser (assuming you have that enabled). Clicking the Feeder bar in the middle takes you to the page ZombieSightings.aspx?type=Feeder. The ability to assign arbitrary URLs to any data point within a series is incredibly useful and enables an endless variety of drill-down reporting scenarios that normally would only be possible in reporting tools such as SQL Server Reporting Services or expensive third-party control suites. (And many of them don't support clickable data points!)

Summary

This chapter provided you with an introduction to ASP.NET Chart Control. You have seen several code samples that illustrate its simplicity, but at the same time, its tremendous power. In many cases developers can now add charting functionality, dashboards, and drill-down reports into their applications without resorting to large enterprise tools such as SQL Server Reporting Services or buying expensive third-party charting control suites.

ASP.NET Chart Control is just one more tool in the ever-growing toolbox of incredibly powerful features and functionality available to developers of ASP.NET 4 applications.

CHAPTER 16

Using the QueryExtender Control

One of ASP.NET's great strengths is the near infinite number of ways in which you can populate your pages with data. Although there have always been low-level options available such as ADO.NET, in recent years it has become more popular to use Object-Relational Mapping (ORM) tools, dynamic data tools, and other abstractions. Most of these abstractions work either at the code-behind level or within other Assemblies.

This chapter introduces you to the QueryExtender control that enables you to modify standard ASP.NET declarative data sources with rich filtering and sorting functionality. This enables the developer to build rich, dynamic, data-driven pages and maintain all the data sorting and filtering logic completely within the ASPx markup without dropping to the code-behind level.

Introduction to the QueryExtender Control

When you retrieve data through a data source control, you traditionally sacrifice the fine-grained control over the query in exchange for the declarative (often design-surface friendly) simplicity of the data source control. The QueryExtender control aims to give you back some of that control while still giving you all the benefits of a declarative data source.

The QueryExtender control gives you the ability to specify filter criteria, sorting options, and even custom queries written in LINQ all in a declarative fashion using a suite of nested child controls that derive from the

ParameterDataSourceExpression class. The next section of this chapter provides an overview of the various types of filtering, sorting, and custom querying you can enable using these controls.

Querying Data with Declarative Syntax

The query extender control is just a container for filter expressions. Each of these filter expressions are sequentially applied to the target query, further filtering and sorting the output of queries from a LINQ or Object data source.

The following sections of the chapter provide you with a tour of the various types of expressions that can be used within a query extender to provide additional sorting and filtering capabilities.

Querying with the `ControlFilterExpression`

This is an expression filter that applies only when you work with a Dynamic Data website. We won't cover a sample of this control in depth. Basically, this filter expression enables you to modify a database query using the data key of an item selected in a data-bound control. In short, this enables you to dynamically filter a query when a user selects an option from a drop-down list.

Querying with the `CustomExpression`

Although the QueryExtender is all about giving you the ability to do your filtering declaratively, occasionally you just need to resort to using a little bit of LINQ to get the job done. However, if you need that bit of LINQ to work in tandem with other expressions already modifying a query, you can make use of the CustomExpression class.

This works simply, you just supply a method to be invoked during the query process that enables you to inject your own modification to the query pipeline. Below is a snippet showing a custom expression and the C# method invoked by this custom expression. Although you wouldn't normally use the custom expression to perform such trivial filtering, this at least gives you an idea of how it can be used.

```
<asp:QueryExtender TargetControlID="weaponDataSource" runat="server">
    <asp:CustomExpression OnQuerying="FilterWeapons" />
</asp:QueryExtender>
```

This declaration of the query extender uses a custom expression to invoke a method called FilterWeapons during the query process. This is far better than using the traditional code-behind method because your custom query modifications are injected into the declarative query modification pipeline, enabling your code to blend seamlessly with all the other declarative sorting and filtering being done.

```
protected void FilterWeapons(object sender, CustomExpressionEventArgs e)
{
    e.Query = from weapon in e.Query.Cast<Weapon>()
        where weapon.SplashDamage && weapon.BlastRadius > 12
        select weapon;
}
```

The preceding code takes the incoming query and modifies it so that whatever expressions are applied afterward will apply only to the set of weapons that meet the criteria we specified.

Querying with the **DynamicFilterExpression**

This is another expression that applies only when you work with an ASP.NET Dynamic Data application. This filter expression builds a database query by using the indicated DynamicFilter control, a control that is part of ASP.NET Dynamic Data framework.

For more information on filtering data using the DynamicFilterExpression in an ASP.NET Dynamic Data application, check out this MSDN link:

http://tinyurl.com/filterrows-dynamicdata

Querying with the **MethodExpression**

The MethodExpression class provides a means by which the developer can specify a custom LINQ query that is defined in a method. This method needs to be static and must take as its first parameter an IQueryable<T> or IEnumerable<T> object. The return value of this method can't change the incoming parameters.

When searching for the method containing the query, the MethodExpression class first checks the class indicated by the TypeName property in the QueryExtender control. If the data source implements IDynamicDataSource, the method is searched for on the DataContext or ObjectContext object property of the data source. Finally, MethodExpression searches for the method in a template control, the base class for the page, or in a user control.

In short, there is a tremendous amount of flexibility in where you can put the custom query method, but the method itself must follow a strict format.

The following markup shows an example of specifying a MethodExpression within a QueryExtender:

```
<asp:QueryExtender ID="QueryExtender1" runat="server"
      TargetControlID="AccountDataSource">
      <asp:MethodExpression MethodName="FilterOutPastDueAccounts" >
      </asp:MethodExpression>
</asp:QueryExtender>
```

16

And you might define a static method in the page (though we recommend explicitly defining the type name so you can avoid filling your code-behinds with additional logic) as follows:

```
public static IQueryable<Product>
        FilterOutPastDueAccounts(IQueryable<BankAccount> query)
{
        return from account in query
                where account.Status != AccountStatuses.PastDue
                select account;
}
```

The return value from this method is passed down the chain of filter expressions. One great advantage of putting code behind these expressions is that they can be easily reused across multiple pages. (This is another reason we recommended specifying the type name of the expression class explicitly rather than putting the expression method in the page's code-behind.)

Sorting with the `OrderByExpression`

The `OrderByExpression` provides developers with a way of specifying a sort expression that can be applied to the query within the query extender control. The two properties of the `OrderByExpression` that control the sorting are the `DataField` and `Direction` properties.

The `DataField` property contains the name of the column on which the sorting will take place, and the `Direction` property indicates which direction the sorting will be done.

```
<asp:QueryExtender runat="server" TargetControlID="AccountsReceivableSource">
    <asp:OrderByExpression DataField="AmountDue" Direction="Descending"/>
</asp:QueryExtender>
```

In the preceding code we sort the accounts receivable rows in descending order by the amount due. This should give us a nice list of the people who owe us money and where they live. This might not be sufficient. What if, for example, for each dollar amount, we want to sort the receivables by the age of the customer? This can enable us to see the oldest person that owes us each amount of money. We can use a `ThenBy` tag as a child of the `OrderByExpression` to accomplish this as shown below:

```
<asp:QueryExtender runat="server" TargetControlID="AccountsReceivableSource">
    <asp:OrderByExpression DataField="AmountDue" Direction="Descending">
        <asp:ThenBy DataField="CustomerAge" Direction="Descending"/>
</asp:QueryExtender>
```

Querying with the `PropertyExpression`

The `PropertyExpression` enables the developer to use the query extender control to filter the result set based on the values of specific columns. Remember that the property expression works only with equality. For example, you cannot use a property expression to filter where the value contained in a column is less than or greater than some other value.

The following example shows how to filter a data source of ransom demands in which the ransom value is selected from a drop-down box:

```
<asp:DropDownList AutoPostBack="true" ID="RansomValues" runat="server">
    <asp:ListItem Value="1000000">1 Meeeeelion Dollars!</asp:ListItem>
    <asp:ListItem Value="1">1 dollar</asp:ListItem>
</asp:DropDownList>
<asp:QueryExtender runat="server" TargetControlID="RansomDataSource">
    <asp:PropertyExpression>
        <asp:ControlParameter ControlID="RansomValues" Name="RansomValue"/>
    </asp:PropertyExpression>
</asp:QueryExtender>
```

There's actually quite a bit of interesting functionality in the preceding code. The first thing you see is that we have a drop-down list containing a list of possible filter values for ransom demands. In this code sample, we hardcoded the values but those could easily be data bound. Next is the query extender, extending a data source called `RansomDataSource`. The query in that data source is filtered to contain only those rows whose `RansomValue` column is exactly equal to the currently selected value of the `RansomValues` drop-down list. This means that if the user were to select the first value in the drop-down list, the page automatically posts back, and the data source automatically filters itself based on the new ransom value.

Control Parameters enable us to continue to use declarative query extension at the same time as pulling valuable information from other controls on the page rather than potentially complicated and messy code-behind classes.

Querying with the `RangeExpression`

If the filter you're looking to apply can be expressed as a range expression, this control can do the trick. A range expression is an expression in which you test whether a value is less than or greater than a target value *or* falls within a target range. This is a versatile expression, as shown in the following sample that filters a data source for rows in which the transaction posting date occurred within the two date periods chosen by the user with two text boxes that have jQuery-based calendar pop-ups feeding them (jQuery code is not included here because it's beyond the scope for this chapter):

```
<asp:QueryExtender runat="server" TargetControlID="AccountsDataSource">
    <asp:RangeExpression DataField="TransactionPostDate" MinType="Inclusive"
        MaxType="Inclusive">
        <asp:ControlParameter ControlID="FromDate" />
        <asp:ControlParameter ControlID="ToDate" />
    </asp:RangeExpression>
</asp:QueryExtender>
```

Querying with the `SearchExpression`

The search expression functionality of the query extender is one of the most powerful expressions available. It enables you to specify a field or list of fields and search those fields by doing a comparison against a search string. This search can be a "starts with", "contains", or "ends with" search. Gone are the days in which the developer has to hand-write these kinds of queries, which is typically an arduous, error-prone process. This expression requires you to specify the `SearchType` and `DataFields` properties, but it does the rest of the magic for you. Optionally, you can use the `ComparsionType` to control the case-sensitivity of the search (depending on whether the underlying data source you used supports this functionality).

As with all these expressions, you can combine them with other expressions to create rich queries without having to drop into your code-behind to do manual sorting and filtering. The following sample illustrates how to use the search expression to provide a full-featured search page (although a real-world, production search page would probably have a better UI!)

```
<form id="searchForm" runat="server">
    Query: <asp:TextBox ID="SearchQueryTextBox" runat="server"/><br/>
    <asp:Button ID="searchButton" runat="server" Text="Search" />
    <asp:LinqDataSource ID="ContactsDataSource"
        ContextTypeName="MyDatabaseDataContext"
        TableName="Contacts" runat="server" />

    <asp:QueryExtender runat="server" TargetControlID="ContactsDataSource">
        <asp:SearchExpression SearchType="Contains"
            DataFields="FirstName,LastName,UserName">
            <asp:ControlParameter ControlID="SearchQueryTextBox" />
        </asp:SearchExpression>
    </asp:QueryExtender>

    <asp:GridView ID="ContactsGrid" runat="server"
        DataSourceID="ContactsDataSource">
    </asp:GridView>
</form>
```

By now most of the markup in the preceding code sample should look familiar; however no code-behind is driving the actual querying of the database. The query extender is automatically going to modify the query (if there is anything in the search box) and filter the results every time a postback occurs. The button press causes a postback but no code in the code-behind needs to be executed because all the search logic has been rigged up declaratively in the .aspx page.

Whether having this "querying as a side-effect" is a good thing is a debate that will probably rage on for quite some time as many developers prefer to explicitly control when and how the query is performed, and obviously proponents of ASP.NET MVC Framework would have the query instigated in a controller action method rather than declaratively in the markup.

Building a Sample Page with the `QueryExtender` Control

Now that we've seen all the different options available to us when using the `QueryExtender` control, let's put this all together with a real data source and some controls on the page and see how it all works as a unit.

In this sample, we point a LINQ data source (a data source for LINQ to SQL contexts) at a context that contains tables for a video game catalog database. When the data source is set up, we just need to create an ASP.NET Web Form page called `GameBrowser.aspx`. This page needs to have a drop-down list that enables users to filter games by Genre and a text box that enables users to search both game title and game description. Take a look at the markup for the GameBrowser.aspx page:

```
<form id="form1" runat="server">
    <div>
        Genre: <asp:DropDownList runat="server" ID="GenreDropDownList"
                DataSourceID="GenreSource" DataTextField="Name"
                DataValueField="ID" AutoPostBack="true" /><br />
        Game Search: <asp:TextBox ID="GameSearchTextBox" runat="server" /><br />

        <asp:GridView runat="server" ID="GamesGrid" DataSourceID="GamesSource"
            AutoGenerateColumns="False" BackColor="LightGoldenrodYellow"
            BorderColor="Tan" BorderWidth="1px" CellPadding="2" ForeColor="Black"
            GridLines="None">
            <AlternatingRowStyle BackColor="PaleGoldenrod" />
            <Columns>
                <asp:BoundField DataField="ID" HeaderText="ID" ReadOnly="True"
                    SortExpression="ID" />
                <asp:BoundField DataField="Title" HeaderText="Title"
➥ReadOnly="True"
                    SortExpression="Title" />
                <asp:BoundField DataField="Description" HeaderText="Description"
```

```
                     ReadOnly="True" SortExpression="Description" />
               <asp:BoundField DataField="GenreID" HeaderText="GenreID"
➡ReadOnly="True"
                     SortExpression="GenreID" />
               <asp:BoundField DataField="GenreName" HeaderText="Genre Name" Read
➡Only="true" />
               <asp:BoundField DataField="ESRB" HeaderText="ESRB" ReadOnly="True"
                     SortExpression="ESRB" />
          </Columns>
          <FooterStyle BackColor="Tan" />
          <HeaderStyle BackColor="Tan" Font-Bold="True" />
          <PagerStyle BackColor="PaleGoldenrod" ForeColor="DarkSlateBlue"
               HorizontalAlign="Center" />
          <SelectedRowStyle BackColor="DarkSlateBlue" ForeColor="GhostWhite" />
          <SortedAscendingCellStyle BackColor="#FAFAE7" />
          <SortedAscendingHeaderStyle BackColor="#DAC09E" />
          <SortedDescendingCellStyle BackColor="#E1DB9C" />
          <SortedDescendingHeaderStyle BackColor="#C2A47B" />
      </asp:GridView>

      <asp:LinqDataSource ID="GamesSource" runat="server"
          ContextTypeName="QueryExtenderApplication.VideoGamesModelDataContext"
          TableName="VideoGames" EntityTypeName=""
          Select="new (Genre.Name as GenreName, ID, Title, Description, GenreID,
➡ESRB)" />
      <asp:LinqDataSource ID="GenreSource" runat="server"
          ContextTypeName="QueryExtenderApplication.VideoGamesModelDataContext"
          TableName="Genres" EntityTypeName="" />

      <asp:QueryExtender runat="server" TargetControlID="GamesSource">
          <asp:PropertyExpression>
              <asp:ControlParameter ControlID="GenreDropDownList" Name="GenreID" />
          </asp:PropertyExpression>
          <asp:SearchExpression ComparisonType="InvariantCultureIgnoreCase"
DataFields="Title,Description" SearchType="Contains">
              <asp:ControlParameter ControlID="GameSearchTextBox" />
          </asp:SearchExpression>
      </asp:QueryExtender>

   </div>
   </form>
```

Aside from the few bits of styling information that came from choosing Autoformat on the GridView, the preceding code isn't all that complex. The first thing we do is create a drop-down list bound to the list of genres in the video games catalog. Second, we create a text box that will eventually filter the list of games.

After the GridView, there are two LINQ data sources. The first data source points to the Genre table in the video game LINQ to SQL model. The second points to the VideoGames table; you might notice that we're actually including a foreign key property (Genre.Name) and adding that to the anonymous type returned by the query.

Finally, we get to the query extender. The first part of the query extender is a PropertyExpression that we use to filter the GenreID property based on the currently selected value of the GenreDropDownList control. When you try this page (after creating a bogus video game catalog), you see that the form automatically reposts and requeries every time you select a new genre. Obviously you can change this behavior for a production application, but it helps drive home the point that all the QueryExtender functionality can be contained solely in the aspx markup.

The second part of the query extender is a SearchExpression. Here we're *further* filtering the result set by searching the Title and Description columns of the VideoGame table for a substring indicated by the current value of the GameSearchTextBox control.

Figure 16.1 shows the output of the page after selecting a genre from the drop-down box.

Figure 16.2 shows the output of the same page after supplying some text on which to filter the games list. Note that there's no button on this page, just hitting enter within the text box will cause a re-query after a postback.

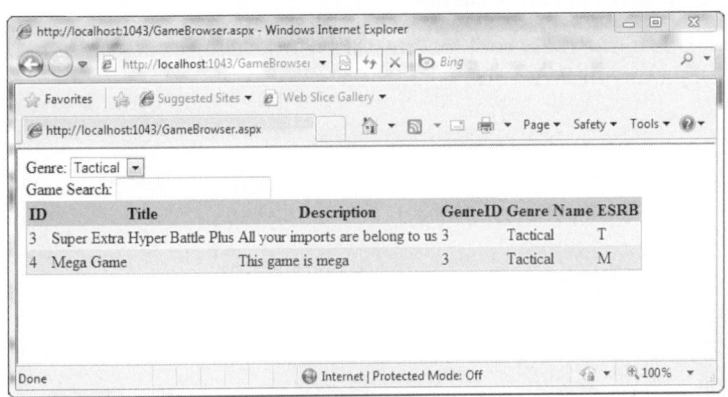

FIGURE 16.1   Filtering using the QueryExtender.

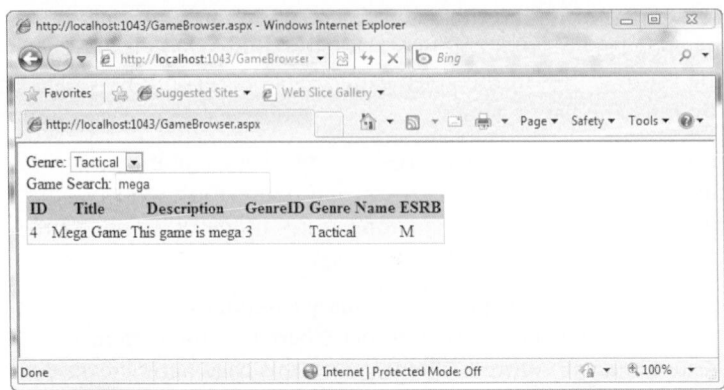

FIGURE 16.2   Filtering using the `QueryExtender` and a SearchExpression.

Summary

This chapter provided you with an overview of building data-driven pages in which the filtering and sorting logic was embedded directly in the page in a declarative fashion using the `QueryExtender` control and its associated expressions.

By enabling you to define your queries and sort expressions declaratively in the markup, the `QueryExtender` also enables you to make those queries dynamic by pulling in values from other controls on the page at runtime. This makes building user-driven forms that perform searches, queries, and sorts incredibly easy.

The `QueryExtender` control is just one more tool for the ASP.NET developer's arsenal for rapidly building powerful, data-driven Web Forms.

Building Components

Components enable you to reuse application logic across multiple pages or even across multiple applications. For example, you can write a method named GetProducts() once and use the method in all the pages in your website. By taking advantage of components, you can make your applications easier to maintain and extend.

For simple applications, you do not need to take advantage of components; however, as soon as your application contains more than a few pages, you'll discover that you are repeating the same work over and over again. Whenever you discover that you need to write the same method more than once, you should immediately rip the method out of your page and add the method to a component.

In this chapter, you learn how to build components in .NET Framework. First, you get an overview of writing components: You learn how to create simple components and use them in the pages in your application. In particular, you learn how to define component methods, properties, and constructors. You also learn how to take advantage of overloading, inheritance, and interfaces.

Next, you learn how to build component libraries that can be shared across multiple applications. You examine different methods of compiling a set of components into assemblies. You also learn how you can add a component library to the Global Assembly Cache.

Finally, we discuss architectural issues involved in using components. The final section of this chapter shows you how to build a simple three-tiered application that is divided into distinct User Interface, Business Logic, and Data Access layers.

> **NOTE**
>
> Let's clarify the terminology. In this book, I use the word *component* as a synonym for the word *class*. Furthermore, by the word *object*, I mean an instance of a class.
>
> I am ignoring a special meaning for the word *component* in .NET Framework. Technically, a component is a class that implements the `System.ComponentModel.IComponent` interface. I am ignoring this special meaning of the word *component* in favor of the common language use of the word.

Building Basic Components

Let's start by building a super simple component. The `HelloWorld` component is contained in Listing 17.1.

LISTING 17.1   HelloWorld.cs

```
public class HelloWorld
{
    public string SayMessage()
    {
        return "Hello World!";
    }
}
```

> **VISUAL WEB DEVELOPER NOTE**
>
> When using Visual Web Developer, you create a component by selecting Website, Add New Item, and then selecting the Class item (see Figure 17.1). The first time you add a component to a project, Visual Web Developer prompts you to create a new folder named App_Code. You want your new component to be added to this folder.

The `HelloWorld` component consists of a single method named `SayMessage()` that returns the string `Hello World!`.

Make sure that you save the `HelloWorld.cs` file to your application's App_Code folder. If you don't save the component to this folder, you can't use the component in your pages. Next, you need to create a page that uses the new component. This page is contained in Listing 17.2.

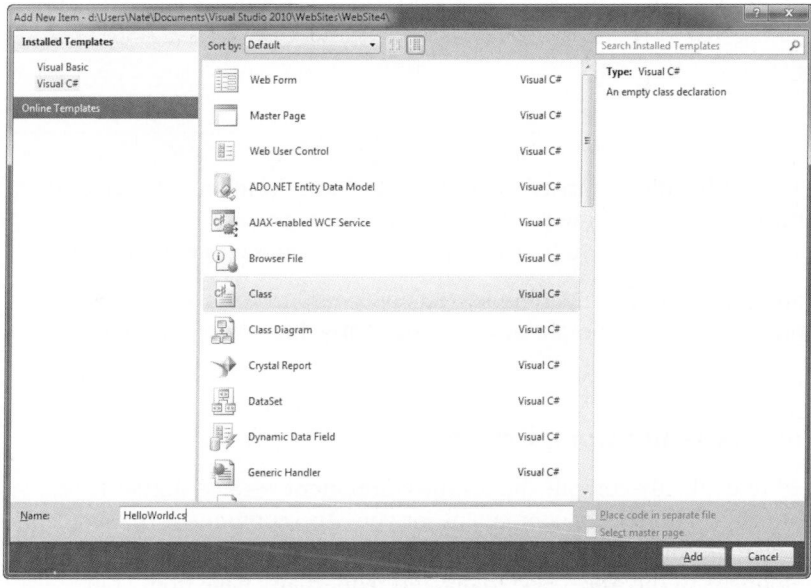

FIGURE 17.1   Creating a new component with Visual Web Developer.

LISTING 17.2   ShowHelloWorld.aspx

```
<%@ Page Language="C#" %>
<!DOCTYPE html PUBLIC "-//W3C//DTD XHTML 1.1//EN"
"http://www.w3.org/TR/xhtml11/DTD/xhtml11.dtd">
<script runat="server">

    void Page_Load()
    {
        HelloWorld objHelloWorld = new HelloWorld();
        lblMessage.Text = objHelloWorld.SayMessage();
    }

</script>
<html xmlns="http://www.w3.org/1999/xhtml" >
<head id="Head1" runat="server">
    <title>Show Hello World</title>
</head>
<body>
    <form id="form1" runat="server">
    <div>

    <asp:Label
        id="lblMessage"
        Runat="server" />
```

```
    </div>
    </form>
</body>
</html>
```

In the Page_Load() event handler, an instance of the HelloWorld component is created. Next, the result returned by a call to the SayMessage() method is assigned to a Label control. When you open the page in your browser, you see the message Hello World!.

This process of creating the component is simple. You don't need to perform any special registration, and you don't need to compile anything explicitly. Everything just works magically.

Components and Dynamic Compilation

You are not required to explicitly compile (build) the component because ASP.NET Framework automatically compiles the component for you. Any component that you add to the App_Code folder is compiled dynamically in the same way as an ASP.NET page. If you add a new component to the App_Code folder and request any page from your website, the contents of the App_Code folder are compiled into a new assembly and saved to the Temporary ASP.NET Files folder, located at the following path:

```
C:\WINDOWS\Microsoft.NET\Framework\[version]\
Temporary ASP.NET Files\[application name]
```

Whenever you modify the component, the existing assembly in the Temporary ASP.NET Files folder is deleted. The App_Code folder is compiled again when you make a new page request.

> **NOTE**
>
> An assembly is the dll file (or dll files) in which components are stored.

You can add as many subfolders to the App_Code folder as you need to organize your components. The ASP.NET Framework finds your component no matter how deeply you nest the component in a subfolder.

One significant drawback of this process of dynamic compilation is that any errors in any component contained in the App_Code folder prevent any pages from executing. Even if a page does not use a particular component, any syntax errors in the component raise an exception when you request the page.

> **TIP**
>
> If a component contains an error, and you want to temporarily hide the component from ASP.NET Framework, change the file extension to an extension that ASP.NET Framework does not recognize, such as `HelloWorld.cs.exclude`. Visual Web Developer uses this method to hide a component when you right-click a component and select the menu option Exclude From Project.

Mixing Different Language Components in the App_Code Folder

You don't have to do anything special if all the components in the App_Code folder are written in the same language. For example, if you use Visual Basic .NET to create all your components, the ASP.NET Framework automatically infers the language of your components and everything just works.

However, if you mix components written in more than one language in the App_Code folder—for example, Visual Basic .NET and C#— you must perform some extra steps.

First, you need to place components written in different languages in different subfolders. You can name the subfolders anything you want. The point is to not mix different language components in the same folder.

Furthermore, you need to modify your web configuration file to recognize the different subfolders. For example, if you create two subfolders in the App_Code folder named VBCode and CSCode, you can use the web configuration file in Listing 17.3 to use components written in both VB.NET and C#.

LISTING 17.3   `Web.Config`

```xml
<?xml version="1.0"?>
<configuration>
  <system.web>
    <compilation>
    <codeSubDirectories>
      <add directoryName="VBCode" />
      <add directoryName="CSCode" />
    </codeSubDirectories>
    </compilation>
  </system.web>
</configuration>
```

When the contents of the App_Code folder are compiled, two assemblies are created: one that corresponds to the VBCode folder and one that corresponds to the CSCode folder. You don't need to indicate the language used for each folder—ASP.NET Framework infers the language for you.

17

There is nothing wrong with mixing components written in different languages in the same ASP.NET page. After a component is compiled, .NET Framework treats VB.NET and C# components in the same way.

Declaring Methods

The simple HelloWorld component in Listing 17.1 contains a single method named SayMessage(), which returns a string value. When writing components with Visual Basic .NET, you create methods by creating either a subroutine or a function. Use a subroutine when a method does not return a value, and use a function when a method does return a value.

The SayMessage() method in Listing 17.1 is an instance method. In other words, you must create a new instance of the HelloWorld class before you can call the SayMessage() method like this:

```
HelloWorld objHelloWorld = new HelloWorld();
lblMessage.Text = objHelloWorld.SayMessage();
```

In the first line, a new instance of the HelloWorld component is created. The SayMessage() method is called from this instance. For this reason, the SayMessage() method is an instance method.

As an alternative to creating an instance method, you can create a static method. The advantage of a static method is that you do not need to create an instance of a component before calling it. For example, the SayMessage() method in the modified HelloWorld component in Listing 17.4 is a static method.

> **NOTE**
>
> Static methods are called *shared methods* in Visual Basic .NET.

LISTING 17.4   StaticHelloWorld.cs

```
public class StaticHelloWorld
{
    public static string SayMessage()
    {
        return "Hello World!";
    }
}
```

The StaticHelloWorld component defined in Listing 17.3 is exactly the same as the HelloWorld component created in Listing 17.1 with one change: The SayMessage() method includes a static modifier.

The page in Listing 17.5 uses the StaticHelloWorld component to display the Hello World! message.

LISTING 17.5   ShowStaticHelloWorld.aspx

```
<%@ Page Language="C#" %>
<!DOCTYPE html PUBLIC "-//W3C//DTD XHTML 1.1//EN"
"http://www.w3.org/TR/xhtml11/DTD/xhtml11.dtd">
<script runat="server">

    void Page_Load()
    {
        lblMessage.Text = StaticHelloWorld.SayMessage();
    }

</script>
<html xmlns="http://www.w3.org/1999/xhtml" >
<head id="Head1" runat="server">
    <title>Show Shared Hello World</title>
</head>
<body>
    <form id="form1" runat="server">
    <div>

    <asp:Label
        id="lblMessage"
        Runat="server" />

    </div>
    </form>
</body>
</html>
```

The page in Listing 17.5 does not create an instance of the StaticHelloWorld component. The SayMessage() method is called directly from the StaticHelloWorld class.

The advantage of using static methods is that they save you typing. You don't have to go through the pain of instantiating a component before calling the method. Many classes in .NET Framework include static methods. For example, String.Format(),Int32.Parse(), and DateTime.DaysInMonth() methods are all static methods.

There is nothing wrong with mixing both static and instance methods in the same component. For example, you might want to create a Product component that has a static GetProducts() method and an instance SaveProduct() method.

The one significant limitation of using a static method is that a static method cannot refer to an instance field or property. In other words, static methods must be stateless.

Declaring Fields and Properties

You can define a property for a component in two ways: the lazy way and the virtuous way. The lazy way to create a property is to create a public field. If you declare any field with the Public access modifier, the field can be accessed from outside the component. For example, the component in Listing 17.6 contains a public field named Message.

LISTING 17.6   FieldHelloWorld.cs

```
public class FieldHelloWorld
{
    public string Message;
    public string SayMessage()
    {
        return Message;
    }
}
```

The Message field is declared near the top of the FieldHelloWorld class definition. The Message field is returned by the SayMessage() method.

The page in Listing 17.7 uses the FieldHelloWorld component to display a message.

LISTING 17.7   ShowFieldHelloWorld.aspx

```
<%@ Page Language="C#" %>
<!DOCTYPE html PUBLIC "-//W3C//DTD XHTML 1.1//EN"
"http://www.w3.org/TR/xhtml11/DTD/xhtml11.dtd">
<script runat="server">

    void Page_Load()
    {
        FieldHelloWorld objFieldHelloWorld = new FieldHelloWorld();
        objFieldHelloWorld.Message = "Good Day!";
        lblMessage.Text = objFieldHelloWorld.SayMessage();
    }

</script>
<html xmlns="http://www.w3.org/1999/xhtml" >
<head id="Head1" runat="server">
    <title>Show Field Hello World</title>
</head>
```

```
<body>
    <form id="form1" runat="server">
    <div>

    <asp:Label
        id="lblMessage"
        Runat="server" />

    </div>
    </form>
</body>
</html>
```

In the `Page_Load()` event handler in Listing 17.7, an instance of the `FieldHelloWorld` class is created, a value is assigned to the `Message` field, and the `SayMessage()` method is called.

There are a couple of serious disadvantages to creating properties by creating public fields. First, .NET Framework recognizes properties as separate entities. Several methods in .NET Framework recognize properties but not fields.

For example, you can refer to component properties and not fields when using the `Eval()` method in a databinding expression. If you want to bind a collection of `Product` objects to a `GridView` control, you should expose the properties of the Product component as true properties and not as fields.

The other disadvantage of fields is that they do not provide you with a chance to validate the value assigned to the field. For example, imagine that a property represents a database column and the column accepts no more than five characters. In that case, you should check whether the value assigned to the property is less than five characters.

The component in Listing 17.8 uses a property instead of a field. (It does things the virtuous way.)

LISTING 17.8   PropertyHelloWorld.cs

```
using System;

public class PropertyHelloWorld
{
    private string _message;

    public string Message
    {
        get
        {
            return _message;
```

17

```
        }
        set
        {
            if (value.Length > 5)
                throw new Exception("Message too long!");
            _message = value;
        }
    }

    public string SayMessage()
    {
        return _message;
    }
}
```

The component in Listing 17.8 contains a property named Message and a private backing field named _message. The Message property contains both a getter (get) and a setter (set). The getter is called when you read the value of the Message property, and the setter is called when you assign a value to the Message property.

The getter simply returns the value of the private _message field. The setter assigns a value to the private _message field. The setter throws an exception if the length of the value assigned to the _message field exceeds five characters.

NOTE

In Listing 17.8, the private field is named _message. The underscore character (_) has no programmatic significance. By convention, private members of a class are named with a leading underscore, but there is nothing wrong with following some other convention.

NOTE

The version of C# included with .NET Framework 3.5 and 4 supports the *automatic properties* feature. Automatic properties provide you with a shorthand syntax for creating a property with a backing field. To learn more about automatic properties, see Chapter 20, "Data Access with LINQ to SQL."

The page in Listing 17.9 uses the PropertyHelloWorld component.

LISTING 17.9   ShowPropertyHelloWorld.aspx

```
<%@ Page Language="C#" %>
<!DOCTYPE html PUBLIC "-//W3C//DTD XHTML 1.1//EN"
"http://www.w3.org/TR/xhtml11/DTD/xhtml11.dtd">
<script runat="server">
    void Page_Load()
    {
        PropertyHelloWorld objPropertyHelloWorld = new PropertyHelloWorld();
        objPropertyHelloWorld.Message = "Hello World!";
        lblMessage.Text = objPropertyHelloWorld.SayMessage();
    }
</script>
<html xmlns="http://www.w3.org/1999/xhtml" >
<head id="Head1" runat="server">
    <title>Show Property Hello World</title>
</head>
<body>
    <form id="form1" runat="server">
    <div>

    <asp:Label
        id="lblMessage"
        Runat="server" />

    </div>
    </form>
</body>
</html>
```

If you open the page in Listing 17.9 in your web browser, you get a big, fat error message (see Figure 17.2). Because a string longer than five characters is assigned to the Message property in the Page_Load() method, the Message property raises an exception.

You can also create read-only properties when the situation warrants it. For example, the component in Listing 17.10 returns the current server time. It would not make sense to assign a value to this property, so the property is declared as read-only.

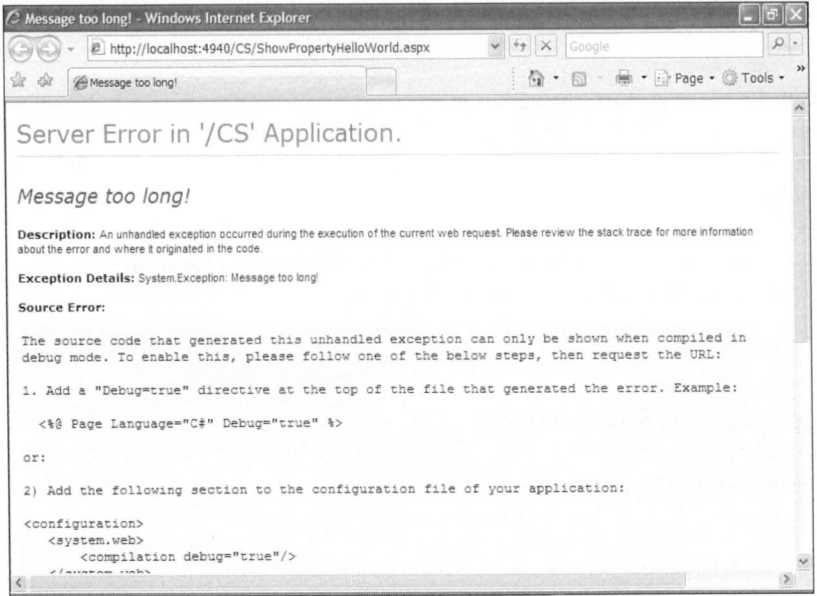

FIGURE 17.2   Assigning more than five characters.

LISTING 17.10   ServerTime.cs

```csharp
using System;


public class ServerTime
{
    public string CurrentTime
    {
        get
        {
            return DateTime.Now.ToString();
        }
    }
}
```

> **NOTE**
>
> You can create static fields and properties in the same way as you create shared methods, by using the `static` keyword. Any value you assign to a static field or property is shared among all instances of a component.
>
> I recommend that you avoid using static fields and properties when building ASP.NET applications. Using static fields and properties raises nasty concurrency issues in a multithreaded environment such as ASP.NET. If you insist on creating a static field or property, make it read-only.

Declaring Constructors

A constructor is a special class method called automatically when you create a new instance of a class. Typically, you use the constructor to initialize private fields contained in the class.

When creating a constructor in C#, you create a method with the same name as the class name. For example, the class in Listing 17.11 displays a random quotation (see Figure 17.3). The collection of random quotations is created in the component's constructor.

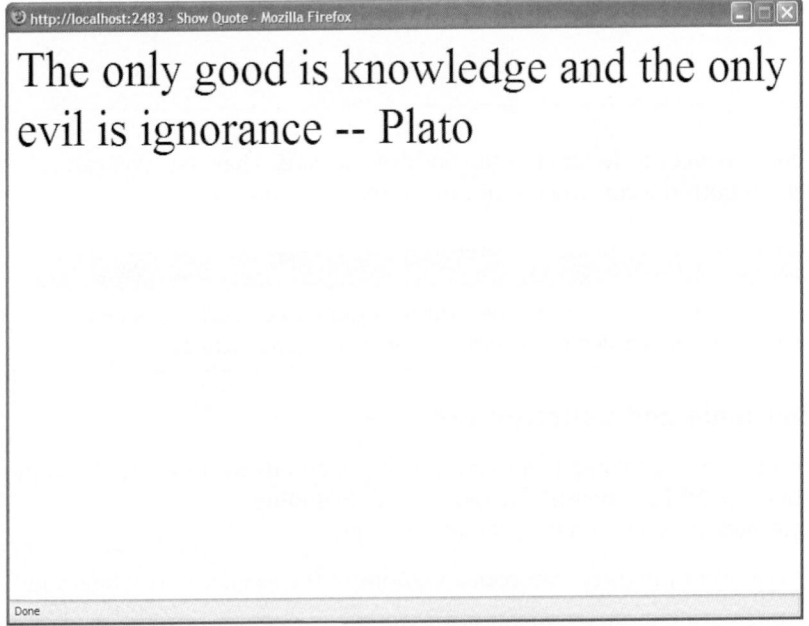

FIGURE 17.3   Displaying a random quotation.

17

LISTING 17.11   `Quote.cs`

```
using System;
using System.Collections.Generic;

public class Quote
{
    private List<string> _quotes = new List<string>();

    public string GetQuote()
    {
        Random rnd = new Random();
        return _quotes[rnd.Next(_quotes.Count)];
    }

    public Quote()
    {
        _quotes.Add("All paid jobs absorb and degrade the mind -- Aristotle");
        _quotes.Add("No evil can happen to a good man, either in life or after
death --Plato");
        _quotes.Add("The only good is knowledge and the only evil is ignorance --
Plato");
    }
}
```

The collection named _quotes is declared in the body of the class. That way, you can refer to the _quotes field in both the constructor and the `GetQuote()` method.

> **NOTE**
>
> You can create static constructors by using the `static` keyword when declaring a constructor. A static constructor is called once before any instance constructors.

Overloading Methods and Constructors

When a method is overloaded, a component contains two methods with exactly the same name. Many methods in .NET Framework are overloaded, including `String.Replace()`,`Random.Next()`, and `Page.FindControl()`.

For example, here is a list of the three overloaded versions of the `Random.Next()` method:

▶ **Next()**—Returns a random number between 0 and 2,147,483,647.

▶ **Next(upperbound)**—Returns a number between 0 and the upper bound.

▶ **Next(lowerbound, upperbound)**—Returns a number between the lower bound and the upper bound.

Because all three methods do the same thing—they all return a random number—it makes sense to overload the Next() method. The methods differ only in their *signatures*. A method signature consists of the order and type of parameters that a method accepts. For example, you can't overload two methods that have exactly the same set of parameters (even if the names of the parameters differ).

Overloading is useful when you want to associate related methods. Overloading is also useful when you want to provide default values for parameters. For example, the StoreProduct component in Listing 17.12 contains three overloaded versions of its SaveProduct() method.

LISTING 17.12   StoreProduct.cs

```csharp
using System;

public class StoreProduct
{
    public void SaveProduct(string name)
    {
        SaveProduct(name, 0, String.Empty);
    }

    public void SaveProduct(string name, decimal price)
    {
        SaveProduct(name, price, String.Empty);
    }

    public void SaveProduct(string name, decimal price, string description)
    {
        // Save name, price, description to database
    }
}
```

You can call any of the three SaveProduct() methods in Listing 17.12 to save a new product. You can supply the new product with a name, a name and a price, or a name, a price, and a description.

VISUAL WEB DEVELOPER NOTE

When typing an overloaded method in Source view, the Intellisense pops up with all the different sets of parameters that you can use with the overloaded method (see Figure 17.4).

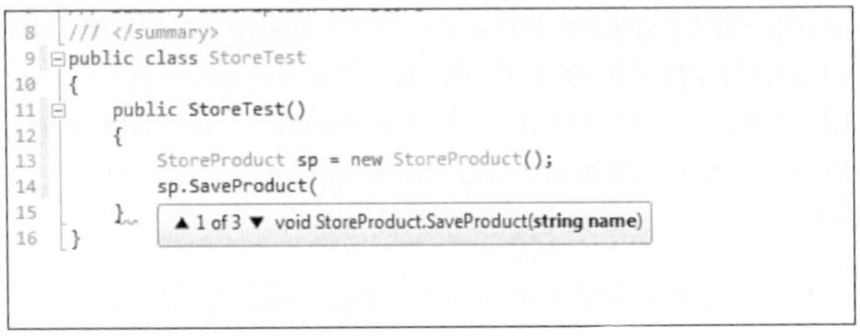

FIGURE 17.4   Typing an overloaded method in Visual Web Developer.

Because a constructor is just a special method, you also can use overloading when declaring constructors for a class. For example, the `ProductConstructor` class in Listing 17.13 contains three overloaded constructors that can be used to initialize the `Product` class.

LISTING 17.13   ProductConstructor.cs

```
using System;


public class ProductConstructor
{
    public ProductConstructor(string name)
        : this(name, 0, String.Empty) { }

    public ProductConstructor(string name, decimal price)
        : this(name, price, String.Empty) { }

    public ProductConstructor(string name, decimal price, string description)
    {
        // Use name, price, and description
    }
}
```

When you instantiate the component in Listing 17.13, you can instantiate it in any of the following ways:

```
ProductConstructor objProduct = new ProductConstructor("Milk");
ProductConstructor objProduct = new ProductConstructor("Milk", 2.99d);
ProductConstructor objProduct = new ProductConstructor("Milk", 2.99d, "While Milk");
```

Declaring Namespaces

A namespace enables you to group logically related classes. You are not required to provide a class with a namespace. To this point, all the components you have seen created have been members of the global namespace. However, several advantages result from grouping components into namespaces.

First, namespaces prevent naming collisions. If two companies produce a component with the same name, namespaces provide you with a method of distinguishing the components.

Second, namespaces make it easier to understand the purpose of a class. If you group all your data access components into a DataAccess namespace and all your business logic components in a BusinessLogic namespace, you can immediately understand the function of a particular class.

In an ASP.NET page, you import a namespace like this:

```
<%@ Import Namespace="System.Collections" %>
```

In a C# component, on the other hand, you import a namespace like this:

```
using System.Collections;
```

You can create your own custom namespaces and group your components into namespaces by using the namespace statement. For example, the component in Listing 17.14 is contained in the AspUnleashed.SampleCode namespace.

LISTING 17.14 Namespaced.cs

```
namespace AspNetUnleashed.SampleCode
{
    public class Namespaced
    {
        public string SaySomething()
        {
            return "Something";
        }
    }
}
```

The file in Listing 17.14 uses the Namespace statement to group the Namespaced component into the AspUnleashed.SampleCode namespace. Components in different files can share the same namespace, and different components in the same file can occupy different namespaces.

The periods in a namespace name have no special significance. The periods are used to break up the words in the namespace, but you could use another character, such as an underscore character, instead.

Microsoft recommends a certain naming convention when creating namespaces:

```
CompanyName.TechnologyName[.Feature][.Design]
```

So, if your company is named Acme Consulting and you are building a data access component, you might add your component to the following namespace:

```
AcmeConsulting.DataAccess
```

Of course this is simply a naming convention. No serious harm will come to you if you ignore it.

Creating Partial Classes

You can define a single component that spans multiple files by taking advantage of a feature of .NET Framework called *partial classes*.

For example, the files in Listings 17.15 and 17.16 contain two halves of the same component.

LISTING 17.15 FirstHalf.cs

```
public partial class Tweedle
{
    private string _message = @"THEY were standing under a tree,
        each with an arm round the other's neck, and Alice knew
        which was which in a moment, because one of them had
        ""DUM"" embroidered on his collar, and the other ""DEE"".";
}
```

LISTING 17.16 SecondHalf.cs

```
public partial class Tweedle
{
    public string GetMessage()
    {
        return _message;
    }
}
```

The private _message field is defined in the first file, but this private field is used in the GetMessage() method in the second file. When the GetMessage() method is called, it returns the value of the private field from the other class. Both files define a class with the same name. The class declaration includes the keyword Partial, which marks the classes as partial classes.

> **NOTE**
>
> Partial classes are the basis for code-behind pages in the ASP.NET Framework. The code-behind file and the presentation page are two partial classes that get compiled into the same class.

Inheritance and Abstract Classes

When one class inherits from a second class, the inherited class automatically includes all the nonprivate methods and properties of its parent class. In other words, what's true of the parent is true of the child, but not the other way around.

Inheritance is used throughout .NET Framework. For example, every ASP.NET page inherits from the base `System.Web.UI.Page` class. The only reason that you can use properties such as the `IsPostback` property in an ASP.NET page is that the page derives from the base Page class.

All classes in .NET Framework derive from the base `System.Object` class. The `Object` class is the great-grandmother of every other class. This means that any methods or properties of the `Object` class, such as the `ToString()` method, are shared by all classes in the Framework.

You can take advantage of inheritance when building your own components. You indicate that one class inherits from a second class when you declare a class. For example, the file in Listing 17.17 includes three components: a `BaseProduct` class, a `ComputerProduct` class, and a `TelevisionProduct` class.

LISTING 17.17   `Inheritance.cs`

```
public class BaseProduct
{
    private decimal _price;

    public decimal Price
    {
        get { return _price; }
        set { _price = value; }
    }

}

public class ComputerProduct : BaseProduct
{
    private string _processor;

    public string Processor
    {
        get { return _processor; }
        set { _processor = value; }
```

17

```
    }

}

public class TelevisionProduct : BaseProduct
{
    private bool _isHDTV;

    public bool IsHDTV
    {
        get { return _isHDTV; }
        set { _isHDTV = value; }
    }

}
```

Both the ComputerProduct and TelevisionProduct components inherit from the BaseProduct component. Because the BaseProduct class includes a Price property, both inherited components automatically inherit this property.

When inheriting one class from another, you also can override methods and properties of the base class. Overriding a method or property is useful when you want to modify the behavior of an existing class.

To override a property or method of a base class, the property or method must be marked with the C# virtual or abstract keyword or the Visual Basic .NET Overridable or MustOverride keyword. Only methods or properties marked with the virtual or abstract keyword can be overridden.

For example, the file in Listing 17.18 contains two components: a ProductBase class and a OnSaleProduct class. The second class inherits from the first class and overrides its Price property. The Price property of the OnSaleProduct component divides the price by half.

LISTING 17.18   OnSaleProduct.cs

```
public class ProductBase
{
    private decimal _price;

    public virtual decimal Price
    {
        get { return _price; }
        set { _price = value; }
    }
}

public class OnSaleProduct : ProductBase
```

```
{
    override public decimal Price
    {
        get { return base.Price / 2; }
        set { base.Price = value; }
    }
}
```

The base keyword (MyBase in Visual Basic) is used in Listing 17.18 to refer to the base class (the ProductBase class).

Finally, you can use the abstract keyword when declaring a class to mark it as a class that requires inheritance. You cannot instantiate an abstract class. To use an abstract class, you must derive a new class from the abstract class and instantiate the derived class.

Abstract classes are the foundation for the ASP.NET Provider Model. Personalization, Membership, Roles, Session State, and Site Maps all use the Provider Model. For example, the MembershipProvider class is the base class for all Membership Providers. The SqlMembershipProvider and ActiveDirectoryMembershipProvider classes both derive from the base MembershipProvider class.

> **NOTE**
>
> Chapter 27, "Using ASP.NET Membership," discusses the MembershipProvider classes in detail, which is responsible for saving and loading membership information such as application usernames and passwords.

The base MembershipProvider class is an abstract class. You cannot use this class directly in your code. Instead, you must use one of its derived classes. However, the base MembershipProvider class provides a common set of methods and properties that all MembershipProvider-derived classes inherit.

The base MembershipProvider class includes a number of methods and properties marked as abstract. A derived MembershipProvider class is required to override these properties and methods.

The file in Listing 17.19 contains two components. The first component, the BaseEmployee component, is an abstract class that contains an abstract property named Salary. The second component, the SalesEmployee, inherits the BaseEmployee component and overrides the Salary property.

LISTING 17.19 Employees.cs

```
public abstract class BaseEmployee
{
    public abstract decimal Salary
    {
        get;
```

```
    }

    public string Company
    {
        get { return "Acme Software"; }
    }
}

public class SalesEmployee : BaseEmployee
{
    public override decimal Salary
    {
        get { return 67000.23m; }
    }
}
```

Declaring Interfaces

An interface is a list of properties and methods that a class must implement. If a class implements an interface, you know that the class includes all the properties and methods contained in the interface.

For example, the file in Listing 17.20 contains an interface named IProduct and two components named MusicProduct and BookProduct.

LISTING 17.20   Products.cs

```
public interface IProduct
{
    decimal Price
    {
        get;
    }

    void SaveProduct();
}

public class MusicProduct : IProduct
{
    public decimal Price
    {
        get { return 12.99m; }
    }
```

```
    public void SaveProduct()
    {
        // Save Music Product
    }
}

public class BookProduct : IProduct
{
    public decimal Price
    {
        get { return 23.99m; }
    }

    public void SaveProduct()
    {
        // Save Book Product
    }
}
```

Both components in Listing 17.17 are declared as implementing the IProduct interface. (The colon can mean implements or inherits.) Furthermore, both components include the SaveProduct() method and the Price property. Both components are required to have this method and property because they are declared as implementing the IProduct interface.

Interfaces are similar to abstract classes with two important differences. First, a component can inherit from only one class. On the other hand, a component can implement many different interfaces.

Second, an abstract class can contain application logic. You can add methods to an abstract class that all derived classes inherit and can use. An interface, on the other hand, cannot contain any logic. An interface is nothing more than a list of methods and properties.

Using Access Modifiers

C# supports the following access modifiers, which you can use when declaring a class, method, or property:

▶ **Public**—A public class, method, or property has no access restrictions.

▶ **Protected**—A protected method or property can be accessed only within the class itself or a derived class.

17

▶ **Internal**—An internal class, method, or property can be accessed only by a component within the same assembly (dll file). Because ASP.NET pages are compiled into different assemblies than the contents of the App_Code folder, you cannot access an internal member of a class outside of the App_Code folder.

▶ **Private**—A private class, method, or property can be accessed only within the class itself.

Visual Basic .NET supports the following access modifiers (also called *access levels*), which you can use when declaring a class, method, or property:

▶ **Public**—A Public class, method, or property has no access restrictions.

▶ **Protected**—A Protected method or property can be accessed only within the class itself or a derived class.

▶ **Friend**—A Friend class, method, or property can be accessed only by a component within the same assembly (dll file). Because ASP.NET pages are compiled into different assemblies than the contents of the App_Code folder, you cannot access a Friend member of a class outside of the App_Code folder.

▶ **Protected Friend**—A Protected Friend method or property can be accessed within the class itself or a derived class, or any other class located in the same assembly.

▶ **Private**—A Private class, method, or property can be accessed only within the class itself.

Using access modifiers is useful when you develop a component library that might be used by other members of your development team (or your future self). For example, you should mark all methods that you don't want to expose from your component as private.

Intellisense and Components

Visual Web Developer automatically pops up with Intellisense when you type the names of classes, properties, or methods in Source view. You can add comments that appear in Intellisense to your custom components to make it easier for other developers to use your components.

If you add XML comments to a component, the contents of the XML comments appear automatically in Intellisense. For example, the component in Listing 17.21 includes XML comments for its class definition, property definitions, and method definition (see Figure 17.5).

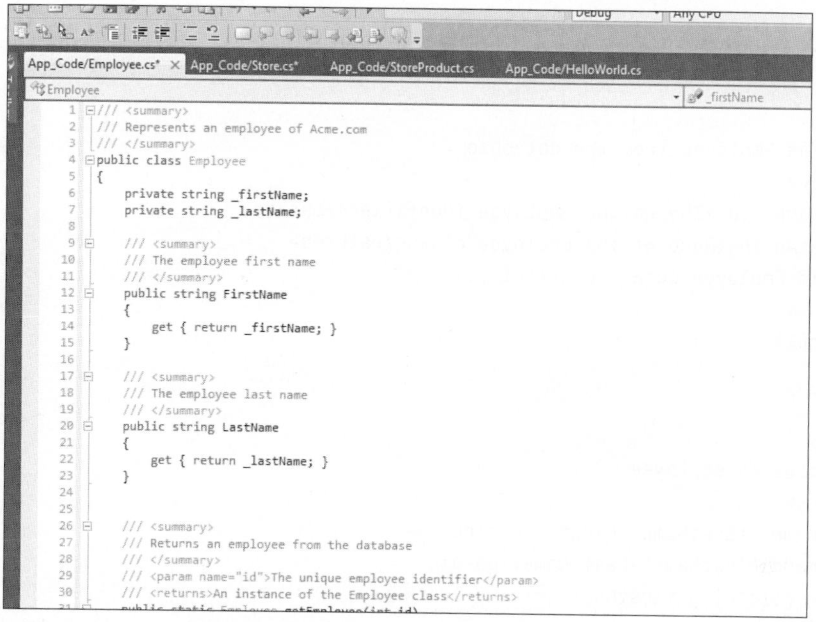

FIGURE 17.5 Adding comments to a component.

LISTING 17.21 Employee.cs

```csharp
/// <summary>
/// Represents an employee of Acme.com
/// </summary>
public class Employee
{
    private string _firstName;
    private string _lastName;

    /// <summary>
    /// The employee first name
    /// </summary>
    public string FirstName
    {
        get { return _firstName; }
    }

    /// <summary>
    /// The employee last name
    /// </summary>
    public string LastName
    {
        get { return _lastName; }
```

```
    }


    /// <summary>
    /// Returns an employee from the database
    /// </summary>
    /// <param name="id">The unique employee identifier</param>
    /// <returns>An instance of the Employee class</returns>
    public static Employee getEmployee(int id)
    {
        return null;
    }


    /// <summary>
    /// Initializes an employee
    /// </summary>
    /// <param name="firstName">First Name</param>
    /// <param name="lastName">Last Name</param>
    public Employee(string firstName, string lastName)
    {
        _firstName = firstName;
        _lastName = lastName;
    }

}
```

NOTE

You can generate an XML documentation file—a file that contains all the XML comments—for the components contained in a folder by using the /doc switch with the C# or Visual Basic command-line compiler. The command-line compiler is discussed in the second part of this chapter, "Building Component Libraries."

Using ASP.NET Intrinsics in a Component

When you add code to an ASP.NET page, you are adding code to an instance of the Page class. The Page class exposes several ASP.NET intrinsic objects such as the Request, Response, Cache, Session, and Trace objects.

If you want to use these objects within a component, you need to do a little more work. Realize that when you create a component, you are not creating an ASP.NET component. In this chapter, we create .NET components, and a .NET component can be used by any type of .NET application, including a Console application or Windows Forms application.

To use the ASP.NET instrinsics in a component, you need to get a reference to the current `HtppContext`. The `HttpContext` object is the one object available behind the scenes through the entire page processing life cycle. You can access the `HttpContext` object from any user control, custom control, or component contained in a page.

> **NOTE**
>
> The `HttpContext` object includes an Items collection. You can add anything to the Items collection and share the thing among all the elements contained in a page.

To get a reference to the current `HttpContext` object, you can use the static (shared) `Current` property included in the `HttpContext` class. For example, the component in Listing 17.22 uses the `HttpContext` object to use both the `Session` and `Trace` objects.

LISTING 17.22   Preferences.cs

```
using System.Web;

public class Preferences
{
    public static string FavoriteColor
    {
        get
        {
            HttpContext context = HttpContext.Current;
            context.Trace.Warn("Getting FavoriteColor");
            if (context.Session["FavoriteColor"] == null)
                return "Blue";
            else
                return (string)context.Session["FavoriteColor"];
        }
        set
        {
            HttpContext context = HttpContext.Current;
            context.Trace.Warn("Setting FavoriteColor");
            context.Session["FavoriteColor"] = value;
        }
    }
}
```

The `Preferences` component contains a single property named `FavoriteColor`. The value of this property is stored in `Session` state. Anytime this property is modified, the `Trace` object writes a warning.

You can use the `Preferences` component in the page contained in Listing 17.23.

LISTING 17.23   ShowPreferences.aspx

```
<%@ Page Language="C#" trace="true" %>
<!DOCTYPE html PUBLIC "-//W3C//DTD XHTML 1.1//EN"
"http://www.w3.org/TR/xhtml11/DTD/xhtml11.dtd">
<script runat="server">

    void Page_PreRender()
    {
        body1.Style["background-color"] = Preferences.FavoriteColor;
    }

    protected void btnSelect_Click(object sender, EventArgs e)
    {
        Preferences.FavoriteColor = ddlFavoriteColor.SelectedItem.Text;
    }
</script>

<html xmlns="http://www.w3.org/1999/xhtml" >
<head id="Head1" runat="server">
    <style type="text/css">
        .content
        {
            width:80%;
            padding:20px;
            background-color:white;
        }
    </style>
    <title>Show Preferences</title>
</head>
<body id="body1" runat="server">
    <form id="form1" runat="server">
    <div class="content">

    <h1>Show Preferences</h1>

    <asp:DropDownList
        id="ddlFavoriteColor"
        Runat="server">
        <asp:ListItem Text="Blue" />
        <asp:ListItem Text="Red" />
        <asp:ListItem Text="Green" />
    </asp:DropDownList>
    <asp:Button
```

```
        id="btnSelect"
        Text="Select"
        Runat="server" OnClick="btnSelect_Click" />

    </div>
    </form>
</body>
</html>
```

After you open the page in Listing 17.23, you can select your favorite color from the DropDownList control. Your favorite color is stored in the Preferences object (see Figure 17.6).

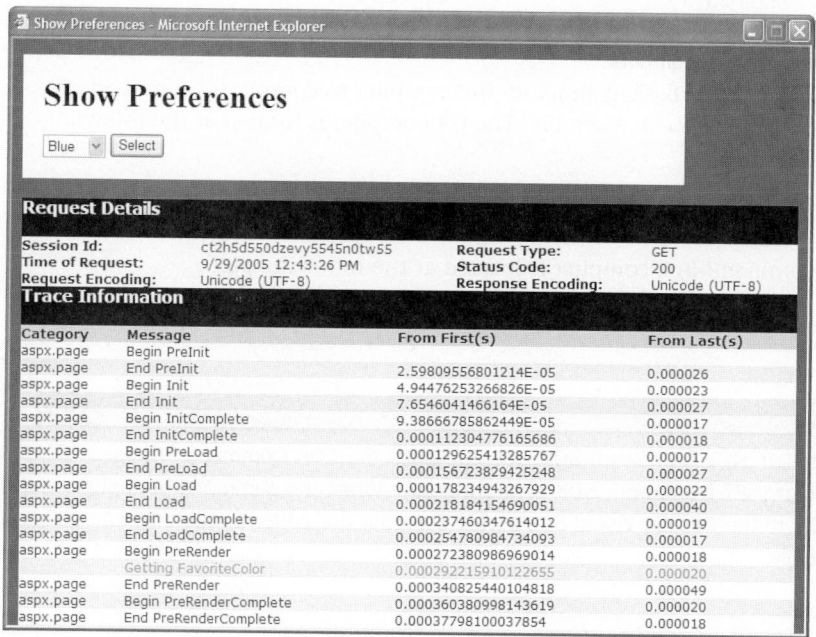

FIGURE 17.6   Selecting a favorite color.

Building Component Libraries

One of the advertised benefits of using components is code reuse. You write a method once, and then you never need to write the same method again.

One problem with the components that have been created to this point is that they have all been application-specific. In other words, you cannot reuse the components across multiple websites without copying all the source code from one App_Code folder to another.

If you want to share components among multiple websites, you can no longer take advantage of dynamic compilation. To share components, you need to compile the components explicitly in a separate assembly.

Compiling Component Libraries

You can use a number of methods to compile a set of components into an assembly:

▶ The command-line compiler

▶ C# or Visual Basic Express

▶ The full version of Visual Studio 2010

These options are explored in turn.

Using the C# Command-Line Compiler

You can use the C# or Visual Basic command-line compiler to compile a source code file, or set of source code files, into an assembly. The C# compiler is located at the following path:

```
C:\Windows\Microsoft.NET\Framework\v4.0.30319\csc.exe
```

The Visual Basic command-line compiler is located at the following path:

```
C:\Windows\Microsoft.NET\Framework\v4.0.30319\vbc.exe
```

> **NOTE**
>
> If you have installed .NET Framework SDK, you can open the SDK Command Prompt from the Microsoft .NET Framework SDK program group. When the command prompt opens, the paths to the C# and Visual Basic .NET compiler are added to the environment automatically.

You can use the `csc.exe` tool to compile any C# source file like this:

```
csc /t:library SomeFile.cs
```

The `/t` (target) option causes the compiler to create a component library and not a Console or Windows application. When you execute this command, a new file named `SomeFile.dll` is created, which is the compiled assembly.

As an alternative to compiling a single file, you can compile all the source code files in a folder (and every subfolder) like this:

```
csc /t:library /recurse:*.cs /out:MyLibrary.dll
```

The /recurse option causes the compiler to compile the contents of all the subfolders. The /out option provides a name for the resulting assembly.

Using Visual C# Express

You can download a trial edition of Visual C# Express from the Microsoft website (http://www.microsoft.com/express/windows/). Visual C# Express enables you to build Windows applications, Console applications, and class libraries.

To create a class library that you can use with an ASP.NET application, you create a Class Library project in Visual C# Express (see Figure 17.7). When you build the project, a new assembly is created.

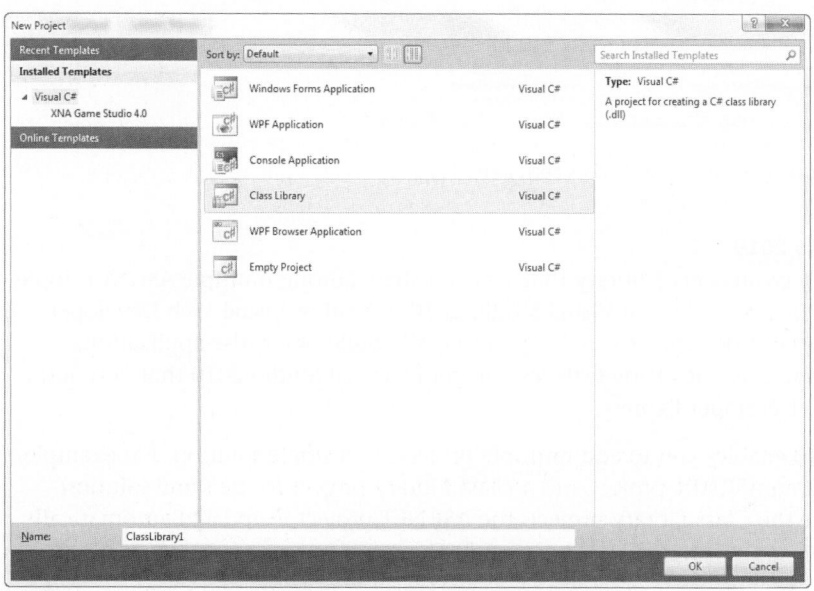

FIGURE 17.7   Creating a Class Library in C# Express.

If you need to use ASP.NET classes in your class library, such as the HttpContext class, you need to add a reference to the System.Web.dll assembly to your Class Library project. Select Project, Add Reference and add the System.Web.dll from the .NET tab (see Figure 17.8).

> **NOTE**
>
> If you are a VB.NET developer, you can download Visual Basic Express from the MSDN website at http://www.microsoft.com/express/windows/.

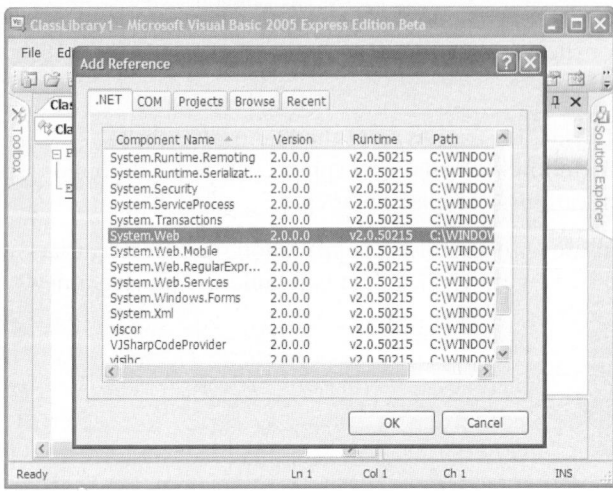

FIGURE 17.8   Adding a reference to `System.Web.dll`.

Using Visual Studio 2010

The easiest way to create a class library that you can share among multiple ASP.NET applications is to use the full version of Visual Studio 2010 instead of Visual Web Developer. Visual Studio 2010 was designed to enable you to easily build enterprise applications. Building class libraries is one of the features you get in Visual Studio 2010 that you don't get in Visual Web Developer Express.

Visual Studio 2010 enables you to add multiple projects to a single solution. For example, you can add both an ASP.NET project and a Class Library project to the same solution. When you update the Class Library project, the ASP.NET project is updated automatically (see Figure 17.9).

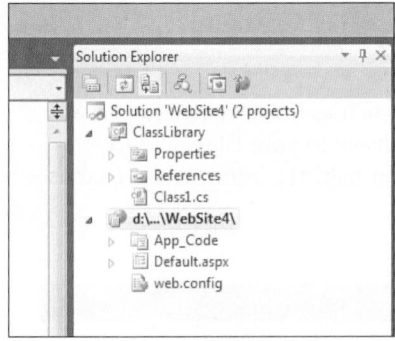

FIGURE 17.9   A solution that contains multiple projects.

Adding a Reference to a Class Library

Now that you understand how you can create a class library in a separate assembly, you need to know how you can use this class library in another project. In other words, how do you use the components contained in an assembly within an ASP.NET page?

You can make an assembly available to an ASP.NET application in two ways. You can add the assembly to the application's /Bin folder or you can add the assembly to the Global Assembly Cache.

Adding an Assembly to the Bin Folder

In general, the best way to use an assembly in an ASP.NET application is to add the assembly to the application's root Bin folder. There is nothing magical about this folder. The ASP.NET Framework automatically checks this folder for any assemblies. If the folder contains an assembly, the assembly is referenced automatically by the ASP.NET application when it is compiled dynamically.

If you use Visual Web Developer, you can select the menu option Website, Add Reference to add a new assembly to your application's Bin folder (see Figure 17.10). Alternatively, you can simply copy an assembly into this folder. (If the folder doesn't exist, just create it.)

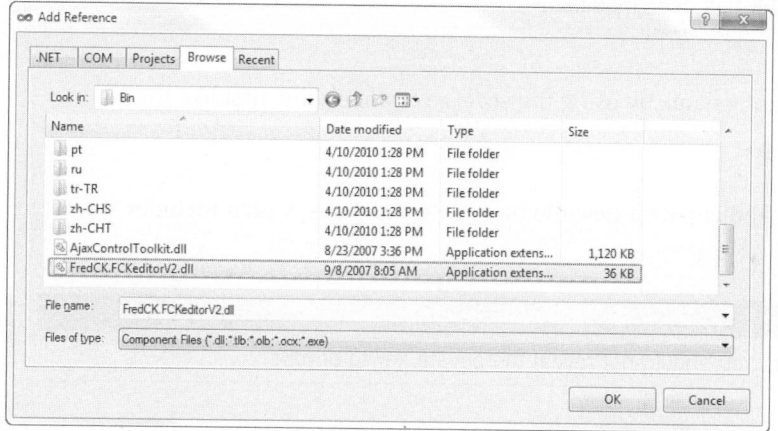

FIGURE 17.10   Adding an assembly reference with Visual Web Developer.

When you add an assembly to an ASP.NET application's Bin folder, the assembly is scoped to the application. This means that you can add different versions of the same assembly to different applications without worrying about any conflicts.

Furthermore, if you add an assembly to the Bin folder, you can take advantage of XCopy deployment. In other words, if you need to move your website to a new server, you can simply copy all the files in your website from one server to another. As long as you copy your Bin folder, the assembly is available at the new location.

Adding an Assembly to the Global Assembly Cache

All the assemblies that make up the .NET Framework class library are contained in the Global Assembly Cache. For example, the Random class is located in the System.dll assembly, and the System.dll assembly is contained in the Global Assembly Cache. Any assembly located in the Global Assembly Cache can be referenced by any application running on a server.

The Global Assembly Cache's physical location is at the following path:

```
C:\WINDOWS\assembly
```

Before you can add an assembly to the Global Assembly Cache, you must add a strong name to the assembly. A strong name is similar to a GUID. You use a strong name to provide your assembly with a universally unique identifier.

> **NOTE**
>
> Technically, a strong name consists of the name, version number, and culture of the assembly. The strong name also includes the public key from a public/private key pair. Finally, the strong name includes a hash of the assembly's contents so that you know whether the assembly has been modified.

You can generate a strong name by using the sn.exe command-line tool like this:

```
sn.exe -k KeyPair.snk
```

Executing this command creates a new file named KeyPair.snk, which includes a new random public/private key pair.

> **WARNING**
>
> Protect your key file. You should not reveal the private key to anyone.

You can compile an assembly that includes a strong name by executing the Visual Basic .NET command-line compiler like this:

```
csc /t:library /keyfile:KeyPair.snk /recurse:*.cs /out:MyLibrary.dll
```

The resulting assembly is strongly named with the public key from the KeyPair.snk file. The /keyfile option associates the key file with the assembly. In this case, the name of the resulting assembly is MyLibrary.dll.

An alternative method of associating a strong name with an assembly is to use the <Assembly: AssemblyKeyFile> attribute. You can add this attribute to any of the source files that get compiled into the assembly. For example, you can drop the file in Listing 17.24 into the folder that you are compiling, and it associates the public key from the KeyPair.snk file with the compiled assembly.

LISTING 17.24   AssemblyInfo.cs

```
using System.Reflection;


[assembly:AssemblyKeyFile("KeyPair.snk")]
[assembly:AssemblyVersion("0.0.0.0")]
```

The file in Listing 17.24 actually includes two attributes. The first attribute associates the KeyPair.snk public key with the assembly. The second attribute associates a version number with the assembly. The version number consists of four sets of numbers: major version, minor version, build number, and revision number.

After you add the file in Listing 17.24 to a folder that contains the source code for your components, use the following command to compile the folder:

```
csc /t:library /recurse:*.cs /out:MyLibrary.dll
```

After you associate a strong name with an assembly, you can use the GacUtil.exe command-line tool to add the assembly to the Global Assembly Cache. Executing the following statement from a command prompt adds the MyLibrary.dll assembly to the Global Assembly Cache:

```
GacUtil.exe /i MyLibrary.dll
```

You can verify that the MyLibrary.dll assembly has been added successfully to the Global Assembly Cache by opening your Global Assembly Cache folder located at the following path:

```
C:\WINDOWS\assembly
```

You should see the MyLibrary.dll assembly listed in the Assembly Name column (see Figure 17.11). Note the Version and the PublicKeyToken columns. You need to know the values of these columns to use the assembly in an application.

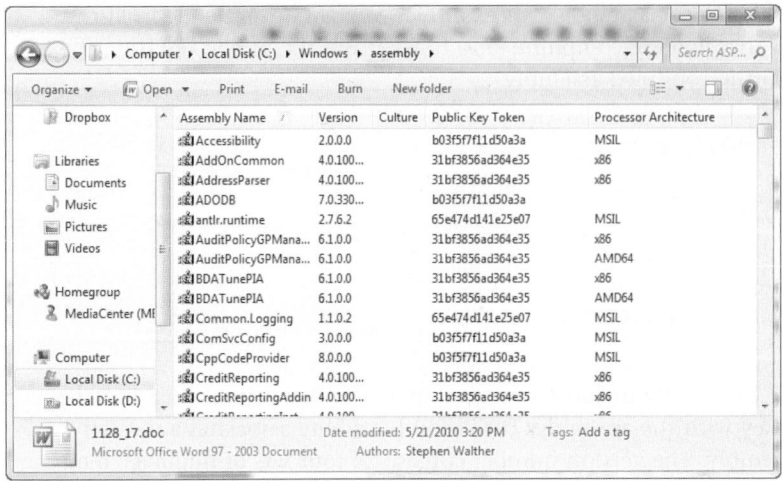

FIGURE 17.11   Viewing the Global Assembly Cache.

After you install an assembly in the Global Assembly Cache, you can use the assembly in your ASP.NET Pages and App_Code components by adding a reference to the assembly in your web configuration file. The web configuration file in Listing 17.25 adds the MyLibrary.dll assembly to your application.

LISTING 17.25   Web.Config

```
<?xml version="1.0"?>
<configuration>
  <system.web>
    <compilation>
      <assemblies>
        <add assembly="MyLibrary,Version=0.0.0.0,Culture=neutral,
          PublicKeyToken=250c66fc9dd31989" />
      </assemblies>
    </compilation>
  </system.web>
</configuration>
```

The web configuration file in Listing 17.25 adds the MyLibrary assembly. You must supply the Version, Culture, and PublicKeyToken associated with the assembly. You need to substitute the correct values for these properties in Listing 17.25 before you use the file with an assembly that you have compiled. (Remember that you can get these values by opening the c:\WINDOWS\assembly folder.)

> **NOTE**
>
> When using Visual C# Express or Visual Studio 2010, you can create a strong name automatically and associate the strong name with an assembly. Right-click the name of your project in the Solution Explorer window and select Properties. Next, select the tab labeled Signing.

In general, you should avoid adding your assemblies to the Global Assembly Cache because using the Global Assembly Cache defeats XCopy deployment. Using the Global Assembly Cache makes it more difficult to back up an application. It also makes it more difficult to move an application from one server to another.

Architectural Considerations

If you embark on a large ASP.NET project, you quickly discover that you spend more time writing code for components than writing code for your pages. This is not a bad thing. Placing as much of your application logic as possible in components makes it easier to maintain and extend your application. However, the process of organizing the components itself can become time consuming. In other words, you start to run into architectural issues concerning the best way to design your web application.

The topic of architecture, like the topics of politics and religion, should not be discussed in polite company. People have passionate opinions about architecture, and discussions on this topic quickly devolve into people throwing things. Be aware that all statements about proper architecture are controversial.

With these disclaimers out of the way, in this section I provide you with an overview of one of the most common architectures for ASP.NET applications. In this section, you learn how to build a three-tiered ASP.NET application.

Building Multitier Applications

One common architecture for an application follows an n-tier design model. When using an n-tier architecture, you encapsulate your application logic into separate layers. In particular, it is recommended that an application should be divided into the following three application layers:

- ▶ User Interface
- ▶ Business Logic
- ▶ Data Access

The idea is that the User Interface layer should contain nothing but user interface elements such as HTML and ASP.NET controls. The User Interface layer should not contain any business logic or data access code.

The Business Logic layer contains all your business rules and validation code. It manages all data access for the User Interface layer.

Finally, the Data Access layer contains all the code for interacting with a database. For example, all the code for interacting with Microsoft SQL Server should be encapsulated in this layer.

The advantage of encapsulating your application logic into different layers is that it makes it easier to modify your application without requiring you to rewrite your entire application. Changes in one layer can be completely isolated from the other layers.

For example, imagine that (one fine day) your company decides to switch from using Microsoft SQL Server to using Oracle as its database server. If you have been careful to create an isolated Data Access layer, you would need to rewrite only your Data Access layer. It might be a major project, but you would not need to start from scratch.

Or imagine that your company decides to create a Silverlight version of an existing ASP.NET application. Again, if you have been careful to isolate your User Interface layer from your Business Logic layer, you can extend your application to support a Silverlight interface without rewriting your entire application. The Siverlight application can use your existing Business Logic and Data Access layers.

This is all abstract, so let's examine a particular sample. We create a simple product management system that enables you to select, insert, update, and delete products. However, we do it the right way by dividing the application into distinct User Interface, Business Logic, and Data Access layers.

Creating the User Interface Layer

The User Interface layer is contained in Listing 17.26. The User Interface layer consists of a single ASP.NET page. This page contains no code whatsoever.

LISTING 17.26   Products.aspx

```
<%@ Page Language="C#" %>
<!DOCTYPE html PUBLIC "-//W3C//DTD XHTML 1.1//EN"
  "http://www.w3.org/TR/xhtml11/DTD/xhtml11.dtd">
<html xmlns="http://www.w3.org/1999/xhtml" >
<head id="Head1" runat="server">
    <style type="text/css">
    html
    {
        background-color:silver;
    }
    .content
    {
        padding:10px;
        background-color:white;
```

```
        }
        .products
        {
            margin-bottom:20px;
        }
        .products td,.products th
        {
            padding:5px;
            border-bottom:solid 1px blue;
        }
        a
        {
            color:blue;
        }
        </style>
        <title>Products</title>
</head>
<body>
    <form id="form1" runat="server">
    <div class="content">

    <asp:GridView
        id="grdProducts"
        DataSourceID="srcProducts"
        DataKeyNames="Id"
        AutoGenerateEditButton="true"
        AutoGenerateDeleteButton="true"
        AutoGenerateColumns="false"
        CssClass="products"
        GridLines="none"
        Runat="server">
        <Columns>
        <asp:BoundField
            DataField="Id"
            ReadOnly="true"
            HeaderText="Id" />
        <asp:BoundField
            DataField="Name"
            HeaderText="Name" />
        <asp:BoundField
            DataField="Price"
            DataFormatString="{0:c}"
            HeaderText="Price" />
        <asp:BoundField
            DataField="Description"
            HeaderText="Description" />
```

```
            </Columns>
    </asp:GridView>

    <fieldset>
    <legend>Add Product</legend>
    <asp:DetailsView
        id="dtlProduct"
        DataSourceID="srcProducts"
        DefaultMode="Insert"
        AutoGenerateInsertButton="true"
        AutoGenerateRows="false"
        Runat="server">
        <Fields>
        <asp:BoundField
            DataField="Name"
            HeaderText="Name:" />
        <asp:BoundField
            DataField="Price"
            HeaderText="Price:"/>
        <asp:BoundField
            DataField="Description"
            HeaderText="Description:" />
        </Fields>
    </asp:DetailsView>
    </fieldset>


    <asp:ObjectDataSource
        id="srcProducts"
        TypeName="AcmeStore.BusinessLogicLayer.Product"
        SelectMethod="SelectAll"
        UpdateMethod="Update"
        InsertMethod="Insert"
        DeleteMethod="Delete"
        Runat="server" />

    </div>
    </form>
</body>
</html>
```

The page in Listing 17.26 contains a GridView, DetailsView, and ObjectDataSource control. The GridView control enables you to view, update, and delete the products contained in the Products database table (see Figure 17.12). The DetailsView enables you to add new products to the database. Both controls use the ObjectDataSource as their data source.

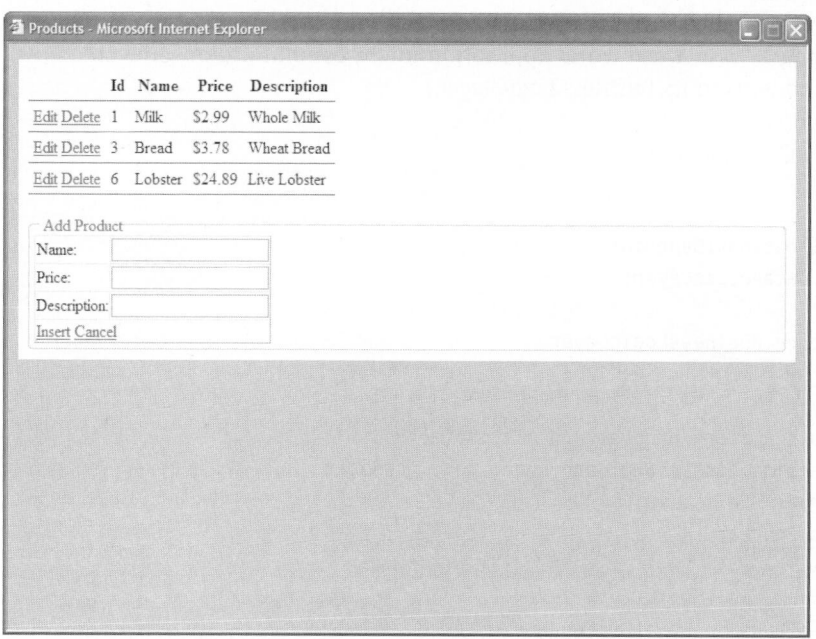

FIGURE 17.12 The Products.aspx page.

> **NOTE**
>
> The next chapter is entirely devoted to the ObjectDataSource control.

The page in Listing 17.26 does not interact with a database directly. Instead, the ObjectDataSource control binds the GridView and DetailsView controls to a component named AcmeStore.BusinessLogicLayer.Product. The Product component is contained in the Business Logic layer.

> **NOTE**
>
> The page in Listing 17.26 does not contain any validation controls. I omitted adding validation controls for reasons of space. In a real application, you would want to toss some RequiredFieldValidator and CompareValidator controls into the page.

Creating the Business Logic Layer

The ASP.NET pages in your application should contain a minimum amount of code. All your application logic should be pushed into separate components contained in either the Business Logic or Data Access layers.

Your ASP.NET pages should not communicate directly with the Data Access layer. Instead, the pages should call the methods contained in the Business Logic layer.

The Business Logic layer consists of a single component named Product, which is
contained in Listing 17.27. (A real-world application might contain dozens or even
hundreds of components in its Business Logic layer.)

LISTING 17.27   BLL/Product.cs

```csharp
using System;
using System.Collections.Generic;
using AcmeStore.DataAccessLayer;

namespace AcmeStore.BusinessLogicLayer
{
    /// <summary>
    /// Represents a store product and all the methods
    /// for selecting, inserting, and updating a product
    /// </summary>
    public class Product
    {
        private int _id = 0;
        private string _name = String.Empty;
        private decimal _price = 0;
        private string _description = String.Empty;

        /// <summary>
        /// Product Unique Identifier
        /// </summary>
        public int Id
        {
            get { return _id; }
        }

        /// <summary>
        /// Product Name
        /// </summary>
        public string Name
        {
            get { return _name; }
        }

        /// <summary>
        /// Product Price
        /// </summary>
        public decimal Price
        {
            get { return _price; }
        }
```

```csharp
/// <summary>
/// Product Description
/// </summary>
public string Description
{
    get { return _description; }
}

/// <summary>
/// Retrieves all products
/// </summary>
/// <returns></returns>
public static List<Product> SelectAll()
{
    SqlDataAccessLayer dataAccessLayer = new SqlDataAccessLayer();
    return dataAccessLayer.ProductSelectAll();
}

/// <summary>
/// Updates a particular product
/// </summary>
/// <param name="id">Product Id</param>
/// <param name="name">Product Name</param>
/// <param name="price">Product Price</param>
/// <param name="description">Product Description</param>
public static void Update(int id, string name, decimal price, string
➥description)
{
    if (id < 1)
        throw new ArgumentException("Product Id must be greater than 0",
➥"id");

    Product productToUpdate = new Product(id, name, price, description);
    productToUpdate.Save();
}

/// <summary>
/// Inserts a new product
/// </summary>
/// <param name="name">Product Name</param>
/// <param name="price">Product Price</param>
/// <param name="description">Product Description</param>
public static void Insert(string name, decimal price, string description)
{
    Product newProduct = new Product(name, price, description);
```

17

```csharp
            newProduct.Save();
        }

        /// <summary>
        /// Deletes an existing product
        /// </summary>
        /// <param name="id">Product Id</param>
        public static void Delete(int id)
        {
            if (id < 1)
                throw new ArgumentException("Product Id must be greater than 0",
➡"id");

            SqlDataAccessLayer dataAccessLayer = new SqlDataAccessLayer();
            dataAccessLayer.ProductDelete(id);
        }

        /// <summary>
        /// Validates product information before saving product
        /// properties to the database
        /// </summary>
        private void Save()
        {
            if (String.IsNullOrEmpty(_name))
                throw new ArgumentException("Product Name not supplied", "name");
            if (_name.Length > 50)
                throw new ArgumentException("Product Name must be less than 50
characters", "name");
            if (String.IsNullOrEmpty(_description))
                throw new ArgumentException("Product Description not supplied",
"description");

            SqlDataAccessLayer dataAccessLayer = new SqlDataAccessLayer();
            if (_id > 0)
                dataAccessLayer.ProductUpdate(this);
            else
                dataAccessLayer.ProductInsert(this);
        }

        /// <summary>
        /// Initializes Product
        /// </summary>
        /// <param name="name">Product Name</param>
        /// <param name="price">Product Price</param>
        /// <param name="description">Product Description</param>
        public Product(string name, decimal price, string description)
```

```
            : this(0, name, price, description) { }

        /// <summary>
        /// Initializes Product
        /// </summary>
        /// <param name="id">Product Id</param>
        /// <param name="name">Product Name</param>
        /// <param name="price">Product Price</param>
        /// <param name="description">Product Description</param>
        public Product(int id, string name, decimal price, string description)
        {
            _id = id;
            _name = name;
            _price = price;
            _description = description;
        }


    }
}
```

The Product component contains four public methods named SelectAll(), Update(),
Insert(), and Delete(). All four of these methods use the SqlDataAccessLayer component to interact with the Products database table. The SqlDataAccessLayer is contained in
the Data Access layer.

For example, the SelectAll() method returns a collection of Product objects. This collection is retrieved from the SqlDataAccessLayer component.

The Insert(), Update(), and Delete() methods validate their parameters before passing
the parameters to the Data Access layer. For example, when you call the Insert() method,
the length of the Name parameter is checked to verify that it is less than 50 characters.

The Business Logic layer does not contain any data access logic. All this logic is contained
in the Data Access layer.

Creating the Data Access Layer

The Data Access layer contains all the specialized code for interacting with a database. The
Data Access layer consists of the single component in Listing 17.28. (A real-world application might contain dozens or even hundreds of components in its Data Access layer.)

LISTING 17.28   DAL\SqlDataAccessLayer.cs

```
using System;
using System.Data;
using System.Data.SqlClient;
using System.Web.Configuration;
```

```csharp
using System.Collections.Generic;
using AcmeStore.BusinessLogicLayer;

namespace AcmeStore.DataAccessLayer
{
    /// <summary>
    /// Data Access Layer for interacting with Microsoft
    /// SQL Server 2008
    /// </summary>
    public class SqlDataAccessLayer
    {
        private static readonly string _connectionString = string.Empty;

        /// <summary>
        /// Selects all products from the database
        /// </summary>
        public List<Product> ProductSelectAll()
        {
            // Create Product collection
            List<Product> colProducts = new List<Product>();

            // Create connection
            SqlConnection con = new SqlConnection(_connectionString);

            // Create command
            SqlCommand cmd = new SqlCommand();
            cmd.Connection = con;
            cmd.CommandText = "SELECT Id,Name,Price,Description FROM Products";

            // Execute command
            using (con)
            {
                con.Open();
                SqlDataReader reader = cmd.ExecuteReader();
                while (reader.Read())
                {
                    colProducts.Add(new Product(
                        (int)reader["Id"],
                        (string)reader["Name"],
                        (decimal)reader["Price"],
                        (string)reader["Description"]));
                }
            }
            return colProducts;
        }
```

```
/// <summary>
/// Inserts a new product into the database
/// </summary>
/// <param name="newProduct">Product</param>
public void ProductInsert(Product newProduct)
{
    // Create connection
    SqlConnection con = new SqlConnection(_connectionString);

    // Create command
    SqlCommand cmd = new SqlCommand();
    cmd.Connection = con;
    cmd.CommandText = "INSERT Products (Name,Price,Description) VALUES
(@Name,@Price,

    // Add parameters
    cmd.Parameters.AddWithValue("@Name", newProduct.Name);
    cmd.Parameters.AddWithValue("@Price", newProduct.Price);
    cmd.Parameters.AddWithValue("@Description", newProduct.Description);

    // Execute command
    using (con)
    {
        con.Open();
        cmd.ExecuteNonQuery();

    }
}

/// <summary>
/// Updates an existing product into the database
/// </summary>
/// <param name="productToUpdate">Product</param>
public void ProductUpdate(Product productToUpdate)
{
    // Create connection
    SqlConnection con = new SqlConnection(_connectionString);

    // Create command
    SqlCommand cmd = new SqlCommand();
    cmd.Connection = con;
    cmd.CommandText = "UPDATE Products SET
Name=@Name,Price=@Price,Description=
    // Add parameters
    cmd.Parameters.AddWithValue("@Name", productToUpdate.Name);
    cmd.Parameters.AddWithValue("@Price", productToUpdate.Price);
```

17

```csharp
        cmd.Parameters.AddWithValue("@Description", productToUpdate.Description);
        cmd.Parameters.AddWithValue("@Id", productToUpdate.Id);

        // Execute command
        using (con)
        {
            con.Open();
            cmd.ExecuteNonQuery();

        }
    }

    /// <summary>
    /// Deletes an existing product in the database
    /// </summary>
    /// <param name="id">Product Id</param>
    public void ProductDelete(int Id)
    {
        // Create connection
        SqlConnection con = new SqlConnection(_connectionString);

        // Create command
        SqlCommand cmd = new SqlCommand();
        cmd.Connection = con;
        cmd.CommandText = "DELETE Products WHERE Id=@Id";

        // Add parameters
        cmd.Parameters.AddWithValue("@Id", Id);

        // Execute command
        using (con)
        {
            con.Open();
            cmd.ExecuteNonQuery();

        }
    }

    /// <summary>
    /// Initialize the data access layer by
    /// loading the database connection string from
    /// the Web.Config file
    /// </summary>
    static SqlDataAccessLayer()
    {
```

```
        _connectionString =
WebConfigurationManager.ConnectionStrings["Store"].ConnectionString;
        if (string.IsNullOrEmpty(_connectionString))
            throw new Exception("No connection string configured in Web.Config
file");
        }
    }
}
```

The SqlDataAccessLayer component in Listing 17.28 grabs the database connection string that it uses when communicating with Microsoft SQL Server in its constructor. The connection string is assigned to a private field so that it can be used by all the component's methods.

The SqlDataAccessLayer component has four public methods: ProductSelectAll(), ProductInsert(), ProductUpdate(), and ProductDelete(). These methods use the ADO.NET classes from the System.Data.SqlClient namespace to communicate with Microsoft SQL Server.

NOTE

We discuss ADO.NET in Chapter 19, "Building Data Access Components with ADO.NET."

NOTE

In this section, the Data Access layer was built using ADO.NET. It could just have as easily been built using LINQ to SQL. We discuss LINQ to SQL in Chapter 20.

17

The SqlDataAccessLayer component is not completely isolated from the components in the Business Logic layer. The ProductSelectAll() method builds a collection of Product objects, which the method returns to the Business Logic layer. You should strive to isolate each layer as much as possible. However, in some cases, you cannot completely avoid mixing objects from different layers.

Summary

In this chapter, you learned how to build components in .NET Framework. In the first part, you were given an overview of component building. You learned how to take advantage of dynamic compilation by using the App_Code folder. You also learned how to create component properties, methods, and constructors. You also examined several advanced topics related to components such as overloading, inheritance, MustInherit classes, and interfaces.

In the second half of this chapter, you learned how to build component libraries. You saw different methods for compiling a set of components into an assembly. You also examined how you can add components to both an application's Bin folder and the Global Assembly Cache.

Finally, you had a chance to consider architectural issues related to building applications with components. You learned how to build a three-tiered application, divided into isolated User Interface, Business Logic, and Data Access layers.

Using the ObjectDataSource Control

The ObjectDataSource control enables you to bind DataBound controls such as the GridView, DetailsView, and FormView controls to a component. You can use the ObjectDataSource control to easily build multitier applications with ASP.NET Framework. Unlike the SqlDataSource control, which mixes data access logic in the User Interface layer, the ObjectDataSource control enables you to cleanly separate your User Interface layer from your Business Logic and Data Access layers.

In this chapter, you learn how to use the ObjectDataSource control to represent different types of objects. For example, you learn how to use the ObjectDataSource control with components that represent database data. You also learn how to use the ObjectDataSource control to represent different types of method parameters.

We tackle a number of advanced topics. For example, you learn how to page, sort, and filter database records represented by the ObjectDataSource control. You learn how to page and sort through large database tables efficiently.

In the final section, you learn how to extend the ObjectDataSource control to represent specialized data sources. You also learn how to extend the ObjectDataSource control with custom parameters.

Representing Objects with the ObjectDataSource Control

The `ObjectDataSource` control includes five main properties:

▶ **TypeName**—The name of the type of object that the `ObjectDataSource` control represents.

▶ **SelectMethod**—The name of a method that the `ObjectDataSource` calls when selecting data.

▶ **UpdateMethod**—The name of a method that the `ObjectDataSource` calls when updating data.

▶ **InsertMethod**—The name of a method that the `ObjectDataSource` calls when inserting data.

▶ **DeleteMethod**—The name of a method that the `ObjectDataSource` calls when deleting data.

An `ObjectDataSource` control can represent any type of object in .NET Framework. This section discusses several types of objects you might want to represent. For example, you learn how to use the `ObjectDataSource` control with components that represent collections, ADO.NET DataReaders, DataSets, LINQ to SQL queries, and web services.

> **NOTE**
>
> You can use the `ObjectDataSource` control to represent any object (any class that derives from the `System.Object` class). If the object does not support the `IEnumerable` interface, the `ObjectDataSource` control automatically wraps the object in a new object that supports the IEnumerable interface. You can even represent an ASP.NET ListBox control with an `ObjectDataSource` (not that a ListBox has any interesting methods).

Binding to a Component

Let's start with a simple component. The component in Listing 18.1 is named `MovieCollection` and contains one method named `GetMovies()`, which returns a collection of movie titles.

LISTING 18.1 MovieCollection.cs

```
using System;
using System.Web.Configuration;
using System.Collections.Generic;

public class MovieCollection
```

```
{
    public List<string> GetMovies()
    {
        List<string> movies = new List<string>();
        movies.Add("Star Wars");
        movies.Add("Independence Day");
        movies.Add("War of the Worlds");
        return movies;
    }


}
```

You can use the page in Listing 18.2 to display the list of movies returned by the GetMovies() method in a GridView control. The page contains an ObjectDataSource control that represents the MovieCollection component.

LISTING 18.2   ShowMovieCollection.aspx

```
<%@ Page Language="C#" %>
<!DOCTYPE html PUBLIC "-//W3C//DTD XHTML 1.1//EN"
    "http://www.w3.org/TR/xhtml11/DTD/xhtml11.dtd">
<html xmlns="http://www.w3.org/1999/xhtml" >
<head id="Head1" runat="server">
    <title>Show Movie Collection</title>
</head>
<body>
    <form id="form1" runat="server">
    <div>

    <asp:GridView
        id="grdMovies"
        DataSourceID="srcMovies"
        Runat="server" />

    <asp:ObjectDataSource
        id="srcMovies"
        TypeName="MovieCollection"
        SelectMethod="GetMovies"
        Runat="server" />

    </div>
    </form>
</body>
</html>
```

18

In Listing 18.2, the `ObjectDataSource` control includes two properties named `TypeName` and `SelectMethod`. The `TypeName` property contains the name of the component that you want to represent with the `ObjectDataSource` control. The `SelectMethod` property represents the method of the component that you want to call when selecting data.

The `GridView` control is bound to the `ObjectDataSource` control through its `DataSourceID` property. When you open the page in Listing 18.2, the list of movies is retrieved from the `MovieCollection` component and displayed in the `GridView`.

The `MovieCollection` component contains instance methods. The `ObjectDataSource` automatically creates a new instance of the `MovieCollection` component before calling its `GetMovies()` method. It automatically destroys the object after it finishes using the object.

You also can use the `ObjectDataSource` control to call shared (static) methods. In that case, the `ObjectDataSource` doesn't need to instantiate a component before calling the method.

Binding to a `DataReader`

Typically, you use the `ObjectDataSource` control to represent database data. The .NET Framework provides you with multiple ways of representing data. This section discusses how you can use an `ObjectDataSource` to represent a `DataReader`.

> **NOTE**
>
> The different ADO.NET objects are compared and contrasted in Chapter 19, "Building Data Access Components with ADO.NET."

The ADO.NET `DataReader` object provides you with a fast, read-only representation of database data. If you need to retrieve database records in the fastest possible way, you should use a `DataReader` object.

For example, the component in Listing 18.3, the `MovieDataReader` component, returns all the movies from the Movies database table by using the `SqlDataReader` object. The component imports the `System.Data.SqlClient` namespace to use this Microsoft SQL Server-specific ADO.NET object.

LISTING 18.3   `MovieDataReader.cs`

```
using System;
using System.Data;
using System.Data.SqlClient;
using System.Web.Configuration;

public class MovieDataReader
{
    private readonly string _conString;
```

```
    public SqlDataReader GetMovies()
    {
        // Create Connection
        SqlConnection con = new SqlConnection(_conString);

        // Create Command
        SqlCommand cmd = new SqlCommand();
        cmd.Connection = con;
        cmd.CommandText = "SELECT Id,Title,Director FROM Movies";

        // Return DataReader
        con.Open();
        return cmd.ExecuteReader(CommandBehavior.CloseConnection);
    }

    public MovieDataReader()
    {
        _conString =
➥WebConfigurationManager.ConnectionStrings["Movies"].ConnectionString;
    }
}
```

The component in Listing 18.3 actually uses three ADO.NET objects: Connection, Command, and DataReader. The SqlCommand object uses the SqlConnection object to connect to the database. The records are returned from the SqlCommand object and represented by the SqlDataReader object.

The WebConfigurationManager class retrieves the database connection string from the web configuration file. To use this class, you need to import the System.Web.Confiugration namespace (and have a reference to the System.Web.dll assembly).

The ObjectDataSource control in Listing 18.4 represents the MovieDataReader object. It binds the movies to a GridView control.

LISTING 18.4   ShowMovieDataReader.aspx

```
<%@ Page Language="C#" %>
<!DOCTYPE html PUBLIC "-//W3C//DTD XHTML 1.1//EN"
  "http://www.w3.org/TR/xhtml11/DTD/xhtml11.dtd">
<html xmlns="http://www.w3.org/1999/xhtml" >
<head id="Head1" runat="server">
    <title>Show Movie DataReader</title>
</head>
<body>
    <form id="form1" runat="server">
```

18

```
<div>

<asp:GridView
    id="grdMovies"
    DataSourceID="srcMovies"
    Runat="server" />

<asp:ObjectDataSource
    id="srcMovies"
    TypeName="MovieDataReader"
    SelectMethod="GetMovies"
    Runat="server" />

</div>
</form>
</body>
</html>
```

Binding to a DataSet

You also can use the ObjectDataSource when you need to represent an ADO.NET DataSet. Using a DataSet is slower than using a DataReader; however, you can perform advanced operations, such as filtering and sorting, on data represented with a DataSet.

The component in Listing 18.5 returns all the records from the Movies database table. However, it uses a DataSet instead of a DataReader object.

LISTING 18.5   MovieDataSet.cs

```csharp
using System;
using System.Data;
using System.Data.SqlClient;
using System.Web.Configuration;

public class MovieDataSet
{
    private readonly string _conString;

    public DataSet GetMovies()
    {
        // Create DataAdapter
        string commandText = "SELECT Id,Title,Director FROM Movies";
        SqlDataAdapter dad = new SqlDataAdapter(commandText, _conString);
```

```
        // Return DataSet
        DataSet dstMovies = new DataSet();
        using (dad)
        {
            dad.Fill(dstMovies);
        }
        return dstMovies;
    }


    public MovieDataSet()
    {
        _conString =
➥WebConfigurationManager.ConnectionStrings["Movies"].ConnectionString;
    }
}
```

The component in Listing 18.5 uses two ADO.NET objects: DataAdapter and DataSet. The SqlDataAdapter represents the SQL select command and populates the DataSet with the results of executing the command. The WebConfigurationManager class reads the database connection string from the web configuration file.

The page in Listing 18.6 binds the list of movies to a DropDownList control.

LISTING 18.6   ShowMovieDataSet.aspx

```
<%@ Page Language="C#" %>
<!DOCTYPE html PUBLIC "-//W3C//DTD XHTML 1.1//EN"
  "http://www.w3.org/TR/xhtml11/DTD/xhtml11.dtd">
<html xmlns="http://www.w3.org/1999/xhtml" >
<head id="Head1" runat="server">
    <title>Show Movie DataSet</title>
</head>
<body>
    <form id="form1" runat="server">
    <div>

    <asp:GridView
        id="grdMovies"
        DataSourceID="srcMovies"
        Runat="server" />

    <asp:ObjectDataSource
        id="srcMovies"
        TypeName="MovieDataReader"
```

18

```
        SelectMethod="GetMovies"
        Runat="server" />

    </div>
    </form>
</body>
</html>
```

Binding to a LINQ to SQL Query

LINQ to SQL is the preferred method of data access in .NET Framework. The expectation is that you will use LINQ to SQL instead of ADO.NET to interact with a database. Chapter 20, "Data Access with LINQ to SQL," is devoted to the topic of LINQ to SQL.

Here's a quick sample of binding an `ObjectDataSource` to a component that represents a LINQ to SQL query. The component that contains the LINQ query is contained in Listing 18.7.

LISTING 18.7   Employee.cs

```
using System.Collections.Generic;
using System.Linq;
using System.Data.Linq;

public partial class Employee
{
    public static IEnumerable<Employee> Select()
    {
        EmployeesDataContext db = new EmployeesDataContext();
        return db.Employees.OrderBy( e=>e.LastName );
    }
}
```

Before you can use the component in Listing 18.7, you first must create the `EmployeesDataContext`. The easiest way to create the `DataContext` is to select Website, Add New Item and select the LINQ to SQL Classes template. Name the LINQ to SQL Classes **Employees**.

After the LINQ to SQL Designer appears, drag the Employees database table onto the Designer surface from the Database Explorer window. At this point, the `EmployeesDataContext` will be ready.

The page in Listing 18.8 contains an ObjectDataSource that represents the Employee class.

LISTING 18.8   ShowLINQ.aspx

```
<%@ Page Language="C#" %>
<!DOCTYPE html PUBLIC "-//W3C//DTD XHTML 1.0 Transitional//EN"
"http://www.w3.org/TR/xhtml1/DTD/xhtml1-transitional.dtd">
<html xmlns="http://www.w3.org/1999/xhtml">
<head runat="server">
    <title>Show LINQ</title>
</head>
<body>
    <form id="form1" runat="server">
    <div>

    <asp:GridView
        id="grdEmployees"
        DataSourceID="srcEmployees"
        runat="server" />

    <asp:ObjectDataSource
        id="srcEmployees"
        TypeName="Employee"
        SelectMethod="Select"
        Runat="server" />

    </div>
    </form>
</body>
</html>
```

Binding to a Web Service

Web services enable you to share information across the Internet. When you communicate with a remote web service, you use a local proxy class to represent the web service located on the remote machine. You can use the ObjectDataSource to represent this proxy class.

For example, the file in Listing 18.9 contains a simple web service that returns the current server time. You can create this file in Visual Web Developer by selecting Web Site, Add New Item, and selecting the Web Service item.

LISTING 18.9   `TimeService.asmx`

```
<%@ WebService Language="C#" Class="TimeService" %>
using System;
using System.Web;
using System.Web.Services;
using System.Web.Services.Protocols;

[WebService(Namespace = "http://tempuri.org/")]
[WebServiceBinding(ConformsTo = WsiProfiles.BasicProfile1_1)]
public class TimeService   : System.Web.Services.WebService {

    [WebMethod]
    public DateTime GetServerTime() {
        return DateTime.Now;
    }

}
```

After you create the web service in Listing 18.9, you can communicate with the service from anywhere in the world (or the galaxy or the universe). Just as long as a computer is connected to the Internet, the computer can call the GetServerTime() method.

Before you can call the web service, you need to create a web service proxy class. If you use Visual Web Developer, select Web Site, Add Web Reference and enter the URL of the TimeService.asmx file. (You can click the Web Services in This Solution link to list all the web services in your current project.) Change the name of the web reference to LocalServices and click Add Reference (see Figure 18.1).

NOTE

If you are not using Visual Web Developer, you can create a web service proxy class from the command line by using the Wsdl.exe (Web Services Description Language) tool.

When you click Add Reference, a new folder is added to your project named App_WebReferences. The App_WebReferences folder contains a subfolder named LocalServices. Finally, your web configuration file is updated to include the URL to the TimeService web service.

Now that we have a consumable web service, we can represent the Web service using the ObjectDataSource control. The page in Listing 18.10 displays the server time using a FormView control bound to an ObjectDataSource control (see Figure 18.2).

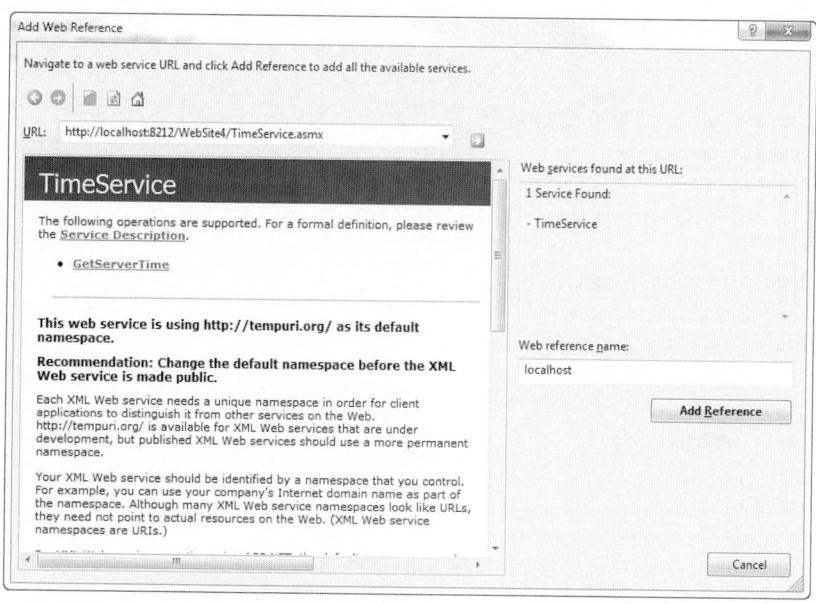

FIGURE 18.1   Adding a Web Reference in Visual Web Developer.

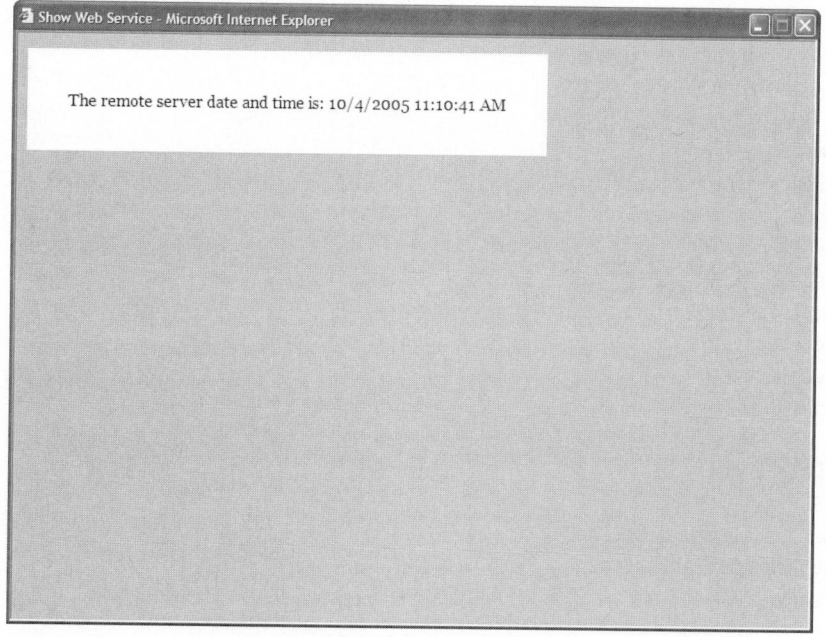

FIGURE 18.2   Retrieving the time from a web service.

LISTING 18.10   ShowWebService.aspx

```
<%@ Page Language="C#" %>
<html xmlns="http://www.w3.org/1999/xhtml" >
<head id="Head1" runat="server">
    <style type="text/css">
        html
        {
            background-color:silver;
        }
        .serverTime
        {
            background-color:white;
            font:16px Georgia,Serif;
        }
        .serverTime td
        {
            padding:40px;
        }
    </style>
    <title>Show Web Service</title>
</head>
<body>
    <form id="form1" runat="server">
    <div>

    <asp:FormView
        id="frmServerTime"
        DataSourceID="srcServerTime"
        CssClass="serverTime"
        Runat="server">
        <ItemTemplate>
        The remote server date and time is: <%# Container.DataItem %>
        </ItemTemplate>
    </asp:FormView>

    <asp:ObjectDataSource
        id="srcServerTime"
        TypeName="LocalServices.TimeService"
        SelectMethod="GetServerTime"
        Runat="server" />

    </div>
    </form>
</body>
</html>
```

The `ObjectDataSource` control's `TypeName` property contains both the namespace and name of the web service proxy class (the web reference). In other words, it contains the fully qualified name of the proxy class. The `SelectMethod` property contains the name of the web method represented by the proxy class.

> **NOTE**
>
> If you open the `ShowWebService.aspx` page from the book's website, you receive an error. Before the page will work correctly, you need to update the web configuration file with the correct path to the web service on your computer.

Using Parameters with the `ObjectDataSource` Control

You can use parameters when calling a method with the `ObjectDataSource` control. The `ObjectDataSource` control includes five parameter collections:

- ▶ **SelectParameters**—Collection of parameters passed to the method represented by the `SelectMethod` property.

- ▶ **InsertParameters**—Collection of parameters passed to the method represented by the `InsertMethod` property.

- ▶ **UpdateParameters**—Collection of parameters passed to the method represented by the `UpdateMethod` property.

- ▶ **DeleteParameters**—Collection of parameters passed to the method represented by the `DeleteParameters` property.

- ▶ **FilterParameters**—Collection of parameters used by the FilterExpression property.

DataBound controls—such as the `GridView`, `DetailsView`, and `FormView` controls—can build the necessary parameter collections for you automatically.

For example, the component in Listing 18.11 enables you to select movies and update a particular movie in the Movies database table. The `UpdateMovie()` method has four parameters: `id`, `title`, `director`, and `dateReleased`.

LISTING 18.11   `Movies.cs`

```
using System;
using System.Data;
using System.Data.SqlClient;
using System.Web.Configuration;

public class Movies
{
    private readonly string _conString;
```

```
    public void UpdateMovie(int id, string title, string director, DateTime
➥dateReleased)
    {
        // Create Command
        SqlConnection con = new SqlConnection(_conString);
        SqlCommand cmd = new SqlCommand();
        cmd.Connection = con;
        cmd.CommandText = "UPDATE Movies SET
Title=@Title,Director=@Director,DateReleased=
        // Add parameters
        cmd.Parameters.AddWithValue("@Title", title);
        cmd.Parameters.AddWithValue("@Director", director);
        cmd.Parameters.AddWithValue("@DateReleased", dateReleased);
        cmd.Parameters.AddWithValue("@Id", id);

        // Execute command
        using (con)
        {
            con.Open();
            cmd.ExecuteNonQuery();
        }
    }

    public SqlDataReader GetMovies()
    {
        // Create Connection
        SqlConnection con = new SqlConnection(_conString);

        // Create Command
        SqlCommand cmd = new SqlCommand();
        cmd.Connection = con;
        cmd.CommandText = "SELECT Id,Title,Director,DateReleased FROM Movies";

        // Return DataReader
        con.Open();
        return cmd.ExecuteReader(CommandBehavior.CloseConnection);
    }

    public Movies()
    {
        _conString =
WebConfigurationManager.ConnectionStrings["Movies"].ConnectionString;
    }
}
```

The page in Listing 18.12 contains a `GridView` and `ObjectDataSource` control. The `ObjectDataSource` control includes an `UpdateMethod` property that points to the `UpdateMovie()` method.

LISTING 18.12   ShowMovies.aspx

```
<%@ Page Language="C#" %>
<!DOCTYPE html PUBLIC "-//W3C//DTD XHTML 1.1//EN"
"http://www.w3.org/TR/xhtml11/DTD/xhtml11.dtd">
<html xmlns="http://www.w3.org/1999/xhtml" >
<head id="Head1" runat="server">
    <title>Show Movies</title>
</head>
<body>
    <form id="form1" runat="server">
    <div>

    <asp:GridView
        id="grdMovies"
        DataSourceID="srcMovies"
        DataKeyNames="Id"
        AutoGenerateEditButton="true"
        Runat="server" />

    <asp:ObjectDataSource
        id="srcMovies"
        TypeName="Movies"
        SelectMethod="GetMovies"
        UpdateMethod="UpdateMovie"
        Runat="server"/>

    </div>
    </form>
</body>
</html>
```

In Listing 18.12, the `GridView` automatically adds the update parameters to the `ObjectDataSource` control's `UpdateParameters` collection. As an alternative, you can declare the parameters used by the `ObjectDataSource` control explicitly. For example, the page in Listing 18.13 declares all the parameters passed to the `UpdateMovie()` method.

LISTING 18.13   ExplicitShowMovies.aspx

```
<%@ Page Language="C#" %>
<!DOCTYPE html PUBLIC "-//W3C//DTD XHTML 1.1//EN"
"http://www.w3.org/TR/xhtml11/DTD/xhtml11.dtd">
```

```
<html xmlns="http://www.w3.org/1999/xhtml" >
<head id="Head1" runat="server">
    <title>Show Movies</title>
</head>
<body>
    <form id="form1" runat="server">
    <div>

    <asp:GridView
        id="grdMovies"
        DataSourceID="srcMovies"
        DataKeyNames="Id"
        AutoGenerateEditButton="true"
        Runat="server" />

    <asp:ObjectDataSource
        id="srcMovies"
        TypeName="Movies"
        SelectMethod="GetMovies"
        UpdateMethod="UpdateMovie"
        Runat="server">
        <UpdateParameters>
        <asp:Parameter Name="title" />
        <asp:Parameter Name="director" />
        <asp:Parameter Name="dateReleased" Type="DateTime" />
        <asp:Parameter Name="id" Type="Int32" />
        </UpdateParameters>
    </asp:ObjectDataSource>

    </div>
    </form>
</body>
</html>
```

The ObjectDataSource uses reflection to match its parameters against the parameters of
the method that it calls. The order of the parameters does not matter, and the case of the
parameters does not matter. However, the one thing that does matter is the names of the
parameters.

You specify the type of a parameter with the Type property, which represents a member of
the TypeCode enumeration. The TypeCode enumeration represents an enumeration of
common .NET Framework data types such as Int32, Decimal, and DateTime. If the
enumeration does not include a data type that you need, you can use the
TypeCode.Object member from the enumeration.

Using Different Parameter Types

You can use all the same types of parameters with the `ObjectDataSource` control that you can use with the `SqlDataSource` control:

- **Parameter**—Represents an arbitrary static value.

- **ControlParameter**—Represents the value of a control or page property.

- **CookieParameter**—Represents the value of a browser cookie.

- **FormParameter**—Represents the value of an HTML form field.

- **ProfileParameter**—Represents the value of a `Profile` property.

- **QueryStringParameter**—Represents the value of a query string field.

- **SessionParameter**—Represents the value of an item stored in Session state.

For example, the page in Listing 18.14 contains a `DropDownList` control and a `GridView` control, which enables you to view movies that match a selected category (see Figure 18.3).

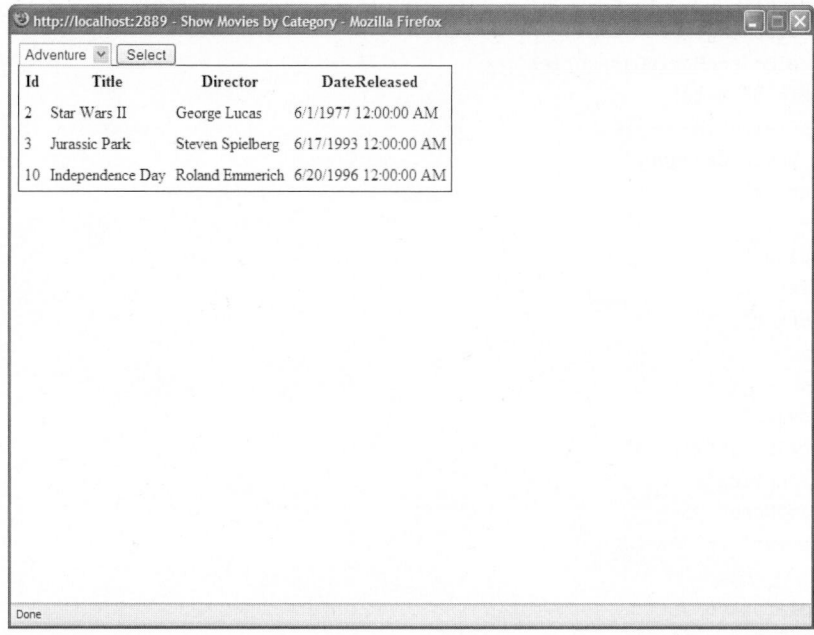

FIGURE 18.3   Displaying movies by category.

LISTING 18.14   `ShowMoviesByCategory.aspx`

```
<%@ Page Language="C#" %>
<!DOCTYPE html PUBLIC "-//W3C//DTD XHTML 1.1//EN"
"http://www.w3.org/TR/xhtml11/DTD/xhtml11.dtd">
<html xmlns="http://www.w3.org/1999/xhtml" >
```

```
<head id="Head1" runat="server">
    <style type="text/css">
    .movies
    {
        border:Solid 1px black;
    }
    .movies td,.movies th
    {
        padding:5px;
    }
    </style>
    <title>Show Movies by Category</title>
</head>
<body>
    <form id="form1" runat="server">
    <div>

    <asp:DropDownList
        id="ddlMovieCategory"
        DataSourceID="srcMovieCategories"
        DataTextField="Name"
        DataValueField="Id"
        ToolTip="Movie Category"
        Runat="server" />
    <asp:Button
        id="btnSelect"
        Text="Select"
        Runat="server" />

    <asp:GridView
        id="grdMovies"
        DataSourceID="srcMovies"
        CssClass="movies"
        GridLines="None"
        Runat="server" />

    <asp:ObjectDataSource
        id="srcMovieCategories"
        TypeName="MovieCategories"
        SelectMethod="GetCategories"
        Runat="server" />

    <asp:ObjectDataSource
        id="srcMovies"
        TypeName="MovieCategories"
        SelectMethod="GetMovies"
```

```
        Runat="server">
        <SelectParameters>
        <asp:ControlParameter
            Name="CategoryId"
            ControlID="ddlMovieCategory" />
        </SelectParameters>
    </asp:ObjectDataSource>

    </div>
    </form>
</body>
</html>
```

The ObjectDataSource control in Listing 18.14 is bound to the component contained in Listing 18.15. The ObjectDataSource control includes a SelectParameters collection. The SelectParameters collection contains a ControlParameter, which represents the current value of the ddlMovieCategory DropDownList control.

LISTING 18.15   MovieCategories.cs

```
using System;
using System.Data;
using System.Data.SqlClient;
using System.Web.Configuration;

public class MovieCategories
{
    private readonly string _conString;

    public SqlDataReader GetMovies(int categoryId)
    {
        // Create Connection
        SqlConnection con = new SqlConnection(_conString);

        // Create Command
        SqlCommand cmd = new SqlCommand();
        cmd.Connection = con;
        cmd.CommandText = "SELECT Id,Title,Director,DateReleased "
            + " FROM Movies WHERE CategoryId=@CategoryId";

        // Add parameters
        cmd.Parameters.AddWithValue("@CategoryId", categoryId);

        // Return DataReader
        con.Open();
```

18

```
            return cmd.ExecuteReader(CommandBehavior.CloseConnection);
    }

    public SqlDataReader GetCategories()
    {
        // Create Connection
        SqlConnection con = new SqlConnection(_conString);

        // Create Command
        SqlCommand cmd = new SqlCommand();
        cmd.Connection = con;
        cmd.CommandText = "SELECT Id,Name FROM MovieCategories";

        // Return DataReader
        con.Open();
        return cmd.ExecuteReader(CommandBehavior.CloseConnection);
    }

    public MovieCategories()
    {
        _conString =
WebConfigurationManager.ConnectionStrings["Movies"].ConnectionString;
    }
}
```

Passing Objects as Parameters

Passing long lists of parameters to methods can make it difficult to maintain an application. If the list of parameters changes, you need to update every method that accepts the list of parameters. Rather than pass a list of parameters to a method, you can pass a particular object. For example, you can pass a CompanyEmployee object to a method used to update an employee, rather than a list of parameters that represent employee properties.

If you specify a value for an ObjectDataSource control's DataObjectTypeName property, you can pass an object rather than a list of parameters to the methods that an ObjectDataSource represents. In that case, the ObjectDataSource parameters represent properties of the object.

For example, the EmployeeData component in Listing 18.16 contains an InsertEmployee() method for creating a new employee. This method is passed an instance of the CompanyEmployee object that represents a particular employee. The CompanyEmployee class also is included in Listing 18.16.

LISTING 18.16 `EmployeeData.cs`

```csharp
using System;
using System.Data;
using System.Data.SqlClient;
using System.Collections.Generic;
using System.Web.Configuration;

public class EmployeeData
{
    string _connectionString;

    public void UpdateEmployee(CompanyEmployee employeeToUpdate)
    {
        // Initialize ADO.NET objects
        SqlConnection con = new SqlConnection(_connectionString);
        SqlCommand cmd = new SqlCommand();
        cmd.CommandText = "UPDATE Employees SET FirstName=@FirstName," +
            "LastName=@LastName,Phone=@Phone WHERE Id=@Id";
        cmd.Connection = con;

        // Create parameters
        cmd.Parameters.AddWithValue("@Id", employeeToUpdate.Id);
        cmd.Parameters.AddWithValue("@FirstName", employeeToUpdate.FirstName);
        cmd.Parameters.AddWithValue("@LastName", employeeToUpdate.LastName);
        cmd.Parameters.AddWithValue("@Phone", employeeToUpdate.Phone);

        // Execute command
        using (con)
        {
            con.Open();
            cmd.ExecuteNonQuery();
        }
    }

    public List<CompanyEmployee> GetEmployees()
    {
        List<CompanyEmployee> employees = new List<CompanyEmployee>();

        SqlConnection con = new SqlConnection(_connectionString);
        SqlCommand cmd = new SqlCommand();
        cmd.CommandText = "SELECT Id,FirstName,LastName,Phone FROM Employees";
        cmd.Connection = con;
        using (con)
        {
            con.Open();
```

18

```csharp
            SqlDataReader reader = cmd.ExecuteReader();
            while (reader.Read())
            {
                CompanyEmployee newEmployee = new CompanyEmployee();
                newEmployee.Id = (int)reader["Id"];
                newEmployee.FirstName = (string)reader["FirstName"];
                newEmployee.LastName = (string)reader["LastName"];
                newEmployee.Phone = (string)reader["Phone"];
                employees.Add(newEmployee);
            }
        }
        return employees;
    }


    public EmployeeData()
    {
        _connectionString =
WebConfigurationManager.ConnectionStrings["Employees"].ConnectionString;
    }
}

public class CompanyEmployee
{
    private int _id;
    private string _firstName;
    private string _lastName;
    private string _phone;

    public int Id
    {
        get { return _id; }
        set { _id = value; }
    }

    public string FirstName
    {
        get { return _firstName; }
        set { _firstName = value; }
    }

    public string LastName
    {
        get { return _lastName; }
        set { _lastName = value; }
    }
```

```
    public string Phone
    {
        get { return _phone; }
        set { _phone = value; }
    }
}
```

The page in Listing 18.17 contains a DetailsView control and an ObjectDataSource control. The DetailsView control enables you to update existing employees in the Employees database table.

LISTING 18.17 UpdateEmployees.aspx

```
<%@ Page Language="C#" %>
<!DOCTYPE html PUBLIC "-//W3C//DTD XHTML 1.1//EN"
"http://www.w3.org/TR/xhtml11/DTD/xhtml11.dtd">
<html xmlns="http://www.w3.org/1999/xhtml" >
<head id="Head1" runat="server">
    <title>Update Employees</title>
</head>
<body>
    <form id="form1" runat="server">
    <div>

    <asp:DetailsView ID="DetailsView1"
        DataSourceID="srcEmployees"
        DataKeyNames="Id"
        AutoGenerateRows="True"
        AutoGenerateEditButton="True"
        AllowPaging="true"
        Runat="server" />

    <asp:ObjectDataSource
        id="srcEmployees"
        TypeName="EmployeeData"
        DataObjectTypeName="CompanyEmployee"
        SelectMethod="GetEmployees"
        UpdateMethod="UpdateEmployee"
        Runat="server" />

    </div>
    </form>
</body>
</html>
```

18

The ObjectDataSource control includes a DataObjectTypeName property. This property contains the name of an object used with the UpdateEmployee() method. When the UpdateEmployee() method is called, an instance of the CompanyEmployee component is created and passed to the method.

> **NOTE**
>
> The DataObjectTypeName property has an effect on only the methods represented by the InsertMethod, UpdateMethod, and DeleteMethod properties. It does not have an effect on the method represented by the SelectMethod property.

There is one important limitation when using the DataObjectTypeName property. The object represented by this property must have a parameterless constructor. For example, you could not use the following CompanyEmployee class with the DataObjectTypeName property:

```
public class CompanyEmployee
{
    private string _firstName;

    public string FirstName
    {
        get
        {
            return _firstName;
        }
    }

    public void CompanyEmployee(string firstName)
    {
        _firstName = firstName;
    }
}
```

The problem with this class is that it initializes its FirstName property in its constructor. Its constructor requires a firstName parameter. Instead, you need to use a class that looks like this:

```
public class CompanyEmployee
{
    private string _firstName;
```

```
public string FirstName
{
    get
    {
        return _firstName;
    }
    set
    {
        _firstName = value;
    }
}
}
```

This class has a parameterless constructor. The `FirstName` property is a read/write property.

If you have the need, you can get around this limitation by handling the `Inserting`, `Updating`, or `Deleting` event. When you handle one of these events, you can pass any object that you need to a method. These events are discussed later in this chapter in the section "Handling `ObjectDataSource` Events."

Paging, Sorting, and Filtering Data with the ObjectDataSource Control

The `ObjectDataSource` control provides you with two options for paging and sorting database data. You can take advantage of either user interface or data source paging and sorting. The first option is easy to configure, and the second option has much better performance. In this section, you learn how to take advantage of both options.

You also learn how to take advantage of the `ObjectDataSource` control's support for filtering. When you combine filtering with caching, you can improve the performance of your data-driven web pages dramatically.

User Interface Paging

Imagine that you want to use a `GridView` control to display the results of a database query in multiple pages. The easiest way to do this is to take advantage of user interface paging.

For example, the page in Listing 18.18 uses a `GridView` and `ObjectDataSource` control to display the records from the Movies database table in multiple pages (see Figure 18.4).

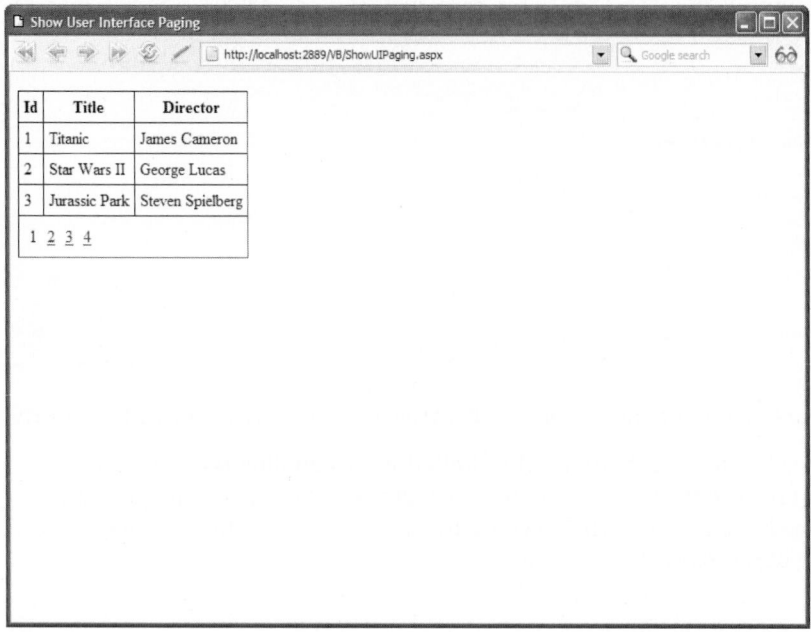

FIGURE 18.4   Displaying multiple pages with user interface paging.

LISTING 18.18   `ShowUIPaging.aspx`

```
<%@ Page Language="C#" %>
<!DOCTYPE html PUBLIC "-//W3C//DTD XHTML 1.1//EN"
"http://www.w3.org/TR/xhtml11/DTD/xhtml11.dtd">
<html xmlns="http://www.w3.org/1999/xhtml" >
<head id="Head1" runat="server">
    <style type="text/css">
        .movies td,.movies th
        {
            padding:5px;
        }
    </style>
    <title>Show User Interface Paging</title>
</head>
<body>
    <form id="form1" runat="server">
    <div>

    <asp:GridView
        id="grdMovies"
        DataSourceID="srcMovies"
        AllowPaging="true"
        PageSize="3"
```

```
            CssClass="movies"
            Runat="server" />

    <asp:ObjectDataSource
        id="srcMovies"
        TypeName="MovieUIPaging"
        SelectMethod="GetMoviesDataSet"
        Runat="server" />

    </div>
    </form>
</body>
</html>
```

The `GridView` control in Listing 18.18 includes an `AllowPaging` property set to the value `True`. Setting this property enables user interface paging.

The `ObjectDataSource` control in Listing 18.18 represents the `MovieUIPaging` component in Listing 18.19. This component includes a `GetMoviesDataSet()` method that returns an ADO.NET `DataSet` object.

To take advantage of user interface paging, you must bind the `GridView` control to the right type of data source., which includes a collection, a `DataSet`, a `DataTable`, and a `DataView`. The right type of data source does not include, for example, a `DataReader`.

LISTING 18.19 MovieUIPaging.cs

```
using System;
using System.Data;
using System.Data.SqlClient;
using System.Web.Configuration;

public class MovieUIPaging
{
    private readonly string _conString;

    public DataSet GetMoviesDataSet()
    {
        // Create DataAdapter
        string commandText = "SELECT Id,Title,Director FROM Movies";
        SqlDataAdapter dad = new SqlDataAdapter(commandText, _conString);

        // Return DataSet
        DataSet dstMovies = new DataSet();
        using (dad)
        {
```

```
            dad.Fill(dstMovies);
        }
        return dstMovies;
    }


    public MovieUIPaging()
    {
        _conString =
➥WebConfigurationManager.ConnectionStrings["Movies"].ConnectionString;
    }
}
```

User interface paging is convenient because you can enable it by setting a single property; however, there is a significant drawback to this type of paging. When user interface paging is enabled, all the movie records must be loaded into server memory. If the Movies database table contains 3 billion records, and you display 3 records a page, all 3 billion records must be loaded to display the 3 records. This places an incredible burden on both the web server and database server. In the next section, you learn how to use data source paging, which enables you to work efficiently with large sets of records.

Data Source Paging

Data source paging enables you to write custom logic for retrieving pages of database records. You can perform the paging in the component, a stored procedure, or a LINQ to SQL query.

If you want the best performance, you should write your paging logic in either a stored procedure or a LINQ query. We examine both approaches in this section.

> **NOTE**
>
> Chapter 20 is devoted to the topic of LINQ.

The page in Listing 18.20 contains an ObjectDataSource control with data source paging enabled.

LISTING 18.20   ShowDSPaging.aspx

```
<%@ Page Language="C#" %>
<!DOCTYPE html PUBLIC "-//W3C//DTD XHTML 1.1//EN"
    "http://www.w3.org/TR/xhtml11/DTD/xhtml11.dtd">
<html xmlns="http://www.w3.org/1999/xhtml" >
<head id="Head1" runat="server">
    <style type="text/css">
```

```
        .movies td,.movies th
        {
            padding:5px;
        }
    </style>
    <title>Show Data Source Paging</title>
</head>
<body>
    <form id="form1" runat="server">
    <div>

    <asp:GridView
        id="grdMovies"
        DataSourceID="srcMovies"
        AllowPaging="true"
        PageSize="3"
        CssClass="movies"
        Runat="server" />

    <asp:ObjectDataSource
        id="srcMovies"
        TypeName="MoviesDSPaging"
        SelectMethod="GetMovies"
        SelectCountMethod="GetMovieCount"
        EnablePaging="True"
        Runat="server" />

    </div>
    </form>
</body>
</html>
```

The ObjectDataSource control includes an EnablePaging property that has the value True.
The ObjectDataSource also includes a SelectCountMethod property that represents the
name of a method that retrieves a record count from the data source.

Furthermore, that the GridView control includes both an AllowPaging and PageSize property. Even when using data source paging, you need to enable the AllowPaging property
for the GridView so that the GridView can render its paging user interface.

When an ObjectDataSource control has its EnablePaging property set to the value True,
the ObjectDataSource passes additional parameters when calling the method represented
by its SelectMethod property. The two additional parameters are named StartRowIndex
and MaximumRows.

Now that we have the page setup for data source paging, we need to create the component. Let's start by using a LINQ to SQL query. This approach is the easiest and recommended way. The component in Listing 18.21 uses LINQ to SQL queries to implement both the GetMovies() and GetMovieCount() methods.

LISTING 18.21   MoviesLINQPaging.cs

```
using System;
using System.Collections.Generic;
using System.Linq;
using System.Data.Linq;
using System.Web;

public class MoviesDSPaging
{
    public static IEnumerable<Movie> GetMovies(int startRowIndex, int maximumRows)
    {
        MyDatabaseDataContext db = new MyDatabaseDataContext();
        return db.Movies.Skip(startRowIndex).Take(maximumRows);
    }

    public static int GetMovieCount()
    {
        HttpContext context = HttpContext.Current;
        if (context.Cache["MovieCount"] == null)
            context.Cache["MovieCount"] = GetMovieCountFromDB();
        return (int)context.Cache["MovieCount"];
    }

    private static int GetMovieCountFromDB()
    {
        MyDatabaseDataContext db = new MyDatabaseDataContext();
        return db.Movies.Count();
    }
}
```

Before you can use the component in Listing 18.21, you need to create a DataContext named MyDatabaseDataContext. You can create this DataContext by selecting Website, Add New Item, and adding a new LINQ to SQL Classes item to your website. Name the new LINQ to SQL Classes item MyDatabase.dbml. Next, after the LINQ to SQL Designer opens, drag the Movies database table from the Database Explorer window onto the Designer surface.

> **NOTE**
>
> Unfortunately, when you drag the Movies database table onto the LINQ to SQL Designer surface, the Designer may create a new entity named Movy. The Designer is attempting to singularize the word and it fails badly. You must rename the entity to Movie in the Properties window.

You are not required to use LINQ to SQL when you want to implement data source paging. As an alternative to LINQ to SQL, you can perform your paging logic within a SQL stored procedure. The component in Listing 18.22 contains ADO.NET code instead of LINQ to SQL queries.

LISTING 18.22   MoviesSQLPaging.cs

```csharp
using System;
using System.Web;
using System.Data;
using System.Data.SqlClient;
using System.Web.Configuration;

public class MoviesDSPaging
{
    private static readonly string _conString;

    public static SqlDataReader GetMovies(int startRowIndex, int maximumRows)
    {
        // Initialize connection
        SqlConnection con = new SqlConnection(_conString);

        // Initialize command
        SqlCommand cmd = new SqlCommand();
        cmd.Connection = con;
        cmd.CommandText = "GetPagedMovies";
        cmd.CommandType = CommandType.StoredProcedure;

        // Add ADO.NET parameters
        cmd.Parameters.AddWithValue("@StartRowIndex", startRowIndex);
        cmd.Parameters.AddWithValue("@MaximumRows", maximumRows);

        // Execute command
        con.Open();
        return cmd.ExecuteReader(CommandBehavior.CloseConnection);
    }
```

18

```
    public static int GetMovieCount()
    {
        HttpContext context = HttpContext.Current;
        if (context.Cache["MovieCount"] == null)
            context.Cache["MovieCount"] = GetMovieCountFromDB();
        return (int)context.Cache["MovieCount"];
    }

    private static int GetMovieCountFromDB()
    {
        int result = 0;

        // Initialize connection
        SqlConnection con = new SqlConnection(_conString);

        // Initialize command
        SqlCommand cmd = new SqlCommand();
        cmd.Connection = con;
        cmd.CommandText = "SELECT Count(*) FROM Movies";

        // Execute command
        using (con)
        {
            con.Open();
            result = (int)cmd.ExecuteScalar();
        }
        return result;
    }


    static MoviesDSPaging()
    {
        _conString =
➥WebConfigurationManager.ConnectionStrings["Movies"].ConnectionString;
    }

}
```

To improve performance, the GetMovieCount() method attempts to retrieve the total count of movie records from the server cache. If the record count cannot be retrieved from the cache, the count is retrieved from the database.

The GetMovies() method calls a stored procedure named GetPagedMovies to retrieve a particular page of movies. The StartRowIndex and MaximumRows parameters are passed to the stored procedure. The GetPagedMovies stored procedure is contained in Listing 18.23.

LISTING 18.23 `GetPagedMovies.sql`

```sql
CREATE PROCEDURE dbo.GetPagedMovies
(
    @StartRowIndex INT,
    @MaximumRows INT
)
AS


-- Create a temp table to store the select results
CREATE TABLE #PageIndex
(
    IndexId INT IDENTITY (1, 1) NOT NULL,
    RecordId INT
)


-- INSERT into the temp table
INSERT INTO #PageIndex (RecordId)
SELECT Id FROM Movies

-- Get a page of movies
SELECT
    Id,
    Title,
    Director,
    DateReleased
FROM
    Movies
    INNER JOIN #PageIndex WITH (nolock)
    ON Movies.Id = #PageIndex.RecordId
WHERE
    #PageIndex.IndexID > @startRowIndex
    AND #PageIndex.IndexID < (@startRowIndex + @maximumRows + 1)
ORDER BY
    #PageIndex.IndexID
```

The `GetPagedMovies` stored procedure returns a particular page of database records. The stored procedure creates a temporary table named #PageIndex that contains two columns: an identity column and a column that contains the primary key values from the Movies database table. The temporary table fills in any holes in the primary key column that might result from deleting records.

Next, the stored procedure retrieves a certain range of records from the #PageIndex table and joins the results with the Movies database table. The end result is that only a single page of database records is returned.

18

When you open the page in Listing 18.20, the `GridView` displays its paging interface, which you can use to navigate between different pages of records (see Figure 18.5).

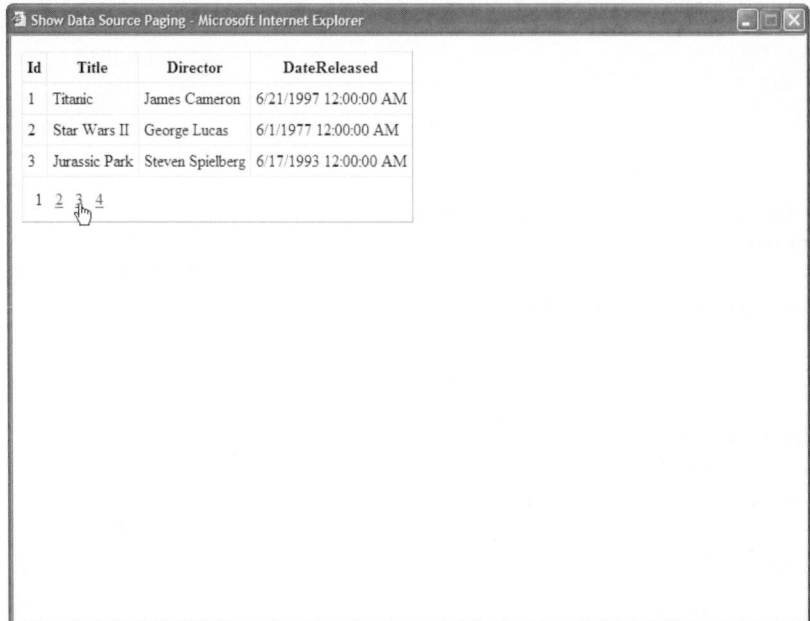

FIGURE 18.5   Displaying multiple pages with data source paging.

If temporary tables make you anxious, you have an alternative when working with Microsoft SQL Server 2005 or 2008. You can take advantage of the new `ROW_NUMBER()` function to select a range of rows. The `ROW_NUMBER()` function automatically calculates the sequential number of a row within a resultset.

The modified stored procedure in Listing 18.24 does the same thing as the stored procedure in Listing 18.23. However, the modified stored procedure avoids any temporary tables.

LISTING 18.24   GetPagedMovies2005.sql

```
CREATE PROCEDURE dbo.GetPagedMovies2005
(
    @StartRowIndex INT,
    @MaximumRows INT
)
AS

WITH OrderedMovies  AS
(
SELECT
    Id,
    ROW_NUMBER() OVER (ORDER BY Id) AS RowNumber
FROM Movies
)

SELECT
    OrderedMovies.RowNumber,
    Movies.Id,
    Movies.Title,
    Movies.Director
FROM
    OrderedMovies
    JOIN Movies
    ON OrderedMovies.Id = Movies.Id
WHERE
    RowNumber BETWEEN (@StartRowIndex + 1) AND (@startRowIndex + @maximumRows + 1)
```

User Interface Sorting

If you need to sort the records displayed by the GridView control, the easiest type of sorting to enable is user interface sorting. When you take advantage of user interface sorting, the records are sorted in the server's memory.

For example, the page in Listing 18.25 contains a GridView that has its AllowSorting property set to the value True. The GridView is bound to an ObjectDataSource that represents the Employees database table (see Figure 18.6).

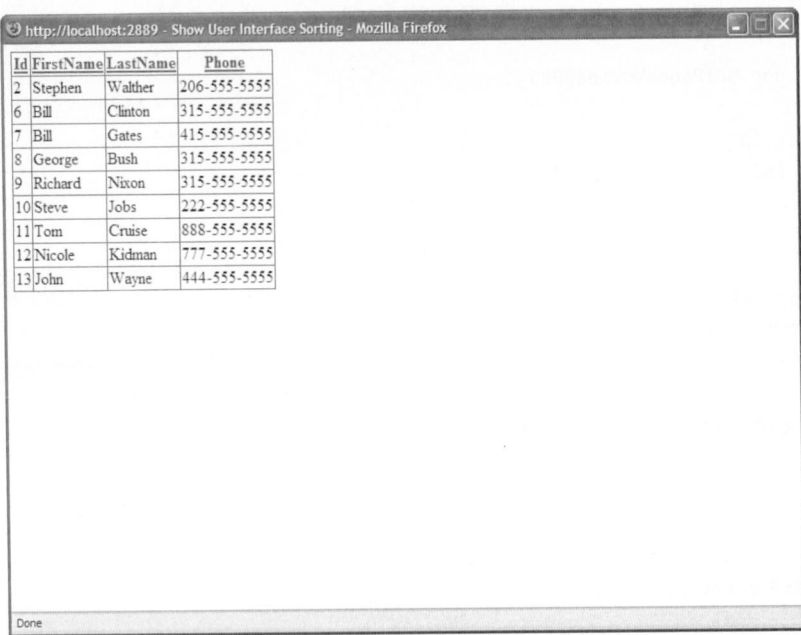

FIGURE 18.6   Sorting records with user interface sorting.

LISTING 18.25   ShowUISorting.aspx

```
<%@ Page Language="C#" %>
<!DOCTYPE html PUBLIC "-//W3C//DTD XHTML 1.1//EN"
"http://www.w3.org/TR/xhtml11/DTD/xhtml11.dtd">
<html xmlns="http://www.w3.org/1999/xhtml" >
<head id="Head1" runat="server">
    <title>Show User Interface Sorting</title>
</head>
<body>
    <form id="form1" runat="server">
    <div>

    <asp:GridView
        id="grdEmployees"
        DataSourceID="srcEmployees"
        AllowSorting="True"
        Runat="server" />

    <asp:ObjectDataSource
        id="srcEmployees"
        TypeName="EmployeesUISorting"
        SelectMethod="GetEmployees"
        Runat="server" />
```

```
    </div>
    </form>
</body>
</html>
```

The `ObjectDataSource` control in Listing 18.25 is bound to the component in Listing 18.26. The `GetEmployees()` method returns an ADO.NET `DataSet` object. When taking advantage of user interface sorting, the `ObjectDataSource` control must represent the right type of data source. The right type of data source includes `DataSet`, `DataTable`, and `DataView` controls.

LISTING 18.26 `EmployeesUISorting.cs`

```csharp
using System;
using System.Data;
using System.Data.SqlClient;
using System.Web.Configuration;

public class EmployeesUISorting
{
    private static readonly string _conString;

    public static DataSet GetEmployees()
    {
        // Initialize ADO.NET objects
        string selectText = "SELECT Id,FirstName,LastName,Phone FROM Employees";
        SqlDataAdapter dad = new SqlDataAdapter(selectText, _conString);
        DataSet dstEmployees = new DataSet();

        // Fill the DataSet
        using (dad)
        {
            dad.Fill(dstEmployees);
        }
        return dstEmployees;
    }

    static EmployeesUISorting()
    {
        _conString =
➥WebConfigurationManager.ConnectionStrings["Employees"].ConnectionString;
    }

}
```

18

User interface sorting is convenient. You can enable this type of sorting by setting a single property of the GridView control. Unfortunately, just as with user interface paging, some serious performance drawbacks result from user interface sorting. All the records from the underlying database must be loaded and sorted in memory. This is a particular problem when you want to enable both sorting and paging at the same time. In the next section, you learn how to implement data source sorting, which avoids this performance issue.

Data Source Sorting

Imagine that you are working with a database table that contains 3 billion records and you want to enable users to both sort the records and page through the records contained in this table. In that case, you want to implement both data source sorting and paging.

The page in Listing 18.27 contains a GridView and ObjectDataSource control. The GridView has both its AllowSorting and AllowPaging properties enabled (see Figure 18.7).

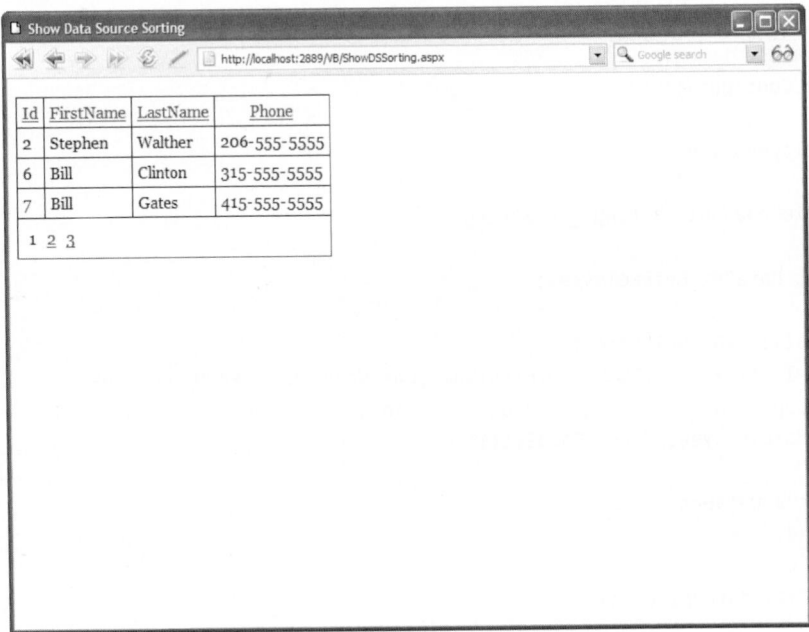

FIGURE 18.7   Paging and sorting database records.

LISTING 18.27   ShowDSSorting.aspx

```
<%@ Page Language="C#" %>
<!DOCTYPE html PUBLIC "-//W3C//DTD XHTML 1.1//EN"
  "http://www.w3.org/TR/xhtml11/DTD/xhtml11.dtd">
<html xmlns="http://www.w3.org/1999/xhtml" >
<head id="Head1" runat="server">
```

```
    <style type="text/css">
    .employees td,.employees th
    {
        font:16px Georgia,Serif;
        padding:5px;
    }
    a
    {
        color:blue;
    }
    </style>
    <title>Show Data Source Sorting</title>
</head>
<body>
    <form id="form1" runat="server">
    <div>

    <asp:GridView
        id="grdEmployees"
        DataSourceID="srcEmployees"
        AllowSorting="true"
        AllowPaging="true"
        PageSize="3"
        CssClass="employees"
        Runat="server" />

    <asp:ObjectDataSource
        id="srcEmployees"
        TypeName="EmployeesDSSorting"
        SelectMethod="GetEmployees"
        SelectCountMethod="GetEmployeeCount"
        EnablePaging="true"
        SortParameterName="sortExpression"
        Runat="server" />

    </div>
    </form>
</body>
</html>
```

The `ObjectDataSource` control in Listing 18.27 represents the `EmployeesDSSorting`
component in Listing 18.28. The `ObjectDataSource` control includes a `SortParameterName`
property. When this property is present, the `ObjectDataSource` control uses data source
sorting instead of user interface sorting.

LISTING 18.28   EmployeesDSSorting.vb

```vb
Imports System
Imports System.Data
Imports System.Data.SqlClient
Imports System.Web.Configuration

Public Class EmployeesDSSorting

    Private Shared ReadOnly _conString As String

    Public Shared Function GetEmployees(ByValsortExpression As String, ByVal
startRowIndex As Integer, ByVal maximumRows As Integer) As SqlDataReader
        ' Initialize connection
        Dim con As New SqlConnection(_conString)

        ' Initialize command
        Dim cmd As New SqlCommand()
        cmd.Connection = con
        cmd.CommandText = "GetSortedEmployees"
        cmd.CommandType = CommandType.StoredProcedure

        ' Create parameters
        cmd.Parameters.AddWithValue("@SortExpression", sortExpression)
        cmd.Parameters.AddWithValue("@StartRowIndex", startRowIndex)
        cmd.Parameters.AddWithValue("@MaximumRows", maximumRows)

        ' Execute command
        con.Open()
        Return cmd.ExecuteReader(CommandBehavior.CloseConnection)
    End Function


    Public Shared Function GetEmployeeCount() As Integer
        Dim context As HttpContext = HttpContext.Current
        If context.Cache("EmployeeCount") Is Nothing Then
            context.Cache("EmployeeCount") = GetEmployeeCountFromDB()
        End If
        Return CType(context.Cache("EmployeeCount"), Integer)
    End Function

    Private Shared Function GetEmployeeCountFromDB() As Integer
        Dim result As Integer = 0
```

```
    ' Initialize connection
    Dim con As SqlConnection = New SqlConnection(_conString)

    ' Initialize command
    Dim cmd As SqlCommand = New SqlCommand()
    cmd.Connection = con
    cmd.CommandText = "SELECT Count(*) FROM Employees"

    ' Execute command
    Using con
        con.Open()
        result = CType(cmd.ExecuteScalar(), Integer)
    End Using
    Return result
End Function



Shared Sub New()
    _conString =
➥WebConfigurationManager.ConnectionStrings("Employees").ConnectionString
    End Sub

End Class
```

The GetEmployees() method in the component in Listing 18.28 calls a stored procedure to sort and page records. The stored procedure, named GetSortedEmployees, returns a sorted page of records from the Employees database table. This stored procedure is contained in Listing 18.29.

LISTING 18.29   GetSortedEmployees.sql

```
CREATE PROCEDURE GetSortedEmployees
(
    @SortExpression NVarChar(100),
    @StartRowIndex INT,
    @MaximumRows INT
)
AS

-- Create a temp table to store the select results
CREATE TABLE #PageIndex
(
    IndexId INT IDENTITY (1, 1) NOT NULL,
    RecordId INT
```

```
)

-- INSERT into the temp table
INSERT INTO #PageIndex (RecordId)
SELECT Id FROM Employees
ORDER BY
CASE WHEN @SortExpression='Id' THEN Id END ASC,
CASE WHEN @SortExpression='Id DESC' THEN Id END DESC,
CASE WHEN @SortExpression='FirstName' THEN FirstName END ASC,
CASE WHEN @SortExpression='FirstName DESC' THEN FirstName END DESC,
CASE WHEN @SortExpression='LastName' THEN LastName END ASC,
CASE WHEN @SortExpression='LastName DESC' THEN LastName END DESC,
CASE WHEN @SortExpression='Phone' THEN Phone END ASC,
CASE WHEN @SortExpression='Phone DESC' THEN Phone END DESC

-- Get a page of records
SELECT
    Id,
    FirstName,
    LastName,
    Phone
FROM
    Employees
    INNER JOIN #PageIndex WITH (nolock)
    ON Employees.Id = #PageIndex.RecordId
WHERE
    #PageIndex.IndexID > @StartRowIndex
    AND #PageIndex.IndexID < (@StartRowIndex + @MaximumRows + 1)
ORDER BY
    #PageIndex.IndexID
```

The stored procedure in Listing 18.29 uses SQL CASE functions to sort the records before they are added to the temporary table. Unfortunately, you can't use a parameter with an ORDER BY clause, so the sort columns must be hard-coded in the CASE functions. Next, a page of records is selected from the temporary table.

NOTE

As an alternative to the data source sorting method described in this section, you can use LINQ to SQL. For more information on LINQ to SQL, see Chapter 20.

Filtering Data

You can supply the ObjectDataSource control with a filter expression. The filter expression is applied to the data returned by the control's select method. A filter is particularly useful when used in combination with caching. You can load all the data into the cache and then apply different filters to the cached data.

> **NOTE**
>
> You learn how to cache data with the ObjectDataSource control in Chapter 29, "Caching Application Pages and Data."

For example, the page in Listing 18.30 contains a DropDownList and GridView control. The DropDownList displays a list of movie categories, and the GridView displays matching movies (see Figure 18.8).

FIGURE 18.8   Filtering movies with the ObjectDataSource control.

LISTING 18.30   ShowFilteredMovies.aspx

```
<%@ Page Language="C#" %>
<!DOCTYPE html PUBLIC "-//W3C//DTD XHTML 1.1//EN"
    "http://www.w3.org/TR/xhtml11/DTD/xhtml11.dtd">
<html xmlns="http://www.w3.org/1999/xhtml" >
<head id="Head1" runat="server">
    <title>Show Filtered Movies</title>
</head>
<body>
    <form id="form1" runat="server">
    <div>

    <asp:DropDownList
        id="ddlMovieCategory"
        DataSourceID="srcMovieCategories"
        DataTextField="Name"
        DataValueField="Id"
        Runat="server" />
    <asp:Button
        id="btnSelect"
        Text="Select"
        Runat="server" />

    <hr />

    <asp:GridView
        id="grdMovies"
        DataSourceID="srcMovies"
        AutoGenerateColumns="false"
        Runat="server">
        <Columns>
        <asp:BoundField
            DataField="Title"
            HeaderText="Movie Title" />
        <asp:BoundField
            DataField="Director"
            HeaderText="Movie Director" />
        </Columns>
    </asp:GridView>

    <asp:ObjectDataSource
        id="srcMovieCategories"
        TypeName="FilterMovies"
        SelectMethod="GetMovieCategories"
```

```
        EnableCaching="true"
        CacheDuration="Infinite"
        Runat="server" />

    <asp:ObjectDataSource
        id="srcMovies"
        TypeName="FilterMovies"
        SelectMethod="GetMovies"
        EnableCaching="true"
        CacheDuration="Infinite"
        FilterExpression="CategoryID={0}"
        Runat="server">
        <FilterParameters>
        <asp:ControlParameter
            Name="Category"
            ControlID="ddlMovieCategory" />
        </FilterParameters>
    </asp:ObjectDataSource>


    </div>
    </form>
</body>
</html>
```

Both `ObjectDataSource` controls in Listing 18.30 have caching enabled. Furthermore, the second `ObjectDataSource` control includes a `FilterExpression` property that filters the cached data, using the selected movie category from the `DropDownList` control.

Both `ObjectDataSource` controls represent the component in Listing 18.31.

LISTING 18.31 FilterMovies.cs

```
using System;
using System.Web;
using System.Data;
using System.Data.SqlClient;
using System.Web.Configuration;

public class FilterMovies
{
    private readonly string _conString;

    public DataSet GetMovies()
    {
        // Initialize connection
```

18

```
        SqlConnection con = new SqlConnection(_conString);

        // Initialize DataAdapter
        string commandText = "SELECT Title,Director,CategoryId FROM Movies";
        SqlDataAdapter dad = new SqlDataAdapter(commandText, con);

        // Return DataSet
        DataSet dstMovies = new DataSet();
        using (con)
        {
            dad.Fill(dstMovies);
        }
        return dstMovies;
    }

    public DataSet GetMovieCategories()
    {
        // Initialize connection
        SqlConnection con = new SqlConnection(_conString);

        // Initialize DataAdapter
        string commandText = "SELECT Id,Name FROM MovieCategories";
        SqlDataAdapter dad = new SqlDataAdapter(commandText, con);

        // Return DataSet
        DataSet dstCategories = new DataSet();
        using (con)
        {
            dad.Fill(dstCategories);
        }
        return dstCategories;
    }

    public FilterMovies()
    {
        _conString =
➥WebConfigurationManager.ConnectionStrings["Movies"].ConnectionString;
    }
}
```

The ObjectDataSource enables you to filter data only when the data is represented by a DataSet, DataTable, or DataView object. This means that if you use filtering, the data must be returned as one of these objects.

> **NOTE**
>
> Behind the scenes, the `ObjectDataSource` control uses the `DataView.RowFilter` property to filter database rows. You can find detailed documentation on proper filter syntax by looking up the `DataColumn.Expression` property in the .NET Framework SDK Documentation.

Handling `ObjectDataSource` Control Events

The `ObjectDataSource` control supports the following events:

- ▶ **Deleting**—Occurs immediately before the method represented by the `DeleteMethod` property is called.

- ▶ **Deleted**—Occurs immediately after the method represented by the `DeleteMethod` property is called.

- ▶ **Inserting**—Occurs immediately before the method represented by the `InsertMethod` property is called.

- ▶ **Inserted**—Occurs immediately after the method represented by the `InsertMethod` property is called.

- ▶ **Selecting**—Occurs immediately before the method represented by the `SelectMethod` property is called.

- ▶ **Selected**—Occurs immediately after the method represented by the `InsertMethod` property is called.

- ▶ **Updating**—Occurs immediately before the method represented by the `InsertMethod` property is called.

- ▶ **Updated**—Occurs immediately after the method represented by the `InsertMethod` property is called.

- ▶ **Filtering**—Occurs immediately before the filter expression is evaluated.

- ▶ **ObjectCreating**—Occurs immediately before the object represented by the `ObjectDataSource` control is created.

- ▶ **ObjectCreated**—Occurs immediately after the object represented by the `ObjectDataSource` control is created.

- ▶ **ObjectDisposing**—Occurs before the object represented by the `ObjectDataSource` control is destroyed.

Most of these events come in pairs. One event happens immediately before a method is called, and one event happens immediately after a method is called. You can handle these events to modify the parameters and objects represented by an `ObjectDataSource` control.

You can also use these events to handle any errors that might result from calling methods with the ObjectDataSource control.

Adding and Modifying Parameters

You can handle the Selecting, Inserting, Updating, and Deleting events to modify the parameters that are passed to the methods called by the ObjectDataSource control. There are several situations in which you might want to do this.

First, if you work with an existing component, you might need to change the names of the parameters passed to the component. For example, instead of passing a parameter named id to an update method, you might want to rename the parameter to movieId.

Second, you might want to pass additional parameters to the method called. For example, you might need to pass the current username, the current IP address, or the current date and time as a parameter to a method.

For example, imagine that you want to create a guestbook and automatically associate the IP address of the user making an entry with each entry in the guestbook. The page in Listing 18.32 illustrates how you can do this with the help of a FormView control and an ObjectDataSource control (see Figure 18.9).

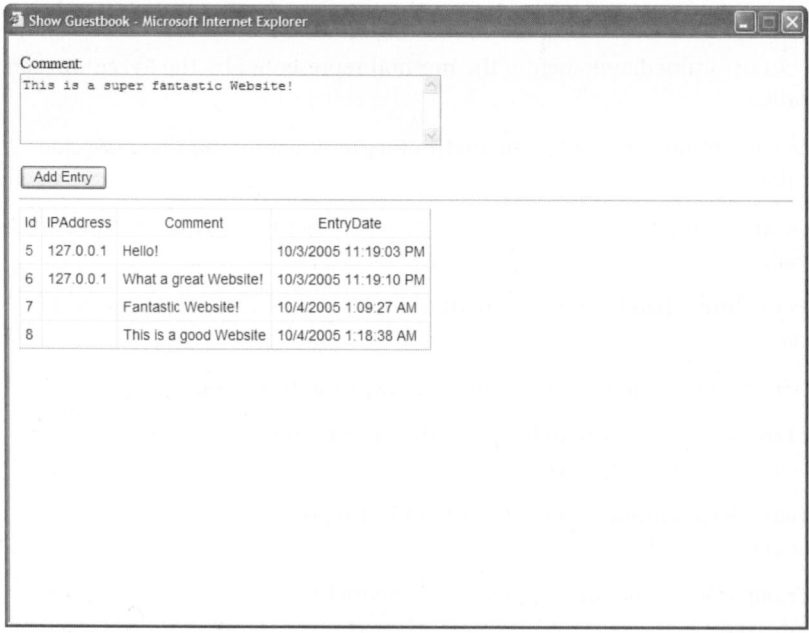

FIGURE 18.9   Displaying a guestbook.

LISTING 18.32   ShowGuestbook.aspx

```
<%@ Page Language="C#" %>
<!DOCTYPE html PUBLIC "-//W3C//DTD XHTML 1.1//EN"
"http://www.w3.org/TR/xhtml11/DTD/xhtml11.dtd">
<script runat="server">

    protected void srcGuestbook_Inserting(object sender,
➥ObjectDataSourceMethodEventArgs e)
    {
        e.InputParameters.Add("IPAddress", Request.UserHostAddress);
    }
</script>
<html xmlns="http://www.w3.org/1999/xhtml">
<head id="Head1" runat="server">
    <style type="text/css">
        .guestbook td,.guestbook th
        {
            padding:5px;
            font:14px Arial,Sans-Serif;
        }
    </style>
    <title>Show Guestbook</title>
</head>
<body>
    <form id="form1" runat="server">
    <div>

    <asp:FormView
        id="frmGuestbook"
        DataSourceID="srcGuestbook"
        DefaultMode="Insert"
        Runat="server">
        <InsertItemTemplate>
        <asp:Label
            ID="lblComment"
            Text="Comment:"
            AssociatedControlID="txtComment"
            Runat="server" />
        <br />
        <asp:TextBox
            id="txtComment"
            Text='<%# Bind("comment") %>'
            TextMode="MultiLine"
            Columns="50"
            Rows="4"
```

```
            Runat="server" />
        <br />
        <asp:Button
            id="btnInsert"
            Text="Add Entry"
            CommandName="Insert"
            Runat="server" />
        </InsertItemTemplate>
    </asp:FormView>

    <hr />

    <asp:GridView
        id="grdGuestbook"
        DataSourceID="srcGuestbook"
        CssClass="guestbook"
        Runat="server" />

    <asp:ObjectDataSource
        id="srcGuestbook"
        TypeName="Guestbook"
        SelectMethod="GetEntries"
        InsertMethod="AddEntry"
        OnInserting="srcGuestbook_Inserting"
        Runat="server" />

    </div>
    </form>
</body>
</html>
```

The page in Listing 18.32 includes an Inserting event handler. When the insert method is called, the IP address of the current user is added to the parameters collection.

The ObjectDataSource control in Listing 18.32 is bound to the Guestbook component in Listing 18.33.

LISTING 18.33   Guestbook.cs

```
using System;
using System.Data;
using System.Data.SqlClient;
using System.Web.Configuration;

public class Guestbook
{
    private string _conString;
```

```
public SqlDataReader GetEntries()
{
    // Initialize connection
    SqlConnection con = new SqlConnection(_conString);

    // Initialize command
    SqlCommand cmd = new SqlCommand();
    cmd.Connection = con;
    cmd.CommandText = "SELECT Id,IPAddress,Comment,EntryDate FROM Guestbook";

    // Execute command
    con.Open();
    return cmd.ExecuteReader(CommandBehavior.CloseConnection);
}

public void AddEntry(string IPAddress, string comment)
{
    // Initialize connection
    SqlConnection con = new SqlConnection(_conString);

    // Initialize command
    SqlCommand cmd = new SqlCommand();
    cmd.Connection = con;
    cmd.CommandText = "INSERT Guestbook (IPAddress,Comment)" +
        " VALUES (@IPAddress, @Comment)";

    // Add ADO.NET parameters
    cmd.Parameters.AddWithValue("@IPAddress", IPAddress);
    cmd.Parameters.AddWithValue("@Comment", comment);

    // Execute command
    using (con)
    {
        con.Open();
        cmd.ExecuteNonQuery();
    }
}

public Guestbook()
{
    _conString =
➥WebConfigurationManager.ConnectionStrings["Guestbook"].ConnectionString;
}

}
```

18

Realize that you can manipulate the parameters collection in any way that you need. You can change the names, types, or values of any of the parameters.

Handling Method Errors

You can handle the Selected, Inserted, Updated, or Deleted events to handle any errors that might result from calling a method. For example, the page in Listing 18.34 handles the Inserting event to capture any errors raised when the method represented by the ObjectDataSource control's InsertMethod property is called.

LISTING 18.34 HandleErrors.aspx

```
<%@ Page Language="C#" %>
<!DOCTYPE html PUBLIC "-//W3C//DTD XHTML 1.1//EN"
"http://www.w3.org/TR/xhtml11/DTD/xhtml11.dtd">
<script runat="server">

    protected void srcMovies_Inserted(object sender,
➥ObjectDataSourceStatusEventArgs e)
    {
        if (e.Exception != null)
        {
            e.ExceptionHandled = true;
            lblError.Text = "Could not insert movie";
        }
    }
</script>

<html xmlns="http://www.w3.org/1999/xhtml" >
<head id="Head1" runat="server">
    <style type="text/css">
        html
        {
            background-color:silver;
        }
        .insertForm
        {
            background-color:white;
        }
        .insertForm td,.insertForm th
        {
            padding:10px;
        }
        .error
        {
            color:red;
```

```
            font:bold 14px Arial,Sans-Serif;
        }
    </style>
    <title>Handle Errors</title>
</head>
<body>
    <form id="form1" runat="server">
    <div>

    <asp:Label
        id="lblError"
        EnableViewState="false"
        CssClass="error"
        Runat="server" />

    <h1>Insert Movie</h1>
    <asp:DetailsView
        id="dtlMovies"
        DataSourceID="srcMovies"
        DefaultMode="Insert"
        AutoGenerateInsertButton="true"
        AutoGenerateRows="false"
        CssClass="insertForm"
        GridLines="None"
        Runat="server">
        <Fields>
        <asp:BoundField
            DataField="Title"
            HeaderText="Title:"/>
        <asp:BoundField
            DataField="Director"
            HeaderText="Director:" />
        </Fields>
    </asp:DetailsView>

    <asp:ObjectDataSource
        id="srcMovies"
        TypeName="InsertMovie"
        InsertMethod="Insert"
        Runat="server" OnInserted="srcMovies_Inserted" />

    </div>
    </form>
</body>
</html>
```

18

In Listing 18.34, the Inserted event handler checks for an exception. If an exception exists, the exception is handled and an error message displays (see Figure 18.10).

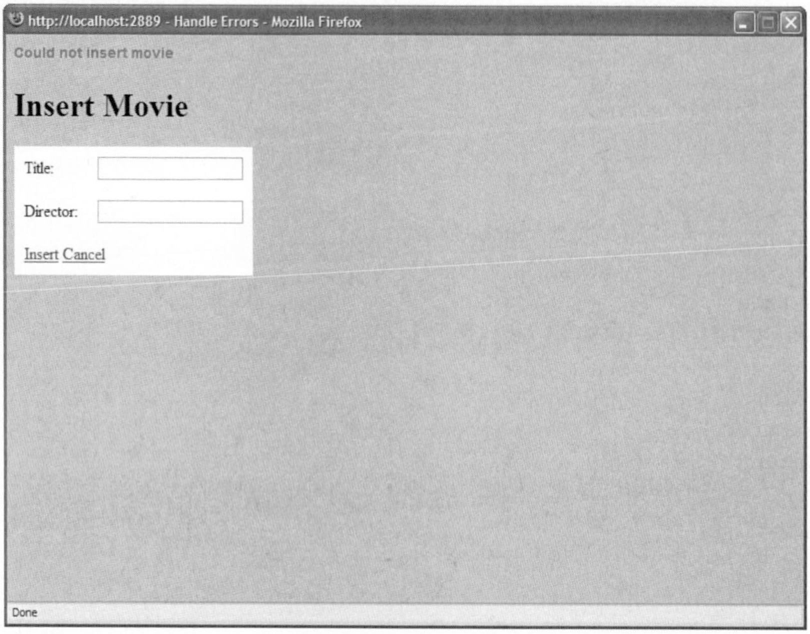

FIGURE 18.10   Handling method errors gracefully.

The page in Listing 18.34 is bound to the component in Listing 18.35.

LISTING 18.35   InsertMovie.cs

```csharp
using System;
using System.Web;
using System.Data;
using System.Data.SqlClient;
using System.Web.Configuration;

public class InsertMovie
{
    private static readonly string _conString;

    public static SqlDataReader GetMovies()
    {
        // Initialize connection
        SqlConnection con = new SqlConnection(_conString);
```

```
    // Initialize command
    SqlCommand cmd = new SqlCommand();
    cmd.Connection = con;
    cmd.CommandText = "SELECT Id,Title,Director FROM Movies";

    // Execute command
    con.Open();
    return cmd.ExecuteReader(CommandBehavior.CloseConnection);
}

public static void Insert(string title, string director)
{
    // Initialize connection
    SqlConnection con = new SqlConnection(_conString);

    // Initialize command
    SqlCommand cmd = new SqlCommand();
    cmd.Connection = con;
    cmd.CommandText = "INSERT Movies (Title,Director)" +
        " VALUES (@Title,@Director)";

    // Add ADO.NET parameters
    cmd.Parameters.AddWithValue("@Title", title);
    cmd.Parameters.AddWithValue("@Director", director);

    // Execute command
    using (con)
    {
        con.Open();
        cmd.ExecuteNonQuery();
    }
}

static InsertMovie()
{
    _conString =
➥WebConfigurationManager.ConnectionStrings["Movies"].ConnectionString;
}

}
```

You can create an exception by entering a new movie record and not supplying a value for one of the fields. For example, the Title column in the Movies database table does not accept null values.

NOTE

Instead of handling errors at the level of the DataSource control, you can handle errors at the level of the DataBound control. For example, the DetailsView control supports an ItemInserted event.

Handling the `ObjectCreating` Event

By default, the ObjectDataSource control can represent only components that have a constructor that does not require any parameters. If you are forced to use a component that does require parameters for its constructor, you can handle the ObjectDataSource control's ObjectCreating event.

For example, the component in Listing 18.36 must be initialized with a movie category parameter. The component returns only movies in the specified category.

LISTING 18.36   MoviesByCategory.cs

```csharp
using System;
using System.Web;
using System.Data;
using System.Data.SqlClient;
using System.Web.Configuration;

public class MoviesByCategory
{
    private readonly string _conString;
    private readonly string _movieCategory;

    public SqlDataReader GetMovies()
    {
        // Initialize connection
        SqlConnection con = new SqlConnection(_conString);

        // Initialize command
        SqlCommand cmd = new SqlCommand();
        cmd.Connection = con;
        cmd.CommandText = "SELECT Title,Director,DateReleased FROM Movies"
            + " JOIN MovieCategories ON Movies.CategoryId=MovieCategories.Id"
            + " WHERE MovieCategories.Name=@CategoryName";

        // Create ADO.NET parameters
        cmd.Parameters.AddWithValue("@CategoryName", _movieCategory);

        // Execute command
        con.Open();
```

```
        return cmd.ExecuteReader(CommandBehavior.CloseConnection);
    }

    public MoviesByCategory(string movieCategory)
    {
        _movieCategory = movieCategory;
        _conString =
➥WebConfigurationManager.ConnectionStrings["Movies"].ConnectionString;
    }
}
```

The page in Listing 18.37 contains an ObjectDataSource control that represents the
MoviesByCategory component. The page includes a handler for the ObjectCreating event
so that it can assign an initialized instance of the MoviesByCategory component to the
ObjectDataSource control.

LISTING 18.37   ShowAdventureMovies.aspx

```
<%@ Page Language="C#" %>
<!DOCTYPE html PUBLIC "-//W3C//DTD XHTML 1.1//EN"
"http://www.w3.org/TR/xhtml11/DTD/xhtml11.dtd">
<script runat="server">

    protected void srcMovies_ObjectCreating(object sender,
➥ObjectDataSourceEventArgs e)
    {
        MoviesByCategory movies = new MoviesByCategory("Adventure");
        e.ObjectInstance = movies;
    }
</script>
<html xmlns="http://www.w3.org/1999/xhtml" >
<head id="Head1" runat="server">
    <title>Adventure Movies</title>
</head>
<body>
    <form id="form1" runat="server">
    <div>

    <h1>Adventure Movies</h1>

    <asp:GridView
        id="grdMovies"
        DataSourceID="srcMovies"
        Runat="server" />
```

```
<asp:ObjectDataSource
    id="srcMovies"
    TypeName="MoviesByCategory"
    SelectMethod="GetMovies"
    OnObjectCreating="srcMovies_ObjectCreating"
    Runat="server" />

    </div>
    </form>
</body>
</html>
```

Even though the `MoviesByCategory` component is initialized in the `ObjectCreating` event handler, you still must assign the name of the component to the `ObjectDataSource` control's `TypeName` property. The `ObjectDataSource` control needs to know what type of object it is representing when it calls its methods.

> **NOTE**
>
> The `ObjectCreating` event is not raised when a shared method is called.

Concurrency and the `ObjectDataSource` Control

Imagine that two users open the same page for editing the records in the movies database table at the same time. By default, if the first user submits changes before the second user, the first user's changes are overwritten. In other words, the last user to submit changes wins.

This default behavior of the `ObjectDataSource` control can be problematic in an environment in which a lot of users work with the same set of data. You can modify this default behavior by modifying the `ObjectDataSource` control's `ConflictDetection` property. This property accepts the following two values:

- ▶ **`CompareAllValues`**—Causes the `ObjectDataSource` control to track both the original and new values of its parameters.

- ▶ **`OverwriteChanges`**—Causes the `ObjectDataSource` to overwrite the original values of its parameters with new values (the default value).

When you set the `ConflictDetection` property to the value `CompareAllValues`, you should add an `OldValuesParameterFormatString` property to the `ObjectDataSource` control. You use this property to indicate how the original values the database columns should be named.

The page in Listing 18.38 contains a GridView and ObjectDataSource control, which you can use to edit the movies in the Movies database table. The ObjectDataSource control includes a ConflictDetection property with the value CompareAllValues and an OldValuesParameterFormatString property with the value original_{0}.

LISTING 18.38   ShowConflictDetection.aspx

```
<%@ Page Language="C#" %>
<!DOCTYPE html PUBLIC "-//W3C//DTD XHTML 1.1//EN"
"http://www.w3.org/TR/xhtml11/DTD/xhtml11.dtd">
<script runat="server">

    protected void srcMovies_Updated(object sender,
➥ObjectDataSourceStatusEventArgs e)
    {
        if (e.Exception != null)
        {
            e.ExceptionHandled = true;
            lblError.Text = "Could not update record";
        }
    }
</script>
<html xmlns="http://www.w3.org/1999/xhtml" >
<head id="Head1" runat="server">
    <style type="text/css">
        .error
        {
            color:red;
            font:bold 16px Arial,Sans-Serif;
        }
        a
        {
            color:blue;
        }
    </style>
    <title>Show Conflict Detection</title>
</head>
<body>
    <form id="form1" runat="server">
    <div>

    <asp:Label
        id="lblError"
        EnableViewState="false"
```

18

```
        CssClass="error"
        Runat="server" />

    <asp:GridView
        id="grdMovies"
        DataSourceID="srcMovies"
        DataKeyNames="Id"
        AutoGenerateEditButton="true"
        Runat="server" />

    <asp:ObjectDataSource
        id="srcMovies"
        ConflictDetection="CompareAllValues"
        OldValuesParameterFormatString="original_{0}"
        TypeName="ConflictedMovies"
        SelectMethod="GetMovies"
        UpdateMethod="UpdateMovie"
        OnUpdated="srcMovies_Updated"
        Runat="server" />

    </div>
    </form>
</body>
</html>
```

The ObjectDataSource control in Listing 18.38 is bound to the component in Listing 18.39.

LISTING 18.39   ConflictedMovies.cs

```
using System;
using System.Data;
using System.Data.SqlClient;
using System.Web.Configuration;

public class ConflictedMovies
{
    private static readonly string _conString;

    public static SqlDataReader GetMovies()
    {
        // Initialize connection
        SqlConnection con = new SqlConnection(_conString);
```

```
        // Initialize command
        SqlCommand cmd = new SqlCommand();
        cmd.Connection = con;
        cmd.CommandText = "SELECT Id,Title,Director FROM Movies";

        // Execute command
        con.Open();
        return cmd.ExecuteReader(CommandBehavior.CloseConnection);
    }

    public static void UpdateMovie(string title, string director,
            string original_title, string original_director, int original_id)
    {
        // Initialize connection
        SqlConnection con = new SqlConnection(_conString);

        // Initialize command
        SqlCommand cmd = new SqlCommand();
        cmd.Connection = con;
        cmd.CommandText = "UPDATE Movies SET Title=@Title,Director=@Director"
            +
 " WHERE Id=@original_Id AND Title=@original_Title AND Director=@original_Director";

        // Create parameters
        cmd.Parameters.AddWithValue("@Title", title);
        cmd.Parameters.AddWithValue("@Director", director);
        cmd.Parameters.AddWithValue("@original_Id", original_id);
        cmd.Parameters.AddWithValue("@original_Title", original_title);
        cmd.Parameters.AddWithValue("@original_Director", original_director);

        using (con)
        {
            con.Open();
            int rowsAffected = cmd.ExecuteNonQuery();
            if (rowsAffected == 0)
                throw new Exception("Could not update movie record");
        }
    }

    static ConflictedMovies()
    {
        _conString =
➥WebConfigurationManager.ConnectionStrings["Movies"].ConnectionString;
    }
}
```

The component in Listing 18.39 includes an `UpdateMovie()` method. This method accepts five parameters: `original_title`, `title`, `original_director`, `director`, and `original_id`.

The `UpdateMovie()` method raises an exception when the original parameter values don't match the current values in the Movies database table. The command executed by the `Command` object looks like this:

```
UPDATE Movies SET Title=@Title, Director=@Director
WHERE Id=@original_id AND Title=@original_Title AND Director=@original_Director
```

This statement updates a row in the database only when the current values from the row match the original values selected from the row. If the original and current values don't match, no records are affected and the `UpdateMovie()` method raises an exception.

Extending the `ObjectDataSource` Control

In this final section, we examine two methods of extending the `ObjectDataSource` control. You learn how to create a custom data source control by deriving a new control from the `ObjectDataSource` control. You also learn how to create custom parameters that can be used with the `ObjectDataSource` and other `DataSource` controls.

Creating a Custom `ObjectDataSource` Control

If you discover that you are declaring an `ObjectDataSource` control with the same properties on multiple pages, it makes sense to derive a new control from the `ObjectDataSource` control that has these properties by default. That way, you can simply declare the derived control in a page.

For example, if you display a list of movies in multiple pages in your website, it would make sense to create a specialized `MovieDataSource` control.

The control in Listing 18.40, named the `MovieDataSource` control, derives from the base `ObjectDataSource` control class. The `MovieDataSource` control represents the `MoviesComponent`, which is also contained in Listing 18.40.

LISTING 18.40   MovieDataSource.cs

```
using System;
using System.Data;
using System.Data.SqlClient;
using System.Web.Configuration;
using System.Web.UI.WebControls;

namespace AspNetUnleashed.Samples
{
```

```
public class MovieDataSource : ObjectDataSource
{
    public MovieDataSource()
    {
        this.TypeName = "AspNetUnleashed.Samples.MoviesComponent";
        this.SelectMethod = "GetMovies";
    }
}

public class MoviesComponent
{
    private readonly string _conString;

    public SqlDataReader GetMovies()
    {
        // Initialize connection
        SqlConnection con = new SqlConnection(_conString);

        // Initialize command
        SqlCommand cmd = new SqlCommand();
        cmd.Connection = con;
        cmd.CommandText = "SELECT Title,Director,DateReleased FROM Movies";

        // Execute command
        con.Open();
        return cmd.ExecuteReader(CommandBehavior.CloseConnection);
    }

    public MoviesComponent()
    {
        _conString =
➥WebConfigurationManager.ConnectionStrings["Movies"].ConnectionString;
    }
}
}
```

The MovieDataSource control initializes the base ObjectDataSource control's TypeName and SelectMethod properties in its constructor. The TypeName is assigned the fully qualified name of the MoviesComponent.

The page in Listing 18.41 illustrates how you can use the MovieDataSource control in a page (see Figure 18.11).

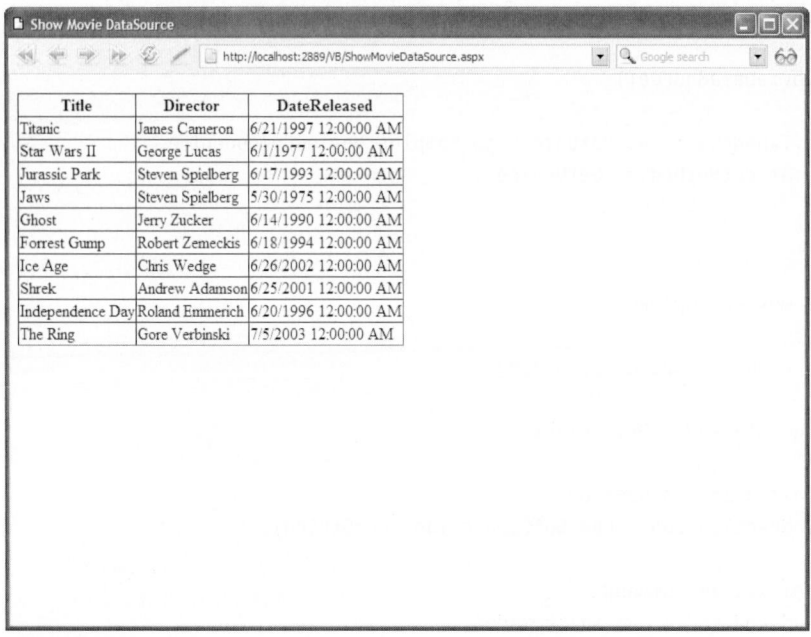

FIGURE 18.11   Using the `MovieDataSource` control to display movies.

LISTING 18.41   ShowMovieDataSource.aspx

```
<%@ Page Language="C#" %>
<%@ Register TagPrefix="custom" Namespace="AspNetUnleashed.Samples" %>
<!DOCTYPE html PUBLIC "-//W3C//DTD XHTML 1.1//EN"
    "http://www.w3.org/TR/xhtml11/DTD/xhtml11.dtd">
<html xmlns="http://www.w3.org/1999/xhtml" >
<head id="Head1" runat="server">
    <title>Show Movie DataSource</title>
</head>
<body>
    <form id="form1" runat="server">
    <div>

    <asp:GridView
        id="grdMovies"
        DataSourceID="srcMovies"
        Runat="server" />

    <custom:MovieDataSource
        id="srcMovies"
        Runat="server" />
```

```
   </div>
   </form>
</body>
</html>
```

The custom control must be registered with a `<%@ Register %>` directive at the top of Listing 18.41. After you register the control, you can simply declare the `MovieDataSource` control in the page to represent the contents of the Movies database table.

> **NOTE**
>
> As an alternative to registering the `MovieDataSource` control in a page, you can register the control for an entire application in the web configuration file within the `<pages>` element.

Creating Custom Parameter Objects

The standard DataSource Parameter objects included in the ASP.NET Framework enable you to represent objects such as query string values, items from Session state, and the values of control properties. If none of the standard Parameter objects satisfy your requirements, you always have the option of creating a custom Parameter object.

You create a custom Parameter object by deriving a new class from the base `Parameter` class. In this section, we create two custom parameters. The first is a `UsernameParameter` that automatically represents the current username. Next is a `PagePropertyParameter` that represents the current value of a property contained in the page.

Creating a Username Parameter

The `UsernameParameter` class is contained in Listing 18.42. The class in Listing 18.42 derives from the Parameter class and overrides the `Evaluate()` method of the base class. The `Evaluate()` method determines what the parameter represents.

LISTING 18.42   UsernameParameter.cs

```csharp
using System;
using System.Web;
using System.Web.UI;
using System.Web.UI.WebControls;

namespace MyControls
{
    public class UsernameParameter : Parameter
    {
        protected override object Evaluate(HttpContext context, Control control)
        {
            if (context != null)
```

```
                return context.User.Identity.Name;
            else
                return null;
        }
    }
}
```

The UsernameParameter returns the current username. The parameter retrieves this information from the current HttpContext passed to the Evaluate() method. The UsernameParameter is used in the page in Listing 18.43.

LISTING 18.43   ShowUsernameParameter.aspx

```
<%@ Page Language="C#" %>
<%@ Register TagPrefix="custom" Namespace="MyControls" %>
<!DOCTYPE html PUBLIC "-//W3C//DTD XHTML 1.1//EN"
    "http://www.w3.org/TR/xhtml11/DTD/xhtml11.dtd">
<html xmlns="http://www.w3.org/1999/xhtml" >
<head id="Head1" runat="server">
    <style type="text/css">
        .guestbook td,.guestbook th
        {
            padding:5px;
            font:14px Arial,Sans-Serif;
        }
    </style>
    <title>Show Username Parameter</title>
</head>
<body>
    <form id="form1" runat="server">
    <div>
    <asp:FormView
        id="frmGuestbook"
        DataSourceID="srcGuestbook"
        DefaultMode="Insert"
        Runat="server">
        <InsertItemTemplate>
        <asp:Label
            ID="lblComment"
            Text="Comment:"
            AssociatedControlID="txtComment"
            Runat="server" />
```

```
        <br />
        <asp:TextBox
            id="txtComment"
            Text='<%# Bind("comment") %>'
            TextMode="MultiLine"
            Columns="50"
            Rows="4"
            Runat="server" />
        <br />
        <asp:Button
            id="btnInsert"
            Text="Add Entry"
            CommandName="Insert"
            Runat="server" />
    </InsertItemTemplate>
</asp:FormView>

<hr />

<asp:GridView
    id="grdGuestbook"
    DataSourceID="srcGuestbook"
    CssClass="guestbook"
    Runat="server" />

<asp:ObjectDataSource
    id="srcGuestbook"
    TypeName="GuestbookComponent"
    SelectMethod="GetEntries"
    InsertMethod="AddEntry"
    Runat="server">
    <InsertParameters>
        <custom:UsernameParameter name="username" />
    </InsertParameters>
</asp:ObjectDataSource>

    </div>
    </form>
</body>
</html>
```

The UsernameParameter is declared in the ObjectDataSource control's InsertParameters collection. When you add a new entry to the guestbook, your username is added automatically (see Figure 18.12).

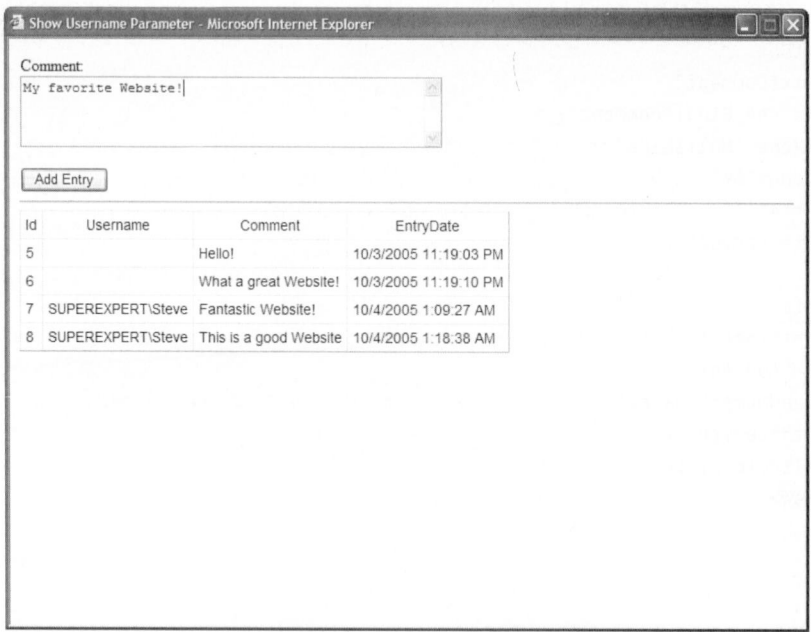

FIGURE 18.12   Inserting records with the `UsernameParameter`.

Creating a Page Property Parameter

`PagePropertyParameter` enables you to represent an arbitrary property of the current page. The property being represented can return whatever type of value you want. The code for the `PagePropertyParameter` is contained in Listing 18.44.

LISTING 18.44   `PagePropertyParameter.cs`

```
using System;
using System.Web;
using System.Web.UI;
using System.Web.UI.WebControls;

namespace MyControls
{
    public class PagePropertyParameter : Parameter
    {
        private string _propertyName;

        protected override object Evaluate(HttpContext context, Control control)
        {
            return DataBinder.Eval(control.Page, PropertyName);
        }
```

```
    public string PropertyName
    {
        get { return _propertyName; }
        set { _propertyName = value; }
    }

}
}
```

The component in Listing 18.44 overrides the `Evaluate` method of the base `Parameter` class. The `DataBinder.Eval()` method is used to return the value of a property of the current page.

The page in Listing 18.45 uses the `PagePropertyParameter` to represent a property of the page named `CurrentUsername`. This property returns the current username.

LISTING 18.45   `ShowPagePropertyParameter.aspx`

```
<%@ Page Language="C#" %>
<%@ Register TagPrefix="custom" Namespace="MyControls" %>
<!DOCTYPE html PUBLIC "-//W3C//DTD XHTML 1.1//EN"
    "http://www.w3.org/TR/xhtml11/DTD/xhtml11.dtd">
<script runat="server">

    Public ReadOnly Property CurrentUsername() As String
        Get
            Return User.Identity.Name
        End Get
    End Property

</script>
<html xmlns="http://www.w3.org/1999/xhtml">
<head id="Head1" runat="server">
    <style type="text/css">
        .guestbook td,.guestbook th
        {
            padding:5px;
            font:14px Arial,Sans-Serif;
        }
    </style>
    <title>Show Page Property Parameter</title>
</head>
<body>
    <form id="form1" runat="server">
    <div>
```

```
<asp:FormView
    id="frmGuestbook"
    DataSourceID="srcGuestbook"
    DefaultMode="Insert"
    Runat="server">
    <InsertItemTemplate>
    <asp:Label
        ID="lblComment"
        Text="Comment:"
        AssociatedControlID="txtComment"
        Runat="server" />
    <br />
    <asp:TextBox
        id="txtComment"
        Text='<%# Bind("comment") %>'
        TextMode="MultiLine"
        Columns="50"
        Rows="4"
        Runat="server" />
    <br />
    <asp:Button
        id="btnInsert"
        Text="Add Entry"
        CommandName="Insert"
        Runat="server" />
    </InsertItemTemplate>
</asp:FormView>

<hr />

<asp:GridView
    id="grdGuestbook"
    DataSourceID="srcGuestbook"
    CssClass="guestbook"
    Runat="server" />

<asp:ObjectDataSource
    id="srcGuestbook"
    TypeName="GuestbookComponent"
    SelectMethod="GetEntries"
    InsertMethod="AddEntry"
    Runat="server">
    <InsertParameters>
    <custom:PagePropertyParameter
        Name="Username"
        PropertyName="CurrentUsername" />
```

```
        </InsertParameters>
    </asp:ObjectDataSource>

    </div>
    </form>
</body>
</html>
```

In Listing 18.45, the `PagePropertyParameter` represents the current username. Because the `PagePropertyParameter` can represent any page property, the parameter could represent any type of value.

Summary

In this chapter, you learned how to use the `ObjectDataSource` control to represent different types of objects. In the first section, you were provided with sample code that demonstrated how you can use the `ObjectDataSource` control to represent a collection, `DataReader`, `DataSet`, a LINQ to SQL query, and a web service.

We also discussed how you can use the `ObjectDataSource` control to page, sort, and filter data. You learned how to implement both user interface paging and data source paging, which enables you to efficiently work with very large sets of records.

Next, we examined how you can handle `ObjectDataSource` control events. You learned how to add and modify the parameters represented by the `ObjectDataSource` control. You also learned how to gracefully handle errors raised when executing an `ObjectDataSource` control method.

Finally, we discussed two methods of extending the `ObjectDataSource` control. You learned how to derive a new control from the base `ObjectDataSource` control to represent specialized data sources such as a Product data source. We also discussed how you can create custom `Parameter` objects that can be used with the `ObjectDataSource` control.

18

CHAPTER 19

Building Data Access Components with ADO.NET

In the previous chapter, you learned how to use the ObjectDataSource control to bind data controls—such as the GridView or DetailsView controls—to a data access component. In this chapter, we shift focus from the ObjectDataSource control to the topic of building data access components.

This chapter provides you with an overview of ADO.NET, which is the main set of classes included in .NET Framework for working with database data. For example, under the covers, the SqlDataSource control uses ADO.NET classes to retrieve data from a SQL Server database.

The classes in ADO.NET Framework support two models of data access: a connected and disconnected model. In the first part, you learn how to take advantage of the connected model of data access. You learn how to use ADO.NET Connection, Command, and DataReader classes to retrieve and modify database data.

In the next part, you learn how to take advantage of the disconnected model of data access represented by ADO.NET DataAdapter, DataTable, DataView, and DataSet classes. You can use these classes to build an in-memory representation of database data.

Finally, at the end of this chapter, we explore two advanced topics. You learn how to take advantage of two important new features included in ADO.NET 2.0. First, you learn how to improve the performance of your database access code by executing asynchronous database commands. You learn how to build asynchronous ASP.NET pages that execute asynchronous ADO.NET commands.

You also learn how to build Microsoft SQL Server database objects, such as stored procedures and user-defined types, by using .NET Framework. For example, you learn how to write a Microsoft SQL Server stored procedure, using C# programming language.

> **NOTE**
>
> If you don't want to get your hands dirty touching any actual SQL or ADO.NET code, skip this chapter and read Chapter 20, "Data Access with LINQ to SQL." LINQ to SQL enables you to access the database without writing any ADO.NET or SQL code.

Connected Data Access

The ADO.NET Framework encompasses a huge number of classes. However, at its heart, it actually consists of the following three classes:

- **Connection**—Enables you to represent a connection to a data source.

- **Command**—Enables you to execute a command against a data source.

- **DataReader**—Enables you to represent data retrieved from a data source.

Most of the other classes in ADO.NET Framework are built from these three classes. These three classes provide you with the fundamental methods of working with database data. They enable you to connect to a database, execute commands against a database, and represent the data returned from a database.

Now that you understand the importance of these three classes, it's safe to tell you that they don't actually exist. ADO.NET uses the Provider model. You use different sets of ADO.NET classes for communicating with different data sources.

For example, there is no such thing as the Connection class. Instead, there are the SqlConnection, OracleConnection, OleDbConnection, and ODBCConnection classes. You use different Connection classes to connect to different data sources.

The different implementations of the Connection, Command, and DataReader classes are grouped into the following namespaces:

- **System.Data.SqlClient**—Contains ADO.NET classes for connecting to Microsoft SQL Server version 7.0 or higher.

- **System.Data.OleDb**—Contains ADO.NET classes for connecting to a data source with an OLEDB provider.

- **System.Data.Odbc**—Contains ADO.NET classes for connecting to a data source with an ODBC driver.

- **System.Data.OracleClient**—Contains ADO.NET classes for connecting to an Oracle database (requires Oracle 8i Release 3/8.1.7 Client or later).

- **System.Data.SqlServerCe**—Contains ADO.NET classes for connecting to SQL Server Mobile.

If you connect to Microsoft SQL Server 7.0 or higher, you should always use the classes from the SqlClient namespace. These classes provide the best performance because they connect directly to SQL Server at the level of the Tabular Data Stream (the low-level protocol that Microsoft SQL Server uses to communicate with applications).

Of course, there are other databases in the world than Microsoft SQL Server. If you are communicating with an Oracle database, you should use the classes from the OracleClient namespace. If you are communicating with another type of database, you need to use the classes from either the OleDb or Odbc namespaces. Just about every database created by man has either an OLEDB provider or an ODBC driver.

Because ADO.NET follows the Provider model, all implementations of the Connection, Command, and DataReader classes inherit from a set of base classes. Here is a list of these base classes:

- ▶ **DbConnection**—The base class for all Connection classes.

- ▶ **DbCommand**—The base class for all Command classes.

- ▶ **DbDataReader**—The base class for all DataReader classes.

These base classes are contained in the System.Data.Common namespace.

All the sample code in this chapter assumes that you work with Microsoft SQL Server. Therefore, all the sample code uses the classes from the SqlClient namespace. However, because ADO.NET uses the Provider model, the methods that you would use to work with another database are similar to the methods described in this chapter.

> **NOTE**
>
> Before you can use the classes from the SqlClient namespaces in your components and pages, you need to import the System.Data.SqlClient namespace.

Before we examine the Connection, Command, and DataReader classes in detail, let's look at how you can build a simple data access component with these classes. The component in Listing 19.1, named Movie1, includes a method named GetAll() that returns every record from the Movies database table.

LISTING 19.1   App_Code\Movie1.cs

```
using System;
using System.Data;
using System.Data.SqlClient;
using System.Web.Configuration;
using System.Collections.Generic;

public class Movie1
{
    private static readonly string _connectionString;
```

19

```
    private string _title;
    private string _director;

    public string Title
    {
        get { return _title; }
        set { _title = value; }
    }

    public string Director
    {
        get { return _director; }
        set { _director = value; }
    }

    public List<Movie1> GetAll()
    {
        List<Movie1> results = new List<Movie1>();
        SqlConnection con = new SqlConnection(_connectionString);
        SqlCommand cmd = new SqlCommand("SELECT Title,Director FROM Movies", con);
        using (con)
        {
            con.Open();
            SqlDataReader reader = cmd.ExecuteReader();
            while (reader.Read())
            {
                Movie1 newMovie = new Movie1();
                newMovie.Title = (string)reader["Title"];
                newMovie.Director = (string)reader["Director"];
                results.Add(newMovie);
            }
        }
        return results;
    }

    static Movie1()
    {
        _connectionString =
WebConfigurationManager.ConnectionStrings["Movies"].ConnectionString;
    }
}
```

In Listing 19.1, a SqlConnection object represents a connection to a Microsoft SQL Server database. A SqlCommand object represents a SQL SELECT command. The results of executing the command are represented with a SqlDataReader.

Each row returned by the SELECT command is retrieved by a call to the SqlDataReader.Read() method from within a While loop. When the last row is retrieved from the SELECT command, the SqlDataReader.Read() method returns False and the While loop ends.

Each row retrieved from the database is added to a List collection. An instance of the Movie1 class represents each record.

The page in Listing 19.2 uses a GridView and ObjectDataSource control to display the records returned by the Movie1 data access component (see Figure 19.1).

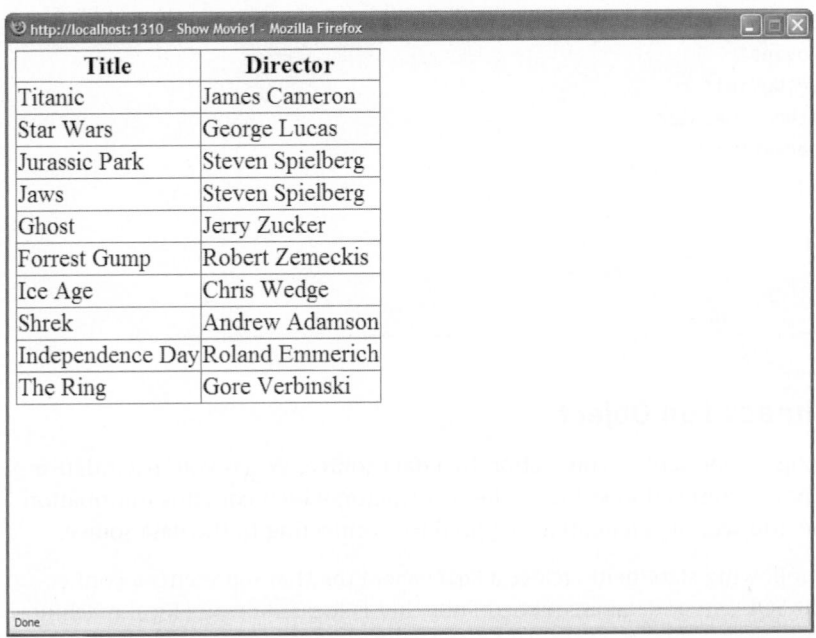

Title	Director
Titanic	James Cameron
Star Wars	George Lucas
Jurassic Park	Steven Spielberg
Jaws	Steven Spielberg
Ghost	Jerry Zucker
Forrest Gump	Robert Zemeckis
Ice Age	Chris Wedge
Shrek	Andrew Adamson
Independence Day	Roland Emmerich
The Ring	Gore Verbinski

FIGURE 19.1   Displaying movie records.

LISTING 19.2   ShowMovie1.aspx

```
<%@ Page Language="C#" %>
<!DOCTYPE html PUBLIC "-//W3C//DTD XHTML 1.0 Transitional//EN"
"http://www.w3.org/TR/xhtml1/DTD/xhtml1-transitional.dtd">
<html xmlns="http://www.w3.org/1999/xhtml" >
<head id="Head1" runat="server">
    <title>Show Movie1</title>
```

19

```
</head>
<body>
    <form id="form1" runat="server">
    <div>

    <asp:GridView
        id="grdMovies"
        DataSourceID="srcMovies"
        Runat="server" />

    <asp:ObjectDataSource
        id="srcMovies"
        TypeName="Movie1"
        SelectMethod="GetAll"
        Runat="server" />

    </div>
    </form>
</body>
</html>
```

Using the Connection Object

The Connection object represents a connection to a data source. When you instantiate a Connection, you pass a connection string to the constructor, which contains information about the location and security credentials required for connecting to the data source.

For example, the following statement creates a SqlConnection that represents a connection to a Microsoft SQL Server database named Pubs that is located on the local machine:

```
SqlConnection con = new SqlConnection("Data Source=localhost;Integrated
➥Security=True;Initial Catalog=Pubs");
```

For legacy reasons, there are a number of ways to write a connection string that does exactly the same thing. For example, the keywords Data Source, Server, Address, Addr, and Network Address are all synonyms. You can use any of these keywords to specify the location of the database server.

> **NOTE**
>
> You can use the SqlConnectionStringBuilder class to convert any connection string into canonical syntax. For example, this class replaces the keyword Server with the keyword Data Source in a connection string.

Before you execute any commands against the data source, you first must open the connection. After you finish executing commands, you should close the connection as quickly as possible.

A database connection is a valuable resource. Strive to open database connections as late as possible, and close database connections as early as possible. Furthermore, always include error handling code to make sure that a database connection gets closed even when there is an exception.

For example, you can take advantage of the Using statement to force a connection to close even when an exception is raised, like this:

```
SqlConnection con = new SqlConnection("Data Source=localhost;
Integrated Security=True;Initial Catalog=Pubs");
SqlCommand cmd = new SqlCommand("INSERT Titles (Title) VALUES ('Some Title')", con);
using (con)
{
  con.Open();
  cmd.ExecuteNonQuery();
}
```

The using statement forces the connection to close, regardless of whether an error occurs when a command is executed against the database. The using statement also disposes of the Connection object. (If you need to reuse the Connection, you need to reinitialize it.)

Alternatively, you can use a try...catch statement to force a connection to close like this:

```
SqlConnection con = new SqlConnection("Data Source=localhost;Integrated
Security=True;Initial Catalog=Pubs");
SqlCommand cmd = new SqlCommand("INSERT Titles (Title) VALUES ('Some Title')", con);
try
{
  con.Open();
  cmd.ExecuteNonQuery();
}
finally
{
  con.Close();
}
```

The finally clause in this try...catch statement forces the database connection to close both when there are no errors and when there are errors.

Retrieving Provider Statistics

When you use the SqlConnection object, you can retrieve statistics about the database commands executed with the connection. For example, you can retrieve statistics on total execution time.

19

The GetAll() method exposed by the component in Listing 19.3 includes a parameter named executionTime. After the database command executes, the value of executionTime is retrieved from the Connection statistics.

LISTING 19.3   App_Code\Movie2.cs

```
using System;
using System.Data;
using System.Data.SqlClient;
using System.Web.Configuration;
using System.Collections;
using System.Collections.Generic;

public class Movie2
{
    private static readonly string _connectionString;

    private string _title;
    private string _director;

    public string Title
    {
        get { return _title; }
        set { _title = value; }
    }

    public string Director
    {
        get { return _director; }
        set { _director = value; }
    }

    public List<Movie2> GetAll(out long executionTime)
    {
        List<Movie2> results = new List<Movie2>();
        SqlConnection con = new SqlConnection(_connectionString);
        SqlCommand cmd = new SqlCommand("WAITFOR DELAY '0:0:03';SELECT Title,Director
FROM Movies", con);
        con.StatisticsEnabled = true;
        using (con)
        {
            con.Open();
            SqlDataReader reader = cmd.ExecuteReader();
            while (reader.Read())
            {
```

```
            Movie2 newMovie = new Movie2();
            newMovie.Title = (string)reader["Title"];
            newMovie.Director = (string)reader["Director"];
            results.Add(newMovie);
        }
    }
    IDictionary stats = con.RetrieveStatistics();
    executionTime = (long)stats["ExecutionTime"];
    return results;
}

static Movie2()
{
    _connectionString =
WebConfigurationManager.ConnectionStrings["Movies"].ConnectionString;
    }
}
```

In Listing 19.3, the SqlConnection.StatisticsEnabled property is set to the value True.
You must enable statistics before you can gather statistics. After the command executes, a
dictionary of statistics is retrieved with the SqlConnection.RetrieveStatistics()
method. Finally, you retrieve the executionTime by looking up the ExecutionTime key in
the dictionary.

NOTE

In Listing 19.3, the SQL WAITFOR statement is used to pause the execution of the
SELECT command for three seconds so that a more interesting execution time is
retrieved from the ExecutionTime statistic. Because the SELECT command is such a
simple command, if you don't add a delay, you often receive an execution time of 0
milliseconds.

The page in Listing 19.4 illustrates how you can use this component to display both the
results of a database query and the database query execution time (see Figure 19.2).

19

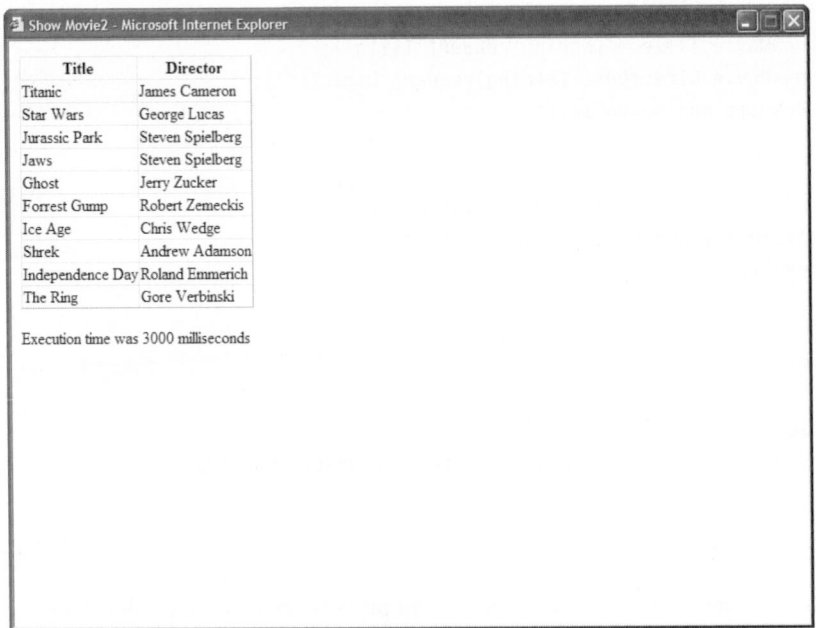

FIGURE 19.2   Displaying execution time statistics.

LISTING 19.4   ShowMovie2.aspx

```
<%@ Page Language="C#" %>
<!DOCTYPE html PUBLIC "-//W3C//DTD XHTML 1.0 Transitional//EN"
"http://www.w3.org/TR/xhtml1/DTD/xhtml1-transitional.dtd">

<script runat="server">

    protected void srcMovies_Selected(object sender,
➥ObjectDataSourceStatusEventArgs e)
    {
        lblExecutionTime.Text = e.OutputParameters["executionTime"].ToString();
    }
</script>

<html xmlns="http://www.w3.org/1999/xhtml" >
<head id="Head1" runat="server">
    <title>Show Movie2</title>
</head>
<body>
```

```
    <form id="form1" runat="server">
    <div>

    <asp:GridView
        id="grdMovies"
        DataSourceID="srcMovies"
        Runat="server" />

    <asp:ObjectDataSource
        id="srcMovies"
        TypeName="Movie2"
        SelectMethod="GetAll"
        Runat="server" OnSelected="srcMovies_Selected">
        <SelectParameters>
        <asp:Parameter Name="executionTime" Type="Int64" Direction="Output" />
        </SelectParameters>
    </asp:ObjectDataSource>

    <br />

    Execution time was
    <asp:Label
        id="lblExecutionTime"
        Runat="server" />
    milliseconds

    </div>
    </form>
</body>
</html>
```

The `SqlConnection` object supports the following properties and methods related to gathering statistics:

- ▶ **StatisticsEnabled**—Enables you to turn on statistics gathering.

- ▶ **RetrieveStatistics()**—Enables you to retrieve statistics represented with an `IDictionary` collection.

- ▶ **ResetStatistics()**—Resets all statistics to 0.

You can call the `RetrieveStatistics()` method multiple times on the same `SqlConnection`. Each time you call the method, you get another snapshot of the Connection statistics.

Here's a list of the statistics that you can gather:

▶ **BuffersReceived**—Returns the number of TDS packets received.

▶ **BuffersSent**—Returns the number of TDS packets sent.

▶ **BytesReceived**—Returns the number of bytes received.

▶ **BytesSent**—Returns the number of bytes sent.

▶ **ConnectionTime**—Returns the total amount of time that the connection has been opened.

▶ **CursorsOpen**—Returns the number of cursors opened.

▶ **ExecutionTime**—Returns the connection execution time in milliseconds.

▶ **IduCount**—Returns the number of INSERT, DELETE, and UPDATE commands executed.

▶ **IduRows**—Returns the number of rows modified by INSERT, DELETE, and UPDATE commands.

▶ **NetworkServerTime**—Returns the amount of time spent waiting for a reply from the database server.

▶ **PreparedExecs**—Returns the number of prepared commands executed.

▶ **Prepares**—Returns the number of statements prepared.

▶ **SelectCount**—Returns the number of SELECT commands executed.

▶ **SelectRows**—Returns the number of rows selected.

▶ **ServerRoundtrips**—Returns the number of commands sent to the database that received a reply.

▶ **SumResultSets**—Returns the number of resultsets retrieved.

▶ **Transactions**—Returns the number of user transactions created.

▶ **UnpreparedExecs**—Returns the number of unprepared commands executed.

The page in Listing 19.5 displays the values of all these statistics in a GridView control (see Figure 19.3).

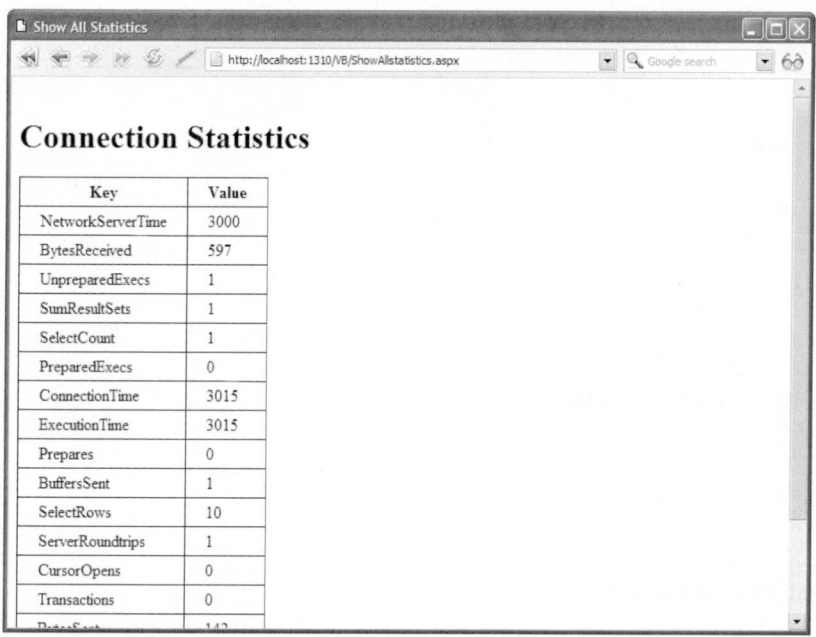

FIGURE 19.3   Displaying all provider statistics.

LISTING 19.5   ShowAllStatistics.aspx

```
<%@ Page Language="C#" %>
<%@ Import Namespace="System.Data.SqlClient" %>
<%@ Import Namespace="System.Web.Configuration" %>
<!DOCTYPE html PUBLIC "-//W3C//DTD XHTML 1.0 Transitional//EN"
"http://www.w3.org/TR/xhtml1/DTD/xhtml1-transitional.dtd">
<script runat="server">

    void Page_Load()
    {
        string connectionString =
WebConfigurationManager.ConnectionStrings["Movies"].ConnectionString;
        SqlConnection con = new SqlConnection(connectionString);
        SqlCommand cmd = new SqlCommand("WAITFOR DELAY '0:0:03';
➥SELECT Title,Director FROM Movies", con);
        con.StatisticsEnabled = true;
        using (con)
        {
            con.Open();
            SqlDataReader reader = cmd.ExecuteReader();
        }
        grdStats.DataSource = con.RetrieveStatistics();
```

19

```
            grdStats.DataBind();
        }

</script>
<html xmlns="http://www.w3.org/1999/xhtml" >
<head id="Head1" runat="server">
    <style type="text/css">
        td,th
        {
            padding:4px 20px;
        }
    </style>
    <title>Show All Statistics</title>
</head>
<body>
    <form id="form1" runat="server">
    <div>

    <h1>Connection Statistics</h1>

    <asp:GridView
        id="grdStats"
        AutoGenerateColumns="false"
        Runat="server">
        <Columns>
        <asp:BoundField DataField="Key" HeaderText="Key" />
        <asp:BoundField DataField="Value" HeaderText="Value" />
        </Columns>
    </asp:GridView>

    </div>
    </form>
</body>
</html>
```

Improving Performance with Connection Pooling

Database connections are precious resources. If you want your ASP.NET application to scale to handle the demands of thousands of users, you need to do everything in your power to prevent database connections from being wasted.

Opening a database connection is a slow operation. Rather than open a new database connection each time you need to connect to a database, you can create a pool of connections that can be reused for multiple database queries. When connection pooling is enabled, closing a connection does not really close the connection to the database server.

Instead, closing the connection releases the database connection back into the pool. That way, the next time a database query is performed, a new connection to the database does not need to be opened.

When you use the `SqlConnection` object, connection pooling is enabled by default. By default, the ADO.NET Framework keeps a maximum of 100 connections opened in a connection pool. You need to be warned about two things in regard to connection pooling. First, when taking advantage of connection pooling, it is still important to close your connections by calling the `SqlConnection.Close()` method. If you don't close a connection, the connection is not returned to the pool. It might take a long time for an unclosed connection to be reclaimed by ADO.NET.

Second, different connection pools are created for different connection strings. In particular, a different connection pool is created for each unique combination of connection string, process, application domain, and Windows identity.

An exact character-by-character match is performed on the connection string. For this reason, you should always store your connection strings in the web configuration file. Don't hardcode connection strings inside your components. If there is a slight variation between two connection strings, separate connection pools are created, which defeats the performance gains that you get from connection pooling.

The `SqlConnection` object supports two methods for clearing connection pools programmatically:

- **`ClearAllPools`**—Enables you to clear all database connections from all connection pools.

- **`ClearPool`**—Enables you to clear all database connections associated with a particular `SqlConnection` object.

These methods are useful when you work with a cluster of database servers. For example, if you take a database server down, you can programmatically clear the connection pool to the database server that no longer exists.

You can control how connections are pooled by using the following attributes in a connection string:

- **`Connection Timeout`**—Enables you to specify the maximum lifetime of a connection in seconds. (The default value is 0, which indicates that connections are immortal.)

- **`Connection Reset`**—Enables you to reset connections automatically when retrieved from the connection pool. (The default value is `True`.)

- **`Enlist`**—Enables you to enlist a connection in the current transaction context. (The default value is `True`.)

- **`Load Balance Timeout`**—Same as `Connection Timeout`.

- **`Max Pool Size`**—Enables you to specify the maximum number of connections kept in the connection pool. (The default value is 100.)

▶ **Min Pool Size**—Enables you to specify the minimum number of connections kept in the connection pool. (The default value is 0.)

▶ **Pooling**—Enables you to turn on or off connection pooling. (The default value is True.)

The page in Listing 19.6 displays a list of all the current user connections to a database in a GridView (see Figure 19.4). The connection string used when connecting to the database creates a minimum connection pool size of 10 connections. (You need to refresh the page at least once to see the 10 connections.)

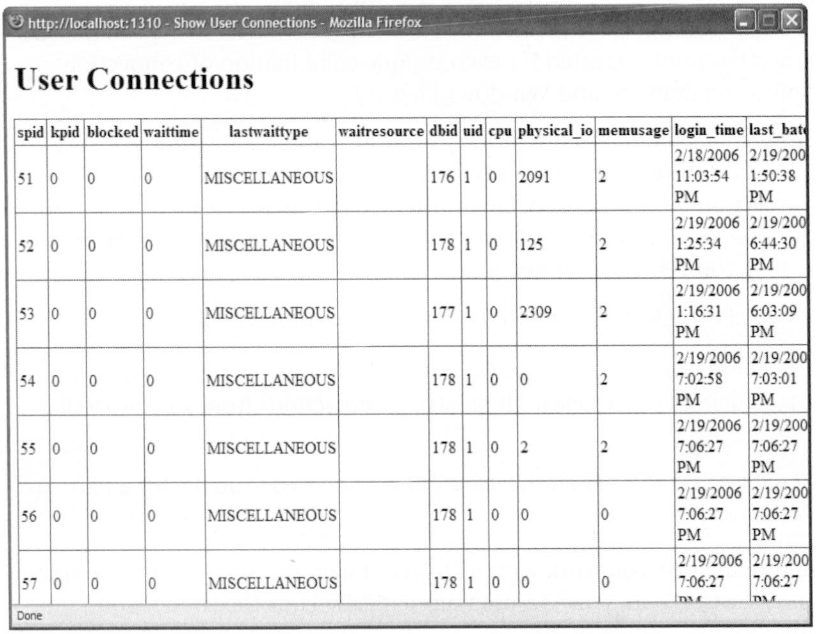

User Connections

spid	kpid	blocked	waittime	lastwaittype	waitresource	dbid	uid	cpu	physical_io	memusage	login_time	last_bat
51	0	0	0	MISCELLANEOUS		176	1	0	2091	2	2/18/2006 11:03:54 PM	2/19/200 1:50:38 PM
52	0	0	0	MISCELLANEOUS		178	1	0	125	2	2/19/2006 1:25:34 PM	2/19/200 6:44:30 PM
53	0	0	0	MISCELLANEOUS		177	1	0	2309	2	2/19/2006 1:16:31 PM	2/19/200 6:03:09 PM
54	0	0	0	MISCELLANEOUS		178	1	0	0	2	2/19/2006 7:02:58 PM	2/19/200 7:03:01 PM
55	0	0	0	MISCELLANEOUS		178	1	0	2	2	2/19/2006 7:06:27 PM	2/19/200 7:06:27 PM
56	0	0	0	MISCELLANEOUS		178	1	0	0	0	2/19/2006 7:06:27 PM	2/19/200 7:06:27 PM
57	0	0	0	MISCELLANEOUS		178	1	0	0	0	2/19/2006 7:06:27 PM	2/19/200 7:06:27 PM

FIGURE 19.4   Displaying user database connections.

LISTING 19.6   ShowUserConnections.aspx

```
<%@ Page Language="C#" %>
<%@ Import Namespace="System.Data.SqlClient" %>
<%@ Import Namespace="System.Web.Configuration" %>
<!DOCTYPE html PUBLIC "-//W3C//DTD XHTML 1.0 Transitional//EN"
"http://www.w3.org/TR/xhtml1/DTD/xhtml1-transitional.dtd">
<script runat="server">

    void Page_Load()
    {
        string connectionString = @"Min Pool Size=10;Data
```

```
Source=.\SQLExpress;Integrated
Security=True;AttachDbFileName=|DataDirectory|MyDatabase.mdf;User Instance=True";
        SqlConnection con = new SqlConnection(connectionString);
        SqlCommand cmd = new SqlCommand("SELECT * FROM master..sysprocesses WHERE
hostname<>''", con);
        using (con)
        {
            con.Open();
            grdStats.DataSource = cmd.ExecuteReader();
            grdStats.DataBind();
        }
    }
</script>
<html xmlns="http://www.w3.org/1999/xhtml" >
<head id="Head1" runat="server">
    <style type="text/css">
        td,th
        {
            padding:2px;
        }
    </style>
    <title>Show User Connections</title>
</head>
<body>
    <form id="form1" runat="server">
    <div>

    <h1>User Connections</h1>

    <asp:GridView
        id="grdStats"
        Runat="server" />

    </div>
    </form>
</body>
</html>
```

Using the Command Object

The Command object represents a command that can be executed against a data source. In this section, you learn how to use the SqlCommand object to execute different types of database commands against Microsoft SQL Server.

19

Executing a Command

You can use the SqlCommand.ExecuteNonQuery() method to execute a SQL command that does not return a set of rows. You can use this method when executing SQL UPDATE, DELETE, and INSERT commands. You can also use this method when executing more specialized commands, such as a CREATE TABLE or DROP DATABASE command.

For example, the component in Listing 19.7 includes Update() and Delete() methods that update and delete movie records.

LISTING 19.7   App_Code\Movie3.cs

```csharp
using System;
using System.Data;
using System.Data.SqlClient;
using System.Web.Configuration;
using System.Collections.Generic;

public class Movie3
{
    private static readonly string _connectionString;

    private int _id;
    private string _title;
    private string _director;

    public int Id
    {
        get { return _id; }
        set { _id = value; }
    }

    public string Title
    {
        get { return _title; }
        set { _title = value; }
    }

    public string Director
    {
        get { return _director; }
        set { _director = value; }
    }

    public void Update(int id, string title, string director)
    {
        SqlConnection con = new SqlConnection(_connectionString);
```

```csharp
        SqlCommand cmd = new SqlCommand("UPDATE MOVIES SET
Title=@Title,Director=@Director WHERE Id=@Id", con);
        cmd.Parameters.AddWithValue("@Title", title);
        cmd.Parameters.AddWithValue("@Director", director);
        cmd.Parameters.AddWithValue("@Id", id);
        using (con)
        {
            con.Open();
            cmd.ExecuteNonQuery();
        }
    }

    public void Delete(int id)
    {
        SqlConnection con = new SqlConnection(_connectionString);
        SqlCommand cmd = new SqlCommand("DELETE MOVIES WHERE Id=@Id", con);
        cmd.Parameters.AddWithValue("@Id", id);
        using (con)
        {
            con.Open();
            cmd.ExecuteNonQuery();
        }
    }

    public List<Movie3> GetAll()
    {
        List<Movie3> results = new List<Movie3>();
        SqlConnection con = new SqlConnection(_connectionString);
        SqlCommand cmd = new SqlCommand("SELECT Id,Title,Director FROM Movies", con);
        using (con)
        {
            con.Open();
            SqlDataReader reader = cmd.ExecuteReader();
            while (reader.Read())
            {
                Movie3 newMovie = new Movie3();
                newMovie.Id = (int)reader["Id"];
                newMovie.Title = (string)reader["Title"];
                newMovie.Director = (string)reader["Director"];
                results.Add(newMovie);
            }
        }
        return results;
    }

    static Movie3()
```

```
    {
        _connectionString =
WebConfigurationManager.ConnectionStrings["Movies"].ConnectionString;
    }
}
```

The page in Listing 19.8 contains a GridView that binds to the data access component in Listing 19.7. The GridView enables you to display, update, and delete database records (see Figure 19.5).

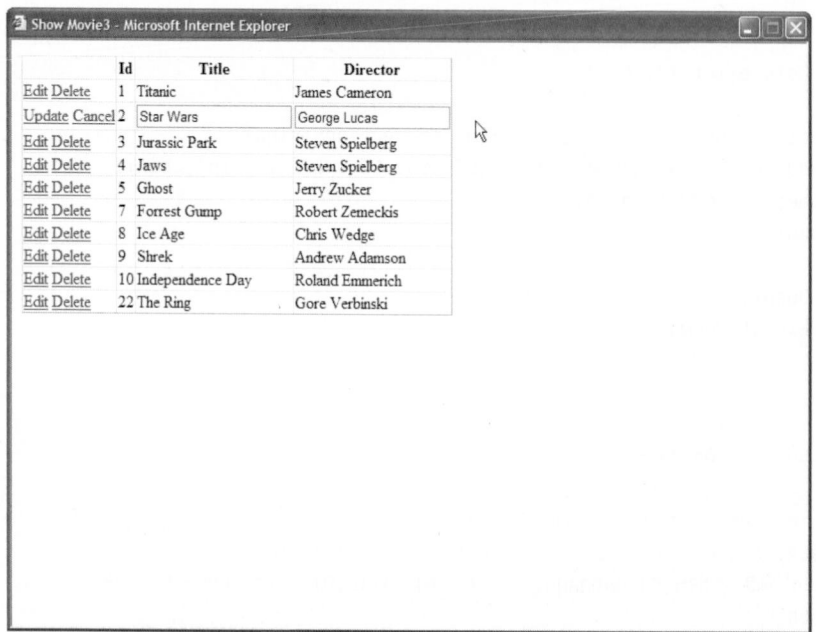

FIGURE 19.5   Updating and deleting database records.

LISTING 19.8   ShowMovie3.aspx

```
<%@ Page Language="C#" %>
<!DOCTYPE html PUBLIC "-//W3C//DTD XHTML 1.0 Transitional//EN"
"http://www.w3.org/TR/xhtml1/DTD/xhtml1-transitional.dtd">
<html xmlns="http://www.w3.org/1999/xhtml" >
<head id="Head1" runat="server">
    <title>Show Movie3</title>
</head>
<body>
    <form id="form1" runat="server">
    <div>
```

```
<asp:GridView
    id="grdMovies"
    DataSourceID="srcMovies"
    DataKeyNames="Id"
    AutoGenerateEditButton="true"
    AutoGenerateDeleteButton="true"
    Runat="server" />

<asp:ObjectDataSource
    id="srcMovies"
    TypeName="Movie3"
    SelectMethod="GetAll"
    UpdateMethod="Update"
    DeleteMethod="Delete"
    Runat="server" />

</div>
</form>
</body>
</html>
```

Executing a Command with Parameters

Most database commands that you execute include parameters. For example, when updating a database record, you need to supply parameters that represent the new values of the database record columns.

WARNING

Never build command parameters through string concatenation because concatenating strings is an open invitation for SQL injection attacks. If a user enters the proper sequence of characters in a form field, and a SQL command is built through concatenation, a user can execute an arbitrary SQL command.

Always explicitly create parameters by creating instances of the SqlParameter object. When a SQL command is executed with explicit parameters, the parameters are passed individually to a SQL Server stored procedure named sp_executesql.

You represent a parameter with the SqlParameter object. You can create a new SqlParameter in multiple ways. The easiest way is to call the SqlCommand.AddWithValue() method like this:

```
SqlCommand cmd = new SqlCommand("INSERT Titles (Title) VALUES (@Title)", con);
cmd.Parameters.AddWithValue("@Title", "ASP.NET 4.0 Unleashed");
```

The first statement creates a SqlCommand object that represents a SQL INSERT command. The command includes a parameter named @Title.

The second statement adds a SqlParameter to the SqlCommand object's Parameters collection. The AddWithValue() method enables you to add a parameter with a certain name and value. In this case, the method supplies the value for the @Title parameter.

When you execute the SqlCommand, the following command is sent to Microsoft SQL Server:

```
exec sp_executesql N'INSERT Titles (Title) VALUES (@Title)',
➥N'@Title nvarchar(17)', @Title = N'ASP.NET 4.0 Unleashed'
```

The SqlCommand object calls the sp_executesql stored procedure when it executes a command. In this case, it passes the type, size, and value of the @Title parameter to the sp_executesql stored procedure.

When you use AddWithValue(), the SqlCommand object infers the type and size of the parameter for you. The method assumes that string values are SQL NVarChar values, integer values are SQL Int values, decimal values are SQL decimal values, and so on.

As an alternative to using the AddWithValue() method, you can create a SqlParameter explicitly and add the SqlParameter to a SqlCommand object's Parameters collection. The advantage of creating a parameter explicitly is that you can specify parameter properties explicitly, such as its name, type, size, precision, scale, and direction.

For example, the following code creates a parameter named @Title with a particular data type, size, and value:

```
SqlCommand cmd = new SqlCommand("INSERT Titles (Title) VALUES (@Title)", con);
SqlParameter paramTitle = new SqlParameter();
paramTitle.ParameterName = "@Title";
paramTitle.SqlDbType = SqlDbType.NVarChar;
paramTitle.Size = 50;
paramTitle.Value = "ASP.NET 4.0 Unleashed";
cmd.Parameters.Add(paramTitle);
```

If this seems like a lot of code to do something simple, you can use one of the overloads of the Add() method to create a new SqlParameter like this:

```
SqlCommand cmd = new SqlCommand("INSERT Test (Title) VALUES (@Title)", con);
cmd.Parameters.Add("@Title", SqlDbType.NVarChar,50).Value = "ASP.NET 4.0
➥Unleashed";
```

In general, in this book and in the code that I write, I use the AddWithValue() method to create parameters. I like the AddWithValue() method because it involves the least typing.

Executing a Command That Represents a Stored Procedure

You can use a SqlCommand object to represent a Microsoft SQL Server stored procedure. For example, you can use the following two statements to create a SqlCommand object that represents a stored procedure named GetTitles:

```
SqlCommand cmd = new SqlCommand("GetTitles", con);
cmd.CommandType = CommandType.StoredProcedure;
```

When you execute this SqlCommand, the GetTitles stored procedure is executed. When you create SqlParameters for a SqlCommand that represents a stored procedure, the SqlParameters represent stored procedure parameters. The modified Movie component in Listing 19.9 uses stored procedures to retrieve and update movie records.

LISTING 19.9   App_Code\Movie4.cs

```csharp
using System;
using System.Data;
using System.Data.SqlClient;
using System.Web.Configuration;
using System.Collections.Generic;

public class Movie4
{
    private static readonly string _connectionString;

    private int _id;
    private string _title;
    private string _director;

    public int Id
    {
        get { return _id; }
        set { _id = value; }
    }

    public string Title
    {
        get { return _title; }
        set { _title = value; }
    }

    public string Director
    {
        get { return _director; }
        set { _director = value; }
    }
```

```csharp
public void Update(int id, string title, string director)
{
    SqlConnection con = new SqlConnection(_connectionString);
    SqlCommand cmd = new SqlCommand("MovieUpdate", con);
    cmd.CommandType = CommandType.StoredProcedure;
    cmd.Parameters.AddWithValue("@Id", id);
    cmd.Parameters.AddWithValue("@Title", title);
    cmd.Parameters.AddWithValue("@Director", director);
    using (con)
    {
        con.Open();
        cmd.ExecuteNonQuery();
    }
}


public List<Movie4> GetAll()
{
    List<Movie4> results = new List<Movie4>();
    SqlConnection con = new SqlConnection(_connectionString);
    SqlCommand cmd = new SqlCommand("MovieSelect", con);
    cmd.CommandType = CommandType.StoredProcedure;
    using (con)
    {
        con.Open();
        SqlDataReader reader = cmd.ExecuteReader();
        while (reader.Read())
        {
            Movie4 newMovie = new Movie4();
            newMovie.Id = (int)reader["Id"];
            newMovie.Title = (string)reader["Title"];
            newMovie.Director = (string)reader["Director"];
            results.Add(newMovie);
        }
    }
    return results;
}

static Movie4()
{
    _connectionString =
WebConfigurationManager.ConnectionStrings["Movies"].ConnectionString;
}
}
```

The component in Listing 19.9 uses the MovieSelect and MovieUpdate stored procedures contained in Listing 19.10.

LISTING 19.10   MovieStoredProcedures.sql

```sql
CREATE PROCEDURE dbo.MovieSelect
AS
SELECT Id, Title, Director FROM Movies

CREATE PROCEDURE dbo.MovieUpdate
(
    @Id int,
    @Title NVarchar(100),
    @Director NVarchar(100)
)
AS
UPDATE Movies SET
    Title = @Title,
    Director = @Director
WHERE Id = @Id
```

The ASP.NET page in Listing 19.11 contains a `GridView` that is bound to the modified `Movie` component. This `GridView` enables you to display and update movie records.

LISTING 19.11   ShowMovie4.aspx

```aspx
<%@ Page Language="C#" %>
<!DOCTYPE html PUBLIC "-//W3C//DTD XHTML 1.0 Transitional//EN"
  "http://www.w3.org/TR/xhtml1/DTD/xhtml1-transitional.dtd">
<html xmlns="http://www.w3.org/1999/xhtml" >
<head id="Head1" runat="server">
    <title>Show Movie4</title>
</head>
<body>
    <form id="form1" runat="server">
    <div>

    <asp:GridView
        id="grdMovies"
        DataSourceID="srcMovies"
        DataKeyNames="Id"
        AutoGenerateEditButton="true"
        Runat="server" />

    <asp:ObjectDataSource
        id="srcMovies"
        TypeName="Movie4"
        SelectMethod="GetAll"
```

19

```
            UpdateMethod="Update"
            Runat="server" />

    </div>
    </form>
</body>
</html>
```

You can use a `SqlParameter` to represent not only stored procedure input parameters, but also to represent stored procedure return values and output parameters. If you need to return an integer value from a stored procedure, you can create a `SqlParameter` that represents a return value. For example, the stored procedure in Listing 19.12 returns the number of rows in the Movies database table.

LISTING 19.12   GetMovieCount.sql

```
CREATE PROCEDURE dbo.GetMovieCount
AS
RETURN (SELECT COUNT(*) FROM Movies)
```

The page in Listing 19.13 displays the return value from the `GetMovieCount` stored procedure with a `Label` control (see Figure 19.6).

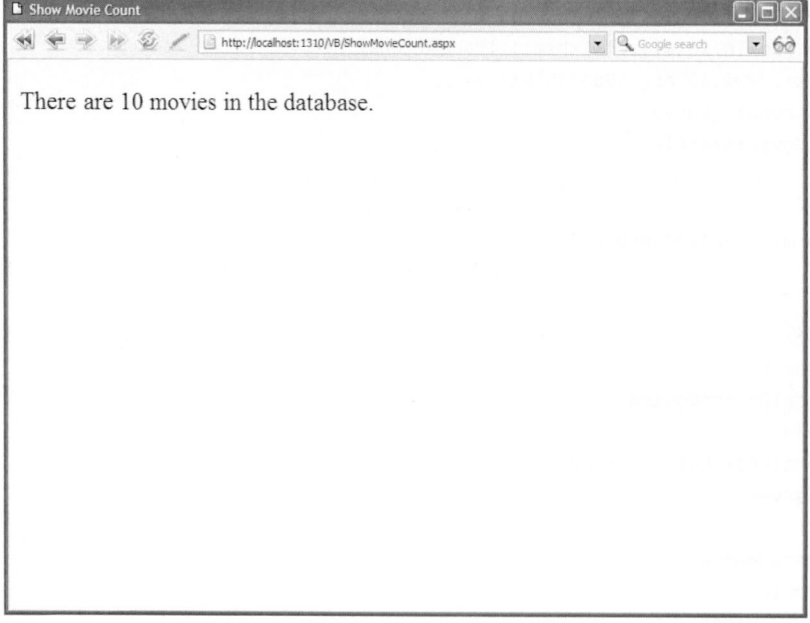

FIGURE 19.6   Displaying a stored procedure return value.

LISTING 19.13   ShowMovieCount.aspx

```csharp
<%@ Page Language="C#" %>
<%@ Import Namespace="System.Data" %>
<%@ Import Namespace="System.Data.SqlClient" %>
<%@ Import Namespace="System.Web.Configuration" %>
<!DOCTYPE html PUBLIC "-//W3C//DTD XHTML 1.0 Transitional//EN"
"http://www.w3.org/TR/xhtml1/DTD/xhtml1-transitional.dtd">
<script runat="server">

    void Page_Load()
    {
        lblMovieCount.Text = GetMovieCount().ToString();
    }


    private int GetMovieCount()
    {
        int result = 0;
        string connectionString =
WebConfigurationManager.ConnectionStrings["Movies"].ConnectionString;
        SqlConnection con = new SqlConnection(connectionString);
        SqlCommand cmd = new SqlCommand("GetMovieCount", con);
        cmd.CommandType = CommandType.StoredProcedure;
        cmd.Parameters.Add("@ReturnVal", SqlDbType.Int).Direction =
➥ParameterDirection.ReturnValue;
        using (con)
        {
            con.Open();
            cmd.ExecuteNonQuery();
            result = (int)cmd.Parameters["@ReturnVal"].Value;
        }
        return result;
    }
</script>
<html xmlns="http://www.w3.org/1999/xhtml" >
<head id="Head1" runat="server">
    <title>Show Movie Count</title>
</head>
<body>
    <form id="form1" runat="server">
    <div>

    There are
    <asp:Label
        id="lblMovieCount"
        Runat="server" />
```

19

```
    movies in the database.

    </div>
    </form>
</body>
</html>
```

In Listing 19.13, a SqlParameter is created that has the name ReturnVal. The name of the SqlParameter is not important. However, the SqlParameter.Direction property is set to the value ReturnValue. After the SqlCommand is executed, the return value can be retrieved by reading the value of this parameter.

A stored procedure has only one return value, and it must be an integer value. If you need to return more than one value, or values of a different data type than an integer, you need to use stored procedure output parameters.

For example, the stored procedure in Listing 19.14 returns movie titles and box office totals. The stored procedure includes an output parameter named @SumBoxOfficeTotals. This output parameter represents a sum of all box office totals.

LISTING 19.14   GetBoxOfficeTotals.sql

```sql
CREATE PROCEDURE dbo.GetBoxOfficeTotals
(
  @SumBoxOfficeTotals Money OUTPUT
)
AS
-- Assign Sum Box Office Totals
SELECT @SumBoxOfficeTotals = SUM(BoxOfficeTotals) FROM Movies

-- Return all rows
SELECT Title, BoxOfficeTotals FROM Movies
```

The data access component in Listing 19.15 contains a method named GetBoxOffice() that calls the GetBoxOfficeTotals stored procedure. The method adds an output parameter to the SqlCommand object.

LISTING 19.15   App_Code\Movie5.cs

```csharp
using System;
using System.Data;
using System.Data.SqlClient;
using System.Web.Configuration;
using System.Collections.Generic;

public class Movie5
```

```csharp
{
    private static readonly string _connectionString;

    private string _title;
    private decimal _boxOfficeTotals;

    public string Title
    {
        get { return _title; }
        set { _title = value; }
    }

    public decimal BoxOfficeTotals
    {
        get { return _boxOfficeTotals; }
        set { _boxOfficeTotals = value; }
    }

    public List<Movie5> GetBoxOffice(out decimal SumBoxOfficeTotals)
    {
        List<Movie5> results = new List<Movie5>();
        SqlConnection con = new SqlConnection(_connectionString);
        SqlCommand cmd = new SqlCommand("GetBoxOfficeTotals", con);
        cmd.CommandType = CommandType.StoredProcedure;
        cmd.Parameters.Add("@SumBoxOfficeTotals", SqlDbType.Money).Direction =
ParameterDirection.Output;
        using (con)
        {
            con.Open();
            SqlDataReader reader = cmd.ExecuteReader();

            while (reader.Read())
            {
                Movie5 newMovie = new Movie5();
                newMovie.Title = (string)reader["Title"];
                newMovie.BoxOfficeTotals = (decimal)reader["BoxOfficeTotals"];
                results.Add(newMovie);
            }
            reader.Close();
            SumBoxOfficeTotals =
➥(decimal)cmd.Parameters["@SumBoxOfficeTotals"].Value;

        }
        return results;
    }
```

```
    static Movie5()
    {
        _connectionString =
WebConfigurationManager.ConnectionStrings["Movies"].ConnectionString;
    }
}
```

In Listing 19.15, the `SqlDataReader` is explicitly closed before the output parameter is read. If you do not close the `SqlDataReader` first, attempting to read the value of the output parameter raises an exception.

Finally, the page in Listing 19.16 displays the movie box office totals in a `GridView`. In addition, it displays the value of the output parameter in a `Label` control (see Figure 19.7).

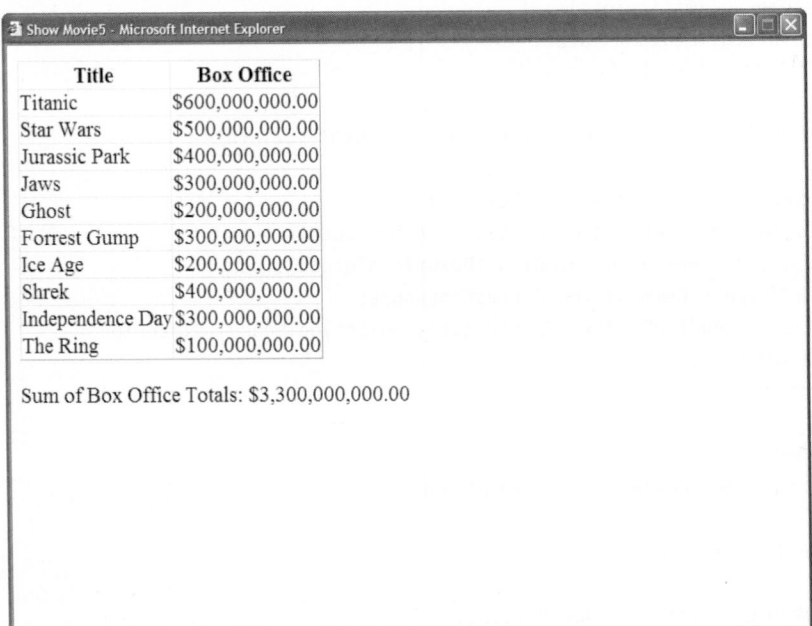

FIGURE 19.7   Displaying an output parameter.

LISTING 19.16   ShowMovie5.aspx

```
<%@ Page Language="C#" %>
<!DOCTYPE html PUBLIC "-//W3C//DTD XHTML 1.0 Transitional//EN"
"http://www.w3.org/TR/xhtml1/DTD/xhtml1-transitional.dtd">
<script runat="server">

    protected void srcMovies_Selected(object sender,
➥ObjectDataSourceStatusEventArgs e)
```

```
        {
            decimal sum = (decimal)e.OutputParameters["SumBoxOfficeTotals"];
            lblSum.Text = sum.ToString("c");
        }
</script>
<html xmlns="http://www.w3.org/1999/xhtml" >
<head id="Head1" runat="server">
    <title>Show Movie5</title>
</head>
<body>
    <form id="form1" runat="server">
    <div>

    <asp:GridView
        id="grdMovies"
        DataSourceID="srcMovies"
        AutoGenerateColumns="false"
        Runat="server">
        <Columns>
        <asp:BoundField DataField="Title" HeaderText="Title" />
        <asp:BoundField
            DataField="BoxOfficeTotals"
            HeaderText="Box Office"
            HtmlEncode="false"
            DataFormatString="{0:c}" />
        </Columns>
    </asp:GridView>
    <br />
    Sum of Box Office Totals:
    <asp:Label
        id="lblSum"
        Runat="server" />

    <asp:ObjectDataSource
        id="srcMovies"
        TypeName="Movie5"
        SelectMethod="GetBoxOffice"
        Runat="server" OnSelected="srcMovies_Selected">
        <SelectParameters>
        <asp:Parameter
            Name="SumBoxOfficeTotals"
            Type="Decimal"
            Direction="Output" />
        </SelectParameters>
    </asp:ObjectDataSource>
```

19

```
    </div>
    </form>
</body>
</html>
```

Returning a Single Value

If you need to return a single value from a database query, you can use the
`SqlCommand.ExecuteScalar()` method. This method always returns the value of the first
column from the first row of a resultset. Even when a query returns hundreds of columns
and billions of rows, everything is ignored except for the value of the first column from
the first row.

For example, the page in Listing 19.17 contains a lookup form. If you enter the title of a
movie, the movie's total box office returns display in a `Label` control (see Figure 19.8).

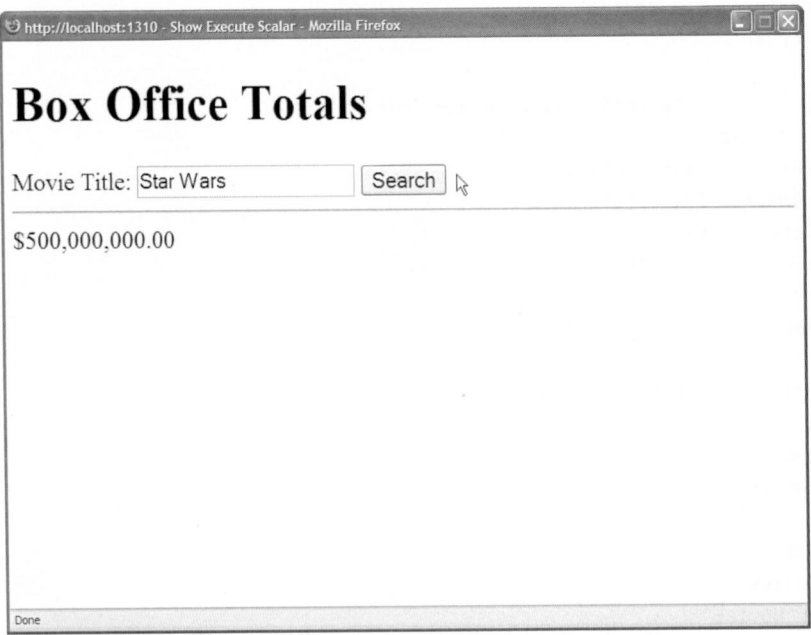

FIGURE 19.8   Retrieving a value with `ExecuteScalar()`.

LISTING 19.17   ShowExecuteScalar.aspx

```
<%@ Page Language="C#" %>
<%@ Import Namespace="System.Data" %>
<%@ Import Namespace="System.Data.SqlClient" %>
<%@ Import Namespace="System.Web.Configuration" %>
<!DOCTYPE html PUBLIC "-//W3C//DTD XHTML 1.0 Transitional//EN"
```

```
"http://www.w3.org/TR/xhtml1/DTD/xhtml1-transitional.dtd">
<script runat="server">

    protected void btnSearch_Click(object sender, EventArgs e)
    {
        string connectionString =
WebConfigurationManager.ConnectionStrings["Movies"].ConnectionString;
        SqlConnection con = new SqlConnection(connectionString);
        SqlCommand cmd = new SqlCommand("SELECT BoxOfficeTotals FROM Movies WHERE
Title=@Title", con);
        cmd.Parameters.AddWithValue("@Title", txtTitle.Text);
        using (con)
        {
            con.Open();
            Object result = cmd.ExecuteScalar();
            if (result != null)
                lblResult.Text = String.Format("{0:c}", result);
            else
                lblResult.Text = "No match!";
        }

    }
</script>
<html xmlns="http://www.w3.org/1999/xhtml" >
<head id="Head1" runat="server">
    <title>Show Execute Scalar</title>
</head>
<body>
    <form id="form1" runat="server">
    <div>

    <h1>Box Office Totals</h1>

    <asp:Label
        id="lblTitle"
        Text="Movie Title:"
        AssociatedControlID="txtTitle"
        Runat="server" />

    <asp:TextBox
        id="txtTitle"
        Runat="server" />

    <asp:Button
        id="btnSearch"
```

```
        Text="Search"
        OnClick="btnSearch_Click"
        Runat="server" />

    <hr />

    <asp:Label
        id="lblResult"
        Runat="server" />

    </div>
    </form>
</body>
</html>
```

The ExecuteScalar() method returns a value of type Object. This means that you must cast the value returned from ExecuteScalar() to a particular type before you do anything with the value. In Listing 19.17, after verifying that a value is returned, the value is cast to a decimal.

You have a choice here. Rather than use the ExecuteScalar() method, you can use an output parameter. You can use either method to return a single value from a database. There is no real difference in performance between using the ExecuteScalar() method with a stored procedure or using an output parameter. The approach you take is largely a matter of preference.

NOTE

For performance comparisons between ExecuteScalar and output parameters, see Priya Dhawan's article at the Microsoft MSDN website (msdn.Microsoft.com), "Performance Comparison: Data Access Techniques."

Returning a Resultset

If you need to return multiple rows of data with a SqlCommand object, you can call the SqlCommand.ExecuteReader() method. This method returns a SqlDataReader that you can use to fetch each row of records from the database.

For example, the data access component in Listing 19.18 contains a method named GetAll() that returns all the movies from the Movies database table. After the ExecuteReader() method is called, each row is retrieved from the SqlDataReader and dumped into a generic List collection.

LISTING 19.18   App_Code\Movie6.cs

```csharp
using System;
using System.Data;
using System.Data.SqlClient;
using System.Web.Configuration;
using System.Collections.Generic;

public class Movie6
{
    private static readonly string _connectionString;

    private string _title;
    private string _director;

    public string Title
    {
        get { return _title; }
        set { _title = value; }
    }

    public string Director
    {
        get { return _director; }
        set { _director = value; }
    }

    public List<Movie6> GetAll()
    {
        List<Movie6> results = new List<Movie6>();
        SqlConnection con = new SqlConnection(_connectionString);
        SqlCommand cmd = new SqlCommand("SELECT Title,Director FROM Movies", con);
        using (con)
        {
            con.Open();
            SqlDataReader reader = cmd.ExecuteReader();
            while (reader.Read())
            {
                Movie6 newMovie = new Movie6();
                newMovie.Title = (string)reader["Title"];
                newMovie.Director = (string)reader["Director"];
                results.Add(newMovie);
            }
        }
        return results;
    }
```

19

```
    static Movie6()
    {
        _connectionString =
WebConfigurationManager.ConnectionStrings["Movies"].ConnectionString;
    }
}
```

The page in Listing 19.19 contains a `GridView` bound to an `ObjectDataSource` that represents the component in Listing 19.18 (see Figure 19.9).

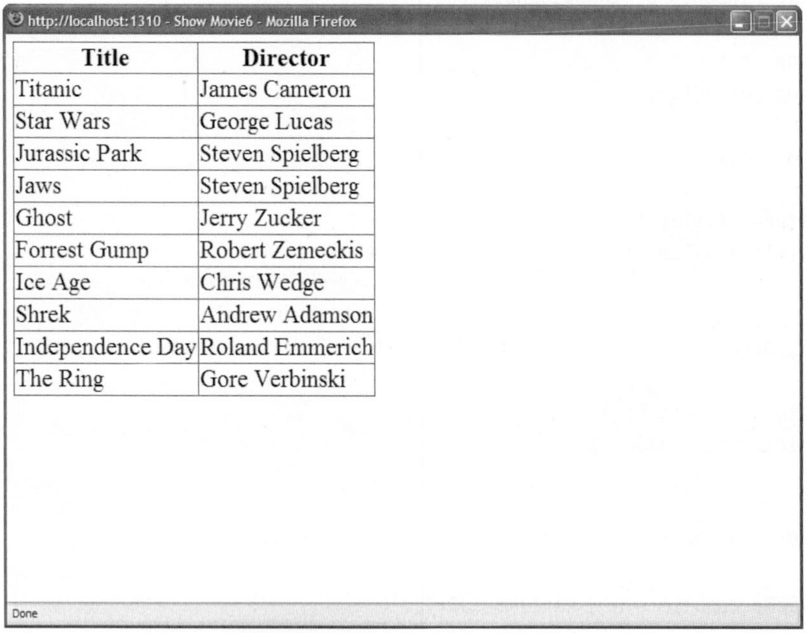

FIGURE 19.9   Returning a resultset.

LISTING 19.19   ShowMovie6.aspx

```
<%@ Page Language="C#" %>
<!DOCTYPE html PUBLIC "-//W3C//DTD XHTML 1.0 Transitional//EN"
    "http://www.w3.org/TR/xhtml1/DTD/xhtml1-transitional.dtd">
<html xmlns="http://www.w3.org/1999/xhtml" >
<head id="Head1" runat="server">
    <title>Show Movie6</title>
</head>
<body>
    <form id="form1" runat="server">
    <div>
```

```
<asp:GridView
    id="grdMovies"
    DataSourceID="srcMovies"
    Runat="server" />

<asp:ObjectDataSource
    id="srcMovies"
    TypeName="Movie6"
    SelectMethod="GetAll"
    Runat="server" />

</div>
</form>
</body>
</html>
```

The component in Listing 19.18 copies all the records from the `SqlDataReader` to a collection before returning the results of the query.

If you want to skip the copying step, and not add the records to a collection, you can pass a `CommandBehavior.CloseConnection` parameter to the `ExecuteReader()` method. This parameter causes the database connection associated with the `SqlDataReader` to close automatically after all the records have been fetched from the `SqlDataReader`.

The component in Listing 19.20 illustrates how you can use `CommandBehavior.CloseConnection` with the `ExecuteReader()` method.

LISTING 19.20   App_Code\Movie7.cs

```
using System;
using System.Data;
using System.Data.SqlClient;
using System.Web.Configuration;
using System.Collections.Generic;

public class Movie7
{
    private static readonly string _connectionString;

    public SqlDataReader GetAll()
    {
        SqlConnection con = new SqlConnection(_connectionString);
        SqlCommand cmd = new SqlCommand("SELECT Title,Director FROM Movies", con);
        con.Open();
        return cmd.ExecuteReader(CommandBehavior.CloseConnection);
    }
```

19

```
    static Movie7()
    {
        _connectionString =
WebConfigurationManager.ConnectionStrings["Movies"].ConnectionString;
    }
}
```

The page in Listing 19.21 displays the records returned from the component in Listing 19.20 in GridView.

LISTING 19.21   ShowMovie7.aspx

```
<%@ Page Language="C#" %>
<!DOCTYPE html PUBLIC "-//W3C//DTD XHTML 1.0 Transitional//EN"
    "http://www.w3.org/TR/xhtml1/DTD/xhtml1-transitional.dtd">
<html xmlns="http://www.w3.org/1999/xhtml" >
<head id="Head1" runat="server">
    <title>Show Movie7</title>
</head>
<body>
    <form id="form1" runat="server">
    <div>

    <asp:GridView
        id="grdMovies"
        DataSourceID="srcMovies"
        Runat="server" />

    <asp:ObjectDataSource
        id="srcMovies"
        TypeName="Movie7"
        SelectMethod="GetAll"
        Runat="server" />

    </div>
    </form>
</body>
</html>
```

The CommandBehavior.CloseConnection parameter enables you to return a SqlDataReader from a method. When all the records are read from the SqlDataReader, the CommandBehavior.CloseConnection parameter causes the SqlConnection object associated with the SqlDataReader to close automatically.

The big disadvantage of using the CommandBehavior.CloseConnection parameter is that it prevents you from adding any exception handling code. You can't use a Using statement or Try...Catch statement with the SqlConnection created in the component in Listing 19.19. A Using statement or Try...Catch statement would force the SqlConnection to close before the SqlDataReader is returned from the method.

Using the DataReader Object

The DataReader object represents the results of a database query. You get a DataReader by calling a Command object's ExecuteReader() method.

You can verify whether a DataReader represents any rows by checking the HasRows property or calling the Read() method. The Read() method returns true when the DataReader can advance to a new row. (Calling this method also advances you to the next row.)

The DataReader represents a single row of data at a time. To get the next row of data, you need to call the Read() method. When you get to the last row, the Read() method returns False.

There are multiple ways to refer to the columns returned by a DataReader. For example, imagine that you use a SqlDataReader named reader to represent the following query:

```
SELECT Title, Director FROM Movies
```

If you want to retrieve the value of the Title column for the current row represented by a DataReader, you can use any of the following methods:

```
string title = (string)reader["Title"];
string title = (string)reader[0];
string title = reader.GetString(0);
SqlString title = reader.GetSqlString(0);
```

The first method returns the Title column by name. The value of the Title column is returned as an Object. Therefore, you must cast the value to a string before you can assign the value to a string variable.

The second method returns the Title column by position. It also returns the value of the Title column as an Object, so you must cast the value before using it.

The third method returns the Title column by position. However, it retrieves the value as a String value. You don't need to cast the value in this case.

Finally, the last method returns the Title column by position; however, it returns the value as a SqlString rather than a normal String. A SqlString represents the value using the specialized data types defined in the System.Data.SqlTypes namespace.

There are trade-offs between the different methods of returning a column value. Retrieving a column by its position rather than its name is faster. However, this technique also makes your code more brittle. If the order of your columns changes in your query, your code no longer works.

19

Returning Multiple Resultsets

A single database query can return multiple resultsets. For example, the following query returns the contents of both the MovieCategories and Movies tables as separate resultsets:

```
SELECT * FROM MoviesCategories;SELECT * FROM Movies
```

A semicolon is used to separate the two queries. Executing multiple queries in one shot can result in better performance. When you execute multiple queries with a single command, you don't tie up multiple database connections.

The component in Listing 19.22 illustrates how you can retrieve multiple resultsets with a single query when using a SqlDataReader. The GetMovieData() method returns two collections: a collection representing MovieCategories and a collection representing Movies.

LISTING 19.22   App_Code\DataLayer1.cs

```csharp
using System;
using System.Data;
using System.Data.SqlClient;
using System.Web.Configuration;
using System.Collections.Generic;

public class DataLayer1
{
    private static readonly string _connectionString;

    public class MovieCategory
    {
        private int _id;
        private string _name;

        public int Id
        {
            get { return _id; }
            set { _id = value; }
        }

        public string Name
        {
            get { return _name; }
            set { _name = value; }
        }
    }

    public class Movie
    {
```

```
        private string _title;
        private int _categoryId;

        public string Title
        {
            get { return _title; }
            set { _title = value; }
        }

        public int CategoryId
        {
            get { return _categoryId; }
            set { _categoryId = value; }
        }
    }

    public static void GetMovieData(
List<DataLayer1.MovieCategory> movieCategories,
List<DataLayer1.Movie> movies)
    {
        string commandText =
"SELECT Id,Name FROM MovieCategories;SELECT Title,CategoryId FROM Movies";
        SqlConnection con = new SqlConnection(_connectionString);
        SqlCommand cmd = new SqlCommand(commandText, con);
        using (con)
        {
            // Execute command
            con.Open();
            SqlDataReader reader = cmd.ExecuteReader();

            // Create movie categories
            while (reader.Read())
            {
                DataLayer1.MovieCategory newCategory =
➥new DataLayer1.MovieCategory();
                newCategory.Id = (int)reader["Id"];
                newCategory.Name = (string)reader["Name"];
                movieCategories.Add(newCategory);
            }

            // Move to next result set
            reader.NextResult();

            // Create movies
            while (reader.Read())
```

```
            {
                DataLayer1.Movie newMovie = new DataLayer1.Movie();
                newMovie.Title = (string)reader["Title"];
                newMovie.CategoryId = (int)reader["CategoryID"];
                movies.Add(newMovie);
            }
        }
    }

    static DataLayer1()
    {
        _connectionString =
WebConfigurationManager.ConnectionStrings["Movies"].ConnectionString;
    }
}
```

The `SqlDataReader.NextResult()` method is called to advance to the next resultset. This method returns either `True` or `False` depending on whether a next resultset exists. In Listing 19.22, it is assumed that there is both a movies category and movies resultset.

The page in Listing 19.23 displays the contents of the two database tables in two `GridView` controls (see Figure 19.10).

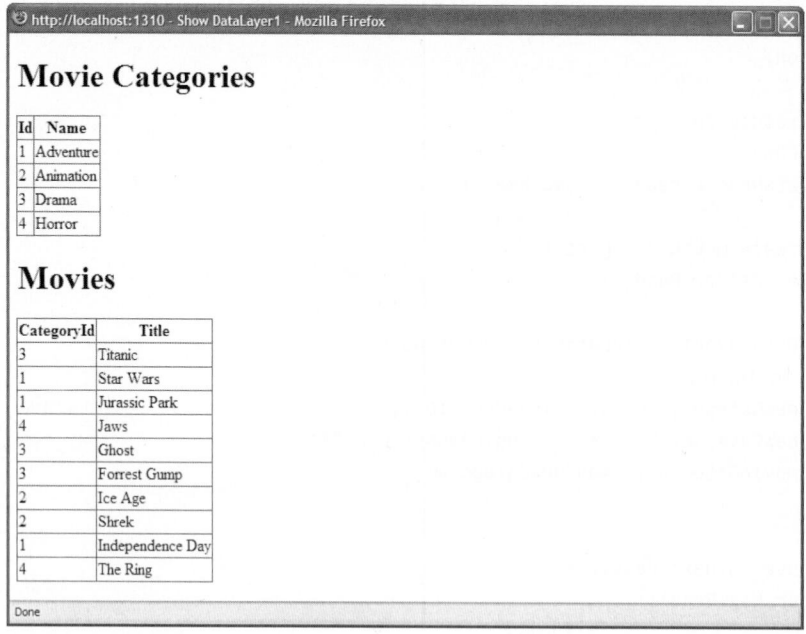

FIGURE 19.10   Displaying two resultsets.

LISTING 19.23   ShowDataLayer1.aspx

```
<%@ Page Language="C#" %>
<%@ Import Namespace="System.Collections.Generic" %>
<!DOCTYPE html PUBLIC "-//W3C//DTD XHTML 1.0 Transitional//EN"
"http://www.w3.org/TR/xhtml1/DTD/xhtml1-transitional.dtd">
<script runat="server">

    void Page_Load()
    {
        // Get database data
        List<DataLayer1.MovieCategory> categories =
➥new List<DataLayer1.MovieCategory>();
        List<DataLayer1.Movie> movies = new List<DataLayer1.Movie>();
        DataLayer1.GetMovieData(categories, movies);

        // Bind the data
        grdCategories.DataSource = categories;
        grdCategories.DataBind();
        grdMovies.DataSource = movies;
        grdMovies.DataBind();
    }
</script>
<html xmlns="http://www.w3.org/1999/xhtml" >
<head id="Head1" runat="server">
    <title>Show DataLayer1</title>
</head>
<body>
    <form id="form1" runat="server">
    <div>

    <h1>Movie Categories</h1>
    <asp:GridView
        id="grdCategories"
        Runat="server" />

    <h1>Movies</h1>
    <asp:GridView
        id="grdMovies"
        Runat="server" />

    </div>
    </form>
</body>
</html>
```

19

Working with Multiple Active Resultsets

ADO.NET 2.0 introduced a new feature named Multiple Active Results Sets (MARS). In the previous version of ADO.NET, a database connection could represent only a single resultset at a time. If you take advantage of MARS, you can represent multiple resultsets with a single database connection. Using MARS is valuable in scenarios in which you need to iterate through a resultset and perform an additional database operation for each record in the resultset. MARS is disabled by default. To enable MARS, you must include a `MultipleActiveResultSets=True` attribute in a connection string.

For example, the page in Listing 19.24 programmatically builds the nodes in a `TreeView` control. The page displays a list of movie categories and, beneath each movie category, it displays a list of matching movies (see Figure 19.11).

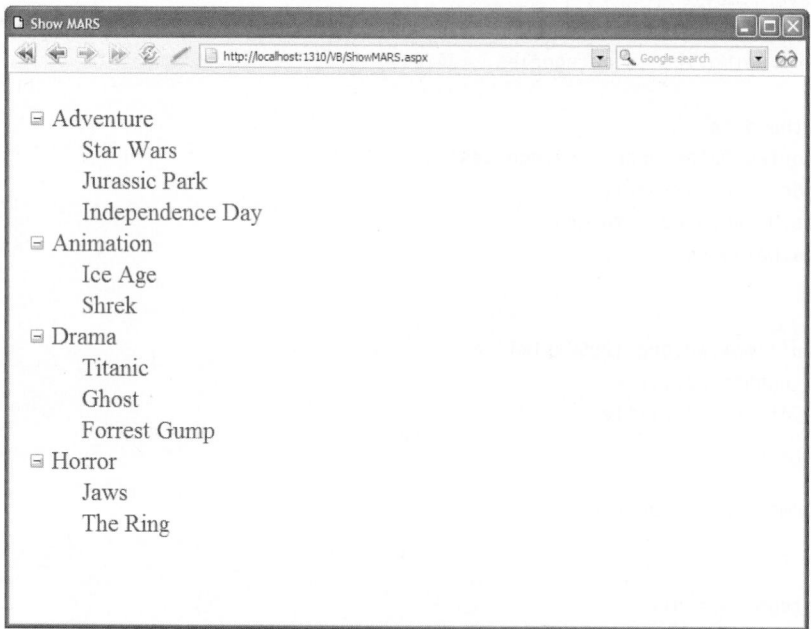

FIGURE 19.11   Fetching database records with MARS enabled.

LISTING 19.24   ShowMARS.aspx

```
<%@ Page Language="C#" %>
<%@ Import Namespace="System.Data" %>
<%@ Import Namespace="System.Data.SqlClient" %>
<!DOCTYPE html PUBLIC "-//W3C//DTD XHTML 1.0 Transitional//EN"
"http://www.w3.org/TR/xhtml1/DTD/xhtml1-transitional.dtd">
<script runat="server">

    void Page_Load()
    {
```

```csharp
    if (!Page.IsPostBack)
        BuildTree();
}

void BuildTree()
{
    // Create MARS connection
    string connectionString = @"MultipleActiveResultSets=True;"
        + @"Data Source=.\SQLExpress;Integrated Security=True;"
        + @"AttachDBFileName=¦DataDirectory¦MyDatabase.mdf;User Instance=True";
    SqlConnection con = new SqlConnection(connectionString);

    // Create Movie Categories command
    string cmdCategoriesText = "SELECT Id,Name FROM MovieCategories";
    SqlCommand cmdCategories = new SqlCommand(cmdCategoriesText, con);

    // Create Movie command
    string cmdMoviesText = "SELECT Title FROM Movies "
        + "WHERE CategoryId=@CategoryID";
    SqlCommand cmdMovies = new SqlCommand(cmdMoviesText, con);
    cmdMovies.Parameters.Add("@CategoryId", SqlDbType.Int);

    using (con)
    {
        con.Open();

        // Iterate through categories
        SqlDataReader categories = cmdCategories.ExecuteReader();
        while (categories.Read())
        {
            // Add category node
            int id = categories.GetInt32(0);
            string name = categories.GetString(1);
            TreeNode catNode = new TreeNode(name);
            TreeView1.Nodes.Add(catNode);

            // Iterate through matching movies
            cmdMovies.Parameters["@CategoryId"].Value = id;
            SqlDataReader movies = cmdMovies.ExecuteReader();
            while (movies.Read())
            {
                // Add movie node
                string title = movies.GetString(0);
                TreeNode movieNode = new TreeNode(title);
                catNode.ChildNodes.Add(movieNode);
```

19

```
                }
                movies.Close();
            }
        }
    }
</script>
<html xmlns="http://www.w3.org/1999/xhtml" >
<head id="Head1" runat="server">
    <title>Show MARS</title>
</head>
<body>
    <form id="form1" runat="server">
    <div>

    <asp:TreeView
        id="TreeView1"
        Runat="server" />

    </div>
    </form>
</body>
</html>
```

The `MultipleActiveResultSets` attribute is included in the connection string used to open the database connection. If MARS were not enabled, you couldn't loop through the interior `SqlDataReader` that represents the matching movies while the containing `SqlDataReader` that represents the movie categories is open.

Disconnected Data Access

The ADO.NET Framework supports two models of data access. In the first part of this chapter, you saw how you can use the `SqlConnection`, `SqlCommand`, and `SqlDataReader` objects to connect to a database and retrieve data. When you read data from a database by using a `SqlDataReader` object, an open connection must be maintained between your application and the database.

In this section, we examine the second model of data access supported by ADO.NET: the disconnected model. When you use the objects discussed in this section, you do not need to keep a connection to the database open.

This section discusses four new ADO.NET objects:

▶ **DataAdapter**—Enables you to transfer data from the physical database to the in-memory database and back again.

▶ **DataTable**—Represents an in-memory database table.

▶ **DataView**—Represents an in-memory database view.

▶ **DataSet**—Represents an in-memory database.

The ADO.NET objects discussed in this section are built on top of the ADO.NET objects discussed in the previous section. For example, behind the scenes, the DataAdapter uses a DataReader to retrieve data from a database.

The advantage of using the objects discussed in this section is that they provide you with more functionality. For example, you can filter and sort the rows represented by a DataView. Furthermore, you can use the DataTable object to track changes made to records and accept or reject the changes.

The big disadvantage of using the objects discussed in this section is that they tend to be slower and more resource intensive. Retrieving 500 records with a DataReader is much faster than retrieving 500 records with a DataAdapter.

NOTE

For detailed performance comparisons between the DataReader and DataAdapter, see Priya Dhawan's article at the Microsoft MSDN website (msdn.Microsoft.com), "Performance Comparison: Data Access Techniques."

Therefore, unless you need to use any of the specialized functionality supported by these objects, my recommendation is that you stick with the objects discussed in the first part of this chapter when accessing a database. In other words, DataReaders are good and DataAdapters are bad.

Using the DataAdapter Object

The DataAdapter acts as the bridge between an in-memory database table and a physical database table. You use the DataAdapter to retrieve data from a database and populate a DataTable. You also use a DataAdapter to push changes that you have made to a DataTable back to the physical database.

The component in Listing 19.25 illustrates how you can use a SqlDataAdapter to populate a DataTable.

19

LISTING 19.25   App_Code\Movie8.cs

```csharp
using System;
using System.Data;
using System.Data.SqlClient;
using System.Web.Configuration;
using System.Collections.Generic;

public class Movie8
{
    private static readonly string _connectionString;

    public DataTable GetAll()
    {
        // Initialize the DataAdapter
        SqlDataAdapter dad = new SqlDataAdapter(
"SELECT Title,Director FROM Movies", _connectionString);

        // Create a DataTable
        DataTable dtblMovies = new DataTable();

        // Populate the DataTable
        dad.Fill(dtblMovies);

        // Return results
        return dtblMovies;
    }

    static Movie8()
    {
        _connectionString =
WebConfigurationManager.ConnectionStrings["Movies"].ConnectionString;
    }
}
```

The page in Listing 19.26 contains a GridView that is bound to an ObjectDataSource that represents the component in Listing 19.25 (see Figure 19.12).

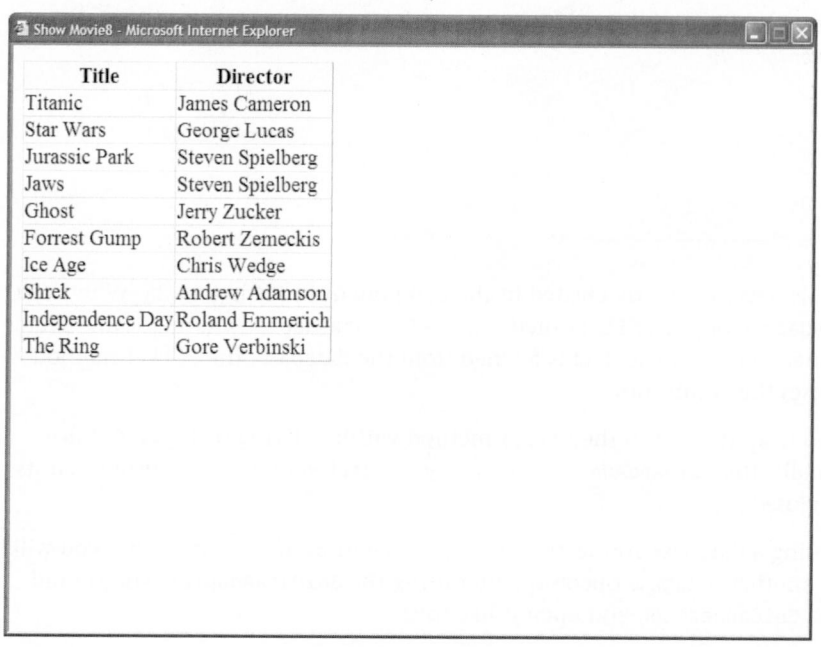

FIGURE 19.12   Displaying data with a DataAdapter.

LISTING 19.26   ShowMovie8.aspx

```
<%@ Page Language="C#" %>
<!DOCTYPE html PUBLIC "-//W3C//DTD XHTML 1.0 Transitional//EN"
  "http://www.w3.org/TR/xhtml1/DTD/xhtml1-transitional.dtd">
<html xmlns="http://www.w3.org/1999/xhtml" >
<head id="Head1" runat="server">
    <title>Show Movie8</title>
</head>
<body>
    <form id="form1" runat="server">
    <div>

    <asp:GridView
        id="grdMovies"
        DataSourceID="srcMovies"
        Runat="server" />

    <asp:ObjectDataSource
        id="srcMovies"
        TypeName="Movie8"
```

```
        SelectMethod="GetAll"
        Runat="server" />

   </div>
   </form>
</body>
</html>
```

A `SqlConnection` is never explicitly created in the component in Listing 19.25. When you call the `SqlDataAdapter` object's `Fill()` method, the `SqlDataAdapter` automatically creates and opens a connection. After the data is fetched from the database, the `Fill()` method automatically closes the connection.

You don't need to wrap the call to the `Fill()` method within a `Using` or `Try...Catch` statement. Internally, the `SqlDataAdapter` uses a `Try...Catch` statement to ensure that its connection gets closed.

Opening and closing a database connection is a slow operation. If you know that you will need to perform another database operation after using the `SqlDataAdapter`, you should explicitly create a `SqlConnection` and open it like this:

```
SqlConnection con = new SqlConnection(...connection string...);
SqlDataAdapter dad = new SqlDataAdapter("SELECT Title,Director FROM Movies", con);
using (con)
{
  con.Open();
  dad.Fill(dtblMovies);
  ... Perform other database operations with connection ...
}
```

If a `SqlConnection` is already open when you call the `Fill()` method, it doesn't close it. In other words, the `Fill()` method maintains the state of the connection.

Performing Batch Updates

You can think of a `SqlDataAdapter` as a collection of four `SqlCommand` objects:

▶ **SelectCommand**—Represents a `SqlCommand` used for selecting data from a database.

▶ **UpdateCommand**—Represents a `SqlCommand` used for updating data in a database.

▶ **InsertCommand**—Represents a `SqlCommand` used for inserting data into a database.

▶ **DeleteCommand**—Represents a `SqlCommand` used for deleting data from a database.

You can use a `DataAdapter` not only when retrieving data from a database, but also when updating, inserting, and deleting data from a database. If you call a `SqlDataAdapter` object's `Update()` method, and pass the method a `DataTable`, the `SqlDataAdapter` calls its `UpdateCommand`, `InsertCommand`, and `DeleteCommand` to make changes to the database.

You can assign a `SqlCommand` object to each of the four properties of the `SqlDataAdapter`. Alternatively, you can use the `SqlCommandBuilder` object to create the `UpdateCommand`, `InsertCommand`, and `DeleteCommand` for you. The `SqlCommandBuilder` class takes a `SqlDataAdapter` that has a `SELECT` command and generates the other three commands automatically.

For example, the page in Listing 19.27 displays all the records from the Movies database table in a spreadsheet created with a `Repeater` control (see Figure 19.13). If you make changes to the data and click the Update button, the Movies database table is updated with the changes.

FIGURE 19.13 Batch updating database records.

LISTING 19.27 ShowDataAdapterUpdate.aspx

```
<%@ Page Language="C#" %>
<%@ Import Namespace="System.Data" %>
<%@ Import Namespace="System.Data.SqlClient" %>
<%@ Import Namespace="System.Web.Configuration" %>
<!DOCTYPE html PUBLIC "-//W3C//DTD XHTML 1.0 Transitional//EN"
"http://www.w3.org/TR/xhtml1/DTD/xhtml1-transitional.dtd">
<script runat="server">

    private SqlDataAdapter dad;
    private DataTable dtblMovies;
```

```csharp
    void Page_Load()
    {
        // Create connection
        string connectionString =
WebConfigurationManager.ConnectionStrings["Movies"].ConnectionString;
        SqlConnection con = new SqlConnection(connectionString);

        // Create Select command
        dad = new SqlDataAdapter("SELECT Id,Title,Director FROM Movies", con);

        // Create Update, Insert, and Delete commands with SqlCommandBuilder
        SqlCommandBuilder builder = new SqlCommandBuilder(dad);

        // Add data to DataTable
        dtblMovies = new DataTable();
        dad.Fill(dtblMovies);

        // Bind data to Repeater
        rptMovies.DataSource = dtblMovies;
        rptMovies.DataBind();
    }

    protected void lnkUpdate_Click(object sender, EventArgs e)
    {
        // Update DataTable with changes
        for (int i=0; i < rptMovies.Items.Count;i++)
        {
            RepeaterItem item = rptMovies.Items[i];
            TextBox txtTitle = (TextBox)item.FindControl("txtTitle");
            TextBox txtDirector = (TextBox)item.FindControl("txtDirector");
            if (dtblMovies.Rows[i]["Title"] != txtTitle.Text)
                dtblMovies.Rows[i]["Title"] = txtTitle.Text;
            if (dtblMovies.Rows[i]["Director"] != txtDirector.Text)
                dtblMovies.Rows[i]["Director"] = txtDirector.Text;
        }

        // Set batch size to maximum size
        dad.UpdateBatchSize = 0;

        // Perform update
        int numUpdated = dad.Update(dtblMovies);
        lblResults.Text = String.Format("Updated {0} rows", numUpdated);
    }
</script>
<html xmlns="http://www.w3.org/1999/xhtml" >
<head id="Head1" runat="server">
```

```
    <title>Show DataAdapter Update</title>
</head>
<body>
    <form id="form1" runat="server">
    <div>

    <asp:Repeater
        id="rptMovies"
        EnableViewState="false"
        Runat="server">
        <HeaderTemplate>
        <table>
        <tr>
            <th>Title</th><th>Director</th>
        </tr>
        </HeaderTemplate>
        <ItemTemplate>
        <tr>
        <td>
        <asp:TextBox
            id="txtTitle"
            Text='<%#Eval("Title")%>'
            Runat="server" />
        </td>
        <td>
        <asp:TextBox
            id="txtDirector"
            Text='<%#Eval("Director")%>'
            Runat="server" />
        </td>
        </tr>
        </ItemTemplate>
        <FooterTemplate>
        </table>
        </FooterTemplate>
    </asp:Repeater>
    <br />

    <asp:LinkButton
        id="lnkUpdate"
        Text="Update Movies"
        Runat="server" OnClick="lnkUpdate_Click" />

    <br /><br />
```

```
    <asp:Label
        id="lblResults"
        EnableViewState="false"
        Runat="server" />

    </div>
    </form>
</body>
</html>
```

The SqlDataAdapter in Listing 19.27 performs a batch update. When a SqlDataAdapter object's UpdateBatchSize property is set to the value 0, the SqlDataAdapter performs all its updates in a single batch. If you want to perform updates in smaller batches, you can set the UpdateBatchSize to a particular size.

Using the DataTable Object

The DataTable object represents an in-memory database table. You can add rows to a DataTable with a SqlDataAdapter, with a SqlDataReader, with an XML file, or programmatically. For example, the page in Listing 19.28 builds a new DataTable programmatically. The contents of the DataTable then display in a GridView control (see Figure 19.14).

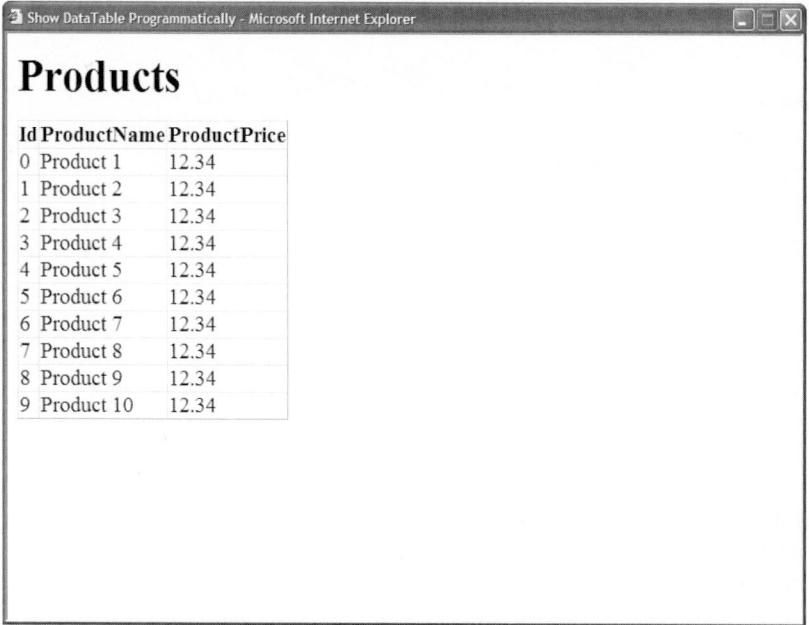

FIGURE 19.14   Displaying a DataTable that was built programmatically.

LISTING 19.28   ShowDataTableProgram.aspx

```
<%@ Page Language="C#" %>
<%@ Import Namespace="System.Data" %>
<!DOCTYPE html PUBLIC "-//W3C//DTD XHTML 1.0 Transitional//EN"
"http://www.w3.org/TR/xhtml1/DTD/xhtml1-transitional.dtd">
<script runat="server">

    void Page_Load()
    {
        // Create the DataTable columns
        DataTable newDataTable = new DataTable();
        newDataTable.Columns.Add("Id", typeof(int));
        newDataTable.Columns.Add("ProductName", typeof(string));
        newDataTable.Columns.Add("ProductPrice", typeof(decimal));

        // Mark the Id column as an autoincrement column
        newDataTable.Columns["Id"].AutoIncrement = true;

        // Add some data rows
        for (int i = 1; i < 11; i++)
        {
            DataRow newRow = newDataTable.NewRow();
            newRow["ProductName"] = "Product " + i.ToString();
            newRow["ProductPrice"] = 12.34m;
            newDataTable.Rows.Add(newRow);
        }

        // Bind DataTable to GridView
        grdProducts.DataSource = newDataTable;
        grdProducts.DataBind();
    }
</script>
<html xmlns="http://www.w3.org/1999/xhtml" >
<head id="Head1" runat="server">
    <title>Show DataTable Programmatically</title>
</head>
<body>
    <form id="form1" runat="server">
    <div>

    <h1>Products</h1>
```

19

```
<asp:GridView
    id="grdProducts"
    Runat="server" />

</div>
</form>
</body>
</html>
```

In Listing 19.28, a DataTable with the following three columns is created: Id, ProductName, and ProductPrice. The data type of each column is specified with a .NET Framework type. For example, the ProductPrice column is created as a decimal column. Alternatively, you could create each column with a SqlType. For example, you could use System.Data.SqlTypes.SqlDecimal for the type of the ProductPrice column.

The Id column is created as an autoincrement column. When you add new rows to the DataTable, the column increments its value automatically.

Selecting DataRows

You can retrieve particular rows from a DataTable by using the DataTable object's Select() method. The Select() method accepts a filter parameter. You can use just about anything that you would use in a SQL WHERE clause with the filter parameter.

When you retrieve an array of rows with the Select() method, you can also specify a sort order for the rows. When specifying a sort order, you can use any expression that you would use with a SQL ORDER BY clause.

For example, the page in Listing 19.29 caches a DataTable in memory with the ASP.NET Cache object. The page contains a TextBox control. When you enter a partial movie title into the TextBox control, a list of matching movies is displayed in a GridView control. The rows are sorted in order of the movie title (see Figure 19.15).

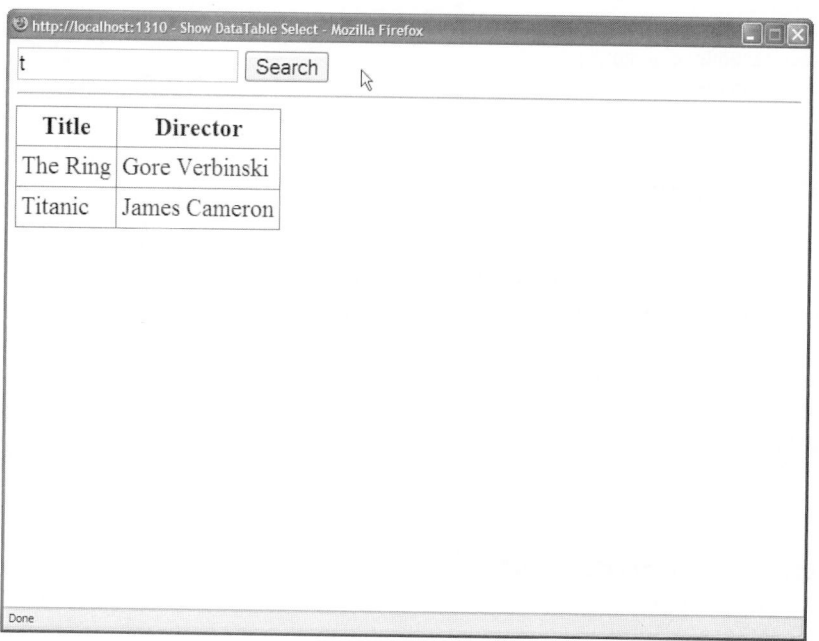

FIGURE 19.15   Selecting matching rows from a cached `DataTable`.

LISTING 19.29   ShowDataTableSelect.aspx

```
<%@ Page Language="C#" %>
<%@ Import Namespace="System.Data" %>
<%@ Import Namespace="System.Data.SqlClient" %>
<%@ Import Namespace="System.Web.Configuration" %>
<!DOCTYPE html PUBLIC "-//W3C//DTD XHTML 1.0 Transitional//EN"
"http://www.w3.org/TR/xhtml1/DTD/xhtml1-transitional.dtd">
<script runat="server">

    protected void btnSearch_Click(object sender, EventArgs e)
    {
        // Get movies DataTable from Cache
        DataTable dtblMovies = (DataTable)Cache["MoviesToFilter"];
        if (dtblMovies == null)
        {
            dtblMovies = GetMoviesFromDB();
            Cache["MoviesToFilter"] = dtblMovies;
        }

        // Select matching rows
        string filter = String.Format("Title LIKE '{0}*'", txtTitle.Text);
        DataRow[] rows = dtblMovies.Select(filter, "Title");
```

19

```
        // Bind to GridView
        grdMovies.DataSource = rows;
        grdMovies.DataBind();
    }

    private DataTable GetMoviesFromDB()
    {
        string connectionString =
WebConfigurationManager.ConnectionStrings["Movies"].ConnectionString;
        SqlDataAdapter dad = new SqlDataAdapter(
"SELECT Title, Director FROM Movies", connectionString);
        DataTable dtblMovies = new DataTable();
        dad.Fill(dtblMovies);
        return dtblMovies;

    }
</script>
<html xmlns="http://www.w3.org/1999/xhtml" >
<head id="Head1" runat="server">
    <style type="text/css">
        th, td
        {
            padding:5px;
        }
    </style>
    <title>Show DataTable Select</title>
</head>
<body>
    <form id="form1" runat="server">
    <div>

    <asp:TextBox
        id="txtTitle"
        Tooltip="Search"
        Runat="server" />
    <asp:Button
        id="btnSearch"
        Text="Search"
        Runat="server" OnClick="btnSearch_Click" />


    <hr />

    <asp:GridView
        id="grdMovies"
        AutoGenerateColumns="false"
```

```
            Runat="server">
            <Columns>
            <asp:TemplateField HeaderText="Title">
            <ItemTemplate>
                <%# ((DataRow)Container.DataItem)["Title"] %>
            </ItemTemplate>
            </asp:TemplateField>
            <asp:TemplateField HeaderText="Director">
            <ItemTemplate>
                <%# ((DataRow)Container.DataItem)["Director"] %>
            </ItemTemplate>
            </asp:TemplateField>
            </Columns>
            </asp:GridView>

    </div>
    </form>
</body>
</html>
```

The `DataTable Select()` method returns an array of `DataRow` objects. There is nothing wrong with binding an array of `DataRow` objects to a `GridView` control. However, you must explicitly cast each data item to a `DataRow` and read within a `GridView` `TemplateField`.

DataRow States and DataRow Versions

When you modify the rows in a `DataTable`, the `DataTable` keeps track of the changes that you make. A `DataTable` maintains both the original and modified version of each row.

Each row in a `DataTable` has a particular `RowState` that has one of the following values:

- ▶ **Unchanged**—The row has not been changed.
- ▶ **Added**—The row has been added.
- ▶ **Modified**—The row has been modified.
- ▶ **Deleted**—The row has been deleted.
- ▶ **Detached**—The row has been created but not added to the `DataTable`.

Each row in a `DataTable` can have more than one version. Each version is represented by one of the following values of the `DataRowVersion` enumeration:

- ▶ **Current**—The current version of the row.
- ▶ **Default**—The default version of the row.
- ▶ **Original**—The original version of the row.
- ▶ **Proposed**—The version of a row that exists during editing.

You can use the DataTable.AcceptChanges() method to copy the current versions of all the rows to the original versions of all the rows. And you can use the DataTable.RejectChanges() method to copy the original versions of all the rows to the current versions of all the rows.

For example, the component in Listing 19.30 includes an AcceptChanges() and RejectChanges() method. The component maintains a DataTable in Session state. If you update a row in the DataTable, the row is updated in memory. If the RejectChanges() method is called, any changes made to the DataTable are rejected. If the AcceptChanges() method is called, the database is updated and all changes are accepted.

LISTING 19.30 App_Code\Movie9.cs

```
using System;
using System.Data;
using System.Data.SqlClient;
using System.Web;
using System.Web.Configuration;

public class Movie9
{
    private SqlDataAdapter dad = new SqlDataAdapter();

    public DataTable GetAll()
    {
        return (DataTable)HttpContext.Current.Session["MoviesToEdit"];
    }

    public void Update(int id, string title, string director)
    {
        DataTable movies = (DataTable)HttpContext.Current.Session["MoviestoEdit"];
        DataRow rowToEdit = movies.Rows.Find(id);
        rowToEdit["title"] = title;
        rowToEdit["director"] = director;
    }

    public void RejectChanges()
    {
        DataTable movies = (DataTable)HttpContext.Current.Session["MoviestoEdit"];
        movies.RejectChanges();
    }
```

```
    public void AcceptChanges()
    {
        DataTable movies = (DataTable)HttpContext.Current.Session["MoviestoEdit"];
        dad.Update(movies);
        movies.AcceptChanges();
    }


    public Movie9()
    {
        // Create Data Adapter
        string connectionString =
WebConfigurationManager.ConnectionStrings["Movies"].ConnectionString;
        dad = new SqlDataAdapter(
"SELECT Id,Title,Director FROM Movies", connectionString);
        SqlCommandBuilder builder = new SqlCommandBuilder(dad);
        dad.UpdateBatchSize = 0;

        HttpContext context = HttpContext.Current;
        if (context.Session["MoviesToEdit"] == null)
        {
            // Add data to DataTable
            DataTable dtblMovies = new DataTable();
            dad.Fill(dtblMovies);
            dtblMovies.PrimaryKey = new DataColumn[] { dtblMovies.Columns["Id"] };
            context.Session["MoviesToEdit"] = dtblMovies;
        }
    }
}
```

The page in Listing 19.31 contains a GridView that is bound to the component in Listing 19.30. The GridView includes a column that indicates whether each row has been changed. The column displays the value of the corresponding DataRow object's RowState property (see Figure 19.16).

19

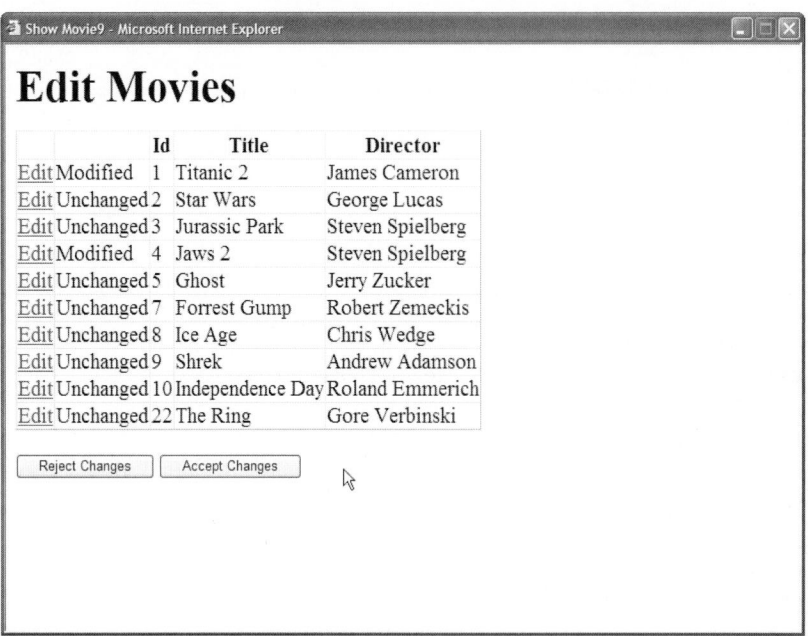

FIGURE 19.16   Tracking data row changes.

LISTING 19.31   ShowMovie9.aspx

```
<%@ Page Language="C#" %>
<%@ Import Namespace="System.Data" %>
<!DOCTYPE html PUBLIC "-//W3C//DTD XHTML 1.0 Transitional//EN"
"http://www.w3.org/TR/xhtml1/DTD/xhtml1-transitional.dtd">
<script runat="server">

    protected void btnReject_Click(object sender, EventArgs e)
    {
        Movie9 movie = new Movie9();
        movie.RejectChanges();
        grdMovies.DataBind();
    }


    protected void btnAccept_Click(object sender, EventArgs e)
    {
        Movie9 movie = new Movie9();
        movie.AcceptChanges();
        grdMovies.DataBind();
    }
</script>
<html xmlns="http://www.w3.org/1999/xhtml" >
```

```
<head id="Head1" runat="server">
    <title>Show Movie9</title>
</head>
<body>
    <form id="form1" runat="server">
    <div>

    <h1>Edit Movies</h1>

    <asp:GridView
        id="grdMovies"
        DataSourceID="srcMovies"
        DataKeyNames="Id"
        AutoGenerateEditButton="true"
        Runat="server">
        <Columns>
        <asp:TemplateField>
        <ItemTemplate>
        <%# ((DataRowView)Container.DataItem).Row.RowState %>
        </ItemTemplate>
        </asp:TemplateField>
        </Columns>
    </asp:GridView>

    <br />

    <asp:Button
        id="btnReject"
        Text="Reject Changes"
        OnClick="btnReject_Click"
        Runat="server" />

    <asp:Button
        id="btnAccept"
        Text="Accept Changes"
        OnClick="btnAccept_Click"
        Runat="server" />

    <asp:ObjectDataSource
        id="srcMovies"
        TypeName="Movie9"
        SelectMethod="GetAll"
        UpdateMethod="Update"
        Runat="server" />

    </div>
```

```
    </form>
</body>
</html>
```

If you click the Accept Changes button, all the changes made to the rows in the GridView are sent to the database. If you click the Reject Changes button, all the rows revert to their original values.

Using the `DataView` Object

The DataView object represents an in-memory database view. You can use a DataView object to create a sortable, filterable view of a DataTable.

The DataView object supports three important properties:

- ▶ **Sort**—Enables you to sort the rows represented by the DataView.
- ▶ **RowFilter**—Enables you to filter the rows represented by the DataView.
- ▶ **RowStateFilter**—Enables you to filter the rows represented by the DataView according to the row state (for example, OriginalRows, CurrentRows, Unchanged).

The easiest way to create a new DataView is to use the DefaultView property exposed by the DataTable class like this:

```
Dim dataView1 As DataView = dataTable1.DefaultView;
```

The DefaultView property returns an unsorted, unfiltered view of the data contained in a DataTable.

You also can directly instantiate a new DataView object by passing a DataTable, filter, sort order, and DataViewRowState filter to the DataView object's constructor, like this:

```
DataView dataView1 = new DataView(dataTable1,
    "BoxOfficeTotals > 100000",
    "Title ASC",
    DataViewRowState.CurrentRows);
```

This statement creates a new DataView from a DataTable that represents the Movies database table. The rows are filtered to include only the movies that have a box office total greater than 100,000 dollars. Also, the rows are sorted by the movie title in ascending order. Finally, all the current rows are represented from the DataTable (as opposed, for instance, to rows that have been deleted).

The page in Listing 19.30 illustrates one way that you can use a DataView. In Listing 19.32, a DataView is cached in Session state. You can sort the cached DataView by clicking on the header links rendered by the GridView control (see Figure 19.17).

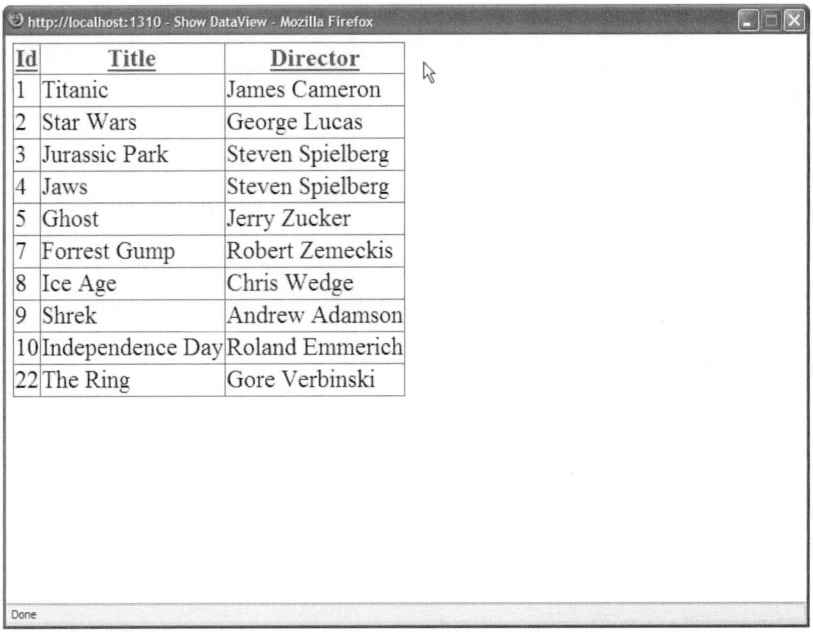

FIGURE 19.17   Sorting a cached DataView.

LISTING 19.32   ShowDataView.aspx

```
<%@ Page Language="C#" %>
<%@ Import Namespace="System.Data" %>
<%@ Import Namespace="System.Data.SqlClient" %>
<%@ Import Namespace="System.Web.Configuration" %>
<!DOCTYPE html PUBLIC "-//W3C//DTD XHTML 1.0 Transitional//EN"
"http://www.w3.org/TR/xhtml1/DTD/xhtml1-transitional.dtd">
<script runat="server">

    void Page_Load()
    {
        if (Session["MoviesToSort"] == null)
        {
            string connectionString =
WebConfigurationManager.ConnectionStrings["Movies"].ConnectionString;
            SqlDataAdapter dad = new SqlDataAdapter(
"SELECT Id,Title,Director FROM Movies", connectionString);
            DataTable dtblMovies = new DataTable();
            dad.Fill(dtblMovies);
            Session["MoviesToSort"] = dtblMovies.DefaultView;
        }

        if (!Page.IsPostBack)
```

19

```
                BindMovies();
    }

    void BindMovies()
    {
        grdMovies.DataSource = Session["MoviesToSort"];
        grdMovies.DataBind();
    }

    protected void grdMovies_Sorting(object sender, GridViewSortEventArgs e)
    {
        DataView dvwMovies = (DataView)Session["MoviesToSort"];
        dvwMovies.Sort = e.SortExpression;
        BindMovies();
    }
</script>

<html xmlns="http://www.w3.org/1999/xhtml" >
<head id="Head1" runat="server">
    <title>Show DataView</title>
</head>
<body>
    <form id="form1" runat="server">
    <div>

    <asp:GridView
        id="grdMovies"
        AllowSorting="true"
        OnSorting="grdMovies_Sorting"
        Runat="server" />

    </div>
    </form>
</body>
</html>
```

Using the DataSet Object

The DataSet object represents an in-memory database. A single DataSet can contain one
or many DataTable objects. You can define parent/child relationships between the
DataTable objects contained in a DataSet.

For example, the page in Listing 19.33 contains a TreeView control. The TreeView displays
a list of movie categories and, beneath each movie category, a list of matching movies (see
Figure 19.18).

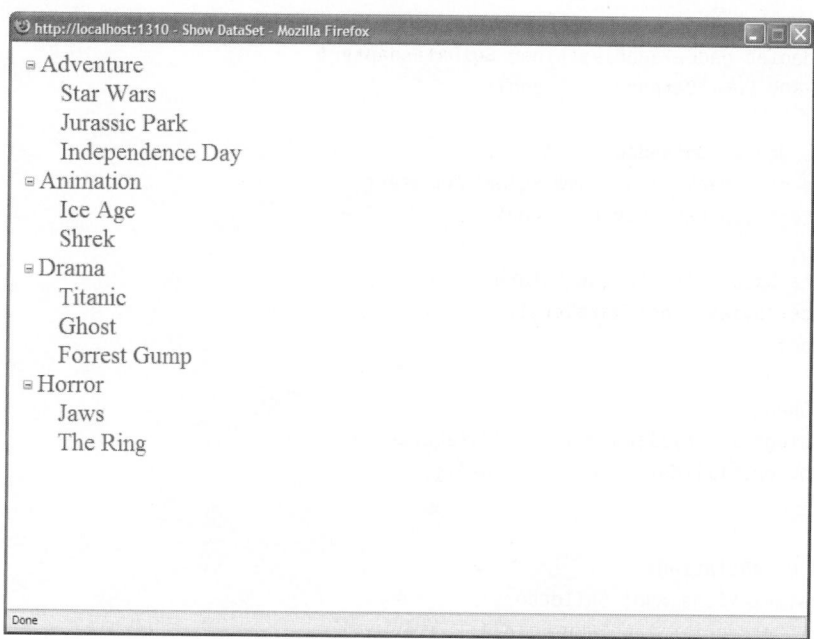

FIGURE 19.18   Building a `TreeView` from a `DataSet`.

LISTING 19.33   ShowDataSet.aspx

```
<%@ Page Language="C#" %>
<%@ Import Namespace="System.Data" %>
<%@ Import Namespace="System.Data.SqlClient" %>
<%@ Import Namespace="System.Web.Configuration" %>
<!DOCTYPE html PUBLIC "-//W3C//DTD XHTML 1.0 Transitional//EN"
"http://www.w3.org/TR/xhtml1/DTD/xhtml1-transitional.dtd">
<script runat="server">

    void Page_Load()
    {
        if (!Page.IsPostBack)
            BuildTree();
    }

    void BuildTree()
    {
        // Create Connection
        string connectionString =
WebConfigurationManager.ConnectionStrings["Movies"].ConnectionString;
        SqlConnection con = new SqlConnection(connectionString);
```

19

```
        // Create Movie Categories DataAdapter
        SqlDataAdapter dadCategories = new SqlDataAdapter(
"SELECT Id,Name FROM MovieCategories", con);

        // Create Movies DataAdapter
        SqlDataAdapter dadMovies = new SqlDataAdapter(
"SELECT Title,CategoryId FROM Movies", con);

        // Add the DataTables to the DataSet
        DataSet dstMovies = new DataSet();
        using (con)
        {
            con.Open();
            dadCategories.Fill(dstMovies, "Categories");
            dadMovies.Fill(dstMovies, "Movies");
        }

        // Add a DataRelation
        dstMovies.Relations.Add("Children",
dstMovies.Tables["Categories"].Columns["Id"],
dstMovies.Tables["Movies"].Columns["CategoryId"]);

        // Add the Movie Category nodes
        foreach (DataRow categoryRow in dstMovies.Tables["Categories"].Rows)
        {
            string name = (string)categoryRow["Name"];
            TreeNode catNode = new TreeNode(name);
            TreeView1.Nodes.Add(catNode);

            // Get matching movies
            DataRow[] movieRows = categoryRow.GetChildRows("Children");
            foreach (DataRow movieRow in movieRows)
            {
                string title = (string)movieRow["Title"];
                TreeNode movieNode = new TreeNode(title);
                catNode.ChildNodes.Add(movieNode);
            }
        }
    }
</script>
<html xmlns="http://www.w3.org/1999/xhtml" >
<head id="Head1" runat="server">
    <title>Show DataSet</title>
</head>
<body>
```

```
<form id="form1" runat="server">
<div>

<asp:TreeView
    id="TreeView1"
    Runat="server" />

</div>
</form>
</body>
</html>
```

The `TreeView` is built programmatically. In the `BuildTree()` method, a `DataSet` is created that contains two `DataTable` objects. The first `DataTable` represents the MovieCategories database table, and the second `DataTable` represents the Movies database table. A parent/child relationship is created between the two `DataTable` objects with the help of a `DataRelation`.

The `DataRelation` is used to get the movies that match each movie category. The `DataRow.GetChildRows()` method is called to retrieve the movies that match a particular movie category.

Executing Asynchronous Database Commands

Normally, when you execute a database command, the thread executing the command must wait until the command finishes before executing any additional code. In other words, normally, when you execute a database command, the thread is blocked.

When you take advantage of asynchronous commands, on the other hand, the database command is executed on another thread so that the current thread can continue performing other work. For example, you can use the current thread to execute yet another database command.

There are two reasons that you might want to use asynchronous database commands when building an ASP.NET page. First, executing multiple database commands simultaneously can significantly improve your application's performance. This is especially true when the database commands are executed against different database servers.

Second, the ASP.NET Framework uses a limited thread pool to service page requests. When ASP.NET Framework receives a request for a page, it assigns a thread to handle the request. If ASP.NET Framework runs out of threads, the request is queued until a thread becomes available. If too many threads are queued, the framework rejects the page request with a 503—Server Too Busy response code.

19

If you execute a database command asynchronously, the current thread is released back into the thread pool so that it can be used to service another page request. While the asynchronous database command is executing, ASP.NET Framework can devote its attention to handling other page requests. When the asynchronous command completes, the framework reassigns a thread to the original request and the page finishes executing.

NOTE

You can configure the ASP.NET thread pool with the `httpRuntime` element in the web configuration file. You can modify the `appRequestQueueLimit`, `minFreeThreads`, and `minLocalRequestFreeThreads` attributes to control how many requests ASP.NET Framework queues before giving up and sending an error.

There are two parts to this task undertaken in this section. A data access component that supports asynchronous ADO.NET methods must be created and an ASP.NET page that executes asynchronously.

Using Asynchronous ADO.NET Methods

There are asynchronous versions of several ADO.NET methods. These methods come in pairs: a `Begin` and `End` method. For example, the `SqlCommand` object supports the following asynchronous methods:

- `BeginExecuteNonQuery()`

- `EndExecuteNonQuery()`

- `BeginExecuteReader()`

- `EndExecuteReader()`

- `BeginExecuteXmlReader()`

- `EndExecuteXmlReader()`

The idea is that when you execute the `Begin` method, the asynchronous task is started on a separate thread. When the method finishes executing, you can use the `End` method to get the results.

To use these asynchronous methods, you must use a special attribute in your connection string: the `Asynchronous Processing=true` attribute.

The data access component in Listing 19.34 contains a `BeginGetMovies()` and `EndGetMovies()` method that fetches movies from the Movies database table asynchronously. These methods use the ADO.NET `BeginExecuteReader()` and `EndExecuteReader()` to fetch a `DataReader` asynchronously.

LISTING 19.34   App_Code\AsyncDataLayer.cs

```csharp
using System;
using System.Data;
using System.Data.SqlClient;
using System.Web.Configuration;
using System.Collections.Generic;

public class AsyncDataLayer
{
    private static readonly string _connectionString;
    private SqlCommand _cmdMovies;

    public IAsyncResult BeginGetMovies(AsyncCallback callback, Object state)
    {
        SqlConnection con = new SqlConnection(_connectionString);
        _cmdMovies = new SqlCommand(
"WAITFOR DELAY '0:0:01';SELECT Title,Director FROM Movies", con);
        con.Open();
        return _cmdMovies.BeginExecuteReader(callback, state,
CommandBehavior.CloseConnection);
    }

    public List<AsyncDataLayer.Movie> EndGetMovies(IAsyncResult result)
    {
        List<AsyncDataLayer.Movie> results = new List<AsyncDataLayer.Movie>();
        SqlDataReader reader = _cmdMovies.EndExecuteReader(result);
        while (reader.Read())
        {
            AsyncDataLayer.Movie newMovie = new AsyncDataLayer.Movie();
            newMovie.Title = (string)reader["Title"];
            newMovie.Director = (string)reader["Director"];
            results.Add(newMovie);
        }
        return results;
    }

    static AsyncDataLayer()
    {
        _connectionString =
WebConfigurationManager.ConnectionStrings["Movies"].ConnectionString
            + ";Asynchronous Processing=true";
    }

    public class Movie
    {
```

19

```
        private string _title;
        private string _director;

        public string Title
        {
            get { return _title; }
            set { _title = value; }
        }

        public string Director
        {
            get { return _director; }
            set { _director = value; }
        }
    }
}
```

Using Asynchronous ASP.NET Pages

When you take advantage of asynchronous ADO.NET methods, you must also enable asynchronous ASP.NET page execution. You enable an asynchronous ASP.NET page by adding the following two attributes to a page directive:

```
<%@ Page Async="true" AsyncTimeout="8" %>
```

The first attribute enables asynchronous page execution. The second attribute specifies a timeout value in seconds. The timeout value specifies the amount of time that the page gives a set of asynchronous tasks to complete before the page continues execution.

After you enable asynchronous page execution, you must set up the asynchronous tasks and register the tasks with the page. You represent each asynchronous task with an instance of the PageAsyncTask object. You register an asynchronous task for a page by calling the Page.RegisterAsyncTask() method.

For example, the page in Listing 19.35 displays the records from the Movies database table in a GridView control. The database records are retrieved asynchronously from the AsyncDataLayer component created in the previous section.

LISTING 19.35 ShowPageAsyncTask.aspx

```
<%@ Page Language="C#" Async="true" AsyncTimeout="5" Trace="true" %>
<%@ Import Namespace="System.Threading" %>
<!DOCTYPE html PUBLIC "-//W3C//DTD XHTML 1.0 Transitional//EN"
"http://www.w3.org/TR/xhtml1/DTD/xhtml1-transitional.dtd">
<script runat="server">
```

```
    private AsyncDataLayer dataLayer = new AsyncDataLayer();


    void Page_Load()
    {
        // Setup asynchronous data execution
        PageAsyncTask task =
 new PageAsyncTask(BeginGetData, EndGetData, TimeoutData, null, true);
        Page.RegisterAsyncTask(task);

        // Fire off asynchronous tasks
        Page.ExecuteRegisteredAsyncTasks();
    }


    IAsyncResult BeginGetData(object sender, EventArgs e,
AsyncCallback callback, object state)
    {
        // Show Page Thread ID
        Trace.Warn("BeginGetData: " + Thread.CurrentThread.GetHashCode());

        // Execute asynchronous command
        return dataLayer.BeginGetMovies(callback, state);
    }


    void EndGetData(IAsyncResult ar)
    {
        // Show Page Thread ID
        Trace.Warn("EndGetDate: " + Thread.CurrentThread.GetHashCode());

        // Bind results
        grdMovies.DataSource = dataLayer.EndGetMovies(ar);
        grdMovies.DataBind();
    }


    void TimeoutData(IAsyncResult ar)
    {
        // Display error message
        lblError.Text = "Could not retrieve data!";
    }
</script>
<html xmlns="http://www.w3.org/1999/xhtml" >
<head id="Head1" runat="server">
    <title>Show Page AsyncTask</title>
</head>
<body>
    <form id="form1" runat="server">
    <div>
```

19

```
    <asp:Label
        id="lblError"
        Runat="server" />

    <asp:GridView
        id="grdMovies"
        Runat="server" />

    </div>
    </form>
</body>
</html>
```

The page in Listing 19.35 creates an instance of the `PageAsyncTask` object that represents the asynchronous task. Next, the `PageAsyncTask` object is registered for the page with the `Page.RegisterAsyncTask()` method. Finally, a call to the `Page.ExecuteRegisteredAsyncTasks()` method executes the task. (If you don't call this method, any asynchronous tasks registered for the page are executed during the `PreRender` event automatically.)

The constructor for the `PageAsyncTask` object accepts the following parameters:

▶ **beginHandler**—The method that executes when the asynchronous task begins.

▶ **endHandler**—The method that executes when the asynchronous task ends.

▶ **timoutHandler**—The method that executes when the asynchronous task runs out of time according to the `Page` directive's `AsyncTimeout` attribute.

▶ **state**—An arbitrary object that represents state information.

▶ **executeInParallel**—A Boolean value that indicates whether multiple asynchronous tasks should execute at the same time or execute in sequence.

You can create multiple `PageAsyncTask` objects and register them for the same page. When you call the `ExecuteRegisteredAsyncTasks()` method, all the registered tasks are executed.

If an asynchronous task does not complete within the time allotted by the `AsyncTimeout` attribute, the `timoutHandler` method executes. For example, the page in Listing 19.35 gives the asynchronous tasks 5 seconds to execute. If the database `SELECT` command does not return a record within the 5 seconds, the `TimeoutData()` method executes.

It is important to understand that the asynchronous task continues to execute even when the task executes longer than the interval of time specified by the `AsyncTimeout` attribute. The `AsyncTimeout` attribute specifies the amount of time that a page is willing to wait before continuing execution. An asynchronous task is not canceled if takes too long.

The page in Listing 19.35 has tracing enabled and is sprinkled liberally with calls to Trace.Warn() so that you can see when different events happen. The Trace.Warn() statements writes out the ID of the current Page thread. The Page thread ID can change between the BeginGetData() and EndGetData() methods (see Figure 19.19).

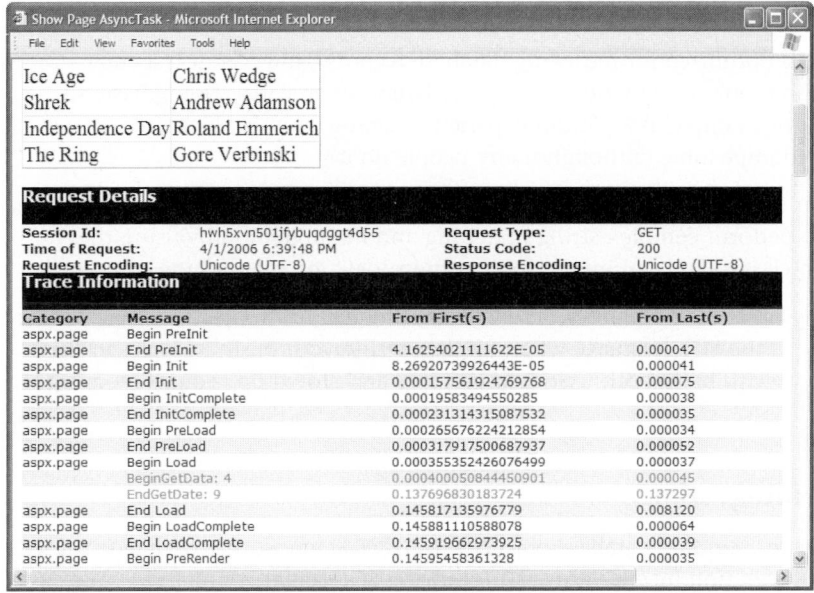

FIGURE 19.19   Trace information for a page executed asynchronously.

You can force the asynchronous task in Listing 19.35 to time out by adding a delay to the database command executed by the AsyncDataLayer.BeginGetMovies() method. For example, the following SELECT statement waits 15 seconds before returning results:

```
WAITFOR DELAY '0:0:15';SELECT Title,Director FROM Movies
```

If you use this modified SELECT statement, the asynchronous task times out and the TimeoutData() method executes. The TimeoutData() method simply displays a message in a Label control.

NOTE

As an alternative to using the Page.RegisterAsyncTask() method to register an asynchronous task, you can use the Page.AddOnPreRenderCompleteAsync() method. However, this latter method does not provide you with as many options.

19

Building Database Objects with the .NET Framework

Microsoft SQL Server 2005 and 2008 (including Microsoft SQL Server Express) supports building database objects with .NET Framework. For example, you can create user-defined types, stored procedures, user-defined functions, and triggers written with the Visual Basic .NET or C# programming language.

The SQL language is optimized for retrieving database records. However, it is a crazy language that doesn't look like any other computer language on earth. Doing basic string parsing with SQL, for example, is a painful experience. Doing complex logic in a stored procedure is next to impossible (although many people do it).

When you work in the .NET Framework, on the other hand, you have access to thousands of classes. You can perform complex string matching and manipulation by using the Regular expression classes. You can implement business logic, no matter how complex.

By taking advantage of the .NET Framework when writing database objects, you no longer have to struggle with the SQL language when implementing your business logic. In this section, you learn how to build both user-defined types and stored procedures by using .NET Framework.

Enabling CLR Integration

By default, support for building database objects with .NET Framework is disabled. You must enable CLR integration by executing the following SQL Server command:

```
sp_configure 'clr enabled', 1
RECONFIGURE
```

When using SQL Express, you can execute these two commands by right-clicking a database in the Database Explorer window and selecting the New Query menu option. Enter the following string:

```
sp_configure 'clr enabled', 1; RECONFIGURE
```

Select Query Designer, Execute SQL to execute the commands (see Figure 19.20). You receive warnings that the query can't be parsed, which you can safely ignore.

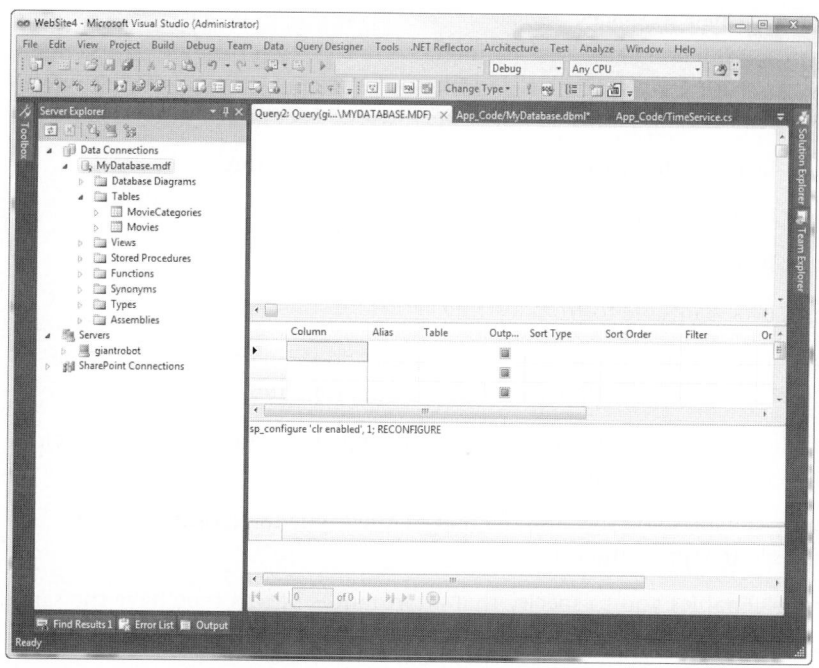

FIGURE 19.20 Executing a database query in Visual Web Developer.

Creating User-Defined Types with .NET Framework

You can create a new user-defined type by creating either a .NET class or .NET structure. After you create a user-defined type, you can use it in exactly the same way as the built-in SQL types such as the Int, NVarChar, or Decimal types. For example, you can create a new type and use the type to define a column in a database table.

To create a user-defined type with the .NET Framework, you must complete each of the following steps:

1. Create an assembly that contains the new type.
2. Register the assembly with SQL Server.
3. Create a type based on the assembly.

We go through each of these steps and walk through the process of creating a new user-defined type. We create a new user-defined type named DBMovie. The DBMovie type represents information about a particular movie. The type includes properties for the Title, Director, and BoxOfficeTotals for the movie.

After we create the DBMovie type, we can use the new type to define a column in a database table. Next, we write ADO.NET code that inserts and retrieves DBMovie objects from the database.

19

Creating the User-Defined Type Assembly

You can create a new user-defined type by creating either a class or a structure. We create the DBMovie type by creating a new .NET class. When creating a class that will be used as a user-defined type, you must meet certain requirements:

▶ The class must be decorated with a `SqlUserDefinedType` attribute.

▶ The class must be able to equal `NULL`.

▶ The class must be serializable to/from a byte array.

▶ The class must be serializable to/from a string.

If you plan to use a class as a user-defined type, you must add the `SqlUserDefinedType` attribute to the class. This attribute supports the following properties:

▶ **Format**—Enables you to specify how a user-defined type is serialized in SQL Server. Possible values are `Native` and `UserDefined`.

▶ **IsByteOrdered**—Enables you to cause the user-defined type to be ordered in the same way as its byte representation.

▶ **IsFixedLength**—Enables you to specify that all instances of this type have the same length.

▶ **MaxByteSize**—Enables you to specify the maximum size of the user-defined type in bytes.

▶ **Name**—Enables you to specify a name for the user-defined type.

▶ **ValidationMethodName**—Enables you to specify the name of a method that is called to verify whether a user-defined type is valid (useful when retrieving a user-defined type from an untrusted source).

The most important of these properties is the `Format` property. You use this property to specify how the user-defined type is serialized. The easiest option is to pick `Native`. In that case, SQL Server handles all the serialization issues, and you don't need to perform any additional work. Unfortunately, you can take advantage of native serialization only for simple classes. If your class exposes a nonvalue type property such as a `String`, you can't use native serialization.

Because the `DBMovie` class includes a `Title` and `Director` property, it's necessary to use `UserDefined` serialization. This means that it's also necessary to implement the `IBinarySerialize` interface to specify how the class gets serialized.

The `DBMovie` class is contained in Listing 19.36.

LISTING 19.36   DBMovie.cs

```
using System;
using System.Text;
using Microsoft.SqlServer.Server;
using System.Data.SqlTypes;
```

```csharp
using System.Runtime.InteropServices;
using System.IO;

[SqlUserDefinedType(Format.UserDefined, MaxByteSize = 512, IsByteOrdered = true)]
public class DBMovie : INullable, IBinarySerialize
{
    private bool _isNull;
    private string _title;
    private string _director;
    private decimal _boxOfficeTotals;

    public bool IsNull
    {
        get { return _isNull; }
    }

    public static DBMovie Null
    {
        get
        {
            DBMovie movie = new DBMovie();
            movie._isNull = true;
            return movie;
        }
    }

    public string Title
    {
        get { return _title; }
        set { _title = value; }
    }


    public string Director
    {
        get { return _director; }
        set { _director = value; }
    }

    [SqlFacet(Precision = 38, Scale = 2)]
    public decimal BoxOfficeTotals
    {
        get { return _boxOfficeTotals; }
        set { _boxOfficeTotals = value; }
    }
```

19

```csharp
[SqlMethod(OnNullCall = false)]
public static DBMovie Parse(SqlString s)
{
    if (s.IsNull)
        return Null;

    DBMovie movie = new DBMovie();
    string[] parts = s.Value.Split(new char[] { ',' });
    movie.Title = parts[0];
    movie.Director = parts[1];
    movie.BoxOfficeTotals = decimal.Parse(parts[2]);
    return movie;
}

public override string ToString()
{
    if (this.IsNull)
        return "NULL";

    StringBuilder builder = new StringBuilder();
    builder.Append(_title);
    builder.Append(",");
    builder.Append(_director);
    builder.Append(",");
    builder.Append(_boxOfficeTotals.ToString());
    return builder.ToString();
}

public void Write(BinaryWriter w)
{
    w.Write(_title);
    w.Write(_director);
    w.Write(_boxOfficeTotals);
}

public void Read(BinaryReader r)
{
    _title = r.ReadString();
    _director = r.ReadString();
    _boxOfficeTotals = r.ReadDecimal();
}

public DBMovie()
{
}
}
```

The class in Listing 19.36 exposes three properties: the movie Title, Director, and BoxOfficeTotals properties. The BoxOfficeTotals property is decorated with a SqlFacet attribute that indicates the precision and scale of the property value. You must include this attribute if you want to perform SQL queries that use comparison operators with this property.

The class in Listing 19.36 also includes both an IsNull and Null property. SQL Server uses a three-valued logic (True,False,Null). All SQL Server types must be nullable.

The DBMovie class also includes both a Parse() and a ToString() method. These methods are required for converting the DBMovie class back and forth to a string representation.

Finally, the DBMovie class includes both a Write() and Read() method. These methods are required by the IBinarySerialize interface. The Write() method serializes the class. The Read() method deserializes the class. These methods must be implemented because the class uses UserDefined serialization.

You need to compile the DBMovie class into a separate assembly (.dll file). After you create (and debug) the class, move the class from your App_Code folder to another folder in your application, such as the root folder. Next, open the Visual Studio 2010 Command prompt and execute the following command:

```
csc /t:library DBMovie.cs
```

This command uses the C# command-line compiler to compile the DBMovie class into an assembly.

Registering the User-Defined Type Assembly with SQL Server

After you create the assembly that contains your user-defined type, you must register the assembly in SQL Server. You can register the DBMovie assembly by executing the following command in a query window:

```
CREATE ASSEMBLY DBMovie
FROM 'C:\DBMovie.dll'
```

You need to provide the right path for the DBMovie.dll file on your hard drive.

After you complete this step, the assembly is added to Microsoft SQL Server. When using Visual Web Developer, you can see the assembly by expanding the Assemblies folder in the Database Explorer window. Alternatively, you can view a list of all the assemblies installed on SQL Server by executing the following query:

```
SELECT * FROM sys.assemblies
```

You can drop any assembly by executing the DROP Assembly command. For example, the following command removes the DBMovie assembly from SQL Server:

```
DROP Assembly DBMovie
```

19

Creating the User-Defined Type

After you have loaded the DBMovie assembly, you can create a new user-defined type from the assembly. Execute the following command:

```
CREATE TYPE dbo.DBMovie EXTERNAL NAME DBMovie.DBMovie
```

If you need to delete the type, you can execute the following command:

```
DROP TYPE DBMovie
```

After you have added the type, you can use it just like any other SQL Server native type. For example, you can create a new database table with the following command:

```
CREATE TABLE DBMovies(Id INT IDENTITY, Movie DBMovie)
```

You can insert a new record into this table with the following command:

```
INSERT DBMovies (Movie)
VALUES ('Star Wars,George Lucas,12.34')
```

Finally, you can perform queries against the table with queries like the following:

```
SELECT Id, Movie FROM DBMovies WHERE  Movie.BoxOfficeTotals > 13.23
SELECT  MAX(Movie.BoxOfficeTotals) FROM DBMovies
SELECT  Movie FROM DBMovies WHERE Movie.Director LIKE 'g%'
```

I find the fact that you can execute queries like this truly amazing.

Building a Data Access Layer with a User-Defined Type

In this final section, let's actually do something with our new user-defined type. We create a new data access component that uses the DBMovie class and an ASP.NET page that interfaces with the component.

Before we can do anything with the DBMovie type, we need to add a reference to the DBMovie.dll assembly to our application. In Visual Web Developer, select Website, Add Reference, and browse to the DBMovie.dll. Alternatively, you can create an application root Bin folder and copy the DBMovie.dll into the Bin folder.

Our new data access component is contained in Listing 19.37.

LISTING 19.37   App_Code\DBDataLayer.cs

```
using System;
using System.Data;
using System.Data.SqlClient;
using System.Web.Configuration;
using System.Collections.Generic;
```

```csharp
public class DBDataLayer
{
    private static readonly string _connectionString;

    public List<DBMovie> GetAll()
    {
        List<DBMovie> results = new List<DBMovie>();
        SqlConnection con = new SqlConnection(_connectionString);
        SqlCommand cmd = new SqlCommand("SELECT Movie FROM DBMovies", con);
        using (con)
        {
            con.Open();
            SqlDataReader reader = cmd.ExecuteReader();
            while (reader.Read())
            {
                DBMovie newMovie = (DBMovie)reader["Movie"];
                results.Add(newMovie);
            }
        }
        return results;
    }

    public void Insert(DBMovie movieToAdd)
    {
        SqlConnection con = new SqlConnection(_connectionString);
        SqlCommand cmd = new SqlCommand("INSERT DBMovies (Movie) VALUES (@Movie)",
➥con);
        cmd.Parameters.Add("@Movie", SqlDbType.Udt);
        cmd.Parameters["@Movie"].UdtTypeName = "DBMovie";
        cmd.Parameters["@Movie"].Value = movieToAdd;
        using (con)
        {
            con.Open();
            cmd.ExecuteNonQuery();
        }
    }

    static DBDataLayer()
    {
        _connectionString =
WebConfigurationManager.ConnectionStrings["Movies"].ConnectionString;
    }
}
```

19

The component in Listing 19.37 contains two methods: `GetAll()` and `Insert()`. The `GetAll()` method retrieves all the `Movie` objects from the DBMovies database table. You can cast the object represented by the `DataReader` directly to a `DBMovie`.

The `Insert()` method adds a new `DBMovie` to the DBMovies database table. The method creates a normal ADO.NET `Command` object. However, a special parameter is added to the command that represents the `DBMovie` object.

When you create a parameter that represents a user-defined type, you must specify a `UdtTypeName` property that represents the name of the user-defined type. In Listing 19.37, the value `DBMovie` is assigned to the `UdtTypeName` property. When the command executes, a new `DBMovie` object is added to the DBMovies database table.

The page in Listing 19.38 contains a `GridView`, `DetailsView`, and `ObjectDataSource` control. The `GridView` displays all the movies from the DBMovies database table. The `DetailsView` control enables you to insert a new `DBMovie` into the database (see Figure 19.21).

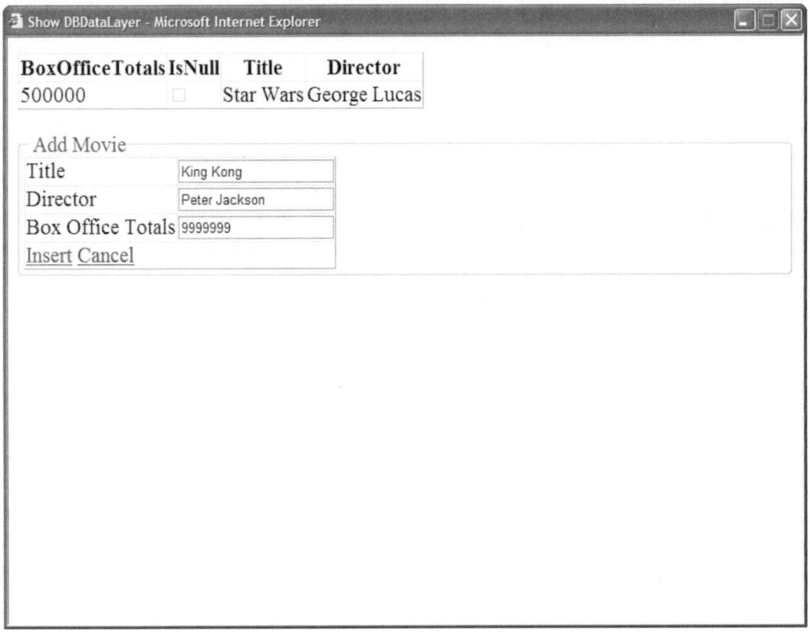

FIGURE 19.21   Displaying and inserting `DBMovie` objects.

LISTING 19.38   ShowDBDataLayer.aspx

```
<%@ Page Language="C#" %>
<!DOCTYPE html PUBLIC "-//W3C//DTD XHTML 1.0 Transitional//EN"
  "http://www.w3.org/TR/xhtml1/DTD/xhtml1-transitional.dtd">
<html xmlns="http://www.w3.org/1999/xhtml" >
<head id="Head1" runat="server">
```

```
    <title>Show DBDataLayer</title>
</head>
<body>
    <form id="form1" runat="server">
    <div>

    <asp:GridView
        id="grdMovies"
        DataSourceID="srcMovies"
        Runat="server" />

    <br />

    <fieldset>
    <legend>Add Movie</legend>
    <asp:DetailsView
        id="dtlMovie"
        DataSourceID="srcMovies"
        DefaultMode="Insert"
        AutoGenerateInsertButton="true"
        AutoGenerateRows="false"
        Runat="server">
        <Fields>
        <asp:BoundField DataField="Title" HeaderText="Title" />
        <asp:BoundField DataField="Director" HeaderText="Director" />
        <asp:BoundField DataField="BoxOfficeTotals"
            HeaderText="Box Office Totals" />
        </Fields>
    </asp:DetailsView>
    </fieldset>

    <asp:ObjectDataSource
        id="srcMovies"
        TypeName="DBDataLayer"
        DataObjectTypeName="DBMovie"
        SelectMethod="GetAll"
        InsertMethod="Insert"
        Runat="server" />

    </div>
    </form>
</body>
</html>
```

19

Creating Stored Procedures with .NET Framework

You can use .NET Framework to build a SQL stored procedure by mapping a stored procedure to a method defined in a class. You must complete the following steps:

▶ Create an assembly that contains the stored procedure method.

▶ Register the assembly with SQL Server.

▶ Create a stored procedure based on the assembly.

In this section, we create two stored procedures with .NET Framework. The first stored procedure, named GetRandomRow(), randomly returns a single row from a database table. The second stored procedure, GetRandomRows(), randomly returns a set of rows from a database table.

Creating the Stored Procedure Assembly

Creating a stored procedure with .NET Framework is easy. All you need to do is decorate a method with the SqlProcedure attribute.

The method used for the stored procedure must satisfy two requirements. The method must be a shared (static) method. Furthermore, the method must be implemented either as a subroutine or as a function that returns an integer value.

Within your method, you can take advantage of the SqlPipe class to send results back to your application. The SqlPipe class supports the following methods:

▶ **Send()**—Enables you to send a DataReader, single-row resultset, or string.

▶ **ExecuteAndSend()**—Enables you to execute a SqlCommand and send the results.

▶ **SendResultsStart()**—Enables you to initiate the sending of a resultset.

▶ **SendResultsRow()**—Enables you to send a single row of a resultset.

▶ **SendResultsEnd()**—Enables you to end the sending of a resultset.

Within the method used for creating the stored procedure, you can use ADO.NET objects such as the SqlCommand, SqlDataReader, and SqlDataAdapter objects in the normal way. However, rather than connect to the database by using a normal connection string, you can create something called a *context connection*. A context connection enables you to connect to the same database server as the stored procedure without authenticating.

Here's how you can initialize a SqlConnection to use a context connection:

```
SqlConnection con = new SqlConnection("context connection=true");
```

You don't specify credentials or the location of the database in the connection string. Remember that the method actually executes within SQL Server. Therefore, you don't need to connect to SQL Server in the normal way.

The class in Listing 19.39 contains two methods named GetRandomRow() and GetRandomRows(). Both methods use a SqlDataAdapter to fill a DataTable with the contents of the Movies database table. The GetRandomRow() method grabs a single row from the DataTable and sends it back to the client. The GetRandomRows() method sends multiple rows back to the client.

LISTING 19.39   RandomRows.cs

```csharp
using System;
using System.Data;
using System.Data.SqlClient;
using Microsoft.SqlServer.Server;

public class RandomRows
{
    [SqlProcedure]
    public static void GetRandomRow()
    {
        // Dump all records from Movies into a DataTable
        SqlDataAdapter dad = new SqlDataAdapter(
"SELECT Id,Title FROM Movies", "context connection=true");
        DataTable dtblMovies = new DataTable();
        dad.Fill(dtblMovies);

        // Grab a random row
        Random rnd = new Random();
        DataRow ranRow = dtblMovies.Rows[rnd.Next(dtblMovies.Rows.Count)];

        // Build a SqlDataRecord that represents the row
        SqlDataRecord result = new SqlDataRecord(
new SqlMetaData("Id", SqlDbType.Int), new SqlMetaData("Title", SqlDbType.NVarChar,
➥100)));
        result.SetSqlInt32(0, (int)ranRow["Id"]);
        result.SetSqlString(1, (string)ranRow["Title"]);

        // Send result
        SqlContext.Pipe.Send(result);
    }

    [SqlProcedure]
    public static void GetRandomRows(int rowsToReturn)
    {
        // Dump all records from Movies into a DataTable
        SqlDataAdapter dad = new SqlDataAdapter(
"SELECT Id,Title FROM Movies", "context connection=true");
        DataTable dtblMovies = new DataTable();
        dad.Fill(dtblMovies);
```

```
        // Send start record
        SqlDataRecord result = new SqlDataRecord(new SqlMetaData("Id",
SqlDbType.Int),new SqlMetaData("Title", SqlDbType.NVarChar, 100));
        SqlContext.Pipe.SendResultsStart(result);

        Random rnd = new Random();
        for (int i = 0; i < rowsToReturn; i++)
        {
            // Grab a random row
            DataRow ranRow = dtblMovies.Rows[rnd.Next(dtblMovies.Rows.Count)];

            // Set the record
            result.SetSqlInt32(0, (int)ranRow["Id"]);
            result.SetSqlString(1, (string)ranRow["Title"]);

            // Send record
            SqlContext.Pipe.SendResultsRow(result);
        }

        // Send end record
        SqlContext.Pipe.SendResultsEnd();
    }

}
```

You need to compile the `RandomRows` class into a separate assembly (`.dll` file). After you create (and debug) the class, move the class from your App_Code folder to another folder in your application, such as the root folder. Next, open the SDK Command prompt and execute the following command:

```
csc /t:library RandomRows.cs
```

This command uses the C# command-line compiler to compile the `RandomRows` class into an assembly.

Registering the Stored Procedure Assembly with SQL Server

After you compile the `RandomRows` assembly, you are ready to deploy the assembly to SQL Server. You can load the assembly into SQL Server by executing the following command:

```
CREATE ASSEMBLY RandomRows
FROM 'C:\RandomRows.dll'
```

You need to supply the proper path to the `RandomRows.dll` assembly on your hard drive. If you need to remove the assembly, you can execute the following command:

```
DROP Assembly RandomRows
```

Creating the Stored Procedures

Now that the assembly is loaded, you can create two stored procedures that correspond to the two methods defined in the assembly. Execute the following two SQL commands:

```
CREATE PROCEDURE GetRandomRow  AS
EXTERNAL NAME RandomRows.RandomRows.GetRandomRow

CREATE PROCEDURE GetRandomRows(@rowsToReturn Int) AS
EXTERNAL NAME RandomRows.RandomRows.GetRandomRows
```

After you execute these two commands, you have two new stored procedures named GetRandomRow and GetRandomRows. You can treat these stored procedures just like normal stored procedures. For example, executing the following command displays three random movies from the Movies database:

```
GetRandomRows 3
```

If you need to delete these stored procedures, you can execute the following two commands:

```
DROP PROCEDURE GetRandomRow
DROP PROCEDURE GetRandomRows
```

Executing a .NET Stored Procedure from an ASP.NET Page

After the two stored procedures have been created, you can use the stored procedures with an ASP.NET page. For example, the component in Listing 19.40 contains two methods that call the two stored procedures.

LISTING 19.40   App_Code\RandomDataLayer.cs

```
using System;
using System.Data;
using System.Data.SqlClient;
using System.Web.Configuration;
using System.Collections.Generic;

public class RandomDataLayer
{
    private static readonly string _connectionString;

    public List<String> GetRandomMovies()
    {
        List<String> results = new List<String>();
        SqlConnection con = new SqlConnection(_connectionString);
        SqlCommand cmd = new SqlCommand("GetRandomRows", con);
        cmd.CommandType = CommandType.StoredProcedure;
        cmd.Parameters.AddWithValue("@rowsToReturn", 5);
```

19

```
    using (con)
    {
        con.Open();
        SqlDataReader reader = cmd.ExecuteReader();
        while (reader.Read())
            results.Add((string)reader["Title"]);
    }
    return results;
}


public static string GetRandomMovie()
{
    string result = String.Empty;
    SqlConnection con = new SqlConnection(_connectionString);
    SqlCommand cmd = new SqlCommand("GetRandomRow", con);
    cmd.CommandType = CommandType.StoredProcedure;
    using (con)
    {
        con.Open();
        SqlDataReader reader = cmd.ExecuteReader();
        if (reader.Read())
            result = (string)reader["Title"];
    }
    return result;
}

static RandomDataLayer()
{
    _connectionString =
WebConfigurationManager.ConnectionStrings["Movies"].ConnectionString;
}

}
```

In Listing 19.40, the GetRandomRow and GetRandomRows stored procedures are executed with the help of SqlCommand objects.

The page in Listing 19.41 contains a GridView and ObjectDataSource control. The ObjectDataSource control represents the RandomDataLayer component. When you request the page, a single random movie title displays in a Label control. Furthermore, a list of five random movie titles displays in the GridView control (see Figure 19.22).

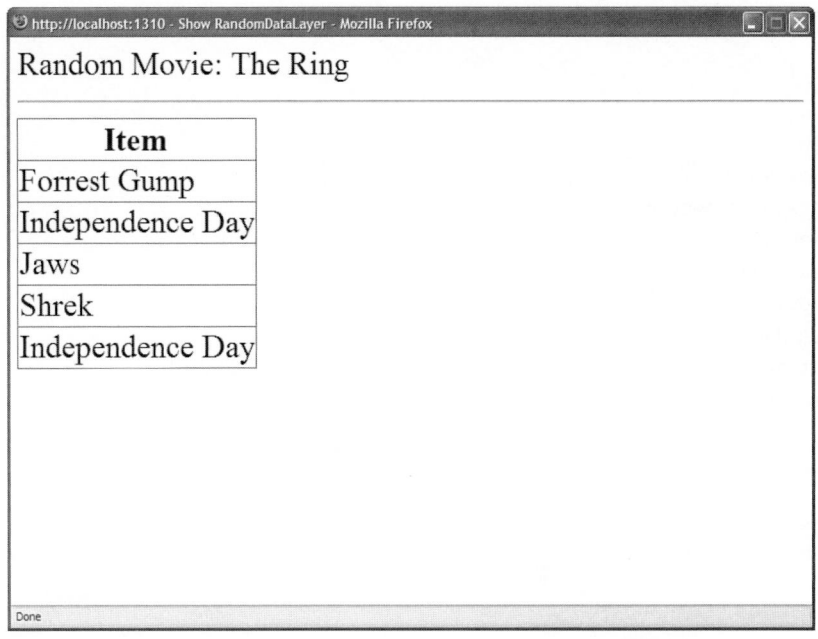

FIGURE 19.22   Calling a .NET stored procedure from an ASP.NET page.

LISTING 19.41   ShowRandomDataLayer.aspx

```
<%@ Page Language="C#" %>
<!DOCTYPE html PUBLIC "-//W3C//DTD XHTML 1.0 Transitional//EN"
"http://www.w3.org/TR/xhtml1/DTD/xhtml1-transitional.dtd">
<script runat="server">

    void Page_Load()
    {
        lblRandomMovie.Text = RandomDataLayer.GetRandomMovie();
    }
</script>
<html xmlns="http://www.w3.org/1999/xhtml" >
<head id="Head1" runat="server">
    <title>Show RandomDataLayer</title>
</head>
<body>
    <form id="form1" runat="server">
    <div>

    Random Movie:
    <asp:Label
        id="lblRandomMovie"
```

19

```
            Runat="server" />

    <hr />

    <asp:GridView
        id="grdMovies"
        DataSourceID="srcMovies"
        Runat="server" />
    <asp:ObjectDataSource
        id="srcMovies"
        TypeName="RandomDataLayer"
        SelectMethod="GetRandomMovies"
        Runat="server" />
    </div>
    </form>
</body>
</html>
```

Summary

This chapter provided you with an overview of ADO.NET. It described how you can use ADO.NET to represent database data with both a connected and disconnected model of data access.

In the first part, you learned how to use the `Connection`, `Command`, and `DataReader` objects to connect to a database, execute commands, and represent the results of a database query. You learned how to retrieve provider statistics such as command execution times. You also learned how to represent stored procedures with the `Command` object. Finally, you learned how to work with multiple active resultsets (MARS).

In the second part, you learned how to work with the `DataAdapter`, `DataTable`, `DataView`, and `DataSet` objects. You learned how you can perform batch updates with the `DataAdapter` object. You also learned how to use the `DataTable` object to represent and edit database rows.

Next, you learned how to improve the data access performance of your ASP.NET pages by executing asynchronous database commands within asynchronous ASP.NET pages.

Finally, you got a chance to tackle the advanced topic of building database objects with .NET Framework. You learned how you can use .NET Framework to build both user-defined types and stored procedures. For example, you learned how to insert and select a custom class from a database table by creating a user-defined type with .NET Framework.

Data Access with LINQ to SQL

A vast chasm separates the way developers work with transient application data and the way developers work with persistent database data. In our applications, we work with objects and properties (created with either C# or VB.NET). In most databases, on the other hand, we work with tables and columns.

This is true even though our applications and our databases represent the very same data. For example, you might have both a class and a database table named Product that represents a list of products you sell through your website. However, the languages we use to interact with these entities are different. The C# and VB.NET languages are different from the SQL language. Larger companies typically have different developers who specialize in C# or VB.NET, on the one hand, or SQL, on the other hand.

A huge amount of developer time is spent performing brain-dead, tedious translations between the object and relational universes. I cringe when I think of the number of hours I've spent declaring classes that contain a one-to-one mapping between properties and database columns. This is time I could have devoted to going to the park with my children, seeing a movie, walking my dog, and so on.

LINQ to SQL promises to finally enable us to put SQL to a well-deserved death. Or more accurately, it promises to make SQL a subterranean language that we never need to interact with again. (SQL is plumbing, and I am not a plumber.) This is a good thing. Death to SQL!

This is a hard chapter. LINQ to SQL is not easy to understand because it relies on several mind-bending features introduced into C#, VB.NET, and .NET Framework. So please, have patience. Take a deep breath. Everything will make sense in the end.

This chapter is divided into four parts. In the first part, I discuss the features introduced in C#, VB.NET, and .NET Framework that support LINQ. Next, you learn how to represent database tables with LINQ to SQL entities. In the following part, I explain how to perform standard SQL commands—such as SELECT, INSERT, UPDATE, and DELETE—with LINQ to SQL. In the final part of this chapter, I demonstrate how you can create a custom entity base class (and integrate form validation into your LINQ entities).

New C# and VB.NET Language Features

To get LINQ to SQL to work, Microsoft had to introduce several new language features to both C# and VB.NET. Many of these features make C# and VB.NET behave more like a dynamic language (think JavaScript). Although the primary motivation for introducing these new features was to support LINQ, the new features are also interesting in their own right.

> **NOTE**
>
> LINQ was introduced in ASP.NET 3.5. These language features will not work on websites targeting .NET Framework 1.1, 2.0, or 3.0.

Understanding Automatic Properties

The first of these language features we explore is *automatic properties*, which unfortunately is supported only by C# and not VB.NET. Automatic properties provide you with a shorthand method for defining a new property. For example, Listing 20.1 contains a class named Product that contains Id, Description, and Price properties.

LISTING 20.1   LanguageChanges\App_Code\AutomaticProperties.cs

```
public class AutomaticProperties
{
    // Automatic Properties

    public int Id { get; set; }

    public string Description { get; set; }


    // Normal Property

    private decimal _Price;
```

```
    public decimal Price
    {
        get { return _Price; }
        set { _Price = value; }
    }
}
```

The first two properties, `Id` and `Description`, unlike the last property, `Price`, do not include getters or setters. The C# compiler creates the getters and setters—and the secret, private, backing fields—for you automatically.

You can't add any logic to the getters and setters for an automatic property. You also can't create read-only automatic properties.

Why are automatic properties relevant to LINQ to SQL? When working with LINQ to SQL, you often use classes to represent nothing more than the list of columns you want to retrieve from the database (the shape of the data) like the select list in a SQL query. In those cases, you just want to do the minimum amount of work possible to create a list of properties, and automatic properties enable you to do this.

NOTE

You can quickly add an automatic property to a class or page when using Visual Web Developer/Visual Studio by typing **prop** and pressing the Tab key twice.

Understanding Initializers

You can use initializers to reduce the amount of work it takes to create a new instance of a class. For example, assume that you have a class that looks like Listing 20.2 (in C#) or like Listing 20.3 (in VB.NET).

LISTING 20.2   LanguageChanges\App_Code\Product.cs

```
public class Product
{
    public int Id { get; set; }

    public string Name { get; set; }

    public decimal Price { get; set; }
}
```

20

LISTING 20.3   LanguageChanges\App_Code\Product.vb

```vb
Public Class Product

    Private _Id As Integer

    Public Property Id() As Integer
        Get
            Return _Id
        End Get
        Set(ByVal value As Integer)
            _Id = value
        End Set
    End Property

    Private _Name As String

    Public Property Name() As String
        Get
            Return _Name
        End Get
        Set(ByVal value As String)
            _Name = value
        End Set
    End Property

    Private _Price As Decimal

    Public Property Price() As Decimal
        Get
            Return _Price
        End Get
        Set(ByVal value As Decimal)
            _Price = value
        End Set
    End Property

End Class
```

The Product class has three public properties (declared by taking advantage of automatic properties in the case of C#—sorry VB.NET).

Now, let's say you want to create an instance of the Product class. Here's how you would do it in .NET Framework 2.0 (with C#):

```
Product product1 = new Product();
product1.Id = 1;
product1.Name = "Laptop Computer";
product1.Price = 800.00m;
```

And here is how you would do it in .NET Framework 2 (with VB.NET):

```
Dim product1 As New Product()
product1.Id = 1
product1.Name = "Laptop Computer"
product1.Price = 800.0
```

It takes four lines of code to initialize this trivial little Product class. That's too much work. By taking advantage of initializers, you can do everything in a single line of code. Here's how you use initializers in C#:

```
Product product2 = new Product {Id=1, Name="Laptop Computer", Price=800.00m};
```

Here's how you use initializers in VB.NET:

```
Dim product2 As New Product() With {.Id = 1, .Name = "Laptop Computer",
    ➥.Price = 800.0}
```

Now, clearly, you could do something similar by declaring a constructor on the Product class that accepts Id, Name, and Price parameters. However, then your class would become more bloated with code because you would need to assign the constructor parameter values to the class properties. Initializers are useful because, by taking advantage of this feature, you can declare agile, little classes and initialize these svelte classes with a minimum of code.

Understanding Type Inference

Here's a feature that makes C# and VB.NET look much more like a dynamic language such as JavaScript: local variable type inference. When you take advantage of type inference, you allow the C# or VB.NET compiler to determine the type of a variable at compile time.

Here's an example of how you use type inference with C#:

```
var message = "Hello World!";
```

And here is how you would use type inference with VB.NET:

```
Dim message = "Hello World!"
```

The message variable is declared without specifying a type. The C# and VB.NET compilers can infer the type of the variable (it's a String) from the value you use to initialize the variable. No performance impact results from using type inference. (The variable is not late bound.) The compiler does all the work of figuring out the data type at compile time.

A new keyword was introduced in ASP.NET 3.5 to support type inference: the var keyword. You declare a variable as type var when you want the compiler to figure out the variable's data type all by itself. You can take advantage of type inference only when you provide a local variable with an initial value. For example, this won't work (C#):

```
var message;
message = "Hello World!";
```

The C# compiler will refuse to compile this code because the message variable is not initialized when it is declared.

The following code will work in VB.NET (but it won't do what you want):

```
Dim message
message = "Hello World!"
```

In this case, VB.NET will treat the message variable as type Object. At runtime, it will cast the value of the variable to a string when you assign the string to the variable. This is not good from a performance perspective.

> **NOTE**
>
> VB.NET includes an Option Infer option that must be enabled for the implicit typing feature to work. You can enable it for a particular class file by adding the line Option Infer On at the top of a code file.

The relevance of type inference to LINQ to SQL will be apparent after you read the next section. In many circumstances when using LINQ to SQL, you won't actually know the name of the type of a variable, so you have to let the compiler infer the type.

Understanding Anonymous Types

Anonymous types is another idea that might be familiar to you from dynamic languages. Anonymous types are useful when you need a transient, fleeting type and you don't want to do the work to create a class.

Here's an example of creating an anonymous type in C#:

```
var customer = new {FirstName = "Stephen", LastName = "Walther"};
```

Here's how you would create the same anonymous type in VB.NET:

```
Dim customer = New With {.FirstName = "Stephen", .LastName = "Walther"}
```

The customer variable is used without specifying a type, which looks very much like JavaScript or VBScript. However, you need to understand that customer does have a type; you just don't know its name: It's anonymous.

In a single line of code, we've managed to both create a new class and initialize its properties. The terseness brings tears to my eyes.

Anonymous types are useful when working with LINQ to SQL because you'll discover that you often need to create new types on-the-fly. For example, you might want to return a class that represents a limited set of database columns when performing a particular query. You need to create a transient class that represents the columns.

Understanding Generics

Generics are not a new feature; however, they are such an important aspect of LINQ to SQL that it is worth using a little space to review this feature.

> **NOTE**
>
> To use generics, you need to import the System.Collections.Generic namespace.

I most often use generics by taking advantage of generic collections. For example, if you want to represent a list of strings, you can declare a list of strings like this (in C#):

```
List<string> stuffToBuy = new List<string>();
stuffToBuy.Add("socks");
stuffToBuy.Add("beer");
stuffToBuy.Add("cigars");
```

Here's how you would declare the list of strings in VB.NET:

```
Dim stuffToBuy As New List(Of String)
stuffToBuy.Add("socks")
stuffToBuy.Add("beer")
stuffToBuy.Add("cigars")
```

And, by taking advantage of collection initializers, you can now declare a strongly typed list of strings in a single line like this (in C#):

```
List<string> stuffToBuy2 = new List<string> {"socks", "beer", "cigars"};
```

20

> **NOTE**
>
> Unfortunately, VB.NET does not support collection intializers or array initializers.

The List class is an example of a generic because you specify the type of object that the class will contain when you declare the List class. In C#, you specify the type in between the alligator mouths (< >), and in VB.NET you use the Of keyword. In the preceding examples, we created a List class that contains strings. Alternatively, we could have created a List class that contains integers or a custom type such as products or customers represented by a Product or Customer class.

A generic collection such as a List is superior to a nongeneric collection such as an ArrayList because a generic is strongly typed. An ArrayList stores everything as an object. A generic stores everything as a particular type. When you pull an item out of an ArrayList, you must cast it to a particular type before you use it. An item pulled from a generic, on the other hand, does not need to be cast to a type.

Generics are not limited solely to collections. You can create generic methods, generic classes, and generic interfaces. For example, when working with ADO.NET classes, I like to convert my data readers into strongly typed List collections. The method GetListFromCommand(), shown in Listing 20.4, takes a command object, executes it, and generates a typed List automatically.

LISTING 20.4   LanguageChanges\App_Code\GenericMethods.cs

```csharp
using System;
using System.Collections.Generic;
using System.Data.SqlClient;

public class GenericMethods
{
    public static List<T> GetListFromCommand<T>(SqlCommand command)
    where T: ICreatable, new()
    {
        List<T> results = new List<T>();
        using (command.Connection)
        {
            command.Connection.Open();
            SqlDataReader reader = command.ExecuteReader();
            while (reader.Read())
            {
                T newThing = new T();
                newThing.Create(reader);
                results.Add( newThing );
            }
        }
        return results;
    }
}
```

```
public interface ICreatable
{
    void Create(SqlDataReader reader);
}
```

The GetListFromCommand() method in Listing 20.4 accepts a SqlCommand object and returns a generic List<T>. The generic type is constrained by the where clause. The generic constraint restricts the types that can be used for T to types that implement the ICreatable interface and types that can be instantiated with new.

The ICreatable interface is also defined in Listing 20.4. The interface requires a class to implement a single method named Create().

Now that we have created a generic method for converting data readers into strongly typed lists, we can use it with any class that implements the ICreatable interface, such as the Movie class in Listing 20.5.

LISTING 20.5 Movie.cs

```
using System;
using System.Data.SqlClient;

public class Movie : ICreatable
{
    public int Id { get; set; }

    public string Title { get; set; }

    public void Create(SqlDataReader reader)
    {
        Id = (int)reader["Id"];
        Title = (string)reader["Title"];
    }

}
```

You can call the generic GetListFromCommand() method with the Movie type like this (the page named ShowGenericMethods.aspx on the book's website uses this code):

```
string conString = WebConfigurationManager.ConnectionStrings["con"].
    ➥ConnectionString;
SqlConnection con = new SqlConnection(conString);
SqlCommand cmd = new SqlCommand("SELECT Id, Title FROM Movie", con);
List<Movie> movies = GenericMethods.GetListFromCommand<Movie>(cmd);
```

20

The beautiful thing about generics here is that you don't have to write the same code to convert a data reader to a generic List for each type. You write the `GetListFromCommand()` method as a generic method once, and you can use the method with any type that meets the generic constraints in the future.

The right way to think of generics is to think of a code template. You can use generics to define a certain pattern of code into which you can plug a particular type.

Understanding Lambda Expressions

Lambda expressions, another language feature introduced with .NET Framework 3.5, provide you with an extremely terse way of defining methods.

Imagine, for example, that you want to programmatically wire up a `Click` event handler to a button control. Listing 20.6 is an example of one way of doing this.

LISTING 20.6   LanguageChanges\NormalMethod.aspx

```
<%@ Page Language="C#" %>
<!DOCTYPE html PUBLIC "-//W3C//DTD XHTML 1.0 Transitional//EN"
"http://www.w3.org/TR/xhtml1/DTD/xhtml1-transitional.dtd">
<script runat="server">

    void Page_Init()
    {
        btn.Click += new EventHandler(btn_Click);
    }

    void btn_Click(object sender, EventArgs e)
    {
        lblResult.Text = DateTime.Now.ToString();
    }
</script>

<html xmlns="http://www.w3.org/1999/xhtml">
<head runat="server">
    <title>Normal Method</title>
</head>
<body>
    <form id="form1" runat="server">
    <div>

    <asp:Button
        id="btn"
        Text="Go!"
        Runat="server" />
```

```
    <asp:Label
        id="lblResult"
        Runat="server" />

    </div>
    </form>
</body>
</html>
```

In Listing 20.6, the `Page_Init()` method associates the Button `Click` event with the `btn_Click()` method. When you click the button, the `btn_Click()` method executes and displays the current date and time. Nothing special here.

In .NET Framework 2.0, the notion of anonymous methods for C# was introduced. The advantage of an anonymous method is that you can declare it inline. For example, Listing 20.7 does the same thing as the previous page, except for that it uses an anonymous method to handle the Button `Click` event.

LISTING 20.7   LanguageChanges\AnonymousMethod.aspx

```
<%@ Page Language="C#" %>
<!DOCTYPE html PUBLIC "-//W3C//DTD XHTML 1.0 Transitional//EN"
 "http://www.w3.org/TR/xhtml1/DTD/xhtml1-transitional.dtd">
<script runat="server">

    void Page_Init()
    {
        btn.Click += delegate(object sender, EventArgs e)
                    {
                            lblResult.Text = DateTime.Now.ToString();
                    };
    }

</script>

<html xmlns="http://www.w3.org/1999/xhtml">
<head id="Head1" runat="server">
    <title>Anonymous Method</title>
</head>
<body>
    <form id="form1" runat="server">
    <div>

    <asp:Button
        id="btn"
```

```
            Text="Go!"
            Runat="server" />

    <asp:Label
        id="lblResult"
        Runat="server" />

    </div>
    </form>
</body>
</html>
```

In Listing 20.7, the `Click` event is handled with a function declared within the `Page_Init()` method.

Anonymous methods are not supported by VB.NET, but VB.NET does support lambda expressions—so don't stop reading if you use VB.NET.

Lambda expressions take the notion of the anonymous method one step further. Lambda expressions reduce the amount of syntax required to define a method to its semantic minimum. Listing 20.8 does the same thing as the previous two listings, except that the page uses a lambda expression.

LISTING 20.8   LanguageChanges\LambdaExpression.aspx

```
<%@ Page Language="C#" %>
<!DOCTYPE html PUBLIC "-//W3C//DTD XHTML 1.0 Transitional//EN"
 "http://www.w3.org/TR/xhtml1/DTD/xhtml1-transitional.dtd">
<script runat="server">

    void Page_Init()
    {
        btn.Click += (sender, e) => lblResult.Text = DateTime.Now.ToString();
    }

</script>

<html xmlns="http://www.w3.org/1999/xhtml">
<head id="Head1" runat="server">
```

```
    <title>Lambda Expressions</title>
</head>
<body>
    <form id="form1" runat="server">
    <div>

    <asp:Button
        id="btn"
        Text="Go!"
        Runat="server" />

    <asp:Label
        id="lblResult"
        Runat="server" />

    </div>
    </form>
</body>
</html>
```

The lambda expression in Listing 20.8 is the one that looks like this:

```
(sender, e) => lblResult.Text = DateTime.Now.ToString();
```

This is just a terse way of writing a method. A lambda expression uses the => operator (the "goes into" operator) to separate a list of method parameters from the method body. The compiler (usually) can infer the data types of the parameters. However, if you want, you can be explicit about the parameter types, like this:

```
(object sender, EventArgs e) => lblResult.Text = DateTime.Now.ToString();
```

It is also worth mentioning that the parentheses around the parameters are optional when there is a single parameter. So, a lambda expression can be terse.

Visual Basic also supports lambda expressions, but in a more limited way. A lambda expression in Visual Basic cannot contain statements; it can only contain expressions.

Here's the syntax in VB for creating a lambda expression:

```
Dim AddNumbers = Function(x, y) x + y
Response.Write(AddNumbers(5, 6))
```

The first statement creates a variable named AddNumbers that represents a lambda expression. The VB syntax Function(x,y) x + y is equivalent to the C# syntax (x,y) => x + y. Next, the lambda function is called with two arguments.

20

Understanding Extension Methods

The idea behind extension methods should also be familiar to anyone who has worked with JavaScript (think prototype). By taking advantage of extension methods, you can add new methods to existing classes. For example, you can make up any method you want and add the method to the String class.

I'm constantly HTML-encoding strings because I am paranoid about JavaScript injection attacks. In .NET Framework 2.0, you HTML-encode a string by calling the Server.HtmlEncode() static method, like this:

```
string evilString = "<script>alert('boom!')<" + "/script>";
ltlMessage.Text = Server.HtmlEncode(evilString);
```

In this statement, the static HtmlEncode() method is called on the Server class. Wouldn't it be nice if we could just call HtmlEncode() on a string directly like this:

```
string evilString = "<script>alert('boom!')<" + "/script>";
ltlMessage.Text = evilString.HtmlEncode();
```

Using extension methods, we can do exactly that. We can add any methods to a class that we feel like. You create an extension method by creating a static class and declaring a static method that has a special first parameter. Listing 20.9 demonstrates how you create an extension method to add the HtmlEncode() method to the String class.

LISTING 20.9   LanguageChanges\MyExtensions.cs

```
public static class MyExtensions
{
    public static string HtmlEncode(this string str)
    {
        return System.Web.HttpUtility.HtmlEncode(str);
    }
}
```

The one and only parameter for the HtmlEncode() method is preceded by the keyword this. The parameter indicates the type that the extension method applies to.

Creating extension methods in VB.NET is similar to creating extension methods in C#. Listing 20.10 contains the same HtmlEncode() method as the previous listing.

LISTING 20.10   LanguageChanges\MyExtensions.cs

```
public static class MyExtensions
{

    public static string HtmlEncode(this string str)
    {
```

```
                  return System.Web.HttpUtility.HtmlEncode(str);
    }
}
```

When working with VB.NET, you must declare an extension method in a module. Furthermore, you mark the extension methods with the `System.Runtime.CompilerServices.Extension` attribute.

Understanding LINQ

Finally, we get to the topic of LINQ—the last topic we need to examine before we can dive into the true subject of this chapter: LINQ to SQL.

LINQ stands for Language Integrated Query and consists of a set of new language features added to both the C# and VB.NET languages that enable you to perform queries. LINQ enables you to use SQL query-like syntax within C# or VB.NET.

Here's a simple example of a LINQ query:

```
var words = new List<string> {"zephyr", "apple", "azure"};


var results = from w in words
  where w.Contains("z")
  select w;
```

The first statement creates a generic List of three strings named "words." The second statement is the LINQ query. The LINQ query resembles a backward SQL statement. It retrieves all the words from the List that contain the letter *z*. After you execute the query, the results variable contains the following list of two words:

```
zephyr
azure
```

You can perform a standard LINQ query against any object that implements the `IEnumerable<T>` interface interface>. An object that implements this interface is called a *sequence*. Notable examples of sequences are both the generic `List` class and the standard `Array` class. (So anything you can dump into an array, you can query with LINQ.)

The C# language supports the following clauses that you can use in a query:

- ▶ **from**—Enables you to specify the data source and a variable for iterating over the data source (a range variable).

- ▶ **where**—Enables you to filter the results of a query.

- ▶ **select**—Enables you to specify the items included in the results of the query.

- ▶ **group**—Enables you to group related values by a common key.

- ▶ **into**—Enables you to store the results of a group or join into a temporary variable.

20

▶ **orderby**—Enables you to order query results in ascending or descending order.

▶ **join**—Enables you to join two data sources using a common key.

▶ **let**—Enables you to create a temporary variable to represent subquery results.

Building a LINQ query is like building a backward SQL query. You start by specifying a `from` clause that indicates where you want to get your data. Next, optionally, you specify a `where` clause that filters your data. Finally, you specify a `select` clause that gives shape to your data (determines the objects and properties you want to return).

Under the covers, standard LINQ queries are translated into method calls on the `System.LINQ.Enumerable` class. The `Enumerable` class contains extension methods applied to any class that implements the `IEnumerable<T>` interface interface>.

So, the query

```
var results = from w in words
  where w.Contains("z")
  select w;
```

is translated into this query by the C# compiler:

```
var results = words.Where( w => w.Contains("z") ).Select( w => w );
```

The first query uses *query syntax*, and the second query uses *method syntax*. The two queries are otherwise identical.

The query using method syntax accepts lambda expressions for its `Where()` and `Select()` methods. The lambda expression used with the `Where()` method filters the results so that only words that contain the letter *z* are returned. The `Select()` method indicates the object and property to return. If we had passed the lambda expression w => w.Length to the `Select()` method, the query would return the length of each word instead of the word itself.

The choice of whether to use query or method syntax when building LINQ queries is purely a matter of preference. Query syntax uses language-specific syntax (C# or VB.NET). Method syntax is language-independent.

I find that I use method syntax more than query syntax because query syntax is a subset of method syntax. In other words, you can do more with method syntax. That said, in some cases, writing a query in method syntax is just too verbose. For example, writing left outer joins with LINQ to SQL is much easier using query syntax than method syntax.

At the end of the day, the choice of whether to use method or query syntax doesn't actually matter because all the query syntax statements get translated by the compiler into method syntax. In the case of standard LINQ, those method calls are calls on methods of the `Enumerable` class.

Look up the `System.Linq.Enumerable` class in the SDK documentation to view the full list of methods that the `Enumerable` class supports. Here is a list of some of the more interesting and useful methods:

- ▶ **Aggregate()**—Enables you to apply a function to every item in a sequence.
- ▶ **Average()**—Returns the average value of every item in a sequence.
- ▶ **Count()**—Returns the count of items from a sequence.
- ▶ **Distinct()**—Returns distinct items from a sequence.
- ▶ **Max()**—Returns the maximum value from a sequence.
- ▶ **Min()**—Returns the minimum value from a sequence.
- ▶ **Select()**—Returns certain items or properties from a sequence.
- ▶ **Single()**—Returns a single value from a sequence.
- ▶ **Skip()**—Enables you to skip a certain number of items in a sequence and return the remaining elements.
- ▶ **Take()**—Enables you to return a certain number of elements from a sequence.
- ▶ **Where()**—Enables you to filter the elements in a sequence.

In this section, we've been discussing standard LINQ (also called LINQ to Objects). LINQ uses the provider model. There are many different implementations of LINQ, including LINQ to SQL, LINQ to XML, LINQ over DataSets, and LINQ to Entities. There are also third-party implementations of LINQ, including LINQ to NHibernate and LINQ to SharePoint. You can use each of these different flavors of LINQ to query different types of data sources, such as XML files, SharePoint lists, and so on.

In this chapter, we are interested in LINQ to SQL because this is the Microsoft version of LINQ designed exclusively for working with database data. So LINQ to SQL is the subject to which we turn now.

Creating LINQ to SQL Entities

LINQ to SQL enables you to perform LINQ queries against database data. Currently, you can use LINQ to SQL with Microsoft SQL Server 2000, Microsoft SQL Server 2005, or Microsoft SQL Server 2008 (including the SQL Server Express editions). Other databases—such as Oracle, DB2, and Access databases—might be supported in the future, but they are not right now.

In this section, you learn how to create LINQ to SQL entities. An *entity* is a C# or VB.NET class that represents a database table (or view). You can use a set of standard custom attributes to map classes and properties to tables and columns. You learn how to create entities both by hand and by using the LINQ to SQL Designer.

Building Entities by Hand

Before you can start performing queries using LINQ to SQL, you need to create one or more entity classes that represent the data you are querying. In this section, you learn how to code these classes by hand.

Imagine that you have the following database table named Movie that you want to perform queries against:

Movie

Column Name	Data Type	Is Identity?
Id	Int	TRUE
Title	NVarchar(100)	FALSE
Director	NVarchar	FALSE
DateReleased	DateTime	FALSE
BoxOfficeTotals	Money	FALSE

You can use the class in Listing 20.11 to represent this table.

LISTING 20.11   Entities\App_Code\Movie.cs

```
using System;
using System.Data.Linq.Mapping;

[Table]
public class Movie
{
    [Column(IsPrimaryKey=true, IsDbGenerated=true)]
    public int Id { get; set; }
```

```
[Column]
public string Title { get; set; }

[Column]
public string Director { get; set; }

[Column]
public DateTime DateReleased { get; set; }

[Column]
public decimal BoxOfficeTotals { get; set; }
}
```

The class in Listing 20.11 contains a property that corresponds to each column in the Movie database table. Each property is decorated with a custom attribute named `Column`. This attribute marks the property as one that represents a database column.

> **NOTE**
>
> The `Column` and `Table` attribute classes live in the `System.Data.Linq.Mapping` namespace.

Furthermore, the class itself is decorated with a `Table` attribute. This attribute marks the class as representing a database table.

The `Column` attribute supports the following properties:

▶ **AutoSync**—Indicates whether the value of the property is synchronized with the value of the database column automatically. Possible values are `OnInsert`, `Always`, and `None`.

▶ **CanBeNull**—Indicates whether the property can represent a null value.

▶ **DbType**—Indicates the database column data type.

▶ **Expression**—Indicates the expression used by a computed database column.

▶ **IsDbGenerated**—Indicates that the value of the property is generated in the database (for example, an identity column).

▶ **IsDiscriminator**—Indicates whether the property holds the discriminator value for an inheritance hierarchy.

▶ **IsPrimaryKey**—Indicates whether the property represents a primary key column.

▶ **IsVersion**—Indicates whether the property represents a column that represents a row version (for example, a timestamp column).

▶ **Name**—Indicates the name of the database column that corresponds to the property.

20

▶ **Storage**—Indicates a field where the value of the property is stored.

▶ **UpdateCheck**—Indicates whether the property participates in optimistic concurrency comparisons.

The `Table` attribute supports the following single property:

▶ **Name**—Indicates the name of the database table that corresponds to the class.

Some comments about these attributes are needed. First, you don't need to specify a `Name` property when your property or class name corresponds to your database column or table name. If, on the other hand, your database table were named Movies and your class were named `Movie`, you would need to supply the `Name` property for the `Table` attribute to map the correct table to the class.

Second, you always want to specify the primary key column by using the `IsPrimaryKey` property. For example, if you don't specify a primary key column, you can't do updates against your database using LINQ.

Finally, even though we didn't do this in our `Movie` class, you almost always want to include a timestamp column in your database table and indicate the timestamp column by using the `IsVersion` property. If you don't do this, LINQ to SQL checks whether the values of all the properties match the values of all the columns before performing an update command to prevent concurrency conflicts. If you specify a version property, LINQ to SQL can check the value of this single property against the database rather than all the columns.

Now that we've created an entity, we can start performing queries against the database using LINQ to SQL. For example, the page in Listing 20.12 contains a form that enables you to search for movies by a particular director.

LISTING 20.12   Entities\SearchMovies.aspx

```
<%@ Page Language="C#" %>
<%@ Import Namespace="System.Web.Configuration" %>
<%@ Import Namespace="System.Linq" %>
<%@ Import Namespace="System.Data.Linq" %>
<!DOCTYPE html PUBLIC "-//W3C//DTD XHTML 1.0 Transitional//EN"
 "http://www.w3.org/TR/xhtml1/DTD/xhtml1-transitional.dtd">
<script runat="server">

    protected void btnSearch_Click(object sender, EventArgs e)
    {
        string conString = WebConfigurationManager.
        ConnectionStrings["Movies"].ConnectionString;
        DataContext db = new DataContext(conString);
        var tMovie = db.GetTable<Movie>();
```

```
                grdMovies.DataSource = tMovie.Where( m => m.Director.Contains(
                    txtDirector.Text) );
                grdMovies.DataBind();
        }
</script>
<html xmlns="http://www.w3.org/1999/xhtml">
<head runat="server">
    <title>SearchMovies.aspx</title>
</head>
<body>
    <form id="form1" runat="server">
    <div>

    <asp:Label
        id="lblDirector"
        Text="Director:"
        AssociatedControlID="txtDirector"
        Runat="server" />
    <asp:TextBox
        id="txtDirector"
        Runat="server" />
    <asp:Button
        id="btnSearch"
        Text="Search"
        OnClick="btnSearch_Click"
        Runat="Server" />

    <br /><br />

    <asp:GridView
        id="grdMovies"
        Runat="server" />

    </div>
    </form>
</body>
</html>
```

When you click the Search button, the btnSearch_Click() method executes the LINQ to SQL query.

First, a DataContext is created by passing a database connection string to the class's constructor. The DataContext is responsible for tracking all the LINQ to SQL entities and representing the database connection.

Next, a variable named tMovie is instantiated that represents a particular database table from the DataContext. Because we pass the Movie entity to the GetTable<T>() method() method>, the method returns a Table<T> object that represents the Movie database table. The Table<T> object implements the IQueryable interface and can, therefore, be queried with a LINQ to SQL query.

Finally, the following LINQ to SQL query is executed:

```
tMovie.Where( m => m.Director.Contains(txtDirector.Text)
```

The lambda expression m => m.Director.Contains(txtDirector.Text) passed to the Where() method returns every movie record from the database in which the Director column contains the text entered into the TextBox control.

We had to import two namespaces to use the LINQ to SQL query: System.Linq and System.Data.Linq.

NOTE

To keep things simple, I use the LINQ to SQL query directly within the ASP.NET page in Listing 20.12. In real life, to avoid mixing user interface and Data Access layers, I would perform the LINQ to SQL query in a separate class and use an ObjectDataSource to represent the class.

Building Entities with the LINQ to SQL Designer

As an alternative to building entities by hand, you can use the LINQ to SQL Designer. You can simply drag database tables from the Database Explorer (Server Explorer) onto the Designer. The Designer generates the entity classes with the correct attributes automatically.

Follow these steps to use the LINQ to SQL Designer:

1. Select Website, Add New Item to open the Add New Item dialog box.
2. Select the LINQ to SQL Classes template, give it the name MyDatabase, and click the Add button.
3. When prompted to create the LINQ to SQL classes in the App_Code folder, click the Yes button.
4. After the LINQ to SQL Designer opens, drag one or more database tables from the Database Explorer/Server Explorer window onto the Designer surface.

You can view the code that the Designer generates by expanding the MyDatabase.dbml node in the App_Code folder and double-clicking the MyDatabase.designer.cs file.

The Designer generates a strongly typed DataContext class named MyDatabaseContext. Each database table that you drag onto the Designer surface gets exposed by the DataContext class as a strongly typed property.

The Designer, furthermore, generates a distinct class for each database table you drag onto the Designer. For example, after you drag the Movie table onto the Designer, a new class named Movie is created in the MyDatabase.designer.cs file.

The page in Listing 20.13 demonstrates how you can use the MyDatabaseContext class when performing a LINQ to SQL query (after dragging the Movies database table onto the LINQ to SQL Designer).

LISTING 20.13   Entities\ListMoviesByBoxOffice.aspx

```
<%@ Page Language="C#" %>
<%@ Import Namespace="System.Linq" %>
<%@ Import Namespace="System.Data.Linq" %>
<!DOCTYPE html PUBLIC "-//W3C//DTD XHTML 1.0 Transitional//EN"
 "http://www.w3.org/TR/xhtml1/DTD/xhtml1-transitional.dtd">
<script runat="server">

    void Page_Load()
    {
        MyDatabaseDataContext db = new MyDatabaseDataContext();
        grd.DataSource = db.Movies.OrderBy(m => m.BoxOfficeTotals);
        grd.DataBind();
    }

</script>
<html xmlns="http://www.w3.org/1999/xhtml">
<head runat="server">
    <title>List Movies by Box Office</title>
</head>
<body>
    <form id="form1" runat="server">
    <div>

    <asp:GridView
        id="grd"
        runat="server" />
```

20

```
        </div>
        </form>
</body>
</html>
```

The page in Listing 20.13 displays a list of all movies in order of the movie's box office totals.

The LINQ to SQL Designer creates partial classes for each table you drag onto the Designer surface. This means that you extend the functionality of each entity by creating a new partial class. For example, the class in Listing 20.14 extends the Movie class that the LINQ to SQL Designer generates.

LISTING 20.14 Entities\App_Code\Movie.cs

```
using System;
using System.Collections.Generic;
using System.Linq;
using System.Data.Linq;

public partial class Movie
{
    public static IEnumerable<Movie> Select()
    {
        MyDatabaseDataContext db = new MyDatabaseDataContext();
        return db.Movies;
    }

    public static IEnumerable<Movie> SelectByBoxOfficeTotals()
    {
        return Select().OrderBy( m => m.BoxOfficeTotals);
    }
}
```

The Movie class in Listing 20.14 is declared as a partial class. It extends the partial class in the MyDatabase.designer.cs file by adding both a Select() method and a SelectByBoxOfficeTotals() method.

> **NOTE**
>
> The SelectByBoxOfficeTotals() method calls the Select() method. It is important to understand that this does not cause two SQL SELECT commands to be executed against the database. Until the GridView control starts iterating through the results of the LINQ to SQL query, you are just building an expression.

The page in Listing 20.15 demonstrates how you represent the `Movie` class with an `ObjectDataSource` control.

LISTING 20.15   Entities\PartialMovie.aspx

```
<%@ Page Language="C#" %>
<!DOCTYPE html PUBLIC "-//W3C//DTD XHTML 1.0 Transitional//EN"
 "http://www.w3.org/TR/xhtml1/DTD/xhtml1-transitional.dtd">
<html xmlns="http://www.w3.org/1999/xhtml">
<head runat="server">
    <title>Partial Movie</title>
</head>
<body>
    <form id="form1" runat="server">
    <div>

    <asp:GridView
        id="grdMovies"
        DataSourceID="srcMovies"
        Runat="server" />

    <asp:ObjectDataSource
        id="srcMovies"
        TypeName="Movie"
        SelectMethod="SelectByBoxOfficeTotals"
        runat="server" />

    </div>
    </form>
</body>
</html>
```

There is no code in the page in Listing 20.15. All the code is where it should be, in the Data Access layer implemented by the `Movie` class.

Building Entity Associations

One entity can be associated with another entity. For example, a `MovieCategory` entity might be associated with one or more `Movie` entities.

If you have defined foreign key relationships between your database tables, these relationships are preserved when you drag your tables onto the LINQ to SQL Designer. The LINQ to SQL Designer generates entity associations based on the foreign key relationships automatically.

20

For example, the `MovieCategory` entity is related to the `Movie` entity through the `Movie` entity's `CategoryId` property. As long as you have defined a foreign key relationship between `Movie.CategoryId` and `MovieCategory.Id`, you can use a query like this following:

```
MyDatabaseDataContext db = new MyDatabaseDataContext();
var category = db.MovieCategories.Single( c => c.Name == "Drama" );
var query = category.Movies;
```

The second statement grabs the Drama movie category. The third statement returns all movies associated with the Drama movie category. In this case, we've followed a one-to-many relationship and got a list of movies that match a movie category. You can also go the opposite direction and retrieve the only movie category that matches a particular movie:

```
string categoryName = db.Movies.Single(m=>m.Id==1).MovieCategory.Name;
```

This query retrieves the name of the movie category associated with the movie that has an ID of 1.

NOTE

Under the covers, the LINQ to SQL Designer creates the entity relationships by adding association attributes to entity properties. The LINQ to SQL Designer also adds some tricky synchronization logic to keep the properties of associated entities synchronized.

Although I wish that I could code all my entities by hand, adding all the logic necessary to get the entity associations to work correctly is too much work. For that reason, I use the LINQ to SQL Designer.

Using the LinqDataSource Control

I want to briefly describe the LinqDataSource control. You can use this control to represent LINQ queries. For example, the page in Listing 20.16 contains a simple search form for searching movies by director. The page uses a `LinqDataSource` to represent the LINQ query.

LISTING 20.16   Entities\ShowLinqDataSource.aspx

```
<%@ Page Language="C#" %>
<!DOCTYPE html PUBLIC "-//W3C//DTD XHTML 1.0 Transitional//EN"
 "http://www.w3.org/TR/xhtml1/DTD/xhtml1-transitional.dtd">
<html xmlns="http://www.w3.org/1999/xhtml">
<head runat="server">
    <title>Show LinqDataSource</title>
</head>
<body>
```

```
<form id="form1" runat="server">
<div>

<asp:Label
    id="lblSearch"
    AssociatedControlID="txtSearch"
    Text="Search:"
    Runat="server" />
<asp:TextBox
    id="txtSearch"
    Runat="server" />
<asp:Button
    id="btnSearch"
    Text="Search"
    Runat="server" />

<br /><br />

<asp:GridView
    id="grd"
    DataSourceID="LinqDataSource1"
    Runat="server" />

    <asp:LinqDataSource
        ID="LinqDataSource1"
        ContextTypeName="MyDatabaseDataContext"
        TableName="Movies"
        Where="Director == @Director"
        OrderBy="DateReleased"
        Select="new (Title, Director)"
        runat="server">
        <whereparameters>
            <asp:controlparameter
                Name="Director"
                ControlID="txtSearch"
                PropertyName="Text"
                Type="String" />
        </whereparameters>
    </asp:LinqDataSource>

</div>
</form>
</body>
</html>
```

The LinqDataSource in Listing 20.16 represents the following LINQ query:

```
var query = db.Movies
   .Where(m => m.Director == txtSearch.Text)
   .OrderBy(m => m.DateReleased)
   .Select(m => new {m.Title, m.Director});
```

You also can use the LinqDataSource to generate Update, Insert, and Delete LINQ queries automatically. Simply set the EnableInsert, EnableUpdate, or EnableDelete property to the value True. For example, the page in Listing 20.17 contains a DetailsView control and a GridView control that you can use to insert, edit, and delete movie records. The inserting, editing, and deleting is performed by the LinqDataSource control.

LISTING 20.17   Entities\EditLinqDataSource.aspx

```
<%@ Page Language="C#" %>
<!DOCTYPE html PUBLIC "-//W3C//DTD XHTML 1.0 Transitional//EN"
 "http://www.w3.org/TR/xhtml1/DTD/xhtml1-transitional.dtd">
<script runat="server">

    protected void frmMovie_ItemInserted
    (
      object sender,
      DetailsViewInsertedEventArgs e
    )
    {
        grdMovies.DataBind();
    }
</script>

<html xmlns="http://www.w3.org/1999/xhtml">
<head runat="server">
    <title>Edit LinqDataSource</title>
</head>
<body>
    <form id="form1" runat="server">
    <div>

    <asp:DetailsView
        id="frmMovie"
        DataSourceID="srcMovies"
        DefaultMode="Insert"
        AutoGenerateRows="false"
        AutoGenerateInsertButton="true"
        Runat="server" OnItemInserted="frmMovie_ItemInserted">
```

```
            <Fields>
            <asp:BoundField DataField="Title" HeaderText="Title" />
            <asp:BoundField DataField="Director" HeaderText="Director" />
            <asp:BoundField DataField="DateReleased" HeaderText="Date Released" />
            </Fields>
        </asp:DetailsView>

        <br /><br />

        <asp:GridView
            id="grdMovies"
            DataKeyNames="Id"
            DataSourceID="srcMovies"
            AllowPaging="true"
            PageSize="5"
            AutoGenerateEditButton="true"
            AutoGenerateDeleteButton="true"
            Runat="server" />

        <asp:LinqDataSource
            id="srcMovies"
            ContextTypeName="MyDatabaseDataContext"
            TableName="Movies"
            OrderBy="Id descending"
            EnableInsert="true"
            EnableUpdate="true"
            EnableDelete="true"
            AutoPage="true"
            Runat="server" />

        </div>
        </form>
</body>
</html>
```

One other thing that you should notice about the LinqDataSource control in Listing 20.17: the LinqDataSource control has an AutoPage attribute set to the value True. When this property has the value True, the LinqDataSource performs data source paging automatically.

I don't use the LinqDataSource control in production applications. Instead, I wrap up all my LINQ queries in a separate class and use the ObjectDataSource control to represent the class. The LinqDataSource control is similar to the SqlDataSource control in that both controls are great for prototyping and doing demos, but they are not appropriate controls to use in production applications.

Performing Standard Database Commands with LINQ to SQL

In this section, you learn how to use LINQ to SQL as a replacement for working directly with SQL. We start by discussing how LINQ to SQL queries differ from standard LINQ queries. Next, we examine how you can perform standard database queries and commands using LINQ to SQL such as Select, Update, Insert, and Delete commands. We'll also discuss how you can create dynamic queries with LINQ. Finally, we investigate the important topic of how you can debug LINQ to SQL queries.

LINQ to Objects Versus LINQ to SQL

You can use standard LINQ (LINQ to Objects) with any object that implements the IEnumerable<T> interface interface>. You can use LINQ to SQL, on the other hand, with any object that implements the IQueryable<T> interface. Standard LINQ is implemented with the extension methods exposed by the System.Linq.Enumerable class. LINQ to SQL, on the other hand, uses the extension methods exposed by the System.Linq.Queryable class. Why the difference?

When you build a query using standard LINQ, the query executes immediately. When you build a query using LINQ to SQL, on the hand, the query does not execute until you start enumerating the results. In other words, the query doesn't execute until you use a foreach loop to walk through the query results.

Consider the following valid LINQ to SQL query:

```
var query = tMovie.Where(m => m.Director == "Steven Spielberg")
                .OrderBy( m => m.BoxOfficeTotals )
                .Select( m => m.Title );
```

This query returns a list of movies directed by Steven Spielberg in order of the movie box office totals. You want LINQ to SQL to execute this query against the database in the most efficient way possible. In particular, you don't want LINQ to SQL to execute each method independently; you want LINQ to SQL to execute one smart database query.

When executing this query, it would be bad if LINQ to SQL (1) grabbed all the Movie records that were directed by Steven Spielberg; (2) sorted the records; and then (3) discarded all the columns except the Title column. You want LINQ to SQL to perform one smart database query that looks like this:

```
SELECT [t0].[Title] FROM [Movie] AS [t0] WHERE [t0].[Director] = @p0
ORDER BY [t0].[BoxOfficeTotals]
```

This SQL query is the exact query that LINQ to SQL performs. LINQ to SQL defers execution of a query until you start iterating through the results of the query. When you build a query, you are in reality building a representation of the query. Technically, you are building an expression tree. That way, LINQ to SQL can translate the query into one efficient SQL statement when it comes time to actually execute it.

To summarize, when you build a query using standard LINQ, the query executes as you build it. When you build a query using LINQ to SQL, you are building a representation of a query that doesn't actually execute until you start iterating through the query's results.

NOTE

When people first start using LINQ, they always worry about how they can build the equivalent of dynamic SQL commands. Later in this section, you learn how to create dynamic LINQ to SQL queries by dynamically building expression trees.

Selecting with LINQ to SQL

If you want to perform a simple, unordered `select`, you can use the following query (assuming that you have an entity named `Movie` that represents the Movies database table):

```
MyDatabaseDataContext db = new MyDatabaseDataContext();
var query = db.Movies;
```

No LINQ extension methods are used in this query. All the items are retrieved from the Movies table. If you prefer, you can use query syntax instead of method syntax, like this:

```
MyDatabaseDataContext db = new MyDatabaseDataContext();
var query = from m in db.Movies select m;
```

Selecting Particular Columns

If you want to select only particular columns, and not all the columns, from a database table, you can create an anonymous type on-the-fly, like this:

```
MyDatabaseDataContext db = new MyDatabaseDataContext();
var query = db.Movies.Select( m => new {m.Id, m.Title} );
```

The expression `new {m.Id, m.Title}` creates an anonymous type that has two properties: `Id` and `Title`. The names of the properties of the anonymous type are inferred. If you want to be more explicit, or if you want to change the names of the anonymous type's properties, you can construct your query like this:

```
MyDatabaseDataContext db = new MyDatabaseDataContext();
var query = db.Movies.Select( m => new {Id = m.Id, MovieTitle = m.Title} );
```

Selecting Particular Rows

If you want to select only particular rows from a database table and not all the rows, you can take advantage of the `Where()` method. The following LINQ to SQL query retrieves all the movies directed by George Lucas with box office totals greater than $100,000:

```
MyDatabaseDataContext db = new MyDatabaseDataContext();
var query = db.Movies
  .Where( m => m.Director == "George Lucas" && m.BoxOfficeTotals > 100000.00m)
  .Select( m => new {m.Title, m.Director, m.BoxOfficeTotals});
```

Remember to always call the Where() method before the Select() method. You need to filter your data with Where() before you shape it with Select().

Selecting Rows in a Particular Order

You can use the following methods to control the order in which rows are returned from a LINQ to SQL query:

- ▶ **OrderBy()**—Returns query results in a particular ascending order.

- ▶ **OrderByDescending()**—Returns query results in a particular descending order.

- ▶ **ThenBy()**—Returns query results using in an additional ascending order.

- ▶ **ThenByDescending()**—Returns query results using an additional descending order.

The OrderBy() and OrderBy() methods return an IOrderedQueryable<T> collection instead of the normal IQueryable<T> collection type collection type>. If you want to perform additional sorting, you need to call either the ThenBy() or ThenByDescending() method.

The following query returns movies in order of release date and then in order of box office totals:

```
MyDatabaseDataContext db = new MyDatabaseDataContext();
var query = db.Movies.OrderBy(m=>m.DateReleased).ThenBy(m=>m.BoxOfficeTotals);
```

Executing this LINQ to SQL query executes the following SQL query:

```
SELECT
  [t0].[Id],
  [t0].[CategoryId],
  [t0].[Title],
  [t0].[Director],
  [t0].[DateReleased],
  [t0].[InTheaters],
  [t0].[BoxOfficeTotals],
  [t0].[Description]
FROM [dbo].[Movie] AS [t0]
ORDER BY [t0].[DateReleased], [t0].[BoxOfficeTotals]
```

Selecting a Single Row

If you want to select a single row from the database, you can use one of the following two query methods:

▶ **Single()**—Selects a single record.

▶ **SingleOrDefault()**—Selects a single record or a default instance.

The first method assumes there is at least one element to be returned. (If not, you get an exception.) The second method returns null (for a reference type) when no matching element is found.

Here's a sample query that retrieves the only record where the movie Id has the value 1:

```
MyDatabaseDataContext db = new MyDatabaseDataContext();
Movie result = db.Movies.SingleOrDefault(m => m.Id == 1);
if (result != null)
  Response.Write(result.Title);
```

This query returns a single object of type Movie. If there is no movie record that matches the query, result is null, and the value of the Movie Title property is not written.

NOTE

When you execute a query that returns a single result, there is no deferred query execution. The LINQ query is translated into a SQL command and executed immediately.

Performing a LIKE Select

You can perform the equivalent of a LIKE Select with LINQ to SQL in several ways. First, you can use String methods such as Length, Substring, Contains, StartsWith, EndsWith, IndexOf, Insert, Remove, Replace, Trim, ToLower, ToUpper, LastIndexOf, PadRight, and PadLeft with LINQ to SQL queries. For example, the following query returns all movies that start with the letter *t*:

```
MyDatabaseDataContext db = new MyDatabaseDataContext();
var query = db.Movies.Where(m=>m.Title.StartsWith("t"));
```

Behind the scenes, this query is translated into a SQL query that uses the LIKE operator:

```
SELECT [t0].[Id], [t0].[CategoryId], [t0].[Title], [t0].[Director],
[t0].[DateReleased], [t0].[InTheaters], [t0].[BoxOfficeTotals], [t0].[Description]
FROM [dbo].[Movie] AS [t0]
WHERE [t0].[Title] LIKE @p0
```

An alternative, more flexible way to make LIKE queries is to use the System.Data.Linq.SqlClient.SqlMethods.Like() method:

```
MyDatabaseDataContext db = new MyDatabaseDataContext();
var query = db.Movies.Where(m=>SqlMethods.Like(m.Title, "t%"));
```

Using the SqlMethods.Like() method is more flexible than using the standard String methods because you can add as many wildcards to the match pattern as you need.

20

NOTE

The SqlMethods class also contains a number of useful methods for expressing the SQL DateDiff() function in a LINQ to SQL Query.

Paging Through Records

Doing database paging right when working with ADO.NET is difficult. The SQL language is not designed to make it easy to retrieve a range of records. Doing database paging using LINQ to SQL queries, on the other hand, is trivial.

You can take advantage of the following two query methods to perform database paging:

▸ **Skip()**—Enables you to skip a certain number of records.

▸ **Take()**—Enables you to take a certain number of records.

For example, the class in Listing 20.18 contains a method named SelectedPaged() that gets a particular page of movie records from the Movie database table.

LISTING 20.18   Standard\App_Code\Movie.cs

```
using System;
using System.Collections.Generic;
using System.Linq;
using System.Data.Linq;

public partial class Movie
{
    public static IEnumerable<Movie> Select()
    {
        MyDatabaseDataContext db = new MyDatabaseDataContext();
        return db.Movies;
    }

    public static IEnumerable< Movie> SelectPaged
    (
      int startRowIndex,
      int maximumRows
    )
    {
        return Select().Skip(startRowIndex).Take(maximumRows);
    }

    public static int SelectCount()
    {
```

```
        return Select().Count();
    }
}
```

I'm assuming, in the case of Listing 20.18, that you have already created a Movie entity by using the LINQ to SQL Designer. The Movie class in Listing 20.18 is a partial class that extends the existing Movie class generated by the Designer.

The ASP.NET page in Listing 20.19 illustrates how you can use the Movie class with the ObjectDataSource control to page through movie records.

LISTING 20.19   Standard\ShowPagedMovies.aspx

```
<%@ Page Language="C#" %>
<!DOCTYPE html PUBLIC "-//W3C//DTD XHTML 1.0 Transitional//EN"
 "http://www.w3.org/TR/xhtml1/DTD/xhtml1-transitional.dtd">
<html xmlns="http://www.w3.org/1999/xhtml">
<head runat="server">
    <title>Show Paged Movies</title>
</head>
<body>
    <form id="form1" runat="server">
    <div>

    <asp:GridView
        id="grdMovies"
        DataSourceID="srcMovies"
        AllowPaging="true"
        PageSize="5"
        Runat="server" />

    <asp:ObjectDataSource
        id="srcMovies"
        TypeName="Movie"
        SelectMethod="SelectPaged"
        SelectCountMethod="SelectCount"
        EnablePaging="true"
        Runat="server" />

    </div>
    </form>
</body>
</html>
```

20

Joining Records from Different Tables

You can perform joins when selecting entities just like you can when joining database tables. For example, imagine that you want to join the Movie and MovieCategory tables on the CategoryId key. Assuming that you have both a Movie and MovieCategory entity, you can use the following query:

```
MyDatabaseDataContext db = new MyDatabaseDataContext();
var query = db.MovieCategories
        .Join(db.Movies, c=>c.Id, m=>m.CategoryId, (c,m)=>new {c.Id,c.Name,m.Title});
```

This LINQ query gets translated into the following SQL command:

```
SELECT [t0].[Id], [t0].[Name], [t1].[Title]
FROM [dbo].[MovieCategory] AS [t0]
INNER JOIN [dbo].[Movie] AS [t1] ON [t0].[Id] = [t1].[CategoryId]
```

This query performs an inner join. If you want to perform an outer join, the syntax is a little more complicated. Here's how you do a left outer join using query syntax:

```
MyDatabaseDataContext db = new MyDatabaseDataContext();
var query = from c in db.MovieCategories
            join m in db.Movies
            on c.Id equals m.CategoryId into cm
            from m in cm.DefaultIfEmpty()
            select new { c.Id, c.Name, m.Title };
```

This LINQ query gets translated into the following SQL SELECT:

```
SELECT [t0].[Id], [t0].[Name], [t1].[Title] AS [value]
FROM [dbo].[MovieCategory] AS [t0]
LEFT OUTER JOIN [dbo].[Movie] AS [t1] ON [t0].[Id] = [t1].[CategoryId]
```

As an alternative to using joins, consider taking advantage of the associations between entities. Remember that the following type of query is perfectly valid:

```
MyDatabaseDataContext db = new MyDatabaseDataContext();
var category = db.MovieCategories.Single( c => c.Name == "Drama" );
var query = category.Movies;
```

Caching Records

Getting caching to work with LINQ to SQL is a little tricky. Remember that a LINQ to SQL query represents a query expression and not the actual query results. The SQL command is not executed, and the results are not retrieved until you start iterating through the query results.

For example, imagine that you declare the following ObjectDataSource control in a page and that this ObjectDataSource control represents a class that returns a LINQ to SQL query:

```
<asp:ObjectDataSource
    id="srcMovies"
    TypeName="Movie"
    SelectMethod="Select"
    EnableCaching="true"
    CacheDuration="9999"
    Runat="server" />
```

This ObjectDataSource has been set up to cache its results. Its EnableCaching and
CacheDuration properties are set. However, what gets cached here is the query expression
and not that actual query results. The SQL select statement that corresponds to the LINQ
to SQL query executes every time the page is requested.

To get caching to work, we need to force the query results and not the query into the cache.
The Movie class in Listing 20.20 contains a SelectCached() method that successfully caches
database data with a LINQ to SQL query.

LISTING 20.20   Standard\App_Code\Movie.cs

```csharp
using System;
using System.Web;
using System.Collections.Generic;
using System.Linq;
using System.Data.Linq;

public partial class Movie
{
    public static IEnumerable<Movie> Select()
    {
        MyDatabaseDataContext db = new MyDatabaseDataContext();
        return db.Movies;
    }

    public static IEnumerable<Movie> SelectCached()
    {
        HttpContext context = HttpContext.Current;
        List<Movie> movies = (List<Movie>)context.Cache["Movies"];
        if (movies == null)
        {
            movies = Select().ToList();
            context.Cache["Movies"] = movies;
            context.Trace.Warn("Retrieving movies from database");
        }
        return movies;
    }
}
```

20

The `SelectCached()` method attempts to retrieve movie records from the cache. If the records can't be retrieved from the cache, the movies are retrieved from the database. The vast majority of the time, the movies are retrieved from the cache.

The trick here is to use the `ToList()` method to convert the `IEnumerable<Movie>` into a `List<Movie>`. When the `List<Movie>` is created, the SQL query associated with the LINQ to SQL query is executed and the actual data is returned.

You can use the class in Listing 20.20 with the ASP.NET page in Listing 20.21.

LISTING 20.21   Standard\ShowCachedMovies.aspx

```
<%@ Page Language="C#" Trace="true" %>
<!DOCTYPE html PUBLIC "-//W3C//DTD XHTML 1.0 Transitional//EN"
 "http://www.w3.org/TR/xhtml1/DTD/xhtml1-transitional.dtd">
<html xmlns="http://www.w3.org/1999/xhtml">
<head runat="server">
    <title>Show Cached Movies</title>
</head>
<body>
    <form id="form1" runat="server">
    <div>

    <asp:GridView
        id="grdMovies"
        DataSourceID="srcMovies"
        Runat="server" />

    <asp:ObjectDataSource
        id="srcMovies"
        TypeName="Movie"
        SelectMethod="SelectCached"
        Runat="server" />

    </div>
    </form>
</body>
</html>
```

The `ObjectDataSource` in Listing 20.21 does not have caching enabled. All the caching happens in the Data Access layer (the `Movie` class).

Inserting with LINQ to SQL

There are two steps to adding and inserting a new record with LINQ to SQL. First, you need to use the `InsertOnSubmit()` method to add an entity to an existing table. Next, you call `SubmitChanges()` on the `DataContext` to execute the SQL `INSERT` statement against the database.

The class in Listing 20.22 illustrates how you can write a method to add a new record into the Movie database table.

LISTING 20.22   Standard\App_Code\Movie.cs

```
using System;
using System.Web;
using System.Collections.Generic;
using System.Linq;
using System.Data.Linq;

public partial class Movie
{
    public static int Insert(Movie movieToInsert)
    {
        MyDatabaseDataContext db = new MyDatabaseDataContext();
        db.Movies.InsertOnSubmit( movieToInsert );
        db.SubmitChanges();
        return movieToInsert.Id;
    }

    public static IEnumerable<Movie> Select()
    {
        MyDatabaseDataContext db = new MyDatabaseDataContext();
        return db.Movies.OrderByDescending(m=>m.Id);
    }

}
```

The `Movie` class includes an `Insert()` method that inserts a new movie into the database. The `Insert()` method returns an integer that represents the identity value of the new record. As soon as `SubmitChanges()` is called, the `Id` property is updated with the new identity value from the database.

20

> **NOTE**
>
> I'm assuming in this section that you have used the LINQ to SQL Designer to create entities for the Movie and MovieCategories database tables.

The page in Listing 20.23 contains a `FormView` control and a `GridView` control. You can use `FormView` to insert new movie records into the database. The `FormView` control is bound to an `ObjectDataSource` control that represents the `Movie` class.

LISTING 20.23   Standard\InsertMovie.aspx

```
<%@ Page Language="C#" Trace="true" %>
<!DOCTYPE html PUBLIC "-//W3C//DTD XHTML 1.0 Transitional//EN"
 "http://www.w3.org/TR/xhtml1/DTD/xhtml1-transitional.dtd">
<html xmlns="http://www.w3.org/1999/xhtml">
<head runat="server">
    <title>Insert Movie</title>
</head>
<body>
    <form id="form1" runat="server">
    <div>

    <asp:FormView
        id="frmMovie"
        DataSourceID="srcMovies"
        DefaultMode="Insert"
        Runat="Server">
        <InsertItemTemplate>
            <asp:Label
                id="lblTitle"
                Text="Title:"
                AssociatedControlID="txtTitle"
                Runat="server" />
            <br />
            <asp:TextBox
                id="txtTitle"
                Text='<%# Bind("Title") %>'
                Runat="server" />

            <br /><br />

            <asp:Label
                id="lblCategory"
                Text="Category:"
                AssociatedControlID="ddlCategory"
                Runat="server" />
            <br />
            <asp:DropDownList
                id="ddlCategory"
                DataSourceId="srcMovieCategories"
```

```
        SelectedValue='<%# Bind("CategoryId") %>'
        DataTextField="Name"
        DataValueField="Id"
        Runat="server" />
<asp:ObjectDataSource
    id="srcMovieCategories"
    TypeName="MovieCategory"
    SelectMethod="Select"
    Runat="Server" />
<br /><br / >

<asp:Label
    id="lblDirector"
    Text="Director:"
    AssociatedControlID="txtDirector"
    Runat="server" />
<br />
<asp:TextBox
    id="txtDirector"
    Text='<%# Bind("Director") %>'
    Runat="server" />

<br /><br />

<asp:Label
    id="lblDescription"
    Text="Description:"
    AssociatedControlID="txtDescription"
    Runat="server" />
<br />
<asp:TextBox
    id="txtDescription"
    Text='<%# Bind("Description") %>'
    TextMode="MultiLine"
    Columns="60"
    Rows="3"
    Runat="server" />

<br /><br />

<asp:Label
    id="lblDateReleased"
    Text="Date Released:"
    AssociatedControlID="txtDateReleased"
    Runat="server" />
```

```
                <br />
                <asp:TextBox
                    id="txtDateReleased"
                    Text='<%# Bind("DateReleased") %>'
                    Runat="server" />

                <br /><br />

                <asp:Button
                    id="btnInsert"
                    Text="Insert"
                    CommandName="Insert"
                    Runat="server" />

            </InsertItemTemplate>
        </asp:FormView>

        <hr />

        <asp:GridView
            id="grdMovies"
            DataSourceID="srcMovies"
            Runat="server" />

        <asp:ObjectDataSource
            id="srcMovies"
            TypeName="Movie"
            DataObjectTypeName="Movie"
            SelectMethod="Select"
            InsertMethod="Insert"
            Runat="server" />

    </div>
    </form>
</body>
</html>
```

The ObjectDataSource control in Listing 20.23 includes a DataObjectTypeName attribute that is set to the value Movie. ObjectDataSource instantiates a new Movie object automatically when calling the Movie.Insert() method.

Updating with LINQ to SQL

You can update a LINQ to SQL entity and the underlying database table by modifying the entity's properties and calling the DataContext's SubmitChanges() method, like this:

```
MyDatabaseDataContext db = new MyDatabaseDataContext();
Movie movieToUpdate = db.Movies.Single(m=>m.Id==1);
movieToUpdate.Title = "King Kong II";
movieToUpdate.Director = "George Lucas";
db.SubmitChanges();
```

This code first grabs the movie that has an Id value of 1. Next, the movie Title and Director properties are modified. Finally, these changes are submitted to the database by calling the SubmitChanges() method.

This code works, but it is not the best code to use when building an ASP.NET page. Typically, when performing an update in ASP.NET, you already have information about the entity in view state. You don't want or need to grab the entity from the database to modify it.

For example, if you use a FormView control to update the database, the FormView control will do a select automatically and store the entity information in view state. You don't want to grab the entity information a second time after the user clicks the Insert button.

Instead, what you want to do is reattach the entity back into the DataContext from view state. You already have the entity; you just want to make the DataContext aware of the entity again.

This approach is illustrated in the class in Listing 20.24.

LISTING 20.24   Standard\App_Code\Movie.cs

```
using System;
using System.Web;
using System.Collections.Generic;
using System.Linq;
using System.Data.Linq;

public partial class Movie
{
    public static void Update(Movie oldMovie, Movie newMovie)
    {
        MyDatabaseDataContext db = new MyDatabaseDataContext();
        db.Movies.Attach(oldMovie);
        oldMovie.Title = newMovie.Title;
        oldMovie.Director = newMovie.Director;
        db.SubmitChanges();
    }

    public static IEnumerable<Movie> Select()
    {
        MyDatabaseDataContext db = new MyDatabaseDataContext();
```

20

```
        return db.Movies;
    }
}
```

The Update() method in Listing 20.24 receives both the original and new version of the Movie entity. First, the old version of the Movie entity is attached to the DataContext. Next, the old entity is updated with changes from the new entity. Finally, SubmitChanges() is called to perform the SQL UPDATE command against the database.

You can use the page in Listing 20.25 with the Update() method.

LISTING 20.25   Standard\UpdateMovie.aspx

```
<%@ Page Language="C#" Trace="true" %>
<!DOCTYPE html PUBLIC "-//W3C//DTD XHTML 1.0 Transitional//EN"
 "http://www.w3.org/TR/xhtml1/DTD/xhtml1-transitional.dtd">
<html xmlns="http://www.w3.org/1999/xhtml">
<head runat="server">
    <title>Update Movie</title>
</head>
<body>
    <form id="form1" runat="server">
    <div>

    <asp:GridView
        id="grdMovies"
        DataSourceID="srcMovies"
        DataKeyNames="Id"
        AutoGenerateEditButton="true"
        Runat="server" />

    <asp:ObjectDataSource
        id="srcMovies"
        TypeName="Movie"
        DataObjectTypeName="Movie"
        SelectMethod="Select"
        UpdateMethod="Update"
        ConflictDetection="CompareAllValues"
        OldValuesParameterFormatString="oldMovie"
        Runat="server" />

    </div>
    </form>
</body>
</html>
```

The `ObjectDataSource` control has both its `ConflictDetection` and `OldValuesParameterFormatString` attributes set. The `ConflictDetection` attribute is set to the value `CompareAllValues`. This value causes the `ObjectDataSource` to store the original movie property values in view state. The `OldValuesParameterFormatString` attribute determines the name of the parameter that represents the old `Movie` entity.

When you update a movie by using the page in Listing 20.25, the following SQL command is sent to the database:

```
UPDATE [dbo].[Movie]
SET [Title] = @p7
WHERE ([Id] = @p0) AND ([CategoryId] = @p1)
AND ([Title] = @p2) AND ([Director] = @p3)
AND ([DateReleased] = @p4) AND (NOT ([InTheaters] = 1))
AND ([BoxOfficeTotals] = @p5) AND ([Description] = @p6)
```

LINQ to SQL compares all the new column values against the old column values. This is done to prevent concurrency conflicts. If someone else makes a change to a record before you have a chance to submit your changes, the record won't be updated with your changes. However, all this comparing of column values seems wasteful and silly.

If you don't want LINQ to SQL to compare all the column values when it does an update, you need to add a version property to your entity. The easiest way to do this is to add a timestamp column to the database table that corresponds to the entity (and re-create the entity in the LINQ to SQL Designer so that it has the new timestamp column property). So, our modified Movie table looks like this:

Movie

Column Name	Data Type	Is Identity?
Id	Int	TRUE
Title	NVarchar(100)	FALSE
Director	NVarchar	FALSE
DateReleased	DateTime	FALSE
BoxOfficeTotals	Money	FALSE
Version	TimeStamp	FALSE

You also need to ensure that the `Version` property gets saved into view state. You can do this by adding the `Version` property to a `DataBound` control's `DataKeyNames` property. This approach is illustrated by the page in Listing 20.26.

20

LISTING 20.26   Standard\UpdateMovieVersion.aspx

```
<%@ Page Language="C#" Trace="true" %>
<!DOCTYPE html PUBLIC "-//W3C//DTD XHTML 1.0 Transitional//EN"
 "http://www.w3.org/TR/xhtml1/DTD/xhtml1-transitional.dtd">
<html xmlns="http://www.w3.org/1999/xhtml">
<head id="Head1" runat="server">
    <title>Update Movie Version</title>
</head>
<body>
    <form id="form1" runat="server">
    <div>

    <asp:GridView
        id="grdMovies"
        DataSourceID="srcMovies"
        DataKeyNames="Id,Version"
        AutoGenerateEditButton="true"
        Runat="server" />

    <asp:ObjectDataSource
        id="srcMovies"
        TypeName="Movie"
        DataObjectTypeName="Movie"
        SelectMethod="Select"
        UpdateMethod="Update"
        ConflictDetection="CompareAllValues"
        OldValuesParameterFormatString="oldMovie"
        Runat="server" />

    </div>
    </form>
</body>
</html>
```

Both the Id and Version properties are assigned to the GridView control's DataKeyNames attribute.

After you make these changes, the update SQL command looks like this:

```
UPDATE [dbo].[Movie]
SET [Title] = @p2
WHERE ([Id] = @p0) AND ([Version] = @p1)
```

Deleting with LINQ to SQL

You can delete an entity with LINQ to SQL by using code like the following:

```
MyDatabaseDataContext db = new MyDatabaseDataContext();
Movie movieToDelete = db.Movies.Single(m=>m.Id==1);
db.Movies.Remove( movieToDelete );
db.SubmitChanges();
```

This code starts by retrieving the record with an Id of 1 from the Movie database table. Next, the Movie entity is removed from the Movies collection. Finally, this change is submitted to the database and the following SQL command executes:

```
DELETE FROM [dbo].[Movie]
WHERE ([Id] = @p0) AND ([Version] = @p1)
```

> **NOTE**
>
> I'm assuming in this section that you have added a Version property to your Movie database table. If not, see the previous section, because you should add a Version property when deleting for the same reasons you should add a Version property when updating.

It seems silly to retrieve a record from the database just so that you can delete it—and it is silly. What you need to do is reattach the Movie entity so that you can delete it. Thus, you can avoid making two calls to the database.

The modified Movie class in Listing 20.27 includes a Delete() method that removes a movie without retrieving it first.

LISTING 20.27   Standard\App_Code\Movie.cs

```
using System;
using System.Web;
using System.Collections.Generic;
using System.Linq;
using System.Data.Linq;

public partial class Movie
{
    public static void Delete(Movie movieToDelete)
    {
        MyDatabaseDataContext db = new MyDatabaseDataContext();
        db.Movies.Attach(movieToDelete);
        db.Movies.DeleteOnSubmit(movieToDelete);
        db.SubmitChanges();
```

20

```
    }

    public static IEnumerable<Movie> Select()
    {
        MyDatabaseDataContext db = new MyDatabaseDataContext();
        return db.Movies;
    }
}
```

You can use the class in Listing 20.27 with the ASP.NET page in Listing 20.28.

LISTING 20.28   Standard\DeleteMovie.aspx

```
<%@ Page Language="C#" Trace="true" %>
<!DOCTYPE html PUBLIC "-//W3C//DTD XHTML 1.0 Transitional//EN"
 "http://www.w3.org/TR/xhtml1/DTD/xhtml1-transitional.dtd">
<html xmlns="http://www.w3.org/1999/xhtml">
<head id="Head1" runat="server">
    <title>Delete Movie</title>
</head>
<body>
    <form id="form1" runat="server">
    <div>

    <asp:GridView
        id="grdMovies"
        DataSourceID="srcMovies"
        DataKeyNames="Id,Version"
        AutoGenerateDeleteButton="true"
        Runat="server" />

    <asp:ObjectDataSource
        id="srcMovies"
        TypeName="Movie"
        DataObjectTypeName="Movie"
        SelectMethod="Select"
        DeleteMethod="Delete"
        ConflictDetection="CompareAllValues"
        OldValuesParameterFormatString="oldMovie"
        Runat="server" />

    </div>
    </form>
</body>
</html>
```

The `ObjectDataSource` control in Listing 20.28 has both its `ConflictDetection` and `OldValuesParameterFormatString` attributes set. The `ObjectDataSource` remembers a `Movie` entity across postbacks. It passes the original `Movie` entity to the `Delete()` method so that the entity and be reattached and deleted.

Dynamic Queries

One concern that everyone has when they start working with LINQ to SQL is the problem of representing dynamic queries. When you create a query by using ADO.NET and SQL, you can dynamically modify the SQL query simply by modifying the string that represents the SQL command. When working with LINQ to SQL, on the other hand, you can't do this because you are not working with strings.

In this section, we explore two methods of executing dynamic queries. You learn how to pass normal SQL commands while using LINQ to SQL. You also learn how to dynamically build LINQ to SQL query expressions.

Executing Dynamic SQL Statements

If you simply want to execute a SQL statement or query, and you don't want to use ADO.NET directly, you can take advantage of the `DataContext` `ExecuteCommand()` and `ExecuteQuery()` methods. The `ExecuteCommand()` method executes a SQL command against a database. The `ExecuteQuery()` method executes a SQL query against a database and returns the results as entities.

The following code illustrates how to use both of these methods:

```
MyDatabaseDataContext db = new MyDatabaseDataContext();
db.ExecuteCommand("INSERT Movie (Title,Director,CategoryId)
  VALUES (@p0,@p1,
var query = db.ExecuteQuery(typeof(Movie), "SELECT * FROM Movie
  WHERE CategoryId=@p0", new object[]{2});
```

Here, the `ExecuteCommand()` method is used to insert a new record into the Movie database table. The `ExecuteQuery()` method is used to grab all the records from the Movie table where the CategoryId column has the value 2.

You indicate parameters by using parameter names like @p0, @p1, @p2, and so on. You do not use named parameters like you would in the case of an ADO.NET command. Parameters are identified by their ordinal position.

Building Query Expressions Dynamically

Resorting to executing SQL statements against the database feels like a type of cheating. The whole point of LINQ to SQL is to get away from working with SQL directly. What we actually want to do is build LINQ to SQL queries dynamically in the same way we can build a SQL command dynamically.

20

You can build LINQ to SQL query expressions dynamically by taking advantage of the System.Linq.Expressions.Expression class. This class contains all the methods for building query expressions dynamically. Here is a (very partial) list of methods supported by this class:

- **Add()**—Creates an expression that represents addition.

- **And()**—Creates an expression that represents a logical AND.

- **Condition()**—Creates an expression that represents a condition.

- **Constant()**—Creates an expression that represents a constant value.

- **Convert()**—Creates an expression that represents a conversion from one type to another.

- **Divide()**—Creates an expression that represents division.

- **Equal()**—Creates an expression that represents whether two expressions are equal.

- **Field()**—Creates an expression that represents a field.

- **Lambda()**—Creates a lambda expression.

- **Multiply()**—Creates an expression that represents multiplication.

- **Or()**—Creates an expression that represents a logical OR.

- **Parameter()**—Creates an expression that represents a function parameter.

- **Property()**—Creates an expression that represents accessing a property.

- **PropertyOrField()**—Creates an expression that represents accessing a property or field.

- **Subtract()**—Creates an expression that represents subtraction.

Again, this is not a complete list of methods supported by the Expression class. However, it should give you some idea of how you can go about building expressions.

Let's discuss a real-world situation in which you need dynamic LINQ to SQL expressions: sorting. If you want to enable sorting when using a GridView control with LINQ to SQL, you have a choice. You can create a switch (SELECT CASE) block to sort by every possible column that a user can click, or you can create a dynamic LINQ to SQL expression.

The class in Listing 20.29 contains a method called GetDynamicSort() that returns a dynamic lambda expression that can be used with either the OrderBy() or OrderByDescending()method.

LISTING 20.29   Standard\App_Code\Movie.cs

```
using System;
using System.Web;
using System.Collections.Generic;
using System.Linq;
```

```
using System.Linq.Expressions;
using System.Data.Linq;
using System.Reflection;

public partial class Movie
{

    public static IEnumerable<Movie> Select(string orderBy)
    {
        string orderByColumn = "Id";
        string orderByDirection = "asc";
        if (!String.IsNullOrEmpty(orderBy))
            ParseOrderBy(orderBy, ref orderByColumn, ref orderByDirection);


        MyDatabaseDataContext db = new MyDatabaseDataContext();
        if (orderByDirection == "asc")
            return db.Movies.OrderBy(GetDynamicSort(orderByColumn));
        else
            return db.Movies.OrderByDescending(GetDynamicSort(orderByColumn));
    }



    public static void ParseOrderBy
    (
      string orderBy,
      ref string orderByColumn,
      ref string orderByDirection
    )
    {
        string[] orderByParts = orderBy.Split(' ');
        orderByColumn = orderByParts[0];
        if (orderByParts.Length > 1)
            orderByDirection = orderByParts[1].ToLower();
    }



    private static Expression<Func<Movie, string>> GetDynamicSort
    (
        string orderByColumn
    )
    {
        // Create expression to represent Movie parameter into lambda expression
        ParameterExpression pMovie = Expression.Parameter(typeof(Movie), "m");
```

```
    // Create expression to access value of order by column
    PropertyInfo propInfo = typeof(Movie).GetProperty(orderByColumn);
    MemberExpression m = Expression.MakeMemberAccess(pMovie, propInfo);

    // Box it
    UnaryExpression b = Expression.TypeAs(m, typeof(object));

    // Convert to string
    MethodInfo convertMethod = typeof(Convert).GetMethod("ToString",
        new Type[] { typeof(object) });
    MethodCallExpression c = Expression.Call(null, convertMethod, b);

    // Return lambda
    return Expression.Lambda<Func<Movie, string>>(c, pMovie);
    }
}
```

The GetDynamicSort() method builds a lambda expression dynamically and creates an expression that looks like this:

```
m => Convert.ToString(m.Id As Object)
```

When the LINQ to SQL query gets translated to SQL, the following SQL command is executed:

```
SELECT [t0].[Id], [t0].[CategoryId], [t0].[Title],
[t0].[Director], [t0].[DateReleased], [t0].[InTheaters],
[t0].[BoxOfficeTotals], [t0].[Description], [t0].[Version]
FROM [dbo].[Movie] AS [t0]
ORDER BY CONVERT(NVarChar(MAX),[t0].[Title])
```

You can use the class in Listing 20.29 with the ASP.NET page in Listing 20.30. When you click a header column in GridView, it is sorted by the column.

LISTING 20.30   Standard\ShowDynamicSort.aspx

```
<%@ Page Language="C#" trace="true" %>
<!DOCTYPE html PUBLIC "-//W3C//DTD XHTML 1.0 Transitional//EN"
 "http://www.w3.org/TR/xhtml1/DTD/xhtml11-transitional.dtd">
<html xmlns="http://www.w3.org/1999/xhtml">
<head runat="server">
    <title>Show Dynamic Sort</title>
</head>
<body>
    <form id="form1" runat="server">
    <div>
```

```
    <asp:GridView
        id="grdMovies"
        DataSourceId="srcMovies"
        AllowSorting="true"
        Runat="server" />

    <asp:ObjectDataSource
        id="srcMovies"
        TypeName="Movie"
        SelectMethod="Select"
        SortParameterName="orderBy"
        Runat="server" />

    </div>
    </form>
</body>
</html>
```

The `GridView` control has its `AllowSorting` attribute set to the value `true` and the
`ObjectDataSource` control has its `SortParameterName` attribute set to the value `orderBy`.
The page is set up to enable data source paging.

> **NOTE**
>
> The `GetDynamicSort()` method described in this section does a sort after converting
> the values of a column to strings. For nonstring data types such as dates and integers,
> doing string sorts produces the wrong results. For example, after sorting, the id column
> is ordered as 10, 2, 22, 29, 3, 30, 31, and so on.
>
> In the final part of this chapter, you learn how to create a custom entity base class that
> implements a more sophisticated version of a dynamic sort that sorts different column
> types correctly.

Debugging LINQ to SQL

For the sake of performance, you had better know what is going on beneath the covers
when you execute LINQ to SQL queries. In particular, it is useful to know how your LINQ
to SQL queries get translated into SQL and when your LINQ to SQL queries execute. In
this section, I describe three methods of debugging LINQ to SQL.

20

Using the LINQ to SQL Debug Visualizer

The LINQ to SQL Debug Visualizer is a useful tool for viewing how a LINQ to SQL query translates into SQL. The LINQ to SQL Debug Visualizer is not included with .NET Framework. You need to download it from the following address: http://www.scottgu.com/blogposts/linqquery/SqlServerQueryVisualizer.zip.

After you download the LINQ to SQL Visualizer, you can use it like other Visualizers in Visual Web Developer and Visual Studio by compiling it and placing the resulting DLL in the My Documents\Visual Studio 2010\Visualizers folder. Then, If you set a breakpoint after a LINQ to SQL query and hover your mouse over the query, you can click the magnifying glass to see the full SQL command into which the query gets translated (see Figure 20.1). You also have the option of executing the SQL query directly from the Visualizer.

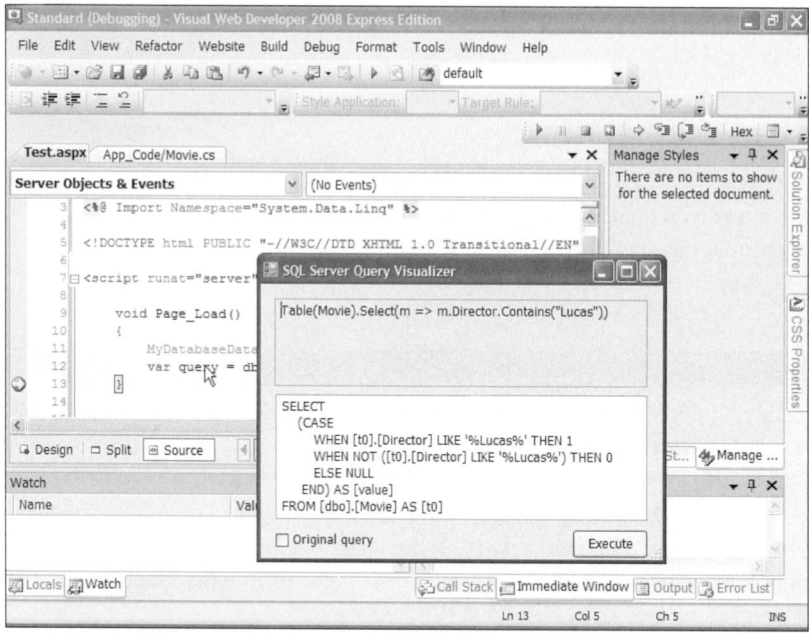

FIGURE 20.1   Using the LINQ to SQL Debug Visualizer.

Logging LINQ to SQL Queries

My favorite method of debugging LINQ to SQL queries is to log all the DataContext output to ASP.NET trace. That way, I can see all the LINQ to SQL queries that execute at the bottom of each of my ASP.NET pages (see Figure 20.2).

The DataContext class includes a Log property. You can assign a TextWriter to the Log property, and DataContext writes to this TextWriter whenever it executes a query.

Unfortunately, the .NET Framework does not include a TextWriter that writes to ASP.NET Trace. Fortunately, it is not that difficult to write one, and I've included the code for a Trace TextWriter in Listing 20.31.

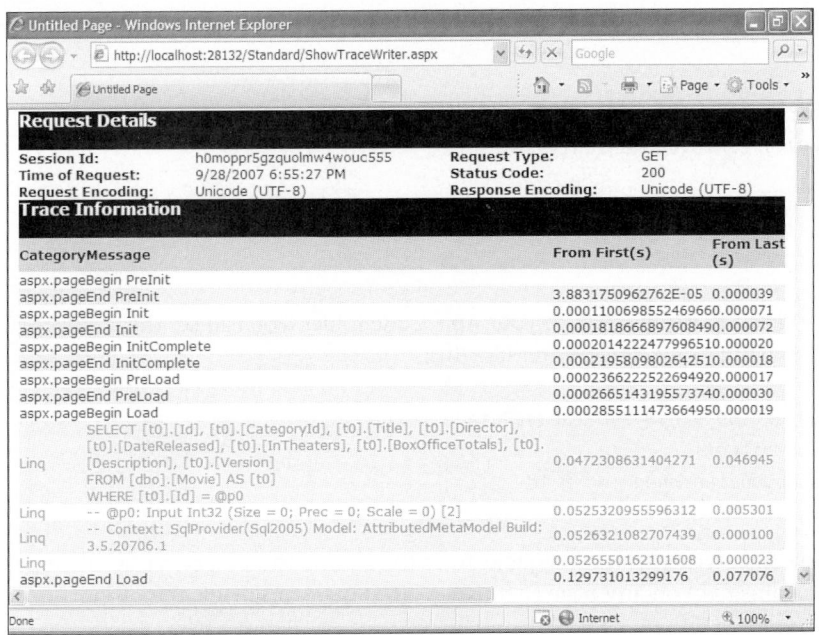

FIGURE 20.2   Logging LINQ to Trace.

LISTING 20.31   Standard\TraceWriter.cs

```
using System;
using System.Text;
using System.Web;
using System.IO;
using System.Globalization;

public class TraceWriter : TextWriter
{
    public override void Write(string value)
    {
        HttpContext.Current.Trace.Warn(value);
    }

    public override void Write(char[] buffer, int index, int count)
    {
        HttpContext.Current.Trace.Warn("Linq", new string(buffer, index, count));
    }

    public override Encoding Encoding
    {
```

20

```
        get { return Encoding.Unicode; }
    }

    public TraceWriter()
        : base(CultureInfo.CurrentCulture)
    {
    }
}
```

After you drop the class in Listing 20.31 in your App_Code folder, you can set the DataContext class to write to the TraceWriter like this:

```
MyDatabaseDataContext db = new MyDatabaseDataContext();
db.Log = new TraceWriter();
grd.DataSource = db.Movies.Where(m=>m.Id==2);
grd.DataBind();
```

After you set up the TraceWriter, you can enable Trace (by adding the Trace="true" attribute to the <%@ Page %> directive) on any page that uses a LINQ query and view the output.

> **NOTE**
>
> The LINQ entity base class we create in the last part of this chapter automatically logs all output to the TraceWriter.

Using the GetCommand Method

Finally, you can use the DataContext.GetCommand() method to get the ADO.NET command object that executes when a LINQ to SQL query executes. After you grab the command object, you can examine its parameters or its command text.

The following code assigns the command text of a command associated with a LINQ to SQL query to a Label control:

```
MyDatabaseDataContext db = new MyDatabaseDataContext();
var query = db.Movies.Where(m=>m.Id==2);

lblQuery.Text = db.GetCommand(query).CommandText;
```

The following SELECT command is displayed in the Label control:

```
SELECT [t0].[Id], [t0].[CategoryId], [t0].[Title], [t0].[Director],
[t0].[DateReleased], [t0].[InTheaters], [t0].[BoxOfficeTotals],
[t0].[Description],
[t0].[Version] FROM [dbo].[Movie] AS [t0] WHERE [t0].[Id] = @p0
```

Creating a Custom LINQ Entity Base Class

In this final part of this chapter, we build a custom LINQ to SQL base class. Our base class contains standard methods for selecting records, inserting records, updating records, and deleting records. It also supports paging and caching. Finally, our base class contains methods for performing validation.

The files for the custom classes can be found on the website that accompanies this book in the folder EntityBaseClasses. This folder contains the following files:

▶ **EntityBase**—A custom base class for LINQ to SQL entities.

▶ **EntityDataSource**—A custom data source control derived from the ObjectDataSource control for representing LINQ to SQL entities.

▶ **EntityValidator**—A custom validation control.

▶ **EntityCallOutValidator**—A custom validation control that displays a call-out validation error message.

▶ **ValidationError**—A class that represents a validation error.

▶ **ValidationErrorCollection**—A collection of validation errors.

▶ **ValidationException**—An exception thrown when there is a validation error.

▶ **TraceWriter**—A class for logging LINQ to SQL queries to ASP.NET trace.

The motivation for writing these classes was to make standard database operations easier when using LINQ to SQL. I discovered that I was writing the exact same queries and commands over and over again whenever I created a new entity. Writing a standard base class made my life easier because it freed me from writing the same repetitive code.

Using the Entity Base Class

Follow these steps to use the custom entity base classes:

1. Create a new website.
2. Add an App_Code folder to your website, and copy the EntityBaseClasses folder to the App_Code folder.
3. Create one or more LINQ to SQL entities with the help of the LINQ to SQL Designer.
4. Add a connection string named con to your database in the web.config file.
5. Create a separate partial class for each LINQ to SQL entity and derive the class from the EntityBase class.
6. Create an empty Validate() method for each entity class.

For example, imagine that you have used the LINQ to SQL Designer to create an entity named Movie. You created the Movie entity by dragging the Movie database table from the Database Explorer (Server Explorer) window onto the LINQ to SQL Designer surface. At this point, you are ready to inherit your new Movie entity from the EntityBase class.

20

Listing 20.32 contains the file that you add to your website to create a `Movie` entity that inherits from the `EntityBase` class.

LISTING 20.32   ShowEntityBase\App_Code\Movie.cs

```
using System;


public partial class Movie : EntityBase<Movie>
{
    protected override void Validate()
    {
    }
}
```

Now that you have derived the `Movie` entity from `EntityBase`, the `Movie` class inherits methods for selecting, inserting, updating, and deleting records.

Performing Standard Data-Access Operations with the `EntityBase` Class

Any entity that you inherit from the `EntityBase` class inherits the following methods automatically:

▶ **Select()**—Selects all entities.

▶ **Select(string orderBy)**—Selects all entities in a certain order.

▶ **SelectCached()**—Selects all entities from the cache.

▶ **SelectCached(string orderBy)**—Selects all entities from the cache in a certain order.

▶ **Select(int startRowIndex, int maximumRows)**—Selects a page of entities.

▶ **Select(int startRowIndex, int maximumRows, orderBy)**—Selects a page of entities in a certain order.

▶ **SelectCount()**—Returns a count of entities.

▶ **SelectCount(string orderBy)**—Returns a count of entities.

▶ **SelectCountCached()**—Returns a count of entities from the cache.

▶ **Get(int? Id)**—Gets a single entity using the entity's identity value.

▶ **Save(T oldEntity, T newEntity)**—Either performs an insert or update depending on whether the identity value is 0.

▶ **Insert(T entityToInsert)**—Inserts a new entity.

▶ **Update(T oldEntity, T newEntity)**—Updates an existing entity.

▶ **Delete(T entityToDelete)**—Deletes an entity.

Two of these methods—Get() and Save()—require that the database table an entity represents include an identity column. The other methods do not make this assumption.

The page in Listing 20.33 illustrates how you can use these methods.

LISTING 20.33   ShowEntityBase\SelectPagedSortedMovies.aspx

```
<%@ Page Language="C#" Trace="true" %>
<!DOCTYPE html PUBLIC "-//W3C//DTD XHTML 1.0 Transitional//EN"
 "http://www.w3.org/TR/xhtml1/DTD/xhtml1-transitional.dtd">
<html xmlns="http://www.w3.org/1999/xhtml">
<head id="Head1" runat="server">
    <title>Select Paged Sorted Movies</title>
</head>
<body>
    <form id="form1" runat="server">
    <div>

    <asp:GridView
        id="grdMovies"
        DataSourceId="srcMovies"
        AllowPaging="true"
        AllowSorting="true"
        Runat="server" />

    <asp:ObjectDataSource
        id="srcMovies"
        TypeName="Movie"
        SelectMethod="Select"
        EnablePaging="true"
        SelectCountMethod="SelectCountCached"
        SortParameterName="orderBy"
        Runat="Server" />

    </div>
    </form>
</body>
</html>
```

The page in Listing 20.33 contains a GridView control bound to an ObjectDataSource control. The ObjectDataSource control represents the Movie entity. The ObjectDataSource is configured to support data source paging and sorting. You get both the Select() and SelectCountCached() methods for free from the EntityBase class.

The EntityBaseClasses folder also contains a control named EntityDataSource, which can be used instead of the normal ObjectDataSource. The EntityDataSource control inherits from the `ObjectDataSource` control and provides default values for several `ObjectDataSource` control properties.

For example, you could swap the `ObjectDataSource` control in Listing 20.33 with the following `EntityDataSource` control:

```
<custom:EntityDataSource
    id="srcMovies"
    TypeName="Movie"
    EnablePaging="true"
    SortParameterName="orderBy"
    Runat="Server" />
```

Why use the `EntityDataSource` control? Less typing. I don't want to program all day; I want to see a movie.

Performing Validation with the `EntityBase` Class

One complaint I've always had about ASP.NET Framework is that validation happens at the wrong place. When building ASP.NET pages, you write the vast majority of your validation code in the user interface layer instead of your business logic layer where your validation code properly belongs.

Performing validation in your user interface layer is bad for two main reasons. First, it means that if you switch user interfaces for your application, you must rewrite all your validation logic. For example, you might want to create a cool Silverlight interface for your application. In that case, you have to write all your validation logic again from scratch. Validation logic should be user interface-independent.

Also, placing your validation logic in your user interface layer means that you have to rewrite the exact same validation logic on each page that you use an entity. This is an extraordinary time waster. I want to write my validation logic for an entity once and use the same logic everywhere.

The `EntityBase` class includes a `Validate()` method that you can use to incorporate validation logic into your entities (and thus, your business logic layer). Listing 20.34 illustrates how you can write the `Movie` class so that it validates the `Title`, `Director`, and `DateReleased` properties.

LISTING 20.34   ShowEntityBase\App_Code\Movie.cs

```
using System;


public partial class Movie : EntityBase<Movie>
{
```

```
protected override void Validate()
{
    // Title is required
    if (!ValidationUtility.SatisfiesRequired(Title))
        ValidationErrors.Add("Title", "Required");
    // Director is required
    if (!ValidationUtility.SatisfiesRequired(Director))
        ValidationErrors.Add("Director", "Required");
    // DateReleased is required
    if (DateReleased == DateTime.MinValue)
        ValidationErrors.Add("DateReleased", "Required");
    // DateReleased can't be more than 10 years ago
    if ((DateTime.Now.Year - DateReleased.Year) > 10)
        ValidationErrors.AddIfNotAlready("DateReleased", "Movie too old");
}
}
```

The Validate() method validates the properties of the Movie entity. The method takes advantage of the ValidationUtility class. The ValidationUtility class contains a set of methods to make it easier to perform standard types of validation:

▶ **SatisfiesRequired()**—Enables you to check whether an expression has a value.

▶ **SatisfiesType()**—Enables you to validate against a regular expression defined in the Web.config file.

▶ **SatisfiesExpression()**—Enables you to validate against a regular expression.

▶ **IsInRole()**—Enables you to check whether the current user is in a particular role.

▶ **IsUserName()**—Enables you to check whether the current user has a particular username.

▶ **ShowValidationErrors()**—Displays validation errors on a page.

The ASP.NET page in Listing 20.35 demonstrates how you take advantage of entity validation when inserting new movie records into the database (see Figure 20.3).

20

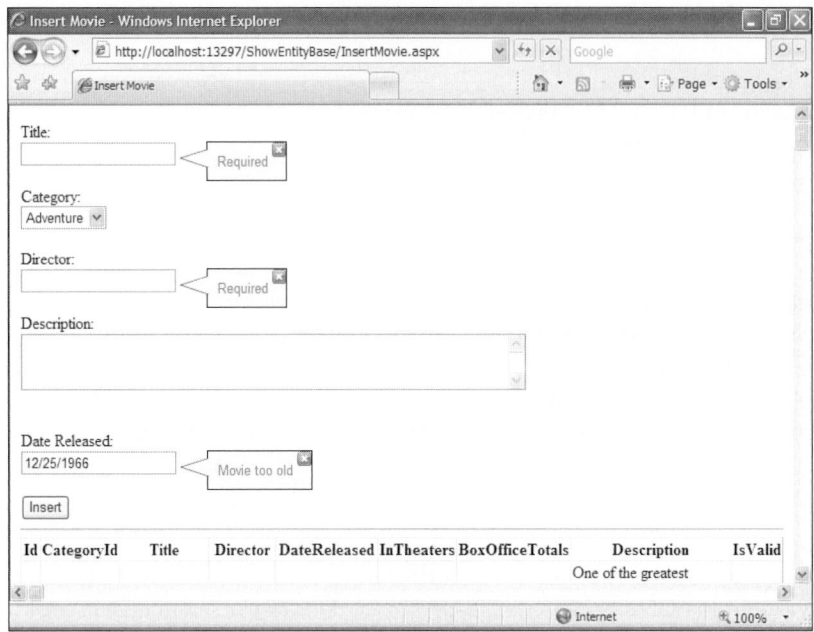

FIGURE 20.3   Performing entity validation.

LISTING 20.35   ShowEntityBase\InsertMovie.aspx

```csharp
<%@ Page Language="C#" Trace="true" %>
<%@ Register TagPrefix="custom" Namespace="Superexpert.Controls" %>
<!DOCTYPE html PUBLIC "-//W3C//DTD XHTML 1.0 Transitional//EN"
 "http://www.w3.org/TR/xhtml1/DTD/xhtml1-transitional.dtd">
<script runat="server">

    protected void frmMovie_ItemInserted
    (
      object sender,
      FormViewInsertedEventArgs e
    )
    {
        if (e.Exception != null)
        {
            e.ExceptionHandled = true;
            e.KeepInInsertMode = true;
            ValidationUtility.ShowValidationErrors(this, e.Exception);
        }
    }

</script>
```

```html
<html xmlns="http://www.w3.org/1999/xhtml">
<head id="Head1" runat="server">
    <title>Insert Movie</title>
</head>
<body>
    <form id="form1" runat="server">
    <div>

    <asp:FormView
        id="frmMovie"
        DataSourceID="srcMovies"
        DefaultMode="Insert"
        OnItemInserted="frmMovie_ItemInserted"
        Runat="Server">
        <InsertItemTemplate>
            <asp:Label
                id="lblTitle"
                Text="Title:"
                AssociatedControlID="txtTitle"
                Runat="server" />
            <br />
            <asp:TextBox
                id="txtTitle"
                Text='<%# Bind("Title") %>'
                Runat="server" />
            <custom:EntityCallOutValidator
                id="valTitle"
                PropertyName="Title"
                Runat="Server" />
            <br /><br />

            <asp:Label
                id="lblCategory"
                Text="Category:"
                AssociatedControlID="ddlCategory"
                Runat="server" />
            <br />
            <asp:DropDownList
                id="ddlCategory"
                DataSourceId="srcMovieCategories"
                SelectedValue='<%# Bind("CategoryId") %>'
                DataTextField="Name"
                DataValueField="Id"
                Runat="server" />
            <asp:ObjectDataSource
                id="srcMovieCategories"
```

20

```
        TypeName="MovieCategory"
        SelectMethod="Select"
        Runat="Server" />
    <br /><br / >

    <asp:Label
        id="lblDirector"
        Text="Director:"
        AssociatedControlID="txtDirector"
        Runat="server" />
    <br />
    <asp:TextBox
        id="txtDirector"
        Text='<%# Bind("Director") %>'
        Runat="server" />
    <custom:EntityCallOutValidator
        id="valDirector"
        PropertyName="Director"
        Runat="Server" />

    <br /><br />

    <asp:Label
        id="lblDescription"
        Text="Description:"
        AssociatedControlID="txtDescription"
        Runat="server" />
    <br />
    <asp:TextBox
        id="txtDescription"
        Text='<%# Bind("Description") %>'
        TextMode="MultiLine"
        Columns="60"
        Rows="3"
        Runat="server" />

    <br /><br />

    <asp:Label
        id="lblDateReleased"
        Text="Date Released:"
        AssociatedControlID="txtDateReleased"
        Runat="server" />
    <br />
    <asp:TextBox
        id="txtDateReleased"
```

```
                    Text='<%# Bind("DateReleased") %>'
                    Runat="server" />
            <custom:EntityCallOutValidator
                id="valDateReleased"
                PropertyName="DateReleased"
                ControlToValidate="txtDateReleased"
                TypeName="date"
                Runat="Server" />
            <br /><br />

            <asp:Button
                id="btnInsert"
                Text="Insert"
                CommandName="Insert"
                Runat="server" />

        </InsertItemTemplate>
    </asp:FormView>

    <hr />

    <asp:GridView
        id="grdMovies"
        DataSourceID="srcMovies"
        Runat="server" />

    <custom:EntityDataSource
        id="srcMovies"
        TypeName="Movie"
        Runat="server" />

    </div>
    </form>
</body>
</html>
```

You should notice several things about the page in Listing 20.35. First, the page includes a method for handling the FormView control's ItemInserted event. This handler checks for an exception. If Movie.Validate() creates one or more validation errors, the Movie entity throws a ValidationException when inserting or updating automatically.

If there is an exception, the exception is passed to the ValidationUtility.ShowValidationErrors() method. The ShowValidationErrors() method finds the EntityCallOutValidator that corresponds to each validation error and displays the correct error message.

The `Validate()` method executes only if a `Movie` entity can be created. If someone enters the wrong type of value into a field, the `ObjectDataSource` can't even create the entity and the `Validate()` method never executes. The `EntityCallOutValidator` associated with the `DateReleased` property includes `ControlToValidate` and `TypeName` properties. This validation control checks whether the value entered into the `DateReleased TextBox` is a valid date even before the `Movie` entity is created.

Summary

We covered a lot of material over the course of this chapter. In the first part, we discussed all the features of C# and VB.NET used to support LINQ, such as anonymous types, extension methods, and lambda expressions.

Next, we discussed LINQ to SQL entities. You learned how to build entities that represent your database objects both by hand and by using the LINQ to SQL Designer. We also briefly examined the `LinqDataSource` control.

In the following part, we discussed how you can perform basic database operations with LINQ to SQL. For example, you learned how to select records, page through records, and cache records. You also learned how to insert, update, and delete database records with LINQ to SQL.

In the final part of this chapter, you learned how to build a custom LINQ to SQL base class. You learned how to use this class to support selecting, inserting, deleting, and updating entities without writing any code. You also learned how to add validation logic to your entities.

Data Access with WCF Data Services

Throughout this section of the book, we covered a wide variety of ways to get data to and from your web forms. In a standard n-tier model, the web application would talk to a middle tier containing business logic, which would in turn talk to a data tier responsible for communicating with the database.

Although this is a perfectly adequate model, to handle the scalability and performance demands of modern distributed applications, we need something a bit more flexible. In large organizations we might have dozens of services exposed by multiple departments and multiple web applications that need to consume those services. In this case, we can't just add a reference to the Business Logic Layer (BLL) and start invoking methods.

This chapter shows you how to use WCF Data Services to facilitate high-performance, scalable, distributed applications by exposing entity models as RESTful web services that can be reused by many applications on many platforms. We provide an overview of the WCF Data Services technology and provide samples of some of the ways your ASP.NET application can consume these services.

Overview of WCF Data Services

When you see data access samples, most of them illustrate making a direct database connection from the web server (even if it's from a data tier) to the database. Although this is fine for illustrative purposes, it's not that practical. In many production environments, firewalls and other security systems prevent direct database connections of any kind. As previously mentioned, in many service-oriented, distributed systems, client code must go through a service to read or write any data.

In the past, developers had to manually create their own service-based facades in front of the database, generally creating headaches and extra work. WCF Data Services aims to solve some of these problems. A WCF Data Service is a standardized service that exposes underlying relational data as a RESTful Web Service. This means that there's no WSDL, no ASMX, just a convention for building URL-based queries and using the AtomPub or JSON protocols for sending data over the wire.

It is beyond the scope of this book to go into too much detail on how to build WCF Data Services or create the underlying Entity Models exposed by WCF Data Services. For more information on these services, read the MSDN documentation at

http://msdn.microsoft.com/en-us/data/bb931106.aspx.

The following two sections show you how to allow your ASP.NET application to communicate with a WCF Data Service, either by using a Service Reference or by using the client-side `DataServiceContext` class directly.

Using Data Services with a Service Reference

If you've used Visual Studio for any length of time, you're probably familiar with the ability to add service references to existing projects. These either discover services in the current solution, or you can enter the URL of a WCF service and the service reference creates a client-side proxy for you. Up until now, this has worked only for regular web services.

With Visual Studio 2010 and WCF Data Services, you can add a Service Reference to a WCF Data Service. This Service Reference can create a special client proxy for you, one that exposes all the entities for the service and handles all the change tracking and other heavy lifting that, as a service consumer, you just don't want to have to deal with manually.

Figure 21.1 shows the screen you see when attempting to add a service reference to a WCF Data Service. Each of the entities exposed by the data service appear as properties on the client proxy generated.

To illustrate how we might consume a WCF Data Service from an ASP.NET application, let's use an example that is a little bit more fun than the typical "Hello World" sample.

Let's say that you work for a fabulously successful video game company and your most popular game, *Zombie Killa*, has an incredible multiplayer mode. You've been asked to make the kill list and scores available on the web. The team that keeps that information won't let you access its database directly for many (very good) reasons. Instead, it set up a WCF Data Service that exposes some of the key entities that you need to create your high scores website.

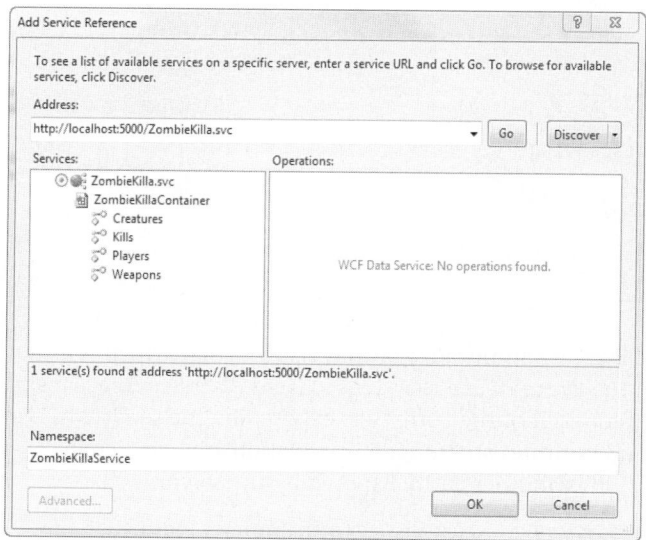

FIGURE 21.1   Adding a service reference to a WCF Data Service.

The first thing to do is add a service reference to its service, which you can see in Figure 21.1. This creates a client-side proxy that enables your code to treat the entities like regular LINQ data sources. Your LINQ queries convert into the WCF Data Services URL syntax, and the data coming back from the service converts into instances of the classes generated when you added the service reference.

Now that you have your service reference, you're ready to access the data service. For this sample, we've been asked to create a My Kills page that shows all the zombies a particular player has killed and the weapons she used.

We created a MyKills.aspx page and then added the code from Listing 21.1 to the Page_Load() method. In addition to enabling us to write LINQ queries against specific entities, we can also invoke custom methods made available on the service. The game team didn't want us to try to create the My Kills filter on our own because it might change over time, so it provided a method on the service called "GetMyKills" that we can execute. The amazing thing is that the result of this custom method execution is still queryable, enabling us to further filter, page, and sort the results.

LISTING 21.1   Page_Load for MyKills.aspx.cs

```
protected void Page_Load(object sender, EventArgs e)
{
    ZombieKillaService.ZombieKillaContainer svc =
        new ZombieKillaService.ZombieKillaContainer(
            new Uri("http://localhost:5000/ZombieKilla.svc"));
        var q = from Kill kill in svc.CreateQuery<Kill>("GetMyKills")
```

```
        .AddQueryOption("playerId", 1)
        .Expand("Weapon")
        .Expand("Player")
        .Expand("Creature")
        orderby kill.KillTime descending
        select kill;
    killsRepeater.DataSource = q;
    killsRepeater.DataBind();
}
```

The first thing we do in this code is create an instance of the service proxy, which is a generated class that inherits from the `System.Data.Services.Client.DataServiceContext` class. This class exposes properties for each of the entity sets exposed by the service. In our case, we have players, weapons, and creatures and foreign key relationships that enable them all to link to the kill log. (A Kill is another entity exposed by the service.)

The custom service context client proxy takes as a constructor parameter a `Uri` that contains the address of the service. In a production scenario, you might use service discovery, a service registry, or `Web.config` files to store the URLs of the services.

The next thing we do is call `CreateQuery<Kill>("GetMyKills")`. There's quite a bit of functionality packed into this one method call. `CreateQuery()` doesn't actually talk to the service; it is merely asking us for the shape of the rows that will be returned from the query (the `Kill` class) and for either the name of a service method to invoke or the name of an entity set to query. If we had simply supplied the string `"Kills"` to the method, we would be querying the Kills entity set directly and not invoking a custom method.

Next you can see that the output of the `CreateQuery()` method is something queryable; so we can chain method calls onto this method in a "fluent" style. We use the `Expand()` method to tell the WCF Data Service that for every `Kill` we return, also expand the specified relationship properties. This enables us to bring over all the data related to an entity in a single method call rather than making a bunch of chatty calls with high overhead and latency. In our case, we want the names of the weapons and creatures that were killed.

If we wanted, we could supply virtually any additional LINQ queries to the end of our statement, but in this case we were happy with sorting the kills in descending order by time so that the players see their most recent kill first.

At this point, the service has *still not been queried*. All we're doing up to this point is building an in-memory expression tree. The service will not actually be called until we, directly or indirectly, invoke `GetEnumerator()` on the query object. For the code in Listing 21.1, we won't make the actual network call until somewhere inside the `DataBind()` method of the repeater control.

Figure 21.2 shows what the `MyKills.aspx` page looks like when fed data from the WCF Data Service.

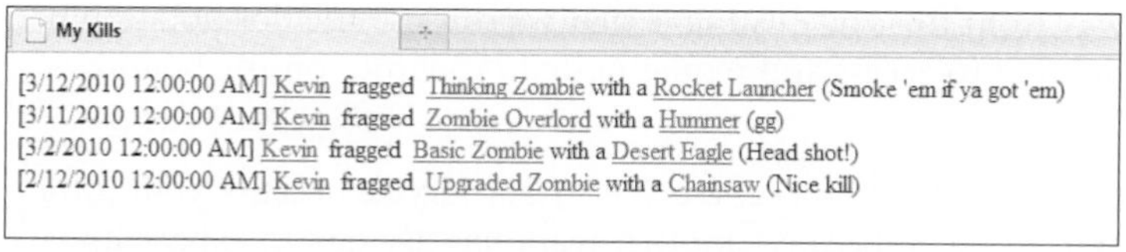

FIGURE 21.2   Displaying "My Kills" with data from WCF Data Service.

The great part about using WCF Data Services is that, with a few minor exceptions, the classes coming back from the service containing results are just specialized C# classes. This means if I want to know the name of the weapon used in a particular kill (and I've pre-expanded the property chain), I can refer to kill.Weapon.Name. Likewise, to find the name of the creature killed, I can refer to kill.Creature.Name.

This property chaining syntax still works with ASP.NET's binding syntax and templating system. The code in Listing 21.2 shows MyKills.aspx; you can see how the DataBinder.Eval() calls work perfectly well with nested properties returned on the entity objects from the WCF Data Service.

LISTING 21.2   MyKills.aspx

```
<form id="form1" runat="server">
    <div>
        <asp:Repeater ID="killsRepeater" runat="server">
            <ItemTemplate>
                [<%# DataBinder.Eval(Container.DataItem, "KillTime") %>]
                <a href='Player.aspx?playerId=
                 <%# DataBinder.Eval(Container.DataItem, "PlayerID") %>'>
                 <%# DataBinder.Eval(Container.DataItem, "Player.Name") %></a>
                  fragged 
                <a href='Create.aspx?creatureId=
                <%# DataBinder.Eval(Container.DataItem, "CreatureID") %>'>
                <%# DataBinder.Eval(Container.DataItem, "Creature.Name") %></a>
                with a
                <a href='Weapon.aspx?weaponId=
                <%# DataBinder.Eval(Container.DataItem, "WeaponID") %>'>
                <%# DataBinder.Eval(Container.DataItem, "Weapon.Name") %></a>
                (<%# DataBinder.Eval(Container.DataItem, "Notes") %>)
                <br />
            </ItemTemplate>
        </asp:Repeater>
    </div>
    </form>
```

The main thing to take away from this code listing is that we can use the dot notation in the data binder's Eval() method to access and render nested properties on the bound item.

The moral of this story is that whether you access a WCF Data Service because your infrastructure prevents direct SQL access or because another team has decided to expose its data that way, it's incredibly simple to create a service reference and start working with the data on that service. Also keep in mind that WCF Data Services aren't just simple query services; you can insert, delete, and update as well, and data services can even be configured to support optimistic concurrency checking, which comes in handy for high-volume intranet applications.

To add a new creature to the system and update a kill using the service reference, we can just use the code shown in Listing 21.3. When querying data, the web service is not contacted until code invokes GetEnumerator() on the query. When modifying data, the change requests are not sent to the service until you invoke the SaveChanges() method on the service context.

LISTING 21.3   Adding and Updating Entities with a WCF Data Service Proxy

```
ZombieKillaService.ZombieKillaContainer svc = new
    ZombieKillaService.ZombieKillaContainer(
        new Uri("http://localhost:5000/ZombieKilla.svc"));
svc.MergeOption =
System.Data.Services.Client.MergeOption.PreserveChanges;
ZombieKillaService.Creature creature = new ZombieKillaService.Creature()
{
            Armor = 215,
            Hitpoints = 512,
            Name = "Fantastically Big Zombie"
};
svc.AddToCreatures(creature);
svc.SaveChanges();
Response.Write("Created a new creature with ID of " +
    creature.ID.ToString());

ZombieKillaService.Player player = svc.Players.FirstOrDefault();
ZombieKillaService.Weapon weapon = svc.Weapons.FirstOrDefault();
ZombieKillaService.Kill kill = new ZombieKillaService.Kill()     {
        KillTime = DateTime.Now,
        PlayerID = player.ID,
        CreatureID = creature.ID,
        WeaponID = weapon.ID,
        Notes = "Awesome shot!"
};
svc.AddToKills(kill);
svc.SaveChanges();
```

From this listing, you can see that the service reference proxy gives us classes that we can instantiate to represent any of the entities hosted by the data service. In addition, we also get methods such as `AddToCreatures()` that queue up all the work necessary to add an entity to an entity set on the server. We can also query for a specific item, make changes to it (or items related to it), and save those changes as well. You can do a few hundred other things with the data service proxy, but this is an ASP.NET book so we're going to stick to the basics for this chapter.

Using Data Services with a Data Context

In the previous section, we built a sample application that displays the kill log from a fictional video game called *Zombie Killa*. This kill log is exposed as a WCF Data Service, and we communicated with that service through an automatically generated proxy class.

In this section, we take a look at how we can talk to the WCF Data Service without using any generated code or classes by using the `DataServiceContext` class directly.

As with the generated proxy, we create an instance of the proxy by providing it with the URL of the WCF Data Service. After that, we can create our own queries (and make changes, inserts, and deletes) by invoking various methods on the context. In the code in Listing 21.4, we call CreateQuery() and pass it the name of the entity set we want to query: Players.

LISTING 21.4   Querying a Data Service Manually with a DataServiceContext

```
// NOTE: Not using auto-generated client proxy, using generic client with POCO
View Models!
DataServiceContext ctx = new DataServiceContext(
    new Uri("http://localhost:5000/ZombieKilla.svc"));
ctx.IgnoreMissingProperties = true;
 var q = from ViewModels.Player player in
            ctx.CreateQuery<ViewModels.Player>("Players")
            .Expand("Kills").Expand("Kills/Weapon").Expand("Kills/Creature")
            where player.ID == Int32.Parse(Request["playerId"])
            select player;
 ViewModels.Player p = q.FirstOrDefault();
StringBuilder sb = new StringBuilder();
sb.Append(p.Name + "<br/>");
foreach (ViewModels.Kill kill in p.Kills)
{    sb.AppendFormat(" Killed {1} with a {2} ({3})<br/>",
            kill.KillTime, kill.Creature.Name, kill.Weapon.Name, kill.Notes);
}
placeHolder.Controls.Add(new LiteralControl(sb.ToString()));
```

The calls to Expand() differ slightly from the previous samples. The beauty of WCF Data Service relationship expansion is that we can expand multiple levels. So, not only can I ask for a player, but I can also ask for that player's kills, *and*, for each of those kills I can obtain the weapon and creature used for that kill. All this comes over the wire as a *single response*; I don't need to make multiple calls to get all the referential and lookup data.

Finally, the code calls FirstOrDefault() to actually send the query over the wire. The DataServiceContext class is so powerful that it knows how to convert the information in the payload from the service into the data type required by the client. When we create the query, we pass it the type ViewModels.Player. This is a Plain Old CLR Object (POCO) class that we created that is little more than a code-based schema that tells the service how to shape the response. Listing 21.5 shows the code for the ViewModels.Player class and the ViewModels.Kill class.

LISTING 21.5   The ViewModels.Player Class and ViewModels.Kill Class

```
public class Player
{
    public int ID { get; set; }
    public string Name { get; set; }

    public ICollection<Kill> Kills { get; set; }
}
public class Kill
{
    public int ID { get; set; }
    public int PlayerID { get; set; }
    public int CreatureID { get; set; }
    public DateTime KillTime { get; set; }
    public string Notes { get; set; }
    public Player Player { get; set; }
    public Creature Creature { get; set; }
    public Weapon Weapon { get; set; }
}
```

If you find that you create or refresh a client-side proxy every time the entity definitions change on the service, creating your own view models might be a better idea. This gives you the added benefit of placing all these view models in a shared assembly that can be used by multiple web applications or multiple service clients.

Another advantage of the view model approach using the raw data service context is that you can decorate these view models with any attributes you want, including those that might be compatible with various client-side validation frameworks or other custom uses for your ASP.NET or ASP.NET MVC applications. With an auto-generated proxy, any changes you make or decorations you add can be wiped out every time you refresh the reference.

The real power here is that you can choose whether you want to access a raw data service context or one created by adding a service reference. Which option you choose and when should be based on how frequently your service entities change and how much extra functionality you want to put into the client-side objects.

Summary

In this chapter you learned a little bit about WCF Data Services and the OData protocol. There are countless strategies for getting data in and out of your ASP.NET application ranging from traditional raw SQL access to service-based data access such as WCF Data Services.

WCF Data Services provide developers with a platform-independent way of querying and manipulating data without needing to know the specifics of the underlying schema or even the underlying data store.

Whether you choose to access a WCF Data Service using a raw data context, a generated data context wrapper, or even through a raw HTTP request, these services provide incredible value and can dramatically increase productivity, code reuse, and even scalability of distributed applications.

For more information on WCF Data Services, check out MSDN's page for them at http://msdn.microsoft.com/en-us/data/bb931106.aspx.

Using the Navigation Controls

In this chapter, you learn how to use the SiteMapPath, Menu, and TreeView controls. You can use all three of these controls to enable users to navigate your website. Furthermore, you can use the Menu and TreeView controls independently of website navigation. You can bind these two controls to other data sources such as XML documents or database data.

This chapter explores different methods of binding the Menu and TreeView controls to different data sources and shows you how to format the rendered output of both of these controls. You also learn how to take advantage of Ajax when working with the TreeView control.

In the final section, we build a SqlHierarchicalDataSource control, which enables you to bind controls such as the TreeView and Menu controls to hierarchical database data.

Understanding Site Maps

Before you learn about the navigation controls, you first need to understand Site Maps. All three navigation controls use Site Maps to retrieve navigation information. A Site Map enables you to represent the navigational relationships between the pages in an application, independent of the actual physical relationship between pages as stored in the file system.

Site Maps use the provider model. In the next chapter, you learn how to create custom Site Map providers to store Site Maps in custom data stores such as database tables. The examples in this chapter take advantage of the default XML Site Map provider, which enables you to store a Site Map in an XML file.

By default, the navigation controls assume the existence of an XML file named Web.sitemap, which is located in the root of your application.

For example, Listing 22.1 contains a simple Site Map.

LISTING 22.1 Web.sitemap

```
<?xml version="1.0" encoding="utf-8" ?>
<siteMap xmlns="http://schemas.microsoft.com/AspNet/SiteMap-File-1.0" >

<siteMapNode
  url="~/Default.aspx"
  title="Home"
  description="The home page of the Website">

  <!-- Product Nodes -->
  <siteMapNode
    title="Products"
    description="Website products">
    <siteMapNode
      url="~/Products/FirstProduct.aspx"
      title="First Product"
      description="The first product" />
    <siteMapNode
      url="~/Products/SecondProduct.aspx"
      title="Second Product"
      description="The second product" />
  </siteMapNode>

  <!-- Services Nodes -->
  <siteMapNode
    title="Services"
    description="Website services">
    <siteMapNode
      url="~/Service/FirstService.aspx"
      title="First Service"
      description="The first service" />
    <siteMapNode
      url="~/Products/SecondService.aspx"
      title="Second Service"
      description="The second service" />
  </siteMapNode>

</siteMapNode>

</siteMap>
```

A Site Map file contains `<siteMapNode>` elements. There can be only one top-level node. In the case of Listing 22.1, the top-level node represents the website's home page.

A `<siteMapNode>` supports three main attributes:

▶ **title**—A brief title that you want to associate with a node.

▶ **description**—A longer description that you want to associate with a node.

▶ **url**—A URL that points to a page or other resource.

The `url` attribute is not required. Both the Products and Services nodes do not include a `url` attribute because these nodes do not represent pages to which you can navigate.

Each `<siteMapNode>` can contain any number of child nodes. In Listing 22.1, both the Products and Services nodes include two child nodes.

The Site Map in Listing 22.1 represents a website that has the following folder and page structure:

```
Default.aspx
Products
  FirstProduct.aspx
  SecondProduct.aspx
Services
  FirstService.aspx
  SecondService.aspx
```

The navigational structure of a website as represented by a Site Map is not required to have any relationship to the navigational structure of a website as stored in the file system. You can create any relationship between the nodes in a Site Map that you want.

Using the `SiteMapPath` Control

The `SiteMapPath` control enables you to navigate easily to any parent page of the current page. It displays the standard breadcrumb trail that you see on many popular websites (see Figure 22.1).

You can use the `SiteMapPath` control simply by declaring the control in a page. The control automatically uses the `Web.sitemap` file located in the root of your application. For example, the page in Listing 22.2 includes the `SiteMapPath` control (see Figure 22.2).

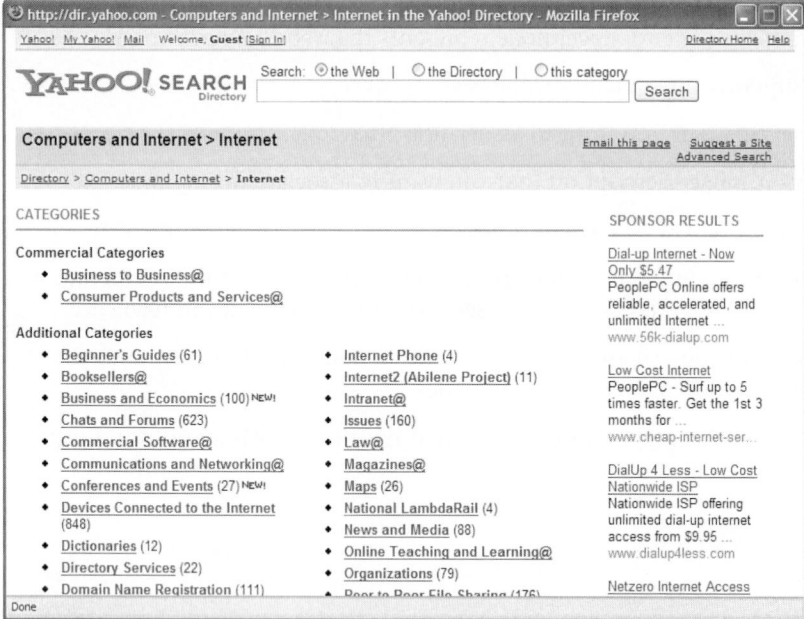

FIGURE 22.1   Breadcrumb trail at Yahoo.com.

FIGURE 22.2   Displaying the SiteMapPath control.

LISTING 22.2   UsingSiteMapPath/DisplaySiteMapPath.aspx

```
<%@ Page Language="C#" %>
<!DOCTYPE html PUBLIC "-//W3C//DTD XHTML 1.1//EN"
 "http://www.w3.org/TR/xhtml11/DTD/xhtml11.dtd">
<html xmlns="http://www.w3.org/1999/xhtml" >
<head id="Head1" runat="server">
    <title>Display SiteMapPath</title>
</head>
<body>
    <form id="form1" runat="server">
    <div>

    <asp:SiteMapPath
        id="SiteMapPath1"
        Runat="server" />

    <hr />

    <h1>Displaying a SiteMapPath Control</h1>

    </div>
    </form>
</body>
</html>
```

You can click the Home link rendered by the SiteMapPath control to navigate to the website's home page. The SiteMapPath uses both the title and description attributes from the <siteMapNode> elements contained in the Web.sitemap file. The title attribute is used for the node (link) text, and the description attribute is used for the node tool tip.

> **NOTE**
>
> Typically, you do not add a SiteMapPath control to individual pages in your website. If you add a SiteMapPath control to a Master Page, you can display the SiteMapPath control automatically on every page. To learn more about Master Pages, see Chapter 5, "Designing Websites with Master Pages."

The SiteMapPath control supports the following properties:

▶ **ParentLevelsDisplay**—Enables you to limit the number of parent nodes displayed. By default, a SiteMapPath control displays all the parent nodes.

▶ **PathDirection**—Enables you to reverse the order of the links displayed by the SiteMapPath control. Possible values are RootToCurrent (the default) or CurrentToRoot.

▶ **PathSeparator**—Enables you to specify the character used to separate the nodes displayed by the `SiteMapPath` control. The default value is >.

▶ **RenderCurrentNodeAsLink**—Enables you to render the `SiteMapPath` node that represents the current page as a link. By default, the current node is not rendered as a link.

▶ **ShowToolTips**—Enables you to disable the display of tool tips.

▶ **SiteMapProvider**—Enables you to specify the name of an alternative Site Map provider to use with the `SiteMapPath` control.

▶ **SkipLinkText**—Enables you to specify more specific text for skipping the links displayed by the `SiteMapPath` control. The default value for this property is `Skip Navigation Links`.

WEB STANDARDS NOTE

All the navigation controls automatically render a skip navigation link to meet accessibility requirements. The skip navigation link is read by a screen reader, but it is not displayed in a normal browser.

If you are interacting with a web page through a screen reader, you don't want to hear the list of navigation links every time you open a page. (It is the equivalent of listening to a phone menu every time you open a page.) The skip navigation link enables users of screen readers to skip the repetitive reading of links.

Formatting the `SiteMapPath` Control

You can use either styles or templates to format the `SiteMapPath` control.

The control supports the following Style objects:

▶ **CurrentNodeStyle**—Formats the `SiteMapPath` node that represents the current page.

▶ **NodeStyle**—Formats every node rendered by the `SiteMapPath` control.

▶ **PathSeparatorStyle**—Formats the text displayed between each `SiteMapPath` node.

▶ **RootNodeStyle**—Formats the root (first) node rendered by the `SiteMapPath` control.

For example, the page in Listing 22.3 takes advantage of all four Style properties to modify the default appearance of the `SiteMapPath` control (see Figure 22.3).

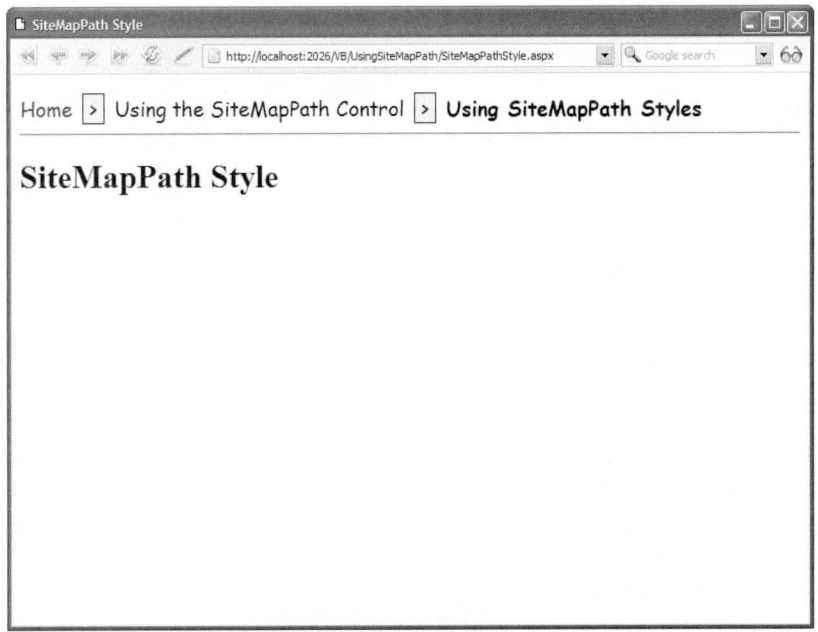

FIGURE 22.3   Using styles with the SiteMapPath control.

LISTING 22.3   UsingSiteMapPath/SiteMapPathStyle.aspx

```
<%@ Page Language="C#" %>
<!DOCTYPE html PUBLIC "-//W3C//DTD XHTML 1.1//EN"
   "http://www.w3.org/TR/xhtml11/DTD/xhtml11.dtd">
<html xmlns="http://www.w3.org/1999/xhtml" >
<head id="Head1" runat="server">
    <style type="text/css">
        .siteMapPath
        {
            font:20px Comic Sans MS,Serif;
        }
        .currentNodeStyle
        {
            font-weight:bold;
        }
        .nodeStyle
        {
            text-decoration:none;
        }
        .pathSeparatorStyle
        {
            background-color:yellow;
```

```
                margin:10px;
                border:Solid 1px black;
            }
            .rootNodeStyle
            {
                text-decoration:none;
            }
        </style>
        <title>SiteMapPath Style</title>
    </head>
<body>
    <form id="form1" runat="server">
    <div>

    <asp:SiteMapPath
        id="SiteMapPath1"
        CssClass="siteMapPath"
        CurrentNodeStyle-CssClass="currentNodeStyle"
        NodeStyle-CssClass="nodeStyle"
        PathSeparatorStyle-CssClass="pathSeparatorStyle"
        RootNodeStyle-CssClass="rootNodeStyle"
        Runat="server" />

    <hr />

    <h1>SiteMapPath Style</h1>

    </div>
    </form>
</body>
</html>
```

Furthermore, you can use templates with the SiteMapPath control to format the appearance of the control (and change its behavior). The SiteMapPath control supports the following templates:

▶ **CurrentNodeTemplate**—For the SiteMapPath node that represents the current page.

▶ **NodeTemplate**—For each SiteMapPath node that is not the current or root node.

▶ **PathSeparatorTemplate**—For the text displayed between each SiteMapPath node.

▶ **RootNodeTemplate**—For the root (first) node rendered by the SiteMapPath control.

For example, the SiteMapPath control in Listing 22.4 includes a NodeTemplate. The NodeTemplate includes a HyperLink control that displays the current SiteMapPath node. The template also displays a count of the child nodes of the current node (see Figure 22.4).

FIGURE 22.4   Using a template with the SiteMapPath control.

LISTING 22.4   UsingSiteMapPath/SiteMapPathTemplates.aspx

```
<%@ Page Language="C#" %>
<!DOCTYPE html PUBLIC "-//W3C//DTD XHTML 1.1//EN"
  "http://www.w3.org/TR/xhtml11/DTD/xhtml11.dtd">
<html xmlns="http://www.w3.org/1999/xhtml" >
<head id="Head1" runat="server">
    <title>SiteMapPath Templates</title>
</head>
<body>
    <form id="form1" runat="server">
    <div>

    <asp:SiteMapPath
        id="SiteMapPath1"
        Runat="server">
        <NodeTemplate>
        <asp:HyperLink
```

```
            id="lnkPage"
            Text='<%# Eval("Title") %>'
            NavigateUrl='<%# Eval("Url") %>'
            ToolTip='<%# Eval("Description") %>'
            Runat="server" />
        [<%# Eval("ChildNodes.Count") %>]
        </NodeTemplate>
    </asp:SiteMapPath>


    <hr />


    <h1>SiteMapPath Templates</h1>



    </div>
    </form>
</body>
</html>
```

Within a template, the data item represents a SiteMapNode. Therefore, you can refer to any of the properties of the SiteMapNode class in a databinding expression.

Using the Menu Control

The Menu control enables you to create two types of menus. You can use the Menu control to create the left-column menu that appears in many websites. In other words, you can use the Menu control to display a vertical list of links.

You also can use the Menu control to create a menu that more closely resembles the drop-down menus that appear in traditional desktop applications. In this case, the Menu control renders a horizontal list of links.

Unlike the SiteMapPath control, the Menu control can represent other types of data than Site Map data. Technically, you can bind a Menu control to any data source that implements the IHiearchicalDataSource or IHiearchicalEnumerable interface.

In this section, you learn how to create different types of menus with the Menu control. First, you learn how to add menu declaratively items to a Menu control. Next, we discuss how the Menu control can be used with the MultiView control to display a tabbed page.

You also examine how you can bind the Menu control to different types of data sources. You learn how to use the Menu control with Site Map data, XML data, and database data.

Declaratively Adding Menu Items

You can display a menu with the Menu control by adding one or more MenuItem objects to its Items property. For example, the page in Listing 22.5 uses a Menu control to create a simple vertical menu (see Figure 22.5).

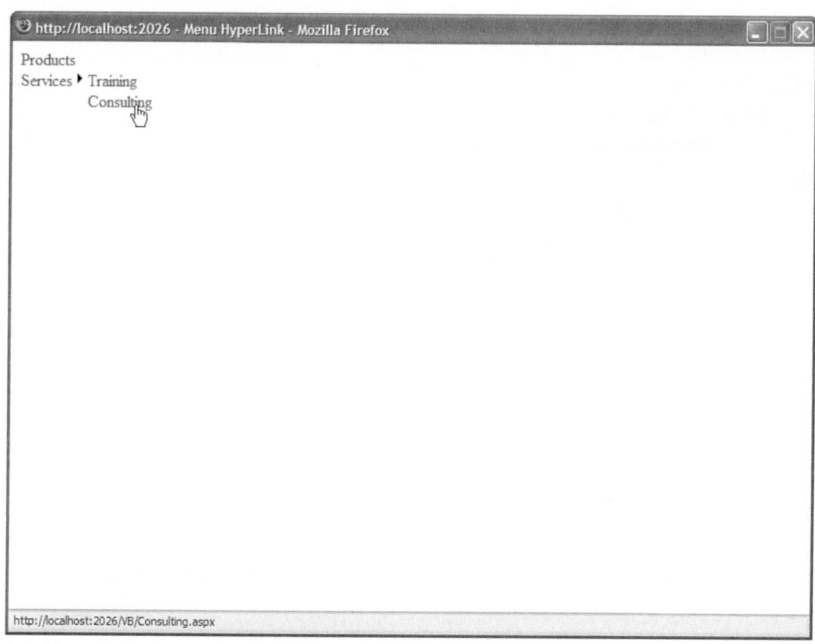

FIGURE 22.5   Displaying a menu with the Menu control.

LISTING 22.5   MenuHyperLink.aspx

```
<%@ Page Language="C#" %>
<!DOCTYPE html PUBLIC "-//W3C//DTD XHTML 1.1//EN"
 "http://www.w3.org/TR/xhtml11/DTD/xhtml11.dtd">
<html xmlns="http://www.w3.org/1999/xhtml" >
<head id="Head1" runat="server">
    <title>Menu HyperLink</title>
</head>
<body>
    <form id="form1" runat="server">
    <div>

    <asp:Menu
        id="Menu1"
```

```
            Runat="server">
            <Items>
                <asp:MenuItem
                    Text="Products"
                    NavigateUrl="Products.aspx" />
                <asp:MenuItem
                    Text="Services"
                    NavigateUrl="Services.aspx">
                    <asp:MenuItem
                        Text="Training"
                        NavigateUrl="Training.aspx" />
                    <asp:MenuItem
                        Text="Consulting"
                        NavigateUrl="Consulting.aspx" />
                </asp:MenuItem>
            </Items>
        </asp:Menu>

        </div>
        </form>
</body>
</html>
```

The Menu in Listing 22.5 is created from MenuItem objects. Each menu item in Listing 22.5 contains a link to another page.

MenuItem objects can be nested. The second MenuItem object—Services—includes two child MenuItem objects. When you hover your mouse over a parent menu item, the child menu items display.

Each MenuItem in Listing 22.5 includes a Text and NavigateUrl property. Rather than use a MenuItem to link to a new page, you also can use a MenuItem to link back to the same page. In other words, each MenuItem can act like a Linkbutton control instead of a HyperLink control.

For example, each MenuItem object in Listing 22.6 includes a Text and Value property. When you click a menu item, the same page is reloaded, and the value of the selected menu item displays (see Figure 22.6).

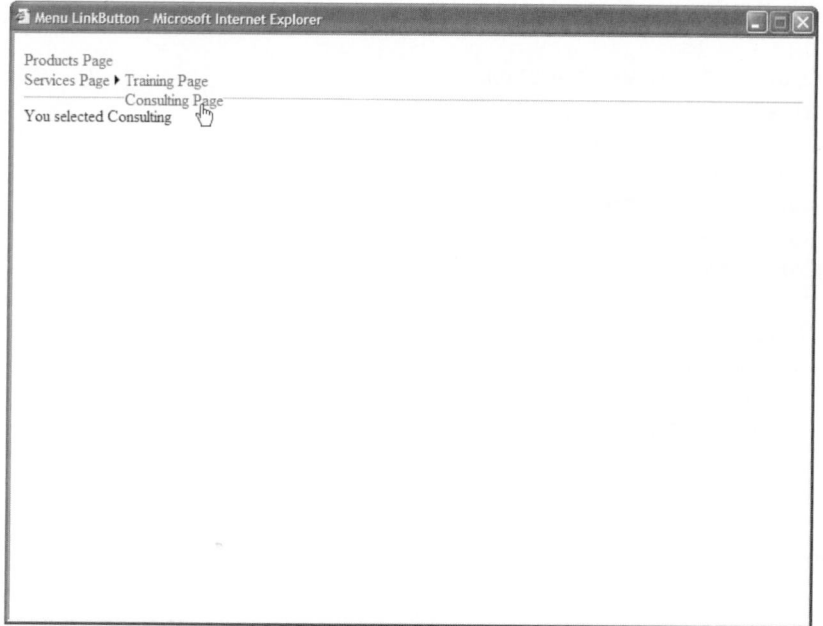

FIGURE 22.6   Selecting menu items.

LISTING 22.6   MenuLinkButton.aspx

```
<%@ Page Language="C#" %>
<!DOCTYPE html PUBLIC "-//W3C//DTD XHTML 1.1//EN"
"http://www.w3.org/TR/xhtml11/DTD/xhtml11.dtd">
<script runat="server">

    protected void Menu1_MenuItemClick(object sender, MenuEventArgs e)
    {
        lblMessage.Text = "You selected " + Menu1.SelectedValue;
    }
</script>
<html xmlns="http://www.w3.org/1999/xhtml" >
<head id="Head1" runat="server">
    <title>Menu LinkButton</title>
</head>
<body>
    <form id="form1" runat="server">
    <div>
```

22

```
<asp:Menu
    id="Menu1"
    OnMenuItemClick="Menu1_MenuItemClick"
    Runat="server">
    <Items>
        <asp:MenuItem
            Text="Products Page"
            Value="Products" />
        <asp:MenuItem
            Text="Services Page"
            Value="Services">
            <asp:MenuItem
                Text="Training Page"
                Value="Training" />
            <asp:MenuItem
                Text="Consulting Page"
                Value="Consulting" />
        </asp:MenuItem>
    </Items>
</asp:Menu>

<hr />

<asp:Label
    id="lblMessage"
    EnableViewState="false"
    Runat="server" />

</div>
</form>
</body>
</html>
```

The page includes a MenuItemClick event handler. When you click a MenuItem (and the MenuItem does not have a NavigateUrl property), the MenuItemClick event is raised.

In Listing 22.6, the MenuItemClick handler displays the value of the selected MenuItem in a Label control.

Using the Menu Control with the MultiView Control

When the Menu control is used with the MultiView control, you can create tabbed pages. You use the Menu control to display the tabs, and the MultiView control to display the content that corresponds to the selected tab.

For example, the page in Listing 22.7 displays three tabs (see Figure 22.7).

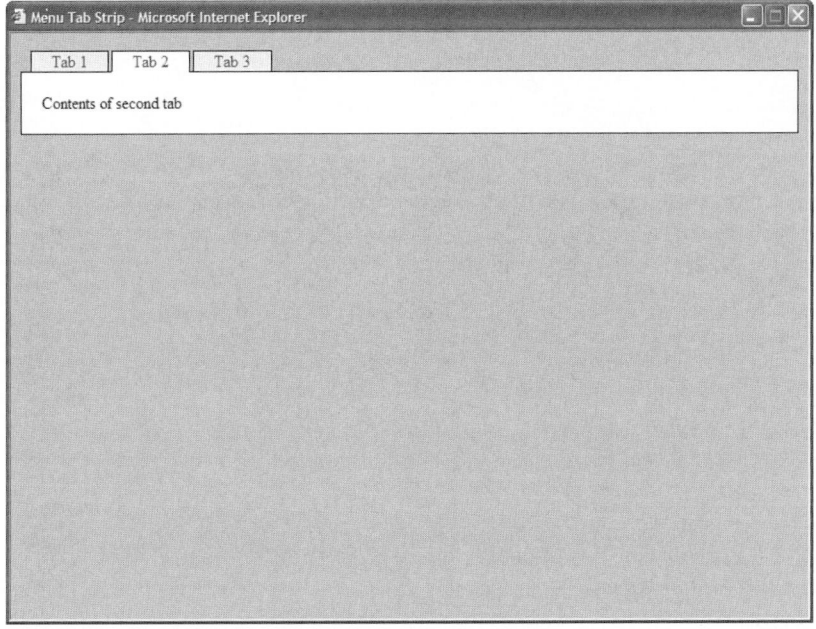

FIGURE 22.7   Displaying a tabbed page.

LISTING 22.7   MenuTabStrip.aspx

```
<%@ Page Language="C#" %>
<!DOCTYPE html PUBLIC "-//W3C//DTD XHTML 1.1//EN"
"http://www.w3.org/TR/xhtml11/DTD/xhtml11.dtd">
<script runat="server">

    protected void menuTabs_MenuItemClick(object sender, MenuEventArgs e)
    {
        multiTabs.ActiveViewIndex = Int32.Parse(menuTabs.SelectedValue);
    }
</script>
<html xmlns="http://www.w3.org/1999/xhtml" >
<head id="Head1" runat="server">
    <style type="text/css">
        html
        {
            background-color:silver;
        }
        .menuTabs
        {
            position:relative;
            top:1px;
```

22

```
            left:10px;
        }
        .tab
        {
            border:Solid 1px black;
            border-bottom:none;
            padding:0px 10px;
            background-color:#eeeeee;
        }
        .selectedTab
        {
            border:Solid 1px black;
            border-bottom:Solid 1px white;
            padding:0px 10px;
            background-color:white;
        }
        .tabBody
        {
            border:Solid 1px black;
            padding:20px;
            background-color:white;
        }
    </style>
    <title>Menu Tab Strip</title>
</head>
<body>
    <form id="form1" runat="server">
    <div>

    <asp:Menu
        id="menuTabs"
        CssClass="menuTabs"
        StaticMenuItemStyle-CssClass="tab"
        StaticSelectedStyle-CssClass="selectedTab"
        Orientation="Horizontal"
        OnMenuItemClick="menuTabs_MenuItemClick"
        Runat="server">
        <Items>
        <asp:MenuItem
            Text="Tab 1"
            Value="0"
            Selected="true" />
        <asp:MenuItem
            Text="Tab 2"
            Value="1"/>
        <asp:MenuItem
```

```
                Text="Tab 3"
                Value="2" />

        </Items>
    </asp:Menu>


    <div class="tabBody">
    <asp:MultiView
        id="multiTabs"
        ActiveViewIndex="0"
        Runat="server">
        <asp:View ID="view1" runat="server">

        Contents of first tab

        </asp:View>
        <asp:View ID="view2" runat="server">

        Contents of second tab

        </asp:View>
        <asp:View ID="view3" runat="server">

        Contents of third tab

        </asp:View>
    </asp:MultiView>
    </div>

    </div>
    </form>
</body>
</html>
```

After you open the page in Listing 22.7 and click a tab, the `MenuItemClick` event is raised. The `MenuItemClick` event handler changes the `ActiveViewIndex` property of the `MultiView` control to display the content of the selected tab.

Binding to a Site Map

Like the `SiteMapPath` control, you can use the `Menu` control with a Site Map. Users can click menu items to navigate to particular pages in your website. Unlike the `SiteMapPath` control, however, the `Menu` control does not automatically bind to a Site Map. You must explicitly bind the `Menu` control to a `SiteMapDataSource` control to display nodes from a Site Map.

For example, the page in Listing 22.8 contains a menu that contains links to all the pages in a website (see Figure 22.8).

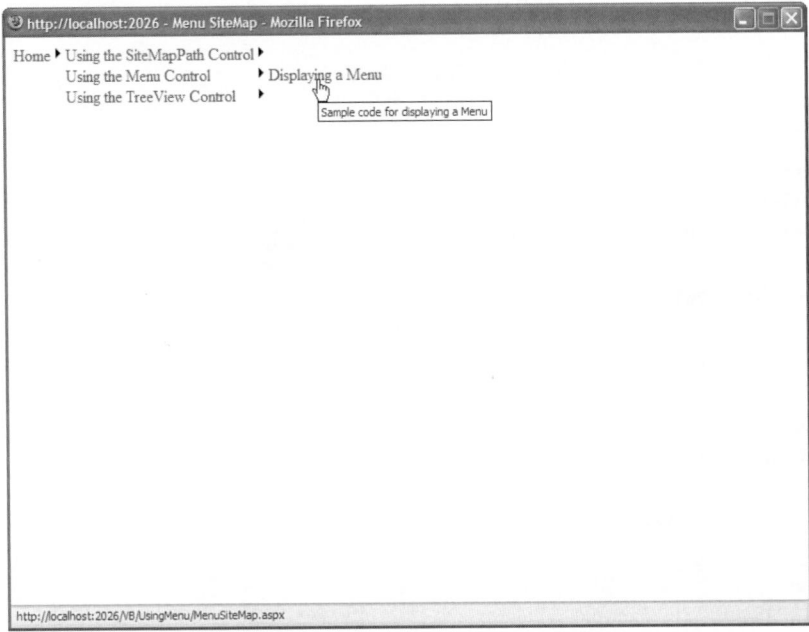

FIGURE 22.8   Displaying a Site Map with a Menu control.

LISTING 22.8   UsingMenu/MenuSiteMap.aspx

```
<%@ Page Language="C#" %>
<!DOCTYPE html PUBLIC "-//W3C//DTD XHTML 1.1//EN"
  "http://www.w3.org/TR/xhtml11/DTD/xhtml11.dtd">
<html xmlns="http://www.w3.org/1999/xhtml" >
<head id="Head1" runat="server">
    <title>Menu SiteMap</title>
</head>
<body>
    <form id="form1" runat="server">
    <div>

    <asp:Menu
        id="Menu1"
        DataSourceID="srcSiteMap"
        Runat="server" />

    <asp:SiteMapDataSource
        id="srcSiteMap"
```

```
        Runat="server" />

    </div>
    </form>
</body>
</html>
```

When you initially open the page in Listing 22.8, the only menu item that appears is the link to the Home page. If you hover your mouse over this link, links to additional pages display.

Normally, you do not want the Home link to display in a navigation menu. Instead, you want to display the second level of menu items. You can use the ShowStartingNode property of the SiteMapDataSource control to hide the topmost node in a Site Map.

For example, the page in Listing 22.9 uses a Menu control that renders a standard left-column navigational menu (see Figure 22.9).

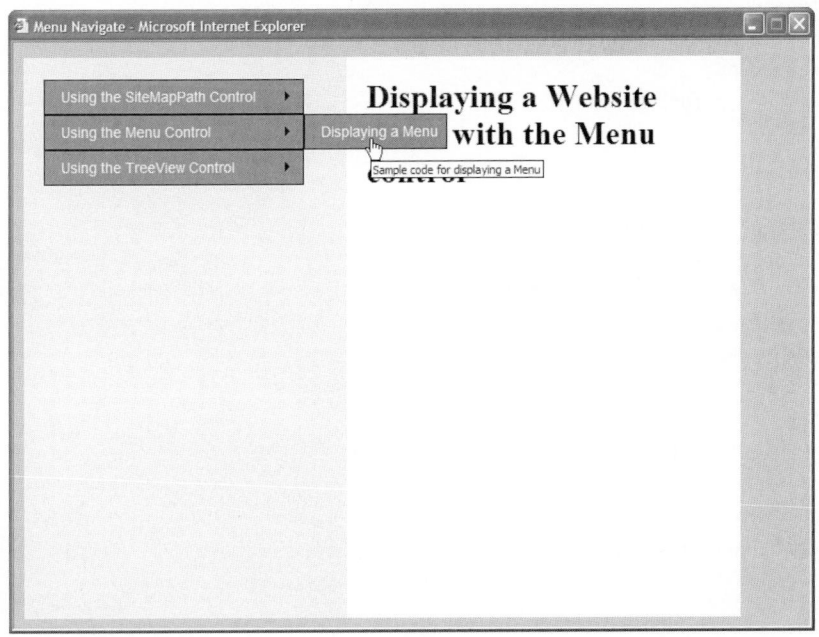

FIGURE 22.9   Displaying a navigation menu.

LISTING 22.9   UsingMenu/MenuNavigate.aspx

```
<%@ Page Language="C#" %>
<!DOCTYPE html PUBLIC "-//W3C//DTD XHTML 1.1//EN"
    "http://www.w3.org/TR/xhtml11/DTD/xhtml11.dtd">
<html xmlns="http://www.w3.org/1999/xhtml" >
```

```
<head id="Head1" runat="server">
    <style type="text/css">
        html
        {
            background-color:silver;
        }
        .navigation
        {
            float:left;
            width:280px;
            height:500px;
            padding:20px;
            background-color:#eeeeee;
        }
        .content
        {
            float:left;
            width:550px;
            height:500px;
            padding:20px;
            background-color:white;
        }
        .menuItem
        {
            border:Outset 1px black;
            background-color:Gray;
            font:14px Arial;
            color:White;
            padding:8px;
        }
    </style>
    <title>Menu Navigate</title>
</head>
<body>
    <form id="form1" runat="server">


    <div class="navigation">

    <asp:Menu
        id="Menu1"
        DataSourceID="srcSiteMap"
        StaticMenuItemStyle-CssClass="menuItem"
        DynamicMenuItemStyle-CssClass="menuItem"
        Runat="server" />
```

```
        <asp:SiteMapDataSource
            id="srcSiteMap"
            ShowStartingNode="false"
            Runat="server" />

    </div>

    <div class="content">

    <h1>Displaying a Website menu with the Menu control</h1>

    </div>


    </form>
</body>
</html>
```

When you open the page in Listing 22.9, the second-level nodes from the Site Map initially display. Furthermore, the Menu control is styled to appear more like a traditional website navigation menu.

Binding to an XML File

As an alternative to binding a Menu control to a SiteMapDataSource control, you can bind the control to an XML document by using the XmlDataSource control. For example, suppose that you have the XML file in Listing 22.10.

LISTING 22.10   Menu.xml

```
<?xml version="1.0" encoding="utf-8" ?>
<menu>
  <appetizer>
    <soup />
    <cheese />
  </appetizer>
  <entree>
    <duck />
    <chicken />
  </entree>
  <dessert>
    <cake />
    <pie />
  </dessert>
</menu>
```

The page in Listing 22.11 displays the contents of Listing 22.10 by using an XmlDataSource control to represent the XML document.

LISTING 22.11   MenuXML.aspx

```
<%@ Page Language="C#" %>
<!DOCTYPE html PUBLIC "-//W3C//DTD XHTML 1.1//EN"
    "http://www.w3.org/TR/xhtml11/DTD/xhtml11.dtd">
<html xmlns="http://www.w3.org/1999/xhtml" >
<head id="Head1" runat="server">
    <title>Menu XML</title>
</head>
<body>
    <form id="form1" runat="server">
    <div>

    <asp:Menu
        id="Menu1"
        DataSourceID="srcMenu"
        Runat="server" />

    <asp:XmlDataSource
        id="srcMenu"
        DataFile="Menu.xml"
        Runat="server" />

    </div>
    </form>
</body>
</html>
```

When using the XmlDataSource control, you can use the XPath property to supply an xpath query that restricts the nodes returned by the XmlDataSource. You also can use either the Transform or TransformFile property to apply an XSLT Style Sheet to the XML document and transform the nodes returned by the XmlDataSource.

The XML file in Listing 22.10 is simple. The nodes do not contain any attributes. When you bind the Menu control to the XML file, the ToString() method is called on each XML file node.

You also can bind the Menu control to more complex XML documents. For example, the item nodes in the XML document in Listing 22.12 include two attributes: text and price.

LISTING 22.12   MenuComplex.xml

```xml
<?xml version="1.0" encoding="utf-8" ?>
<menu>
  <category text="appetizer">
    <item text="soup" price="12.56" />
    <item text="cheese" price="17.23" />
  </category>
  <category text="entree">
    <item text="duck" price="89.21" />
    <item text="chicken" price="34.56" />
  </category>
  <category text="dessert">
    <item text="cake" price="23.43" />
    <item text="pie" price="115.46" />
  </category>
</menu>
```

When you bind to the XML document in Listing 22.12, you must specify one or more menu item bindings. The menu item bindings specify the relationship between node attributes and the menu items displayed by the Menu control.

The Menu control in Listing 22.13 includes MenuItemBinding subtags (see Figure 22.10).

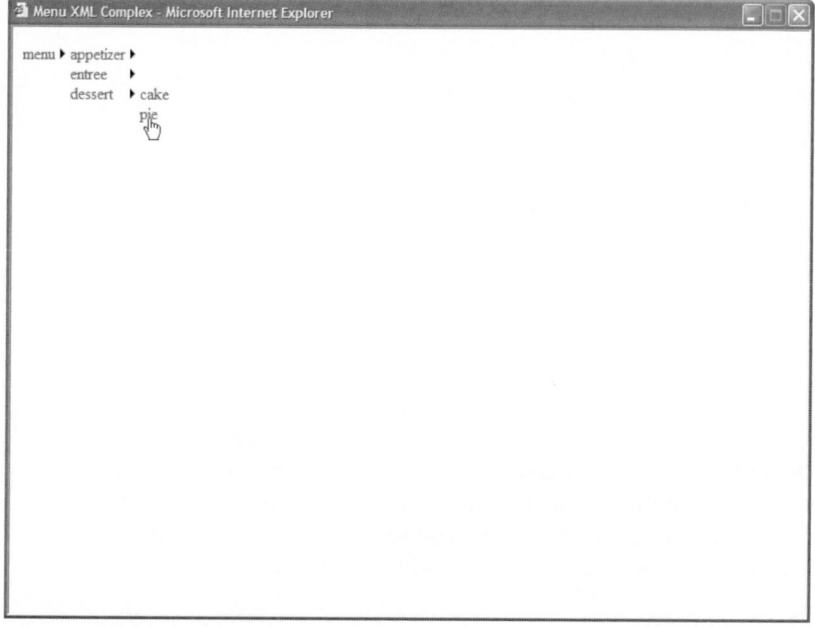

FIGURE 22.10   Displaying an XML document with the Menu control.

LISTING 22.13   MenuXMLComplex.aspx

```
<%@ Page Language="C#" %>
<!DOCTYPE html PUBLIC "-//W3C//DTD XHTML 1.1//EN"
    "http://www.w3.org/TR/xhtml11/DTD/xhtml11.dtd">
<html xmlns="http://www.w3.org/1999/xhtml" >
<head id="Head1" runat="server">
    <title>Menu XML Complex</title>
</head>
<body>
    <form id="form1" runat="server">
    <div>

    <asp:Menu
        id="Menu1"
        DataSourceID="srcMenu"
        Runat="server">
        <DataBindings>
        <asp:MenuItemBinding
            DataMember="category"
            TextField="text" />
        <asp:MenuItemBinding
            DataMember="item"
            TextField="text"
            ValueField="price" />
        </DataBindings>
    </asp:Menu>

    <asp:XmlDataSource
        id="srcMenu"
        DataFile="MenuComplex.xml"
        Runat="server" />

    </div>
    </form>
</body>
</html>
```

The Menu control includes a <DataBindings> element. This element includes two
MenuItemBinding subtags. The first subtag represents the relationship between the category nodes in the XML file and the menu items. The second subtag represents the relationship between the item nodes in the XML file and the menu items.

Binding to Database Data

You can't bind a Menu control directly to database data. Neither the SqlDataSource nor ObjectDataSource controls implement the IHierachicalDataSource interface. Therefore, if you want to represent database data with the Menu control, you need to perform some more work.

One option is to create your own SqlHiearachicalDataSource control. You can do this either by deriving from the base HiearchicalDataSourceControl class or implementing the IHiearchicalDataSource interface. You take this approach in the final section of this chapter, when a custom SqlHierarchicalDataSource control is built.

A second option is to build the menu items programmatically in the Menu control. This is the approach followed here.

Imagine that you want to represent the contents of the following database table with a Menu control:

CategoryId	ParentId	Name
1	null	Beverages
2	null	Fruit
3	1	Milk
4	1	Juice
5	4	Apple Juice
6	4	Orange Juice
7	2	Apples
8	2	Pears

This database table represents product categories. The categories are nested with the help of the ParentId column. For example, the Orange Juice category is nested below the Juice category, and the Juice category is nested below the Beverages category.

The page in Listing 22.14 illustrates how you can display this database table with a Menu control (see Figure 22.11).

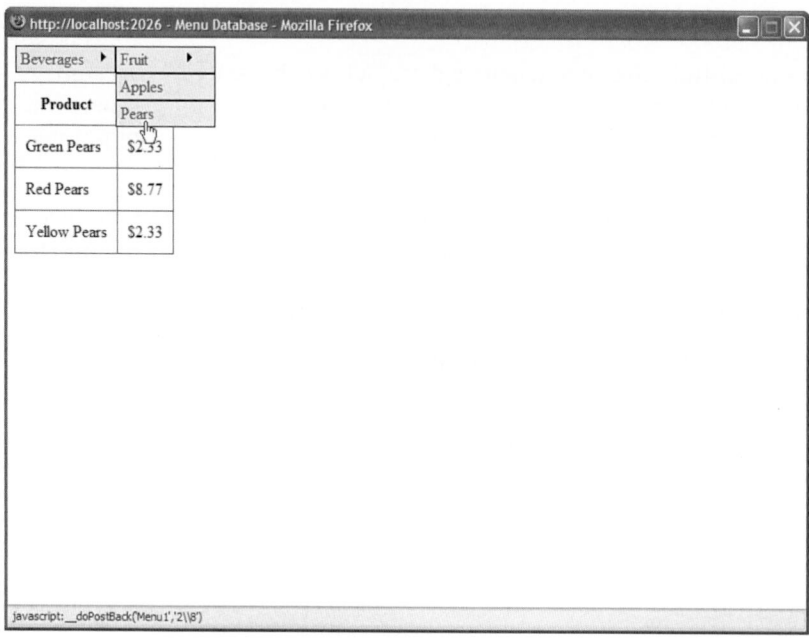

FIGURE 22.11   Displaying database data with the Menu control.

LISTING 22.14   MenuDatabase.aspx

```
<%@ Page Language="C#" %>
<%@ Import Namespace="System.Web.Configuration" %>
<%@ Import Namespace="System.Data" %>
<%@ Import Namespace="System.Data.SqlClient" %>
<!DOCTYPE html PUBLIC "-//W3C//DTD XHTML 1.1//EN"
"http://www.w3.org/TR/xhtml11/DTD/xhtml11.dtd">
<script runat="server">


    /// <summary>
    /// Only populate the menu when the page first loads
    /// </summary>
    void Page_Load()
    {
        if (!Page.IsPostBack)
            PopulateMenu();
    }


    /// <summary>
    /// Get the data from the database and create the top-level
    /// menu items
    /// </summary>
```

```
    private void PopulateMenu()
    {
        DataTable menuData = GetMenuData();
        AddTopMenuItems(menuData);
    }


    /// <summary>
    /// Use a DataAdapter and DataTable to grab the database data
    /// </summary>
    /// <returns></returns>
    private DataTable GetMenuData()
    {
        // Get Categories table
        string selectCommand = "SELECT CategoryId,ParentId,Name FROM Categories";
        string conString =
WebConfigurationManager.ConnectionStrings["Categories"].ConnectionString;
        SqlDataAdapter dad = new SqlDataAdapter(selectCommand, conString);
        DataTable dtblCategories = new DataTable();
        dad.Fill(dtblCategories);
        return dtblCategories;
    }


    /// <summary>
    /// Filter the data to get only the rows that have a
    /// null ParentID (these are the top-level menu items)
    /// </summary>
    private void AddTopMenuItems(DataTable menuData)
    {
        DataView view = new DataView(menuData);
        view.RowFilter = "ParentID IS NULL";
        foreach (DataRowView row in view)
        {
            MenuItem newMenuItem = new MenuItem(row["Name"].ToString(),
row["CategoryId"].ToString());
            Menu1.Items.Add(newMenuItem);
            AddChildMenuItems(menuData, newMenuItem);
        }

    }


    /// <summary>
    /// Recursively add child menu items by filtering by ParentID
    /// </summary>
    private void AddChildMenuItems(DataTable menuData, MenuItem parentMenuItem)
    {
        DataView view = new DataView(menuData);
```

```
            view.RowFilter = "ParentID=" + parentMenuItem.Value;
            foreach (DataRowView row in view)
            {
                MenuItem newMenuItem = new MenuItem(row["Name"].ToString(),
row["CategoryId"].ToString());
                parentMenuItem.ChildItems.Add(newMenuItem);
                AddChildMenuItems(menuData, newMenuItem);
            }
        }

</script>
<html xmlns="http://www.w3.org/1999/xhtml" >
<head id="Head1" runat="server">
    <style type="text/css">
        .menuItem
        {
            border:Solid 1px black;
            width:100px;
            padding:2px;
            background-color:#eeeeee;
        }
        .menuItem a
        {
            color:blue;
        }
        .grid
        {
            margin-top:10px;
        }

        .grid td, .grid th
        {
            padding:10px;
        }
    </style>
    <title>Menu Database</title>
</head>
<body>
    <form id="form1" runat="server">
    <div>

    <asp:Menu
        id="Menu1"
        Orientation="horizontal"
        StaticMenuItemStyle-CssClass="menuItem"
```

```
            DynamicMenuItemStyle-CssClass="menuItem"
            Runat="server" />

    <asp:GridView
        id="grdProducts"
        DataSourceID="srcProducts"
        CssClass="grid"
        AutoGenerateColumns="false"
        Runat="server">
        <Columns>
        <asp:BoundField
            DataField="ProductName"
            HeaderText="Product" />
        <asp:BoundField
            DataField="Price"
            HeaderText="Price"
            DataFormatString="{0:c}" />
        </Columns>
    </asp:GridView>

    <asp:SqlDataSource
        id="srcProducts"
        ConnectionString="<%$ ConnectionStrings:Categories %>"
        SelectCommand="SELECT ProductName,Price FROM Products
            WHERE CategoryId=@CategoryId"
        Runat="server">
        <SelectParameters>
        <asp:ControlParameter
            Name="CategoryId"
            ControlID="Menu1" />
        </SelectParameters>
    </asp:SqlDataSource>


    </div>
    </form>
</body>
</html>
```

The menu items are added to the Menu control in the PopulateMenu() method. This method first grabs a DataTable that contains the contents of the Categories database table. Next, it creates a menu item for each row that does not have a parent row (each row where the ParentId column has the value null).

The child menu items for each menu item are added recursively. The ParentId column is used to filter the contents of the Categories DataTable.

The page in Listing 22.14 also includes a GridView control that displays a list of products that match the category selected in the menu. GridView is bound to a SqlDataSource control, which includes a ControlParameter that filters the products based on the selected menu item.

Formatting the Menu Control

The Menu control supports an abundance of properties that can be used to format the appearance of the control. Many of these properties have an effect on static menu items, and many of these properties have an effect on dynamic menu items. Static menu items are menu items that always appear. Dynamic menu items are menu items that appear only when you hover your mouse over another menu item.

First, the Menu control supports the following general properties related to formatting:

- ▶ **DisappearAfter**—Enables you to specify the amount of time, in milliseconds, that a dynamic menu item is displayed after a user moves the mouse away from the menu item.

- ▶ **DynamicBottomSeparatorImageUrl**—Enables you to specify the URL to an image that appears under each dynamic menu item.

- ▶ **DynamicEnableDefaultPopOutImage**—Enables you to disable the image (triangle) that indicates that a dynamic menu item has child menu items.

- ▶ **DynamicHorizontalOffset**—Enables you to specify the number of pixels that a dynamic menu item is shifted relative to its parent menu item.

- ▶ **DynamicItemFormatString**—Enables you to format the text displayed in a dynamic menu item.

- ▶ **DynamicPopOutImageTextFormatString**—Enables you to format the alt text displayed for the popout image.

- ▶ **DynamicPopOutImageUrl**—Enables you to specify the URL for the dynamic popout image. (By default, a triangle is displayed.)

- ▶ **DynamicTopSeparatorImageUrl**—Enables you to specify the URL to an image that appears above each dynamic menu item.

- ▶ **DynamicVerticalOffset**—Enables you to specify the number of pixels that a dynamic menu item is shifted relative to its parent menu item.

- ▶ **ItemWrap**—Enables you to specify whether the text in menu items should wrap.

- ▶ **MaximumDynamicDisplayLevels**—Enables you to specify the maximum number of levels of dynamic menu items to display.

- ▶ **Orientation**—Enables you to display a menu horizontally or vertically. (The default value is Vertical.)

- ▶ **ScollDownImageUrl**—Enables you to specify the URL to an image that is displayed and that enables you to scroll down through menu items.

▶ **ScrollDownText**—Enables you to specify alt text for the ScrollDown image.

▶ **ScrollUpImageUrl**—Enables you to specify the URL to an image that is displayed and that enables you to scroll up through menu items.

▶ **ScrollUpText**—Enables you to specify alt text for the ScrollUp image.

▶ **SkipLinkText**—Enables you to modify the text displayed by the skip link. (The skip link enables blind users to skip past the contents of a menu.)

▶ **StaticBottomSeparatorImageUrl**—Enables you to specify the URL to an image that appears below each static menu item.

▶ **StaticDisplayLevels**—Enables you to specify the number of static levels of menu items to display.

▶ **StaticEnableDefaultPopOutImage**—Enables you to disable the default popout image that indicates that a menu item has child menu items.

▶ **StaticItemFormatString**—Enables you to format the text displayed in each static menu item.

▶ **StaticImagePopOutFormatString**—Enables you to specify the alt text displayed by the popout image.

▶ **StaticPopOutImageUrl**—Enables you to specify the URL for the popout image.

▶ **StaticSubMenuIndent**—Enables you to specify the number of pixels that a static menu item is indented relative to its parent menu item.

▶ **StaticTopSeparatorImageUrl**—Enables you to specify the URL to an image that appears above each static menu item.

▶ **Target**—Enables you to specify the window in which a new page opens when you click a menu item.

This list includes several interesting properties. For example, you can specify images for scrolling up and down through a list of menu items. These images appear when you constrain the height of either the static or dynamic menu.

The Menu control also exposes several Style objects. You can use these Style objects as hooks to which you can attach Cascading Style Sheet (CSS) classes:

▶ **DynamicHoverStyle**—Style applied to a dynamic menu item when you hover your mouse over it.

▶ **DynamicMenuItemStyle**—Style applied to each dynamic menu item.

▶ **DynamicMenuStyle**—Style applied to the container tag for the dynamic menu.

▶ **DynamicSelectedStyle**—Style applied to the selected dynamic menu item.

▶ **StaticHoverStyle**—Style applied to a static menu item when you hover your mouse over it.

▶ **StaticMenuItemStyle**—Style applied to each static menu item.

▶ **StaticMenuStyle**—Style applied to the container tag for the static menu.

▶ **StaticSelectedStyle**—Style applied to the selected static menu item.

Furthermore, you can apply styles to menu items based on their level in the menu. For example, you might want the font size to get progressively smaller depending on how deeply nested a menu item is within a menu. You can use three properties of the Menu control to format menu items, depending on their level:

▶ **LevelMenuItemStyles**—Contains a collection of MenuItemStyle controls, which correspond to different menu levels

▶ **LevelSelectedStyles**—Contains a collection of MenuItemStyle controls, which correspond to different menu levels of selected menu items

▶ **LevelSubMenuStyles**—Contains a collection of MenuItemStyle controls, which correspond to different menu levels of static menu items

For example, the page in Listing 22.15 illustrates how you can apply different formatting to menu items that appear at different menu levels (see Figure 22.12).

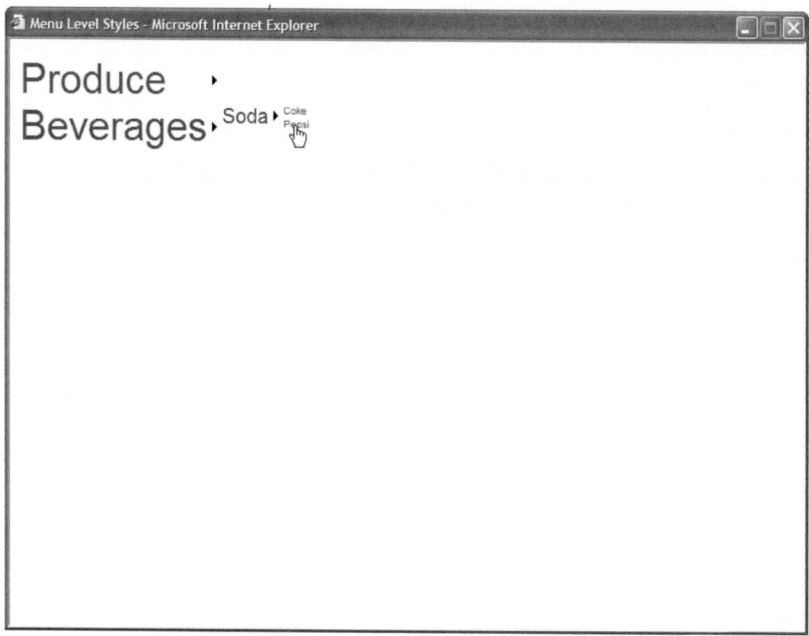

FIGURE 22.12   Applying styles to different menu levels.

LISTING 22.15   MenuLevelStyles.aspx

```
<%@ Page Language="C#" %>
<!DOCTYPE html PUBLIC "-//W3C//DTD XHTML 1.1//EN"
  "http://www.w3.org/TR/xhtml11/DTD/xhtml11.dtd">
<html xmlns="http://www.w3.org/1999/xhtml" >
<head id="Head1" runat="server">
```

```
    <style type="text/css">
        .menuLevel1
        {
            font:40px Arial,Sans-Serif;
        }
        .menuLevel2
        {
            font:20px Arial,Sans-Serif;
        }
        .menuLevel3
        {
            font:10px Arial,Sans-Serif;
        }
    </style>
    <title>Menu Level Styles</title>
</head>
<body>
    <form id="form1" runat="server">
    <div>

    <asp:Menu
        id="Menu1"
        Runat="server">
        <LevelMenuItemStyles>
            <asp:MenuItemStyle CssClass="menuLevel1" />
            <asp:MenuItemStyle CssClass="menuLevel2" />
            <asp:MenuItemStyle CssClass="menuLevel3" />
        </LevelMenuItemStyles>
        <Items>
        <asp:MenuItem Text="Produce">
            <asp:MenuItem Text="Apples" />
            <asp:MenuItem Text="Oranges" />
        </asp:MenuItem>
        <asp:MenuItem Text="Beverages">
            <asp:MenuItem Text="Soda">
                <asp:MenuItem Text="Coke" />
                <asp:MenuItem Text="Pepsi" />
            </asp:MenuItem>
        </asp:MenuItem>
        </Items>
    </asp:Menu>

    </div>
    </form>
</body>
</html>
```

22

The MenuItemStyle controls are applied to the menu level that corresponds to their order of declaration. The first MenuItemStyle is applied to the first menu level, the second MenuItemStyle is applied to the second menu level, and so on.

Finally, the MenuItem class itself includes several useful formatting properties:

▶ **ImageUrl**—Enables you to specify the URL for an image that is displayed next to a menu item.

▶ **PopOutImageUrl**—Enables you to specify the URL for an image that is displayed when a menu item contains child menu items.

▶ **SeparatorImageUrl**—Enables you to specify the URL for an image that appears below a menu item.

▶ **Selectable**—Enables you to prevent users from selecting (clicking) a menu item.

▶ **Selected**—Enables you to specify whether a menu item is selected.

▶ **Target**—Enables you to specify the name of the window that opens when you click a menu item.

For example, the page in Listing 22.16 displays a menu that resembles a traditional desktop application menu (see Figure 22.13).

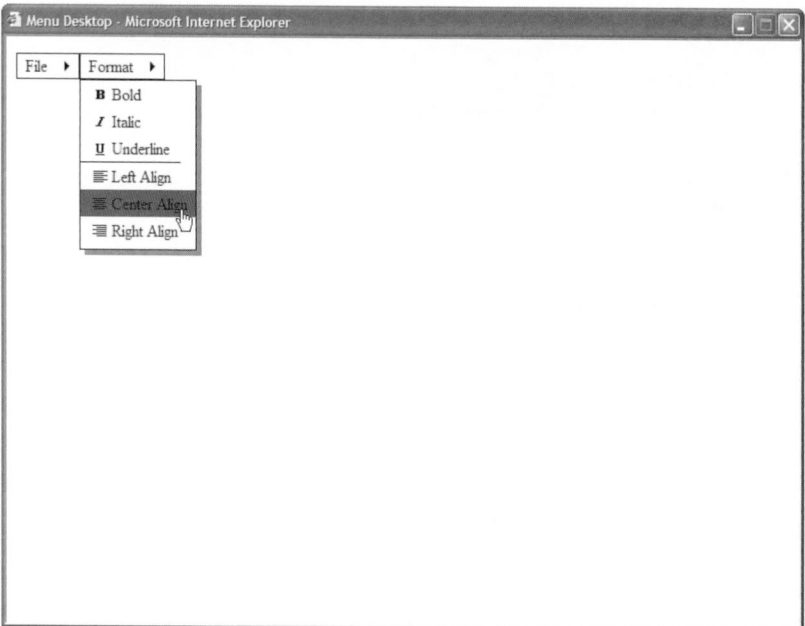

FIGURE 22.13 Displaying a desktop application menu.

LISTING 22.16   MenuDesktop.aspx

```
<%@ Page Language="C#" %>
<!DOCTYPE html PUBLIC "-//W3C//DTD XHTML 1.1//EN"
    "http://www.w3.org/TR/xhtml11/DTD/xhtml11.dtd">
<html xmlns="http://www.w3.org/1999/xhtml" >
<head id="Head1" runat="server">
    <style type="text/css">
        .staticMenuItem
        {
            color:black;
            border:solid 1px black;
            padding:2px 4px;
        }
        .menuHover
        {
            color:white;
            background-color:blue;
        }
        .dynamicMenuItem
        {
            color:black;
            padding:2px 4px;
        }
        .dynamicMenu
        {
            border:Solid 1px black;
            filter:progid:DXImageTransform.Microsoft.dropshadow(OffX=5, OffY=5,
 Color='gray', Positive='true')"
        }
    </style>
    <title>Menu Desktop</title>
</head>
<body>
    <form id="form1" runat="server">
    <div>

    <asp:Menu
        id="Menu1"
        Orientation="Horizontal"
        StaticMenuItemStyle-CssClass="staticMenuItem"
        StaticHoverStyle-CssClass="menuHover"
        DynamicHoverStyle-CssClass="menuHover"
        DynamicMenuItemStyle-CssClass="dynamicMenuItem"
        DynamicMenuStyle-CssClass="dynamicMenu"
        Runat="server">
```

```
    <Items>
    <asp:MenuItem
        Text="File"
        Selectable="false">
        <asp:MenuItem
            Text="Save" />
        <asp:MenuItem
            Text="Open" />
    </asp:MenuItem>
    <asp:MenuItem
        Text="Format"
        Selectable="false">
        <asp:MenuItem
            Text="Bold"
            ImageUrl="Images/Bold.gif" />
        <asp:MenuItem
            Text="Italic"
            ImageUrl="Images/Italic.gif" />
        <asp:MenuItem
            Text="Underline"
            ImageUrl="Images/Underline.gif"
            SeparatorImageUrl="Images/Divider.gif" />
        <asp:MenuItem
            Text="Left Align"
            ImageUrl="Images/JustifyLeft.gif" />
        <asp:MenuItem
            Text="Center Align"
            ImageUrl="Images/JustifyCenter.gif" />
        <asp:MenuItem
            Text="Right Align"
            ImageUrl="Images/JustifyRight.gif" />
    </asp:MenuItem>
    </Items>
</asp:Menu>

</div>
</form>
</body>
</html>
```

Using Templates with the Menu Control

The Menu control supports templates. You can use templates to completely customize the appearance of the Menu control.

The Menu control supports the following two templates:

▶ **DynamicItemTemplate**—Applied to dynamic menu items.

▶ **StaticItemTemplate**—Applied to static menu items.

The page in Listing 22.17 uses both templates to display menu items. The templates display a count of child items for each menu item (see Figure 22.14).

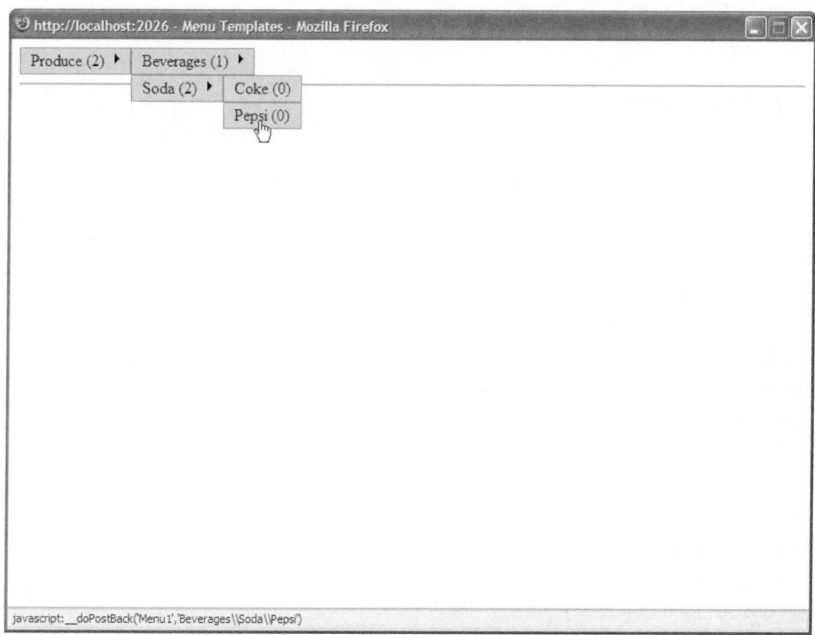

FIGURE 22.14   Using templates with the Menu control.

LISTING 22.17   MenuTemplates.aspx

```
<%@ Page Language="C#" %>
<!DOCTYPE html PUBLIC "-//W3C//DTD XHTML 1.1//EN"
"http://www.w3.org/TR/xhtml11/DTD/xhtml11.dtd">
<script runat="server">

    protected void Menu1_MenuItemClick(object sender, MenuEventArgs e)
    {
        lblMessage.Text = Menu1.SelectedValue;
    }
</script>
<html xmlns="http://www.w3.org/1999/xhtml" >
<head id="Head1" runat="server">
    <style type="text/css">
        .menuItem
```

```
            {
                color:black;
                border:Solid 1px Gray;
                background-color:#c9c9c9;
                padding:2px 5px;
            }
        </style>
        <title>Menu Templates</title>
</head>
<body>
        <form id="form1" runat="server">
        <div>

        <asp:Menu
            id="Menu1"
            OnMenuItemClick="Menu1_MenuItemClick"
            Orientation="Horizontal"
            StaticMenuItemStyle-CssClass="menuItem"
            DynamicMenuItemStyle-CssClass="menuItem"
            Runat="server">
            <StaticItemTemplate>
            <%# Eval("Text") %>
            (<%# Eval("ChildItems.Count") %>)
            </StaticItemTemplate>
            <DynamicItemTemplate>
            <%# Eval("Text") %>
            (<%# Eval("ChildItems.Count") %>)
            </DynamicItemTemplate>
            <Items>
            <asp:MenuItem Text="Produce">
                <asp:MenuItem Text="Apples" />
                <asp:MenuItem Text="Oranges" />
            </asp:MenuItem>
            <asp:MenuItem Text="Beverages">
                <asp:MenuItem Text="Soda">
                    <asp:MenuItem Text="Coke" />
                    <asp:MenuItem Text="Pepsi" />
                </asp:MenuItem>
            </asp:MenuItem>
            </Items>
        </asp:Menu>
```

```
    <hr />

    <asp:Label
        id="lblMessage"
        EnableViewState="false"
        Runat="server" />

    </div>
    </form>
</body>
</html>
```

You do not need to create `LinkButton` controls in the templates. The content of the template is wrapped in a link automatically when it is appropriate.

Using the `TreeView` Control

The `TreeView` control is similar to the `Menu` control. Like the `Menu` control, you can use the `TreeView` control to display hierarchical data. The `TreeView` control binds to any data source that implements the `IHierarchicalDataSource` or `IHiearchicalEnumerable` interface.

In this section, you learn how to add items declaratively to the `TreeView` control. You also learn how to bind a `TreeView` control to hierarchical data sources such as the `SiteMapDataSource` and `XmlDataSource` controls.

You also see how you can use the `TreeView` control with database data. A `TreeView` is built programmatically from database data.

Finally, you learn how you can use AJAX with the `TreeView` control to display large sets of data efficiently. By taking advantage of AJAX, you can update a `TreeView` without posting a page back to the server.

Declaratively Adding Tree Nodes

A `TreeView` control is made up of `TreeNode` objects. You can build a `TreeView` control by declaring `TreeNode` objects in the `TreeView` control's Items collection.

For example, Listing 22.18 contains a `TreeView` which renders a nested set of links to pages (see Figure 22.15).

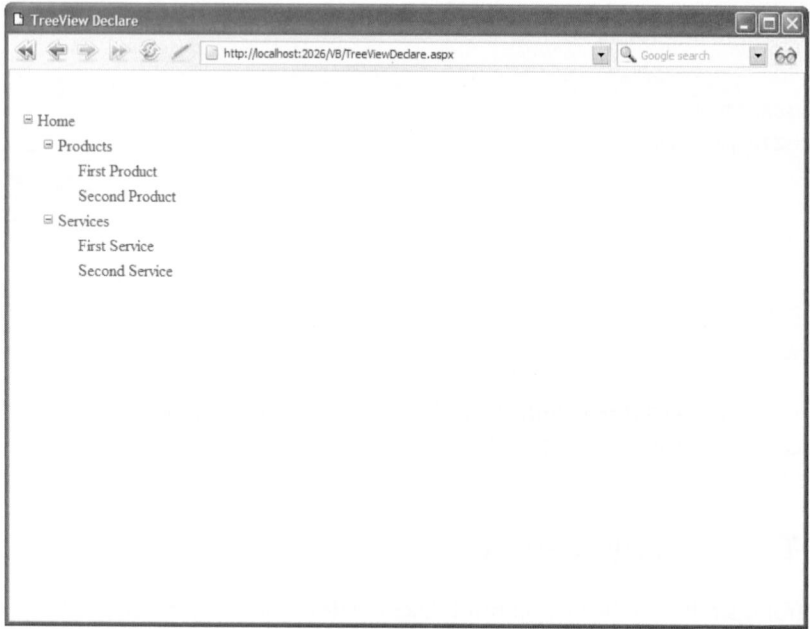

FIGURE 22.15   Displaying a TreeView control.

LISTING 22.18   TreeViewDeclare.aspx

```
<%@ Page Language="C#" %>
<!DOCTYPE html PUBLIC "-//W3C//DTD XHTML 1.1//EN"
    "http://www.w3.org/TR/xhtml11/DTD/xhtml11.dtd">
<html xmlns="http://www.w3.org/1999/xhtml" >
<head id="Head1" runat="server">
    <title>TreeView Declare</title>
</head>
<body>
    <form id="form1" runat="server">
    <div>

    <asp:TreeView
        id="TreeView1"
        Runat="server">
        <Nodes>
        <asp:TreeNode
            Text="Home"
```

```
            NavigateUrl="~/Default.aspx">
            <asp:TreeNode
                Text="Products">
                <asp:TreeNode
                    Text="First Product"
                    NavigateUrl="~/Products/FirstProduct.aspx" />
                <asp:TreeNode
                    Text="Second Product"
                    NavigateUrl="~/Products/SecondProduct.aspx" />
            </asp:TreeNode>
            <asp:TreeNode
                Text="Services">
                <asp:TreeNode
                    Text="First Service"
                    NavigateUrl="~/Services/FirstService.aspx" />
                <asp:TreeNode
                    Text="Second Service"
                    NavigateUrl="~/Services/SecondService.aspx" />
            </asp:TreeNode>
        </asp:TreeNode>
        </Nodes>
    </asp:TreeView>


    </div>
    </form>
</body>
</html>
```

Some of the TreeNodes in Listing 22.18 include a Text property, and some of the TreeNodes include both a Text and NavigateUrl property. You can click the TreeNodes that include a NavigateUrl property to link to a new page.

You also can associate a Value property with a TreeNode. This is useful when you want to post back to the same page. For example, the page in Listing 22.19 enables you to display the value of the selected TreeNode in a Label control (see Figure 22.16).

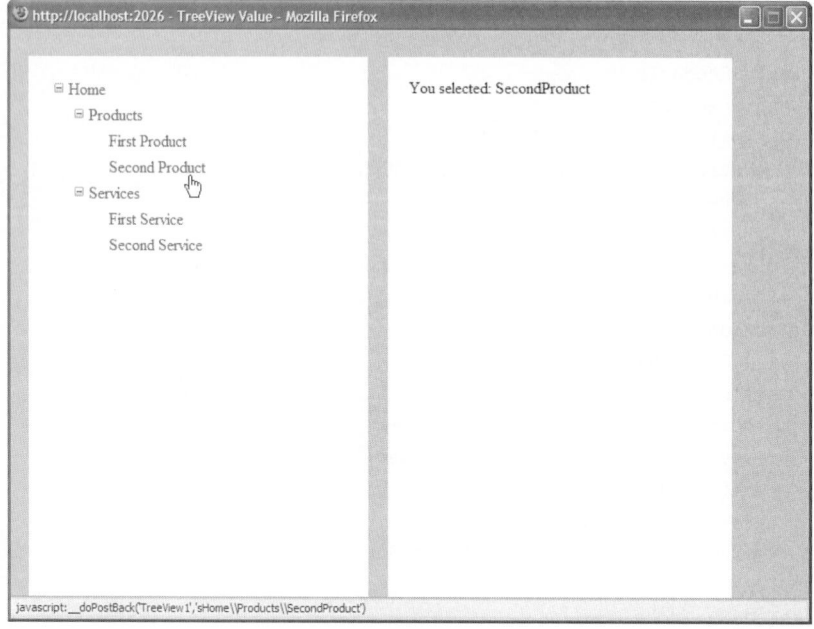

FIGURE 22.16   Selecting a `TreeView` node.

LISTING 22.19   TreeViewValue.aspx

```
<%@ Page Language="C#" %>
<!DOCTYPE html PUBLIC "-//W3C//DTD XHTML 1.1//EN"
"http://www.w3.org/TR/xhtml11/DTD/xhtml11.dtd">

<script runat="server">

    protected void TreeView1_SelectedNodeChanged(object sender, EventArgs e)
    {
        lblMessage.Text = TreeView1.SelectedValue;
    }
</script>
<html xmlns="http://www.w3.org/1999/xhtml" >
<head id="Head1" runat="server">
    <style type="text/css">
        html
        {
            background-color:silver;
        }
        .content
        {
            float:left;
```

```
            width:350px;
            height:500px;
            padding:20px;
            margin:10px;
            background-color:white;
        }
    </style>
    <title>TreeView Value</title>
</head>
<body>
    <form id="form1" runat="server">

    <div class="content">
    <asp:TreeView
        id="TreeView1"
        OnSelectedNodeChanged="TreeView1_SelectedNodeChanged"
        Runat="server" >
        <Nodes>
        <asp:TreeNode
            Text="Home"
            Value="Home">
            <asp:TreeNode
                Text="Products">
                <asp:TreeNode
                    Text="First Product"
                    Value="FirstProduct" />
                <asp:TreeNode
                    Text="Second Product"
                    Value="SecondProduct" />
            </asp:TreeNode>
            <asp:TreeNode
                Text="Services">
                <asp:TreeNode
                    Text="First Service"
                    Value="FirstService" />
                <asp:TreeNode
                    Text="Second Service"
                    Value="SecondService" />
            </asp:TreeNode>
        </asp:TreeNode>
        </Nodes>
    </asp:TreeView>
    </div>
```

22

```
<div class="content">
You selected:
<asp:Label
    id="lblMessage"
    EnableViewState="false"
    Runat="server" />
</div>

</form>
</body>
</html>
```

The page in Listing 22.19 includes a SelectedNodeChanged event handler. When you select a new node, the SelectedNodeChanged event handler displays the value of the selected TreeNode in a Label control.

Displaying Check Boxes with the TreeView Control

You can display check boxes next to each node in a TreeView control by assigning a value to the ShowCheckBoxes property. This property accepts the following values:

- ▶ All
- ▶ Leaf
- ▶ None
- ▶ Parent
- ▶ Root

You can use a bitwise combination of these values when specifying the nodes to display with check boxes.

The page in Listing 22.20 illustrates the ShowCheckBoxes property (see Figure 22.17).

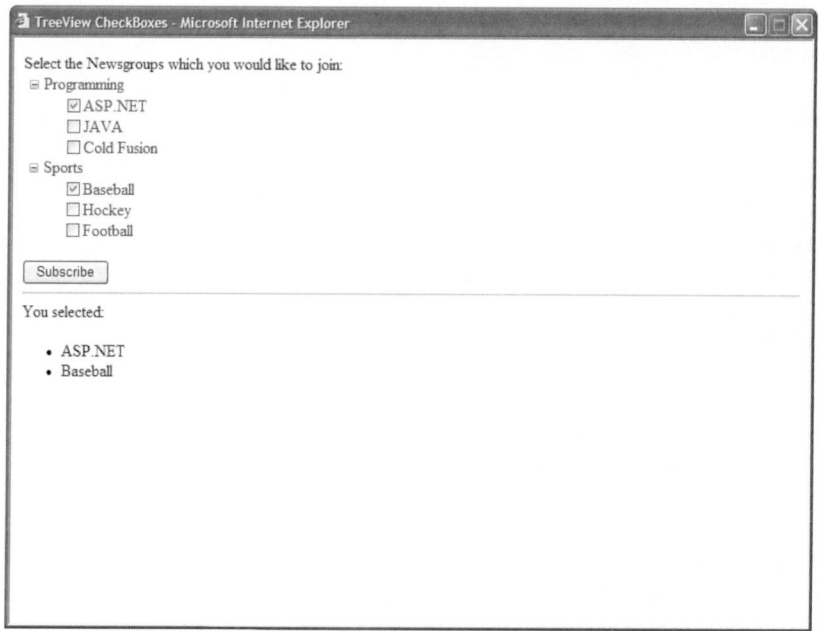

FIGURE 22.17   Displaying TreeView check boxes.

LISTING 22.20   TreeViewCheckBoxes.aspx

```
<%@ Page Language="C#" %>
<!DOCTYPE html PUBLIC "-//W3C//DTD XHTML 1.1//EN"
"http://www.w3.org/TR/xhtml11/DTD/xhtml11.dtd">
<script runat="server">

    protected void btnSubscribe_Click(object sender, EventArgs e)
    {
        foreach (TreeNode node in TreeView1.CheckedNodes)
            bltSubscribed.Items.Add(node.Text);
    }
</script>
<html xmlns="http://www.w3.org/1999/xhtml" >
<head id="Head1" runat="server">
    <title>TreeView CheckBoxes</title>
</head>
<body>
    <form id="form1" runat="server">
    <div>
```

22

```
Select the Newsgroups which you
would like to join:

<br />

<asp:TreeView
    id="TreeView1"
    ShowCheckBoxes="Leaf"
    Runat="server">
    <Nodes>
    <asp:TreeNode
        Text="Programming">
        <asp:TreeNode Text="ASP.NET" />
        <asp:TreeNode Text="JAVA" />
        <asp:TreeNode Text="Cold Fusion" />
    </asp:TreeNode>
    <asp:TreeNode
        Text="Sports">
        <asp:TreeNode Text="Baseball" />
        <asp:TreeNode Text="Hockey" />
        <asp:TreeNode Text="Football" />
    </asp:TreeNode>
    </Nodes>
</asp:TreeView>

<br />

<asp:Button
    id="btnSubscribe"
    Text="Subscribe"
    OnClick="btnSubscribe_Click"
    Runat="server" />

<hr />

You selected:

<asp:BulletedList
    id="bltSubscribed"
    EnableViewState="false"
    Runat="server" />

</div>
</form>
</body>
</html>
```

The page in Listing 22.20 displays nested newsgroups. You can subscribe to the newsgroups by clicking the Subscribe button.

When you click the Subscribe button, the CheckedNodes property returns a list of all the checked TreeNodes. This list displays in a BulletedList control.

Binding to a Site Map

You can use a TreeView control as a navigation element in your pages by binding the TreeView to a Site Map. The page in Listing 22.21 demonstrates how you can bind a TreeView to a SiteMapDataSource control (see Figure 22.18).

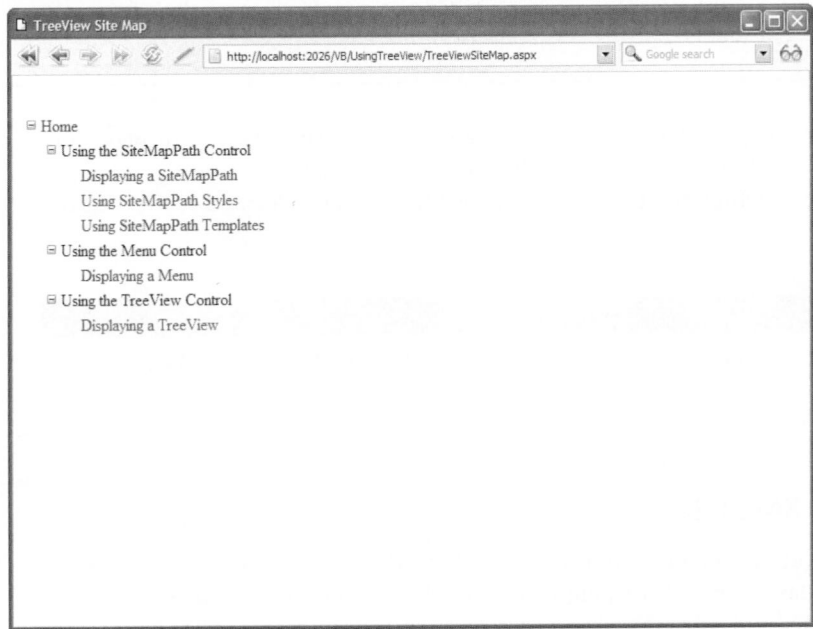

FIGURE 22.18   Displaying a Site Map with a TreeView control.

LISTING 22.21   UsingTreeView/TreeViewSiteMap.aspx

```
<%@ Page Language="C#" %>
<!DOCTYPE html PUBLIC "-//W3C//DTD XHTML 1.1//EN"
 "http://www.w3.org/TR/xhtml11/DTD/xhtml11.dtd">
<html xmlns="http://www.w3.org/1999/xhtml" >
<head id="Head1" runat="server">
    <title>TreeView Site Map</title>
</head>
<body>
    <form id="form1" runat="server">
    <div>
```

```
    <asp:TreeView
        id="TreeView1"
        DataSourceID="srcSiteMap"
        Runat="server" />

    <asp:SiteMapDataSource
        id="srcSiteMap"
        Runat="server" />

    </div>
    </form>
</body>
</html>
```

When you open the page in Listing 22.21, all the nodes from the Site Map display automatically in the TreeView control. By default, the SiteMapDataSource uses the XmlSiteMapProvider, which represents a file named Web.sitemap located at the root of an application.

> **NOTE**
>
> You can add a TreeView and SiteMapDataSource control to a Master Page to show the TreeView in multiple pages. To learn more about Master Pages, see Chapter 5.

Binding to an XML File

Because an XmlDataSource control returns hierarchical data, you can bind a TreeView directly to an XmlDataSource. For example, imagine that you need to display the XML document contained in Listing 22.22.

LISTING 22.22　Movies.xml

```xml
<?xml version="1.0" encoding="utf-8" ?>
<movies>
  <action>
    <StarWars />
    <IndependenceDay />
  </action>
  <horror>
    <Jaws />
    <NightmareBeforeChristmas />
  </horror>
</movies>
```

The page in Listing 22.23 illustrates how you can display the contents of this XML document with a `TreeView` control.

LISTING 22.23   TreeViewXml.aspx

```
<%@ Page Language="C#" %>
<!DOCTYPE html PUBLIC "-//W3C//DTD XHTML 1.1//EN"
 "http://www.w3.org/TR/xhtml11/DTD/xhtml11.dtd">
<html xmlns="http://www.w3.org/1999/xhtml" >
<head id="Head1" runat="server">
    <title>TreeView XML</title>
</head>
<body>
    <form id="form1" runat="server">
    <div>

    <asp:TreeView
        id="TreeView1"
        DataSourceID="srcMovies"
        Runat="server" />

     <asp:XmlDataSource
        id="srcMovies"
        DataFile="~/Movies.xml"
        Runat="server" />

    </div>
    </form>
</body>
</html>
```

The `Movies.xml` document in Listing 22.22 is extremely simple. The elements do not include any attributes. You can display more complicated XML documents with the `TreeView` control by declaring one or more `TreeNodeBinding` elements.

For example, the nodes in the XML document in Listing 22.24 include `id` and `text` attributes.

LISTING 22.24   MoviesComplex.xml

```
<?xml version="1.0" encoding="utf-8" ?>
<movies>
  <category id="category1" text="Action">
    <movie id="movie1" text="Star Wars" />
    <movie id="movie2" text="Independence Day" />
  </category>
```

```
  <category id="category2" text="Horror">
    <movie id="movie3" text="Jaws" />
    <movie id="movie4" text="Nightmare Before Christmas" />
  </category>
</movies>
```

The page in Listing 22.25 displays the contents of the XML document in Listing 22.24.

LISTING 22.25   TreeViewXMLComplex.aspx

```
<%@ Page Language="C#" %>
<!DOCTYPE html PUBLIC "-//W3C//DTD XHTML 1.1//EN"
  "http://www.w3.org/TR/xhtml11/DTD/xhtml11.dtd">
<html xmlns="http://www.w3.org/1999/xhtml" >
<head id="Head1" runat="server">
    <title>TreeView XML Complex</title>
</head>
<body>
    <form id="form1" runat="server">
    <div>

    <asp:TreeView
        id="TreeView1"
        DataSourceID="srcMovies"
        Runat="server">
        <DataBindings>
        <asp:TreeNodeBinding
            DataMember="category"
            TextField="text"
            ValueField="id" />
        <asp:TreeNodeBinding
            DataMember="movie"
            TextField="text"
            ValueField="id" />
        </DataBindings>
    </asp:TreeView>

    <asp:XmlDataSource
        id="srcMovies"
        DataFile="~/MoviesComplex.xml"
        Runat="server" />

    </div>
    </form>
</body>
</html>
```

The TreeView in Listing 22.25 includes a DataBindings subtag. This tag includes two TreeNodeBinding elements. The first TreeNodeBinding specifies the relationship between <category> nodes in the XML document and TreeView nodes. The second TreeNodeBinding specifies the relationship between <movie> nodes and TreeView nodes.

Binding to Database Data

You cannot bind a TreeView control directly to a SqlDataSource or ObjectDataSource control because neither of these two controls exposes hierarchical data. If you want to display database data with the TreeView control, you have a choice: create a custom SqlHierarchicalDataSource control or programmatically bind the TreeView to the database data.

The hard option is to build a SQL hierarchical DataSource control. You can do this by deriving a new control from the base HierarchicalDataSourceControl class or by implementing the IHierarchicalDataSource interface. We explore this option in the final section.

The second option is to build the TreeView control programmatically from a set of database records. This is the approach that we follow in this section.

Imagine that you have a database table that looks like this:

MessageId	ParentId	Subject
1	null	How do you use the Menu control?
2	null	What is the TreeView control?
3	1	RE:How do you use the Menu control?
4	1	RE:How do you use the Menu control?
5	2	RE:What is the TreeView control?
6	5	RE:RE:What is the TreeView control?

This database table represents a discussion forum. The relationship between the messages is determined by the ParentId column. The messages that have a null ParentID represent the threads, and the other messages represent replies to the threads.

The page in Listing 22.26 uses a TreeView control to display the contents of the Discuss database table (see Figure 22.19).

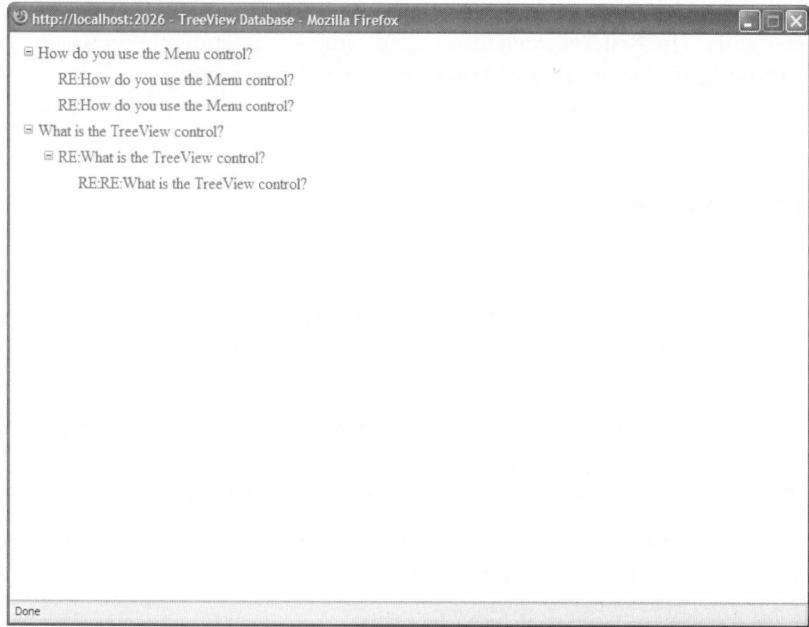

FIGURE 22.19   Displaying database data with a `TreeView` control.

LISTING 22.26   `TreeViewDatabase.aspx`

```
<%@ Page Language="C#" %>
<%@ Import Namespace="System.Web.Configuration" %>
<%@ Import Namespace="System.Data" %>
<%@ Import Namespace="System.Data.SqlClient" %>
<!DOCTYPE html PUBLIC "-//W3C//DTD XHTML 1.1//EN"
"http://www.w3.org/TR/xhtml11/DTD/xhtml11.dtd">
<script runat="server">

    /// <summary>
    /// Only populate the TreeView when the page first loads
    /// </summary>
    void Page_Load()
    {
        if (!Page.IsPostBack)
            PopulateTreeView();
    }

    /// <summary>
    /// Get the data from the database and create the top-level
    /// TreeView items
    /// </summary>
```

```
    private void PopulateTreeView()
    {
        DataTable treeViewData = GetTreeViewData();
        AddTopTreeViewNodes(treeViewData);
    }


    /// <summary>
    /// Use a DataAdapter and DataTable to grab the database data
    /// </summary>
    /// <returns></returns>
    private DataTable GetTreeViewData()
    {
        // Get Discuss table
        string selectCommand = "SELECT MessageId,ParentId,Subject FROM Discuss";
        string conString =
WebConfigurationManager.ConnectionStrings["Discuss"].ConnectionString;
        SqlDataAdapter dad = new SqlDataAdapter(selectCommand, conString);
        DataTable dtblDiscuss = new DataTable();
        dad.Fill(dtblDiscuss);
        return dtblDiscuss;
    }


    /// <summary>
    /// Filter the data to get only the rows that have a
    /// null ParentID (these are the top-level TreeView items)
    /// </summary>
    private void AddTopTreeViewNodes(DataTable treeViewData)
    {
        DataView view = new DataView(treeViewData);
        view.RowFilter = "ParentID IS NULL";
        foreach (DataRowView row in view)
        {
            TreeNode newNode = new TreeNode(row["Subject"].ToString(),
row["MessageId"].ToString());
            TreeView1.Nodes.Add(newNode);
            AddChildTreeViewNodes(treeViewData, newNode);
        }

    }

    /// <summary>
    /// Recursively add child TreeView items by filtering by ParentID
    /// </summary>
    private void AddChildTreeViewNodes(DataTable treeViewData,
TreeNode parentTreeViewNode)
    {
```

```
        DataView view = new DataView(treeViewData);
        view.RowFilter = "ParentID=" + parentTreeViewNode.Value;
        foreach (DataRowView row in view)
        {
            TreeNode newNode = new TreeNode(row["Subject"].ToString(),
row["MessageId"].ToString());
            parentTreeViewNode.ChildNodes.Add(newNode);
            AddChildTreeViewNodes(treeViewData, newNode);
        }
    }

</script>
<html xmlns="http://www.w3.org/1999/xhtml" >
<head id="Head1" runat="server">
    <style type="text/css">
    </style>
    <title>TreeView Database</title>
</head>
<body>
    <form id="form1" runat="server">
    <div>

    <asp:TreeView
        id="TreeView1"
        Runat="server" />

    </div>
    </form>
</body>
</html>
```

The page in Listing 22.26 filters the contents of the Discuss database table by its ParentID column. First, the top-level nodes are added to the TreeView. Next, the child nodes are recursively added to the TreeView with the help of the AddChildTreeViewNodes() method.

Using Populate On Demand and AJAX

You can use the TreeView control even when working with a large set of data. For example, the Microsoft MSDN website (msdn.Microsoft.com) has links to thousands of articles. This website uses a tree view to display the nested links to the articles.

Because thousands of articles are hosted at the MSDN website, not all the tree nodes are downloaded to the browser when you open a page. Instead, additional nodes are downloaded to your browser only when you expand a particular node.

You can use a feature named Populate On Demand with the TreeView control. When you enable the PopulateOnDemand property for a Tree node, child nodes are not added to the parent node until the parent node is expanded.

For example, the page in Listing 22.27 contains an infinitely expanding TreeView. Each time you expand a Tree node, five new child nodes display. Each time you expand a child node, five more child nodes display, and so on (see Figure 22.20).

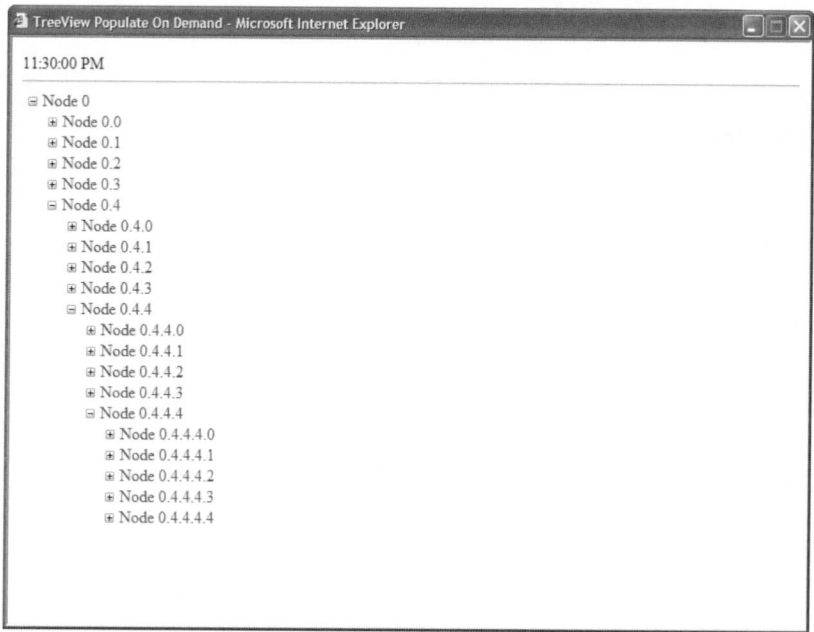

FIGURE 22.20 An infinitely expanding TreeView control.

LISTING 22.27 TreeViewPopulateOnDemand.aspx

```
<%@ Page Language="C#" %>
<!DOCTYPE html PUBLIC "-//W3C//DTD XHTML 1.1//EN"
"http://www.w3.org/TR/xhtml11/DTD/xhtml11.dtd">
<script runat="server">

    void TreeView1_TreeNodePopulate(object s, TreeNodeEventArgs e)
    {
        for (int i=0;i<5;i++)
        {
            TreeNode newNode = new TreeNode();
            newNode.Text = String.Format("{0}.{1}", e.Node.Text, i);
            newNode.PopulateOnDemand = true;
            e.Node.ChildNodes.Add(newNode);
        }
```

```
        }

</script>
<html xmlns="http://www.w3.org/1999/xhtml" >
<head id="Head1" runat="server">
    <title>TreeView Populate On Demand</title>
</head>
<body>
    <form id="form1" runat="server">
    <div>

    <%=DateTime.Now.ToString("T") %>

    <hr />

    <asp:TreeView
        ID="TreeView1"
        ExpandDepth="0"
        OnTreeNodePopulate="TreeView1_TreeNodePopulate"
        Runat="server">
        <Nodes>
        <asp:TreeNode
            PopulateOnDemand="true"
            Text="Node 0" />
        </Nodes>
    </asp:TreeView>

    </div>
    </form>
</body>
</html>
```

The TreeView in Listing 22.27 includes a single statically declared TreeNode. This TreeNode includes a PopulateOnDemand property set to the value True.

Additionally, the TreeView control itself includes a TreeNodePopulate event handler. When you expand a TreeNode that has its PopulateOnDemand property enabled, the TreeNodePopulate event handler executes. In the case of Listing 22.27, the event handler adds five new TreeNodes to the TreeNode that was expanded.

When you use the Populate On Demand feature, the page containing the TreeView is not posted back to the server when you expand a TreeNode. Instead, the browser uses AJAX (Asynchronous JavaScript and XML) to communicate with the web server. The additional TreeNodes are retrieved from the server, without performing a postback.

The page in Listing 22.27 displays the current time when you open the page. The time is not updated when you expand a particular TreeNode. The time is not updated because the

only content in the page that is updated when you expand a node is the `TreeView`
content. AJAX can have a dramatic impact on performance because it does not require the
entire page to be re-rendered each time you expand a `TreeNode`.

> **NOTE**
>
> If, for some reason, you don't want to use AJAX with Populate On Demand, you can
> assign the value `False` to the `TreeView` control's `PopulateNodesFromClient` property.

The page in Listing 22.28 contains a more realistic sample of using Populate On Demand
and AJAX. This page uses a `TreeView` control to display the contents of the Discuss database table (see Figure 22.21).

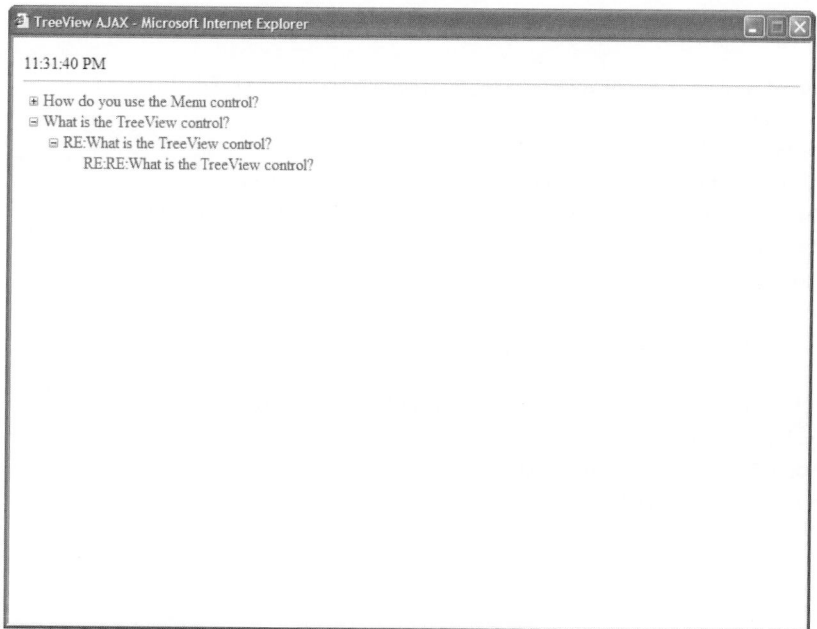

FIGURE 22.21   Displaying database data with AJAX.

LISTING 22.28   `TreeViewAJAX.aspx`

```
<%@ Page Language="C#" %>
<%@ Import Namespace="System.Web.Configuration" %>
<%@ Import Namespace="System.Data" %>
<%@ Import Namespace="System.Data.SqlClient" %>
<!DOCTYPE html PUBLIC "-//W3C//DTD XHTML 1.1//EN"
"http://www.w3.org/TR/xhtml11/DTD/xhtml11.dtd">
<script runat="server">
```

```csharp
/// <summary>
/// Only populate the TreeView when the page first loads
/// </summary>
void Page_Load()
{
    if (!Page.IsPostBack)
        PopulateTopNodes();
}



/// <summary>
/// Get the top level nodes (nodes with a null ParentId)
/// </summary>
private void PopulateTopNodes()
{
    string selectCommand = "SELECT MessageId,ParentId,Subject FROM Discuss
 WHERE ParentId IS NULL";
    string conString =
WebConfigurationManager.ConnectionStrings["Discuss"].ConnectionString;
    SqlDataAdapter dad = new SqlDataAdapter(selectCommand, conString);
    DataTable dtblMessages = new DataTable();
    dad.Fill(dtblMessages);

    foreach (DataRow row in dtblMessages.Rows)
    {
        TreeNode newNode = new TreeNode(row["Subject"].ToString(),
row["MessageId"].ToString());
        newNode.PopulateOnDemand = true;
        TreeView1.Nodes.Add(newNode);
    }
}


/// <summary>
/// Get the child nodes of the expanded node
/// </summary>
protected void TreeView1_TreeNodePopulate(object sender, TreeNodeEventArgs e)
{
    string selectCommand = "SELECT MessageId,ParentId,Subject FROM Discuss
WHERE ParentId=@ParentId";
    string conString =
WebConfigurationManager.ConnectionStrings["Discuss"].ConnectionString;
    SqlDataAdapter dad = new SqlDataAdapter(selectCommand, conString);
    dad.SelectCommand.Parameters.AddWithValue("@ParentId", e.Node.Value);
    DataTable dtblMessages = new DataTable();
    dad.Fill(dtblMessages);
```

```
        foreach (DataRow row in dtblMessages.Rows)
        {
            TreeNode newNode = new TreeNode(row["Subject"].ToString(),
row["MessageId"].ToString());
            newNode.PopulateOnDemand = true;
            e.Node.ChildNodes.Add(newNode);
        }
    }
}

</script>
<html xmlns="http://www.w3.org/1999/xhtml" >
<head id="Head1" runat="server">
    <style type="text/css">
    </style>
    <title>TreeView AJAX</title>
</head>
<body>
    <form id="form1" runat="server">
    <div>

    <%= DateTime.Now.ToString("T") %>

    <hr />

    <asp:TreeView
        id="TreeView1"
        ExpandDepth="0"
        OnTreeNodePopulate="TreeView1_TreeNodePopulate"
        Runat="server" />

    </div>
    </form>
</body>
</html>
```

When the page in Listing 22.28 first opens, only the first-level message subjects display. These messages are retrieved by the `PopulateTopNodes()` method.

When you expand a thread, the matching replies are retrieved for the thread. These replies are retrieved in the `TreeView1_TreeNodePopulate()` event handler.

The `TreeView` in Listing 22.28 performs well even when working with a large set of data. At any time, only the child messages of a message are retrieved from the database. At no time are all the messages retrieved from the database.

When the page is used with a modern browser, AJAX retrieves the messages from the web server. The page does not need to be posted back to the web server when you expand a particular message thread.

Formatting the `TreeView` Control

The `TreeView` control supports an abundance of properties that have an effect on how the `TreeView` is formatted.

Following are some of the more useful properties of a `TreeView` control, which modify its appearance (this is not a complete list):

▶ **CollapseImageToolTip**—Enables you to specify the title attribute for the collapse image.

▶ **CollapseImageUrl**—Enables you to specify a URL to an image for the collapse image.

▶ **ExpandDepth**—Enables you to specify the number of `TreeNode` levels to display initially.

▶ **ExpandImageToolTip**—Enables you to specify the title attribute for the expand image.

▶ **ExpandImageUrl**—Enables you to specify the URL to an image for the expand image.

▶ **ImageSet**—Enables you to specify a set of images to use with the `TreeView` control.

▶ **LineImagesFolder**—Enables you to specify a folder that contains line images.

▶ **MaxDataBindDepth**—Enables you to specify the maximum levels of `TreeView` levels to display when binding to a data source.

▶ **NodeIndent**—Enables you to specify the number of pixels to indent a child Tree node.

▶ **NodeWrap**—Enables you to specify whether or not text is wrapped in a Tree node.

▶ **NoExpandImageUrl**—Enables you to specify the URL to an image for the `NoExpand` image (typically, an invisible spacer image).

▶ **ShowCheckBoxes**—Enables you to display check boxes next to each Tree node. Possible values are `All`, `Leaf`, `None`, `Parent`, and `Root`.

▶ **ShowExpandCollapse**—Enables you to disable the expand and collapse icons that appear next to each expandable node.

▶ **ShowLines**—Enables you to show connecting lines between Tree nodes.

▶ **SkipLinkText**—Enables you to specify the text used for skipping the contents of the `TreeView` control. (The Skip Link contains hidden text that is accessible only to users of assistive devices.)

▶ **Target**—Enables you to specify the name of the window that opens when you navigate to a URL with the `TreeView` control.

The two most interesting properties in this list are the `ImageSet` and the `ShowLines` properties. You can set the `ImageSet` property to any of the following values to modify the images displayed by the `TreeView` control:

▶ Arrows

▶ BulletedList

▶ BulletedList2

▶ BulletedList3

▶ BulletedList4

▶ Contacts

▶ Custom

▶ Events

▶ Faq

▶ Inbox

▶ Msdn

▶ News

▶ Simple

▶ Simple2

▶ WindowsHelp

▶ XPFileExplorer

The `ShowLines` property causes connecting line images to be rendered between `TreeView` nodes. Displaying lines between Tree nodes can make it easier to visually discern the nested relationships between nodes. If you want to create custom lines, you can specify a value for the `LinesImagesFolder` property.

VISUAL WEB DEVELOPER NOTE

Visual Web Developer includes a `TreeView` Line Image Generator that enables you to create custom connecting lines. You can open this tool in Design view by selecting the `TreeView` control and opening the Tasks dialog box and selecting Customize Line Images.

The page in Listing 22.29 illustrates how to use both the `ImageSet` and `ShowLines` properties (see Figure 22.22).

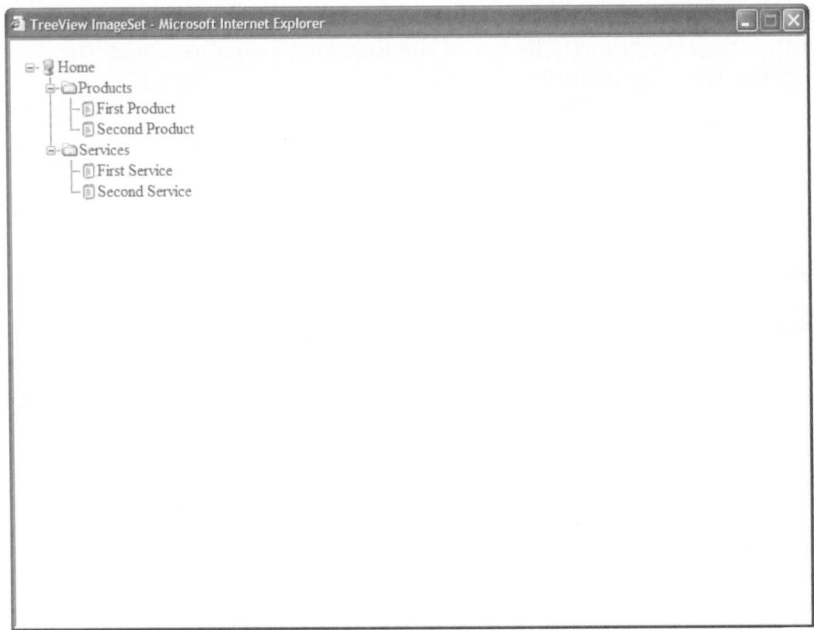

FIGURE 22.22   Formatting a `TreeView` with an image set and lines.

LISTING 22.29   TreeViewImageSet.aspx

```
<%@ Page Language="C#" %>
<!DOCTYPE html PUBLIC "-//W3C//DTD XHTML 1.1//EN"
    "http://www.w3.org/TR/xhtml11/DTD/xhtml11.dtd">
<html xmlns="http://www.w3.org/1999/xhtml" >
<head id="Head1" runat="server">
    <title>TreeView ImageSet</title>
</head>
<body>
    <form id="form1" runat="server">
    <div>

    <asp:TreeView
        id="TreeView1"
        ImageSet="XPFileExplorer"
        ShowLines="true"
        Runat="server">
        <Nodes>
        <asp:TreeNode
            Text="Home">
            <asp:TreeNode Text="Products">
                <asp:TreeNode Text="First Product" />
```

```
                <asp:TreeNode Text="Second Product" />
            </asp:TreeNode>
            <asp:TreeNode Text="Services">
                <asp:TreeNode Text="First Service" />
                <asp:TreeNode Text="Second Service" />
            </asp:TreeNode>
        </asp:TreeNode>
        </Nodes>
    </asp:TreeView>


    </div>
    </form>
</body>
</html>
```

The `TreeNode` object itself also supports several properties that have an effect on the appearance of its containing `TreeView`. Following is a list of the most useful properties of the `TreeNode` object:

▶ **Checked**—Enables you to check the check box that appears next to the Tree node.

▶ **Expanded**—Enables you to initially expand a node.

▶ **ImageToolTip**—Enables you to associate alt text with a Tree node image.

▶ **ImageUrl**—Enables you to specify an image that appears next to a Tree node.

▶ **NavigateUrl**—Enables you to specify the URL to which the current Tree node links.

▶ **SelectAction**—Enables you to specify the action that occurs when you click a Tree node. Possible values are `Expand`, `None`, `Select`, or `SelectExpand`.

▶ **Selected**—Enables you to specify whether the current Tree node is selected.

▶ **ShowCheckBox**—Enables you to display a check box for the current Tree node.

▶ **Target**—Enables you to specify the name of the window that opens when you navigate to a URL.

▶ **ToolTip**—Enables you to specify a title attribute for the current Tree node.

You can style the `TreeView` control by attaching Cascading Style Sheet classes to the `Style` object exposed by the `TreeView` control. The `TreeView` control supports the following `Style` objects:

▶ **HoverNodeStyle**—Applied to a Tree node when you hover your mouse over a node.

▶ **LeafNodeStyle**—Applied to leaf Tree nodes (Tree nodes without child nodes).

▶ **NodeStyle**—Applied to Tree nodes by default.

▶ **ParentNodeStyle**—Applied to parent nodes (Tree nodes with child nodes).

▶ **RootNodeStyle**—Applied to root nodes (Tree nodes with no parent nodes).

▶ **SelectedNodeStyle**—Applied to the selected node.

For example, the page in Listing 22.30 uses several of these Style objects to format a TreeView control (see Figure 22.23).

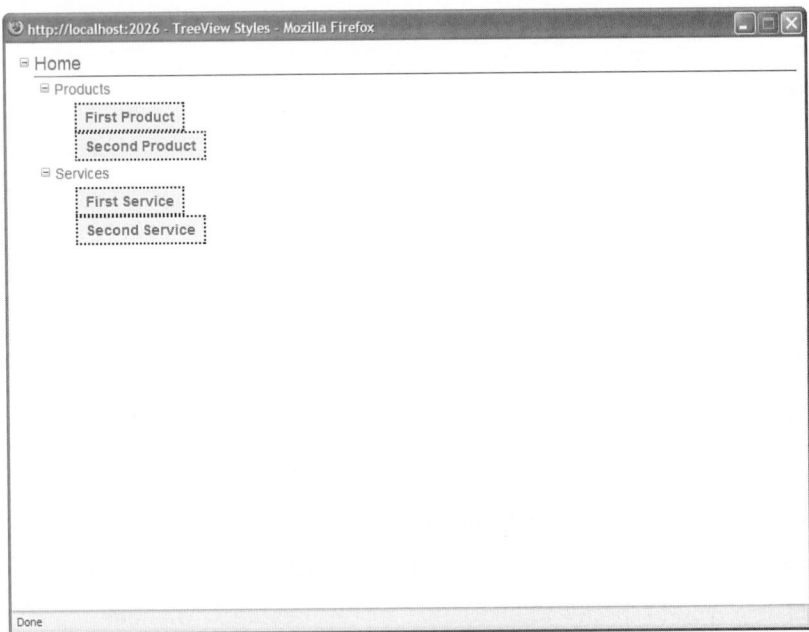

FIGURE 22.23   Using Styles with the TreeView control.

LISTING 22.30   TreeViewStyles.aspx

```
<%@ Page Language="C#" %>
<!DOCTYPE html PUBLIC "-//W3C//DTD XHTML 1.1//EN"
 "http://www.w3.org/TR/xhtml11/DTD/xhtml11.dtd">
<html xmlns="http://www.w3.org/1999/xhtml" >
<head id="Head1" runat="server">
    <style type="text/css">
        .treeNode
        {
            color:blue;
            font:14px Arial, Sans-Serif;
        }
        .rootNode
        {
            font-size:18px;
            width:100%;
            border-bottom:Solid 1px black;
```

```
        }
        .leafNode
        {
            border:Dotted 2px black;
            padding:4px;
            background-color:#eeeeee;
            font-weight:bold;
        }
    </style>
    <title>TreeView Styles</title>
</head>
<body>
    <form id="form1" runat="server">
    <div>

    <asp:TreeView
        id="TreeView1"
        NodeStyle-CssClass="treeNode"
        RootNodeStyle-CssClass="rootNode"
        LeafNodeStyle-CssClass="leafNode"
        Runat="server">
        <Nodes>
        <asp:TreeNode
            Text="Home">
            <asp:TreeNode Text="Products">
                <asp:TreeNode Text="First Product" />
                <asp:TreeNode Text="Second Product" />
            </asp:TreeNode>
            <asp:TreeNode Text="Services">
                <asp:TreeNode Text="First Service" />
                <asp:TreeNode Text="Second Service" />
            </asp:TreeNode>
        </asp:TreeNode>
        </Nodes>
    </asp:TreeView>

    </div>
    </form>
</body>
</html>
```

Furthermore, you can apply styles to particular Tree node levels by taking advantage of the TreeView control's LevelStyles property. The page in Listing 22.31 uses the LevelStyles property to format first level nodes differently than second level nodes and third level nodes (see Figure 22.24).

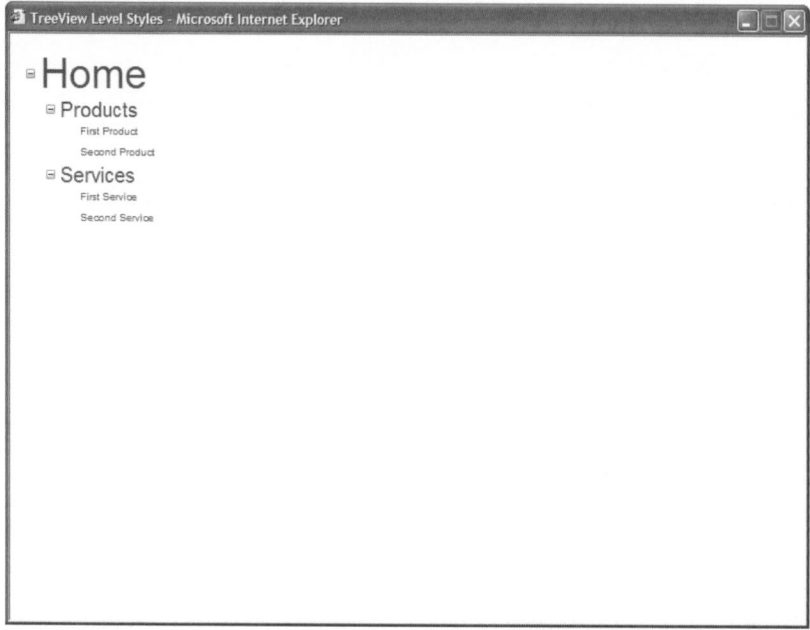

FIGURE 22.24   Applying styles to different TreeView node levels.

LISTING 22.31   TreeViewLevelStyles.aspx

```
<%@ Page Language="C#" %>
<!DOCTYPE html PUBLIC "-//W3C//DTD XHTML 1.1//EN"
    "http://www.w3.org/TR/xhtml11/DTD/xhtml11.dtd">
<html xmlns="http://www.w3.org/1999/xhtml" >
<head id="Head1" runat="server">
    <style type="text/css">
        .nodeLevel1
        {
            font:40px Arial,Sans-Serif;
        }
        .nodeLevel2
        {
            font:20px Arial,Sans-Serif;
        }
        .nodeLevel3
        {
            font:10px Arial,Sans-Serif;
        }
    </style>
    <title>TreeView Level Styles</title>
</head>
<body>
```

```
<form id="form1" runat="server">
<div>

<asp:TreeView
    id="TreeView1"
    Runat="server">
    <LevelStyles>
    <asp:TreeNodeStyle CssClass="nodeLevel1" />
    <asp:TreeNodeStyle CssClass="nodeLevel2" />
    <asp:TreeNodeStyle CssClass="nodeLevel3" />
    </LevelStyles>
    <Nodes>
    <asp:TreeNode
        Text="Home">
        <asp:TreeNode Text="Products">
            <asp:TreeNode Text="First Product" />
            <asp:TreeNode Text="Second Product" />
        </asp:TreeNode>
        <asp:TreeNode Text="Services">
            <asp:TreeNode Text="First Service" />
            <asp:TreeNode Text="Second Service" />
        </asp:TreeNode>
    </asp:TreeNode>
    </Nodes>
</asp:TreeView>

</div>
</form>
</body>
</html>
```

Building a SQL Hierarchical Data Source Control

In this final section of this chapter, we build a SqlHierarchicalDataSource control. This custom control enables you to declaratively and (thus) easily bind controls such as the Menu and TreeView controls to data retrieved from a database.

NOTE

The code samples in this section can be found in the SqlHierarchicalDataSourceVB and SqlHierarchicalDataSourceCS applications in the accompanying source code on the book's website.

The page in Listing 22.32 illustrates how you can use the SqlHierarchicalDataSource control to bind a Menu control to a database table that contains nested categories.

LISTING 22.32   ShowMenu.aspx

```
<%@ Page Language="C#" %>
<%@ Register TagPrefix="custom" Namespace="AspNetUnleashed" %>
<!DOCTYPE html PUBLIC "-//W3C//DTD XHTML 1.1//EN"
"http://www.w3.org/TR/xhtml11/DTD/xhtml11.dtd">
<script runat="server">

    protected void Menu1_MenuItemClick(object sender, MenuEventArgs e)
    {
        lblSelected.Text = Menu1.SelectedValue;
    }
</script>
<html xmlns="http://www.w3.org/1999/xhtml" >
<head id="Head1" runat="server">
    <style type="text/css">
        .menu
        {
            border:solid 1px black;
            padding:4px;
        }
    </style>
    <title>Show Menu</title>
</head>
<body>
    <form id="form1" runat="server">
    <div>

    <asp:Menu
        id="Menu1"
        DataSourceId="srcCategories"
        OnMenuItemClick="Menu1_MenuItemClick"
        Orientation="Horizontal"
        DynamicMenuStyle-CssClass="menu"
        Runat="server">
        <DataBindings>
            <asp:MenuItemBinding TextField="Name" ValueField="Name" />
        </DataBindings>
    </asp:Menu>

    <custom:SqlHierarchicalDataSource
        id="srcCategories"
        ConnectionString='<%$ ConnectionStrings:Categories %>'
```

```
            DataKeyName="CategoryId"
            DataParentKeyName="ParentId"
            SelectCommand="SELECT CategoryId, ParentId, Name FROM Categories"
            Runat="server" />

        <hr />

        <asp:Label
            id="lblSelected"
            Runat="server" />

    </div>
    </form>
</body>
</html>
```

When you open the page in Listing 22.32, all the rows from the Categories table display in the Menu control.

The SqlHierarchicalDataSource control includes two properties: DataKeyName and DataParentKeyName. The DataKeyName property represents the name of a database column that contains a unique value for each database table row. The DataParentKeyName column represents the name of a database column that relates each row to its parent row.

Furthermore, the Menu control includes a MenuItemBinding, which associates the database Name column with the Menu item Text property and the Name column with the Menu item Value property.

You also can use the SqlHierarchicalDataSource control when working with the TreeView control. The page in Listing 22.33 displays all the rows from the Discuss database table in a TreeView control.

LISTING 22.33   ShowTreeView.aspx

```
<%@ Page Language="C#" %>
<%@ Register TagPrefix="custom" Namespace="AspNetUnleashed" %>
<!DOCTYPE html PUBLIC "-//W3C//DTD XHTML 1.1//EN"
"http://www.w3.org/TR/xhtml11/DTD/xhtml11.dtd">
<script runat="server">

    protected void TreeView1_SelectedNodeChanged(object sender, EventArgs e)
    {
        lblSelected.Text = TreeView1.SelectedValue;
    }
</script>
<html xmlns="http://www.w3.org/1999/xhtml" >
<head id="Head1" runat="server">
```

```
    <title>Show TreeView</title>
</head>
<body>
    <form id="form1" runat="server">
    <div>

    <asp:TreeView
        id="TreeView1"
        DataSourceID="srcDiscuss"
        OnSelectedNodeChanged="TreeView1_SelectedNodeChanged"
        ImageSet="News"
        Runat="server">
        <DataBindings>
            <asp:TreeNodeBinding
                TextField="Subject"
                ValueField="MessageId" />
        </DataBindings>
    </asp:TreeView>

    <custom:SqlHierarchicalDataSource
        id="srcDiscuss"
        ConnectionString='<%$ ConnectionStrings:Discuss %>'
        DataKeyName="MessageId"
        DataParentKeyName="ParentId"
        SelectCommand="SELECT MessageId,ParentId,Subject FROM Discuss"
        Runat="server" />

    <hr />

    You selected message number:
    <asp:Label
        id="lblSelected"
        Runat="server" />

    </div>
    </form>
</body>
</html>
```

When you open the page in Listing 22.33, the contents of the Discuss database table display in the TreeView control.

All the code for the SqlHierarchicalDataSource control is included on the book's website. The control is composed out of five separate classes:

▶ **SqlHierarchicalDataSource**—Represents the actual control. It inherits from the base SqlDataSource control and implements the IHierarchicalDataSource interface.

▶ **SqlHierarchicalDataSourceView**—Represents the hierarchical data returned by the control. It inherits from the base HierarchicalDataSourceView class.

▶ **SqlHierarchicalEnumerable**—Represents a collection of SqlNodes.

▶ **SqlNode**—Represents a particular database row from the data source. It includes methods for retrieving child and parent rows.

▶ **SqlNodePropertyDescriptor**—Inherits from the base PropertyDescriptor class. It converts the database columns represented by a SqlNode into class properties so that you can bind to the columns using TreeView and Menu control DataBindings.

Summary

In this chapter, you learned how to use the SiteMapPath, Menu, and TreeView controls. First, you learned how to use the SiteMapPath control to display a breadcrumb trail. You learned how to format the SiteMapPath control with styles and templates.

Next, you explored the Menu control. You learned how to create both vertical and horizontal menus. You also learned how you can bind a Menu control to different data sources such as Site Maps, XML documents, and database data.

The TreeView control was also discussed. You learned how to display check boxes with a TreeView control. You also learned how to bind a TreeView control to different data sources such as Site Maps, XML documents, and database data. You learned how to display a large set of Tree nodes efficiently by using AJAX and the TreeView control.

Finally, we created a custom SqlHierarchicalDataSource control that enables you to easily bind controls such as the Menu and TreeView controls to hierarchical database data.

Using Site Maps

This chapter jumps into the details of Site Maps. First, you learn how to use the SiteMapDataSource control to represent a Site Map on a page. For example, you learn how to use the SiteMapDataSource control to display a list of all the pages contained in a folder.

Next, you explore the SiteMap and SiteMapNode classes. You learn how to create new Site Map nodes dynamically. You also learn how to programmatically retrieve Site Map nodes and display the properties of a node in a page.

This chapter also examines several advanced features of Site Maps. For example, you learn how to show different Site Maps to different users depending on their roles. You also learn how you can extend Site Maps with custom attributes.

You also learn how to create custom Site Map providers. The first custom Site Map provider—the AutoSiteMapProvider—automatically builds a Site Map based on the folder and page structure of your website. The second custom Site Map provider—the SqlSiteMapProvider—enables you to store a Site Map in a Microsoft SQL Server database table.

Finally, you learn how to generate Google SiteMaps from ASP.NET Site Maps automatically. You can use a Google SiteMap to improve the way that your website is indexed by the Google search engine.

Using the `SiteMapDataSource` Control

The `SiteMapDataSource` control enables you to represent a Site Map declaratively in a page. You can bind navigation controls such as the `TreeView` and `Menu` controls to a `SiteMapDataSource` control. You also can bind other controls such as the `GridView` or `DropDownList` control to a `SiteMapDataSource` control.

Imagine, for example, that your website contains the `Web.sitemap` file in Listing 23.1. Because the default `SiteMapProvider` is the `XmlSiteMapProvider`, the `SiteMapDataSource` control automatically represents the contents of this XML file.

> **NOTE**
>
> The code samples in this section are located in the `SiteMaps` application on the website for this book.

LISTING 23.1   `Web.sitemap`

```
<?xml version="1.0" encoding="utf-8" ?>
<siteMap xmlns="http://schemas.microsoft.com/AspNet/SiteMap-File-1.0" >
<siteMapNode
  url="Default.aspx"
  title="Home"
  description="The Home Page">
  <siteMapNode
    url="Products/Default.aspx"
    title="Our Products"
    description="Products that we offer">
    <siteMapNode
      url="Products/FirstProduct.aspx"
      title="First Product"
      description="The description of the First Product" />
    <siteMapNode
      url="Products/SecondProduct.aspx"
      title="Second Product"
      description="The description of the Second Product" />
  </siteMapNode>
  <siteMapNode
    url="Services/Default.aspx"
    title="Our Services"
    description="Services that we offer">
    <siteMapNode
      url="Services/FirstService.aspx"
      title="First Service"
      description="The description of the First Service"
```

```
      metaDescription="The first service" />
    <siteMapNode
      url="Services/SecondService.aspx"
      title="Second Service"
      description="The description of the Second Service" />
  </siteMapNode>
</siteMapNode>
</siteMap>
```

The Site Map file in Listing 23.1 represents a website with the following folder and page structure:

```
Default.aspx
Products
    FirstProduct.aspx
    SecondProduct.aspx
Services
    FirstService.aspx
    SecondService.aspx
```

The page in Listing 23.2 illustrates how you can represent a Site Map by binding a TreeView control to the SiteMapDataSource control.

LISTING 23.2   Default.aspx

```
<%@ Page Language="C#" %>
<!DOCTYPE html PUBLIC "-//W3C//DTD XHTML 1.1//EN" "http://www.w3.org/TR/
xhtml11/DTD/xhtml11.dtd">
<html xmlns="http://www.w3.org/1999/xhtml" >
<head id="Head1" runat="server">
    <title>Home</title>
</head>
<body>
    <form id="form1" runat="server">
    <div>

    <asp:SiteMapPath
        id="SiteMapPath1"
        Runat="server" />

    <hr />

    <asp:TreeView
        id="TreeView1"
        DataSourceID="srcSiteMap"
        Runat="server" />
```

```
    <asp:SiteMapDataSource
        id="srcSiteMap"
        Runat="server" />

    </div>
    </form>
</body>
</html>
```

When you open the page in Listing 23.2, all the elements from the `Web.sitemap` file display in the `TreeView` control with the help of the `SiteMapDataSource` control (see Figure 23.1).

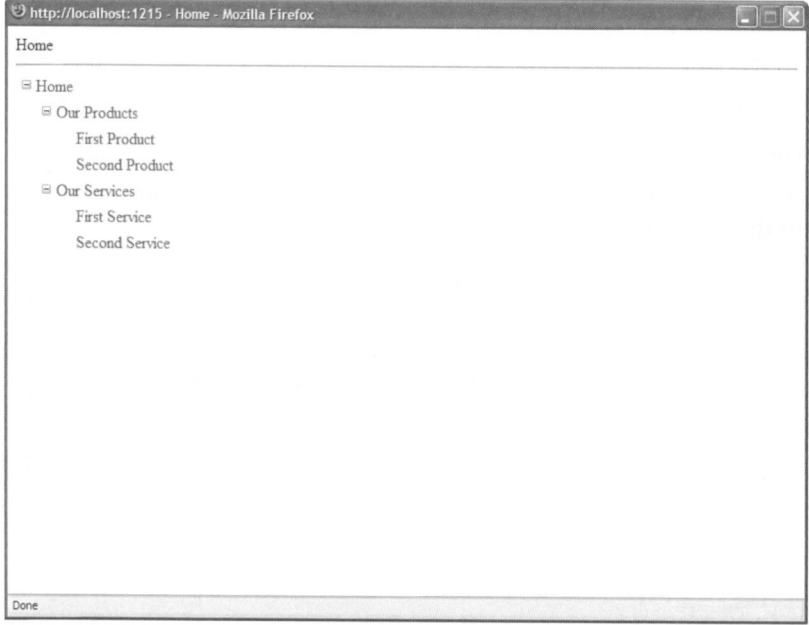

FIGURE 23.1   Displaying a Site Map with a `TreeView` control.

Setting `SiteMapDataSource` Properties

The `SiteMapDataSource` control includes several valuable properties that you can set to modify the nodes that the control returns:

▶ **ShowStartingNode**—Enables you to hide the starting node.

▶ **StartFromCurrentNode**—Enables you to return all nodes starting from the current node.

▶ **StartingNodeOffset**—Enables you to specify a positive or negative offset from the current node.

▶ **StartingNodeUrl**—Enables you to return all nodes, starting at a node associated with a specified URL.

The most useful of these properties is the ShowStartingNode property. Normally, when you display a list of nodes with a Menu or TreeView control, you do not want to display the starting node (the link to the home page). The page in Listing 23.3 illustrates how you can bind a Menu control to a SiteMapDataSource that has the value False assigned to its ShowStartingNode property.

LISTING 23.3   Services/Default.aspx

```
<%@ Page Language="C#" %>
<!DOCTYPE html PUBLIC "-//W3C//DTD XHTML 1.1//EN" "http://www.w3.org/TR/
xhtml11/DTD/xhtml11.dtd">
<html xmlns="http://www.w3.org/1999/xhtml" >
<head id="Head1" runat="server">
    <style type="text/css">
        .menuItem
        {
            border:solid 1px black;
            background-color:#eeeeee;
            padding:4px;
            margin:1px 0px;
        }
    </style>
    <title>Our Services</title>
</head>
<body>
    <form id="form1" runat="server">
    <div>

    <asp:SiteMapPath
        id="SiteMapPath1"
        Runat="server" />

    <hr />

    <asp:Menu
        id="Menu1"
        DataSourceID="srcSiteMap"
        StaticMenuItemStyle-CssClass="menuItem"
        DynamicMenuItemStyle-CssClass="menuItem"
        Runat="server" />
```

```
    <asp:SiteMapDataSource
        id="srcSiteMap"
        ShowStartingNode="false"
        Runat="server" />

    </div>
    </form>
</body>
</html>
```

When you open the page in Listing 23.3, only the second-level nodes and descendent nodes display (see Figure 23.2).

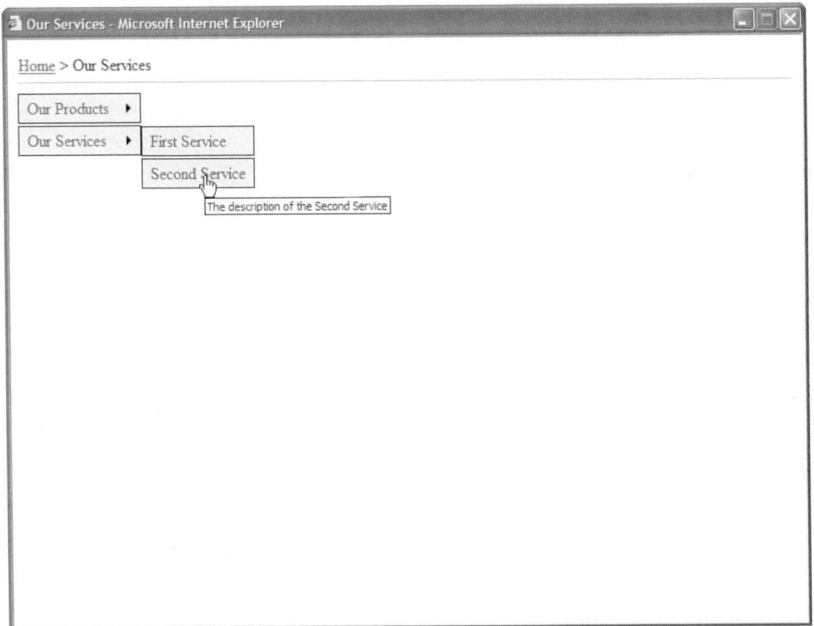

FIGURE 23.2   Hiding the starting node.

The StartFromCurrentNode property is useful when you want to display a list of all nodes below the current node. For example, the page in Listing 23.4 is the Default.aspx page contained in the Products folder. It displays a list of all the product pages contained in the folder.

LISTING 23.4   Products/Default.aspx

```
<%@ Page Language="C#" %>
<!DOCTYPE html PUBLIC "-//W3C//DTD XHTML 1.1//EN" "http://www.w3.org/TR/
xhtml11/DTD/xhtml11.dtd">
<html xmlns="http://www.w3.org/1999/xhtml" >
<head id="Head1" runat="server">
    <style type="text/css">
        html
        {
            font:16px Georgia,Serif;
        }
        .productList li
        {
            margin:5px;
        }
    </style>
    <title>Our Products</title>
</head>
<body>
    <form id="form1" runat="server">
    <div>

    <h1>Products</h1>

    <asp:BulletedList
        id="bltProducts"
        DisplayMode="HyperLink"
        DataTextField="Title"
        DataValueField="Url"
        DataSourceID="srcSiteMap"
        CssClass="productList"
        Runat="server" />

    <asp:SiteMapDataSource
        id="srcSiteMap"
        ShowStartingNode="false"
        StartFromCurrentNode="true"
        Runat="server" />

    </div>
    </form>
</body>
</html>
```

The page in Listing 23.4 contains a BulletedList control bound to a SiteMapDataSource control. Because the SiteMapDataSource control has its StartFromCurrentNode property set to the value True and its ShowStartingNode property set to the value False, all immediate child nodes of the current node display (see Figure 23.3).

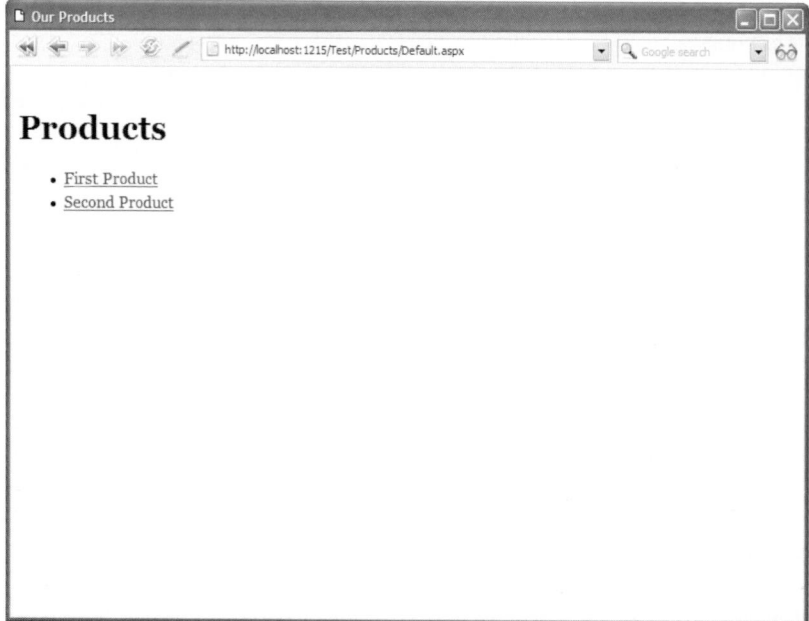

FIGURE 23.3   Displaying the contents of a folder.

Using the SiteMap Class

Under the covers, the SiteMapDataSource control represents the contents of the SiteMap class. The SiteMap class represents an application's Site Map regardless of whether the Site Map is stored in an XML file, a database, or some other data source. The class is a memory-resident representation of Site Map data.

All the properties exposed by the SiteMap class are shared (static) properties:

▶ **CurrentNode**—Enables you to retrieve the SiteMapNode that corresponds to the current page.

▶ **Enabled**—Enables you to determine whether the Site Map is enabled.

▶ **Provider**—Enables you to retrieve the default SiteMapProvider.

▶ **Providers**—Enables you to retrieve all the configured SiteMapProviders.

▶ **RootNode**—Enables you to retrieve the root SiteMapNode.

The `CurrentNode` and `RootNode` properties return a `SiteMapNode` object. Because a Site Map can contain only one root node, and the root node contains all the other nodes as children, the `RootNode` property enables you to iterate through all the nodes in a Site Map.

The `Provider` property returns the default `SiteMapProvider`. You can use this property to access all the properties and methods of the `SiteMapProvider` class, such as the `FindSiteMapNode()` and `GetParentNode()` methods.

The `SiteMap` class also supports a single event:

▶ `SiteMapResolve`—Raised when the current node is accessed.

You can handle this event to modify the node returned when the current node is retrieved. For example, the `Global.asax` file in Listing 23.5 automatically adds a new node when the current page does not include a node in the Site Map.

LISTING 23.5   `Global.asax`

```
<%@ Application Language="C#" %>
<%@ Import Namespace="System.IO" %>
<script runat="server">

    void Application_Start(Object sender, EventArgs e)
    {
        SiteMap.SiteMapResolve += new
➥SiteMapResolveEventHandler(SiteMap_SiteMapResolve);
    }


    SiteMapNode SiteMap_SiteMapResolve(object sender, SiteMapResolveEventArgs e)
    {
        if (SiteMap.CurrentNode == null)
        {
            string url = e.Context.Request.Path;
            string title = Path.GetFileNameWithoutExtension(url);
            SiteMapNode newNode = new SiteMapNode(e.Provider, url, url, title);
            newNode.ParentNode = SiteMap.RootNode;
            return newNode;
        }
        return SiteMap.CurrentNode;
    }
</script>
```

The `Application_Start()` event handler in Listing 23.5 executes only once when the application first starts. The handler adds a `SiteMapResolve` event handler to the `SiteMap` class.

Whenever any control retrieves the current node, the `SiteMap_SiteMapResolve()` method executes. If there is no node that corresponds to a page, the method creates a new node and returns it.

The About.aspx page in Listing 23.6 is not included in the Web.sitemap file; however, this page includes a SiteMapPath control. The SiteMapPath control works correctly because the About.aspx page is dynamically added to the Site Map when you access the page (see Figure 23.4).

FIGURE 23.4   Adding nodes to a Site Map dynamically.

LISTING 23.6   About.aspx

```
<%@ Page Language="C#" %>
<!DOCTYPE html PUBLIC "-//W3C//DTD XHTML 1.1//EN" "http://www.w3.org/TR/
xhtml11/DTD/xhtml11.dtd">
<html xmlns="http://www.w3.org/1999/xhtml" >
<head id="Head1" runat="server">
    <title>About</title>
</head>
<body>
    <form id="form1" runat="server">
    <div>

    <asp:SiteMapPath
        id="SiteMapPath1"
        Runat="server" />
```

```
    <hr />

    <h1>About Our Company</h1>

    </div>
    </form>
</body>
</html>
```

Using the `SiteMapNode` Class

All pages and folders in a Site Map are represented by instances of the `SiteMapNode` class. The `SiteMapNode` class contains the following properties:

▶ **`ChildNodes`**—Returns the child nodes of the current node.

▶ **`Description`**—Returns the description of the current node.

▶ **`HasChildNodes`**—Returns `True` when the current node has child nodes.

▶ **`Item`**—Returns a custom attribute (or resource string).

▶ **`Key`**—Returns a unique identifier for the current node.

▶ **`NextSibling`**—Returns the next sibling of the current node.

▶ **`ParentNode`**—Returns the parent node of the current node.

▶ **`PreviousSibling`**—Returns the previous sibling of the current node.

▶ **`Provider`**—Returns the `SiteMapProvider` associated with the current node.

▶ **`ReadOnly`**—Returns true when a node is read-only.

▶ **`ResourceKey`**—Returns the resource key associated with the current node (enables localization).

▶ **`Roles`**—Returns the user roles associated with the current node.

▶ **`RootNode`**—Returns the Site Map root node.

▶ **`Title`**—Returns the title associated with the current node.

▶ **`Url`**—Returns the URL associated with the current node.

The `SiteMapNode` class also supports the following methods:

▶ **`Clone()`**—Returns a clone of the current node.

▶ **`GetAllNodes()`**—Returns all descendent nodes of the current node.

▶ **`GetDataSourceView()`**—Returns a `SiteMapDataSourceView` object.

▶ **`GetHierarchicalDataSourceView()`**—Returns a `SiteMapHierarchicalDataSourceView`.

▶ **IsAccessibleToUser()**—Returns True when the current user has permissions to view the current node.

▶ **IsDescendantOf()**—Returns True when the current node is a descendant of a particular node.

By taking advantage of the SiteMap and SiteMapNode classes, you can work directly with Site Maps in a page. For example, imagine that you want to display the value of the SiteMapNode title attribute in both the browser's title bar and in the body of the page. Listing 23.7 demonstrates how you can retrieve the value of the Title property associated with the current page programmatically.

LISTING 23.7   Products/FirstProduct.aspx

```
<%@ Page Language="C#" %>
<!DOCTYPE html PUBLIC "-//W3C//DTD XHTML 1.1//EN"
"http://www.w3.org/TR/xhtml11/DTD/xhtml11.dtd">
<script runat="server">
    void Page_Load()
    {
        if (!Page.IsPostBack)
        {
            SiteMapNode currentNode = SiteMap.CurrentNode;
            this.Title = currentNode.Title;
            ltlBodyTitle.Text = currentNode.Title;
            lblDescription.Text = currentNode.Description;
        }
    }

</script>
<html xmlns="http://www.w3.org/1999/xhtml" >
<head id="Head1" runat="server">
    <title>First Product</title>
</head>
<body>
    <form id="form1" runat="server">
    <div>

    <h1><asp:Literal ID="ltlBodyTitle" runat="server" /></h1>

    <asp:Label
        id="lblDescription"
        Runat="server" />
```

```
    </div>
    </form>
</body>
</html>
```

When you open the page in Listing 23.7, the Page_Load() event handler grabs the current SiteMapNode and modifies the Page Title property. The handler also assigns the value of the Title property to a Literal control contained in the body of the page. Finally, the value of the SiteMapNode's Description property is assigned to a Label control (see Figure 23.5).

FIGURE 23.5   Retrieving Site Map node properties.

> **NOTE**
>
> It would make sense to place the code in Listing 23.7 in a Master Page. To learn more about Master Pages, see Chapter 5, "Designing Websites with Master Pages."

Advanced Site Map Configuration

This section explores several advanced features of Site Maps. For example, you learn how to display different SiteMap nodes, depending on the roles associated with the current user. You also learn how to create multiple Site Maps for a single application. Finally, you learn how you can extend Site Maps with custom attributes.

Using Security Trimming

You might want to display different navigation links to different users, depending on their roles. For example, if a user is a member of the Administrators role, you might want to display links to pages for administrating the website. However, you might want to hide these links from other users.

To display different links to different users depending on their roles, you must enable a feature of Site Maps named Security Trimming. This feature is disabled by default. The web configuration file in Listing 23.8 enables Security Trimming.

LISTING 23.8   Web.Config

```
<?xml version="1.0"?>
<configuration>
  <system.web>

    <authentication mode="Windows" />
    <roleManager enabled="true" />

    <siteMap defaultProvider="MySiteMapProvider">
      <providers>
        <add
          name="MySiteMapProvider"
          type="System.Web.XmlSiteMapProvider"
          securityTrimmingEnabled="true"
          siteMapFile="Web.sitemap" />

      </providers>
    </siteMap>

  </system.web>
</configuration>
```

The configuration file in Listing 23.8 includes a <siteMap> element that configures a new SiteMapProvider named MySiteMapProvider. The new provider enables Security Trimming with its securityTrimmingEnabled property.

After you enable Security Trimming, any pages a user is not allowed to view are automatically hidden. For example, imagine that your website includes a folder named Admin that contains the web configuration file in Listing 23.9.

LISTING 23.9   Web.Config

```
<?xml version="1.0"?>
<configuration xmlns="http://schemas.microsoft.com/.NetConfiguration/v2.0">
<system.web>
```

```
    <authorization>
      <allow users="WebAdmin" />
      <deny users="*" />
    </authorization>

  </system.web>
</configuration>
```

The configuration file in Listing 23.9 prevents anyone who is not a member of the WebAdmin role from viewing pages in the same folder (and below) as the configuration file. Even if the Web.sitemap file includes nodes that represent pages in the Admin folder, the links don't appear for anyone except members of the WebAdmin role.

23

Another option is to explicitly associate roles with nodes in a Site Map. This is useful in two situations. First, if your website contains links to another website, you can hide or display these links based on the user role. Second, if you explicitly associate roles with pages, you hide page links even when a user has permission to view a page.

The Web.sitemap file in Listing 23.10 contains links to the Microsoft, Google, and Yahoo websites. A different set of roles is associated with each link.

LISTING 23.10 Web.sitemap

```
<?xml version="1.0" encoding="utf-8" ?>
<siteMap xmlns="http://schemas.microsoft.com/AspNet/SiteMap-File-1.0" >
  <siteMapNode
    title="External Links"
    description="Links to external Websites"
    roles="RoleA,RoleB,RoleC">
    <siteMapNode
      title="Google"
      url="http://www.Google.com"
      description="The Google Website"
      roles="RoleA" />
    <siteMapNode
      title="Microsoft"
      url="http://www.Microsoft.com"
      description="The Microsoft Website"
      roles="RoleB" />
    <siteMapNode
      title="Yahoo"
      url="http://www.Yahoo.com"
      description="The Yahoo Website"
      roles="RoleC" />
  </siteMapNode>
</siteMap>
```

The page in Listing 23.11 enables you to add yourself and remove yourself from different roles. Different links appear in the TreeView control, depending on which roles you select.

LISTING 23.11   ShowSecurityTrimming.aspx

```
<%@ Page Language="C#" %>
<!DOCTYPE html PUBLIC "-//W3C//DTD XHTML 1.1//EN"
"http://www.w3.org/TR/xhtml11/DTD/xhtml11.dtd">
<script runat="server">

    void Page_Load()
    {
        if (!Page.IsPostBack)
        {
            foreach (ListItem item in cblSelectRoles.Items)
                if (!Roles.RoleExists(item.Text))
                {
                    Roles.CreateRole(item.Text);
                    Roles.AddUserToRole(User.Identity.Name, item.Text);
                }
        }
    }


    protected void btnSelect_Click(object sender, EventArgs e)
    {
        foreach (ListItem item in cblSelectRoles.Items)
        {
            if (item.Selected)
            {
                if (!User.IsInRole(item.Text))
                    Roles.AddUserToRole(User.Identity.Name, item.Text);
            }
            else
            {
                if (User.IsInRole(item.Text))
                    Roles.RemoveUserFromRole(User.Identity.Name, item.Text);
            }
        }
        Response.Redirect(Request.Path);
    }


    void Page_PreRender()
    {
        foreach (ListItem item in cblSelectRoles.Items)
            item.Selected = User.IsInRole(item.Text);
    }
</script>
```

```html
<html xmlns="http://www.w3.org/1999/xhtml" >
<head id="Head1" runat="server">
    <style type="text/css">
        html
        {
            background-color:silver;
        }
        .column
        {
            float:left;
            width:300px;
            border:Solid 1px black;
            background-color:white;
            padding:10px;
        }
    </style>
    <title>Show Security Trimming</title>
</head>
<body>
    <form id="form1" runat="server">

    <div class="column">

    <asp:Label
        id="lblSelectRoles"
        Text="Select Roles:"
        AssociatedControlID="cblSelectRoles"
        Runat="server" />

    <br />

    <asp:CheckBoxList
        id="cblSelectRoles"
        Runat="server">
        <asp:ListItem Text="RoleA" />
        <asp:ListItem Text="RoleB" />
        <asp:ListItem Text="RoleC" />
    </asp:CheckBoxList>

    <asp:Button
        id="btnSelect"
        Text="Select"
        OnClick="btnSelect_Click"
        Runat="server" />

    </div>
```

```
    <div class="column">

    <asp:TreeView
        id="TreeView1"
        DataSourceID="srcSiteMap"
        Runat="server" />

    <asp:SiteMapDataSource
        id="srcSiteMap"
        Runat="server" />

    </div>

    </form>
</body>
</html>
```

When you first open the page in Listing 23.11, the Page_Load() handler creates three roles—RoleA, RoleB, and RoleC—and adds the current user to each role.

The CheckBoxList control in the body of the page enables you to select the roles that you want to join. Different links to external websites appear, depending on which roles you select (see Figure 23.6).

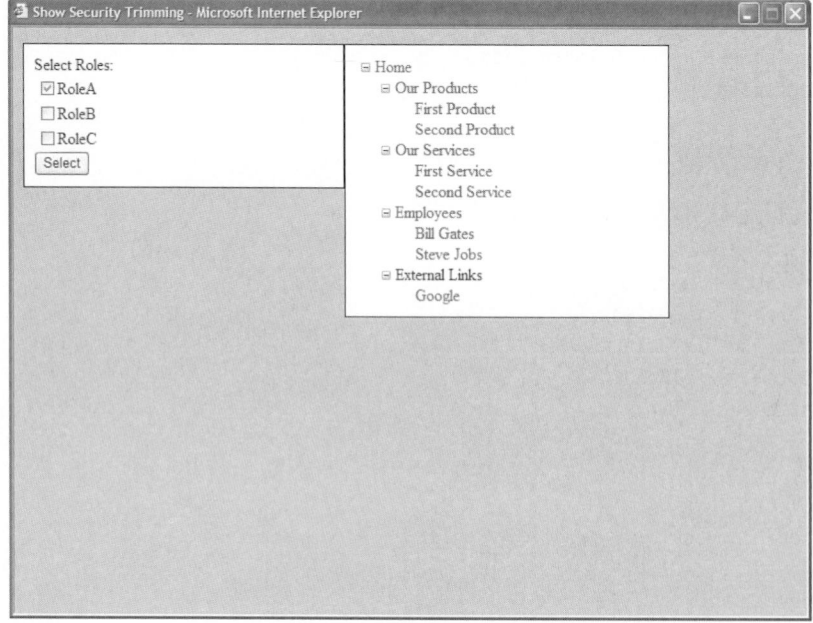

FIGURE 23.6   Hiding Site Map nodes by user role.

Merging Multiple Site Maps

To make it easier to manage a large application, you can store Site Maps in more than one location and merge the Site Maps at runtime. For example, if you use the default SiteMapProvider—the XmlSiteMapProvider— you can create multiple sitemap files that describe the navigation structure of different sections of your website.

For example, the Web.sitemap file in Listing 23.12 includes a node that points to another sitemap file.

LISTING 23.12   Web.sitemap

```xml
<?xml version="1.0" encoding="utf-8" ?>
<siteMap xmlns="http://schemas.microsoft.com/AspNet/SiteMap-File-1.0" >
<siteMapNode
  url="Default.aspx"
  title="Home"
  description="The Home Page">
  <siteMapNode
    url="Products/Default.aspx"
    title="Our Products"
    description="Products that we offer">
    <siteMapNode
      url="Products/FirstProduct.aspx"
      title="First Product"
      description="The description of the First Product" />
    <siteMapNode
      url="Products/SecondProduct.aspx"
      title="Second Product"
      description="The description of the Second Product" />
  </siteMapNode>
  <siteMapNode
    url="Services"
    title="Our Services"
    description="Services that we offer">
    <siteMapNode
      url="Services/FirstService.aspx"
      title="First Service"
      description="The description of the First Service"
      metaDescription="The first service" />
    <siteMapNode
      url="Services/SecondService.aspx"
      title="Second Service"
      description="The description of the Second Service" />
  </siteMapNode>
```

23

```
  <siteMapNode
    siteMapFile="Employees/Employees.sitemap" />
</siteMapNode>
</siteMap>
```

The sitemap in Listing 23.12 includes the following node:

```
<siteMapNode siteMapFile="Employees/Employees.sitemap" />
```

This node includes a `siteMapFile` attribute that points to a sitemap located in the Employees subdirectory of the current application. The contents of the `Employees.sitemap` are automatically merged with the default `Web.sitemap`.

The `Employees.sitemap` is contained in Listing 23.13.

LISTING 23.13   Employees/Employees.sitemap

```
<?xml version="1.0" encoding="utf-8" ?>
<siteMap xmlns="http://schemas.microsoft.com/AspNet/SiteMap-File-1.0" >
  <siteMapNode
    url="Employees/Default.aspx"
    title="Employees"
    description="Contains descriptions of employees">
    <siteMapNode
      url="Employees/BillGates.aspx"
      title="Bill Gates"
      description="Bill Gates Page" />
    <siteMapNode
      url="Employees/SteveJobs.aspx"
      title="Steve Jobs"
      description="Steve Jobs Page" />
  </siteMapNode>
</siteMap>
```

There is nothing special about the sitemap in Listing 23.13. It contains a description of the two pages in the Employees subdirectory.

This is a great feature for working with large websites. Each section of the website can be managed by a different developer. When the website is accessed by a user, the contents of the different sitemaps are seamlessly stitched together.

NOTE

You also can associate different `SiteMapProviders` with different nodes in a sitemap file by taking advantage of the `provider` attribute. For example, a Site Map might be stored in a database table for one section of your website and stored in an XML file for another section of your website.

Creating Custom Site Map Attributes

You can extend a Site Map with your own custom attributes. You can use a custom attribute to represent any type of information that you want.

For example, imagine that you want to associate <meta> Description tags with each page in your web application to make it easier for search engines to index your website. In that case, you can add a metaDescription attribute to the nodes in a Web.sitemap file.

The Web.sitemap file in Listing 23.14 includes metaDescription attributes for the two Services pages.

LISTING 23.14   Web.sitemap

```
<?xml version="1.0" encoding="utf-8" ?>
<siteMap xmlns="http://schemas.microsoft.com/AspNet/SiteMap-File-1.0" >
  <siteMapNode
    url="Default.aspx"
    title="Home"
    description="The Home Page">
    <siteMapNode
      url="Products/Default.aspx"
      title="Our Products"
      description="Products that we offer">
      <siteMapNode
        url="Products/FirstProduct.aspx"
        title="First Product"
        description="The description of the First Product" />
      <siteMapNode
        url="Products/SecondProduct.aspx"
        title="Second Product"
        description="The description of the Second Product" />
    </siteMapNode>
    <siteMapNode
      url="Services/Default.aspx"
      title="Our Services"
      description="Services that we offer">
      <siteMapNode
        url="Services/FirstService.aspx"
        title="First Service"
        description="The description of the First Service"
        metaDescription="The first service" />
      <siteMapNode
        url="Services/SecondService.aspx"
        title="Second Service"
        description="The description of the Second Service"
        metaDescription="The second service"  />
```

23

```
    </siteMapNode>
  </siteMapNode>
</siteMap>
```

Any custom attributes that you add to a Site Map are exposed by instances of the SiteMapNode class. For example, the page in Listing 23.15 retrieves the value of the metaDescription attribute from the current node and displays the value in an actual <meta> tag.

LISTING 23.15   Services/FirstService.aspx

```
<%@ Page Language="C#" %>
<!DOCTYPE html PUBLIC "-//W3C//DTD XHTML 1.1//EN"
"http://www.w3.org/TR/xhtml11/DTD/xhtml11.dtd">
<script runat="server">

    void Page_Load()
    {
        HtmlMeta meta = new HtmlMeta();
        meta.Name = "Description";
        meta.Content = SiteMap.CurrentNode["metaDescription"];
        head1.Controls.Add(meta);
    }
</script>
<html xmlns="http://www.w3.org/1999/xhtml" >
<head id="head1" runat="server">
    <title>First Service</title>
</head>
<body>
    <form id="form1" runat="server">
    <div>

    <h1>The First Service</h1>

    </div>
    </form>
</body>
</html>
```

After you open the page in Listing 23.15 in a web browser, you can select View, Source to see the <meta> tag added to the source of the page (see Figure 23.7).

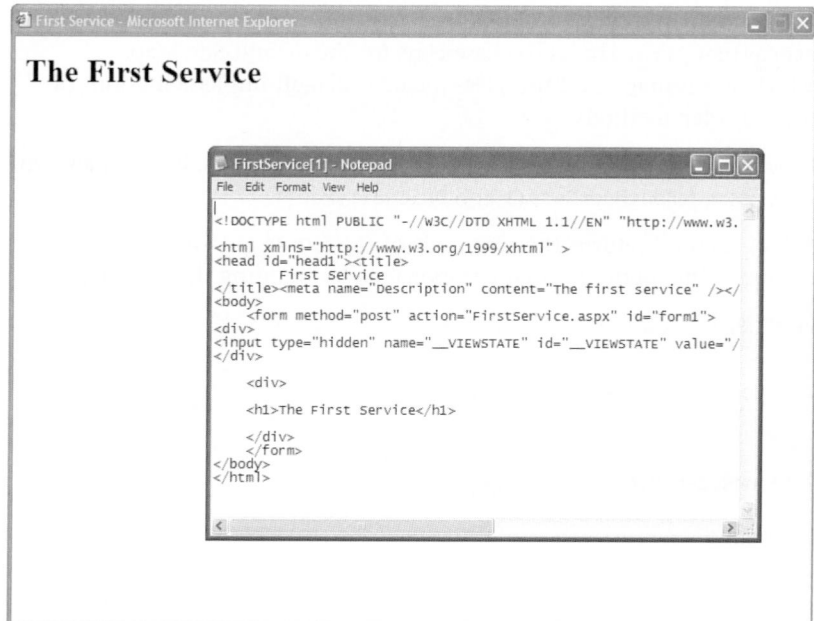

FIGURE 23.7   Extending a Site Map with a <meta> tag.

It is important to emphasize that you can do anything you want with custom SiteMapNode attributes. You can represent page titles, section titles, product icons, or anything else with a custom attribute.

Creating Custom Site Map Providers

Site Maps use the provider model. This means that you can easily modify or extend the way Site Maps work by creating your own Site Map provider.

In this section, we create two custom Site Map providers. First, we create the AutoSiteMapProvider. This provider automatically builds a Site Map based on the file and folder structure of a website.

Next, we create a SqlSiteMapProvider. This provider enables you to store a Site Map in a Microsoft SQL Server database table instead of an XML file.

Creating the `AutoSiteMapProvider`

All Site Map providers inherit from the base `SiteMapProvider` class. If you want to create your own Site Map provider, you can override the methods of this base class.

However, in most cases it makes more sense to derive a custom Site Map provider from the base `StaticSiteMapProvider` class. This is the base class for the default Site Map provider—the `XmlSiteMapProvider`—and this class includes default implementations of many of the `SiteMapProvider` methods.

This `AutoSiteMapProvider` derives from the `StaticSiteMapProvider` class. It overrides two methods of the base class: `GetRootNodeCore()` and `BuildSiteMap()`.

The `GetRootNodeCore()` method returns the root node of the Site Map. The `BuildSiteMap()` method is the method actually responsible for building the Site Map.

The AutoSiteMapProvider is contained in Listing 23.16.

LISTING 23.16   App_Code/AutoSiteMapProvider.cs

```
using System;
using System.Collections.Generic;
using System.IO;
using System.Web;
using System.Web.Caching;

namespace AspNetUnleashed
{
    public class AutoSiteMapProvider : StaticSiteMapProvider
    {
        private SiteMapNode _rootNode;
        private static List<string> _excluded = new List<string>();
        private List<string> _dependencies = new List<string>();

        /// <summary>
        /// These folder and pages won't be added
        /// to the Site Map
        /// </summary>
        static AutoSiteMapProvider()
        {
            _excluded.Add("app_code");
            _excluded.Add("app_data");
            _excluded.Add("app_themes");
            _excluded.Add("bin");
        }
```

```
/// <summary>
/// Return the root node of the Site Map
/// </summary>
protected override SiteMapNode GetRootNodeCore()
{
    return BuildSiteMap();
}


/// <summary>
/// Where all of the work of building the Site Map happens
/// </summary>
public override SiteMapNode BuildSiteMap()
{
    // Only allow the Site Map to be created by a single thread
    lock (this)
    {
        // Attempt to get Root Node from Cache
        HttpContext context = HttpContext.Current;
        _rootNode = (SiteMapNode)context.Cache["RootNode"];
        if (_rootNode == null)
        {
            // Clear current Site Map
            Clear();

            // Create root node
            string folderUrl = HttpRuntime.AppDomainAppVirtualPath;
            string defaultUrl = folderUrl + "/Default.aspx";
            _rootNode = new SiteMapNode(this, folderUrl, defaultUrl, "Home");
            AddNode(_rootNode);

            // Create child nodes
            AddChildNodes(_rootNode);
            _dependencies.Add(HttpRuntime.AppDomainAppPath);

            // Add root node to cache with file dependencies
            CacheDependency fileDependency =
                new CacheDependency(_dependencies.ToArray());
            context.Cache.Insert("RootNode", _rootNode, fileDependency);
        }
        return _rootNode;
    }
}

/// <summary>
/// Add child folders and pages to the Site Map
```

```
    /// </summary>
    private void AddChildNodes(SiteMapNode parentNode)
    {

        AddChildFolders(parentNode);
        AddChildPages(parentNode);
    }

    /// <summary>
    /// Add child folders to the Site Map
    /// </summary>
    /// <param name="parentNode"></param>
    private void AddChildFolders(SiteMapNode parentNode)
    {
        HttpContext context = HttpContext.Current;
        string parentFolderPath = context.Server.MapPath(parentNode.Key);
        DirectoryInfo folderInfo = new DirectoryInfo(parentFolderPath);

        // Get sub folders
        DirectoryInfo[] folders = folderInfo.GetDirectories();
        foreach (DirectoryInfo folder in folders)
        {
            if (!_excluded.Contains(folder.Name.ToLower()))
            {
                string folderUrl = parentNode.Key + "/" + folder.Name;
                SiteMapNode folderNode =
                  new SiteMapNode(this, folderUrl, null, GetName(folder.Name));
                AddNode(folderNode, parentNode);
                AddChildNodes(folderNode);
                _dependencies.Add(folder.FullName);
            }
        }
    }

    /// <summary>
    /// Add child pages to the Site Map
    /// </summary>
    private void AddChildPages(SiteMapNode parentNode)
    {
        HttpContext context = HttpContext.Current;
        string parentFolderPath = context.Server.MapPath(parentNode.Key);
        DirectoryInfo folderInfo = new DirectoryInfo(parentFolderPath);

        FileInfo[] pages = folderInfo.GetFiles("*.aspx");
        foreach (FileInfo page in pages)
        {
```

```
            if (!_excluded.Contains(page.Name.ToLower()))
            {
                string pageUrl = parentNode.Key + "/" + page.Name;
                if (String.Compare(pageUrl, _rootNode.Url, true) !=0)
                {
                    SiteMapNode pageNode =
                      new SiteMapNode(this, pageUrl, pageUrl,
➥GetName(page.Name));

                    AddNode(pageNode, parentNode);
                }
            }
        }
    }
}

    /// <summary>
    /// Fix the name of the page or folder
    /// by removing the extension and replacing
    /// underscores with spaces
    /// </summary>
    private string GetName(string name)
    {
        name = Path.GetFileNameWithoutExtension(name);
        return name.Replace("_", " ");
    }
    }
}
```

Almost all the work in Listing 23.16 happens in the `BuildSiteMap()` method. This method recursively iterates through all the folders and pages in the current web application creating `SiteMapNodes`. When the method completes its work, a Site Map that reflects the folder and page structure of the website is created.

You should notice two special aspects of the code in Listing 23.16. First, file dependencies are created for each folder. If you add a new folder or page to your website, the `BuildSiteMap()` method is automatically called the next time you request a page.

Second, the constructor for the `AutoSiteMapProvider` class creates a list of excluded files. For example, this list includes the `App_Code` and Bin folders. You do not want these files to appear in a Site Map. If there are other special files that you want to hide, you need to add the filenames to the list of excluded files in the constructor.

After you create the `AutoSiteMapProvider` class, you need to configure your application to use the custom Site Map provider. You can use the configuration file in Listing 23.17 to enable the `AutoSiteMapProvider`.

LISTING 23.17   Web.Config

```
<?xml version="1.0"?>
<configuration xmlns="http://schemas.microsoft.com/.NetConfiguration/v2.0">
    <system.web>

        <siteMap defaultProvider="MyAutoSiteMapProvider">
            <providers>
                <add
                    name="MyAutoSiteMapProvider"
                    type="AspNetUnleashed.AutoSiteMapProvider" />
            </providers>
        </siteMap>

    </system.web>
</configuration>
```

The configuration file in Listing 23.17 configures the AutoSiteMapProvider as the application's default provider.

You can try out the AutoSiteMapProvider by requesting the Default.aspx page from the AutoSiteMapProviderApp Web application contained in the source code on the book's website. This application does not include a Web.sitemap file. The Site Map is automatically generated from the structure of the website (see Figure 23.8).

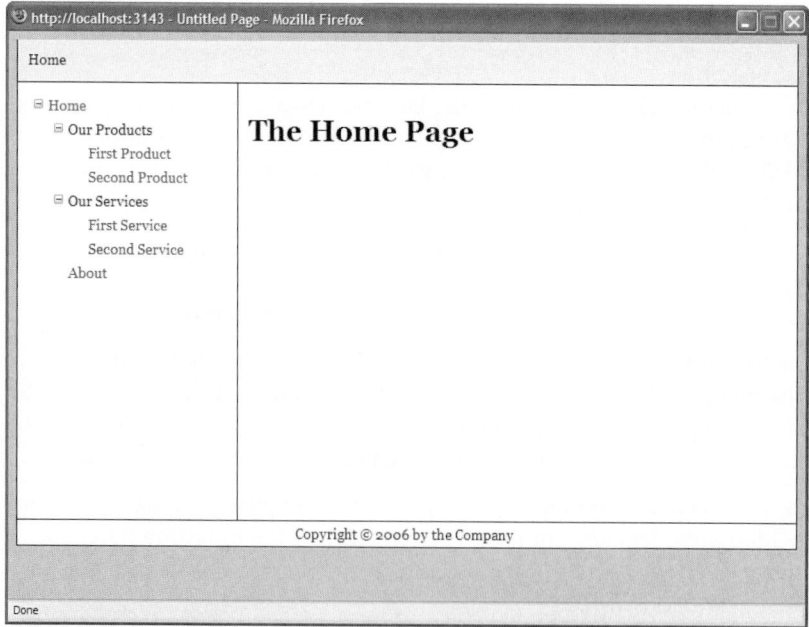

FIGURE 23.8   Displaying an automatically generated Site Map.

Creating the `SqlSiteMapProvider`

For certain applications it makes more sense to store a Site Map in a database table than an XML file. In this section, you can see the creation of the `SqlSiteMapProvider`, which stores a Site Map in a Microsoft SQL Server database.

To use the `SqlSiteMapProvider` class, you must create a SQL database table named SiteMap. Furthermore, the SiteMap database table must look like this:

Id	ParentId	Url	Title	Description
1	null	Default.aspx	Home	Home Page
2	1		Products	Products
3	2	Products/FirstProduct.aspx	First Product	First Product
4	2	Products/SecondProduct.aspx	Second Product	Second Product
6	1		Services	Services
7	6	Services/FirstService.aspx	First Service	First Service

Each row in the SiteMap table represents a particular Site Map node. The relationship between the nodes is represented by the ParentId column. The row that represents the root node has a ParentId column with the value null. Every other row is either a child of the root node or the child of some other node.

The code for the `SqlSiteMapProvider` is contained in Listing 23.18.

LISTING 23.18   App_Code\SqlSiteMapProvider.cs

```
using System;
using System.Collections.Specialized;
using System.Web.Configuration;
using System.Data;
using System.Data.SqlClient;
using System.Web;
using System.Web.Caching;

namespace AspNetUnleashed
{
    /// <summary>
    /// Summary description for SqlSiteMapProvider
    /// </summary>
    public class SqlSiteMapProvider : StaticSiteMapProvider
    {
        private bool _isInitialized = false;
```

```
    private string _connectionString;
    private SiteMapNode _rootNode;

    public override void Initialize(string name, NameValueCollection attributes)
    {
        if (_isInitialized)
            return;

        base.Initialize(name, attributes);

        string connectionStringName = attributes["connectionStringName"];
        if (String.IsNullOrEmpty(connectionStringName))
            throw new Exception("You must provide a connectionStringName
➥attribute");

        _connectionString =
            WebConfigurationManager.ConnectionStrings[connectionStringName].
            ConnectionString;
        if (String.IsNullOrEmpty(_connectionString))
            throw new Exception("Could not find connection string " +
➥connectionStringName);

        _isInitialized = true;
    }

    protected override SiteMapNode GetRootNodeCore()
    {
        return BuildSiteMap();
    }

    public override SiteMapNode BuildSiteMap()
    {
        // Only allow the Site Map to be created by a single thread
        lock (this)
        {
            // Attempt to get Root Node from Cache
            HttpContext context = HttpContext.Current;
            _rootNode = (SiteMapNode)context.Cache["RootNode"];

            if (_rootNode == null)
            {
                HttpContext.Current.Trace.Warn("Loading from database");

                // Clear current Site Map
                Clear();
```

```
            // Load the database data
            DataTable tblSiteMap = GetSiteMapFromDB();

            // Get the root node
            _rootNode = GetRootNode(tblSiteMap);
            AddNode(_rootNode);

            // Build the child nodes
            BuildSiteMapRecurse(tblSiteMap, _rootNode);

            // Add root node to cache with database dependency
            SqlCacheDependency sqlDepend =
                new SqlCacheDependency("SiteMapDB", "SiteMap");
            context.Cache.Insert("RootNode", _rootNode, sqlDepend);
        }
        return _rootNode;
    }
}


private DataTable GetSiteMapFromDB()
{
    string selectCommand = "SELECT Id,ParentId,Url,Title,Description FROM
➥SiteMap";
    SqlDataAdapter dad = new SqlDataAdapter(selectCommand,
➥_connectionString);
    DataTable tblSiteMap = new DataTable();
    dad.Fill(tblSiteMap);
    return tblSiteMap;
}


private SiteMapNode GetRootNode(DataTable siteMapTable)
{
    DataRow[] results = siteMapTable.Select("ParentId IS NULL");
    if (results.Length == 0)
        throw new Exception("No root node in database");
    DataRow rootRow = results[0];
    return new SiteMapNode(this, rootRow["Id"].ToString(),
        rootRow["url"].ToString(), rootRow["title"].ToString(),
        rootRow["description"].ToString());
}

private void BuildSiteMapRecurse(DataTable siteMapTable, SiteMapNode
➥parentNode)
{
```

```
                    DataRow[] results = siteMapTable.Select("ParentId=" + parentNode.Key);
                    foreach (DataRow row in results)
                    {
                        SiteMapNode node = new SiteMapNode(this, row["Id"].ToString(),
                            row["url"].ToString(), row["title"].ToString(),
                            row["description"].ToString());
                        AddNode(node, parentNode);
                        BuildSiteMapRecurse(siteMapTable, node);
                    }
                }
            }

        }
    }
```

Like the custom Site Map provider that was created in the previous section, the
SqlSiteMapProvider derives from the base StaticSiteMapProvider class. The
SqlSiteMapProvider class overrides three methods of the base class: Initialize(),
GetRootNodeCore(), and BuildSiteMap().

The Initialize() method retrieves a database connection string from the web configuration file. If a database connection string cannot be retrieved, the method throws a big,
fat exception.

Almost all the work happens in the BuildSiteMap() method. This method loads the
contents of the SiteMap database table into an ADO.NET DataTable. Next, it recursively
builds the Site Map nodes from the DataTable.

There is one special aspect of the code in Listing 23.18. It uses a SQL cache dependency
to automatically rebuild the Site Map when the contents of the SiteMap database table
are changed.

To enable SQL cache dependencies for a database, you must configure the database with
either the enableNotifications tool or the aspnet_regsql tool. Use the
enableNotifications tool when enabling SQL cache dependencies for a SQL Express database table, and use the aspnet_regsql tool when enabling SQL cache dependencies for the
full version of Microsoft SQL Server.

NOTE

To learn more about configuring SQL cache dependencies, see Chapter 29, "Caching
Application Pages and Data."

To enable SQL cache dependencies for a SQL Express database named SiteMapDB that
contains a table named SiteMap, browse to the folder that contains the SiteMapDB.mdf
file and execute the following command from a Command Prompt:

```
enableNotifications "SiteMapDB.mdf" "SiteMap"
```

You can configure your website to use the `SqlSiteMapProvider` class with the Web configuration file in Listing 23.19.

LISTING 23.19   Web.Config

```
<?xml version="1.0"?>
<configuration>
  <connectionStrings>
    <add
      name="conSiteMap"
      connectionString="Data Source=.\SQLExpress;Integrated
 Security=True;AttachDbFileName=¦DataDirectory¦SiteMapDB.mdf;User Instance=True"/>
  </connectionStrings>

    <system.web>
      <siteMap defaultProvider="myProvider">
        <providers>
          <add
            name="myProvider"
            type="AspNetUnleashed.SqlSiteMapProvider"
            connectionStringName="conSiteMap" />

        </providers>
      </siteMap>

      <caching>
      <sqlCacheDependency enabled = "true" pollTime = "5000" >
        <databases>
          <add name="SiteMapDB"
               connectionStringName="conSiteMap"
          />
        </databases>
      </sqlCacheDependency>
      </caching>

    </system.web>
</configuration>
```

The configuration file in Listing 23.19 accomplishes several tasks. First, it configures the `SqlSiteMapProvider` as the default Site Map provider. The provider includes a `connectionStringName` attribute that points to the connection string for the local SQL Express database named SiteMapDB.

The configuration file also enables SQL cache dependency polling. The application is configured to poll the SiteMapDB database for changes every 5 seconds. In other words, if you make a change to the SiteMap database table, the Site Map is updated to reflect the change within 5 seconds.

You can try out the SqlSiteMapProvider by opening the Default.aspx page included in the SqlSiteMapProviderApp web application on the website that accompanies this book. If you modify the SiteMap database table, the changes are automatically reflected in the Site Map (see Figure 23.9).

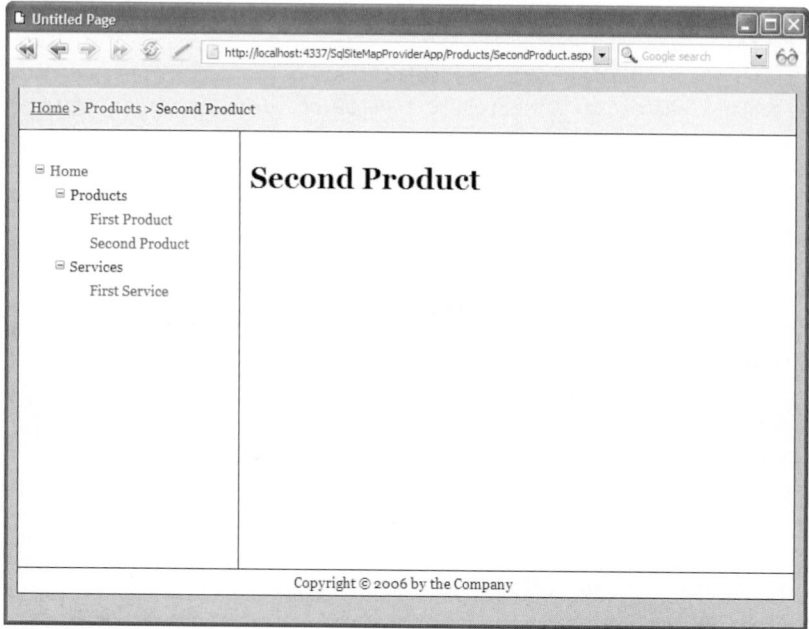

FIGURE 23.9   Displaying a Site Map from a Microsoft SQL database.

Generating a Google SiteMap File

Google provides a free service, named Google SiteMaps, that you can use to monitor and improve the way that Google indexes the pages on your website. For example, you can use Google SiteMaps to discover which Google search queries have returned pages from your website and the ranking of your pages in Google search results. You also can use Google SiteMaps to view any problems that the Google crawler encounters when indexing your site.

You can sign up for Google SiteMaps by visiting the following URL:

http://www.google.com/webmasters/sitemaps

To use Google SiteMaps, you must provide Google with the URL of a Google SiteMap file hosted on your website. The Google SiteMap file is an XML file that contains a list of URLs you want Google to index.

The Google SiteMap XML file has the following format:

```
<?xml version="1.0" encoding="UTF-8"?>
<urlset xmlns="http://www.google.com/schemas/sitemap/0.84">
  <url>
    <loc>http://www.example.com/</loc>
    <lastmod>2005-01-01</lastmod>
  </url>
  <url>
    <loc>http://www.example.com/sample.html/</loc>
    <lastmod>2006-03-11</lastmod>
  </url>
</urlset>
```

The Google SiteMap file contains a simple list of `<url>` elements that contain `<loc>` elements representing the location of the URL and `<lastmod>` elements representing the last modified date of the URL.

NOTE

The Google SiteMap file also can contain `<changefreq>` and `<priority>` elements. The `<changefreq>` element indicates how frequently a URL changes, and the `<priority>` element represents the priority of a URL relative to other URLs in your site. These elements are optional and are ignored here.

You can generate a Google SiteMap file automatically from an ASP.NET SiteMap. The HTTP Handler in Listing 23.20 generates a Google SiteMap that conforms to Google's requirements for a valid SiteMap file.

LISTING 23.20   `PublicSiteMap.ashx`

```csharp
<%@ WebHandler Language="C#" Class="PublicSiteMap" %>
using System;
using System.Web;
using System.Xml;
using System.Text;
using System.IO;

public class PublicSiteMap : IHttpHandler {

    private XmlWriter _xmlWriter;

    public void ProcessRequest (HttpContext context) {
        context.Response.ContentType = "text/xml";
```

23

```
XmlWriterSettings settings = new XmlWriterSettings();
settings.Encoding = Encoding.UTF8;
settings.Indent = true;
_xmlWriter = XmlWriter.Create(context.Response.OutputStream,settings);
_xmlWriter.WriteStartDocument();
_xmlWriter.WriteStartElement("urlset","http://www.google.com/schemas/
➥sitemap/0.84");

    // Add root node
    AddUrl(SiteMap.RootNode);

    // Add all other nodes
    SiteMapNodeCollection nodes = SiteMap.RootNode.GetAllNodes();
    foreach (SiteMapNode node in nodes)
        AddUrl(node);

_xmlWriter.WriteEndElement();
_xmlWriter.WriteEndDocument();
_xmlWriter.Flush();
}

private void AddUrl(SiteMapNode node)
{
    // Skip empty Urls
    if (String.IsNullOrEmpty(node.Url))
        return;
    // Skip remote nodes
    if (node.Url.StartsWith("http", true, null))
        return;
    // Open url tag
    _xmlWriter.WriteStartElement("url");
    // Write location
    _xmlWriter.WriteStartElement("loc");
    _xmlWriter.WriteString(GetFullUrl(node.Url));
    _xmlWriter.WriteEndElement();
    // Write last modified
    _xmlWriter.WriteStartElement("lastmod");
    _xmlWriter.WriteString(GetLastModified(node.Url));
    _xmlWriter.WriteEndElement();
    // Close url tag
    _xmlWriter.WriteEndElement();
}

private string GetFullUrl(string url)
```

```
    {
        HttpContext context = HttpContext.Current;
        string server =
            context.Request.Url.GetComponents(UriComponents.SchemeAndServer,
                UriFormat.UriEscaped);
        return Combine(server, url);
    }

    private string Combine(string baseUrl, string url)
    {
        baseUrl = baseUrl.TrimEnd(new char[] {'/'});
        url = url.TrimStart(new char[] { '/' });
        return baseUrl + "/" + url;
    }

    private string GetLastModified(string url)
    {
        HttpContext context = HttpContext.Current;
        string physicalPath = context.Server.MapPath(url);
        return File.GetLastWriteTimeUtc(physicalPath).ToString("s") + "Z";
    }

    public bool IsReusable {
        get {
            return true;
        }
    }
}
```

The HTTP Handler in Listing 23.20 generates an XML file by iterating through each of the nodes in an ASP.NET Site Map. The XML file is created with the help of the XmlWriter class. This class generates each of the XML tags.

NOTE

You can think of an HTTP Handler as a lightweight ASP.NET page. You learn about HTTP Handlers in Chapter 31, "Working with the HTTP Runtime."

The file in Listing 23.21 contains the XML file returned by the PublicSiteMap.ashx handler when the Handler is called from the sample application contained on the website that accompanies this book. (The file has been abridged to save space.)

LISTING 23.21   PublicSiteMap.ashx Results

```xml
<?xml version="1.0" encoding="utf-8"?>
<urlset xmlns="http://www.google.com/schemas/sitemap/0.84">
  <url>
    <loc>http://localhost:2905/SiteMaps/Default.aspx</loc>
    <lastmod>2005-10-30T03:13:58Z</lastmod>
  </url>
  <url>
    <loc>http://localhost:2905/SiteMaps/Products/Default.aspx</loc>
    <lastmod>2005-10-28T21:48:04Z</lastmod>
  </url>
  <url>
    <loc>http://localhost:2905/SiteMaps/Services</loc>
    <lastmod>2005-10-30T04:31:57Z</lastmod>
  </url>
  <url>
    <loc>http://localhost:2905/SiteMaps/Employees/Default.aspx</loc>
    <lastmod>1601-01-01T00:00:00Z</lastmod>
  </url>
  <url>
    <loc>http://localhost:2905/SiteMaps/Products/FirstProduct.aspx</loc>
    <lastmod>2005-10-30T03:43:52Z</lastmod>
  </url>
</urlset>
```

When you sign up at the Google SiteMaps website, submit the URL of the PublicSiteMap.ashx file when you are asked to enter your SiteMap URL. The Google service retrieves your SiteMap from the handler automatically.

Summary

In this chapter, you learned how to work with Site Maps. The first section discussed the SiteMapDataSource control. You learned how to declaratively represent different sets of nodes in a Site Map with this control.

Next, the SiteMap and SiteMapNode classes were examined. You learned how to create new Site Map nodes dynamically by handling the SiteMapResolve event. You also learned how to programmatically retrieve the current Site Map node in a page.

The next section discussed several advanced features of Site Maps. You learned how to display different Site Map nodes to different users depending on their roles. You also learned how to merge SiteMap files located in different subfolders. Finally, you learned how to extend Site Maps with custom attributes.

We also built two custom Site Map providers. We created an `AutoSiteMapProvider` that automatically builds a Site Map that reflects the folder and page structure of a website. We also created a `SqlSiteMapProvider` that stores a Site Map in a Microsoft SQL Server database table.

Finally, you learned how to use ASP.NET Site Maps with Google SiteMaps. In the final section of this chapter, you learned how to create a custom HTTP Handler that converts an ASP.NET Site Map into a Google SiteMap so that you can improve the way that Google indexes your website's pages.

23

Advanced Navigation

Websites tend to be organic—they grow and change over time. This can create problems when other applications link to your application. You need some way of modifying your website without breaking all the existing links to your website.

In this chapter, you learn how to remap URLs. In other words, you learn how to serve a different page than the page a user requests. In the first section of the chapter, you learn how to remap URLs in the web configuration file.

Next, you learn how to remap URLs by creating a custom HTTP module. Using a module is useful when you need to support wildcard matches and other types of pattern matching when remapping a URL.

Finally, you learn how to use the VirtualPathProvider class to remap URLs. You learn how you can store all your website pages in a database. In the last section of this chapter, a simple Content Management System (CMS) is built with the VirtualPathProvider class.

All these techniques are different than the techniques that use the new ASP.NET 4 Routing Engine. If your goal is to provide "permalink" type functionality or specifically map URLs to pieces of content (rather than .aspx pages), these techniques are for you. However, if your goal is to provide a more SEO-friendly, user-friendly, and possibly REST-friendly URL pattern *for your entire website*, you should *not* use the techniques in this chapter and instead skip to the chapter on the URL Routing Engine.

Remapping URLs

The simplest way to remap a URL is to specify the remapping in your application's web configuration file. For example, the web configuration file in Listing 24.1 remaps the Home.aspx page to the Default.aspx page.

LISTING 24.1   Web.Config

```
<?xml version="1.0"?>
<configuration>
<system.web>
  <urlMappings>
    <add
      url="~/Home.aspx"
      mappedUrl="~/Default.aspx"/>
  </urlMappings>
</system.web>
</configuration>
```

The configuration file in Listing 24.1 contains a <urlMappings> element. This element can contain one or more elements that remap a page from a URL to a mapped Url.

The mappedUrl attribute can contain query strings. However, it cannot contain wildcards. You can use the <urlMappings> element only when performing simple page-to-page mappings.

After you add the web configuration file in Listing 24.1 to your application, any requests for the Home.aspx page are modified automatically to requests for the Default.aspx page. It doesn't matter whether the Home.aspx page actually exists. If the Home.aspx page does exist, you can never open the page.

> **NOTE**
>
> The tilde character (~) has a special meaning when used with a path. It represents the current application root. A forward slash (/) at the start of a URL, on the other hand, represents the website root.
>
> You can use the tilde only with properties of ASP.NET controls. For example, you can use it with the ASP.NET Image control's ImageUrl property, but you cannot use it with the HTML <img> src attribute.
>
> In code, you can use the tilde character with a path by using the Page.ResolveUrl() method. This method automatically expands the tilde to the application root.

When working with remapped URLs, you often need to determine the original URL that a user requested. For example, you might want to display a message that tells users to update their bookmarks (favorites) to point to the new URL.

You can use the following to determine the current URL:

- **Request.RawUrl**—Returns the original URL (before being remapped).

- **Request.Path**—Returns the current URL (after being remapped).

- **Request.AppRelativeCurrentExecutionFilePath**—Returns the application relative URL (after being remapped).

The last property automatically replaces the name of the web application with a tilde (~) character.

For example, the Default.aspx page in Listing 24.2 illustrates all three properties.

LISTING 24.2   Default.aspx

```
<%@ Page Language="C#" %>
<!DOCTYPE html PUBLIC "-//W3C//DTD XHTML 1.1//EN"
"http://www.w3.org/TR/xhtml11/DTD/xhtml11.dtd">
<script runat="server">

    void Page_Load()
    {
        if (String.Compare(Request.Path, Request.RawUrl, true) != 0)
            lblMessage.Text = "The URL to this page has changed, " +
                "please update your bookmarks.";
    }

</script>
<html xmlns="http://www.w3.org/1999/xhtml" >
<head runat="server">
    <style type="text/css">
        html
        {
            font:14px Georgia,Serif;
        }
        .message
        {
            border:Dotted 2px red;
            background-color:yellow;
        }
    </style>
    <title>Default Page</title>
</head>
<body>
    <form id="form1" runat="server">
    <div>
```

24

```
<h1>The Default Page</h1>

<p>
<asp:Label
    id="lblMessage"
    CssClass="message"
    Runat="server" />
</p>

The original request was for:
<blockquote>
    <%=Request.RawUrl%>
</blockquote>
which got remapped to:
<blockquote>
    <%= Request.Path %>
</blockquote>
and the application relative version is:
<blockquote>
    <%= Request.AppRelativeCurrentExecutionFilePath %>
</blockquote>

    </div>
    </form>
</body>
</html>
```

If you request the Home.aspx page, the request is remapped to the Default.aspx page by the web configuration file in Listing 24.1. The Page_Load() event handler displays a message asking users to update their bookmarks when the RawUrl does not match the path (see Figure 24.1).

Each property displayed in the body of the page displays a different value:

```
Request.RawUrl = /UrlMappingsApp/Home.aspx
Request.Path = /UrlMappingsApp/Default.aspx
Request.AppRelativeCurrentExecutionFilePath = ~/Default.aspx
```

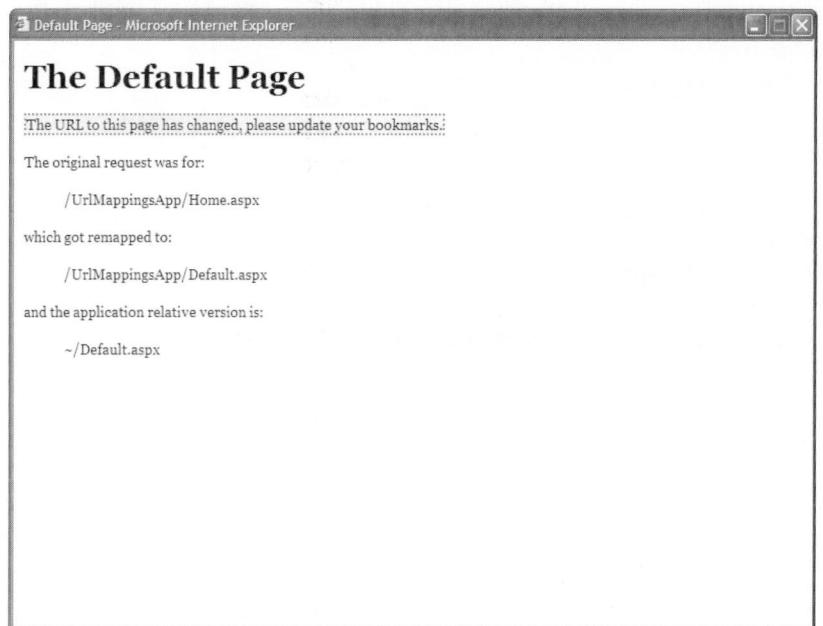

The Default Page

The URL to this page has changed, please update your bookmarks.

The original request was for:

/UrlMappingsApp/Home.aspx

which got remapped to:

/UrlMappingsApp/Default.aspx

and the application relative version is:

~/Default.aspx

FIGURE 24.1   Remapping the Home page.

Creating a Custom `UrlRemapper` Module

The `<urlMappings>` configuration element discussed in the previous section performs a simple task. It remaps one page to another. However, you quickly discover that you need to perform more complex remappings.

For example, imagine that you have a database that contains a table of product categories and a table of products. You want your website's users to request a URL that contains a product category and to see matching products. For example, if someone requests the `/Products/Soda.aspx` page, you want to display all the products in the Soda category. If someone requests the `/Products/Milk.aspx` page, you want to display all the products in the Milk category.

In that case, you need to use a wildcard when matching URLs. When someone requests any path that matches the pattern `/Products/*`, you want to redirect the user to a page where you can display matching products for the category specified in the path.

In this section, we create a custom HTTP module that remaps one URL to another. The module supports regular expression matching. Therefore it supports wildcard matches.

The code for the custom module—named `UrlRemapper`—is contained in Listing 24.3.

LISTING 24.3   UrlRemapper.cs

```
using System;
using System.Web;
```

```
using System.Xml;
using System.Web.Caching;
using System.Text.RegularExpressions;

namespace AspNetUnleashed
{
    public class UrlRemapper : IHttpModule
    {
        public void Init(HttpApplication app)
        {
            app.BeginRequest += new EventHandler(app_BeginRequest);
        }

        public void app_BeginRequest(Object s, EventArgs e)
        {
            // Get HTTP Context
            HttpApplication app = (HttpApplication)s;
            HttpContext context = app.Context;

            // Get current URL
            string currentUrl = context.Request.AppRelativeCurrentExecutionFilePath;

            // Get URL Mappings
            XmlDocument urlMappings = GetUrlMappings(context);

            // Compare current URL against each URL from mappings file
            XmlNodeList nodes = urlMappings.SelectNodes("//add");
            foreach (XmlNode node in nodes)
            {
                string url = node.Attributes["url"].Value;
                string mappedUrl = node.Attributes["mappedUrl"].Value;
                if (Regex.Match(currentUrl, url, RegexOptions.IgnoreCase).Success)
                    context.RewritePath(mappedUrl);
            }
        }

        private XmlDocument GetUrlMappings(HttpContext context)
        {
            XmlDocument urlMappings = (XmlDocument)context.Cache["UrlMappings"];
            if (urlMappings == null)
            {
                urlMappings = new XmlDocument();
                string path = context.Server.MapPath("~/UrlMappings.config");
                urlMappings.Load(path);
                CacheDependency fileDepend = new CacheDependency(path);
                context.Cache.Insert("UrlMappings", urlMappings, fileDepend);
```

```
            }
            return urlMappings;
        }

        public void Dispose() { }

    }
}
```

The class in Listing 24.3 implements the `IHttpModule` interface. An HTTP module is a special class that executes whenever you make a page request. HTTP Modules are discussed in detail in Chapter 31, "Working with the HTTP Runtime."

The module in Listing 24.3 includes an `Init()` method. This method adds an event handler for the Application `BeginRequest` event. The `BeginRequest` event is the first event raised when you request a page.

The `BeginRequest` handler gets a list of URL remappings from an XML file named `UrlMappings.config`. The contents of this XML file are cached in memory until the `UrlMappings.config` file is changed on the hard drive.

Next, the module iterates through each remapping from the XML file and performs a regular expression match against the current URL. If the match is successful, the `Context.RewritePath()` method is used to change the current path to the remapped path.

Before you can use the module in Listing 24.3 in an application, you must first register the module in your application's web configuration file. The web configuration file in Listing 24.4 contains an `<httpModules>` element that includes the `UrlRemapper` module.

LISTING 24.4 Web.Config

```
<?xml version="1.0"?>
<configuration xmlns="http://schemas.microsoft.com/.NetConfiguration/v2.0">
<system.web>

  <httpModules>
    <add
      name="UrlRemapper"
      type="AspNetUnleashed.UrlRemapper" />
  </httpModules>

</system.web>
</configuration>
```

A sample `UrlMappings.config` file is contained in Listing 24.5.

LISTING 24.5   `UrlMappings.config`

```xml
<?xml version="1.0"?>
<urlMappings>
  <add
    url="~/Home.aspx"
    mappedUrl="~/Default.aspx" />
  <add
    url="/Products/.*"
    mappedUrl="~/Products/Default.aspx" />
</urlMappings>
```

The XML file in Listing 24.5 contains two remappings. First, it remaps any request for the Home.aspx page to the Default.aspx page. Second, it remaps any request for any page in the Products directory to the Default.aspx page located in the Products folder.

The second mapping uses a regular expression to match the incoming URL. The .* expression matches any sequence of characters.

The Default.aspx page in the Products folder is contained in Listing 24.6.

LISTING 24.6   `Products/Default.aspx`

```aspx
<%@ Page Language="C#" %>
<%@ Import Namespace="System.IO" %>
<!DOCTYPE html PUBLIC "-//W3C//DTD XHTML 1.1//EN"
"http://www.w3.org/TR/xhtml11/DTD/xhtml11.dtd">
<script runat="server">

    void Page_Load()
    {
        if (!Page.IsPostBack)
        {
            string category = Path.GetFileNameWithoutExtension(Request.RawUrl);
            ltlCategory.Text = category;
            srcProducts.SelectParameters["Category"].DefaultValue = category;
        }
    }
</script>
<html xmlns="http://www.w3.org/1999/xhtml" >
<head id="Head1" runat="server">
    <style type="text/css">
        .grid td,.grid th
        {
            padding:4px;
            border-bottom:solid 1px black;
```

```
            }
        </style>
        <title>Products</title>
</head>
<body>
    <form id="form1" runat="server">
    <div>

    <h1>
    <asp:Literal
        ID="ltlCategory"
        runat="server" />
    </h1>

    <asp:GridView
        id="grdProducts"
        DataSourceID="srcProducts"
        CssClass="grid"
        GridLines="None"
        AutoGenerateColumns="false"
        Runat="server">
        <Columns>
        <asp:BoundField
            HeaderText="Product Name"
            DataField="Name" />
        <asp:BoundField
            HeaderText="Price"
            DataField="Price"
            DataFormatString="{0:c}" />
        </Columns>
    </asp:GridView>


    <asp:SqlDataSource
        id="srcProducts"
        ConnectionString="<%$ ConnectionStrings:Products %>"
        SelectCommand="SELECT Products.* FROM Products
            JOIN Categories ON Products.CategoryId=Categories.Id
            WHERE Categories.Name=@Category"
        Runat="server">
        <SelectParameters>
        <asp:Parameter Name="Category" />
        </SelectParameters>
    </asp:SqlDataSource>
```

```
    </div>
    </form>
</body>
</html>
```

The Page_Load() event handler in Listing 24.6 grabs the path of the original request, using the Request.RawUrl property. Next, it extracts the filename from the path, using the System.IO.Path.GetFileNameWithoutExtension() method. Finally, it assigns the name of the page (the category name) to a Label and SqlDataSource control. Products that match the category display in a GridView control.

For example, if you request the /Products/Soda.aspx page, all the products in the Soda category display (see Figure 24.2). If you request the /Products/Milk.aspx page, all products in the Milk category display.

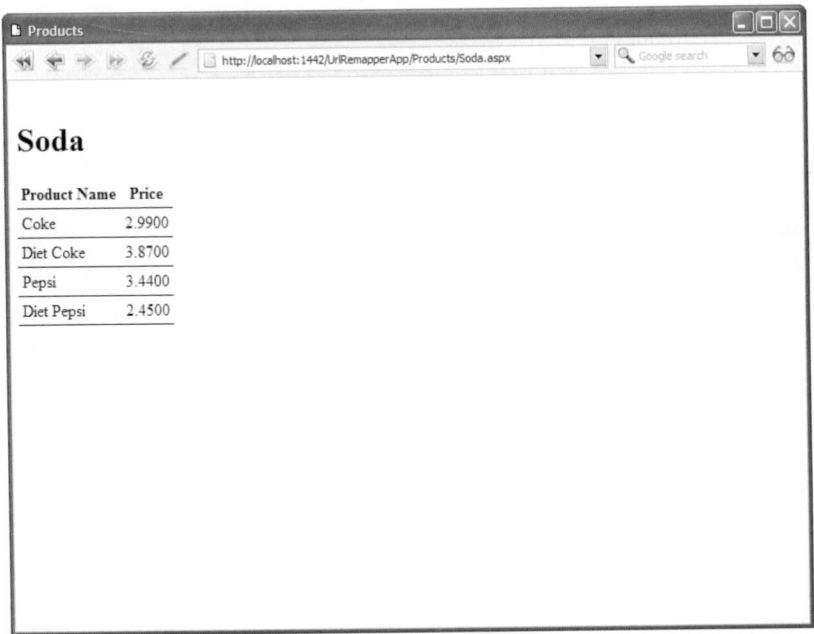

FIGURE 24.2   Displaying matching products.

Using the VirtualPathProvider Class

The VirtualPathProvider class enables you to abstract the pages in a web application from the file system. In other words, it enables you to store your ASP.NET pages any way you please.

For example, you can use the VirtualPathProvider class to store all the pages in your application in a database. This would be an appropriate choice when you need to build a

Content Management System. If you store pages in a database, users can update the pages easily in an application through an HTML form interface and save the changes to the database.

In this section, we present you with some basic information about the `VirtualPathProvider` class. We do not go into too much detail or provide a lengthy code example because for many modern scenarios you probably want to use the new Routing Engine rather than the VPP. The VPP is ideal if you want to take specific URLs and provide access to underlying content (rather than invoke ASPx pages). If you want nice URLs that invoke ASPx pages, your best bet is to use the new routing engine.

Limitations of the `VirtualPathProvider` Class

Unfortunately, you can't use the `VirtualPathProvider` with every type of file. In particular, the following types of files must always be located on the file system:

▶ `Global.asax` file

▶ `Web.Config` files

▶ App_Data folder

▶ App_Code folder

▶ App_GlobalResources folder

▶ App_LocalResource folders

▶ Bin folder

Every other type of file is fair game. This includes ASP.NET pages, User controls, Themes, and Master Pages.

Understanding the `VirtualPathProvider` Class

The `VirtualPathProvider` class is a `MustInherit` (abstract) class. It contains the following methods, which you can override:

▶ **`CombineVirtualPaths()`**—Returns a combined path from two paths.

▶ **`DirectoryExists()`**—Returns `true` when a directory exists.

▶ **`FileExists()`**—Returns `true` when a file exists.

▶ **`GetCacheDependency()`**—Returns a cache dependency object that indicates when a file has been changed.

▶ **`GetCacheKey()`**—Returns the key used by the cache dependency.

▶ **`GetDirectory()`**—Returns a VirtualDirectory.

▶ **`GetFile()`**—Returns a VirtualFile.

▶ **`GetFileHash()`**—Returns a hash of the files used by the cache dependency.

▶ **`OpenFile()`**—Returns the contents of a file.

Typically, you override the FileExists() and GetFile() methods to retrieve a file from your data store. If you want to represent directories, you also need to override the DirectoryExists() and GetDirectory() methods.

Several of these methods are related to caching. The VirtualPathProvider needs to know when a file has been modified so that it can retrieve the new version of the file and compile it. By default, the ASP.NET Framework uses a file dependency to determine when a file has been modified on the hard drive. However, in this situation a SqlCacheDependency is used because the files will be stored in a database.

The VirtualPathProvider also includes a useful property:

▶ **Previous**—Returns the previously registered VirtualPathProvider.

The Previous property enables you to use the default VirtualPathProvider. For example, if you want to store some files in the file system and other files in the database, you can use the Previous property to avoid rewriting all the logic for working with files in the file system.

The GetFile() method returns an instance of the VirtualFile class. When using the VirtualPathProvider, you must create a new class that inherits from the VirtualFile class. This class contains the following properties:

▶ **IsDirectory**—Always returns False.

▶ **Name**—Returns the name of the file.

▶ **VirtualPath**—Returns the virtual path of the file.

The VirtualFile class also contains the following method:

▶ **Open()**—Returns the contents of the file.

Typically, when creating a class that inherits from the VirtualFile class, you override the Open() method. For example, we override this method to get the contents of a file from a database table in the code sample built in this section.

The GetDirectory() method returns an instance of the VirtualDirectory class. This class contains the following properties:

▶ **Children**—Returns all the files and directories that are children of the current directory.

▶ **Directories**—Returns all the directories that are children of the current directory.

▶ **Files**—Returns all the files that are children of the current directory.

▶ **IsDirectory**—Always returns True.

▶ **Name**—Returns the name of the directory.

▶ **VirtualPath**—Returns the virtual path of the directory.

There is another class in the ASP.NET Framework that you want to use when working with the `VirtualPathProvider` class. The `VirtualPathUtility` class contains several useful methods for working with virtual paths:

▶ **AppendTrailingSlash()**—Returns a path with at most one forward slash appended to the end of the path.

▶ **Combine()**—Returns the combination of two virtual paths.

▶ **GetDirectory()**—Returns the directory portion of a path.

▶ **GetExtension()**—Returns the file extension of a path.

▶ **GetFileName()**—Returns the filename from a path.

▶ **IsAbsolute()**—Returns True when a path starts with a forward slash.

▶ **IsAppRelative()**—Returns True when a path starts with a tilde (~).

▶ **MakeRelative()**—Returns a relative path from an application-relative path.

▶ **RemoveTrailingSlash()**—Removes trailing slash from the end of a path.

▶ **ToAbsolute()**—Returns a path that starts with a forward slash.

▶ **ToAppRelative()**—Returns a path that starts with a tilde (~).

By taking advantage of the `VirtualPathUtility` class, you can avoid doing a lot of tedious string parsing on paths.

Registering a `VirtualPathProvider` Class

Before you can use an instance of the `VirtualPathProvider` class, you must register it for your application. You can register a `VirtualPathProvider` instance with the `HostingEnvironment.RegisterVirtualPathProvider()` method.

You need to register the `VirtualPathProvider` when an application first initializes. You can do this by creating a shared method named `AppInitialize()` and adding the method to any class contained in the App_Code folder. The `AppInitialize()` method is automatically called by the ASP.NET Framework when an application starts.

For example, the following `AppInitialize` method registers a `VirtualPathProvider` named `MyVirtualPathProvider`:

```
public static void AppInitialize()
{
  MyVirtualPathProvider myProvider = new MyVirtualPathProvider();
  HostingEnvironment.RegisterVirtualPathProvider(myProvider);
}
```

Summary

This chapter explored several advanced topics related to website navigation. In the first two sections, you learned how to map URLs from one path to another. In the first section, you learned how to configure remappings in the Web configuration file. In the second section, you learned how to build a custom HTTP module, which enables you to use wild-card matches when remapping a URL.

In the final section of this chapter, you learned how to abstract pages in your application from the file system by using the `VirtualPathProvider` class. The techniques described in this chapter remain in this book mostly for backward compatibility with previous versions of ASP.NET. They still work in ASP.NET 4, but you might want to consider using the new Routing Engine if your goal is to provide powerful, flexible URL schemes that still invoke underlying ASPx pages. If you are simply pointing one location to another, or providing a URL scheme on top of nonexecutable content files, this chapter still applies to your situation.

Using the ASP.NET URL Routing Engine

One of the many new features introduced in ASP.NET 4 is the concept of URL routing. This chapter provides you with an introduction to URL routing and why it should concern you as an ASP.NET Web Forms developer, then continues with examples of various scenarios in which URL routing truly shines, and finishes with coverage of a few advanced usages of URL routing.

When you finish with this chapter, you should have a firm grasp on the technology that makes URL routing work as well as when you might (or might not) want to utilize it in your own applications.

Introduction to URL Routing

URL routing, in general terms, is a system that enables the developer to build in dynamism, flexibility, and (hopefully) readability to the URLs that access the various parts of a web application.

We've all seen URLs like the following:

```
http://www.myapplication.com/server/client/apps/app2/
userdata.aspx?mode=1&system=22
&user=abc8341290c3120c1&sessionid=
2312cxjsfk3xj123&action=3123x31pb
&jibberish=continuing&urlcomplexity=needless
```

And we all know how ugly they are. Not only are they difficult to cut and paste, but they're also not very memorable or not clean, and users never know whether they can feel free to copy them, Digg them, share them on Facebook, or whatever. The reason for this is that, to an end user, a complicated-looking URL is an unusable or unsharable URL. They assume that there's so much cruft jammed into the URL that it couldn't possibly be portable. URL routing enables us to simplify those URLs, up to and including giving us the ability to build RESTful style URLs and even hide the .aspx extension entirely. We no longer even need a 1:1 mapping between the URL and physical page on disk.

The first and foremost reason why URL routing should matter to you is that simple URLs make for calm users. The simpler your URL, the simpler people are going to assume your site is to use. Sure, this is often a bad assumption on the user's part, but if you're given an opportunity to make your users feel more welcome, shouldn't you take it?

Secondly, simple and easy URLs make for better Search Engine Optimization (SEO). An ASPx page that serves up a different product page when the query string varies by a `productid` parameter might look something like this:

```
http://my.store.com/product_detail.aspx?productid=12
```

This is certainly more user-friendly than the previous URL, but is it search-engine friendly? Can a search engine crawler tell that more products are available on this same filename? There are all kinds of tricks you can do, including publishing a page that produces a master list of links to all products, but even those links aren't the best links.

What if each product detail page URL could include the short name of the product and the category to which it belonged? In this case, the URL carries information that might help make that URL more discoverable via search engines:

```
http://my.store.com/products/dvdplayers/toshiba/sd1600
```

This URL, although simple, has packed a truckload of information into it that can not only be used by end users (they immediately know they're looking at the URL for a Toshiba DVD player, model number SD-1600) but also provides search engine crawlers with a lot of context. Both human and web crawler alike can assume that if they use the /products/dvdplayers URL they will get all DVD players, and the /products/dvdplayers/toshiba URL should provide all Toshiba DVD players.

Finally, dynamically routing between URL and physical page gives you the flexibility to use URL parameters to do things that might otherwise be cumbersome, difficult, or even impossible without routing. For example, take the following two URLs:

```
http://my.app.com/blog/2010/08/12
```

and

```
http://my.app.com/products/tags/discount/new/black
```

The first one enables you to supply a date directly on the URL, but you don't need to worry about figuring out what the query string parameter names are for the components—just put the date in the URL with slashes. This reduces a lot of complexity for the underlying blog page and for end users.

The second URL enables you to supply an infinite list of tags directly on the URL. This enables power users to start adding tag after tag to the end of a URL to further limit their list of products—functionality available to users without the developer even having to provide a GUI for it.

Basic URL Routing Scenarios

Now that you've had an introduction to what URL routing is and why you might want to use it, let's take a look at some of the basics of how to use URL routing in your Web Forms application. The ASP.NET MVC Framework also makes use of the URL routing engine, but it does so in a slightly different way. The MVC Framework uses the routing engine to map routes to controllers and actions with parameters whereas ASP.NET Web Forms applications use the routing engine to map routes to physical files on disk and supply parameters to those pages.

Mapping Basic URLs

The first thing that needs to be done to use the URL routing engine is to register your route maps. A route map is just a mapping from a *route expression* to a physical file on disk (or a controller/action combination in the case of ASP.NET MVC Framework).

These routes are registered at application startup time and the registration is typically wrapped in its own method, as shown in the following code snippet taken from a Global.asax.cs file:

```
void Application_Start(object sender, EventArgs e)
{
    // Code that runs on application startup
    InitializeRoutes(RouteTable.Routes);
}
private void InitializeRoutes(RouteCollection routes)
{
    // ... perform route registration
    routes.MapPageRoute(.... );
}
```

The simplest and most basic type of route is one in which you map a static route directly to an ASPx page without any parameters. You typically see this when the target page takes no parameters and has fairly simple functionality such as a login, logout, or about page. The following code shows how to use the MapPageRoute method of the RouteCollection class to add basic route mappings:

```
routes.MapPageRoute("", "about", "~/About.aspx"); // anonymous route
routes.MapPageRoute("login", "login", "~/Login.aspx"); // named route (login)
routes.MapPageRoute("", "logout", "~/Logoff.aspx");
```

The effect of these simple route mappings is that users can now use the URL
`http://server/about`, and they will be given the content from the About.aspx page. The
URL in the browser appears as "/about". If that page were to post back to itself as many
ASP.NET Web Forms pages do, the post back would be sent to the "/about" URL, but the
About.aspx page would still be invoked.

NOTE

No matter what you have in a route rule, if the URL requested by the user corresponds
to a physical file on disk, the routing rule will be ignored. This means any constraints
and defaults defined by that rule will also be ignored. As a matter of practice (and good
style), you should avoid writing route rules and contain the ".aspx" file extension to
avoid accidental conflicts between physical files and routes.

Mapping URLs with Parameters

Static route mappings come in handy, but any application that has any kind of dynamic
nature or is driven by an underlying data source is, at some point, going to need parameters passed on the query string. Mapping parameters within a route expression and
making those parameters available to the target page is actually quite simple. Thankfully
we don't (yet) need to worry about regular expressions!

Let's assume that you're creating a web application that has blogging functionality. Rather
than force users to create (or look at) some horribly complicated URL syntax that might
even include the GUID of the blog post, you can use URL routing to simplify that URL
syntax.

NOTE

You may be thinking that no one would ever throw the GUID of a blog post entry in the
blog URL, but we have actually seen it multiple times. Never underestimate the capability of the Internet to breed bad user experience, and take every opportunity you can to
rid the Internet of such!

A common convention used by many blogging platforms is to embed a date directly in
the URL, enabling end users, GUIs, and crawlers to easily select the content they want. To
do this, we need to direct traffic to URLs like this:

`http://my.app.com/blog/2010/05/12`

to our blog rendering page (Blog.aspx). We've seen how to send static (never changing)
URLs to individual ASPx pages, but how do we send dynamic URLs to those pages?

To do this without the routing engine, we'd have to create a low-level HttpHandler to
inspect the URLs, parse them, convert them into query string parameters, and then finally
load up the appropriate page. Thankfully it's much easier to just use the following code in
our InitializeRoutes method:

```
// URL pattern: blog/2010/05/12 routes to blog.aspx
routes.MapPageRoute("blog", "blog/{year}/{month}/{day}", "~/Blog.aspx");
```

The words inside the curly braces are now named parameters within the routing engine and, when captured, will be made available to the Blog.aspx page. At this point you might be tempted to try and access these parameters as part of the Request.QueryString object. Don't! Parameters passed through the URL routing engine are made available inside the Page.RouteData property and *not* as part of the query string, as shown in the following code:

```
protected void Page_Load(object sender, EventArgs e)
{
    string year = RouteData.Values["year"] as string;
    string month = RouteData.Values["month"] as string;
    string day = RouteData.Values["day"] as string;

    // Perform blog processing based on date parameter
}
```

As you see as you progress through the chapter, this is just the beginning of what can be done with route expressions.

NOTE

Parameters captured by the routing engine that show up in the RouteData dictionary are always stored as strings when used with ASP.NET Web Forms, even if you have constrained their data types via regular expressions (shown later in the chapter). As a result, it is up to you to convert them to their final destination types after getting them from the RouteData dictionary. ASP.NET MVC does a little extra work on your behalf to convert parameters into the data types the controllers expect.

Mapping URLs with Multiple Segments

The technique in the preceding section is great if you know ahead of time exactly which parameters are going to be in the URL and how many of them there are going to be. But what do you do if you don't know how many parameters you're going to have, or you want people to pass a list of data on the URL without using cumbersome query string syntax?

For example, let's say that you have an application that exposes data that can have a deeply nested hierarchy and you want users to drill into that hierarchy directly from the URL. Thankfully, the URL routing engine gives us the ability to map a list of parameters. An example of such a URL might enable the user to drill down to a location geographically, such as

```
http://my.app.com/location/Earth/USA/NY/NYC/TimesSquare
```

or as we'll see in the next code sample, we can supply a list of tags to filter data in a flat hierarchy:

```
http://my.app.com/tags/free/ammo/guns
```

(should return everything tagged with free, ammo, and guns, though we might be a little scared to see those results).

Multiple parameters can be supplied to a mapping by putting an asterisk in front of the named parameter:

```
// URL pattern with variable segments
routes.MapPageRoute("products-by-tag",
    "products/tags/{*tagnames}",
    "~/ProductsByTag.aspx");
```

And then in the `ProductsByTag.aspx.cs` we can obtain the list of values passed on the URL as a slash-delimited list:

```
string tagNames = RouteData.Values["tagnames"] as string;
string[] tagList = tagNames.Split('/');
Response.Write(string.Format(
    "You wanted products that have the following tags: {0}",
    string.Join(" : ", tagList)));
```

Linking to Other Pages with Routes

So far we've looked at a bunch of ways we can get a user from a URL to a page, but what about going the other way? When the user is on an ASP.NET Web Form, how do we create links to other pages in a way that respects the URL routing scheme without giving each page "magic" knowledge of how the URLs are formatted?

Basically what we want is to keep all the URL routing logic inside the single initialization method at application startup. We never want individual Web Forms to be creating links with hard-coded strings or string concatenation because those pages would cease to work properly if the URL route maps changed.

Ideally, we want to create URLs dynamically by supplying parameters and, optionally, the name of the route map. We can do this either declaratively in the ASPx markup or we can build the URL programmatically in the code behind.

First, let's take a look at how we can link to another page using the asp:HyperLink server control tag:

```
<asp:HyperLink ID="testLink" runat="server"
      NavigateUrl=
      "<%$ RouteUrl:RouteName=products-by-tag,tagnames=new/discounted %>">New and
DiscountedProducts
</asp:HyperLink>
```

This markup relies on the `RouteUrlExpressionBuilder` class to perform the appropriate route map lookup, apply the supplied parameters to the expression, and return a virtual path that respects the route. In the preceding code, the link returned will be for the /products/tags/new/discounted relative path. We supplied the `tagnames` parameter directly; we did not manually construct the URL fragments. This insulates the Web Form from changes to the URL mapping. If one day we get tired of using "products/tags" and decide to change the mapping to "products/list/bytags" as the prefix, we won't have to change any of this code—it will just work.

If we want to generate a route-aware URL programmatically, we can do so using the following code (the `codeGeneratedLink` object is just a hyperlink control):

```
RouteValueDictionary parameters = new RouteValueDictionary()
{
    { "tagnames", "new/discounted" }
};

VirtualPathData vpd = RouteTable.Routes.GetVirtualPath(
    null, "products-by-tag", parameters);
codeGeneratedLink.NavigateUrl = vpd.VirtualPath;
```

> **NOTE**
>
> Although these techniques make working with the routing engine seamless, they also have an added benefit: the removal of hard-coded URLs. Hard-coded URLs are the bane of many a website, and by the very act of adopting the use of URL routing in your website, your team will be forced to work without hard-coded URLs. A great functional test would be to add a random word to all the route paths to see if your site continues to function. As we all know, every time you remove a magic string from your code, an angel gets its wings.

Advanced URL Routing

So far you've seen examples of how to use URL routing to deal with static routes, routes with known parameters, and even routes with lists of parameters of unknown sizes. In this next section we examine several other advanced scenarios that truly show off the power and flexibility of the ASP.NET URL routing system.

Using Routes with Default Parameters

Another powerful feature of the URL routing system is the capability to supply some meaningful defaults for route parameters. For example, you might have a product category page that displays products within that category. If the user doesn't specify a category, you might want to pick a default one.

In the following route configuration, we have a category browser page that we can reach with the "/category/{name}" route pattern. If the user doesn't supply a category name, we supply a default:

```
// URL pattern with defaults
routes.MapPageRoute("category-browse",
    "category/{categoryname}",
    "~/Category.aspx",
    true,
    new RouteValueDictionary()
    {
        {"categoryname", "explosives"}
    });
```

In this case, the default supplied is the "explosives" category. The target page doesn't need to know that it was invoked with a default value; it can simply grab the category name from the `RouteData` dictionary.

Supplying defaults is useful both for creating default landing options for hitting pages without parameters, but also so that the target page doesn't need to be cluttered up with conditional statements checking to see whether particular values have been supplied in route data.

Using Constrained Routes

For a lot of situations, the type of route patterns that we have discussed thus far are sufficient. If you want static routes, or routes with simple parameters (with or without defaults), you are all set.

However, if you want to further constrain your route patterns so that only after certain conditions are met should your route be invoked, you're also in luck. One of the overloads of the `MapPageRoute` method that we haven't yet discussed actually takes a dictionary of constraints to route parameters. These constraints come in the form of regular expressions. (We warned you earlier that we'd have to talk about them eventually.)

At their simplest level you can use these regular expressions to limit the size of parameters so that when passing a state code on the URL, the code must be only two characters and must not contain numbers. Anyone familiar with regular expressions also knows that you can create incredibly powerful expressions that do far more than just simple validation. Regular expressions are outside the scope of this book, so we're going to use some simple expressions to illustrate their use in constraining route patterns.

The code below adds a new route to our blog system. This pattern restricts the year to no more than 4 digits, but the year can also be missing. The day and month parameters receive similar treatment, both enabling between 0 (missing) and 2 digits each. Because we're forcing them to be digits through the regular expression constraints means that the route will not be used if any non-numeric characters are passed on the URL.

NOTE

Remember that just because we use regular expressions to enforce a rule on our parameters limiting the data to only digits, that doesn't mean the parameters will be converted to integers for us. On the target page, we still need to perform the appropriate data conversion from strings.

```
// URL pattern with constraints
routes.MapPageRoute(
    routeName: "constrained-blog",
    routeUrl: "cblog/{year}/{month}/{day}",
    physicalFile: "~/Blog.aspx",
    checkPhysicalUrlAccess: true,
    defaults: new RouteValueDictionary() {
            { "year", DateTime.Now.Year.ToString() },
            { "month", DateTime.Now.Month.ToString() },
            { "day", DateTime.Now.Day.ToString() }
    },
    constraints: new RouteValueDictionary() {
            { "year", @"\d{0,4}" },
            { "month", @"\d{0,2}" },
            { "day", @"\d{0,2}" }
    }
);
```

In a small amount of code, we accomplish quite a bit. The first thing you see is that we supplied some default values for this route. The default values are set to the year, month, and day when the application started. Keep in mind that these won't change, so if your application has a long uptime, these values could lose their usefulness. However, they do the trick for this particular demo.

The next thing to look at is the RouteValueDictionary containing the constraints. The year parameter is mapped to a regular expression indicating it can be a digit between 0 and 4 digits. The month and day parameters are constrained to digits between 0 and 2 digits. In a real-world scenario you might choose better regular expressions but, as we said, regular expressions are outside the scope of this book, and plenty of great resources are on the Internet including a great site at http://www.regular-expressions.info.

Another thing you might have noticed is that all the method arguments have names. This is a great new feature of .NET 4 that makes method overloads with large numbers of arguments vastly more readable. Without the named arguments, you would have difficulty deciphering what the two dictionaries were and why they contained those values. If you find yourself dropping to a multiline method invocation because of a large number of arguments, also consider using named arguments to make your code that much easier to read.

Security Concerns with Routes

At this point you might be wondering how the URL routing system integrates with ASP.NET's declarative, location-based security system. It actually integrates quite well. You might have noticed that in several of the samples in this chapter we have been passing a parameter called `checkPhysicalUrlAccess` when creating route patterns.

This parameter, when true, tells ASP.NET that it should enforce location-based security after determining which ASPx page to call in response to a given pattern. This means that if you have a pattern that looks like this:

```
http://my.app.com/blog/2010/01/02
```

and maps to the following location:

```
/contentsystem/blogapp/posts.aspx
```

you can define a <location> element in your web.config to secure the physical location the same way you would normally secure that location, and permissions will be checked before the user gets to that page.

If the web.config-based security system doesn't work for you, you can always enforce individual permission checks at the page level either by hooking into the page life cycle or by placing code in the code-behind—all tactics that you would use with a traditional ASP.NET application.

Summary

This chapter has provided you with an introduction and a thorough overview of the ASP.NET URL routing engine and how to use it. It provides flexibility and power for developers, user-friendly URLs, and even a URL syntax that can provide added value and additional information to search engine crawlers. All this adds up to a powerful system that can make your website more powerful and easier to use by humans and computers alike.

If you're like us, at this point after having discovered the new routing engine, you're probably wondering where this tool has been all your life. Our exercise for you now is to go forth and create route maps and websites with friendly, easy-to-use URL syntax.

Using the Login Controls

You can use the ASP.NET Login controls to easily build a user registration system for your website. You can use the Login controls to display user registration forms, login forms, change password forms, and password reminder forms.

By default, the Login controls use ASP.NET Membership to authenticate users, create new users, and change user properties. When you use the Login controls, you are not required to write any code when performing these tasks.

> **NOTE**
>
> ASP.NET Membership is discussed in detail in the following chapter.

In the first part of this chapter, you are provided with an overview of the Login controls. You learn how to password-protect a section of your website and enable users to register and log in to your website.

In the remainder of this chapter, you learn how to use each of the following Login controls in detail:

▶ **Login**—Enables you to display a user login form.

▶ **CreateUserWizard**—Enables you to display a user registration form.

▶ **LoginStatus**—Enables you to display either a log in or log out link, depending on a user's authentication status.

▶ **LoginName**—Enables you to display the current user's registered username.

▶ **ChangePassword**—Enables you to display a form that allows users to change their passwords.

▶ **PasswordRecovery**—Enables you to display a form that allows users to receive an email containing their password.

▶ **LoginView**—Enables you to display different content to different users depending on the their authentication status or role.

Overview of the Login Controls

You won't have any fun using the Login controls unless you have confidential information to protect. Therefore, let's start by creating a page that needs password protection.

Create a new folder in your application named SecretFiles and add the page in Listing 26.1 to the SecretFiles folder.

LISTING 26.1   SecretFiles\Secret.aspx

```
<%@ Page Language="C#" %>
<!DOCTYPE html PUBLIC "-//W3C//DTD XHTML 1.0 Transitional//EN"
    "http://www.w3.org/TR/xhtml1/DTD/xhtml1-transitional.dtd">
<html xmlns="http://www.w3.org/1999/xhtml" >
<head id="Head1" runat="server">
    <title>Secret</title>
</head>
<body>
    <form id="form1" runat="server">
    <div>

    <h1>This Page is Secret!</h1>

    </div>
    </form>
</body>
</html>
```

There is nothing special about the page in Listing 26.1. It just displays the message This Page is Secret!.

To password-protect the Secret.aspx page, you need to make two configuration changes to your application: You need to configure both authentication and authorization.

First, you need to enable the proper type of authentication for your application. By default, Windows authentication is enabled. To use the Login controls, you need to enable Forms authentication by adding the web configuration file in Listing 26.2 to the root of your application.

LISTING 26.2 `Web.Config`

```
<?xml version="1.0" encoding="utf-8"?>
<configuration>
  <system.web>
    <authentication mode="Forms" />
  </system.web>
</configuration>
```

The web configuration file in Listing 26.2 contains an authentication element that includes a mode attribute. The mode attribute has the value Forms.

> **NOTE**
>
> Authentication and authorization is discussed in more detail in Chapter 27, "Using ASP.NET Membership."

By default, all users have access to all pages in an application. If you want to restrict access to the pages in a folder, you need to configure authorization for the folder.

If you add the web configuration file in Listing 26.3 to the SecretFiles folder, anonymous users are prevented from accessing any pages in the folder.

LISTING 26.3 `SecretFiles\Web.Config`

```
<?xml version="1.0"?>
<configuration>
  <system.web>
    <authorization>
      <deny users="?"/>
    </authorization>
  </system.web>
</configuration>
```

The web configuration file in Listing 26.3 contains an authorization element. This element contains a list of authorization rules for the folder. The single authorization rule in Listing 26.3 prevents anonymous users from accessing pages in the folder. (The ? represents anonymous users.)

> **VISUAL WEB DEVELOPER NOTE**
>
> If you prefer, you can use the Web Site Administration Tool to configure authentication and authorization. This tool provides you with a form interface for performing these configuration changes. When using Visual Web Developer, you can open the Web Site Administration Tool by selecting Website, ASP.NET Configuration.

If you attempt to request the Secret.aspx page after adding the web configuration file in Listing 26.3, you are redirected to a page named Login.aspx automatically. Therefore, the next page that we need to create is the Login.aspx page. (By default, this page must be located in the root of your application.)

The Login.aspx page in Listing 26.4 contains a Login control. The Login control automatically generates a login form (see Figure 26.1).

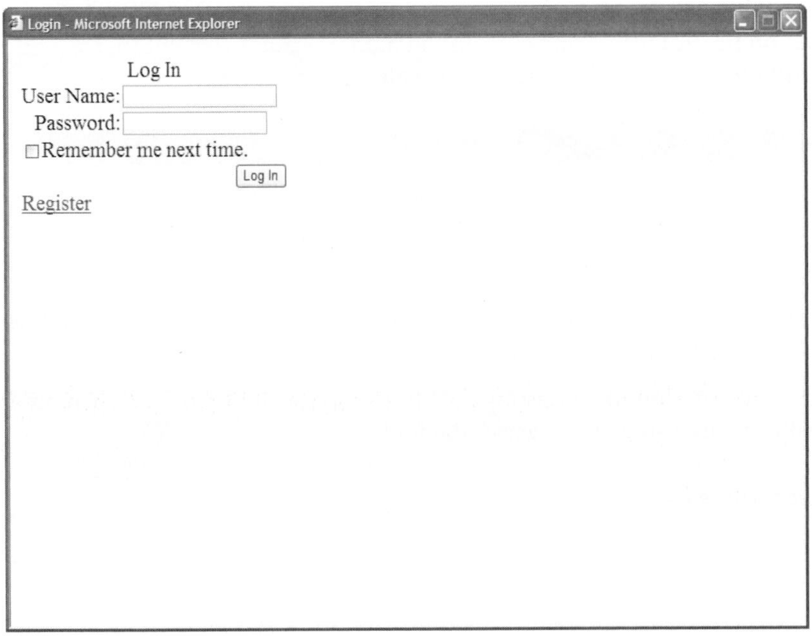

FIGURE 26.1   Displaying a Login form.

LISTING 26.4   Login.aspx

```
<%@ Page Language="C#" %>
<!DOCTYPE html PUBLIC "-//W3C//DTD XHTML 1.0 Transitional//EN"
    "http://www.w3.org/TR/xhtml1/DTD/xhtml1-transitional.dtd">
<html xmlns="http://www.w3.org/1999/xhtml" >
<head id="Head1" runat="server">
    <title>Login</title>
</head>
<body>
    <form id="form1" runat="server">
    <div>
```

```
    <asp:Login
        id="Login1"
        CreateUserText="Register"
        CreateUserUrl="~/Register.aspx"
        Runat="server" />

    </div>
    </form>
</body>
</html>
```

The `Login` control includes a `CreateUserText` and `CreateUserUrl` property. Adding these properties to the `Login` control causes the control to display a link to a page that enables a new user to register for your application. The `Login` control in Listing 26.4 links to a page named `Register.aspx`. This page is contained in Listing 26.5.

LISTING 26.5 `Register.aspx`

```
<%@ Page Language="C#" %>
<!DOCTYPE html PUBLIC "-//W3C//DTD XHTML 1.0 Transitional//EN"
  "http://www.w3.org/TR/xhtml1/DTD/xhtml1-transitional.dtd">
<html xmlns="http://www.w3.org/1999/xhtml" >
<head id="Head1" runat="server">
    <title>Register</title>
</head>
<body>
    <form id="form1" runat="server">
    <div>

    <asp:CreateUserWizard
        id="CreateUserWizard1"
        ContinueDestinationPageUrl="~/SecretFiles/Secret.aspx"
        Runat="server" />

    </div>
    </form>
</body>
</html>
```

The `Register.aspx` page contains a `CreateUserWizard` control. This control automatically generates a user registration form (see Figure 26.2). After you submit the form, a new user is created, and you are redirected back to the `Secret.aspx` page.

26

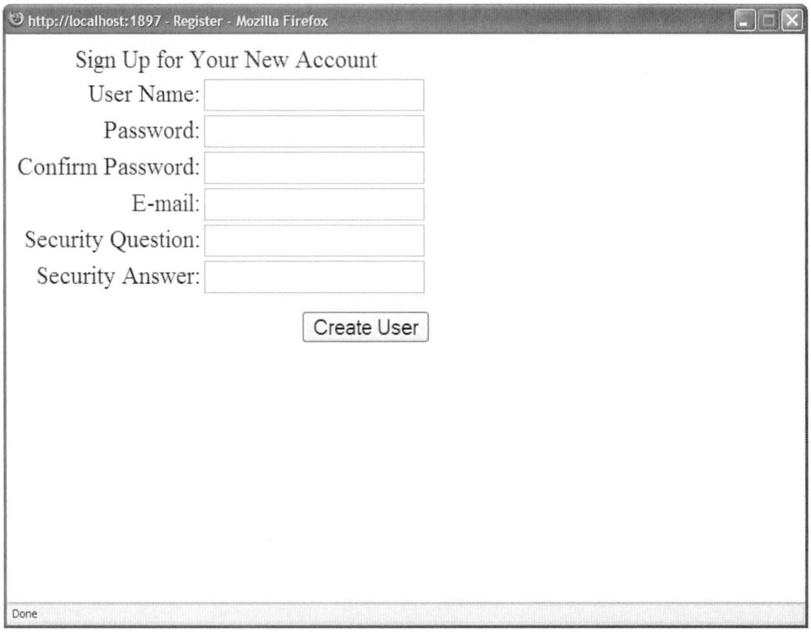

FIGURE 26.2   Displaying a registration form.

> **WARNING**
>
> The default ASP.NET Membership provider requires you to create a password that contains at least seven characters, and at least one of the characters must be nonalphanumeric (not a letter and not a number). So, secret_ is a valid password, but secret9 is not. In the next chapter, you learn how to change these default password complexity requirements.

That's all there is to it. We have created a complete user registration system without writing a single line of code. All the messy details of storing usernames and passwords are taken care of by ASP.NET Framework in the background.

Using the Login Control

The Login control renders a standard user login form. By default, the Login control uses ASP.NET Membership to authenticate users. However, as you see in a moment, you can customize how the Login control authenticates users.

The Login control supports a large number of properties that enable you to customize the appearance and behavior of the control (too many properties to list here). The page in Listing 26.6 illustrates how you can modify several of the Login control's properties to customize the form rendered by the control (see Figure 26.3).

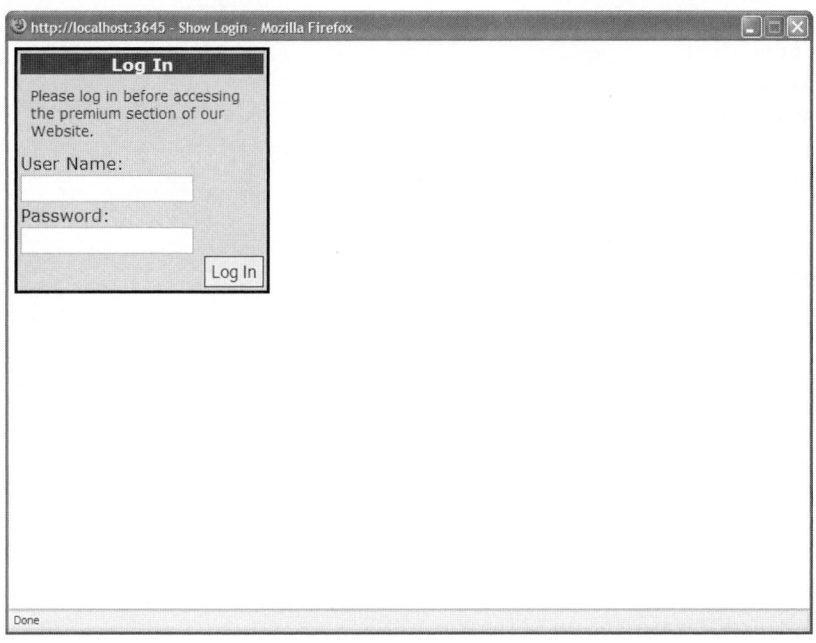

FIGURE 26.3   Customizing the Login form.

LISTING 26.6   ShowLogin.aspx

```
<%@ Page Language="C#" %>
<!DOCTYPE html PUBLIC "-//W3C//DTD XHTML 1.0 Transitional//EN"
  "http://www.w3.org/TR/xhtml1/DTD/xhtml1-transitional.dtd">
<html xmlns="http://www.w3.org/1999/xhtml" >
<head id="Head1" runat="server">
    <style type="text/css">
        .login
        {
            width:250px;
            font:14px Verdana,Sans-Serif;
            background-color:lightblue;
            border:solid 3px black;
            padding:4px;
        }
        .login_title
        {
            background-color:darkblue;
            color:white;
            font-weight:bold;
        }
        .login_instructions
```

```
        {
            font-size:12px;
            text-align:left;
            padding:10px;
        }
        .login_button
        {
            border:solid 1px black;
            padding:3px;
        }
    </style>
    <title>Show Login</title>
</head>
<body>
    <form id="form1" runat="server">
    <div>

    <asp:Login
        id="Login1"
        InstructionText="Please log in before
            accessing the premium section of our Website."
        TitleText="Log In"
        TextLayout="TextOnTop"
        LoginButtonText="Log In"
        DisplayRememberMe="false"
        CssClass="login"
        TitleTextStyle-CssClass="login_title"
        InstructionTextStyle-CssClass="login_instructions"
        LoginButtonStyle-CssClass="login_button"
        Runat="server" />

    </div>
    </form>
</body>
</html>
```

The page in Listing 26.6 uses Cascading Style Sheets (CSS) to change the appearance of the login form rendered by the Login control. By taking advantage of Cascading Style Sheets, you can customize the appearance of the Login control in any way that you can imagine.

NOTE

For the complete list of properties supported by the Login control, see the Microsoft .NET Framework SDK Documentation.

Automatically Redirecting a User to the Referring Page

If you request a page that you are not authorized to view, the ASP.NET Framework automatically redirects you to the Login.aspx page. After you log in successfully, you are redirected back to the original page that you requested.

When you are redirected to the Login.aspx page, a query string parameter named ReturnUrl is automatically added to the page request. This query string parameter contains the path of the page that you originally requested. The Login control uses the ReturnUrl parameter when redirecting you back to the original page.

You need to be aware of two special circumstances. First, if you request the Login.aspx page directly, a ReturnUrl parameter is not passed to the Login.aspx page. In that case, after you successfully log in, you are redirected to the Default.aspx page.

Second, if you add the Login control to a page other than the Login.aspx page, the ReturnUrl query string parameter is ignored. In this case, you need to set the Login control's DestinationPageUrl property. When you successfully log in, you are redirected to the URL represented by this property. If you don't supply a value for the DestinationPageUrl property, the same page is reloaded.

Automatically Hiding the Login Control from Authenticated Users

Some websites display a login form at the top of every page. That way, registered users can log in at any time to view additional content. The easiest way to add a Login control to all the pages in an application is to take advantage of Master Pages. If you add a Login control to a Master Page, the Login control is included in every content page that uses the Master Page.

You can change the layout of the Login control by modifying the Login control's Orientation property. If you set this property to the value Horizontal, the Username and Password text boxes are rendered in the same row.

If you include a Login control in all your pages, you should also modify the Login control's VisibleWhenLoggedIn property. If you set this property to the value False, the Login control is not displayed when a user has already authenticated.

For example, the Master Page in Listing 26.7 contains a Login control that has both its Orientation and VisibleWhenLoggedIn properties set.

LISTING 26.7   LoginMaster.master

```
<%@ Master Language="C#" %>
<!DOCTYPE html PUBLIC "-//W3C//DTD XHTML 1.0 Transitional//EN"
   "http://www.w3.org/TR/xhtml1/DTD/xhtml1-transitional.dtd">
<html xmlns="http://www.w3.org/1999/xhtml" >
<head id="Head1" runat="server">
```

```
<style type="text/css">
    html
    {
        background-color:silver;
    }
    .content
    {
        margin:auto;
        width:650px;
        border:solid 1px black;
        background-color:white;
        padding:10px;
    }
    .login
    {
        font:10px Arial,Sans-Serif;
        margin-left:auto;
    }
    .login input
    {
        font:10px Arial,Sans-Serif;
    }
</style>
<title>My Website</title>
</head>
<body>
    <form id="form1" runat="server">
    <div class="content">
    <asp:Login
        id="Login1"
        Orientation="Horizontal"
        VisibleWhenLoggedIn="false"
        DisplayRememberMe="false"
        TitleText=""
        CssClass="login"
        Runat="server" />
        <hr />
        <asp:contentplaceholder
            id="ContentPlaceHolder1"
            runat="server">
        </asp:contentplaceholder>
    </div>
    </form>
</body>
</html>
```

The content page in Listing 26.8 uses the Master Page in Listing 26.7 (see Figure 26.4). When you open the page in a browser, the Login control is hidden after you successfully log in to the application.

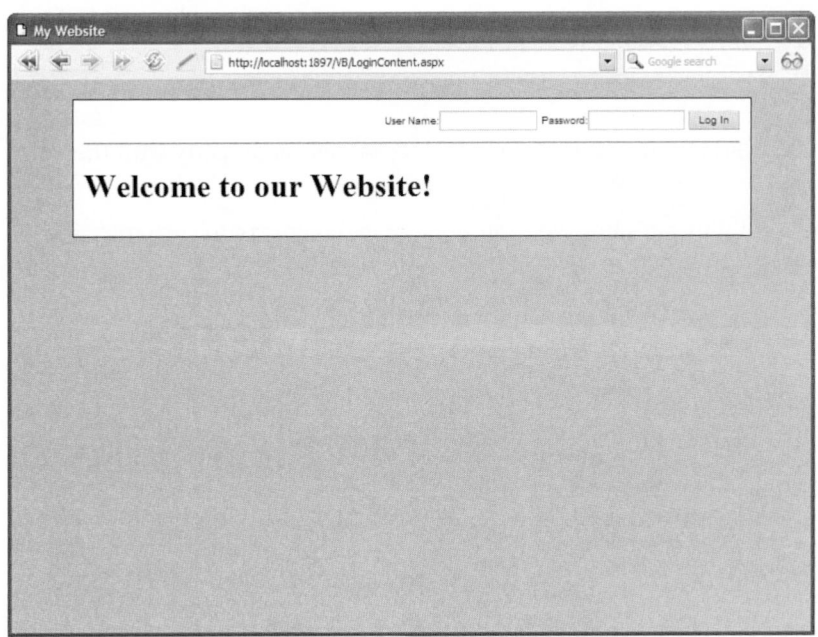

FIGURE 26.4   Adding the Login control to a Master Page.

LISTING 26.8   LoginContent.aspx

```
<%@ Page Language="C#" MasterPageFile="~/LoginMaster.master" %>
<asp:Content
    ID="Content1"
    ContentPlaceHolderID="ContentPlaceHolder1"
    Runat="Server">

    <h1>Welcome to our Website!</h1>

</asp:Content>
```

Using a Template with the Login Control

If you need to completely customize the appearance of the Login control, you can use a template. The Login control includes a LayoutTemplate property that enables you to customize the layout of the controls rendered by the Login control.

When you create a Layout template, you can add controls to the template that have the following IDs:

- ▶ UserName

- ▶ Password

- ▶ RememberMe

- ▶ FailureText

You also need to add a Button control that includes a CommandName property with the value Login.

The page in Listing 26.9 illustrates how you can use a LayoutTemplate to customize the appearance of the Login control (see Figure 26.5).

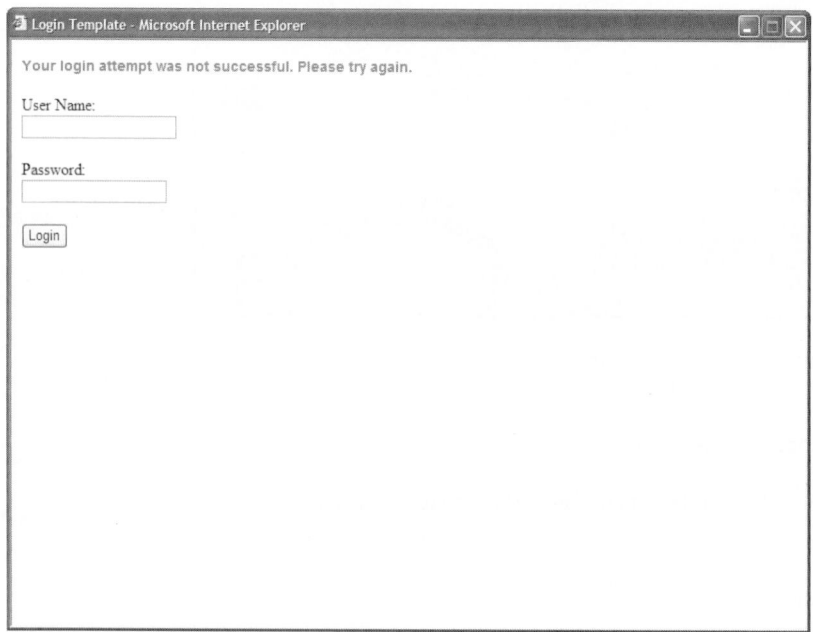

FIGURE 26.5   Using a template with the Login control.

LISTING 26.9   LoginTemplate.aspx

```
<%@ Page Language="C#" %>
<!DOCTYPE html PUBLIC "-//W3C//DTD XHTML 1.0 Transitional//EN"
  "http://www.w3.org/TR/xhtml1/DTD/xhtml1-transitional.dtd">
<html xmlns="http://www.w3.org/1999/xhtml" >
<head id="Head1" runat="server">
    <style type="text/css">
        .loginError
```

```
            {
                color:red;
                font:bold 14px Arial,Sans-Serif;
            }
        </style>
        <title>Login Template</title>
    </head>
    <body>
        <form id="form1" runat="server">
        <div>

        <asp:Login
            id="Login1"
            Runat="server">
            <LayoutTemplate>
            <asp:Label
                id="FailureText"
                EnableViewState="false"
                CssClass="loginError"
                Runat="server" />

            <br />
            <asp:Label
                id="lblUserName"
                AssociatedControlID="UserName"
                Text="User Name:"
                Runat="server" />
            <br />
            <asp:TextBox
                id="UserName"
                Runat="server" />

            <br /><br />
            <asp:Label
                id="lblPassword"
                AssociatedControlID="Password"
                Text="Password:"
                Runat="server" />
            <br />
            <asp:TextBox
                id="Password"
                TextMode="Password"
                Runat="server" />

            <br /><br />
            <asp:Button
```

```
                id="btnLogin"
                Text="Login"
                CommandName="Login"
                Runat="server" />
        </LayoutTemplate>
    </asp:Login>

    </div>
    </form>
</body>
</html>
```

Performing Custom Authentication with the Login Control

By default, the Login control uses ASP.NET Membership to authenticate a username and password. If you need to change this default behavior, you can handle the Login control's Authenticate event.

Imagine, for example, that you are building a simple application and you want to store a list of usernames and passwords in the web configuration file. The web configuration file in Listing 26.10 contains the credentials for two users named Bill and Ted.

LISTING 26.10   Web.Config

```
<?xml version="1.0" encoding="utf-8"?>
<configuration>
  <system.web>
    <authentication mode="Forms">
      <forms>
        <credentials passwordFormat="Clear">
          <user name="Bill" password="secret" />
          <user name="Ted" password="secret" />
        </credentials>
      </forms>
    </authentication>
  </system.web>
</configuration>
```

The page in Listing 26.11 contains a Login control that authenticates users against the list of usernames and passwords stored in the web configuration file.

LISTING 26.11   LoginCustom.aspx

```
<%@ Page Language="C#" %>
<!DOCTYPE html PUBLIC "-//W3C//DTD XHTML 1.0 Transitional//EN"
                "http://www.w3.org/TR/xhtml1/DTD/xhtml1-transitional.dtd">
<script runat="server">
    protected void Login1_Authenticate(object sender, AuthenticateEventArgs e)
    {
        string userName = Login1.UserName;
        string password = Login1.Password;
        e.Authenticated = FormsAuthentication.Authenticate(userName, password);
    }
</script>
<html xmlns="http://www.w3.org/1999/xhtml" >
<head id="Head1" runat="server">
    <title>Login Custom</title>
</head>
<body>
    <form id="form1" runat="server">
    <div>

    <asp:Login
        id="Login1"
        OnAuthenticate="Login1_Authenticate"
        Runat="server" />

    </div>
    </form>
</body>
</html>
```

The page in Listing 26.11 includes a method that handles the Login control's
Authenticate event. The second parameter passed to the Authenticate event handler is an
instance of the AuthenticateEventArgs class. This class includes the following property:

▶ Authenticated

If you assign the value True to this property, the Login control authenticates the user.

In Listing 26.11, the FormsAuthentication.Authenticate() method is called to check for
a username and password in the web configuration file that matches the username and
password entered into the login form. The value returned from this method is assigned to
the AuthenticateEventArgs.Authenticated property.

Using the `CreateUserWizard` Control

The `CreateUserWizard` control renders a user registration form. If a user successfully submits the form, a new user is added to your website. In the background, the `CreateUserWizard` control uses ASP.NET membership to create the new user.

The `CreateUserWizard` control supports a large number of properties (too many to list here) that enable you to modify the appearance and behavior of the control. For example, the page in Listing 26.12 uses several of the `CreateUserWizard` properties to customize the appearance of the form rendered by the control.

LISTING 26.12   ShowCreateUserWizard.aspx

```
<%@ Page Language="C#" %>
<!DOCTYPE html PUBLIC "-//W3C//DTD XHTML 1.0 Transitional//EN"
  "http://www.w3.org/TR/xhtml1/DTD/xhtml1-transitional.dtd">
<html xmlns="http://www.w3.org/1999/xhtml" >
<head id="Head1" runat="server">
    <style type="text/css">
        .createUser
        {
            width:350px;
            font:14px Verdana,Sans-Serif;
            background-color:lightblue;
            border:solid 3px black;
            padding:4px;
        }
        .createUser_title
        {
            background-color:darkblue;
            color:white;
            font-weight:bold;
        }
        .createUser_instructions
        {
            font-size:12px;
            text-align:left;
            padding:10px;
        }
        .createUser_button
        {
            border:solid 1px black;
            padding:3px;
        }
    </style>
    <title>Show CreateUserWizard</title>
</head>
```

```
<body>
    <form id="form1" runat="server">
    <div>

    <asp:CreateUserWizard
        id="CreateUserWizard1"
        ContinueDestinationPageUrl="~/Default.aspx"
        InstructionText="Please complete the following form
            to register at this Website."
        CompleteSuccessText="Your new account has been
            created. Thank you for registering."
        CssClass="createUser"
        TitleTextStyle-CssClass="createUser_title"
        InstructionTextStyle-CssClass="createUser_instructions"
        CreateUserButtonStyle-CssClass="createUser_button"
        ContinueButtonStyle-CssClass="createUser_button"
        Runat="server" />


    </div>
    </form>
</body>
</html>
```

The CreateUserWizard control in Listing 26.12 is formatted with Cascading Style Sheets
(see Figure 26.6). The control's ContinueDestinationPageUrl property is set to the value
"~/Default.aspx". After you successfully register, you are redirected to the
Default.aspx page.

> **NOTE**
>
> For the complete list of properties supported by the CreateUserWizard control, see
> the Microsoft .NET Framework SDK Documentation.

Configuring Create User Form Fields

By default, the CreateUserWizard control displays the following form fields:

- ▶ Username
- ▶ Password
- ▶ Confirm Password
- ▶ Email
- ▶ Security Question
- ▶ Security Answer

FIGURE 26.6   Formatting the `CreateUserWizard` control.

These are the default form fields. The last three fields are optional.

If you don't want to require a user to enter either an email address or a security question and answer, you need to modify the configuration of the default membership provider. The web configuration file in Listing 26.13 makes both an email address and security question and answer optional.

LISTING 26.13   Web.Config

```
<?xml version="1.0" encoding="utf-8"?>
<configuration>
  <system.web>

    <authentication mode="Forms" />

    <membership defaultProvider="MyMembership">
      <providers>
        <add
          name="MyMembership"
          type="System.Web.Security.SqlMembershipProvider"
          connectionStringName="LocalSqlServer"
          requiresQuestionAndAnswer="false"
          requiresUniqueEmail="false" />
```

```
    </providers>
  </membership>

  </system.web>
</configuration>
```

If you add the web configuration file in Listing 26.13 to your application, the CreateUserWizard control does not render fields for a security question and answer. However, the CreateUserWizard control still renders an email field. If you don't want the email form field to be rendered, you must perform an additional step. You must set the CreateUserWizard control's RequireEmail property to the value False.

If you add the page in Listing 26.14 to an application that contains the web configuration file in Listing 26.13, the email, security question, and security answer form fields are not displayed (see Figure 26.7).

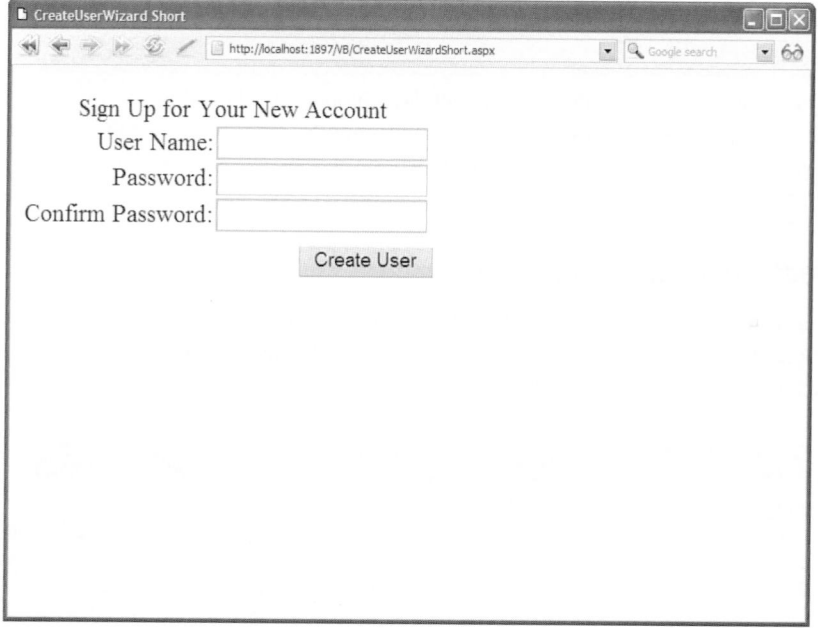

FIGURE 26.7   An abbreviated registration form.

LISTING 26.14   CreateUserWizardShort.aspx

```
<%@ Page Language="C#" %>
<!DOCTYPE html PUBLIC "-//W3C//DTD XHTML 1.0 Transitional//EN"
  "http://www.w3.org/TR/xhtml1/DTD/xhtml1-transitional.dtd">
<html xmlns="http://www.w3.org/1999/xhtml" >
<head id="Head1" runat="server">
```

```
    <title>CreateUserWizard Short</title>
</head>
<body>
    <form id="form1" runat="server">
    <div>

    <asp:CreateUserWizard
        id="CreateUserWizard1"
        RequireEmail="false"
        Runat="server" />

    </div>
    </form>
</body>
</html>
```

> **WARNING**
>
> Don't set the CreateUserWizard control's RequireEmail property to the value False
> when the membership provider's requiresUniqueEmail property is set to the value
> True. In other words, don't require an email address when you haven't provided a user
> with a method for entering an email address.

Sending a Create User Email Message

You can set up the CreateUserWizard control so that it automatically sends an email
when a new user registers. For example, you can send an email that contains the new
user's registered username and password to that user's email account.

> **WARNING**
>
> Sending an unencrypted email across the Internet with a user's password is danger-
> ous. However, it also is a common practice to include a password in a registration con-
> firmation email.

The page in Listing 26.15 includes a MailDefinition property that specifies the properties
of the email that is sent to a user after the user successfully registers.

LISTING 26.15   CreateUserWizardEmail.aspx

```
<%@ Page Language="C#" %>
<!DOCTYPE html PUBLIC "-//W3C//DTD XHTML 1.0 Transitional//EN"
  "http://www.w3.org/TR/xhtml1/DTD/xhtml1-transitional.dtd">
<html xmlns="http://www.w3.org/1999/xhtml" >
```

```
<head id="Head1" runat="server">
    <title>CreateUserWizard Email</title>
</head>
<body>
    <form id="form1" runat="server">
    <div>

    <asp:CreateUserWizard
        id="CreateUserWizard1"
        Runat="server">
        <MailDefinition
            BodyFileName="Register.txt"
            Subject="Registration Confirmation"
            From="Admin@YourSite.com" />
    </asp:CreateUserWizard>

    </div>
    </form>
</body>
</html>
```

The `MailDefinition` class supports the following properties:

▶ **BodyFileName**—Enables you to specify the path to the email message.

▶ **CC**—Enables you to send a carbon copy of the email message.

▶ **EmbeddedObjects**—Enables you to embed objects, such as images, in the email message.

▶ **From**—Enables you to specify the FROM email address.

▶ **IsBodyHtml**—Enables you to send an HTML email message.

▶ **Priority**—Enables you to specify the priority of the email message. Possible values are High, Low, and Normal.

▶ **Subject**—Enables you to specify the subject of the email message.

The `MailDefinition` associated with the `CreateUserWizard` control in Listing 26.15 sends the contents of the text file in Listing 26.16.

LISTING 26.16 Register.txt

```
Thank you for registering!


Here is your new username and password:

    username: <% UserName %>
    password: <% Password %>
```

The email message in Listing 26.16 includes two special expressions: <% UserName %> and <% Password %>. When the email is sent, the user's registered username and password are substituted for these expressions (see Figure 26.8).

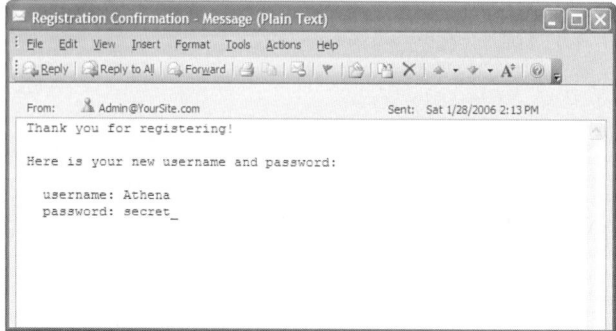

FIGURE 26.8   Receiving a registration email.

The MailDefinition class uses the email server configured by the smtp element in the web configuration file. For example, the web configuration file in Listing 26.17 illustrates how you can configure the MailDefinition class to use the local SMTP server included with Internet Information Services. (You can enable the local SMTP Server by opening Internet Information Services from the Administrative Tools folder.)

LISTING 26.17   Web.Config

```xml
<?xml version="1.0" encoding="utf-8"?>
<configuration>
  <system.net>
    <mailSettings>
      <smtp deliveryMethod="PickupDirectoryFromIis"/>
    </mailSettings>
  </system.net>
  <system.web>
    <authentication mode="Forms" />
  </system.web>
</configuration>
```

If you need to connect to a mail server located on another machine, you can use the web configuration file in Listing 26.18. In Listing 26.18, the smtp element includes a network element that specifies a mail host, username, and password.

LISTING 26.18 Web.Config

```
<?xml version="1.0" encoding="utf-8"?>
<configuration>
  <system.net>
    <mailSettings>
      <smtp>
        <network
            host="mail.YourServer.com"
            userName="admin"
            password="secret" />
      </smtp>
    </mailSettings>
  </system.net>
  <system.web>
    <authentication mode="Forms" />
  </system.web>
</configuration>
```

NOTE

If you need to customize the email message sent by the CreateUserWizard control, you can handle the CreateUserWizard control's SendingMail event. See the CreateUserWizardCodeConfirmation.aspx page in the next section.

Automatically Redirecting a User to the Referring Page

When you successfully log in from the Login.aspx page, you automatically are redirected back to the original page you requested. The CreateUserWizard control, on the other hand, does not redirect you back anywhere. If you want the CreateUserWizard control to work in the same way as the Login control, you need to write some code.

The Login control in Listing 26.19 includes a link to a user registration page named CreateUserWizardReturn.aspx. In the Page_Load() event handler, the value of the ReturnUrl query string parameter is added to the link to the registration page.

LISTING 26.19 LoginReturn.aspx

```
<%@ Page Language="C#" %>
<!DOCTYPE html PUBLIC "-//W3C//DTD XHTML 1.0 Transitional//EN"
    "http://www.w3.org/TR/xhtml1/DTD/xhtml1-transitional.dtd">
```

```
<script runat="server">

    protected void Page_Load(object sender, EventArgs e)
    {
        if (!Page.IsPostBack)
        {
            string dest = Request.QueryString["ReturnUrl"];
            Login1.CreateUserUrl =
                "~/CreateUserWizardReturn.aspx?ReturnUrl=" + Server.UrlEncode(dest);
        }
    }
</script>
<html xmlns="http://www.w3.org/1999/xhtml" >
<head id="Head1" runat="server">
    <title>Login Return</title>
</head>
<body>
    <form id="form1" runat="server">
    <div>

    <asp:Login
        id="Login1"
        CreateUserText="Register"
        CreateUserUrl="~/CreateUserWizardReturn.aspx"
        Runat="server" />

    </div>
    </form>
</body>
</html>
```

Before you use the page in Listing 26.19, you need to rename the page to Login.aspx. If a user requests a page that the user is not authorized to access, the user is automatically redirected to the Login.aspx page. The ReturnUrl parameter is automatically added to the request for Login.aspx.

The page in Listing 26.20 contains a CreateUserWizard control. This page also contains a Page_Load() event handler. The value of the ReturnUrl query string parameter is used to redirect the user back to the originally requested page.

LISTING 26.20 CreateUserWizardReturn.aspx

```
<%@ Page Language="C#" %>
<!DOCTYPE html PUBLIC "-//W3C//DTD XHTML 1.0 Transitional//EN"
"http://www.w3.org/TR/xhtml1/DTD/xhtml1-transitional.dtd">
<script runat="server">
```

```
    void Page_Load()
    {
        if (!Page.IsPostBack)
        {
            string dest = "~/Default.aspx";
            if (!String.IsNullOrEmpty(Request.QueryString["ReturnURL"]))
                dest = Request.QueryString["ReturnURL"];
            CreateUserWizard1.ContinueDestinationPageUrl = dest;
        }
    }
</script>
<html xmlns="http://www.w3.org/1999/xhtml" >
<head id="Head1" runat="server">
    <title>CreateUserWizard Return</title>
</head>
<body>
    <form id="form1" runat="server">
    <div>

    <asp:CreateUserWizard
        id="CreateUserWizard1"
        Runat="server" />

    </div>
    </form>
</body>
</html>
```

Automatically Generating a Password

Some websites require you to complete multiple steps when registering. For example, you must complete the following steps when registering for a new account at eBay:

1. Complete the registration form.
2. Receive an email with a confirmation code.
3. Enter the confirmation code into a form.

This method of registration enables you to verify a user's email address. If someone enters an invalid email address, the confirmation code is never received.

If you need to implement this registration scenario, you need to know about the following three properties of the CreateUserWizard control:

▶ **AutoGeneratePassword**—Enables the CreateUserWizard control to generate a new password automatically.

▶ **DisableCreatedUser**—Enables you to disable the new user account created by the CreateUserWizard control.

▶ **LoginCreatedUser**—Enables you to prevent a new user from being logged in automatically.

You can send two types of confirmation email messages. First, you can generate a new password automatically and send the password to the user. In that case, you want to enable the AutoGeneratePassword property and disable the LoginCreatedUser properties.

Alternatively, you can allow a new user to enter her own password and send a distinct confirmation code in the confirmation email message. In that case, you want to enable the DisableCreatedUser property and disable the LoginCreatedUser property. Let's examine each of these scenarios in turn.

The page in Listing 26.21 contains a CreateUserWizard control that does not render a password form field. The control has its AutoGeneratePassword property enabled and its LoginCreatedUser property disabled. After you complete the form rendered by the CreateUserWizard control, you can click the Continue button to open the Login.aspx page.

LISTING 26.21   CreateUserWizardPasswordConfirmation.aspx

```
<%@ Page Language="C#" %>
<!DOCTYPE html PUBLIC "-//W3C//DTD XHTML 1.0 Transitional//EN"
   "http://www.w3.org/TR/xhtml1/DTD/xhtml1-transitional.dtd">
<html xmlns="http://www.w3.org/1999/xhtml" >
<head id="Head1" runat="server">
    <title>CreateUserWizard Password Confirmation</title>
</head>
<body>
    <form id="form1" runat="server">
    <div>

    <asp:CreateUserWizard
        id="CreateUserWizard1"
        CompleteSuccessText="A confirmation email
            containing your new password has been
            sent to your email address."
        AutoGeneratePassword="true"
        LoginCreatedUser="false"
        ContinueDestinationPageUrl="~/Login.aspx"
        Runat="server">
        <MailDefinition
            From="Admin@YourSite.com"
            BodyFileName="PasswordConfirmation.htm"
            IsBodyHtml="true"
            Subject="Registration Confirmation" />
    </asp:CreateUserWizard>
```

```
        </div>
    </form>
</body>
</html>
```

The CreateUserWizard control in Listing 26.21 sends the email message contained in
Listing 26.22.

LISTING 26.22   PasswordConfirmation.htm

```
<!DOCTYPE html PUBLIC "-//W3C//DTD XHTML 1.0 Transitional//EN"
    "http://www.w3.org/TR/xhtml1/DTD/xhtml1-transitional.dtd">
<html xmlns="http://www.w3.org/1999/xhtml" >
<head>
    <title>Password Confirmation</title>
</head>
<body>

    Your new password is <% Password %>.

</body>
</html>
```

The email message in Listing 26.22 includes the automatically generated password. When
the new user receives the automatically generated password in her inbox, she can enter
the password in the Login.aspx page.

In the second scenario, the user gets to choose his password. However, the user's account
is disabled until he enters his confirmation code.

The CreateUserWizard control in Listing 26.23 has its DisableCreateUser property
enabled and its LoginCreatedUser property disabled.

LISTING 26.23   CreateUserWizardCodeConfirmation.aspx

```
<%@ Page Language="C#" %>
<!DOCTYPE html PUBLIC "-//W3C//DTD XHTML 1.0 Transitional//EN"
 "http://www.w3.org/TR/xhtml1/DTD/xhtml1-transitional.dtd">
<script runat="server">
```

26

```
    protected void CreateUserWizard1_SendingMail(object sender,
MailMessageEventArgs e)
    {
        MembershipUser user = Membership.GetUser(CreateUserWizard1.UserName);
        string code = user.ProviderUserKey.ToString();
        e.Message.Body = e.Message.Body.Replace("<%ConfirmationCode%>", code);
    }
</script>
<html xmlns="http://www.w3.org/1999/xhtml" >
<head id="Head1" runat="server">
    <title>CreateUserWizard Code Confirmation</title>
</head>
<body>
    <form id="form1" runat="server">
    <div>

    <asp:CreateUserWizard
        id="CreateUserWizard1"
        CompleteSuccessText="A confirmation email
            containing your new password has been
            sent to your email address."
        DisableCreatedUser="true"
        ContinueDestinationPageUrl="~/ConfirmCode.aspx"
        OnSendingMail="CreateUserWizard1_SendingMail"
        Runat="server">
        <MailDefinition
            From="Admin@YourSite.com"
            BodyFileName="CodeConfirmation.htm"
            IsBodyHtml="true"
            Subject="Registration Confirmation" />
    </asp:CreateUserWizard>

    </div>
    </form>
</body>
</html>
```

The page in Listing 26.23 includes a SendingMail event handler. The confirmation code is the unique key assigned to the new user by the membership provider (a GUID). The confirmation code is substituted into the email message before the message is sent. The email message is contained in Listing 26.24.

LISTING 26.24   CodeConfirmation.htm

```
<!DOCTYPE html PUBLIC "-//W3C//DTD XHTML 1.0 Transitional//EN"
  "http://www.w3.org/TR/xhtml1/DTD/xhtml1-transitional.dtd">
<html xmlns="http://www.w3.org/1999/xhtml" >
<head>
    <title>Code Confirmation</title>
</head>
<body>

<%UserName%>,
your confirmation code is <%ConfirmationCode%>

</body>
</html>
```

After you complete the form rendered by the CreateUserWizard control, you can click the Continue button to open the ConfirmCode.aspx page in Listing 26.25 (see Figure 26.9).

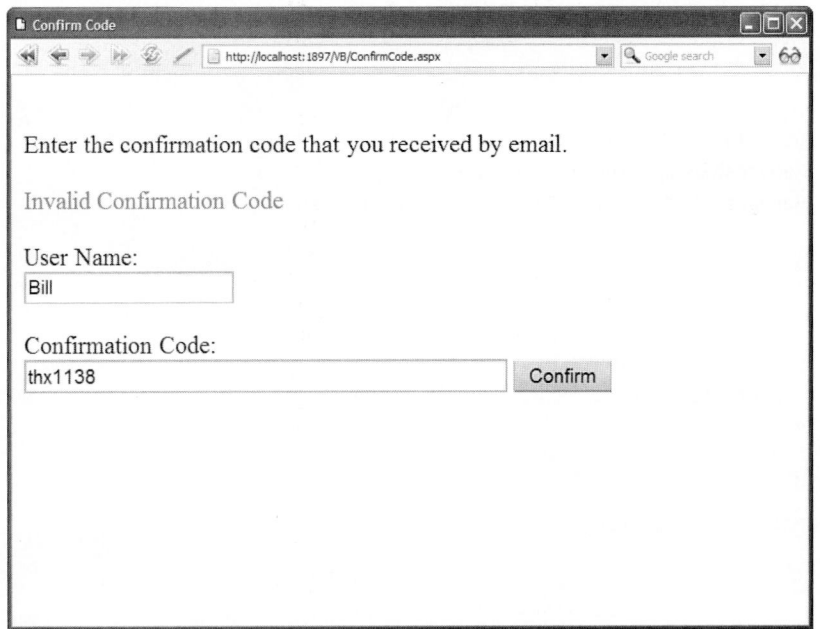

FIGURE 26.9   Entering a confirmation code.

LISTING 26.25   ConfirmCode.aspx

```
<%@ Page Language="C#" %>
<!DOCTYPE html PUBLIC "-//W3C//DTD XHTML 1.0 Transitional//EN"
    "http://www.w3.org/TR/xhtml1/DTD/xhtml1-transitional.dtd">
<script runat="server">

    protected void btnConfirm_Click(object sender, EventArgs e)
    {
        MembershipUser user = Membership.GetUser(txtUserName.Text);
        if (user == null)
        {
            lblError.Text = "Invalid User Name";
        }
        else
        {
            string providerCode = user.ProviderUserKey.ToString();
            string userCode = txtConfirmationCode.Text.Trim();
            if (providerCode != userCode)
            {
                lblError.Text = "Invalid Confirmation Code";
            }
            else
            {
                user.IsApproved = true;
                Membership.UpdateUser(user);
                Response.Redirect("~/SecretFiles/Secret.aspx");
            }
        }
    }
</script>
<html xmlns="http://www.w3.org/1999/xhtml" >
<head id="Head1" runat="server">
    <title>Confirm Code</title>
</head>
<body>
    <form id="form1" runat="server">
    <div>

    <p>
    Enter the confirmation code that you received by email.
    </p>

    <asp:Label
        id="lblError"
        EnableViewState="false"
```

```
            ForeColor="Red"
            Runat="server" />

        <br /><br />
        <asp:Label
            id="lblUserName"
            Text="User Name:"
            AssociatedControlID="txtUserName"
            Runat="server" />
        <br />
        <asp:TextBox
            id="txtUserName"
            Runat="server" />

        <br /><br />
        <asp:Label
            id="lblConfirmationCode"
            Text="Confirmation Code:"
            AssociatedControlID="txtConfirmationCode"
            Runat="server" />
        <br />
        <asp:TextBox
            id="txtConfirmationCode"
            Columns="50"
            Runat="server" />
        <asp:Button
            id="btnConfirm"
            Text="Confirm"
            OnClick="btnConfirm_Click"
            Runat="server" />

        </div>
        </form>
</body>
</html>
```

If the user enters the correct username and confirmation code, his account is enabled. The
`MembershipUser.IsApproved` property is assigned the value `True` and the updated user
information is saved with the `Membership.UpdateUser()` method.

Using Templates with the `CreateUserWizard` Control

If you need to customize the appearance of the form rendered by the `CreateUserWizard`
control, you can create templates for the `CreateUserWizardStep` and the
`CompleteWizardStep`. For example, the page in Listing 26.26 displays a drop-down list to
display options for the security question (see Figure 26.10).

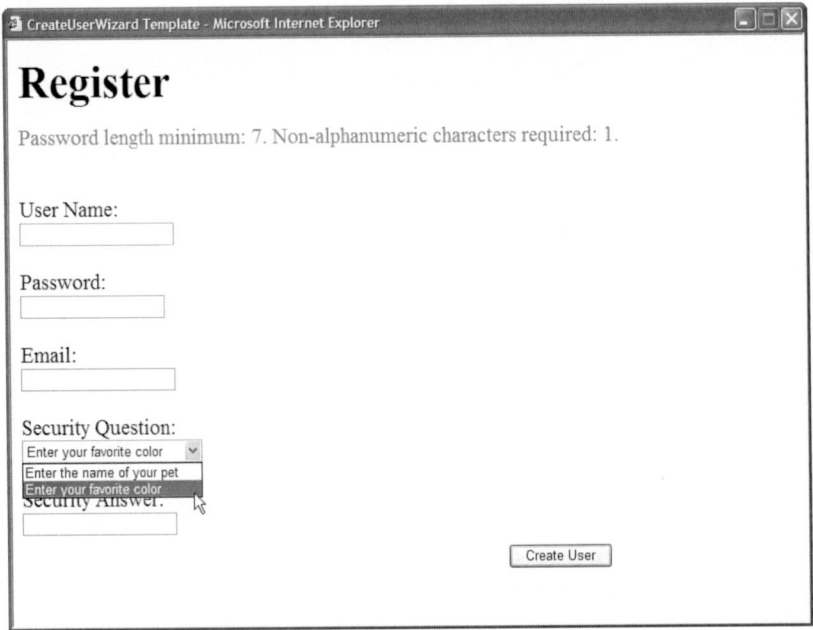

FIGURE 26.10   Customizing the `CreateUserWizard` control with templates.

LISTING 26.26   CreateUserWizardTemplate.aspx

```
<%@ Page Language="C#" %>
<!DOCTYPE html PUBLIC "-//W3C//DTD XHTML 1.0 Transitional//EN"
  "http://www.w3.org/TR/xhtml1/DTD/xhtml1-transitional.dtd">
<html xmlns="http://www.w3.org/1999/xhtml" >
<head id="Head1" runat="server">
    <title>CreateUserWizard Template</title>
</head>
<body>
    <form id="form1" runat="server">
    <div>

    <asp:CreateUserWizard
        id="CreateUserWizard1"
        Runat="server">
        <WizardSteps>
        <asp:CreateUserWizardStep>
        <ContentTemplate>
        <h1>Register</h1>

        <asp:Label
            id="ErrorMessage"
```

```
            ForeColor="Red"
            Runat="server" />

    <br /><br />
    <asp:Label
        id="lblUserName"
        Text="User Name:"
        AssociatedControlID="UserName"
        Runat="server" />
    <br />
    <asp:TextBox
        id="UserName"
        Runat="server" />

    <br /><br />
    <asp:Label
        id="lblPassword"
        Text="Password:"
        AssociatedControlID="Password"
        Runat="server" />
    <br />
    <asp:TextBox
        id="Password"
        TextMode="Password"
        Runat="server" />

    <br /><br />
    <asp:Label
        id="lblEmail"
        Text="Email:"
        AssociatedControlID="Email"
        Runat="server" />
    <br />
    <asp:TextBox
        id="Email"
        Runat="server" />

    <br /><br />
    <asp:Label
        id="lblQuestion"
        Text="Security Question:"
        AssociatedControlID="Question"
        Runat="server" />
    <br />
    <asp:DropDownList
        id="Question"
```

26

```
                Runat="server">
                <asp:ListItem
                    Text="Enter the name of your pet"
                    Value="Pet Name" />
                <asp:ListItem
                    Text="Enter your favorite color"
                    Value="Favorite Color" />
            </asp:DropDownList>

            <br /><br />
            <asp:Label
                id="lblAnswer"
                Text="Security Answer:"
                AssociatedControlID="Answer"
                Runat="server" />
            <br />
            <asp:TextBox
                id="Answer"
                Runat="server" />
        </ContentTemplate>
        </asp:CreateUserWizardStep>
        <asp:CompleteWizardStep>
        <ContentTemplate>
            Your account was successfully created.
        </ContentTemplate>
        </asp:CompleteWizardStep>
        </WizardSteps>
    </asp:CreateUserWizard>

    </div>
    </form>
</body>
</html>
```

In the CreateUserWizardStep, you can add controls with the following IDs:

- UserName

- Password

- Email

- ConfirmPassword

- Question

- Answer

- ErrorMessage

Of course, you can add any other controls that you need. For example, you can request additional information when a new user registers and store the information in a separate database table (see the next section).

In the CreateUserWizardStep, you also can add Button controls that contain CommandName properties with the following values:

▶ CreateUser

▶ Cancel

Adding Steps to the CreateUserWizard Control

The CreateUserWizard control inherits from the base Wizard control. That means that you can use all the properties supported by the Wizard control when using the CreateUserWizard control. In particular, you can extend the CreateUserWizard control with additional wizard steps.

For example, imagine that you want to require new users to enter their first and last names. The page in Listing 26.27 contains an additional WizardStep that includes both first and last name form fields.

LISTING 26.27 CreateUserWizardExtra.aspx

```
<%@ Page Language="C#" %>
<%@ Import Namespace="System.Data.SqlClient" %>
<%@ Import Namespace="System.Web.Configuration" %>
<!DOCTYPE html PUBLIC "-//W3C//DTD XHTML 1.0 Transitional//EN"
    "http://www.w3.org/TR/xhtml1/DTD/xhtml1-transitional.dtd">

<script runat="server">

    protected void CreateUserWizard1_CreatedUser(object sender, EventArgs e)
    {
        CreateUserProfile(CreateUserWizard1.UserName,txtFirstName.Text,txtLastName.
Text);
    }

    private void CreateUserProfile(string userName, string firstName, string
lastName)
    {
        string conString =
          WebConfigurationManager.ConnectionStrings["UserProfiles"].ConnectionString;
        SqlConnection con = new SqlConnection(conString);
        SqlCommand cmd =
          new SqlCommand(
 "INSERT UserProfiles (UserName,FirstName,LastName)
VALUES(@UserName,@FirstName,con);
```

26

```
        cmd.Parameters.AddWithValue("@UserName", userName);
        cmd.Parameters.AddWithValue("@FirstName", firstName);
        cmd.Parameters.AddWithValue("@LastName", lastName);
        using (con)
        {
            con.Open();
            cmd.ExecuteNonQuery();
        }
    }

</script>

<html xmlns="http://www.w3.org/1999/xhtml" >
<head id="Head1" runat="server">
    <title>CreateUserWizard Extra</title>
</head>
<body>
    <form id="form1" runat="server">
    <div>

    <asp:CreateUserWizard
        id="CreateUserWizard1"
        Runat="server" OnCreatedUser="CreateUserWizard1_CreatedUser">
        <WizardSteps>
        <asp:WizardStep>
            <asp:Label
                id="lblFirstName"
                Text="First Name:"
                AssociatedControlID="txtFirstName"
                Runat="server" />
            <br />
            <asp:TextBox
                id="txtFirstName"
                Runat="server" />

            <br /><br />
            <asp:Label
                id="lblLastName"
                Text="Last Name:"
                AssociatedControlID="txtLastName"
                Runat="server" />
            <br />
            <asp:TextBox
                id="txtLastName"
                Runat="server" />
        </asp:WizardStep>
```

```
        <asp:CreateUserWizardStep />
        </WizardSteps>
    </asp:CreateUserWizard>

    </div>
    </form>
</body>
</html>
```

The page in Listing 26.27 includes a CreatedUser event handler that executes after the new user is created. This handler adds the new user's first and last name to a database named UserProfilesDB.

Using the LoginStatus Control

The LoginStatus control displays either a Login link or a Logout link, depending on your authentication status. When you click the Login link, you are transferred to the Login.aspx page. When you click the Logout link, you are logged out of the website.

The page in Listing 26.28 contains a LoginStatus control (see Figure 26.11).

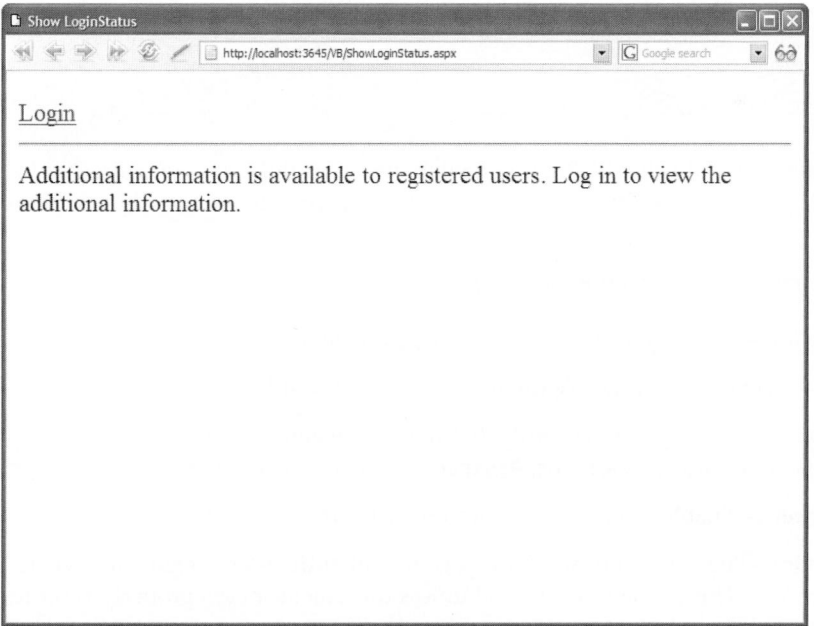

FIGURE 26.11   Displaying a Login link with the LoginStatus control.

LISTING 26.28   ShowLoginStatus.aspx

```
<%@ Page Language="C#" %>
<!DOCTYPE html PUBLIC "-//W3C//DTD XHTML 1.0 Transitional//EN"
  "http://www.w3.org/TR/xhtml1/DTD/xhtml1-transitional.dtd">
<html xmlns="http://www.w3.org/1999/xhtml" >
<head id="Head1" runat="server">
    <title>Show LoginStatus</title>
</head>
<body>
    <form id="form1" runat="server">
    <div>

    <asp:LoginStatus
        id="LoginStatus1"
        Runat="server" />

    <hr />

    Additional information is available to registered users. Log in to view
    the additional information.


    </div>
    </form>
</body>
</html>
```

After you open the page in Listing 26.28, if you click the Login link, you are redirected to the Login page. If you enter a valid username and password, you are redirected back to the ShowLoginStatus.aspx page.

The LoginStatus control supports the following properties:

▶ **LoginImageUrl**—Enables you to specify an image for the Login link.

▶ **LoginText**—Enables you to specify the text for the Login link.

▶ **LogoutAction**—Enables you to control what happens when the Logout link is clicked. Possible values are Redirect, RedirectToLoginPage, and Refresh.

▶ **LogoutImageUrl**—Enables you to specify an image for the Logout link.

▶ **LogoutPageUrl**—Enables you to specify a page to which the user is redirected when the user logs out. This property is ignored unless the LogoutAction property is set to the value Redirect.

▶ **LogoutText**—Enables you to specify the text for the Logout link.

The LoginStatus control also supports the following two events:

▶ **LoggingOut**—Raised before the user is logged out.

▶ **LoggedOut**—Raised after the user is logged out.

Using the LoginName Control

The LoginName control displays the current user's registered username. If the current user is not authenticated, the LoginName control renders nothing.

The page in Listing 26.29 contains both a LoginName and LoginStatus control.

LISTING 26.29   ShowLoginName.aspx

```
<%@ Page Language="C#" %>
<!DOCTYPE html PUBLIC "-//W3C//DTD XHTML 1.0 Transitional//EN"
   "http://www.w3.org/TR/xhtml1/DTD/xhtml1-transitional.dtd">
<html xmlns="http://www.w3.org/1999/xhtml" >
<head id="Head1" runat="server">
    <title>Show LoginName</title>
</head>
<body>
    <form id="form1" runat="server">
    <div>

    <asp:LoginName
        id="LoginName1"
        FormatString="{0} /"
        Runat="server" />

    <asp:LoginStatus
        id="LoginStatus1"
        Runat="server" />

    <hr />

    Additional information is available to registered users. Log in to view
    the additional information.

    </div>
    </form>
</body>
</html>
```

26

When you first open the page in Listing 26.29, the LoginName control displays nothing. However, if you login by clicking the Login link, the LoginName control displays your username (see Figure 26.12).

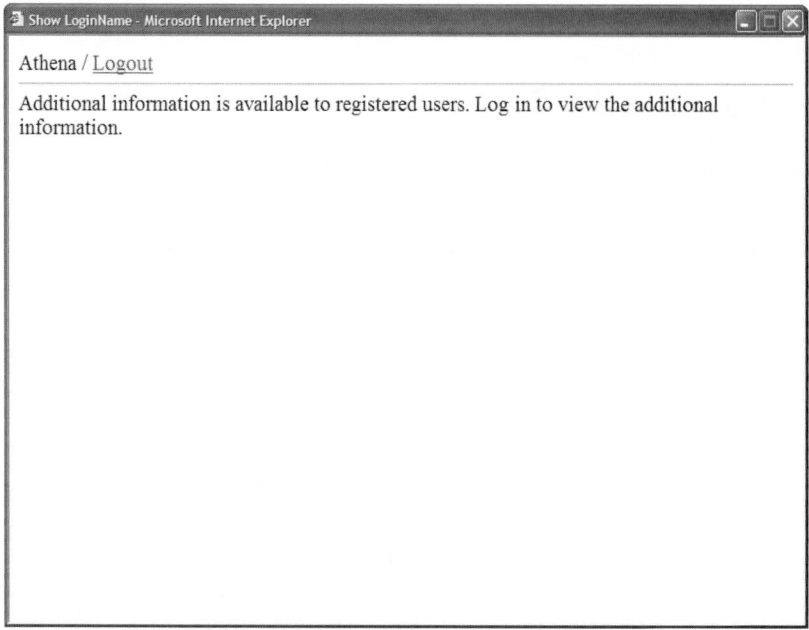

FIGURE 26.12   Displaying the current username with the LoginName control.

The LoginName control supports the following property:

▶ **FormatString**—Enables you to format the username when the username is rendered.

Using the ChangePassword Control

The ChangePassword control enables a user (or administrator) to change a user password. The page in Listing 26.30 illustrates how you can use this control.

LISTING 26.30   ShowChangePassword.aspx

```
<%@ Page Language="C#" %>
<!DOCTYPE html PUBLIC "-//W3C//DTD XHTML 1.0 Transitional//EN"
 "http://www.w3.org/TR/xhtml1/DTD/xhtml1-transitional.dtd">
<html xmlns="http://www.w3.org/1999/xhtml" >
<head id="Head1" runat="server">
    <style type="text/css">
        .changePassword
```

```
            {
                font:14px Verdana,Sans-Serif;
                background-color:lightblue;
                border:solid 3px black;
                padding:4px;
            }
            .changePassword_title
            {
                background-color:darkblue;
                color:white;
                font-weight:bold;
            }
            .changePassword_instructions
            {
                font-size:12px;
                text-align:left;
                padding:10px;
            }
            .changePassword_button
            {
                border:solid 1px black;
                padding:3px;
            }
    </style>
    <title>Show ChangePassword</title>
</head>
<body>
    <form id="form1" runat="server">
    <div>

    <asp:LoginName ID="LoginName1" runat="server" />

    <asp:ChangePassword
        id="ChangePassword1"
        InstructionText="Complete this form to create
            a new password."
        DisplayUserName="true"
        ContinueDestinationPageUrl="~/Default.aspx"
        CancelDestinationPageUrl="~/Default.aspx"
        CssClass="changePassword"
        TitleTextStyle-CssClass="changePassword_title"
        InstructionTextStyle-CssClass="changePassword_instructions"
        ChangePasswordButtonStyle-CssClass="changePassword_button"
        CancelButtonStyle-CssClass="changePassword_button"
        ContinueButtonStyle-CssClass="changePassword_button"
        Runat="server" />
```

26

```
    </div>
    </form>
</body>
</html>
```

The form in Listing 26.30 includes form fields for entering your username, old password, and new password (see Figure 26.13). After you submit the form, your old password is changed to the new password.

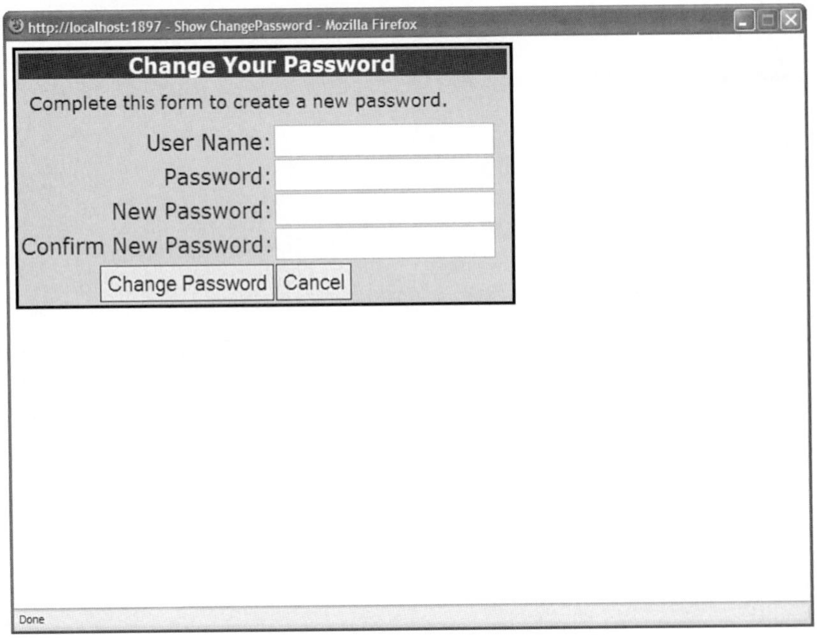

FIGURE 26.13   Changing your password with the ChangePassword control.

The ChangePassword control in Listing 26.30 includes a DisplayUserName property. When this property is enabled, the username form field is rendered. You don't need to include the DisplayUserName property when you place the page within a password-protected section of your web application. In that case, the ChangePassword control uses the name of the current user automatically.

Sending a Change Password Email

After the user changes his password, you can use the ChangePassword control to automatically send an email message that contains the new password. The page in Listing 26.31 contains a ChangePassword control that automatically sends an email.

NOTE

You can send a user's password in an email message even when the password is encrypted or hashed by the membership provider.

LISTING 26.31   ChangePasswordEmail.aspx

```
<%@ Page Language="C#" %>
<!DOCTYPE html PUBLIC "-//W3C//DTD XHTML 1.0 Transitional//EN"
  "http://www.w3.org/TR/xhtml1/DTD/xhtml1-transitional.dtd">
<html xmlns="http://www.w3.org/1999/xhtml" >
<head id="Head1" runat="server">
    <title>ChangePassword Email</title>
</head>
<body>
    <form id="form1" runat="server">
    <div>

    <asp:ChangePassword
        id="ChangePassword1"
        DisplayUserName="true"
        Runat="server">
        <MailDefinition
            From="Admin@YourSite.com"
            BodyFileName="ChangePassword.txt"
            Subject="Your New Password" />
    </asp:ChangePassword>

    </div>
    </form>
</body>
</html>
```

The ChangePassword control in Listing 26.31 includes a MailDefinition property that defines the email sent by the control. The ChangePassword control emails the message contained in Listing 26.32.

LISTING 26.32   ChangePassword.txt

```
<%UserName%>,
your new password is <%Password%>.
```

The email message in Listing 26.32 includes two special expressions: `<% UserName %>` and `<% Password %>`. When the email is sent, the user's existing username and new password are substituted for these expressions.

Using Templates with the `ChangePassword` Control

If you need to completely modify the appearance of the `ChangePassword` control, you can use templates to format the control. The `ChangePassword` control supports both a `ChangePasswordTemplate` and a `SuccessTemplate`.

The page in Listing 26.33 illustrates how you can use both the templates supported by the `ChangePassword` control (see Figure 26.14).

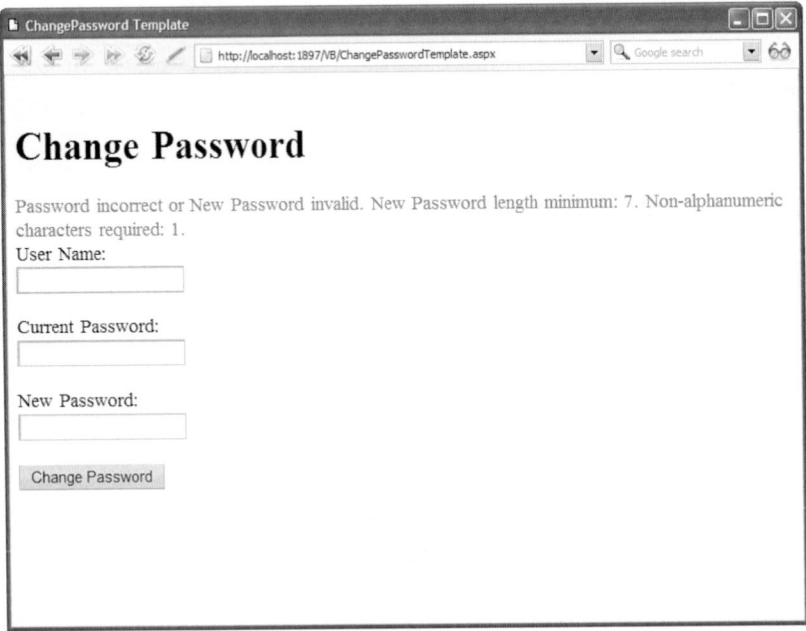

FIGURE 26.14   Customizing the `ChangePassword` control with templates.

LISTING 26.33   ChangePasswordTemplate.aspx

```
<%@ Page Language="C#" %>
<!DOCTYPE html PUBLIC "-//W3C//DTD XHTML 1.0 Transitional//EN"
  "http://www.w3.org/TR/xhtml1/DTD/xhtml1-transitional.dtd">
<html xmlns="http://www.w3.org/1999/xhtml" >
<head id="Head1" runat="server">
    <title>ChangePassword Template</title>
</head>
<body>
    <form id="form1" runat="server">
    <div>

    <asp:ChangePassword
        id="ChangePassword1"
        DisplayUserName="true"
        Runat="server">
        <ChangePasswordTemplate>
            <h1>Change Password</h1>
            <asp:Label
                id="FailureText"
                EnableViewState="false"
                ForeColor="Red"
                Runat="server" />
            <br />
            <asp:Label
                id="lblUserName"
                Text="User Name:"
                AssociatedControlID="UserName"
                Runat="server" />
            <br />
            <asp:TextBox
                id="UserName"
                Runat="server" />
            <br /><br />
            <asp:Label
                id="lblCurrentPassword"
                Text="Current Password:"
                AssociatedControlID="CurrentPassword"
                Runat="server" />
            <br />
            <asp:TextBox
                id="CurrentPassword"
                TextMode="Password"
                Runat="server" />
            <br /><br />
```

26

```
            <asp:Label
                id="lblNewPassword"
                Text="New Password:"
                AssociatedControlID="NewPassword"
                Runat="server" />
            <br />
            <asp:TextBox
                id="NewPassword"
                TextMode="Password"
                Runat="server" />
            <br /><br />
            <asp:Button
                id="btnChangePassword"
                Text="Change Password"
                CommandName="ChangePassword"
                Runat="server" />
        </ChangePasswordTemplate>
        <SuccessTemplate>
            Your password has been changed!
        </SuccessTemplate>
    </asp:ChangePassword>

    </div>
    </form>
</body>
</html>
```

You can use controls with the following IDs in the `ChangePasswordTemplate` template:

▶ UserName

▶ CurrentPassword

▶ ConfirmPassword

▶ NewPassword

▶ FailureText

You also can add `Button` controls with the following values for the `CommandName` property:

▶ ChangePassword

▶ Cancel

▶ Continue

Using the `PasswordRecovery` Control

If a user forgets her password, she can use the `PasswordRecovery` control to email herself her password. The `PasswordRecovery` control either sends the user's original password or resets the password and sends the new password.

The page in Listing 26.34 contains a `PasswordRecovery` control.

LISTING 26.34 ShowPasswordRecovery.aspx

```
<%@ Page Language="C#" %>
<!DOCTYPE html PUBLIC "-//W3C//DTD XHTML 1.0 Transitional//EN"
  "http://www.w3.org/TR/xhtml1/DTD/xhtml1-transitional.dtd">
<html xmlns="http://www.w3.org/1999/xhtml" >
<head id="Head1" runat="server">
    <style type="text/css">
        .passwordRecovery
        {
            font:14px Verdana,Sans-Serif;
            background-color:lightblue;
            border:solid 3px black;
            padding:4px;
        }
        .passwordRecovery_title
        {
            background-color:darkblue;
            color:white;
            font-weight:bold;
        }
        .passwordRecovery_instructions
        {
            font-size:12px;
            text-align:left;
            padding:10px;
        }
        .passwordRecovery_button
        {
            border:solid 1px black;
            padding:3px;
        }
    </style>
    <title>Show PasswordRecovery</title>
</head>
<body>
    <form id="form1" runat="server">
    <div>
```

26

```
<asp:PasswordRecovery
    id="PasswordRecovery1"
    CssClass="passwordRecovery"
    TitleTextStyle-CssClass="passwordRecovery_title"
    InstructionTextStyle-CssClass="passwordRecovery_instructions"
    SubmitButtonStyle-CssClass="passwordRecovery_button"
    Runat="server">
    <MailDefinition
        From="Admin@YourSite.com"
        Subject="Password Reminder" />
</asp:PasswordRecovery>

</div>
</form>
</body>
</html>
```

After you open the page in Listing 26.34 in your web browser, you are first asked to enter your username (see Figure 26.15). Next, you are asked to enter the answer to the security question that you entered when registering. Finally, a password is emailed to your registered email account.

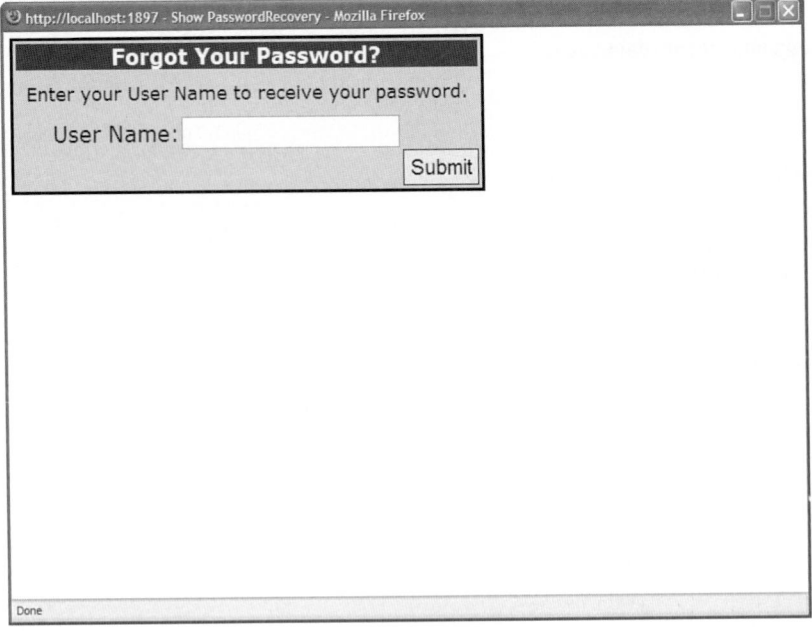

FIGURE 26.15   Retrieving a lost password with the PasswordRecovery control.

> **NOTE**
>
> Before you use the `PasswordRecovery` control, you must specify your mail server settings in your application's web configuration file. See the earlier section in this chapter, "Sending a Create User Email Message."

By default, the `PasswordRecovery` control first resets your password before sending you the password. In the next section, you learn how to send a user's original password.

Sending the Original Password

By default, the `PasswordRecovery` control does not send a user's original password. If you don't want the `PasswordRecovery` control to reset a user's password before sending it, you must change the configuration of the membership provider. Three configuration settings matter: `passwordFormat`, `enablePasswordRetrieval`, and `enablePasswordReset`.

By default, the `passwordFormat` attribute has the value `Hashed`. When passwords are hashed, the `PasswordRecovery` control cannot send a user's original password. This limitation makes sense because when passwords are hashed, the actual passwords are never stored anywhere. If you want to send a user his original password, you need to set the `passwordFormat` attribute to either the value `Clear` or `Encrypted`.

By default, the `enablePasswordRetrieval` attribute has the value `False`. Therefore, if you want to send a user his original password, you must enable this property in the web configuration file.

Finally, by default, the `enablePasswordReset` attribute has the value `True`. Regardless of the value of the `passwordFormat` or `enablePasswordRetrieval` attributes, you can always reset a user's password and email the new password to the user.

The web configuration file in Listing 26.35 contains the necessary configuration settings to enable a user's original password to be sent.

LISTING 26.35   Web.Config

```
<?xml version="1.0" encoding="utf-8"?>
<configuration>
  <system.web>
    <authentication mode="Forms" />

    <membership defaultProvider="MyMembership">
      <providers>
        <add
          name="MyMembership"
          type="System.Web.Security.SqlMembershipProvider"
          connectionStringName="LocalSqlServer"
```

26

```
            passwordFormat="Clear"
            enablePasswordRetrieval="true"
            />
        </providers>
      </membership>

    </system.web>
</configuration>
```

The configuration file in Listing 26.35 causes passwords to be stored in plain text rather than hashed. Furthermore, password retrieval is enabled.

Requiring a Security Question and Answer

When you use the `CreateUserWizard` control to register, you are required to select a security question and answer. The `PasswordRecovery` control displays a form that contains the security question. If you cannot enter the correct security answer, your password is not sent.

If you do not want to require users to answer a security question before receiving their passwords, you can modify the configuration of the membership provider. The web configuration file in Listing 26.36 assigns the value `false` to the `requiresQuestionAndAnswer` attribute.

LISTING 26.36   Web.Config

```
<?xml version="1.0" encoding="utf-8"?>
<configuration>
  <system.web>
    <authentication mode="Forms" />

    <membership defaultProvider="MyMembership">
      <providers>
        <add
          name="MyMembership"
          type="System.Web.Security.SqlMembershipProvider"
          connectionStringName="LocalSqlServer"
          requiresQuestionAndAnswer="false"
          />
      </providers>
    </membership>

  </system.web>
</configuration>
```

Using Templates with the `PasswordRecovery` Control

If you need to completely customize the appearance of the `PasswordRecovery` control, you can use templates. The `PasswordRecovery` control supports the following three types of templates:

▶ `UserNameTemplate`

▶ `QuestionTemplate`

▶ `SuccessTemplate`

The page in Listing 26.37 illustrates how you can use all three of these templates.

LISTING 26.37   `PasswordRecoveryTemplate.aspx`

```
<%@ Page Language="C#" %>
<!DOCTYPE html PUBLIC "-//W3C//DTD XHTML 1.0 Transitional//EN"
    "http://www.w3.org/TR/xhtml1/DTD/xhtml1-transitional.dtd">
<html xmlns="http://www.w3.org/1999/xhtml" >
<head id="Head1" runat="server">
    <style type="text/css">
        html
        {
            font:12px Arial,Sans-Serif;
        }
        h1
        {
            font:bold 16px Arial,Sans-Serif;
            color:DarkGray;
        }
    </style>
    <title>PasswordRecovery Template</title>
</head>
<body>
    <form id="form1" runat="server">
    <div>

    <asp:PasswordRecovery
        id="PasswordRecovery1"
        Runat="server">
        <MailDefinition
            From="Admin@YourSite.com"
            Subject="Password Reminder"
            BodyFileName="PasswordRecovery.txt" />
        <UserNameTemplate>
```

```
<h1>User Name</h1>
<asp:Label
    id="FailureText"
    EnableViewState="false"
    ForeColor="Red"
    Runat="server" />
<br />
<asp:Label
    id="lblUserName"
    Text="Enter your user name:"
    AssociatedControlID="UserName"
    Runat="server" />
<br />
<asp:TextBox
    id="UserName"
    Runat="server" />
<br />
<asp:Button
    id="btnSubmit"
    Text="Next"
    CommandName="Submit"
    Runat="server" />
</UserNameTemplate>
<QuestionTemplate>
<h1>Security Question</h1>
<asp:Label
    id="FailureText"
    EnableViewState="false"
    ForeColor="Red"
    Runat="server" />
<br />
<asp:Label
    id="Question"
    Text="Enter your user name:"
    AssociatedControlID="Answer"
    Runat="server" />
<br />
<asp:TextBox
    id="Answer"
    Runat="server" />
<br />
<asp:Button
    id="btnSubmit"
    Text="Next"
    CommandName="Submit"
    Runat="server" />
```

```
        </QuestionTemplate>
        <SuccessTemplate>
        <h1>Success</h1>
        An email has been sent to your registered
        email account that contains your user name
        and password.
        </SuccessTemplate>
    </asp:PasswordRecovery>

    </div>
    </form>
</body>
</html>
```

The `UserNameTemplate` must contain a control with an ID of `UserName`. You also can include a control with an ID of `FailureText` when you want to display error messages. This template also must contain a `Button` control with a `CommandName` that has the value `Submit`.

The `QuestionTemplate` must contain a control with an ID of `Question` and a control with an ID of `Answer`. Optionally, you can include a `FailureText` control when you want to display error messages. It also must have a `Button` control with a `CommandName` that has the value `Submit`.

The `SuccessTemplate`, on the other hand, does not require any special controls.

The `PasswordRecovery` control in Listing 26.37 includes a `MailDefinition` property that references a custom email message. The message is contained in Listing 26.38.

LISTING 26.38 PasswordRecovery.txt

```
Here's your login information:

  user name: <%UserName%>
   password: <%Password%>
```

The email message in Listing 26.38 contains substitution expressions for both the username and password.

Using the `LoginView` Control

The `LoginView` control enables you to display different content to different users depending on their authentication status. For example, the page in Listing 26.39 displays different content for authenticated users and anonymous users (see Figure 26.16).

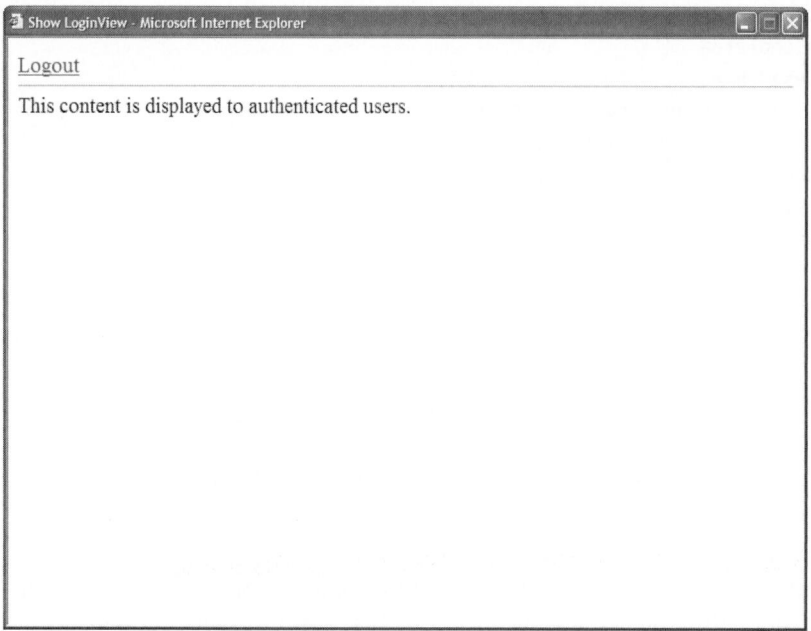

FIGURE 26.16   Displaying content to authenticated users with the `LoginView` control.

LISTING 26.39   ShowLoginView.aspx

```
<%@ Page Language="C#" %>
<!DOCTYPE html PUBLIC "-//W3C//DTD XHTML 1.0 Transitional//EN"
    "http://www.w3.org/TR/xhtml1/DTD/xhtml1-transitional.dtd">
<html xmlns="http://www.w3.org/1999/xhtml" >
<head id="Head1" runat="server">
    <title>Show LoginView</title>
</head>
<body>
    <form id="form1" runat="server">
    <div>

    <asp:LoginStatus
        id="LoginStatus"
        Runat="server" />
    <hr />

    <asp:LoginView
        id="LoginView1"
        Runat="server">
        <AnonymousTemplate>
        This content is displayed to anonymous users.
```

```
        </AnonymousTemplate>
        <LoggedInTemplate>
        This content is displayed to authenticated users.
        </LoggedInTemplate>
    </asp:LoginView>

    </div>
    </form>
</body>
</html>
```

The LoginView control in Listing 26.39 contains two templates: an AnonymousTemplate and a LoggedInTemplate. Only one of the two templates is displayed at a time.

The page also includes a LoginStatus control. You can use this control to log in and log out quickly.

> **NOTE**
>
> You can use the LoginView control with Windows authentication as well as Forms authentication.

Using Roles with the LoginView Control

You also can use the LoginView control to display different content to users who belong to different roles. The page in Listing 26.40 contains a LoginView that contains two RoleGroup controls. The first RoleGroup contains content that is displayed to members of the Administrator role. The second RoleGroup contains content that is displayed to members of the Manager and Worker roles.

LISTING 26.40   LoginViewRoles.aspx

```
<%@ Page Language="C#" %>
<!DOCTYPE html PUBLIC "-//W3C//DTD XHTML 1.0 Transitional//EN"
    "http://www.w3.org/TR/xhtml1/DTD/xhtml1-transitional.dtd">
<script runat="server">

    protected void Page_Load(object sender, EventArgs e)
    {
        MembershipCreateStatus status;
        // Create Bill
        Membership.CreateUser("Bill","secret_","bill@somewhere.com",
          "dog","rover",true,out status);
        // Create Ted
        Membership.CreateUser("Ted", "secret_", "ted@somewhere.com",
          "dog", "rover", true,out status);
```

26

```
        // Create Fred
        Membership.CreateUser("Fred", "secret_", "fred@somewhere.com",
            "dog", "rover", true, out, status);
        // Create Administrator Role
        if (!Roles.RoleExists("Administrator"))
        {
            Roles.CreateRole("Administrator");
            Roles.AddUserToRole("Bill", "Administrator");
        }
        // Create Manager Role
        if (!Roles.RoleExists("Manager"))
        {
            Roles.CreateRole("Manager");
            Roles.AddUserToRole("Bill", "Manager");
            Roles.AddUserToRole("Ted", "Manager");
        }
        // Create Worker Role
        if (!Roles.RoleExists("Worker"))
        {
            Roles.CreateRole("Worker");
            Roles.AddUserToRole("Fred", "Worker");
        }
    }
}
</script>
<html xmlns="http://www.w3.org/1999/xhtml" >
<head id="Head1" runat="server">
    <title>LoginView Roles</title>
</head>
<body>
    <form id="form1" runat="server">
    <div>

    <asp:LoginStatus
        id="LoginStatus"
        Runat="server" />
    <hr />

    <asp:LoginView
        id="LoginView1"
        Runat="server">
        <RoleGroups>
        <asp:RoleGroup Roles="Administrator">
        <ContentTemplate>
```

```
        This content is displayed to Administrators.
        </ContentTemplate>
        </asp:RoleGroup>
        <asp:RoleGroup Roles="Manager,Worker">
        <ContentTemplate>
        This content is displayed to Managers
        and Workers.
        </ContentTemplate>
        </asp:RoleGroup>
        </RoleGroups>
    </asp:LoginView>

    </div>
    </form>
</body>
</html>
```

The Page_Load() handler in Listing 26.40 creates three users named Bill, Ted, and Fred. Bill is added to both the Administrator and Manager roles; Ted is added to the Manager role; and Fred is added to the Worker role.

The content of only one RoleGroup is displayed by the LoginView control at a time. If a user matches more than one RoleGroup, the content of the first RoleGroup matched is displayed and the other RoleGroups are ignored.

Before you can use the page in Listing 26.40, you must enable roles in the web configuration file. The file in Listing 26.41 contains the necessary roleManager element.

LISTING 26.41   Web.Config

```
<?xml version="1.0" encoding="utf-8"?>
<configuration>
  <system.web>

    <authentication mode="Forms" />

    <roleManager enabled="true" />

  </system.web>
</configuration>
```

26

Summary

This chapter was devoted to the ASP.NET Login controls. In the first section, you were provided with an overview of the Login controls. You learned how to create both a Login and Registration page.

Next, we examined each of the Login controls one by one. You learned how to use the Login control to authenticate users and the CreateUserWizard control to register new users. You also learned how to send an email to new users automatically.

We also examined the LoginStatus and LoginView controls. You learned how to display either a Login or Logout link with the LoginStatus control. You learned how to display the current user's name with the LoginName control.

You also learned how to change passwords and send password reminders by using the ChangePassword and PasswordRecovery controls. You learned how to customize both of these controls by using templates.

Finally, you learned how to use the LoginView control to display different content to different users, depending on their authentication status. We also discussed how you can use roles with the LoginView control.

Using ASP.NET Membership

In the previous chapter, you learned how to use the Login controls to create an entire user registration system. This chapter looks under the covers and examines the security frameworks on which the Login controls are built.

The ASP.NET Framework includes four frameworks related to security:

▶ **ASP.NET Authentication**—Enables you to identify users.

▶ **ASP.NET Authorization**—Enables you to authorize users to request particular resources.

▶ **ASP.NET Membership**—Enables you to represent users and modify their properties.

▶ **Role Manager**—Enables you to represent user roles and modify their properties.

In this chapter, you learn how to configure authentication, authorization, ASP.NET Membership, and the Role Manager. You learn how to enable Forms authentication and configure advanced Forms authentication features such as cookieless authentication and cross-application authentication.

You learn how to configure authorization to control access to resources. We explore several advanced features of authorization. For example, you learn how to password-protect images and other files and pages.

You also learn how to configure different Membership providers, create custom Membership providers, and work with the properties and methods of the Membership class.

For example, you learn how to build a custom XmlMembershipProvider that stores membership information in an XML file.

Finally, we examine the Role Manager. You learn how to create user roles and add and remove users from a particular role. You also learn how to configure the different Role providers included in ASP.NET Framework.

Configuring Authentication

Authentication refers to the process of identifying who you are. The ASP.NET Framework supports three types of authentication:

- ▶ Windows
- ▶ .NET Passport
- ▶ Forms

A particular application can have only one type of authentication enabled. You can't, for example, enable both Windows and Forms authentication at the same time.

Windows authentication is enabled by default. When Windows authentication is enabled, users are identified by their Microsoft Windows account names. Roles correspond to Microsoft Windows groups. Windows authentication delegates the responsibility of identifying users to Internet Information Server. Internet Information Server can be configured to use Basic, Integrated Windows, or Digest authentication.

.NET Passport authentication is the same type of authentication used at Microsoft websites such as MSN and Hotmail. If you want to allow users to log in to your application by using their existing Hotmail usernames and passwords, you can enable .NET Passport authentication.

> **NOTE**
>
> You must download and install the Microsoft .NET Passport SDK, register with Microsoft, and pay Microsoft a fee before you can use .NET Passport authentication. For more information, see the MSDN website (msdn.microsoft.com).

The final type of authentication is Forms authentication. When Forms authentication is enabled, users are typically identified by a cookie (but see the next section). When a user is authenticated, an encrypted cookie is added to the user's browser. As the user moves from page to page, the user is identified by the cookie.

When Forms authentication is enabled, user and role information is stored in a custom data store. You can store user information anywhere that you want. For example, you can store usernames and passwords in a database, an XML file, or even a plain text file.

In ASP.NET 1.x, after enabling Forms authentication, you had to write all the code for storing and retrieving user information. When building an ASP.NET 4 application, on the other hand, you can let ASP.NET Membership do all this work for you. ASP.NET Membership can handle all the details of storing and retrieving user and role information.

You enable a particular type of authentication for an application in an application's root web configuration file. The file in Listing 27.1 enables Forms authentication.

LISTING 27.1   Web.Config

```
<?xml version="1.0"?>
<configuration>
    <system.web>

        <authentication mode="Forms" />

    </system.web>
</configuration>
```

In Listing 27.1, the authentication element's mode attribute is set to the value Forms. The possible values for the mode attribute are None, Windows, Forms, and Passport.

> **NOTE**
>
> Windows, Forms, and Passport authentication are implemented with HTTP Modules. If you need to implement a custom authentication scheme, you can create a custom HTTP Module. For more information on HTTP Modules, see Chapter 31, "Working with the HTTP Runtime."

> **VISUAL WEB DEVELOPER NOTE**
>
> If you prefer, you can enable a particular type of authentication by using the Web Site Administration Tool. This tool provides you with a form interface for modifying the web configuration file. You can open the Web Site Administration Tool by selecting Website, ASP.NET Configuration.

Configuring Forms Authentication

Several configuration options are specific to Forms authentication:

▸ **cookieless**—Enables you to use Forms authentication even when a browser does not support cookies. Possible values are UseCookies, UseUri, AutoDetect, and UseDeviceProfile. The default value is UseDeviceProfile.

▸ **defaultUrl**—Enables you to specify the page to which a user is redirected after being authenticated. The default value is Default.aspx.

▸ **domain**—Enables you to specify the domain associated with the authentication cookie. The default value is an empty string.

- ▶ **enableCrossAppRedirects**—Enables you to authenticate users across applications by passing an authentication ticket in a query string. The default value is `false`.

- ▶ **loginUrl**—Enables you to specify the path to the Login page. The default value is `Login.aspx`.

- ▶ **name**—Enables you to specify the name of the authentication cookie. The default value is `.ASPXAUTH`.

- ▶ **path**—Enables you to specify the path associated with the authentication cookie. The default value is `/`.

- ▶ **protection**—Enables you to specify how the authentication cookie is encrypted. Possible values are `All`, `Encryption`, `None`, and `Validation`. The default value is `All`.

- ▶ **requiresSSL**—Enables you to require an SSL (Secure Sockets Layer) connection when transmitting the authentication cookie. The default value is `false`.

- ▶ **slidingExpiration**—Enables you to prevent the authentication cookie from expiring as long as a user continues to make requests within an interval of time. Possible values are `True` and `False`. The default value is `True`.

- ▶ **timeout**—Enables you to specify the amount of time in minutes before the authentication cookie expires. The default value is `30`.

Several of these configuration settings are related to the authentication cookie. For example, you can use the web configuration file in Listing 27.2 to change the name of the authentication cookie.

LISTING 27.2   Web.Config

```xml
<?xml version="1.0"?>
<configuration>

    <system.web>
      <authentication mode="Forms">
        <forms name="MyApp" />
      </authentication>

    </system.web>
</configuration>
```

Several of these options require additional explanation. In the following sections, you learn how to enable cookieless authentication, modify the cookie expiration policy, and enable authentication across applications.

Using Cookieless Forms Authentication

Normally, Forms authentication uses a cookie to identify a user. However, Forms authentication also supports a feature named cookieless authentication. When cookieless authentication is enabled, a user can be identified without a browser cookie.

By taking advantage of cookieless authentication, you can use Forms Authentication and ASP.NET Membership to authenticate users even when someone uses a browser that does not support cookies or a browser with cookies disabled.

When cookieless authentication is enabled, a user can be identified by a unique token added to a page's URL. If a user uses relative URLs to link from one page to another, the token is passed from page to page automatically and the user can be identified across multiple page requests.

When you request a page that requires authentication and cookieless authentication is enabled, the URL in the browser address bar looks like this:

```
http://localhost:2500/Original/(F(WfAnevWxFyuN4SpenRclAEh_lY6OKWVllOKdQkRk
tOqV7cfcrgUJ2NKxNhH9dTA7fgzZ-cZwyr4ojyU6EnarC-bbf8g4sl6m4k5kk6Nmcsg1))
/SecretFiles/Secret2.aspx
```

That long, ugly code in the URL is the user's encoded authentication ticket.

You configure cookieless authentication by assigning a value to the cookieless attribute of the forms element in the web configuration file. The cookieless attribute accepts any of the following four values:

▶ **UseCookies**—Always use an authentication cookie.

▶ **UseUri**—Never use an authentication cookie.

▶ **AutoDetect**—Automatically detect when to use an authentication cookie.

▶ **UseDeviceProfile**—Use the device profile to determine when to use an authentication cookie.

The default value is UseDeviceProfile. By default, ASP.NET Framework issues a cookie only when a particular type of device supports cookies. The ASP.NET Framework maintains a database of device capabilities in a set of files contained in the following folder:

```
\WINDOWS\Microsoft.NET\Framework\v2.0.50727\CONFIG\Browsers
```

By default, ASP.NET Framework never uses cookieless authentication with a browser such as Microsoft Internet Explorer. According to the device profile for Internet Explorer, Internet Explorer supports cookies, so cookieless authentication is not used. The Framework doesn't use cookieless authentication even when cookies are disabled in a browser.

If you want ASP.NET Framework to automatically detect whether a browser supports cookies, you need to set the cookieless attribute to the value AutoDetect. When

27

AutoDetect is enabled, ASP.NET Framework checks whether a browser sends an HTTP COOKIE header. If the COOKIE header is present, an authentication cookie is assigned to the browser. Otherwise, ASP.NET Framework uses cookieless authentication.

The web configuration file in Listing 27.3 enables AutoDetect.

LISTING 27.3   Web.Config

```
<?xml version="1.0"?>
<configuration>
    <system.web>
      <authentication mode="Forms">
        <forms cookieless="AutoDetect"/>
      </authentication>
    </system.web>
</configuration>
```

Using Sliding Expiration with Forms Authentication

By default, Forms authentication uses a sliding expiration policy. As long as a user lets no more than 30 minutes pass without requesting a page, the user continues to be authenticated. However, if the user does not request a page for 30 minutes, the user is logged out automatically.

If you have strict security requirements, you can use an absolute expiration policy rather than a sliding expiration policy. In other words, you can force a user to log in again after a particular interval of time.

The web configuration file in Listing 27.4 forces a user to log in again every minute.

LISTING 27.4   Web.Config

```
<?xml version="1.0"?>
<configuration>
    <system.web>
      <authentication mode="Forms">
        <forms slidingExpiration="false" timeout="1" />
      </authentication>
    </system.web>
</configuration>
```

Using Forms Authentication Across Applications

By default, Forms authentication is application relative. In other words, if you log in to one application, you aren't logged in to any other application—even when the other application is located on the same web server.

This creates problems in two situations. First, you don't want to require the employees of your company to log in multiple times as they move between different applications hosted by your company. An employee should log in once and use any application provided by your company automatically.

Second, if you host a web farm, you don't want to force a user to log in whenever a request is served by a different web server. From the perspective of a user, a web farm should seem just like a single server.

By default, the Forms authentication cookie is encrypted and signed. Furthermore, by default, each application generates a unique decryption and validation key. Therefore, by default, you can't share the same authentication cookie across applications.

You specify encryption and validation options with the machineKey element in the web configuration file. Here are the default settings for this element:

```
<machineKey
    decryption="Auto"
    validation="SHA1"
    decryptionKey="AutoGenerate,IsolateApps"
    validationKey="AutoGenerate,IsolateApps" />
```

The decryption attribute specifies the algorithm used to encrypt and decrypt the forms authentication cookie. Possible values are Auto, AES (the government standard encryption algorithm), and 3DES (Triple DES). By default, the decryption attribute is set to Auto, which causes the ASP.NET Framework to select the encryption algorithm based on the capabilities of the web server.

The validation attribute specifies the hash or encryption algorithm used when an authentication cookie is signed. Possible values are AES, MD5, SHA1, and TripleDES.

The decryptionKey attribute represents the key used to encrypt and decrypt the authentication cookie. The validationKey represents the key used when the authentication cookie is signed. By default, both attributes are set to the value AutoGenerate, which causes ASP.NET Framework to generate a random key and store it in the LSA (your web server's Local Security Authority).

Notice that both the decryptionKey and validationKey attributes include an IsolateApps modifier. When the IsolateApps modifier is present, a unique key is created for each application on the same web server.

If you want to share the same authentication cookie across every application hosted on the same web server, you can override the default machineKey element in the machine root web configuration file and remove the IsolateApps attribute from both the decryptionKey and validationKey attributes. You can add the following machineKey element anywhere within the system.web section in the web configuration file:

27

```
<machineKey
  decryption="Auto"
  validation="SHA1"
  decryptionKey="AutoGenerate"
  validationKey="AutoGenerate" />
```

The root web configuration file is located at the following path:

```
C:\WINDOWS\Microsoft.NET\Framework\[version]\CONFIG\Web.Config
```

On the other hand, if you need to share the same authentication cookie across separate web servers, you need to specify the decryptionKey and validationKey manually. You cannot allow ASP.NET Framework to generate these keys automatically because you need to share the keys across the different web servers.

For example, the following machineKey element contains explicit decryption and validation keys:

```
<machineKey
  decryption="AES"
  validation="SHA1"
  decryptionKey="306C1FA852AB3B0115150DD8BA30821CDFD125538A0C606DACA53DBB3C3E0AD2"
  validationKey="61A8E04A146AFFAB81B6AD19654F99EA7370807F18F5002725DAB98B8EFD19C711
➥337E26948E26D1D174B159973EA0BE8CC9CAA6AAF513BF84E44B2247792265" />
```

When using AES, you need to set the decryption key to a random sequence of 64 hex characters. When using SHA1, you need to set the decryption key to a random sequence of 128 hex characters. You can use the page in Listing 27.5 to generate these random character sequences for you (see Figure 27.1).

LISTING 27.5 GenerateKeys.aspx

```
<%@ Page Language="C#" %>
<%@ Import Namespace="System.Security.Cryptography" %>
<!DOCTYPE html PUBLIC "-//W3C//DTD XHTML 1.0 Transitional//EN"
    "http://www.w3.org/TR/xhtml1/DTD/xhtml1-transitional.dtd">

<script runat="server">

    void Page_Load()
    {
        lblAES.Text = GetSequence(64);
        lblSHA1.Text = GetSequence(128);
    }

    private string GetSequence(int length)
    {
        byte[] buffer = new byte[length/2];
```

```
        RNGCryptoServiceProvider provider = new RNGCryptoServiceProvider();
        provider.GetBytes(buffer);
        StringBuilder builder = new StringBuilder(length);
        for (int i = 0; i < buffer.Length; i++)
            builder.Append(string.Format("{0:X2}", buffer[i]));
        return builder.ToString();
    }
</script>
<html xmlns="http://www.w3.org/1999/xhtml" >
<head id="Head1" runat="server">
    <title>Generate Keys</title>
</head>
<body>
    <form id="form1" runat="server">
    <div>

    AES:
    <asp:Label
        id="lblAES"
        Runat="server" />
    <br /><br />
    SHA1:
    <asp:Label
        id="lblSHA1"
        Runat="server" />

    </div>
    </form>
</body>
</html>
```

The page in Listing 27.5 uses the RNGCryptoServiceProvider to generate the random sequence of characters. The GetBytes() method returns a cryptographically strong sequence of random values.

NOTE

The GenerateKeys.aspx page is based on a code sample from an article titled "How To: Configure MachineKey in ASP.NET 2.0," located at the Microsoft MSDN website (msdn.microsoft.com).

FIGURE 27.1   Generating cryptographically strong keys.

You can add a machineKey element with explicit keys to either the machine root web configuration file or to particular application web configuration files. If you don't want to share the same keys across all the applications on a web server, you should add the machineKey element only to the applications that you need to share.

Using Forms Authentication Across Domains

In the previous section, you learned how to share the same authentication cookie across applications located on the same server or a different server. But how do you share the same authentication cookie across domains?

A browser cookie is always domain relative. For example, the Amazon website cannot read cookies set by the Barnes & Noble website, which is a good thing. However, you might discover that you need to share authentication information across websites with different domains.

You can work around this problem by passing an authentication ticket in a query string parameter rather than in a cookie. There is nothing to prevent you from passing query strings between domains.

To enable this scenario, you must configure your applications to accept authentication tickets passed in a query string. The web configuration file in Listing 27.6 includes an enableCrossAppRedirects attribute that enables sharing authentication tickets across domains.

LISTING 27.6 Web.config

```
<?xml version="1.0"?>
<configuration>
  <system.web>
    <authentication mode="Forms">
      <forms enableCrossAppRedirects="true" />
    </authentication>

    <machineKey
      decryption="AES"
      validation="SHA1"
      decryptionKey="306C1FA852AB3B0115150DD8BA30821CDFD125538A0C606DACA5
➥3DBB3C3E0AD2"
      validationKey="61A8E04A146AFFAB81B6AD19654F99EA7370807F18F5002725DAB98B8E
➥FD19C711337E26948E26D1D174B159973EA0BE8CC9CAA6AAF513BF84E44B2247792265" />

  </system.web>
</configuration>
```

If you add the web configuration file in Listing 27.6 to two applications located in different domains, the two applications can share the same authentication ticket.

> **WARNING**
>
> Make sure that you change the validation and encryption keys in Listing 27.6. You can use the GenerateKeys.aspx page discussed in the previous section to generate new random keys.

When you link or redirect from one application to another, you must pass the authentication ticket in a query string parameter. The page in Listing 27.7 adds the necessary query string parameter to a hyperlink.

LISTING 27.7 QueryStringAuthenticate.aspx

```
<%@ Page Language="C#" %>
<!DOCTYPE html PUBLIC "-//W3C//DTD XHTML 1.0 Transitional//EN"
    "http://www.w3.org/TR/xhtml1/DTD/xhtml1-transitional.dtd">
<script runat="server">

    void Page_Load()
    {
        string cookieName = FormsAuthentication.FormsCookieName;
        string cookieValue =
      FormsAuthentication.GetAuthCookie(User.Identity.Name, false).Value;
```

27

```
            lnkOtherDomain.NavigateUrl += String.Format("?{0}={1}", cookieName,
➥cookieValue);
    }
</script>
<html xmlns="http://www.w3.org/1999/xhtml" >
<head id="Head1" runat="server">
    <title>Query String Authenticate</title>
</head>
<body>
    <form id="form1" runat="server">
    <div>

    <asp:HyperLink
        id="lnkOtherDomain"
        Text="Link to Other Domain"
        NavigateUrl="http://www.OtherDomain.com/Secret.aspx"
        Runat="server" />

    </div>
    </form>
</body>
</html>
</html>
```

Using the `FormsAuthentication` Class

The main application programming interface for interacting with Forms authentication is
the FormsAuthentication class. This class supports the following properties:

▶ **CookieDomain**—Returns the domain associated with the authentication cookie.

▶ **CookieMode**—Returns the cookieless authentication mode. Possible values are
AutoDetect, UseCookies, UseDeviceProfile, and UseUri.

▶ **CookiesSupported**—Returns True when a browser supports cookies and Forms
authentication is configured to use cookies.

▶ **DefaultUrl**—Returns the URL of the page to which a user is redirected after being
authenticated.

▶ **EnableCrossAppRedirects**—Returns True when an authentication ticket can be
removed from a query string.

▶ **FormsCookieName**—Returns the name of the authentication cookie.

▶ **FormsCookiePath**—Returns the path associated with the authentication cookie.

▶ **LoginUrl**—Returns the URL of the page to which a user is redirected when being
authenticated.

▶ **RequireSSL**—Returns True when the authentication cookie must be transmitted with SSL (the Secure Sockets Layer).

▶ **SlidingExpiration**—Returns True when the authentication cookie uses a sliding expiration policy.

These properties return the configuration settings for Forms authentication from the web configuration file.

The FormsAuthentication class supports the following methods:

▶ **Authenticate**—Enables you to validate a username and password against a list of usernames and passwords stored in the web configuration file.

▶ **Decrypt**—Enables you to decrypt an authentication cookie.

▶ **GetAuthCookie**—Enables you to retrieve an authentication cookie.

▶ **GetRedirectUrl**—Enables you to retrieve the path to the original page that caused the redirect to the Login page.

▶ **HashPasswordForStoringInConfigFile**—Enables you to hash a password so that it can be stored in the web configuration file.

▶ **RedirectFromLoginPage**—Enables you to redirect a user back to the original page requested before the user was redirected to the Login page.

▶ **RedirectToLoginPage**—Enables you to redirect the user to the Login page.

▶ **RenewTicketIfOld**—Enables you to update the expiration time of an authentication cookie.

▶ **SetAuthCookie**—Enables you to create and issue an authentication cookie.

▶ **SignOut**—Enables you to remove an authentication cookie and log out a user.

You can use the methods and properties of the FormsAuthentication class to build a user registration and authentication system without using ASP.NET Membership. For example, the web configuration file in Listing 27.8 contains a list of usernames and passwords.

LISTING 27.8 Web.Config

```xml
<?xml version="1.0"?>
<configuration>
  <system.web>

    <authentication mode="Forms">
      <forms>
        <credentials passwordFormat="Clear">
          <user name="Bill" password="secret" />
          <user name="Jane" password="secret" />
          <user name="Fred" password="secret" />
        </credentials>
```

27

```
      </forms>
    </authentication>

  </system.web>
</configuration>
```

The web configuration file in Listing 27.8 contains a `forms` element that contains a `credentials` element. The `credentials` element includes a list of usernames and passwords.

Notice that the `credentials` element includes a `passwordFormat` attribute that is set to the value `Clear`. If you prefer, rather than store passwords in clear text, you can store password hash values. That way, anyone working on the web server can't see everyone else's passwords. The other two possible values for the `passwordFormat` attribute are `MD5` and `SHA1`.

> **NOTE**
>
> If you need to hash a password so you can store it in the web configuration file, you can use the (appropriately named) `FormsAuthentication.HashPasswordForStoring InConfigFile()` method. This method accepts a clear text password and the name of a hash algorithm, and it returns a hashed version of the password.

The Login page in Listing 27.9 contains a User Name and a Password text box (see Figure 27.2).

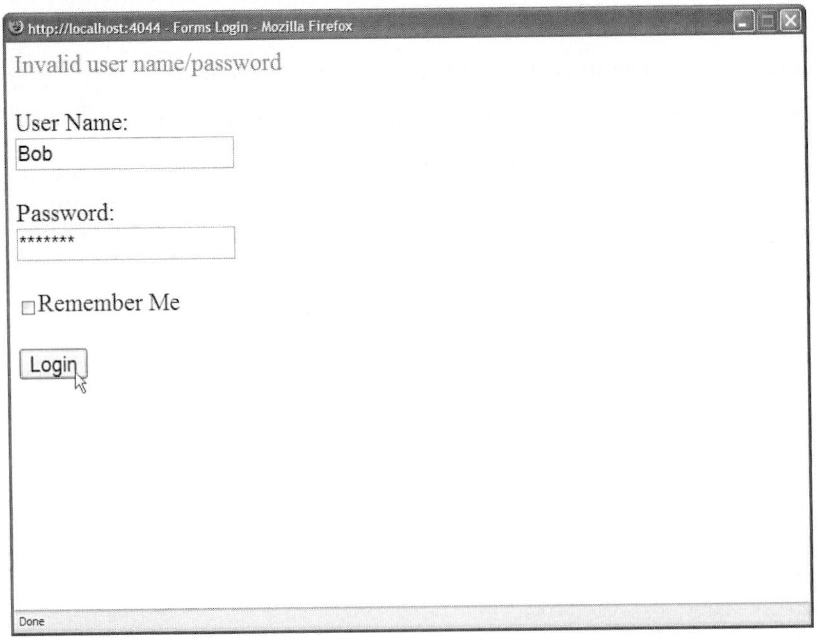

FIGURE 27.2   Authenticating against web configuration credentials.

LISTING 27.9 FormsLogin.aspx

```
<%@ Page Language="C#" %>
<!DOCTYPE html PUBLIC "-//W3C//DTD XHTML 1.0 Transitional//EN"
"http://www.w3.org/TR/xhtml1/DTD/xhtml1-transitional.dtd">
<script runat="server">

    protected void btnLogin_Click(object sender, EventArgs e)
    {
        if (FormsAuthentication.Authenticate(txtUserName.Text,txtPassword.Text))
            FormsAuthentication.RedirectFromLoginPage(
                txtUserName.Text, chkRememberMe.Checked);
        else
            lblError.Text = "Invalid user name/password";
    }
</script>
<html xmlns="http://www.w3.org/1999/xhtml" >
<head id="Head1" runat="server">
    <title>Forms Login</title>
</head>
<body>
    <form id="form1" runat="server">
    <div>

    <asp:Label
        id="lblError"
        EnableViewState="false"
        ForeColor="Red"
        Runat="server" />

    <br /><br />
    <asp:Label
        id="lblUserName"
        Text="User Name:"
        AssociatedControlID="txtUserName"
        Runat="server" />
    <br />
    <asp:TextBox
        id="txtUserName"
        Runat="server" />
    <br /><br />
    <asp:Label
        id="lblPassword"
        Text="Password:"
        AssociatedControlID="txtPassword"
        Runat="server" />
```

```
    <br />
    <asp:TextBox
        id="txtPassword"
        TextMode="Password"
        Runat="server" />
    <br /><br />
    <asp:CheckBox
        id="chkRememberMe"
        Text="Remember Me"
        Runat="server" />
    <br /><br />
    <asp:Button
        id="btnLogin"
        Text="Login"
        OnClick="btnLogin_Click"
        Runat="server" />

    </div>
    </form>
</body>
</html>
```

When you click the Login button, the `btnLogin_Click()` handler executes and the `FormsAuthentication.Authenticate()` method checks whether the username and password entered into the `TextBox` controls match a username and password in the web configuration file. If the user successfully authenticates, the `FormsAuthentication.RedirectFromLoginPage()` method is called.

The `RedirectFromLoginPage()` method does two things. The method adds an authentication cookie to the user's browser. The method also redirects the user back to whatever page the user originally requested. If the user requests the Login page directly, the user is redirected to the `Default.aspx` page.

The second parameter passed to the `RedirectFromLoginPage()` method indicates whether you want to create a session or persistent cookie. If you create a persistent cookie, a user does not need to log in when the user returns to the website in the future.

Using the User Class

You can use the `Page.User` or the `HttpContext.User` property to retrieve information about the current user. The `Page.User` property exposes a `Principal` object that supports the following method:

▶ **IsInRole**—Enables you to check whether a user is a member of a particular role.

For example, when Windows authentication is enabled, you can use the `IsInRole()` method to check whether a user is a member of a particular Microsoft Windows group such as the BUILTIN\Administrators group:

```
if (User.IsInRole("BUILTIN\Administrators"))
{
    // Do some Administrator only operation
}
```

> **NOTE**
>
> If the Role Manager is enabled, you must configure the Role Manager to use the `WindowsTokenRoleProvider` before you can use the `User.IsInRole()` method with Windows groups.

The `Principal` object also includes an `Identity` property that enables you to get information about the current user's identity. The `Identity` object supports the following three properties:

- ▶ **AuthenticationType**—Enables you to determine how the user was authenticated. Examples of possible values are `Forms`, `Basic`, and `NTLM`.

- ▶ **IsAuthenticated**—Enables you to determine whether a user is authenticated.

- ▶ **Name**—Enables you to retrieve the user's name.

If you want to get the name of the current user, you can use logic that looks like this:

```
Dim name As String = User.Identity.Name
```

If a user is not authenticated, the `User.Identity.Name` property returns an empty string.

Configuring Authorization

Authorization refers to the process of identifying the resources that you are allowed to access. You control authorization by adding an authorization element to a web configuration file.

Authorization works the same way regardless of the type of authentication that is enabled. In other words, you configure authorization in the same way when using Forms, Windows, and .NET Passport authentication.

Typically, you place all the pages that you want to password-protect in a separate folder. If you add a web configuration file to the folder, the settings in the web configuration file apply to all pages in the folder and all subfolders.

For example, if you add the web configuration file in Listing 27.10 to a folder, then unauthenticated users are blocked from accessing pages in the folder.

LISTING 27.10   SecretFiles\Web.Config

```xml
<?xml version="1.0"?>
<configuration>
    <system.web>

        <authorization>
          <deny users="?"/>
        </authorization>

    </system.web>
</configuration>
```

If you add the file in Listing 27.10 to a folder, unauthenticated users cannot access any pages in the folder. When Forms authentication is enabled, unauthenticated users are automatically redirected to the Login page.

The web configuration file in Listing 27.10 contains an authorization element that contains a single authorization rule. The configuration file denies access to anonymous users. The ? symbol represents anonymous (unauthenticated) users.

You can use the following two special symbols with the users attribute:

▶ ?—Represents unauthenticated users.

▶ *—Represents all users (unauthenticated or authenticated).

You also can assign a particular username, or comma-delimited list of usernames, to the deny element. For example, the authorization element in Listing 27.11 enables access for a user named Jane, but denies access to anyone else (even authenticated users).

LISTING 27.11   SecretFiles\Web.Config

```xml
<?xml version="1.0"?>
<configuration>
    <system.web>

        <authorization>
          <allow users="Jane" />
          <deny users="*" />
        </authorization>

    </system.web>
</configuration>
```

The order of the authorization rules is important. The ASP.NET Framework uses a first-match algorithm. If you switched the allow and deny rules in Listing 27.11, no one, not even Jane, would be allowed to access the pages in the folder.

NOTE

You can prevent anonymous users from accessing any page in an application by adding an authorization element to the application root web configuration file. In that case, anonymous users are still allowed to access the Login page. (Otherwise, no one could log in when using Forms authentication.)

VISUAL WEB DEVELOPER NOTE

If you prefer, you can configure authorization rules by using the Web Site Administration Tool. This tool provides you with a form interface for configuring authorization rules for different folders. You can open the Web Site Administration Tool by selecting Website, ASP.NET Configuration.

Authorizing by Role

When creating authorization rules, you can authorize by user role. For example, the web configuration file in Listing 27.12 prevents access to any pages in a folder by anyone except members of the Administrators role.

LISTING 27.12   SecretFiles\Web.Config

```
<?xml version="1.0"?>
<configuration>
    <system.web>

        <authorization>
          <allow roles="Administrator"/>
          <deny users="*"/>

        </authorization>

    </system.web>
</configuration>
```

When Forms authentication is enabled, the role refers to a custom role. In the final section of this chapter, "Using the Role Manager," you learn how to configure and create custom roles. When Windows authentication is enabled, the role refers to a Microsoft Windows group.

Authorizing Files by Location

By default, authorization rules are applied to all pages in a folder and all subfolders. However, you also have the option of using the location element with the authorization element. The location element enables you to apply a set of authorization rules to a folder or page at a particular path.

For example, imagine that you want to password-protect one, and only one, page in a folder. In that case, you can use the location element to specify the path of the single page. The web configuration file in Listing 27.13 password-protects a page named Secret.aspx.

LISTING 27.13 Web.Config Protecting a File

```xml
<?xml version="1.0"?>
<configuration>

  <system.web>
    <authentication mode="Forms" />
  </system.web>

  <location path="Secret.aspx">
    <system.web>
      <authorization>
        <deny users="?" />
      </authorization>
    </system.web>
  </location>

</configuration>
```

You also can use the location element to apply configuration settings to a particular subfolder. For example, the web configuration file in Listing 27.14 password-protects a folder named SecretFiles.

LISTING 27.14 Web.Config Protecting a Folder

```xml
<?xml version="1.0"?>
<configuration>

  <system.web>
    <authentication mode="Forms" />
  </system.web>

  <location path="SecretFiles">
    <system.web>
```

```
      <authorization>
        <deny users="?"/>
      </authorization>
    </system.web>
  </location>

</configuration>
```

Using Authorization with Images and Other File Types

Authorization rules are applied only to files mapped into the ASP.NET Framework. The Visual Web Developer web server maps all file types to ASP.NET Framework. Internet Information Server, on the other hand, maps only particular file types to ASP.NET Framework.

If you use Internet Information Services, and you add an image to a password-protected folder, users aren't blocked from requesting the image. By default, authorization rules apply only to ASP.NET file types such as ASP.NET pages. Files such as images, Microsoft Word documents, and classic ASP pages are ignored by ASP.NET Framework.

If you need to password-protect a particular type of static file, such as an image or Microsoft Word document, you need to map the file's extension to the ASP.NET ISAPI extension.

For example, follow these steps to enable authorization for .gif image files:

1. Open Internet Information Services by selecting Start, Control Panel, Administrative Tools, Internet Information Services (IIS) Manager.
2. In the tree on the left, click a particular website or virtual directory. A list of configuration icons appears in the main content area.
3. Open the Mappings page by double-clicking the Handler Mappings icon located under the IIS configuration group. The Handler Mappings dialog window appears (see Figure 27.3).
4. Click the Add Script Map button to open the Add Script Map dialog box.
5. In the Request Path field, enter ***.gif**.
6. In the Executable field, enter the path to the ASP.NET ISAPI DLL. (You can copy and paste this path from the Application Mapping for the .aspx extension.)
7. In the Name field, enter a mapping name such as GIF-ISAPI-4.0.

After you complete these steps, requests for .gif images are passed to ASP.NET Framework. You can then use authentication and authorization rules with .gif images.

You can complete the same sequence of steps to password-protect other static file types, such as Microsoft Word documents, Excel spreadsheets, or video files.

27

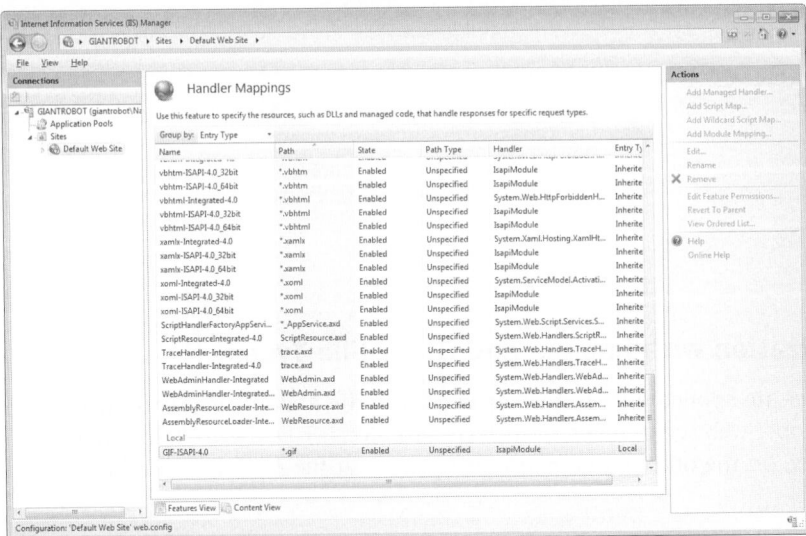

FIGURE 27.3 The Mappings configuration in Internet Information Services (Windows 7).

Using ASP.NET Membership

ASP.NET Membership enables you to create new users, delete users, and edit user properties. It's the framework used behind the scenes by the Login controls.

ASP.NET Membership picks up where Forms authentication leaves off. Forms authentication provides you with a way of identifying users. ASP.NET Membership is responsible for representing the user information.

ASP.NET Membership uses the provider model. The ASP.NET Framework includes two Membership providers:

▶ **SqlMembershipProvider**—Stores user information in a Microsoft SQL Server database.

▶ **ActiveDirectoryMembershipProvider**—Stores user information in the Active Directory or an Active Directory Application Mode server.

In this section, you learn how to use the ASP.NET Membership application programming interface. You learn how to use the Membership class to modify membership information programmatically.

You also learn how to configure both the SqlMembershipProvider and the ActiveDirectoryMembershipProvider. For example, you learn how to modify the requirements for a valid membership password.

Finally, we build a custom Membership provider. It is an XmlMembershipProvider that stores membership information in an XML file.

NOTE

Chapter 36, "Building Custom Controls," discusses custom control building.

LISTING 27.16   UsersOnline.cs

```csharp
using System;
using System.Web.Security;
using System.Web.UI;
using System.Web.UI.WebControls;

namespace myControls
{
    /// <summary>
    /// Displays Number of Users Online
    /// </summary>
    public class UsersOnline : WebControl
    {
        protected override void RenderContents(HtmlTextWriter writer)
        {
            writer.Write(Membership.GetNumberOfUsersOnline());
        }
    }
}
```

The page in Listing 27.17 uses the UsersOnline control to display the number of users currently online (see Figure 27.5).

LISTING 27.17   ShowUsersOnline.aspx

```aspx
<%@ Page Language="C#" %>
<%@ Register TagPrefix="custom" Namespace="myControls" %>
<!DOCTYPE html PUBLIC "-//W3C//DTD XHTML 1.0 Transitional//EN"
  "http://www.w3.org/TR/xhtml1/DTD/xhtml1-transitional.dtd">
<html xmlns="http://www.w3.org/1999/xhtml" >
<head id="Head1" runat="server">
    <title>Show UsersOnline</title>
</head>
<body>
    <form id="form1" runat="server">
    <div>
```

27

```
    How many people are online?
    <br />
    <custom:UsersOnline
        id="UsersOnline1"
        Runat="server" />

    </div>
    </form>
</body>
</html>
```

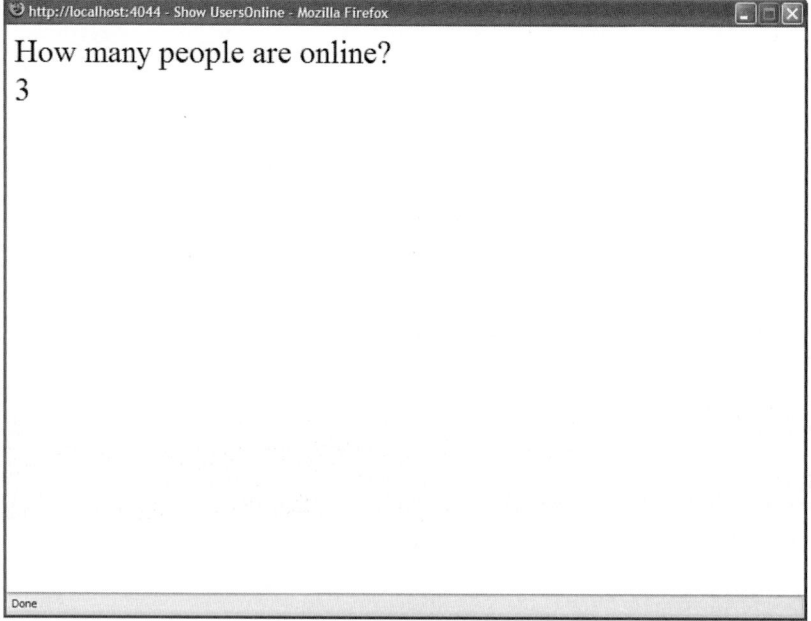

How many people are online?
3

FIGURE 27.5   Display number of users online.

NOTE

A user is considered online if his username was used in a call to the ValidateUser(), UpdateUser(), or GetUser() method in the last 15 minutes. You can modify the default time interval of 15 minutes by modifying the userIsOnlineTimeWindow attribute of the membership element in the web configuration file.

Several of the methods of the Membership class return one or more MembershipUser objects. The MembershipUser object represents a particular website member. This class supports the following properties:

- ▶ **Comment**—Enables you to associate a comment with the user.

- ▶ **CreationDate**—Enables you to get the date when the user was created.

- ▶ **Email**—Enables you to get or set the user's email address.

- ▶ **IsApproved**—Enables you to get or set whether the user is approved and her account is active.

- ▶ **IsLockedOut**—Enables you to get the user's lockout status.

- ▶ **IsOnline**—Enables you to determine whether the user is online.

- ▶ **LastActivityDate**—Enables you to get or set the date of the user's last activity. This date is updated automatically with a call to CreateUser(), ValidateUser(), or GetUser().

- ▶ **LastLockoutDate**—Enables you to get the date that the user was last locked out.

- ▶ **LastLoginDate**—Enables you to get the date that the user last logged in.

- ▶ **LastPasswordChangedDate**—Enables you to get the date that the user last changed her password.

- ▶ **PasswordQuestion**—Enables you to get the user's password question.

- ▶ **ProviderName**—Enables you to retrieve the name of the Membership provider associated with this user.

- ▶ **ProviderUserKey**—Enables you to retrieve a unique key associated with the user. In the case of the SqlMembershipProvider, this is the value of a GUID column.

- ▶ **UserName**—Enables you to get the name of the user.

Notice that the MembershipUser class does not contain a property for the user's password or password answer. This is intentional. If you need to change a user's password, you need to call a method.

The MembershipUser class supports the following methods:

- ▶ **ChangePassword**—Enables you to change a user's password.

- ▶ **ChangePasswordQuestionAndAnswer**—Enables you to change a user's password question and answer.

- ▶ **GetPassword**—Enables you to get a user's password.

- ▶ **ResetPassword**—Enables you to reset a user's password to a randomly generated password.

- ▶ **UnlockUser**—Enables you to unlock a user account that has been locked out.

27

Encrypting and Hashing User Passwords

Both of the default Membership providers included in the ASP.NET Framework enable you to store user passwords in three ways:

▶ **Clear**—Passwords are stored in clear text.

▶ **Encrypted**—Passwords are encrypted before they are stored.

▶ **Hashed**—Passwords are not stored. Only the hash values of passwords are stored. (This is the default value.)

You configure how passwords are stored by setting the `passwordFormat` attribute in the web configuration file. For example, the web configuration file in Listing 27.18 configures the `SqlMembershipProvider` to store passwords in plain text.

LISTING 27.18   Web.Config

```xml
<?xml version="1.0"?>
<configuration>
    <system.web>
      <authentication mode="Forms" />

      <membership defaultProvider="MyProvider">
        <providers>
          <add
            name="MyProvider"
            type="System.Web.Security.SqlMembershipProvider"
            passwordFormat="Clear"
            connectionStringName="LocalSqlServer"/>
        </providers>

      </membership>
    </system.web>
</configuration>
```

The default value of the `passwordFormat` attribute is `Hashed`. By default, actual passwords are not stored anywhere. A hash value is generated for a password and the hash value is stored.

NOTE

A hash algorithm generates a unique value for each input. The distinctive thing about a hash algorithm is that it works in only one direction. You can easily generate a hash value from any value. However, you cannot easily determine the original value from a hash value.

The advantage of storing hash values is that even if your website is compromised by a hacker, the hacker cannot steal anyone's passwords. The disadvantage of using hash values is that you also cannot retrieve user passwords. For example, you cannot use the PasswordRecovery control to email a user his original password.

Instead of hashing passwords, you can encrypt the passwords. The disadvantage of encrypting passwords is that it is more processor-intensive than hashing passwords. The advantage of encrypting passwords is that you can retrieve user passwords.

The web configuration file in Listing 27.19 configures the SqlMembershipProvider to encrypt passwords. The web configuration file includes a machineKey element. You must supply an explicit decryptionKey when encrypting passwords.

NOTE

For more information on the machineKey element, see the "Using Forms Authentication Across Applications" section, earlier in this chapter.

LISTING 27.19   Web.Config

```xml
<?xml version="1.0"?>
<configuration>
  <system.web>
    <authentication mode="Forms" />

    <membership defaultProvider="MyProvider">
      <providers>
        <add
          name="MyProvider"
          type="System.Web.Security.SqlMembershipProvider"
          passwordFormat="Encrypted"
          connectionStringName="LocalSqlServer"/>
      </providers>
    </membership>

    <machineKey
        decryption="AES"
        decryptionKey="306C1FA852AB3B0115150DD8BA30821CDFD1
➥25538A0C606DACA53DBB3C3E0AD2" />

  </system.web>
</configuration>
```

27

> **WARNING**
>
> Make sure that you change the value of the decryptionKey attribute before using the web configuration file in Listing 27.19. You can generate a new decryptionKey with the GenerateKeys.aspx page described in the "Using Forms Authentication Across Applications" section, earlier in this chapter.

Modifying User Password Requirements

By default, passwords are required to contain at least 7 characters and 1 nonalphanumeric character (a character that is not a letter or a number such as *,_, or !). You can set three Membership provider attributes that determine password policy:

▶ **minRequiredPasswordLength**—The minimum required password length. (The default value is 7.)

▶ **minRequiredNonalphanumericCharacters**—The minimum number of non-alphanumeric characters (The default value is 1.)

▶ **passwordStrengthRegularExpression**—The regular expression pattern that a valid password must match (The default value is an empty string.)

The minRequiredNonAlphanumericCharacters attribute confuses everyone. Website users are not familiar with the requirement that they must enter a nonalphanumeric character. The web configuration file in Listing 27.20 illustrates how you can disable this requirement when using the SqlMembershipProvider.

LISTING 27.20 Web.Config

```
<?xml version="1.0"?>
<configuration>
  <system.web>
    <authentication mode="Forms" />

    <membership defaultProvider="MyProvider">
      <providers>
        <add
          name="MyProvider"
          type="System.Web.Security.SqlMembershipProvider"
          minRequiredNonalphanumericCharacters="0"
          connectionStringName="LocalSqlServer"/>
      </providers>
    </membership>


  </system.web>
</configuration>
```

Locking Out Bad Users

By default, if you enter a bad password more than five times within 10 minutes, your account is automatically locked out. In other words, it is disabled.

Also, if you enter the wrong answer for the password answer more than five times in a 10-minute interval, your account is locked out. You get five attempts at your password and five attempts at your password answer. (These two things are tracked independently.)

Two configuration settings control when an account gets locked out:

▶ **maxInvalidPasswordAttempts**—The maximum number of bad passwords or bad password answers that you are allowed to enter (The default value is 5.)

▶ **passwordAttemptWindow**—The time interval in minutes in which entering bad passwords or bad password answers results in being locked out.

For example, the web configuration file in Listing 27.21 modifies the default settings to enable you to enter a maximum of three bad passwords or bad password answers in 1 hour.

LISTING 27.21   Web.Config

```xml
<?xml version="1.0"?>
<configuration>
  <system.web>
    <authentication mode="Forms" />

    <membership defaultProvider="MyProvider">
      <providers>
        <add
          name="MyProvider"
          type="System.Web.Security.SqlMembershipProvider"
          maxInvalidPasswordAttempts="3"
          passwordAttemptWindow="60"
          connectionStringName="LocalSqlServer"/>
      </providers>
    </membership>

  </system.web>
</configuration>
```

After a user has been locked out, you must call the `MembershipUser.UnlockUser()` method to reenable the user account. The page in Listing 27.22 enables you to enter a username and remove a lock (see Figure 27.6).

27

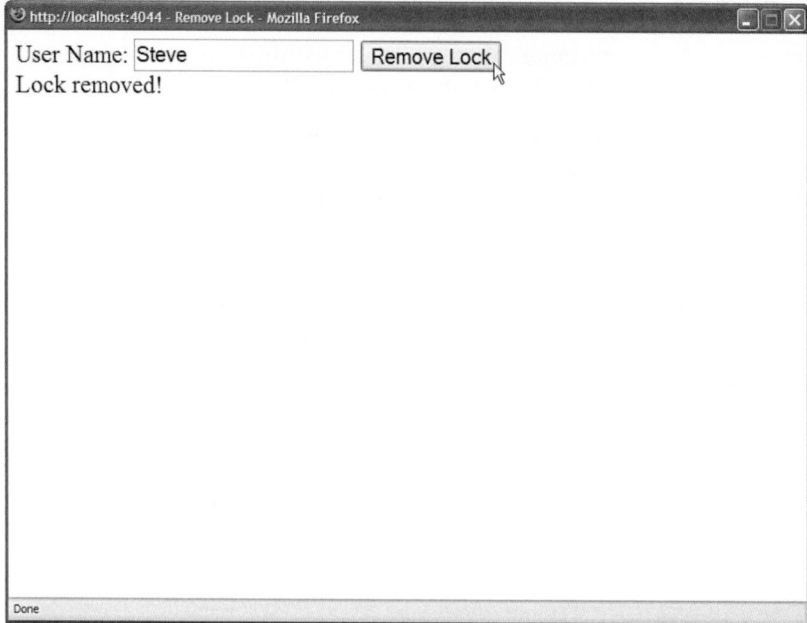

FIGURE 27.6   Removing a user lock.

LISTING 27.22   RemoveLock.aspx

```
<%@ Page Language="C#" %>
<!DOCTYPE html PUBLIC "-//W3C//DTD XHTML 1.0 Transitional//EN"
    "http://www.w3.org/TR/xhtml1/DTD/xhtml1-transitional.dtd">
<script runat="server">

    protected void btnRemove_Click(object sender, EventArgs e)
    {
        MembershipUser userToUnlock = Membership.GetUser(txtUserName.Text);
        if (userToUnlock == null)
        {
            lblMessage.Text = "User not found!";
        }
        else
        {
            userToUnlock.UnlockUser();
            lblMessage.Text = "Lock removed!";
        }
    }
</script>
```

```
<html xmlns="http://www.w3.org/1999/xhtml" >
<head runat="server">
    <title>Remove Lock</title>
</head>
<body>
    <form id="form1" runat="server">
    <div>

    <asp:Label
        id="lblUserName"
        Text="User Name:"
        AssociatedControlID="txtUserName"
        Runat="server" />
    <asp:TextBox
        id="txtUserName"
        Runat="server" />
    <asp:Button
        id="btnRemove"
        Text="Remove Lock"
        Runat="server" OnClick="btnRemove_Click" />
    <br />
    <asp:Label
        id="lblMessage"
        EnableViewState="false"
        Runat="server" />
    </div>
    </form>
</body>
</html>
```

Configuring the `SQLMembershipProvider`

The `SqlMembershipProvider` is the default Membership provider. Unless otherwise config-ured, it stores membership information in the local `ASPNETDB.mdf` Microsoft SQL Server Express database located in your application's App_Data folder. This database is created for you automatically the first time that you use Membership.

If you want to store membership information in some other Microsoft SQL Server data-base, you need to perform the following two tasks:

▶ Add the necessary database objects to the Microsoft SQL Server database.

▶ Configure your application to use the new database.

To complete the first task, you can use the `aspnet_regiis` command-line tool. This tool is located in the following folder:

`\Windows\Microsoft.NET\Framework\v4.0.30319`

> **NOTE**
>
> If you open the Visual Studio Command Prompt, you don't need to navigate to the Microsoft.NET folder before using the `aspnet_regsql` tool because that tool is already in the path

If you execute the `aspnet_regsql` tool without supplying any parameters, the ASP.NET SQL Server Setup Wizard appears (see Figure 27.7). You can use this wizard to select a database and install the Membership objects automatically.

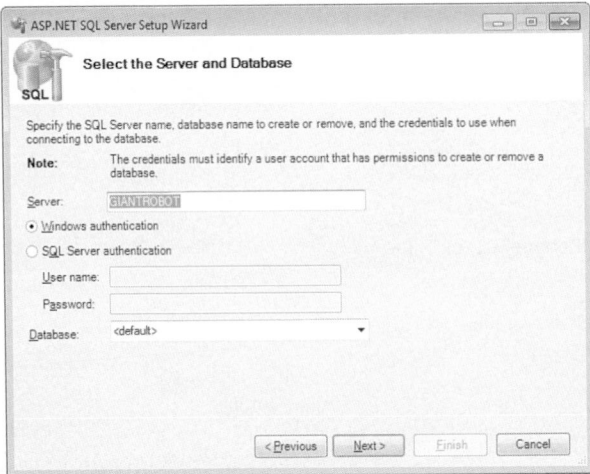

FIGURE 27.7   Using the ASP.NET SQL Setup Wizard.

If you prefer, rather than use the `aspnet_reqsql` tool, you can execute the following two SQL batch files to install Membership:

```
\WINDOWS\Microsoft.NET\Framework\v4.0.30319\InstallCommon.sql
\WINDOWS\Microsoft.NET\Framework\v4.0.30319\InstallMembership.sql
```

If you don't want to install.NET Framework on your database server, you can execute these SQL batch files.

After you have configured your database to support ASP.NET Membership, you must configure your application to connect to your database when using Membership. The web configuration file in Listing 27.23 connects to a database named MyDatabase located on a server named MyServer.

LISTING 27.23 Web.Config

```
<?xml version="1.0"?>
<configuration>
  <connectionStrings>
    <add name="MyConnection" connectionString="Data Source=MyServer;Integrated
➥Security=True;Initial Catalog=MyDatabase"/>
  </connectionStrings>

  <system.web>
    <authentication mode="Forms" />

    <membership defaultProvider="MyMembershipProvider" >
      <providers>
        <add
          name="MyMembershipProvider"
          type="System.Web.Security.SqlMembershipProvider"
          connectionStringName="MyConnection" />
      </providers>
    </membership>
  </system.web>
</configuration>
```

In Listing 27.23, a new default Membership provider named MyMembershipProvider is configured. The new Membership provider uses a connection string name that has the value MyConnection. The MyConnection connection string is defined in the connectionStrings element near the top of the configuration file. This connection string represents a connection to a database named MyDatabase located on a server named MyServer.

Configuring the ActiveDirectoryMembershipProvider

The other Membership provider included in ASP.NET Framework is the ActiveDirectoryMembershipProvider. You can use this provider to store user information in Active Directory or AD LDS (Active Directory Lightweight Directory Services).

AD LDS is a lightweight version of Active Directory. You can download AD LDS from the Microsoft website (www.microsoft.com/adam). AD LDS is compatible with both Windows Vista and Windows 7.

If you want to use ASP.NET Membership with AD LDS, you need to complete the following two steps:

1. Create an AD LDS instance and create the required classes.
2. Configure your application to use the ActiveDirectoryMembershipProvider and connect to the ADAM instance.

27

The following sections examine each of these steps in turn.

Configuring AD LDS

First, you need to set up a new instance of AD LDS. After downloading and installing AD LDS, follow these steps:

1. Launch the Active Directory Lightweight Directory Services Setup Wizard by selecting Active Directory Lightweight Directory Services Setup Wizard from Control Panel, Administrative Tools (see Figure 27.8).

FIGURE 27.8   Creating a new AD LDS instance.

2. In the Setup Options step, select the option to create a unique instance.
3. In the Instance Name step, enter the name **WebUsersInstance.**
4. In the Ports step, use the default LDAP and SSL port numbers (389 and 636).
5. In the Application Directory Partition step, create a new directory application partition named `O=WebUsersDirectory`.
6. In the File Locations step, use the default data file locations.
7. In the Service Account Selection step, select Network Service Account.
8. In the AD LDS Administrators step, select Currently Logged on User for the administrator account.
9. In the Importing LDIF Files step, select `MS-AZMan.ldf`, `MS-InetOrgPerson.ldf`, `MS-User.ldf`, `MS-UserProxy.ldf`.

After you complete the preceding steps, a new AD LDS instance named `WebUsersInstance` is created. The next step is to configure an AD LDS administrator account. Follow these steps:

WARNING

If you are using Windows XP, and you don't have an SSL certificate installed, you need to perform an additional configuration step. Otherwise, you receive an error when you attempt to reset a user password.

By default, you are not allowed to perform password operations over a non-secured connection to an AD LDS instance. You can disable this requirement by using the `dsmgmt.exe` tool included with AD LDS. Open the AD LDS Tools Command Prompt and type the following series of commands:

1. Type **dsmgmt**.
2. Type **ds behavior**.
3. Type **connections**.
4. Type **connect to server localhost:389**.
5. Type **quit**.
6. Type **allow passwd op on unsecured connection**.
7. Type **quit**.

If you don't use an SSL connection, passwords are transmitted in plain text. Don't do this in the case of a production application.

---

1. Open the AD LDS ADSI Edit application from the Control Panel, Administrative Tools (see Figure 27.9).

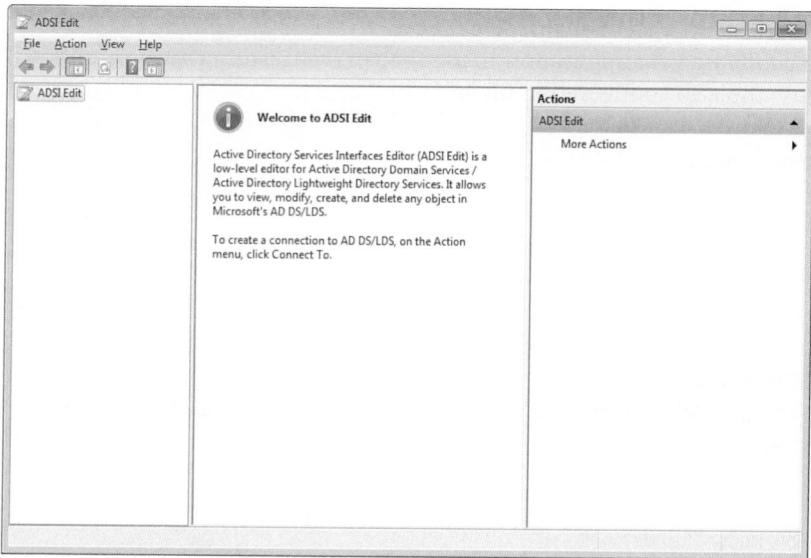

FIGURE 27.9   Using ADLDS ADSI Edit.

2. Open the Connection Settings dialog box by selecting Action, Connect To.

3. In the Connection Settings dialog box, select the option to connect to a node by using a distinguished name, and enter the name **O=WebUsersDirectory. In the** Computer group, choose Select or Type a Domain or Server and enter localhost in the field. Click OK.

4. Expand the new connection and select the **O=WebUsersDirectory** node.

5. Select Action, New, Object.

6. In the Create Object dialog box, select the organizationalUnit class and name the new class WebUsers.

7. Select the OU=WebUsers node and select Action, New, Object.

8. In the Create Object dialog box, select the user class and name the new class **ADLDSAdministrator.**

9. Select CN=ADLDSAdministrator and select Action, Reset Password and enter the password **secret.**

10. Select the CN=Roles node and double-click the CN-Administrators node.

11. Double-click the Member attribute and add the distinguished name for the ADLDSAdministrator ADAM account (CN=ADLDSAdministrator,OU=WebUsers, O=WebUsersDirectory).

After you complete this series of steps, an ADLDSAdministrator account is configured. You need to use this account when connecting to the ADLDS instance from the ActiveDirectoryMembershipProvider.

Configuring the ActiveDirectoryMembershipProvider

The next step is to configure your application to use the ActiveDirectoryMembership provider. You can use the web configuration file in Listing 27.24.

LISTING 27.24   Web.Config

```
<?xml version="1.0"?>
<configuration>

  <connectionStrings>
    <add
      name="ADLDSConnection"
      connectionString="LDAP://localhost:389/OU=WebUsers,O=WebUsersDirectory"/>
  </connectionStrings>

  <system.web>
    <authentication mode="Forms" />

    <membership defaultProvider="MyMembershipProvider">
      <providers>
        <add
```

```
            name="MyMembershipProvider"
            type="System.Web.Security.ActiveDirectoryMembershipProvider"
            connectionStringName="ADLDSConnection"
            connectionProtection="None"
            connectionUsername="CN=ADLDSAdministrator,OU=WebUsers,O=WebUsersDirectory"
            connectionPassword="secret_"
            enableSearchMethods="true" />

    </providers>
  </membership>
</system.web>
</configuration>
```

The web configuration file in Listing 27.24 configures a new default Membership provider named `MyMembershipProvider`. This provider is an instance of the `ActiveDirectoryMembershipProvider`.

Several of the attributes used with the `ActiveDirectoryMembershipProvider` require additional explanation. The `connectionStringName` attribute points to the connection string defined in the `connectionStrings` section. This connection string connects to a local ADAM instance that listens on port 389.

The `connectionProtection` attribute is set to the value `None`. If you don't modify this attribute, you are required to use an SSL connection. If you do use an SSL connection, you need to change the port used in the connection string (typically port 636).

The `connectionUsername` and `connectionPassword` attributes use the `ADLDSAdministrator` account that you configured in the previous section. When you don't use an SSL connection, you must provide both a `connectionUsername` and `connectionPassword` attribute.

Finally, notice that the provider declaration includes an `enableSearchMethods` attribute. If you want to configure users by using the Web Site Administration Tool, you must include this attribute.

The `ActiveDirectoryMembershipProvider` class supports several attributes specific to working with Active Directory:

▶ **connectionStringName**—Enables you to specify the name of the connection to the Active Directory Server in the `connectionStrings` section.

▶ **connectionUsername**—Enables you to specify the Active Directory account used to connect to Active Directory.

▶ **connectionPassword**—Enables you to specify the Active Directory password used to connect to Active Directory.

▶ **connectionProtection**—Enables you to specify whether or not the connection is encrypted. Possible values are `None` and `Secure`.

27

▶ **enableSearchMethods**—Enables the `ActiveDirectoryMembershipProvider` class to use additional methods. You must enable this attribute when using the Web Site Administration Tool.

▶ **attributeMapPasswordQuestion**—Enables you to map the Membership security question to an Active Directory attribute.

▶ **attributeMapPasswordAnswer**—Enables you to map the Membership security answer to an Active Directory attribute.

▶ **attributeMapFailedPasswordAnswerCount**—Enables you to map the Membership `MaxInvalidPasswordAttempts` property to an Active Directory attribute.

▶ **attributeMapFailedPasswordAnswerTime**—Enables you to map the Membership `PasswordAttemptWindow` property to an Active Directory attribute.

▶ **attributeMapFailedPasswordAnswerLockoutTime**—Enables you to map the Membership `PasswordAnswerAttemptLockoutDuration` property to an Active Directory attribute.

After you finish these configuration steps, you can use the `ActiveDirectoryMembership Provider` in precisely the same way that you can use the `SqlMembershipProvider`. When you use the `Login` control, users are validated against Active Directory. When you use the `CreateUserWizard` control, new users are created in Active Directory.

Creating a Custom Membership Provider

Because ASP.NET Membership uses the provider model, you can easily extend ASP.NET membership by creating a custom Membership provider. There are two main situations in which you might need to create a custom Membership provider.

First, imagine that you have an existing ASP.NET 1.x or ASP classic application. You are currently storing membership information in your own custom set of database tables. Furthermore, your table schemas don't easily map to the table schemas used by the `SqlMembershipProvider`.

In this situation, it makes sense to create a custom Membership provider that reflects your existing database schema. If you create a custom Membership provider, you can use your existing database tables with ASP.NET Membership.

Second, imagine that you need to store membership information in a data store other than Microsoft SQL Server or Active Directory. For example, your organization might be committed to Oracle or DB2. In that case, you need to create a custom Membership provider to work with the custom data store.

In this section, we create a simple custom Membership provider: an `XmlMembershipProvider` that stores membership information in an XML file.

Unfortunately, the code for the XmlMembershipProvider is too long to place here. The code is included on the book's website in a file named XmlMembershipProvider.cs, located in the App_Code folder.

The XmlMembershipProvider class inherits from the abstract MembershipProvider class. This class has more than 25 properties and methods that you are required to implement. For example, you are required to implement the ValidateUser() method. The Login control calls this method when it validates a username and password.

You also are required to implement the CreateUser() method. This method is called by the CreateUserWizard control when a new user is created.

The web configuration file used to set up the XmlMembershipProvider is contained in Listing 27.25.

LISTING 27.25   Web.Config

```xml
<?xml version="1.0"?>
<configuration>
    <system.web>

        <authentication mode="Forms" />

        <membership defaultProvider="MyMembershipProvider">
          <providers>
            <add
              name="MyMembershipProvider"
              type="AspNetUnleashed.XmlMembershipProvider"
              dataFile="~/App_Data/Membership.xml"
              requiresQuestionAndAnswer="false"
              enablePasswordRetrieval="true"
              enablePasswordReset="true"
              passwordFormat="Clear" />
          </providers>
        </membership>

    </system.web>
</configuration>
```

Notice that the XmlMembershipProvider supports a number of attributes. For example, it supports a passwordFormat attribute that enables you to specify whether passwords are stored as hash values or as plain text. (It does not support encrypted passwords.)

The XmlMembershipProvider stores membership information in an XML file named Membership.xml, located in the App_Data folder. If you want, you can add users to the file by hand. Alternatively, you can use the `CreateUserWizard` control or the Web Site Administration Tool to create new users.

A sample of the `Membership.xml` file is contained in Listing 27.26.

LISTING 27.26   App_Data\Membership.xml

```
<credentials>
  <user name="Steve" password="secret" email="steve@somewhere.com" />
  <user name="Andrew" password="secret" email="andrew@somewhere.com" />
</credentials>
```

The sample code folder on the book's website includes a `Register.aspx`, `Login.aspx`, and `ChangePassword.aspx` page. You can use these pages to try out different features of the `XmlMembershipProvider`.

> **WARNING**
>
> Dynamic XPath queries are open to XPath Injection Attacks in the same way that dynamic SQL queries are open to SQL Injection Attacks. When writing the `XmlMembershipProvider` class, I avoided using methods such as the `SelectSingleNode()` method to avoid XPath Injection Attack issues, even though using this method would result in leaner and faster code. Sometimes, it is better to be safe than fast.

Using the Role Manager

Instead of configuring authorization for particular users, you can group users into roles and assign authorization rules to the roles. For example, you might want to password-protect a section of your website so that only members of the Administrators role can access the pages in that section.

Like ASP.NET Membership, the Role Manager is built on the existing ASP.NET authentication framework. You configure role authorization rules by adding an authorization element to one or more web configuration files.

Furthermore, like ASP.NET Membership, the Role Manager uses the provider model. You can customize where role information is stored by configuring a particular Role provider.

The ASP.NET Framework includes three role providers:

▶ **SqlRoleProvider**—Enables you to store role information in a Microsoft SQL Server database.

▶ **WindowsTokenRoleProvider**—Enables you to use Microsoft Windows groups to represent role information.

▶ **AuthorizationStoreRoleProvider**—Enables you to use Authorization Manager to store role information in an XML file, Active Directory, or Activity Directory Lightweight Directory Services (ADLDS).

In the following sections, you learn how to configure each of these Role providers. You also learn how to manage role information programmatically by working with the Roles application programming interface.

Configuring the `SqlRoleProvider`

The `SqlRoleProvider` is the default role provider. You can use the `SqlRoleProvider` to store role information in a Microsoft SQL Server database. The `SqlRoleProvider` enables you to create custom roles. You can make up any roles that you need.

You can use the `SqlRoleProvider` with either Forms authentication or Windows authentication. When Forms authentication is enabled, you can use ASP.NET Membership to represent users and assign the users to particular roles. When Windows authentication is enabled, you assign particular Windows user accounts to custom roles. I assume, in this section, that you use Forms authentication.

> **WARNING**
>
> The Web Site Administration Tool does not support assigning users to roles when Windows authentication is enabled. When Windows authentication is enabled, you must assign users to roles programmatically.

The web configuration file in Listing 27.27 enables the `SqlRoleProvider`.

LISTING 27.27   Web.Config

```
<?xml version="1.0" encoding="utf-8"?>
<configuration>
    <system.web>
        <roleManager enabled="true" />
        <authentication mode="Forms" />
    </system.web>
</configuration>
```

The Role Manager is disabled by default. The configuration file in Listing 27.27 simply enables the Role Manager. Notice that the configuration file also enables Forms authentication.

If you don't want to type the file in Listing 27.27, you can let the Web Site Administration Tool create the file for you. Open the Web Site Administration Tool in Visual Web

Developer by selecting Website, ASP.NET Configuration. Next, click the Security tab and the Enable roles link (see Figure 27.10).

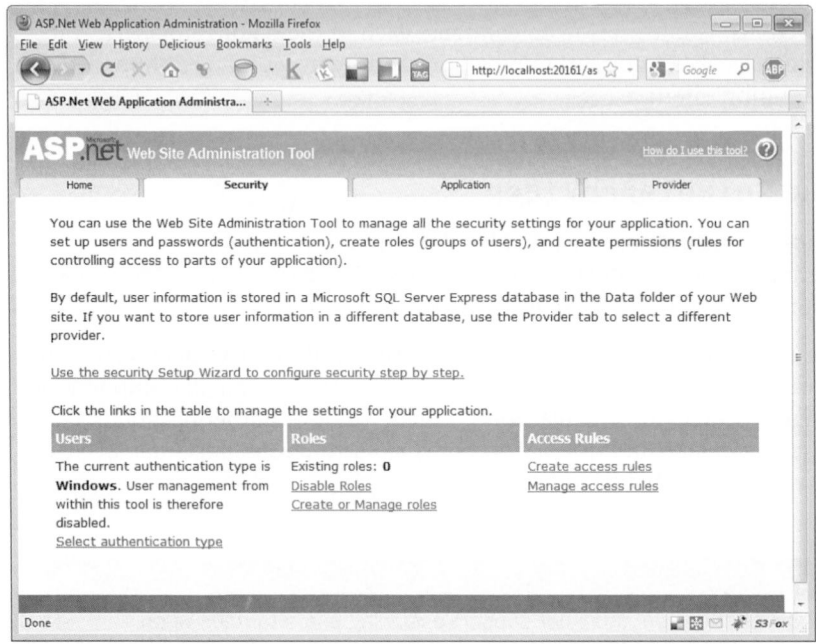

FIGURE 27.10   Enabling Roles with the Web Site Administration Tool.

After you enable the Role Manager, you need to create some roles. You can create roles in two ways. You can use the Web Site Administration Tool or you can create the roles programmatically.

Open the Web Site Administration Tool and click the Create or Manage Roles link located under the Security tab. At this point, you can start creating roles. I'll assume that you have created a role named Managers.

After you create a set of roles, you need to assign users to the roles. Again, you can do this by using the Web Site Administration Tool or you can assign users to roles programmatically.

If you have not created any users for your application, create a user now by clicking the Create User link under the Security tab. Notice that you can assign a user to one or more roles when you create the user (see Figure 27.11). You can click the Create or Manage Roles link to assign roles to users at a later date.

After you finish creating your roles and assigning users to the roles, you can use the roles in the authentication section of a web configuration file. For example, imagine that your website includes a folder named SecretFiles and you want only members of the Managers role to be able to access the pages in that folder. The web configuration file in Listing 27.28 blocks access to anyone except members of the Managers role to the SecretFiles folder.

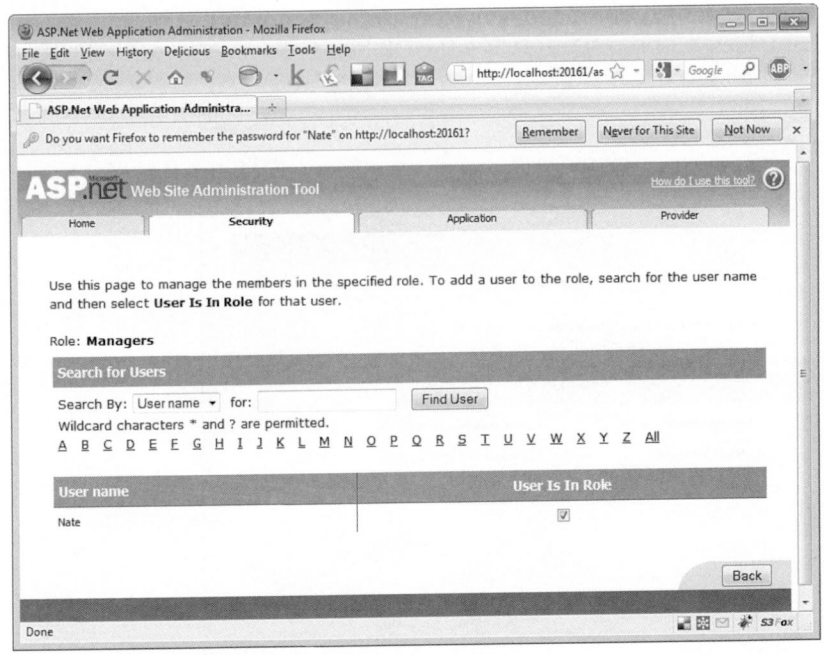

FIGURE 27.11   Assigning a new user to a role.

LISTING 27.28   Web.Config

```
<?xml version="1.0"?>
<configuration>
    <system.web>

      <authorization>
        <allow roles="Managers"/>
        <deny users="*"/>
      </authorization>

    </system.web>
</configuration>
```

The configuration file in Listing 27.28 authorizes Managers and denies access to everyone else.

If you prefer, you can manage authorization with the Web Site Administration Tool. Behind the scenes, this tool creates web configuration files that contain authorization elements (in other words, it does the same thing as we just did).

Under the Security tab, click the Create Access Rules link. Select the SecretFiles folder from the tree view, the Managers role, Allow (see Figure 27.12). Click the OK button to create the rule. Next, create a second access rule to deny access to users not in the Managers role. Select the SecretFiles folder, All Users, Deny. Click the OK button to add the new rule.

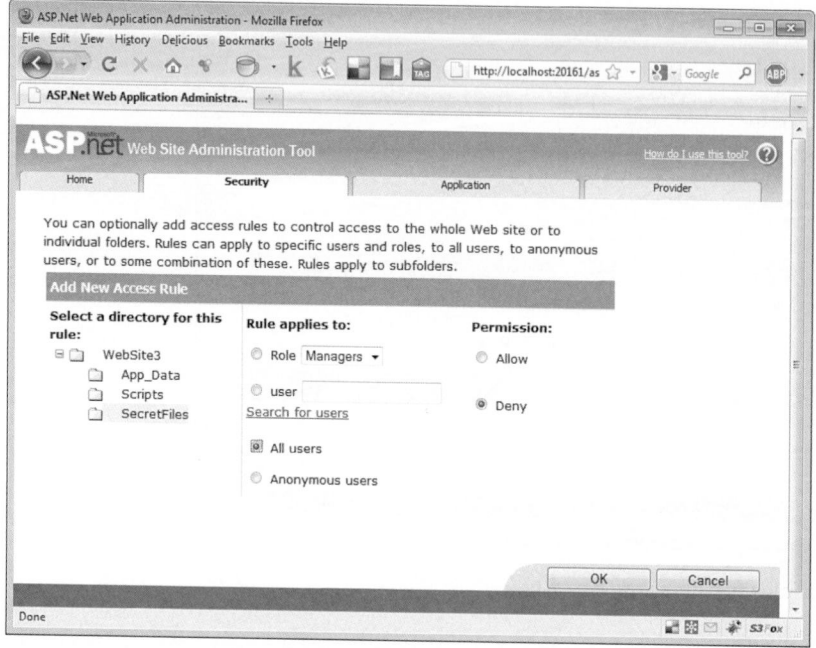

FIGURE 27.12   Creating authorization rules.

Using a Different Database with the SqlRoleProvider

By default, the SqlRoleProvider uses the same Microsoft SQL Server Express database as ASP.NET Membership: the AspNetDB.mdf database. This database is created for you automatically in your application's root App_Data folder.

If you want to store role information in another Microsoft SQL Server database, then you must perform the following two configuration steps.

▶ Configure the database so that it contains the necessary database objects.

▶ Configure your application to use the new database.

Before you can store role information in a database, you need to add the necessary tables and stored procedures to the database. The easiest way to add these objects is to use the aspnet_regsql command-line tool. This tool is located in the following folder:

```
\WINDOWS\Microsoft.NET\Framework\[version]
```

NOTE

You don't need to navigate to the Microsoft.NET folder when you open the SDK Command Prompt.

If you execute `aspnet_regsql` without any parameters, the ASP.NET SQL Server Setup Wizard opens (see Figure 27.13). You can use this wizard to connect to a database and add the necessary database objects automatically.

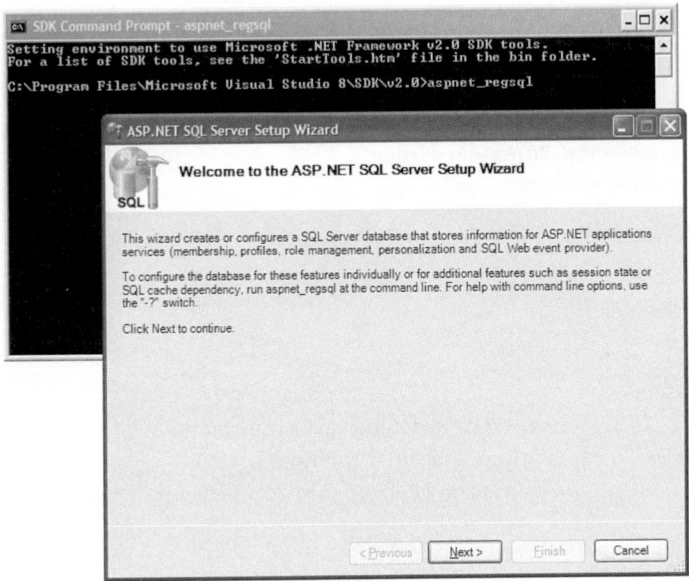

FIGURE 27.13   Using the SQL Server Setup Wizard.

Alternatively, you can set up a database by executing the following two SQL batch files.

▶ `InstallCommon.sql`

▶ `InstallRoles.sql`

These batch files are located in the same folder as the `aspnet_regsql` tool.

After you set up your database, you need to configure a new `SqlRoleProvider` that includes the proper connection string for your database. The web configuration file in Listing 27.29 configures a new provider named `MyRoleProvider` that connects to a database named MyDatabase located on a server named MyServer.

LISTING 27.29   Web.Config

```
<?xml version="1.0" encoding="utf-8"?>
<configuration>
  <connectionStrings>
    <add
      name="MyConnection"
      connectionString="Data Source=MyServer;
➥Integrated Security=True;Initial Catalog=MyDatabase"/>
```

```
    </connectionStrings>

    <system.web>
        <authentication mode="Forms" />

        <roleManager enabled="true" defaultProvider="MyRoleProvider">
            <providers>
                <add
                    name="MyRoleProvider"
                    type="System.Web.Security.SqlRoleProvider"
                    connectionStringName="MyConnection"/>
            </providers>
        </roleManager>

    </system.web>
</configuration>
```

The configuration file in Listing 27.29 creates a new default `RoleManager` named `MyRoleProvider`. Notice that the `MyRoleProvider` provider includes a `connectionStringName` attribute that points to the `MyConnection` connection.

Configuring the `WindowsTokenRoleProvider`

When you use the `WindowsTokenRoleProvider`, roles correspond to Microsoft Windows groups. You must enable Windows authentication when using the `WindowsTokenRoleProvider`. You cannot use Forms authentication or ASP.NET Membership with the `WindowsTokenRoleProvider`.

The configuration file in Listing 27.30 configures the `WindowsTokenRoleProvider` as the default provider.

LISTING 27.30   Web.Config

```
<?xml version="1.0" encoding="utf-8"?>
<configuration>
    <system.web>
        <authentication mode="Windows" />

        <roleManager enabled="true" defaultProvider="MyRoleProvider">
            <providers>
                <add
                    name="MyRoleProvider"
                    type="System.Web.Security.WindowsTokenRoleProvider" />
            </providers>
        </roleManager>
```

```
    </system.web>
</configuration>
```

The page in Listing 27.31 contains a `LoginView` control. The `LoginView` control displays different content to the members of the Windows Administrators group than it displays to everyone else (see Figure 27.14).

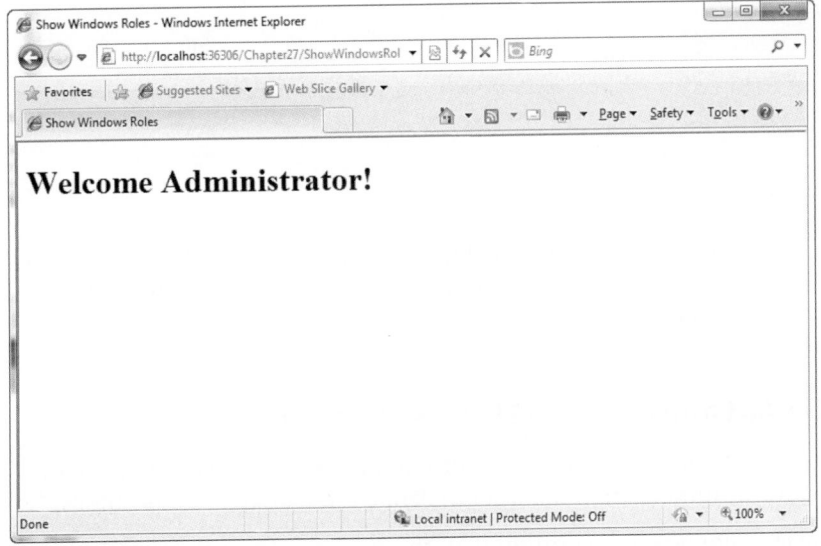

FIGURE 27.14 Displaying different content to members of the Windows Administrators group.

LISTING 27.31 ShowWindowsRoles.aspx

```
<%@ Page Language="C#" %>
<!DOCTYPE html PUBLIC "-//W3C//DTD XHTML 1.0 Transitional//EN"
  "http://www.w3.org/TR/xhtml1/DTD/xhtml1-transitional.dtd">
<html xmlns="http://www.w3.org/1999/xhtml" >
<head id="Head1" runat="server">
    <title>Show Windows Roles</title>
</head>
<body>
    <form id="form1" runat="server">
    <div>

    <asp:LoginView
        id="LoginView1"
        Runat="server">
        <RoleGroups>
        <asp:RoleGroup Roles="BUILTIN\Administrators">
```

```
        <ContentTemplate>
        <h1>Welcome Administrator!</h1>
        </ContentTemplate>
    </asp:RoleGroup>
    </RoleGroups>
    <LoggedInTemplate>
        <h1>Welcome Average User!</h1>
    </LoggedInTemplate>
    </asp:LoginView>

    </div>
    </form>
</body>
</html>
```

If you request the page in Listing 27.31 after enabling the WindowsTokenRoleProvider, you
see the content displayed by the LoginView control only when you are a member of the
Windows Administrators group.

Configuring the AuthorizationStoreRoleProvider

Authorization Manager (AzMan) is a component of Windows Server 2003 and Windows
Server 2008. You can use Authorization Manager to define roles, tasks, and operations.

Authorization Manager supports more features than the authorization framework included
in ASP.NET Framework. For example, Authorization Manager supports role inheritance,
which enables you to easily define new roles based on existing roles.

Authorization Manager can store role information in three different ways. You can create
an authorization store by using an XML file, by using Active Directory, or by using Active
Directory Lightweight Directory Services (AD LDS).

Before you use Authorization Manager with the ASP.NET Framework, you need to create
an authorization store. Role information is stored in an XML file local to the application.
Follow these steps:

1. Launch Authorization Manager by executing the command AzMan.msc from a
command prompt (see Figure 27.15).
2. Switch Authorization Manager into Developer mode by selecting Action, Options
and selecting Developer mode.
3. Open the New Authorization Store dialog box by selecting Action, New
Authorization Store.
4. Select the XML file option and enter the path to your application's App_Data folder
for the Store Name field. For example:

```
c:\Websites\MyWebsite\App_Data\WebRoles.xml
```

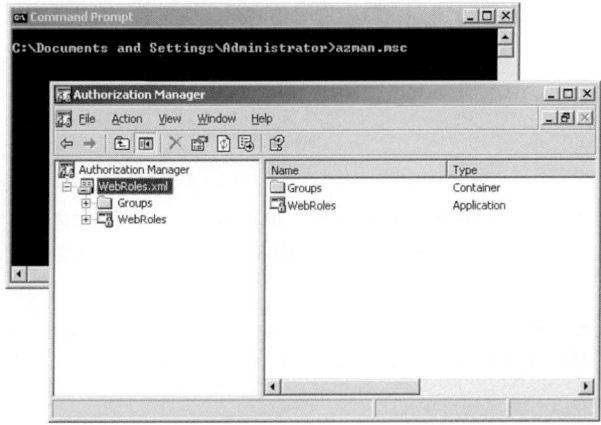

FIGURE 27.15   Using Authorization Manager.

5. Create a new Authorization Manager application by right-clicking the name of your authorization store and selecting New Application. Enter the name WebRoles for your application (you can leave the other fields blank).

After you complete these steps, a new XML file is added to your application. This XML file contains the authorization store.

Next, you need to configure the ASP.NET Role Manager to use the authorization store. The web configuration file in Listing 27.32 uses the WebRoles.xml authorization store.

LISTING 27.32   Web.Config

```xml
<?xml version="1.0" encoding="utf-8"?>
<configuration>
  <connectionStrings>
    <add
      name="AZConnection"
      connectionString="msxml://~/App_Data/WebRoles.xml"/>
  </connectionStrings>

  <system.web>
    <authentication mode="Windows" />

    <roleManager enabled="true" defaultProvider="MyRoleProvider">
      <providers>
        <add
          name="MyRoleProvider"
          type="System.Web.Security.AuthorizationStoreRoleProvider"
          connectionStringName="AZConnection"
          applicationName="WebRoles"
          />
```

27

```
    </providers>
  </roleManager>

 </system.web>
</configuration>
```

You should notice a couple of things about the configuration file in Listing 27.32. First, notice that the connection string uses the prefix `msxml:` to indicate that the connection string represents a connection to an XML file.

Second, notice that the `AuthorizationStoreRoleProvider` includes an `applicationName` attribute. This attribute must contain the name of the Authorization Manager application that you created in the preceding steps.

After you complete these configuration steps, you can use the Authorization Manager just as you do the default `SqlMembershipProvider`. You can define new roles by using either the Web Site Administration Tool or the Authorization Manager interface (see Figure 27.16).

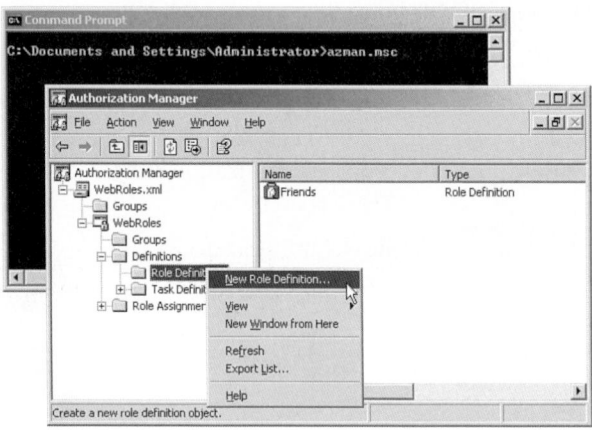

FIGURE 27.16   Creating a new role definition with Authorization Manager.

Caching Roles in a Browser Cookie

To improve your application's performance, you can cache user roles in a browser cookie. That way, the Role Manager does not have to perform a query against the Role provider each and every time a user visits a page.

Caching roles in cookies is disabled by default. You can enable this feature with the web configuration file in Listing 27.33.

LISTING 27.33 Web.Config

```xml
<?xml version="1.0" encoding="utf-8"?>
<configuration>
    <system.web>
      <roleManager
        enabled="true"
        cacheRolesInCookie="true"
        createPersistentCookie="true" />
    </system.web>
</configuration>
```

The web configuration in Listing 27.33 enables role caching. Furthermore, it causes the roles to be cached in a persistent cookie rather than a session cookie.

> **WARNING**
>
> When you cache roles in a cookie, there is the potential that a user's cached roles can become out of sync with a user's actual roles. If you update users' roles on the server, they don't get updated on the browser. You can call the `Roles.DeleteCookie()` method to delete the cached cookies.

You can set a number of attributes related to the roles cookie:

- **cacheRolesInCookie**—Enables you to cache user roles in a browser cookie (the default value is `false`).

- **cookieName**—Enables you to specify the name for the roles cookie (the default value is `.ASPXROLES`).

- **cookiePath**—Enables you to specify the path associated with the cookie. (The default value is `/`.).

- **cookieProtection**—Enables you to encrypt and validate the roles cookie. Possible values are `All`, `Encryption`, `None`, and `Validation` (the default value is `All`).

- **cookieRequireSSL**—Enables you to require that the roles cookie be transmitted over a Secure Sockets Layer connection. (The default value is `False`.).

- **cookieSlidingExpiration**—Enables you to prevent a cookie from expiring just as long as a user continues to request pages. (The default value is `True`.)

- **cookieTimeout**—Enables you to specify the amount of time in minutes before a cookie times out. (The default value is `30`.)

- **createPersistentCookie**—Enables you to create a persistent rather than a session cookie. (The default value is `False`.)

27

▶ **domain**—Enables you to specify the domain associated with the cookie. (The default value is an empty string.)

▶ **maxCachedResults**—Enables you to specify the maximum number of roles that are cached in a cookie. (The default is 25.)

Using the Roles Application Programming Interface

The Roles class exposes the main application programming interface for manipulating roles. If you need to create roles programmatically, delete roles, or assign users to roles; then you use the methods of the Roles class.

The Roles class includes the following methods:

▶ **AddUsersToRole**—Enables you to add an array of users to a role.

▶ **AddUsersToRoles**—Enables you to add an array of users to an array of roles.

▶ **AddUserToRole**—Enables you to add a user to a role.

▶ **AddUserToRoles**—Enables you to add a user to an array of roles.

▶ **CreateRole**—Enables you to create a new role.

▶ **DeleteCookie**—Enables you to delete the roles cookie.

▶ **DeleteRole**—Enables you to delete a particular role.

▶ **FindUsersInRole**—Enables you to return a list of users in a role that has a particular username.

▶ **GetAllRoles**—Enables you to retrieve a list of all roles.

▶ **GetRolesForUser**—Enables you to get a list of all roles to which a user belongs.

▶ **GetUsersInRole**—Enables you to get a list of users in a particular role.

▶ **IsUserInRole**—Enables you to determine whether a particular user is a member of a particular role.

▶ **RemoveUserFromRole**—Enables you to remove a particular user from a particular role.

▶ **RemoveUserFromRoles**—Enables you to remove a particular user from an array of roles.

▶ **RemoveUsersFromRole**—Enables you to remove an array of users from a particular role.

▶ **RemoveUsersFromRoles**—Enables you to remove an array of users from an array of roles.

▶ **RoleExists**—Enables you to determine whether a particular role exists.

The page in Listing 27.34 illustrates how you can use the methods of the Roles class. The Page_Load() method creates two roles named Sales and Managers (if they don't already exist). Next, it assigns the current user to both roles. The body of the page contains a GridView that displays all the roles to which the current user belongs (see Figure 27.17).

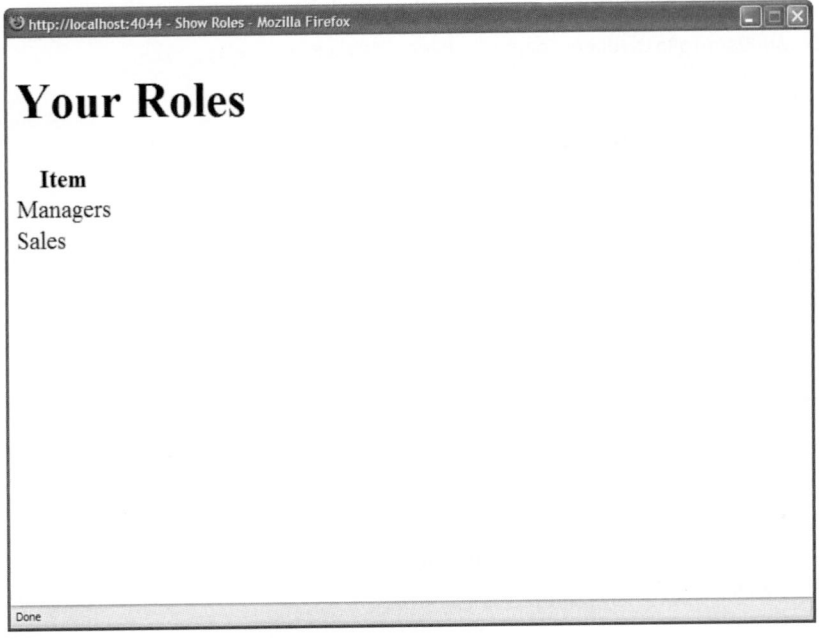

FIGURE 27.17   Displaying a user's roles.

LISTING 27.34   ShowRoles.aspx

```
<%@ Page Language="C#" %>
<!DOCTYPE html PUBLIC "-//W3C//DTD XHTML 1.0 Transitional//EN"
    "http://www.w3.org/TR/xhtml1/DTD/xhtml1-transitional.dtd">
<script runat="server">
    void Page_Load()
    {
        // If user is not authenticated, redirect to Login page
        if (!Request.IsAuthenticated)
        {
            FormsAuthentication.RedirectToLoginPage();
            Response.End();
        }
        // Create two roles
        if (!Roles.RoleExists("Managers"))
            Roles.CreateRole("Managers");
        if (!Roles.RoleExists("Sales"))
            Roles.CreateRole("Sales");

        // Add current user to both roles
        if (!Roles.IsUserInRole("Managers"))
            Roles.AddUserToRole(User.Identity.Name, "Managers");
```

27

```
            if (!Roles.IsUserInRole("Sales"))
                Roles.AddUserToRole(User.Identity.Name, "Sales");
    }
</script>
<html xmlns="http://www.w3.org/1999/xhtml" >
<head id="Head1" runat="server">
    <title>Show Roles</title>
</head>
<body>
    <form id="form1" runat="server">
    <div>

    <h1>Your Roles</h1>

    <asp:GridView
        id="grdRoles"
        DataSourceID="srcRoles"
        EmptyDataText="You are not a member of any roles"
        GridLines="none"
        Runat="server" />

    <asp:ObjectDataSource
        id="srcRoles"
        TypeName="System.Web.Security.Roles"
        SelectMethod="GetRolesForUser"
        Runat="server" />

    </div>
    </form>
</body>
</html>
```

Summary

In this chapter, you learned about the four security frameworks included in ASP.NET Framework. In the first part, you learned how to authenticate users by enabling both Forms and Windows authentication. You learned how to take advantage of several advanced features of authentication such as cookieless authentication and cross-application authentication.

You also learned how to authorize users to access particular resources. You not only learned how to control access to ASP.NET pages, but also how you can control access to image files and other files or pages.

Next, you learned how to use ASP.NET Membership to represent user information. You learned how to use the `Membership` class to create users, delete users, and modify user properties programmatically. You also explored the two Membership providers included with ASP.NET Framework: `SqlMembershipProvider` and `ActiveDirectoryMembership Provider`. Finally, we created a custom `MembershipProvider`: the `XmlMembershipProvider`.

The final section was devoted to the Role Manager. You learned how to configure the three Role providers included in ASP.NET Framework: `SqlRoleProvider`, `WindowsTokenRoleProvider`, and `AuthorizationStoreRoleProvider`. You also learned how to take advantage of the `Roles` class to create roles, delete roles, and assign users to roles programmatically.

27

CHAPTER **28**

Maintaining Application State

Developers who are new to programming for the web always have difficulty understanding the problem of maintaining state. The HTTP protocol, the fundamental protocol of the World Wide Web, is a stateless protocol. What this means is that from a web server's perspective, every request is from a new user. The HTTP protocol does not provide you with any method of determining whether any two requests are made by the same person.

However, maintaining state is important in just about any web application. The paradigmatic example is a shopping cart. If you want to associate a shopping cart with a user over multiple page requests, you need some method of maintaining state.

This chapter looks at three methods included in ASP.NET 4 Framework for associating data with a particular user over multiple page requests. In the first section, you learn how to create and manipulate browser cookies. A browser cookie enables you to associate a little bit of text with each website user.

Next, you learn how to take advantage of Session state, which enables you to associate an arbitrary object with any user. For example, you can store a shopping cart object in Session state.

You learn how take advantage of cookieless Session state so that you can use Session state even when a browser has cookies disabled. You also learn how to make Session state more robust by enabling out-of-process Session state.

Finally, we examine a feature introduced with ASP.NET 2.0 the `Profile` object. The `Profile` object provides you with a method of creating a strongly typed and persistent form of session state.

You learn different methods of defining a profile. You also learn how to use the `Profile` object from within a component. Finally, you learn how to implement a custom `Profile` provider.

Using Browser Cookies

Cookies were introduced into the world with the first version of the Netscape browser. The developers at Netscape invented cookies to solve a problem that plagued the Internet at the time. There was no way to make money because there was no way to create a shopping cart.

Here's how cookies work. When a web server creates a cookie, an additional HTTP header is sent to the browser when a page is served to the browser. The HTTP header looks like this:

```
Set-Cookie: message=Hello
```

This `Set-Cookie` header causes the browser to create a cookie named `message` that has the value `Hello`.

After a cookie has been created on a browser, whenever the browser requests a page from the same application in the future, the browser sends a header that looks like this:

```
Cookie: message=Hello
```

The `Cookie` header contains all the cookies that have been set by the web server. The cookies are sent back to the web server each time a request is made from the browser. A cookie is nothing more than a little bit of text. You can store only string values when using a cookie.

You actually can create two types of cookies: session cookies and persistent cookies. A session cookie exists only in memory. If a user closes the web browser, the session cookie disappears forever.

A persistent cookie, on the other hand, can last for months or even years. When you create a persistent cookie, the cookie is stored permanently by the user's browser on the user's computer. Internet Explorer, for example, stores cookies in a set of text files contained in the following folder:

```
\Documents and Settings\[user]\Cookies
```

The Mozilla Firefox browser, on the other hand, stores cookies in the following file:

```
\Documents and Settings\[user]\Application Data\Mozilla\Firefox\Profiles\
➥[random folder name]\Cookies.txt
```

Because different browsers store cookies in different locations, cookies are browser-relative. If you request a page that creates a cookie when using Internet Explorer, the cookie doesn't exist when you open Firefox or Opera. Furthermore, both Internet Explorer and Firefox store cookies in clear text. You should never store sensitive information—such as Social Security numbers or credit card numbers in a cookie.

> **NOTE**
>
> Where does the name *cookie* come from? According to the original Netscape cookie specification, the term cookie was selected "for no compelling reason." However, the name most likely derives from the UNIX world in which a "magic cookie" is an opaque token passed between programs.

Cookie Security Restrictions

Cookies raise security concerns. When you create a persistent cookie, you are modifying a file on a visitor's computer. There are people who sit around all day dreaming up evil things that they can do to your computer. To prevent cookies from doing horrible things to people's computers, browsers enforce a number of security restrictions on cookies.

First, all cookies are domain-relative. If the Amazon website sets a cookie, the Barnes & Noble website cannot read the cookie. When a browser creates a cookie, the browser records the domain associated with the cookie and doesn't send the cookie to another domain.

> **NOTE**
>
> An image contained in a web page might be served from another domain than the web page itself. Therefore, when the browser makes a request for the image, a cookie can be set from the other domain. Companies, such as DoubleClick, that display and track advertisements on multiple websites take advantage of this loophole to track advertisement statistics across multiple websites. This type of cookie is called a third-party cookie.

The other important restriction that browsers place on cookies is a restriction on size. A single domain cannot store more than 4,096 bytes. This size restriction encompasses the size of both the cookie names and the cookie values.

> **NOTE**
>
> Internet Explorer supports a feature named the `userData` behavior, which enables you to persist far more data than a cookie (10,240KB for an intranet site and 1,024 for an Internet site). To learn more about the `userData` behavior, visit the Microsoft MSDN website (msdn.microsoft.com).

Finally, most browsers restrict the number of cookies that can be set by a single domain to no more than 20 cookies (but not Internet Explorer). If you attempt to set more than 20 cookies, the oldest cookies are automatically deleted.

Because of all the security concerns related to cookies, all modern browsers provide users with the option of disabling cookies. This means that unless you are building an Intranet application and you control every user's browser, you should attempt to not rely on cookies. Strive to use cookies only when storing noncrucial information.

That said, many parts of ASP.NET Framework rely on cookies. For example, Web Parts, Forms Authentication, `Session` state, and anonymous Profiles all depend on cookies by default. If you depend on one of these features, there is no reason not to use cookies.

Furthermore, many websites rely on cookies. Many sections of the Yahoo! and MSDN websites you cannot visit without having cookies enabled. In other words, requiring visitors to have cookies enabled to use your website is not an entirely unreasonable requirement.

Creating Cookies

You create a new cookie by adding a cookie to the `Response.Cookies` collection, which contains all the cookies sent from the web server to the web browser. For example, the page in Listing 28.1 enables you to create a new cookie named `Message`. The page contains a form that enables you to enter the value of the `Message` cookie (see Figure 28.1).

FIGURE 28.1   Creating a new cookie.

LISTING 28.1   SetCookie.aspx

```
<%@ Page Language="C#" %>
<!DOCTYPE html PUBLIC "-//W3C//DTD XHTML 1.0 Transitional//EN"
"http://www.w3.org/TR/xhtml1/DTD/xhtml1-transitional.dtd">
<script runat="server">

    protected void btnAdd_Click(object sender, EventArgs e)
    {
        Response.Cookies["message"].Value = txtCookieValue.Text;
    }
</script>
<html xmlns="http://www.w3.org/1999/xhtml" >
<head id="Head1" runat="server">
    <title>Set Cookie</title>
</head>
<body>
    <form id="form1" runat="server">
    <div>

    <asp:Label
        id="lblCookieValue"
        Text="Cookie Value:"
```

28

```
        AssociatedControlID="txtCookieValue"
        Runat="server" />
    <asp:TextBox
        id="txtCookieValue"
        Runat="server" />
    <asp:Button
        id="btnAdd"
        Text="Add Value"
        OnClick="btnAdd_Click"
        Runat="server" />

    </div>
    </form>
</body>
</html>
```

Be warned that cookie names are case-sensitive. Setting a cookie named message is different from setting a cookie named Message.

If you want to modify the value of the cookie created by the page in Listing 28.1, you can open the page and enter a new value for the message cookie. When the web server sends its response to the browser, the modified value of the cookie is set on the browser.

The page in Listing 28.1 creates a session cookie. The cookie disappears when you close your web browser. If you want to create a persistent cookie, you need to specify an expiration date for the cookie.

The page in Listing 28.2 creates a persistent cookie.

LISTING 28.2   SetPersistentCookie.aspx

```
<%@ Page Language="C#" %>
<!DOCTYPE html PUBLIC "-//W3C//DTD XHTML 1.0 Transitional//EN"
    "http://www.w3.org/TR/xhtml1/DTD/xhtml1-transitional.dtd">
<script runat="server">

    void Page_Load()
    {
        // Get current value of cookie
        int counter = 0;
        if (Request.Cookies["counter"] != null)
            counter = Int32.Parse(Request.Cookies["counter"].Value);

        // Increment counter
        counter++;
```

```
        // Add persistent cookie to browser
        Response.Cookies["counter"].Value = counter.ToString();
        Response.Cookies["counter"].Expires = DateTime.Now.AddYears(2);

        // Display value of counter cookie
        lblCounter.Text = counter.ToString();
    }
</script>
<html xmlns="http://www.w3.org/1999/xhtml" >
<head id="Head1" runat="server">
    <title>Set Persistent Cookie</title>
</head>
<body>
    <form id="form1" runat="server">
    <div>

    You have visited this page
    <asp:Label
        id="lblCounter"
        Runat="server" />
    times!

    </div>
    </form>
</body>
</html>
```

The page in Listing 28.2 tracks the number of times that you request the page. A persistent cookie named counter tracks page requests. The counter cookie's Expires property is set to 2 years in the future. When you set a particular expiration date for a cookie, the cookie is stored as a persistent cookie.

Reading Cookies

You use the Response.Cookies collection to create and modify cookies. You use the Request.Cookies collection to retrieve a cookie's value.

For example, the page in Listing 28.3 retrieves the message cookie's value.

LISTING 28.3   GetCookie.aspx

```
<%@ Page Language="C#" %>
<!DOCTYPE html PUBLIC "-//W3C//DTD XHTML 1.0 Transitional//EN"
    "http://www.w3.org/TR/xhtml1/DTD/xhtml1-transitional.dtd">
<script runat="server">

    void Page_Load()
    {
        if (Request.Cookies["message"] != null)
            lblCookieValue.Text = Request.Cookies["message"].Value;
    }

</script>
<html xmlns="http://www.w3.org/1999/xhtml" >
<head id="Head1" runat="server">
    <title>Get Cookie</title>
</head>
<body>
    <form id="form1" runat="server">
    <div>

    The value of the message cookie is:
    <asp:Label
        id="lblCookieValue"
        Runat="server" />

    </div>
    </form>
</body>
</html>
```

In Listing 28.3, the IsNothing() function checks whether the cookie exists before reading its value. If you don't include this check, you might get a null reference exception. Also, don't forget that cookie names are case-sensitive.

The page in Listing 28.4 lists all cookies contained in the Request.Cookies collection (see Figure 28.2).

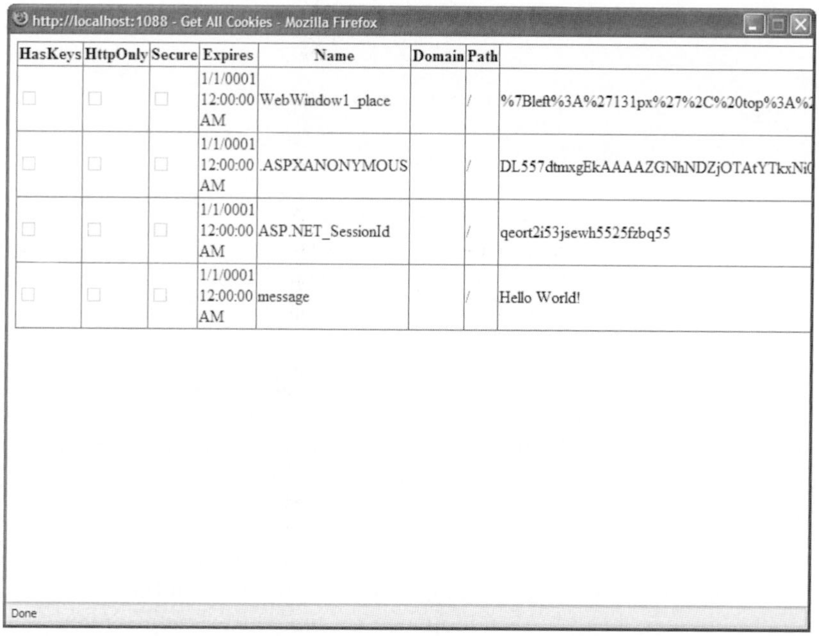

HasKeys	HttpOnly	Secure	Expires	Name	Domain	Path	
☐	☐	☐	1/1/0001 12:00:00 AM	WebWindow1_place		/	%7Bleft%3A%27131px%27%2C%20top%3A%2
☐	☐	☐	1/1/0001 12:00:00 AM	.ASPXANONYMOUS		/	DL557dtmxgEkAAAAZGNhNDZjOTAtYTkxNi0
☐	☐	☐	1/1/0001 12:00:00 AM	ASP.NET_SessionId		/	qeort2i53jsewh5525fzbq55
☐	☐	☐	1/1/0001 12:00:00 AM	message		/	Hello World!

Done

FIGURE 28.2   Displaying a list of all cookies.

LISTING 28.4   GetAllCookies.aspx

```
<%@ Page Language="C#" %>
<!DOCTYPE html PUBLIC "-//W3C//DTD XHTML 1.0 Transitional//EN"
    "http://www.w3.org/TR/xhtml1/DTD/xhtml1-transitional.dtd">
<script runat="server">

    void Page_Load()
    {

        ArrayList colCookies = new ArrayList();
        for (int i = 0; i < Request.Cookies.Count; i++)
            colCookies.Add(Request.Cookies[i]);

        grdCookies.DataSource = colCookies;
        grdCookies.DataBind();
    }
</script>
<html xmlns="http://www.w3.org/1999/xhtml" >
<head id="Head1" runat="server">
    <title>Get All Cookies</title>
</head>
<body>
    <form id="form1" runat="server">
```

28

```
    <div>

    <asp:GridView
        id="grdCookies"
        Runat="server"/>

    </div>
    </form>
</body>
</html>
```

The only meaningful information that you get back from iterating through the `Request.Cookies` collection is the `HasKeys`, `Name`, and `Value` properties. The other columns show incorrect information. For example, the `Expires` column always displays a minimal date. Browsers don't communicate these additional properties with page requests, so you can't retrieve these property values.

When using the `Request.Cookies` collection, you need to understand that a `For...Each` loop returns different values than a `For...Next` loop. If you iterate through the `Request.Cookies` collection with a `For...Each` loop, you get the cookie names. If you iterate through the collection with a `For...Next` loop, you get instances of the `HttpCookie` class (described in the next section).

Setting Cookie Properties

Cookies are represented with the `HttpCookie` class. When you create or read a cookie, you can use any of the properties of this class:

- ▶ **Domain**—Enables you to specify the domain associated with the cookie. The default value is the current domain.

- ▶ **Expires**—Enables you to create a persistent cookie by specifying an expiration date.

- ▶ **HasKeys**—Enables you to determine whether a cookie is a multi-valued cookie (see the section "Working with Multivalued Cookies" later in this chapter).

- ▶ **HttpOnly**—Enables you to prevent a cookie from being accessed by JavaScript.

- ▶ **Name**—Enables you to specify a name for a cookie.

- ▶ **Path**—Enables you to specify the path associated with a cookie. The default value is /.

- ▶ **Secure**—Enables you to require a cookie to be transmitted across a Secure Sockets Layer (SSL) connection.

- ▶ **Value**—Enables you to get or set a cookie value.

- ▶ **Values**—Enables you to get or set a particular value when working with a multivalued cookie. (See the section "Working with Multivalued Cookies" later in this chapter.)

A couple of these properties require additional explanation. For example, you might find the `Domain` property confusing because you can't change the domain associated with a cookie.

The `Domain` property is useful when your organization includes subdomains. If you want to set a cookie that can be read by the `Sales.MyCompany.com`, `Managers.MyCompany.com`, and `Support.MyCompany.com` domains, you can set the `Domain` property to the value `.MyCompany.com`. (Notice the leading period.) You can't, however, use this property to associate a cookie with an entirely different domain.

The `HttpOnly` property enables you to specify whether a cookie can be accessed from JavaScript code. This property works only with Internet Explorer 6 (Service Pack 1) and above. The property was introduced to help prevent cross-site scripting attacks.

The `Path` property enables you to scope cookies to a particular path. For example, if you host multiple applications in the same domain, and you do not want the applications to share the same cookies, you can use the `Path` property to prevent one application from reading another application's cookies.

The `Path` property sounds useful. Unfortunately, you should never use it. Internet Explorer performs a case-sensitive match against the path. If a user uses a different case when typing the path to a page into the address bar, the cookie isn't sent. In other words, the following two paths don't match:

```
http://localhost/original/GetAllCookies.aspx
http://localhost/ORIGINAL/GetAllCookies.aspx
```

Deleting Cookies

The method for deleting cookies is not intuitive. To delete an existing cookie, you must set its expiration date to a date in the past.

The page in Listing 28.5 illustrates how you can delete a single cookie. The page contains a form field for the cookie name. When you submit the form, the cookie with the specified name is deleted.

LISTING 28.5 `DeleteCookie.aspx`

```
<%@ Page Language="C#" %>
<!DOCTYPE html PUBLIC "-//W3C//DTD XHTML 1.0 Transitional//EN"
    "http://www.w3.org/TR/xhtml1/DTD/xhtml1-transitional.dtd">
<script runat="server">

    protected void btnDelete_Click(object sender, EventArgs e)
    {
        Response.Cookies[txtCookieName.Text].Expires = DateTime.Now.AddDays(-1);
    }
</script>
```

```
<html xmlns="http://www.w3.org/1999/xhtml" >
<head id="Head1" runat="server">
    <title>Delete Cookie</title>
</head>
<body>
    <form id="form1" runat="server">
    <div>

    <asp:Label
        id="lblCookieName"
        Text="Cookie Name:"
        AssociatedControlID="txtCookieName"
        Runat="server" />
    <asp:TextBox
        id="txtCookieName"
        Runat="server" />
    <asp:Button
        id="btnDelete"
        Text="Delete Cookie"
        OnClick="btnDelete_Click"
        Runat="server" />

    </div>
    </form>
</body>
</html>
```

The particular date that you specify when deleting a cookie doesn't matter as long as it is in the past. In Listing 28.5, the expiration date is set to one day ago.

The page in Listing 28.6 deletes all cookies sent from the browser to the current domain (and path).

LISTING 28.6 DeleteAllCookies.aspx

```
<%@ Page Language="C#" %>
<!DOCTYPE html PUBLIC "-//W3C//DTD XHTML 1.0 Transitional//EN"
    "http://www.w3.org/TR/xhtml1/DTD/xhtml1-transitional.dtd">
<script runat="server">

    void Page_Load()
    {
        string[] cookies = Request.Cookies.AllKeys;
        foreach (string cookie in cookies)
```

```
        {
            BulletedList1.Items.Add("Deleting " + cookie);
            Response.Cookies[cookie].Expires = DateTime.Now.AddDays(-1);
        }
    }
</script>
<html xmlns="http://www.w3.org/1999/xhtml" >
<head id="Head1" runat="server">
    <title>Delete All Cookies</title>
</head>
<body>
    <form id="form1" runat="server">
    <div>

    <h1>Delete All Cookies</h1>

    <asp:BulletedList
        id="BulletedList1"
        EnableViewState="false"
        Runat="server" />

    </div>
    </form>
</body>
</html>
```

The page in Listing 28.6 loops through all the cookie names from the Request.Cookies collection and deletes each cookie.

Working with Multivalued Cookies

According to the cookie specifications, browsers should not store more than 20 cookies from a single domain. You can work around this limitation by creating multivalued cookies.

A multivalued cookie is a single cookie that contains subkeys. You can create as many subkeys as you need.

For example, the page in Listing 28.7 creates a multivalued cookie named preferences. The preferences cookie stores a first name, last name, and favorite color (see Figure 28.3).

28

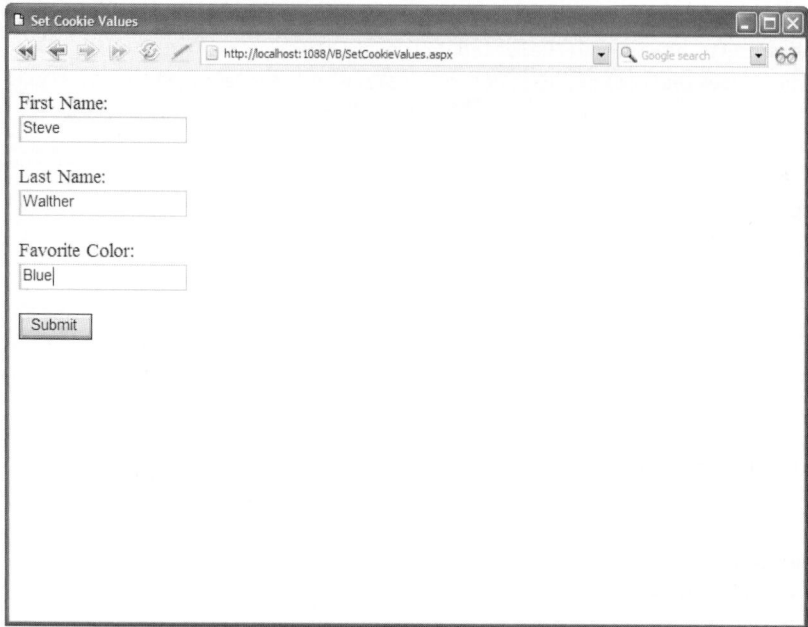

FIGURE 28.3   Creating a multivalued cookie.

LISTING 28.7   SetCookieValues.aspx

```
<%@ Page Language="C#" %>
<!DOCTYPE html PUBLIC "-//W3C//DTD XHTML 1.0 Transitional//EN"
    "http://www.w3.org/TR/xhtml1/DTD/xhtml1-transitional.dtd">
<script runat="server">

    void btnSubmit_Click(Object s, EventArgs e)
    {
        Response.Cookies["preferences"]["firstName"] = txtFirstName.Text;
        Response.Cookies["preferences"]["lastName"] = txtLastName.Text;
        Response.Cookies["preferences"]["favoriteColor"] = txtFavoriteColor.Text;
        Response.Cookies["preferences"].Expires = DateTime.MaxValue;
    }
</script>
<html xmlns="http://www.w3.org/1999/xhtml" >
<head id="Head1" runat="server">
    <title>Set Cookie Values</title>
</head>
<body>
    <form id="form1" runat="server">
    <div>
```

```
<asp:Label
    id="lblFirstName"
    Text="First Name:"
    AssociatedControlID="txtFirstName"
    Runat="server" />
<br />
<asp:TextBox
    id="txtFirstName"
    Runat="server" />
<br /><br />
<asp:Label
    id="lblLastName"
    Text="Last Name:"
    AssociatedControlID="txtFirstName"
    Runat="server" />
<br />
<asp:TextBox
    id="txtLastName"
    Runat="server" />
<br /><br />
<asp:Label
    id="lblFavoriteColor"
    Text="Favorite Color:"
    AssociatedControlID="txtFavoriteColor"
    Runat="server" />
<br />
<asp:TextBox
    id="txtFavoriteColor"
    Runat="server" />
<br /><br />
<asp:Button
    id="btnSubmit"
    Text="Submit"
    OnClick="btnSubmit_Click"
    Runat="server" />


</div>
</form>
</body>
</html>
```

28

When you submit the page in Listing 28.7, the following HTTP header is sent to the browser:

```
Set-Cookie: preferences=firstName=Steve&lastName=Walther&favoriteColor=green;
expires=Fri, 31-Dec-9999 23:59:59 GMT; path=/
```

The page in Listing 28.8 reads the values from the preferences cookie.

LISTING 28.8   GetCookieValues.aspx

```
<%@ Page Language="C#" %>
<!DOCTYPE html PUBLIC "-//W3C//DTD XHTML 1.0 Transitional//EN"
    "http://www.w3.org/TR/xhtml1/DTD/xhtml1-transitional.dtd">
<script runat="server">

    void Page_Load()
    {
        if (Request.Cookies["preferences"] != null)
        {
            lblFirstName.Text = Request.Cookies["preferences"]["firstName"];
            lblLastName.Text = Request.Cookies["preferences"]["lastName"];
            lblFavoriteColor.Text = Request.Cookies["preferences"]["favoriteColor"];
        }
    }
</script>
<html xmlns="http://www.w3.org/1999/xhtml" >
<head id="Head1" runat="server">
    <title>Get Cookie Values</title>
</head>
<body>
    <form id="form1" runat="server">
    <div>

    First Name:
    <asp:Label
        id="lblFirstName"
        Runat="server" />
    <br />
    Last Name:
    <asp:Label
        id="lblLastName"
        Runat="server" />
    <br />
    Favorite Color:
    <asp:Label
        id="lblFavoriteColor"
        Runat="server" />
```

```
      </div>
      </form>
</body>
</html>
```

You can use the `HttpCookie.HasKeys` property to detect whether a cookie is a normal cookie or a multivalued cookie.

Using Session State

You can't use a cookie to store a shopping cart. A cookie is just too small and too simple. To enable you to work around the limitations of cookies, ASP.NET Framework supports a feature called `Session` state.

Like cookies, items stored in `Session` state are scoped to a particular user. You can use `Session` state to store user preferences or other user-specific data across multiple page requests.

Unlike cookies, `Session` state has no size limitations. If you had a compelling need, you could store gigabytes of data in `Session` state. Furthermore, unlike cookies, `Session` state can represent more complex objects than simple strings of text. You can store any object in `Session` state. For example, you can store a `DataSet` or a custom shopping cart object in `Session` state.

You add items to `Session` state by using the `Session` object. For example, the page in Listing 28.9 adds a new item named `message` to `Session` state that has the value `Hello World!`.

LISTING 28.9   SessionSet.aspx

```
<%@ Page Language="C#" %>
<!DOCTYPE html PUBLIC "-//W3C//DTD XHTML 1.0 Transitional//EN"
    "http://www.w3.org/TR/xhtml1/DTD/xhtml1-transitional.dtd">
<script runat="server">

    void Page_Load()
    {
        Session["message"] = "Hello World!";
    }
</script>
<html xmlns="http://www.w3.org/1999/xhtml" >
<head id="Head1" runat="server">
    <title>Session Set</title>
</head>
<body>
    <form id="form1" runat="server">
```

```
    <div>

    <h1>Session item added!</h1>

    </div>
    </form>
</body>
</html>
```

In the Page_Load() event handler in Listing 28.9, a new item is added to the Session object. You can use the Session object just as you would use a Hashtable collection.

The page in Listing 28.10 illustrates how you can retrieve the value of an item that you have stored in Session state.

LISTING 28.10   SessionGet.aspx

```
<%@ Page Language="C#" %>
<!DOCTYPE html PUBLIC "-//W3C//DTD XHTML 1.0 Transitional//EN"
    "http://www.w3.org/TR/xhtml1/DTD/xhtml1-transitional.dtd">
<script runat="server">

    void Page_Load()
    {
        lblMessage.Text = Session["message"].ToString();
    }
</script>
<html xmlns="http://www.w3.org/1999/xhtml" >
<head id="Head1" runat="server">
    <title>Session Get</title>
</head>
<body>
    <form id="form1" runat="server">
    <div>

    <asp:Label
        id="lblMessage"
        Runat="server" />

    </div>
    </form>
</body>
</html>
```

When you use Session state, a session cookie named ASP.NET_SessionId is added to your browser automatically. This cookie contains a unique identifier. It is used to track you as you move from page to page.

When you add items to the Session object, the items are stored on the web server and not the web browser. The ASP.NET_SessionId cookie associates the correct data with the correct user.

By default, if cookies are disabled, Session state does not work. You don't receive an error, but items that you add to Session state aren't available when you attempt to retrieve them in later page requests. (You learn how to enable cookieless Session state later in this section.)

> **WARNING**
>
> Be careful not to abuse Session state by overusing it. A separate copy of each item added to Session state is created for each user who requests the page. If you place a DataSet with 400 records into Session state in a page, and 500 users request the page, you have 500 copies of that DataSet in memory.

By default, ASP.NET Framework assumes that a user has left the website when the user has not requested a page for more than 20 minutes. At that point, any data stored in Session state for the user is discarded.

Storing Database Data in Session State

You can use Session state to create a user-relative cache. For example, you can load data for a user and enable the user to sort or filter the data.

The page in Listing 28.11 loads a DataView into Session state. The user can sort the contents of the DataView by using a GridView control (see Figure 28.4).

28

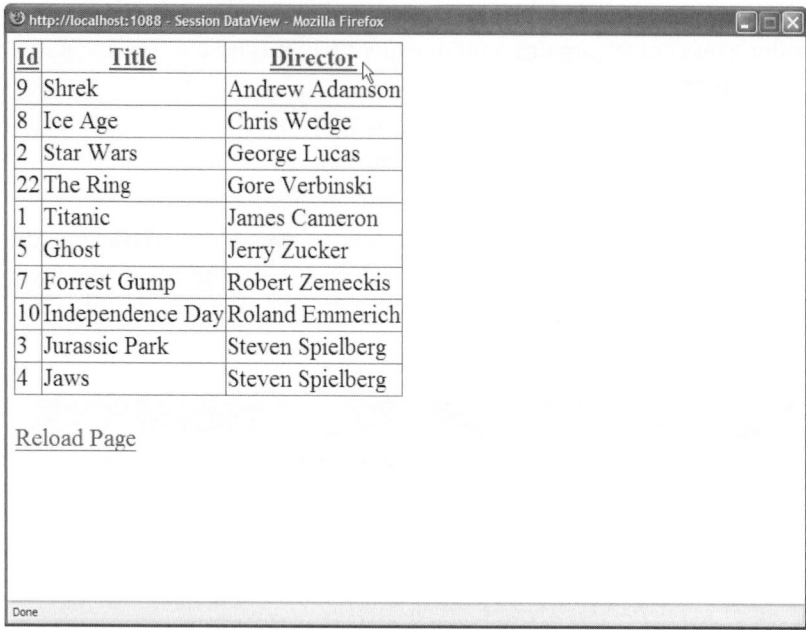

FIGURE 28.4   Sorting a DataView stored in Session state.

LISTING 28.11   SessionDataView.aspx

```
<%@ Page Language="C#" %>
<%@ Import Namespace="System.Data" %>
<%@ Import Namespace="System.Data.SqlClient" %>
<%@ Import Namespace="System.Web.Configuration" %>
<!DOCTYPE html PUBLIC "-//W3C//DTD XHTML 1.0 Transitional//EN"
    "http://www.w3.org/TR/xhtml1/DTD/xhtml1-transitional.dtd">
<script runat="server">

    DataView dvMovies;

    /// <summary>
    /// Load the Movies
    /// </summary>
    void Page_Load()
    {
        dvMovies = (DataView)Session["Movies"];
        if (dvMovies == null)
        {
            string conString =
    WebConfigurationManager.ConnectionStrings["Movies"].ConnectionString;
            SqlDataAdapter dad =
```

```
        new SqlDataAdapter("SELECT Id,Title,Director FROM Movies", conString);
            DataTable dtblMovies = new DataTable();
            dad.Fill(dtblMovies);
            dvMovies = new DataView(dtblMovies);
            Session["Movies"] = dvMovies;
        }
    }


    /// <summary>
    /// Sort the Movies
    /// </summary>
    protected void grdMovies_Sorting(object sender, GridViewSortEventArgs e)
    {
        dvMovies.Sort = e.SortExpression;
    }


    /// <summary>
    /// Render the Movies
    /// </summary>
    void Page_PreRender()
    {
        grdMovies.DataSource = dvMovies;
        grdMovies.DataBind();
    }
</script>
<html xmlns="http://www.w3.org/1999/xhtml" >
<head id="Head1" runat="server">
    <title>Session DataView</title>
</head>
<body>
    <form id="form1" runat="server">
    <div>

    <asp:GridView
        id="grdMovies"
        AllowSorting="true"
        EnableViewState="false"
        OnSorting="grdMovies_Sorting"
        Runat="server" />
    <br />
    <asp:LinkButton
        id="lnkReload"
        Text="Reload Page"
        Runat="server" />

    </div>
```

28

```
    </form>
</body>
</html>
```

In Listing 28.11, a DataView object is stored in Session state. When you sort the GridView control, the DataView is sorted.

The page in Listing 28.11 includes a link that enables you to reload the page. The sort order of the records displayed by the GridView is remembered across page requests. The sort order is remembered even if you navigate to another page before returning to the page.

Using the Session Object

The main application programming interface for working with Session state is the HttpSessionState class. This object is exposed by the Page.Session, Context.Session, UserControl.Session, WebService.Session, and Application.Session properties. This means that you can access Session state from just about anywhere.

This HttpSessionState class supports the following properties (this is not a complete list):

- ▸ **CookieMode**—Enables you to specify whether cookieless sessions are enabled. Possible values are AutoDetect, UseCookies, UseDeviceProfile, and UseUri.

- ▸ **Count**—Enables you to retrieve the number of items in Session state.

- ▸ **IsCookieless**—Enables you to determine whether cookieless sessions are enabled.

- ▸ **IsNewSession**—Enables you to determine whether a new user session was created with the current request.

- ▸ **IsReadOnly**—Enables you to determine whether the Session state is read-only.

- ▸ **Keys**—Enables you to retrieve a list of item names stored in Session state.

- ▸ **Mode**—Enables you to determine the current Session state store provider. Possible values are Custom, InProc, Off, SqlServer, and StateServer.

- ▸ **SessionID**—Enables you to retrieve the unique session identifier.

- ▸ **Timeout**—Enables you to specify the amount of time in minutes before the web server assumes that the user has left and discards the session. The maximum value is 525,600 (1 year).

The HttpSessionState object also supports the following methods:

- ▸ **Abandon**—Enables you to end a user session.

- ▸ **Clear**—Enables you to clear all items from Session state.

- ▸ **Remove**—Enables you to remove a particular item from Session state.

The Abandon() method enables you to end a user session programmatically. For example, you might want to end a user session automatically when a user logs out from your application to clear away all of a user's session state information.

Handling Session Events

There are two events related to Session state that you can handle in the Global.asax file: Session Start and Session End.

The Session Start event is raised whenever a new user session begins. You can handle this event to load user information from the database. For example, you can handle the Session Start event to load the user's shopping cart.

The Session End event is raised when a session ends. A session comes to an end when it times out because of user inactivity or when it is explicitly ended with the Session.Abandon() method. You can handle the Session End event, for example, when you want to automatically save the user's shopping cart to a database table.

The Global.asax file in Listing 28.12 demonstrates how you can handle both the Session Start and End events.

LISTING 28.12   Global.asax

```
<%@ Application Language="C#" %>
<script runat="server">
    void Application_Start(object sender, EventArgs e)
    {
        Application["SessionCount"] = 0;
    }

    void Session_Start(object sender, EventArgs e)
    {
        Application.Lock();
        int count = (int)Application["SessionCount"];
        Application["SessionCount"] = count + 1;
        Application.UnLock();
    }

    void Session_End(object sender, EventArgs e)
    {
        Application.Lock();
        int count = (int)Application["SessionCount"];
        Application["SessionCount"] = count - 1;
        Application.UnLock();
    }
</script>
```

28

In Listing 28.12, the Global.asax file tracks the number of active sessions. Whenever a new session begins, the Session Start event is raised and the SessionCount variable is incremented by one. When a session ends, the Session End event is raised and the SessionCount variable is decremented by one.

The SessionCount variable is stored in Application state, which contains items shared among all users of a web application. The Application object is locked before it is modified. You must lock and unlock the Application object because multiple users could potentially access the same item in Application state at the same time.

> **NOTE**
>
> Application state is little used in ASP.NET applications. In most cases, you should use the Cache object instead of Application state because the Cache object is designed to manage memory automatically.

The page in Listing 28.13 displays the number of active sessions with a Label control (see Figure 28.5).

FIGURE 28.5   Displaying a count of user sessions.

LISTING 28.13 ShowSessionCount.aspx

```
<%@ Page Language="C#" %>
<!DOCTYPE html PUBLIC "-//W3C//DTD XHTML 1.0 Transitional//EN"
    "http://www.w3.org/TR/xhtml1/DTD/xhtml1-transitional.dtd">
<script runat="server">

    void Page_Load()
    {
        lblSessionCount.Text = Application["SessionCount"].ToString();
    }
</script>
<html xmlns="http://www.w3.org/1999/xhtml" >
<head id="Head1" runat="server">
    <title>Show Session Count</title>
</head>
<body>
    <form id="form1" runat="server">
    <div>

    Total Application Sessions:
    <asp:Label
        id="lblSessionCount"
        Runat="server" />

    </div>
    </form>
</body>
</html>
```

WARNING

The Session End event is not raised by all session store providers. The event is raised by the InProc session store provider (the default provider), but it is not raised by the StateServer or SQLServer state providers.

Controlling When a Session Times Out

By default, ASP.NET Framework assumes that a user has left an application after 20 minutes have passed without the user requesting a page. In some situations, you want to modify the default timeout value.

For example, imagine that you are creating a college admissions website and the website includes a form that enables an applicant to enter a long essay. In that situation, you would not want the user session to timeout after 20 minutes. Please, give the poor college applicants at least 1 hour to write their essays. The disadvantage of increasing the Session timeout is that more memory is consumed by your application. The longer the Session timeout, the more server memory is potentially consumed.

You can specify the Session timeout in the web configuration file or you can set the Session timeout programmatically. For example, the web configuration file in Listing 28.14 changes the Session timeout value to 60 (1 hour).

LISTING 28.14   Web.Config

```
<?xml version="1.0"?>
<configuration>
<system.web>

  <sessionState timeout="60" />

</system.web>
</configuration>
```

You can modify the Session timeout value programmatically with the Timeout property of the Session object. For example, the following statement changes the timeout value from the default of 20 minutes to 60 minutes.

```
Session.Timeout = 60;
```

After you execute this statement, the timeout value is modified for the remainder of the user session. This is true even when the user visits other pages.

Using Cookieless Session State

By default, Session state depends on cookies. The ASP.NET Framework uses the ASP.NET_SessionId cookie to identity a user across page requests so that the correct data can be associated with the correct user. If a user disables cookies in the browser, Session state doesn't work.

If you want Session state to work even when cookies are disabled, you can take advantage of cookieless sessions. When cookieless sessions are enabled, a user's session ID is added to the page URL.

Here's a sample of what a page URL looks like when cookieless sessions are enabled:

```
http://localhost:4945/Original/(S(5pnh11553sszre45oevthxnn))/SomePage.aspx
```

The strange-looking code in this URL is the current user's Session ID. It is the same value as the one you get from the Session.SessionID property.

You enable cookieless sessions by modifying the sessionState element in the web configuration file. The sessionState element includes a cookieless attribute that accepts the following values:

- **AutoDetect**—The Session ID is stored in a cookie when a browser has cookies enabled. Otherwise, the cookie is added to the URL.

- **UseCookies**—The Session ID is always stored in a cookie (the default value).

- **UseDeviceProfile**—The Session ID is stored in a cookie when a browser supports cookies. Otherwise, the cookie is added to the URL.

- **UseUri**—The Session ID is always added to the URL.

When you set cookieless to the value UseDeviceProfile, ASP.NET Framework determines whether the browser supports cookies by looking up the browser's capabilities from a set of files contained in the following folder:

\WINDOWS\Microsoft.NET\Framework\[version]\CONFIG\Browsers

If, according to these files, a browser supports cookies, the ASP.NET Framework uses a cookie to store the Session ID. The Framework attempts to add a cookie even when a user has disabled cookies in the browser.

When cookieless is set to the value AutoDetect, the framework checks for the existence of the HTTP Cookie header. If the Cookie header is detected, the framework stores the Session ID in a cookie. Otherwise, the framework falls back to storing the Session ID in the page URL.

The web configuration file in Listing 28.15 enables cookieless sessions by assigning the value AutoDetect to the cookieless attribute.

LISTING 28.15 Web.Config

```xml
<?xml version="1.0"?>
<configuration>
<system.web>

  <sessionState
    cookieless="AutoDetect"
    regenerateExpiredSessionId="true" />

</system.web>
</configuration>
```

28

> **NOTE**
>
> The easiest way to test cookieless sessions is to use the Mozilla Firefox browser because this browser enables you to easily disable cookies. Select the menu option Tools, Options. Select the Privacy tab and uncheck Allow Sites to Set Cookies.

The configuration file in Listing 28.15 also includes a `regenerateExpiredSessionId` attribute. When you enable cookieless session state, you should also enable this attribute because it can help prevent users from inadvertently sharing session state.

For example, imagine that someone posts a link in a discussion forum to an ASP.NET website that has cookieless sessions enabled. The link includes the Session ID. If someone follows the link after the original session has timed out, a new Session is started automatically. However, if multiple people follow the link at the same time, all the people share the same Session ID and, therefore, they share the same `Session` state, which is a major security problem.

On the other hand, when `regenerateExpiredSessionId` is enabled and a session times out, the Session ID in the URL regenerates when a person requests the page. A redirect back to the same page is performed to change the Session ID in the URL. If a link is posted in a discussion forum, or sent to multiple users in an email, each user who follows the link is assigned a new Session ID.

When you enable cookieless sessions, you need to be careful to use relative URLs when linking between pages in your application. If you don't use a relative URL, the Session ID cannot be added to the URL automatically.

For example, when linking to another page in your website, use a URL that looks like this (a relative URL):

```
/SomeFolder/SomePage.aspx
```

Do not use a URL that looks like this (an absolute URL):

```
http://SomeSite.com/SomeFolder/SomePage.aspx
```

If, for some reason, you need to use an absolute URL, you can add the Session ID to the URL by using the `Response.ApplyAppPathModifier()` method. This method takes an absolute URL and returns the URL with a Session ID embedded in it.

Configuring a Session State Store

By default, `Session` state is stored in memory in the same process as the ASP.NET process. There are two significant disadvantages to storing `Session` state in the ASP.NET process.

First, in-process `Session` state is fragile. If your application restarts, all `Session` state is lost. A number of different events can cause an application restart. For example, modifying the web configuration file or errors in your application both can cause an application restart.

Second, in-process Session state is not scalable. When Session state is stored in-process, it is stored on a particular web server. In other words, you can't use in-process Session state with a web farm.

If you need to implement a more robust version of Session state, ASP.NET Framework supplies you with a number of options. You can configure ASP.NET Framework to store Session state in an alternative location by modifying the Session state mode.

You can set the Session state mode to any of the following values:

▶ **Off**—Disables Session state.

▶ **InProc**—Stores Session state in the same process as the ASP.NET process.

▶ **StateServer**—Stores Session state in a Windows NT process, which is distinct from the ASP.NET process.

▶ **SQLServer**—Stores Session state in a SQL Server database.

▶ **Custom**—Stores Session state in a custom location.

By default, the Session state mode is set to the value InProc. This is done for performance reasons. In-process Session state results in the best performance. However, it sacrifices robustness and scalability.

When you set the Session state mode to either StateServer or SQLServer, you get robustness and scalability at the price of performance. Storing Session state out-of-process results in worse performance because Session state information must be passed back and forth over your network.

Finally, you can create a custom Session state store provider by inheriting a new class from the SessionStateStoreProviderBase class. In that case, you can store Session state any place that you want. For example, you can create a Session state store provider that stores Session state in an Oracle or FoxPro database.

Configuring State Server Session State

When you enable State Server Session state, Session state information is stored in a separate Windows NT Service. The Windows NT Service can be located on the same server as your web server, or it can be located on another server in your network.

If you store Session state in the memory of a separate Windows NT Service, Session state information survives even when your ASP.NET application doesn't. For example, if your ASP.NET application crashes, your Session state information is not lost because it is stored in a separate process.

Furthermore, you can create a web farm when you store state information by using a Windows NT Service. You can designate one server in your network as your state server. All the web servers in your web farm can use the central state server to store Session state.

28

You must complete the following two steps to use State Server Session state:

1. Start the ASP.NET State Service.
2. Configure your application to use the ASP.NET State Service.

You can start the ASP.NET State Service by opening the Services applet located at Start, Administrative Tools (see Figure 28.6). After you open the Services applet, double-click the ASP.NET State Service and click Start to run the service. You also should change the Startup type of the service to the value Automatic so that the service starts automatically every time that you reboot your machine.

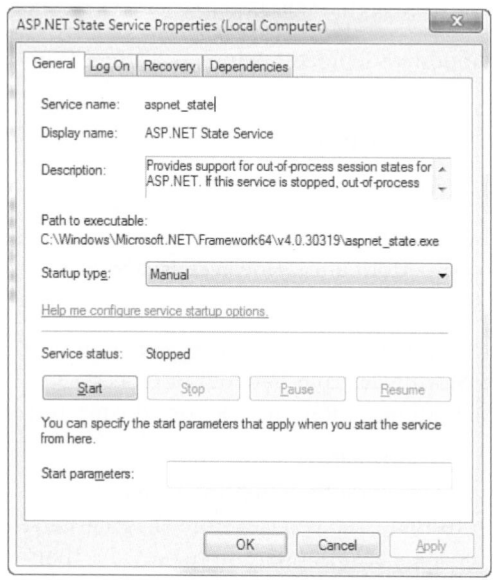

FIGURE 28.6   Starting the ASP.NET State service.

If you want to run the ASP.NET State Service on a separate server on your network, you must edit a Registry setting on the server that hosts the ASP.NET State Service. By default, the ASP.NET State Service does not accept remote connections. To allow remote connections, execute RegEdit from a command prompt and set the following Registry key to the value 1:

```
HKEY_LOCAL_MACHINE\SYSTEM\CurrentControlSet\Services\aspnet_state\
➥Parameters\AllowRemoteConnection
```

After you start the ASP.NET State Service, you need to configure your ASP.NET application to use it. The web configuration file in Listing 28.16 enables State Server Session State.

LISTING 28.16 Web.Config

```
<?xml version="1.0"?>
<configuration>
    <system.web>

       <sessionState
          mode="StateServer"
          stateConnectionString="tcpip=localhost:42424"
          stateNetworkTimeout="10"   />

       <machineKey
          decryption="AES"
          validation="SHA1"
          decryptionKey="306C1FA852AB3B0115150DD8BA30821
➥CDFD125538A0C606DACA53DBB3C3E0AD2"
          validationKey="61A8E04A146AFFAB81B6AD19654F
➥99EA7370807F18F5002725DAB98B8EFD19C711337E2
➥6948E26D1D174B159973EA0BE8CC9CAA6AAF513BF84E44B2247792265" />

    </system.web>
</configuration>
```

The web configuration file in Listing 28.16 modifies three attributes of the `sessionState` element. First, the `mode` attribute is set to the value `StateServer`. Next, the `stateConnectionString` attribute is used to specify the location of the ASP.NET State Server. In Listing 28.16, a connection is created to the local server on port 42428. Finally, the `stateNetworkTimeout` attribute specifies a connection timeout in seconds.

NOTE

You can configure the ASP.NET State Server to use a different port by modifying the following Registry value:

`HKEY_LOCAL_MACHINE\SYSTEM\CurrentControlSet\Services\aspnet_state\`
➥`Parameters\Port`

You need to stop and restart the ASP.NET State Service with the Services applet after making this modification.

The web configuration in Listing 28.16 includes a `machineKey` element. If you are setting up a web farm, and you need to use the same State Server to store `Session` state for multiple servers, you are required to specify explicit encryption and validation keys. On the other hand, you don't need to include a `machineKey` element when the ASP.NET State Server is hosted on the same machine as your ASP.NET application.

28

WARNING

Don't use the web configuration file in Listing 28.16 without modifying the values of both the `decryptionKey` and `validationKey` attributes. Those values must be secret. You can use the `GenerateKeys.aspx` page discussed in Chapter 27, "Using ASP.NET Membership," to generate new values for these attributes.

After you complete these configuration steps, `Session` state information is stored in the ASP.NET State Server automatically. You don't need to modify any of your application code when you switch to out-of-process `Session` state.

Configuring SQL Server `Session` **State**

If you want to store `Session` state in the most reliable way possible, you can store `Session` state in a Microsoft SQL Server database. Because you can set up failover SQL Server clusters, `Session` state stored in SQL Server should survive just about anything, including a major nuclear war.

You must complete the following two steps to enable SQL Server `Session` state:

1. Configure your database to support SQL Server `Session` state.
2. Configure your application to use SQL Server `Session` state.

You can use the `aspnet_regsql` tool to add the necessary tables and stored procedures to your database to support SQL Server Session state. The `aspnet_regsql` tool is located in the following path:

```
\WINDOWS\Microsoft.NET\Framework\[version]\aspnet_regsql.exe
```

NOTE

If you open the Visual Studio Command Prompt, you don't need to navigate to the Microsoft.NET folder to use the `aspnet_regsql` tool.

Executing the following command enables SQL Server Session state for a database server named YourServer.

```
aspnet_regsql -C "Data Source=YourServer;Integrated Security=True" -ssadd
```

When you execute this command, a new database is created on your database server named ASPState. The ASPState database contains all the stored procedures used by `Session` state. However, by default, `Session` state information is stored in the TempDB database. When your database server restarts, the TempDB database is cleared automatically.

If you want to use SQL Server Session state with a failover cluster of SQL Servers, you can't store `Session` state in the TempDB database. Also, if you want `Session` state to survive database restarts, you can't store the state information in the TempDB database.

If you execute the following command, Session state is stored in the ASPState database instead of the TempDB database:

```
aspnet_regsql -C "Data Source=YourServer;Integrated Security=True" -ssadd -sstype p
```

This command includes a -sstype p switch. The p stands for persistent. Session state stored in the ASPState database is called persistent Session state because it survives database server restarts.

Finally, you can store Session state in a custom database. The following command stores Session state in a database named MySessionDB:

```
aspnet_regsql -C "Data Source=YourServer;Integrated Security=True"
➥-ssadd -sstype c -d MySessionDB
```

Executing this command creates a new database named MySessionDB that contains both the tables and stored procedures for storing Session state. The -sstype switch has the value c for custom. The command also includes a -d switch that enables you to specify the name of the new database.

If you want to remove the Session state tables and stored procedures from a server, you can execute the following command:

```
aspnet_regsql -C "Data Source=YourServer;Integrated Security=True" -ssremove
```

Executing this command removes the ASPState database. It does not remove a custom Session state database. You must remove a custom database manually.

After you configure your database server to support Session state, you must configure your ASP.NET application to connect to your database. You can use the web configuration file in Listing 28.17 to connect to a database named YourServer.

LISTING 28.17 Web.Config

```xml
<?xml version="1.0"?>
<configuration>
    <system.web>

       <sessionState
         mode="SQLServer"
         sqlConnectionString="Data Source=YourServer;Integrated Security=True"
         sqlCommandTimeout="30" />

       <machineKey
         decryption="AES"
         validation="SHA1"
         decryptionKey="306C1FA852AB3B0115150DD8BA30821CDFD125538A0C606DACA
➥53DBB3C3E0AD2"
             validationKey="61A8E04A146AFFAB81B6AD19654F99EA7370807F18F5002725D
```

28

➥AB98B8EFD19C711337E26948E26D1D174B159973EA0BE8CC9CAA6AAF513BF84E44
➥B2247792265" />

```
    </system.web>
</configuration>
```

The sessionState element includes three attributes. The mode attribute is set to the value SQLServer to enable SQL Server Session state. The second attribute, sqlConnectionString, contains the connection string to the Session state database. Finally, the sqlCommandTimeout specifies the maximum amount of time in seconds before a command that retrieves or stores Session state times out.

The configuration file in Listing 28.17 includes a machineKey element. If your Session state database is located on a different machine than your ASP.NET application, you are required to include a machineKey element that contains explicit encryption and validation keys.

> **WARNING**
>
> Don't use the web configuration file in Listing 28.16 or 28.17 without modifying the values of both the decryptionKey and validationKey attributes. Those values must be secret. You can use the GenerateKeys.aspx page discussed in Chapter 27 to generate new values for these attributes.

If you select the option to store Session state in a custom database when executing the aspnet_regsql tool, you need to specify the name of the custom database in your configuration file. You can use the web configuration file in Listing 28.18.

LISTING 28.18   Web.config

```
<?xml version="1.0"?>
<configuration>
    <system.web>

      <sessionState
        mode="SQLServer"
        sqlConnectionString="Data Source=YourServer;
Integrated Security=True;database=MySessionDB"
        sqlCommandTimeout="30"
        allowCustomSqlDatabase="true"/>

      <machineKey
        decryption="AES"
        validation="SHA1"
        decryptionKey="306C1FA852AB3B0115150DD8BA30821CDFD125538A0C606DACA
```

➥53DBB3C3E0AD2"
        validationKey="61A8E04A146AFFAB81B6AD19654F99EA7370807F18F5002725D
➥AB98B8EFD19C711337E26948E26D1D174B159973EA0BE8CC9CAA6AAF513BF84E44
➥B2247792265" />

```
    </system.web>
</configuration>
```

The sessionState element in the configuration file in Listing 28.18 includes an allowCustomSqlDatabase attribute. Furthermore, the sqlConnectionString attribute contains the name of the custom database.

Enabling SQL Server session state has no effect on how you write your application code. You can initially build your application using in-process Session state and, when you have the need, you can switch to SQL Server Session state.

> **NOTE**
>
> ASP.NET 4 introduced a new option to compress session state for the out-of-process providers (SQL Server and State Server). You can enable compression when using these providers by setting the compressionEnabled option to true.
>
> ```
>   <sessionState
>     mode="SqlServer"
>     sqlConnectionString="data source=dbserver;Initial Catalog=aspnetstate"
>     allowCustomSqlDatabase="true"
>     compressionEnabled="true"
>   />
> ```
>
> This compresses the session state before storing it, which can substantially improve performance.

Using Profiles

The ASP.NET Framework provides you with an alternative to using cookies or Session state to store user information: the Profile object. The Profile object provides you with a strongly typed, persistent form of session state.

You create a Profile by defining a list of Profile properties in your application root web configuration file. The ASP.NET Framework dynamically compiles a class that contains these properties in the background. For example, the web configuration file in Listing 28.19 defines a Profile that contains three properties: firstName, lastName, and numberOfVisits.

LISTING 28.19   Web.Config

```xml
<?xml version="1.0"?>
<configuration>
<system.web>

  <profile>
    <properties>
      <add name="firstName" />
      <add name="lastName" />
      <add name="numberOfVisits" type="Int32" defaultValue="0" />
    </properties>
  </profile>


</system.web>
</configuration>
```

When you define a Profile property, you can use any of the following attributes:

▶ **name**—Enables you to specify the name of the property.

▶ **type**—Enables you to specify the type of the property. The type can be any custom type, including a custom component that you define in the App_Code folder. (The default type is string.)

▶ **defaultValue**—Enables you to specify a default value for the property.

▶ **readOnly**—Enables you to create a read-only property. (The default value is false.)

▶ **serializeAs**—Enables you to specify how a property is persisted into a static representation. Possible values are Binary, ProviderSpecific, String, and Xml. (The default value is ProviderSpecific.)

▶ **allowAnonymous**—Enables you to allow anonymous users to read and set the property. (The default value is false.)

▶ **provider**—Enables you to associate the property with a particular Profile provider.

▶ **customProviderData**—Enables you to pass custom data to a Profile provider.

After you define a Profile in the web configuration file, you can use the Profile object to modify the Profile properties. For example, the page in Listing 28.20 enables you to modify the firstName and lastName properties with a form. Furthermore, the page automatically updates the numberOfVisits property each time the page is requested (see Figure 28.7).

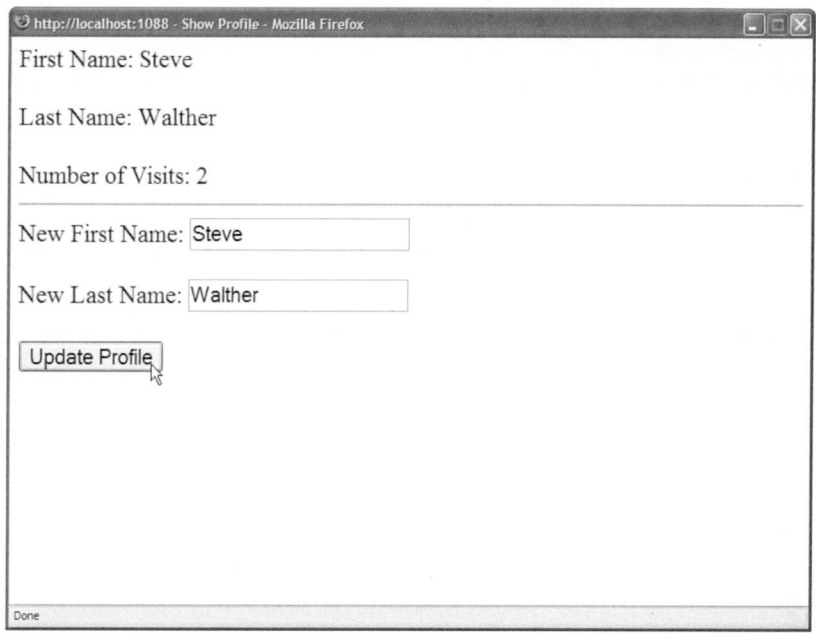

FIGURE 28.7   Displaying Profile information.

LISTING 28.20   ShowProfile.aspx

```
<%@ Page Language="C#" %>
<!DOCTYPE html PUBLIC "-//W3C//DTD XHTML 1.0 Transitional//EN"
    "http://www.w3.org/TR/xhtml1/DTD/xhtml1-transitional.dtd">
<script runat="server">

    void Page_PreRender()
    {
        lblFirstname.Text = Profile.firstName;
        lblLastName.Text = Profile.lastName;

        Profile.numberOfVisits++;
        lblNumberOfVisits.Text = Profile.numberOfVisits.ToString();
    }

    protected void btnUpdate_Click(object sender, EventArgs e)
    {
        Profile.firstName = txtNewFirstName.Text;
        Profile.lastName = txtNewLastName.Text;
    }
</script>
```

28

```
<html xmlns="http://www.w3.org/1999/xhtml" >
<head id="Head1" runat="server">
    <title>Show Profile</title>
</head>
<body>
    <form id="form1" runat="server">
    <div>

    First Name:
    <asp:Label
        id="lblFirstname"
        Runat="server" />
    <br /><br />
    Last Name:
    <asp:Label
        id="lblLastName"
        Runat="server" />
    <br /><br />
    Number of Visits:
    <asp:Label
        id="lblNumberOfVisits"
        Runat="server" />

    <hr />

    <asp:Label
        id="lblNewFirstName"
        Text="New First Name:"
        AssociatedControlID="txtNewFirstName"
        Runat="server" />
    <asp:TextBox
        id="txtNewFirstName"
        Runat="server" />
    <br /><br />
    <asp:Label
        id="lblNewLastName"
        Text="New Last Name:"
        AssociatedControlID="txtNewLastName"
        Runat="server" />
    <asp:TextBox
        id="txtNewLastName"
        Runat="server" />
    <br /><br />
    <asp:Button
        id="btnUpdate"
        Text="Update Profile"
```

```
        OnClick="btnUpdate_Click"
        Runat="server" />

    </div>
    </form>
</body>
</html>
```

Profile properties are exposed as strongly typed properties. The numberOfVisits property, for example, is exposed as an integer property because you defined it as an integer property.

It is important to understand that Profile properties are persistent. If you set a Profile property for a user, and that user does not return to your website for 500 years, the property retains its value. Unlike Session state, when you assign a value to a Profile property, the value does not evaporate after a user leaves your website.

The Profile object uses the Provider model. The default Profile provider is the SqlProfileProvider. By default, this provider stores the Profile data in a Microsoft SQL Server 2008 Express database named ASPNETDB.mdf, located in your application's App_Data folder. If the database does not exist, it is created automatically the first time that you use the Profile object.

By default, you cannot store Profile information for an anonymous user. The ASP.NET Framework uses your authenticated identity to associate Profile information with you. You can use the Profile object with any of the standard types of authentication supported by ASP.NET Framework, including both Forms and Windows authentication. (Windows authentication is enabled by default.)

> **NOTE**
>
> Later in this section, you learn how to store Profile information for anonymous users.

28

Creating Profile Groups

If you need to define a lot of Profile properties, you can make the properties more manageable by organizing the properties into groups. For example, the web configuration file in Listing 28.21 defines two groups named Preferences and ContactInfo.

LISTING 28.21 Web.Config

```
<?xml version="1.0"?>
<configuration>
<system.web>

  <profile>
```

```
    <properties>
      <group name="Preferences">
        <add name="BackColor" defaultValue="lightblue"/>
        <add name="Font" defaultValue="Arial"/>
      </group>
      <group name="ContactInfo">
        <add name="Email" defaultValue="Your Email"/>
        <add name="Phone" defaultValue="Your Phone"/>
      </group>
    </properties>
  </profile>

</system.web>
</configuration>
```

The page in Listing 28.22 illustrates how you can set and read properties in different groups.

LISTING 28.22   ShowProfileGroups.aspx

```csharp
<%@ Page Language="C#" %>
<%@ Import Namespace="System.Drawing" %>
<!DOCTYPE html PUBLIC "-//W3C//DTD XHTML 1.0 Transitional//EN"
    "http://www.w3.org/TR/xhtml1/DTD/xhtml1-transitional.dtd">
<script runat="server">

    void Page_Load()
    {
        // Display Contact Info
        lblEmail.Text = Profile.ContactInfo.Email;
        lblPhone.Text = Profile.ContactInfo.Phone;

        // Apply Preferences
        Style pageStyle = new Style();
        pageStyle.BackColor = ColorTranslator.FromHtml(Profile.Preferences.
➥BackColor);
        pageStyle.Font.Name = Profile.Preferences.Font;
        Header.StyleSheet.CreateStyleRule(pageStyle, null, "html");
    }
</script>
<html xmlns="http://www.w3.org/1999/xhtml" >
<head id="Head1" runat="server">
    <title>Untitled Page</title>
</head>
<body>
```

```
        <form id="form1" runat="server">
        <div>

        Email:
        <asp:Label
            id="lblEmail"
            Runat="server" />
        <br /><br />
        Phone:
        <asp:Label
            id="lblPhone"
            Runat="server" />

        </div>
        </form>
</body>
</html>
```

Supporting Anonymous Users

By default, anonymous users cannot modify Profile properties. The problem is that ASP.NET Framework has no method of associating Profile data with a particular user unless the user is authenticated.

If you want to enable anonymous users to modify Profile properties, you must enable a feature of ASP.NET Framework called Anonymous Identification. When Anonymous Identification is enabled, a unique identifier (a GUID) is assigned to anonymous users and stored in a persistent browser cookie.

> **NOTE**
>
> You can enable cookieless anonymous identifiers. Cookieless anonymous identifiers work just like cookieless sessions: The anonymous identifier is added to the page URL instead of a cookie. You enable cookieless anonymous identifiers by setting the cookie-less attribute of the anonymousIdentification element in the web configuration file to the value UseURI or AutoDetect.

Furthermore, you must mark all Profile properties that you want anonymous users to modify with the allowAnonymous attribute. For example, the web configuration file in Listing 28.23 enables Anonymous Identification and defines a Profile property that can be modified by anonymous users.

LISTING 28.23   Web.Config

```
<?xml version="1.0"?>
<configuration>
<system.web>

  <authentication mode="Forms" />

  <anonymousIdentification enabled="true" />

  <profile>
    <properties>
      <add
        name="numberOfVisits"
        type="Int32"
        defaultValue="0"
        allowAnonymous="true" />
    </properties>
  </profile>

</system.web>
</configuration>
```

The numberOfVisits property defined in Listing 28.23 includes the allowAnonymous attribute. The web configuration file also enables Forms authentication. When Forms authentication is enabled, and you don't log in, you are an anonymous user.

The page in Listing 28.24 illustrates how you modify a Profile property when Anonymous Identification is enabled.

LISTING 28.24   ShowAnonymousIdentification.aspx

```
<%@ Page Language="C#" %>
<!DOCTYPE html PUBLIC "-//W3C//DTD XHTML 1.0 Transitional//EN"
    "http://www.w3.org/TR/xhtml1/DTD/xhtml1-transitional.dtd">
<script runat="server">

    void Page_PreRender()
    {
        lblUserName.Text = Profile.UserName;
        lblIsAnonymous.Text = Profile.IsAnonymous.ToString();
        Profile.numberOfVisits++;
        lblNumberOfVisits.Text = Profile.numberOfVisits.ToString();
    }
```

```
    protected void btnLogin_Click(object sender, EventArgs e)
    {
        FormsAuthentication.SetAuthCookie("Bob", false);
        Response.Redirect(Request.Path);
    }

    protected void btnLogout_Click(object sender, EventArgs e)
    {
        FormsAuthentication.SignOut();
        Response.Redirect(Request.Path);
    }
</script>
<html xmlns="http://www.w3.org/1999/xhtml" >
<head id="Head1" runat="server">
    <title>Show Anonymous Identification</title>
</head>
<body>
    <form id="form1" runat="server">
    <div>

    User Name:
    <asp:Label
        id="lblUserName"
        Runat="server" />
    <br />
    Is Anonymous:
    <asp:Label
        id="lblIsAnonymous"
        Runat="server" />
    <br />
    Number Of Visits:
    <asp:Label
        id="lblNumberOfVisits"
        Runat="server" />

    <hr />
    <asp:Button
        id="btnReload"
        Text="Reload"
        Runat="server" />

    <asp:Button
        id="btnLogin"
        Text="Login"
        OnClick="btnLogin_Click"
```

28

```
        Runat="server" />

    <asp:Button
        id="btnLogout"
        Text="Logout"
        OnClick="btnLogout_Click"
        Runat="server" />

    </div>
    </form>
</body>
</html>
```

Each time that you request the page in Listing 28.24, the numberOfVisits Profile property is incremented and displayed. The page includes three buttons: Reload, Login, and Logout (see Figure 28.8).

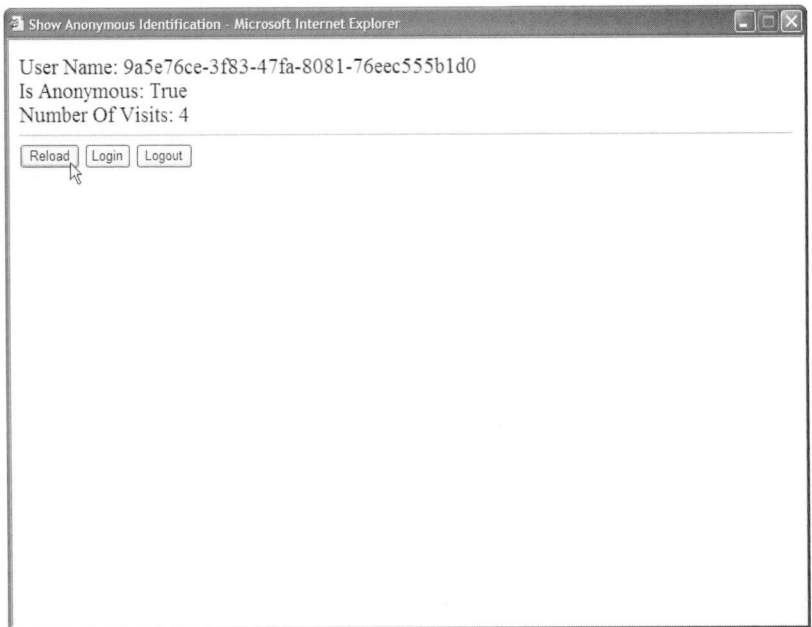

FIGURE 28.8   Creating an anonymous profile.

The page also displays the value of the Profile.UserName property. This property represents either the current username or the anonymous identifier. The value of the numberOfVisits Profile property is tied to the value of the Profile.UserName property.

You can click the Reload button to quickly reload the page and increment the value of the numberOfVisits property. If you click the Login button, the Profile.UserName property changes to the value Bob. The numberOfVisits property is reset.

If you click the Logout button, the Profile.UserName property switches back to your anonymous identifier. The numberOfVisits property reverts to its previous value.

Migrating Anonymous Profiles

In the previous section, you saw that all profile information is lost when a user transitions from anonymous to authenticated. For example, if you store a shopping cart in the Profile object and a user logs in, all the shopping cart items are lost.

You can preserve the value of Profile properties when a user transitions from anonymous to authenticated by handling the MigrateAnonymous event in the Global.asax file. This event is raised when an anonymous user that has a profile logs in.

For example, the MigrateAnonymous event handler in Listing 28.25 automatically copies the values of all anonymous Profile properties to the user's current authenticated profile.

LISTING 28.25   Global.asax

```
<%@ Application Language="C#" %>
<script runat="server">

    public void Profile_OnMigrateAnonymous(object sender, ProfileMigrateEventArgs
➥args)
    {
        // Get anonymous profile
        ProfileCommon anonProfile = Profile.GetProfile(args.AnonymousID);

        // Copy anonymous properties to authenticated
        foreach (SettingsProperty prop in ProfileBase.Properties)
            Profile[prop.Name] = anonProfile[prop.Name];

        // Kill the anonymous profile
        ProfileManager.DeleteProfile(args.AnonymousID);
        AnonymousIdentificationModule.ClearAnonymousIdentifier();
    }

</script>
```

The anonymous Profile associated with the user is retrieved when the user's anonymous identifier is passed to the Profile.GetProfile() method. Next, each Profile property is copied from the anonymous Profile to the current Profile. Finally, the anonymous Profile is deleted and the anonymous identifier is destroyed. (If you don't destroy the

28

anonymous identifier, the `MigrateAnonymous` event continues to be raised with each page request after the user authenticates.)

Inheriting a Profile from a Custom Class

Instead of defining a list of `Profile` properties in the web configuration file, you can define `Profile` properties in a separate class. For example, the class in Listing 28.26 contains two properties named `FirstName` and `LastName`.

LISTING 28.26   App_Code\SiteProfile.cs

```
using System;
using System.Web.Profile;

public class SiteProfile : ProfileBase
{
    private string _firstName = "Your First Name";
    private string _lastName = "Your Last Name";

    [SettingsAllowAnonymous(true)]
    public string FirstName
    {
        get { return _firstName; }
        set { _firstName = value; }
    }

    [SettingsAllowAnonymous(true)]
    public string LastName
    {
        get { return _lastName; }
        set { _lastName = value; }
    }
}
```

The class in Listing 28.26 inherits from the `BaseProfile` class.

After you declare a class, you can use it to define a profile by inheriting the `Profile` object from the class in the web configuration file. The web configuration file in Listing 28.27 uses the `inherits` attribute to inherit the `Profile` from the `SiteProfile` class.

LISTING 28.27   Web.Config

```
<?xml version="1.0"?>
<configuration>
<system.web>

  <anonymousIdentification enabled="true" />

  <profile inherits="SiteProfile" />

</system.web>
</configuration>
```

After you inherit a `Profile` in the web configuration file, you can use the `Profile` in the normal way. You can set or read any of the properties that you defined in the `SiteProfile` class by accessing the properties through the `Profile` object.

> **NOTE**
>
> The downloadable code from the website that accompanies this book includes a page named `ShowSiteProfile.aspx`, which displays the `Profile` properties defined in Listing 28.27.

> **NOTE**
>
> If you inherit `Profile` properties from a class and define `Profile` properties in the web configuration file, the two sets of `Profile` properties are merged.

When you define `Profile` properties in a class, you can decorate the properties with the following attributes:

- ▶ **SettingsAllowAnonymous**—Enables you to allow anonymous users to read and set the property.

- ▶ **ProfileProvider**—Enables you to associate the property with a particular `Profile` provider.

- ▶ **CustomProviderData**—Enables you to pass custom data to a `Profile` provider.

For example, both properties declared in the `SiteProfile` class in Listing 28.27 include the `SettingsAllowAnonymous` attribute, which allows anonymous users to read and modify the properties.

28

Creating Complex Profile Properties

To this point, we used the Profile properties to represent simple types such as strings and integers. You can use Profile properties to represent more complex types such as a custom ShoppingCart class.

For example, the class in Listing 28.28 represents a simple shopping cart.

LISTING 28.28   App_Code\ShoppingCart.cs

```
using System;
using System.Collections.Generic;
using System.Web.Profile;

namespace AspNetUnleashed
{
    public class ShoppingCart
    {
        private List<CartItem> _items = new List<CartItem>();

        public List<CartItem> Items
        {
            get { return _items; }
        }
    }

    public class CartItem
    {
        private string _name;
        private decimal _price;
        private string _description;

        public string Name
        {
            get { return _name; }
            set { _name = value; }
        }

        public decimal Price
        {
            get { return _price; }
            set { _price = value; }
        }
```

```
    public string Description
    {
        get { return _description; }
        set { _description = value; }
    }

    public CartItem() { }

    public CartItem(string name, decimal price, string description)
    {
        _name = name;
        _price = price;
        _description = description;
    }
    }
}
```

The file in Listing 28.28 actually contains two classes: ShoppingCart and CartItem. The ShoppingCart class exposes a collection of CartItem objects.

The web configuration file in Listing 28.29 defines a Profile property named ShoppingCart that represents the ShoppingCart class. The type attribute is set to the fully qualified name of the ShoppingCart class.

LISTING 28.29   Web.Config

```
<?xml version="1.0"?>
<configuration>
<system.web>

  <profile>
    <properties>
      <add name="ShoppingCart" type="AspNetUnleashed.ShoppingCart" />
    </properties>
  </profile>

</system.web>
</configuration>
```

Finally, the page in Listing 28.30 uses the Profile.ShoppingCart property. The contents of the ShoppingCart are bound and displayed in a GridView control. The page also contains a form that enables you to add new items to the ShoppingCart (see Figure 28.9).

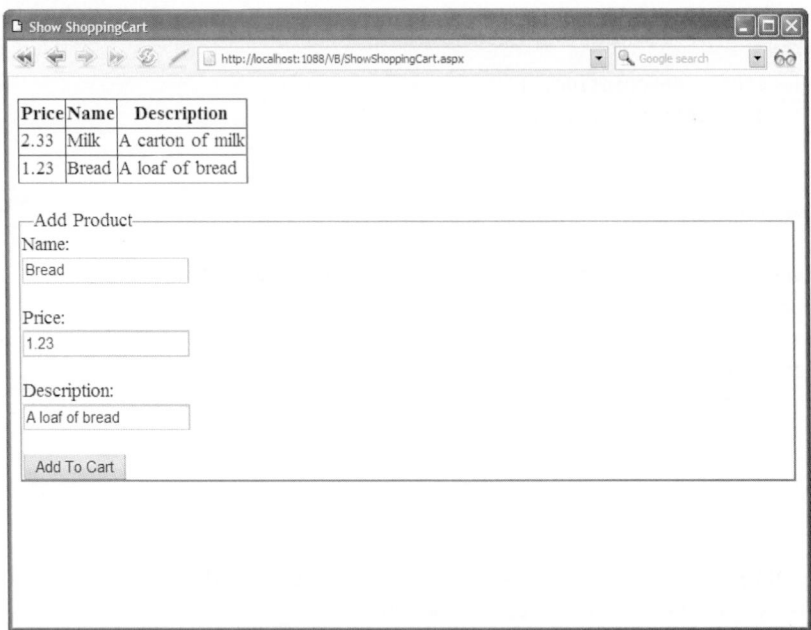

FIGURE 28.9   Storing a shopping cart in a profile.

LISTING 28.30   ShowShoppingCart.aspx

```
<%@ Page Language="C#" %>
<%@ Import Namespace="AspNetUnleashed" %>
<!DOCTYPE html PUBLIC "-//W3C//DTD XHTML 1.0 Transitional//EN"
     "http://www.w3.org/TR/xhtml1/DTD/xhtml1-transitional.dtd">
<script runat="server">

    void Page_PreRender()
    {
        grdShoppingCart.DataSource = Profile.ShoppingCart.Items;
        grdShoppingCart.DataBind();
    }

    protected void btnAdd_Click(object sender, EventArgs e)
    {
        CartItem newItem =
            new CartItem(txtName.Text, decimal.Parse(txtPrice.Text),
➥txtDescription.Text);
        Profile.ShoppingCart.Items.Add(newItem);
    }
</script>
<html xmlns="http://www.w3.org/1999/xhtml" >
```

```
<head id="Head1" runat="server">
    <title>Show ShoppingCart</title>
</head>
<body>
    <form id="form1" runat="server">
    <div>

    <asp:GridView
        id="grdShoppingCart"
        EmptyDataText="There are no items in your shopping cart"
        Runat="server" />

    <br />

    <fieldset>
    <legend>Add Product</legend>
    <asp:Label
        id="lblName"
        Text="Name:"
        AssociatedControlID="txtName"
        Runat="server" />
    <br />
    <asp:TextBox
        id="txtName"
        Runat="server" />
    <br /><br />
    <asp:Label
        id="lblPrice"
        Text="Price:"
        AssociatedControlID="txtPrice"
        Runat="server" />
    <br />
    <asp:TextBox
        id="txtPrice"
        Runat="server" />
    <br /><br />
    <asp:Label
        id="lblDescription"
        Text="Description:"
        AssociatedControlID="txtDescription"
        Runat="server" />
    <br />
    <asp:TextBox
        id="txtDescription"
        Runat="server" />
```

28

```
    <br /><br />
    <asp:Button
        id="btnAdd"
        Text="Add To Cart"
        Runat="server" OnClick="btnAdd_Click" />
    </fieldset>

    </div>
    </form>
</body>
</html>
```

If you want to take control over how complex properties are stored, you can modify the value of the serializeAs attribute associated with a Profile property. The serializeAs attribute accepts the following four values:

▶ Binary

▶ ProviderSpecific

▶ String

▶ Xml

The default value, when using the SqlProfileProvider, is ProviderSpecific. In other words, the SqlProfileProvider decides on the best method for storing properties. In general, simple types are serialized as strings and complex types are serialized with the XML Serializer.

One disadvantage of the XML Serializer is that it produces a more bloated representation of a property than the Binary Serializer. For example, the results of serializing the ShoppingCart class with the XML Serializer are contained in Listing 28.31:

LISTING 28.31   Serialized Shopping Cart

```
<?xml version="1.0" encoding="utf-16"?>
<ShoppingCart xmlns:xsi=http://www.w3.org/2001/XMLSchema-instance
 xmlns:xsd="http://www.w3.org/2001/XMLSchema">
  <Items>
    <CartItem>
      <Name>First Product</Name>
      <Price>2.99</Price>
      <Description>The First Product</Description>
    </CartItem>
    <CartItem>
      <Name>Second Product</Name>
      <Price>2.99</Price>
      <Description>The Second Product</Description>
```

```
      </CartItem>
    </Items>
</ShoppingCart>
```

If you want to serialize a Profile property with the Binary Serializer (and save some database space), you need to do two things. First, you need to indicate in the web configuration file that the Profile property should be serialized with the Binary Serializer. Furthermore, you need to mark the class that the Profile property represents as serializable.

The modified ShoppingClass (named BinaryShoppingCart) in Listing 28.32 includes a Serializable attribute. Both the BinaryShoppingCart and BinaryCartItem classes are decorated with the Serializable attribute.

LISTING 28.32   App_Code\BinaryShoppingCart.cs

```
using System;
using System.Collections.Generic;
using System.Web.Profile;

namespace AspNetUnleashed
{
    [Serializable]
    public class BinaryShoppingCart
    {
        private List<BinaryCartItem> _items = new List<BinaryCartItem>();

        public List<BinaryCartItem> Items
        {
            get { return _items; }
        }
    }

    [Serializable]
    public class BinaryCartItem
    {
        private string _name;
        private decimal _price;
        private string _description;

        public string Name
        {
            get { return _name; }
            set { _name = value; }
        }
```

```
    public decimal Price
    {
        get { return _price; }
        set { _price = value; }
    }

    public string Description
    {
        get { return _description; }
        set { _description = value; }
    }

    public BinaryCartItem() { }

    public BinaryCartItem(string name, decimal price, string description)
    {
        _name = name;
        _price = price;
        _description = description;
    }
  }
}
```

The Profile in the web configuration file in Listing 28.33 includes a property that represents the BinaryShoppingCart class. The property includes a serializeAs attribute that has the value Binary. If you don't include this attribute, the BinaryShoppingCart will be serialized as XML.

LISTING 28.33   Web.Config

```
<?xml version="1.0"?>
<configuration>
<system.web>

  <profile>
    <properties>
      <add
        name="ShoppingCart"
        type="AspNetUnleashed.BinaryShoppingCart"
        serializeAs="Binary" />
    </properties>
  </profile>

</system.web>
</configuration>
```

> **NOTE**
>
> The code download from the website that accompanies this book includes a page named `ShowBinaryShoppingCart.aspx` that displays the `BinaryShoppingCart`.

Saving Profiles Automatically

A profile is loaded from its profile provider the first time that a property from the profile is accessed. For example, if you use a `Profile` property in a `Page_Load()` handler, the profile is loaded during the Page Load event. If you use a `Profile` property in a `Page_PreRender()` handler, the `Profile` is loaded during the page `PreRender` event.

If a `Profile` property is modified, the `Profile` is saved automatically at the end of page execution. The ASP.NET Framework can detect automatically when certain types of properties are changed but not others. In general, ASP.NET Framework can detect changes made to simple types but not to complex types.

For example, if you access a property that exposes a simple type such as a string, integer, or Datetime, ASP.NET Framework can detect when the property has been changed. In that case, the framework sets the `Profile.IsDirty` property to the value `true`. At the end of page execution, if a profile is marked as dirty, the profile is saved automatically.

The ASP.NET Framework cannot detect when a `Profile` property that represents a complex type has been modified. For example, if your profile includes a property that represents a custom `ShoppingCart` class, the ASP.NET Framework has no way of determining when the contents of the `ShoppingCart` class have been changed.

The ASP.NET Framework errs on the side of caution. If you access a complex `Profile` property at all—even if you simply read the property—ASP.NET Framework sets the `Profile.IsDirty` property to the value `true`. In other words, if you read a complex property, the profile is always saved at the end of page execution.

Because storing a profile at the end of each page execution can be an expensive operation, ASP.NET Framework provides you with two methods of controlling when a profile is saved.

First, you can take the responsibility of determining when a profile is saved. The web configuration file in Listing 28.34 disables the automatic saving of profiles by setting the `autoSaveEnabled` property to the value `false`.

LISTING 28.34 Web.Config

```
<?xml version="1.0"?>
<configuration>
  <system.web>

  <profile automaticSaveEnabled="false">
    <properties>
      <add name="ShoppingCart" type="AspNetUnleashed.ShoppingCart"/>
```

28

```
        </properties>
      </profile>

</system.web>
</configuration>
```

After you disable the automatic saving of profiles, you must explicitly call the Profile.Save() method to save a profile after you modify it. For example, the btnAdd_Click() method in Listing 28.35 explicitly calls the Profile.Save() method when a new item has been added to the shopping cart.

LISTING 28.35   ShowExplicitSave.aspx

```
<%@ Page Language="C#" %>
<%@ Import Namespace="AspNetUnleashed" %>
<!DOCTYPE html PUBLIC "-//W3C//DTD XHTML 1.0 Transitional//EN"
    "http://www.w3.org/TR/xhtml1/DTD/xhtml1-transitional.dtd">
<script runat="server">

    void Page_PreRender()
    {
        grdShoppingCart.DataSource = Profile.ShoppingCart.Items;
        grdShoppingCart.DataBind();
    }

    protected void btnAdd_Click(object sender, EventArgs e)
    {
        CartItem newItem =
            new CartItem(txtName.Text, decimal.Parse(txtPrice.Text),
➥txtDescription.Text);
        Profile.ShoppingCart.Items.Add(newItem);

        // Explicitly Save Shopping Cart
        Profile.Save();
    }
</script>
<html xmlns="http://www.w3.org/1999/xhtml" >
<head id="Head1" runat="server">
    <title>Show Explicit Save</title>
</head>
<body>
    <form id="form1" runat="server">
    <div>
```

```
<asp:GridView
    id="grdShoppingCart"
    EmptyDataText="There are no items in your shopping cart"
    Runat="server" />

<br />

<fieldset>
<legend>Add Product</legend>
<asp:Label
    id="lblName"
    Text="Name:"
    AssociatedControlID="txtName"
    Runat="server" />
<br />
<asp:TextBox
    id="txtName"
    Runat="server" />
<br /><br />
<asp:Label
    id="lblPrice"
    Text="Price:"
    AssociatedControlID="txtPrice"
    Runat="server" />
<br />
<asp:TextBox
    id="txtPrice"
    Runat="server" />
<br /><br />
<asp:Label
    id="lblDescription"
    Text="Description:"
    AssociatedControlID="txtDescription"
    Runat="server" />
<br />
<asp:TextBox
    id="txtDescription"
    Runat="server" />
<br /><br />
<asp:Button
    id="btnAdd"
    Text="Add To Cart"
    OnClick="btnAdd_Click"
```

```
        Runat="server" />
    </fieldset>

    </div>
    </form>
</body>
</html>
```

As an alternative to disabling the automatic saving of profiles, you can write custom logic to control when a profile is saved by handling the ProfileAutoSaving event in the Global.asax file. For example, the Global.asax file in Listing 28.36 saves a profile only when the Profile.ShoppingCart.HasChanged property has been assigned the value True.

LISTING 28.36   Global.asax

```
<%@ Application Language="C#" %>


<script runat="server">

    public void Profile_ProfileAutoSaving(object s, ProfileAutoSaveEventArgs e)
    {
        if (Profile.ShoppingCart.HasChanged)
            e.ContinueWithProfileAutoSave = true;
        else
            e.ContinueWithProfileAutoSave = false;
    }

</script>
```

NOTE

The code download from the website that accompanies this book includes the shopping cart class and ASP.NET page that accompany the Global.asax file in Listing 28.36. The class is named ShoppingCartHasChanged.cs and the page is named ShowShoppingCartHasChanged.aspx. You need to modify the web configuration file so that the profile inherits from the ShoppingCartHasChanged class.

Accessing Profiles from Components

You can access the `Profile` object from within a component by referring to the `HttpContext.Profile` property. However, you must cast the value of this property to an instance of the `ProfileCommon` object before you access its properties.

For example, the web configuration file in Listing 28.37 defines a `Profile` property named `firstName`.

LISTING 28.37   Web.Config

```
<?xml version="1.0"?>
<configuration>
  <system.web>

  <profile>
    <properties>
      <add name="firstName" defaultValue="Steve" />
    </properties>
  </profile>

</system.web>
</configuration>
```

The component in Listing 28.38 grabs the value of the `firstName` `Profile` property. The `Profile` object retrieved from the current `HttpContext` object must be typecast to a `ProfileCommon` object.

LISTING 28.38   App_Code\ProfileComponent.cs

```
using System;
using System.Web;
using System.Web.Profile;

/// <summary>
/// Retrieves first name from Profile
/// </summary>
public class ProfileComponent
{
    public static string GetFirstNameFromProfile()
    {
        ProfileCommon profile = (ProfileCommon)HttpContext.Current.Profile;
        return profile.firstName;
    }
}
```

28

> **WARNING**
>
> To avoid conflicts with other code samples in this chapter, the component in Listing 28.38 is named `ProfileComponent.cs_listing38` in the code download from the website that accompanies this book. You need to rename the file to `ProfileComponent.cs` before you use the component.

Finally, the page in Listing 28.39 illustrates how you can call the `ProfileComponent` from within an ASP.NET page to retrieve and display the `firstName` attribute.

LISTING 28.39   ShowProfileComponent.aspx

```
<%@ Page Language="C#" %>
<!DOCTYPE html PUBLIC "-//W3C//DTD XHTML 1.0 Transitional//EN"
    "http://www.w3.org/TR/xhtml1/DTD/xhtml1-transitional.dtd">
<script runat="server">

    void Page_Load()
    {
        lblFirstName.Text = ProfileComponent.GetFirstNameFromProfile();
    }

</script>
<html xmlns="http://www.w3.org/1999/xhtml" >
<head id="Head1" runat="server">
    <title>Show Profile Component</title>
</head>
<body>
    <form id="form1" runat="server">
    <div>

    First Name:
    <asp:Label
        id="lblFirstName"
        Runat="server" />

    </div>
    </form>
</body>
</html>
</html>
```

Using the Profile Manager

Unlike Session state, profile data does not evaporate when a user leaves your application. Over time, as more users visit your application, the amount of data stored by the Profile object can become huge. If you allow anonymous profiles, the situation becomes even worse.

The ASP.NET Framework includes a class named the ProfileManager class that enables you to delete old profiles. This class supports the following methods:

▶ **DeleteInactiveProfiles**—Enables you to delete profiles that have not been used since a specified date.

▶ **DeleteProfile**—Enables you to delete a profile associated with a specified username.

▶ **DeleteProfiles**—Enables you to delete profiles that match an array of usernames or collection of ProfileInfo objects.

▶ **FindInactiveProfilesByUserName**—Enables you to retrieve all profiles associated with a specified username that have been inactive since a specified date.

▶ **FindProfilesByUserName**—Enables you to retrieve all profiles associated with a specified user.

▶ **GetAllInactiveProfiles**—Enables you to retrieve all profiles that have been inactive since a specified date.

▶ **GetAllProfiles**—Enables you to retrieve every profile.

▶ **GetNumberOfInactiveProfiles**—Enables you to retrieve a count of profiles that have been inactive since a specified date.

▶ **GetNumberOfProfiles**—Enables you to retrieve a count of the total number of profiles.

You can use the ProfileManager class from within a console application and execute the DeleteInactiveProfiles() method on a periodic basis to delete inactive profiles. Alternatively, you can create an administrative page in your web application that enables you to manage profile data.

The page in Listing 28.40 illustrates how you can use the ProfileManager class to remove inactive profiles (see Figure 28.10).

28

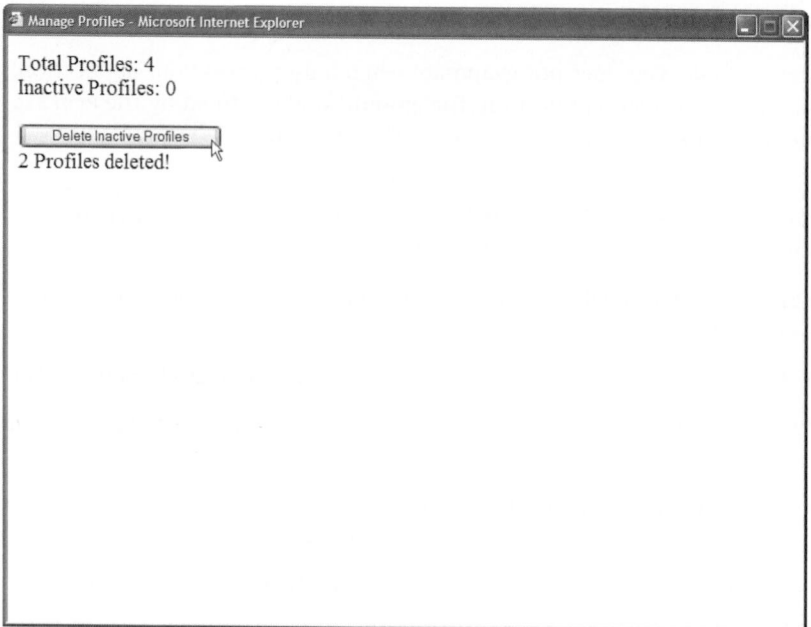

FIGURE 28.10   Deleting inactive profiles.

LISTING 28.40   ManageProfiles.aspx

```
<%@ Page Language="C#" %>
<!DOCTYPE html PUBLIC "-//W3C//DTD XHTML 1.0 Transitional//EN"
    "http://www.w3.org/TR/xhtml1/DTD/xhtml1-transitional.dtd">
<script runat="server">

    DateTime inactiveDate = DateTime.Now.AddMonths(-3);

    void Page_PreRender()
    {
        lblProfiles.Text =
      ProfileManager.GetNumberOfProfiles(
        ProfileAuthenticationOption.All).ToString();
        lblInactiveProfiles.Text =
      ProfileManager.GetNumberOfInactiveProfiles(
          ProfileAuthenticationOption.All, inactiveDate).ToString();
    }

    protected void btnDelete_Click(object sender, EventArgs e)
    {
        int results =
            ProfileManager.DeleteInactiveProfiles(
```

```
            ProfileAuthenticationOption.All, inactiveDate);
        lblResults.Text = String.Format("{0} Profiles deleted!", results);
    }
</script>
<html xmlns="http://www.w3.org/1999/xhtml" >
<head id="Head1" runat="server">
    <title>Manage Profiles</title>
</head>
<body>
    <form id="form1" runat="server">
    <div>

    Total Profiles:
    <asp:Label
        id="lblProfiles"
        Runat="server" />
    <br />
    Inactive Profiles:
    <asp:Label
        id="lblInactiveProfiles"
        Runat="server" />
    <br /><br />

    <asp:Button
        id="btnDelete"
        Text="Delete Inactive Profiles"
        Runat="server" OnClick="btnDelete_Click" />
    <br />
    <asp:Label
        id="lblResults"
        EnableViewState="false"
        Runat="server" />

    </div>
    </form>
</body>
</html>
```

The page in Listing 28.40 displays the total number of profiles and the total number of inactive profiles. An inactive profile is a profile that has not been accessed for more than 3 months. The page also includes a Delete Inactive Profiles button that enables you to remove the old profiles.

Configuring the Profile Provider

By default, profile data is stored in a Microsoft SQL Server Express database named ASPNETDB.mdf, located in your application's root App_Data folder. If you want to store profile data in another database in your network, you need to perform the following two tasks:

1. Add the necessary database objects required by the profile object to the database.
2. Configure your application to connect to the database.

You can add the necessary database tables and stored procedures required by the Profile object to a database by executing the aspnet_regsql command-line tool. The aspnet_regsql tool is located at the following path:

```
\WINDOWS\Microsoft.NET\Framework\[version]\aspnet_regsql.exe
```

> **NOTE**
>
> If you open the Visual Studio Command Prompt, you do not need to navigate to the Microsoft.NET directory to execute the aspnet_regsql tool.

If you execute this tool without supplying any parameters, the ASP.NET SQL Server Setup Wizard launches. This wizard guides you through the process of connecting to a database and adding the necessary database objects.

As an alternative to using the aspnet_regsql tool, you can install the necessary database objects by executing the following two SQL batch files:

```
\WINDOWS\Microsoft.NET\Framework\[version]\InstallCommon.sql
\WINDOWS\Microsoft.NET\Framework\[version]\InstallProfile.sql
```

After you set up your database, you need to configure the default profile provider to connect to the database. The web configuration file in Listing 28.41 connects to a database named MyDatabase on a server named MyServer

LISTING 28.41   Web.Config

```
<?xml version="1.0"?>
<configuration>
  <connectionStrings>
    <add
      name="conProfile"
      connectionString="Data Source=MyServer;
Integrated Security=true;database=MyDatabase"/>
  </connectionStrings>
  <system.web>
```

```
    <profile defaultProvider="MyProfileProvider">
      <properties>
        <add name="firstName" />
        <add name="lastName" />
      </properties>
      <providers>
        <add
          name="MyProfileProvider"
          type="System.Web.Profile.SqlProfileProvider"
          connectionStringName="conProfile"/>
      </providers>
    </profile>

  </system.web>
</configuration>
```

After you complete these configuration steps, all profile data is stored in a custom database.

Creating a Custom Profile Provider

The Profile object uses the Provider Model. The ASP.NET Framework includes a single profile provider, the SqlProfileProvider, that stores profile data in a Microsoft SQL Server database. In this section, you learn how to build a custom profile provider.

One problem with the default SqlProfileProvider is that it serializes an entire profile into a single blob and stores the blob in a database table column. This means that you can't execute SQL queries against the properties in a profile. In other words, the default SqlProfileProvider makes it extremely difficult to generate reports off the properties stored in a profile.

In this section, we create a new profile provider that is modestly named the BetterProfileProvider. The BetterProfileProvider stores each Profile property in a separate database column.

Unfortunately, the code for the BetterProfileProvider is too long to place in this book. However, the entire source code is included on the website that accompanies this book.

The BetterProfileProvider inherits from the base ProfileProvider class. The two most important methods that must be overridden in the base ProfileProvider class are the GetPropertyValues() and SetPropertyValues() methods. These methods are responsible for loading and saving a profile for a particular user.

Imagine that you want to use the BetterProfileProvider to represent a profile that contains the following three properties: FirstName, LastName, and NumberOfVisits. Before you can use the BetterProfileProvider, you must create a database table that contains three columns that correspond to these Profile properties. In addition, the database table must contain an int column named ProfileID.

28

You can create the necessary database table with the following SQL command:

```sql
CREATE TABLE ProfileData
{
  ProfileID Int,
  FirstName NVarChar(50),
  LastName NVarChar(50),
  NumberOfVisits Int
}
```

Next, you need to create a database table named Profiles. This table is used to describe the properties of each profile. You can create the Profiles table with the following SQL command:

```sql
CREATE TABLE Profiles
(
  UniqueID IDENTITY NOT NULL PRIMARY KEY,
  UserName NVarchar(255) NOT NULL,
  ApplicationName NVarchar(255) NOT NULL,
  IsAnonymous BIT,
  LastActivityDate DateTime,
  LastUpdatedDate DateTime,
)
```

After you create these two database tables, you are ready to use the BetterProfileProvider. The web configuration file in Listing 28.42 configures the BetterProfileProvider as the default profile provider.

LISTING 28.42   Web.Config

```xml
<?xml version="1.0"?>
<configuration>
  <connectionStrings>
    <add
      name="conProfile"
      connectionString=
"Data Source=.\SQLExpress;Integrated
➥Security=true;AttachDBFileName=¦DataDirectory¦ProfilesDB.mdf;User Instance=true"
/>
  </connectionStrings>
  <system.web>

    <profile defaultProvider="MyProfileProvider">
      <properties>
        <add name="FirstName" />
        <add name="LastName" />
        <add name="NumberOfVisits" type="Int32" />
```

```
        </properties>
        <providers>
          <add
            name="MyProfileProvider"
            type="AspNetUnleashed.BetterProfileProvider"
            connectionStringName="conProfile"
            profileTableName="ProfileData" />
        </providers>
      </profile>

    </system.web>
</configuration>
```

The BetterProfileProvider is configured with both a connectionStringName and profileTableName attribute. The connectionStringName points to the database that contains the two database tables that were created earlier. The profileTableName property contains the name of the table that contains the profile data. (This attribute defaults to the value ProfileData, so it isn't necessary here.)

After you configure the BetterProfileProvider, you can use it in a similar manner to the default SqlProfileProvider. For example, the page in Listing 28.43 displays the values of the FirstName, LastName, and NumberOfVisits profile properties and enables you to modify the FirstName and LastName properties.

> **WARNING**
>
> The BetterProfileProvider has several important limitations. It does not support serialization, so you cannot use it with complex types such as a custom shopping cart class. It also does not support default values for Profile properties.

LISTING 28.43   ShowBetterProfileProvider.aspx

```
<%@ Page Language="C#" %>
<!DOCTYPE html PUBLIC "-//W3C//DTD XHTML 1.0 Transitional//EN"
    "http://www.w3.org/TR/xhtml1/DTD/xhtml1-transitional.dtd">
<script runat="server">

    void Page_PreRender()
    {
        Profile.NumberOfVisits++;
        lblNumberOfVisits.Text = Profile.NumberOfVisits.ToString();

        lblFirstName.Text = Profile.FirstName;
        lblLastName.Text = Profile.LastName;
    }
```

28

```
    protected void btnUpdate_Click(object sender, EventArgs e)
    {
        Profile.FirstName = txtNewFirstName.Text;
        Profile.LastName = txtNewLastName.Text;
    }
</script>
<html xmlns="http://www.w3.org/1999/xhtml" >
<head id="Head1" runat="server">
    <title>Show BetterProfileProvider</title>
</head>
<body>
    <form id="form1" runat="server">
    <div>

    Number of Visits:
    <asp:Label
        id="lblNumberOfVisits"
        Runat="server" />
    <br />
    First Name:
    <asp:Label
        id="lblFirstName"
        Runat="server" />
    <br />
    Last Name:
    <asp:Label
        id="lblLastName"
        Runat="server" />

    <hr />

    <asp:Label
        id="lblNewFirstName"
        Text="First Name:"
        AssociatedControlID="txtNewFirstName"
        Runat="server" />
    <asp:TextBox
        id="txtNewFirstName"
        Runat="server" />
    <br />
    <asp:Label
        id="lblNewLastname"
        Text="Last Name:"
        AssociatedControlID="txtNewLastName"
        Runat="server" />
    <asp:TextBox
```

```
        id="txtNewLastName"
        Runat="server" />
    <br />
    <asp:Button
        id="btnUpdate"
        Text="Update"
        OnClick="btnUpdate_Click"
        Runat="server" />

    </div>
    </form>
</body>
</html>
```

The main advantage of the BetterProfileProvider is that you can perform SQL queries against the data stored in the ProfileData table. For example, the page in Listing 28.44 displays the contents of the ProfileData table in a GridView control (see Figure 28.11). You can't do this when using the default SqlProfileProvider because the SqlProfileProvider stores profile data in a blob.

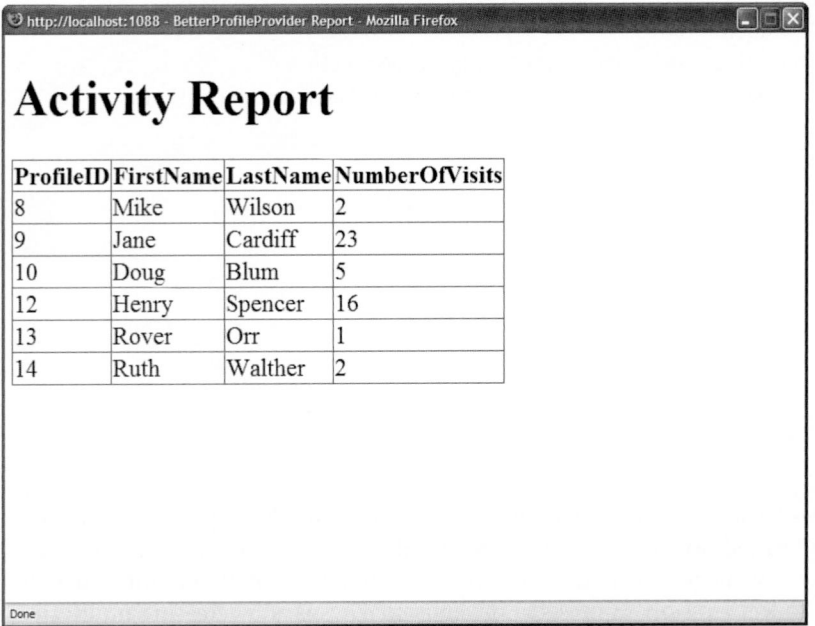

FIGURE 28.11   Displaying a profile report.

LISTING 28.44   `BetterProfileProviderReport.aspx`

```
<%@ Page Language="C#" %>
<!DOCTYPE html PUBLIC "-//W3C//DTD XHTML 1.0 Transitional//EN"
    "http://www.w3.org/TR/xhtml1/DTD/xhtml1-transitional.dtd">
<html xmlns="http://www.w3.org/1999/xhtml" >
<head id="Head1" runat="server">
    <title>BetterProfileProvider Report</title>
</head>
<body>
    <form id="form1" runat="server">
    <div>

    <h1>Activity Report</h1>

    <asp:GridView
        id="grdProfiles"
        DataSourceID="srcProfiles"
        Runat="server" />

    <asp:SqlDataSource
        id="srcProfiles"
        ConnectionString="<%$ ConnectionStrings:conProfile %>"
        SelectCommand="SELECT ProfileID,FirstName,LastName,NumberOfVisits
            FROM ProfileData"
        Runat="server" />

    </div>
    </form>
</body>
</html>
```

Summary

In this chapter, you learned how to maintain state in your ASP.NET applications. In the first section, you learned how to create, modify, and delete browser cookies. You learned how you can take advantage of cookies when you need to add a small amount of data to a browser. You also learned how to preserve precious cookie space by creating multivalued cookies.

Next, we examined the topic of Session state. You learned how to take advantage of Session state to store larger amounts of data than can be stored in a cookie. You also learned how to configure cookieless Session state so that Session state works even when a browser has cookies disabled. We also discussed how to make Session state more robust by storing Session state data in a Windows NT Service or a Microsoft SQL Server database table.

Finally, you learned how to use the Profile object to create a typed and persistent form of Session state. You learned how to enable anonymous profiles. In the final section of this chapter, we built a custom Profile provider that enables you to store Profile properties in separate database table columns.

28

Caching Application Pages and Data

The slowest operation that you can perform in an ASP.NET page is database access. Opening a database connection and retrieving data is a slow operation. The best way to improve the performance of your data access code is not to access the database at all.

By taking advantage of caching, you can cache your database records in memory. Retrieving data from a database is slow. Retrieving data from the cache, on the other hand, is lightning fast.

In this chapter, you learn about the different caching mechanisms supported by ASP.NET Framework, which provides you with an overwhelming number of caching options. We attempt to clarify all these caching options over the course of this chapter.

In the final section of this chapter, you learn how to use SQL Cache Dependencies, which enable you to reload cached data automatically when data changes in a database table. You learn how to use both polling and push SQL Cache Dependencies.

Overview of Caching

The ASP.NET 4 Framework supports the following types of caching:

- Page Output Caching
- Partial Page Caching
- DataSource Caching
- Data Caching

Page Output Caching enables you to cache the entire rendered contents of a page in memory (everything that you see when you select View Source in your web browser). The next time that any user requests the same page, the page is retrieved from the cache.

Page Output Caching caches an entire page. In some situations, this might create problems. For example, if you want to display different banner advertisements randomly in a page, and you cache the entire page, the same banner advertisement displays with each page request.

> **NOTE**
>
> The `AdRotator` control included in ASP.NET Framework takes advantage of a feature called post-cache substitution to randomly display different advertisements even when a page is cached. Post-cache substitution is described later in this chapter.

Partial Page Caching enables you to get around this problem by enabling you to cache only particular regions of a page. By taking advantage of Partial Page Caching, you can apply different caching policies to different areas of a page.

You use DataSource Caching with the different ASP.NET `DataSource` controls such as the `SqlDataSource` and `ObjectDataSource` controls. When you enable caching with a `DataSource` control, the `DataSource` control caches the data that it represents.

Finally, Data Caching is the fundamental caching mechanism. Behind the scenes, all the other types of caching use Data Caching. You can use Data Caching to cache arbitrary objects in memory. For example, you can use Data Caching to cache a DataSet across multiple pages in a web application.

In the following sections, you learn how to use each of these different types of caching in detail.

> **NOTE**
>
> Caching LINQ to SQL queries raises special issues, which are addressed in Chapter 20, "Data Access with LINQ to SQL."

> **NOTE**
>
> When configuring and debugging caching, having a tool that enables you to monitor the HTTP traffic between web server and browser is extremely helpful. You can download the free Fiddler tool, which enables you to view the raw request and response HTTP traffic, from http://www.FiddlerTool.com.

Using Page Output Caching

You enable Page Output Caching by adding an `<%@ OutputCache %>` directive to a page. For example, the page in Listing 29.1 caches its contents for 15 seconds.

LISTING 29.1   CachePageOutput.aspx

```
<%@ Page Language="C#" %>
<%@ OutputCache Duration="15" VaryByParam="none" %>
<!DOCTYPE html PUBLIC "-//W3C//DTD XHTML 1.0 Transitional//EN"
    "http://www.w3.org/TR/xhtml1/DTD/xhtml1-transitional.dtd">
<script runat="server">

    void Page_Load()
    {
        lblTime.Text = DateTime.Now.ToString("T");
    }

</script>
<html xmlns="http://www.w3.org/1999/xhtml" >
<head id="Head1" runat="server">
    <title>Cache Page Output</title>
</head>
<body>
    <form id="form1" runat="server">
    <div>

    <asp:Label
        id="lblTime"
        Runat="server" />

    </div>
    </form>
</body>
</html>
```

The page in Listing 29.1 displays the current server time in a `Label` control. The page also includes an `<%@ OutputCache %>` directive. If you refresh the page multiple times, you notice that the time is not updated until at least 15 seconds have passed.

When you cache a page, the contents of the page are not regenerated each time you request the page. The .NET class that corresponds to the page is not executed with each page request. The rendered contents of the page are cached for every user that requests the page. The page is cached in multiple locations. By default, the page is cached on the browser, any proxy servers, and on the web server.

In Listing 29.1, the page is cached for 15 seconds. You can assign a much larger number to the duration attribute. For example, if you assign the value 86400 to the duration parameter, the page is cached for a day.

> **NOTE**
>
> There is no guarantee that a page will be cached for the amount of time that you specify. When server memory resources become low, items are automatically evicted from the cache.

Varying the Output Cache by Parameter

Imagine that you need to create a separate master and details page. The master page displays a list of movies. When you click a movie title, the details page displays detailed information on the movie selected.

When you create a master/details page, you typically pass a query string parameter between the master and details page to indicate the particular movie to display in the details page. If you cache the output of the details page, however, everyone will see the first movie selected.

You can get around this problem by using the VaryByParam attribute. The VaryByParam attribute causes a new instance of a page to be cached when a different parameter is passed to the page. (The parameter can be either a query string parameter or a form parameter.)

For example, the page in Listing 29.2 contains a master page that displays a list of movie titles as links.

LISTING 29.2 Master.aspx

```
<%@ Page Language="C#" %>
<!DOCTYPE html PUBLIC "-//W3C//DTD XHTML 1.0 Transitional//EN"
 "http://www.w3.org/TR/xhtml1/DTD/xhtml1-transitional.dtd">
<html xmlns="http://www.w3.org/1999/xhtml" >
<head id="Head1" runat="server">
    <title>Master</title>
</head>
<body>
```

```
<form id="form1" runat="server">
<div>

<asp:GridView
    id="grdMovies"
    DataSourceID="srcMovies"
    AutoGenerateColumns="false"
    ShowHeader="false"
    GridLines="none"
    Runat="server">
    <Columns>
    <asp:HyperLinkField
        DataTextField="Title"
        DataNavigateUrlFields="Id"
        DataNavigateUrlFormatString="~/Details.aspx?id={0}" />
    </Columns>
</asp:GridView>

<asp:SqlDataSource
    id="srcMovies"
    ConnectionString="<%$ ConnectionStrings:Movies %>"
    SelectCommand="SELECT Id,Title FROM Movies"
    Runat="server" />

</div>
</form>
</body>
</html>
```

If you hover your mouse over the links displayed in Listing 29.2, you can see the query string parameter passed by each link in the browser status bar (see Figure 29.1). For example, the first movie link includes a query string parameter with the value 1, the second link includes a query string parameter with the value 2, and so on. When you click a movie link, this query string parameter is passed to the details page in Listing 29.3.

29

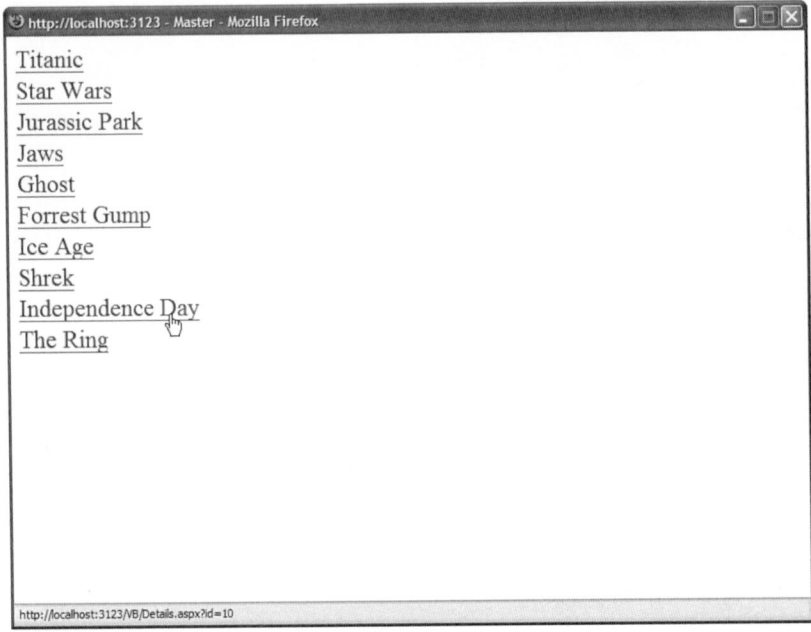

FIGURE 29.1   Displaying the Master page.

LISTING 29.3   Details.aspx

```
<%@ Page Language="C#" %>
<%@ OutputCache Duration="3600" VaryByParam="id" %>
<!DOCTYPE html PUBLIC "-//W3C//DTD XHTML 1.0 Transitional//EN"
    "http://www.w3.org/TR/xhtml1/DTD/xhtml1-transitional.dtd">
<html xmlns="http://www.w3.org/1999/xhtml" >
<head id="Head1" runat="server">
    <title>Details</title>
</head>
<body>
    <form id="form1" runat="server">
    <div>

    <%= DateTime.Now.ToString("T") %>

    <hr />

    <asp:DetailsView
        id="dtlMovie"
        DataSourceID="srcMovies"
        Runat="server" />
```

```
<asp:SqlDataSource
    id="srcMovies"
    ConnectionString="<%$ ConnectionStrings:Movies %>"
    SelectCommand="SELECT * FROM Movies
        WHERE Id=@Id"
    Runat="server">
    <SelectParameters>
        <asp:QueryStringParameter
            Name="Id"
            Type="int32"
            QueryStringField="Id" />
    </SelectParameters>
</asp:SqlDataSource>

    </div>
    </form>
</body>
</html>
```

The page in Listing 29.3 uses a DetailsView to display detailed information on the movie selected from the master page (see Figure 29.2). The DetailsView is bound to a SqlDataSource control that includes a QueryStringParameter SELECT parameter that represents the id query string parameter.

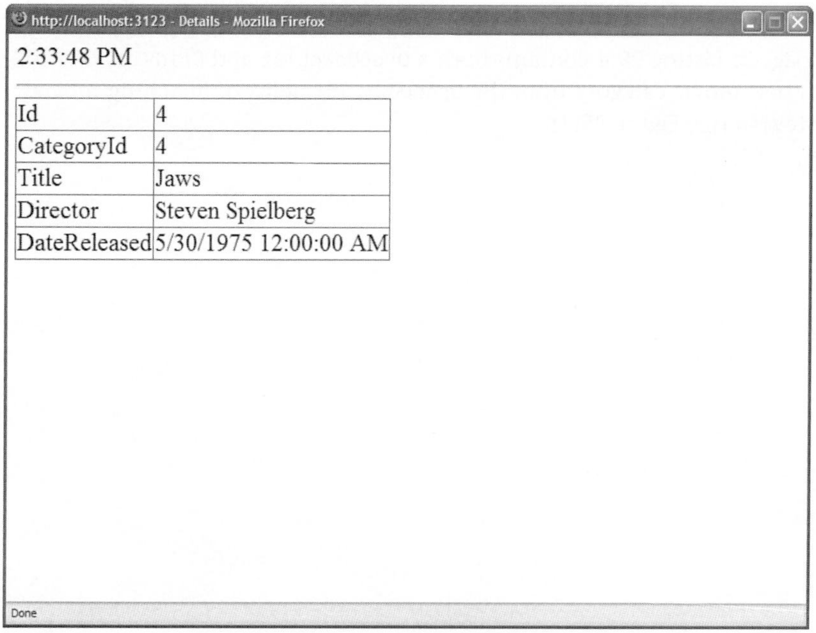

FIGURE 29.2 Displaying the Details page.

The Details.aspx page includes an <%@ OutputCache %> directive. The VaryByParam attribute in the <%@ OutputCache %> directive has the value id. If you request the Details.aspx page with a different value for the id query string parameter, a different cached version of the page is created.

It is important to understand that using VaryByParam results in more caching and not less caching. Each time a different id parameter is passed to the Details.aspx page, another version of the same page is cached in memory.

The Details.aspx page displays the current time. The time does not change when you request the Details.aspx page with the same query string parameter.

You can assign two special values to the VaryByParam attribute:

▶ **none**—Causes any query string or form parameters to be ignored. Only one version of the page is cached.

▶ *****—Causes a new cached version of the page to be created whenever there is a change in any query string or form parameter passed to the page.

You also can assign a semicolon-delimited list of parameters to the VaryByParam attribute when you want to create different cached versions of a page, depending on the values of more than one parameter.

Varying the Output Cache by Control

The VaryByControl attribute enables you to generate different cached versions of a page depending on the value of a particular control in the page. This attribute is useful when you need to create a single-page Master/Details form.

For example, the page in Listing 29.4 contains both a DropDownList and GridView control. When you select a new movie category from the DropDownList, a list of matching movies displays in the GridView (see Figure 29.3).

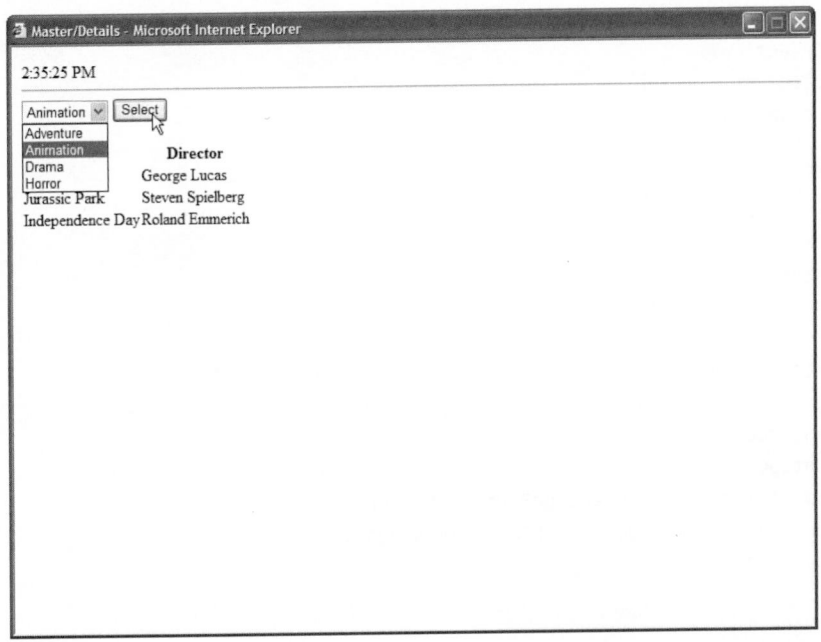

FIGURE 29.3   Displaying a single-page Master/Details form.

LISTING 29.4   MasterDetails.aspx

```
<%@ Page Language="C#" %>
<%@ OutputCache Duration="3600" VaryByControl="dropCategories" %>
<!DOCTYPE html PUBLIC "-//W3C//DTD XHTML 1.0 Transitional//EN"
   "http://www.w3.org/TR/xhtml1/DTD/xhtml1-transitional.dtd">
<html xmlns="http://www.w3.org/1999/xhtml" >
<head id="Head1" runat="server">
    <title>Master/Details</title>
</head>
<body>
    <form id="form1" runat="server">
    <div>

    <%= DateTime.Now.ToString("T") %>
    <hr />

    <asp:DropDownList
        id="dropCategories"
        DataSourceID="srcCategories"
        DataTextField="Name"
        DataValueField="Id"
        Runat="server" />
```

29

```
<asp:Button
    id="btnSelect"
    Text="Select"
    Runat="server" />

<br /><br />

<asp:GridView
    id="grdMovies"
    DataSourceID="srcMovies"
    GridLines="none"
    Runat="server" />

<asp:SqlDataSource
    id="srcCategories"
    ConnectionString="<%$ ConnectionStrings:Movies %>"
    SelectCommand="SELECT Id,Name FROM MovieCategories"
    Runat="server" />

<asp:SqlDataSource
    id="srcMovies"
    ConnectionString="<%$ ConnectionStrings:Movies %>"
    SelectCommand="SELECT Title,Director FROM Movies
        WHERE CategoryId=@CategoryId"
    Runat="server">
    <SelectParameters>
    <asp:ControlParameter
        Name="CategoryId"
        ControlID="dropCategories" />
    </SelectParameters>
</asp:SqlDataSource>

</div>
</form>
</body>
</html>
```

The page in Listing 29.4 contains an <%@ OutputCache %> directive. This directive includes a VaryByControl parameter. The ID of the DropDownList control is assigned to this parameter.

If you neglected to add the VaryByControl attribute, the same list of movies would display in the GridView regardless of which movie category is selected. The VaryByControl attribute causes different cached versions of the page to be created whenever the DropDownList represents a different value.

Varying the Output Cache by Header

Another option is to use the VaryByHeader attribute to create different cached versions of a page when the value of a particular browser header changes. Several standard browser headers are transmitted with each page request, including

▶ **Accept-Language**—Represents a prioritized list of languages that represent the preferred human language of the user making the request.

▶ **User-Agent**—Represents the type of device making the request.

▶ **Cookie**—Represents the browser cookies created in the current domain.

For example, the page in Listing 29.5 includes an <%@ OutputCache %> directive that has a VaryByHeader attribute with the value User-Agent. When you request the page with different browsers, different versions of the page are cached.

LISTING 29.5   VaryByHeader.aspx

```
<%@ Page Language="C#" %>
<%@ OutputCache Duration="3600" VaryByParam="none" VaryByHeader="User-Agent"  %>
<!DOCTYPE html PUBLIC "-//W3C//DTD XHTML 1.0 Transitional//EN"
  "http://www.w3.org/TR/xhtml1/DTD/xhtml1-transitional.dtd">
<html xmlns="http://www.w3.org/1999/xhtml" >
<head id="Head1" runat="server">
    <title>Vary By Header</title>
</head>
<body>
    <form id="form1" runat="server">
    <div>

    <%= DateTime.Now.ToString("T") %>

    <hr />

    <%= Request.UserAgent %>

    </div>
    </form>
</body>
</html>
```

I don't recommend using the VaryByHeader attribute with the User-Agent header. The problem with this attribute is that it is too fine-grained. If there is any variation in the User-Agent header, a different cached version of a page is generated.

29

Consider the User-Agent header sent by the Internet Explorer browser installed on my computer. It looks like this:

```
Mozilla/4.0 (compatible; MSIE 8.0; Windows NT 6.1; .NET CLR 2.0.50727; .NET
CLR 3.5.30729; .NET CLR 3.0.30729; .NET4.0C; .NET4.0E)
```

This header includes the major and minor version of the browser, the platform (Windows 7) and the versions of .NET Framework installed on my machine. If someone else requests the same page with a slight difference in the User-Agent header, a different cached version of the page is generated. In other words, the web server must do more work rather than less, which defeats the point of caching.

Instead of using the VaryByHeader attribute, I recommend that you use the VaryByCustom attribute described in the next two sections.

Varying the Output Cache by Browser

A better way to create different cached versions of a page that depend on the type of browser used to request the page is to use the VaryByCustom attribute. This attribute accepts the special value browser. When VaryByCustom has the value browser, only two attributes of the browser are considered important: the type of browser and its major version.

For example, a page request from Internet Explorer results in a different cached version of the page than does one from Firefox. A page request from Internet Explorer 8 rather than Internet Explorer 6 also results in a different cached version. Any other variations in the User-Agent header are ignored.

The page in Listing 29.6 illustrates how you can use the VaryByCustom attribute with the value browser. The page displays the current time and the value of the User-Agent header. If you request the page with Internet Explorer and request the page with Firefox, different cached versions of the page are created.

LISTING 29.6   VaryByBrowser.aspx

```
<%@ Page Language="C#" %>
<%@ OutputCache Duration="3600" VaryByParam="none" VaryByCustom="browser"  %>
<!DOCTYPE html PUBLIC "-//W3C//DTD XHTML 1.0 Transitional//EN"
    "http://www.w3.org/TR/xhtml1/DTD/xhtml1-transitional.dtd">
<html xmlns="http://www.w3.org/1999/xhtml" >
<head id="Head1" runat="server">
    <title>Vary By Browser</title>
</head>
<body>
    <form id="form1" runat="server">
    <div>

    <%= DateTime.Now.ToString("T") %>

    <hr />
```

```
    <%= Request.UserAgent %>

    </div>
    </form>
</body>
</html>
```

Varying the Output Cache by a Custom Function

The VaryByCustom attribute is named the VaryByCustom attribute for a reason. You can specify a custom function that determines when a different cached version of a page is generated.

You can use any criteria that you want with the custom function. You can create different cached versions of a page depending on the browser minor version, the browser DOM support, the time of day, or even the weather.

You create the custom function in the Global.asax file by overriding the GetVaryByCustomString() method. For example, the Global.asax file in Listing 29.7 illustrates how you can override the GetVaryByCustomString() method to create different cached versions of a page depending on a particular feature of a browser. If the VaryByCustom attribute in a page has the value css, the function returns a string representing whether the current browser supports Cascading Style Sheets (CSS).

LISTING 29.7   Global.asax

```
<%@ Application Language="C#" %>
<script runat="server">

    public override string GetVaryByCustomString(HttpContext context, string custom)
    {
        if (String.Compare(custom, "css") == 0)
        {
            return Request.Browser.SupportsCss.ToString();
        }
        return base.GetVaryByCustomString(context, custom);
    }

</script>
```

The page in Listing 29.8 displays one of two Panel controls. The first Panel contains text formatted with a CSS style, and the second Panel contains text formatted with (outdated) HTML. Depending on whether a browser supports CSS, either the first or second Panel displays.

29

LISTING 29.8   VaryByCustom.aspx

```
<%@ Page Language="C#" %>
<%@ OutputCache Duration="3600" VaryByParam="none" VaryByCustom="css" %>
<!DOCTYPE html PUBLIC "-//W3C//DTD XHTML 1.0 Transitional//EN"
    "http://www.w3.org/TR/xhtml1/DTD/xhtml1-transitional.dtd">
<script runat="server">

    void Page_Load()
    {
        if (Request.Browser.SupportsCss)
            pnlCss.Visible = true;
        else
            pnlNotCss.Visible = true;
    }
</script>
<html xmlns="http://www.w3.org/1999/xhtml" >
<head id="Head1" runat="server">
    <title>Vary By Custom</title>
</head>
<body>
    <form id="form1" runat="server">
    <div>

    <asp:Panel
        id="pnlCss"
        Visible="false"
        Runat="server">
        <span style="font-weight:bold">Hello!</span>
    </asp:Panel>

    <asp:Panel
        id="pnlNotCss"
        Visible="false"
        Runat="server">
        <b>Hello!</b>
    </asp:Panel>

    </div>
    </form>
</body>
</html>
```

The page contains an <%@ OutputCache %> directive with a VaryByCustom attribute set to the value css. Two different cached versions of the same page are generated: one version for CSS browsers and another version for non-CSS browsers.

Specifying the Cache Location

You can use the Location attribute of the <%@ OutputCache %> directive to specify where a page is cached. This attribute accepts the following values:

- ▶ **Any**—The page is cached on the browser, proxy servers, and web server (the default value).

- ▶ **Client**—The page is cached only on the browser.

- ▶ **Downstream**—The page is cached on the browser and any proxy servers, but not the web server.

- ▶ **None**—The page is not cached.

- ▶ **Server**—The page is cached on the web server, but not the browser or any proxy servers.

- ▶ **ServerAndClient**—The page is cached on the browser and web server, but not on any proxy servers.

By default, when you use Page Output Caching, a page is cached in three locations: the web server, any proxy servers, and the browser. There are situations in which you might need to modify this default behavior. For example, if you cache private information, you don't want to cache the information on the web server or any proxy servers.

For example, the page in Listing 29.9 caches a page only on the browser and not on any proxy servers or the web server. The page displays a random number (see Figure 29.4).

29

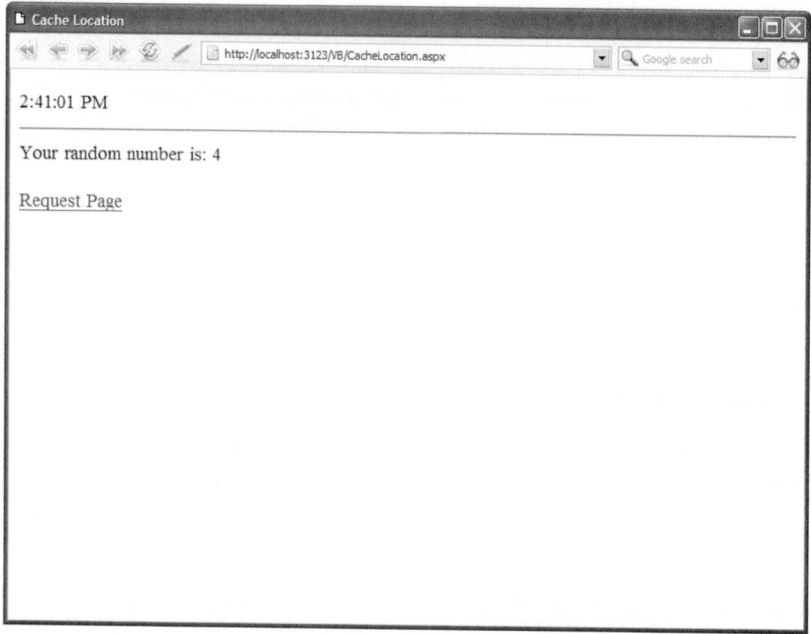

FIGURE 29.4   Caching a page on the browser.

LISTING 29.9   CacheLocation.aspx

```
<%@ Page Language="C#" %>
<%@ OutputCache Duration="3600" VaryByParam="none" Location="Client" %>
<!DOCTYPE html PUBLIC "-//W3C//DTD XHTML 1.0 Transitional//EN"
    "http://www.w3.org/TR/xhtml1/DTD/xhtml1-transitional.dtd">
<script runat="server">

    void Page_Load()
    {
        Random rnd = new Random();
        lblRandom.Text = rnd.Next(10).ToString();
    }
</script>
<html xmlns="http://www.w3.org/1999/xhtml" >
<head id="Head1" runat="server">
    <title>Cache Location</title>
</head>
<body>
    <form id="form1" runat="server">
    <div>
```

```
<%= DateTime.Now.ToString("T") %>
<hr />

Your random number is:
<asp:Label
    id="lblRandom"
    Runat="server" />

<br /><br />
<a href="CacheLocation.aspx">Request Page</a>

</div>
</form>
</body>
</html>
```

If you click the link located at the bottom of the page in Listing 29.9 and request the same page, the page is retrieved from the browser cache and the same random number displays. If you reload the page in your web browser by clicking your browser's Reload button, the page is reloaded from the web server and a new random number displays. The page is cached only in your local browser cache and nowhere else.

> **NOTE**
>
> Behind the scenes, ASP.NET Framework uses the `Cache-Control` HTTP header to specify where a page is cached. This header is defined in RFC 2616, "Hypertext Transfer Protocol—HTTP/1.1."

Creating a Page Output Cache File Dependency

You can create a dependency between a cached page and a file (or set of files) on your hard drive. When the file is modified, the cached page is automatically dropped and regenerated with the next page request.

For example, the page in Listing 29.10 displays the contents of an XML file in a `GridView`. The page is cached until the XML file is modified (see Figure 29.5).

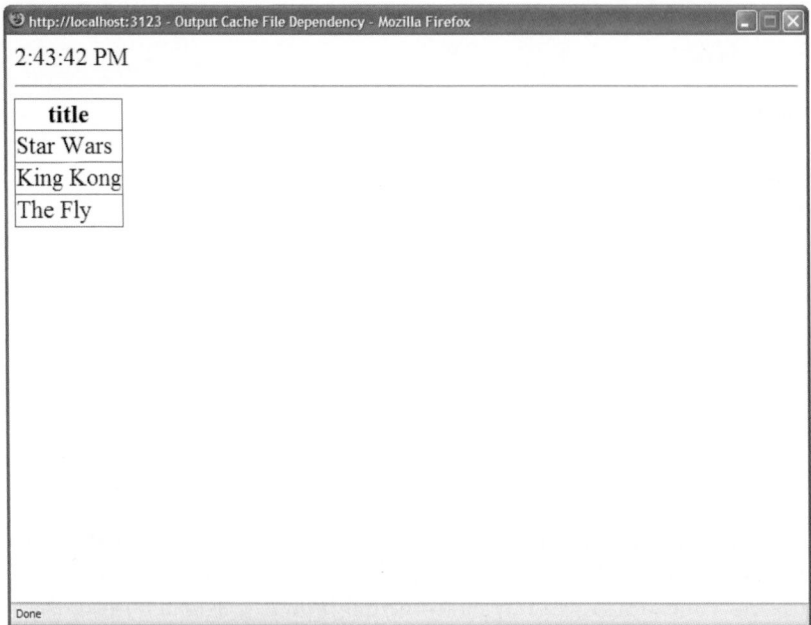

FIGURE 29.5   Caching a page with a file dependency.

LISTING 29.10   `OutputCacheFileDependency.aspx`

```
<%@ Page Language="C#" %>
<%@ OutputCache Duration="9999" VaryByParam="none" %>
<!DOCTYPE html PUBLIC "-//W3C//DTD XHTML 1.0 Transitional//EN"
    "http://www.w3.org/TR/xhtml1/DTD/xhtml1-transitional.dtd">
<script runat="server">

    void Page_Load()
    {
        Response.AddFileDependency(MapPath("Movies.xml"));
    }
</script>
<html xmlns="http://www.w3.org/1999/xhtml" >
<head id="Head1" runat="server">
    <title>Output Cache File Dependency</title>
</head>
<body>
    <form id="form1" runat="server">
    <div>

    <%= DateTime.Now.ToString("T") %>
    <hr />
```

```
    <asp:GridView
        id="grdMovies"
        DataSourceID="srcMovies"
        Runat="server" />

    <asp:XmlDataSource
        id="srcMovies"
        DataFile="Movies.xml"
        Runat="server" />

    </div>
    </form>
</body>
</html>
```

The page in Listing 29.10 displays the current time. The time does not change until you modify the `Movies.xml` XML file. The page in Listing 29.10 uses the `Response.AddFileDependency()` method to create a dependency between the cached page and a single file on disk. If you need to create a dependency on multiple files, you can use the `AddFileDependencies()` method instead.

Expiring the Page Output Cache Programmatically

You can remove a page from the cache programmatically by using the `Response.RemoveOutputCacheItem()` method. For example, imagine that you are caching a page that displays a list of products. Furthermore, imagine that your website includes a separate page for adding a new product. In that case, you want to remove the first page programmatically from the cache when the list of products is updated.

The page in Listing 29.11 uses a `GridView` control to display a list of movies. The page is cached for 1 hour with an `<%@ OutputCache %>` directive.

LISTING 29.11 MovieList.aspx

```
<%@ Page Language="C#" %>
<%@ OutputCache Duration="3600" VaryByParam="none" %>
<!DOCTYPE html PUBLIC "-//W3C//DTD XHTML 1.0 Transitional//EN"
  "http://www.w3.org/TR/xhtml1/DTD/xhtml1-transitional.dtd">
<html xmlns="http://www.w3.org/1999/xhtml" >
<head id="Head1" runat="server">
    <title>Movie List</title>
</head>
<body>
    <form id="form1" runat="server">
    <div>
```

29

```
    <%= DateTime.Now.ToString("T") %>
    <hr />

    <asp:GridView
        id="grdMovies"
        DataSourceID="srcMovies"
        Runat="server" />

    <asp:SqlDataSource
        id="srcMovies"
        ConnectionString="<%$ ConnectionStrings:Movies %>"
        SelectCommand="SELECT Title, Director FROM Movies"
        Runat="server" />

    <br /><br />
    <a href="AddMovie.aspx">Add Movie</a>

    </div>
    </form>
</body>
</html>
```

The page in Listing 29.12 contains a `DetailsView` control that enables you to add a new movie. When you insert a new movie into the database, the `Response.RemoveOutputCacheItem()` method is called to remove the `MovieList.aspx` page from the cache. Because this method accepts only a "virtual absolute" path, the `Page.ResolveUrl()` method converts the tilde into the application root path.

LISTING 29.12   AddMovie.aspx

```
<%@ Page Language="C#" %>
<!DOCTYPE html PUBLIC "-//W3C//DTD XHTML 1.0 Transitional//EN"
    "http://www.w3.org/TR/xhtml1/DTD/xhtml1-transitional.dtd">
<script runat="server">

    protected void dtlMovie_ItemInserted(object sender,
➡DetailsViewInsertedEventArgs e)
    {
        HttpResponse.RemoveOutputCacheItem(Page.ResolveUrl("~/MovieList.aspx"));
        Response.Redirect("~/MovieList.aspx");
    }
</script>
<html xmlns="http://www.w3.org/1999/xhtml" >
<head id="Head1" runat="server">
    <title>Add Movie</title>
```

```
</head>
<body>
    <form id="form1" runat="server">
    <div>

    <h1>Add Movie</h1>

    <asp:DetailsView
        id="dtlMovie"
        DefaultMode="Insert"
        DataSourceID="srcMovies"
        AutoGenerateRows="false"
        AutoGenerateInsertButton="true"
        Runat="server" OnItemInserted="dtlMovie_ItemInserted">
        <Fields>
        <asp:BoundField
            DataField="Title"
            HeaderText="Title:" />
        <asp:BoundField
            DataField="Director"
            HeaderText="Director:" />
        </Fields>
    </asp:DetailsView>

    <asp:SqlDataSource
        id="srcMovies"
        ConnectionString="<%$ ConnectionStrings:Movies %>"
        InsertCommand="INSERT Movies (Title, Director)
            VALUES (@Title, @Director)"
        Runat="server" />

    </div>
    </form>
</body>
</html>
```

The Response.RemoveOutputCacheItem() method enables you to remove only one page from the cache at a time. If you need to remove multiple pages, you can create a *key dependency*, which enables you to create a dependency between one item in the cache and another item. When the second item is removed from the cache, the first item is removed automatically.

For example, the page in Listing 29.13 also displays a list of movies. However, the page is cached with a dependency on an item in the cache named Movies.

LISTING 29.13   MovieListKeyDependency.aspx

```
<%@ Page Language="C#" %>
<%@ OutputCache Duration="3600" VaryByParam="none" %>
<!DOCTYPE html PUBLIC "-//W3C//DTD XHTML 1.0 Transitional//EN"
    "http://www.w3.org/TR/xhtml1/DTD/xhtml1-transitional.dtd">
<script runat="server">

    protected void Page_Load(object sender, EventArgs e)
    {
        Cache.Insert("Movies", DateTime.Now);
        Response.AddCacheItemDependency("Movies");
    }
</script>
<html xmlns="http://www.w3.org/1999/xhtml" >
<head id="Head1" runat="server">
    <title>Movie List Key Dependency</title>
</head>
<body>
    <form id="form1" runat="server">
    <div>

    <%= DateTime.Now.ToString("T") %>
    <hr />

    <asp:GridView
        id="grdMovies"
        DataSourceID="srcMovies"
        Runat="server" />

    <asp:SqlDataSource
        id="srcMovies"
        ConnectionString="<%$ ConnectionStrings:Movies %>"
        SelectCommand="SELECT Title, Director FROM Movies"
        Runat="server" />

  <br /><br />
  <a href="AddMovieKeyDependency.aspx">Add Movie</a>

    </div>
    </form>
</body>
</html>
```

The page in Listing 29.14 enables you to add a new movie to the Movies database table. When the new movie is inserted, the Movies item is removed, and any pages dependent on the Movies item are dropped from the cache automatically.

LISTING 29.14   AddMovieKeyDependency.aspx

```
<%@ Page Language="C#" %>
<!DOCTYPE html PUBLIC "-//W3C//DTD XHTML 1.0 Transitional//EN"
    "http://www.w3.org/TR/xhtml1/DTD/xhtml1-transitional.dtd">
<script runat="server">

    protected void dtlMovie_ItemInserted(object sender,
➥DetailsViewInsertedEventArgs e)
    {
        Cache.Remove("Movies");
        Response.Redirect("~/MovieListKeyDependency.aspx");
    }
</script>
<html xmlns="http://www.w3.org/1999/xhtml" >
<head id="Head1" runat="server">
    <title>Add Movie Key Dependency</title>
</head>
<body>
    <form id="form1" runat="server">
    <div>

    <h1>Add Movie</h1>

    <asp:DetailsView
        id="dtlMovie"
        DefaultMode="Insert"
        DataSourceID="srcMovies"
        AutoGenerateRows="false"
        AutoGenerateInsertButton="true"
        Runat="server" OnItemInserted="dtlMovie_ItemInserted">
        <Fields>
        <asp:BoundField
            DataField="Title"
            HeaderText="Title:" />
        <asp:BoundField
            DataField="Director"
            HeaderText="Director:" />
        </Fields>
    </asp:DetailsView>
```

29

```
    <asp:SqlDataSource
        id="srcMovies"
        ConnectionString="<%$ ConnectionStrings:Movies %>"
        InsertCommand="INSERT Movies (Title, Director)
            VALUES (@Title, @Director)"
        Runat="server" />

    </div>
    </form>
</body>
</html>
```

Manipulating the Page Output Cache Programmatically

If you need more control over how ASP.NET Framework caches pages, then you can work directly with the HttpCachePolicy class. This class is exposed by the Response.Cache property.

The HttpCachePolicy class includes properties and methods that enable you to perform programmatically all the tasks that you can perform with the <%@ OutputCache %> directive. You also can use the methods of this class to manipulate the HTTP cache headers that are sent to proxy servers and browsers.

This class supports the following properties:

▶ **VaryByHeaders**—Gets the list of headers that are used to vary cache output.

▶ **VaryByParams**—Gets the list of query string and form parameters used to vary cache output.

The HttpCachePolicy class also supports the following methods:

▶ **AddValidationCallback**—Enables you to create a method called automatically before a page is retrieved from the cache.

▶ **AppendCacheExtension**—Enables you to add custom text to the Cache-Control HTTP header.

▶ **SetAllowResponseInBrowserHistory**—Enables you to prevent a page from appearing in the browser history cache.

▶ **SetCacheability**—Enables you to set the Cache-Control header and the server cache.

▶ **SetETag**—Enables you to set the ETag HTTP header.

▶ **SetETagFromFileDependencies**—Enables you to set the ETag HTTP header from the time stamps of all files on which the page is dependent.

▶ **SetExpires**—Enables you to set the Expires HTTP header.

- ▶ **SetLastModified**—Enables you to set the Last-Modified HTTP header.

- ▶ **SetLastModifiedFromFileDependencies**—Enables you to set the Last-Modified HTTP header from the time stamps of all files on which the page is dependent.

- ▶ **SetMaxAge**—Enables you to set the Cache-Control:max-age HTTP header.

- ▶ **SetNoServerCaching**—Enables you to disable web server caching.

- ▶ **SetNoStore**—Enables you to send a Cache-Control:no-store HTTP header.

- ▶ **SetNoTransform**—Enables you to send a Cache-Control:no-transform HTTP header.

- ▶ **SetOmitVaryStar**—Enables you to not send the vary:* HTTP header.

- ▶ **SetProxyMaxAge**—Enables you to set the Cache-Control:s-maxage HTTP header.

- ▶ **SetRevalidation**—Enables you to set the Cache-Control HTTP header to either must-revalidation or proxy-revalidate.

- ▶ **SetSlidingExpiration**—Enables you to set a sliding expiration policy.

- ▶ **SetValidUntilExpires**—Enables you to prevent a page from expiring from the web server cache when a browser sends a Cache-Control header.

- ▶ **SetVaryByCustom**—Enables you to set the string passed to the GetVaryByCustomString() method in the Global.asax file.

For example, the page in Listing 29.15 programmatically places a page in the output cache. The page is cached on the browser, proxy servers, and web server for 15 seconds.

LISTING 29.15   ProgramOutputCache.aspx

```
<%@ Page Language="C#" %>
<!DOCTYPE html PUBLIC "-//W3C//DTD XHTML 1.0 Transitional//EN"
    "http://www.w3.org/TR/xhtml1/DTD/xhtml1-transitional.dtd">
<script runat="server">

    void Page_Load()
    {
        Response.Cache.SetCacheability(HttpCacheability.Public);
        Response.Cache.SetExpires(DateTime.Now.AddSeconds(15));
        Response.Cache.SetMaxAge(TimeSpan.FromSeconds(15));
        Response.Cache.SetValidUntilExpires(true);
        Response.Cache.SetLastModified(DateTime.Now);
        Response.Cache.SetOmitVaryStar(true);
    }
</script>
<html xmlns="http://www.w3.org/1999/xhtml" >
<head id="Head1" runat="server">
    <title>Program OutputCache</title>
```

29

```
</head>
<body>
    <form id="form1" runat="server">
    <div>

    <%= DateTime.Now.ToString("T") %>

    <br /><br />
    <a href="ProgramOutputCache.aspx">Request this Page</a>

    </div>
    </form>
</body>
</html>
```

Clearly, it is more difficult to enable Page Output Caching programmatically than declaratively. You need to call many methods to cache a page in the same way as you can with a single <%@ OutputCache %> directive. However, programmatically manipulating the cache provides you with fine-grained control over the HTTP headers sent to proxy servers and browsers.

Creating Page Output Cache Profiles

Instead of configuring Page Output Caching for each page in an application, you can configure Page Output Caching in a web configuration file and apply the settings to multiple pages. You can create a Cache Profile. Creating Cache Profiles makes your website easier to manage.

For example, the web configuration file in Listing 29.16 contains the definition for a Cache Profile named Cache1Hour that caches a page for one hour.

LISTING 29.16   Web.Config

```
<?xml version="1.0"?>
<configuration>
  <system.web>
    <caching>
      <outputCacheSettings>
        <outputCacheProfiles>
          <add name="Cache1Hour" duration="3600" varyByParam="none" />
        </outputCacheProfiles>
      </outputCacheSettings>
    </caching>
  </system.web>
</configuration>
```

The page in Listing 29.17 uses the Cache1Hour profile. This profile is set with the `<%@ OutputCache %>` directive's CacheProfile attribute.

LISTING 29.17   OutputCacheProfile.aspx

```
<%@ Page Language="C#" %>
<%@ OutputCache CacheProfile="Cache1Hour" %>
<!DOCTYPE html PUBLIC "-//W3C//DTD XHTML 1.0 Transitional//EN"
  "http://www.w3.org/TR/xhtml1/DTD/xhtml1-transitional.dtd">
<html xmlns="http://www.w3.org/1999/xhtml" >
<head id="Head1" runat="server">
    <title>Output Cache Profile</title>
</head>
<body>
    <form id="form1" runat="server">
    <div>

    <%= DateTime.Now.ToString("T") %>

    </div>
    </form>
</body>
</html>
```

You can set the same caching properties in a Cache Profile as you can set in an individual page's `<%@ OutputCache %>` directive. For example, you can set varyByParam, varyByControl, varyByHeader, and even varyByCustom attributes in a Cache Profile.

> **NOTE**
>
> ASP.NET 4 introduces a new feature called *Extensible Output Caching*, which enables you to configure a custom output-cache provider that utilizes whatever storage medium you choose—local disks, cloud-based storage, and so on. To learn more about developing a custom output-cache provider, check out the MSDN website (http://msdn.microsoft.com).

29

Using Partial Page Caching

In the previous section of this chapter, you learned how to cache the entire output of a page. In this section, you learn how to take advantage of Partial Page Caching to cache particular regions of a page.

Partial Page Caching makes sense when a page contains both dynamic and static content. For example, you might want to cache a set of database records displayed in a page but not cache a random list of news items displayed in the same page.

In this section, you learn about two methods for enabling Partial Page Caching. You can use post-cache substitution to cache an entire page except for a particular region. You can use User Controls to cache particular regions in a page, but not the entire page.

Using Post-Cache Substitution

In some cases, you might want to cache an entire page except for one small area. For example, you might want to display the current username dynamically at the top of a page but cache the remainder of a page. In these cases, you can take advantage of a feature of ASP.NET Framework called *post-cache substitution*.

Post-cache substitution is used internally by the AdRotator control. Even when you use Page Output Caching to cache a page that contains an AdRotator control, the content rendered by the AdRotator control is not cached.

You can use post-cache substitution either declaratively or programmatically. If you want to use post-cache substitution declaratively, you can use the ASP.NET Substitution control. For example, the page in Listing 29.18 uses the Substitution control to display the current time on a page that has been output cached (see Figure 29.6).

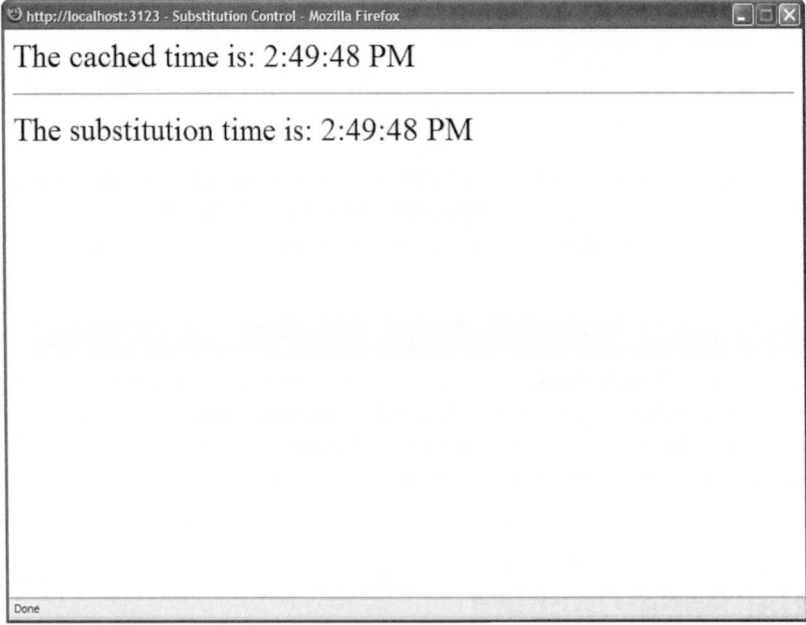

FIGURE 29.6   Using the **Substitution** control.

LISTING 29.18 SubstitutionControl.aspx

```
<%@ Page Language="C#" %>
<%@ OutputCache Duration="15" VaryByParam="none" %>
<!DOCTYPE html PUBLIC "-//W3C//DTD XHTML 1.0 Transitional//EN"
    "http://www.w3.org/TR/xhtml1/DTD/xhtml1-transitional.dtd">
<script runat="server">

    public static string GetTime(HttpContext context)
    {
        return DateTime.Now.ToString("T");
    }
</script>
<html xmlns="http://www.w3.org/1999/xhtml" >
<head id="Head1" runat="server">
    <title>Substitution Control</title>
</head>
<body>
    <form id="form1" runat="server">
    <div>

    The cached time is: <%= DateTime.Now.ToString("T") %>
    <hr />
    The substitution time is:
    <asp:Substitution
        id="Substitution1"
        MethodName="GetTime"
        Runat="server" />

    </div>
    </form>
</body>
</html>
```

In Listing 29.18, the time is displayed twice. The time displayed in the body of the page is output cached. The time displayed by the Substitution control is not cached.

The Substitution control has one important property: MethodName. The MethodName property accepts the name of a method defined in the page. The method must be a shared (static) method because an instance of the class is not created when the page is output cached.

Alternatively, you can use post-cache substitution programmatically by using the Response.WriteSubstitution() method. This method is illustrated in the page in Listing 29.19.

29

LISTING 29.19   ShowWriteSubstitution.aspx

```
<%@ Page Language="C#" %>
<%@ OutputCache Duration="15" VaryByParam="none" %>
<!DOCTYPE html PUBLIC "-//W3C//DTD XHTML 1.0 Transitional//EN"
    "http://www.w3.org/TR/xhtml1/DTD/xhtml1-transitional.dtd">
<script runat="server">

    public static string GetTime(HttpContext context)
    {
        return DateTime.Now.ToString("T");
    }
</script>
<html xmlns="http://www.w3.org/1999/xhtml" >
<head id="Head1" runat="server">
    <title>Show WriteSubstitution</title>
</head>
<body>
    <form id="form1" runat="server">
    <div>

    The cached time is: <%= DateTime.Now.ToString("T") %>
    <hr />
    The substitution time is:
    <% Response.WriteSubstitution(GetTime); %>

    </div>
    </form>
</body>
</html>
```

There are two advantages to using the WriteSubstitution() method. First, the method referenced by the WriteSubstitution() method does not have to be a method of the current class. The method can be either an instance or shared method on any class.

The second advantage of the WriteSubstitution() method is that you can use it within a custom control to perform post-cache substitutions. For example, the NewsRotator control in Listing 29.20 uses the WriteSubstitution() method when displaying a random news item. If you use this control in a page that has been output cached, the NewsRotator control continues to display news items randomly.

LISTING 29.20   NewsRotator.cs

```
using System;
using System.Data;
using System.Web;
```

```
using System.Web.UI;
using System.Web.UI.WebControls;
using System.Collections.Generic;

namespace myControls
{
    public class NewsRotator : WebControl
    {

        public static string GetNews(HttpContext context)
        {
            List<String> news = new List<string>();
            news.Add("Martians attack!");
            news.Add("Moon collides with earth!");
            news.Add("Life on Jupiter!");

            Random rnd = new Random();
            return news[rnd.Next(news.Count)];
        }

        protected override void RenderContents(HtmlTextWriter writer)
        {
            Context.Response.WriteSubstitution(GetNews);
        }

    }
}
```

> **NOTE**
>
> Building custom controls is discussed in detail in Chapter 36, "Building Custom Controls."

The book's website includes a page named ShowNewsRotator.aspx. If you open this page, all the content of the page is cached except for the random news item displayed by the NewsRotator control (see Figure 29.7).

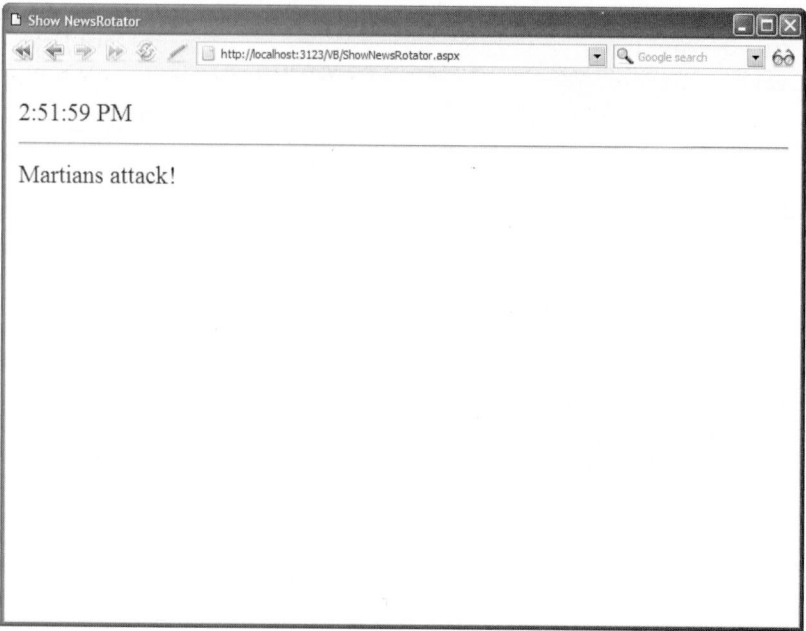

FIGURE 29.7   Displaying dynamic news items in a cached page.

When you use post-cache substitution (declaratively or programmatically) caching no longer happens beyond the web server. Using post-cache substitution causes a Cache-Control:no-cache HTTP header to be included in the HTTP response, which disables caching on proxy servers and browsers. This limitation is understandable because the substitution content must be generated dynamically with each page request.

Caching with a User Control

Using post-cache substitution is appropriate only when working with a string of text or HTML. If you need to perform more complex partial page caching, you should take advantage of User Controls.

You can cache the rendered contents of a User Control in memory in the same way as you can cache an ASP.NET page. When you add an <%@ OutputCache %> directive to a User Control, the rendered output of the User Control is cached.

> **NOTE**
>
> When you cache a User Control, the content is cached on the web server and not on any proxy servers or web browsers. When a web browser or proxy server caches a page, it always caches an entire page.

For example, the Movies User Control in Listing 29.21 displays all the rows from the Movies database table. Furthermore, it includes an `OutputCache` directive, which causes the contents of the User Control to be cached in memory for a maximum of 10 minutes (600 seconds).

LISTING 29.21   `Movies.ascx`

```
<%@ Control Language="C#" ClassName="Movies" %>
<%@ OutputCache Duration="600" VaryByParam="none" %>

User Control Time:
<%= DateTime.Now.ToString("T") %>

<asp:GridView
    id="grdMovies"
    DataSourceID="srcMovies"
    Runat="server" />

<asp:SqlDataSource
    id="srcMovies"
    ConnectionString="<%$ ConnectionStrings:Movies %>"
    SelectCommand="SELECT Title,Director FROM Movies"
    Runat="server" />
```

The User Control in Listing 29.21 displays the records from the Movies database table with a `GridView` control. It also displays the current time. Because the control includes an `OutputCache` directive, the entire rendered output of the control is cached in memory.

The page in Listing 29.22 includes the `Movies` User Control in the body of the page. It also displays the current time at the top of the page. When you refresh the page, the time displayed by the `Movies` control changes, but not the time displayed in the body of the page (see Figure 29.8).

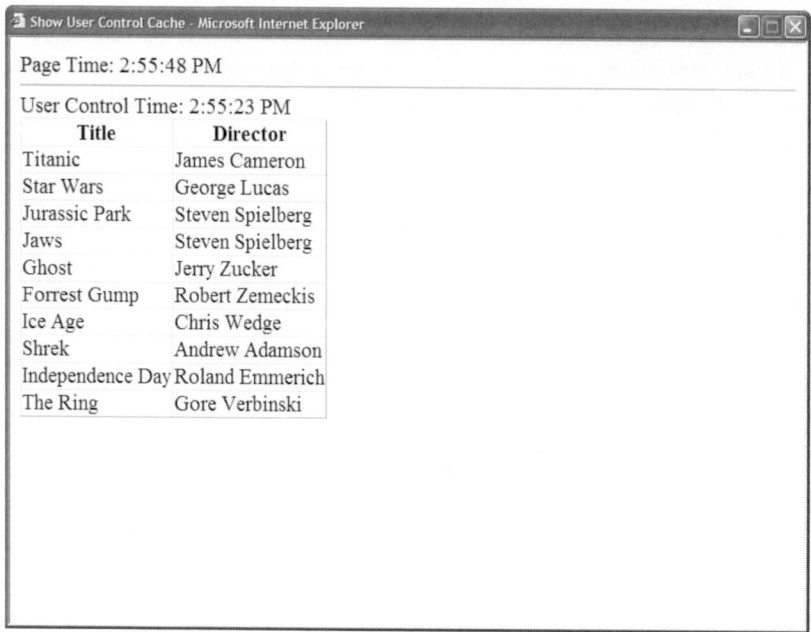

FIGURE 29.8   Caching the output of a User Control.

LISTING 29.22   ShowUserControlCache.aspx

```
<%@ Page Language="C#" %>
<%@ Register TagPrefix="user" TagName="Movies" Src="~/Movies.ascx" %>
<!DOCTYPE html PUBLIC "-//W3C//DTD XHTML 1.1//EN"
 "http://www.w3.org/TR/xhtml11/DTD/xhtml11.dtd">
<html xmlns="http://www.w3.org/1999/xhtml" >
<head id="Head1" runat="server">
    <title>Show User Control Cache</title>
</head>
<body>
    <form id="form1" runat="server">
    <div>

    Page Time:
    <%= DateTime.Now.ToString("T") %>
    <hr />

    <user:Movies
        id="Movies1"
        Runat="server" />
```

```
        </div>
      </form>
  </body>
</html>
```

You can use the following attributes with an `<%@ OutputCache %>` directive declared in a User Control:

- ▶ **Duration**—The amount of time in seconds that the rendered content of the User Control is cached.

- ▶ **Shared**—Enables you to share the same cached version of the User Control across multiple pages.

- ▶ **VaryByParam**—Enables you to create different cached versions of a User Control, depending on the values of one or more query string or form parameters. You can specify multiple parameters by supplying a semicolon-delimited list of query string or form parameter names.

- ▶ **VaryByControl**—Enables you to create different cached versions of a User Control, depending on the value of a control. You can specify multiple controls by supplying a semicolon-delimited list of control IDs.

- ▶ **VaryByCustom**—Enables you to specify a custom string used by a custom cache policy. (You also can supply the special value browser, which causes different cached versions of the control to be created when the type and major version of the browser differs.)

Because each User Control that you add to a page can have different caching policies, and because you can nest User Controls with different caching policies, you can build pages that have fiendishly complex caching policies. There is nothing wrong with doing this; you should take advantage of this caching functionality whenever possible to improve the performance of your applications.

> **WARNING**
>
> Be careful when setting properties of a cached User Control. If you attempt to set the property of a User Control programmatically when the content of the control is served from the cache, you get a `NullReference` exception. Before setting a property of a cached control, first check whether the control actually exists like this:
>
> ```
> if (myControl != null)
>     myControl.SomeProperty = "some value";
> ```

29

Sharing a User Control Output Cache

By default, instances of the same User Control located on different pages do not share the same cache. For example, if you add the same Movies User Control to more than one page, the contents of each user control is cached separately.

If you want to cache the same User Control content across multiple pages, you need to include the Shared attribute when adding the <%@ OutputCache %> directive to a User Control. For example, the modified Movies User Control in Listing 29.23 includes the Shared attribute.

LISTING 29.23   SharedMovies.ascx

```
<%@ Control Language="C#" ClassName="SharedMovies" %>
<%@ OutputCache Duration="600" VaryByParam="none" Shared="true" %>

User Control Time:
<%= DateTime.Now.ToString() %>

<asp:GridView
    id="grdMovies"
    DataSourceID="srcMovies"
    Runat="server" />

<asp:SqlDataSource
    id="srcMovies"
    ConnectionString="<%$ ConnectionStrings:Movies %>"
    SelectCommand="SELECT Title,Director FROM Movies"
    Runat="server" />
```

Using the Shared attribute is almost always a good idea. You can save a significant amount of server memory by taking advantage of this attribute.

Manipulating a User Control Cache Programmatically

When you include an <%@ OutputCache %> directive in a User Control, you can modify programmatically how the User Control is cached. The User Control CachePolicy property exposes an instance of the ControlCachePolicy class, which supports the following properties:

- ▶ **Cached**—Enables you to enable or disable caching.

- ▶ **Dependency**—Enables you to get or set a cache dependency for the User Control.

- ▶ **Duration**—Enables you to get or set the amount of time (in seconds) that content is cached.

- **SupportsCaching**—Enables you to check whether the control supports caching.

- **VaryByControl**—Enables you to create different cached versions of the control, depending on the value of a control.

- **VaryByParams**—Enables you to create different cached versions of the control, depending on the value of a query string or form parameter.

The ControlCachePolicy class also supports the following methods:

- **SetExpires**—Enables you to set the expiration time for the cache.

- **SetSlidingExpiration**—Enables you to set a sliding expiration cache policy.

- **SetVaryByCustom**—Enables you to specify a custom string used by a custom cache policy. (You also can supply the special value browser, which causes different cached versions of the control to be created when the type and major version of the browser differs.)

For example, the User Control in Listing 29.24 uses a sliding expiration policy of 1 minute. When you specify a sliding expiration policy, a User Control is cached just as long as you continue to request the User Control within the specified interval of time.

LISTING 29.24   SlidingUserCache.ascx

```
<%@ Control Language="C#" ClassName="SlidingUserCache" %>
<%@ OutputCache Duration="10" VaryByParam="none" %>
<script runat="server">

    void Page_Load()
    {
        CachePolicy.SetSlidingExpiration(true);
        CachePolicy.Duration = TimeSpan.FromMinutes(1);
    }

</script>


User Control Time:
<%= DateTime.Now.ToString("T") %>
```

The book's website includes a page named ShowSlidingUserCache.aspx, which contains the SlidingUserCache control. If you keep requesting this page, and do not let more than 1 minute pass between requests, the User Control isn't dropped from the cache.

29

Creating a User Control Cache File Dependency

You can use the `CacheControlPolicy.Dependency` property to create a dependency between a cached User Control and a file (or set of files) on the file system. When the file is modified, the User Control is dropped from the cache automatically and reloaded with the next page request.

For example, the User Control in Listing 29.25 displays all the movies from the `Movies.xml` file in a `GridView` control. The User Control includes a `Page_Load()` handler that creates a dependency on the `Movies.xml` file.

LISTING 29.25   `MovieFileDependency.ascx`

```
<%@ Control Language="C#" ClassName="MovieFileDependency" %>
<%@ OutputCache Duration="9999" VaryByParam="none" %>
<script runat="server">

    void Page_Load()
    {
        CacheDependency depend = new CacheDependency(MapPath("~/Movies.xml"));
        this.CachePolicy.Dependency = depend;
    }
</script>
User Control Time:
<%= DateTime.Now.ToString("T") %>
<hr />

<asp:GridView
    id="grdMovies"
    DataSourceID="srcMovies"
    Runat="server" />

<asp:XmlDataSource
    id="srcMovies"
    DataFile="Movies.xml"
    Runat="server" />
```

The code download on the website that accompanies this book includes a page named `ShowMovieFileDependency`, which displays the `MovieFileDependency` User Control (see Figure 29.9). If you open the page, the User Control is automatically cached until you modify the `Movies.xml` file.

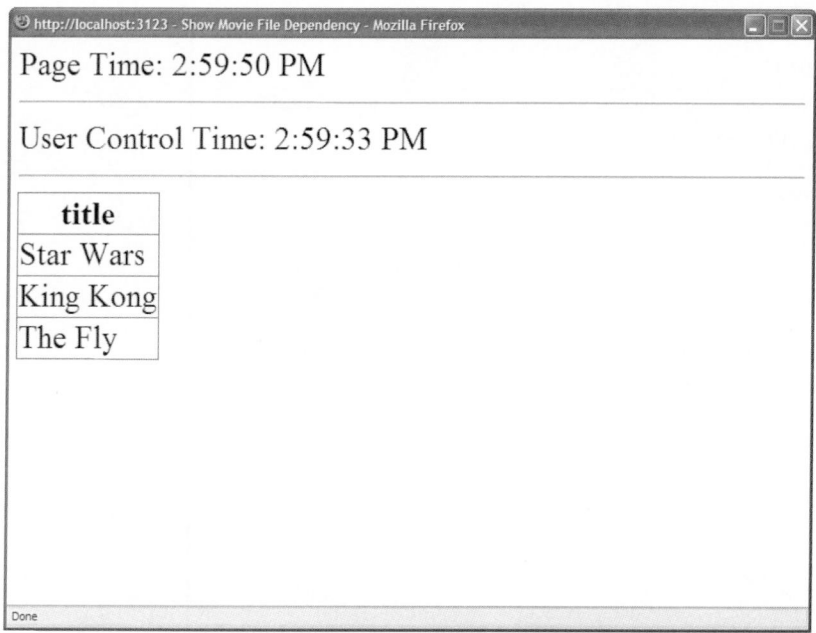

FIGURE 29.9   Displaying a User Control with a file dependency.

Caching Dynamically Loaded User Controls

You can load a User Control dynamically by using the `Page.LoadControl()` method. You can cache dynamically loaded User Controls in the same way that you can cache User Controls declared in a page. If a User Control includes an `<%@ OutputCache %>` directive, the User Control will be cached regardless of whether the control was added to a page declaratively or programmatically.

However, you need to be aware that when a cached User Control is loaded dynamically, ASP.NET Framework automatically wraps the User Control in an instance of the `PartialCachingControl` class. Therefore, you need to cast the control returned by the `Page.LoadControl()` method to an instance of the `PartialCachingControl` class.

For example, the page in Listing 29.26 dynamically adds the `Movies` User Control in its `Page_Load()` event handler. The `Page_Load()` method overrides the default cache duration specified in the User Control's `<%@ OutputCache %>` directive. The cache duration is changed to 15 seconds (see Figure 29.10).

29

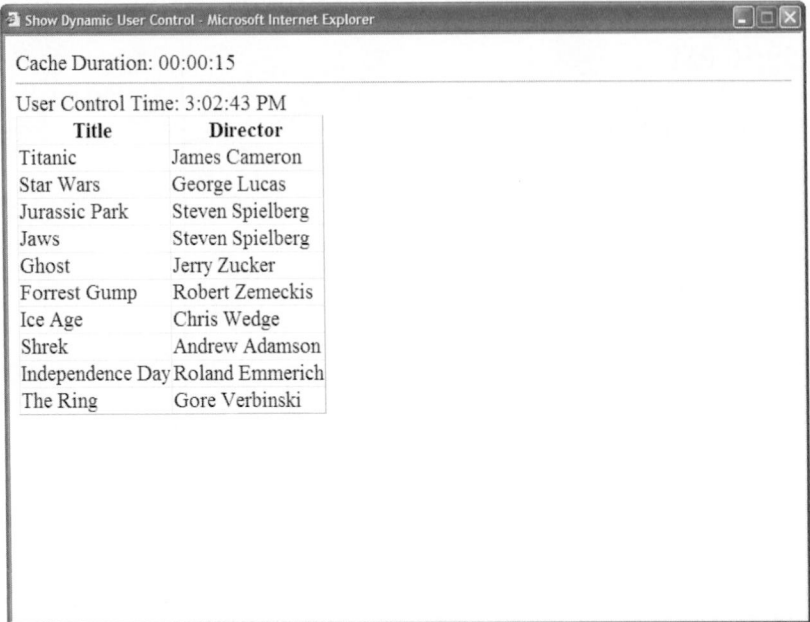

FIGURE 29.10   Programmatically caching a User Control.

LISTING 29.26   ShowDynamicUserControl.aspx

```
<%@ Page Language="C#" %>
<!DOCTYPE html PUBLIC "-//W3C//DTD XHTML 1.1//EN"
    "http://www.w3.org/TR/xhtml11/DTD/xhtml11.dtd">
<script runat="server">

    void Page_Load()
    {
        // Load the control
        PartialCachingControl cacheMe =
         (PartialCachingControl)Page.LoadControl("Movies.ascx");

        // Change cache duration to 15 seconds
        cacheMe.CachePolicy.SetExpires(DateTime.Now.AddSeconds(15));

        // Add control to page
        PlaceHolder1.Controls.Add(cacheMe);

        // Display control cache duration
        lblCacheDuration.Text = cacheMe.CachePolicy.Duration.ToString();
    }
</script>
```

```
<html xmlns="http://www.w3.org/1999/xhtml" >
<head id="Head1" runat="server">
    <title>Show Dynamic User Control</title>
</head>
<body>
    <form id="form1" runat="server">
    <div>

    Cache Duration:
    <asp:Label
        id="lblCacheDuration"
        Runat="server" />
    <hr />

    <asp:PlaceHolder
        id="PlaceHolder1"
        Runat="server" />

    </div>
    </form>
</body>
</html>
```

In Listing 29.26, the default cache duration is modified by modifying the PartialCachingControl's CachePolicy property. This property returns an instance of the same ControlCachePolicy class described in the two previous sections of this chapter.

You can refer to the User Control contained with an instance of the PartialCachingControl class by using the class's CachedControl property. Normally, this property returns the value Nothing (null) because when the User Control is cached, it is never actually created.

Using DataSource Caching

Instead of caching at the page or User Control level, you can cache at the level of a DataSource control. Three of the four standard ASP.NET DataSource controls—SqlDataSource, ObjectDataSource, and XmlDataSource—include properties that enable you to cache the data that the DataSource control represents. (The LinqDataSource control does not support caching.)

One advantage of using the DataSource controls when caching is that the DataSource controls can reload data automatically when the data is updated. For example, if you use a SqlDataSource control to both select and update a set of database records, the SqlDataSource control is smart enough to reload the cached data after an update.

The `DataSource` controls are also smart enough to share the same data across multiple pages. For example, when using the `SqlDataSource` control, a unique entry is created in the `Cache` object for each combination of the following `SqlDataSource` properties: `SelectCommand`, `SelectParameters`, and `ConnectionString`. If these properties are identical for two `SqlDataSource` controls located on two different pages, the two controls share the same cached data.

> **NOTE**
>
> DataSource caching does not work with LINQ to SQL queries. To learn about caching LINQ to SQL queries, see Chapter 20, "Data Access with LINQ to SQL."

In this section, you learn how to use the `SqlDataSource`, `ObjectDataSource`, and `XmlDataSource` controls to cache data. You learn how to set either an absolute or sliding expiration policy. Finally, you learn how to create a cache key dependency that you can use to expire the cache programmatically.

Using an Absolute Cache Expiration Policy

When you use an absolute cache expiration policy, the data that a `DataSource` represents is cached in memory for a particular duration of time. Using an absolute cache expiration policy is useful when you know that your data does not change that often. For example, if you know that the records contained in a database table are modified only once a day, there is no reason to keep grabbing the same records each and every time someone requests a web page.

> **WARNING**
>
> When caching with the `SqlDataSource` control, the `SqlDataSource` control's `DataSourceMode` property must be set to the value `DataSet` (the default value) rather than `DataReader`.

The page in Listing 29.27 displays a list of movies cached in memory. The page uses a `SqlDataSource` control to cache the data.

LISTING 29.27   `DataSourceAbsoluteCache.aspx`

```
<%@ Page Language="C#" %>
<!DOCTYPE html PUBLIC "-//W3C//DTD XHTML 1.1//EN"
   "http://www.w3.org/TR/xhtml11/DTD/xhtml11.dtd">
<html xmlns="http://www.w3.org/1999/xhtml" >
<head id="Head1" runat="server">
    <title>DataSource Absolute Cache</title>
</head>
```

```
<body>
    <form id="form1" runat="server">
    <div>

    <asp:GridView
        id="grdMovies"
        DataSourceID="srcMovies"
        Runat="server" />

    <asp:SqlDataSource
        id="srcMovies"
        EnableCaching="True"
        CacheDuration="3600"
        SelectCommand="SELECT * FROM Movies"
        ConnectionString="<%$ ConnectionStrings:Movies %>"
        Runat="server" />

    </div>
    </form>
</body>
</html>
```

In Listing 29.27, two properties of the SqlDataSource control related to caching are set. First, the EnableCaching property is set to the value True. Next, the CacheDuration property is set to the value 3,600 seconds (1 hour). The movies are cached in memory for a maximum of 1 hour. If you don't supply a value for the CacheDuration property, the default value is Infinite.

You need to understand that there is no guarantee that the SqlDataSource control will cache data for the amount of time specified by its CacheDuration property. Behind the scenes, DataSource controls use the Cache object for caching. This object supports scavenging. When memory resources become low, the Cache object automatically removes items from the cache.

You can test whether the page in Listing 29.27 is working by opening the page and temporarily turning off your database server. You can turn off SQL Server Express by opening the SQL Configuration Manager located in the Microsoft SQL Server 2008 program group and stopping the SQL Server service (see Figure 29.11). If you refresh the page, the data displays even though the database server is unavailable.

29

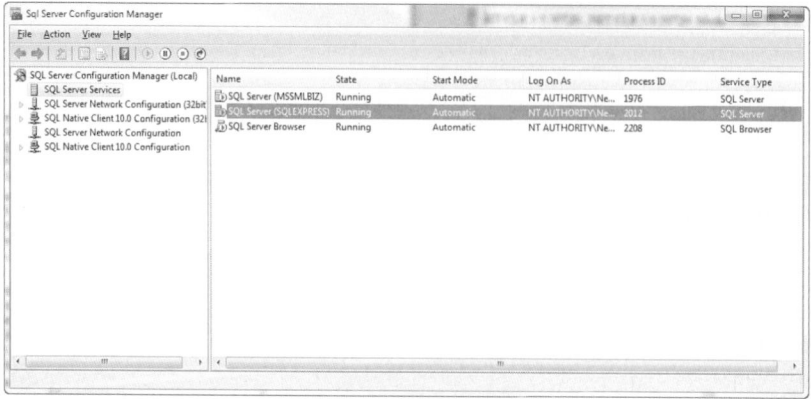

FIGURE 29.11   The SQL Configuration Manager.

Using a Sliding Cache Expiration Policy

If you need to cache a lot of data, it makes more sense to use a sliding expiration policy rather than an absolute expiration policy. When you use a sliding expiration policy, data remains in the cache as long as the data continues to be requested within a certain interval.

For example, imagine that you have been asked to rewrite the Amazon website with ASP.NET. The Amazon website displays information on billions of books. You couldn't cache all this book information in memory. However, if you use a sliding expiration policy, you can cache the most frequently requested books automatically.

The page in Listing 29.28 illustrates how you can enable a sliding cache expiration policy. The cache duration is set to 15 seconds. As long as no more than 15 seconds pass before you request the page, the movies are kept cached in memory.

LISTING 29.28   DataSourceSlidingCache.aspx

```
<%@ Page Language="C#" %>
<!DOCTYPE html PUBLIC "-//W3C//DTD XHTML 1.1//EN"
    "http://www.w3.org/TR/xhtml11/DTD/xhtml11.dtd">
<script runat="server">

    protected void srcMovies_Selecting(object sender,
➥SqlDataSourceSelectingEventArgs e)
    {
        lblMessage.Text = "Selecting data from database";
    }
```

```
    </script>
<html xmlns="http://www.w3.org/1999/xhtml" >
<head id="Head1" runat="server">
    <title>DataSource Sliding Cache</title>
</head>
<body>
    <form id="form1" runat="server">
    <div>

    <p>
    <asp:Label
        id="lblMessage"
        EnableViewState="false"
        Runat="server" />
    </p>

    <asp:GridView
        id="grdMovies"
        DataSourceID="srcMovies"
        Runat="server" />

    <asp:SqlDataSource
        id="srcMovies"
        EnableCaching="True"
        CacheExpirationPolicy="Sliding"
        CacheDuration="15"
        SelectCommand="SELECT * FROM Movies"
        ConnectionString="<%$ ConnectionStrings:Movies %>"
        OnSelecting="srcMovies_Selecting"
        Runat="server" />

    </div>
    </form>
</body>
</html>
```

The page in Listing 29.28 includes a srcMovies_Selecting() event handler. This handler is called only when the movies are retrieved from the database rather than from memory. In other words, you can use this event handler to detect when the movies are dropped from the cache (see Figure 29.12).

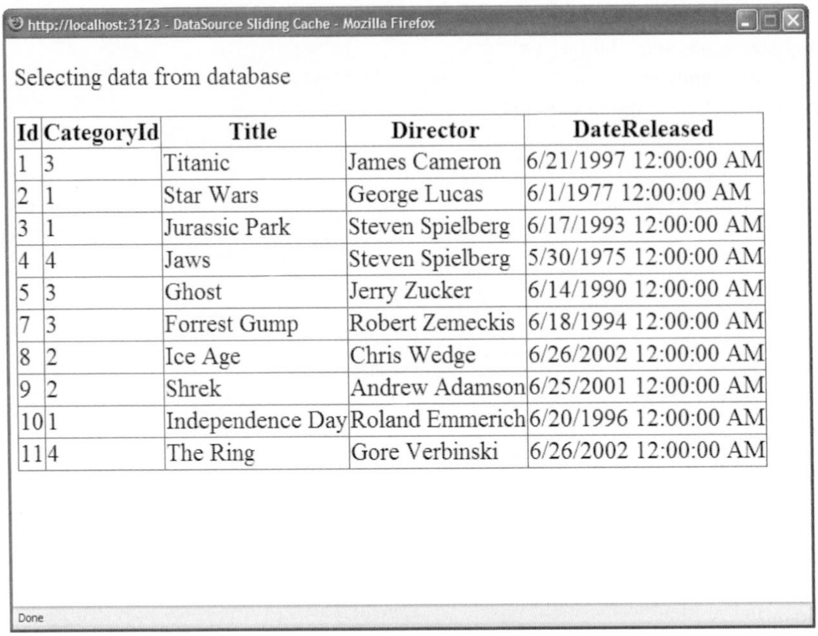

FIGURE 29.12   Using a sliding expiration policy with a DataSource control.

Caching with the ObjectDataSource Control

The ObjectDataSource control supports the same caching properties as the SqlDataSource control. You can cache the data that an ObjectDataSource control represents by setting its EnableCaching, CacheDuration, and (optionally) CacheExpirationPolicy properties.

> **NOTE**
>
> Multiple ObjectDataSource controls can share the same cached data. To share the same cache, the ObjectDataSource controls must have identical TypeName, SelectMethod, and SelectParameters properties.

For example, the page in Listing 29.29 uses an ObjectDataSource control to represent the Movies database table. The ObjectDataSource is bound to a component named Movie that includes a method named GetMovies() that returns all the records from the Movies database table.

LISTING 29.29 ShowObjectDataSourceCaching.aspx

```
<%@ Page Language="C#" %>
<!DOCTYPE html PUBLIC "-//W3C//DTD XHTML 1.0 Transitional//EN"
    "http://www.w3.org/TR/xhtml1/DTD/xhtml1-transitional.dtd">
<script runat="server">

    protected void srcMovies_Selecting(object sender,
➥ObjectDataSourceSelectingEventArgs e)
    {
        lblMessage.Text = "Selecting data from component";
    }
</script>
<html xmlns="http://www.w3.org/1999/xhtml" >
<head id="Head1" runat="server">
    <title>Show ObjectDataSource Caching</title>
</head>
<body>
    <form id="form1" runat="server">
    <div>

    <asp:Label
        id="lblMessage"
        EnableViewState="false"
        Runat="server" />
    <br /><br />

    <asp:GridView
        id="grdMovies"
        DataSourceID="srcMovies"
        Runat="server" />

    <asp:ObjectDataSource
        id="srcMovies"
        EnableCaching="true"
        CacheDuration="15"
        TypeName="Movie"
        SelectMethod="GetMovies"
        OnSelecting="srcMovies_Selecting"
        Runat="server" />

    </div>
    </form>
</body>
</html>
```

29

The ObjectDataSource control in Listing 29.29 includes an event handler for its Selecting event. The event handler displays a message in a Label control. Because the Selecting event is not raised when data is retrieved from the cache, you can use this method to determine when data is retrieved from the cache or the Movie component.

The Movie component is contained in Listing 29.30.

LISTING 29.30 Movie.cs

```
using System;
using System.Data;
using System.Data.SqlClient;
using System.Web.Configuration;

public class Movie
{
    public static DataTable GetMovies()
    {
        string conString =
        WebConfigurationManager.ConnectionStrings["Movies"].ConnectionString;
        SqlDataAdapter dad =
            new SqlDataAdapter("SELECT Title,Director FROM Movies", conString);
        DataTable movies = new DataTable();
        dad.Fill(movies);
        return movies;
    }
}
```

The GetMovies() method returns a DataTable. When using the ObjectDataSource control, you can cache certain types of data but not others. For example, you can cache data represented with a DataSet, DataTable, DataView, or collection. However, you cannot cache data represented by a DataReader. If you attempt to bind to a method that returns a DataReader, an exception is thrown.

Caching with the XmlDataSource Control

Unlike the SqlDataSource and ObjectDataSource controls, the XmlDataSource control has caching enabled by default. The XmlDataSource automatically creates a file dependency on the XML file that it represents. If the XML file is modified, the XmlDataSource control automatically reloads the modified XML file.

For example, the page in Listing 29.31 contains an XmlDataSource control that represents the Movies.xml file. If you modify the Movies.xml file, the contents of the files automatically reload.

LISTING 29.31   ShowXmlDataSourceCaching.aspx

```
<%@ Page Language="C#" %>
<!DOCTYPE html PUBLIC "-//W3C//DTD XHTML 1.0 Transitional//EN"
 "http://www.w3.org/TR/xhtml1/DTD/xhtml1-transitional.dtd">
<html xmlns="http://www.w3.org/1999/xhtml" >
<head id="Head1" runat="server">
    <title>Show XmlDataSource Caching</title>
</head>
<body>
    <form id="form1" runat="server">
    <div>

    <asp:GridView
        id="grdMovies"
        DataSourceID="srcMovies"
        Runat="server" />

    <asp:XmlDataSource
        id="srcMovies"
        DataFile="Movies.xml"
        Runat="server" />

    </div>
    </form>
</body>
</html>
```

Creating a DataSource Control Key Dependency

Imagine that your web application has multiple pages that display different sets of records from the Movies database table; however, you have one page that enables a user to enter a new movie. In that case, you need some method of signaling to all your DataSource controls that the Movies database table has changed.

You can create a key dependency between the DataSource controls in your application and an item in the cache. That way, if you remove the item from the cache, all the DataSource controls reload their data.

The page in Listing 29.32 contains a SqlDataSource control that displays the contents of the Movies database table. The SqlDataSource caches its data for an infinite duration.

29

LISTING 29.32   DataSourceKeyDependency.aspx

```
<%@ Page Language="C#" %>
<!DOCTYPE html PUBLIC "-//W3C//DTD XHTML 1.1//EN"
    "http://www.w3.org/TR/xhtml11/DTD/xhtml11.dtd">
<script runat="server">

    protected void srcMovies_Selecting(object sender,
➥SqlDataSourceSelectingEventArgs e)
    {
        lblMessage.Text = "Selecting data from database";
    }
</script>


<html xmlns="http://www.w3.org/1999/xhtml" >
<head id="Head1" runat="server">
    <title>DataSource Key Dependency</title>
</head>
<body>
    <form id="form1" runat="server">
    <div>

    <p>
    <asp:Label
        id="lblMessage"
        EnableViewState="false"
        Runat="server" />
    </p>

    <asp:GridView
        id="grdMovies"
        DataSourceID="srcMovies"
        Runat="server" />

    <asp:SqlDataSource
        id="srcMovies"
        EnableCaching="True"
        CacheDuration="Infinite"
        CacheKeyDependency="MovieKey"
        SelectCommand="SELECT * FROM Movies"
        ConnectionString="<%$ ConnectionStrings:Movies %>"
        OnSelecting="srcMovies_Selecting"
        Runat="server" />

    <br /><br />
```

```
        <a href="AddMovieDataSourceKeyDependency.aspx">Add Movie</a>

    </div>
    </form>
</body>
</html>
```

The SqlDataSource control in Listing 29.32 includes a CacheKeyDependency property that has the value MovieKey. This property creates a dependency between the DataSource control's cached data and an item in the cache named MovieKey.

The Global.asax file in Listing 29.33 creates the initial MovieKey cache item. The value of the cache item doesn't really matter. In Listing 29.33, the MovieKey cache item is set to the current date and time.

LISTING 29.33   Global.asax

```
<%@ Application Language="C#" %>
<script runat="server">

    void Application_Start(object sender, EventArgs e)
    {
        HttpContext context = HttpContext.Current;
        context.Cache.Insert(
            "MovieKey",
            DateTime.Now,
            null,
            DateTime.MaxValue,
            Cache.NoSlidingExpiration,
            CacheItemPriority.NotRemovable,
            null);
    }
</script>
```

The page in Listing 29.34 contains a DetailsView control that enables you to insert a new record. The DetailsView control's ItemInserted event is handled. When you insert a new record, the MovieKey item is reinserted into the cache, and every DataSource control that is dependent on this key reloads automatically.

29

LISTING 29.34   AddMovieDataSourceKeyDependency.aspx

```
<%@ Page Language="C#" %>
<!DOCTYPE html PUBLIC "-//W3C//DTD XHTML 1.0 Transitional//EN"
    "http://www.w3.org/TR/xhtml1/DTD/xhtml1-transitional.dtd">
<script runat="server">

    protected void dtlMovie_ItemInserted(object sender,
➥DetailsViewInsertedEventArgs e)
    {
        Cache.Insert("MovieKey", DateTime.Now);
        Response.Redirect("~/DataSourceKeyDependency.aspx");
    }
</script>
<html xmlns="http://www.w3.org/1999/xhtml" >
<head id="Head1" runat="server">
    <title>Add Movie Key Dependency</title>
</head>
<body>
    <form id="form1" runat="server">
    <div>

    <h1>Add Movie</h1>

    <asp:DetailsView
        id="dtlMovie"
        DefaultMode="Insert"
        DataSourceID="srcMovies"
        AutoGenerateRows="false"
        AutoGenerateInsertButton="true"
        OnItemInserted="dtlMovie_ItemInserted"
        Runat="server">
        <Fields>
        <asp:BoundField
            DataField="Title"
            HeaderText="Title:" />
        <asp:BoundField
            DataField="Director"
            HeaderText="Director:" />
        </Fields>
    </asp:DetailsView>

    <asp:SqlDataSource
        id="srcMovies"
```

```
        ConnectionString="<%$ ConnectionStrings:Movies %>"
        InsertCommand="INSERT Movies (Title, Director)
            VALUES (@Title, @Director)"
        Runat="server" />

    </div>
    </form>
</body>
</html>
```

Using Data Caching

Behind the scenes, all the various caching mechanisms included in ASP.NET Framework use the Cache object. In other words, the Cache object is the fundamental mechanism for all caching in ASP.NET Framework.

One instance of the Cache object is created for each ASP.NET application. Any items you add to the cache can be accessed by any other page, control, or component contained in the same application (virtual directory).

In this section, you learn how to use the properties and methods of the Cache object. You learn how to add items to the cache, set cache expiration policies, and create cache item dependencies.

Using the Cache Application Programming Interface

The Cache object exposes the main application programming interface for caching. This object supports the following properties:

- ▶ **Count**—Represents the number of items in the cache.

- ▶ **EffectivePrivateBytesLimit**—Represents the size of the cache in kilobytes.

The Cache object also supports the following methods:

- ▶ **Add**—Enables you to add a new item to the cache. If the item already exists, this method fails.

- ▶ **Get**—Enables you to return a particular item from the cache.

- ▶ **GetEnumerator**—Enables you to iterate through all the items in the cache.

- ▶ **Insert**—Enables you to insert a new item into the cache. If the item already exists, this method replaces it.

- ▶ **Remove**—Enables you to remove an item from the cache.

For example, the page in Listing 29.35 displays all the items currently contained in the cache (see Figure 29.13).

29

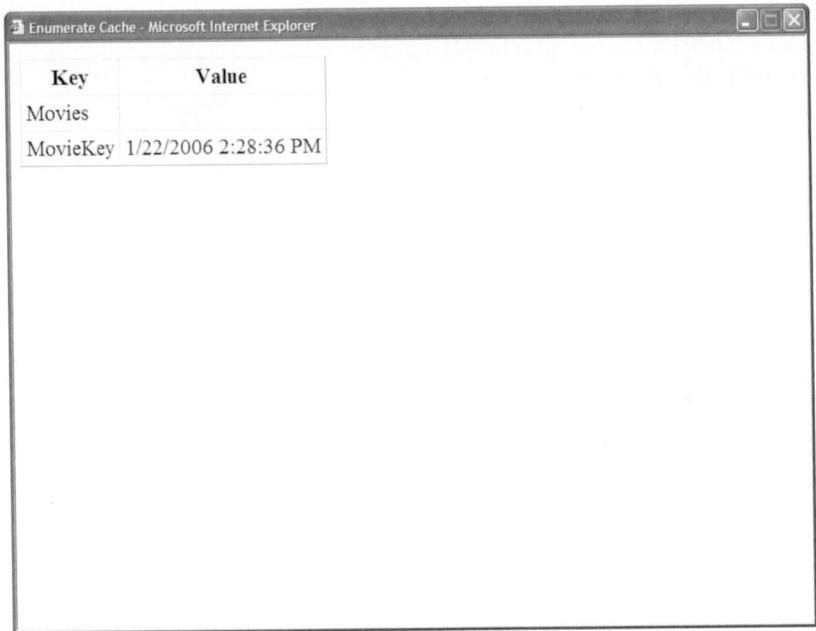

FIGURE 29.13   Displaying the cache's contents.

LISTING 29.35   EnumerateCache.aspx

```
<%@ Page Language="C#" %>
<!DOCTYPE html PUBLIC "-//W3C//DTD XHTML 1.0 Transitional//EN"
    "http://www.w3.org/TR/xhtml1/DTD/xhtml1-transitional.dtd">
<script runat="server">

    public class CacheItem
    {
        private string _key;
        private object _value;

        public string Key
        {
            get { return _key; }
        }

        public string Value
        {
            get { return _value.ToString(); }
        }
```

```
        public CacheItem(string key, object value)
        {
            _key = key;
            _value = value;
        }
    }

    void Page_Load()
    {
        ArrayList items = new ArrayList();
        foreach (DictionaryEntry item in Cache)
            items.Add(new CacheItem(item.Key.ToString(),item.Value));

        grdCache.DataSource = items;
        grdCache.DataBind();
    }
</script>
<html xmlns="http://www.w3.org/1999/xhtml" >
<head id="Head1" runat="server">
    <style type="text/css">
        .grid td, .grid th
        {
            padding:5px;
        }
    </style>
    <title>Enumerate Cache</title>
</head>
<body>
    <form id="form1" runat="server">
    <div>

    <asp:GridView
        id="grdCache"
        CssClass="grid"
        Runat="server" />

    </div>
    </form>
</body>
</html>
```

29

The page in Listing 29.35 displays only items that have been added to the cache by the methods of the Cache object. For example, it does not display a list of pages that have been output cached. Output cached pages are stored in the internal cache (the secret cache maintained by the ASP.NET Framework).

Adding Items to the Cache

You can add items to the cache by using the `Insert()` method. There are several over-loaded versions of the `Insert()` method. The maximally overloaded version of the `Insert()` method accepts the following parameters:

▶ **key**—Enables you to specify the name of the new item.

▶ **value**—Enables you to specify the value of the new item.

▶ **dependencies**—Enables you to specify one or more cache dependencies, such as a file, key, or SQL dependency.

▶ **absoluteExpiration**—Enables you to specify an absolute expiration time for the cached item. If you don't need to specify a value for this property, use the static field `Cache.NoAbsoluteExpiration`.

▶ **slidingExpiration**—Enables you to specify a sliding expiration interval for the cached item. If you don't need to specify a value for this property, use the static field `Cache.NoSlidingExpiration`.

▶ **priority**—Enables you to specify the priority of the cached item. Possible values are `AboveNormal`, `BelowNormal`, `Default`, `High`, `Low`, `Normal`, and `NotRemovable`.

▶ **onRemoveCallback**—Enables you to specify a method called automatically before the item is removed from the cache.

When using the cache, you need to understand that items that you add to the cache might not be there when you attempt to retrieve the item in the future. The cache supports scavenging. When memory resources become low, items are automatically evicted from the cache.

Before using any item that you retrieve from the cache, you should always check whether the item is `Nothing` (null). If an item has been removed, you retrieve `Nothing` when you attempt to retrieve it from the cache in the future. You can add almost any object to the cache. For example, you can add custom components, `DataSets`, `DataTables`, `ArrayLists`, and `Lists` to the cache.

You shouldn't add items to the cache that depend on an external resource. For example, it does not make sense to add a `SqlDataReader` or a `FileStream` to the cache. When using a `SqlDataReader`, you need to copy the contents of the `SqlDataReader` into a static representation such as an `ArrayList` or `List` collection.

Adding Items with an Absolute Expiration Policy

When you insert items in the cache, you can specify a time when the items expire. If you want an item to remain in the cache for an extended period of time, you should always specify an expiration time for the item.

The page in Listing 29.36 illustrates how you can add an item to the cache with an absolute expiration policy. The item is added to the cache for 1 hour.

LISTING 29.36   ShowAbsoluteExpiration.aspx

```
<%@ Page Language="C#" Trace="true" %>
<%@ Import Namespace="System.Data" %>
<%@ Import Namespace="System.Data.SqlClient" %>
<%@ Import Namespace="System.Web.Configuration" %>
<!DOCTYPE html PUBLIC "-//W3C//DTD XHTML 1.0 Transitional//EN"
    "http://www.w3.org/TR/xhtml1/DTD/xhtml1-transitional.dtd">
<script runat="server">

    void Page_Load()
    {
        // Get movies from Cache
        DataTable movies = (DataTable)Cache["Movies"];

        // If movies not in cache, recreate movies
        if (movies == null)
        {
            movies = GetMoviesFromDB();
            Cache.Insert("Movies", movies, null,
              DateTime.Now.AddHours(1), Cache.NoSlidingExpiration);
        }

        grdMovies.DataSource = movies;
        grdMovies.DataBind();
    }

    private DataTable GetMoviesFromDB()
    {
        Trace.Warn("Getting movies from database");
        string conString =
          WebConfigurationManager.ConnectionStrings["Movies"].ConnectionString;
        SqlDataAdapter dad =
            new SqlDataAdapter("SELECT Title,Director FROM Movies", conString);
        DataTable movies = new DataTable();
        dad.Fill(movies);
        return movies;
    }
</script>
<html xmlns="http://www.w3.org/1999/xhtml" >
<head id="Head1" runat="server">
    <title>Show Absolute Expiration</title>
</head>
<body>
    <form id="form1" runat="server">
    <div>
```

29

```
    <asp:GridView
        id="grdMovies"
        Runat="server" />

    </div>
    </form>
</body>
</html>
```

The first time the page in Listing 29.36 is requested, nothing is retrieved from the cache. In that case, a new DataTable is created that represents the Movies database table. The DataTable is inserted into the cache. The next time the page is requested, the DataTable can be retrieved from the cache, and there is no need to access the database.

The DataTable remains in the cache for 1 hour or until memory pressures force the DataTable to be evicted from the cache. In either case, the logic of the page dictates that the DataTable will be added back to the cache when the page is next requested.

Tracing is enabled for the page in Listing 29.36 so that you can see when the Movies database table loads from the cache and when the table loads from the database. The GetMoviesFromDB() method writes a Trace message whenever it executes (see Figure 29.14).

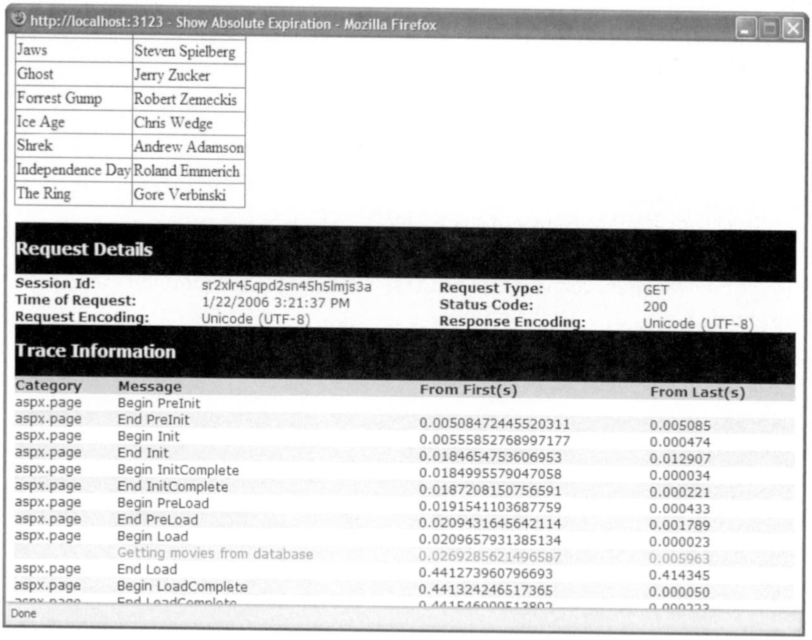

FIGURE 29.14   Adding an item to the cache with an absolute expiration policy.

Adding Items with a Sliding Expiration Policy

When you specify a sliding expiration policy, items remain in the cache just as long as they continue to be requested within a specified interval of time. For example, if you specify a sliding expiration policy of 5 minutes, the item remains in the Cache just as long as no more than 5 minutes pass without the item being requested.

Using a sliding expiration policy makes sense when you have too many items to add to the cache. A sliding expiration policy keeps the most requested items in memory and the remaining items are dropped from memory automatically.

The page in Listing 29.37 illustrates how you can add a DataSet to the cache with a sliding expiration policy of 5 minutes.

LISTING 29.37   ShowSlidingExpiration.aspx

```
<%@ Page Language="C#" Trace="true" %>
<%@ Import Namespace="System.Data" %>
<%@ Import Namespace="System.Data.SqlClient" %>
<%@ Import Namespace="System.Web.Configuration" %>
<!DOCTYPE html PUBLIC "-//W3C//DTD XHTML 1.0 Transitional//EN"
    "http://www.w3.org/TR/xhtml1/DTD/xhtml1-transitional.dtd">
<script runat="server">

    void Page_Load()
    {
        // Get movies from Cache
        DataSet movies = (DataSet)Cache["Movies"];

        // If movies not in cache, recreate movies
        if (movies == null)
        {
            movies = GetMoviesFromDB();
            Cache.Insert("Movies", movies, null,
                Cache.NoAbsoluteExpiration, TimeSpan.FromMinutes(5));
        }

        grdMovies.DataSource = movies;
        grdMovies.DataBind();
    }

    private DataSet GetMoviesFromDB()
    {
        Trace.Warn("Getting movies from database");
        string conString =
            WebConfigurationManager.ConnectionStrings["Movies"].ConnectionString;
        SqlDataAdapter dad =
```

```
            new SqlDataAdapter("SELECT Title,Director FROM Movies", conString);
        DataSet movies = new DataSet();
        dad.Fill(movies);
        return movies;
    }
</script>
<html xmlns="http://www.w3.org/1999/xhtml" >
<head id="Head1" runat="server">
    <title>Show Sliding Expiration</title>
</head>
<body>
    <form id="form1" runat="server">
    <div>

    <asp:GridView
        id="grdMovies"
        Runat="server" />

    </div>
    </form>
</body>
</html>
```

In Listing 29.37, when the DataSet is added to the cache with the Insert() method, its
absoluteExpiration parameter is set to the value Cache.NoAbsoluteExpiration, and its
slidingExpiration parameter is set to an interval of 5 minutes.

Adding Items with Dependencies

When you add an item to the Cache object, you can make the item dependent on an
external object. If the external object is modified, the item is automatically dropped from
the cache.

The ASP.NET Framework includes three cache dependency classes:

▶ **CacheDependency**—Enables you to create a dependency on a file or other cache key.

▶ **SqlCacheDependency**—Enables you to create a dependency on a Microsoft SQL Server
database table or the result of a SQL Server 2005 query.

▶ **AggregateCacheDependency**—Enables you to create a dependency using multiple
CacheDependency objects. For example, you can combine file and SQL dependencies
with this object.

The CacheDependency class is the base class. The other two classes derive from this class.
The CacheDependency class supports the following properties:

▶ **HasChanged**—Enables you to detect when the dependency object has changed.

▶ **UtcLastModified**—Enables you to retrieve the time when the dependency object last changed.

The CacheDependency object also supports the following method:

▶ **GetUniqueID**—Enables you to retrieve a unique identifier for the dependency object.

NOTE

You can create a custom cache dependency class by deriving a new class from the base CacheDependency class.

The SqlCacheDependency class is discussed in detail in the final section of this chapter. In this section, I want to show you how you can use the base CacheDependency class to create a file dependency on an XML file.

The page in Listing 29.38 creates a dependency on an XML file named Movies.xml. If you modify the Movies.xml file, the cache is reloaded with the modified file automatically.

LISTING 29.38   ShowFileDependency.aspx

```
<%@ Page Language="C#" Trace="true" %>
<%@ Import Namespace="System.Data" %>
<%@ Import Namespace="System.Data.SqlClient" %>
<!DOCTYPE html PUBLIC "-//W3C//DTD XHTML 1.0 Transitional//EN"
  "http://www.w3.org/TR/xhtml1/DTD/xhtml1-transitional.dtd">
<script runat="server">

    void Page_Load()
    {
        DataSet movies = (DataSet)Cache["Movies"];
        if (movies == null)
        {
            Trace.Warn("Retrieving movies from file system");
            movies = new DataSet();
            movies.ReadXml(MapPath("~/Movies.xml"));
            CacheDependency fileDepend = new
➥CacheDependency(MapPath("~/Movies.xml"));
            Cache.Insert("Movies", movies, fileDepend);
        }
        grdMovies.DataSource = movies;
        grdMovies.DataBind();
    }
</script>
```

29

```
<html xmlns="http://www.w3.org/1999/xhtml" >
<head id="Head1" runat="server">
    <title>Show File Dependency</title>
</head>
<body>
    <form id="form1" runat="server">
    <div>

    <asp:GridView
        id="grdMovies"
        Runat="server" />

    </div>
    </form>
</body>
</html>
```

Specifying Cache Item Priorities

When you add an item to the Cache, you can specify a particular priority for the item. Specifying a priority provides you with some control over when an item gets evicted from the Cache. For example, you can indicate that one cached item is more important than other cache items so that when memory resources become low, the important item is not evicted as quickly as other items.

You can specify any of the following values of the CacheItemPriority enumeration to indicate the priority of a cached item:

- ▶ AboveNormal

- ▶ BelowNormal

- ▶ Default

- ▶ High

- ▶ Low

- ▶ Normal

- ▶ NotRemovable

For example, the following line of code adds an item to the cache with a maximum absolute expiration time and a cache item priority of NotRemovable:

```
Cache.Insert("ImportantItem", DateTime.Now, null, DateTime.MaxValue,
➥ Cache.NoSlidingExpiration, CacheItemPriority.NotRemovable, null);
```

Configuring the Cache

You can configure the size of the cache by using the web configuration file. You specify cache settings with the cache element. This element supports the following attributes:

▶ **disableMemoryCollection**—Enables you to prevent items from being removed from the cache when memory resources become low.

▶ **disableExpiration**—Enables you to prevent items from being removed from the cache when the items expire.

▶ **privateBytesLimit**—Enables you to specify the total amount of memory that can be consumed by your application and its cache before items are removed.

▶ **percentagePhysicalMemoryUsedLimit**—Enables you to specify the total percentage of memory that can be consumed by your application and its cache before items are removed.

▶ **privateBytesPollTime**—Enables you to specify the time interval for checking the application's memory usage.

You can't set the size of the cache directly. However, you can specify limits on the overall memory that your application consumes, which indirectly limits the size of the cache.

By default, both the privateBytesLimit and percentPhysicalMemoryUsedLimit attributes have the value 0, which indicates that ASP.NET Framework should determine the correct values for these attributes automatically.

The web configuration file in Listing 29.39 changes the memory limit of your application to 100,000 kilobytes and disables the expiration of items in the cache.

LISTING 29.39 Web.Config

```
<?xml version="1.0"?>
<configuration>
    <system.web>
      <caching>
        <cache privateBytesLimit="100000" disableExpiration="true"/>
      </caching>
    </system.web>
</configuration>
```

The page in Listing 29.40 displays your application's current private bytes limit (see Figure 29.15):

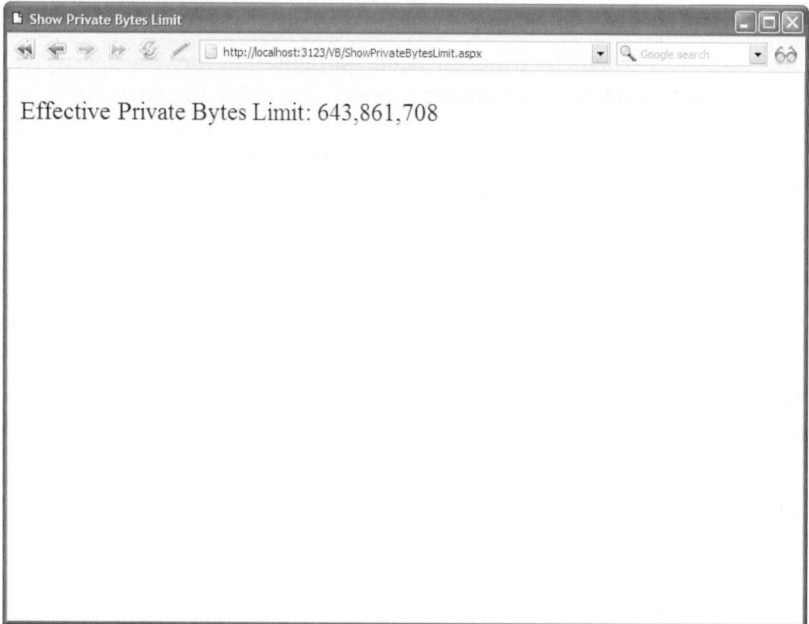

FIGURE 29.15   Displaying the maximum application and cache size.

LISTING 29.40   ShowPrivateBytesLimit.aspx

```
<%@ Page Language="C#" %>
<!DOCTYPE html PUBLIC "-//W3C//DTD XHTML 1.0 Transitional//EN"
  "http://www.w3.org/TR/xhtml1/DTD/xhtml1-transitional.dtd">
<script runat="server">

    void Page_Load()
    {
        lblPrivateBytes.Text = Cache.EffectivePrivateBytesLimit.ToString("n0");
    }
</script>
<html xmlns="http://www.w3.org/1999/xhtml" >
<head id="Head1" runat="server">
    <title>Show Private Bytes Limit</title>
</head>
<body>
    <form id="form1" runat="server">
    <div>

    Effective Private Bytes Limit:
    <asp:Label
        id="lblPrivateBytes"
```

```
        Runat="server" />

    </div>
    </form>
</body>
</html>
```

Using SQL Cache Dependencies

One of the most powerful features supported by ASP.NET Framework is SQL cache dependencies. This feature enables you to reload cached database data automatically whenever the data in the underlying databases changes.

There is a trade-off when you use either an absolute or sliding cache expiration policy. The trade-off is between performance and stale data. For example, if you cache data in memory for 20 seconds, the data displayed on your web pages might be 20 seconds out of date. In the case of most applications, displaying slightly stale data does not actually matter. For example, if you build a discussion forum, everyone can live with the fact that new posts might not appear immediately.

However, there are certain types of applications in which you cannot afford to display any stale data at all. For example, if you create a stock trading website or an auction website, every second might count.

The ASP.NET Framework's support for SQL cache dependencies enables you to take advantage of caching but minimize stale data. When you use a SQL cache dependency, you can automatically detect when data has changed in the underlying database and refresh the data in the cache.

The ASP.NET Framework supports two types of SQL cache dependencies: Polling and Push. You can use Polling SQL cache dependencies with any recent version of Microsoft SQL Server, including Microsoft SQL Server 2008 Express, Microsoft SQL Server 2005 Express, Microsoft SQL Server 2000, and Microsoft SQL Server 7.0. The second type of cache dependency, Push SQL cache dependencies, works with only Microsoft SQL Server 2008 or Microsoft SQL Server 2005 (including the Express editions) because it requires the SQL Server Service Broker.

You can use either type of SQL cache dependencies with Page Output Caching, DataSource Control Caching, and Data Caching. The following sections examine each scenario.

Using Polling SQL Cache Dependencies

A Polling SQL cache dependency is the most flexible type of SQL cache dependency, and I recommend that you use Polling rather than Push SQL cache dependencies for most applications. You can use a Polling SQL cache dependency to detect any type of modification to a database table.

29

Behind the scenes, a Polling SQL cache dependency uses a database trigger. When a table is modified, the trigger fires, and a row in a database table named AspNet_SqlCacheTablesForChangeNotification is updated to record that the table has been changed.

The ASP.NET Framework uses a background thread to poll this database table for changes on a periodic basis. If there has been a change, any item in the cache that is dependent on the database table is dropped from the cache.

If you use a Polling SQL cache dependency, you can eliminate the majority of your database traffic. Unless a database table changes, the only traffic between your web server and the database server is the query that checks for changes in the AspNet_SqlCacheTablesForChangeNotification table.

Because a Polling SQL cache dependency must poll the database for changes, an item cached with a SQL Polling cache dependency won't be dropped from the cache immediately after there is a change in the database. The polling interval determines the staleness of your cached data. You can configure the polling interval to be any value you need.

Configuring Polling SQL Cache Dependencies

Before you can use a Polling SQL cache dependency, you must perform two configuration steps:

1. You must enable SQL cache dependencies for a database and one or more database tables.

2. You must configure SQL cache dependencies in your web configuration file.

Let's examine each of these steps.

Configuring a Database for Polling SQL Cache Dependencies

You can configure a SQL Server database to support Polling SQL cache dependencies by using a class in the Framework named the SqlCacheDependencyAdmin class. This class has the following methods:

▶ **DisableNotifications**—Enables you to disable a database for Polling SQL cache dependencies; removes all tables and stored procedures used by Polling SQL cache dependencies.

▶ **DisableTableForNotification**—Enables you to disable a particular database table for Polling SQL cache dependencies.

▶ **EnableNotifications**—Enables a database for Polling SQL cache dependencies by adding all the necessary database objects.

▶ **EnableTableForNotifications**—Enables a particular database table for Polling SQL cache dependencies.

▶ **GetTablesEnabledForNotifications**—Enables you to retrieve all tables enabled for Polling SQL cache dependencies.

You should not use the `SqlCacheDependencyAdmin` class in an ASP.NET page because calling the methods of this class requires database permissions to create tables, stored procedures, and triggers. For security reasons, the ASP.NET process should not be given these permissions. Instead, you should use the `SqlCacheDependencyAdmin` class in a command-line tool.

The ASP.NET Framework includes a command-line tool named `aspnet_regsql` that enables you to configure a database to support Polling SQL cache dependencies. This tool works with Microsoft SQL Server 7.0, Microsoft SQL Server 2000, Microsoft SQL Server 2005, and Microsoft SQL Server 2008. Unfortunately, the `aspnet_regsql` command-line tool does not work with a local instance of Microsoft SQL Server. (But we'll fix this limitation in a moment.)

The `aspnet_regsql` tool is located in the following folder:

```
c:\Windows\Microsoft.NET\Framework\[version]
```

> **NOTE**
>
> If you open the SDK Command Prompt from the Microsoft .NET Framework SDK Program group, you do not need to navigate to the Microsoft.NET folder to execute the `aspnet_regsql` command-line tool.

Executing the following command enables the Pubs database for SQL cache dependencies:

```
aspnet_regsql -C "Data Source=localhost;Integrated Security=True;
➥Initial Catalog=Pubs" -ed
```

This command creates the AspNet_SqlCacheTablesForChangeNotification database table and adds a set of stored procedures to the database specified in the connection string.

After you enable a database, you can enable a particular table for SQL cache dependencies with the following command:

```
aspnet_regsql -C "Data Source=localhost;Integrated Security=True;
➥Initial Catalog=Pubs" -et -t Titles
```

This command enables the Titles database table for SQL cache dependencies. It creates a new trigger for the Titles database table and adds a new entry in the AspNet_SqlCacheTablesForChangeNotification table.

29

Unfortunately, you cannot use the standard `aspnet_regsql` tool to enable a local SQL Server 2008 Express or SQL Server 2005 Express database for Polling SQL cache dependencies. The aspnet_regsql tool does not enable you to use the `AttachDBFileName` parameter in the connection string. To get around this limitation, I've written a custom command-line tool named `enableNotifications` that works with a local SQL Express database. This tool is included in the code download from the website that accompanies this book.

To use the `enableNotifications` tool, you need to open a command prompt and navigate to the folder that contains your local SQL Express database table. Next, execute the command with the name of the database file and the name of the database table that you want to enable for Polling SQL cache dependencies. For example, the following command enables the Movies database table located in the `MyDatabase.mdf` database:

```
enableNotifications "MyDatabase.mdf" "Movies"
```

The `enableNotifications` tool works only with a local instance of Microsoft SQL Server Express 2005 or Microsoft SQL Server Express 2008. You cannot use the tool with other versions of Microsoft SQL Server.

WARNING

When using the `enableNotifications` tool, you must navigate to the same folder as the database that you want to enable for Polling SQL cache dependencies.

Configuring an Application for Polling SQL Cache Dependencies

After you set up a database to support Polling SQL cache dependencies, you must configure your application to poll the database. You configure Polling SQL cache dependencies with the `sqlCacheDependency` subelement of the caching element in the web configuration file.

For example, the file in Listing 29.41 causes your application to poll the AspNet_SqlCacheTablesForChangeNotification table every 5 seconds (5,000 milliseconds) for changes.

LISTING 29.41 Web.Config

```
<?xml version="1.0"?>
<configuration>

  <connectionStrings>
    <add name="Movies" connectionString="Data Source=.\SQLEXPRESS;
      AttachDbFilename=¦DataDirectory¦MyDatabase.mdf;Integrated Security=True;
User Instance=True" />
  </connectionStrings>
```

```
  <system.web>
    <caching>
      <sqlCacheDependency enabled="true" pollTime="5000">
        <databases>
          <add
            name="MyDatabase"
            connectionStringName="Movies" />
        </databases>
      </sqlCacheDependency>
    </caching>
  </system.web>
</configuration>
```

Using Polling SQL Cache Dependencies with Page Output Caching

After you configure Polling SQL cache dependencies, you can use a SQL dependency with Page Output Caching. For example, the page in Listing 29.42 is output cached until you modify the Movies database table.

LISTING 29.42   PollingSQLOutputCache.aspx

```
<%@ Page Language="C#" %>
<%@ OutputCache Duration="9999" VaryByParam="none"
  SqlDependency="MyDatabase:Movies" %>
<!DOCTYPE html PUBLIC "-//W3C//DTD XHTML 1.0 Transitional//EN"
  "http://www.w3.org/TR/xhtml1/DTD/xhtml1-transitional.dtd">
<html xmlns="http://www.w3.org/1999/xhtml" >
<head id="Head1" runat="server">
    <title>Polling SQL Output Cache</title>
</head>
<body>
    <form id="form1" runat="server">
    <div>

    <%= DateTime.Now.ToString("T") %>
    <hr />

    <asp:GridView
        id="grdMovies"
        DataSourceID="srcMovies"
        Runat="server" />

    <asp:SqlDataSource
        id="srcMovies"
```

29

```
        ConnectionString="<%$ ConnectionStrings:Movies %>"
        SelectCommand="SELECT Title, Director FROM Movies"
        Runat="server" />

    </div>
    </form>
</body>
</html>
```

The page in Listing 29.42 includes an `<%@ OutputCache %>` directive with a `SqlDependency` attribute. The value of the `SqlDependency` attribute is the name of the database enabled for SQL dependencies in the web configuration file, followed by the name of a database table.

If you open the page in Listing 29.42 in your browser and click your browser's Reload button multiple times, you notice that the time displayed does not change. The page is output cached (see Figure 29.16).

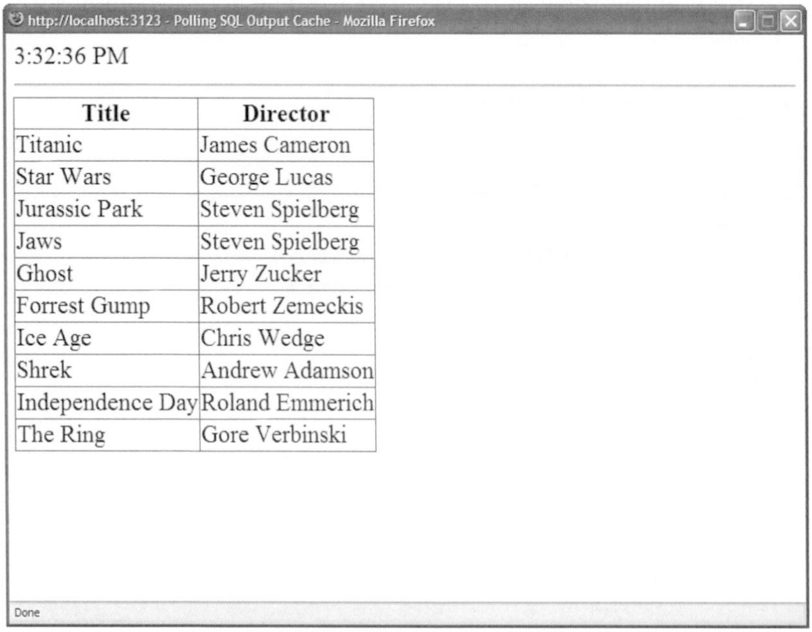

3:32:36 PM

Title	Director
Titanic	James Cameron
Star Wars	George Lucas
Jurassic Park	Steven Spielberg
Jaws	Steven Spielberg
Ghost	Jerry Zucker
Forrest Gump	Robert Zemeckis
Ice Age	Chris Wedge
Shrek	Andrew Adamson
Independence Day	Roland Emmerich
The Ring	Gore Verbinski

FIGURE 29.16   Using Page Output Caching with a Polling SQL cache dependency.

However, if you modify the Movies database, the page is dropped from the cache automatically (within 5 seconds). The next time you click the Reload button, the modified data displays.

If you want to make a page dependent on multiple database tables, you can assign a semicolon-delimited list of database and table names to the `SqlDependency` attribute.

> **NOTE**
>
> You also can use Polling SQL cache dependencies with an `<%@ OutputCache %>` directive included in a User Control. In other words, you can use Polling SQL cache dependencies with Partial Page Caching.

Using Polling SQL Cache Dependencies with DataSource Caching

You can use Polling SQL cache dependencies with both the `SqlDataSource` and `ObjectDataSource` controls by setting the `SqlCacheDependency` property. For example, the page in Listing 29.43 caches the output of a `SqlDataSource` control until the Movies database table is modified.

LISTING 29.43   PollingSQLDataSourceCache.aspx

```
<%@ Page Language="C#" %>
<!DOCTYPE html PUBLIC "-//W3C//DTD XHTML 1.0 Transitional//EN"
   "http://www.w3.org/TR/xhtml1/DTD/xhtml1-transitional.dtd">
<script runat="server">

    protected void srcMovies_Selecting(object sender,
➥SqlDataSourceSelectingEventArgs e)
    {
        lblMessage.Text = "Retrieving data from database";
    }
</script>
<html xmlns="http://www.w3.org/1999/xhtml" >
<head id="Head1" runat="server">
    <title>Polling SQL DataSource Cache</title>
</head>
<body>
    <form id="form1" runat="server">
    <div>

    <asp:Label
        id="lblMessage"
        EnableViewState="false"
        Runat="server" />
    <hr />

    <asp:GridView
        id="grdMovies"
        DataSourceID="srcMovies"
        Runat="server" />

    <asp:SqlDataSource
```

29

```
        id="srcMovies"
        ConnectionString="<%$ ConnectionStrings:Movies %>"
        SelectCommand="SELECT Title, Director FROM Movies"
        EnableCaching="true"
        SqlCacheDependency="MyDatabase:Movies"
        OnSelecting="srcMovies_Selecting"
        Runat="server" />

    </div>
    </form>
</body>
</html>
```

In Listing 29.43, the `SqlDataSource` control includes both an `EnableCaching` property and a `SqlCacheDependency` property. A database name and table name are assigned to the `SqlCacheDependency` property. (The database name must correspond to the database name configured in the `<sqlCacheDependency>` section of the web configuration file.)

If you need to monitor multiple database tables, you can assign a semicolon-delimited list of database and table names to the `SqlCacheDependency` property.

Using Polling SQL Cache Dependencies with Data Caching

You also can use Polling SQL cache dependencies when working with the `Cache` object. You represent a Polling SQL cache dependency with the `SqlCacheDependency` object.

For example, the page in Listing 29.44 creates a `SqlCacheDependency` object that represents the Movies database table. When a `DataTable` is added to the `Cache` object, the `DataTable` is added with the `SqlCacheDependency` object.

LISTING 29.44   PollingSQLDataCache.aspx

```
<%@ Page Language="C#" Trace="true" %>
<%@ Import Namespace="System.Data" %>
<%@ Import Namespace="System.Data.SqlClient" %>
<%@ Import Namespace="System.Web.Configuration" %>
<!DOCTYPE html PUBLIC "-//W3C//DTD XHTML 1.0 Transitional//EN"
  "http://www.w3.org/TR/xhtml1/DTD/xhtml1-transitional.dtd">
<script runat="server">

    void Page_Load()
    {
        DataTable movies = (DataTable)Cache["Movies"];
        if (movies == null)
        {
```

```
            movies = GetMoviesFromDB();
            SqlCacheDependency sqlDepend =
                new SqlCacheDependency("MyDatabase", "Movies");
            Cache.Insert("Movies", movies, sqlDepend);
        }
        grdMovies.DataSource = movies;
        grdMovies.DataBind();
    }

    private DataTable GetMoviesFromDB()
    {
        Trace.Warn("Retrieving data from database");
        string conString =
            WebConfigurationManager.ConnectionStrings["Movies"].ConnectionString;
        SqlDataAdapter dad =
            new SqlDataAdapter("SELECT Title,Director FROM Movies", conString);
        DataTable movies = new DataTable();
        dad.Fill(movies);
        return movies;
    }
</script>
<html xmlns="http://www.w3.org/1999/xhtml" >
<head id="Head1" runat="server">
    <title>Polling SQL Data Cache</title>
</head>
<body>
    <form id="form1" runat="server">
    <div>

    <asp:GridView
        id="grdMovies"
        Runat="server" />

    </div>
    </form>
</body>
</html>
```

In Listing 29.44, an instance of the SqlCacheDependency class is created. A database name and table name are passed to the constructor for the SqlCacheDependency class. This class is used as a parameter with the Cache.Insert() method when the DataTable is added to the Cache.

NOTE

If you need to create dependencies on multiple database tables, you need to create multiple `SqlCacheDependency` objects and represent the multiple dependencies with an instance of the `AggregateCacheDependency` class.

Using Push SQL Cache Dependencies

When using Microsoft SQL Server 2008 or Microsoft SQL Server 2005, you have the option of using Push SQL cache dependencies rather than Polling SQL cache dependencies. These databases include a feature called query notifications, which uses the Microsoft SQL Server Service Broker in the background. The Service Broker can automatically send a message to an application when data changes in the database.

WARNING

You can create two types of databases with SQL Server Express: a Local or a Server database. You should not use Push dependencies with a Local database. You should use Push dependencies only with a Server database.

You cannot create new Server databases when using Visual Web Developer. You can create a Server database by using the full version of Visual Studio 2010 or by downloading Microsoft SQL Server Management Studio Express from the Microsoft MSDN website (msdn.microsoft.com).

The advantage of using Push dependencies rather than Polling dependencies is that your ASP.NET application does not need to continuously poll your database for changes. When a change happens, your database is responsible for notifying your application of the change.

However, there are significant limitations on the types of queries that you can use with Push dependencies. Following are some of the more significant limitations:

▶ The query must use two-part table names (for example, dbo.Movies instead of Movies) to refer to tables.

▶ The query must contain an explicit list of column names. (You cannot use *.)

▶ The query cannot reference a view, derived table, temporary table, or table variable.

▶ The query cannot reference large object types such as `Text`, `NText`, and `Image` columns.

▶ The query cannot contain a subquery, outer join, or self join.

▶ The query cannot use the `DISTINCT`, `COMPUTE`, `COMPUTE BY`, or `INSERT` keywords.

▶ The query cannot use many aggregate functions including `AVG`, `COUNT(*)`, `MAX`, and `MIN`.

This is not a complete list of query limitations. For the complete list, refer to the Creating a Query for Notification topic in the SQL Server 2005 Books Online or the MSDN website (msdn.microsoft.com).

For example, the following simple query won't work:

```
SELECT * FROM Movies
```

This query won't work for two reasons. First, you cannot use the asterisk (*) to represent columns. Second, you must supply a two-part table name. The following query, on the other hand, works:

```
SELECT Title, Director FROM dbo.Movies
```

You can use Push SQL cache dependencies with stored procedures; however, each SELECT statement in the stored procedure must meet all the requirements just listed.

Configuring Push SQL Cache Dependencies

You must perform two configuration steps to enable Push SQL cache dependencies:

1. Configure your database by enabling the SQL Server Service Broker.
2. Configure your application by starting the notification listener.

In this section, you learn how to perform both of these configuration steps.

WARNING

Unfortunately, when a Push SQL cache dependency fails, it fails silently, without adding an error message to the Event Log. This makes the situation especially difficult to debug. I recommend that after you make the configuration changes discussed in this section that you restart both your web server and database server.

Configuring a Database for Push SQL Cache Dependencies

Before you can use Push SQL cache dependencies, you must enable the Microsoft SQL Server Service Broker. You can check whether the Service Broker is activated for a particular database by executing the following SQL query:

```
SELECT name, is_broker_enabled FROM sys.databases
```

If the Service Broker is not enabled for a database, you can enable it by executing an ALTER DATABASE command. For example, the following SQL command enables the Service Broker for a database named MyMovies:

```
ALTER DATABASE MyMovies SET ENABLE_BROKER
```

29

Finally, the ASP.NET process must be supplied with adequate permissions to subscribe to query notifications. When an ASP.NET page is served from Internet Information Server, the page executes in the context of the NETWORK SERVICE account (for Microsoft Windows Server 2003) or the ASPNET account (for other operating systems such as Windows XP).

Executing the following SQL command provides the local ASPNET account on a server named YOURSERVER with the required permissions:

```
GRANT SUBSCRIBE QUERY NOTIFICATIONS TO "YOURSERVER\ASPNET"
```

When you request an ASP.NET page when using the Visual Web Developer web server, an ASP.NET page executes in the security context of your current user account. Therefore, when using a file system website, you need to grant SUBSCRIBE QUERY NOTIFICATIONS permissions to your current account.

> **NOTE**
>
> Push SQL cache dependencies do not use the SQL Server Notification Services.

Configuring an Application for Push SQL Cache Dependencies

Before you can receive change notifications in your application, you must enable the query notification listener. You can enable the listener with the Global.asax file in Listing 29.45.

LISTING 29.45   Global.asax

```
<%@ Application Language="C#" %>
<%@ Import Namespace="System.Data.SqlClient" %>
<%@ Import Namespace="System.Web.Configuration" %>
<script runat="server">

    void Application_Start(object sender, EventArgs e)
    {
        // Enable Push SQL cache dependencies
        string conString =
          WebConfigurationManager.ConnectionStrings["MyMovies"].ConnectionString;
        SqlDependency.Start(conString);
    }
</script>
```

The Application_Start handler executes once when your application first starts. In Listing 29.45, the SqlDependency.Start() method is called with a connection string to a SQL Express server database named MyMovies.

> **WARNING**
>
> The code in Listing 29.45 is commented out in the `Global.asax` file in the code download from the website that accompanies this book so that it won't interfere with all the previous code samples discussed in this chapter. You need to remove the comments to use the code samples in the following sections.

Using Push SQL Cache Dependencies with Page Output Caching

You can use Push SQL cache dependencies when caching an entire ASP.NET page. If the results of any SQL command contained in the page changes, the page is dropped automatically from the cache.

The `SqlCommand` object includes a property named the `NotificationAutoEnlist` property. This property has the value `True` by default. When `NotificationAutoEnlist` is enabled, a Push cache dependency is created between the page and the command automatically.

For example, the page in Listing 29.46 includes an `<%@ OutputCache %>` directive that includes a `SqlDependency` attribute. This attribute is set to the special value `CommandNotification`.

LISTING 29.46   PushSQLOutputCache.aspx

```
<%@ Page Language="C#" %>
<%@ OutputCache Duration="9999" VaryByParam="none"
  SqlDependency="CommandNotification" %>
<!DOCTYPE html PUBLIC "-//W3C//DTD XHTML 1.0 Transitional//EN"
  "http://www.w3.org/TR/xhtml1/DTD/xhtml1-transitional.dtd">
<html xmlns="http://www.w3.org/1999/xhtml" >
<head id="Head1" runat="server">
    <title>Push SQL Output Cache</title>
</head>
<body>
    <form id="form1" runat="server">
    <div>

    <%= DateTime.Now.ToString("T") %>
    <hr />

    <asp:GridView
        id="grdMovies"
        DataSourceID="srcMovies"
        Runat="server" />

    <asp:SqlDataSource
        id="srcMovies"
        ConnectionString="<%$ ConnectionStrings:MyMovies %>"
```

```
        SelectCommand="SELECT Title, Director FROM dbo.Movies"
        Runat="server" />

    </div>
    </form>
</body>
</html>
```

The page in Listing 29.46 includes a `SqlDataSource` control that retrieves all the records from the Movies database table. The `SqlDataSource` control uses a SQL query that explicitly lists column names and uses a two-part table name. These are requirements when using Push dependencies.

The page in Listing 29.46 displays the current time. If you request the page in your browser, and refresh the page, the time does not change. The time does not change until you modify the Movies database table.

WARNING

The page in Listing 29.46 connects to a Server database named MyMovies. You should not use Push dependencies with a Local SQL Express database. The page uses a database table named Movies, which was created with the following SQL command:

```
CREATE TABLE Movies
(
    Id int IDENTITY NOT NULL,
    Title nvarchar(100) NOT NULL,
    Director nvarchar(50) NOT NULL,
    EntryDate datetime NOT NULL DEFAULT GetDate()
)
```

WARNING

You cannot use Push SQL cache dependencies with an `<%@ OutputCache %>` directive included in a User Control. In other words, you cannot use Push SQL cache dependencies with Partial Page Caching.

Using Push SQL Cache Dependencies with `DataSource` Caching

You also can use Push SQL cache dependencies with both the `SqlDataSource` and `ObjectDataSource` controls by setting the `SqlCacheDependency` property. When using Push rather than Polling dependencies, you need to set the `SqlCacheDependency` property to the value `CommandNotification`.

For example, the page in Listing 29.47 contains a `SqlDataSource` control that has both its `EnableCaching` and `SqlDependency` properties set.

LISTING 29.47   PushSQLDataSourceCache.aspx

```
<%@ Page Language="C#" %>
<!DOCTYPE html PUBLIC "-//W3C//DTD XHTML 1.0 Transitional//EN"
    "http://www.w3.org/TR/xhtml1/DTD/xhtml1-transitional.dtd">
<script runat="server">

    protected void srcMovies_Selecting(object sender,
➥SqlDataSourceSelectingEventArgs e)
    {
        lblMessage.Text = "Retrieving data from database";
    }
</script>
<html xmlns="http://www.w3.org/1999/xhtml" >
<head id="Head1" runat="server">
    <title>Push SQL DataSource Cache</title>
</head>
<body>
    <form id="form1" runat="server">
    <div>

    <asp:Label
        id="lblMessage"
        EnableViewState="false"
        Runat="server" />
    <hr />

    <asp:GridView
        id="grdMovies"
        DataSourceID="srcMovies"
        Runat="server" />

    <asp:SqlDataSource
        id="srcMovies"
        ConnectionString="<%$ ConnectionStrings:MyMovies %>"
        SelectCommand="SELECT Title, Director FROM dbo.Movies"
        EnableCaching="true"
        SqlCacheDependency="CommandNotification"
        OnSelecting="srcMovies_Selecting"
        Runat="server" />

    </div>
    </form>
```

29

```
</body>
</html>
```

In Listing 29.47, the SqlDataSource control includes a Selecting event handler. Because this event is raised when the data cannot be retrieved from the cache, you can use this event to determine when the data is retrieved from the cache or the database server (see Figure 29.17).

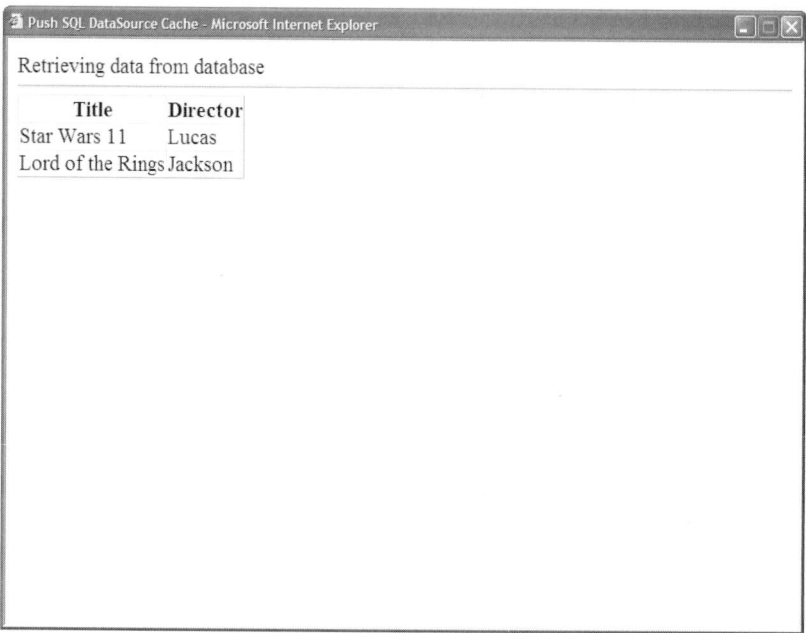

FIGURE 29.17   Using Push SQL cache dependencies with a DataSource control.

WARNING

The page in Listing 29.47 connects to a Server database named MyMovies. You should not use Push dependencies with a Local SQL Express database. The page uses a database table named Movies, which was created with the following SQL command:

```
CREATE TABLE Movies
(
  Id int IDENTITY NOT NULL,
  Title nvarchar(100) NOT NULL,
  Director nvarchar(50) NOT NULL,
  EntryDate datetime NOT NULL DEFAULT GetDate()
)
```

Using Push SQL Cache Dependencies with Data Caching

You can use Push SQL cache dependencies when working with the Cache object. You represent a Push SQL cache dependency with an instance of the SqlCacheDependency class.

For example, in the Page_Load() handler in Listing 29.48, a DataTable is added to the cache that represents the contents of the Movies database table. The DataTable displays in a GridView control.

LISTING 29.48   PushSQLDataCache.aspx

```
<%@ Page Language="C#" Trace="true" %>
<%@ Import Namespace="System.Data" %>
<%@ Import Namespace="System.Data.SqlClient" %>
<%@ Import Namespace="System.Web.Configuration" %>
<!DOCTYPE html PUBLIC "-//W3C//DTD XHTML 1.0 Transitional//EN"
    "http://www.w3.org/TR/xhtml1/DTD/xhtml1-transitional.dtd">
<script runat="server">

    void Page_Load()
    {
        DataTable movies = (DataTable)Cache["Movies"];
        if (movies == null)
        {
            Trace.Warn("Retrieving data from database");
            string conString =
             WebConfigurationManager.ConnectionStrings["MyMovies"].ConnectionString;
            SqlDataAdapter dad =
                new SqlDataAdapter("SELECT Title,Director FROM dbo.Movies",
conString);
            SqlCacheDependency sqlDepend = new SqlCacheDependency(dad.SelectCommand);
            movies = new DataTable();
            dad.Fill(movies);

            Cache.Insert("Movies", movies, sqlDepend);
        }
        grdMovies.DataSource = movies;
        grdMovies.DataBind();
    }
</script>
<html xmlns="http://www.w3.org/1999/xhtml" >
<head id="Head1" runat="server">
    <title>Push SQL Data Cache</title>
</head>
<body>
    <form id="form1" runat="server">
```

29

```
    <div>

    <asp:GridView
        id="grdMovies"
        Runat="server" />

    </div>
    </form>
</body>
</html>
```

An instance of the `SqlCacheDependency` class is created. A `SqlCommand` object is passed to the constructor for the `SqlCacheDependency` class. If the results of the `SqlCommand` change, the `DataTable` will be dropped automatically from the cache.

The order of the commands here is important. You need to create the `SqlCacheDependency` object before you execute the command. If you call the `Fill()` method before you create the `SqlCacheDependency` object, the dependency is ignored.

WARNING

The page in Listing 29.48 connects to a Server database named MyMovies. You should not use Push dependencies with a Local SQL Express database. The page uses a database table named Movies, which was created with the following SQL command:

```
CREATE TABLE Movies
(
    Id int IDENTITY NOT NULL,
    Title nvarchar(100) NOT NULL,
    Director nvarchar(50) NOT NULL,
    EntryDate datetime NOT NULL DEFAULT GetDate()
)
```

Summary

In this chapter, you learned how to improve the performance of your ASP.NET applications by taking advantage of caching. In the first part of this chapter, you learned how to use each of the different types of caching technologies supported by ASP.NET Framework.

First, you learned how to use Page Output Caching to cache the entire rendered contents of a page. You learned how to create different cached versions of the same page when the page is requested with different parameters, headers, and browsers. You also learned how to remove pages programmatically from the Page Output Cache. Finally, we discussed how you can define Cache Profiles in a web configuration file.

Next, you learned how to use Partial Page Caching to apply different caching policies to different regions in a page. You learned how to use post-cache substitution to dynamically inject content into a page that has been output cached. You also learned how to use User Controls to cache different areas of a page.

We also discussed how you can cache data by using the different DataSource controls. You learned how to enable caching when working with the SqlDataSource, ObjectDataSource, and XmlDataSource controls.

Next, you learned how to use the Cache object to cache items programmatically. You learned how to add items to the cache with different expiration policies and dependencies. You also learned how to configure the maximum size of the cache in the web configuration file.

Finally, we discussed SQL cache dependencies. You learned how to use SQL cache dependencies to reload database data in the cache automatically when the data in the underlying database changes. You learned how to use both Polling and Push SQL cache dependencies with Page Output Caching, DataSource Caching, and the Cache object.

29

CHAPTER 30

Localizing Applications for Multiple Languages

You can localize an ASP.NET website so that it supports multiple languages and cultures. For example, you might need to create both an English language and Spanish language version of the same website.

One approach to localization is to simply create multiple copies of the same website and translate each copy into a different language. This was a common approach when building ASP Classic (or even ASP.NET 1.1) websites. The problem with this approach is it creates a website maintenance nightmare. Whenever you need to make a change to the website—no matter how simple—you must make the change in each copy of the website.

When building ASP.NET applications, you do not need to create multiple copies of a website to support multiple languages. Instead, you can take advantage of resource files. A resource file contains language-specific content. For example, one resource file might contain a Spanish version of all the text in your website, and a second resource file might contain the Indonesian version of all the text in your website.

In this chapter, you learn how to localize ASP.NET applications. First, you learn how to set the culture of the current page. You learn how to use both the Culture and UICulture properties. You also learn how to detect users' preferred languages automatically through their browser settings.

Next, local resources are explored. A local resource contains content scoped to a particular file such as an ASP.NET page. You learn how to use both implicit and explicit resource expressions.

This chapter also examines global resources, which contain content that can be used in any page within an application. For example, you can place the title of your website in a global resource file.

Finally, the ASP.NET Localize control is discussed. You learn how to use this control in your pages to localize big chunks of page text.

Setting the Current Culture

Two main properties of the Page class have an effect on localization:

▶ UICulture

▶ Culture

The UICulture property specifies which resource files are loaded for the page. The resource files can contain all the text content of your pages translated into a particular language. You can set this property to any standard culture name. This property is discussed in detail during the discussion of using local and global resources later in this chapter.

The Culture property, on the other hand, determines how strings such as dates, numerals, and currency amounts are formatted. It also determines how values are compared and sorted. For example, by modifying the Culture property, you can display dates with language-specific month names such as January (English), Januar (German), or Enero (Spanish).

Both the UICulture and Culture properties accept standard culture names for their values. Culture names follow the RFC 1766 and RFC 3066 standards maintained by the Internet Engineering Task Force (IETF). The IETF website is located at www.IETF.org.

Following are some common culture names:

▶ de-DE = German (Germany)

▶ en-US = English (United States)

▶ en-GB = English (United Kingdom)

▶ es-MX = Spanish (Mexico)

▶ id-ID = Indonesian (Indonesia)

▶ zh-CN = Chinese (China)

Each culture name consists of two parts. The first part represents the language code, and the second part represents the country/region code. If you specify a culture name and do not provide a country/region code—for example, en—you have specified something called a *neutral culture*. If you provide both a language code and a country/region code—for example, en-US—you have specified something called a *specific culture*.

The Culture property must always be set to a specific culture. This makes sense because, for example, different English speakers use different currency symbols. The UICulture property, on the other hand, can be set to either a neutral or specific culture name. Text written in Canadian English is pretty much the same as text written in U.S. English.

You can set the UICulture and Culture properties to the same value or different values. For example, if you create an online store, you might want to set the UICulture property to the value de-DE to display German product descriptions. However, you might want to set the Culture property to the value en-US to display product prices in U.S. currency amounts.

Setting a Culture Manually

You can set either the UICulture or Culture properties by using the <%@ Page %> directive. For example, the page in Listing 30.1 sets both properties to the value id-ID (Indonesian).

LISTING 30.1   Bagus.aspx

```
<%@ Page Language="C#" Culture="id-ID" UICulture="id-ID" %>
<!DOCTYPE html PUBLIC "-//W3C//DTD XHTML 1.1//EN"
"http://www.w3.org/TR/xhtml11/DTD/xhtml11.dtd">
<script runat="server">

    void Page_Load()
    {
        lblDate.Text = DateTime.Now.ToString("D");
        lblPrice.Text = (512.33m).ToString("c");
    }
</script>
<html xmlns="http://www.w3.org/1999/xhtml" >
<head id="Head1" runat="server">
    <title>Bagus</title>
</head>
<body>
    <form id="form1" runat="server">
    <div>

    Today's date is:
    <br />
    <asp:Label
```

30

```
            id="lblDate"
            Runat="server" />

    <hr />
    The price of the product is:
    <br />
    <asp:Label
            id="lblPrice"
            Runat="server" />

    </div>
    </form>
</body>
</html>
```

The page in Listing 30.1 displays a date and a currency amount. Because the Culture property is set to the value id-ID in the <%@ Page %> directive, both the date and currency amount are formatted with Indonesian cultural conventions (see Figure 30.1).

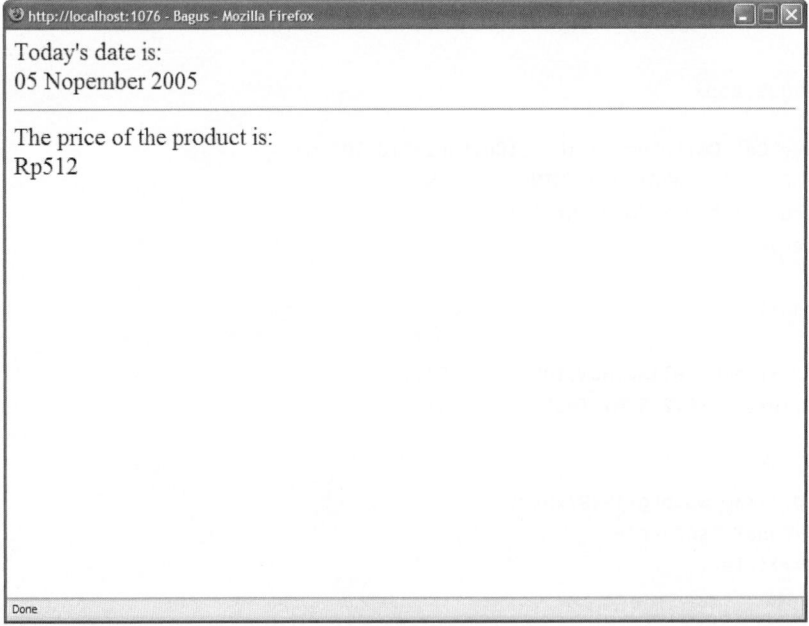

FIGURE 30.1   Displaying a localized date and price.

The date is displayed like this:

    05 March 2010

The currency amount is displayed as an Indonesian Rupiah amount like this:

    Rp512

> **NOTE**
>
> Setting the Culture does not actually convert a currency amount. Setting a particular culture formats only the currency as appropriate for a particular culture. If you need to convert currency amounts, you need to use a Web service: Conversion rates change minute by minute. See, for example, www.xmethods.com.

Instead of using the `<%@ Page %>` directive to set the `Culture` or `UICulture` properties, you can set these properties programmatically. For example, the page in Listing 30.2 enables you to select a particular culture from a drop-down list of cultures (see Figure 30.2).

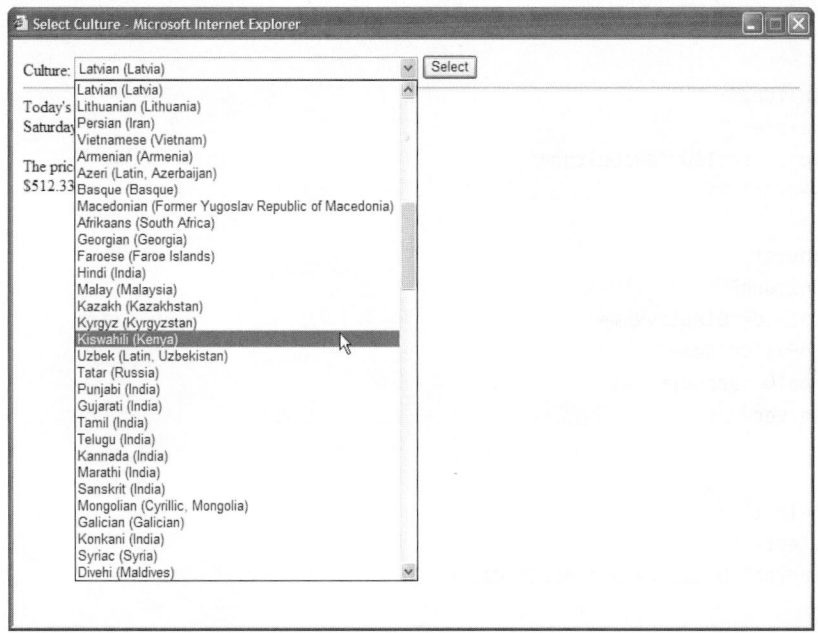

FIGURE 30.2   Selecting a culture from a `DropDownList` control.

LISTING 30.2   SelectCulture.aspx

```
<%@ Page Language="C#" %>
<!DOCTYPE html PUBLIC "-//W3C//DTD XHTML 1.1//EN"
"http://www.w3.org/TR/xhtml11/DTD/xhtml11.dtd">
<script runat="server">
    protected void btnSelect_Click(object sender, EventArgs e)
    {
        Culture = ddlCulture.SelectedValue;
```

```
    }

    void Page_PreRender()
    {
        lblDate.Text = DateTime.Now.ToString("D");
        lblPrice.Text = (512.33m).ToString("c");
    }
</script>
<html xmlns="http://www.w3.org/1999/xhtml" >
<head id="Head1" runat="server">
    <title>Select Culture</title>
</head>
<body>
    <form id="form1" runat="server">
    <div>

    <asp:Label
        id="lblCulture"
        Text="Culture:"
        AssociatedControlID="ddlCulture"
        Runat="server" />

    <asp:DropDownList
        id="ddlCulture"
        DataTextField="DisplayName"
        DataValueField="Name"
        DataSourceID="srcCultures"
        Runat="server" />

    <asp:Button
        id="btnSelect"
        Text="Select"
        Runat="server" OnClick="btnSelect_Click" />


    <asp:ObjectDataSource
        id="srcCultures"
        TypeName="System.Globalization.CultureInfo"
        SelectMethod="GetCultures"
        Runat="server">
        <SelectParameters>
            <asp:Parameter Name="types" DefaultValue="SpecificCultures" />
        </SelectParameters>
    </asp:ObjectDataSource>
```

```
        <hr />

        Today's date is:
        <br />
        <asp:Label
            id="lblDate"
            Runat="server" />

        <br /><br />

        The price of the product is:
        <br />
        <asp:Label
            id="lblPrice"
            Runat="server" />

        </div>
        </form>
</body>
</html>
```

The `DropDownList` control in Listing 30.2 is bound to an `ObjectDataSource` control, which retrieves a list of all the culture names supported by .NET Framework. The culture names are retrieved during a call to the `GetCultures()` method of the `CultureInfo` class.

When you click the button to select a culture, the `btnSelect_Click()` method executes and assigns the name of the selected culture to the page's `Culture` property. When you select a new culture, the formatting applied to the date and currency amount changes.

Several websites on the Internet display a page that requires the user to select a language before entering the main website. For example, the Federal Express website (www.FedEx.com) requires you to select a country before entering the website.

You can take advantage of the `Profile` object to store a user's preferred culture. That way, a user needs to select a culture only once, and the culture is then used any time the user returns to your website in the future. The page in Listing 30.3 illustrates this approach.

LISTING 30.3   SelectCultureProfile.aspx

```
<%@ Page Language="C#" %>
<!DOCTYPE html PUBLIC "-//W3C//DTD XHTML 1.1//EN"
"http://www.w3.org/TR/xhtml11/DTD/xhtml11.dtd">
<script runat="server">

    protected override void InitializeCulture()
    {
        Culture = Profile.UserCulture;
```

```
            UICulture = Profile.UserUICulture;
    }


    protected void btnSelect_Click(object sender, EventArgs e)
    {
        Profile.UserCulture = ddlCulture.SelectedValue;
        Profile.UserUICulture = ddlCulture.SelectedValue;
        Response.Redirect(Request.Path);
    }

    void Page_PreRender()
    {
        lblDate.Text = DateTime.Now.ToString("D");
        lblPrice.Text = (512.33m).ToString("c");
    }
</script>
<html xmlns="http://www.w3.org/1999/xhtml" >
<head id="Head1" runat="server">
    <title>Select Culture Profile</title>
</head>
<body>
    <form id="form1" runat="server">
    <div>

    <asp:Label
        id="lblCulture"
        Text="Culture:"
        AssociatedControlID="ddlCulture"
        Runat="server" />

    <asp:DropDownList
        id="ddlCulture"
        DataTextField="DisplayName"
        DataValueField="Name"
        DataSourceID="srcCultures"
        Runat="server" />

    <asp:Button
        id="btnSelect"
        Text="Select"
        Runat="server" OnClick="btnSelect_Click" />
```

```
<asp:ObjectDataSource
    id="srcCultures"
    TypeName="System.Globalization.CultureInfo"
    SelectMethod="GetCultures"
    Runat="server">
    <SelectParameters>
        <asp:Parameter Name="types" DefaultValue="SpecificCultures" />
    </SelectParameters>
</asp:ObjectDataSource>

<hr />

Today's date is:
<br />
<asp:Label
    id="lblDate"
    Runat="server" />

<br /><br />

The price of the product is:
<br />
<asp:Label
    id="lblPrice"
    Runat="server" />

</div>
</form>
</body>
</html>
```

Consider two things about the page in Listing 30.3. First, the culture is set in the `InitializeCulture()` method, which overrides the `InitializeCulture()` method of the base `Page` class and sets the `UICulture` and `Culture` properties by using the `Profile` object.

Second, the `btnSelect_Click()` handler updates the properties of the `Profile` object and redirects the page back to itself, which is done so that the `InitializeCulture()` method executes after a user changes the selected culture.

The page in Listing 30.3 uses the `Profile` defined in the web configuration file contained in Listing 30.4.

LISTING 30.4   Web.Config

```
<?xml version="1.0"?>
<configuration xmlns="http://schemas.microsoft.com/.NetConfiguration/v2.0">
  <system.web>
    <anonymousIdentification enabled="true"/>

    <profile>
      <properties>
        <add
          name="UserCulture"
          defaultValue="en-US" />
        <add
          name="UserUICulture"
          defaultValue="en"/>
      </properties>
    </profile>
  </system.web>
</configuration>
```

The web configuration file in Listing 30.4 includes an anonymousIdentification element. Including this element causes a profile to be created for a user even if the user has not been authenticated.

Automatically Detecting a Culture

In the previous section, you learned how to set the UICulture and Culture properties by allowing the user to select a particular culture from a DropDownList control. Instead of requiring users to select their culture, you can automatically detect users' cultures through their browser settings.

Whenever a browser makes a request for a web page, the browser sends an Accept-Language header, which contains a list of the user's preferred languages.

You can set your preferred languages when using Microsoft Internet Explorer or Mozilla Firefox by selecting Tools, Internet Options and clicking the Languages button. You can then create an ordered list of your preferred languages (see Figure 30.3). When using Opera, select Tools, Preferences and click the Details button (see Figure 30.4).

You can retrieve the value of the Accept-Language header by using the Request.UserLanguages property. For example, the page in Listing 30.5 displays a list of the languages retrieved from a browser's Accept-Language header (see Figure 30.5).

FIGURE 30.3   Setting your preferred language with Internet Explorer.

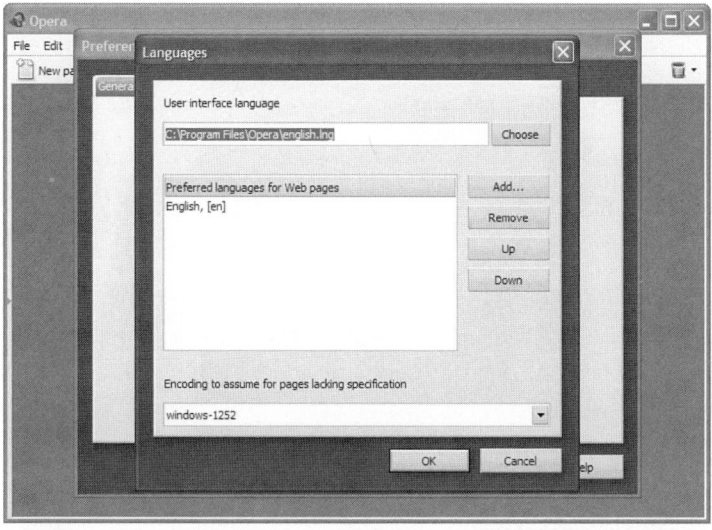

FIGURE 30.4   Setting your preferred language with Opera.

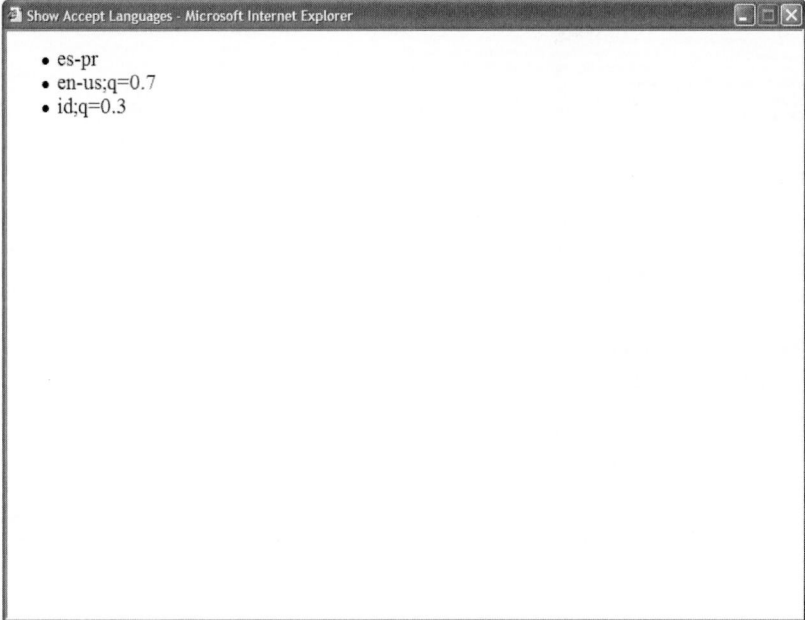

FIGURE 30.5   Displaying a browser's language settings.

LISTING 30.5   ShowAcceptLanguages.aspx

```
<%@ Page Language="C#" %>
<!DOCTYPE html PUBLIC "-//W3C//DTD XHTML 1.1//EN"
"http://www.w3.org/TR/xhtml11/DTD/xhtml11.dtd">
<script runat="server">

    void Page_Load()
    {
        bltAcceptLanguages.DataSource = Request.UserLanguages;
        bltAcceptLanguages.DataBind();
    }

</script>
<html xmlns="http://www.w3.org/1999/xhtml" >
<head id="Head1" runat="server">
    <title>Show Accept Languages</title>
</head>
<body>
    <form id="form1" runat="server">
    <div>
```

```
<asp:BulletedList
    id="bltAcceptLanguages"
    Runat="server" />

</div>
</form>
</body>
</html>
```

If you want to set the `Culture` or `UICulture` properties automatically by detecting the browser's Accept-Language header, you can set either of these properties to the value auto. For example, the page in Listing 30.6 automatically displays the date and currency amount according to the user's preferred language.

LISTING 30.6   SelectCultureAuto.aspx

```
<%@ Page Language="C#" Culture="auto:en-US" UICulture="auto:en-US"%>
<!DOCTYPE html PUBLIC "-//W3C//DTD XHTML 1.1//EN"
"http://www.w3.org/TR/xhtml11/DTD/xhtml11.dtd">
<script runat="server">

    void Page_PreRender()
    {
        lblDate.Text = DateTime.Now.ToString("D");
        lblPrice.Text = (512.33m).ToString("c");
    }
</script>
<html xmlns="http://www.w3.org/1999/xhtml" >
<head id="Head1" runat="server">
    <title>Select Culture Auto</title>
</head>
<body>
    <form id="form1" runat="server">
    <div>

    Today's date is:
    <br />
    <asp:Label
        id="lblDate"
        Runat="server" />

    <br /><br />
```

```
    The price of the product is:
    <br />
    <asp:Label
        id="lblPrice"
        Runat="server" />

    </div>
    </form>
</body>
</html>
```

In the <%@ Page %> directive in Listing 30.6, both the Culture and UICulture attributes are set to the value auto:en-US. The culture name that appears after the colon enables you to specify a default culture when a language preference cannot be detected from the browser.

> **WARNING**
>
> Don't assume that all values of the Accept-Language header retrieved from a browser are valid culture names. Most browsers enable users to enter a "user-defined" language, which might not be valid.

Setting the Culture in the Web Configuration File

Rather than set the Culture and UICulture properties in each page, you can set these properties once in the web configuration file. Typically, you should take this approach because it makes your website easier to maintain.

The web configuration file in Listing 30.7 sets the Culture and UICulture properties to the value de-DE (German).

LISTING 30.7   Web.Config

```
<?xml version="1.0"?>
<configuration xmlns="http://schemas.microsoft.com/.NetConfiguration/v2.0">
<system.web>

  <globalization
    culture="de-DE"
    uiCulture="de-DE" />

</system.web>
</configuration>
```

If you prefer, you can use the value auto in the web configuration file if you want the culture to be automatically detected based on the value of the browser Accept-Language header. If you need to override the configuration settings in the web configuration file in a particular page, you can simply set the Culture and UICulture properties in the page.

Culture and ASP.NET Controls

The value of the Culture property automatically has an effect on the rendering behavior of ASP.NET controls such as the Calendar control. For example, Listing 30.8 uses the ASP.NET Calendar control to display a calendar (see Figure 30.6).

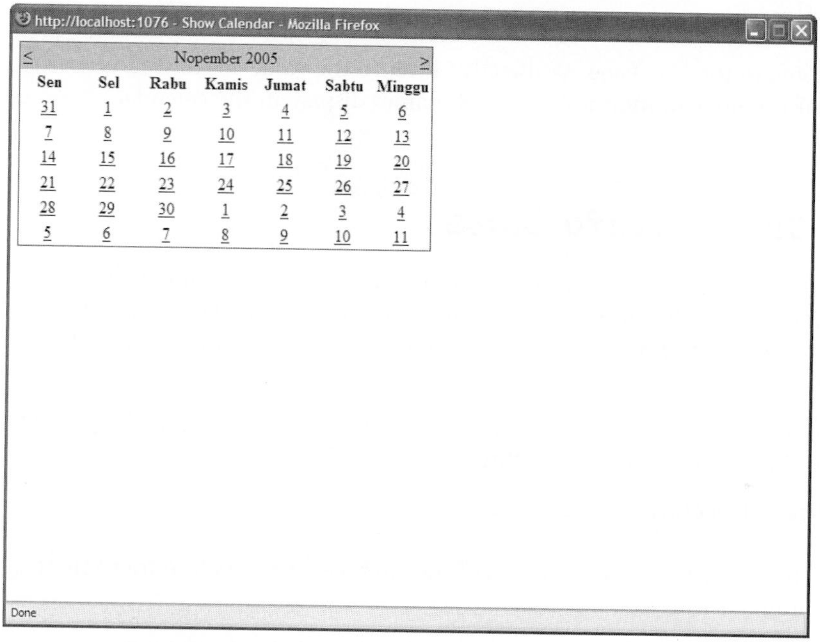

FIGURE 30.6   Displaying a localized Calendar control.

LISTING 30.8   ShowCalendar.aspx

```
<%@ Page Language="C#" Culture="id-ID" %>
<!DOCTYPE html PUBLIC "-//W3C//DTD XHTML 1.1//EN"
"http://www.w3.org/TR/xhtml11/DTD/xhtml11.dtd">
<html xmlns="http://www.w3.org/1999/xhtml" >
<head id="Head1" runat="server">
    <title>Show Calendar</title>
</head>
<body>
```

```
    <form id="form1" runat="server">
    <div>

    <asp:Calendar
        id="Calendar1"
        Runat="server" />

    </div>
    </form>
</body>
</html>
```

The `Culture` attribute in the `<%@ Page %>` directive is set to the value `id-ID` (Indonesian). When the calendar is rendered, Indonesian month names display in the calendar.

Using the `CultureInfo` Class

The `CultureInfo` class contains information about more than 150 different cultures. You can use the methods of this class in your code to retrieve information about a specific culture and use the information when formatting values such as dates, numbers, and currency amounts.

To represent a culture with the `CultureInfo` class, you can instantiate the class by passing a culture name to the class constructor like this:

```
Dim culture As New CultureInfo("de-DE")
```

You can also use any of the following methods of the `CultureInfo` class to retrieve information about a culture or cultures:

▶ **CreateSpecificCulture**—Enables you to create a `CultureInfo` object by supplying the name of a specific culture.

▶ **GetCultureInfo**—Enables you to create a `CultureInfo` object by supplying an identifier, culture name, or `CompareInfo` and `TextInfo` object.

▶ **GetCultureInfoByIetfLanguageTag**—Enables you to create a `CultureInfo` object efficiently by supplying a culture name.

▶ **GetCultures**—Enables you to retrieve an array of cultures.

The `CultureInfo` class lives in the `System.Globalization` namespace. Before you can use the `CultureInfo` class, you need to import this namespace.

Using the `CultureInfo` Class to Format String Values

To this point, the culture has been set at the level of an individual ASP.NET page or the level of an entire ASP.NET application. However, you might need to take advantage of locale-specific formatting at a more granular level. You can use the `CultureInfo` class to format a particular value independent of the `Culture` set for the page.

When you use the `ToString()` method to format dates, times, numbers, and currency amounts, you can supply an additional parameter that formats the value in accordance with a specific culture. For example, the page in Listing 30.9 formats two sets of date and time values.

LISTING 30.9   ToStringCulture.aspx

```
<%@ Page Language="C#" %>
<%@ Import Namespace="System.Globalization" %>
<!DOCTYPE html PUBLIC "-//W3C//DTD XHTML 1.1//EN"
"http://www.w3.org/TR/xhtml11/DTD/xhtml11.dtd">
<script runat="server">

    void Page_Load()
    {
        // Get German Culture Info
        CultureInfo gCulture = new CultureInfo("de-DE");

        // Use culture when formatting strings
        lblGermanDate.Text = DateTime.Now.ToString("D", gCulture);
        lblGermanPrice.Text = (512.33m).ToString("c", gCulture);

        // Get Indonesian Culture Info
        CultureInfo iCulture = new CultureInfo("id-ID");

        // Use culture when formatting strings
        lblIndonesianDate.Text = DateTime.Now.ToString("D", iCulture);
        lblIndonesianPrice.Text = (512.33m).ToString("c", iCulture);
    }
</script>
<html xmlns="http://www.w3.org/1999/xhtml" >
<head id="Head1" runat="server">
    <title>ToString Culture</title>
</head>
<body>
    <form id="form1" runat="server">
    <div>
```

30

```
<h1>German</h1>

Today's date is:
<br />
<asp:Label
    id="lblGermanDate"
    Runat="server" />

<br /><br />

The price of the product is:
<br />
<asp:Label
    id="lblGermanPrice"
    Runat="server" />



<h1>Indonesian</h1>

Today's date is:
<br />
<asp:Label
    id="lblIndonesianDate"
    Runat="server" />

<br /><br />

The price of the product is:
<br />
<asp:Label
    id="lblIndonesianPrice"
    Runat="server" />


    </div>
    </form>
</body>
</html>
```

The first date and time is formatted with German cultural conventions, and the second date and time is formatted with Indonesian cultural conventions (see Figure 30.7). Two CultureInfo objects, corresponding to two cultures, are created in the Page_Load() method.

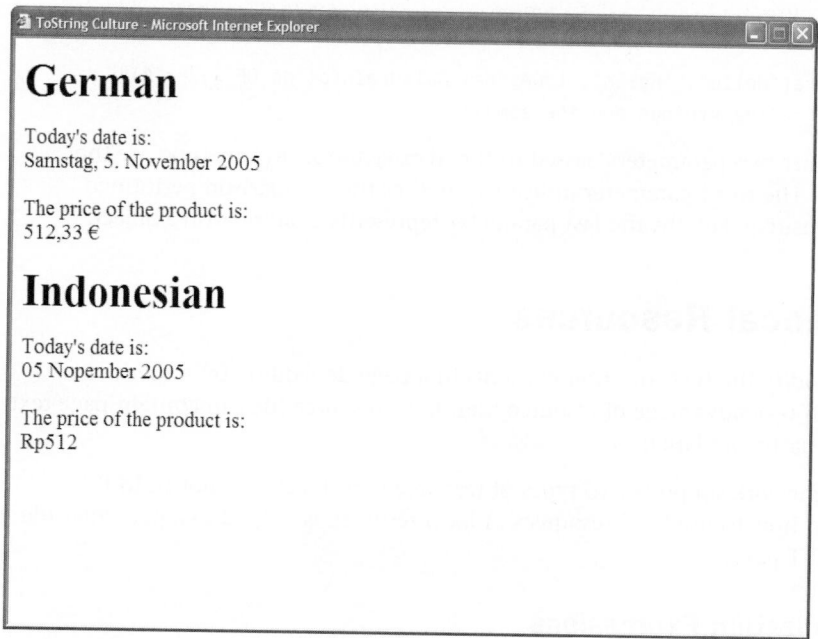

FIGURE 30.7   Formatting with the ToString() method.

Comparing and Sorting String Values

Different cultures follow different conventions when comparing and sorting string values. If you need to compare or sort string values in your code, you should use the String.Compare() method and optionally supply the method with an instance of the CultureInfo object.

The String.Compare() method returns one of the following values:

▶ **Negative Integer**—The first string is less than the second string.

▶ **Zero**—The first string is equal to the second string.

▶ **Positive Integer**—The first string is greater than the second string.

For example, the following conditional compares two strings, using the current culture set for the page:

```
if (String.Compare("Hello", "Hello") == 0)
  lblResult.Text = "The strings are the same!";
```

30

The following conditional uses a specific culture to perform a string comparison:

```
if (String.Compare("Hello", "Hello", true, new CultureInfo("de-DE")) == 0)
  lblResult.Text = "The strings are the same!";
```

In this case, the first two parameters passed to the `String.Compare()` method are the strings compared. The third parameter indicates whether the comparison performed should be case-sensitive. Finally, the last parameter represents a `CultureInfo` object.

Creating Local Resources

If you need to modify the text (or other content) in a page depending on a user's language, you can take advantage of resource files. Each resource file can contain page text translated into a particular language.

The ASP.NET Framework supports two types of resource files: local and global. In this section, you learn how to use local resources. A local resource is scoped to a particular file such as an ASP.NET page.

Explicit Localization Expressions

The page in Listing 30.10 is a simple page. It contains a button labeled Click Here! and displays the text Thank You! after you click the button.

LISTING 30.10   SimplePage.aspx

```
<%@ Page Language="C#" %>
<!DOCTYPE html PUBLIC "-//W3C//DTD XHTML 1.1//EN"
"http://www.w3.org/TR/xhtml11/DTD/xhtml11.dtd">
<script runat="server">

    protected void btnSubmit_Click(object sender, EventArgs e)
    {
        lblMessage.Visible = true;
    }
</script>
<html xmlns="http://www.w3.org/1999/xhtml" >
<head id="Head1" runat="server">
    <title>Simple Page</title>
</head>
<body>
    <form id="form1" runat="server">
    <div>

    <asp:Button
        id="btnSubmit"
```

```
            Text="Click Here!"
            OnClick="btnSubmit_Click"
            Runat="server" />

    <br /><br />

    <asp:Label
        id="lblMessage"
        Text="Thank You!"
        Visible="false"
        Runat="server" />

    </div>
    </form>
</body>
</html>
```

The page in Listing 30.10 displays the same text regardless of the language of the user visiting the page. If you want to display text in different languages for different users, you need to make a few modifications to the page.

The page in Listing 30.11 is a localizable version of the same page.

LISTING 30.11   LocalizablePage.aspx

```
<%@ Page Language="C#" UICulture="auto" %>
<!DOCTYPE html PUBLIC "-//W3C//DTD XHTML 1.1//EN"
"http://www.w3.org/TR/xhtml11/DTD/xhtml11.dtd">
<script runat="server">

    protected void btnSubmit_Click(object sender, EventArgs e)
    {
        lblMessage.Visible = true;
    }
</script>
<html xmlns="http://www.w3.org/1999/xhtml" >
<head id="Head1" runat="server">
    <title>Localizable Page</title>
</head>
<body>
    <form id="form1" runat="server">
    <div>

    <asp:Button
        id="btnSubmit"
        Text="<%$ Resources:ClickHere %>"
```

30

```
            OnClick="btnSubmit_Click"
            Runat="server" />


    <br /><br />

    <asp:Label
        id="lblMessage"
        Text="<%$ Resources:ThankYou %>"
        Visible="false"
        Runat="server" />

    </div>
    </form>
</body>
</html>
```

Two types of changes were made to the page in Listing 30.11. First, the `<%@ Page %>` directive includes a `UICulture` attribute that is set to the value `auto`. When a user requests the page, a resource file that matches the user's preferred browser language loads automatically.

NOTE

Don't confuse the Page `UICulture` property with the Page `Culture` property. The `UICulture` property determines which resource files load for the page. The `Culture` property, on the other hand, determines how date, number, and currency values are formatted.

Second, both the Button and Label controls have been modified. The Button control is declared like this:

```
<asp:Button
    id="btnSubmit"
    Text="<%$ Resources:ClickHere %>"
    OnClick="btnSubmit_Click"
    Runat="server" />
```

The value of the `Text` property is a resource expression. This resource expression retrieves the value of an entry named `ClickHere` from the loaded resource file. This resource expression is considered to be an *explicit* resource expression because the property is explicitly set to the value of a particular resource entry.

After you localize a page, you can associate a resource file with the page. All the resource files that you want to associate with a page must be added to a special folder named App_LocalResources. You create the App_LocalResources folder in the same folder as the page that you want to localize. For example, if the page is located in the root of your application, you would add the App_LocalResources folder to the root folder.

You associate a resource file in the App_LocalResources folder with a particular page by using the following file-naming convention:

```
page name.[culture name].resx
```

For example, all the following resource files are associated with the `LocalizablePage.aspx` page:

```
LocalizablePage.aspx.resx
LocalizablePage.aspx.es-PR.resx
LocalizablePage.aspx.es.resx
```

The first resource file is the default resource file. If none of the other resource files match the user's language settings, the contents of the default resource file are used.

The second resource filename includes the specific culture name es-PR (Puerto Rican Spanish). If a user's browser is set to Puerto Rican Spanish, the contents of this resource file are loaded.

Finally, the third resource filename includes the neutral culture name es (Spanish). If a user's preferred language is Spanish, but not Puerto Rican Spanish, the contents of this resource file are loaded.

You create a resource file when using Visual Web Developing by right-clicking an App_LocalResources folder, selecting Add New Item, and Assembly Resource file. Visual Web Developer automatically displays an editor for the resource file. The editor enables you to enter name and value pairs. For example, the `LocalizablePage.aspx.es.resx` resource file contains the two name/value pairs in Listing 30.12.

LISTING 30.12   `App_LocalResources\LocalizablePage.aspx.es.resx`

Name	Value
ClickHere	chasque aquí
ThankYou	¡Gracias!

Behind the scenes, resource files are XML files. You can open a resource file in Notepad and edit its contents. The ASP.NET Framework dynamically compiles resource files into assemblies in the background.

Implicit Localization Expressions

As an alternative to using explicit localization expressions, you can use an implicit localization expression. An implicit localization expression enables you to localize multiple control properties with one resource key.

The page in Listing 30.13 uses implicit localization expressions.

30

LISTING 30.13 `LocalizablePageImplicit.aspx`

```
<%@ Page Language="C#" UICulture="auto" %>
<!DOCTYPE html PUBLIC "-//W3C//DTD XHTML 1.1//EN"
"http://www.w3.org/TR/xhtml11/DTD/xhtml11.dtd">
<script runat="server">

    protected void btnSubmit_Click(object sender, EventArgs e)
    {
        lblMessage.Visible = true;
    }
</script>
<html xmlns="http://www.w3.org/1999/xhtml" >
<head id="Head1" runat="server">
    <title>Localizable Page Implicit</title>
</head>
<body>
    <form id="form1" runat="server">
    <div>

    <asp:Button
        id="btnSubmit"
        meta:resourceKey="btnSubmit"
        Text="Click Me!"
        ToolTip="Click to show message"
        OnClick="btnSubmit_Click"
        Runat="server" />

    <br /><br />

    <asp:Label
        id="lblMessage"
        meta:resourceKey="lblMessage"
        Text="Thank You!"
        Visible="false"
        Runat="server" />

    </div>
    </form>
</body>
</html>
```

Both the Button and Label control include a `meta:resourceKey` property. The value of this property represents a resource key in a local resource file. For example, the resource file in Listing 30.14 contains three entries.

LISTING 30.14   App_LocalResources\LocalizablePageImplicit.aspx.es.resx

Name	Value
btnSubmit.Text	chasque aquí
btnSubmit.ToolTip	Chasque aquí para demostrar el mensaje
lblMessage.Text	¡Gracias!

The first two entries set the Text and ToolTip properties of the btnSubmit control. The third entry sets the value of the Text property of the lblMessage property.

> **WARNING**
>
> When you are ready to start localizing a page, always create a default localization file (for example, LocalizablePageImplicit.aspx.resx). If you don't create a default localization file, other culture-specific localization files are ignored.

There are two advantages to using implicit localization expressions instead of using explicit localization expressions. First, implicit expressions enable you to override multiple control properties by associating a single resource key with the control.

Second, by taking advantage of implicit localization expressions, you can easily localize an existing website. You simply need to add the meta:resourceKey attribute to any control that you need to localize.

Using Local Resources with Page Properties

You can use resource expressions when setting page properties such as the page title. For example, the page in Listing 30.15 uses an explicit resource expression to set the page title.

LISTING 30.15   PageExplicit.aspx

```
<%@ Page Language="C#" UICulture="auto" %>
<!DOCTYPE html PUBLIC "-//W3C//DTD XHTML 1.1//EN"
    "http://www.w3.org/TR/xhtml11/DTD/xhtml11.dtd">
<html xmlns="http://www.w3.org/1999/xhtml" >
<head id="Head1" runat="server">
    <title><asp:Literal Text="<%$ Resources:Title %>" runat="Server" /></title>
</head>
<body>
    <form id="form1" runat="server">
    <div>

    <h1>Page Explicit Localization</h1>
```

```
    </div>
    </form>
</body>
</html>
```

In Listing 30.15, the page title is created with a `Literal` control, which contains an explicit resource expression for the value of its `Text` property. You also can use implicit resource expressions when setting the page title. This approach is illustrated by the page in Listing 30.16.

LISTING 30.16   PageImplicit.aspx

```
<%@ Page Language="C#" UICulture="auto" meta:resourceKey="page" %>
<!DOCTYPE html PUBLIC "-//W3C//DTD XHTML 1.1//EN"
    "http://www.w3.org/TR/xhtml11/DTD/xhtml11.dtd">
<html xmlns="http://www.w3.org/1999/xhtml" >
<head id="Head1" runat="server">
    <title>Page Title</title>
</head>
<body>
    <form id="form1" runat="server">
    <div>

    <h1>Page Implicit Localization</h1>

    </div>
    </form>
</body>
</html>
```

The `<%@ Page %>` directive includes a `meta:resourceKey` attribute. If a local resource includes a `page.Title` entry, the value of this entry is used for the title displayed by the page.

Retrieving Local Resources Programmatically

If you need to retrieve a local resource in your page code, you can use the `GetLocalResourceObject()` method. For example, the page in Listing 30.17 grabs a welcome message from a resource file. The welcome message is used to format some text, and then the formatted text displays in a `Label` control.

LISTING 30.17   ProgramLocal.aspx

```
<%@ Page Language="C#" %>
<!DOCTYPE html PUBLIC "-//W3C//DTD XHTML 1.1//EN"
"http://www.w3.org/TR/xhtml11/DTD/xhtml11.dtd">
```

```
<script runat="server">

    void Page_Load()
    {
        string welcomeMessage = (string)GetLocalResourceObject("welcomeMessage");
        lblMessage.Text = String.Format(welcomeMessage, "Steve");
    }

</script>
<html xmlns="http://www.w3.org/1999/xhtml" >
<head id="Head1" runat="server">
    <title>Program Local Resource</title>
</head>
<body>
    <form id="form1" runat="server">
    <div>

    <asp:Label
        id="lblMessage"
        Runat="server" />

    </div>
    </form>
</body>
</html>
```

The result returned from `GetLocalResourceObject()` must be cast to a string value. As the method name implies, the method returns an object and not a string value. The resource file associated with the page in Listing 30.17, named `ProgramLocal.aspx.es.resx`, is contained in Listing 30.18.

LISTING 30.18 `App_LocalResources\ProgramLocal.aspx.es.resx`

Name	Value
welcomeMessage	Welcome {0} to our website!

If someone's browser is set to Spanish as the preferred language, and the user requests the page, the welcome message is retrieved from this resource file, the name Steve is added to the string, and the result displays in the browser (see Figure 30.8).

You also can retrieve local resources in a component. Within a component, use the shared `HttpContext.GetLocalResourceObject()` method. For example, the component in Listing 30.19 grabs the entry named `ClickHere` from the local resource file that corresponds to the page named `LocalizablePage.aspx`.

FIGURE 30.8   Retrieving a local resource programmatically.

LISTING 30.19   LocalComponent.cs

```
using System;
using System.Web;

public class LocalComponent
{
    public static string getResource()
    {
        return (string)HttpContext.GetLocalResourceObject("~/LocalizablePage.aspx",
➥"ClickHere");
    }
}
```

Creating Global Resources

A local resource is scoped to a particular page. A global resource, on the other hand, can be used by any page in an application. Any localized content that you need to share among multiple pages in your website should be added to a global resource file.

You create global resource files by adding the files to a special folder named App_GlobalResources. This folder must be located in the root of your application.

For example, the file in Listing 30.20 is a global resource file.

LISTING 30.20   App_GlobalResources\Site.resx

Name	Value
Title	My website
Copyright	Copyright © 2006 by the Company

The page in Listing 30.21 uses the entries from the global resource file (see Figure 30.9).

LISTING 30.21   ShowGlobalPage.aspx

```
<%@ Page Language="C#" %>
<!DOCTYPE html PUBLIC "-//W3C//DTD XHTML 1.1//EN"
    "http://www.w3.org/TR/xhtml11/DTD/xhtml11.dtd">
<html xmlns="http://www.w3.org/1999/xhtml" >
<head id="Head1" runat="server">
    <title>
    <asp:Literal
        id="ltlTitle"
        Text="<%$ Resources:Site,Title %>"
        Runat="Server" />
    </title>
</head>
<body>
    <form id="form1" runat="server">
    <div>

    <br />Page Content
    <br />Page Content
    <br />Page Content
    <br />Page Content

    <hr />
    <asp:Literal
        id="ltlCopyright"
        Text="<%$ Resources:Site,Copyright %>"
        Runat="Server" />

    </div>
    </form>
</body>
</html>
```

30

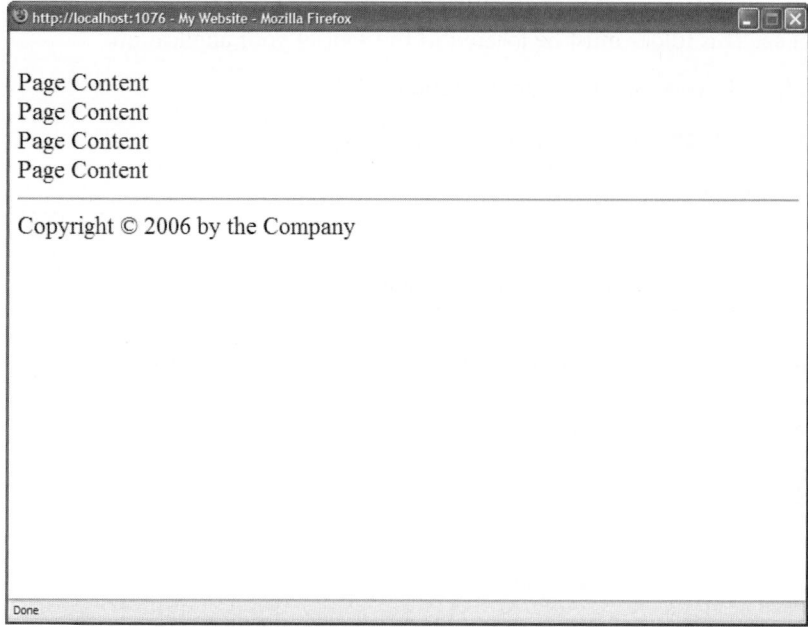

FIGURE 30.9   Displaying global resource entries.

Just as you can with a local resource file, you can localize a global resource file by adding culture names to the file name. For example, the page in Listing 30.22 is localized to Spanish.

LISTING 30.22   App_GlobalResources\Site.es.resx

Name	Value
Title	Mi Website
Copyright	Copyright © 2006 de la compañía

If you modify the UICulture attribute contained in the <%@ Page %> directive in Listing 30.21 to the value es, the resource file in Listing 30.22 will be used with the page. Alternatively, you can set UICulture to the value auto and change your browser's language settings.

Retrieving Global Resources Programmatically

You can retrieve a global resource entry programmatically from any page by using the GetGlobalResourceObject() method. For example, the page in Listing 30.23 grabs the Title entry from the Site resource file and displays the value of the entry in a Label control.

LISTING 30.23 ProgramGlobal.aspx

```
<%@ Page Language="C#" UICulture="auto" %>
<!DOCTYPE html PUBLIC "-//W3C//DTD XHTML 1.1//EN"
"http://www.w3.org/TR/xhtml11/DTD/xhtml11.dtd">
<script runat="server">

    void Page_Load()
    {
        lblMessage.Text = (string)GetGlobalResourceObject("Site", "Title");
    }
</script>
<html xmlns="http://www.w3.org/1999/xhtml" >
<head id="Head1" runat="server">
    <title>Program Global</title>
</head>
<body>
    <form id="form1" runat="server">
    <div>

    <asp:Label
        id="lblMessage"
        Runat="server" />

    </div>
    </form>
</body>
</html>
```

The `GetGlobalResourceObject()` method requires two parameters: the name of the resource class and the name of an entry. The resource class corresponds to the global resource filename.

Using Strongly Typed Localization Expressions

The ASP.NET Framework automatically converts global resources into compiled classes behind the scenes. This enables you to use strongly typed expressions when working with global resources in your code. When you create a resource, a new class is added automatically to the Resources namespace. The class exposes all the entries of the resource file as properties.

For example, the page in Listing 30.24 retrieves the Title entry from the Site global resource file (`Site.resx` and its culture-specific variations).

LISTING 30.24   ProgramGlobalTyped.aspx

```
<%@ Page Language="C#" UICulture="auto" %>
<!DOCTYPE html PUBLIC "-//W3C//DTD XHTML 1.1//EN"
"http://www.w3.org/TR/xhtml11/DTD/xhtml11.dtd">
<script runat="server">

    void Page_Load()
    {
        lblMessage.Text = Resources.Site.Title;
    }
</script>
<html xmlns="http://www.w3.org/1999/xhtml" >
<head id="Head1" runat="server">
    <title>Program Global Typed</title>
</head>
<body>
    <form id="form1" runat="server">
    <div>

    <asp:Label
        id="lblMessage"
        Runat="server" />

    </div>
    </form>
</body>
</html>
```

You can use the following expression magically to refer to the Title entry in the Site resource file:

```
lblMessage.Text = Resources.Site.Title
```

Using the Localize Control

The ASP.NET Framework includes a control named the Localize control, which is included in Framework to make it easier to localize big chunks of text in a page.

For example, the page in Listing 30.25 uses the Localize control in the body of the page.

LISTING 30.25 ShowLocalizeControl.aspx

```
<%@ Page Language="C#" UICulture="auto" %>
<!DOCTYPE html PUBLIC "-//W3C//DTD XHTML 1.1//EN"
    "http://www.w3.org/TR/xhtml11/DTD/xhtml11.dtd">
<html xmlns="http://www.w3.org/1999/xhtml" >
<head id="Head1" runat="server">
    <title>Show Localize Control</title>
</head>
<body>
    <form id="form1" runat="server">
    <div>

    <asp:Localize
        ID="locBodyText"
        meta:resourceKey="locBodyText"
        Runat="server">
        Here is the page body text
    </asp:Localize>

    <br /><br />

    <asp:Literal
        ID="ltlBodyText"
        runat="server">
        Here is some literal text
    </asp:Literal>

    </div>
    </form>
</body>
</html>
```

The Localize control is similar to the Literal control (it derives from the Literal control). In Source View, there is nothing that distinguishes the two controls. The difference between the Localize control and Literal control is apparent only in Design View. Unlike the Literal control, the contents of the Localize control can be edited directly on the Designer surface in Design View (see Figure 30.10).

30

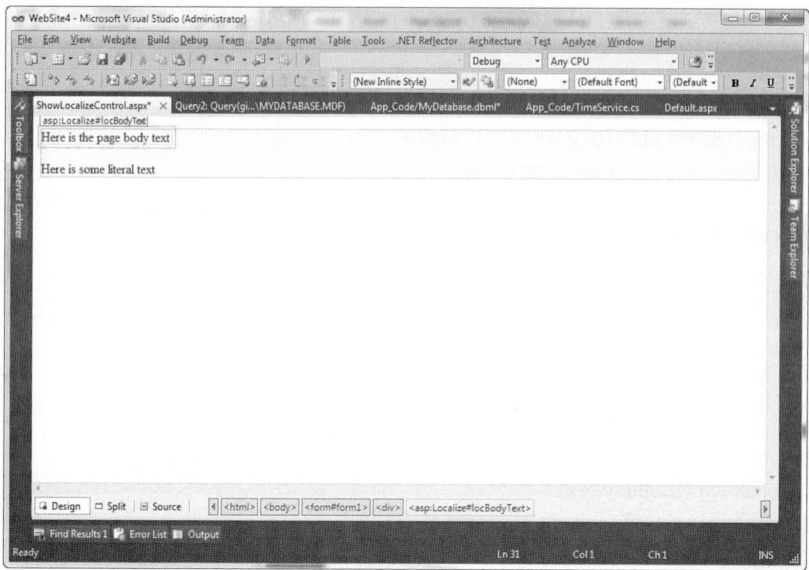

FIGURE 30.10   Using the `Localize` control in Design View.

Summary

In this chapter, you learned how to localize websites for different languages and culture. In the first section, you learned how to use the `Culture` and `UICulture` properties to set the current culture for the page. You also learned how to set these properties automatically by detecting a browser's preferred language settings.

Next, you learned how to create local resource files that you can apply to particular pages (and other files). You learned how to use both explicit and implicit localization expressions. You also saw how you can programmatically retrieve local resource entries in your code.

You then studied the topic of global resource files, which contain entries that can be used within any page in a website. You learned to use explicit resource expressions with global resources and how to retrieve global resource entries programmatically.

Finally, you had a brief look at the ASP.NET `Localize` control. You learned how to use this control to localize big chunks of text in a page.

Working with the HTTP Runtime

This chapter tackles a number of advanced topics by digging deeper into the mechanics of how an ASP.NET page is processed. In this first section, you learn how to create a custom BuildProvider, which is a .NET class that generates source code from a file automatically. You learn how to create a custom BuildProvider that builds custom data access components automatically.

Next, you learn how to create a custom ExpressionBuilder, which is responsible for parsing an expression into code. For example, when you use the <%$ ConnectionStrings: MyDatabase %> syntax to refer to a connection string, you use the ConnectionStringExpressionBuilder in the background. In this chapter, you learn how to build a custom ExpressionBuilder that looks up values from an XML file.

You also learn how to work with HTTP Handlers. An HTTP Handler is a .NET class that executes whenever a request is made for a file at a certain path. For example, you can use a custom HTTP Handler to retrieve an image from a database table whenever someone requests a file with the extension .gif or .jpeg.

Finally, you will see how to create custom HTTP Modules. An HTTP Module is a .NET class that executes with each and every request. For example, you can implement a custom authentication system by creating a custom HTTP Module. You also can use a custom HTTP Module to create a custom logging module.

Creating a Custom `BuildProvider`

When you write an ASP.NET page and save the page to your computer's file system, the ASP.NET page gets compiled dynamically into a .NET class in the background. The page is compiled dynamically by a `BuildProvider`.

The ASP.NET Framework includes a number of `BuildProviders`. Each `BuildProvider` is responsible for compiling a file with a particular extension located in a particular type of folder. For example, there are `BuildProviders` for Themes, Master Pages, User Controls, and Web Services.

When a `BuildProvider` builds, it builds a new class in the Temporary ASP.NET Files folder. Any class added to the folder becomes available to your application automatically. When you use Visual Web Developer, any public properties and methods of the class appear in Intellisense.

You can create your own `BuildProviders`. This can be useful in a variety of different scenarios. For example, imagine that you find yourself building a lot of ASP.NET pages that display forms. You can tediously build each ASP.NET page by hand by adding all the necessary form and validation controls. Alternatively, you can create a new `BuildProvider` that takes an XML file and generates the form pages for you automatically.

Or imagine that you are spending a lot of time building data access components. For example, every time you need to access a database table, you create a new component that exposes properties that correspond to each of the columns in the database table. In this case, it would make sense to create a custom `BuildProvider` that generates the data access component automatically.

Creating a Simple `BuildProvider`

Let's start by creating a simple `BuildProvider`. The new `BuildProvider` will be named the `SimpleBuildProvider`. Whenever you create a file that has the extension `.simple`, the `SimpleBuilderProvider` builds a new class with the same name as the file in the background. The dynamically compiled class also includes a single method named `DoSomething()` that doesn't actually do anything.

The `SimpleBuildProvider` is contained in Listing 31.1.

LISTING 31.1   `App_Code\CustomBuildProviders\SimpleBuildProvider.cs`

```
using System;
using System.Web.Compilation;
using System.CodeDom;
using System.IO;

namespace AspNetUnleashed
{
    public class SimpleBuildProvider : BuildProvider
```

```
    {
        public override void GenerateCode(AssemblyBuilder ab)
        {
            string fileName = Path.GetFileNameWithoutExtension(this.VirtualPath);
            string snippet = "public class " + fileName + @"
                {
                    public static void DoSomething(){}
                }";
            ab.AddCodeCompileUnit(this, new CodeSnippetCompileUnit(snippet));
        }


    }
}
```

All `BuildProviders` must inherit from the base `BuildProvider` class. Typically, you override the `BuildProvider` class `GenerateCode()` method. This method is responsible for generating the class that gets added to the Temporary ASP.NET Files folder.

An instance of the `AssemblyBuilder` class is passed to the `GenerateCode()` method. You add the class that you want to create to this `AssemblyBuilder` by calling the `AssemblyBuilder.AddCodeCompileUnit()` method.

In Listing 31.1, a `CodeSnippetCompileUnit` is used to represent the source code for the class. Any code that you represent with the `CodeSnippetCompileUnit` is added, verbatim, to the dynamically generated class. This approach is problematic.

Unfortunately, you can use the `SimpleBuildProvider` in Listing 31.1 only when building a C# application;.it doesn't work with a Visual Basic .NET application. Because the code represented by the `CodeSnippetCompileUnit` is C# code, using the `SimpleBuildProvider` with a Visual Basic .NET application would result in compilation errors. The `SimpleBuildProvider` would inject C# code into a Visual Basic .NET assembly.

The proper way to write the `SimpleBuildProvider` class would be to use the `CodeDom`, which enables you to represent .NET code in a language neutral manner. When you represent a block of code with the `CodeDom`, the code can be converted to either C# or Visual Basic .NET code automatically. You learn how to use the `CodeDom` when we build a more complicated `BuildProvider` in the next section. For now, just realize that we are taking a shortcut to keep things simple.

When you add the `SimpleBuildProvider` to your project, it is important that you add the file to a separate subfolder in your App_Code folder and you mark the folder as a separate code folder in the web configuration file. The `SimpleBuildProvider` is located in the sample code on the book's website.

You must add a `BuildProvider` to a separate subfolder because a `BuildProvider` must be compiled into a different assembly than the other code in the App_Code folder. This makes sense because a `BuildProvider` is actually responsible for compiling the other code in the App_Code folder.

The web configuration file in Listing 31.2 defines the CustomBuildProviders folder and registers the `SimpleBuildProvider`.

LISTING 31.2   Web.Config

```
<?xml version="1.0"?>
<configuration>
    <system.web>

      <compilation>
        <codeSubDirectories>
          <add directoryName="CustomBuildProviders"/>
        </codeSubDirectories>
        <buildProviders>
          <add extension=".simple" type="AspNetUnleashed.SimpleBuildProvider" />
        </buildProviders>
      </compilation>

    </system.web>
</configuration>
```

The web configuration file in Listing 31.2 associates the `SimpleBuildProvider` with the file extension `.simple`. Whenever you add a file with the `.simple` extension to the App_Code folder, the `SimpleBuildProvider` automatically compiles a new class based on the file.

> **NOTE**
>
> Build Providers execute at different times depending on the type of folder. Build Providers associated with the App_Code folder execute immediately after a new file is saved. Build Providers associated with the Web or App_Data folders execute when a file is requested.

For example, adding the file in Listing 31.3 to your App_Code folder causes the `SimpleBuildProvider` to create a new class named Mike.

LISTING 31.3   App_Code\Mike.simple

```
Hello!
Hello!
Hello!
```

The actual content of the file that you create doesn't matter. The `SimpleBuildProvider` ignores everything about the file except for the name of the file.

You can see the new file created by the `SimpleBuildProvider` by navigating to the Sources_App_Code folder contained in the folder that corresponds to your application in the Temporary ASP.NET Files folder. The contents of the auto-generated file are contained in Listing 31.4.

LISTING 31.4 mike.simple.72cecc2a.cs

```
#pragma checksum "C:\Chapter27\Code\CS\App_Code\Mike.simple"
➡"{406ea660-64cf-4c82-b6f0-42d48172a799}" "AD2E00BE337DD88E4E4B07F6B4580617"
public class Mike
{
  public static void DoSomething(){}
}
```

Any class added to the Temporary ASP.NET Files folder is available in your application automatically. For example, the page in Listing 31.5 uses the `Mike` class.

LISTING 31.5 ShowSimpleBuildProvider.aspx

```
<%@ Page Language="C#" %>
<!DOCTYPE html PUBLIC "-//W3C//DTD XHTML 1.0 Transitional//EN"
"http://www.w3.org/TR/xhtml1/DTD/xhtml1-transitional.dtd">
<script runat="server">

    void Page_Load()
    {
        Mike.DoSomething();
    }
</script>
<html xmlns="http://www.w3.org/1999/xhtml" >
<head id="Head1" runat="server">
    <title>Show SimpleBuildProvider</title>
</head>
<body>
    <form id="form1" runat="server">
    <div>

    </div>
    </form>
</body>
</html>
```

The Mike class appears in Intellisense. For example, if you type Mike followed by a period, the DoSomething() method appears (see Figure 31.1).

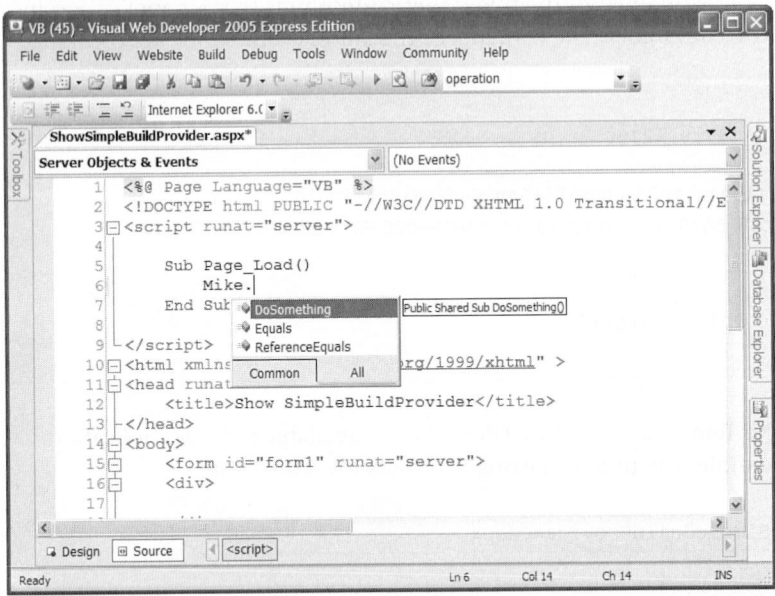

FIGURE 31.1   Using a BuildProvider to generate a class dynamically.

Creating a Data Access Component BuildProvider

In the previous section, we created a simple but useless BuildProvider. In this section, we create a complicated but useful BuildProvider.

In this section, we create a DataBuildProvider, which generates a data access component automatically from an XML file. For example, if you add the XML file in Listing 31.6 to your project, the DataBuildProvider generates the class in Listing 31.7 automatically.

LISTING 31.6   App_Code\Movie.data

```
<Movies>
  <add name="Title" />
  <add name="Director" />
  <add name="BoxOfficeTotals" type="Decimal" />
</Movies>
```

LISTING 31.7   movie.data.72cecc2a.cs

```csharp
#pragma checksum "C:\Documents and Settings\Steve\My Documents\ASP.NET 3.5
Unleashed\Chapter27\Code\CS\App_Code\Movie.data" "{406ea660-64cf-4c82-b6f0-
42d48172a799}""2E0F31E6B8F9D4B8687F94F0305E6D15"
//------------------------------------------------------------------------
// <auto-generated>
//     This code was generated by a tool.
//     Runtime Version:2.0.50731.1378
//
//     Changes to this file may cause incorrect behavior and will be lost if
//     the code is regenerated.
// </auto-generated>
//------------------------------------------------------------------------

namespace Data {
    using System;

    public partial class Movie {

        private string _Title;
        private string _Director;
        private Decimal _BoxOfficeTotals;

        public Movie() {
        }

        public virtual string Title {
            get {
                return this._Title;
            }
            set {
                this._Title = value;
            }
        }

        public virtual string Director {
            get {
                return this._Director;
            }
            set {
                this._Director = value;
            }
        }
```

```
        public virtual Decimal BoxOfficeTotals {
            get {
                return this._BoxOfficeTotals;
            }
            set {
                this._BoxOfficeTotals = value;
            }
        }


        /// <summary>Returns List of Movie</summary>
        public static System.Collections.Generic.List<Movie>
Select(System.Data.SqlClient.SqlConnection con) {
            System.Collections.Generic.List<Movie> results = new
System.Collections.Generic.List<Movie>();
            System.Data.SqlClient.SqlCommand cmd = new
System.Data.SqlClient.SqlCommand();
            cmd.Connection = con;
            string cmdText = "SELECT Title,Director,BoxOfficeTotals FROM Movies";
            cmd.CommandText = cmdText;
            System.Data.SqlClient.SqlDataReader reader = cmd.ExecuteReader();
            int counter;
            for (counter = 0; reader.Read(); counter = (counter + 1)) {
                Movie record = new Movie();
                record.Title = ((string)(reader["Title"]));
                record.Director = ((string)(reader["Director"]));
                record.BoxOfficeTotals = ((Decimal)(reader["BoxOfficeTotals"]));
                results.Add(record);
            }
            return results;
        }


        /// <summary>Returns List of Movie</summary>
        public static System.Collections.Generic.List<Movie> Select(string
connectionStringName) {
            System.Collections.Generic.List<Movie> results = new
System.Collections.Generic.List<Movie>();
            System.Configuration.ConnectionStringSettings conStringSettings =
System.Web.Configuration.WebConfigurationManager.ConnectionStrings[connectionString
➡Name];
            string conString = conStringSettings.ConnectionString;
            System.Data.SqlClient.SqlConnection con = new
System.Data.SqlClient.SqlConnection();
            con.ConnectionString = conString;
            try {
                con.Open();
                results = Movie.Select(con);
```

```
            }
            finally {
                con.Close();
            }
            return results;
        }
    }
}
```

The XML file in Listing 31.6 contains the name of a database table (Movies) and contains a list of columns from the database table. When you add the file in Listing 31.6 to your project, the class in Listing 31.7 is generated automatically.

The data access component in Listing 31.7 contains a property that corresponds to each of the columns listed in the `Movie.data` file. Furthermore, each property has the data type specified in the `Movie.data` file.

Furthermore, the Movie data access component includes two `Select()` methods. You can retrieve all the records from the Movies database table in two ways: by passing an open `SqlConnection` object to the `Select()` method or by passing the name of a connection string defined in the web configuration file to the `Select()` method.

The page in Listing 31.8 illustrates how you can use the Movie data access component within an ASP.NET page (see Figure 31.2).

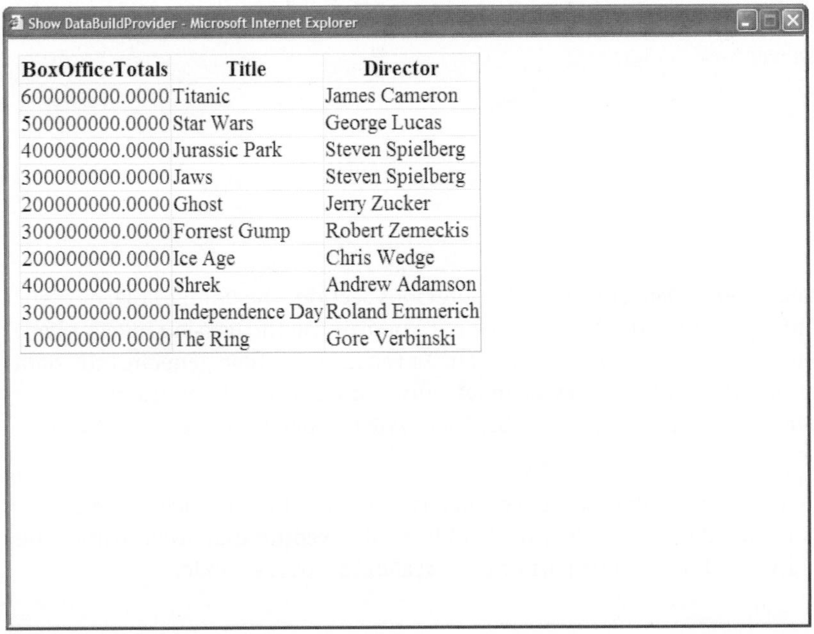

BoxOfficeTotals	Title	Director
600000000.0000	Titanic	James Cameron
500000000.0000	Star Wars	George Lucas
400000000.0000	Jurassic Park	Steven Spielberg
300000000.0000	Jaws	Steven Spielberg
200000000.0000	Ghost	Jerry Zucker
300000000.0000	Forrest Gump	Robert Zemeckis
200000000.0000	Ice Age	Chris Wedge
400000000.0000	Shrek	Andrew Adamson
300000000.0000	Independence Day	Roland Emmerich
100000000.0000	The Ring	Gore Verbinski

FIGURE 31.2   Displaying data returned by a dynamically generated data access component.

LISTING 31.8   ShowDataBuildProvider.aspx

```
<%@ Page Language="C#" %>
<!DOCTYPE html PUBLIC "-//W3C//DTD XHTML 1.0 Transitional//EN"
"http://www.w3.org/TR/xhtml1/DTD/xhtml1-transitional.dtd">

<script runat="server">

    void Page_Load()
    {
        grdMovies.DataSource = Data.Movie.Select("Movies");
        grdMovies.DataBind();
    }

</script>

<html xmlns="http://www.w3.org/1999/xhtml" >
<head id="Head1" runat="server">
    <title>Untitled Page</title>
</head>
<body>
    <form id="form1" runat="server">
    <div>

    <asp:GridView
        id="grdMovies"
        Runat="server" />

    </div>
    </form>
</body>
</html>
```

Unlike the SimpleBuildProvider created in the previous section, the DataBuildProvider uses the CodeDom to represent code. This means that you can use the DataBuildProvider in both Visual Basic .NET and C# applications. The DataBuildProvider generates the data access component in different languages automatically. For example, if you use the DataBuildProvider in a C# application, the BuildProvider generates the code in Listing 31.6 in C#.

Unfortunately, the code for the DataBuildProvider is much too long to include here. The entire code is included on the code download from the website that accompanies the book. The file in Listing 31.9 contains part of the DataBuildProvider code.

LISTING 31.9   DataBuildProvider.cs (Partial)

```csharp
using System;
using System.Collections.Generic;
using System.Web.Compilation;
using System.CodeDom;
using System.Xml;
using System.IO;
using System.Web.Hosting;

namespace AspNetUnleashed
{
    public class DataBuildProvider : BuildProvider
    {
        string _className;

        public override void GenerateCode(AssemblyBuilder ab)
        {
            // Load the XML file
            XmlDocument xmlData = new XmlDocument();
            xmlData.Load(HostingEnvironment.MapPath(this.VirtualPath));

            // Generate code from XML document
            CodeCompileUnit dataCode = GetDataCode(xmlData);

            // Add the code
            ab.AddCodeCompileUnit(this, dataCode);
        }

        private CodeCompileUnit GetDataCode(XmlDocument xmlData)
        {
            // Add class
            _className = Path.GetFileNameWithoutExtension(this.VirtualPath);
            CodeTypeDeclaration dataType = new CodeTypeDeclaration(_className);
            dataType.IsPartial = true;

            // Add constructor
            AddConstructor(dataType);

            // Add properties
            AddProperties(dataType, xmlData);

            // Add Select method
            AddSelect(dataType, xmlData);
```

```
                // Add Select with conString overload
                AddSelectConString(dataType, xmlData);

                // Create namespace
                CodeNamespace dataNS = new CodeNamespace("Data");

                // Add class to namespace
                dataNS.Types.Add(dataType);

                // Create code unit
                CodeCompileUnit dataCode = new CodeCompileUnit();

                // Add namespace to code unit
                dataCode.Namespaces.Add(dataNS);

                // Add default namespaces
                dataNS.Imports.Add(new CodeNamespaceImport("System"));

                return dataCode;
            }
        }
    }
```

The `DataBuildProvider`'s `GenerateCode()` method loads a `.data` file into an `XmlDocument`. The `VirtualPath` property represents the path of the file being built. For example, if you add a file named `Products.data` to your project, the `VirtualPath` property would represent the path to the `Products.data` file.

Next, the code for the data access component is created from the XML file by the `GetDataCode()` method, which makes heavy use of the `CodeDom` to generate the code in a language-neutral manner. Working with the `CodeDom` is a strange and tedious experience. You must build up a block of code by building a code tree. In Listing 31.9, a `CodeCompileUnit` named `dataCode` is created. A `CodeNamespace` named `dataNS` that represents a namespace is created and added to the `CodeCompileUnit`. And a `CodeTypeDeclaration` named `datatype` that represents a class is added to the namespace. After the class is created, the methods and properties are added to the class block by block.

Creating a Custom `ExpressionBuilder`

An `ExpressionBuilder` class generates one expression from another expression. Typically, you use an `ExpressionBuilder` to look up a particular value given a particular key.

The ASP.NET Framework includes the following `ExpressionBuilder` classes:

▶ **`AppSettingsExpressionBuilder`**—Retrieves values from the `appSettings` section of the web configuration file.

▶ **ConnectionStringsExpressionBuilder**—Retrieves values from the connectionStrings section of the web configuration file.

▶ **ResourceExpressionBuilder**—Retrieves values from resource files.

The ConnectionStringsExpressionBuilder has been used throughout this book whenever a connection string has needed to be retrieved.

You use the following syntax when working with an ExpressionBuilder:

```
<%$ ConnectionStrings:MyDatabase %>
```

The <%$ and %> tags mark an expression that should be parsed by an ExpressionBuilder. The prefix ConnectionStrings is mapped to the particular ExpressionBuilder class responsible for parsing the expression. ExpressionBuilders must always be used with control properties. For example, you cannot display a connection string in a page like this:

```
<%$ ConnectionStrings:MyDatabase %>
```

Instead, you must display the connection string like this:

```
<asp:Literal
  Id="ltlConnectionString"
  Text='<%$ ConnectionStrings:MyDatabase %>'
  Runat="server" />
```

You can create a custom ExpressionBuilder when none of the existing ExpressionBuilder classes do what you need. For example, you might want to store your application settings in a custom section of the web configuration file. In that case, you might want to create a custom ExpressionBuilder that grabs values from the custom configuration section.

Creating a Lookup ExpressionBuilder

In this section, you learn how to extend ASP.NET Framework by building a custom ExpressionBuilder class. We create a Lookup ExpressionBuilder that looks up string values from an XML file.

The LookupExpressionBuilder class is contained in Listing 31.10.

LISTING 31.10   App_Code\LookupExpressionBuilder.cs

```
using System;
using System.CodeDom;
using System.Web.UI;
using System.ComponentModel;
using System.Web.Compilation;
using System.Xml;
using System.Web.Hosting;
```

```
using System.Web.Caching;

namespace AspNetUnleashed
{
    public class LookupExpressionBuilder : ExpressionBuilder
    {
        public override CodeExpression GetCodeExpression(BoundPropertyEntry entry,
object parsedData, ExpressionBuilderContext context)
        {
            CodeTypeReferenceExpression refMe = new
CodeTypeReferenceExpression(base.GetType());
            CodePrimitiveExpression expression = new
CodePrimitiveExpression(entry.Expression);
            return new CodeMethodInvokeExpression(refMe, "GetEvalData", new
CodeExpression[] { expression });
        }

        public override object EvaluateExpression(object target, BoundPropertyEntry
entry, object parsedData, ExpressionBuilderContext context)
        {
            return GetEvalData(entry.Expression);
        }

        public override bool SupportsEvaluate
        {
            get
            {
                return true;
            }
        }

        public static string GetEvalData(string expression)
        {
            XmlDocument lookupDoc =(XmlDocument)HostingEnvironment.Cache["Lookup"];
            if (lookupDoc == null)
            {
                lookupDoc = new XmlDocument();
                string lookupFileName = HostingEnvironment.MapPath("~/Lookup.
➥config");
                lookupDoc.Load(lookupFileName);
                CacheDependency fileDepend = new CacheDependency(lookupFileName);
                HostingEnvironment.Cache.Insert("Lookup", lookupDoc, fileDepend);
            }
```

```
        string search = String.Format("//add[@key='{0}']", expression);
        XmlNode match = lookupDoc.SelectSingleNode(search);
        if (match != null)
            return match.Attributes["value"].Value;
        return "[no match]";
    }


    }
}
```

Before you can use the LookupExpressionBuilder class, you need to register it in the web configuration file. The web configuration file in Listing 31.11 includes an <expressionBuilders> section that registers the LookupExpressionBuilder class for the prefix lookup.

LISTING 31.11   Web.Config

```
<?xml version="1.0"?>
<configuration>
  <system.web>
    <compilation>
      <expressionBuilders>
        <add expressionPrefix="lookup"
            type="AspNetUnleashed.LookupExpressionBuilder" />
      </expressionBuilders>
    </compilation>
  </system.web>
</configuration>
```

The LookupExpressionBuilder uses an XML file named Lookup.config to contain a database of lookup values. This file contains key and value pairs. A sample Lookup.config file is contained in Listing 31.12.

LISTING 31.12   Lookup.config

```
<?xml version="1.0"?>
<lookup>
  <add key="WelcomeMessage" value="Welcome to our Web site!" />
  <add key="Copyright" value="All content copyrighted by the company." />
</lookup>
```

Finally, the page in Listing 31.13 uses the LookupExpressionBuilder. It contains a Literal control that displays the value of a lookup expression named WelcomeMessage (see Figure 31.3).

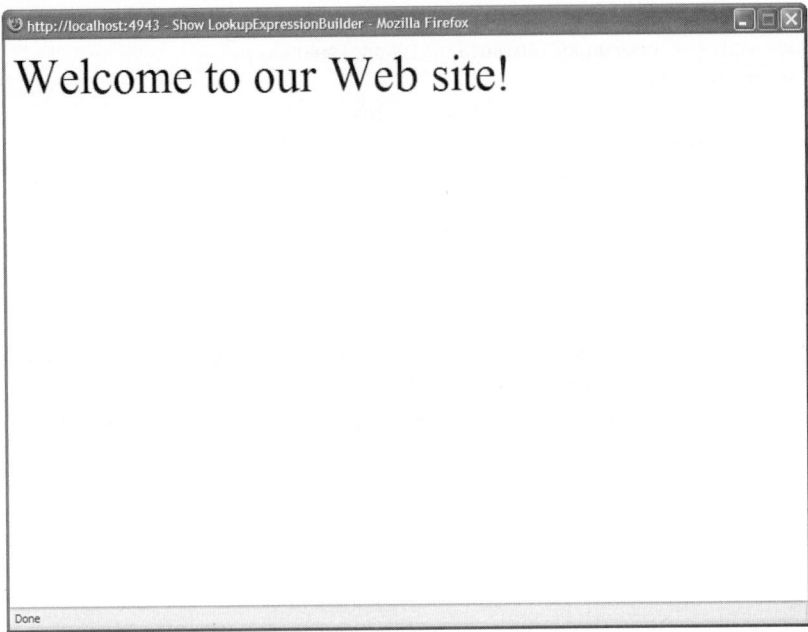

FIGURE 31.3   Displaying text generated by an ExpressionBuilder.

LISTING 31.13   ShowLookupExpressionBuilder.aspx

```
<%@ Page Language="C#" %>
<!DOCTYPE html PUBLIC "-//W3C//DTD XHTML 1.0 Transitional//EN"
  "http://www.w3.org/TR/xhtml1/DTD/xhtml1-transitional.dtd">
<html xmlns="http://www.w3.org/1999/xhtml" >
<head id="Head1" runat="server">
    <title>Show LookupExpressionBuilder</title>
</head>
<body>
    <form id="form1" runat="server">
    <div>

    <asp:Literal ID="Literal1"
        Text="<%$ lookup:WelcomeMessage %>"
        runat="Server" />

    </div>
    </form>
</body>
</html>
```

You create a custom ExpressionBuilder by inheriting a new class from the base ExpressionBuilder class. The ExpressionBuilder class has the following methods:

▶ **GetCodeExpression**—Returns the code that evaluates an expression.

▶ **EvaluateExpression**—Evaluates the expression in the case of no-compile ASP.NET pages.

▶ **ParseExpression**—Returns a parsed version of the expression.

The ExpressionBuilder class also supports the following property:

▶ **SupportsEvaluate**—When true, the ExpressionBuilder can be used in no-compile ASP.NET pages.

When you use an ExpressionBuilder in a normal ASP.NET page, the ExpressionBuilder returns code that is integrated into the compiled ASP.NET page. The GetCodeExpression() method returns a block of code injected into the compiled ASP.NET page class that gets created in the Temporary ASP.NET Files folder.

Because an ExpressionBuilder might be used with either a Visual Basic .NET or C# ASP.NET page, the code returned by the GetCodeExpression() method must be language neutral. This means that you must represent the code that gets executed with the CodeDom.

In Listing 31.11, the GetCodeExpression() method returns an instance of the CodeMethodInvokeExpression class. This class represents an expression that invokes a class method. In this case, the CodeMethodInvokeExpression class represents the expression LookupExpressionBuilder.GetEvalData(). In other words, the ExpressionBuilder adds code to the compiled ASP.NET page class that invokes the GetEvalData() method contained in Listing 31.10.

As an alternative to creating a normal ASP.NET page, you can create something called a *no-compile* ASP.NET page, which is not compiled dynamically. You create a no-compile ASP.NET page by adding the following attribute to a <%@ Page %> directive:

```
<%@ Page CompilationMode="Never" %>
```

NOTE

No-compile ASP.NET pages are discussed in Chapter 1, "Overview of ASP.NET."

If you want an ExpressionBuilder to work with no-compile ASP.NET pages, you must return the value True from the ExpressionBuilder.SupportsEvaluate property and implement the EvaluateExpression() method. The EvaluateExpression is executed at runtime when the no-compile ASP.NET page is requested. In Listing 31.11, the EvaluateExpression() method simply calls the GetEvalData() method.

Creating HTTP Handlers

An HTTP Handler is a .NET class that executes whenever you make a request for a file at a certain path. Each type of resource that you can request from an ASP.NET application has a corresponding handler. For example, when you request an ASP.NET page, the Page class executes. The Page class is actually an HTTP Handler because it implements the IHttpHandler interface.

Other examples of HTTP Handlers are the TraceHandler class, which displays application-level trace information when you request the Trace.axd page, and the ForbiddenHandler class, which displays an Access Forbidden message when you attempt to request source code files from the browser.

You can implement your own HTTP handlers. For example, imagine that you want to store all your images in a database table;however, you want use normal HTML <img> tags to display images in your web pages. In that case, you can map any file that has a .gif or .jpeg extension to a custom image HTTP handler. The image HTTP handler can retrieve images from a database automatically whenever an image request is made.

Or imagine that you want to expose an RSS feed from your website. In that case, you can create an RSS HTTP Handler that displays a list of blog entries or articles hosted on your website. You can create an HTTP Handler in two ways. You can either create something called a Generic Handler, or you can implement the IHttpHandler interface in a custom class. This section explores both methods of creating an HTTP Handler.

Creating a Generic Handler

The easiest way to create a new HTTP Handler is to create a Generic Handler. When you create a Generic Handler, you create a file that ends with the extension .ashx. Whenever you request the .ashx file, the Generic Handler executes.

You can think of a Generic Handler as a lightweight ASP.NET page. A Generic Handler is like an ASP.NET page that contains a single method that renders content to the browser. You can't add any controls declaratively to a Generic Handler. A Generic Handler also doesn't support events such as the Page Load or Page PreRender events.

In this section, we create a Generic Handler that dynamically generates an image from a string of text. For example, if you pass the string Hello World! to the handler, the handler returns an image of the text Hello World!.

The Generic Handler is contained in Listing 31.14.

LISTING 31.14   ImageTextHandler.ashx

```
<%@ WebHandler Language="C#" Class="ImageTextHandler" %>


using System;
using System.Web;
using System.Drawing;
```

```csharp
using System.Drawing.Imaging;

public class ImageTextHandler : IHttpHandler
{

    public void ProcessRequest(HttpContext context)
    {
        // Get parameters from querystring
        string text = context.Request.QueryString["text"];
        string font = context.Request.QueryString["font"];
        string size = context.Request.QueryString["size"];

        // Create Font
        Font fntText = new Font(font, float.Parse(size));

        // Calculate image width and height
        Bitmap bmp = new Bitmap(10, 10);
        Graphics g = Graphics.FromImage(bmp);
        SizeF bmpSize = g.MeasureString(text, fntText);
        int width = (int)Math.Ceiling(bmpSize.Width);
        int height = (int)Math.Ceiling(bmpSize.Height);
        bmp = new Bitmap(bmp, width, height);
        g.Dispose();

        // Draw the text
        g = Graphics.FromImage(bmp);
        g.Clear(Color.White);
        g.DrawString(text, fntText, Brushes.Black, new PointF(0, 0));
        g.Dispose();

        // Save bitmap to output stream
        bmp.Save(context.Response.OutputStream, ImageFormat.Gif);
    }

    public bool IsReusable
    {
        get
        {
            return true;
        }
    }

}
```

The `ImageTextHandler` in Listing 31.14 includes one method and one property. The `ProcessRequest()` method is responsible for outputting any content that the handler renders to the browser.

In Listing 31.14, the image text, font, and size are retrieved from query string fields. You specify the image that you want to return from the handler by making a request that looks like this:

```
/ImageTextHandler.ashx?text=Hello&font=Arial&size=30
```

Next, a bitmap is created with the help of the classes from the System.Drawing namespace. The bitmap is actually created twice. The first one measures the size of the bitmap required for generating an image that contains the text. Next, a new bitmap of the correct size is created, and the text is drawn on the bitmap. After the bitmap has been created, it is saved to the `HttpResponse` object's `OutputStream` so that it can be rendered to the browser.

The handler in Listing 31.14 also includes an `IsReusable` property, which indicates whether the same handler can be reused over multiple requests. You can improve your application's performance by returning the value `True`. Because the handler isn't maintaining any state information, there is nothing wrong with releasing it back into the pool so that it can be used with a future request.

The page in Listing 31.15 illustrates how you can use the `ImageTextHandler.ashx` file. This page contains three HTML `<img>` tags that pass different query strings to the handler (see Figure 31.4).

FIGURE 31.4   Displaying text images with an HTTP Handler.

LISTING 31.15   ShowImageTextHandler.aspx

```
<%@ Page Language="C#" %>
<!DOCTYPE html PUBLIC "-//W3C//DTD XHTML 1.0 Transitional//EN"
  "http://www.w3.org/TR/xhtml1/DTD/xhtml1-transitional.dtd">
<html xmlns="http://www.w3.org/1999/xhtml" >
<head id="Head1" runat="server">
    <title>Show ImageTextHandler</title>
</head>
<body>
    <form id="form1" runat="server">
    <div>

    <img src="ImageTextHandler.ashx?text=Some Text&font=WebDings&size=42" />
    <br />
    <img src="ImageTextHandler.ashx?text=Some Text&font=Comic Sans MS&size=42" />
    <br />
    <img src="ImageTextHandler.ashx?text=Some Text&font=Courier New&size=42" />

    </div>
    </form>
</body>
</html>
```

Implementing the `IHttpHandler` Interface

The big disadvantage of a Generic Handler is that you cannot map a Generic Handler to a particular page path. For example, you cannot execute a Generic Handler whenever someone requests a file with the extension `.gif`. If you need more control over when an HTTP Handler executes, you can create a class that implements the `IHttpHandler` interface.

For example, the class in Listing 31.16 represents an Image HTTP Handler. This handler retrieves an image from a database table and renders the image to the browser.

LISTING 31.16   App_Code\ImageHandler.cs

```
using System;
using System.Web;
using System.Data;
using System.Data.SqlClient;
using System.Web.Configuration;

namespace AspNetUnleashed
{
    public class ImageHandler : IHttpHandler
```

```csharp
    {
        const string connectionStringName = "Images";

        public void ProcessRequest(HttpContext context)
        {
            // Don't buffer response
            context.Response.Buffer = false;

            // Get file name
            string fileName = VirtualPathUtility.GetFileName(context.Request.Path);

            // Get image from database
            string conString =
WebConfigurationManager.ConnectionStrings[connectionStringName].ConnectionString;
            SqlConnection con = new SqlConnection(conString);
            SqlCommand cmd = new SqlCommand("SELECT Image FROM Images WHERE
FileName=@FileName", con);
            cmd.Parameters.AddWithValue("@fileName", fileName);
            using (con)
            {
                con.Open();
                SqlDataReader reader =
cmd.ExecuteReader(CommandBehavior.SequentialAccess);
                if (reader.Read())
                {
                    int bufferSize = 8040;
                    byte[] chunk = new byte[bufferSize];
                    long retCount;
                    long startIndex = 0;
                    retCount = reader.GetBytes(0, startIndex, chunk, 0, bufferSize);
                    while (retCount == bufferSize)
                    {
                        context.Response.BinaryWrite(chunk);

                        startIndex += bufferSize;
                         retCount = reader.GetBytes(0, startIndex, chunk, 0,
➥bufferSize);
                    }
                    byte[] actualChunk = new Byte[retCount - 1];
                    Buffer.BlockCopy(chunk, 0, actualChunk, 0, (int)retCount - 1);
                    context.Response.BinaryWrite(actualChunk);
                }
            }

        }
```

```
        public bool IsReusable
        {
            get { return true; }
        }
    }
}
```

After you create a class that implements the IHttpHandler interface, you need to register the class in the web configuration file. The web configuration file in Listing 31.17 includes an httpHandlers section that associates the .gif, .jpeg, and .jpg extensions with the Image handler.

LISTING 31.17   Web.Config

```
<?xml version="1.0"?>
<configuration>
  <connectionStrings>
    <add name="Images"
      connectionString="Data Source=.\SQLExpress;Integrated
          Security=True;AttachDBFileName=¦DataDirectory¦ImagesDB.mdf;
          User Instance=True"/>
  </connectionStrings>
    <system.web>

      <httpHandlers>
        <add path="*.gif" verb="*"
          type="AspNetUnleashed.ImageHandler" validate="false" />
        <add path="*.jpeg" verb="*"
          type="AspNetUnleashed.ImageHandler" validate="false" />
        <add path="*.jpg" verb="*"
          type="AspNetUnleashed.ImageHandler" validate="false" />
      </httpHandlers>

    </system.web>
</configuration>
```

When you register a handler, you specify the following four attributes:

- ▶ **path**—Enables you to specify the path associated with the handler. You can use wildcards in the path expression.

- ▶ **verb**—Enables you to specify the HTTP verbs, such as GET or POST, associated with the handler. You can specify multiple verbs in a comma-separated list. You can represent any verb with the * wildcard.

- ▶ **type**—Enables you to specify the name of the class that implements the handler.

▶ **validate**—Enables you to specify whether the handler is loaded during application startup. When true, the handler is loaded at startup. When false, the handler is not loaded until a request associated with the handler is made. This second option can improve your application's performance when a handler is never used.

The page in Listing 31.18 uses the ImageHandler to render its images. The page enables you to upload new images to a database named ImagesDB. The page also displays existing images (see Figure 31.5).

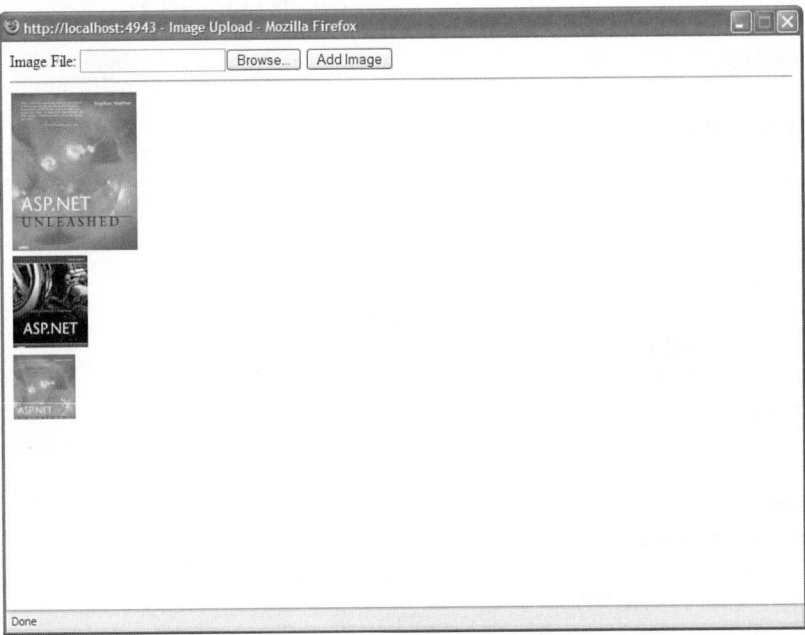

FIGURE 31.5   Displaying images with the ImageHandler.

LISTING 31.18   ImageUpload.aspx

```csharp
<%@ Page Language="C#" %>
<!DOCTYPE html PUBLIC "-//W3C//DTD XHTML 1.0 Transitional//EN"
"http://www.w3.org/TR/xhtml1/DTD/xhtml1-transitional.dtd">
<script runat="server">

    protected void btnAdd_Click(object sender, EventArgs e)
    {
        if (upFile.HasFile)
        {
                srcImages.Insert();
        }
    }
```

```
</script>
<html xmlns="http://www.w3.org/1999/xhtml" >
<head id="Head1" runat="server">
    <style type="text/css">
        .fileList li
        {
            margin-bottom:5px;
        }
    </style>
    <title>Image Upload</title>
</head>
<body>
    <form id="form1" runat="server">
    <div>

    <asp:Label
        id="lblFile"
        Text="Image File:"
        AssociatedControlID="upFile"
        Runat="server" />
    <asp:FileUpload
        id="upFile"
        Runat="server" />
    <asp:Button
        id="btnAdd"
        Text="Add Image"
        OnClick="btnAdd_Click"
        Runat="server" />
    <hr />

    <asp:GridView
        id="grdImages"
        DataSourceID="srcImages"
        AutoGenerateColumns="false"
        ShowHeader="false"
        GridLines="None"
        Runat="server">
        <Columns>
        <asp:ImageField
            DataImageUrlField="FileName"
            DataAlternateTextField="FileName" />
        </Columns>
    </asp:GridView>

    <asp:SqlDataSource
        id="srcImages"
```

```
        ConnectionString="<%$ ConnectionStrings:Images %>"
        SelectCommand="SELECT FileName FROM Images"
        InsertCommand="INSERT Images (FileName,Image) VALUES (@FileName,@FileBytes)"
        Runat="server">
        <InsertParameters>
            <asp:ControlParameter Name="FileName" ControlID="upFile"
PropertyName="FileName" />
            <asp:ControlParameter Name="FileBytes" ControlID="upFile"
PropertyName="FileBytes" />
        </InsertParameters>
    </asp:SqlDataSource>

    </div>
    </form>
</body>
</html>
```

Creating an Asynchronous HTTP Handler

When you create an HTTP Handler by creating either a Generic Handler or implementing the IHttpHandler interface, you are creating a synchronous handler. In this section, you learn how to create an asynchronous handler.

The advantage of creating an asynchronous handler is scalability. The ASP.NET Framework maintains a limited pool of threads that are used to service requests. When ASP.NET Framework receives a request for a file, it assigns a thread to handle the request. If ASP.NET Framework runs out of threads, the request is queued until a thread becomes available. If too many threads are queued, the framework rejects the page request with a 503—Server Too Busy response code.

If you execute an HTTP Handler asynchronously, the current thread is released back into the thread pool so that it can be used to service another page request. While the asynchronous handler is executing, ASP.NET Framework can devote its attention to handling other requests. When the asynchronous handler completes its work, the framework reassigns a thread to the original request, and the handler can render content to the browser.

> **NOTE**
>
> You can configure the ASP.NET thread pool with the httpRuntime element in the web configuration file. You can modify the appRequestQueueLimit, minFreeThreads, and minLocalRequestFreeThreads attributes to control how many requests ASP.NET Framework queues before giving up and sending an error.

You create an asynchronous HTTP handler by implementing the IHttpAsyncHandler interface, which derives from the IHttpHandler interface and adds two additional methods:

> ▶ **BeginProcessRequest**—Called to start the asynchronous task.

> ▶ **EndProcessRequest**—Called when the asynchronous task completes.

For example, the file in Listing 31.19 contains an asynchronous handler that grabs an RSS feed from the ASP.NET website.

LISTING 31.19   App_Code\RSSHandler.cs

```csharp
using System;
using System.Web;
using System.Net;
using System.IO;

namespace AspNetUnleashed
{
    public class RSSHandler : IHttpAsyncHandler
    {
        private HttpContext _context;
        private WebRequest _request;

        public IAsyncResult BeginProcessRequest(HttpContext context,
            AsyncCallback cb, object extraData)
        {
            // Store context
            _context = context;

            // Initiate call to RSS feed
            _request = WebRequest.Create("http://www.asp.net/rss/spotlight");
            return _request.BeginGetResponse(cb, extraData);
        }

        public void EndProcessRequest(IAsyncResult result)
        {
            // Get the RSS feed
            string rss = String.Empty;
            WebResponse response = _request.EndGetResponse(result);
            using (response)
            {
                StreamReader reader = new StreamReader(response.GetResponseStream());
                rss = reader.ReadToEnd();
            }
            _context.Response.Write(rss);
        }

        public bool IsReusable
```

```
        {
            get { return true; }
        }

        public void ProcessRequest(HttpContext context)
        {
            throw new Exception("The ProcessRequest method is not implemented.");
        }
    }
}
```

The handler in Listing 31.19 implements both the BeginProcessRequest() and EndProcessRequest() methods required by the IHttpAsyncHandler interface.

The BeginProcessRequest() method uses the WebRequest class to request the page that contains the RSS headlines from the MSDN website. The WebRequest.BeginGetResponse() method retrieves the remote page asynchronously.

When the BeginGetResponse() method completes, the handler's EndProcessRequest() method is called. This method retrieves the page and renders the contents of the page to the browser.

Before you can use the RSSHandler, you need to register it in your web configuration file. The web configuration file in Listing 31.20 includes an <httpHandlers> section that registers the RSSHandler and associates the handler with the .rss extension.

LISTING 31.20   Web.Config

```xml
<?xml version="1.0"?>
<configuration>
    <system.web>

        <httpHandlers>
          <add path="*.rss" verb="*" type="AspNetUnleashed.RSSHandler"/>
        </httpHandlers>

    </system.web>
</configuration>
```

After you register the RSSHandler, you can execute the handler by making a request for any file that ends with the extension .rss. If you have a news reader, such as SharpReader, you can enter a path like the following in the reader's address bar:

```
http://localhost:2026/YourApp/news.rss
```

The page in Listing 31.21 contains a `GridView` and `XmlDataSource` control. The `XmlDataSource` control calls the `RssHandler` to retrieve the headlines displayed in the `GridView` control (see Figure 31.6).

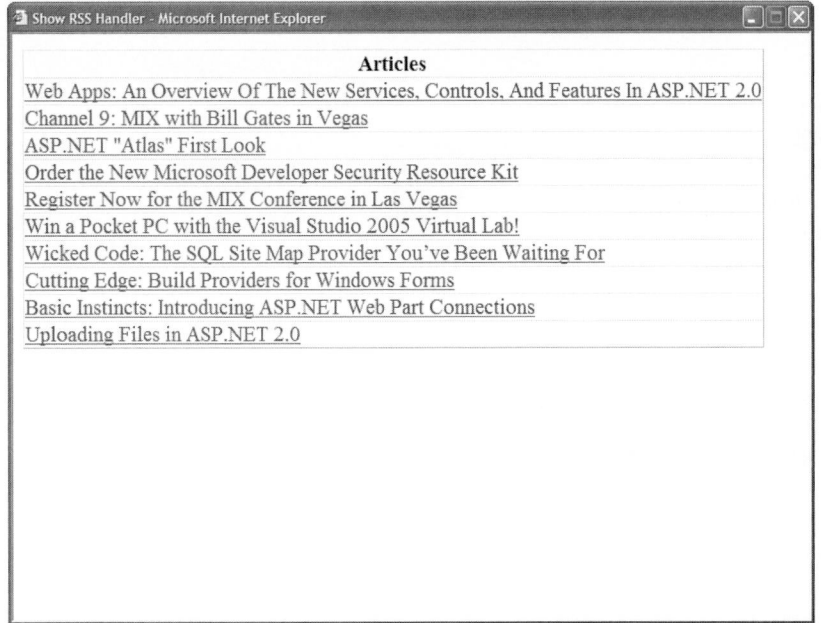

FIGURE 31.6   Retrieving an RSS feed asynchronously.

LISTING 31.21   ShowRSSHandler.aspx

```csharp
<%@ Page Language="C#" %>
<%@ Import Namespace="System.IO" %>
<!DOCTYPE html PUBLIC "-//W3C//DTD XHTML 1.0 Transitional//EN"
"http://www.w3.org/TR/xhtml1/DTD/xhtml1-transitional.dtd">
<script runat="server">

    void Page_Load()
    {
        string pagePath = Request.Url.OriginalString;
        string rssPath = Path.ChangeExtension(pagePath, ".rss");
        srcRSS.DataFile = rssPath;
    }
</script>
```

```
<html xmlns="http://www.w3.org/1999/xhtml" >
<head id="Head1" runat="server">
    <title>Show RSS Handler</title>
</head>
<body>
    <form id="form1" runat="server">
    <div>

    <asp:GridView
        id="grdRSS"
        DataSourceID="srcRSS"
        AutoGenerateColumns="false"
        Runat="server">
        <Columns>
        <asp:TemplateField HeaderText="Articles">
        <ItemTemplate>
            <asp:HyperLink
                id="lnkRSS"
                Text='<%# XPath("title") %>'
                NavigateUrl='<%# XPath("link") %>'
                Runat="server" />
        </ItemTemplate>
        </asp:TemplateField>
        </Columns>
    </asp:GridView>

    <asp:XmlDataSource
        id="srcRSS"
        XPath="//item"
        Runat="server" />

    </div>
    </form>
</body>
</html>
```

Working with HTTP Applications and HTTP Modules

Whenever you request an ASP.NET page, ASP.NET Framework assigns an instance of the HttpApplication class to the request. This class performs the following actions in the following order:

1. Raises the BeginRequest event

2. Raises the AuthenticateRequest event

3. Raises the `AuthorizeRequest` event

4. Calls the `ProcessRequest()` method of the `Page` class

5. Raises the `EndRequest` event

> **NOTE**
>
> This is not a complete list of `HttpApplication` events. There are a lot of them!

The entire page execution lifecycle happens during the fourth step. For example, the `Page` `Init`, `Load`, and `PreRender` events all happen when the `Page` class `ProcessRequest()` method is called. The `HttpApplication` object is responsible for raising application events. These application events happen both before and after a page is executed.

You might want to handle one of the application events for several reasons. For example, you might want to implement a custom authentication scheme. In that case, you would need to handle the `AuthenticateRequest` event to identify the user. Or you might want to create a custom logging module that tracks the pages that your website users visit. In that case, you might want to handle the `BeginRequest` event to record the pages being requested.

If you want to handle `HttpApplication` events, there are two ways to do it. You can create a `Global.asax` file or you can create one or more custom HTTP Modules.

Creating a `Global.asax` File

By default, the ASP.NET Framework maintains a pool of `HttpApplication` objects to service incoming page requests. A separate `HttpApplication` instance is assigned to each request.

If you prefer, you can create a custom `HttpApplication` class. That way, an instance of your custom class is assigned to each page request.

You can create custom properties in your derived class. These properties can be accessed from any page, control, or component. You also can handle any application events in your custom `HttpApplication` class.

You create a custom `HttpApplication` class by creating a special file named `Global.asax` in the root of your application. Every application can have one and only one of these files. For example, the `Global.asax` file in Listing 31.22 can be used to track the number of page requests made for any page.

LISTING 31.22   Global.asax

```
<%@ Application Language="C#" %>
<%@ Import Namespace="System.Data" %>
<%@ Import Namespace="System.Data.SqlClient" %>
<%@ Import Namespace="System.Web.Configuration" %>
<script runat="server">
```

```
    private string _conString;
    private SqlConnection _con;
    private SqlCommand _cmdSelect;
    private SqlCommand _cmdInsert;

    public override void Init()
    {
        // initialize connection
        _conString =
➥WebConfigurationManager.ConnectionStrings["Log"].ConnectionString;
        _con = new SqlConnection(_conString);

        // initialize select command
        _cmdSelect = new SqlCommand("SELECT COUNT(*) FROM Log WHERE Path=@Path",
➥_con);
        _cmdSelect.Parameters.Add("@Path", SqlDbType.NVarChar, 500);

        // initialize insert command
        _cmdInsert = new SqlCommand("INSERT Log (Path) VALUES (@Path)", _con);
        _cmdInsert.Parameters.Add("@Path", SqlDbType.NVarChar, 500);
    }

    public int NumberOfRequests
    {
        get
        {
            int result = 0;
            _cmdSelect.Parameters["@Path"].Value =
Request.AppRelativeCurrentExecutionFilePath;
            try
            {
                _con.Open();
                result = (int)_cmdSelect.ExecuteScalar();
            }
            finally
            {
                _con.Close();
            }
            return result;
        }
    }

    void Application_BeginRequest(object sender, EventArgs e)
    {
        // Record new request
```

```
        _cmdInsert.Parameters["@Path"].Value =
Request.AppRelativeCurrentExecutionFilePath;
        try
        {
            _con.Open();
            _cmdInsert.ExecuteNonQuery();
        }
        finally
        {
            _con.Close();
        }
    }
}
</script>
```

The Global.asax page in Listing 31.22 handles the Application BeginRequest() event. You can handle any application event by following the naming pattern Application_EventName where EventName is the name of the HttpApplication event.

In Listing 31.22, the Application_BeginRequest() handler records the path of the page requested. A SqlCommand object records the page path to a database table named Log. The Global.asax file also extends the base HttpApplication class with a custom property named NumberOfRequests. This property retrieves the number of requests made for the page at the current path.

Finally, the Global.asax includes an Init() method that overrides the base HttpApplication's Init() method. In Listing 31.22, the Init() method initializes the SqlConnection and two SqlCommand objects used in the Global.asax file. The Init() method is called when the class represented by the Global.asax is initialized. It is called only once, when the class is first created.

> **WARNING**
>
> The same instance of the HttpApplication object is reused for multiple page requests (although never for multiple page requests at the same time). Any value that you assign to a property in a Global.asax file is maintained over the multiple page requests.

The page in Listing 31.23 displays the value of the custom property exposed by the Global.asax file (see Figure 31.7). The ApplicationInstance property is used to refer to the instance of the HttpApplication class associated with the page. Because the Global.asax file is compiled dynamically in the background, any properties that you declare in the Global.asax file are exposed as strongly typed properties.

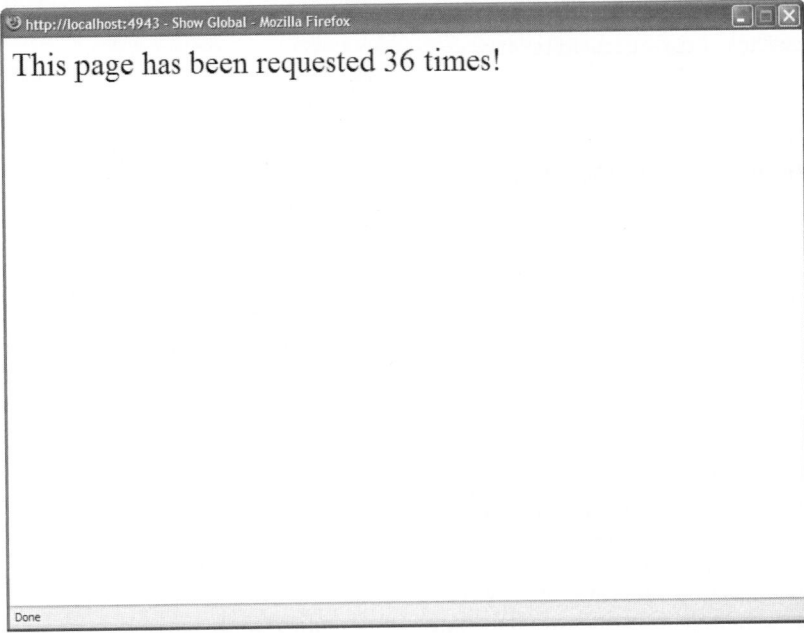

FIGURE 31.7   Displaying the `NumberOfRequests` property.

LISTING 31.23   ShowGlobal.aspx

```
<%@ Page Language="C#" %>
<!DOCTYPE html PUBLIC "-//W3C//DTD XHTML 1.0 Transitional//EN"
"http://www.w3.org/TR/xhtml1/DTD/xhtml1-transitional.dtd">
<html xmlns="http://www.w3.org/1999/xhtml" >
<head id="Head1" runat="server">
    <title>Show Global</title>
</head>
<body>
    <form id="form1" runat="server">
    <div>

    This page has been requested
    <%= this.ApplicationInstance.NumberOfRequests %>
    times!

    </div>
    </form>
</body>
</html>
```

Creating Custom HTTP Modules

An HTTP Module is a .NET class that executes with each and every page request. You can use an HTTP Module to handle any of the `HttpApplication` events that you can handle in the `Global.asax` file.

Behind the scenes, ASP.NET Framework uses HTTP Modules to implement many of the standard features of the framework. For example, ASP.NET Framework uses the `FormsAuthenticationModule` to implement Forms authentication and the `WindowsAuthenticationModule` to implement Windows authentication.

Session state is implemented with an HTTP Module named the `SessionStateModule`. Page output caching is implemented with an HTTP Module named the `OutputCacheModule`, and the `Profile` object is implemented with an HTTP Module named the `ProfileModule`.

When a new instance of an `HttpApplication` class is created, the `HttpApplication` loads all the HTTP Modules configured in the web configuration file. Each HTTP Module subscribes to one or more `HttpApplication` events. For example, when the `HttpApplication` object raises its `AuthenticateRequest` event, the `FormsAuthenticationModule` executes its code to authenticate the current user.

In this section, we create a simple authentication HTTP Module. The HTTP Module doesn't enable you to request a page unless you include the proper query string with the request. The code for the custom HTTP Module is contained in Listing 31.24.

LISTING 31.24   App_Code\QueryStringAuthenticationModule.cs

```
using System;
using System.Web;

namespace AspNetUnleashed
{
    public class QueryStringAuthenticationModule : IHttpModule
    {
        public void Init(HttpApplication app)
        {
            app.AuthorizeRequest += new EventHandler(AuthorizeRequest);
        }

        private void AuthorizeRequest(Object sender, EventArgs e)
        {
            // Get context
            HttpApplication app = (HttpApplication)sender;
            HttpContext context = app.Context;

            // If the request is for Login.aspx, exit
```

```
            string path = context.Request.AppRelativeCurrentExecutionFilePath;
            if (String.Compare(path, "~/login.aspx", true) == 0)
                return;

            // Check for password
            bool authenticated = false;
            if (context.Request.QueryString["password"] != null)
            {
                if (context.Request.QueryString["password"] == "secret")
                    authenticated = true;
            }

            // If not authenticated, redirect to login.aspx
            if (!authenticated)
                context.Response.Redirect("~/Login.aspx");
        }

        public void Dispose() { }
    }
}
```

The class in Listing 31.24 implements the IHttpModule interface. This interface includes two methods:

- **Init**—Enables you to subscribe to HttpApplication events.

- **Dispose**—Enables you to clean up any resources used by the HTTP Module.

In Listing 31.25, the Init() method adds an event handler for the HttpApplication AuthorizeRequest event. When the HttpApplication raises the AuthorizeRequest event, the HTTP Module's AuthorizeRequest() method executes.

The AuthorizeRequest() method checks for a password=secret query string. If the query string does not exist, the user is redirected to the Login.aspx page. (The method also checks whether the user is requesting the Login.aspx page to avoid a vicious circle.)

Before you can use the QueryStringAuthenticationModule, you must register the HTTP Module in the web configuration file. The web configuration file in Listing 31.25 includes an <httpModules> section that registers the module.

LISTING 31.25   Web.Config

```
<?xml version="1.0"?>
<configuration>
    <system.web>

        <httpModules>
```

```
        <add name="QueryStringAuthenticationModule"
            type="AspNetUnleashed.QueryStringAuthenticationModule"/>
    </httpModules>

    </system.web>
</configuration>
```

After you register the HTTP Module, if you attempt to request any page without including the `password=secret` query string, you are redirected to the `Login.aspx` page. (If the `Login.aspx` page doesn't exist, you receive a `404--Not Found` error message.)

Summary

In this chapter, you learned how to extend the ASP.NET Framework by extending different parts of the HTTP Runtime. In the first section, you learned how to create a custom `BuildProvider`. For example, you learned how to create a `BuildProvider` that dynamically generates a data access component from an XML file.

Next, you explored the topic of `ExpressionBuilders`. You learned how to use an `ExpressionBuilder` to automatically replace one expression with another. For example, we created a custom `ExpressionBuilder` that enables you to look up a value from an XML file.

The topic of HTTP Handlers was also explored. You learned two methods of creating custom HTTP Handlers. You learned how to create a Generic Handler and how to create an HTTP Handler by implementing the `IHttpHandler` interface. You also saw how you can improve the scalability of your ASP.NET applications by implementing asynchronous HTTP Handlers.

Finally, you learned two methods of handling application-wide events. You learned how to create a custom `HttpApplication` by creating a `Global.asax` file. You also learned how to handle application events by implementing a custom HTTP Module.

CHAPTER 32

Building Dynamic Data Applications

ASP.NET Dynamic Data originally appeared in .NET Framework 3.5 Service Pack 1 release and its templates came with Visual Studio 2008 SP1. This chapter provides you with an overview of ASP.NET Dynamic Data and walks you through the process of building an application with it and discuss when you might (and might not) build a dynamic data application.

When you finish this chapter you should have a good idea of what it's like to build dynamic data applications and the productivity benefits they provide for developers, and you can compare and contrast this framework with traditional Web Forms and ASP.NET MVC Framework.

Introducing ASP.NET Dynamic Data

The hallmark of every good programmer is the ability to locate redundant code and factor it out into a reusable module or library. Many people these days equate good programming skills with writing far *less* lines of code than we used to while still producing incredible applications.

When we build ASP.NET applications that sit on top of a data store of some kind, there are always a set of common tasks that we need to provide a UI for. Although the data models can vary from application to application, several common patterns emerge in virtually any data-driven application. Just a few of these patterns are listed here:

▶ **Entity Lists**—Display a list of rows in a table.

▶ **Detail Form**—Displays the details of a single entity.

▶ **Edit Form**—Enables the user to edit the details of a single entity.

▶ **Create**—Adds a new entity to a list.

▶ **Delete**—Deletes an entity from a list.

▶ **Navigation**—Provides Search, Filter, Sort, and Paginate lists of entities.

These tasks are common to virtually all web applications regardless of the underlying data model. The ASP.NET Dynamic Data framework takes this into account and, out-of-the-box, gives you scaffolding and templates that can provide all this functionality for you without you writing more than a few lines of code. In the next section, you see how to build a dynamic data application, and you see the features and functionality provided for you as a starting point.

Building a Dynamic Data Application

Before we start building a sample application, we need something to build. In the spirit of keeping things simple so that we can focus this chapter solely on dynamic data, the application must also be simple.

We call it ZombiePedia, a website for cataloguing the appearances of various zombies. This way, during the zombie apocalypse, we can all hit ZombiePedia from our smart phones to log zombies we've seen and look up repeat zombies to find their vital statistics. After all, we need to know if we can touch a zombie with bare hands or if it's a virus carrier, don't we?

Without dynamic data, we would have to hand-code the page that displays the list of zombie sightings, the sighting detail and edit forms, the ability to create new sightings, and the pages that add, remove, and edit zombie types, and a bunch more plumbing. Doing this by hand, even with a rapid development framework like the MVC Framework, would be tedious and time-consuming. If our goal is to produce a functioning prototype that we can use as the launching point to start building our production application, we should use dynamic data.

To start, let's create a new web application. Open up Visual Studio 2010 and create a new project. Under the Installed Templates panel in the Web category, click ASP.NET Dynamic Data Entities Web Application (shown in Figure 32.1). Call the application whatever you like, but ZombiePedia might be a good choice.

This particular template creates an ASP.NET Dynamic Data website that comes pre-equipped with code, scaffolding, and references to build a dynamic user interface on top of ADO.NET Entity Framework Entity Data Model (EDM).

Before we go any further, we need to add the entity data model to our project. You can mock this up quickly by creating two simple tables in a SQL database: ZombieType (ID, Name, Description) and ZombieSighting (ID, Name, Longitude, Latitude, and so on). Figure 32.2 shows the dialog box with which you are presented after right-clicking the project and choosing to add a new ADO.NET Entity Model and choosing Generate from Database.

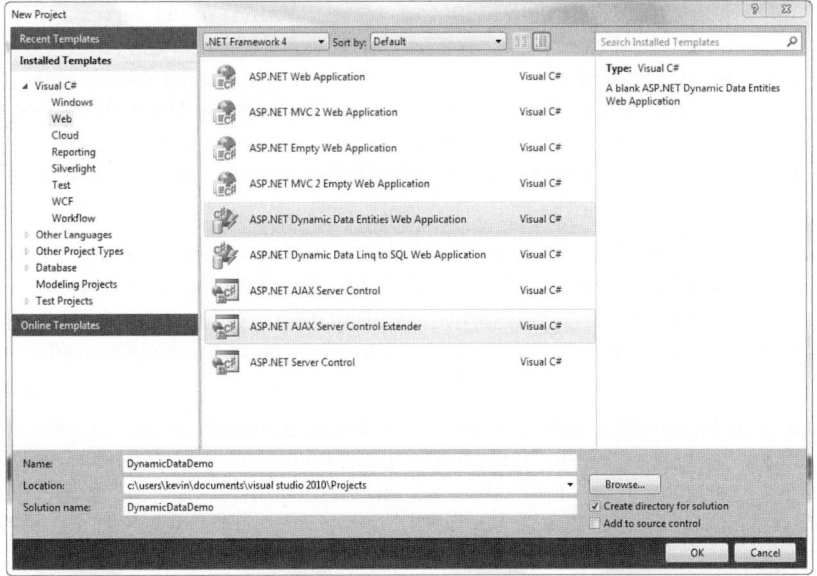

FIGURE 32.1   Creating a new ASP.NET Dynamic Data Entries Project.

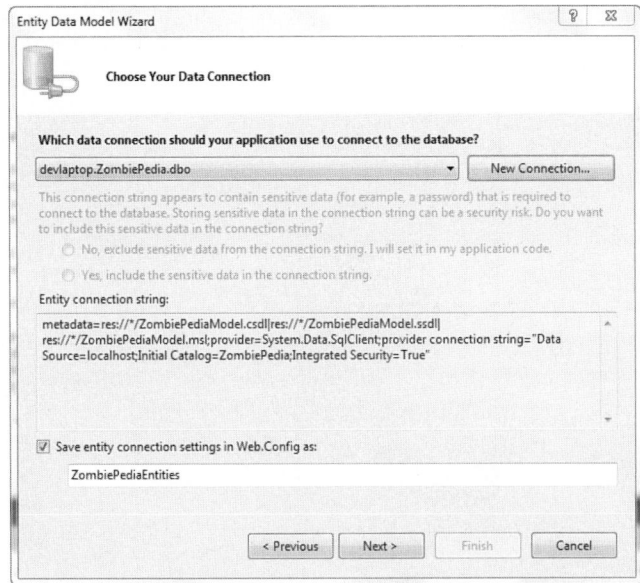

FIGURE 32.2   Adding an ADO.NET Entity Data Model by Generating from Database.

With a dynamic data website created and an entity data model added to the project, we're almost ready to run the application—no code written yet! First, let's take a look at the project that Visual Studio 2010 created for us.

The key folder of importance here is the `DynamicData` folder. A content folder serves as a root folder for all your content and media. The `EntityTemplates` folder contains user controls that apply to screens that deal with an individual entity. This folder comes with files for rendering an entity, editing an entity, and inserting a new entity. These files work against *any* entity type and are generic. This is a great starting point, but you can also customize these later and tailor the UI more specifically to your schema, as you see later in the chapter.

Also worth looking at is the `FieldTemplates` folder, which contains user controls for rendering read-only and edit-mode views of individual fields. There is a field here for virtually every type of column-level data you can think of including enumerated types, email addresses, dates, decimals, and even foreign-key controls such as `ForeignKey` and `ManyToMany`.

You can't see it clearly in Figure 32.3, but `PageTemplates` folder contains default templates for all the different types of pages: Details, Edit, Insert, Delete, List, and ListDetails. It is no coincidence that a page template exists for each of the different types of reusable data-driven application patterns we mentioned at the beginning of the chapter.

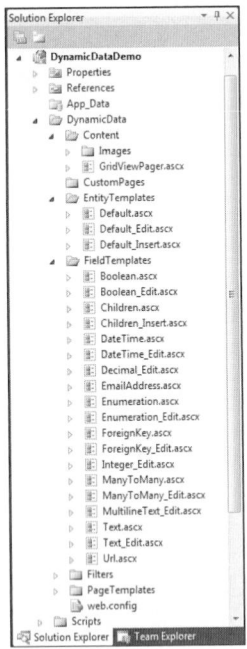

FIGURE 32.3   Default Project Created By ASP.NET Dynamic Data Template.

Before we can run the application as it stands, we need to tell the dynamic data framework about our entity model. To do that, open up the `Global.asax.cs` file.

A commented outline of code calls the `DefaultModel.RegisterContext` method. After uncommenting, it looks something like this:

```
DefaultModel.RegisterContext(
    typeof(Entities),
    new ContextConfiguration() { ScaffoldAllTables = true });
```

In our situation, the name of the entity model context created was called `Entities`, so that's what we passed as the first parameter to the method. The `ScaffoldAllTables` parameter instructs dynamic data to enable all the tables in our entity model to be scaffolded. That is, each table will have its own fully functioning UI that enables for listing, detail viewing, editing, inserting, and deleting. We can choose not to scaffold all tables and manually control which tables are scaffolded if we want.

With this in place, and assuming that the entities connection string is sitting in our `Web.config` file properly, we can then run the application. When we run the application, the home page (shown in Figure 32.4) presents us with a list of tables. This list of tables, as mentioned previously, is either all the tables in the model or is manually defined by code. In our case we have two tables: `ZombieTypes` and `ZombieSightings`. Note that these table names were pluralized by the Entity Framework—SQL Server thinks these tables are called `ZombieType` and `ZombieSighting`.

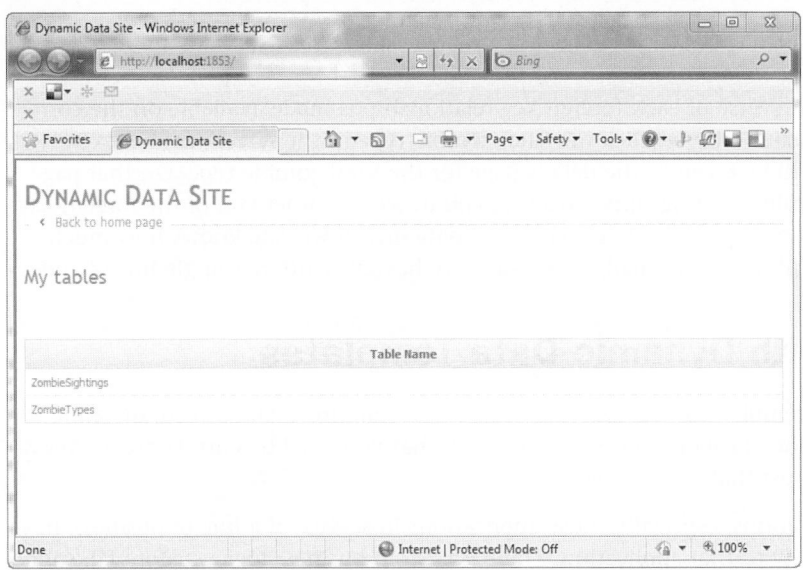

FIGURE 32.4   List of Scaffolded Tables in Dynamic Data Application.

Clicking the `ZombieSightings` link takes us to the list display page for the zombie sightings table. The URL for this is /ZombieSightings/List.aspx. Our application does not contain a `ZombieSightings` folder. The combination of the URL Routing engine (see Chapter 26, "Using the Login Controls,") and dynamic data work together to merge the information in the URL with the dynamic data templates.

Figure 32.5 shows the list view. Not only do we have a pagination-enabled grid view showing the rows of data, but also we can filter on columns (even columns that are foreign keys!) and sort by clicking the column headers.

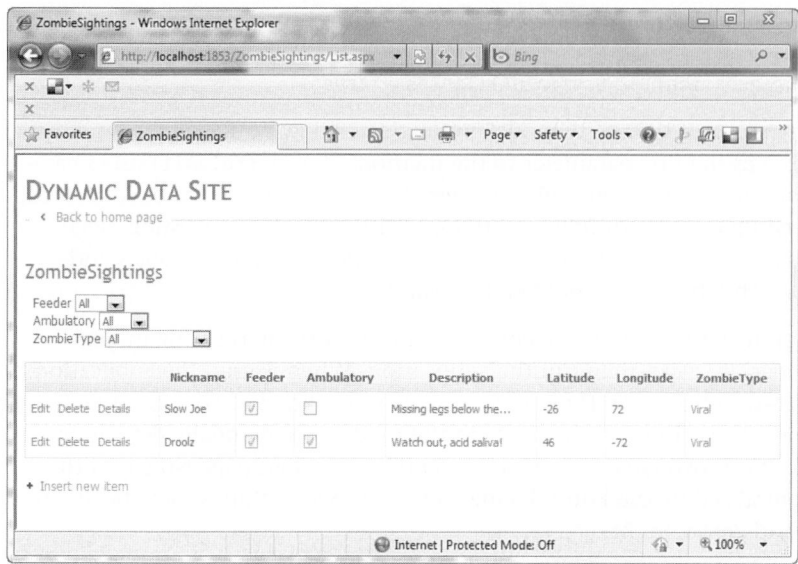

FIGURE 32.5   Displaying Data in an Entity List Scaffold view.

Automatically, the reverse of each foreign key relationship is made available on the corresponding entity page. So if you click the Viral zombie type in the screen, as shown in Figure 32.5, you will be taken to the details page for the Viral zombie type. On that page there is a View ZombieSightings link, enabling you to see the other end of the foreign key relationship. Any developer who has ever built a data-driven website knows how much code and manual labor this normally takes—and we haven't written a single line of code!

Working with Dynamic Data Templates

Using the default templates is a great place to start for building a data-driven, dynamic web application. They provide all the functionality that you need to start. However, they should be used as just that—a starting point.

Typical web applications, especially those applications in service of a line of business, have specific functionality to that application. There is custom business logic, custom UI, subtle tweaks to the way controls work, and the overall user experience. All this combines to make a compelling user experience and an excellent web application. To do that with a dynamic data application, you need to know how to create your own templates and customize the shared templates.

Following are two types of template changes you can make:

> ▶ **Shared Templates**—Apply to all entities within an application. Making a change here can cause the change to appear in the UI everywhere in the application.

> ▶ **Custom Templates**—Apply only to a specific entity and override the shared templates when the dynamic data framework finds them.

Making Shared Template Changes

If you make changes to the user controls in the `FieldTemplates`, `PageTemplates`, `EntityTemplates`, or `Filters` directory, those changes apply to *all* entities for which your application provides scaffolding.

To see how this works in action, let's modify the list template to pretty up the message that we get when no records are found. This message displays when there are no records and when the search criteria returns no results. To help clarify that, we change the text a little.

Open the `List.aspx` page in the PageTemplates folder, and scroll down to the GridView1 grid view control and locate the `EmptyDataTemplate` element. Replace it with the following:

```
<EmptyDataTemplate>
    There are currently no <%= table.DisplayName%> found.
</EmptyDataTemplate>
```

Now when we run the application, no matter which table we view, we see this new display text when we attempt to set a filter that returns 0 rows or if the table is empty.

Obviously in a production application, the level of customization is much higher. The great thing about these templates is that because they apply automatically to all tables, it becomes incredibly easy to make sweeping changes to the look, feel, and functionality of your application regardless of the underlying data model. These custom templates, because of their loosely coupled nature, can even be reused among multiple applications within the same organization to create a strong, branded feel and shared functionality.

Creating Type and Entity-Specific Templates

Having the ability to make changes to every piece of your website with a single code change is powerful but also not necessarily the most prudent way to make changes. It brings up the old hitting-a-nail-with-a-sledgehammer analogy. After you make your subtle changes to the shared templates, you might want to make changes to the templates for a single entity.

To do this, you make use of the `CustomPages` folder. For this exercise, we modify the list template for the `ZombieSightings` table so that we are not using auto-generated columns and we have a bit more control over how this grid displays.

To start, create a new folder called `ZombieSightings` under the `CustomPages` folder. Make a copy of the `List.aspx` page from the `PageTemplates` folder, and copy it to the `ZombieSightings` folder.

Now open up the `List.aspx` page in your new `ZombieSightings` folder. At this point we have build errors because there is a type name conflict. Change the Inherits property at the top of the page to `ZombieList`; then in the `List.aspx.cs` file, change the class name to `ZombieList`. This now prevents the custom list template from having a name collision with the shared list template at compile time.

Modify the markup for List.aspx for our custom list so that it looks like the following code:

```
<%@ Page Language="C#" MasterPageFile="~/Site.master"
    CodeBehind="List.aspx.cs" Inherits="DynamicDataDemo.ZombieList" %>
<%@ Register src="~/DynamicData/Content/GridViewPager.ascx"
 tagname="GridViewPager" tagprefix="asp" %>
<asp:Content ID="headContent" ContentPlaceHolderID="head" Runat="Server">
</asp:Content>
<asp:Content ID="Content1" ContentPlaceHolderID="ContentPlaceHolder1"
➡Runat="Server">
    <asp:DynamicDataManager ID="DynamicDataManager1" runat="server"
➡AutoLoadForeignKeys="true">
        <DataControls>
            <asp:DataControlReference ControlID="GridView1" />
        </DataControls>
    </asp:DynamicDataManager>
    <h2 class="DDSubHeader">Zombie Sightings!</h2>

    <asp:UpdatePanel ID="UpdatePanel1" runat="server">
        <ContentTemplate>
            <div class="DD">
                <asp:ValidationSummary
                    ID="ValidationSummary1" runat="server" EnableClientScript="true"
                        HeaderText="List of validation errors" CssClass="DDValidator" />
                <asp:DynamicValidator runat="server"
                    ID="GridViewValidator" ControlToValidate="GridView1"
                        Display="None" CssClass="DDValidator" />

                <asp:QueryableFilterRepeater runat="server" ID="FilterRepeater">
                    <ItemTemplate>
                        <asp:Label runat="server" Text='<%# Eval("DisplayName") %>'
                            OnPreRender="Label_PreRender" />
                        <asp:DynamicFilter runat="server" ID="DynamicFilter"
                            OnFilterChanged="DynamicFilter_FilterChanged" /><br />
                    </ItemTemplate>
                </asp:QueryableFilterRepeater>
                <br />
            </div>
            <asp:GridView ID="GridView1" runat="server"
                DataSourceID="GridDataSource" EnablePersistedSelection="true"
                AllowPaging="True" AllowSorting="True" CssClass="DDGridView"
                AutoGenerateColumns="false"
                RowStyle-CssClass="td" HeaderStyle-CssClass="th" CellPadding="6">
                <Columns>
                    <asp:TemplateField>
```

```
                        <ItemTemplate>
                            <asp:DynamicHyperLink runat="server" Action="Edit"
➥Text="Edit"
                            /> <asp:LinkButton runat="server"
                        CommandName="Delete" Text="Delete"
                                OnClientClick='
                    return confirm("Are you sure you want to delete this item?");'
                            /> <asp:DynamicHyperLink runat="server"
➥Text="Details" />
                        </ItemTemplate>
                    </asp:TemplateField>
                    <asp:DynamicField DataField="Nickname" />
                    <asp:DynamicField DataField="ZombieType" HeaderText="Zombie Type"
                        ItemStyle-HorizontalAlign="Center"/>
                    <asp:DynamicField DataField="Description" />
                    <asp:DynamicField DataField="Feeder" HeaderText="Feeder?"
                        ItemStyle-HorizontalAlign="Center" />
                    <asp:DynamicField DataField="Ambulatory" HeaderText="Ambulatory?"
                        ItemStyle-HorizontalAlign="Center"/>
                </Columns>
                <AlternatingRowStyle BackColor="LightGoldenrodYellow" />
                <PagerStyle CssClass="DDFooter"/>
                <PagerTemplate>
                    <asp:GridViewPager runat="server" />
                </PagerTemplate>
                <EmptyDataTemplate>
                    There are currently no <%= table.DisplayName%> found.
                </EmptyDataTemplate>
            </asp:GridView>
            <asp:EntityDataSource ID="GridDataSource" runat="server"
➥EnableDelete="true" />
            <asp:QueryExtender TargetControlID="GridDataSource"
                ID="GridQueryExtender" runat="server">
                <asp:DynamicFilterExpression ControlID="FilterRepeater" />
            </asp:QueryExtender>
            <br />
            <div class="DDBottomHyperLink">
                <asp:DynamicHyperLink ID="InsertHyperLink" runat="server"
                Action="Insert">
             <img runat="server" src="~/DynamicData/Content/Images/plus.gif"
                alt="Insert new item" />Insert new item</asp:DynamicHyperLink>
            </div>
        </ContentTemplate>
    </asp:UpdatePanel>
</asp:Content>
```

After having made these changes, we can run the application and click the ZombieSightings link from the home page. This presents a UI that looks like the one shown in Figure 32.6. Go back to the main page; then click on the ZombieTypes link to verify that it still conforms to the globally shared list template.

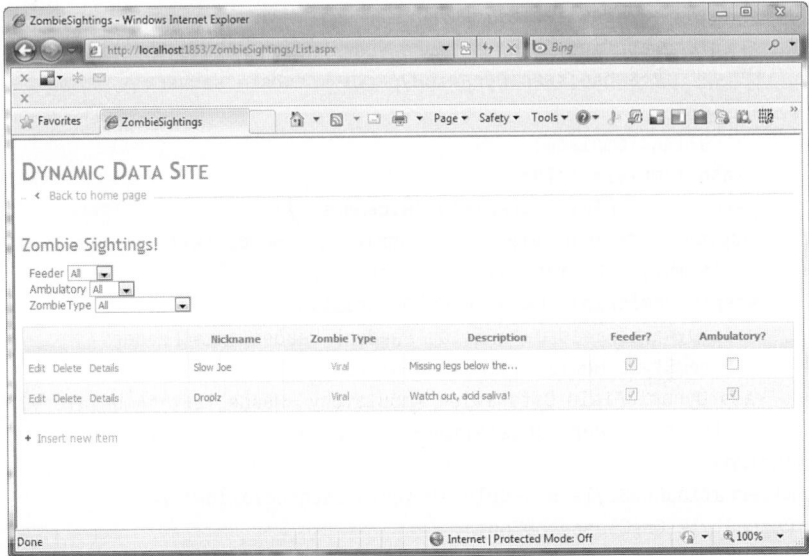

FIGURE 32.6   Custom Entity-Specific List template.

What we've just done is just the tip of the iceberg. If we stay within the structure of the dynamic data template system, we can create incredibly powerful, reusable templates that dramatically increase the productivity of developers and decrease the time gap between database schema creation and the corresponding web UI.

Summary

This chapter has provided you with an overview of the ASP.NET Dynamic Data system. This framework enables you to rapidly build web applications with extremely powerful, interactive, data-driven user interfaces with little-to-no initial coding. Starting from the basic scaffolding, you can stack subtle and rapid customizations over time to take your application from a test scaffold to a full-fledged production application.

ASP.NET Dynamic Data is just one more tool in the ASP.NET 4 developer's toolbox, making ASP.NET an appealing choice for building just about any kind of web application under virtually any circumstances.

Building ASP.NET MVC Applications

ASP.NET Web Forms was originally created to give Windows Forms developers a familiar paradigm when developing web applications. Web Forms creates abstractions and provides the underlying plumbing to enable developers to create event handlers for things such as click-and-selection changed events. Some developers felt that this abstraction incurred too much overhead and complicated the act of building web applications.

Many of those who felt that way were fans of a Model View Controller (MVC) pattern. This pattern goes by several other names, but most commonly is referred to as MVC or MVP (Model-View-Presenter). This chapter provides you with an introduction to ASP.NET MVC Framework, a new alternative to Web Forms development that comes built into Visual Studio 2010. If you are intrigued by MVC development after reading this chapter, SAMS Publishing offers several books that give you all the detail you need for this new framework.

Introducing the ASP.NET MVC Framework

MVC is all about giving developers the ability to create web applications in a quick, lean, and agile fashion. This means that the core tenets of this MVC Framework are testability, rapid development, and extensibility. Anything that you want the MVC Framework to do that it doesn't do now, you can extend on your own through any number of extension points.

Key to making an MVC application testable and extensible is a clear separation of concerns. In other words, all the functional parts of an MVC application have clear responsibilities that are hard and fast rules, not conventions or guidelines. For example, with a Web Forms application it is up to the developers to decide whether they're going to put code in a code-behind file or in the ASPx page, or if they've been around the block a few times, in a separate class library. With the MVC Framework, there are no code-behind files, only Models, Views, and Controllers.

Models

In short, models are data. The model is the abstraction of your application's business logic, rules, and the information stored and retrieved by your application. Models basically define the entities with which your users interact, the rules for those interactions, and information about the data type and constraints. You need to know that the models here refer to the models supplying information to the views, and these models do not necessarily need to be the same as the objects pulled directly from your database. For example, the Order model rendered by a view in your application might not look exactly like the Order table in your database.

Views

The view is the markup sent to the browser. Some code can be inside the view to dynamically pull information from the model, but the view is never anything more than dynamically rendered HTML. There should never be any business logic embedded in a view. The view displays the results of executed business logic by referring to the model but should never execute the business logic itself. When you think about the ultimate goal of separation of concerns—keeping duties and responsibilities clear and separate—the idea of keeping business logic out of the view makes sense.

Controllers

The responsibility of the controller is to handle an incoming request, interact with the data sources as needed (web services, cloud services, or raw database access), decide which view is appropriate based on the request, and finally render the view. The controller makes sure that the view has access to the model and then tells the MVC framework to render it. In the next few sections you see how controllers interact with models and views in a sample application.

Creating Your First ASP.NET MVC Application

To start learning about what an MVC application looks like, the easiest thing to do is just create one. Open Visual Studio 2010 and open the Create Project dialog. Select Web from the installed templates panel on the left, and you should then see a ASP.NET MVC 2 Web

Application template, as shown in Figure 33.1. Give the project a name and a directory and then click OK.

After you click OK, you are asked if you want to create a unit test project (shown in Figure 33.2). As previously mentioned, one of the key tenets of ASP.NET MVC Framework is testability. If you answer yes, a project will be added to the solution that provides a test framework for unit testing your controllers. If you are interested in learning more about unit testing and how it applies to the ASP.NET MVC Framework, see the end of the chapter for additional learning resources.

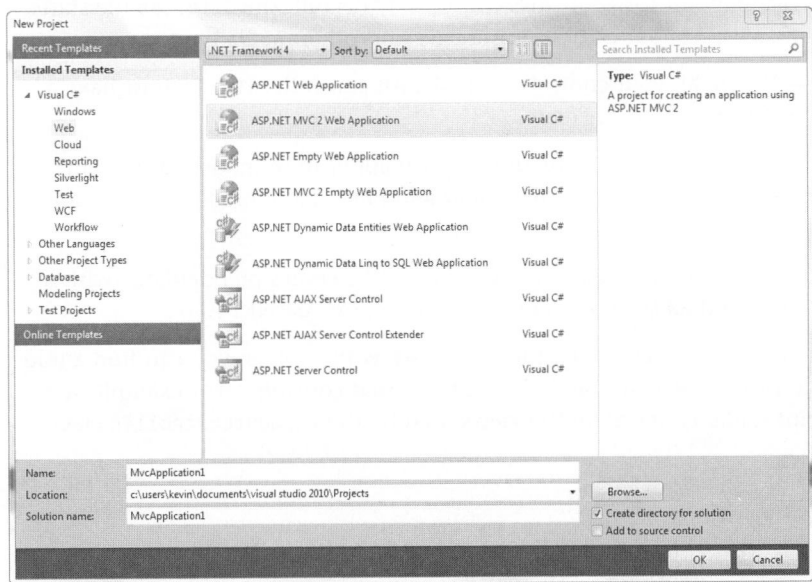

FIGURE 33.1   Visual Studio 2010 New Project dialog.

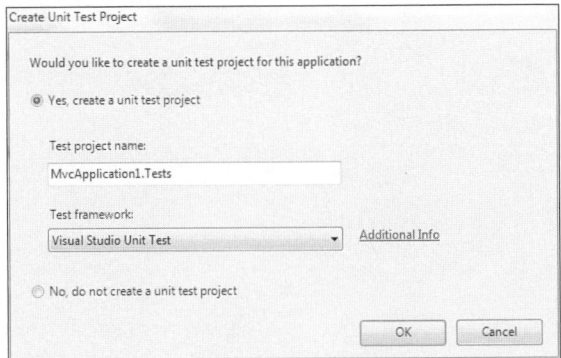

FIGURE 33.2   New MVC Project dialog, prompting for unit test project creation.

The MVC template is going to create the core pieces of your application and some basic scaffolding such as a controller and set of views for enabling users to create accounts and log in using the ASP.NET Membership Provider.

NOTE

One of the great things about ASP.NET MVC Framework is that it can utilize virtually any ASP.NET facility, including the entire provider model. This enables you to create MVC applications with session state, roles, membership, forms authentication, and much more.

The stock project structure includes some prepopulated folders:

▶ **Content**—Starting point for your site's content. By default, the `Site.css` file starts here, and you can add subdirectories for images and other media types.

▶ **Controllers**—Where all your controllers reside. All controller classes must have a Controller postfix, as shown in Figure 33.3.

▶ **Models**—A handy starting point for all your web application models. Many enterprise applications start by deleting this folder and placing the models in a reusable class library.

▶ **Scripts**—Where all your JavaScript resides. This folder comes prepopulated with a version of jQuery and all the scripts required to support ASP.NET Ajax.

▶ **Views**—The root of the view folder hierarchy. Below this folder, you can find a folder for each controller, named exactly the same as that controller. For example, a Views/Account folder contains all the views used by the `AccountController` class.

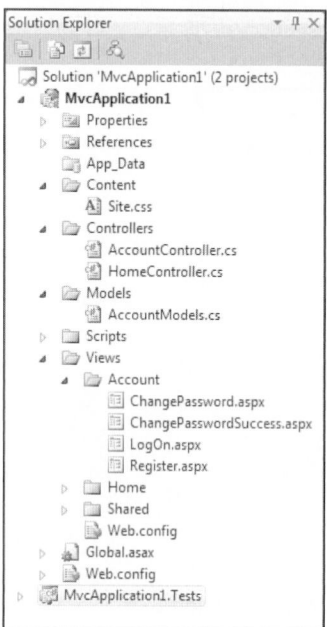

FIGURE 33.3 Stock ASP.NET MVC 2 project structure in Solution Explorer.

Figure 33.3 shows a screenshot of the stock project structure after creating a new ASP.NET MVC project.

At this point, because the default project template contains enough scaffolding for you to start, you can press F5 and watch the application run. Note that the application supports forms authentication, new user creation, and user login out-of-the-box.

Figure 33.4 shows what it looks like when you run the default ASP.NET MVC project.

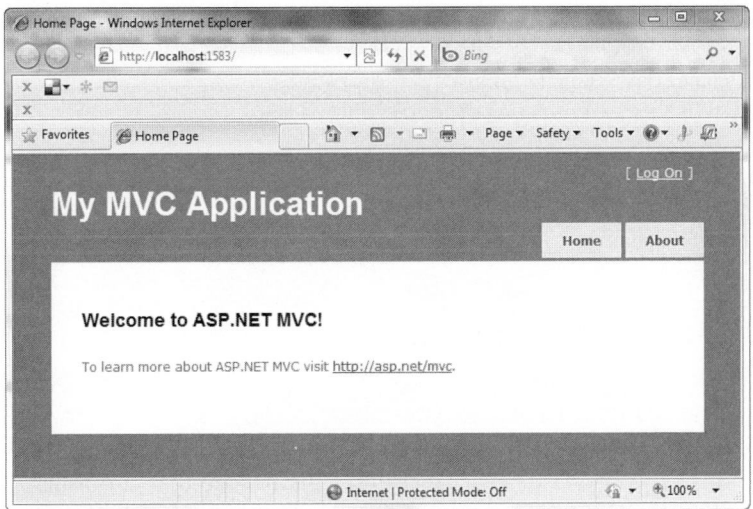

FIGURE 33.4   Default ASP.NET MVC 2 application.

In the next section you create your own MVC page that shows you how MVC's internal plumbing works.

Building an MVC Page

This section walks you through the basics of creating a new ASP.NET MVC page. By going through this process you can hopefully get a good feel for how the MVC framework works at a high level.

The first thing we to need is a controller. To create a new controller, right-click the `Controllers` folder in the project created in the previous section, and choose Add and Controller. This brings up a dialog asking you for the controller name and also asks if you want to create stub methods for Create, Update, Delete, and Details. Leave that check box unchecked so we can create our methods manually; call the controller `DemoController`. When you're ready, click the Add button.

What you are presented with is an empty MVC controller that looks like the following code:

```
using System;
using System.Collections.Generic;
using System.Linq;
using System.Web;
using System.Web.Mvc;

namespace MvcApplication1.Controllers
{
    public class DemoController : Controller
    {
        //
        // GET: /Demo/

        public ActionResult Index()
        {
            return View();
        }


    }
}
```

Right now, we have a controller called DemoController and a method on that controller called Index. This means that the URLs /demo and /demo/index both work and both execute that method. This is due to the default URL routing configuration. To see the routing configuration in action, open the Global.asax.cs file.

If we try to press these URLs, we get an error because no view corresponds to the Index method. The error message that you get from trying to access this URL is so informative to a new MVC developer that we included it as Figure 33.5.

In this message you can see how the MVC Framework is attempting to automatically locate a view based on the name of the method invoked and the name of the controller.

Now let's create a view. To do that, create a new folder called Demo under the Views folder. Then, right-click the Demo folder and choose Add; then select View. Here you see several options, including creating a strongly typed view, choosing which type of stock view content should be provided, and the view name. For now, leave all the defaults and name the view Index.

This brings up an HTML editing surface for the new view. Note that there is no code-behind for this view—this is by design. If you remember in previous section, separation of concerns tells us that putting a code-behind below a view is a dangerous temptation to start embedding business logic in the view, so code-behinds are left out entirely. If there's work to be done, it should be done in the controller (fetch and update) or in the model (business logic and data representation).

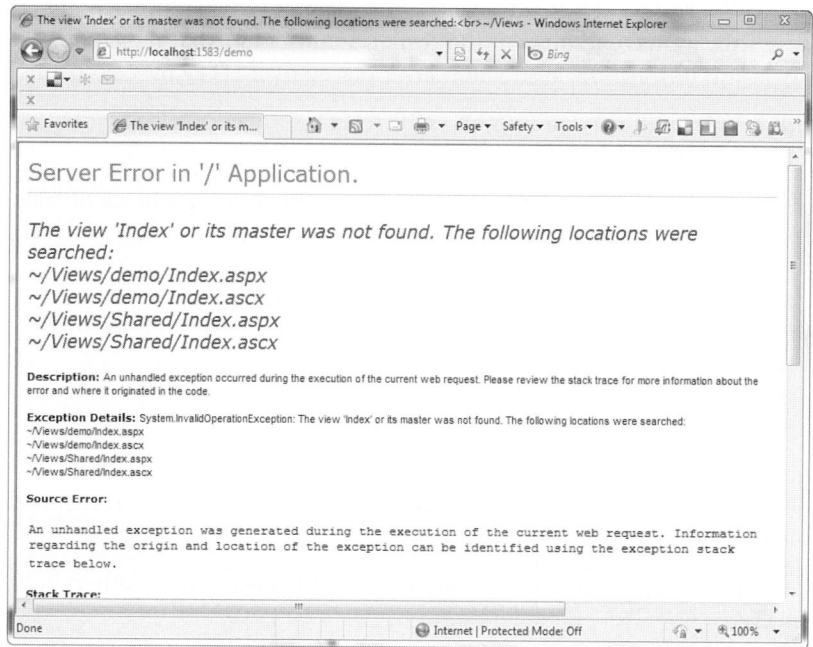

FIGURE 33.5   Accessing a controller without a corresponding view.

Now when you run the application and navigate to the /demo or /demo/index URLs, you should see the default content.

As a brief taste of the kind of incredibly powerful functionality you can get from MVC views, add the following line of code somewhere below the word Index in the second content placeholder:

```
<%= Html.ActionLink("Click here to go home", "Index", "Home") %>
```

This HTML extender actually renders an HTML anchor element. The huge benefit here is that it renders a link to the Index method on the Home controller; the developer doesn't need to (and shouldn't!) know about the specific URL. This is just one of dozens of HTML extenders that make creating dynamic views in MVC both powerful and easy.

Accepting Form Input

Invariably, after seeing a little bit of what MVC is and how it works, developers immediately begin wondering how to invoke server-side events or how to manipulate data and accept input from users. First, you need to remember that in the MVC framework, there is no concept of server-side events. There are no server controls and no concept of postback and invoking server-side events.

So if you don't have postbacks and server-side events, how do you provide interactivity for your users? To answer this, we have to dust off the corner of our brains that remembers what HTML actually is and unlearn the abstraction layer placed over HTTP by Web Forms.

To demonstrate both MVC's simplicity and power, let's create a simple form and write a controller method that responds to that form.

To start, open the Index.aspx page in the Demo folder and add the following block of code below the Index text:

```
<% using (Html.BeginForm("DoSomething", "Demo", FormMethod.Post)) { %>
        Enter your favorite color:
        <%= Html.TextBox("favoriteColor", "Blue") %><br />
        <input type="submit" id="submit" value="Submit" />
    <% } %>
```

Here we use another HTML extender, the BeginForm method to tell the MVC Framework that we plan to POST the contents of the user-submitted form to whatever URL is mapped to the Demo controller's DoSomething method.

Because we post to the DoSomething method, we should probably create that method in the DemoController class:

```
[HttpPost]
public ActionResult DoSomething(string favoriteColor)
{
    ViewData["color"] = favoriteColor;
    return View();
}
```

There is an incredibly powerful model binding subsystem that is part of ASP.NET MVC that can take form values and either turn them into method parameters as shown here or even convert them into model classes. For example, if all the form values in a form belong to a Customer class, you can actually pass an instance of the Customer class to the method to which your form posts, and the MVC model binder takes care of mapping everything accordingly. It is a huge timesaver and creates incredibly readable code.

Now let's just create the view. Repeat the process we used last time by right-clicking the Demo folder in the Views folder and add a new view called DoSomething. Put the following markup in the file:

```
<%= ViewData["color"] %>
```

Now when you request the page at the /demo URL, you are prompted to enter your favorite color. When you do so and click the Submit button, your browser makes an HTTP POST request to /demo/DoSomething, which invokes the code you just added to the DoSomething() method. This sets a variable in the ViewData dictionary. (A facility for providing information from the controller to the view; more can be found on this by checking out the resources at the end of the chapter.) This variable is then accessed from the DoSomething.aspx view, displaying your favorite color, as shown in Figure 33.6.

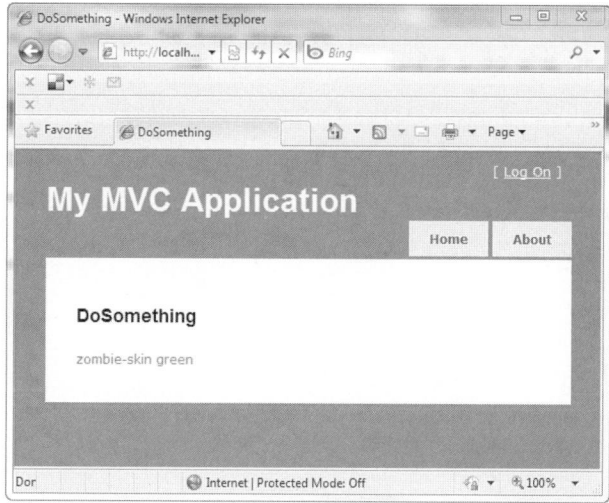

FIGURE 33.6   Results of posting a form to a Controller method.

Summary

This chapter provided you with a small taste of what it's like to build web applications using ASP.NET MVC Framework, which strives for simplicity, ease of maintenance, high testability and reliability, and scalability. If these things interest you and you aren't a big fan of postback-based development, perhaps you should look into MVC development.

This chapter barely scratches the surface of what you can do with ASP.NET MVC Framework but showed you some of the things possible while still being completely compatible with existing ASP.NET functionality such as the provider models, session state, forms authentication, and more.

> **NOTE**
>
> This chapter barely scratches the surface of ASP.NET MVC Framework and all of the advanced functionality you can leverage from it. For a detailed approach to ASP.NET MVC, read *ASP.NET MVC Framework Unleashed* from Sams Publishing or check out the official ASP.NET MVC Framework website at http://www.asp.net/mvc. The MVC Framework has historically released new versions faster than Visual Studio, so keep an eye on the official website for the latest version and the publicly available source code if you're into that sort of thing.

Configuring Applications

In this chapter, you learn how to configure your ASP.NET applications. In the first section, you are provided with an overview of the different sections contained in a web configuration file. You also learn how to modify web configuration files by using both the Web Site Administration Tool and the ASP.NET Microsoft Management Console Snap-In.

Next, you learn how to manipulate configuration settings programmatically with the Configuration API. We discuss how you can both retrieve and modify configuration settings. You also learn how to work with configuration settings located at a remote website.

You also learn how to add custom configuration sections to the web configuration file. You learn how to register custom configuration sections and interact with custom configuration sections with the Configuration API.

Finally, we discuss the important topic of protecting your configuration files. You learn how to encrypt different sections of a configuration file so that they cannot be read by human eyes. You also learn how you can deploy an encrypted configuration file from one server to another.

Overview of Website Configuration

ASP.NET uses a hierarchical system of configuration. At the top of the hierarchy is the Machine.config file. This file contains all the default configuration settings for ASP.NET applications and all other types of applications built with the .NET Framework.

The Machine.config file is located at the following path:

\WINDOWS\Microsoft.NET\Framework\[version]\CONFIG\Machine.config

This same folder also contains a Web.config file. The Web.config file contains settings that serve as defaults for all ASP.NET applications running on the machine. The Web.config file overrides particular settings in the Machine.config file.

NOTE

The \CONFIG folder includes the following six files:

- ▶ **Machine.config**—Contains the actual configuration settings.
- ▶ **Machine.config.default**—Contains the default values for all configuration settings.
- ▶ **Machine.config.comments**—Contains comments on each configuration setting.
- ▶ **Web.config**—Contains the actual configuration settings.
- ▶ **Web.config.default**—Contains the default values for all configuration settings.
- ▶ **Web.config.comments**—Contains comments on each configuration setting.

Only the Machine.config and Web.config files are actually used. The other files are for the purpose of documentation.

You can place a Web.config file in the root folder of a website, such as the wwwroot folder. A Web.config file located in the root folder of a website contains settings that apply to all applications contained in the website.

You also can place a Web.config file in the root of a particular application. In that case, the Web.config file has application scope.

Finally, you can place a Web.config file in an application subfolder. In that case, the Web.config file applies to all pages in that folder and below.

When an ASP.NET application starts, this hierarchy of configuration files merges and caches in memory. A file dependency is created between the cached configuration settings and the file system. If you make a change to any of the configuration files in the hierarchy, the new configuration settings are loaded into memory automatically.

When an ASP.NET page reads a configuration setting, the setting is read from memory. This means that the ASP.NET Framework can read configuration settings, such as connection strings, efficiently.

Furthermore, when you make a change to a configuration setting, you don't need to stop and restart an application manually for the new setting to take effect. The ASP.NET Framework reloads the cached configuration settings automatically when the configuration settings are changed on the file system. (The one exception to this is modifications to the processModel section.)

WARNING

Modifying most configuration settings results in an application restart. Any data stored using the cache or in-process `Session` state is lost and must be reloaded. You can get around this issue by using external configuration files. See the section "Placing Configuration Settings in an External File" later in this chapter. Additionally, this rarely poses a problem in production environments because developers are typically not modifying these files directly on production servers.

The configuration files are XML files. You can modify configuration settings by opening the `Machine.config` file or a `Web.config` file and modifying a setting in Notepad. Alternatively, you can change many of the configuration settings (but not all) by using either the Web Site Administration Tool or the ASP.NET Microsoft Management Console Snap-In.

Using the Web Site Administration Tool

If you use Visual Web Developer (or Visual Studio .NET), you can modify certain configuration settings with the Web Site Administration Tool. This tool provides you with a form interface for making configuration changes (see Figure 34.1).

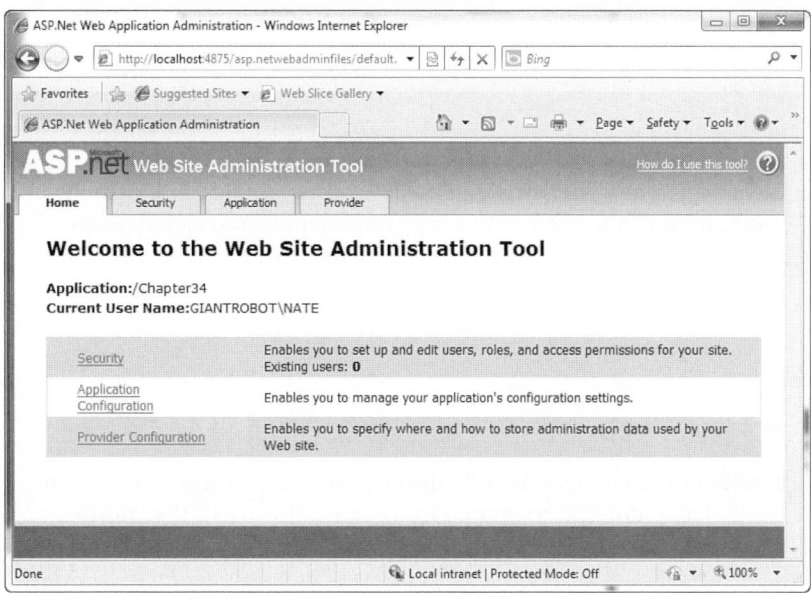

FIGURE 34.1   Opening the Web Site Administration Tool.

You open the Web Site Administration Tool by selecting Project and then clicking ASP.NET Configuration. Selecting this option opens a browser window that contains the tool.

The Web Site Administration Tool has the following four tabs:

▶ **Home**—Contains links to the other tabs.

▶ **Security**—Enables you to configure authentication, authorization, and the Role Manager.

▶ **Application**—Enables you to create and manage application settings, configure SMTP settings, and enable application tracing, debugging, and error pages. You also can use this tab to take your application offline.

▶ **Provider**—Enables you to select a provider for Membership and the Role Manager.

Under the Application tab, you can click the link to take your application offline. When you click this link, the following httpRuntime element is added to your web configuration file:

```
<httpRuntime enable="false" />
```

This setting causes the Application Domain associated with the ASP.NET application to refuse any requests. When an application is offline, all requests result in a 404—Not Found error message. You might want to take your application offline, for example, to prevent people from requesting pages while you perform updates to your application.

> **NOTE**
>
> You also can take an ASP.NET application offline by adding a file with the name
> app_offline.htm to the root of your application.

The Web Site Administration Tool is implemented as an ASP.NET application. Behind the scenes, it uses the Configuration API discussed later in this chapter. You can view the entire source code for the Web Site Administration Tool by navigating to the following folder:

```
\WINDOWS\Microsoft.NET\Framework\[version]\ASP.NETWebAdminFiles
```

Using the ASP.NET Microsoft Management Console Snap-In

You also can make configuration changes with IIS directly. The latest versions of Internet Information Services (IIS) have ASP.NET configuration options directly in the console. Previous versions of IIS had snap-in property sheets that provided limited configuration. When you click either a website or an application in the left-side browser, the following ASP.NET options are available for that selection:

▶ .NET Authorization Rules

▶ .NET Compilation

▶ .NET Error Pages

▶ .NET Globalization

- ▶ .NET Profile

- ▶ .NET Trust Levels

- ▶ Application Settings

- ▶ Connection Strings

- ▶ Machine Key

- ▶ Pages and Controls

- ▶ Session State

- ▶ SMTP E-mail

Behind the scenes, IIS is directly manipulating the Web.config files for sites and applications. If you ever had to manually tweak some difficult settings in these files, then you can certainly appreciate that IIS now lets you make these changes directly within IIS (see Figure 34.2).

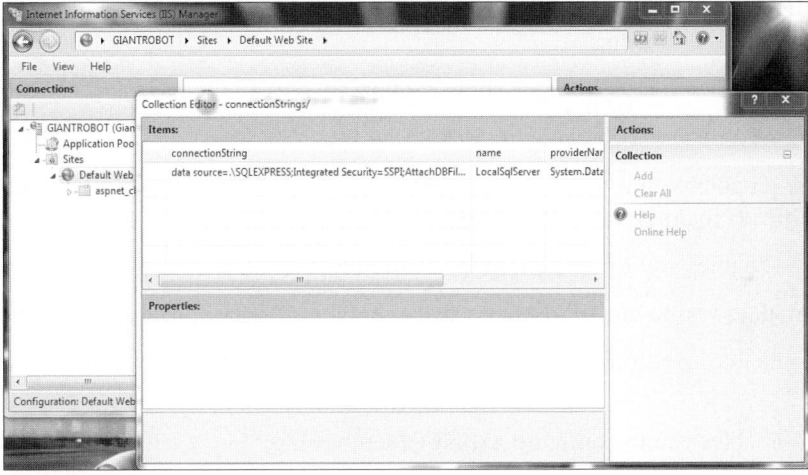

FIGURE 34.2   Configuration options available within IIS.

ASP.NET Configuration Sections

All the configuration sections in the Machine.config or Web.config file related to ASP.NET are contained in the <system.web> section group. Here is a complete list of the 36 ASP.NET configuration sections and a brief explanation of the purpose of each section:

- ▶ **anonymousIdentification**—Enables you to configure anonymous user identification, which is used, for example, by the Profile object.

- ▶ **authentication**—Enables you to configure authentication.

- ▶ **authorization**—Enables you to configure authorization.

▶ **browserCaps**—Enables you to configure the lookup of browser capabilities.

▶ **caching**—Enables you to configure caching policies.

▶ **clientTarget**—Enables you to configure aliases for different clients (browsers).

▶ **compilation**—Enables you to configure how ASP.NET applications are compiled. For example, you can specify whether an application is compiled in debug mode.

▶ **customErrors**—Enables you to configure custom error pages.

▶ **deployment**—Enables you to specify whether an ASP.NET application is deployed in retail mode.

▶ **deviceFilters**—Enables you to configure device filters.

▶ **globalization**—Enables you to configure the Culture, UICulture, and other attributes related to building multilingual web applications.

▶ **healthMonitoring**—Enables you to configure Health Monitoring. See the final section of this chapter.

▶ **hostingEnvironment**—Enables you to configure ASP.NET application properties such as the application idle timeout.

▶ **httpCookies**—Enables you to configure how cookies are sent to the browser.

▶ **httpHandlers**—Enables you to configure HTTP Handlers.

▶ **httpRuntime**—Enables you to configure properties of the HTTP Runtime, such as the number of threads maintained in the thread pool.

▶ **httpModules**—Enables you to configure HTTP Modules.

▶ **identity**—Enables you to configure the identity of the ASP.NET application account.

▶ **machineKey**—Enables you to configure encryption keys used by Membership and Session state.

▶ **membership**—Enables you to configure ASP.NET Membership.

▶ **mobileControls**—Enables you to configure adapters used with ASP.NET mobile controls.

▶ **pages**—Enables you to configure page properties such as the website Master Page and Theme. See Chapter 5, "Designing Websites with Master Pages," and Chapter 6, "Designing Websites with Themes."

▶ **processModel**—Enables you to configure the ASP.NET process.

▶ **profile**—Enables you to configure the Profile object.

▶ **roleManager**—Enables you to configure the Role Manager.

▶ **securityPolicy**—Enables you to map security policy files to trust levels.

▶ **sessionPageState**—Enables you to configure how mobile devices store Session state.

- ▶ **sessionState**—Enables you to configure `Session` state.

- ▶ **siteMap**—Enables you to configure Site Maps.

- ▶ **trace**—Enables you to configure page and application tracing.

- ▶ **trust**—Enables you to configure Code Access Security (CAS) for an ASP.NET application.

- ▶ **urlMappings**—Enables you to remap page requests to new pages.

- ▶ **webControls**—Enables you to specify the location of client-script files used by web controls.

- ▶ **webParts**—Enables you to configure Web Parts.

- ▶ **webServices**—Enables you to configure web services.

- ▶ **xhtmlConformance**—Enables you to configure the level of XHTML conformance of the XHTML rendered by web controls.

Applying Configuration Settings to a Particular Path

By default, the settings in a `Machine.config` or `Web.config` file are applied to all pages in the same folder and below. However, if you have the need, you can also apply configuration settings to a particular path. For example, you can apply configuration settings to a particular subfolder or even a particular page.

You apply configuration settings to a particular path by using the `<location>` element. For example, the web configuration file in Listing 34.1 enables password-protection for a single file named `Secret.aspx`.

LISTING 34.1 Web.config

```xml
<?xml version="1.0"?>
<configuration >

  <system.web>
    <authentication mode="Forms" />
  </system.web>

  <location path="Secret.aspx">
    <system.web>
      <authorization>
        <deny users="?" />
      </authorization>
    </system.web>
  </location>

</configuration>
```

34

If you attempt to request the Secret.aspx page, you are redirected to the Login.aspx page. However, none of the other files in the same application are password protected by the configuration file.

The <location> element must be added as an immediate child of the <configuration> element. You can't, for example, add the <location> element within a <system.web> element. You must surround the <system.web> element with the <location> element.

> **NOTE**
>
> You can create the web configuration file in Listing 34.1 by right-clicking the project in Solution Explorer, choosing Add New Item, and selecting the Web Configuration File template. Alternatively, you can add the appSettings section by using either the Web Site Administration Tool or IIS. Both tools enable you to enter values for the appSettings section through a user-friendly interface.

Locking Configuration Settings

You can lock configuration settings so that they cannot be overridden at a lower level in the configuration hierarchy. For example, you might want to require that no application running on your production server executes in debug mode. In that case, you can lock the debug configuration setting in a website Web.config file, the root Web.config file, or the Machine.config file.

> **TIP**
>
> As an alternative to locking the compilation section to prevent a production website being deployed in debug mode, you can take advantage of the deployment element. Adding the following element to the system.web section of the machine.config disables debug mode, enables remote custom errors, and disables trace:
>
> ```
>     <deployment retail="true" />
> ```

You can lock a configuration setting in multiple ways. The Web.config file in Listing 34.2 illustrates how you can lock a setting by using the allowOverride="false" attribute of the <location> element.

LISTING 34.2   Web.config

```
<?xml version="1.0"?>
<configuration >

  <location allowOverride="false">
    <system.web>
      <compilation debug="false" />
    </system.web>
```

```
    </location>

</configuration>
```

The configuration file in Listing 34.2 locks the compilation element. If you attempt to add a configuration file that sets the debug attribute to the value true, and the configuration file is located below the configuration file in Listing 34.2, an exception is raised (see Figure 34.3).

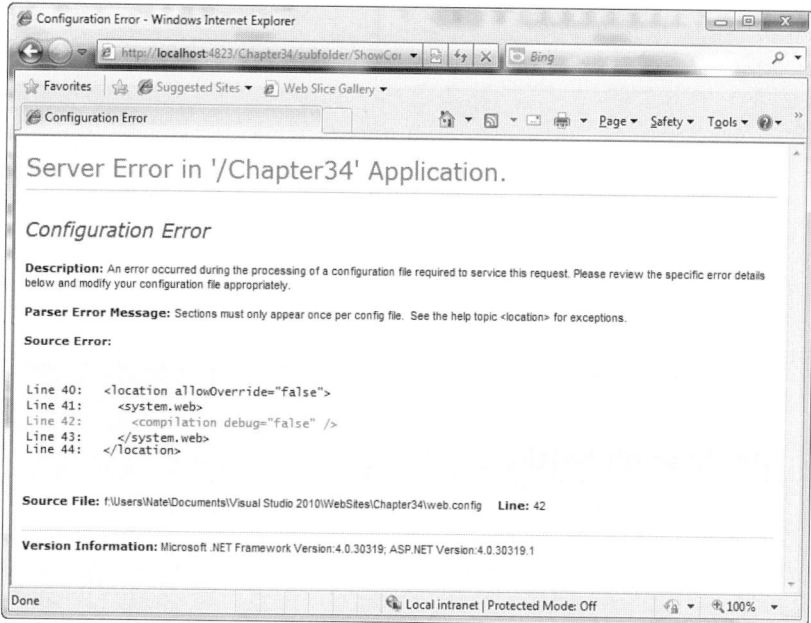

FIGURE 34.3   Attempting to override a locked configuration section.

One problem with the configuration file in Listing 34.2 is that it locks the entire compilation element. If you attempt to change any attribute of the compilation element at a lower level in the configuration hierarchy, an exception is raised.

You can add any of the following attributes to a particular configuration element to lock either the entire element or one or more of its attributes:

▶ **lockAllAttributesExcept**—Enables you to lock all attributes except those listed as the value of this attribute. You can specify multiple attributes to exclude in a comma-delimited list.

▶ **lockAllElementsExcept**—Enables you to lock all child elements of the current element except those listed as the value of this attribute. You can specify multiple elements to exclude in a comma-delimited list.

▶ **lockAttributes**—Enables you to lock multiple attributes. You can specify the attributes to lock in a comma-delimited list.

▶ **lockElements** —Enables you to lock multiple child elements. You can specify the child elements to lock in a comma-delimited list.

▶ **lockItem**—Enables you to lock the current element.

For example, the web configuration file in Listing 34.3 locks the debug attribute, and only the debug attribute, of the <compilation> element.

LISTING 34.3 Web.config

```
<?xml version="1.0"?>
<configuration >


    <system.web>
      <compilation debug="false" lockAttributes="debug" />
    </system.web>


</configuration>
```

Adding Custom Application Settings

You can easily add custom configuration settings to the web configuration file by taking advantage of the appSettings section, which section contains a list of key and value pairs. For example, the web configuration file in Listing 34.4 contains a welcome message and a copyright notice.

LISTING 34.4 Web.config

```
<?xml version="1.0"?>
<configuration>
  <appSettings>
    <add key="welcome" value="Welcome to our Web site!" />
    <add key="copyright" value="Copyright (c) 2007 by the company" />
  </appSettings>
</configuration>
```

You can retrieve values from the appSettings section either programmatically or declaratively. The page in Listing 34.5 illustrates both approaches (see Figure 34.4).

FIGURE 34.4   Displaying values from the `appSettings` configuration section.

LISTING 34.5   `ShowAppSettings.aspx`

```
<%@ Page Language="C#" %>
<%@ Import Namespace="System.Web.Configuration" %>
<!DOCTYPE html PUBLIC "-//W3C//DTD XHTML 1.0 Transitional//EN"
"http://www.w3.org/TR/xhtml1/DTD/xhtml1-transitional.dtd">
<script runat="server">

    void Page_Load()
    {
        lblWelcome.Text = WebConfigurationManager.AppSettings["welcome"];
    }

</script>
<html xmlns="http://www.w3.org/1999/xhtml" >
<head id="Head1" runat="server">
    <title>Show AppSettings</title>
</head>
<body>
    <form id="form1" runat="server">
    <div>
```

```
<asp:Label
    id="lblWelcome"
    Runat="server" />

<hr />

<asp:Literal
    id="ltlCopyright"
    Text="<%$ AppSettings:copyright %>"
    Runat="server" />

</div>
</form>
</body>
</html>
```

In Listing 34.5, the welcome message is retrieved programmatically from the `WebConfigurationManager.AppSettings` property. The value retrieved is assigned to a `Label` control. The `System.Web.Configuration` namespace must be imported before you can use the `WebConfigurationManager` class.

You retrieve the copyright notice declaratively by using the `AppSettingsExpressionBuilder`. The following expression retrieves the value of the copyright key:

```
<%$ AppSettings: copyright %>
```

Placing Configuration Settings in an External File

You can place particular configuration sections in an external file. You might want to do this for a couple of reasons. First, you can make a configuration file more manageable by dividing it into multiple files. Also, when you place configuration information in a separate file, you can prevent application restarts when you change a configuration setting.

Every configuration element includes a `configSource` attribute. You can assign a path to a file as the value of the `configSource` attribute. For example, the web configuration file in Listing 34.6 uses the `configSource` attribute in its `<appSettings>` element.

LISTING 34.6 Web.config

```
<?xml version="1.0"?>
<configuration>
  <appSettings configSource="appSettings.config" />
</configuration>
```

The `appSettings` are stored in the external file, as shown in Listing 34.7.

LISTING 34.7   appSettings.config

```xml
<?xml version="1.0"?>
<appSettings>
  <add key="message" value="Hello World!" />
</appSettings>
```

Normally, modifying a web configuration file results in your ASP.NET application restarting. Any data stored in Session State or the `Cache` object is lost. However, the `appSettings` section is declared in the `Machine.config` file with a `restartOnExternalChanges="false"` attribute. This attribute prevents your application from restarting when a change is made to the `appSettings` section in an external configuration file. If you modify the file in Listing 34.6, for example, your application won't restart.

> **NOTE**
>
> The book's website includes a page named `ShowAppStartTime.aspx`, which displays the time that the current ASP.NET application started. You can use this file to detect when a modification made to a web configuration file caused an application restart. (The application start time is retrieved in the `Application_Start()` event handler in the `Global.asax` file.)

Using the Configuration API

The Configuration API enables you to retrieve and modify configuration settings. You can use the Configuration API to modify web configuration files on the local machine or a remote machine.

If you are responsible for maintaining a large number of websites, the Configuration API can make your life much easier. You can build administrative tools that enable you to quickly make configuration changes to multiple applications. You can use the Configuration API in an ASP.NET page, or you can build command-line tools or Windows Forms applications that use the Configuration API.

The Configuration API is exposed by the `WebConfigurationManager` class (located in the `System.Web.Configuration` namespace). This class supports the following properties:

▶ **AppSettings**—Exposes all the settings from the `appSettings` section.

▶ **ConnectionStrings**—Exposes all the settings from the `connectionStrings` section.

The WebConfigurationManager also supports the following methods:

- ▶ **GetSection**—Retrieves a configuration section relative to the current page or a supplied virtual path.

- ▶ **GetWebApplicationSection**—Retrieves a configuration section from the current web application root web configuration file.

- ▶ **OpenMachineConfiguration**—Retrieves a Machine.config file on either the local machine or a remote server.

- ▶ **OpenMappedMachineConfiguration**—Retrieves a Machine.config file by using a particular file mapping.

- ▶ **OpenMappedWebConfiguration**—Retrieves a web configuration file by using a particular file mapping.

- ▶ **OpenWebConfiguration**—Retrieves a Web.config file on either the local machine or a remote server.

Almost every configuration section in the web configuration file has a corresponding class in .NET Framework that represents the configuration section. These classes provide you with a strongly typed representation of each configuration section.

For example, corresponding to the <authentication> section in the web configuration file, there is a System.Web.Configuration.AuthenticationSection class. Corresponding to the <pages> section in the web configuration file, there is a System.Web.Configuration.PagesSection class. Each of these classes expose properties that correspond to all the attributes you can set in the web configuration file.

Reading Configuration Sections from the Current Application

When an ASP.NET application starts, the application merges all the configuration settings in the configuration hierarchy to create one representation of the configuration settings. A particular configuration setting might have different values at different levels in the hierarchy. You can use the methods of the WebConfigurationManager class to get the value of a configuration setting at any level in the hierarchy.

The WebConfigurationManager.GetWebApplicationSection() method always retrieves a configuration setting from the application root Web.config file. For example, the page in Listing 34.8 displays whether debugging is enabled.

LISTING 34.8   ShowConfigApp.aspx

```
<%@ Page Language="C#" %>
<%@ Import Namespace="System.Web.Configuration" %>
<!DOCTYPE html PUBLIC "-//W3C//DTD XHTML 1.0 Transitional//EN"
"http://www.w3.org/TR/xhtml1/DTD/xhtml1-transitional.dtd">
<script runat="server">
```

```
    void Page_Load()
    {
        CompilationSection section =
(CompilationSection)WebConfigurationManager.GetWebApplicationSection("system.web/co
mpilation");
        lblDebug.Text = section.Debug.ToString();
    }
</script>
<html xmlns="http://www.w3.org/1999/xhtml" >
<head id="Head1" runat="server">
    <title>Show Config App</title>
</head>
<body>
    <form id="form1" runat="server">
    <div>

    Debug Mode:
    <asp:Label
        id="lblDebug"
        Runat="server" />

    </div>
    </form>
</body>
</html>
```

The GetWebApplication() method returns an object. You must cast the value returned by this method to a particular configuration section type. In Listing 34.8, the value returned by this method is cast to an instance of the CompilationSection type.

Realize that you can get the same result when the page in Listing 34.8 is located in different subfolders. For example, debugging might not be enabled in a root configuration file, but it might be enabled in a configuration file in a particular subfolder. However, if you call the GetWebApplicationSection() method, the method always returns the configuration setting for the application root Web.config file.

If you want to get the value of a configuration setting relative to the folder in which the page executes, you can use the GetSection() method instead of the GetWebApplicationSection() method. The page in Listing 34.9 is located in a subfolder. The page displays the value of the debug setting retrieved from both the GetWebApplicationSection() method and the GetSection() method (see Figure 34.5).

FIGURE 34.5   Retrieving a configuration setting with the GetSection() and
GetWebApplicationSection() methods.

LISTING 34.9   SubFolder\ShowConfigRelative.aspx

```
<%@ Page Language="C#" %>
<%@ Import Namespace="System.Web.Configuration" %>
<!DOCTYPE html PUBLIC "-//W3C//DTD XHTML 1.0 Transitional//EN"
"http://www.w3.org/TR/xhtml1/DTD/xhtml1-transitional.dtd">
<script runat="server">

    void Page_Load()
    {
        CompilationSection section =
(CompilationSection)WebConfigurationManager.GetSection("system.web/compilation");
        lblDebug1.Text = section.Debug.ToString();

        section =
(CompilationSection)WebConfigurationManager.GetWebApplicationSection("system.web/co
mpilation");
        lblDebug2.Text = section.Debug.ToString();
    }
```

```
</script>
<html xmlns="http://www.w3.org/1999/xhtml" >
<head id="Head1" runat="server">
    <title>Show Config Relative</title>
</head>
<body>
    <form id="form1" runat="server">
    <div>

    GetSection Debug:
    <asp:Label
        id="lblDebug1"
        Runat="server" />

    <br /><br />

    GetWebApplicationSection Debug:
    <asp:Label
        id="lblDebug2"
        Runat="server" />

    </div>
    </form>
</body>
</html>
```

When you request the page in Listing 34.9, different values display by the `GetSection()` method and `GetWebApplicationSection()` method. The method displays the configuration setting relative to the current directory. The second method displays the configuration setting from the application root `Web.config` file.

If you want to retrieve the value of a configuration setting for a particular path, you can use the overload of the `GetSection()` method that accepts a path parameter. The page in Listing 34.10 iterates through all the immediate subfolders contained in the current application and displays whether debugging is enabled (see Figure 34.6).

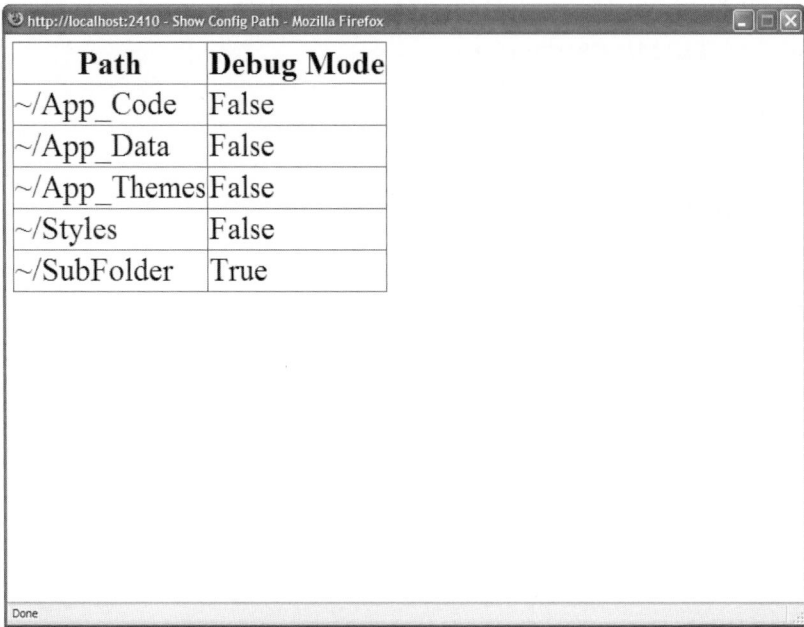

FIGURE 34.6   Displaying configuration settings for each subfolder in an application.

LISTING 34.10   ShowConfigPath.aspx

```
<%@ Page Language="C#" %>
<%@ Import Namespace="System.IO" %>
<%@ Import Namespace="System.Web.Configuration" %>
<%@ Import Namespace="System.Collections.Generic" %>
<!DOCTYPE html PUBLIC "-//W3C//DTD XHTML 1.0 Transitional//EN"
"http://www.w3.org/TR/xhtml1/DTD/xhtml1-transitional.dtd">
<script runat="server">

    void Page_Load()
    {
        Dictionary<string, bool> results = new Dictionary<string, bool>();
        DirectoryInfo rootDir = new DirectoryInfo(Request.PhysicalApplicationPath);
        DirectoryInfo[] dirs = rootDir.GetDirectories();
        foreach (DirectoryInfo dir in dirs)
        {
            string path = "~/" + dir.Name;
            CompilationSection section =
(CompilationSection)WebConfigurationManager.GetSection("system.web/compilation",
path);
```

```
            results.Add(path, section.Debug);
        }
        grdResults.DataSource = results;
        grdResults.DataBind();
    }
</script>
<html xmlns="http://www.w3.org/1999/xhtml" >
<head id="Head1" runat="server">
    <title>Show Config Path</title>
</head>
<body>
    <form id="form1" runat="server">
    <div>

    <asp:GridView
        id="grdResults"
        AutoGenerateColumns="false"
        Runat="server">
        <Columns>
        <asp:BoundField DataField="Key" HeaderText="Path" />
        <asp:BoundField DataField="Value" HeaderText="Debug Mode" />
        </Columns>
    </asp:GridView>

    </div>
    </form>
</body>
</html>
```

Opening a Configuration File

If you want to open a particular configuration file, you can use one of the Open methods exposed by the WebConfigurationManager class. For example, the page in Listing 34.11 uses the OpenMachineConfiguration() method to open the Machine.config file and display the default value for the authentication mode setting.

LISTING 34.11   ShowConfigMachine.aspx

```
<%@ Page Language="C#" %>
<%@ Import Namespace="System.Web.Configuration" %>
<!DOCTYPE html PUBLIC "-//W3C//DTD XHTML 1.0 Transitional//EN"
"http://www.w3.org/TR/xhtml1/DTD/xhtml1-transitional.dtd">
<script runat="server">
```

```
    void Page_Load()
    {
        Configuration config = WebConfigurationManager.OpenMachineConfiguration();
        AuthenticationSection section =
(AuthenticationSection)config.GetSection("system.web/authentication");
        lblMode.Text = section.Mode.ToString();
    }
</script>
<html xmlns="http://www.w3.org/1999/xhtml" >
<head id="Head1" runat="server">
    <title>Show Config Machine</title>
</head>
<body>
    <form id="form1" runat="server">
    <div>

    Authentication Mode Default Value:
    <asp:Label
        id="lblMode"
        Runat="server" />

    </div>
    </form>
</body>
</html>
```

You can use the `WebConfigurationManager` class to display configuration information for other websites located on the same server. For example, the page in Listing 34.12 displays a list of all the virtual directories contained in the default website. You can select a virtual directory and view the authentication mode associated with the virtual directory (see Figure 34.7).

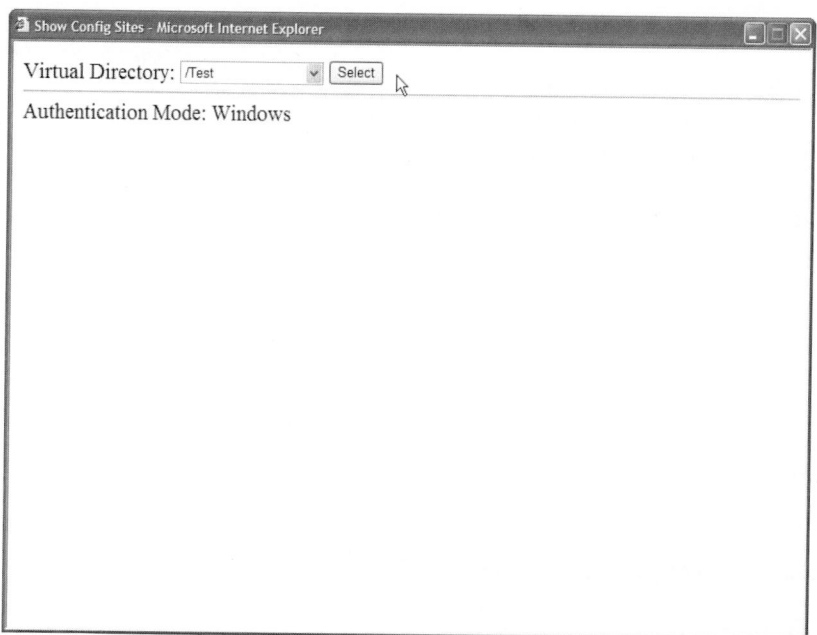

FIGURE 34.7   Displaying configuration information for any application hosted on a server.

LISTING 34.12   ShowConfigSites.aspx

```
<%@ Page Language="C#" %>
<%@ Import Namespace="System.Web.Configuration" %>
<%@ Import Namespace="System.DirectoryServices" %>
<%@ Import Namespace="System.Collections.Generic" %>
<!DOCTYPE html PUBLIC "-//W3C//DTD XHTML 1.0 Transitional//EN"
"http://www.w3.org/TR/xhtml1/DTD/xhtml1-transitional.dtd">

<script runat="server">

    const string sitePath = "IIS://localhost/W3SVC/1/ROOT";

    void Page_Load()
    {
        if (!Page.IsPostBack)
        {
            dropVDirs.DataSource = GetVirtualDirectories();
            dropVDirs.DataBind();
        }
    }
```

```
    private List<String> GetVirtualDirectories()
    {
        List<String> dirs = new List<string>();
        DirectoryEntry site = new DirectoryEntry(sitePath);
        DirectoryEntries vdirs = site.Children;

        foreach (DirectoryEntry vdir in vdirs)
        {
            if (vdir.SchemaClassName == "IIsWebVirtualDir")
            {
                string vPath = vdir.Path.Remove(0, sitePath.Length);
                dirs.Add(vPath);
            }
        }
        return dirs;
    }

    protected void btnSelect_Click(object sender, EventArgs e)
    {
        Configuration config =
WebConfigurationManager.OpenWebConfiguration(dropVDirs.SelectedValue);
        AuthenticationSection section =
(AuthenticationSection)config.GetSection("system.web/authentication");
        lblAuthenticationMode.Text = section.Mode.ToString();
    }
</script>
<html xmlns="http://www.w3.org/1999/xhtml" >
<head id="Head1" runat="server">
    <title>Show Config Sites</title>
</head>
<body>
    <form id="form1" runat="server">
    <div>

    <asp:Label
        id="lblVirtualDirectory"
        Text="Virtual Directory:"
        AssociatedControlID="dropVDirs"
        Runat="server" />
    <asp:DropDownList
        id="dropVDirs"
        Runat="server" />
    <asp:Button
        id="btnSelect"
        Text="Select"
        OnClick="btnSelect_Click"
```

```
            Runat="server" />

        <hr />

        Authentication Mode:
        <asp:Label
            id="lblAuthenticationMode"
            Runat="server" />

        </div>
        </form>
</body>
</html>
```

The list of virtual directories is retrieved with the classes from the
System.DirectoryServices namespace. When you select a virtual directory, the
OpenWebConfiguration() method is called with the path to the virtual directory to get the
configuration information.

> **WARNING**
>
> Before you can use the classes from the System.DirectoryServices namespace, you
> must add a reference to the System.DirectoryServices.dll assembly. In Visual
> Web Developer, select Website, Add Reference. Also, depending on the security set-
> tings for the site and code running the directory services code, it might fail to connect
> to the domain controller. Make sure your code runs under a properly authorized identity.

Opening a Configuration File on a Remote Server

You can use the WebConfigurationManager class to open Machine.config or Web.config
files located on remote web servers. However, before you can do this, you must perform
one configuration step. You must enable the remote server to accept remote configuration
connections by executing the following command from a command prompt:

```
aspnet_regiis -config+
```

To disable remove configuration connections, execute the following command:

```
aspnet_regiis -config-
```

The aspnet_regiis tool is located in the following path:

```
\WINDOWS\Microsoft.NET\Framework\[version]\aspnet_regiis.exe
```

NOTE

If you open the SDK Command Prompt or the Visual Studio Command Prompt, you don't need to navigate to the Microsoft.NET folder to execute the `aspnet_regiis` tool.

After you make this modification to a remote server, you can retrieve (and modify) configuration settings on the remote server by using one of the Open methods exposed by the `WebConfigurationManager` class. For example, the page in Listing 34.13 contains a form that enables you to enter a server, username, and password. When you submit the form, the page connects to the remote server and retrieves its `Machine.config` file. The page displays the current value of the remote server's authentication mode (see Figure 34.8).

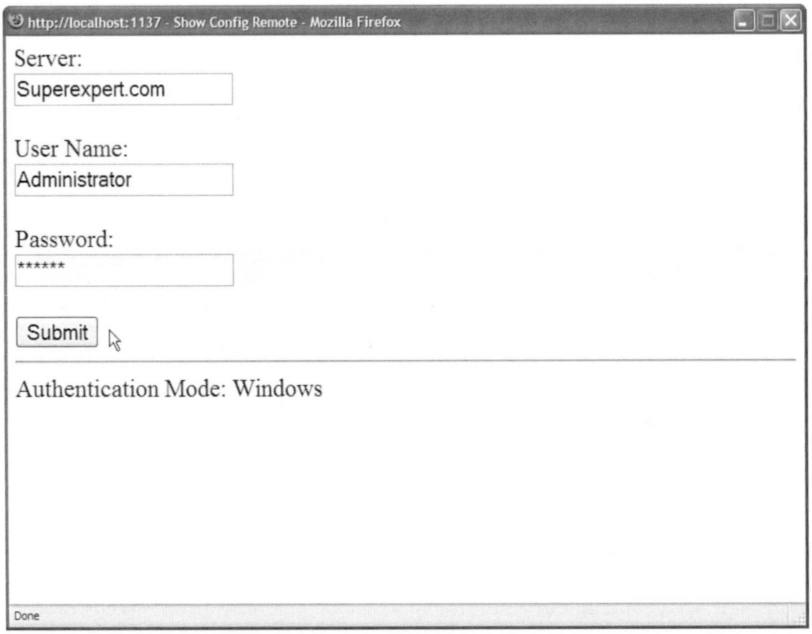

FIGURE 34.8   Changing configuration settings for a remote server.

LISTING 34.13   ShowConfigRemote.aspx

```
<%@ Page Language="C#" %>
<%@ Import Namespace="System.Web.Configuration" %>
<!DOCTYPE html PUBLIC "-//W3C//DTD XHTML 1.0 Transitional//EN"
"http://www.w3.org/TR/xhtml1/DTD/xhtml1-transitional.dtd">
<script runat="server">

    protected void btnSubmit_Click(object sender, EventArgs e)
    {
        try
```

```
        {
            Configuration config = WebConfigurationManager.OpenMachine
➥Configuration(null, txtServer.Text, txtUserName.Text, txtPassword.Text);
            AuthenticationSection section = (AuthenticationSection)config.
➥GetSection("system.web/authentication");
            lblAuthenticationMode.Text = section.Mode.ToString();
        }
        catch (Exception ex)
        {
            lblAuthenticationMode.Text = ex.Message;
        }
    }
</script>
<html xmlns="http://www.w3.org/1999/xhtml" >
<head id="Head1" runat="server">
    <title>Show Config Remote</title>
</head>
<body>
    <form id="form1" runat="server">
    <div>

    <asp:Label
        id="lblServer"
        Text="Server:"
        AssociatedControlID="txtServer"
        Runat="server" />
    <br />
    <asp:TextBox
        id="txtServer"
        Runat="server" />
    <br /><br />
    <asp:Label
        id="lblUserName"
        Text="User Name:"
        AssociatedControlID="txtUserName"
        Runat="server" />
    <br />
    <asp:TextBox
        id="txtUserName"
        Runat="server" />
    <br /><br />
    <asp:Label
        id="lblPassword"
        Text="Password:"
        AssociatedControlID="txtPassword"
        Runat="server" />
```

34

```
    <br />
     <asp:TextBox
        id="txtPassword"
        TextMode="Password"
        Runat="server" />
    <br /><br />
    <asp:Button
        id="btnSubmit"
        Text="Submit"
        OnClick="btnSubmit_Click"
        Runat="server" />

    <hr />

    Authentication Mode:
    <asp:Label
        id="lblAuthenticationMode"
        Runat="server" />

    </div>
    </form>
</body>
</html>
```

You can use the page in Listing 34.13 even when the web server is located in some distant part of the Internet. You can enter a domain name or IP address in the server field.

Using the Configuration Class

When you use one of the `WebConfigurationManager` Open methods—such as the `OpenMachineConfiguration()` or `OpenWebConfiguration()` methods—the method returns an instance of the `Configuration` class. This class supports the following properties:

▶ **AppSettings**—Returns the `appSettings` configuration section.

▶ **ConnectionStrings**—Returns the `connectionStrings` configuration section.

▶ **EvaluationContext**—Returns an instance of the `ContextInformation` class that enables you to determine the context of the configuration information.

▶ **FilePath**—Returns the physical file path to the configuration file.

▶ **HasFile**—Returns `True` when there is a file that corresponds to the configuration information.

▶ **Locations**—Returns a list of locations defined by the configuration.

▶ **NamespaceDeclared**—Returns `True` when the configuration file includes a namespace declaration.

- ▶ **RootSectionGroup**—Returns the root section group.

- ▶ **SectionGroups**—Returns the child section groups contained by this configuration.

- ▶ **Sections**—Returns the child sections contained by this configuration.

The Configuration class also supports the following methods:

- ▶ **GetSection**—Enables you to return the specified configuration section.

- ▶ **GetSectionGroup**—Enables you to return the specified configuration section group.

- ▶ **Save**—Enables you to save any configuration changes.

- ▶ **SaveAs**—Enables you to save the configuration as a new file.

A configuration file contains two basic types of entities: section groups and sections. For example, the <system.web> element in a configuration file represents a section group. The <system.web> section group contains child sections such as the <authentication> and <httpRuntime> sections.

You can use the Configuration.RootSectionGroup property to get the primary section group in a configuration file. You can use the SectionGroups property to return all of a section group's child section groups and the Sections property to return all of a section group's child sections.

For example, the page in Listing 34.14 recursively displays the contents of the Machine.config file in a TreeView control (see Figure 34.9).

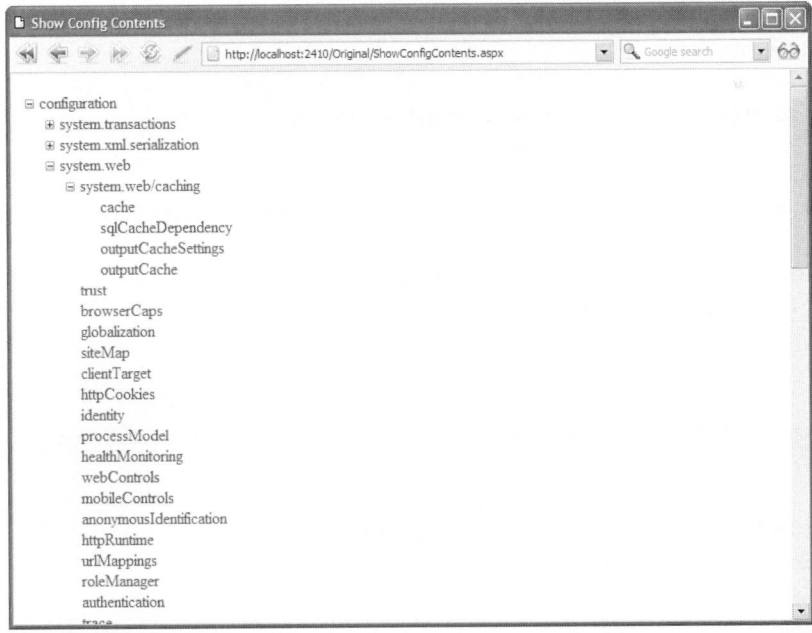

FIGURE 34.9   Displaying all configuration sections from the system.web configuration section group.

LISTING 34.14   ShowConfigContents.aspx

```
<%@ Page Language="C#" %>
<%@ Import Namespace="System.Web.Configuration" %>
<!DOCTYPE html PUBLIC "-//W3C//DTD XHTML 1.0 Transitional//EN"
"http://www.w3.org/TR/xhtml1/DTD/xhtml1-transitional.dtd">
<script runat="server">

    void Page_Load()
    {
        // Add first node
        TreeNode parentNode = new TreeNode("configuration");
        TreeView1.Nodes.Add(parentNode);

        // Start from the root section group
        Configuration config = WebConfigurationManager.OpenMachineConfiguration();

        // Show child section groups
        AddChildSectionGroups(parentNode, config.RootSectionGroup);

        // Show child sections
        AddChildSections(parentNode, config.RootSectionGroup);
    }

    private void AddChildSectionGroups(TreeNode parentNode, ConfigurationSectionGroup
parentConfigSectionGroup)
    {
        foreach (ConfigurationSectionGroup configSectionGroup
➥in parentConfigSectionGroup.SectionGroups)
        {
            TreeNode childNode = new TreeNode(configSectionGroup.SectionGroupName);
            parentNode.ChildNodes.Add(childNode);
            AddChildSectionGroups(childNode, configSectionGroup);
            AddChildSections(childNode, configSectionGroup);
        }
    }

    private void AddChildSections(TreeNode parentNode, ConfigurationSectionGroup
parentConfigSectionGroup)
    {
        foreach (ConfigurationSection configSection in
parentConfigSectionGroup.Sections)
        {
```

```
            TreeNode childNode = new
TreeNode(configSection.SectionInformation.Name);
            parentNode.ChildNodes.Add(childNode);
        }
    }
</script>
<html xmlns="http://www.w3.org/1999/xhtml" >
<head id="Head1" runat="server">
    <title>Show Config Contents</title>
</head>
<body>
    <form id="form1" runat="server">
    <div>

    <asp:TreeView
        id="TreeView1"
        Runat="server" />

    </div>
    </form>
</body>
</html>
```

Modifying Configuration Sections

You can use the WebConfigurationManager class not only when opening a configuration file to read the values of various configuration settings, but you also can use the WebConfigurationManager class to modify existing configuration settings or add new ones.

The Configuration class supports two methods for saving configuration information: the Save() and SaveAs() methods. For example, the page in Listing 34.15 enables you to turn on and off debugging for an application (see Figure 34.10).

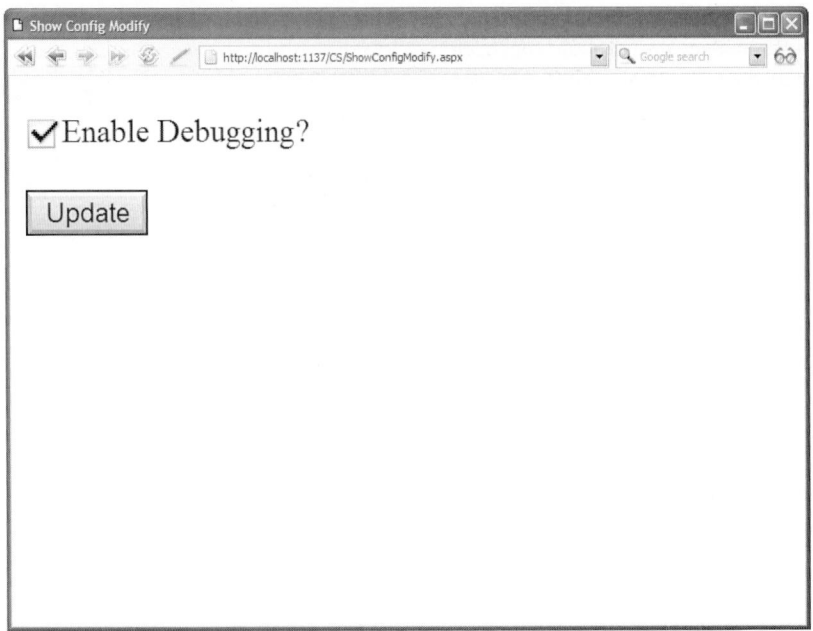

FIGURE 34.10   Modifying the value of the Debug configuration setting.

LISTING 34.15   ShowConfigModify.aspx

```
<%@ Page Language="C#" %>
<%@ Import Namespace="System.Web.Configuration" %>
<!DOCTYPE html PUBLIC "-//W3C//DTD XHTML 1.0 Transitional//EN"
"http://www.w3.org/TR/xhtml1/DTD/xhtml1-transitional.dtd">
<script runat="server">

    void Page_Load()
    {
        if (!Page.IsPostBack)
        {
            Configuration config =
WebConfigurationManager.OpenWebConfiguration(Request.ApplicationPath);
            CompilationSection section =
(CompilationSection)config.GetSection("system.web/compilation");
            chkDebug.Checked = section.Debug;
        }
    }

    protected void btnUpdate_Click(object sender, EventArgs e)
    {
```

```
        Configuration config =
WebConfigurationManager.OpenWebConfiguration(Request.ApplicationPath);
        CompilationSection section =
(CompilationSection)config.GetSection("system.web/compilation");
        section.Debug = chkDebug.Checked;
        config.Save(ConfigurationSaveMode.Modified);
    }
</script>
<html xmlns="http://www.w3.org/1999/xhtml" >
<head id="Head1" runat="server">
    <title>Show Config Modify</title>
</head>
<body>
    <form id="form1" runat="server">
    <div>

    <asp:CheckBox
        id="chkDebug"
        Text="Enable Debugging?"
        Runat="server" />
    <br /><br />
    <asp:Button
        id="btnUpdate"
        Text="Update"
        OnClick="btnUpdate_Click"
        Runat="server" />

    </div>
    </form>
</body>
</html>
```

The page in Listing 34.15 loads the application root Web.config file with the help of the OpenWebConfiguration() method. (The Nothing parameter causes the root Web.config file to be loaded.) Next, the value of the Compilation.Debug property is modified. Finally, the Save() method is called to save this change.

When you call the Save() method, you can pass a ConfigurationSaveMode parameter to the method. This parameter can have the following values:

▶ **Full**—Saves all configuration settings, regardless of whether they have been modified.

▶ **Minimal**—Saves only those configuration settings that are different from their inherited value.

▶ **Modified**—Saves only those configuration settings that have been modified.

To use the Save() or SaveAs() methods, the account associated with the page must have Write permissions for the folder in which the configuration file is saved. By default, when pages are served from Internet Information Server, ASP.NET pages execute in the security context of the NETWORK SERVICE account (for Windows Server 2003) or the ASPNET account (for other operating systems). By default, neither of these accounts have permissions to save configuration changes.

> **NOTE**
>
> To make things more confusing, when pages are served from the web server included with Visual Web Developer, the pages are always served in the security context of the current user.

There are multiple ways that you can get around this permission problem. First, remember that you can use many of the methods of the WebConfigurationManager class from a console application or a Windows Forms application. If you build this type of application, you can sidestep these security issues.

Another option is to enable per-request impersonation for your ASP.NET application. When impersonation is enabled, an ASP.NET page executes within the security context of the user making the page request. If the user account has permissions to write to the file system, the page has permissions to write to the file system.

The web configuration file in Listing 34.16 enables impersonation.

LISTING 34.16   Web.config

```
<?xml version="1.0"?>
<configuration>
    <system.web>
      <identity impersonate="true" />
    </system.web>
</configuration>
```

If you add the configuration file in Listing 34.16 to the same folder that contains the file in Listing 34.15, you can make modifications to configuration files.

> **WARNING**
>
> Most changes to a configuration file result in an application restart. When an ASP.NET application restarts, all data stored in memory is blown away. For example, all data cached in the Cache object or Session state is lost. Also keep in mind that allowing remote configuration changes on a production server can result in a big security hole, so this type of arrangement is only advisable for development and testing environments.

Provisioning a New Website

When you provision new websites, you often need to create a new virtual directory. The Configuration API doesn't provide you with any help here; however, you can create new virtual directories (and applications) by taking advantage of the classes in the System.DirectoryServices namespace. These classes enable you to use Active Directory Services Interface (ADSI) to modify properties of Internet Information Server.

> **NOTE**
>
> You can also manipulate Internet Information Server properties by using Windows Management Instrumentation (WMI). For more information, see the topic "Using WMI to Configure IIS" at the Microsoft MSDN website (msdn.microsoft.com).

Before you can use the classes from the System.DirectoryServices namespace, you need to add a reference to the System.DirectoryServices.dll assembly. In Visual Web Developer, select Website, Add Reference, and select System.DirectoryServices.dll.

For example, the page in Listing 34.17 enables you to provision a new ASP.NET application (see Figure 34.11). The page creates a new virtual directory and a new application. The page also creates a new web configuration file in the virtual directory that contains the default language and debug settings you specify.

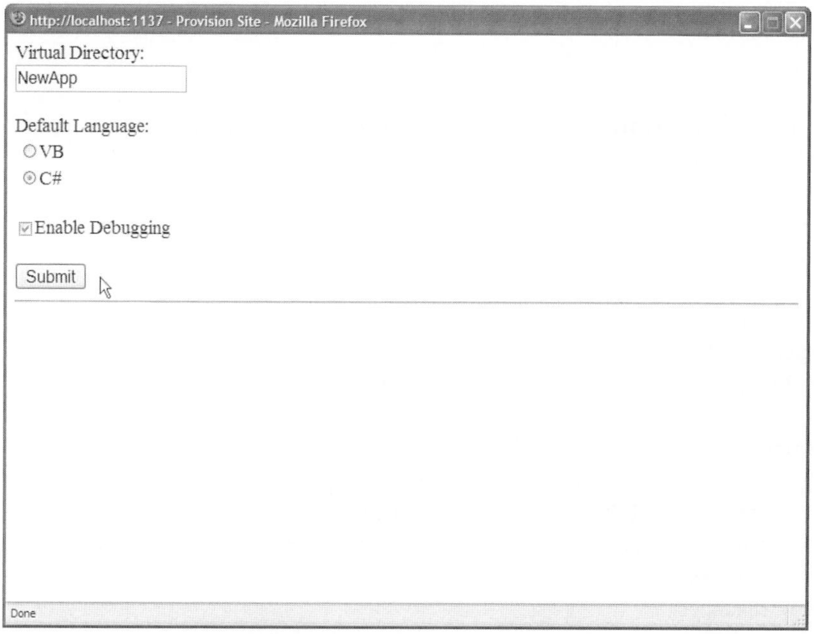

FIGURE 34.11   Creating a new ASP.NET application.

LISTING 34.17   ProvisionSite.aspx

```csharp
<%@ Page Language="C#" %>
<%@ Import Namespace="System.IO" %>
<%@ Import Namespace="System.DirectoryServices" %>
<%@ Import Namespace="System.Web.Configuration" %>
<!DOCTYPE html PUBLIC "-//W3C//DTD XHTML 1.0 Transitional//EN"
"http://www.w3.org/TR/xhtml1/DTD/xhtml1-transitional.dtd">

<script runat="server">

    const string wwwroot = @"c:\Inetpub";
    const string sitePath = @"IIS://localhost/W3SVC/1/ROOT";

    protected void btnSubmit_Click(object sender, EventArgs e)
    {
        string newFolder = Path.Combine(wwwroot, txtVirtualDir.Text);

        CreateVirtualDirectory(newFolder, txtVirtualDir.Text, txtVirtualDir.Text);
        CreateConfiguration(txtVirtualDir.Text);

        // Show link to new site
        lnkNewSite.NavigateUrl = "http://localhost/" + txtVirtualDir.Text;
        lnkNewSite.Target = "_top";
        lnkNewSite.Visible = true;
    }

    private void CreateVirtualDirectory(string folderPath, string virtualDirectory-
Name,string appFriendlyName)
    {
        // Create new Folder
        Directory.CreateDirectory(folderPath);

        // Create Virtual Directory
        DirectoryEntry vRoot = new DirectoryEntry(sitePath);
        DirectoryEntry vDir = vRoot.Children.Add(virtualDirectoryName,
"IIsWebVirtualDir");
        vDir.CommitChanges();
        vDir.Properties["Path"].Value = folderPath;
        vDir.Properties["DefaultDoc"].Value = "Default.aspx";
        vDir.Properties["DirBrowseFlags"].Value = 2147483648;
        vDir.CommitChanges();
        vRoot.CommitChanges();

        // Create Application (Isolated)
        vDir.Invoke("AppCreate2", 1);
```

```
        vDir.Properties["AppFriendlyName"].Value = appFriendlyName;
        vDir.CommitChanges();
    }

    private void CreateConfiguration(string virtualPath)
    {
        // Open configuration
        Configuration config = WebConfigurationManager.OpenWebConfiguration("/" +
virtualPath);

        // Set language and debug setting
        CompilationSection section =
(CompilationSection)config.GetSection("system.web/compilation");
        section.DefaultLanguage = rdlLanguage.SelectedItem.Text;
        section.Debug = chkDebug.Checked;

        // Save configuration
        config.Save(ConfigurationSaveMode.Modified);
    }
</script>
<html xmlns="http://www.w3.org/1999/xhtml" >
<head id="Head1" runat="server">
    <title>Provision Site</title>
</head>
<body>
    <form id="form1" runat="server">
    <div>

    <asp:Label
        id="lblVirtualDir"
        Text="Virtual Directory:"
        AssociatedControlID="txtVirtualDir"
        Runat="server" />
    <br />
    <asp:TextBox
        id="txtVirtualDir"
        Runat="server" />
    <br /><br />
    <asp:Label
        id="lblLanguage"
        Text="Default Language:"
        AssociatedControlID="rdlLanguage"
        Runat="server" />
    <asp:RadioButtonList
        id="rdlLanguage"
        Runat="server">
```

34

```
        <asp:ListItem Text="VB" Selected="True" />
        <asp:ListItem Text="C#" />
    </asp:RadioButtonList>
    <br />
    <asp:CheckBox
        id="chkDebug"
        Text="Enable Debugging"
        Runat="server" />
    <br /><br />
    <asp:Button
        id="btnSubmit"
        Text="Submit"
        OnClick="btnSubmit_Click"
        Runat="server" />

    <hr />
    <asp:HyperLink
        id="lnkNewSite"
        Visible="false"
        Text="Go to New Site"
        Runat="server" />

    </div>
    </form>
</body>
</html>
```

To use the page in Listing 34.17, you need adequate permissions. You can enable per-request impersonation by adding the file in Listing 34.16 to the same folder as the page in Listing 34.17.

> **NOTE**
>
> Internet Information Server includes several sample ADSI scripts. Look in your `Inetpub\AdminScripts` folder.

Creating Custom Configuration Sections

You can add custom configuration sections to a web configuration file. You can use a custom configuration section to store whatever information you want.

For example, if you need to manage a large number of database connection strings, you might want to create a custom database connection string configuration section. Or if you want to follow the Provider Model and implement a custom provider, you need to create a custom configuration section for your provider.

You create a custom configuration section by inheriting a new class from the base ConfigurationSection class. For example, the class in Listing 34.18 represents a simple custom configuration section.

LISTING 34.18   App_Code\DesignSection.cs

```csharp
using System;
using System.Configuration;
using System.Drawing;

namespace AspNetUnleashed
{
    public class DesignSection : ConfigurationSection
    {
        [ConfigurationProperty("backcolor", DefaultValue = "lightblue", IsRequired = true)]
        public Color BackColor
        {
            get { return (Color)this["backcolor"]; }
            set { this["backcolor"] = value; }
        }

        [ConfigurationProperty("styleSheetUrl", DefaultValue =
"~/styles/style.css",IsRequired = true)]
        [RegexStringValidator(".css$")]
        public string StyleSheetUrl
        {
            get { return (string)this["styleSheetUrl"]; }
            set { this["styleSheetUrl"] = value; }
        }

        public DesignSection(Color backcolor, string styleSheetUrl)
        {
            this.BackColor = backcolor;
            this.StyleSheetUrl = styleSheetUrl;
        }

        public DesignSection()
        {
        }
    }
}
```

34

The class in Listing 34.18 represents a Design configuration section. This section has two properties: BackColor and StyleSheetUrl. Both properties are decorated with ConfigurationProperty attributes. The ConfigurationProperty attribute maps the property to an element attribute in the configuration file. When you declare the ConfigurationProperty attribute, you can use the following parameters:

▶ **Name**—Enables you to specify the name of the attribute in the configuration file that corresponds to the property.

▶ **DefaultValue**—Enables you to specify the default value of the property.

▶ **IsDefaultCollection**—Enables you to specify whether the property represents the default collection of an element.

▶ **IsKey**—Enables you to specify whether the property represents a key for a collection of configuration elements.

▶ **IsRequired**—Enables you to specify whether this property must have a value.

▶ **Options**—Enables you to use flags to specify the values of the above options.

You also can use validators when defining configuration properties. For example, in Listing 34.18, RegexStringValidator checks whether the value of the StyleSheetUrl property ends with a .css extension.

You can use the following validators with configuration properties:

▶ **CallbackValidator**—Enables you to specify a custom method to use to validate a property value.

▶ **IntegerValidator**—Enables you to validate whether a property value is an integer value (System.Int32).

▶ **LongValidator**—Enables you to validate whether a property value is a long value (System.Int64).

▶ **PositiveTimeSpanValidator**—Enables you to validate whether a property value is a valid time span.

▶ **RegexStringValidator**—Enables you to validate a property value against a regular expression pattern.

▶ **StringValidator**—Enables you to validate a property value that represents a string against a minimum length, maximum length, and list of invalid characters.

▶ **SubClassTypeValidator**—Enables you to validate whether the value of a property is inherited from a particular class.

▶ **TimeSpanValidator**—Enables you to validate a property value that represents a time span against a minimum and maximum value.

WARNING

When you use validators such as the `RegexStringValidator`, make sure that you provide a property with a default value by using the `DefaultValue` parameter with the `ConfigurationProperty` attribute.

After you create a custom configuration section, you need to register it in a configuration file before you can use it. The web configuration file in Listing 34.19 adds the `DesignSection` configuration section to the `system.web` section.

LISTING 34.19   Web.config

```
<configuration>
  <configSections>
    <sectionGroup name="system.web">
    <section
        name="design"
        type="AspNetUnleashed.DesignSection"
        allowLocation="true"
        allowDefinition="Everywhere" />
    </sectionGroup>
  </configSections>
  <system.web>
    <design
      backcolor="red"
      styleSheetUrl="~/styles/style.css" />
  </system.web>
</configuration>
```

You are not required to add a custom configuration section to any particular configuration section group. For that matter, you are not required to add a custom configuration section to any configuration section group at all.

After you register a custom configuration section, you can use it just like any of the standard configuration sections. You can use the methods of the `WebConfigurationManager` class to retrieve and modify the custom section.

For example, the page in Listing 34.20 uses the custom configuration section just created to retrieve the page background color and style sheet (see Figure 34.12).

34

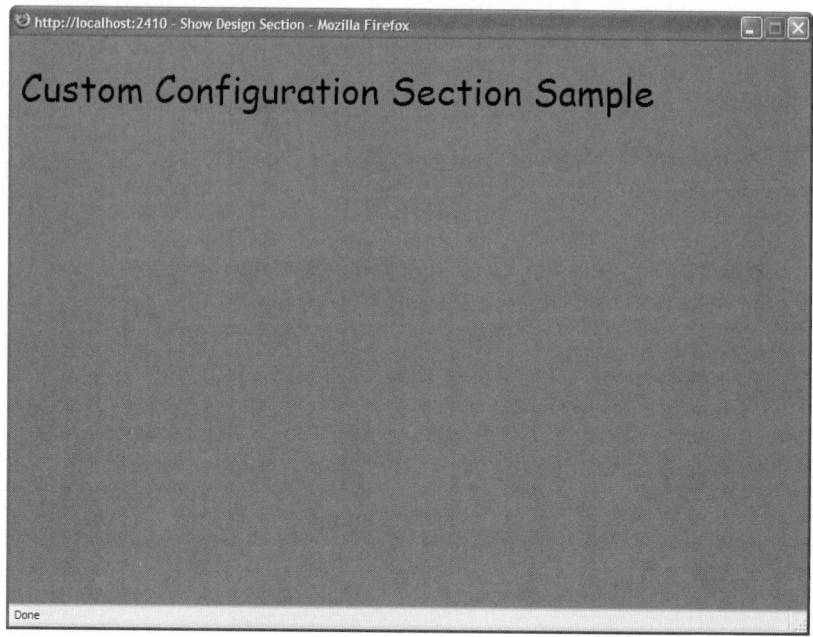

FIGURE 34.12   Using the custom configuration section to modify the page style and background color.

LISTING 34.20   ShowDesignSection.aspx

```
<%@ Page Language="C#" %>
<%@ Import Namespace="AspNetUnleashed" %>
<%@ Import Namespace="System.Web.Configuration" %>
<!DOCTYPE html PUBLIC "-//W3C//DTD XHTML 1.0 Transitional//EN"
"http://www.w3.org/TR/xhtml1/DTD/xhtml1-transitional.dtd">
<script runat="server">

    void Page_Load()
    {
        // Get configuration
        DesignSection section = (DesignSection)WebConfigurationManager.
➥GetWebApplicationSection("system.web/design");

        // Set Background Color
        htmlBody.Attributes["bgcolor"] =
System.Drawing.ColorTranslator.ToHtml(section.BackColor);

        // Set style sheet
        HtmlLink link = new HtmlLink();
        link.Href = section.StyleSheetUrl;
        link.Attributes.Add("rel", "stylesheet");
```

```
            link.Attributes.Add("type", "text/css");
            Page.Header.Controls.Add(link);
        }
    </script>
    <html xmlns="http://www.w3.org/1999/xhtml" >
    <head id="Head1" runat="server">
        <title>Show Design Section</title>
    </head>
    <body id="htmlBody" runat="server">
        <form id="form1" runat="server">
        <div>

        <h1>Custom Configuration Section Sample</h1>

        </div>
        </form>
    </body>
    </html>
```

Creating a Configuration Element Collection

A configuration element can contain a collection of child elements. For example, if you need to create a custom configuration section to configure a provider, you use child elements to represent the list of providers.

The class in Listing 34.21 represents a configuration section for a ShoppingCart. The configuration section includes three properties: MaximumItems, DefaultProvider, and Providers. The Providers property represents a collection of shopping cart providers.

LISTING 34.21 App_Code\ShoppingCartSection.cs

```
using System;
using System.Configuration;

namespace AspNetUnleashed
{
    public class ShoppingCartSection : ConfigurationSection
    {
        [ConfigurationProperty("maximumItems", DefaultValue = 100, IsRequired =
➥true)]
        public int MaximumItems
        {
            get { return (int)this["maximumItems"]; }
            set { this["maximumItems"] = value; }
        }
```

```
        [ConfigurationProperty("defaultProvider")]
        public string DefaultProvider
        {
            get { return (string)this["defaultProvider"]; }
            set { this["defaultProvider"] = value; }
        }


        [ConfigurationProperty("providers", IsDefaultCollection = false)]
        public ProviderSettingsCollection Providers
        {
            get { return (ProviderSettingsCollection)this["providers"]; }
        }


        public ShoppingCartSection(int maximumItems, string defaultProvider)
        {
            this.MaximumItems = maximumItems;
            this.DefaultProvider = defaultProvider;
        }


        public ShoppingCartSection()
        {
        }
    }
}
```

The `Providers` property returns an instance of the `ProviderSettingsCollection` class.
This class is contained in the `System.Configuration` namespace.

The web configuration file in Listing 34.22 illustrates how you can use the
`ShoppingCartSection`.

LISTING 34.22   Web.config

```
<configuration>
  <configSections>
    <sectionGroup name="system.web">
      <section
        name="shoppingCart"
        type="AspNetUnleashed.ShoppingCartSection"
        allowLocation="true"
        allowDefinition="Everywhere" />
    </sectionGroup>
  </configSections>
<system.web>

  <shoppingCart
    maximumItems="50"
```

```
      defaultProvider="SqlShoppingCartProvider">
      <providers>
        <add
          name="SqlShoppingCartProvider"
          type="AspNetUnleashed.SqlShoppingCartProvider" />
        <add
          name="XmlShoppingCartProvider"
          type="AspNetUnleashed.XmlShoppingCartProvider" />
      </providers>
    </shoppingCart>

  </system.web>
  </configuration>
```

The ShoppingCartSection class takes advantage of an existing class in the .NET Framework: the ProviderSettingsCollection class. If you have the need, you can create a custom configuration element collection class.

The AdminUsersSection class in Listing 34.23 enables you to represent a list of users. The class includes a property named Users that exposes an instance of the AdminUsersCollection class. The AdminUsersCollection represents a collection of configuration elements. The AdminUsersCollection class is also defined in Listing 34.23.

LISTING 34.23   App_Code\AdminUsersSection.cs

```
using System;
using System.Configuration;

namespace AspNetUnleashed
{
    public class AdminUsersSection : ConfigurationSection
    {
        [ConfigurationProperty("", IsDefaultCollection = true)]
        public AdminUsersCollection Users
        {
            get { return (AdminUsersCollection)this[""]; }
        }

        public AdminUsersSection()
        {
        }
    }

    public class AdminUsersCollection : ConfigurationElementCollection
    {
        protected override ConfigurationElement CreateNewElement()
```

34

```
    {
        return new AdminUser();
    }

    protected override object GetElementKey(ConfigurationElement element)
    {
        return ((AdminUser)element).Name;
    }

    public AdminUsersCollection()
    {
        this.AddElementName = "user";
    }
    }

    public class AdminUser : ConfigurationElement
    {
        [ConfigurationProperty("name", IsRequired = true, IsKey = true)]
        public string Name
        {
            get { return (string)this["name"]; }
            set { this["name"] = value; }
        }

        [ConfigurationProperty("password", IsRequired = true)]
        public string Password
        {
            get { return (string)this["password"]; }
            set { this["password"] = value; }
        }
    }
}
```

The ConfigurationProperty attribute that decorates the Users property sets the name of the configuration attribute to an empty string. It also marks the property as representing the section's default collection. These options enable you to avoid having to create a subtag for the user collection. The user collection appears immediately below the main <adminUsers> section tag.

The web configuration file in Listing 34.24 illustrates how you can use the AdminUsersSection class.

LISTING 34.24 Web.config

```
<configuration>
<configSections>
```

```
  <sectionGroup name="system.web">
    <section
      name="adminUsers"
      type="AspNetUnleashed.AdminUsersSection"
      allowLocation="true"
      allowDefinition="Everywhere" />
  </sectionGroup>
</configSections>
<system.web>

  <adminUsers>
    <user name="Bob" password="secret" />
    <user name="Fred" password="secret" />
  </adminUsers>

</system.web>
</configuration>
```

The ASP.NET page in Listing 34.25 displays all the users from the adminUsers section in a BulletedList control (see Figure 34.13).

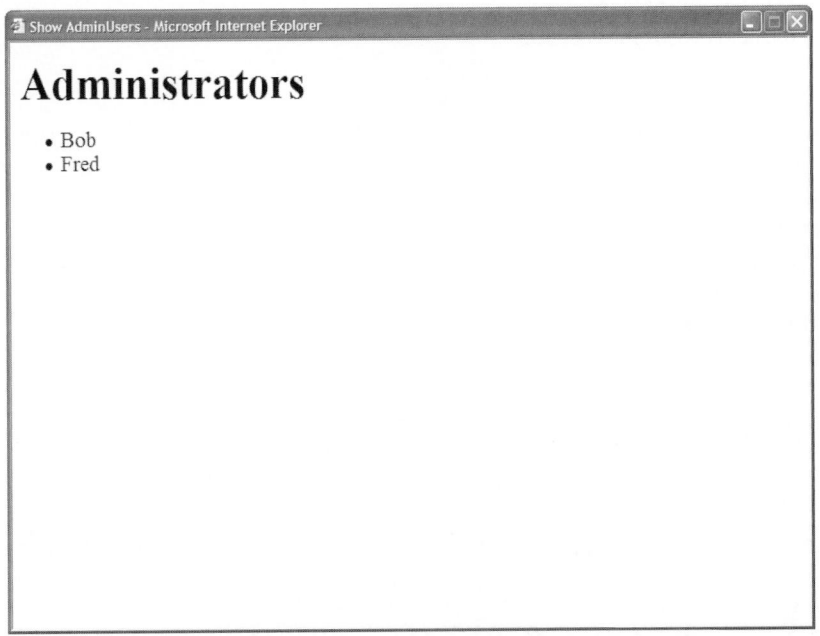

FIGURE 34.13 Displaying the contents of the adminUsers section in a BulletedList control.

LISTING 34.25   ShowAdminUsersSection.aspx

```
<%@ Page Language="C#" %>
<%@ Import Namespace="AspNetUnleashed" %>
<%@ Import Namespace="System.Web.Configuration" %>
<!DOCTYPE html PUBLIC "-//W3C//DTD XHTML 1.0 Transitional//EN"
"http://www.w3.org/TR/xhtml1/DTD/xhtml1-transitional.dtd">
<script runat="server">

    void Page_Load()
    {
        // Get configuration
        AdminUsersSection section =
(AdminUsersSection)WebConfigurationManager.GetWebApplicationSection("system.web/
adminUsers");

        // Bind section to GridView
        bltAdminUsers.DataSource = section.Users;
        bltAdminUsers.DataBind();
    }
</script>
<html xmlns="http://www.w3.org/1999/xhtml" >
<head id="Head1" runat="server">
    <title>Show AdminUsersSection</title>
</head>
<body>
    <form id="form1" runat="server">
    <div>

    <h1>Administrators</h1>
    <asp:BulletedList
        id="bltAdminUsers"
        DataTextField="Name"
        Runat="server" />

    </div>
    </form>
</body>
</html>
```

Creating Encrypted Configuration Sections

If you need to protect sensitive information stored in a configuration file, you can encrypt the information. For example, you should always encrypt the connectionStrings section of a configuration file to prevent your database connection strings from being stolen by unauthorized intruders.

You can encrypt just about any section in the web configuration file. You can encrypt any of the sections in the `system.web` section group with the sole exception of the `processModel` section. You also can encrypt a custom configuration section.

The .NET Framework uses the Provider Model for encrypting configuration sections. The Framework ships with two `ProtectedConfigurationProviders`: the `RsaProtectedConfigurationProvider` and the `DpapiProtectedConfigurationProvider`.

`RsaProtectedConfigurationProvider` protects sensitive information stored in a configuration file. It uses the RSA algorithm to protect a configuration section. The RSA algorithm uses public key cryptography. It depends on that no one has discovered an efficient method to factor large prime numbers.

The second provider, the `DpapiProtectedConfigurationProvider`, uses the Data Protection API (DPAPI) to encrypt a configuration section. The DPAPI is built into the Windows operating system (Microsoft Windows 2000 and later). It uses either Triple-DES or AES (the United States Government-standard encryption algorithm) to encrypt data.

`RsaProtectedConfigurationProvider` is the default provider and is the one that you should almost always use. The advantage of `RsaProtectedConfigurationProvider` is that this provider supports exporting and importing encryption keys. This means that you can move an application that contains an encrypted configuration file from one web server to a new web server. For example, you can encrypt a configuration section on your development web server and deploy the application to a production server.

If you use the `DpapiProtectedConfigurationProvider` to encrypt a configuration section, on the other hand, you cannot decrypt the configuration section on another web server. If you need to move the configuration file from one server to another, you need to first decrypt the configuration file on the source server and re-encrypt the configuration file on the destination server.

WEB STANDARDS NOTE

The .NET Framework uses the World Wide Web Consortium (W3C) recommendation for encrypting XML files. This recommendation is located at www.w3.org/TR/2002/REC-xmlenc-core-20021210.

You can use encryption not only with configuration files, but also with other XML files. To learn more about encrypting XML files, look up the `EncryptedXml` class in the Microsoft .NET Framework SDK Documentation.

Encrypting Sections with the `aspnet_regiis` Tool

The easiest way to encrypt a section in the web configuration file is to use the `aspnet_regiis` command-line tool located at the following path:

```
\WINDOWS\Microsoft.NET\Framework\[version]\aspnet_regiis.exe
```

If you want to encrypt a particular section of a configuration file, you can use the `-pef` option when executing the `aspnet_regiis` tool. For example, the following command encrypts the `connectionStrings` section of a configuration file located in a folder named MyWebApp:

```
aspnet_regiis -pef connectionStrings c:\Websites\MyWebApp
```

If you prefer, rather than specify the location of a web application by its file system path, you can use its virtual path. The following command encrypts the `connectionStrings` section of a configuration file located in a virtual directory named /MyApp:

```
aspnet_regiis -pe connectionStrings -app /MyApp
```

The `-app` option is used to specify the application's virtual path.

You can decrypt a configuration section by using the `-pdf` option. The following command decrypts a configuration file located in a folder named MyWebApp:

```
aspnet_regiis -pdf connectionStrings c:\Websites\MyWebApp
```

You also can decrypt a configuration section by specifying a virtual directory. The following command uses the `-pd` option with the `-app` option:

```
aspnet_regiis -pd connectionStrings -app /MyApp
```

When you encrypt a configuration section, you can specify `ProtectedConfigurationProvider` to use to encrypt the section. The `Machine.config` file configures two providers: `RsaProtectedConfigurationProvider` and `DataProtectionConfigurationProvider`. The `RsaProtectedConfigurationProvider` provider is used by default.

If you execute the following command, the `connectionStrings` section is encrypted with `DataProtectionConfigurationProvider`:

```
aspnet_regiis -pe connectionStrings -app /MyApp -prov ProtectedConfigurationProvider
```

This command includes a `-prov` option that enables you to specify the `ProtectedConfigurationProvider`.

Encrypting Sections Programmatically

Instead of using the `aspnet_regiis` tool to encrypt configuration sections, you can use the Configuration API. Specifically, you can encrypt a configuration section by calling the `SectionInformation.ProtectSection()` method.

For example, the ASP.NET page in Listing 34.26 displays all the sections contained in the `system.web` section group in a `GridView` control. You can click Protect to encrypt a section and UnProtect to decrypt a section (see Figure 34.14).

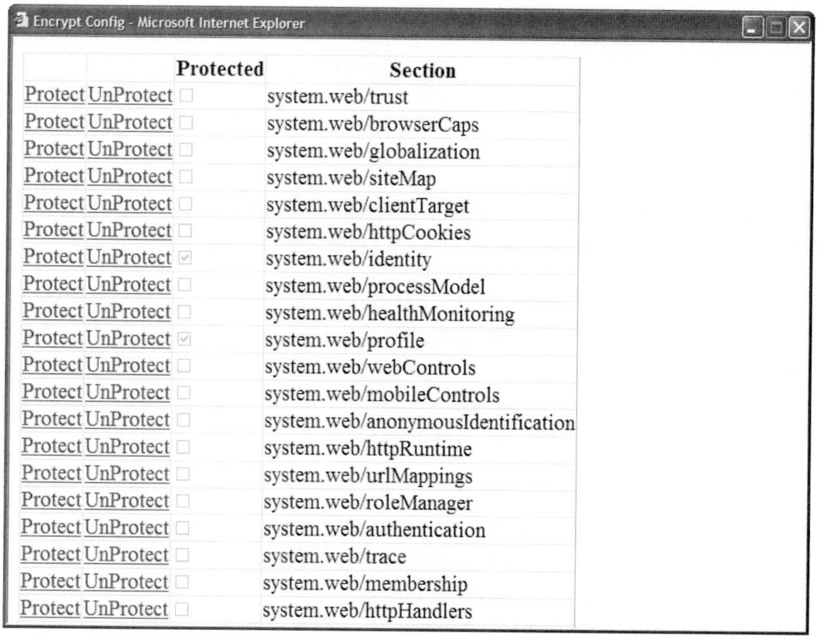

		Protected	Section
Protect	UnProtect	☐	system.web/trust
Protect	UnProtect	☐	system.web/browserCaps
Protect	UnProtect	☐	system.web/globalization
Protect	UnProtect	☐	system.web/siteMap
Protect	UnProtect	☐	system.web/clientTarget
Protect	UnProtect	☐	system.web/httpCookies
Protect	UnProtect	☑	system.web/identity
Protect	UnProtect	☐	system.web/processModel
Protect	UnProtect	☐	system.web/healthMonitoring
Protect	UnProtect	☑	system.web/profile
Protect	UnProtect	☐	system.web/webControls
Protect	UnProtect	☐	system.web/mobileControls
Protect	UnProtect	☐	system.web/anonymousIdentification
Protect	UnProtect	☐	system.web/httpRuntime
Protect	UnProtect	☐	system.web/urlMappings
Protect	UnProtect	☐	system.web/roleManager
Protect	UnProtect	☐	system.web/authentication
Protect	UnProtect	☐	system.web/trace
Protect	UnProtect	☐	system.web/membership
Protect	UnProtect	☐	system.web/httpHandlers

FIGURE 34.14 Encrypting and decrypting configuration sections.

LISTING 34.26 EncryptConfig.aspx

```
<%@ Page Language="C#" %>
<%@ Import Namespace="System.Web.Configuration" %>
<%@ Import Namespace="System.Collections.Generic" %>
<!DOCTYPE html PUBLIC "-//W3C//DTD XHTML 1.0 Transitional//EN"
"http://www.w3.org/TR/xhtml1/DTD/xhtml1-transitional.dtd">
<script runat="server">

    void Page_Load()
    {
        if (!Page.IsPostBack)
            BindSections();
    }

    protected void grdSections_RowCommand(object sender, GridViewCommandEventArgs e)
    {
        int rowIndex = Int32.Parse((string)e.CommandArgument);
        string sectionName = (string)grdSections.DataKeys[rowIndex].Value;
        if (e.CommandName == "Protect")
            ProtectSection(sectionName);
        if (e.CommandName == "UnProtect")
            UnProtectSection(sectionName);
```

```
        BindSections();
    }

    private void ProtectSection(string sectionName)
    {
        Configuration config =
WebConfigurationManager.OpenWebConfiguration(Request.ApplicationPath);
        ConfigurationSection section = config.GetSection(sectionName);
        section.SectionInformation.ProtectSection
➥("RsaProtectedConfigurationProvider");
        config.Save(ConfigurationSaveMode.Modified);
    }

    private void UnProtectSection(string sectionName)
    {
        Configuration config =
WebConfigurationManager.OpenWebConfiguration(Request.ApplicationPath);
        ConfigurationSection section = config.GetSection(sectionName);
        section.SectionInformation.UnprotectSection();
        config.Save(ConfigurationSaveMode.Modified);
    }

    private void BindSections()
    {
        Configuration config =
WebConfigurationManager.OpenWebConfiguration(Request.ApplicationPath);
        List<SectionInformation> colSections = new List<SectionInformation>();
        foreach (ConfigurationSection section in
config.SectionGroups["system.web"].Sections)
            colSections.Add(section.SectionInformation);
        grdSections.DataSource = colSections;
        grdSections.DataBind();
    }

</script>
<html xmlns="http://www.w3.org/1999/xhtml" >
<head id="Head1" runat="server">
    <title>Encrypt Config</title>
</head>
<body>
    <form id="form1" runat="server">
    <div>

    <asp:GridView
        id="grdSections"
        DataKeyNames="SectionName"
```

```
        AutoGenerateColumns="false"
        OnRowCommand="grdSections_RowCommand"
        Runat="server" >
        <Columns>
        <asp:ButtonField ButtonType="Link" Text="Protect" CommandName="Protect" />
        <asp:ButtonField ButtonType="Link" Text="UnProtect"
➥CommandName="UnProtect" />
        <asp:CheckBoxField DataField="IsProtected" HeaderText="Protected" />
        <asp:BoundField DataField="SectionName" HeaderText="Section" />
        </Columns>
    </asp:GridView>

    </div>
    </form>
</body>
</html>
```

When you click the Protect link, the grdSection_RowCommand() event handler executes and calls the ProtectSection() method. This method calls the SectionInformation.ProtectSection() method to encrypt the selected section. The name of ProtectedConfigurationProvider is passed to the ProtectSection() method.

WARNING

The page in Listing 34.26 saves the configuration file. By default, the ASPNET and NETWORK SERVICE accounts do not have permission to write to the file system. If you want the page in Listing 34.26 to execute within the security context of the user requesting the page, you can enable per-request impersonation by adding the configuration file in Listing 34.26 to the root of your application.

Deploying Encrypted Web Configuration Files

If you need to copy an encrypted configuration file from one server to a new server, you must copy the keys used to encrypt the configuration file to the new server. Otherwise, your application can't read encrypted sections of the configuration file on the new server.

WARNING

You can't copy an encrypted configuration file from one server to another when you use the DpapiProtectedConfigurationProvider. This section assumes that you use the RsaProtectedConfigurationProvider.

34

By default, the `RsaProtectedConfigurationProvider` uses a public/private key pair stored in a key container named `NetFrameworkConfigurationKey`. This key container is located at the following path:

`\Documents and Settings\All Users\Application Data\Microsoft\Crypto\RSA\MachineKeys`

If you want to deploy an application that contains an encrypted configuration file to a new server, you must configure a new key container and import the key container to the new server. You must complete five configuration steps:

1. Create a new key container.
2. Configure your application to use the new key container.
3. Export the keys from the origin server.
4. Import the keys on the destination server.
5. Grant access to the key container to your ASP.NET application.

You need to perform this sequence of configuration steps only once. After you set up both servers to use the same encryption keys, you can copy ASP.NET applications back and forth between the two servers and read the encrypted configuration sections. Let's examine each of these steps.

First, you need to create a new key container because the default key container, the `NetFrameworkConfigurationKey` key container, does not support exporting both the public and private encryption keys. Execute the following command from a command prompt:

`aspnet_regiis -pc "SharedKeys" -exp`

This command creates a new key container named `SharedKeys`. The `-exp` option makes any keys added to the container exportable.

After you create the new key container, you must configure your application to use it. The web configuration file in Listing 34.27 configures `RsaProtectedConfigurationProvider` to use the `SharedKeys` key container.

LISTING 34.27   Web.config

```
  <?xml version="1.0"?>
<configuration>
  <configProtectedData
    defaultProvider="MyProtectedConfigurationProvider">
    <providers>
    <add
      name="MyProtectedConfigurationProvider"
      type="System.Configuration.RsaProtectedConfigurationProvider"
      cspProviderName=""
      useMachineContainer="true"
      useOAEP="false"
      keyContainerName="SharedKeys" />
```

```
    </providers>
  </configProtectedData>

  <connectionStrings>
    <add
      name="Movies"
      connectionString="Data Source=DataServer;Integrated Security=true;
        Initial Catalog=MyDB" />
  </connectionStrings>
</configuration>
```

The configuration file in Listing 34.27 includes a configProtectedData section. This section is used to configure a new ProtectedConfigurationProvider named MyProtectedConfigurationProvider. This provider includes a keyContainerName attribute that points to the SharedKeys key container.

The next step is to export the keys contained in the SharedKeys key container to an XML file. You can export the contents of the SharedKeys key container by executing the following command:

```
aspnet_regiis -px "SharedKeys" keys.xml -pri
```

Executing this command creates a new XML file named keys.xml. The -pri option causes both the private and public key—and not only the public key—to be exported to the XML file.

> **WARNING**
>
> The XML key file contains secret information (the keys to the kingdom). After importing the XML file, you should immediately destroy the XML file (or stick the XML file on a CD and lock the CD away in a safe location).

After you create keys.xml file on the origin server, you need to copy the file to the destination server and import the encryption keys. Execute the following command on the destination server to create a new key container and import the encryption keys:

```
aspnet_regiis -pi "SharedKeys" keys.xml
```

The final step is to grant access to the key container to your ASP.NET application. By default, a page served from Internet Information Server executes within the security context of either the NETWORK SERVICE account (Windows 2003 Server) or the ASPNET account (other operating systems). You can grant access to the SharedKeys key container to the ASPNET account by executing the following command:

```
aspnet_regiis -pa "SharedKeys" "ASPNET"
```

34

Executing this command modifies the ACLs for the SharedKeys key container so that the ASPNET account has access to the encryption keys.

After you complete this final step, you can transfer ASP.NET applications with encrypted configuration files back and forth between the two servers. An application on one server can read configuration files that were encrypted on the other server.

NOTE

As an alternative to using the aspnet_regiis tool, you can transfer encryption keys with the help of the RsaProtectedConfigurationProvider class. The RsaProtectedConfigurationProvider class contains methods for exporting and importing keys to and from XML files programmatically.

Summary

This chapter was devoted to the topic of configuration. In the first section, you were provided with an overview of the configuration sections used by ASP.NET Framework. You learned how to lock configuration sections to prevent sections from being modified. You also learned how to place configuration sections in external files.

Next, we tackled the topic of the Configuration API. You learned how to read and modify configuration files programmatically. You also learned how to provision new ASP.NET applications by creating new virtual directories and configuration files.

You learned how to create custom configuration sections and how to create both simple custom configuration sections and custom configuration sections that contain custom collections of configuration elements.

Finally, we discussed the topic of encryption. You learned how to encrypt a configuration section by using the aspnet_regiis command-line tool. You also learned how to encrypt configuration sections programmatically. In the final section, you also learned how to deploy encrypted configuration files from a development server to a production server.

Deploying ASP.NET Web Applications

Many developers have been in the situation in which they have spent a tremendous amount of effort building a web application but when it comes time to deploy it, things fall apart. Some teams don't spend enough time planning for deployment, other times the deployment is just hindered by poor or inadequate technology.

This chapter shows you how new features in ASP.NET 4 ease the burden of web application deployment. After reading this chapter, you should quickly and easily deploy ASP.NET 4 applications to your development, testing, staging, and production environments—hopefully without any of the pain and suffering this process caused with previous versions.

Packaging Web Applications

When ASP.NET was first released, one of its most lauded features was Xcopy deployment. This basically referred to the ability of a developer to copy files from one location to the other, and the application should work. This was a response to the often complicated web deployment process of legacy ASP applications.

Copying files to deploy a web application is still a benefit, but today's web applications have become far more than just a collection of .aspx files and the site's compiled DLL file. Modern web applications carry a tremendous amount of "baggage" and modern developers need a way of bundling all that baggage with an application to deploy it smoothly and quickly.

Today's web applications can consist of any or all of the following:

- Content (aspx, ascx, images, compiled binaries, media, XML files, and so on)

- Databases

- Assemblies that need to be in the Global Assembly Cache (GAC)

- Registry and Configuration Settings

- Security settings (certificates, CAS policy, and such)

- IIS Configuration (security, custom error pages, and more)

This is just the tip of the iceberg. Any web application of sufficient complexity requires a large amount of ancillary "stuff." Up until now, developers have had no real good way of packaging this stuff in a single, simplified way.

Some developers reading this book might have had experience with building web applications in Java. And Java web application developers have long had a facility known as WAR (Web Archive) files. These files are basically ZIP archives that contain (usually) everything that a particular web site needs to function, including security policy, configuration files, and bundled content and media.

Visual Studio 2010 now gives developers the ability to create such single file bundles directly from within the IDE. (Although it can be done from the command line and from within MSBuild as well!)

Before you deploy a web application, you're actually going to need a web application—so if you want to follow along you can simply create a new ASP.NET Web Application in Visual Studio 2010. Make sure it uses IIS as the web host server and not Visual Studio; this can help demonstrate the capability to deploy IIS configuration settings later.

After you create the application, right-click the project in Solution Explorer and choose properties. Click the Package/Publish Web vertical tab . This displays the screen that enables you to configure how your application is going to be packaged. Figure 35.1 shows a sample of this screen.

A bunch of options are on this screen, but some of the more important ones are listed here:

- **Items to Deploy**—This enables you to choose whether you just want items necessary to run the application or whether you want source code and debug symbols deployed as well.

- **Include All Databases**—We discuss this option later in the chapter.

- **Include all IIS Settings**—Because the application runs under IIS (remember we mentioned you should configure your app to run under IIS?) the deployment bundler can actually grab the IIS settings for your application during the packaging process. These settings will be preserved by the target IIS server upon deployment.

▶ **Create Deployment Package as a ZIP File**—You can choose to build a deployment package as a single file or as a folder hierarchy. In general you probably always want to use the ZIP file because it is easier to move around between servers. A folder hierarchy enables you to perform file- and folder-level diff comparisons, however.

▶ **IIS Site/Application Name**—You can prespecify the name of the application (or site) that will be deployed and the physical path for deployment. As you see shortly, the administrator importing this package can override this values if they choose.

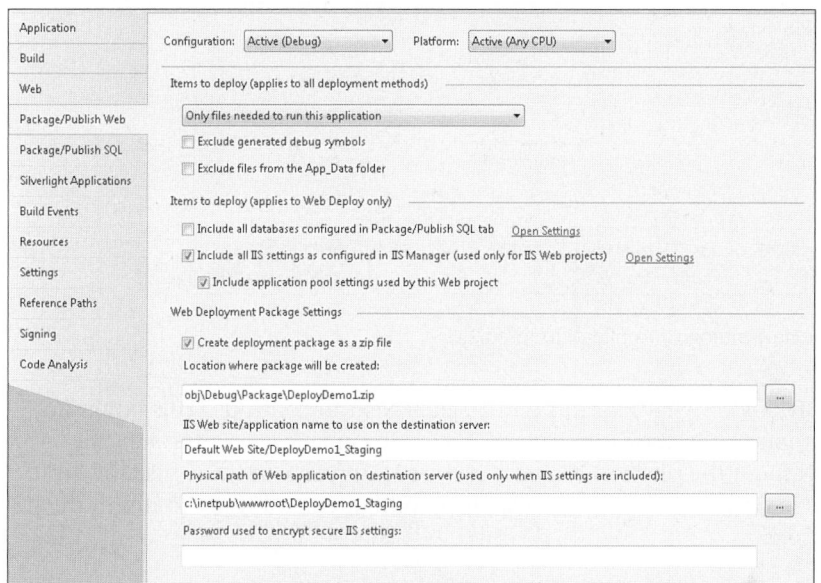

FIGURE 35.1   The Package/Publish Web Properties screen.

To actually build the deployment package, right-click the project in Solution Explorer and choose the Build Deployment Package option. This runs a build step, and you should see Publish Succeeded at the bottom of your build log. Open up the folder you chose as the package destination, and you should see the ZIP file you built.

If you crack open that ZIP file with your favorite ZIP tool or with Windows Explorer, you can see there's a Content folder and a few XML files, notably `archive.xml` (used for the archive itself), `parameters.xml` (used for IIS settings, and so on), and `systeminfo.xml` (contains a list of installed components).

Next, let's move to the destination machine (you can do this from your development workstation as well if you don't have a staging server handy) and import the application.

To do that, open up the IIS Management console (Under Administrative Tools, Internet Information Services (IIS) Manager), right-click the Default Web Site node, and select Deploy; then select Import Application. After you browse to the location of the ZIP file, you see an information dialog showing the contents of the deployment package, including the content and IIS settings. You now have the ability to ignore individual bits of content or IIS settings. Under Advanced Settings you also have the option of setting the

`WhatIf` flag, which enable you to do a mock import (shown in Figure 35.2). The `WhatIf` flag is extremely handy when doing new application imports on production servers.

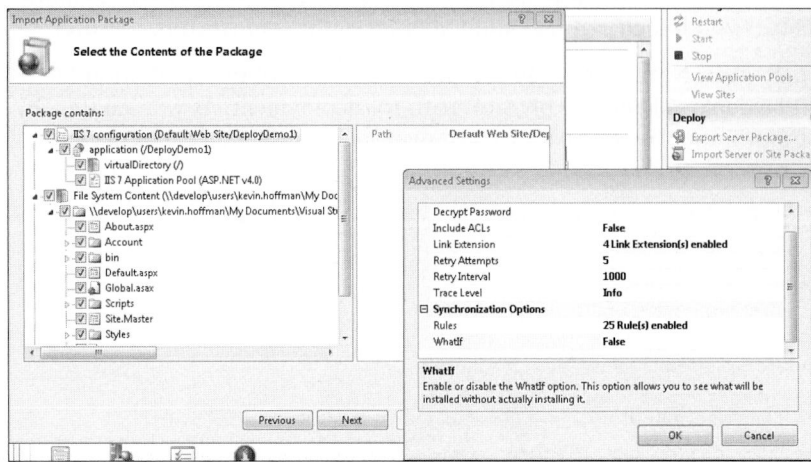

FIGURE 35.2   Preview dialog of Application Import.

When you're satisfied with what's on this screen, click Next to continue. This brings up the final confirmation screen shown in Figure 35.3, which enables you to specify the name of the application, the physical location of the files, and so on. After clicking Next, you see a progress bar; then the application appears configured and ready to run in the IIS Management console.

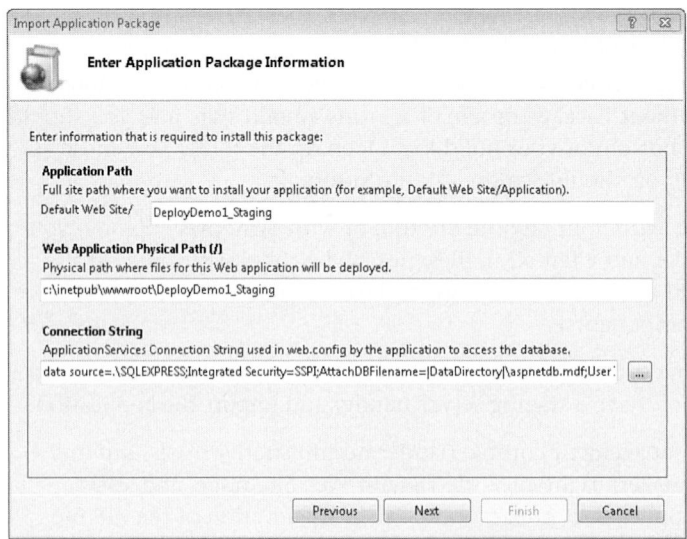

FIGURE 35.3   Confirming details of Web Deployment Package Import.

This is an absolutely priceless utility to have. Now developers can create deployment packages and give them to the administrators who have secured control over QA, Staging, and Production environments. All these people have to do is import the deployment package and all the files, content, prerequisites, and configuration necessary for that application will be put where they belong.

Using Web.config Transformations

So far we've seen that with Visual Studio 2010 we can create new web deployment packages that drastically simplify the deployment of applications to interim environments such as QA and Staging, but what about the configuration? Application settings, connection strings, web service endpoints, and hundreds of other pieces of configuration all typically vary depending on whether the application is running on a developer workstation, in QA, in Staging, or in Production. So how do we take advantage of the great web deployment tools but still have varying configuration files?

Before Visual Studio 2010, we would write custom build scripts that would replace our Web.config files with custom files specific to certain environments. Now, having a Web.config file specialized for specific build targets is actually built into Visual Studio.

For each of your build configurations (by default VS2010 comes with Debug and Release, but you can create as many as you like), you can have a Web.config file. This file isn't a complete copy of the file but is actually a list of transformations you want to make to the original. This is actually a smart strategy because the bulk of the config file typically stays the same across environments with small changes to things such as service endpoints, connection strings, and app settings.

To see this in action, let's add a build configuration to the empty ASP.NET project we deployed in the previous section. To do this, right-click the solution in Solution Explorer and bring up the Configuration Manager (see Figure 35.4). Click the drop-down arrow next to the configuration for the web application (probably says Debug at the moment) and select New.... Call the new configuration Staging, and base it on the Release configuration.

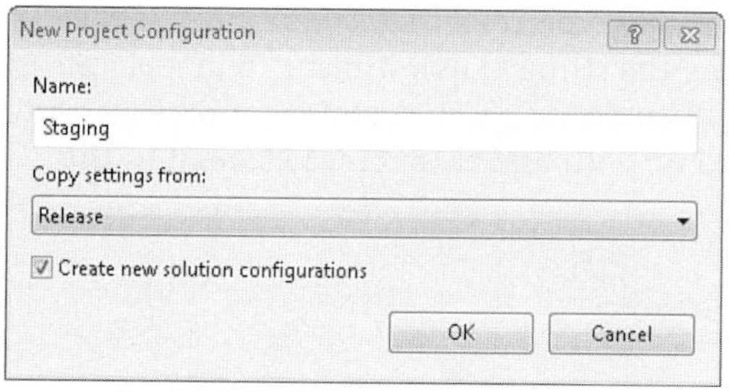

FIGURE 35.4   Creating a Staging configuration.

After you have a staging configuration created, you can right-click the Web.config file and select Add config transforms, as shown in Figure 35.5. This is the only way to create the Web.config transformation files. If you manually create a Web.staging.config file without going through this menu item, it won't compile properly and will not properly transform your Web.config file.

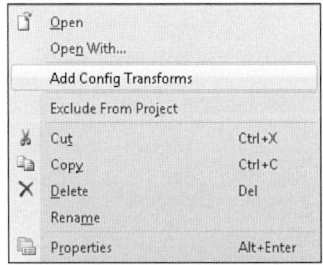

FIGURE 35.5   Adding configuration transforms.

Open up the main Web.config file and add a new app setting as shown here:

```
<appSettings>
    <add key="Environment" value="DevWorkstation"/>
</appSettings>
```

Now for the fun part—creating the transformation. Double-click the Web.staging.config file to bring it up in the IDE. Add the following code below the commented out sample involving a connection string:

```
<appSettings>
    <add key="Environment" value="Staging"
        xdt:Transform="SetAttributes" xdt:Locator="Match(key)"/>
  </appSettings>
```

The full syntax of the transformation language would be too much to include in this chapter; however, a link to detailed MSDN documentation directly is in the sample config file, http://go.microsoft.com/fwlink/?LinkId=125889. The code we just put into the file searches the root Web.config for a key matching the string "Environment" and replace the value with the one from the staging file. If we then create a web deployment package with Staging being our active configuration, we end up with an appSettings element in the deployed Web.config that looks like this:

```
<appSettings>
    <add key="Environment" value="Staging" />
</appSettings>
```

The power we get from the combination of transformable configuration files on a per-build-configuration basis and the web deployment packages is incredible. We can now create individual package files that are targeted at a specific environment and have confidence that the app will contain all its content, binaries, prerequisites, *and* configuration suited for that environment.

Deploying Databases

Although it's certainly a huge productivity increase and a time and stress saver, it sure would be great if we could correlate our database migrations with our application deployments.

The folks at Microsoft have thought of this as well. There is a Package/Publish SQL tab on the project properties page now. This enables you to create a list of database deployments in a grid. For each of those deployments, you can define a source database and a destination database. You can also choose whether the deployment includes schema only, data only, or both. Also keep in mind that all this information is also on a per-configuration basis, so the list of databases and their source/target pairs will be different depending on whether you create a production deployment or staging deployment.

Figure 35.6 shows a screenshot of this new Publish/Package SQL screen.

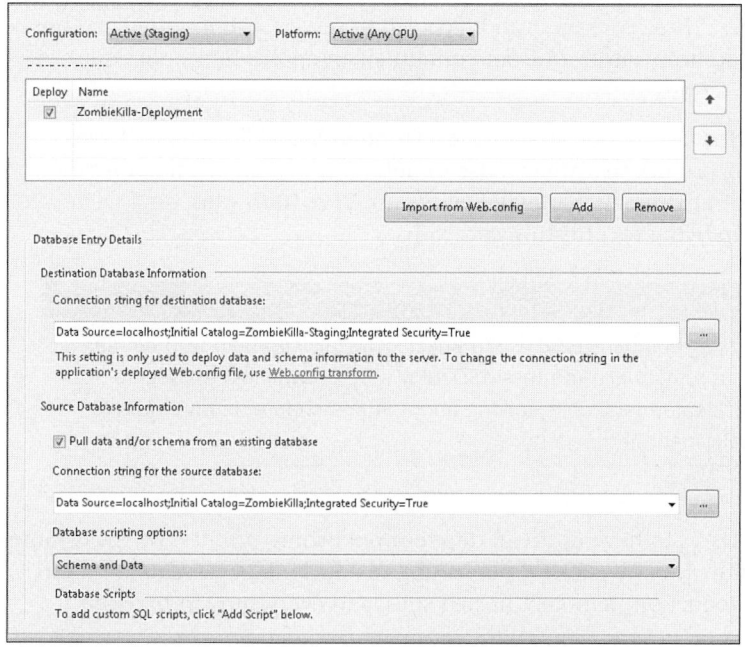

FIGURE 35.6   The Publish/Package SQL screen.

In this scenario, we have a web application that we built called Zombie Killa, a social network for zombie killers. At the top of the figure you can see a grid where we can define *all* the databases that we want to include in the deployment, so we're not limited to just one database. Also, keep in mind that these databases are independent of any database projects you might have in your solution.

For each of the databases in the grid, we can then configure the options shown in the lower half of Figure 35.6. We can define the connection string for the source database and the connection string for the destination database. We can also configure what is copied from one to the other: schema, data, or both. Finally, we can also add custom SQL scripts that do specific migration-related tasks because even the best databases have thorns in them that create bumps or stalls for migration processes.

Now when we build a deployment package, it contain all the information necessary to ensure that when the web application is fully deployed in the target environment; *all its required databases* will be available as well, containing exactly the data and schema that we want them to have.

One-Click Publishing Web Applications

In the previous section, we gave you an overview of how to create portable, self-contained web deployment packages. These packages can be copied to servers and installed on those servers by developers or administrators and can contain all an application's prerequisites, even database migration scripts.

Microsoft actually took this facility one step further. Through Visual Studio 2010, we can actually create publishing profiles that we can use to publish a web application *directly from the IDE*. This comes in extremely handy when we use VS2010 to work on a web application that we're deploying to a hosting company.

> **NOTE**
>
> When we talk about hosting company here, we're specifically talking about web hosting companies that provide a remote IIS with the MSDeploy service available for secure deployment. The type of deployment we're talking about in this chapter is unrelated to Windows Azure and deployment in the cloud.

Visual Studio 2010 enables us to have up to 50 different publishing profiles, which is more than enough room to allow for one-clicking publishing to a local IIS, a development environment, staging, QA, production, remotely hosted sites, and everything in between.

One-Click publication is just a layer on top of the web deployment configuration you saw in the previous section. It takes all the information from the Package/Publish Web and the Package/Publish SQL property pages and performs the packaging process and the remote deployment in one step.

To trigger the one-click publish process, you can right-click the project and choose Publish (yes, we know that's actually two clicks), or you can push up a single button in the Publish toolbar that defaults to a position at the top of your IDE. Figure 35.7 shows what happens when you click this button.

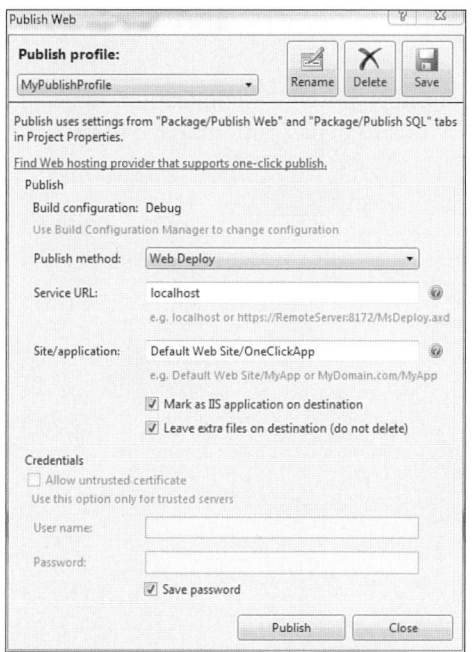

FIGURE 35.7   Creating a publish profile.

As mentioned, you can deploy to a local IIS or a remote one within your own organization or a remote one hosted by a third party. The only requirement is that the web deployment tool be installed on the destination server. If you install Visual Studio 2010 on top of a machine with IIS7, you already have the web deployment tool installed. If you don't have it installed (version 1.1, at the time this book was written), you can get it from http://www.iis.net/expand/WebDeploy. This site has a link that you can use to install the tool using the Web Platform Installer and a wealth of documentation and videos to give you more information on the web deployment tool than is in scope for this book.

If you have nightmarish flashbacks of deployment using FrontPage Extensions and twitch at the memory of the difficulties and heartburn caused by those days, you can rest easy—deployment with MSDeploy is, nothing like deployment using FrontPage extensions.

Summary

ASP.NET 4 brings with it quite a few new features to make the act of developing websites easier, more reliable, even faster and more scalable. However, as an added bonus, we now also have the ability to create web deployment packages that bundle up our web applications along with all their configuration, dependencies, and prerequisites. These packages can be deployed to IIS servers by developers, administrators, or command-line scripts and dramatically ease the burden of deploying web applications.

In addition, we also have the ability to create one-click publication profiles that enable us to take these web packages and deploy them on-demand just by clicking a button inside Visual Studio.

When you have gotten over the joy of building your new ASP.NET 4 application, it's going to get even more fun when you see how easy it is to deploy and manage these applications.

Building Custom Controls

In this chapter, you learn how to extend ASP.NET Framework by building custom controls. You learn how to create controls in exactly the same way that Microsoft developed the standard ASP.NET controls, such as the TextBox and Button controls. Although the standard toolbox of controls available to developers is full of useful controls, you might need something more specific for your application, or you might intend to build controls available throughout your organization or for resale to other developers.

Overview of Custom Control Building

Answer two questions before writing a custom control:

▶ What type of control do I want to write?

▶ From what class do I inherit?

The two basic types of controls are fully rendered and composite controls. When you build a fully rendered control, you start from scratch. You specify all the HTML content that the control renders to the browser.

When you create a composite control, on the other hand, you build a new control from existing controls. For example, you can create a composite AddressForm control from existing TextBox and RequiredFieldValidator controls. When you create a composite control, you bundle together existing controls as a new control and potentially add new behaviors and properties.

The second question that you must address is the choice of the base control for your new control. You can inherit a new control from any existing ASP.NET control. For example, if you want to create a better `GridView` control, you can inherit a new control from the `GridView` control and add additional properties and methods to your custom `GridView` control.

Typically, when building a basic control, you inherit your new control from one of the following base classes (or from a control that derives from one of these):

▶ `System.Web.UI.Control`

▶ `System.Web.UI.WebControls.WebControl`

▶ `System.Web.UI.WebControls.CompositeControl`

The `CompositeControl` class inherits from the `WebControl` class, which inherits from the `Control` class. Each of these base classes adds additional functionality.

The base class for all controls in ASP.NET Framework is the `System.Web.UI.Control` class. Every control, including the `TextBox` and `GridView` controls, ultimately derives from this control. This means that all the properties, methods, and events of the `System.Web.UI.Control` class are shared by all controls in the Framework.

All Web controls inherit from the base `System.Web.UI.WebControls.WebControl` class. The difference between the `Control` class and `WebControl` class is that controls that derive from the `WebControl` class always have opening and closing tags. Because a `WebControl` has an opening and closing tag, you also get more formatting options. For example, the `WebControl` class includes `BackColor`, `Font`, and `ForeColor` properties.

For example, the ASP.NET `Literal` control inherits from the base `Control` class, whereas the `Label` control inherits from the base `WebControl` class. The `Repeater` control inherits from the base `Control` class, whereas the `GridView` control (ultimately) inherits from the `WebControl` class.

Finally, the `System.Web.UI.WebControls.CompositeControl` should be used as the base class for any composite control. The `CompositeControl` automatically creates a naming container for its child controls. It also includes an overridden `Controls` property that forces child controls to appear in Design view.

Building Fully Rendered Controls

Let's start by creating a simple fully rendered control. When you create a fully rendered control, you take on the responsibility of specifying all the HTML content that the control renders to the browser.

The file in Listing 36.1 contains a fully rendered control that derives from the base `Control` class.

LISTING 36.1   `FullyRenderedControl.cs`

```csharp
using System.Web.UI;


namespace myControls
{
    public class FullyRenderedControl : Control
    {
        private string _Text;

        public string Text
        {
            get { return _Text; }
            set { _Text = value; }
        }

        protected override void Render(HtmlTextWriter writer)
        {
            writer.Write(_Text);
        }
    }
}
```

NOTE

Add the control in Listing 36.1 to your App_Code folder. Any code added to the App_Code folder is compiled dynamically.

The control in Listing 36.1 inherits from the base `Control` class, overriding the base class `Render()` method. The control simply displays whatever value that you assign to its `Text` property. The value of the `Text` property is written to the browser with the `HtmlTextWriter` class's `Write()` method.

The file in Listing 36.2 illustrates how you can use the new control in a page.

LISTING 36.2   `ShowFullyRenderedControl.aspx`

```
<%@ Page Language="C#" %>
<%@ Register TagPrefix="custom" Namespace="myControls" %>
<!DOCTYPE html PUBLIC "-//W3C//DTD XHTML 1.0 Transitional//EN"
➥"http://www.w3.org/TR/xhtml1/DTD/xhtml1-transitional.dtd">
<html xmlns="http://www.w3.org/1999/xhtml" >
<head id="Head1" runat="server">
```

36

```
    <title>Show Fully Rendered Control</title>
</head>
<body>
    <form id="form1" runat="server">
    <div>

    <custom:FullyRenderedControl
        ID="FullyRenderedControl1"
        Text="Hello World!"
        runat="Server" />

    </div>
    </form>
</body>
</html>
```

NOTE

In Listing 36.2, the custom control is registered in the page through use of the `<%@ Register %>` directive. Alternatively, you can register the control for an entire website by registering the control in the `<pages>` section of the web configuration file.

If you open the page in Listing 36.2 in a browser and select View Source, you can see the HTML rendered by the control. The control simply renders the string `"Hello World!"`.

Rather than inherit from the base `Control` class, you can create a fully rendered control by inheriting a new control from the base `WebControl` class. When inheriting from the `WebControl` class, you override the `RenderContents()` method instead of the `Render()` method.

For example, the control in Listing 36.3 contains a simple, fully rendered control that inherits from the `WebControl` class.

LISTING 36.3   FullyRenderedWebControl.cs

```
using System.Web.UI;
using System.Web.UI.WebControls;

namespace myControls
{
    public class FullyRenderedWebControl : WebControl
    {
        private string _Text;

        public string Text
```

```
        {
            get { return _Text; }
            set { _Text = value; }
        }

        protected override void RenderContents(HtmlTextWriter writer)
        {
            writer.Write(_Text);
        }
    }
}
```

The page in Listing 36.4 illustrates how you can use the new control (see Figure 36.1). The BackColor, BorderStyle, and Font properties are set. Because the control in Listing 36.3 derives from the base WebControl class, you get these properties for free.

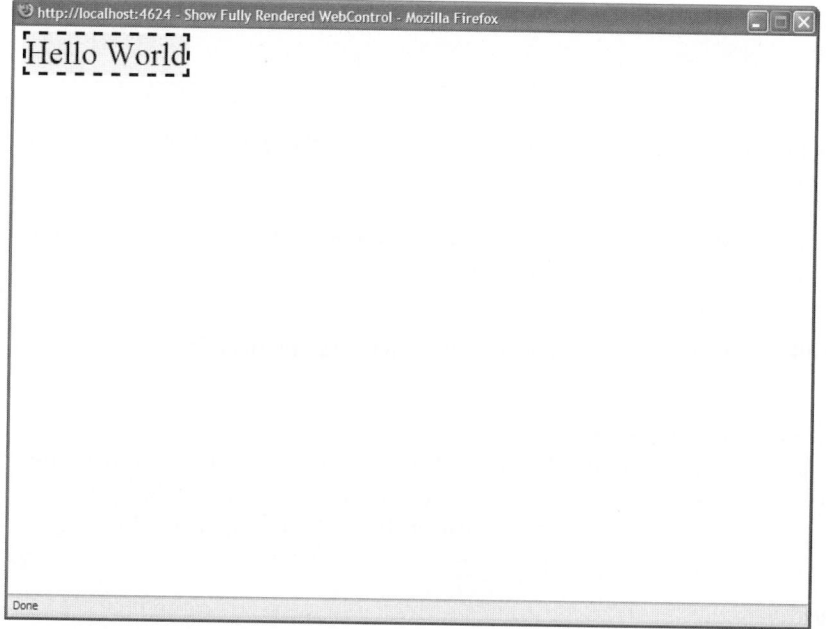

FIGURE 36.1   Displaying a fully rendered WebControl.

LISTING 36.4   ShowFullyRenderedWebControl.aspx

```
<%@ Page Language="C#" %>
<%@ Register TagPrefix="custom" Namespace="myControls" %>
<!DOCTYPE html PUBLIC "-//W3C//DTD XHTML 1.0 Transitional//EN"
➥"http://www.w3.org/TR/xhtml1/DTD/xhtml1-transitional.dtd">
<html xmlns="http://www.w3.org/1999/xhtml" >
```

```
<head id="Head1" runat="server">
    <title>Show Fully Rendered WebControl</title>
</head>
<body>
    <form id="form1" runat="server">
    <div>

    <custom:FullyRenderedWebControl
        ID="FullyrenderedWebControl1"
        Text="Hello World"
        BackColor="Yellow"
        BorderStyle="Dashed"
        Font-Size="32px"
        Runat="Server" />

    </div>
    </form>
</body>
</html>
```

After opening the page in Listing 36.4, if you select View Source in your browser, you can
see the rendered output of the control. It looks like this:

```
<span id="FullyrenderedWebControl1" style="display:inline-block;
➥background-color:Yellow;border-style:Dashed;
➥font-size:32px;">Hello World</span>
```

A WebControl, unlike a control, renders an enclosing <span> tag by default.

Understanding the `HtmlTextWriter` Class

When you create a fully rendered control, you use the `HtmlTextWriter` class to write the
HTML content to the browser. The `HtmlTextWriter` class was specifically designed to
make it easier to render HTML. Here is a partial list of the methods supported by this
class:

▶ **`AddAttribute()`**—Adds an HTML attribute to. the tag rendered by calling
   `RenderBeginTag()`.

▶ **`AddStyleAttribute()`**—Adds a CSS attribute to the tag rendered by a call to
   `RenderBeginTag()`.

▶ **`RenderBeginTag()`**—Renders an opening HTML tag.

▶ **`RenderEndTag()`**—Renders a closing HTML tag.

▶ **`Write()`**—Renders a string to the browser.

▶ **`WriteBreak()`**—Renders a `<br />` tag to the browser.

You can call the `AddAttribute()` or the `AddStyleAttribute()` method as many times as you please before calling `RenderBeginTag()`. When you call `RenderBeginTag()`, all the attributes are added to the opening HTML tag.

The methods of the `HtmlTextWriter` class can use the following enumerations:

▶ **HtmlTextWriterTag**—Contains a list of the most common HTML tags.

▶ **HtmlTextWriterAttribute**—Contains a list of the most common HTML attributes.

▶ **HtmlTextWriterStyle**—Contains a list of the most Cascading Style Sheet attributes.

When using the methods of the `HtmlTextWriter` class, you should strive to use these enumerations to represent HTML tags and attributes. If a particular tag or attribute is missing from one of the enumerations, you can pass a string value instead.

For example, the control in Listing 36.5 renders a table of HTML colors by using an HTML table (see Figure 36.2). The `RenderContents()` method takes advantage of the methods of the `HtmlTextWriter` class to render the HTML table.

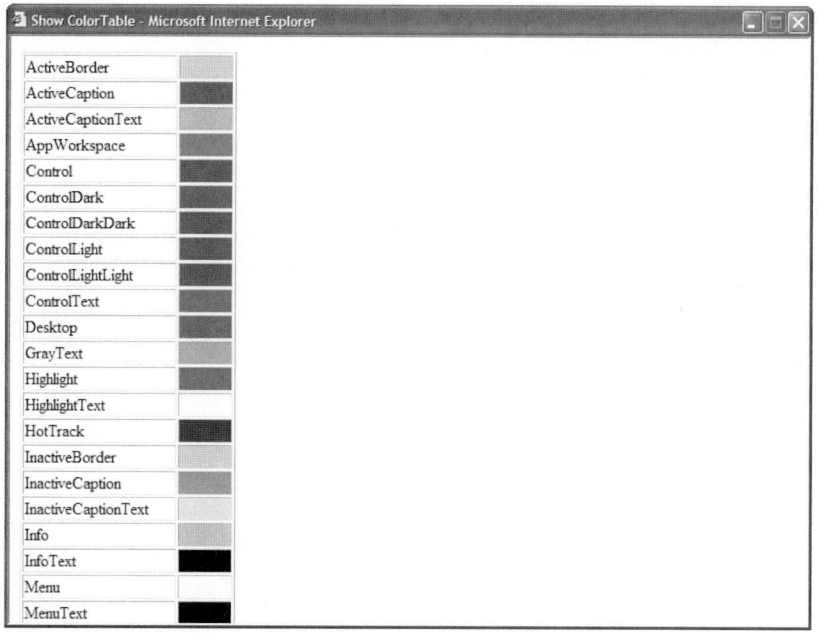

FIGURE 36.2   Displaying a table of HTML colors.

LISTING 36.5   `ColorTable.cs`

```
using System;
using System.Web.UI;
using System.Web.UI.WebControls;
using System.Drawing;
```

```
namespace myControls
{
    public class ColorTable : WebControl
    {
        protected override void RenderContents(HtmlTextWriter writer)
        {
            // Get list of colors
            KnownColor[] colors = (KnownColor[])Enum.GetValues(typeof(KnownColor));

            // Render opening table tag
            writer.AddAttribute(HtmlTextWriterAttribute.Border, "1");
            writer.RenderBeginTag(HtmlTextWriterTag.Table);

            // Render table body
            foreach (KnownColor colorName in colors)
            {
                writer.RenderBeginTag(HtmlTextWriterTag.Tr);

                // Render first column
                writer.RenderBeginTag(HtmlTextWriterTag.Td);
                writer.Write(colorName);
                writer.RenderEndTag();

                // Render second column
                writer.AddAttribute(HtmlTextWriterAttribute.Width, "50px");
                writer.AddAttribute(HtmlTextWriterAttribute.Bgcolor,
                  colorName.ToString());
                writer.RenderBeginTag(HtmlTextWriterTag.Td);
                writer.Write(" ");
                writer.RenderEndTag();

                writer.RenderEndTag();
            }

            // close table
            writer.RenderEndTag();
        }
    }
}
```

You should notice a number of things about the control in Listing 36.5. First, the
AddAttribute() method is called to add the table border attribute. When the
RenderBeginTag() method is called, the table border attribute is added to the opening
table tag.

Furthermore, you do not specify the tag when calling the `RenderEndTag()` method. This method automatically closes the last tag opened with the `RenderBeginTag()` method.

The control in Listing 36.6, the `DropShadow` control, illustrates how you can use the `AddStyleAttribute()` method of the `HtmlTextWriter` class to add Cascading Style Sheet (CSS) attributes to an HTML tag.

LISTING 36.6   DropShadow.cs

```
using System.Web.UI;
using System.Web.UI.WebControls;

namespace myControls
{
    public class DropShadow : WebControl
    {
        private string _Text;

        public string Text
        {
            get { return _Text; }
            set { _Text = value; }
        }

        protected override void RenderContents(HtmlTextWriter writer)
        {
            writer.AddStyleAttribute(
              HtmlTextWriterStyle.Filter,
                "dropShadow(color=#AAAAAA,offX=3,offY=3);width:500px");
            writer.RenderBeginTag(HtmlTextWriterTag.Div);
            writer.Write(_Text);
            writer.RenderEndTag();
        }
    }
}
```

36

The control in Listing 36.6 renders a drop shadow behind whatever text you assign to the control's Text property (see Figure 36.3). The drop shadow is created with the help of an Internet Explorer DropShadow filter.

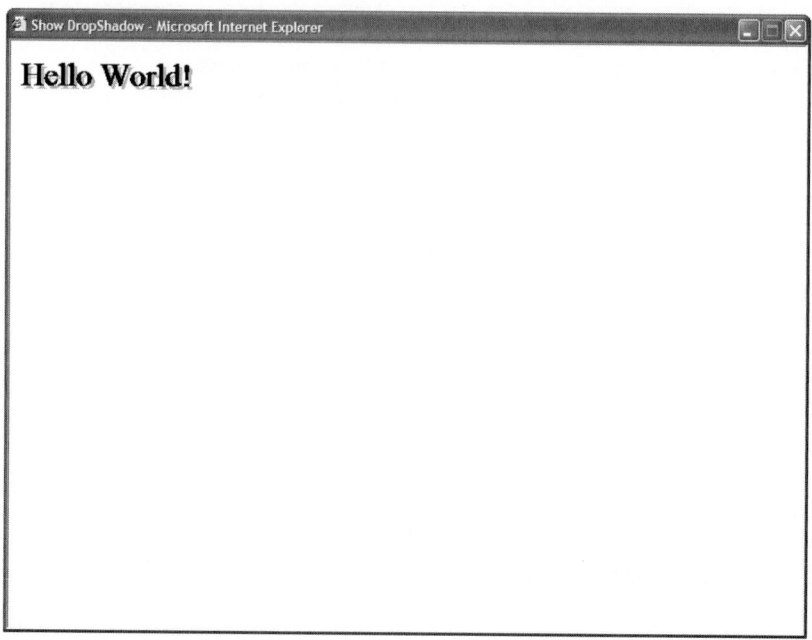

FIGURE 36.3   Displaying a drop shadow with the DropShadow control.

The Filter attribute is added to the <div> tag with a call to the AddStyleAttribute() method. The AddStyleAttribute() method works just like the AddAttribute() method, except that the AddStyleAttribute() method adds a CSS attribute instead of an HTML attribute.

WEB STANDARDS NOTE

Filters are an Internet Explorer extension to the CSS standard. They don't work with Firefox or Opera. Firefox has its own extensions to CSS with its -moz style rules.

Specifying the Containing WebControl Tag

By default, a WebControl renders an HTML <span> tag around its contents. You can specify a different tag by overriding the WebControl's TagKey property. For example, the control in Listing 36.7 renders its contents within an HTML <div> tag.

LISTING 36.7   Glow.cs

```csharp
using System.Web.UI;
using System.Web.UI.WebControls;

namespace myControls
{
    public class Glow : WebControl
    {
        private string _Text;

        public string Text
        {
            get { return _Text; }
            set { _Text = value; }
        }

        protected override HtmlTextWriterTag TagKey
        {
            get
            {
                return HtmlTextWriterTag.Div;
            }
        }

        protected override void AddAttributesToRender(HtmlTextWriter writer)
        {
            writer.AddStyleAttribute(
              HtmlTextWriterStyle.Filter, "glow(Color=#ffd700,Strength=10)");
            base.AddAttributesToRender(writer);
        }

        protected override void RenderContents(HtmlTextWriter writer)
        {
            writer.Write(_Text);
        }

        public Glow()
        {
            this.Width = Unit.Parse("500px");
        }

    }
}
```

The control in Listing 36.7 displays a glowing effect around any text that you assign to its Text property. The control takes advantage of the Internet Explorer Glow filter to create the glow effect (see Figure 36.4). In a real production application, you would want to either provide an alternate rendering for other browsers, or stick to more CSS-compliant rendering.

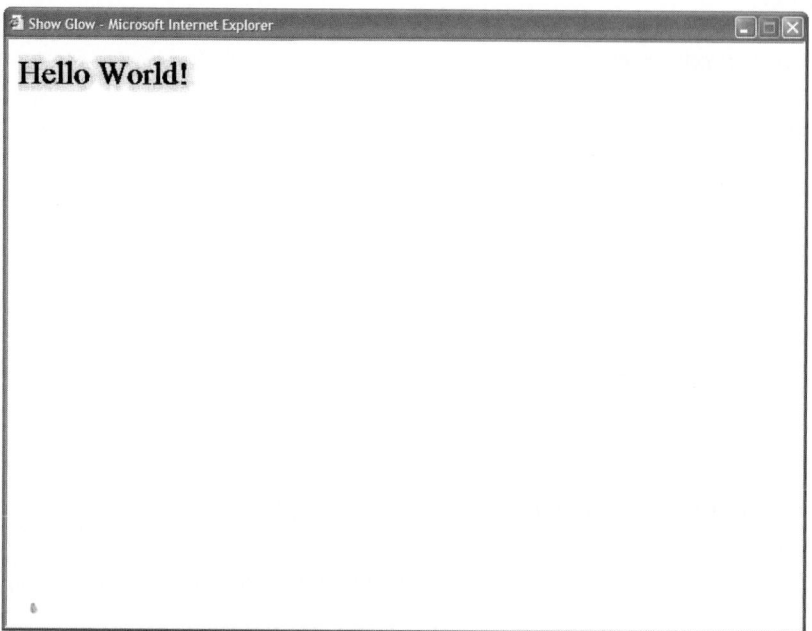

FIGURE 36.4   Displaying glowing text with the Glow control.

The control overrides the base WebControl's TagKey property. Because the overridden property returns a <div> tag, the WebControl renders a <div> tag.

> **NOTE**
>
> You can use several methods to modify the tag rendered by a WebControl. You can override the TagName property instead of the TagKey property. The TagName property enables you to specify an arbitrary string for the tag. (It doesn't limit you to the HtmlTextWriterTag enumeration.) You also can specify the tag rendered by a WebControl in the WebControl's constructor. Finally, you can override a WebControl's RenderBeginTag() and RenderEndTag() methods and completely customize the opening and closing tags.

Furthermore, the control in Listing 36.7 overrides the AddAttributesToRender() method. If you override this method, you can add HTML or CSS attributes to the opening HTML tag rendered by the control. When overriding this method, be careful to call the base `AddAttributesToRender()` method or the standard control attributes, such as the control ID, won't be rendered.

Building Composite Controls

If you don't want to start from scratch when building a custom control, you can build a composite control. When you create a composite control, you create a new control from existing controls.

Every ASP.NET control has a `Controls` property that represents all its child controls. If you add child controls to a control, the child controls are automatically rendered when the parent control is rendered.

When you create a composite control, you typically override a control's `CreateChildControls()` method. This method is called when a control builds its collection of child controls.

For example, the control in Listing 36.8 combines a `TextBox` control and `RequiredFieldValidator` control.

LISTING 36.8 RequiredTextBox.cs

```
using System;
using System.Web.UI.WebControls;

namespace myControls
{
    public class RequiredTextBox : CompositeControl
    {
        private TextBox input;
        private RequiredFieldValidator validator;

        public string Text
        {
            get
            {
                EnsureChildControls();
                return input.Text;
            }
            set
            {
                EnsureChildControls();
                input.Text = value;
            }
        }
```

36

```
protected override void CreateChildControls()
{
    input = new TextBox();
    input.ID = "input";
    this.Controls.Add(input);

    validator = new RequiredFieldValidator();
    validator.ID = "valInput";
    validator.ControlToValidate = input.ID;
    validator.ErrorMessage = "(Required)";
    validator.Display = ValidatorDisplay.Dynamic;
    this.Controls.Add(validator);
}
}
}
```

The control in Listing 36.8 inherits from the base `CompositeControl` class. Furthermore, rather than override the base control's `RenderContents()` method, the control overrides the base control's `CreateChildControls()` method.

You should notice one other special thing in Listing 36.8. The `EnsureChildControls()` method is called in both the `Get` and `Set` methods of the `Text` property. The `EnsureChildControls()` method forces the `CreateChildControls()` method to be called; however, it prevents the `CreateChildControls()` method from being called more than once.

The Text property gets or sets a property of a child control (the `TextBox` control). If you attempt to use the `Text` property before the `CreateChildControls()` method is called, you receive a null reference exception. The child controls must be created before you can access any of the child control properties.

The page in Listing 36.9 illustrates how you can use the `RequiredTextBox` control in a page.

LISTING 36.9 ShowRequiredTextBox.aspx

```
<%@ Page Language="C#" Trace="true" %>
<%@ Register TagPrefix="custom" Namespace="myControls" %>
<!DOCTYPE html PUBLIC
    "-//W3C//DTD XHTML 1.0 Transitional//EN"
    "http://www.w3.org/TR/xhtml1/DTD/xhtml1-transitional.dtd">
<script runat="server">

    protected void btnSubmit_Click(object sender, EventArgs e)
    {
```

```
            lblResults.Text = txtUserName.Text;
        }
</script>
<html xmlns="http://www.w3.org/1999/xhtml" >
<head id="Head1" runat="server">
    <title>Show RequiredTextBox</title>
</head>
<body>
    <form id="form1" runat="server">
    <div>

    <asp:Label
        ID="lblUserName"
        Text="User Name:"
        AssociatedControlID="txtUserName"
        Runat="server" />

    <custom:RequiredTextBox
        ID="txtUserName"
        Runat="Server" />

    <br />

    <asp:Button
        ID="btnSubmit"
        Text="Submit"
        Runat="server" OnClick="btnSubmit_Click" />

    <hr />

    <asp:Label
        id="lblResults"
        Runat="server" />

    </div>
    </form>
</body>
</html>
```

The page in Listing 36.9 has tracing enabled. If you look at the control tree for the page, you see that the RequiredTextBox control includes both a TextBox and RequiredFieldValidator control as child controls.

Building Hybrid Controls

In practice, you rarely build pure composite controls. In most cases in which you override a control's CreateChildControls() method, you also override the control's RenderContents() method to specify the layout of the child controls.

For example, the control in Listing 36.10 represents a Login control. In the control's CreateChildControls() method, two TextBox controls are added to the control's collection of child controls.

LISTING 36.10   Login.cs

```
using System;
using System.Web.UI;
using System.Web.UI.WebControls;

namespace myControls
{
    public class Login : CompositeControl
    {
        private TextBox txtUserName;
        private TextBox txtPassword;

        public string UserName
        {
            get
            {
                EnsureChildControls();
                return txtUserName.Text;
            }

            set
            {
                EnsureChildControls();
                txtUserName.Text = value;
            }
        }

        public string Password
        {
            get
            {
                EnsureChildControls();
                return txtPassword.Text;
            }

            set
```

```
        {
            EnsureChildControls();
            txtPassword.Text = value;
        }
    }

    protected override void CreateChildControls()
    {
        txtUserName = new TextBox();
        txtUserName.ID = "txtUserName";
        this.Controls.Add(txtUserName);

        txtPassword = new TextBox();
        txtPassword.ID = "txtPassword";
        txtPassword.TextMode = TextBoxMode.Password;
        this.Controls.Add(txtPassword);
    }

    protected override void RenderContents(HtmlTextWriter writer)
    {
        writer.RenderBeginTag(HtmlTextWriterTag.Tr);

        // Render UserName Label
        writer.RenderBeginTag(HtmlTextWriterTag.Td);
        writer.AddAttribute(HtmlTextWriterAttribute.For, txtUserName.ClientID);
        writer.RenderBeginTag(HtmlTextWriterTag.Label);
        writer.Write("User Name:");
        writer.RenderEndTag(); // Label
        writer.RenderEndTag(); // TD

        // Render UserName TextBox
        writer.RenderBeginTag(HtmlTextWriterTag.Td);
        txtUserName.RenderControl(writer);
        writer.RenderEndTag(); // TD

        writer.RenderEndTag();
        writer.RenderBeginTag(HtmlTextWriterTag.Tr);

        // Render Password Label
        writer.RenderBeginTag(HtmlTextWriterTag.Td);
        writer.AddAttribute(HtmlTextWriterAttribute.For, txtPassword.ClientID);
        writer.RenderBeginTag(HtmlTextWriterTag.Label);
        writer.Write("Password:");
        writer.RenderEndTag(); // Label
        writer.RenderEndTag(); // TD
```

36

```
            // Render Password TextBox
            writer.RenderBeginTag(HtmlTextWriterTag.Td);
            txtPassword.RenderControl(writer);
            writer.RenderEndTag(); // TD

            writer.RenderEndTag(); // TR
        }

        protected override HtmlTextWriterTag TagKey
        {
            get
            {
                return HtmlTextWriterTag.Table;
            }
        }


    }
}
```

In Listing 36.10, the RenderContents() method is overridden to layout the two TextBox
controls. The TextBox controls are rendered within an HTML table (see Figure 36.5). Each
TextBox is rendered by calling the RenderControl() method.

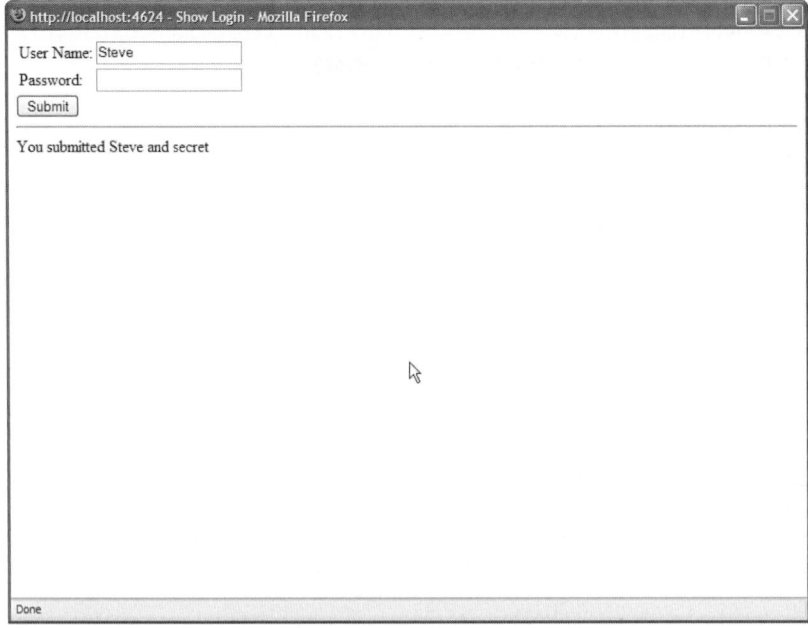

FIGURE 36.5   Performing layout with an HTML table.

The default `RenderContents()` method simply calls the `RenderControl()` method for each child control. If you override the `RenderContents()` method, you have more control over the layout of the control.

The `Login` control in Listing 36.10 uses an HTML table for layout. From a web standards perspective, using HTML tables for layout is frowned upon. The modified `Login` control in Listing 36.11 uses <div> tags instead of a <table> tag for layout.

LISTING 36.11 LoginStandards.cs

```csharp
using System;
using System.Web.UI;
using System.Web.UI.WebControls;

namespace myControls
{
    public class LoginStandards : CompositeControl
    {
        private TextBox txtUserName;
        private TextBox txtPassword;

        public string UserName
        {
            get
            {
                EnsureChildControls();
                return txtUserName.Text;
            }

            set
            {
                EnsureChildControls();
                txtUserName.Text = value;
            }
        }

        public string Password
        {
            get
            {
                EnsureChildControls();
                return txtPassword.Text;
            }

            set
            {
```

```
        EnsureChildControls();
        txtPassword.Text = value;
    }
}

protected override void CreateChildControls()
{
    txtUserName = new TextBox();
    txtUserName.ID = "txtUserName";
    this.Controls.Add(txtUserName);

    txtPassword = new TextBox();
    txtPassword.ID = "txtPassword";
    txtPassword.TextMode = TextBoxMode.Password;
    this.Controls.Add(txtPassword);
}

protected override void RenderContents(HtmlTextWriter writer)
{
    writer.AddStyleAttribute("float", "left");
    writer.RenderBeginTag(HtmlTextWriterTag.Div);
    writer.AddStyleAttribute(HtmlTextWriterStyle.Padding, "3px");
    writer.RenderBeginTag(HtmlTextWriterTag.Div);
    writer.AddAttribute(HtmlTextWriterAttribute.For, txtUserName.ClientID);
    writer.RenderBeginTag(HtmlTextWriterTag.Label);
    writer.Write("User Name:");
    writer.RenderEndTag();
    writer.RenderEndTag();

    writer.AddStyleAttribute(HtmlTextWriterStyle.Padding, "3px");
    writer.RenderBeginTag(HtmlTextWriterTag.Div);
    writer.AddAttribute(HtmlTextWriterAttribute.For, txtPassword.ClientID);
    writer.RenderBeginTag(HtmlTextWriterTag.Label);
    writer.Write("Password:");
    writer.RenderEndTag();
    writer.RenderEndTag();
    writer.RenderEndTag();

    writer.AddStyleAttribute("float", "left");
    writer.RenderBeginTag(HtmlTextWriterTag.Div);
    writer.AddStyleAttribute(HtmlTextWriterStyle.Padding, "3px");
    writer.RenderBeginTag(HtmlTextWriterTag.Div);
    txtUserName.RenderControl(writer);
    writer.RenderEndTag();
```

```
            writer.AddStyleAttribute(HtmlTextWriterStyle.Padding, "3px");
            writer.RenderBeginTag(HtmlTextWriterTag.Div);
            txtPassword.RenderControl(writer);
            writer.RenderEndTag();
            writer.RenderEndTag();

            writer.Write("<br style='clear:left' />");
        }

        protected override HtmlTextWriterTag TagKey
        {
            get
            {
                return HtmlTextWriterTag.Div;
            }
        }

    }
}
```

The control in Listing 36.11 works quite nicely in all recent browsers (Internet Explorer 6, Firefox, Opera 8) without requiring an HTML table for layout (see Figure 36.6).

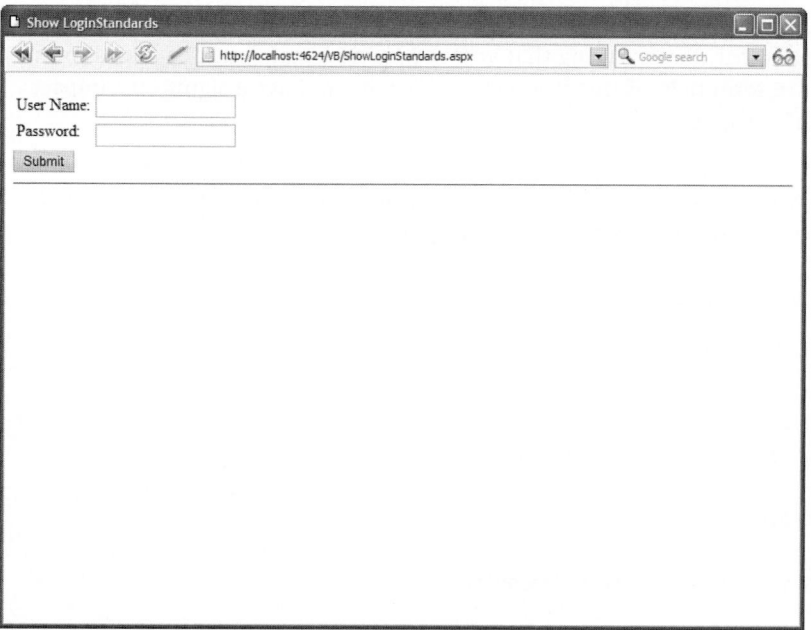

FIGURE 36.6   Performing CSS layout.

View State and Control State

The standard ASP.NET controls retain the values of their properties across postbacks. For example, if you change the text displayed by a Label control, the Label control continues to display the new text even if you repeatedly post the page containing the Label control back to the server.

The ASP.NET Framework takes advantage of a hidden form field named __VIEWSTATE to preserve the state of control properties across postbacks. If you want your controls to preserve the values of their properties, you need to add the values of your control properties to this hidden form field using the appropriate APIs—never access this hidden form field directly.

The ASP.NET Framework supports two methods of preserving values across postbacks. You can take advantage of either View State or Control State.

Supporting View State

You can use the ViewState property of the Control or Page class to add values to View State. The ViewState property exposes a dictionary of key and value pairs. For example, the following statement adds the string Hello World! to View State:

```
ViewState["message"] = "Hello World!"
```

Technically, you can add an instance of any serializable class to View State. In practice, however, you should add only simple values to View State, such as Strings, DateTimes, and Integers. Remember that anything that you add to View State must be added to the hidden __VIEWSTATE form field. If this field gets too big, it can have a significant impact on your page's performance.

The control in Listing 36.12 has two properties: Text and ViewStateText. The first property does not use View State, and the second property does use View State. The value of the ViewStateText property is preserved across postbacks automatically.

LISTING 36.12 ViewStateControl.cs

```
using System;
using System.Web;
using System.Web.UI;
using System.Web.UI.WebControls;

namespace myControls
{
    public class ViewStateControl : WebControl
    {
        private string _text;

        public string Text
```

```
    {
        get { return _text; }
        set { _text = value; }
    }

    public string ViewStateText
    {
        get
        {
            if (ViewState["ViewStateText"] == null)
                return String.Empty;
            else
                return (string)ViewState["ViewStateText"];
        }
        set { ViewState["ViewStateText"] = value; }
    }

    protected override void RenderContents(HtmlTextWriter writer)
    {
        writer.Write("Text: " + Text);
        writer.WriteBreak();
        writer.Write("ViewStateText: " + ViewStateText);
        writer.WriteBreak();
    }

}
}
```

The ViewStateText property uses the Control's ViewState collection to preserve whatever value is assigned to the ViewStateText property across postbacks. When you add a value to the ViewState collection, the value is stuffed into the hidden __VIEWSTATE form field automatically.

WARNING

View State is loaded after the Page InitComplete event, and View State is saved after the Page PreRenderComplete event. This means that you should not attempt to retrieve a value from View State before or during the InitComplete event. You also should not attempt to add a value to View State after the PreRenderComplete event.

The page in Listing 36.13 includes ViewStateControl. The text Hello World! is assigned to both control properties in the Page_Load() handler. However, if you post the page back to itself by clicking the button, only the value of the ViewStateText property is preserved across postbacks.

LISTING 36.13   ShowViewState.aspx

```
<%@ Page Language="C#" %>
<%@ Register TagPrefix="custom" Namespace="myControls" %>
<!DOCTYPE html PUBLIC
    "-//W3C//DTD XHTML 1.0 Transitional//EN"
    "http://www.w3.org/TR/xhtml1/DTD/xhtml1-transitional.dtd">
<script runat="server">

    void Page_Load()
    {
        if (!Page.IsPostBack)
        {
            ViewStateControl1.Text = "Hello World!";
            ViewStateControl1.ViewStateText = "Hello World!";
        }
    }

</script>
<html xmlns="http://www.w3.org/1999/xhtml" >
<head runat="server">
    <title>Show View  State</title>
</head>
<body>
    <form id="form1" runat="server">
    <div>

    <custom:ViewStateControl
        id="ViewStateControl1"
        Runat="server" />

    <asp:Button
        id="btnSubmit"
        Text="Submit"
        Runat="server" />

    </div>
    </form>
</body>
</html>
```

Supporting Control State

The ASP.NET Framework includes a feature named Control State, which is similar to View State. Just like View State, any values that you add to Control State are preserved in the hidden __VIEWSTATE form field. However, unlike View State, Control State cannot be disabled. Control State is intended to be used only for storing crucial information across postbacks.

Control State was introduced to address a problem that developers encountered in the first version of ASP.NET Framework. You can disable View State for any control by assigning the value False to a control's EnableViewState property. Often, this is a good idea for performance reasons; however, disabling View State also made several controls nonfunctional.

For example, by default a GridView control retains the values of all the records that it displays in View State. If you display 500 database records with a GridView control, by default all 500 records are stuffed into the hidden __VIEWSTATE form field. To improve performance, you might want to disable View State for the GridView.

However, a GridView uses the __VIEWSTATE form field to remember crucial information required for the proper functioning of the control, such as the current page number and the currently selected row. You don't want the GridView to forget this critical information even when View State is disabled.

The concept of Control State was introduced to enable you to save critical information in the hidden __VIEWSTATE form field even when View State is disabled. Microsoft makes it slightly more difficult to use Control State because they don't want you to overuse this feature. You should use it only when storing super critical information.

For example, the control in Listing 36.14 includes two properties named ViewStateText and ControlStateText. View State preserves the value of the first property, and Control State preserves the value of the second property.

LISTING 36.14 ControlStateControl.cs

```
using System;
using System.Web;
using System.Web.UI;
using System.Web.UI.WebControls;

namespace myControls
{

    public class ControlStateControl : WebControl
    {

        private string _controlStateText;

        public string ViewStateText
        {
```

36

```csharp
        get
        {
            if (ViewState["ViewStateText"] == null)
                return String.Empty;
            else
                return (string)ViewState["ViewStateText"];
        }
        set { ViewState["ViewStateText"] = value; }
    }

    public string ControlStateText
    {
        get { return _controlStateText; }
        set { _controlStateText = value; }
    }

    protected override void OnInit(EventArgs e)
    {
        Page.RegisterRequiresControlState(this);
        base.OnInit(e);
    }

    protected override object SaveControlState()
    {
        return _controlStateText;
    }

    protected override void LoadControlState(object savedState)
    {
        _controlStateText = (string)savedState;
    }

    protected override void RenderContents(HtmlTextWriter writer)
    {
        writer.Write("ViewStateText: " + ViewStateText);
        writer.WriteBreak();
        writer.Write("ControlStateText: " + ControlStateText);
        writer.WriteBreak();
    }

    }
}
```

The control in Listing 36.14 overrides the base Control class's `OnInit()`, `SaveControlState()`, and `LoadControlState()` methods. In the `OnInit()` method, the `RegisterRequiresControlState()` method is called to indicate that the control needs to take advantage of Control State.

The `SaveControlState()` and `LoadControlState()` methods are responsible for saving and loading the Control State. Control State is saved as an object. The object is serialized by ASP.NET Framework into the hidden `__VIEWSTATE` form field automatically.

The page in Listing 36.15 illustrates the difference between View State and Control State. In the `Page_Load()` handler, the value `Hello World!` is assigned to both properties of the `ControlStateControl`. The control has View State disabled; however, if you click the button and post the page back to itself, the value of the `ControlStateText` property is not lost.

LISTING 36.15   ShowControlState.aspx

```
<%@ Page Language="C#" %>
<%@ Register TagPrefix="custom" Namespace="myControls" %>
<!DOCTYPE html PUBLIC
   "-//W3C//DTD XHTML 1.0 Transitional//EN"
   "http://www.w3.org/TR/xhtml1/DTD/xhtml1-transitional.dtd">
<script runat="server">

    void Page_Load()
    {
        if (!Page.IsPostBack)
        {
            ControlStateControl1.ViewStateText = "Hello World!";
            ControlStateControl1.ControlStateText = "Hello World!";
        }
    }

</script>
<html xmlns="http://www.w3.org/1999/xhtml" >
<head id="Head1" runat="server">
    <title>Show Control  State</title>
</head>
<body>
    <form id="form1" runat="server">
    <div>

    <custom:ControlStateControl
        id="ControlStateControl1"
        EnableViewState="false"
        Runat="server" />

    <asp:Button
```

36

```
        id="btnSubmit"
        Text="Submit"
        Runat="server" />

    </div>
    </form>
</body>
</html>
```

Processing Postback Data and Events

The ASP.NET Framework is built around web forms and controls pass information from the browser to the server by submitting a form to the server. This process of posting a form back to the server is called a *postback*.

When an ASP.NET page processes a form that has been posted back to the server, two types of information can be passed to the controls in the page. First, if a control initiates a postback, a server-side event can be raised when the form is posted to the server. For example, if you click a Button control, a Click event is raised on the server when the form containing the Button is posted back to the server. This event is called a *postback event*.

Second, the form data contained in the web form can be passed to a control. For example, when you submit a form that contains a TextBox control, the form data is passed to the TextBox control when the web form is submitted to the server. This form data is called the *postback data*.

When building a custom control, you might need to process either postback data or a postback event. In this section, you learn how to implement the required control interfaces for processing postbacks.

Handling Postback Data

If your control needs to process form data submitted to the server, you need to implement the IPostbackDataHandler interface. This interface includes the following two methods:

▶ **LoadPostData()**—Receives the form fields posted from the browser.

▶ **RaisePostDataChangedEvent()**—Enables you to raise an event indicating that the value of a form field has been changed.

For example, the control in Listing 36.16 is a simple TextBox control that implements the IPostbackDataHandler interface to preserve the state of an input field across postbacks.

LISTING 36.16   CustomTextBox.cs

```csharp
using System;
using System.Web.UI;
using System.Web.UI.WebControls;

namespace myControls
{
    public class CustomTextBox : WebControl, IPostBackDataHandler
    {
        public event EventHandler TextChanged;

        public string Text
        {
            get
            {
                if (ViewState["Text"] == null)
                    return String.Empty;
                else
                    return (string)ViewState["Text"];
            }

            set { ViewState["Text"] = value; }
        }

        protected override void AddAttributesToRender(HtmlTextWriter writer)
        {
            writer.AddAttribute(HtmlTextWriterAttribute.Type, "text");
            writer.AddAttribute(HtmlTextWriterAttribute.Value, Text);
            writer.AddAttribute(HtmlTextWriterAttribute.Name, this.UniqueID);
            base.AddAttributesToRender(writer);
        }

        protected override HtmlTextWriterTag TagKey
        {
            get
            {
                return HtmlTextWriterTag.Input;
            }
        }

        public bool LoadPostData(string postDataKey,
          System.Collections.Specialized.NameValueCollection postCollection)
        {
            if (postCollection[postDataKey] != Text)
            {
```

36

```
                Text = postCollection[postDataKey];
                return true;
            }
            return false;
        }

        public void RaisePostDataChangedEvent()
        {
            if (TextChanged != null)
                TextChanged(this, EventArgs.Empty);
        }
    }
}
```

The LoadPostData() receives the form fields posted from the browser. The method in
Listing 36.16 is passed a collection of all the form fields posted to the server. The
postDataKey represents the name of the field that corresponds to the current control.

NOTE

If the name of a form field rendered by a control does not match the name of the control, you need to notify the page containing the control to pass the form data to the control. You can call the Page.RegisterRequiresPostBack() method inside (or before)
the control's PreRender() event to notify the page that the control is interested in
receiving the postback data. In other words, if you discover that your control's
LoadPostData() method is never called, call the Page.RegisterRequiresPostBack()
method in your control.

If the value of the form field has changed—in other words, it does not match the current
value of the control's Text property—the Text property is updated and the method returns
the value True. Otherwise, the method returns the value False.

When the LoadPostData() method returns True, the RaisePostDataChangedEvent()
method is executed. Typically, you implement this method to raise a change event. In
Listing 36.16, this method is used to raise the TextChanged event, indicating that the
contents of the TextBox have been changed.

The page in Listing 36.17 illustrates how you can use the custom TextBox control in a
page (see Figure 36.7).

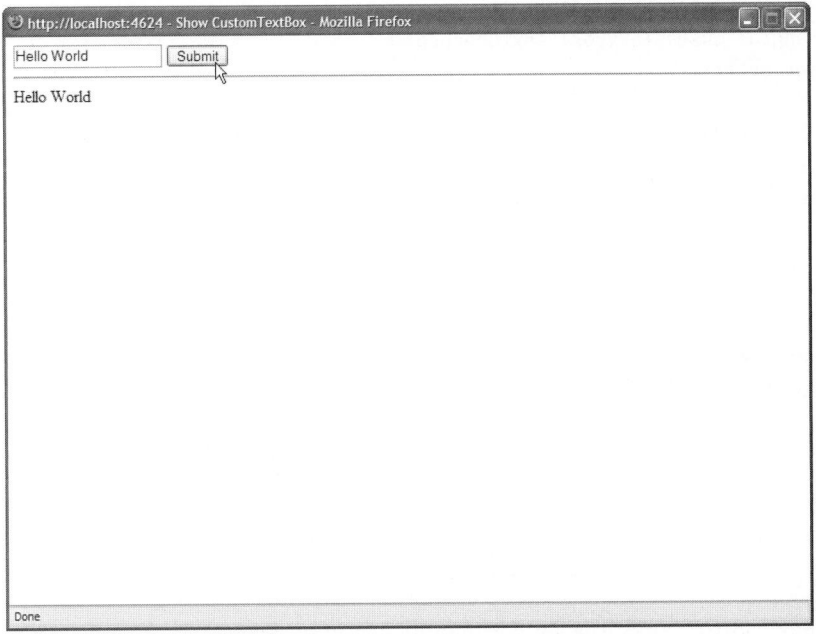

FIGURE 36.7   Handling postback data.

LISTING 36.17   ShowCustomTextBox.aspx

```
<%@ Page Language="C#" %>
<%@ Register TagPrefix="custom" Namespace="myControls" %>
<!DOCTYPE html PUBLIC
  "-//W3C//DTD XHTML 1.0 Transitional//EN"
  "http://www.w3.org/TR/xhtml1/DTD/xhtml1-transitional.dtd">
<script runat="server">

    protected void CustomTextBox1_TextChanged(object sender, EventArgs e)
    {
        lblResults.Text = CustomTextBox1.Text;
    }
</script>
<html xmlns="http://www.w3.org/1999/xhtml" >
<head id="Head1" runat="server">
    <title>Show CustomTextBox</title>
</head>
<body>
    <form id="form1" runat="server">
    <div>

    <custom:CustomTextBox
```

```
        id="CustomTextBox1"
        OnTextChanged="CustomTextBox1_TextChanged"
        Runat="server" />

    <asp:Button id="btnSubmit"
        Text="Submit"
        Runat="server" />

    <hr />

    <asp:Label
        id="lblResults"
        Runat="server" />

    </div>
    </form>
</body>
</html>
```

The custom TextBox control works in a similar manner as the standard ASP.NET TextBox control. The control preserves its state across postbacks and raises a TextChanged event when its contents have been modified.

> **NOTE**
>
> You will discover that you need to implement the IPostbackDataHandler interface quite often when building custom JavaScript controls. A common method of passing data from a JavaScript control back to the server is to use a hidden form field. You can process the contents of the hidden form field by using the IPostBackDataHandler interface.

Handling Postback Events

Only one control in a page at a time can cause a form to be submitted back to the server. When a control initiates a postback, the control can raise a postback event.

To process a postback event, you need to implement the IPostBackEventHandler interface. This interface includes a single method:

▶ **RaisePostBackEvent()**—Called on the server when a control initiates a postback.

The control in Listing 36.18 illustrates how you can implement the IPostBackEventHandler interface.

LISTING 36.18   CustomLinkButton.cs

```csharp
using System;
using System.Web.UI;
using System.Web.UI.WebControls;

namespace myControls
{
    public class CustomLinkButton : WebControl, IPostBackEventHandler
    {
        public event EventHandler Click;

        private string _Text;

        public string Text
        {
            get { return _Text; }
            set { _Text = value; }
        }

        protected override void AddAttributesToRender(HtmlTextWriter writer)
        {
            string eRef =
              Page.ClientScript.GetPostBackClientHyperlink(this, String.Empty);
            writer.AddAttribute(HtmlTextWriterAttribute.Href, eRef);
            base.AddAttributesToRender(writer);
        }

        protected override HtmlTextWriterTag TagKey
        {
            get
            {
                return HtmlTextWriterTag.A;
            }
        }

        protected override void RenderContents(HtmlTextWriter writer)
        {
            writer.Write(_Text);
        }


        public void RaisePostBackEvent(string eventArgument)
        {
            if (Click != null)
                Click(this, EventArgs.Empty);
```

36

```
        }
    }
}
```

The control in Listing 36.18 is a simple custom `LinkButton` control. It works much like the standard ASP.NET `LinkButton` control. When you click the link rendered by the control on the browser, the form containing the control is posted back to the server, and the `RaisePostBackEvent()` method is called. In Listing 36.18, the `RaisePostBackEvent()` method simply raises the `Click` event.

The `Page.ClientScript.GetPostBackClientHyperlink()` method is called in the control's `AddAttributesToRender()` method. The `GetPostBackClientHyperLink()` method returns the JavaScript that initiates the form postback in the browser. When this method is called in Listing 36.18, it returns the following JavaScript:

```
javascript:__doPostBack('CustomLinkButton1','')
```

The `__doPostBack()` JavaScript method calls the client-side form `submit()` method, which causes the form to be submitted back to the web server. (You can see all this by selecting View Source in your web browser.)

NOTE

There is a closely related method to the `GetPostBackClientHyperLink()` method named the `GetPostBackEventReference()` method. The `GetPostBackClientHyperLink()` method includes the `"JavaScript:"` prefix, whereas the `GetPostBackEventReference()` does not.

The page in Listing 36.19 demonstrates how you can use the custom `LinkButton` in an ASP.NET page.

LISTING 36.19   ShowCustomLinkButton.aspx

```
<%@ Page Language="C#" %>
<%@ Register TagPrefix="custom" Namespace="myControls" %>
<!DOCTYPE html PUBLIC
    "-//W3C//DTD XHTML 1.0 Transitional//EN"
    "http://www.w3.org/TR/xhtml1/DTD/xhtml1-transitional.dtd">
<script runat="server">

    protected void CustomLinkButton1_Click(object sender, EventArgs e)
    {
        lblResults.Text = txtUserName.Text;
    }
```

```
</script>
<html xmlns="http://www.w3.org/1999/xhtml" >
<head id="Head1" runat="server">
    <title>Show CustomLinkButton</title>
</head>
<body>
    <form id="form1" runat="server">
    <div>

    <asp:Label
        id="lblUserName"
        Text="User Name:"
        AssociatedControlID="txtUserName"
        Runat="server" />
    <asp:TextBox
        id="txtUserName"
        Runat="server" />

    <br /><br />

    <custom:CustomLinkButton
        id="CustomLinkButton1"
        Text="Submit"
        OnClick="CustomLinkButton1_Click"
        runat="server" />

    <hr />

    <asp:Label
        id="lblResults"
        EnableViewState="false"
        Runat="server" />

    </div>
    </form>
</body>
</html>
```

The page in Listing 36.19 contains a TextBox control and the custom LinkButton control. When you click the LinkButton, the form is posted back to the server. The Click handler displays the value of the TextBox control's Text property in a Label control (see Figure 36.8).

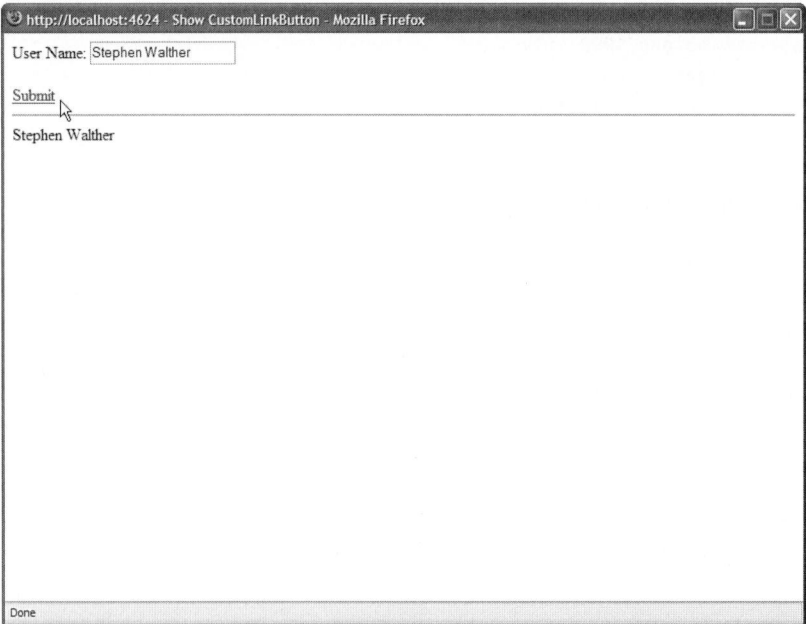

FIGURE 36.8   Using the `CustomLinkButton` control.

Passing Postback Event Arguments

When you call the `GetPostBackClientHyperLink()` method, you can supply the method with an optional argument. The argument is passed from the browser to the server when a postback is initiated. The value of the argument is passed to the `RaisePostBackEvent()` method on the server.

Imagine, for example, that you want to create a custom pager control that you could use with the `GridView` control. You want the custom control to display a list of page numbers you can click to navigate to a particular page of records displayed by a `GridView`.

To create this control, you need to render multiple links that initiate a postback event. Each link needs to pass the correct page number.

Listing 36.20 contains the custom pager control.

LISTING 36.20   `Pager.cs`

```
using System;
using System.Web.UI;
using System.Web.UI.WebControls;

namespace myControls
{
```

```csharp
public class Pager : WebControl, IPostBackEventHandler
{
    string _controlToPage;

    public string ControlToPage
    {
        get { return _controlToPage; }
        set { _controlToPage = value; }
    }

    protected override void RenderContents(HtmlTextWriter writer)
    {
        GridView grid = GetControlToPage();

        for (int i = 0; i < grid.PageCount; i++)
        {
            string eRef =
        Page.ClientScript.GetPostBackClientHyperlink(this, i.ToString());
            writer.Write("[");
            if (i == grid.PageIndex)
                writer.AddStyleAttribute(HtmlTextWriterStyle.FontWeight, "bold");
            writer.AddAttribute(HtmlTextWriterAttribute.Href, eRef);
            writer.RenderBeginTag(HtmlTextWriterTag.A);
            writer.Write("{0}", i + 1);
            writer.RenderEndTag();
            writer.Write("] ");
        }
    }

    private GridView GetControlToPage()
    {
        if (String.IsNullOrEmpty(_controlToPage))
            throw new Exception("Must set ControlToPage property");
        return (GridView)Page.FindControl(_controlToPage);
    }

    public void RaisePostBackEvent(string eventArgument)
    {
        GridView grid = GetControlToPage();
        grid.PageIndex = Int32.Parse(eventArgument);
    }
}
```

36

In Listing 36.20, the RenderContents() method renders the page numbers. Each page number is rendered as a link. When you click a link, the associated GridView control changes the page that it displays (see Figure 36.9).

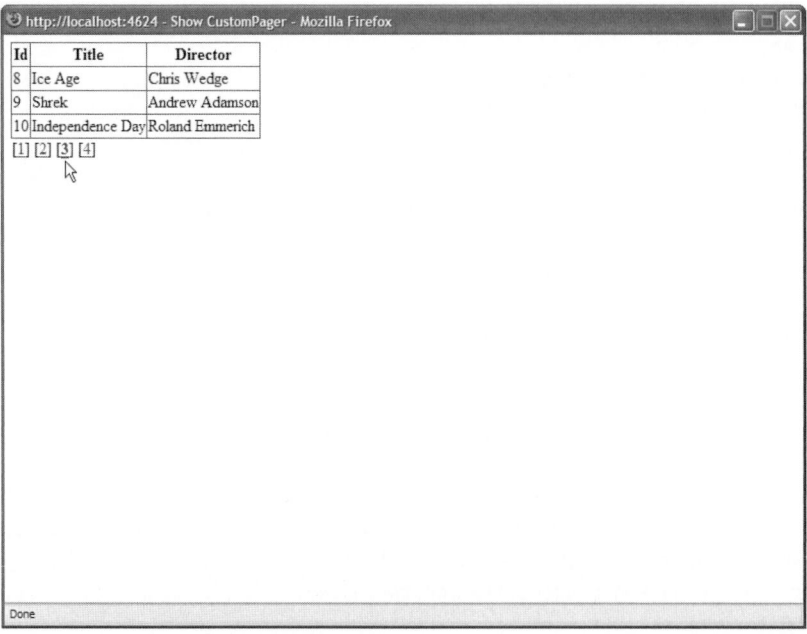

FIGURE 36.9   Using the Pager control.

The href attribute for each link is created by calling the GetPostBackClientHyperLink() method. The page number is passed as an argument to this method. When the pager is rendered to the browser, the following series of links is rendered:

```
[<a href="javascript:__doPostBack('Pager1','0')" style="font-weight:bold;">1</a>]
[<a href="javascript:__doPostBack('Pager1','1')">2</a>]
[<a href="javascript:__doPostBack('Pager1','2')">3</a>]
[<a href="javascript:__doPostBack('Pager1','3')">4</a>]
```

When you click a page number link, the corresponding page number is posted back to the server. The RaisePostBackEvent() method receives the page number and changes the page displayed by its associated GridView.

The page in Listing 36.21 illustrates how you can use the pager control to navigate to different pages of records displayed by a GridView control.

LISTING 36.21   `ShowPager.aspx`

```
<%@ Page Language="C#" %>
<%@ Register TagPrefix="custom" Namespace="myControls" %>
<!DOCTYPE html PUBLIC "-//W3C//DTD XHTML 1.0 Transitional//EN"
➥"http://www.w3.org/TR/xhtml1/DTD/xhtml1-transitional.dtd">
<html xmlns="http://www.w3.org/1999/xhtml" >
<head id="Head1" runat="server">
    <title>Show CustomPager</title>
</head>
<body>
    <form id="form1" runat="server">
    <div>

    <asp:GridView
        id="GridView1"
        DataSourceID="srcMovies"
        AllowPaging="true"
        PageSize="3"
        PagerSettings-Visible="false"
        Runat="server" />

    <custom:Pager
        id="Pager1"
        ControlToPage="GridView1"
        Runat="server" />

    <asp:SqlDataSource
        id="srcMovies"
        ConnectionString="Data Source=.\SQLExpress;Integrated Security=True;
            AttachDbFileName=¦DataDirectory¦MyDatabase.mdf;User Instance=True"
        SelectCommand="SELECT Id,Title,Director FROM Movies"
        Runat="server" />

    </div>
    </form>
</body>
</html>
```

36

Using Postback Options

Postbacks are more complicated than you might think. A postback can involve cross-page posts, validation groups, and programmatic control of control focus. To implement these advanced features in a custom control, you need to specify advanced postback options.

You specify advanced postback options by taking advantage of the `PostBackOptions` class. This class has the following properties:

▶ **ActionUrl**—Enables you to specify the page where form data is posted.

▶ **Argument**—Enables you to specify a postback argument.

▶ **AutoPostBack**—Enables you to add JavaScript necessary for implementing an AutoPostBack event.

▶ **ClientSubmit**—Enables you to initiate the postback through client-side script.

▶ **PerformValidation**—Enables you to specify whether validation is performed (set by the CausesValidation property).

▶ **RequiresJavaScriptProtocol**—Enables you to generate the JavaScript: prefix.

▶ **TargetControl**—Enables you to specify the control responsible for initiating the postback.

▶ **TrackFocus**—Enables you to scroll the page back to its current position and return focus to the control after a postback.

▶ **ValidationGroup**—Enables you to specify the validation group associated with the control.

Imagine that you need to create a form that enables users to place a product order. However, imagine that you want to create an advanced options check box. When someone clicks the advanced options check box, the current form data is submitted to a new page that includes a more complex form.

The `AdvancedCheckBox` control in Listing 36.22 supports cross-page posts. When you click the check box, the form data is submitted to the page indicated by its `PostBackUrl` property.

> **NOTE**
>
> Cross-page posts are covered during the discussion of `Button` controls in Chapter 2, "Using the Standard Controls."

LISTING 36.22   AdvancedCheckBox.cs

```
using System;
using System.Web.UI;
using System.Web.UI.WebControls;

namespace myControls
{
    public class AdvancedCheckBox : WebControl
    {
```

```csharp
private string _Text;
private string _PostBackUrl;

public string Text
{
    get { return _Text; }
    set { _Text = value; }
}

public string PostBackUrl
{
    get { return _PostBackUrl; }
    set { _PostBackUrl = value; }
}

protected override void AddAttributesToRender(HtmlTextWriter writer)
{
    PostBackOptions options = new PostBackOptions(this);
    options.ActionUrl = _PostBackUrl;

    string eRef = Page.ClientScript.GetPostBackEventReference(options);

    writer.AddAttribute(HtmlTextWriterAttribute.Onclick, eRef);
    writer.AddAttribute(HtmlTextWriterAttribute.Name, this.UniqueID);
    writer.AddAttribute(HtmlTextWriterAttribute.Type, "checkbox");


    base.AddAttributesToRender(writer);
}

protected override void RenderContents(HtmlTextWriter writer)
{
    if (!String.IsNullOrEmpty(_Text))
    {
        writer.AddAttribute(HtmlTextWriterAttribute.For, this.ClientID);
        writer.RenderBeginTag(HtmlTextWriterTag.Label);
        writer.Write(_Text);
        writer.RenderEndTag();
    }
}

protected override HtmlTextWriterTag TagKey
{
    get
    {
        return HtmlTextWriterTag.Input;
```

36

```
            }
        }
    }
}
```

In the `AddAttributesToRender()` method in Listing 36.22, an instance of the `PostBackOptions` class is created. The `ActionUrl` property is modified to support cross-page posts. The instance of the `PostBackOptions` class is passed to the `GetPostBackEventReference()` method to generate the JavaScript for initiating the postback.

The page in Listing 36.23 illustrates how you can use the `AdvancedCheckBox` control to submit form data to a new page when you click the check box (see Figure 36.10). The `AdvancedCheckBox` control's `PostBackUrl` property is set to the value `ShowAdvancedOptions.aspx`. When you click the check box, the form data is posted to this page.

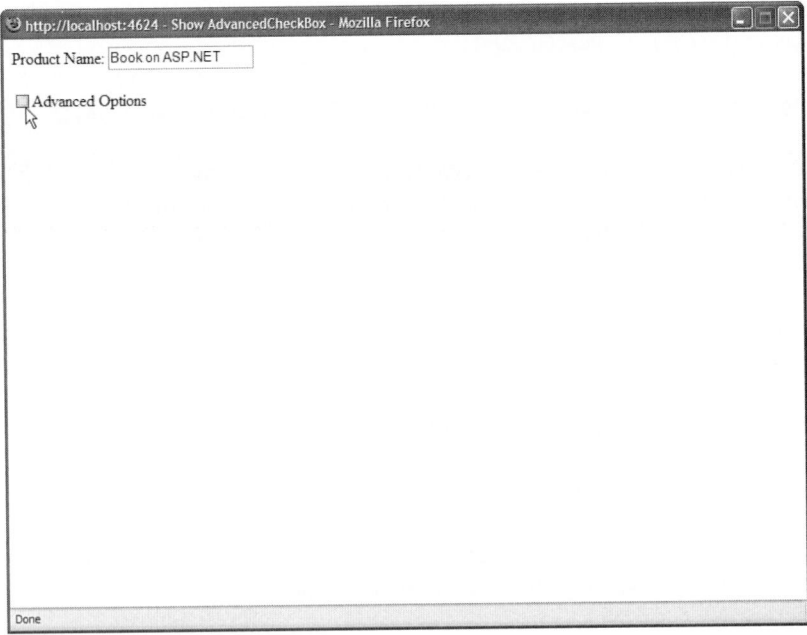

FIGURE 36.10   Using the `AdvancedCheckBox` control.

LISTING 36.23   `ShowAdvancedCheckBox.aspx`

```
<%@ Page Language="C#" %>
<%@ Register TagPrefix="custom" Namespace="myControls" %>
<!DOCTYPE html PUBLIC
    "-//W3C//DTD XHTML 1.0 Transitional//EN"
```

```
            "http://www.w3.org/TR/xhtml1/DTD/xhtml1-transitional.dtd">
<script runat="server">

    public string ProductName
    {
        get { return txtProductName.Text; }
    }
</script>
<html xmlns="http://www.w3.org/1999/xhtml" >
<head id="Head1" runat="server">
    <title>Show AdvancedCheckBox</title>
</head>
<body>
    <form id="form1" runat="server">
    <div>

    <asp:Label
        id="lblProductName"
        Text="Product Name:"
        AssociatedControlID="txtProductName"
        Runat="server" />

    <asp:TextBox
        id="txtProductName"
        Runat="server" />

    <br /><br />

    <custom:AdvancedCheckBox
        id="AdvancedCheckBox1"
        Text="Advanced Options"
        PostBackUrl="AdvancedOptions.aspx"
        Runat="server" />

    </div>
    </form>
</body>
</html>
```

36

Working with Control Property Collections

When you build more complex controls, you often need to represent a collection of items. For example, the standard ASP.NET DropDownList control contains one or more ListItem controls that represent individual options in the DropDownList. The GridView control can contain one or more DataBoundField controls that represent particular columns to display.

In this section, we build several controls that represent a collection of items. We build multiple content rotator controls that randomly display HTML content, and a server-side tab control that renders a tabbed view of content.

Using the ParseChildren Attribute

When building a control that contains a collection of child controls, you need to be aware of a ParseChildren attribute, which determines how the content contained in a control is parsed.

When the ParseChildren attribute has the value True, content contained in the control is parsed as properties of the containing control. If the control contains child controls, the child controls are parsed as properties of the containing control. (The attribute should have been named the ParseChildrenAsProperties attribute.)

When the ParseChildren attribute has the value False, no attempt is made to parse a control's child controls as properties. The content contained in the control is left alone.

The default value of the ParseChildren attribute is False. However, the WebControl class overrides this default value and sets the ParseChildren attribute to the value to True. Therefore, you should assume that ParseChildren is False when used with a control that inherits directly from the System.Web.UI.Control class, but assume that ParseChildren is True when used with a control that inherits from the System.Web.UI.WebControls.WebControl class.

Imagine, for example, that you need to create a content rotator control that randomly displays content in a page. There are two ways of creating this control, depending on whether ParseChildren has the value True or False.

The control in Listing 36.24 illustrates how you can create a content rotator control when ParseChildren has the value False.

LISTING 36.24   ContentRotator.cs

```
using System;
using System.Web.UI;
using System.Web.UI.WebControls;

namespace myControls
{
```

```
[ParseChildren(false)]
public class ContentRotator : WebControl
{
    protected override void AddParsedSubObject(object obj)
    {
        if (obj is Content)
            base.AddParsedSubObject(obj);
    }

    protected override void RenderContents(HtmlTextWriter writer)
    {
        Random rnd = new Random();
        int index = rnd.Next(this.Controls.Count);
        this.Controls[index].RenderControl(writer);
    }
}

public class Content : Control
{
}
}
```

The file in Listing 36.24 actually contains two controls: ContentRotator and a Content. The ContentRotator control randomly selects a single Content control from its child controls and renders the Content control to the browser. This all happens in the control's RenderContents() method.

The ParseChildren attribute has the value False in Listing 36.24. If you neglected to add this attribute, the Content controls would be parsed as properties of the ContentRotator control, and you would get an exception.

NOTE

The AddParsedSubObject() method is discussed in the next section.

The page in Listing 36.25 illustrates how you can use the ContentRotator and Content controls (see Figure 36.11).

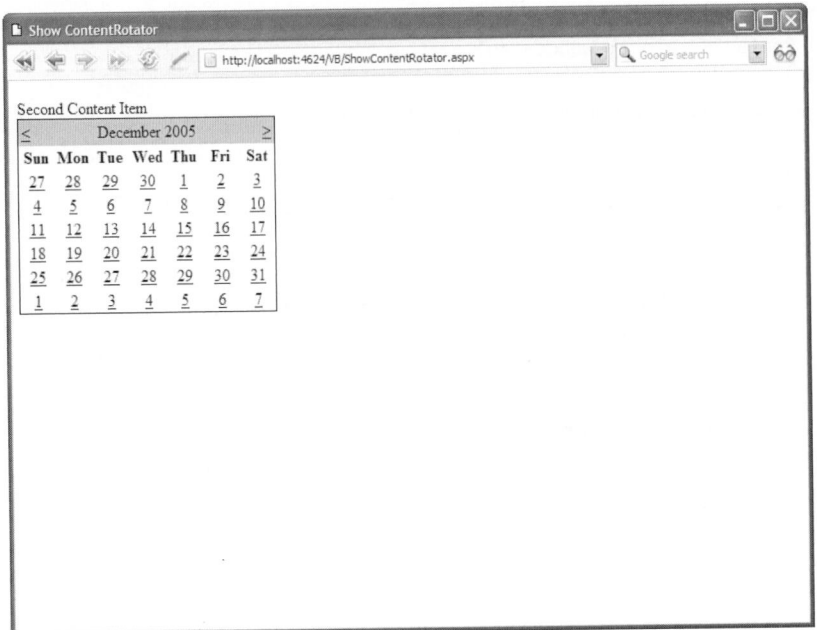

FIGURE 36.11   Randomly displaying content with the ContentRotator control.

LISTING 36.25   ShowContentRotator.aspx

```
<%@ Page Language="C#" %>
<%@ Register TagPrefix="custom" Namespace="myControls" %>
<!DOCTYPE html PUBLIC "-//W3C//DTD XHTML 1.0 Transitional//EN"
➥"http://www.w3.org/TR/xhtml1/DTD/xhtml1-transitional.dtd">
<html xmlns="http://www.w3.org/1999/xhtml" >
<head id="Head1" runat="server">
    <title>Show ContentRotator</title>
</head>
<body>
    <form id="form1" runat="server">
    <div>

    <custom:ContentRotator
        id="ContentRotator1"
        Runat="server">
        <custom:Content
            id="Content1"
            Runat="server">
            First Content Item
        </custom:Content>
        <custom:Content
```

```
                id="Content2"
                Runat="server">
                Second Content Item
                <asp:Calendar
                    id="Calendar1"
                    Runat="server" />
            </custom:Content>
            <custom:Content
                id="Content3"
                Runat="server">
                Third Content Item
            </custom:Content>
        </custom:ContentRotator>

        </div>
        </form>
</body>
</html>
```

If `ParseChildren` is not set to the value `False`, you need to add a property to your control that corresponds to the child controls contained in the control. For example, the control in Listing 36.26 includes an `Items` property that represents the `Item` controls contained in the control.

LISTING 36.26   ItemRotator.cs

```
using System;
using System.Collections;
using System.Web.UI;
using System.Web.UI.WebControls;
using System.ComponentModel;

namespace myControls
{
    [ParseChildren(true, "Items")]
    public class ItemRotator : CompositeControl
    {
        private ArrayList _items = new ArrayList();

        [Browsable(false)]
        public ArrayList Items
        {
            get { return _items; }
        }
```

```
        protected override void CreateChildControls()
        {
            Random rnd = new Random();
            int index = rnd.Next(_items.Count);
            Control item = (Control)_items[index];
            this.Controls.Add(item);
        }
    }

    public class Item : Control
    {

    }
}
```

In Listing 36.26, the second value passed to the ParseChildren attribute is the name of a control property. The contents of the ItemRotator are parsed as items of the collection represented by the specified property.

Unlike the ContentRotator control, the controls contained in the ItemRotator control are not automatically parsed into child controls. After the CreateChildControls() method executes, the ItemRotator control contains only one child control (the randomly selected Item control).

The page in Listing 36.27 illustrates how you can use the ItemRotator control to randomly display page content.

LISTING 36.27   ShowItemRotator.aspx

```
<%@ Page Language="C#" Trace="true" %>
<%@ Register TagPrefix="custom" Namespace="myControls" %>
<!DOCTYPE html PUBLIC "-//W3C//DTD XHTML 1.0 Transitional//EN"
➡"http://www.w3.org/TR/xhtml1/DTD/xhtml1-transitional.dtd">
<html xmlns="http://www.w3.org/1999/xhtml" >
<head id="Head1" runat="server">
    <title>Show ItemRotator</title>
</head>
<body>
    <form id="form1" runat="server">
    <div>

    <custom:ItemRotator
        id="ItemRotator1"
        Runat="server">
        <custom:item ID="Item1" runat="server">
            First Item
```

```
        </custom:item>
        <custom:item ID="Item2" runat="server">
            Second Item
            <asp:Calendar
                id="Calendar1"
                Runat="server" />
        </custom:item>
        <custom:item ID="Item3" runat="server">
            Third Item
        </custom:item>
    </custom:ItemRotator>

    </div>
    </form>
</body>
</html>
```

There is no requirement that the contents of a control must be parsed as controls. When building a control that represents a collection of items, you can also represent the items as objects. For example, the ImageRotator control in Listing 36.28 contains ImageItem objects. The ImageItem class does not represent a control.

LISTING 36.28   ImageRotator.cs

```
using System;
using System.Collections;
using System.Web.UI;
using System.Web.UI.WebControls;
using System.ComponentModel;

namespace myControls
{
    [ParseChildren(true, "ImageItems")]
    public class ImageRotator : WebControl
    {
        private ArrayList _imageItems = new ArrayList();

        public ArrayList ImageItems
        {
            get
            {
                return _imageItems;
            }
        }
```

```
        protected override void RenderContents(HtmlTextWriter writer)
        {
            if (_imageItems.Count > 0)
            {
                Random rnd = new Random();
                ImageItem img =
➡(ImageItem)_imageItems[rnd.Next(_imageItems.Count)];
                writer.AddAttribute(HtmlTextWriterAttribute.Src, img.ImageUrl);
                writer.AddAttribute(HtmlTextWriterAttribute.Alt, img.AlternateText);
                writer.RenderBeginTag(HtmlTextWriterTag.Img);
                writer.RenderEndTag();
            }
        }
    }

    public class ImageItem
    {
        private string _imageUrl;
        private string _alternateText;

        public string ImageUrl
        {
            get { return _imageUrl; }
            set { _imageUrl = value; }
        }

        public string AlternateText
        {
            get { return _alternateText; }
            set { _alternateText = value; }
        }
    }
}
```

The ImageItem class is just a class and does not derive from the base Control class. Because the ImageItem class does nothing more than represent a couple of properties, there is no reason to make it a full-blown control.

The page in Listing 36.29 illustrates how you can use the ImageRotator control to display different images randomly.

LISTING 36.29   ShowImageRotator.aspx

```
<%@ Page Language="C#" Trace="true" %>
<%@ Register TagPrefix="custom" Namespace="myControls" %>
<!DOCTYPE html PUBLIC "-//W3C//DTD XHTML 1.0 Transitional//EN"
➥"http://www.w3.org/TR/xhtml1/DTD/xhtml1-transitional.dtd">
<html xmlns="http://www.w3.org/1999/xhtml" >
<head id="Head1" runat="server">
    <title>Show ImageRotator</title>
</head>
<body>
    <form id="form1" runat="server">
    <div>

    <custom:ImageRotator
        id="ImageRotator1"
        Runat="server">
        <custom:ImageItem ImageUrl="Image1.gif" AlternateText="Image 1" />
        <custom:ImageItem ImageUrl="Image2.gif" AlternateText="Image 2" />
        <custom:ImageItem ImageUrl="Image3.gif" AlternateText="Image 3" />
    </custom:ImageRotator>

    </div>
    </form>
</body>
</html>
```

The page in Listing 36.29 has tracing enabled. If you look in the Control Tree section, you see that the ImageRotator control does not contain any child controls (see Figure 36.12).

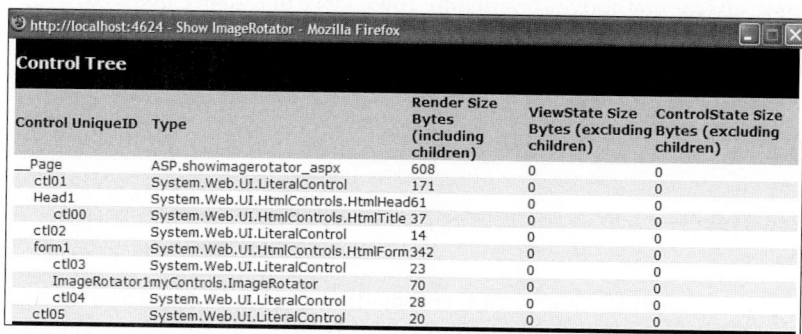

Control UniqueID	Type	Render Size Bytes (including children)	ViewState Size Bytes (excluding children)	ControlState Size Bytes (excluding children)
__Page	ASP.showimagerotator_aspx	608	0	0
ctl01	System.Web.UI.LiteralControl	171	0	0
Head1	System.Web.UI.HtmlControls.HtmlHead	61	0	0
ctl00	System.Web.UI.HtmlControls.HtmlTitle	37	0	0
ctl02	System.Web.UI.LiteralControl	14	0	0
form1	System.Web.UI.HtmlControls.HtmlForm	342	0	0
ctl03	System.Web.UI.LiteralControl	23	0	0
ImageRotator1	myControls.ImageRotator	70	0	0
ctl04	System.Web.UI.LiteralControl	28	0	0
ctl05	System.Web.UI.LiteralControl	20	0	0

FIGURE 36.12   The ShowImageRotator.aspx page control tree.

Using the `AddParsedSubObject()` Method

When the `ParseChildren` attribute has the value `false`, the contents of a control are automatically added to the control's collection of child controls (represented by the `Controls` property). You need understand that all content contained in the control, even carriage returns and spaces, are added to the controls collection.

Any content contained in a control that does not represent a server-side control is parsed into a `Literal` control. In some cases, you might want to allow only a certain type of control to be added to the `Controls` collection.

The `AddParsedSubObject()` method is called as each control is added to the Controls collection. By overriding the `AddParsedSubObject()` method, you can block certain types of controls—such as `Literal` controls—from being added to the `Controls` collection.

For example, the `ContentRotator` control in Listing 36.20 overrides the base `AddParsedSubObject()` method and prevents anything that is not a `Content` control from being added to the `ContentRotator` `Controls` collection. If you removed the `AddParsedSubObject()` method from this control, all the carriage returns and spaces between the `Content` controls would be added to the `Controls` collection as `Literal` controls.

Using a `ControlBuilder`

The `AddParsedSubObject()` method enables you to specify which parsed controls get added to a Controls collection. Sometimes, you must take even more control over the parsing of a control.

When the ASP.NET Framework parses a page, the Framework uses a special type of class called a `ControlBuilder` class. You can modify the way in which the content of a control is parsed by associating a custom `ControlBuilder` with a control.

Here's a list of the most useful methods supported by the `ControlBuilder` class:

- ▶ `AllowWhiteSpaceLiterals()`—Enables you to trim white space from the contents of a control.

- ▶ `AppendLiteralString()`—Enables you trim all literal content from the contents of a control.

- ▶ `GetChildControlType()`—Enables you to specify how a particular tag gets parsed into a control.

The `GetChildControlType()` method is the most useful method and enables you to map tags to controls. You can use the `GetChildControlType()` method to map any tag to any control.

For example, the file in Listing 36.30 contains a `ServerTabs` control that renders multiple tabs (see Figure 36.13). Each tab is represented by a `Tab` control.

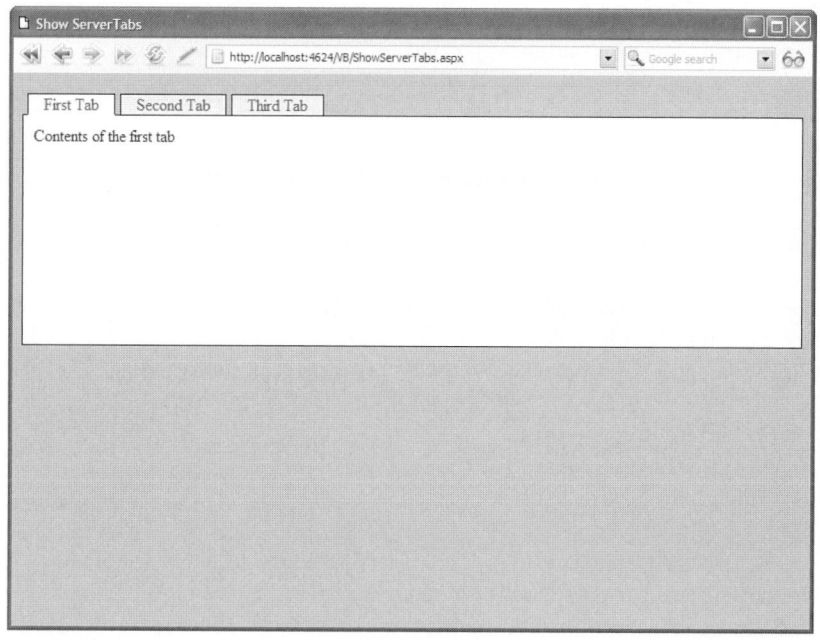

FIGURE 36.13   Using the ServerTabs control.

LISTING 36.30   ServerTabs.cs

```csharp
using System;
using System.Collections;
using System.Web.UI;
using System.Web.UI.WebControls;

namespace myControls
{
    [ControlBuilder(typeof(ServerTabsBuilder))]
    [ParseChildren(false)]
    public class ServerTabs : WebControl, IPostBackEventHandler
    {
        public int SelectedTabIndex
        {
            get
            {
                if (ViewState["SelectedTabIndex"] == null)
                    return 0;
                else
                    return (int)ViewState["SelectedTabIndex"];
            }
            set
```

```
        {
            ViewState["SelectedTabIndex"] = value;
        }
    }


    protected override void RenderContents(HtmlTextWriter writer)
    {
        for (int i = 0; i < this.Controls.Count; i++)
        {
            ServerTab tab = (ServerTab)this.Controls[i];
            string eRef =
        Page.ClientScript.GetPostBackClientHyperlink(this, i.ToString());

            if (SelectedTabIndex == i)
                writer.AddAttribute(
        HtmlTextWriterAttribute.Class, "tab selectedTab");
            else
                writer.AddAttribute(HtmlTextWriterAttribute.Class, "tab");
            writer.RenderBeginTag(HtmlTextWriterTag.Div);
            writer.AddAttribute(HtmlTextWriterAttribute.Href, eRef);
            writer.RenderBeginTag(HtmlTextWriterTag.A);
            writer.Write(tab.Text);
            writer.RenderEndTag(); // A
            writer.RenderEndTag(); // Tab DIV
        }
        writer.Write("<br style='clear:both' />");

        writer.AddAttribute(HtmlTextWriterAttribute.Class, "tabContents");
        writer.RenderBeginTag(HtmlTextWriterTag.Div);
        this.Controls[SelectedTabIndex].RenderControl(writer);
        writer.RenderEndTag(); // Tab Contents DIV
    }


    protected override void AddParsedSubObject(object obj)
    {
        if (obj is ServerTab)
            base.AddParsedSubObject(obj);
    }


    protected override HtmlTextWriterTag TagKey
    {
        get
        {
            return HtmlTextWriterTag.Div;
        }
    }
```

```
        public void RaisePostBackEvent(string eventArgument)
        {
            SelectedTabIndex = Int32.Parse(eventArgument);
        }
    }

    public class ServerTabsBuilder : ControlBuilder
    {
        public override Type GetChildControlType(string tagName, IDictionary attribs)
        {
            if (String.Compare(tagName, "tab", true) == 0)
                return typeof(ServerTab);
            else
                return null;
        }
    }

    public class ServerTab : Control
    {
        private string _Text;

        public string Text
        {
            get { return _Text; }
            set { _Text = value; }
        }
    }
}
```

36

The `ServerTabs` class is decorated with a `ControlBuilder` attribute. This attribute associates the `ServerTabs` control with a `ControlBuilder` class named `ServerTabsBuilder`.

The `ServerTabsBuilder` class overrides the base `ControlBuilder` `GetChildControlType()` method. The overridden method maps the `<tab>` tag to the `Tab` control. Because of this mapping, you do not need to use a prefix or use the `runat="server"` attribute when declaring a tab within the `ServerTabs` control.

The page in Listing 36.31 illustrates how you can use the `ServerTabs` control.

LISTING 36.31   ShowServerTabs.aspx

```
<%@ Page Language="C#" %>
<%@ Register TagPrefix="custom" Namespace="myControls" %>
<!DOCTYPE html PUBLIC "-//W3C//DTD XHTML 1.0 Transitional//EN"
➥"http://www.w3.org/TR/xhtml1/DTD/xhtml1-transitional.dtd">
```

```
<html xmlns="http://www.w3.org/1999/xhtml" >
<head id="Head1" runat="server">
    <style type="text/css">
        html
        {
            background-color:silver;
        }
        .tab
        {
            float:left;
            position:relative;
            top:1px;
            background-color:#eeeeee;
            border:solid 1px black;
            padding:0px 15px;
            margin-left:5px;
        }
        .tab a
        {
            text-decoration:none;
        }
        .selectedTab
        {
            background-color:white;
            border-bottom:solid 1px white;
        }
        .tabContents
        {
            border:solid 1px black;
            background-color:white;
            padding:10px;
            height:200px;
        }
    </style>
    <title>Show ServerTabs</title>
</head>
<body>
    <form id="form1" runat="server">
    <div>

    <custom:ServerTabs
        ID="ServerTabs1"
        Runat="Server">
        <tab Text="First Tab">
          Contents of the first tab
        </tab>
```

```
        <tab Text="Second Tab">
          Contents of the second tab
        </tab>
        <tab Text="Third Tab">
          Contents of the third tab
        </tab>
    </custom:ServerTabs>

    </div>
    </form>
</body>
</html>
```

The `ControlBuilder` enables you to declare instances of the `Tab` control by using the `<tab>` tag instead of using a `<custom:Tab runat="server">` tab.

Creating a Better Designer Experience

Up to this point, we've ignored the Design view experience. In other words, we've ignored the question of how our custom controls appear in the Visual Web Developer or Visual Studio .NET Design view.

You can modify the appearance of your control in Design view in two ways. You can apply design-time attributes to the control, or you can associate a `ControlDesigner` with your control. We explore both methods in this section.

Applying Design-Time Attributes to a Control

Design-time attributes enable you to modify how control properties appear in Design view. Some attributes are applied to the control itself, whereas other attributes are applied to particular properties of a control.

Here is the list of the design-time attributes you can apply to a control:

- ▶ **DefaultEvent**—Enables you to specify the default event for a control. When you double-click a control in Visual Web Developer or Visual Studio .NET, an event handler is automatically created for the default event.

- ▶ **DefaultProperty**—Enables you to specify the default property for a control. When you open the Property window for a control, this property is highlighted by default.

- ▶ **PersistChildren**—Enables you to specify whether child controls or properties are persisted as control attributes or control contents.

- ▶ **ToolboxData**—Enables you to specify the tag added to a page when a control is dragged from the toolbox.

▶ **ToolboxItem**—Enables you to block a control from appearing in the Toolbox.

Here is the list of design-time attributes you can apply to a control property:

▶ **Bindable**—Enables you to indicate to display a Databindings dialog box for the property.

▶ **Browsable**—Enables you to block a property from appearing in the Properties window.

▶ **Category**—Enables you to specify the category associated with the property. The property appears under this category in the Properties window.

▶ **DefaultValue**—Enables you to specify a default value for the property. When you right-click a property in the Properties window, you can select Reset to the return the property to its default value.

▶ **Description**—Enables you to specify the description associated with the property. The description appears in the Properties window when the property is selected.

▶ **DesignerSerializationVisibility**—Enables you to specify how changes to a property are serialized. Possible values are Visible, Hidden, and Content.

▶ **Editor**—Enables you to specify a custom editor for editing the property in Design view.

▶ **EditorBrowsable**—Enables you to block a property from appearing in Intellisense.

▶ **NotifyParentProperty**—Enables you to specify that changes to a subproperty should be propagated to the parent property.

▶ **PersistenceMode**—Enables you to specify whether a property is persisted as a control attribute or control content. Possible values are Attribute, EncodedInnerDefaultProperty, InnerDefaultProperty, and InnerProperty.

▶ **TypeConverter**—Enables you to associate a custom type converter with a property. A type converter converts a property between a string representation and a type (or vice versa).

The Editor attribute enables you to associate a particular editor with a property. Certain types in the Framework have default editors. For example, a property that represents a System.Drawing.Color value is automatically associated with the ColorEditor. The ColorEditor displays a color picker (see Figure 36.14). To view the list of editors included in .NET Framework, look up the UITypeEditor class in the .NET Framework SDK Documentation.

The MovieView control contained in Listing 36.32 illustrates how you can use several of these attributes. The control displays a single movie.

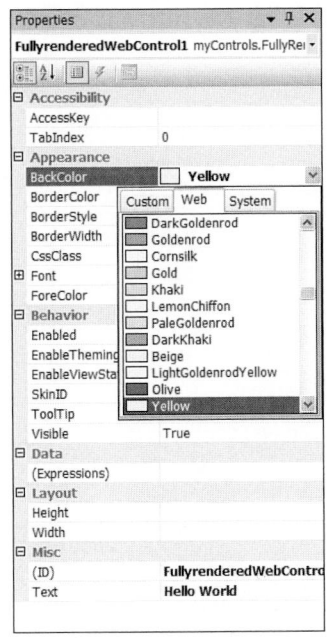

FIGURE 36.14   Using the ColorEditor to pick a color.

LISTING 36.32   MovieView.cs

```csharp
using System;
using System.Web.UI;
using System.Web.UI.WebControls;
using System.ComponentModel;

namespace myControls
{
    [DefaultProperty("Title")]
    public class MovieView : WebControl
    {

        private string _title = "Movie Title";
        private string _description = "Movie Description";

        [Category("Movie")]
        [Description("Movie Title")]
        public string Title
        {
```

```
        get { return _title; }
        set { _title = value; }
    }


    [Category("Movie")]
    [Description("Movie Description")]
    public string Description
    {
        get { return _description; }
        set { _description = value; }
    }



    protected override void RenderContents(HtmlTextWriter writer)
    {
        writer.RenderBeginTag(HtmlTextWriterTag.H1);
        writer.Write(_title);
        writer.RenderEndTag();

        writer.Write(_description);
    }

    protected override HtmlTextWriterTag TagKey
    {
        get
        {
            return HtmlTextWriterTag.Div;
        }
    }
}
}
```

The page in Listing 36.33 contains the MovieView control. Open the page in Design view to see the effect of the various design-time attributes. For example, a category and description are associated with both the Title and Description properties in the Properties window (see Figure 36.15).

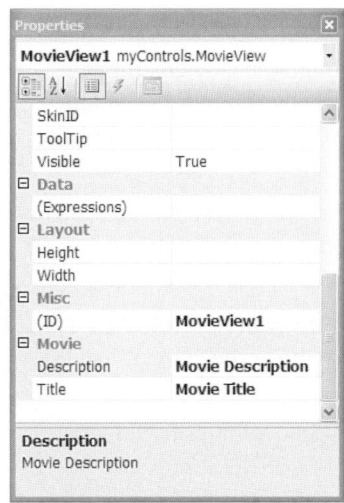

FIGURE 36.15   The MovieView control in Design view.

LISTING 36.33   ShowMovieView.aspx

```
<%@ Page Language="C#" %>
<%@ Register TagPrefix="custom" Namespace="myControls" %>
<!DOCTYPE html PUBLIC "-//W3C//DTD XHTML 1.0 Transitional//EN"
➥"http://www.w3.org/TR/xhtml1/DTD/xhtml1-transitional.dtd">
<html xmlns="http://www.w3.org/1999/xhtml" >
<head id="Head1" runat="server">
    <title>Show MovieView</title>
</head>
<body>
    <form id="form1" runat="server">
    <div>

    <custom:MovieView
        id="MovieView1"
        Runat="server" />

    </div>
    </form>
</body>
</html>
```

36

Creating Control Designers

You can modify the appearance of your custom controls in Design view by creating a ControlDesigner. The ASP.NET Framework enables you to implement a number of fancy features when you implement a ControlDesigner. This section focuses on just two of these advanced features.

First, you learn how to create a ContainerControlDesigner. A ContainerControlDesigner enables you to drag and drop other controls from the Toolbox onto your control in Design view.

You also learn how to add Smart Tags (also called Action Lists) to your control. When a control supports Smart Tags, a menu of common tasks pop up above the control in Design view.

Creating a Container `ControlDesigner`

If you associate a custom control with a ContainerControlDesigner, you can add child controls to your control in Design view. For example, the file in Listing 36.34 contains a GradientPanel control. This control displays a gradient background behind its contents (see Figure 36.16).

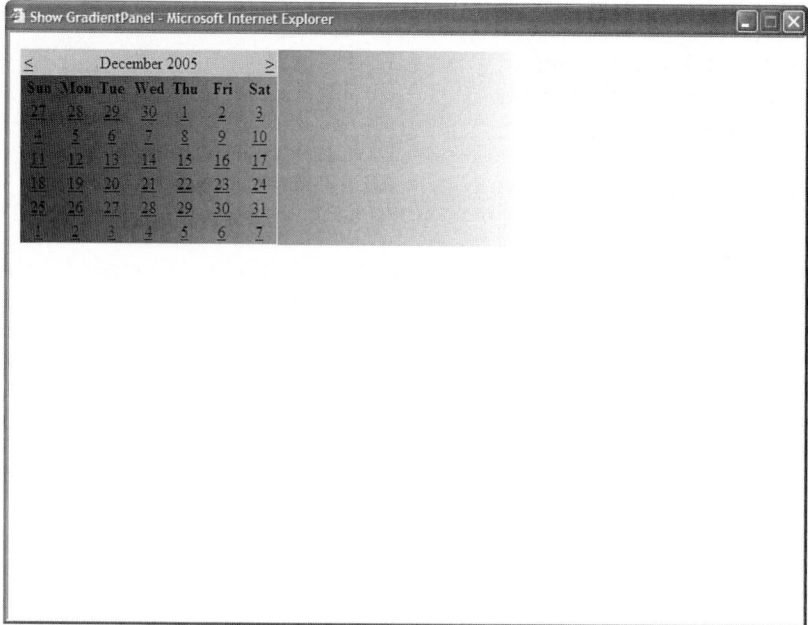

FIGURE 36.16   Displaying the GradientPanel control.

LISTING 36.34   GradientPanel.cs

```csharp
using System;
using System.Web.UI;
using System.Web.UI.WebControls;
using System.Web.UI.Design;
using System.ComponentModel;
using System.Drawing;

namespace myControls
{
    [Designer(typeof(GradientPanelDesigner))]
    [ParseChildren(false)]
    public class GradientPanel : WebControl
    {
        private GradientDirection _direction = GradientDirection.Horizontal;
        private Color _startColor = Color.DarkBlue;
        private Color _endColor = Color.White;

        public GradientDirection Direction
        {
            get { return _direction; }
            set { _direction = value; }
        }

        public Color StartColor
        {
            get { return _startColor; }
            set { _startColor = value; }
        }

        public Color EndColor
        {
            get { return _endColor; }
            set { _endColor = value; }
        }

        protected override void AddAttributesToRender(HtmlTextWriter writer)
        {
            writer.AddStyleAttribute(HtmlTextWriterStyle.Filter, this.GetFilter
➥String());
            base.AddAttributesToRender(writer);
        }

        public string GetFilterString()
        {
```

```
            return String.Format(
"progid:DXImageTransform.Microsoft.Gradient(gradientType={0},startColorStr={1},
➥endColorStr={2})", _
    direction.ToString("d"),
    ColorTranslator.ToHtml(_startColor), ColorTranslator.ToHtml(_endColor));
        }

        public GradientPanel()
        {
            this.Width = Unit.Parse("500px");
        }

        protected override HtmlTextWriterTag TagKey
        {
            get
            {
                return HtmlTextWriterTag.Div;
            }
        }
    }

    public enum GradientDirection
    {
        Vertical = 0,
        Horizontal = 1
    }

    public class GradientPanelDesigner : ContainerControlDesigner
    {
        protected override void AddDesignTimeCssAttributes(
          System.Collections.IDictionary styleAttributes)
        {
            GradientPanel gPanel = (GradientPanel)this.Component;
            styleAttributes.Add("filter", gPanel.GetFilterString());
            base.AddDesignTimeCssAttributes(styleAttributes);
        }
    }
}
```

The GradientPanel control uses an Internet Explorer filter to create the gradient back-ground. The filter is applied in the AddAttributesToRender() method. You can set the StartColor, EndColor, and Direction properties to control the appearance of the gradient background.

The `GradientPanel` control is decorated with a `ControlDesigner` attribute. This attribute associates the `GradientPanelDesigner` class with the `GradientPanel` control.

The `GradientPanelDesigner` is also included in Listing 36.34. One method is overridden in the `GradientPanelDesigner` class. The `AddDesignTimeCssAttributes()` method is used to apply the gradient background in Design view.

WARNING

The file in Listing 36.34 doesn't compile unless you add a reference to the `System.Design.dll` assembly to your application. You can add the necessary reference by selecting Website, Add Reference and selecting the `System.Design` assembly.

The page in Listing 36.35 illustrates how you can declare the `GradientPanel` in a page. However, to understand the effect of the `ContainerControlDesigner`, you need to open the page in Design view in either Visual Web Developer or Visual Studio .NET.

LISTING 36.35   ShowGradientPanel.aspx

```
<%@ Page Language="C#" %>
<%@ Register TagPrefix="custom" Namespace="myControls" %>
<!DOCTYPE html PUBLIC "-//W3C//DTD XHTML 1.0 Transitional//EN"
➥"http://www.w3.org/TR/xhtml1/DTD/xhtml1-transitional.dtd">
<html xmlns="http://www.w3.org/1999/xhtml" >
<head id="Head1" runat="server">
    <title>Show GradientPanel</title>
</head>
<body>
    <form id="form1" runat="server">
    <div>

    <custom:GradientPanel
        id="GradientPanel1"
        Runat="server">
        <asp:Calendar
            ID="Calendar1"
            runat="server" />
    </custom:GradientPanel>

    </div>
    </form>
</body>
</html>
```

36

When you open the page in Listing 36.35 in Design view, you can drag other controls from the toolbox onto the GradientPanel control. For example, if you drag a Calendar control onto the GradientPanel control, the Calendar control is added automatically to the control collection of the GradientPanel (see Figure 36.17).

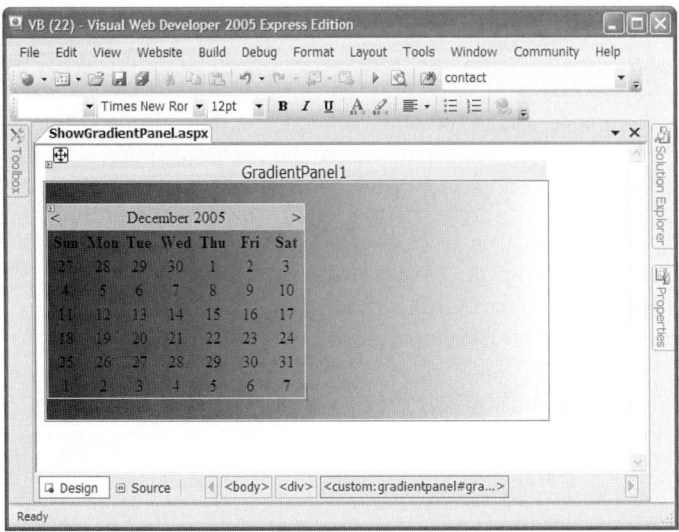

FIGURE 36.17   Editing the GradientPanel control in Design view.

Adding Smart Tasks

If you add a GridView control to a page when you are in Design view, a menu of common tasks appears above the GridView. For example, you can select a Smart Task to enable sorting or paging.

You can add your own Smart Tasks to a custom control by inheriting a new class from the base DesignerActionList class.

For example, the file in Listing 36.36 contains three classes. It contains a custom control, named the SmartImage control, which enables you to rotate and mirror images. It also contains a ControlDesigner. Finally, it contains a DesignerActionList class that contains two Smart Tasks.

LISTING 36.36   SmartImage.cs

```
using System;
using System.Web.UI;
using System.Web.UI.WebControls;
using System.Web.UI.Design;
using System.ComponentModel;
using System.ComponentModel.Design;
```

```
namespace myControls
{
    [Designer(typeof(SmartImageDesigner))]
    public class SmartImage : WebControl
    {
        string _imageUrl;
        string _alternateText;
        int _rotation = 0;
        bool _mirror = false;

        public string ImageUrl
        {
            get { return _imageUrl; }
            set { _imageUrl = value; }
        }

        public string AlternateText
        {
            get { return _alternateText; }
            set { _alternateText = value; }
        }

        public int Rotation
        {
            get { return _rotation; }
            set { _rotation = value; }
        }

        public bool Mirror
        {
            get { return _mirror; }
            set { _mirror = value; }
        }

        protected override HtmlTextWriterTag TagKey
        {
            get
            {
                return HtmlTextWriterTag.Img;
            }
        }

        private string GetFilterString()
        {
            string _mirrorValue = "0";
```

36

```
            if (_mirror)
                _mirrorValue = "1";

            return
String.Format(
"progid:DXImageTransform.Microsoft.BasicImage(Rotation={0},Mirror={1})",
  _rotation, _mirrorValue);
        }

        protected override void AddAttributesToRender(HtmlTextWriter writer)
        {
            writer.AddStyleAttribute(HtmlTextWriterStyle.Filter, this.GetFilter
➥String());
            writer.AddAttribute(HtmlTextWriterAttribute.Src, _imageUrl);
            writer.AddAttribute(HtmlTextWriterAttribute.Alt, _alternateText);


            base.AddAttributesToRender(writer);
        }
    }

    public class SmartImageDesigner : ControlDesigner
    {
        public override DesignerActionListCollection ActionLists
        {
            get
            {
                DesignerActionListCollection actionLists =
                  new DesignerActionListCollection();
                actionLists.AddRange(base.ActionLists);
                actionLists.Add(new SmartImageActionList(this));
                return actionLists;
            }
        }
    }

    public class SmartImageActionList : DesignerActionList
    {

        private DesignerActionItemCollection items;
        private SmartImageDesigner _parent;

        public SmartImageActionList(SmartImageDesigner parent)
            : base(parent.Component)
        {
```

```
                _parent = parent;
        }


        public void Rotate()
        {
            TransactedChangeCallback toCall = new TransactedChangeCallback(DoRotate);
            ControlDesigner.InvokeTransactedChange(this.Component, toCall,
                "Rotate", "Rotate image 90 degrees");
        }


        public void Mirror()
        {
            TransactedChangeCallback toCall = new TransactedChangeCallback(DoMirror);
            ControlDesigner.InvokeTransactedChange(this.Component, toCall, "Mirror",
                    "Mirror Image");
        }


        public override DesignerActionItemCollection GetSortedActionItems()
        {
            if (items == null)
            {
                items = new DesignerActionItemCollection();
                items.Add(new DesignerActionMethodItem(this, "Rotate",
                    "Rotate Image", true));
                items.Add(new DesignerActionMethodItem(this, "Mirror", "Mirror
Image", true));
            }
            return items;
        }


        public bool DoRotate(object arg)
        {
            SmartImage img = (SmartImage)this.Component;
            img.Rotation += 1;
            if (img.Rotation > 3)
                img.Rotation = 0;
            _parent.UpdateDesignTimeHtml();
            return true;
        }


        public bool DoMirror(object arg)
        {
            SmartImage img = (SmartImage)this.Component;
            img.Mirror = !img.Mirror;
            _parent.UpdateDesignTimeHtml();
```

36

```
            return true;
        }
    }
}
```

The `SmartImage` control takes advantage of an Internet Explorer filter named the `BasicImage` filter. This filter enables you to manipulate images by rotating, mirroring, and changing the opacity of images. In Listing 36.36, the filter is applied in the `AddAttributesToRender()` method.

The `SmartImage` control is associated with a `ControlDesigner` named the `SmartImageDesigner` through the control's `Designer` attribute. The `SmartImageDesigner` class overrides the base class's `ActionLists` property to expose a custom `DesignerActionList`.

The `DesignerActionList` is the final class declared in Listing 36.36. This class contains four methods named `Rotate()`, `DoRotate()`, `Mirror()`, and `DoMirror()`. The `GetSortedActionItems()` method exposes the Rotate and Mirror actions.

When all is said and done, the custom `ActionList` enables you to display Rotate and Mirror Smart Tags for the `SmartImage` control in Design view. When you open a page in the browser after clicking the Rotate action in Design view, the image is rotated (see Figure 36.18).

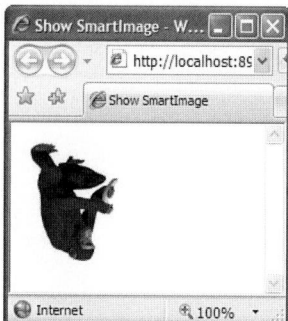

FIGURE 36.18 Adding Smart Tags to a control.

NOTE

You can view the `SmartImage` control by opening the `ShowSmartImage.aspx` page included in the downloadable code on the website that accompanies this book.

Summary

In this chapter, you learned how to build basic controls in ASP.NET Framework. First, you learned how to create both fully rendered and composite controls. You also learned how to combine the features of fully rendered and composite controls by creating hybrid controls.

You learned how to preserve the values of control properties in View State. You learned the difference between View State and Control State and how to use both features of the framework.

Next, you learned how to handle postback data and events. You saw how you can process form data submitted to the server. You also learned how you can raise a server-side event that is initiated by a postback.

This chapter examined the topic of building controls that represent a collection of items. You learned how to use the `ParseChildren` attribute to parse the inner content of a control in different ways. You also learned how to alter the parsing of a control's content by overriding the `AddParsedSubObject()` method and by creating custom `ControlBuilders`.

Finally, you saw two methods of modifying the appearance of a control in Design view. You learned how to apply design-time attributes to a control and its properties. You also learned how to associate a `ControlDesigner` with a custom control.

Building Templated Databound Controls

The ASP.NET Framework is a framework. If you don't like anything about the framework, you always have the option of extending it. In particular, if you discover that the standard databound controls in the framework don't do everything you need, you can create a custom databound control.

In this chapter, you learn how to create custom controls that work like the ASP.NET GridView, DetailsView, ListView, and FormView controls. In the first part of this chapter, you learn how to create controls that support templates. You learn how to implement controls that support both standard templates and two-way databinding templates. You also learn how to supply a control with a default template.

The last part of this chapter is devoted to the topic of databound controls. You learn about the new base control classes included in the framework that were supplied to make it easier to create custom databound controls. We create a custom templated databound control.

Creating Templated Controls

A template enables you to customize the layout of a control. Furthermore, a template can contain expressions that are not evaluated until runtime.

The ASP.NET Framework supports two types of templates. First, you can create a one-way databinding template. You use a one-way databinding template to display data items. In a one-way databinding template, you use the Eval() expression to display the value of a data item.

Second, you have the option of creating a two-way databinding template. A two-way databinding template can not only display data items, but also can update data items. You can use the Bind() expression in a two-way databinding template to both display a data item and extract the value of a data item.

Typically, you use templates with a databound control. For example, the GridView, Repeater, DataList, FormView, and DetailsView controls all support an ItemTemplate that enables you to format the data items that these controls display. However, you can use a template even when you are not displaying a set of data items. For example, the Login control supports a LayoutTemplate that enables you to customize the appearance of the Login form.

This part of this chapter concentrates on creating nondatabound controls that support templates. In the next part of this chapter, you learn how to use templates with databound controls.

Implementing the ITemplate Interface

You create a one-way databinding template by adding a property to a control that returns an object that implements the ITemplate interface. The ITemplate interface includes one method:

▶ **InstantiateIn**—Instantiates the contents of a template in a particular control.

You are not required to implement the InstantiateIn() method. The ASP.NET Framework creates the method for you automatically. You call the InstantiateIn method in your control to add the contents of a template to your control.

For example, the control in Listing 37.1 represents an article. The Article control includes a template named ItemTemplate, which lays out the elements of the article: title, author, and contents.

LISTING 37.1   Article.cs

```
using System;
using System.Web;
using System.Web.UI;
using System.Web.UI.WebControls;

namespace myControls
{
    public class Article : CompositeControl
    {

        private string _title;
        private string _author;
        private string _contents;
```

```
    private ITemplate _itemTemplate;

    public string Title
    {
        get { return _title; }
        set { _title = value; }
    }

    public string Author
    {
        get { return _author; }
        set { _author = value; }
    }

    public string Contents
    {
        get { return _contents; }
        set { _contents = value; }
    }

    [TemplateContainer(typeof(Article))]
    [PersistenceMode(PersistenceMode.InnerProperty)]
    public ITemplate ItemTemplate
    {
        get { return _itemTemplate; }
        set { _itemTemplate = value; }
    }

    protected override void CreateChildControls()
    {
        _itemTemplate.InstantiateIn(this);
    }
    }

}
```

The Article control contains a property named ItemTemplate that returns an object that implements the ITemplate interface. This property is decorated with two attributes: TemplateContainer and PersistenceMode.

The TemplateContainer attribute specifies the type of control that contains the template. For the Article control, the template is contained in the Article control. Therefore, the Article control's type is passed to the TemplateContainer attribute.

The PersistenceMode attribute indicates how a property is persisted in an ASP.NET page. The possible values are Attribute, EncodedInnerDefaultProperty, InnerDefaultProperty, and InnerProperty. We want to declare the ItemTemplate like this:

```
<custom:Article
  runat="server">
  <ItemTemplate>
  ... template contents ...
  </ItemTemplate>
</custom:Article>
```

Because we want to declare the ItemTemplate inside the Article control, the PersistenceMode attribute needs to be set to the value InnerProperty.

The Article control overrides the base WebControl class's CreateChildControls() method. The ItemTemplate is added as a child control to the Article control. Any controls contained in the template become child controls of the current control.

The page in Listing 37.2 illustrates how you can use the Article control and its ItemTemplate.

LISTING 37.2   ShowArticle.aspx

```
<%@ Page Language="C#" %>
<%@ Register TagPrefix="custom" Namespace="myControls" %>
<!DOCTYPE html PUBLIC "-//W3C//DTD XHTML 1.0 Transitional//EN"
"http://www.w3.org/TR/xhtml1/DTD/xhtml1-transitional.dtd">
<script runat="server">

    void Page_Load()
    {
        Article1.Title = "Creating Templated Databound Controls";
        Article1.Author = "Stephen Walther";
        Article1.Contents = "Blah, blah, blah, blah...";
        Article1.DataBind();
    }

</script>
<html xmlns="http://www.w3.org/1999/xhtml" >
<head id="Head1" runat="server">
    <title>Show Article</title>
</head>
<body>
    <form id="form1" runat="server">
    <div>

    <custom:Article
```

```
            id="Article1"
            Runat="server">
            <ItemTemplate>

            <h1><%# Container.Title %></h1>
            <em>By <%# Container.Author %></em>
            <br /><br />
            <%# Container.Contents %>

            </ItemTemplate>
      </custom:Article>

      </div>
      </form>
</body>
</html>
```

When you open the page in Listing 32.2, the contents of the ItemTemplate display (see
Figure 37.1).

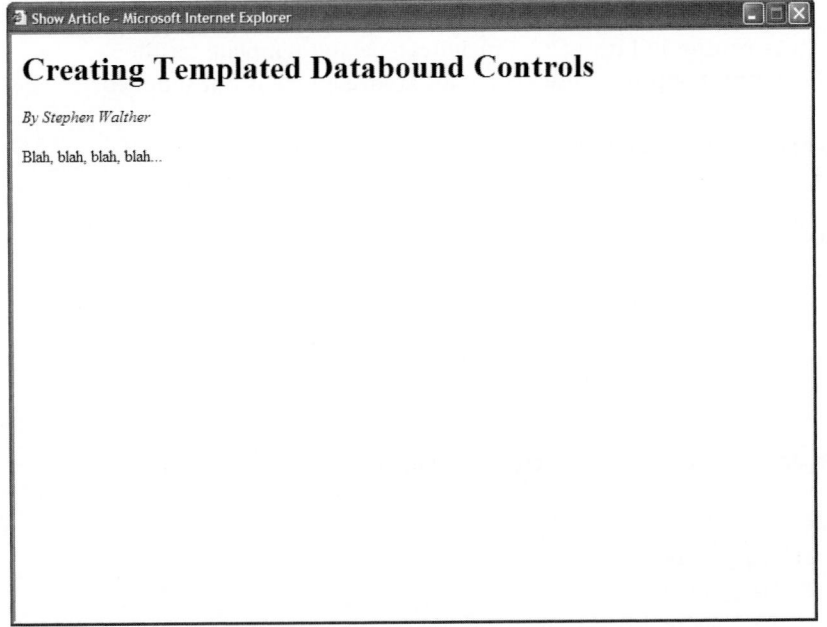

FIGURE 37.1   Using a template to display an article.

In the Page_Load() method, the Title, Author, and Contents properties of the article are set. These properties are used within databinding expressions within the Article control's ItemTemplate. For example, the value of the Title property displays with the following databinding expression:

```
<%# Container.Title %>
```

The Container keyword refers to the current *binding container*. In this case, the binding container is the Article control. Therefore, you can refer to any property of the Article control by using the Container keyword.

The Article control's DataBind() method is called at the end of the Page_Load() method. Don't forget to call this method when you include databinding expressions in a template. If you don't call this method, the databinding expressions are never evaluated and displayed.

Creating a Default Template

The previous section discussed the ITemplate interface's InstantiateIn() method. Normally, you don't implement the InstantiateIn() method; you let ASP.NET Framework do it for you. However, if you want to supply a control with a default template, you need to implement this method.

The modified Article control in Listing 37.3 includes a default template for the ItemTemplate. The default template is used when an ItemTemplate is not supplied.

LISTING 37.3   ArticleWithDefault.cs

```
using System;
using System.Web;
using System.Web.UI;
using System.Web.UI.WebControls;

namespace myControls
{

    public class ArticleWithDefault : CompositeControl
    {

        private string _title;
        private string _author;
        private string _contents;

        private ITemplate _itemTemplate;

        public string Title
        {
```

```
        get { return _title; }
        set { _title = value; }
    }

    public string Author
    {
        get { return _author; }
        set { _author = value; }
    }

    public string Contents
    {
        get { return _contents; }
        set { _contents = value; }
    }

    [TemplateContainer(typeof(ArticleWithDefault))]
    [PersistenceMode(PersistenceMode.InnerProperty)]
    public ITemplate ItemTemplate
    {
        get { return _itemTemplate; }
        set { _itemTemplate = value; }
    }

    protected override void CreateChildControls()
    {
        if (_itemTemplate == null)
            _itemTemplate = new ArticleDefaultTemplate();
        _itemTemplate.InstantiateIn(this);
    }
}

public class ArticleDefaultTemplate : ITemplate
{
    public void InstantiateIn(Control container)
    {
        Label lblTitle = new Label();
        lblTitle.DataBinding += new EventHandler(lblTitle_DataBinding);

        Label lblAuthor = new Label();
        lblAuthor.DataBinding += new EventHandler(lblAuthor_DataBinding);

        Label lblContents = new Label();
        lblContents.DataBinding += new EventHandler(lblContents_DataBinding);
```

37

```
            container.Controls.Add(lblTitle);
            container.Controls.Add(new LiteralControl("<br />"));
            container.Controls.Add(lblAuthor);
            container.Controls.Add(new LiteralControl("<br />"));
            container.Controls.Add(lblContents);
        }


        void lblTitle_DataBinding(object sender, EventArgs e)
        {
            Label lblTitle = (Label)sender;
            ArticleWithDefault container =
➥(ArticleWithDefault)lblTitle.NamingContainer;
            lblTitle.Text = container.Title;
        }


        void lblAuthor_DataBinding(object sender, EventArgs e)
        {
            Label lblAuthor = (Label)sender;
            ArticleWithDefault container =
➥(ArticleWithDefault)lblAuthor.NamingContainer;
            lblAuthor.Text = container.Author;
        }


        void lblContents_DataBinding(object sender, EventArgs e)
        {
            Label lblContents = (Label)sender;
            ArticleWithDefault container =
➥(ArticleWithDefault)lblContents.NamingContainer;
            lblContents.Text = container.Contents;
        }


    }


}
```

The control in Listing 37.3 is similar to the control created in the previous section;
however, the CreateChildControls() method has been modified. The new version of the
CreateChildControls() method tests whether there is an ItemTemplate. If no
ItemTemplate exists, an instance of the ArticleDefaultTemplate class is created.

The ArticleDefaultTemplate class, which is also included in Listing 37.3, implements the
ITemplate interface. In particular, the class implements the InstantiateIn() method,
which creates all the controls that appear in the template.

In Listing 37.3, three Label controls are created that correspond to the Title, Author, and
Contents properties. The DataBinding event is handled for all three of these Label

controls. When the DataBind() method is called, the DataBinding event is raised for each child control in the Article control. At that time, the values of the Title, Author, and Contents properties are assigned to the Text properties of the Label controls.

The page in Listing 37.4 illustrates how you can use the modified Article control.

LISTING 37.4   ShowArticleWithDefault.aspx

```
<%@ Page Language="C#" %>
<%@ Register TagPrefix="custom" Namespace="myControls" %>
<!DOCTYPE html PUBLIC "-//W3C//DTD XHTML 1.0 Transitional//EN"
"http://www.w3.org/TR/xhtml1/DTD/xhtml1-transitional.dtd">
<script runat="server">

    void Page_Load()
    {
        ArticleWithDefault1.Title = "Creating Templated Databound Controls";
        ArticleWithDefault1.Author = "Stephen Walther";
        ArticleWithDefault1.Contents = "Blah, blah, blah, blah...";
        ArticleWithDefault1.DataBind();
    }

</script>
<html xmlns="http://www.w3.org/1999/xhtml" >
<head id="Head1" runat="server">
    <title>Show Article with Default Template</title>
</head>
<body>
    <form id="form1" runat="server">
    <div>

    <custom:ArticleWithDefault
        id="ArticleWithDefault1"
        Runat="server" />

    </div>
    </form>
</body>
</html>
```

The ArticleWithDefault control in Listing 37.4 does not include an ItemTemplate. When the page displays in a browser, the contents of the ItemTemplate are supplied by the ArticleDefaultTemplate class (see Figure 37.2).

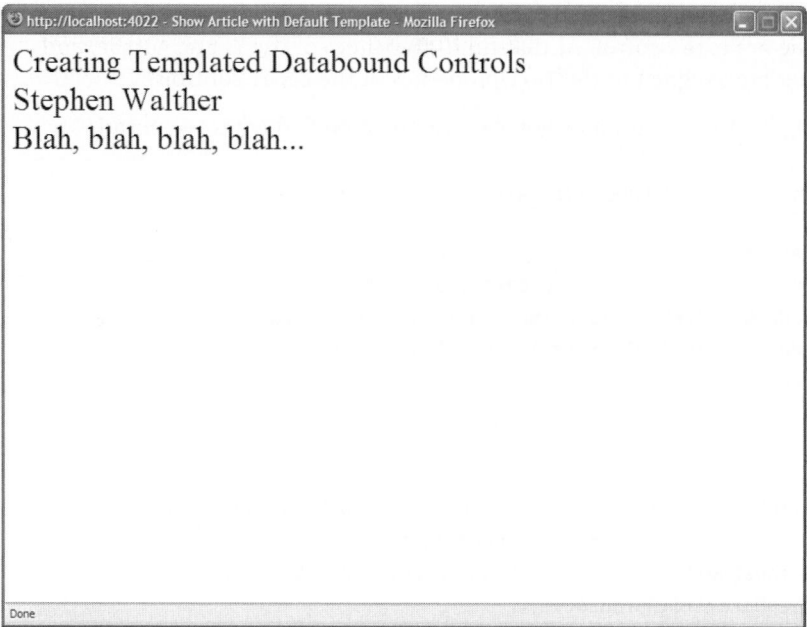

FIGURE 37.2   Displaying an article with a default template.

Supporting Simplified Databinding

The databinding expressions used in the previous two sections might seem a little odd. For example, we used the following databinding expression to refer to the Title property:

```
<%# Container.Title %>
```

When you use a databinding expression with one of the standard ASP.NET controls, such as the GridView control, you typically use a databinding expression that looks like this:

```
<%# Eval("Title") %>
```

Why the difference? The standard ASP.NET controls support a simplified databinding syntax. If you want to support this simplified syntax in your custom controls, you must implement the IDataItemContainer interface.

The IDataItemContainer includes the following three properties, which you are required to implement:

▶ **DataItem**—Returns the value of the data item.

▶ **DataItemIndex**—Returns the index of the data item from its data source.

▶ **DisplayIndex**—Returns the index of the data item as it is displayed in a control.

Typically, you implement the IDataItemContainer when creating a databound control. For example, you wrap up each record retrieved from a database table in an object that implements the IDataItemContainer interface. That way, you can use a simplified data-binding expression to refer to the value of a particular database record column.

In this section, we create a nondatabound control that supports the simplified databinding syntax. The control is named the Product control, and is included in Listing 37.5.

LISTING 37.5 Product.cs

```
using System;
using System.Web;
using System.Web.UI;
using System.Web.UI.WebControls;

namespace myControls
{
    public class Product : CompositeControl
    {
        private ITemplate _itemTemplate;
        private ProductItem _item;

        public string Name
        {
            get
            {
                EnsureChildControls();
                return _item.Name;
            }
            set
            {
                EnsureChildControls();
                _item.Name = value;
            }
        }

        public Decimal Price
        {
            get
            {
                EnsureChildControls();
                return _item.Price;
            }
            set
            {
                EnsureChildControls();
```

```csharp
                _item.Price = value;
            }
        }

        [TemplateContainer(typeof(ProductItem))]
        [PersistenceMode(PersistenceMode.InnerProperty)]
        public ITemplate ItemTemplate
        {
            get { return _itemTemplate; }
            set { _itemTemplate = value; }
        }

        protected override void CreateChildControls()
        {
            _item = new ProductItem();
            _itemTemplate.InstantiateIn(_item);
            Controls.Add(_item);
        }
    }

    public class ProductItem : WebControl, IDataItemContainer
    {
        private string _name;
        private decimal _price;

        public string Name
        {
            get { return _name; }
            set { _name = value; }
        }

        public decimal Price
        {
            get { return _price; }
            set { _price = value; }
        }

        public object DataItem
        {
            get
            {
                return this;
            }
        }
```

```
        public int DataItemIndex
        {
            get { return 0; }
        }

        public int DisplayIndex
        {
            get { return 0; }
        }
    }

}
```

The file in Listing 37.5 actually contains two classes: Product and ProductItem. The Product control includes an ItemTemplate property. The TemplateContainer attribute that decorates this property associates the ProductItem class with the ItemTemplate.

In the CreateChildControls() method, the ItemTemplate is instantiated into the ProductItem class, which in turn, is added to the controls collection of the Product class.

The ProductItem class implements the IDataItemContainer interface. Implementing the DataItemIndex and DisplayIndex properties is a little silly because there is only one data item. However, you are required to implement all the properties of an interface.

The page in Listing 37.6 illustrates how you can use the Product control with the simplified databinding syntax.

LISTING 37.6   ShowProduct.aspx

```
<%@ Page Language="C#" %>
<%@ Register TagPrefix="custom" Namespace="myControls" %>
<!DOCTYPE html PUBLIC "-//W3C//DTD XHTML 1.0 Transitional//EN"
"http://www.w3.org/TR/xhtml1/DTD/xhtml1-transitional.dtd">

<script runat="server">

    void Page_Load()
    {
        Product1.Name = "Laptop Computer";
        Product1.Price = 1254.12m;
        Product1.DataBind();
    }

</script>

<html xmlns="http://www.w3.org/1999/xhtml" >
```

```
<head id="Head1" runat="server">
    <title>Show Product</title>
</head>
<body>
    <form id="form1" runat="server">
    <div>

    <custom:Product
        id="Product1"
        Runat="Server">
        <ItemTemplate>
        Name: <%# Eval("Name") %>
        <br />
        Price: <%# Eval("Price", "{0:c}") %>
        </ItemTemplate>
    </custom:Product>

    </div>
    </form>
</body>
</html>
```

Notice that the Eval() method is used in the Product control's ItemTemplate. For example, the expression Eval("Name") displays the product name. If you prefer, you can still use the Container.Name syntax. However, the Eval() syntax is more familiar to ASP.NET developers.

Supporting Two-Way Databinding

Two-way databinding is a feature introduced with ASP.NET 2.0 Framework. Two-way databinding enables you to extract values from a template. You can use a two-way databinding expression not only to display the value of a data item, but also to update the value of a data item.

You create a template that supports two-way databinding expressions by creating a property that returns an object that implements the IBindableTemplate interface. This interface inherits from the ITemplate interface. It has the following two methods:

▶ **InstantiateIn**—Instantiates the contents of a template in a particular control.

▶ **ExtractValues**—Returns a collection of databinding expression values from a template.

For example, the ProductForm control in Listing 37.7 represents a form for editing an existing product. The control includes a property named EditItemTemplate that represents a two-way databinding template.

LISTING 37.7 ProductForm.cs

```csharp
using System;
using System.Web;
using System.Web.UI;
using System.Web.UI.WebControls;
using System.ComponentModel;
using System.Collections.Specialized;

namespace myControls
{

    public class ProductForm : CompositeControl
    {
        public event EventHandler ProductUpdated;

        private IBindableTemplate _editItemTemplate;
        private ProductFormItem _item;
        private IOrderedDictionary _results;

        public IOrderedDictionary Results
        {
            get { return _results; }
        }

        public string Name
        {
            get
            {
                EnsureChildControls();
                return _item.Name;
            }
            set
            {
                EnsureChildControls();
                _item.Name = value;
            }
        }

        public decimal Price
        {
            get
            {
                EnsureChildControls();
                return _item.Price;
            }
```

37

```
        set
        {
            EnsureChildControls();
            _item.Price = value;
        }
    }

    [TemplateContainer(typeof(ProductFormItem), BindingDirection.TwoWay)]
    [PersistenceMode(PersistenceMode.InnerProperty)]
    public IBindableTemplate EditItemTemplate
    {
        get { return _editItemTemplate; }
        set { _editItemTemplate = value; }
    }

    protected override void CreateChildControls()
    {
        _item = new ProductFormItem();
        _editItemTemplate.InstantiateIn(_item);
        Controls.Add(_item);
    }

    protected override bool OnBubbleEvent(object source, EventArgs args)
    {
        _results = _editItemTemplate.ExtractValues(_item);
        if (ProductUpdated != null)
            ProductUpdated(this, EventArgs.Empty);
        return true;
    }
}

public class ProductFormItem : WebControl, IDataItemContainer
{
    private string _name;
    private decimal _price;

    public string Name
    {
        get { return _name; }
        set { _name = value; }
    }

    public decimal Price
    {
        get { return _price; }
```

```
            set { _price = value; }
        }

        public object DataItem
        {
            get { return this; }
        }

        public int DataItemIndex
        {
            get { return 0; }
        }

        public int DisplayIndex
        {
            get { return 0; }
        }


    }
}
```

The EditItemTemplate property does two special things. First, the property returns an object that implements the IBindableTemplate interface. Second, the TemplateContainer attribute that decorates the property includes a BindingDirection parameter. You can assign one of two possible values to BindingDirection: OneWay and TwoWay.

The ProductForm includes an OnBubbleEvent() method, which is called when a child control of the ProductForm control raises an event. For example, if someone clicks a Button control contained in the EditItemTemplate, the OnBubbleEvent() method is called.

In Listing 37.7, the OnBubbleEvent() method calls the EditItemTemplate's ExtractValues() method. This method is supplied by ASP.NET Framework because the EditItemTemplate is marked as a two-way databinding template.

The ExtractValues() method returns an OrderedDictionary collection that contains name/value pairs that correspond to each of the databinding expressions contained in the EditItemTemplate. The ProductForm control exposes this collection of values with its Results property. After the values are extracted, the control raises a ProductUpdated event.

The page in Listing 37.8 illustrates how you can use the ProductForm control to update the properties of a product.

LISTING 37.8   ShowProductForm.aspx

```
<%@ Page Language="C#" %>
<%@ Register TagPrefix="custom" Namespace="myControls" %>
<!DOCTYPE html PUBLIC "-//W3C//DTD XHTML 1.0 Transitional//EN"
"http://www.w3.org/TR/xhtml1/DTD/xhtml1-transitional.dtd">

<script runat="server">

    void Page_Load()
    {
        if (!Page.IsPostBack)
        {
            ProductForm1.Name = "Laptop";
            ProductForm1.Price = 433.12m;
            ProductForm1.DataBind();
        }
    }

    protected void ProductForm1_ProductUpdated(object sender, EventArgs e)
    {
        lblName.Text = ProductForm1.Results["Name"].ToString();
        lblPrice.Text = ProductForm1.Results["Price"].ToString();
    }
</script>

<html xmlns="http://www.w3.org/1999/xhtml" >
<head id="Head1" runat="server">
    <title>Show ProductForm</title>
</head>
<body>
    <form id="form1" runat="server">
    <div>

    <custom:ProductForm
        id="ProductForm1"
        Runat="server" OnProductUpdated="ProductForm1_ProductUpdated">
        <EditItemTemplate>

        <asp:Label
            id="lblName"
            Text="Product Name:"
            AssociatedControlID="txtName"
            Runat="server" />
        <asp:TextBox
            id="txtName"
```

```
            Text='<%# Bind("Name") %>'
            Runat="server" />
        <br /><br />
        <asp:Label
            id="lblPrice"
            Text="Product Price:"
            AssociatedControlID="txtPrice"
            Runat="server" />
        <asp:TextBox
            id="txtPrice"
            Text='<%# Bind("Price") %>'
            Runat="server" />
        <br /><br />
        <asp:Button
            id="btnUpdate"
            Text="Update"
            Runat="server" />

    </EditItemTemplate>
    </custom:ProductForm>

    <hr />
    New Product Name:
    <asp:Label
        id="lblName"
        Runat="server" />

    <br /><br />

    New Product Price:
    <asp:Label
        id="lblPrice"
        Runat="server" />

    </div>
    </form>
</body>
</html>
```

In the Page_Load() method in Listing 37.8, the ProductForm Name and Price properties are set. Next, the DataBind() is called to cause the ProductForm control to evaluate its databinding expressions.

The ProductForm control's EditItemTemplate includes Bind() expressions instead of Eval() expressions. You use Bind() expressions in a two-way databinding template.

The EditItemTemplate includes a Button control. When you click the Button control, the ProductForm control's OnBubbleEvent() method executes, the values are retrieved from the EditItemTemplate, and the ProductUpdated event is raised.

The page in Listing 37.8 handles the ProductUpdated event and displays the new values with two Label controls (see Figure 37.3).

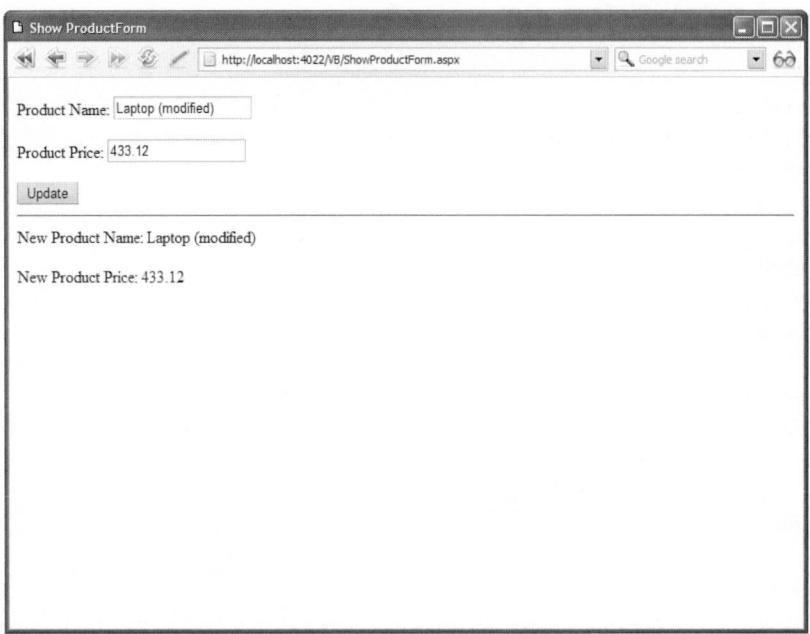

FIGURE 37.3   Using a two-way databinding template.

Creating Templated Databound Controls

In this section, you learn how to build templated databound controls. A databound control can be bound to a DataSource control such as the SqlDataSource or ObjectDataSource controls.

The ASP.NET Framework provides you with a number of base classes that you can use when creating a custom databound control. So, let's look at some tables and figures. Table 37.1 lists the base control classes for all the standard ASP.NET databound controls. Figure 37.4 displays the inheritance hierarchy of all the new databound controls in ASP.NET Framework. Typically, you inherit from one of the leaf nodes. You create a control that derives from the base CompositeDataBoundControl, HierarchicalDataBoundControl, or ListControl class.

TABLE 37.1   Base Databound Control Classes

Control	Base Control
ListView	DataBoundControl
GridView, DetailsView, FormView	CompositeDataBoundControl
Menu, TreeView	HierarchicalDataBoundControl
DropDownList, ListBox RadioButtonList, CheckBoxList, BulletedList	ListControl
DataList, DataGrid	BaseDataList
Repeater	Control

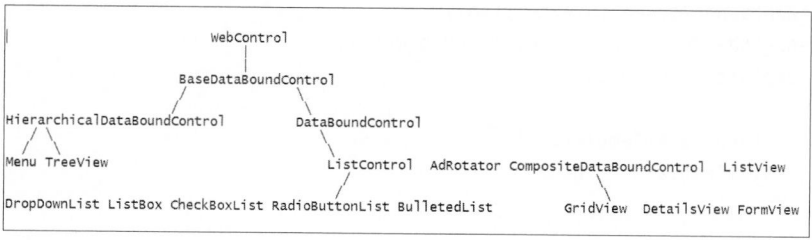

FIGURE 37.4   Databound control inheritance hierarchy.

This chapter concentrates on inheriting new controls from the base CompositeDataBoundControl class. This is the easiest base class to use when you want to display one or more database records and use templates.

> **NOTE**
>
> You learned how to create controls that inherit from the base ListControl class in Chapter 10, "Using List Controls."

Creating a `DivView` Control

Let's start simple. In this section, we create a custom databound control named the DivView control, which displays a set of data items (database records) in HTML <div> tags.

The DivView control inherits from the base CompositeDataBoundControl class and overrides a single method of the base class. The DivView control overrides the base class's CreateChildControls() method.

The DivView control is contained in Listing 37.9.

LISTING 37.9   DivView.cs

```csharp
using System;
using System.Collections;
using System.Web;
using System.Web.UI;
using System.Web.UI.WebControls;

namespace AspNetUnleashed
{
    public class DivView : CompositeDataBoundControl
    {
        private ITemplate _itemTemplate;

        [TemplateContainer(typeof(DivViewItem))]
        [PersistenceMode(PersistenceMode.InnerProperty)]
        public ITemplate ItemTemplate
        {
            get { return _itemTemplate; }
            set { _itemTemplate = value; }
        }

        protected override int CreateChildControls(IEnumerable dataSource, bool
dataBinding)
        {
            int counter = 0;
            foreach (object dataItem in dataSource)
            {
                DivViewItem contentItem = new DivViewItem(dataItem, counter);
                _itemTemplate.InstantiateIn(contentItem);
                Controls.Add(contentItem);
                counter++;
            }
            DataBind(false);
            return counter;
        }

        protected override HtmlTextWriterTag TagKey
        {
            get
            {
                return HtmlTextWriterTag.Div;
            }
        }
    }
```

```
public class DivViewItem : WebControl, IDataItemContainer
{
    private object _dataItem;
    private int _index;


    public object DataItem
    {
        get { return _dataItem; }
    }

    public int DataItemIndex
    {
        get { return _index; }
    }

    public int DisplayIndex
    {
        get { return _index; }
    }

    protected override HtmlTextWriterTag TagKey
    {
        get
        {
            return HtmlTextWriterTag.Div;
        }
    }

    public DivViewItem(object dataItem, int index)
    {
        _dataItem = dataItem;
        _index = index;
    }


}
}
```

The DivView control supports an ItemTemplate used to format each of its data items. You are required to supply an ItemTemplate when you use the DivView control.

All the work happens in the CreateChildControls() method. This is not the same CreateChildControls() method included in the base System.Web.UI.Control class. The DivView control overrides the CompositeDataBounControl's CreateChildControls() method.

The `CreateChildControls()` method accepts the following two parameters:

▶ **dataSource**—Represents all the data items from the data source.

▶ **dataBinding**—Represents whether the `CreateChildControls()` method is called when the data items are retrieved from the data source.

The `CreateChildControls()` method is called every time that the `DivView` control renders its data items. When the control is first bound to a `DataSource` control, the `dataSource` parameter represents the data items retrieved from the `DataSource` control. After a postback, the `dataSource` parameter contains a collection of null values, but the correct number of null values.

After a postback, the contents of the data items can be retrieved from View State. As long as the correct number of child controls is created, the Framework can rebuild the contents of the databound control.

You can use the `dataBinding` parameter to determine whether the data items from the data source actually represent anything. Typically, the `dataBinding` parameter has the value `True` when the page first loads and the value `False` after each postback.

The `DataBind()` method is called after the child controls are created. You must call the `DataBind()` method when a template includes databinding expressions. Otherwise, the databinding expressions are never evaluated.

The page in Listing 37.10 illustrates how you can bind the `DivView` control to a `SqlDataSource` control.

LISTING 37.10   ShowDivView.aspx

```
<%@ Page Language="C#" %>
<%@ Register TagPrefix="custom" Namespace="AspNetUnleashed" %>
<!DOCTYPE html PUBLIC "-//W3C//DTD XHTML 1.0 Transitional//EN"
    "http://www.w3.org/TR/xhtml1/DTD/xhtml1-transitional.dtd">
<html xmlns="http://www.w3.org/1999/xhtml" >
<head id="Head1" runat="server">
    <style type="text/css">
        .movies
        {
            width:500px;
        }
        .movies div
        {
            border:solid 1px black;
            padding:10px;
            margin:10px;
```

```
        }
    </style>
    <title>Show DivView</title>
</head>
<body>
    <form id="form1" runat="server">
    <div>

    <custom:DivView
        id="lstMovies"
        DataSourceID="srcMovies"
        CssClass="movies"
        Runat="Server">
        <ItemTemplate>
        <h1><%# Eval("Title") %></h1>
        Director: <%# Eval("Director") %>
        </ItemTemplate>
    </custom:DivView>


    <asp:SqlDataSource
        id="srcMovies"
        ConnectionString="<%$ ConnectionStrings:Movies %>"
        SelectCommand="SELECT Title, Director FROM Movies"
        Runat="server" />

    <br />
    <asp:LinkButton
        id="lnkReload"
        Text="Reload"
        Runat="server" />

    </div>
    </form>
</body>
</html>
```

In Listing 37.10, the SqlDataSource control represents the Movies database table. The DivView control includes an ItemTemplate that formats each of the columns from this database table (see Figure 37.5).

FIGURE 37.5   Displaying database records with the `DivView` control.

Summary

This chapter was devoted to the topic of building templated databound controls. In the first part, you learned how to support templates in your custom controls. You learned how to create templates that support both one-way and two-way databinding expressions. You also learned how to create a default template for a control.

The second half of this chapter focused on the topic of building databound controls. You learned how to create a simple `DivView` control that displays the records from a database table in a series of HTML `<div>` tags.

Using Server-Side ASP.NET AJAX

Users of modern web applications have changed quite a bit since the first days of the web. When the web was new and when functional, commercial websites were few and far between, the users of web applications were a generally complacent and easy-to-please audience.

Today, web application users don't just want more, they demand more. They demand that websites be fast, responsive, and interactive. They don't want an entire page to reload just because a small piece needs to be changed. Most important, they don't want to sit and wait in front of an unresponsive user interface while background processing takes place.

To meet the increasing demands of web users, a new technology called AJAX (Asynchronous JavaScript and XML) was created. This enabled already-rendered web pages to make asynchronous calls and retrieve XML, which could then be used to modify the existing page. The first evidence of this type of technology actually showed up in Microsoft Outlook's web access product. Since then, web application users have been demanding unprecedented levels of interactivity and responsiveness.

The key to giving users this responsiveness lies in the combination of asynchronous messaging calls and JavaScript (or jQuery or any number of JavaScript-based frameworks). In this chapter you learn about one small piece of this puzzle: Microsoft's server-side Ajax controls such as the UpdatePanel, a control that enables postbacks within a region of the page to modify only that portion of the page and not interrupt the user's overall experience. We also provide an overview of two controls that support the UpdatePanel: the Timer and the UpdateProgress.

The Ajax Vision

ASP.NET is a *server-side* technology for building web applications. Almost all the work happens on the web server and not the web browser. Whenever you perform an action in an ASP.NET page—such as clicking a button or sorting a GridView—the entire page must be posted back to the web server. Any significant action on a page results in a postback.

If you think about it, this is incredibly inefficient. When you perform a postback in an ASP.NET page, the entire page must be transported across the Internet from browser to server. Next, the .NET class that corresponds to the page must re-render the entire page again from scratch. Finally, the finished page must be sent back across the Internet to the browser. This whole long, slow, agonizing process must occur even if you are updating a tiny section of the page.

Using a server-side technology such as ASP.NET results in a bad user experience. Every time a user performs some action on a page, the universe temporarily freezes. Whenever you perform a postback, the browser locks, the page jumps, and the users must wait patiently twiddling their thumbs while the page is reconstructed. All of us have grown accustomed to this awful user experience; however, we would never design our desktop applications in the same way.

When the members of the ASP.NET team invented ASP.NET in the late 1990s, there was good reason to embrace the server side. Getting a page that was written in JavaScript to work consistently across different browsers, and even across different versions of the same browser, was difficult. The server side was safe and reliable.

However, we've reached a tipping point. Web developers are discovering that if they want to build truly great applications, they need to leave the safety of the server side and enter the wilds of the client side. Today's popular web applications such as Facebook, Google Gmail, and YouTube all rely heavily on Ajax-based functionality.

An Ajax application is a client-side web application written using native browser technologies such as JavaScript and the DOM. A pure Ajax application is a web application that consists of a single page and performs all its communications with the web server through web service calls.

> **NOTE**
>
> Applications that use client-side technologies such as Flash, Flex, Java applets, and Silverlight don't count as Ajax applications because these are proprietary technologies. An Ajax application must use native browser technologies.

Unlike a server-side web application, an Ajax application can be responsive to user interaction. If a user clicks a button in a server-side web application, the button Click event doesn't actually happen until the page gets posted back to the server. In a server-side application, the button Click event gets shifted in time and space. In a client-side Ajax application, on the other hand, the button `Click` event happens when it happens: right on the browser.

In an Ajax application, the user interface layer is located in the browser (where it should be). The business logic and data access layers are located on the server. The user interface layer accesses the business logic layer through web services.

Server-Side Ajax Versus Client-Side Ajax

Microsoft has a complicated relationship with Ajax. On the one hand, the company wants to provide its existing ASP.NET developers with an easy way to implement Ajax functionality without having to learn JavaScript. On the other hand, Microsoft recognizes that the client is a powerful area to enable developers. Therefore, it wants to provide web developers with the tools they need to build pure client-side Ajax applications. For these reasons, Microsoft has both a server-side Ajax framework and a client-side Ajax framework.

If you want to retrofit an existing ASP.NET application to take advantage of Ajax, you can take advantage of Microsoft's server-side AJAX framework. To take advantage of the server-side framework, you don't need to write a single line of JavaScript code. You can continue to build ASP.NET pages with server-side controls in the standard way. You learn how to take advantage of the server-side AJAX framework in this chapter.

The advantage of the server-side framework is that it provides existing ASP.NET developers with a painless method of doing Ajax. The disadvantage of the server-side framework is that it doesn't escape all the problems associated with a server-side framework. You still have to run back to the server whenever you perform any client-side action.

The Microsoft client-side AJAX framework (which we discuss in Chapter 40, "Client-Side AJAX with jQuery") embraces the client side. When building applications with the Microsoft client-side AJAX framework, you must build the application by using JavaScript. The advantage of building applications with the client-side framework is that you can build rich and responsive web applications. You can build web applications with the same rich interactivity as a desktop application.

Debugging Ajax Applications

Before we start discussing the Microsoft AJAX frameworks, you need to be aware of two crucial debugging tools. Debugging Ajax applications presents challenges not present in a normal server-side application. If an Ajax call fails, you won't necessarily know. You need a way of monitoring the Ajax calls that happen between the browser and server.

The first tool is Fiddler. You can download this tool (for free) at http://www.fiddlertool. com. Fiddler enables you to view HTTP requests and responses, including Ajax calls. Fiddler works by installing itself as a proxy between your web browser and the rest of the universe. You can use Fiddler with Internet Explorer, Mozilla Firefox, Opera, Safari, and just about any other browser.

After you install Fiddler, from Microsoft Internet Explorer, you can launch the tool by selecting Tools, Fiddler2. After Fiddler launches, every browser request and response is recorded in the Fiddler Web Sessions pane. You can click a request and then click the Session Inspector tab to see the full request and response (see Figure 38.1).

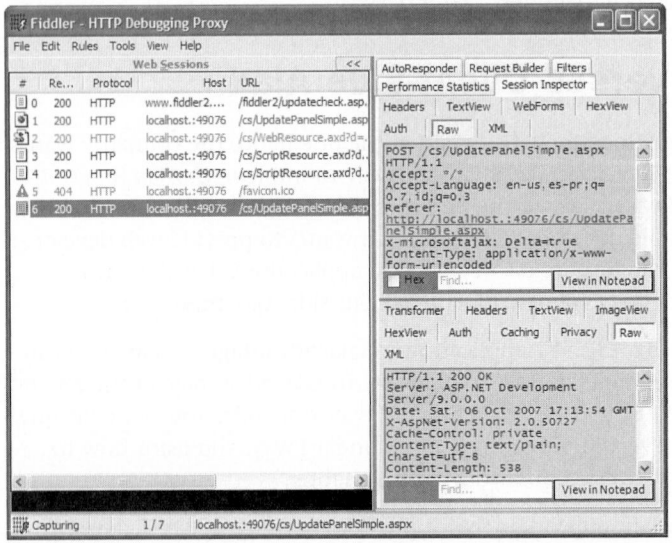

FIGURE 38.1   Using Fiddler to inspect an Ajax request and response.

NOTE

If you can't get Fiddler to capture page requests from localhost, try adding a period directly after localhost in the browser address bar. For example, make a request that looks like this:

http://localhost.:6916/Original/Feedback.aspx

The other critical Ajax debugging tool is Firebug, which is a free Firefox extension. You can download Firebug by launching Firefox and selecting Tools, Add-ons. Next, click the Get Extensions link. Finally, enter **Firebug** into the search box and follow the installation instructions.

Firebug, like Fiddler, enables you to monitor Ajax calls, but it enables you to do much more. After you install Firebug, you can click the bug icon at the bottom right of the Firefox browser to open Firebug (see Figure 38.2).

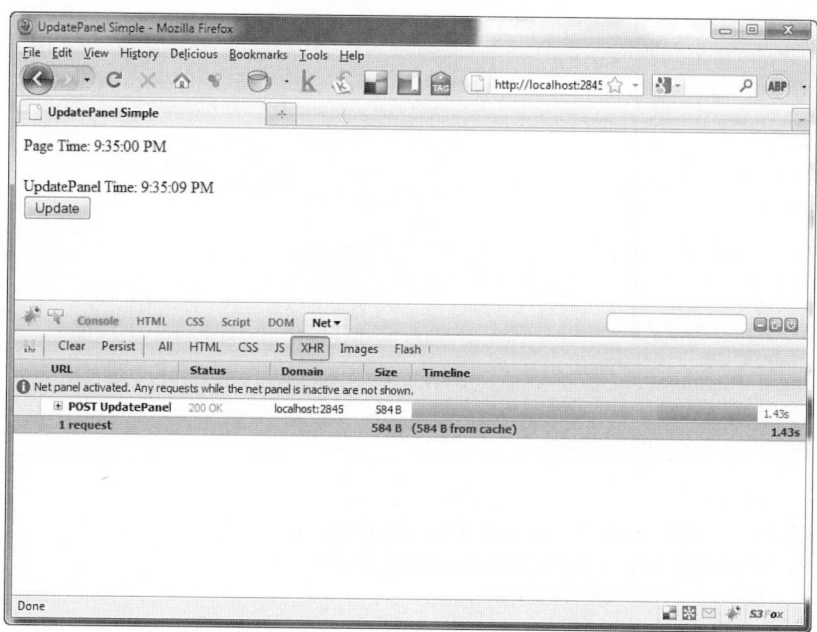

FIGURE 38.2   Using Firebug in Mozilla Firefox.

Firebug has several useful features for debugging JavaScript applications. For example, it enables you to set breakpoints in JavaScript scripts, inspect DOM elements, and determine which CSS rules apply to which elements in a page. Right now, however, I want you to notice that you can use Firebug to monitor Ajax requests and responses. If you click the Net tab and the XHR tab, every Ajax call appears in the Firebug window. You can click a particular Ajax request to see the full request and response interaction between browser and server.

Using the UpdatePanel Control

Microsoft's server-side AJAX framework consists of one main control: UpdatePanel. The UpdatePanel control enables you to update a portion of a page without updating the entire page. In other words, it enables you to perform partial-page rendering.

Let's start with a super-simple example of a page that uses the UpdatePanel control. The page in Listing 38.1 contains a ScriptManager control and an UpdatePanel control. The UpdatePanel control contains a single Button control. When you click the button, only the content contained in the UpdatePanel control is refreshed (see Figure 38.3).

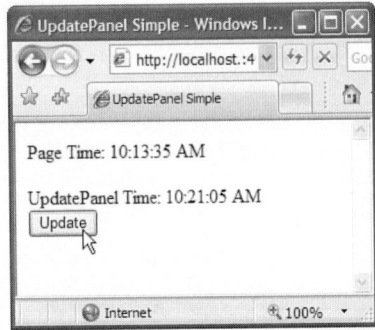

FIGURE 38.3   Using the UpdatePanel control.

LISTING 38.1   UpdatePanelSimple.aspx

```
<%@ Page Language="C#" %>
<!DOCTYPE html PUBLIC "-//W3C//DTD XHTML 1.0 Transitional//EN"
"http://www.w3.org/TR/xhtml1/DTD/xhtml1-transitional.dtd">
<html xmlns="http://www.w3.org/1999/xhtml">
<head runat="server">
    <title>UpdatePanel Simple</title>
</head>
<body>
    <form id="form1" runat="server">

    <asp:ScriptManager ID="ScriptManager1" runat="server" />

    Page Time: <%= DateTime.Now.ToString("T") %>
    <br /><br />

    <asp:UpdatePanel
        id="up1"
        runat="server">
        <ContentTemplate>
        UpdatePanel Time: <%= DateTime.Now.ToString("T") %>
        <br />
        <asp:Button
            id="btn"
            Text="Update"
            runat="server" />
        </ContentTemplate>
    </asp:UpdatePanel>

    </form>
</body>
</html>
```

The page in Listing 38.1 displays the current time both inside and outside the
`UpdatePanel` control. When you click the button, only the time within the `UpdatePanel`
control is refreshed.

Let's look at a more realistic example that just begs for some Ajax (see Figure 38.4). The
page in Listing 38.2 does not use any of the ASP.NET AJAX controls. It contains two
cascading `DropDownList` controls. The first `DropDownList` enables you to pick a state, and
the second `DropDownList` enables you to pick a city. The list of cities changes depending
on the state selected.

FIGURE 38.4   A page with cascading `DropDownList` controls.

LISTING 38.2   `CascadingDropDownsNoAjax.aspx`

```
<%@ Page Language="C#" %>
<!DOCTYPE html PUBLIC "-//W3C//DTD XHTML 1.0 Transitional//EN"
"http://www.w3.org/TR/xhtml1/DTD/xhtml1-transitional.dtd">
<html xmlns="http://www.w3.org/1999/xhtml">
<head runat="server">
    <title>Cascading DropDownList Controls</title>
</head>
<body>
    <form id="form1" runat="server">
    <div>

    <asp:Label
        id="lblState"
        Text="State:"
        AssociatedControlID="ddlState"
        Runat="server" />
    <asp:DropDownList
        id="ddlState"
        DataSourceID="srcState"
        DataTextField="State"
        DataValueField="State"
```

```
            AutoPostBack="true"
            Runat="server" />
        <asp:SqlDataSource
            id="srcState"
            ConnectionString='<%$ ConnectionStrings:con %>'
            SelectCommand="SELECT State FROM State
                ORDER BY State"
            Runat="server" />

        <br /><br />


        <asp:Label
            id="Label1"
            Text="City:"
            AssociatedControlID="ddlCity"
            Runat="server" />
        <asp:DropDownList
            id="ddlCity"
            DataSourceID="srcCity"
            DataTextField="City"
            AutoPostBack="true"
            Runat="server" />
        <asp:SqlDataSource
            id="srcCity"
            ConnectionString='<%$ ConnectionStrings:con %>'
            SelectCommand="SELECT City FROM City
                WHERE State=@State
                ORDER BY City"
            Runat="server">
            <SelectParameters>
                <asp:ControlParameter Name="State" ControlID="ddlState" />
            </SelectParameters>
        </asp:SqlDataSource>

    </div>
    </form>
</body>
</html>
```

When you select a state using the first DropDownList control, there is a click, and the page posts back to itself to populate the second DropDownList control with matching cities. Clearly, the user experience here is less than optimal. All work must stop while the page performs a postback.

Let's fix up this page with some Ajax. The page in Listing 38.3 is exactly the same as the page in Listing 38.2, except for two changes. First, the page now contains a `ScriptManager` control. Second, and more important, the `DropDownList` controls in Listing 38.3 are wrapped inside an `UpdatePanel` control.

LISTING 38.3 `CascadingDropDownsAjax.aspx`

```
<%@ Page Language="C#" %>
<!DOCTYPE html PUBLIC "-//W3C//DTD XHTML 1.0 Transitional//EN"
"http://www.w3.org/TR/xhtml1/DTD/xhtml1-transitional.dtd">
<html xmlns="http://www.w3.org/1999/xhtml">
<head id="Head1" runat="server">
    <title>Cascading DropDownList Controls</title>
</head>
<body>
    <form id="form1" runat="server">
    <div>

    <asp:ScriptManager
        id="sm1"
        Runat="server" />

    <asp:UpdatePanel
        id="UpdatePanel1"
        Runat="server">
        <ContentTemplate>

    <asp:Label
        id="lblState"
        Text="State:"
        AssociatedControlID="ddlState"
        Runat="server" />
    <asp:DropDownList
        id="ddlState"
        DataSourceID="srcState"
        DataTextField="State"
        DataValueField="State"
        AutoPostBack="true"
        Runat="server" />
    <asp:SqlDataSource
        id="srcState"
        ConnectionString='<%$ ConnectionStrings:con %>'
        SelectCommand="SELECT State FROM State
            ORDER BY State"
        Runat="server" />
```

```
    <br /><br />


    <asp:Label
        id="Label1"
        Text="City:"
        AssociatedControlID="ddlCity"
        Runat="server" />
    <asp:DropDownList
        id="ddlCity"
        DataSourceID="srcCity"
        DataTextField="City"
        AutoPostBack="true"
        Runat="server" />
    <asp:SqlDataSource
        id="srcCity"
        ConnectionString='<%$ ConnectionStrings:con %>'
        SelectCommand="SELECT City FROM City
            WHERE State=@State
            ORDER BY City"
        Runat="server">
        <SelectParameters>
            <asp:ControlParameter Name="State" ControlID="ddlState" />
        </SelectParameters>
    </asp:SqlDataSource>

    </ContentTemplate>
    </asp:UpdatePanel>

    </div>
    </form>
</body>
</html>
```

In Listing 38.3, when you select a new state with the first DropDownList control, matching cities display in the second DropDownList control. However, there is no click and there is no noticeable postback. The browser doesn't freeze, and the page does not jump. Everything happens smoothly and professionally through the magic of Ajax.

The ScriptManager control in Listing 38.3 adds the necessary JavaScript scripts to enable Ajax. Anytime you create a page that uses Ajax, regardless of whether you are doing server-side or client-side Ajax, you'll add a ScriptManager control to the page.

The UpdatePanel control is the control that is doing all the Ajax work here. It hijacks the normal postback that would happen when you select a new item in the first DropDownList control. The UpdatePanel hijacks the normal postback and performs a "sneaky" postback to grab the new content in the background.

Let's look at another page that takes advantage of the UpdatePanel control. The page in Listing 38.4 represents a simple customer feedback form (see Figure 38.5). The page contains a FormView control and a GridView control. The FormView control renders the insert form, and the GridView control is used to display previous customer responses. You can sort the contents of GridView in order of the different columns.

FIGURE 38.5   Entering customer feedback into an Ajax-enabled form.

LISTING 38.4   Feedback.aspx

```aspx
<%@ Page Language="C#" %>
<!DOCTYPE html PUBLIC "-//W3C//DTD XHTML 1.0 Transitional//EN"
"http://www.w3.org/TR/xhtml1/DTD/xhtml1-transitional.dtd">
<html xmlns="http://www.w3.org/1999/xhtml">
<head runat="server">
    <title>Feedback</title>
</head>
<body>
    <form id="form1" runat="server">
    <div>

    <asp:ScriptManager
        id="sm1"
        Runat="server" />
```

```
<asp:UpdatePanel
    id="up1"
    Runat="server">
    <ContentTemplate>

<asp:FormView
    id="frmFeedback"
    DataSourceId="srcFeedback"
    DefaultMode="Insert"
    Runat="server">
    <InsertItemTemplate>

    <asp:Label
        id="lblName"
        Text="Name:"
        AssociatedControlID="txtName"
        Runat="server" />
    <asp:RequiredFieldValidator
        id="valName"
        Text="Required"
        ControlToValidate="txtName"
        Runat="server" />
    <br />
    <asp:TextBox
        id="txtName"
        Text='<%# Bind("Name") %>'
        Runat="server" />
    <br /><br />
    <asp:Label
        id="lblComment"
        Text="Comment:"
        AssociatedControlID="txtComment"
        Runat="server" />
    <asp:RequiredFieldValidator
        id="valComment"
        Text="Required"
        ControlToValidate="txtComment"
        Runat="server" />
    <br />
    <asp:TextBox
        id="txtComment"
        Text='<%# Bind("Comment") %>'
        TextMode="MultiLine"
        Columns="50"
        Rows="3"
        Runat="server" />
```

```
        <br /><br />
        <asp:Button
            id="btnSubmit"
            Text="Submit"
            CommandName="Insert"
            Runat="server" />
        </InsertItemTemplate>
    </asp:FormView>

    <br /><br />

    <asp:GridView
        id="grdFeedback"
        DataSourceID="srcFeedback"
        AllowSorting="true"
        Runat="server" />

    </ContentTemplate>
    </asp:UpdatePanel>


    <asp:SqlDataSource
        id="srcFeedback"
        ConnectionString='<%$ ConnectionStrings:con %>'
        SelectCommand="SELECT Id,Name,Comment,DateSubmitted
            FROM Feedback"
        InsertCommand="INSERT Feedback (Name,Comment)
            VALUES (@Name,@Comment)"
        Runat="server" />

    </div>
    </form>
</body>
</html>
```

Because the UpdatePanel control in Listing 38.4 contains both the FormView and GridView, you can interact with the page without performing a single postback. When you submit the form, the form data is submitted back to the server using Ajax. When you sort the columns in the GridView, the sorted rows are retrieved from the server through an Ajax call.

The UpdatePanel control has six important properties:

▶ **ChildrenAsTriggers**—Gets or sets a Boolean value that indicates whether child controls should trigger an asynchronous postback automatically.

▶ **ContentTemplateContainer**—Gets the container for the UpdatePanel control's ContentTemplate. You can add controls to the ContentTemplate programmatically using this property.

▶ **IsInPartialRendering**—Gets a Boolean value indicating whether the UpdatePanel is rendered in response to an asynchronous postback.

▶ **RenderMode**—Gets or sets a value that indicates whether the contents of an UpdatePanel should be enclosed in an HTML <div> or <span> tag. Possible values are Block (the default) and Inline.

▶ **Triggers**—Gets a list of controls that trigger the UpdatePanel to perform either an asynchronous or synchronous postback.

▶ **UpdateMode**—Gets or sets a value indicating when the content of the UpdatePanel is updated. Possible values are Always (the default) and Conditional.

The UpdatePanel also supports the following single important method:

▶ **Update()**—Causes the UpdatePanel to update its contents.

You learn how to take advantage of these properties and methods in the following sections.

Specifying UpdatePanel Triggers

By default, an UpdatePanel hijacks any postbacks that any of its child controls performs. For example, if a Button control is contained in an UpdatePanel, the UpdatePanel hijacks the button Click event and performs an Ajax call instead of the normal postback.

You can cause an UpdatePanel to refresh its contents from a control located outside of the UpdatePanel by specifying a trigger. For example, the page in Listing 38.5 contains a Button control outside of an UpdatePanel that causes the UpdatePanel to refresh its content.

LISTING 38.5 TriggerUpdatePanel.aspx

```
<%@ Page Language="C#" %>
<!DOCTYPE html PUBLIC "-//W3C//DTD XHTML 1.0 Transitional//EN"
"http://www.w3.org/TR/xhtml1/DTD/xhtml1-transitional.dtd">
<html xmlns="http://www.w3.org/1999/xhtml">
<head runat="server">
    <title>Trigger Update Panel</title>
</head>
<body>
    <form id="form1" runat="server">
    <div>
```

```
    <asp:ScriptManager
        id="sm1"
        Runat="server" />

    Page Time: <%= DateTime.Now.ToString("T") %>
    <br />
    <asp:Button
        id="btnUpdate"
        Text="Update"
        Runat="server" />

    <asp:UpdatePanel
        id="up1"
        Runat="server">
        <Triggers>
            <asp:AsyncPostBackTrigger
                ControlID="btnUpdate"
                EventName="Click" />
        </Triggers>
        <ContentTemplate>

        Update Panel Time: <%= DateTime.Now.ToString("T") %>

        </ContentTemplate>
    </asp:UpdatePanel>

    </div>
    </form>
</body>
</html>
```

38

The UpdatePanel in Listing 38.5 includes a Triggers subelement that contains a single AsyncPostBackTrigger. This trigger points to the Button control located outside of the UpdatePanel named btnUpdate. Because the UpdatePanel contains this trigger, clicking the Button control causes the UpdatePanel to refresh its contents.

If you want, you can prevent the UpdatePanel from refreshing its contents unless you have explicitly created a trigger. If you set the UpdatePanel control's ChildrenAsTriggers property to the value false, you must explicitly create a trigger to update the contents of the UpdatePanel.

The UpdatePanel supports two types of triggers: AsyncPostBackTrigger and PostBackTrigger. The AsyncPostBackTrigger causes an asynchronous (Ajax) postback. The PostBackTrigger causes a normal entire-page postback.

You'll rarely use a PostBackTrigger. The only situation in which it makes sense to use a PostBackTrigger is when you need to mix buttons that cause asynchronous postbacks and normal postbacks in the same UpdatePanel control. For example, because you cannot perform a file upload without performing a normal entire-page postback, if a file-upload button is contained in an UpdatePanel, you need to create a PostBackTrigger for the file-upload button.

Nesting UpdatePanel Controls

One UpdatePanel can contain another UpdatePanel. You can nest UpdatePanels to your heart's content, just like Russian nesting dolls.

Nesting UpdatePanel controls is useful when you want to control how much of a page gets refreshed during an asynchronous postback. Sometimes, you might need to update only a tiny portion of a page, and other times you might need to update the entire page.

For example, the page in Listing 38.6 contains two nested UpdatePanels. The outer UpdatePanel contains a DropDownList, FormView, and ListView control. The inner UpdatePanel contains only the ListView control (see Figure 38.6).

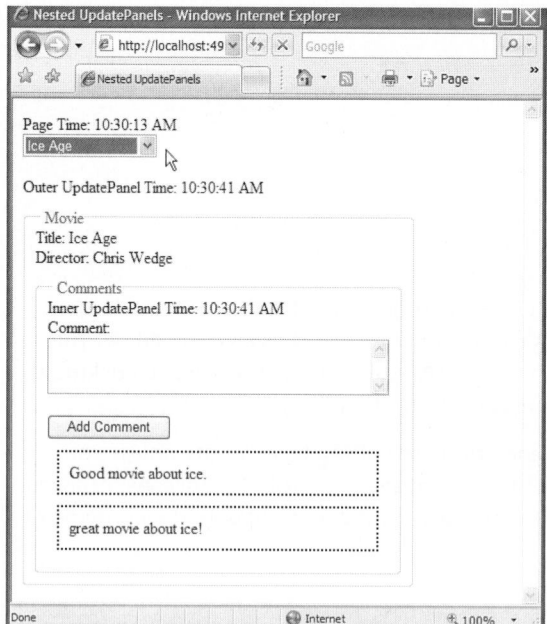

FIGURE 38.6   Page with nested UpdatePanel controls.

LISTING 38.6   NestedUpdatePanels.aspx

```
<%@ Page Language="C#" %>
<!DOCTYPE html PUBLIC "-//W3C//DTD XHTML 1.0 Transitional//EN"
"http://www.w3.org/TR/xhtml1/DTD/xhtml1-transitional.dtd">
<html xmlns="http://www.w3.org/1999/xhtml">
<head runat="server">
    <title>Nested UpdatePanels</title>
    <style type="text/css">
        fieldset
        {
            padding: 10px;
        }
        .comment
        {
            padding: 10px;
            border: dotted 2px black;
            margin: 10px;
        }
    </style>
</head>
<body>
    <form id="form1" runat="server">
    <div>

    <asp:ScriptManager
        id="sm1"
        Runat="server" />

    Page Time: <%= DateTime.Now.ToString("T") %>
    <br />

    <asp:DropDownList
        id="ddlMovie"
        DataSourceID="srcMovies"
        DataValueField="Id"
        DataTextField="Title"
        AutoPostBack="true"
        Runat="server" />
    <asp:SqlDataSource
        id="srcMovies"
        ConnectionString='<%$ ConnectionStrings:con %>'
        SelectCommand="SELECT Id, Title FROM Movie"
        Runat="server" />

    <br /><br />
```

38

```
<asp:UpdatePanel ID="upOuter" UpdateMode="Conditional" runat="server">
<Triggers>
    <asp:AsyncPostBackTrigger ControlID="ddlMovie" />
</Triggers>
<ContentTemplate>

Outer UpdatePanel Time: <%= DateTime.Now.ToString("T") %>
<br />

<asp:FormView
    id="frmMovie"
    DataSourceID="srcMovie"
    Runat="server">
    <ItemTemplate>
    <fieldset>
    <legend>Movie</legend>
    Title: <%# Eval("Title") %>
    <br />
    Director: <%# Eval("Director") %>

    <asp:UpdatePanel ID="upInner" runat="server">
    <ContentTemplate>
    <asp:ListView
        id="lstMovieComments"
        DataSourceID="srcMovieComments"
        InsertItemPosition="FirstItem"
        Runat="server">
        <LayoutTemplate>
            <fieldset>
            <legend>Comments</legend>
            Inner UpdatePanel Time: <%= DateTime.Now.ToString("T") %>
            <div id="itemContainer" runat="server">
            </div>
            </fieldset>
        </LayoutTemplate>
        <ItemTemplate>
            <div class="comment">
            <%# Eval("Comment") %>
            </div>
        </ItemTemplate>
        <InsertItemTemplate>
        <asp:Label
            id="lblComment"
            Text="Comment:"
            AssociatedControlID="txtComment"
```

```
                    Runat="server" />
            <br />
            <asp:TextBox
                id="txtComment"
                Text='<%# Bind("Comment") %>'
                TextMode="MultiLine"
                Columns="40"
                Rows="3"
                Runat="server" />
            <br />
            <asp:Button
                id="btnInsert"
                Text="Add Comment"
                CommandName="Insert"
                Runat="server" />
        </InsertItemTemplate>
    </asp:ListView>
    </ContentTemplate>
    </asp:UpdatePanel>
    <asp:SqlDataSource
        id="srcMovieComments"
        ConnectionString='<%$ ConnectionStrings:con %>'
        SelectCommand="SELECT Id, Comment
            FROM MovieComment
            WHERE MovieId=@MovieId"
        InsertCommand="INSERT MovieComment (Comment,MovieId)
            VALUES (@Comment,@MovieId)"
        Runat="server">
        <SelectParameters>
            <asp:ControlParameter Name="MovieId" ControlID="ddlMovie" />
        </SelectParameters>
        <InsertParameters>
            <asp:ControlParameter Name="MovieId" ControlID="ddlMovie" />
        </InsertParameters>
    </asp:SqlDataSource>
    </fieldset>
    </ItemTemplate>
</asp:FormView>
</ContentTemplate>
</asp:UpdatePanel>
<asp:SqlDataSource
    id="srcMovie"
    ConnectionString='<%$ ConnectionStrings:con %>'
    SelectCommand="SELECT Id, Title, Director
        FROM Movie
        WHERE Id=@Id"
```

38

```
        Runat="server">
        <SelectParameters>
            <asp:ControlParameter Name="Id" ControlID="ddlMovie" />
        </SelectParameters>
    </asp:SqlDataSource>

    </div>
    </form>
</body>
</html>
```

When you select a movie by using the DropDownList control, the entire page is updated. When you add a new comment to the movie with the ListView control, on the other hand, only the comments portion of the page is updated.

There are two UpdatePanel controls. The first UpdatePanel control has an ID of upOuter. It includes a trigger that points to the DropDownList control used to select a movie. This UpdatePanel control has its UpdateMode property set to the value Conditional. If the UpdateMode property was not set to this value, the outer UpdatePanel would refresh its content when the Add Comment button contained in the inner UpdatePanel control was clicked.

The inner UpdatePanel is named upInner. This UpdatePanel surrounds the ListView used to display the form for adding and displaying movie comments. When you add a new movie comment, only the comments area of the page is updated and not the entire page.

The page, the outer UpdatePanel, and the inner UpdatePanel all display the current time. When you select a new movie, the time displayed by both the outer and inner UpdatePanel—but not the page—changes. When you add a new comment, only the time displayed by the inner UpdatePanel changes.

In general, for performance reasons, you should place the smallest possible area that you need to update inside of an UpdatePanel control. The larger the area contained in an UpdatePanel, the more content that must be passed across the Internet when the UpdatePanel is updated. By nesting UpdatePanel controls, you have more granular control over the content that gets updated in a page.

Updating UpdatePanels Programmatically

The UpdatePanel control includes an Update() method. You can use this method to update the content of an UpdatePanel programmatically during an asynchronous postback.

Two properties determine when an UpdatePanel control updates its contents: UpdateMode and ChildrenAsTriggers. If you set the UpdateMode property to the value Conditional and you set ChildrenAsTriggers to the value false (and you don't define any triggers), the only way to update an UpdatePanel control's content is by calling the Update() method.

For example, the page in Listing 38.7 enables you to search movies by title. The page contains two UpdatePanel controls. The first UpdatePanel control contains a TextBox control and a Button control. The second UpdatePanel control contains a GridView control, which uses a Movie class (which can be found in the source code on the book's website) to communicate with the datbase. When you click the button, the Button Click event is raised on the server through an asynchronous postback. The second UpdatePanel that contains the GridView of results is updated if, and only if, any results are found that match the search query.

LISTING 38.7   UpdateUpdatePanel.aspx

```
<%@ Page Language="C#" %>
<!DOCTYPE html PUBLIC "-//W3C//DTD XHTML 1.0 Transitional//EN"
"http://www.w3.org/TR/xhtml1/DTD/xhtml1-transitional.dtd">
<script runat="server">
    protected void btnSearch_Click(object sender, EventArgs e)
    {
        ArrayList results = Movie.Search(txtSearch.Text);
        if (results.Count > 0)
        {
            grdResults.DataSource = results;
            grdResults.DataBind();
            upResults.Update();
        }
    }
</script>
<html xmlns="http://www.w3.org/1999/xhtml">
<head runat="server">
    <title>Update UpdatePanel</title>
</head>
<body>
    <form id="form1" runat="server">
    <div>

    <asp:ScriptManager
        id="sm1"
        Runat="server" />

    <asp:UpdatePanel
        id="upSearch"
        Runat="server">
        <ContentTemplate>
        <asp:TextBox
            id="txtSearch"
```

```
            Runat="server" />
        <asp:Button
            id="btnSearch"
            Text="Search"
            OnClick="btnSearch_Click"
            Runat="server" />
        </ContentTemplate>
    </asp:UpdatePanel>

    <asp:UpdatePanel
        id="upResults"
        UpdateMode="Conditional"
        Runat="server">
        <ContentTemplate>
        Results Time: <%= DateTime.Now.ToString("T") %>
        <br />
        <asp:GridView
            id="grdResults"
            runat="server" />
        </ContentTemplate>
    </asp:UpdatePanel>

    </div>
    </form>
</body>
</html>
```

UpdatePanels and JavaScript

You must take special care when using JavaScript with UpdatePanel controls. If you use the standard methods of the ClientScriptManager class for working with JavaScript, they will fail when called during an asynchronous request.

For example, I often use the Page.ClientScript.RegisterStartupScript() method from my server-side code to inject a JavaScript script into a page dynamically. The page in Listing 38.8 contains a Delete All Files button. When you click the button, and the FileHelper.DeleteAll() method returns true, a JavaScript alert box displays the message All Files Deleted Successfully! (see Figure 38.7).

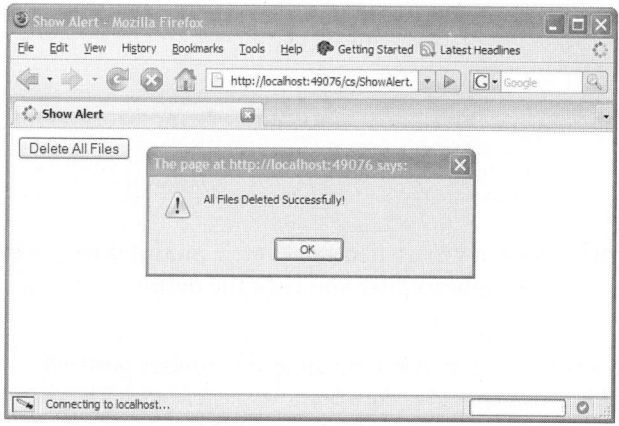

FIGURE 38.7   Displaying a JavaScript alert.

LISTING 38.8   ShowAlert.aspx

```
<%@ Page Language="C#" %>
<!DOCTYPE html PUBLIC "-//W3C//DTD XHTML 1.0 Transitional//EN"
"http://www.w3.org/TR/xhtml1/DTD/xhtml1-transitional.dtd">
<script runat="server">

    protected void btnDeleteAll_Click(object sender, EventArgs e)
    {
        if (FileHelper.DeleteAll() == true)
        {
            string script = @"alert('All Files Deleted Successfully!');";
            Page.ClientScript.RegisterStartupScript(this.GetType(), "filesDeleted",
            ➥script, true);
        }
    }
</script>
<html xmlns="http://www.w3.org/1999/xhtml">
<head runat="server">
    <title>Show Alert</title>
</head>
<body>
    <form id="form1" runat="server">
    <div>

    <asp:Button
        id="btnDeleteAll"
        Text="Delete All Files"
        OnClick="btnDeleteAll_Click"
```

```
        Runat="server" />

    </div>
    </form>
</body>
</html>
```

Unfortunately, the page in Listing 38.8 does not work when the Button control is wrapped in an UpdatePanel. The JavaScript alert never appears after you click the button. The page fails silently.

If you need to inject JavaScript into a page when performing an asynchronous postback, you need to take advantage of the methods exposed by the ScriptManager class. The ScriptManager class duplicates all the standard JavaScript methods of the ClientScriptManager class, including the following:

▶ **RegisterArrayDeclaration()**—Enables you to add a JavaScript array to the page.

▶ **RegisterClientScriptBlock()**—Enables you to add an inline JavaScript script right after the opening <form> tag.

▶ **RegisterClientScriptInclude()**—Enables you to add a JavaScript <script src=""> tag to a page.

▶ **RegisterClientScriptResource()**—Enables you to add a reference to a JavaScript file embedded in an assembly.

▶ **RegisterExpandoAttribute()**—Enables you to register a tag expando.

▶ **RegisterOnSubmitStatement()**—Enables you to register a JavaScript script that is executed when the form is submitted.

▶ **RegisterStartupScript()**—Enables you to add an inline JavaScript script right before the closing <form> tag.

The page in Listing 38.9 demonstrates how you can add JavaScript from the server to a page when performing an asynchronous postback.

LISTING 38.9   ShowAlertUpdatePanel.aspx

```
<%@ Page Language="C#" %>
<!DOCTYPE html PUBLIC "-//W3C//DTD XHTML 1.0 Transitional//EN"
"http://www.w3.org/TR/xhtml1/DTD/xhtml1-transitional.dtd">
<script runat="server">

    protected void btnDeleteAll_Click(object sender, EventArgs e)
    {
        if (FileHelper.DeleteAll() == true)
        {
```

```
              string script = @"alert('All Files Deleted Successfully!');";
              ScriptManager.RegisterStartupScript(this, this.GetType(), "filesDeleted",
              ➥script, true);
          }
      }
</script>
<html xmlns="http://www.w3.org/1999/xhtml">
<head id="Head1" runat="server">
    <title>Show Alert UpdatePanel</title>
</head>
<body>
    <form id="form1" runat="server">
    <div>

    <asp:ScriptManager
        id="sm1"
        Runat="server" />

    <asp:UpdatePanel id="up1" runat="server">
    <ContentTemplate>
    UpdatePanel Time: <%= DateTime.Now.ToString("T") %>
    <br />
    <asp:Button
        id="btnDeleteAll"
        Text="Delete All Files"
        OnClick="btnDeleteAll_Click"
        Runat="server" />

    </ContentTemplate>
    </asp:UpdatePanel>

    </div>
    </form>
</body>
</html>
```

In Listing 38.9, the Button control is wrapped in an UpdatePanel. When you click the
button, the ScriptManager.RegisterStartupScript() method adds the JavaScript alert to
the page dynamically.

UpdatePanel Server-Side Page Execution Life Cycle

You need to understand that a server-side page goes through its normal page execution life
cycle when you perform an asynchronous postback. The Page PreInit, Init, Load, and
PreRender events are raised for an asynchronous postback in just the same way as these
events are raised for a normal postback.

The page in Listing 38.10 logs each server event and displays the log in a `BulletedList` control (see Figure 38.8).

FIGURE 38.8   Viewing an asynchronous postback's server lifecycle.

LISTING 38.10   ServerLifecycle.aspx

```
<%@ Page Language="C#" %>
<!DOCTYPE html PUBLIC "-//W3C//DTD XHTML 1.0 Transitional//EN"
"http://www.w3.org/TR/xhtml1/DTD/xhtml1-transitional.dtd">
<script runat="server">

    public ArrayList _log = new ArrayList();

    void Page_PreInit()
    {
        _log.Add("PreInit " + sm1.IsInAsyncPostBack);
    }

    void Page_Init()
    {
        _log.Add("Init " + sm1.IsInAsyncPostBack);
    }

    void Page_Load()
    {
        _log.Add("Load " + sm1.IsInAsyncPostBack);
    }

    void Page_PreRender()
    {
        _log.Add("PreRender " + sm1.IsInAsyncPostBack);

        // Show Lifecycle log
        bltLog.DataSource = _log;
```

```
            bltLog.DataBind();
        }
    </script>

    <html xmlns="http://www.w3.org/1999/xhtml">
    <head runat="server">
        <title>Server Lifecycle</title>
    </head>
    <body>
        <form id="form1" runat="server">
        <div>

        <asp:ScriptManager
            id="sm1"
            runat="server" />

        <asp:UpdatePanel
            id="up1"
            runat="server">
            <ContentTemplate>
            <asp:Button
                id="btnLog"
                Text="Show Server Page Lifecycle"
                Runat="server" />
            <asp:BulletedList
                id="bltLog"
                Runat="server" />

            </ContentTemplate>
        </asp:UpdatePanel>

        </div>
        </form>
    </body>
    </html>
```

When you first open the page in Listing 38.10, each page event is listed in the BulletedList control. Next to each event, you see the word *False*. The ScriptManager.IsInAsyncPostBack property displays whether the page is processed within a normal postback or an asynchronous postback.

The page includes an UpdatePanel that contains a Button control. Clicking the button initiates an asynchronous postback. After you click the button, the exact same list of events appears in the BulletedList control. The exact same events are raised during an asynchronous postback as are raised during a normal postback.

> **NOTE**
>
> `ScriptManager.IsInAsyncPostBack` has the value `False` when the `PreInit` event is raised during an asynchronous postback. This `IsInAsyncPostBack` property is updated after this event. (So it is just wrong.)

UpdatePanel Client-Side Page Execution Life Cycle

A page that contains a `ScriptManager` control not only has a server-side page execution life cycle, it also has a client-side page execution life cycle. The following series of events happen on the client-side:

- ▶ `Application.init`—Raised when a page is first requested. This event is not raised during an asynchronous postback.

- ▶ `PageRequestManager.initializeRequest`—Raised before an asynchronous request to the server starts.

- ▶ `PageRequestManager.beginRequest`—Raised before an asynchronous request to the server starts.

- ▶ `PageRequestManager.pageLoading`—Raised after an asynchronous response is received from the server but before `UpdatePanel` content is updated.

- ▶ `PageRequestManager.pageLoaded`—Raised after an asynchronous response is received from the server and after `UpdatePanel` content is updated. Also raised during the initial page request.

- ▶ `Application.load`—Raised during both normal and asynchronous postbacks.

- ▶ `PageRequestManager.endRequest`—Raised after an asynchronous response both when there is and when there isn't an error.

- ▶ `Application.unload`—Raised before the user leaves or reloads the page.

Two client-side objects raise client life-cycle events: `Sys.Application` object and `Sys.WebForms.PageRequestManager`. The `Sys.Application` events happen in a page regardless of whether the page contains `UpdatePanel` controls. The `Sys.WebForms.PageRequestManager` events are tied to `UpdatePanels`.

The page in Listing 38.11 illustrates when each of these client-side events occurs. The page takes advantage of ASP.NET AJAX's client-side trace support. When each client event occurs, `Sys.Debug.trace()` is used to write a message to the Trace Console. Figure 38.9 shows the page after the Async Postback button is clicked.

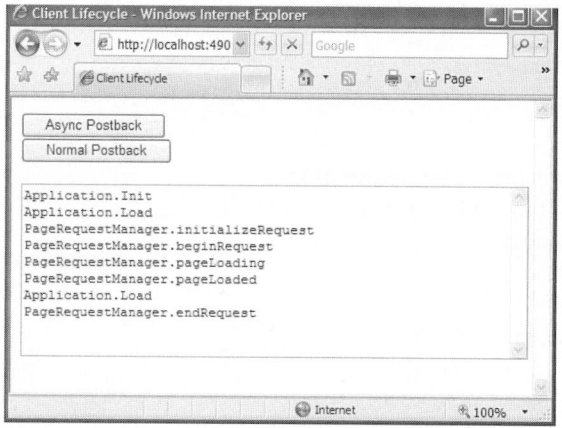

FIGURE 38.9   Viewing an asynchronous page's client execution lifecycle.

LISTING 38.11   ClientLifecycle.aspx

```
<%@ Page Language="C#" %>
<!DOCTYPE html PUBLIC "-//W3C//DTD XHTML 1.0 Transitional//EN"
"http://www.w3.org/TR/xhtml1/DTD/xhtml1-transitional.dtd">
<html xmlns="http://www.w3.org/1999/xhtml">
<head runat="server">
    <title>Client Lifecycle</title>
</head>
<body>
    <form id="form1" runat="server">
    <div>
        <asp:ScriptManager ID="ScriptManager1" runat="server" />

        <asp:UpdatePanel ID="up1" runat="server">
        <ContentTemplate>
            <asp:Button ID="btnAsync" Text="Async Postback" runat="server" />
        </ContentTemplate>
        </asp:UpdatePanel>
        <asp:Button ID="Button1" Text="Normal Postback" runat="server" />

        <br /><br />
        <textarea id="TraceConsole" cols="60" rows="10"></textarea>

    </div>
    </form>
</body>
<script type="text/javascript">

  Sys.Application.add_init(application_init);
```

```
function application_init()
{
  Sys.Debug.trace("Application.Init");

  var prm = Sys.WebForms.PageRequestManager.getInstance();
  prm.add_initializeRequest( prm_initializeRequest );
  prm.add_beginRequest( prm_beginRequest );
  prm.add_pageLoading( prm_pageLoading );
  prm.add_pageLoaded( prm_pageLoaded );
  prm.add_endRequest( prm_endRequest );
}

function pageLoad()
{
  Sys.Debug.trace("Application.Load");
}

function prm_initializeRequest()
{
  Sys.Debug.trace("PageRequestManager.initializeRequest");
}

function prm_beginRequest()
{
  Sys.Debug.trace("PageRequestManager.beginRequest");
}

function prm_pageLoading()
{
  Sys.Debug.trace("PageRequestManager.pageLoading");
}

function prm_pageLoaded()
{
  Sys.Debug.trace("PageRequestManager.pageLoaded");
}

function prm_endRequest()
{
  Sys.Debug.trace("PageRequestManager.endRequest");
}

function pageUnload()
{
  alert("Application.Unload");
```

```
    }

</script>
</html>
```

Because we are discussing client-side events, we have moved over into the JavaScript world. The script in Listing 38.11 has to be written in JavaScript because it executes within the browser and not on the server.

Different information is available during each client-side event. You can access the event information by reading the properties of the second parameter passed to the event handler. What follows is the event information passed to each event handler.

InitializeRequestEventArgs

Passed to the `PageRequestManager.initializeRequest` event handler. Supports the following properties:

▶ **cancel**—Enables you to cancel the current asynchronous postback.

▶ **postBackElement**—The element that caused the asynchronous postback.

▶ **request**—The request object used to perform the asynchronous postback.

BeginRequestEventArgs

Passed to the `PageRequestManager.beginRequest` event handler. Supports the following properties:

▶ **postBackElement**—The element that caused the asynchronous postback.

▶ **request**—The request object used to perform the asynchronous postback.

PageLoadingEventArgs

Passed to the `PageRequestManager.pageLoading` event handler. Supports the following properties:

▶ **dataItems**—The data items registered with the `ScriptManager.RegisterDataItem()` method.

▶ **panelsDeleting**—The array of `UpdatePanel` elements being deleted.

▶ **panelsUpdating**—The array of `UpdatePanel` elements being updated.

PageLoadedEventArgs

Passed to the `PageRequestManager.pageLoaded` event handler. Supports the following properties:

▶ **dataItems**—The data items registered with the `ScriptManager.RegisterDataItem()` method.

▶ **panelsCreated**—The array of `UpdatePanel` elements created.

▶ **panelsUpdated**—The array of `UpdatePanel` elements updated.

ApplicationLoadEventArgs

Passed to the `Application.load` event handler. Supports the following properties:

- ▶ **components**—The array of components created since the last time the `Application.load` event was raised.

- ▶ **isPartialLoad**—Indicates whether the page is executing in the context of an asynchronous postback.

EndRequestEventArgs

Passed to the `PageRequestManager.endRequest` event handler. Supports the following properties:

- ▶ **dataItems**—The data items registered with the `ScriptManager.RegisterDataItem()` method.

- ▶ **error**—The error, if any, that occurred during the asynchronous postback.

- ▶ **errorHandled**—Enables you to suppress the error.

- ▶ **response**—The response associated with the asynchronous postback.

> **NOTE**
>
> You can detect whether a page is executing within the context on an asynchronous post-back within client code by using the `PageRequestManager.isInAsyncPostBack` property.

The page in Listing 38.12 illustrates how you can take advantage of these event properties. The page contains two `UpdatePanel` controls. During an asynchronous call, the border of the active `UpdatePanel` turns the color orange. When the asynchronous call completes, the border of the updated `UpdatePanel` turns green.

> **NOTE**
>
> Later in this chapter, you learn how to use the `UpdateProgress` control to display an `UpdatePanel`'s progress. The method described in this section of handling client events directly is useful when you want to display a custom progress indicator.

LISTING 38.12   UpdatePanelCustomProgress.aspx

```
<%@ Page Language="C#" %>
<!DOCTYPE html PUBLIC "-//W3C//DTD XHTML 1.0 Transitional//EN"
"http://www.w3.org/TR/xhtml1/DTD/xhtml1-transitional.dtd">
<script runat="server">

    protected void btnSubmit_Click(object sender, EventArgs e)
    {
        System.Threading.Thread.Sleep(2000); // sleep 2 seconds
```

```
            }

</script>
<html xmlns="http://www.w3.org/1999/xhtml">
<head runat="server">
    <title>UpdatePanelCustomProgress</title>
    <style type="text/css">
        .normal
        {
            width:300px;
            padding:10px;
            margin:10px;
            border: solid 4px black;
        }

        .updating
        {
            width:300px;
            padding:10px;
            margin:10px;
            border: solid 4px orange;
        }

        .updated
        {
            width:300px;
            padding:10px;
            margin:10px;
            border: solid 4px green;
        }
    </style>
</head>
<body>
    <form id="form1" runat="server">

    <asp:ScriptManager ID="ScriptManager1" runat="server" />

    <div id="panelContainer">
    <asp:UpdatePanel id="up1" UpdateMode="Conditional" runat="server">
    <ContentTemplate>
        <%= DateTime.Now.ToString("T") %>
        <asp:Button
            id="btnSubmit1"
            Text="Submit 1"
            OnClick="btnSubmit_Click"
            Runat="server" />
```

```
    </ContentTemplate>
    </asp:UpdatePanel>

    <asp:UpdatePanel id="up2" UpdateMode="Conditional" runat="server">
    <ContentTemplate>
        <%= DateTime.Now.ToString("T") %>
        <asp:Button
            id="btnSubmit2"
            Text="Submit 2"
            OnClick="btnSubmit_Click"
            Runat="server" />
    </ContentTemplate>
    </asp:UpdatePanel>
    </div>
    </form>
    <script type="text/javascript">
    var prm = Sys.WebForms.PageRequestManager.getInstance();
    prm.add_beginRequest(prm_beginRequest);
    prm.add_pageLoaded(prm_pageLoaded);

    function prm_beginRequest(sender, args)
    {
        var container = args.get_postBackElement().parentNode;
        container.className = 'updating';
    }

    function prm_pageLoaded(sender, args)
    {
        var panelsCreated = args.get_panelsCreated();
        for (var k=0;k<panelsCreated.length;k++)
            panelsCreated[k].className = 'normal';

        var panelsUpdated = args.get_panelsUpdated();
        for (var k=0;k<panelsUpdated.length;k++)
            panelsUpdated[k].className = 'updated';
    }

    </script>
</body>
</html>
```

When the page in Listing 38.12 first loads in your browser, the `PageRequestManager` `pageLoaded` event is raised and the `prm_pageLoaded` event handler executes. This event handler assigns a default CSS class (named `normal`) to each of the `UpdatePanel` controls in

the page. The list of `UpdatePanels` is retrieved from the
`PageLoadedEventArgs.panelsCreated` property.

If you click the first button, the border around the first button turns orange until the
asynchronous postback completes and the border turns green. The same thing happens
when you click the second button.

When you click a button, the `PageRequestManager` `beginRequest` event is raised and the
border around the button turns orange. After the response is returned from the server, the
`PageRequestManager` `pageLoaded` event is raised and the border around the button turns
green. The list of updated UpdatePanels is retrieved from the
`PageLoadedEventArgs.updated` property.

What happens if you click both buttons in rapid succession? In that case, you are attempting to perform two simultaneous asynchronous postbacks. Unfortunately, the `UpdatePanel`
does not support multiple simultaneous asynchronous postbacks. By default, the last postback performed will abort all previous postbacks.

Canceling the Current Asynchronous Postback

As you learned in the previous section, you can perform at most one asynchronous postback in a page at a time. By default, the last postback wins. If you initiate a new postback
while a previous postback is being processed, the previous postback is aborted.

If you want to reverse this logic, and give precedence to the first postback over future
postbacks, you can cancel every postback that occurs after the first postback until the first
postback completes. The page in Listing 38.13 illustrates how to cancel an asynchronous
postback in the event handler for the `PageRequestManager.initializeRequest` event (see
Figure 38.10).

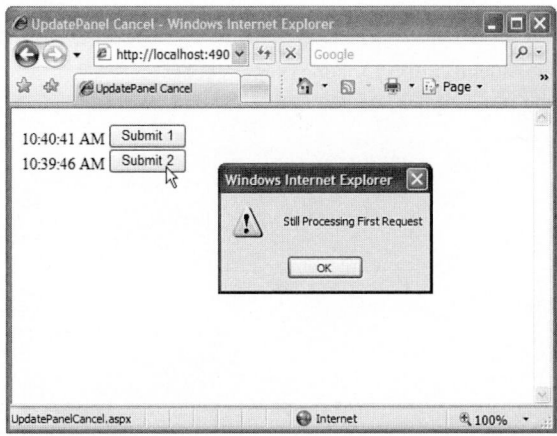

FIGURE 38.10   Canceling an asynchronous postback.

LISTING 38.13   UpdatePanelCancel.aspx

```
<%@ Page Language="C#" %>
<!DOCTYPE html PUBLIC "-//W3C//DTD XHTML 1.0 Transitional//EN"
"http://www.w3.org/TR/xhtml1/DTD/xhtml1-transitional.dtd">
<script runat="server">

    protected void btnSubmit_Click(object sender, EventArgs e)
    {
        System.Threading.Thread.Sleep(3000); // sleep 3 seconds
    }
</script>
<html xmlns="http://www.w3.org/1999/xhtml">
<head runat="server">
    <title>UpdatePanel Cancel</title>
</head>
<body>
    <form id="form1" runat="server">
    <asp:ScriptManager ID="ScriptManager1" runat="server" />

    <asp:UpdatePanel ID="up1" UpdateMode="Conditional" runat="server">
    <ContentTemplate>
        <%= DateTime.Now.ToString("T") %>
        <asp:Button
            id="btnSubmit1"
            Text="Submit 1"
            OnClick="btnSubmit_Click"
            Runat="server"/>
    </ContentTemplate>
    </asp:UpdatePanel>

    <asp:UpdatePanel ID="up2" UpdateMode="Conditional" runat="server">
    <ContentTemplate>
        <%= DateTime.Now.ToString("T") %>
        <asp:Button
            id="btnSubmit2"
            Text="Submit 2"
            OnClick="btnSubmit_Click"
            Runat="server" />
    </ContentTemplate>
    </asp:UpdatePanel>

    </form>
    <script type="text/javascript">
```

```
    var prm = Sys.WebForms.PageRequestManager.getInstance();
    prm.add_initializeRequest( prm_initializeRequest );

    function prm_initializeRequest(sender, args)
    {
        if (prm.get_isInAsyncPostBack())
        {
            alert('Still Processing First Request');
            args.set_cancel(true);
        }
    }
    </script>

</body>
</html>
```

Using similar logic, you can always give precedence to one UpdatePanel over another. Listing 38.14 contains client-script that always gives precedence to the btnSubmit1 button over any other button that causes an asynchronous postback in the page. (The entire page is included in the source code on the book's website).

LISTING 38.14   UpdatePanelPrecedence.aspx

```
<script type="text/javascript">

    var prm = Sys.WebForms.PageRequestManager.getInstance();
    prm.add_initializeRequest( prm_initializeRequest );

    var prevPostBackElementId;

    function prm_initializeRequest(sender, args)
    {
        if (prm.get_isInAsyncPostBack())
        {
            if (prevPostBackElementId == 'btnSubmit1')
            {
                alert('Still Processing btnSubmit1 Request');
                args.set_cancel(true);
            }
        }
        prevPostBackElementId = args.get_postBackElement().id;
    }
</script>
```

38

If you click the second button (btnSubmit2) immediately after clicking the first button (btnSubmit1), the second asynchronous postback is canceled.

Aborting the Previous Asynchronous Postback

You can explicitly abort a previous asynchronous postback by using the PageRequestManager abortPostBack() method. Explicitly aborting a postback is useful when you want to associate a Cancel button with an asynchronous postback (see Figure 38.11).

FIGURE 38.11   Aborting an asynchronous postback with a Cancel button.

For example, the page in Listing 38.15 contains two buttons. The first button retrieves your fortune. The oracle, however, is slow. It takes 3 seconds for the oracle to deliver a new fortune. If you want to cancel the new fortune during these 3 seconds, you can click the Cancel button.

LISTING 38.15   UpdatePanelAbort.aspx

```
<%@ Page Language="C#" %>
<!DOCTYPE html PUBLIC "-//W3C//DTD XHTML 1.0 Transitional//EN"
"http://www.w3.org/TR/xhtml1/DTD/xhtml1-transitional.dtd">
<script runat="server">

    protected void btnGetFortune_Click(object sender, EventArgs e)
    {
        System.Threading.Thread.Sleep(3000); // wait 3 seconds
        lblFortune.Text = String.Format("At {0:T}, the oracle says: ",
        DateTime.Now);
        Random rnd = new Random();
        switch (rnd.Next(4))
```

```
            {
                case 0:
                    lblFortune.Text += "You're doomed!";
                    break;
                case 1:
                    lblFortune.Text += "Good luck is around the corner.";
                    break;
                case 2:
                    lblFortune.Text += "Don't leave home.";
                    break;
                case 3:
                    lblFortune.Text += "Buy stock today.";
                    break;
            }
    }
</script>
<html xmlns="http://www.w3.org/1999/xhtml">
<head runat="server">
    <title>UpdatePanel Abort</title>
</head>
<body>
    <form id="form1" runat="server">
    <div>
        <asp:ScriptManager ID="ScriptManager1" runat="server" />

        <asp:UpdatePanel ID="up1" runat="server">
        <ContentTemplate>
            <asp:Button
                id="btnGetFortune"
                Text="Get Fortune"
                OnClick="btnGetFortune_Click"
                Runat="server" />
            <asp:Button
                id="btnCancel"
                Text="Cancel"
                Enabled="false"
                Runat="server" />
                <br />
                <asp:Label ID="lblFortune" runat="server" />
        </ContentTemplate>
        </asp:UpdatePanel>

    </div>
    </form>
    <script type="text/javascript">
```

38

```
    var prm = Sys.WebForms.PageRequestManager.getInstance();
    prm.add_initializeRequest(prm_initializeRequest);

    function prm_initializeRequest(sender, args)
    {
        if (args.get_postBackElement().id == 'btnCancel')
        {
            prm.abortPostBack();
            alert("Fortune Aborted!");
        }
        else
        {
            $get('btnCancel').disabled = false;
        }
    }
    </script>
</body>
</html>
```

Passing Additional Information During an Asynchronous Postback

You can pass additional items from the web server to the web browser during an asynchronous postback. Passing additional items is useful when the area that you need to update
on a page does not fall into a neat little rectangle. For example, you might want to update
a page's title or a page's meta tags based on the results of an asynchronous query.

The page in Listing 38.16 contains a DetailsView control that you can use to navigate the
contents of the Movie database table. The DetailsView control is contained inside of an
UpdatePanel control so that a postback does not happen when you navigate to a new movie.

LISTING 38.16   UpdatePanelDataItem.aspx

```
<%@ Page Language="C#" %>
<!DOCTYPE html PUBLIC "-//W3C//DTD XHTML 1.0 Transitional//EN"
"http://www.w3.org/TR/xhtml1/DTD/xhtml1-transitional.dtd">
<script runat="server">

    protected void dtlMovie_DataBound(object sender, EventArgs e)
    {
        string movieTitle = (string)DataBinder.Eval(dtlMovie.DataItem, "Title");

        if (sm1.IsInAsyncPostBack)
        {
            sm1.RegisterDataItem(Head1, movieTitle);
        }
```

```
        else
        {
            Head1.Title = movieTitle;
            hTitle.InnerHtml = movieTitle;
        }
    }
</script>
<html xmlns="http://www.w3.org/1999/xhtml">
<head id="Head1" runat="server">
    <title>UpdatePanel DataItem</title>
</head>
<body>
    <form id="form1" runat="server">
    <div>

    <asp:ScriptManager
        id="sm1"
        Runat="server" />

    <h1 id="hTitle" runat="server"></h1>


    <asp:UpdatePanel
        id="upSearch"
        Runat="server">
        <ContentTemplate>

        <asp:DetailsView
            id="dtlMovie"
            DataSourceID="srcMovies"
            AllowPaging="true"
            Runat="server" OnDataBound="dtlMovie_DataBound" />

        </ContentTemplate>
    </asp:UpdatePanel>

    <asp:SqlDataSource
        id="srcMovies"
        ConnectionString='<%$ ConnectionStrings:con %>'
        SelectCommand="SELECT Id,Title,Director FROM Movie"
        Runat="server" />

    </div>
    </form>
    <script type="text/javascript">
```

38

```
    var prm = Sys.WebForms.PageRequestManager.getInstance();
    prm.add_pageLoaded( prm_pageLoaded );

    function prm_pageLoaded(sender, args)
    {
        if (prm.get_isInAsyncPostBack())
        {
            var movieTitle = args.get_dataItems()['Head1'];
            // assign browser title bar
            document.title = movieTitle;
            // assign heading
            $get('hTitle').innerHTML = movieTitle;
        }
    }
    </script>
</body>
</html>
```

When you navigate to a new movie, both the browser title bar, and the page heading are updated to display the title of the new movie (see Figure 38.12). The title and heading are updated by passing a data item that represents the movie title during the asynchronous postback.

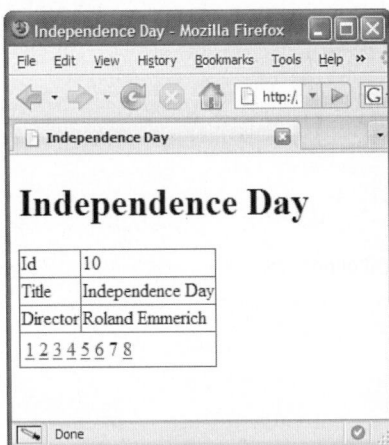

FIGURE 38.12   Updating a page's header and title asynchronously.

Handling UpdatePanel Errors Gracefully

Sometimes things go terribly wrong. The Internet gets clogged, an application's database server goes down, and so on. How do you recover from these types of errors gracefully in an Ajax application?

By default, if an error occurs during an asynchronous postback, a JavaScript alert box appears that displays an error message. This is a jarring experience in a production application.

You have several options for avoiding this default experience: You can configure a custom error page; you can handle the error on the server side; or you can handle the error on the client side. Let's examine each of these options.

First, if you configure a custom error page for your application, by default the custom error page applies to asynchronous postback errors. You enable a custom error page by adding the following element to the system.web section of your web configuration file:

```
<customErrors mode="On" defaultRedirect="ErrorPage.aspx" />
```

This element enables a custom error page for both local and remote requests. Any unhandled exceptions in any page cause the browser to be redirected to a page named ErrorPage.aspx.

The page in Listing 38.17 throws an exception when you click the button located in the UpdatePanel control. If you open the page in Listing 38.17 with a custom error page enabled, the browser is redirected to the ErrorPage.aspx page automatically.

LISTING 38.17   UpdatePanelError.aspx

```
<%@ Page Language="C#" %>
<!DOCTYPE html PUBLIC "-//W3C//DTD XHTML 1.0 Transitional//EN"
"http://www.w3.org/TR/xhtml1/DTD/xhtml1-transitional.dtd">
<script runat="server">

    protected void btnSubmit_Click(object sender, EventArgs e)
    {
        throw new Exception("Server Error");
    }
</script>
<html xmlns="http://www.w3.org/1999/xhtml">
<head runat="server">
    <title>UpdatePanel Error</title>
</head>
<body>
    <form id="form1" runat="server">

    <asp:ScriptManager
        id="sm1"
        Runat="server" />

    <asp:UpdatePanel
        id="up1"
        runat="server">
```

38

```
        <ContentTemplate>

        <asp:Button
            id="btnSubmit"
            Text="Submit"
            OnClick="btnSubmit_Click"
            Runat="server" />

        </ContentTemplate>
    </asp:UpdatePanel>

    </form>
</body>
</html>
```

You can disable custom error pages in the case of an asynchronous postback by adding an `AllowCustomErrorRedirect` attribute to the `ScriptManager` tag, like this:

```
<asp:ScriptManager
    id="sm1"
    AllowCustomErrorsRedirect="false"
    Runat="server" />
```

Instead of redirecting the user to an error page, you can customize the error message that the user sees. You can customize the error on both the server and the client.

On the server, you can handle the `ScriptManager` control's `AsyncPostBackError` event to customize the error message transmitted to the client. For example, the page in Listing 38.18 modifies the error message to be a generic one.

LISTING 38.18   UpdatePanelErrorServer.aspx

```
<%@ Page Language="C#" %>
<!DOCTYPE html PUBLIC "-//W3C//DTD XHTML 1.0 Transitional//EN"
"http://www.w3.org/TR/xhtml1/DTD/xhtml1-transitional.dtd">
<script runat="server">

    protected void btnSubmit_Click(object sender, EventArgs e)
    {
        throw new Exception("Server Error");
    }

    protected void sm1_AsyncPostBackError(object sender,
    ➥AsyncPostBackErrorEventArgs e)
```

```
        {
            sm1.AsyncPostBackErrorMessage = "A server error occurred";
        }
</script>
<html xmlns="http://www.w3.org/1999/xhtml">
<head id="Head1" runat="server">
    <title>UpdatePanel Error Server</title>
</head>
<body>
    <form id="form1" runat="server">

    <asp:ScriptManager
        id="sm1"
        OnAsyncPostBackError="sm1_AsyncPostBackError"
        Runat="server" />

    <asp:UpdatePanel
        id="up1"
        runat="server">
        <ContentTemplate>

        <asp:Button
            id="btnSubmit"
            Text="Submit"
            OnClick="btnSubmit_Click"
            Runat="server" />

        </ContentTemplate>
    </asp:UpdatePanel>

    </form>
</body>
</html>
```

38

The page in Listing 38.18 cloaks the actual server-side error message with a generic message. The error message displayed by the page is still not professional. Most likely, you'll want to customize the error message even more when the error is displayed on the client.

The page in Listing 38.19 illustrates how UpdatePanelErrorServer.aspx you can customize an error message on the client. The page displays an error message directly above the UpdatePanel when an asynchronous postback fails (see Figure 38.13).

FIGURE 38.13   Customizing a client-side error message.

LISTING 38.19   UpdatePanelErrorClient.aspx

```
<%@ Page Language="C#" %>
<!DOCTYPE html PUBLIC "-//W3C//DTD XHTML 1.0 Transitional//EN"
"http://www.w3.org/TR/xhtml1/DTD/xhtml1-transitional.dtd">
<script runat="server">

    protected void btnSubmit_Click(object sender, EventArgs e)
    {
        throw new Exception("Server Error");
    }

    protected void sm1_AsyncPostBackError(object sender,
    ➥AsyncPostBackErrorEventArgs e)
    {
        sm1.AsyncPostBackErrorMessage = "A server error occurred";
    }
</script>
<html xmlns="http://www.w3.org/1999/xhtml">
<head id="Head1" runat="server">
    <title>UpdatePanel Error Server</title>
    <style type="text/css">

    .errorMessage
    {
        background-color: Yellow;
        color: Red;
    }

    </style>
</head>
<body>
```

```
<form id="form1" runat="server">

<asp:ScriptManager
    id="sm1"
    OnAsyncPostBackError="sm1_AsyncPostBackError"
    Runat="server" />

<span id="spanError" class="errorMessage"></span>

<asp:UpdatePanel
    id="up1"
    runat="server">
    <ContentTemplate>

    <asp:Button
        id="btnSubmit"
        Text="Submit"
        OnClick="btnSubmit_Click"
        Runat="server" />

    </ContentTemplate>
</asp:UpdatePanel>

</form>
<script type="text/javascript">

var prm = Sys.WebForms.PageRequestManager.getInstance();
prm.add_endRequest( prm_endRequest );

function prm_endRequest(sender, args)
{
    var spanError = $get("spanError");
    if (args.get_error())
    {
        args.set_errorHandled(true);
        spanError.innerHTML = "Could not complete your request";
    }
    else
    {
        spanError.innerHTML = "";
    }
}

</script>
</body>
</html>
```

38

Before leaving this section, I need to mention one last property supported by the ScriptManager control related to errors: AsyncPostBackTimeOut. This property determines the amount of time in seconds before an asynchronous postback times out. The default value is 90 seconds. You might want to set this value to a briefer duration.

UpdatePanel Performance

The UpdatePanel hides the normal page postback by performing an asynchronous (sneaky) postback. Even though you can use the UpdatePanel to trick your users into believing that a postback is not occurring, it is important that you do not trick yourself.

You can use either of the two debugging tools discussed earlier in this chapter to view the Ajax request and response that occur during an asynchronous postback. For example, Listing 38.20 contains a typical Ajax request, and Listing 38.21 contains a typical Ajax response.

LISTING 38.20   Ajax Request

```
sm1=up1%7CgrdFeedback&__EVENTTARGET=grdFeedback&__EVENTARGUMENT=Sort%24Name&__VIEWS
TATE=%2FwEPDwUKLTk4MzMyODc2MQ9kFgICAw9kFgICAw9kFgJmD2QWBAIBDzwrAAoBAA8WBB4LXyFEYXRh
Qm91bmRnHgtfIUl0ZW1Db3VudGZkFgJmD2QWBGYPDxYCHgdWaXNpYmxlaGRkAgIPDxYCHwJoZGQCAw88KwA
NAgAPFgQfAGcfAQIEZAwUKwAEFggeBE5hbWUFAklkHgpJc1JlYWRPbmx5aB4EVHlwZRkrAR4JRGF0YUZpZW
xkBQJJJZBYIHwMFBE5hbWUfBGgfBRkrAh8GBQROYW1lFggfAwUHQ29tbWVudB8EaB8FGSsCHwYFB0NvbW1lb
nQWCB8DBQ1EYXRlU3VibW10dGVkVkHwRoHwUZKVxTeXN0ZW0uRGF0ZVRpbWUsIG1zY29ybGliLCBWZXJzaW9u
PTIuMC4wLjAsIEN1bHR1cmU9bmV1dHJhbCwgUHVibGljS2V5VG9rZW49Yjc3YTVjNTYxOTM0ZTA4OR8GBQ1
EYXRlU3VibW10dGVkFgJmD2QWCgIBD2QWCGYPDxYCHgRUZXh0BQE0ZGQCAQ8PFgIfBwUFU3RldmVkZA-
ICDw8WAh8HBRJJIZXJ1IG1zIG15IGNvbW11bnRkZAIDDw8WAh8HBRQxMC8zLzIwMDcgNDo1MjowNCBQTWRk-
AgIPZBYIZg8PFgIfBwUBM2RkAgEPDxYCHwcFA0JvYmRkAgIPDxYCHwcFFUhleSwgd2hhdCBhYm91dCBBBamF
4P2RkAgMPDxYCHwcFFDEwLzMvMjAwNyA0OjE5OjI1IFBNZGQCAw9kFghmDw8WAh8HBQExZGQCAQ8PFgIfB-
wUFc3RldmVkZAICDw8WAh8HBRVXaGF0IGEgZ3JlYXQgd2Vic210ZSFkZAIDDw8WAh8HBRQxMC8zLzIwMD-
cgNDowOTo1NiBQTWRkAgQPZBYIZg8PFgIfBwUBM2RkAgEPDxYCHwcFBXN0ZXZlZGQCAg8PFgIfBwVaV293L
CBpdCBpcyB3cml0dGVuIGVudGlyZWx5IHdpdGggTGlucT8gVGhhdCBtdXN0IGhhdmUgUgc2F2ZWQgeW91IGEg
bG90IG9mIGRldmVsb3B3ZW50IHRpbWUhZGQCAw8PFgIfBwUUMTAvMy8yMDA3IDQ6MDk6NTYgUE1kZA-
IFDw8WAh8CaGRkGAIFC2dyZEZlZWRiYWNrDzwrAAkCBAUHQ29tbWVudAgCAWQFC2ZybUZlZWRiYWNrDx-
QrAAdkZAICZGQWAGRkuZs7yL%2Fem%2BLQG%2FRqUcYBa9aTsI4%3D&frmFeedback%24txtName=&frmFe
edback%24txtComment=&__EVENTVALIDATION=%2FwEWCALS%2BMLfAgKVvojNBgKio6JkAp7t150BAtnw
1uUHApCu1%2B4GAoKl7PcLAoGY7eABIj9XtltK55e8Og9%2BNK4DglwM43M%3D&
```

LISTING 38.21   Ajax Response

```
2124|updatePanel|up1|
```

```
    <table cellspacing="0" border="0" id="frmFeedback"
      style="border-collapse:collapse;">
    <tr>
```

```
     <td colspan="2">

         <label for="frmFeedback_txtName" id="frmFeedback_lblName">Name:</label>
         <span id="frmFeedback_valName" style="color:Red;visibility:hidden;">
         ➥Required</span>
         <br />
         <input name="frmFeedback$txtName" type="text" id="frmFeedback_txtName" />
         <br /><br />
         <label for="frmFeedback_txtComment" id="frmFeedback_lblComment">
         ➥Comment:</label>
         <span id="frmFeedback_valComment" style="color:Red;visibility:hidden;">
         ➥Required</span>
         <br />
         <textarea name="frmFeedback$txtComment" rows="3" cols="50"
           id="frmFeedback_txtComment"></textarea>
         <br /><br />
         <input type="submit" name="frmFeedback$btnSubmit" value="Submit"
           onclick="javascript:WebForm_DoPostBackWithOptions
           (new WebForm_PostBackOptions(&quot;frmFeedback$btnSubmit&quot;,
           &quot;&quot;, true, &quot;&quot;, &quot;&quot;, false, false))"
           id="frmFeedback_btnSubmit" />
     </td>
   </tr>
</table>

   <br /><br />

   <div>
   <table cellspacing="0" rules="all" border="1" id="grdFeedback"
          style="border-collapse:collapse;">
     <tr>
         <th scope="col"><a href="javascript:__
                     doPostBack('grdFeedback','Sort$Id')">Id</a></th>
                     <th scope="col"><a href="javascript:__doPostBack
                     ('grdFeedback','Sort$Name')">Name</a></th><th
➥scope="col">
                     <a href="javascript:__doPostBack
                     ('grdFeedback','Sort$Comment')">Comment</a></th>
                     <th scope="col"><a href="javascript:__doPostBack
                     ('grdFeedback','Sort$DateSubmitted')">
                      DateSubmitted</a></th>
     </tr><tr>
         <td>3</td><td>Bob</td><td>Hey, what about Ajax?
                     </td><td>10/3/2007 4:19:25 PM</td>
     </tr><tr>
         <td>1</td><td>steve</td><td>What a great website!
```

```
                          </td><td>10/3/2007 4:09:56 PM</td>
        </tr><tr>
            <td>2</td><td>steve</td><td>Wow, it is written entirely
                          with Linq? That must have saved you a lot of
                          development time!</td><td>10/3/2007 4:09:56 PM</td>
        </tr><tr>
            <td>4</td><td>Steve</td><td>Here is my comment
                          </td><td>10/3/2007 4:52:04 PM</td>
        </tr>
    </table>
</div>
```

¦0¦hiddenField¦__EVENTTARGET¦¦0¦hiddenField¦__EVENTARGUMENT¦¦1264¦hidden-
Field¦__VIEWSTATE¦/wEPDwUKLTk4MzMyODc2MQ9kFgICAw9kFgICAw9kFgJmD2QWBAIBDzwrAAoBAA8WB
B4LXyFEYXRhQm91bmRnHgtfIUl0ZW1Db3VudGZkFgJmD2QWBGYPDxYCHgdWaXNpYmxlaGRkAgIPDxYCH-
wJoZGQCAw88KwANAgAPFgQfAGcfAQIEZAwUKwAEFggeBE5hbWUFAklkHgpJc1JlYWRPbmx5aB4EVHlwZRkr
AR4JRGF0YUZpZWxkBQJJZBYIHwMFBE5hbWUfBGgfBRkrAh8GBQROYW1lFggfAwUHQ29tbWVudB8EaB8FGSs
CHwyFB0NvbW1lbnQWCB8DBQ1EYXRlU3VibWl0dGVkHwRoHwUZKVxTeXN0ZW0uRGF0ZVRpbWUsIG1zY29ybG
liLCBWZXJzaW9uPTIuMC4wLjAsIEN1bHR1cmU9bmV1dHJhbCwgUHVibGljS2V5VG9rZW49Yjc3YTVjNTYx-
OTM0ZTA4OR8GBQ1EYXRlU3VibWl0dGVkFgJmD2QWAICgIBD2QWCGYPDxYCHgRUZXh0BQEzZGQCAQ8PFgIfB-
wUDQm9iZGQCAg8PFgIfBwUVSGV5LCB3aGF0IGFib3V0IEFqYXg/ZGQCAw8PFgIfBwUUMTAvMy8yMDA3IDQ6
MTk6MjUgUE1kZAICD2QWCGYPDxYCHwcFATFkZAIBDw8WAh8HBQVzdGV2ZWRkAgIPDxYCHwcFFVdvdYXQgyS-
BncmVhdCB3ZWJzaXRlIWRkAgMPDxYCHwcFFDEwLzMvMjAwNyA0OjA5OjU2IFBNZGQCAw9kFghmDw8WAh8HB
QEyZGQCAQ8PFgIfBwUFc3RldmVkZAICDw8WAh8HBVpXb3csIGl0IGlzIHdyaXR0ZW4gZW50aXJlbHkgd2l0
aCBMaW5xPyBUaGF0IG11c3QgaGF2ZSBzYXZlZCB5b3UgYSBsb3Qgb2YgZGV2ZWxvcG1lbnQgdGltZSS-
FkZAIDDw8WAh8HBRQxMC8zLzIwMDcgNDowOTo1NiBQTWRkAgQPZBYIZg8PFgIfBwUBNGRkAgEPDxYCHwcF-
BVN0ZXZlZGQCAg8PFgIfBwUSSGVyZSBpcyBteSBjb21tZW50ZGQCAw8PFgIfBwUUMTAvMy8yMDA3IDQ6NTI
6MDQgUE1kZAIFDw8WAh8CaGRkGAIFC2dyZEZlZWRiYWNrDzwrAAkCBAUETmFtZZQgCAWQFC2ZybUZlZWRiY-
WNrDxQrAAdkZAICZGQWAGRkVKO/p/Z+TKr7wPvuagKWmQ2FfIY=¦96¦hiddenField¦__EVENTVALIDA-
TION¦/wEWCAKuyYyNBQKVvojNBgKio6JkAp7t150BAtnw1uUHApCu1+4GAoKl7PcLAoGY7eABqkyic8N4ML
Im8nwM1bpWblCsXyA=¦0¦asyncPostBackControlIDs¦¦¦0¦postBackControlIDs¦¦¦4¦updatePan-
elIDs¦¦tup1¦0¦childUpdatePanelIDs¦¦¦3¦panelsToRefreshIDs¦¦up1¦2¦asyncPostBackTime-
out¦¦90¦13¦formAction¦¦Feedback.aspx¦8¦pageTitle¦¦Feedback¦46¦arrayDeclaration¦Page
_Validators¦document.getElementById("frmFeedback_valName")¦49¦arrayDeclaration¦Page
_Validators¦document.getElementById("frmFeedback_valComment")¦139¦scriptBlock¦Scrip
tPath¦/Original/ScriptResource.axd?d=pGcnA3xf7SUaukdr-
behbvslg2hOq48wA9WuXk0fdM20k9xho9i9m9JZzVPbP2-
5l3cHqVSeROczjHZXGFjpag2&t=633231592768281250¦367¦scriptBlock¦ScriptContentWithTags
¦{"text":"\r\n\u003c!-—\r\nvar Page_ValidationActive = false;\r\nif (typeof(Valida-
torOnLoad) == \"function\") {\r\n   ValidatorOnLoad();\r\n}\r\n\r\nfunction Val-
idatorOnSubmit() {\r\n   if (Page_ValidationActive) {\r\n   return
ValidatorCommonOnSubmit();\r\n   }\r\n   else {\r\n   return true;\r\n
}\r\n}\r\n// -—\u003e\r\n","type":"text/javascript"}¦90¦onSubmit¦¦if (typeof(Val-
idatorOnSubmit) == "function" && ValidatorOnSubmit() == false) return
false;¦21¦expando¦document.getElementById('frmFeedback_valName')['controltovalidate']¦"frmFeedback_txtName"¦39¦expando¦document.getElementById('frmFeedback_val-

```
Name')['evaluationfunction']¦"RequiredFieldValidatorEvaluateIsValid"¦2¦expando¦doc-
ument.getElementById('frmFeedback_valName')['initialvalue']¦""¦24¦expando¦docu-
ment.getElementById('frmFeedback_valComment')['controltovalidate']¦"frmFeedback_txt
Comment"¦39¦expando¦document.getElementById('frmFeedback_valComment')['evaluation-
function']¦"RequiredFieldValidatorEvaluateIsValid"¦2¦expando¦document.getElement-
ById('frmFeedback_valComment')['initialvalue']¦""¦78¦scriptDispose¦up1¦Array.remove
(Page_Validators, document.getElementById('frmFeedback_valName'));¦81¦scriptDis-
pose¦up1¦Array.remove(Page_Validators, document.getElementById('frmFeedback_valCom-
ment'));¦
```

The Ajax request and response in Listing 38.20 and Listing 38.21, respectively, were captured using Fiddler after sorting by the Name column in the Feedback.aspx page.

I'm including the full request and response traffic to make a point. No one would describe either the request or response as tiny. A lot of text must be passed back and forth from the browser to the server and back again when an UpdatePanel control refreshes its content.

A big chunk of both the request and response consists of ViewState, which is passed to the server during an asynchronous postback, just like it is passed during a normal post-back. The server-side page executes just like it executes during a normal postback. Therefore, the server-side page needs the ViewState to execute correctly.

To improve the performance of asynchronous postbacks performed by an UpdatePanel, consider disabling ViewState for the controls contained within the UpdatePanel. Every ASP.NET control has an EnableViewState property. You can always set this property to the value False to disable ViewState.

The following table compares the size of the asynchronous request and response with the GridView control's ViewState enabled and disabled:

Ajax Request/Response Size

	ViewState Enabled	ViewState Disabled
Request	2,066	1,067
Response	5,720	4,719

As the table clarifies, you save about 1,000 bytes for both the request and response by disabling ViewState.

The disadvantage of disabling ViewState for a control such as a GridView is that it forces GridView to make a new database call whenever you sort or page GridView. However, one easy way to reduce the load on your database server is to take advantage of caching. If you cache all the records displayed by GridView on the server, and disable ViewState; then you reduce your network traffic and you don't place any additional load on your database server.

38

> **NOTE**
>
> To learn more about caching, see Chapter 29, "Caching Application Pages and Data."

When working with the UpdatePanel, you should never forget that the server-side page undergoes its normal page execution life cycle whenever an asynchronous postback occurs. If you perform an expensive database lookup in your Page_Load() method, that lookup occurs with each asynchronous call to your server.

You can avoid performing unnecessary server-side work during an asynchronous postback by taking advantage of the ScriptManager control's IsInAsyncPostBack property. You can use this property to detect whether the page is executing in the context of a normal postback or an asynchronous postback.

Using the Timer Control

The ASP.NET AJAX Timer control enables you to refresh an UpdatePanel (or the entire page) on a timed basis. The Timer control has one important property:

▶ **Interval**—The amount of time, in milliseconds, between Tick events. The default value is 60,000 (1 minute).

The Timer control raises a Tick event every so many milliseconds, depending on the value of its Interval property.

If you don't associate the Timer control with an UpdatePanel, the Timer posts the entire page back to the server performing a normal postback. For example, the page in Listing 38.22 posts the entire page back to the server every 2 seconds.

LISTING 38.22   TimerPage.aspx

```
<%@ Page Language="C#" %>
<!DOCTYPE html PUBLIC "-//W3C//DTD XHTML 1.0 Transitional//EN"
"http://www.w3.org/TR/xhtml1/DTD/xhtml1-transitional.dtd">
<html xmlns="http://www.w3.org/1999/xhtml">
<head runat="server">
    <title>Timer Page</title>
</head>
<body>
    <form id="form1" runat="server">
    <div>
    <asp:ScriptManager ID="ScriptManager1" runat="server" />

    <asp:Timer ID="Timer1" Interval="2000" runat="server" />
```

```
    The time is <%= DateTime.Now.ToString("T") %>

    </div>
    </form>
</body>
</html>
```

A more typical use of the `Timer` control is to refresh an `UpdatePanel` control's content on a timed basis. For example, the page in Listing 38.23 displays a random quotation every 2 seconds (see Figure 38.14).

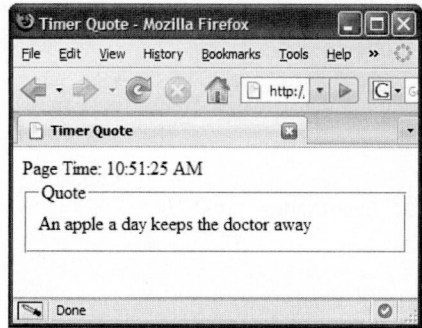

FIGURE 38.14   Refreshing the control content using `Timer` control.

LISTING 38.23   `TimerQuote.aspx`

```
<%@ Page Language="C#" %>
<%@ Import Namespace="System.Collections.Generic" %>
<!DOCTYPE html PUBLIC "-//W3C//DTD XHTML 1.0 Transitional//EN"
"http://www.w3.org/TR/xhtml1/DTD/xhtml1-transitional.dtd">
<script runat="server">

    protected void Page_Load(object sender, EventArgs e)
    {
        List<string> quotes = new List<string>();
        quotes.Add("A fool and his money are soon parted");
        quotes.Add("A penny saved is a penny earned");
        quotes.Add("An apple a day keeps the doctor away");

        Random rnd = new Random();
        lblQuote.Text = quotes[rnd.Next(quotes.Count)];
    }
</script>
```

38

```
<html xmlns="http://www.w3.org/1999/xhtml">
<head id="Head1" runat="server">
    <title>Timer Quote</title>
</head>
<body>
    <form id="form1" runat="server">
    <div>
    <asp:ScriptManager ID="ScriptManager1" runat="server" />


    <asp:Timer ID="Timer1" Interval="2000" runat="server" />


    Page Time: <%= DateTime.Now.ToString("T") %>


    <fieldset>
    <legend>Quote</legend>
    <asp:UpdatePanel ID="up1" runat="server">
    <Triggers>
        <asp:AsyncPostBackTrigger ControlID="Timer1" EventName="Tick" />
    </Triggers>
    <ContentTemplate>
        <asp:Label ID="lblQuote" runat="server" />
    </ContentTemplate>
    </asp:UpdatePanel>
    </fieldset>


    </div>
    </form>
</body>
</html>
```

The Timer control in Listing 38.23 is configured as a trigger for the UpdatePanel control.
When the Timer raises its Tick event, the UpdatePanel control refreshes its content by
performing an asynchronous postback and grabbing a new quotation to display.

The final example of the Timer control is contained in Listing 38.24. In this example, a
Timer control refreshes a discussion forum's messages every 5 seconds. If you leave your
browser window open, you see new messages as they are posted by other members of the
forum (see Figure 38.15).

FIGURE 38.15   Database messages being updated asynchronously.

LISTING 38.24   TimerMessages.aspx

```
<%@ Page Language="C#" %>
<!DOCTYPE html PUBLIC "-//W3C//DTD XHTML 1.0 Transitional//EN"
"http://www.w3.org/TR/xhtml1/DTD/xhtml1-transitional.dtd">
<html xmlns="http://www.w3.org/1999/xhtml">
<head runat="server">
    <title>Timer Messages</title>
    <style type="text/css">

    .message
    {
        margin-left: 20px;
        font-style:italic;
    }

    </style>
</head>
<body>
    <form id="form1" runat="server">

    <asp:ScriptManager ID="sm1" runat="server" />

    <asp:Timer ID="Timer1" Interval="5000" runat="server" />

    <asp:UpdatePanel ID="up1" runat="server">
    <Triggers>
        <asp:AsyncPostBackTrigger ControlID="Timer1" EventName="Tick" />
```

38

```
        </Triggers>
        <ContentTemplate>
        Last Refresh <%= DateTime.Now.ToString("T") %>
        <hr />
        <asp:ListView
            id="lstMessages"
            DataSourceID="srcMessages"
            Runat="server">
            <LayoutTemplate>
                <div id="itemContainer" runat="server">
                </div>
            </LayoutTemplate>
            <ItemTemplate>
                <div>
                    Posted by <%# Eval("PostedBy") %>
                    <div class="message">
                    <%# Eval("Post") %>
                    </div>
                </div>
            </ItemTemplate>
        </asp:ListView>
        </ContentTemplate>
        </asp:UpdatePanel>

        <asp:ObjectDataSource
            id="srcMessages"
            TypeName="Message"
            SelectMethod="Select"
            Runat="server" />

    </form>
</body>
</html>
```

The page in Listing 38.24 contains a `ListView` that gets refreshed every 5 seconds. Be aware that every person who has this page open in a browser will cause a database call to be made every 5 seconds. This data is an excellent candidate for caching.

Using the UpdateProgress Control

The last control that we need to examine in this chapter is the `UpdateProgress` control. This control enables you to display a progress indicator while an `UpdatePanel` is updating its content.

During a normal postback, the browser displays its progress in downloading new content by spinning an icon or displaying a progress bar. During an asynchronous postback, on the other hand, there is no visual indication of progress. You can use the UpdateProgress control to give the users some sense that something is happening during an asynchronous postback.

> **NOTE**
>
> In the next chapter, we examine an alternative method of displaying UpdatePanel progress. You learn how to use the UpdatePanelAnimation control to display an animation while an UpdatePanel's content is refreshed.

The page in Listing 38.25 illustrates how to use the UpdateProgress control. If you click the button, an animation spins while the asynchronous postback is performed (see Figure 38.16).

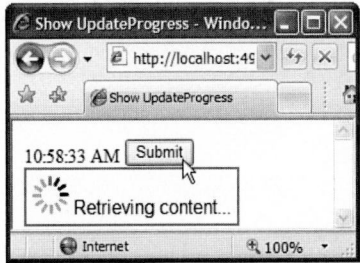

FIGURE 38.16   Viewing a spinning asynchronous progress indicator.

LISTING 38.25   ShowUpdateProgress.aspx

```
<%@ Page Language="C#" %>
<!DOCTYPE html PUBLIC "-//W3C//DTD XHTML 1.0 Transitional//EN"
"http://www.w3.org/TR/xhtml1/DTD/xhtml1-transitional.dtd">
<script runat="server">

    protected void btnSubmit_Click(object sender, EventArgs e)
    {
        System.Threading.Thread.Sleep(5000);
    }
</script>
<html xmlns="http://www.w3.org/1999/xhtml">
<head runat="server">
    <title>Show UpdateProgress</title>
    <style type="text/css">
    .progress
```

```
        {
            font-family:Arial;
            position: absolute;
            background-color:lightyellow;
            border:solid 2px red;
            padding:5px;
        }
        </style>
    </head>
    <body>
        <form id="form1" runat="server">
        <div>
            <asp:ScriptManager ID="ScriptManager1" runat="server" />
            <asp:UpdatePanel ID="up1" runat="server">
            <ContentTemplate>
                <%= DateTime.Now.ToString("T") %>
                <asp:Button
                    id="btnSubmit"
                    Text="Submit"
                    Runat="server" OnClick="btnSubmit_Click" />
            </ContentTemplate>
            </asp:UpdatePanel>
            <asp:UpdateProgress
                ID="progress1"
                AssociatedUpdatePanelID="up1"
                runat="server">
                <ProgressTemplate>
                    <div class="progress">
                    <asp:Image
                        id="imgProgress"
                        ImageUrl="~/Images/Progress.gif"
                        Runat="server" />
                        Retrieving content...
                    </div>
                </ProgressTemplate>
            </asp:UpdateProgress>

        </div>
        </form>
    </body>
    </html>
```

When you click the button in Listing 38.25, the response is delayed for 5 seconds so you have a chance to see the progress indicator. The delay simulates a network delay.

> **NOTE**
>
> Several websites enable you to generate fancy animator progress indicator icons. Here is the address to one of my favorites:
>
> http://www.ajaxload.info

The UpdateProgress control supports the following three properties:

▶ **AssociatedUpdatePanelID**—The UpdateProgress control displays progress for this UpdatePanel control.

▶ **DisplayAfter**—The amount of time, in milliseconds, before the UpdateProgress control displays content. The default is 500 milliseconds (half a second).

▶ **DynamicLayout**—When this property is set to true (the default), the UpdateProgress control is initially hidden with the Cascading Style Sheet (CSS) attribute display:none. When this property is set to false, the UpdateProgress control is hidden with the CSS attribute visibility:hidden.

Summary

In this chapter, you learned how to use the primary server-side ASP.NET AJAX control: UpdatePanel. The bulk of this chapter was devoted to discussing the different features of this control. You learned how to specify triggers for an UpdatePanel. You also learned about how the UpdatePanel control participates in a page's server-side and client-side page execution life cycle. We also examined how you can handle errors gracefully when using the UpdatePanel control.

In the final parts of this chapter, you learned how to use two controls that support the UpdatePanel control. First, you learned how to use the Timer control to refresh an UpdatePanel on a timed basis. Second, you learned how to use the UpdateProgress control to give the user something to watch during an UpdatePanel control's asynchronous postback.

38

Using the ASP.NET AJAX Control Toolkit

The ASP.NET AJAX Control Toolkit consists of more than 40 server-side Ajax controls that you can use in your ASP.NET applications. You can take advantage of the controls to create website special effects such as animations, rounded corners, and modal pop-ups. You can also use the controls for more serious applications such as implementing auto-complete and masked edit text fields.

The controls in the ASP.NET AJAX Control Toolkit are Ajax controls in the broad sense of the word *Ajax*. All the Toolkit controls use client-side JavaScript. However, most of the controls do not perform asynchronous postbacks. So, they are Ajax controls in the sense that they take advantage of a lot of JavaScript.

Almost all the controls in the Toolkit are extender controls. The controls extend the functionality of existing ASP.NET controls, such as the standard `TextBox` and `Panel` controls, with new functionality. Almost all the Toolkit controls have a `TargetControlID` property that you use to point to a control to extend.

In the first part of this chapter, you learn how to install and use the Toolkit controls in an ASP.NET application. Next, you are provided with a brief overview of each of the controls. Finally, we examine six of the controls in more detail: AutoComplete, DragPanel, FilteredTextBox, MaskedEdit, Animation, and UpdatePanelAnimation.

Using the ASP.NET AJAX Control Toolkit

The ASP.NET AJAX Control Toolkit is not included with ASP.NET 4 Framework. The Toolkit is continuously updated; a new release of the Toolkit is available every couple months. The Toolkit is maintained as a project at Microsoft CodePlex. You can download the latest release of the ASP.NET AJAX Control Toolkit at http://ajaxcontroltoolkit.codeplex.com/.

The "download" link will give you the 3.5 version of the toolkit, which won't work with our ASP.NET 4 websites. To get the toolkit that's compatible with .NET 4, click the "other downloads" link.

When you download the Toolkit, you have the choice of either (1) downloading the controls and the source code or (2) downloading the controls only. You need to unzip the download onto your hard drive.

As part of the download, you get a sample website that demonstrates each of the Toolkit controls. You can open the sample website by launching Visual Web Developer, selecting File, Open Website and browsing to the SampleWebSite folder in the unzipped download.

The ASP.NET AJAX Control Toolkit is not installed in the Global Assembly Cache. You must copy the AjaxControlToolkit.dll assembly from the /Bin folder of the SampleWebSite to the /Bin folder in your application. You can do this in multiple ways:

▶ **Copy the assembly by hand**—You can simply copy the AjaxControlToolkit.dll assembly from the SampleWebSite /Bin folder to a /Bin folder located in a new website.

▶ **Add an assembly reference**—Follow these steps:

  1. Within Visual Web Developer, select Website, Add Reference.

  2. Select the Browse tab.

  3. Browse to the AjaxControlToolkit.dll assembly located in the SampleWebSite /Bin folder.

▶ **Add the Toolkit to your Toolbox (see Figure 39.1)**—You can add the ASP.NET AJAX Control Toolkit to the Visual Web Developer Toolbox by following these steps:

  1. Within Visual Web Developer, create a new ASP.NET page.

  2. Right-click in the Toolbox window and select Add Tab. Create a new tab named Toolkit.

  3. Right-click under the new tab and select Choose Items.

  4. Click the Browse button located at the bottom of the .NET Framework Components tab.

  5. Browse to the /Bin folder of the SampleWebSite and select the AjaxControlToolkit.dll assembly.

  6. When you drag a control from the Toolbox onto a page, the AjaxControlToolkit.dll is copied to the Website /Bin folder automatically.

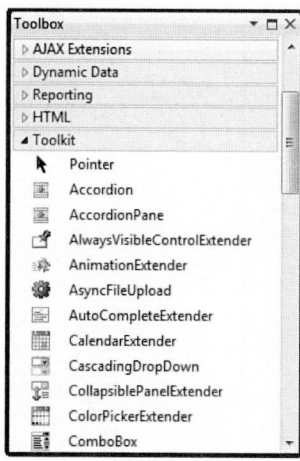

FIGURE 39.1   Adding the ASP.NET AJAX Control Toolkit to the Toolbox.

The majority of the controls in the ASP.NET AJAX Control Toolkit are extender controls. Visual Web Developer provides additional designer features for working with extender controls. For example, if you add a standard `TextBox` control to the Designer, an Add Extender link appears in the Common TextBox Tasks dialog box (See Figure 39.2).

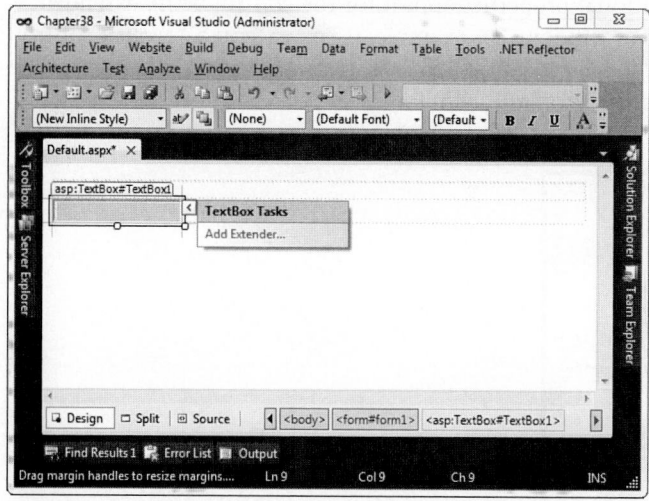

FIGURE 39.2   The Add Extender task.

If you click the Add Extender link, a dialog box appears that enables you to pick an extender that can be applied to the TextBox control (see Figure 39.3). Different extenders appear for different controls. For example, because you can apply a `ConfirmButton` extender to a Button control but not a `TextBox` control, the `ConfirmButton` extender appears only when you click Add Extender for the Button control.

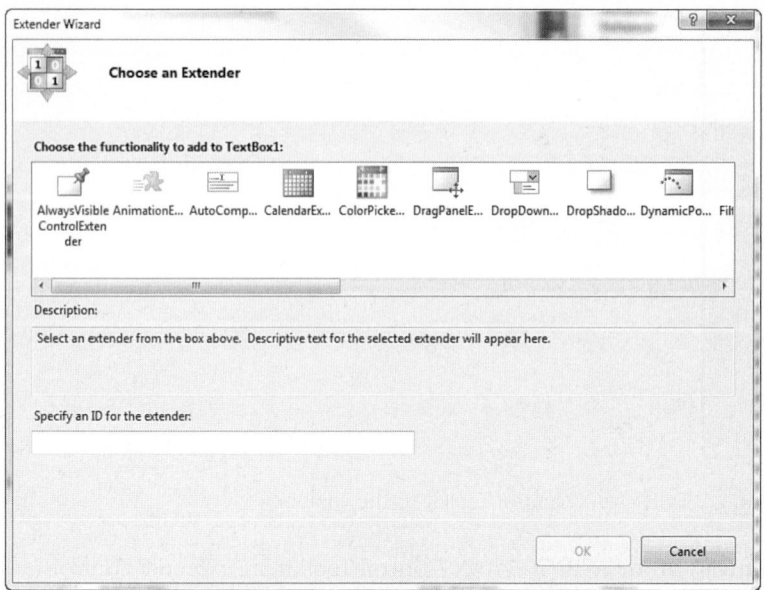

FIGURE 39.3   Selecting an extender control.

When you extend a control, additional properties appear for the control being extended in the extended control's Properties window. For example, if you extend a TextBox control with the AutoComplete extender, the AutoComplete extender control's properties appear when you open the TextBox control's Properties window (see Figure 39.4).

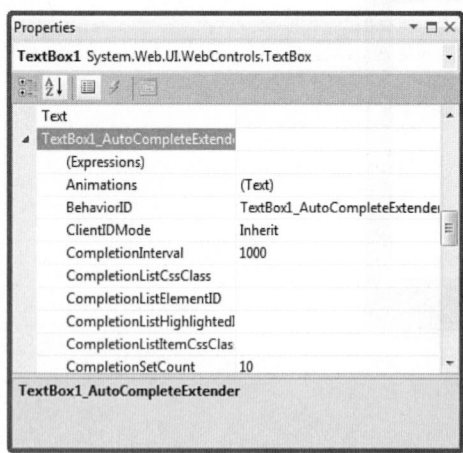

FIGURE 39.4   Viewing extender control properties.

Overview of the Toolkit Controls

This section, provides you with a brief overview of each of the current Toolkit controls. I recommend that you open the ASP.NET AJAX Control Toolkit sample website and experiment with the controls while reading this chapter.

▶ **Accordion**—Enables you to create a Microsoft Outlook-like expanding and collapsing menu. The `Accordion` control can contain one or more `AccordionPane` controls. One `AccordionPane` can be selected at a time. The selected pane is expanded; the other panes are collapsed.

▶ **AlwaysVisibleControl**—Enables you to display content that is fixed at one location in the browser window even when you scroll the window. The control works like the `position:fixed` Cascading Style Sheet (CSS) attribute. However, unlike the CSS attribute, `AlwaysVisibleControl` works with Microsoft Internet Explorer 6.0.

▶ **Animation**—Enables you to add fancy animation effects to your website. For example, you can move, resize, and fade elements in a page. We examine the `Animation` control in detail in the section "Using the Animation Control."

▶ **AsyncFileUpload**—Enables you to upload files asynchronously to the server.

▶ **AutoComplete**—Enables you to display suggestions as a user types text into a text field. We discuss this control in detail in the section "Using the AutoComplete Control." (This control is used in the sample application described in the last chapter.)

▶ **Calendar**—Displays a pop-up calendar next to `TextBox`. It enables you to select a year, month, and date by clicking dates in a pop-up calendar.

▶ **CascadingDropDown**—Enables you to make the list of items displayed in one `DropDownList` control dependent on the list of items displayed in another `DropDownList` control. The `DropDownList` items are updated by performing an asynchronous postback.

▶ **CollapsiblePanel**—Enables you to hide or display content contained in a Panel control. When you click its header, the content either appears or disappears.

▶ **ColorPicker**—Provides an interactive pop-up control that enables you to graphically choose colors.

▶ **ComboBox**—Is similar to a traditional ASP.NET `DropDownList`, except it provides functionality similar to the `ComboBox` control found in Windows Forms, such as the ability to type in free-form text.

▶ **ConfirmButton**—Enables you to display a confirmation dialog box when a user clicks a button. The confirmation dialog box can be the default JavaScript confirmation box. Alternatively, you can associate a modal dialog box with the `ConfirmButton` control.

▶ **DragPanel**—Enables you to create a panel that you can drag with your mouse around the page. It enables you to create a virtual floating window. We discuss the DragPanel control in the section "Using the DragPanel Control."

▶ **DropDown**—Enables you to create a SharePoint-style drop-down menu.

▶ **DropShadow**—Enables you to add a drop shadow to a Panel control. You can set properties of the drop shadow, such as its width and opacity.

▶ **DynamicPopulate**—Enables you to dynamically populate the contents of a control, such as a Label control, by performing an asynchronous call to the server. You can set up the DynamicPopulate control so that the asynchronous request is triggered by another control such as a Button control.

▶ **FilteredTextBox**—Enables you to prevent certain characters from being entered into TextBox. The FilteredTextBox is discussed in the section "Using the FilteredTextBox Control."

▶ **HoverMenu**—Displays a pop-up menu when you hover over another control.

▶ **HTMLEditor**—Enables you to easily create HTML through a rich WYSIWYG editor. A toolbar is provided with controls for formatting, color selections, cut and paste, and more.

▶ **ListSearch**—Enables you to perform an incremental search against the items in either a ListBox or DropDownList control.

▶ **MaskedEdit**—Forces a user to enter a certain pattern of characters into a TextBox control. The MaskedEdit control is discussed in the section "Using the MaskedEdit Control."

▶ **ModalPopup**—Enables you to display a modal pop-up. When the modal pop-up appears, the remainder of the page is grayed out, preventing you from interacting with the page.

▶ **MultiHandleSlider**—Enables you to select multiple values through a graphical slider interface.

▶ **MutuallyExclusiveCheckBox**—Enables you to treat a set of CheckBox controls like a set of RadioButton controls. Only one CheckBox can be selected at a time.

▶ **NoBot**—Attempts to prevent spam robots from posting advertisements to your website. The control attempts to detect whether a human or robot is posting content.

▶ **NumericUpDown**—Enables you to display up and down buttons next to a TextBox control. When you click the up and down buttons, you can cycle through a set of numbers or other items such as month names or flavors of ice cream.

▶ **PagingBulletedList**—Enables you to display different content depending on the bullet clicked in a BulletedList control.

▶ **PasswordStrength**—Enables you to display a pop-up box that indicates the security strength of a password as a user selects a new password. (This control is used in the sample application described in the last chapter.)

▶ **PopupControl**—Displays a pop-up window.

▶ **Rating**—Enables you to rate an item on a scale. (This control is used in the sample application described in the last chapter.)

▶ **ReorderList**—Enables you to render an interactive list of items that supports reordering through drag and drop.

▶ **ResizableControl**—Enables you to resize images and other content contained on a web page.

▶ **RoundedCorners**—Enables you to add rounded corners around an element on a page.

▶ **SeaDragon**—Provides functionality to interact with an image, such as zooming in, zooming out, and making the image fill the entire browser window.

▶ **Slider**—Enables you to create either a horizontal or vertical slider for selecting a particular value in a range of values.

▶ **SlideShow**—Displays a slide show of images. The control can render Next, Previous, Play, and Stop buttons.

▶ **Tabs**—Enables you to create a tabbed interface. Switching tabs does not require a postback.

▶ **TextBoxWatermark**—Enables you to display background text inside of a `TextBox` control. When focus is given to `TextBox`, the background text disappears.

▶ **ToggleButton**—Enables you to customize the appearance of a `CheckBox` control. Instead of displaying a check box, you can display a thumbs-up or thumbs-down image.

▶ **UpdatePanelAnimation**—Enables you to display an animation while `UpdatePanel` is performing an asynchronous postback. We discuss the `UpdatePanelAnimation` control in the section "Using the `UpdatePanelAnimation` Control."

▶ **ValidatorCallout**—Can be used with any of the standard ASP.NET validation controls to create a callout effect when a validation error occurs.

In the following sections, we examine six of the controls in more detail: `AutoComplete`, `DragPanel`, `FilteredTextBox`, `MaskedEdit`, `Animation`, and `UpdatePanelAnimation`.

Using the AutoComplete Control

The one control I use most often from the ASP.NET AJAX Control Toolkit is the `AutoComplete` control, which enables you to convert a standard ASP.NET TextBox control into something resembling a combo box. As you enter text into the `TextBox` control, a list of matching options displays beneath the control (see Figure 39.5).

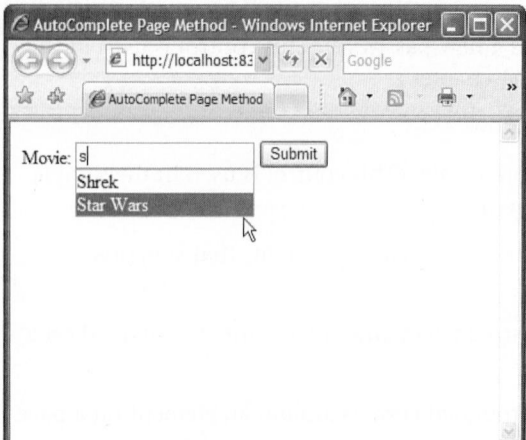

FIGURE 39.5   Using the `AutoComplete` extender control.

The cool thing about the `AutoComplete` control is that it retrieves the matching options from the web server, using an Ajax call, while you type. You can use the `AutoComplete` control to efficiently search through a database of billions of items because the entire database of items never needs to be downloaded to the browser.

The `AutoComplete` control is smart enough to cache items on the client. If you enter the same text into a `TextBox` control that you enter previously, the `AutoComplete` control can grab the suggestions from its cache instead of performing another Ajax call to retrieve the same information.

In this section, you learn how to use the `AutoComplete` extender control. You learn how to expose the items displayed by the `AutoComplete` control from a web method contained in the same page as the `AutoComplete` control and from a web method exposed by a separate web service. Finally, you learn how to associate hidden values (such as primary keys) with each item displayed by the `AutoComplete` control.

Using the `AutoCompleteExtender` with a Page Method

If you don't need to use suggestions in more than one page, it makes sense to expose the list of auto-complete suggestions from a page method. You can create a web method that is a static method on a page.

For example, the page in Listing 39.1 contains an `AutoComplete` extender control, which displays movie title suggestions while the user enters a movie title into a `TextBox` control.

LISTING 39.1   `AutoCompletePageMethod.aspx`

```
<%@ Page Language="C#" %>
<%@ Register TagPrefix="ajax" Namespace="AjaxControlToolkit"
 Assembly="AjaxControlToolkit"  %>
<%@ Import Namespace="System.Linq" %>
```

```
<!DOCTYPE html PUBLIC "-//W3C//DTD XHTML 1.0 Transitional//EN"
 "http://www.w3.org/TR/xhtml1/DTD/xhtml1-transitional.dtd">
<script runat="server">
    [System.Web.Services.WebMethod]
    public static string[] GetSuggestions(string prefixText, int count)
    {
        MyDatabaseDataContext db = new MyDatabaseDataContext();
        return db.Movies
            .Where( m => m.Title.StartsWith(prefixText) )
            .OrderBy( m => m.Title )
            .Select( m => m.Title)
            .Take(count)
            .ToArray();
    }


    protected void btnSubmit_Click(object sender, EventArgs e)
    {
        lblSelectedMovieTitle.Text = txtMovieTitle.Text;
    }
</script>
<html xmlns="http://www.w3.org/1999/xhtml">
<head runat="server">
    <title>AutoComplete Page Method</title>
</head>
<body>
    <form id="form1" runat="server">
    <div>

    <asp:ScriptManager ID="sm1" runat="server" />

    <asp:Label
        id="lblMovieTitle"
        Text="Movie:"
        AssociatedControlID="txtMovieTitle"
        Runat="server" />
    <asp:TextBox
        id="txtMovieTitle"
        AutoComplete="off"
        Runat="server" />
    <ajax:AutoCompleteExtender
        id="ace1"
        TargetControlID="txtMovieTitle"
        ServiceMethod="GetSuggestions"
        MinimumPrefixLength="1"
        runat="server" />
    <asp:Button
```

39

```
            id="btnSubmit"
            Text="Submit"
            OnClick="btnSubmit_Click"
            Runat="server" />

        <br /><br />

        <asp:Label
            id="lblSelectedMovieTitle"
            runat="server" />

        </div>
        </form>
</body>
</html>
```

In Listing 39.1, the AutoComplete extender control is declared like this:

```
<ajax:AutoCompleteExtender
    id="ace1"
    TargetControlID="txtMovieTitle"
    ServiceMethod="GetSuggestions"
    MinimumPrefixLength="1"
    runat="server" />
```

The TargetControlID property refers to the control that is extended. In this case, the AutoComplete extender extends a TextBox control named txtMovieTitle with auto-complete functionality.

> **NOTE**
>
> Notice that the extended TextBox control includes an AutoComplete="off" attribute. This attribute is necessary to disable the built-in browser auto-complete for Internet Explorer and Firefox. Realize that there is an important difference between AutoComplete="off" and AutoComplete="false".

The MinimumPrefixLength property represents the number of characters that must be entered before suggestions displays. The default value for this property is 3. I've changed the default to 1 so that suggestions appear immediately after you start typing.

The ServiceMethod property refers to the name of a web method. In this case, the web method is defined in the same page as the AutoComplete control as a static page method. The GetSuggestions() method looks like this:

```
[System.Web.Services.WebMethod]
public static string[] GetSuggestions(string prefixText, int count)
```

```
{
    MyDatabaseDataContext db = new MyDatabaseDataContext();
    return db.Movies
        .Where( m => m.Title.StartsWith(prefixText) )
        .OrderBy( m => m.Title )
        .Select( m => m.Title)
        .Take(count)
        .ToArray();
}
```

The GetSuggestions() method is declared as a static method—this is a requirement. Furthermore, notice that the method is decorated with the WebMethod attribute.

The GetSuggestions() method must have prefixText and count parameters. The prefixText parameter represents the text entered into the TextBox being extended so far. The count parameter represents the number of suggestions to return.

The GetSuggestions() method returns matching movie titles from the Movie database table. A LINQ to SQL query retrieves movie records that start with the prefix text.

> **NOTE**
>
> To learn more about LINQ to SQL, see Chapter 20, "Data Access with LINQ to SQL."

Using the AutoCompleteExtender with a Web Service Method

If you prefer, you can retrieve the auto-complete suggestions from a separate web service instead of a page method. For example, the web service in Listing 39.2, the FileService web service, retrieves a list of matching filenames from the file system.

LISTING 39.2   FileService.asmx

```
<%@ WebService Language="C#" Class="FileService" %>


using System;
using System.Web;
using System.Web.Services;
using System.Web.Services.Protocols;
using System.IO;
using System.Linq;

[WebService(Namespace = "http://tempuri.org/")]
[WebServiceBinding(ConformsTo = WsiProfiles.BasicProfile1_1)]
[System.Web.Script.Services.ScriptService]
public class FileService  : System.Web.Services.WebService {

    [WebMethod]
```

```
    public string[] GetSuggestions(string prefixText, int count)
    {
        DirectoryInfo dir = new DirectoryInfo("c:\\windows");
        return dir
            .GetFiles()
            .Where( f => f.Name.StartsWith(prefixText) )
            .Select( f => f.Name )
            .ToArray();
    }


}
```

The web service in Listing 39.2 includes a web method named GetSuggestions() that returns a list of filenames that match the prefix text passed to the web method. A LINQ query is used to return the matching results.

The FileService class is decorated with a ScriptService attribute. This attribute is required when exposing a web method to an Ajax request. If you don't include the ScriptService attribute, the web service cannot be called from the client side.

The page in Listing 39.3 contains an AutoComplete extender control that calls the web service.

LISTING 39.3   AutoCompleteWebService.aspx

```
<%@ Page Language="C#" %>
<%@ Register TagPrefix="ajax" Namespace="AjaxControlToolkit"
 Assembly="AjaxControlToolkit"  %>
<!DOCTYPE html PUBLIC "-//W3C//DTD XHTML 1.0 Transitional//EN"
 "http://www.w3.org/TR/xhtml1/DTD/xhtml1-transitional.dtd">
<script runat="server">
    protected void btnSubmit_Click(object sender, EventArgs e)
    {
        lblSelectedFileName.Text = txtFileName.Text;
    }
</script>
<html xmlns="http://www.w3.org/1999/xhtml">
<head runat="server">
    <title>Show AutoComplete Web Service</title>
</head>
<body>
    <form id="form1" runat="server">
    <div>

    <asp:ScriptManager ID="sm1" runat="server" />
```

```
<asp:Label
    id="lblFileName"
    Text="File Name:"
    AssociatedControlID="txtFileName"
    Runat="server" />
<asp:TextBox
    id="txtFileName"
    AutoComplete="off"
    Runat="server" />
<ajax:AutoCompleteExtender
    id="ace1"
    TargetControlID="txtFileName"
    ServiceMethod="GetSuggestions"
    ServicePath="~/FileService.asmx"
    MinimumPrefixLength="1"
    runat="server" />
<asp:Button
    id="btnSubmit"
    Text="Submit"
    OnClick="btnSubmit_Click"
    Runat="server"/>

<br /><br />

<asp:Label
    id="lblSelectedFileName"
    runat="server" />


    </div>
    </form>
</body>
</html>
```

As you enter text into TextBox rendered by the page in Listing 39.3, a list of matching file-names is retrieved by calling the GetSuggestions() method declared in the web service. The AutoComplete control is declared like this:

```
<ajax:AutoCompleteExtender
    id="ace1"
    TargetControlID="txtFileName"
    ServiceMethod="GetSuggestions"
    ServicePath="~/FileService.asmx"
    MinimumPrefixLength="1"
    runat="server" />
```

39

The `AutoComplete` control is declared with values assigned to its `ServiceMethod` and `ServicePath` properties. `ServicePath` represents the path to the web service.

Using Text and Value Pairs with the `AutoCompleteExtender`

In the previous two sections, you saw how you can use the `AutoComplete` control to display suggestions as you enter text into a `TextBox` control. For example, you saw how you can display matching movie titles as you type. After entering a title in `TextBox`, you might want to retrieve the entire movie database record.

However, you run into a problem here. The `GetSuggestions()` method retrieves the movie titles from the database and not the movie IDs. You need the movie ID to do a lookup for the matching movie database record. You need some way of retrieving both the movie title and movie ID when using the `AutoComplete` control.

The `AutoComplete` control includes a static method named `CreateAutoCompleteItem()` that returns a single string that represents a text and value pair. You can use this method when returning a string array from the `GetSuggestions()` method to include a primary key with each suggestion.

A `TextBox` control, however, can represent only a single value. To represent the ID of the selected movie, you need to add a hidden form field to your page. You can update the value of the hidden field whenever a user selects a new suggestion.

The page in Listing 39.4 illustrates how you can retrieve the primary key associated with the suggestion that a user selects when using the `AutoComplete` control.

LISTING 39.4   `AutoCompleteTextValue.aspx`

```
<%@ Page Language="C#" %>
<%@ Register TagPrefix="ajax" Namespace="AjaxControlToolkit"
 Assembly="AjaxControlToolkit"  %>
<%@ Import Namespace="System.Collections.Generic" %>
<%@ Import Namespace="System.Linq" %>
<!DOCTYPE html PUBLIC "-//W3C//DTD XHTML 1.0 Transitional//EN"
 "http://www.w3.org/TR/xhtml1/DTD/xhtml1-transitional.dtd">
<script runat="server">
    [System.Web.Services.WebMethod]
    public static string[] GetSuggestions(string prefixText, int count)
    {
        MyDatabaseDataContext db = new MyDatabaseDataContext();
        List<Movie> movies = db.Movies
            .Where( m => m.Title.StartsWith(prefixText) )
            .OrderBy( m => m.Title )
            .Take(count)
            .ToList();
```

```
        return movies
            .Select( m => AutoCompleteExtender.CreateAutoCompleteItem(
                m.Title, m.Id.ToString()))
            .ToArray();
    }


    protected void btnSubmit_Click(object sender, EventArgs e)
    {
        lblSelectedMovieTitle.Text = txtMovieTitle.Text;
        lblSelectedMovieId.Text = ace1Value.Value;
    }
</script>
<html xmlns="http://www.w3.org/1999/xhtml">
<head id="Head1" runat="server">
    <title>AutoComplete Page Method</title>
    <script type="text/javascript">

    function ace1_itemSelected(sender, e)
    {
        var ace1Value = $get('<%= ace1Value.ClientID %>');
        ace1Value.value = e.get_value();
    }

    </script>

</head>
<body>
    <form id="form1" runat="server">
    <div>

    <asp:ScriptManager ID="sm1" runat="server" />

    <asp:Label
        id="lblMovieTitle"
        Text="Movie:"
        AssociatedControlID="txtMovieTitle"
        Runat="server" />
    <asp:TextBox
        id="txtMovieTitle"
        AutoComplete="off"
        Runat="server" />
    <ajax:AutoCompleteExtender
        id="ace1"
        TargetControlID="txtMovieTitle"
```

```
            ServiceMethod="GetSuggestions"
            MinimumPrefixLength="1"
            OnClientItemSelected="ace1_itemSelected"
            FirstRowSelected="true"
            runat="server" />
        <asp:HiddenField
            id="ace1Value"
            Runat="server" />
        <asp:Button
            id="btnSubmit"
            Text="Submit"
            OnClick="btnSubmit_Click"
            Runat="server" />

        <br /><br />

        Title:
        <asp:Label
            id="lblSelectedMovieTitle"
            runat="server" />

        <br /><br />

        Primary Key:
        <asp:Label
            id="lblSelectedMovieId"
            runat="server" />


        </div>
        </form>
</body>
</html>
```

Several aspects of the page in Listing 39.4 require explanation. Let's start with the GetSuggestions() web method. This method is declared like this:

```
[System.Web.Services.WebMethod]
public static string[] GetSuggestions(string prefixText, int count)
{
    MyDatabaseDataContext db = new MyDatabaseDataContext();
    List<Movie> movies = db.Movies
        .Where( m => m.Title.StartsWith(prefixText) )
```

```
        .OrderBy( m => m.Title )
        .Take(count)
        .ToList();
    return movies
        .Select( m => AutoCompleteExtender.CreateAutoCompleteItem(
            m.Title, m.Id.ToString()))
        .ToArray();
}
```

The GetSuggestions() web method consists of two LINQ queries. The first LINQ query, a LINQ to SQL query, retrieves matching movies from the database. The second LINQ query, a standard LINQ query, calls the AutoCompleteExtender.CreateAutoCompleteItem() method for each movie. This method combines the movie Title and Id into a single string.

The AutoComplete extender is declared in the page with an associated HiddenField control, like this:

```
<ajax:AutoCompleteExtender
    id="ace1"
    TargetControlID="txtMovieTitle"
    ServiceMethod="GetSuggestions"
    MinimumPrefixLength="1"
    OnClientItemSelected="ace1_itemSelected"
    FirstRowSelected="true"
    runat="server" />
<asp:HiddenField
    id="ace1Value"
    Runat="server" />
```

The AutoComplete extender control includes an OnClientItemSelected property. When a new suggestion is selected, the ace1_itemSelected() JavaScript method executes. The ace1_itemSelected() method updates the value of the HiddenField with the value of the selected suggestion. This JavaScript method looks like this:

```
function ace1_itemSelected(sender, e)
{
    var ace1Value = $get('<%= ace1Value.ClientID %>');
    ace1Value.value = e.get_value();
}
```

39

The second parameter passed to the JavaScript method includes a value property that represents the primary key of the selected suggestion. The primary key is assigned to the HiddenField so that it can be read when the page is posted back to the server. When you select a movie and click the Submit button, both the title of the selected movie and the primary key associated with the selected movie are displayed in Label controls (see Figure 39.6).

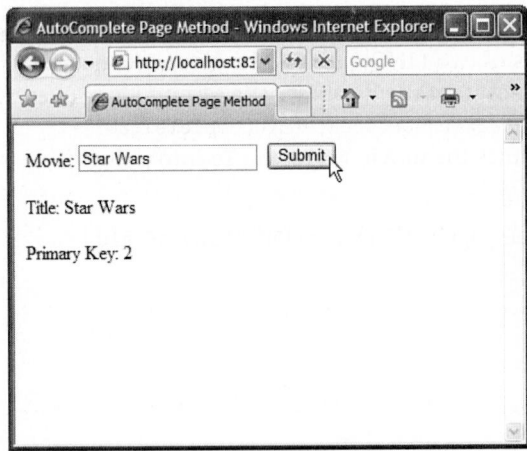

FIGURE 39.6   Selecting a primary key value with auto-complete.

Using the `DragPanel` Control

The `DragPanel` extender control enables you to create a virtual window for your web application. The `DragPanel` can be used to extend the Panel control so that you can drag the Panel around the page.

The `DragPanel` extender has the following properties:

- ▶ **`TargetControlID`**—The ID of the Panel control to drag.
- ▶ **`DragHandleID`**—The ID of the control that the user clicks to drag the Panel control.

The page in Listing 39.5 contains a `GridView` control that lists the current movies in the Movie database table. When you click the Add Movie link, a draggable window appears that contains a form for inserting a new movie (see Figure 39.7).

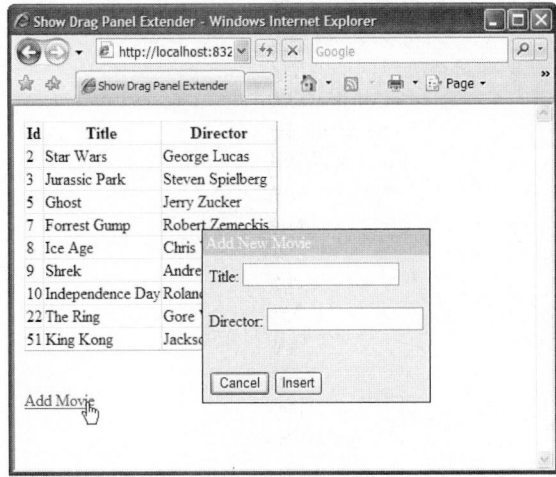

FIGURE 39.7   A virtual pop-up window created with the `DragPanel` control.

LISTING 39.5   ShowDragPanel.aspx

```
<%@ Page Language="C#" %>
<%@ Register TagPrefix="ajax" Namespace="AjaxControlToolkit"
 Assembly="AjaxControlToolkit"  %>
<!DOCTYPE html PUBLIC "-//W3C//DTD XHTML 1.0 Transitional//EN"
 "http://www.w3.org/TR/xhtml1/DTD/xhtml1-transitional.dtd">
<html xmlns="http://www.w3.org/1999/xhtml">
<head runat="server">
    <title>Show Drag Panel Extender</title>
    <style type="text/css">

    .pnlAdd
    {
        display: none;
        border: solid 1px black;
        background-color: #eeeeee;
    }

    .pnlDrag
    {
        background-color: #cccccc;
        color: White;
        cursor:move;
        padding: 3px;
    }

    .pnlContents
    {
```

```
            padding: 5px;
        }

    </style>
</head>
<body>
    <form id="form1" runat="server">
    <div>

    <asp:ScriptManager id="sm1" Runat="server" />

    <asp:GridView
        id="grdMovies"
        DataSourceID="srcMovies"
        Runat="server" />

    <asp:Panel ID="pnlAdd" CssClass="pnlAdd" runat="server">
        <asp:Panel ID="pnlDrag" CssClass="pnlDrag" runat="server">
        Add New Movie
        </asp:Panel>
        <div class="pnlContents">
        <asp:FormView
            ID="frmMovie"
            DataSourceID="srcMovies"
            DefaultMode="Insert"
            runat="server">
        <InsertItemTemplate>

        <asp:Label
            id="lblTitle"
            AssociatedControlID="txtTitle"
            Text="Title:"
            Runat="server" />
        <asp:TextBox
            id="txtTitle"
            Text='<%# Bind("Title") %>'
            Runat="server" />

        <br /><br />

        <asp:Label
            id="lblDirector"
            AssociatedControlID="txtDirector"
            Text="Director:"
            Runat="server" />
        <asp:TextBox
```

```
            id="txtDirector"
            Text='<%# Bind("Director") %>'
            Runat="server" />

    <br /><br />

    <asp:Button
        id="btnCancel"
        Text="Cancel"
        CommandName="Cancel"
        Runat="server" />
    <asp:Button
        id="btnInsert"
        Text="Insert"
        CommandName="Insert"
        Runat="server" />

    </InsertItemTemplate>
    </asp:FormView>
    </div>
</asp:Panel>
<ajax:DragPanelExtender
    id="dpe1"
    TargetControlID="pnlAdd"
    DragHandleID="pnlDrag"
    Runat="server" />

<br /><br />

<a
    href="javascript:void(0)"
    onclick="$get('pnlAdd').style.display='block';">Add Movie</a>


<asp:ObjectDataSource
    id="srcMovies"
    TypeName="Movie"
    SelectMethod="Select"
    InsertMethod="Insert"
    Runat="server" />

    </div>
    </form>
</body>
</html>
```

39

In Listing 39.5, the `DragPanel` extender control is declared like this:

```
<ajax:DragPanelExtender
    id="dpe1"
    TargetControlID="pnlAdd"
    DragHandleID="pnlDrag"
    Runat="server" />
```

Both the `TargetControlID` and `DragHandleID` properties point at Panel controls. The outer Panel, `pnlAdd`, is the Panel that gets dragged. The inner Panel, `pnlDrag`, is the Panel that you click to drag the outer Panel control.

When you first open the page, the Panel does not appear. The Cascading Style Sheet (CSS) rule associated with the Panel hides the Panel with `display:none`. The page includes the following link that displays the draggable Panel:

```
<a
    href="javascript:void(0)"
    onclick="$get('pnlAdd').style.display='block';">Add Movie</a>
```

The `$get()` method is an alias for the `document.getElementById()` method. When you click the link, the display style for the `pnlAdd` Panel is set to block, and the Panel and its contents appear.

Using the `FilteredTextBox` Control

The `FilteredTextBox` extender control enables you to prevent users from entering the wrong type of content into `TextBox`. You can use the `FilteredTextBox` extender control, for example, to create `TextBox` that accepts only numbers.

The page in Listing 39.6 illustrates how to use the `FilteredTextBox` control. The page contains two `TextBox` controls. The first `TextBox` accepts only numbers. The second `TextBox` accepts lowercase letters, underscores, and exclamation marks.

LISTING 39.6   ShowFilteredTextBox.aspx

```
<%@ Page Language="C#" %>
<%@ Register TagPrefix="ajax" Namespace="AjaxControlToolkit"
  Assembly="AjaxControlToolkit"  %>
<!DOCTYPE html PUBLIC "-//W3C//DTD XHTML 1.0 Transitional//EN"
  "http://www.w3.org/TR/xhtml1/DTD/xhtml1-transitional.dtd">
<html xmlns="http://www.w3.org/1999/xhtml">
<head runat="server">
    <title>Show Filtered TextBox</title>
</head>
<body>
```

```
<form id="form1" runat="server">
<div>
    <asp:ScriptManager ID="ScriptManager1" runat="server" />

    <asp:Label
        id="lblNumeric"
        Text="Enter a Number:"
        AssociatedControlID="txtNumeric"
        Runat="server" />
    <br />
    <asp:TextBox
        id="txtNumeric"
        Runat="server" />
    <ajax:FilteredTextBoxExtender
        id="fte1"
        TargetControlID="txtNumeric"
        FilterType="Numbers"
        Runat="server" />

    <br /><br />

    <asp:Label
        id="lblProductCode"
        Text="Enter a Product Code:"
        AssociatedControlID="txtProductCode"
        Runat="server" />
    <br />
    <asp:TextBox
        id="txtProductCode"
        Runat="server" />
    <ajax:FilteredTextBoxExtender
        id="fte2"
        TargetControlID="txtProductCode"
        FilterType="LowercaseLetters,Custom"
        FilterMode="ValidChars"
        ValidChars="_!"
        Runat="server" />
    <br />
    (A product code can contain only lower-case characters,
    underscores, exclamation marks, and no spaces)

</div>
</form>
</body>
</html>
```

39

You specify the type of characters that a TextBox extended with the FilteredTextBox control accepts by setting the FilterType property. This property accepts the following constants: Numbers, LowercaseLetters, UppercaseLetters, and Custom. You can assign more than one of these constants to the FilterType property by separating the constants with a comma.

If at least one of the FilterType constants is Custom, you can create either a list of valid characters or list of invalid characters for the filter. The second FilteredText control in Listing 39.6 has its FilterMode property set to the value ValidChars. The ValidChars property lists two valid characters (_ and !) that a user can enter in addition to lowercase letters.

Using the MaskedEdit Control

The MaskedEdit extender control renders a user interface that guides you as to what type of input a TextBox control accepts. For example, you can use the MaskedEdit control to force a user to enter a date, a number, or a currency amount in a certain format.

The page in Listing 39.7 includes a movie date released field. This field requires a date in the format mm/dd/yyyy. The MaskedEdit control enforces that format (see Figure 39.8).

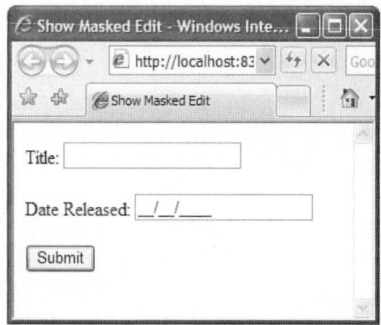

FIGURE 39.8   Using the MaskedEdit control when entering a date.

LISTING 39.7   ShowMaskedEdit.aspx

```
<%@ Page Language="C#" %>
<%@ Register TagPrefix="ajax" Namespace="AjaxControlToolkit"
 Assembly="AjaxControlToolkit"  %>
<!DOCTYPE html PUBLIC "-//W3C//DTD XHTML 1.0 Transitional//EN"
 "http://www.w3.org/TR/xhtml1/DTD/xhtml1-transitional.dtd">
<html xmlns="http://www.w3.org/1999/xhtml">
<head runat="server">
    <title>Show Masked Edit</title>
```

```
</head>
<body>
    <form id="form1" runat="server">
    <div>
        <asp:ScriptManager ID="ScriptManager1" runat="server" />

        <asp:Label
            id="lblTitle"
            Text="Title:"
            AssociatedControlID="txtTitle"
            Runat="server" />
        <asp:TextBox
            id="txtTitle"
            Runat="server" />

        <br /><br />

        <asp:Label
            id="lblDateReleased"
            Text="Date Released:"
            AssociatedControlID="txtDateReleased"
            Runat="server" />
        <asp:TextBox
            id="txtDateReleased"
            Runat="server" />
        <ajax:MaskedEditExtender
            id="me1"
            TargetControlID="txtDateReleased"
            Mask="99/99/9999"
            MaskType="Date"
            runat="Server" />

        <br /><br />

        <asp:Button
            id="btnSubmit"
            Text="Submit"
            Runat="server" />

    </div>
    </form>
</body>
</html>
```

The `MaskedEdit` control has three important properties:

- **TargetControlID**—The `TextBox` to extend.
- **Mask**—The mask to apply to the `TextBox`.
- **MaskType**—The type of mask to apply. Possible values are `None`, `Number`, `Date`, `Time`, and `DateTime`.

The `TargetControlID` and `Mask` properties are required. You should also set the `MaskType` property if you want the resulting text to be formatted correctly.

The `Mask` property accepts a character pattern. You can use the following special characters:

- 9—Only a numeric character.
- L—Only a letter.
- $—Only a letter or a space.
- C—Only a custom character (case-sensitive).
- A—Only a letter or a custom character.
- N—Only a numeric or custom character.
- ?—Any character.
- /—Date separator.
- :—Time separator.
- .—Decimal separator.
- ,—Thousands separator.
- \—Escape character.
- {—Initial delimiter for repetition of masks.
- }—Final delimiter for repetition of masks.

The final two special characters listed are curly braces. They enable you to specify how many times a character is allowed to be repeated. For example, you can use the following `TextBox` and `MaskedEdit` controls to force someone to enter a Social Security number in the format 555-55-5555:

```
<asp:TextBox
    id="txtSSN"
    Runat="server" />
<ajax:MaskedEditExtender
    id="MaskedEditExtender1"
    TargetControlID="txtSSN"
    Mask="9{3}-9{2}-9{4}"
    runat="Server" />
```

The character pattern 9{3} requires the user to enter three numbers in a row.

NOTE

The ASP.NET AJAX Control Toolkit also includes a `MaskedEditValidator` control that accompanies the `MaskedEdit` control. You can take advantage of the `MaskedEditValidator` control to provide the user with validation error messages when a user enters the wrong type of value into a TextBox extended with the `MaskedEdit` control.

Using the Animation Control

The Microsoft ASP.NET AJAX Control Toolkit includes a rich, declarative animation framework. You can use this framework to create animation special effects in your pages. For example, you can fade, move, and resize elements in a page. These animations are created without the benefit of Flash or Silverlight. The effects are written entirely in JavaScript.

Several of the Toolkit controls support the animation framework. For example, earlier in this chapter, we discussed the `AutoComplete` extender control. You can use the animation framework to create an animation when the list of suggestions appear and disappear. For instance, you might want the list of suggestions to fade in and out of view.

In this section, you learn about the `Animation` extender control. This control enables you to target one or more elements in a page and play an animation. The page in Listing 39.8 uses the `Animation` control to move a Panel control into the center of the page and then fade it out.

LISTING 39.8   ShowAnimationSimple.aspx

```
<%@ Page Language="C#" %>
<%@ Register TagPrefix="ajax" Namespace="AjaxControlToolkit"
 Assembly="AjaxControlToolkit"  %>
<!DOCTYPE html PUBLIC "-//W3C//DTD XHTML 1.0 Transitional//EN"
 "http://www.w3.org/TR/xhtml1/DTD/xhtml1-transitional.dtd">
<html xmlns="http://www.w3.org/1999/xhtml">
<head runat="server">
    <title>Show Animation Simple</title>
    <style type="text/css">

    #pnl
    {
        position:absolute;
        padding:3px;
        background-color: #eeeeee;
```

39

```
            border:solid 1px black;
        }

    </style>
</head>
<body>
    <form id="form1" runat="server">
    <div>
        <asp:ScriptManager ID="ScriptManager1" runat="server" />

        <asp:Panel
            ID="pnl"
            runat="server">
            <h3>I feel so animated!</h3>
        </asp:Panel>

        <ajax:AnimationExtender
            ID="ae1"
            TargetControlID="pnl"
            runat="server">
            <Animations>
            <OnLoad>
                <Sequence>
                <Move
                    Horizontal="300"
                    Vertical="300"
                    Duration="1"
                    Fps="20" />
                <FadeOut
                    Duration="1"
                    Fps="20" />
                </Sequence>
            </OnLoad>
            </Animations>
        </ajax:AnimationExtender>

    </div>
    </form>
</body>
</html>
```

In Listing 39.8, the Animation control targets a Panel control named pnl. The Panel control is moved to the center of the page and then is faded out.

Notice that the page in Listing 39.8 includes an inline style that sets several style attributes of the Panel control. In particular, the Panel control is given an absolute position. This is a requirement when using the Move animation.

When you create an animation, you must specify the event that triggers the animation. You can use any of the following events:

- **OnLoad**—Animation plays when the page loads.

- **OnClick**—Animation plays when the target control is clicked.

- **OnMouseOver**—Animation plays when you move your mouse over the target.

- **OnMouseOut**—Animation plays when you move your mouse away from the target.

- **OnHoverOver**—Animation plays when you hover your mouse over the target (stops any OnHoverOut animation).

- **OnHoverOut**—Animation plays when you hover your mouse away from the target (stops any OnHoverOver animation).

In the page in Listing 39.8, the animation starts as soon as the page loads.

An animation can consist of a set of animation effects that play in sequence or play in parallel. In Listing 39.8, the animation plays in sequence. First, the Panel was moved and then it was faded.

The ability to play animations in parallel is powerful because it provides you with a method of composing more complex animations out of simpler ones. For example, the Panel contained in the page in Listing 39.9 fades into view at the same time as it grows in size.

LISTING 39.9 ShowAnimationComposite.aspx

```
<%@ Page Language="C#" %>
<%@ Register TagPrefix="ajax" Namespace="AjaxControlToolkit"
 Assembly="AjaxControlToolkit"  %>
<!DOCTYPE html PUBLIC "-//W3C//DTD XHTML 1.0 Transitional//EN"
 "http://www.w3.org/TR/xhtml1/DTD/xhtml1-transitional.dtd">
<html xmlns="http://www.w3.org/1999/xhtml">
<head id="Head1" runat="server">
    <title>Show Animation Composite</title>
    <style type="text/css">

    #pnl
    {
        display:none;
```

```
            position:absolute;
            width:1px;
            height:1px;
            left:200px;
            top:200px;
            padding:3px;
            background-color: #eeeeee;
            border:solid 1px black;
        }

    </style>
</head>
<body>
    <form id="form1" runat="server">
    <div>
        <asp:ScriptManager ID="ScriptManager1" runat="server" />

        <asp:Button
            id="btn"
            Text="Play"
            OnClientClick="return false;"
            Runat="server" />

        <asp:Panel
            ID="pnl"
            runat="server">
            <h3>I feel so animated!</h3>
        </asp:Panel>

        <ajax:AnimationExtender
            ID="ae1"
            TargetControlID="btn"
            runat="server">
            <Animations>
            <OnClick>
              <Sequence AnimationTarget="pnl">
                <EnableAction
                    AnimationTarget="btn"
                    Enabled="false" />
                <StyleAction
                    Attribute="display"
                    Value="block"/>
                <Parallel>
                <FadeIn
                    Duration="1"
                    Fps="20" />
```

```
              <Scale
                  Duration="1"
                  Fps="20"
                  ScaleFactor="30.0"
                  Center="true" />
              </Parallel>
            </Sequence>
          </OnClick>
          </Animations>
      </ajax:AnimationExtender>

    </div>
    </form>
</body>
</html>
```

When you click the button rendered by the page in Listing 39.9, the following sequence of animations are rendered

- **EnableAction**—This animation is used to disable the button that started the animation.

- **StyleAction**—This animation is used to display the Panel control. When the page first opens, the Panel control has a style of display:none.

- **FadeIn**—This animation is used to fade the Panel into view.

- **Scale**—This animation is used to grow the Panel into view.

The FadeIn and Scale animations are contained in a `<Parallel>` tag, which causes these two animation effects to play simultaneously.

The animation framework supports the following types of animations:

- **Parallel Animation**—Plays a set of animations in parallel.

- **Sequence Animation**—Plays a set of animations in sequence.

- **Condition Animation**—Plays an animation when a JavaScript expression evaluates to true; otherwise, it plays another animation (the else clause).

- **Case Animation**—Plays one animation from a list of animations depending on the evaluation of a JavaScript expression.

- **Fade Animation**—Plays either a fade-in or fade-out animation.

- **FadeIn Animation**—Plays a fade-in animation.

- **FadeOut Animation**—Plays a fade-out animation.

- **Pulse Animation**—Plays fade-in and fade-out animations in rapid succession.

▶ **Discrete Animation**—Plays an animation by setting a property of the target element to a sequence of values.

▶ **Interpolated Animation**—Plays an animation by changing a property gradually between a range of values represented by `startValue` and `endValue`.

▶ **Color Animation**—Plays an animation by changing a property gradually between a range of values represented by a start color and an end color.

▶ **Length Animation**—Plays an animation by changing a property gradually between a range of values representing a start and end unit of length.

▶ **Move Animation**—Plays an animation by moving an element (either relatively or absolutely) across the page.

▶ **Resize Animation**—Plays an animation by resizing an element by changing the element's width and height.

▶ **Scale Animation**—Plays an animation by resizing an element by using a scale factor.

▶ **Enable Action**—An action that disables or enables an element on the page (such as a Button control).

▶ **Hide Action**—An action that hides an element by setting `display:none`.

▶ **Style Action**—An action that applies a style attribute to an element.

▶ **Opacity Action**—An action that modified the transparency of an element.

▶ **Script Action**—An action that executes a JavaScript script.

To learn more about the properties that you can use with each of these different types of animations, refer to the Animation Reference included with the ASP.NET AJAX Control Toolkit SampleWebSite website.

Using the UpdatePanelAnimation Control

The final Toolkit control that we need to discuss in this chapter is the UpdatePanelAnimation extender control. This control can play an animation both when an UpdatePanel is initiating an asynchronous postback and when postback results are returned from the web server.

Performing some type of animation while an UpdatePanel is performing an asynchronous postback provides the user with a way to know that your web application hasn't frozen. The animation indicates that some work is being done in the background.

The page in Listing 39.10 demonstrates how you can use the `UpdatePanelAnimation` control to create a yellow fade effect while an `UpdatePanel` is performing an update.

LISTING 39.10   ShowUpdatePanelAnimation.aspx

```
<%@ Page Language="C#" %>
<%@ Register TagPrefix="ajax" Namespace="AjaxControlToolkit"
 Assembly="AjaxControlToolkit"  %>
<!DOCTYPE html PUBLIC "-//W3C//DTD XHTML 1.0 Transitional//EN"
 "http://www.w3.org/TR/xhtml1/DTD/xhtml1-transitional.dtd">
<script runat="server">

    protected void btnSubmit_Click(object sender, EventArgs e)
    {
        System.Threading.Thread.Sleep(2000);
        lblSelectedColor.Text = txtFavoriteColor.Text;
    }
</script>

<html xmlns="http://www.w3.org/1999/xhtml">
<head runat="server">
    <title>Show UpdatePanel Animation</title>
</head>
<body>
    <form id="form1" runat="server">
    <div>
        <asp:ScriptManager ID="ScriptManager1" runat="server" />

        <%-- First Update Panel --%>

        <asp:UpdatePanel ID="up1" runat="server">
        <ContentTemplate>

        <asp:Label
            id="lblFavoriteColor"
            Text="Enter Your Favorite Color:"
            Runat="server" />
        <asp:TextBox
```

```
        id="txtFavoriteColor"
        Runat="server" />
    <asp:Button
        id="btnSubmit"
        Text="Submit"
        Runat="server" OnClick="btnSubmit_Click" />

    </ContentTemplate>
    </asp:UpdatePanel>
    <ajax:UpdatePanelAnimationExtender
        id="upae1"
        TargetControlID="up1"
        runat="server">
    <Animations>
        <OnUpdating>
        <Color
            Duration="0.5"
            Fps="20"
            Property="style"
            PropertyKey="backgroundColor"
            StartValue="#FFFFFF"
            EndValue="#FFFF90" />

        </OnUpdating>
        <OnUpdated>
        <Color
            Duration="1"
            Fps="20"
            Property="style"
            PropertyKey="backgroundColor"
            StartValue="#FFFF90"
            EndValue="#FFFFFF" />
        </OnUpdated>
    </Animations>
    </ajax:UpdatePanelAnimationExtender>

    <p> </p>

    <%-- Second Update Panel --%>
    <asp:UpdatePanel ID="up2" runat="server">
    <ContentTemplate>

    You selected:
    <asp:Label
        id="lblSelectedColor"
        Runat="server" />
```

```
        </ContentTemplate>
        </asp:UpdatePanel>
        <ajax:UpdatePanelAnimationExtender
            id="UpdatePanelAnimationExtender1"
            TargetControlID="up2"
            runat="server">
        <Animations>
            <OnUpdating>
            <Color
                Duration="0.5"
                Fps="20"
                Property="style"
                PropertyKey="backgroundColor"
                StartValue="#FFFFFF"
                EndValue="#FFFF90" />

            </OnUpdating>
            <OnUpdated>
            <Color
                Duration="3"
                Fps="20"
                Property="style"
                PropertyKey="backgroundColor"
                StartValue="#FFFF90"
                EndValue="#FFFFFF" />
            </OnUpdated>
        </Animations>
        </ajax:UpdatePanelAnimationExtender>

    </div>
    </form>
</body>
</html>
```

The page in Listing 39.10 contains two UpdatePanel controls. The first UpdatePanel control contains a form that asks you to enter your favorite color. When you submit the form, the color that you entered appears in a Label control that is contained in the second UpdatePanel control.

The yellow fade effect is applied to both UpdatePanel controls. When you submit the form, the background colors of both UpdatePanel controls fade to yellow. Then, gradually, the background colors fade back to white.

There are two good reasons to use a yellow fade effect in the page in Listing 39.10. First, this animation effect is used with the first UpdatePanel to show that work is being done.

During an asynchronous postback, a user cannot look at the browser progress bar to detect progress. You need to provide the user with some indication of work.

The second `UpdatePanelAnimation` control applies a yellow fade effect to the `UpdatePanel` that displays the value that the user entered into the form. The other reason to use a yellow fade effect is to highlight the areas of a page that have been updated. Because Ajax enables you to quietly update different regions of a page, you need some way of drawing a user's attention to the areas that have been updated. The `UpdatePanelAnimation` control provides you with an easy way to grab the user's attention and focus it on areas of the page that have been changed.

> **NOTE**
>
> The yellow fade effect was invented and popularized by Matthew Linderman at 37signals. You can read the original description of this technique at the following address: http://www.37signals.com/svn/archives/000558.php.

Summary

This chapter provided you with an overview of the ASP.NET AJAX Control Toolkit. In the first part of this chapter, you were provided with a brief overview of each of the controls currently contained in the Toolkit. Next, we focused on six of the controls: `AutoComplete`, `DragPanel`, `FilteredTextBox`, `MaskedEdit`, `Animation`, and `UpdatePanelAnimation`.

You learned how to use the `AutoComplete` control to display auto-complete suggestions while a user is entering text into a `TextBox`. You learned how to expose the suggestions from a web method contained in a page and a web method contained in a separate web service. You also learned how to associate a primary key value with each suggestion.

Next, we examined the `DragPanel` control. You learned how to use the `DragPanel` control to create a pop-up, draggable virtual window.

We then looked at two controls that can be used to restrict user input into a `TextBox`. You learned how to use the `FilteredTextBox` control to allow only certain characters to be entered in a TextBox. You also learned how to use the `MaskedEdit` control to provide a user interface that indicates the type of content a TextBox accepts.

Finally, we explored the topic of animation. You were provided with an overview of the rich, declarative animation framework included with the ASP.NET AJAX Control Toolkit. You also learned how to play an animation while an `UpdatePanel` control performs an asynchronous postback.

Client-Side Ajax with jQuery

In this chapter, you learn how to build "pure" Ajax applications that execute on the browser instead of the server. In previous versions of ASP.NET, the primary method of writing client-side code was to use the Microsoft AJAX library. This library provided extensions to JavaScript to make it resemble .NET languages such as C# and VB.NET.

The corporate vice president of .NET Platform, Scott Guthrie, announced in March 2010, that it was taking a different approach to client-side development. A JavaScript library called jQuery is now the recommended method to build client-side functionality. In ASP.NET 4, you can still use the Microsoft AJAX library to develop client-side applications, but it is now part of the Ajax Toolkit instead of built into ASP.NET Framework.

In the first part of this chapter, you learn about the jQuery library and how it works. You dive into two core features of jQuery: events and selectors. You also build your first application that executes completely on the client-side.

Next, we get to the heart of client-side Ajax. You learn how to perform Ajax calls from the browser to the server. You learn how to call both web methods exposed by an ASP.NET web service and web methods exposed by an ASP.NET page.

What Is jQuery?

jQuery is an extremely fast, lightweight JavaScript library that simplifies many aspects of client-side web development. You can use jQuery for almost any client-side functionality that you can think of—event handling, animations, drag-and-drop functionality, asynchronous web service calls, and much more. Furthermore, jQuery supports a robust plug-in model that enables developers to write their own extensions to implement whatever functionality they want. There are already hundreds of powerful jQuery plug-ins available.

jQuery is CSS3-compliant and works on almost all browsers—Internet Explorer 6.0+, FireFox 2+, Safari 3.0+, Opera 9.0, and Google Chrome. This means that you can write one set of code and not have to worry about handling the specifics of different browser implementations; each line of jQuery works exactly the same on all browsers.

The jQuery library is used on an incredible number of popular websites. Google, Dell, Bank of America, Digg.com, Netflix, WordPress, and even the White House are some examples of websites that rely on jQuery for client-side functionality.

Using the jQuery Library

The supporting code for jQuery, is contained in a single JavaScript file named `jquery-<version>.js`. At the time this book was written, the latest jQuery version is 1.4.1, so the filename is `jquery-1.4.1.js`. This file is included automatically in the Scripts folder when you create a website project using the ASP.NET Website template in Visual Studio 2010.

You'll also see two other files in the Scripts directory—`jquery-<version>.min.js` and `jquery-<version>-vsdoc.js` (see Figure 40.1).

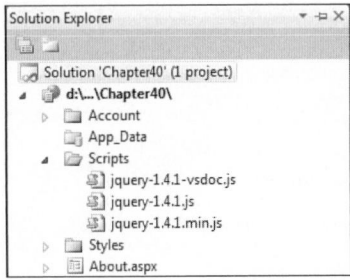

FIGURE 40.1   The jQuery library files within an ASP.NET project.

The "min" file is a "minified" version of the jQuery library. It can be compared to the two different versions of .NET builds: Debug and Release. The Debug contains more information so that you can track down errors but is ultimately slower. Similarly, the minified version of jQuery is a lot faster but is unreadable for debugging purposes. The minified version of jQuery is only 24KB, whereas the development version is 155KB—more than six times the size. For production applications, you should use the minified version of jQuery. For all the following examples, we use the larger, slower developer version of jQuery so that you can debug the applications.

> **NOTE**
>
> The Microsoft AJAX libraries also have separate development and minified versions. The minified version is 83KB—more than three times the size of the minified version of jQuery!

The vsdoc file provides jQuery IntelliSense within Visual Studio. Visual Web Developer attempts to provide all jQuery methods and objects in the pop-up window as you write your JavaScript. This is quite an accomplishment considering that jQuery (and JavaScript, in general) is dynamic, and a variable might change its data type at any time at runtime.

It is easy to add jQuery to any web page. You need to add only one line of HTML:

```
<script type="text/javascript" src="./Scripts/jquery-1.4n.1.js"></script>
```

Simply add this to your page, and you have the full jQuery library available to you. You don't need to explicitly add a reference to the vsdoc file—as long as the filename matches the jQuery filename up to the -vsdoc.js, the IntelliSense file will be interpreted automatically (see Figure 40.2).

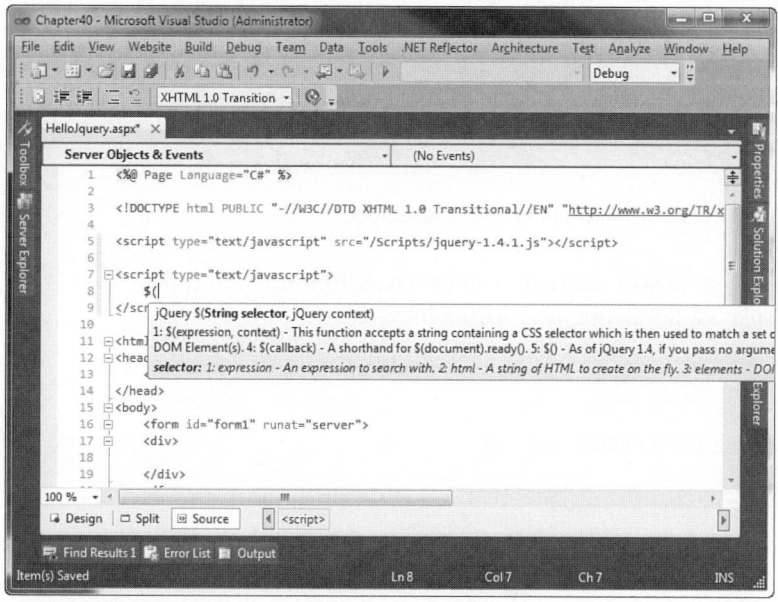

FIGURE 40.2   Adding jQuery to a page and jQuery IntelliSense.

Creating a jQuery File

Before we do anything else, we need to discuss how you create an external JavaScript file and reference it in a Web Form page. Although you can add JavaScript directly to a page by wrapping it in <script> tags, it is better to separate your client-side logic into its own file. You create a JavaScript file by selecting Website, Add New Item and selecting the Jscript File option (see Figure 40.3).

40

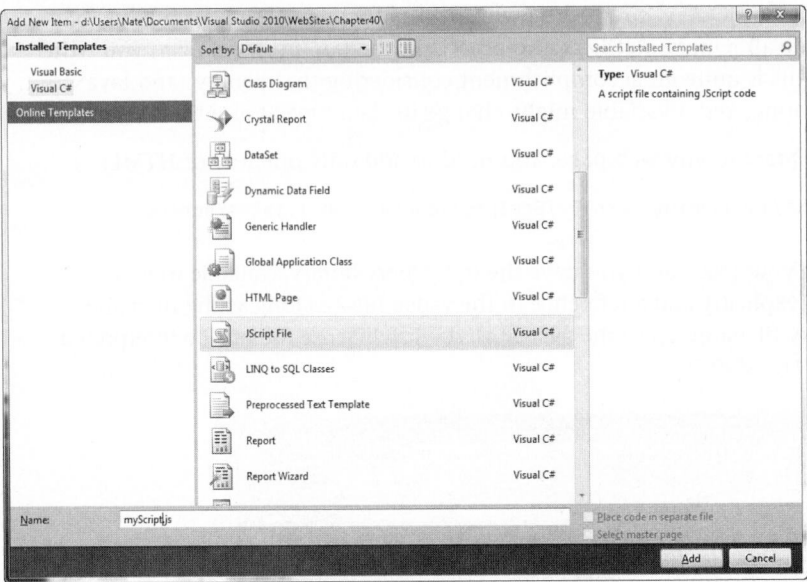

FIGURE 40.3   Creating a script file with Visual Web Developer.

For example, the file in Listing 40.1 contains a single JavaScript function called sayMessage() that displays a JavaScript alert with a message.

LISTING 40.1   myScript.js

```
/// <reference path="/Scripts/jquery-1.4.1.js"/>


function sayMessage() {
    alert("Hello World!");
}

$(document).ready(function () {
    sayMessage();
});
```

By default, Visual Studio will put this file in the root of your website. To keep things organized, you should move this file in the "scripts" folder of your project.

You should notice two special things about this file. First, at the bottom of the file is a call to a jQuery method: $(document).ready(). The significance of this method is explained in the next section.

Second, you notice a comment at the top of the file that references the jQuery library. This reference gives you full jQuery Intellisense in your JavaScript file, even though the jQuery library isn't explicitly referenced in your actual JavaScript code.

After you create an external JavaScript file, you can use it in an ASP.NET AJAX-enabled page by creating a script reference. The page in Listing 40.2 illustrates how you add a script reference to the myLibrary.js library.

LISTING 40.2   HelloJquery.aspx

```
<%@ Page Language="C#" %>


<!DOCTYPE html PUBLIC "-//W3C//DTD XHTML 1.0 Transitional//EN"
"http://www.w3.org/TR/xhtml1/DTD/xhtml1-transitional.dtd">

<script type="text/javascript" src="./Scripts/jquery-1.4.1.js"></script>
<script type="text/javascript" src="./Scripts/myScript.js"></script>

<html xmlns="http://www.w3.org/1999/xhtml">
<head runat="server">
    <title></title>
</head>
<body>
    <form id="form1" runat="server">
    <div>

    </div>
    </form>
</body>
</html>
```

You can see that all we're doing is adding another script reference to our new myScript.js file. Other than that, we're not adding any additional code to the page. From this simple six-line script and the reference to it, we're already adding client-side functionality to our page.

The $ Method and $(document).ready()

The heart of jQuery lies is a single method called jQuery(). To make things easier for developers, the same method can be called by using the $ character. The dollar-sign is a valid character in JavaScript, so it alone can be used as a method name.

The $() method is used to *select* objects in your web page. In general, it is similar to the JavaScript method getElementById, except it's much more flexible. We cover selectors in detail in the next section, but for now, understand that the $() method is used in every jQuery method.

The $(document).ready() call that we used in the previous example is your first example of a jQuery event. jQuery events are similar to ASP.NET events because they fire at certain points during an application's execution. The `$(document).ready()` event fires when the Domain Object Model (DOM) is loaded. Generally, you can put most of your jQuery code in this event:

```
$(document).ready(function() {
      // your jQuery code goes here
}
```

By doing so, you're ensuring that your page is ready before it runs your code. Otherwise, your logic might start executing before the page has completed loading, and your code might not work as expected.

In Listing 40.2, our script tells the browser to execute the `sayMessage()` method when the document is ready. When you execute the page, you can see the alert box pop up as soon as you open the page. Although it appears to pop up right away, the browser is actually waiting until any other page-preparing logic has completed and is ensuring that the DOM is fully loaded. When those conditions are met, the code in `$(document).ready()` fires and you see the alert box.

jQuery Selectors

Selectors are a core piece of the jQuery library. jQuery code follows this basic methodology:

> Select an element.
>
> Do something with it.

As we mentioned above, the `$()` is the method that you use to select elements. For `$(document).ready()`, we're actually selecting the "document" and defining what to do when the `ready()` event fires.

You can select any element (or multiple elements) on your page. Following are three basic ways of selecting elements:

- ▶ **By ID**—Matches a single element with the element ID. The ID you provide should be prefaced by a # character. For example, `$("#myId")` would match `<div id="myId">`.

- ▶ **By CSS Class**—Matches all elements with the provides CSS class. The class you provide should be prefaced with a . character. For example, `$(".navigationListItem")` would match `<li class="navigationListItem">`.

- ▶ **By Element**—Matches all elements by tag name. For example, `$("div")` would match `<div id="myId1">` and `<div id="myId2">`.

After selecting an element (or elements), you need to do something with it. For example, you can define what should execute when you click an element by using the "click" function. Listing 40.3 demonstrates this:

LISTING 40.3   jqueryClick.js

```
/// <reference path="/Scripts/jquery-1.4.1.js"/>


function spanClicked() {
    $("#colorSpan").addClass("redClass");
}

$(document).ready(function () {
    $("#clickSpan").click(spanClicked);
});
```

This code has two sections of jQuery. First, we define a function called "spanClicked" that selects the element with the ID "colorSpan". It then adds a CSS class to that element called "redClass"Second, we define the $(document).ready() code. When the document finishes loading, we select the element with an ID of "clickSpan" and tell it to execute the "spanClicked" function whenever that element is clicked.

Notice how we use inline function()syntax in the $(document).ready code. This is called an *anonymous function* in JavaScript and enables you to define functions inside of your logic without needing to explicitly define and name it. It is often used with jQuery and enables you to nest all your logic in a single call instead of defining a method for each one. It dramatically improves the readability and fluidity of your code as well.

The page in Listing 40.4 defines the span elements along with the CSS class and demonstrates the jQuery selectors.

LISTING 40.4   jqueryClick.aspx

```
<%@ Page Language="C#" %>


<!DOCTYPE html PUBLIC "-//W3C//DTD XHTML 1.0 Transitional//EN"
"http://www.w3.org/TR/xhtml1/DTD/xhtml1-transitional.dtd">

<script type="text/javascript" src="./Scripts/jquery-1.4.1.js"></script>
<script type="text/javascript" src="./Scripts/jqueryClick.js"></script>

<html xmlns="http://www.w3.org/1999/xhtml">
<head id="Head1" runat="server">
    <title></title>
```

40

```
<style type="text/css">
.redClass
{
    color: Red;
}

</style>
</head>
<body>
    <form id="form1" runat="server">
    <div>
        <p><span id="clickSpan">This is the span that we will click.</span></p>
        <p><span id="colorSpan">This will turn red when we click on it.</span></p>
    </div>
    </form>
</body>
</html>
```

There is an amazing amount of events and functions available in jQuery to apply to your selected objects. For a complete list, visit the documentation and tutorial sections at http://www.jquery.com.

Calling Web Services from the Client

The heart of Ajax is the capability to send and retrieve information from the web server without needing to post back a page to the web server. Ajax is all about performing "sneaky" postbacks.

The vision behind a pure Ajax application is that it should consist of a single page. All updates to the single page after it has been loaded should be performed by calling web services. You should never need to perform a postback because any postback results in a bad user experience. (The page jumps and the universe freezes.)

The jQuery library provides support for calling web services directly from the client (the web browser) with a built-in function called $.ajax. In this section, you learn two methods of exposing a web method to an AJAX page. You learn how to call a web method from a separate web service and how to call a web method exposed by the page.

Calling an External Web Service

Let's start simple. We create a Quotation web service that randomly returns a quotation from a list of quotations. Next, we create an AJAX page that contains a button. When you click the button, a random quotation displays in a <span> tag (see Figure 40.4).

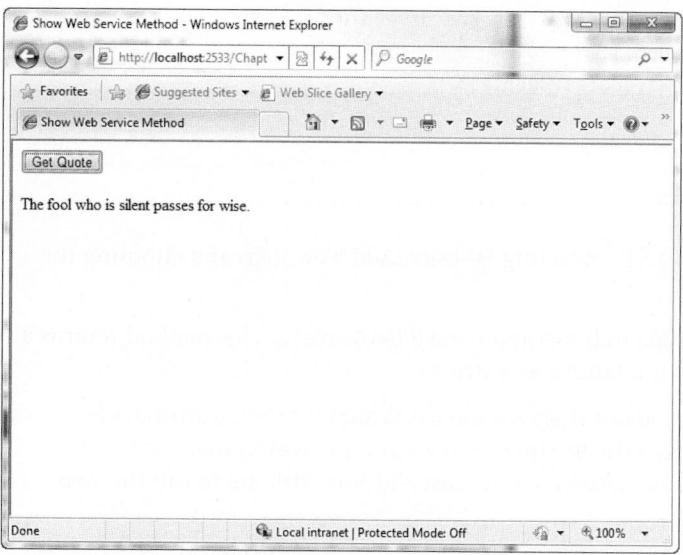

FIGURE 40.4   Retrieving a random quotation from the server.

The first step is to create the web service, which is contained in Listing 40.5.

LISTING 40.5   QuotationService.asmx

```
<%@ WebService Language="C#" Class="QuotationService" %>

using System;
using System.Web;
using System.Web.Services;
using System.Web.Services.Protocols;
using System.Web.Script.Services;
using System.Collections.Generic;

[WebService(Namespace = "http://tempuri.org/")]
[WebServiceBinding(ConformsTo = WsiProfiles.BasicProfile1_1)]
[ScriptService]
public class QuotationService  : System.Web.Services.WebService
{

    [WebMethod]
    public string GetQuote()
    {
        List<string> quotes = new List<string>();
        quotes.Add("The fool who is silent passes for wise.");
        quotes.Add("The early bird catches the worm.");
```

40

```
        quotes.Add("If wishes were true, shepherds would be kings.");
        Random rnd = new Random();
        return quotes[rnd.Next(quotes.Count)];
    }

}
```

You create the file in Listing 40.5 by selecting Website, Add New Item and choosing the Web Service item.

The web service contains a single web method named GetQuote(). This method returns a single quotation from a list of quotations as a string.

There is only one thing special about this web service. A ScriptService attribute is applied to the web service class. (The ScriptService attribute lives in the System.Web.Script.Services namespace.) You must add this attribute to call the web service from an AJAX page.

Now that we have created the web service, we can call it from an AJAX page. The page in Listing 40.6 calls the web service to display a random quotation.

LISTING 40.6   ShowWebServiceMethod.aspx

```
<%@ Page Language="C#" %>
<!DOCTYPE html PUBLIC "-//W3C//DTD XHTML 1.0 Transitional//EN"
 "http://www.w3.org/TR/xhtml1/DTD/xhtml1-transitional.dtd">
<html xmlns="http://www.w3.org/1999/xhtml">
<head id="Head1" runat="server">
    <title>Show Web Service Method</title>
    <script type="text/javascript" src="./Scripts/jquery-1.4.1.js"></script>

    <script type="text/javascript">

        $(document).ready(function () {
            $("#btnGet").click(function () {
                $.ajax({
                    type: "POST",
                    dataType: "json",
                    contentType: "application/json",
                    url: "QuotationService.asmx/GetQuote",
                    success: function (data) {
                        $("#spanQuote").html(data.d);
                    },
                    error: function () {
                        alert("The call to the web service failed.");
                    }
```

```
                })
            });
        });

    </script>
</head>
<body>
    <form id="form1" runat="server">
    <div>

        <input id="btnGet" type="button" value="Get Quote" />
        <br /><br />
        <span id="spanQuote"></span>

    </div>
    </form>
</body>
</html>
```

You should note several things in this page. To begin, the first thing we do in the `$(document).ready()` call is add a click event handler to the `"btnGet"` element. This click event makes one function call to the `$.ajax` function.

The `$.ajax` jQuery function makes an asynchronous call to a URL. In this case, we call the web service method that we defined at QuotationService.asmx/GetQuote. If this asynchronous call is successful, the "success" parameter's function gets called, which selects the "spanQuote" and fills it with the data that was returned by using the "html" jQuery function.

We also pass in a data type and content data type of "json" to our web service. JSON stands for JavaScript Object Notation and is a lightweight format that enables you to define an unordered set of name/value pairs. This data is contained in the `"d"` property of data—when we call the `"html"` jQuery function, we pass in `"data.d"` as the parameter so all the data is pushed into the span. When web services first started being utilized, XML was used almost exclusively to send data back and forth. Today, JSON is quickly becoming the standard because large amounts of data can be sent back and forth without the extra overhead of XML.

When you call a web method with `$.ajax`, you can pass a reference to both a success and an error method. If the web method call is successful, the success method is called. Otherwise, the error method is called.

In Listing 40.6, if the `$.ajax` call is successful, the quotation displays in a <span> tag in the body of the page.

40

Calling a Static Page Method

If you do not plan to call a web method from multiple pages, don't perform all the work of creating a separate web service. Instead, you can expose a static method from the same AJAX page calling the web method.

For example, the page in Listing 40.7 includes a server method named GetQuote().

LISTING 40.7   ShowPageMethod.aspx

```
<%@ Page Language="C#" %>
<!DOCTYPE html PUBLIC "-//W3C//DTD XHTML 1.0 Transitional//EN"
 "http://www.w3.org/TR/xhtml1/DTD/xhtml1-transitional.dtd">

 <script runat="server">
     [System.Web.Services.WebMethod]
     public static string GetQuote()
     {
         List<string> quotes = new List<string>();
         quotes.Add("The fool who is silent passes for wise.");
         quotes.Add("The early bird catches the worm.");
         quotes.Add("If wishes were true, shepherds would be kings.");
         Random rnd = new Random();
         return quotes[rnd.Next(quotes.Count)];
     }
 </script>

<html xmlns="http://www.w3.org/1999/xhtml">
<head id="Head1" runat="server">
    <title>Show Web Service Method</title>
    <script type="text/javascript" src="./Scripts/jquery-1.4.1.js"></script>

    <script type="text/javascript">

        $(document).ready(function () {
            $("#btnGet").click(function () {
                $.ajax({
                    type: "POST",
                    dataType: "json",
                    contentType: "application/json",
                    url: "ShowPageMethod.aspx/GetQuote",
                    success: function (data) {
                        $("#spanQuote").html(data.d);
                    },
                    error: function () {
                        alert("The call to the web service failed.");
                    }
```

```
                })
            });
        });

    </script>
</head>
<body>
    <form id="form1" runat="server">
    <div>

        <input id="btnGet" type="button" value="Get Quote" />
        <br /><br />
        <span id="spanQuote"></span>

    </div>
    </form>
</body>
</html>
```

Just like in the previous section, you can call a page method in the exact same manner as a web service. We pass in the URL and method name of our GetQuote() method to the $.ajax call, and our success and error references do the rest. This is handy when you develop page-specific functionality that doesn't require the extra work of building a separate web service.

Summary

In the first part of this chapter, you learned about the jQuery library and what it has to offer. You learned about the $(document).ready() event and how to select elements with the $() jQuery function.

In the next part, you learned how to call web services from the browser. You learned how to call a web method in an external web service and a static web method exposed from a server-side page.

jQuery is a powerful tool that makes it incredibly easy to add client-based functionality to your web applications with little code. We have barely scratched the surface of what jQuery can do—it is a great way to improve the user experience of your applications, so spend some time to learn everything it has to offer.

40

Index

Symbols

A

CacheDependency, 1394

CircleHotSpot, 106

component libraries, 749-757

Configuration, 1536-1537

ConflictedMovies, 830-831

constructors, 733-736

Control, 1576

ControlBuilder, 1626, 1629-1631

ControlCachePolicy, 1370-1371

creating, 722, 724

CultureInfo, 1434-1438

custom components, inheriting profiles from, 1308-1309

data access. See data access components

DBMovie, 920

definition of, 722

different language components, mixing in App_Code folder, 725-726

DpapiProtectedConfigurationProvider, 1557

dynamic compilation, 724-725

EmployeeData, 791-793

EmployeesDSSorting, 810

ExpressionBuilders, 1464-1469

FieldHelloWorld, 728-729

fields
    declaring, 728-731
    shared fields, 733

File, 10

FilterMovies, 815-816

FormsAuthentication, 1216-1220

Framework Class Library. See Framework Class Library

Graphics, 10

Guestbook, 820

HelloWorld, 722, 724

HtmlTextWriter, 1580-1584

HTTP Handlers, 1470
    anonymous HTTP Handlers, 1478-1481
    Generic Handlers, creating, 1470-1473
    IHttpHandler interface, 1475-1476
    IHttpHandler interface, implementing, 1473

HttpApplication, 1482-1483
    custom HTTP Modules, creating, 1487-1489
    Global.asax files, 1483, 1485

HttpCachePolicy, 1358-1360

HttpCookie, 1272-1273

HttpPostedFile, 180

HttpSessionState, 1284-1285

inheritance, 739-741

InsertMovie, 824-825

Intellisense, 744, 746

interfaces, declaring, 742-743

MailDefinition, 1167

Membership, 1227-1230

MembershipProvider, 741

MembershipUser, 1230-1231

methods
    declaring, 726-728
    overloading, 734-736
    shared methods, 726, 728
    signatures, 735

Movie, 1382

Movie4, 865-868

Movie5, 870-872

MovieCollection, 772-773

MovieDataReader, 774-775

MovieDataSet, 776-778

Movies, 783, 785-786

MoviesByCategory, 826-827

MoviesDSPaging, 800-802

MustInherit classes, 739-741

namespaces, declaring, 736-738

PagePropertyParameter, 838-839, 841

partial classes, 42, 738

PolygonHotSpot, 106

PostBackOptions, 1613, 1616

Preferences, 747, 749

ProductConstructor, 736

ProfileManager, 1323, 1325

properties
    declaring, 728-731
    shared properties, 733

D

How can we make this index more useful? Email us at indexes@samspublishing.com

files

authorizing by location, 1224-1225

generating source code from. *See* BuildProviders

jQuery, creating, 1771-1773

large files, uploading, 189-190, 193, 195

  buffering thresholds, 189

  FileUploadLarge.ashx page, 194

  FileUploadLarge.aspx page, 190, 193

placing configuration settings in, 1522-1523

saving

  to database, 185, 188-190, 193

  to filesystem, 181, 184

web configuration, 13, 1096

Web.sitemap, 1097

XML files, storing advertisements in, 208, 210, 212

Files property, 1134

FileService class, 1744

FileService.asmx file, 1743

filesystem, saving files to, 181, 184

FileUpload control, 180

files

  large files, uploading, 189-195

  saving to databases, 185, 188-190, 193

  saving to filesystems, 181, 184

HttpPostedFile class, 180

methods, 180

properties, 180

FileUploadDatabase.aspx page, 185, 187

FileUploadFile.aspx page, 181, 183

FileUploadLarge.ashx page, 194

FileUploadLarge.aspx page, 190, 193

Fill( ) method, 892, 1416

FilterChart.aspx page, 697

FilteredTextBox control, 1738, 1754, 1756

FilterExpression property, 397

filtering, 813

Chart Control, 694, 696, 698

data, ObjectDataSource control, 813-816

rows, 395-397

Filtering event, 403, 817

FilterMovies component, 815-816

FilterMovies.cs file, 815-816

FilterParameters collection, 783

filters

QueryExtender control, 711-719

transition, 627

FilterTopN method, 696

FinancialFormula method, 701, 704

FindContent.aspx file, 262-263

FindControl( ) method, 39, 98, 261-263, 555

FindInactiveProfilesByUserName( ) method, 1323

FindMaster.master file, 261-262

FindProfilesByUserName( ) method, 1323

FindUsersByEmail( ) method, 1227

FindUsersByName( ) method, 1227

FindUsersInRole( ) method, 1258

FinishButtonClick event, 227

FinishDestinationPageUrl property (Wizard control), 226

FinishNavigationTemplate, 226

Firebug, 1676

FirstHalf.cs file, 738

FirstPage.aspx page, 7, 35, 37

FirstPageCodeBehind.aspx page, 40-42

FirstPageCodeBehind.aspx.cs file, 41

FirstPageImageUrl property (PagerSettings class), 506, 581, 608

FirstPageText property (PagerSettings class), 506, 581, 608

fixed values, comparing form fields against, 148

Float.css file, 287-288

floating layouts, 287-288

Focus( ) method, 180

Button control, 86

CheckBox control, 78

ImageButton control, 93

ImageMap control, 111

LinkButton control, 89

H

O

P

WebConfigurationManager class, 1523

Wizard control, 226

Property( ) method, 984

PropertyContent.aspx file, 259, 261

PropertyExpression, 715, 719

PropertyHelloWorld component, 730-731

PropertyHelloWorld.cs file, 729

PropertyMaster.master file, 258-259

PropertyName property

ControlParameter object, 410

ProfileParameter object, 420

PropertyOrField( ) method, 984

PropertyRandomImage control, 304

PropertyRandomImage User control, 305

PropertyRandomImage.ascx file, 304-305

Proposed value, 901

Protected access, 743-744

Protected Friends, 744

protection configuration option (Forms authentication), 1208

ProtectSection( ) method, 1558, 1561

provider attribute, 1298

Provider property

SiteMap class, 1090

SiteMapNode class, 1093

provider statistics, retrieving, 849-856

displaying in GridView control, 855-856

list of statistics, 854

Movie2 component, 850, 852

ResetStatistics( ) method, 853

RetrieveStatistics( ) method, 853

ProviderName property, 386, 1231

providers, creating Site Maps providers

AutoSiteMapProvider, 1106, 1109-1110

SqlSiteMapProvider, 1111, 1114, 1116

Providers property, 1090, 1552

ProviderSettingsCollection class, 1553

ProviderSpecific value, 1314

ProviderUserKey property (MembershipUser class), 1231

provisioning new websites, 1543, 1546

ProvisionSite.aspx page, 1544

Public access, 743-744

PublicSiteMap.ashx page, 1117, 1119

PublicSiteMap.ashx results, 1120

Publish/Package SQL screen, 1571

Pulse Animation, 1763

Push SQL cache dependencies, 1408-1409

configuring applications for, 1410

configuring databases for, 1409-1410

Data Caching, 1415-1416

DataSource Caching, 1412, 1414

Page Output Caching, 1411-1412

PushSQLDataCache.aspx page, 1415-1416

PushSQLDataSourceCache.aspx page, 1413-1414

PushSQLOutputCache.aspx page, 1411-1412

Q

queries

associations, 959-960

dynamic, 983-987

entities, building, 952-959

expressions, 983

jQuery

$( ) method, 1773-1774

$(document).ready( ) method, 1773-1774

creating files, 1771-1773

libraries, 1770-1771

overview of, 1769

selectors, 1774-1776

LinqDataSource control, 960, 962-963

SQL, cache dependencies, 1408

query syntax, 950

QueryExtender control, 711-719

querying, 712

ControlFilterExpression, 712

CustomExpression, 712

DynamicFilterExpression, 713

How can we make this index more useful? Email us at indexes@samspublishing.com

How can we make this index more useful? Email us at indexes@samspublishing.com

T

V

How can we make this index more useful? Email us at indexes@samspublishing.com

X–Z

then, with his animal guides, would be shown a community of spirits responsible for sickness in the world. Later the shaman would 'fly' in spirit form to the top of an enormous tree that would explain to him: 'I am the tree that makes all people capable of living.' The tree spirit would then provide the shaman with a branch with three offshoots that could be used in the construction of three special drums: one for performing shamanic rituals over women in childbirth, the second for treating the sick and the third for aiding those who were dying. In Siberia the drum itself had a special role because it was on the rhythmic drumbeat that the shaman 'rode' into a state of ecstasy. And the idea of shamanism as a 'journey' into the metaphysical world is a feature not only of Nanay cosmology, but of shamanic cultures generally.

It therefore comes as no surprise that among the Jivaro of Eastern Ecuador, for example, the normal everyday world is considered to be false or a 'lie', while the truth about the real nature of things is to be found only by entering the 'supernatural' world. Undertaking this vision quest, clearly, is the role of the shaman.

BECOMING A SHAMAN

Shamanism is a magical vocation. Some shamans adopt their role in society as part of an ancestral lineage, while others are called to the path through dreams or spirit-visions. The Chukchee of Siberia say that future shamans have a certain look in their eyes which indicates that they can see beyond the domain of everyday reality to the realms of spirit which lie beyond. And perhaps because this visionary capacity is restricted to just a few, shamans have often found themselves somewhat on the edge of society – rather like visionary eccentrics. Often introverted and sometimes smitten themselves by disease or misfortune, potential shamans by definition function in parallel mental universes and, as a result, some psychiatrists have compared them to schizophrenics. There is, however, a crucial difference between shamans and schizophrenics. Schizophrenics move in and out of different mental states continually and without control,

thus dwelling in a world of experiential chaos, while shamans have to learn to integrate their visionary capacities and subject them to the individual will. For this reason, the noted scholar of comparative religion, Mircea Eliade, referred to the shaman or medicine man as one 'who has succeeded in curing himself'. With this self-mastery comes the ability to undertake spirit-journeys, to drive away evil spirits and to cure the sick.

Often during the initiatory process of becoming a shaman there are special revelations. The North American Gitksan Indian Isaac Tens began falling into trance states when he was 30 and frequently experienced terrifying visions. On one occasion, animal spirits and snake-like

Luisah Teish (above) is a voodoo priestess of African, Haitian, Native American and French ancestry. A priestess of Oshun, 'Mother of the Spirit', she uses healing trance.

Drums and percussive instruments have traditionally played a central role in shamanism because they provide the rhythms of sound on which the shaman 'rides' into an altered state of consciousness.

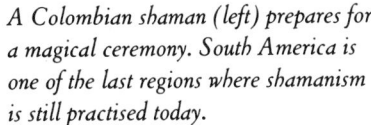

A Colombian shaman (left) prepares for a magical ceremony. South America is one of the last regions where shamanism is still practised today.

trees seemed to be chasing him, and an owl tried to attack him and lift him up. Later, on a hunting trip, Tens again saw an owl and shot it, but was unable to locate its body. He fell into a trance. His body began to 'boil' and 'quiver' and he found he was singing spontaneously:

A chant was coming out of me without my being able to do anything to stop it. Many things appeared to me presently: huge birds and other animals. They were calling me. I saw a meskyawawderh (a kind of bird) and a mesqag-weeuk (bullhead fish). These were visible only to me, not to the others in my house. Such visions happen when a man is about to become a halaait; they occur of their own accord. The songs force themselves out, complete, without any attempt to compose them. But I learned and memorised these songs by repeating them.

Similarly, the Paviotso shaman Dick Mahwee had his first shamanic visions while dreaming in a cave. Aged around 50, Mahwee was in a state of 'conscious sleep' and had a mystical encounter with a tall, thin Indian holding an eagle tail-feather. The Indian instructed him in ways of curing sickness. Mahwee now enters a trance state to perform shamanic healing:

I smoke before I go into the trance. While I am in the trance no one makes any noise. I go out to see what will happen to the patient. When I see a whirlwind I know that it caused the sickness. If I see the patient walking on grass and flowers it means that he will get well; he will soon be up and walking. When I see the patient among fresh flowers and he picks them it means that he will recover. It the flowers are withered or look as if the frost had killed them, I know that the patient will die. Sometimes in a trance I see the patient walking on the ground. If he leaves footprints I know that he will live, but if there are no tracks, I cannot cure him.

REGALIA AND RITUALS

As noted earlier, the shaman was perceived as a master of ecstasy: the shaman's role was to fly in the spirit vision to where the gods were, for it was here that the revelations were received. And since the shaman was able to travel from one dimension of reality to another, it was understandable that his rituals and clothing would embody all that was sacred or mythically relevant within the given culture.

Sometimes shamans would decorate their clothing with motifs relating to their magical animal allies, or with relevant symbols from their mythology.

Traditional Japanese shamans wore caps of eagle and owl feathers and their cloaks were adorned with stuffed snakes. Siberian Yakut shamans wore kaftans embellished with a solar disc – thought to be the opening through the earth leading to the Underworld – while Goldi shamans wore coats depicting the Cosmic Tree and magical animals like bears and leopards. Buryats wore costumes laden with iron ornaments, symbolizing the iron bones of immortality, and also used motifs representing the bears, serpents and lizards that they had befriended as their helper spirits.

This bone was used by Batak shamans from Sumatra to read magical chants. It is carved with a spirit figure, magical symbols and pentacles.

Shamans, as we have already noted, imitate birds and animals in their dances. Yakuts could imitate the lapwing, falcon, eagle and cuckoo, while Kirghiz shamans learned not only bird songs but also how to imitate the sounds of their

wings in flight. Zuni Pueblo Indians still summon their Beast Gods in ceremonies involving dancing, rattling and drumming. Wearing ritual masks, they work themselves into a state of frenzy where they feel they are becoming the animals themselves through an act of ritual identification. According to anthropologist Dr Michael Harner, who has observed them, the Zuni dancers are doing much more than simply impersonating animal forms. Transported into an altered state of consciousness by the dancing, drumming, rattling and whirr of bull-roarers, the shaman 'becomes for the time being the actual

This Eskimo woodcarving represents a shaman in the middle of a seance, with his two animal helper-spirits nearby. His shaman drum is close at hand.

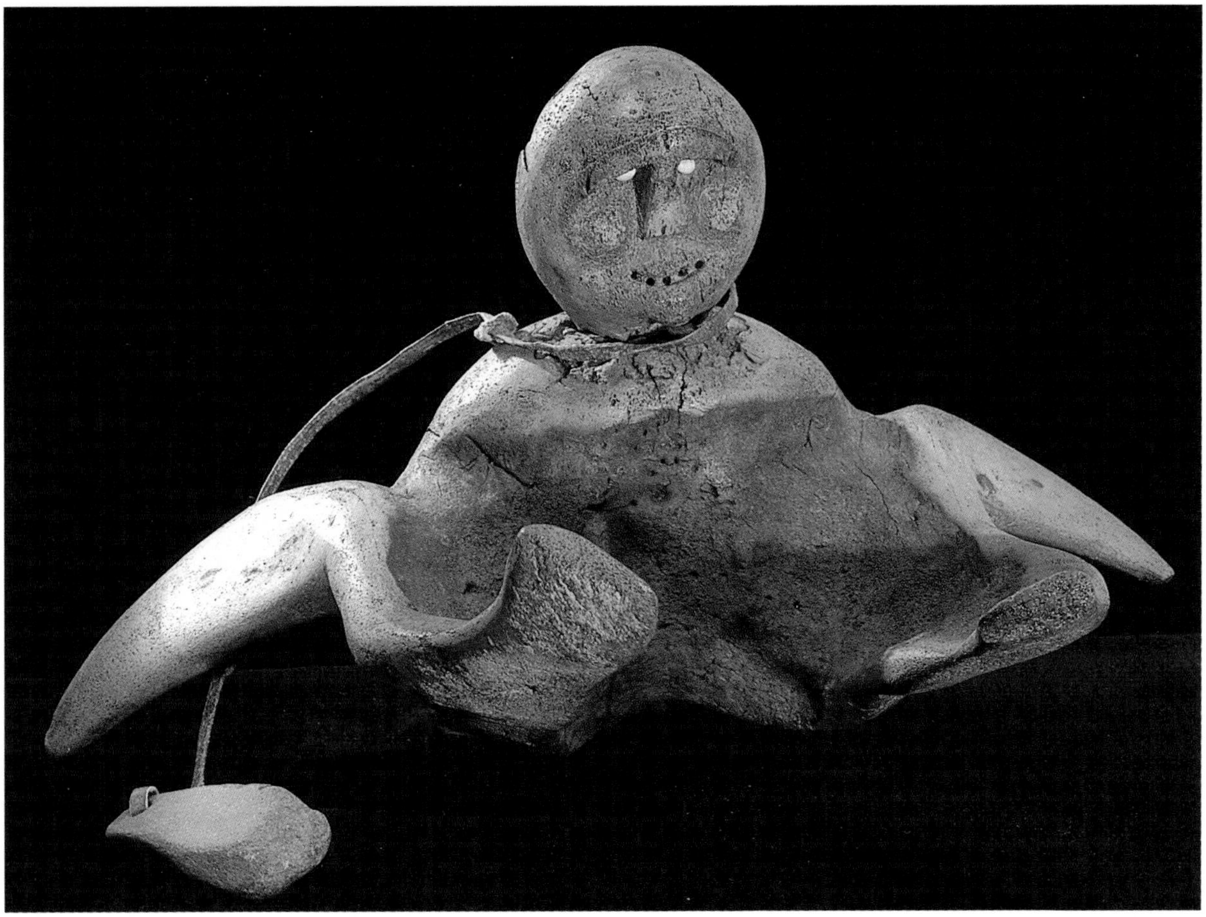

An Eskimo figurine from Point Hope, Alaska. Here we see a shaman engaged in leaving his body in spirit form to fly into the celestial realms. The figurine is fashioned from whale vertebrae, walrus ivory, wood, seal hide and stone.

embodiment of the spirit which is believed to reside in the mask'.

As one can see from accounts like this, the drum plays a vital role in shamanic practice: it is literally the 'vehicle' that carries the shaman into the magical world. The rhythmic sound of the drumbeat acts as a focusing device for the shaman, enabling him to enter the trance state in a controlled way. Some shamans also embellish their drums in ways that are symbolically significant. Lapp shamans decorate their drums with motifs like the Cosmic Tree, the Sun, the Moon or a rainbow, while traditional Evenks fashioned their drum rims from sacred larch.

SACRED PLANTS, HELPER SPIRITS AND DIVINATION

In divining the origins of sickness, some healer-shamans have frequent recourse to sacred mind-altering plants and helper spirits, or 'familiars'.

The Mazatec Indians of Mexico, who have female shamans as their healers, make use of sacred psilocybe mushrooms; the shamans use the altered state of consciousness induced by the mushrooms to determine the cause of the sickness or affliction. Among the Mazatecs, both the patient and the shaman take the sacred mushrooms so that the sick person may in due course hear the healing words which issue forth from the spirit world, and thereby share directly in the cure.

When the adventurer and former banker Gordon Wasson visited the Sierra Mazateca in 1955, he made contact with the renowned shaman Maria Sabina. Maria had become well known in the town of Huatla for assisting people who were ill, suffering some sort of loss or theft, or wishing to recover from the effects of an accident. Wasson obtained permission to attend a *velada*, or all-night healing vigil. During the *velada* Maria took thirteen pairs of mushrooms while the other participants took five or six pairs each, the idea being that the mushrooms would eventually 'speak' through the voice of the shaman. The spirits of the sacred mushroom were invoked and, at a very special point during

the evening, divinatory pronouncements were made. As Maria Sabina explained to Gordon Wasson: 'I see the Word fall, come down from above, as though they were little luminous objects falling from heaven. The Word falls on the Holy Table, on my body: with my hand I catch them. Word by Word.'

A similar use of sacred psychedelic plants is found in the divinatory ceremonies of Peruvian shaman Eduardo Calderón. Like Maria Sabina, Calderón blends Christianity and native Indian traditions. Born in 1930, he grew up in a Spanish-speaking, Roman Catholic family, but at the age of 24 began an apprenticeship with a *curandero* who was the uncle of his second wife. This healer made ritual use of the psychedelic San Pedro cactus and also had an altar, or *mesa*, containing various magical 'power objects'. After successfully treating a sick person through his newly learned shamanic techniques, Calderón became a *curandero* in his own right.

According to Calderón, the visionary cactus enables him to contact healing energies in the Cosmos and allows him to interpret the magical influences afflicting his patients. Calderón's *mesa* includes symbolic zones pertaining to the polarities of good and evil, and also has a middle zone where the opposing forces are held in balance. The left zone is ruled by Satan, the right by Jesus Christ, and various artefacts and images of the saints are used in the divinatory ritual.

During a healing session Calderón drinks a San Pedro infusion and in due course this 'activates' the artefacts on the magical altar, enabling him to 'see' the cause of witchcraft or bad luck affecting his patient. Once diagnosed, such evil influences can be ritually exorcized. Well educated as he is, Calderón was able to describe the process to anthropologist Douglas Sharon in terms familiar to the Western mind:

The subconscious is a superior part (of man) ... a kind of bag where the individual has stored all his memories.... By means of the magical plants and the chants and the search for the roots of the problem, the subconscious of the individual is opened like a flower.

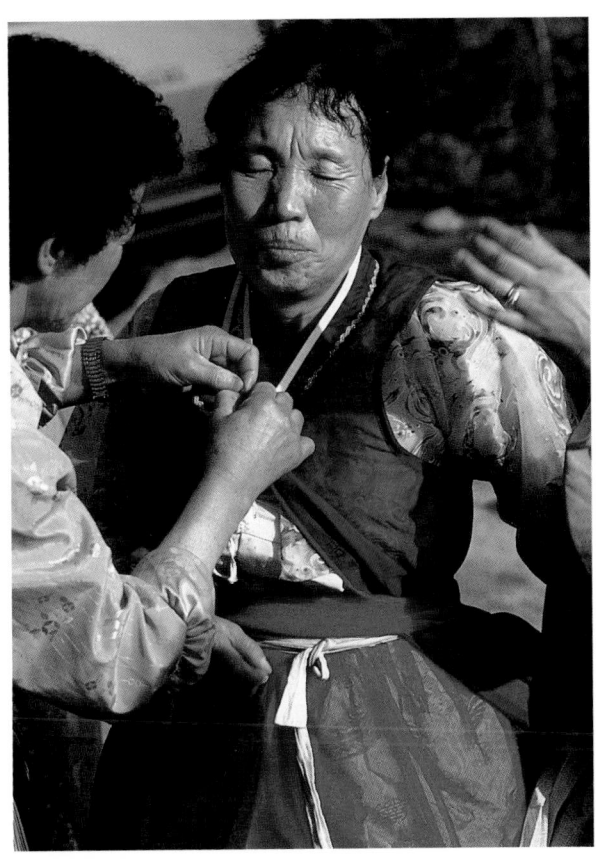

A South Korean shaman in trance. In Korea, shamanism predated the arrival of Buddhism, and was introduced from the Altaic and Tungusic regions of Central and Northern Asia.

Dr Michael Harner (below) with his shaman drum. Harner, a former anthropology professor, introduced shamanism to contemporary psychological understanding and has been a major influence in bringing shamanism to the West.

If sacred plants are often a vital ingredient in shamanic healing rituals, so too are magical helper spirits or 'allies'. There are many different terms for these entities – they are variously known as 'familiars', 'guardian spirits', 'dream healers' or 'power animals' - but it is generally agreed by scholars of comparative religion that healer-shamans need spirit guides of one form or another in their divinatory practices. As Michael Harner has written: 'A shaman may be defined as a man or woman who is in direct contact with the spirit world through a trance state and has one or more spirits at his command to carry out his bidding for good or evil.' These allies appear to the shaman in dreams and visions and on some occasions can be purchased or inherited from other shamans or family elders. Allies can be summoned into action through songs and dances and often require ritualistic offerings. Some shamans have even claimed to be married to their spirit guides!

The divinatory functions of helper spirits are diverse. They might be sent by the shaman into the patient's body in order to detect the cause of sickness, or they might be despatched in order to locate missing objects. Healer spirits may also accompany the shaman on the visionary journey to the magical world.

The Yurok Indians of north-western California still practise shamanic healing using spirit guides. Yurok healer Tela Lake describes a shaman as 'a holistic healer who uses the physical and spiritual forces of Nature to effect a cure'. She believes that the soul is the very essence of a human being, and that the body, mind and soul are held together by a force-field of power or spirit. It is this energy field that can be treated by the shaman through spirit divination.

Patients abstain from drugs, sex and alcohol for four days prior to a healing ceremony with Tela Lake: they are then considered 'clean'. After the patient arrives, Tela goes outside to consult with her familiar spirits and then accepts or rejects the patient for the healing ceremony (refusal usually arising only when the patient contravenes the spiritual laws of the Yurok in some way). Immediately before the actual ceremony, all participants are required to bathe and various plants and herbal medicines are used to purify the patient.

As the ceremony begins, the shaman sits in front of her patient, facing east, and invokes her spirits through song and prayer. According to Tela, the spirits will feel welcome if the area is 'clean' and they assist her in identifying the cause of the patient's problems. She says that some spirits can fly backwards in time to seek the origins of disease, while other 'interpreter' spirits can divine information received magically in different languages. Included among Tela's helper spirits are a woodpecker (able to remove pain from the patient's body) and a humming-bird (able to suck out poison). She also summons bear and wolf allies to fight off sickness and a spirit fish to eat away at illness, as the need arises.

The Shoshoni medicine-man, Tudy Roberts, on the other hand, told Professor Ake Hult-krantz in the 1950s that he had spirit helpers of both animal and human appearance. Once he had a dream-vision where he saw three bear spirits, one of which claimed to be immune to bullets and offered one of his ears to the shaman as a protection. Later Roberts found a dead bear, cut off its ear, and began to wear it during the important Sun Dance ceremony, which was performed by the Shoshoni as a thanksgiving to the Supreme Being.

Roberts also had contact with three hu-manoid spirit beings after performing a Sun Dance and then falling asleep in the foothills of Fort Washakie. These spirits looked like Indians but wore feathers in their hats and had 'very clean clothes'. Roberts

learned that they were lightning spirits and that they would help him in his healing practices. The spirits showed him how to perform shamanic divination using an eagle tail and eagle wing, and he subsequently gained the power to cure diseases like colds, measles and paralysis. However Roberts never sought to cure anybody unless he received instructions from his helper spirits in shamanic dream-vision.

The divinatory practices of shamans like Tela Lake and Tudy Roberts epitomize a point made earlier: that it is in the world of spirit that we gain the most profound perspectives on the true nature of our life, our health and our well-being on the planet.

From the viewpoint of the modern reader, keen to understand this most ancient of all religious and divinatory systems, we can think of shamanism as a means of recognizing the spiritual dimension in Nature and of awakening the magical potentialities within our very being. Shamanism reminds us that we all share a common destiny on the planet, since we are all born of the Earth Mother. If we can begin to attune ourselves to a holistic understanding of both Nature and Cosmos, we will find ourselves entering into a spiritual tradition which is as old as humanity itself.

In shamanism the drum is literally the vehicle for transporting the healer or magician into a state of trance. This shaman's drum is from the Magar tribe of Nepal.

THE
CIRCUMPOLAR
REGION

In the long, cold nights of the Far North, when no one could be certain if the sun would ever rise again once it had set, it became especially important to know what the future held in store. For this reason the divinatory methods described in this section are particularly detailed and precise. They range from the detailed study of animal bones, through the observance of rings or bone fragments gyrating on a beaten drum-skin, to the questioning of dead spirits. We also encounter the presence of animal 'totems' or helpers, both personal and tribal, who gave assistance to the diviners in their search for the hidden reasons behind daily events.

Here again we meet the class of official diviners who are named shamans, whose work consists in maintaining a close and harmonious relationship with the natural world – a thread in the tapestry of divination which reappears again in many of the methods described in this book.

As we saw in Chapter One, the shamans possessed many skills, of which divination was only one. In the subarctic regions, and in the lands which stretched to the south, west and east into modern-day Russia, Siberia and Eurasia, where the nomadic tribes moved with the seasons and whose whole life was geared towards the observance of natural events, the shamans became especially skilled in the reading of hidden, inner meanings in the thousand and one variations of sky, clouds, winds, and animal presence and migration.

They also made direct contact with spirits of the great dead, of shamans who had gone into the other worlds and could thus be consulted on a variety of topics of which they now possessed an even deeper knowledge. Thus the definition of the diviner's art is here already widened. The shamans of the frozen North divined the causes of illness and death among both human patients and the vast reindeer herds, the best places to make camp for the wandering tribes they served, and the future fortunes of new-born children.

The many layers of the inner worlds to which the shaman travelled in search of inner truth were as complex and multi-layered as rock formations. Each level possessed a different significance and was to be visited for a different reason. Yet all were linked by a central pole of meaning, a world-tree that grew through all the worlds. Thus the shaman-diviner travelled in trance or other altered state of consciousness into the inner realms and returned with wisdom and knowledge, which he or she then passed on to the tribe.

We learn that divination is much more than foretelling the future – a fact that will be encountered again and again throughout this book – but that it is rather an intimate part of our lives, touching us at many levels, from the dreams we seek to have interpreted to the decisions we make about where and how we live, and the very objects with which we choose to surround ourselves.

CHAPTER TWO

THE FROZEN NORTH

Divination Among the Peoples of the Arctic and Eurasia

Alan Haymes

Three kinds of divination were once widely practised throughout Eurasia: ecstatic or intuitive divination, whereby the necessary information is obtained by a shaman who acts on behalf of the tribe by mediating with the world of spirits; inductive divination, involving the reading of signs according to preconceived systematic procedures; and interpretative divination, which combines aspects of the other two and would include, for example, the understanding of dreams.

Eurasia covers a vast expanse of the surface of the Earth, with the Ural Mountains accepted as a natural frontier between Europe and Siberia, which stretches all the way to the Bering Sea in the east and down to the borders of China and Mongolia in the south. In places, climatic conditions can be extreme, with winter lasting as long as ten months and temperatures dropping to 70°C below zero. During the brief ten week summer, however, there is a dramatic turn around with temperatures rising to levels of 40°C above freezing.

Over 30 different native peoples are still to be found in Siberia, but their collective number is small, at around the million mark, when compared to the total population of the region which is about 30 million. The traditional occupations of the indigenous peoples loosely displayed a north/south divide, with fishing, hunting and reindeer herding being practised in the north and nomadic pastoralism and agriculture in the south. The closeness to animals in the wild and the often desperate need to hunt for food simultaneously accommodated a strong

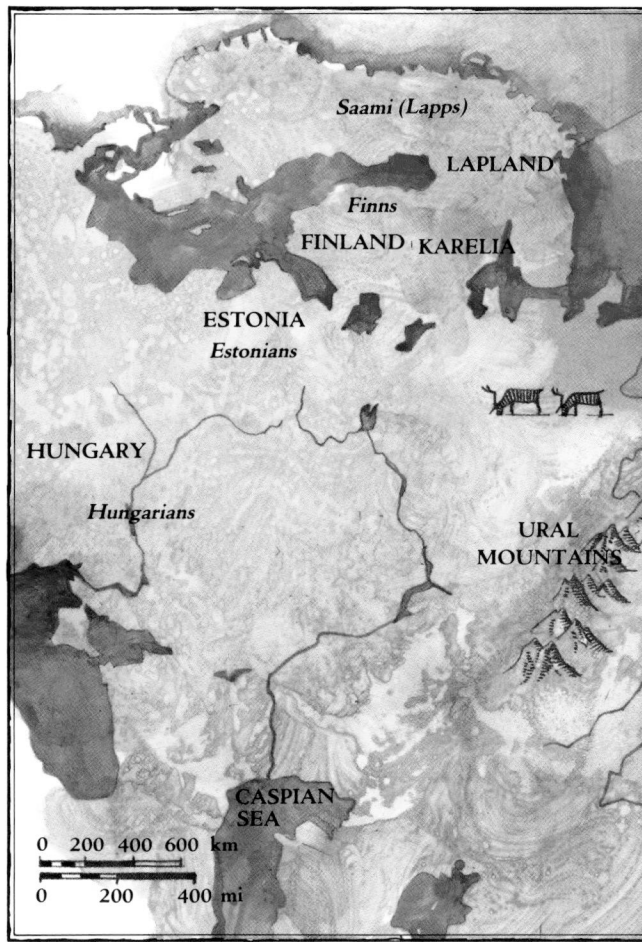

respect and reverence for certain animals, most notably the bear. This animal was regarded as being particularly special by many Northern Eurasian peoples because it was believed to have a soul and thus be close to humanity, if not an ancestor in another guise. As a result elaborate bear-hunting rites evolved to reconcile the problem of killing a sacred animal for food: the

THE PEOPLE OF THE NORTH

At least three specific varieties of vegetation are encountered across the vast land mass of Eurasia, including the Tundra of the polar north, the coniferous forests of the Taiga and the scrubland of the Steppes towards the south. The Ural mountain range, which partly dissects the region from north to south and acts as a natural frontier between Europe to the west and Siberia to the east, also lends its name to one of the two main groups of languages that are spoken in the region, that is 'Uralic'. Categorization on linguistic grounds is a useful method of identifying the various indigenous peoples encountered in Eurasia. The other prominent language family is the 'Altaic', which similarly takes its title from a mountain range, the Altai

mountains, which lies to the south where Siberia meets Mongolia. A third, but much smaller linguistic grouping, that of 'Palaeo-Siberian', covers the ancient unrelated languages of four peoples, including the Kets of the River Yenisey district. Most of the 24 million Uralic speakers reside in areas to the west of the Urals, and include the Finns, Estonians, Saami (Lapps) and Hungarians. Those that inhabit the Siberian territories are mainly the Samoyed, Mansi (Voguls) and Khanti (Ostyaks). Siberian speakers of the Altaic languages number about a million and are normally categorized into three groups, examples of which are the Turkic-speaking Sakhas (Yakuts) and Tuvans, the Mongolic-speaking Buryats and the Tungusic-speaking Evenki.

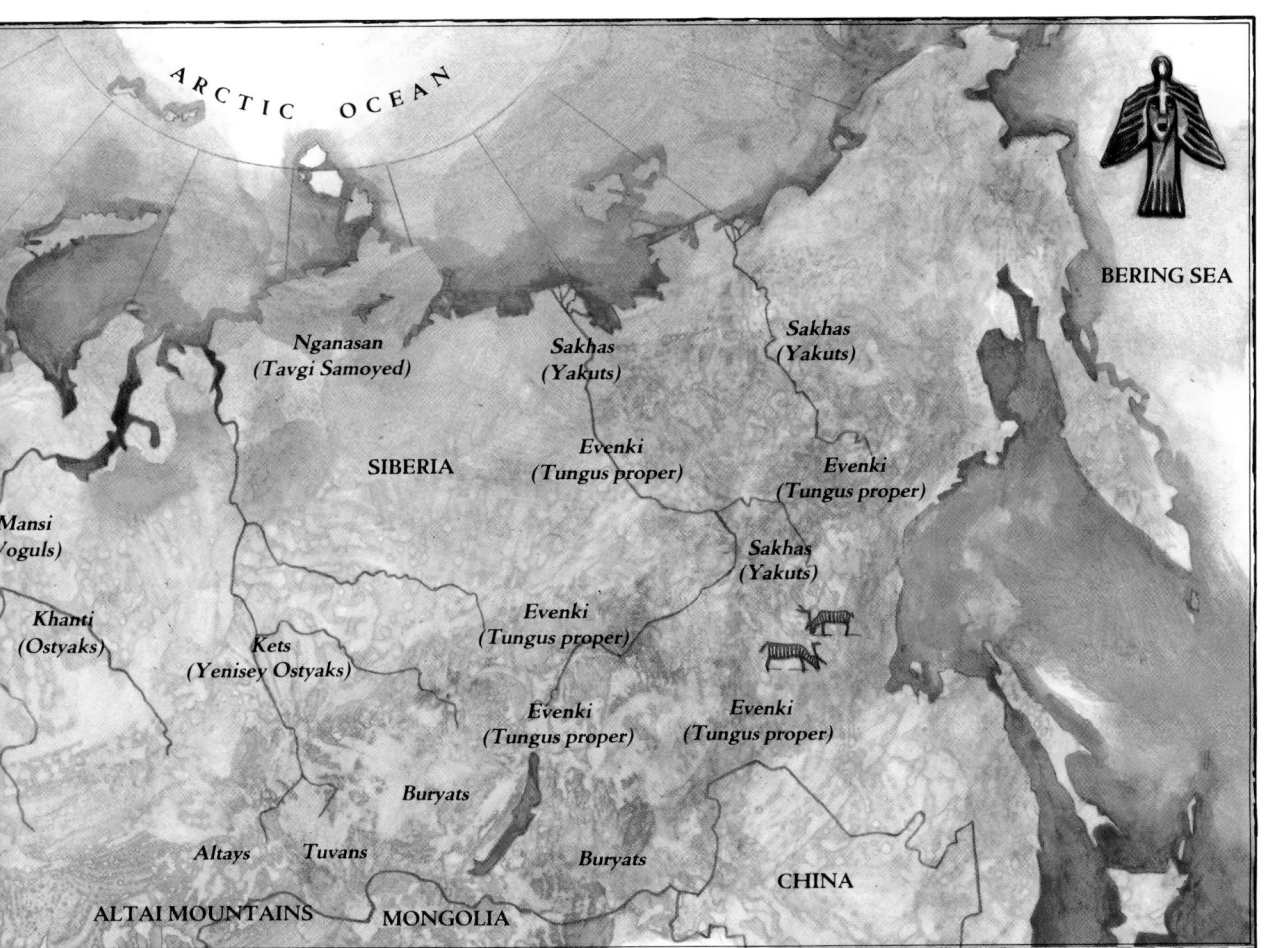

spirit of the bear had to be placated and appeased, perhaps by blaming others, because it was feared that it would take revenge when it realized its physical misfortune. Totemic clan animals also played a significant part in many tribes' identification of themselves within their surroundings, and the influence of ancestral spirits guided many of their day-to-day activities.

ECSTATIC DIVINATION

The bedrock of the spiritual well-being of most of the communities in Siberia was the figure of the shaman, although in many areas the encroaching influences of other religious systems, such as Russian Orthodox Christianity, Islam, and Buddhism, were also felt. The term shaman is indigenous to Siberia and is derived through the Russian from the Tungusic languages, of which the Evenki variants *xaman* and *saman* are prime examples.

Central to the definition of Eurasian shamanism was the leading part played by spirits. It thus follows that ecstatic divination was very much the prerogative of the shaman because it involved soul flight and spirit mediation. Divination of this kind was used to seek the causes of illness, to locate lost possessions, to determine the success of the hunt, to gauge the future prosperity of the community and to obtain from the spirits knowledge of the sacrifices required to ensure successful outcomes. Fundamental to the shaman undertaking this form of divination was the belief that each person has at least two main souls, a body soul and a free soul. The body soul was active during waking consciousness and covered functions such as, breathing, the pulse, emotions and volition. The free soul was active during altered states of consciousness and thus under certain conditions wandered free from the body. These states covered the dream of the sleeper, the coma of the sick and the trance of the shaman. The free soul was often regarded as residing in the head and was crucial to the beliefs in ancestral rebirth; it thus had an element of immortality about it.

The Otherworld to which the free soul of the shaman journeys during an ecstatic trance can be one of two realms, the Upperworld or the Lowerworld. Together with the middle earth of physical manifestation there are thus three worlds for the shaman to be active in. Linking these three worlds is normally a Cosmic Tree or a Cosmic River. In journeying to them, the shaman is in effect returning to the sacred centre of space and the primordial time of the first ancestral shaman. Above the World Tree shines the Pole Star, which as the 'nail of heaven' is the hook upon which the sky realm hangs. The macrocosm of the World Tree with the three worlds is often symbolized in microcosmic form by the *yurta* (a skin tent common to the area) with a central pole pointing up towards the smoke hole.

The Lowerworld tends to be the domain of the dead and is often regarded as the obverse of the land of the living with everything occurring in reverse. Thus it is upside down and backwards, with the dead getting 'younger' every day until they return to the point of their original conception. In addition to the dead, numerous spirits of disease also inhabit the Underworld and it is to these that the shaman travels when divining for the location of a stolen soul of a sick patient. In the Upperworld reside the spirits benevolent to humanity.

Ultimately it is the spirits, very often those of the ancestors, that elect a new shaman, even in those cultures which had hereditary shamanic families. To resist the call of the spirits was to court serious illness and death. In the Evenki tradition the free soul of the elected person was guided by the ancestors down to the Underworld where it was eaten by the great clan mother animal and then reborn as a shamanic soul. In some traditions the souls of future shamans lived as young birds in nests upon the branches of the World Tree, awaiting rebirth in the human plane. Very often the Underworld transformation of the shaman took the form of an attack by the spirits who stripped away flesh and dismembered the skeleton, only for the bones to be reset and the body remade.

In journeys to the Otherworld the shaman's free soul could take on the form of an ancestral tutelary spirit, which was usually that of a deceased shaman, or that of a clan totem animal. To some extent and depending on the culture, the shaman gained empowerment from the Underworld and received wisdom from the Upperworld. Since spirits were generally regarded as being ambivalent towards humanity, the shaman had to protect the community by mastering and controlling them. These spirits

The skins of Saami shaman drums were decorated with important symbols from Saami cosmology and helped the shamans by guiding them on their journeys to other worlds. These drums show, from left to right, the three levels of the cosmos, the upper, middle and lower worlds; the four cardinal directions and the four intermediate directions for use during the eight seasons of the Saami year; and the Sun surrounded by other celestial bodies.

became the shaman's spirit helpers and in turn aided the shaman in his or her work when summoned during rituals and divinations. These spirit helpers also took on various guises, such as the forms of fish, wild animals and birds. When calling upon and in certain cases incarnating the spirits the shaman was always in control and never possessed by them.

Chants were often sung in strange animal or bird-like voices to induce an altered state of consciousness in the shaman, but the sound of the steady beating of a drum was probably the principal method used for falling into an ecstatic trance. In the Altaic-speaking cultures of Siberia the shaman resorted to forms of ecstatic divination in order to find the materials to make a drum. Thus the Tuvan shaman conducted an oracle to locate the special tree which would furnish the wood for the drum frame, whilst the Evenki shaman relied on dreams to find the reindeer which would supply the hide needed for the drum skin. The shaman's drum was rich in symbolism since the wood could represent the shaman's particular World Tree and the skin the shaman's animal soul guardian. Depending on the culture, the shaman often 'rode' his drum as a reindeer or horse to the Otherworld, the drumbeats representing both the heartbeats and the hoof-beats.

The outer surface of the skin of a Saami drum tended to be richly decorated with the images of the indigenous cosmology and thus acted as a map to guide the shaman on his journeys between the worlds. It is likely that the drums were viewed from different angles depending on the time of year, and particular star alignments may have indicated when gateways were open to facilitate the shaman's journey to the Otherworld. Special markings were also to be found inside many drums indicating tribal and clan sigils and sacred symbols known only to the shamans themselves. One other significant feature of the drums were various holes which acted as entrances for the shaman's free soul to travel through during its ecstatic flight.

In performing one of his or her most important functions, that of healer, the shaman often had to use ecstatic divination to locate the whereabouts of a patient's lost soul. Illnesses were deemed to result from two major causes, soul loss and spirit intrusion, with the former occurring during a loss of consciousness, as in a coma, and the latter applying to ailments of a physical nature. The shaman who travelled to the realm of the dead was always in great danger of losing his own soul and thus exercised his spirit helpers to protect him. The spirits of the Underworld inevitably demanded sacrifices to be performed in exchange for anything given up by them. In the *Kalevala*, the national epic of Finland, a character who shows strong shamanistic traits, Lemminkäinen, lost his soul in the

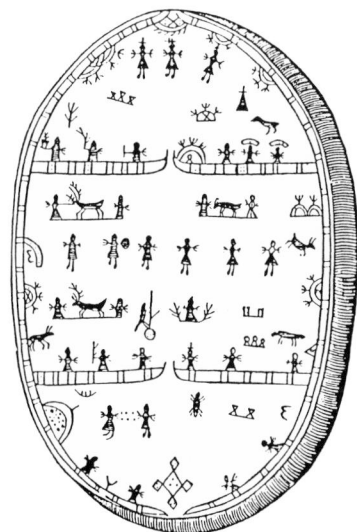
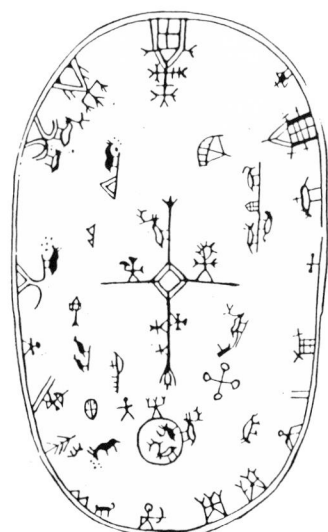

River of the Dead and is dismembered in the process. His mother became aware of his fate when blood oozed from her son's brush, the bristles probably coming from an animal that represented Lemminkäinen's animal soul guardian. Taking on the mantle of a shaman, she eventually located her son's lost soul and journeyed to the Rapids of Death, where, using a rake, she collected up the various parts of his body. With the help of charms and ointments she reassembled Lemminkäinen's body and restored his soul, and thus in effect brought him back to life.

READING THE SIGNS

Whereas ecstatic divination tended to play a central role in the ritual performance of the shaman, inductive methods of divination were very often carried out by the shaman towards the end of the ceremony for the benefit of other members of the community or the community in general. One form of inductive divination is the casting of lots, which involved the cutting of slithers of wood from the branches of an alder tree. This was used by Väinämöinen, a principal character in the *Kalevala*, to locate the whereabouts of the Sun and Moon which had both been hidden by Louhi, the mistress of Pohjola, a magical land to the north.

Elsewhere in the *Kalevala* Louhi ordered her serving maid to throw rowan twigs into the fire so that she could divine from the types of sap that oozed out of the wood the purposes of the approaching Väinämöinen and Ilmarinen. If blood flowed from the twigs then war would follow, if it was water then there would be peace, and if it was honey then a wedding would ensue. In this case it was honey that dripped from the rowan and this prompted Louhi to recommend that her daughter marry Väinämöinen.

A curious method of divination is mentioned in the Estonian *Kalevipoeg*, the national epic of Estonia, involving both the spinning of a brooch on a thread and the simultaneous reading of the flight patterns of an 'alder-beetle'. Flight by the beetle in a southerly direction was deemed fortunate, with the opposite applying if the

A scene from the Kalevala, *in which Lemminkäinen's mother used ecstatic divination to locate her son's soul in the underworld and restore him to life.*

direction was northwards. In this part of the epic, Kalev was lying seriously ill forcing his wife Linda to use divination to ascertain whether assistance could be called upon. She took hold of a brooch and spun it around on a thread, and at the same time sent an alder beetle on a series of four journeys, each of seven days length, to seek aid from, in turn, the Moon, the evening star, the Sun, and the wind. On each occasion the brooch span for seven days, but the whole exercise was to no avail because Kalev died before the beetle returned from its fourth flight. Presumably the brooch would cease to spin if the beetle suffered a mishap during flight, thus resulting in the divination being aborted.

Among many of the Siberian Altaic speakers, the bow was used as a method of divination. This could take the form of looking into a fire along the length of a bow string or by listening to the sound made by the string as the tension was changed. A third way was to balance the bow by holding the bow string in the middle with the thumb and forefinger and then interpret the extent of any swing made by the bow in response to the questions put. The bow was of great symbolic significance in Siberian culture and some have regarded it as a precursor to the shaman's drum when it was used as a one-stringed instrument to induce an altered state.

Certainly on the underside of some of the drums used by Altaic shamans was a bar representing the bow string. The shooting of arrows was also practised as a method of divination, with outcomes being determined by the flight and distance of the arrows being fired. The arrow contained much symbolic significance as it represented both the speed of ecstatic flight and shamanic action at a distance. The shooting of a chain of arrows symbolized the bridge to the Otherworld, which the shaman needed to cross in order to journey to the realm of spirits.

A by-product of the bear hunt was a divination method entailing the use of the bear's right paw. The Kets believed that the bear possessed the soul of a dead relative and so when the animal was hunted down, killed and subsequently taken back to the settlement, it had to receive treatment befitting a guest of honour. Since it was regarded as a deceased relative its name had to be known so that it could be properly welcomed. The bear's right paw was cut off and tossed up in the air as a name was called out. This was carried out three times and when the paw landed pad side up was it deemed that the correct name had been divined. At the end of the feast the paw became a talisman.

The tossing up of an object a number of times and the subsequent divining of an outcome from the way that the object landed is probably the simplest method of divination used by the Eurasian peoples. Many divined in this way using the drumstick. When doubts lingered after an ecstatic divination concerning the fate of a sick person, the Samoyed shaman of the Nganasan tribe would toss the drumstick up three times to further divine the outcome. Landing face upwards was regarded as a good omen in this case.

The Khanti (Ostyaks) and the Mansi (Voguls) used divination during a pregnancy to ascertain the health of the mother and the expected child. As soon as a woman became pregnant she made from birchwood a thumb-sized female figurine called a *sos*. This doll had a ribbon tied around its waist and the ends were used to suspend the *sos* between three fingers.

Siberian shamans use the bow as an instrument of divination by balancing it from the middle of the bow string, and then observing and interpreting the extent of any sway made by the bow in response to particular questions – one of a number of ways in which bows and arrows can be used as tools for divination purposes.

As the birth approached, the expectant mother would divine from the movements of the suspended doll whether she would survive and the health of the child. Hanging motionless or twitching erratically was deemed inauspicious, whereas a smooth swaying was a good omen.

Babies were believed to have the souls of ancestors reborn and so the name of the person who had in effect returned to the fold had to be determined. This form of divination was carried out by the eldest woman on the father's side, who placed a knife under the cradle containing the child and then attempted to lift the cradle off the floor each time a name was shouted out. Only when the correct name was called out did the cradle become too heavy to move, since the additional weight was a sign of the presence of the soul of the reborn ancestor.

The drum was also used by some Eurasian peoples, most notably the Saamis of Lapland, for divination purposes. The main method was to place a brass ring or a piece of antler on the membrane of the drum and then to start beating the drum frantically with the special antler drumstick. The movement of the ring across the images on the surface of the drum was keenly observed and the sound of the vibrating membrane was also noted. When the ring ceased to move in spite of the drumming, the image that it covered was taken to indicate the outcome to the immediate problem posed.

Amongst the *táltos* of Hungary a leather-covered sieve was often used for divining, with grains of maize thrown onto the surface and the outcomes read from the resulting positions.

There were various other ways of divining with rings. The Sakhas (Yakut) shamans were reputed to foretell a person's future by simply moving a ring around on the palm of the enquirer's hand. Of more importance was the role of the *eheken*, or 'spirit of hunting', which was represented by an irregular oval ring of antler horn covered with calfskin. Before the hunt, the northern Sakhas would smear the skin with fat and hold the ring near to a fire. When the fat melted in the heat and the face of the skin glowed, it was perceived that the spirit of the hunt was amongst them. The ring was tossed up and if it landed face upwards success in the hunt was assured. Landing face downwards meant that any hunting planned for that day had to be cancelled.

Scapulimancy, or the art of divination by shoulder-blade, was a method much favoured by the Altaic-speaking peoples. Sheep, goats and deer were generally the animals selected to supply the shoulder-blades. The bone was cleaned, warmed by a fire and smeared with fat. A northern Yakut diviner waved the bone around himself three times, spat on it each time and recited an incantation. He put some burning coals on the bone and fanned them to make them glow. As soon as the blade started to crack the coals were removed and the resultant lines were interpreted according to the accepted meanings. When the divination was completed the shoulder-blade was protected from subsequent desecration.

A method involving pieces of bone cut from the hooves of a deer was used by the northern Sakhas. The request was first whispered onto one of the bone pieces before it was waved around three times by the diviner. Next all the bone pieces were placed in three piles and then three bits at a time were taken away until only four were left in each section. The bones that were removed were laid out in the form of a human figure, which was then used as the divining map. The remaining bone pieces were thrown at the human image and the outcome determined from the resultant positions.

The use of bones for divination was particularly apt because to many of the Eurasian cultures bones symbolized the continual regeneration of life. The soul was possibly deemed to reside in the marrow and so the bones of animals killed in the hunt were carefully collected together and buried, thus enabling the animals to be reborn again from their essence. This practise mirrors the dismembering and resetting of the shaman's skeleton during some initiations in the Underworld. The skeleton was depicted on the ritual costumes of many Siberian shamans, thus emphasizing its symbolic power.

THE CELTIC AND NORSE WORLD

The number of parallels between the divinatory systems of the Norse and Celtic peoples is remarkable and perhaps suggests one reason why, when the two races came into conflict in the sixth century AD, they were in time able to fuse to become the Anglo-Saxon race. Both practised the art of throwing lots, and the description of the Norse augurs, drawn from the account of the Roman writer Tacitus, could equally well stand as a description of *Crannchur*, or 'Throwing the Woods', described in the chapter on the Celts.

Aside from this, there are strong parallels between the Norse Runic and Celtic Ogam alphabets – though each originated as an individual system and belongs to its own cultural milieu, despite various attempts in recent times to confuse the two.

Again, the reading of auguries from the flight and cries of birds seems to have been common to both peoples, and there are numerous references in the literature of the Celts and the Norse which testify to the sacredness of animals generally and the magical power of birds in particular.

We might also mention, while discussing such similarities, the importance attached to the reading of dreams by both peoples: both employed professional augurs to undergo a kind of temple sleep from which they returned with word of future events or the answer to a specific question.

Within a wider framework of world-wide divinatory techniques, we may note the close similarity between the accounts of Celtic diviners reading from the shoulder-blades of dead animals and those of the peoples of the Circumpolar region, who still practised this type of augury up to very recent times. The horse augury used by the Norse was, according to recent evidence, in all probability also practised in ancient Scotland.

Such common features help to reinforce the belief that at one time there existed a few basic divinatory systems using stones, twigs and the observance of natural events such as the fall of a leaf, the shapes of clouds, or the ever changing pattern of the stars. With the passage of time, these methods became more sophisticated and mutated into many different forms.

In the world of the Celtic and Norse peoples, as in the Circumpolar regions, we are able to look through a window in time to when divinatory systems were actually undergoing a period of development. We can therefore see the wide variety of types of divination practised by these people; as well as the common elements in their methods.

CHAPTER THREE

BY STICK AND STONE

Celtic Methods of Divination

John Matthews

The Celtic world once stretched from the far east of Europe to the edge of the Atlantic; now it is limited to Wales, Scotland, Ireland, Brittany and parts of Gallicia. The fascination with future events which existed among the people who lived in these areas from around the third century BC finds expression in many ways. Practitioners of the various arts of divination are recorded from the earliest times and are still recognized as part of a continuing tradition – though now it is those who possess 'the second sight' who predict the future, and the old methods of divining are virtually forgotten. However, references to a number of methods survive. We find these in medieval accounts of the 'Bardic schools' of Britain and Ireland, where such skills were taught as part of a 25-year curriculum. From them we can get a clear picture of how these methods worked and how they were practised, and gain fresh insight into the rich heritage of the Celtic tradition.

Among the systems and methods of which we find mention are divination by the throwing of *Ogam Sticks*; *Nealdoracht* or Cloud Reading; several kinds of *Incubatory Sleep*, in which the precognitive dreams of individuals were studied and interpreted; and three mysterious methods of divining events known by the enigmatic titles of *Imbas Forosnai* (Enlightened Manifestation), *Tenm Laida* (Illumination by Song) and *Dichetal do Chennaib* (Meditation on the Finger Ends). In addition are several methods of augury practised among the Gaels of Scotland. If we look closely at each of these we find that there is a surprising commonality to each and every one.

THE CELTIC WORLD

The Celts originated in the heartland of Europe, from where they migrated steadily westward, founding colonies in Spain, Gaul, Britain and Ireland. In time they migrated to Scotland and then back across the European continent as far as Italy and Greece, sacking Rome in 390 BC. A joyful and creative people, quick-tempered, energetic and great warriors, their art, religion and mythology had a powerful influence on the Western world; but they were more of a loose-knit confederacy than a united people, and when they met the might of the Roman Empire they gave way before it. Today the descendants of the original Celtic race can be found in Scotland, Ireland and Wales, as well as Brittany and parts of Spain. Their fascination with divining the future remains in the heritage of tradition and a strong belief in the 'Second Sight'.

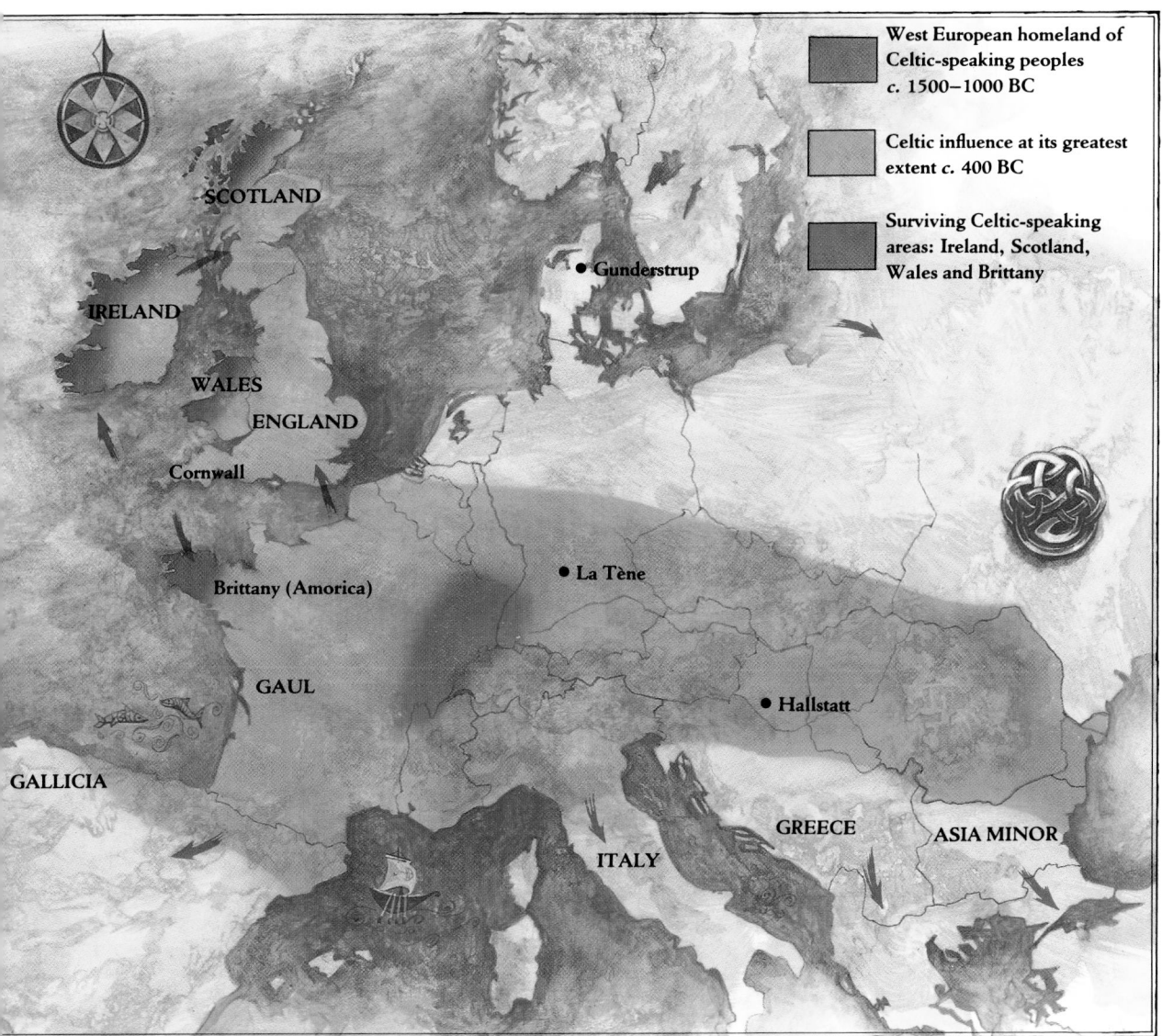

	West European homeland of Celtic-speaking peoples c. 1500–1000 BC
	Celtic influence at its greatest extent c. 400 BC
	Surviving Celtic-speaking areas: Ireland, Scotland, Wales and Brittany

OGAM: SECRET LANGUAGE OF THE POETS

Principle among the methods of divination that we know about is the use of Ogam (Ogham), a form of archaic alphabet put to many and varied uses. It has been called 'the Secret Language of the Poets' and formed an important part of the Bardic teachings in both Wales and Ireland. Hundreds of standing stones have been dis-

Across much of Ireland, Wales and Scotland, like curious fingers pointing to the sky, are large numbers of stones carved with inscriptions in Ogam. Using the edge of the stone as a stave, the combinations of lines that make up the letters are carved along the edges. They may have acted as grave markers or boundary stones. The one shown here is from Ireland.

covered bearing inscriptions in Ogam, some of which refer to famous heroes, while others are believed to have been boundary markers. But the uses of Ogam go far beyond this, being capable of sophisticated application and great subtlety of allusion. In the hands of a master it could be made to convey a wide range of meanings, and was almost certainly used to convey secret messages in a kind of code.

The Ogam alphabet consists of 20 letters, arranged in groups of five, which are constructed from series of straight lines incised across a single stave (five more letters of a more complex structure are thought to have been added some time after the original number). It

THE OGAM ALPHABET

OGAM NAME	LETTER	TREE
Beithe	b	birch
Luis	l	elm/rowan
Fearn	f	alder
Saile	s	willow
Nuin	n	ash
(h) Uathe	h	whitethorn/hawthorn
Duir	d	oak
Tinne	t	holly/elderberry
Coll	h	hazel
Quert	q	quicken/aspen/apple
Muinn	m	vine/mulberry
Gort	g	fir/ivy
(N) Getal	ng	broom/fern
Straif	str	willowbrake/blackthorn
Ruis	r	elder
Ailm	a	fir/pine
Ohn	o	furze/ash/gorse
Ur	u	thorn/heather

OGAM NAME	LETTER	TREE
Edhadh	e	yew/aspen
Ido	i	service tree/yew
Ebadh	eba	elecampane/aspen
Oir	oi	spindle tree
Uilleand	ui	ivy/honeysuckle
Iphin	io	pine/gooseberry
Emancoll/Phagos	ae	witch-hazel/beech

In the table above the names most generally attributed to the letters of the tree alphabet are shown along with their associated trees. (There is still some disagreement between the various attributions.)

To create a personal Ogam set, the author has collected sticks of various trees during his travels, and incised the appropriate Ogam letter at one end on a carved flattened surface. In this way an original and authentic system is available for divinatory use.

was a simple matter to carve these enigmatic letters on the edge of stones, and it is from this source that the structure of the alphabet has been derived. The origin of the letters is given mythological status in several old Irish texts, among them *Cormac's Glossary*, which, although it was not compiled until the Middle Ages, is known to contain much earlier material. The passage in question reads as follows:

What are the place, time, person, and cause of the invention of Ogam? ... In the time of Bres, son of Elatha ...Ogma, a man well skilled in speech and in poetry, invented the Ogam. The cause of its invention [was] as a proof of his ingenuity, and that the speech should belong to the learned apart, to the exclusion of rustics and herdsmen.... The father of Ogam is Ogma, the mother of Ogam is the hand or knife of Ogma.... (Translation by W. Stokes.)

The figure of Ogma (sometimes called Ogmios) is well attested throughout Irish and Gaulish mythology. There, rather than being described as a man, he is very clearly identified as one of the Tuatha de Danaan, the primal gods of Ireland. Although the details of his discovery of the Ogam letters remain obscure, we may imagine that at one time there must have existed a story which told of his quest for the alphabet in much the same way as the Norse Odin is represented as having discovered the runes (see Chapter Four, The Message of the Runes).

Certainly Ogma was a master of the poetic mysteries, and it is in this area that Ogam finds its primary use. Each of the letters has a name, and is associated with a wide range of natural objects. The most famous example of this is the Tree Alphabet, in which each of the letters is identified with a tree. This has led some commentators to assume the existence of a complex tree 'calendar', with each month identified by an Ogam 'stave' (row) of letters. Whether or not there is any truth in this assumption it is an important example of the way in which the letters seem to have been used. The

names most generally attributed to the letters of the Tree Alphabet are shown opposite.

This points to the possible use of the letters in divining the future, though once again the evidence for their exact use is scarce. It would appear that twigs of wood from the various trees were inscribed with the appropriate letters and that these were then 'thrown' at random, the positions in which they fell and the relationships to one another then being read and interpreted.

How this was done is suggested by the many lists of Ogam correspondences found in a variety of ancient sources. Among others we find 'Sow Ogam', 'Bird Ogam', 'River Ogam', 'King Ogam', 'Colour Ogam' and 'Food Ogam'. It is evident from this that a truly vast range of associations existed, all of which had to be memorized by the Celtic shaman-poets, whose interpretive skills meant that Ogam divination was indeed a specialized activity.

'Finger Ogam' was used by those who possessed the knowledge of the alphabet and its hidden references. This involved using one finger as a vertical or horizontal stave against which combinations of other digits could be laid

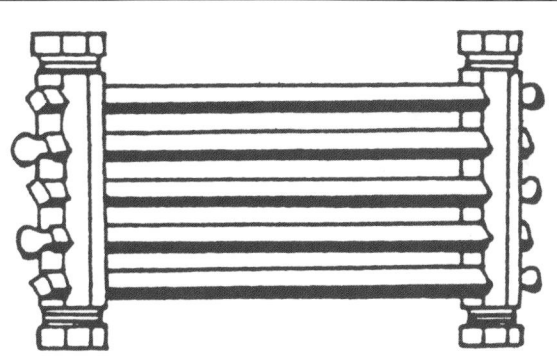

SPINNING THE FUTURE

In the Peithynen framework used by the Welsh Bards, five rods squared off to provide four surfaces, each carrying a carved Ogam letter, were placed into a wooden frame. By striking the rods with the palm of the hand, they were spun to give a combination of letters for interpretation. We must treat the authenticity of the Peithynen with caution, however, as it can be traced back no further than the eighteenth century, and may have been the invention of the great Welsh antiquarian and forger Iolo Morgannwg.

to spell out the Ogam letters. In this way messages could be passed that were undetectable by those who knew nothing of Ogam. The throwing of the sticks, called *Crannchur* or 'Casting the Woods', is referred to in a medieval text called the *Senchus Mor*, where it is said that when a decision was to be made, or a question asked, three 'lots' or slips of wood were placed in a bag, shaken and drawn forth again one at a time. According to the order in which they came forth (and, we may assume, the Ogam letter carved thereon), a decision to the question proposed was to be understood.

A later, almost certainly nineteenth-century system, is called *Coelbrenn*, 'Wood-Letters'. Despite its apparent lateness, the fact that the name of the system contains two ancient Celtic names, 'Coel' and 'Brenn' (possibly Bran, the Celtic God of Inspiration), suggests that it may derive from a much earlier source.

Other methods included the use of wooden dice, carved with *coelbrenns* on each side. These could then be palmed, shaken and thrown in a similar manner to conventional dice, but they could also be used by those informed in their symbolic values either to pass secret messages, or to foretell events in the future.

Taken together these references suggest that the Ogams were used as a divinatory system, and that this consisted in various methods of arriving at random combinations of the letters, which could then be interpreted by the skilled bard or shaman-poet.

That these methods, or ones similar to them, may also have been in use among the Druids is also a possibility, though we have only Julius Caesar's somewhat unreliable testimony to go on. Logic suggests that the Druids, who were certainly the keepers of the native wisdom in these islands, would have possessed ways of reading the future, but this is not enough to support the many fantastic theories proposed as to the methods they used. At least two specific means of divining the future may, with greater certainty, be attributed to Druidic practice. These are the reading of dreams and the interpretation of shapes in the clouds.

DREAM READING

Far and away the second most common method of divination practised by the Celts was the interpretation of dreams. Over and again we find references in the literature to people who possessed the ability to dream the future. This took a more specific shape in the accounts we have of Incubatory Sleep. This method seems to have originated in Classical Greece and to have sprung up independently within the Celtic world. It involved the person with a question regarding either past, present or future events, or with a problem to be solved, visiting a special temple dedicated to a particular god or goddess, in which a building containing a number of separate chambers was set aside. Here the querent was ritually prepared (probably by taking a purifying bath and being laved in sacred oils) and then left to sleep. If they had prepared themselves properly, and were in a correct state

During Incubatory Sleep the subject lay within a darkened chamber and received a healing dream or sometimes as visitation from a god. This is a depiction by Anglo-Danish artist Monica Sjöö.

of mind, they then received a dream, or sometimes a visitation from the deity of the place, in which the question they had proposed was answered. They were attended by priests or priestesses who were skilled in the interpretation of such dreams, rather like the oracles at Delphi or Eleusis in Greece, which also required interpretation.

Evidence for such practice among the Celts has been found at more than one site in Britain and Ireland. The best known is at Lydney in Gloucestershire, where a number of votive offerings have been found, as well as the foundations of a later temple complex consisting of numerous sleep-chambers clearly modelled on the type discovered in Greece and dedicated to Asklepios, the god of healing.

Related to this method of precognitive dreaming is a mysterious ceremony known as *Tarb Feis*, 'Bull Sleep'. This involved a trained shaman or priest being put to sleep in a darkened hut on a cured bull's hide. Invariably this seems to have produced the required trance state from which the practitioner emerged some hours later with the words of prophecy on his lips. A sufficiently similar description of this method exists from as late as the seventeenth century, suggesting the strength of this tradition and its survival and continuance until comparatively recent times.

READING THE CLOUDS

The reading of clouds is probably one of the oldest and most commonly practised methods of divination in the world. Among the Celts this method of precognition seems to have been carried to a fine art, judging by the existence of a specialized group of people whose task it was to practise the art of *Neladoracht*, 'Divination by clouds'. That this was a form of practice common to the Druids is shown in an ancient manuscript now in a Dublin library, in which it is told how a certain king asked his Druid to read the future for him. The priest did so by climbing to the top of *Crocna-Druad*, 'Druid's Hill', 'where he remained the night, returning at sunrise. He then addressed the king with these

words: "Are you asleep, O king of Erin and Alban? ....I have consulted the clouds ...and have discovered that you shall make a conquest of Alban, Britain and Gaul", which accordingly he did soon after.' (Translation by P.W. Joyce.)

FRITH

The *frith* (pronounced 'free') was a method of augury practised until recently in the Western Highlands and Islands of Scotland. Those practising the *frith* were usually people with the 'sight'. They were called *frithirs*, a title that has descended into modern usage as a surname: Freer. The Freers were the hereditary state augurs for the kings of Scotland. The method of augury was as follows: the *frithir* would fast on the first Monday of every quarter, and would stand before sunrise, bare-headed, bare-footed and blindfolded on the doorstep. She would put a hand on either side of the doorposts and make an invocation. On removing the blindfold, she would then make a prediction based upon the first thing she saw. An extensive list of possible sightings and their correspondences would have been part of the training of a *frithir*, but these are not available in any written text.

This was only one of several methods of augury practised among the Gaels of Scotland in particular. Although most of the information regarding them comes from comparatively recent times, the existence of these methods in folklore tradition suggests a much earlier point of origin.

SLINNEANCHACHD: SIGNS FROM THE SHOULDER

Slinneanchachd derives from the Gaelic word for shoulder, *slinnean*. The method involved the slaughter of an animal, usually a black sheep or a pig (the latter was sacred to the Celts). When the flesh had been boiled from the bones, the shoulder-blade was then studied and certain marks that appeared thereon were interpreted. An account dating from 1746 describes a soldier at the battle of Culloden predicting victory for the Hanoverian army after reading the shoulder-blade of a sheep.

DEUCHAINN: FIRST SIGHT

This is one of several types of augury involving the sight of significant objects, people or animals. It literally means 'trial' or 'proof' and in order to discover the outcome of some significant forthcoming event, such as a wedding, the person requiring to know this went up a hill or cairn which was too steep for an animal to climb. On the way down, or subsequently returning home, the first creature to be met with indicated what kind of person one might marry. Similarly, if it was required to know what kind of fortune might attend upon one at the start of a new year, the enquirer would walk to the end of their house, outside, with eyes shut. On opening them, the first thing to be seen was the omen sought for.

A similar form of augury was *Manadh*, generally translated simply as 'luck', which involved the observance of certain birds or animals that were said to bring either good or bad luck. Thus a cuckoo's call was said to predict the death of a child, while a cock crowing at midnight meant news coming next day. Each of these methods, though seemingly random, required skilled interpretation.

IMBAS FOROSNA: ENLIGHTENED MANIFESTATION

Perhaps the most mysterious of Celtic divinatory methods that we know something about is *Imbas Forosna*, which may be translated as 'Enlightened Manifestation' or more simply 'Illumination' and which is described in various Celtic texts as being widely practised among the Celts of Britain and Ireland. The technique involved entering a completely darkened place and spending some time alone and in a state of sensory deprivation. At the end of a specified time – ranging from several hours to three days – the seer was brought forth into bright light, which might either be sunshine or the light of a fire. Either way, the effect of the long enclaustration in darkness, followed by the sudden exposure to brilliant illumination, seems to have set free the tongue and enabled the diviner to utter inspired words and answers relevant to the

question he or she had originally entered the dark place to discover.

DICHETEL DO CHENNAIB: MEDITATION ON THE FINGER ENDS

A number of explanations of this practice have been put forward in the face of sparse textual information. The most likely is that it refers to the use of Finger Ogam combined with a type of meditation that led the seer to conceive an inspired answer to the question asked. An alternate theory is that the words may be translated as 'The Cracking Open of the Nuts of Wisdom', these being the hazels that grew above the mystical Well of Segais in the Celtic Otherworld. Salmon swam in this well and were believed to eat the nuts, for which reason to catch and eat a salmon was considered one road to extreme illumination, and the great Irish hero Fionn MacCumhail is said to have acquired his considerable wisdom by this means.

TENM LAIDA: ILLUMINATION BY SONG

This refers to the chant of the shamans by which they passed into a trance state that enabled them to journey into the inner realms and bring back information not readily available to the rest of humankind. The account in *Cormac's Glossary* suggests a more elaborate ritual, in which the seer first chewed a piece of raw meat, which he then placed on the threshold of his dwelling, before entering an altered state of consciousness. It has been suggested that this may refer to the fact that when raw meat is chewed or consumed it releases endocrines in the brain, thus generally enhancing consciousness.

These then are the principal methods of divination practised by the Celts. We can be confident that a people with such a highly developed interest in the reading of the future had other methods. The information remaining may be scarce, but it is certainly sufficient to inform us of their dedicated pursuit of knowledge by these and other means.

CHAPTER FOUR

THE MESSAGE OF THE RUNES

Divination in the Ancient Germanic World

Peter Taylor

The Roman orator and author Tacitus, writing in the first century AD, gives us in his *Germania 10* an account of the divinatory practices of the ancient Germanic peoples:

For divination and the casting of lots they have the highest regard. Their procedure in casting lots is always the same. They cut off a branch of a nut-bearing tree and slice it into strips; these they mark with different signs and throw them completely at random onto a white cloth. Then the priest of the state, if the consultation is a public one, or the father of the family if it is private, offers a prayer to the gods, and looking up at the sky picks up three strips, one at a time, and reads their meaning from the signs previously scored on them. If the lots forbid an enterprise, there is no deliberation that day on the matter in question; if they allow it, confirmation by the taking of auspices is required. (Penguin translation)

The signs marked on the strips of wood were probably similar to those holy-signs known to us as rune-staves. Although Tacitus had observed

The runic inscription on the eighth-century silver-gilt mount shown above, found in the River Thames in London, probably forms a chant.

this particular divinatory procedure being carried out by men, he makes it clear that the ancient Germanic people held the prophetic abilities of women in the highest possible regard: 'they believe that there resides in woman an element of holiness and a gift of prophecy; and so they do not scorn to ask their advice, or lightly disregard their replies' (*Germania 8*). Tacitus concludes *Germania 10* with an outline of various forms of augury which would have been used for the 'taking of auspices', the first being 'seeking information from the cries and flight of birds'. The patterns formed by birds flying would have played a part in determining the shapes of the rune-staves. Tacitus also tells us that pure white horses were kept at public expense in sacred woods and groves; they were yoked to sacred chariots, and note was taken of their neighs and snorts. The horse omens inspired great trust, 'not only among the common people, but even among the nobles and priests, who think that they themselves are but servants of the gods, whereas the horses are privy to the gods' counsels.' Sleipnir, the horse of Óđinn, had teeth that were graven with Runes, and the name of the nineteenth Rune is *ehwaz*, the horse.

In *Eiríks Saga Rauđa 4*, there is a remarkable

description of an oracular priestess known as the *Volva* or *Seidkona*, who travelled around the country giving weather forecasts and prophetic advice. In the divinatory ceremony of *Seidr*, the *Volva* visited the Otherworld in trance, whence she was called back by chanting to give voice to her prophetic utterances. There are similarities here to certain shamanic practices of the Eskimo, Lapp and Finno-Ugric peoples (see Chapter Two, The Frozen North).

Seidr is closely connected with the cult of the fertility goddess Freyja/Vanadis. On special occasions, the high seat was raised up on a sacred burial mound and those consulting the *Volva* were clad in boar helms and masks: the ancestors and the goddess herself spoke through the *Volva* from the Underworld.

The peoples of the ancient Germanic North also paid much attention to visions received in dreams. In an Underworld practice called *Útiseta*, they slept on the hide of a totemic beast in a pigsty, a sacred forest grove, or on a burial mound. This enabled oracular contact with the tribal ancestors or with female fertility powers.

RUNES

(In what follows it should be noted that 'Ur-Runes' refers to Runes before their systematization; 'Runes' to the essential oracular mystery beyond each symbol; 'rune-staves' or 'rune-signs' to the carven or inscribed shapes; and 'rune-names' to the mnemonic song-words which are the sonic keys to the Runes.)

The divinatory practices so far mentioned are those of a people living in close harmony with the environment, the ancestors, the seasonal and stellar cycles and the deities. All of these aspects coalesce in the mysterious symbols known as Runes, which provide us with the tools for a uniquely environmental form of divination. The word 'Rune,' which occurs in various forms in both Germanic and Celtic languages, means 'a Mystery' or 'holy secret' that is 'whispered'.

RUNE ORIGINS

Ancestral lore sings of an ancient tribe known as the Völsungr, who wandered out of the far

North with the last great Ice. They were guardians of the primordial forests and holysteads, and of the ancient trackways, the dragon paths, linking them. These 'Children of Freedom' offered help to any suffering deep need, bondage or oppression, thus engendering fear among human oppressors. Their direct memory of the timeless hoard of Ur-Runes provided them with the wisdom, power and compassion needed to carry out these tasks.

It was also the task of the Völsungr to seed knowledge of the Ur-Runes among those of the newer tribes who would maintain their Mysteries for the future need of the Land. This task complete, the Völsungr withdrew into the deepest and most hidden holy heart-woods of the diminishing Northern Forests, and passed beyond human knowledge.

THE GERMANIC 'FUÞARK'

In the fifth century BC, certain alphabets came into use in the Alpine Regions, known variously as North Etruscan, North Italic or Alpine. During the course of the following century, the *Alpengermanen* are thought to have come into contact with these alphabets and made some use of them. Evidence for this exists in the form of a bronze helmet, dating from the third century BC, found at Negau in Steiermark, south of the Danube. It is inscribed with a text in a Germanic language, but using Alpine letters. The text reads: *HARIGASTI TEIWA* – to the god Harigast (Wōdanaz).

ᐱᐴᐱᐰᐅᐻᐍᐎᐞᐉᐆᐃᐴᐔᐅᐱᐴ

THE JOURNEY OF THE RUNES

The Völsungr fetched the Runes southward, treading out in the Land the pathway of the White Wyrm (dragon), and marking its backbone with the Runes. The shape of this growth in the wisdom of Land guardianship can be seen in the rune-staves on the map and expressed by the following key words, which represent the Runes in the order in which they appear on the map: free the Land; nurture; turn and let flow the blood of the Land; seek that which is; hear the holy Rede; kindle the inner fire; give; wish; hallow; follow the Pole Star; water the roots of the World Tree.

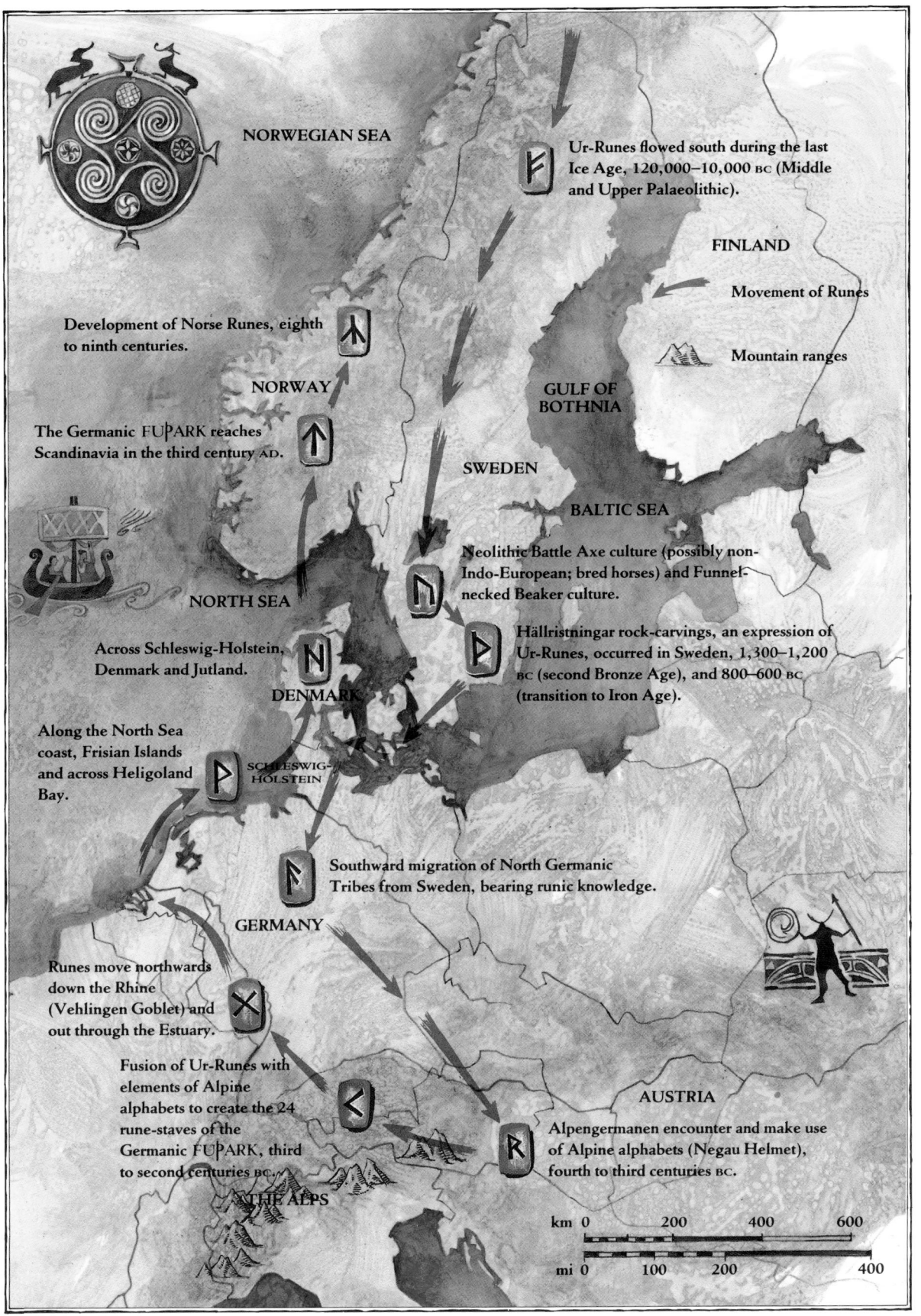

Ur-Runes flowed south during the last
Ice Age, 120,000–10,000 BC (Middle
and Upper Palaeolithic).

FINLAND

Movement of Runes

Mountain ranges

NORWEGIAN SEA

GULF OF
BOTHNIA

Development of Norse Runes, eighth
to ninth centuries.

NORWAY

SWEDEN

BALTIC SEA

The Germanic FUÞARK reaches
Scandinavia in the third century AD.

Neolithic Battle Axe culture (possibly non-
Indo-European; bred horses) and Funnel-
necked Beaker culture.

NORTH SEA

Hällristningar rock-carvings, an expression of
Ur-Runes, occurred in Sweden, 1,300–1,200
BC (second Bronze Age), and 800–600 BC
(transition to Iron Age).

Across Schleswig-Holstein,
Denmark and Jutland.

DENMARK

Along the North Sea
coast, Frisian Islands
and across Heligoland
Bay.

SCHLESWIG-
HOLSTEIN

Southward migration of North Germanic
Tribes from Sweden, bearing runic knowledge.

GERMANY

Runes move northwards
down the Rhine
(Vehlingen Goblet) and
out through the Estuary.

Fusion of Ur-Runes with
elements of Alpine
alphabets to create the 24
rune-staves of the
Germanic FUÞARK, third
to second centuries BC.

AUSTRIA

Alpengermanen encounter and make use
of Alpine alphabets (Negau Helmet),
fourth to third centuries BC.

THE ALPS

km	0		200		400		600

mi	0		100		200		400

There occurred at this point a remarkable fusion between the Germanic Ur-Runes and letters from the Alpine alphabets, resulting in the creation of the 24 Germanic rune-staves known to us. The reason for this fusion may have been to preserve the Runes for times when magical symbols would increasingly be used for written communications and records. But it should be said that, even after this systematization, rune-staves continued to be used primarily for magical purposes rather than for writing, and never developed a cursive form.

The 24 Germanic Runes – known as the 'FUÞARK' from the letter values of the first six Runes – are divided into three families (or *ættir*) of eight Runes. Each family of eight Runes can be linked to the eight directions on the horizon, to the seasonal festivals, and to various cycles of time and stars. To inscribe an object with the complete FUÞARK was a magical act of considerable potency.

The following pages (38 to 40) show the 24 Germanic rune-staves (together with the Anglo-Frisian form where it differs); the rune-name in Proto-Germanic and Old English; and the letter-value.

Also given for each Rune is a series of words, generated from the 'ancestral' Indo-European roots of the mnemonic rune-names, and from other Indo-European roots which are resonant in sound and meaning. (For a full appreciation of this magico-linguistic aspect of runic knowledge, it would be necessary to give the Indo-European roots and their derivatives in both Germanic and Old English. There is, however, only space here for derivatives in modern English.)

It should be emphasized that these words are not 'oracular meanings' of the Runes, but are extensions of the rune-names, to be meditated upon and uttered. Thereby are the sonic keys forged that will unlock the doors to the oracular and prophetic mysteries of the Runes themselves. It is important to distinguish between the Runes and the mnemonic names attached to them. The names are not only mnemonics, but also a means of stimulating the deep oracular

memory of the Runes themselves.

(Derivatives in capital letters have equivalents in other Germanic languages; those in lower-case have derived from Indo-European by different linguistic paths. Each numbered group of words derives from one Indo-European root. An asterisk indicates that the word has been reconstructed from the information available.)

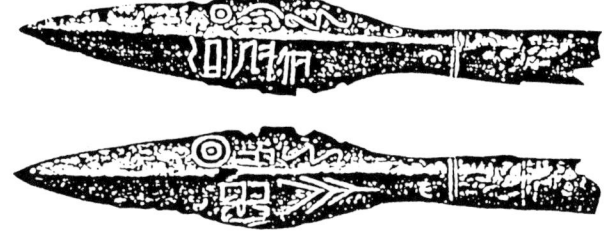

A formal expression of the 'Ur-Runes' is the Hällristningar rock-carvings (top), found in particular abundance in Sweden, dating from two periods: 1300–1200 BC (second Bronze Age), and 800–600 BC (transition to the Iron Age). Such pictorial symbols, together with their associated song-names and magical lore, were the ancestral inheritance of the North Germanic peoples migrating south from Scandinavia. They are to be seen above, inscribed together with Runes, on a lance-tip dating from the third century AD, found at Kovel, south-east of Brest.

This Swedish rune-stone from the Viking period was carved c. 1020 by Åsmund Karesson of Osla in Uppland. The inscription reads: 'BJÖRN, ÖDULF, GUNNAR AND HOLMDIS RAISED THIS STONE TO ULF, GINLOG'S HUSBAND, AND ÅSMUND HEWED [IT].'

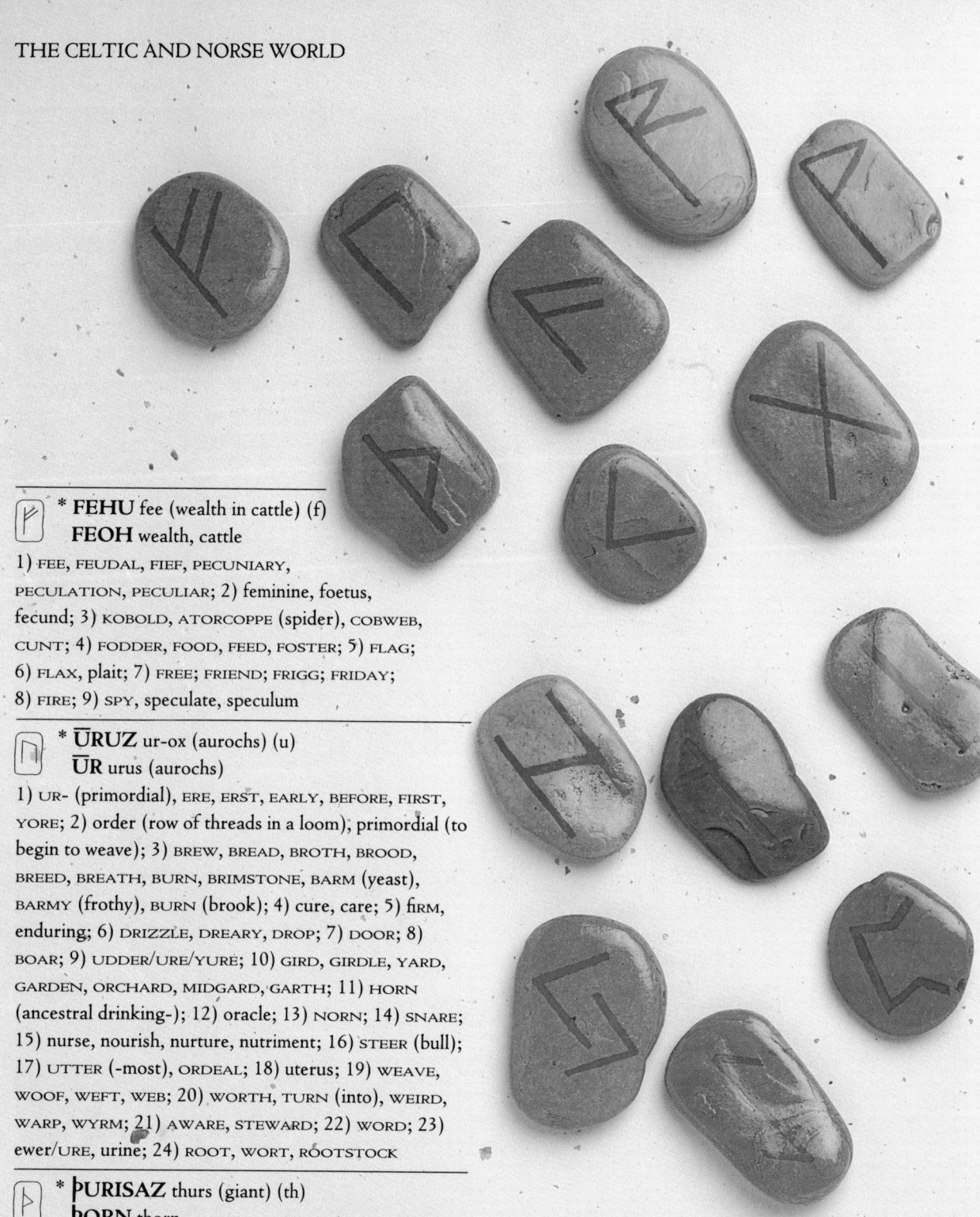

* FEHU fee (wealth in cattle) (f)
FEOH wealth, cattle

1) FEE, FEUDAL, FIEF, PECUNIARY, PECULATION, PECULIAR; 2) feminine, foetus, fecund; 3) KOBOLD, ATORCOPPE (spider), COBWEB, CUNT; 4) FODDER, FOOD, FEED, FOSTER; 5) FLAG; 6) FLAX, plait; 7) FREE; FRIEND; FRIGG; FRIDAY; 8) FIRE; 9) SPY, speculate, speculum

* ŪRUZ ur-ox (aurochs) (u)
ŪR urus (aurochs)

1) UR- (primordial), ERE, ERST, EARLY, BEFORE, FIRST, YORE; 2) order (row of threads in a loom); primordial (to begin to weave); 3) BREW, BREAD, BROTH, BROOD, BREED, BREATH, BURN, BRIMSTONE, BARM (yeast), BARMY (frothy), BURN (brook); 4) cure, care; 5) firm, enduring; 6) DRIZZLE, DREARY, DROP; 7) DOOR; 8) BOAR; 9) UDDER/URE/YURE; 10) GIRD, GIRDLE, YARD, GARDEN, ORCHARD, MIDGARD, GARTH; 11) HORN (ancestral drinking-); 12) oracle; 13) NORN; 14) SNARE; 15) nurse, nourish, nurture, nutriment; 16) STEER (bull); 17) UTTER (-most), ORDEAL; 18) uterus; 19) WEAVE, WOOF, WEFT, WEB; 20) WORTH, TURN (into), WEIRD, WARP, WYRM; 21) AWARE, STEWARD; 22) WORD; 23) ewer/URE, urine; 24) ROOT, WORT, ROOTSTOCK

* ÞURISAZ thurs (giant) (th)
ÞORN thorn

1) THURS, STORM; 2) THORN; 3) THUNDER, THURSDAY; 4) THRESH, DRILL, TURN, TWIST, THREAD; 5) THRILL, THROUGH

* ANSUZ Áss/Ásynja (Holy Power or wielder of divine breath: 'Asura') (a)
ŌS mouth (o)

1) OS (mouth of womb, divine utterance); 2) ASH (from fire); 3) IS, YES, SOOTH; 4) ASH (tree)

* RAIÐŌ riding (r)
RĀD riding

1) RIDE, RIDING, ROAD, RAID, READY, STRAIGHT; 2) READ, REDE, RIDDLE ('riddle my rede'), RITE, 'RTA' (cosmic order); 3) TREE, TROW, TRUE, TRUST, TRUTH, TROTH, TAR; 4) RAW; 5) RIGHT, REALM, RULE, RECKON; 6) RED, ROWAN, RADDLE/RUDDLE, RUDDOCK, RUBRIC, RUST; 7) ROOT

* **KAUNAZ** ulcer
* **KĒNAZ** resinous pinewood (torch)
  (cf. German 'kien')
* **KANŌ** skiff (k)
  CĒN or **CEĀN** resinous pinewood (torch) (c)

1) PINE, PITCH; 2) IGNEOUS; 3) CHINE, CLEFT, CHINK, SCION, KITH; 4) (Indo-European '* gen-'): KIN, KING, KIND, CHILD; 5) KNEE, KNEEL; 6) KNOW, CAN, CUNNING, KEN, KENNING, COUTH, KITH (kith & kin), KEEN (brave); 7) QUEEN; 8) CANDLE, CANDOUR, INCANDESCENT, INCENDIARY, INCENSE; 9) SHINE, SHEEN, SHIMMER, KINDLE; 10) HEAP, HIP, HIVE, HIGH (cf. Lithuanian 'kaukas': swelling, boil, 'kaukarus': hill and Germanic 'Xau-xaz': High, a name of Wōđanaz), KNAP, KNOB, KNELL, KNOLL, KNOT, KNIFE, KNEAD; 11) GROUNDSEL ('pus-absorber'); 12) CAUSTIC, CAUTERIZE; 13) CAN (watering-), COBLE (boat for salmon fishing); 14) SHIP, SKIFF

* **GEƀŌ** gift (g)
  GYFU gift

1) GIVE, FORGIVE, GIFT (for a wedding), GAVEL (tribute);
2) GOOD, TOGETHER, GATHER, GAD

* **WUNJŌ** 'winsome', joy (w)
  WYN joy (clan-), pasture

1) WIN, WINSOME, WONT, WEAN, WEEN, WISH, VENOM, VENERY, VANADIS; 2) WIND, WEND, WANDER, WAND, WANDERER, VANDALS

* **HAGALAZ** hail, sleet (h)
  HÆGL hail

1) HAIL; 2) GALLOWS, WINDLASS; 3) HAGGARD, HEDGE, HAWTHORN, QUAY; 4) HALE, WHOLESOME, WASSAIL, HEAL, HEALTH, HOLY, HALLOW; 5) HEL, HALL, HELE, HOLE, HOLLOW, HULL/HUSK, HAUGH, HELM (ritual mask); 6) HILL, HOLM; 7) HOLT, HALT (lame); 8) HOLLY; 9) HEW, HAY, HAYWARD, HAG

* **NAUÞIZ** need, necessity (n)
  NŸD need

1) NEED, NECESSITY, NARWHAL, NAUGHT/NOUGHT, EXHAUSTION; 2) NAUSEA, NAUTICAL, NAUTILUS, NAVAL, NAVE, NAVIGATE, NAVY, ARGONAUT

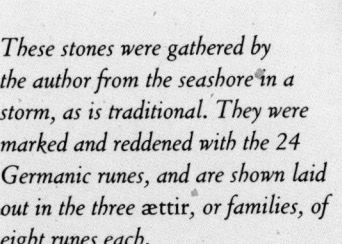

These stones were gathered by the author from the seashore in a storm, as is traditional. They were marked and reddened with the 24 Germanic runes, and are shown laid out in the three ættir, or families, of eight runes each.

* ĪSA ice (i)
ĪS ice

1) ICE; 2) IRON (Celtic '* īsarno', the holy metal);
3) ICICLE

* JĒRA year, harvest (j – as the y in year)
GĒR (fruitful) year or harvest (g)

1) YEAR; 2) HARVEST, pluck, carp (recite, brag)

* EIHWAZ yew (æ)
ĒOH yew-tree (eo)

1) YEW (+ reddish and motley)

* PERÞ thorp (suggestion only) (p)
PEORÐ

(this rune-name has yet to be satisfactorily translated, but
it is likely to relate to PERCHT, goddess of the Wild Hunt
and spinning) 1) THORP (village), TERP (village-mound);
2) EARTH; 3) BOAR (Indo-European '* eper-'); 4)
IRMINSUL; 5) HEARTH; 6) RUN, RUNNEL, EMBER DAY,
RENNET, RILL; 7) RAFTER, RAFT; 8) SPEAR, SPAR; 9)
SPROUT, SPURT, SPRIT, SPREAD, sperm; 10) BERTHA:
'the White Lady', Frau Wode

* ALHIZ elk
* ALGIZ protection (z)
EOLHX-SECG elk (-sedge) (x)

1) ELM, ALDER, ELK; 2) ELL (45"), ELLEN, 'OUR LADY'S
ELLWAND'; 3) ELF, ELDRITCH; 4) SCYTHE, SICKLE,
SEDGE, SAXON; 5) SAY, SAW (a saying), SAGA, SKALD

* SŌWULŌ sun (s)
SIGEL sun

1) SUN, SOL; 2) OE. SIGE (victory); 3) SWINE, SOW

* TEIWAZ Tīw (Shining One or deity of Pole
Star, Deiwos, Tuisto) (t)
TĪR Tīw/Tig

1) TUESDAY; 2) OE. STRÆLE (arrow); 3) STREW; 4)
STAR

* BERKANA birch twig (ƀ)
BEORC birch tree (b)

1) BRIGHT, BIRCH ('the White Tree'); 2) BEAVER, BEAR

* EHWAZ 'equine', horse (e)
EH horse

1) equine, equerry, equestrian, equitation

* MANNAZ man (not male gender: human) (m)
MAN human

1) HUMAN/S, WOMAN (OE. 'wīfman'), MAN (OE.
'wæpnman'); 2) MOUND, (hand); 3) MIND, MEMORY,
REMEMBER, MINDFUL, OHG. 'MINNA': love

* LAGUZ lake (water, sea) (l)
LAGU water, sea

1) LAKE, LOCH; 2) LAW, LAY

* INGUZ Ing (god of fertility) (ng)
ING Ing

1) groin; 2) kidney

* ÐAGAZ day (đ)
DÆG day (d)

1) DAY; DAWN; 2) TIDE, TIDINGS, daimon, DEAL,
ORDEAL; 3) DAIRY, DOUGH, paradise; 4) DEW, HONEY-
DEW

* ŌÞILA odal (sacred ancestral land) (o)
ĒÞEL inherited land (œ) (cf. Frankish '* fehuŏd',
which reveals the close link between the Mysteries
of the first and last Runes)

1) ALL, PECULIAR; 2) ALLODIUM, ODAL, UDAL (although
these three words have become associated with false
notions of the ownership or holding of land, they in
reality refer to the holy guardianship and sacredness of
the Land. This is the key to the Mysteries of the Runes);
3) ÆÐELING (prince), EDELWEISS; 4) WŌÐANAZ,
ÓÐINN, WÓDEN

The Germanic rune-staves were not the end of
the Runes' journey. At the end of the second
century BC, there were present in the Alpine
regions Germanic survivors of the Battles of
Vercellae (the Cimbri) and Aquae Sextiae (the
Teutons). The Cimbri stayed in the southern
foothills of the Alps before recrossing to
Germany, and may have learned the Runes from
the *Alpengermanen*, later passing them on to the
Suevi.

During the first century BC, the Runes
journeyed northwards down the Rhine, possibly
carried by the Cimbri, Suevi or Teutons,
meanwhile also being taken eastwards by the
Marcomanni of the Upper Rhine. The Rhine
journey of the Runes is evidenced by a first
century BC goblet found at Vehlingen on the
Lower Rhine, inscribed with the following potent
runic formula:

And so the Runes flowed out of the Rhine
Estuary, along the North Sea coastal routes by
way of the Frisian Islands and Heligoland Bay,
and from there across Schleswig-Holstein to

reach Denmark, Jutland and, by the third century AD, Scandinavia.

An early Scandinavian runic find is the lance-tip from Øvre Stabu in Norway, dated AD 200. The Runes inscribed thereon are: ᚱᚨᚢᚾᛁᛃᚨᛉ *raunijaz*, the tester. From the second century onwards, rune-staves were increasingly to occur on objects of metal, stone and bone, particularly in the regions close to the Baltic Sea.

The magical 'FUÞARK' order of the rune-staves first appears on a Gothic grave-slab at Kylver in Gotland around 400 AD (see Contents page), and on a golden medallion from Vadstena in Sweden (c. 550), which also shows the three families of Runes divided by double dots.

It also appears, in modified form, on an eighth-century Saxon 'scramasax', or short sword, found on the bed of the Thames in London. The Saxons first gained knowledge of the Runes in Schleswig-Holstein and north-west Germany; and later in Friesland there developed the 28 rune-staves of the 'FUÞORC', which the Saxons brought to England during, at the latest, the sixth century. The 'FUÞORC' continued to develop, reaching a total of 33 rune-staves in early ninth-century Northumbria.

NORSE RUNES

The use of the Germanic 'FUÞARK' came to an end early in the ninth century. After a period of transition, an entirely Scandinavian rune-row came into being, which in its development was at least partially independent of its predecessor. Unlike the Anglo-Frisian rune-staves, which gradually increased in number, the Norse Runes represent a magical concentration of the runic energies into only 16 staves. The earliest record of purely Norse rune-staves is an inscription on a fibula from Strand in Norway, dated 800. The inscription reads: '*siglis n a (nauđa) hle*', the ornament is a protection against distress.

The Norse rune-staves, names and letter values, together with images derived from the Norwegian and Icelandic rune-poems (thirteenth and fifteenth centuries), provide further keys for unlocking the mysteries of the Runes.

Old English golden ring (eighth century), found on Greymoor Hill in Cumbria, England. The engraving is likely to be a runic chart or magical formula.

ᚠ	**FÉ** *cattle, sheep, property, money (f, b) (wolf in forest; sea-fire; serpent-path; gold)*
ᚢ	**ÚR** *drizzle, flakes of metal (u, y, w, ø, au) (slag; reindeer runs over hard-frozen snow; weeping of clouds; shower)*
ᚦ	**ÞURS** *giant (th – hard and soft) (giant: cliff dweller)*
ᚬ ᚨ	**ÓSS** *mouth of river or firth (ą, ó) (scabbard of swords; god: ancient creator, king of Asgard, Lord of Valhalla)*
ᚱ	**REIÐ** *riding, chariot (r) (Regin forged best sword)*
ᚴ	**KAUN** *sore, boil (k, g, ng) (ulcer; death: pale corpse; painful spot, dwelling of putrefaction)*
ᚼ	**HAGALL** *hail (h) (coldest of grains; Creator of primeval world; driving sleet; sickness of serpents)*
ᚾ ᚿ	**NAUÐ** *need, difficulty, distress, poverty (n) (naked man chilled by frost; distress of bond-woman; oppression; hard labour; service)*

	ÍSS
	ice (on sea or water) (i, e) (ice: the broad bridge; bark of rivers, roof of wave; wild boar)

	ÁR
	year, good season (a) (harvest; good summer; fully ripe crops)

	SÓL
	sun, sun goddess (s) (sun: light of the world; divine judgement; shield of sky; shining ray; destroyer of ice)

	TÝR
	Týr (divinity of lode-star) (t, d, nt, nd) (one-handed Áss; smith has oft to blow the bellows; leavings of wolf, king of temples)

	BJARKAN
	birch (b, v, p, mb, mp) (greenest-leaved of branches; Loki lucky in deception; fir tree)

	MAÐR
	person, human (m) (increase of mould; great the claw of hawk; joy of humanity; adorner of ships)

	LǪGR
	sea, water (1) (water: falls from mountain side; ornaments of gold; welling stream; broad geyser; land of fish; lake)

	ÝR
	yew tree, bow of yew (R, y) (greenest of winter trees; sputters when burns; bent bow; brittle iron; giant of the arrow)

During the course of their heroic voyages (eighth to twelfth centuries), the Vikings seeded runic knowledge from the Arctic and North America (Newfoundland) to the Mediterranean. Inscriptions have been found as far apart as Greenland, Venice, Orkney and the Isle of Man.

Runes remained in use to a very late period in the North: sixteenth-century inscriptions have been found in Gotland; and in seventeenth-century Iceland, Christians deemed it necessary to burn people to death merely for the possession of rune-staves. Runic calendars were still in use in remote regions of Sweden in the nineteenth century.

ANCIENT TRIBAL USES OF RUNES

The wise women and men used the Runes on behalf of the tribe for these reasons: to determine the tasks to be carried out; to divine the pleasure and intentions of the deities for the tribe; to alter consciousness; and to bring about external events.

At a birth, the Runes were cast to find the name and life-path of the child. Runes were also used to assist members of the tribe when returning to the ancestors at death and to determine the course of tribal migrations.

They were used by the tribal magicians on their ecstatic journeys into the Underworld, as a means of gaining knowledge, for healing, and to bring back gifts to the tribe, such as wisdom, inspiration or courage. Rune-chants were used for the conception, gestation and birth of a child, and also for the celebration of the seasonal festivals.

If healing was needed, the Runes were cast and used as gateways in order to remember the means of healing that particular injury or sickness. This is going neither into the past nor into the future: it is entering into that condition where everything actually is, the eternal present moment.

A METHOD OF RUNIC DIVINATION

If you come to the realization that you have forgotten the reason for your presence on Earth, the Runes can be used to restore that memory. By using the Runes as gateways, you descend to the Underworld to regain lost knowledge and to find the spiritual tools that will enable you to carry out the task that you remember.

The Runes are not for fortune-telling in the modern sense. Wanting to know whether good or bad things are going to happen to you is alien to the consciousness out of which the Runes emerged. Runes can, however, help us towards achieving wholeness and act as a mouthpiece for the gods, goddesses, ancestors and non-human beings who will help us with the task of environmental regeneration. When casting the Runes, you are allowing the formation of a pattern, a map of the relationship between this world and the other worlds within Creation.

The method of runic divination given here is based upon the image of the Nine Worlds of Creation on the Web of Wyrd (Wyrd meaning the pattern of cosmic destiny), which is eternally spun between root and branch of Yggdrasil, the Tree of Cosmic Axis, by the dark weaving goddess Urðr. There is no suggestion that this is an ancient method, but it will be found to be in resonance with the nature of the Runes.

Ideally, the web pattern should be painted or embroidered on a white cloth, but this is not essential. If a specific question is being asked, ensure that it is framed with clarity and reduced to its essential kernel of meaning. The method may also be used with no question, in which case questions rather than answers are likely to be generated.

Commence the divination by kindling a sacred flame and making a short invocation to one of the Norse deities associated with Runes. Chanting based on rune-names might also be done at this point. Become aware of the eight directions on the horizon, of the sacredness of the Land, and of the central axis – pointing towards the Pole Star – about which all the worlds turn.

The rune-staves or stones (the signs are traditionally coloured red) can either be taken out of their bag, one at a time, and placed according to the numerical sequence on the diagram (or any other sequence that you are inspired to use); or, if preferred and a rune-cloth is being used, all the staves or stones may be cast onto the cloth, and the nine falling closest to the circles be allowed to form the pattern.

The nine circles form a map of the Nine Worlds of Creation delineated in Norse mythology. Their significance in this context is briefly indicated as follows:

1 *MIÐGARÐR* – Middle Earth: the land or environment; here might be encountered the earth goddess Nerthus and the ancestors.
2 *NIFLHEIMR* – the World of Mists and Ice, location of *Hvergelmir*, the Roaring Cauldron, which nourishes one of the roots of Yggdrasil:

Key to the map of the Nine Worlds of Creation on the Web of Wyrd
1 Middle Earth (the land or environment)
2 The World of Mists and Ice
3 Giant World
4 The World of Fire
5 The World of the Vanir
6 The World of the Elven Smiths
7 The World of the Star Elves
8 The World of the Dark Goddesses of Spinning and Weaving
9 The Realm of the Aesir and Asynjur

an expression of the primordial realm of Cosmic Ice; here might be encountered the vast nurturing forces of the cow Auðumbla, from whose teats flowed the galaxies.

3 *JǪTUNHEIMR* – Giant World, location of *Mímisbrunnr*, the Well of Memory, which nourishes one of the roots of Yggdrasil: an expression of the vast primordial beings known as *Asuras*; here might be encountered the giantess Gerd, beloved of Freyr, of whom it is sung in *Skírnismál*: 'Her arms glistened so they reflected all the heavens and seas.'

4 *MUSPELLSHEIMR* – the World of Fire: an expression of the primordial realm of Cosmic Fire; here might be encountered 'the Keeper of the Oracular Flame'.

5 *VANAHEIMR* – the World of the Vanir (fertility

deities): here might be encountered Idun, keeper of the Golden Apples of Immortality, who carved Runes on the tongue of Bragi, god of poetry.

6 SVARTALFHEIMR – the World of the Elven Smiths: the realm of 'sub-atomic space'; here might be encountered Sunna, the feminine power of the Sun shining in Earth, and Íwaldi, guardian of the primordial Mead Cauldron and father of the Elven Smiths. They give teaching concerning the laws of chemistry.

7 LJOSSALFHEIMR – the World of the Star Elves: the realm of 'stellar space'; here might be encountered the Vanadis (Freyja) and her brother Freyr, Lady and Lord of the Star Elves. They give teaching concerning the laws of biology.

8 HELHEIMR – the World of the Dark Goddess of Spinning and Weaving: the deepest realm of the Underworld; here might be encountered Urðr, who eternally weaves the Web of Wyrd.

9 ÁSGARÐR – Realm of the Æsir and Asynjur, location of Urðabrunnr, the Well of Fate, which nourishes one of the roots of Yggdrasil: here might be encountered Frigg (who 'knows men's fates though she does not prophesy') and Óðinn seated on their thrones, from where they are able to look out over all the worlds. They give teaching concerning the laws of physics.

10 Return to the Land: at this point, the first stone can be reconsidered in the light of the entire pattern; and if appropriate, a tenth stone may be cast to indicate a process of regeneration in the Land.

Conclude the divination by bidding thanks to any beings contacted and by reaffirming the sacredness of the Cosmic Axis, the eight directions on the horizon and the Land. Return the rune-staves to their bag and extinguish the flame.

There are Ogams as well as Runes carved on this rune-stone. The rune-signs read: 'THÓRGRÍMR CARVED THIS CROSS'; the Ogams read: 'A BLESSING UPON THÓRGRÍMR.' This is an example of a type of rune-stone where the talismanic potency is concentrated in the Runes forming the power-name (THÓRGRÍMR) of the magician who made the carving.

Viking runic inscription in Maeshowe, Orkney, made by 'that man most skilled in runecraft west over the sea' during the winter of 1151–2. The bottom row consists of kvistrūnir *(branch runes). The number of branches to the left of the upright indicates which of the three families the rune-sign belongs to; and the number of branches to the right tells us which rune-sign within the family is to be read.*

EUROPE AND THE WEST

In the West the great civilizations of Greece, Rome, Mesopotamia, Egypt and Babylon developed their own divinatory systems, which generally became more complex with the passage of time. Thus in the classical world a number of state-funded oracles were established at the great religious centres of Delphi, Delos, Dodona and Rome; while in Mesopotamia the study of the stars and planets evolved gradually into the exact science we know today as astrology. In Babylon, meanwhile, the study of omens became increasingly sophisticated, with vast collections of significant events recorded and tabulated. At the same time, throughout the classical world, extispicy, the study of entrails, flourished (see Chapter Seven).

The melting pot of the Near East gave birth to Tarot, a symbolic card game which grew to be perhaps the quintessential divinatory system of the West. And this in turn was influenced by Cabbala, the Jewish mystical system which, though it had nothing to do with foretelling the future, did give rise to one such system, Galgal, which is discussed in Chapter Eight.

In every case these were far more formalized than the random casting of rune stones or Ogam sticks, or the counting of bones and stones, which developed into numerology and geomancy on the one hand, whilst continuing to be used in shamanistic fashion by grass-roots diviners of the kind discussed in Chapter Nine, later in this section.

Within all the complex divergences between the main methods of Western divination, certain common threads continue to emerge: the belief that it was possible to enter into a state of being in which one could communicate directly with the spirit world (oracles); the belief that there existed a store of wisdom deriving from most ancient times, and which it was possible to tap into through the study of complex symbols and correspondences (Tarot, Galgal); and that the movement of planets and the positions of constellations at birth affected the lives of everyone (astrology).

And still, while such systems as these became ever more complex and refined, the practice of the ancient shamanic techniques of divination – the observance of natural events in the world which surrounds us – continued largely unchanged and unabated. Village wise women throughout the European world continued to study the flights of birds, the lines in the palms of hands, the embers of spent fires and all the variations in the patterns of the weather, just as today their descendants read patterns in tea-leaves and the vague shapes that appear in the cloudy depths of crystal balls.

In palace and court, as in village hut and roadside, wizards, astrologers and fortune-tellers delved ever deeper into the hidden secrets of creation. Their methods were increasingly dissimilar, but they still sought the same thing – to find out what the future held in store.

CHAPTER FIVE

THE KEYS OF TAROT

Divination by Cartomancy

Rachel Pollack

The Tarot is the classic divination system of Western European culture. Although more people know astrology, astrology originated in Asia, while, as far as we know, the Tarot began in Italy in the Renaissance. The Tarot's importance comes from more than its legendary accuracy as a tool of prophecy. Its symbolic pictures outline a deep spiritual teaching, and in recent decades Tarot readers and commentators have explored the Tarot as an almost infinite source of psychological understanding.

No one knows the exact origin of the Tarot, a problem that only adds to the mystery surrounding it. We do not even know the origin of the word. *Les Tarots* is the French name for a card game, an ancestor of bridge, known in Italy as *Tarocchi*. No information has come down to us as to why the game's players used those particular terms, although there is a Taro River in Northern Italy, not far from the Swiss border.

Many people have put forward theories of the Tarot's origin. These include Cabbala (see below), Egyptian initiation practices, Tantra (Indian esotericism), allegorical poems and processions, medieval Celtic traditions, underground Christian heresies, masters of Atlantis, Chaldean phases of the Moon, and so on. Most of these theories share a common assumption: that the Tarot contains so much coded wisdom it *must* originate in some ancient secret doctrine.

Historically, we know of the Tarot first as a card game. Cards of any kind first appeared in Europe in the fourteenth century, possibly brought by Crusaders from the Middle East. In the middle of the fifteenth century an artist named Bonifacio Bembo painted a set of Tarot cards as a wedding present for a marriage between the Sforza family and the Visconti family of Milano, Italy. One hundred and fifty years earlier, in 1300, Church officials burned to death one Maria Visconti, whom a sect of heretics had elected as the first woman pope. The classic Tarot contains a card titled the Female Pope.

The Renaissance was a time very given to allegories, spiritual development, alchemy and occult ideas (not unlike our own time). Whatever the Tarot's origins, the cards certainly contain allegorical images: Death, the Last Judgement, the Christian virtues of Temperance and Strength, the Wheel of Fortune, and so on.

When the Romanies ('Gypsies') came to Europe from North Africa they discovered the Tarot and began using it for fortune-telling.

Many people today still believe that the Romanies invented the Tarot, or that they brought it to Europe from Egypt. (The word 'Gypsy' derives from the mistaken belief that the Romanies, who in fact originated in India, come from Egypt.) Despite this early use in divination, the Tarot still existed primarily as a game. In fact, *Les Tarots* is still played today through much of Southern Europe and French-influenced Northern Africa.

In 1781 a man named Antoine Court de Gebelin made a startling pronouncement. In the course of a multi-volume study of occult teachings, Court de Gebelin claimed that he had discovered the 'book of Thoth', a legendary book of universal knowledge created by the Egyptian god Thoth for his magician disciples (according to Egyptian myth, Thoth was the inventor of magic and writing). This book did not lay buried in some secret library, but existed in plain view, as the game of Tarot. Inspired by Court de Gebelin, an occultist who called himself Etteila (his name, Aliette, spelled backwards) created a Tarot deck devoted to divination rather than game-playing.

In the mid-nineteenth century Eliphas Lévi (the occult name of Alphonse Louis Constant) extended Court de Gebelin's suggestions into a system. While continuing to use Egyptian images, Lévi linked the Tarot primarily to Cabbala (an idea first put forward by Court de Gebelin), a vastly complex Jewish system of mysticism, meditation, cosmogony, theosophy and magical practices. Originating in medieval Spain, Cabbala developed into the main structure of Christian as well as Jewish occultism in Europe.

The links between Cabbala and Tarot are certainly impressive. Cabbala derives from meditation on the 22 letters of the Hebrew alphabet (see Chapter Eight, Divination on the Tree of Life). The Tarot contains 22 trump cards. Cabbala teaches that God created the Cosmos in four steps, or 'worlds'. The Tarot contains four suits. Cabbala focuses on two primary images, the four-letter name of God in Hebrew, and the Tree of Life, with its ten

'Sephiroth', emanations of the light of God. The four suits of the Tarot each contain four 'court' cards, along with cards numbered from one to ten. No wonder Antoine Court de Gebelin and Eliphas Lévi considered the Tarot a systematic expression of Cabbalist wisdom. And yet, as far as we know, in all the thousands of pages of Cabbalist writing, no mention exists of anything like Tarot cards.

At the turn of the century an esoteric group named the Order of the Golden Dawn developed Lévi's ideas further. They linked the cards to magical rituals, and especially to astrology. The Order of the Golden Dawn existed for only a few years, but its influence continues today. Two of its members later designed the two most popular Tarot packs of the twentieth century. Arthur Edward Waite created the 'Rider' pack with painter Pamela Colman Smith. This pack has sold millions of copies world-wide. A great many contemporary Tarot creators base their pictures on Smith's drawings. Aleister Crowley designed *The Book of Thoth*, painted by Lady Frieda Harris. Although not as accessible as the Rider, Harris's elegant art and Crowley's dense symbolism have given this pack enormous influence.

The Tarot consists of two parts: the 22 trump cards, known as the Major Arcana (Arcana means secrets), and the four suits, collectively called the Minor Arcana. Traditionally, only the Major Arcana contained scenes and people. These are the allegorical images mentioned above. The Minor Arcana usually showed only the correct number of symbols from the particular suit. That is, the Ten of Cups would show ten cups arranged in a pattern, the Two of Swords depicted two crossed swords, and so on.

The Rider pack changed this, which is one reason for its great popularity. In Smith's paintings every card shows a scene. The Ten of Cups displays a family celebrating under a rainbow. The Two of Swords portrays a blindfolded woman holding a sword in each hand. This new begining – adopted by most contemporary decks – fundamentally changed

Tarot divination. Previously, the Minor cards carried formulaic interpretations, phrases like 'journey by water' or 'a message, hidden plans'. The Rider pack enabled diviners to interpret the events and actions shown in the pictures.

READING THE TAROT CARDS

There are three ways to divine with Tarot. The first involves memorizing the meanings (or looking them up) and applying them strictly to the cards. 'You will take a journey' or 'You will meet an older man who will give you a gift', and so on. In the second, the diviner analyses the scenes in the cards and their relation to the person's life. The diviner may look at what the people in the pictures are doing, how the action changes from one picture to another, and which symbols recur in the different cards. The diviner may stress psychological qualities rather than events. Finally, the 'psychic' approach involves giving no meanings at all to the cards, instead using them as triggers for internal revelations, for flashes of insight and knowledge. In practice, most modern readers combine elements of all these approaches. They will know a set of meanings for the cards, they will look carefully at the pictures and how they compare with each other, and they will allow understanding to come to them as they look at the images.

The modern approach to Tarot has brought together the spiritual and divinatory interpretations. Previously, those people who sought

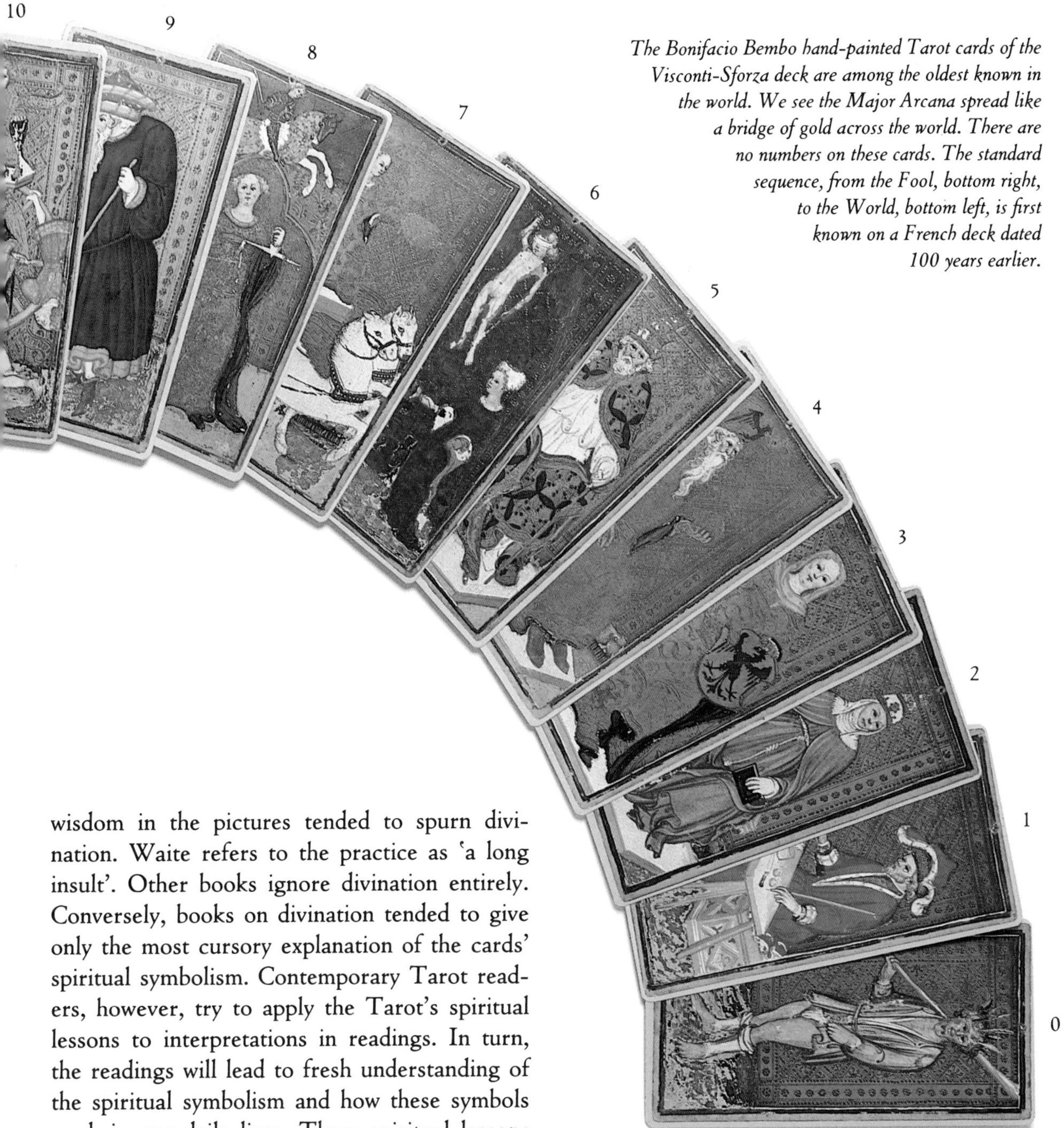

The numbers 10, 9, 8, 7, 6, 5, 4, 3, 2, 1, 0 label the cards spread in an arc.

The Bonifacio Bembo hand-painted Tarot cards of the Visconti-Sforza deck are among the oldest known in the world. We see the Major Arcana spread like a bridge of gold across the world. There are no numbers on these cards. The standard sequence, from the Fool, bottom right, to the World, bottom left, is first known on a French deck dated 100 years earlier.

wisdom in the pictures tended to spurn divination. Waite refers to the practice as 'a long insult'. Other books ignore divination entirely. Conversely, books on divination tended to give only the most cursory explanation of the cards' spiritual symbolism. Contemporary Tarot readers, however, try to apply the Tarot's spiritual lessons to interpretations in readings. In turn, the readings will lead to fresh understanding of the spiritual symbolism and how these symbols work in our daily lives. These spiritual lessons derived primarily from the Major Arcana.

The Major Arcana are shown here in their generally agreed order:

0 The Fool (some place this card at the end, or between 20 and 21)

1 The Magician, also called the Juggler

2 The High Priestess, also called the Female Pope

3 The Empress

4 The Emperor

5 The Hierophant, also called the Pope

6 The Lovers

7 The Chariot

8 Justice (in some modern decks Strength is 8 and Justice is 11)

9 The Hermit

10 The Wheel of Fortune

11 Strength

12 The Hanged Man

13 Death

14 Temperance

15 The Devil

16 The Tower

17 The Star

18 The Moon

19 The Sun

20 Judgement

21 The World

In general, most commentators agree that the Major Arcana depicts the soul in its journey from birth to enlightenment. Arguments centre on the specific stages of the journey, and on the particular doctrine – Cabbala, Egyptian, Celtic, etc. – outlined in the symbolism. For instance, many people have described the Magician as 'the male principle' and the High Priestess as 'the female'. But just what do these terms mean? Are they simply light and darkness, or the positive and negative poles of electromagnetism? Do they describe actual men and women? And is the Magician derived from the Egyptian god Thoth, and the High Priestess from the goddess Isis? Or do they symbolize the first two connecting pathways on the Cabbalist Tree of Life (or the

The Rider pack has become the world's most popular Tarot. Here it is shown in a simple, four-card spread. The four can be the four elements, or the four seasons of the year.

second and third, if the Fool signifies the first)? Or do they portray roles human beings can play, such as a ritual magician and the priestess of an occult order? Or perhaps modern descendants of tribal shamans and diviners? The Tarot gains much of its power from the fact that all of these interpretations exist simultaneously.

Unlike the *I Ching*, the Tarot images bear no official text. Even the names and numbers of the cards apparently developed some time after the earliest known paintings. The lack of an orthodox doctrine allows us to accept the accumulated wisdom of past interpretations while opening us to fresh possibilities each time we look at the pictures. And even though the cards now come in a specific order we can change that order simply by shuffling the pack. New juxtapositions open the way to new ideas.

The Minor Arcana consists of four suits of 14 cards each: Ace–10, plus the four 'Court' cards, Page, Knight, Queen, and King. The names of the suits have changed over the years. Most common are:

Wands, also called Staves, Rods, etc.

Cups

Swords

Pentacles, called Coins in earlier packs

Traditionally, Tarot commentators have paid more attention to the Major Arcana than the Minor. Most modern interpreters link the Minor suits to the four 'elements' of medieval philosophy and modern astrology. These elements are fire, water, air and earth. Some arguments exist over which suits belong to which elements. The most common attribution runs Wands=Fire, Cups=Water, Swords=Air, Pentacles=Earth. Some contemporary decks have renamed the suits in line with the elements, for example, Stones instead of Pentacles, Flames instead of Wands.

Divining with Tarot involves 'reading' the cards. Some people do this by turning over cards at random and seeing what inspiration rises from them. Most, however, lay the cards down in specific patterns, known as 'spreads', or 'layouts'. Hundreds of these spreads exist. Some serve particular purposes, for instance a 'year

spread' to look at issues likely to arise in the coming 12 months. Or various relationship spreads targeted to the particular problems and issues of romantic involvements. Or spreads to help people understand and recover from alcoholism and other special problems. Some spreads derive from particular shapes: a spread in the form of a six-pointed star, or a spread outlining a human body (with the 'brain' card showing what a person thinks, the 'heart' card what the person feels, and so on).

The Tarot de Marseilles has become the classic Tarot. We see them here in a 12-card spread with several possible interpretations. We can see each card as representing one month of the coming year, for example. Alternatively, we can interpret them within the context of the 12 houses of the Zodiac.

Whatever the spread, the principle remains simple. Each position in the spread carries its own meaning, such as 'past influences', 'unconscious desires', and so on. Since each card bears a meaning as well, the interpretation combines the card and the position. For example, the Five

TAROT READING USING THE CELTIC CROSS SPREAD

Question: The querent, a woman, has the possibility of a new relationship. What is the best way to react? Deck used: the Rider pack.

1 Central issue: the Fool. This indicates the person's desire to leap into this new relationship. She has an impulsive quality and an openness, which may lead to love but which also may get her in trouble.

2 Crossing influence: 4 of Swords. This card shows a counter desire to the Fool. The querent has been hurt in the past and feels a need to heal. Having such a clear conflict between this card and the Fool has led to her indecision.

6 Approaching influence: Star. This continues the theme of liberation. The person will experience a renewed optimism. She will stop holding back and will express herself very openly.

7 Self: 2 of Cups. She is ready for a genuine commitment with an equal partner.

8 Others: Page of Wands. The traditional meanings for this card include a faithful lover. It therefore indicates that the other person can be trusted and is eager for this relationship. The card is a good match for the Fool.

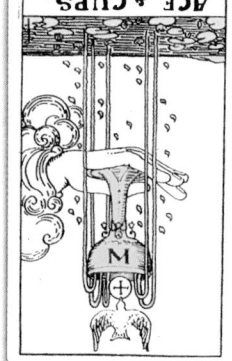

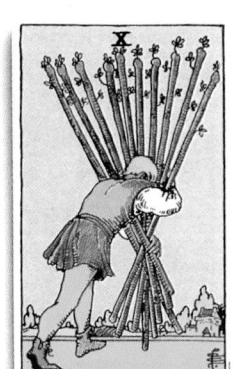

3 Basis (influence of the past): Lovers reversed. This indicates a love relationship that went badly and is the cause of the hesitation.

4 Recent developments: 8 of Swords reversed. The reversed card says that this woman has begun to free herself emotionally from the damaging effects of the past relationship. This card and the Fool together indicate a liberation and a chance for a new beginning.

5 Possible developments: 10 of Wands. The 10 suggests the person has a tendency to take on herself all the burdens of maintaining a relationship. She will have to be aware of this attitude to make the new relationship work.

9 Hopes and fears: Ace of Cups reversed. The Ace is the gift of love and happiness. Reversed, it says the person fears the relationship will turn out badly, and that love will be an illusory hope. This fear is what holds her back. The reading is telling her it comes from past hurts, and not from the actual situation.

10 Outcome: 7 of Wands reversed. The card advises the woman to take action. Along with the cards which have come before (such as the 8 of Swords, the Star and the Page of Wands), it tells her that love is not an illusion and she can follow her feelings with confidence.

of Cups usually signifies loss. In 'past influences' the card would indicate a previous loss which still affects the person's life. In 'future events' the same card would show the possibility of facing such a loss in the coming time. And in 'influences of others' it might show someone else suffering from a loss.

Some Tarot commentators and teachers recommend various rituals for reading the cards. These might include ways to hold them, phrases to say while mixing them or laying them out, and so on. However, the basic procedure remains simple. The 'querent' (the person seeking the reading) mixes the cards. Often, they will end the shuffle by separating the pack into three piles. The reader then lays out the cards in the particular spread. Turning each card face up, the reader interprets their meanings in the light of whatever questions the querent has brought to the reading.

The power of the reading lies first of all in the reader's ability to see and communicate the message shown in the cards and their combinations. Secondly – and perhaps more importantly – the power lies in the querent's response to the pictures.

In traditional fortune-telling the querent said very little. The reader was supposed to discover hidden knowledge and predict future events. Many Tarot readers still follow this approach, and many people who go for a Tarot reading expect such revelations. However, in the past few decades the emphasis has shifted to self-knowledge for the querent, and the possibility of using the Tarot as inspiration for positive change. In such a model, the reader first seeks to help the querent understand the issues involved in the situation, and then to make good choices and act on them. Of course, this method still requires the reader to trust that the cards will reveal truths not apparent on the surface. The difference is a matter of emphasis. For instance, if a querent asks 'Will my husband remain faithful to me?' the reader may avoid making a prediction and instead help the querent to look more closely at the problems in her marriage, at the reasons for her worry or insecurity.

As a result of these shifts many readers involve the querent much more directly in the choice of an appropriate spread and the interpretation of the cards. Some readers do not use any standard spread patterns, but will make up a spread on the spot based on the querent's issues and questions. When interpreting the cards, the reader will still explain the symbolism and rely on her or his own intuition as to the meanings. But she or he also may ask the querent, 'What does this picture say to you?' or 'Does this scene remind you of something you've experienced in your own life?' The reader will then take the querent's responses, combine them with the traditional meanings and the reader's own inspirations, and finally help the querent understand the possibilities and choices arising out of the reading as a whole. Some readers will end the reading with a meditation on a particular card, or by asking such questions as 'Which card symbolizes for you what you want to achieve in this situation?' In these ways, the reader attempts to take the reading beyond predictions. The cards and their symbolism become tools for the querent to gain more control of her or his life.

The Tarot is not only the most developed and complex of Western divinatory systems, it is also the most dynamic. New Tarot packs appear constantly, and many of these have taken the Tarot – and Tarot divination – in new directions (see the Appendix, Modern Restatements). For example, a number of new packs adapt the traditional Tarot pictures to a particular cultural context. These include a Native American Tarot, a Norse Tarot, an Aztec Tarot, and so on. Divination with these cards involves the reader with the concepts and traditions of those cultures.

Readers also have found new ways to use existing packs. These include dream interpretation, psychodrama, fiction writing, even musical composition through divination (the process involves assigning a note to each card, and then choosing cards at random). Whatever the Tarot's origins, it has evolved into a powerful tool for knowledge and inspiration.

CHAPTER SIX

SHAPES IN THE STARS

Patterns of Western Astrology

Prudence Jones

Astrology is a method of correlating events on earth with the positions of the planets in the heavens, in order to explain the significance of these events and to predict future ones. Astrologers think that earthly events are timed by the cycles of the celestial bodies, and that each of these celestial bodies – the Sun, Moon, planets and other phenomena such as asteroids and comets – is associated with a particular kind of event or situation. The planet Mars, for example, is connected with matters of initiative, pugnacity, breakages and disruption, with social groups such as gangs of young men, and with engineers, surgeons and soldiers. The two-year cycle of its apparent path around the Earth coincides, interestingly enough, with the standard length of posting in the armed forces in the UK. Such curious coincidences are the routine stuff of the astrologer's trade, and the skill of astrology lies not only in predicting when such coincidences are likely to happen, but in explaining why an apparently random, meaningless event was (or will be) in fact meaningful and able to serve the greater wisdom and understanding of those whom it involves.

Astrology is a unique mixture of precise scientific method (observation, measurement, prediction and verification or falsification) and the religious, magical or (more politely) 'synchronistic' outlook used in the other divinatory arts. Astrologers do not simply attempt to correlate events on Earth with the cycles of the celestial bodies, as applied astronomers do (for example in meteorology). They also assume that each moment, particularly the 'birth' moment of any entity, from a human being to a building to a political party, has a potentially fated quality which will fix the nature of that entity for the rest of its lifetime. Certain moments are seen as intrinsically powerful, whether they correspond with a 'birth' or not, in particular the times of eclipses, solstices and equinoxes.

AN ANCIENT ART

Most ancient cultures used a certain amount of applied astronomy in order to regulate their calendars, from the simple observation of the lunar cycle and the seasonal variation in the sunrise point on the local horizon, to the more elaborate calculation of the solstices, the equinoxes and the true solar year (exactly 365 days, 6 hours, 9 minutes and 9.5 seconds). Many ancient cultures also included some method of interpreting celestial events such as eclipses, which were thought to be omens – direct communications from the divine powers to those who could interpret them. Modern Western astrology, however, descends directly from just one of these cultures: the celestial omen-lore of ancient Mesopotamia.

The Mesopotamians – the Sumerians, Akkadians, Babylonians and Assyrians who lived in what is now Iraq, the land between the rivers Euphrates and Tigris – were assiduous inter-

This cuneiform tablet is one of the early Babylonian records of celestial omens. It was carved in the reign of King Ammisaduqa, c. 1700 BC, and records observations of the planet Venus. Hundreds of such astronomical records have been preserved in stone.

preters of omens. Hundreds of clay tablets, inscribed between the nineteenth and first centuries BC, have come down to us, recording the observation and interpretation of various classes of omen. These omens included the shapes formed by molten lead when poured into cold water, the pattern of veins on the liver of a sacrificed animal (see Chapter Eight, Consulting the Oracles) and, relevantly for our purposes here, the appearance of the stars, eclipses and planets in the night sky. Here is one of the celestial omens:

There will be an eclipse which is evil for Elam, Aharou, lucky for the king my lord, rest happy. It will be seen without Venus, to the king my lord I say there will be an eclipse. (Translation by Dorothea Wender.)

Although celestial omens were recorded by reference to their position in the night sky, for example 'in the east' or 'against the constellation of the Fishes', there is no evidence that regular cycles of occurrence were taken into account. Each omen seems to have been interpreted individually, like tea-leaves in a teacup, rather than being seen as a particular instance of a regularly occurring natural cycle, as it is in astrology proper.

SCIENTIFIC METHOD AND THE EMERGENCE OF WESTERN ASTROLOGY

What turned Babylonian omen-reading into astrology was its increasing association with scientific method. A curiosity about the existence of mechanical processes which unfold according to intrinsic rational laws, independently of the whims of personal choice, whether divine or human, seems to have grown in the eastern Mediterranean during the last 800 years BC. The Greeks are its most famous exponents, but in Mesopotamia as well we see empirical method developing, with the so-called Astronomical Diaries beginning in the mid-seventh century BC. The 18.6-year eclipse cycle was calculated with some exactitude by scholars in

Athens and in Babylon, and it was a Greek, Euktemon, who first identified the solstice and equinox points at about the same time (the mid-fifth century), thus creating a framework of observation within which an exact solar calendar could be drawn up. This framework of observation, known as the ecliptic, or Sun's annual path against the constellations as seen from Earth, is also the framework of modern astrology.

The earlier celestial observations, whether for omen-reading or for calculation of the seasons, had been located in the sphere of the local observer, the set of orientations based on the four compass points which surrounds a person looking at the heavens from anywhere on Earth.

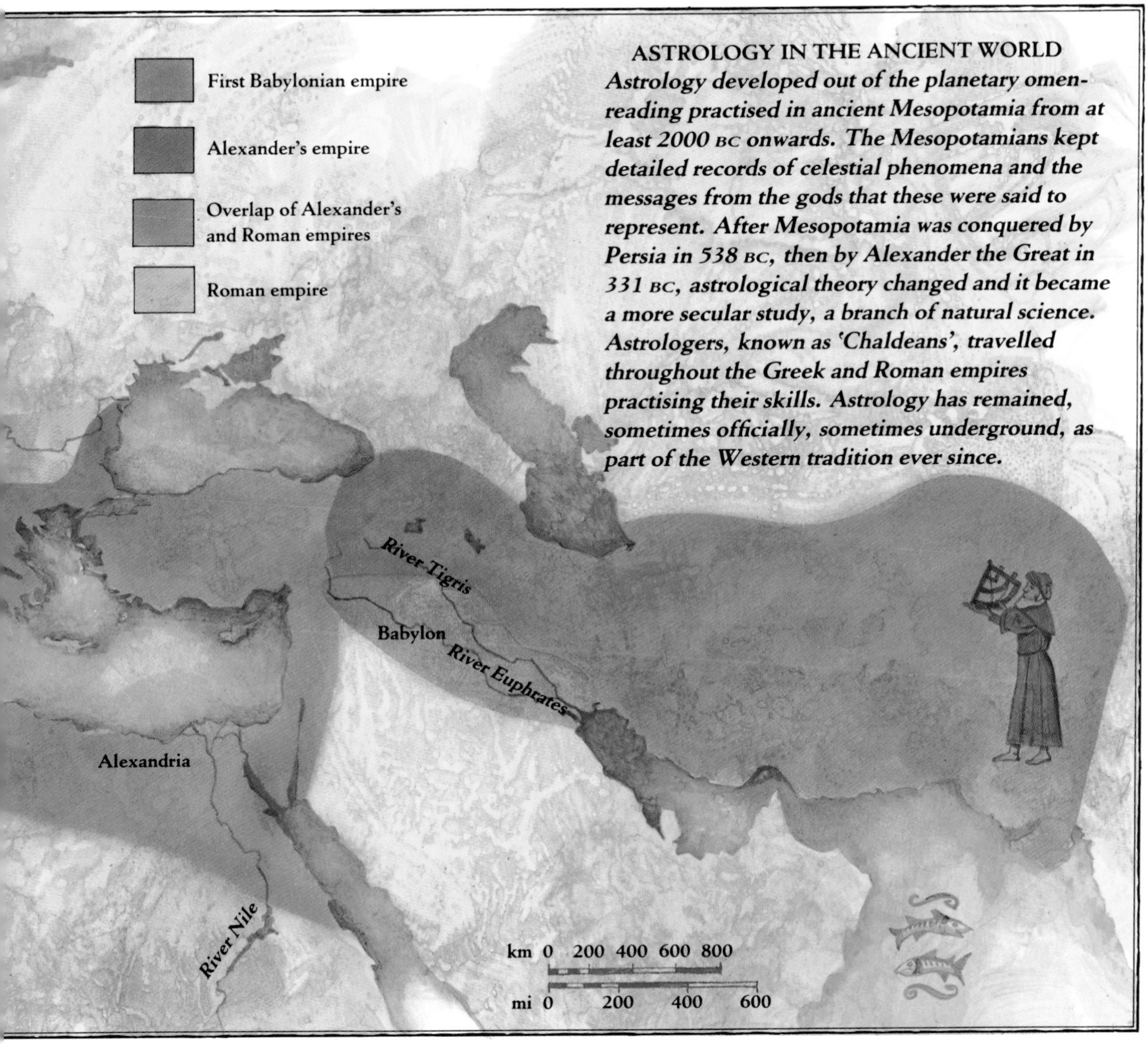

First Babylonian empire

Alexander's empire

Overlap of Alexander's
and Roman empires

Roman empire

ASTROLOGY IN THE ANCIENT WORLD
Astrology developed out of the planetary omen-reading practised in ancient Mesopotamia from at least 2000 BC onwards. The Mesopotamians kept detailed records of celestial phenomena and the messages from the gods that these were said to represent. After Mesopotamia was conquered by Persia in 538 BC, then by Alexander the Great in 331 BC, astrological theory changed and it became a more secular study, a branch of natural science. Astrologers, known as 'Chaldeans', travelled throughout the Greek and Roman empires practising their skills. Astrology has remained, sometimes officially, sometimes underground, as part of the Western tradition ever since.

River Tigris

Babylon

River Euphrates

Alexandria

River Nile

km 0   200 400 600 800

mi 0   200   400   600

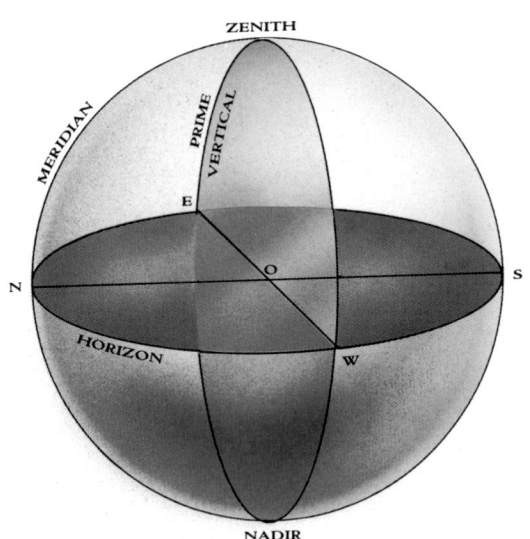

ZENITH

MERIDIAN

PRIME VERTICAL

E

N   O   S

HORIZON

W

NADIR

The six spatial co-ordinates of any location on Earth (the four compass directions, above and below) are the earliest framework for locating celestial phenomena. This is the observer's sphere. The earliest Babylonian omen text, apparently foretelling the destruction of Ur by Enneatum in 2400 BC, tells the king: 'You shall look to the South and observe the eclipse.' Much later, in about 750 BC, the poet Hesiod times the seasons in this way:

> When Orion and the Dog Star move
> Into the mid-sky, and Arcturus sees
> The rosy-fingered Dawn, then Perses, pluck
> The clustered grapes, and bring your harvest home.

With the discovery that the Sun's path (the ecliptic) is inclined to the Earth's equator at about 23¹/₂°, the Greeks were able to identify the constellations which marked its highest and lowest points (the two solstice signs, Cancer and Capricorn), and the points where it cuts the equator in the spring and autumn (the equinoxes, Aries and Libra). These four, together with the celestial pole and its opposite point in the southern sky, allowed planets to be located against the fixed co-ordinates of celestial space, not simply against individual constellations in the local sphere of observation.

With the mapping of the ecliptic onto the fixed points of the solstices and equinoxes, what is called the celestial sphere could be calculated. Planets could be located in the celestial sphere, i.e. relative to the solstice and equinox points, rather than simply relative to the local sphere of the four compass directions, zenith (the point directly above the observer at right angles to the horizon) and nadir (the point directly below). The way that this was done was simply by dividing up the Sun's annual path into 12 × 30° sectors, calculated originally from the point of the summer solstice, but later, as is still the case today, from the spring equinox. The 30° arc following the spring equinox was called after the constellation which occupied it at the time, i.e. Aries, the Ram, the next arc was called after the next constellation, Taurus, the Bull, and so on.

This system of dividing the Sun's annual path into 12 sectors, which also defined the 12 months of the original solar calendar, was developed at the same time that the solstice and equinox points were located in the sky. Because of what is known as the precession of the equinoxes, i.e. the slow wobble of the earth's axis over about 26,000 years, the signs of the Zodiac, the 30° arcs beginning with the spring equinox point, no longer coincide with the constellations after which they were named. When early astrologers referred to a particular sign, such as the sign of the Fishes (Pisces), sometimes they meant the constellation called the Fishes, sometimes (as nowadays) the 12th 30° arc of the ecliptic following the equinox. Until the Greek astrologer Ptolemy, writing in the first century AD, decided in favour of the latter, astrologers' usage was variable. Nowadays, however, Western astrology follows the so-called 'tropical' pattern, with the signs measured from the 'tropics' or seasonal turning-points marked by the solstices and equinoxes, whereas astrology in India locates the planets by reference to the actual constellations (see Chapter Eighteen, Star Lore in the East).

After the fall of the Roman Empire, leading theologians in the Church, which had continued the Imperial plan of dominating Europe through a universal civilization, unfortunately condemned the predictive aspect of astrology. The art went into decline for many years in Christian Europe, being pursued almost entirely outside Christendom by the Arabs and the Jews. Then, when the Christians clashed with the Arabs in eighth-century Spain, the emperor Charlemagne took up the study of astrology himself, as well as employing a full-time astrologer. Astrology remained among the regular political resources of the crowned heads of Europe, although periodically debated and restricted by the Church, until after the Reformation, when it slowly fell into disrepute in mainland Europe,

not being revived until the Theosophical Movement of the 1880s. Strangely enough, the years following the Reformation were the time when astrology began to be popular (as opposed to élitist) in Britain. Astrologers were busy dealing with personal queries and with political predictions throughout the seventeenth century, and during the Age of Reason in the following two centuries astrology retained near-respectability among the common people, with regular sales of almanacs, textbooks and even magazines.

Astrology remains popular in the West today, particularly in the simplified fortune-telling form of the 'Sun-sign' column, but also among a growing number of people who are looking for a more elaborate philosophy to explain their place in the universe. Like the Hindu and Buddhist systems of thought, which have also been adopted by Westerners (and which themselves accept astrology's validity), astrology satisfies both the age-old need for philosophical explanation and the modern demand for scientific justification. It is, however, shunned by both the religious and the scientific Establishments, being too fatalistic for Christians and for atheists alike, and being (so far) insufficiently validated to satisfy the scientific community. Astrology challenges the cruder forms of Western belief in absolute individual self-determination, but as yet it has not found a language that will allow it to be incorporated into mainstream Western thought. It therefore remains part of a lively and articulate subculture.

ASTROLOGICAL INTERPRETATION
A horoscope is an accurate diagram of the positions of the Sun, Moon, the planets Mercury, Venus, Mars, Jupiter, Saturn, Uranus, Neptune and Pluto, located by reference to the ecliptic (the Sun's annual path against the constellations as seen from Earth) as this intersects the local sphere of the observer.

The basics of astrology are summarized in beginners' textbooks. Their synthesis into a chart reading demands skill and experience, and astrological theory is constantly being modified through feedback from practitioners.

THE PLANETS

These celestial bodies are the motive forces of the horoscope, the people, groups, forces, drives and emotions that make things happen in our everyday world. They were originally seen by the Babylonians as deities, and are named after these deities in their Roman form. Each has a particular symbol that represents it in the horoscope diagram.

SUN ☉	Genuineness, authenticity, nobility. Ostentation and magnificence. The monarch, presiding authority.
MOON ☽	Instincts, reactions, needs. Mothers, brewers, those who work by the sea. Populism. The general public.
MERCURY ☿	Observation, communication, skilful knowledge or action. Letters, telephone calls, short journeys, cars. Solicitors, broadcasters, journalists, statisticians, small businesses.
VENUS ♀	Attractiveness, beauty, victory, attainment, love. Purses, cash in hand. Jewels, works of art, young women. Sculptors, painters, singers, dancers.
MARS ♂	Pugnacity, vigour, initiative, courage. Competitiveness. Iron, weapons, young men. The armed forces, surgeons, butchers, engineers.
JUPITER ♃	Magnanimity, generosity, aspirations and success. Judges, teachers, ecclesiastics, merchants and foreign travellers. Large gentle animals. The legal establishment, educated or informed opinion.
SATURN ♄	Sternness, inflexibility, limitations. Lead, deserts, bones and borders. Old men, farm labourers, beggars, hermits. Hierarchies, control mechanisms.
URANUS ♅	Genius, inventiveness, disruption. Electricity and computer technology. Space technology, aircraft. Revolutionaries, inventors, earthquakes.
NEPTUNE ♆	Compassion, idealism, merging and dissolution. The ocean, mist, pharmaceuticals. Musicians, dancers, the fine arts. Visionaries, alcoholics, dependent and helpless people. Socialism.
PLUTO ♇	Hidden power, transformation, destruction and regeneration. Biological imperatives. The underworld, miners, sewage workers, criminals. Surgeons and psychiatrists. Big business.

THE HOUSES

These are divisions of the local sphere of the observer (see the diagram on page 57), in which both planets and signs are located. They are usually shown on the horoscope diagram as sectors of the circle. There are many ways of dividing up the local sphere, and their relative merits are a subject of increasing debate. Four constant points are important: the ascendant, the point where the ecliptic cuts the horizon in the east; the descendant, its opposite point in the west; the midheaven, or MC, the highest point of the ecliptic (which in northern hemisphere charts is usually high in the southern sky); and its opposite point, the lower midheaven or IC, the lowest point of the ecliptic. These points and the 12 spaces between them (in most systems of division), which are the houses, identify the area of life within which the signs and planets are active.

FIRST HOUSE	Beginnings, physical appearance, self-interest.
SECOND HOUSE	Possessions, resources, values.
THIRD HOUSE	Neighbourhood, siblings, all communications and local travel.
FOURTH HOUSE	Home, origins, land. Father, ancestors. Unconscious resources, buried treasure.
FIFTH HOUSE	Creativity, children, recreation, pleasures, play. The arts.
SIXTH HOUSE	Health and illness, routine and maintenance activities including work. Workers, carers.
SEVENTH HOUSE	Partnership or enmity. The opposite of self: spouse or partner, and enemies.
EIGHTH HOUSE	Shared resources. Other people's values. Loans and credit. Taxes. Letting go of pure self-interest.
NINTH HOUSE	International communication. Philosophy, dreams and visions. Lawyers, ecclesiastics.
TENTH HOUSE	Prestige and standing in the community. Career. Authority and responsibilities. People in charge.
ELEVENTH HOUSE	Ideals, hopes, hobbies, friends. Legislative assemblies.
TWELFTH HOUSE	Unconscious impulses, hidden enemies, solitude, sleep and meditation. Institutions and confinement.

THE SIGNS

The signs are divisions of the celestial sphere: 30° divisions of the ecliptic, beginning from the spring equinox point. They add information about the nature of the houses and the planets in them. Thus, for example, the planet Jupiter in the sign Aries in the fifth house indicates success and the expansion of understanding (Jupiter) through a vigorous, enterprising attitude (Aries) to creativity or recreation (fifth house).

ARIES	♈	With initiative, aggressively, impulsively.
TAURUS	♉	Steadily, thoroughly, with gusto.
GEMINI	♊	Rapidly, skilfully, with versatility.
CANCER	♋	Emotively, protectively, with feeling.
LEO	♌	Magnificently, with style, in an overbearing manner.
VIRGO	♍	Prudently, with an eye to detail.
LIBRA	♎	Elegantly, fairly, rationally.
SCORPIO	♏	Intensely, passionately, with secrecy.
SAGITTARIUS	♐	Magnanimously, idealistically, without animosity.
CAPRICORN	♑	Methodically, with determination, authoritatively.
AQUARIUS	♒	Objectively, democratically, through communication.
PISCES	♓	Vaguely, passively, with sensitivity.

THE ASPECTS

The angular relationships between the planets, as seen from Earth, describe the interaction of the forces which the planets represent. When two planets are in roughly the same place in the sky ('conjunction'), their forces are said to merge; for example, Moon conjunct Mars gives a militant attitude to mothering, or perhaps a nurturing attitude to initiative. Planets separated by 90° ('square') frustrate each other's influence, planets 120° apart ('trine') work smoothly and effortlessly together, and planets opposite each other in the Zodiac are expressed through contrast, whether by enmity or by partnership and co-operation.

APPLICATIONS OF ASTROLOGY

NATAL HOROSCOPES

The bulk of a modern astrologer's work is concerned with personal horoscopes for individuals. The natal chart, i.e. the horoscope for the moment of birth, tells the astrologer what sort of person he or she is dealing with, with what talents, what liabilities, what characteristic relationships and life situations. Then, by calculating the movements of the planets as they leave their natal positions, the astrologer can also see how this natal potential unfolds, and in particular on what dates certain aspects of the natal blueprint will be emphasized (the predictive side of astrology). Whether these developments of the natal pattern manifest in the person's life as a change of outlook, a change of friends or situation, or as a seemingly external 'accident', the astrologer cannot say. For most astrologers, the so-called 'outside' world is simply a reflection of the so-called 'inner' world. Both are manifestations of the unfolding of the cosmic pattern, which is measured by the cycles of the stars and planets and a phase of which is embodied in each individual's natal chart.

HORARY CHARTS

Astrology can be used in a more specifically divinatory way, to answer questions such as 'Where are my lost keys?' The horoscope is cast for the moment of asking the question, and the position of the planets and signs are interpreted according to the highly specific rules of horary, in much the same way as the yarrow stalks or coins of the *I Ching* are read. The expression 'to cast a horoscope' is derived from the medieval method of determining some kind of ascendant, in the days before regular tables were available, by casting stones, the resulting geomantic figures each being taken to represent a particular part of the Zodiac. The bulk of astrologers' work in the English astrological renaissance of the seventeenth century (by which time accurate ascendants were generally calculated) seems to have been horary, and this technique was revived in the early 1980s.

MUNDANE ASTROLOGY

The astrology of the 'mundus', the physical world ruled by science and mass psychology, is usually contrasted with that of the psyche, the individual soul, which is generally considered to have at least some free will and moral responsibility. In modern terms, mundane astrology is concerned with the collective, with groups and organizations, particularly with nations, empires and other political groupings. Nations and organizations have natal horoscopes just as individuals do, and these can be analysed by the same techniques. In addition, eclipses, solstice and equinox horoscopes, and the cycles of the planets through the signs and relative to each other can be interpreted as giving what we would nowadays call a psychological climate to the times. The study of mundane astrology received a boost in the 1980s as the availability of computer technology has made the rapid analysis of horoscopes possible.

EVENT CHARTS

A horoscope for the occurrence of a particular event, whether a physical one such as an earthquake, or a mental one such as an inspiration or discovery, will show the astrological factors operating in that place at that time. For instance, the horoscope for the bombing of the conference of Britain's ruling Conservative Party in October 1984 shows a conjunction of Mars and Jupiter – someone taking the law into their own hands. Such astrological factors are nowadays interpreted as the unconscious forces of mass psychology, which become embodied in pressure groups as well as in the personal psychology of charismatic leaders. The analysis of event charts gives a useful insight into the hidden background of the events, and can help people to deal skilfully and accurately with their effects. In particular, the chart for the time when a person falls ill and takes to their bed ('decumbiture') has traditionally been used to diagnose and predict the course of an illness. The use of decumbiture charts for medical diagnosis is, however, restricted by law in many Western countries today.

ELECTIONAL ASTROLOGY

Because the natal chart describes the nature of an entity for the whole of its life, astrologers have often been asked to choose, or 'elect', the most favourable possible time to begin an enterprise, found a company – or even to time conception or induce a birth. The most famous example of a (probable) election is that for the Royal Observatory at Greenwich, drawn up by the Astronomer Royal, Flamsteed, in 1675. More recently, in the USA, the astrologer Joan Quigley elected the times for various meetings, journeys, signings, etc., on which the course of President Reagan's presidency hung. The success of her endeavours is obvious: Ronald Reagan stayed in office for the maximum two terms, remained hugely popular throughout, presided over *détente* with the Soviet Union, and successfully disproved allegations similar to those that had plunged Richard Nixon into utter disgrace. Despite this recent example of the art, the theory of electional astrology has not been developed in any detail during the twentieth century.

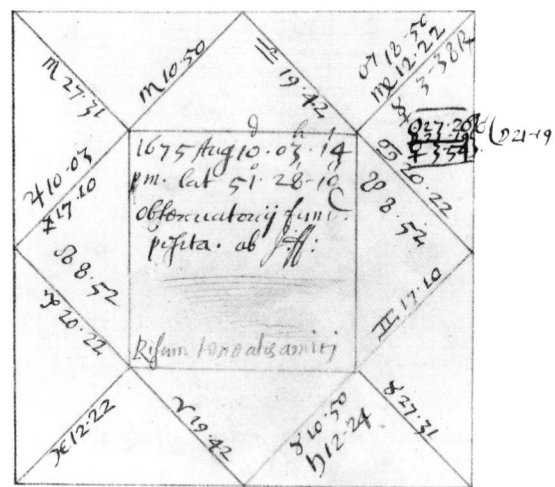

This horoscope was drawn up (in the square format of the times, now replaced by circular diagrams) by the first Astronomer Royal, John Flamsteed. It records the moment when the Royal Observatory's foundation stone was laid: 10 August 1675, 3.14 p.m. Was the time chosen deliberately, or was the horoscope merely done on impulse? Flamsteed's comment, 'May this keep you laughing, my friends', is ambiguous, just as we might expect from serious Saturn in the horoscope's fifth house of games and pleasantries.

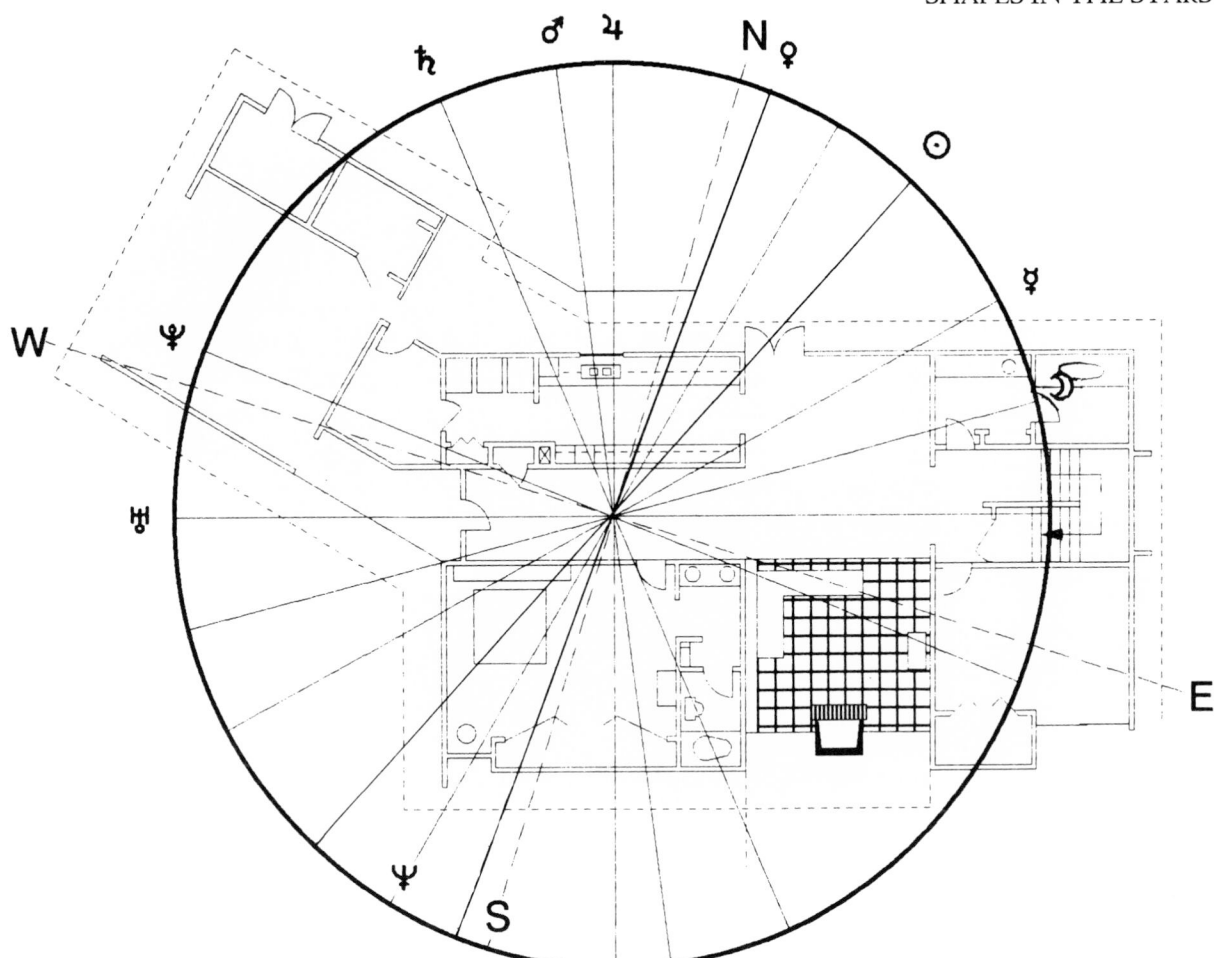

LOCAL SPACE ASTROLOGY

This is an ancient branch of astrology, familiar in China as an aspect of Feng Shui (see Chapter Seventeen, Dragon Lines in the Land), which has become available again through computer technology. The horoscope diagram normally locates planets on the plane of the ecliptic, but the local space chart shows where the perpendiculars of the planets' altitudes cut the local horizon. The local space derivative of the natal horoscope, for example, gives its owner a set of expectations about any place where they live. Energy, strenuousness and strife lie on the Mars line, and the person who wants excitement should go in that direction from their present home in order to find it. One person was amazed to find that her Mars line led directly to the port where she was called up for her annual military service. Within the home, the various activities of life are best located according to their lines of planetary rulership, or, as Ben Jonson's Abel Drugger put it:

Here the circular map of the local horizon, with azimuths showing the sighting lines to and from the planets in a natal horoscope, is superimposed on a floor plan of the horoscope owner's house. Notice the Moon line going through the kitchen, an ideal location for it, and the Uranus line going through the staircase. This is less suitable: light bulbs in the hall and on the stairs will probably have a short life, and the stairwell might behave as a natural lightning conductor for as long as the owner of that particular horoscope lives in the house.

I would know by art, sir, of your worship,
Which way I should make my door, by necromancy,
And where my shelves, and which should be for boxes,
And which for pots. I would be glad to thrive, sir,
And I was wished to your worship by a gentleman
. . . that says you know men's planets.

This ancient application of astrology has been brought up to date by modern researchers since the 1970s, but is as yet little used in routine practice.

ASTRO*CARTO*GRAPHY

By contrast, a different application of astrology to the landscape, made possible only through accurate geographical surveying and easily accessible computer mathematics, has become widely used over the last 15 years. The Astro*Carto*Graphy map is a two-dimensional summary of all possible local observation spheres (see the diagram of the observer's sphere). It shows all the places on Earth where, for example, the planet Jupiter was seen at the midheaven at the time of the chart owner's birth, the places where it would therefore be easy for them to make a career (midheaven) as a teacher, entrepreneur or ecclesiastic (Jupiter). In places where, by contrast, Uranus was rising, the person would appear to others as an erratic, eccentric, probably brilliant individual who would disrupt any situation they came into. Astro*Carto*Graphy thus makes it easy for people to choose (or at least to know) the astrological effect of their new location when they move house.

The technique is also used in mundane astrology to locate the prevailing astrological influences at each seasonal ingress (solstice or equinox). It gives mundane astrologers an idea of what kind of events to expect in the different areas of the world. For example, the winter solstice A*C*G chart for 1978, forecasting the year 1979, showed Venus, the planet which traditionally rules Islam, and Uranus, the planet of revolution, at the midheaven in Iran. It was, of course, during the following 12 months that the Shah was deposed and an Islamic republic took his place.

At the exact moment of the winter solstice, 1978, certain locations on Earth saw one or more of the 10 planets either rising, culminating, setting, or at inverse culmination. This map displays those locations, with rising and setting planets identified by 'R' and 'S' against their glyphs (at the end of the curved lines), planets at upper and lower culmination noted at the top and bottom respectively of their straight lines. Hence, for example, a person born at the exact moment of the winter solstice 1978 in southern Mexico, with the sensitive, impressionable Moon rising, would lay themselves open to some abrasive experiences by relocating to western Scotland, which would put flinty, no-nonsense Saturn at the midheaven point which describes authority figures. Note the culminating position of Venus and Uranus in Iran, analysed in the text.

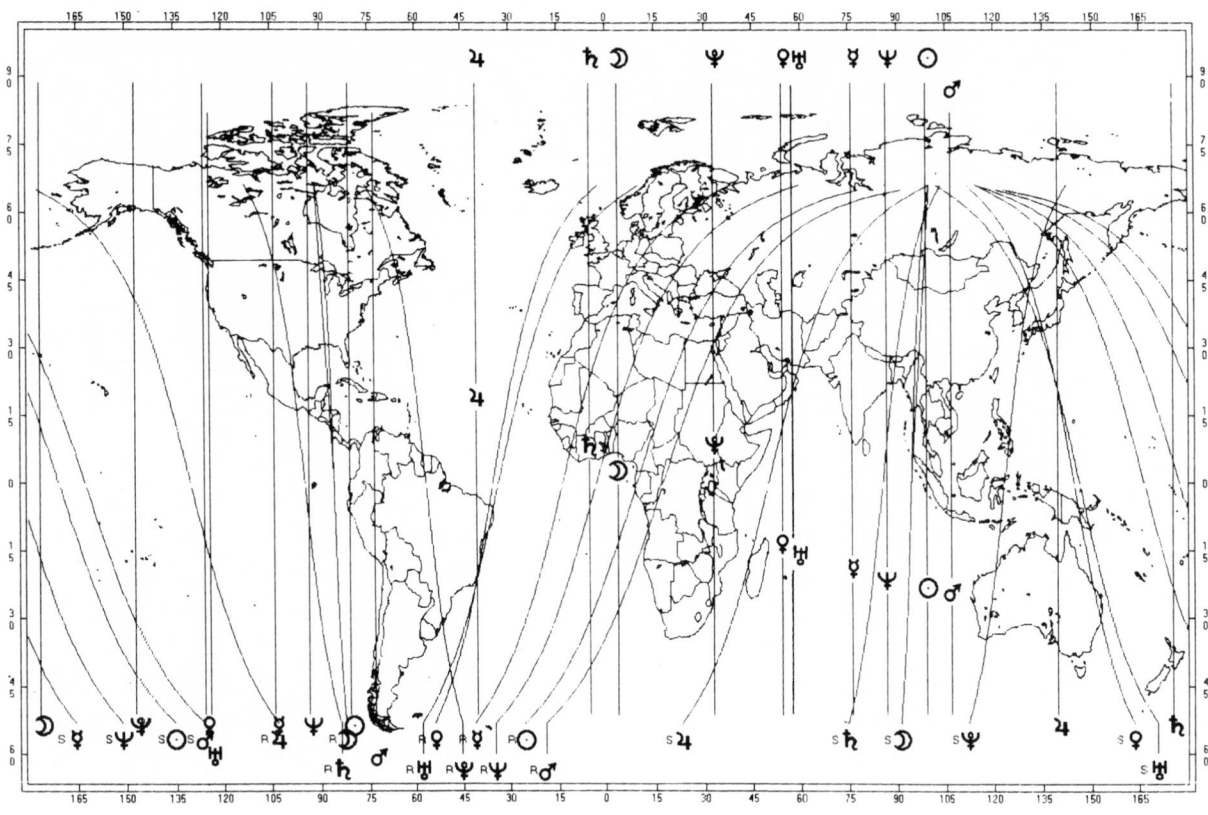

CHAPTER SEVEN

CONSULTING THE ORACLES

The Classic Systems of Greece and Rome

Robert Temple

When we think of ancient Greece and Rome we tend to think of the great classical philosophers such as Plato and Aristotle, the supremacy of the intellect and the rule of reason. It is not generally realized that divination was an important part of classical life and was practised on a daily basis. We could even go so far as to say that the whole of classical civilization was based on divination as the foundation of all its actions. No major decision of state, such as going to war, was made without consulting the gods through divination. Few personal undertakings, such as financial investment, getting married or making a journey, were embarked upon without divination. Even the great Socrates consulted the oracle at Delphi.

The classical civilizations had many forms of divination which they used constantly: divination by lightning, by the flights of birds (augury), by the chance words uttered by idiots or passers-by (cledonism), by thunderbolts, by the manner in which chickens pecked at corn, and so on. Divination by lightning and augury by the flights of birds were both very complex systems. The sky was generally divided up into 16 sections: if birds flew from one section to another, that signified one thing; if they then flew from that section to another, it meant something else, and so on. The same applied to streaks of lightning. There were 'textbooks' to consult so that people could look these things up. In a surviving ancient Greek dream book by Artemidorus, there are hundreds of different dreams listed alongside their prophetic meanings.

Interior forms of divination, lacking in official sanction and prestige, were practised by wandering fortune-tellers. Farmers had much folklore about what they called 'omens', namely calves born with two heads or even children with webbed fingers, all of which portended various sorts of coming events and disasters. Other methods included an early form of roulette, which was connected with the oracle at Delphi and gave answers to enquiries rather than winners in a gambling game; both lots and dice were also used to consult the future. The Greeks were keen on an early form of crystal-gazing, whereby maidens gazed into pools of water or bowls of liquid and sought visions of the future. The Babylonians had voluminous Omen Books, many fragments of which survive, and much of

Greek terracotta from South Italy, c. 480 BC. A diviner is about to remove the entrails from a sacrificial pig in order to consult the future.

65

that lore entered into folk wisdom, which probably survives in peasant societies today. There is certainly a very strong tradition in modern Greece among the country folk about fairies, the evil eye and prophecy.

EXTISPICY: AN EXAMINATION OF ENTRAILS

It is often assumed that the main divination system of the Greeks and Romans, as well as of the Assyrians and Babylonians, was astrology. But in fact astrology was a very late technique, and it can be said without the slightest doubt that the main divination system of the classical cultures was extispicy, which is divination by the entrails of sacrificial animals.

Extispicy was a mania with the Greeks, Romans and Etruscans. Of the last, Cicero, who was himself an official Roman augur, said in his book *On Divination*: 'the whole Etruscan nation has gone stark mad on the subject of entrails.' The animal that was sacrificed was usually a lamb, although occasionally oxen were used, especially by the Romans.

Extispicy was in fact the main divination system of Western man for many thousands of years, and because of its remote origins in Stone Age antiquity or earlier, the millennia of its continuous use, and its widespread geographical extent, it can probably be regarded as the main divination system to have been used on this planet during the entire history of humanity.

I re-created the ancient extispicy techniques by going to an abattoir and personally removing the entrails of freshly slaughtered lambs, following the directions of the ancient Babylonian tablets which set the pattern for the later Greeks and Romans. Generally, in the modern age, only butchers can be expected to know much about entrails as they emerge from animals, but I decided it was necessary to re-create the ancient setting in order to see just what it was that the ancients were doing. In this way I was able to resolve many enigmas.

The two main organs used in divination were the liver and the intestines. I discovered that if you pull the liver out of a freshly slaughtered lamb it will act as a perfect mirror; I could see my face in it clearly for fifteen or twenty minutes, after which it went dull and ceased to act as a reflector. Because the ancients were somewhat literal-minded when they wanted to figure out what internal organs were for, they decided the purpose of the liver in the body was *to act as a mirror* of the divine rays that the gods were thought to be shining down on us continually. The liver was therefore thought to be the seat of the soul. There is plenty in such sources as Plato and Plutarch on this subject to satisfy the most curious. Since the gods have foreknowledge, it follows that the divine rays bring us intimations of the future if we can only discern them. So the premise of extispicy was that if you scrutinize the liver of a sacrificial animal carefully enough, it will yield foreknowledge traces left behind by the divine rays which have streamed into it up until the moment of the sacrifice. The Babylonians divided the lamb's liver up into 55 separate 'zones' where, if marks were found, they portended various things. The Greeks tended to look for broader indicators such as the presence or absence of various main fissures and protrusions. The most important was the 'head', or 'lobe' or 'finger' as the Jews

This Babylonian baked-clay model of a sheep's liver, c. 2000 BC, would have been used for reference and instruction. Lying across the liver on the right is the gall bladder. The liver is divided into 55 sections for divination purposes and covered with cuneiform texts commenting on the sections.

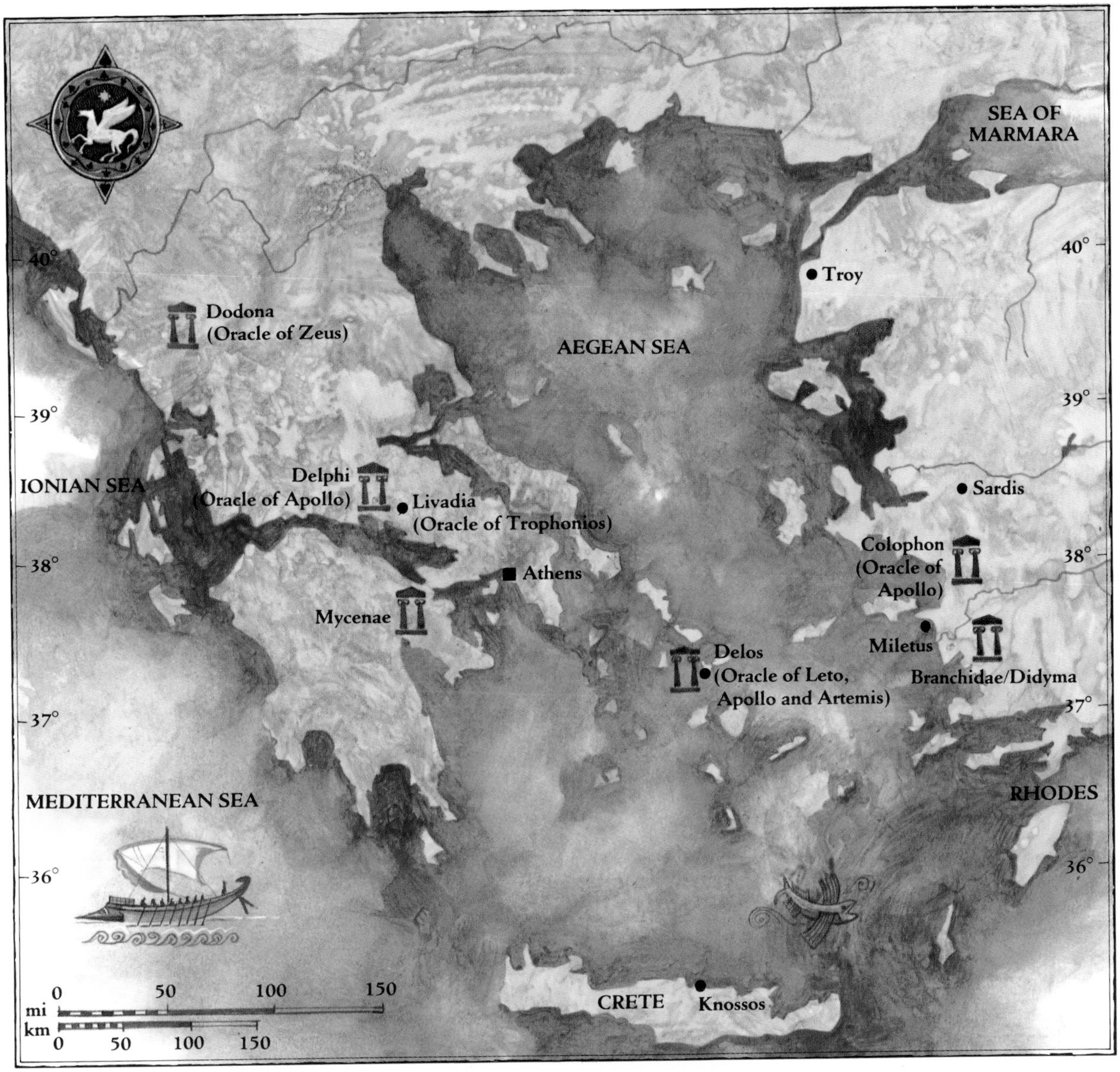

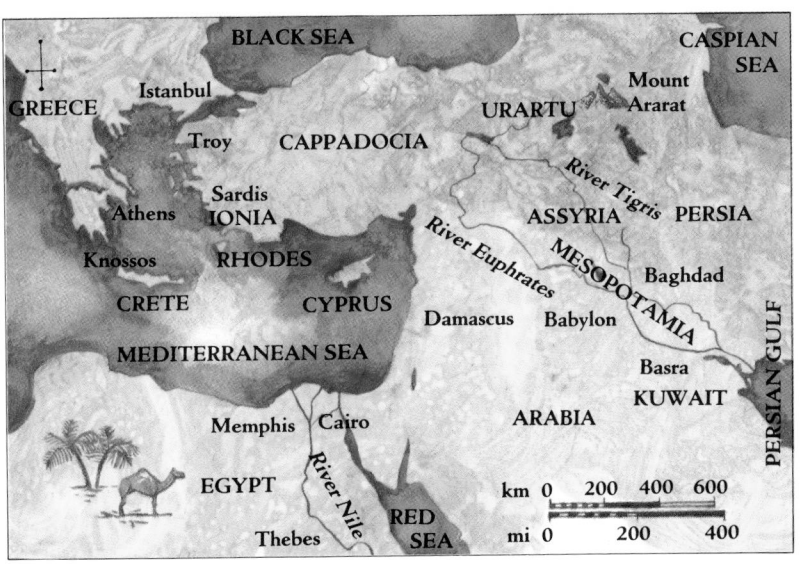

SACRED SITES OF THE ORACLES

*The main oracle centres of the Greeks
were established at particular geodetic
locations, marking latitude lines. Hence
Dodona, Delphi and Delos are one
degree apart (39° 30', 38° 30', 37°
30') in succession, and were matched by
corresponding Eastern oracle centres on
the same latitude lines: Metsamor beside
Mount Ararat (see inset map), an oracle
near Sardis beside Mount Sipylus, and
the Oracle of Apollo at Branchidae/
Didyma near Miletus (also 39° 30',
38° 30', and 37° 30'). The oracle
centres preceded the age of classical
Greece, and the sacred sites may in
turn have preceded any oracular function.*

still call it; its absence was a dreadful sign, and it was said to have been absent just before the deaths of both Julius Caesar and Alexander the Great. Its anatomical name is the *processus pyramidalis*, and it is shaped like a protruding tetrahedron, which was considered significant by the Pythagoreans and the Platonists, for whom the shape was the elemental particle of fire.

The scrutiny of the intestines also revealed mystical connections. The lamb's intestines, when laid flat for inspection, form a spiralling labyrinth which has been depicted on stones and in clay for millennia as a sacred symbol. The pattern was also connected to the orbital motions of the planets, and the writings of Martianus Capella make this connection explicit. The Etruscans were the ones who, in Roman times, were the experts in extispicy, and they especially drew these connections between celestial motions and the complex pattern of the coiled intestines.

The retrograde motions of Mercury in particular were connected with the twist-and-return pattern of the intestinal spiral; this connection was made as early as 2750 BC by the Sumerians of the Middle East, who based their 'Mask of Huwawa' on intestinal convolutions, and this Mask was also meant to represent the planet Mercury.

Divination by the intestines was based upon a

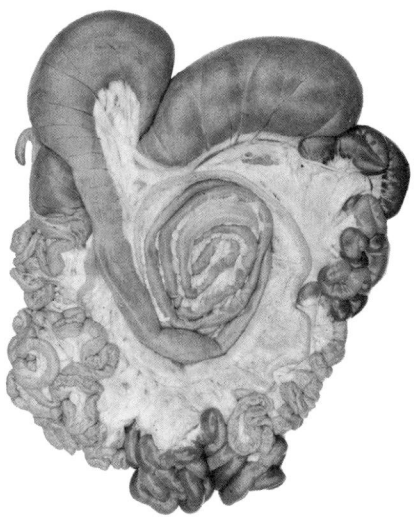

The intestines and caecum of an unhealthy lamb. In the centre is the 'spiral colon', which was the part consulted by the Babylonians, Greeks and Romans for prophecy. In this instance a single arc of the spiral colon is inflamed as a result of gastro-enteritis, causing it to become practically invisible. The 'count' of the arcs, which can be plainly seen, is thus an odd number, which was considered an unhappy omen.

close examination of which arcs of the spiral may have been inflamed by infection, such as in gastro-enteritis. When an arc of intestines is inflamed, as I have personally seen, it goes white and matches the colour of the surrounding intestinal fat, thereby becoming essentially invisible. The 'count' of the arcs then becomes odd rather than even in many cases, which yields an unfavourable prognosis for the future.

In both the intestines and the liver, disease will have been at work, causing the unfavourable signs. The disease, and therefore the inauspicious signs, will often have come from unwholesomeness of the environment. In very ancient times our nomad ancestors used such

indicators as cues to move on to healthier pastures. This earliest tradition is explicitly preserved in the text of Vitruvius, the Roman architectural writer, for whom the choice of a sound geographical location was the necessary preliminary to building anything at all. Inspection of the entrails of animals thus comes down in the end to using the technique of the autopsy to look for signs of internal disease, which may indicate that things in the environment are not as well as they seem.

THE ORACLES: SEERS OR FRAUDS?

Amongst the Greeks the form of divination of second importance after extispicy was certainly the use of oracles. Whereas extispicy was revered as of primary value, and practised by most people very frequently indeed, the institutional and formal divinatory establishment was represented by the oracle centres, primary among them being Delphi. Delphi, Dodona and Delos were the primary oracle sites used by the Minoans prior to 1200 BC in Greece proper.

The original purpose of these sites seems not to have been for oracular uses primarily, but rather for geodetic ones, that is, for measuring the Earth. The oracles were founded as sacred expressions of key points established by surveying techniques that marked out latitude lines. For instance, Dodona, Delphi and Delos form a descending scale of geodetic points precisely one degree of latitude apart. The geodetic points seem to have been correlated with musical notes in the heptatonic diatonic scale (which archaeologists have established existed as early as 2500 BC), somewhat in the manner that the later Pythagoreans revered the musical notes and spoke of a 'harmony of the spheres'. It is therefore presumed that the original purpose of the oracle sites was connected with a reverence

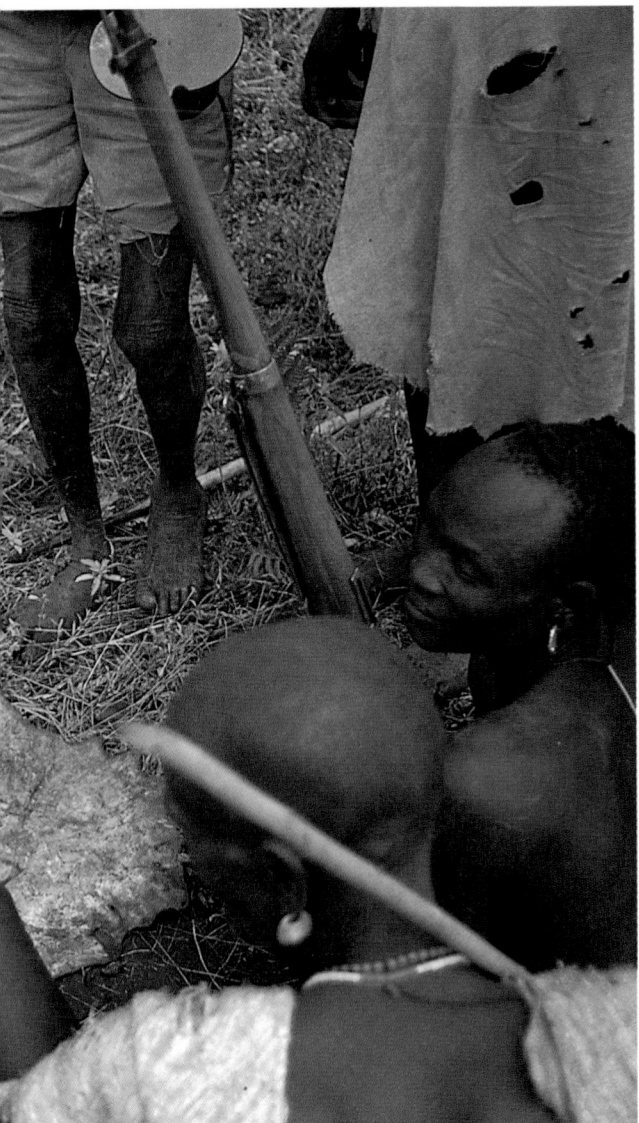

In contemporary Ethiopia the intestines of animals are still consulted by the native inhabitants as indicators of future events. The Mursi tribe are a cattle tribe, so divination by entrails is easily accessible to them. This is a survival of the ancient practice of extispicy, which has been continuously used for several thousand years, longer than any other form of divination.

for the earth spirit, and that the meticulous measurements were not merely for navigational purposes, but for elucidating the deep mysteries of the measurement of the Earth as a sphere and its cosmic motions, which to the ancients were the profoundest mysteries of all. As the centuries wore on, however, the oracles achieved increasing prominence and the geodetic function was forgotten.

The oracle at Dodona had the official primacy, with Zeus as its patron, but because it was so distant and difficult to reach in the far north-west of Greece, Delphi took on the role of the major arbiter of Greek affairs in classical times. In connection with the manner in which the oracle of Delphi worked, there is much misinformation, some of it purposely circulated by the priests at the time. It was claimed that the sybil, or prophetess, sat on a tripod over a chasm in the earth from which intoxicating fumes (supposed to arise from the rotting corpse of a mythological monster called Python) rose up to send her into a prophetic trance. She would then utter poems which told the enquirer what his future held. In practice, the utterances of the sybil were taken down and systematically rendered in verse by poets resident for the purpose. But as the French excavators discovered earlier this century when they commenced their digs at Delphi, no chasm in the earth existed. In fact the original site of the Delphic oracle was two miles (three kilometres) further up the mountain in a small cavern. The classical site, which had been adopted as easier of access, was a secondary one and not the 'real thing', a fact that its custodians were probably anxious to keep to themselves.

The whole tale was probably invented as a cover-story to explain the strange smell of the intoxicating fumes from burning drug-plants. Inhaling fumes or swallowing drugs can induce states which bring visions of various kinds. Shamans all over the world from the earliest times have done this in order to obtain insights and glimpses of the future. There is much clear archaeological evidence that the Minoans used opium routinely in their religious rituals. The sybil of Delphi was fumigated by drug plants and

possibly swallowed them as well. Iamblichus tells us that the priest of the oracle of Apollo at Colophon drank a drugged potion before prophesying, and that the prophetess of the oracle of Apollo at Branchidae passed out after inhaling drugged fumes from boiling potions, after which she could prophesy in a trance.

There is no doubt that states of trance and self-hypnosis, whether drug-induced or not, were used frequently in connection with many of the ancient oracles. This practise existed in Egypt as well, and the foundation of the main Greek oracles may have been done in connection with the Egyptians, for Herodotus records a tradition that Dodona was founded from Egyp-

At the dramatic and remote site of the ancient Greek Oracle of Dodona, in the north-west of Greece, the Oracle of Zeus was situated. The original site was probably on the nearby Mount Tomaros. The answers to questions about the future were said to be conveyed by the rustling of the leaves in Zeus's sacred oak trees, and were interpreted by the priests.

The Castalian Spring, situated at the entrance to the Castalian Gorge, is one of several springs at Delphi. Although water from it was apparently used in preparing the drugged potions for the prophesying sybil, the Spring of Kassotis above the temple is supposed to have been the actual divinatory spring proper during classical times. But the Castalian Spring takes its name from another spring two miles higher up the mountain, where the original site of the oracle was prior to 1000 BC.

tian Thebes, and the oracle at Delos is thought to have been founded by the son of Cecrops, an Egyptian who became King of Athens, in 1558 BC. A good deal of evidence survives from Egypt, Mesopotamia and Greece about trance inductions. One Hellenistic papyrus from Egypt suggests words that will invariably produce a prophetic trance and advises: 'Say the formula seven times into the man's ear, and right away he will fall down. Sit down on the bricks and make your enquiry, and he will describe everything with truth.' At certain periods in the history of Delphi there were probably sybils who had genuine prophetic visions. The difficulty arose when such a sybil died and could not be replaced; the institution could not simply be shut down, so stronger drugs would be used and eventually organized fraud was the only answer.

It was also a regular practice amongst the Greeks to drug those who came to consult certain of the oracles. This was not the case at Dodona or Delphi, but it was most definitely the case at the oracle of Trophonios at Lebadea, now known as Livadia. Pausanius has left a minute description of this harrowing experience. After fasting and being made to drink mysterious potions, the drugged client was led to a chute down which he slid into the underground chambers where he was assailed on all sides by a mass of serpents. In a state of utter terror and total suggestibility, he would hear someone tell him a prophetic message. Often he would stay underground for days, where cells evidently existed to enable clients to 'sleep it off'. If the client expressed scepticism he might be murdered and never 'reappear from the Underworld'. The actual drugs regularly used were extremely powerful and included henbane, thorn apple, and black and white hellebore. Henbane was so important that Pliny tells us its name was *apollinaris*, named after Apollo, patron god of Delphi and of prophecy in general.

The most eerie and bizarre of all the ancient classical oracle centres was undoubtedly the pre-Roman oracle of the Dead at Baia on the western coast of Italy. It is near the present city of Naples, and was linked with the oracular cave and sybil of nearby Cuma, which is reputed to have been the earliest of the Greek settlements on the Italian peninsula. In 1967 a retired English engineer named Robert F. Paget rediscovered the fantastic underground sanctuary of the Baian oracle, which was blocked up in the reign of Augustus. The underground complex has never been opened to the public, and only a handful of scholars and archaeologists have ever been allowed access. What is so extraordinary in this artificial underground complex carved a fifth of a mile into the solid rock is that it actually contains an *artificial River Styx* across which clients were rowed in a coracle. They were presumably meant to believe that they were genuinely visiting the Underworld. Seances appear to have been staged in the inner sanctum. The description of the descent into Hades given in Book VI of Virgil's *Aeneid* is in fact a description of the descent into the Baian oracle, near which Virgil lived for some time. The Inner Sanctum has never been fully cleared of the rubble with which it was filled by Agrippa, a henchman of Augustus who had a special hatred for the oracle for some personal reason, and swore that no one would ever use it again.

Much of the oracular set-up in Greece was therefore phoney. A network of carrier-pigeons and carrier-swallows carried secret messages from all over the Mediterranean world to Delphi and the other oracular centres, notifying the priests of the latest events, the results of battles, the deaths of kings, and so forth. These were then 'uttered by the god' as prophecies. The 'prophetic doves' so often used as symbols of the oracle centres were the bird-telegraphy which made accurate political prophecies possible and gave centres such as Delphi immense wealth and political power. Delphi took the side of Sparta against Athens in the Peloponnesian War, and one reason may have been that the Spartans were so conservative in their religious piety that they were easier to fool. But the phoniness of the oracular institutions was a peculiar form of pious fraud, which was often perpetrated by intellectuals 'for the good of the masses', and it would be wrong to think that the only motives were

sordid. For after all, one High Priest of Delphi was the author Plutarch, and of him at least we can be quite certain that he was as upright and honest a man as ancient Greece ever produced. Indeed, much of what we know of Delphic lore comes from his profound and learned writings. He lived during Roman times, though he wrote in Greek, and already much of the history of Delphi in the earlier Greek classical era was as remote to him as it is to us.

Oracular responses were often phrased in enigmatic form or posed as riddles. While maintaining arch-conservative positions with regard to cult matters, these responses by the oracles often stretched the minds of the Greeks in creative ways and stimulated fresh modes of thought, even occasionally setting mathematical problems! As the philosopher Aristotle, who made a special study of riddles oracular and otherwise, said of them: 'The thoughts were startling and they did not fit in with the ideas already held.' It is because the Greeks were courageous enough to think fresh thoughts that we still honour them today, and it takes no act of divination to predict that we will continue to do so as long as there are thinking men about.

Lake Avernus (top), near Cuma and Baia in Italy, is within the crater of an extinct volcano. The ancient Greek geographer, Strabo, wrote of it: 'The inhabitants affirm that birds, flying over the lake, fall into the water, being stifled by the vapours rising from it . . . the oracle of the dead was situated somewhere here. . . .'

The cave of the Sybil of Cuma in Italy (middle), not far from the location of the Oracle of the Dead at Baia, was visited by countless enquirers in antiquity. The prophesying Sybil sat in the far niche. Her replies to questions are said to have been written on leaves laid on the floor; when the door was opened, the wind blew the leaves into confusion, symbolizing the state of our knowledge of the future. Cuma was a Greek settlement in Italy, established long before the rise of Rome. This cavern was excavated in 1932.

On one side of this Etruscan bronze (left), c. sixth century BC, an augur scans the skies to study the flights of birds for clues to the future. On the other side, a diviner studies the liver of a sacrificial animal to predict the future by the divinatory science of extispicy.

CHAPTER EIGHT

THE TREE OF LIFE

Galgal, A Cabbalistic Method

Cherry Gilchrist

The letters are without question the root of all wisdom and knowledge, and they themselves are the substance of prophecy. In a prophetic vision, they appear as if they were solid bodies, actually speaking to the individual.

Rabbi Abraham Abulafia, *Life of the Future World*, 1280

The Hebrew alphabet is a sacred language. Its 22 letters are seen as the key to the secrets of creation; every letter has a meaning, and is a word in its own right. Letters within words can be reordered, giving rise to new meanings. This is more easily done in Hebrew than in most languages, and can be used as a way of reinterpreting holy scriptures. The letters themselves are said to have power, and in deep contemplation may be visualized turning into fire or angelic beings, as the esoteric texts tell us, bringing prophetic revelation to the meditator. Letters are the spirit through which God speaks to man, and through which man may understand and even influence the world.

In the medieval schools of Jewish Cabbala, letter magic and meditation was carried on to an extremely advanced degree, and many texts of instruction were circulated secretly, for fear of endangering the uninitiated. Cabbala, though at that time a part of Judaism, was nevertheless regarded with suspicion by many of the orthodox, as it leaned towards the occult and the mystical, and towards a direct personal experience of the divine.

Galgal is a relatively new flowering of the Cabbalistic tradition, but it lies in direct descent from these earlier schools. It is, in a sense, a divination system that took hundreds of years to grow. Combining the Hebrew letters and the Tree of Life, the two main lines of Cabbalistic teaching, Galgal has evolved from that first burning concern with prophecy and revelation and with discovering hidden knowledge through letter permutation and Tree magic. We can see here how spiritual impulses may still be at work centuries later, producing new tangible evidence of their existence as time goes on. Because Galgal cannot be divorced from the Cabbalistic tradition itself, it will be helpful to look at certain aspects of this first before turning to the divination system in detail.

CABBALA: THE HIDDEN TRADITION

Like most schools of wisdom, only so much can be charted. Cabbala is chiefly an oral tradition, the teachings handed on from teacher to pupil, and what finds its way into the books is only a part. The scholars are prepared to authenticate the existence of Cabbala only from the medieval period onwards, where it took root, following the dispersion of the Jews, in North Africa, Spain, Italy and other parts of Europe. But it is considered to be much older, and may not, in fact, have originated within Judaism at all, for

The symbol held aloft on this carving from the Egyptian temple of Kom Ombo, constructed about 300–200 BC, represents 'order and stability'. It bears a marked resemblance to the Cabbalistic Tree of Life, hinting at Cabbala's long history, which may have wound its way through various religious mythologies.

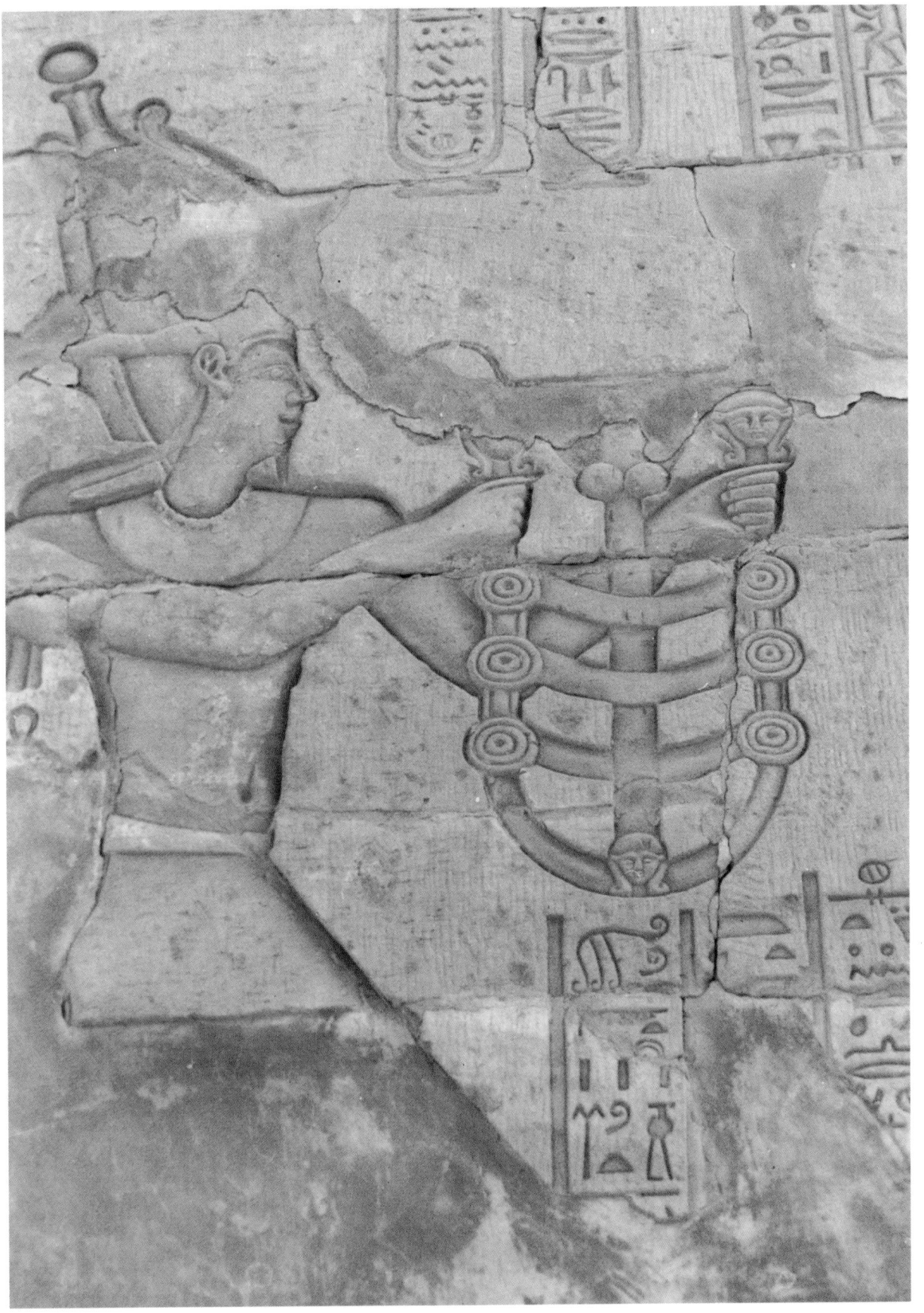

the symbolic representation of the Cabbalistic Tree of Life is found in a very similar form in certain Assyrian and Egyptian carved reliefs.

Cabbala is a way of knowledge; like other schools of wisdom it may find a home within orthodox religion, but it is not bound to remain there. It is recognized by many as having a universality, so that it is possible to understand the various major religions within its framework. The power of Cabbala to cross cultural boundaries was witnessed in Renaissance times, when its teachings were eagerly seized upon by men such as Giordano Bruno and Marsilio Ficino, leading lights in the philosophic and artistic renewal of Christian Italy; and since then a strongly Westernized, Christian form of Cabbala has developed.

Cabbala means 'to receive'. This implies that each human being is capable of receiving directly from God; but how we receive is dependent upon how we are, and so it also implies that we may have to do a little work upon ourselves first before we can expect this to happen. Most Cabbalistic schools promote a thorough training, which encourages individuals to meditate, to observe, and to work with both their hearts and their minds. This can also include ritual and magical work, and visualizations known nowadays as 'path-working', where images are allowed to arise as the practitioner concentrates on one particular path of the Tree of Life. Although the work of such schools is usually carried out behind closed doors, participants today are encouraged to live and work in the world. Cabbala might have attracted more religious recluses in earlier times, but the need for integrating worldly and heavenly experience has always been recognized.

'Receiving' also implies a structure, so just as you need a prism to refract light, and a radio set to pick up transmissions, Cabbala provides a framework that finely tunes the sensibilities, generating more experience and offering a means of understanding it. The Tree of Life and the Hebrew alphabet are the structures most commonly used by Cabbalists, sometimes together, sometimes independently.

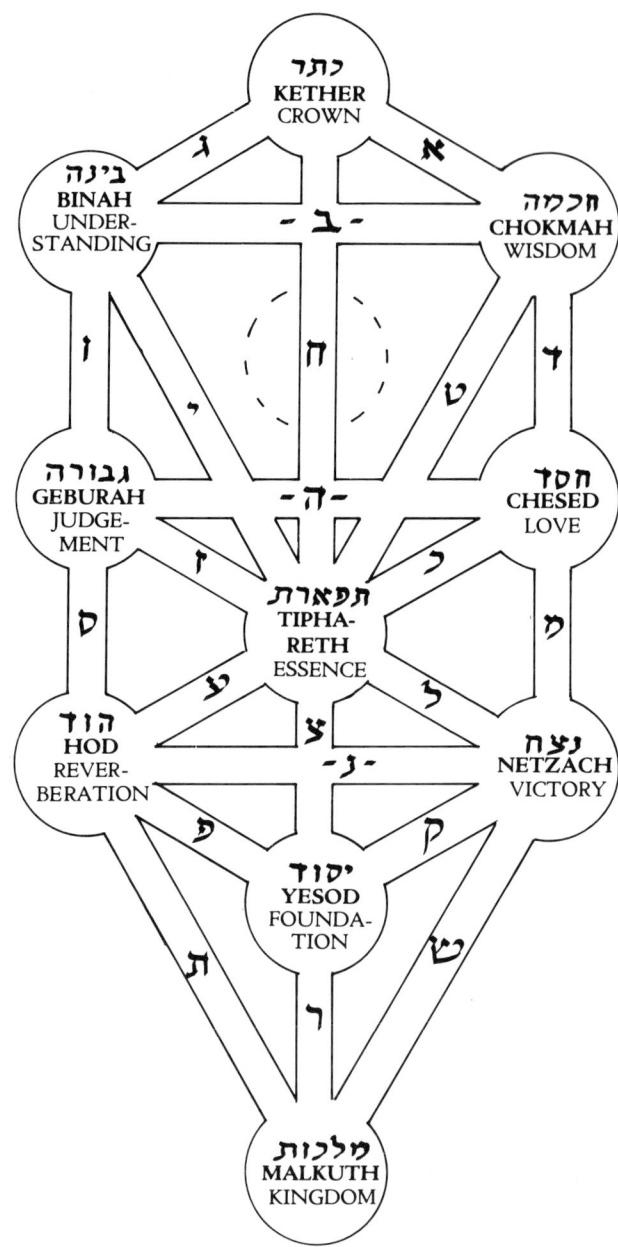

The Tree is a map of creation which has been in a process of continuous development for at least 1,000 years, and probably much longer. Although representations vary, it is usually portrayed as a glyph, a stylized form with ten Sephiroth (spheres) marking the ten different levels of creation, starting with Kether, the Crown, and finishing with Malkuth, the Kingdom. Twenty-two paths connect the Sephiroth, which are arranged on the three pillars of Force, Consciousness and Form. The three highest emanations, of Kether (the Crown), Chokmah (Wisdom) and Binah (Understanding), are the supernal triad of forces which shape the whole of life. The Lightning Flash of Creation then passes through the hidden Sephira of Daath (the Abyss) to reach the manifest world of Chesed (Love) and Geburah (Judgement), the two great rulers of human life. With Tiphareth (Essence), this creates the 'soul'

א	ALEPH	OX (TAME)
ב	BETH	HOUSE
ג	GIMEL	CAMEL (FRUITION)
ד	DALETH	DOOR
ה	HEH	WINDOW (BE)
ו	VAV	HOOK (NAIL)
ז	ZAYIN	SWORD (WEAPON)
ח	CHET	FENCE (FEAR)
ט	TET	SERPENT (MUD)
י	YOD	HAND
כ	CAPH	PALM OF HAND
ל	LAMED	GOAD (LEARN)
מ	MEM	WATER
נ	NUN	FISH
ס	SAMEKH	SUPPORT
ע	AYIN	EYE
פ	PEH	MOUTH
צ	TSADI	FISH HOOK (JUST)
ק	KOOPH	BACK OF HEAD (MONKEY)
ר	RESH	HEAD
ש	SHIN	TOOTH
ת	TAV	SIGN

triad, which must be activated and purified in our journey through this world. Next come Netzach (Victory), signifying feelings and desires, and Hod (Reverberation), signifying mental powers of communication and analysis. Yesod, on the central pillar of consciousness like Tiphareth, is our personality and our foundation in the world, and Malkuth, which is often said to be the hardest Sephira of all to understand, is the physical world of the senses.

The Hebrew alphabet (above) is shown with the transliteration and meaning of each letter. The letters themselves have power and are understood to be a way to unlock the secrets of the universe, bringing revelation to those who contemplate them.

The Tree is both a map of the universe and of the individual; 'as above so below' is a favourite maxim of Cabbalists, and it is said that we each contain the complete Tree within ourselves. It lends itself readily as a kind of Jacob's Ladder which we can climb towards the source of creation, each step bringing new experiences, new challenges and responsibilities. Each Sephira has attracted a wealth of correspondences to itself: astrological, cosmological and, in modern times, scientific and psychological. There are colours, images, qualities ascribed to each one which are used in various forms of Sephirothic meditation, or as a basis for ritual magic, depending upon the orientation of the practitioner.

The tradition of working with Hebrew letters, the sacred alphabet, is obviously more pertinent within Jewish Cabbala, though it certainly has not been neglected in Western Mystery schools. It will not have escaped the eagle-eyed that with 22 paths upon the Tree, and 22 letters in the Hebrew alphabet, we have an excellent opportunity to marry the two. This is, in fact, the basis of Galgal. There are also versions of Cabbala that concentrate more intensely upon the letters, and these are direct ancestors of the Galgal system as they imply an active use of the letters, rather than simply ascribing them to the paths.

THE SOURCE OF GALGAL DIVINATION

The main antecedents of Galgal are the teachings of Abraham Abulafia (*b.* 1240 and quoted above) and Chaim Vital (1543–1620). The *Sefer Yetzirah*, one of the key medieval Cabbalistic texts, emphasizes how the world is created through the permutation of letters. These fundamental permutations can thus be said to form a series of divine names, and it is these which constitute the backbone of Abulafia's work. (His name has recently gained new popularity through being given to the endlessly-permutating computer in Umberto Eco's best-selling novel *Foucault's Pendulum*.)

Abulafia's intense, magical system of medi-

Older forms of Jewish divination include the interpretation of dreams. Here Joseph is seen giving advice to the puzzled Egyptian Pharaoh as to the prophetic meaning of his dreams. Any specific ancient techniques associated with such divination are lost to us today.

tation, involving breathing techniques and ritual movements, outraged his more conventional contemporaries. His claim to true prophecy was denied on the grounds that prophecy could only occur in the Holy Land; his reply, characteristically, was that he had attained the Holy Land of the Spirit and could thus claim to be a prophet. His outlook was broad, and he stated that any language could be used for mystical purposes, not just Hebrew, and that Christians as well as Jews could attain spiritual enlightenment. However, he plainly believed Judaism to be the best religion, since his most perilous exploit on record was when he set out on a mission to convert the Pope, an adventure from which he was lucky to return alive!

Rabbi Chaim Vital, born in 1543 and thus heralding a later development of Cabbala, was a man of brilliant intelligence and extraordinary learning. His interests extended to alchemy, astrology and all current forms of divination. His methods were directed towards gaining entry to the Gates of Understanding, another key Cabbalistic concept associated with the Sephira of Binah, the Great Mother, and they included ritual purification, mantric repetition of holy texts, and visualization of a Holy Name in letters of white fire tinged with the colour of the appropriate Sephira. After careful preparation, the initiate is told to:

Strengthen yourself with a powerful yearning, meditating on the supernal universe. There you should attach yourself to the Root of your soul and to the Supernal Lights. It should seem as if your soul had left your body and had ascended on high. Imagine yourself standing in the supernal universe.

Like Abulafia, Vital recognized the potential dangers of his system, and left instructions on discriminating between fantasy and revelation.

The work of these two schools, along with the tradition of work with the Tree of Life, are the main source of inspiration for Galgal. Cabbalistic astrology is also woven in; Vital's interest in astrology has already been mentioned, and a long association between the planets and Sephiroth exists – both, in one sense, are 'heavenly spheres'. The elegant framework of the Tree of Life, with its geometric structure and different numberings (10 Sephiroth, 22 paths, three pillars, four worlds, and so on) lends itself to astrological interpretations, astrology being itself based upon pattern and number. Galgal uses a method, common among Cabbalists, of equating the Sun with the central Sephira of Tiphareth, the Moon with Yesod, Earth with Malkuth, and the planets with the outer Sephiroth of the Tree. Unique to Galgal, however, is the ascription of the 12 houses of the zodiac with 12 triads upon the Tree of Life (see page 76).

Galgal was first published as a set of 56 cards with an accompanying text in 1972 (Scot o' the Covert, London). The immediate cause of its creation was a discovery made by its originators, Wilfred Davies and Gila Zur, while experimenting with letter permutation in the time-honoured fashion. Until then, no system of placing the letters upon the Tree had proved entirely satisfactory. Cabbalists of different schools argued the merits of different orderings, and some went so far as to say that any letter on any path would give at least some illumination – a statement hard indeed to disagree with.

However, two traditional oral teachings of Cabbala provided the clue that was to result in Galgal. Firstly: 'The Tree emanates forth in the order of the Lightning Flash' (the order of the Sephiroth as given above); and secondly: 'The Tree is complete at every point'. Thus, if it is taken that the Tree begins with Kether and ends at Malkuth, and if at every new Sephira the potential pathways to the pre-existing Sephiroth are mapped in, in descending order, this gives a numbering of 1–22 for the paths, and a placing for the letters following their natural order through the alphabet.

The proof of the validity of this method came when the two researchers began to form the 'wheels' of Galgal. Each card consists of a segment of the Tree which is given a circular shape; the name Galgal itself means wheel, and the term has been used in Cabbala since the Middle Ages to refer to a particular technique of permutating letters. The outer rim of the wheel will thus contain a short sequence of letters, one for each path that forms the rim. These particular combinations of letters began to throw out a remarkable series of meanings; without any extra manipulation, in nearly every case the sequence of letters contained several words within it. Other possible orderings of the letters upon the paths were tried, with minimal results being achieved.

HOW GALGAL WORKS

In Galgal, four of the meanings from the letters around the circumference of each wheel create four separate cards. These are in each case assigned to the four worlds, named in Cabbala as Assiah, the physical, Yetzirah, the formative or psychological, Briah, the creative, and Aziluth, the abstract. In astrology they are known as earth, water, fire and air. So, for instance, for a wheel with Tiphareth (translated as Know: Adorn) as its centre, and with five Sephiroth at the rim (named Crown, Wisdom, Mercy, Judgement and Understand), we have four cards: in ascending order of worlds they are the Gambler, Concern, Pride and the Society. Another, with Yesod (Found: Experience) at the centre, gives rise to the Locksmith, the Eater, the Witness and the Wanderer.

The complete set of 56 cards parallels the number in the Tarot pack, but here the resemblance ends, for whereas the Tarot is vividly imaged, portrayed in bright colours, Galgal is a series of patterns drawn in stark black and white, framed against the deep red of the board on which the cards are laid out. Just as the Cabbalistic letter meditation was designed to draw one through to deeper and deeper levels of understanding, so too Galgal leads the practitioner past the imaginative and intuitive level to the place of 'true thought', the place of the abstract, in the sense that sacred geometry is abstract. Not everyone finds it easy to use for this reason.

Each Galgal card has as its centre one of the

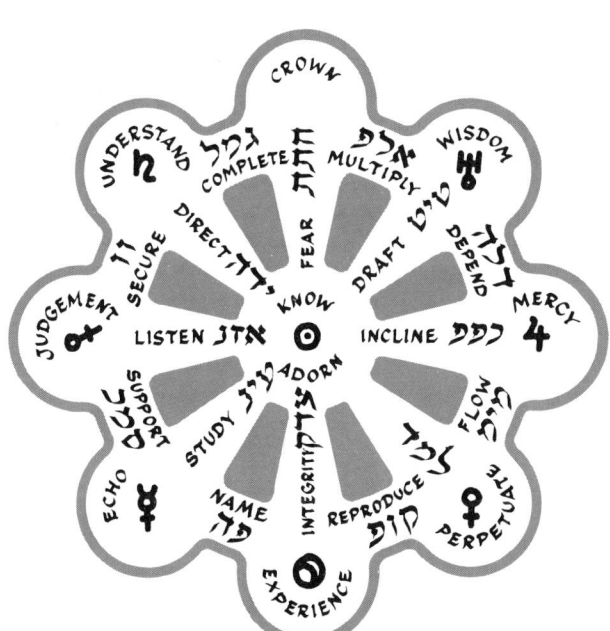

This is one of the 14 wheels of Galgal. Each wheel appears on four cards, once for each element.

Sephiroth from the pillar of consciousness. This means that the divination reading itself centres upon the human capacity to create and, if necessary, to make changes. This offers hope, as opposed to a fate-bound, mechanized view of the universe. The whole Tree, with its letters and Sephiroth, shows us the complete map of creation; the Galgal layout, each card a partial representation of this, shows us the world we have created at this moment in time.

Fourteen cards are laid out with 12 placed around the outside of the board, a schema which equates the mundane houses of astrology (see Chapter Six, Shapes in the Stars) with the twelve external triads of the Tree of Life. Two central cards give the essence and the appearance of the matter enquired about, the Tiphareth and the Yesod of the situation. The twelve astrological houses, which are also used for divination in certain forms of geomancy (see Chapter Twenty-three, Ancient Secrets of the Earth), cover every aspect of human worldly life: family, money, work, ideals, lovers, speculation, travel, health, and so on. Economic, social and psychological aspects are incorporated too and so the houses provide a comprehensive basis for framing the matter to be answered.

The interpretation of each card is thus partly defined in terms of the 'house' it is placed in. The manual that accompanies Galgal gives a clear guide to using the system, and some hints as to the essential meaning of each card, but, as with other major divination systems, the real art of interpretation lies with the practitioner. The title of each card taken at face value is enough to kindle a response, and it is certainly not necessary to be a student of Cabbala to use Galgal, but those wishing to penetrate further can take account of the 'element' of each (earth, water, fire or air), the portion of the Tree represented in the wheel, and the words engraved on each separate path, which are derived from the root meaning of the single letter that belongs there.

Galgal can therefore be used not only as a system of divination, but as a way of entering into the living tradition of the Cabbala. If we

think of certain major divination systems, such as astrology and the *I Ching*, as having an out-flow and an in-flow, it can be seen that we can either stay on the tip of the out-flow, using the system simply for practical purposes, or we can choose to be drawn in on the in-flow, following the system right to its very heart and finding it thus a way of knowledge as well as a way of reading the past, the present and the future.

The author, Cherry Gilchrist, lays out the cards for a Galgal reading, in the order of the Lightning Flash of Creation. The board is inscribed with correspondences that help the practitioner to read the 'story' that the cards spell out, according to Cabbalistic and astrological symbolism.

CHAPTER NINE

WISE WOMEN COUNSELLORS

Popular Methods of Divination

Marian Green

In this age of instant communication with friends, relatives and events around the world, it is easy to forget that in the past people had to rely on the services of sensitives, seers, oracles and clairvoyants to glean any information about distant events. From the courts of kings down to the humblest peasant whose loved ones were away at war, there was a desire to know what was happening and to be kept abreast of battles, invasions or the coming of a flood. Because the technologies we take for granted did not exist, all kinds of methods, rational and irrational, were used. Thus both couriers on horseback and those who could fly beyond their bodies gathered information, and conveyed it through time and space to those who needed to know.

In many parts of the world, the training of seers and the places where they practised their arts were within the confines of religious temples or royal palaces, permitting access to only a chosen few. The Wise Women of the past may originally have been chosen as oracles or seers in the temples of the Classical world – chosen because they had a different capacity for far-seeing than men, perhaps due to that inherently female sense of awareness that enables such women to keep track of their children or loved ones when those people are out of sight.

Over time, this capacity to see beyond the immediate view became the province of Gypsies and country women, who learned their skills from other women in their families: by watching mother or grandma reading a palm and later enquiring as to what the symbols marked on their own hands meant. These women did not study books, nor did they write them; most of the accounts of folk fortune-tellers come from notes in their clients' diaries and day-books. For this reason, there are few books that detail their simple, intuitive, but extremely accurate and varied arts of divination and far-sight. Being 'weather wise' or able to 'talk to animals' were abilities women would inherit and then build upon. Most of the methods that have come down to us as amusements and folksy ways of foretelling the future have provided extraordinarily exact and relevant information that could not have been discovered in any other way.

Many of the methods that have gradually made their way down into the mystic arts of Gypsies, wise women, witches and fortune-tellers are ones in which the practitioner causes her vision to be focused on other levels of reality by means of a speculum or scrying glass, by the random scatter of tea-leaves, pebbles or other small objects, or by the shapes formed when molten wax is poured into water. In all cases, her attention has to be redirected away from the everyday world into that cross-dimensional space within the pattern or glass. To achieve this altered level of perception, the scryer (that is one who 'descrys' or far-sees) has to shift her consciousness quite deliberately so that other times and places may be shown to her. The pictures do not actually appear within the sphere of the crystal ball itself or in the tea-leaves, but in the mind of the fortune-teller. That art can be learned by most people, given patience and concentration.

SCRYING WITH A CRYSTAL BALL
OR OTHER SPECULUM

Since the earliest times certain individuals have discovered that, whilst in a dreamy state, they can begin to see images, shapes, symbols, numbers, figures or complete events apparently reflected in some shining surface. Cave-paintings in France, Australia, South Africa and elsewhere seem to show animals and human figures surrounded with 'haloes' or jagged auras, and this is exactly how many modern seers perceive images within a scrying glass. The pictures seen within the shiny surface are not real, not ordinary reflections, but always differ in intensity, colour or some other feature.

Still, dark pools of water, black stones, such as coal or jet, and wet slabs of slate have been

A collection of scrying instruments (from the top, anti-clockwise): 1 A lighted candle; 2 A glass of dark wine; 3 A concave black mirror; 4 Coloured and clear glass marbles; 5 A crystal of natural clear quartz; 6 A glass or crystal ball on its stand.

the mirror in which 'psychic' visions may be projected. The embers of fires, the flames of burning candles or lamps, the shimmer of the sun on a river, or even a wetted finger-nail may have been the oldest glittering media which helped those with the innate skill to discover other sights within the mind. At Wookey Hole Caves in Somerset, England, recent archaeological excavations uncovered a woman's skeleton dating back to the Stone Age. With her bones was an artificially polished sphere of crystalline granite about the size of a baseball. This appeared to have no other use than as a magical instrument, with which, in the confines of the dark cave, lit by a flickering fire, she may have been able to see visions of the whereabouts of game, and many fossilized animal bones lay scattered alongside hers.

In ancient Egypt there were sacred lotus pools used by priests for scrying, and shallow bowls carved of dark stone have been found in many parts of the world. When filled with water, ink or dark red wine they too became mirrors in which the future could be descryed. The crystal sphere that modern practitioners use is more recent; the earliest examples, used primarily for divination, date from about AD 1500.

To make any such speculum work you need to be able to distract your awareness of the world around you and become mentally and physically still. Often a period of quiet contemplation with the eyes closed will attune the psychic vision to see within the glass or crystal or black mirror when the eyes are opened again. Almost anything can be used: a bowl of water, a wine glass painted black on the outside, a polished sphere of dark or transparent quartz, lead crystal or even a hollow, glass sphere. Within the ball, which acts as a doorway through time and space, pictures will begin to swim out of a swirling mist. Often it is hard to relax enough to see even the swirling fog of astral matter, but eventually, given endurance, a darker area will appear within, and through that time-tunnel, or window of the mind, letters, shapes, symbols, images and information will begin to flow.

This engraved gold disc was made by John Dee, the astrologer and advisor to Queen Elizabeth I, and worn as a magical symbol to enhance the abilities of the scryer. It shows the four protective watch towers of a magical circle.

The author, using an eighteenth-century glass speculum backed by black velvet, seeks answers to questions. Reflections of light have to be ignored so that inner visions can appear within or beyond the sphere. It is necessary to change the level of awareness to achieve effective results.

A heart shows the love in your life, of which you will become more aware. This can be a future partner or children's affections if close to a toy symbol.

A snake shows underhand behaviour in business or professional work and you should be careful of trusting someone. If it is coming towards the top of the cup the threat implied is getting worse soon.

A dagger shows you have an enemy or rival who will make a sudden attack. It could be a new colleague or jealous underling who envies your position and will try to harm your reputation or self-esteem.

A moon, in this case waxing, shows an increase within a project, or new customers. A full moon can indicate a potential romance within a month. A waning crescent can indicate the end of difficulties, or minor, delaying troubles.

A clover leaf shows good luck, even if other symbols in the cup are less positive. It is especially lucky if there are four leaves. The nearer the top of the cup, the faster good fortune will reach you, cancelling other difficulties.

A broom is a positive indicator. If you are a witch it shows interesting journeys. If you are thinking of moving house a change is on the way. Spring-cleaning or brushing away difficulties is suggested.

A Victorian tea-leaf reader's cup and saucer, marked with common symbols and planetary and Zodiac signs, gave a deeper meaning to any tea-leaf patterns that had settled there after the ritual that preceded a reading.

When the client had drunk her cup of tea, made from loose leaves, she would consider the question to which she sought answers. She would take the cup in her left hand, swirl it clockwise three times and upturn its contents into the saucer. Sometimes this was repeated again, to ensure that all the wet tea-leaves had taken up the most auspicious positions for the tasseomancer to interpret.

A horseshoe is a symbol of good luck. If money or travel symbols accompany it, they show the area in which Fortune is smiling upon you.

A cat's head indicates peace and contentment, perhaps the chance to settle down. If the whole cat is in a fighting pose, it can mean strife or conflict. The shape of this symbol determines the good or bad implications.

Initials point you to look at anyone to whom they apply. If other symbols are those of love or contentment, this could be a life partner; or, if business signs, then that would be the affected area of your life.

Parallel lines point to a long journey. The longer and straighter, the more pleasant the journey, and symbols like palm trees or exotic objects could show a delightful holiday destination.

A saw can show a break with a friend or situation. It can also indicate hard personal work, which can also cut you off from the people with whom you usually spend time.

An anchor shows success, especially if close to the handle or rim. It indicates stability and success in home or work, but it is less fortunate if broken or surrounded by broken lines.

TEA-LEAF READING

Tasseomancy – the art of divining with tea-leaves – was introduced into Europe only as recently as the eighteenth century, for that was when the practice of drinking tea as a hot beverage drifted westwards from its original home in China and India. The observation of random patterns of small things has been part of the shaman's system of divination from ancient times; seeing patterns in tea-leaves is an eroded form of the shamanic priest or priestess's art. It is something our grandmothers used to do, or the Gypsy woman calling at the door, for nearly all tea-leaf readers are women.

It is probably because of the kind of questions one might ask over a cup of tea that it has fallen to female diviners to learn and carry on this art. The ritual method of using whole leaf tea in a pot without a filter, poured into a shallow-bowled cup and drunk whilst considering the question in the mind of the querent is still performed according to a traditional rite. When most of the tea has been consumed, another little ritual follows, in which the questioner swirls the cup three times clockwise, then tips it into the saucer. The tea-leaf reader then looks into the bowl of the cup at the patterns made by the residual leaves. Their positions towards the rim or bowl concern time, the quarter of the cup in which they fall gives an indication of the area of life they affect, and the clarity of the symbols adds weight to the interpretation.

The kind of tea we drink in the West provides the raw materials for the sorts of symbols that we can relate to: birds signifying journeys, a house for security, a dagger for danger, a tree for growth, a horseshoe for good luck, or a nail hinting at trouble. There are thousands of symbols, signs, shapes, letters and representations that have a definite interpretation. Because of the intimacy with which this divination would be performed – in the home, usually among friends – the questions are normally about love, family, home, career, progress in activities and partnership matters. Most traditional symbols produced by tasseomancy in the West respond to these questions.

In China, where the art developed perhaps 2,000 years ago and the tea is more stick-like and twiggy, the symbols discovered in the emptied bowl are more like the ideograms used in Chinese writing: not letters as we know them, but hieroglyphs with a pictorial meaning. The symbols could also form as the 64 hexagrams of the *I Ching*. In India the patterns are both symbolic and in letter form, as they traditionally use a more leafy form of tea, and the symbols are used in conjunction with astrology to predict the timing of future events.

Today all manner of teas are available and both Indian and China tea-leaves, as well as herbal teas and coffee grounds, can be used ritually to produce a pattern of scattered symbols from which the outcome of wishes or the train of events can be determined by someone with the skill to read them.

PALMISTRY

The 'form' of things has often been used to symbolize wider concepts, so in this way the human hand – the lines upon the palm, the shapes of the fingers, the colour and texture of the nails – has, from ancient times, been used to discover the nature of the individual whose hands are being examined. Although the fact that the whorls, loops and bridges of lines at the fingertips of every human being are unique has been known only since the middle of the last century, diviners have always known how distinct every hand is. Cave walls across the Earth are decorated with hands: handprints in red or white ochre, outlines and hand-shaped paintings.

In the Old Testament of the Bible it is written 'God sealeth up the hand of every man; that all men may know his work' (Job 37:7), but in far more ancient Vedic texts from India and in Chinese scripts some 3,000 years old, allusions to telling a man's fate from the shape, lines and patterns on his hand have been deciphered. In the West, it is the writings of the Greek philosopher Aristotle that first confirm people's interest in their hands and the existence of those especially skilled in reading the palm for its future prognostications. Aristotle is believed to have gained his knowledge on the matter of hand-reading from earlier Egyptian texts, found on an altar dedicated to Thoth (Hermes), the god of wisdom and writing, which he described in a letter to Alexander the Great. In classical Rome there were hand diviners, some lauded by Pliny, others satirized by the playwright Juvenal.

Once again the wandering Gypsies may have brought this most portable form of divination to the common people during the Dark Ages. When books became more readily available there were a number of texts in Latin, Greek, Sanskrit, Hebrew, German and, later, English detailing the significance of the lines, mounts, phalanges and shape of the hand. In the sixteenth and seventeenth centuries a wide variety of books by scientists, alchemists and philosophers contained material on palmistry and the hand. In Britain the art of hand-reading may have existed since the time of the Druids, who seem to have had a kind of language or method of communication known as Finger Ogam, based on the phalanges, palm and movements of the hand, by which they could silently talk to each other in the presence of others without betraying their secrets (see Chapter Three, By Stick and Stone).

Much of the symbolism of palmistry is based on astrology, with mounds on the palm and individual fingers attributed to planets and their symbolism. The ring finger, for example, is associated with Apollo, the Sun god: the wedding ring – usually made of gold, the metal of the sun – is placed there during marriage because the ancients believed a line of energy ran directly from that finger to the heart.

The lines show the many markings that need to be taken into account when a reading is given. Traditionally, the pattern of lines, grooves, wrinkles and soft cushions of flesh on the left hand (in right-handed people) represents the raw talents, the inherited traits and the potential of the individual, while his right hand shows what he has done with them. If you look at your own hands you will see distinct differences in the clarity, depth and patterns of the lines on each hand, although the general layout will be similar.

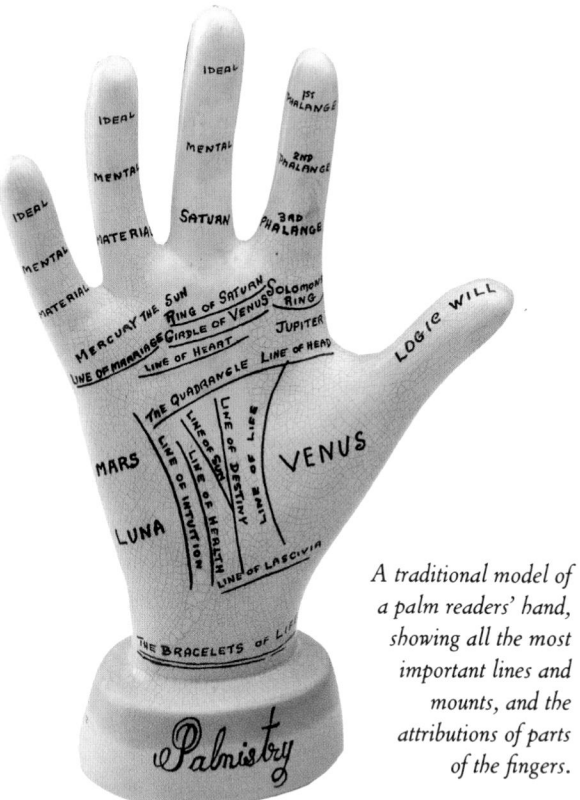

A traditional model of a palm readers' hand, showing all the most important lines and mounts, and the attributions of parts of the fingers.

People who suffer from Down's Syndrome have a combined head and heart line, a reflection of the way that their thinking tends to come from their feelings. Other characteristics such as colour, the texture of the nails, the shape of the mounts and the numbers of fine lines can be seen as clear indications of disease or potential illness. Like some other seemingly improbable forms of alternative diagnosis, this is being scientifically studied to see whether it can yield results before conventional methods are used.

The overall shape of the hand gives guidance as to the practical nature of the individual, and there are generally considered to be eight forms: the elemental or simple hand; the spatulate or active hand; the conical or temperamental hand; the square or practical hand; the philosophic hand with knotty joints; the pointed or spiritually idealistic hand; the hand with two basic characteristics; and the truly mixed hand. The shape of the palm is also important, and whether it is narrow or square, regularly shaped or curvy all determine specific aspects of the owner's personality, or predict future trends in his affairs.

The primary lines are: Heart, telling of love; Head, showing practicality and intelligence; and Life, showing how long the individual might be expected to live and the times of danger from ill health or accidents. The line of Destiny, in the centre of the palm, may indicate factors beyond the control of the person, or influences on him. The mounts of Venus, the Moon and Mars indicate aspects of strength: Venus is physical vitality and sensuality; the Moon shows sensitivity, creativity and inner or psychic strength; while Mars shows courage. The other mounts associated with the planets are Jupiter, showing self-confidence and self-esteem; Saturn, showing the stabilizing effects of relationships and business partnerships; the Sun, showing artistry and imagination; and Mercury, showing a wide span of interests, including science, eloquence, enterprise and business acumen. These mounts may have indented rings, chains, stars, crosses or squares on them, some enhancing the owner's abilities, others showing difficulties on their path through life.

The study of each individual feature on both hands – the interconnections of the lines, the softness of mounts, the varying lengths of the phalanges of the fingers, the flexibility of the thumb – all add up to an extremely complex subject. Every land has its traditions and there are numerous books of interpretation of each feature. Part of the essential skill of any divination, however, is the personal interaction between the reader and the client. There has to be trust and honesty on both sides. Because the palm reader actually has to hold the hands of her client, there is a very close connection through which a great deal of background information can be gained psychically, and this can greatly expand the reading. Confidence is essential, and this seems to be the main reason why most palmists are women: it gives female clients assurance and also pleases young men, who like to hold hands with wise or witty seeresses.

Readings still take place at fairs where Gypsy readers ply their traditional skills of 'dikkering' or fortune-telling, or in the parlour where friends meet to chat about their futures.

A palm reader in Mali uses the same method of close touch and examination with his client as that used by European and Indian palmists. The palmist spreads out his client's hand to point to features concerning marriage or family.

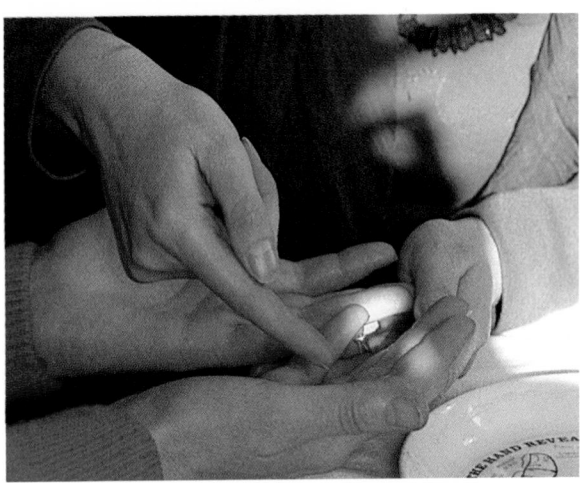

In this consultation, the author, Marian Green, shows a client some of the important lines and markings on her hands. It is the sense of psychic touch, as well as the inherent meanings of these signs, which gives value and depth to any such reading.

CHAPTER TEN

THE SEASONAL ROUND

The Folklore of Divination in Britain

Jennifer Westwood

At different times and in different places divination has been the province of experts: shamans, soothsayers, prophets, priests, astrologers, Gypsies and village Wise Women and Cunning Men. Today this strain of professional divination survives – indeed flourishes – but so does the traditional divination of the peasantry, even if somewhat less conspicuously. These country folk were only occasionally able to afford the services of the local 'Star Reader' and mostly sought for themselves through portents and signs some certainty in an uncertain future. Country people, and people in isolated work groups such as fishermen and miners, have been less touched by outside influences than the rest of the community and have remained more conservative. Consequently, divinations known in sixteenth-century England were still practised in the nineteenth, and even in the twentieth century old divinatory formulae may be part of our daily lives without our knowing it.

WEATHER PROGNOSTICATION

Weather 'saws' mostly fall into the category of divinations that have been absorbed into proverbial lore: 'Red sky at night, shepherd's delight', for example. This is a prediction based on observation, as are many prognostications taken, in the manner of the Roman augurs, from the flight of birds: if swallows skim low to the ground, storms will spoil the crops, but if they fly high, there will be drought.

Such saws were the product of collective experience reaching back many years, handed on as a rule of thumb to the greenhorn, as were

prognostications based on the weather of a particular day of the year. If St Paul's Day (25 January) was wet, corn would be dear, and if it rained on St Swithun's (15 July), 40 days of rain would follow. This type of weather forecasting on the basis of observed natural phenomena was useful to a wide audience and found a place in print in, for example, the prognostications published by John Claridge, 'the Shepherd of Banbury', *The Shepheards Legacy: or, John Clearidge, his forty years experience of the weather* (1670).

It is doubtful whether countrymen separated this fundamentally rational lore from much that had a quite different intellectual basis. It cannot have been forecasting based on observation, for example, but a presumption of the benign influence radiated by a doubly holy day over the whole of the next twelvemonth when farmers predicted a good year if Christmas Day fell on a Sunday.

THE DIVINATORY RHYMES OF BRITAIN

Divination was once practised all over Britain and many of the rituals were accompanied by a rhyme. Most of those on the map are explained in the text of this chapter. 'Oak before Ash' is a typical weather prognostication, and the invocation 'O good St Faith' was recited on 6 October, St Faith's Day, by girls performing the Dumb Cake ceremony. 'If you love me, bounce and fly' accompanies an old Hallowe'en charm. Though hazelnuts are used in the ritual described in the text, this version uses apple pips. If the sweetheart is faithful, the pip will burst on the fire, otherwise burn quietly. 'If you love me, cling all round me' accompanied the old Oxfordshire game of 'lovelaces' played with four blades of grass. The blades were held in one hand, and knotted at each end. The omens were read according to whether they formed a ring, came apart, or fell separately.

If you love me, bounce and fly,
If you hate me, lie and die.

Hempseed, I sow. Hempseed, grow.
He that is my true love
Come after me and mow.

Oak before Ash
We'll only have a splash,
Ash before Oak
We're in for a soak.

SCOTLAND

I pare this pippin round and round again
My sweetheart's name to flourish on the plain,
I fling the unbroken paring o'er my head,
My sweetheart's letter on the ground is read.

Even, even ash,
I pluck thee off the tree;
The first young man that I do meet,
My love he shall be.

NORTHUMBERLAND

NORTHERN
IRELAND

Bishy, Bishy Barnabee,
Tell me when my wedding be;
If it be tomorrow day,
Take your wings and fly away.
Fly away east, fly away west,
Show me where lives the one
I love best.

New Moon, New Moon, New Moon, I hail thee,
If ever I marry a man, or a man marry me,
This night may I him see;
And may his apparel not frighten me.

YORKSHIRE

By St Peter and St Paul,
If Robert has stolen William's goods,
Turn about riddle and shears and all.

IRISH SEA

HUNTINGDONSHIRE

Here is the boot,
Where is the foot?

WALES

ENGLAND

OXFORDSHIRE

This knot I knit,
To know the thing, I know not yet,
That I may see,
The man that shall my husband be,
How he goes, and what he wears,
And what he does, all days, and years.

ENGLISH CHANNEL

If you love me, cling all round me,
If you hate me, pull off quite,
If you neither love nor hate me,
Come in two at last.

O good St Faith, be kind tonight
And bring to me my heart's delight
Let me my future husband view
And be my vision chaste and true.

km 0   50   100   150

mi 0   50   100   150

THE SIEVE AND SHEARS

A commonly practised divination was the Sieve and Shears, used to discover thieves. The points of the shears were thrust into the wooden rim of the sieve so that the handles stood upright and the sieve hung from the points. Two people supported the handles with the middle fingers of their right hands. Once the sieve was suspended, the names of suspects were recited:

By St Peter and St Paul,

If (such-and-such) has stolen (so-and-so's) goods,

Turn about riddle and shears and all.

When the thief's name was mentioned, the sieve turned or fell to the ground. Faith in the method was absolute.

DIVINATION OF LENGTH OF LIFE

Although even treasure-divining by the raising of spirits was long tolerated at official levels, forecasting the length of the king's reign was not. As important in politics as calculating through opinion polls the likely 'life' of a government is today, it was the province of the professional astrologer and expressly forbidden by law, as in popular estimation it came perilously near conjuring to take the king's life. Several astrologers were executed for it and in 1581 Parliament made it a statutory felony to cast nativities or calculate by prophecy how long Queen Elizabeth I would live. None the less such prediction continued: the Gunpowder Plotters employed it, and the astrologer John Heydon was allegedly imprisoned for predicting the death of Cromwell.

Outside the propertied classes – where there would be impatient heirs – people were less concerned with life expectancy as such than with the very real chances of dying in the coming year. To ascertain that likelihood, there was both a generalized reading of death omens – the howling of a dog round the house or the hooting of owls, or birds beating their wings against the window near a sick-bed – and more specific divinations.

Most often the recommended dates for divinations of any kind were the 'eves' or vigils before certain feast days of the pre-Reformation Church calendar, especially St Agnes's Eve (20 January), St Mark's Eve (24 April), St John's or Midsummer Eve (23 June) and All Hallows' Eve or Hallowe'en (31 October). All Hallows, the Christian feast of the dead, falls on 1 November, the beginning of the old Celtic year. In Wales *Nos Galangaeaf*, Winter's Eve, was one of the three Ghost Nights (*y Tair Ysbrydnos*) – the others being May Eve (30 April) and St John's Eve – when the spirits of the dead, the 'fetches' (doubles) of the living and the fairies walked the Earth. Because the dead were believed to know the future, all over Britain these three were particular nights for divination.

'Watching in the church porch' itself was most often practised on St Mark's Eve. The procedure was to go to the porch and wait for an hour before and an hour after midnight. At some moment during the vigil, the forms of those in the parish destined to die in the ensuing twelvemonth would appear.

'Cauff-riddling' was the Yorkshire name for a divination likewise performed mainly on St Mark's Eve, whose purpose was specific enquiry into one's own future. The enquirer went to a barn at midnight and, leaving the doors standing wide, riddled chaff (i.e. sifted husks of corn). If nothing was seen while he did so, the omen was good; but if a coffin carried by two bearers passed across the doorway, he would die within the twelvemonth.

Anecdotes like this – whether true or 'witness legends' designed to support a belief – raise the question of auto-suggestion, one reason perhaps why divining the future was commonly regarded as risky. Whether people thought of such ceremonies as the raising of apparitions (i.e. witchcraft) or as blasphemy (prying into the secrets of God) is unclear. Few, perhaps, drew distinctions.

MARRIAGE DIVINATIONS

Well into this century, marriage was the only career open to most women. Because of this, of all forms of popular divination the ones that survive in the most variety are those to do with marriage, and most were performed by girls.

Many of the rituals resemble conjurations, though often they leave some doubt as to whether the future partner is to be seen in the flesh, in a dream or as a 'fetch' or *doppelgänger*. In Northumberland, a girl had to find an ash leaf with an even number of leaflets and say:

> *Even, even ash,*
> *I pluck thee off the tree*
> *The first young man that I do meet,*
> *My love he shall be.*

She then put it in her left shoe. The first man she met after that would be her husband. This is apparently an encounter in the flesh, but what of the man who scattered ashes along a quiet lane on Hallowe'en in the expectation of seeing his destined wife following the trail?

A divination from north-west England takes the form of a salutation to the Moon. When the first New Moon of the year was seen, a girl was to take a brush in one hand and a comb in the other, and go in silence and secrecy into the garden. There she was to say:

> *New Moon, New Moon, New Moon, I hail thee.*
> *If ever I marry a man, or a man marry me,*
> *This night may I him see;*
> *And may his apparel not frighten me.*

She was then to return to the house in silence and go to bed, whereupon she would see her future husband in a dream, though the lingering apprehension in this charm suggests that originally he was expected as a fetch.

This was certainly so in a very old ritual once practised all over the country. Going at midnight to the churchyard, the enquirer (usually female) had to walk round the church sowing hempseed and saying:

> *Hempseed, I sow. Hempseed, grow.*
> *He that is my true love*
> *Come after me and mow.*

Looking back on the stroke of twelve (from the church clock), she would either see a coffin – meaning that she would die an old maid – or else a man's form would appear behind her with a scythe, mowing. St Mark's Eve, Midsummer Eve, Hallowe'en and Christmas Eve were all

suitable dates for the divination.

A man could find out who he would marry by going out to his barn and winnowing corn three nights running at midnight with both doors open. On the third night he would see the apparition of his future wife.

Midnight was also the critical time in the making of the Dumb Cake usually confined to Christmas Eve, St Agnes's Eve, St Mark's Eve or Hallowe'en. The Dumb Cake was a simple bannock (a round, flat loaf) – the traditional formula was an eggshell full of salt, one of wheat flour, and one of barley-meal. It had to be prepared alone, fasting and in ritual silence – hence the name. In Oxfordshire, girls pricked their initials on it and left it on the hearthstone to bake. Then they went to bed, leaving the door of the house open. At midnight the future husband's fetch was expected to enter through the door and add his initials. In the North of England, solitariness was not a requirement: two or three girls met together to bake the cake, divided it equally, and walked backwards upstairs holding it in their hands. They ate it just before getting into bed, in the hope of seeing the man they would marry in a dream.

The eating of the cake was probably originally required everywhere as the mechanism for inducing dreams and visions. In some parts of Northumberland, instead of the Dumb Cake, the girls ate an eggshell filled with salt, and on Tyneside men consumed a red herring, bones and all, for the same purpose.

MAGICAL ELEMENTS IN MARRIAGE DIVINATION

Darkness, secrecy, silence, the expectations raised by performance at the witching hour and on special 'ghost nights' - all played a part in creating the right context for these ceremonials. Others depended on magical factors. An old marriage divination recorded by Aubrey in the seventeenth century and still in use in the nineteenth could be used to see either a future wife or a husband, but only if you were away from home. 'You must', says Aubrey, 'lie in another county, and knit the left garter about the right-legged stocking (let the other garter and stocking alone) and as you rehearse these following verses, at every comma, knit a knot.'

> *This knot I knit,*
> *To know the thing, I know not yet,*
> *That I may see,*
> *The man (woman) that shall my husband (wife) be,*
> *How he goes, and what he wears,*
> *And what he does, all days, and years.*

The magic of knots – often employed in witchcraft – is involved here, as well the garter's possession of some sexual meaning: a bride's garters were snatched for luck at weddings.

In Wales, enquirers would walk seven times round the house carrying a boot, saying 'Here is the boot, where is the foot?' expecting to see the future partner appear. In Glamorgan in the 1950s a girl would scratch her boyfriend's initials on a leaf and put it inside her shoe. After a day and night, if the initials appeared plainer, she would take it as a sign that he was the one she would marry. In both rituals, the significant feature is the shoe, traditionally connected with marriage.

Plant material with magical significance was also often used. In Huntingdonshire, on May Eve, a girl would hang a branch of flowering May (hawthorn blossom) on a signpost at a crossroads and leave it there all night. In the morning she would look to see which way the wind had blown it, in the belief that her future husband would come from that direction. Not only was the crossroads traditionally a no-man's-land between the everyday and the supernatural, but the hawthorn was a fairy tree: their coming together is not coincidence.

John Gay, author of *The Beggar's Opera*, gives in *The Shepherd's Week* in 1714 a version of a game probably already old in his day. The enquirer suits his action to the words:

> *I pare this pippin [apple] round and round again*
> *My sweetheart's name to flourish on the plain.*
> *I fling the unbroken paring o'er my head,*
> *My sweetheart's letter on the ground is read.*

This is still played as a game in Scotland at Hallowe'en and by children at any time of the year, but an underlying seriousness is shown by the fact that the peel is thrown over the left shoulder – the (in the original sense) *fatal* side. The apple was regarded as a magical fruit.

In some places Hallowe'en was known as Nutcrack Night. If a girl wanted to be sure her lover was true, she took two hazelnuts and set them on the bars of the grate or on a log in the fire. If they burnt away together, he was faithful; if they flew apart, faithless.

DIVINATION AND CHILDREN'S GAMES

It is likely that a playful element was present in some marriage divinations from the first, and that it was the seemingly innocent, Arcadian appearance of such customs that has allowed so many to survive. Children still play 'He loves me, he loves me not' by pulling the petals off a daisy, one of several divinations of a simple counting-out kind. While some test the affections of a sweetheart, others sift through possibilities, like 'Tinker, tailor', originally played with cherry-stones: 'Tinker, tailor, soldier, sailor, rich man, poor man, beggar man, thief.'

Even more specific is the address to 'Bishy Barnabee', the ladybird, for obscure reasons named after St Barnabas. Blowing a ladybird off his or her hand, the enquirer says:

> *Bishy, Bishy Barnabee,*
> *Tell me when my wedding be;*
> *If it be tomorrow day,*
> *Take your wings and fly away.*

If he or she also wants to know the direction the lover will come from, action and words are the same, with the addition of:

> *Fly away east, fly away west,*
> *Show me where lives the one I love best.*

Marriage divination still flourished in the 1950s, when Welsh schoolgirls believed that if you counted nine stars on nine successive nights, on the ninth night you would dream of your future boyfriend. It remains to be seen if in the long term the force of the old drives will be enough to withstand the sexual revolution.

AFRICA

On the African continent divinatory systems have probably had a more continuous existence than in almost any other part of the world. The systems described in the two chapters that follow derive from very ancient times, possibly as far back as the Stone Age, and, remarkably in a time when Western influence is increasingly felt, they are still widely practised today.

As in the Celtic and Norse systems discussed in Chapters Two and Three, there is a direct link to deity. The diviners are not simply looking to the natural world, or to random events, or even to spirits, but directly to the gods; though it is also evident that they were in most instances either 'priests' or 'doctors', and thus fit within the category of shamans.

One also catches glimpses, in the accounts of anthropologists, of traditions that relate to 'families' of diviners, who passed on the knowledge of their skills from generation to generation. Although such instances are less well documented in the European world, it is more than likely that the same traditions were upheld within Western culture.

The similarities that obtain within individual tribes in the names attributed to the bones used for divination point to an ancient and widespread usage, and it is interesting to speculate whether bone divination was arrived at individually or was imported. There are clear similarities between Ifa and the various systems of geomancy, especially Sikidy and Raml (see Chapter Twenty-three), which is not surprising since these entered the West through the gate of North Africa. Other similarities are to be seen between the use of divination symbols drawn in sand and the allusive marks from which Saami diviners foretell events in the Far North (see Chapter Two).

The sheer diversity of places in which variations of the bone oracle are found suggests that this method is, indeed, the oldest and most basic of all the divination systems. It is in fact found in areas as widely separated as Europe, Scandinavia, Australia, New Zealand and the Americas, as well as all over Africa and throughout the East.

Although both of the chapters that follow concentrate on the particularly rich area of Southern Africa, similar systems exist throughout the rest of the continent. Aside from tribal variations, they are substantially the same as those described here.

CHAPTER ELEVEN

ORACLES IN BONE

Divination in Southern Africa

Kunderke Kevlin

In 1507 the Portuguese missionary Joano dos Santos observed the throwing of four 'bones' for the purpose of divination in Mozambique. Today, despite repeated attempts by white missionaries and governments in the colonial era to stamp out the practice, this same divinatory system is still widely prevalent in the industrial cities and rural areas of Southern and South Central Africa. The bone diviner continues to be a familiar figure, consulted whenever misfortunes threaten or have occurred, or whenever there is a need to have certainty about future events. People will consult him (it is usually a man) with questions such as 'What is the cause of my illness? Is there witchcraft involved? If there is, who is the witch?' or 'Will my cattle multiply and my crops be bountiful this year' or 'What will be the outcome of the court case?' As it is believed that virtually all misfortune is caused by witchcraft, most questions ultimately come down to a basic anxiety about witchcraft.

THE ORIGINS OF BONE DIVINATION

The tribal peoples of the vast area that comprises Southern and South Central Africa are not of the same cultural stock, so where and with whom this divinatory system originated is an intriguing question. The answer is hard to establish as it goes back in time long before written records existed. We can know only more recent events with certainty: that in the nineteenth century, for instance, the custom was brought to what is now Zambia by a migrating tribe from the Transvaal.

It has been suggested by some authors that the custom of bone divination of the first type described below originated with the old Zimbabwe culture and/or from the Arab trading influence in this same area. They supply no firm evidence for their view, but I found information in the ethnographic writing which does provide some circumstantial evidence.

It is certain, for example, that the names of the principal bones are of archaic origin and refer to cultural heroes or ancestor gods. The tribes of the Venda and Lemba, who live in the Transvaal province of South Africa, have traditions that link them strongly to the names used for the bones. In a famous legend it is told how Mwali, the great god, king of heaven, but also the ancestor god of the Royal Singo clan of the Venda, had a son called Tshilume and one of Tshilume's successors was called Hwami. Hwami and Tshilume are the names of two of the principal bones of the divination set among the Venda and Lemba and most of the tribes recorded as having the custom. The Venda names for the other two principal bones, Thwalima and Lumwe, are also widely distributed among the other tribes.

We know that the Venda and Lemba migrated together from Zimbabwe to the Transvaal (Zimbabwe was the magnificent capital of an ancient kingdom from which present-day Zimbabwe takes its name), and that the Lemba are a tribe of mixed origin, resulting from the intermarriage of Arabs and Africans. Other tribes make frequent reference to Lemba and Venda in the 'praises' attached to the bones, which tends to confirm them as the originators of the system.

In this chapter I focus mainly on the traditions of bone divination among the Sotho, Tswana, Venda and Lovedu tribes, who live in the South African provinces of the Transvaal and Orange Free State and in Botswana and Lesotho. The tribes further north, such as the Shona, differ quite significantly in their culture, although the basic principles of their system of bone divination appear similar. Other South African tribes, such as the Swazi, Zulu and Xhosa, who live in Swaziland, Natal, Transkei and the Cape Province, are again quite different culturally and tend to use a different form of bone divination, of which there are fewer eyewitness accounts. They also place greater emphasis on another form of divination, based on clairvoyance and usually carried out by women.

THE BONES

There are two different types of bones, which are used either separately or in conjunction with

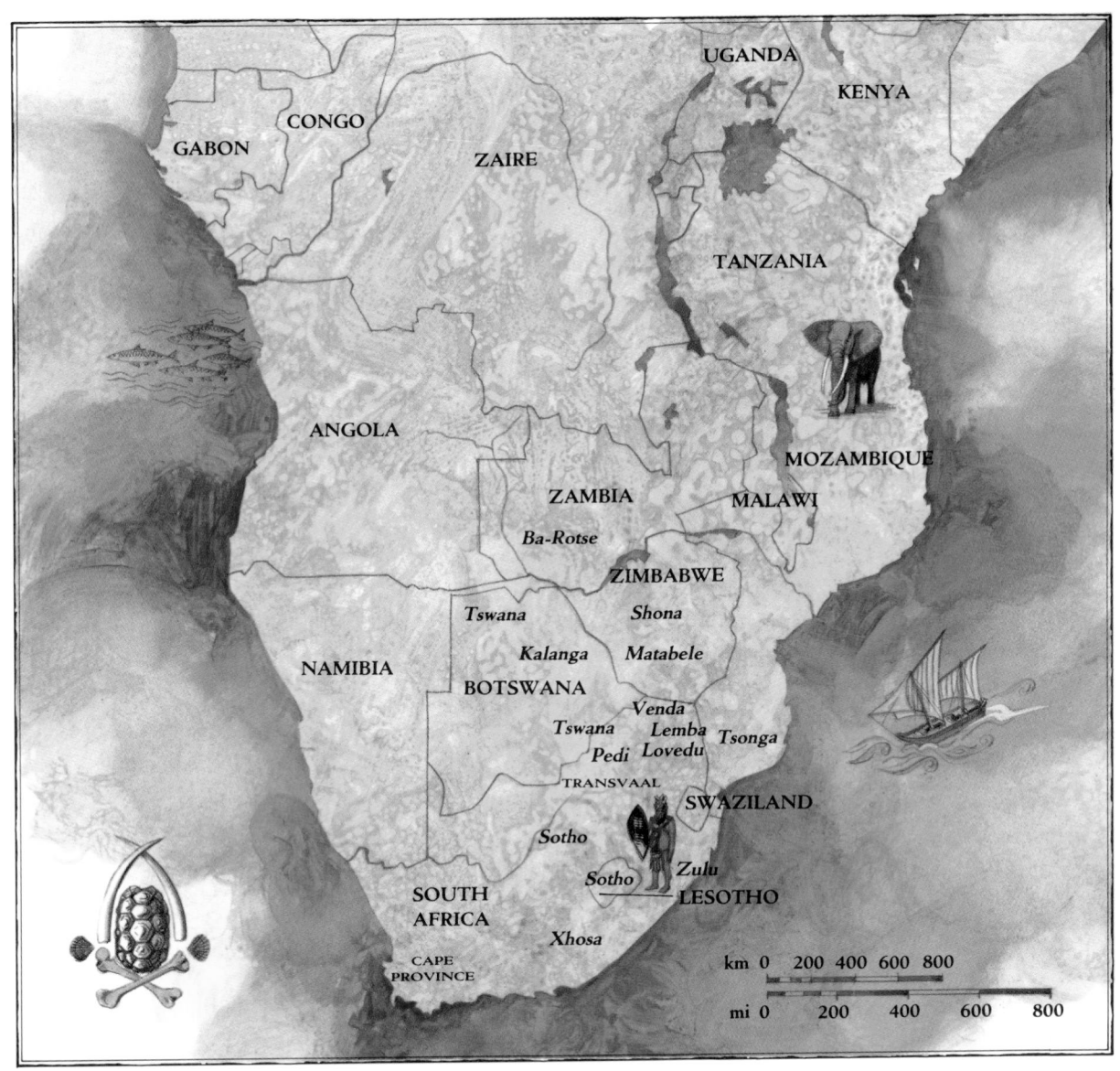

THE SPREAD OF BONE DIVINATION
Bone divination probably originated in Zimbabwe. It became established in Southern Africa through the migration of tribes southwards and the acceptance of the custom by the tribes already resident there. Today it is found as far north as Zambia and as far south as the Cape Province.

each other. There are thus also two different forms of bone divination.

The first is divination by means of a set of four bones, which are differentiated into a senior male, a junior male, a senior female and a junior female. These bones consist either all four of ivory, bone, horn (of cattle) or wood, or two of the bones may be cut from the tip of the hoof of an ox or cow and thus be pyramid-shaped. Each of the bones has a positive, decorated side and a negative, undecorated side, so that they can form 16 different combinations when thrown together on the ground. Each combination or 'fall' has a name, a 'praise' (the poem that is recited when the fall is identified) and a standard general interpretation, and the diviner interprets this meaning in relation to the problems at hand. Thus the system is based on three oppositions – male/female, senior/junior and positive/negative – and the meanings produced by combinations of these categories.

The second is divination by means of a large number (up to 60) of *astragali* (knucklebones) of various animals and sometimes also a few other objects, such as seashells, tortoiseshell and special stones. In general the aim is to have a male and female bone of each species, with a few significant exceptions: for instance, among the Lovedu the antbear is represented by only one bone as it digs in the ground where the dead are buried and is thus associated with the ancestors. Again, each bone has a positive and negative side so that the diviner can 'read' the fall in terms of the position of the bones in relation to each other and according to which side faces up.

The Nguni peoples and the tribes of Southern Mozambique use only this second form of divination, while the Sotho, Tswana, Venda, Lovedu, Matabele and Kalanga use both types of bones, but consider the *astragali* of secondary significance.

THE DIVINER

The person who wants to be a bone diviner usually does this in combination with learning the skills of doctoring. The better-known diviners are also herbalists and base their

diagnosis, not on an examination of the patient, but on what the bones tell them.

Anyone who wishes to learn the skills of the doctor-diviner may ask a diviner to instruct him. As a rule the diviner, before commencing to teach another person, will consult his divining bones to ascertain if the prospective pupil is worthy of admission into the profession. If the bones reply in the affirmative, but only then, the pupil is taught how to divine. He learns the names of the divining bones and the meanings of

96

the various positions and combinations in which they fall, with the appropriate praises to each.

At first the teacher uses his own divining set, but after some time he tells the pupil to kill an ox, from whose bones he carves a set of the four principal pieces. The bones must be cut out of the raw flesh and doctored with various medicines. An appeal is made to the ancestors to give the bones the power of divination. The process may involve the use of white objects or substances, for example, placing the bones under white ash, or under white leaves on a growing tree beneath white moonlight. In some tribes the apprentice drinks a concoction of water in which the bones plus various roots, powders and the

Seeking advice on his health, a Tswana man has thrown the bones. The diviner – dressed in white, the colour of the spirits – studies the throw and will soon give a reading. The presence of a female healer indicates that she will also be involved in effecting a cure once the diagnosis has been made. In this case only a few of the pieces of a divining set have been used, i.e. two ivory tablets, six astragali *and one cowrie shell.*

flesh of a white goat have been boiled, so that he will eventually understand 'inside his heart' how to read the bones.

The period of instruction may be from one to three years, according to the ability of the pupil and the extent of the teacher's knowledge. The pupil may also extend his training by becoming an apprentice to other diviners after his initial training has been completed.

Learning bone divination is in many ways a logical process, rather than one requiring psychic ability. Definite rules of interpretation are taught and it is the bones, not the diviner, who are in direct contact with the spirit world. The diviner has to learn the rules in order to understand what the bones are telling him. Although the application of these rules to particular cases also requires intuition and creativity, as the rules have to be interpreted according to the complexity of each case, it is not requisite that the diviner himself develops psychic abilities.

THE MEANING OF THE BONES

The bones are believed to have an intrinsic power, which is strengthened, but not determined, by the ritual doctoring they have received. Different suggestions have been made as to where their power derives from. Some say they reveal the will of God, others that the ancestors speak through them, yet others that they reveal a more or less impersonal cosmic power. It is likely that all these viewpoints are true. The Bantu concept of God is very different from the Christian one, so that the first and the last suggestions are one and the same thing. And, as noted earlier, the ancestors are asked to 'strengthen' the bones and impart of their wisdom to them, but that does not mean that they are the ultimate source of the divining power. The ancestors are part of and bound by the same cosmic and moral order as man is. It should be noted that the term *bola* or *bala* or *bula*, which is used to refer to the divining set, has also been translated as 'the word', implying a relatively impersonal cosmic power.

The power of the bones lies in the fact that they represent important categories that are used in the ordering of the social and cultural world. It could also be argued that these same categories or ordering principles are found at the cosmic and natural levels. In other words, there are principles of order in the universe which manifest at both the human and non-human levels.

As mentioned previously, the divinatory set is based on the oppositions of male and female and junior and senior. These are also the key principles of the social order and cultural activities. The division between and the complementarity of male and female pervades nearly every social and ritual activity. Much of tribal life is divided into male and female spheres of influence, competence and experience. Often there were prohibitions against crossing from one sphere to another and where the two unavoidably met, as in sexual activity and procreation, there was considered to be both great danger and great creative potential. Symbolism constantly reinforces this basic division. For instance, when a boy is born the father will be told by a man hitting him with a stick across the shoulders, but if it is a girl a woman will pour a calabash of water over him. The earth is female, the sky is male; the left side of the hut is female, the right side of the hut is male; and so on. Even diviners were typically divided into the male diviners who used the bones and the female diviners who instead used clairvoyance.

The senior/junior opposition is equally significant. The whole of society is ranked within the sphere of each sex – the ranking often falls away when it applies to people of a different gender. Siblings of the same sex are ranked as senior and junior to each other, and this is extended to lineages, villages and totemic groups.

These rules are the basis of the kinship system and the bones are directly linked to specific positions within the family. Thus the simplest designation is father, mother, son, daughter – but this can be extended according to the case presented. Thus, the senior male bone can represent the paternal ancestors, the grandfather, the father's brother, the chief or simply a senior or elderly man. The junior male can represent the mother's brother, the maternal ancestors or any junior ranking male.

The meaning of the *astragalus* bones varies between clusters of tribes. With those tribes that have totemic groups they represent them, with the others they represent social categories. An account of the bones used by the Lovedu tribe illustrates that the full divinatory set represents the Lovedu social universe:

The Lovedu set is fairly stereotyped, consisting of about forty pieces, most but not all of which are bones.... Dominating the usual Lovedu set are four flat pieces of ivory or bone, two male and two female, which fall in sixteen different combinations.... There are other sets of four: pieces from the ventral surface of a tortoise, each with two easily distinguishable sides, and shells, two Olwa standing for males and two Cypraea standing for females. Having thrown the dice, the diviner looks first at the ivory pieces and gives the praises of their disposition, which indicates the general situation....But this general situation must be related to the lie of certain other bones, particularly malope, *the knuckle-bone of the steenbuck- ...from which, as representing the chief, the diviner next orientates the situation. The procedure thereafter involves linking this situation, on the one hand, with events of specific prognostications of good or evil and, on the other, with people playing a part in these events.* Thakadu *or* mudimo, *the talus of an antbear, represents the ancestors, who, like the antbear, live underground, shows whether they are angry or not, and is diagnostic of the health or life of a person, which in the last resort lies in ancestral hands.* Dau, *the phalanx of a lion,* phiri, *the knee-bone of the hyena ... and* tshweni, *male and female knee-bones of the baboon, all stand for the evil power of witches and their familiars.... Two or three sheep bones stand for important or respected people, such as district or village heads, and goat bones ...for mere commoners....Different totems are shown by the bones of the animals revered.* (E. Krige, The Realm of the Rain Queen, 1943, pp. 226–7.)

THE PRAISE-POEMS AND THEIR READING

The four principal bones of the divinatory set combine into 16 different falls, each of which has its own name and praise-poem. The names of the bones and the falls show a striking similarity among the different tribes, if allowance is made for linguistic variation. This suggests that the meanings and interpretations of each fall might also have a single system of meaning. Unfortunately, this does not appear to be the case. Many praise-poems are virtually impossible to understand for a cultural outsider, and it can only be hoped that one day an African researcher/diviner will give a more understandable and thorough account. The meanings of some falls are, however, relatively accessible to Western diviners.

The fall in which all the four principle (senior male) bones fall positive is called *Mphirifiri* or *Mufirifiri*. It indicates too much action or feverish activity and is associated with fire and 'hotness', which is considered a dangerously overenergetic state.

The following is a Sotho praise for this fall:

Unrest of a multitude makes the dust rise; they have cut the cord that goes through the nostrils of the ox. At Phalaborwa, near the Olifants river, where the blacksmiths live, sounds the hammer, the morning bird sings, in the east the day shines.

This fall is generally interpreted as a negative one, associated with strife, illness, death and witchcraft. A patient whose health is in question, for instance, will die; or there will be quarrels between the people and attempts to bewitch each other.

The fall that is negative for the senior male and female and positive for the junior male and female is called *Thlapadima* among the Kgatla, a Tswana tribe. The praise goes:

I am the cheater of the children, of the children who have no parents, of the rain; it is a person who cannot cross the river, it says one who sinks in and jumps out, it says the biter in the river (water) when there is no rhinoceros or crocodile. What are you washing frog, why do you wash as if you will be taken by the rhinoceros or crocodile. The reeds are on the bank of the river, you are in the water, when the river takes you it will sweep you away, roots and all, and sweep you into the big rivers; it says we are just the same, you will be burned outside in the grass, and my body will be burned but when the first rains fall I shall grow again. (From the research notes of Professor Isaac Schapera.)

The first part of this praise has been said to refer to illegitimate sex, but no comment is supplied for the clearly much more profound statement about life and death in the latter part. This fall is also considered a negative one: it might mean that the patient will recover, but his blood has thickened and he is shivering; or a wife is deceiving her husband with other men in his absence; or a pregnant woman keeps miscarrying.

The meaning of the fall can differ according to what category of problem is presented. A fall that is generally negative may be propitious for one type of problem, for example rainfall in the case of *Mufirifiri*.

BONE DIVINATION IN A CHANGING WORLD

Bone divination originated in a tribal culture that was founded on close contact with the natural world. Today, the wild animals are confined to game reserves, and industrial cities dominate the economy. Many Africans now live their whole lives in an urban environment and even more spend the greater part of their time working in the cities and mines as migrant labourers. Tribal culture has undergone profound changes in the twentieth century, and these changes will inevitably have led to new developments in the symbolism and interpretation of the bones. It is unlikely, however, that the reasons why people consult a diviner have changed. The belief in witchcraft is certainly as strong as ever, and in fact the incidence of witchcraft accusations may have increased as a

Although lifestyle and customs have changed within many African tribes, belief in the power of divination remains strong. Here, Zulu mystic and diviner Laduma Madela prepares for a reading.

result of the psychological insecurities of this time of rapid social change. Today's African still turns to the diviner when beset by anxieties or difficulties, and so the sight of the diviner taking out his little bag of bones and shaking them out onto the ground remains a common one.

Note
I want to express my gratitude to Professor Isaac Schapera, who kindly allowed me to study his unpublished research notes concerning Kgatla divination.

CHAPTER TWELVE

IFA

A Yoruba System of Oracular Worship

John Turpin and Judith Gleason

Ifa, teacher of gods, of men, and the means of communication between them, is an oracular worship-and-belief system rooted in the spiritual history of the Yoruba people of south-western Nigeria. Despite social change, consultation of Ifa through its traditionally instructed practitioners continues to be a vital part of Yoruba life. Variants and derivatives of Ifa exist most notably in the Republic of Benin (formerly Dahomey) and in Togo. Across the Atlantic, Cuba became the stronghold of Ifa-in-diaspora, and today hundreds of Ifa priests, trained in Cuba and Africa, are practising throughout the United States.

There are five principal deities or divine beings associated with Ifa. Orunmila is the deity who manifests the spiritual essence of Ifa. Throughout the divination literature of Ifa one finds Orunmila verbally linked to a mysterious spirit or principle known as Ela, 'the preserver'. An indispensable companion of the divination process is Elégba, trickster spirit and messenger, who conveys the necessary offerings and sacrifices for well-being that human beings make, in accordance with oracular prescription, to the ancestors and to the various gods of the Yoruba pantheon. A second crucial companion of the process is Osanyin, divine herbalist and medicinal healer. Olodumare, the Yoruba creator, also known as Olorun, 'owner of the heavens', although out of respect invoked and at times depicted in the sacred verses of Ifa, cannot be said to play an active role in the divination process, even on the sacrificial level of placation; for Olodumare is beyond responding to gifts of food and drink from humans.

The containers of Ifa's wisdom are called Odu, and they can be described in various ways. All practitioners consider the 16 major Odu to be divine personalities in their own right, and there are some practitioners who so conceive the entire group of 256 Odu. Because an extensive and elaborate traditional oral literature is associated with each Odu, they can be thought of as sacred 'books' belonging to a library housed in the collective memory of Ifa priests, who are known as *Babaláwo*, or 'fathers of secrets'. We can also imagine Odu that appear in the process of divination as signatures of prototypical events, apt to occur and recur in a

A divining tray (Opon Ifa) with the face of Eshu, intercessor, guardian and messenger, at the top of the board. This tray is from Ijebu, Nigeria, and has a diameter of 14 inches.

variety of ways in the experience of human beings. At the most tangible level, Odu are graphic figures: a series of 256 octograms resulting from the casting and notation of Ifa's lots.

I I	II II	II II	I I
I I	II II	I I	II II
I I	II II	I I	II II
I I	II II	II II	I I
1	**2**	**3**	**4**
Èjìogbè	Ọ̀yẹ̀kú Méjì	Ìwòrì Méjì	Òdí Méjì

I I	II II	I I	II II
I I	II II	II II	II II
II II	I I	II II	II II
II II	I I	II II	I I
5	**6**	**7**	**8**
Ìrosùn Méjì	Ọ̀wọ́nrín Méjì	Ọ̀bàrà Méjì	Òkànràn Méjì

I I	II II	II II	II II
I I	I I	I I	II II
I I	I I	II II	I I
II II	I I	II II	II II
9	**10**	**11**	**12**
Ògúndá Méjì	Òsá Méjì	Ìká Méjì	Òtúrúpọ̀n Méjì

I I	I I	I I	II II
II II	I I	II II	I I
I I	II II	I I	II II
I I	I I	II II	I I
13	**14**	**15**	**16**
Òtúrá Méjì	Ìrẹtẹ̀ Méjì	Ọ̀sé Méjì	Òfún Méjì

In this diagram the major Odu are listed in their usual ranking order. Each of the 16 configurations taken separately (rather than in a pair, as is the case here) may combine with any of the remaining 15, thus generating 240 more Odu, each with its own core meanings and attendant obligations.

ORIGINS

What is the origin of Ifa? According to myth, Ọrunmila came down to Earth at the beginning of time along with the other divinities, but in a period of great disorder (dramatized by the disrespectful bahaviour of his youngest son) the divinity of oracular wisdom retreated. Later, responsive to universal entreaty, Ọrunmila sent the Odu down to make order among gods and people in his stead.

This emphasis on order and reorganization

Babalorixa Balbino, founder of Ile Ase Opo Aganju (a Yoruba cult house) in Salvador, Brazil, performing a divination in February 1983 with cowrie shells, whose combinations coincide with those of Ifa. The rim of the divining tray is symbolically represented by necklaces of all the Orisha (Yoruba divinities).

may well be a coded way of referring to an incorporation by the earliest Ifa priests of an archaic and indigenous system of cowrie-shell divination known today as Dilogun. Dilogun, which in turn has incorporated much of the Ifa nomenclature and which contains recognizable permutations of many of its paradigmatic stories, continues to be practised widely by priests and priestesses of the various divinities

IFA IN AFRICA AND IN EXILE

Ifa divination originated among the Yoruba people, ten million of whom presently live in south-western Nigeria and parts of the neighbouring republics of Benin (formerly Dahomey) and Togo. Ifa was probably practised in Dahomey as early as the late seventeenth century. During the slave-trading era, Yoruba diviners were carried to Cuba in sufficient numbers to keep the practice alive there. In recent times Cuban Babaláwo in exile have introduced Ifa to the continental United States; and even more recently many African-Americans have been going directly to Nigeria for training. In Nigeria, Cuba and elsewhere in the Caribbean a system of cowrie-shell divination called Dilogun, with cultural and metaphysical links to Ifa, is standard practice. Other forms of cowrie-shell divination, based on a different numerical system, are widespread in West Africa, as is the Islamic method of 'sand cutting'.

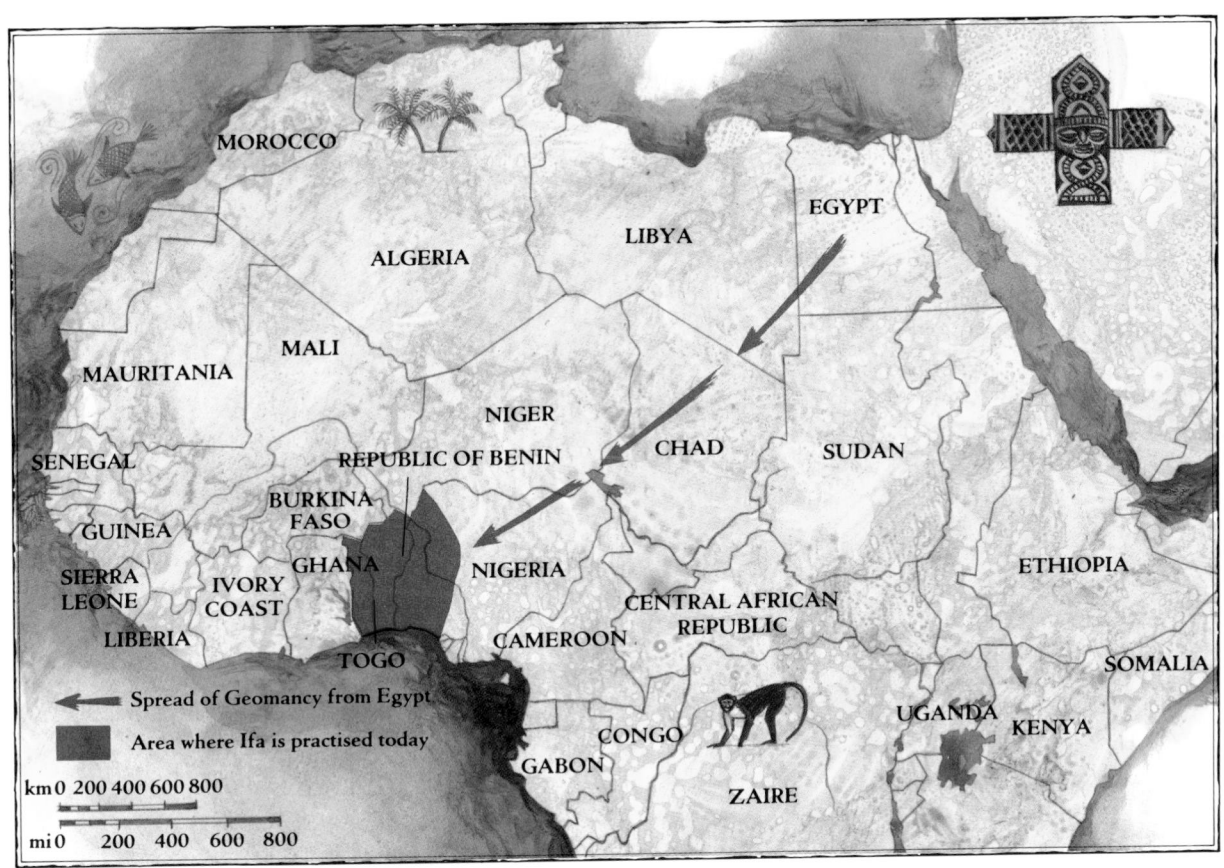

Spread of Geomancy from Egypt

Area where Ifa is practised today

km 0 200 400 600 800

mi 0 200 400 600 800

both in Africa and in the new world. The myth of reorganization by imposition from 'above' of an elaborate geomantic system associated with the masculine *logos* may be supplemented by the traditional attribution of cowrie-shell divination to a feminine divinity, Oshun, from whose mediums every Ifa priest is expected to select a wife. From what we know of the migration of the ancient science of geomancy, it seems that 'above' can also be read as north. The random selection of odd or even remainders to generate 16 signs of four dimensions each is as generic to geomancy as is the writing of these signs upon the face (or simulated surface) of the Earth (see Chapter Twenty-three, Ancient Secrets of the Earth).

Even though Ifa's belief system, value system, procedures and literature are entirely its own, some traces of its probable origins as a divinatory technology remain. Orunmila's name may well be a synthesis of the Yoruba word for 'heaven' (*òrun*) and the Arabic word for 'sand' (*ram'l*); and the name Ifa itself may be derived from the Arabic word for 'omen' (*fa'l*). Those most important of omens, bird pressages, are in Arabic called *iyafa*. Here perhaps we have the kernel of Ifa myths about the original Odu, a goddess, arriving on Earth with 'bird power', a euphemism for witchcraft, which may here be defined as the ability to respond intuitively and effectively to whatever a crisis demands.

AN IFA DIVINATION

The manner in which the Ifa oracle is 'opened' may be described as follows. The Ifa priest will seat himself, facing east, on a mat that has been placed on the ground or on the floor. He will then arrange the divinatory artefacts about him. The tray will be placed directly in front of him near a shallow wooden bowl containing the palm nuts. From a small sealed vessel, stored in the commodious covered bowl, he will take wood dust and sprinkle it onto the tray. Using the middle finger of his right hand, the diviner will draw a line from the top of the tray to the bottom and from right to left. Intersecting at the midpoint, these marks form a cross with equidistant branches. A small bowl of cool water will be placed beside the vessel bearing the palm nuts. Then, taking the divining wand in his right hand, while continuously tapping it lightly against the tray, the *Babaláwo* will begin to recite a series of invocations, one of which is as follows:

Olódùmarè
'Unique and permanent container of Being'
Olòjó oni mo júbà
I give deepest respect to the Owner of this day
Ati waiyé ojo, ìbà
And to the worldly forces existing today, my homage
Ati là òrun, ìbà
And to dawning in the heavens, my homage
Ìbà o loni, ìbà o
Praise be to this day, o praise
Ìbà tó tó tó f'onílè àìye
Infinite praise to our great mother, o earth
Onílè mo júbà
Spirit within the earth, my homage . . . .

Further opening incantations are intended to awaken and propitiate the holy spirit of Ifa, the oracle deity Orunmila, the sacred constellation of all divinities and the spirit of the deified ancestors. The priest then takes the bowl of cool water and sprinkles it over the sacred palm nuts. Lifting them from the vessel one at a time, he

CONTINUED ON PAGE 106

SACRED ARTEFACTS IN IFA DIVINATION

1 Sixteen consecrated palm nuts gathered from a special tree (Elaeis guineensis). Palm nuts chosen for divination have four 'eyes' at their base and therefore 'see' in all cardinal directions.

2 A wooden tray upon which the Odu figures are marked. This tray is usually round, but may be rectangular. Carvings along the rim include a schematic central face (facing the diviner across the board), which represents the presence of Elégba, the messenger, guardian of the crossroads and the trickster or 'uncertainty principle' inherent in the workings of fate. Serpentine markings represent the play of fortune.

3 Wood dust from a certain tree (Baphia nitida) which, having been gnawed by termites, dissolves into a beautiful representation of natural entropy. A pinch of the dust, which has been sprinkled on the divining board and had Odu signs marked upon it, and is considered to be imbued with the transformative power of the oracle, is either touched to the client's forehead or given to him sacramentally to swallow.

4 A divining chain containing eight seed halves (Schrebera golungensis). Although the palm-nut procedure is the more sacred and the one used for special consulations, the divining chain, which is said to 'chatter' faster, is in practice the more common vehicle of Ifa divination. The Ifa priest holds it by the centre string or chain, swings it away from himself and towards the client, then lets it fall upon the mat. The two halves of the chain are read from right to left (from the client's perspective). If a seed falls with its convex surface facing up it receives a notation of two marks ($||$), while a concave surface uppermost receives one ($|$). The 'head' of the Odu is that closest to the centre of the connecting chain.

5 A divining wand, carved either from an elephant's tusk or from a piece of wood shaped like one, which is tapped against the divining tray to invoke the spirit of the oracle.

A detail of the divining wand shows the extended body of a chameleon in the position of an ancestor's beard. The chameleon, associated with the divinity of moral purity and exemplary character, travels slowly but arrives with the redemptive message.

6 An assortment of small symbolic objects of vegetable, animal or mineral substance – tokens used in clarifying the intention of Ifa in particular situations. Of these, a bone (signifying 'no' and, depending on the context, ancestors, death, or children) and two cowrie shells tied together (which means 'yes', as well as money or illness, again depending on the context) are the tokens most actively engaged during consultations.

7 and **8** Carved containers (for the palm nuts, divining chain, small objects and certain sacramental ingredients) in the shape of a covered bowl or sculpted cup on a stem.

9 Although it is not used in the divining process itself, no description of the *Babaláwo*'s paraphernalia would be complete without mention of the diviner's bag, often beautifully beaded, which he wears over his shoulder when he walks out of his own residence. Inside the bag are the essential items of his profession, like the palm nuts and the divining chain, ready for a house-call.

All of these artefacts must be consecrated before use as effective transmitters of oracular energy.

This ritual bowl from Ekiti, Nigeria, might contain the palm nuts of Ifa. The cock is considered to be a messenger of spirits. On the lid a forest cat devours a smaller animal.

calls in succession the names of the 16 primary Odu. Holding the palm nuts in his left hand, he takes one from the 16, touches it to the forehead of the client, and while so doing recites a prayer of affirmation and supplication. Replacing this single palm nut, he utters these final invocatory phrases in order to 'open the way' for the oracular spirit:

Emi ọ̀run sọ̀kalẹ̀ wá
Heaven, descend to us
Wá gbe imu ilẹ̀ yi
Make this house your home
Sọ̀kalẹ̀ pẹ̀lú agbára
Descend with complete power
Wá mi mímọn wá
Come freshness come!

With his right hand the Ifa priest covers the palm nuts held in his left hand. Now with joined hands containing the palm nuts he touches the four cardinal points of the tray, and subsequently with a circular counter-clockwise motion of

Portrait of Dosso Solo, a hunters' diviner, from Lafiabougou quarter, San, Mali, in March 1983. Solo uses 12 rather than 16 cowries and a geomantic 'sand cutting' method whose markings are allied to those of Ifa.

his right hand effaces the crossed lines he had previously marked in the wood dust. As he does so, the priest chants:

Arére. Atótó. Ifá fé fọ ohùn. E dákẹ́.
Silence. Quiet. Ifa wishes to speak.
Let there be silence.

Immediately, with his right hand, the priest attempts to grasp all of the 16 palm nuts from his left hand. If all are in fact grasped, he will make no mark in the dust on the divination tray. He will transfer the nuts back to the left hand and grasp them again. If only one nut remains in his left hand, he will make a double mark ($\|$) in the wood dust. If only two remain, he will make a single mark ($|$). If more than two remain he will begin again. This procedure will continue until a full Odu of eight indices is marked on the tray in the following manner: beginning at the top of the board, the paired markings are made in two columns, first right then left (see diagram on page 102); and as they are written, so they are read – from right to left.

When a person consults Ifa he has a 'presenting problem' which he does not initially tell the diviner, but upon which he focuses by silently declaring its nature to a coin or shell and then placing it on the board. It is a problem – perhaps an important decision to make, or a journey to be embarked upon, perhaps an illness or social maladjustment – which the diviner will assist him in solving in four stages, of which the unfolding of the Odu as described above is the first. By putting the isolated client's case into a generic situational context, the revelation of the appropriate Odu beings preliminary relief, comparable to that felt by a suffering patient experiencing diagnosis of a named and hence intelligible and treatable malady. In effect, Ifa is saying: of the 256 possible windows looking out onto Being, this is the one before which you now stand with a quandary, life crisis, or affliction

The late lamented Araba of Lagos, Chief Fagbemi Ajanaku. Araba means 'Great Spreading Tree' and is the title given to the chief diviner of a city. Ajanaku was also a doctor of traditional medicine. This photograph was taken in 1977.

endemic to this 'place' and under scrutiny of or attack by certain invisible forces, which will have to be placated according to their own individual requirements.

As soon as the Odu is inscribed on the board, its name is pronounced and the Odu is praised in order to activate it. At once the diviner begins to recite texts which are traditionally a part of that particular Odu's canon. These texts include stories in a folkloric vein whose protagonists are always clients (human beings with curious, instructive names; sometimes gods; sometimes animals or natural phenomena, like a pond or a tree; sometimes utensils or other familiar objects) who long ago consulted Ifa for various reasons, and who, depending on whether or not they made the specified sacrifices, were or were not given satisfaction and a bettered or even joyous condition. It is up to the client to identify and listen to the story most pertinent to his own situation.

Having recognized an analogous case, the client then opens his heart to the diviner who now uses the tokens to question Ifa further on the hidden implications of the problem, and thus fine-tune the diagnosis. Conversation with the client also aids in this interpretive phase during which the metaphors of the chosen story-road of the Odu become transparent indications of specific difficulties in the client's attitude and environment.

The *Babaláwo* now specifies the sacrificial ingredients called for by the Odu at hand. Most of these are food substances. Should the client's situation indeed be serious, perhaps more so than he realized, a fowl or four-footed animal might have to lose its life in order to preserve his or that of a family member. Often symbolic items like a cloth of a certain colour are specified. The sooner the offerings are made to the appropriate spiritual forces, the better. Should the client refuse or neglect the obligation, there is nothing more the diviner-priest can do. But as soon as he complies, then a herbal remedy is concocted from leaves or roots associated with the particular Odu and given to the client either to drink or to bathe with.

Thus are resistances clogging the flow between inner self ('head' in Yoruba parlance), behavioural self (social harmony being essential in Yoruba context) and the invisible world temporarily dissipated. The slow-working part of the cure is the paradigmatic story chosen by the client himself from the many recited by the diviner, a story accompanied by a song or chant which enables him to remember and to reflect upon his situation as mirrored in Ifa's indispensable wisdom.

Integral to an understanding of Ifa are the interconnected Yoruba notions of 'head' and destiny. In short, the Yoruba believe that one chooses one's 'head' or inner personality before birth, and this head implies a certain path, including fortune or misfortune, in life. It is possible to consult the oracle and be given an Odu-symbol of one's character and fate combined. By consistent consultation of Ifa and scrupulous observation of obligations to one's 'head-ruling' deity and to one's ancestors, as well as dutiful following of all other truly inspired (as opposed to quack) advice, even a problematic head can get itself together and provide its bodily owner with a satisfactory earthly existence this time around. Consultation on behalf of a new-born baby can get it properly orientated so far as the visible and invisible worlds are concerned. For example, perhaps a certain ancestor has chosen to come back into the world through the medium of this new-born baby, who should be named accordingly. Or perhaps a certain divinity has chosen the child as its putative worshipper. Although various Odu turn up during a life-long series of consultations, one is born under a certain constellation of forces and it is important that this natal Odu be known, and that its idiosyncratic dietary and behavioural prescriptions be observed as soon as possible. Furthermore, certain temperamental characteristics, appropriate to those born under particular Odu-patterns, are better respected, even indulged, at the onset of life rather than retrospectively, after a degree of parental or societal violence may already have been done to the young person's nature.

THE AMERICAS

The difficulties involved in attempting to describe the divinatory methods of the Native Americans are immediately apparent when one considers that there were, until the coming of white people, over 600 separate tribes, each with their own cultural variations. There are still some 487 recognized tribal groups; but among these perhaps only two per cent of the people still carry 'medicine', retaining the old ways which have been stamped out by years of persecution and re-education.

The Native American way of life is based upon a deep relationship to the natural world. As Jamie Sams has remarked, *everything* in the world of the Great Mystery has a story to tell, and it is by observing it that one becomes aware of trends and movements within the pattern of being. Thus the story of divination in North America is at the same time superbly simple and endlessly complex, just as the patterns of the created world are both simple and complex.

Above all, it is the recognition of the interrelatedness of all things and all beings, and of their divine origin, which marks out the Native American tradition and enables those who follow its ways to utilize the signs and languages of the natural world to divine their place in the scheme of the Great Mystery. The beings who inhabit the natural world are themselves sacred, so, in accordance with Native tradition, we have capitalized their names to show that they are Sacred Beings and not simply stones, animals or things.

There are clear echoes here of the old native spiritual traditions of Europe and the Far North, just as there are powerful connections to the traditions of Australia and New Zealand. All these cultural groups share a belief in the sacredness of all things and in the close observation of natural trends as a means of discovering the answers to ages old questions of meaning and progress.

In ancient Mesoamerica (today's Mexico and Central America), a more complex and formalized set of traditions took shape. Careful observations of star patterns and influences by the Mayan, Aztec, Toltec, Zapotec and Mixtec peoples evolved into an intricate astrological and divinatory calendric system that has been kept alive for more than 2,000 years in oral tradition, despite, as in the case of the northern Amerindian world, efforts to suppress or destroy all traces of the native way of life. (In the South, where the great culture was that of the Incas, a more limited form of divination – by animal entrails – flourished, similar to that practised in the classical world – see Chapter Seven).

In the Mesoamerican astro-calendar we may see links with both Tarot (Chapter Five) and astrology (Chapter Six), as well as with the runic alphabets of the Celts and the Norse (Chapters Three and Four). Similarly, in the method of counting out beans or crystals, we are reminded both of the bone oracles of Africa (Chapter Eleven) and of the techniques of geomancy (Chapter Twenty-three).

CHAPTER THIRTEEN

SACRED MEDICINE

Native North-American Divination Systems

Jamie Sams

From the earliest rememberings of our oral traditions until modern times, Native American people have looked to the Earth Mother and Nature for signs, portents, omens and guidance. Our systems of divination have always been more a way of life than a philosophy or religion. The Red Race, which can be defined as the indigenous people of the Americas, has been given the guardianship of Natural Law and the Medicines of Earth, Medicines meaning the strengths, talents and healing ways of being that humankind could find in the natural world. These Medicines would allow the Original People (human beings) to learn how to survive and how to grow spiritually in physical bodies. It was up to our Elders to see that these teachings were passed from generation to generation so that human Two-leggeds would know how to walk on the Earth in beauty and balance, being in harmony with all living things. We have always considered all life-forms on our Mother Planet to be our relatives and our equals. For centuries, we have sought to learn the languages of every life-form in order to know how to live life on Earth with gratitude for all the lessons each teacher in Nature brings.

Native American divination covers the whole of North, Central and South America. The North American continent alone has over 487 recognized Tribes, and although each Tribe has its own separate Tradition, many common practices link each Nation or Tribe with the others. The common threads that are found in every Tribe are the links to the Great Mystery (the Creator), the Earth Mother, Father Sky,

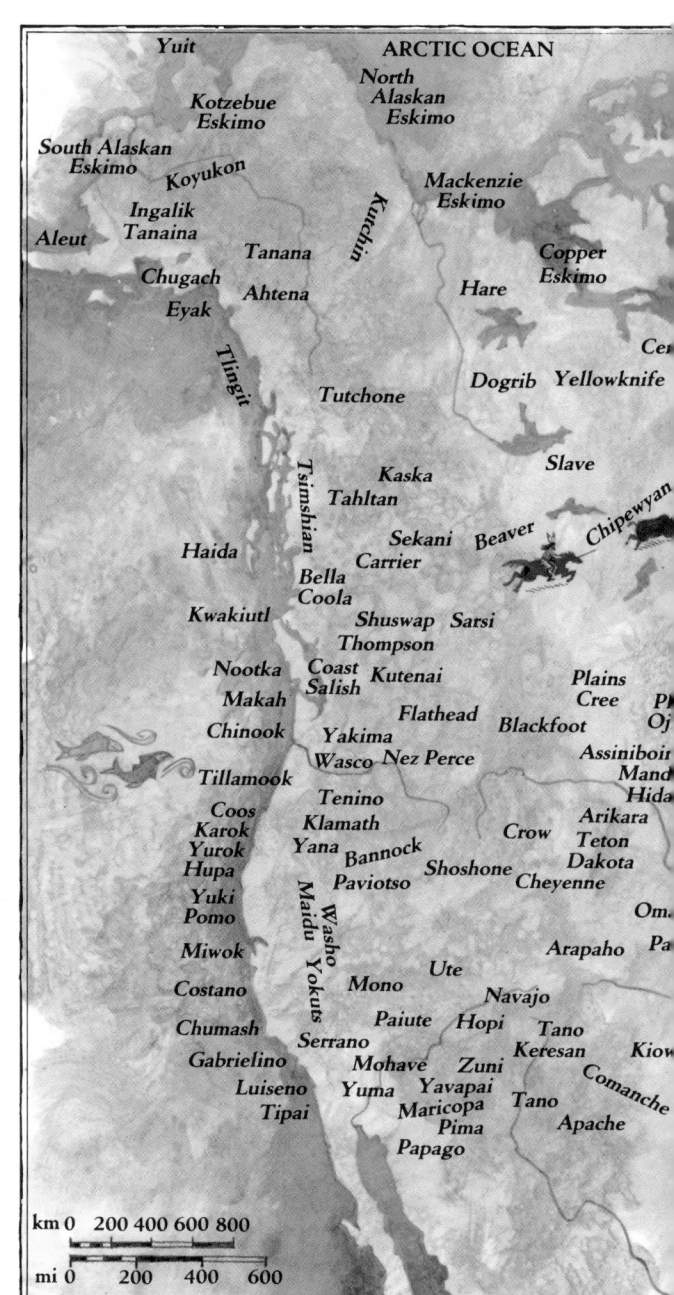

Grandfather Sun, Grandmother Moon and all of Nature. Although some Tribes assign the Sun, Moon and Sky to different identities – early Cherokee teachings spoke of Grandmother Sun and Grandfather Moon – the meaning is the same, and the only thing that is different is the relationship with the human being.

In my training, my Elders have taught me that we are here to walk the Earth in order to bring our spiritual natures into alignment with our physical bodies. We do this by manifesting the Great Mystery's Eternal Flame of Love through our thoughts and actions on the physical plane. This is Divine balance and requires many lessons to be learned. How we learn those lessons depends upon how we see and honour the Sacredness of all life. To accomplish this goal of Sacredness in our lives we must follow a Sacred Path, also called the Beauty Way.

In my Tradition, we believe that sometimes the Great Mystery can be a Divine Trickster and that the joke is how we humans are tricked into growing, learning and evolving. Since Divine and divination have the same root word, it is easy to see how everything the Great Mystery created can be a blueprint or map for human beings to use for growth. We believe that all humans have the same mission in their Earthwalks (physical life). This mission is for each individual to discover his or her gifts, talents and abilities, then to develop those gifts fully and share them with humanity in order to aid the whole of Creation. Our systems of divination are based upon teaching human beings how to understand those lessons of spiritual growth. Unlike many other systems of divination, which point the seeker to romance, success, fame or impending doom, the Native American culture holds a Sacred Point of View, using the signs and languages of Nature to point the way to 'right relationship' with self, family, Nation, Clan, Tribe, Nature and the Great Mystery. Everything else is merely an illusion.

The Dreamtime is the parallel reality or Spirit World where all the tangible, breakable, physical things of life can be stripped away until only the essence remains. We believe that this essence is the Eternal Flame of Love. It is in the Dreamtime that we can see beyond the illusions

TRIBAL LANDS OF THE NATIVE PEOPLE
This map shows the original homelands that were given to the Indian Tribes of North America by the Great Mystery. Each Tribe was given the guardianship of the Earth Mother in their location, in order to preserve the abundance of life for as long as the grass grew, the rivers flowed and the sun shone. Most Tribes were relocated during the Trail of Tears in the 1870s.

and into our essence, which is total connection to all things, bonded with the glue of Great Mystery's fire. To get to the Dreamtime or beyond physical illusion, we use the maps of Nature, the call of our Ancestors' voices, the languages of the trees and stones, and the lessons of the Creature-teachers. We believe that all things that have ever existed in a location are still in that location. The only thing that separates us from those realities is a thin membrane which is composed of our illusory concept of time. In using the lessons of Nature and the guidance provided by those Allies (Allies being any force or living thing in Nature which can teach us), we can come into spiritual balance and bridge the abyss of illusion. When we move into the Oneness of all things, the eternal truths of the world of Spirit and the world of physicality are blended and made known to us.

ANIMAL MEDICINE

Animals are our Creature-teachers and protective spirits. They carry certain strengths which we call Medicines. These Medicines comprise the talents, abilities and instincts that each Totem (Power Animal) embodies. These gifts can assist humans in learning how to live in the physical world. Since Native Americans honour the fact that we are spiritual beings, housed in human bodies, and that we are born into physical life to learn about being human, it is logical that our Creature counterparts should be our teachers. The Totems are a reflection of our animal nature or physicalness, just as the Great Mystery is the Source of our spiritual beings.

In the times of our Ancestors, Native people would walk through the woodlands and observe the Creatures in order to gain the knowledge they needed to survive. If the Birds ate a certain berry, it was okay for human consumption. If the Creatures could drink from a stream, it was pure enough for the Two-leggeds to drink. Sometimes an albino animal would appear in a dream and would be the Spirit Totem for the human Dreamer. Other times, an animal would come to a Two-legged human in a way that was out of

the ordinary, such as an Eagle circling the person five times and then alighting a few feet away without fear and looking into the person's eyes for a moment before flying away. These signs, found through dreams or unusual experiences, were sure messages that the Creature in question was allying itself to a human being in order to teach or to protect that person during his or her Earthwalk (lifetime).

Some examples of the Medicines of the Creature-teachers are: Buffalo – Bringer of abundance; Lynx – Knower of Secrets; Rabbit –

The Rainbow Lizard is the Power Animal who is the Guardian of the Whirling Rainbow Dream Prophecy of the North American Indians. This prophecy came from divining the visions found in the Dreamtime that spoke of the Fifth World of Peace, uniting all races and life-forms on our planet as one.

This standing stone represents the Medicine Woman who is covered in her blanket, looking toward the mountains. The sun shines on the back of her head and shoulders, warming the silent guardian who watches and waits while the women in the Tipi journey into the Dreamtime seeking visions.

Ability to confront fear, bringer of fertility and teacher of how to listen; Deer – Gentleness; and Raven – Teacher of how to use Magic. There are as many Totem Medicines as there species of wildlife on our planet and in our oceans.

Since all life-forms have strengths and challenges, so do the Medicines of animals. For instance, Buffalo is abundance and the challenge is fear of scarcity. There is no bad Medicine, only the challenges which hone the skills each Medicine brings. If we heal our fear of scarcity, we will open to the abundance the Great Mystery brings. The Medicine of each animal therefore has both a dignified and a contrary meaning. Human beings tend to learn through opposites and, since both sides of any question are always present, we have to see the challenges as well as the solutions to learning life's lessons. When, in our human stubbornness, we see life from only one viewpoint, we limit our capacity to find alternatives. Our Creature-teachers have the mission of bringing new and non-threatening viewpoints into our lives in order to enrich our human experience. (See Appendix, Modern Restatements, on pages 211–12, for more information about the Medicine of animals in the *Medicine Cards* and for a full description of the *Sacred Path Cards*.)

THE BEAUTY WAY

The rituals, ceremonies, Traditions and teachings have been gleaned by our Native American Ancestors from centuries of living in harmony with the Earth Mother. All of these Knowing Systems (traditions of wisdom) hold meanings that suggest and instruct, but do not ever force anyone to follow another human being. We use the symbols of Nature in order to enlighten each individual so that each person makes their own decisions. Our understanding is that the Spirit World and the Great Mystery

These typical Indian items include: (top) antique Medicine Bowl used to brew herbal remedies, (bottom right to left) Papago basket filled with Medicine objects (stones and animal hide), Isleta Pueblo pottery vase, Ute Medicine Pouch painted with a Buffalo skull, and a one-sided drum used for healing.

This Seneca mask is a Traditional Harvest Mask used in ceremony to return thanks to the Creator for the abundance of crops harvested. It is woven of corn husks and sports a corn-cob nose, reminding the Indian People that being grateful for the blessings received is a philosophy that will 'grow corn'.

This Sweat Lodge Altar is made of a tree stump with the Sacred Hoop painted around a Turtle, symbolizing the Earth Mother. The Sacred Healing Rattles on the Altar are (right to left): Cherokee Turtle Rattle, Seneca Horn Rattle, Yaqui Gourd Rattle and Lakota Rawhide Buffalo Rattle. The petroglyph stones are copies of the Sacred Petroglyphs found on mountains, containing the picto-history of the Red Race.

This Huichole Tribal mask is made by pressing each seed bead into the thin coat of beeswax that covers the carved wooden face. The deity, Mescal, is the spirit of the Peyote plant. The Huicholes and their practice of Peyote Ceremonies gave birth to the Native American Church in North America after the Trail of Tears in the 1870s. Peyote is used along with deep prayer to enter the Dreamtime.

work with each person individually, using unique methods of applying spirit to physical life. The decisions made in a person's life are therefore between that person and the Creative Source and bring the rewards as well as the more difficult personal lessons.

If a human being has lost connection to the Great Mystery or the Earth Mother it is a tragic event because that person is no longer connected to the Pathway of Beauty. In this instance it is easy for humans to lose faith, reasoning abilities and intuitive gifts and then to follow a crooked trail. Our Native American way of life not only provides ceremonies that will assist a person in reconnecting with the Creator and All Our Relations, but also gives every person the right to return to the Beauty Way. The Beauty Way is a way of being that never puts anything outside the self. If we are connected to the other members of the Planetary Family such as the Stone People and Plant People, we are never alone. All Native American people see everything as being alive and having spirit and consciousness. Because of this knowing, every living creature in the Planetary Family is a relative of the Original People, the human beings. Our brothers and sisters in the animal kingdom and our relations such as the Cloud People will hear our hearts through *Hail-oh-way-ain*, the language of love, and send us the omens and signs we need in order to reclaim our love of living life and return to the Sacred Path.

Every part of Nature has a language that can point out the signposts which will keep us on a Path of Beauty. The language of the Stones, for example, can be found etched on the faces of the Stone People all over our Earth. Anyone can pick up a Stone and examine the symbols or marks that occur naturally there in order to find what that Stone Person can teach. The markings also show the natural talents of the human who found the Stone Person, even if the seeker has hidden those talents from him or herself.

For instance, a straight vertical line on a Stone means the power of Spirit to conquer all challenges found in the material world. Two arrows crossing and forming an X with the arrowheads pointing up represents the power of mutual respect and friendship. A square represents firm foundations and organizational abilities. A diamond shape represents life, unity and equality for eternity, as well as freedom from fear. The diamond shape also denotes that the seeker has the protection of the Four Winds and is protected in every direction he or she may travel in life. (For more information about the Stone People, see *Other Council Fires Were Here Before Ours* by Jamie Sams and Twylah Nitsch.)

THE MEDICINE WHEEL

All 487 Traditions and Tribes in North America have their own Medicine Wheels and their own significances for the directions, but overall they are very similar. On the Seneca Medicine Wheel (opposite) there are 12 directions laid out like the face of a clock. Each direction has a colour, a Cycle of Truth and a birth month, and represents a pathway any human being may follow to find inner peace, as well as a way to become a peacemaker for the world. This Medicine Wheel can also act as a map or dictionary which will allow a person to understand the languages of the Plant People, the Stone People, the Creature-beings and the elements of Nature, as well as the Medicine objects that Nature gives to each person who asks for assistance.

Each direction has a set of lessons and teaches something about understanding truth more fully. If we draw a line from any position on the wheel to the position directly opposite, we find a Pathway to inner Peace. These Pathways of Peace are the reflections we each receive from life. When we learn any set of lessons represented by one direction on the wheel and then learn the lessons of the opposite direction, we can heal any inner conflict which would keep us from being our personal best. When we find an object in Nature which sends us its message through the colour it carries, we are given the opportunity to find the answer we need for our personal growth.

Each colour on the wheel is a key to the Medicine or gifts, talents and abilities the found

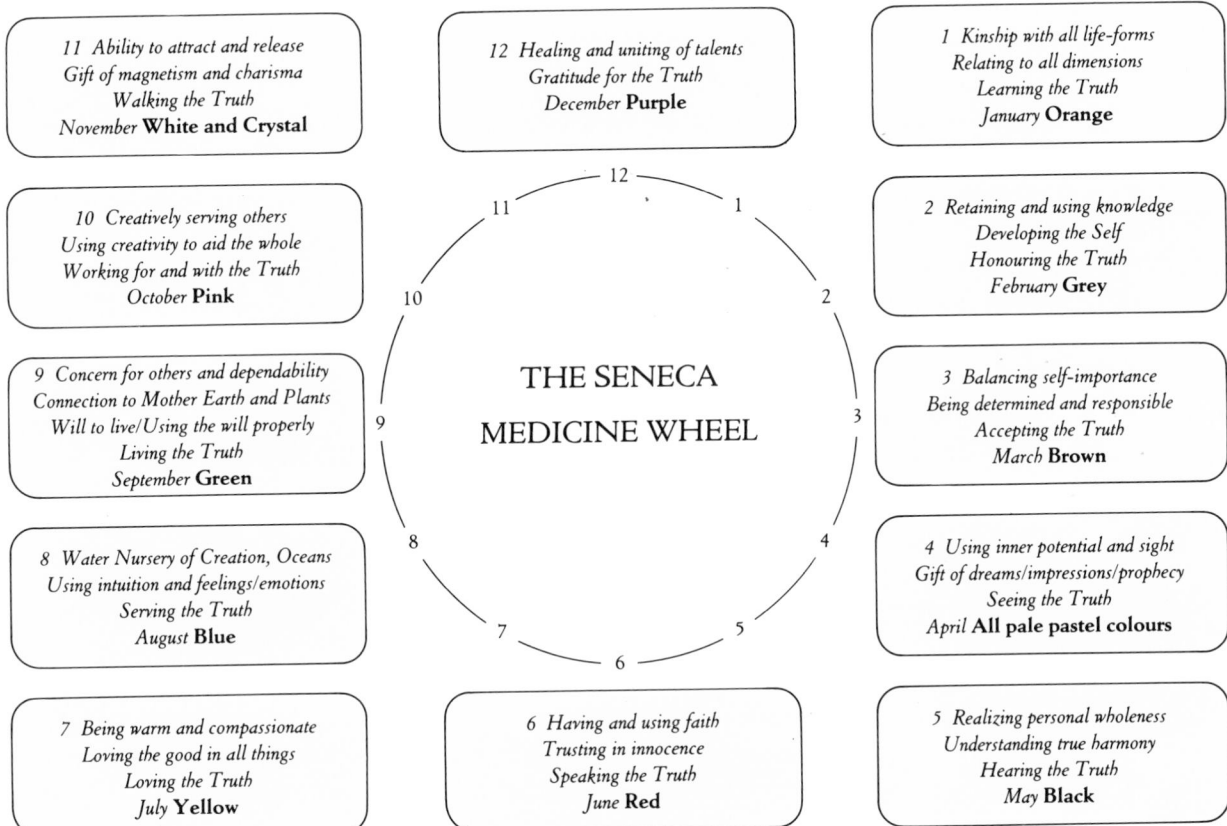

11 Ability to attract and release
Gift of magnetism and charisma
Walking the Truth
November **White and Crystal**

12 Healing and uniting of talents
Gratitude for the Truth
December **Purple**

1 Kinship with all life-forms
Relating to all dimensions
Learning the Truth
January **Orange**

10 Creatively serving others
Using creativity to aid the whole
Working for and with the Truth
October **Pink**

2 Retaining and using knowledge
Developing the Self
Honouring the Truth
February **Grey**

9 Concern for others and dependability
Connection to Mother Earth and Plants
Will to live/Using the will properly
Living the Truth
September **Green**

3 Balancing self-importance
Being determined and responsible
Accepting the Truth
March **Brown**

8 Water Nursery of Creation, Oceans
Using intuition and feelings/emotions
Serving the Truth
August **Blue**

4 Using inner potential and sight
Gift of dreams/impressions/prophecy
Seeing the Truth
April **All pale pastel colours**

7 Being warm and compassionate
Loving the good in all things
Loving the Truth
July **Yellow**

6 Having and using faith
Trusting in innocence
Speaking the Truth
June **Red**

5 Realizing personal wholeness
Understanding true harmony
Hearing the Truth
May **Black**

THE SENECA
MEDICINE WHEEL

object carries. In this manner, anyone can go into Nature and find a feather, a stone, a shell, a leaf, a seed or a piece of bark that could provide an answer or direction to aid that person in making sense of any given situation. Actual in-depth teachings or messages might be felt or heard if the seeker used his or her intuition to sit in silence with the found object and listen. This highly evolved sense of perception is normally developed over many years through specific training as a Seer or Dreamer and is not usually accomplished overnight. The basics of how to interpret the general lessons are, however, easily understood simply by looking at the colours in the found object and then finding the colour on this chart.

If, for instance, a person came upon a stone with a green colour to it (position 9), the stone could teach the proper use of the will and how to increase the life force or will to live. The stone could also teach the person how to Live the Truth, which is that direction's Cycle of Truth. The month is September and so this stone could

be particularly helpful for someone born in that month. The Pathway of Peace that this stone would teach begins at September and goes straight across the wheel to March, which represents Accepting the Truth. Therefore, the Pathway of Peace for the person finding a green stone would be organizing their life so that accepting and living their personal truth can be easily accomplished.

If a person went for a walk by the sea and was looking for some direction or clarity and asked the Allies of nature for assistance, the permission to help the seeker would be given and the door to discovery would be open. In a sacred manner, the asking gives permission to Nature's Allies, whom we know to be the helpers of the Great Mystery and the Earth Mother. Let us imagine that this person then came upon an unusual shell that was on his or her path. The person would then give thanks for the sign and give an offering to the Earth in the place where the shell was found. This offering is traditionally tobacco in our Native teachings, but could be a lock of the seeker's hair, cornmeal, corn pollen, saliva or some other object that was special to the seeker. Before removing the shell, the seeker would ask if the shell wanted to be moved from its Sacred Space on the beach in order to go home with the human being. If the person then felt uncomfortable or ill at ease, the shell has said no. If the answer was yes, the person would feel good about removing the shell.

The colours of the shell could be located on the Seneca Wheel and the general lessons understood. If the shell did not wish to be removed but was willing to give the lessons needed, the person could sit in that location and examine the shell, see its colours and look up the

Jamie Sams' grandmother, Twylah Nitsch, seen here in beaded ceremonial garments, is a Seneca elder of the Wolf Clan Teaching Lodge.

connections and lessons upon arriving home. This simple method of observing the obvious becomes quite easy once a person learns the wheel and applies that wisdom to anything that crosses his or her path. This is one basic form of using the elements of nature as an oracle, which has been used in different forms by my people for centuries.

Our Native American systems of divination are as countless as there are parts to Creation. Each language from some part of our natural world represents a relationship we, Two-legged humans, have to Nature. I cannot be a spokesperson for the whole Red Race, but I can speak from my Sacred Point of View and share the lessons which have been handed down to me. Every Tribe and Nation has its own system of divining or understanding the Creatures and other Relations of our Earth Mother. To cover even one Tradition in depth would overwhelm most non-Native people. Our understandings, our oral traditions and our wisdom of Earth Medicine is 160,000 years older than any written history on this planet and begins approximately 220,000 years before most events recorded in the Old Testament of the Judaeo-Christian religious tradition.

My Elders have taught me that the most Sacred of all our ceremonies is the Give-away. This rite teaches us how to give from the heart with no strings attached. I know from experience that the wisdom is to be shared, to be given away, or those Traditions will die with the last person who was a Guardian of 'the remembering'. It is in this spirit that I share the rich legacy which has been passed to me and I trust that those who learn these languages of our Relations will, in turn, share this wisdom so that all races may learn the Medicines that will heal the hearts of humankind and bring full understanding and peace to our planet.

The understanding of the languages of All Our Relations – animal, plant, stone, shell – or Clan Chiefs of Air, Earth, Water and Fire is no small subject, but I am happy to have been able to share a small part of these Knowing Systems with the readers of *The World Atlas of Divination*.

CHAPTER FOURTEEN

SUN, TIME AND SYMBOLISM

Astrological Divination in Ancient Mesoamerica

Bruce Scofield

Around the time of the early Greeks, and possibly even earlier, an astrological divinatory calendar originated in Mesoamerica, today's Mexico and northern Central America. Later, during the rise and fall of the Maya, the cycle was elaborated upon and perpetuated. When the Spanish arrived in the early sixteenth century, they found a culture that was deeply enmeshed in these same concepts, then perhaps 2,000 or more years old. Today, in the remote Maya villages of rural Guatemala and Mexico, an oral tradition persists in keeping the ancient knowledge alive, albeit in altered and somewhat simplified form. After two and a half millennia, the rise and fall of numerous empires, and constant efforts on the part of Christians to eliminate it, the 260-day astrological divinatory calendar still lives.

TIME: THE BUILDING BLOCK OF REALITY

In Mesoamerica, astrology and divination were linked intimately. At the core of both activities was a cycle of 20 named days. Beginning with a day called Alligator, and ending with one called Flower, the 20 days symbolized various stages of life, much like the 22 Major Arcana cards of the Tarot or the Runes. Because the four directions (north, south, east, west) and their symbolism is so closely woven into the cycle, it might be said that the 20 days are really five cycles of the four directions. Because this cycle was a calendar of sorts, every birth occurs during the influence of one of the days. In this sense, the system is astrological. However, like the Tarot, Runes or

I Ching, the symbolism of the cycle was also utilized as a divinatory system.

An interesting comparison might be made to the Near Eastern seven-day week in use throughout the world today. Our week is actually a remnant of a kind of time-based astrology. The original astrological meanings and usage of the seven-day week have faded during modern times, but the planetary names of the days in the Latin languages points towards an earlier astrological use. During much of Western history, human births and the fate of the new year were judged according to the day of the week they fell on. Today, only a nursery rhyme survives that offers an astrological interpretation for a child born on each day of the week. But the point here is that our seven-day week and the Mesoamerican 20-day count were both attempts to pin symbolic meanings on a cycle of days. In essence both are sets of signs based on time, not space.

The 20 named days are only part of a much bigger picture. A second cycle of 13 days must be added to understand even the rudiments of the system. Just as one day is a sign in the Mesoamerican tradition, so also is a period of 13 days. In fact, the 13-day period or count was probably the most-used astrological framework for interpretation of sky-events, in the same way that the Babylonian zodiac is used by Western astrologers. Now consider the following. Thirteen cycles of 20 days is equal to 20 cycles of 13 days. This permutation takes a total of 260 days and this number is the key to the system. The combined 13- and 20-day cycles are considered

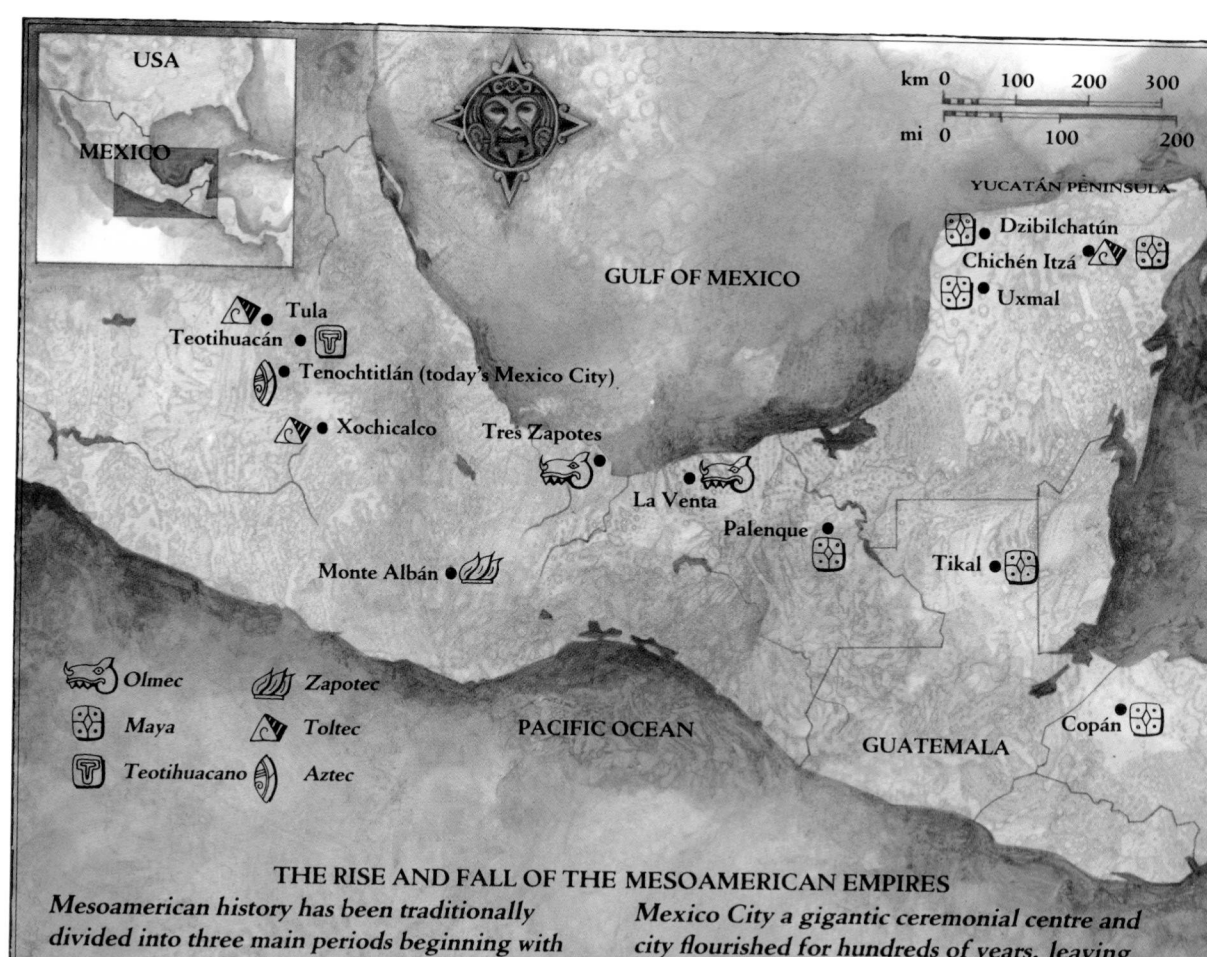

THE RISE AND FALL OF THE MESOAMERICAN EMPIRES

Mesoamerican history has been traditionally divided into three main periods beginning with what is called the Preclassic or Formative Period. Although this period began around 1800 BC, fully fledged civilization made its first appearance about 1,000 years later along the eastern coast of Mexico. A culture later called Olmec thrived during these times and left behind ceremonial centres, pyramids and remarkably sophisticated sculpture. It was from them that the first symbolic writing and the first notions of the 260-day calendar arose.

The Classic Period, dating from roughly 200 BC to AD 900, saw the flowering of Mesoamerican culture in two different areas. In the Guatamalan south and Mexico's Yucatan Peninsula the Maya built dramatic ceremonial centers, many of which stand today and are a mecca for tourists to the region. It was the Maya who developed the 260-day count into a complex astrological-numerological master key to the universe, though only tantalizing fragments of these ideas survived massive book-burnings by Spanish friars.

Approximately contemporary with the Maya was the culture of Teotihuacan. Near present-day Mexico City a gigantic ceremonial centre and city flourished for hundreds of years, leaving behind two huge pyramids and miles of ancient walls, buildings and roadways. Its influence was felt well into the Maya world. Midway between the Maya and the city of Teotihuacan was Monte Alban, the site of Zapotec culture, which in many ways stood on its own terms. Sometime around AD 750 Teotihuacan burned and was abandoned. Not long afterwards the latest Maya centres in Yucatan collapsed. It was during the Classic Period that the worship of the god Quetzalcoatl (feathered serpent), believed to be the creator of the 260-day count, became established.

The Postclassic Period began around AD 900 with a renaissance of both Classic cultures. In the region around Mexico City the Toltecs built a capital at Tula and then began a period of empire building. Their reach extended to the old Maya city of Chichen Itza, stimulating a resurgence of Maya culture. Last came the Aztecs, who built their capital city on the site of today's Mexico City. Like their predecessors, the Toltecs, they were empire builders and carriers, not creators, of a more ancient culture.

the internal parts of the 260-day astrological divinatory calendar of ancient Mesoamerica. But these figures are more than just a count of days, they are also the master numbers for an intellectual and religious tradition that probably saw number as the key to everything.

Four, 13, 20 and 260 – these are the building blocks of reality as it was mapped in Mesoamerica. These ideas appear to be based on both astronomical and biological facts. Four probably comes from the naming of the four directions, and these are defined by the movements of the Sun at the horizon as it is observed throughout the seasonal year. The Sun in its daily movement across the sky creates the day. The day is the corner-stone, or primary measure, of time itself. For the Maya, day, Sun and time were one and the same and one word, *kin*, was used for all three. It is an interesting fact that it takes the Sun about 13 days to cover the same space as the Moon does in one day. A nine-month human gestation is nine cycles of Moon and Sun or about 266 days, a figure very close to 260 days. The planet Venus averages about 263 days for its appearances as morning and evening star. If one uses the fingers and toes for counting, than a count of 20 becomes basic. Other astronomical and numerological explanations have been offered to explain the origination of the key components of the Mesoamerican system, but none has emerged uncontested and universally accepted. Exactly how the 260-day count came to be is still a mystery.

DIVINING BY THE DAY-SIGNS

In ancient times the 260-day astrological calendar was utilized in the timing of political and religious events, and also in the interpretation of one's fate, thought to be sealed at birth. The Maya word for the 260-day count was *tzolkin*, the Aztec *Tonalpouhalli*. Functioning like an ephemeris, a book called *tonalamatl*, or 'book of fate', was referred to by priests and practitioners of astrology and divination. In the case of a birth, parents would take their new-born child to a *tonalpoulque* (reader) to find out what *tonalli* (day-sign) influenced their child. After the

Spanish conquest, the Christian friars strove to destroy this tradition and in order to do so they recorded some details of it so that future friars would know what to look for. Some of this material survives, and although it came to the friars third hand and years after the conquest, it does reveal much about the importance of the 260-day astrological calendar in Aztec society.

The 260-day count was also a master divination device much like the *I Ching*. With its 20 key symbols and 13 variants of each, a total of 260 answers for a question were possible. It is not known exactly how divinations were conducted during pre-Columbian times, but much is known about the tradition as it survives today. The Quiche Maya who live in remote sections of Guatemala have a tradition of shamans or 'day-keepers' who pass on knowledge of the 260-day count orally. They provide a useful service to the community by determining times for rituals and handling personal problems for individuals. Divinations are done with crystals, beans and their memory of the calendar. The procedure is roughly as follows. After the question has been asked, the day-keeper grabs a handful of beans and crystals from a bag and

Discovered in 1790 beneath a street in Mexico City, the Aztec calendar stone has become a symbol of Mexico itself. It is actually a sophisticated cosmogram depicting the cycles of the ages. Five creation cycles occupy the centre, with the fifth and current cycle encompassing the other four. Around this centre is a ring containing the 20 day-signs.

In recent years, scholars have learned to read the complex Mayan hieroglyphs that tell the dynastic histories of ancient empires. This is a detail of a door lintel, part of the 'hieroglyphic stairway' at Naranjo, Guatemala.

lays them on a table. These are sorted into piles of four until they are exhausted. The last pile is critical. If there are two or four beans, then a divination is possible, if one or three, the divination is abandoned. If a reading is possible, then the number of piles are counted and added to the current day-sign in effect. For example, if there are 45 piles, then the day-sign 45 days ahead of the present day is used as the symbol for interpretation. Readings often involve repeating this process several times.

The notions about the 20 day-signs recorded by the Spanish friars leave much to be desired. They are sparse in most cases and extremist in others, a reflection of the Aztec world in shambles after the conquest. The meanings of the day-signs according to contemporary Quiche Maya day-keepers are likewise limited and reflect the realities of their present-day existence. Then there is the problem of correlating the Mesoamerican calendar with the Christian one, a problem that archaeoastronomers and archaeologists have struggled with for decades. I have spent a number of years attempting to put the 20 core symbols on a solid footing without distorting the system. I have taken a pragmatic approach, one that utilizes every available source of information, but emphasizes usefulness, not just idealistic symmetry. A consensus is emerging among a number of astrologers who have examined the results of this reconstruction that supports the definitions and meanings presented.

THE WHEELS OF TIME

The cycles of 13 and 20 days combined to produce the master unit of 260 days. But the Mesoamerican effort to unify time, number and nature did not end there. Because the 260-day count was symbolic and not tied to the seasons, it could not be used as a civil calendar, so one of 365 days was used for that purpose. However, after 52 years of 365 days, there would be

This corpulent shaman, from Mexico around 200 BC, is apparently reaching into his bag of beans and crystals to do a divination.

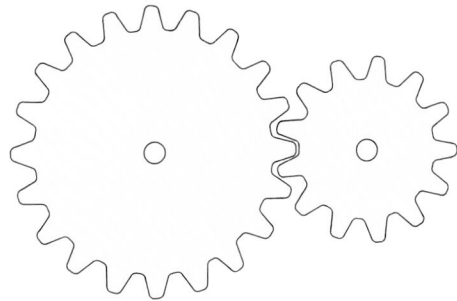

Teotihuacán covered an area of 8 square miles. Ahead, the 'street of the Dead' extends for 2 miles, passing in front of the 'Pyramid of the Sun', one of several large monuments precisely aligned in both an astronomical and a geomantic sense.

In the Mesoamerican concept of time, 13 cycles of 20 days is equivalent to 20 cycles of 13 days: in 260 days the day-signs coincide and the cycle begins again.

exactly 73 cycles of 260 days and the two counts would combine. This figure, 52 years, was the length of a Mesoamerican 'century' and important renewal rituals were held at the start of each new cycle. The planet Venus has a cycle of 584 days, which happens to dovetail with the 365-day year in the ratio 5:8. After 104 years (2 × 52), the Venus year, the 365-day year and the 260-day year meet precisely. The numerological aspects of these interrelationships are truly astonishing.

The Maya developed a type of mundane astrology that was the 260-day count writ large. A count of 7,200 days called a *katun*, a figure that closely approximates the cycle of Jupiter and Saturn (i.e the time between their conjunctions), was the corner-stone of a creation epoch of 5,125 years. Within this period cycled 20 groups of 13 *katuns* and 13 groups of 20 *katuns* called *baktuns*. Five creation cycles very nearly equals the length of the Earth's precessional cycle, a cycle of approximately 25,700 years that is caused by a wobbling of the Earth's pole which Westerners divide into twelfths and call the astrological ages. Interestingly, the latest creation cycle of the Maya is to end in the year 2012, and in 1993 the 260th and last of the *katuns* will begin.

THE 20 DAY-SIGNS OR *TONALLI*

The astrological attributions of the 20 day-signs below were derived from a sampling of 400 persons and an analysis of the surviving ancient sources. The calendar correlation recommended is that of Goodman–Martinez–Thompson, the most respected among scholars and still in use in remote villages. The day 1–Alligator correlates with 9 August 1992.

In ancient times the 260-day astrological calendar began with the sign 1–Alligator. The next sign was 2–Wind. Then came 3–House, 4–Lizard, 5–Serpent, 6–Death, 7–Deer, 8–Rabbit, 9–Water, 10–Dog, 11–Monkey, 12–Grass and 13–Reed. The next sign, 1–Ocelot, started the 13–day cycle over again and was followed by 2–Eagle, 3–Vulture, 4–Earthquake, 5–Knife, 6–Rain, and 7–Flower, thus completing the 20 named days. It was 8–Alligator, the first of the signs, that came next. In essence then, both the sign Alligator and any sign linked with the number 1 (as in 1–Ocelot, above, for example) function as the head of a sequence. Only once every 260 days does 1–Alligator come up.

Alligator
(Maya = *Imix*, Aztec = *Cipactli*)

Direction: East
Divination: Primitive beginnings, maternal concern
Astrological imprint: Energetic, practical, creative and initiating, but also dominating and parental towards others. Strong nurturing instincts, quite sensitive and private. Experiences or feels rejection from family or parents. Often founders of businesses or associations.

Wind
(Maya = *Ik*, Aztec = *Ehecatl*)

Direction: North
Divination: Diversification, communication
Astrological imprint: Mentally active and communicative, versatile and multi-faceted. Idealistic and romantic, fashion conscious or artistic. Somewhat non-committal or indecisive. Problems with responsibility and obligation.

House
(Maya = *Akbal*, Aztec = *Calli*)

Direction: West
Divination: Strength, resistance to change
Astrological imprint: Powerful, often physically dominating. Organized, patient, with much endurance. Hard worker. Logical approach to problems but also traditional and mentally rigid. Concern for security in home and family. Introspective, needs solitude.

Lizard
(Maya = *Kan*, Aztec = *Cuetzpallin*)

Direction: South
Divination: Procreation and dispersion
Astrological imprint: Interest in leadership and performance. Self-esteem an important issue. Influential, with reputation for being different. Fanatical interests and high standards. Strongly influenced by sexual matters.

Serpent
(Maya = *Chicchan*, Aztec = *Coatl*)

Direction: East
Divination: Changes and transformations
Astrological imprint: Strong-willed, high-powered, extremist. Mysterious, charismatic, dramatic, with 'sex appeal'. Strong emotional reactions cause great upheavals in relationships. Intelligent, well-informed, fanatical and obsessive.

Death
(Maya = *Cimi*, Aztec = *Miquitztli*)

Direction: North
Divination: Belief and sacrifice
Astrological imprint: A sign of politics, obligations, sacrifice and faith. Involved or interested in civic affairs. Not natural leaders and will accept secondary roles or positions. Traditional in faith or religion. Materialistic, concerned with domestic security and real estate. Close experiences with death.

Deer
(Maya = *Manik*, Aztec = *Mazatl*)

Direction: West
Divination: Meetings and joinings
Astrological imprint: Peaceful, inspiring and generous, but also outspoken, deviant and dominating. Not overly interested in leadership. Strong feelings for family and friends. Needs companionship. Interests or abilities in the arts. Sensual, sexual, intuitive and sensitive to the concerns of others.

Rabbit
(Maya = *Lamat*, Aztec = *Tochtli*)

Direction: South
Divination: Conflict, advantage
Astrological imprint: Energetic, busy, nervous. Contrary. A fighter and joker. Needs physical activity and exercise. Often extremely intelligent, but also paranoid and wild. Liking for performance, games and risk-taking. Appreciates music and humour, sometimes self-destructive.

Water
(Maya=*Muluc*, Aztec=*Atl*)

Direction: East

Divination: Compulsive actions

Astrological imprint: Strong emotions. Powerful imagination and psychic. Romantic and performance conscious. Dominates others with emotions. Struggles with responsibility and self-control. Sexual.

Dog
(Maya=*Oc*, Aztec=*Itzcuintli*)

Direction: North

Divination: Guidance and movement

Astrological imprint: Loyal and consistent. Good team player. Needs variety. Likes leadership, but will wait for turn. Thoughtful, political and artistic. Struggles with emotional maturity.

Monkey
(Maya=*Chuen*, Aztec=*Ozomatli*)

Direction: West

Divination: Ego, performance

Astrological imprint: Needs attention. Likes centre stage, performing, artistry, etc. Multiple interests, curious, communicative. Quick learner. Emotionally distant but sexually active. Seeks leadership positions.

Grass
(Maya=*Eb*, Aztec=*Malinalli*)

Direction: South

Divination: Crisis and healing

Astrological imprint: Calm on the surface. Slow to anger, courteous and kind. Sensitive, touchy, easily hurt. Represses bad feelings. Hard worker, ambitious.

Reed
(Maya=*Ben*, Aztec=*Acatl*)

Direction: East

Divination: Power and authority

Astrological imprint: Popular, accomplished and generally competent. Will fight for principles and take on challenges. Capable of intense work but knows how to relax. Concerned with human nature.

Ocelot
(Maya=*Ix*, Aztec=*Ocelotl*)

Direction: North

Divination: Secrecy and entanglement

Astrological imprint: Private, sensitive and psychic. Aggressive streak but avoids confrontations. Becomes deeply involved in relationships. Good counsellor. Often concerned with religion or spirituality.

Eagle
(Maya=*Men*, Aztec=*Cuauhtli*)

Direction: West

Divination: Perspective

Astrological imprint: Independent with own ideas about life. Scientific and exacting mind. Perfectionist yet open to ideas. Ambitious and escapist. Popular.

Vulture
(Maya=*Cib*, Aztec=*Cozcacuauhtli*)

Direction: South

Divination: Rejection

Astrological imprint: Serious, realistic and pragmatic. Hardened to life, callous at times. Status-conscious, authoritative, although sometimes dominated by others. Has high standards. Competent and critical.

Earthquake
(Maya=*Caban*, Aztec=*Ollin*)

Direction: East

Divination: Balance

Astrological imprint: Mentally active, rationalizing and clever. Usually liberal and progressive. Sense of humour. Seeks leadership but is usually controversial.

Knife
(Maya=*Etz'nab*, Aztec=*Tecpatl*)

Direction: North

Divination: Choice

Astrological imprint: Practical, with good co-ordination. Extremely social but struggles in close relationships. Polite and often indecisive.

Rain
(Maya=*Cauac*, Aztec=*Quiahuitl*)

Direction: West

Divination: Purification

Astrological imprint: Youthful, restless, mentally active and friendly. Imitates rather than initiates. Multi-faceted. Over-compensates for insecurities. Drawn to religion or philosophy. Concern for others. Concerned with healing.

Flower
(Maya=*Ahau*, Aztec=*Xochitl*)

Direction: South

Divination: Perfection

Astrological imprint: A resistant idealist. Socially awkward, but well intentioned. Interests in art and beauty. Difficulties in close relationships due to expectations. Stubborn, but devoted to friends and lovers. Easily hurt.

This 'cosmogram' (right) shows the 20 day-signs as they cycle through the four directions. The symbolism is that of the Mixtec calendar from the Codex Fejervary-Mayer. The border is marked with 260 small circles at intervals of 13, marked by each of the 20 signs. This progression begins within the upper right-hand corner and moves counter clockwise. Year bearers prominently occupy the four corners of the design. The signs are Alligator, Jaguar, Deer, Flower, Reed, Death, Rain, Grass, Serpent, Knife, Monkey, Lizard, Earthquake, Dog, House, Vulture, Water, Wind, Eagle, Rabbit. This is the order of the 13-day periods. The four arms of the cross and the centre symbolize the five regions of the world. East is at the top, south to the right, west at the bottom and north on the left. The Sun is located in the east. Xiuhtecuhtli, the lord of central fire, is in the centre being fed blood from the rest of the diagram. He is the first of the Nine Lords of the Night. The other eight are (clockwise from east in order) Pilcintecuhtli, Iztli, Mictlantecuhtli, Cinteotl, Tlazolteotl, Chalchiuhtilicue, Tlaloc, Tlazolteotl.

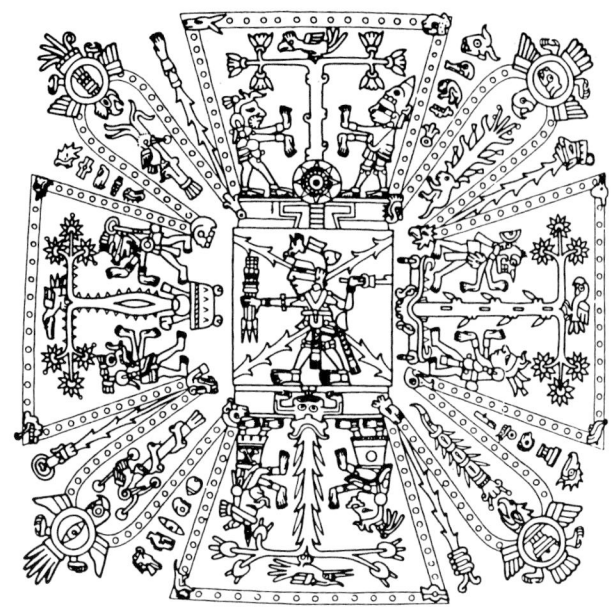

The Caracol at Chichén Itzá (above) is believed to have been an observatory. The circular tower at the top of the structure has sightlines to significant rising and setting positions of the Sun and Venus. In the background is 'El Castillo', the pyramid.

THE EASTERN WORLD

India, China, Japan and Tibet – the oldest civilizations anywhere in the world – possess a proliferation of divinatory systems, many of which were established while the rest of the world was still in a primitive state. In almost every case these systems derive from ancient oral tradition and consist of layers and accretions from different periods of the culture.

In the West when a sign or premonition of the future is sought by divinatory methods, it is by no means a foregone conclusion that such an answer will be forthcoming. In the East, and particularly in China, heaven is expected to make its will known in any one of a bewildering number of ways. This reflects a degree of fatalism, apparent particularly in the kinds of divination practised in the Far East. The future is a course laid down for each and every person; he, or she, must follow the way, and though an individual may obtain glimpses of future events, these often cannot be changed.

Several of the systems discussed here deal with energies that have been polarized into complementary opposites (the yin and yang which form the basis of the Chinese system of *I Ching*, Chapter Sixteen). These energies are seen as representing the natural law of the universe and the changing patterns of existence.

In almost all of the traditions in this book we have seen that natural law is an important element of divination. In Feng Shui, for example, the right relationship of everything to everything is of paramount importance in achieving a harmonious environment. In Indian astrology the human form is seen as a microcosm of the universe, and the stars which influence parts of the body are thus a divine reflection. The 'benific' and 'malific' planets in Indian astrology are polarized in the same way as the yin and yang energies in the *I Ching*. In both the *I Ching* and Feng Shui we encounter the observation of animals, birds and nature in general and the understanding that the patterns inherent within them are meaningful to the reading of future events. The same may be said of Mah Jongg, which is related to bone oracles, to Tarot and to the *I Ching*, all of which represent the significance of 'random' or 'chance' events.

Tibetan divination, with its emphasis on the reading of omens in the flight and cries of birds and in the actions of animals, shares this connection with the natural world, which is full of intimations of the divine. Tibet both influenced and was influenced by the culture and belief systems of India and China, and so the teachings of Buddhism, which contain many of the beliefs described in this section, may be seen to underlie the divinatory techniques in these countries. The fact that religious belief still occupies a central place goes a long way towards explaining why there is a deeper sense of the efficacy of divination in the East than in most other parts of the world today.

CHAPTER FIFTEEN

THE WAY OF THE EMPEROR

The Oracle and Game of Mah Jongg

Derek Walters

Take a stroll through a city's Chinatown one hot summer's afternoon and you may be puzzled by a strange clattering noise, seeming to come from every direction. Look up, beyond the shops and restaurants, to the open windows above, and you might spot the source of the curious sound. What might have been mistaken for the shuttling of a very old loom, or the clicking of a dozen antique typewriters, will be the sound of Chinese workers at their favourite pastime: the game of Mah Jongg. Hundreds of the bamboo and bone tiles, sliding and colliding over the polished surface of every available table, are producing the intriguing and distinctive rattle that the Chinese call 'the Twittering of the Sparrows'.

Almost exclusively known as a gambling game today, Mah Jongg is the modern descendant of one of the world's most ancient forms of divination, with a history full of astonishing twists, turns and side-roads. The Chinese equivalent of playing cards and the Tarot, Mah Jongg's antecedents are several centuries older than its Western cousins and, incredible though it may seem, its evolution is related to such widely different concepts as the game of chess, the navigator's compass and paper currency.

THE MAH JONGG TILES

The standard set consists of 144 pieces, about the size of a finger joint. Westerners call the pieces 'tiles', although the Chinese word for them is the same as the word for cards or dominoes – *pai*. Today, the tiles are usually made of plastic, but they may be made from wood, bamboo, cardboard, bone or any convenient material. Antique sets are usually handmade, with a bone or ivory face jointed into a polished bamboo back, which gives them a distinctive curved shape, missing from the more convenient, but soulless, modern plastic ones.

The face of the tile is carved or embossed with a name or value. Sometimes this will be a Chinese character, or a symbol, while a few of the tiles will have a simple picture of a flower or other figure, the quality varying considerably from one set to another. Although the number of unfamiliar signs may be intimidating to the uninitiated, the tiles' names are actually much more straightforward than they might appear at first glance.

The traditional game of Mah Jongg has not been eradicated in communist China, despite it being frowned upon by the authorities. Although these players in Kunming, Yunnan province, may be oblivious to the game's mystic origins, they will be familiar with its ancient symbolism.

To begin with, apart from eight tiles called the Flowers or Guardians, which are distinctly different from the others, each of the tiles is replicated four times, forming four 'packs' of 34 tiles. Each of the four packs comprises three suits (bamboos, circles or discs, and characters) of nine tiles each, 27 in all; four directions (often called the 'four winds'); and three colours (called 'dragons' by western players).

To summarize, the complete set consists of:
One of each of the eight Guardians or Flowers
Four of each of the following:
Bamboo suit (1 to 9)
Circles suit (1 to 9)
Characters suit (1 to 9)
Directions (East, South, West, North)
Colours (Green, Red, White)

The suits are marked along similar lines to ordinary playing cards or Tarot cards, but instead of hearts, spades, diamonds and clubs, the tiles show bamboo stalks, circles, and, in the case of the 'characters', a Chinese number, followed by the symbol *Wan*, meaning 10,000. Uniquely, the 1 Bamboo tile shows a bird of uncertain species. There is, however, an interesting difference between the design of playing cards and Mah Jongg suit tiles. Although the Mah Jongg tiles are engraved in red, green and black, these colours are not associated with any particular suit in the same way that hearts and diamonds are always red, or spades and clubs black.

The four direction tiles are marked, in black, with the Chinese characters for East, South, West and North, while some sets, made for export, also have E, S, W, or N marked in one corner of each tile.

The three remaining tiles, the colours, are shown by the Chinese character *Fa*, meaning 'Commence', engraved in green (and therefore called the 'Green Dragon' by western players); the character for 'Centre' in red; and a tile which is either completely black or with just an empty frame (sometimes referred to as the 'White Dragon').

THE EIGHT GUARDIANS

The remaining eight tiles form two sets representing the four seasons, Spring, Summer, Autumn and Winter. These may be shown symbolically by flowers appropriate to the season – usually plum blossom for Spring, orchid for Summer, chrysanthemum for Autumn and evergreen bamboo for Winter – while the other four guardians may be shown by seasonal occupations, such as the Fisherman, Woodcutter, Farmer and Scholar. But there are many regional variations in these 'flower' tiles. Their inclusion is almost an anomaly and some players discard them as being superfluous. But in some parts of the Far East, particularly in Japan, there are sets of cards used for fortune-telling and leisure games which are composed exclusively of flower cards.

THE SYMBOLISM OF MAH JONGG

Even in the heat of a gambling session for high stakes, the mystical origins of Mah Jongg are never forgotten. The four players sit in positions known as East, South, West and North, but because the four directions are meant to represent the four quarters of the heavens (a mirror image of the Earth), East and West are reversed in relation to North and South. In Chinese philosophy, the four directions are related to the four seasons, shown by the Guardian tiles, while the four directions plus the Centre relate to the five elements of Chinese philosophy: Wood (Spring or East), Fire (Summer or South), Metal (Autumn or West), Water (Winter or North), with the remaining element, Earth, being represented both by the Centre tile and by the playing area itself. Even the colours used for the tiles are symbolic: the colours green, red, black and white are the colours associated with the elements, seasons and directions: green for East, Wood, and the Spring; red for South, Fire and the Summer; black for North, Water and Winter; and White for West, Metal and Autumn. Furthermore, just as the four directions represent the four seasons, so the number of tiles in a player's hand – 13 – represents the number of lunar months in a year.

The fact that there are nine tiles in each suit is highly significant. For the Chinese nine is a mystic number. An arrangement of the numbers one to nine was said to have appeared on the back of a tortoise – which emerged from the River Lo, and inspired China's first philosopher, Fu Hsi, with the understanding of the Cosmos. Today, just as over 2,000 years ago, Chinese mystics practise a system of nine-house numerology according to precepts traditionally ascribed to the great sage.

THE HISTORY OF MAH JONGG

Games of chance were known in ancient China, but their origins are inseparable from methods of divination. In Tibet, for example, as recently as the last century, dice and counters were used exclusively for foretelling future events, and not for gambling (see Chapter Nineteen, Mirrors of the Sky). In Chinese religions the purpose of divination was, and still remains, a method of obtaining an answer from the gods. This reveals a fundamental difference between Western and Eastern attitudes to the celestial world. When the Westerner offers a prayer, publicly it may be a form of thanksgiving for favours received, or privately a petition to ask for further favours. Very infrequently, in cases of dire distress, the petitioner may ask for a 'sign' to indicate a course of action, although usually the form and meaning of the sign is left for the heavenly authorities to decide. But for the Chinese worshipper, such signs are expected as a matter of course, and prayer is presumed to be a two-way form of communication. Through some form of sortilege, or the casting of lots, heaven is able to reveal its will, and consequently the course that destiny must take.

Although today the concept that a petition may achieve a response through lots is absent from Western religious practice, it was not always so. In the Bible, Aaron is said to have carried 'Urim and Thummim' in his breastplate, and we are told that the Urim and Thummim were used for judgement before the Lord (Exodus 28:30 and Leviticus 8:8). Their use must have been so familiar that the patriarchs did not bother to record a description of them, nor the way that they were used, and it was only when the Urim and Thummim failed to respond that the demented Saul was constrained to visit the Witch of Endor (I Samuel 28:6–7). What the Urim and Thummim were can only be guessed at, but it is entirely probable that they were similar to the two ancient traditional methods that are still found being used in Chinese temples today. These are the two blocks of wood called *chiao pai* and the bundle of sticks known as *chim*.

The *chiao pai* are two comma-shaped blocks, one side curved and the other flat, which are thrown on to the ground. Whether the blocks both fall curved sides up (yin), flat sides up (yang), or with one curved and one flat uppermost is regarded as a positive, negative or neutral response, although interpretation does vary from one part of China to another.

A yes-no answer, albeit frank and concise, does not give detailed advice in difficult situations. In such cases, petitioners use the *chim* for more sophisticated responses. *Chim* consist of bundles of sticks or bamboo slips, which are shaken in a horizontally held cylinder until one of the slips falls out. The slip bears a number or sign similar to domino spots, the number being a reference to a verse in a mystic book which can be interpreted in the light of the question put to the oracle. Modern versions of the oracle often use up to 100 sticks, and the mystic responses may be from texts that are only a few centuries old; but the original form of the sticks were marked with only one of four signs, even though there may have been as many as 64 sticks in a bundle.

In another method of consulting the oracle, the signs were marked on special divining dice. At some very early date, some bored bystander must have conceived the notion of debasing the divining dice into a game of chance, and the popularity of the invention is self-evident. But once the dice had lost their spiritual values, they soon became the source of contention. Dice are too easily prone to manipulation, and an accidental – or purposeful – jolt at a critical

*Divining sticks (*chim*) and divining blocks (*chiao pai*) at the Lung Shan (Dragon Mountain) temple, near Taipei. Unlike most divining sticks, the ones used at this temple are about a metre long. The rods are shuffled about, one is selected, and the* chiao pai *are then cast to see if the correct one has been chosen.*

moment could dispose of a fortune. To avoid this problem, the gaming signs were transferred back to slips of wood, like *chim*, or on to more substantial blocks of clay, the precursor of dominoes. But before we see what became of the dominoes, we find another intriguing thread woven into the tapestry of Mah Jongg's history.

Several centuries before the building of the Great Wall of China, and before the separation of astronomy and astrology, astronomers were busy recording the movements of the planets, and cataloguing the positions of the stars. To this end, a simple form of planisphere was invented to show the daily movement of the celestial sphere in relation to its annual rotation. Because the Earth is symbolically square, and the heavens circular, the planisphere took the form of a disc rotating on a square base. The edge of the square was marked with the names of the 28 Chinese constellations through which the Sun, Moon and planets passed, while at the centre of the disc a pointer was formed from the seven stars of the Great Bear, known to the Chinese as the Ladle. This constellation was regarded as supremely important by Chinese astronomers; its handle pointed to the first of the Chinese constellations, and its edge pointed to celestial north, while the entire constellation sweeps round the heavens like the hands of a cosmic clock. By placing counters to represent the planets at appropriate positions on the planisphere, early astronomers were able to plot their courses and calculate their future positions. This act of moving pieces about on a board was the inspiration for board games such as Chinese chess and another ancient Chinese game called *Liu Po*. Although the rules of *Liu Po* have now been lost, in its heyday, 2,000 years ago, it was a very popular pastime, and models that have been discovered at archaeological sites reveal it to be an ancestor of Mah Jongg.

The elegance of the planisphere led to its

The more usual way of consulting the oracle is shown by this worshipper at a temple in Hong Kong. He first casts the chiao pai *and, on receiving a favourable answer, shakes the box of* chim *until one of the bamboo slips falls out.*

being used as a model for several other contrivances. When the magnetic power of lodestone was discovered, it seemed to be perfectly valid to cast the lodestone in the shape of the Ladle, since this constellation always pointed to the north. And the compass plate, instead of being marked simply by the cardinal points, was marked with the same mystic astronomical signs as were found on the planisphere. Thus it is that, even today, Chinese junks plying their courses through the South Pacific navigate with the aid of an instrument originally designed for the use of astrologers, sages and magicians.

The advance of Chinese technology was to produce yet another surprise. Perhaps the most influential discovery of all time was the invention of printing. But its impact was not confined to the publication of books and writings on an undreamt-of scale: it also revolutionized commerce through the introduction of paper currency, and balanced that with the more frivolous creation of playing cards, several centuries

The game of Liu Po is portrayed in a clay funerary model discovered in a tomb of the Han dynasty (second to first centuries BC). This ancient pastime is the forerunner of cards, dominoes, and even chess.

before the Tarot was devised in the West. The ease of printing meant that designers had ample scope to modify existing games, and today several varieties of playing cards are to be found, including Mah Jongg itself. Yet the Chinese never relinquished their fondness for the solid, tactile quality of the domino-like pieces of the Mah Jongg. And, as noted earlier, although the Chinese word for playing cards (*pai*) is the same as the word for Mah Jongg pieces, playing cards are often more disparagingly referred to as 'portable cards'.

Alas, however, today the ancient oracular function of Mah Jongg has all but been over-shadowed by the gambler, and it is now only at the end of a gaming session that the matriarch of the family might gather the pieces together to divine what the future may hold. Yet

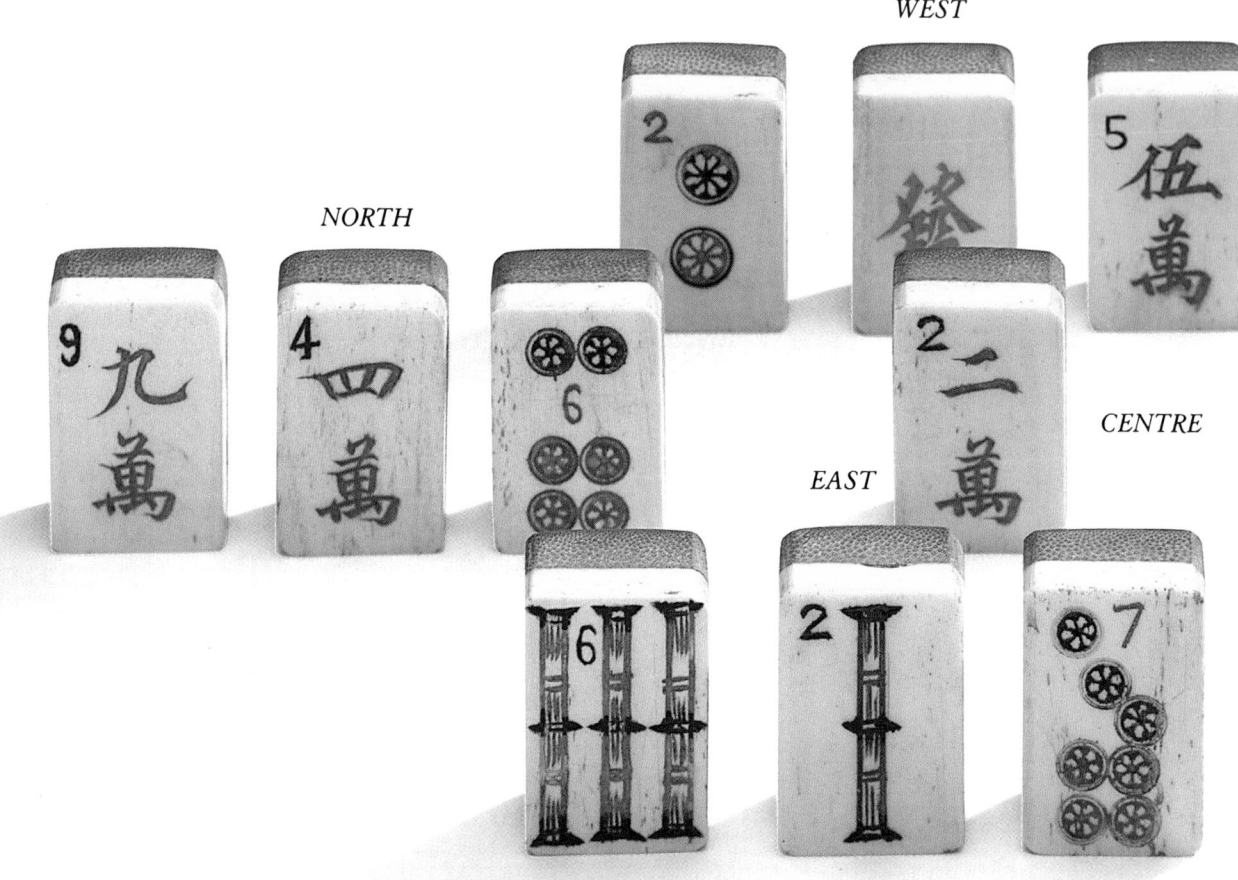

These tiles were selected by a lady planning to travel. The central tile, 2 Wan (Sword), shows a choice to be made. The three tiles in the foreground, 6, 2 and 7 Bamboo, are all 'watery tiles', relating directly to the question. To the right, the tiles in the 'south' represent the immediate future, and the red 'Centre' tile reveals that immediate objectives will be attained, confirmed by the Door (1 Wan) opening to the favourable

South tile. Problems are shown by the distant tiles, particularly the Pine (2 Circles), representing a younger male, and the House (5 Wan). The final tiles, on the left, show a change in circumstances: 9 Wan represents the end of an episode, 4 Wan rest or retirement, and the Peach (6 Circles) extravagance. The lady was a travel courier, worried about leaving her son at home while she went to the Bahamas for the winter!

SYMBOLISM OF THE MAH JONGG TILES

BAMBOO TILES

1 **Peacock** Self, pride, success.
2 **Duck** Devotion, partnership.
3 **Toad** Recovery from sickness.
4 **Carp** Determination. Long life.
5 **Lotus** New life, vision. A baby.
6 **Water** Travel, correspondence.
7 **Tortoise** Learning. Illegitimacy.
8 **Fungus** Virtue. Eccentricity.
9 **Willow** Tact. Resilience.

CIRCLE TILES

1 **Pearl** Honour, refinement. An older woman.
2 **Pine** Strength, literature. A young man.

3 **Phoenix** Good news.
4 **Jade** Worth, good deeds.
5 **Dragon** Good fortune.
6 **Peach** Fine arts. A young lady.
7 **Insect** Craft, skill, manual work.
8 **Tiger** Authority. An older man.
9 **Unicorn** Ability to see ahead.

WAN (CHINESE NUMERALS)

1 **Open door** New opportunities.
2 **Sword** A choice, a decision. Twins.
3 **Earth** Land, the countryside. Relocation.
4 **Lute** Music, leisure.
5 **House** A building, real estate, the home.
6 **Fire** Loss, danger.

7 **Stars** Dreams, ambitions, imagination.
8 **Knot** Tying or untying.
9 **Heaven** Spiritual matters. A ceremony.

DIRECTIONS

East The Self.
South Good fortune, growth, progress.
West The objective or partner.
North Difficulties. Shortage.

COLOURS

Green (Go) Go ahead, don't delay.
Red (Centre) Achievement of ambition.
White Documents. Ghosts.

the inseparable tie between games of chance and the oracle of lot-casting leaves no doubt as to the reason why the Chinese are notorious for being such inveterate gamblers. Nowhere else does chance play such a large part in both religious and social life.

READING MAH JONGG TILES

Many people who have used Mah Jongg find that it has a specific advantage over the Tarot. Although the variety of Mah Jongg tiles is more limited, since for the most part each tile is repeated four times, it is this very repetition which intensifies the message delivered by the oracle. If a tile appears at the beginning of a reading and then reappears later, its significance is heightened and this directs the reader to examine such factors as the tiles that are close by and the time-scale involved.

When setting the tiles out for a reading, 13 tiles are taken, as in the game of Mah Jongg, and set out in sets of fours, representing the four seasons, with one central tile representing the question of the moment. The three tiles nearest the reader represent the present situation, those to the right the immediate future, those furthest away the objective and the hazards which have to be faced, while the four at the left refer to the more distant future, or the situation as it will be in a year's time. Should one of the eight Guardian tiles be selected, another tile is drawn and placed beside it. The Guardian reveals the existence of a difficulty, and its solution.

SOUTH

CHAPTER SIXTEEN

THE CHINESE BOOK OF CHANGES

Ancient Wisdom from the *I Ching*

Nigel Pennick

The *I Ching* is the ancient Chinese Book of Changes. It is a text that gives the user an insight into the forces, literally the 'changes', operating at any particular moment in time. The *I Ching* is the crystallization into writing in antiquity of the even more ancient oral tradition of divination. In traditional divination, patterns seen in natural things were used as indicators of immediate conditions in the eternal flow of events in time. In China, the patterns that diviners saw in Nature were standardized and related to a book of readings – the *I Ching* – thereby putting these patterns into a formal framework which is still useful today.

YANG AND YIN: THE ORIGIN OF THE *I CHING*

According to the Confucian and Taoist religions, when the *Great Extreme* (*Tai Ji*) came into being at the beginning of all existence it produced the two complementary opposites, yang and yin. These represent odd and even, plus and minus, male and female, light and darkness, day and night, and so on. Literally, the ancient meaning of yin was 'the shaded, north side of a hill', when yang meant 'the sunny, south side of a hill'. Yang controls heaven and all things positive, active, masculine, hard, moving and living. Yin controls the Earth and all things

The Former Heaven Sequence of trigrams on a nineteenth-century luck-bringing talisman was used in Feng Shui to ward off evil influences. The Former Heaven Sequence is the cosmic ideal, while the Later Heaven Sequence is its earthly application. The tiger symbolizes the west. Its corresponding trigram is K'an.

negative, passive, dark, soft, still and non-living. Traditionally, yang is shown as a solid, single continuous line, and yin as a broken line, in two distinct pieces.

yang   yin

In this belief-system, the eternal changes of existence are ascribed to the waxing and waning of the relative qualities of yang and yin. Any particular circumstance contains a specific balance of these qualities, and they can be determined by consulting the *I Ching*.

The four seasons clearly demonstrate the working of this yang-yin principle: in winter, yin is at its maximum and yang at its minimum. Then in springtime, yang and yin are equal, with yang waxing and yin waning. Summertime has the maximum yang; then autumn has again a balance of yang and yin, with yang waning and yin waxing. Finally, in the next winter, yin is

Chinese sages interpret the yang-yin symbol. This painting is on a Chinese ceramic dish, bearing the identification mark of K'ang Hai (1661–1722).

THE EIGHT TRIGRAMS: THEIR NAMES, MEANINGS AND CORRESPONDENCES

Ch'ien represents heaven, creative originality in all things. It signifies a change for the better, substitution or variation to achieve harmony. Its three unbroken lines represent vitality, strength and good fortune.

K'un represents the Earth and feminine things. Its three broken lines signify the ultimate in yin qualities. It is the complementary opposite of *Ch'ien*.

Chen represents thunder, the movement and development of things. Its two broken lines and one solid one signify apprehension and alterations in the status quo.

Sun denotes penetration (wind and wood). It represents pliability and influence, and the growth of vegetation.

K'an, which means 'pit', signifies danger, and also flowing water. It is connected with the mind, thought and concentration. The unbroken line at the centre represents inner strength, but this is countered by the broken outer lines.

Li denotes separation (fire and lightning), but in divination it signifies beauty and firmness. Its form, two solid lines enclosing a broken line, represents adherence.

Ken, meaning 'mountain', represents stopped action, either a blockage to progress, or a well-earned rest during some process.

Tui represents happiness, joy and satisfaction, manifested as achievement and progress. Its weak yin line is compensated for by two strong, unbroken yang lines.

again at its maximum. This general principle applies to all things. The Chinese symbol of existence, the yin-yang, shows this essential unity. The dark yin has within it a 'seed' of light yang, whilst the light yang has its complementary 'seed' of dark yin.

During the creation process, yang and yin gave birth to four primary symbols. These are each represented by two lines:

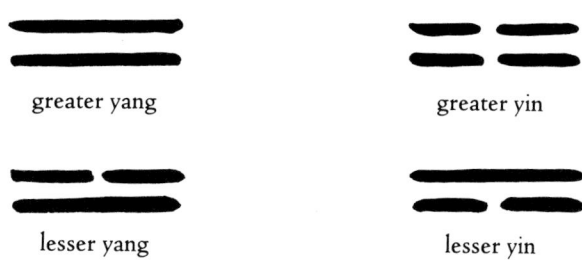

greater yang · greater yin

lesser yang · lesser yin

To these primary symbols were added a further line, of either yin or yang, creating the eight trigrams. These trigrams have names and specific relations to one another: they are related to the eight directions of space; they determine the divination of fortune in the *I Ching* and the orientation of buildings in the Chinese art of placement, Feng Shui (see Chapter Seventeen).

According to legend, the diagrams of the *I Ching* were invented by an inspired man. This parallels exactly the legendary origin of the Ogam script with Ogma and geomancy with Idris (see Chapters Three and Twenty-three). In the case of the *I Ching*, its originator was Fu Hsi, fabled first emperor of China, who also invented weaving and fishing nets. He devised the trigrams after examining the basic patterns underlying all things in the world. One of the *I Ching* commentaries, *The Great Appendix*, describes this revelation:

In ancient times, when Fu Hsi ruled all things under heaven, he looked up to contemplate the bright forms in the sky, then looked down to contemplate the patterns forming on the earth. He contemplated the patterns of birds and animals and the properties of their habitats. Near at hand, he found in his own body things for consideration, and also observed distant things in general. Thus he devised the eight trigrams, in order to clarify the

heavenly processes in Nature, and to understand the relations of all things.

A related story tells how Fu Hsi discovered the first eight trigrams by studying the patterns on a tortoise shell. In the archaic Lungshan period in China, tortoise shells were used in divination. A tortoise shell was heated in a fire until it cracked and the pattern of cracks was then interpreted by a trained diviner. In creating the trigrams, Fu Hsi made some order of these random patterns according to Chinese cosmic theory.

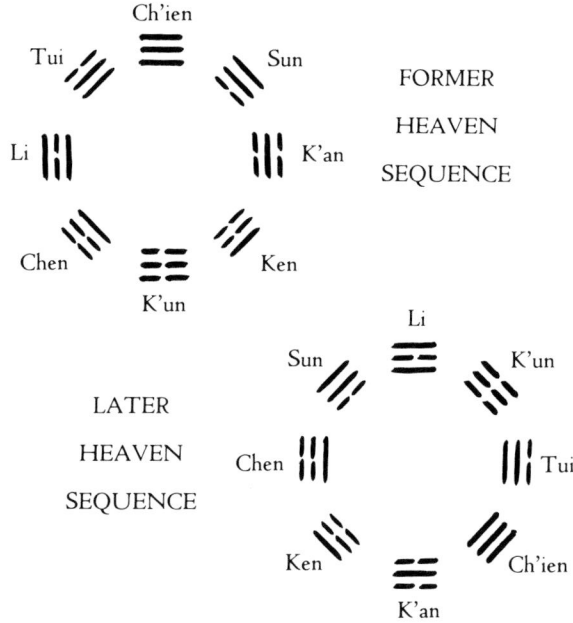

Customarily, the basic eight trigrams are laid out in the form of an octagon. Two layouts are used: the older is the Former Heaven Sequence, which is attributed to Fu Hsi, and the subsequent one is the Later Heaven Sequence, which is attributed to King Wen, first ruler of the Chou dynasty.

According to tradition, the full development of the *I Ching* took place in 1143 BC, when a feudal lord named Wen (who subsequently became King Wen) was imprisoned by the emperor and threatened with death. During his time in prison, he used his enforced solitude to expand and refine the *Book of Changes*, relating divined patterns to specific texts. He did this by doubling up the trigrams to make six-line hexagrams, and allotting each one to a corresponding text. Each hexagram combined the meanings of two trigrams, and thus described a specific interaction of qualities. The 64 hexagrams of the *I Ching* comprise all the possible combinations of paired trigrams.

Later, Wen's son, the Duke of Chou, added further material to the book. Chou's addition of 384 commentaries became an integral part of the divinatory text. They allowed more detailed readings, using a divination starting with the four primary symbols.

The oracle then took on its present form, where the divination results in the creation of a hexagram containing certain elements that refer to a unique 'energy' or quality of existence. In total, the *I Ching* permits 11,520 possible situations to be described. These are said to express every possible physical, social and psychological condition. They are explained in the corresponding text in the *Book of Changes*.

The final form of the *I Ching* consists of King Wen's 64 hexagrams and their accompanying descriptions; the Duke of Chou's further interpretations of the lines; and additional Confucian commentaries. Fortunately, it escaped the wholesale burning of books ordered by Emperor Ch'in Shih Huang Ti in 213 BC. In the year AD 175, the texts of the *Five Confucian Classics*, including the *I Ching*, were engraved on stone. It was revised during the Sung dynasty (960–1279), when a commentary by the philosopher Chu Hsi (1130–1200) was added. The present standard edition, on which Western translations are based, is the K'ang Hsi edition, which was published in 1715.

THE *I CHING* THROUGH THE AGES

Legends apart, it is likely that the text of the *I Ching* dates from the Chou dynasty (c. 1000 BC). It developed greatly during the Han dynasty (202 BC–AD 220), when the diagrams were classified systematically according to cosmological-religious principles. This is a direct parallel of what happened in other parts of the world, where early spontaneous techniques were the basis for later formal systems. But in contrast to the West, where divination is not considered a legitimate part of the culture, the *I Ching* became an integral part of traditional Chinese life

The eight trigrams are often used together in a charm called Pak Kua *(both trigrams and hexagrams are called* Kua*), which is often used as a talisman in Feng Shui to ward off harm. Surrounding the Yang and Yin motif, the trigrams appear on flags and plaques and also form the surrounding for geomantic mirrors set up at bad places to reflect away harmful spirits or energies. As in the Vintana of Madagascar, which links the oracle of geomancy (for prediction) with locational geomancy (for good and bad places in the landscape), the* Pak Kua *links the trigrams with Feng Shui. The form of the eight trigrams makes them a relative of the 16 tetragrams of Western geomancy, as both have a combination of odd and even.*

and thought, and remains so today. Once based solely in China, it has since spread to all parts of the globe.

Throughout history, the *I Ching* has been used by Chinese generals in the conduct of war. In the twentieth century, the Chinese Nationalist leader Chiang Kai-Shek praised the value of the *I Ching* as both an oracle and a record of the ultimate values of Chinese life. The *I Ching* was also used in warfare by his opponent, the Communist leader Mao Zedong, whose forces eventually overcame those of the Nationalists in the Chinese Civil War. Although most 'esoteric' belief-systems were rejected by Maoism, the *I Ching* seems to have been exempt from suppression because it works.

Western interest in the *I Ching* began in the

nineteenth century. In 1834, *Y-King, antiquissimus Sinarum Liber*, by P. Regis, was published at Paris. This was the first translation of the *I Ching*, by Jesuit missionaries, into a Western language. In 1889, C. de Harlez published a French translation at Brussels: *Le Yih-King, Texte Primitif: Rétabli, Traduit et Commenté*. An English edition was published by James Legge at Oxford in 1899. But the most influential work in the West was the edition translated by Richard Wilhelm, *I Ging: das Buch der Wandlungen*, published in German at Jena in 1924. Wilhelm's translation had a seminal foreword by psychologist C.G. Jung, whose insights into the *I Ching* transformed Western awareness of its nature and use. Jung was the first Westerner to recognize its universal relevance. When he used it, he found 'undeniably remarkable results',

This Neolithic oracle bone bears inscriptions in early Chinese characters. The I Ching *was developed from earlier divination techniques that used bones or tortoise shells. The patterns on the shells or bones were formalized into the trigrams and hexagrams used today.*

inexplicable yet meaningful connections with his own thought patterns. Since Jung's day, the *I Ching* has taken its place in the West alongside other ancient traditional means of self-knowledge. Today, it is used in occultism, mathematics, psychology, and business studies.

CASTING THE HEXAGRAMS

The traditional way to generate the hexagrams uses stalks of the yarrow plant (*Achillea millefolium*). The divination begins with 50 long stalks of yarrow. First, the diviner takes one of them away, leaving 49 (7 × 7, an important 'square number' in divination). This is put on one side. Then the remaining 49 are divided into two random piles. Once this is done, four stalks are removed from one pile, then the other, in turn, until three, two, one or no stalks are left in each pile. The diviner then counts the stalks remaining. From this, he or she obtains various numbers which are interpreted as the four primary symbols: old yang (—⊖—), old yin (—×—), young yang (———) and young yin (— —). The whole procedure is done a further five times, producing six lines – the hexagram – which can be either old lines, young lines, or a mixture of both. The hexagram is looked up in the book, and the answer to the question is read.

Confucian and Taoist teachings tell that when a power reaches its apex or culmination, becoming 'old', it is then transformed into its opposite. Thus an 'old yang' line is in the process of moving from yang to yin. When an 'old' line appears in a hexagram, it creates a second hexagram as the line moves from, for example, yang to yin. The second hexagram must be taken into account when consulting the text, and the 'moving' lines are particularly important for the reading.

Another way of generating hexagrams uses coins. Many *I Ching* users like to use old Chinese cash coins. These round coins with square central holes were originally ordinary currency, but nowadays they are sold for oracular use. The side of the coin with four characters is the yang side and has a value of three. The reverse has a value of two. The three coins are cast six times, producing a value of six, seven, eight or nine at each throw. Each number corresponds to a quality of yang or yin: a six is old yin, seven is young yang, eight is young yin and nine old yang. It is equally valid to use Western-style coins in *I Ching* divination. Here, the 'head' side is taken as positive (yang, value 3) and the 'tail' as negative (yin, value 2).

	Trigram	Family	Part of body	Compass direction	Element	Season	Natural feature
☰	*Ch'ien*	father	head	NW	metal	late autumn/ early winter	heaven
☷	*K'un*	mother	belly	SW	earth	late summer/ early autumn	earth
☳	*Chen*	eldest son	foot	E	wood	spring	thunder
☴	*Sun*	eldest daughter	thighs	SE	wood	late spring/ early summer	wind
☵	*K'an*	middle son	ear	N	water	winter	moon
☲	*Li*	middle daughter	eye	S	fire	summer	sun
☶	*Ken*	youngest son	hand	NE	wood	late winter/ early spring	mountain
☱	*Tui*	youngest daughter	mouth	W	water/ metal	autumn	lake

The trigrams have many correspondences: they express family relationships, natural features, parts of the human body, directions, seasons and elements. The two sequences have their own connections, too. The Former Heaven Sequence is used to express the seasons (the passing of time), while orientation and location are expressed through the Later Heaven Sequence.

This table shows the correspondences of the trigrams according to these sequences.

A simpler method of making hexagrams uses the Six Wands Method. This uses six special wands, painted black with a white bar across one side. They are thrown onto the ground or a table-top, then are picked up beginning with the rod nearest to the caster. Those that show the white bar are yin, and those that do not are yang. The drawback of this method is that only one hexagram is produced. There can be no moving lines, so the Duke of Chou's commentary is not available for use.

The *I Ching* also lends itself to modern computer technology. There are even hand-held, battery-powered *I Ching* computers which give instant readings anywhere.

However they are generated, the hexagrams are accumulated from the bottom upwards, as in the traditional way of writing Chinese characters. This is in accord with Nature, because all things grow from the ground upwards. The first line generated is thus the lower line, and the sixth, final one, the upper line. Like the trigrams, each hexagram has a name and a basic meaning.

The 64 hexagrams are laid out here in sequence, with the first at the top left. Each column is read from the top downwards, so hexagram 8 is at the bottom of the left-hand column, hexagram 9 is at the top of the next column to the right, and so on.

1 *Ch'ien*, creativity.
2 *K'un*, quiescence.
3 *Chun*, difficulties at the beginning (birth pangs).
4 *Meng*, youth (inexperience).
5 *Hsu*, nourishment (contemplation).
6 *Sung*, conflict.
7 *Shih*, the army.
8 *Pi*, unity.
9 *Hsiao Ch'u*, restraint (by the weak).
10 *Lu*, treading.
11 *T'ai*, peace.
12 *P'i*, disharmony (stagnation).
13 *T'ung Jen*, social harmony.
14 *Ta Yu*, wealth.
15 *Ch'ien*, modesty.
16 *Yu*, enthusiasm (calm confidence).
17 *Sui*, adaptive following.
18 *Ku*, reparation (decay).
19 *Lin*, conduct (getting ahead).
20 *Kuan*, consolidation (contemplation).
21 *Shih Ho*, biting through.
22 *Pi*, gracefulness (adornment).

23 *Po*, breaking-down (shedding).
24 *Fu*, return.
25 *Wu Wang*, simplicity (simple integrity).
26 *Ta Ch'u*, restrained power.
27 *I*, nourishment.
28 *Ta Kuo*, excess.
29 *K'an*, the deep (the perilous chasm).
30 *Li*, fire (brilliant beauty).
31 *Hsien*, stimulus (mutual attraction).
32 *Heng*, continuance.
33 *Tun*, retreat.
34 *Ta Chuang*, great power (vigorous strength).
35 *Chin*, progress.
36 *Min I*, advancing darkness.
37 *Chia Jen*, family.
38 *K'uei*, disunity (opposites).
39 *Chien*, obstruction.
40 *Hsieh*, liberation.
41 *Sun*, decrease.
42 *I*, increase.
43 *Kuai*, determination (renewed advance).
44 *Kou*, temptation (sudden

encounters).
45 *Ts'ui*, harmoniousness (collecting together).
46 *Sheng*, pushing upwards (ascending).
47 *K'un*, oppression (exhausting restriction).
48 *Ching*, the well.
49 *Ko*, revolution.
50 *Ting*, the cauldron.
51 *Chen*, thunderclap.
52 *Ken*, keeping still.
53 *Chien*, progressive development (gradual advance).
54 *Kuei Mei*, the marrying maiden.
55 *Feng*, fullness (abundant prosperity).
56 *Lu*, the travelling stranger.
57 *Sun*, the penetrating wind.
58 *Tui*, joyousness.
59 *Huan*, dispersion.
60 *Chieh*, limitation.
61 *Chung Fu*, truth.
62 *Hsiao Kua*, small successes.
63 *Chi Chi*, completion achieved.
64 *Wei Chi*, before completion.

CHAPTER SEVENTEEN

DRAGON LINES IN THE LAND

Feng Shui

Derek Walters

Feng Shui is the name of an ancient Chinese philosophy which relates every aspect of our lives to our surroundings. Literally, Feng Shui translates as 'wind and water', but there is no exact Western equivalent for the expression. The Chinese understand it to mean an environment that brings peace of mind, good health, long life, happiness and, ultimately, prosperity. Whether it is the geographical location, or the man-made buildings around us, the position of the furniture, or even a carefully posed single flower in a vase, all these produce or affect the prevailing Feng Shui, for good or for harm, as the following story shows.

The seven newly-built houses tucked away in a quiet corner of a private housing estate had every amenity that a young married couple could want. Modern, comfortable and within easy reach of the city, they would have been the pride of their eager new owners when they first crossed the threshold. Yet within months of the seven houses being occupied, five of the couples who had such golden hopes for their future lives had parted and gone their separate ways. It was as if this one enclave, unlike the other streets and roads of the neighbourhood, held some grim and sombre secret that blighted the happiness of those who had unwittingly made their homes there. But why?

This sad series of events took place in a residential suburb of England's second largest city. There seemed no rational explanation. Yet if it had happened anywhere in the Chinese-speaking world, the reason would have been evident, and uncontested. The location's Feng Shui was bad. But what may be apparent to the Chinese eye may not be so easy for the Western mind to comprehend. Explain Feng Shui in rational terms, and the Western sceptic dismisses it as plain common sense. Explain it in terms of Chinese philosophical belief, and the sceptic dismisses it as superstition.

When a Feng Shui expert was asked to inspect the area, he asserted that because the road at the back of the estate ran into a wider one, which in turn ran into a major trunk road, all the *ch'i*, or positive force, was being drained away. Next he looked at the homes themselves, and was disturbed to find that the stairs faced

A woodcut illustration from the Yellow Emperor Classic, perhaps the oldest extant Feng Shui text, shows a house facing north-east, with a side entrance north-west, producing the favourable Ch'i locations 'Generating Breath' and 'Lengthened Years' respectively.

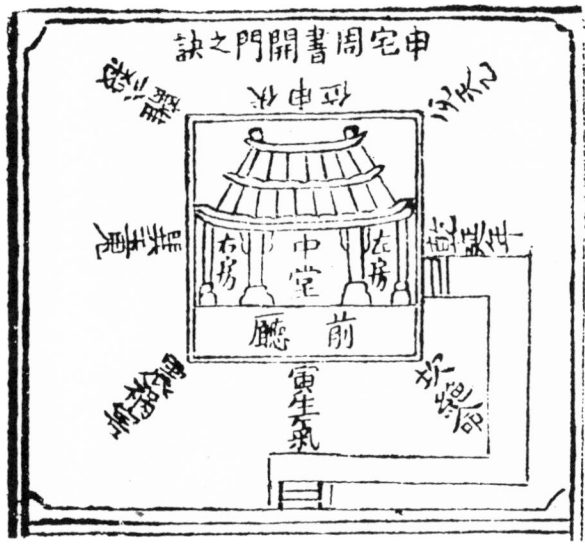

143

the main entrance – again causing the homes' own energy to cascade out of the house. But standing by the window, it was possible to indentify another, subtly psychological reason for the 'weak energy' in the house. Anyone staying in the house for any length of time could not fail to be aware of the constant flow of traffic – moving always away from the house. Subconsciously, a feeling of unease and restlessness would be generated, leading to a desire to get away, perhaps from the house, perhaps from everything that it represented: marriage, family, even the home.

But, the remarkable thing about this example is that, while the rational, psychological explanation applied only to this particular case, the elementary precepts advanced by the Feng Shui expert would apply in a much wider variety of situations. It is a guiding principle of conventional scientific research that when there are several possible theories to account for a particular phenomenon, the simpler and more universal theory is the one most likely to be true.

Feng Shui is a complex subject, with as many facets as, say, music – something which is partly an art and partly a science, but mostly an intrinsic quality that is beyond definition. If the scenery surrounding a village has rolling hills, trickling streams, a waterfall and naturally sculpted rocks, the environment may be said to have good Feng Shui. If, then, electricity pylons are erected in front of the house, or a new motorway cuts a gash through a wooded valley, the Feng Shui is likely to be destroyed – but not just because the landscape is now less pleasing to the eye. The principles of Feng Shui reveal the consequences that follow its destruction: fire, accident, illness, misfortune or separation may pursue those obliged to live in the regions where the Feng Shui has been toppled. Fortunately, Feng Shui techniques not only reveal what kind of locations are beneficial, but also how it is possible to rectify or at least improve a situation that lacks the essential qualities to produce a harmonious environment.

Until a few years ago, it might have been supposed that Feng Shui practices were confined to the Chinese-speaking world, but the impact is much more widespread. It comes as no surprise that Feng Shui principles are respected from Bangkok to Tokyo and from Ulan Bator to Jakarta, given the unifying factor of Buddhist influence in the nations adjoining China; but perhaps less predictable is its appearance in Madagascar and East Africa, where even the most primitive dwellings are constructed according to Feng Shui principles, even to the point of having the Eight Diagrams, an ancient secret talisman, carved on the lintel (see Chapter Twenty-three, Ancient Secrets of the Earth).

Now, with the growth of interest in philosophies beyond our own, interest in Feng Shui is world-wide, and Western-based businesses in Europe and America frequently find it prudent to call in the services of a consultant versed in the practice and mysteries of Feng Shui.

THE HISTORY OF FENG SHUI

The first known textbook on Feng Shui was compiled in the ninth century AD by the sage Yang Yun-sung, but he wrote principally about the Feng Shui produced by the fantastically vivid landscapes of the Kuei-lin region. His precepts are therefore known as the 'form school' of Feng Shui. Not long afterwards, other scholars, surrounded by less visually arresting scenery, compiled manuals of Feng Shui which were based on the ritual significance of the compass points: ideas which had been enshrined a thousand or more years before in the sacred Book of Rites. This aspect of Feng Shui was consequently known as the 'compass school'.

Until recent years, commentators on Chinese traditional customs had assumed that Feng Shui was – in terms of China's history – a comparatively recent innovation. But archaeological excavations have recently unearthed compass plates dating from the first century BC which are identical in detail to illustrations in books written a thousand years later. This reveals that although Yang Yun-sung might have been the first known author of a book expounding the principles of Feng Shui, the practice and oral traditions were already extremely ancient.

The Form and Compass schools are mutually dependent, and though there is a mystical side to Feng Shui, its foundation being based on the Chinese scriptures, at the core lies a good deal of common sense. The earliest Feng Shui consultants were in fact the equivalent of today's surveyors and valuers.

Thus, the ideal site for a farmstead would be on the slope of a hill, neither at the peak, where there would be a shortage of water, nor at its foot, which would make it difficult to defend. It would be close to running water, and face south for the sunshine while being protected from the wind from the north. But although not every house could be aligned north-south in a perfect environment, it was presumed that such a setting would ensure security, prosperity and so, ultimately, happiness.

There is, however, in addition to the Form and Compass schools, another canon of traditions, which sceptical Western observers scathingly regard as a collection of superstitions. These precepts have no classical foundation and

The prosperity of Hong Kong is said to be due to the favourable Feng Shui produced by the twin influences of the Dragon Mountains of Kowloon and the surrounding ocean. But overdevelopment has sapped the strength of the Dragon influences, leaving the future of Hong Kong in peril.

defy objective explanation; neither do they have any common thread relating them together. Yet these *ad hoc* prescriptions are widely known among the Chinese and universally accepted. So whereas the Feng Shui master might give a scholarly analysis of the surroundings, and carefully plot the location and orientation according to precise Feng Shui laws, the client could feel very disappointed if the consultant did not also leave behind a sealed packet of mystic ingredients, a talisman or two, and burn a few obligatory sticks of incense to placate the wayward spirits.

YANG AND YIN FENG SHUI

The study of buildings in relation to their environment is known as yang or positive Feng Shui. Although this is the more obvious aspect of Feng Shui, for the Chinese there is another, vitally important aspect of Feng Shui: yin or negative Feng Shui, which applies, not to houses for the living, but to the dwellings of the dead. This aspect of Feng Shui is a study in itself, covering funeral rites and ceremonies, the correct alignment of tombs, and the selection of dates for burial. Closely related is a whole genre of magical myths and legends woven round the abilities of the yin Feng Shui master to summon the corpses of the newly deceased in order that, zombie-like, they could perform his bidding. Although this is the material from which countless Chinese horror movies are built, the source of the belief is surprisingly benign. If an elder relative had died in a far-off city, poor families may not have been able to afford the cost of transporting the deceased for interment in the ancestral grave. The family would therefore call on the services of a skilled Taoist master of yin Feng Shui, and, provided that the animating force had not yet completely left the corpse, the sorceror could command the corpse's physical body to make its own way to the desirable tomb which had been prepared for it.

THE LOCATION

When a site is being assessed to find its potential Feng Shui qualities, the first step is to look at the surrounding landscape. In the ideal situation, there would be an open space in front of the building, with rolling hills behind. The main feature of the landscape would be the Dragon, a prominent hill or mountain, and various features of the hill would be identified by the Feng Shui consultant as the Dragon's head, body, and limbs, while streams and rivulets would be regarded as its veins. The community that lived in the benign gaze of the Dragon would be certain to become wealthy. Indeed, if it were not for the presence of the Nine Dragons (in Cantonese, *Kowloon*) to the north of Hong Kong, that city would never have achieved its present prosperity.

There are many places where the terrain is flat and featureless, yet there is still good fortune inherent in the patterns of rivers, lakes and waterways that surround the area. In cities, the meanderings of watercourses may be imitated by the flow of traffic through busy thoroughfares. Similarly, the silhouettes of the roofs of buildings on the skyline will have as much significance in an urban landscape as the shapes of hills in a rural setting.

THE INFLUENCE OF FIVE

To understand more fully the significance of the shapes on the skyline, whether natural or man-made, it is important to be familiar with the underlying philosophy of the Five Elements. ('Elements' may not be an accurate translation of the Chinese technical term, but it has been sanctioned by long usage.)

The five elements, or forces, are called Wood, Fire, Earth, Metal and Water. Four of these five elements are related to the four cardinal points, with Earth being at the centre. The Four Cardinal points are in turn related to four seasons, each of which has its own symbolic colour and shape. Thus wood, which encompasses all growing vegetative life, is the element related to the Spring, the beginning of the year, the sunrise and the eastern direction. The appropriate colour is bluish-green, like the green of plants, or the Great Sea to the east of China, while the associated shape is tall and narrow, like the trunk of a tree.

Fire, shown by the heat of the sun, is the element of midday, the Summer, the South, animal life and the colour red. Its symbolic shape is triangular, the sharp points of the triangle being likened to flames.

Earth, at the centre, is not associated with any direction or season, but is symbolized by flat shapes and the colour ochre, like the earth of central China. It represents stability and all earthenware materials.

Metal is the element of Autumn, signifying either swords or agricultural implements. The appropriate colour is silvery white, like the element itself, but also like the snows of the Himalayan mountains to the west of China. Metal is represented by circular shapes, perhaps in allusion to metal coins.

The astonishing scenery of Kuei-lin has inspired Chinese poets and painters for centuries. It was here that Yang Yun-sung first outlined the principles of 'form school' Feng Shui, equating the shapes of the hills to the astrological Dragon and Tiger.

Finally, the element Water represents Winter, night and the colour black, and symbolizes all fluid situations, including speech and communication. Because Water lacks form, irregular shapes denote the Water element.

If a particular shape dominates the location, the related element influences both natural and human events. For example, acutely angled triangles would put the affected area in danger of accident through fire, unless there were other, balancing features. To this end, it is important to realize that each element is able to 'produce', or reinforce, the next in the sequence: Wood – Fire – Earth – Metal – Water – Wood. Conversely, each element destroys and neutralizes the effect of the next but one in the series; thus Wood destroys Earth, but is itself destroyed by Metal.

WOOD
burns,
producing
FIRE
produces ash or
EARTH
from which is mined
METAL
which melts, like
WATER
which nourishes
WOOD

WOOD
takes away the
nourishment from
EARTH
muddies and pollutes
WATER
which extinguishes
FIRE
which melts
METAL
which chops down
WOOD

Thus a building with a sharply pointed roof, representing the element Fire, in an environment mainly surrounded by tall trees, or buildings with columns and pillars, would be in a Wood environment. As Wood 'produces' Fire, the situation is stimulating. Feng Shui scholars aver that this type of location produces very intelligent children, while several manufacturing and commercial enterprises also benefit from this combination of elements.

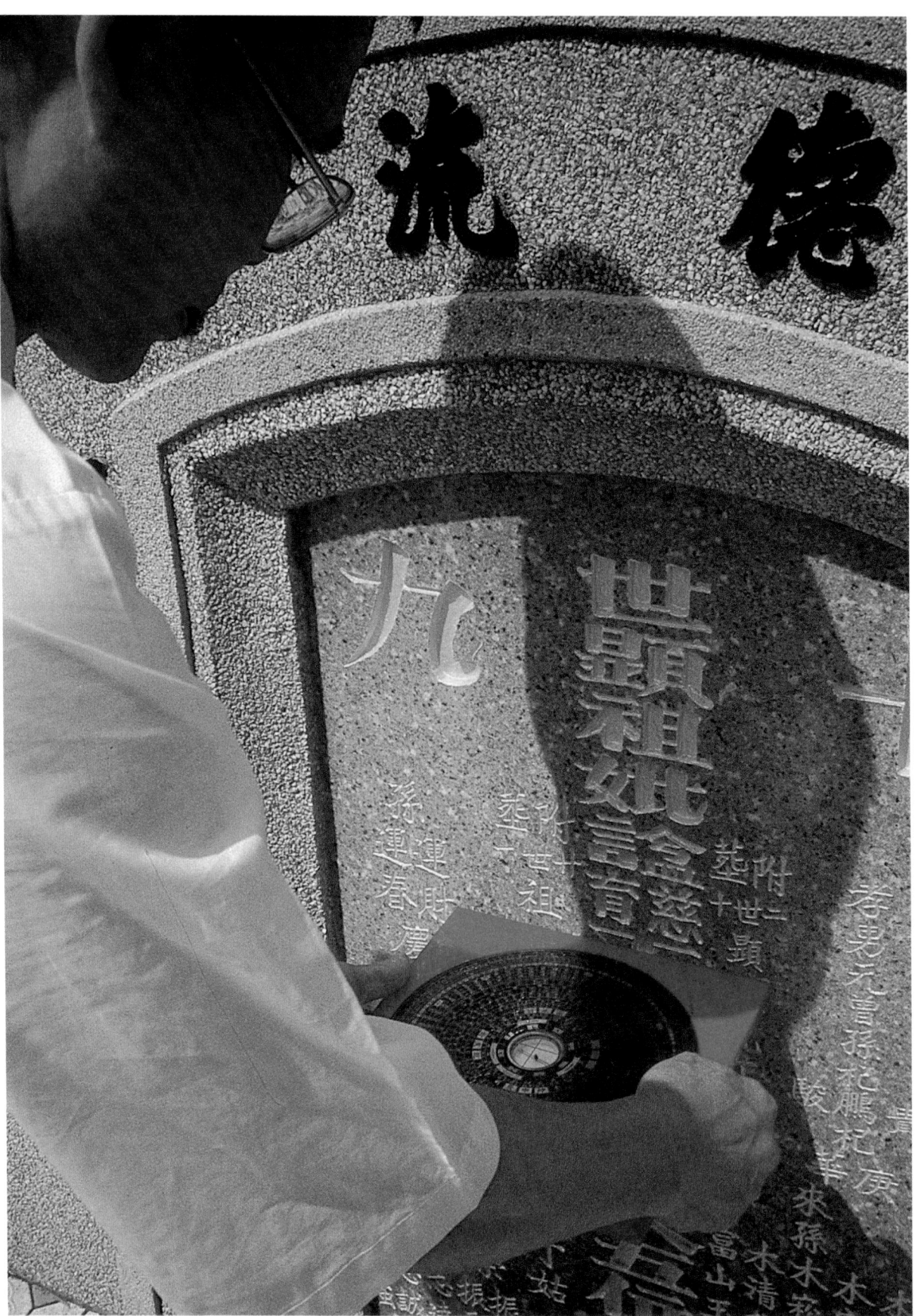

THE EASTERN WORLD

A professional geomancer uses the Lo P'an to ascertain the orientation of a tomb, at Ping Tung in southern Taiwan. If the tomb has good Feng Shui this will ensure that the ancestors will be content, and this in turn will bring merit and good fortune to their descendants.

FLOW GENTLE *CH'I*

Having taken into account the surrounding environment, the orientation of the building and various other features, the consultant will then enter the building to advise on the interior. At some point the Feng Shui master is bound to consult the *LoP'an*, through which it is possible to locate the ideal positions for various functions such as the study, the bedroom, or the correct siting of doors and windows.

The *LoP'an* is a specially designed compass. It is to the Feng Shui master what the stethoscope is to the doctor, the virtual insignia of his calling. The face of the compass dial is divided into several circles, each sub-divided into numerous further divisions representing, not only different compass points, but lucky and unlucky directions, the hours, months and days associated with each compass point, and even the constellation exerting the greatest influence at that moment and in that direction.

The web-like arrangement of divisions resembled a net to the Chinese, who thus called it the 'net plate' – in Chinese, *LoP'an*. The saucer-shaped 'net plate' sits in a square base which has two cross-threads running over the pivot of the compass needle. When a site is under inspection, the sides of the square base are aligned with the walls of the room or building. The circular plate housing the compass needle is then turned until the south point on the dial lines up with the compass needle (Chinese compasses point to the south, not the north). The cross-threads on the base then indicate the various favourable or unfavourable times associated with the orientation of the building, enabling the consultant to suggest the correct positioning of the entrance, or the ideal moment for the building's inauguration.

There must, for example, be a good flow of *Ch'i*. This is something peculiar to Chinese philosophy and consequently defies adequate translation. Loosely speaking, *Ch'i* is a current of good, healthy energy through the building.

Ch'i meanders and flows in curves: it should bubble effortlessly through the building, without ending in enclosed areas, where it stifles and consequently exerts a bad influence. While it may be likened to the flow of fresh air through a house, *Ch'i* is not just fresh air, for it can be deflected from, or along, its course by the means of suitably positioned mirrors. It is unwise for *Ch'i* to flow straight through a house without being able to pass on its revitalizing forces: a corridor or hallway which runs straight to the rear from the front entrance is such a case, as the *Ch'i* fails to permeate the rooms.

Similarly, reception rooms which have windows at both ends lose their *Ch'i*. In effect, there is no comfortable focal point where it is possible to sit without having a window at one's back – subconsciously creating a feeling of unease. The solution is simple: blinds should be drawn over one of the windows during the day, so that light enters from only one direction. Alternatively, the room should be partitioned or otherwise divided into two smaller areas.

In China, a garden provides the ideal opportunity to balance the Feng Shui of the locality with its surrounding scenery. For this reason, the English landscaped garden has a much more favourable Feng Shui than the formal, continental style.

SECRET ARROWS

The converse of *Ch'i* currents, which flow in undulating lines, are *Sha*, which shoot along straight lines like an arrow. The Chinese aversion to straight lines was one of the reasons why railways were slow to develop in China. If straight *Sha*-transporting lines, such as are produced by roads, paths and telegraph wires, are unavoidable, they must approach the house obliquely, in order for the *Sha* to be deflected.

Sha can also be produced by angles pointing at the house: these might be found in the sharp corners of other buildings, or roads which suddenly turn, forming a bend which is like an arrowhead. Such secret arrows are sure portents of impending accident.

A path that curves towards a house is preferred to one that runs straight up to the entrance. Winding or zig-zag paths are able to deflect the adverse influences of harmful Sha, *which always travels in straight lines.*

MIRROR ON THE WALL

Mirrors are often used to encourage the flow of *Ch'i* and to dissipate harmful *Sha*. Mirrors have always fascinated the Chinese, and were regarded as a door to the world beyond. Indeed, it was customary for the backs of mirrors to be decorated with cosmic symbols, so much so that the designs on the backs of Chinese mirrors are an authentic chronicle of the history of Chinese cosmological thought.

The mirror most often employed today for Feng Shui purposes is in an octagonal frame, on which are depicted the Eight Trigrams – a

powerful demonifuge and talisman. The actual mirror is often concave or convex, the better to dissipate harmful *Sha*. Mirrors, however, are not favoured in bedrooms, because they stimulate the *Ch'i*, thus provoking a restless sleep. It is also regarded as dangerous for the dreamer's soul to catch its reflection in a mirror, lest it take fright and leave the body.

THE EIGHT TRIGRAMS AND THEIR SYMBOLISM

The Eight Trigrams, found among the religious symbolism of nations from East Africa to Japan, are simply the eight possible arrangements of three lines, whole or broken (see Chapter Sixteen, The Chinese Book of Changes). They have been recorded in inscriptions which are several thousand years old.

Li — South. Fire and heat. Middle daughter. Heating; the kitchen; furnaces and ovens.

K'un — South-west. Nourishment. Mother. Medical centres, welfare, children's rooms.

Tui — West. Joy, laughter. Youngest daughter. Recreation, entertainment.

Ch'ien — North-west. Heaven. Authority. Father. Strength. Management, design, training.

K'an — North. Wheels, rotation, danger. Middle son. Workshops, garages, machinery.

Ken — North-east. Obstacles. Mountains. Youngest son. Entrances, security, barriers.

Chen — East. Thunder. Movement, speed. Eldest son. Transport, roads, distribution.

Sun — South-east. Trade, growth. Eldest daughter. Continuous operation: assembly lines and routine.

CHAPTER EIGHTEEN

STAR LORE IN THE EAST

Sidereal Astrology

Valerie J. Roebuck

Sidereal astrology, an astrology based on the fixed stars which is widely practised today in the countries of South and Southeast Asia, developed in the Indian subcontinent as part of the world-picture shared by Hindus, Buddhists and Jains. It owed its origin to two main sources, one of them indigenous, the other derived from cultures to the West.

The earliest Indian star-lore is to be found in the Vedas, four collections of hymns and prayers, composed from about 1500 BC on. The Vedas, written in often mysterious and riddling language, are full of awe and wonder at the power of the gods, combined with a strong sense of questioning of the meaning of things. In both respects they contain the seeds of later Hinduism. Many of the gods and goddesses of the Vedas are connected with the phenomena of Nature: earth and sky, fire and wind, dawn and night. The people of India 3,000 years ago, living in small settlements in a vast land, were acutely aware of how fully they depended on these powers for their survival.

They relied on the Sun for heat, and the light by which they worked, though in the Indian climate its power could also be destructive. The Moon was the measurer of time, its cool light a welcome sight after the heat of the day. The fixed stars too were revered: some of them were regarded as holy men and women, once mortal, but now living in the sky. Notable among them were Dhruva, 'the Fixed' or Pole Star, and the Seven Sages of the Great Bear. Agastya, a sage who took Vedic teachings to South India, was identified with the southern star Canopus. (The

planets, it appears, had not yet acquired any special significance: perhaps they were thought of as bright, moving stars.)

Most important among the stars were the lunar mansions, the constellations among which the Moon appeared to move in the course of its monthly journey. Originally the mansions varied in size according to their actual appearance in the sky, but by about 400 BC they had been systematized into a lunar Zodiac of 27 equal mansions, which could be used for making accurate measurements of celestial positions. Although the Indians may have learned some of their science from the Babylonians, the lunar mansion system seems to be purely Indian in origin.

Through centuries of observation, the Vedic star-lore developed into *jyotiṣa*, the study of the heavenly bodies. The early *jyotiṣins* (practitioners of *jyotiṣa*) combined the functions of astronomers, astrologers, mathematicians and meteorologists. They had not only to create a reliable calendar, based on the movements of the Sun and Moon, but also to watch for omens in the sky, and forecast the weather and outbreaks of disease. Their work was concerned with matters that affected the community as a whole, it was not yet with drawing up individual horoscopes.

The change from the Vedic star-lore to a developed system of astrology was largely inspired by the Greeks, whom the Indians called 'Yavanas' or Ionians. In the early centuries of the Christian era there were a number of Greek settlements in India. Best known now are probably those of Gandhāra, which covered parts of the present-day Afghanistan, Pakistan and north-west India, but there were others in the west coast areas of Gujarat and Maharashtra, important ports for the sea-trade between the Indian and Graeco-Roman cultural spheres.

The earliest Greek influence on Indian *jyotiṣa* seems to have come to western India from Alexandria, which was the main centre of science for late Greek civilization. Around AD 140, Yavaneśvara, 'Lord of the Greeks', translated a Greek astrological text into Sanskrit. This is now lost, but its influence can be traced in surviving works by Sphujidhvaja, in the mid-third century, and Mīnarāja, in the fourth. All these men seem to have been rulers among the Greek communities of western India. Sphujidhvaja's astrology is very close to that of the Alexandrian Greeks, though it already includes a certain amount that is purely Indian, such as references to the lunar mansions. Mīnarāja's, though it uses the Greek structure, is recognizably Indian astrology as it is known today.

For in taking over the Greek system, the Indian astrologers did not keep it unchanged, but adapted it to their own cosmology. Although they adopted the 12-sign Zodiac, they did not abandon their own system of lunar mansions, but found a way of reconciling the two. Previously they had counted the mansions from Kṛttikā, the Pleiades, but they now made Aśvinī (the two stars β and γ Arietis) the first mansion, so that both signs and mansions were measured from the same point.

THE DEVELOPMENT AND INFLUENCE OF INDIAN ASTROLOGY

The Indian Subcontinent, also known as South Asia, has been a centre of civilization since at least 3000 BC. It is similar in size to Europe (excluding Russia), and has a comparable variety of terrain, climate, language and people. Despite this variety, the area possesses a strong cultural unity, which has persisted throughout recorded history. An outstanding feature of South Asian civilization is its ability to absorb ideas from other cultures, but in doing so to develop them and give them a character of its own. Best known among its gifts to the world are its distinctive achievements in religion, philosophy and the arts. Less appreciated, perhaps, are its discoveries in mathematics and the sciences, including the 'Arabic' – really Indian – system of numbers which, by superseding the unwieldy Roman system, made modern mathematics possible.

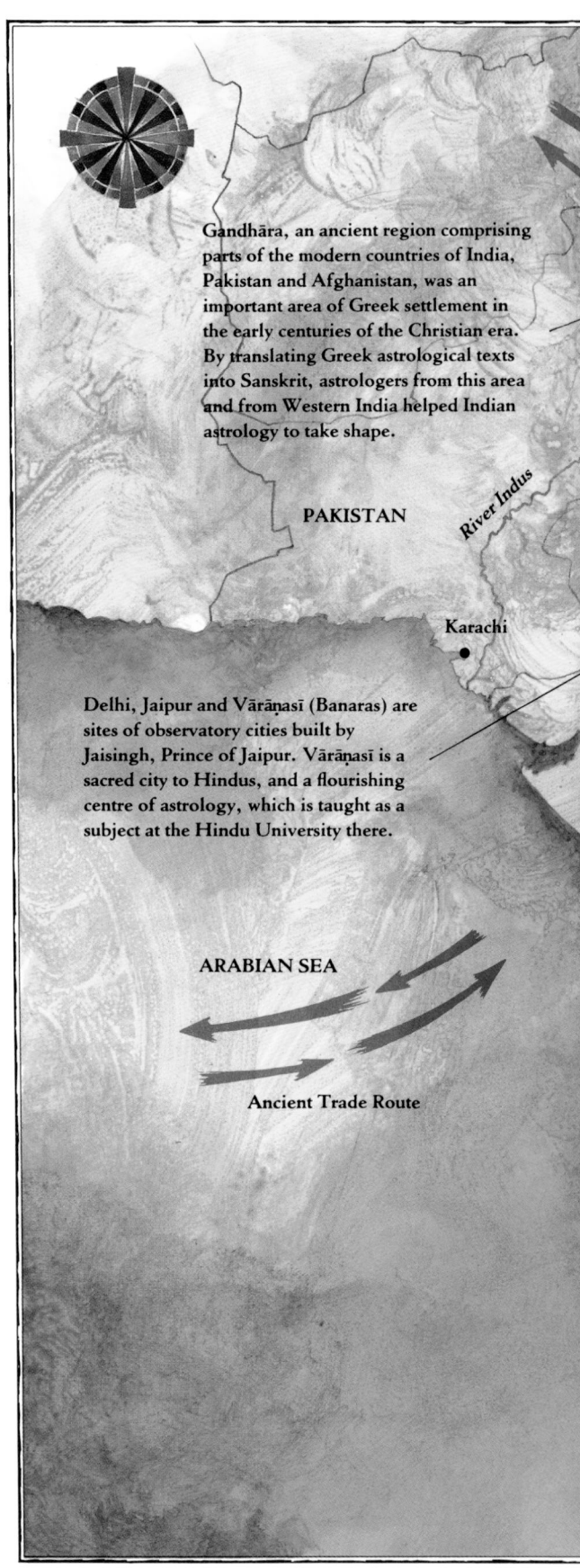

Gandhāra, an ancient region comprising parts of the modern countries of India, Pakistan and Afghanistan, was an important area of Greek settlement in the early centuries of the Christian era. By translating Greek astrological texts into Sanskrit, astrologers from this area and from Western India helped Indian astrology to take shape.

PAKISTAN

River Indus

Karachi

Delhi, Jaipur and Vārāṇasī (Banaras) are sites of observatory cities built by Jaisingh, Prince of Jaipur. Vārāṇasī is a sacred city to Hindus, and a flourishing centre of astrology, which is taught as a subject at the Hindu University there.

ARABIAN SEA

Ancient Trade Route

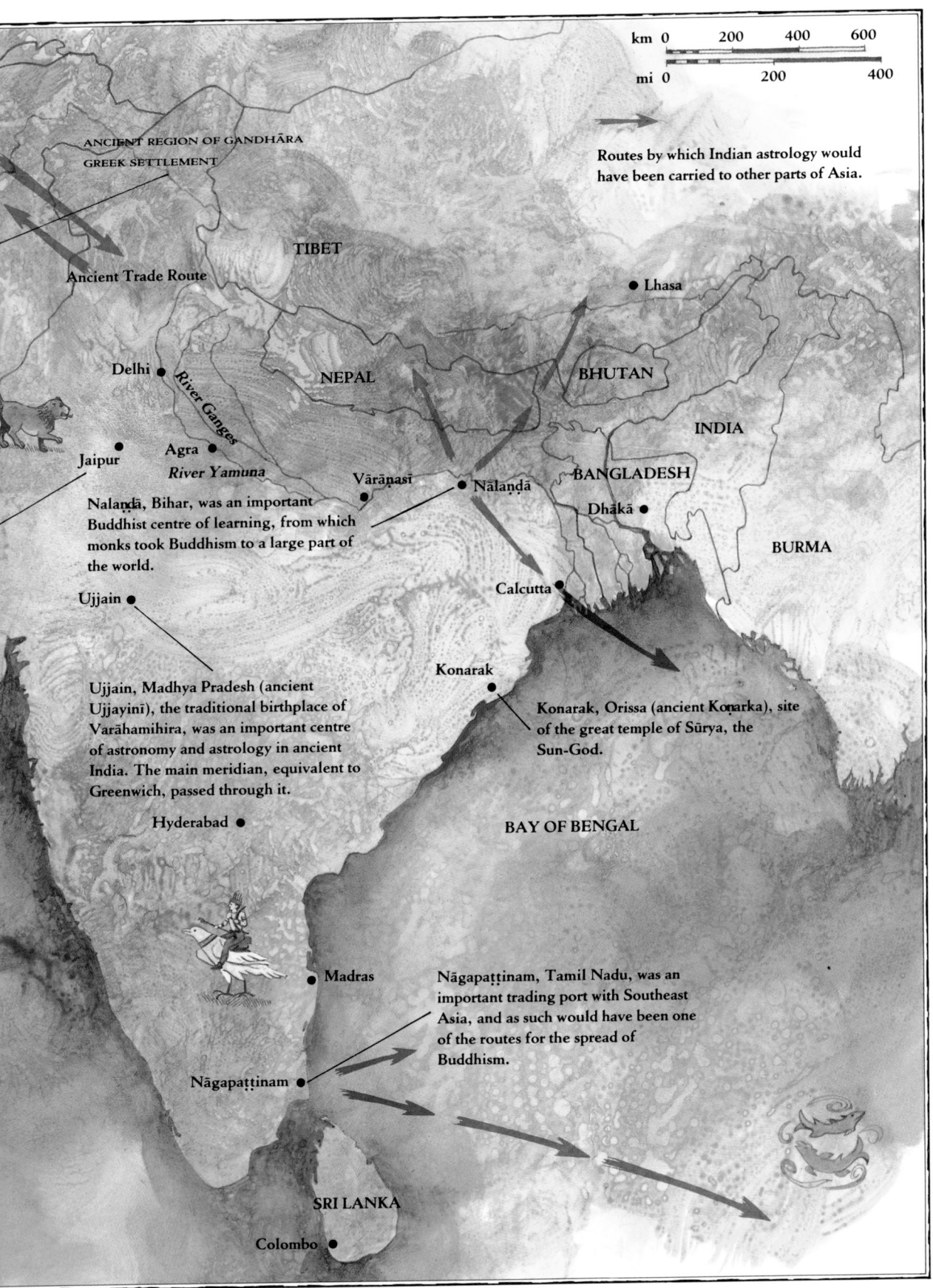

Routes by which Indian astrology would have been carried to other parts of Asia.

Nalandā, Bihar, was an important Buddhist centre of learning, from which monks took Buddhism to a large part of the world.

Ujjain, Madhya Pradesh (ancient Ujjayinī), the traditional birthplace of Varāhamihira, was an important centre of astronomy and astrology in ancient India. The main meridian, equivalent to Greenwich, passed through it.

Konarak, Orissa (ancient Koṇarka), site of the great temple of Sūrya, the Sun-God.

Nāgapaṭṭinam, Tamil Nadu, was an important trading port with Southeast Asia, and as such would have been one of the routes for the spread of Buddhism.

A more fundamental adaptation was the use of a different Zodiac system. Although Greek astrologers were by now using the tropical Zodiac (see Chapter Six, Shapes in the Stars), the Indians soon returned to the more ancient sidereal Zodiac, in keeping with the greater importance they gave to the fixed stars.

Later Indian astrologers used a system of sidereal astrology into which both Greek and Vedic elements had been fully assimilated. By common consent, the greatest of them all was Varāhamihira, believed to have been court astrologer to one of the Gupta emperors around the middle of the sixth century. Varāhamihira wrote on every aspect of *jyotiṣa*, effectively giving Indian astrology the form in which it has been practised ever since. His works are still studied by Indian astrologers today.

The main development since Varāhamihira's time has been the growth in importance of the lunar nodes, Rāhu and Ketu. These are the points at which the apparent paths of the Sun and Moon intersect, and eclipses can occur. By about the ninth century they had come to be treated as dark planets on a par with the seven visible ones.

This change seems to have been influenced by the spiritual movement known as Tantra, which found astrology congenial to its view of each human being as a microcosm, reflecting the greater universe or macrocosm. The Tantric cult of the Nine Planets, visualized as gods, seems to have reached its height in the mid-thirteenth century with the building of the Sun Temple at Konarak, Orissa. It was conceived as a colossal chariot of the Sun, and adorned with magnificent sculptures, including figures of the Sun-God and the planetary deities.

Indian astrology has both influenced and been influenced by the thought of many other civilizations. It spread to the Buddhist cultures of Tibet and Southeast Asia, where it combined with local traditions to appear in new and distinctive forms. It affected the astrology of the Islamic world, and was influenced by it in turn, though mainly in matters of detail; the basic structure had by now become fixed.

Through the Islamic world, a few of the ideas of Indian astrology reached medieval and Renaissance Europe, but the main influence in that direction began much later, when, from the nineteenth century on, Western thinkers became interested in Eastern philosophy. In recent times, in the hands of Western astrologers, Indian astrology has helped to generate new forms of sidereal and harmonic astrology.

THE SIDEREAL ZODIAC

Both Indian and Western astrology chart the movements of the planets in relation to the ecliptic, the apparent path of the Sun through the sky, which they divide up into a Zodiac of

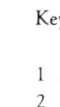

Key

1 Aries
2 Taurus
3 Gemini
4 Cancer
5 Leo
6 Virgo
7 Libra
8 Scorpio
9 Sagittarius
10 Capricorn
11 Aquarius
12 Pisces

This Lotus and Zodiac, c. twelfth century, is from Pattancheruvu, Andhra Pradesh. The stone cylinder is topped by a lotus surrounded by the signs of the Zodiac. The signs run clockwise, beginning with the Ram at the bottom (see key).

The temple of Sūrya, the Sun-God, at Konarak, Orissa, was built in the reign of King Narasiṃhadeva (1238–64). Even in ruins, it stands over 30 metres high, and was originally twice that height.

twelve equal signs. However, they begin their Zodiacs from two different points.

The Western system uses a tropical Zodiac, based on the seasons of the solar year, while the Indian system uses a sidereal Zodiac, based on the fixed stars. 0° Aries in the tropical Zodiac corresponds to the position of the Sun at the spring equinox (the 'vernal point'). 0° Aries in the sidereal Zodiac is the point among the fixed stars at which the Sun is thought to enter the constellation of the Ram. The Western signs,

unlike the Indian ones, have long ceased to coincide with the constellations from which they take their names.

The Zodiac and the Planets: *an engraving based on an eighteenth-century Indian painting. In the centre Sūrya, the Sun-God, rides a chariot drawn by seven horses (the days of the week). Surrounding him are the deities of the Moon (no. 5 on the diagram), Mars (6), Mercury (7), Jupiter (8), Venus (9), Saturn (2), Rāhu (3) and Ketu (4). The outer ring shows the signs of the Zodiac. From* The Hindu Pantheon *(1810) by Edward Moor, a pioneer of Indian studies in the West.*

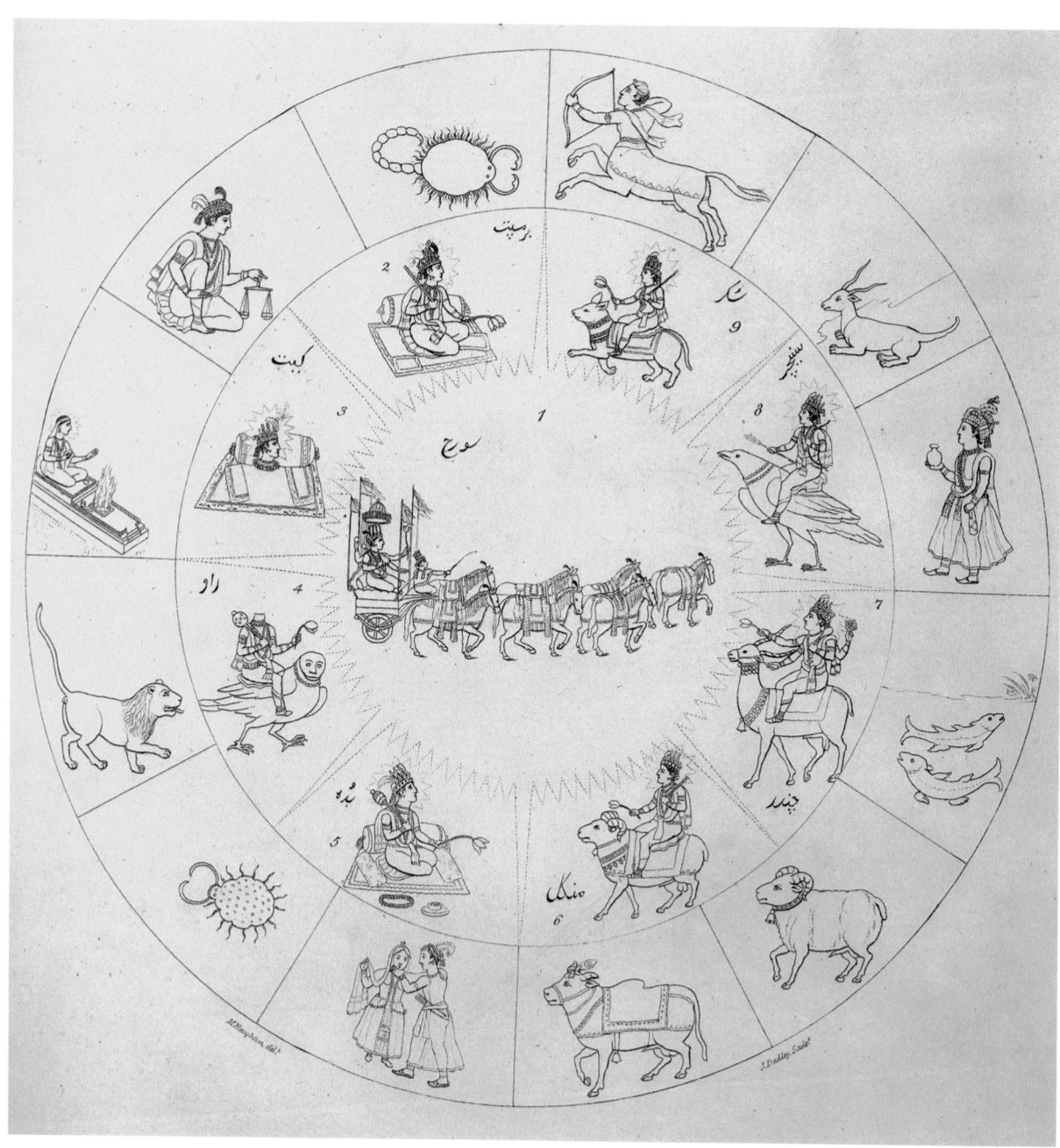

The discrepancy is caused by the *precession of the equinoxes* (see Chapter Six, Shapes in the Stars). Not only does the Earth turn on its own axis, but, because of the gravitational pull of the Sun and Moon on its bulging equator, the axis itself revolves, like that of a spinning top which is slowing down. As a result, each of the Earth's Poles is turning in relations to the stars, completing a full circle every 25,800 years. As the Poles turn, the positions of the equinoxes move too, in the opposite direction to the movement of the Sun and planets, at the rate of 50" of arc per year, or a degree every 72 years.

The difference between the tropical and sidereal systems at any given time is called the *ayanāṃśa*, a Sanskrit term that has been adopted by Western astrologers. When calculating an Indian-style chart, the astrologer should work out the positions of the planets, the Ascendant, etc., from the ephemeris in the usual way, but complete the calculation by subtracting the appropriate *ayanāṃśa* (generally considered to be in the region of 24°) from each.

Even without the telescope, Indian jyotiṣins of former times made observations of remarkable accuracy, using measuring instruments of great size. The Jaipur Observatory is one of three built in the late-seventeenth century for the astrologer-prince Jaisingh. The Rāśivalaya Yantra *(above) was used to calculate the position of the Sun. The view of the Observatory (below) is from the top of the tallest instrument.*

THE SIGNS OF THE ZODIAC (*RĀŚI*):

Indian names and symbols, with Western equivalents.

1 *Meṣa*, the Ram: Aries
2 *Vṛsabha*, the Bull: Taurus
3 *Mithuna*, the Couple, the woman holding a *Vīnā* (stringed instrument) and the man a mace: Gemini
4 *Karkata*, the Crab: Cancer
5 *Simha*, the Lion: Leo
6 *Kanyā*, the Maiden, often depicted in a boat, and holding a lamp and grain: *Virgo*
7 *Tulā*, the Scales, often shown as a merchant weighing his goods in the market-place: Libra
8 *Vṛścika*, the Scorpion: Scorpio
9 *Dhanus*, the Bow, often, as in the West, a centaur archer: Sagittarius
10 *Makara*, the Sea-monster, a mythical aquatic beast, typically resembling an ornate crocodile with an elephant's trunk, although the astrological version is often shown as a deer with a fish's tail: Capricorn
11 *Kumbha*, the Water-pot, sometimes, as in the West, shown as a man emptying a water-pot carried on his shoulder: Aquarius
12 *Mīna*, the Fishes: Pisces.

In texts in English, the Indian signs are generally called by the names of their Western equivalents: a convenient custom so long as it is remembered that it is the sidereal, not the tropical, Aries or Taurus that is meant.

THE HOUSES (*BHĀVA*)

The houses are reckoned from the Ascendant, the point of the ecliptic rising at the time of the birth or event. The method most commonly used is a form of the Equal House system, in which each house is an exact 30° portion of the Ecliptic;

however, the Ascendant marks the centre of the first house, not, as in Western astrology, its cusp. The areas of life covered by the houses are similar, but not identical, in the two systems:

1 Ascendant: the body, appearance and personality
2 Wealth: property, family, speech
3 Brothers: brothers and sisters, courage, food
4 Kin: the early life, roots, and above all the mother
5 Sons: offspring, intelligence, actions done in past lives
6 Enemies, or Wounds: ill health and other obstacles
7 Wife: the marriage-partner, love, respect
8 Death: the life-span, death, and future rebirth
9 Religion: the spiritual teacher, the father and the proper way of life
10 Work: career, status, knowledge
11 Gain: income, prosperity, success
12 Loss: expenditure, misfortune, travel.

THE PLANETS (*GRAHA*)

The planets are named in the order of their days of the week, an ancient Babylonian sequence preserved in both European and Indian languages. All have masculine names, and are pictured in art as male gods. For astrological purposes, however, the Moon, Venus and Rāhu are regarded as feminine planets, and Mercury, Saturn and Ketu as neuter.

Sūrya or *Ravi*: the Sun
Candra or *Soma*: the Moon
Maṅgala 'Auspicious', or *Aṅgāraka*, 'Burning Charcoal': Mars
Budha, 'Knower': Mercury
Bṛhaspati, 'Lord of Sacred Speech', or *Guru*, 'Spiritual Teacher': Jupiter

Śukra, 'White' or 'Sperm': Venus
Śani, 'Slow', or *Śanaiścara*, 'Slow-goer': Saturn.

The list of nine planets is completed by the two lunar nodes, pictured in myth as Eclipse Demons pursuing the Sun and Moon: *Rāhu*, 'Seizer': the North Node *Ketu*, 'Banner', 'Sign': the South Node.

The planets discovered in historical times, Uranus, Neptune and Pluto, have not yet acquired a settled place in Indian astrology.

Planets are said to be strong in their signs of rulership, which are the same as in the Western system: the Sun rules Leo, the Moon rules Cancer, Mercury rules Gemini and Virgo, Venus rules Taurus and Libra, Mars rules Aries and Scorpio, Jupiter rules Pisces and Sagittarius, and Saturn rules Aquarius and Capricorn. But they are stronger still in their signs of exaltation, in which their energy is most harmoniously expressed: the Sun in Aries, the Moon in Taurus, Mars in Capricorn, Mercury in Virgo, Jupiter in Cancer, Venus in Pisces, and Saturn in Libra.

For the purpose of prediction, some planets are said to be 'benefic' or 'lucky', and others 'malefic' or 'unlucky'. Jupiter and Venus are benefic, the Sun, Mars, Saturn, Rāhu and Ketu malefic. The Moon is benefic when waxing or full, malefic when waning or new. Mercury is benefic in conjunction with benefic planets, and malefic with malefics: on its own it is slightly benefic. Strong planets are well disposed, and when in exaltation, even malefics are benign.

Aspects and conjunctions are always measured sign-to-sign, so that any planet in Aries is in opposition to any planet in Libra. Rāhu and Ketu do not form aspects, only conjunctions. No account is taken of 'easy' and 'difficult' aspects, only of the nature and compatibility of the aspecting planets.

THE LUNAR MANSIONS
(NAKSATRA)

Just as a sign of the Zodiac represents the Sun's movement in a month, a lunar mansion corresponds to the Moon's movement in a day. The Moon takes about 27.3 days to circle the ecliptic, and Indian astrology generally divides the ecliptic into 27 equal mansions, though for certain purposes a 28-fold system may be used, an extra mansion being inserted between numbers 21 and 22. In myth and iconography, the mansions are visualized as the wives of the Moon-God, whom he visits night by night. In a birth-chart, the mansion occupied by the Moon is particularly significant, especially if it is full, waxing, or strongly placed.

1 0° Aries: *Aśvinī*, 'Possessing Horses', 'the Horsewoman': a horse's head
2 13° 20' Aries: *Bharanī*, 'Bearing': female sexual organ
3 26° 40' Aries: *Kṛttikā*, 'the Cutters': a weapon or a flame
4 10° Taurus: *Rohinī*, 'the Growing (or Red) One': a temple, an ox-cart, or a cow's head
5 23°20' Taurus: *Mṛgaśiras*, 'the Deer's Head': a deer's head
6 6° 40' Gemini: *Ārdrā*, 'the Moist One': a tear-drop
7 20° Gemini: *Punarvasū*, 'the Two Good-Again': a quiver of arrows
8 3° 20' Cancer: *Puṣya*, 'Nourishing': a cow's udder
9 16° 40' Cancer: *Āśleṣā*, 'the Clinging': a coiled snake
10 0° Leo: *Maghā*, 'the Great', 'the Bountiful': a royal throne-room
11 13° 20' Leo: *Pūrvaphalgunī*, 'the Former Reddish (or Small) One': a swinging hammock
12 26° 40' Leo: *Uttaraphalgunī*, 'the Latter Reddish (or Small) One': a bed or couch
13 10° Virgo: *Hasta*, 'the Hand': a hand
14 23° 20' Virgo: *Citrā*, 'Bright', 'Many-coloured', 'Wonderful': a bright jewel
15 6° 40' Libra: *Svāti*, 'Self-going': a young shoot blown by the wind
16 20° Libra: *Viśākhā*, the 'Forked' or 'Two-branched' (or *Rādhā* 'Delightful'): a gateway decorated with leaves
17 3° 20' Scorpio: *Anurādhā*, 'Additional Rādhā', 'After-Rādhā': a staff, or a row of offerings to the gods
18 16° 40' Scorpio: *Jyeṣṭhā*, 'the Eldest': a circular talisman
19 0° Sagittarius: *Mūla*, 'the Root': a tied bunch of roots
20 13° 20' Sagittarius: *Pūrvāsādhā*, 'the Former Unconquered': a winnowing basket or fan
21 26° 40' Sagittarius: *Uttarāṣādhā*, 'the Latter Unconquered': an elephant's tusk
Intercalary Mansion. Abhijit, 'the Victorious': a triangle or three-cornered nut
22 10° Capricorn: *Śravaṇa*, 'Hearing' or 'Limping': three footprints side by side
23 23° 20' Capricorn: *Śraviṣṭhā*, 'the Most Famous' (or *Dhaniṣṭhā*, 'the Wealthiest'): a musical drum
24 6° 40' Aquarius: *Śatabhiṣaj*, 'The Hundred Physicians': a circle enclosing a space
25 20° Aquarius: *Pūrvabhadrapadā*, 'the Former Lucky Feet': the first end of a bed (the head?)
26 3° 20' Pisces: *Uttarabhadrapadā*, 'the Latter Lucky Feet': the other end of the bed
27 16° 40' Pisces: *Revatī*, 'Wealthy': a drum.

The lunar mansion and Zodiac systems are reconciled by dividing the ecliptic into 108 *navāmśas* or ninth-signs, each of which is also a quarter of a mansion. The *navāmśas* are allotted in order to the rulers of the 12 signs of the Zodiac, nine times repeated, and are often used for drawing subsidiary charts. The use of *navāmśas* and other subdivisions of signs by Indian astrologers helped to inspire the recent development of harmonic astrology, in which additional charts are calculated from the main one.

Rāhu and Ketu, the Lunar Nodes, are pictured as eclipse demons who seek to devour the Sun and Moon. Here Rāhu, fanged and ferocious, grasps two slices of Moon, while a serpent-tailed Ketu holds a sword and (in the missing hand) a bowl of fire. These are part of a set of Nine Planets from the Sūrya Temple, Konarak, now in the British Museum.

INDIAN ASTROLOGY TODAY

Because they have part of their heritage in common, there is much in the Indian system that a Western astrologer will find familiar: far more so than in the case of, say, the Chinese system. However, the ways in which it is used reflect differences in the nature of Indian and Western society. Whereas modern Western astrology has to a great extent rejected prediction, and concentrated on individual psychology, Asian astrologers are still prepared to talk about benefic and malefic planets, and to forecast the events of the client's life. In this respect, their way is closer to the Western astrology of earlier times.

Unlike their Western counterparts, Indian astrologers may even attempt to forecast the time of a client's death. For Asian people, death is not the taboo subject it may be elsewhere; indeed it is important to prepare for it properly in order to face it in a calm state of mind. The truth of reincarnation is taken for granted, and some Indian astrology books give rules for working out from the birth-chart where we spent our last life and, from the chart of the time of death, in what kind of realm we are likely to be born in the next one. This approach is not as fatalistic as it may appear, since in the South Asian religions the events that happen to us are believed to be the result of our past actions, either in this life or a previous one. By living well in the present life, whatever the circumstances, we can build up a store of merit which will bring about happier rebirths in the future.

People in India or Southeast Asia might go to an astrologer for advice over any kind of problem. An entrepreneur might ask about the prospects for an investment, a farmer might want to know where to look for a missing animal, and of course anyone might want help in resolving difficulties in the family. Some would go to an astrologer in the market-place, but others would have a personal astrologer whom they consulted regularly, just as they might have a personal physician.

Both men and women practise as astrologers. The knowledge is handed down in certain families of the Brahmin (priestly) class, but it is also possible to study it at university. Some priests or monks are learned in astrology, and may use it in giving advice to their followers.

As well as dealing with mundane problems, Indian astrology provides a framework for relating the human body and mind to the Cosmos as a whole. The universe is pictured as *Kālapuruṣa*, the Time Man, who symbolizes both the Creator and every human being. His body is composed of the signs of the Zodiac: Aries is his head, Taurus his face and neck, Gemini his shoulders and arms, Cancer his chest, Leo his heart, Virgo his belly, Libra his hips and navel, Scorpio his sexual and excretory organs, Sagittarius his thighs, Capricorn his knees, Aquarius his lower legs, and Pisces his feet.

The planets represent his inner qualities. The Sun is his true self, the Moon his mind, Mars his courage, Mercury his speech, Jupiter his knowledge and happiness, Venus his desire, and Saturn his sorrow. The strength of the planets within the birth-chart is said to show the strength of those qualities within the individual, with the exception of Saturn: a strong Saturn means *less* sorrow, because it brings understanding. Viewed on this level, all the signs and all the planets are equally 'benefic' and equally holy.

Some Indian astrologers combine their art with other methods of divination. This one, working in a street in Calcutta, seeks omens in the behaviour of the birds, seen in a cage beside him.

CHAPTER NINETEEN

MIRRORS IN THE SKY

Tibetan Methods of Divination

Jay L. Goldberg

Clouds drift among high mountain peaks, silence spreads across vast plateaus, and the ear strains at the sound of ethereal winds. This is the kingdom of Tibet, the Roof of the World, the Land of Snows, long known to the world only through a veil of mystical obscurity. This once-forgotten land has been a place of interest for the spiritually minded for many years, held in high regard as a place of mystery and wonder. This is not just the outsider's point of view, but in many ways is held by the Tibetan people. For them, the world truly is a place of awe, in both a terrifying and a bewildering sense. To make some order of it, or at least to obtain a feeling of security, Tibetans have always sought the aid and reassurance of divination.

There are a large variety of divinatory systems in Tibet: astrology, mediumship, reading omens in bodies of water, viewing images reflected in mirrors or on thumb-nails, tying knotted cords, calling forth visions in dreams, casting dice, and interpreting naturally occurring phenomena such as the colour and placement of rainbows, the direction or type of thunderous sounds, or the direction and time of calls of black birds. This does not exhaust the list, but it does give an idea of the extent to which Tibetans sought divinatory knowledge.

Some of these forms of divination are indigenous to Tibet itself, but a great influence was also exerted by both India and China. The indigenous religion of Bon was the sole belief system in Tibet for centuries, and it had a number of its own divinatory systems. However, with the arising of Buddhism in Tibet, this entire belief system underwent a drastic change.

It was under the leadership of King Srongtsan Gampo (AD 617–650) that Buddhism was introduced into Tibet. He had two wives, one from Nepal and one from China, each of whom influenced him to such an extent that he converted to Buddhism. He sent translators to India to obtain Buddhist texts and teachings. This started a flow of cultural interchanges that eventually revolutionized the religious beliefs and outlooks of Tibet.

A century later, under the rulership of Tri Srong Detsen, a large cultural exchange of Tibetans going to India and Indian teachers coming to Tibet occurred. During this period, the vast collection of Indian Buddhist scriptures were translated into Tibetan, and many Tibetans travelled to India to obtain the knowledge of Buddhism first hand. However, it was not only from India that the religious beliefs of Tibet were influenced, but from China as well. Chan (Zen) monks wandered through Tibet spreading their own form of Buddhism. Finally, according to Tibetan historical chronicles, King Tri Srong Detsen wanted to settle the question of which form of Buddhism should be embraced by the Tibetans. For this purpose he ordered a grand debate to be held. Accordingly, in about AD 750, a debate between the Indian Master Kamalashila and the Chinese Master Hwa Shan was held for several days. The debate ended in favour of Kamalashila and Indian Buddhism was decreed the official religion of Tibet. This did not mean, though, that the Chinese religious beliefs were obliterated in Tibet. Their influence continued

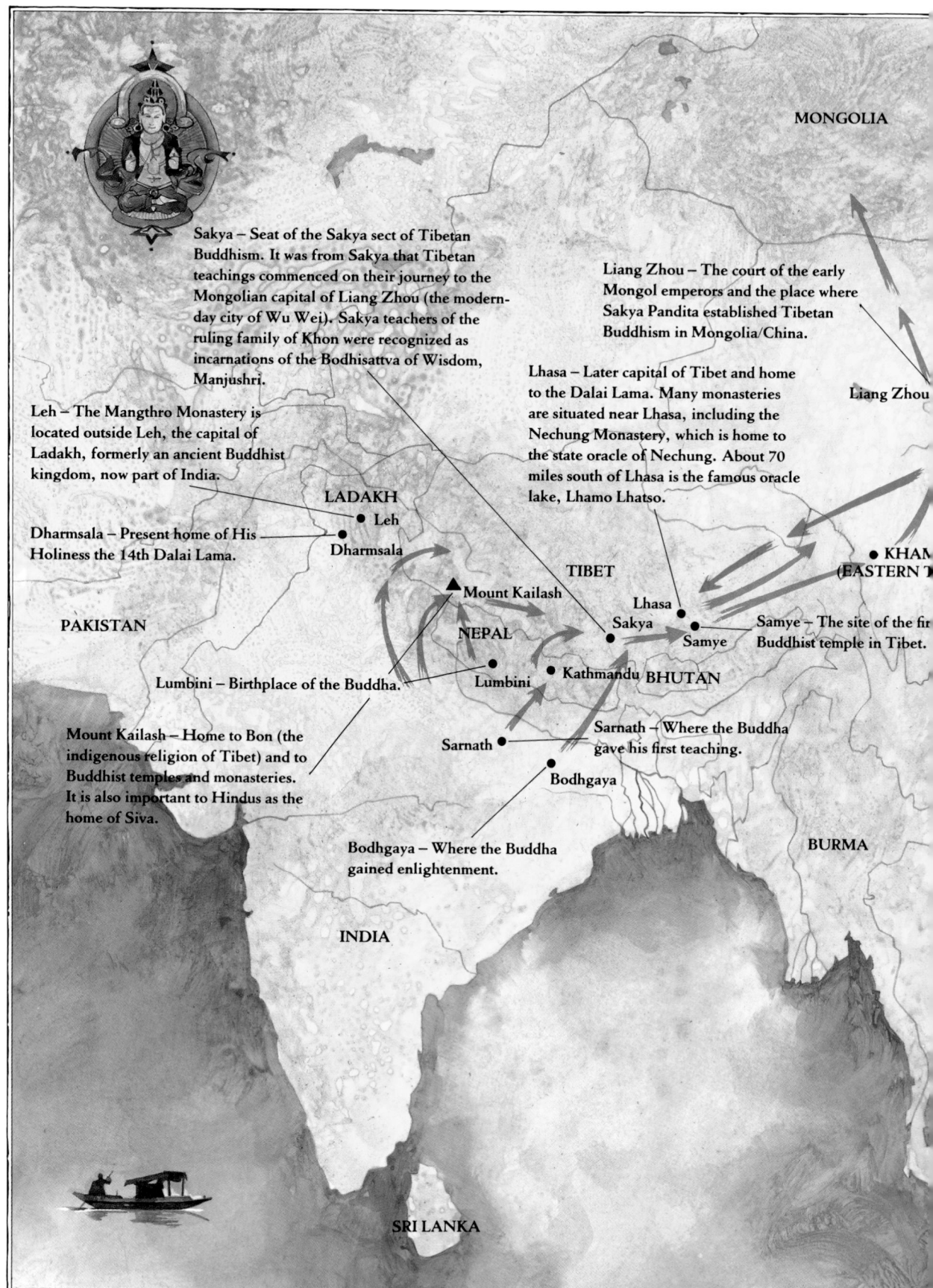

Sakya – Seat of the Sakya sect of Tibetan Buddhism. It was from Sakya that Tibetan teachings commenced on their journey to the Mongolian capital of Liang Zhou (the modern-day city of Wu Wei). Sakya teachers of the ruling family of Khon were recognized as incarnations of the Bodhisattva of Wisdom, Manjushri.

Leh – The Mangthro Monastery is located outside Leh, the capital of Ladakh, formerly an ancient Buddhist kingdom, now part of India.

Dharmsala – Present home of His Holiness the 14th Dalai Lama.

Lumbini – Birthplace of the Buddha.

Mount Kailash – Home to Bon (the indigenous religion of Tibet) and to Buddhist temples and monasteries. It is also important to Hindus as the home of Siva.

Liang Zhou – The court of the early Mongol emperors and the place where Sakya Pandita established Tibetan Buddhism in Mongolia/China.

Lhasa – Later capital of Tibet and home to the Dalai Lama. Many monasteries are situated near Lhasa, including the Nechung Monastery, which is home to the state oracle of Nechung. About 70 miles south of Lhasa is the famous oracle lake, Lhamo Lhatso.

Samye – The site of the fir Buddhist temple in Tibet.

Sarnath – Where the Buddha gave his first teaching.

Bodhgaya – Where the Buddha gained enlightenment.

MONGOLIA

Liang Zhou

KHAM
(EASTERN T

LADAKH

Leh

Dharmsala

PAKISTAN

Mount Kailash

TIBET

Lhasa

Sakya

NEPAL

Lumbini

Kathmandu

Samye

BHUTAN

Sarnath

Bodhgaya

BURMA

INDIA

SRI LANKA

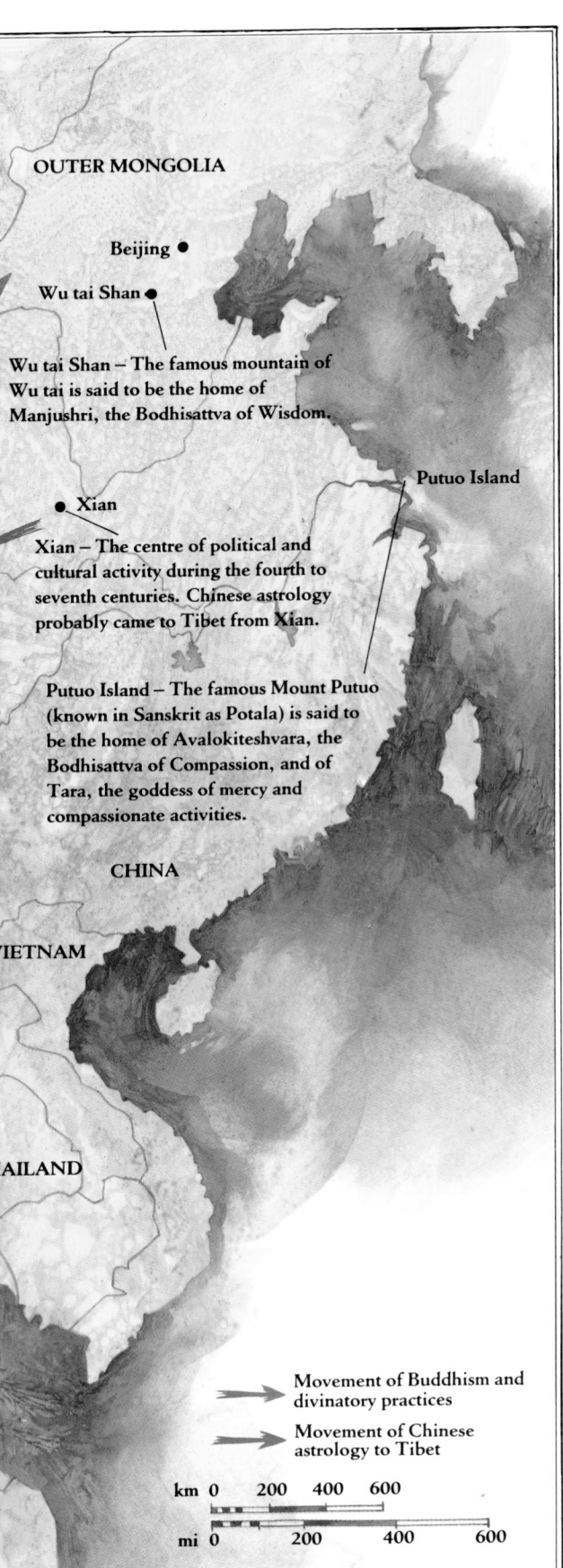

OUTER MONGOLIA

Beijing ●

Wu tai Shan ●

Wu tai Shan – The famous mountain of
Wu tai is said to be the home of
Manjushri, the Bodhisattva of Wisdom.

● Xian

Xian – The centre of political and
cultural activity during the fourth to
seventh centuries. Chinese astrology
probably came to Tibet from Xian.

Putuo Island

Putuo Island – The famous Mount Putuo
(known in Sanskrit as Potala) is said to
be the home of Avalokiteshvara, the
Bodhisattva of Compassion, and of
Tara, the goddess of mercy and
compassionate activities.

CHINA

VIETNAM

THAILAND

→ Movement of Buddhism and
divinatory practices

→ Movement of Chinese
astrology to Tibet

km 0   200   400   600

mi 0   200   400   600

to be felt in subsequent years (this being
symbolically represented by the story of Hwa
Shan leaving one of his shoes behind when he
departed for China).

The new religion did not become fully
entrenched until the arrival of the Indian
Tantric Master, Guru Padma Sambhava, around
775. Through his mystical power and acumen,
he demonstrated the Vajrayana school which
was the most esoteric form of Buddhism
promulgated in India. Its use of deity worship,
meditative visualizations of Buddhas and other
supramundane beings, yoga and elaborate ritual-
ism appealed to the Tibetan mentality.

One of the main goals of the Vajrayana is
compassion. This is the belief that the practitioner must work to allay the sufferings of
others. Although this was primarily accomplished through acts of charity, morality,
meditation and wisdom, other techniques that
might benefit others were also taught. And
among these teachings are found many different
forms of divination.

By the eleventh and twelfth centuries, Buddhism had become the religion of the masses as
well as of the royalty. At this same time China
and large portions of central Asia were ruled by
the Mongols. In the middle of the twelfth
century, the Mongols, wishing to consolidate
power over Tibet and to bring a cultural and
religious veneer to their empire, invited the

WHERE SHAMANISM AND BUDDHISM MEET

*Tibet lies between the two great civilizations of India and
China. Although Tibet possessed its own shamanistic system,
called Bon, it was greatly influenced by the Buddhist beliefs of
India and China. As early as the seventh century, Buddhist
monks travelled to Tibet to spread their religious ideas and to
meditate in the solitude of the vast mountain ranges of this
Himalayan kingdom. Royal patronage encouraged Tibetans to
travel to India for the purpose of translating and studying
Buddhist scriptures. Other forms of knowledge, such as poetry,
logic and astrology, were also learned and brought back to
Tibet. Along the way, various divinatory systems were acquired
and passed from one culture to another. Several of these forms
of divination were integrated into the Tibetan belief-system and
were later transmitted to Mongolia and parts of China.
Throughout Tibet, India, Nepal and Bhutan there are
hundreds of Tibetan Buddhist temples and monasteries.*

grand Lama of the Sakya Sect, Sakya Pandita, to their capital of Liang Zhou (in the north central part of modern China). However, it was the priest-king relationship between Sakya Pandita's nephew, Chogyal Phagpa, and the Mongolian emperor Kublai Khan that confirmed the conversion of the Mongolian empire to Buddhism. During the next 50 years or so, all the Buddhist scriptures that had been translated into Tibetan from Indian Sanskrit were now translated into Mongolian, and the Vajrayana school of Buddhism spread north and east from Tibet.

DIVINATORY SYSTEMS IN TIBET

It is not possible to explain here all the different types of divinatory systems in Tibet. However, I would like to make mention of a few, show a common basis for many of them, and elaborate on a specific system. As mentioned earlier, divinatory systems in Tibet had three sources: their own indigenous forms, those from India, and those from China. Some of these systems incorporated from outside Tibet did not, however, retain their 'pure' form since they were sifted through Tibetan beliefs and ultimately came out with a Tibetan flavour.

ASTROLOGY

Astrology has been popular through the centuries in Tibet and two distinct systems were practiced, one originating in India and the other in China. The Indian form was known as 'white astrology' and the Chinese as 'black astrology'. These terms came from the Tibetan names for the two countries, India being known as the 'vast white continent' because the majority of people there wear white clothes and China being the 'vast black continent' because the majority of its people wear dark clothes.

The Indian form of astrology was learned by fewer people and was considered to be a more complicated system than the Chinese. Unlike the Chinese, which relies primarily on the elements and animal symbols, Indian astrology deals with more detailed calculations of planet positions within a complex constellatory matrix (see Chapter Eighteen, Star Lore in the East).

The Chinese system used in Tibet is very similar to that found in China. It was commonly utilized in Tibetan almanacs and was very popular among the monastic community (who were the main interpreters for the lay community).

This system uses animals to represent years, months and days (which are divided into 12 two-hour periods). The 12 animals are: rat, ox, tiger, hare, dragon, snake, horse, sheep, monkey, bird, dog and pig. In addition to these, the five elements of wood, fire, earth, iron and water are also considered. The Tibetan calendar is divided into 60-year cycles; this is accomplished by combining an animal and an element together to represent one year. For example, the year

beginning in February 1991 was known as the Iron Sheep Year, while 1992 is the Water Monkey Year, and 1993 the Water Bird Year.

When astrological calculations are sought, it is the interplay between different animals and elements in one's life that determines the types of results one encounters. Births, marriages, annual readings, life readings and especially death are the most important occasions for the use of astrology. No Tibetan funeral is carried out without first seeking the advice of an astrologer in matters such as how to dispose of the body, rituals to be conducted on behalf of the departed so that they will obtain a good rebirth, and rituals or prayers to be conducted on behalf of the surviving relatives. Yearly almanacs are published with general astrological readings that indicate the type of year it will be for a person's life force, physical body, power, luck and intelligence.

DIVINING OMENS

Tibetans look upon the world around them, both the mental and the physical world, for signs to divine the fortunes of their lives or specific

One of the methods for seeking omens was to invoke the guardian spirit of a lake and request that it bring forth visions on the lake's surface. Information about the rebirth of the Dalai Lamas was sought in this manner. This lake is in central Tibet.

occasions. Whenever someone leaves on a long journey, signs are always sought. For example, upon embarking on a trip, if a person or vehicle laden with goods is seen, this is considered a good sign, while seeing an empty vehicle is considered unfortunate. The following are previously unpublished excerpts I translated from a Tibetan text, known as *The Illuminating Mirror*, edited by Lang Dor Lama Rinpoche. Some of these texts come from Tibetan writings, while some are Tibetan translations of Sanskrit texts.

OMENS IN DREAMS

Dreams that appear in the pre-dawn part of the night should be considered important for determining the occurrence of good or bad results.

Dreaming of climbing to the top of a high mountain means one will obtain a high rank or position. Dreaming of the sun shining without any clouds means the arising of bliss and happiness. Dreaming of vast crops, grains, honey or ripened fruit, obtaining food and clothes or using a treasure indicates that one will gain wealth. Dreaming of donning good clothes means one will receive praise and respect from others. Dreaming of donning armour means one will not be harmed by disease or evil spirits. If one dreams of sitting in a nice house then good fortune and good luck will occur. Dreaming of carrying a weapon in one's hand means that one's opposing enemies will not harm one. If one dreams of being adorned with ornaments then one will become famous. Dreaming of happily arriving at the other side of a river means one will accomplish whatever one wishes. Blowing or playing musical instruments such as cymbals, drums and conch shells means the arising of fame in the world for oneself. In brief, if one dreams of beautiful forms and feels happy and joyful at the time of awakening, then these indicate the certain obtainment of joyful results.

Dreams of blizzards and crossing a swamp which one falls into, going into a filthy place, wearing clothes stained by excrement, wearing filthy clothes, filth falling from the sky or finding filthy things indicates some type of obscuration for oneself. Making use of gold dust, riding a saddleless horse or donkey and being naked indicate one's own death. Seeing one's reflection in a mirror crying, wearing clothes with no collar or no hat or going on a vacation indicates the arising of suffering. Wearing tattered clothes or rags, eating and drinking filthy substances, insects sticking to one's body and being held by creatures such as wolves is explained to be the arising of an illness. Collections of barley, parched barley, beans or many empty containers, or dreams of pieces of bows and arrows indicate being gossiped about or that people sing your praises, which causes you to become puffed up about yourself and so turn into a bad person. Being pierced by a weapon, being pursued by soldiers, floods, fire or lightning, seeing hail storms, or falling into a pit indicates being harmed by others. Having one's body bound, going beneath the ground, being held in prison or cutting one's head or body portends harm by curses or black magic. Dreaming of being naked and riding on a donkey in a southern direction or dreaming solely of red flowers indicates an obstacle to one's life (i.e. a sudden death). If on awakening one feels unhappy, this shows that the dream is a sign of an unhappy occurrence.

OMENS IN APPEARANCES

If ravens or stinging insects make a nest or hive in one's house, then it is explained that a sudden fright or death will occur. If meat falls from the mouth of a flesh-eating bird, the place where the meat fell will experience some form of punishment. If branches and leaves grow on a dried-up tree, it is said to mean that fighting among the inhabitants of that area will occur. If one sees bent weapons and bright rays from a fire, or if the times for cold and hot weather are reversed, then many harmful events will occur that year. If in the womb a child is heard to talk, cry or laugh then destruction for that area will occur.

OMENS IN THE CRIES OF RAVENS

The sounds of ravens are examined in relation to the time of day and the direction from which the sound comes. For example, if we consider the period from noon to 3.00 p.m., then we would see: if a raven makes a noise in the east wealth will be gained; if the noise comes from the south-east a quarrel will ensue; if noise is made in the south a great wind will be coming; if the noise comes from the south-west an enemy will be coming; if the noise comes from a western direction a woman will be coming; if from the north-west someone close to you will come; if made in the north a good friend will be coming; if the noise is made in the north-east there will

This is a holy image of Guru Padmasambhava, the great Indian Buddhist master. It was through his efforts that the Vajrayana form of Buddhism was established in Tibet during the eighth century. A master of meditation and of Tantric practices, he built the first Buddhist temple in Tibet at Samye.

be a fire that causes damage; if the noise is from above the ruler of the land will grant you something near to your heart.

ENLIGHTENED BEINGS, DEITIES AND SPIRITS

Within the Vajrayana school of Buddhism, distinctions are made among the many classes of enlightened beings, deities, spirits and worldly sentient beings. The most important and holy of these are the Buddhas (such as the Buddha Shakyamuni who gained enlightenment under the Bodhi tree in India more than 2,500 years ago) and the Bodhisattvas (those training to become fully enlightened Buddhas and who have already gained some of the stages leading to that final stage of perfect Buddhahood). Some examples of these Bodhisattvas are Manjushri, Avalokiteshvara, Vajrapani and Tara.

Another class of beings, known as Protectors of the Religion, are deities with a very fierce appearance. These deities have promised to aid and protect from obstacles those practising the spiritual path. Some of the Protectors are wrathful manifestations of enlightened beings. Others were malevolent spirits who have been converted to the Buddha's teaching and have assumed the role of Protectors. For example, when Guru Padma Sambhava built the first Buddhist temple in Tibet at Samye, he encountered great interference from the local spirits who resided there. They were displeased with this new religion and caused great obstacles to the temple being built. To overcome this, Guru Padma Sambhava subdued the spirits of that locale through his spiritual and magical powers, converted them to the Buddhist faith and established them as Protectors of the Religion. The Protectors are worshipped at the temple and special offerings are made to them daily.

In the worldly realms, besides sentient beings of the celestial, human, animal and nether worlds, there are also spirits of the earth, of bodies of water, of mountains and other locations that receive offerings to appease them. Although these are not looked upon as gods or supramundane beings, they are viewed as having power to harm or benefit others.

From the point of view of divination, some of these beings from the various classes are linked to divinatory systems. For example, the Bodhisattva of Wisdom, Manjushri, is the patron saint of astrology. Below, we examine his relationship to a system of divination that uses dice. The female Bodhisattva of Transcendental Activities, Tara, is sought for divination through dreams. Palden Lhamo, a Protectress, is associated with a number of divinatory systems.

DREAM DIVINATION

A person usually goes into a week-long meditation retreat to invoke the blessings of Tara. During this week the meditator visualizes a form of Tara and recites a special mantra of hers thousands of times. Then he or she receives a sign during the retreat that Tara's gift of dream divination has been granted. Endowed with that attainment, when that person wishes to seek the answer to some problem, he will briefly meditate upon Tara just before going to sleep and will clearly think of the question at that time. During his sleep, Tara will provide him with a dream vision to answer the question he had in mind. I personally know a Tibetan nun presently living in Nepal who has great proficiency in this dream divination method. Many times she has been approached by others seeking solutions to their problems, and who have testified to receiving accurate and beneficial advice.

MEDIUMSHIP

The Protectors of the Religion are a very common source of aid for divinations. Their assistance comes in a variety of ways, but the two most renowned are mediumship and dice divination. Each monastery in Tibet has its own special Protector. At some of these monasteries, the Protector takes possession of a chosen monk (who is usually trained for the position) and, speaking through that monk, gives predictions for the year for that monastery and its monks. The Protector also entertains specific questions that anyone wishes to bring forth. The most famous 'oracle protector' of Tibet is the state

oracle who is commonly called the Nechung Oracle. Prior to the Chinese Communist takeover of Tibet in 1959, this oracle was located in the Nechung Monastery near Lhasa, the capital of Tibet. On a regular basis, the Nechung Oracle prognosticated the future events of the country, and was always consulted on matters of state. He was also consulted for very special occasions, such as locating the reincarnation of the Dalai Lama, the spiritual and temporal ruler of Tibet, upon his passing away. The present Nechung Oracle lives in Dharmsala, India, near the residence of His Holiness the 14th Dalai Lama, who is living in exile. (For an excellent presentation of the history and rituals surrounding the Nechung Oracle, see John F. Avedon's *In Exile From The Land of Snows*.)

Another instance of this type of mediumship is presently found in Mangthro Monastery in Ladakh, India. A Tibetan monk by the name of Trungpa Dorje Palsang left his homeland in eastern Tibet during the fifteenth century and travelled through western Tibet, finally settling in Ladakh, which is now part of the Northern Indian province of Kashmir. A local spirit from his hometown attached itself to him and begged to tag along no matter where he went. He was a well-accomplished monk, and when he finally settled in Ladakh a number of monks approached him and became his followers. Finally, a monastery was established there under his leadership. He decided to establish the spirit that followed him as 'Protector of the Religion' for that monastery, and so the monks offered it special rituals on a daily basis. As an aid to the monastery, the 'Protector', known as Rongtsen Kawa Karpo, takes possession of a monk in order to give advice. A system was established for a monk to act as a medium for the spirit for a five-year period. The monk must first go into a meditation retreat for a year. Then, during part of the new year celebration, which lasts for the first 15 days of the first month of the Tibetan lunar calendar (usually around middle to late February), the Protector takes possession of the monk's body. During the first part of this, he performs harrowing feats, such as slashing his tongue with a knife and running quickly on the edge of the monastery's outer wall, which drops, sheer down the side of a mountain. Then he gives his annual predictions for the monastery. Both monks and laypeople seek his advice.

VISIONS ARISING IN BODIES OF WATER

Another form of divination in Tibet utilizes lakes or other bodies of water. In parts of central Tibet, there are famous lakes where visions are seen. The practice is to make offerings to the Protector or spirit of that locale and request their assistance in granting a vision. The most famous of these lakes is Lhamo Lhatso. Here, officials of the government have come to find help to locate the reincarnation of the Dalai Lama. John F. Avedon describes one such event:

In the spring of 1935, Tibet's newly appointed Regent, Reting Rinpoche, joined by a senior minister of the old ruler's cabinet, journeyed to the sacred lake of Lhamo Lhatso, seeking a vision.... The Thirteenth Dalai Lama himself had been discovered by means of a dramatic vision of his birthplace, seen by hundreds and lasting for a week, in the centre of its waters.

After spending some days in prayer at nearby Chokhorgyal Monastery, the Regent's party rode their ponies to the base of the rocky slope overlooking the lake. Proceeding upward on foot, they reached the top of a sheer ridge, whereupon they dispersed in different directions, each to seek his own vision. Alone among them, Reting Rinpoche witnessed a remarkable sight. On staring at the clear alpine waters, he discerned three letters from the Tibetan alphabet float into view: Ah, Ka and Ma. The image of a great three-storied monastery, capped by gold and jade rooftops, followed. A white road led east from the monastery to a house before a small hill, its roof strikingly fringed in turqoise-coloured tiles, a brown and white spotted dog in the courtyard. (In Exile From The Land of Snows, pp.4–5).

Besides extracting visions from bodies of water,

there is also a practice of seeking for them on mirrors or even on one's thumb-nail. Having first recited a special Sanskrit mantra, which has been passed down from teacher to disciple for centuries, the practitioner will blow upon a mirror or his thumb-nail, causing a vision to appear. The problem with this method, according to a number of Tibetan lamas, is that though they have the power of the mantra which causes the vision to appear, they don't have the ability to see the vision. They must rely upon others who have the capability of seeing the vision (in many instances, young children are found to have this ability). Due to this, they find the method unreliable.

THE CASTING OF DICE

Probably the most popular and relied upon method of divination used today among Tibetans is the casting of dice. Lamas from all the traditions of Tibetan Buddhism engage in this practice. Since the teachers are always striving to help others, they cast the dice for the faithful in order to advise them on how to deal with the problems which they face. I have seen lines of people waiting before a lama's residence solely for the purpose of having a dice divination performed. Concerning the purpose of dice divination, His Holiness Sakya Trizin, the spiritual head of the Sakya sect of Tibetan Buddhism, wrote in his introduction to *MO: Tibetan Divination System,*

There are two primary functions of the MO [dice divination]. First of all, it is a system that allows us to help ourselves to see a situation or event clearly. Secondly, if we use it for others with the proper motivation of performing a selfless act of giving – as has been extensively done by many of the great teachers of Tibet – it is a system that enhances our practice of Bodhisattva's path. There is also a secondary function of the MO. The central, most profound teaching of the Buddha is Pratitya Samutpada, which may be translated as interdependent origination or codependent arising. This teaching simultaneously explains the essence of the interplay of causes and conditions on the relative, worldly level of reality and the essence of emptiness or selflessness on the ultimate level of reality. Although diligent efforts are needed in concentration and insight to attain a realization of interdependent origination, a system such as MO *reveals a glimpse of the interdependence and casual play of the world in which we live and may hopefully induce one to investigate it on a deeper level.*

There are several different systems of this form of divination, but the one that relies upon the Protectress Palden Lhamo and the one that relies upon the Buddhist saint of wisdom, Manjushri, are preferred. The system that invokes Palden Lhamo uses three dice with the usual dots running from one through six on them. There are 15 possible answers, and each answer is divided into different categories, such as one's life forces, wealth, illness, etc.

The one that invokes the Bodhisattva Manjushri uses one dice upon which the last six of the seven syllables of Manjushri's mantra, OM AH RA PA TSA NA DHIH, are written. About this form of dice divination His Holiness Sakya Trizin had this to say:

Many methodologies of MO *have been utilized in Tibet. The system here, compiled by the great master Jamgon Mipham from the sacred Tantras expounded by the Buddha, obtains its authority from the spiritual power and wisdom of Manjushri – the Bodhisattva who embodies the transcendental knowledge of all the Buddhas. It is Manjushri's speech as epitomized in his holy mantra,* OM AH RA PA TSA NA DHIH, *and the sanctity of his all-pervasive wisdom that empower one to obtain an accurate answer that reflects the interplay of conditions concerning the situation and its outcome. In the* Manjushri Nama Samgiti (Chanting the Names of Manjushri), *the Buddha himself extolled the great qualities of Manjushri and stated that the mantra of Manjushri,* OM AH RA PA TSA NA DHIH, *is an expression of the wisdom experienced by all enlightened beings. Therefore, by relying upon the compassionate blessings of Manjushri and the power of his*

Manjushri is considered the embodiment of the wisdom of all the Buddhas. His knowledge and wisdom are all-pervasive, and so his blessings are sought by all alike. Whether for an insight into the Buddha's wisdom or a glimpse into the inner workings of this world, prayers are made to him.

mantra, you should have no doubt that the wisdom of all enlightened beings is manifesting itself in the throw of the dice.

For a further description of MO: *Tibetan Divination System* and its method of use, see Appendix: Modern Restatements, on page 211.

The scope and variety of divinatory systems in Tibet is truly vast, and a few of these have been covered in scant detail. Tibet's unique forms of divination grew to evolve into a potent force that affected its entire population. From Tibet it travelled to Mongolia and China, and today in many countries of the world, both East and West, you can find Tibetans and others utilizing these notable, rich and ancient forms of divination.

AUSTRALIA
AND
NEW ZEALAND

The Australian continent contains the oldest surviving cultural link with the Stone Age, and in the Aboriginal people we see a primal race still practising the earliest form of spiritual activity, a totally shamanistic world-view that parallels that of some of the other cultures we have seen, such as the Norse, Celtic, Lapp and Amerindian traditions.

As in many other cultures, the professional services of an augur, called a *mekigar*, are required to invoke the oracular elements in creation. Change is enacted through ritual, and once again, as so often before, we see that it is the *land* itself that supplies the necessary ingredient for divinatory practice. It is the intimate relationship of the *mekigar* with the elements, animal life and creation that enables him to penetrate the spirit world and to return with answers to his questions. Indeed, as James Cowan indicates, it seems that the augurs are in almost constant dialogue with the inner world, which in Australian tradition is embodied in the Dreamtime, the time of the ancestors, mighty individuals who have attained mythical, even divine status, and who make their continued presence felt in the shape of the landscape itself.

Among the Maori of New Zealand the same holds true. As in the case of the Australian Aborigines, the Maori originated in Asia, and brought with them something of the racial memory of that land. Between them they give a picture containing some of the most ancient cultural references we possess, one of which, divination, is shown to be of central importance to both peoples.

The parallels between Maori and Celtic traditions have been noticed before. Both were a warrior race, who sought to propitiate the gods before battle and used prognostication to foretell the outcome. The remarkable similarities between certain of the Maori divination methods mentioned here and those of the Celts discussed in Chapter Two cannot go unnoticed: both peoples believed in the second sight, in the signs provided by animals and birds, and in the throwing of marked sticks to foretell the future. As far as we know the Maori are unique in using kites to divine events to come, while the complicated *niu* rite is, so far as we are aware, unlike anything practised elsewhere in the world.

The common links between these antipodean cultures, as between so many of those we have discussed, therefore lie in the importance of communication with the ancestors and gods, and in an understanding of the significance of the patterns supplied by nature.

CHAPTER TWENTY

WILD STONES

Aboriginal Sorcery in Divination

James G. Cowan

The Aboriginal tradition of Australia is the oldest unbroken contact we have with our Stone Age forebears. For over 50,000 years the Aborigines have been living on the Australian continent, practising a semi-nomadic existence over a period spanning at least two Ice Ages. Many of their myths and stories tell of two major migrations from the Asian mainland, before such journeys were curtailed by rising sea levels. Arriving in Australia by way of island-hopping and short canoe voyages, the original settlers came into contact with a lonely land-scape populated by large animals, some of which are still with us today, such as the kangaroo and duck-billed platypus.

Their early culture and belief-systems were coloured by the philosophic concepts they brought from Asia. But the landscape they encountered would have been vastly different from any previously experienced; it is so powerful that these settlers would have spent many generations coming to terms with its spiritual dimension. Eventually, all divinatory activity was necessarily conditioned by the land, its earth-centred power (*djang*) and the mythology surrounding it.

THE DREAMING

Central to the Aboriginal belief-system is the Dreaming. The Dreaming means 'the time of the ancestors'. It is a primordial condition that transcends time and represents a body of spiritual lore pertaining to the creation of the world. The principle of manifestation is governed by Sky Heroes, those mythical beings who made the landscape, who passed on custom and law to the Aborigines, and who live on as visible icons in tribal territory in the form of 'frozen' motifs made up of unusual landforms, sacred water-holes and trees, which themselves embody a metaphysical or Dreaming presence.

The Aborigine's relationship with the Dreaming is the centre of his life. No other reality holds so much significance, not even his tribal or family relationships. His totemic being – his sense of ancestry – is derived from the Dreaming, his kinship ties find their origins there, and his ultimate destination at death is his return to it as his primordial source. He does not worship the Dreaming so much as acknowledge his inseparability from it as the basis of his spiritual essence.

Much of the Aborigine's ritual life revolves around making contact with the Dreaming and the Dreaming ancestors. Although a deeply spiritual being, he acknowledges the demands of this world. Indeed, one is struck by the relationship between all the elements in this cosmic drama: man, animals, birds, insects, flora, and the wide land which both possesses and is possessed by an Aborigine while he is alive. An Aborigine acknowledges that he 'belongs' to a stretch of country because of his dream affiliations: his father may have dreamed

A tribal custodian guards the sacred churinga *boards at a cave dedicated to the Great Snake in Central Australia. These boards are used in all ritual activity as invocational devices. The cave symbolizes the vulva of a Maletji woman. On the far right we see the Great Snake's penis about to fertilize the Dog-woman.*

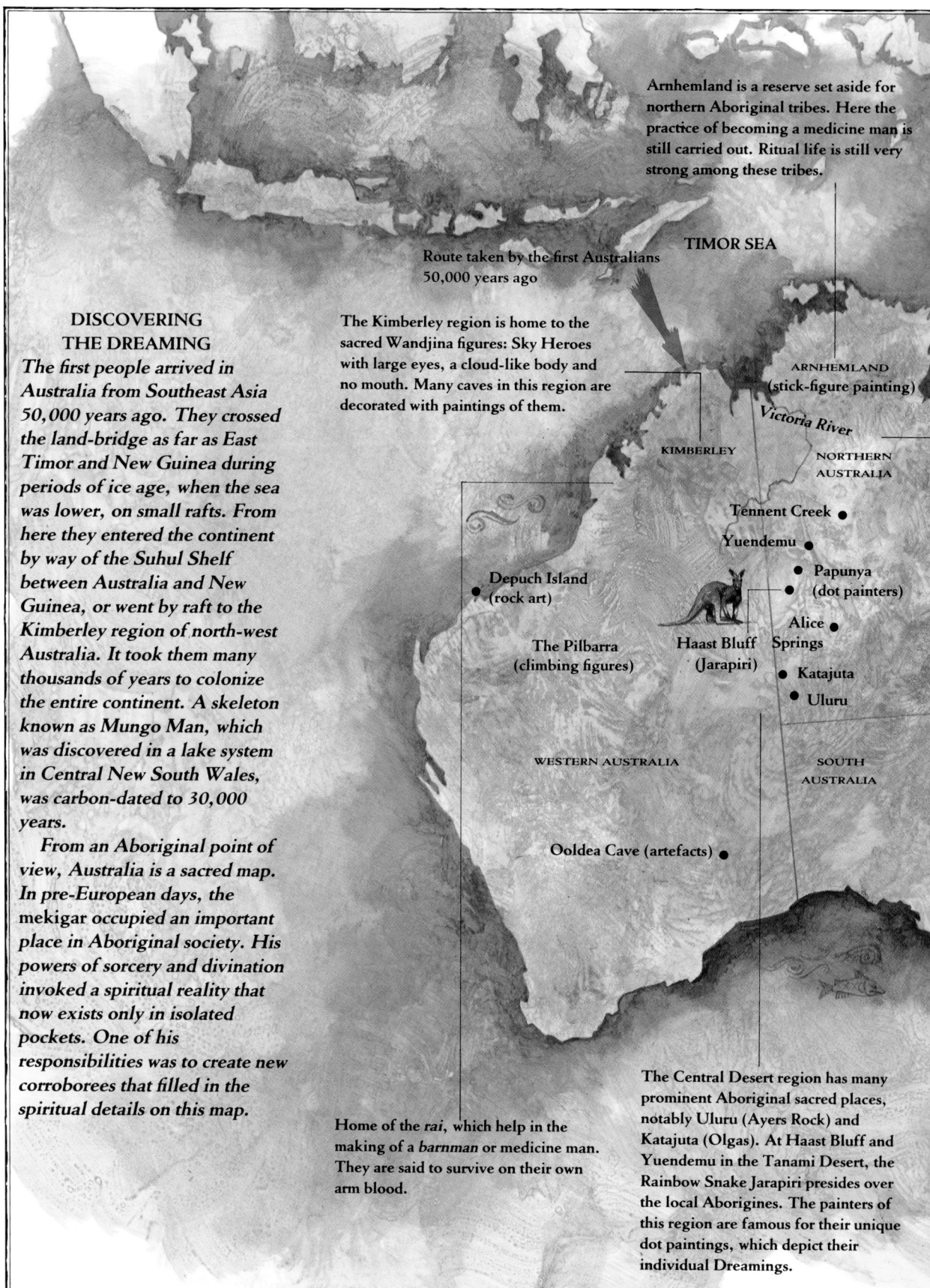

Arnhemland is a reserve set aside for northern Aboriginal tribes. Here the practice of becoming a medicine man is still carried out. Ritual life is still very strong among these tribes.

Route taken by the first Australians 50,000 years ago

TIMOR SEA

The Kimberley region is home to the sacred Wandjina figures: Sky Heroes with large eyes, a cloud-like body and no mouth. Many caves in this region are decorated with paintings of them.

ARNHEMLAND
(stick-figure painting)

Victoria River

KIMBERLEY

NORTHERN
AUSTRALIA

Tennent Creek ●

Yuendemu ●

● Papunya
(dot painters)

Depuch Island
(rock art) ●

Alice ●
Springs

The Pilbarra
(climbing figures)

Haast Bluff
(Jarapiri)

● Katajuta

● Uluru

WESTERN AUSTRALIA

SOUTH
AUSTRALIA

Ooldea Cave (artefacts) ●

DISCOVERING
THE DREAMING

The first people arrived in Australia from Southeast Asia 50,000 years ago. They crossed the land-bridge as far as East Timor and New Guinea during periods of ice age, when the sea was lower, on small rafts. From here they entered the continent by way of the Suhul Shelf between Australia and New Guinea, or went by raft to the Kimberley region of north-west Australia. It took them many thousands of years to colonize the entire continent. A skeleton known as Mungo Man, which was discovered in a lake system in Central New South Wales, was carbon-dated to 30,000 years.

From an Aboriginal point of view, Australia is a sacred map. In pre-European days, the mekigar occupied an important place in Aboriginal society. His powers of sorcery and divination invoked a spiritual reality that now exists only in isolated pockets. One of his responsibilities was to create new corroborees that filled in the spiritual details on this map.

Home of the *rai*, which help in the making of a *barnman* or medicine man. They are said to survive on their own arm blood.

The Central Desert region has many prominent Aboriginal sacred places, notably Uluru (Ayers Rock) and Katajuta (Olgas). At Haast Bluff and Yuendemu in the Tanami Desert, the Rainbow Snake Jarapiri presides over the local Aborigines. The painters of this region are famous for their unique dot paintings, which depict their individual Dreamings.

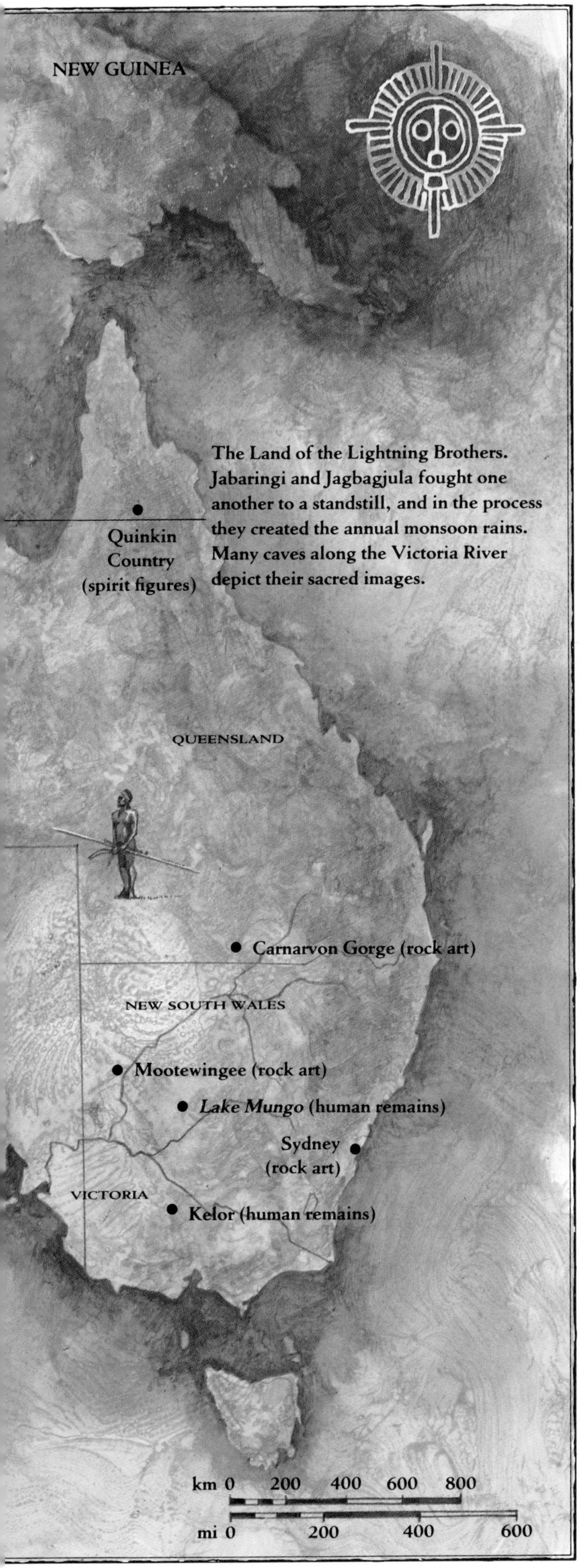

The Land of the Lightning Brothers. Jabaringi and Jagbagjula fought one another to a standstill, and in the process they created the annual monsoon rains. Many caves along the Victoria River depict their sacred images.

NEW GUINEA

Quinkin Country (spirit figures)

QUEENSLAND

● Carnarvon Gorge (rock art)

NEW SOUTH WALES

● Mootewingee (rock art)
● *Lake Mungo* (human remains)
Sydney ●
(rock art)

VICTORIA

● Kelor (human remains)

km 0   200   400   600   800

mi 0   200   400   600

of his conception in this territory, or his spirit-child (*muri*) may have entered his mother's womb there. Later, his totemic origin will also bind him to his country in such a way that he becomes the hereditary custodian of it until his death. These key-men become responsible for retaining the sacred lore, the dance and songs relating to their region, as well as the mythic background inherent in the land itself. Without their knowledge, no landscape, whether actual or Dreaming, can be evoked by others. It follows that if a hereditary line dies out, as it has done in many parts of Australia today, the Dreaming of that particular region dies with it. As a result the land dies to the world of men and becomes 'rubbish country', an object of scorn and derision, finally a desanctified landscape.

A Binbinga medicine man or karadji *from the MacArthur River region in Central Australia, at around the turn of the century, carries on his back a bark-wrapped bundle containing items for ritual use. This man acknowledged encountering spirits that killed him and then finally restored him to life during his period of initiation.*

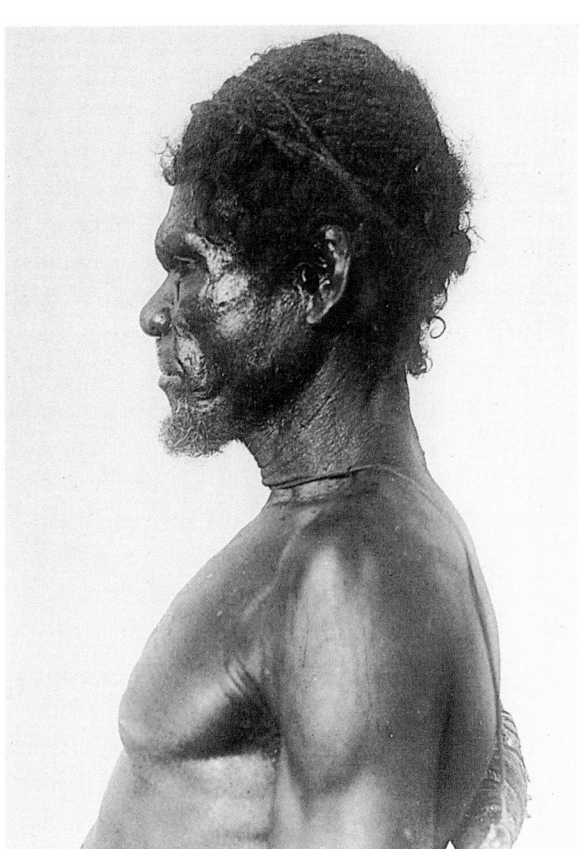

THE *MEKIGAR:* MAN OF MAGIC

A core belief in Aboriginal spirituality is that one can cross over into the Otherworld through ritual action. Divinatory activity is therefore of great importance in the ritual life of the individual and the tribe, and a central figure in this activity is the *mekigar*. The *mekigar* or *karadji* (his name varies depending on his tribe) is a man who is set apart from his contemporaries by the nature of his vocation, his intelligence and his special powers. As a young boy he is often physically different and may be recognized 'by the light radiating from his eyes', as one commentator observed. By and large, his office is inherited from his father, although it is acknowledged that the powers of a *mekigar* cannot be handed on by a father, but rather acquired only from the great Baiami (All-father) himself. While a father or practising *mekigar* may have the authority to initiate a postulant into the secrets of his craft, he can only do so on the understanding that the candidate has already been made aware of his vocation by way of visionary contact with his Dreaming ancestors.

Circumstantial and oral testimony suggests that a would-be *mekigar* undergoes a form of initiation that consists of ritual death at the hands of *Oruncha* spirits, accompanied by prolonged bouts of meditation in the wilderness. Ritual killing involves the use of quartz crystals which are pressed into the postulant's legs and breastbone. He then lies down on the ground while the officiants jerk their hands towards him, all the while holding other crystals which are later rubbed into his scalp. Meanwhile a hole is cut under his forefinger, into which crystals are inserted. Finally the postulant is asked to eat meat and drink water that has been impregnated with crystals. Sometimes a crystal is inserted in a hole in his tongue. Grease is rubbed all over his body and a sacred representation of the *Oruncha* painted on his chest and forehead. He is told to remain in the men's camp until his wounds have healed. He also has to observe certain food taboos, sleep with a fire between himself and his wife, and hold himself aloof from everyone, otherwise the power that has entered him on

This cave painting at a Wardaman cave in Northern Australia shows copulating spirit-figures. Such caves are ritual centres that the tribes visit on their annual wanderings. The paintings are often extremely old, although retouched as a part of ritual. Sacred sex is an important ritual activity among northern tribes, who worship Kunapipi, a female Great Snake.

initiation might leave him altogether.

The first phase of his initiation now over, a *mekigar* continues his education under the guidance of his mentor. Finer details in the arts of bone-pointing (the act of condemning a man to death), sorcery and diagnostic techniques in the cure of illness and psychic disorder are all taught to him. These are the more practical aspects of his craft and underlie the important social contribution the man makes to his community in the role of doctor. They do not, however, convey fully the spiritual metamorphosis he has undergone in his pursuit of the power associated with the ritual insertion of quartz crystals. These artefacts, along with australite rocks and unusual stones and bones, are regarded as power-bearers of rich symbolic significance. Among the eastern tribes these are known as 'wild stones' and are said to embody the Great Spirit himself. The quartz crystal owes its extraordinary prestige to its celestial origin, as originally Baiami's throne was said to be made of crystal. Quartz crystals are, in a sense, a form of 'solidified light'.

Accompanying his transition, a *mekigar* was often said to grow feathers on his arms which, after a few days, developed into wings. The growing of feathers as an expression of spiritual transformation lends credence to the idea that the *mekigar* is more than a medicine man; he is a keeper of sacred lore by the nature of his spiritual attainments.

A great deal of emphasis is placed upon

Aranda tribesmen perform a corroboree in April 1901. Deeply committed to ritual life, Aborigines regularly come together to perform sacred dances in accordance with their totemic origins. The dancers' bodies are decorated with patterns denoting the symbolic presence of the Sky Hero to whom the dance belongs. Ritual activity is focused on necessities such as rain increase or ensuring a plentiful supply of animals in a region.

Jagbagjula and Jabaringi, the two sacred Lightning Brothers of Wardaman spirit lore, are responsible for making rain each season and are therefore at the centre of extensive ritual practices. Their ferocious battle over the wife of one brother brings on lightning and rain, so important for the land's renewal. This is one of many cave paintings in Northern Australia that represent these sacred beings.

breathing techniques among *mekigar*. One report suggests that a *mekigar* used to sit on the bottom of the river for days at a time, talking with the spirits. He was able to hold his breath for the entire period of his immersion, returning to the surface with bloodshot eyes and covered in mud. Such accounts may not be factual in a physiological sense (although it would be risky to discount them entirely), but they do indicate a preoccupation with breathing techniques similar to those practised in other spiritual disciplines.

DEVELOPING THE INNER EYE

In his role as doctor, a *mekigar* is often called upon to use his 'inner eye' to diagnose ailments. One *mekigar*, Mowaldjali, gives us a clear outline of the functional use of the 'inner eye'.

The diagnostician's eye, that is a magic eye, is the one with which he checks the liver, urine, the gall bladder, the heart and the intestines. He checks these completely. 'Ah yes,' he says. 'The trouble is in the back of the neck!' He sees perfectly ... they call him the expert. He is trained by the rai *[spirits]. In the beginning he is unable to see very far. His sight is still dim. As yet he does not know [understand]. So the* rai, *they send a spirit-animal or insect out to him. Then his eyes begin to open and he is astonished. That's the way he begins to see further and further. He has become an expert.*

This 'third eye' indicates spiritual rather than physical vision. A *mekigar* is capable of discerning illness by way of an interior power not available to others.

A *mekigar* develops this power during meditation. It is during contemplative phases that he is able to enter the spirit world and converse with the Sky Heroes. One text details the importance of meditation among these men:

When you see an old man sitting by himself over there, do not disturb him for he will growl at you. Do not play near him, because he is sitting down with his thoughts in order to see. He is gathering his thoughts so that he can feel and hear. Perhaps he then lies down, getting into a special posture so

that he can see while sleeping [i.e. meditating]. He sees indistinct visions and hears persons [the rai*] talk in them. He gets up and looks for those he has seen; but not seeing them, he sits down again in the prescribed manner so as to see what he has seen before.*

Here we have a vividly descriptive account of a *mekigar's* encounter with visionary experience. In the act of meditation he leaves himself, and is able to enter the imaginal realm where divination can occur.

A DIVINE LANGUAGE

The contact Aborigines make with the Otherworld, the Dreaming, is carefully choreographed. A man cannot converse with Sky Heroes except by way of ritual activity. He is not free to engage in exclusive dialogue with the spirits, since they belong to all men and in themselves are immune from any form of singular discourse. The 'other language' he learns to speak when conversing with the Sky Heroes is more often than not a priestly language quite distinct from the one he might use on an everyday basis. Language is a vital part of invocation, of divination, and a man who has reached an advanced initiatory phase in his life is entitled to speak this 'language of the gods'. Others defer to him in these matters, knowing that he alone has attained a 'third eye', the gift of the *rai*. Such men are known as 'men of high degree', partaking of a special spiritual quality which we might associate with sainthood.

DIVINATION AS A TRIBAL ACTIVITY

Since Aborigines do not believe they can influence the future except through ritual activity, there is little call for the *mekigar* to foretell the future. Influencing the future is largely a collective activity participated in by the elders of the tribe, involving complex rituals which may span many months. The mythic life surrounding the landscape is so important that, to the outsider at least, Aborigines appear to be constantly engaged in a Dreaming dialogue with the Sky Heroes. The dances and songs, the incantations and body-paintings, even the ritual ground where such events take place, all are made a part of the symbolic essence of sacred expression. Divination *per se* becomes a collective act of all elders who desire to ensure that the cosmic flow is maintained.

The divinatory act for Aborigines is therefore much more than an isolated event. An Aborigine's whole life is an act of divination since he rarely acknowledges any separation between himself and the Dreaming. Although the *mekigar* may be a man of visionary experience *par excellence*, it does not mean that his talents are allowed to obscure the role played by his fellow tribesmen in any rite of passage. Each body of knowledge complements the other. Mediumistic lore, the lore of the shaman, may be in the hands of the *mekigar*, but ritual lore, the lore of the prescribed manifestation of Sky Heroes in this world, is in the hands of every dancer, songster and story-teller who is able to enact their appearance during important ceremonies pertaining to his totemic existence. It is this complementary relationship between the individual and the tribe that makes divination among the Aborigines such an all-embracing affair. All men have the right to experience the reality of the Dreaming, and sharing this imaginal realm becomes an act of brotherliness, a demonstration of congeniality among men.

The Aborigine was – and to a certain extent still is – loathe to see himself as passive in his relationship with the Sky Heroes. Although they are world-creators and objects of veneration, their activity did not cease at the time of the Dreaming; their role as materializers still continues. Aborigines see themselves as participants in this primordial event, and so have the power to initiate change through ritual action. It is this form of divination that an Aborigine adheres to: to augment a fruitful landscape, whether as a food source or as the principal theatre of cosmic drama, delineates his importance both as a part of Nature and as a man, for he knows that it is his concern which makes the land fruitful. It is his songs and his ceremonies

This Gagadju tribesman is in his totemic country near Kakadu, Northern Australia. His country is determined by his conception, and remains his throughout his life. It is then passed on to a new custodian in the same way.

that contribute to the land's spiritual power. As one old tribesman remarked, 'When we sing the sacred songs, the animals listen and are happy. When we don't sing them they go away and the land becomes barren.'

For the Aborigine, ritual action makes the difference between a world that is continually revitalized – and a world that is spiritually dead.

CHAPTER TWENTY-ONE

ANCESTORS, GODS AND MEN

Maori Methods of Divination

David Simmons

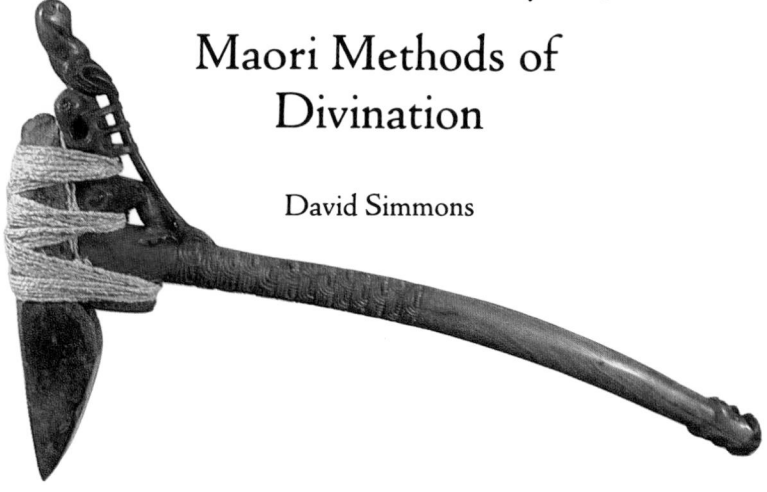

In order to understand ancient and modern Maori divination it is necessary to have some understanding of the way Maori view the world. While most Maori are now members of Christian or Christian-derived churches and other world religions, ancient beliefs remain part of their world-view. The place of the ancestors, who may influence and direct the actions of their descendants, is just one example of ancient belief which continues to be relevant today.

THE MAORI WORLD

The world of the Maori consists of three realms. The original realm is *Te Kore* (the Nothingness), in which all is in potential and from which come the *wai ora*, the waters of life, here undivided. In this realm were created the primal parents, Rangi the Sky Father and Papa the Earth Mother. They copulated and the birth of their first child ushered in the next realm, *Te Po* (The Night), in which their children, the gods, live. The children separated their parents, whose tight embrace did not allow them room to live.

Above the Sky Father are 10 or 12 heavens in which the gods live. Beneath the Earth Mother is the Underworld, also said by some to be divided into levels in which live the descendants of the gods, including man after death. The creation of man by the god Tiki, or Tane according to some tribes, involved adding the life force of man to the already existing life force of the gods. When man dies he can enter the realm of the gods either proceeding by the entrance under Cape Reinga in the far north to Rarohenga, the Underworld; or, if he is a high chief or first-born of the senior genealogical line, he is taken by spirit canoe to the heavens where his eyes become stars.

The realm in which humankind lives is *Te Ao Marama* (this world), the world of light, which lies between Earth and Sky. The waters of life flow into this world and are part of all things, down to the rocks of the earth and the crystals in them. Here those waters are divided into the dark waters of the sky and the clear waters of the great deep. It was on the great waters of the

Iriperi, a sacred ancestral adze (above), has a genealogy going back to its maker 25 generations ago. The adze was rehafted when a new high chief was installed to succeed to his grandfather. The old handle was taken off and buried with the previous holder. The adze is a fearful thing if used in divination because its mere presence may kill the wrongdoer.

THE COMING OF THE MAORI

Maui, the demigod, sailed on the waters of the deep. With a hook made from his grandmother's jawbone, he fished up the island known as Te Ika a Maui, the Fish of Maui – the North Island of New Zealand. Then came Kupe, who found the fish still alive. He killed it and made it suitable for men to live on. He named it Aotearoa, Land of the Long White Cloud. From the other islands in the Pacific came the ancestors sailing in their great canoes. They settled the land, and here they completed the migration that had taken their ancestors from east to west, from the Solomons to Easter Island, Hawaii, Tahiti and the Cook Islands. Here they became Maori.

Hikurangi Mountain, on which Maui's canoe is said to rest, is itself an ancient name, for it is the mountain on which the first light fell at the separation of Earth and Sky. For the thousand years that men have lived here, so have these stories been told.

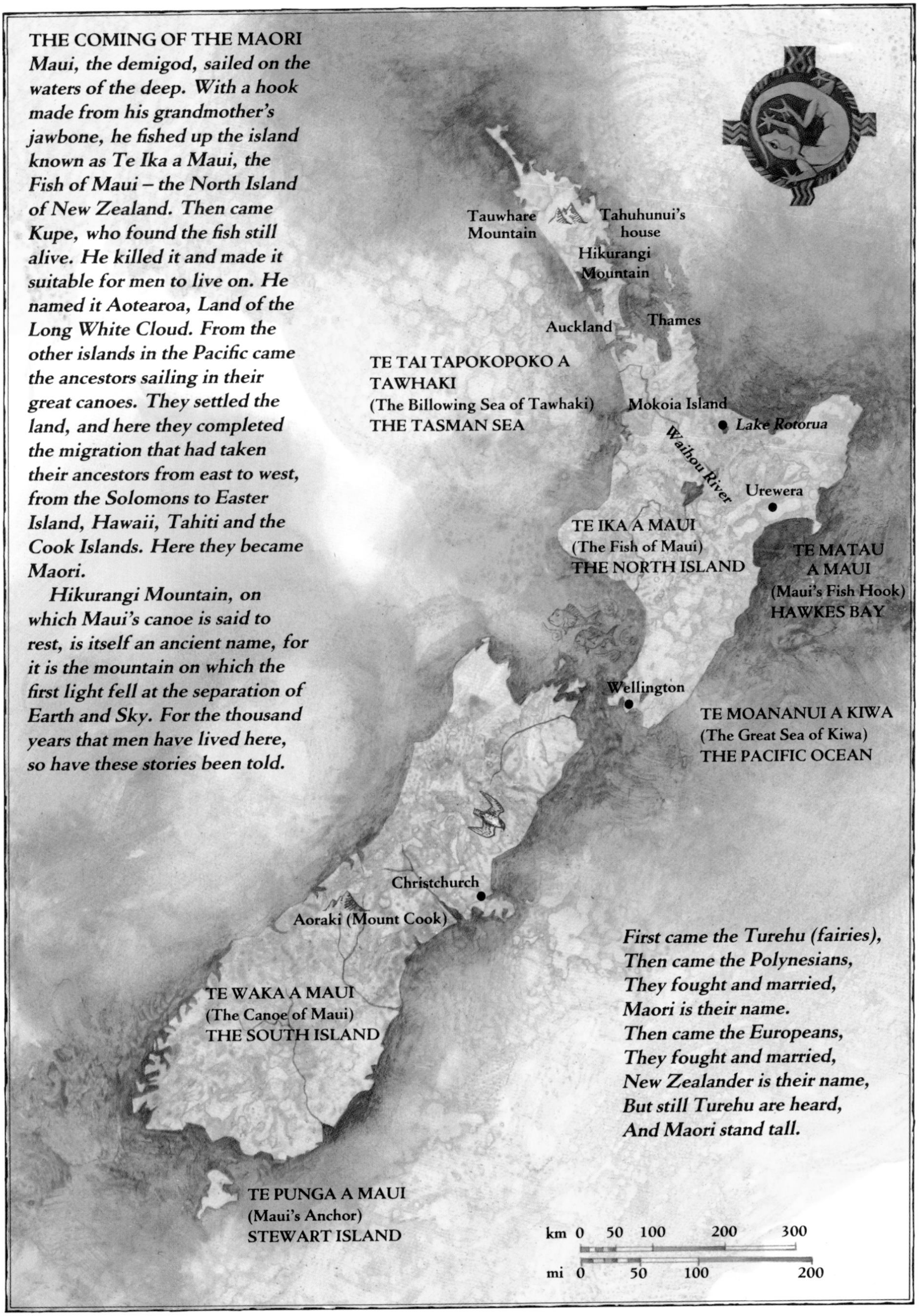

Tauwhare Mountain

Tahuhunui's house

Hikurangi Mountain

Auckland

Thames

TE TAI TAPOKOPOKO A TAWHAKI
(The Billowing Sea of Tawhaki)
THE TASMAN SEA

Mokoia Island

Waihou River

● *Lake Rotorua*

Urewera

TE IKA A MAUI
(The Fish of Maui)
THE NORTH ISLAND

TE MATAU A MAUI
(Maui's Fish Hook)
HAWKES BAY

Wellington

TE MOANANUI A KIWA
(The Great Sea of Kiwa)
THE PACIFIC OCEAN

Christchurch

Aoraki (Mount Cook)

TE WAKA A MAUI
(The Canoe of Maui)
THE SOUTH ISLAND

First came the Turehu (fairies),
Then came the Polynesians,
They fought and married,
Maori is their name.
Then came the Europeans,
They fought and married,
New Zealander is their name,
But still Turehu are heard,
And Maori stand tall.

TE PUNGA A MAUI
(Maui's Anchor)
STEWART ISLAND

km 0   50 100   200   300

mi 0   50   100   200

deep that the demigod Maui sailed to fish up these islands: Te Ika a Maui, the Fish of Maui, is the fish which is the North Island of New Zealand. (From above, the North Island looks like a sting-ray.) His canoe remains on a mountain, Hikurangi, on which the first light fell when Earth and Sky were separated.

Today a chief standing on the tribal meeting place, the *marae*, will pay homage to Earth, Sky, the gods, the ancestors and the sacred tribal mountains and rivers as part of the ritual of greeting visitors. The ancestors, who are present with the visitors on the *marae* to protect their descendants, and the newly dead, who are with them, are greeted by the home people. The visitors also greet the ancestors and newly dead of the *marae*, and the ancestors of both sides are farewelled and asked to return to the other world. The living are greeted and the final expression of grief for the dead, the *hongi* or touching noses, completes the ritual.

THE GUARDIAN ANCESTORS

Communication between the three realms and between the gods, the demigods, the ancestors and their descendants is a normal occurrence. The ancestors guard and guide their descendants quite directly by personal intervention and sometimes by personal appearances. For example a great priest, a *tohunga*, was eating with friends when his nose twitched violently. He stopped eating and over the next three days prepared himself for death, for this was a sign from his ancestors. On the third evening the sun lay a golden path over the sea and his spirit followed to the homeland.

Tohunga means expert. In this context it could be defined as spiritual expert, or more pejoratively as witch-doctor – but that is a speciality of certain *tohunga makutu*, i.e. black magic experts. *Tohunga matakite* were and are seers. A graduate of the college of learning, the son or in some instances the daughter (i.e. the eldest born) of a chief was taught spiritual matters in order to ask for the goodwill of the gods and ancestors. As a direct descendant of the gods that person had *mana*, or spiritual power, and was in conse-

quence *tapu*, or sacred. Such people are seen as having a special relationship with the ancestors and gods, and can interpret the omens and signs that are directed towards them.

A person may also be a seer because he shows that he is able to find lost treasures or put right transgressions of *tapu*. These people may be male or female and are also often healers. There is also the *tohunga rongoa*, the expert in Maori medicines and massage, who learns the craft from grandparents. Ordinary people are also aware of omens and portents, and there are often knowledgeable 'aunties' who will be rung up. Children are still being trained in the arts of the *tohunga*.

DREAMS

The ancestors, and perhaps the gods, also send dreams in which great faith is placed. The *kuia*, or elderly women, are often those consulted when a particularly troubling dream is experienced. There are on record a number of instances where an expedition was abandoned because of dreams. A chief called Tahuhunui was so named because the land and the house his father was building were abandoned because of a dream, leaving only the *tahuhu*, or ridge pole, to be seen as the canoe sailed away. Some ladies today are also particularly good at dreaming of winners in horse races.

BODY TWITCHES

Twitches and starts while sleeping can be sure signs of evil things to come, although precise interpretations may vary. Both arms thrown across the chest and gurgling could each foretell killing, the first in war, the second as murder. For some people, signs in the body on the left side are lucky, for others the right side is lucky. In most tribes the left side is the female side, the spiritual side, but in some it is the reverse, and the left side is that of the male line. More usually, the right side is the male side, the side of the human life force, of war and warriors. Most genealogical lines have more *mana* (prestige) on the male line, but again this may not be true of certain tribes or individuals.

SPIRIT GUARDIANS

Chiefs' families, small tribal units or often whole tribes have ancestral or spirit guardians. Certain birds are thought of as descending into the Otherworld at night, returning in the morning. Some are messengers from the heavens, like the Hokioi, a great bird which never lands, and whose cry is heard in the sky when a high chief is about to die. The bush falcon is a messenger from earth to the heavens and was used in ritual: the bird was imprisoned by its flight feathers when the ridge pole was placed on the front post in a new ceremonial house; if it freed itself it was good news that it carried to the gods; if not, the house was abandoned.

A fantail laughed when Maui the demigod attempted to ensure the retention of immortality, so the appearance of a fantail is considered to be a sign that death is to occur, that a relative has died, or that the ancestors are present and must be recognized lest misfortune befall. For war parties in the old days, hearing an owl was a sign that the hearer would die. Many people still regard the cry of the owl as a sign of death to come. The guardian spirit of one chiefly family of Te Ati Awa is a peculiar white owl that

Matuatonga, a tribal fertility symbol, stands among the gardens on the island of Mokoia in Lake Rotorua. This ancestral image of great mana is said to have been brought to New Zealand by the ancestors of the Arawa Tribes. It is a tribal heirloom and as such had divinatory powers. The island is also called Te Motutapu a Tinirau, sacred island of Tinirau, which links it to the island of the same name in the otherworld, where the waters of life flow to give fertility to fish. Tinirau is the god of fish.

A godstick representing Hukere. He was particularly concerned with things that belonged in the Earth Mother and therefore was the god who oversaw the return of the bodies of men to the earth. Hukere was one of a set of three dealing with the sea, cultivations and death. It is held in Auckland Museum.

appears when the senior member is to die. In the Urewera tribe Ngati Whare, a particular ancestress appears as a giant cormorant hovering over the village, a sign that the chief will die or, in the olden days, be attacked or lose a battle. The cries of birds heard on the left side or the right could be lucky or unlucky.

Other manifestations of the spirit world, which are sometimes but not always ancestral, are the *tipua kura* (strange objects) and the *taniwha* (mythical monsters). *Tipua kura* are named and their appearance *can* be good but is usually a warning. Many of them are natural objects which behave in unnatural ways: Papakauri, for example, is a log that floats in the Waihou River near Thames and moves up the river against the current, thus presaging the death of a chief.

SECOND SIGHT

The gift of *matakite*, or second sight, presaging death or calamity, is a fairly usual occurrence. Misfortune and death are often attributed to the breaking of the laws of *tapu* (sacredness), by which the ancestral remains and sacred treasures are protected. A divinatory dance, a *haka tutohu*, was sometimes done to determine the culprit. If the wrong was shown to be a transgression by another tribe, then war may have resulted. The death of the culprit was often the only way to redress the wrong. It was the *tohunga*, or divinatory expert, who divined the wrong and recommended the steps to be taken, a function that continues to this day.

THE WILL OF THE GODS

Communication with the gods living in the 10 or 12 heavens is a two-way process. Men acknowledge the *mana* or prestige of the gods. Tane is god of the forest and birds, Tangaroa is god of the sea, Tawhirimatea god of winds, Tumatauenga god of man and of war, and so on. Then there are the local gods who may be tribal or family. The task of men is to observe good manners towards these beings whose bounty, in the form of their children, is their everyday food. In return, the gods allow the harvest and make

the land and sea fruitful – always provided that humans, who are also their descendants, employ all their skill in any task undertaken. The gods make their wishes known by celestial or natural phenomena. Lightning, thunder, wind and rain are all personified as children of the Sky Father and Earth Mother.

NATURAL PHENOMENA

Each tribe has sacred peaks where lightning is seen and portents read. Many sung poems heard on the *marae* start like this lament for Te Huhu.

Tera te uira e hiko i te rangi,
E whawhai rua ana na runga Tauwhare,
Kaore ianei, ko te tohu o te mate.

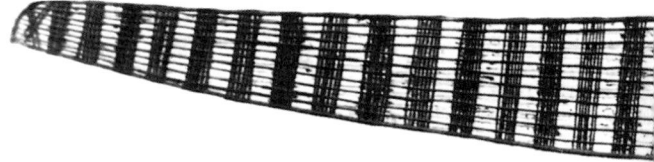

There is the lightning flashing in the sky,
Hunting the lightning pit on Tauwhare [mountain],
It is for today a sign of the death [of Te Huhu].

The way the lightning flashes, whether straight down, which is bad for the locals, away towards another tribe, which is bad for them and good for the locals, or as broad summer lightning without thunder which portends war, and the place where the lightning starts and finishes are all noted and interpreted.

A red glow in the sky in front of a party is very ominous. Similarly, a low rainbow in front of a person or party will cause them to turn back, as will fragments of rainbow. A high-arched rainbow almost forming a circle is the best sign there can be.

Old-time *tohunga* are said to have been able to send messages by natural signs such as a ring around the Moon or a ring around the Sun, and these are still good signs.

DIVINATORY RITES

Before embarking on an enterprise it was, and still is, wise and polite to invoke the blessing of the spiritual powers. However, good manners can be backed up by knowing that the task is likely to succeed. Various divinatory rites were used in the old days to ascertain the outcome of any new undertaking.

These rites were particularly concerned with war: whether the tribe would be victorious or suffer defeat, and who out of their chiefs would be killed. The *niu* and *raurau* rites were often used for this.

War divination was sometimes done by man-shaped kites (middle); omens were drawn by the way they flew over the battleground or village.

Casting lots in the niu *and* raurau *rites was done by the* tohunga *(top and bottom). In the* raurau *rite a small mound was made and named for the tribes, and green twigs of* karamu *were placed in each. In front of these, small sticks were placed on the ground. Invocations were said. The small sticks would then move towards the twigs, and leaves would drop off to show how many would be killed. The* niu *takes two or more forms. The* tohunga *spread a mat on the ground, then took fern stalks in his hand and named each one of them for the chiefs who were to go on the war party. Each stick was tied with a piece of flax. Another set − without the flax ties − was named for the chiefs of the opposing tribes.   The enemy chief sticks were then stuck upright through the mat. The* tohunga *took up the sticks with the ties and threw one of them at a stick without a tie. If it dropped to the left of the upright stick, the chief would fall. If it dropped to the right he would survive. This was done for all the chiefs. Another* niu *rite involved placing sticks in the ground and balancing named sticks with flax ties on them on each. The* tohunga *then waited for these to fall to the left or right.*

FORMS OF THE GODS

Gods can communicate with men by sending their *aria*, or semblance, often as lizards. The green gecko is a sign of death, while illness was thought to be caused by a god in the form of a lizard gnawing at the body. *Tohunga* used to produce lizards from a sick person's body as proof that the illness was conquered by prayer, and then give medicine. *Aria* may also be in the shape of dogs, birds, insects (particularly the green mantis), trees, rocks, weapons, rainbows, comets and stars. All of these manifestations are regarded as portents.

OBJECTS OF *MANA*

Ancestral treasures, images of the gods, symbols of chieftanship and many other items had *mana*, or power, of their own and could be used (and some are still used) to ask the goodwill of the gods. For exactly the same reason they can be used in divinatory rites. Such an item may turn over, move sideways, or otherwise answer the questions asked by those who have the right to ask, the legitimate holders and descendants of the *mana* of the gods. Their task is to ensure the continuation of, and if necessary restore, the balance between the realms of existence.

Living in the world of today for Maori people involves embracing and looking back to the past. The Maori vision of time is of a group looking back to what has gone before and backing into the unknown future. The dead are thought of as going before, returning to the past yet at the same time preparing the future place for their relatives and descendants.

The continuation of this world-view is illustrated by the following story. As noted earlier, when a person or group goes onto the *marae* (ceremonial meeting place) of another tribal group they are never alone, for their dead are with them to protect them from harm. Both sides are very conscious of any omens or portents that may appear. Quite recently, when a small party was waiting to be called and welcomed onto a *marae*, the local elders looked out and decided they did not need to do very much as the group appeared to be of little importance and mainly European.

Just then there was a short, sharp shower which fell out of a clear sky only on the *marae* courtyard. The elders immediately called for their women and the other people around the *marae* to come and help welcome the visitors. These were *waewae tapu*, sacred footsteps, and the ancestral spirits were telling their descendants to welcome them properly lest evil befall.

*A house lintel from Hauraki depicts the birth of
the gods from the Earth Mother. At the sides are* manaia,
*which represent the spirit world and are probably a
combination of bird and lizard.*

WORLD-WIDE SYSTEMS

We have seen points of similarity between many of the divinatory systems. Some are almost globally disseminated, and for this reason they are discussed here separately.

Numerology, for example, can be seen to have arisen more or less spontaneously in Greece, Assyria, Egypt and the greater part of Europe. In most instances there seems to be a recurring pattern of discovery that numbers equate to the natural patterns observable in the universe. This, of course, gave them magical significance and provided those who possessed the wisdom to understand them with superior qualities. The importance of crystals throughout much of the world may also have played a part in the origin of the science of numbers, since crystalline forms themselves display a numerical quality and are seen as the foundation of much of created matter. The antiquity of the examples collected by Norman Shine to illustrate his chapter indicates that numerology is one of the oldest divinatory systems in the world.

Geomancy, which has spread throughout the world and underlies many of the divinatory systems we have discussed, itself relies heavily on numerical patterns, though it is perhaps more related to the profound understanding of the elements and natural cycles – a theme that we have encountered again and again in this study.

Geomancy is also related to the work of the classical augurs (Chapter Seven) and to the practitioners of Feng Shui, whose earth-orientated skills are part of the geomantic heritage. When we read the description of the basic methods used by geomancers to foretell future events or to decide upon the positioning of a building, we may well be reminded of the methods used by more than half the diviners we have followed throughout this collection.

Dowsing may perhaps be considered the 'odd man out' in this section, yet the ability to divine lost objects, and to discover the relationships of one thing to another, is very much part of the diviner's art. Like numerology and geomancy it is known to have flourished in many different areas of the world – as, indeed, it still does today. Dowsers operate in all kinds of ways, seeking things as diverse as the discovery of murder victims, the recovery of lost works of art or (traditionally) hidden springs of water.

The degree of interest in divination throughout the world continues unabated and has even, in the last few years, begun to expand. Hence in the appendix to this collection Eileen Campbell discusses a few of the many new or newly rediscovered systems which are arousing interest all over the world. Several of these have grown out of a consideration of the ancient systems we have examined above; they are restatements or fresh developments which have emerged from the old. Their existence makes it clear that we are as eager today as were our ancestors to know the answer to the question with which we began: What *does* the future hold in store?

CHAPTER TWENTY-TWO

COUNTING ON THE FUTURE

The Art and Science of Numerology

Norman Shine

Numerology, the science of numbers, has its origins early in the history of man. Among the Aryans and Greeks, the Assyrians and Egyptians, the Chinese and the early prehistoric Europeans, we find evidence of a symbolic system that was concerned with something more than mere enumeration.

Behind the Cosmos there is an intelligence which we see expressed in Nature. God appears to be mathematical, and in Nature we have the geometric expression of Divine intelligence. Crystallization takes place according to definite laws: water, for example, crystallizes at an angle of 60°. The universe can therefore be seen as the crystallized imagination of God, as a divine thought-form. By the study of numbers we can learn the laws of divine expression, from the constitution of the universe down to the most trivial occurrences.

One of the earliest attempts at a numerological representation of time and space is the arrangement of nine small, round cavities carved in the rock in the pre-historic Jean Anglier cave near Noisy-sur-Ecole in France, which is reminiscent of the early Chinese numerological 'maps'. The *I Ching*, the Book of Changes, is the earliest Chinese reference to a number system. The Chinese described the difference between odd and even numbers, allocating to the odd numbers heavenly qualities, and to the even numbers earthly qualities. The texts associated with the *I Ching* include a 'magic square' where the sum of the digits horizontally, vertically and diagonally always adds up to 15. These 'magic squares' are found at various times and in a

number of different cultures. The Vedic Square is a table of multiplication numbers and, as the name implies, is associated with the early Sanskrit texts, the Vedas. The basis for the calculations of the Vedic Square is the multiplication table from one to nine, but instead of using the double numbers obtained by the multiplication of single numbers, they are reduced here to single numbers, e.g. $6 \times 6 = 36 = 9$ (see overleaf). Note that in the Vedic Square, with the exception of the numbers 3, 6 and 9, each number appears six times. Numbers 3 and 6 appear twelve times. Number 9 appears twenty-one times. By joining the mid-points of the squares where the number 1 repeats itself, the pattern for number 1 is formed. The designs obtained from the Vedic Square have been used as decorations in holy places by both Moslem and Hindu craftsmen throughout the ages.

The sixth-century BC Greek philosopher Pythagoras made a very considerable contribution to numerology. His work on mathematics was primarily orientated towards religion and philosophy, as witnessed by his statement in the *Sacred Discourses*: 'Number is the ruler of form and ideas and is the cause of gods and demons.' This statement echoes the Chinese observation from the beginning of the second millennium BC: 'The sum total of heavenly numbers and earthly numbers is 55. It is this ...which sets gods and demons in movement.' Pythagoras related the sequence of numbers to the sequence of letters in the Greek alphabet so that alpha = 1, beta = 2, gamma = 3, and so on. Pythagoras operated only with the number sequence 123456789; the

Hebrews, in the development of the Cabbala, operated with the number sequence 1 to 22. The 22 letters in the Hebrew alphabet served as the basis for a numerology which incorporated a very broad range of associated concepts.

NUMBERS AND PLANETS

A key to understanding numerology is found in the sequence of the days of the week. The global acceptance of the seven-day week suggests that there is a symbolic meaning to the number sequence 1234567. What we find is that the sequence of the days – whose names are derived from those of the planets – is the same as the sequence of the planets in early Hindu astrology.

1 Sun (Sunday)
2 Moon (Monday)
3 Mars (Tuesday)
4 Mercury (Wednesday)

5 Jupiter (Thursday)
6 Venus (Friday)
7 Saturn (Saturday)

The basis of numerology is this relationship of numbers to planets. The correlation between number and planet is far from arbitrary: the associations we form with the different numbers harmonize well with the attributions given astrologically to the planets. Keywords and examples of these associations are:

1 Unity. The personal resources of the individual. Divine presence. Ego. Synthesis. Sun.

2 Polarity. Duality. Good/bad; day/night; either/or. The mind. Emotions. Antithesis. Dilemma. Choice. Ambivalence. Moon.

3 Action. Personal creativity. The Divine triangle: Heaven, man, Earth. The Holy Trinities of God the Father, Son and Holy Ghost; Brahma, Vishnu and Shiva. Thought, word and action. Mars.

4 The number of the world. The concrete. Practice. The stable square. The four seasons. The four directions. The four elements. The lower intellect and instincts. The quantitative. Order and classification. The first arithmetic square (2x2). Mercury.

5 The five senses. Five toes. Five fingers. Learning through the senses. Expansion. Jupiter.

6 The double triangle. The Star of David. Higher intellectual creativity. The abstract. Perfection. The world created in six days. Beauty. Harmony. Sense of discrimination. Imagination. Venus (rules the sexual organs) and Uranus (rules the sexual glands).

7 The limit of matter. Time. Chronos, the Greek god of time. The colours of the rainbow. The seven tones of the musical scale. The seven days of the week. The seven cardinal virtues and deadly sins. The seven seals of the Book of Revelations. Stability and endurance. Duration of the material. Saturn.

To complete the correlation of numbers with astrological phenomena we can take two important symbols of Hindu astrology, the lunar nodes. We can correlate the number 8 with the north lunar node. The north node of the Moon is now commonly accepted as an indicator of the individual's fate in a specific lifetime. The number 9 can be correlated with the south lunar node. The south node of the Moon is acknowledged as an indicator of individual karma, the unresolved residue of earlier lives.

The number 8 has always been a mystic number, with its association with infinity (∞) and being beyond the force of time. The number 8 symbolizes the material, the temporary, whereas the number 9 symbolizes truth and love, the Divine, the eternal reality. Their other associations are:

8 The double square. The first arithmetic cube (2x2x2). The number of dissolution. The law of cyclic evolution. As a cubic number it adds the new dimension of timeless (beyond 7) space. In contrast to 2 (either/or), this number symbolizes the absolute reality of matter, which is bound by time. Thus, it symbolizes good *and* bad, right *and* wrong, night *and* day. All these are bound by time. Because of its shape it is also associated with

the caduceus (staff) carried by Mercury. It illustrates the balance between opposing forces, or the equilibrium between the spiritual powers and the powers of nature. It is associated with Pluto as well as with the north node of the Moon. It represents the breakdown of the barrier between the material and the spiritual, in order to complete transformation.

9 The triple three (3x3). A complete picture of the three worlds: the physical (1, 2, 3), the intellectual (4, 5, 6), and the spiritual (7, 8, 9). The last of the symbols in the numerical sequence before it returns to unity, raised to a higher level (10). For the Hebrews 9 is the symbol of truth, for the Hindus it is the number of Brahman. It is associated with the planet Neptune (Neptune is the ruler of the last of the astrological signs, Pisces, symbolizing the relinquishing of the ego) as well as with the south node of the Moon.

For the numerologist there are, then, only nine numbers from which all calculations concerning the material world are made. By a simple method of addition all numbers beyond 9 can be reduced

1	2	3	4	5	6	7	8	9
2	4	6	8	10	12	14	16	18
3	6	9	12	15	18	21	24	27
4	8	12	16	20	24	28	32	36
5	10	15	20	25	30	35	40	45
6	12	18	24	30	36	42	48	54
7	14	21	28	35	42	49	56	63
8	16	24	32	40	48	56	64	72
9	18	27	36	45	54	63	72	81

5. The Cabbala's complex correlation system is based on the Hebrew alphabet. Today it is mostly used in conjunction with the Tarot.

Hebrew Letter	English Letter	Number	Planetary or Zodiacal Ruler
Aleph	A	1	Mercury
Beth	B	2	Virgo
Gimel	G	3	Libra
Daleth	D	4	Scorpio
He	E	5	Jupiter
Vau	V U W	6	Venus
Zain	Z	7	Sagittarius
Cheth	H	8	Capricorn
Teth	Th	9	Aquarius
Jod	I J Y	10	Uranus
Caph	C K	11	Neptune
Lamed	L	12	Pisces
Mem	M	13	Aries
Nun	N	14	Taurus
Sameck	X	15	Saturn
Ayin	O	16	Mars
Pe	F P	17	Gemini
Tzaddi	Ts Tz	18	Cancer
Quoph	Q	19	Leo
Resh	R	20	Moon
Shin	S	21	Sun
Tau	T	22	Earth

NUMEROLOGY AROUND THE WORLD

Numerology is truly a world-wide phenomenon and lies behind many other systems of divination. The mystical possibilities inherent in numbers have fascinated people throughout the ages, although the precise forms of numerological science depend on the cultures in which they originate, as the examples on the map indicate.

This detail from the prehistoric Jean Anglier cave near Noisy-sur-Ecole in France appears to illustrate an attempt at ordering time and space.

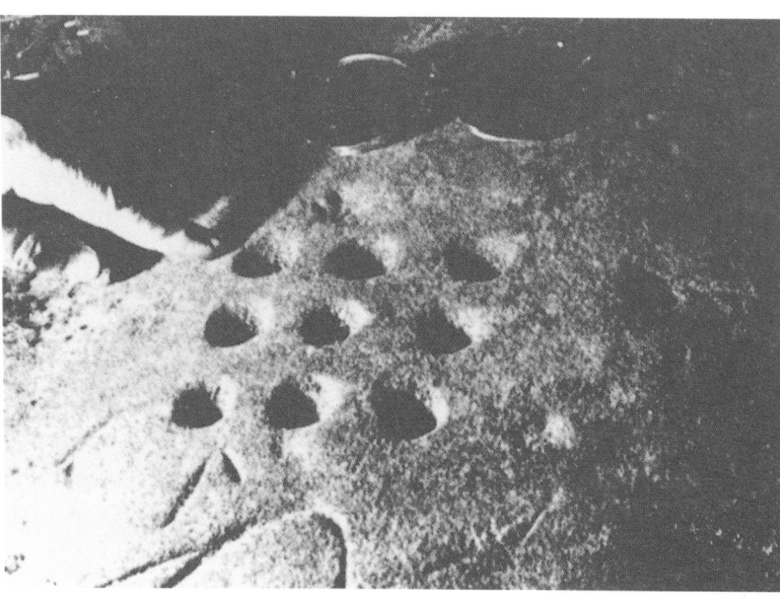

1. The Vedic Square is a table of multiplication numbers: the table on the left is used as a base for calculating the Vedic Square on the right. The double numbers of the multiplication table (left) are reduced to single numbers, e.g. $6 \times 6 = 36 = 3 + 6 = 9$.

1	2	3	4	5	6	7	8	9
2	4	6	8	1	3	5	7	9
3	6	9	3	6	9	3	6	9
4	8	3	7	2	6	1	5	9
5	1	6	2	7	3	8	4	9
6	3	9	6	3	9	6	3	9
7	5	3	1	8	6	4	2	9
8	7	6	5	4	3	2	1	9
9	9	9	9	9	9	9	9	9

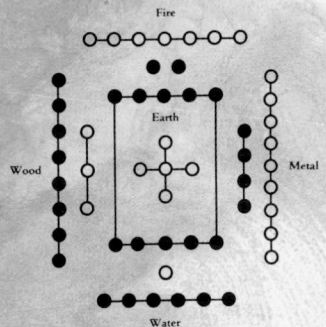

2. This diagram, known as *Ho T'u*, the Yellow River Map, dating from the second millennium BC, shows the development out of odd and even numbers of the 'five stages of change' (usually incorrectly called elements).

4   9   2

3   5   7

8   1   6

4. This diagram shows an important 'magic square', where the sum of the digits horizontally, vertically and diagonally is 15 in each case. This square is found throughout Europe during the Middle Ages.

3. This arrangement, also found in texts associated with the *I Ching*, is known as the *Lo Shu*, the Writing from the River Lo. It is here stated that 'the sum total of heavenly numbers and earthly numbers is 55. It is this that . . . sets demons and gods in movement.'

to single whole numbers. The number 10 is not a single whole number, it is actually only a 1 with a zero.

Zero is not a number and thus has no numerological value. The Western world has not recognized zero as long as the Eastern world: both the Indian and the Chinese cultures used the zero during the Stone Age period of the Western world. Beginners are advised to be careful when interpreting the role of zero numerologically, as it has certain negative attributes when found in dates.

NUMEROLOGY IN PRACTICE

The application of the numerological correlates in the Cabbala is complex, so those who are new to numerology are advised to apply Pythagoras' system. Pythagoras employed a pragmatic and logical approach:

1	2	3	4	5	6	7	8	9
A	B	C	D	E	F	G	H	I
J	K	L	M	N	O	P	Q	R
S	T	U	V	W	X	Y	Z	

Thus AJS = 1, BKT = 2, and so on.

The principle is that one sequence (numbers) is correlated with the other sequence (here, the alphabet). This principle can also be employed should we wish to relate colours to numbers. Here, however, we must decide whether we should employ the seven colours of the rainbow, in which case the association of colour with number follows the sequence 1234567. According to the modern colour therapist Marie Louise Lacy, a key to the colours and their numerological vibrations is:

1 Red	4 Green	7 Violet
2 Orange	5 Blue	8 Silver
3 Yellow	6 Indigo	9 Gold

If we bear in mind that there are over 20 different house systems in astrology, we should not be surprised that there are many different systems within numerology. The systems must not, however, be mixed. If we use a system in one way, then it must be followed consistently at all times with the same name or date.

NUMEROLOGY WITH DATES

The birth date, time and place are equally valid for divining purposes in numerology. The example here shows the numerological analysis of the birth date 28 August 1954.

The *day of birth* is symbolic of the way the individual sees him or herself. This *psychic number* is obtained by making a single whole number of the day of the month, here $28 = 2 + 8 = 10 = 1 + 0 = 1$.

The *destiny* or *fate number* is where the individual can see what he or she has deserved. It is the single whole number obtained from the addition of the day, month and year of birth: 28 August $1954 = 2+8+8+1+9+5+4 = 37 = 3+7 = 10 = 1+0 = 1$.

NUMEROLOGICAL ANALYSIS OF NAMES

The *name number* is a synthesis of both psychic and destiny numbers and illustrates how the individual will react to specific situations. The name number may be seen as a whole (personal name(s) plus family or surname) or may be treated specifically as personal name (symbolizing the individual's personal relationship to others and society in general).

The name number is illustrated as a single whole number obtained by the addition of the number equivalents of the letters of the name. For example, Birgitte Shine $=2+9+9+7+9+2+2+5+1+8+9+5+5 = 73 = 7+3 = 10 = 1$.

Once the numerologist has the psychic, destiny and name numbers it is possible to assess the way in which these numbers work together. In the above example we can see that all three numbers are 1. Quite clearly this is an illustration of great intensity of energy in one particular area: a narrow front with great depth. Where all three numbers are different (for example: psychic number 6, fate number 7 and name number 8) we find a broad energy front that is more shallow. Interpretation may vary, but it must rest on the classical understanding of number symbolism.

Most numerological systems simply add all the digits to arrive at a name number, as in the example above. An interpretation here is simple: the name is 'read' numerologically as a '1'. The analysis will be as limited as an astrological analysis of the Sun-sign: born on 8 October I am seen as being born under the sign of Libra, and all other relevant astrological data are ignored. An interpretation of the basic characteristics of number 1s is that they are resourceful and talented. They have a clear sense of their own identity, are self-sufficient and have stable values. They also have leadership abilities. The negative traits are that they are wilful, inconsiderate and tend to complacency.

Obviously, the sum of the digits description just given is too simple. When we look at the name diagram shown below, we can see that in fact there is very little 1 in the name Birgitte Shine. It is found only once. In the diagram this is illustrated by one circle around the number 1. On the other hand, number 2 and number 5 are both found three times, 9 is found four times, and 7 and 8 are each found once. A fuller analysis of the name should thus take into account these other features of the personality.

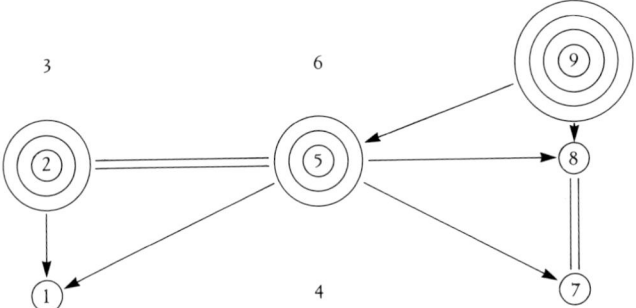

Birgitte Shine: 2,9,9,7,9,2,2,5,1,8,9,5,5

An analysis of the name could include the following observations:

Number	Characteristic	Frequency	Manifestation (personal)
1	Awareness of personal resources	1	Relatively low self-confidence. Needs to build this up by meeting new challenges with open mind and use of instincts.
2	Awareness of feelings and emotions	3	High emotionality. Feminine emotional responses.
3	Awareness of personal creativity	0	Low awareness. No conscious controls. Impetuosity. Rashness. Ruled by emotions (high 2 and low 1).
4	Awareness of concrete, logical and intellectual processes	0	Neither practical nor logical. Non-intellectual but highly instinctive and intelligent (note high emotionality – 2).
5	Awareness of senses	3	Relatively high. Sensuality linked closely to emotions (2 and 5 have same frequency).
6	Awareness of abstract, imaginative, intellectual processes	0	Low imagination awareness. High intuitive abilities.
7	Awareness of material limitations (time and space)	1	Well developed. Matches awareness of own resources. Risk of sense of inadequacy. Limits of action (low awareness of activity ability).
8	Awareness of eternity (materiality/ spirituality)	1	Well developed but subject to emotions (high) and compulsive unconscious urges and reaction patterns (see 9 below).
9	Awareness of inborn talents and compulsive urges	4	A main motive force in the personality working through feelings (intense) and with spiritual awareness and the setting of limits. Dominated by unconscious mechanisms.

The lines and arrows in the diagram show the direction and intensity of the energy flow. Where the number 2 is high and the number 1 is low it shows that the individual's emotions are stronger than her awareness of her resources. Emotions are used to develop resources.

Where there is a low frequency of a number (fewer circles) and, most of all, where a number is not represented in a name, that number attracts most energy from the surrounding numbers, and much energy is used in attempting to exploit the hidden resources in the number(s) lacking. We tend to be controlled by those energies we are not conscious of. In the energy pattern of Birgitte Shine, the absence of a number 3 means that emotional self-control is necessary for her to become aware of her strong (but concealed) ability to act and think creatively. If she uses her massive awareness of her inborn subconscious and unconscious powers (high frequency number 9) to her own advantage, she can cease to respond automatically to emotional situations by compulsive action and near-compulsive setting of limits. (Low frequency 7 and no 3s attract too much 9 energy.)

As we can see, the name number (by addition) is 1, which is identical with her psychic number (based on birthdate) and her fate number (based on total birth data). Her true psychic picture of herself is of a resourceful person. Her life is exciting and full of challenges. But when we see her name analysis in detail we see that she is inhibited by lacking a functional awareness of her powers. This is mainly as a result of (a) compulsive behaviour and (b) over-emotionality.

APPLICATIONS OF NUMEROLOGY

Numerology is useful in rapid analysis of personal qualities and behavioural patterns. By combining and comparing names the numerologist is able to describe compatibility potential. Such analyses are used in marriage counselling, personnel and staff management (who will work best with whom) and parent counselling (in ascertaining why some parents have great difficulties with their children).

Numerology is also useful for a rapid investigation of the change in an individual's energy pattern in the case of name change (by marriage, adoption, etc.). The numerologist is of great assistance in helping those who, in an identity crisis, are able to find solutions to their problems by finding a new name to reflect a new development in their life.

There is, as has been indicated, a certain overlapping between numerology and astrology. The knowledge of the planetary cycles (in both Western and Hindu astrology) is invaluable in determining prognoses for future events. For this reason, a good numerologist should also have knowledge of astrology, psychology, palmistry and graphology. Where a client wishes to change his or her name, the numerologist is, by an investigation of a birth chart (horoscope), able to confirm to the client the wiseness of his or her choice. The choice of names, however, is best left to the client.

LUCKY NUMBERS?

Almost everyone has his or her 'lucky' number or numbers. And it is a fact that individuals respond especially strongly to certain numbers. Some numbers we can call friendly numbers, others we can call neutral numbers, and finally there are numbers we might just as well call enemy numbers. 'Lucky' or friendly numbers are useful in finding what house number to live in, which lottery ticket to buy, which numbers to play on in roulette and racing. In his practice the numerologist can give advice on such matters on the basis of birthdays and names. Certain dates are also luckier for an individual than others.

The means of calculating such numbers are relatively complex and lie outside the scope of this article. The value of such advice is far from being frivolous: although the numerologist cannot bring luck where no luck is merited, he can reduce the risk of the client bringing bad luck on himself by not maximizing his awareness of the potential of a given situation. The 'lucky' person is one who listens to an inner voice, the instincts and intuition. Those who are not too good at this can always find a numerologist.

CHAPTER TWENTY-THREE

ANCIENT SECRETS OF THE EARTH

The Oracle of Geomancy

Nigel Pennick

Geomancy is one of the systems of divination that use aspects of the four elements. The other three elemental systems are aeromancy, using the air; pyromancy, using fire; and hydromancy, using water. Correspondingly, geomancy gives its messages by or through the earth. The word geomancy comes from the Greek words *Ge*, Gaia, Mother Earth, and *manteia*, divination; or, alternatively, the second part of the word may come from *magos*, knowledge. It is thus knowledge of earthly things, for, according to traditional belief, geomancy works through the agency of the Earth Goddess or through the elemental spirits of the Earth.

Today, the word geomancy refers to two distinct yet related forms of divination. They are oracular geomancy, which deals with prediction, and locational geomancy, the esoteric science of placement, which looks for good and bad places in the landscape. In the East, locational geomancy has several related forms. The most important are Vastuvidya (India), Yattara (Burma) and Feng Shui (China) (see Chapter Seventeen). In the West, locational geomancy includes the practices of Greek, Etruscan and Roman augurs, and the work of the 'locators' of medieval and baroque Europe, men who founded cities, cathedrals and churches.

Throughout history, geomantic patterns have been made by almost any available method. Among the most common methods are: scattering handfuls of earth on the ground; throwing seeds, nuts or sea-shells onto a special tray; pricking marks on paper with a pin, or making dots with a pen. A larger version of the pin or pen marks can be made using a tray of sand or on the earth with a rod, a technique closely related to *rhabdomancy*, which is a form of dowsing. Special dice or divination chains are also used occasionally. What these techniques have in common is that, from marks made unconsciously, patterns are created which can be interpreted by the experienced geomant.

THE HISTORY AND SPREAD OF GEOMANCY

Because of its wide-ranging techniques, the origin of geomancy is uncertain. Although ancient Greek and Latin writings refer to geomancy, they do not give comprehensive descriptions, which makes it difficult to reconstruct precise details of techniques. It is known that during the siege of Syracuse the geometer Archimedes (278–212 BC) drew figures in the sand to predict the outcome of the battle; but precisely what he was doing is unknown.

The most coherent and developed system of geomancy arose among the Arabs in North Africa. Arab geomancy is known as Raml, from *'ilm al-raml* (the science of sand), and is the type of geomancy used today all over the world. It seems to have been formalized into the present system around the eighth century AD. It may have been devised in Alexandria, derived from ancient Greek or Egyptian methods, but this is not historically proven.

As with many other divination systems (for example the Ogams and the *I Ching* – see Chapters Three and Sixteen), the discovery of geomancy is attributed to a single inspired man. The Arab tradition ascribes it to the prophet Idris (the Islamic name for the Egyptian sage Hermes Trismegistus, founder of alchemy), who was taught the art by the angel Gabriel. Alternative 'originators' of geomancy are said to have been the Jewish prophet Daniel and the Indian Tum-Tum el-Hindi.

As a means of foretelling the future, Raml fits in well with Islamic belief in predestination, and the initial spread of geomancy from North Africa reflects Islamic conquests and influence. There are two distinct areas of geomantic practice in sub-Saharan Africa – eastern and western. To the east is Madagascar, where Arab colonies existed in the ninth century. They were

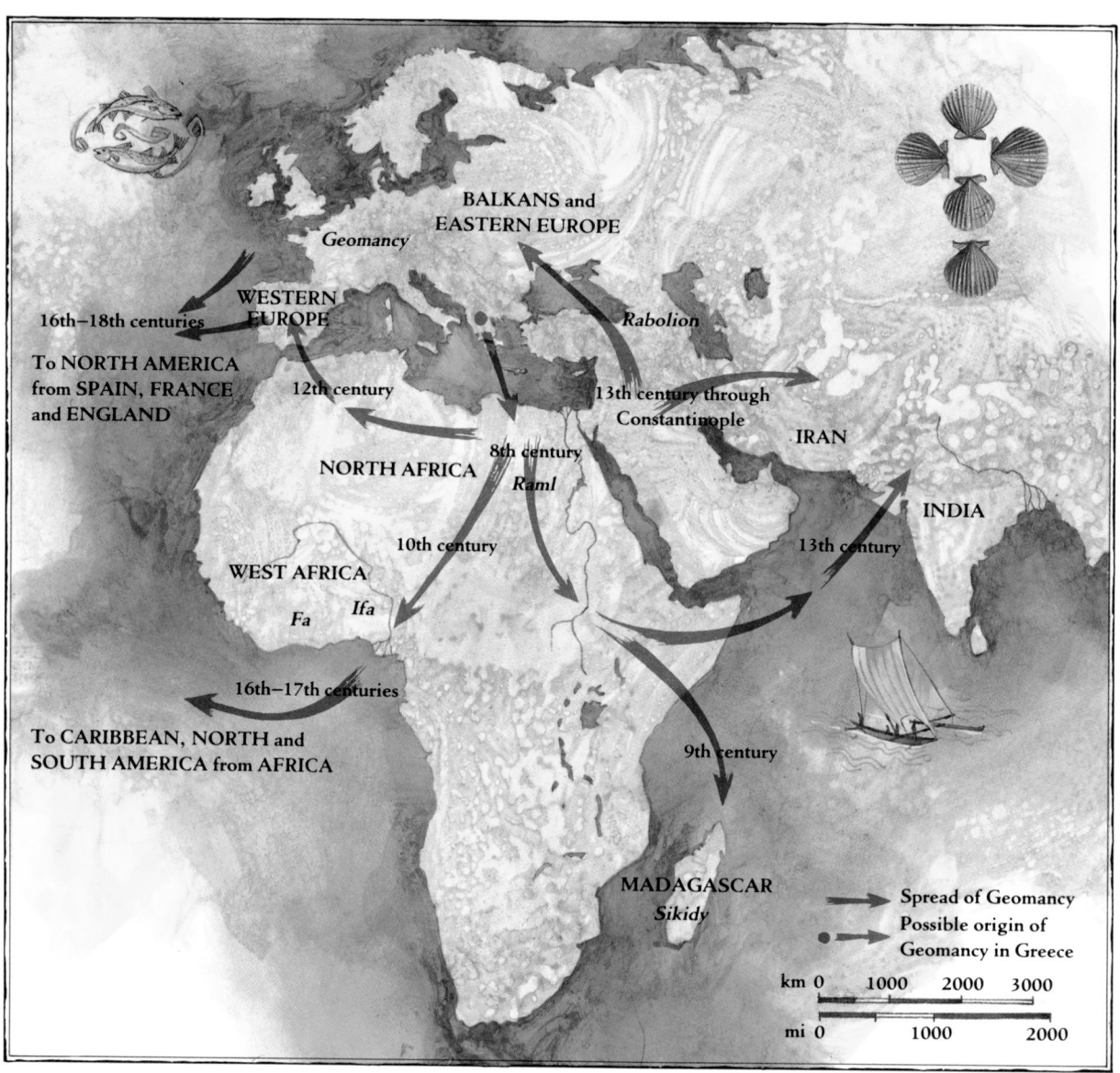

THE SPREAD OF GEOMANCY

The Oracle of Geomancy may have been used in ancient Greece but its present form almost certainly originated after the Arab conquest of Egypt. As Islam expanded further into Africa during the ninth century, geomancy followed. In West Africa, it became Fa and Ifa, while in Madagascar it became Sikidy. The Arabs also took it to Islamic Spain, whence it came into Christian Western Europe. At the other end of the Mediterranean Sea, it entered Eastern Europe through Constantinople, where it became Rabolion. In the thirteenth century, geomancy reached India by land through Iran and by sea from Arabia and East Africa. After Columbus, geomancy was taken to the New World from Africa by slaves and from Western Europe by the conquerors.

the means by which Raml entered Malagasy culture and became Sikidy. Later, it was synthesized with the Malay magico-religious tradition of Bintana and Chinese ideas about Feng Shui to make a distinctly Malagasy system, Vintana.

The second area of sub-Saharan geomancy is in West Africa, which Raml reached overland via the Sahara. In the countries around the Gulf of Guinea, it became Fa and Ifa (see Chapter Twelve). It is likely that these contacts occurred around the tenth century.

Geomancy also spread north of the Mediterranean by two distinct routes. First, it came into Western Europe from Islamic Spain and spread through Christian scholarly writings. The first Latin texts, *Ars Geomantiae* and *Geomantia Nova*, were written in Aragon around 1140, with information from Arabic sources. The author of these works was Hugh of Santalla, who was the first writer to describe Raml as *Geomantia*, giving it its modern name. Some time later, Arab geomancy entered Christian Europe by a second route, through the Eastern Roman Empire. There, the Byzantine Greeks called it Rabolion.

In medieval Europe, geomancy was a popular form of divination. Following Hugh of Santalla, other intellectuals wrote about geomantic divination, adding their own interpretations to a growing European literature on the subject; most notable were Gerard of Cremona (1114–87); Plato of Tivoli (*c.* 1140), Michael Scot (*c.* 1175–*c.* 1235) and Albertus Magnus (1193–1280). Geomancy was also part of the medieval Jewish tradition in Europe, where it was known as Goral Ha-hol (the lot by sand), or Hokhmah Ha-nekuddot (the science of points).

Sometimes, along with astrology, astronomy and alchemy, geomancy was condemned by the Church as heretical. In his *Parson's Tale* (1386), Geoffrey Chaucer notes:

What do we say of those who believe in divinations, as by the flight or sounds of birds, of beasts, of sortilege, by geomancy, by dreams, by creaking of doors, or cracking of houses, by gnawing of rats, and such manner of wretchedness? Certainly, all this is forbidden by God and all the Holy Church. (Author modernization)

But at other times, churchmen have been avid followers of geomancy, and it has flourished. Perhaps its high point was the sixteenth century, in both the Arab world and Europe. Heinrich Cornelius Agrippa (1468–1535), Europe's most famous Renaissance magus, connected geomancy with astrology. In the English edition of his *Fourth Book of Occult Philosophy* (London, 1655), Agrippa gives the following definition:

Geomancy is an art of divination … [which] consisteth especially in certain points whereof certain figures are deducted according to the reason or rule of equality or inequality, likeness or unlikeness; which figures are also reduced to the celestial figures, assuming their natures and properties, according to the course and forms of the signs and planets.

Connecting the geomantic figures with corresponding astrological signs subsequently became an important subsidiary of geomancy, with parallels in the Sikidy of Madagascar, where geomancy is an integral part of astrology and geolocation. Writing in 1558, the Italian geomant Christopher Cattan was explicit in the connection:

Geomancy is a science and art which consisteth of points, pricks and lines, made instead of the four elements, and of the stars and planets of heaven, called the Science of the Earth …every prick [point] signifieth a star, and every line an element, and every figure, the four quarters of the world.… Wherefore it is easy to know that geomancy is none other thing but astrology.…

Geomancy is also mentioned in an astrological context by Dante in his *Purgatorio*: 'In the hours when the day's heat …can no longer temper the cold of the Moon, when the geomancers see their Fortuna Major rise in the east before dawn.…' (Canto XIX).

During the Renaissance period, geomancy was taken to the colonies in the Americas, first by Spanish conquistadors, later by English and French magicians. The African version, Ifa, was also taken to the New World by people transported there to work as slaves. Today it remains part of their descendants' culture in the United States, Haiti, Cuba and Brazil.

In nineteenth-century Europe, a version of geomancy using a book called *Napoleon's Book of Fate* gained popularity. It is a kind of Western *I Ching* (see Chapter Sixteen). Figures consisting of five lines rather than four are created by geomantic methods, and each figure corresponds to a reading from the book. Despite the fact that Napoleon never used it, and it has been called a fake, it still works.

During the twentieth century, geomancy continues to flourish in traditional societies as well as modern ones. It was an important part of the magical tradition of the Hermetic Order of the Golden Dawn, the most influential order of modern magic, and from this school have come several important publications on geomancy (see Further Reading).

HOW IT WORKS

As an oracle, geomancy gives its messages by forming certain distinct patterns. There are 16 possible geomantic figures (tetragrams), each composed of dots (or alternatively stars, points or lines). Each geomantic figure has a name and a corresponding meaning, and may be interpreted either alone or in combination with the other figures.

The Dogon geomant (left), of Mali, West Africa, creates his geomantic figures directly on the ground. He uses sand in a specially prepared sacred enclosure. Ground nuts, magically linked with the element of earth, are used to make the actual geomantic figures.

Dogon geomants (right) interpret animal tracks across a geomantic pattern left overnight. The type of animal making the track, as well as its position on the geomantic grid, is significant. Animal tracks can be used as an oracle by themselves, or may give useful additional information to a divination performed on the previous day.

The principles used in creating the tetragrams of geomancy are the same as those for making the hexagrams of the *I Ching* with yarrow stalks. Technically, these oracles work on the mathematical principle known as 'sensitive dependence on initial conditions', where the final result depends significantly on the first move. Both geomancy and the *I Ching* use binary mathematics. Geomancy has 16 (2^4) figures, whilst the *I Ching* has 64 (2^6). Both start with a series of alternative choices that narrow down the options, step by step, until only one of the possibilities remains.

Each culture has its own names for the geomantic figures, but, wherever they are used, the meaning of each figure is the same. In Europe, it is customary to use the Latin names for the geomantic figures. They are arranged in their complementary or opposite pairs (see overleaf).

199

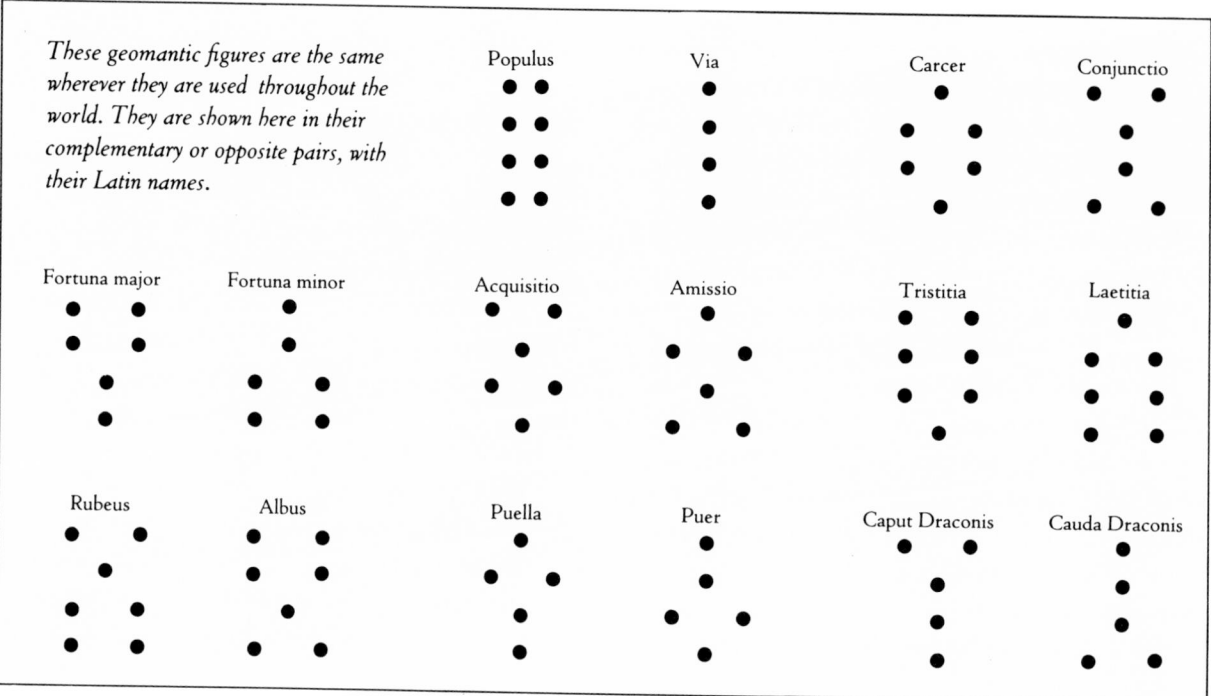

These geomantic figures are the same wherever they are used throughout the world. They are shown here in their complementary or opposite pairs, with their Latin names.

Populus · Via · Carcer · Conjunctio

Fortuna major · Fortuna minor · Acquisitio · Amissio · Tristitia · Laetitia

Rubeus · Albus · Puella · Puer · Caput Draconis · Cauda Draconis

THE UNIVERSAL MEANING OF THE GEOMANTIC FIGURES

POPULUS (THE PEOPLE): an assembly, union, society, crowd, gang, congregation. This figure has a changeable character. Sometimes it can be good and sometimes bad, relative to the other figures in the reading.

VIA (THE WAY): path, street, highway, journey, direction, ways and means, the way of (the questioner's) life. Via has an unfavourable effect on other good figures, but it is beneficial when the question is about travel.

CONJUNCTIO (UNION): connection, recovery of lost things, gathering together, reunion, collection, contracts. Conjunctio is on the positive side of neutral.

CARCER (PRISON): a prison, cell, confinement, servitude, binding, delay.

FORTUNA MAJOR (THE GREATER FORTUNE): good luck, fortune, success, victory, safe property, a good position in society,

entry into good things. An extremely good figure.

FORTUNA MINOR (THE LESSER FORTUNE): assistance from others, protection from harm. A beneficial figure, but not so good as Fortuna Major.

ACQUISITIO (GAIN): profitable business, extension of existing property, success, gains from a request or investigation, great benefit.

AMISSIO (LOSS): things taken away, possibly loss through illness, or through theft of property or financial problems.

TRISTITIA (SADNESS): sadness, misery, melancholy, humiliation, dwindling resources, poverty, a change for the worse.

LAETITIA (JOY): delight, gladness, beauty, grace, sanity, balance, good health, matters of the head. This is a very good geomantic figure.

RUBEUS (RED): passion, vice,

temper, destructive fire, a stop sign. A warning to stop now.

ALBUS (WHITE): dazzling beauty, illumination, wisdom, sagaciousness, profitability. Good results in business and all actions of entry.

PUELLA (GIRL): a girl, daughter, young wife, nurse, a pleasant character, purity, cleanliness. This may appear to be a good figure, but it can be deceptive, as fine external appearances may hide unpleasantness.

PUER (BOY): a boy, son, servant, employee, rashness, inconsiderateness, combativeness. A negative figure, except in combat or love.

CAPUT DRACONIS (DRAGON'S HEAD): a place of entry, a doorway to the heavenly Upperworld.

CAUDA DRACONIS (DRAGON'S TAIL): a way out, the Underworld, possible problems.

USING THE ORACLE

Before starting, think seriously about the question you are asking. Write it down. Then, bearing the question in mind, make a line of dots at random. Repeat this until you have 16 lines of dots. Then count the number of dots in each line and write the numbers down. An odd number gives a single point in the geomantic figure, and an even number gives two points. The 16 lines give four geomantic figures, the Mothers, in all.

Next, four further figures, the Daughters, are made from the four Mothers. The first Daughter is made from the top lines of the four Mothers. The second Daughter is made up from the second line of the four Mother figures in the same way. The third Daughter is made from the third line, and the final Daughter is composed of the bottom line of the four Mother Figures.

Then, four Nephews are made. The first Nephew figure is made by adding together the corresponding points of the first two Mothers. If the sum of points is odd, then that line of the Nephew has one point. If it is even, then there are two points in that line. The second Nephew figure is made by adding together the other two Mothers. The third Nephew is made by adding the first two Daughters, and the fourth Nephew by adding the third and fourth Daughters. There are now 12 geomantic figures in all – four Mothers, four Daughters and four Nephews. The next step is to make two more figures, the Witnesses. The first is created by adding the first and second Nephew figures together. The second comes from adding the third and fourth Nephews. Finally, add together the two Witnesses to make the Judge. The process of geomantic divination means that the Judge will be one of eight figures. These are *Acquisitio, Amissio, Carcer, Conjunctio, Fortuna Major, Fortuna Minor, Populus* and *Via*. None of the other figures can ever be the Judge. The resulting geomantic figures are interpreted in the light of the original question.

In the example shown opposite, the question was whether a new business venture should be started. The lines of dots made at random combine to make the final geomantic figure, or Judge, which in this case is *Via*. This is not a particularly favourable outcome, but is also not negative enough to abandon the enterprise.

• • • • •	5
• • • • • •	6
• • • • •	5
• • • • •	5
• • • • • •	7
• • • • • •	6
• • • • • •	6
• • • • •	5
• • • • •	5
• • • • • •	6
• • • • • • •	7
• • • • • •	6
• • • • •	5
• • • • • • •	7
• • • • • • •	7
• • • • • • •	7

	Puella	Carcer	Amissio	Via
Mothers				

	Via	Tristitia	Puella	Puer
Daughters				

	Albus	Acquisitio	Cauda Draconis	Conjunctio
Nephews				

	Caput Draconis	Laetitia	Via
Witnesses			Judge

CHAPTER TWENTY-FOUR

DOWSING THE WAY

Divining with Pendulum and Rod

Sig Lonegren

Dowsing is the ability to find objects, or the answers to questions, through the use of both the rational and the intuitive aspects of our being. Also called raedesthesia or, perhaps more significantly, divining, dowsing uses a tool that indicates 'yes' or 'no', or the direction to, or specific location of, a target. There are four basic types of dowsing tools: Y-rods, the pendulum, L-rods and the bobber.

Perhaps the best-known dowsing device is the Y-rod, or forked stick. Primarily used by water dowsers, traditionally a Y-rod is cut from an apple or willow tree, although many competent diviners today use plastic because it doesn't break under the constant twisting of the downward pull of the rod. This forked stick is held in both hands, thumbs outwards, with the tip of the 'Y' pointing upwards. This is called the search position. The tip of the rod then goes down sharply when the dowser is over the target.

A pendulum, also known as a plumb bob, can be any well-balanced weight on the end of a thread or light chain. Each dowser sets up his own code to interpret the movements of the pendulum. For some, back and forth means 'yes' (like nodding one's head in affirmation) and an oscillation from side to side means 'no'. For others, a clockwise rotation is 'yes' and counterclockwise means 'no'. As there are other possibilities and combinations of pendulum movement, each dowser has to find his own signals for 'yes' and 'no'. Pendulums are used by many different kinds of dowsers, from those who look for water to those who use divining to help resolve personal problems.

L-rods are bent coat-hangers or lengths of welding rod held in the hands like six-guns in the old cowboy movies. When you get over your target, the rods swing either out or in depending what you have programmed them to do. L-rods are used by water dowsers and by those interested in the Earth Energies found at sacred sites. L-rods are also used by healers, as they are very effective at locating disease in the body.

The fourth dowsing tool is the bobber. Imagine that you are holding a fishing pole at the wrong end. It will bob up and down to tell you 'yes' and go from side to side to tell you 'no'. The bobber is used primarily by oil dowsers who call themselves 'doodlebugs'.

THE HISTORY OF DOWSING

No one knows for certain where dowsing first originated. In the Tassili-n-Ajjer caves, on a plateau in the Sahara desert in south-eastern Algeria near the Libyan border, there are pictoglyphs that could be up to 8,000 years old of a group of people watching someone holding what appears to be a forked stick (Y-rod). This could be the oldest depiction of dowsing.

Various mythological figures are credited with inventing dowsing tools, or at least bringing them to humans. For example, both the Egyptian god Thoth and the Greek inventor Daedalus,

Cornish dowser Hamish Miller, a blacksmith by trade, made these L-rods at his forge to use while tracking the Earth Energies of the famous Michael Line in England, a geomantic corridor that runs from St Michael's Mount in Land's End north-eastward, passing through several churches of St Michael, Glastonbury Tor, Avebury and other ancient holy sites.

who built the Cretan labyrinth, are credited with inventing the plumb bob (i.e. pendulum).

In the latter part of the third millennium BC, a Chinese adventurer by the name of Yü apparently travelled to the United States, went down the Grand Canyon and ended up on the west coast of Mexico before returning to China where he became the emperor. Emperor Yü is the earliest recorded dowser in history whom we know by name. In the Freer Gallery in Washington, DC, there is a Han Dynasty bas-relief that shows Emperor Yü with the following inscription, 'Yü of the Hsia Dynasty was a master of the science of the earth and in those matters concerning water veins and springs; he was well acquainted with the Yin principle and, when required, built dams.'

Although the Bible in more than one place severely censures dowsers and diviners, we are also told two stories where Moses finds water with the use of his rod – the magical one he used to create the plagues in Egypt that convinced Pharaoh to let his people go. One divining story occurs in Exodus (17:1–6) in the Wilderness of Sin in western Sinai at the beginning of the Hebrews' 40 years in the wilderness; the other happens just before they reached the Promised Land. At this second time (in Numbers 20:1–12), the people of Israel were in the Wilderness of Zin in what is now called the Negev Desert. They were tired of their two generations of wandering, and they had once again run out of water. They came to Moses and his brother Aaron and complained bitterly and seemed ready to rebel against Moses' leadership.

Then Moses and Aaron went from the presence of the assembly to the door of the tent of the meeting, and fell on their faces. And the glory of the Lord appeared to them, and the Lord said to Moses, 'Take the rod, and assemble the congregation, you and Aaron your brother, and tell the rock before their eyes to yield its water....' And Moses took the rod from before the Lord, as he commanded him.

And Moses and Aaron gathered the assembly together before the rock, and he said to them,

'Hear now, you rebels; shall we bring forth water for you out of this rock?' And Moses lifted up his hand and struck the rock twice, and water came forth abundantly, and the congregation drank, and their cattle (drank also).

Dowsing has always been a threat to established religions because the layperson can tune in directly to the spiritual realms without going through the priesthood as intermediaries. While this is empowering to the individual, it disempowers the priestly hierarchy. This was one of the reasons that the Christian Church suppressed many forms of dowsing during the Inquisition. Fortunately, several kinds of dowsing were not able to be exterminated. Dowsing can be used for all kinds of targets, but 'water witching', or the ability to find water, is

There are many connections that linguistically tie dowsing with spiritual realms. The French word is 'le sourcier'. In the United States, some call it 'water witching'. Dowsing puts us in touch with things that we can otherwise not see.

Some dowsers believe that the material their tools are made of is important. These L-rods are copper. The Y-rod is not the old, forked apple-stick of yore, but a modern one of metal that provides the same pull (reaction) every time.

indispensable, so it was one dowsing skill that made it through that time of persecution.

Another kind of dowsing that was not suppressed by the Church was written about by the sixteenth-century magician Georgius Agricola. In 1556, in *De Re Metallica* (On Metals), Agricola described how miners in Germany were using dowsing to find underground veins of metal. The German miners later brought their dowsing skills to Britain to help British miners locate tin in Devon and Cornwall.

DOWSING FOR ENVIRONMENTAL HEALTH

In the twentieth century dowsing has flourished once again. Science and rationalism had led Western man to the conclusion that dowsing was just superstition, and therefore not a threat. In the 1920s in Germany, however, it was noticed that people in certain houses – generation after generation – got cancer, while people in neighbouring houses did not. This was true even if different families moved into these '*krebs*' (cancer) houses. Medical doctors were mystified by this phenomenon, until dowsers were called in and reported significant numbers of underground veins of water crossing under the *krebs* houses but not under adjoining homes. It has since been found by many dowsers around the world that spending time over crossing veins of water may induce various kinds of degenerative diseases like cancer and arthritis, as well as colic in babies and sleeplessness.

Erich Schuck, watched by a farmer, dowses on Mindanao Island, Philippines, in search of the hiding place of Second World War Matsushita gold. Schuck was working with psychic archaeologist Umberto di Grazia.

Before they go out onto the site, many dowsers first employ map dowsing. Here a dowser looks for a suitable site to drill a well. He uses the pin in his left hand as a pointer and watches the responses in his pendulum.

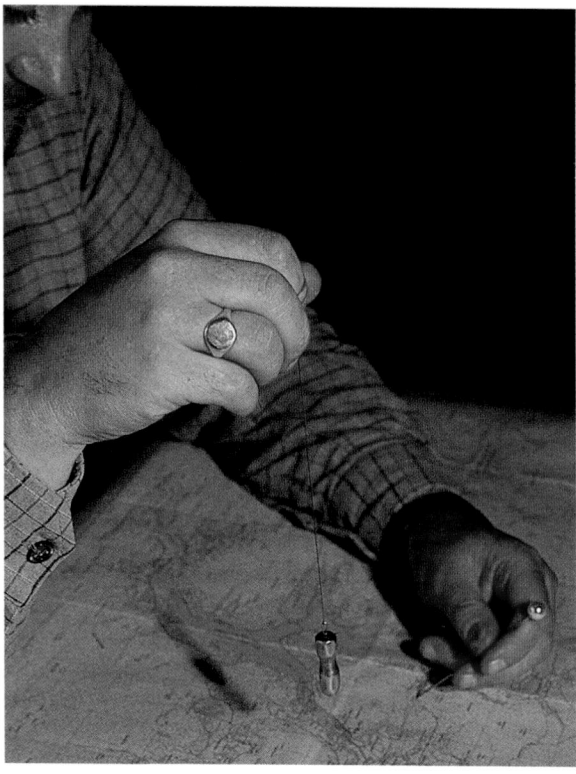

Today there is a great deal of interest in environmental healing, and various remedial techniques have been developed, from putting loops of wire around the frame of the bed where the veins of water cross underneath (the Lakhovsky loop), through putting blue tape on the floor over the veins, to actually driving metal rods into the heart of the veins of water as they enter and exit the house. This last is a form of Earth acupuncture and needs to be done with a great deal of care, preferably under the supervision of an expert dowser. It is my belief that all of these techniques work on a magical level to neutralize the negative effects of the veins.

DIVINING THE EARTH'S SPIRITUAL ENERGY

Reginald Allender Smith was the Keeper of the Egyptian and British Antiquities for the British Museum. After he retired from his job in the 1930s, this respected archaeologist shocked his academic colleagues when articles written by him began to appear in the *Journal of the British Society of Dowsers* saying that he was also a dowser, and that he was finding underground veins of water at sacred sites in Britain.

In 1969, a book by British dowser Guy Underwood, *The Pattern of the Past*, was published posthumously by the executors of his estate. It was the first book devoted to what one dowser found at sacred sites. Underwood dowsed all kinds of curving patterns that in one way or another conformed to the site itself. He had various names for these lines: aquastats, track lines and water lines, to name but a few. While this book has been widely read by dowsers studying what has come to be known as the Earth Energies, not many have pursued Underwood's findings; however, many have found that Allender Smith's veins of water are integrally connected with sacred space.

Underground water is only one of the things that dowsers find at sacred sites. Another type of energy that is found by many dowsers is based on the work of another Englishman, Alfred Watkins. During the early decades of this century he discovered that ancient sacred sites

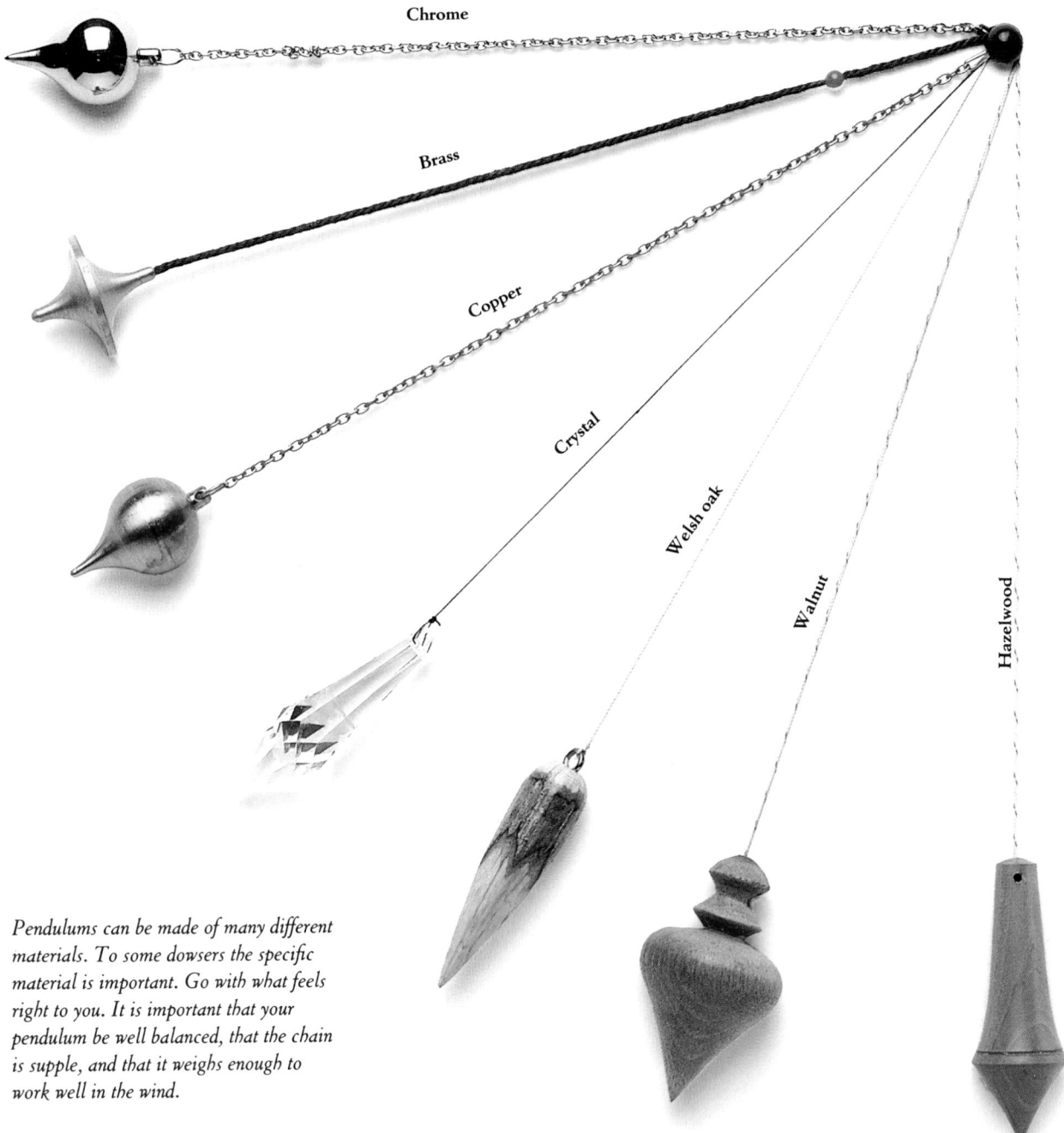

Chrome

Brass

Copper

Crystal

Welsh oak

Walnut

Hazelwood

Pendulums can be made of many different materials. To some dowsers the specific material is important. Go with what feels right to you. It is important that your pendulum be well balanced, that the chain is supple, and that it weighs enough to work well in the wind.

are connected along straight lines in the land. He called these alignments 'leys' and wrote about them in his book, *The Old Straight Track*. While Watkins himself was not a dowser, many people have found energy associated with these leys. In the 1930s, for example, Glastonbury psychic Dion Fortune wrote about straight lines of energy that she perceived, and in the late 1960s American dowser Terry Ross brought the notion of dowseable leys to the United States.

These straight lines of energy, six to eight feet wide, are now called energy leys to differentiate them from Watkins' alignments of holy sites; while energy leys often run concurrently with Watkins' leys, sometimes they do not. Energy leys are described as having yang (masculine) energy, while underground water has yin (feminine) energy.

British dowser Tom Graves has dowsed for energy patterns at a number of sacred sites in recent years. He has found 'overgrounds' that seem to resemble energy leys, and inside stone circles he has found concentric rings of energy which he initially called haloes. He has since come to feel that, instead of rings, what he was actually finding was a spiral of energy going round and round, in towards the centre. Cornish dowser Hamish Miller also finds spirals at sacred sites.

Other dowsers have found different patterns of energy at sacred sites, including Maltese crosses, clusters of circles similar to a bunch of grapes, grids of straight lines.

DOWSING TODAY

So, given all these different experiences, what exactly is it that dowsers find at sacred sites? I have been dowsing for over 30 years now, and have been using this skill at sacred sites for about 20 years. I consistently find Reginald Allender Smith's undergound veins of water and Terry Ross's energy leys crossing at the centre of sacred spaces as far apart as Machu Picchu in Peru, the circular underground kivas of the Anasazi in the American south-west, the underground stone chambers of New England, the stone circles and long barrows of Britain, the high altar of Chartres Cathedral in France, and the stone labyrinths of Sweden. While I am consistent in my findings, it would be less than candid of me if I did not also say that very few other Earth Energy dowsers find what I do. Divination by dowsing is an extremely individual

thing. Each dowser seems to find something different. As a result, I have come to the conclusion that, unless they were trained by the same teacher, no two dowsers will find the same thing in sacred space.

This, I believe, is the challenge that dowsing faces in the 1990s. We all 'see' the energies differently. We all bring to the sacred our own individual level of consciousness. We also all come with our own expectations and, as a result, we each see different parts of the whole. This is anathema to modern science where repeatability is the key. A scientist would say, 'I ought to be able to find exactly the same thing that you do at a given sacred site.' But this just is not the case.

It's the same with any form of divination. No two people would read the tea-leaves in the bottom of a cup in exactly the same way (unless, perhaps, they too were trained by the same teacher). No two readers of Tarot cards would read a given spread in exactly the same way. Divination is an art, not a science, and divining in sacred space leads the dowser to exactly what he or she needs.

Sacred spaces are places on this Earth where the location itself enhances the possibility of spiritual growth. If I were new to dowsing and I came to a sacred space like one of the places mentioned in this chapter, I would take out my dowsing tool of choice and say, 'Point to the spot on this site where it would benefit me the most to be right now.' Then I'd go there and see what happens.

MODERN RESTATEMENTS

An Overview of Contemporary Systems

Eileen Campbell

As the modern world has become ever more complex, we have as human beings become less in touch with the rhythms of life and our inner selves. While much of our technology provides us with the illusion of being in control of our lives, we know that unexpected change and upheaval are constants that cannot be controlled. Divination tools, however, can be rather like the weather forecast for the sailor. They can help us navigate our lives, increasing our awareness about favourable and unfavourable times – past, present and future. Divination helps us to use our intuition so that we can harmonize our actions and face what may befall us or indeed deal with what has already happened. At one level fortune-telling (human beings naturally tend to want to know what might happen to them), at its highest level divination is about what is best for psychological and spiritual growth. Even when times are difficult, there is always positive action which can be taken.

In recent years many completely newly devised systems, based on old lore, have been made available. Ironically, it is we in the West who have been busily devising new systems, while in some parts of the world the ancient systems continue to be used.

Almost every method of divination is a philosophy about the world presented in a series of symbols. Ancient cultures provide the basis for many of the new systems of divination, and I will review some examples of these in this chapter (derived from the Germanic tribes of pre-Christian Europe, the Celts, the Greeks, the Tibetans and the Native Americans).

Some new divination methods are intentionally more popular in appeal, though often grounded in an older philosophy or esoteric art. So I look at *The Astrology Kit, Know Yourself Through Colour, The Crystal Oracle, The Phoenix Cards, The Pendulum Kit* and *The Russian Gypsy Fortune-Telling Cards*.

Finally, since Tarot has proved one of the most popular divination systems of all, and since there has been a proliferation of Tarot decks in recent years, this chapter gives a flavour of some of the most exciting decks now available.

SYSTEMS BASED ON ANCIENT CULTURES

RUNES

Runes were the magical alphabet used by the Germanic tribes of pre-Christian Europe to ward off enemies and diseases, or to promote good health or fertility. Today in their revived form they are helpful in all kinds of problem solving.

Two rune sets have been developed in recent years, the first and probably the most successful being *The Book of Runes* by Ralph Blum and the more recent one being *Rune Stones* by D. Jason Cooper. Each consists of 25 rune stones (24 lettered and one blank) and both include accompanying books which give detailed descriptions of the history of runes and the various methods of using them. Several spreads are given in D. Jason Cooper's book, including the Celtic Spread invented by A.E. Waite for the Tarot. Ralph Blum also gives a number of spreads, such as the Three Rune Spread, the Runic Cross, and Rune Poker. D. Jason Cooper's accompanying book gives instructions for the making of magical talismans and practical exercises for ritual magic using runes. Both give details of how to make a personal rune set.

There are two main methods of using the rune stones. Either put them in a bag or container and shake them, focusing on the question, and then pull out however many are required for a particular spread. Or stand in a circle marked on the ground, focus on the question and toss the rune stones, and see where they land. The closer they are to you, the more significant they are in answering your question. They are interpreted according to where they fall in relation to the inquirer and to other rune stones.

CELTIC ORACLES

To the Celts all trees were sacred. Every tree was an image of the Cosmic Tree, which was itself a symbol of the universe with its three worlds, representing the underlying basis of Celtic spirituality. The qualities and virtues of the major sacred trees were incorporated into an alphabet of twenty letters, the Ogams (see Chapter Three, By Stick and Stone).

The Ogam alphabet is one of the oldest systems of writing still in existence. It was almost certainly used by the Druids as long ago as the sixth century BC, although they probably inherited it from an even older tradition. At some stage the letters of the alphabet were given names, taken from trees or plants.

There is evidence to suggest that Ogam was used in divination, and working from this Colin and Liz Murray created *The Celtic Tree Oracle*, an excellent modern system of divination using a variety of meanings for each of the letters. These are presented as a set of 25 cards, painted by Vanessa Card and showing the tree or plant in question together with its Ogam letter. These are shuffled and laid out in a square. Cards are then turned over at random to produce a reading which

is entered on a record sheet ready for detailed interpretation. According to the positions of the cards on a spread-sheet, various meanings are set forth and internal patterns of relationship drawn up.

Another modern interpretation of Ogam divination is *The Celtic Oracle* by Nigel Jackson and Nigel Pennick, again containing 25 cards: twenty cards represent the tree-letters of the Ogam alphabet; one card – the White Roebuck – represents a Celtic tree, and stands for the mistletoe, the holiest plant of the Druids; four other cards are the Four Holy Treasures of the gods of Celtic tradition, corresponding to the four elements, and are like the four Tarot suits.

The Ogam letters are ordered magically – B L N F S H D T C Q M G Ng St R A O U E I – and the meaning of one letter leads on to the next. Each letter has a name, which is the traditional Irish name of a tree. It also has a number of correspondences, for example the first Ogam letter is Beth, the letter B, which represents the birch tree. Its deities are the White Goddess, Belin; its bird is the pheasant; its animal the white cow; its herb is the Fly Agaric mushroom; its colour is white; its uses are for cradles, broomsticks and yule logs.

The book accompanying the deck in *The Celtic Oracle* gives a description of all 25 cards, with correspondences and meanings, upright and reversed, and provides the necessary information on interpretation. A number of spreads are given, from the simple Three Weavers Spread through to more complicated spreads like the Thirteen Treasures Spread.

OLYMPUS: SELF-DISCOVERY AND THE GREEK ARCHETYPES

This is a do-it-yourself psychoanalysis system which anyone can use. Devised by Murry Hope, it

makes the ancient Greek wisdom available to everyone who would like to know themselves better.

Within Greek mythology is embedded a profound understanding of human psychology. In *Olympus* Murry Hope breaks down the psychological meaning of the various myths and characters and translates them into modern terms, providing a system to help us discover the real truth about ourselves, our friends and our associates.

Olympus was the home of the gods, but it represents a state of mind that can be achieved when we have overcome the imbalances which are naturally associated with the human condition. The gods had a right to reside on Olympus because of the deeds and labours which enabled them to achieve immortality, immortality here meaning a state of mental equilibrium or self-mastery.

Olympus contains 36 cards illustrated by Anthea Toorchen, together with a guide book. The 36 cards comprise:

The Twelve Olympians – who represent the major gods of Olympus (Zeus, Hera, etc.), exemplifying archetypal principles.
The Three Tutors – who represent the lessons we need to assimilate in life and the instructions that might prove of benefit to us (in classical mythology, both mortals and immortals were tutored by non-humans who often assumed the form of fabulous beasts like Chiron the centaur, Silenus the satyr or the goat-footed Pan).
The Four Heroes – who represent the four humours: sanguine, choleric, phlegmatic and melancholic. Although most of us are a mixture of all four types, one may be more appropriate than the others.
The Seventeen Indicators – who represent a variety of mythological characters such as Gorgons, Sirens, Fates, etc. These will help highlight some hopes and fears.

There are two methods of consulting *Olympus*: The Greek Key – used for a mini self-analysis or to gain insight into a problem or question; The Maze, or Labyrinth – used for an in-depth analysis or to ascertain future trends.

THE CELTIC BOOK OF THE DEAD

The Celtic stories of the Voyage to the Otherworld, known as the '*immrama*' (mystical voyages), are comparable to the better known Egyptian and Tibetan books of the dead. These stories, with their guardians and entities who sit at the boundaries between life and death and guard, guide and challenge, can teach us about death, and ease the transition between the states of living and dying. They also teach us better ways of living, and can now be used as a divination tool by those facing problems or decisions in life.

Caitlín Matthews has used the Voyage of Maelduin to devise *The Celtic Book of the Dead*. Maelduin travels across the water to the West, in keeping with Celtic tradition, to discover his destiny. Like Homer's *Odyssey*, this is a voyage of self-discovery. The 42 cards of the Immram deck, exquisitely executed by Danuta Mayer, depict the experiences of the voyage of the soul and the otherworldly islands, and so we have images both magnificent and terrifying, e.g. the Islands of Singing Birds and Plenteous Salmon and the Islands of Cannibal Horses and Fiery Pigs. These cards are laid out on the reading cloth, according to the spread used.

In the accompanying book there is a full translation of the Voyage of Maelduin, plus a shortened prose retelling and commentary. Each card is reproduced in the book and the Celtic background and the divinatory meaning are provided together with a challenge for the querent to address. There are 33 otherworldly destinations and two guide cards which represent the soul friends of the voyager who show us the otherworldly wonders. In addition there are seven gift cards, each of which represents an empowering aspect of the Otherworld. There are two ways of consulting *The Celtic Book of the Dead*: choose the Outward Passage (Immram One), which has nine positions arranged as a journey, when seeking an answer to a problem or situation; and choose the Homeward Passage (Immram Two), which reverses the course of Immram One, when you have a good idea of the circumstances surrounding the situation, but feel uncertain how to proceed.

The Celtic Book of the Dead is intended as a guide to be consulted in times of crisis and explores the inner quest for meaning. However, it can also be used in two further ways: for shamanic journeying, to find empowerment and assistance, to seek information and to help bring healing from the Otherworld into this; and for soul-leading, to conduct the dying person from this world to the other so that fear of the unknown is lessened.

MO: TIBETAN DIVINATION SYSTEM

The Tibetans have consulted oracles of various kinds throughout their history and the teachings of the Buddha are part and parcel of the life of the Tibetans. MO, which is one of the ways an answer to a predicament or an insight into a problem can be gained, should not be seen as separate from the teachings of the Buddha.

The system of MO is compiled from the sacred scriptures by the great saint and scholar, Jamgon Mipham. It comprises a divination manual, translated from the Tibetan by Jay L. Goldberg and Lobsang Dakpa, together with 36 MO cards (beautifully illustrated by Doya Nardin), and one Tibetan dice. The method calls for you first to visualize the form of Manjushri, the Bodhisattva of Wisdom, in the sky in front of you and to invoke his blessing so that you can receive a clear answer to your enquiry. Having recited his mantra (sacred sound) and another mantra, provided in the divination manual, you throw the dice twice, and thus obtain one of the possible 36 answers.

MEDICINE CARDS AND SACRED PATH CARDS

Realizing that most human beings in the modern world are out of touch with Nature, Jamie Sams and David Carson decided to create a set of cards with pictures on them that would key the seeker back into the traditional wisdom that comes from contact with the natural world. They therefore devised the first system of Native American divination based on the teachings of the animals. The *Medicine Cards* are beautifully illustrated with 44 animals that have been used by Native Americans as guides and teachers. The primary strength or characteristic of each animal is described in the accompanying book.

A Medicine Card can be drawn as a lesson for the day, or for a longer period of time (for example at the start of a new year). The questioner can also pick several cards to lay out as a spread. Each animal's lesson sheds new understanding on any given situation, and will assist the seeker in coming to decisions or choosing how to grow.

The *Sacred Path Cards*, created by Jamie Sams, cover the initiation steps that every human being has to learn on the path to wholeness. The 44 cards in this pack have Native American symbols that each hold a special Medicine. There is a history of each one so that the reader can understand how the Medicine of each symbol came into being. The Counting Coup card, for example, is an old tradition in which victory over an enemy was celebrated. In modern times our victories are different, and might include breaking a habit or developing our intuition.

These two packs can be used in conjunction with each other to create double meanings that give a deeper level of understanding. For example, the Raven Medicine Card (which teaches that magic is a shift in consciousness) combined with the Counting Coup Sacred Path Card shows that the seeker has been victorious in shifting an old way of looking at things and perhaps reclaimed the magic of being alive due to this new attitude.

A VOICE FROM THE EARTH: THE CARDS OF WINDS AND CHANGES

This is a new divination system created by Judith Pintar, a story-teller and musician, who served a four-year apprenticeship with an Ojibwe medicine woman.

Drawing on ideas and images from the Native American peoples of the Great Lakes and Canada, whose traditions demonstrate an awareness of the unique spiritual wisdom of the Earth and the importance of its preservation, Judith Pintar has designed the 49-card deck to be used as a tool to regain balance in our lives.

The deck comprises seven suits, or Winds, representing the seven directions: East, South, West, North, Earth, Great Spirit, and Here and Now. There are seven cards, or Changes, in each suit. They also represent the seven directions, but are named for the spiritual energy of that direction: Vision, Incarnation, Transformation, Transcendence, Gaia, All That Is, Stillness.

There are seven primary cards in the deck. A primary card occurs when both the Wind and Change of a card represent the same direction, so the primary card of Vision is the

East/Vision card, and so on.

The deck is accompanied by a book which has a detailed guide to the Cards of Winds and Changes with instructions on how to interpret, and also contains stories, advice and songs. The questioner can use a spread of seven cards, or pick a card at random.

POPULAR DIVINATION SYSTEMS

THE ASTROLOGY KIT

We all know what our Sun-sign is and will probably read what a particular columnist in a newspaper or magazine predicts for the week, but this is a far cry from astrology proper, which is both a science and an art. Yet not all of us are in a position to visit an astrologer and have our chart drawn up and interpreted. However, with *The Astrology Kit*, based on the work of Grant Lewi (a very successful astrologer in his day), everyone can cast their own horoscope in about 15 minutes, without having to have any astrological knowledge.

The Astrology Kit consists of: an introductory book, 'How to Cast a Horoscope', which contains the Table of Years (or Ephemeris, as it is known in astrological circles) covering the years 1900–1999, with a page for each year, showing the aspects between the Sun, Moon and planets for each day; a printed Personal Notepad, on which to write down details about the positions of the Sun and Moon in the chart and the basic conjunctions and aspects, so that it can then be looked up in the Book of Readings; a Zodiac Wheel, a colourful circular device divided into the 12 signs with 36 numbered divisions, with a moving inner circle containing squares and triangles, accompanied by a special marker pen for writing in the position of the planets; A Book of Readings – the horoscope interpretations.

The kit is fun and easy to use both for oneself and for friends. All you need to know is your birthdate.

KNOW YOURSELF THROUGH COLOUR

We are all affected by colour far more than we realize, and there are many ways in which colour can be used to benefit ourselves and others. The Ancient Egyptians knew all about the healing power of colour and the virtues of the seven rays:

Red Ray	The Spirit of Life
Orange Ray	The Spirit of Health and Purity
Yellow Ray	The Spirit of Knowledge and Wisdom
Green Ray	The Spirit of Evolution
Blue Ray	The Spirit of Truth
Indigo Ray	The Spirit of Power with Knowledge
Violet Ray	The Spirit of Sacrifice and High Ideals

Marie Louise Lacy, an experienced colour therapist, devised this divination tool of 28 Colour Keys, through which we can learn more about ourselves. The Colour Keys are 28 coloured cards, seven of which are one colour, five of which have a clear top and a colour below, and 16 of which show dual colours. The cards can be used for divinatory readings, through which we can discover where our attributes lie and can remedy deficiencies occurring in any of the four realms – physical, emotional, mental and spiritual.

Accompanying the 28 colour cards is a full-colour chart and a book. The book describes methods of bringing colour into our lives, the ways of using colour for healing, the deeper meaning of numbers when linked to the colours, how decor and design can help transform negative energy, and the influence of different colours throughout the day. Methods of reading and instructions for interpretation are provided.

THE CRYSTAL ORACLE

Throughout history crystals have been endowed with powers both to heal and protect. Worn in jewellery and armour, adorning crowns and sceptres, many myths and legends are associated with crystals.

Devised by Leroy Montana, Linda Waldron and Kathleen Jonah, *The Crystal Oracle* can be used to answer questions, seek guidance or provide a message for the day ahead. It comprises five semi-precious stones, to which various qualities are attributed:

amethyst   spirituality, justice, creativity
aquamarine happiness, clarity
carnelian   self, current conditions
rose quartz health, prosperity
tourmaline power, activity

The Crystal Oracle contains a velvet casting cloth divided into 15 sections and a book giving full instructions on how to use and interpret it.

Crystals are unique in that they have a geometrically perfect atomic structure, and they also have electrical properties, something which modern technology has capitalized on. This electric potential is tapped in the Crystal Oracle, each of the five crystals having a complementary function:

amethyst   receiver
aquamarine tuner
carnelian   earth
rose quartz transmitter
tourmaline amplifier

Leroy Montana has described the Crystal Oracle as a New Age radio set! When the crystals are held in the hand, they receive electrical impulses from the brain, and then conduct that energy to the casting cloth. Whether this is the case or not, the Crystal Oracle is certainly great fun to use. It is consulted by holding the crystals in one hand, palm down, a few inches above the cloth. The question is asked of the crystals, which are then allowed to drop on to the cloth. Each one will fall on or near 15 points of reference or the centre. According to where the crystals land (there are rules for where and how they fall), there is a message or reading. There are 140 possible readings contained in the accompanying book.

THE PHOENIX CARDS

This is the first method of divination created specifically for exploring past-life influences. We all experience particular affinities for different places, times and cultures, and it may be that this has been carried over from some previous existence. Unexplained fears may be based on karmic memories, puzzling aspects of our personalities may be a hangover from something unresolved in an earlier incarnation. In all kinds of ways we are influenced by our past lives.

The Phoenix Cards were created by psychic and artist Susan Sheppard and illustrated by Toni Taylor. The 28 cards draw on ancient monuments and symbols of many cultures, and each represents a spiritual symbol. They are designed to trigger memories and feelings from previous lifetimes, and thus help unravel past-life experiences. They are consulted by choosing seven cards to which you feel drawn, and then meditating on them.

THE PENDULUM KIT

Dowsing is a way of balancing our rational and intuitive selves. Also called divining, dowsing generally employs a swinging pendulum to find answers to questions.

This divination kit contains a brass pendulum and a cord. It also contains an instruction book by Sig Lonegren, complete with charts, maps and exercises. Finding underground water, recovering a lost object, forecasting the weather, discovering which foods are best for your health or which particular healing remedy to use – all these are possible using *The Pendulum Kit*.

RUSSIAN GYPSY FORTUNE-TELLING CARDS

This is one of the most beautiful of recent divination packages. Based on the authentic Gypsy teachings of nineteenth-century Russia, the 25 large-format cards are illustrated in the Russian 'Palekh' style by Kathleen M. Skelly and Svetlana Alexandrovna Touchkoff.

The cards divide diagonally into four quarters, and when they are laid out in five rows and swivelled, they can form a picture card from two quarters. There are 50 complete pictures, and the meaning of each picture is contained in the elegant hardback book packaged together with the cards.

Svetlana Alexandrovna Touchkoff acquired the cards from her mother (her grandmother had also used such cards). They originated from the south-western part of Russia and are a blend of Gypsy wisdom and Russian folklore, using simple and universal symbols:

animals e.g. fox, bear, dog
natural landscape e.g. mountains, forest, moon
Christian images (though not exclusively so) e.g. lily, bread, angel

The person asking the question lays out five rows of five cards each, turning the cards in any direction to see if they form pictures with the adjacent cards. Particular attention is paid to the last card, which consolidates the meaning of the reading. The accompanying book provides an interpretation for the picture itself and for each of the four positions in which the picture lies.

TAROT DECKS

Often used to foretell the future, like all divination methods Tarot is also a powerful tool for exploring the subconscious. Prior to the 1970s there were really only two main Tarot decks in general use – the Tarot de Marseilles and the Rider-Waite deck, named after the publisher and A.E. Waite. In the past 20 years an enormous range of Tarot decks have been developed and are widely available. Tarot has proved to be very adaptable because it consists of images rather than text.

ESOTERIC TAROTS

From the end of the eighteenth century when Antoine Court de Gebelin claimed that the Tarot formed an ancient Egyptian book of wisdom, the Book of Thoth, there has been a steady stream of claims linking Tarot with various esoteric systems – with Cabbala, Rosicrucianism and with Masonic and Theosophical ideas. Members of the Order of the Golden Dawn had to create their own decks using MacGregor Mather's original deck (painted by Moira Mathers). The Thoth Tarot of Aleister Crowley and Lady Frieda Harris was published as a deck in 1969, although the paintings existed long before that.

The Magical Tarot, designed by Anthony Clark, is based primarily on Aleister Crowley, but also on John Dee's ideas, as well as being influenced by a quite different divination system, the *I Ching*. Anthony Clark has also collaborated on a more recent deck for the Servants of the Light, one of the leading schools of magical practice. The deck was begun by Jo Gill, who painted the Major Arcana. Under Dolores Ashcroft-Nowicki's direction (Dolores being the current head of the Servants of the Light), Anthony Clark completed the deck, combining magical and Cabbalistic insights.

The Enochian Tarot was created by Gerald and Betty Schueler and painted by Sallie Ann Glassman.

Based upon the principles of Enochian magic (a special branch of magic begun by John Dee and Edward Kelly), this deck actually has 86 cards rather than the usual 78. There are 30 regions or Aethyrs for the Major Arcana (instead of 22) and four suits for the Minor Arcana.

CULTURAL TAROTS

A recent development has been the devising of cultural Tarots, including cultures which had no previous connection with Tarot. Tarot is very much a Western system of divination, so it is fascinating that it can be taken and adapted to the symbols of quite different cultural traditions.

One of the first cultural Tarots to appear was Peter Balin's *Xultun Maya Tarot* in 1976. The cards are designed in the vivid and elaborate style of Mayan art, and something quite unique about this deck is the fact that the cards of the Major Arcana join together to make a single picture.

Another recent pack is *The Australian Contemporary Dreamtime Tarot*, devised by Keith and Daicon Courtney-Peto. This is based on the imagery and symbolism of the Australian Aborigines. The number of cards remains unchanged, and the division into Major and Minor Arcana and four suits is traditional, but the cards have acquired new names, drawn from the mythology of the Dreamtime. Thus the Fool is now called Karadji, the Lovers become Wejas and Strength is Thalera. The suits have become Muggils (Swords), Kundas (Staves), Coolamons (Cups) and Wariats (Pentacles). Full divinatory meanings are given in the accompanying booklet; for the Major Arcana this is extended to include gems, animals, plants or herbs, elements, musical notes, etc.

Since 1976 all kinds of cultural Tarots have appeared, from Egyptian, to Norse, to Tibetan (*The*

Secret Dakini Oracle) to Japanese (*Ukiyoe Tarot*). In *The Native American Tarot*, designed by Magda and J.A. Gonzalez, we have the lore of many of the native tribes of North America gathered in one deck: Apache, Arapaho, Cherokee, Cheyenne, Chippiwa, Comanche, Hopi, Huron, Inuit, Iroquois, Kiowa, Navaho, Pagamo, Pima, Pueblo, Shawnee, Sioux and Yaqui – and this is a partial listing!

MYTH AND STORY-TELLING TAROTS

Some recent decks are based on myth and story. *The Celtic Tarot*, designed by Courtney Davis, draws on Celtic myth and legend. The popular *Merlin Tarot*, designed by Bob Stewart and illustrated by Miranda Gray, again uses Celtic imagery and myth in showing the esoteric myths of the British tradition, but is also very much designed as a story-telling Tarot.

Another myth-orientated Tarot is *The Mythic Tarot*, devised by Juliet Sharman-Burke and Liz Greene and illustrated by Tricia Newell. This takes its inspiration entirely from Greek myths. It consists of the usual 78 cards, divided into Major and Minor Arcana, each of which retains its normal title. However, the designs show deities and heroes/heroines from classical tradition, so that the Fool becomes the god Dionysus, Justice is Athena with her owl, and the Heirophant is the wise centaur Chiron.

The Jungian Tarot is an unusual deck, devised by the distinguished Tarot expert Robert Wang. It derives from the system of psychological archetypes discovered by the great Swiss psychologist C.G. Jung (1875–1961). These correspond to certain basic patterns seen as present within every individual, regardless of culture or background. The cards retain their traditional names and order, but are interpreted in Jungian terms. Thus the Empress and Emperor are designated the Father and Mother, while Death becomes 'Mother as Gateway' and the Star is the Virgin Daughter. The four suits represent different stages on the Jungian path to individuation, which we might understand as enlightenment. The Five of Cups is thus designated as Troubles, and the Seven of Swords as Love. The marriage of these two important systems provides a set of visual glyphs of the modern psychological movement, as well as showing once again how varied and deep-rooted the Tarot symbolism is. The accompanying handbook includes a 34-week course in personal study, aimed at opening up an inner awareness of individual archetypes.

Undoubtedly the best example of a myth and story-telling Tarot is *The Arthurian Tarot*. Designed by Western tradition experts John and Caitlín Matthews, and again illustrated by Miranda Gray (although this time in a more mature style), *The Arthurian Tarot* is based on the legends, history and tradition of Arthurian Britain. The Arthurian stories are not just literary inventions but arise from the mythic and oral traditions of Britain. The Greater Powers (the Major Arcana) feature such characters as the Lady of the Lake, the Wounded King, the Green Knight, whilst the Lesser Powers (the Minor Arcana), the Suits of Swords, Spear, Grail and Stone, are the empowering objects of the Quest.

WOMEN'S TAROTS
Again the fact that the Tarot works through images rather than text has enabled it to be taken up and designed by women for women. Concerned with feminine values, these Tarots describe the experiences of women and hark back to an earlier, pre-patriarchal period of history.

Vicki Noble's *Motherpeace* deck is perhaps the best known, its very roundness symbolizing a different approach to life. It is full of images, drawn by Karen Vogel, of ancient goddesses, and seeks a woman-centred spirituality. The *Barbara Walker Tarot* comes from the illustrations she created for her book *Secrets of the Tarot*. Again, goddesses and ancient rituals feature, as well as figures from the Grail stories. An exciting new Tarot is *The Shining Woman Tarot*, devised and designed by Rachel Pollack, based on the world-wide traditions of shamanism.

PUBLICATION DETAILS OF THE SYSTEMS DESCRIBED

Ashcroft-Nowicki, Dolores, *The Servants of the Light Tarot*, London, Aquarian, 1991.

Balin, Peter, *The Xultún Tarot: The Maya Tarot Deck*, Wilmot, Wisconsin, Arcana Publishing, 1976.

Blum, Ralph, *The New Book of Runes*, London, Headline, 1990.

Clark, Anthony, *The Magical Tarot*, London, Aquarian, 1992.

Cooper, D. Jason, *Rune Stones: A Comprehensive Introduction to the Art of Runecraft*, London, Aquarian, 1990.

Courtney-Peto, Keith and Daicon, *The Australian Contemporary Dreamtime Tarot*, Queensland, Goldrope, 1991.

Davis, Courtney, *The Celtic Tarot*, London, Aquarian, 1990.

Goldberg, Jay L. and Dakpa, Lobsang, MO: *Tibetan Divination System*, Ithaca, New York, Snow Lion, 1990.

Hope, Murry, *Olympus: Self-Discovery and the Greek Archetypes*, London, Aquarian, 1991.

Jackson, Nigel and Pennick, Nigel, *The Celtic Oracle*, London, Aquarian, 1992.

Lacey, Marie Louise, *Know Yourself Through Colour*, London, Aquarian, 1989.

Lonegren, Sig, *The Pendulum Kit*, New York, Simon & Schuster, 1990; London, Virgin, 1992.

Matthews, Caitlín, *The Celtic Book of the Dead*, New York, St Martins Press, 1992; London, Aquarian, 1992.

Matthews, John and Caitlín, *The Arthurian Tarot*, London, Aquarian, 1990.

Montana, Leroy, Waldron, Linda and Jonah, Kathleen, *The Crystal Oracle*, London, Aquarian, 1989.

Murray, Liz and Colin, *The Celtic Tree Oracle*, London, Rider, 1988.

Noble, Vicki, *The Motherpeace Tarot*, New York, US Games, 1981.

Pintar, Judith, *A Voice from the Earth: The Cards of Winds and Changes*, London, Unwin Hyman, 1990; New York, Stirling, 1990.

Pollack, Rachel, *The Shining Woman Tarot*, London, Aquarian, 1992.

Sams, Jamie, *Sacred Path Cards: The Discovery of Self Through Native Teachings*, San Francisco, HarperCollins, 1990.

Sams, Jamie and Carson, David, *Medicine Cards: The Discovery of Power Through the Ways of Animals*, Santa Fe, Bear and Co., 1988.

Schuel, Gerald and Betty, *The Enochian Tarot*, St Paul, Minnesota, Llewellyn, 1989.

Sharman-Burke, Juliet and Greene, Liz, *The Mythic Tarot*, London, Rider, 1986.

Sheppard, Susan, *The Phoenix Cards: Reading and Interpreting Past-Life Influences with the Phoenix Deck*, Rochester, Vermont, Destiny, 1990.

Skelly, Kathleen M. and Touchkoff, Svetlana Alexandrovna, *Russian Gypsy Fortune-Telling Cards*, San Francisco, HarperCollins, 1990.

Stewart, R.J., *The Merlin Tarot*, London, Aquarian, 1988.

Walker, Barbara, *The Barbara Walker Tarot*, New York, US Games, 1986.

Wang, Robert, *Jungian Tarot Set*, Neuhausen, Urania Verlag, 1988.

THE CONTRIBUTORS

Eileen Campbell read history at the University of Reading in the 1960s. Since that time she has travelled extensively and studied all kinds of traditions and philosophies. A leading New Age publisher, she has been responsible for the publication of many important books and has published many of the modern divination systems. She has written and broadcast on the New Age and has compiled a series of successful inspirational anthologies, which include *A Dancing Star* (1991) and *A Lively Flame* (1992).

James G. Cowan is a distinguished author and poet. He has spent much of his life exploring the world of traditional peoples such as the Berbers, the Tuareg, the Torres Strait Islanders, the Iban of Borneo, the Rajputs of the Sind and the Monks of Mount Athos. For the past ten years he has documented the spiritual life of the Australian Aborigines. In books such as *Mysteries of the Dreaming, Sacred Places, Letters from a Wild State* and *The Elements of Aboriginal Tradition* he unveiled their rich metaphysical perspective. He has lectured in England, the USA and India on similar themes. Other recent books include *The Painted Shore* and a translation of Rumi's odes to Shems of Tabriz, *Where Two Oceans Meet*.

Nevill Drury is a specialist in occult mythology, magical philosophy and shamanism. He has contributed numerous articles to periodicals and journals and is the author of over 20 books on esoteric thought, many of them published internationally. His books include *Don Juan, Mescalito and Modern Magic, Inner Visions, The Shaman and the Magician, The Elements of Shamanism* and, most recently, *The Visionary Human*. He holds a Master of Arts degree in anthropology.

Cherry Gilchrist is concerned with bringing back ancient knowledge into the light of day. Her books on alchemy, astrology, divination and feminine symbolism all reflect this. Cherry is both an author and a singer, directing the professional early music ensemble, Arcadia. She was the first to write about the connection between alchemy and the birth of baroque music, and her latest book investigates the nature of performance itself. Cherry holds a degree in English and anthropology from Cambridge University.

Judith Gleason received her PhD in comparative literature from Columbia University in 1963. Her thesis on African novels in English and French was subsequently published by Northwestern University. Combining field work with scholarly investigation, she has published several books on West African as well as Caribbean religion and oral traditions, most recently *Oya: In Praise of an African Goddess*. She lives and practises a Jungian-oriented psychotherapy in New York City.

Jay L. Goldberg is a Buddhist scholar and practitioner who has spent 17 years living in Asia, where he trained in Buddhist thought and the Tibetan language. He received his Masters degree in Indian philosophy at Banaras Hindu University and

studied at the Sakya College where he engaged in translations of Tibetan texts. His recent books include *MO: Tibetan Divination System* and *The Beautiful Ornament of the Three Visions*, and he has previously had other books and texts of Tibetan translations published. He has translated for many Tibetan lamas during their lecture tours of Asia and North America, so his knowledge of Tibetan culture, customs and beliefs is extensive.

Marian Green is a leading exponent of the Western magical arts. She has edited *Quest*, a quarterly magazine on magical traditions, since 1970, and is the author of many books, including *Magic for the Aquarian Age, The Elements of Natural Magic, The Elements of Ritual Magic* and *A Witch Alone*. She runs training courses in the UK, USA and Europe on magic, divination, Celtic mythology, the Grail and Arthurian legends and witchcraft. She has broadcast on radio and television.

Alan Haymes' study of medieval history at university generated a deep interest in the underlying cultures of Northern Eurasia and initiated his research into the mythologies and shamanic traditions of the Indo-European, Uralic, Altaic and Paleo-Siberian speaking peoples. The importance of the wisdom of the ancestors and the links with the distant past has led him to appreciate the teachings of the 'perennial philosophy' and in particular the writings of the French thinker, René Guénon.

Prudence Jones has lectured widely on astrology and its history, and has conducted original research into ancient astronomy and calendars. She has contributed to books on astrology and has edited her own collection, *Creative Astrology: Experiential Understanding of the Birth Chart*. She is a practising psychotherapist, a Pagan priestess and a theologian. She edited, with Caitlín Matthews, *Voices from the Circle: The Heritage of Western Paganism* and is writing a history of Pagan Europe with Nigel Pennick.

Kunderke Kevlin (previously Kooijman) studied social anthropology at the Universities of Durban and Johannesburg, South Africa, and cultural anthropology at the University of Leiden. She did 18 months fieldwork among a Tswana tribe in Botswana, focusing on social-economic change. At Leiden University she changed her subject to the world-view, symbolism and religion of the Southern African tribes, particularly their divination systems.

Sig Lonegren was taught by his mother to dowse in 1960. He has been a student of sacred enclosures since the early 1970s, and has a Masters degree in Sacred Space, the study of pre-Protestant Reformation spiritual centres. He is the author of the *Earth Mysteries Handbook: Wholistic Non-Intrusive Data Gathering Techniques*, which discusses sacred geometry, archaeoastronomy and dowsing, *Spiritual Dowsing, The Pendulum Kit* and *Labyrinths: Ancient Myths and Modern Uses*.

John Matthews was born in the north of England in 1948. He has been a full-time writer for 12 years and has made the Arthurian field his own territory, exploring the grail mysteries, Arthurian legends and esoteric wisdom in his numerous books. His most recent publications include *Ladies of the Lake: A Study of the Feminine Archetypes in the Arthurian Tradition*, *Taliesin: Shamanism and the Bardic Mysteries in Britain and Ireland* and *Choirs of the God: Revisioning Masculinity*. He is an established lecturer and gives many talks in Europe and America.

Nigel Pennick is a writer and lecturer on ancient and modern mysteries, an authority on northern European geomancy, runemaster, practising geomant and traditional symbolic craftsman. A founder and co-ordinator of the Institute for Geomantic Research, he organized five Cambridge geomantic symposia and has co-ordinated an international conference on labyrinths. He has written many books, including *Secret Lore of Runes and Other Ancient Alphabets* and *The Celtic Oracle*.

Rachel Pollack was born in Brooklyn, New York. She has studied the Tarot for 20 years and has taught classes and workshops in England, USA and Europe. She is the author of several books, including *78 Degrees of Wisdom*, *The Open Labyrinth* and *The New Tarot*. She has also devised her own pack, *The Shining Woman Tarot*.

Valerie J. Roebuck read oriental studies at the University of Cambridge and is a specialist in the art and religion of India. She teaches Sanskrit and Comparative Religion, and has a keen interest in astrology, astronomy, myth and language. Her publications include *The Circle of Stars: An Introduction to Indian Astrology* and entries for *Who's Who of World Religion*.

Jamie Sams is a Native American medicine teacher and a member of the Wolf Clan teaching lodge of the Seneca Nation. She is of Iroquois and Choctaw descent, and has been trained in Seneca, Mayan, Aztec and Choctaw medicine. She has taught in England, France, Egypt, Kenya, Mexico, Peru and Guatemala, as well as in the United States. Her books include *Midnight Song: Quest for the Vanished Ones*, *Medicine Cards: The Discovery of Power Through the Ways of Animals* (with David Carson), *Sacred Path Cards: The Discovery of Self Through Native Teachings*, *Other Council Fires Were Here Before Ours* (with Twylah Nitsch) and *The Thirteen Original Clan Mothers: The Story of the Sisterhood and the Legacy of Woman*.

Bruce Scofield has earned a living as an astrological consultant since 1980. He maintains a private practice in Massachusetts, working with his clients by telephone and mail. He is the author of several books on astrology, including two on Mesoamerican astrology.

Norman Shine was born in London and has lived in Copenhagen since 1963. After graduating in history and psychology he became a civil service interpreter. He was subsequently associate professor of literature at the University of Cophenhagen and associate professor of intepreting and applied linguistics at the Copenhagen School of Economics. He is now a consultant numerologist and writer.

David Simmons was born in 1930 in New Zealand. He attended university in Auckland, Wellington, Paris and Rennes, obtaining a Master of Arts degree in anthropology and a Diploma in Celtic Studies. On his return to New Zealand he taught in secondary schools before taking up a post as Keeper in Anthropology at Otago Museum, Dunedin. He moved to Auckland Museum to become Ethnologist and later Assistant Director of Auckland Institute and Museum until 1986. He was co-curator of the Te Maori Exhibition which toured the USA, and he has been associated with many Maori projects. He has published books on Maori history and culture.

Peter Taylor is an exponent of the practical aspects of the perennial Magic Tradition, having a particular interest in the current resurgence of the Starry Wisdom – which, he believes, provides us with the means to return scientific endeavour to a proper basis in spiritual reality. He works with various magical symbol systems, including the Runes. The raw material for much of his writing comes from experimental magical work carried out in small groups.

Robert Temple is the author of seven books, which have been translated into a total of 43 languages. His first book, *The Sirius Mystery*, was a best-seller and dealt with mysterious aspects of the ancient world. *Conversations with Eternity* contained the first popular account of the techniques of extispicy (divination by the entrails). Temple's extensive studies in the subjects of trance and hypnosis appeared in his book *Open to Suggestion*. His latest book, *He Who Saw Everything*, is a modern translation of the Epic of Gilgamesh, with notes and commentary. Temple is also a television producer with his own independent production company.

John Turpin is a minister of Ifa, a Babaláwo, in the tradition of the Yoruba of southwest Nigeria. He was ordained in Ijabu Remo, Nigeria, in 1980. This ordination was the culmination of a six-year period of study and training in the United States, Europe and Africa, and began the period of his active ministry in the United States. In 1991 he founded the Temple Orunmila and the Center for Ifa Studies in Oakland, California.

Derek Walters was born in Manchester in 1936, and lives in Manchester and London. In later life, after many years of fringe interest in Chinese culture, he has devoted his entire time to the study of Chinese astrology and philosophy. He is the author of several books, and has travelled widely throughout Southeast Asia. He is regarded as one of the Western world's foremost authorities on traditional Chinese divination, and has been admitted to the Hong Kong fraternity of diviners.

Jennifer Westwood has made a lifelong study of myth, legend, folktale and folklore. She graduated from Oxford and Cambridge universities in Anglo-Saxon and medieval Icelandic literature, and has since gone on to write several books on myth, folklore and legend. Her most recent publications include *Albion: A Guide to Legendary Britain* and *The Atlas of Legendary Places*. She gives frequent lectures and has appeared several times on radio and television.

FURTHER READING

CHAPTER ONE
SEERS AND HEALERS
(Shamanism)

Doore, G. (ed.), *Shaman's Path*, Boston, Shambhala, 1988.

Drury, N., *The Elements of Shamanism*, Shaftesbury, Element Books, 1989.

Eliade, M., *Shamanism*, New Jersey, Princeton University Press, 1972.

Furst, P.T. (ed.), *Flesh of the Gods*, London, Allen & Unwin, 1972.

Halifax, J. (ed.), *Shamanic Voices*, New York, Dutton, 1979.

Halifax, J., *Shaman: the Wounded Healer*, New York, Crossroad, 1982.

Harner, M. (ed.), *Hallucinogens and Shamanism*, New York, Oxford University Press, 1973.

Harner, M., *The Way of the Shaman*, San Francisco, Harper & Row, 1980.

Kalweit, H., *Dreamtime and Inner Space*, Boston, Shambhala, 1988.

Nicholson, S. (ed.), *Shamanism*, Illinois, Quest Books, 1987.

Wasson, R.G., *The Wondrous Mushroom*, New York, McGraw Hill, 1980.

CHAPTER TWO
THE FROZEN NORTH
(Arctic systems)

Bäckman, Louise and Hultkrantz, Åke, *Studies in Lapp Shamanism*, Stockholm, Stockholm Studies in Comparative Religion no.16, 1978.

Diszegi, Vilmos and Hoppál, Mihály (eds), *Shamanism in Siberia*, Budapest, Akademiai Kiado, 1978.

Hajdú, Petér (ed.), *Ancient Cultures of the Uralian Peoples*, Budapest, Corvina Press, 1976.

Hoppál, Mihály (ed.), *Shamanism in Eurasia*, Göttingen, Herodot, 1984.

Michael, Henry N. (ed.), *Studies in Siberian Shamanism*, Toronto, University of Toronto Press, 1963.

Oinas, Felix J., *Studies in Finnic Folklore*, Helsinki, Finnish Literature Society, 1985.

Pentikäinen, Juha, *Kalevala Mythology*, Indiana, Indiana University Press, 1989.

CHAPTER THREE
BY STICK AND STONE
(Celtic methods)

Calder, G., *Auraicept Na N-Eces (The Scholar's Primer)*, Edinburgh, John Grant, 1917.

Davidson, H.E. (ed.), *The Seer in Celtic and Other Traditions*, Edinburgh, John Donald, 1990.

Matthews, J., *The Celtic Shaman*, Shaftesbury, Element Books, 1991.

Matthews, J., *Taliesin: Shamanism and the Bardic Mysteries in Britain and Ireland*, London, Aquarian, 1991.

Matthews, J. 'Incubatory Sleep and Precognitive Dreaming in the Celtic World', *Psychology and the Spiritual Traditions*, ed. R.J. Stewart, Shaftesbury, Element Books, 1991.

Pennick, N., *The Secret Lore of Runes and Other Ancient Alphabets*, London, Rider, 1991.

Sutherland, E., *Ravens and Black Rain: the Story of Highland Second Sight*, London, Constable, 1985.

CHAPTER FOUR
THE MESSAGE OF THE RUNES
(Runes)

Byock, Jesse L., *The Saga of the Volsungs* (Introduction and Translation), Berkeley, University of California Press, 1990.

Elliott, R.W.V., *Runes*, Manchester, Manchester University Press, 1980.

Faulkes, Anthony (translator), *Edda*, Snorri Sturlson, London, Everyman Classics, J.M. Dent & Sons, 1987.

Hollander, Lee M., (translator), *The Poetic Edda*, Austin, University of Texas Press, 1990.

Pennick, Nigel, *Practical Magic in the Northern Tradition*, London, Aquarian, 1989.

Turville-Petre, E.O.G., *Myth and Religion in the North*, London, Weidenfeld & Nicolson, 1964.

CHAPTER FIVE
THE KEYS OF TAROT
(Tarot)

Fairfield, Gail, *Choice-Centered Tarot*, North Hollywood, California, Newcastle, 1985.

Foster Case, Paul, *The Tarot*, New York, Macoy, 1947.

Greer, Mary K., *Tarot For Yourself*, North Hollywood, California, Newcastle, 1984; UK edition: *Tarot Transformations*, London, Aquarian, 1987.

Kaplan, Stuart J., *Encyclopedia of Tarot*, Vols I-III, New York, US Games Systems Inc., vol. I 1978, vol. II 1985, vol. III 1986.

Knight, Gareth, *The Treasure House of Images*, London, Aquarian, 1986.

Pollack, Rachel, *Seventy-eight Degrees of Wisdom*, Parts 1 and 2, London, Aquarian, 1980 and 1983.

Pollack, Rachel, *The New Tarot*, London, Aquarian, 1989.

CHAPTER SIX
PATTERNS OF WESTERN ASTROLOGY
(Western astrology)

Baigent, M., Campion, N. and Harvey, C., *Mundane Astrology*, London, Aquarian, 1991.

Barclay, Olivia, *Horary Astrology Rediscovered*, Pennsylvania, Whitford Press, 1990.

Campion, Nicholas, *An Introduction to the History of Astrology*, London, ISCWA, 1982.

Cozzi, Steve, *Planets in Locality*, St Paul, Minnesota, Llewellyn, 1988.

Doane, Doris Chase, *Profit by Electional Astrology*, Tempe, Arizona, American Federation of Astrologers, 1990.

Huntley, Janice, *The Elements of Astrology*, Shaftesbury, Element Books, 1991.

Parker, Derek and Julia, *The New Compleat Astrologer*, London, Mitchell Beazley, 1990.

Ridder-Patrick, Jane, *A Handbook of Medical Astrology*, London, Arkana, 1990.

CHAPTER SEVEN
CONSULTING THE ORACLES
(Classic systems)

Artemidorus, *The Interpretation of Dreams (Oneirocritica)*, trans. Robert J. White, New Jersey, Noyes Press, 1975.

Cicero, *On Divination (De Divinatione)*, trans. in vol. 154 of the Loeb Classical Library series, London, Heinemann, 1923.

Fontenrose, Joseph, *The Delphic Oracle*, Berkeley, University of California Press, 1978.

Meer, L.B. van der, *The Bronze Liver of Piacenza*, Amsterdam, J.C. Gieben, 1987.

Parke, H.W. and Wormell, D.E.W., *The Delphic Oracle*, Oxford, Blackwell, 1939; new edition 1956.

Plutarch, *The E at Delphi, Oracles at Delphi No Longer Given in Verse* and *Obsolescence of Oracles*, trans. in vol. 306 of the Loeb Classical Library series, London, Heinemann, 1936.

Temple, Robert K.G., *Conversations With Eternity*, London, Rider, 1984.

Vitruvius, *On Architecture*, trans. in vols 251 and 280 of the Loeb Classical Library series, London, Heinemann, 1931 and 1934.

Weinstock, Stefan, 'Martianus Capella and the Cosmic System of the Etruscans', *Journal of Roman Studies*, London, Society for the Promotion of Roman Studies, vol. XXXVI, 1930, p. 122.

CHAPTER EIGHT
THE TREE OF LIFE
(Galgal)

Gilchrist, Cherry, *Divination: The Search for Meaning*, London, Dryad Press, 1987.

Halevi, Z'ev ben Shimon, *Kabbalah: Tradition of Hidden Knowledge*, London, Thames & Hudson, 1979.

Kaplan, Aryeh, *Meditation and Kabbalah*, York Beach, Maine, Samuel Weiser, 1982.

Knight, Gareth, *A Practical Guide to Qabalistic Symbolism*, Watford, Herts, Helios Books, 1965.

Parfitt, Will, *The Living Qabalah*, Shaftesbury, Element Books, 1988.

Scholem, Gerschom, *Major Trends in Jewish Mysticism*, New York, Schocken Books, 1971.

CHAPTER NINE
WISE WOMEN COUNSELLORS
(Popular methods)

Glass, Justine, *The Story of Fulfilled Prophecy*, London, Cassell, 1969.

Green, Marian, *A Calendar of Festivals*, Shaftesbury, Element Books, 1992.

Green, Marian, *A Witch Alone*, London, Aquarian, 1990.

Harding, M. Ester, *Women's Mysteries*, London, Rider, 1971; New York, Putnam, 1972.

Tindall, Gillian, *A Handbook on Witches*, London, Panther Books, 1967.

Valiente, Doreen, *Natural Magic*, London, Hale, 1975.

CHAPTER TEN
THE SEASONAL ROUND
(Folklore)

Aubrey, John, *Three Prose Works*, ed. John Buchanan-Brown, Fontwell, Centaur Press, 1972.

Hole, Christina, *English Folklore*, 2nd edition, revised, London, B.T. Batsford, 1944–5.

Leach, Maria and Fried, Jerome (eds), *Funk and Wagnall's Standard Dictionary of Folklore, Mythology and Legend*, New York, Harper & Row, 1984.

Opie, Iona and Peter, *The Lore and Language of Schoolchildren*, Oxford, Clarendon Press, 1959.

Radford, E. and M.A., *Encyclopaedia of Superstitions*, edited and revised by Christina Hole, London, Hutchinson, 1961.

Thomas, Keith, *Religion and the Decline of Magic*, Harmondsworth, Peregrine Books, 1978.

CHAPTER ELEVEN
ORACLES IN BONE
(Southern Africa)

Dornan, Rev. S.S., 'Divination and Divining Bones', *South African Journal of Science*, vol. XX, pp.504–11, 1923–4.

Hunt, N.A., 'Some Notes on the Witchdoctor's Bones', *Nada*, XXVII, pp.40–46, 1950; XXXI, pp.16–23, 1954; XXXIX, pp.14–16, 1962.

Junod, H.A., 'La Divination au moyen de Tablettes d'Ivoire chez les Pedis', *Bull. Soc. Neuchat. Geogr.*, 34, pp.38–56, 1925.

Krige, E.J. and Krige, J.D., *The Realm of the Rain Queen*, London, International African Institute, 1943.

Peek, M., (ed.), *African Divination Systems: Ways of Knowing*, Indiana, Indiana University Press, 1991.

Roberts, N., 'Bantu Methods of Divination: a Comparative Study', *South African Journal of Science*, vol. XIII, pp.397–408, 1917.

Tracey, H., 'The Hakata of Southern Rhodesia', *Nada*, XL, pp.105–7, 1963.

CHAPTER TWELVE
IFA
(A Yoruba system of oracular worship)

Abimbola, Wande, *Ifa Divination Poetry*, New York, Nok Publishers, 1977.

Bascom, William, *Ifa Divination*, Bloomington, Indiana University Press, 1969.

Fahd, Toufic, *La Divination Arab*, Leiden, Brill, 1966.

Idowu, E. Bolaji, *Olodumare: God in Yoruba Belief*, New York, Praeger, 1963.

Maupoil, Bernard, 'La Géomancie à l'Ancienne Côte des Esclaves', *Travaux et Mémoires de l'Institut d'Ethnologie*, XLII, Paris, 1943.

CHAPTER THIRTEEN
SACRED MEDICINE
(Native American systems)

Lake, Bobby Grislybear, *Native Healer*, Wheaton, Illinois, Theosophical Publishing House, 1991.

McGaa, Ed (Eagleman), *Mother Earth Spirituality*, San Francisco, HarperCollins, 1990.

Medicine Eagle, Brooke, *Buffalo Woman Came Singing*, New York, Ballantine, 1991.

Sams, Jamie, *Sacred Path Cards: The Discovery of Self Through Native Teachings*, San Francisco, HarperCollins, 1990.

Sams, Jamie and **Nitsch, Twylah**, *Other Council Fires Were Here Before Ours*, San Francisco, HarperCollins, 1991.

Sams, Jamie and **Carson, David**, *Medicine Cards: The Discovery of Power Through the Ways of Animals*, Santa Fe, Bear & Co., 1988.

A comprehensive list of books about Native Americans can be obtained from the University of Oklahoma Press, Norman, Oklahoma 73019, USA.

CHAPTER FOURTEEN
SUN, TIME AND SYMBOLISM
(Mesoamerican astrology)

Arguelles, Jose A., *The Mayan Factor*, Sante Fe, New Mexico, Bear & Co., 1987.

Aveni, Anthony F., *Skywatchers of Ancient Mexico*, Austin, University of Texas Press, 1980.

Aveni, Anthony F., *Empires of Time*, New York, Basic Books, 1989.

Burland, C.A., *The Gods of Mexico*, New York, Putnam, 1967.

Edmonson, Monro S., *The Book of the Year: Middle American Calendrical Systems*, Salt Lake City, University of Utah Press, 1988.

Sahagun, Fray Bernardino de, *Florentine Codex: A General History of the Things of New Spain, Books 4 and 5*, trans. C.E. Dibble and A.J.O. Anderson, Ogden, University of Utah Press, 1957.

Schele, Linda and **Freidel, David**, *A Forest of Kings: The Untold Story of the Ancient Maya*, New York, William Morrow, 1990.

Scofield, Bruce and **Cordova, Angela**, *The Aztec Circle of Destiny*, St Paul, Minnesota, Llewellyn, 1988.

Scofield, Bruce, *Day Signs: Native American Astrology from Ancient Mexico*, Amherst, Massachusetts, One Reed Publications, 1991.

Tedlock, Barbara, *Time and the Highland Maya*, Albuquerque, University of New Mexico Press, 1982.

Thompson, J. Eric S., *Maya Hieroglyphic Writing: An Introduction*, Norman, University of Oklahoma Press, 1960.

Two programs on Aztec astrology, including one that prints reports, are available from Astrolabe Software, Box 1750-R, Brewster, MA 02631, USA.

CHAPTER FIFTEEN
THE WAY OF THE EMPEROR
(Mah Jongg)

Loewe, Michael, *Ways to Paradise*, London, Allen & Unwin, 1979.

Millington, A.D., *The Complete Book of Mah Jongg*, London, Barker, 1977.

Walters, Derek, *Your Future Revealed by Mah Jongg*, London, Aquarian, 1982.

CHAPTER SIXTEEN
THE CHINESE BOOK OF CHANGES
(I Ching)

Blofeld, John, *I Ching*, London, George Allen & Unwin, 1965.

Legge, James, *The I Ching*, New York, Dover, 1963.

Loewe, Michael and **Blacker, Carmen** (eds), *Divination and Oracles*, London, George Allen & Unwin, 1979.

Moore, Stephen, *The Trigrams of Han: Inner Structures of the I Ching*: London, Aquarian, 1989.

Temple, Robert, *Conversations with Eternity: Ancient Man's Attempts to Know the Future*, London, Rider, 1984.

Wilhelm, Richard, *The I Ching or Book of Changes*, London, Penguin/Arkana, first edition 1951.

CHAPTER SEVENTEEN
DRAGON LINES IN THE LAND
(Feng Shui)

Eitel, E.J., *Feng Shui*, Trubner, 1873; reprinted Bristol, Pentacle Books, 1979.

Feuchtwang, Stephan, *An Anthropological Analysis of Chinese Geomancy*, Vientiane, Laos, Editions Vithagna, 1974.

Pirazzoli-T'Serstevens, Michele, *Living Architecture: Chinese*, London, Macdonald, 1972.

Walters, Derek, *Chinese Geomancy*, Shaftesbury, Element Books, 1991.

Walters, Derek, *The Feng Shui Handbook*, London, Aquarian, 1991.

CHAPTER EIGHTEEN
STAR LORE IN THE EAST
(Sidereal astrology)

Bhat, M. Ramakrishna, *Fundamentals of Astrology*, New Delhi, Motilal Banarsidass, 1967.

Filbey J. and Filbey P., *The Astrologer's Companion*, London, Aquarian, 1986.

Oken, Alan, *Astrology; Evolution and Revolution; A Path to Higher Consciousness through Astrology*, New York, Toronto and London, Bantam, 1976.

Marinelli, Luciana, *Astrologia Indiana: Teoria e Pratica*, Rome, Edizione Mediterranee, 1983.

Pingree, David, *Jyotiḥśāstra: Astral and Mathematical Literature*, Otto Harrassowitz, in Jan Gonda, *A History of Indian Literature*, vol. VI, fasc. 4, Wiesbaden, 1981.

Quaritch Wales, H.G., *Divination in Thailand: the Hopes and Fears of a Southeast Asian People*, London, Curzon Press, 1983.

Robson, Vivian E., *The Fixed Stars and Constellations in Astrology*, London, Aquarian, 1969.

Roebuck, Valerie J., *The Circle of Stars: an Introduction to Indian Astrology*, Shaftesbury, Element Books, 1992.

CHAPTER NINETEEN
MIRRORS IN THE SKY
(Tibetan divination)

Avedon, John F., *In Exile From The Land Of Snows*, New York, Alfred A. Knopf, 1984.

De Nebesky-Wojkowitz, Rene, *Oracles and Demons of Tibet*, The Hague, Mouton & Co., Publ., 1956.

Goldberg, Jay L. and **Lobsang, Dakpa**, *MO: Tibetan Divination System*, Ithaca, NY, Snow Lion Publications, 1990.

Snellgrove, David and **Richardson, Hugh**, *A Cultural History of Tibet*, Boulder, CO, Prajna Press, 1980.

Stein, R.A., *Tibetan Civilization*, Stanford, Stanford University Press, CA, 1972.

Waddell, Austine L., *Tibetan Buddhism*, New York, Dover Publications, 1972.

CHAPTER TWENTY
WILD STONES
(Aboriginal divination)

Berndt, R.M. and **C.H.**, *The World of the First Australians*, Sydney, Ure Smith, 1976.

Cowan, James, *Mysteries of the Dreaming*, Bridport, Prism Press, 1988.

Cowan, James, *Letters from a Wild State*, Shaftesbury,

Element Books, 1990; New York, Bell Tower, 1992.

Cowan, James, *Sacred Places in Australia*, Sydney, Simon & Schuster, 1991.

Cowan, James, *The Elements of Aboriginal Tradition*, Shaftesbury, Element Books, 1992.

Elkin, A.P., *Aboriginal Men of High Degree*, Brisbane, University of Queensland Press, 1974.

CHAPTER TWENTY-ONE
ANCESTORS, GODS AND MEN
(Maori methods)

Oppenheim, Roger *Maori Death Customs*, Wellington, A.H. & A.W. Reed, 1973.

Servant, Catherin, *Customs and Habits of the New Zealanders 1838–1842* (ed. D.R. Simmons), Wellington, A.H. & A.W. Reed, 1973.

Simmons, David, 'Iconography of New Zealand Maori Religion', *Iconography of Religions II.I*, Leiden, E.J. Brill, 1986.

Stafford, Donald, *Te Arawa*, Auckland, Reed Books, 1991.

Te Rangi Hiroa (Sir Peter Buck), *The Coming of the Maori*, Wellington, Maori Purposes Fund Board, 1977.

CHAPTER TWENTY-TWO
COUNTING THE FUTURE
(Numerology)

Cheiro, Count Louis Hamon, *Cheiro's Book of Numbers: The Complete Science of Numerology*, New York, Prentice Hall Press, 1988.

Drayer, Ruth, *Numerology: The Language of Life*, El Paso, Texas, Skidmore-Roth Publishing, 1990.

Javane, Faith and **Bunker, Dusty**, *Numerology and the Divine Triangle*, West Chester, Penn., Whitford Press, 1979.

Johari, Harish, *Numerology with Tantra, Ayurveda, and Astrology: A Key to Human Behaviour*, Rochester, Vermont, Destiny Books, 1990.

Konraad, Sandor, *Numerology: Key to the Tarot*, Rochester, Vermont, Destiny Books, 1990.

CHAPTER TWENTY-THREE
ANCIENT SECRETS OF THE EARTH
(Geomancy)

Crowley, Aleister, *Magick in Theory and Practice*, Paris, Lecram, 1929.

Pennick, Nigel, *Madagascar Divination*, Cambridge, Fenris-Wolf, 1975.

Pennick, Nigel, *Secret Games of the Gods*, York Beach, Maine, Samuel Weiser, 1992.

Regardie, Francis Israel, *A Practical Guide to Geomantic Divination*, London, Aquarian, 1972.

Skinner, Stephen, *Terrestrial Astrology: Divination by Geomancy*, London, Routledge & Kegan Paul, 1980.

CHAPTER TWENTY-FOUR
DOWSING THE WAY
(Dowsing)

Agricola, Georgius, *De Re Metallica (On Metals)*, New York, Dover Publications, 1950; translated by Herbert Clark Hoover and Lou Henry Hoover.

Bird, Christopher, *The Divining Hand*, New York, E.P. Dutton, 1979.

Graves, Tom, *Needles of Stone Revisited*, Glastonbury, Gothic Image, 1986.

Graves, Tom (ed.), *Dowsing and Archaeology*, Wellingborough, Turnstone Press, 1908; a selection of articles from the *Journal of the British Society of Dowsers*.

Lonegren, Sig, *The Pendulum Kit*, New York, Simon & Schuster, 1990; Melbourne, Lothian, 1990; London, Virgin, 1992.

Lonegren, Sig, *Spiritual Dowsing*, Glastonbury, Gothic Image, 1986.

Ross, Edward T. and **Wright, Richard D.**, *The Divining Mind*, Rochester, Vermont, Destiny Books, 1990.

Underwood, Guy, *The Pattern of the Past*, New York, Abelard-Schuman, 1973.

Watkins, Alfred, *The Old Straight Track*, London, Abacus, 1974.

INDEX